May 18–22, 2015
Florence, Italy

Association for
Computing Machinery

Advancing Computing as a Science & Profession

WWW
2015
FLORENCE, ITALY

WWW'15

Proceedings of the 24th International Conference on World Wide Web

Sponsored by:

IW3C2

In co-operation with:

ACM SIGWEB

IW3C3

Notice to Past Authors of IW3C3 Published Articles
ACM intends to create a complete electronic archive of all articles and/or other material previously published by ACM. If you have written a work that has been previously published by ACM in any journal or conference proceedings prior to 1978, or any SIG Newsletter at any time, and you do NOT want this work to appear in the ACM Digital Library, please inform permissions@acm.org, stating the title of the work, the author(s), and where and when published.

ISBN: 978-1-4503-3469-3 (Digital)

ISBN: 978-1-4503-3860-8 (Print)

Printed in the USA

WWW'15 General Chairs' Welcome

It is our great pleasure to welcome you to the 24th International World Wide Web Conference (WWW 2015) which will be held on May 18-22, 2015 in Florence, Italy. The annual World Wide Web Conference is the premier international forum to present and discuss progress in research, development, standards, and applications of the topics related to the Web. WWW is organized by the International World Wide Web Conference Steering Committee (IW3C2) in collaboration with local conference organizers of the host country. WWW 2015 offers a unique opportunity for sharing the latest insights of academic and industrial research, as well as to experience the unique environment of Florence, a city at the heart of artistic, cultural, and scientific developments since many centuries.

WWW 2015 will offer high quality technical activities, including research sessions, poster sessions, workshops, tutorials, demonstrations, an industry track, a Web Science track, a W3C track, panels, and a Ph.D. symposium. Co-located events include the 2nd edition of the Bigdata Innovators Gathering (BIG 2015), a novel Entrepreneurs Track (ET), the Digital Disease Detection Conference (DDD), the Digital Health Conference (DH), Digital Marketing 2015 -- Made in Italy on the Web (DM 2015), and the Web for All conference (W4A). WWW 2015 will also be collocated with the International Conference on Mobile Systems, Services and Applications (MobiSys 2015).

We hope you will be pleased with the quality of this year's program, featuring three keynote speeches by world-class experts. The Research track presents 131 high quality papers; 72 posters of the Poster track report short summaries of research; the Demo track shows 28 appealing demos; the Ph.D. Symposium track reports 9 presentations of doctoral students; the Industry track consists of 8 speeches from prominent industrial researchers; the Web Science track presents 12 papers and 14 posters on novel interdisciplinary research; W3C track is composed of sessions on the latest Web standards and emerging technologies; the Panel consists of a plenary panel discussing several relevant issues related to the impact of Web technologies on society. In addition to the tracks and special programs, workshops and tutorials are organized to report on-going work and to provide in-depth knowledge on important subjects; 26 workshops are organized to present contributed papers and several invited speeches; 14 tutorials are organized as lectures by experts. The detailed program is spelled out in the conference proceedings and in the companion proceedings for your future reference.

This conference is the result of the support and dedicated efforts of many individuals and institutions, all of whom are acknowledged in the subsequent pages of these proceedings. We would especially like to thank the authors, speakers, and panelists for providing the excellent technical content of the conference. In shaping the 2015 program, the chairs of the tracks and special programs worked with a large network of program committee members and external reviewers, and their collaboration with the members of the local organizing committee has been invaluable. We would also like to thank our sponsors for their generous financial contributions, and IW3C2, whose guidelines served as a valuable resource in preparing the conference. Special thanks to Wendy Hall, Chair of IW3C2, for her continued support and to Prabhakar Raghavan for his invaluable advice on all aspects of the organization of WWW 2015 that he generously provided as IW3C2 liason; research track co-chairs Chengxiang Zhai, and Krishna Gummadi for handling the large volume of submissions and assembling an excellent research paper program. We also thank the W3C Consortium and its Italian office, and the Institute of Cognitive Sciences and

Technologies of the Italian Research Council. Last but not least, we acknowledge the contribution of Sandra Celoni and Viviana Vitali from Professional Conference Organizer O.I.C. Florence for the highly professional work done on all aspects of the local organization of WWW 2015, as well as the Florence Convention Bureau that bootstrapped the plans for the first Italian WWW in Florence. We hope that this conference will contribute novel insights, valuable experiences, and opportunities to connect with colleagues and collaborators, and that you will have a pleasant time during your stay in Florence.

The WWW 2015 General Chairs

Aldo Gangemi
National Research Council, Italy

Stefano Leonardi
Sapienza University of Rome

Alessandro Panconesi
Sapienza University of Rome

WWW'15 Program Chairs' Welcome

We are delighted to present the technical program of the 24th International World Wide Web Conference (WWW 2015), held from May 18 to 22, 2015 in Florence, Italy. Since its inception in 1994, the International World Wide Web Conference has been the premier venue for researchers, academics, businesses, and standards organizations to convene and discuss the latest Web research and technologies.

This year, we have received a record number of 929 submissions for the research program, distributed over the following 11 Web-related technical areas: (1) Behavior Analysis and Personalization, (2) Crowdsourcing Systems and Social Media, (3) Content Analysis, (4) Internet Economics and Monetization, (5) Pervasive Web and Mobility, (6) Security and Privacy, (7) Semantic Web, (8) Social Networks and Graph Analysis, Web Infrastructure -- Data Centers, (9) Content Delivery Networks, (10) Web Mining, and (11) Web Search Systems and Applications. All submissions underwent a rigorous reviewing process, where at least three expert Program Committee (PC) members reviewed each submission and a fourth expert lead the discussion of the reviews. In total, a highly skilled and diverse team of 554 PC members were involved in the reviewing process and they collectively produced over 3000 reviews. The PC members were recruited by area chairs, who also oversaw the reviewing of the submissions in their area, made initial recommendations to accept or reject the submissions in their area, and participated in a two-day area chair meeting held in Kaiserslautern, Germany. The final acceptance decisions were made at the meeting, where the recommendations of the area chairs were discussed and voted on by all area chairs and the PC chairs. Submissions, where area chairs were conflicted, were handled separately PC chairs. The outcome of the meeting was to accept a total of 131 (14.1%) papers for the research program. We believe that these 131 accepted papers represent some of the best Web-related research conducted over the last year and we are confident that they would lead to fruitful discussions and new ideas at the conference.

It would not have been possible to put together this research program without the tireless efforts of a number of volunteers. We wish to thank everybody who contributed to the technical program, including the authors who submitted papers to WWW 2015, and the area chairs, PC members, and external reviewers who contributed their time and expertise. We extend special thanks to the general chairs Aldo Gangemi, Stefano Leonardi, and Alessandro Panconesi for their constant support and for assembling an excellent organizing team that put together an exciting conference program. We are grateful to the PC Chairs of WWW 2014, particularly Andrei Broder, for sharing their experiences and providing very helpful advice. We hope that both conference attendees and the readers of the proceedings would find the resulting program interesting and rewarding.

Krishna P. Gummadi

WWW 2015 Program Co-Chair
Max Planck Institute for Software Systems
Germany

ChengXiang Zhai

WWW 2015 Program Co-Chair
University of Illinois at Urbana-Champaign
U.S.A.

Table of Contents

WWW 2015 Organization & Committees

GENERAL CHAIRS Aldo Gangemi, National Research Council, Italy & Paris 13 University-CNRS, France
Stefano Leonardi, Sapienza University of Rome, Italy
Alessandro Panconesi, Sapienza University of Rome, Italy

LOCAL ORGANIZING COMMITTEE

W3C TRACK CHAIR Marie-Claire Forgue, W3C, France

PUBLICITY & SOCIAL MEDIA CHAIRS Flavio Chierichetti, Sapienza University of Rome, Italy
Gabriella Pasi, University of Milano-Bicocca, Italy
Daniele Quercia, Yahoo Labs, Barcelona, Spain

WEB PRESENCE CHAIR Aris Anagnostopoulos, Sapienza University of Rome, Italy

PRESS CHAIR Marco Magrini, Florence, Italy

FINANCE CHAIRS Stefano Leonardi, Sapienza University of Rome, Italy
Viviana Vitali, OIC-International Congress Organization, Florence, Italy

REGISTRATION CHAIR Luca Becchetti, Sapienza University of Rome, Italy

SPONSORSHIP CHAIRS Alessandro Panconesi, Sapienza University of Rome, Italy
Paola Velardi, Sapienza University of Rome, Italy

EXHIBITION CHAIRS Aldo Gangemi, National Research Council, Italy & Paris 13 University-CNRS, France
Gioacchino La Vecchia, W3C, Italy

LOCAL ARRANGEMENTS CHAIR Sandra Celoni, OIC-International Congress Organization, Florence, Italy

EVENT MOBILE APPLICATIONS CHAIR Emanuele Panizzi, Sapienza University of Rome, Italy

MARKETING CHAIRS Carlotta Ferrari, Florence Conference Bureau, Florence, Italy
Viviana Vitali, OIC-International Congress Organization, Florence, Italy
Gerry Turano, Rome, Italy

GRAPHICS CHAIR

COLOCATED EVENTS CHAIRS Andrei Broder, Google Inc., USA
Ciro Cattuto, ISI Foundation, Turin, Italy
Stefano Leonardi, Sapienza University of Rome, Italy

PROCEEDINGS AND METADATA CHAIRS
Eva Blomqvist, University of Linköping, Sweden
Paolo Boldi, University of Milano, Italy
Valentina Presutti, National Research Council, Italy
Li Ding, Memect LLC, USA

PANEL CHAIRS
Aris Anagnostopoulos, Sapienza University of Rome, Italy
Fabrizio Silvestri, Yahoo Labs, Barcelona, Spain

VOLUNTEERS CHAIRS
Sebastien Forget, TD Bank, Canada
Nicola Tonellotto, National Research Council, Italy

STUDENT TRAVEL GRANT CHAIRS
Filippo Geraci, National Research Council, Italy
Marco Pellegrini, National Research Council, Italy

Program Committee Members

BEHAVIORAL ANALYSIS AND PERSONALIZATION

Mikhail Ageev, Moscow State University, Russia
Eugene Agichtein, Emory University, USA
Amr Ahmed, Google, USA
Omar Alonso, Microsoft Bing, USA
Jaime Arguello, University of North Carolina at Chapel Hill, USA
Peter Bailey, Microsoft Bing, Australia
Linas Baltrunas, Telefonica Research, Spain
Nicholas Belkin, Rutgers University, USA
Ralf Bierig, Vienna University of Technology, Austria
Peter Brusilovsky, University of Pittsburgh, USA
Pablo Castells, Universidad Autonoma de Madrid, Spain
Ed Chi, Google, USA
Wei Chu, Microsoft Bing, USA
Michael Cole, Rutgers University, USA
Nick Craswell, Microsoft Bing, USA
Paolo Cremonesi, Politecnico di Milano, Italy
Alex Deng, Microsoft Bing, USA
Chabane Djeraba, LIFL, University of Sciences and Technologies of Lille, France
Debora Donato, StumbleUpon, USA
Doug Downey, Northwestern University, USA
Georges Dupret, Yahoo!, USA
Andy Edmonds, Ebay, USA
Carsten Eickhoff, ETHZ, Switzerland
Hui Fang, Nayang Technological University, Singapore
Henry Feild, Endicott College, USA
Qi Guo, Microsoft Bing, USA
Ido Guy, Yahoo!, Israel
Jiawei Han, University of Illinois at Urbana Champaign, USA
Ahmed Hassan Awadallah, Microsoft Research, USA
Victor Hu, Microsoft Bing, USA
Jeff Huang, Brown University, USA
Pan Hui, Hong Kong University of Science and Technology, Hong Kong
Alejandro Jaimes, Yahoo!, Spain
Dieter Jannach, TU Dortmund, Germany
Robert Jäschke, L3S Research Center, Germany
Jiepu Jiang, University of Massachusetts, USA
Rosie Jones, Microsoft, USA
Joemon Jose, University of Glasgow, UK
Bhargav Kanagal, Google, USA
Diane Kelly, University of North Carolina at Chapel Hill, USA
Youngho Kim, University of Massachusetts, USA
Alex Kotov, Wayne State University, USA
Dmitry Lagun, Emory University, USA
Mounia Lalmas, Yahoo!, Spain

BEHAVIORAL ANALYSIS AND PERSONALIZATION (Continued)

Kristen Lefevre, Google, USA
Jingjing Liu, University of South Carolina, USA
Weike Pan, Shenzhen University, China
Dan Pelleg, Yahoo!, Israel
Kira Radinsky, SalesPredict, Israel
Karthik Raman, Cornell University, USA
Oleg Rokhenko, Yahoo!, Israel
Pavel Serdyukov, Yandex, Russia
Milad Shokouhi, Microsoft Bing, UK
Fabrizio Silvestri, Yahoo!, Spain
Mark Smucker, University of Waterloo, Canada
Oren Somekh, Yahoo!, Israel
Markus Strohmaier, University of Koblenz-Landau, Germany
Idan Szpektor, Yahoo!, Israel
Paul Thomas, CSIRO, Australia
Nava Tintarev, University of Aberdeen, UK
Hanghang Tong, CUNY, USA
Robert Villa, University of Sheffield, UK
Jian Wang, LinkedIn, USA
Jun Wang, University College London, UK
Robert West, Stanford University, USA
Emine Yilmaz, University College London, UK
Lanbo Zhang, Twitter, USA
Mi Zhang, Fudan University, China

CROWDSOURCING SYSTEMS AND SOCIAL MEDIA

Jussara Almeida, UFMG
Marcos Baez, University of Trento
Roja Bandari, UCLA
Fabio Casati, University of Trento
Justin Cheng
Michele Coscia, National Research Council, Pisa
Munmun De Choudhury, Georgia Institute of Technology
Yashar Ganjali, University of Toronto
Daniel Gatica-Perez, Idiap and EPFL
Daniel Gayo Avello, University of Oviedo
Werner Geyer, IBM T.J. Watson Research
Manuel Gomez-Rodriguez
Sandra Gonzalez-Bailon, University of Pennsylvania
Bahareh Heravi
Andreas Hotho, University of Wuerzburg
Yun Huang, Syracuse University
Panos Ipeirotis, New York University
Venky Iyer
Anupam Joshi
David Jurgens, McGill University
Brian Keegan, Northeastern University
Emre Kiciman, Microsoft Research

CROWDSOURCING SYSTEMS AND SOCIAL MEDIA (Continued)

Patty Kostkova, City ehealth Research Centre (CeRC), City University, London
Ee-Peng Lim, Singapore Management University
Yu-Ru Lin, University of Pittsburgh
Peter Marbach
Winter Mason, Facebook
Michael Mathioudakis
Julian Mcauley, UC San Diego
Panagiotis Metaxas, Wellesley College
Tanushree Mitra, Georgia Institute of Technology
Andres Monroy-Hernandez
Sue Moon, KAIST
Michael Muller, IBM Research
Aditya Pal, IBM
Stelios Paparizos, Microsoft Research
Walter Quattrociocchi, Labss,Institute of Cognitive Sciences and Technologies
Daniele Quercia, Yahoo Labs
Bruno Ribeiro, Carnegie Mellon University
Daniel Romero, University of Michigan
Derek Ruths, McGill University
Antonio Scala
Anna Squicciarini, The Pennsylvania State University
Markus Strohmaier, University of Koblenz-Landau
Arun Sundararajan, New York University
Siddhart Suri
Maja Vukovic, IBM Research
Claudia Wagner, GESIS-Leibniz Institute for the Social Sciences
Ingmar Weber, Qatar Computing Research Institute
Cong Yu, Google Research
Haiyi Zhu, Carnegie Mellon University

CONTENT ANALYSIS

Steven Bethard, University of Alabama at Birmingham
Yunbo Cao, Microsoft Research Asia
Taylor Cassidy, US Army Research Lab/IBM/CUNY
Wanxiang Che, Harbin Institute of Technology
Zhiyuan Chen, University of Illinois at Chicago
Hsin-Hsi Chen, National Taiwan University
Gao Cong, Nanyang Technological University
Eduard Dragut, Temple University
Koji Eguchi, Kobe University
Anthony Fader, University of Washington
Boi Faltings, EPFL
Radu Florian, IBM TJ Watson Research Center
Ralph Grishman, New York University
Ben Hachey, University of Sydney
Sanda Harabagiu, University of Texas at Dallas
Hongzhao Huang, Rensselaer Polytechnic Institute
Minlie Huang, Tsinghua University
Seung-Won Hwang, POSTECH

CONTENT ANALYSIS (Continued)

Jing Jiang, Singapore Management University
Dan Jurafsky, Stanford University
Wai Lam, The Chinese University of Hong Kong
Hang Li, Huawei Technologies
Fangtao Li, Google Research
Juanzi Li, Tsinghua University
Qi Li, Queens College and Graduate Center, CUNY
Sujian Li, Peking university
Hao Li, Rensselaer Polytechnic Institute
Ee-Peng Lim, Singapore Management University
Chin-Yew Lin, Microsoft Research Asia
Wei Liu, IBM Thomas J. Watson Research Center
Zhiyuan Liu, Tsinghua University
Kang Liu, Institute of Automation, Chinese Academy of Sciences
Ting Liu, Harbin Institute of Technology
David McClosky, IBM Research
Samaneh Moghaddam, Simon Fraser University
Alessandro Moschitti, University of Trento
Vincent Ng, University of Texas at Dallas
Sinno Jialin Pan, i2r, a*star, Singapore
Emily Pitler, Google
Tieyun Qian, Wuhan University
Delip Rao, Johns Hopkins University
Alan Ritter, University of Washington
Hinrich Schütze, University of Munich
Satoshi Sekine, New York University
Benoit Favre, Laboratoire d'Informatique Fondamentale de Marseille
Shuming Shi, Microsoft Research Asia
Kyuseok Shim, Seoul National University
Partha Talukdar, Indian Institute of Science
Yoshimasa Tsuruoka, The University of Tokyo
Benjamin Van Durme, Johns Hopkins University
V.G.Vinod Vydiswaran, University of Michigan
Xiaojun Wan, Peking University
Houfeng Wang, Peking University
Chi Wang, University of Illinois at Urbana-Champaign
Michael Wiegand, Saarland University
Kam-Fai Wong, The Chinese University of Hong Kong
Wei Xu, New York University
Nianwen Xue, Brandeis University
Xin Zhao, Peking University and Singapore Management University
Dongyan Zhao, Peking University
Jun Zhao, Institute of Automation, Chinese Academy of Sciences
Guodong Zhou, Soochow University
Xiaoyan Zhu, Tsinghua University
Imed Zitouni, Microsoft
Chengqing Zong, Institute of Automation, Chinese Academy of Sciences

INTERNET ECONOMICS AND MONETIZATION

Shipra Agrawal, Microsoft Research
Eytan Bakshy, Facebook
Liad Blumrosen, Hebrew University
Pranav Dandekar, Stanford
Xiaotie Deng, Shanghai Jiaotong University
Arpita Ghosh, Cornell
Gagan Goel, Google Research
Paul Goldberg, Oxford
Ralf Herbrich, Amazon
Nicole Immorlica, Microsoft Research
Krishnamurthy Iyer, Cornell
Kamal Jain, eBay Research
Radu Jurca, Google
Peter Key, Microsoft Research
Scott Kominers, Harvard
Vahab Mirrokni, Google
Markus Mobius, Microsoft Research
Hamid Nazerzadeh, USC
David Pennock, Microsoft Research
R. Preston McAfee, Microsoft
Tao Qin, Microsoft Research
Dou Shen, Baidu
Richard Steinberg, London School of Economics
Mukund Sundararajan, Stanford University
Neel Sundaresan, eBay Research
Steve Tadelis, Berkeley
Sergei Vassilvitskii, Google Research
Gabriel Weintraub, Columbia Business Schoo

PERVASIVE WEB AND MOBILITY

Aruna Balasubramian, University of Washington
Maria Ebling, IBM
Romit Roy Choudhury, University of Illinois at Urbana Champaign
Urs Hengartner, University of Waterloo
Wenjun Hu, Yale University
Eyal de Lara, University of Toronto
Cecilia Mascolo, University of Cambridge
Archan Misra, Singapore Management University (SMU)
Rama Ramasubramanian
Lenin Ravindranath Sivalingam, Microsoft Research
Stefan Saroiu, Microsoft Research
Souvik Sen, HP Labs
Matt Welsh, Google
Guoliang Xing, Michigan State University
Lin Zhong, Rice University

SECURITY AND PRIVACY

Davide Balzarotti, Eurecom
Rainer Boehme, University of Münster
Joseph Bonneau, Princeton University
Delphine Christin, University of Bonn
Sergej Dechand, University of Bonn
Tamara Denning, University of Utah
Adam Doupe
Dirk Dr. Wetter, OWASP German Chapter
Serge Egelman, UC Berkeley
Sascha Fahl, Leibniz University Hannover
Bernd Freisleben, University of Marburg
Thorsten Holz, Ruhr-Universität Bochum
Markus Jakobsson, Fatskunk
Suman Jana, University of Texas at Austin
Mike Just, Glasgow Caledonian University
Patrick Gage Kelley, University of New Mexico
Engin Kirda, Northeastern University
Katharina Krombholz, SBA Research
Christopher Kruegel, University of California, Santa Barbara
Zhenkai Liang, National University of Singapore
Heather Lipford, UNC Charlotte
Benjamin Livshits, Microsoft Research
Long Lu, Stony Brook University
Prateek Mittal, Princeton University
Esfandiar Mohammadi, Saarland University
Tyler Moore, Southern Methodist University
Nick Nikiforakis, Stony Brook University
Adrian Perrig, ETH Zurich
Konrad Rieck, University of Göttingen
Elaine Shi, PARC
Kapil Singh, IBM T.J. Watson Research Center
Robin Sommer, ICSI/LBNL
Xiaofeng Wang, Indiana University, USA
Christo Wilson, Northeastern University
Haifeng Yu, National University of Singapore
Mary Ellen Zurko, Cisco Systems

SEMANTIC WEB

Harith Alani, KMi, The Open University
Pramod Anantharam, Kno.e.sis Center
Kemafor Anyanwu, North Carolina State University
Marcelo Arenas, PUC Chile
Lora Aroyo, VU University Amsterdam
Sören Auer, University of Bonn & Fraunhofer IAIS
Isabelle Augenstein, Dept of Computer Science, The University of Sheffield
Sean Bechhofer, University of Manchester
Abraham Bernstein, University of Zurich
Roi Blanco, Yahoo! Research
Pierre-Antoine Champin, LIRIS
Key-Sun Choi, KAIST
Philipp Cimiano, University of Bielefeld
Oscar Corcho, Universidad Politécnica de Madrid
Philippe Cudré-Mauroux, U. of Fribourg
Claudia D'Amato, University of Bari
Mathieu D'Aquin, Knowledge Media Institute, the Open University
Brian Davis, DERI NUIG
Miriam Fernandez, Knowledge Media Institute
Lorenz Fischer, University of Zurich
Fabien Gandon, Inria
Paul Groth, VU University Amsterdam
Tudor Groza, School of ITEE, The University of Queensland
Andreas Harth, AIFB, Karlsruhe Institute of Technology
Tom Heath, Open Data Institute
Aidan Hogan, DCC, Universidad de Chile
Matthew Horridge, Stanford University
Lalana Kagal, MIT
Pavel Klinov, University of Ulm
Jacek Kopecky, University of Portsmouth
Spyros Kotoulas, IBM Research
Freddy Lecue, IBM Research
David Martin, SRI International
Diana Maynard, University of Sheffield
Robert Meusel, University of Mannheim
Dunja Mladenic, Jozef Stefan Institute
Axel-Cyrille Ngonga Ngomo, University of Leipzig
Nadeschda Nikitina, Oxford University
Josiane Parreira, Siemens
Peter Patel-Schneider, Nuance
Terry Payne, University of Liverpool
Dimitris Plexousakis, Institute of Computer Science, FORTH
Axel Polleres, Vienna University of Economics and Business – WU Wien
Valentina Presutti, STLab (ISTC-CNR)
Guilin Qi, Southeast University
Riccardo Rosati, DIS, Sapienza Universita' di Roma

SEMANTIC WEB (Continuied)

Manuel Salvadores, Stanford University
Cristina Sarasua, Universität Koblenz – Landau
Uli Sattler, University of Manchester
Ansgar Scherp, Kiel University and Leibniz Information Center for Economics, Kiel, Germany
Stefan Schlobach, Vrije Universiteit Amsterdam
Daniel Schwabe, Dept. of Informatics, PUC-Rio
Oshani Seneviratne, Massachusetts Institute of Technology
Juan F. Sequeda, Dept of Computer Science, The University of Texas at Austin
Amit Sheth, Wright State
Elena Simperl, University of Southampton
Kavitha Srinivas, IBM Research
Steffen Staab, University of Koblenz-Landau
Gerd Stumme,
Hideaki Takeda, National Institute of Informatics
Kerry Taylor, CSIRO & Australian National University
Raphaël Troncy, EURECOM
Tania Tudorache, Stanford University
Giovanni Tummarello, DERI, National University of Ireland galway
Jacopo Urbani, Vrije Universiteit Amsterdam
Victoria Uren, Aston University
Jacco van Ossenbruggen, CWI & VU University Amsterdam
Ruben Verborgh, Ghent University – iMinds
Johanna Völker, University of Mannheim
Chris Welty, IBM Research
Amapali Zaveri, AKSW Group, University of Leipzig
Antoine Zimmermann, École des Mines de Saint-Étienne

SOCIAL NETWORKS AND GRAPH ANALYSIS

Bruno Abrahao, Cornell University
Yong-Yeol Ahn, Indiana University Bloomington
Luca Maria Aiello, Yahoo Labs
Leman Akoglu, Stony Brook University
Aris Anagnostopoulos, Sapienza University of Rome
Luca Becchetti, University of Rome "La Sapienza"
Fabricio Benevenuto, Federal University of Minas Gerais
Paolo Boldi, Università degli Studi di Milano
Francesco Bonchi, Yahoo! Research
Ceren Budak, UCSB
James Caverlee, Texas A&M University
Yang Chen, Duke University
Wei Chen, Microsoft Research Asia
Hong Cheng, The Chinese University of Hong Kong
Aaron Clauset, University of Colorado Boulder
Gao Cong, Nanyang Technological University
Yafei Dai, Peking University
Atish Das Sarma, eBay Research Labs

SOCIAL NETWORKS AND GRAPH ANALYSIS (Continued)

Anirban Dasgupta, Purdue University
Emilio Ferrara, Indiana University Bloomington
Pierre Fraigniaud, CNRS and University of Paris 7
Sabrina Gaito, Università degli Studi di Milano
Aristides Gionis, Aalto University
Bruno Gonçalves, Aix-Marseille Université
Amit Goyal, University of Maryland
Stephan Günnemann, Carnegie Mellon University
Jake Hofman, Microsoft Research
Panos Kalnis, King Abdullah University of Science and Technology
Ioannis Koutis, University of Puerto Rico-Rio Piedras
Ponnurangam Kumaraguru, IIITD
Haewoon Kwak, QCRI
Theodoros Lappas, Stevens Institute of Technology
Matthieu Latapy, CNRS
Silvio Lattanzi, Google
Kristina Lerman, University of Southern California
David Liben-Nowell, Carleton College
Yu-Ru Lin, University of Pittsburgh
Nelly Litvak, University of Twente
Mohammad Mahdian, Google
Michael Mahoney, Stanford University
Madhav Marathe, Virginia Tech
Vahab Mirrokni, Google Research
Alan Mislove, Northeastern University
Sebastian Moreno, Purdue University
Mirco Musolesi, University of Birmingham
Alice Oh, KAIST
Ali Pinar, Sandia National Laboratories
Derek Ruths, McGill University
Alessandra Sala, Alcatel-Lucent Bell Labs
Grant Schoenebeck, University of Michigan
Aneesh Sharma, Twitter
Mauro Sozio, Télécom ParisTech
Nikolaj Tatti, Aalto University
Evimaria Terzi, Boston University
Panayiotis Tsaparas, University of Ioannina
Charalampos Tsourakakis, Carnegie Mellon University
Johan Ugander, Cornell University
Antti Ukkonen, Helsinki Institute for Information Technology
Sebastiano Vigna, University of Milan
Sarita Yardi Schoenebeck, University of Michigan
Georgios Zervas, Boston University School of Management
Ben Zhao, UC Santa Barbara
Heather Zheng, UC Santa Barbara

WEB INFRASTRUCTURE: DATACENTERS, CONTENT DELIVERY NETWORKS, AND CLOUD COMPUTING

Mahesh Balakrishnan
Paolo Costa, Microsoft Research
Flavio Junqueira, Microsoft Research
Evangelia Kalyvianaki, City University London
Wyatt Lloyd, USC / Facebook
Jacob R. Lorch, Microsoft Research
Derek Murray, Unaffiliated
Peter Pietzuch, Imperial College London
Pablo Rodriguez, Telefonica
Marco Serafini, Qatar Computing Research Institute
Alexander Shraer, Google
Yee Jiun Song, Facebook
Bernard Wong, University of Waterloo

WEB MINING

Charu Aggarwal, IBM
Azin Ashkan, Technicolor Labs
Timothy Baldwin, The University of Melbourne
Roberto Bayardo, Google Research
Michael Bendersky, Google, Inc.
Mikhail Bilenko, Microsoft
Rui Cai, Microsoft Research, Asia
Vineet Chaoji, Amazon
Ovi Dan, Microsoft
Dennis Fetterly
Qi He, LinkedIn
Liangjie Hong, Yahoo! Labs
Xia (Ben) Hu, Arizona State University
Daxin Jiang, Microsoft Research Asia
Yunliang Jiang, Twitter
Arnd Christian König, Microsoft Research
Yehuda Koren, Google
Wai Lam, The Chinese University of Hong Kong
Hady Lauw, Singapore Management University
Chengkai Li, University of Texas at Arlington
Huan Liu, Professor, Arizona State University
Yue Lu, Twitter Inc.
Michael Lyu, the Chinese University of Hong Kong
Hao Ma, Microsoft Research
Yutaka Matsuo, University of Tokyo
Srujana Merugu, Amazon
Dunja Mladenic, Jozef Stefan Institute
Bamshad Mobasher, DePaul University
Arjun Mukherjee, University of Illinois, Chicago
Olfa Nasraoui, University of Louisville
Alexandros Ntoulas, Zynga
Spiros Papadimitriou, Rutgers University

WEB MINING (Continued)

Srinivasan Parthasarathy
Jian Pei, Simon Fraser University
Simone Paolo Ponzetto, University of Mannheim
Naren Ramakrishnan, Virginia Tech
Rajeev Rastogi, Yahoo!
Tamas Sarlos, Google
H. Andrew Schwartz, University of Pennsylvania
Myra Spiliopoulou, U. Magdeburg
Yizhou Sun, Northeastern University
Neel Sundaresan, eBay Research Labs
Chenhao Tan, Cornell University
Jian Tang, Peking University
Cindi Thompson
Masashi Toyoda, University of Tokyo
Jianyong Wang, Tsinghua University
Ke Wang, Simon Fraser University
Jian Wang, LinkedIn Corporation
Hongning Wang, Dept of Computer Science at University of Virginia
Shuang-Hong Yang, Twitter Inc.
Philip Yu, University of Illinois at Chicago
Jeffery Xu Yu, Dept of Systems Engineering & Engineering Management, Chinese University of Hong Kong
Zhe Zhao, University of Michigan, Ann Arbor
Feida Zhu, Singapore Management University

WEB SEARCH SYSTEMS AND APPLICATIONS

James Allan, UMass Amherst, USA
Omar Alonso, Microsoft, USA
Ziv Bar-Yossef, Google, Israel
Behshad Behzadi, Google, Swizerland
Edward Bortnikov, Yahoo Labs, Israel
B. Barla Cambazoglu, Yahoo Labs, Spain
Kevin Chang, University of Illinois at Urbana-Champaign, USA
Xueqi Cheng, Chinese Academy of Sciences, China
Arjen de Vries, CWI, Netherlands
Fernando Diaz, Microsoft Research, USA
Marcus Fontoura, Google, USA
C. Lee Giles, Pennsylvania State University, USA
Nadav Golbandi, Yahoo Labs, USA
Luis Gravano, Columbia University, USA
Maxim Gurevich, RelateIQ, USA
Xu Hongbo, Chinese Academy of Sciences, China
Xuanjing Huang, Fudan University, China
Amruta Joshi, UCLA, USA
Jaap Kamps, University of Amsterdam, Netherlands
Oren Kurland, Technion – Israel Institute of Technology, Israel
Rui Li, University of Illinois at Urbana-Champaign, USA

WEB SEARCH SYSTEMS AND APPLICATIONS (Comtinued)

Ee-Peng Lim, Singapore Management University, Singapore
Hongfei Lin, Dalian University of Technology, China
Wei-Ying Ma, Microsoft Research, China
Ilya Markov, University of Lugano, Switzerland
Wolfgang Nejdl, Leibniz Universität Hannover, Germany
Hua Ouyang, Yahoo Labs, USA
Uri Schonfeld, Yahoo Labs, USA
Torsten Suel New York University, USA
Neel Sundaresan, eBay Research Labs, USA
Stratis Viglas, University of Edinburgh, UK
Wouter Weerkamp, 904Labs, Netherlands
Michael Welch, UCLA, USA
Ran Wolff, Yahoo Labs, Israel
Makoto Yamada, Yahoo Labs, USA
Hengshuai Yao, University of Alberta, Canada
Emine Yilmaz, Microsoft Research, UK
Min Zhang, Tsinghua University, China

The Web as a Jungle: Non-Linear Dynamical Systems for Co-evolving Online Activities

Yasuko Matsubara
Kumamoto University
yasuko@cs.kumamoto-u.ac.jp

Yasushi Sakurai
Kumamoto University
yasushi@cs.kumamoto-u.ac.jp

Christos Faloutsos
Carnegie Mellon University
christos@cs.cmu.edu

ABSTRACT

Given a large collection of co-evolving online activities, such as searches for the keywords "Xbox", "PlayStation" and "Wii", how can we find patterns and rules? Are these keywords related? If so, are they competing against each other? Can we forecast the volume of user activity for the coming month?

We conjecture that online activities compete for user attention in the same way that species in an ecosystem compete for food. We present ECOWEB, (i.e., Ecosystem on the Web), which is an intuitive model designed as a non-linear dynamical system for mining large-scale co-evolving online activities. Our second contribution is a novel, *parameter-free*, and *scalable* fitting algorithm, ECOWEB-FIT, that estimates the parameters of ECOWEB.

Extensive experiments on real data show that ECOWEB is *effective*, in that it can capture long-range dynamics and meaningful patterns such as seasonalities, and *practical*, in that it can provide accurate long-range forecasts. ECOWEB consistently outperforms existing methods in terms of both accuracy and execution speed.

Categories and Subject Descriptors: H.2.8 [**Database management**]: Database applications–*Data mining*

Keywords: Ecosystem; Time-series; Non-linear; Parameter-free;

1. INTRODUCTION

The increasing volume of online user activity represents a vital new opportunity for data scientists and analysts to measure the collective behavior of social, economic, and other important evolutions [57, 56, 27, 13].

Given real-time, online user activity sequences, such as the search volume for the keywords "Xbox" and "PlayStation", how can we find patterns and rules to perform, e.g., sociological, behavioral, and even marketing research? If we know nothing about the sequences, we could (and should) try using Fourier, Wavelets, AR, Kalman filters and the other time series analysis tools. However, we are told that the sequences correspond to online user activity (e.g. the search volume for a keyword) — Can we do better than the existing methods?

This is exactly the idea behind our work. We conjecture that the volume per keyword/activity will behave like a species in an "ecosystem". It will compete with other species for food and also exhibit seasonal behavior. Here we propose that "food" corresponds to user resources: given a set of users and their resources (e.g., attention, time, money), the d keywords/activities compete for the user resources.

In this paper, we present an intuitive model, namely ECOWEB, which provides a good description of large collections of co-evolving online activities. [1] In short, the problem we wish to solve is as follows:

INFORMAL PROBLEM 1. *Given a large collection of co-evolving sequences $X = \{\boldsymbol{x}_1, \cdots, \boldsymbol{x}_d\}$, which consists of d keywords/activities of duration n, where each record $x_i(t)$ corresponds to a user activity (e.g., queries, time/dollars spent) for keyword i at time tick t, we want to*

- *detect competition (e.g., "Xbox" vs. "PlayStation")*
- *find seasonal events (e.g., Christmas, summer vacations)*
- *forecast future dynamics*

Preview of our results. Figure 1 shows our discoveries related to the video game industry consisting of $d = 4$ activities, namely, the search volumes for "Xbox" ($\boldsymbol{x}_1$), "PS2, PS3" ($\boldsymbol{x}_2$), "Wii" ($\boldsymbol{x}_3$), and "Android" ($\boldsymbol{x}_4$), taken from *Google*, [2] and spanning over a decade (2004-2014), with weekly measurements. ECOWEB discovered the following important patterns:

- *Long-term fitting:* Figure 1 (a) shows the original volume of the four activities/keywords as circles, and our fitted model as solid lines. Notice that our fit is even visually very good, and it detects seasonalities and up- or down-trends: For example, our model fitted the success of "Wii" (which launched in 2006 and apparently drew attention from the competing "Xbox"). Similarly, it fitted the fall in the popularity of "Wii" in 2011, which coincided with the ascent of "Android", possibly indicating that mobile and social games attracted the attention of Wii gamers.
- *Interspecies interaction:* Recently, video games have been facing increasing competition (from online/social games), and our model automatically identifies this latent competition: Figure 1 (b) shows the interaction network that captures the interaction between the four activities/keywords. Edges indicate interaction/competition between two keywords; the thicker the edge, the stronger the interaction. For example, the red edge from "Wii" to "Android" indicates that the latter is drawing attention away from "Wii". Similarly, "Xbox" has strong connections to "PlayStation" and "Wii" (blue edges), summarizing the fact that the attention for "Xbox" was anti-correlated with "Wii" and "PlayStation", during 2007-2010.

[1] Available at
http://www.cs.kumamoto-u.ac.jp/~yasuko/software.html
[2] http://www.google.com/trends/

WWW 2015, May 18–22, 2015, Florence, Italy.
ACM 978-1-4503-3469-3/15/05.
http://dx.doi.org/10.1145/2736277.2741092.

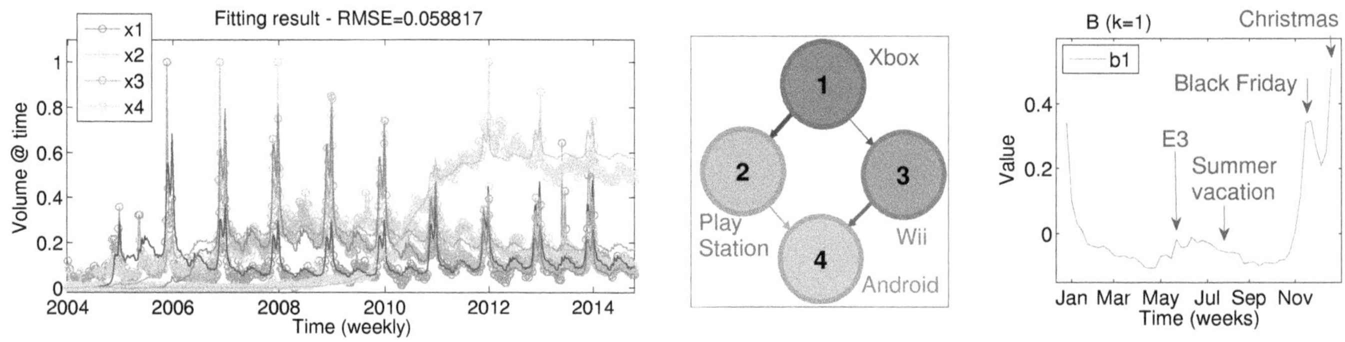

(a) Fitting result (solid lines) vs. original data (in circles) (b) Interaction network (c) seasonal activities

Figure 1: Modeling power of EcoWeb: (a) Our model (solid lines) fits the original data (in circles) very well, and (b) it reveals latent interaction networks, such as "Xbox" vs. "PlayStation" and "Wii" vs. "Android", as well as (c) seasonal activities (i.e., they all peak on Black Friday and at Christmas). Moreover, our fitting algorithm is *fully automatic*, requiring no user intervention.

- *Seasonal activities:* Figure 1 (c) succinctly summarizes the seasonality of all four keywords. There is a clear yearly periodicity, with peaks every November ("Black Friday") and December (Christmas); a small peak in June (coinciding with the Electronic Entertainment Expo (E3), an annual trade show for video games); and sustained, medium-level activity during the summer vacations.

Contributions. We propose EcoWeb, a succinct, yet powerful model, which is inspired by the competition between biological species, and which captures the evolution of multiple online activities. EcoWeb has the following desirable properties:

1. **Effective**: EcoWeb captures long-range dynamics, important patterns and seasonalities that agree with human intuition.
2. **Automatic**: EcoWeb-Fit requires no training set, no parameters to tune, no user intervention.
3. **Scalable**: It is carefully designed to be linear on the input size.
4. **Practical**: It can provide long-term forecasting, outperforming existing methods (Sections 6 and 7).

Outline. The rest of the paper is organized in the conventional way: Section 2 discusses related work and Section 3 describes some fundamental concepts. In Section 4 and Section 5, we describe our proposed model and algorithms. Sections 6 and 7 describe our experimental results and applications. We conclude in section 8.

2. RELATED WORK

The related work falls into the following large subgroups:

Similarity search and forecasting: There is a lot of interest in mining time series and data streams [42, 1, 20, 53, 11, 48]. Traditional approaches applied to data mining include auto-regression (AR), linear dynamical systems (LDS), Kalman filters (KF) and their variants [18, 30, 51]. Similarity search and pattern discovery in time sequences have also attracted huge interest [52, 25, 50, 48, 9].

Large-scale sequence mining: Here, TriMine [33] is a scalable method for forecasting co-evolving multiple (thousands of) sequences, while, FUNNEL [35] is a non-linear model for spatially coevolving epidemic tensors. [32] developed a fully-automatic mining algorithm for co-evolving sequences. Rakthanmanon et al. [46] proposed a similarity search algorithm for "trillions of time series" under the DTW distance. Yang et al. [55] developed a new model for mining time-evolving event sequences. As regards parameter-free mining, the work in [5, 7] focused on summarization and clustering based on the MDL principle.

Table 1: Capabilities of approaches. Only our approach meets all specifications.

	LV	DWT	AR++	AutoPlait	EcoWeb
Domain knowledge	√				√
Co-evolution	√			√	√
Periodicity		√	√	√	√
Parameter free				√	√
Forecasting			√		√

Social media analysis: Analyses of social media and online user behavior has attracted considerable interest [44, 24, 22, 49, 31, 10, 28, 3]. Gruhl et al. [15] explored online "chatter" (e.g., blogging) activity, and measured the actual sales ranks on Amazon.com. Ginsberg et al. [13] examined a large number of search engine queries tracking influenza epidemics. They reported that the evolutions of search engine keywords are highly correlated with actual flu virus activity. The work reported in [8, 45, 14] studied keyword volume, to predict consumer behavior.

Spikes and propagation: The work in [34] studied the rise and fall patterns in the information diffusion process through online social media. The work in [12] investigated the effect of revisits on content popularity, while [47] focused on the daily number of active users. Prakash et al. [43] described a case where two competing products/ideas spreading over the network, and provided a theoretical analysis of the propagation model (winner takes all: WTA) for arbitrary graph topology.

Economic models: Leontief [26] developed the "input-output model", which represents an economy as d interdependent industries (i.e., sectors). This model represents an economy as a system of equations, with producer-consumer relationships (analogous to prey-predator equations).

Contrast with competitors. Table 1 illustrates the relative advantages of our method. Only our EcoWeb matches all requirements, while,

- The Lotka-Volterra (LV) model [36], the logistic function (LF) [6], the susceptible-infected (SI) model [2], and other non-linear equations [17, 38, 43, 35] incorporate domain knowledge, however, they are not intended to capture co-evolving user activities and seasonal patterns.
- Wavelets and Fourier transforms (i.e., DWT, DFT, DCT) focus on a single time sequence, and cannot detect interaction between multiple co-evolving sequences.
- The traditional AR, ARIMA and related forecasting methods including AWSOM [40], PLiF [30] and TriMine [33] are *fundamentally* unsuitable for our setting, because they are based

on linear equations, while we employ *non*-linear equations. Moreover, (a) they can not incorporate domain knowledge, and (b) most of them require parameter tuning.

- AUTOPLAIT [32], SWAB [21] and pHMM [54] have the ability to capture the dynamics of sequences and perform segmentation, however, they cannot model the long-range evolution of multiple time series.

In short, none of the existing methods focuses specifically on the automatic mining of non-linear dynamics in co-evolving online activities.

3. BACKGROUND - ECOLOGICAL CONSIDERATIONS

Let us consider a biological ecosystem by analogy with a jungle where herbivores feed on plants, carnivores feed on other animals, and so on. How many spider monkeys should we expect to have in the next time tick, given the current count of spider monkeys, bananas, squirrel monkeys, etc? This is exactly the focus of population ecology, namely, to develop mathematical models to predict the evolution of the population of each species [39, 38].

Competition between species. There are two major mechanisms that the equations try to model: (a) un-restricted growth, i.e., with infinite resources, every squirrel monkey generates r offspring in each time tick, and (b) competition, i.e., with finite resources, the "carrying capacity" K of the environment is the maximum number of squirrel monkeys it can support.

There is competition between the members of the same species (two squirrel monkeys competing for fruit), as well as between different species (e.g., squirrel monkey vs. spider monkey, all competing for fruit). This competition is what keeps the population size of a species from exploding exponentially: If an ecosystem has too many squirrel monkeys and too few fruits, competition for those resources increases, throttling the growth of the squirrel monkey population.

One of the simplest models that captures the above phenomena is the Lotka-Volterra population model of competition [37]. It describes the interaction of d species with the following non-linear differential equations:

$$\frac{dP_i}{dt} = r_i P_i \left(1 - \frac{\sum_{j=1}^{d} a_{ij} P_j}{K_i}\right), \quad (i = 1, 2, \dots, d) \qquad (1)$$

where,

- P_i: Population size of species i.
- r_i: Intrinsic growth rate of species i, i.e., the rate of reproduction in the absence of density regulation ($r_i \geq 0$).
- K_i: Carrying capacity of species i when the other species are absent ($K_i \geq 0$).
- a_{ii}: Intraspecies competition, i.e., competition for resources between members of the same population ($a_{ii} = 1$).
- a_{ij}: Interspecies competition, i.e., competition between two different species ($a_{ij} \geq 0$).

Here, time t is considered continuous and dP_i/dt is the derivative. For each species i, the number of offspring per parent increases linearly with the size of the current population P_i, and it corresponds to the intrinsic growth rate r_i.

In the Lotka-Volterra equation, it is assumed that multiple (i.e., d) species are competing for some common resources. For example, Figure 2 (a) shows the interaction between wild animals in the jungle. [3] Assume that these species share some of the resources (e.g., fruits). The number of individuals using the resources of species i can be described as: $a_{i1}P_1 + \cdots a_{ij}P_j \cdots P_i + \cdots a_{id}P_d = \sum_{j=1}^{d} a_{ij}P_j$. Here, $a_{ij} (i \neq j)$ is called "interspecies competition", which measures the effect an individual of species j has on an individual of species i. [4]

[3] Image courtesy of xura, criminalatt, David Castillo Dominici, happykanppy at FreeDigitalPhotos.net.

4. PROPOSED MODEL

In this section, we present our proposed model, namely, ECOWEB. Consider that we have a collection of activity volumes X of d keywords, with duration n. That is, we have $X = \{\boldsymbol{x}_1, \cdots, \boldsymbol{x}_i, \cdots, \boldsymbol{x}_d\}$, where $\boldsymbol{x}_i$ is a sequence of keyword i, (i.e., $\boldsymbol{x}_i = \{x_i(t)\}_{t=1}^{n}$). Given a set of co-evolving time series X, our goal is to (a) capture the evolutions of X, (b) find the hidden relationship between each sequence, and (c) forecast future dynamics.

So, how can we describe the evolutions of multiple keywords, and spot interactions between two different keywords? What exactly is the relationship, say, between Xbox and Wii, or Facebook and LinkedIn? Are there any differences or similarities? Do they compete with each other, like wild animals?

Ecosystem on the web - intuition behind our model. So, what is an ecosystem on the web? Can we find similar phenomena in virtual communities? If so, what kind of species live on the web? How does the population size of each species evolve over time? — Our answers are that: (a) there are an infinite number of "virtual species" living on the web (as in a "jungle"), and (b) they evolve naturally over time by interacting with other species.

Figure 2 (b) shows an ecosystem on the web. Similar to the biological community, which consists of multiple species (e.g., monkeys and macaws, as shown in Figure 2 (a)), there is a community of virtual species on the web (e.g., Xbox and PlayStation, as shown in Figure 2 (b)).

Here, we provide two important analogies with respect to the ecosystem on the web.

- **Keyword/activity (i.e., species)**: No keyword can survive on the web if no one is paying attention to that topic. It behaves like a living organism. The relationship between keywords and users (e.g., between Wii and kids) is similar to the relationship between species and food resources (e.g., between squirrel monkeys and fruits or between capybaras and grass). No species can survive without resources.
- **User resources (i.e., food resources)**: Similar to an ecological system, there are a finite number of users and their resources on the web. The user resources could be anything, such as user interest/attention, or an amount of the time and money they spend. Users cannot use their time/money for multiple purposes simultaneously. [5] As shown in Figure 2 (b), there are some groups of users, such as kids, teenagers and adults. For example, kids love video games, e.g., Xbox, PlayStation and Wii, while most adults prefer Android.

Although important, the above analogies are not immediately applicable to our setting. We need a few more concepts. Specifically, we want to describe the following three properties:

- **(G1)**: Non-linear evolution of keywords/activities
- **(G2)**: Interaction coefficients between keywords
- **(G3)**: Seasonality of user activities

[4] There are several variations of the Lotka-Volterra model, e.g., the predator-prey/parasitism model. However, in this paper, we only focus on the simplest case where $a_{ij} \geq 0$ $(i \neq j)$ for all species i and j (i.e., neutralism/amensalism/competition).

[5] For example, given N users, there are $N \times 24$ hours/resources per day, or fewer, depending on the keyword and the demographic group it appeals to.

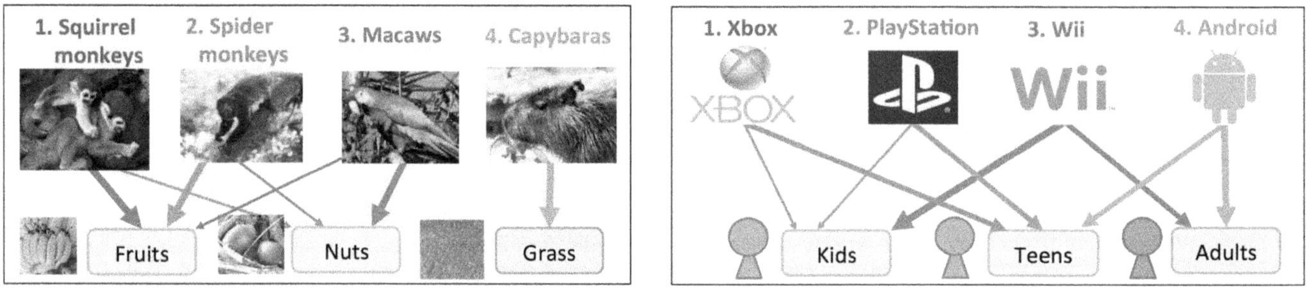

(a) Ecosystem in the jungle (b) Ecosystem on the web

Figure 2: Illustration of jungle vs. web: (a) Ecosystem in the jungle (e.g., Amazon rainforest): squirrel monkeys partially share their food with spider monkeys and macaws, while capybaras are isolated (i.e., they have no competitors here); (b) Ecosystem on the web (e.g., game industry): the main targets of Xbox, PlayStation and Wii are kids and teenagers, while most adults are interested in Android games rather than Xbox and PlayStation.

Table 2: Analogy: Jungle vs. web.

Jungle	Web
Species (e.g., squirrel monkeys)	Keywords/activities (e.g., Wii/Xbox)
Food resources (e.g., fruits)	User resources (e.g., kids/adults)
Population	Popularity
Climate/season	Annual events (e.g., Christmas)

In a real ecosystem, the population of each species varies continuously over time. It depends on the reproduction rate per generation and the number of offspring produced in a lifetime by each individual. The same thing happens on the web: the popularity size of each keyword evolves over time. The popularity size corresponds to the aggregated volume of each user interest/attention. If a new product (say, Android) is attractive, the users would spend more time on it, or recommend it to their friends. Similarly, their friends would influence other users, and eventually, this would lead to an exponential growth in popularity size. To handle (**G1**), we propose using a non-linear difference equation.

For (**G2**), we assume that there are latent interactions between two different keywords. For example, in Figure 1 (a), the sequences of Xbox (i.e., $\boldsymbol{x}_1$) and PlayStation (i.e., $\boldsymbol{x}_2$) behave in opposite ways: When the volume of PlayStation increases, the volume of Xbox decreases considerably (please see Figure 1 (a) from 2007 to 2010). That is, there must be competition/interaction between these two keywords.

We should also note that online activities have certain annual patterns, i.e., seasonality (**G3**). For example, in Figure 1 (a), all the sequences have a huge spike at Christmas. This is because the users modulate their activities based on a yearly cycle. Similar behavior is observed with wild animals in that their activities may depend on climate and season.

Table 2 describes our basic analogy, namely, the jungle ecosystem applied to the web. We conjecture that users of the web behave in the same way as wild animals in the jungle in that they interact and compete with each other for resources.

Next, we introduce our model in steps of increasing complexity.

4.1 EcoWeb-individual (G1)

We begin with the simplest case, where we have a single sequence/keyword, i.e., there is no interspecies interaction/competition.

Let K be the quantity of available user resources that might be used (i.e., paid attention) as regards this keyword, and p represent the quantity of user resources that have already been used as regards this keyword at time tick $t = 0$ (i.e., initial condition).

In our model, we assume that the keyword/activity follows some very simple local rules:

Table 3: Symbols and definitions.

Symbol	Definition
d	Number of unique keywords/activities (i.e., species)
n	Duration of sequences
X	d co-evolving time sequences (i.e., $X = \{\boldsymbol{x}_1, \ldots, \boldsymbol{x}_d\}$)
$\boldsymbol{x}_i$	Sequence of keyword i (i.e., $\boldsymbol{x}_i = \{x_i(1), \ldots, x_i(n)\}$)
$x_i(t)$	Volume of keyword i at time tick t
$P_i(t)$	Popularity size of keyword i at time tick t
$C_i(t)$	Estimated volume of keyword i at time tick t
$\boldsymbol{p}$	Initial popularity size i.e., $\{p_i\}_{i=1}^{d}$
$\boldsymbol{r}$	Growth rate i.e., $\{r_i\}_{i=1}^{d}$
$\boldsymbol{K}$	Carrying capacity i.e., $\{K_i\}_{i=1}^{d}$
$\mathbf{A}$	Interaction matrix ($d \times d$) i.e., $\mathbf{A} = \{a_{ij}\}_{i,j=1}^{d,d}$
n_p	Period (i.e., 52 weeks)
k	Number of hidden seasonalities
$\mathbf{E}$	Seasonal activities ($d \times n$) i.e., $\mathbf{E} = \{e_i(t)\}_{i,t=1}^{d,n}$
$\mathbf{W}$	Participation matrix ($d \times k$) i.e., $\mathbf{W} = \{w_{ij}\}_{i,j=1}^{d,k}$
$\mathbf{B}$	Seasonality matrix ($k \times n_p$) i.e., $\mathbf{B} = \{b_j(\tau)\}_{j,\tau=1}^{k,n_p}$

- It maintains its current popularity size (i.e., user attention) unless there is intra/interspecies competition.
- For each time tick t, it obtains new user resources, and the popularity size increases by a constant percentage r.

Let $P(t)$ be the popularity size of the keyword at time tick t. The evolution of a single keyword is described by the following difference equation:

$$P(t+1) = P(t)\left[1 + r\left(1 - \frac{P(t)}{K}\right)\right], \tag{2}$$

with the initial condition $P(0) = p$, where,

- $P(t)$: Popularity size of the keyword at time tick t, i.e., the aggregated volume of user attention to the keyword. [6]
- p: Initial condition, i.e., popularity size at time tick $t = 0$.
- r: growth rate, i.e., the attractiveness/strength (i.e., impact) of the keyword.
- K: Carrying capacity, i.e., maximum popularity size of the keyword (= available user resources).

Note that the term: $\left[1 + r\left(1 - \frac{P(t)}{K}\right)\right]$ corresponds to the contribution of the current popularity to the next popularity growth, where $\left(1 - \frac{P(t)}{K}\right)$ is the percentage of available user resources for the keyword at time tick t. If the keyword runs out of user re-

[6] In this paper, we assume that $P(t)$ is the popularity density of a keyword, i.e., $0 \leq P(t) \leq 1$, however, our equations can also handle other settings, such as the actual numbers of keyword appearances.

sources (i.e., $P(t) = K$), the expanding popularity will hit a constraint. Also note that Equation 2 is a discrete version of the Lotka-Volterra differential equation, (Equation 1), when it has a single species ($d = 1$).

4.2 EcoWeb-interaction (G2)

We now move on to the next step, namely, spotting an interaction between co-evolving keywords (**G2**). In general, some keywords are competing for some common user resources. Obviously, there is some kind of competition between video game consoles, such as Xbox and PlayStation. Most users choose one of the consoles based on their preferences (e.g., price and available game titles).

MODEL 1 (ECOWEB-INTERACTION). *Let $P_i(t)$ be the popularity size of keyword i at time tick t. Our interaction model is governed by the following equations,*

$$P_i(t+1) = P_i(t)\left[1 + r_i\left(1 - \frac{\sum_{j=1}^{d} a_{ij}P_j(t)}{K_i}\right)\right], \quad (i = 1, \cdots, d), \quad (3)$$

where, $r_i > 0, K_i > 0, a_{ii} = 1, a_{ij} \geq 0$, and $P_i(0) = p_i$.

In Model 1, it is assumed that competing keywords share some of the same user resources. At time tick t, the percentage of potential (i.e., available) user resources for keyword i [7] can be described as,

$$\left(1 - \frac{\sum_{j=1}^{d} a_{ij}P_j(t)}{K_i}\right), \quad (4)$$

where, a_{ij} is the interaction coefficient, which describes the effect rate of keyword j on keyword i.

Please note that if there is no interspecies interaction/competition, (that is, $a_{ij} = 0\ (i \neq j)$), this model is identical to Equation 2 (i.e., "neutralism"). In contrast, if $a_{ij} = a_{ji} = 1$ for keywords i, j, this means that two keywords i, j compete with each other, by sharing exactly the same user resource group. If $a_{ij} = 1, a_{ji} = 0$, the model describes an asymmetric competitive interaction, which is known as "amensalism". In this case, keyword i is strongly affected by keyword j, while keyword j is almost unaffected by keyword i.

EXAMPLE 1. *Figure 1 (b) shows the interaction between $d = 4$ keywords, where we have an interaction matrix:*

$$\mathbf{A} = \begin{bmatrix} 1 & 0.5 & 0.1 & 0 \\ 0 & 1 & 0 & 0.1 \\ 0 & 0 & 1 & 0.3 \\ 0 & 0 & 0 & 1 \end{bmatrix}.$$

Here, Xbox $\boldsymbol{x}_1$ is affected by PlayStation $\boldsymbol{x}_2$, (i.e., $a_{12} = 0.5$) and Wii $\boldsymbol{x}_3$, (i.e., $a_{13} = 0.1$), while PlayStation and Wii are affected by Android $\boldsymbol{x}_4$, (i.e., $a_{24} = 0.1$, $a_{34} = 0.3$). Xbox and Android do not interact directly with each other (i.e., $a_{14} = a_{41} = 0$).

4.3 With seasonality (G3)

Thus far, we have discussed how to describe the long-range dynamics of d co-evolving sequences. Although important, it is not sufficient to capture the real keyword evolutions. Each keyword (e.g., Xbox and Amazon) always has a certain number of users (i.e., popularity), however, the users change their behavior dynamically, according to various seasonal events (e.g., Amazon.com has many visitors on Black Friday). We can observe similar behavior in an ecological system, where activities depend on season and climate: for example, most monkeys are active during warm and sunny days, while they sleep at night. Most importantly, these activities are often correlated with other related species/keywords, e.g., the sales of most retailers including Amazon peak on Black Friday. That is, there must be some groups of "hidden" seasonal activities, (e.g., seasonal retail sales).

So how can we reflect this phenomenon in our equation? We want a powerful yet simple model that can capture seasonal patterns (**G3**) in real co-evolving sequences, as well as long-range non-linear evolutions. We provide an answer below.

MODEL 2 (ECOWEB-FULL). *Let $C_i(t)$ be the estimated volume of keyword i at time tick t. Our full model captures seasonal user activities with the following equations:*

$$C_i(t) = P_i(t)\left[1 + e_i(t)\right] \quad (i = 1, \cdots, d), \quad (5)$$

where $e_i(t)$ describes seasonal activities of keyword i over time.

The estimated volume $C_i(t)$ describes how many times keyword i appears at time tick t, and depends on the latent popularity size $P_i(t)$ and seasonal activities $\mathbf{E} = \{e_i(t)\}_{i,t=1}^{d,n}$. Each element in $\mathbf{E}$ describes the relative value of the potential popularity size versus the actual keyword volume, and it corresponds to seasonal events, holidays, etc. If there is no seasonal pattern in keyword i at time t, (i.e., $e_i(t) = 0$), the keyword volume is equal to the popularity size (i.e., $C_i(t) = P_i(t)$).

Compact representation of seasonality. With respect to seasonal activities $\mathbf{E}$, we need $(d \times n)$ parameters to describe the entire dataset X, and this is not feasible in our case. We want to avoid redundancy, and so it should be compressed into a small set of parameters. We are interested in capturing (a) yearly periodic patterns (e.g., Black Friday) as well as (b) hidden groups of seasonal activities (e.g., retail sales). So how can we deal with this issue? We propose *decomposing* $\mathbf{E}$, to achieve much better modeling. Specifically, we decompose $\mathbf{E}$ into two matrices, namely, seasonality matrix $\mathbf{B}$ of size $(k \times n_p)$ and participation matrix $\mathbf{W}$ of size $(d \times k)$. Here, $\mathbf{B}$ represents a set of k seasonal components of period n_p, while $\mathbf{W}$ describes the participation weight of each sequence for each seasonal component. Consequently, the seasonal activities $\mathbf{E} = \{e_i(t)\}_{i,t=1}^{d,n}$ can be described as the following function:

$$e_i(t) \simeq f(i, t|\mathbf{W}, \mathbf{B}) = \sum_{j=1}^{k} w_{ij} b_j(\tau) \quad (\tau = [t \mod n_p]) \quad (6)$$

where,

- n_p: Period (say, 52 weeks in one year).
- k: Number of latent seasonal components.
- $\mathbf{W} = \{w_{ij}\}_{i,j=1}^{d,k}$: Participation matrix, i.e., participation weight of keyword i for the j-th seasonal component.
- $\mathbf{B} = \{b_j(\tau)\}_{j,\tau=1}^{k,n_p}$: Seasonality matrix, i.e., temporal activity at time tick τ for the j-th seasonal component.

Note that the number of components k should be estimated automatically, and we will describe this in the next section.

EcoWeb: full model parameter set. Figure 3 shows our modeling framework. Given a set of d co-evolving sequences X, our goal is to find important patterns with respect to three aspects: **(G1)** individual properties, i.e., initial popularity size: $\boldsymbol{p} = \{p_i\}_{i=1}^{d}$, growth rate: $\boldsymbol{r} = \{r_i\}_{i=1}^{d}$, carrying capacity: $\boldsymbol{K} = \{K_i\}_{i=1}^{d}$; **(G2)** interaction matrix: $\mathbf{A} = \{a_{ij}\}_{i,j=1}^{d,d}$; **(G3)** a set of k seasonal activities, which consists of participation matrix $\mathbf{W}$ and seasonality matrix $\mathbf{B}$.

[7] We can also say: the amount of available user resources for keyword i with a limited size of maximum popularity size K_i is: $K_i - \sum_{j=1}^{d} a_{ij}P_j(t)$.

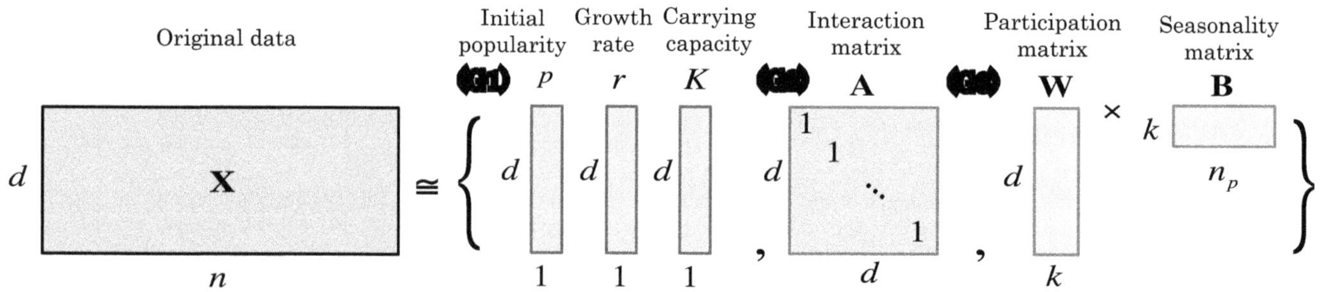

Figure 3: Illustration of EcoWeb structure. Given a set of d sequences X of length n, we extract (G1) individual properties, i.e., initial popularity size: p, growth rate: r, carrying capacity: K, (G2) interaction matrix: A, as well as (G3) a set of k seasonal components, i.e., participation matrix: W and seasonality matrix: B.

Definition 1 (Complete set of EcoWeb). *Let $\mathcal{S}$ be a complete set of parameters (namely, $\mathcal{S} = \{\boldsymbol{p}, \boldsymbol{r}, \boldsymbol{K}, \mathbf{A}, \mathbf{W}, \mathbf{B}\}$) that describe the individual/interactive/seasonal patterns of X.*

5. OPTIMIZATION ALGORITHM

In the previous section, we have seen how we can describe the evolutions of multiple sequences with respect to three properties that we observed with real time series data. Now, we want to figure out *how to estimate* an optimal parameter set. Specifically, we need to answer the following two questions: (1) How can we find an optimal set of seasonal components, (i.e., $\mathbf{W}, \mathbf{B}$)? (2) How can we efficiently and effectively estimate full parameter set $\mathcal{S}$ that best captures the important patterns in X? Each question is dealt with in the following subsections.

5.1 Automatic seasonal component analysis

Let us begin with the first question, namely, how to find an appropriate set of seasonal components $\mathbf{W}$ and $\mathbf{B}$. Here, we divide the question into two parts:

- *Seasonal component detection:* Find good seasonal matrices $\mathbf{W}$ and $\mathbf{B}$, when given a fixed number of components k.
- *Automatic component analysis:* Search for the best number of components among all possible k values ($k = 1, 2, \dots$).

Seasonal component detection. Assume that we are given X, and *also* a set of base model parameters for our model, i.e., $\{\boldsymbol{p}, \boldsymbol{r}, \boldsymbol{K}, \mathbf{A}\}$. According to Models 1 and 2, each element in $\mathbf{E}$ can be simply computed by:

$$e_i(t) = \frac{x_i(t) - P_i(t)}{P_i(t)} \quad (i = 1, \dots, d; t = 1, \dots, n). \qquad (7)$$

After computing $\mathbf{E}$ of size $(d \times n)$, our next step is to decompose it into an optimal set consisting of $\mathbf{W}$ and $\mathbf{B}$.

The most straightforward solution would be to assume that there is a set of $k = d$ different temporal activities of length n for all d sequences. However, this solution requires $(d \times n)$ parameters to capture the entire sequence set X. Also, it gives a very poor representation, and cannot capture seasonal dynamics among multiple keywords.

We thus propose an efficient and effective algorithm that can find an optimal set of k distinct seasonal patterns among all sequences X. Figure 4 illustrates our approach. Given a set of seasonal activities $\mathbf{E}$ of size $(d \times n)$, our algorithm splits each sequence into non-overlapping subsequences of length n_p, and constructs a matrix $\hat{\mathbf{E}}$ of size $([d \times \lceil n/n_p \rceil] \times n_p)$. It then finds a set of k components from $\hat{\mathbf{E}}$ and creates a seasonality matrix $\mathbf{B}$ of size $(k \times n_p)$. After finding $\mathbf{B}$, it estimates a participation matrix $\mathbf{W}$ of size $(d \times k)$ so that we can reconstruct the original matrix $\mathbf{E}$ as described in Equation 6, (i.e., $\mathbf{E} \simeq f(\mathbf{W}, \mathbf{B})$).

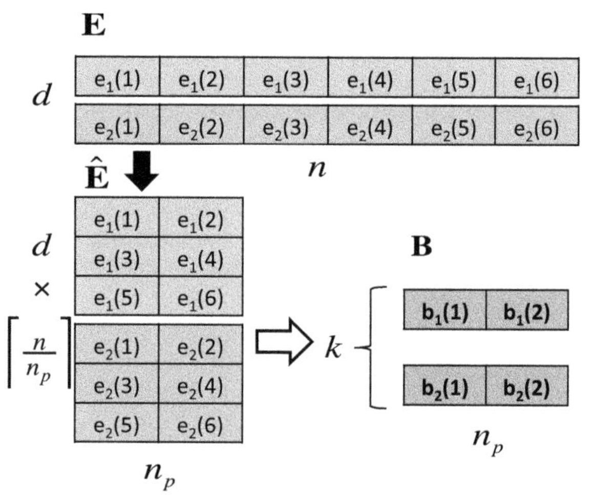

Figure 4: Illustration of seasonal component analysis (for $n_p = 2$). Given a set of seasonal activities E of size $(d \times n)$, it creates a matrix $\hat{\mathbf{E}}$ of $d \times \lceil n/n_p \rceil$ disjoint windows. It then finds their k major components, i.e., B $(k \times n_p)$.

There is an important issue here: what is the best way of finding typical seasonal components $\mathbf{B}$ in $\hat{\mathbf{E}}$? The first idea would be to perform principal component analysis (PCA) [19] as employed in [23, 41]. However, PCA has pitfalls: it uses an orthogonal transformation. Given an input matrix $\hat{\mathbf{E}}$, it tries to find the best component that goes through $\hat{\mathbf{E}}$; and then the second best component (orthogonal to the first), and so on, until it obtains k components. That is, it cannot capture "real" activities. We thus propose employing independent component analysis (ICA) [16], which is also known as blind source separation (BSS). Unlike PCA, it finds a set of k components that are both statistically independent and non-Gaussian. That is, it seeks components that are the most independent from each other.

Automatic component analysis. As regards seasonal component analysis, we need to determine the number of components, k. We thus provide an intuitive coding scheme, which enables our algorithm to find appropriate sizes for $\mathbf{W}$ and $\mathbf{B}$, *automatically*. Our coding scheme is based on the minimum description length (MDL) principle. In short, it follows the assumption that the more we can compress the data, the more we can learn about its underlying patterns.

The description complexity of model parameter set $\mathcal{S}$ consists of the following terms: The number of dimensions d and time ticks

n require $\log^*(d) + \log^*(n)$ bits. [8] The initial popularity size, growth rate, carrying capacity i.e., $\{\boldsymbol{p}, \boldsymbol{r}, \boldsymbol{K}\}$ and the interaction matrix $\mathbf{A}$ require $d \times 3$ and $(d \times d - d)$ parameters, respectively, i.e., $Cost_M(\boldsymbol{p}, \boldsymbol{r}, \boldsymbol{K}) + Cost_M(\mathbf{A}) = c_F \cdot d(3 + d - 1)$, where c_F is the floating point cost[9]. Similarly, the model description cost of k seasonal components is $Cost_M(k, \mathbf{W}, \mathbf{B}) = \log^*(k) + \log^*(n_p) + c_F(dk + kn_p)$.

Once we have decided the full parameter set $\mathcal{S}$, we can encode the original data X using Huffman coding [4], i.e., a number of bits is assigned to each value in X, which is the logarithm of the inverse of the probability (i.e., the negative log-likelihood) of the value. The encoding cost of X given $\mathcal{S}$ is computed by:

$$Cost_C(X|\mathcal{S}) = \sum_{i,t=1}^{d,n} \log_2 p^{-1}_{Gauss(\mu,\sigma^2)}(x_i(t) - C_i(t)),$$

where, $x_i(t)$ and $C_i(t)$ are the original and estimated volumes of keyword i at time tick t (i.e., Model 2). Also, μ and σ^2 are the mean and variance of the distance between the original and estimated values. [10]

The total code length for X with respect to a given parameter set $\mathcal{S}$ can be described as follows:

$$\begin{aligned} Cost_T(X; \mathcal{S}) &= \log^*(d) + \log^*(n) + Cost_M(\boldsymbol{p}, \boldsymbol{r}, \boldsymbol{K}) \\ &+ Cost_M(\mathbf{A}) + Cost_M(k, \mathbf{W}, \mathbf{B}) + Cost_C(X|\mathcal{S}) \qquad (8) \end{aligned}$$

Consequently, our algorithm automatically determines the optimal number of seasonal components k_{opt} according to the above function, i.e., $k_{opt} = \arg\min_k Cost_T(X; \mathcal{S})$.

5.2 Multi-step fitting algorithm

We have described how to find seasonal activities $\{\mathbf{W}, \mathbf{B}\}$ in X, when a set of base parameters $\{\boldsymbol{p}, \boldsymbol{r}, \boldsymbol{K}, \mathbf{A}\}$ were given. Next, we tackle the most important and challenging question, namely, how to efficiently and effectively estimate a full parameter set $\mathcal{S}$. We would like to estimate (**G1**) individual parameters $\{\boldsymbol{p}, \boldsymbol{r}, \boldsymbol{K}\}$, (**G2**) interaction matrix $\mathbf{A}$ and (**G3**) seasonal activities $\{\mathbf{W}, \mathbf{B}\}$, *simultaneously*.

So how do we go about finding the optimal solution $\mathcal{S}$? The most straightforward approach would be simply to estimate all the parameters in $\mathcal{S}$ simultaneously. This approach requires us to estimate $(3d + (d^2 - d) + k(d + n_p))$ parameters for each iteration. It also requires us to compare all possible solutions for a different number k $(1 \le k \le d)$. This method is both extremely expensive and ineffective in that it is difficult to optimize all the parameters directly.

We thus propose an efficient algorithm, StepFit, which divides a parameter set $\mathcal{S}$ into two subsets $\{\boldsymbol{p}, \boldsymbol{r}, \boldsymbol{K}, \mathbf{A}\}$, and $\{\mathbf{W}, \mathbf{B}\}$, and estimates the parameters alternately (see Algorithm 1). The first step assumes that there is no seasonality, i.e., $k = 0$, and estimates the base parameters. In the next step, the base parameters are fixed, and $\mathbf{B}$ and $\mathbf{W}$ are computed using automatic seasonal component analysis as described in subsection 5.1. Here, we use the *Levenberg-Marquardt (LM)* [29] algorithm to minimize the cost function (i.e., Equation 8). The algorithm continues to estimate the parameters until convergence.

However, StepFit still needs to update the parameters of interaction matrix $\mathbf{A}$ of size $(d \times d)$, as well as all d individual parameters i.e., $\{\boldsymbol{p}, \boldsymbol{r}, \boldsymbol{K}\}$ for every iteration. In other words, StepFit tries to find the best solution $\mathcal{S}$ among all possible combinations of d keywords. One subtle but important issue is that, compared with the linear model, it is difficult to find the optimal parameter set for non-linear equations. So, how can we efficiently and effectively estimate all the parameters $\mathcal{S}$? We want to find the optimal solution in terms of both the individual and interactive parameters.

Algorithm 1 StepFit (X)

```
Input: Co-evolving sequences X (d × n)
Output: Full parameter set, i.e., S = {p, r, K, A, W, B}
W = B = 0; /* Initialize seasonal activities (k = 0) */
while improving the parameters do
    /* (I) Base parameter fitting (G1), (G2) */
    {p, r, K, A} = arg min_{p',r',K',A'} Cost_T(X; p', r', K', A', W, B);
    /* (II) Seasonal parameter fitting (G3) */
    {W, B} = arg min_{W',B'} Cost_T(X; p, r, K, A, W', B');
end while
return S = {p, r, K, A, W, B};
```

Algorithm 2 EcoWeb-Fit (X)

```
Input: Co-evolving sequences X (d × n)
Output: Full parameter set, i.e., S = {p, r, K, A, W, B}
A = I_d; /* Initialize A, i.e., identity matrix of size (d × d) */
/* (I) Single fitting (G1), (G3) */
for i = 1 : d do
    /* Estimate individual parameters of keyword i */
    S_i = StepFit(x_i);
end for
/* (II) Pair fitting (G1), (G2), (G3) */
while improving the parameters do
    /* Find the most unfitted sequence x_i */
    i = arg max_{1≤i'≤d} Cost_T(x_{i'}; S);
    /* Estimate parameters of pair (i, j) */
    for j = 1 : d do
        S'_ij = StepFit(x_i, x_j);
    end for
    /* Find the most affecting sequence x_j on x_i */
    j = arg min_{j'} Cost_T(x_i, x_{j'}; S'_{ij'});
    /* Update best pair parameters */
    Update S_ij = S'_ij;
end while
/* (III) Full fitting (G1), (G2), (G3) */
S = arg min_{S'} Cost_T(X; S');
return S;
```

Algorithm - EcoWeb-Fit. We thus extend StepFit and introduce a partitioning approach for analyzing a large number of keywords, which yields a dramatic reduction in the computation cost. Algorithm 2 describes the overall procedure. The idea is that instead of fitting all the parameters of X simultaneously, it first assumes that there is no interspecies competition, (that is, it sets $\mathbf{A} = \mathbf{I}_d$, i.e., $a_{ij} = 0$ $(i \neq j)$), and estimates a model parameter set $\mathcal{S}_i = \{p_i, r_i, K_i, w_{ii}, b_i\}$ for each individual sequence x_i $(i = 1, \ldots, d)$, separately using StepFit. In the next step, it assumes that there is competition between two keywords i and j. Specifically, for each iteration, the algorithm tries to find the best pair (x_i, x_j) so that it minimizes the cost function i.e., $Cost_T(x_i, x_j|\mathcal{S}_{ij})$. It continues pair-fitting until convergence. Finally, the algorithm optimizes the full parameter set $\mathcal{S}$ using the entire sequence set X.

6. EXPERIMENTS

In this section we demonstrate the effectiveness of EcoWeb with real data. The experiments were designed to answer the following questions:

[8] Here, $\log^*$ is the universal code length for integers.

[9] We digitize the floating number into $c_F = 8$ bits.

[10] Here, μ, σ^2 need $2c_F$ bits, but we can eliminate them because they are constant values and independent of our modeling.

- Q1 *Effectiveness*: How successful is our method in spotting meaningful patterns in given input sequences?
- Q2 *Accuracy*: How well does our method match the data?
- Q3 *Scalability*: How does our method scale in terms of computational time?

6.1 Q1: Effectiveness

We now demonstrate the power of our model in terms of capturing important and informative patterns of online activities. We performed experiments on sequence sets of keywords/activities from five areas on *GoogleTrend*. Note that the dataset is scaled so that each sequence has a peak volume of 1.0.

#1. Video games. The result for this area has already been presented in Figure 1 of section 1. Our method captures long-range evolving dynamics between three game consoles (i.e., Xbox, PlayStation and Wii), and the appearance of Android, as well as important annual events, e.g., Black Friday and Christmas.

#2. Programming languages. Figure 5 (a) shows our discoveries on "C", "R" and "MATLAB".

- *Long-range evolution and interaction*: Figure 5 (a-i) shows the fitting results (lines) and the original sequences (circles). Again, our method fits the real data very well. Moreover, it captures the interaction: Figure 5 (a-ii) shows the interaction network, indicating competition between the "C" programming language and the "R" statistical system, while "MATLAB" seems not to be involved. Indeed, the time sequences show that the interest in "R" has increased constantly since 2004, at the expense of "C" - possibly, due to an emphasis on big data analytics.
- *Seasonal activities*: Figure 5 (a-iii) shows the full parameter set of EcoWeb (darker gray corresponds to a higher value). With respect to the seasonal activities ($\mathbf{W}$ and $\mathbf{B}$, shown at the bottom), our method discovered, to our surprise, that there is a strong correlation with the academic calendar. For example, during the spring, summer and winter breaks, the attention paid to each keyword (especially, MATLAB) decreases significantly: Apparently, most of those issuing queries, are students (as opposed to professional programmers), and they enjoy their vacation, instead of coding.

#3. Social media. Figure 5 (b) shows the fitting result for the social media activities: "Tumblr", "Facebook" and "LinkedIn".

- *Long-range evolution and interaction*: Most social media sites have been attracting searches only recently (say, after 2008 - $\boldsymbol{p} \approx 0$, see (b-iii)). For example, Tumblr is a blog platform that was founded in 2007, and it has been attracting huge numbers of users (i.e., the growth rate r of Tumblr is steep). Figure 5 (b-ii) shows that there is competition between Tumblr and Facebook, but there is no competitor for LinkedIn.
- *Seasonal activities*: The bottom figure (b-iii) shows that there is an opposite seasonality as regards social media: during Christmas and New Year's day, the number of Facebook users increases, while the number using LinkedIn drops significantly. This is probably because the former is used for private purposes, while the latter is a business-oriented SNS.

#4. Apparel companies. Figure 5 (c) shows the result for four heavily-searched fashion-related companies: *Nordstrom* (an upscale department store); *Kohl's* (a discount retailer) *JCPenney* (a mid-range department store, with CEO problems) and *Forever21* (which focuses on young girls, and recently added a line of bigger sizes).

- *Long-range evolution and interaction*: Our method captures the competition between Kohl's and Nordstrom, and between JCPenney and Forever21. Arguably due to the recession (2008 onwards), shoppers moved away from upscale Nordstrom and towards discount-priced Kohl's (which also engaged in some brilliant marketing: offering discounts for seniors, and issuing its own credit card to encourage increased customer loyalty). Similarly, Forever21 grew significantly, probably due to their decision to add a line of bigger sizes; thus, it apparently lured attention away from JCPenney, which was damaged by poor decisions made by the new CEO, Ron Johnson, who was eventually fired.
- *Seasonal activities*: All keywords have clear patterns of annual activity. There is a huge spike on Black Friday: the biggest sale event of the year. There is also a small spike in August, which is the *"back to school"* period.

#5. Retail companies. Figure 5 (d) shows the results for the top six retail companies.

- *Long-range evolution and interaction*: Clearly, every keyword is steadily increasing, with Best Buy being the only exception (arguably suffering, due to the success of online retailers). There is no clear interaction, except between Home Depot and Lowes, which are home improvement and appliance retailers, or, *do it yourself (DIY)* stores. In Figure 5 (d-i), our method captures both the individual and interaction dynamics of retail activities.
- *Seasonal activities*: As described in (d-iii), our method *automatically* discovered *two* hidden seasonal patterns (i.e., $k = 2$) in retail companies. The first component (b_1, in light brown) corresponds to Home Depot and Lowes, and the second component (b_2, in purple) corresponds to Amazon, Walmart, Best Buy and Costco. In addition to a huge clear spike on Black Friday in both components, there are multiple spikes in Home Depot and Lowes, corresponding to the national holidays in summer (see b_1): Memorial Day (last Monday in May), Independence Day (4th of July) and Labor Day (first Monday in September).

6.2 Q2: Model accuracy

Next, we discuss the quality of our approach in terms of fitting accuracy. We compared EcoWeb-Fit with the standard *LV* model. To evaluate the effect of our efficient fitting algorithms, we also compared them with a special version of our method: EcoWeb-Plain, which uses only StepFit to estimate model parameters. Figure 6 shows the root mean square error (RMSE) between the original and estimated volumes for five sequence sets (#1-#5). A lower value indicates a better fitting accuracy. As shown in the figure, our approach achieved high fitting accuracy. Since the *LV* model cannot capture seasonal patterns, it was strongly affected by multiple spikes and failed to capture co-evolving dynamics. EcoWeb-Plain has the ability to capture periodic patterns, but it was not completely successful in capturing complicated dynamics and interactions between multiple sequences.

6.3 Q3: Scalability

We also evaluated the scalability of our method. Figure 7 shows the average computational cost of EcoWeb-Fit. We varied the dataset size from five to ten years. Our method achieved a large reduction in terms of computation time as well as fitting error for every sequence set. We observed that EcoWeb-Fit was linear with respect to data length n, and was up to 20 times faster than EcoWeb-Plain. EcoWeb-Fit was also up to 7 times faster than the *LV* model, even though our method has the ability to capture seasonal dynamics.

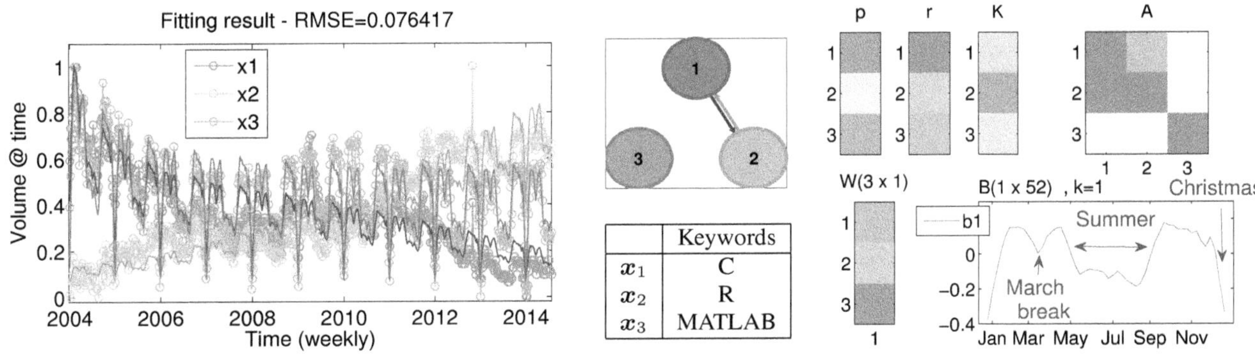

(a-i) Fitting result vs. original data (a-ii) Interaction (a-iii) Full parameter set

(a) Fitting result for the programming language activities.

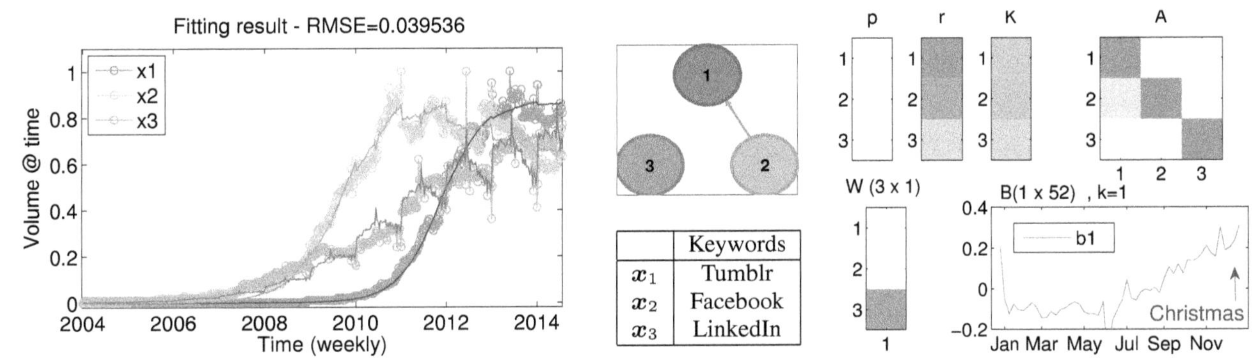

(b-i) Fitting result vs. original data (b-ii) Interaction (b-iii) Full parameter set

(b) Fitting result for the social media activities.

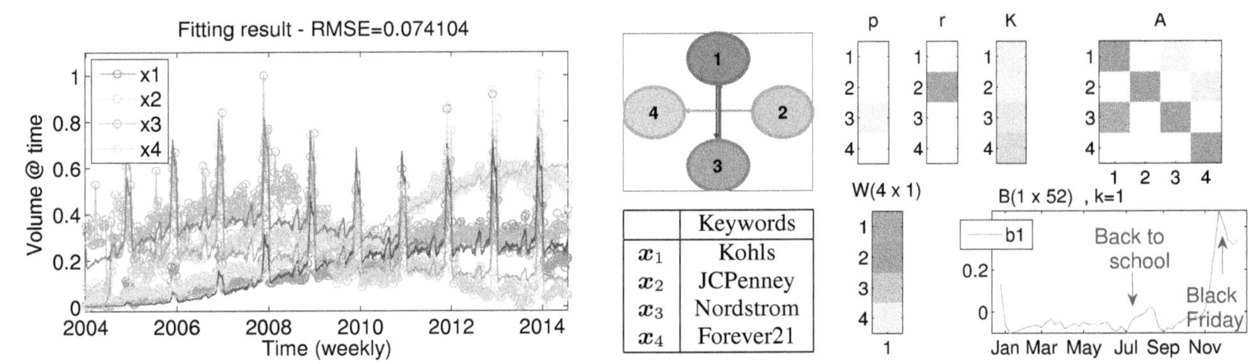

(c-i) Fitting result vs. original data (c-ii) Interaction (c-iii) Full parameter set

(c) Fitting result for the apparel company activities.

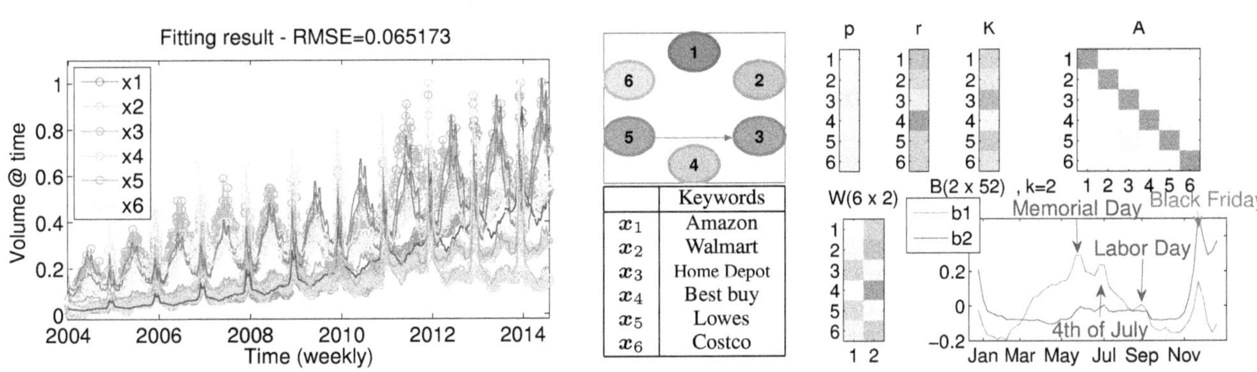

(d-i) Fitting result vs. original data (d-ii) Interaction (d-iii) Full parameter set

(d) Fitting result for the retail companies.

Figure 5: Fitting results of EcoWeb for four areas, i.e., (a) Programming languages, (b) social media, (c) apparel and (d) retail companies. Our model (solid lines) fits the original data (in circles) very well; spots competitors (indicated by edges); and spots the strongest seasonal patterns. See text for more observations.

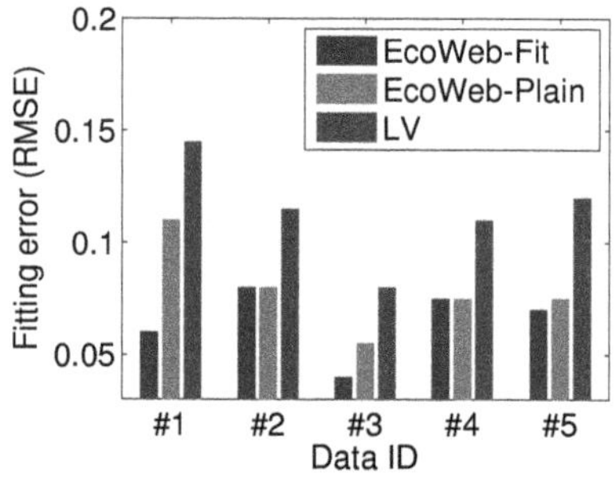

Figure 6: Accuracy of EcoWeb-Fit: Fitting error (RMSE) between original and estimated volume for five sequence sets (#1-#5) (lower is better).

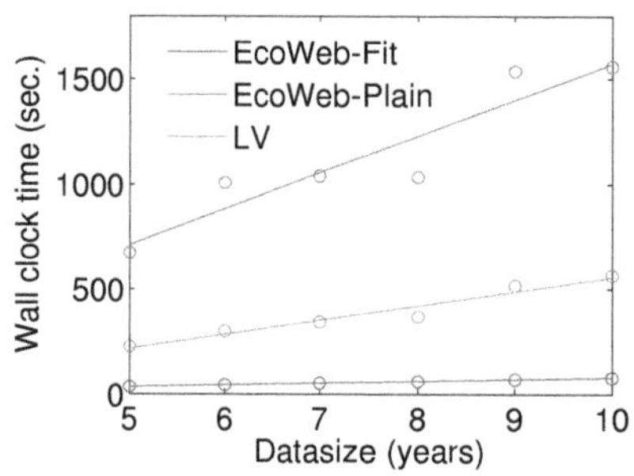

Figure 7: EcoWeb-Fit scales linearly: Wall clock time vs. dataset size (years). EcoWeb-Fit is 7 times faster than *LV* and 20 times faster than EcoWeb-Plain.

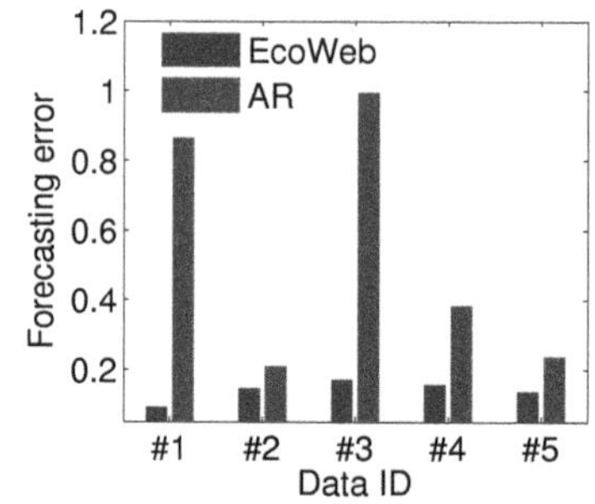

Figure 8: Forecasting error for each sequence set (#1-#5). Lower is better. Our method achieves high forecasting accuracy for every sequence set.

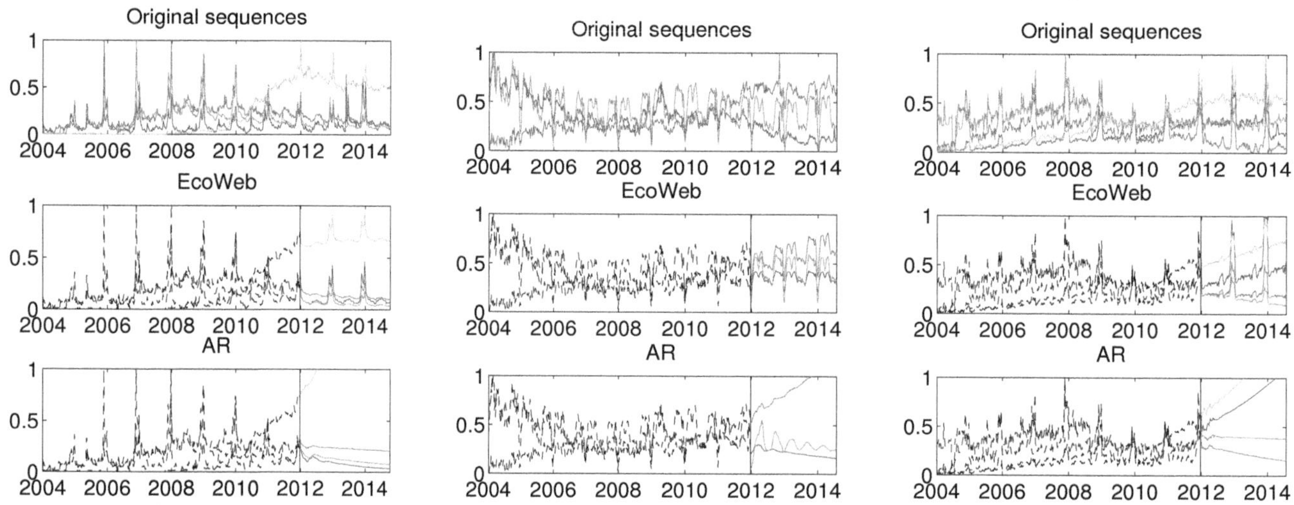

(a) Video games (#1) (b) Programming languages (#2) (c) Apparel companies (#4)

Figure 9: Forecasting future evolutions. Top: original sequence set. Middle and bottom: EcoWeb clearly outperforms *AR*. Both methods train the model parameters using $2/3$ of each sequence set, and then start forecasting (at the vertical line, i.e., 2012).

7. EcoWeb AT WORK - FORECASTING

Here, we describe the most important application of EcoWeb, namely, forecasting the future dynamics of co-evolving activities. Figure 8 shows the forecasting accuracy of five sequence sets (i.e., #1-#5) and Figure 9 shows results of our forecasting in relation to three sequence sets: (#1, #2 and #4). We trained the model parameters by using the $2/3$ values for each sequence set (black lines in Figure 9), and then forecasted the following years (colored lines, from 2012). We compared EcoWeb with the auto regressive (*AR*) model. For a fair comparison, we used coefficients that were the same size as our model parameters. In Figure 9, the top, middle and bottom rows show the original sequences, and the forecast results of EcoWeb and *AR*, respectively. As shown in Figure 9, our method successfully forecasted the long-range evolution of each sequence, as well as seasonal spikes, while *AR* failed to capture the non-linear evolutions.

The forecasting error (RMSE) between the original and the forecasted volume of each dataset is shown in Figure 8. A lower value indicates a better forecasting accuracy. Unlike *AR*, our method achieves high forecasting accuracy for every sequence set.

8. CONCLUSIONS

We presented EcoWeb, an intuitive model for mining large scale co-evolving online activities. Our main idea is that online activities behave like species in an ecological system in that they compete for resources (such as user attention), and they evolve over time according to a non-linear dynamical system. Our proposed method has the following appealing properties:

1. **Effective**: it detects important patterns, hidden interactions and seasonalities that match human intuition.
2. **Automatic**: it needs no parameter tuning, thanks to our coding scheme.
3. **Scalable**: it is linear on the input size.
4. **Practical**: it can undertake long-range forecasting and outperforms existing methods (Section 7).

Acknowledgement. The authors would like to thank Christina Cowan for her help with interpreting the patterns of apparel companies. This work was supported by JSPS KAKENHI Grant-in-Aid for Scientific Research Number 26730060, 24500138, 26280112, 25·7946. This material is based upon work supported by the National Science Foundation under Grants No. CNS-1314632 and IIS-1408924; and by the Army Research Laboratory (ARL) under Cooperative Agreement Number W911NF-09-2-0053; and by a Google Focused Research Award. Any opinions, findings, and conclusions or recommendations expressed in this material are those of the author(s) and do not necessarily reflect the views of the National Science Foundation, ARL, or other funding parties. The U.S. Government is authorized to reproduce and distribute reprints for Government purposes notwithstanding any copyright notation here on.

9. REFERENCES

[1] C. C. Aggarwal. The setwise stream classification problem. In *KDD*, pages 432–441, 2014.

[2] R. M. Anderson and R. M. May. *Infectious Diseases of Humans Dynamics and Control*. Oxford University Press, 1992.

[3] A. Beutel, B. A. Prakash, R. Rosenfeld, and C. Faloutsos. Interacting viruses in networks: can both survive? In *KDD*, pages 426–434, 2012.

[4] C. Böhm, C. Faloutsos, J.-Y. Pan, and C. Plant. Ric: Parameter-free noise-robust clustering. *TKDD*, 1(3), 2007.

[5] C. Böhm, C. Faloutsos, and C. Plant. Outlier-robust clustering using independent components. In *SIGMOD*, pages 185–198, 2008.

[6] F. Brauer and C. Castillo-Chavez. *Mathematical models in population biology and epidemiology*, volume 40. Springer Verlag, New York, 2001.

[7] D. Chakrabarti, S. Papadimitriou, D. S. Modha, and C. Faloutsos. Fully automatic cross-associations. In *KDD*, pages 79–88, 2004.

[8] H. Choi and H. R. Varian. Predicting the present with google trends. *The Economic Record*, 88(s1):2–9, 2012.

[9] I. N. Davidson, S. Gilpin, O. T. Carmichael, and P. B. Walker. Network discovery via constrained tensor analysis of fmri data. In *KDD*, pages 194–202, 2013.

[10] M. Eirinaki and M. Vazirgiannis. Web mining for web personalization. *ACM Trans. Internet Techn.*, 3(1):1–27, 2003.

[11] J. Ferlez, C. Faloutsos, J. Leskovec, D. Mladenic, and M. Grobelnik. Monitoring network evolution using MDL. In *ICDE*, pages 1328–1330.

[12] F. Figueiredo, J. M. Almeida, Y. Matsubara, B. Ribeiro, and C. Faloutsos. Revisit behavior in social media: The phoenix-r model and discoveries. In *PKDD*, pages 386–401, 2014.

[13] J. Ginsberg, M. Mohebbi, R. Patel, L. Brammer, M. Smolinski, and L. Brilliant. Detecting influenza epidemics using search engine query data. *Nature*, 457:1012–1014, 2009.

[14] S. Goel, J. Hofman, S. Lahaie, D. Pennock, and D. Watts. Predicting consumer behavior with web search. *PNAS*, 2010.

[15] D. Gruhl, R. Guha, R. Kumar, J. Novak, and A. Tomkins. The predictive power of online chatter. In *KDD*, pages 78–87, 2005.

[16] A. Hyvärinen and E. Oja. Independent component analysis: Algorithms and applications. *Neural Netw.*, 13(4-5):411–430, 2000.

[17] E. Jackson. *Perspectives of Nonlinear Dynamics:*. Cambridge University Press, 1992.

[18] A. Jain, E. Y. Chang, and Y.-F. Wang. Adaptive stream resource management using kalman filters. In *SIGMOD*, pages 11–22, 2004.

[19] I. Jolliffe. *Principal Component Analysis*. Springer Verlag, 1986.

[20] R. L. Jr., A. Veloso, A. M. Pereira, W. M. Jr., R. Ferreira, and S. Parthasarathy. Economically-efficient sentiment stream analysis. In *SIGIR*, pages 637–646, 2014.

[21] E. J. Keogh, S. Chu, D. Hart, and M. J. Pazzani. An online algorithm for segmenting time series. In *ICDM*, pages 289–296, 2001.

[22] Y. Koren. Factorization meets the neighborhood: a multifaceted collaborative filtering model. In *KDD*, pages 426–434, 2008.

[23] F. Korn, H. V. Jagadish, and C. Faloutsos. Efficiently supporting ad hoc queries in large datasets of time sequences. In *SIGMOD 1997*, pages 289–300, 1997.

[24] R. Kumar, M. Mahdian, and M. McGlohon. Dynamics of conversations. In *KDD*, pages 553–562, 2010.

[25] J.-G. Lee, J. Han, and K.-Y. Whang. Trajectory clustering: a partition-and-group framework. In *SIGMOD*, pages 593–604, 2007.

[26] W. Leontief. *Input-output economics*. Oxford University Press, 1986.

[27] J. Leskovec, L. Backstrom, and J. M. Kleinberg. Meme-tracking and the dynamics of the news cycle. In *KDD*, pages 497–506, 2009.

[28] J. Leskovec, L. Backstrom, R. Kumar, and A. Tomkins. Microscopic evolution of social networks. In *KDD*, pages 462–470, 2008.

[29] K. Levenberg. A method for the solution of certain non-linear problems in least squares. *Quarterly Journal of Applied Mathmatics*, II(2):164–168, 1944.

[30] L. Li, B. A. Prakash, and C. Faloutsos. Parsimonious linear fingerprinting for time series. *PVLDB*, 3(1):385–396, 2010.

[31] Y. Lu, P. Tsaparas, A. Ntoulas, and L. Polanyi. Exploiting social context for review quality prediction. In *WWW*, pages 691–700, 2010.

[32] Y. Matsubara, Y. Sakurai, and C. Faloutsos. Autoplait: Automatic mining of co-evolving time sequences. In *SIGMOD*, 2014.

[33] Y. Matsubara, Y. Sakurai, C. Faloutsos, T. Iwata, and M. Yoshikawa. Fast mining and forecasting of complex time-stamped events. In *KDD*, pages 271–279, 2012.

[34] Y. Matsubara, Y. Sakurai, B. A. Prakash, L. Li, and C. Faloutsos. Rise and fall patterns of information diffusion: model and implications. In *KDD*, pages 6–14, 2012.

[35] Y. Matsubara, Y. Sakurai, W. G. van Panhuis, and C. Faloutsos. FUNNEL: automatic mining of spatially coevolving epidemics. In *KDD*, pages 105–114, 2014.

[36] R. M. May. Qualitative stability in model ecosystems. *Ecology*, 54(3):638–641, 1973.

[37] J. Murray. *Mathematical Biology II: Spatial Models and Biomedical Applications*. Intercisciplinary Applied Mathematics: Mathematical Biology. Springer, 2003.

[38] M. Nowak. *Evolutionary Dynamics*. Harvard University Press, 2006.

[39] E. Odum and G. Barrett. *Fundamentals of Ecology*. Thomson Brooks/Cole, 2005.

[40] S. Papadimitriou, A. Brockwell, and C. Faloutsos. Adaptive, hands-off stream mining. In *VLDB*, pages 560–571, 2003.

[41] S. Papadimitriou, J. Sun, and C. Faloutsos. Streaming pattern discovery in multiple time-series. In *VLDB*, pages 697–708, 2005.

[42] S. Papadimitriou and P. S. Yu. Optimal multi-scale patterns in time series streams. In *SIGMOD*, pages 647–658, 2006.

[43] B. A. Prakash, A. Beutel, R. Rosenfeld, and C. Faloutsos. Winner takes all: competing viruses or ideas on fair-play networks. In *WWW*, pages 1037–1046, 2012.

[44] B. A. Prakash, D. Chakrabarti, M. Faloutsos, N. Valler, and C. Faloutsos. Threshold conditions for arbitrary cascade models on arbitrary networks. In *ICDM*, pages 537–546, 2011.

[45] T. Preis, H. S. Moat, and H. E. Stanley. Quantifying trading behavior in financial markets using google trends. *Sci. Rep.*, 3, 04 2013.

[46] T. Rakthanmanon, B. J. L. Campana, A. Mueen, G. E. A. P. A. Batista, M. B. Westover, Q. Zhu, J. Zakaria, and E. J. Keogh. Searching and mining trillions of time series subsequences under dynamic time warping. In *KDD*, pages 262–270, 2012.

[47] B. Ribeiro. Modeling and predicting the growth and death of membership-based websites. In *WWW*, pages 653–664, 2014.

[48] Y. Sakurai, S. Papadimitriou, and C. Faloutsos. Braid: Stream mining through group lag correlations. In *SIGMOD*, pages 599–610, 2005.

[49] E. Shmueli, A. Kagian, Y. Koren, and R. Lempel. Care to comment?: recommendations for commenting on news stories. In *WWW*, pages 429–438, 2012.

[50] J. Sun, D. Tao, and C. Faloutsos. Beyond streams and graphs: dynamic tensor analysis. In *KDD*, pages 374–383, 2006.

[51] Y. Tao, C. Faloutsos, D. Papadias, and B. Liu. Prediction and indexing of moving objects with unknown motion patterns. In *SIGMOD*, pages 611–622, 2004.

[52] M. Vlachos, D. Gunopulos, and G. Kollios. Discovering similar multidimensional trajectories. In *ICDE*, pages 673–684, 2002.

[53] H. Wang, J. Yin, J. Pei, P. S. Yu, and J. X. Yu. Suppressing model overfitting in mining concept-drifting data streams. In *KDD*, pages 736–741, 2006.

[54] P. Wang, H. Wang, and W. Wang. Finding semantics in time series. In *SIGMOD Conference*, pages 385–396, 2011.

[55] J. Yang, J. J. McAuley, J. Leskovec, P. LePendu, and N. Shah. Finding progression stages in time-evolving event sequences. In *WWW*, pages 783–794, 2014.

[56] R. Zafarani and H. Liu. Connecting users across social media sites: a behavioral-modeling approach. In *KDD*, pages 41–49, 2013.

[57] Y. Zhao, N. Sundaresan, Z. Shen, and P. S. Yu. Anatomy of a web-scale resale market: a data mining approach. In *WWW*, pages 1533–1544, 2013.

Spanning Edge Centrality: Large-scale Computation and Applications

Charalampos Mavroforakis
Boston University
cmav@cs.bu.edu

Richard Garcia-Lebron
University of Texas
San Antonio
richard.garcialebron@utsa.edu

Ioannis Koutis
University of Puerto Rico
Rio Piedras
ioannis.koutis@upr.edu

Evimaria Terzi
Boston University
evimaria@cs.bu.edu

ABSTRACT

The spanning centrality of an edge e in an undirected graph G is the fraction of the spanning trees of G that contain e. Despite its appealing definition and apparent value in certain applications in computational biology, spanning centrality hasn't so far received a wider attention as a measure of edge centrality. We may partially attribute this to the perceived complexity of computing it, which appears to be prohibitive for very large networks. Contrary to this intuition, spanning centrality can in fact be approximated arbitrary well by very efficient near-linear time algorithms due to Spielman and Srivastava, combined with progress in linear system solvers. In this article we bring theory into practice, with careful and optimized implementations that allow the **fast computation** of spanning centrality in very large graphs with millions of nodes. With this computational tool in our disposition, we demonstrate experimentally that spanning centrality is in fact a **useful tool** for the analysis of large networks. Specifically, we show that, relative to common centrality measures, spanning centrality is more effective in identifying edges whose removal causes a higher disruption in an information propagation procedure, while being very resilient to noise, in terms of both the edges scores and the resulting edge ranking.

Categories and Subject Descriptors

H.2.8 [**Database Management**]: Database Applications—*Data mining*; G.2.2 [**Discrete Mathematics**]: Graph Theory—*Graph algorithms, Trees*

Keywords

edge centrality; spanning trees; graph algorithms; social networks

WWW 2015, May 18–22, 2015, Florence, Italy.
ACM 978-1-4503-3469-3/15/05.
http://dx.doi.org/10.1145/2736277.2741125 .

1. INTRODUCTION

Measures of edge centrality are usually defined on the basis of some assumption about how information propagates or how traffic flows in a network. For example, the betweenness centrality of an edge is defined as the fraction of shortest paths that contain it; the underlying assumption being that information or traffic travels in shortest paths [7]. Although more complicated measures of centrality are conceivable, betweenness centrality is simple *by design*: its goal is to yield a computable measure of importance, which can quickly provide valuable information about the network.

Operating under the requirement for simplicity, all edge-importance measures are subject to weaknesses. Betweenness centrality is no exception, having partially motivated a number of other measures (Section 2). It's clear for example that information doesn't always prefer shortest paths; we have all experienced situations when it makes sense to explore slightly *longer* road paths in the presence of traffic. However, it is not clear how to modify betweenness to accommodate such *randomness*. At the same time, betweenness centrality can be *unstable*; the addition of even one 'shortcut' link can dramatically change the scores of edges in the network [27]. Yet, betweenness centrality is at its core very sensible: information may not always take shortest paths, but it *rarely* takes much longer paths.

These considerations lead us to focus on a *simple* and natural alternative model, where information propagates along paths on *randomly* selected *spanning trees*. The idea can actually be viewed as a relaxation of the shortest-paths propagation model: information is 'allowed' to randomly explore longer paths, which however contribute less in the importance measure, because the associated spanning trees are less frequent, as (in some sense) is reflected by the NP-hardness of finding long paths. A number of findings lend support to this intuition: In social networks, information propagates following tree-shaped cascades [15, 26]. Similarly, in computer networks, packages are distributed in the network through tree-shaped structures [18, 28].

We thus define the spanning centrality of an edge e as the fraction of the spanning trees of the graph that contain e. Spanning centrality as a measure for evaluating the significance of edges was introduced in the network analysis literature by Texeira *et al.* [33] in the context of evaluating phylogenetic trees. Computing spanning centrality, by definition involves counting spanning trees, a task that can be carried out in polynomial time using Kirchhoff's classical matrix-tree theorem [29]. Using this observation, Texeira *et al.* described an exact algorithm for computing the spanning centrality of all m edges in an n-node graph in $O(mn^{3/2})$ time. Despite its appealing definition, spanning centrality hasn't so far received wider attention as a measure of edge importance. This may be partially because, even with the clever observation in [33], the required computation time appears to be prohibitive for most networks of interest.

In this work we remove the aforementioned computational obstacle. We describe a **fast implementation** of an algorithm for spanning centrality that requires $O(m \log^2 n)$ time, or even less in practice (Section 5). The algorithm is *randomized* and it computes *approximations* to spanning centralities, but with strict theoretical guarantees. In practice, for a network consisting of 1.5 million nodes, we can compute spanning centrality values that are within 5% of the exact ones in 30 minutes. The algorithm is based on the fact that the spanning centrality of an edge is equal to its *effective resistance* when the graph is construed as a an electrical resistive network. The core component of our implementation is a fast linear system solver for Laplacian matrices [25]. The computation of spanning centrality is also crucially based on the remarkable work of Spielman and Srivastava [31]. Leveraging these two existing algorithmic tools is however not sufficient: our ability to experiment with large-scale networks also relies on a set of **computational speedups**, which include parallelization, exploitation of the input graph structure, and space-efficient implementations. Incidentally, our implementations allow the faster computation of a larger class of *electrical* centralities (Section 6).

With this computational tool in our disposition we embark in the first experimental analysis of spanning centrality as a measure of edge importance, including comparisons with a number of previously proposed centrality measures (Section 7). Our experimental evaluation demonstrates the **practical utility** of spanning centrality for analyzing very large graphs stemming from different application domains. More specifically, we demonstrate its *resilience* to noise, i.e. additions and deletions of edges. Our experiments illustrate that spanning centrality is significantly more resilient than other edge-importance measures, in terms of both the edges scores and the the resulting edge ranking. Thus, the edges with high spanning centrality scores are robust to noisy graphs or graphs that change over time. Further, we investigate the ability of spanning centrality to capture edge-importance with respect to more realistic *information-propagation processes* that don't readily yield computable measures. Our experiments show that removing edges with high spanning centrality incurs significant disruptions in the underlying information-propagation process, more so than other edge-importance measures. This suggests that an effective and computationally efficient way for disrupting the propagation of an item in a network is cutting the links with high spanning centrality.

2. RELATED WORK

In the graph-mining literature, there exists a plethora of measures for quantifying the importance of network nodes or edges [1, 4, 6, 7, 8, 10, 12, 13, 19, 21, 27, 30, 33]. Here, we limit our review to edge-importance measures.

Betweeness centrality remains very popular, and its simplicity can lead to relatively fast implementations despite its quadratic running time. As a consequence, a lot of work has been devoted in its fast computation. The simplest approach leads to an $O(nm)$ time algorithm for unweighted graphs ($O(nm+n^2 \log n)$ if the graph is weighted), where n (resp. m) is the number of nodes (resp. edges) in the graph [7]. The main bottleneck of that computation lies in finding the all-pairs shortest paths. Existing algorithms for speeding up this computation rely on reducing the number of such shortest-path computations. For example, Brandes and Pich [9] propose sampling pairs of source-destination pairs. Then, they experimentally evaluate the accuracy of different source-destination sampling schemes, including random sampling. Geisberger *et al.* [14] also propose sampling source–destination pairs. The only difference is that, in their case, the contribution of every sampled pair to the centrality of a node depends on the distance of that node from the nodes in the selected pair. Instead of sampling random source-destination pairs, Bader *et al.* [2] sample only sources from which they form a DFS traversal of the input graph. Therefore, the shortest-paths from the selected source to all other nodes are retrieved. The key of their method is that the sampling of such sources is adaptive, based on the exploration (through DFS trees) that has already been made. The trade-off between the speedups and the accuracy in the resulting methods is clear as these methods do not provide any approximation guarantees.

Current-flow centrality is another edge-centrality measure proposed by Brandes and Fleischer [8]. Current-flow assigns high scores to edges that participate in many short paths connecting pairs of nodes. We show that both spanning and current-flow centralities belong in the same class of *electrical* centrality measures and we describe a speedup of the original algorithm (proposed by Brandes and Fleischer). In a more recent work, De Meo *et al.* [10] propose *k-path centrality* as a faster-to-compute alternative to current-flow centrality. This centrality counts the number of times an edge is visited by simple random walks of length at most k starting from every node in the network. We note that on their largest reported dataset consisting of 1.1 million nodes and 4.9 million edges their algorithm requires about 6 hours (for very small values of k). We can deal with very similar datasets in less than 1 hour.

3. PRELIMINARIES

We will assume that the input consists of a connected and undirected graph $G = (V, E)$ with n nodes (i.e., $|V| = n$) and m edges (i.e., $|E| = m$). When we deal with matrices, we will be using MATLAB notation. That is, for matrix X, we will use $X(i, :)$ (resp. $X(:, j)$) to refer to the i-th row (resp. j-th column) of X.

Graphs as electrical networks: Throughout the paper, we will view the input graph as a resistive network, i.e., an electrical circuit where every edge is a resistor with fixed (e.g., unit) resistance. By attaching the poles of a battery to different nodes in the network, we will seek computational methods for evaluating the current that passes through the different edges.

The Graph Laplacian matrix: Given a graph $G = (V, E)$, the Laplacian of G is an $n \times n$ matrix L such that, if $\deg(v)$ is the degree of node v in the graph G, then $L(i, i) = \deg(i)$ for every i and $L(i, j) = -1$ if $(i, j) \in E$; otherwise $L(i, j) = 0$.

The incidence matrix: Given graph $G = (V, E)$, we define the *edge-incidence matrix* B of G to be an $m \times n$ matrix such that each row of B corresponds to an edge in E and each column of B corresponds to a node in V. The entries $B(e, v)$ for $e \in E$ and $v \in V$ take values in $\{-1, 0, 1\}$ as follows: $B(e, v) = 1$ if v is the destination of edge e, $B(e, v) = -1$ if v is the origin of e and $B(e, v) = 0$ otherwise. For undirected graphs, the direction of each edge is specified arbitrarily.

Fast linear solvers: Our methods rely on the Combinatorial Multigrid (CMG) solver [25]. CMG is based on a set of *combinatorial preconditioning* methods that have yielded provably very fast linear system solvers for Laplacian matrices and the more general class of symmetric diagonally dominant (SDD) matrices [23, 24]. SDD systems are of the form $Ax = b$ where A is an $n \times n$ matrix that is symmetric and diagonally dominant: i.e., for every i, $A(i,i) \geq \sum_{j \neq i} |A(i,j)|$. For such systems, the solver finds a solution $\overline{x}$ such that $\|\overline{x} - x\|_A = \epsilon \|x\|_A$, where $\| \cdot \|_A$ is the A-norm of a vector, i.e., $\|x\| = \sqrt{x^T A x}$. If m is the number of non-zero entries of the system matrix A, the theoretically guaranteed solvers run in $O(m \log n \log(1/\epsilon))$ time, but the CMG solver has an even better empirical running time of $O(m \log(1/\epsilon))$.

4. SPANNING CENTRALITY

The spanning centrality of an edge assigns to the edge an importance score based on the number of spanning trees the edge participates in. That is, important edges participate in many spanning trees. Formally, the measure has been defined recently by Teixeira *et al.* [33] as follows:

DEFINITION 1 (SPANNING). *Given a graph $G = (V, E)$ which is connected, undirected and unweighted, the* SPANNING *centrality of an edge e, denoted by* SC(e)*, is defined as the fraction of spanning trees of G that contain this edge.*

By definition, SC$(e) \in (0, 1]$. In cases where we want to specify the graph G used for the computation of the SC of an edge e, we extend the set of arguments of SC with an extra argument: SC(e, G).

Intuition: In order to develop some intuition, it is interesting to discuss which edges are assigned high SC scores: the only edges that achieve the highest possible SC score of 1 are *bridges*, i.e., edges that, if removed, make G disconnected. This is means that they participate in all possible spanning trees. The extreme case of bridges helps demonstrate the notion of importance captured by the SC scores for the rest of the edges. Assuming that spanning trees encode candidate pathways through which information propagates , then edges with high SC are those that, once removed, would incur a significant burden on the remaining edges.

Spanning centrality as an electrical measure: Our algorithms for computing the SPANNING centrality efficiently rely on the connection between the SC scores and the *effective resistances* of edges. The notion of effective resistance comes from viewing the input graph as an electrical circuit [11], in which each edge is a resistor with unit resistance. The effective resistance $R(u, v)$ between two nodes u, v of the graph — that may or may not be directly connected — is equal to the potential difference between nodes u and v when a unit of current is injected in one vertex (e.g., u) and extracted at the other (e.g., v).

In fact, it can be shown [5, 11] that for any graph $G = (V, E)$ and edge $e \in E$, the effective resistance of e, denoted by $R(e)$, is equal to the probability that edge e appears in a random spanning tree of G. This means that SC$(e) = R(e)$. This fact makes the theory of resistive electrical networks [11] available to us. The details of these computations are given in the next section.

Spanning centrality for weighted graphs: We note here that all the definitions and the results we explain in the next sections also hold for weighted graphs under the following definition of SPANNING centrality: Given a weighted graph $G = (V, E, w)$, where $w(e)$ is the weight of edge e, the weighted SPANNING centrality of e is again defined as the fraction of all trees of G in which e participates in, but, in this case, the importance of each tree is weighted by its weight. Specifically, the SPANNING centrality in weighted graphs is computed as: $\sum_{T \in \mathcal{T}_e} w(T) / \sum_{T \in \mathcal{T}} w(T)$. Here, $\mathcal{T}$ refers to the set of all spanning trees of G, while $\mathcal{T}_e$ is the set of spanning trees containing edge e. Also, $w(T)$ denotes the weight of a single tree T and is defined as the *product* of the weights of its edges, i.e., $w(T) = \prod_{e \in T} w(e)$. In other words, when the edge weight corresponds to the probability of the existence of that edge, $w(T)$ corresponds to the likelihood of T. The weighted SPANNING centrality maintains the probabilistic interpretation of its unweighted version; it corresponds to the probability that edge e appears in a spanning tree of G, when the spanning trees are sampled with probability proportional to their likelihood $w(T)$.

All the algorithms that we introduce in the next section can be used for weighted graphs with the above definition of SPANNING centrality. The only modification one has to make is to form the $m \times m$ diagonal weight matrix W, such that $W(e, e) = w(e)$, and then define the weighted graph Laplacian as $L = B^T W B$. This matrix can then be used as an input to all of the algorithms that we describe below.

5. COMPUTING SPANNING CENTRALITY

In this section, we present our algorithm for evaluating the spanning centrality of all the edges in a graph. For that, we first discuss existing tools and how they are currently used. Then, we show how the SDD solvers proposed by Koutis *et al.* [24, 23] can speed up existing algorithms. Finally, we present a set of speedups that we can apply to these tools towards an efficient and practical implementation.

5.1 Tools

Existing algorithms for computing the SPANNING centrality are based on the celebrated Kirchoff's matrix-tree theorem [17, 34]. The best known such algorithm has running time $O(mn^{3/2})$ [33], which makes it impossible to use even on networks with a few thousands of nodes and edges.

Random projections for spanning centrality: The equivalence between SC(e) and the effective resistance of edge e, denoted by $R(e)$, allows us to take advantage of existing algorithms for computing the latter. The effective resistances of all edges $\{u, v\}$ are the diagonal elements of the $m \times m$ matrix R computed as [11]:

$$R = BL^{\dagger}B^T, \tag{1}$$

where B is the incidence matrix and $L^{\dagger}$ is the pseudoinverse of the Laplacian matrix L of G. Unfortunately, this computation requires $O(n^3)$ time.

Equation (1) provides us with a useful intuition: the effective resistance of an edge $e = \{u, v\}$ can be re-written as the distance between two vectors that only depend on nodes u and v. To see this consider the following notation: for node $v \in V$ assume an $n \times 1$ unit vector e_v with value one in its v-th position and zeros everywhere else (i.e., $e_v(v) = 1$ and $e_v(v') = 0$ for $v \neq v'$). Using Equation (1), we can write the effective resistance $R(e)$ between nodes $u, v \in V$ as follows:

$$R(e) \;=\; (e_u - e_v)^T L^\dagger (e_u - e_v) = \left\| BL^\dagger (e_u - e_v) \right\|_2^2.$$

Thus, the effective resistances of edges $e = \{u, v\}$ can be viewed as pairwise distances between vectors in $\{BL^\dagger e_v\}_{v \in V}$.

This viewpoint of effective resistance as the L_2^2 distance of these vectors, allows us to use the Johnson-Lindenstraus Lemma [20]. The pairwise distances are still preserved if we project the vectors into a lower-dimensional space, spanned by $O(\log n)$ random vectors. This observation led to Algorithm 1, which was first proposed by Spielman and Srivastava [31]. We refer to this algorithm with the name `TreeC`.

Algorithm 1 The `TreeC` algorithm.

Input: $G = (V, E)$.
Output: $R(e)$ for every $e = \{u, v\} \in E$
1: $Z = [\,]$, $L =$ Laplacian of G
2: Construct random projection matrix Q of size $k \times m$
3: Compute $Y = QB$
4: **for** $i = 1 \ldots k$ **do**
5: Approximate z_i by solving: $Lz_i = Y(:, i)$
6: $Z = [Z; z_i^T]$
7: return $R(e) = \|Z(:, u) - Z(:, v)\|_2^2$

In Line 2, a random $\{0, \pm 1/\sqrt{k}\}$ matrix Q of size $k \times m$ is created. This is the projection matrix for $k = O(\log n)$, according to the Johnson-Lindenstrauss Lemma. Using this, we could simply project matrix $BL^\dagger$ on the k random vectors defined by the rows of Q, i.e., computing $QBL^\dagger$. However, this would not help in terms of running time, as it would require computing $L^\dagger$ which takes $O(n^3)$ steps. Lines 3 and 5 approximate $QBL^\dagger$, without computing the pseudoinverse of L: first, $Y = QB$ is computed in time $O(2m \log n)$ — this is because B is sparse and has only $2m$ non-zero entries. Then, Line 5 finds an approximation of the *rows* z_i of matrix $QBL^\dagger$ by (approximately) solving the system $Lz_i = y_i$, where y_i is the i-th row of Y. Therefore, the result of the `TreeC` algorithm is the set of rows of matrix $Z = [z_1^T, \ldots, z_k^T]$, which is an approximation of $QBL^\dagger$. By the Johnson-Lindenstrauss lemma we know that, if $k = O(\log n)$, the `TreeC` algorithm will guarantee that the estimates $\tilde{R}(e)$ of $R(e)$ satisfy

$$(1 - \epsilon)R(e) \leq \tilde{R}(e) \leq (1 + \epsilon)R(e),$$

with probability at least $1 - 1/n$. We call ϵ the *error parameter* of the algorithm. Now, if the running time required to solve the linear system in Line 5 is $I(n, m)$, then the total running time of the `TreeC` algorithm is $O(I(n, m) \log n)$.

Incorporating SDD solvers: Now, if we settle for approximate solutions to the linear systems solved by `TreeC` and we deploy the SDD solver proposed by Koutis *et al.* [24, 23], then we have that $I(n, m) = \tilde{O}(m \log n)$, therefore achieving a running time of $\tilde{O}\left(m \log^2 n \log\left(\frac{1}{\epsilon}\right)\right)$. Additionally, with probability $(1 - 1/n)$, the estimates $\tilde{R}(e)$ of $R(e)$ satisfy

$$(1 - \epsilon)^2 R(e) \leq \tilde{R}(e) \leq (1 + \epsilon)^2 R(e). \qquad (2)$$

We refer to the version of the `TreeC` algorithm that uses such solvers as the `Fast-TreeC` algorithm. The running time of `Fast-TreeC` increases linearly with the number of edges and logarithmically with the number of nodes. This dependency manifests itself clearly in our experiments in Section 7.

5.2 Speedups

We now describe three observations that lead to significant improvements in the space and runtime requirements of `Fast-TreeC`.

Space-efficient implementation: First, we observe that intermediate variables Y and Z of Algorithm 1 need not be stored in $k \times n$ matrices but, instead, vectors y and z of size $1 \times n$ are sufficient. The pseudocode that implements this observation is shown in Algorithm 2. In this case, the algorithm proceeds in $k = O(\log n)$ iterations. In each iteration, a single random vector q (i.e., a row of the matrix Q from Algorithm 1) is created and used for projecting the nodes. The effective resistance of edge $e = \{u, v\}$ is computed additively — in each iteration the portion of the effective resistance score that is due to the particular dimension is added to the total effective resistance score (Line 6 of Algorithm 2).

Algorithm 2 The space-efficient version of `Fast-TreeC`.

Input: $G = (V, E)$.
Output: $R(e)$ for every $e = \{u, v\} \in E$
1: $L =$ Laplacian of G
2: **for** $i = 1 \ldots k$ **do**
3: Construct a vector q of size $1 \times m$
4: Compute $y = qB$
5: Approximate z by solving: $Lz = y$
6: return $R(e) = R(e) + \|z(u) - z(v)\|_2^2$

Parallel implementation: Algorithm 2 reveals also that `Fast-TreeC` is amenable to parallelization. The execution of every iteration of the `for` loop (Line 2 of Algorithm 2) can be done independently and in parallel, in different cores, and the results can be combined. This leads to another running-time improvement: in a parallel system with $O(\log n)$ cores, the running time of the parallel version of the `Fast-TreeC` algorithm is $\tilde{O}\left(m \log n \log\left(\frac{1}{\epsilon}\right)\right)$. In all our experiments we make use of this parallelization.

Reducing the size of the input to the 2-core: As it has been observed in Section 4, the *bridges* of a graph participate in all the spanning trees of the graph and thus have SC score equal to 1. Although we know how to extract bridges efficiently [32], assigning to those edges SC score of 1 and applying the `Fast-TreeC` algorithm on each disconnected component would not give us the correct result. It is not clear how to combine the SC scores from the different connected components. However, we observe that this can still be done for a subset of the bridges.

Let us first provide some intuition before making a more general statement. Consider an input graph $G = (V, E)$ and an edge $e = \{u, v\}$ connecting node v of degree one to the rest of the network via node u. Clearly e participates in all spanning trees of G and, therefore, $\text{SC}(e, G) = 1$. Now assume that edge e and node v are removed from G, resulting

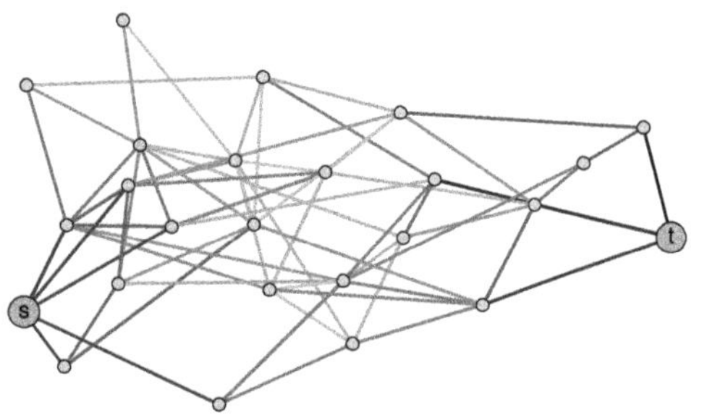

Figure 1: A network, viewed as an electrical resistive circuit. The thickness of an edge represents the amount of current it carries, if a battery is attached to nodes s and t.

into graph $G' = (V \setminus \{v\}, E \setminus \{e\})$. Since e was connecting a node of degree 1 to the rest of G, the *number* of spanning trees in G' is equal to the number of spanning trees in G. Thus, $\mathrm{SC}(e', G') = \mathrm{SC}(e', G)$ for every edge $e' \in E \setminus \{e\}$.

Now the key observation is that the above argument can be applied recursively. Formally, consider the input graph $G = (V, E)$ and let $C_2(G) = (V', E')$ be the 2-*core* of G, i.e., the subgraph of G that has the following property: the degree of every node $v \in V'$ in $C_2(G)$ is *at least* 2. Then, we have the following observation:

LEMMA 1. *If $G = (V, E)$ is a connected graph with 2-core $C_2(G) = (V', E')$, then for every edge $e \in E'$*

$$\mathrm{SC}(e, C_2(G)) = \mathrm{SC}(e, G).$$

The above suggests the following speedup for `Fast-TreeC`: given a graph $G = (V, E)$, first extract the 2-core $C_2(G) = (V', E')$. Then, for every edge $e \in E'$ compute $\mathrm{SC}(e)$ using the `Fast-TreeC` algorithm with input $C_2(G)$. For every $e \in E \setminus E'$, set $\mathrm{SC}(e) = 1$.

The computational savings of such a scheme depend on the time required to extract $C_2(G)$ from G. At a high level, this can be done by recursively removing from G nodes with degree 1 and their incident edges. This algorithm, which we call `Extract2Core`, runs in time $O(m)$ [3]. Our experiments (Section 7) indicate that extracting $C_2(G)$ and applying `Fast-TreeC` on this subgraph is more efficient than running `Fast-TreeC` on the original graph, i.e., the time required for running `Extract2Core` is much less than the speedup achieved by reducing the input size. By default, we use this speedup in all our experiments.

6. A GENERAL FRAMEWORK

In this section, we show that SPANNING centrality is an instance of a general class of edge-centrality measures, which we call *electrical measures* of edge centrality. We introduce a framework that offers a unified view to all the existing measures and leads to novel ones. Finally, we demonstrate how SDD solvers can be utilized within this framework.

6.1 Electrical measures of centrality

The common characteristic of the electrical measures of centrality is that they view the input graph G as a resistive circuit, i.e., an electrical network where every edge is a resistor of constant (e.g., unit) resistance. To get a better understanding of these measures, consider Figure 1. Suppose that we hook the poles of a battery to nodes s and t and apply a voltage difference sufficient to drive one unit of current (1A) from s to t. Doing that, each node in the network will get a voltage value and electrical current will flow essentially *everywhere*. At a high level, the electrical measures quantify the importance of an edge by *aggregating the values of the flows* that pass through it over different choices for pairs of nodes s and t. In fact, specific combinations of aggregation schemes and battery placements lead to different definitions of edge-importance measures.

More formally, consider two fixed nodes s and t on which we apply a voltage difference sufficient to drive one unit of current (1A) from s to t. Let the (s,t)-*flow* of edge $e = \{u, v\}$, denoted by $f_{st}(u, v)$, be the flow that passes through edge e in this configuration. We can now derive the following instances of electrical measures of edge centrality:

SPANNING **centrality:** For spanning centrality, we only consider a single battery placement and get the following alternative definition of the centrality of edge $e = \{u, v\}$:

$$\mathrm{SC}(e = \{u, v\}) = f_{uv}(u, v).$$

CURRENTFLOW **centrality:** If we consider the *average* flow that passes through an edge, where the average is taken over all distinct pairs of nodes (s,t), then we get another centrality measure known as current-flow:

$$\mathrm{CFC}(e = \{u, v\}) \triangleq \frac{1}{\binom{n}{2}} \sum_{(s,t)} f_{st}(u, v).$$

This measure was first proposed by Brandes and Fleisher [8].

From the combinatorial perspective, CURRENTFLOW considers an edge as important if it is used by many paths in the graph, while SPANNING focuses on the participation of edges in trees. The idea of counting paths is also central in the definition of *betweenness centrality* [7]. However, betweenness centrality takes into consideration only the shortest paths between the source-destination pairs. Therefore, if an edge does not participate in many shortest paths, it will have low betweenness score. This is the case even if that edge is still part of many relatively *short* paths. More importantly, the betweenness score of an edge may change by the addition of a small number of edges to the graph (e.g., edges that create triangles) [27]. Clearly, the CURRENTFLOW centrality does not suffer from such unstable behavior since it takes into account the importance of the edge in all the paths that connect all source-destination pairs.

β-CURRENTFLOW **centrality:** Instead of plugging a single battery in two endpoints (s,t), we can consider plugging β batteries into β pairs of distinct endpoints $\langle s_i, t_i \rangle$. For any such placement of β batteries, we can again measure the current that flows through an edge $e = \{u, v\}$ and denote it by $f_{\langle s_i, t_i \rangle}(u, v)$. Then, we define the β-CURRENTFLOW centrality of an edge as:

$$\beta\text{-}\mathrm{CFC}(e = \{u, v\}) = \frac{1}{|C_b|} \sum_{\langle s_i, t_i \rangle \in C_b} f_{\langle s_i, t_i \rangle}(u, v),$$

where C_b denotes the set of all feasible placements of β batteries in the electrical network defined by G. We can view β-CURRENTFLOW as a generalization of CURRENTFLOW; the two measures are identical when $\beta = 1$.

6.2 Computing electrical measures

In order to compute the centralities we described above, we need to be able to compute the flows $f_{st}(u,v)$. Using basic theory of electrical resistive networks, the computation of these flows for a fixed pair (s,t) can be done by solving the Laplacian linear system $Lx = b$. The right hand side of the system is a vector with the total residual flows on the nodes. Specifically, we let $b(s) = 1, b(t) = -1$ and $b(u) = 0$ for all $u \neq s,t$. This is because one unit of current enters s, one unit of current leaves s and a net current of 0 enters and leaves every other node by Kirchoff's law. As we have already discussed, setting a voltage difference between s and t assigns voltages to all the other nodes. The values of these voltages are given in the solution vector x. Then,

$$f_{st}(u,v) = |x(u) - x(v)| \tag{3}$$

The algorithm of Brandes and Fleisher [8]: From the above, the computation of one set of flows for a fixed pair (s,t) requires the solution of one linear system. Of course. we need $\binom{n}{2}$ linear systems in order to account for all pairs s and t. As shown by Brandes and Fleisher [8], it is enough to find the pseudo-inverse $L^{\dagger}$ of the Laplacian L *once*; then the scores can be computed in $O(mn \log n)$ time. In fact, this computation expresses the solution of each of the $\binom{n}{2}$ linear systems as a simple 'lightweight' linear combination of the solution of n systems that can be found in the columns of $L^{\dagger}$. Brandes and Fleisher point out that the pseudo-inverse can be computed via solving n linear systems in $O(mn^{3/2} \log n)$.

Proposed speedups: Using our state-of-the-art solver for SDD, the running time of finding $L^{\dagger}$ drops to $O(mn \log n)$, matching the post-processing part that actually computes the scores. Of course, this running time remains quadratic.

This worst-case running time can be improved in practice through sampling and parallelism. With sampling one can construct an estimator of a measure, say CFC, denoted by $\overline{\text{CFC}}$ as follows: instead of considering all pairs (s,t) we can only consider a set S_k of k pairs (s,t) that are selected uniformly at random. Similarly to Brandes and Fleisher [8] we define

$$\overline{\beta\text{-CFC}}(e = \{u,v\}) \triangleq \frac{1}{k} \sum_{(s,t)\in S_k} f_{st}(u,v), \tag{4}$$

which is an unbiased estimator of β-CFC(e).

Note that for each (s,t) pair one has to solve a linear system $Lx = b$ in order to obtain the values $f_{st}(u,v)$ of Equation (3). It is for those systems that we use the state-of-the art SDD solver. At the same time we observe that these systems can be solved independently for different vectors b, therefore parallelism can be exploited here too.

We call the algorithm that takes advantage of the state-of-the art SDD solver and the parallelism of `Fast-FlowC`. We evaluate the efficiency of this algorithm in Section 7.4.

7. EXPERIMENTS

In this section, we experimentally evaluate our methods for computing the spanning centrality and we study its properties with respect to edge additions/deletions and information propagation. For the evaluation, we use a large collection of datasets of different sizes, which come from a diverse set of domains.

Experimental setup: We implemented both `Fast-TreeC` and `Fast-FlowC` using a combination of Python, Matlab and C code. The CMG solver [25] is written mostly in C and can be invoked from Matlab. At the same time, in order to make our methods easily accessible, we compiled them as a Python library on top of the popular *networkx*[1] package [16]. The code is available online[2].

We ran all our experiments on a machine with 4 *Intel Xeon E5-4617 @ 2.9GHz*, with 512*GB* of memory. We need to note here that none of our algorithms pushed the memory of the machine near its limit. For `Fast-TreeC` and `Fast-FlowC` we used 12 hardware threads.

Datasets: In order to demonstrate the applicability of our algorithms on different types of data, we used a large collection of real-world datasets of varying sizes, coming from different application domains. Table 1 provides a comprehensive description of these datasets shown in increasing size (in terms of the number of edges). The smallest dataset consists of approximately 4×10^3 nodes, while the largest one has almost 3.8×10^6 nodes.

For each dataset, the first two columns of Table 1 report the number of nodes and the number of edges in the *Largest Connected Component* (LCC) of the graph that correspond to this dataset. The third and fourth columns report the number of nodes and edges in the 2-core of each dataset. The 2-core of a graph is extracted using the algorithm of Batagelj *et al.* [3]. The statistics of these last two columns will be revisited when we explore the significance of applying `Extract2Core` in the running time of `Fast-TreeC`.

In addition to their varying sizes, the datasets also come from a wide set of application domains, including collaboration networks (`HepTh`, `GrQc`, `DBLP` and `Patents`), social networks (`wiki-Vote`, `Slashdot`, `Epinions`, `Orkut` and `Youtube`), communication networks, (`Gnutella08`, `Gnutella31`, `skitter` and `Oregon`) and road networks (`roadNet-TX`). All the above datasets are publicly available through the *Stanford Large Network Dataset Collection* (SNAP). [3] For consistency, we maintain the names of the datasets from the original SNAP website. Since our methods only apply to undirected graphs, if the original graphs were directed or had self-loops, we ignored the directions of the edges as well as the self loops.

7.1 Experiments for SPANNING

Accuracy-efficiency tradeoff: Our first experiment aims to convey the practical semantics of the accuracy-efficiency tradeoff offered by the `Fast-TreeC` algorithm. For this, we recorded the running time of the `Fast-TreeC` algorithm for different values of the error parameter ϵ (see Equation (2)) and for different datasets. Note that the running times reported for this experiment are obtained after applying all the three speedups that we discuss in Section 5.2.

The results are shown in Figure 2; for better readability the figure shows the results we obtained only for a subset of our datasets (from different applications and with different sizes); the trends in other datasets are very similar. As expected, the running time of `Fast-TreeC` decreases as the value of ϵ, the error parameter, increases. Given that the

[1] http://networkx.github.io/
[2] http://cs-people.bu.edu/cmav/centralities
[3] http://snap.stanford.edu/data

Table 1: Statistics of the collection of datasets used in our experiments.

Dataset name	#Nodes in LCC	#Edges in LCC	#Nodes in the 2-Core	#Edges in the 2-Core
GrQc	4 158	13 422	3 413	12 677
Gnutella08	6 299	20 776	4 535	19 012
Oregon	11 174	23 409	7 228	19 463
HepTh	8 638	24 806	7 059	23 227
wiki-Vote	7 066	100 736	4 786	98 456
Gnutella31	62 561	147 878	33 816	119 133
Epinions	75 877	405 739	37 300	367 162
Slashdot	82 168	504 230	52 181	474 243
Amazon	334 863	925 872	305 892	896 901
DBLP	317 080	1 049 866	271 646	1 004 432
roadNet-TX	1 351 137	1 878 201	1 068 728	1 596 792
Youtube	1 134 890	2 987 624	470 164	2 322 898
skitter	1 694 616	11 094 209	1 463 934	10 863 527
Patents	3 764 117	16 511 740	3 093 271	15 840 895

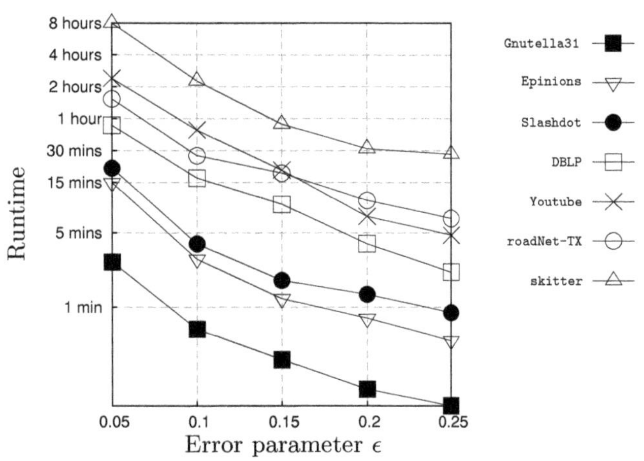

Figure 2: Accuracy-efficiency tradeoff; y-axis (logarithmic scale): running time of the Fast-TreeC algorithm; x-axis: error parameter ϵ.

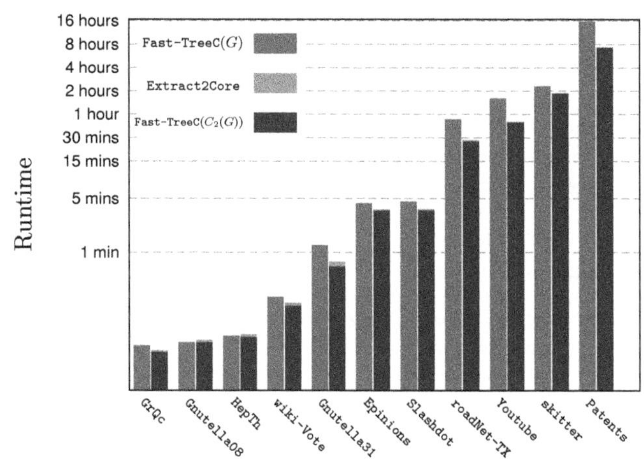

Figure 3: Limiting the computation on the 2-core shows a measurable improvement in the running time of Fast-TreeC.

y-axis in Figure 2 is logarithmic, this decrease in the running time is, as expected, exponential. Even for our largest datasets (e.g., skitter and roadNet-TX), the running time of Fast-TreeC even for very small values of ϵ (e.g., $\epsilon = 0.05$) was never more than 8 hours. Also, for $\epsilon = 0.15$, which is a very reasonable accuracy requirement , Fast-TreeC calculates the spanning centrality of all the edges in the graphs in less than 1 hour.

Also, despite the fact that the roadNet-TX and skitter datasets have almost the same number of nodes, skitter runs significantly faster than roadNet-TX for the same value of ϵ. This is due to the fact that skitter has approximately 5 times more edges than the corresponding graph of roadNet-TX and that the running time of Fast-TreeC is linear to the number of edges yet logarithmic to the number of nodes of the input graph.

Effect of the 2-core speedup: Here, we explore the impact of reducing the size of the input to the 2-core of the original graph on the running time of Fast-TreeC. For this, we fix the value of the error parameter $\epsilon = 0.1$, and run the Fast-TreeC algorithm twice; once using as input the original graph G and then using as input the 2-core of the same graph, denoted by $C_2(G)$. Then, we report the running times of both these executions. We separately also compute the time required to extract $C_2(G)$ from G using the Extract2Core routine described in Section 5.2.

Figure 3 shows the runtime for all these operations. In the figure, we use Fast-TreeC(G) (resp. Fast-TreeC($C_2(G)$)) to denote the running time of Fast-TreeC on input G (resp. $C_2(G)$). We also use Extract2Core to denote the running time of Extract2Core for the corresponding input. For each of these datasets, we computed the SC scores of the edges, before (left) and after (right), and we report the running time in the y-axis using logarithmic scale.

Note that on top of the box that represents the runtime of Fast-TreeC($C_2(G)$), we have also stacked a box with size relative to the time it took us to find that 2-core subgraph. It is hard to discern this box, because the time spent for Extract2Core is minimal compared to the time it took to compute the SPANNING centralities. Only in the case of smaller graphs is this box visible, but again, in these cases, the total runtime does not exceed a minute. For instance, for Patents (our largest graph) spending less than 5 minutes to find the 2-core of the graph lowered the runtime of Fast-

TreeC down to less than 8 hours, which is less than half of the original. Moreover, the difference between the height of the left and the right bar for the different datasets behaves similarly. Hence, as the size of the dataset and the runtime of Fast-TreeC grow exponentially, so does the speedup.

7.2 Resilience under noise

In this experiment, we evaluate the resilience of SPANNING centrality to noise that comes in the form of adding and deleting edges in the original graph. We also compare the resilience of SPANNING to the resilience of CURRENTFLOW centrality [8] and BETWEENNESS centrality [7, 12], which are the most commonly used measures of edge centrality.

Noise: Given the original graph $G = (V, E)$ we form its noisy version of $G' = (V, E')$ by either *adding* or *deleting* edges. We consider three methods for edge addition: (a) **random** that picks two disconnected nodes at random and creates an edge, (b) **heavy** that selects two nodes with probability proportional to the sum of their degrees and (c) **light** that selects two nodes with probability inversely proportional to the sum of their degrees. Note that adding edges with **heavy** imitates graph evolution under the scale-free models, while the addition of edges with **light** imitates the evolution of newly-added nodes in an evolving network. The edge deletion is performed similarly; we delete an already existing edge (a) randomly, (b) with probability proportional to the sum of the degrees of its endpoints or (c) with probability inversely proportional to the sum of the degrees of its endpoints.

The number of edges ℓ added to or deleted from G is a parameter to our experiment – expressed as a percentage of the number of original edges in G.

Evaluation: We evaluate the resilience of a centrality measure both in terms of the values it assigns to edges that are both in G and G', as well as the ranking that these values induce.

Formally, given a graph $G = (V, E)$ and its noisy version $G' = (V, E')$, let e be an edge in $E \cap E'$. If c_e is the centrality score of the edge in G and c'_e the value of the same score in G', then we define the relative change in the value of e as:

$$\texttt{RelChange}(e, G, G') = \frac{|c_e - c'_e|}{c_e}.$$

In order to aggregate over all edges in E, we define the average relative change of c with respect to G and G' as

$$\texttt{AvgRC}(G, G') = \frac{1}{|E \cap E'|} \sum_{e \in E \cap E'} \texttt{RelChange}(e).$$

This evaluation metric captures the average relative change in the value of the centrality scores in G and G'. Observe that for edge additions, $E \cap E' = E$, while, for edge deletions $E \cap E' = E'$. In general, $\texttt{AvgRC}(G, G')$ takes values in $[0, \infty)$ and smaller values imply a more resilient centrality measure.

In order to evaluate how the ranking of the edges according to a centrality measure changes in G and G' — ignoring the actual values of the measure — we proceed as follows: first we generate the sets of edges that contain the top-k% edges in G and G', denoted by $I(G, k)$ and $I(G', k)$ resp. Then, we compare these sets using their Jaccard similarity. That is, we define:

$$\texttt{JaccSim}(G, G', k) = \frac{|I(G,k) \cap I(G',k)|}{|I(G,k) \cup I(G',k)|}.$$

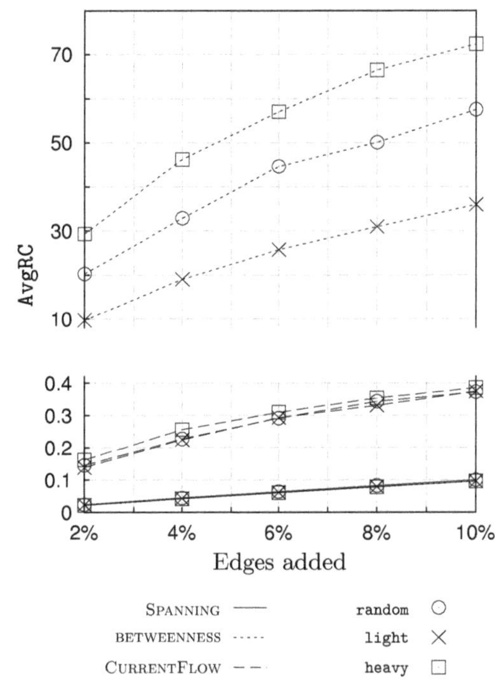

Figure 4: Average relative change in the edge importance scores. The x-axis shows the percentage of noisy edges added to the original **HepTh** graph.

JaccSim takes values in $[0, 1]$. Large values of Jaccard similarity mean that the sets $I(G, k)$ and $I(G', k)$ are similar. Consequently, larger values of JaccSim indicate higher resilience of the measure under study.

Results: Figures 4 and 5 show the noise resilience of SPANNING, CURRENTFLOW and BETWEENNESS centrality under edge addition. This is measured using both **AvgRC** (Fig. 4) as well as **JaccSim** (Fig. 5). The results that are shown are for the **HepTh** network, but the trend was the same in all the datasets that we tried. Note that while we use the fastest known algorithms for both CURRENTFLOW [8] and BETWEENNESS [7] (implemented in NetworkX), these algorithms remain a bottleneck, so we cannot present comparative experiments for larger networks. The edge additions are performed using all the three sampling methods we mentioned above, i.e. **random**, **heavy** and **light**. The shown results are averages over 10 different independent runs.

In both figures the x-axis corresponds to the number of edges being added to form E' as a fraction of the number of edges in $G = (V, E)$. For Figure 5, we picked $k = 10$ for the percentage of the highest-ranking edges whose behavior we want to explore; results for other values of k have very similar trends.

Overall, we observe that as we add more edges, the **AvgRC** increases for all the centralities, while **JaccSim**(G, G', k) decreases. This is expected, since we increasingly alter the structure of the graph. What is surprising though is how significantly smaller the values of **AvgRC** for SPANNING are, especially when compared to the corresponding values for BETWEENNESS, for the same number of edge additions. As shown in Figure 4, SPANNING has, in the worst case, **AvgRC**

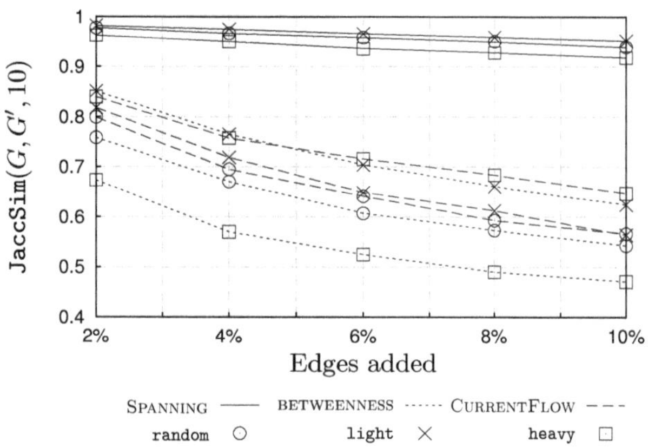

Figure 5: Jaccard similarity between the top 10%-scoring edges in the original and the noisy graph. Note how resilient the SPANNING centrality is to noise.

of value less than 0.1. In contrast, **AvgRC** of BETWEENNESS reaches up to 71.5 for the **light** sampling. This indicates that the values of SPANNING centrality are much more stable under the edge addition schemes we consider than the values of BETWEENNESS centrality. We also observe that CURRENTFLOW exhibits behavior between 2× and 4× worse than SPANNING, which is still much better than BETWEENNESS.

The results shown in Figure 5 show that the ranking of edges implied by the SPANNING measure is also much more stable than the ranking implied by either BETWEENNESS or CURRENTFLOW. More specifically, for $k = 10$, we observe that **JaccSim** has, in the worst case, score equal to 0.91 – which is very close to 1. The corresponding values for both BETWEENNESS and CURRENTFLOW are significantly lower, at 0.47 and 0.57 respectively. In addition to the above, we observed that, even when adding a 10% noise to the graph edges, more than 95% of the edges in $I(G, 10)$ are still deemed important by SPANNING. Note that the trends observed for $\texttt{JaccSim}(G, G', k)$ are similar for values of k that are smaller than 10%. Due to the similarity of these results to the ones we present here, we omitted them.

Overall, the resilience of SPANNING under edge additions demonstrates that even when SPANNING is computed over evolving graphs, it need not be recomputed frequently. In fact, our experiments indicate that even when 10% more edges are added in the original graph, both the centrality values as well the ranking of edges implied by the SPANNING centrality remain almost the same. Note that, although we only show here the results for edge additions, our findings for edge deletions are very similar and thus we omit them.

Resilience of β-CURRENTFLOW: In addition to the experiments we presented below, we also investigated the resilience of β-CURRENTFLOW. Our results are summarized as follows: for larger values of β, the **AvgRC** decreases to values that are smaller than the values we observe for BETWEENNESS. However even the smallest values are in the range [3, 5], thus never as small as the values we observe for SPANNING. The values of **JaccSim** on the other hand are consistently around 0.5. Although these results are not extensive, we conclude that the SPANNING centrality is significantly more resilient than β-CURRENTFLOW under edge additions and deletions.

7.3 Edge-importance measures and information propagation

A natural question to consider is the following: what do all the different edge-importance measures capture and how do they relate to each other? Here, we describe an experiment that allows us to quantitatively answer this question. On a high level, we do so by investigating how edges ranked as important (or less important) affect the result of an information-propagation process in the network.

Methodology: Given a network $G = (V, E)$, we compute the spread of an information propagation process, by picking 5% of the nodes of the graph, running the popular independent cascade model [22] using these nodes as seeds and computing the expected number of infected nodes in the end of this process. By repeating the experiment 20 times and taking the average we compute the SPREAD(G).

For any edge-importance measure, we compute the scores of all edges according to this measure, rank the edges in decreasing order of this score and then pick a set of ℓ edges, where $\ell = 0.02|E|$, such that they are at positions $((k-1)\ell + 1)\ldots k\ell$, for $k = 1, \ldots, |E|/\ell$. We refer to the set of edges picked for any k as E_k. For every k, we then remove the edges in E_k, forming graph G_k, and then compute SPREAD(G_k). In order to quantify the influence that the set E_k has on the information-propagation process we compute:

$$\Delta_k = \text{SPREAD}(G) - \text{SPREAD}(G_k).$$

Clearly, larger the values of Δ_k imply a larger effect of the removed edges E_k on the propagation process.

We experiment with the following four measures of importance: SPANNING, CURRENTFLOW, BETWEENNESS and RANDOM. Recall that the betweenness score of an edge is the fraction of all pairs shortest paths that go through this edge [12]. RANDOM simply assigns a random order on the edges in E.

Results: Figure 6 shows the values of Δ_k in the case of the **HepTh** network, for $k = 1, \ldots, 49$ when sets E_k are determined by the different importance measures. Overall we observe that the trend of Δ_k varies across measures. More specifically, in the case of SPANNING centrality (Figure 6a), Δ_k takes larger values for small k and appears to drop consistently until $k = 30$. This behavior can be explained by the definition of the SPANNING centrality – an edge is important if it is part of many spanning trees in the network – and the fact that the propagation of information in a graph can be represented as a spanning tree. CURRENTFLOW and BETWEENNESS (Figures 6b and 6c) behave differently. They appear to give medium importance scores to edges that have high impact on the spread. For CFC, these are the edges in E_k for $k \in [38, 43]$ and, for BETWEENNESS, the edges for $k \in [13, 18]$. These edges correspond to the peaks we see in Figures 6b and 6c. Observe that, for BETWEENNESS, this peak appears for smaller values of k, indicating that in this particular graph, there are edges that participate in relatively many shortest paths and, once removed, they disconnect the network, hindering the propagation process. Finally, the results for RANDOM show no specific pattern, indicating that what we observed in Figures 6a–6c is statistically significant.

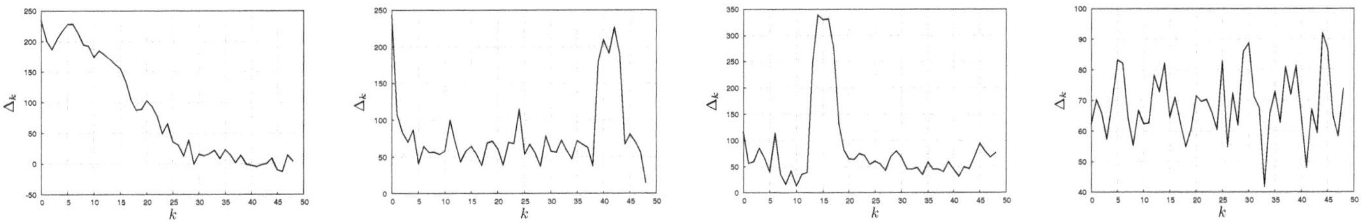

(a) SPANNING (b) CURRENTFLOW (c) BETWEENNESS (d) RANDOM

Figure 6: The values Δ_k as a function of k for the different importance measures.

7.4 Experiments with CURRENTFLOW

In this last experiment, we give some indicative examples of the efficiency of **Fast-FlowC**, which we described in the end of Section 6.

One of the major problems that **Fast-FlowC** has to solve is finding the right number of samples k that will be used for the evaluation of Equation (4). In practice we deal with this as follows: we run **Fast-FlowC** in epochs, each epoch consisting of 1000 independent samples of (s,t) pairs. For the rest of the discussion we will use **Fast-FlowC**(i) to refer to **Fast-FlowC** that stops after i epochs. If we use F^* to denote the ground-truth centrality values, computed via an exhaustive algorithm that goes through all (s,t) pairs, and F^i to denote the output of **Fast-FlowC**(i), then we could decide to stop when $\texttt{CorrD}(F^*, F^i)$ is reasonably small. Here, $\texttt{CorrD}(F, F')$ is the correlation distance between the two vectors F and F', and is computed as 1 minus their correlation coefficient. Thus, $\texttt{CorrD}(F, F') \in [0,2]$.

In the absence of ground-truth, we use the *self-correlation index* $\tau = \texttt{CorrD}(F^i, F^{i-1})$ to decide whether the number of samples is sufficient. We terminate when τ is close to 0.

In order not to bias our experiments with the large number of edges that have very small centrality scores, we only consider the top-10% scored edges in F^i and F^{i-1} and we compute $\texttt{CorrD}(F^{i-1}, F^i)$ projected on the union of these sets of edges. After all, importance measures aim at finding the highly scoring edges.

Also, in our experiments we found that drawing 1000 samples of (s,t) pairs between any two consecutive iterations of **Fast-FlowC**(i) is adequate to guarantee that the correlation between F^i and F^{i-1} is due to the convergence of the sampling procedure and not the closeness of the readings.

Ideally, we would like $\texttt{CorrD}(F^i, F^*)$ to be small for values of i for which τ is also small. Our experiments with small datasets indicate that this is the case. As a result, τ can be used as a proxy for convergence of **Fast-FlowC** for larger datasets.

In Table 2, we report the running time of β-**Fast-FlowC** for $\tau < 0.02$ as well as the running time for the exact computation of CURRENTFLOW (from NetworkX) for three different datasets: **GrQc**, **Oregon** and **Epinions**. Note that for **Epinions**, the largest of the three datasets, the exact algorithm does not terminate within a reasonable time. On the other hand for the medium-size dataset, i.e., **Oregon**, **Fast-FlowC** takes only 2-3 minutes (depending on the choice of β), while the exact algorithm requires time close to 5 hours.

Dataset	Fast-FlowC algorithm ($\beta = 1$)	($\beta = 5$)	($\beta = 20$)	Exact algorithm
GrQc	2.1 mins	1.3 mins	1.3 mins	20 mins
Oregon	3.3 mins	1.9 mins	1.4 mins	4h 40mins
Epinions	12h 23mins	5h 26mins	3h	n/a

Table 2: Time until termination of **Fast-FlowC** and the exact algorithm. We terminate for $\tau < 0.02$.

8. CONCLUSIONS

In this paper, we studied the problem of efficiently computing the SPANNING centrality of edges in large graphs. More specifically, we described a randomized approximate algorithm that builds upon seminal work in the theory community on the effective resistances of graphs and on efficiently solving laplacian linear systems. While the algorithm we describe exploits these ideas, we also introduce efficient speedups, that we deploy in order to achieve scalability even for very large graphs. Overall, our experimental evaluation gives ample empirical evidence of the efficiency of the proposed algorithm and its ability to handle large graphs. Indicatively, our method can compute the SPANNING centrality of all the edges of a graph with more than 1.5 million nodes and 11 million edges in less than 30 minutes, while offering low error guarantees. In addition to that, our experiments explored the properties of SPANNING and showed that (i) it is resilient to noise and (ii) ranks the edges according to their participation in an information-propagation process. In an attempt to generalize the ideas behind SPANNING centrality, we showed that it is an instance of a class of edge-importance measures, which we call *electrical measures*. In the paper, we showed multiple instances of such measures and demonstrated how the algorithmic tools we relied upon for the computation of SPANNING can also be used for efficiently computing these measures.

Acknowledgments: The authors would like to thank Petros Drineas, George Kollios and Malik Magdon-Ismail for useful discussions on topics related to this paper. This research was supported by: NSF CAREER #1253393, NSF grants: CNS #1017529, III #1218437, IIS #1320542 and gifts from Microsoft and Hariri Institute of Computing. I. Koutis is supported by NSF CAREER CCF-1149048. Part of this work was undertaken while I. Koutis was visiting ICERM (Institute of Computational and Experimental Research in Mathematics).

9. REFERENCES

[1] J. M. Anthonisse. *The rush in a directed graph.* SMC, 1971.

[2] D. A. Bader, S. Kintali, K. Madduri, and M. Mihail. Approximating betweenness centrality. In *WAW*, 2007.

[3] V. Batagelj and M. Zaversnik. An o(m) algorithm for cores decomposition of networks. *CoRR*, 2003.

[4] A. Bavelas. A mathematical model for group structure. *Human Organizations*, 7, 1948.

[5] B. Bollobas. *Modern Graph Theory.* Springer, 1998.

[6] S. P. Borgatti. Centrality and network flow. *Social Networks*, 27, Jan. 2005.

[7] U. Brandes. A faster algorithm for betweenness centrality. *Journal of Mathematical Sociology*, 25(2), 2001.

[8] U. Brandes and D. Fleischer. Centrality measures based on current flow. In *STACS*, 2005.

[9] U. Brandes and C. Pich. Centrality estimation in large networks. *International Journal of Bifurcation and Chaos*, 17(7), 2007.

[10] P. De Meo, E. Ferrara, G. Fiumara, and A. Ricciardello. A novel measure of edge centrality in social networks. *Knowledge-based Systems*, 30, 2012.

[11] P. Doyle and J. Snell. *Random walks and electric networks.* Math. Assoc. America., Washington, 1984.

[12] L. C. Freeman. A Set of Measures of Centrality Based on Betweenness. *Sociometry*, 40(1), Mar. 1977.

[13] L. C. Freeman, S. P. Borgatti, and D. R. White. Centrality in valued graphs: A measure of betweenness based on network flow. *Social networks*, 13(2), 1991.

[14] R. Geisberger, P. Sanders, and D. Schultes. Better approximation of betweenness centrality. In *ALENEX*, 2008.

[15] M. Gomez-Rodriguez, J. Leskovec, and A. Krause. Inferring networks of diffusion and influence. *TKDD*, 5(4), 2012.

[16] A. A. Hagberg, D. A. Schult, and P. J. Swart. Exploring network structure, dynamics, and function using NetworkX. In *Proceedings of the 7th Python in Science Conference (SciPy2008)*, Aug. 2008.

[17] J. M. Harris, J. L. Hirst, and M. J. Mossinghoff. *Combinatorics and Graph Theory.* Undergraduate Texts in Mathematics, Springer, 2008.

[18] C. Huitema. *Routing in the Internet.* Prentice Hall, 2000.

[19] V. Ishakian, D. Erdös, E. Terzi, and A. Bestavros. Framework for the evaluation and management of network centrality. In *SDM*, 2012.

[20] W. Johnson and J. Lindenstrauss. Extensions of lipschitz mappings into a hilbert space. In *Conference in modern analysis and probability*, 1982.

[21] U. Kang, S. Papadimitriou, J. Sun, and H. Tong. Centralities in large networks: Algorithms and observations. In *SDM*, 2011.

[22] D. Kempe, J. Kleinberg, and É. Tardos. Maximizing the spread of influence through a social network. In *Proceedings of the ninth ACM SIGKDD international conference on Knowledge discovery and data mining.* ACM, 2003.

[23] I. Koutis, G. L. Miller, and R. Peng. A nearly-m log n time solver for sdd linear systems. In *FOCS*, 2011.

[24] I. Koutis, G. L. Miller, and R. Peng. A fast solver for a class of linear systems. *Commun. ACM*, 55(10), 2012.

[25] I. Koutis, G. L. Miller, and D. Tolliver. Combinatorial preconditioners and multilevel solvers for problems in computer vision and image processing. *Computer Vision and Image Understanding*, 115(12), 2011.

[26] T. Lappas, E. Terzi, D. Gunopulos, and H. Mannila. Finding effectors in social networks. In *KDD*, 2010.

[27] M. Newman. A measure of betweenness centrality based on random walks. *Social networks*, 27(1), 2005.

[28] R. J. Perlman. An algorithm for distributed computation of a spanningtree in an extended lan. In *SIGCOMM*, 1985.

[29] G. Royle and C. Godsil. *Algebraic Graph Theory.* Graduate Texts in Mathematics. Springer Verlag, 1997.

[30] A. Shimbel. Structural parameters of communication networks. *Bulletin of Mathematical Biology*, 15, 1953.

[31] D. A. Spielman and N. Srivastava. Graph sparsification by effective resistances. *SIAM J. Comput.*, 40(6), 2011.

[32] R. E. Tarjan. A note on finding the bridges of a graph. *Inf. Process. Lett.*, 2(6), 1974.

[33] A. S. Teixeira, P. T. Monteiro, J. A. Carrico, M. Ramirez, and A. P. Francisco. Spanning edge betweenness. In *Workshop on Mining and Learning with Graphs*, 2013.

[34] W. Tutte. *Graph Theory.* Cambridge University Press, 2001.

No Escape from Reality: Security and Privacy of Augmented Reality Browsers

Richard McPherson
University of Texas at Austin
richard@cs.utexas.edu

Suman Jana
University of Texas at Austin
suman@cs.utexas.edu

Vitaly Shmatikov
University of Texas at Austin
shmat@cs.utexas.edu

ABSTRACT

Augmented reality (AR) browsers are an emerging category of mobile applications that add interactive virtual objects to the user's view of the physical world. This paper gives the first system-level evaluation of their security and privacy properties.

We start by analyzing the functional requirements that AR browsers must support in order to present AR content. We then investigate the security architecture of Junaio, Layar, and Wikitude browsers, which are running today on over 30 million mobile devices, and identify new categories of security and privacy vulnerabilities unique to AR browsers. Finally, we provide the first engineering guidelines for securely implementing AR functionality.

1 Introduction

Augmented reality (AR) technologies enhance users' perception of the world by blending interactive virtual objects with the visual representation of actual objects in real time [2, 3]. Traditional AR applications range from medical visualization to aircraft navigation, but only recently have consumer mobile devices become sufficiently powerful to run AR software.

AR applications have three stages: sensing input, transforming sensed objects (e.g., adding virtual objects), and rendering the transformed objects to the user. Modern AR platforms ease the burden of implementing these tasks. By far the most popular platforms are *AR browsers* like Junaio, Layar, and Wikitude, available as SDKs or standalone mobile apps. Junaio has more than 20 million users and over 20,000 content developers who have created more than 210,000 AR "channels" [14]. Layar has 1.5 million users and 9,000 content developers [18]. Wikitude has 13 million users [29] and over 30,000 content developers.

All existing AR browsers are based on Web browsers and are similar to them in the sense that they, too, fetch and display interactive content from websites ("channels," in AR parlance). In addition to rendering HTML and executing JavaScript, AR browsers provide support for the three key tasks necessary for AR functionality: sensing, transforming, and displaying transformed objects. They enable AR channels to (1) access sensors on the mobile device, including the onboard camera and GPS location, (2) create and manipulate a variety of 2D and 3D interactive virtual objects, and (3) display virtual objects on top of the camera feed, realistically blending them with real objects. The resulting AR content combines image recognition, geolocation, interactive virtual objects, conventional Web content, and control code written in JavaScript (see an example in Fig. 1).

Figure 1: A Layar-based mobile app [7].

The basic architecture of AR services is shown in Fig. 2. From the security and privacy perspective, its key aspect is that the AR browsers provide augmentation mechanisms, but the actual AR content comes from channels created by independent developers. Just like a conventional Web browser is an interface between the user and Web content from independent websites, an AR browser is an interface between the user and independent AR content. An AR browser is thus responsible for ensuring that malicious AR content cannot access content from other sources, nor damage or abuse the user's system outside the browser.

A major difference between Web browsers and AR browsers is the business model. Web browsers are typically part of the standard software distribution, and their developers are paid by the licensing fees from OEMs and OS owners and by the search engines. This model works because there is already a wealth of Web content. AR browsers, however, need a different model because there is not much AR content available today. Their sources of revenue include advertising injected into AR content, registration fees from content developers, and revenue sharing for paid content. This business model has an impact on the architecture of AR services: unlike Web content, which is accessed directly from the Web browser, requests to load third-party AR content must go through the AR service provider, as shown in Fig. 2.

Our contributions. We perform the first systematic analysis of the security and privacy properties of AR browsers and how they differ from Web browsers. Untrusted AR content presents new, unique types of threats, yet—in contrast to Web-browser specifications—the latest Augmented Reality Markup Language (ARML) specification [19] barely mentions security or privacy, and they are often overlooked in the design of the existing AR browsers.

WWW 2015, May 18–22, 2015, Florence, Italy.
ACM 978-1-4503-3469-3/15/05.
http://dx.doi.org/10.1145/2736277.2741657.

We start by analyzing the **functional requirements** needed to support the sensing, transforming, and rendering of AR content. These include new ways of combining AR objects and conventional HTML content from multiple origins, new APIs for accessing objects outside the browser, new mechanisms for controlling the display of AR and HTML objects, and new ways of launching content.

Then, for each functional requirement, we investigate how it is implemented by the existing AR browsers. All AR browsers are based on Web browsers, which do not support AR functionality, forcing AR browsers to resort to ad-hoc cross-origin mechanisms, APIs that open holes in the browser sandbox, custom techniques for composing visual content from different origins, and non-standard delegation schemes for authentication credentials.

Architectural flaws in these mechanisms result in security and privacy vulnerabilities. We explore the threat model of AR browsers and demonstrate several **new categories of threats** caused by the AR browsers' unique combination of high-volume visual data gathering, image-triggered code execution, outsourced image processing, and merging images from the onboard camera with third-party content. For example, individual-specific items such as license plates can automatically launch malicious AR content, enabling fully automated stalking and tracking; malicious AR channels can abuse image-triggered code execution; and a conventional webpage can hijack the AR browser installed on the user's mobile device and use it to gain unauthorized access to the device's camera and GPS without the user's permission. We also show AR browsers amplify existing threats such as cross-site scripting, clickjacking, cookie stealing, and leakage of private information.

For each design flaw, we present our **recommendations**. Some are easy to fix, others require a substantial re-design, but none are mere "bugs." They all stem from the fact that standard system components used in today's mobile and Web applications are insufficient to securely support AR functionality. For each functional requirement of the AR browsers, we explain which features and system abstractions are needed to implement it properly

2 AR Services

AR services are deployed by AR *service providers* such as Junaio and Layar. These companies supply AR client software (we use the term *AR browser*) to users and maintain dedicated AR servers through which users access third-party AR content (see Fig. 2). AR *content providers* are independent developers who create AR content, host it on their own servers, and register this content with AR service providers. We use the term *channel* generically for any AR content, but the actual terminology differs from service to service (e.g., channels are called *layers* in Layar).

By analogy with conventional Web, AR service providers are similar to Web-browser developers, while AR channels are similar to Web applications. There are important differences, however. AR providers make money by charging for SDK licenses, features such as cloud storage for AR channels, and per-user fees from third-party apps that connect to their services. All providers analyzed in this paper allow a limited use of free channels, but some charge for commercial channels and/or may insert banner ads into free channels. Therefore, they typically require that browsers initiate access to third-party channels via providers' own servers.

2.1 Functional requirements

Access to native resources on the user's device. The AR browser must have access to the onboard camera and GPS location to recognize images and locations that launch AR content, and to correctly add AR objects to the camera feed.

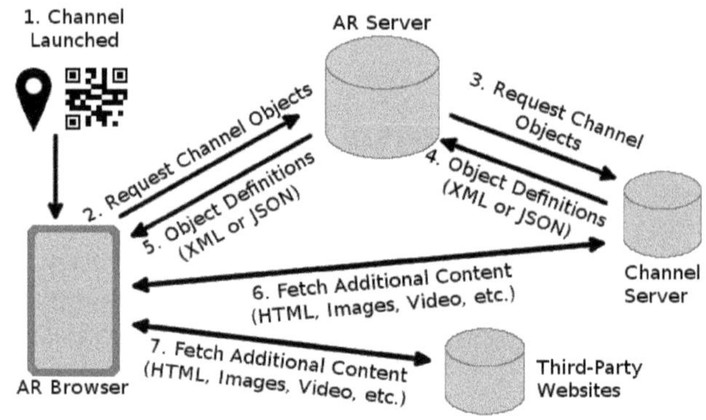

Figure 2: Architecture of a typical AR service.

Support for interactive, non-HTML AR content. In addition to HTML content such as images and text, AR content may include 2D and 3D models and animations that cannot be described in HTML. AR channels thus include service-specific XML or JSON defining how to place and render these objects.

Image-triggered code execution. AR browsers access content in non-standard ways: they send images from the device's camera to their servers, which attempt to recognize certain pictures and QR codes and automatically launch the associated AR channels.

Outsourced image processing. Image recognition is a computationally heavy task that may not be feasible on low-powered mobile devices and often involves proprietary algorithms. Furthermore, image-based code execution requires the server to extract the trigger image from the camera feed and match it against a proprietary database of registered images. Therefore, AR browsers send images from the phone's camera to the AR provider for processing.

Visual composition of AR content. The AR browser is responsible for constructing a visual stack that combines non-HTML AR content, such as interactive 3D models, with HTML content from multiple origins (e.g., online ads) on top of the camera feed.

Indirect retrieval of AR content. Instead of directly fetching AR content from its developers, AR browsers typically submit requests via the AR provider's server. This enables providers to charge fees for registration and usage, inject advertising, etc.

2.2 Components of AR services

AR browsers. Fig. 3 shows the generic architecture of an AR browser, including (1) one or more instances of an embedded Web browser such as WebView, (2) a "native" component with direct access to OS-managed resources such as the camera and GPS location, and (3) ad-hoc mechanisms for gluing these pieces together.

AR channels. An AR channel is roughly similar to a website. It defines an augmented reality experience by specifying AR content to display and how to display it. This content may include AR objects linked to a geolocation ("points of interest" or POI), HTML pages, audio, video, etc., as well as JavaScript to control these objects. The channel may also specify the actions to take when a certain object comes into view or is clicked by the user.

For example, an AR channel may overlay historical pictures when viewing landmarks,[1] show reviews for nearby restaurants,[2] or control an avatar running around the scene.[3] A channel may directly incorporate third-party content—for instance, include online ads in

[1] `http://layar.it/YuDzik`
[2] Wikitude Restaurants
[3] `junaio://channels/?id=127275`

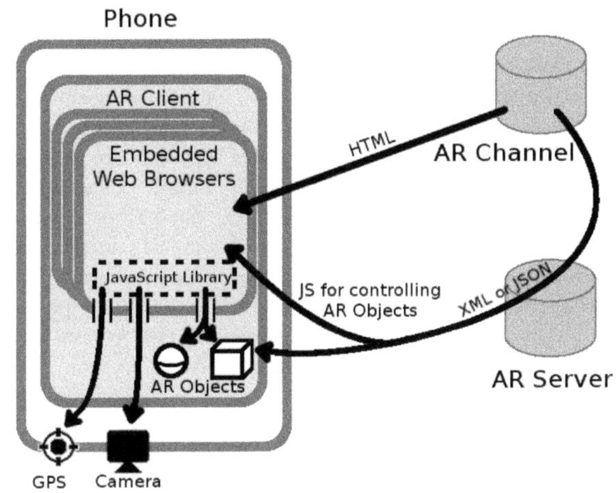

Figure 3: Architecture of an AR browser.

its HTML—or instruct the AR browser to load a third-party webpage when the user performs a certain action.

A user launches a channel by selecting it from a list provided by the AR browser (based on the geolocation or most popular channels) or by scanning an image.

AR servers. As explained in Section 2.1, requests to load a channel are sent by the AR browser to the AR provider's server, not directly to the channel server (see Fig. 2). Each request includes some combination of the channel's id, the location of the device, and other data. The AR server forwards the request to a server that the channel owner registered with the AR provider. The AR server may also handle the authentication of users to channels (Section 9). The response from the channel with the XML or JSON definitions of AR objects is forwarded via the AR server, too. Subsequent requests may be sent by the browser directly to the channel server.

2.3 Specific AR browsers

We focus on the most popular AR browsers. **Junaio** is an AR browser developed by Metaio to augment both print media and geolocation-based environments (Fig. 4). **Layar** focuses primarily on adding AR features to print media such as magazines and newspapers (Fig. 5), but also supports geolocation-based AR. AR content for Layar is served by *layers*, but we will refer to them as *channels* for terminological consistency. **Wikitude** is another AR browser, but some of its features did not execute correctly in our testing, thus we discuss only the features we were able to evaluate.

Unlike HTML, AR content is browser-specific, i.e., a Junaio browser can only display Junaio channels. Augmented Reality Markup Language (ARML) is a proposed standard that unifies the XML format of AR objects [19].

3 Threat Model

We are concerned with five classes of attackers.

AR attackers. Just like a standard Web attacker, an AR attacker controls the malicious content of his AR channel and may trick or entice users into visiting it. He cannot observe users' network communications with other destinations, nor execute any code on their machines other than JavaScript served by his own channel.

Unlike conventional Web browsers, AR browsers automatically launch a channel whenever they scan a picture or QR code associated with it. This introduces a new attack vector: since the attacker can choose any image for his channel, he can trick users' browsers into automatically launching malicious content by placing this image in a public place (e.g., as a sticker on a wall).

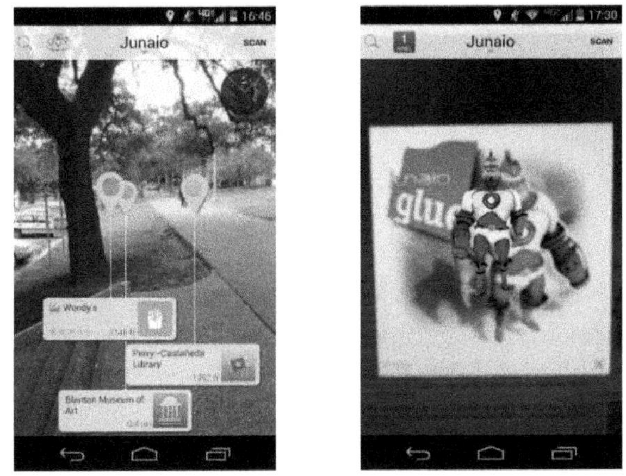

(a) (b)

Figure 4: 4a is a Junaio channel showing nearby places of interest. 4b is a channel showing a 3D model placed over the Junaio logo.

Ad attackers. AR channels can include third-party content such as syndicated ads. An "ad attacker" tricks a trusted website or AR channel into incorporating his malicious content, e.g., via ad brokers. We assume that ads can run arbitrary JavaScript, but are confined into iframes when rendered by the AR browser.

Web attackers. The focus of this paper is on malicious AR content, but we also investigate how the mere presence of AR browsers on the device can be exploited by conventional Web attackers (Section 4.2). A Web attacker controls his own website (but not the network) and may lure users to it via enticing content, ads, etc.

Curious AR services. We assume that AR browsers are benign (the issues raised by malicious mobile apps are well beyond our scope), but we do investigate privacy risks caused by user-specific visual data collected by AR services.

Network attackers. We briefly analyze privacy threats posed by network attackers. Either through man-in-the-middle attacks or by being on the same network as the victim, a network attacker can listen in on the communications between the AR browser and the AR provider, AR channel owners, and third-party servers.

4 Out-of-sandbox Native Access

AR browsers cannot function without access to the camera and GPS location. Both are required to launch AR channels and to correctly add AR objects to the camera feed. Consequently, all AR browsers equip JavaScript with some form of access to native device resources outside the browser. Script access to AR objects is also required by the ARML 2.0 specification [19, Section 9.1].

These custom APIs effectively open holes in the Web-browser sandbox, intended to support native access by the channel's own JavaScript. Unfortunately, the WebView embedded browser where this JavaScript is executed does not provide any way to restrict access to these APIs. Consequently, they can be accessed by any Web content regardless of its origin.

Another common functionality is launching AR browsers via custom URLs. This is needed for interoperability [21, Section 5]: for example, one AR browser may launch another AR browser to render proprietary content that is not supported by the first browser.

4.1 Doing it wrong

The control code of Junaio channels is written in JavaScript and executed in an embedded WebView. This WebView is extended with custom APIs for accessing the camera, reading and changing the Junaio-reported geolocation, controlling the device's light, making

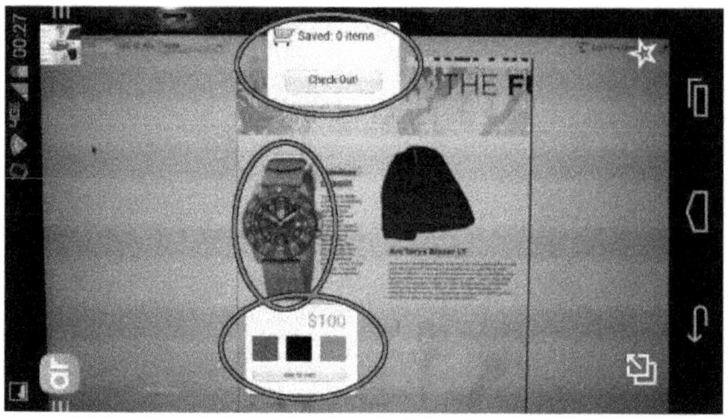

Figure 5: A Layar channel running on a scanned magazine page. The AR objects are circled. Clicking any color below the 3D watch model changes its color. The user can also add the watch to his or her shopping cart.

requests to the channel server, opening conventional Web-browser windows, or loading a different channel.

These APIs are accessed via AREL, a JavaScript library that encodes commands in pseudo-URIs. For example, *arel://media/website/?action=open&external=true&url=http%3a%2f%2f www.google.com* instructs the Junaio app to launch Google.com in a conventional browser. To pass this pseudo-URI from WebView to the Junaio app, the channel's Web code pushes it to the global "commandQueue" and sets *window.location* to *"arel://requests Pending"*. The Junaio app intercepts the URL load event, reads the command off the queue, and performs the requested action. In Junaio on Android, however, any content—regardless of its origin and even if running inside an iframe—can bypass AREL and execute native commands directly, without user permission, by setting *window.location* to the corresponding pseudo-URI.

4.2 Risks

In this section, we are concerned with (1) conventional Web attackers, whose malicious pages are viewed by mobile users in conventional browsers, (2) "ad attackers," whose untrusted HTML is incorporated into trusted AR channels but confined into iframes, and (3) AR attackers who directly control malicious AR channels.

Conventional Web content breaking out of the sandbox. Conventional webpages cannot access the camera or other native resources outside the browser unless explicitly authorized by the user. Unfortunately, the AR browser's access rights can be hijacked by malicious webpages to gain this access without involving the user.

Suppose the user has the Junaio app installed on his Android phone. The user accidentally visits a malicious webpage in a *regular Web browser* (e.g., Android's default system browser) by clicking on an ad, a link in a spam message, etc. The malicious page contains a URL of the form *junaio://channel=*... and a script in the page forces the browser to open this URL. This generates an Android intent, which automatically starts the Junaio app and launches any channel chosen by the attacker, e.g., the attacker's own channel. Like all Junaio channels, the attacker's channel automatically has access to the device's camera, can take pictures of the user and its surroundings, etc. Layar, too, can be automatically launched from a conventional webpage via a pseudo-URI.

This attack completely bypasses OS access control. Even though the user granted camera access only to Junaio or Layar, this access has now been hijacked by a conventional webpage. The attack can even be stealthy. Having read images from the camera, the attacker's channel can relaunch the regular Web browser and immediately redirect the user to the page he was initially browsing.

This vulnerability is *generic* because the ability to automatically launch an AR browser is required for interoperability [21]. The presence of a single AR browser on the user's device can thus be exploited by any conventional webpage to bypass user permissions.

Malicious ads breaking out of the sandbox. Because native-access rights are not restricted to the channel's own origin, any iframe can hijack them. In Section 5.2, we describe how native-access capabilities can be used by a malicious ad to perform a cross-site scripting attack against any origin of its choosing.

Furthermore, malicious third-party iframes included into a trusted channel can redirect the entire AR browser to a malicious channel. For example, in Layar, a script in an iframe can use a *layar://* command to switch the browser to a different channel. In Junaio, the switchChannel command in AREL (also accessible from an iframe) has the same effect. This can be exploited for undetectable phishing: a malicious iframe can automatically switch the browser to a visually indistinguishable malicious channel.

Malicious AR content abusing native access. The ability of AR channels to access resources outside the browser sandbox presents privacy risks to their users. In Junaio, as long as the channel's transparent overlay (Section 5.1) continues to run in the background, it can surreptitiously grab images from the camera and send them to the channel server even after the user moved away from the place where he launched the channel. The user's location can be tracked in a similar fashion in Junaio, Layar, and Wikitude.

4.3 How to do it right

Interfaces to native resources must be protected by origin-based access control, lest they are hijacked by untrusted iframes. Recent solutions to the problem of unauthorized native access by third-party origins in mobile apps, e.g., NoFrak by Georgiev et al. [9], may be applicable to AR browsers. Furthermore, AR browsers should be re-designed to support fine-grained native-access permissions. For example, instead of unfettered access to a camera, the channel would be restricted to accessing it only via pre-defined system abstractions such as "recognizers" [12] for specific objects.

To prevent conventional webpages from gaining unauthorized access to the camera and other resources by launching the AR browser and directing it to the attacker's channel, the user should be asked for confirmation whenever the AR browser is invoked automatically (this presents interface-design and usability challenges).

5 Support for Non-HTML AR Content

In addition to HTML content such as images and text, interactive AR content includes videos, animations, and 2D and 3D models with unique visual presentation requirements. These AR objects cannot be described in HTML alone, thus AR services rely on XML or JSON definitions to specify how to place and render these objects, and on JavaScript to control these objects at runtime.

Just like conventional websites, AR channels may combine content from different origins. AR browsers must therefore confine untrusted content. In conventional Web browsers, the same-origin policy (SOP) ensures that content from a given origin—defined by the protocol (HTTP or HTTPS), domain name, and port number—cannot access the non-trivial attributes of any content from a different origin [27]. Web browsers also provide origin-based isolation mechanisms such as iframes and structured cross-origin communication mechanisms such as postMessage.

In AR browsers, interactive, non-HTML AR objects make the confinement problem much harder because these objects must be described in XML or JSON, which are not governed by the SOP. Therefore, the AR browser cannot rely on the underlying Web browser to provide isolation between origins.

5.1 Doing it wrong

Junaio. In Junaio, AR objects are defined in an XML page returned by the channel server. Junaio supports floating clickable

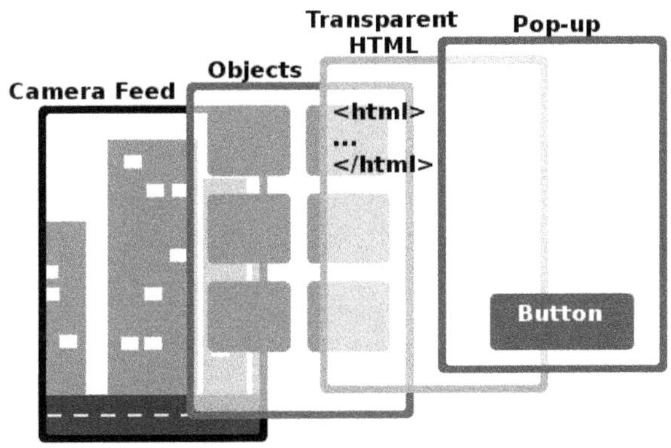

Figure 6: Junaio's visual stack. AR objects are on top of the camera feed, the transparent overlay on top of the objects. If an object is clicked, a popup appears at the very top.

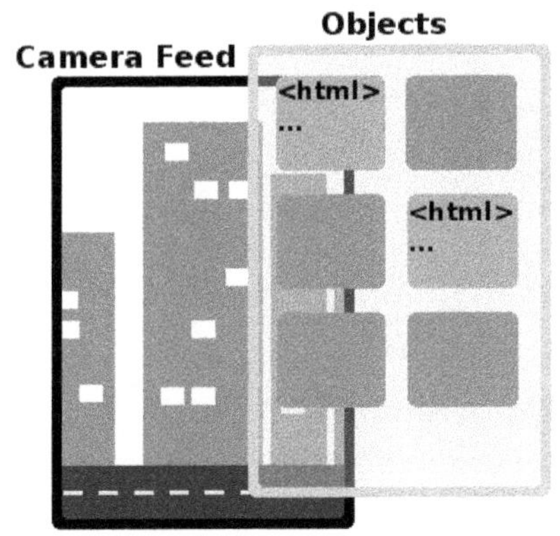

Figure 7: Layar's visual stack. AR objects, which can include HTML pages, are overlaid on the camera feed.

objects ("points of interest"), 3D models, floating pictures, movies, and 360-degree panoramas (Figs. 4a and 4b). The Junaio browser renders these objects in the visual stack shown in Fig. 6.

On top of the AR objects, Junaio places a transparent window implemented using WebView (Android) or UIWebView (iOS). We call it the *transparent HTML overlay*. This overlay provides GUI functionality to channels and enables them to control AR objects outside WebView via special browser interfaces and a custom JavaScript library called AREL (Section 4.1). These interfaces can be used to create, destroy, animate, move, or resize AR objects, to read and modify their parameters such as id, name, geolocation, and the associated popup, and to handle events based on channel state, object state, or user's interaction with the object (e.g., channel ready, object loaded, sound finished playing, object rotated).

The URL of the transparent overlay is specified in the XML page and may belong to a different origin than the AR channel itself. This URL cannot be viewed by the user. The channel—and any third-party content included in the channel—can also supply JavaScript that will be executed inside the transparent page.

Clicking a link in the transparent overlay loads the destination in the same window, replacing the old page. JavaScript in the transparent overlay can also open an opaque window with a conventional embedded Web browser. Another way to open an opaque window is via a popup (Section 5.2). JavaScript continues to run in the background after opening the window.

Layar. The Layar browser displays AR objects on top of the visual feed from the device's camera (Fig. 7). The objects can be HTML webpages, 2D images, 3D models, or videos, and can have actions associated with them, such as placing a phone call, sending an SMS or email, launching a website, loading or refreshing channels, sharing the channel on Facebook or Twitter, and loading movies and music. Actions are specified in the object definition via pseudo-URIs such as 'tel:', 'sms:', 'mailto:', 'layar://' , 'layarshare://'.

Wikitude. Wikitude is architecturally similar to Junaio. AR content includes a transparent webpage that shows a GUI and controls AR objects via a custom JavaScript library called ARchitect. Object types include *HtmlDrawable*, intended to display HTML content. HtmlDrawables have an evalJavaScript function that can be used to execute JavaScript inside a drawable (it worked only sporadically in our testing on Android 4.4.2).

5.2 Risks

In this section, we are concerned with AR attackers, who may incorporate trusted content into their malicious AR channels, and "ad attackers," whose malicious content (e.g., online ads) is incorporated into trusted AR channels but confined into iframes.

Cross-site scripting. The XML definition of an AR object in Junaio can have a *popup* field with a textual description and an array of buttons. When such an object is clicked, a partially transparent window with the popup's description and buttons is opened on top of the transparent overlay (Fig. 6). Each button contains either a URL, or JavaScript code. When a button is clicked, the associated URL is loaded in an opaque window. If the button contains JavaScript, it is executed in the transparent overlay—even if the origin of the content in the overlay is different from the origin of the channel that provided the script.

This setup opens a hole in the same-origin policy. A malicious channel can specify any origin for the transparent page and associate an arbitrary script with a button. When the button is clicked, this script is injected into the transparent page and gains unrestricted access to all content from this page's origin—see Fig. 8a. This cross-site scripting (XSS) vulnerability can be exploited, for example, to modify the victim's DOM (see Fig. 8b) or steal cookies.

HtmlDrawable objects in Wikitude contain an even simpler XSS vulnerability. A malicious channel can specify any URL for an HtmlDrawable object and use evalJavaScript to inject an arbitrary script into this object.

Universal cross-site scripting. The above XSS attacks assume that the channel is malicious. Unfortunately, even if (1) the channel itself is benign, (2) all untrusted, third-party content, such as online ads, is correctly confined to iframes, and (3) the embedded Web browser running the channel's HTML correctly enforces the SOP, confined third-party content in Junaio can perform XSS attacks against *any* origin of its choosing.

Consider a benign Junaio channel that includes an AR object with a popup button and suppose that the channel's transparent HTML page contains an ad in an iframe (Fig. 9a). Malicious JavaScript hidden in such an ad can (1) use AREL commands (Section 4.1) to change the script associated with the popup, and (2) change the URL of the transparent overlay to the victim page (Fig. 9b). When the button is clicked, the attack script is executed in the victim page (Fig. 9c). This is a *universal XSS vulnerability*: a malicious ad can inject an arbitrary script into any origin whatsoever.

As a proof of concept, we have implemented this attack against Twitter. Our channel includes an HTML page and one geolocation object associated with a popup. At first, this popup simply launches `google.com`. The channel's HTML page contains an iframe with a button. When clicked, this button executes JavaScript which issues an AREL command to Junaio to associate the popup with an attack script, then changes the URL of the transparent page to Twitter with an attacker-chosen tweet text. When the user opens the

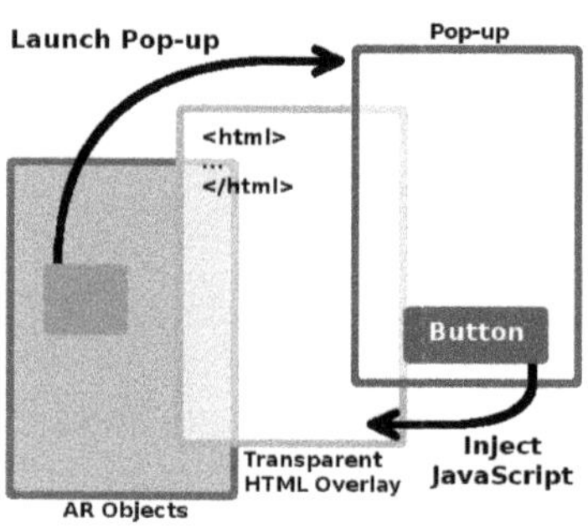

(a) XSS vector.

(b) Exploiting XSS.

Figure 8: Cross-site scripting (XSS) in Junaio

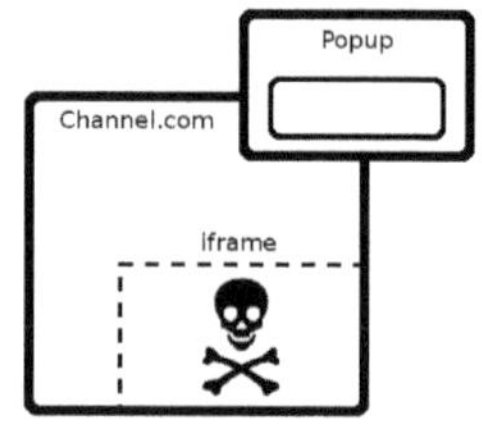

(a) Step 1

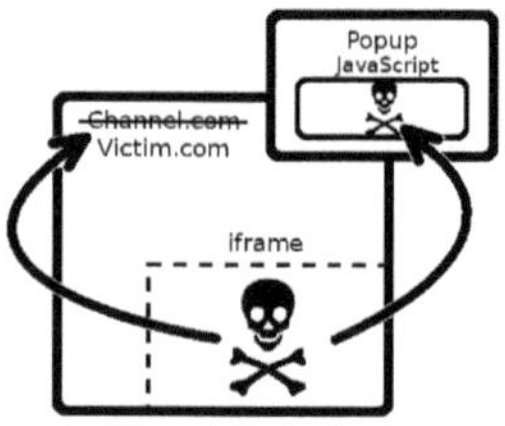

(b) Step 2

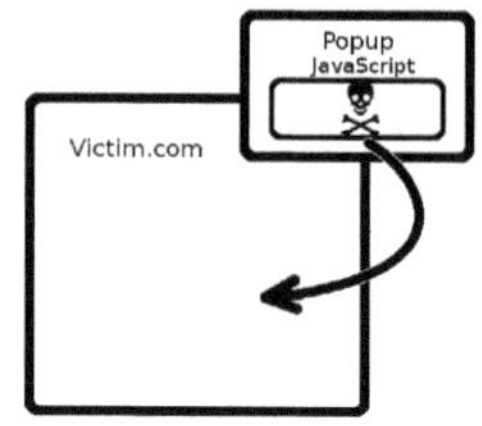

(c) Step 3

Figure 9: Universal XSS vulnerability in Junaio.

popup and clicks the button, Junaio unwittingly injects the script into the Twitter page, where it submits the attacker's tweet.

Other capabilities available to malicious code in an iframe include launching an opaque browser window, turning on and off the camera and the light, removing all AR objects, switching channels, and launching audio and video files.

5.3 How to do it right

Quick patches. The cross-site scripting vulnerabilities described above are caused in part by the fact that the origin of HTML incorporated into an AR channel may be different from the channel's own origin. One plausible defense is for the AR browser to ensure that the two origins are the same; another is to sanitize XML so that it does not contain scripts, which is a notoriously difficult problem [4]. Both defenses require the AR browser to carefully reason about the origins of content specified in custom XML definitions, thus replicating a complex piece of Web-browser functionality. Furthermore, both defenses disable important functional features of AR browsers (such as controlling the appearance of AR objects from another origin) and may break existing applications.

In Wikitude, where evalJavaScript allows channels to inject scripts into an HtmlDrawable regardless of its origin, restricting the origin is not feasible because HtmlDrawable is intended to display content from origins other than the channel itself.

Principled solutions. The root cause of many security holes described in this section is that AR objects cannot be described in HTML, thus AR browsers must use custom mechanisms to enable HTML content to control these objects. Standardizing AR object description languages, including them in HTML5 via either tags, or a special document type, (e.g., *channel*), and adding support for these new HTML5 features into browsers would allow AR content to execute entirely within WebView, eliminating the need for XML and some of the ad-hoc browser interfaces.

Unfortunately, assigning origins to these tags is not trivial. In the existing AR browsers, all AR objects are treated as if their origin is the domain where the main AR channel is hosted. Since these objects may contain JavaScript, this is extremely dangerous.

The alternative is to extend the same-origin policy to AR tags. These tags are intended to support 3D models, animations, UI elements, etc. which may come from different domains but are intended to work smoothly together to produce a unified AR experience. A naive extension of the SOP would isolate the AR HTML tags based on their domains, but this would prevent them from communicating. The developers would then have to implement cross-origin communication mechanisms, which is fraught with peril [26]. Enforcement of the SOP is complicated further by the fact that several of these new tags may need plugins to be rendered (similar to Flash).

Lacking HTML5 support for AR, WebView can at least provide origin-restricted APIs that render arbitrary objects on top of camera images and let JavaScript inside WebView control these objects.

6 Image-Triggered Code Execution

The ability to scan their surroundings and to recognize and track images is fundamental in AR browsers [19, Section 7.5.1.2]. This enables new methods for invoking AR content: for example, a Junaio or Layar channel can be launched simply by scanning a picture or QR code associated with the channel.

6.1 Doing it wrong

When the user is viewing his surroundings through the Junaio or Layar browser, the AR service is continuously analyzing the camera feed. As soon as it recognizes an image associated with some channel, it automatically launches and executes the channel's content, without any confirmation prompts. The user cannot preview the URL or any other information about the content, with one exception: for QR codes (but not pictures), Layar previews the URL by showing it as a button before launching the channel. Unfortunately, its URL parser is broken (Fig. 10). For example, if the URL in the QR code is *http:////attacker.com*, it will not be displayed in the preview, but the browser will launch AR content hosted at *http://attacker.com*. In Junaio, *after* a channel is fully loaded, the user can see its description and the developer's name.

6.2 Risks

In this section, we are primarily concerned with AR attackers who can choose any picture or QR code as the automatic trigger for their malicious channels. For some (but not all) attacks, the attacker needs to physically place these images in public places.

Fully automated, stealthy, large-scale tracking. Because not all AR services vet pictures associated with AR channels, they can be used for automated stalking and tracking. For example, Layar's image recognition algorithm is sufficiently precise to distinguish between license plate numbers. An AR attacker can register a Layar channel associated with the photo of a specific license plate. Whenever any of the millions of Layar users scan their surroundings and the license plate is prominent in the camera's view, the channel is launched automatically and the plate's location, along with its entire visual environment, is sent to the channel's owner,

Figure 10: Both codes launch the same channel, but Layar fails to parse the code on the right and does not show the URL.

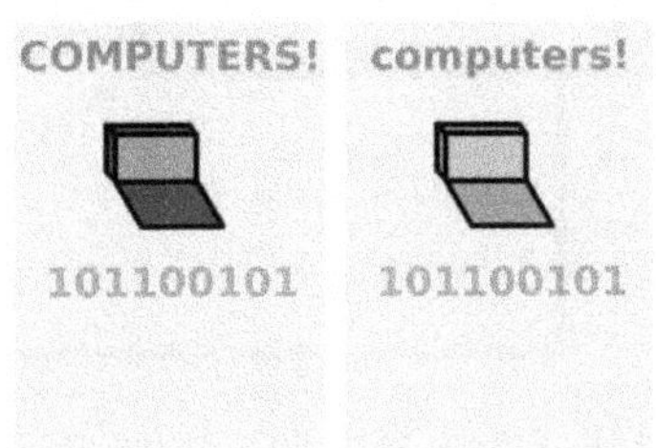

Figure 11: Depending on the angle, each poster nondeterministically launches its own channel or the channel associated with the other poster.

enabling him to track the plate's movements. Other sensitive items can be tracked in a similar fashion.

Automatically launching malicious content. As mentioned above, when an image is recognized by the AR service's (black-box) recognition algorithm, the code of the associated channel executes without user confirmation or channel identification. If a scanned image contains sub-images associated with different channels or a familiar image in an unusual environment or an image that is similar yet subtly different from a familiar image, the user cannot know ahead of time what channel will be launched.

Image recognition algorithms suffer from false positives and are inevitably nondeterministic from the user's point of view [30]. Unfortunately, user interfaces of the AR browsers are derived from the underlying Web browsers and do not inform the user about spurious matches and other potential problems with visual identification.

This can be exploited by an AR attacker in two ways: (1) register an image trigger that is very similar to an image already associated with a trusted channel, or (2) combine a malicious channel's trigger with a trusted channel's trigger into a single composite image. In either scenario, the AR browser may be tricked into automatically launching the malicious channel when scanning the attacker's image on a building wall, bus shelter, etc.

In Layar, the same picture may be associated with multiple channels. For example, we have been able to register our channel with the same movie-poster image as one of Layar's demo channels. If there are multiple channels associated with a picture, the user can open a menu in the corner to see channel names and switch between them. It is possible, however, to create visually similar images that automatically and nondeterministically launch different channels without the browser presenting the channel selection menu to the user. Each poster in Fig. 11 nondeterministically launches the channel associated with the poster or the (completely different) channel associated with the other poster. At many viewing angles and lighting, the channel selection menu is not offered.

(a) (b) (c) (d)

Figure 12: Different combinations of the Junaio mascot and QR code launch different channels.

Furthermore, a malicious channel can suppress the channel selection menu using the native-access capabilities described in Section 4.2. A *layar://[channelname]* pseudo-URI instructs the browser to launch a channel. In this case, the browser does not show other channels associated with the image. Consider a malicious channel that associates itself with the same image as a benign channel. If the user previews the malicious channel before flipping to the benign channel, the first object loaded from the malicious channel can reload the entire channel using *layar://[channelname]* and the other, benign channel will no longer be visible to the user.

The other risk is composite images that include a trusted image in an unexpected visual environment. When faced with a composite image, Junaio's choice of the channel to launch depends on the camera angle and distance. For example, the images in Figs. 12a and 12b launch different channels depending on whether the mascot or the QR code is more prominent. Sometimes, changing the angle of the camera by a few degrees changes which channel is launched. The image in Fig. 12c automatically launches the channel associated with the mascot when scanned from a close distance, and the one associated with the QR code when scanned from further away. Fig. 12d launches the channel associated with the QR code, even though the mascot is visible. This means that even after scanning a familiar image, a user cannot be sure that the automatically launched channel is the one he expects.

6.3 How to do it right

The risk of an AR attacker registering an image trigger that is specific to an individual (e.g., a license plate) is inherent in AR services. A service may attempt to filter out such images during channel registration, but this requires deep semantic analysis of the submitted images and will be inevitably bypassable. This inherent risk is exacerbated by the fact that AR content is executed immediately after the image is scanned.

First, AR browsers should inform the user about the origin of AR content before launching it (at the very least, display the developer's name and basic information about the channel). Second, automatic, image-triggered code execution is fraught with danger and should be used sparingly—for example, only with trusted channels—and not with every image that happens to fall into the camera's field of vision. Third, AR browsers should develop better user interfaces that inform users about the possibility of spurious image matches and nondeterministic launches of unexpected content.

7 Outsourced Image Processing

AR browsers must continuously analyze the device's camera feed in order to recognize automatic content triggers and to anchor or position AR objects on the screen.

7.1 Doing it wrong

AR browsers such as Junaio and Layar do not process the captured images on the device; instead, they send them to central AR servers. There are several reasons to outsource image processing. First, for

Figure 13: An image sent by the Layar browser over HTTP so that the Layar server can recognize content triggers. Note the accidentally captured credit card.

business reasons—injecting ads, charging content providers, keeping usage statistics, etc.—all AR content retrieval is mediated by the AR service. Second, to facilitate image-based channel launching, recognition of trigger images is done at the server. Because this involves matching against proprietary databases using proprietary algorithms, centralized image processing helps protect intellectual property and removes the need to replicate and update the service's image database on millions of devices. Third, many image recognition algorithms are computationally intensive and would heavily task low-powered mobile devices.

7.2 Risks

In this section, we are concerned with (1) network attackers who observe network traffic between the device and the provider's AR server, and (2) the AR service itself.

Accidental overcollection of sensitive data is a big risk in this setting. For example, the Layar browser sends raw camera images to the server over unencrypted HTTP and includes the phone's location into the GET request for the channel's JSON. Combining images with location data is a serious privacy concern for many users [10]. All sensitive items in the image (see Fig. 13) and request are leaked to any Wi-Fi eavesdropper.

Even if network communications are secure, the AR service inevitably collects a tremendous amount of raw visual data about its users' physical environment. This is an inherent design flaw of all existing AR services. The users must trust them to safeguard captured images, which contain a lot of sensitive information that is completely irrelevant to the AR functionality: screens, credit cards, license plates, etc. Furthermore, a user has no way to learn which data is sent to AR servers. For example, in addition to the unencrypted camera images sent at the start of each scan and the geolocation, the Layar browser occasionally sends a log message to the server with the phone's make, model, and OS version number.

7.3 How to do it right

When image recognition is outsourced to the server, a secure protocol should be used to prevent accidental leakage of irrelevant information in the images. If the server is attempting to recognize a channel trigger on a magazine page, there is no need for it to "see" the physical objects surrounding the page.

This is a difficult problem, but there has been some recent progress. Osadchy et al. described a prototype system for secure outsourced face matching [20]. This system cannot be directly applied in AR browsers, however, because images matched by AR browsers may appear in different lighting, under different angles, etc. Another approach is taken by Darkly [13], which can perform simple computer vision tasks without access to raw image details.

8 Visual Composition

To render images, text, 2D and 3D models, and HTML content from multiple origins on top of the camera feed, AR browsers maintain complex visual stacks. Junaio and Layar's visual stacks are described in Section 5.1.

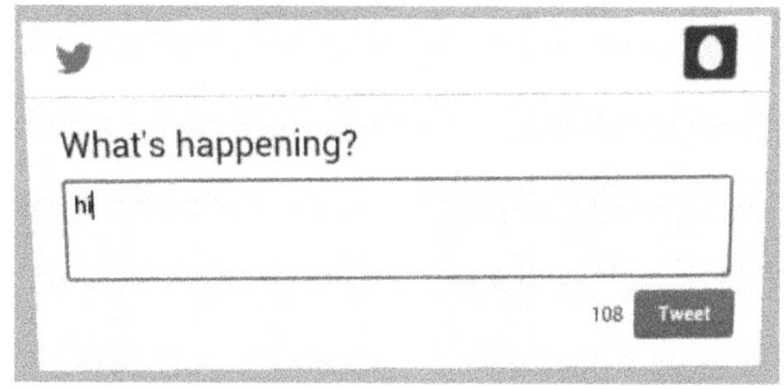

(a) Overlapped HTML widgets in Layar. The widget with "hi" is cut off before its Tweet button.

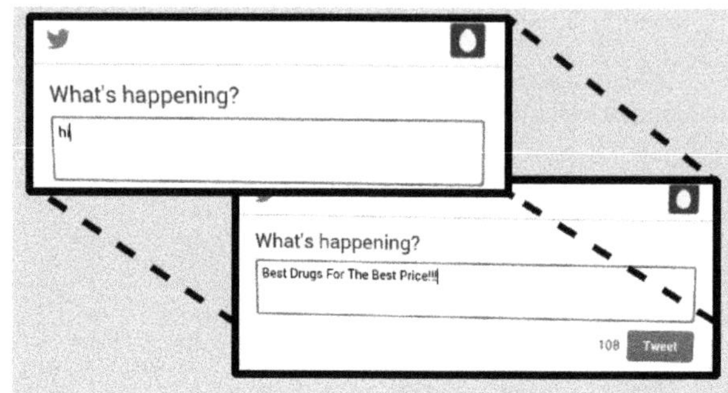

(b) The two HTML widgets expanded. In the attack, the bottom widget is not fully shown (its tweet text is covered and not visible to the user).

Figure 14: Clickjacking in Layar.

In Layar, a channel can use a webpage as an AR object, called an *HTML widget*. Each widget opens in its own WebView and does not display URLs or Web-browser buttons. HTML widgets may not be covered by other types of AR objects, but can be overlaid on each other to create a visual AR experience.

8.1 Doing it wrong

Conventional Web browsers provide the *iframe* abstraction that allows composition of HTML content from different origins. To defend against clickjacking, a webpage can ensure that it is not framed by a page from a different origin, via either framebusting [25] (moving itself to the top frame), or X-Frame-Option [31].

AR browsers must deal with both HTML and non-HTML content, and thus resort to custom mechanisms to implement the functional equivalent of *iframe*. Consequently, standard defenses based on framebusting or X-Frame-Option no longer work. For example, as described above, Layar puts each instance of HTML content into its own WebView instance. Each instance acts like an *iframe* and can be overlaid on other instances. Therefore, a malicious AR channel can overlay content from another origin (B) on top of its own content (A) without B being technically "framed" by A.

8.2 Risks

In this section, we are concerned with an AR attacker whose channel combines his own malicious HTML content with trusted HTML content from other origins.

By cleverly overlaying HTML widgets from different origins, a malicious channel can "hijack" the user's clicks. The user sees a button that appears to belong to some window, but the click is actually captured by a different window. For example, Fig. 14a shows a malicious Layar channel that overlays two Twitter windows. The user may think that the visible "Tweet" button submits the "hi" tweet, but it actually belongs to the bottom window and thus submits the invisible, malicious tweet. Because the victim page is in

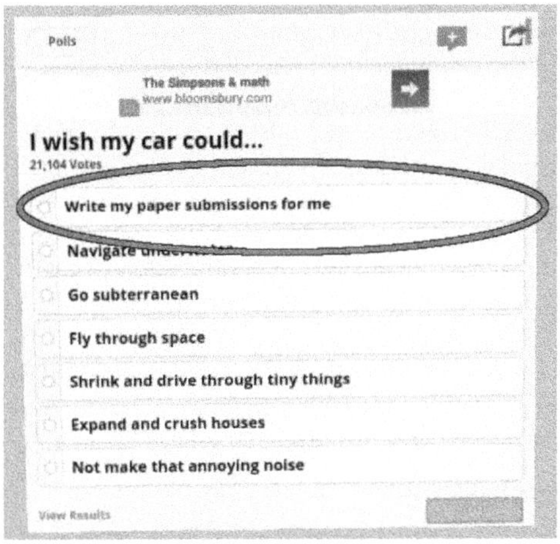

Figure 15: Overlapped HTML widgets in Layar. The first option is in a different widget and, surprisingly, not part of the actual Slashdot poll.

the top/main frame of its own WebView instance, it cannot prevent this attack or even detect when it is being framed in this way.

8.3 How to do it right

Defenses against clickjacking in AR browsers would benefit from a whole-browser equivalent of X-Frame-Option. Layar already prevents non-widget objects from covering widgets, but there is no way for HTML content to specify that its widget—or any WebView in which it is displayed—should not overlap with other widgets.

In general, using conventional browsers such as WebView to render AR content is dangerous because it forces AR browsers to use ad-hoc mechanisms for visually combining content from different origins. A principled solution to clickjacking in AR browsers should involve a clean-slate redesign of their user interfaces.

9 Indirect Retrieval of AR Content

AR content comes from independent third-party developers. While in theory the AR browser could fetch this content directly from the developers' servers, in practice the business models of AR services require them to track usage, charge fees for channel registration, inject advertising, and, in general, tightly monitor the interaction between their browsers and third-party content. Consequently, content requests must pass through the AR provider's own servers.

9.1 Doing it wrong

Some AR browsers enable third-party channels to authenticate users or keep track of users' preferences between their visits. For example, Layar supports a cookie-based user authentication scheme that can be deployed by geolocation channels (Fig. 16). When requesting a channel, the Layar browser sends a POST request to the Layar server and attaches the cookies associated with the channel's origin. The Layar server then attaches these cookies to the GET request it forwards to the channel server.

Cookie security depends on the binding between the cookie and its origin. A conventional Web browser keeps this binding and automatically attaches the cookie to every request sent to its origin. In Layar, channel launches are mediated by the Layar server, which must maintain the same cookie-origin binding as the Layar browser.

The Layar browser learns the origin of the channel from the Layar server. When the browser first loads the channel, the cookies are set by the channel's authentication page and thus correctly bound to the channel's origin at that time. If this origin changes later (e.g., the channel moves to a different domain), the Layar server notes the change and forwards all browser requests to the new location. Critically, the Layar server does *not* notify the browsers connected

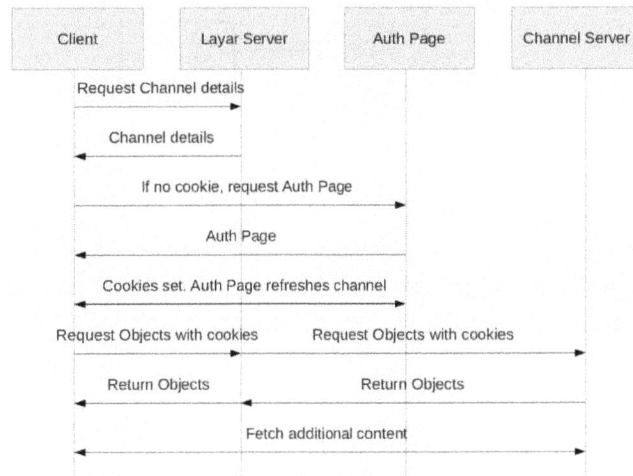

Figure 16: User authentication in Layar.

to the channel that the channel's origin has changed. The browsers continue to attach the cookies from the old origin to their requests, and the Layar server obliviously forwards them to the new origin.

9.2 Risks

In this section, we are concerned with AR attackers who lie about their channels' URLs. By "desynchronizing" the Layar browser's and the Layar server's understanding of the channel's origin, a malicious channel can steal cookies from *any* origin (Fig. 17).

For example, the attacker initially tells Layar that the URL of his channel is *https://www.twitter.com.* When a user launches the channel, the Layar browser attaches Twitter cookies to every channel update request. Next, the attacker changes his channel's URL to *https://attacker.com.* The Layar server registers the change, but the browsers connected to the channel continue to attach Twitter cookies to every channel update request. The Layar server forwards these requests, cookies attached, to *https://attacker.com*, and the attacker steals all of its users' Twitter cookies.

This attack works for any domain of the attacker's choosing (we tested it for Twitter and Facebook). Note that many AR channels are integrated with online social networks, thus the user is likely to be logged into Facebook and Twitter through his AR browser.

9.3 How to do it right

The first defense is to avoid replicating the state of the browser on the Layar server. The browser may request the URL of the channel server from the Layar server, but subsequent communication should be conducted directly between the browser and the channel server. The same-origin policy within the browser will then ensure that cookies are disclosed only to their origins. This defense, however, may break Layar's business model.

The second defense is for the Layar server to ensure that it agrees with the browser about the channel server's URL. This defense requires re-engineering the protocol between the browser, Layar server, and channel server.

The final defense is to use an authentication protocol that supports delegation, e.g., OAuth. In current Layar, channels may use OAuth 1.0 to authenticate the Layar server. This protects benign AR developers from spoofed Layar servers, but not legitimate Layar servers from malicious developers, and thus does not help against the cookie-stealing attack.

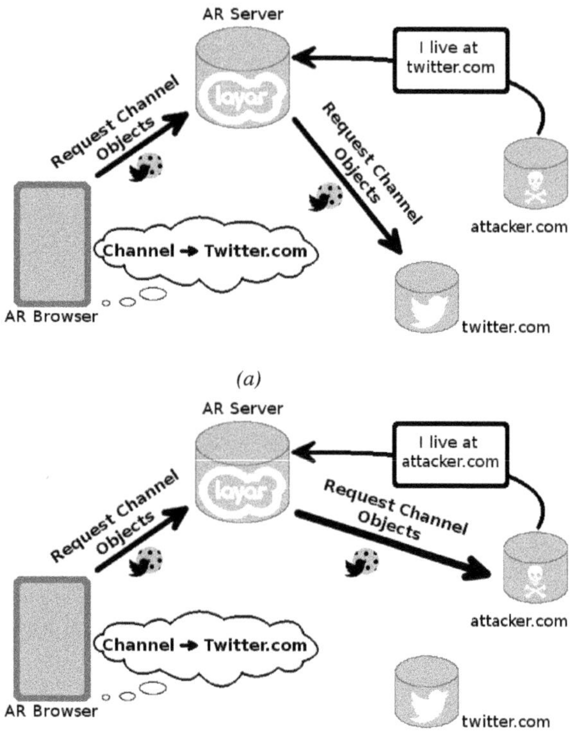

(b)

Figure 17: Layar cookie stealing attack.

10 Related Work

Azuma et al. [2, 3] identified three major properties of AR systems, exhibited by all AR browsers in our study: combining real and virtual objects, real-time interactivity, and support for 3D blending of virtual and real objects. Several papers suggested adding augmented reality to mobile applications such as tour guides [1, 8]. Spohrer et al. [28] explored the idea of associating information with real-world objects using "WorldBoard channels." Just like AR channels analyzed in this paper, "WorldBoard channels" can display HTML-encoded information overlaid on real-world objects. Kooper et al. [16] used the term "real world-wide web" for the combined information space created by merging real-world objects with the HTML content of the WWW. ARML [19] is a proposed standard for defining geospatial AR objects through XML.

Roesner et al. [22, 23] have surveyed various security, privacy, and legal concerns arising from the widespread use of AR technologies. By contrast, we analyze the technical architecture of popular, deployed AR platforms. With the exception of clickjacking and general privacy concerns, none of the issues we discovered are mentioned in these papers.

Several recent papers focused on privacy concerns arising from the unrestricted access to sensor data by untrusted third-party applications. Darkly [13] prevents certain privacy violations by applications based on the OpenCV computer vision library; D'Antoni et al. [6] and Jana et al. [12] show how to confine AR applications by adding fine-grained permissions to the OS. These systems are concerned with protecting users from untrusted applications, whereas we investigate whether and how trusted AR applications protect users from untrusted content (i.e., our threat model is similar to the standard threat model of Web browsers).

Some of our attacks involve pictures or QR codes placed in a public area to trick AR browsers into launching a malicious AR channel. Lookout Mobile Security used a QR code to force Google Glass to connect to an attacker-controlled Wi-Fi access point.[4] Both attacks employ malicious QR codes, but the similarities end there. The attacks described in Section 6.2 exploit the deficiencies of user interfaces in AR browsers, not software vulnerabilities. Other related work includes security threats involving QR codes [15] and the use of QR codes for malware distribution and phishing [17]. Dabrowski et al. [5] recently demonstrated numerous attacks involving hiding a QR code inside of another QR code, similar to our our attacks in Section 6.2.

Clickjacking attacks against conventional Web content were analyzed in [11, 24, 25]. In Section 8.2, we explained that our clickjacking attacks and defenses are somewhat different because of the architectural differences between Web browsers and AR browsers.

11 Conclusions

Augmented reality (AR) browsers are a new technology with exciting potential. We presented the first in-depth analysis of their security and privacy properties, identified multiple architectural flaws, and proposed short-term fixes for specific vulnerabilities as well as directions for future research on building secure AR browsers.

We have reported our findings to Junaio, Layar, and Wikitude. Junaio informed us that they will incorporate our results into their latest internal build. Wikitude was aware of the security flaw in HtmlDrawable (Section 5.2) and is looking into adding security mechanisms. Layar never responded to us.

Acknowledgments. This work was partially supported by the NSF grants CNS-0746888 and CNS-1223396, a Google research award, NIH grant R01 LM011028-01 from the National Library of Medicine, and Google PhD Fellowship to Suman Jana.

12 References

[1] G. Abowd, C. Atkeson, J. Hong, S. Long, R. Kooper, and M. Pinkerton. Cyberguide: A mobile context-aware tour guide. *Wireless Networks*, 3(5), 1997.

[2] R. T. Azuma. A survey of augmented reality. *Presence: Teleoperators and Virtual Environments*, 6(4):355–385, 1997.

[3] R. T. Azuma, Y. Baillot, R. Behringer, S. Feiner, S. Julier, and B. MacIntyre. Recent advances in augmented reality. *Computer Graphics and Applications*, 21(6):34–47, 2001.

[4] D. Bates, A. Barth, and C. Jackson. Regular expressions considered harmful in client-side XSS filters. In *WWW*, 2010.

[5] A. Dabrowski, K. Krombholz, J. Ullrich, and E. Weippl. QR inception: Barcode-in-barcode attacks. In *SPSM*, 2014.

[6] L. D'Antoni, A. Dunn, S. Jana, T. Kohno, B. Livshits, D. Molnar, A. Moshchuk, E. Ofek, F. Roesner, S. Saponas, M. Veanes, and H. J. Wang. Operating system support for augmented reality applications. In *HotOS*, 2013.

[7] Layar launches "world's first augmented reality store". `http://eurodroid.com/2010/04/28/layar-launches-worlds-first-augmented-reality-store`, 2010.

[8] S. Feiner, B. MacIntyre, T. Höllerer, and A. Webster. A touring machine: Prototyping 3D mobile augmented reality systems for exploring the urban environment. *Personal Technologies*, 1(4), 1997.

[9] M. Georgiev, S. Jana, and V. Shmatikov. Breaking and fixing origin-based access control in hybrid Web/mobile application frameworks. In *NDSS*, 2014.

[10] B. Henne, M. Harbach, and M. Smith. Location privacy revisited: Factors of privacy decisions. In *CHI*, 2013.

[11] L.-S. Huang, A. Moshchuk, H. J. Wang, S. Schechter, and C. Jackson. Clickjacking: Attacks and defenses. In *USENIX Security*, 2012.

[4] `http://www.techweekeurope.co.uk/news/google-glass-security-vulnerability-internet-of-things-122073`

[12] S. Jana, D. Molnar, A. Moshchuk, A. Dunn, B. Livshits, H. J. Wang, and E. Ofek. Enabling fine-grained permissions for augmented reality applications with recognizers. In *USENIX Security*, 2013.

[13] S. Jana, A. Narayanan, and V. Shmatikov. A scanner Darkly: Protecting user privacy from perceptual applications. In *S&P*, 2013.

[14] Become a Junaio developer. http://www.slideshare.net/metaio_AR/why-to-become-a-junaio-developer, 2013.

[15] A. Kharraz, E. Kirda, W. Robertson, D. Balzarotti, and A. Francillon. Optical delusions: A study of malicious QR codes in the wild. In *DSN*, 2014.

[16] R. Kooper and B. B. MacIntyre. Browsing the real-world wide web: Maintaining awareness of virtual information in an AR information space. *International Journal of Human-Computer Interaction*, 16(3), 2003.

[17] K. Krombholz, P. Frühwirt, P. Kieseberg, I. Kapsalis, M. Huber, and E. Weippl. QR code security: A survey of attacks and challenges for usable security. In *HCI*, 2014.

[18] Layar introduction for developers. http://www.slideshare.net/layarmobile/layar-introduction-for-developers, 2011.

[19] Open Geospatial Consortium. OGC augmented reality markup language 2.0 (ARML 2.0) [candidate standard]. http://www.opengeospatial.org/projects/groups/arml2.0swg, 2013.

[20] M. Osadchy, B. Pinkas, A. Jarrous, and B. Moskovich. SCiFI - A system for secure face identification. In *S&P*, 2010.

[21] C. Perey. A proposal for AR browser interoperability. http://www.perey.com/ARStandards/AR_Browser_Interoperability_Architecture_Jan_21_2014_v1_2.pdf, 2014.

[22] F. Roesner, T. Kohno, T. Denning, R. Calo, and B. C. Newell. Augmented reality: Hard problems of law and policy. In *UPSIDE*, 2014.

[23] F. Roesner, T. Kohno, and D. Molnar. Security and privacy for augmented reality systems. In *Communications of the ACM*, volume 57, pages 88–96, 2014.

[24] G. Rydstedt, E. Bursztein, and D. Boneh. Framing attacks on smart phones and dumb routers: Tap-jacking and geo-localization. In *WOOT*, 2010.

[25] G. Rydstedt, E. Bursztein, D. Boneh, and C. Jackson. Busting frame busting: A study of clickjacking vulnerabilities at popular sites. In *W2SP*, 2010.

[26] S. Son and V. Shmatikov. The postman always rings twice: Attacking and defending postMessage in HTML5 websites. In *NDSS*, 2013.

[27] Same origin policy. http://www.w3.org/Security/wiki/Same_Origin_Policy.

[28] J. Spohrer. Information in places. *IBM Systems Journal*, 38(4):602–628, 1999.

[29] Wikitude for agencies. http://www.slideshare.net/wikitude/wikitude-media-portfolio-presentation, 2012.

[30] Z. Wu, Q. Ke, M. Isard, and J. Sun. Bundling features for large scale partial-duplicate web image search. In *CVPR*, 2009.

[31] The X-Frame-Options response header. https://developer.mozilla.org/en-US/docs/HTTP/X-Frame-Options.

Discovering Meta-Paths in Large Heterogeneous Information Networks

Changping Meng*
Purdue University
West Lafayette, US
meng40@purdue.edu

Reynold Cheng
University of Hong Kong
Pokfulam Road, Hong Kong
ckcheng@cs.hku.hk

Silviu Maniu*
Noah's Ark Lab, Huawei
Science Park, Hong Kong
silviu.maniu@huawei.com

Pierre Senellart
Télécom ParisTech; CNRS LTCI
& NUS; CNRS IPAL
pierre@senellart.com

Wangda Zhang
University of Hong Kong
Pokfulam Road, Hong Kong
wdzhang2@cs.hku.hk

ABSTRACT

The Heterogeneous Information Network (HIN) is a graph data model in which nodes and edges are annotated with class and relationship labels. Large and complex datasets, such as Yago or DBLP, can be modeled as HINs. Recent work has studied how to make use of these rich information sources. In particular, *meta-paths*, which represent sequences of node classes and edge types between two nodes in a HIN, have been proposed for such tasks as information retrieval, decision making, and product recommendation. Current methods assume meta-paths are found by domain experts. However, in a large and complex HIN, retrieving meta-paths manually can be tedious and difficult. We thus study how to discover meta-paths automatically. Specifically, users are asked to provide example pairs of nodes that exhibit high proximity. We then investigate how to generate meta-paths that can best explain the relationship between these node pairs. Since this problem is computationally intractable, we propose a greedy algorithm to select the most relevant meta-paths. We also present a data structure to enable efficient execution of this algorithm. We further incorporate hierarchical relationships among node classes in our solutions. Extensive experiments on real-world HIN show that our approach captures important meta-paths in an efficient and scalable manner.

1. INTRODUCTION

Heterogeneous Information Networks (HINs), such as *Yago* [17] and *DBpedia* [2], has attracted plenty of attention in recent years. These graph data sources, which contains a gigantic number of inter-related facts, enables discovery of interesting knowledge. Yago, for instance, stores over 10 million entities and 120 million facts [17]. Figure 1 illustrates a knowledge base, a kind of HIN, which captures the relationships among entities (or graph nodes). Each node and edge is associated with a "label", indicative of the node class and edge type, respectively. For example, *Barack Obama* (node 1) has class labels USPresident and Writer. One of his offsprings is *Malia Obama* (node 5), as indicated by the hasChild edge. A *class hierarchy* describes the relationships among node class labels, as shown in Figure 1(a).

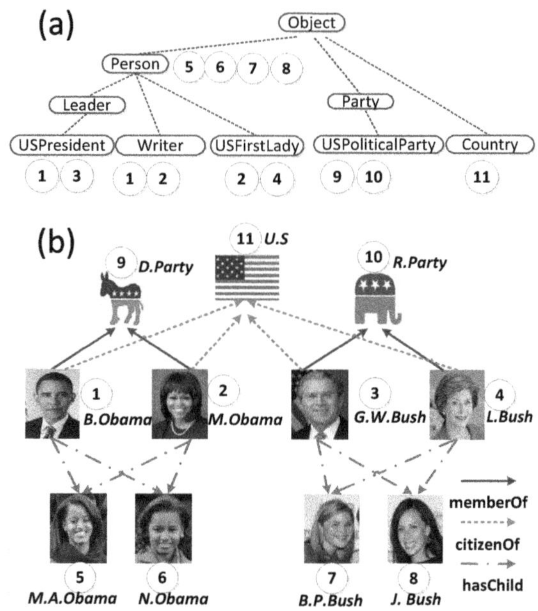

Figure 1: HIN with class hierarchy

The problem of understanding the vast amount of information modeled in HINs has received a lot of interest. In particular, the concept of *meta-paths* has been proposed [10, 19, 20] to explain how nodes are related. A meta-path is a sequence of node classes and edge types between two given nodes. In Figure 1, *Barack Obama* and *Michelle Obama* are connected by the following three different meta-paths:[1]

$$\mathsf{USPresident} \xrightarrow{\mathsf{hasChild}} \mathsf{Person} \xrightarrow{\mathsf{hasChild}^{-1}} \mathsf{USFirstLady},$$

$$\mathsf{USPresident} \xrightarrow{\mathsf{memberOf}} \mathsf{USPoliticalParty} \xrightarrow{\mathsf{memberOf}^{-1}} \mathsf{USFirstLady},$$

$$\mathsf{USPresident} \xrightarrow{\mathsf{citizenOf}} \mathsf{Country} \xrightarrow{\mathsf{citizenOf}^{-1}} \mathsf{USFirstLady}.$$

*Work mainly done while the authors were affiliated with University of Hong Kong.

[1] We use $\mathsf{hasChild}^{-1}$ to denote the opposite direction of the edge labeled hasChild.

WWW 2015, May 18–22, 2015, Florence, Italy.
ACM 978-1-4503-3469-3/15/05.
http://dx.doi.org/10.1145/2736277.2741123 .

Meta-paths can be used to predict the closeness, or *similarity*, among graph nodes. This is especially useful when an edge between two nodes does not exist. As in Figure 1, assume, for the sake of argument, that there is no edge between *Barack Obama* and *Michelle Obama*. However, the two nodes are closely related, as illustrated by the three meta-paths above. Notice that a meta-path can have a path length of more than one. Thus, it can be used to explain sophisticated relationships among nodes that cannot be depicted by a single edge. Recently, researchers have studied how to use meta-paths between two heterogeneous graph nodes to quantify their similarity. They have proposed *meta-path–based similarity measures* (e.g., *path count* (PC) [19], *path constraint random walk* (PCRW) [10], and *HeteSim* (HS) [16]). These metrics on meta-paths between two nodes can be used for link prediction, product recommendation, and decision making. For example, in bibliography networks (e.g., *DBLP* [11]), these measures can be used to predict relationships among authors and research topics. In a recommendation system that stores salesperson, customer, and product information, these similarity values can be used to suggest products to be promoted to customers, and advise salespersons about potential customers [10, 19, 20].

Prior works. Although meta-paths are useful, the important issue of how to generate them has not been well studied. Most existing work assumes that meta-paths are provided by domain experts. While this assumption may be true for a relatively simple HIN (e.g., DBLP [11]), we question its validity for larger ones such as Yago and DBpedia. For these cases, millions of nodes and edges are annotated with thousands of labels, and node class labels exhibit complex hierarchical relationships (as in Figure 1). Moreover, long meta-paths can be extremely difficult to discover, especially if this is done without the aid of machines. The only meta-path generation solution is proposed in [10], and yields meta-paths within a fixed length l. However, it is not clear how l should be set. As we found in our experiments, the performance and effectiveness of their approach is very sensitive to l. In [5], a method called AMIE was proposed to mine association rules from HIN. While association rules are similar to meta-paths, the output of AMIE is "global", i.e., the individual preferences of a user are not considered. On the contrary, our method can be *customized*; a user can provide her opinions about the meta-paths to be generated, through *example node pairs*, as we discuss next. Moreover, AMIE does not use in any special manner the hierarchy of node classes, which we found to be very important in understanding relationships.

Our goal is to develop a systematic and user-friendly solution for efficiently discovering important meta-paths in large knowledge bases. In our approach, users provide example pairs of nodes that exhibit high proximity (e.g., *George W. Bush* and *Laura Bush*). They do not need to specify a maximum length l. Meta-paths that best explain the similarity between these node pairs are then automatically generated. A simple way to do this is to enumerate all the possible meta-paths and the possible meta-path subsets between the given node pairs, and select those that have the highest similarity. Unfortunately, this solution is impractical. As pointed out in [10], the number of possible meta-paths for a given heterogeneous graph grows exponentially with the length of a meta-path. Even if all these meta-paths are known, selecting the most important subsets among them is an NP-complete problem [10]. There is thus a need for a better approach that avoids enumerating all possible meta-paths.

Our solutions. We develop the *Forward Stagewise Path Generation* algorithm (or FSPG), which derives meta-paths that best predict the similarity between the given node pairs. Inspired by machine learning algorithms used for feature selection [4], FSPG contains greedy strategies that generate the most relevant subset of meta-paths under a given regression model. Another advantage of FSPG is that it supports existing meta-path-based similarity measures – PC and PCRW. This is because FSPG adopts our proposed metric, called *Biased Path Constrained Random Walk*, or *BPCRW*, which generalizes PC and PCRW. We will explain how parameters of BPCRW can be tuned to get the best out of these two measures. To facilitate the efficient execution of FSPG, we investigate a data structure called the GreedyTree. This data structure is easily constructed and efficiently supports the online generation of relevant meta-paths. We further explain how to extend our solution to incorporate class hierarchy information in our solutions.

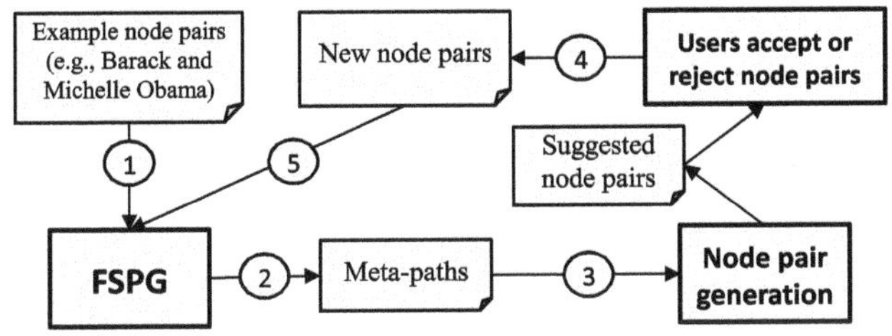

Figure 2: System framework

We have performed extensive experiments on two real knowledge bases, namely DBLP and Yago. Our results show FSPG allows for a significant improvement in the accuracy of link prediction – between 10% and 15%. Moreover, FSPG detects new meta-paths not provided by experts, and this leads to better results than only using the meta-paths provided by experts. We show that FSPG computes meta-paths in an efficient and scalable manner, and achieves an improvement in time of up to two orders of magnitude. We further demonstrate that class hierarchy information significantly increases accuracy of the similarity model, with negligible overhead. We show that FSPG discovers more association rules than AMIE. We further perform a case study, where human users provide opinions on generated meta-paths; FSPG did well in this experiment.

Figure 2 illustrates our high-level approach for discovering meta-paths. In Step 1, users provide example pairs to FSPG. This algorithm generates meta-paths (Step 2), which are then used to generate new node pairs (Step 3), e.g., via similarity search and join operations [18, 27]. From these node pairs, users select those that are indeed similar (Step 4). The accepted node pairs are then input to FSPG to iteratively refine the meta-paths generated (Step 5). An advantage of this framework is flexibility: users can review and change the meta-paths generated in Step 2; they can also provide new example pairs later after the meta-paths are generated. In this paper, we focus on the design and implementation of FSPG (Step 2).

The rest of this paper is organized as follows. We introduce the formal settings and similarity measures in Section 2. We present FSPG and GreedyTree in Section 3, and evaluate them experimentally in Section 4. We review the related work in Section 5, and conclude in Section 6.

2. META-PATH BASED SIMILARITY

We now discuss the formal model of HINs and our problem settings. We then review existing meta-path-based similarity functions, and present a method to generalize them.

2.1 Problem Definition

We model the heterogeneous information network as in [20]:

DEFINITION 1 (**HETEROGENEOUS INFORMATION NETWORK**). *A Heterogeneous Information Network is a directed graph* $G =$

(V,E,Φ,Ψ), *where* V *is the set of nodes (or entities) of the graph;* $E \subseteq V \times V$ *is the set of edges connecting the nodes in* V*; and* Φ *and* Ψ *are functions for labeling nodes and edges. We have* $\Phi : V \to 2^A$, *where* A *is the set of node classes, and* $\Psi : E \to 2^R$, *where* R *is the set of edge types.*

Many graph datasets can be modeled as HIN such as: ontologies (Yago [17], DBPedia [2]), and bibliographic networks (DBLP [11]). Here, we mainly work with knowledge bases (KB) as an instance of HINs.

EXAMPLE 1. *Let us revisit the HIN in Figure 1, where a triple of the form: (Barack Obama,* hasChild*, Natasha Obama) can be represented as an edge having type:* Ψ*(Barack Obama, Natasha Obama)* $=$ {hasChild}. *Each entity can be mapped to multiple types:* Φ*(Barack Obama)* $=$ {USPresident, Writer, Person}.

Moreover, in most HINs on the Web – Yago and DBpedia being prime examples – the classes of the entities are organized in a *hierarchical* manner. For instance, USPresident is a subclass of Leader, and Leader is a subclass of Person. All the classes have a single root, e.g., Object. They are usually organized in KBs as nodes in the graph, linked with edges of type subclassOf. Figure 1 shows an example of hierarchical organization of node classes. This hierarchical organization can affect how one chooses the classes of nodes in a KB, as we shall see later.

Given a path in G between two entities, there is a corresponding *meta-path* that can be derived:

DEFINITION 2 (**META-PATH** [20]). *Given a HIN* $G = (V,E,\Phi,\Psi)$, *a meta-path* $\Pi^{1\ldots n}$ *is a sequence of node class sets* $\mathsf{C}_1,\ldots,\mathsf{C}_n$, *connected by link types* $\mathsf{e}_1,\ldots,\mathsf{e}_{n-1}$: $\Pi^{1\ldots n} = \mathsf{C}_1 \xrightarrow{\mathsf{e}_1} \ldots \mathsf{C}_i \xrightarrow{\mathsf{e}_i} \ldots \mathsf{C}_n$.

We say that a path $P = v_1 \xrightarrow{\mathsf{e}_1} \ldots v_i \xrightarrow{\mathsf{e}_i} \ldots v_n$ satisfies a meta-path $\Pi = \mathsf{C}_1 \xrightarrow{\mathsf{e}_1} \ldots \mathsf{C}_i \xrightarrow{\mathsf{e}_i} \ldots \mathsf{C}_n$ if $\forall i \in \{1,\ldots,n\}$, $\mathsf{C}_i \cap \Phi(v_i) \neq \emptyset$, and $\forall i \in \{1,\ldots,n-1\}$, $\{v_i, v_{i+1}\} \in E$ and $\mathsf{e}_i \in \Psi(v_i, v_{i+1})$. In other words, each entity on the path has a class that exists in the corresponding class set on the meta-path, and each edge on the path has a corresponding type.

EXAMPLE 2. *In Figure 1,* USPresident $\xrightarrow{\text{hasChild}}$ Person $\xrightarrow{\text{hasChild}^{-1}}$ USFirstLady *is satisfied by the path Barack Obama* $\xrightarrow{\text{hasChild}}$ *Natasha Obama* $\xrightarrow{\text{hasChild}^{-1}}$ *MichelleObama. Another meta-path that is satisfied by a path between these two nodes is* USPresident $\xrightarrow{\text{memberOf}}$ USPoliticalParty $\xrightarrow{\text{memberOf}^{-1}}$ USFirstLady, *since Barack and Michelle Obama are both members of the Democratic Party.*

Two entities can have paths that satisfy different meta-paths between them. The challenge then is finding them and including them in a model that can describe accurately the relationship between the nodes. Moreover, we wish to do this when *multiple* pairs are given:

PROBLEM 1 (**RELEVANT META-PATHS**). *Given a HIN* $G = (V,E,\Phi,\Psi)$ *and a set of* e *example node pairs* $\Lambda = \{(s_i,t_i) \mid 1 \leqslant i \leqslant e\}$, *find a set of* p *meta-paths* $\Theta = \{\Pi_i \mid 1 \leqslant i \leqslant p\}$ *which accurately predicts* Λ *for a given similarity scoring function* $\sigma(s,t \mid \Theta)$.

For instance, in Yago, the user can provide several pairs of entities of types Person and Country. A citizenOf link between entities of these types shows that a person is a citizen of a country. When this link is missing, the examples might implicitly suggest a relationship of residency in a country, as explained by a combination of meta-paths Person $\xrightarrow{\text{livedIn}}$ Country and Person $\xrightarrow{\text{worksAt}}$ Institution $\xrightarrow{\text{locatedIn}}$ Country.

The challenge is then: (i) to find *all* and *only* the relevant meta-paths, and (ii) to train a model able to predict the examples pairs. Each path between the entities in the examples pairs that is satisfied by a meta-path in the model contributes to the *similarity* between the example entities. Next, we study meta-path based similarity measures.

2.2 Similarity Function σ

We now explain how to use a combination of meta-paths to derive a similarity measure between two entities in a HIN. The *similarity score* between two entities s and t is a real number, computed by an aggregate function F of the similarity scores for each meta-path of a set Θ: $\sigma(s,t \mid \Theta) = \mathrm{F}(\{\sigma(s,t \mid \Pi_i) \mid 1 \leqslant i \leqslant p\})$, where $\sigma(s,t \mid \Pi_i)$ is a similarity score measuring how "strong" the connection between two entities s and t *given meta-path* Π_i, $\Theta = \{\Pi_1,\ldots,\Pi_p\}$, and F is an aggregate function over the meta-path scores.

Let us start by explaining how to compute $\sigma(s,t \mid \Pi)$, and discuss the function F later. We first review the state of the art of meta-path–based similarity definitions on HINs, and then introduce our general formulation of these similarity measures.

Path Count (PC) [19]. The simplest form of similarity between two nodes is the count of the different paths which satisfy a given meta-path Π. The intuition behind this measure is that the larger the number of paths satisfy a given configuration is, the more similar the entities are.

Path-Constrained Random Walk (PCRW) [10]. For a meta-path $\Pi = \mathsf{C}_1 \xrightarrow{\mathsf{e}_1} \ldots \mathsf{C}_i \xrightarrow{\mathsf{e}_i} \ldots \mathsf{C}_n$, the similarity score between two entities s and t is defined by the random walk starting at s and following only paths satisfying Π. It is defined recursively as follows, with a slight modification to allow for choosing node classes:

$$\sigma(v_i,t \mid \Pi^{i\ldots n}) = \frac{1}{|\rho_{\mathsf{e}_i}(v_i,\mathsf{C}_{i+1})|} \sum_{x \in \rho_{\mathsf{e}_i}(v_i,\mathsf{C}_{i+1})} \sigma(x,t \mid \Pi^{i+1\ldots n}),$$

$$\sigma(t,t \mid \Pi^{n\ldots n}) = 1,$$

where $\rho_{\mathsf{e}_i}(v_i,\mathsf{C}_{i+1})$ is the set of nodes x which have classes in C_{i+1} and are linked by an edge of type e_i from v_i, and $\Pi^{i\ldots n}$ is the meta-path Π truncated to the sub-path between C_i and C_n. The evaluation starts at $\sigma(s,t \mid \Pi) = \sigma(s,t \mid \Pi^{1\ldots n})$. Essentially, PCRW indicates the probability that a walker constrained on a particular meta-path reaches the target node.

PC emphasizes the absolute number of paths satisfying a meta-path while PCRW weighs the paths based on the neighbourhoods of nodes along them. Both measures can be generalized in a single measure, the *Biased Path Constrained Random Walk (BPCRW)*, defined in a manner similar to PCRW as follows:

$$\sigma(v_i,t \mid \Pi^{i\ldots n}) = \frac{1}{|\rho_{\mathsf{e}_i}(u_i,\mathsf{C}_{i+1})|^{\alpha}} \sum_{x \in \rho_{\mathsf{e}_i}(v_i,\mathsf{C}_{i+1})} \sigma(x,t|\Pi^{i+1\ldots n}), \tag{2.1}$$

$$\sigma(t,t \mid \Pi^{n\ldots n}) = 1.$$

When $\alpha = 0$, BPCRW is the same as PC; when $\alpha = 1$, the same as PCRW. If $\alpha \in (0,1)$, α balances the number of meta-paths to be counted and the contribution of neighbors. Particularly, when α is large, we care more about the number of similar neighbors for a node; when α is small, we place more emphasis on the number of paths between two nodes. We will evaluate the effect of α on BPCRW experimentally in Section 4.

Remarks. Our solutions do not consider two recently proposed metrics, *PathSim* and *HeteSim*. The *PathSim* measure [20] obtains similar nodes (or the so-called "peer objects") for single symmetric meta-paths. It is not clear how *PathSim* can handle non-symmetric meta-paths, which are common in KBs. The *HeteSim* metric [15, 16] measures the relevance of a single meta-path. Since it does not have the form of BPCRW (Equation 2.1), it is not supported by our FSPG solution. We experimentally compare BPCRW and *HeteSim* for a given single meta-path in Section 4. An interesting future work is to extend FSPG to support *HeteSim*.

2.3 Similarity Aggregate Function F

Following the previous work on meta-path–based link prediction [10, 19], we use a linear regression model for F, which trains a linear model of the form:

$$\sigma(s,t \mid \Theta) = \sum_{1 \leqslant j \leqslant p} w_j \cdot \sigma(s,t \mid \Pi_j) + w_0, \qquad (2.2)$$

where $w_0, \ldots, w_p$ are real-valued coefficients. The function F forms the basis of our meta-path selection algorithm.

3. GENERATING META-PATHS

We now study efficient algorithms for solving Problem 1. As a matter of fact, an optimal solution for this problem is likely to be intractable [24]. Even if the paths are known in advance, selecting only the most relevant paths is difficult: it has been proved in [1, 24] that the problem is NP-hard, and it cannot be approximated within a constant factor unless P=NP. Therefore, we study efficient algorithms that do well in the average case. Since relevant paths may not be known initially, we propose a greedy framework that starts from a regression model with no meta-paths. We then insert meta-paths to the model, until a desired accuracy is attained. This method is inspired by the design of *forward selection algorithms* [9] in machine learning. As we will explain, forward selection enables meta-paths to be generated as needed.

Algorithm Framework. Our solution consists of two phases. The first phase (Section 3.1) generates meta-paths with only edge types. To support this step efficiently, we develop an appropriate data structure (Section 3.2). In the second phase (Section 3.3), we augment the meta-paths generated in Phase 1 with node class information, by considering the node class hierarchy. Let us now study these in detail.

3.1 Phase 1: Link-Only Path Generation

This phase generates meta-paths with only edge types, by using *Forward Stagewise Path Generation* (or FSPG). We greedily select the next most relevant meta-path, and add it as a feature to the regression model, until the model can fit the example pairs. Specifically, we build a regression model for the input example pairs; it uses meta-paths (with only link types) as features and assigns a weight for each feature. We train this model based on a modified version of the Least-Angle Regression [4] (LARS). This method tests the addition of each feature against the model constructed, repeatedly adding the feature that improves the model the most, until no more features can be added. While LARS needs to know the whole feature space at the beginning of regression which means you need to enumerate all possible meta paths, we propose a heuristic to avoid this.

To support LARS and to avoid generating irrelevant meta-paths, we propose a greedy method that iteratively returns the meta-path with the largest correlation with the partially constructed model. We initialize the model with the first meta-path found by our greedy method. Then, at each stage, we continue testing the next meta-path, by computing its correlation to the currently constructed model. As in LARS, the criterion for choosing a feature is correlation – each time we choose the feature that has the largest correlation with the expected output at this step, so that we can approach the expected output fastest. At each stage, we insert the meta-path that has the largest correlation value with the current residual (explained below), based on a standard cosine function:

$$\cos(\mathbf{m}, \mathbf{r}) = \frac{\mathbf{m} \cdot \mathbf{r}}{\|\mathbf{m}\| \times \|\mathbf{r}\|} \qquad (3.1)$$

where $\mathbf{m}$ is the *resulting vector* of a certain meta-path Π on the training examples (each entry of $\mathbf{m}$ is a BPCRW score $\sigma(s,t \mid \Pi)$ for input pair (s,t)), and $\mathbf{r}$ is the vector of *residual values*, denoting the difference between the values of the ground truth examples (input pairs) and the model results $\mathbf{m}$. Initially, $\mathbf{r}$ is equal to the ground truth $\{1, \ldots, 1, -1, \ldots, -1\}$ of length $|\Lambda|$ with values 1 for positive example pairs, and -1 for negative example pairs.

We now explain the process of generating training data. We require the user to provide *positive* examples only. One does not need to state *negative* examples, which can be difficult. However, if only positive examples are used, the resulting meta-paths may characterize how the node pairs are connected by the *largest* number of meta-paths, instead of how they are *uniquely* connected. Consider two positive examples: (*B. Obama*, *M. Obama*), and (*G. W. Bush*, *L. Bush*), which can be predicted by the three meta-paths: 1) they have the same children, 2) they belong to the same political party, and 3) they are both US citizens. Although all these meta-paths describe the relationship of the two node pairs, meta-path 1) is more rare and important than meta-path 3). To reflect this, our algorithm generates negative node pairs that are pertinent to the positive examples.

One simple way to generate negative examples is to randomly select nodes pairs from the KB. Unfortunately, these examples may be totally irrelevant. For instance, a random pair (*J. Cameron, Avatar*) is unrelated to the positive examples above. In our solution, the number of negative examples is the same as that of the positive ones. We randomly extract entities that share the same *Lowest Common Ancestor* (or *LCA*) label in the class hierarchy as the entities present in the positive pairs. In Figure 1, the LCA of the entities used in our examples, namely *B. Obama* and *G. W. Bush*, is USPresident. We then randomly select nodes that have the LCA USPresident (e.g., *B. Clinton* and *R. Reagan* in Figure 3). Similarly, since the LCA of *M. Obama* and *L. Bush* is USFirstLady (Figure 1), two candidates for negative examples are *B. Ford* and *B. Bush* (Figure 3). These selected nodes are then combined randomly to form negative examples: *(B. Clinton, B. Ford)* and *(R. Reagan, B. Bush)*. Although this process might give us some false negative pairs, this chance is shown to be low in our experiments.

Algorithm 1 details the procedure of obtaining the set of meta-paths with their weights, for an input vector of positive example pairs Λ. We denote all selected meta-paths and their scores in a feature matrix: $X = (\mathbf{m_0}, \ldots, \mathbf{m_k})$. In this matrix, each column $\mathbf{m_k}$ is the BPCRW scores of some meta path for all examples in Λ, and k is the number of meta paths generated. For each meta-path feature, we return its weight in another vector $\mathbf{w}$. After initializing the residual and weight vectors in Step 1, we obtain the first meta-path by invoking GreedyTree in Step 2. This method, which we will explain, returns the meta-path with the largest correlation value. Steps 4–11, we iterate with the meta-path with the next largest correlation.

Note that LARS iterates until every feature has been processed. In our case, the number of features (meta-paths) is unknown, and it is difficult to generate them efficiently. Hence, we modify LARS, and incrementally build the regression model by using a new stopping condition: we iterate until the residual $\mathbf{r}$ is negligible (i.e., $|\mathbf{r}| \leqslant \varepsilon$ in Step 4). In our implementation, traversing the entire space of meta-paths just to find that no path has been found is practically

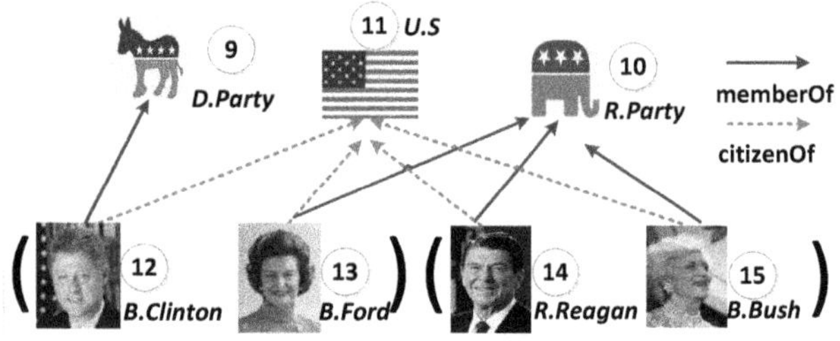

Figure 3: Selected negative example pairs

impossible. So, we also establish a *maximal number of iterations* – 50 in our experiments – that forces the algorithm to stop even if convergence has not been achieved. This is enough, since most models contain a lot of small meta-paths; having more than 50 features start to add noise to the model. In our experiments, this threshold is rarely reached; `FSPG` terminates within 20 iterations.

In each iteration, we obtain the next meta-path (Step 6) having the largest correlation with $\mathbf{r}$, and put it to matrix X (Step 7). Next, we compute the correlation of newly added meta-path feature with the current residual (Steps 8), obtaining direction vector $\mathbf{u}$ and stepsize γ:

$$\mathbf{u} = X(X^TX)^{-1}(\mathbf{1}^T(X^TX)^{-1}\mathbf{1})^{1/2}\mathbf{1} \tag{3.2}$$

$$\gamma = \min_{0 \leqslant j < k}^{+} \left\{ \frac{corr - \cos(\mathbf{m_j}, \mathbf{r})}{(\mathbf{1}^T(X^TX\mathbf{1})^{1/2}) - \mathbf{m_j}^T\mathbf{u}}, \frac{corr + \cos(\mathbf{m_j}, \mathbf{r})}{(\mathbf{1}^T(X^TX\mathbf{1})^{1/2} + \mathbf{m_j}^T\mathbf{u}} \right\}$$

where $\mathbf{1}$ is a vector of 1's of length k and $\min^+$ is the minimal positive value. While these equations appear in `LARS` [4], we made two changes. First, we use the existing feature matrix X to heuristically represent the entire feature matrix. Second, when computing γ, we also only consider the existing meta-path features vectors, or $(\mathbf{m_j})_{0 \leqslant j < k}$ in the kth iteration.

Algorithm 1: $\texttt{FSPG}(G, \Lambda)$

Input: network G, example pairs Λ
Output: meta-paths $\Pi_{0,\dots,k}$, path weight vector $\mathbf{w}$

1 $\mathbf{r} \leftarrow \{1,\dots,-1\}$; $w \leftarrow 0$; $k \leftarrow 0$;
2 $\Pi_0, \mathbf{m_0} \leftarrow$ GreedyTree$(G, \Lambda, \mathbf{r})$;
3 $k \leftarrow 0$;
4 **while** $|\mathbf{r}| > \varepsilon$ **do**
5 $\quad k \leftarrow k+1$;
6 $\quad \Pi_k, \mathbf{m_k} \leftarrow$ GreedyTree$(G, \Lambda, \mathbf{r})$;
7 $\quad X \leftarrow X \cup \mathbf{m_k}$;
8 $\quad corr \leftarrow \cos(\mathbf{m_k}, \mathbf{r})$;
9 $\quad$ compute $\mathbf{u}$, γ using Eq. (3.2) ;
10 $\quad \mathbf{r} \leftarrow \mathbf{r} - X\mathbf{u}\gamma$;
11 $\quad \mathbf{w} \leftarrow \mathbf{w} + \mathbf{u}\gamma$;
12 **return** $\Pi_{0,\dots,k}, \mathbf{w}$

3.2 The GreedyTree Structure

Next, we study how to find the meta-path $\mathbf{m_k}$ with the largest correlation, by applying the `GreedyTree` algorithm. `GreedyTree` has three major advantages. First, it can reduce the search space by applying search heuristics. Second, when starting from multiple example nodes, it minimizes the redundancy in computing the common path sequences that may appear, by using the tree structure to store such paths. Third, the tree structure can be re-used for multiple expansions in the run of the algorithm.

Let us illustrate the algorithm by using the previous example. The positive example pairs are $\{(1,2),(3,4)\}$ in Figure 1 and negative example pairs are $\{(12,13),(14,15)\}$ in Figure 3. The algorithm

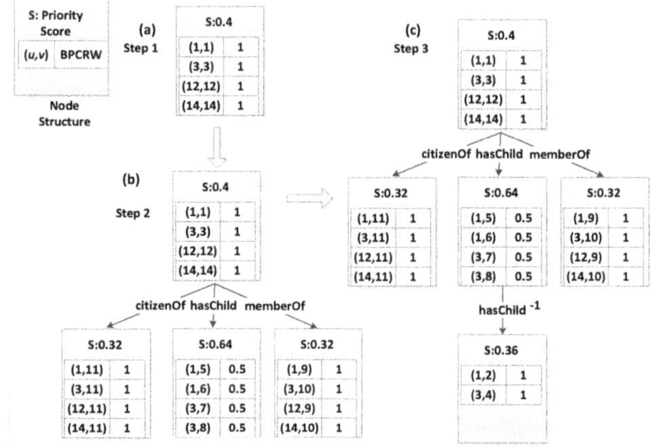

Figure 4: GreedyTree

works by expanding a tree structure, where each tree edge is annotated with an edge type, and each tree node stores a list of node pairs with their BPCRW values and a *priority score S*. Here, the list stores tuples in the form $\langle (u,v), \sigma(u,v \mid \Pi) \rangle$ where (u,v) represents a path in the graph by its starting and current graph nodes, respectively; Π is the edge-only meta-path starting from u to v. The edges of the tree are edge types in the graph. $\sigma(u,v \mid \Pi)$ is the BPCRW score for this meta-path. We compute the value of S as a heuristic on the correlation value, as follows:

$$S = \frac{\sum_{u+} \sigma(u,v \mid \Pi) \cdot \mathbf{r}(u,*)}{\sqrt{\sum_u \sigma(u,v \mid \Pi)^2} \times |\mathbf{r}|} \cdot \beta^L, \tag{3.3}$$

where $\mathbf{r}$ is the current residual vector, $u+$ signifies the starting node u in (u,v) which belongs to positive examples (for instance, $u+ \in \{1,3\}$ in Figure 4), and $\mathbf{r}(u,*)$ is the largest value in the residual vector for example pairs starting from u (initially $\mathbf{r}(u,*) = 1$). β is a decay factor ranging from 0 to 1, and L is the length of current meta path. Unlike the homogeneous graph, there is no guarantee that the current node is on the correct route to reach the target nodes of the example pairs. We add this decay factor β, to avoid the meta path expanding to an infinite length. As shown in Figure 4(a) with $\beta = 0.8$, initially the root of the GreedyTree contains all the starting nodes in the input example pairs, and has $S = 0.4$. After one step of moving in the graph in Figure 4, it passes through three types of edges – citizenOf, hasChild, and memberOf – and generates three new tree nodes in the GreedyTree (Figure 4(b)). It also computes the priority score and all the BPCRW values. Then, it greedily selects the tree node with the largest priority to expand – in this example, we continue to expand the node through hasChild^{-1} link, since it has the largest priority score $S = 0.64$.

After this expansion, we see in Figure 4(c) that $(1,2)$ and $(3,4)$ are already an input pair. Thus, we find a link-only meta-path Π: $? \xrightarrow{\text{hasChild}} ? \xrightarrow{\text{hasChild}^{-1}} ?$ and we compute the actual value of the correlation, as well as the resulting vector m on example pairs. If this value of S is larger than the priority scores of the other two tree leaf nodes (the upper bounds of their own correlations, i.e., 0.32), then Π is the best meta-path currently found and is then returned along with its $\mathbf{m}$ vector. If other priority scores are larger, then we continue to expand the tree node with the largest score, and repeat this procedure until this condition is satisfied or the tree cannot be expanded.

We preserve the expanded tree structure for subsequent iterations of Algorithm 1. Before resuming tree expansions, we need to first update the priority scores of the leaf nodes, since the residual vector **r** has been changed by the addition of a new meta-path feature. By a linear scan of the node pair list in a leaf node, we can efficiently compute the summation in Equation (3.3), and update the value of S. Then, we continue to expand the tree starting from the node with highest S.

Algorithm 2: `GreedyTree`$(G, \Lambda, \mathbf{r})$

```
   Input: KB G, example pairs Λ, residual vector r
   Output: meta-path Π having largest correlation with r, and its result
           vector m
   Data: pattern tree T
 1 update priority scores of leaf nodes in T with r;
 2 while T can be expanded do
 3     M ← node with largest score S in T;
 4     m ← {0,...,0};
 5     foreach tuple p in M do
 6         if p.(u,v) ∈ Λ then
 7             m(u,v) ← σ(u,v | Π) ;
 8     if m has non-zero entry then
 9         M.S ← cos(m,r) (Eq. (3.1));
10         if M.S ≥ max_{T.leaf} S then
11             Π ← the meta-path from root to M;
12             break;
13     else
14         foreach tuple p in M do
15             foreach out-neighbor w of p.v on graph G do
16                 e ← link type from p.v to w;
17                 if M has no child N linked by e then
18                     create new child tree node N of M ;
19                 Π ← the meta-path from root to N;
20                 insert tuple ⟨(p.u,w), σ(p.u,w | Π)⟩ to N;
21                 update N.S according to Eq. (3.3);
22 return Π, m
```

We present the detailed steps of `GreedyTree` in Algorithm 2. First, we check and update the priority scores of leaf nodes changed by new residual vector **r** (Step 1). Then, we expand the tree by moving to out-neighbor nodes on the graph until a meta-path can be found or the graph is completely traversed (Steps 2–21). We target the tree node with largest priority (Step 3) and examine whether its tuples are example pairs (Step 6). If so, we store BPCRW scores in **m** (Step 7), compute the actual correlation value as $M.S$ (Step 9), and determine if we have found a proper meta-path (Steps 10–12). If no example pairs are encountered (Step 13), then we extend each node pair by moving to an out-neighbor (Step 15). We insert this new pair with its BPCRW score to a child node (Steps 17–20), and update its priority score (Step 21).

3.3 Phase 2: Node Class Generation

Existing methods (e.g., [10, 20]) often assume that each KB node has only one class. In complex and real KBs, nodes can have multiple classes. For instance, Barack Obama is not only a president, but also a lawyer and writer. As introduced, these node classes are organized in a hierarchy. For example, in Yago (see Figure 1), Leader and Writer are subclasses of Person. This increases the number of possible paths for satisfying a meta-path. In the previous section, the meta-paths generated do not specify node classes. Here we present ways to assign node classes.

One option is to simply disregard the node classes. So the meta path contains only edge types generated in Phase 1, without any node class constraints. However, the link-only meta-path is generally too common in a large KB, thus introducing more false positive results. For instance, ? $\xrightarrow{\text{liveIn}}$? is a much more common meta-path than Scientist $\xrightarrow{\text{liveIn}}$ CapitalCity. Since link-only meta-paths are less specific to input pairs, they will eventually impair the result quality.

A better method is to choose the classes which are the Lowest Common Ancestor (LCA) in the type hierarchy. For instance, in Figure 1(a), the LCA of USPresident and Writer is Person. Another example is that the LCA of Harvard and Yale is IvyLeague. This way, if given some pairs of persons who graduated from Harvard and Yale, we can generate meta-paths showing they both graduated from IvyLeague. Thus, for every KB node satisfying a certain meta-path node, we generate LCAs for all its possible classes, and use them in the model. The LCAs of KB nodes can simply be recorded in each node of the GreedyTree. Thus, while we expand the GreedyTree, we just need to find the LCA of the current node and its parent node. This approach has the advantage of preserving the same weights as the ones trained in Algorithm 1, at the cost of only a bottom-up traversal in the class hierarchy.

Finally, we can combine the score of the classes on the hierarchy in a tf-idf-like manner, for a given label φ: $score(\varphi) = \frac{tf(\varphi)}{\log of(\varphi)}$, where $tf(\varphi)$ is the count, or frequency, of the label φ in the positive examples, and $of(\varphi)$ the overall count of φ in the entire KB.

For instance, in the first node of the GreedyTree in Figure 4, tf(USPresident) is 2 since it contains nodes 1 and 3 – as the labels of nodes can be easily obtained from the type hierarchy in Figure 1(a). On the other hand, of(USPresident) is 42, since there are 42 nodes which have label USPresident in the entire KB, and then $score$(USPresident) $= 1.23$, which is much higher than other labels for these example nodes. In terms of performance, of can be easily pre-computed by counting all the labels in the HIN, as a pre-processing step.

We show in the next section that this selection mechanism improves considerably the accuracy of the similarity model.

4. EXPERIMENTS

Datasets and setup. In this section, we perform experiments on two representative datasets for online HIN: DBLP and Yago.

DBLP [11] is a bibliographic information network which is frequently used in the study of heterogeneous networks. Our dataset [20, 25]is a subset containing scientific papers in four areas: databases, data mining, artificial intelligence, and information retrieval. The dataset has four classes of nodes: Paper, Author, Topic, and Venue. It also has four edge types: authorOf, publishedIn, containsTopic, and cites. It contains 14,376 papers, 14,475 authors, 8,920 topics, and 20 venues. There are 170,794 links in total.

Yago is a large-scale knowledge base derived from Wikipedia, WordNet, and GeoNames [17]. In our experiments, we use the "CORE Facts" part of this dataset, which contains 4 million facts (network links) of 125 types, made from 2.1 million entities. These entities have 365,000 node classes, organized in a hierarchy tree. A fact is a triple of the form: (Entity, relationship, Entity), e.g., (*Barack Obama*, hasChild, *Malia Obama*).

We validate our algorithm's efficiency and effectiveness mainly by performing link prediction tasks (additional experiments on rule mining and a user study are also presented at the end of this section). We stress that our models are not only usable for link prediction, but for a variety of other tasks, such as search and similarity joins. We chose link prediction for the evaluation because it provides for a measurable and objective way to evaluate the similarity models and algorithms.

For a certain type of link in Yago, for instance citizenOf, we remove all such links and try to predict them with the model that our `FSPG` algorithm learns. We randomly select a number of pairs of objects as training data, and validate the model using a test set of an equal number of pairs. In our experiments, we set the value of ε in Algorithm 1 to 0.01. We have found that even low values of

Table 1: 5 most relevant meta-paths for Yago - citizenOf

meta-path	w
Person $\xrightarrow{\text{bornIn}}$ City $\xrightarrow{\text{locatedIn}}$ Country	5.477
Person $\xrightarrow{\text{livesIn}}$ Country	0.361
Person $\xrightarrow{\text{graduateOf}}$ University $\xrightarrow{\text{locatedIn}}$ Country	0.023
Person $\xrightarrow{\text{diedIn}}$ City $\xrightarrow{\text{locatedIn}}$ Country	0.245
Person $\xrightarrow{\text{bornIn}}$ City $\xrightarrow{\text{happenedIn}^{-1}}$ Event $\xrightarrow{\text{happenedIn}}$ Country	0.198

this parameter allow for a reasonable number of features selected, usually lower than 20. If ε is set to a higher value, the models will be smaller but also less accurate. We compared FSPG with PCRW to models which generate paths of finite length in $\{1,2,3,4\}$, as used in [10]. The PCRW models use the logistic regression model to combine these meta-paths, in order to be coherent with previous work in the area and to allow fair comparisons. For node class selection (Section 3.3), we use the LCA of entities' classes. Finally, unless otherwise specified, the similarity function was BPCRW with a value for α of 0.5. We found this value approximates both PC and PCRW well, and also that it helps to keep the vector of meta-path similarity values normalized. We use β as 0.6 in GreeyTree to avoid the meta path expanding infinitely.

Effectiveness. We present in Figure 5 the results for link prediction for three types of links: citizenOf and advisorOf for Yago, and authorOf for DBLP. For each of these links, we generated 100 training and 100 test pairs, as described above. Each figure shows the Receiver Operating Characteristic (ROC) curve, where the larger area signifies a larger accuracy in prediction.

The figure shows that fixed-length PCRW suffers from several issues. When the maximum length is too small (1 or 2), meta-paths cannot connect example pairs, and as such the model is not better than a random guess and the model will have low recall. When the maximum length is too big, the model introduces too many meta-paths. For length 3, there are 135 meta-paths, and over 2,000 for length 4. In DBLP, length 4 (measured by link hop) meta-paths – equivalent to the method presented in [20] – for authorship prediction work poorly when training pairs are randomly chosen, due to the low number of paths connecting them.

FSPG is clearly better in predicting the links, and it generates only a limited number of meta-paths. For instance, the citizenOf link in Yago has a model of only 15 meta-paths. Moreover, these meta-paths are highly relevant and serve as good explanation of the similarity links. Table 1 shows the most relevant 5 meta-paths for the citizenOf similarity model. Unsurprisingly, the meta-path illustrating the fact that a person has been born in a city of a country is the best predictor of citizenship, but other, longer, paths are also highly relevant. Compared with PCRW with maximum length 2, it has higher recall because it also detected longer important meta-paths, for instance, Person $\xrightarrow{\text{bornIn}}$ City $\xrightarrow{\text{happenedIn}^{-1}}$ Event $\xrightarrow{\text{happenedIn}}$ Country. We found that in Yago some facts are missing. For instance, a fact denoted by the direct link Paris $\xrightarrow{\text{locatedIn}}$ France is missing. [2] In this case, our algorithm can be useful to predict it via longer paths, such as City $\xrightarrow{\text{happenedIn}^{-1}}$ Event $\xrightarrow{\text{happenedIn}}$ Country.

Whereas considering direct links is widely done when querying ontologies, multi-hop meta-paths can in some cases improve query result accuracy. For instance, in citizenOf prediction (Figure 5), only one type of direct links between people and country exists, namely, liveIn. As a result, most information in predicting the citizenship is lost when limiting to direct connections, causing low recall and AUC score. For advisorOf prediction, there is even no direct link between the example pairs. This means resorting to multi-hop meta-paths is necessary.

[2]Although other 2-hop links from Paris to France exist, they were not ranked as high as City $\xrightarrow{\text{happenedIn}^{-1}}$ Event $\xrightarrow{\text{happenedIn}}$ Country.

Efficiency. Figure 6 show the running time of FSPG compared to models with fixed length, and when varying the number of example pairs given as input. It can be observed that generally, the algorithm running time increases sub-linearly in the number of example pairs. The increase is due to the PCRW random walks which need to be performed concurrently for each example pair, but the number of meta-paths in the model does not increase at the same rate.

In Yago, the algorithm performs better than models of paths longer than 2 by a factor of up to 2 orders of magnitude. However, the models of short path length have limited predictive power, despite their better running time. In comparison, our algorithm is capable of finding even longer paths, for an increase in accuracy without much sacrifice in running time.

In DBLP, the running time of FSPG is comparable to length 5 for smaller test set sizes, and comparable to length 4 for larger example set sizes. This is not unexpected, considering that the DBLP KB is very small in size – both as number of types and as graph size – and fixed length models will have reasonably sized number of features. However, even if the running time is worse, we already saw that FSPG on DBLP has generally better accuracy, making it very useful even in very small KBs.

Input set size and precision@k. We turn now to evaluating the influence of the input set size on the accuracy of the models. We compare in terms of Area Under the Curve (AUC) two methods, our FSPG algorithm and PCRW of length 2. We chose length 2 because it was consistently the best performer out of all fixed length models in Yago. The evaluation was done on the same Yago node classes, advisorOf and citizenOf. In Figure 7 and Figure 8, "a-FSPG" represents the advisorOf prediction using FSPG while "c-FSPG" represents for citizenOf prediction using FSPG. The same abbreviation rule also applies to "a-PCRW" and "c-PCRW".

Figure 7 shows the results. It can be seen that the set size does not greatly influence the accuracy of the model, which suggests that even in more realistic scenarios in which users or experts give very few examples the models will be reliable. It can also be seen that FSPG keeps its advantage over PCRW of fixed length, regardless of the input set size. Please note that, for each positive input set size, we have generated an equal number of negative example using the methodology described before.

Figure 8 shows the difference between FSPG and PCRW of path length 2, with an input set size of 100 negative and positive pairs, in the following scenario: we sort the results by their similarity and check the number of true positives at a given value of k in the sorted list. FPSG achieved considerably high precision of predicted pairs at low values of k, suggesting that this method is practically usable especially since similarity search results sets are usually low in numbers. For cases in which prediction is easy – e.g., citizenOf – PCRW becomes competitive only at high values of k. This does not happen in the case of advisorOf, as it is harder to predict.

Improving expert meta-paths. Our method can also be used to improve on expert meta-path models, and we show here how it behaves for authorship prediction in DBLP. In our experiments, we started from the meta-paths defined by experts in DBLP, as explained in [20]. Starting from the already existing model of meta-paths, we first build the corresponding GreedyTree, we compute the residual vector r and "resume" the execution of FSPG.

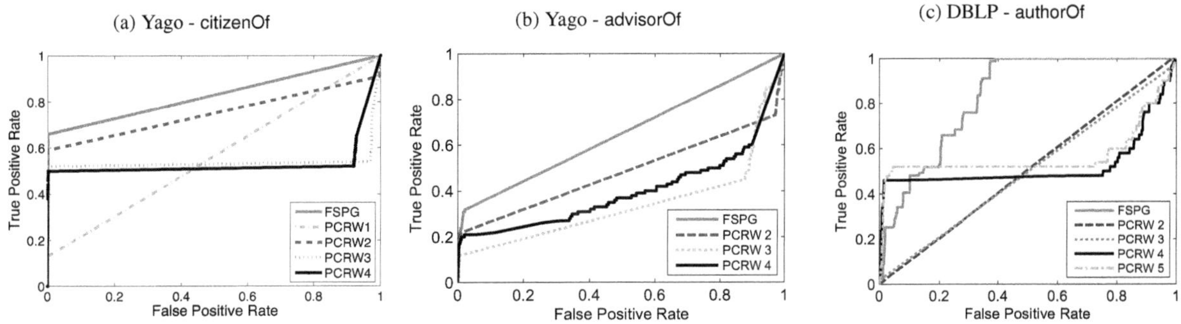

Figure 5: ROC for link prediction

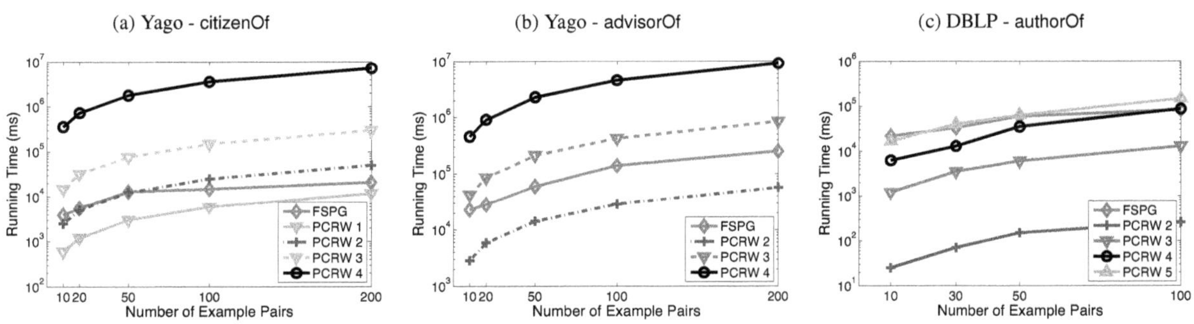

Figure 6: Running time of `FSPG`

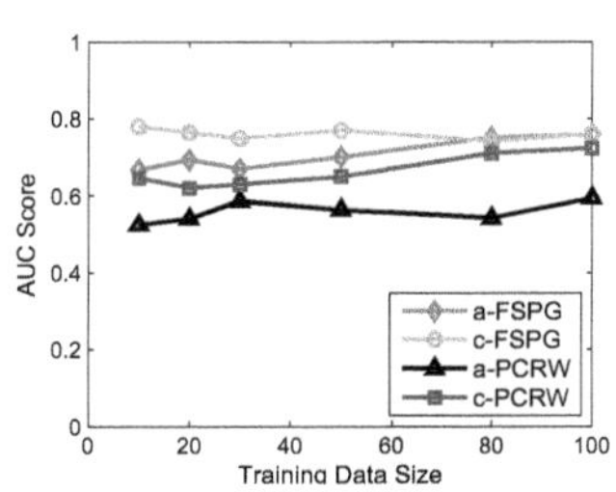

Figure 7: AUC for varying number of example pairs

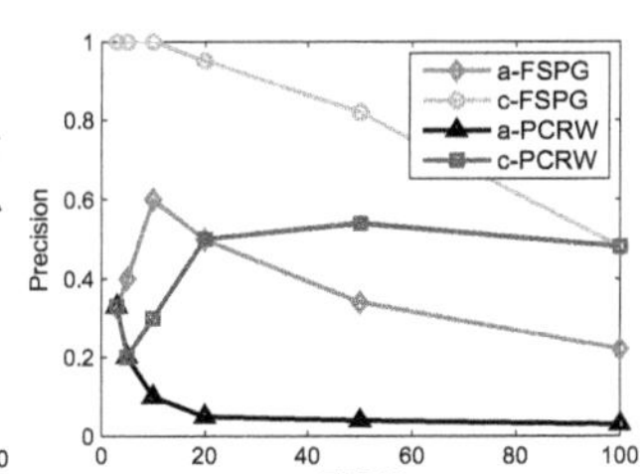

Figure 8: Precision@k

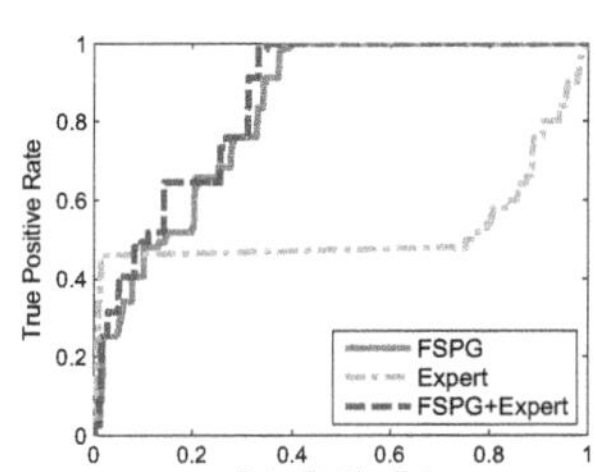

Figure 9: ROC of `Expert`

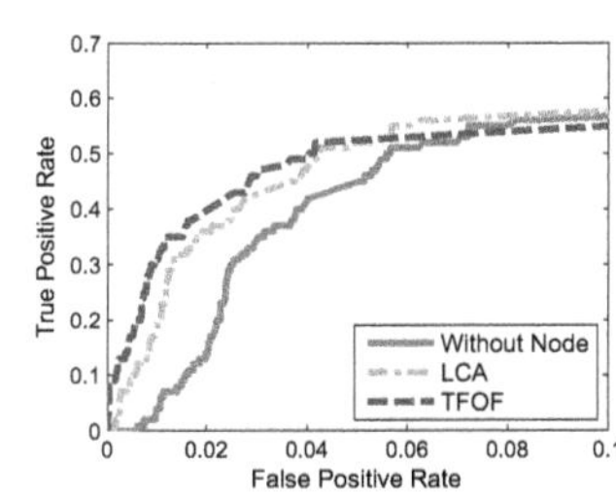

Figure 10: ROC of label selection

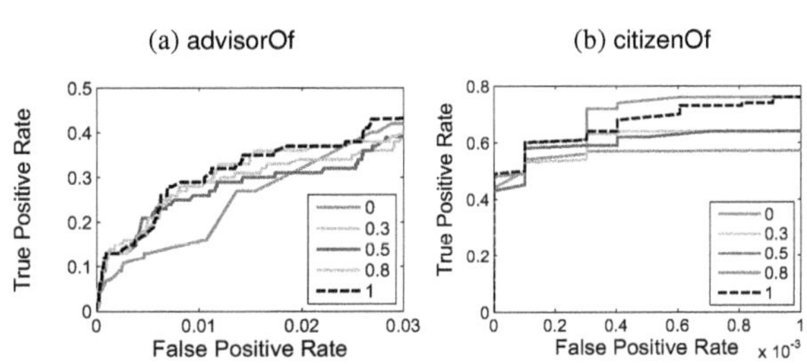

Figure 11: ROC of BPCRW for various α values

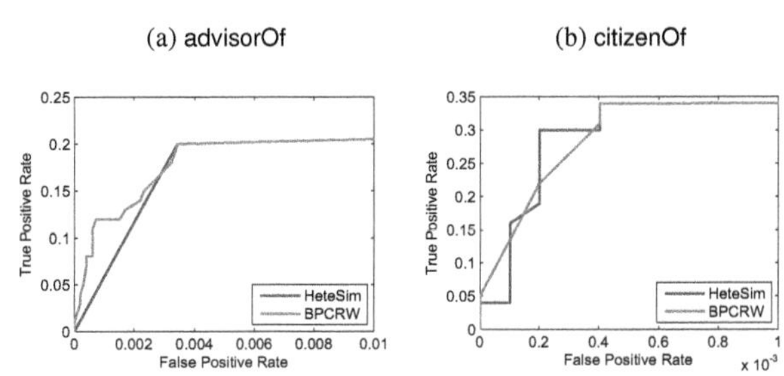

Figure 12: ROC of HeteSim on a single meta-path

We show the resulting ROC curves in Figure 9. It can be seen that starting from expert meta-paths slightly improves the accuracy of FSPG, but greatly improves the accuracy of the expert-only model. This is because the algorithm is able to generate relatively long meta-paths, which are missed by experts, as partially shown in Table 2. This result shows that the algorithm can readily be employed as an expert tool, to suggest meta-paths which might be missed by experts.

Class label selection. Figure 10 shows the accuracy of our model, depending on which class selection from Section 3.1 is chosen. Each training set was generated as before, with corresponding negative pairs. It can be seen that not restricting the class nodes on meta-paths significantly impacts the accuracy. The *tfof* method of generating class labels is better for high precision queries, but LCA is better than it for higher recall rates.

Influence of α. To illustrate the difference between the choice of α values, we illustrate in Figure 11 their power in predicting links of Yago, given a value of α for the BPCRW, for two types of links: advisorOf and citizenOf. The choice of α has a considerable impact on the link effectiveness. It also shows that – even in the same knowledge base – there is no single choice of α which always "wins" over the other similarity models, and it highly depends on the example pairs being given by users. For instance, the best value for advisorOf seems to be 0.8, while for citizenOf it is 1 because they have the largest AUC score.

Due to the low running times of FSPG the best value of α can simply be generated by a loop over reasonable values of α increments, e.g., every 0.1, and choosing the model which has the best fit with the training pairs.

HeteSim. Figure 12 compares BPCRW and *HeteSim* [15, 16] in terms of relationship prediction. As explained in Section 2.2, *HeteSim* is not supported in FSPG, and we study *HeteSim* on one single meta-path only. We select Person $\xrightarrow{\text{bornIn}}$ City $\xrightarrow{\text{locatedIn}}$ Country for citizenship prediction, since it is the most important meta-path (Table 1). For advisor prediction, we use Person $\xrightarrow{\text{graduateFrom}}$ University $\xrightarrow{\text{workAt}^{-1}}$ Scientist, since it is also the most important one as found from another experiment. We observe that BPCRW is comparable to *HeteSim*. Moreover, the prediction quality is much worse using a single meta-path than considering multiple meta-paths. In Figure 5, for citizenship prediction, using a single meta-path yields 34% recall, while using multiple meta-path generates 65% recall. This shows why it is important to use multiple meta-paths, as adopted by our approach.

AMIE. The FSPG method can also be used for mining association rules in heterogeneous graphs, since the meta-paths associated to a given node pair can be interpreted as an association rule for that pair. To evaluate this use case, we compare FSPG with AMIE, which is used to generate association rules in knowledge bases.

We generate the association rules for the citizenOf, advisorOf and ivyLeagueAlumnus links [3], and show the ROC curve results in Figure 13. We first evaluate the association rules by performing link prediction, i.e., we use the association rules generated by AMIE and combine them through logistic regression – just as with the paths generated with FSPG. Our method shows generally better ROC curves for citizenOf and advisorOf. For citizenOf, AMIE produces 8 association rules, while FSPG can produce 3 more association rules such as Object $\xrightarrow{wasBorn}$ Object $\xrightarrow{locatedIn}$ Object $\xrightarrow{locatedIn}$ Object. For advisorOf, AMIE produces 4 association rules and FSPG adds 4 more, such as Object $\xrightarrow{worksAt}$ Object $\xrightarrow{graduatedFrom}$ Object. Table 3 shows other association rules missed by AMIE and generated by FSPG for advisorOf.

[3]This link does not exist in YAGO. We simulate it by creating a link between every pairs of graduates from Ivy League universities.

Table 3: Missed association rules in AMIE for advisorOf

meta-path
Person $\xrightarrow{\text{influence}^{-1}}$ Person
Person $\xrightarrow{\text{diedIn}}$ City $\xrightarrow{\text{diedIn}^{-1}}$ Person
Person $\xrightarrow{\text{workAt}}$ University $\xrightarrow{\text{graduatedFrom}}$ Person
Person $\xrightarrow{\text{liveIn}}$ Country $\xrightarrow{\text{isCitizenOf}^{-1}}$ Person

However, the most important advantage for FSPG lies in its ability to generate rules for the personalized case, where few pairs are given as input. We illustrate this on the link ivyLeagueAlumnus – which does not exist in YAGO. We input these pairs connected by this virtual link ivyLeagueAlumnus. AMIE will look for global rules, and thus generates general rules which fail to distinguish Ivy League alumni from the alumni of any other university. In contrast, our method achieved a ROC of 0.989, and was able to generate more specific association rules such as

Object $\xrightarrow{graduateFrom}$ IvyLeague $\xrightarrow{graduateFrom^{-1}}$ Object or Object $\xrightarrow{isAffiliatedTo}$ Organization $\xrightarrow{isAffiliatedTo^{-1}}$ Object.

User study. Finally, we conduct a user study to determine whether meta-paths learned by FSPG are of interest to users.

We use the data from the Time Magazine's "100 Most Important People of the 20th Century" [21]. Ten volunteers, who are students and research assistants of the CS department of HKU, are asked to select pairs of similar persons. The volunteers have selected 10 pairs of people which are similar, e.g., pairs such as (Franklin D. Roosevelt, Theodore Roosevelt) and (Mao Zedong, Ho Chi Minh). Based on the input pairs, we use FSPG to generate the meta-paths. After the model is trained, we shuffle the most relevant meta-paths with randomly selected, but reasonable, meta-paths and ask the same volunteers to rank them into three categories: *Relevant, Somewhat Relevant, Not Relevant.* We assign each answer a point value of 1 for *Relevant*, 0.5 for *Somewhat Relevant* and 0 for *Not Relevant.* We then average the ranking over all question for the FSPG-returned meta-paths and the most well-ranked random meta-path for each question. The FSPG generated meta-path score average was $0.471(\sigma = 0.229)$ and for the random paths it was $0.285(\sigma = 0.100)$. Statistical significance was estimated using the one-tailed Student's t-test, yielding a p-value of 0.09. This value is satisfactory, taking into account the fact that the users were not always familiar with the historical figures.

At a qualitative level, the result also showed that our generated meta-paths rank consistently higher than the random meta paths. For instance, the most important meta path between Franklin D. Roosevelt and Theodore Roosevelt is A $\xrightarrow{isPoliticianOf}$ country $\xrightarrow{isPoliticianOf^{-1}}$ B, and the most important meta path between Mao Zedong and Ho Chi Minh is A $\xrightarrow{influence^{-1}}$ person $\xrightarrow{influence}$ B.

5. RELATED WORK

Knowledge bases. Yago [17] is a semantic knowledge base derived from Wikipedia, with more than 10 million entities (or nodes) of different types. Links among these entities represent more than 120 million facts about them. Constructed from Wikipedia and the Web in a similar way, DBpedia [2] is another widely used knowledge base. Since both entities and links have a variety of types, a simple homogeneous graph (with only one type of node

Table 2: Missed meta-paths by experts in DBLP authorship prediction

meta-path
$\text{Author} \xrightarrow{authorOf} \text{Paper} \xrightarrow{cites} \text{Paper} \xrightarrow{publishedIn} \text{Venue} \xrightarrow{publishedIn^{-1}} \text{Paper} \xrightarrow{cites} \text{Paper} \xrightarrow{authorOf^{-1}} \text{Author}$
$\text{Author} \xrightarrow{authorOf} \text{Paper} \xrightarrow{cites} \text{Paper} \xrightarrow{containsTopic} \text{Topic} \xrightarrow{containsTopic^{-1}} \text{Paper} \xrightarrow{cites} \text{Paper} \xrightarrow{authorOf^{-1}} \text{Author}$
$\text{Author} \xrightarrow{authorOf} \text{Paper} \xrightarrow{cites} \text{Paper} \xrightarrow{publishedIn} \text{Venue} \xrightarrow{publishedIn^{-1}} \text{Paper} \xrightarrow{containsTopic} \text{Topic} \xrightarrow{containsTopic^{-1}} \text{Paper} \xrightarrow{authorOf^{-1}} \text{Author}$

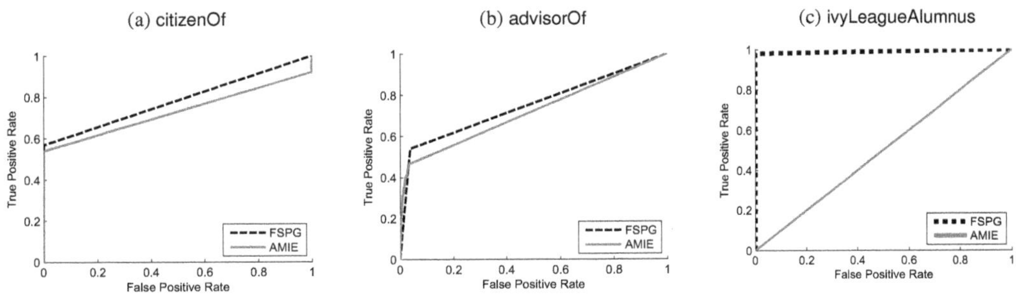

Figure 13: ROC of FSPG and AMIE

or edge) is unable to capture the rich information contained in a knowledge base.

Generating Meta-Paths. The issue of generating good meta-paths has not been satisfactorily addressed. A simple method is to first enumerate all possible meta-paths, by traversing the schema graph [20], and then use the paths as features to train a regression model that best fits the user-provided example pairs. However, the cost of generating all path patterns is prohibitive when the number of node types and edge types is large. Second, the high dimensionality of the resulting data means that, for each feature and example pair, we need to generate the similarity measures by performing the random walks described in Section 2.2. Moreover, the number of features is highly likely to introduce noise due to the curse of dimensionality [6]. On the contrary, our method only generates *relevant* meta-paths. The same authors in [20] also suggest to hire domain experts to define meta-paths. As we have explained, this may not be feasible for very large HIN. Another problem with this approach is that the paths defined in this way are *global*. In our solution, users can participate in the process of generating meta-paths by suggesting example pairs.

Another approach for generating meta-paths is proposed by [10]. Their solution enumerate all the meta-paths within a fixed length l. However, it is not clear how l should be set. More importantly, l can significantly affect the meta-paths generated: (i) if l is large, then many redundant meta-paths may be returned, leading to curse-of-dimensionality effects; and (ii) if l is small, important meta-paths with length larger than l might be missed. Our experiments have shown that the running time of the meta-path generation process grows exponentially with length l. Moreover, the accuracy can also drop with increase in l. Our solution does not require users to provide the value of l.

Link Prediction. Since the main focus of our work is to generate meta-paths, we only use link prediction to quantify our advantage compared with the existing meta-path generation methods, as demonstrated in Section 4. Compared with [14], our method predicts the relationship between different entities, rather than predicting the types of entities. [13] used the factorization of a three-way tensor to perform relational learning; it only considered simple node types and is not applicable to our experiment which has both complex node classes and edge types.

Node similarity. To measure the proximity between graph nodes, neighborhood-based metrics such as *common neighbors* and Jaccard's coefficient were proposed [12]. Other widely-used graph-theoretic measures that are based on random walks between nodes include *personalized PageRank* [3], *SimRank* [8], *hitting times* [27], and *random walk with restart* [22]. These measures do not consider the class labels of nodes and edges present in a HIN. Several similarity metrics have been designed for HIN: *path count* (PC) [19] and *path constraint random walk* (PCRW) [10]. We propose a general form of these two metrics, called the BPCRW. As discussed in Section 2.2, *PathSim* [20] and *HeteSim* [15, 16] are two other recently-proposed meta-path-based measures.

Query by example. We studied the problem of using example node pairs to generate meta-paths. These node pairs can also be used to facilitate query evaluation. In [7], Jayaram et al. examined how to find query graphs that can yield node pairs. It would be interesting to see how our meta-path–based similarity metrics can be used to enhance their solutions. In [23, 26], the problem of generating queries from user-provided example query results in a relational database was investigated.

6. CONCLUSIONS

We examined the problem of generating meta-paths from a given set of node pairs, using a general form of meta-path-based measures. We proposed the `FSPG` algorithm, and developed `GreedyTree` to facilitate its execution. Our experiments showed that `FSPG` generates important meta-paths efficiently. In the future, we will study the theoretical feasibility of meta-path selection for other non-linear similarity functions. We will also examine query algorithms for similarity search and join on large HINs, based on meta-path similarity measures.

Acknowledgments

Reynold Cheng, Silviu Maniu, Changping Meng, and Wangda Zhang were supported by RGC (Project HKU 711110) and HKU (Project 201311159095). We thank the reviewers for their comments.

7. REFERENCES

[1] E. Amaldi and V. Kann. On the approximability of minimizing nonzero variables or unsatisfied relations in linear systems. *Theor. Comp. Sci.*, 209(1-2), 1998.

[2] S. Auer, C. Bizer, G. Kobilarov, J. Lehmann, R. Cyganiak, and Z. Ives. DBpedia: a nucleus for a Web of open data. In *The Semantic Web*. Springer, 2007.

[3] S. Chakrabarti. Dynamic personalized PagRank in entity-relation graphs. In *WWW*, 2007.

[4] B. Efron, T. Hastie, I. Johnstone, and R. Tibshirani. Least angle regression. *Annals of Statistics*, 32(2), 2004.

[5] L. A. Galárraga, C. Teflioudi, K. Hose, and F. Suchanek. AMIE: Association rule mining under incomplete evidence in ontological knowledge bases. In *WWW*, 2013.

[6] G. F. Hughes. On the mean accuracy of statistical pattern recognizers. *IEEE Trans. Information Theory*, 14(1), 1968.

[7] N. Jayaram, A. Khan, C. Li, X. Yan, and R. Elmasri. Querying knowledge graphs by example entity tuples. *CoRR*, abs/1311.2100, 2013.

[8] G. Jeh and J. Widom. SimRank: a measure of structural-context similarity. In *KDD*, 2002.

[9] D. Koller. Toward optimal feature selection. In *ICML*, 1996.

[10] N. Lao and W. W. Cohen. Relational retrieval using a combination of path-constrained random walks. *Mach. Learn.*, 81(1), 2010.

[11] M. Ley. DBLP: some lessons learned. *PVLDB*, 2(2), 2009.

[12] D. Liben-Nowell and J. Kleinberg. The link-prediction problem for social networks. *J. Assoc. Inf. Sci. Technol.*, 58(7), 2007.

[13] M. Nickel, V. Tresp, and H.-P. Kriegel. A three-way model for collective learning on multi-relational data. In *ICML*, 2011.

[14] M. Nickel, V. Tresp, and H.-P. Kriegel. Factorizing YAGO: Scalable machine learning for linked data. In *WWW*, 2012.

[15] C. Shi, X. Kong, Y. Huang, P. S. Yu, and B. Wu. Hetesim: A general framework for relevance measure in heterogeneous networks. *TKDE*, 2014.

[16] C. Shi, X. Kong, P. Yu, S. Xie, and B. Wu. Relevance search in heterogeneous networks. *EDBT*, 2012.

[17] F. M. Suchanek, G. Kasneci, and G. Weikum. Yago: A core of semantic knowledge. In *WWW*, New York, NY, USA, 2007.

[18] L. Sun, R. Cheng, X. Li, D. W. Cheung, and J. Han. On link-based similarity join. *PVLDB*, 4(11), 2011.

[19] Y. Sun, R. Barber, M. Gupt, C. Aggarwal, and J. Han. Co-author relationship prediction in heterogeneous bibliographic networks. In *ASONAM*, 2011.

[20] Y. Sun, J. Han, X. Yan, P. S. Yu, and T. Wu. PathSim: Meta path-based top-k similarity search in heterogeneous information networks. *PVLDB*, 4(11), 2011.

[21] TIME. One Century, 100 Remarkable People. `http://content.time.com/time/specials/packages/0,28757,2020772,00.html`, 2008.

[22] H. Tong, C. Faloutsos, and J.-Y. Pan. Fast random walk with restart and its applications. *ICDM*, 2006.

[23] Q. T. Tran, C.-Y. Chan, and S. Parthasarathy. Query by output. In *SIGMOD*, 2009.

[24] K. S. Van Horn and T. R. Martinez. The minimum feature set problem. *Neural Networks*, 7(3), 1994.

[25] X. Yu, Q. Gu, M. Zhou, and J. Han. Citation prediction in heterogeneous bibliographic networks. In *SDM*, 2012.

[26] M. Zhang, H. Elmeleegy, C. M. Procopiuc, and D. Srivastava. Reverse engineering complex join queries. In *SIGMOD*, 2013.

[27] W. Zhang, R. Cheng, and B. Kao. Evaluating multi-way joins over discounted hitting time. *ICDE*, 2014.

From "Selena Gomez" to "Marlon Brando": Understanding Explorative Entity Search

Iris Miliaraki
Yahoo Labs
Barcelona, Spain
irismili@yahoo-inc.com

Roi Blanco
Yahoo Labs
Barcelona, Spain
roi@yahoo-inc.com

Mounia Lalmas
Yahoo Labs
London, UK
mounia@acm.org

ABSTRACT

Consider a user who submits a search query "Shakira" having a specific search goal in mind (such as her age) but at the same time willing to explore information for other entities related to her, such as comparable singers. In previous work, a system called Spark, was developed to provide such search experience. Given a query submitted to the Yahoo search engine, Spark provides related entity suggestions for the query, exploiting, among else, public knowledge bases from the Semantic Web. We refer to this search scenario as *explorative entity search*. The effectiveness and efficiency of the approach has been demonstrated in previous work. The way users interact with these related entity suggestions and whether this interaction can be predicted have however not been studied. In this paper, we perform a large-scale analysis into how users interact with the entity results returned by Spark. We characterize the users, queries and sessions that appear to promote an explorative behavior. Based on this analysis, we develop a set of query and user-based features that reflect the click behavior of users and explore their effectiveness in the context of a prediction task.

Categories and Subject Descriptors

H.3.3 [**Information Search and Retrieval**]: Search process; H.1.2 [**User/Machine Systems**]: Human information processing

Keywords

related entity; Yahoo Spark system; log analysis; user click behavior; explorative search

1. INTRODUCTION

Search engines are rapidly evolving from the ubiquitous *ten blue links* that have dominated Web search results for over fifteen years. One main driver for enhancing the capabilities of search systems has been the ability to incorporate structured data in their search results page [4, 12]. In general, when a user submits a query to a search engine their corresponding information need can be categorized at a high level as navigational or informational [5]. In the latter case, there are many situations in which users know exactly what they are looking for and would like immediate answers, whereas in other cases they are willing to explore to extend their knowledge, satisfy their curiosity or simply for the fun of it [13]. This situation happens, for example, when learning about people in the news, following a long term interest in music, movies or sports or when exploring destinations for future travel. As an example, consider a user who submits a search query "Shakira". The user may have a specific search goal in mind (such as the age of Shakira, some recent news about her or her next concerts). At the same time that user may be willing to explore other choices given to her, such as other artists related to Shakira, including those who have performed or sang with her.

In the realm of Web search, knowledge bases (KBs) contain information about different real-world objects or concepts commonly referred to as *entities*. Given that KBs generally store typed relationships between entities (such as "*born_in*" for entities *Shakira* and *Colombia*), they can be represented as a graph using entities as nodes and relations as edges, and are also known as *knowledge graphs* (KGs). Search engines can exploit such KGs not only for displaying additional facts and direct information about the central entity in a query, but also to provide extended suggestions for users who would like to browse. Queries containing entities correspond to the most popular type of queries [35] and are typically referred as *named entity queries* or simply *entity queries*. Given that the system is able to identify the real-world entity that is being referenced in an entity query and link it to a knowledge base, then it can provide recommendations of related entities based on the relationships explicitly encoded in the knowledge base.

As an example, consider the search result page in Figure 1 which displays the results on Yahoo Search for the entity query "barcelona spain". Besides the main search result links representing document results and images, we can see on the right panel suggestions for points of interest in Barcelona. This requires an understanding that this query represents the city of Barcelona, and a ranking over the points of interest, which is performed over the entities neighboring *Barcelona* in a KG. This is exactly what a system called Spark is doing [3]. Spark provides extended browsing capabilities through the knowledge graph exploiting public knowledge bases from the Semantic Web, in combination with proprietary data, to provide related entity suggestions for web search queries.

WWW 2015, May 18–22, 2015, Florence, Italy.
ACM 978-1-4503-3469-3/15/05.
http://dx.doi.org/10.1145/2736277.2741284.

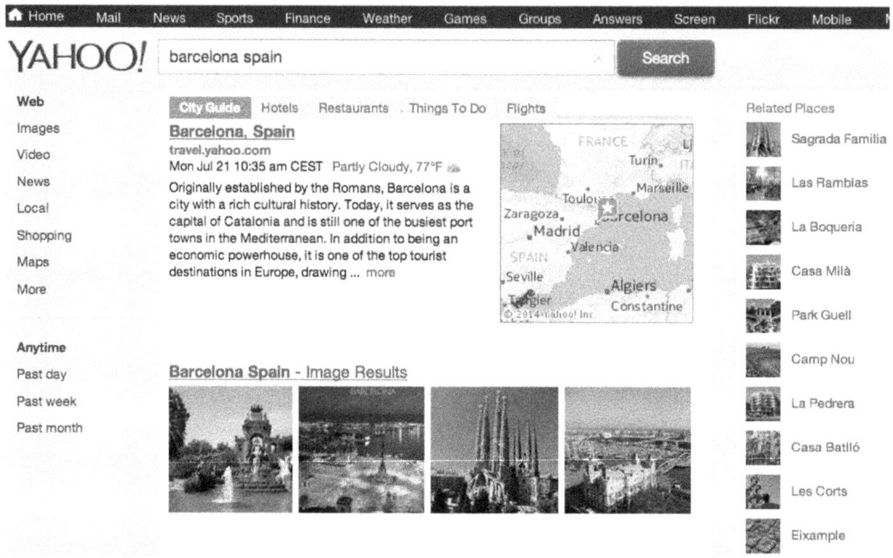

Figure 1: Search result page for the query *"barcelona spain"*. Spark results (related places) appear on the right.

So, what has the young actress "Selena Gomez" to do with "Marlon Brando"? This is a path that can be potentially explored by a user following suggestions made by Spark. Starting from the entity query "selena gomez", Spark is triggered recommending several related entities for exploring, one being *Kevin James*, which itself also triggers Spark to suggest *Henry Winkler*; this process continues with the following sequence of clicks on recommended entities, *Robin Williams*, *Al Pacino*, and *Robert de Niro*, to finally reach *Marlon Brando*. The relationship between each pair of these entities, here persons, comes from them appearing in the same event, belonging to the same industry, involved in the same film, and so on. This sequence of queries and clicks was one that was actually followed by users, and is an example of what we refer to as an *explorative entity search*.

While entity ranking systems have evolved significantly in terms of more effective and efficient algorithms for generating entity recommendations, no previous work has studied how users interact and engage with these systems and under which circumstances they are willing to follow an explorative path not directly related to their information need. This paper attempts to fill this missing gap, which has not been addressed before in the literature, focusing on how users interact with results returned by existing Web scale entity recommendation systems. We perform a large-scale analysis on search logs of $2M$ users on the existing Spark system [3].

We analyze the types of queries and entities that users interact with, exploring who are the users interacting with Spark results, the characteristics of their sessions, and the interplay between the typical search results and Spark entity recommendation results. Our analysis clearly indicates that Spark is able to promote an explorative behavior. Examples of such cases arise with long user sessions and entity queries that lack any surrounding context indicating a specific need (e.g., "images"). Based on our analysis, we develop a set of query and user-based features that reflect the click behavior of the users and explore their impact in the context of click prediction on Spark (i.e., predicting future interactions with entity recommendations). We find that the previous history of users, session duration and query-click through rate are the most discriminating features for predicting whether a user will click on a recommended entity or not.

2. RELATED WORK

Often, the user's initial interest can be uniquely linked to an entity in a KB, and in this case it is natural to recommend the explicitly linked entities for further exploration. Many useful facts about *entities* (people, locations, organizations, or products) and their relationships can be found in data sources such as Wikipedia or Freebase, while others need to be extracted from unstructured text. In real world knowledge bases, however, the number of linked entities may be very large and not all linked entities are equally relevant therefore making ranking related entities a must.

All major search engines currently display *entity recommendations* in the context of a web search session. The focus of our study is Yahoo's Spark system [3]. Spark extracts several signals from a variety of data sources, including user sessions, Twitter and Flickr, using a large cluster of computers running Hadoop. These signals are combined with a machine-learned ranking model to produce a final recommendation of entities to user queries, which is currently powering Yahoo Search results pages.

The problem of discovering interesting relations from unstructured text has led to a surge in research on the topic of *entity search* [8, 15, 20, 24, 26]. Entity search is viewed as an ideal paradigm to support explorative search. It provides semantically rich answers, i.e., entities and their relations, which are often considered more suitable for search exploration than individual web pages. Spark [3] falls in this type of systems.

Methods for generating query recommendations have focused on the analysis of query logs at the level of entire query strings or tokens, without any concern for the linguistic or semantic structure of the query strings [18]. However, more recent work has recognized that queries have internal structures and can be classified based on their semantic intent [21, 25, 16]. These observations have led to the development of the area of semantic search [4]. The broad area of

Table 1: Spark input graph

Domain	# of entities	# of relations
Movie	205,197	9,642,124
TV	88,004	17,126,890
Music	294,319	77,673,434
Notability	585,765	89,702
Sport	75,088	1,281,867,144
Geo	2,195,370	4,655,696
Total	3,443,743	1,391,054,990

semantic search in general refers to finding information in knowledge bases using unstructured, keyword queries typical for search engines; Spark makes explicit use of semantic web technologies [2].

Various evaluation efforts like INEX Entity and Linked Data tracks,[1] TREC Entity track,[2] and SemSearch challenge[3] have been carried out to assess the effectiveness of entity search approaches. Their focus was mainly with respect to evaluating how well the proposed techniques worked, in terms of delivering the right results for a given query. To the best of our knowledge, there has not been any large scale evaluation looking at how users engage with such results. This is the focus of this paper studying user behaviors for queries for which Spark returns recommended entities, for users to browse during their search session.

There has been many works studying user behavior with search engines. These studies examined query log data to elicit search patterns and other signals that can inform about various aspects of the search process [9, 17]. For instance, click-through data has been extensively used to assess how satisfied (or unsatisfied) users are with search results returned to them, mostly in terms of their relevance, e.g. [28, 32]. Query intent [17], user frustration [10] and search engine switching [33] have also been studied. Finally, tracking user search behavior over time (so-called historical data) has been shown to lead to better prediction of future search behavior, e.g. [6, 27, 31]. In this paper, we also study user search behavior to gain similar insights. Our context is however different; we look at how users behave when presented search results, here entities, that are served to them to promote exploration. All the above studies studied user behavior when users were presented search results that were served to "solve" their information need.

Explorative search[4] addresses the problem of less well-defined information need: users are unfamiliar with the problem domain, or the search tasks require some exploration [22, 34]. It also includes scenarios where users are enjoying exploring without a specific search objective in mind, they just want to get an update, or be entertained during their spare time. Searching for fun[5] or having fun while searching involves activities such as online shopping with nothing to buy, reading online, watching funny videos, and even clicking on images that have little relation with the original information needs [30]. Various works looked at approaches to promote and evaluate explorative search [14, 36]. This paper is also concerned with explorative search, and focuses on how users interact with entities returned to them *in addition* to the search results, enticing them to explore.

Although recommendations similar to Spark appear on the result pages of Google and Bing, details of these systems and their large-scale evaluation have not been published. Spark has been described in previous work [3, 19], where the focus was largely on ranking. The system has evolved considerably since then, and is now ready to be studied in terms of what type of engagement it promotes, and whether user behavior patterns can be identified. This paper studies how users interact with results returned by Spark, in terms of the submitted queries, the user demographics, and the interplay between typical search results and Spark entity recommendation.

3. SPARK: AN ENTITY RECOMMENDER SYSTEM

Given the large number of related entities that are usually available in a knowledge base, Spark selects the most relevant ones to show based on the current query of the user. Unlike the standard task addressed in entity search, where most related work has focused [8, 15, 20, 24, 26], Spark does not try to find information directly related to the user's *current query* but to recommend possible *future queries* to explore. Hence, Spark aims to promote exploration search within the remit of entity recommendation, which we refer to as *explorative entity search*.

The main component of Spark is its knowledge base, represented as a large entity graph. Spark takes this graph as input, and applies a ranking function to extract a weighted subgraph consisting of the most important entities, their most important related entities, and their respective types. This entity graph is drawn from a larger Yahoo Knowledge Graph, a unified knowledge base that provides key information about all the entities that are deemed worthwhile, and how they relate to each others. Entities, relations, and information about them are automatically extracted from multiple data sources on an ongoing basis. Data sources consist of Web extractions, structured data feeds, and editorial content. Both open data sources and closed data sources from paid providers are leveraged. Reference data sources such as Wikipedia and Freebase provide background information for a wide variety of domains whereas domain-specific data sources provide rich information for domains such as Movie, TV, Music, or Sport.

The knowledge base is modeled as a property graph with a common ontology, which was developed over 2 years by the Yahoo editorial team and is aligned with schema.org. Today's knowledge graph focuses on the domains of interest of key Yahoo sites, including the News domain (various types of entities), the Movie domain (movies, actors, directors, etc.), the TV domain (TV shows, actors, hosts, etc.), the Music domain (albums, music artists, etc.), the Sport domain (leagues, teams, athletes, etc.), and the Geo domain (points of interests, etc.). Overall, the graph that Spark uses as input consists of 3.5M entities and 1.4B direct and indirect relations from the Movie, TV, Music, Sport and Geo domains. See table 1 for details.

For every triple (subject, relation, object) in the knowledge base, Spark extracts over 100 features belonging to three main categories, i.e., co-occurrence, popularity, and graph-theoretic ones. Co-occurrence features are motivated

[1] `http://www.inex.otago.ac.nz/tracks/entity-ranking/entity-ranking.asp`
[2] `http://ilps.science.uva.nl/trec-entity/`
[3] `http://semsearch.yahoo.com/`
[4] The term "exploratory" search is also used [22].
[5] A workshop Searching4Fun focusing on pleasure-driven, rather than task-driven, search. See `http://www.cs.nott.ac.uk/~mlw/s4f2014/`.

by the fact that entities that frequently occur together in a given set of observations (sets of short text pieces) are more likely to be related to each other. Spark uses Yahoo Search, Twitter, and Flickr as sources to extract the co-occurrence information. For example, for the query "flight from barcelona to madrid", "Barcelona" and "Madrid" are identified as two entities that occur together. In case of Twitter and Flickr, the occurrence frequencies are extracted from tweets and user tags associated with photos, respectively.

Popularity features represent the frequency of an entity in a given data source. Examples include the number of matching results in Yahoo Search, when the entity string is used as a query, as well as frequency information with respect to queries, query sessions, tweets, and photo tags. Finally, the graph-theoretic features include graphs metrics, for example the number of shared vertices (common neighbors) between two entities. The extracted feature vectors are the sole input to the ranking process. Spark uses learning to rank approaches to derive an efficient ranking function for entities related to a query entity. The system employs Stochastic Gradient Boosted Decision Trees (GBDT) for deriving the learning (ranking) function [11].

Figure 1 shows the related entity recommendations made by Spark in Yahoo Web Search for the query "barcelona spain". This is a place, so Spark returns "related places". These are the typical places that are visited by millions of people, as they correspond to the city's top attractions. After clicking one of the related entities a new query is launched with the related entity leading to a new search result page, which can potentially contain more recommendations by Spark based on the new query.

The effectiveness and efficiency of the Spark system has been described recently in [3]. We study how users interact with the related entity recommendations returned by Spark as it performing a large-scale analysis on search logs of $2M$ users. We characterize the users, queries and sessions that appear to promote an explorative behavior.

4. ANALYSIS

We performed a large-scale analysis exploring the click behavior of users submitting entity queries that trigger Spark. We first examine how query characteristics affect the click probability on related entities focusing on the click-through rate of the query, the type of the entity, and the surrounding context of the entity in the query. Then, we study the users, investigate the impact of their demographics (age and gender) on the observed click behavior, and attempt to characterize sessions (e.g., in terms of duration) that lead to a successful interaction with Spark (i.e., at least one click on a related entity). We also distinguish between different navigation patterns of users while interacting with Spark. Last, we examine whether time has an effect on user behavior (i.e., in terms of the day of visit or time of visit) and report also other interesting trends discovered.

4.1 Dataset, metric and scope

We collected a sample of 2M users focusing on their activity on queries that trigger Spark to recommend related entities. We only consider queries issued at least 100 times.

Spark aims to promote exploration. This means that when a set of recommended entities are returned to the user, a successful outcome is a click by the user on at least one of them; the user is exploring. A key metric to measure this is *click-through rate (CTR)*, which is commonly used to evaluate user satisfaction in search [1] or online advertising [29]. For a given query, we define the *search CTR* (respectively the *Spark CTR*) as the total number of clicks on a search (respectively Spark) result returned as an answer to this query divided by the total number of times that the query was issued (respectively, triggered Spark). The latter is also referred to as a *view*, and corresponds to the event that a particular item has been displayed on the search page (an entity or a document result). Likewise, a user can also be characterized by a click-through rate observed over a time period given the queries she has issued and her performed clicks.

Our analysis could include other metrics, such as click dwell time, to differentiate for instance long versus short clicks or time between consecutive clicks. We leave this for future work, as, in this paper, we want to understand what makes users click on the entities returned to them by Spark. We therefore focus on CTR, as our metric to study user exploration with Spark results.

We also restrict ourselves to sessions where Spark was triggered to recommend entities for users to explore as part of their search session. As discussed in the previous section, not all queries submitted by users lead to entities returned by Spark. Although it would be interesting to compare users' "explorative behavior" when returned or not returned Spark results, our focus is to gain an understanding on what makes users explore the entities recommended to them by Spark, and whether this can be predicted.

Finally, for confidentiality reasons we normalize all raw CTR values via a linear transformation and report only relative CTR values.[6]

4.2 Query-based analysis

Consider a user issuing an entity query which leads to a search result page like the one in Figure 1. We distinguish between the following user actions: (1) the user clicks on one or more search results situated in the central page panel (*search click* on organic results), (2) the user clicks on one or more related entities suggested by Spark on the right page panel (*Spark click*), (3) the user does not click. We look at these actions with respect to CTR, entity type and entity context.

Search versus Spark CTR. We look into the relationship between search and Spark click-through rate per query. The results are plotted in Figure 2(a), where the CTR values are plotted after eliminating outliers in the upper deciles (i.e., points referring to less than 2% of the observations) and normalizing the values by the remaining maximum one. We can observe the following cases. First, queries having a relatively low CTR for search results tend to also have a low CTR for Spark results. Then, we identify a mutual growth area where we find queries with relatively high search and Spark CTR. Finally, queries with the highest search CTR values tend to have the lowest values of Spark CTR. Overall this indicates that queries with an average search CTR (neither low nor high) are those for which the returned Spark recommended entities are more likely to "attract" user attention. However, as the plot depicts, the search CTR does not directly indicate its Spark CTR value.

[6]Unless otherwise stated, we normalize by the maximum value observed in each plot.

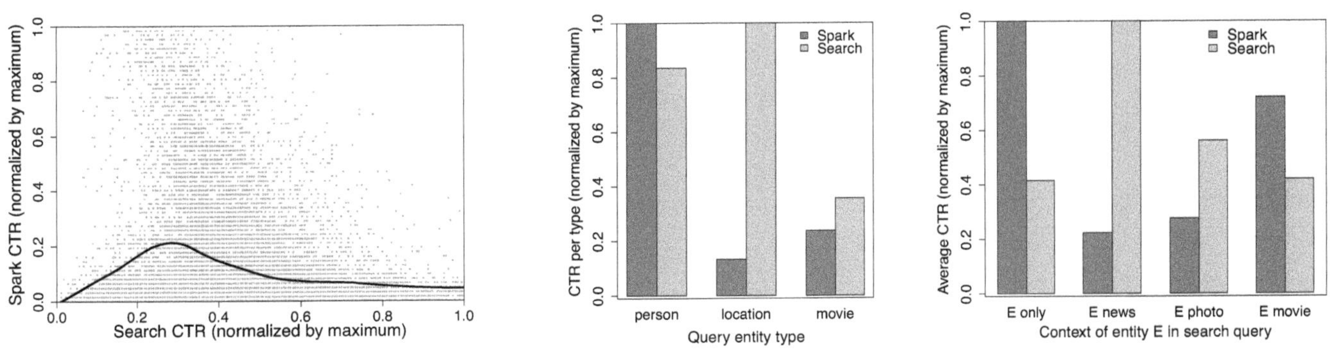

(a) CTR per query (b) CTR per entity type (c) CTR per query context

Figure 2: Query-based analysis

CTR across entity types. In Spark, each entity is associated with a type, such as "person", "location" and "movie". We focus on these types in this study since these are the most common ones. We study now how the click-through rate varies across these entity types. The results are reported in Figure 2(b). We note how some types of entities (persons, movies) are more prone to receive clicks than others (locations). This might be due to the fact that some entity types are intrinsically more likely to spur an explorative intent than others. All reported average values are significantly different (t-test, $p < 0.001$).

Effect of entity context on query. We study how the surrounding context of an entity in a submitted query affects the click behavior of users (see Figure 2(c)). The notion of context in an entity query was used in [35] to build a taxonomy of web search intents for entity queries. As an example, consider the query "jennifer aniston photo", with the intent to discover pictures of Jennifer Aniston (i.e., the surrounding context is "photo"). In this case, Spark may be triggered recommending a set of related entities, as in the case of a query containing only the entity "jennifer aniston". As we observe in Figure 2(c), the user who submits an entity query without any surrounding context is more likely to click on Spark results (denoted as "E only"). However, a user who submits an entity query with the surrounding context such as "news" or "photo" is less likely to click on a Spark result. This might be explained by the fact that users in the latter case are already looking for a specialized set of results within the context of that particular entity (i.e., the actress) and the odds of being willing to explore other related entities (i.e., other actors) are lower. The same holds for the context "news"; returning related entities when users are interested in reading about news does not seem to trigger an explorative behavior through Spark entities. Last, the context "movie", aiming most probably to identify the entity of a query (e.g., "walk the line movie"), leads to a relatively higher CTR on Spark. All reported average values are significantly different (t-test, $p < 0.001$).

To conclude, queries with average CTR are more likely to have their Spark recommended entities clicked, the entity type (person versus location) affects whether the corresponding Spark recommended entities are clicked, and finally, queries associated with a genre (e.g., news) or media context (e.g., image) are less likely to have their Spark recommended entities clicked.

4.3 User-based analysis

We continue our analysis from the user's perspective. First, we study whether the demographics of the users affect their click behavior on Spark and also explore whether specific characteristics of a user session such as its overall duration affect this behavior. In the former case, we consider only a subset of users who have disclosed this information (age and gender) as part of the registration process while obtaining an account with Yahoo.

Spark & search CTR by demographics. In Figure 3(a), we depict the average CTR values for search and Spark results across users of different ages. The plotted values are normalized by the maximum average value separately for search and Spark CTR values. As we observe, there is a different effect on search versus Spark click-through rate as the age increases. In case of Spark, users of a younger age tend to have a relatively higher CTR than the users of the other groups. The results for Search CTR are complementary to this; users from the older age groups tend to click more on search results. Figure 3(b) depicts the difference of the Spark and search CTR rates between male and female users. While for search no difference is observed, for Spark, male users tend to exhibit a higher CTR than female users.

Session duration effect. Figure 3(c) shows how the duration of a user session affects the average Spark CTR and the average search CTR of the corresponding session. Spark and search CTR values are normalized by their standard score and shifted by a constant value for visualization purposes. Shorter sessions have the higher search CTR; users come, find what they are looking for and leave. They are satisfied with the results. As the session length increases, search CTR diminishes, likely because users are trying various queries to find the information they are looking for. After a while, the CTR again increases slowly, which may suggest either a stubborn user, a complex information need, or users who are simply exploring.

The behavior is different for Spark CTR. The longer the session, the higher the CTR. This suggests that when a user clicks on a Spark result she is willing to explore the

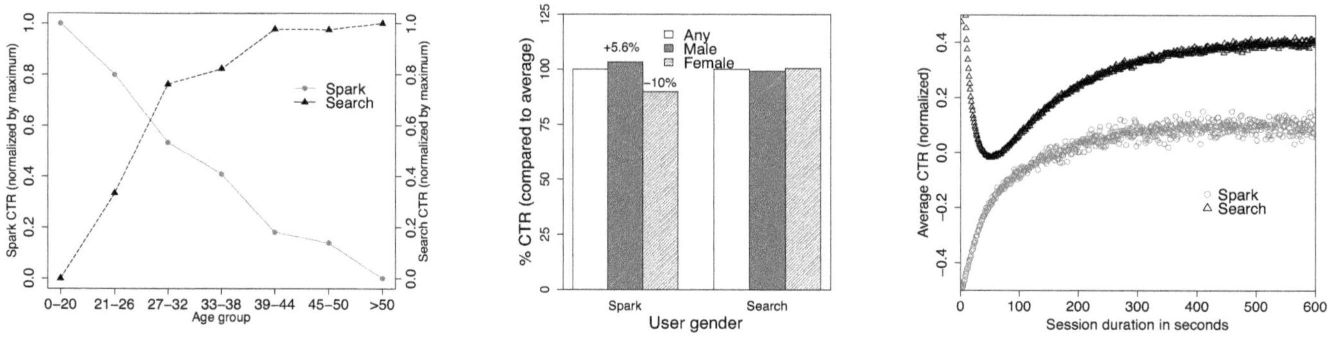

(a) CTR across age groups

(b) CTR across gender

(c) Session duration effect

Figure 3: User-based analysis

Query entity	Entity type	Pattern type	Navigation pattern
Tennis	Sport	star	{Serena Williams, Maria Sharapova}
Barcelona	Location	star	{La Sagrada Familia, Park Guell, Tibidabo}
Marlon Brando	Person	star	{Elizabeth Taylor, Al Pacino, Sophia Loren, Charlie Chaplin}
Scent of a woman	Movie	path	Al Pacino ⇒ Marlon Brando
Basketball	Sport	path	Carmelo Anthony ⇒ Lebron James ⇒ Dwight Howard
Samuel Jackson	Person	path	Bruce Willis ⇒ John Travolta ⇒ Nicolas Cage
Catherine Zeta Jones	Person	path	Julia Roberts ⇒ Natalie Portman ⇒ Scarlett Johansson

Table 2: Example of user navigation patterns using Spark

recommendation, and may continue to do so for a while. The fact that we observe a difference in the curves of search CTR and Spark CTR clearly shows that Spark is indeed returning results that entice users to explore; when users do so, they become more engaged as they interact with the Spark recommendations; it is not anymore about satisfying an information need, but satisfying curiosity.

User navigation patterns. Finally, we studied how users interact with Spark in terms of navigation. We distinguish between *star* and *path* behavior where the former refers to the case where a user tends to click on many related entities for a given entity query (increasing *breadth*) and the latter refers to the case where a user tends to follow a path of related entities issuing different successive queries (increasing *depth*). Different example navigation patterns are shown in Table 2. An example of a star navigation pattern begins from the entity query "Barcelona" and continues with three different related entities, i.e., "La Sagrada Familia", "Park Guell" and "Tibidabo". An example of a path navigation pattern begins with the query entity "Catherine Zeta Jones", continues with "Julia Roberts", "Natalie Portman", and finally ends with "Scarlett Johansson".

The distribution of users' navigation patterns according to their breadth and depth properties are summarized in Tables 3 and 4. We also include the separate distributions for entities of type person and type location. In general, there is a tendency towards a path navigation pattern from users in 13% of the cases compared to only 4% for star navigation patterns. This suggests that users, when returning to the initial search result page after clicking on a Spark result, are less likely to engage in further exploration. They were enticed to click, but now they are back to what they were doing, i.e., a search. On the other hand, when they continue clicking on further entities, they are engaged in exploration. This difference could help to classify whether users are ready to explore or are more focused on solving their information needs.

To conclude, demographics have some effect on CTR. However, in the context of gender, it is not clear if this comes from the type of queries triggering Spark (to return entities) or from the user gender itself. We return to age when we discuss trends. However, what is clear is that Spark results have the potential to lead users in explorative behavior; when they start engaging with Spark search results, it is more likely that the session is longer and the navigation deeper.

4.4 Day of the week effect

We now study whether Spark and search CTR varies for different days of the week or different times of the day. The results are shown in Figures 4(a) and 4(b). For both search and Spark, CTR is significantly higher on weekends (t-test, $p < 0.001$). We recall here that our dataset only contains sessions where the query triggered Spark to recommend entities. Therefore, this indicates that the types of queries that triggered Spark are those more likely to lead to users interacting with the results over the weekend than weekdays. This is not surprising as the entities, and their relationships, covered by Spark (i.e., stored in Spark knowledge base) relate to persons, locations, movies and sports, many of which have an "entertainment" or "leisure" nature.

Moreover, the difference in CTR between weekdays and weekends is more accentuated with Spark CTR in the afternoon and at night. Users are more likely to click on Spark results during these parts of the day on weekends. For the morning, it is the inverse (a stronger difference is observed with Search CTR). Interestingly, both the Spark CTR and the search CTR do not increase significantly from weekdays and weekends in the evening (there is hardly any increase for Search CTR).

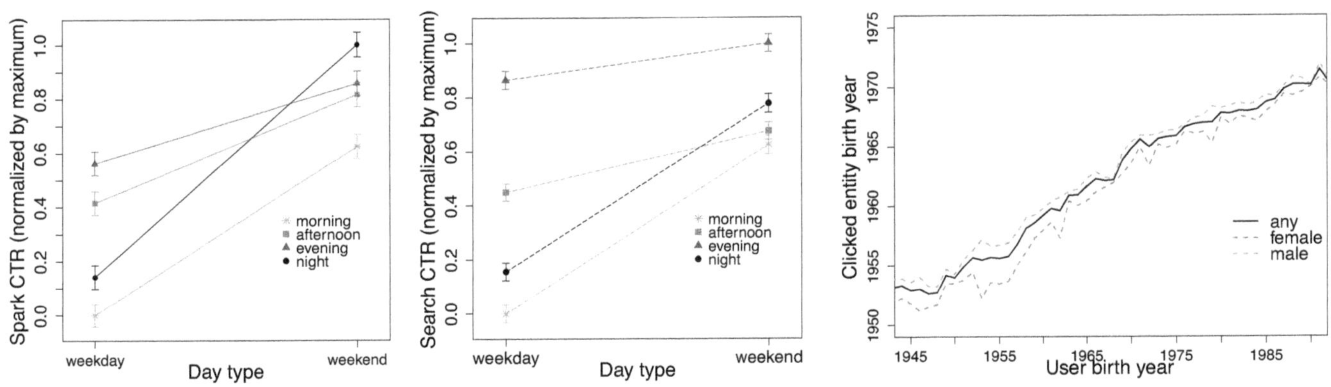

(a) Spark CTR (normalized) (b) Search CTR (normalized) (c) Birth year correlation

Figure 4: Time effect (time of day & day type) and *birth year* correlation

Breadth	All types	Person	Location
1	95.36%	95.46%	95.27%
2	4.10%	3.63%	4.21%
≥ 3	0.54%	0.91%	0.53%

Table 3: Distribution of *star* navigation patterns

Depth	All types	Person	Location
1	72.2%	67.9%	86.6%
2	13.3%	15.1%	7.5%
≥ 3	14.5%	17%	5.9%

Table 4: Distribution of *path* navigation patterns

Overall, the "entertainment" or "leisure" nature of the queries that trigger Spark (e.g. actress, movie) results in users who are more likely to engage with the Spark results (and search results) when their entertainment and leisure activities are planned (a movie trip on the weekend) or happening (browsing the web in the evening). Weekday mornings seem to be a "no-go" for explorative search.

4.5 Other trends

We also looked at many other relationships, between demographics and types of queries (e.g., male users tend to have a higher CTR on sports-related entities), and report one particularly interesting and significant relationship. In Figure 4(c), we plot the age of the users against the age of the person entities that they click on. Values on y-axis are averages of the ages of the entities clicked by users of a specific age (x-axis). To eliminate outliers and potential noise, we only consider ages for which we have at least 100 observations. We observe that a strong correlation exists, clearly showing that users are enticed to explore people of a closer age to them (Pearson correlation is equal to 0.859 with $p < 0.0001$). For instance, younger users tend to click less frequently on results returned to them about persons older than them. This suggests that users, when exploring the recommended entities, seem to choose people with which they can relate, because of their "comparable" ages. We also note the same pattern is observed across genders. If we include user ages with at least 10 observations (introducing potentially more noise), correlation drops to 0.62.

Returning to Figure 3(a), we saw that users of a younger age tend to have a relatively higher CTR than the users of the other groups. It would be interesting to see whether increasing the coverage of Spark, by including entities for which older users would relate, could increase their interaction with Spark (e.g., increasing the CTR on Spark results from older users).

4.6 Discussion

In this section we studied user behavior, with respect to user clicks on related entities suggested by Spark. Users submit a query to solve an information need. Spark results are not there to fulfill this need, but to entice users to explore entities that are related to their initial query. Our analysis clearly shows that Spark is able to promote this explorative behavior. Users are more inclined to navigate through the recommendations for certain types of queries, especially when no specific context is specified (such as "pictures"), with a higher CTR observed during weekends. When users decide to engage with a Spark recommendation, they often end up navigating through the recommendations, clearly engaging in explorative search. Contrary to standard search behavior, where a satisfactory experience is when users find the information they are looking for as soon as possible (the search sessions are short), users interacting with Spark entity recommendations seem to happily explore through these results, leading to longer sessions. Next, we look at how these insights can be used to build a model that can predict whether users will click on Spark results.

5. PREDICTION TASK

We studied the click behavior of users after issuing an entity query for which Spark recommends a set of related entities. Our analysis focused on CTR and how it is affected by the characteristics of the user, the session and the issued entity query. We now consider the problem of predicting whether a user will click or not on a related entity after issuing an query. We tackle this task by exploiting features, user- and query-based ones, inspired by our previous analysis.

5.1 Experimental setup

Dataset. We use a sample of 100k users from Yahoo search logs, from which we collect their actions over a period of 6

Feature	Description	Type
Q1	Total views of entity query	Numeric
Q2	Total clicks on related entities of entity query	Numeric
Q3	Click-through rate of entity query on Spark	Numeric
Q4	Category of search and Spark click-through rate (*low, medium, high*)	Ordinal
Q5	Type of entity (e.g., person, location, movie)	Categorical
Q6	Whether any context surrounds the entity in query string	Binary
U1	Click-through rate of user on Spark	Numeric
U2	Previous user actions ($h = 1, 2, 3$)	Categorical
U3	Session length (*short, medium, long*)	Ordinal

Table 5: Feature sets (Q contains query-based features, U contains user-based features)

months. We only consider actions related to entity queries triggering Spark. To capture the notion of "new users" interacting with Spark for the first time, we only consider users that do not have any action related to Spark during a period of one month and then at some point perform a click on a related entity suggested by Spark. After identifying such users we consider all their succeeding actions. For this task we collect up to $h = 4$ succeeding interactions per user, aiming to exploit at most $h = 3$ succeeding interactions as indicators of the user's future behavior and attempting to predict the last. An interaction consists of the query issued by the user and the action that followed (a click on a Spark result, a click on a search result, or no click at all). We consider two different samples of 100k users varying the number of *required* historical actions from 0 to exactly 3. In the first dataset, denoted as $D1$, we may include users without any or with up to 3 historical actions. In the second, denoted as $D2$, we only consider users for which 3 of their previous actions are known.

Prediction task & method. Given a user, her previous interactions, and an issued entity query, we want to predict whether the user will interact with the Spark module or not. Since our focus is on predicting Spark interactions, we consider this as the "positive event" and any other interaction is considered as the "negative event" (e.g., a click only on organic search results). We do not distinguish between a single click on a related entity or multiple clicks and consider an interaction leading to at least one click as a positive instance. We focus only on interactions concerning entity queries triggering Spark and ignore any other activity of the user. We make use of logistic regression [23] for learning and perform 5-fold cross-validation averaging all reported metrics.

Evaluation metrics. For performance evaluation we use the metrics of precision or positive predictive value (i.e., the ratio of correct positive predictions, denoted as PPV), negative predictive value (i.e., the ratio of correct negative predictions, denoted as NPV), recall or sensitivity (i.e., the ratio of positive observations correctly predicted, denoted as REC), specificity (or else recall for negative labeled instances, denoted as $SPEC$), accuracy (denoted as ACC) and area under the curve (AUC) of a ROC curve. Since our dataset is unbalanced, we use the metric of macro-averaged accuracy ($ACC = PPV \cdot 0.5 + NPV \cdot 0.5$) allowing us to give equal weight to the prediction ability of our method for each class.

5.2 Features

The set of features used for our prediction task are listed in Table 5. Recall that given a user issuing an entity query we want to predict whether the user will click or not on the Spark module (positive vs. negative class). We categorize our features into two sets, query-based ($Q1 - Q6$) and user-based ($U1 - U3$). The set Q of query-based features includes two groups of features related to the issued query. The first group contains query-specific historical features such total number of views (how many times the query has been issued), number of clicks and CTR. These are standard features used in many search-related prediction tasks. The second group includes the query type and the context, as these were shown to have an effect on CTR in Section 4.2. The set U contains features related to the user and includes her past behavior with respect to the Spark module such as her past click-through rate, and previous interaction when returned Spark results. U also includes the current session length (feature $U3$), which, as discussed in Section 4.3, is a good indicator of users being in "explorative mood". $U3$ captures the length of the session up to the time of the action of the user which we aim to predict (inspired by Figure 3(c)).

Besides Spark CTR (see feature $Q3$), we also consider a more coarse-grained representation (see feature $Q4$). We assign both the search and the Spark click-through rate of the query into three bins (low, medium, and high) according to the distribution of their values. This is based also on Figure 2(a), where we saw that queries with an average search CTR (neither low nor high) are those for which the returned Spark recommended entities are more likely to get clicked. As such, each entity query can be characterized by two *CTR classes*, e.g., a *medium* Spark CTR and a *high* Search CTR. These classes are then exploited to characterize the previous actions of the users (see feature $U2$ in Table 5). In total, we can distinguish between 18 types of actions (i.e., 3*3*2, where Spark/search CTR have 3 different labelings each and there are two possible user events, a click on Spark or not). The intuition behind this is to be able to differentiate between a user who clicks on a related entity after issuing a query with a high click-through rate on Spark and the user who clicks on Spark when the click-through rate of the query is low. A user who is likely to click on Spark more often than the average user can be considered a more engaged user and we aim to capture such cases.

5.3 Results

The results for the different sets of features (Q, U, and $Q + U$) are summarized in Table 6. We include the performance results for D1, where the minimum number of previous available actions per user is 0 ($h \geq 0$), and for D2, where exactly 3 actions are available for each user ($h = 3$).

Overall performance per feature set (D1). In dataset D1, the user-based features (U) achieve a higher performance, increasing both in terms of precision and recall, compared to the query-based features (Q). Precision is 19.1% higher when we use the user-based features against the query-based ones.

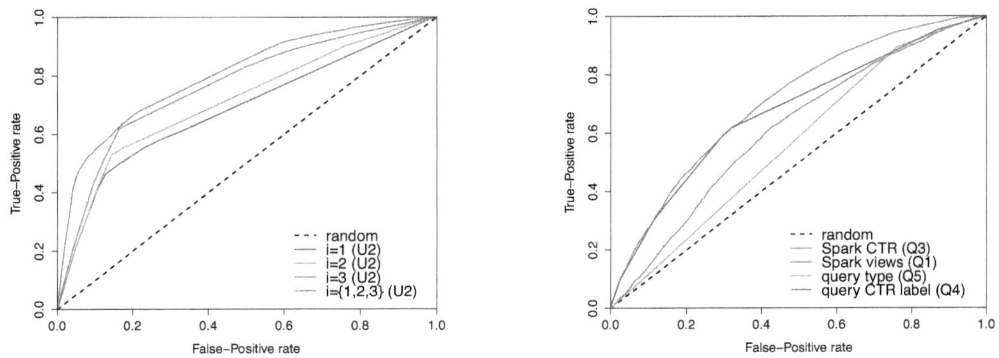

(a) AUC curves for features $U2$

(b) AUC curves for features $Q1$,$Q3$,$Q4$,$Q5$

Figure 5: Features performance for prediction task

Feature set	Dataset	PPV	NPV	REC	SPEC	ACC	AUC
Q	D1	0.512	0.809	0.054	**0.987**	0.660	0.695
U	D1	0.703	**0.875**	0.445	0.954	0.789	0.803
Q+U	D1	**0.707**	**0.875**	**0.447**	0.954	**0.791**	**0.811**
Q	D2	0.616	0.799	0.512	0.858	0.707	0.783
U	D2	0.701	0.874	0.719	0.864	0.787	0.856
Q+U	D2	**0.704**	**0.875**	**0.722**	**0.865**	**0.789**	**0.862**

Table 6: Results for different sets of features (Q, U, $Q+U$) and datasets D1, D2 (minimum actions $h \geq 0$ and $h = 3$)

The recall achieved by Q only is extremely low (<1%) exhibiting the difficulty of predicting the positive instances when no user-based information is available. Exploiting user-based features leads to an increase of 39%. In general, predicting negative instances is an easier task and as such the query-based approach performs relatively well (80% NPV for Q vs. 87.5% NPV for U). The macro-averaged accuracy metric is relatively high, around 79% for U and $Q+U$ features sets, while it drops to 66% for the case of Q. Exploiting both user-based and query-based features ($Q+U$) does not yield any additional gains in terms of performance, exhibiting a similar performance as when only features of U are used. We report, although we do not include the separate measurements, that the individual contribution of the historical features $U3$ with respect to the other user-based features ($U1$ and $U2$), is around 18% improvement in PPV and 5% improvement in NPV. This suggests that session length is a good indicator of whether users will click or not on Spark.

Overall performance per feature set (D2). Continuing with dataset D2, we observe a similar trend where U outperforms Q in terms of all metrics (even for specificity where in $D1$, U's performance was 95.4% vs. 98.7% for Q). On this dataset all feature sets achieve a higher recall (ranging from 51% for Q to 72.2% for $Q+U$). This is most likely due to the inclusion of less variance in the dataset since we only allow users with exactly 3 actions in their past behavior. Precision remains around 70% for both Q and $Q+U$ feature sets.

Effect of individual features (U). To quantify the effect of the inclusion of user's previous actions as indicators of their future behavior we plot the corresponding AUC curves for $i=1$, $i=2$, and $i=3$, where $i=1$ refers to the first available action of the user, $i=2$ refers to the next, and $i=3$ refers to the most recent action of the user. Each line in Figure 5(a) shows the AUC performance when each of these actions is used as a single feature for prediction. A larger area under the ROC curve corresponds to a better performance. We also include the AUC curve when all actions are included ($i=1,2,3$). We can observe that the more recent an action is ($\text{AUC}_{i=1} = 0.690$, $\text{AUC}_{i=2} = 0.719$, and $\text{AUC}_{i=3} = 0.761$), the more accurate the prediction. This suggests that users who are more recently engaged with the Spark module are more likely to continue engaging with it. In other words, users who have clicked on Spark are easier to be enticed to explore its recommended entities when triggered. Alternatively, this may be related to the relatively frequent path navigation patterns observed by the users (see Table 4).

Effect of individual features (Q). We also dig further into the effect of specific features in Q, specifically Spark CTR ($Q3$), Spark views ($Q1$), query CTR category ($Q4$) and query type ($Q5$). The results are shown in Figure 5(b). Interestingly, we see that features related to Spark CTR are the most discriminating to predict the future click behavior of the user.

Demographics. We also experimented with demographic features (gender and age). The addition of these features did not add any significant improvement and as such we do not include them in our analysis. This was particularly surprising as we observed an effect of age in CTR. Note that in other contexts, such as in the case of predicting click-through rate for sponsored ads [7], demographics have been proven to be important indicators. The extent to which the fact that demographics do not help in the prediction task is caused by the coverage of Spark knowledge base should be investigated.

5.4 Discussion

We developed features based on the characteristics of queries and users that reflect the click behavior on related entities recommended by Spark given a query and a user who issues that query. These features were inspired by our analysis of CTR reported in Section 4. Using logistic regression, our results demonstrate that user-based features improve significantly the accuracy for the prediction task compared to using only query-based features. The main contribution for this improvement originates from the historical information on past user click behavior. We also demonstrate that the most significant action is the most recent one. Session length can help in the prediction, indicating that users who spend time on the search application may be in "explorative mood" and are more likely to interact with entities recommended to them by the Spark engine. However, in all cases, recall is relatively low showing that overall the particulars under which a user will engage with the Spark module and a recommended entity are diverse and cannot be captured easily. In all cases, predicting the negative instances is a relatively easier task than predicting the positive ones.

6. CONCLUSIONS

Many entity search systems have been proposed and evaluated through several evaluation initiatives in which the focus was on whether the proposed approaches were effective in returning the most relevant entities given a query. In this paper we also focus on evaluation, but with two main differences. First, we study which relationships promote explorative search exploiting the Spark system, which has been deployed large-scale as part of Yahoo Search, as a use case. Given a query submitted to Yahoo search engine, Spark displays related entity suggestions exploiting Yahoo knowledge graph. Secondly, we perform a large-scale evaluation of Spark, with real information needs that then translate into queries by actual users of Yahoo Search. Our focus is on the queries that trigger Spark to recommend entities.

Analyzing a sample of $2M$ users, we studied how users interact with results returned by Spark, in terms of submitted queries, user demographics, investigating also the interplay between typical search results and Spark recommendations. We looked at how users behave when presented search results, here entities. This resulted in a very different picture compared to studying user behavior when users were presented search results that were served to "solve" their information need. Our results show that Spark is able to promote an explorative behavior. Often, when users decide to engage with a Spark recommendation they end up navigating through the recommendations engaging in explorative search as our introductory example suggests, where users navigated from "Selena Gomez" to "Marlon Brando". Among other findings, we show that longer sessions result in a higher explorative activity and engagement, and that when users navigate through Spark they favour following paths of *different* entities rather than exploring multiple entities related to a *single* entity.

Based on our previous analysis, we design a prediction task aiming to predict when users will click on recommended entities and engage in explorative behavior. We develop a set of features based on the characteristics of queries and users that reflect the click behavior on related entities recommended by Spark given a query and a user who issued it. We showed that user-based features improves significantly the accuracy compared to using only query-based features. The main contribution for this improvement originates from the historical information on past user behavior related to their interaction with Spark results. We also demonstrated that the most significant feature, for predicting of a future click, is the most recent interaction. However, recall is relatively low showing that the specifics under which a user will interact with Spark are diverse and cannot be easily captured easily.

Future work. In this work, we focused on the interplay between search results and Spark recommended entities. Given the content-rich result pages of modern search engines, users will interact with other components of the page like its ads and other results such as images and so on. All these compete for user attention and it will be important to situate the explorative search experience promoted by such systems like Spark within the full search context, and not only with respect to the standard search results, as done in this paper. Also, Spark returns entities from a regularly updated KB. However, we do not study the effect of the coverage, i.e., which entities and relationships are stored in the KB. Future work will look into this issue and into the impact of displaying a more diverse or a larger set of entities to the user and how these elements impact their explorative behavior. Finally, our work focused on queries for which Spark returned entities as recommendations for users to explore. It will be important to study how doing so promotes exploration, compared to not returning any such recommendations.

7. REFERENCES

[1] R. A. Baeza-Yates and B. A. Ribeiro-Neto. *Modern Information Retrieval - the concepts and technology behind search, Second edition.* Pearson Education Ltd., Harlow, England, 2011.

[2] T. Berners-Lee, J. Hendler, O. Lassila, et al. The semantic web. *Scientific american*, 284(5):28–37, 2001.

[3] R. Blanco, B. B. Cambazoglu, P. Mika, and N. Torzec. Entity Recommendations in Web Search. In *The Semantic Web–ISWC 2013*, pages 33–48. Springer, 2013.

[4] R. Blanco, P. Mika, and S. Vigna. Effective and efficient entity search in RDF data. In *Proceedings of the 10th International Conference on The Semantic Web - Volume Part I*, ISWC'11, pages 83–97, 2011.

[5] A. Z. Broder. A taxonomy of web search. *SIGIR Forum*, 36(2):3–10, 2002.

[6] B. Carterette, E. Kanoulas, and E. Yilmaz. Simulating simple user behavior for system effectiveness evaluation. In *Proceedings of the 20th ACM International Conference on Information and Knowledge Management*, CIKM '11, pages 611–620, 2011.

[7] H. Cheng and E. Cantú-Paz. Personalized click prediction in sponsored search. In *Proceedings of the third ACM international conference on Web search and data mining*, pages 351–360. ACM, 2010.

[8] T. Cheng, X. Yan, and K. C.-C. Chang. Entityrank: searching entities directly and holistically. In *VLDB*, 2007.

[9] D. Downey, S. Dumais, and E. Horvitz. Models of searching and browsing: Languages, studies, and applications. In *Proceedings of the 20th International Joint Conference on Artifical Intelligence*, IJCAI'07, pages 2740–2747, 2007.

[10] H. A. Feild, J. Allan, and R. Jones. Predicting searcher frustration. In *Proceedings of the 33rd International ACM SIGIR Conference on Research and Development in Information Retrieval*, SIGIR '10, pages 34–41, 2010.

[11] J. H. Friedman. Greedy function approximation: a gradient boosting machine. *Annals of Statistics*, pages 1189–1232, 2001.

[12] K. Haas, P. Mika, P. Tarjan, and R. Blanco. Enhanced results for web search. In *Proceedings of the 34th International ACM SIGIR Conference on Research and Development in Information Retrieval*, SIGIR '11, pages 725–734, New York, NY, USA, 2011. ACM.

[13] M. Harvey, M. Wilson, and K. Church. Workshop on searching for fun 2014. In *Fifth Information Interaction in Context Symposium, IIiX '14, Regensburg, Germany, August 26-29, 2014*, 2014.

[14] A. Hassan and R. W. White. Task tours: Helping users tackle complex search tasks. In *Proceedings of the 21st ACM International Conference on Information and Knowledge Management*, CIKM '12, pages 1885–1889, 2012.

[15] J. Hoffart, M. A. Yosef, I. Bordino, H. Fürstenau, M. Pinkal, M. Spaniol, B. Taneva, S. Thater, and G. Weikum. Robust disambiguation of named entities in text. In *EMNLP*, 2011.

[16] L. Hollink, P. Mika, and R. Blanco. Web usage mining with semantic analysis. In *Proceedings of the 22nd International Conference on World Wide Web*, WWW '13, pages 561–570, 2013.

[17] B. J. Jansen, D. L. Booth, and A. Spink. Determining the user intent of web search engine queries. In *Proceedings of the 16th International Conference on World Wide Web*, WWW '07, pages 1149–1150, 2007.

[18] R. Jones, B. Rey, O. Madani, and W. Greiner. Generating query substitutions. In L. Carr, D. D. Roure, A. Iyengar, C. A. Goble, and M. Dahlin, editors, *WWW*, pages 387–396. ACM, 2006.

[19] C. Kang, S. Vadrevu, R. Zhang, R. van Zwol, L. G. Pueyo, N. Torzec, J. He, and Y. Chang. Ranking related entities for web search queries. In S. Srinivasan, K. Ramamritham, A. Kumar, M. P. Ravindra, E. Bertino, and R. Kumar, editors, *WWW (Companion Volume)*, pages 67–68. ACM, 2011.

[20] S. Kulkarni, A. Singh, G. Ramakrishnan, and S. Chakrabarti. Collective annotation of Wikipedia entities in web text. In *KDD*, 2009.

[21] T. Lin, P. Pantel, M. Gamon, A. Kannan, and A. Fuxman. Active objects: actions for entity-centric search. In A. Mille, F. L. Gandon, J. Misselis, M. Rabinovich, and S. Staab, editors, *WWW*, pages 589–598. ACM, 2012.

[22] G. Marchionini. Exploratory search: From finding to understanding. *Commun. ACM*, 49(4):41–46, Apr. 2006.

[23] P. McCullagh and J. A. Nelder. Generalized linear models. 1989.

[24] R. Mihalcea and A. Csomai. Wikify!: linking documents to encyclopedic knowledge. In *CIKM*, 2007.

[25] P. Mika, E. Meij, and H. Zaragoza. Investigating the semantic gap through query log analysis. In A. Bernstein, D. R. Karger, T. Heath, L. Feigenbaum, D. Maynard, E. Motta, and K. Thirunarayan, editors, *International Semantic Web Conference*, volume 5823 of *Lecture Notes in Computer Science*, pages 441–455. Springer, 2009.

[26] D. Milne and I. H. Witten. Learning to link with Wikipedia. In *CIKM*, 2008.

[27] K. Radinsky, K. Svore, S. Dumais, J. Teevan, A. Bocharov, and E. Horvitz. Modeling and predicting behavioral dynamics on the web. In *Proceedings of the 21st International Conference on World Wide Web*, WWW '12, pages 599–608, 2012.

[28] F. Radlinski, M. Kurup, and T. Joachims. How does clickthrough data reflect retrieval quality? In *Proceedings of the 17th ACM Conference on Information and Knowledge Management*, CIKM '08, pages 43–52, 2008.

[29] M. Richardson, E. Dominowska, and R. Ragno. Predicting clicks: estimating the click-through rate for new ads. In *Proceedings of the 16th international conference on World Wide Web*, pages 521–530. ACM, 2007.

[30] M. Slaney. Precision-recall is wrong for multimedia. *IEEE Multimedia*, 18(3):4–7, 2011.

[31] Y. Song, X. Shi, and X. Fu. Evaluating and predicting user engagement change with degraded search relevance. In *Proceedings of the 22Nd International Conference on World Wide Web*, WWW '13, pages 1213–1224, 2013.

[32] K. Wang, T. Walker, and Z. Zheng. Pskip: Estimating relevance ranking quality from web search clickthrough data. In *Proceedings of the 15th ACM SIGKDD International Conference on Knowledge Discovery and Data Mining*, KDD '09, pages 1355–1364, 2009.

[33] R. W. White and S. T. Dumais. Characterizing and predicting search engine switching behavior. In *Proceedings of the 18th ACM Conference on Information and Knowledge Management*, CIKM '09, pages 87–96, 2009.

[34] R. W. White and R. A. Roth. Exploratory search: Beyond the query-response paradigm. *Synthesis Lectures on Information Concepts, Retrieval, and Services*, 1(1):1–98, 2009.

[35] X. Yin and S. Shah. Building taxonomy of web search intents for name entity queries. In *Proceedings of the 19th international conference on World wide web*, pages 1001–1010. ACM, 2010.

[36] X. Yuan and R. White. Building the trail best traveled: Effects of domain knowledge on web search trailblazing. In *Proceedings of the SIGCHI Conference on Human Factors in Computing Systems*, CHI '12, pages 1795–1804, 2012.

Children Seen But Not Heard: When Parents Compromise Children's Online Privacy

Tehila Minkus
New York University
tehila@nyu.edu

Kelvin Liu
NYU Shanghai
kelvin.liu@nyu.edu

Keith W. Ross
NYU and NYU Shanghai
keithwross@nyu.edu

ABSTRACT

Children's online privacy has garnered much attention in media, legislation, and industry. Adults are concerned that children may not adequately protect themselves online. However, relatively little discussion has focused on the privacy breaches that may occur to children at the hands of others, namely, their parents and relatives. When adults post information online, they may reveal personal information about their children to other people, online services, data brokers, or surveillant authorities. This information can be gathered in an automated fashion and then linked with other online and offline sources, creating detailed profiles which can be continually enhanced throughout the children's lives.

In this paper, we conduct a study to see how widespread these behaviors are among adults on Facebook and Instagram. We use a number of methods. Firstly, we automate a process to examine 2,383 adult users on Facebook for evidence of children in their public photo albums. Using the associated comments in combination with publicly available voter registration records, we are able to infer children's names, faces, birth dates, and addresses. Secondly, in order to understand what additional information is available to Facebook and the users' friends, we survey 357 adult Facebook users about their behaviors and attitudes with regard to posting their children's information online. Thirdly, we analyze 1,089 users on Instagram to infer facts about their children.

Finally, we make recommendations for privacy-conscious parents and suggest an interface change through which Facebook can nudge parents towards better stewardship of their children's privacy.

Categories and Subject Descriptors

H.1.2 [**Information Systems**]: Models and Principles—*User/Machine Systems, human factors*; K.4.1 [**Computers and Society**]: Public Policy Issues—*Privacy*

WWW 2015, May 18–22, 2015, Florence, Italy.
ACM 978-1-4503-3469-3/15/05.
http://dx.doi.org/10.1145/2736277.2741124.

Keywords

Online social networks; privacy; human factors; measurement

1. INTRODUCTION

Technological advances present the modern parent with novel concerns. How much exposure should a child have to technology? Can children be trusted to retain appropriate privacy in a networked world? However, few parents view their own social media usage as a threat to their children. But as a new generation of adults joins the ranks of parents, mentions and photos of children and babies are popping up on Facebook, Instagram, and other social media with increasing frequency [7]. Facebook has become a "modern day baby book" [22], with the number of parents who post pictures of their children falling in the range of 66% [33] to 98% [4]. Are parents inadvertently compromising their children's privacy?

In this paper, we measure adults' sharing of children's personally identifiable information in online social networks, namely, Facebook and Instagram. This matter deserves attention for two reasons. Firstly, online social networks are public areas – since children are vulnerable, their information should not be publicly visible and archivable. This is a concern recognized by many parents [2]. Secondly, when parents post their children's information on Facebook, Instagram, or another social network, even in a non-public manner, they are effectively supplying the service provider with detailed information about the children. This limits children's ability to hide their online presences should they later wish to do so.

Specifically, we consider to what extent babies and young children – who do not even have their own Facebook accounts – can have their privacy compromised due to their parents' online behavior, and to what extent these privacy violations can be carried out in an automated fashion. We first apply off-the-shelf age detection software to the adults' public Facebook photos to automatically discover photos containing children. We then attempt to identify names and birthdays for the children through automated textual analysis. We find that for a large number of parents, one can learn the names and faces of their children; for many children, one can learn their birthdates.

By linking this information with publicly available data, one can obtain even more vivid profiles of young children. We demonstrate this by analyzing a set of adults for whom we have obtained the corresponding voter registration records. After detecting children on the public profile pages of these adults, we can further determine the addresses of the families, the parents' birthdays and the parents' political affiliations. Such a seed profile could then be continually enhanced throughout the child's life by data brokers, government surveillance agencies, or Facebook itself. We extend this approach to Instagram, and we find that many parents are sharing not only their child's image but his birthday and name as well.

The automated attack described above is restricted to using public Facebook posts. Friends of a parent, Facebook itself, and organizations with access to one's Internet traffic can often see much more. As we cannot access the friends-only content, we cannot directly assess the full extent of what parents share online about their children. In order to gain a more complete picture of parental behavior online, we conduct a survey of parents who use Facebook. We find that the majority of parents report sharing their children's faces and names on Facebook, and many also report posting their children's birthdates.

This paper makes the following contributions:

1. Measure the occurrence of images of children posted by adults on Facebook.

2. Demonstrate how an attacker could infer, in an automated manner, attributes about children based on the posts of adults on Facebook.

3. Further demonstrate how this information can be linked with public records to create more detailed profiles of children.

4. Conduct a survey of parents on Facebook to learn about their posting habits with regard to their children.

5. Examine Instagram to determine how widespread parental oversharing is in this increasingly popular online social network.

6. Recommend better practices to parents and Facebook to protect children's privacy.

The structure of this paper is as follows: in Section 2, we discuss the threats facing children whose parents are active in online social networks as well as the legal and ethical considerations of this project. In Section 3, we present a method to gather a database of children whose likenesses and other information have been posted on Facebook without their participation. In Section 4, we survey parents who use Facebook to learn about their posting behaviors and privacy attitudes with regard to their children. In Section 5, we conduct a similar analysis using the Instagram photo-based social network. In Section 6, we discuss the ramifications of our findings and make some recommendations to parents and Facebook to ensure better privacy for children. Section 7 presents related work. Finally, in Section 8, we conclude.

2. PRELIMINARIES

In this section, we outline the different threats posed to a child whose information is shared on Facebook or Instagram. We also discuss the legal and ethical considerations involved in conducting this research.

2.1 Threats to Children on Online Social Networks

When parents post photos of children to Facebook or Instagram, they likely have only positive intentions: for example, to share updates about their family and life with grandparents, or to chronicle their lives' events [6]. However, the children may bear collateral risk as a result. We describe four threats to a child whose information is posted on Facebook:

- **Stranger danger.** When parents share information publicly about their children, they allow strangers to learn important facts about their children. For example, a public photo of a child with the caption "Happy birthday, Olivia!" provides an observer with knowledge of the child's face, name, and birthday. This could be exploited by criminals or predators local to the child, or by an identity thief who wishes to infer the child's personally identifiable information.

- **Overexposure to acquaintances.** Though media accounts often focus on children's abduction at the hand of strangers, it is far more common that children's kidnappers are from their family's social circles; a 1997 study by the FBI found that 76% of kidnappings and 90% of all violent crimes against juveniles were perpetrated by relatives or acquaintances [14]. As such, sharing personal information about one's child is not necessarily safe even when a parent has friends-only or friends-of-friends settings on their Facebook posts. Additionally, since many adult users of Facebook have 200 or more Facebook friends [31], these posts are less private than they realize. The same applies to a parent who has elected to use the privacy settings on Instagram.

- **Data Brokers.** Data brokers build profiles about people and sell them to advertisers, spammers, malware distributors, employment agencies, and college admission offices. Because the babies' and children's merchandise market is in the hundreds of billion dollars in the US alone, it is not surprising that data brokers are already seeking to compile dossiers on children [32] [30]. Using the information that parents post about their children, data brokers can create mini-profiles that can be continually enhanced throughout an individual's lifetime.

- **Surveillance.** In addition to the threats posed by other users, information posted to online social networks is subject to the threat of surveillance. By sharing a child's likeness and identifying information, a parent exposes his child to surveillance by the service provider and other parties, such as the NSA. This this can be problematic if children later wish to minimize or erase their digital footprints.

To measure the level of these risks, we undertake two methodologies. In the first methodology, we automate the analysis of public Facebook and Instagram pages to search for photos of children and accompanying personal information. This captures two of the four risks enumerated above, by demonstrating what information an unaffiliated viewer (e.g. a stranger or data broker) can glean about a child based on his parent's Facebook page. However, due to the

Facebook privacy settings, it does not provide a full view of the parent's posting behavior. In the second methodology, we conduct a survey of parents to learn about their self-reported habits with regard to their children on Facebook. Since parents are reporting their own behavior, this approach is not subject to the privacy-setting limitations of the first methodology. This allows us to assess what a friend, a surveillant authority, or Facebook itself might be able to infer about the children of the Facebook user.

2.2 Ethical and Legal Considerations

To conduct this research, we programmed crawlers that visited public pages on Facebook and Instagram and downloaded their contents. We then automated content extraction to detect faces, names and other information in the public comments.

Performing real-life research in online privacy can be ethically sensitive. Two stakeholders must be considered: the online service provider and the user. While crawling data from online service providers imposes a load upon their servers, we attempted to minimize the load by using a single process to sequentially download pages.

We emphasize that this research benefits Facebook and Instagram users by bringing to light an important aspect of children's online privacy. Any inferences we made were based on publicly available data. We intentionally limited the number of profiles analyzed in order to minimize the risk to any individual user. For the same reason, we also limited our analysis to a user's most recent posts.

3. AUTOMATED FACEBOOK ANALYSIS

According to Facebook's help pages, users must be at least 13 years old to join the social network[1]. Nevertheless, many children have an indirect social presence on Facebook through the photos and comments posted about them by adults. In this section, we seek to quantify the extent of this phenomenon by crawling the public Facebook posts of adults to see if they have posted photos and information about their children.

3.1 Methodology

Here, we describe the methodology we followed to discover posts about children on Facebook. See Figure 1 for a diagram of the process.

As basis for our exploration, we begin with a list of 2,383 Facebook users in a suburban city on the East Coast in the USA. This city has 20-30,000 households and a median household income in the $70-100,000 range, and its population is about 70% white, 10% African American, and 15% Asian. As we describe below, each one of these users has been matched with high certainty to a particular registered voter in a voter registration list [10]. Therefore, each user on the list is 18 or older.

For each user on the list, we collect the 20 most recent photos posted to the user's account. (This is the number of photos initially shown on a user's Facebook photos page.) We then analyze the photos using Face++[2], an online API which provides an age estimate for the faces detected in the photos. If a face's age estimate is beneath a certain threshold, we flag this photo as containing a child.

[1]https://www.facebook.com/help/210644045634222
[2]http://www.faceplusplus.com/

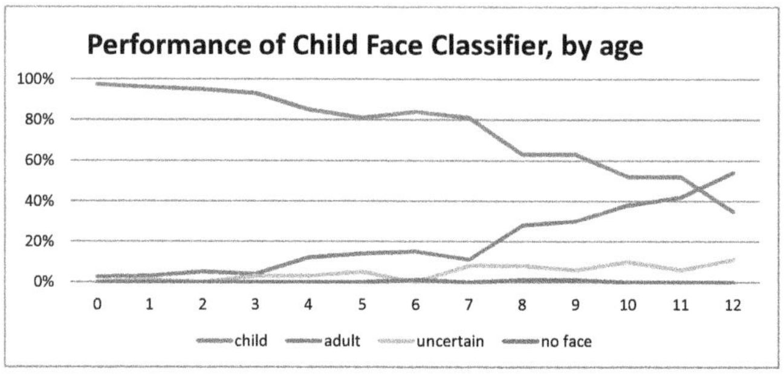

Figure 2: The performance of the Face++ age classification tool at each age, as judged by a human. Among the images that Face++ labeled as including children, some included only adults, people of uncertain ages, or no faces at all. We show the results for each age; the child-detection accuracy dips below 80% for ages eight and older.

Though face recognition and detection has become increasingly accurate, age estimation is still a hard problem; even humans may have a hard time guessing precise ages from a photo. In order to eliminate false positives among our flagged images, we examine only the images that contain a person whose age was estimated as seven or younger. We found through experimentation that this number helped limit false positives (i.e. young-looking teenagers or adults) while still returning most of the actual children in the sample. We established this threshold by labeling 100 random samples from each tagged age bucket and then calculating the proportion of false positives returned by the API. We used four labels: "child", "adult", "uncertain", and "no face pictured" (since some of the photos were incorrectly labeled as containing faces). In order to retain accuracy of at least 80% (without including faces of uncertain age), we opted to use only the photos that had been tagged with an age in the range of zero to seven, since these were less likely to be false positives. Figure 2 displays the results from each age group.

3.2 Results

From the 2,383 Facebook users, we collected 26,602 total photos from the photo pages of the accounts, for an average of 10.5 photos per account. The overall results are displayed in Table 1.

Of these 26,602 photos, Face++ estimated that 2,251 (8.5%) contained a child between zero and seven years old. 575 of these had public comments from which we could deduce a name for the child using the Stanford NER tool[3] [13]. In addition, 60 of the photos included the word "birthday" in the captions or comments and thus revealed the child's date of birth.

In terms of accounts, 807 of the overall 2,383 accounts (34.8%) contained at least one photo of a child. Since children usually share their parent's last name, we are able to infer the last name for all the children in the photos. Of these 807 accounts, 45.2% (365 accounts) had posted or received a comment mentioning the child's first name, and 6.2% (50 accounts) had also revealed the child's date of birth. For 45 of the accounts, all three pieces of identifying information

[3]http://nlp.stanford.edu/software/CRF-NER.shtml

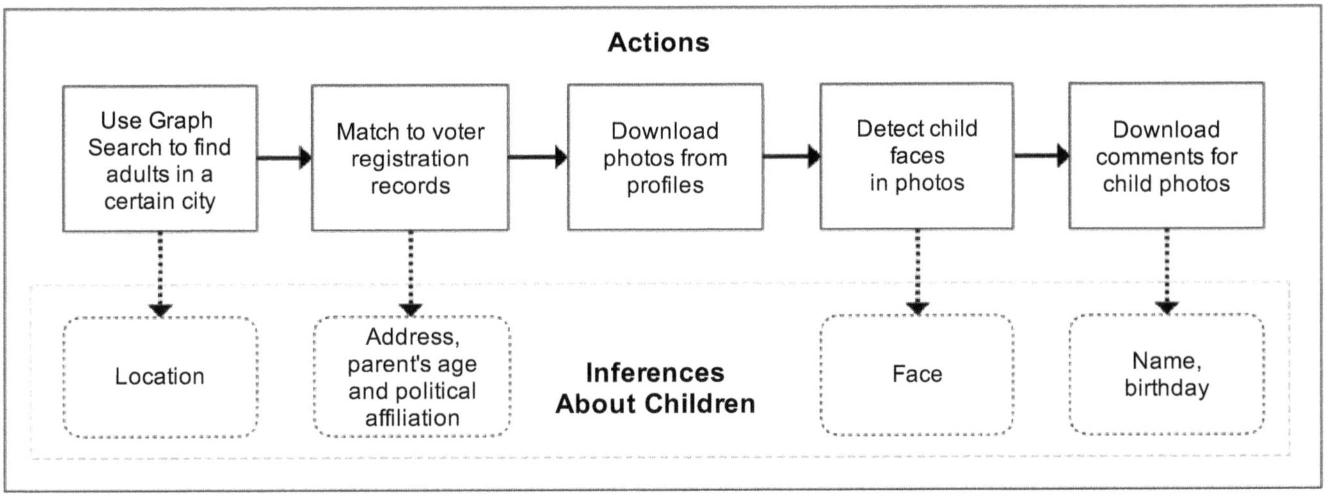

Figure 1: The process for downloading and inferring traits about children whose photos are posted on Facebook.

	Facebook	Instagram
Accounts		
Total collected	2,383	1,089
Sharing child photo	807	1,089
Sharing child name	365	689
Sharing child birthday	50	292
Photos		
Total collected	26,602	21,379
Child in photo	2,251	6,134
Name in comments	575	988
Birthday in comments	60	411

Table 1: The number of accounts and photos for each category examined in both Facebook and Instagram.

regarding a child – photo, name, and date of birth – were available in the parent's public photo albums.

Additionally, by examining the information in the parent's public Facebook pages, we can extend the profiles of the children by profiling their families. Additional information that can potentially be obtained for a child (who does not have a Facebook account) include the names and Facebook pages of both parents, siblings, and grandparents. These can be obtained by accessing the friend list of the parent. Moreover, one can infer the parents' religious and political affiliations, which are often adopted by their children, by the content of their status updates. The attacker can also augment his knowledge of the child by using the profiles of extended family members, if they have posted facts that were not included in the parents' public profiles.

3.3 Linking with Public Records

It is often possible to link Facebook accounts with other sources of offline and online information. For example, as described by Dey et al.[10], one can identify many of the Facebook users in a target town by using a combination of the Facebook graph search API, Facebook friends lists, and the voter registration list for the city. For the target suburban city considered in this paper, this technique was applied to obtain approximately 25,000 Facebook users who reside in the target city. Some of these Facebook users have the same name, and some these users' names match to multiple people in the voter list.

The 2,383 users studied here are a subset of the 25,000 likely-residents, with the following additional properties: (i) each of the 2,383 users has a unique name; (ii) each user recorded on Facebook that his hometown or current city is the target city; (iii) each user has at least five friends in the set of 25,000 likely-residents; and (iv) each user's name is an exact match with one name in the voter registration list of the target city. Owing to these properties, we believe that most (if not all) of the 2,383 Facebook users have been correctly linked to people in the voter registration lists.

Each record in a voter registration list corresponds to a person and contains the person's name, birth date, gender, political affiliation, and *address*. Thus, by linking a parent's Facebook page with his voter registration records, the attacker can further obtain the address of the child, which has clear potential for dangerous outcomes. Moreover, the attacker can obtain the political affiliations and birth dates of the child's parents; this would be informative to a data broker or surveillant authority.

In summary, when a parent posts photos of his or her children to Facebook, and the parent can be matched to a voter registration record, then the attacker can minimally obtain the child's face, last name, address, parents' names, parents' birthdays and parents' political affiliations. Additionally, the attacker may be able to determine the child's first name, birth date, and any additional information made publicly available in the parents' Facebook pages, such as parents' religion or employment. And as mentioned earlier, a Facebook friend of the parent, and Facebook itself, can significantly enhance such a profile with the information the parent shares only with Facebook friends.

3.4 Analysis of Users Posting Child Photos

Among the users who shared a child's photo, each user shared an average of 2.8 child photos within the user's 20 most recent photos.

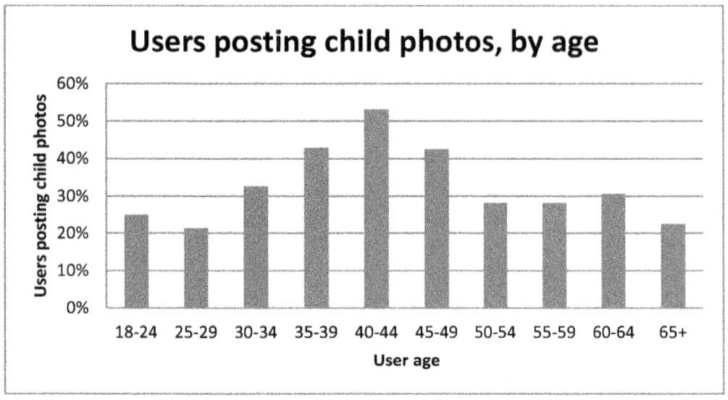

Figure 3: The percentage of users in each age group who shared photos of children on Facebook.

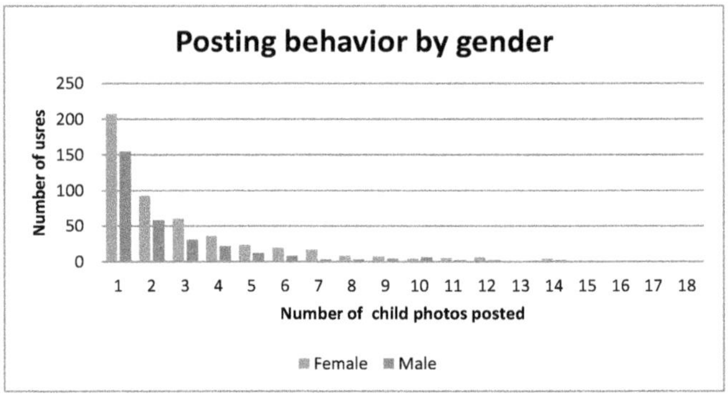

Figure 4: The number of women and men who shared photos of children on Facebook.

Which users account for the majority of the photo sharing? We analyzed several traits in our dataset to find what types of users were sharing photos of children. We note our relevant findings here:

Age.

In Figure 3, we show the percentage of users in each age group who shared child photos, using the set of 2,383 users. As we might expect, photo sharing is highest among users aged 30 to 50, as most parents in this community fall into this age bracket. The median age of the users who shared child photos is 41. Note that a significant fraction of users over 60 are sharing photos of children. We conjecture that the oldest users are sharing photos of their grandchildren.

Gender.

In our dataset of 2,383 users, more women shared child photos than men. 46% of the women in our sample shared a child's photo, as opposed to 23% of men. They also tended to share more photos per user. Among people who had shared child photos, women shared 2.9 photos on average while men shared 2.6. Figure 4 shows the distribution of photo sharing among men and women, respectively.

Politics.

We also examined users' political affiliations, as recorded in their voter registrations. The sample is dominated by political independents and Democrats, since the town profiled leans Democratic. As such, there are relatively few Republicans in the sample. Political affiliation did not make a large difference in whether users shared at least one photo of a child. In our sample, 34% of Democrats, 30% of Republicans, and 33% of independents had shared at least one photo of a child.

3.5 Examples of Oversharing Parents

We found several cogent examples of oversharing parents in our sample. In this section, we showcase some anecdotes to demonstrate more clearly the power that parents wield over their children's privacy. For their protection, we redact any identifying details and merely elaborate the categories known, using false names.

"Laura", age 7: full name and birthdate known. Her family consists of her mother (name and birthdate known), father (name and birthdate known), and an older sister. Her mother works in fashion retailing, and the family's street address is known. Her father is a registered Republican, and her mother is a political independent.

"Jerry", age 0: full name and birthdate known. His family consists of his father (name and birthdate known), mother (name known), and an older sister (name and birthdate known). The father's past and current occupations are known, and he is a football fan and political independent.

"Rebecca", age 2: full name and birthdate known. Her family consists of her father (name and birthdate known), mother (name and birthdate known), two older sisters, and an older brother. Her father is a lawyer and a Republican, and her mother is a political independent.

The data gleaned from a parent's Facebook profile can be rather personal; when conjoined with offline data sources, the information one learns about a child can be highly sensitive. Our work makes clear that this information could be valuable to data brokers, surveillant authorities, or unsavory adults. Parents may unwittingly do their children a disservice when they share too much information.

3.6 Limitations

The automated approach described in this paper for determining the presence of children on a Facebook page is easily scaled. However, it suffers from one major drawback: it can only detect publicly available posts. As a result, it fails to accurately model the threat of malicious acquaintances (who may be able to view friends-only posts) or of surveillant authorities (who can view a user's full posts, either through network traffic analysis, server backdoors, or data requests). To better explore these risks, we conduct a survey in Section 4 where parents report their overall Facebook usage with regard to their children's information.

Additionally, this approach assumes that adults only post photos of their own children on Facebook. In reality, though, adults may post photos of their nieces and nephews, students, friends or even child celebrities. This could be remedied by some heuristics; for example, by using a measure similar to TF-IDF for each face's unique ID, we may more safely determine if the child is a famous person or a family member specific to the account owner. However, we were unable to implement this or other similar heuristics due to lack of groundtruth data.

A similar point can be made regarding name detection. A conversation in the comments of a photo may mention names other than that of the child. We did not filter for this effect in our experiment due to a lack of groundtruth data. However, an attacker with greater resources and access to more data, such as the social network provider or the NSA, would be able to employ more sophisticated unsupervised learning techniques to guess the correct name with higher accuracy.

Finally, we emphasize that this approach provides only a lower bound on how many parents may be exposing their children's personal information online. As we analyzed only the most recent public posts, it is likely that many more parents are actually sharing child-related information than those we detected. Our intention in the experiment was not to actually expose the children, but rather to prove that it could be accomplished. Notwithstanding the limitations of our approach, our research brings to light a new aspect of children's privacy which has not yet been measured at a large scale in the literature. By demonstrating the information that an attacker (or service provider) can gain about a child through adults' online activities, we hope to bring attention to the impact that a parent has on his child's online privacy.

4. SURVEY OF PARENTS ON FACEBOOK

In order to gain deeper insight into parents' sharing behaviors on Facebook, we conducted an online survey of parents who use Facebook. We used Amazon Mechanical Turk, a crowdsourcing platform, to recruit subjects and directed them to a survey hosted on the Qualtrics platform. We restricted our survey to respondents in the United States. Through a series of demographic questions, we narrowed down our respondent pool to Facebook users who are parents of at least one child under age 13 (the age at which Facebook allows teenagers to create their own accounts).

In order to ensure accurate reporting, we included attention-measuring questions wherein the respondent was directed to select a specific response. Respondents who did not follow the directions were assumed to be inattentive and were excluded from the final analysis.

Since this survey uses self-reported data, it provides a more comprehensive picture of parents' posting behaviors on Facebook. Unlike the scraping approach, it is not limited to public posts; rather, parents reported their overall Facebook usage patterns.

Demographics and Family Makeup.

After filtering for attentiveness, we received 357 responses. 48% of the respondents were male, and 52% were female. A majority (52%) of respondents reported that they had one child; 31% reported 2 children; and 17% of respondents reported 3 or more children.

Behavior on Facebook.

Respondents were directed to check their setting for posts to Facebook. 13% of the users had their posts set to public, and another 77% had chosen friends. See Figure 5 for a full breakdown of the choices.

Though choosing "friends" may appear to preserve a large amount of privacy by limiting one's audience, the parents

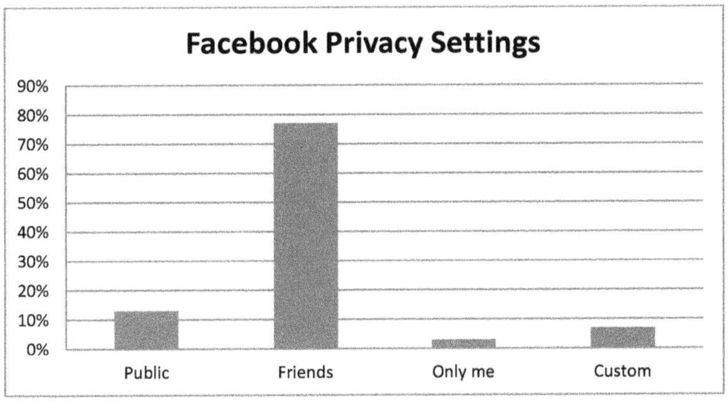

Figure 5: The self-reported Facebook privacy settings chosen by parents of children younger than 13.

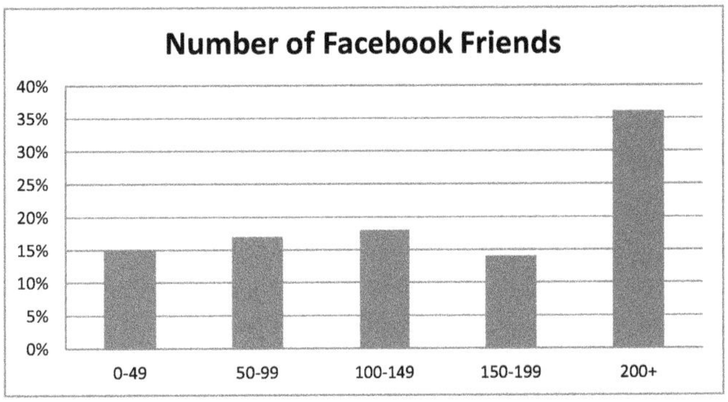

Figure 6: The self-reported Facebook friend count for parents of children younger than 13.

in our survey reported high numbers of friends consistent with findings of other research [31]. The plurality of parents (36%) reported having 200 or more friends, with fully half of respondents reporting a number of friends in the range of 150 and higher. (See Figure 6 for details.) This indicates that even parents who are posting on a friends-only basis are still sharing their photos and comments with large numbers of people.

How much information do parents on Facebook report sharing about their kids? 82% of respondents said they had posted a picture of their child at least once. 77% of the parents said they had mentioned their child's name in a post on Facebook, and 54% of parents said they had mentioned their child's birthday or date of birth. A summary of their responses can be seen in Figure 7.

36 parents - 10% overall - admitted to posting all three of these pieces of information: a photo, name, and birthday. These pieces of personally identifiable information combine to create strong identifiers for their children. (Notably, some parents might not realize that a "Happy birthday" post reveals their child's birthday. Therefore, this number may be underreported.)

Privacy Attitudes.

We included questions in our survey to deduce whether parents were concerned about their children's privacy. We found that parents trended towards moderate regard for privacy, both for themselves and for their children. On a Likert

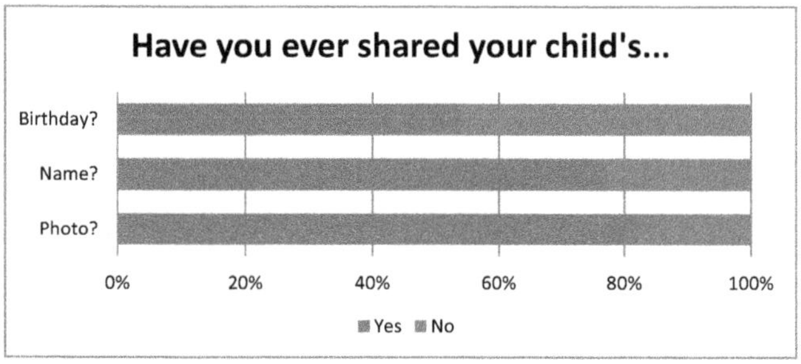

Figure 7: The responses of parents who were asked about their Facebook sharing behaviors.

scale from 1 to 5, parents rated their personal privacy concerns as 3.75, and their privacy concerns for their children as 3.8. Contrary to our expectations, parents were not significantly more concerned for their children's privacy than for their own, as shown by a paired t-test of the scores.

We also asked parents if they believed that they had posted something about their children which could be embarrassing. 11% of parents answered yes, 35% answered no, and 54% were unsure.

Discussion of Findings.

Recall from Section 3 that 35% of the 2,383 Facebook users in our sample publicly shared at least one photo of a child. In particular, among the users in the parenting age group of 30 to 49, 43% shared a photo of a child on their public pages. Although these percentages are substantial, we find that when we ask users to self-report their overall Facebook behavior (not only their public postings), the sharing rates becomes even higher. 82% of the survey respondents said that they share photos of their children. The respondents also indicate significantly more sharing of their children's names and date of birth than what we observed from the public pages of the 2,383 adults. We can therefore conclude that although a substantial percentage of parents are compromising the privacy of their children in their public Facebook pages, significantly more are doing so among Facebook friends. As we note in Section 1, these friends-only photos can still pose a privacy threat to their children.

5. AUTOMATED INSTAGRAM ANALYSIS

As the fastest-growing social site [26], Instagram is rapidly becoming the go-to service for sharing images and photos. As of November 2014, Instagram has more than 200 million active users, and an average of 60 million pictures are uploaded daily [1].

Unlike Facebook, Instagram profiles and posts are fully public by default, and other users can follow the account without approval. Instagram follows a broadcast model (similar to Twitter) unless users specifically change their settings. Instagram's terms of service also state that users must be at least 13 years old[4].

In this section, we describe our analysis of more than 1,000 Instagram accounts. We examine Instagram users who are likely to be parents to find photos and information about their children and predict what an outside viewer may be able to infer about the children.

[4]`http://instagram.com/about/legal/terms/`

5.1 Methods

To find Instagram accounts that were likely to be parents, we used the Instagram API to search for parenting-related hashtags, such as **#mybigboy**, **#mybiggirl**, **#growingtoofast**, **#stopgrowing**, **#sleepingbaby**, **#mylittleprince**, **#mylittleprincess**, **#toddlerbirthday**, and **#firstbirthday**.

This returned a list of photos corresponding to the keywords, along with their associated accounts. A manual analysis of the accounts revealed that not all were relevant; to account for this, we excluded accounts that were associated with less than two of the parenting keywords. We assume that accounts using two or more parenting-related keywords are likely to belong to parents.

After filtering, we downloaded the most recent posts for each of the remaining 1,089 accounts. We then queried the Face++ API for estimates of the ages of the photo subjects. Again, we consider all photos with an estimated age of seven or younger to belong to children. We then proceeded to infer personally identifiable information from the associated comments. If posts contained the words "birthday" or "born," they revealed the child's date of birth. We once again used the Stanford NER tool to extract proper names from the comments after employing some simple sanitation techniques to the text.

5.2 Results

Overall, we considered 1,089 Instagram accounts. We downloaded a total of 21,379 photos, approximately 20 photos per account (as the Instagram API returns the 20 most recent photos by default). The overall results can be viewed in Table 1.

Of the 21,379 photos, 6,134 (28%) were labeled as containing the face of a child. 6,070 (99%) of the child photos included comments or tags. In 988 of these photos, we were able to detect a proper name. Thus, we inferred a name for 16% of the child photos analyzed.

Among the child photos, 317 (5%) mentioned a birthday in the comments. Another 94 photos (2%) mentioned the word "born", which can be used to infer a date of birth. As such, we were able to infer a date of birth for 7% of the child photos.

With respect to accounts, all of the accounts had at least one photo with a child. This indicates that our filtering method (described above in Section 5.1) to locate parents was very accurate. Of the 1082 accounts, 689 (63%) mentioned a child's name in at least one photo. 292 accounts (27% overall) referenced a birth date. 19% of the accounts overall (or 209 individual accounts) referenced both a child's name and date of birth.

Since we do not have auxiliary information about Instagram users, we present a more basic analysis of users' posting behaviors. Among users who posted child photos, the average number of child posts detected in their 20 most recent posts was 5.6, and the median was 5. A distribution of how many photos each user posted can be seen in Figure 8.

5.3 Limitations

Like the Facebook profiling attack, this approach scales quite easily. However, in the process it also suffers from some uncertainty; for example, we cannot verify that the names detected in comments actually belong to the child pictured. Nonetheless, as we state in Section 3.6, a more

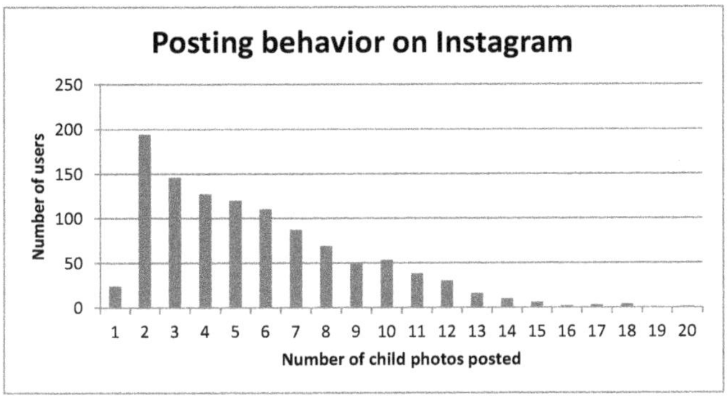

Figure 8: A histogram of the number of child photos shared by users on Instagram.

determined and informed attacker could employ measures to estimate the probability of a specific name belonging to the child. As such, the amount of data shared on Instagram profiles is a matter of concern.

5.4 Comparison of Facebook and Instagram

We find significant variance between the results for inferring children's information on Facebook and Instagram. On Instagram, posts are fully public by default, and the search function for hashtags facilitates finding accounts which belong to parents. Due to these features, it is easier to directly discover children and their data.

Among Facebook users who publicly post a child's photo, less than 50% share the child's name and less than 10% share the child's date of birth. But as shown in Table 1, these numbers are significantly higher for Instagram, with 63% and 27% of the users sharing a child's name and birthday, respectively. We believe that this is largely due to Facebook's more private default sharing settings, whereas Instagram sharing is fully public by default. Indeed, given the Instagram results and the survey results in Section 4, it appears that parents are quite casual about sharing their children's photos, names, and dates of birth in both Facebook and Instagram. However, owing to the difference in the default privacy settings, the information is more accessible to the public when posted on Instagram.

On the other hand, since Facebook encourages users to post many personal attributes on their profiles, more datapoints can be inferred from a Facebook profile. Additionally, the use of Facebook's Graph Search allows an attacker to target a specific geographical area, which in turn enables the profile to be matched more easily to offline data sources such as voter records. Finally, with Instagram, it is not always as easy to infer the last name of a child, as Instagram users often register with pseudonyms.

6. DISCUSSION

In this section, we discuss takeaways from our findings. We also recommend more private behaviors to parents who use these online social tools. Finally, we suggest a Facebook design modification to better protect the privacy of children who are posted on the social network.

6.1 Giving Kids a Chance at Privacy

For children nowadays, navigating the boundaries between public and private is tougher than ever before. While some scholars claim that as "digital natives", adolescents have shed any concern for privacy, teens and children still do care about privacy, as shown by Boyd [5]. Rather, their non-private behaviors are often symptoms of immaturity or ignorance of the specific technologies that can help maintain their desired levels of privacy.

However, we are seeing a move towards more private behavior online, even among children. Applications such as Snapchat, which circumvent the permanence of most digital communications, are very popular among adolescents and teens, since they allow users to share intimate moments without the drama or long-term consequences of persistent messaging applications [5]. Moreover, privacy tools are beginning to become more usable; in particular, Facebook's Privacy Checkup tool urges users to review and update their privacy settings [15].

Currently, adult users of Facebook and Instagram have provided their data by choice, presumably having decided that any potential loss of privacy is worth the utility of a convenient and well-populated social tool. However, the children of these adults have provided no such consent. When a parent shares a child's information online, the child is exposed to non-negligible privacy risk without receiving the attendant benefits of social networking. This is problematic inherently, and it also can reduce a child's privacy agency later in life when the main online service providers are already aware of his presence, personal information, and familial ties.

6.2 Recommendations to Parents

We make the following recommendations to parents who want to preserve their children's online privacy while continuing to use online social networks:

- **Check your Facebook privacy settings.** By using more private settings, parents can limit the audience of potential viewers. Though the service provider (namely, Facebook and any ancillary applications) will still host the data, this can protect children from stranger danger or unsavory acquaintances.
- **Make your Instagram account private.** When a user makes his Instagram private, other users must be approved before viewing the photos on the account. This whitelisting method would allow a parent to share photos with grandparents and other relatives while protecting his child from stranger danger, though again it would not hide the data from the service provider.
- **Think before you share.** A parent can serve as an advocate for his child's privacy by imagining himself in her shoes. How would the parent feel if someone else had shared embarrassing incidents or personal information from his youth in a permanent and semi-public forum?
- **Avoid sharing personally identifiable information whenever possible.** To reduce the likelihood of an adversary learning the child's full identity, we recommend that parents avoid sharing personal information about their children whenever possible. For example, parents should not post children's cell numbers, full names, or birthdates.
- **Encrypt uploaded photos.** Tools such as Cryptagram [34] help users to encrypt any photos uploaded

Figure 9: A mockup interface that Facebook could implement to nudge users towards more private sharing with regard to children's photos.

to Facebook. The photo's owner can then share the key with any user he chooses, allowing them to view it. This hides the photo from unwanted viewers and from surveillant authorities. However, like many applications using cryptography, we recognize that this may not be the most intuitive tool for the average user since it also requires that their friends and family adopt its usage.

Realistically, using any free online service will entail some trade-offs. However, it is important that parents consider the risks before engaging in online sharing about their children.

6.3 Recommendations to Facebook

How can Facebook better protect the privacy of the children who are posted on Facebook by parents or other adults? Similar to the work of Wang et al. [35], we suggest a privacy-preserving mechanism that nudges users to consider more private sharing behaviors with regard to children. If a child's face is detected in a photo, a message can be displayed to encourage the user to select more private settings for the post; see Figure 9 for a graphical example.

Alternatively, Facebook could implement a policy to automatically restrict photos containing children to a more private sharing setting. This would be similar to a past policy regarding teens, whose posts could only be shown to friends-only audiences [21].

7. RELATED WORK

Families and Facebook.

As human interactions move increasingly to the digital realm, research has explored how this affects family dynamics. Burke et al. [6] examine family conversations to find that family member's roles extend into their Facebook conversations; for example, parents of adult children are likely to ask them to call or inquire how the grandchildren are faring. Morris [28] found that new mothers exhibit specific behavioral patterns on Facebook and discusses how these findings can be leveraged to better support women at this critical transition. Kumar and Schoenebeck [22] interviewed 22 mothers of young children and found that mothers often encountered social pressure to share photos of their children. Jomhari et al. [20] described the interactions of mothers in online blogs and social networks as using the new media to tell stories about their children. In a 2012 survey, Bartholomew et al. [4] found that 95% of new mothers and 89% of new fathers had shared images of their babies online.

The medical community has also conducted research on how social media usage can affect children. O'Keeffe et al. [29] point to benefits of social media, such as socialization and enhanced learning opportunities, but they also indicate several risks that apprehend youths on social media. For example, youths may experience cyberbullying, privacy risks, advertising influences, and "Facebook depression," a phenomenon where teens and preteens develop symptoms of depression after excessive social media usage.

Third-party risks to privacy.

Considerable research has demonstrated that a person's privacy can be weakened by the actions of others. In a famous paper, Jernigan and Mistree [19] found that people's sexual orientation could be accurately predicted by the sexual orientation of their friends on Facebook. Similar results were found for age [11], gender [37], and political associations [23], where users' private traits could be predicted by their friends' information.

Children's online privacy.

As access to Internet-connected devices grows, there has been a growing conversation about keeping children safe online. This was formalized with the passage of COPPA, the Children's Online Privacy Protection Act, in the USA. COPPA limits the amount of information that websites may collect about users under age 13 [36]. However, Hargittai et al. [16] found that in many cases, this motivated children to lie about their age with parental consent in order to gain access to more services or features. Dey et al. [9] showed that by lying about their ages, children inadvertently reduced the privacy of their friends who had honestly entered their age. Additionally, Livingstone and Helsper [25] found the surprising result that parental attempts to monitor and limit children's online behavior were not associated with a reduction in overall online risk to the children.

Cranor et al. [8] examined parents' attitudes about their teens' online privacy and found that overall, parents did not take their teens' claims to privacy as seriously as the teens did. However, both Ahern et al. [2] and Kumar and Schoenbeck [22] found that parents practiced some self-censorship, choosing not to share naked or negative photos of their children on Facebook.

Instagram.

As Instagram becomes ever more popular, the research community has started to examine it more closely. Ferrara et al. [12] analyzed its community structure and popular topics, and Manikonda et al. [27] explored user locations and activities. Hu et al. [18] manually coded the content of 50 user profiles to determine what types of content are posted by users. Bakshi et al. [3] found that photos with faces accrued more likes on Instagram. Another work, by Hosseinmardi et al. [17], looked at cyber-bullying on Instagram. While Litt and Hargittai studied users' privacy preferences with regard to online photo sharing [24], we are aware of no work exploring the technical aspects of privacy on Instagram or the role of children whose photos are posted on Instagram.

Our Contribution.

Past research about children's privacy has focused on two main threats: children's carelessness, or malicious third parties. In this paper, we show that even well-meaning parents can unwittingly compromise their child's privacy by sharing seemingly innocuous updates on Facebook and Instagram. We measure this though two large-scale crawl-based experiment as well as a survey of Facebook users with children under age 13 and determine that the practice of parental oversharing on Facebook can have serious implications.

8. CONCLUSION

What role do parents play in their children's online privacy? In this paper, we show that parents and other adults can inadvertently compromise the privacy of children by oversharing on online social networks. We describe four threats and implement two experiments to quantify the extent of parental oversharing. Firstly, we run an automated analysis of public Facebook pages to discover evidence of children in adults' photo albums and comments. We show how, when correlated to offline data sources, the photos of children on Facebook can trigger a chain reaction of privacy violations. We also conduct a survey to examine parent's self-reported behaviors and attitudes about their children's data on Facebook. We find that many adults are sharing personally identifiable information regarding their children on Facebook, thus weakening their children's privacy with regard to strangers, acquaintances, and surveillant authorities. We then extend the automated analysis to Instagram. Finally, we propose better practices for parents and suggest that Facebook change its interface to encourage better privacy stewardship on the part of parents.

Acknowledgements

This work was supported in part by the NSF (under grants CNS-1318659 and DGE-0966187). The views and conclusions contained in this document are those of the authors and should not be interpreted as necessarily representing the official policies, either expressed or implied, of any of the sponsors.

9. REFERENCES

[1] Instagram press. *http://instagram.com/press/.*

[2] S. Ahern, D. Eckles, N. S. Good, S. King, M. Naaman, and R. Nair. Over-exposed?: privacy patterns and considerations in online and mobile photo sharing. In *Proceedings of the SIGCHI conference on Human factors in computing systems*, pages 357–366. ACM, 2007.

[3] S. Bakhshi, D. A. Shamma, and E. Gilbert. Faces engage us: photos with faces attract more likes and comments on instagram. In *Proceedings of the 32nd annual ACM conference on Human factors in computing systems*, pages 965–974. ACM, 2014.

[4] M. K. Bartholomew, S. J. Schoppe-Sullivan, M. Glassman, C. M. Kamp Dush, and J. M. Sullivan. New parents' facebook use at the transition to parenthood. *Family relations*, 61(3):455–469, 2012.

[5] D. Boyd. *It's Complicated: the social lives of networked teens.* Yale University Press, 2014.

[6] M. Burke, L. A. Adamic, and K. Marciniak. Families on facebook. In *ICWSM*, 2013.

[7] A. Considine. Making facebook less infantile. *New York Times*, August 9 2012.

[8] L. F. Cranor, A. L. Durity, A. Marsh, and B. Ur. Parents' and teens' perspectives on privacy in a technology-filled world. In *Symposium on Usable Privacy and Security (SOUPS)*, 2014.

[9] R. Dey, Y. Ding, and K. W. Ross. Profiling high-school students with facebook: how online privacy laws can actually increase minors' risk. In *Proceedings of the 2013 conference on Internet measurement conference*, pages 405–416. ACM, 2013.

[10] R. Dey, Y. Ding, and K. W. Ross. Profiling city residents using publicly available information. Technical report, New York University, Computer Science and Engineering, October 2014.

[11] R. Dey, C. Tang, K. Ross, and N. Saxena. Estimating age privacy leakage in online social networks. In *INFOCOM, 2012 Proceedings IEEE*, pages 2836–2840. IEEE, 2012.

[12] E. Ferrara, R. Interdonato, and A. Tagarelli. Online popularity and topical interests through the lens of instagram. In *Proceedings of the 25th ACM conference on Hypertext and social media*, pages 24–34. ACM, 2014.

[13] J. R. Finkel, T. Grenager, and C. Manning. Incorporating non-local information into information extraction systems by gibbs sampling. In *Proceedings of the 43rd Annual Meeting on Association for Computational Linguistics*, pages 363–370. Association for Computational Linguistics, 2005.

[14] D. Finkelhor and R. Ormrod. *Kidnaping of Juveniles: Patterns from NIBRS.* US Department of Justice, Office of Justice Programs, Office of Juvenile Justice and Delinquency Prevention, 2000.

[15] J. Guyn. Facebook rolling out privacy checkup for users. *USA Today*, September 4 2014.

[16] E. Hargittai, J. Schultz, J. Palfrey, et al. Why parents help their children lie to facebook about age: Unintended consequences of the 'children's online privacy protection act'. *First Monday*, 16(11), 2011.

[17] H. Hosseinmardi, S. Li, Z. Yang, Q. Lv, R. I. Rafiq, R. Han, and S. Mishra. A comparison of common users across instagram and ask.fm to better understand cyberbullying. *ArXiv Preprints*, 2014.

[18] Y. Hu, L. Manikonda, and S. Kambhampati. What we instagram: A first analysis of instagram photo content and user types. In *Proceedings of ICWSM.* AAAI, 2014.

[19] C. Jernigan and B. F. Mistree. Gaydar: Facebook friendships expose sexual orientation. *First Monday*, 14(10), 2009.

[20] N. Jomhari, V. M. Gonzalez, and S. H. Kurniawan. See the apple of my eye: baby storytelling in social space. In *Proceedings of the 23rd British HCI Group Annual Conference on People and Computers: Celebrating People and Technology*, pages 238–243. British Computer Society, 2009.

[21] H. Kelly. Facebook changes privacy settings for teens. *CNN*, October 31, 2013.

[22] P. Kumar and S. Schoenebeck. The modern day baby book: Enacting good mothering and stewarding privacy on facebook. In *Computer Supported Cooperative Work and Social Computing (CSCW '15)*. ACM, 2015.

[23] J. Lindamood, R. Heatherly, M. Kantarcioglu, and B. Thuraisingham. Inferring private information using social network data. In *Proceedings of the 18th international conference on World wide web*, pages 1145–1146. ACM, 2009.

[24] E. Litt and E. Hargittai. Smile, snap, and share? a nuanced approach to privacy and online photo-sharing. *Poetics*, 42:1–21, 2014.

[25] S. Livingstone and E. J. Helsper. Parental mediation of children's internet use. *Journal of broadcasting & electronic media*, 52(4):581–599, 2008.

[26] I. Lunden. Instagram is the fastest-growing social site globally, mobile devices rule over pcs for access. *TechCrunch*, January 21, 2014.

[27] L. Manikonda, Y. Hu, and S. Kambhampati. Analyzing user activities, demographics, social network structure and user-generated content on instagram. *ArXiv Preprints*, 2014.

[28] M. R. Morris. Social networking site use by mothers of young children. In *Proceedings of the 17th ACM conference on Computer supported cooperative work & social computing*, pages 1272–1282. ACM, 2014.

[29] G. S. O'Keeffe, K. Clarke-Pearson, et al. The impact of social media on children, adolescents, and families. *Pediatrics*, 127(4):800–804, 2011.

[30] N. Singer. Senator opens investigation of data brokers. *New York Times*, October 10, 2012.

[31] A. Smith. 6 new facts about facebook. *Pew Research Center*, February 3, 2014.

[32] S. Stecklow. On the web, children face intensive tracking. *Wall Street Journal*, September 17, 2010.

[33] A. Sultan and J. Miller. Facebook parenting is destroying our children's privacy. *CNN*, May 25 2012.

[34] M. Tierney, I. Spiro, C. Bregler, and L. Subramanian. Cryptagram: photo privacy for online social media. In *Proceedings of the first ACM conference on Online social networks*, pages 75–88. ACM, 2013.

[35] Y. Wang, P. G. Leon, K. Scott, X. Chen, A. Acquisti, and L. F. Cranor. Privacy nudges for social media: an exploratory facebook study. In *Privacy and Security in Online Social Media (PSOSM)*. ACM, 2013.

[36] J. Warmund. Can coppa work-an analysis of the parental consent measures in the children's online privacy protection act. *Fordham Intell. Prop. Media & Ent. LJ*, 11:189, 2000.

[37] E. Zheleva and L. Getoor. To join or not to join: the illusion of privacy in social networks with mixed public and private user profiles. In *Proceedings of the 18th international conference on World wide web*, pages 531–540. ACM, 2009.

TrueView: Harnessing the Power of Multiple Review Sites

Amanda J. Minnich
aminnich@cs.unm.edu

Nikan Chavoshi
chavoshi@cs.unm.edu

Abdullah Mueen
mueen@cs.unm.edu

Shuang Luan
sluan@cs.unm.edu

Michalis Faloutsos
michalis@cs.unm.edu

ABSTRACT

Online reviews on products and services can be very useful for customers, but they need to be protected from manipulation. So far, most studies have focused on analyzing online reviews from a single hosting site. How could one leverage information from multiple review hosting sites? This is the key question in our work. In response, we develop a systematic methodology to merge, compare, and evaluate reviews from multiple hosting sites. We focus on hotel reviews and use more than 15 million reviews from more than 3.5 million users spanning three prominent travel sites. Our work consists of three thrusts: (a) we develop novel features capable of identifying cross-site discrepancies effectively, (b) we conduct arguably the first extensive study of cross-site variations using real data, and develop a hotel identity-matching method with 93% accuracy, (c) we introduce the **TrueView score**, as a proof of concept that cross-site analysis can better inform the end user. Our results show that: (1) we detect 7 times more suspicious hotels by using multiple sites compared to using the three sites in isolation, and (2) we find that 20% of all hotels appearing in all three sites seem to have low trustworthiness score.

Our work is an early effort that explores the advantages and the challenges in using multiple reviewing sites towards more informed decision making.

Categories and Subject Descriptors:: H.3.3 [**Information Search & Retrieval**]: Relevance feedback; Selection process; Search process; Information filtering.
Keywords: Opinion Spam; Multi-Site Features; Review Mining; Anomaly Detection; Hotels; Trust

1. INTRODUCTION

How do you use online reviews before booking a hotel, especially if the hotel appears on multiple review sites? This is the overarching question that motivates this work. On the one hand, online reviews provide an unprecedented mechanism for customers to inform potential customers. On the other hand, reviews can suffer from: (a) relevance, as the needs and expectations of customers varies, and (b) fraudulent behavior, from "biased" users or the product providers themselves. As a result, it is not easy for customers to interpret and use such reviews. One often relies either on the overall rating or laboriously goes through many reviews to identify relevance and trustworthiness.

How can we leverage reviews from multiple review sites to make more informed decisions and detect fraud? The use of multiple review sites is the key differentiating factor for our work. Currently, the existence of multiple review sites can add to the confusion of the user. Each of these sites may give a different view of a hotel, and it can be difficult for the consumer to know whom to trust. We focus on reviews of hotels for reasons we discuss below, and we frame the problem as follows: We are given several review sites that review a set of partially overlapping hotels. The reviews typically include a score, user comments, time of review and possibly a user-id. The required output is a trustworthiness score for the reviews of a hotel that take into consideration the reviews from each site. We use the term **suspicious hotel** to refer to hotels whose reviews seem to have been manipulated, e.g. padded with fake reviews. Note that we only focus on trustworthiness and not the relevance of reviews for a particular user, e.g. whether a hotel is a pet-friendly, which is an important but distinct problem.

We focus on hotel reviews for a combination of reasons. First, the hospitality industry exhibits relative stability and consistency. Proximity to the beach does not change, unlike product properties which quickly lose their attractiveness, let alone that the products themselves may be replaced altogether by newer models. Second, hotel properties provide some structure and ubiquitousness. Hotels are consistently evaluated on a relatively limited number of factors (cleanliness, service, location, noise, comfort) as opposed to say electronic goods which can vary significantly depending on the interests and intent of the user (e.g. think digital cameras, or TVs). Our work could easily be expanded to reviews of other "well-defined and persistent" services, such as restaurants. Thus, our overall framework and fundamental functions are a great starting point for expanding our work to other commercial sectors, even if some sector-specific adjustments are required. Specifically, we intend to expand our work to restaurants in the near future.

Most previous work so far has focused on analyzing a single review site, and typically, focus on temporal [7], textual [13], behavioral [16], distributional [8] and graphical features

WWW 2015, May 18–22, 2015, Florence, Italy.
ACM 978-1-4503-3469-3/15/05.
http://dx.doi.org/10.1145/2736277.2741655.

[5] to detect fraudulent reviews. In section 7, we discuss the existing work in more detail.

As our key contribution, we develop a systematic methodology to analyze, compare, and synthesize reviews from multiple review sites. The key novelty of our work lies in its focus on multiple review sites. Another key contribution is a systematic method to match hotel identities across different sites. First, we introduce and evaluate features that capture cross-site discrepancies effectively. Second, we conduct arguably the first extensive study of cross-site discrepancies using real data. Third, we provide the **TrueView score**, a non-trivial synthesis of multi-site reviews, that assesses the trustworthiness of a group of reviews. We provide TrueView as a proof of concept that a cross-site analysis can significantly improve the information that the user sees. In our study, we use more than 15M reviews from more than 3.5M users spanning three prominent travel sites, Tripadvisor, Hotels.com, Booking.com spanning five years for each site.

We highlight our contributions and key results below.

a. A systematic approach to cross-site review evaluation using behavioral features. We propose a comprehensive methodology for comparing and synthesizing reviews from different sites. We use 142 features that go beyond simple rating analysis to consider a set of behavioral and contextual features including review-centric, reviewer-centric, and hotel-centric features. Our features capture temporal, spatial, behavioral, and graph-based characteristics, which provides a multi-faceted view of the reviewing process of a hotel. A key feature of the work is that we evaluate the trustworthiness of the overall review in one site using **cross-site features** leveraging information from the other sites. We find that using cross-site features nearly double the number of suspicious hotels that we find in our experiments.

b. An extensive study of cross-site review differences. We apply our approach to our 15M reviews spanning three sites. As a necessary step, we develop an automated method to match hotel identities on different sites, which is a non-trivial problem. Our study provides several interesting observations:

1. Our identity-matching method matches hotels with 93% accuracy which we validate manually. This method could be of independent interest even outside the scope of this work.

2. There are big differences in the overall score of a hotel across different sites. We find that 10.4% of common hotels from Booking.com and TripAdvisor.com, 9.3% from Hotels.com and TripAdvisor.com, exhibit significantly different rating characteristics, which is usually a sign of suspicious behavior.

3. Using multiple sites can help us detect 7 times more suspicious hotels than the union of suspicious hotels found for each site in isolation.

c. Developing a cross-site scoring system: TrueView. We develop the TrueView score as a proof of concept that leveraging multiple sites can be very informative and change our assessment of the hotels significantly. TrueView is a sophisticated: (a) temporal, contextual, and behavioral features from each site, and (b) cross-site features across the sites. By applying TrueView, we find that 20% of all hotels appearing in all three sites seem to have low trustworthiness score (TrueView score less than 0.75). Although there may be better ways to combine cross-site reviews, we argue that TrueView already demonstrates the potential of such an approach.

Our work in perspective. Our work is arguably the first effort that focuses on the synthesis of reviews from different sites. Our goal is to raise the awareness of the opportunity and the challenges related to this problem. At the same time, our approach provides a foundation for follow up studies in the following directions: (a) detection of fraudulent behaviors, (b) assessing the trustworthiness of review sites, since some may have policies that enable misbehavior, and (c) creating effective review aggregation solutions. Ultimately, the collective wisdom of the users is valuable and empowering, and we would like to protect this from fraudulent behaviors.

2. LOCATION DISAMBIGUATION

We crawled TripAdvisor.com, Hotels.com, and Booking.com. We collected all the reviews for some hotels in these sites. For each review, we collected its text, reviewer-name, date-time and rating. For each hotel, we collected its address. A summary of the whole dataset is given in Table 1.

The three websites have a lot of hotels in common and thus, provide rich information about those hotels together. We focus on location disambiguation problem across these three websites.

2.1 Challenges

The most important challenge in location disambiguation is that hotel names are not unique. Therefore, a full name and address is needed to uniquely identify a hotel. Unfortunately, addresses are also not standard across websites, and the differences between sites are seemingly random. Differences can be as simple as *Street* versus *St.* versus *St* or as complex as *Hotel Atlântico Búzios Convention & Resort - Estrada da Usina, s/n, Humaita, Búzios, CEP 28950-000* and *Hotel Atlantico Buzios Convention and Resort, strada da Usina 294Morro do Humait, Buzios, RJ, 28950-000, Brazil.* For international addresses, words can be in different orders, names can be formatted differently, country names can be excluded, and numbers can be morphed. Addresses can even use waypoints as reference, such as *1000 Yang Gao Road N Pudong Near Pilot Free Trade Zone Gate 3*, which are not standard across websites. Even US addresses, which one might assume follow a standard format, are not immune. For example: *Hilton New Orleans Riverside, Two Poydras Street, New Orleans Central Business District, New Orleans, LA 70130* and *Hilton New Orleans Riverside, 2 Poydras St, New Orleans, LA 70130, United States.* We can look at these two addresses and tell that they are describing the same hotel, but their differences are non-trivial: the use of 'Two' versus 2 and the inclusion of 'New Orleans Central Business District'. Another domestic example: *Mauna Kea Beach Hotel, 62-100 Mauna Kea Beach Drive, Waikoloa, HI 96743* and *Mauna Kea Beach Hotel, 62-100 Mauna Kea Beach Dr, Kamuela, HI, 96743 United States.* These two addresses have every field in common but one: one city is listed as Waikoloa and the other as Kamuela. How much weight should be given to each field? Due to the variety of differences possible, this is a difficult problem to automate.

2.2 Disambiguation techniques

We use a combination of hotel name analysis and geodesic distance to disambiguate hotels. Geodesic distance ensures that the addresses are located in the same place, despite differences in formatting, and name comparison makes sure the hotels' names are similar enough to likely refer to the same business.

Hotel name comparison To compare two hotel names, we divise a similarity measure comparing the number of letters they have in common. The similarity measure we use is the length of the set intersection of the hotel names divided by the length of the longer name. This measure is faster to compute than edit distance and succeeds in the face of small spelling differences or omitted words. This measure on its own has very high precision but low recall, so when combined with geodesic distance we are able to loosen this matching requirement for good results.

Geodesic distance To compare the physical location of the hotels, we employe geocoding. Using the Google Geocoding API, we translate hotel addresses into latitude and longitude coordinates for all of our hotels. This API works well with strangely formatted addresses, both domestic and international. We use a cluster of computers to speed up the coordinate generation process as there is a limit on the number of requests per day. We then calculate the geodesic distance between two sets of latitude and longitudes. To do this we first convert latitude and longitude to spherical coordinates in radians, compute the arc length, then multiply this by the radius of earth in miles to get the distance in miles between the two addresses.

Combining measures: By combining geodesic distance with a distance measure of the hotel names, we are able to have efficient, high-precision matching. To find the ideal distance maximum and similarity minimum, we explored the parameter space for distances from 90 miles to 0 miles and similarities from .1 to .9. By sampling 30 hotels at each parameter combination and manually checking matching fidelity, we found a local maximum in precision at a geodesic distance max of 1 mile and a name similarity minimum of 0.66. Since we want high-quality matching results, we err on the side of caution with our matching constraints.

Results of disambiguation Using these constraints, we find 13,100 total matches. 848 hotels were matched across all three sites, 1007 between Booking.com and Hotels.com, 655 between Booking.com and TripAdvisor.com, and 10,590 between Hotels.com and TripAdvisor.com. Booking.com is a much newer site, and we hypothesize that is the reason for its reduced coverage.

3. NOVEL FEATURE SET

Hotels show various inconsistencies within and across hosting sites. In this section, we present several such inconsistencies that are not discussed previously in the literature and derive relevant features for our trustworthiness scoring. We categorize our features in a similar way to Jindal et al. [9]: reviewer-centric features, review-centric features and hotel-centric features. Features are either generated using one site or multiple sites after the hotels are joined based on location. All the single-site features are combined to put them in the context of multiple sites.

A note worth mentioning is that the location information of these hotels provide an unprecedented opportunity to validate goodness of the reviewers and reviews. All of our novel features described below show promising capabilities in identifying suspicious behavior, and most of the time it is possible to spot such behavior for our novel location disambiguation and merging.

In the reminder of the paper, we will use HDC for Hotels.com, TA for TripAdvisor.com and BDC for Booking.com.

3.1 Reviewer-Centric Features

We identify three new scenarios involving inconsistent and unlikely reviews and capture these scenarios through reviewer-centric features. Since it is not possible to disambiguate users across sites, all of the reviewer-centric features are based on individual sites.

3.1.1 Spatial Inconsistency

We focus on identifying reviewing behaviors that are spatially inconsistent. We find a user named "AmishBoy" who reviewed 34 hotels in Amish Country located in Lancaster, PA over 5 years. Lancaster County spans only 984 square miles, meaning that many of the hotels this user reviewed are right next door to each other. He gave 32 out of these 34 hotels 4 or 5 star ratings, which means he was pleased with his stay. Why then would he continually switch to new hotels? Even if he is simply visiting the area for business or pleasure every couple of months, his pattern of continually switching to new hotels is suspicious. Whether innocent or not, the reviews of this user should be discounted on the grounds that he does not represent a 'typical' traveler visiting this area.

We create a feature that identifies if a user has such a bias to a specific location and accumulate the contributions of such reviewers to every hotel. This feature is first calculated as the maximum count of the number of reviews a reviewer made in a given zip-code. If this value is greater than a threshold, typically 5, the reviewer is marked as a suspicious user. To propagate the feature up to the hotel level, we then sum the number of reviews each hotel has that came from suspicious users. If a hotel has many reviewers who have such spatial preference, it strongly suggests potential review manipulation by the hotel.

3.1.2 Temporal Inconsistency

Another type of suspicious behavior of a reviewer is writing many reviews on the same day. Typically a traveler may review a set of businesses after he comes back from a trip. However, the frequency of such trips and the spatial distribution of the businesses can provide valuable insights. For example, a user named "tonyk81" reviewed 25 businesses on January 22, 2006, which are located across 15 states. Additionally, 21 of these reviews are "first time reviews" for the respective hotels. The reviews describe visit dates starting from May, 2005 till January, 2006 and *all* of the reviews have the words *great* and *good* in the titles. Furthermore, many sentences in the review titles and text are repeated verbatim, for example "Cleanliness seems to be a high priority at this hotel and the rooms are in like new condition." and "This hotel lives up to Marriotts high standards of quality." The user has only reviewed 3 hotels in the last eight years after this burst, all on the same day in 2007. Putting these pieces of evidence together, it is clear that tonyk81 is likely a spam account.

	Booking.com	Hotels.com	TripAdvisor.com
Number of reviews	11,275,833	9,050,133	3,167,035
Number of hotels	52,696	155,763	51,395
Number of unique usernames	1,462,460	1,020,054	1,426,252
Average number of reviews	213.98	74.3	68.71
Average rating	3.35	3.07	3.99
Percent empty reviews	24.4%	19.6%	0.0039%
Date range	09-30-2009 - 05-17-2014	02/01/2006 - 06-01-2014	02/28/2001 - 09/08/2013
Geographic range	International	International	United States

Table 1: Simple Statistics of the three datasets collected from three prominent travel websites.

Figure 1: (top) Locations of the hotels the user AmishBoy reviewed around Lancaster, PA in TA (bottom) A snapshot of the reviews tonyk81 wrote in TA. Note the frequent occurrences of January 22, 2006.

Singleton bursts have been identified as potential indicator of manipulating hotels in [22]. The above example suggests non-singleton bursts can show evidence of spamming users as well. If a hotel has a large number of such reviewers, it likely has manipulated its reviews. To calculate this feature, we find the maximum number of reviews a reviewer left in a given day. If this is greater than a threshold, typically 3, that user is marked as suspicious. We then propagate up to the hotel level as described above, by summing the number of reviews each hotel has that came from suspicious users.

3.1.3 Graphical Inconsistency

Bipartite cliques in user-store graphs can identify groups of users that boost a set of stores by doing a number of small transactions in the form of positive reviews [6]. Inspired by this, we create a feature to capture information about the cliques a reviewer participates in. We restrict ourselves only to cliques of size two and search for the maximum number of hotels a user has reviewed in common with any other user. We find several cases where such a clique points to an abnormal pattern in reviews. One such case we identify is two users who have reviewed over 95% of the hotels in common on nearly the same dates, usually off by one day. Upon researching the reviewers further we discovered that they are married! While a valid reason for such behavior, this shows that our method for finding anomalous behavior by identifying bipartite cliques is successful. Another example is two users from Germany, who have reviewed 117 of the same restaurants, hotels, or landmarks all over the world in the past 5 years out of 189 and 186, respectively. Furthermore, they each are 'first to review' (meaning they were one of the first five reviewers of that location in their native language) for 136 and 144 locations. They also have surprising synchronicity in both the review dates and stay dates for the hotels they have in common. These facts indicate that these may be two accounts may be held by the same person, which is the behavior of a paid spammer.

3.2 Hotel-Centric Features

Hotel-centric features are relatively more successful in identifying outliers (see Experiments). As before, we have three types of inconsistencies for hotels.

3.2.1 Temporal Bursts and Oscillations

Bursts of positive reviews for a hotel specifically aimed to increase the average rating is well identified in the literature. We find several such cases where there are bursts of singleton reviews with an increase in the average ratings. Typically such behavior is prevalent in the early years of the inception of a hotel in the hosting site. Figure 2 shows an example of such a burst. Bursts were calculated by taking the difference between maximum number of reviews in a day and average number of reviews in a day for each hotel.

In addition to bursts, we show cases of oscillation in ratings that are targeted to keep a high rating at the top of the "new-to-old" sorted list. We created two features to characterize oscillation: the number of times a 5 star review was immediately followed by a 1 star review for each hotel, and the number of times a 1 star review was immediately followed by a 5 star review for each hotel. These summed feature values capture the level of oscillation of ratings for a given hotel.

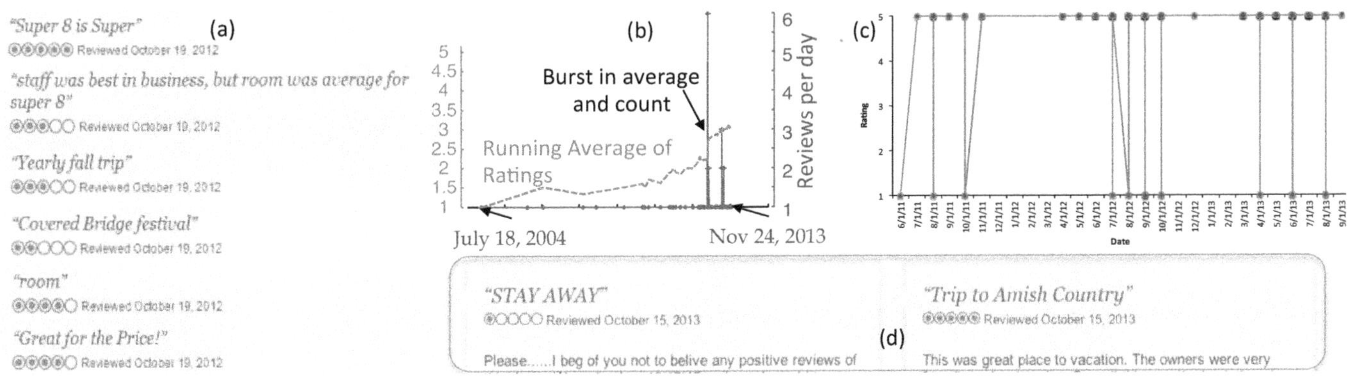

Figure 2: (a) Six reviews for Super 8 hotel in Indiana in the same day (October 19, 2012), all positive, and five of them are singleton reviews where the authors have not reviewed again in TA. (b) The number of reviews per day for a this hotel jumps to 6 on that day which was sufficient to give the hotel a 0.5 star boost in the average rating showing in red. (c) Immediate 5-star ratings after 1-star ratings are frequent in some hotels such as Cherry Lane Motor Inn in Amish Country. (d) Examples of two successive opposite reviews on the same day from two reviewers.

An example of oscillating ratings is shown in Figure 2. We see that eight out of ten 1 star ratings were followed immediately by 5 star ratings.

3.2.2 Temporal Correlation

Temporal correlation between number of ratings of a hotel in different sites is a valuable indicator of consistent customer satisfaction. Commonly, a hotel should have very similar behavior across sites in terms of number of ratings. For example, any hotel in Myrtle Beach, SC shows a high number of ratings per day in summer,decreasing in the winter. Since the number of occupants at hotels in Myrtle Beach, SC [2] decreases from 80% in the summer to 30% in the winter, this pattern makes sense; the number of ratings per day follows the average occupants of the hotel and such behavior is consistent across sites. In Figure 4, we show hotels and their number of ratings per day in HDC and TA. We see the top two hotels have summer peaks in both of the sites. However, Bluewater Resort has dense summer ratings in TA but no significant peak/density in HDC, especially in summer of 2012.

Such discrepancy in temporal behavior can exist for several reasons, each of which are worth considering when it comes to evaluating hotels. The hotel might have received more poor ratings in the summer which were omitted by the hosting site, or the hotel could have sponsored some winter reviews. There can be extreme cases such as the hotel was closed for construction, but irrespective of the real reason, a lack of correlation across sites is a significant indicator for spotting misbehavior. We calculate Pearson's correlation coefficient between the time series of number of ratings per day from two sites. We use only the overlapping time duration for calculation. If the overlap is too small, we naively assume perfect correlation.

3.2.3 Rating Distributions

In [8], authors have suggested that the shape of rating distribution has a strong tie to the spamming hotels. Typically, a "J" shaped distribution has a large number of 5-star and 1-star ratings but a small number of 4-, 3-, and 2-star ratings. Such a distribution may occur if users review only when they are extremely happy or disappointed. However, it is suspicious to have nearly equal numbers of people who hated and loved a hotel. This suggests that one of those rating groups has been artificially inflated by spam reviews. Whereas in [8] they had to compare distributions between hotels, we take a multi-site approach to validate the consistency of distributions across sites for individual hotels. To find this value we calculate the Pearson's correlation coefficient between the rating distributions of a hotel across different sites, represented by two vectors of counts of integer ratings. We also directly compare the distributions of the ratings by using the one-sided p-value from the Mann Whitney U Test as a feature.

Figure 4 shows the correlation coefficients of the distributions between HDC and TA. We take a threshold of -0.9 and locate all the hotels that show less than -0.9 correlation. As shown in Figure 3, we find an interesting co-location pattern for negatively correlated hotels around Atlanta, GA which is more densely populated with such hotels than any major urban area or popular vacation spot, such as Las Vegas, NV or Los Angeles, CA. Around 5% of the hotels in GA show negative correlation, which is much greater than that (1%) in CA and NV.

3.3 Review-Centric Features

Review-centric features are based on the texts of the reviews and their titles. We do not use any natural language processing techniques to spot a spam review by only text, rather rather focus on structural properties of reviews.

3.3.1 Empty Reviews

Reviewers often write empty reviews with no title and no comment. The incentive for such reviews is that they can be submitted without typing. We find an abundance of empty reviews in HDC and BDC, with 20% and 25% empty reviews, respectively, while TA has only 3% empty reviews. In addition to these reviews being potentially suspicious, we find that hosting sites treat these reviews differently. For example, in HDC, empty reviews were visible during the time when we collected the data; however, HDC now hides the empty reviews, while keeping counts of them in their over-

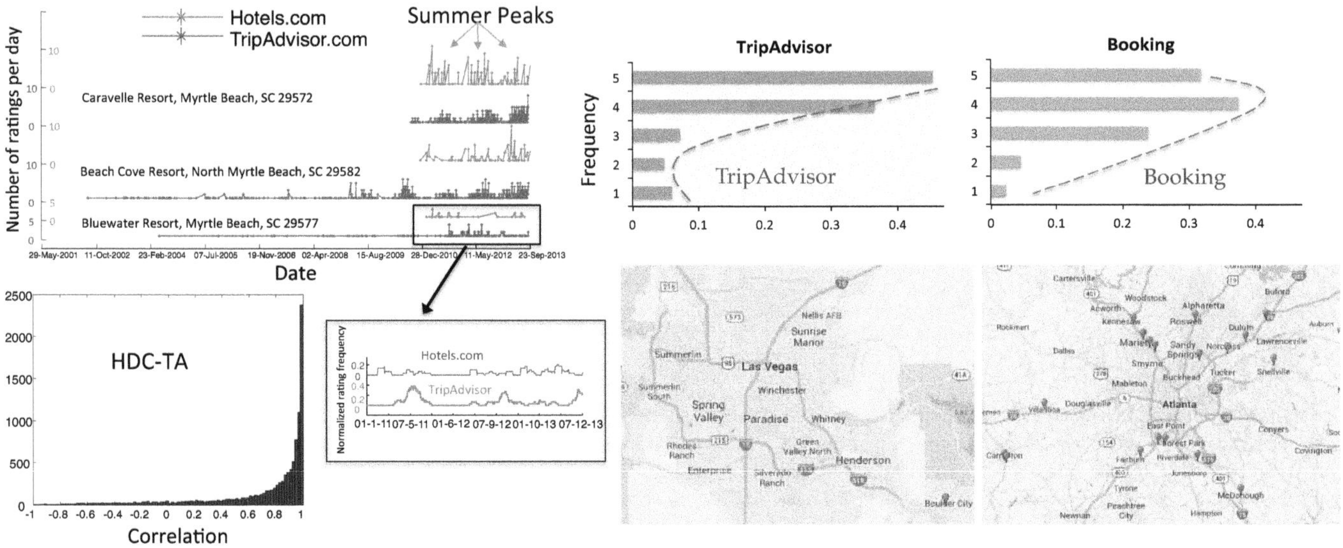

Figure 3: (left) The time series of number of ratings per day for three hotels in Myrtle Beach, SC. The top two hotels show summer peaks in both TA and HDC. The bottom hotel does not show any summer effect in HDC. (center) Distribution of correlation between ratings of hotels in TA and HDC. (top right) Distribution of ratings for the same hotel in two websites showing negative correlation. (bottom right) Negatively correlated hotels are more abundant in the vicinity of Atlanta, GA and almost non-existent in Las Vegas, NV area where both the cities have more than three hundred hotels.

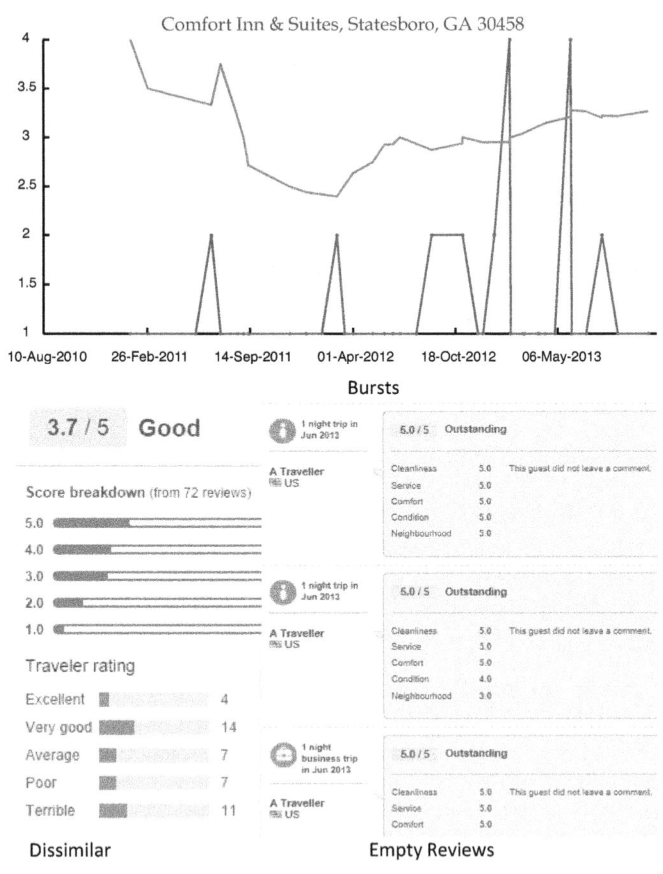

Figure 4: Dissimilar distribution of ratings, temporal bursts in number of ratings per day and frequent empty reviews for the same hotel in Statesboro, GA.

all review tallies. For example, Excalibur Hotel and Casino in Las Vegas, NV has 2500 empty reviews out of 13,144 reviews in HDC, but none of them is visible through the website. Such behavior of hiding consumer reviews has been reported several times in [1] and clearly such an omission is not fair to consumers.

There exist some hotels that have a significantly greater proportion of empty reviews than average. For example, Comfort Suites Newark in New Jersey has 86 empty reviews out of 193 reviews which is more than 44% of the reviews. We find 66 hotels that have only empty reviews in HDC. BDC has a similar-sized body of empty reviews. Sometimes multiple features together describe a suspicious hotel. In Figure 3, we show a hotel having three suspicious behavior captured by three of our features.

3.3.2 Matching Reviews

Inspired by tonyk81's matching review text described above, we create a feature that captures the proportion of sentences any pair of reviews from the same reviewer share to the total number of reviews that reviewer made. While repeating the occasional phrase is to be expected, having reviews that share the majority of the sentences, or are completely identical, is not. We calculate this score by comparing pairwise all reviews made by a given user. We keep a count of the number of sentences these reviews share, and then divide this value by the total number of reviews a reviewer wrote. We then attach this score to each review a reviewer left. For each hotel we aggregate this score for all of its reviews to characterize the lack of uniqueness of its review set. A hotel with many reviewers who use the same sentences repeatedly, suggests that the hotel is soliciting many spam reviews.

3.4 Cross-Site Feature Preparation

We generate 90 features including the novel features described in the previous section for each hotel in each site. In addition to these single-site features, which we use to calculate a TrueView score, we calculate 52 cross-site features for the hotels that exist in multiple sites. These cross-site features are combination of similar single-site features from many sites. Cross-site features can identify discrepancies that a hotel has between a pair of sites, for example, a difference in the percentages of empty reviews.

We combine the single-site features in three different ways. First, we take ratios for scalar values, such as number of reviews. Some of the scalars are only meaningful relatively, such as number of 5-star ratings. We use relative frequencies when taking the ratio of these scalar features. Second, we take correlation coefficients for sequences, such as numbers of high to low ratings. And third, we take the p-value of the Mann-Whitney U test for distributions, such as the distributions of review lengths in words.

The next step is to normalize these features to make them reasonably close to standard normal distribution. The intention is to treat each feature as independent and identically distributed. Some of the features require a log transformation to be converted to standard normal because of their exponential fall out, for example, counts of rating scores, counts of empty reviews, and text similarity scores. After log transformations, we normalize each feature by Z-score. For a complete list of features and their values for all of the hotels please visit the supporting page [3].

4. TRUSTWORTHINESS SCORE

Our work is fundamentally different from existing works. We do not wish to evaluate if a review is fake or untruthful as most existing works do. We believe it is very difficult to achieve high *recall* in identifying review fraud, mostly because of the dynamics of the fraudsters and the lack of labeled data. Even if we assume hypothetically that we can achieve high recall and prevent fake reviews from being shown to the readers, the hotels and sites that promote fraudsters are not penalized and site users are not notified of which hotels are trying to lie to their customers.

We believe that a better approach to this problem is to evaluate hotels and sites to find which ones promote untruthful reviews, and to produce a trustworthiness score to present to the user. We think such scores are more beneficial to the review readers as they can use these scores in their ultimate judgment.

4.1 Outlier Scores

Once all the features are available, we take three approaches to rank the hotels with outlier scores. We use global density-based score, a local outlier factor, and a hierarchical cluster-based score. We describe each technique in this section.

4.1.1 Global Density-based Score

We calculate *how different a hotel is from the centroid of hotels in the feature space.* We take the mode of each feature and form a hypothetical hotel which lies in the center of a large "normal" cluster. We use the simple intuition that most hotels are playing fair and only a small fraction of hotels are generating fake and untruthful reviews. If a hotel is largely dissimilar to the mode/centroid hotel, the hotel might disagree in many features with the mode, which makes its reviews less trustworthy.

We use the concept of density connectedness to form a large cluster of points (i.e. hotels) carrying the mode. A point is a *core point* if it has k or more points within ϵ distance in the Euclidean space. Two points are density-connected if there is a sequence of core points from one to another where every point is within ϵ-neighborhood of the previous point. Thus, any point that is not in the core cluster is an outlier and the degree of outlying is proportional to the distance from the nearest core point. This method is inspired from the original density based clustering algorithm, DBSCAN. This method has a unique advantage that the core cluster can be of any shape and based on the two parameters (i.e. ϵ and k) we can control the size of the core cluster and thus, the size of the outlying cluster.

4.1.2 Local Outlier Factor (LOF)

The global method assumes that all normal hotels form a core cluster. However, there can be alternative structures with numerous small clusters of normal hotels with varying densities in the feature space. We use local outlier factor to score outliers. Local outlier factor uses the notion of k-distance ($dist_k(x)$) which is defined as the distance to the k-th nearest neighbor of a point. Local reachability distance (lrd_k) of x is the average of the reachability distances from x's neighbors to x. Here $N_k(x)$ is the set of k-nearest neighbors of x.

$$lrd_k(x) = \frac{||N_k(x)||}{\sum_{y \in N_k(x)} \max(dist_k(y), dist(x,y))}$$

The LOF of a point x is the average of the ratios of the *local reachability* of x and its k-nearest neighbors. LOF can capture several normal clusters of arbitrary densities that makes it robust for any data domain. Formally, LOF is defined as below

$$LOF_k(x) = \frac{\sum_{y \in N_k(x)} \frac{lrd_k(y)}{lrd_k(x)}}{||N_k(x)||}$$

4.1.3 Hierarchical Cluster-based Score

Both of the density-based methods above use k-neighborhoods to estimate densities or connectivities. Our third approach differs from that and uses a hierarchical clustering approach. We cluster the data hierarchically using the *single linkage* method. The single linkage method starts with singleton clusters. The method evaluates pairs of clusters based on the *minimum distance* between any pair of points that form the two clusters and merges the closest two clusters at every step. This simple bottom-up strategy can produce a dendrogram over the points without any input parameters.

Once the complete hierarchy is built, a set of clusters can be obtained by cutting the hierarchy at a cutoff level. Here again, we assume there is a global normal cluster that contains most hotels and any hotel not in this cluster is an outlier. Under this assumption, we can tune the cutoff level to get a certain percentage of points in the set of outliers.

4.2 TrueView Scores

The three above approaches produce three different outlier scores. A big challenge is that the scores are not at the same scale. Before combining individual scores, we need to regularize and normalize the outlier scores. We take the approach of [11][19] to normalize the outlier scores from each of the above approaches using logarithmic inversion and gaussian scaling.

Let a hotel be x and the outlier score of x is $S(x)$. We do a log transform $z = -\log S(x)/S_{max}$ for each hotel x and scale it using a gaussian distribution to produce a probability $P(x)$ of the hotel x being an outlier. Such a probability score is useful because it is bounded within [0,1] and can easily be converted to a *trustworthiness score* by a simple linear inversion.

$$P(x) = \max(0, erf(\frac{z-\mu_z}{\sqrt{2}\sigma_z}))$$
$$TV(x) = 1 - P(x)$$

Here, $TV(x)$ is the **TrueView** score. The TrueView score describes the probability of a hotel's reviews being truthful and is unitless. As described above, we can now produce TrueView scores from any feature set of these hotels. We define two intermediate scores that can be created as well as the overall TrueView score. First, **TV1** is produced only using features from *one* site. Second, **TV2** is produced using an union of features from *all* sites. Third, the **TrueView** score is produced using the union of all single-site features and the cross-site features from all three sites. Each outlier detection algorithm produces its own scores, and we average them to get the overall **TrueView** score. We provide empirical evidence in Experiments section that **TrueView** identifies successfully identifies outliers.

There are two weaknesses of the above approaches. First, the score of a hotel can change if other hotels connect it to the core cluster. Second, there can be hotels which are unusually good labeled as untrustworthy. These cases are pathological and become rare with more reviews per hotel.

5. EXPERIMENTS

We start with our reproducibility statement, all of the experiments in this section are exactly reproducible with the code and data provided in the supporting page [3]. We also have additional materials such as presentation slides, csv sheets of raw numbers, and more experiments.

5.1 Parameter Sensitivity

The three algorithms we use for outlier detection have a set of parameters to tune. Based on the values of these parameters, we can have different sized sets of outliers. We experiment to test the sensitivities of these parameters and select values for subsequent experiments.

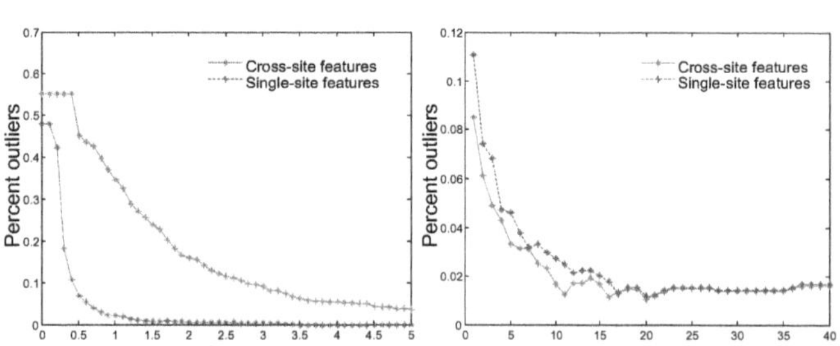

Figure 5: (left) Percentage of outliers detected in the density-based method as we vary ϵ. (right) The same as we vary neighborhood size K in LOF method.

In the global density-based method, we have ϵ and k as parameters. We fix $k = 10$ and vary ϵ and record the percentage of the dataset labeled as outlier. In the local outlier factor method, we have the neighborhood size k as the parameter. In the hierarchical method we use the cutoff value as the parameter and record the percentage of the dataset labeled as outlier. Figure 5 shows the behavior of mode-distance and LOF methods. We select the parameters such that we can rank order 30% of the hotels using all three methods. This number is an arbitrary choice and can be different in other systems.

5.2 Feature Importance

We evaluate feature importance in the calculation of the TrueView score. We use two different and independent approaches to evaluate the features.

5.2.1 *Spectral Feature Selection*

We use the method in [23] to evaluate the importance of our 142 features. The method identifies redundancy in the feature values and properly demotes dependent features. The result is shown in Figure 6, where more than 100 features show very uniform importance scores, which supports the validity of our feature set. In addition, we categorize the features into cross-site and single-site classes. We see that the most important features are cross-site features showing the importance of multiple-site data for evaluating hotels. Note that, the feature selection algorithm does not take into account the ultimate usage of these features in the algorithm, which is outlier detection in this work.

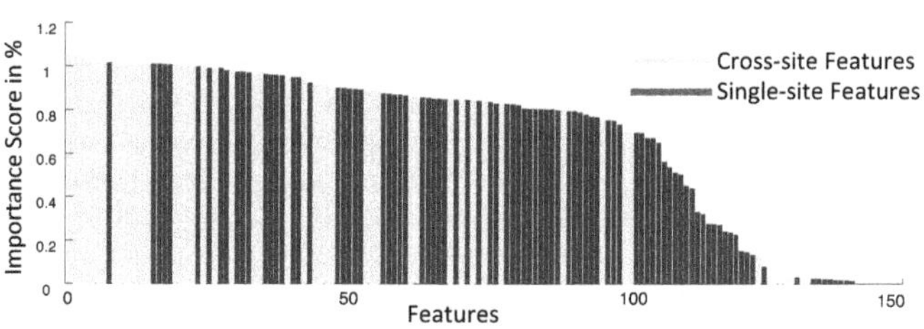

Figure 6: Feature importance percent score for 142 features. Cross-site features are more important than single-site features.

5.2.2 *Distance from Mode*

In this approach, we consider the outliers produced by the global density-based approach. We pick the most different feature of an outlier with respect to the mode of that feature as the representative for that outlier. We see a massive shift in importance of our cross-site features, especially the star rating based cross-site features that become important for more than half of the outliers. In Figure 7, we show the results for other feature categories as described in section 3.

5.3 Validation

Since the algorithm for computing TrueView score is unsupervised, and we do not have labeled data that identifies fraud hotels, we cannot directly validate with ground truth information. Therefore we take two alternate approaches to validate the soundness of our method.

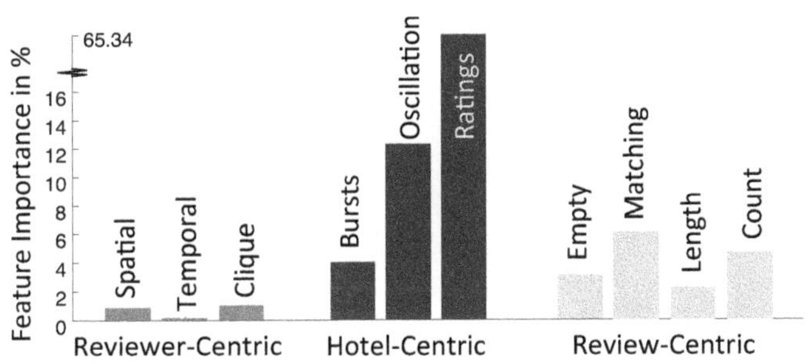

Figure 7: Relative importance of review-,reviewer- and hotel-centric features based on the distance from the centroid.

5.3.1 Sanity Check on Synthetic Frauds

First we generate a synthetic set of outlying hotels to validate that our global density-based approach correctly identifies outliers. To create these outliers, we copy the center point representing the mode of all features and mutate random feature values, randomly setting them to either the ninety-fifth or the fifth percentile. We then calculate their TrueView score based on the global density-based method described above. This experiment is repeated 100 times. We find the distributions of TrueView scores are heavily skewed towards zero, showing that on the whole, they were given very low TrueView scores. Thus our algorithm passes this sanity check, classifying 100% of our synthetic data as outliers and giving them correspondingly low TrueView scores.

5.3.2 Evaluation of Extreme Features

Second, we validate that the hotels with low TrueView scores show a significant difference in the number of extreme feature values from the hotels with high TrueView scores. To calculate this we find the number of features that are below the fifth percentile or above the ninety-fifth percentile for each hotel. We use the Wilcoxon rank-sum test to determine whether the 40 most trustworthy hotels significantly differ in the number of extreme features from the 40 least trustworthy accounts. A p-value of < 0.05 rejects the null hypothesis, and asserts that the two populations are distinct. Table 2 lists the p-values for each outlier algorithm and each feature subset. The cross-site and combined single-site feature sets show statistically significant results for every algorithm, meaning that these feature sets are effective in differentiating outliers. It also means that hotels given high TrueView scores are indeed trustworthy, as most of them have only a few extreme features.

	LOF	Mode Density	Linkage
Cross-site	**3.93E-07**	**1.63E-08**	**4.60E-11**
Single-site	**1.63E-06**	**8.04E-15**	**1.08E-12**
Booking.com	**1.49E-05**	0.419	**0.019**
Hotels.com	0.308	**4.41E-04**	**0.038**
TripAdvisor.com	0.379	0.052	**0.002**

Table 2: p-values of Wilcoxon rank-sum test. Bold faced values mean that there is a significant difference between the top and bottom 40.

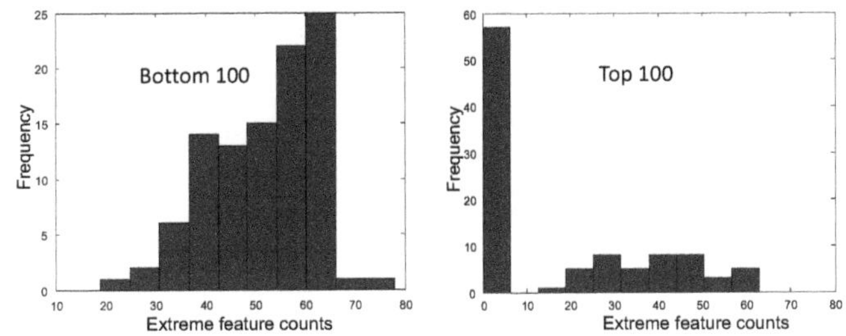

Figure 8: (left) Distribution of the number of extreme features (95th percentile) in the bottom 100 hotels in TrueView ordering (right) Distribution of the same in the top 100 hotels in TrueView ordering. Distributions are significantly different.

6. CASE STUDIES

We want to provide some initial ideas on how the TrueView score could be used in practice. We identify two possibilities: (a) enable the site owner to detect misbehaving hotels, and (b) by the end user.

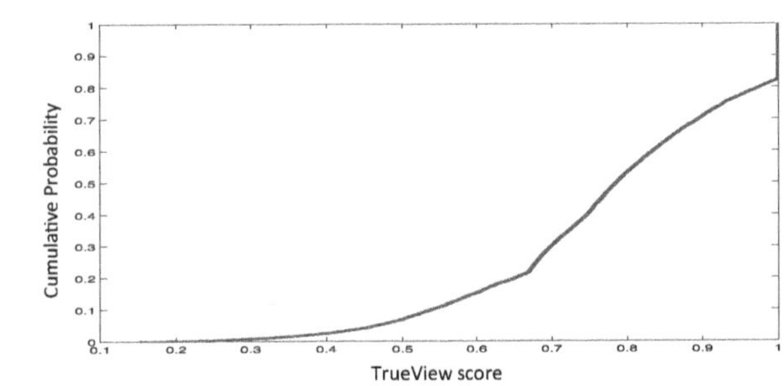

Figure 9: Empirical cumulative distribution function of TrueView scores.

A. TrueView for the site administrator. The usage here is fairly straightforward as a way to identify misbehaving hotels. The administrator can apply TrueView on the data from his own site alone, in which case TrueView resolves to TV1. Assuming cross-site cooperation, the administrator could use data from other sites.

B. TrueView for the end user. The TrueView score could help the user select hotels that are more likely to have non-altered scores. In other words, the user can be more confident that a rating of say 3.5 stars is the true reflection of unbiased customers. TrueView could be used again when a single site is available, but its power lies in its ability to combine reviews from multiple sites.

We see two basic ways the TrueView could be used. (a) as a way to re-rank hotels, by altering the the rate of the hotels, and (b) as a filtering mechanism, in which hotels with unreliable TrueView score are not even shown to the user.

a. Weighted rating using TrueView. There are many ways that to modify the rating of a hotel based on the trustworthiness score. The full input is the rating from each site, the number of reviews per site, the trustworthiness of each site (TV1), and the TrueView across all sites. One approach would be to take the average rating and multiply it by the trustworthiness score, but this method's simplicity is not a proof of effectiveness without extensive study.

Hotel	HDC Stars	T1-HDC	TA Stars	TV1-TA	TV2	**TrueView**	**Trustworthy?**
Super 8 Terre Haut	3.30	1.0	3.00	0.235	0.734	**1.0**	✓
Excalibur Hotel and Casino	3.60	0.846	3.50	0.850	0.951	**0.761**	✓
Comfort Suites Newark	3.80	0.688	3.00	0.705	0.773	**1.0**	✓
Paradise Resort, Myrtle Beach	4.20	1.0	4.00	0.573	0.699	**1.0**	✓
Bluewater Resort, Myrtle Beach	2.90	1.0	3.00	0.735	0.790	**0.462**	**X**
Comfort Inn & Suites, Statesboro	3.60	1.0	3.60	0.783	0.669	**0.264**	**X**

Table 3: TrueView scores for suspicious hotels. (Stars is the average overall rating)

b. Filtering using TrueView. In this method, we need only to find the cut-off threshold of trustworthiness **TV-thres** which forms the cut-off point for hotels with a score less than the threshold. The filtering threshold needs to balance the ability to remove suspicious hotels with its false positive rate, which would reduce the overall choice for the end user. This is the fundamental trade-off that needs to be considered. We present some initial thoughts on how we could develop a threshold like this.

Disclaimer: The discussion below is not intended to be indicative of and not a conclusive and thorough determination of a filtering method. For that, a more extensive analysis is needed to derive a conclusive statement. In addition, the user-facing service and even the user herself can have significant impact on how "strict" the filtering process should be.

Calibration: known suspicious hotels. First, we show the distribution of hotels having a TrueView score less than a threshold in Figure 9 . Obviously, we cannot just mark the bottom 25% as being untrustworthy. However, we can evaluate how well our scoring process works for a known set of misbehaving hotels. If we filter out the bottom 25%, we need a threshold of 0.7. We present results for the 6 suspicious hotels that were identified in Section 3 in Table 3. We see a threshold of 0.7 would give us 33% precision. In other words, filtering out hotels with a a score of less than 0.7 would ensure that 2/6 known malicious hotels are filtered, while reducing the overall choice of hotels by 25%.

For the sake of this case study, one can argue that 0.7 could be a reasonable threshold. In a real deployment, this needs to be based on a much large labeled dataset.

Case study: Finding hotels in Amish Country. We choose the top 20 hotels in Amish Country, Lancaster County, PA from Hotels.com and TripAdvisor. We choose hotels in Amish Country because during our initial investigation many potentially suspicious hotels were present. Amish Country is a small area with many competing hotels trying to access a similar market, so the competition is fierce. We calculate the TrueView scores for those that are part of our matched dataset. We find that two hotels have scores below our threshold of 0.7. We manually assess these two hotels, and we find that they do show suspicious behavior.

7. RELATED WORK

Existing works focus on identifying fraud reviews and reviewers, while we focus on businesses such as hotels that promote fraudulent reviews. Existing work can be categorized based on the methodologies they adopt to detect frauds. Fraud detection using Graphical/Network structure is studied in [5][6][20] where authors exploit network effects and clique structures among reviewers and products to identify fraud. Text-based detection of fraud is studied to spot a fake review without having the context of the reviewer and reviewed product [17][9][13]. Temporal patterns, such as bursts, have been identified as fraudulent behavior of businesses [22][7].

There has been work on joining multiple criteria from single sources to better detect fraud [21]. Various types of fraud have been identified in the literature: groups of fraudsters [16][15], unusual behavioral footprints [14], unusual distributional footprints [8], unexpected rules [10] and unusual rating behaviors [12].

Existing works deal with diverse set of review data in both supervised and unsupervised manners. In [5] 15,094 apps are ranked based on network effects. In [21] 45 hotels are ranked based on an unsupervised hedge algorithm. In [8] , 4000 hotels located in 21 big cities are analyzed to identify distributional anomalies. In [9] reviews on 700,000 products for a month are analyzed using review-, reviewer-, and product-centric features. In [18], 7,345 car repair shops are crawled to collect 270,121 reviews and the data of their 195,417 reviewers.

Our work considers 15 million reviews for over 10 years on three websites and thus considers significantly more data than existing works do. None of the existing work considers reviews from multiple sites to understand fraudulent behavior. Our work is fundamentally different from most existing work, since our focus in in evaluating hotels/businesses instead of reviews.

The closest commercial competitor of TrueView is TrustYou score [4] which calculates a trustworthiness score for a hotel based on the reviews about that hotel in multiple sites. TrustYou is fundamentally different in that it scores the goodness of the hotel itself based mainly on semantic text analysis, while TrueView scores the trustworthiness of the hotel based on a wide range of features.

8. CONCLUSION

The goal of our work is to show the significant benefits we can have by combining reviews from multiple review sites. As our key contribution, we develop a systematic methodology to cross-compare, and synthesize reviews from multiple review sites. The novelty of our approach relies one the introduction and assessment of 142 features that capture single-site and cross-site discrepancies effectively. Our approach culminates with the introduction of the TrueView score, in three different variants, as a proof of concept that the synthesis of multi-site reviews, can provide important and usable information to the end user. We conduct arguably the first extensive study of cross-site discrepancies using real data from 15M reviews from more than 3.5M users spanning three prominent travel sites. We find that there are significant variations in reviews, and we find evidence of review manipulation.

9. FUNDING STATEMENT

Amanda Minnich is supported by the NSF Graduate Research Fellowship under Grant No. DGE-0237002 and the Program in Interdisciplinary Biomedical and Biological Sciences through the University of New Mexico award number T32EB009414 from the National Institute of Biomedical Imaging and Bioengineering. This work was also supported by NSF SaTC Grant No. 1314935.

10. REFERENCES

[1] Consumer complaints & reviews. http://www.consumeraffairs.com/travel/hotelsdotcom.html?page=2.

[2] Myrtle beach area chamber of commerce, page 10. http://www.myrtlebeachareachamber.com/research/docs/20statabstract.pdf.

[3] Supporting webpage containing data, slides and code. www.cs.unm.edu/~aminnich/trueview.

[4] Trustscore: The measurement of online reputation management - trustyou. http://www.trustyou.com/.

[5] L. Akoglu, R. Chandy, and C. Faloutsos. Opinion fraud detection in online reviews by network effects. In *ICWSM'13*, pages 2–11, 2013.

[6] D. H. Chau, S. Pandit, and C. Faloutsos. Detecting fraudulent personalities in networks of online auctioneers. PKDD'06, pages 103–114, 2006.

[7] G. Fei, A. Mukherjee, B. Liu, M. Hsu, M. Castellanos, and R. Ghosh. Exploiting burstiness in reviews for review spammer detection. In *ICWSM'13*, pages 175–184, 2013.

[8] S. Feng, L. Xing, A. Gogar, and Y. Choi. Distributional footprints of deceptive product reviews. In *ICWSM'12*, pages 98–105, 2012.

[9] N. Jindal and B. Liu. Opinion spam and analysis. WSDM '08, pages 219–230.

[10] N. Jindal, B. Liu, and E.-P. Lim. Finding unusual review patterns using unexpected rules. CIKM '10, pages 1549–1552, 2010.

[11] H.-P. Kriegel, P. Kroger, E. Schubert, and A. Zimek. Interpreting and unifying outlier scores. In *SDM*, pages 13–24.

[12] E.-P. Lim, V.-A. Nguyen, N. Jindal, B. Liu, and H. W. Lauw. Detecting product review spammers using rating behaviors. CIKM '10, pages 939–948.

[13] A. Morales, H. Sun, and X. Yan. Synthetic review spamming and defense. WWW '13 Companion, pages 155–156.

[14] A. Mukherjee, A. Kumar, B. Liu, J. Wang, M. Hsu, M. Castellanos, and R. Ghosh. Spotting opinion spammers using behavioral footprints. KDD '13, pages 632–640.

[15] A. Mukherjee, B. Liu, and N. Glance. Spotting fake reviewer groups in consumer reviews. WWW '12, pages 191–200, 2012.

[16] A. Mukherjee, B. Liu, J. Wang, N. Glance, and N. Jindal. Detecting group review spam. WWW '11, pages 93–94.

[17] M. Ott, Y. Choi, C. Cardie, and J. T. Hancock. Finding deceptive opinion spam by any stretch of the imagination. HLT '11, pages 309–319, 2011.

[18] M. Rahman, B. Carbunar, J. Ballesteros, G. Burri, and D. H. P. Chau. Turning the tide: Curbing deceptive yelp behaviors. In *SDM*, pages 244–252, 2014.

[19] E. Schubert, R. Wojdanowski, A. Zimek, and H. Kriegel. On evaluation of outlier rankings and outlier scores. In *SDM*, pages 1047–1058, 2012.

[20] G. Wang, S. Xie, B. Liu, and P. S. Yu. Review graph based online store review spammer detection. ICDM '11, pages 1242–1247.

[21] G. Wu, D. Greene, and P. Cunningham. Merging multiple criteria to identify suspicious reviews. RecSys '10, pages 241–244, 2010.

[22] S. Xie, G. Wang, S. Lin, and P. S. Yu. Review spam detection via temporal pattern discovery. KDD '12, pages 823–831, 2012.

[23] Z. Zhao and H. Liu. Spectral feature selection for supervised and unsupervised learning. ICML '07, pages 1151–1157, 2007.

QUOTUS: The Structure of Political Media Coverage as Revealed by Quoting Patterns

Vlad Niculae[*†]
Cornell University
vlad@cs.cornell.edu

Caroline Suen[*]
Stanford University
cysuen@stanford.edu

Justine Zhang[*†]
Stanford University
justinez@stanford.edu

Cristian Danescu-Niculescu-Mizil[†]
Cornell University
cristian@cs.cornell.edu

Jure Leskovec
Stanford University
jure@cs.stanford.edu

ABSTRACT

Given the extremely large pool of events and stories available, media outlets need to focus on a subset of issues and aspects to convey to their audience. Outlets are often accused of exhibiting a systematic bias in this selection process, with different outlets portraying different versions of reality. However, in the absence of objective measures and empirical evidence, the direction and extent of systematicity remains widely disputed.

In this paper we propose a framework based on quoting patterns for quantifying and characterizing the degree to which media outlets exhibit systematic bias. We apply this framework to a massive dataset of news articles spanning the six years of Obama's presidency and all of his speeches, and reveal that a systematic pattern does indeed emerge from the outlet's quoting behavior. Moreover, we show that this pattern can be successfully exploited in an unsupervised prediction setting, to determine which new quotes an outlet will select to broadcast. By encoding bias patterns in a low-rank space we provide an analysis of the structure of political media coverage. This reveals a latent media bias space that aligns surprisingly well with political ideology and outlet type. A linguistic analysis exposes striking differences across these latent dimensions, showing how the different types of media outlets portray different realities even when reporting on the same events. For example, outlets mapped to the mainstream conservative side of the latent space focus on quotes that portray a presidential persona disproportionately characterized by negativity.

Categories and Subject Descriptors: H.2.8 [**Database Management**]: Database applications—*Data mining*

General Terms: Algorithms; Experimentation.

Keywords: Media bias; Quotes; News media; Political science.

[*]The first three authors contributed equally and are ordered alphabetically. The last two authors are also ordered alphabetically.

[†]The research described herein was conducted in part while these authors were at the Max Planck Institute for Software Systems.

WWW 2015, May 18–22, 2015, Florence, Italy.
ACM 978-1-4503-3469-3/15/05.
http://dx.doi.org/10.1145/2736277.2741688.

1. INTRODUCTION

The public relies heavily on mass media outlets for accessing important information on current events. Given the intrinsic space and time constraints these outlets face, some filtering of events, stories and aspects to broadcast is unavoidable.

The majority of media outlets claim to be balanced in their coverage, selecting issues purely based on their newsworthiness. However, journalism watchdogs and political think-tanks often accuse outlets of exhibiting systematic bias in the selection process, leaning either towards serving the interests of the owners and journalists or towards appeasing the preferences of their intended audience. This phenomenon, generally called media bias, has been extensively studied in political science, economics and communication literature (for a survey see [26]). Theoretical accounts provide a taxonomy of media bias based on the level at which the selection takes place: e.g., what issues and aspects are covered (issue and facts bias), how facts are presented (framing bias) or how they are commented on (ideological stand bias). Importantly, the dimensions along which bias operates can be very diverse: although the most commonly discussed dimension aligns with political ideology (e.g., liberal vs. conservative bias) other dimensions such as mainstream bias, corporate bias, power bias, and advertising bias are also important and perceived as inadequate journalism practices.

Bias is a highly subjective phenomenon that is hard to quantify—something that is considered unfairly biased by some might be regarded as balanced by others. For example, a recent Gallup survey [22] shows not only that the majority of Americans (57%) perceive media as being biased, but also that the perception of bias varies vastly depending on their self-declared ideology: 73% of conservatives perceive the media as having a liberal bias, while only 11% of liberals perceive it as having a liberal bias (and 33% perceive it as having a conservative bias). As a consequence, the extent and direction of bias for individual media outlets remains highly disputed.[1]

The subjective nature of this phenomenon and the absence of large scale objectively labeled data hindered quantitative analyses [13], and consequently most existing empirical studies of media bias are small focused analyses [6, 25, 28]. A few notable computational studies circumvent these limitations by relying on proxies such as the similarity between media outlets and the members of congress [8, 11, 20] or U. S. Supreme Court Justices [13]. Still, the reliance on such proxies constrains the analysis to predetermined

[1]In response to numerous accusations, the 21st Century Fox CEO Rupert Murdoch has declared "I challenge anybody to show me an example of bias in Fox News Channel." (Salon, 3/1/01).

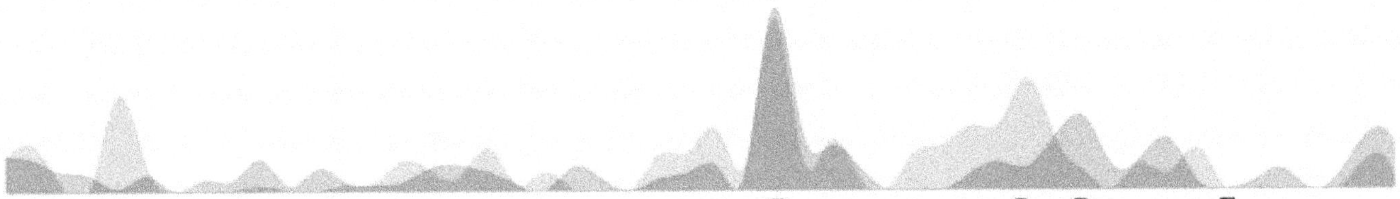

Figure 1: Volume of quotations for each word from a fragment of the 2010 State of the Union Address split by political leaning: conservative outlets shown in red and liberal outlets shown in blue. Quotes from the marked positions are reproduced in Table 1 and shown in the QUOTUS visualization in Figure 2.

Position	Quote from the 2010 State of the Union Address
A	And in the last year, hundreds of al Qaeda's fighters and affiliates, including many senior leaders, have been captured or killed—far more than in 2008.
B	I will work with Congress and our military to finally repeal the law that denies gay Americans the right to serve the country they love because of who they are. It's the right thing to do.
C	Each time lobbyists game the system or politicians tear each other down instead of lifting this country up, we lose faith. The more that TV pundits reduce serious debates to silly arguments, big issues into sound bites, our citizens turn away.
D	Democracy in a nation of 300 million people can be noisy and messy and complicated. And when you try to do big things and make big changes, it stirs passions and controversy. That's just how it is.
E	But I wake up every day knowing that they are nothing compared to the setbacks that families all across this country have faced this year.

Table 1: Quotes corresponding to the positions marked in Figure 1.

dimension of bias, and conditions the value of the results on the accuracy of the proxy assumptions [7, 18].

Present work: unsupervised framework. We present a framework for quantifying the systematic bias exhibited by media outlets, without relying on any annotation and without predetermining the dimensions of bias. The basic operating principle of this framework is that quoting patterns exhibited by individual outlets can reveal media bias. Quotes are especially suitable since they correspond to an outlet's explicit choices of whether to cover or not specific parts a larger statement. In this sense, quotes have the potential to provide precise insight into the decision process behind media coverage.

Ultimately, the goal of the proposed framework is to quantify to what extent quoting decisions follow systematic patterns that go beyond the relative importance (or newsworthiness) of the quotes, and to characterize the dimensions of this bias.

As a motivating example, Figure 1 illustrates media quotations from a fragment of the U.S. President, Barack Obama's 2010 State of the Union Address. The text is ordered along the x axis, and the y axis corresponds to the number of times a particular part of the Address was quoted. We display quoting volume by outlets considered[2] to be liberal (blue) or conservative (red). We observe both similarities and differences in what parts of the address get quoted. For example, the quote at position B (reproduced in Table 1) is highly cited by both sides, while the quote at position A is cited by conservative outlets and largely ignored by liberal outlets.[3] To a certain extent, the audience of the liberal media experienced a different State of the Union Address than the audience of the conservative group. Are these variations just random fluctuations, or are they the result of a systematically biased selection process? Do different media outlets portray consistently different realities even when reporting on the same events?

To study and identify the presence of systematic bias at a large scale, we start from a massive collection of six billion news articles [16] (over 20TB of compressed data) which spans the six years of Barack Obama's tenure in office as the President of the United States (POTUS), between 2009 and 2014. We use the 2,274 public speeches made by Obama during this period (including state of the union addresses, weekly presidential addresses and various press conferences). We match quotes from Obama's speeches to our news articles and build an outlet-to-quote bipartite graph linking 275 media outlets to the over 267,000 quotes which they reproduce. The graph allows us to study the structure of political media coverage over a long period of time and over a diverse set of public issues, while at the same time maintaining uniformity with respect to the person who is quoted.

Focused analysis. Before applying our unsupervised framework to the entire data, we first perform a small-scale focused analysis on a carefully constructed subset of labeled outlet leanings, in order to gain intuition about the nature of the data. We label outlets based on liberal and conservative leaning, as well as on whether or not

[2]While our core methodology is completely unsupervised and not limited to the conservative–liberal direction, we use a small set of manual labels for interpretation (as detailed in Section 3).

[3]We invite the reader to explore more such examples using the online visualization tool we release with this paper: `http://snap.stanford.edu/quotus/vis`

their leaning is self-declared. An empirical investigation of various characteristics of the outlets and of their articles reveals differences that further motivate the need for an unsupervised approach that is not tied to a predetermined dimension of bias.

Large-scale analysis. To quantify the degree to which the outlet-to-quote bipartite graph encodes a systematic pattern that extends beyond the simple newsworthiness of a quote, we use an unsupervised prediction paradigm.[4] The task is to predict whether a given outlet will select a new quote, based on its previous quoting pattern. We show that, indeed, the patterns encoded in the outlet-to-quote graph can be exploited efficiently via a matrix factorization approach akin to that used by recommender systems. Furthermore, this approach brings significant improvement over baselines that only encode the popularity of the quote and the propensity of the outlet to pick up quotes, showing that these can not fully explain the systematic pattern that drives content selection.

Factorizing the outlet-to-quote matrix provides new insights into the structure of the political media coverage. First, we find that our labeled liberal and conservative outlets are separated in the space defined by the first two latent dimensions. Moreover, a post-hoc analysis of the outlets mapped to the extremes of this space reveals a strong alignment between these two latent dimensions and media type (mainstream vs. independent) and political ideology. The separation between outlets along these dimensions is surprisingly clear, considering that the method is completely unsupervised.

By mapping the quotes onto the same latent space, our method also reveals how the systematic patterns of the media operate at a linguistic level. For example, outlets on the conservative side of the (latent) ideological spectrum are more likely to select Obama's quotes that contain more negations and negative sentiment, portraying an overly negative character.

To summarize the main contributions of this paper:

- we introduce a completely unsupervised framework for analyzing the patterns behind the media's selection of what to cover;
- we apply this framework to a large dataset of presidential speeches and media coverage thereof which we make publicly available together with an online visualization tool (Section 2);
- we reveal systematic biases that are predictive of an outlet's quoting choices (Section 4.1);
- we show that the most important dimensions of bias align with the ideological spectrum and outlet type (Section 4.2);
- we characterize these two dimensions linguistically, exposing striking differences in the way in which different outlets portray reality (Section 4.3).

2. METHODOLOGY

Our analysis framework relies on a bipartite graph that encodes various outlets' selections of quotes to cite. First, we introduce the general methodology for building such a bipartite graph from transcript and news article data. We then apply this methodology to the particular setting in which we instantiate this graph: with speeches delivered by President Obama and a massive collection of news articles.

[4]Our approach is unsupervised in the sense of not using any annotation or prior knowlegde about the bias or leaning of either news outlets or quote content.

2.1 Building an outlet-to-quote graph

Matching. We begin with the two datasets that we wish to match: a set of source statements (in our case, presidential speech transcripts), and a set of news articles. We identify the quotes in each article, and search for a candidate speech and corresponding location within the speech from which the quote originates. We allow approximate matches and align article quotes to the speeches word by word.

In order to avoid false positives, we set a lower bound l on the number of words required in each quote. For each remaining quote, we then examine the speeches that occur before the quote's corresponding article's timestamp to find a match. Since more recent speeches are more likely to be quoted, for performance reasons we search the latest speech first, and proceed backwards. Because matches that are too distant in time are more likely to be spurious, we also limit the set of candidates to speeches that occur at most timespan t before the quote.

We find approximate matches using a variant of the Needleman-Wunsch dynamic programming algorithm for matching strings using substring edit distance. We use an empirically determined similarity threshold s to determine whether a quote matches or not.[5] The output of our matching process is an alignment between article quotes and source statements from the transcripts.

Identifying quote clusters. News outlets often quote the same part of a speech in different ways. Variations result when articles select different subparts of the same statement, or choose different paraphrases of the quote. Sometimes these variations can be semantic while most of the times they are purely syntactic (e.g., resolution of pronouns). For our purposes, we want to consider all variations of a quote as a unique quote phrase that the media outlets choose to distribute. To accomplish this, we group two different quotes into the same *quote cluster* if their matched locations within a transcript overlap on at least five words.

The resulting output is a series of quote clusters, each of which is affiliated with a specific area of the statement transcript. The majority of our analysis considers quotes at the cluster level, instead of looking at individual quote variants.

Article deduplication. To most clearly highlight any relationships between quote selection and editorial slant, we wish to ensure that each quote used in analysis is deliberately chosen by the news outlet that published the corresponding article. However, it is a common practice among news outlets to republish content generated by other organizations. Notably, most news outlets will frequently post articles generated by wire services. Such curated content, while endorsed by the outlet, is not necessarily reflective of the outlet's editorial stance, and we can better differentiate outlet quoting patterns after removing them. Duplicate articles need not necessarily be perfectly identical, so we employ fuzzy string matching using length-normalized Levenshtein edit distance. Among each set of duplicate articles, we keep the one published first.

Outlet-to-quote bipartite graph. The output after executing our pipeline above is a set of (outlet, quote phrase) pairs.[6] As a final step, we turn these pairs into a directed bipartite graph G, with outlets and quote clusters as the two disjoint node sets. An edge $u \rightarrow v$ exists in G if outlet u has an article that picks up a variant of quote v.

[5]In our implementation, we use $l = 6$, $t = 7$ days, and $s = -0.4$.
[6]Some news outlets cite the same quote multiple times across different articles. To minimize the effect of multiple quoting, we keep only the chronologically earliest quote, and disregard the rest.

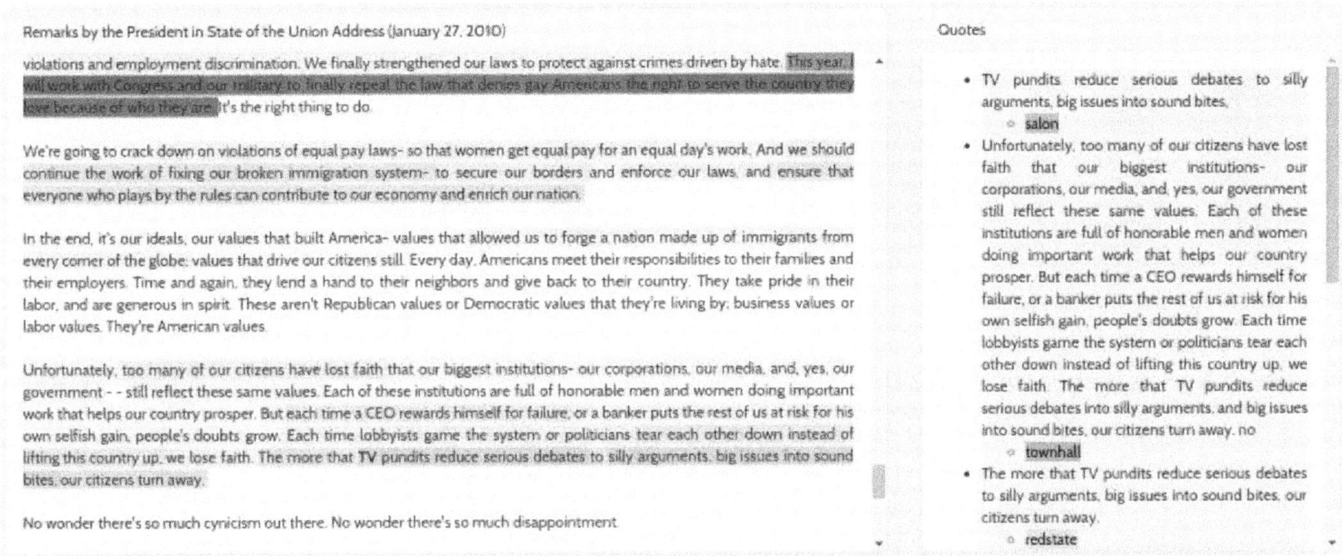

Figure 2: Visualization of the fragment of 2010 State of the Union Address represented in Figure 1 between markers B and C. The left panel shows text highlighted according to quotation volume and slant. The right panel shows all variants of a selected quote cluster. An interactive visualization for the entire dataset is available online at `http://snap.stanford.edu/quotus/vis/`.

Number of news outlets	275
Number of presidential speeches	2,274
Number of unique articles	222,240
Number of unique quotes	267,737
Number of quote clusters	53,504
Number of unique (outlet, cluster) pairs	228,893

Table 2: Statistics of the news article and presidential speech dataset used.

2.2 Dataset description

We construct a database of presidential speeches by crawling the archives of public broadcast transcripts from the White House's web site.[7] In this way we obtain full transcripts of speeches delivered by White House–affiliated personnel, spanning from 2009 to 2014. For the purposes of our analyses, we focus on the paragraphs that are specifically spoken by President Obama. Our news article collection consists of articles spanning from 2009 to 2014; each entry includes the article's title, timestamp, URL, and content. Overall the collection contains over six billion articles. To work with a more manageable amount of data, we run our quote matching pipeline on articles only if they contain the string "Obama", and were produced by one of 275 media outlets from a list that was manually compiled; news outlets on this list were identified as likely to produce content related to politics. Overall, this reduces the collection to roughly 200GB of compressed news article data. Further statistics about the processed data are displayed in Table 2.

Visualization. Finally, we make the matched data publicly available and provide an online visualization to serve as an interface for qualitative investigations of the data.[8]

Figure 2 shows a screenshot of this visualization. Quoted passages have been color-coded with color intensity corresponding to the volume of quotation, and shade corresponding to editorial slant (described in Section 3.1). The right panel displays variations of a selected quote—grouped in one of the quote clusters—as represented by various outlets. Each quote is hyperlinked to the articles containing it. We provide this visualization as a potential tool with which political scientists and other researchers can develop more insight about the structure of political media coverage.

[7] `http://whitehouse.gov`

[8] `http://snap.stanford.edu/quotus/`

3. SMALL-SCALE FOCUSED ANALYSIS

To gain intuition about our data and to better understand the biases that occur in the political news landscape, we first focus our analyses on a small subset of news outlets for which there is an established or suspected bias according to political science research [2, 9, 11]. We conduct an empirical analysis to compare outlets in different label categories in terms of their coverage of the presidential speeches. Then, by interpreting this data as a bipartite graph, we perform a rewiring experiment to quantify the degree to which outlet categories relate to each other. In doing so, we motivate the need for an unsupervised approach to study the structure of political media bias at scale (Section 4).

3.1 Outlet selection

As discussed in the introduction, obtaining reliable labels of outlet political leaning is a challenge that has hindered quantitative analysis of this phenomenon. One of the most common dichotomies considered in the literature is that between liberal and conservative ideologies. We refer to political science research to construct a list of twenty-two outlets which we group in four categories: *declared conservative, suspected conservative, suspected liberal,* and *declared liberal.* Our selection criteria is as follows:

- If an outlet declares itself to be liberal or conservative, or the owner explicitly declares a leaning, we refer to the outlet as declared conservative (dC) or declared liberal (dL). We refer to such outlets as *declared outlets.*
- If several bias-related political science studies [2, 9, 11] consistently suggest that an outlet is liberal or conservative, but

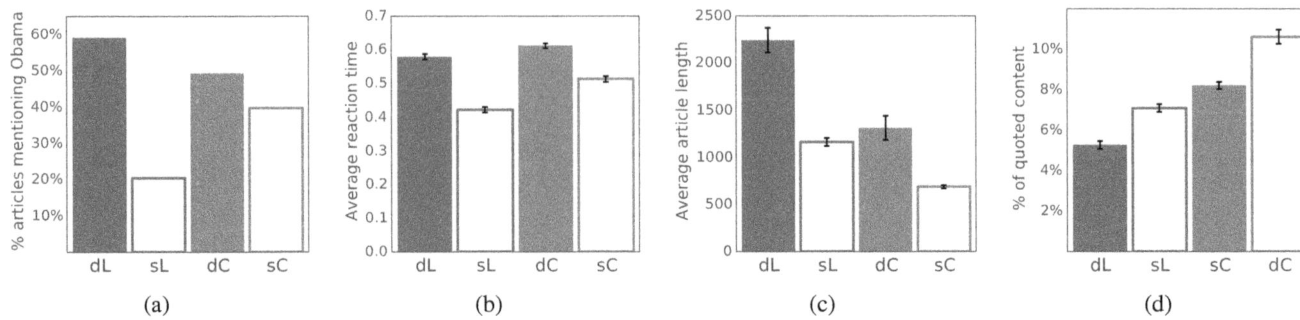

Figure 3: Differences between outlet categories: (a) the fraction of articles mentioning the president; (b) the normalized reaction time to presidential speeches; (c) the average word count of an article; (d) the percentage of quoted content in an article. Filled bars correspond to outlets with declared political slants, and unfilled bars to suspected ones. Error bars indicate standard error.

the outlet itself does not have a declared leaning, we label it as suspected liberal (sL) or suspected conservative (sC). We refer to such outlets as *suspected outlets*.

The labeled outlets considered in this sections is shown in Table 3.

3.2 Outlet and article characteristics

We first perform an empirical analysis to explore the relation between outlet categories. We analyze both general characteristics of the outlets, as well as properties of the articles citing the president.

Percentage of articles discussing Obama. First, we simply measure the percentage of all articles of a given outlet that mention "Obama". Figure 3(a) shows that the fraction of articles discussing the president is generally higher for declared outlets (both liberal and conservative; filled bars) than for suspected ones (unfilled bars). This aligns with the intuition that outlets with a clear ideological affiliation are more likely to discuss political issues.

Reaction time. Declared and suspected outlets also differ in how early they cover popular speech segments. Many sound bites from Obama's more popular speeches, such as the annual state of the union address, are cited by a multitude of outlets. Here we consider quotes that were cited by at least five of the labeled outlets; for each such quote we sort the citing outlets into a relative time ranking between 0 and 1, to normalize for cluster size, where a smaller number indicates a shorter *reaction time*. Aggregated results by outlet category are shown in Figure 3(b). We note that suspected outlets, especially liberal ones, tend to report quotes faster than those with declared ideology.

Article length. We expect the observed difference in reaction time between different categories of outlets to be reflected in the type of articles they publish. The first article feature we investigate is length in words, shown in Figure 3(c). We observe that declared outlets (especially liberal ones) publish substantially longer articles; this difference is potentially related to the longer time that these outlets take to cover the respective speeches.

Fraction of quoted content. To better understand the article-length differences, we examine the composition of the articles in terms of quoted content. In particular, we consider the fraction of words in the article that are quoted from a presidential speech. Figure 3(d) shows that the (generally shorter) declared conservative articles have a considerably higher proportion of presidential content than most declared liberal articles, indicating a different approach to storytelling that relies more on quotes and less on exposition.

Declared Conservative (dC)	**Declared Liberal (dL)**
Daily Caller	Crooks and Liars
National Review	Daily Kos
PJ Media	Mother Jones
Real Clear Politics	The Nation
Reason	Washington Monthly
The Blaze	
Weekly Standard	**Suspected Liberal (sL)**
Town Hall	CBS News
	Chicago Tribune
Suspected Conservative (sC)	CNN
CS Monitor	Huffington Post
Fox News	LA Times
Washington Times	NY Times

Table 3: Labeled outlet categories.

Summary. Our exploration of the characteristics of a small set of labeled outlets reveals differences that go beyond the commonly studied liberal-conservative divide. In particular, we find more substantial differences between self-declared outlets and suspected outlets in terms of their propensity of discussing Obama, their reaction time to new presidential speeches and the length of the articles citing these speeches. Next we will investigate whether these differences also carry over to quoting patterns, and discuss how these observations further motivate an unsupervised approach to the study of media bias.

3.3 Outlet-to-quote graph analysis

We now explore the differences in the quoting patterns of outlets from the four labeled categories. To this end, we explore the structure of the bipartite graph G connecting media outlets to the quotes they cite (introduced in Section 2.1), focusing only the sub-graph induced by the labeled outlets.

We attempt to measure the quoting pattern similarity of outlets from category B to those from category A as the likelihood of a source from category B to cite a quote, given that the respective quote is also cited by some outlet in category A. In terms of the outlet-to-quote graph G, we can quantify this as the average proportion of quotes cited by outlets in A that are also cited by outlets in B:

$$M_G(B|A) = \frac{1}{|o(A)|} \sum_{(u,v)\in o(A)} \frac{1}{|i(v)|} \sum_{(a,b)\in i(v)} \mathbf{1}[a \in B, u \neq a],$$

		A			
		dC	sC	sL	dL
	dC	-3.5	-6.1	-9.7	-3.4
B	sC	0.7	1.4	0.1	1.0
	sL	1.1	5.6	6.1	3.5
	dL	2.1	-3.4	2.4	-3.0

Table 4: Surprise, $S_G(B|A)$, measures how much more likely category B outlets are to cite quotes reported by A outlets, compared to a hypothetical scenario where quoting is random.

where $o(A)$ denotes the set of outbound edges in G with the outlet node residing in A, and $i(v)$ denotes the set of inbound edges in G with v as the destination quote node. We will call $M_G(B|A)$ the *proportion-score* of B given A.

The proportion-score is not directly informative of the quoting pattern similarity since it is skewed by differences in relative sizes of the outlets in each category. To account for these effects, we empirically estimate how unexpected $M_G(B|A)$ is given the observed degree distribution. We construct random graphs by rewiring the edges of the original bipartite graph [23], such that for a large number of iterations we select edges $u_1 \rightarrow v_1$ and $u_2 \rightarrow v_2$ to remove, where $u_1 \neq u_2$ and $v_1 \neq v_2$, and replace these edges with $u_2 \rightarrow v_1$ and $u_1 \rightarrow v_2$.

We use the randomly rewired graphs to build a hypothetical scenario where quoting happens at random, apart from trivial outlet-size effects. We can then quantify the deviation from this scenario using the *surprise* measure, which we defined as follows. Let R denote the set of all rewired graphs; given the original graph G the surprise $S_G(B|A)$ for categories A and B is:

$$S_G(B|A) = \frac{M_G(B|A) - \mathbf{E}_{r \in R} M_r(B|A)}{\sqrt{\mathbf{Var}_{r \in R} M_r(B|A)}}.$$

In other words, surprise measures the average difference between the proportion-score calculated in the original graph G, and the one expected in the randomly rewired graphs, normalized by the standard deviation. Surprise is, therefore, an asymmetric measure of similarity between the quoting patterns of outlets in two given categories, that is not biased by the size of the outlets.

The surprise values between our four considered categories are shown in Table 4. A negative surprise score $S_G(B|A)$ indicates (in units of standard deviation) how much lower the proportion of quotes reported by outlets in A that are also cited by outlets by B is than in a hypothetical scenario where quotes are cited at random. For example, the fact that $S_G(dC|sC)$ is negative indicates that declared conservative outlets are much less likely to cite quotes reported by suspected conservative outlets than by chance, in spite of their suspected ideological similarity. Furthermore, we observe that declared liberal outlets are actually disproportionately more likely to cite quotes that are also reported by declared conservative outlets, in spite of their declared opposing ideologies.

Interestingly, for both categories of declared outlets, we find a high degree of within-category heterogeneity in terms of quoting patterns, with $S_G(dC|dC)$ and $S_G(dL|dL)$ being negative. The reverse is true for suspected outlets: both $S_G(sC|sC)$ and $S_G(sL|sL)$ have positive values that indicate within category homogeneity (e.g., suspected liberal outlets are very likely to cite quotes that other suspected liberal outlets cite). These observations bring additional evidence suggestive of the difference in nature between declared and suspected outlets.

Method	P	R	F_1	MCC
quote popularity	0.07	0.29	0.11	0.12
+ outlet propensity	0.08	0.34	0.13	0.14
matrix completion	**0.25**	0.33	**0.28**	**0.27**

Table 5: Classification performance of matrix completion, compared to the baselines in terms of precision, recall, F_1 score and Matthew's correlation coefficient. Bold scores are significantly better (based on 99% bootstrapped confidence intervals).

Summary. The surprise measure analysis not only confirms that there are systematic patterns in the underlying structure of the outlet-to-quote graph, but also shows that these patterns go beyond a naive liberal-conservative divide. In fact, as also shown by our analysis of outlet and article characteristics, the declared-suspected distinction is often more salient. These results emphasize the limitation of a naive supervised approach to classifying outlets according to ideologies: the outlets which we can confidently label as being liberal or conservative are different in nature from those that we would ideally like to classify. This motivates our unsupervised framework for revealing the structure of political media coverage, which we discuss next.

4. LARGE-SCALE ANALYSIS

In this section we present a fully unsupervised framework for characterizing media bias. Importantly, this framework does not depend on predefined dimensions of bias, and instead uncovers the structure of political media discourse directly from quoting patterns. In order to evaluate our model and confirm the systematicity of media coverage, we formulate the binary prediction task of whether a source will pick up a quote. We then use the low-rank embedding uncovered by our prediction method to analyze and interpret the emerging principal latent dimensions of bias and characterize them linguistically.

4.1 Prediction: matrix completion

We attempt to model the latent dimensions that drive media coverage in a predictive framework that we can objectively evaluate. The task is to predict, for a given media outlet and a given quote from a presidential speech, whether the outlet will choose to report the quote or not.

Formally, we define $X = (x_{ij})$ to be the outlet-by-quote adjacency matrix such that $x_{ij} = 1$ if outlet i cites quote-cluster j and $x_{ij} = 0$ otherwise. In our task, we leave out a subset of the entries, and aim to recover them based on the other entries.

Inspired by recommender systems that reveal latent dimensions of user preferences and item attributes, we use a *low-rank matrix completion* approach. By applying this methodology to news outlets and quotes, we attempt to uncover the dimensions along which quotes vary and along which news outlets manifest their preference for certain types of quotes.

Baselines. We consider, independently, two baselines that do not take media bias into account: the popularity of a quote $\mu_j^q = \mathbf{E}_i x_{ij}$ and the propensity of a news outlet to report quotes from presidential speeches, $\mu_i^s = \mathbf{E}_j x_{ij}$ (where $\mathbf{E}$ is the sample mean).

A simple hypothesis is that quotes are cited only based on their newsworthiness, such that important quotes are cited more often:

$$\hat{x}_{ij} \propto \mu_j^q.$$

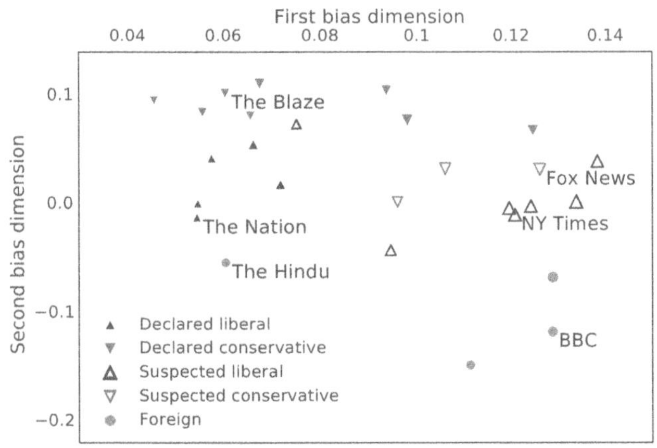

Figure 4: Projection of some of the media outlets onto the first two latent dimensions. Filled and colored markers are outlets with self-declared political slant, such as *The Blaze* and *The Nation*, while unfilled markers are more popular outlets for which slants are suspected, such as *Fox News* and the *New York Times*. Grey circles are international news outlets such as *BBC* and *Hindu Times*. Marker sizes are proportional to the propensity of quoting Obama.

A step further is to also take into account the propensity of an outlet to quote Obama at all:

$$\hat{x}_{ij} \propto \mu_j^q + \mu_i^s.$$

In a world without any media bias, this baseline would be very hard to beat, since all outlets would cover the content proportionally to its importance and to their own capacity, without showing any systematic preference to any particular kind of content.

Low-rank approximation. More realistically, there are multiple dimensions that drive media coverage. To make use of this, we search for a low-rank approximation $\hat{X} \approx \tilde{X}$, where $\tilde{X}$ is constructed as follows:

We start by taking into account quote frequency in the weighted matrix $\bar{X} = (\bar{x}_{ij})$ defined as:

$$\bar{x}_{ij} = \frac{x_{ij}}{\sqrt{\sum x_{:,j}}}.$$

Then, we build a row-normalized $\tilde{X} = (\tilde{x}_{ij})$:

$$\tilde{x}_{ij} = \frac{\bar{x}_{ij}}{||\bar{X}_i||_2}.$$

We estimate $\hat{X}$ as to best reconstruct the observed values (*a*), while keeping the estimate low-rank by regularizing the ℓ_1 norm of its singular values, also known as its *nuclear norm* (*b*) [21]:

$$\text{minimize}_{\hat{X}} \underbrace{\frac{1}{2}||P_\Omega(\tilde{X}) - P_\Omega(\hat{X})||_F^2}_{(a)} + \underbrace{\lambda||\hat{X}||_*}_{(b)},$$

where P_Ω is the element-wise projection over the space of observed values of $\tilde{X}$. To solve the minimization problem, we use a fast alternating least squares method [12].

Results. We leave out 500,000 entries of the outlet-by-quote matrix (out of 14.7 million) and divide them into equal development and test sets. The class distribution is heavily imbalanced, with the positive class (quoting) occurring only about 1.6% of the time. In order to evaluate our model in a binary decision framework, we use Matthew's correlation coefficient as the principal performance metric. We tune the amount of regularization λ and the cutoff threshold on the development set. The selected model has rank 3. Table 5 reports the system's predictive performance on the test set. The latent low-rank model significantly outperforms both the quote popularity baseline as well as the baseline including outlet propensity, showing that the choices made by the media when covering political discourse are not solely explained by newsworthiness and available space. The performance of our model is twice that of the baselines in terms of both F_1 and Matthew's correlation coefficient, and three times better in terms of precision, confirming that the latent quoting pattern bias is systematic and structured. Motivated by our results, next we attempt to characterize the dimension of bias with a spectral and linguistic analysis of the latent low-rank embedding.

High	Middle	Low
weaselzippers.us	motherjones.com	news.com.au
patriotpost.us	nypost.com	news.smh.com.au
hotair.com	economist.com	ottawacitizen.com
freerepublic.com	macleans.ca	nationalpost.com
thegatewaypundit.com	barrons.com	theage.com.au
lonelyconservative.com	whorunsgov.com	canada.com
rightwingnews.com	csmonitor.com	calgaryherald.com
patriotupdate.com	cbsnews.com	edmontonjournal.com
dailycaller.com	latimes.com	aljazeera.net
cnsnews.com	cnn.com	vancouversun.com
wnd.com	villagevoice.com	brisbanetimes.com.au
nationalreview.com	salon.com	montrealgazette.com
americanthinker.com	armytimes.com	bbc.co.uk
theblaze.com	democrats.org	thesun.co.uk
iowntheworld.com	tnr.com	telegraph.co.uk
pjmedia.com	rt.com	dailyrecord.co.uk
angrywhitedude.com	prnewswire.com	independent.co.uk
ace.mu.nu	barackobama.com	theglobeandmail.com

Table 6: Top-most, central and bottom-most news outlets according to the second latent dimension.

4.2 Low-rank analysis

Armed with a low-rank space which captures the predictable quoting behavior patterns of media, we attempt to interpret the latent dimensions and gain insights about these patterns. This low-rank space is given by the singular value decomposition (SVD):

$$\tilde{X} = USV^T,$$

where the rows of U (respectively V) embed outlets (respectively quotes) in the latent space.

We start by looking at the mapping of the labeled outlets, as listed in Table 3, in the space spanned by the latent dimensions. Figure 4 shows that the first two latent dimensions cluster the outlets in interpretable ways. Outlets with high values along the first axis appear to be more mainstream, while outlets with lower values more independent.[9] Along the second dimension, declared conservative outlets all have higher values than declared liberal outlets. International news outlets such as the BBC and Al Jazeera have lower scores. Going beyond our labeled outlets, we look in detail at the projection of news outlets along this dimension in Table 6, showing the outlets with the highest and the lowest dimen-

[9]This characterization is maintained after rewiring the bipartite graph in a way that controls for the number of quotes that each outlet contributes to the data. This dimension is therefore not entirely explained by outlet quoting propensity.

	First dimension of bias
High	The principle that people of all faiths are welcome in this country, and will not be treated differently by their government, is essential to who we are.
	The United States is not, and will never be, at war with Islam. In fact, our partnership with the Muslim world is critical.
	At a time when our discourse has become so sharply polarized [...] it's important for us to pause for a moment and make sure that we are talking with each other in a way that heals, not a way that wounds.
Low	Tonight, we are turning the east room into a bona fide country music hall.
	You guys get two presidents for one, which is a pretty good deal.
	Now, nothing wrong with an art history degree—I love art history.

	Second dimension of bias
High	Those of you who are watching certain news channels, on which I'm not very popular, and you see folks waving tea bags around...
	If we don't work even harder than we did in 2008, then we're going to have a government that tells the American people, "you're on your own."
	By the way, if you've got health insurance, you're not getting hit by a tax.
Middle	Congress passed a temporary fix. A band-aid. But these cuts are scheduled to keep falling across other parts of the government that provide vital services for the American people.
	Keep in mind, nobody is asking them to raise income tax rates. All we're asking is for them to consider closing tax loopholes and deductions.
	The truth is, you could figure out on the back of an envelope how to get this done. The question is one of political will.
Low	By the end of the next year, all U.S. troops will be out of Iraq.
	We come together here in Copenhagen because climate change poses a grave and growing danger to our people.
	Wow, we must come together to end this war successfully.

Table 7: Example quotes by President Obama mapped to top two dimensions of quoting pattern bias.

sion score, as well as outlets in the middle. A post-hoc investigation reveals that all the top outlets can be identified with the conservative ideology. Furthermore, some of the highest ranked outlets on this dimension are self-declared conservative outlets that we did not consider in our manual categorization from Table 3, for example weaselzippers.us, hotair.com and rightwingnews.com. The region around zero, displayed in the second column of Table 6, uncovers some self-declared liberal outlets not considered before, such as democrats.com and President Obama's own blog, barackobama.com, as well as some outlets that are often accused of having a liberal slant, like cbsnews.com and latimes.com. Finally, the outlets with the most negative scores around this dimension are all international media outlets. Given that our framework is completely unsupervised, we find the alignment between the latent dimension and ideology to be surprisingly strong.

4.3 Latent projection of linguistic features

So far we have seen that there are systematic differences in the quoting patterns of different types of media outlets. Since all the quotes we consider are from the same speaker, any systematic linguistic differences that arise have the effect of portraying a different persona of the president by different types of news outlets. By choosing to selectively report certain kinds of quotes by Obama, outlets are able to shape their audience's perception of how the president speaks and what issues he chooses to speak about.

To characterize the effect of this selection, we make use of the fact that the singular value decomposition of $\tilde{X} = USV^T$ provides not only a way of mapping news outlets, but also presidential quotes to the aforementioned latent space. A selection of quotes that map to relevant areas of the space (and that are cited at least five times) is shown in Table 7.

The quote embedding allows us to perform a linguistic analysis of the presidential quotes and interpret the results in the latent bias space. Even though the latent representation is learned in a completely language-agnostic way (starting only from the outlet-quote graph), we find important language-related aspects.

Sentiment. We applied Stanford's sentiment analyzer [30] on the presidential speeches and explore the relationship between the latent dimensions and average sentiment of the paragraph surrounding the quote. We find a negative correlation between the second dimension and sentiment values: the quotes with high values along this dimension, roughly corresponding to outlets ideologically aligned as conservative, come from paragraphs with more negative sentiment (Spearman $\rho = -0.32, p < 10^{-7}$). Figure 5(a) shows how positive and negative sentiment is distributed along the first two latent dimensions. A diagonal effect is apparent, suggesting that outlets clustered in the international and independent region portray a more positive Obama, while more mainstream and conservative outlets tend to reflect more negativity from the president's speeches.

Negation. We also study how the presence of lexical negation (the word *not* and the contraction *n't*) in a quote relates to the probability of media outlets from different regions of the latent bias space to cite that quote. While lexical negation is in some cases related to sentiment, it also corresponds to instances where the president contradicts or refutes a point, potentially relating to controversy. Figure 5(b) shows the likelihood of quotes to contain negation in different areas of the latent space. The effect is similar: quotes with negation seem more likely in the region corresponding to mainstream conservative outlets, possibly because of highlighting the controversial aspects in the president's discourse.

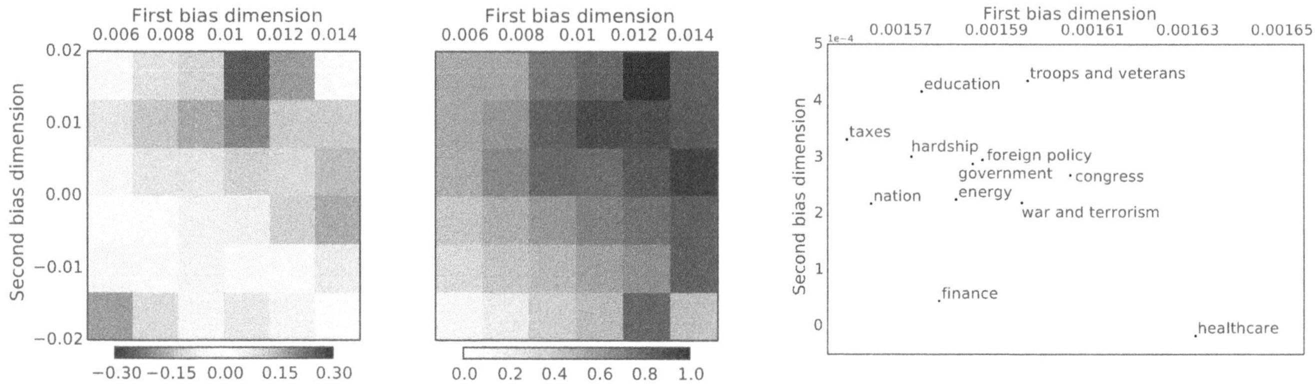

(a) Sentiment (b) Negation (c) Topics

Figure 5: Linguistic features projected on the first two latent dimensions: (a) sentiment of the quoted paragraphs; (b) proportion of quotes that contain negation; (c) dominant topics discussed. Refer to Figure 4 for an interpretation of the latent space in terms of media outlet anchors.

Topic analysis. We train a topic model using Latent Dirichet Allocation [3] on all paragraphs from the presidential speeches. We manually label the topics and discard the ones related to the non-political "background" of the speeches, such as introducing other people and organizing question and answer sessions. We construct a topic–quote matrix $T = (t_{ij})$ such that $t_{ij} = 1$ if the paragraph surrounding quote j in the original speech has topic i as the dominant topic,[10] and 0 otherwise. We scale T so that the rows (topics) sum to 1, obtaining $\tilde{T}$, which we then project to the SVD latent space introduced earlier by solving for L_T in $\tilde{T} = L_T S V^T$. Since V is orthonormal, the projection is given by $L_T = \tilde{T} V S^{-1}$. Figure 5(c) shows the arrangement of the dominant topics in the latent space. Quotes about the troops and war veterans are ranked on the top of the second dimension, corresponding to more conservative outlets, while financial and healthcare quotes occupy the other end of the axis. Healthcare is distanced from other topics on the first axis, suggesting it is a topic of greater interest to mainstream news outlets rather than the more focused, independent media.

Lexical analysis. We attempt to capture a finer-grained linguistic characterization of the space by looking at salient words and bigrams. We restrict our analysis to words and bigrams occurring in at least 100 and at most 1000 quotes. We construct a binary bag-of-words matrix W where $(w_{ij}) = 1$ iff. word or bigram i occurs in quote j. Same as with topics, we scale the rows of W (corresponding to word frequency) to obtain $\tilde{W}$ and project onto the SVD latent space as $L_W = \tilde{W} V S^{-1}$. Among the words that are projected highest on the first axis, we find *republicans*, *cut*, *deficit* and *spending*. Among the center of the ranking we find words and phrases such as *financial crisis*, *foreign oil*, *solar*, *small business*, and *Bin Laden*. The phrase *chemical weapons* also appears near the middle, possibly as an effect of liberal outlets being critical of the decisions former Bush administration. On the negative end of the spectrum, corresponding to international outlets, we find words such as *countries*, *international*, *relationship*, *alliance* and country names such as *Iran*, *China*, *Pakistan*, and *Afghanistan*.

Overall, the mapping of linguistic properties of the quotes in the latent bias space is surprisingly consistent, and suggest that outlets in different regions of this space consistently portray different presidential personae to their audience.

[10] We define a topic to be dominant if its weight is larger by an arbitrary threshold than the second highest weight. We manually label the topics using the ten most characteristic words.

5. FURTHER RELATED WORK

Media bias. Our work relates to an extensive body of literature—spanning across political science, economics and communication studies—that gives theoretical and empirical accounts of media bias and its effects. We refer the reader to a recent comprehensive survey of media bias [26], and focus here on the studies that are most relevant to our approach.

Selection patterns. Several small-scale studies investigate subjects that media outlets select to cover by relying on hand annotated slant labels. For instance, by tracing the media coverage of 32 hand-picked scandal stories, it was shown that outlets with a conservative slant are more likely to cover scandals involving liberal politicians, and vice-versa [27]. Another study [2] focuses on the choices that five online news outlets make with respect to which stories to display in their top news section, and reports that conservative outlets show signs of partisan filtering. In contrast, by relying on an unsupervised methodology, our work explores selection patterns in data involving orders of magnitude more selector agents and items to be selected. Closer to our approach are methods that show political polarization starting from linking patterns in blogs [1] or from the structure of the retweet graph in Twitter [5]. These approaches operate on a predefined liberal-conservative dimension, and assume available political labels. Furthermore, the structure they exploit does not directly apply to the setting of news media articles.

Language and ideology. Recently, natural language processing techniques were applied to identify ideologies in a variety of large scale text collections, including congressional debates [14, 24], presidential debates [19], academic papers [15], books [29], and Twitter posts [4, 33, 34]. All this work operates on a predefined dimension of conservative–liberal political ideology using known slant labels; in the news media domain slant is seldom declared or proven with certainty and thus we need to resort to an unsupervised methodology.

Quote tracking. Recent work has focused quoting practices [31] and on the task of efficiently tracking and matching quote snippets as they evolve, both over a set period of time [16], as well as over an longer, variable period of time [32]. We adapt theis task in order to news article quotes with presidential speech segments and build our outlet-to-quote graph.

6. CONCLUSION

We propose an unsupervised framework for uncovering and characterizing media bias starting from quoting patterns. We apply this framework to a dataset of matched news articles and presidential speech transcripts, which we make publicly available together with an online visualization that can facilitate further exploration.

There is systematic bias in the quoting patterns of different types of news sources. We find that the bias goes beyond simple newsworthiness and space limitation effects, and we objectively quantify this by showing our model to be predictive of quoting activity, without making any *a priori* assumptions regarding the dimension of bias and without requiring labeling of the news domains. When comparing the unsupervised model with self-declared political slants, we find that an important dimension of bias is roughly aligned with an ideology spectrum ranging from conservative, passing through liberal, to the international media outlets.

By selectively choosing to report certain types of quotes by the same speaker, the media has the power to portray different personae of the speaker. Thus, an audience only following one type of media may witness a presidential persona that is different from the one portrayed by other types of media or from what the president tries to project. By conducting a linguistic analysis on the latent dimensions revealed by our framework, we find that differences go beyond topic selection, and that mainstream conservative outlets portray a persona that is characterized by negativism, both in terms of negative sentiment and in use of lexical negation.

Future work. Throughout our analysis, we don't take into account potential changes in a media outlet's behavior over time. Modeling temporal effects could reveal idealogical shifts and differences in issue framing.

Furthermore, natural language techniques can be better tuned to insights from political science in order to produce tools and resources more suited for analyzing political discourse [10]. For instance, exploratory analysis shows that state-of-the-art sentiment analysis tools fail to capture subtle nuances in political commentary and we expect that fine-grained opinion mining can achieve this better [17].

Finally, news sources often take the liberty of skipping or altering certain words when quoting. While these changes are often made to improve readability, we speculate that systematic patterns in such edits could uncover different dimensions of media bias.

Acknowledgements

We would like to acknowledge the valuable input provided by Mathieu Blondel, Flavio Chierichetti, Justin Grimmer, Scott Kilpatrick, Lillian Lee, Alex Niculescu-Mizil, Fabian Pedregosa, Noah Smith and Rebecca Weiss. We are also thankful to the anonymous reviewers for their valuable comments and suggestions. This research has been supported in part by NSF IIS-1016909, NSF IIS-1149837, NSF IIS-1159679, NSF CNS-1010921, DARPA SMISC, Boeing, Facebook, Spinn3r, Volkswagen, and Yahoo.

7. REFERENCES

[1] L. A. Adamic and N. Glance. The political blogosphere and the 2004 US election: divided they blog. In *Proceedings of LinKDD*, 2005.

[2] M. A. Baum and T. Groeling. New media and the polarization of American political discourse. *Political Communication*, 25(4):345–365, 2008.

[3] D. M. Blei, A. Y. Ng, and M. I. Jordan. Latent Dirichlet allocation. *Journal of Machine Learning Research*, 3:993–1022, 2003.

[4] R. Cohen and D. Ruths. Classifying political orientation on Twitter: It's not easy! In *Proceedings of ICWSM*, 2013.

[5] M. D. Conover, B. Goncalves, J. Ratkiewicz, A. Flammini, and F. Menczer. Predicting the political alignment of Twitter users. *IEEE Xplore*, pages 192–199, 2011.

[6] R. J. Dalton, P. A. Beck, and R. Huckfeldt. Partisan cues and the media: Information flows in the 1992 presidential election. *American Political Science Review*, pages 111–126, 1998.

[7] J. T. Gasper. Shifting ideologies? Re-examining media bias. *International Quarterly Journal of Political Science*, 6(1):85–102, 2011.

[8] M. Gentzkow and J. Shapiro. What drives media slant? Evidence from U.S. daily newspapers. *Econometrica*, 78(1):35–71, 2010.

[9] M. Gentzkow and J. M. Shapiro. Ideological segregation online and offline. *National Bureau of Economic Research*, 2010.

[10] J. Grimmer and B. M. Stewart. Text as Data: The Promise and Pitfalls of Automatic Content Analysis Methods for Political Texts. *Political Analysis*, 21(3):267–297, 2013.

[11] T. Groseclose and J. Milyo. A measure of media bias. *The Quarterly Journal of Economics*, 120(4):1191–1237, 2005.

[12] T. Hastie, R. Mazumder, J. Lee, and R. Zadeh. Matrix completion and low-rank SVD via fast alternating least squares. *arXiv preprint arXiv:1410.2596*, 2014.

[13] D. E. Ho. Measuring explicit political positions of media. *Quarterly Journal of Political Science*, 3(4):353–377, 2008.

[14] M. Iyyer, P. Enns, J. Boyd-Graber, and P. Resnik. Political ideology detection using recursive neural networks. In *Proceedings of ACL*, 2014.

[15] Z. Jelveh, B. Kogut, and S. Naidu. Detecting latent ideology in expert text: Evidence from academic papers in economics. In *Proceedings of EMNLP*, 2014.

[16] J. Leskovec, L. Backstrom, and J. Kleinberg. Meme-tracking and the dynamics of the news cycle. In *Proceedings of ACM KDD*, 2009.

[17] J. Li and E. Hovy. Sentiment analysis on the People's Daily. In *Proceedings of EMNLP*, 2014.

[18] M. Liberman. Multiplying ideologies considered harmful. Language Log, 2005.

[19] W.-H. Lin, E. Xing, and A. Hauptmann. A joint topic and perspective model for ideological discourse. In *Machine Learning and Knowledge Discovery in Databases*, pages 17–32. Springer Berlin Heidelberg, 2008.

[20] Y.-R. Lin, J. P. Bagrow, and D. Lazer. More voices than ever? Quantifying media bias in networks. In *Proceedings of ICWSM*, 2011.

[21] R. Mazumder, T. Hastie, and R. Tibshirani. Spectral regularization algorithms for learning large incomplete matrices. *Journal of Machine Learning Research*, 11:2287–2322, 2010.

[22] L. Morales. Distrust in U.S. media edges up to record high. Gallup Politics, 2010.

[23] M. E. Newman, S. H. Strogatz, and D. J. Watts. Random graphs with arbitrary degree distributions and their applications. *Physical Review E*, 64(2):026118, 2001.

[24] V.-A. Nguyen, J. Boyd-Graber, and P. Resnik. Lexical and hierarchical topic regression. In *Proceedings of NIPS*, 2013.

[25] J. S. Peake. Presidents and front-page news: How America's newspapers cover the Bush administration. *The Harvard International Journal of Press/Politics*, 12(4):52–70, 2007.

[26] A. Prat and D. Strömberg. The political economy of mass media. In *Advances in Economics and Econometrics: Tenth World Congress*. Cambridge University Press, 2013.

[27] R. Puglisi and J. M. Snyder. Newspaper coverage of political scandals. *The Journal of Politics*, 73(03):931–950, 2011.

[28] A. J. Schiffer. Assessing partisan bias in political news: The case (s) of local senate election coverage. *Political Communication*, 23(1):23–39, 2006.

[29] Y. Sim, B. Acree, J. H. Gross, and N. A. Smith. Measuring ideological proportions in political speeches. In *Proceedings of EMNLP*, 2013.

[30] R. Socher, A. Perelygin, J. Y. Wu, J. Chuang, C. D. Manning, A. Y. Ng, and C. Potts. Recursive deep models for semantic compositionality over a sentiment treebank. In *Proceedings of EMNLP*, 2013.

[31] S. Soni, T. Mitra, E. Gilbert, and J. Eisenstein. Modeling Factuality Judgments in Social Media Text. In *Proceedings of ACL (short papers)*, 2014.

[32] C. Suen, S. Huang, P. Ekscombatchai, and J. Leskovec. Nifty: A system for large scale information flow tracking and clustering. In *Proceedings of WWW*, 2012.

[33] S. Volkova, G. Coppersmith, and B. Van Durme. Inferring user political preferences from streaming communications. In *Proceedings of ACL*, 2014.

[34] F. M. F. Wong, C. W. Tan, S. Sen, and M. Chiang. Quantifying Political Leaning from Tweets and Retweets. In *ICWSM*, 2013.

Energy and Performance of Smartphone Radio Bundling in Outdoor Environments

†Ana Nika, †Yibo Zhu, §Ning Ding, §Abhilash Jindal, §Y. Charlie Hu, *Xia Zhou
†Ben Y. Zhao and †Haitao Zheng
†UC Santa Barbara, *Dartmouth College, §Purdue University
†{anika, yibo, ravenben, htzheng}@cs.ucsb.edu, *xia@cs.dartmouth.edu, §{ding34,jindal0,ychu}@purdue.edu

ABSTRACT

Most of today's mobile devices come equipped with both cellular LTE and WiFi wireless radios, making radio bundling (simultaneous data transfers over multiple interfaces) both appealing and practical. Despite recent studies documenting the benefits of radio bundling with MPTCP, many fundamental questions remain about potential gains from radio bundling, or the relationship between performance and energy consumption in these scenarios.

In this study, we seek to answer these questions using extensive measurements to empirically characterize both energy and performance for radio bundling approaches. In doing so, we quantify potential gains of bundling using MPTCP versus an ideal protocol. We study the links between traffic partitioning and bundling performance, and use a novel componentized energy model to quantify the energy consumed by CPUs (and radios) during traffic management. Our results show that MPTCP achieves only a fraction of the total performance gain possible, and that its energy-agnostic design leads to considerable power consumption by the CPU. We conclude that not only there is room for improved bundling performance, but an energy-aware bundling protocol is likely to achieve a much better tradeoff between performance and power consumption.

Categories and Subject Descriptors

C.4 [**Performance of Systems**]: Measurement techniques, Modeling techniques; C.2.3 [**Network Operations**]: Network management

Keywords

Radio Bundling; Energy Consumption; Throughput Performance

1. INTRODUCTION

Connectivity options for mobile devices have dramatically evolved in the last decade. First, for today's mobile devices, multiple wireless interfaces *e.g.* cellular, WiFi and Bluetooth, are the norm, not the exception. Second, cellular LTE is not only widely deployed, but offers peak download rates that match or surpass modern WiFi speeds. In a world of ever-increasing demands for improved network performance, these factors make the concept of *radio bundling* both practical and highly appealing.

A flow using radio bundling transfers data simultaneously over multiple wireless networks [1, 2, 20, 26, 35, 27], and works best at locations where WiFi and LTE performance is comparable. Today's mobile data access is dominated by public or outdoor locations, where WiFi cannot match the performance of residential/private environments due to range limitations and uncontrolled contention between public WiFi users. Our own measurements across five US cities show that smartphones' outdoor WiFi throughput varies significantly between 0.21Mbps and 14.5Mbps, while LTE throughput at the same locations mostly range between 1Mbps to as high as 16Mbps. Another measurement study has shown that the median LTE throughput is 4-5 times higher than that of WiFi while the performance of the 3G family largely lags behind LTE [21].

While it is tempting to draw early conclusions about the efficacy and practicality of radio bundling for mobile devices, many fundamental questions remain. First, what are the performance limits of radio bundling under constraints of realistic environments? What is the *maximum* benefit that can be provided by bundling on today's devices, assuming we had an ideal transport protocol to take advantage of available bandwidth? Second, what are the energy costs of achieving that performance gain, given the increasing power demands of today's mobile applications? What role, if any, does traffic management and the CPU play in the energy profile of radio bundling protocols? Answers to these fundamental questions will shed light on the true relationship between energy consumption and bundling performance, and enable us not only to understand the performance and energy profile of current protocols, but to predict the behavior of future protocols.

The goals of our work sets it apart from prior work in several ways. First, where we seek to understand the fundamental limits of radio bundling, prior work on radio bundling consistently rely on experiments with MPTCP [31] as the default transport protocol. These studies provide a single data point in the performance vs. energy tradeoff space. And since MPTCP was not designed for wireless interfaces or considering energy constraints, these results often underestimate the potential benefits of bundling. Second, we seek to build a detailed and accurate *componentized* energy model for mobile devices, which would allow us to attribute energy consumption to specific components like the CPU. This is critical to a true understanding of the CPU's role in energy consumption in bundling scenarios. Finally, given the close relationship between energy consumption and performance, we consider it critical to characterize energy and performance on full protocol implementations on actual mobile devices.

Measurement Methodology. Our measurement study includes three key steps. *First*, we instrumented multiple LTE-capable An-

WWW 2015, May 18–22, 2015, Florence, Italy.
ACM 978-1-4503-3469-3/15/05.
http://dx.doi.org/10.1145/2736277.2741635.

droid smartphones to operate simultaneously on both LTE and WiFi networks, and developed an Android application that enables data transfers using bundling. We performed measurements at 63 outdoor locations in 5 US cities, characterizing energy and network performance for both radio bundling and single radio methods. *Second*, for both bundling and single radio methods, we developed accurate power models to characterize total and individual contributions of both the dual-core CPU and network interfaces (WiFi and LTE). *Finally*, we performed detailed analysis to identify critical issues in implementing smartphone radio bundling, *e.g.* traffic partitioning. We also implemented and compared a protocol-level solution (MPTCP [31]) against an application-level solution on both energy and network performance.

We summarize our key findings below.

- *Performance*: We empirically characterize energy and performance of radio bundling protocols in the wild, and compare two different bundling implementations (optimal bundling that maximizes throughput and MPTCP). Bundling always outperforms single radio access methods (*e.g.*, best radio, radio switching) in network throughput. More importantly, performance gain varies significantly across different RF environment conditions, and is sensitive to the relative throughput between WiFi and LTE links.
- *Energy Consumption*: We provide the first detailed power model on radio bundling that characterizes contributions of individual components (dual-core CPU and two radio interfaces). Bundling dual radios increases instantaneous power draw, but total energy is lowered by reduction in transfer times. More importantly, we show that the CPU can be a key contributor to energy consumption, and must be carefully considered in any energy-aware bundling solution. When modeling energy consumption in bundling protocols, our energy profiler achieves <8% error rate, compared to 17% in the state of the art [23].
- *Performance vs. Energy Tradeoff*: Finally, our measurements and analysis show that performance gains from bundling are heavily dependent on traffic partitioning algorithms, and naive approaches can actually perform worse than single radio operations. Most importantly, MPTCP achieves only between 40%-85% of the total gains possible from bundling, and incurs a considerable energy cost in its CPU utilization. Clearly, there is both a need and an opportunity to design an energy-aware radio bundling protocol with an improved energy-performance tradeoff.

Limitations and Future Work. Our measurement study has several limitations that we plan to address in future work. *First*, because bundling is rarely used today, we only study its performance from a single user perspective without considering its network-level impact in case of wide adoption. We believe that our results can stimulate development and adoption of bundling systems, and build the groundwork for studies of network impact. *Second*, we did not consider network service costs, which can affect a user's decision on bundling and limit the amount of data transfer on LTE. We plan to investigate how bundling performs subject to this constraint in a separate study. *Finally*, while our methodology is general, our study focused on the two most popular Android phone models. We believe conclusions from our energy and performance analyses are indicative of typical smartphones today, and we are planning to expand our study to other phone/OS models.

The rest of our paper is organized as follows. First, we describe in Section 2 our methodology for enabling radio bundling, as well as our two implementations for traffic partitioning (optimal-throughput and MPTCP). Next in Section 3, we describe in detail our novel energy model for decomposing energy consumption between the CPU and network interfaces, and validate it using experimental measurements. In Section 4, we describe our data collection and dataset. This is followed by detailed analysis of performance and energy consumption in Sections 5 and 6. Finally, we describe related work in Section 7 and conclude (Section 8).

2. ENABLING & OPTIMIZING BUNDLING

Our goal is to empirically examine the performance of smartphone radio bundling at scale. In this section, we highlight the two key components of radio bundling, *turning on both radios simultaneously* and *partitioning traffic between the two radios*. We also describe our Android experimentations that evaluate radio bundling with different traffic partitioning approaches.

2.1 Turning on Both Radios

By default, modern smartphone operating systems (Android, iOS, and Windows Mobile) do not allow simultaneous use of cellular and WiFi networks. Even when the cellular connection is set to "always enabled," a smartphone will always automatically stop forwarding data packets to the cellular interface when it establishes a WiFi connection.

Using Android phones, we overcome this restriction by leveraging a small set of undocumented Android APIs, *i.e.* core API calls implemented in the *ConnectivityManager* class. The key is an API call that forces the cellular network to remain on even after a WiFi connection is made. Using these APIs, we reconfigured the Android operating system to split the routing table and forward data traffic to both WiFi and cellular radio interfaces. Depending on which source IP address they use, packets are forwarded through either the WiFi interface or the cellular interface.

On top of this modification, we developed an Android application that enables bundling-based data transfers using parallel HTTP[1] connections over both WiFi and LTE. We use the Apache HTTP Java library to open HTTP connections, since it allows us to specify a local network interface when opening an HTTP connection. We create two threads to manage the two parallel HTTP connections. To download (or upload) files concurrently on both interfaces, we set one local address to the cellular network IP and the other to the WiFi network IP. We partition HTTP downloads (or uploads) on the granularity of bytes, by specifying the start and end points of the requested segment in the HTTP header. To monitor each transfer, we also add an extra monitoring thread that continuously logs, every 100ms, LTE and WiFi signal strength, CPU frequency and usage; we also record downloaded (and uploaded) bytes by running two parallel *tcpdump* commands that listen to the two radio interfaces respectively. Later in §3 we show that these traces are used to project energy consumption of the data transfer.

2.2 Traffic Partitioning

The second component is partitioning data traffic between the two radio interfaces. This can be implemented as a stand-alone scheduler, or integrated into the transport protocol. In our experiments, we use the stand-alone scheduler to evaluate bundling with the optimal traffic partitioning that maximizes throughput, and compare it to MPTCP, which embeds traffic partitioning in TCP.

Optimal. The stand-alone scheduler determines the amount of data to transfer on each radio. The simplest approach is to equally partition the transfer amount between the two radios. But the data transfer ends when the weaker radio finishes its transmission. Instead, to maximize bundling throughput, an optimal sched-

[1]The majority of mobile applications and streaming services (*e.g.* YouTube and Netflix) use HTTP [22, 25].

uler should partition traffic such that both radios finish their assigned transfer at the same time.

Using the bundling application described in the above, we can emulate bundling with optimal traffic partitioning. Specifically, in each measurement we transfer a large chunk of data on each radio, and record the corresponding packet traces. We then "play-back" these traces based on the traffic partitioning algorithm till the total downloaded (or uploaded) bytes from both radios reaches the target transfer size. This play-back analysis enables us to identify, for each data transfer, the throughput (and delay) performance as well as the energy drain. We will discuss this further in §4.1.

MPTCP. An alternative is to integrate traffic partitioning into the transport layer protocol. Existing works [13, 23] have studied MPTCP [31] as a method to using multiple radios simultaneously. MPTCP is a transport layer protocol for multipath communications. It partitions data transfer on the fly by observing each radio's buffer status. In §5 and §6 we compare the performance and energy of MPTCP to those of optimal bundling described in the above.

To do so, we must first port MPTCP to smartphones. While prior efforts have ported MPTCP to two Android phone models [3], both models are outdated and do not support LTE. Instead, we were able to port MPTCP to the popular Galaxy Note phone by configuring the phone to Android 4.0.4, Linux kernel 3.0.8 and instrumenting all the required changes to realize MPTCP. To support data transfer in MPTCP, we set up an HTTP server on port 8080 because cellular carriers (AT&T in our case) remove all TCP header options on port 80. Finally, we note that a recent measurement study [13] has shown that the choice of the radio for the primary subflow, *i.e.* the radio to turn on first, can affect MPTCP performance. However, there is no existing mechanism on how to choose this radio optimally. Thus, for our experiments we follow the default configuration in the original MPTCP implementation [3].

3. AN ACCURATE ENERGY MODEL

Another goal of our study is to understand the energy drain of radio bundling and radio selection. In this section, we describe the methodology we used to capture the energy drain of each data transfer using either radio bundling or selection.

3.1 Key Features

Accurately measuring the energy drain of radio bundling on phones in the wild is challenging. One option is to use a power meter (as in [13]). However, such an approach suffers two drawbacks: (a) the power meter is difficult to carry in field experiments and (b) it can only report the energy drain of the entire phone. Instead, we develop an accurate power model that captures the energy drain of critical phone components used in radio bundling, *i.e.*, the CPU and network interfaces, during each data transfer. Using this model, we can accurately project energy consumption of each data transfer from the CPU log and packet trace. Our projection achieves an error rate of <8%, compared to 17% reported by [23].

Compared with previous works studying radio bundling or radio selection, our proposed energy model includes two key new features that significantly boost the model's accuracy.

Accurately Accounting for CPU Drain. In all of the recent studies on modeling power draw of cellular network interfaces (*e.g.*, [7, 21, 24, 30]) and MPTCP [23], none identified the portion of the power consumed by the CPU during data transfers, *i.e.* from interrupt handling and network stack processing. As we will show in our experiments, the CPU power draw accounts for a significant portion of the total energy consumption during data transfers (up to 39% for radio bundling and even 80% for WiFi-only), and hence not modeling the CPU power drain during data transfer can lead to significant error in power modeling[2].

We develop accurate power models for the dual-core CPU and WiFi and LTE interfaces for the phones used in our experiments. These models allow us to not only accurately derive the total energy drain of data transfers but also study the energy-throughput tradeoffs of radio bundling versus using a single radio. Our model validation below shows that incorporating CPU power modeling improves energy estimation error of data transfers to be within 8.3%.

Incorporating Signal Strength. A recent work [15] showed that the power draw of cellular and WiFi interfaces is significantly affected by the wireless signal strength. But, none of the recent work on radio selection or bundling [23] took into consideration the impact of wireless signal strength on the accuracy of power modeling. In contrast, we develop accurate signal-strength-aware power models for LTE and WiFi for the phones used in our experiments and use them in our study of energy drain of data transfers in the wild.

3.2 Model Details

CPU Power Modeling. To capture the CPU power draw during data transfers we first developed a power model for the dual-core CPUs used in the two smartphones. In training the model, we used the power meter to measure the power draw of the CPU under different frequencies with only one core turned on, while running microbenchmarks. We then repeated the process with both cores turned on. Table 2 in Appendix A shows the CPU power draw at 100% CPU utilization for both phones under a range of frequencies. Single-core results are shown with Core1 turned off.

To use the CPU model in data transfer experiments, we logged the frequencies of the two cores as well as each core's utilization once every 100ms during data transfers. Then in post-processing, we predicted the CPU power over each 100ms time interval based on the logged CPU frequency and utilization, *i.e.* as the power draw at that frequency under 100% utilization weighted by its actual utilization. Finally, we summed up the energy consumed by the CPU in each 100ms bin to arrive at the total CPU energy consumption for the entire data transfer.

WiFi and LTE Power Modeling. WiFi and LTE interfaces have multiple power states (see Appendix A) and the power draw and duration at each state and state transitions are affected by the wireless signal strength in significant ways [15]. To develop signal-strength-aware WiFi and LTE power models for our phones, we followed the procedure in [15]. Specifically, in training the models, we connected the phone to the power meter and ran data transfer microbenchmarks. While the power meter collects the power profile, we also recorded the traffic via tcpdump alongside signal strength values via Android APIs as well as core frequencies and the CPU utilization. We varied the signal strength received by the phone by adjusting the distance between the phone and the AP for WiFi experiments and changing the location of the phone for LTE experiments. In post-processing, we synchronized the power profile from the power meter, tcpdump and signal strength traces. We derived the power draw by the radio interface(s) by subtracting the CPU power from the total power. We inferred the different power states of LTE and WiFi following the procedure in [21, 15] and derived the various parameters of the signal-strength-aware power state machine for each interface (see Appendix A).

To use the power models to estimate the power draw by different interfaces during data transfer experiments, we collected *tcpdump* data and signal strength traces on each interface during data transfers. Then in post-processing, we drove our power state machines

[2]In fact, the authors of [23] reported 17% error in power modeling.

Table 1: Average prediction error of total energy on Galaxy S III

Transfer Size (MB)	0.5	1	2	4	5
Error under					
WiFi	5.5%	4.0%	7.2%	8.1%	5.4%
LTE	7.6%	1.0%	8.1%	2.6%	3.0%
Bundling	7.0%	1.7%	3.0%	3.9%	8.3%

using our tcpdump traces, and recorded the total energy consumed by each interface as it transitions between its power states.

3.3 Model Validation

We validated the above CPU/WiFi/LTE power models as follows. We use the same app as used in our measurement experiments to perform 0.5MB, 1MB, 2MB, 4MB, and 5MB data transfers, under WiFi only, LTE only, and bundling the two, respectively, at 10 random locations on the two measurement phones. During each download (or upload), the power meter is connected to the phone to read the actual power draw, and the CPU frequencies, tcpdump and signal strength traces are collected. We calculate the accuracy of the power models by comparing the predicted total energy drain against that of the power meter reading.

Table 1 shows the results for Galaxy SIII phones. The results for Galaxy Note are similar and omitted. We observe that the average prediction errors vary between 4–8.1%, 1–8.1%, and 1.7–8.3%, under the three radio scenarios respectively.

Difference from Existing Power Models. Our power models for individual radios differ from those in [21]. One key cause is the difference in phones used in the measurement: [21] used an HTC phone (Qualcomm Snapdragon S2 MSM8655 SoC, Android 2.2.1 OS) while we use two newer models: Samsung Galaxy Note (Qualcomm Snapdragon S3 MSM8660 SoC, Android 4.0.4 OS) and Samsung Galaxy SIII (Snapdragon S4 MSM8960 SoC, Android 4.0.4 OS). The other cause is the newer LTE deployment. For example, an author of [21] has confirmed with us they now also observe zero tail power for LTE on their HTC phone (which was 1000mW in [21]), same as in our LTE model (Table 3).

4. DATA COLLECTION

Before presenting the results of our throughput and energy analysis, we first describe the underlying data collection process that allow us to explore and compare radio bundling and selection efficiently. We then describe the resulting dataset used for our analysis.

4.1 Efficient Data Collection

To evaluate radio bundling/selection, we seek to compare six different options in radio usage: *LTE-only*, *WiFi-only*, *Best Radio* [14] (*i.e.* using the better radio), *Radio Switching* [26], MPTCP, and *Bundling* (with optimal data partitioning).

To do so, we face two immediate challenges. *First*, we need to ensure a fair, consistent comparison across all six options. One might use six collocated smartphones, one for each option, to perform data transfer simultaneously. This, however, introduces local traffic contention in both LTE and WiFi networks that pollutes the results. An alternative is to sequentially test each option in isolation, which can also introduce discrepancy due to temporal variations in both signal quality and network traffic. *Second*, it is important to understand the impact of transfer file size, which has been shown to largely affect the MPTCP performance [23, 13]. Yet experimenting with individual file sizes is extremely time consuming and faces the same temporal discrepancy problem.

Coupling Measurements with Replay Analysis. We address these challenges by combining sequential measurements with packet trace "replay" analysis. Specifically, we perform multiple rounds of data transfer experiments in each location. In each round of experiments, we configure the smartphones to operate in one of the three modes sequentially ("Bundling", "MPTCP", "single-radio") and record detailed packet traces. For "single-radio" we use two identical and collocated smartphones, each with only one radio on and performing data transfer (download or upload) of size xMB in total. For "MPTCP" we turn on both radios and perform data transfer of xMB in total. For "Bundling" we turn on both radios and run our bundling application to download (or upload) xMB on each individual radio[3]. For our study, we chose $x = 5MB$ so that the maximum transfer size is $5MB$. For all the experiments/locations, we observed that the three sequential experiments were separated by at most $5s$-$10s$. This time lag is small and thus the variation in network traffic condition should be small. We also examined signal strength variability during our experiments to confirm that signal strength patterns for both radio interfaces remained nearly identical across the three experiments.

Next, we perform "replay" analysis on the collected packet traces, from which we derive throughput and energy performance at varying transfer sizes. Given a target file transfer size y ($y \leq 5MB$), we identify the corresponding segment of packet traces by terminating the "replay" at the time point where the total transfer reaches y. Applying the same methodology, we characterize performance of radio switching [26] and radio selection [14] by determining the target file transfer size on each radio accordingly. For these two options, we consider their ideal realization that maximizes the average throughput. That is, we assume they all make the optimal decision on the choice of radio or traffic partitioning between the two radios. For Best Radio we compare the average throughput of WiFi-only and LTE-only and pick the radio with the better throughput. For Radio Switching we monitor the instantaneous throughput of both radios continuously to make the optimal switching decision. We use the switching overhead measured by [26].

4.2 Dataset

Our efforts produced data transfer measurements at 63 *outdoor* locations in 5 US cities, Boston (MA), Chicago (IL), Lafayette (IN), Miami (FL), Santa Barbara (CA), between March and October 2013. Our experiments used two Android phones: Galaxy Note and Galaxy SIII[4]. Among all the measurement locations, 32 locations were using Galaxy Note and 31 using Galaxy SIII. At each location, we performed 6 rounds of data transfer measurements, 3 for download and 3 for upload. This produced a total of 378 measurement instances where each instance contains the packet traces for all six radio usage options.

All measurement locations had LTE cellular services and public WiFi connections, *i.e.* outdoor malls, coffee shops and campus networks. We used the AT&T LTE network in all the experiments. While both phones support 802.11a/b/g/n in 2.4GHz and 5GHz, we found that all WiFi connections in our experiments used 802.11b/g/n in 2.4GHz. We performed all experiments with only our measurement applications running and no applications running in the background.

Representing RF conditions. Our measurements at locations across multiple cities allow us to evaluate radio bundling/selection

[3]The extra data transfer for "Bundling" is to ensure that we can always emulate bundling with optimal traffic partitioning.

[4]While there are differet varieties of Android LTE-capable phones, our experiments used the above two smartphones because at the time of our experiments they were the two *most popular Android phones* and their radio chipsets were the two *most used chipsets* among all LTE-capable Android phones [4].

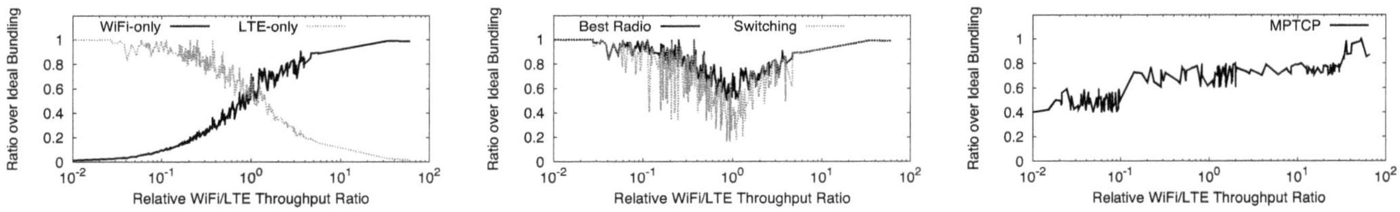

(a) Static selection vs. Bundling, avg throughput (b) Online selection vs. Bundling, avg throughput (c) MPTCP vs. Bundling, avg throughput

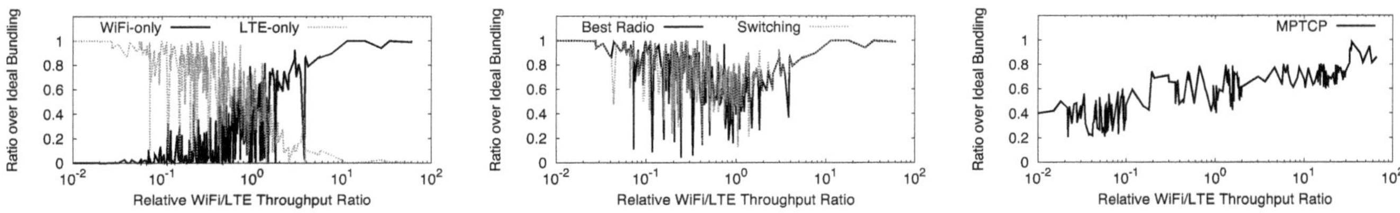

(d) Static selection vs. Bundling, tail throughput (e) Online selection vs. Bundling, tail throughput (f) MPTCP vs. Bundling, tail throughput

Figure 1: Comparing the five radio usage options with Bundling in terms of average and tail throughput. The result is shown as the ratio of throughput over Bundling R_X for option X vs. the relative WiFi/LTE throughput q.

under different RF conditions. We capture these conditions in terms of the *relative quality* of the two radios. That is, we compute the average throughput of WiFi and LTE, and define the relative quality as $q = \frac{thpt_{WiFi}}{thpt_{LTE}}$. For example, $q = 10^{-2}$ means that WiFi throughput is 100x weaker than LTE, and $q = 10^2$ means that WiFi is 100x faster than LTE in average.

Next, we perform detailed analysis on this dataset to understand the throughput and energy performance of radio bundling over radio selection and MPTCP.

5. THROUGHPUT ANALYSIS

We now present our analysis on bundling throughput. Our goal is to understand whether radio bundling provides large advantages in data throughput over radio selection, and if so, where the gain comes from. In addition, we also seek to identify whether today's bundling implementation, *i.e.* MPTCP, can fulfill this potential.

Throughput (or Delay) Metrics. For this, we evaluate the six radio usage options based on two throughput metrics. The first metric is *average throughput*, computed as the total transfer amount divided by the total transfer time. The second metric is *tail throughput*, computed as the bottom 10 percentile value of the instantaneous throughput during the data transfer, where the instantaneous throughput is computed every $100ms$. Essentially, the average throughput directly reflects the overall download (or upload) delay, while the tail throughput reflects the maximum instantaneous delay in each direction.

Using the dataset described in §4, we compare the five radio usage options (LTE-only, WiFi-only, Best Radio, Radio Switching, MPTCP) to Bundling (with optimal data partitioning) in terms of the normalized ratio over Bundling:

$$R_X = \frac{THOUGHPUT_X}{THOUGHPUT_{bundling}}, \quad (1)$$

where X is one of the five options. As mentioned in §4, we apply sequential measurements with replay data analysis such that the comparison across different options is fair and consistent. We mix the results of the two smartphones as well as download and upload scenarios because they lead to the same pattern in R_X.

5.1 Bundling vs. Radio Selection

We first compare Bundling to static radio selection, *i.e.* LTE-only and WiFi-only, and online radio selection, *i.e.* Best Radio and Radio Switching. In Figure 1 we plot the R_X results against q, the relative WiFi/LTE quality, for both the average and tail throughput. We have tested different data transfer sizes between 512K and 5MB, and found that they led to similar trends (discussed later in §5.3 and Figure 3). For brevity we only show the results for 5MB.

Improvement over Static Radio Selection. Figure 1(a) shows that in terms of average throughput, the R_X of the two static radio selection options are both strongly correlated with q, *i.e.* $R_{LTE-only} \approx \frac{1}{1+q}$ and $R_{WiFi-only} \approx \frac{q}{1+q}$. This is because the throughput of Bundling is pretty much the sum of the LTE radio throughput and the WiFi throughput.

On the other hand, Figure 1(d) shows that in terms of tail throughput, the gain of Bundling is much more evident and displays a larger variance over q. For example, the gain can reach more than 19x when LTE is 5-10x stronger than WiFi. This is because during data transfer, each individual radio often experiences temporal variations in signal quality, *e.g.* due to channel fading or interference. Even after averaging over 100ms, the corresponding "instantaneous" throughput trace can still contain deep holes. Bundling, on the other hand, can effectively suppress these deep holes by using both radios simultaneously.

Improvement over Online Radio Selection. For *Best Radio* that always picks the stronger radio for data transfer, the R_X of average throughput is the upper bound of WiFi-only and LTE-only: $R_X \approx \max(\frac{1}{1+q}, \frac{q}{1+q})$. In this case, Bundling is the most beneficial (*i.e.* with 2x throughput gain) when the two radios have similar throughput ($q = 1$). In terms of tail throughput, the gain of Bundling can be significant (>10x) regardless of q. This is because Best Radio still uses the same radio for the entire data transfer who can experience deep fades over time.

When it comes to *Radio Switching* which selects the stronger radio on the fly, the gain of Bundling can reach 5x for average throughput and 10x for tail throughput (see Figure 1(b)(e)). This is somewhat surprising since Radio Switching should perform better than Best Radio. We found that this is due to the overhead of Radio Switching. As shown by [26], the minimum time to switch from cellular to WiFi is 1212ms and from WiFi to cellular 196ms, during which data transmission is disabled. As a reference, we also compared Bundling to instantaneous Radio Switching, *i.e.* zero switching delay, and found that Bundling still achieves up to 2x throughput gain.

Source of Bundling Gain. Our results show that radio Bundling can significantly boost smartphone throughput. Next we dig deeper in our results to understand the key triggers for such improvement. Specifically, we seek to understand whether Bundling can fully utilize both radios. One concern is that Bundling could negatively affect the performance of each single radio, *e.g.* due to CPU competition or radio interference.

To answer this question, we compare each radio's individual throughput with and without bundling using our measurements on WiFi-only, LTE-only and Bundling[5]. Our results (omitted for brevity) confirm that for both WiFi and LTE radios, throughput remains similar with and without bundling. This shows that at least for two popular Android phones [5, 6], bundling LTE and WiFi radios does not negatively impact each radio's performance. That is, the throughput achieved by Bundling is the sum of each radio's throughput operating in isolation.

We suspect that the observed radio independence is due to two factors. *First*, the carrier frequencies of LTE (700/1700MHz) and WiFi (2.4GHz) are widely separated, so the two co-located radios do not physically interfere with each other. *Second*, modern smartphones have two CPU cores, and multi-threaded applications such as our bundling application minimize CPU contention by spreading load across cores. We confirm this via observing the CPU utilization on the two cores (Core 0 and Core 1) of Galaxy Note and Galaxy SIII phones. Specifically, we observe that for all the experiments without bundling, Core 0 is utilized while Core 1 is rarely used. Yet during bundling, Core 1's utilization increases largely while that of Core 0 remains unaffected.

5.2 Bundling vs. MPTCP

Figure 1(c) and (f) compare MPTCP to Bundling with optimal traffic partitioning. In terms of average throughput, MPTCP is able to achieve 40%-85% of the optimal bundling performance. The gap is slightly larger for tail throughput. A more detailed analysis on the traces reveals that the performance gap is mostly caused by the fact that MPTCP often "sacrifices" its throughput to maintain fairness between MPTCP and non-MPTCP clients. For example, if one radio path becomes congested, MPTCP immediately lowers the data transfer on this path more than that of conventional TCP designs. Thus, the current MPTCP design is unable to fully utilize both radios during bundling.

We also observe that compared to radio selection, MPTCP is insensitive to the relative RF condition between WiFi and LTE. This comes from the fact that MPTCP can utilize two radios simultaneously that compensate each other during deep fades. However, when the difference between LTE and WiFi radios is large ($q < 10^{-1}$ and $q > 10^{1}$), online radio selection outperforms MPTCP largely. This is partially because our online radio selection assumes optimal choice of radio to use while MPTCP uses a sub-optimal traffic partitioning algorithm.

Importance of Traffic Partitioning. To further understand the impact of traffic partitioning on Bundling performance, we repeat our analysis using three sub-optimal traffic partitioning algorithms:

- *Even*: It simply partitions the data transfer into two equal parts, one for each radio.
- *Naive*: It first sends a small amount of data, *e.g.* 100KB[6] on the two radios to estimate their throughputs. It then partitions data based on the ratio of the two throughput values.

[5]As discussed earlier in §4, while these measurements take place sequentially, we only consider data where the signal strength pattern remains similar across all three measurements.

[6]We tried 200KB and 300KB and they led to similar results.

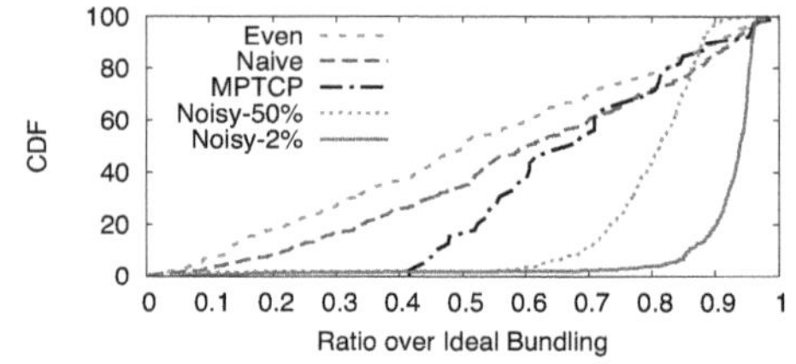

Figure 2: Impact of traffic partitioning in bundling implementation.

- *Noisy*: It assumes a *noisy* estimate of the average throughput for each radio over time, and uses this metric to estimate the transfer amount for each interface. For this, we add zero-mean Gaussian noise on the actual average throughput and set its standard deviation to be 2% (and 50%) of the actual average throughput.

Figure 2 compares the above algorithms and MPTCP to the Bundling with optimal traffic partitioning. We make three key observations. *First*, algorithms like "even" that do not consider the current radio quality perform poorly. In fact it is often worse than single radio methods. *Second*, bundling performance is sensitive to errors in projecting each radio's throughput. Among Naive, Noisy-2% and Noisy-50%, Naive performs the worst because it uses the instantaneous throughput measured in the first 400-600ms to estimate the average throughput over time, leading to the largest prediction error. For 90% of the measurement instances, Noisy-2% achieves at least 85% of the optimal bundling throughput, while Noisy-50% achieves at least 70%. This again demonstrates the importance of accurate throughput estimation in implementing bundling. Finally, by partitioning traffic on the fly based on buffer status, MPTCP lies in between Naive and Noisy-50%. Thus, there is definitely room for further improvement.

5.3 Impact of Data Transfer Size

We also carry out our throughput analysis under transfer data size between 512KB to 5MB. We chose these file sizes because recent measurement studies have shown that smartphone traffic is dominated by large media flows that consist of data chunks of 1MB or larger [22]. For example, typical YouTube files are divided in blocks of size 512KB, while Netflix transfers blocks of either 1.8MB or 5.2MB in size [12].

Figure 3 plots, for the five transfer sizes between 512KB and 5MB, the CDF of R_X (for average throughput) across all measurement instances. We observe similar trends in tail throughput and omit the results for brevity. For both MPTCP and the four configurations of radio selection, the statistics of R_X remain consistent across all transfer sizes. The values of R_X are slightly higher for 512KB and 1MB transfers, but quickly converge as the transfer size grows. This is mostly because TCP slow start prevents the bundling link to be fully utilized and the effect is more visible for small transfers.

5.4 Summary of Results

Overall, our results indicate that the gain of radio Bundling over radio selection and MPTCP is consistent across transfer sizes above 512KB. Thus, Bundling, with optimal traffic partitioning, can consistently boost throughput for most smartphone media applications that demand high throughput. The bundling gain comes from two factors, *radio independence*, *i.e.* the LTE and WiFi operate independently from each other, and *optimal traffic partitioning* that accurately projects radio throughput over time to fully utilize both radios.

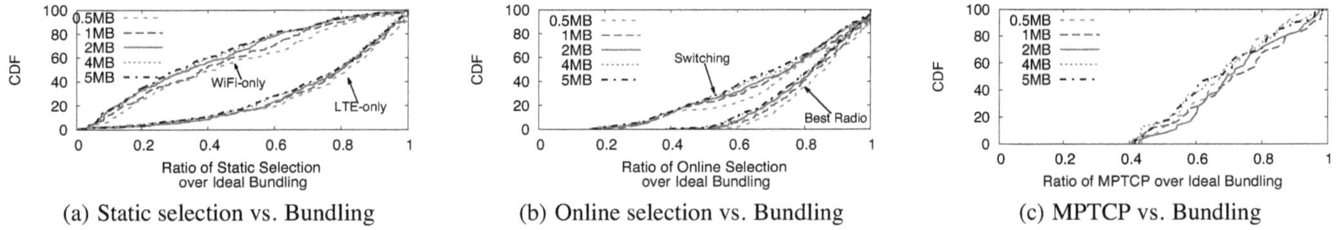

(a) Static selection vs. Bundling (b) Online selection vs. Bundling (c) MPTCP vs. Bundling

Figure 3: CDF of the ratio of throughput over Bundling R_X for option X (LTE-only, WiFi-only, Radio Switching, Best Radio, and MPTCP) for five different file sizes: 0.5MB, 1MB, 2MB, 4MB, 5MB.

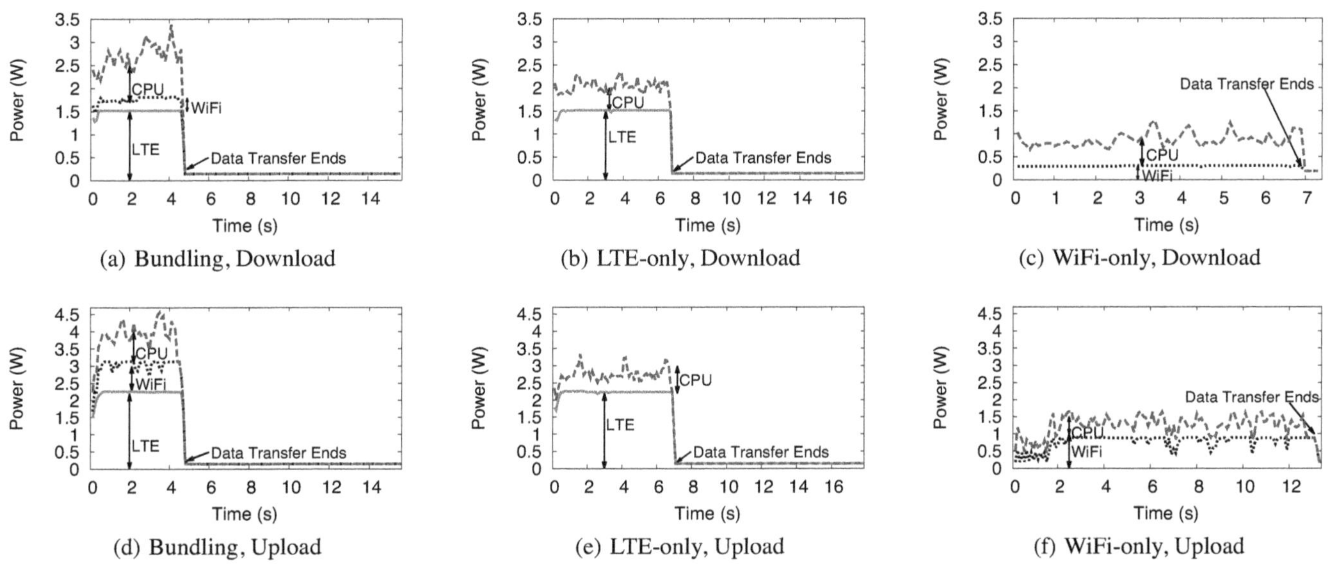

(a) Bundling, Download (b) LTE-only, Download (c) WiFi-only, Download

(d) Bundling, Upload (e) LTE-only, Upload (f) WiFi-only, Upload

Figure 4: A sample plot of power draw of Bundling, LTE-only and WiFi-only in terms of WiFi radio, LTE radio and CPU for a random measurement location while downloading/uploading 5MB. We stack the power draw of the three components to illustrate both the individual contributions and the total power draw value during each transfer. The spikes of LTE and WiFi energy tails do not appear in these figures because they were averaged out in each 100ms interval.

6. ENERGY ANALYSIS

Our measurements in §5 show that bundling LTE and WiFi radios can largely boost smartphone throughput. Yet one may wonder whether such improvement comes with a heavy cost in energy consumed by activating one additional radio. In this section, we perform a detailed analysis of energy consumption on radio bundling using the energy model described in §3. Different from existing models [21, 23], our model separates the energy consumed by CPU and WiFi/LTE radios. This not only improves accuracy of energy estimation (error rate $< 8\%$ compared to 17% in [23]), but also allows fine-grained analysis of radio bundling and selection.

We present results on both instantaneous power draw and total energy drain per transfer for five radio usage options: LTE-only, WiFi-only, Best Radio, MPTCP, and Bundling (with optimal data partitioning). We are unable to examine Radio Switching because there is no available implementation for real-time switching between LTE and WiFi[7]. We leave this to future work. The logging needed for energy estimation was collected along with all the throughput measurements.

6.1 Componentized Power Draw

To provide context for our discussion on the total energy consumption per transfer, we first study how different smartphone components contribute to energy consumption. Using the energy profiler described in §3, we break down energy consumption into three major components related to bundling: *WiFi radio*, *LTE radio* and *CPU*. We then extract the instantaneous power draw (energy consumption in each 100ms slot) per component during each data transfer. We do not include any result on screen energy cost since the data transfer can be done with screen on or off. Figure 4 presents a sample power draw result for bundling with optimal traffic partitioning, LTE-only and WiFi-only, obtained by transferring 5MB data using a Galaxy Note phone at a randomly chosen location.

Next we analyze the three components in details.

LTE vs. WiFi Radio. Across our experiments with both phones we found that the LTE radio consumes at least 50% of the total power draw (see Figure 5(a) that plots the normalized contribution of the LTE radio). On average, it consumes 5+ times more power than the WiFi radio. For example, in the download example of Figure 4, the LTE radio takes 1.5W power draw while WiFi takes only 0.25W, and for uploads, LTE takes 2.2W while WiFi uses 0.75W. Therefore, *LTE is the heaviest energy drainer across the three components*. This observation aligns with existing works [15, 21].

CPU Contribution. For both dual-core smartphones, CPU consumes a significant amount of energy. Figure 5(b) plots the CDF of the normalized CPU energy cost over all the measurement instances. We mix the results of the two smartphones since they are similar. Overall, the median value is 20% for LTE-only and

[7] To the best of our knowledge, the Android version of radio switching [26] only applies to 3G/WiFi and is not available publically.

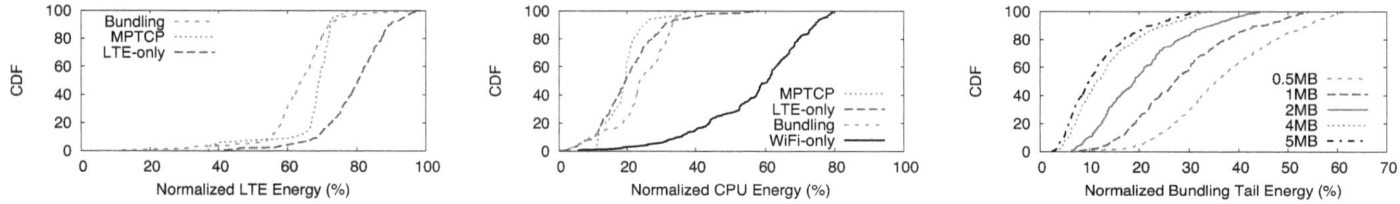

(a) LTE Radio (b) CPU (c) LTE Tail

Figure 5: Contribution of LTE radio, CPU and LTE tail to the overall energy drain.

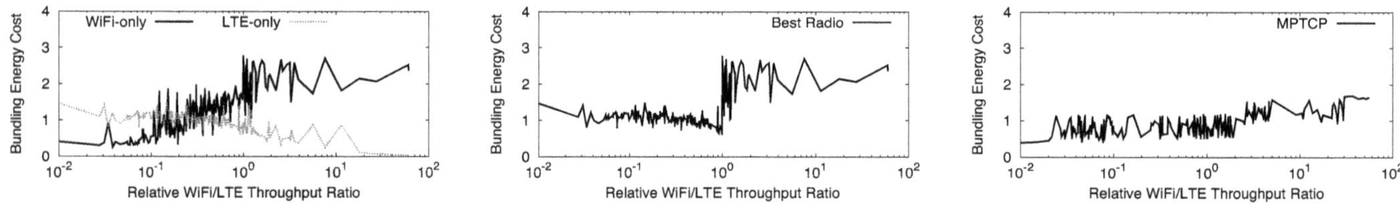

(a) Energy Cost over LTE-only & WiFi-only (b) Energy Cost over Best Radio (c) Energy Cost over MPTCP

Figure 6: Energy cost of radio bundling over LTE-only, WiFi-only, Best Radio, as well as MPTCP across all measurement instances.

MPTCP, 23% for Bundling, and rises to 60% for WiFi-only, while the maximum value can reach 80% for WiFi-only. To the best of our knowledge, this is the *first* field measurement over many locations that shows data transfers can consume significant CPU energy, using popular multi-core smartphones. More importantly, our result shows that *an accurate energy model must not ignore the CPU contribution*.

We also observe that Bundling's CPU power draw is approximately the sum of those of WiFi-only and LTE-only. This can be explained by our measurements on CPU utilization (in §5.1). When only a single radio is active, CPU Core 0 is utilized while Core 1 is rarely used. During Bundling, Core 1 becomes active while Core 0's utilization remains unaffected.

Radio Energy Tail. Both LTE and WiFi radios stay in moderate power state for a period of time after the data transfer finishes [29]. This is the tail state and lasts 11s for LTE and 210ms for WiFi [21]. The power draw displays sudden spikes (of length 40ms) during the tail state. They are averaged out by the 100ms display interval and thus not visible in Figure 4.

As shown by Figure 5(c), our key finding here is that *the energy contribution of these tails, especially the LTE tail, depends on transfer size*. For small files ($\leq$1MB), the LTE tail contributes to up to 60% of energy in the bundling mode (with a median of 25-35%). As the data size increases, the contribution reduces to no more than 30% (with a median of 10%)[8].

6.2 Energy Consumption per Transfer

Next we study the total energy consumption of a data transfer, by first comparing Bundling to radio selection and then to MPTCP. We use the metric of the *normalized energy cost of Bundling over non-Bundling*:

$$Cost_X = \frac{ENERGY_{Bundling}}{ENERGY_X} \tag{2}$$

where X is a non-Bundling strategy. If $Cost_X > 1$, then Bundling consumes more energy than strategy X.

Bundling vs. Radio Selection. Figure 6(a)(b) plot the value of $Cost_X$ vs. the ratio of WiFi and LTE average throughput, for 5MB transfers. Later we will show the impact of transfer size in Figure 7. We mix the results of the two phones as well as download and upload scenarios since they are similar.

We make three key observations. *First*, Bundling consumes less energy compared with LTE-only, despite turning on the extra WiFi radio. This is because Bundling improves the transfer throughput so that the transfer ends earlier. As a result, the energy saving due to reduced transmission time compensates the extra power draw of the WiFi radio. To further illustrate this, we plot in Figure 8 Bundling's energy cost as a function of its throughput gain (inverse of the throughput ratio R_X defined in §5). We see that in general the energy cost scales inversely with the throughput gain.

Second, compared to WiFi-only, Bundling's energy cost fluctuates around 1 when the WiFi-radio is weaker, but increases to more than 2 when the WiFi radio achieves higher throughput than the LTE radio. Again this is due to the fact that Bundling's throughput gain over WiFi-only is higher when WiFi is weaker. The resulting shortened transfer time effectively reduces energy drain despite the fact that Bundling turns on the energy-hungry LTE radio (Figure 8).

Finally, the energy cost over Best Radio follows a bimodal curve: it equals to the cost over LTE-only when the WiFi radio is weak and jumps to that of WiFi-only once the WiFi radio becomes stronger than the LTE radio.

Overall, these results show that the energy consumption of radio Bundling is on par with that of radio selection. Although Bundling uses an extra radio and thus consumes more power draw (radio+CPU), its throughput improvement reduces data transfer time and effectively compensates the increase in power draw.

Bundling vs. MPTCP. Next we compare the energy consumption of optimal Bundling and MPTCP. We note that by partitioning traffic at the transport layer, MPTCP only uses one HTTP connection while optimal Bundling uses two parallel HTTP connections, one for each radio.

Figure 6(c) plots the Bundling energy cost over MPTCP for 5MB data download. Interestingly, the value fluctuates between 0.4 and 1.6, indicating that MPTCP can sometimes save energy! This is unexpected since our throughput results in §5 show that Bundling always outperforms MPTCP in throughput, so MPTCP must run longer to complete the transfer. After studying the energy traces carefully, we find that the key cause is that Bundling consumes more CPU energy by maintaining two parallel HTTP connections with two threads, which activates two CPU cores. MPTCP, on the

[8] As discussed in §3, this result, coming from the new LTE deployment, differs from [21] which observed a much larger energy tail.

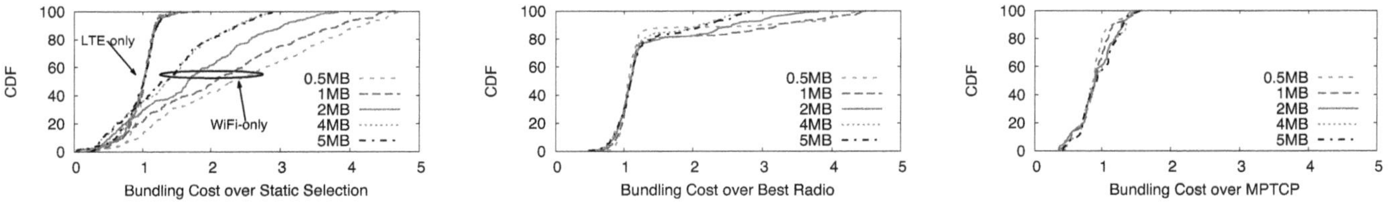

(a) Energy Cost over Static Selection (b) Energy Cost over Best Radio (c) Energy Cost over MPTCP

Figure 7: CDF of Bundling energy cost over LTE-only, WiFi-only, Best Radio, and MPTCP for different file sizes.

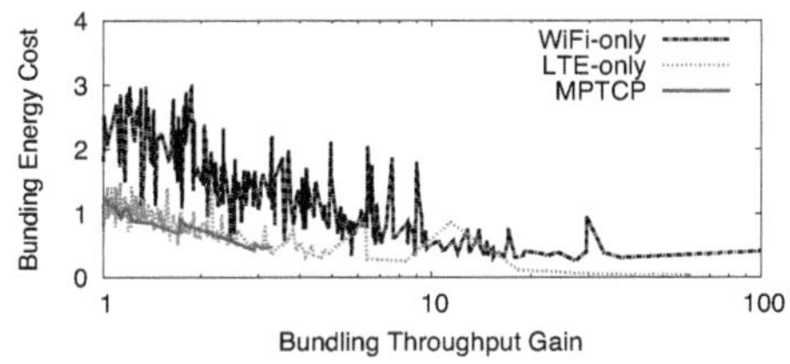

Figure 8: Bundling's energy cost vs. its throughput gain.

other hand, only manages a single thread and runs in a single core. We confirm this by comparing the CPU power draw of the two modes. So, while MPTCP turns on both radios like Bundling, its reduction in CPU usage can lead to savings in the overall energy consumption. As shown in Figure 8, this saving becomes visible when Bundling's throughput gain is small, *i.e.* between 1 and 2, but gets wiped out as Bundling's throughput gain increases.

Impact of Data Transfer Size. We repeated the above energy analysis for different data transfer sizes: 512KB, 1MB, 2MB, 4MB, and 5MB. Figure 7 plots the CDF of energy cost across all the measurements. Overall, the values of energy cost remain consistent across these data transfer sizes, except for the cost of bundling over WiFi-only. This is because the impact of LTE energy tail rises as the transfer size becomes smaller. Compared to WiFi-only, Bundling's extra LTE energy tail becomes a significant overhead in energy. Yet even for small transfers of 512KB, Bundling consumes at most 4.5x energy over WiFi-only (with a median of 2.5).

6.3 Summary of Results

Our analysis on energy consumption shows that Bundling, by using two radios, has a higher instantaneous power draw than single radio methods. Yet such increase in power draw is effectively compensated by the shortened data transfer time (due to Bundling's throughput gain). As a result, Bundling achieves a similar total energy consumption per transfer compared to LTE-only and at most 4.5x more energy than WiFi-only and Best Radio (due to the high energy cost of the LTE radio).

MPTCP and Bundling achieve similar energy consumption since they both use two radios simultaneously. However, MPTCP, by using a single thread implementation, reduces CPU usage and thus CPU power draw. This often turns into energy savings per data transfer. This result suggests that one must account for the CPU contribution when evaluating and designing radio bundling. We are able to make this observation because our energy model can accurately project the energy consumed by CPU and radio interfaces separately.

Designing Energy-efficient Bundling. Our goal in this paper is to understand the energy cost behind Bundling's throughput improvement. Thus, we target an optimal Bundling design that maximizes throughput without considering energy consumption. However, we believe that insights from our study will be valuable in the design of an energy-aware radio bundling protocol with an improved energy-performance tradeoff. We leave this for future work.

7. RELATED WORK

Multi-Radio Usage. Existing works have studied how to select the best network for each flow when multiple networks are available [8, 9, 10, 19]. A recent survey summarizes techniques on multi-radio aggregation [17]. To select the best interface for each application, existing works have considered application requirements [18, 14] and energy [26]. Recent works have studied concurrent use of 3G/WiMAX and WiFi radios on laptops [31, 20, 35, 36] and smartphones [35, 34]. [35] considers bundling WiFi/WiMAX, while [34] proposes to offload TCP ACKs from WiFi to 3G to improve TCP performance. There are also two Android apps that use both cellular 3G/4G and WiFi interfaces [1, 2].

Our work leverages insights from existing studies, but differs significantly from them by measuring and characterizing energy and performance of bundling smartphone LTE/WiFi radios at many locations. To our best knowledge, this is the first empirical study on this subject. Finally, our work also provides the first detailed, validated power model on various components during radio bundling.

MPTCP. Recent works have evaluated MPTCP throughput and energy performance. [27] studied MPTCP handover between 3G/WiFi on a Nokia N950 smartphone and measures energy consumption at one location. Chen et al. [12] analyzed MPTCP performance for different flow sizes using laptops. Deng et. al [13] studied flow-level MPTCP performance under different traffic patterns. They ran MPTCP on a laptop that sends flows to two tethered smartphones and measured energy using a power meter. Lim et al. [23] proposed a power model for MPTCP and examined MPTCP energy consumption for different file sizes. The error rate of the proposed power model is 17%.

Our work differs from these prior works in three key aspects. First, we target bundling with optimal traffic partitioning to explore the full benefit of bundling over radio selection. We also examine whether MPTCP can fulfill the bunding gain. Second, we ported MPTCP to smartphones and performed measurements at scale. Third, we developed an accurate energy model that captures the contribution of individual components (CPU and radio interfaces). Our energy model achieves an error rate of 8%.

Smartphone Energy Characterization. Prior works have examined smartphone energy consumption in a single radio operation mode [11, 33, 37, 24, 28, 30]. Recent work also developed specific power models for WiFi, 3G, GSM, and LTE [7, 15, 21, 32, 16]. Our study leverages insights from these existing studies on power measurements and profiles. The unique contribution of our work is to develop (and verify) detailed power models for both CPU and individual radio components that apply to both radio bundling and single radio operations. Our work considers the two of today's most used Android phone models, and reveals power usage patterns that differ significantly from prior works.

Table 2: **Dual-core CPU power model for Galaxy Note and Galaxy SIII, sampled on 6 frequencies for each core. The unit of power is mW.**

Galaxy Note							
Core0 (Mhz)	Core1 (Mhz)						
	0	384	594	810	1026	1242	1512
384	263	363	440	577	677	907	1129
594	322	366	492	629	655	966	1184
810	470	574	629	710	729	1047	1273
1026	562	670	729	810	847	1132	1365
1242	781	903	958	1051	1132	1262	1480
1512	781	1117	1177	1269	1354	1476	1680
Galaxy SIII							
Core0 (Mhz)	Core1 (Mhz)						
	0	384	594	810	1026	1242	1512
384	296	744	766	818	873	977	1047
594	359	766	814	866	921	1036	1103
810	411	818	866	918	973	1080	1154
1026	455	873	921	977	1029	1136	1217
1242	555	981	1029	1084	1140	1199	1277
1512	633	1062	1106	1158	1221	1273	1351

8. CONCLUSION

In this paper, we reassess the relationship between energy consumption and performance in smartphone radio bundling scenarios. Instead of bundling with MPTCP, we study the more general problem of maximal performance gain in ideal scenarios. Results show that MPTCP achieves only a portion of the total performance gain possible. We build an accurate componentized power model that identifies the significant role mobile CPUs play in energy usage.

There are two key takeaways from our study. First, an energy-agnostic MPTCP achieves only a fraction of the possible performance gains in a radio bundling scenario. Second, given our insights into the role of CPU in power consumption, there is ample room for a new bundling protocol that provides a better tradeoff between performance and energy usage.

Acknowledgments. This project was supported in part by NSF grants IIS-1321083, CNS-1224100, AST-1443956, NeTSE-1065456 and CCF-1320764. Any opinions, findings, and conclusions or recommendations expressed in this material are those of the authors and do not necessarily reflect the views of any funding agencies.

Appendix A: Details of Power Models

Dual-Core CPU Power Model. Table 2 shows the power model for the dual-core CPUs on the two phones used in our study, *i.e.*, the power draw when the two cores are at different combinations of frequencies, derived by following the procedure described in §3.

LTE and WiFi Power Models. The LTE interface on smartphones has four power states. The power states and their transitions are shown in Figure 9(a): (1) *IDLE:* The interface is in idle states when the User Equipment (UE) does not send or receive any data. It consumes little power and periodically wakes up to check whether there are incoming data buffered at the network. (2) *CR:* When the UE sends or receives any data, the interface enters the Continuous Reception (CR) state and consumes high power. (3) *Short DRX:* After the UE finishes data transfer and becomes idle for 200ms, the interface enters the Short DRX state, consumes little power but wakes up frequently to check for incoming traffic. (3) *Long DRX:* The interface enters this state after staying in Short DRX for 400ms without receiving any data. Long DRX is similar to Short DRX except that the wakeup interval becomes longer. Finally, if the UE stays in Long DRX for 11s without receiving any data, the interface returns to the IDLE state; otherwise, any data transfer in Short or Long DRX states will trigger the interface to enter the CR state.

Table 3: **Parameters of signal-strength-aware power models for WiFi and LTE on Galaxy Note and SIII. The unit of Tx/Rx/Tail power is mW.**

WiFi						
RSSI (dBm)	Galaxy Note			Galaxy SIII		
	Tx	Rx	Tail	Tx	Rx	Tail
-50	373.7	214.6	185.0	333.0	262.7	185.0
-60	862.1	292.3	185.0	444.0	281.2	185.0
-70	906.5	292.3	185.0	518.0	314.5	185.0
-80	869.5	358.9	185.0	662.3	373.7	185.0
-90	884.3	314.5	185.0	643.8	355.2	185.0
The duration of WiFi tail for both phones is 210ms.						

Galaxy Note LTE			
	Power(mW)	Duration(ms)	Periodicity(ms)
LTE promotion	950.0	300	N/A
Short DRX	947.2	36	100
Long DRX	932.4	40	320
LTE tail base	0	11000	N/A
DRX in IDLE	780.7	25	1280
Galaxy SIII LTE			
	Power(mW)	Duration(ms)	Periodicity(ms)
LTE promotion	1200.0	300	N/A
Short DRX	788.1	41	100
Long DRX	788.1	45	320
LTE tail base	0	11000	N/A
DRX in IDLE	569.8	32	1280

	Note LTE		SIII LTE	
RSRP (dBm)	Tx (mW)	Rx (mW)	Tx (mW)	Rx (mW)
-90	2160.8	1391.2	2264.4	1280.2
-100	2312.5	1646.5	2275.5	1535.5
-110	1861.1	1949.9	2282.9	2327.3

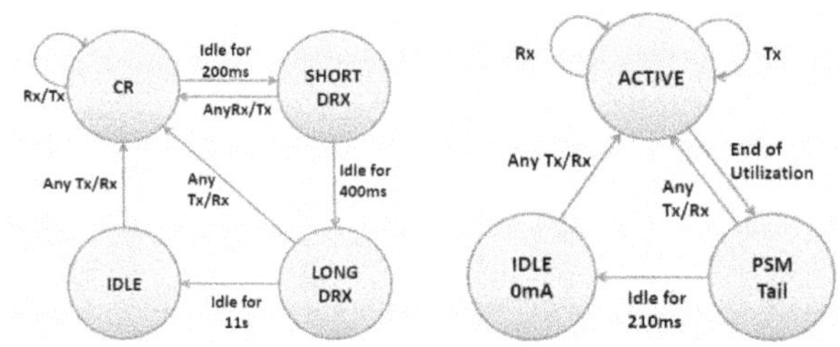

(a) LTE (b) WiFi

Figure 9: WiFi and LTE state machines for Galaxy Note and SIII.

Figure 10 plots the LTE power states on Galaxy SIII in a 100KB download under good signal strength (-90dBm).

The WiFi interface also has four power states: Tx, Rx, Tail, and Idle (Figure 9(b)). The interface is in the Idle state when there is no traffic, and enters the Tx (Rx) state when it starts sending (receiving) data. After data transfer, the interface stays in the Tail state for 210ms before returning to the Idle state. The interface consumes very little power in the Idle state, moderate power in the Tail state, and high power in the Tx and Rx states.

For both LTE and WiFi interfaces, the power draw and duration at each state and state transitions are affected by the wireless signal strength [15]. We derive all the parameters in the power state machines for the WiFi and LTE interfaces for the Galaxy Note and Samsung Galaxy SIII phones, shown in Table 3.

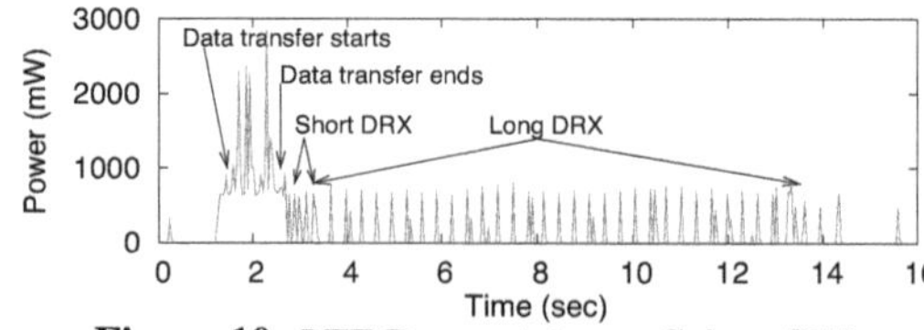

Figure 10: LTE Power states on Galaxy SIII

9. REFERENCES

[1] https://play.google.com/store/apps/details?id=it.opbyte.superdownload_lite&hl=en.

[2] http://www.shoelacewireless.com/pages/videobee.

[3] http://multipath-tcp.org/pmwiki.php/Users/Android.

[4] http://androidandme.com/2012/08/smartphones-2/qualcomm-explains-the-system-of-tiers-for-snapdragon-s4/.

[5] http://www.theverge.com/2013/1/14/3874576/samsung-sells-over-100-million-galaxy-s-devices.

[6] http://news.cnet.com/8301-1035_3-57493718-94/samsung-10m-galaxy-notes-sold-in-nine-months/.

[7] BALASUBRAMANIAN, N., BALASUBRAMANIAN, A., AND VENKATARAMANI, A. Energy consumption in mobile phones: a measurement study and implications for network applications. In *IMC* (2009).

[8] BHULAI, S., HOEKSTRA, G., AND VAN DER MEI, R. Optimal concurrent access strategies in mobile communication networks. In *ITC* (2010).

[9] BHULAI, S., HOEKSTRA, G. J., BOSMAN, J. W., AND VAN DER MEI, R. D. Dynamic traffic splitting to parallel wireless networks with partial information: A bayesian approach. *Perform. Eval. 69*, 1 (2012), 41–52.

[10] BOSMAN, J. W., HOEKSTRA, G. J., VAN DER MEI, R. D., AND BHULAI, S. A simple index rule for efficient traffic splitting over parallel wireless networks with partial information. *Perform. Eval. 70*, 10 (2013).

[11] CARROLL, A., AND HEISER, G. An analysis of power consumption in a smartphone. In *ATC* (2010).

[12] CHEN, Y.-C., LIM, Y.-S., GIBBENS, R. J., NAHUM, E. M., KHALILI, R., AND TOWSLEY, D. A measurement-based study of multipath TCP performance over wireless networks. In *IMC* (2013).

[13] DENG, S., NETRAVALI, R., SIVARAMAN, A., AND BALAKRISHNAN, H. WiFi, LTE or both? measuring mulit-homed wireless internet performance. In *IMC* (2014).

[14] DENG, S., SIVARAMAN, A., AND BALAKRISHNAN, H. All your network are belong to us: A transport framework for mobile network selection. In *HotMobile* (2014).

[15] DING, N., WAGNER, D., CHEN, X., PATHAK, A., HU, Y. C., AND RICE, A. Characterizing and modeling the impact of wireless signal strength on smartphone battery drain. In *SIGMETRICS* (2013).

[16] GARCIA-SAAVEDRA, A., SERRANO, P., BANCHS, A., AND BIANCHI, G. Energy consumption anatomy of 802.11 devices and its implication on modeling and design. In *CoNEXT* (2012).

[17] HABAK, K., HARRAS, K. A., AND YOUSSEF, M. Bandwidth aggregation techniques in heterogeneous multi-homed devices: A survey. *CoRR* (2013).

[18] HIGGINS, B. D., REDA, A., ALPEROVICH, T., FLINN, J., GIULI, T. J., NOBLE, B., AND WATSON, D. Intentional networking: Opportunistic exploitation of mobile network diversity. In *MobiCom* (2010).

[19] HOEKSTRA, G. J., VAN DER MEI, R. D., AND BOSMAN, J. W. Efficient traffic splitting in parallel tcp-based networks: modeling and experimental validation. In *ITC* (2013).

[20] HOU, X., DESHPANDE, P., AND DAS, S. R. Moving bits from 3G to metro-scale WiFi for vehicular network access: an integrated transport layer solution. In *ICNP* (2011).

[21] HUANG, J., QIAN, F., GERBER, A., MAO, Z. M., SEN, S., AND SPATSCHECK, O. A close examination of performance and power characteristics of 4G LTE networks. In *MobiSys* (2012).

[22] HUANG, J., QIAN, F., GUO, Y., ZHOU, Y., XU, Q., MAO, Z. M., SEN, S., AND SPATSCHECK, O. An in-depth study of LTE: effect of network protocol and application behavior on performance. In *SIGCOMM* (2013).

[23] LIM, Y.-S., CHEN, Y.-C., NAHUM, E. M., TOWSLEY, D., AND GIBBENS, R. J. How green is multipath tcp for mobile devices. In *AllThingsCellular* (2014).

[24] MITTAL, R., KANSAL, A., AND CHANDRA, R. Empowering developers to estimate app energy consumption. In *MobiCom* (2012).

[25] NAM, H., KIM, B. H., CALIN, D., AND SCHULZRINNE, H. G. Mobile video is inefficient: A traffic analysis. Tech. rep., Department of Computer Science, Columbia University, 2013.

[26] NIRJON, S., NICOARA, A., HSU, C.-H., SINGH, J. P., AND STANKOVIC, J. A. Multinets: A system for real-time switching between multiple network interfaces on mobile devices. In *TECS* (2013).

[27] PAASCH, C., DETAL, G., DUCHENE, F., RAICIU, C., AND BONAVENTURE, O. Exploring mobile/wifi handover with multipath tcp. In *CellNet* (2012).

[28] PATHAK, A., HU, Y. C., AND ZHANG, M. Where is the energy spent inside my app?: fine grained energy accounting on smartphones with eprof. In *EuroSys* (2012).

[29] PATHAK, A., HU, Y. C., ZHANG, M., BAHL, P., AND WANG, Y.-M. Fine-grained power modeling for smartphones using system call tracing. In *EuroSys* (2011).

[30] QIAN, F., WANG, Z., GERBER, A., MAO, Z., SEN, S., AND SPATSCHECK, O. Profiling resource usage for mobile applications: a cross-layer approach. In *MobiSys* (2011).

[31] RAICIU, C., PAASCH, C., BARRE, S., FORD, A., HONDA, M., DUCHENE, F., BONAVENTURE, O., AND HANDLEY, M. How hard can it be? designing and implementing a deployable multipath tcp. In *NSDI* (2012).

[32] SCHULMAN, A., NAVDA, V., RAMJEE, R., SPRING, N., DESHPANDE, P., GRUNEWALD, C., JAIN, K., AND PADMANABHAN, V. N. Bartendr: A practical approach to energy-aware cellular data scheduling. In *MobiCom* (2010).

[33] SHYE, A., SCHOLBROK, B., AND MEMIK, G. Into the wild: studying real user activity patterns to guide power optimizations for mobile architectures. In *MICRO 42* (2009).

[34] TSAO, C.-L., AND SIVAKUMAR, R. On effectively exploiting multiple wireless interfaces in mobile hosts. In *CoNEXT* (2009).

[35] YAP, K.-K., HUANG, T.-Y., KOBAYASHI, M., YIAKOUMIS, Y., MCKEOWN, N., KATTI, S., AND PARULKAR, G. Making use of all the networks around us: A case study in android. In *CellNet* (2012).

[36] YAP, K.-K., HUANG, T.-Y., YIAKOUMIS, Y., CHINCHALI, S., MCKEOWN, N., AND KATTI, S. Scheduling packets over multiple interfaces while respecting user preferences. In *CoNEXT* (2013).

[37] ZHANG, L., BIRJODH, T., QIAN, Z., WANG, Z., DICK, R. P., MAO, Z. M., AND YANG, L. Accurate online power estimation and automatic battery behavior based power model generation for smartphones. In *CODES+ISSS* (2010).

PriVaricator: Deceiving Fingerprinters with Little White Lies

Nick Nikiforakis
Department of Computer Science
Stony Brook University
nick@cs.stonybrook.edu

Wouter Joosen
iMinds-DistriNet, KU Leuven,
3001 Leuven, Belgium
wouter.joosen@cs.kuleuven.be

Benjamin Livshits
Microsoft Research
livshits@microsoft.com

ABSTRACT

Researchers have shown that, in recent years, unwanted web tracking is on the rise, with browser-based fingerprinting being adopted by more and more websites as a viable alternative to third-party cookies.

In this paper we propose PriVaricator, a solution to the problem of browser-based fingerprinting. A key insight is that when it comes to web tracking, the real problem with fingerprinting is not *uniqueness* of a fingerprint, it is *linkability*, i.e., the ability to connect the same fingerprint across multiple visits. Thus, making fingerprints non-deterministic also makes them hard to link across browsing sessions. In PriVaricator we use the power of randomization to "break" linkability by exploring a space of parameterized randomization policies. We evaluate our techniques in terms of being able to prevent fingerprinting and not breaking existing (benign) sites. The best of our randomization policies renders *all* the fingerprinters we tested ineffective, while causing minimal damage on a set of 1,000 Alexa sites on which we tested, with no noticeable performance overhead.

Categories and Subject Descriptors

K.6.5 [**Security and Protection (D.4.6, K.4.2)**]: Invasive software

Keywords

tracking; fingerprinting; randomization

1. INTRODUCTION

Browser-based fingerprinting, proposed as a theoretical threat to online privacy several years ago, has emerged as a full-fledged alternative to traditional cookie-based tracking. Recent work has demonstrated the growing proliferation of JavaScript-based fingerprinting on the web [2, 20]. Today, companies such as BlueCava [7], ThreatMetrix [23] and iovation [15] routinely fingerprint millions of web users.

WWW 2015, May 18–22, 2015, Florence, Italy.
ACM 978-1-4503-3469-3/15/05.
http://dx.doi.org/10.1145/2736277.2741090.

However, despite several attempts, mostly involving privacy-enhancing browser extensions, there has been a dearth of comprehensive privacy-enhancing technologies addressing in-browser fingerprinting. In this paper, we propose a comprehensive approach to prevent reliable fingerprinting in the browser, called PriVaricator.

Key insight: Much has been made of the fact that it is possible to derive a unique fingerprint of a user, primarily via JavaScript as shown by the Panopticlick project [12]. The main insight behind PriVaricator is the realization that the culprit behind fingerprinting is not the fact that a user's fingerprint is *unique*, but that it is *linkable*, *i.e.*, it can be reliably associated with the same user over multiple visits. While popular prevention techniques have attempted to make the fingerprints of large groups of users look *the same* [24], the key insight our paper explores involves doing the *opposite*. PriVaricator modifies the browser to make every visit appear different to a fingerprinting site, resulting in a *different* fingerprint that cannot be easily linked to a fingerprint from another visit, thus frustrating tracking attempts.

Randomization policies: In this paper we explore a space of *randomization policies* designed to produce unique fingerprints. The basis of our approach is to change the way the browser represents certain important properties, such as `offsetHeight` (used to measure the presence of fonts) and plugins, to the JavaScript environment. We observe that creatively misrepresenting — or lying — about these values introduces an element of non-determinism, which generally makes fingerprints unlinkable over visits.

Note that the randomization is not as easy as it might sound: as discussed by Nikiforakis et al. [20], producing practically impossible combinations of, say, browser headers and the `navigator` object, can actually *reduce* user privacy. Intuitively, blatant lying is *not* such a good idea, since it can significantly degrade the user experience by, for instance, presenting Firefox-optimized sites to users of IE, leading to visual discrepancies or calls into missing APIs. However, *subtly* misrepresenting key properties of the browser environment goes a long way towards combating fingerprinters. In summary, a randomization policy should 1) produce unlinkable fingerprints and 2) not break existing sites.

Practical focus: In this paper we concentrate our attention on randomizing plugins and fonts, as these dominate in the current generation of fingerprinters (Table 1). We, however, consider the approach presented here to be fully extendable to other fingerprinting vectors if that becomes necessary. Since today's browsers update themselves as frequently as once a week, the list of randomization policies can be expanded over time if needed. The issue of extensibility over time is discussed in Section 6.

Deployment: We have implemented PriVaricator on top of the Chromium web browser. We position PriVaricator as an enhancement to the private browsing mode already present in the majority of browsers. Existing private modes help prevent stateful tracking via cookies; PriVaricator focuses on preventing stateless tracking. We believe that it is better to integrate PriVaricator into the browser itself as opposed to providing it via an extension. One of the reasons for this, is the fact that most privacy extensions so far have only enjoyed a small deployment base, which in fact often makes it *easier* for the fingerprinter to identify the user [20].

Evaluation: We discovered that a number of our policies are able to render the fingerprinters we tested ineffective, while creating minimal damage to benign sites. In particular, the best of our policies renders *all* the fingerprinters we tested on ineffective, while only altering the visual appearance of, on average, 0.7% of the content offered by the top 1,000 Alexa sites. Using three JavaScript benchmark suites, we show that the modifications needed to implement PriVaricator on top of the Chromium browser cause a negligible performance overhead.

The reader may improve their intuition by watching two short "before/after" demo videos that show how PriVaricator helps against BlueCava, one of the most widely used fingerprinting services. In the first video BlueCava fingerprints a "vanilla" browser (`https://vimeo.com/95340734`). In the second video, BlueCava is failing to fingerprint against PriVaricator (`https://vimeo.com/95366100`).

2. BACKGROUND

Recent studies have discovered that fingerprinting is emerging as a real alternative to traditional cookie-based tracking [1, 2, 20]. A device *fingerprint* is a set of system attributes that are usually combined in the form of a string. This combination of attributes is generally designed to be unique with a high likelihood and, as such, can function as a device identifier. Attributes that range over a broader set of values (*e.g.*, the list of fonts and plugins) are more identifying than values shared by many devices (*e.g.*, version of the operating system). Stability is a desirable property in a fingerprinting strategy; choosing attributes with values that are more stable over time (*i.e.*, that change only infrequently or very gradually) facilitate reliable identification, compared to those that change frequently and unpredictably.

Web-based device fingerprinting is the process of collecting sufficient information through the browser to perform stateless device identification. The collected information is generally obtained via JavaScript and includes the device's screen size, the versions of installed browser plugins, and the list of installed fonts. Figure 1 shows how modern fingerprinters can use the differences in the sizes of strings rendered with different fonts to collect a user's list of fonts, bypassing the need of explicit font-providing APIs. Due to space limitations, we refer the interested reader to some of our previous work [20] for a more thorough explanation of the font-detecting capabilities of modern fingerprinters.

2.1 Why Fingerprint?

When it comes to the motivation behind web-based device fingerprinting, two reasons have emerged as most common.

```
function getFonts(){
    /* Long list of fonts */
    var fonts = ["cursive","monospace","serif","sans-
        serif","fantasy","Arial","Arial Black","Arial
         Narrow",...]

    /* Measuring ground truth */
    var ground_truth = getFontMeasurement("sans");
    var discovered_fonts = []

    /* Testing for each font family */
    for(var i=0; i < fonts.length; i++){
        c_measurement = getFontMeasurement(fonts[i]);
        if (c_measurement[0] != ground_truth[0] ||
            c_measurement[1] != ground_truth[1]){
            discovered_fonts.push(fonts[i]);
        }
    }
    return discovered_fonts;
}
```

Figure 1: Font detection through JavaScript

Third-party tracking: Probably the most common use of fingerprinting involves tracking the user across multiple, possibly unrelated, web sites to construct an interest profile for the user; this profile can then be employed to deliver targeted ads. As has been argued before, fingerprinting is an effective and stealthy alternative to stateful cookie-based user tracking. In a sense, the better fingerprinting works, the more information is learned about the user with a higher degree of reliability, leading to better ad targeting and thus to higher conversion rates for the advertisers. This creates a direct incentive for ad delivery networks to invest in better fingerprinting strategies, especially given that fingerprinters might not necessarily obey browser-provided Do-Not-Track (DNT) headers [2].

Fraud prevention: Third-party tracking, an activity that has provoked much outrage on the part of both privacy advocates and some users, is not the only motivation behind fingerprinting. It is sometimes argued that fingerprints can be used for fraud prevention. We refer the interested reader to some of the literature from the fingerprinting companies themselves [15, 22, 23] for further details. We should note that it is not obvious that collected fingerprints cannot be also sold to third parties or abused for tracking purposes by the companies that collect them.

In connection to fraud prevention, advocates of fingerprinting claim that a device fingerprint is a powerful tool for finding related transactions either as an identifier in itself or as a means of finding transactions with related characteristics. Fingerprints also can be used to find out when accounts are being illegally shared by more than one persons. The gathered fingerprints can be augmented with device reputation information and be used to blacklist fraudulent users and their activities.

Opt-out: While some of the aforementioned fingerprinting companies offer opt-out pages for the user, it is highly non-obvious what a successful opt-out really means. Ironically, to know that a user has opted-out of tracking, the fingerprinters still first need to compute the fingerprint (assuming cookies are disabled) and then, if they are honest, proceed to disregard information from that session.

Compared to stopping stateful tracking that can be achieved at the client-side, via disabling or clearing cookies, and the help of many extensions, this server-side approach to opt-

Fingerprinting provider	Script name	Plugin enumeration	Screen properties	Uses canvas	Access to offsetWidth	Access to offsetHeight
BlueCava	`BCAC5.js`	✓	✓	✗	63	63
Perferencement	`tagv22.pkmin.js`	✓	✓	✗	155	155
CoinBase	`application-9a3a[...].js`	✓	✓	✗	592	197
MaxMind	`device.js`	✓	✓	✗	261	27
Inside graphs	`ig.js`	✓	✓	✗	1,050	48

Table 1: Techniques used by various fingerprinters in the wild.

ing out is not satisfying because, ultimately, the user needs to trust the fingerprinting server. With PriVaricator, *reliable* fingerprinting is rendered impossible in the first place.

3. OVERVIEW

At the heart of PriVaricator is a strategy for misrepresenting the way parts of the browser environment are presented to the JavaScript language runtime. Previous studies of fingerprinters in the wild [2] have identified certain parts of the browser environment reflected into JavaScript as key to producing a reliable fingerprint. These properties range from common ones such as **navigator.userAgent** to ones that are significantly more obscure such as **getBoundingClientRect** which may be used to test for the presence of particular fonts on a user's machine, instead of the **offsetHeight** and **offsetWidth** attributes of DOM elements. Of course, our wish is to misrepresent environment properties of features that would be most damaging to fingerprinters without breaking existing code. As such, lying about **navigator.userAgent** is generally not a good idea: this may very well cause the server to send HTML code designed for a different browser. However, subtly changing the results of offset measurements turns out to be a better option.

Table 1 lists some of the representative fingerprinters found in the wild, showing which fingerprinting features they use [2]. While none of these fingerprinting companies employ canvas-based fingerprinting, as described in [18], concurrent work by Acar et al. [1] showed that other tracking companies have started making use of it. Even though our current prototype of PriVaricator does not address canvas-based fingerprinting, it is straightforward to add support for it, as further elaborated in Section 6.

Based on this information, combined with statistics about which features provide the highest number of bits of identifying information, in this paper, we primarily focus on randomizing 1) plugins and 2) fonts. Each of these provide more than 21 bits of identifying information, according to Panopticlick [12].

3.1 Randomization Policies

Our strategy in PriVaricator is to intercept each of the accesses to DOM properties of interest and augment the values returned to the JavaScript environment using a set of *randomization policies*. A wide range of randomization policies may apply in principle; for example, for integer values of properties such as **offsetWidth**, a slight change to the returned value is enough. For a property that is more structural and complex, such as the **toDataURL** function used in canvas-based fingerprinting that returns the current state of the canvas as an image [18], a different randomization policy may be used; an example policy for images may add slight visual *noise* to the returned image.

Policies for offset measurements: For the values of **offsetHeight**, **offsetWidth**, and **getBoundingClientRect** in PriVaricator, we propose the following randomization policies: a) Zero; b) Random(0..100); and c) $\pm$ 5% Noise. When these policies are active, instead of returning the original offset value, they return zero, a random number between 0 and 100, and the original number $\pm$5% noise, respectively. What these policies have in common is that they perform arithmetic operations on numbers with deterministic and non-deterministic results. While one can probably envision many more randomization policies, we focused on those that generate plausible offset values (e.g. no generation of negative numbers) as well as those that will create enough noise to confuse fingerprinting efforts. For instance, for the third policy, if the percentage of noise added to an offset is too little, then, for small offset values, it may be rounded off to the same original integer value and become ineffective.

These policies are controlled by a *lying threshold* (denoted as θ) and a *lying probability* (denoted as $P(lie)$). θ controls how fast PriVaricator starts lying, *i.e.*, after how many accesses to **offsetWidth** or **offsetHeight** values, will the policy kick in. $P(lie)$ specifies the probability of lying, *after* the θ threshold has been surpassed.

Policies for plugins: For the randomization of plugins, we define a probability $P(plug\_hide)$ as the probability of hiding each individual entry in the plugin list of a browser, whenever the **navigator.plugins** list is populated.

Example: As an example, a configuration of

$$\begin{aligned} \text{Rand\_Policy} &= \text{Zero}, \\ \theta &= 50, \\ P(lie) &= 20\%, \\ P(plug\_hide) &= 30\% \end{aligned}$$

instructs PriVaricator to start lying after 50 offset accesses, to only lie in 20% of the cases, to respond with the value 0 when lying, and to hide approximately 30% of the browser's plugins. In Section 5 we investigate which combinations of values provide the best tradeoff between the production of unlinkable fingerprints and the breakage of benign websites.

3.2 Breakage Concerns

Building an effective fingerprinting prevention tool involves balancing the effectiveness of preventing fingerprinters and breaking real sites. To better understand the latter, we crawled the top 10,000 Alexa sites to determine which ones use properties that are of interest to fingerprinters.

Access to property **offsetHeight** tends to be pretty telling. Overall, 82.3% of scripts have 0 accesses to **offsetHeight**. However, 1.87% of scripts have more than 50 accesses when visited at runtime. We summarize the results of our crawl in Table 2, sorted by the number of runtime accesses to **offsetHeight**. Fortunately, the majority of sites seem to be ranked not very high. However, some of the sites listed,

		Screen				Navigator									HTML element		
Alexa Rank	Domain	colorDepth	height	pixelDepth	width	mimeType	platform	language	userAgent	appName	vendor	appCodeName	appVersion	plugins	getBounding-ClientRect	offsetWidth	offsetHeight
6,444	bunte.de	0	1	0	1	0	0	2	8	0	0	0	0	1	2	205,115	202,909
8,039	nzz.ch	3	34	1	34	4	4	4	176	5	0	0	5	4	248	187,881	187,349
191	spiegel.de	2	4	0	4	0	0	0	15	3	0	0	1	4	7	154,265	149,293
4,037	wistia.com	1	2	0	2	0	0	3	81	0	0	0	0	0	0	109,347	109,299
1,369	zeit.de	0	4	1	4	0	0	2	8	3	2	0	0	5	1,318	70,025	72,268
8,894	menards.com	0	0	0	0	0	0	0	3,783	0	0	0	0	0	37	43,847	38,715
4,754	groupon.fr	0	0	0	0	0	0	0	1	0	0	0	0	0	15	150,717	36,627
7,488	xinmin.cn	0	0	0	1	0	0	0	70,380	0	0	0	3	0	4,426	34,229	31,996
2,320	celebuzz.com	2	55	0	55	4	2	0	23	0	0	0	0	4	326	27,831	27,779
1,370	wetter.com	4	30	0	30	6	1	8	18	5	0	0	1	7	212	22,578	21,764

Table 2: How widely are various fingerprintable browser properties used in the wild.

such as `spiegel.de`, are clearly important and we should take care not to break them in PriVaricator.

4. IMPLEMENTATION

In Section 3 we discussed the possible randomization policies that can be applied on the browser interfaces that are commonly abused for fingerprinting purposes. Since web-based device fingerprinting happens on the client side, the aforementioned policies could, in theory, be applied via an HTTP proxy, a browser extension, or built into the browser itself. We ultimately chose to instrument the browser itself, although we first examined the other approaches.

Strawman approach: JavaScript-level interception: During preliminary experimentation, we attempted to detect accesses to fingerprintable properties by using getters, as defined in ECMAScript5, on the objects and attributes of choice, *e.g.*, `navigator.plugins`. At first glance, given the amount of obfuscation routinely found in JavaScript code, this seems a better strategy than attempting to instrument JavaScript code at the source level (e.g. via an HTTP proxy). The JavaScript code that defined these getters was injected in a page using a browser extension.

During that time, however, we encountered many browser-specific issues that eventually steered us towards modifying the browser itself. For instance, in order to be able to lie about the `offsetWidth` and `offsetHeight` of any given element, we need to intercept the requests of these attributes on all elements on a page, since we cannot *a priori* know which element(s) are going to be used for font detection. Unlike the `navigator` and `screen` objects which are created by the browser and thus always available, HTML elements are created initially when parsing a page's HTML code, as well as on-demand, whenever a programmer wishes to do so through JavaScript. As such, we need to intercept the creation of all HTML elements and define getters upon their creation.

The natural way to do this, is to "poison" the correct object prototype, so that all future JavaScript objects that inherit from that prototype will also inherit the getters. We discovered that although our prototype poisoning was working in Mozilla Firefox, it failed to work as expected in Google Chrome. By investigating the issue, we discovered that in Chrome, the `offsetWidth` and `offsetHeight` properties are not part of the `HTMLElement` prototype, but rather they are defined and initialized upon the creation of new elements. Interestingly, this is not the case for the the `getBoundingClientRect` method which also returns an element's `offsetWidth` and `offsetHeight`, and yet is defined in the expected prototype.

Browser	JSBench	SunSpider	Kraken
Chromium	72.31 ±0.40	139.20 ±1.00	1,146 ±20.48
PriVaricator	72.10 ±0.31	138.70 ±0.49	1,142 ±20.09

Table 3: Performance comparison of "vanilla" Chromium and Chromium equipped with PriVaricator. All measurements are in *ms*.

In addition to this browser-specific behavior, the use of getters also suffers from transparency issues. That is, a (malicious) script can check for the existence of getters using, among others, the `Object.getOwnPropertyDescriptor` method. Achieving transparency at the language level is fundamentally difficult [14].

Our implementation: For the reasons of better compatibility and transparency, we ultimately chose to implement our randomization policies within the browser, by changing the appropriate C++ code in the classes responsible for creating the `navigator` object, and the ones measuring the dimensions of elements. These changes are, by nature, very local; our full prototype involves modifications to a total of seven files in the WebKit implementation of the Chromium browser, version 34.0.1768.0 (242762).

5. EVALUATION

The goal of PriVaricator's evaluation is three-fold. In addition to ensuring that the overhead of PriVaricator is minimal (Section 5.1), we want to maximize the effectiveness of fingerprinting prevention (Section 5.2), while minimizing the overall damage to the way users perceive the web (Section 5.3). When it comes to privacy-enhancing technologies, this tradeoff is not entirely new. For example, Mozilla Firefox decided to misreport (to JavaScript programs) the computed styles for links in order to prevent history leaks [5], after they had been demonstrated on a large scale.

5.1 Performance Overhead

In order to assess the performance overhead of PriVaricator, we used three independently-developed JavaScript benchmark suites: SunSpider version 1.0.2, Kraken version 1.1, and JSBench version 2013.1. Even though these benchmark suites already take repeated measurements, we also executed each suite five times, clearing the browser's cache in between runs. The experiments were run on a desktop machine, running a recent Ubuntu Linux distribution, with an Intel Core i5-3570 CPU @ 3.40 GHz processor, and 8 GB of RAM.

Table 3 shows the average benchmark execution times (in *ms*) and standard deviations for an unmodified version of the Chromium browser, and for the same Chromium browser with our modifications present and enabled. To calculate the upper bound of PriVaricator's overhead, we used the lying policy with the most computations (± 5% Noise) configured with the worst (from a performance point of view) parameter settings, i.e., θ equal to zero and $P(lie)$ equal to 100%. All three benchmarks reported that our runs with PriVaricator executed, on average, slightly *faster* than the ones of the unmodified browser. Given the standard deviation of our measurements, our instrumentation is not, in reality, speeding up the browser; instead, these measurements show that the added overhead of PriVaricator is so negligible that it does not exceed the inherent noise in the reported execution time of browser benchmarks.

5.2 Preventing Fingerprinting

While one can fully analyze the client-side JavaScript code of fingerprinters, the way in which a user's fingerprintable attributes are combined and mapped to a fingerprint (also known as a *device identifier*) is not necessarily a client-side operation. In order to assess how our randomization policies affect a fingerprinter's ability of identifying us, we chose four services that can be used as black-box oracles. Some of these revealed the device identifier as part of the opt-out process, while with others more investigation was required. Unfortunately, finding fingerprinters that are willing to disclose information about their internal workings is a major challenge and it took us some time to understand how to test these four fingerprinters. For this evaluation, we measured how PriVaricator stands against BlueCava, Coinbase, PetPortal, and fingerprintjs, as explained below.

BlueCava: Similar to other third-party trackers, BlueCava provides an opt-out page (`http://bluecava.com/opt-out`) for users who wish to opt-out of tracking by BlueCava. On this page, users are fingerprinted and their fingerprintable attributes are sent to BlueCava's server. The server then responds with a device identifier, *e.g.*, `18B1-EBFC-A3F0-6D81-6DE8-D8DA-CA56-A22B`, and whether this device identifier has already opted-out in the past. The details of how a user's fingerprintable attributes are combined into a device identifier are proprietary and are unknown to us.

PetPortal: Boda *et al.* have created a cross-browser fingerprinting suite as part of their research in browser fingerprinting [9], available at `http://fingerprint.pet-portal.eu/`. As in the case of BlueCava, the user's fingerprintable attributes are delivered to the server, which then sends back a device identifier and whether the device identifier belongs to a new, or returning, user.

Coinbase: Even though Coinbase does not provide an opt-out page, the algorithm for deriving a device identifier from a user's fingerprintable attributes is part of their client-side JavaScript code. More specifically, when a site includes remote JavaScript code for obtaining Coinbase's "Pay with Bitcoin" button, the remote code creates an `iframe`, in which the fingerprinting code runs [10]. Once the fingerprint is computed, it is MD5-ed and then set as a cookie on the user's machine. When the user clicks on the payment button, her fingerprint will be automatically submitted to the Coinbase server via the user's cookies.

fingerprintjs: Finally, fingerprintjs is an open-source fingerprinting library which, like Coinbase, runs fully on the client-side. fingerprintjs is inspired by Panopticlick [12] and contains most of its features. Interestingly, fingerprintjs is also the only library, that we encountered, that fingerprints a user's machine using the HTML5 canvas as proposed by Mowery *et al.* [18]. It should be noted that it is not yet entirely clear how effective canvas-based fingerprinting is, in practice [4]. Lastly, note that fingerprintjs does not support JavaScript-based font detection.

5.2.1 Experimental Setup

In all four cases, the individual fingerprinting providers gave us a way of assessing the efficacy of PriVaricator, simply by visiting each provider multiple times using different randomization settings, and recording the fingerprint provided by each oracle. To explore the space of possible policies in detail, we performed an automated experiment where we visited each fingerprinting provider 1,331 times, to account for 11^3 parameter combinations, where each parameter of our randomized policy (lying threshold, lying probability, and plugin-hiding probability) ranged from 0 to 100 in increments of 10.

Before we present the results of this experiment we would like to elaborate on two of our decisions.

Panopticlick: We chose against the use of Panopticlick [11] since the feedback that it provides to users is of a semi-qualitative nature, *e.g.*, "You are unique among 4 million users". This type of statement does not allow us to compare the fingerprints received from multiple visits, and thus does not allow us to reason about the effect that our parameterized randomization policies have against it. In addition, since all the sets of attributes collected by the studied fingerprinters are supersets of Panopticlick, we have no reason to expect that our results would have been dramatically different, had we been able to include Panopticlick in our study.

Focusing on the ± 5% Noise policy: Even though we propose multiple lying policies about offsets, in this section, we only show the effect of PriVaricator's ± 5% Noise policy, on the four aforementioned fingerprinters. This decision is made in favor of more compact presentation of our results, and in light of the fact that, as described in detail in Section 5.3, the ± 5% Noise policy incurs the least amount of breakage on legitimate websites thus is the policy that strikes the desired balance between thwarting fingerprinting and maintaining the usability of benign web pages. Do note, however, that all policies have similar results due to the effect of randomization on the way fingerprinters detect the installed fonts.

This is because, as shown in the font-detecting JavaScript snippet (Figure 1), fingerprinting providers first establish ground truth using a font-family that they expect to be present on all devices (*e.g.* sans), and then compare the `offsetWidth` and `offsetHeight` of text using other font-families against that ground truth. PriVaricator will cause deviations from that ground truth and may even poison the fingerprinters' ground truth itself, if the ground truth is acquired *after* the lying threshold (θ) of our policies is

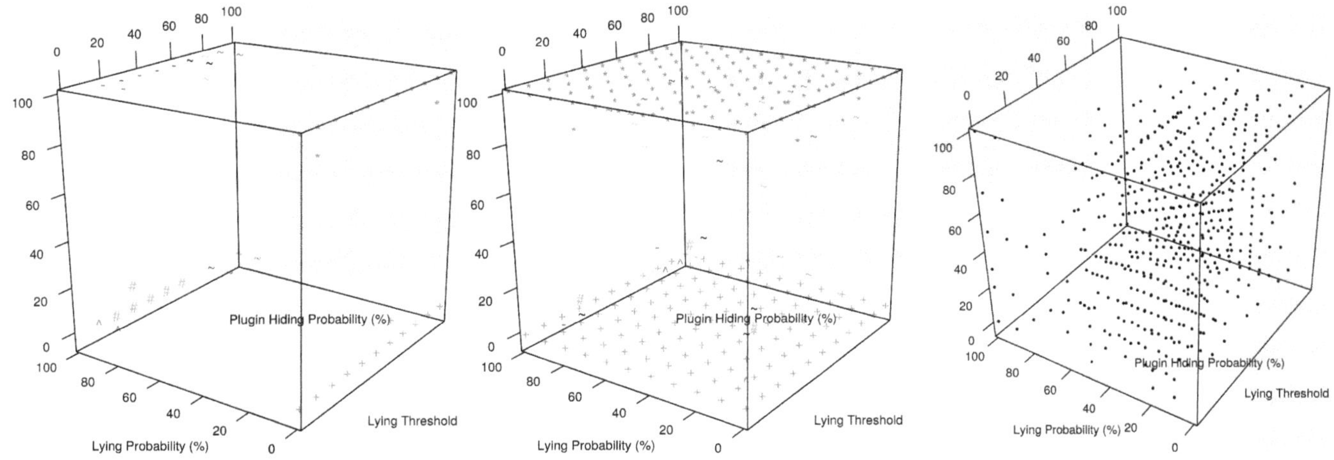

(a) BlueCava (b) fingerprintjs (c) PetPortal

Figure 2: Distribution of device identifiers across three different fingerprinters. For graphs (a) and (b), we show the points where the fingerprinters recognized us as the same user, i.e., PriVaricator failed. For graph (c) we show the points where PetPortal did *not* recognize us as the same user, i.e., PriVaricator succeeded.

surpassed. As such, all of our lying policies will cause the fingerprinter to believe that our machine has fonts that it actually does not have (false positives).

5.2.2 Results

The results of this set of experiments are shown in Figure 2. In all three scatter-plots, the x-axis represents the probability of lying, the y-axis represents the lying threshold, while the z-axis represents the probability of hiding each individual plugin in our browser's list of plugins. For the first two graphs, colors and symbols represent *clusters* of fingerprints, *e.g.*, all green plus signs denote the same fingerprint, within a given service.

BlueCava: For BlueCava, in Figure 2a one can see that their fingerprinting algorithm can only track us mostly along the edges of the graph. For example, when our plugin-hiding probability is 0, *i.e.*, we always show all plugins, and the lying probability is also 0, i.e., we never lie, we get the same fingerprints (green plus-signs at the "bottom" of the graph).

What is also interesting is how fingerprints change when the lying threshold is less than 60, or greater than 60. One reasonable explanation for this effect is that when our threshold is lower than 60, we then poison the ground truth of the JavaScript-based font detection algorithm, which leads to having an increased number of fonts marked as "present." This change of fingerprint is visible both when the plugin probability is 0% (bottom-left of the graph), as well as when the plugin-hiding probability is 100% (top-left of the graph).

At the same time, it is also evident that most of the cube is empty, that is, in all points other than the ones present, every fingerprint was *unique*, yielding 96.32% of all fingerprints being unique. This shows how fragile BlueCava's identification is against our randomization policies.

fingerprintjs and Coinbase: For fingerprintjs, Figure 2b, the arrangement of points is visibly different from BlueCava's. Since this library does not support for JavaScript-based font detection, our choices of lying probability and lying threshold have no effect. What has the most influence is the value of the plugin-hiding probability. It is evident that fingerprintjs can only track us either when we have no plugins showing, *i.e.*, hiding probability equals 100%, or all plugins showing, *i.e.*, hiding probability is 0%.

In nearly all intermediate points (78.36% of the total set of collected fingerprints), randomness works in our favor by returning different sets of plugins, which, in turn, result in different fingerprints. These results show how important it is to *combine* randomization approaches in order to deter fingerprinters who do not utilize all fingerprintable attributes of a user's browsing environment. In Section 6 we briefly discuss why, given the current state of the art in fingerprinting, a fingerprinter *cannot* avoid extracting both fonts and plugins, while maintaining meaningful results. Coinbase's results were very similar to fingerprintjs's; we briefly discuss them in the Appendix.

PetPortal: Lastly, Figure 2c, shows the results of our experiment against PetPortal. Note that for this figure, because of the large number of clusters, to make the results more readable, we show all the configurations that resulted in *unique fingerprints*, instead of showing clusters of same fingerprints. It is evident that PetPortal succeeds more in tracking us than BlueCava, Coinbase, and fingerprintjs.

In contrast with the other three services, we were able to get unique fingerprints in "only" 37.83% of the 1,331 parameter combinations. One can notice from this graph that we defeat tracking when the lying probability is in the range of 10% to 60%. When the lying probability exceeds 60% we begin lying too often, which likely results in having most fonts marked as "present." There, we also see a lack of effect from the plugin-hiding probability which cannot recover us from being accurately fingerprinted. This likely means that PetPortal places more weight on the discovered fonts, and less on the claimed plugins.

Summary: Overall, our experiments showed that, while the specific choices of each fingerprinter affect the uniqueness of our fingerprints, PriVaricator was able to deceive all of them for a large fraction of the tested combination settings. Moreover, the presence of clusters of identical fingerprints demonstrates that most fingerprinting providers derive a fingerprint by following a more complicated approach than just hashing all fingerprintable attributes together. Comparatively speaking, PetPortal was most resistant to PriVaricator.

5.3 Assessing the Breakage

In the previous section, we demonstrated that PriVaricator was able to withstand fingerprinting by measuring the number of unique fingerprints received, for a total of 1,331 settings combinations. By computing the intersection of the points resulting in unique fingerprints across all four fingerprinting providers, (essentially identical to PetPortal's results), we obtain a range of settings, all of which provide prevention from reliable fingerprinting. In this section, we assess the level of breakage of benign sites for each of those parameter combinations.

Experimental setup: An element's offset properties (accessible through `offsetWidth` and `offsetHeight`) provide information to a JavaScript program about the size of that element, as is currently rendered on a user's screen. When PriVaricator lies about these values, it creates a potential for visual breakage. For example, by reporting that an element is smaller than it actually is, PriVaricator could cause the page to place it in a smaller container, hiding part of its content from the user. Numerically, we define *breakage* as the fraction of pixels that are different when a site is loaded with a vanilla browser (PriVaricator turned off) and with PriVaricator.

To assess the breakage, we instrumented Chromium to visit the main pages of the top 1,000 Alexa sites, for 48 different combinations of lying probability and lying threshold; these were the parameter combinations that resulted in unique fingerprints, as described in the previous section. To contain the dimensionality of this experiment, we statically assigned the plugin-hide probability to zero (showing all plugins) since we reasoned that the main pages of the most popular sites of the web likely behave the same for users with different plugins. At every site visit, the browser waited for 25 seconds and then captured a screenshot (1,050x850 pixels) of the rendered content.

In order to separate between visual differences caused by PriVaricator, and visual differences caused by the inherent variation of a site, *e.g.*, ads, image carousels, and newly posted content, we collected a new vanilla-browser screenshot every ten visits of a page, resulting in a total of five extra screenshots. Since any visual variation detected on these five screenshots can be attributed to a website's dynamic content, we computed a visual mask of differences appearing on them, and used it when comparing a screenshot captured using a specific policy parameter combination, to the vanilla one. This mask can be applied to all PriVaricator screenshots to exclude the naturally varying parts of a page from subsequent breakage comparisons. For illustration, Figure 3 shows three different vanilla-browser screenshots of `tumblr.com` and the computed mask.

Finally, while in the previous section the choice of randomization policy was not as important, in this section, different policies are likely to produce different visual results, *e.g.*, receiving a value that is 5% off the expected one, versus receiving a value that is completely random. Thus, the entire experiment had to be repeated for every randomization policy: (a) Random(0..100); b) Zero; and c) ± 5% Noise). Overall, we collected a total of approximately 159,000 images, occupying 54 GB of disk space, which we compared in order to quantify the breakage caused by PriVaricator.

Results: The results of our breakage experiments are first detailed in Figure 4 and then summarized in Table 4. Table 4a presents the minimum, average, and maximum breakage for all three policies when considering the fractions of different pixels across all sites. Since we noticed that, in some cases, the computed masks were too *large*, we also calculated the breakage of sites when ignoring sites that had masks with size larger than 30% of the total image; this is shown in Table 4b. This way, we ignore sites that would give PriVaricator an unfair advantage by hiding real breakage under a site's natural variation. While the latter set of numbers is slightly larger than the former, it is evident, not only that the ± 5% Noise policy incurs the least breakage but that the breakage itself is, on average, less than 1%.

Policy	Min	Mean	Max %
Random(0..100)	0.8%	1.4%	2.1%
Zero	0.4%	0.8%	1.3%
± 5% Noise	**0.4%**	0.6%	0.9%

(a) Summary of breakage results.

Policy	Min	Mean	Max %
Random(0..100)	0.8%	1.5%	2.3%
Zero	0.4%	0.9%	1.4%
± 5% Noise	**0.4%**	0.7%	1.0%

(b) Breakage when ignoring pages with masked content greater than 30% (approx. 84% of pages remaining).

Table 4: Breakage summary with and without including sites with large masks.

Every point in Figure 4 is the average breakage of all 1,000 Alexa sites visited with PriVaricator using a specific $\langle P(lie), \theta \rangle$ configuration, and one of our three lying policies. For instance, in Figure 4b, the average breakage of sites when visited by PriVaricator configured with a lying probability equal to 10% and a lying threshold of 30 accesses is 0.004, under the Zero policy. That is, the sites visited by PriVaricator with that specific combination of settings had, on average, 0.4% different pixels when compared to the vanilla screenshots.

For the breakage caused by the Random(0..100) policy (Figure 4a) and Zero policy (Figure 4b), one can discern a positive relationship between the lying probability and the resulting breakage. This relationship makes intuitive sense. The more often PriVaricator lies using these policies, the more often a website receives an unexpected value of 0, or a random number between 0 and 100. On the other hand, this relationship is significantly weaker in ± 5% Noise policy results (Figure 4c). We argue that this is because the modified offset value is relatively close to the value that a script would otherwise expect, thus minimizing the number of sites breaking because of such small modifications.

Inspecting breakage: To understand how a user would experience potential breakage, we manually reviewed the 100 screenshots (under the ± 5% Noise policy) with the largest reported breakage. In this analysis, we discovered that in only 8 cases, the differences could be attributed to PriVaricator. The rest of the screenshots (92/100) were very different from the vanilla screenshots due to a site's inherent variations and errors, not captured in any of the five vanilla screenshots. In many cases, the sites would show an "in-page" pop-up asking the user to participate in a survey. Usually, this pop-up would add a semi-transparent gray overlay over the page,

Figure 3: The first three screenshots show `tumblr.com` and its ever-changing backgrounds. The last image is an automatically-generated mask for assessing the true breakage caused by PriVaricator. Black areas denote masked-out content.

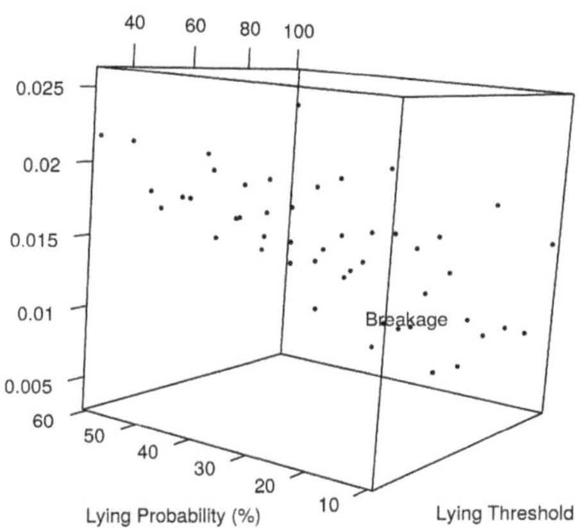

(a) Random(0..100) policy

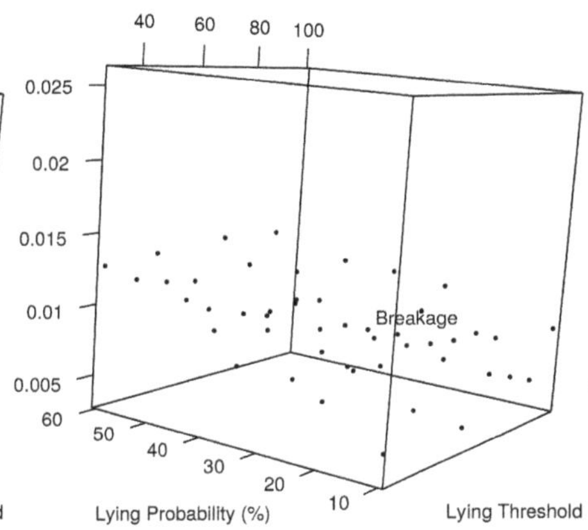

(b) Zero policy

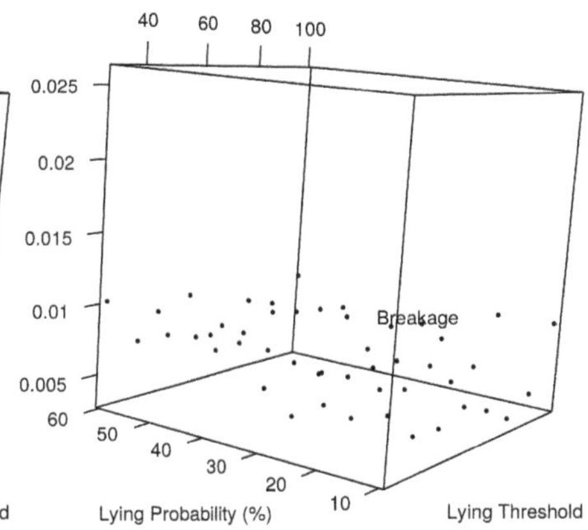

(c) ± 5% Noise policy

Figure 4: Breakage caused by PriVaricator, given a series of possible configurations and a randomization policy

causing our automatic comparison algorithms to report a very large visual difference.

Next to surveys, the reported breakage was due to missing or not-fully loaded ads, error-pages and image carousels. In one case, PriVaricator had caused a slight stretch of a site's background image. While this led to a large computed breakage, users would not notice the change if they could not compare the page with the original non-stretched version. Finally, we manually inspected the sites making the most use of offset accesses (listed in Table 2) by visiting them with PriVaricator and clicking on a few links on each site. All sites were operational and usable, with the only difference being the location and movement of some objects, e.g., moving ads, whose motion and placement was slightly affected by the randomization policies of PriVaricator.

Summary: Overall, the results of our breakage experiments show that the negative effect that PriVaricator has on a user's browsing experience is negligible. Moreover, our manual analysis revealed that we have likely overestimated the breakage since most of the pages with the highest reported breakage turned out to be false positives.

Our low breakage results also allow us to avoid the temptation of cherry-picking configurations for the ± 5% Noise policy, something which could lead to issues related to overfitting. Instead, any of the many parameter configurations could be picked for deployment, e.g., picking one at random when a user starts a private mode session. We opine that an average breakage of 0.7% (likely an upper bound with the actual damage as much as $10x$ less) provides an acceptable trade-off for the extra privacy that the user gains in return.

6. DISCUSSION

Explicit fingerprinting: Note that we do not claim to solve the *entire* problem of web-based device fingerprinting with PriVaricator. The focus of our work is on explicit attempts to fingerprint users via capturing the details of the browser environment. We do *not* attempt to provide protection against sophisticated side-channels such as browser performance [17] which may be used as part of fingerprinting. Our focus is on *explicit fingerprinting*, *i.e.*, JavaScript-based fingerprinting which operates by computing a function of environment variables exposed within the browser, as these are exclusively used in by the popular fingerprinters.

6.1 Comparing to Existing Approaches

Most existing attempts to combat fingerprinting rely on making multiple users look identical. In terms of sophistication, browser extensions that spoof a browser's user agent, such as UserAgent Switcher and UserAgent RG, can be viewed as the most straightforward fingerprinting countermeasure. These extensions attempt to hide the true nature of a browser and show another, possibly more mainstream and less identifying, version. Unfortunately, however, these extensions are trivially bypassable as explained by Nikiforakis *et al.* [20], since an attacker can deduce the original version of the browser by searching for vendor- and version-specific functionality.

On the other side of the spectrum, the Tor browser makes cross-cutting changes to present the same browser attributes for all Tor users so that a probing website may not be able to differentiate between different users of the Tor network.

While Tor happily sacrifices usability for anonymity by disabling all plugins, reporting false screen dimensions, and limiting the number of fonts that any given page can use, we reason that this may not be the goal for most online users. We argue that PriVaricator is the middle-of-the-road option that will allow benign web pages to be rendered with minimum breakage (*e.g.*, no limits in font loading, no unnecessary changes in screen dimensions), while defeating the fingerprinting efforts, as demonstrated in Section 5.2.

6.2 Deployment challenges

The key advantages of PriVaricator are its negligible overhead and the relative ease of porting. It is easy to underestimate the importance of low overhead, but given the current emphasis on browser performance, it is unlikely that a privacy solution that suffers a large performance hit will be deployed. Our design of PriVaricator has emphasized minimal modifications to existing technology, which leads to small overhead and negligible porting costs; overall, the automatically generated patch of our modifications to Chromium (including comments) is only 947 lines long.

Transparency: As with any defense strategy there is a question of *transparency*. We do not claim to preserve transparency in PriVaricator; indeed, this is a tough property to maintain for just about any runtime protection mechanism.

Specifically, since PriVaricator is using randomness to report different values for popular fingerprintable attributes, a motivated fingerprinter could test for the presence of unexpected randomness, *e.g.*, by inquiring about the dimensions of an element 100 times, and then checking for differences in responses. Similarly, a statistical attack may collect multiple readings and average them over a large number of samples, in an effort to approximate the real measurement.

Lie cache: One possible solution that alleviates this transparency issue and thwart some of the statistical attacks is setting up a "lie cache", a mechanism where the browser would report the *same* false value for multiple inquires about the same, unmodified element. To break linkability, the lie cache should be reset at the beginning of every new private mode session, *i.e.*, when a user is opening a private mode tab or window of her browser. This would enhance the transparency at the cost of linkability within the same private mode session. We leave the exploration of this solution and its tradeoffs for future work.

6.3 Making PriVaricator Extensible and Future-Proof

Withstanding small changes: In Section 5.2 we showed that PriVaricator's randomization policies can thwart all modern commercial and open-source fingerprinting projects we have access to. In this paper, we primarily cover two fingerprinting vectors: plugins and fonts. Given that these two vectors contain the highest discriminating power, it is to the advantage of the fingerprinter to use *both.*

One, however, could argue that fingerprinters will adapt to PriVaricator and change their strategy. If, for instance, a fingerprinting library were to stop using plugin information and would only rely on fonts, PriVaricator still offers a large set of combinations for the Lying Probability and Lying threshold parameters resulting in different fonts detected, and thus different fingerprints for the same user.

In a similar fashion, PriVaricator can adapt to a fingerprinter that does not use font information, as was demonstrated in Figure 2b, since the fingerprintjs library does not use fonts. It is also important to stress that every time that a fingerprinter consciously forsakes a fingerprinting vector, he is increasing the probability of collisions of fingerprints of different people. For example, two users may have the same browser plugins but may have installed applications that included different fonts and thus will have different fonts detected by the fingerprinting scripts.

Lastly, if a fingerprinter decides to use neither fonts nor plugins, he will be abandoning the two most powerful identifying attributes of modern browsers. Thus, in this case, while the fingerprint that PriVaricator will provide may be stable, it will have little discriminating power, rendering such an approach useless as a tracking mechanism.

Future fingerprinting vectors: Just like with most defense mechanisms, more sophisticated attacks often are developed in response to them. Security literature is full of such examples, with major attacks, such as buffer overflows and cross-site scripting, evolving significantly over the years, with attacks and defenses adapting to each other. We, unfortunately, cannot foresee new fingerprintable vectors that might appear in the coming years — in the same way that Eckersley could not foresee the use of timing attacks against JavaScript engines [17]. Note, however, that as long as either plugins or fonts are included as part of a user's fingerprint and relied upon to provide meaningful information to the fingerprinting party, the current version of PriVaricator is likely to provide adequate randomization.

Extensibility of PriVaricator: Next to protecting against the current generation of fingerprinting attacks, one of the goals of PriVaricator is to provide a platform for supporting evolving defenses as new fingerprinting vectors emerge. For example, canvas-based fingerprinting, can be thwarted by adding small amounts of noise to the image returned via `getImageData`. Based on our experience in implementing the existing randomization policies, we believe that adding canvas support to PriVaricator will not differ in any substantial way, in terms of the extent of the changes (topical changes in a small number of canvas-specific functions to probabilistically modify pixel values) and performance overhead. Moreover, the effect of adding, say, 5% random noise to a handful of pixels in the canvas, will break the linkability of canvas-fingerprints while being imperceptible to users. Thus we consider it unlikely that the implementation of canvas-support in PriVaricator would significantly change our current performance and usability results.

Fluid browser updates enable changing PriVaricator policies: Given that today's browsers have migrated to an almost weekly update cadence (at least in the case of Firefox and Chrome), shipping updated randomization policies is an easy task. Note that similar updates are shipped to other browser-hosted security mechanisms such as XSS filters, malware filters, and tracking protection lists (TPLs). Extensions such as ad blockers [3] also update their blacklists on a regular basis. As such, we feel that PriVaricator provides an extensible platform for stateless fingerprinting defenses. All of the above examples constitute much more sizable changes compared to small PriVaricator policy updates.

7. RELATED WORK

In this section, we provide an overview of literature focusing on browser fingerprinting.

History of fingerprinting: The work of Mayer [16] and Eckersley [12] presents large-scale studies that show the possibility of effective stateless web tracking via only the attributes of a user's browsing environment. These studies prompted some follow-up efforts [13, 25] to build better fingerprinting libraries. Yen *et al.* [27] performed a fingerprinting study by analyzing month-long logs of Bing and Hotmail and showed that the combination of the User-agent HTTP header with a client's IP address were enough to track approximately 80% of the hosts in their dataset.

While the majority of fingerprinting efforts have focused on fonts and plugins, Mowery and Shacham proposed fingerprinting through the rendering of text and WebGL scenes to a `<canvas>` element [18]. Different browsers will display text and graphics in a different way which, however small, can be used to differentiate and track users. The downsides to this method are that these technologies are only available in the latest versions of modern browsers and that the canvas-generated entropy is not sufficient for it to be used as the only fingerprinted attribute. This is, in practice, exemplified by the statement of AddThis, the company responsible for 95% of the canvas-based fingerprinting that Acar et al. [1] discovered in a recent study. In a follow-up interview, AddThis claimed about canvas-based fingerprinting that "It's not uniquely identifying enough." [4]

Extensions: As analyzed by Nikiforakis *et al.* [20] and discussed in Section 6, browser extensions that spoof a browser's User Agent, may actually be counter-productive, since they considerably narrow down the population of possible users to fingerprint, in addition to frequently reporting impossible combinations of environment variables. PriVaricator goes deeper than these extensions, focusing on portions of the environment that can be spoofed to break fingerprinters, while not significantly affecting other sites.

FireGloves, proposed by Boda *et al.* [8, 9] but no longer supported, was a browser extension that attempted to frustrate fingerprinting attempts by faking the screen resolution and timezone, presenting an empty `navigator.plugins` list, limiting the number of font families allowed to load per tab, and randomizing the return value of `offsetWidth` and `offsetHeight` of elements. As we showed in Section 5.2, presenting an empty list of plugins is as bad as presenting a full list of plugins, since the majority of browsers support at least one plugin. In contrast, PriVaricator chooses to randomize the existing list of plugins which results in a large number of different plugin combinations. The randomized offset value of FireGloves is a random value between 0 and 1,000. As shown in our evaluation of site breakage, Section 5.3, this randomization approach produces the most breakage. Moreover, our randomized values were constrained to a range of 0 to 100, meaning that if one assumes a positive correlation between the size of the set of possible offset values and breakage, FireGloves has the potential to cause considerably more breakage. Contrastingly, in PriVaricator, we sought to find the best balance between defeating fingerprinters and minimizing breakage, by systematically testing our randomization policies against both, and arriving at a range of suitable parameters. Lastly, since FireGloves performs its operations through getters and setters, it suffers from the transparency and compatibility problems we mentioned in Section 4.

In recent work, Besson et al. [6] modeled the problem of privacy protection against fingerprinting and provided upper bounds for the identifiability of each user under different randomization algorithms and usability constraints.

Side channels: Researchers have proposed a variety of side channels for browser fingerprinting which have not yet been discovered to be used in practice. Mowery *et al.* [17] proposed the use of benchmark execution time as a way of fingerprinting JavaScript implementations, under the assumption that specific versions of JavaScript engines will perform in a consistent way. Closely related is the work of Mulazzani *et al.* who used the errors produced by JavaScript engines when executing standard test suites to differentiate between browsers [19]. Olejnik *et al.* [21] show that web history can also be used as a way of fingerprinting for tracking purposes. The authors make this observation by analyzing a corpus of data from when the CSS-visited history bug was still present in browsers. Today, however, all browsers have corrected this issue, so extraction of user history is not as straightforward, especially without user interaction [26]. We are not aware of wide-scale fingerprinting on the web using any of these side channels. This is part of the reason why chose to focus on explicit fingerprint in PriVaricator.

8. CONCLUSION

This paper proposes PriVaricator, an addition to privacy modes present in modern browsers. The goal of PriVaricator is to combat stateless tracking, which is being done primarily using device-fingerprinting JavaScript code. We use careful randomization as a way to make subsequent visits to the same fingerprinter difficult to link together. We evaluate several families of *randomization functions* to find those that result in the best balance between fingerprinting prevention and breaking existing sites. While our implementation has focused on randomizing font- and plugin-related properties, we demonstrate how our approach can be made general with pluggable randomization policies.

Our best randomization policies reliably prevent *all* fingerprinting when tested with several well-known device fingerprinting providers, while incurring minimal damage on the content of the Alexa top 1,000 sites. Furthermore, we found the runtime overhead of PriVaricator to be negligible and discussed how PriVaricator can be used as a platform where randomization-based countermeasures can be straightforwardly incorporated as new fingerprinting vectors emerge.

Acknowledgments: We thank the anonymous reviewers for their valuable comments, and Linode for providing us with virtual machines that made our large-scale experiments possible. For KU Leuven, this research was performed with the financial support of the Prevention against Crime Programme of the European Union (B-CCENTRE), the Research Fund KU Leuven, the IWT project SPION and the EU FP7 project NESSoS.

9. REFERENCES

[1] G. Acar, C. Eubank, S. Englehardt, M. Juarez, A. Narayanan, and C. Diaz. In *Proceedings of the 21st ACM Conference on Computer and Communications Security (CCS)*, 2014.

[2] G. Acar, M. Juarez, N. Nikiforakis, C. Diaz, S. Gürses, F. Piessens, and B. Preneel. FPDetective: Dusting the Web for fingerprinters. In *Proceedings of the ACM Conference on Computer and Communications Security (CCS)*, 2013.

[3] Adblock plus - for annoyance-free web surfing. `http://adblockplus.org`.

[4] J. Angwin. Meet the Online Tracking Device That is Virtually Impossible to Block. `http://www.propublica.org/article/meet-the-online-tracking-device-that-is-virtually-impossible-to-block`.

[5] D. Baron. Preventing attacks on a user's history through CSS:visited selectors. `http://dbaron.org/mozilla/visited-privacy`, 2010.

[6] F. Besson, N. Bielova, and T. Jensen. Browser Randomisation against Fingerprinting: A Quantitative Information Flow Approach. In *Proceedings of the 19th Nordic Conference on Secure IT Systems (NordSec)*, pages 181–196, 2014.

[7] BlueCava. Measuring Mobile Advertising ROI Using BlueCava Device Identification. 2011.

[8] K. Boda. Firegloves. `http://fingerprint.pet-portal.eu/?menu=6`.

[9] K. Boda, A. M. Földes, G. G. Gulyás, and S. Imre. User tracking on the web via cross-browser fingerprinting. In *Proceedings of the Nordic Conference on Information Security Technology for Applications (NordSec)*, 2012.

[10] Bitcoin Payment Buttons - Bitcoin Merchant Tools. `https://coinbase.com/docs/merchant_tools/payment_buttons`.

[11] P. Eckersley. The Panopticlick project. `https://panopticlick.eff.org/`.

[12] P. Eckersley. How Unique Is Your Browser? In *Proceedings of the Privacy Enhancing Technologies Symposium (PETS)*, pages 1–17, 2010.

[13] E. Flood and J. Karlsson. Browser fingerprinting, 2012.

[14] C. Fournet, N. Swamy, J. Chen, P.-E. Dagand, P.-Y. Strub, and B. Livshits. Fully abstract compilation to javascript. In *Proceedings of the Symposium on Principles of Programming Languages (POPL)*, 2013.

[15] iovation. Solving online credit fraud using device identification and reputation. 2007.

[16] J. R. Mayer. Any person... a pamphleteer. Senior Thesis, Stanford University, 2009.

[17] K. Mowery, D. Bogenreif, S. Yilek, and H. Shacham. Fingerprinting information in JavaScript implementations. In H. Wang, editor, *Proceedings of W2SP 2011*. IEEE Computer Society, May 2011.

[18] K. Mowery and H. Shacham. Pixel perfect: Fingerprinting canvas in HTML5. In *Proceedings of the Workshop on Web 2.0 Security and Privacy (W2SP)*. IEEE Computer Society, May 2012.

[19] M. Mulazzani, P. Reschl, M. Huber, M. Leithner, S. Schrittwieser, and E. Weippl. Fast and reliable browser identification with javascript engine fingerprinting. In *Web 2.0 Workshop on Security and Privacy (W2SP)*, May 2013.

[20] N. Nikiforakis, A. Kapravelos, W. Joosen, C. Kruegel, F. Piessens, and G. Vigna. Cookieless monster: Exploring the ecosystem of web-based device fingerprinting. In *Proceedings of the IEEE Symposium on Security and Privacy*, pages 541–555, 2013.

[21] Ł. Olejnik, C. Castelluccia, and A. Janc. Why Johnny Can't Browse in Peace: On the Uniqueness of Web Browsing History Patterns. In *Proceedings of the Workshop on Hot Topics in Privacy Enhancing Technologies (HOTPETS)*.

[22] K. Sivaramakrishnan. The Drawbridge Cross Device Matching Technology.

[23] ThreatMetrix. Device Fingerprinting and Fraud Protection Whitepaper.

[24] Tor: Cross-Origin Fingerprinting Unlinkability. `https://www.torproject.org/projects/torbrowser/design/#fingerprinting-linkability`.

[25] V. Vasilyev. fingerprintjs library. `https://github.com/Valve/fingerprintjs`, 2013.

[26] Z. Weinberg, E. Y. Chen, P. R. Jayaraman, and C. Jackson. I still know what you visited last summer: Leaking browsing history via user interaction and side channel attacks. In *Proceedings of the IEEE Symposium on Security and Privacy*, 2011.

[27] T.-F. Yen, Y. Xie, F. Yu, R. P. Yu, and M. Abadi. Host fingerprinting and tracking on the Web: Privacy and security implications. In *Proceddings of the Network and Distributed System Security Symposium (NDSS)*, 2012.

APPENDIX

Coinbase

Figure 5 shows the distribution of non-unique device identifiers when testing PriVaricator (with the ± 5% Noise policy active) against Coinbase. Colors and symbols represent clusters of identical values, e.g., all green plus-signs denote the same device identifier as generated and reported by Coinbase. As was the case with fingerprintjs (discussed in Section 5.2), PriVaricator deceives Coinbase in the majority of cases (78.81% of the extracted device identifiers were unique).

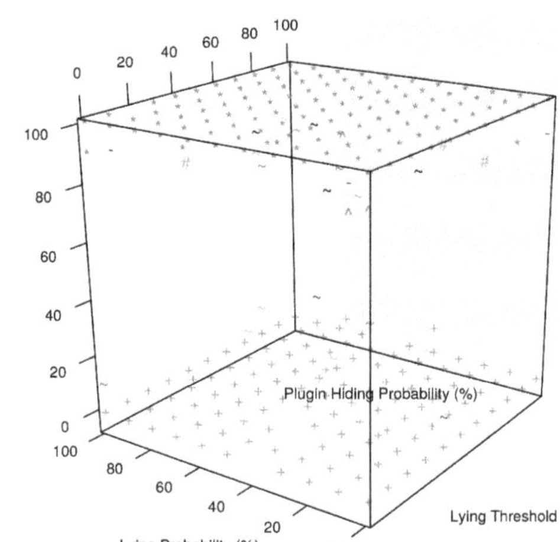

Figure 5: Distribution of non-unique device identifiers of PriVaricator against the Coinbase service.

Diagnoses, Decisions, and Outcomes: Web Search as Decision Support for Cancer

Michael J. Paul*
Johns Hopkins University
3400 N. Charles Street
Baltimore, MD 21218
mpaul@cs.jhu.edu

Ryen W. White
Microsoft Research
One Microsoft Way
Redmond, WA 98052
ryenw@microsoft.com

Eric Horvitz
Microsoft Research
One Microsoft Way
Redmond, WA 98052
horvitz@microsoft.com

ABSTRACT

People diagnosed with a serious illness often turn to the Web for their rising information needs, especially when decisions are required. We analyze the search and browsing behavior of searchers who show a surge of interest in prostate cancer. Prostate cancer is the most common serious cancer in men and is a leading cause of cancer-related death. Diagnoses of prostate cancer typically involve reflection and decision making about treatment based on assessments of preferences and outcomes. We annotated timelines of treatment-related queries from nearly 300 searchers with tags indicating different phases of treatment, including decision making, preparation, and recovery. Using this corpus, we present a variety of analyses toward the goal of understanding search and decision making about treatments. We characterize search queries and the content of accessed pages for different treatment phases, model search behavior during the decision-making phase, and create an aggregate alignment of treatment timelines illustrated with a variety of visualizations. The experiments provide insights about how people who are engaged in intensive searches about prostate cancer over an extended period of time pursue and access information from the Web.

Categories and Subject Descriptors: H.2.8 [Database management]: Database applications—*data mining*

Keywords: medical search; decision making; cancer

1. INTRODUCTION

Upon diagnosis of a major illness, people frequently turn to the Web for information about the course and prognosis of the disease, and to better understand treatments and outcomes [6, 19, 27, 36]. We seek to understand the use of Web search as a medical decision support system by patients who have been diagnosed with a significant disease. In particular, we study the use of Web search to support the decisions of searchers who show salient signs of having been recently diagnosed with prostate cancer. We aim to characterize and enhance the ability of Web search engines to provide decision support for different phases of the illness.

We focus on prostate cancer for several reasons. Prostate cancer is typically slow-growing, leaving patients and physicians with time to reflect on the best course of action. There is no medical consensus about the best treatment option, as the primary options all have similar mortality rates, each with their own tradeoffs and side effects [24]. The choice of treatments for prostate cancer is therefore particularly sensitive to consideration of patients' preferences about outcomes and to the assessed likelihoods of achieving different outcomes. For these reasons, prostate cancer is an "archetypal condition" for the use of decision aids [25].

Guidance on decisions is provided primarily via consultation with a patient's physician and larger care team. Formal decision-making materials may be available through patients' physicians. However, Web search is becoming a common supplement to traditional decision aids [29, 4]. In a 2011 survey of prostate cancer patients, the Internet was found to be the second most common information source for making treatment decisions, after "doctor's recommendation" [37]. An earlier survey found that more than half of the respondents who had searched the Web prior to deciding on a treatment reported that information reviewed online had influenced their decision [32]. Search for information on major illnesses includes information gathering about treatments and outcomes, including characterization of uncertainties about outcomes for different treatments. Beyond providing information about illness, search and retrieval sessions serve as opportunities for interactive assessment of preferences about outcomes and risk. Thus, we are particularly interested in how people learn about different therapeutic options, including how they progress over time in navigating trees of possibilities.

To pursue insights about search and retrieval as medical decision support, we adapt methods developed in a prior study on the use of Web search for pursuing information on breast cancer [31]. In that work, classifiers were constructed from annotated logs to infer that a searcher had likely received a diagnosis of breast cancer. An ontology of different kinds of information needs was introduced to characterize the dynamics of information-seeking for a large set of searchers aligned by an inferred date of diagnosis. We harness similar methods to seek insights about prostate cancer, but focus on decision making and other search activities aligned with different phases of treatment. Specifically, we

*Work conducted during a Microsoft Research internship.

WWW 2015, May 18–22, 2015, Florence, Italy.
ACM 978-1-4503-3469-3/15/05.
http://dx.doi.org/10.1145/2736277.2741662.

perform studies that extend previous work in a number of ways and make the following contributions:

- We create a hierarchy of treatments and associated search terms, as well as an annotated corpus of 272 timelines of treatment search queries.
- We present a characterization of different phases of treatment search, exemplified by n-grams from queries and the content of visited webpages associated with each phase in the annotated corpus. We further characterize the phases and their progression over time by creating a multiple sequence alignment of timelines. We create a series of visualizations illustrating how the phases and queries evolve over time, based on the alignment.
- Focusing specifically on queries tagged as pursuit of decision support, we analyze the number and specificity of treatments that are searched over time, the treatments that co-occur in comparative searches, and transitions among the treatments at the focus of attention in successive queries. We identify and visualize typical sequences of treatment queries traversed by searchers by applying a spanning-tree algorithm to a graph of query transitions.

After presenting analyses and findings on the use of the Web for decision support, we discuss implications and directions for the design of search and retrieval systems that help people to better understand diagnoses and treatment decisions moving forward.

2. RELATED WORK

The Web is an important source of health-related information for many people. According to a 2013 survey, 59% of American adults had used the Web to find health information in the year preceding the survey, 35% of those adults engaged in self-diagnosis, and over half of these self-diagnosing searchers then discussed the matter with a clinician [14]. Despite the potential benefits, concerns have been raised about the quality of online health information [9] including cancer information [17]. A survey of oncologists noted that Web use can "simultaneously make patients more hopeful, confused, anxious, and knowledgeable." [19] In a large-scale survey of the use of search for self-diagnosis, White and Horvitz [42] found that almost 40% of participants experienced increased anxiety from searching health information online.

Such challenges highlight the criticality of understanding how patients use the Web, including the nature and dynamics of queries, and the content delivered in response to queries. To better understand how people pursue health information, studies have examined online health search using a variety of methods, including interviews [33], surveys [38], and analyses of large-scale search log data [3, 1, 20, 5, 43]. Search logs analyses can provide insights about how people use search engines [41], predict future search actions and interests [23, 10, 11], and detect real-world events and activities [34]. Applications of search log data in the health and medical domains include the detection of influenza [16] and the discovery of side effects of medications [44]. Studies of online information-seeking for cancer [6, 19] have characterized how cancer patients use Web resources and have proposed patient taxonomies describing how people employ retrieved health information. In the realm of search and retrieval on cancer, Bader et al [2] categorized cancer-related search queries from three months in 2001. More recently, Ofran et al. [27] used search log data to identify five phases of cancer search activity and showed that the phases mirror those associated with coping and grief that had been previously documented in the literature.

Information access about treatment options has been found to be important for cancer patients facing difficult therapeutic decisions. Cancer patients typically seek access to all relevant information [35, 15]. Valuable information about treatments and outcomes can come via reviewing testimonials from those afflicted with similar conditions [28]. Beyond providing information about treatment options, sharing health experiences online can help people to feel supported and to better engage with health services [46]. Formal decision aids [26] have been used to help patients decide among treatment alternatives, by providing information that helps to resolve or to clarify their uncertainties [25]. A study found that working with decision aids for prostate cancer could influence decisions about treatment strategy [39].

3. TREATMENT TIMELINES

We focus on the analysis of **treatment timelines** extracted from search query logs. A treatment timeline for prostate cancer is a time-stamped sequence of search queries that contain terms pertaining to prostate cancer treatment, where sequences of queries are associated with unique, anonymized user identifiers. The set of treatment timelines was created by first identifying relevant search histories via a series of filters that are described in detail in Section 4. We tag the queries in the treatment timelines with labels indicating the assessed phase of treatment, including whether the searcher appears to be seeking information for an initial or a follow-on, secondary treatment, and whether the queries appear to be aimed at seeking information decisions about a treatment, preparation for a chosen treatment, or recovery from a treatment, as described in Section 4.4.

In Section 5, we present a series of experimental analyses of the treatment timelines. We characterize the content associated with different phases of information pursuit and show how these phases evolve over time for a set of searchers who are temporally aligned by inferred date of diagnosis.

3.1 Treatment Hierarchy

In order to extract treatment timelines from search histories, we identify a set of search terms that searchers tend to use to refer to prostate cancer treatment options. As queries range from very general (e.g. "cancer treatment") to very specific (e.g. "low dose radiation seed implants"), we organized the terms into a hierarchical ontology of known treatments, moving from broad categories down to detailed therapies. Such a treatment hierarchy enables us to analyze treatment timelines in terms of categories of treatments as well as the raw text used to describe options. We can characterize the different types of treatments that are searched and the degree of specificity of queries, based on the depth of the query terms in the hierarchy.

Table 1 shows the treatment hierarchy and the terms associated with each category. The treatment hierarchy was constructed by an extensive review of the literature on the management of prostate cancer. Categories in the treatment hierarchy reflect current standard treatment options for prostate cancer. "Observation" is a treatment option that refers to a decision to forgo treatment for the time being; the two common methods of observation are typically

Level 0	Level 1	Level 2	Level 3	Search terms
Treatment	–	–	–	treatment(s)
Treatment	Surgery	–	–	surgery, prostatectomy, prostate removal, remove prostate
Treatment	Surgery	Open	–	open [Surgery]
Treatment	Surgery	Laparoscopic	–	laparoscopic, minimally invasive
Treatment	Surgery	Laparoscopic	Robotic	robot, robotic, da( )vinci
Treatment	Radiation	–	–	radiation
Treatment	Radiation	Brachytherapy	–	brachytherapy, brachy, seed(s)
Treatment	Radiation	Brachytherapy	LDR	low dose [Brachytherapy], ldr
Treatment	Radiation	Brachytherapy	HDR	high dose [Brachytherapy], hdr
Treatment	Radiation	External	–	external [Radiation], external beam, ebrt
Treatment	Radiation	External	3DRT	3drt, 3dcrt, conformal
Treatment	Radiation	External	IMRT	imrt, intensity-modulated, igrt, calypso
Treatment	Radiation	External	SBRT	sbrt, stereotactic body, cyber( )knife, gamma( )knife, x-knife
Treatment	Radiation	External	Proton	proton, pencil beam
Treatment	Radiation	Drugs	Radium 223	radium 223, radium dichloride, xofigo
Treatment	Hormone therapy	–	–	hormone/hormonal therapy, hormone/hormonal treatment
Treatment	Hormone therapy	LHRH	...	*various hormone-therapeutic drugs are categorized*
Treatment	Hormone therapy	Anti-Androgen	...	*various hormone-therapeutic drugs are categorized*
Treatment	Chemotherapy	–	–	chemotherapy, chemo
Treatment	Chemotherapy	Drugs	...	*various chemotherapeutic drugs are categorized*
Treatment	HIFU	–	–	hifu, high-intensity
Treatment	Cryotherapy	–	–	cryotherapy, cryosurgery, cryoablation, cryo
Treatment	Observation	None	–	no treatment, without treatment
Treatment	Observation	Waiting	–	waiting [Treatment]
Treatment	Observation	Surveillance	–	active surveillance

Table 1: Four-level treatment hierarchy. For space, we do not display several specific drugs at level 3. Brackets indicate co-occurrence constraints with the term. For example "open [Surgery]" indicates that the term "open" is considered as an entry only if it occurs in the same query as a term in the Surgery category.

referred to as "watchful waiting" and "active surveillance" by clinicians. These options may be recommended when the cancer is low grade and the risks of treatment are assessed as outweighing the risks of the disease [21]. HIFU (high-intensity focused ultrasound) and cryotherapy are newer experimental treatments that are less common, though still found to be frequently searched. Another type of treatment, immunotherapy (affecting the patient's immune response), is rarely found in queries in our dataset, and is not included in our analysis.

4. DATASET CREATION

We now review the extraction and tagging of data for the study, including the formulation of relevant search terms, labeling of searchers as likely facing prostate cancer decisions, and annotating phases of long-term timelines.

4.1 Ontology of Relevant Terms

To identify relevant search queries for the study, we relied on a manually-curated ontology of terms of interest. Terms are organized in a four-level hierarchy and include terms related to screening methods, diagnosis (e.g. "biopsy"), cancer staging and grading information (e.g. "stage II", "low grade"), and various treatment options. The formulation of relevant query terms is similar to efforts to construct an ontology for search and retrieval for breast cancer [31], and is distinct from the treatment ontology in Table 1.

4.2 Search and Browsing Logs

The data for this study comes from a proprietary set of anonymized logs from consenting users of the Internet Explorer Web browser. The data includes time-stamped search queries issued through the browser (primarily via interactions with the Microsoft Bing search engine) and time-stamped webpage visits. Each log entry includes a unique anonymized user identifier. The data spans an 18-month period from March 2013 to August 2014.

The initial dataset consists of logs collected from users whose queries include the bigram "prostate cancer" at least three times during this time period. This policy was employed as an initial high-recall filter to identify search histories that would likely be relevant to the study. Given our focus on treatment-related search, we filtered the set for search histories including queries containing treatment-related terms listed in Table 1 (excluding the most general term, "treatment"). This extraction procedure yielded a set of 3,066 search histories.

4.3 Experiential vs. Exploratory Searchers

A key initial task with the extracted data is to identify a high-precision set of search histories from the 3,066 candidate histories. Ideally, the resulting focused set would contain only histories of those who actually experienced a diagnosis of prostate cancer—either personally, or via the intensive searching performed with regard to the diagnosis of a close family member or friend. However, we cannot conclude with certainty whether a searcher is in this situation based only on information in the logs. We consider searchers as *experiential* versus less-involved *exploratory* searchers based on an assessment of *sustained* and *focused* interest in prostate cancer. We exclude search histories that are inconsistent with a cancer diagnosis. Following an annotation of logs as being experiential versus exploratory, we train a classifier (described below) on a small set of labeled histories to identify experiential searchers among the set of candidates in an automated manner.

We annotated a sample of 100 histories with binary relevance tags using the criteria outlined above. One of the authors (EH), with formal medical and decision analysis train-

Phase	# histories	# queries
Initial decision	174	2008
Initial preparation	126	882
Initial post-treatment	140	1232
Secondary decision	84	769
Secondary preparation	24	114
Secondary post-treatment	18	85
Total	272	5090

Table 2: Number of search histories and search queries labeled with each phase in the dataset.

ing (including decision analyses for the treatment of prostate cancer), provided insights on the coding criteria. Beyond leveraging knowledge of prostate cancer and its treatment, we considered distinctions that capture sustained and intensive focus of attention. As examples, a search history with a brief burst of interest that fades away is considered negative because the searcher does not show sustained interest. Histories that include searches for many different diseases are also labeled negative, as people grappling with a new diagnosis are likely to focus on a single illness and its challenges and trajectory. We also exclude searchers who appear to be medical professionals, as their queries include such searches as billing codes or instructions for administering a treatment. The goal was to rule out histories that were not plausibly experiential, in order to reduce noise in the analyzed data, even if we cannot know the ground truth.

Each history was independently coded by two annotators (the first author and one of the two other authors). In cases of disagreement, the final labels were resolved after discussion among the annotators. In some cases, annotators did not commit to an initial label, and instead marked a history as ambiguous to be resolved upon discussion. Annotators were shown all anonymized search sessions containing medical terms contained in the ontology (described in Section 4.1), including terms related to diagnosis, staging, and treatment, as well as other terms such as a set of symptoms and names of diseases. In the final set of annotations, 63% of histories were tagged as experiential.

These annotated histories (combined with similar annotations for breast cancer) were used to train a classifier to identify experiential cancer search histories [31]. The classifier uses a variety of lexical, distributional, and temporal pattern features, and is estimated to have 96% precision and 78% recall (AUC .891) from 5-fold cross validation. After applying the classifier to the 3,066 candidate histories, we identified 1,413 experiential histories.

We then applied an additional filter condition to the positively classified histories: Given our focus on decision support and the process of decision making about treatments, we only include in the final dataset those search histories that contain terms indicative of information-gathering and deliberation about treatment: "vs", "better", "best", "pros", "cons", "which", "option(s)", "should i". This final step yielded a corpus of 272 histories, which we then annotated with additional information, described in the next subsection.

4.4 Annotation of Treatment Timelines

Last, we annotated the treatment timelines—the experiential search histories projected down to only those queries containing treatment terms—with richer tags to allow for finer-grained analysis. The queries are tagged as belonging to different phases of the treatment process that we had observed as common patterns in the timelines. We were particularly interested in tagging queries that appeared to indicate decision making, but we also tagged other phases of treatment-related queries for queries that appeared to come before and after a treatment had occurred.

Each query was annotated with two labels. The first is one of three states of the treatment deliberation process:

- **Decision:** Queries that appear to be used to help a searcher decide between or learn more about different treatment options. These queries would sometimes contain explicit indicators that the searcher is considering different options (e.g. "best treatment options", "which is better", "pros and cons"). Queries for many different treatments in the same timeframe are considered decision queries.
- **Preparation:** Queries about a treatment that appears to be scheduled but before the treatment has taken place (e.g. "what to expect"). If a search history focuses on a single treatment for many days (as opposed to exploring multiple options), we consider these queries preparatory.
- **Post-treatment:** Queries that appear to take place after a treatment has commenced or completed. These may seek information about recovery, or queries regarding side effects that are experienced. Some queries include specific timing references (e.g., "3 weeks after surgery") which can help with determining this label.

The second label captures whether the context of a search session is an initial or follow-up treatment:

- **Initial:** The first round treatment that the searcher is considering, typically surgery or radiation.
- **Secondary:** Any treatment that follows an initial treatment, typically adjuvant radiation, hormone therapy, or chemotherapy for more advanced cancer. Secondary status is often clear from queries with explicit indicators like the term "adjuvant" or including such terms as "after surgery".

The cross-product of these tags defines a total of six different phases of treatment-related search.

The queries were categorized assuming that they were issued by patients experiencing cancer and in reference to treatment for a specific patient, who may be the searcher himself or a family member deeply involved in decisions about the illness. The goal was to group the search activity based on common characteristics that are observable in the data and consistent with a typical patient timeline.

Ambiguous queries were tagged with multiple phases. If more than one phase was included, the phases were ranked based on which phase the annotator believed was most likely. Queries that did not fit these phase labels were not annotated. The tagging of the phases was done by the first author and a second professional annotator formally trained in linguistics. The first annotator reviewed the secondary annotations to ensure consistency of tagging procedures.

Table 2 provides the number of queries labeled with each phase as well as the number of search histories with at least one query labeled with the phase. In the case of ambiguous annotations, only the most likely label was counted in this table. Additionally, the 272 histories contained 33,945 queries that were not annotated with these phase labels.

5. ANALYZING TREATMENT PATTERNS

We now discuss methods and results on characterizing the different phases of treatment as well as the dynamics of the progression of searchers through the phases over time.

5.1 Phase Characterization

We characterize different annotated phases of searcher timelines by identifying n-grams—from search queries and webpage bodies—and domain names that are most associated with retrieval in each phase. We wish to identify features that are *salient*—both probable and representative of the phase [8]. We achieve this with a two-component mixture model that mixes phase-specific feature distributions with a phase-independent background distribution which accounts for common features that are not representative of any particular phase [45].

With this model, the probability of a feature i (an n-gram or a domain name) in the text associated with phase k is a mixture of two parameters θ:

$$P(\text{feature} = i|\text{phase} = k) = \lambda\theta_i^B + (1-\lambda)\theta_i^k \quad (1)$$

Each θ^k is a distribution over features specific to the phase k, while θ^B is a background distribution over features independent of phase, and λ is the mixing weight. Then, we examine the θ^k distributions to find salient feature associations with phase k, because these distributions will put the most mass on n-grams that are probable within the phase but are not better explained by the background distribution.

Experiment Details.

We created a model for each class of features (search and page n-grams, and page domain names) from the annotated queries. We modeled bigrams and trigrams. Features derived from webpage content include the pages visited during the same search session following an annotated query (i.e., on the post-query navigational trail), which is possible since we used browser logs for our analysis. To extract page content, we used the method described in [40], which extracts lines of HTML such that the ratio of text tokens to tags tokens is at least one standard deviation above the mean ratio. This is a simple heuristic for identifying the core content in the page, rather than supplementary text such as navigation menus and page footers.

The parameter posteriors for the mixture model are inferred using Gibbs sampling. We averaged the parameter values from every 100 sampling iterations, collected from 4000 iterations after a 2000-iteration burn-in. The θ parameters were given Dirichlet(0.01) priors, and λ was given a Beta(9000, 1000) prior, so that high values of λ (favoring the background distribution) are *a priori* more likely, resulting in stronger feature associations.[1]

When encoding feature values for the mixture model (i.e., the number of times each feature is observed within each class label), we used fractional values when annotators included multiple labels for a query. Since annotators provide labels in order of likelihood, we set the fraction to be twice as high for the more probable label. For example, two labels results in counts of $\frac{2}{3}$ and $\frac{1}{3}$ for features in that query.

[1]We used existing software for cross-collection Latent Dirichlet Allocation (ccLDA) [30], a topic model that learns topics for multiple collections of text as well as collection-independent background topics. This two-component model is a special case of ccLDA with only one topic.

Results.

Table 3 shows the top features for each phase, displaying the highest probability n-grams and domain names under each θ^k. For space and simplicity, the table only displays bigrams and not trigrams.

We see that the general query "treatment options" is associated with both the initial and secondary decision phases. The initial decision phase is also associated with queries containing the trigram "pros and cons", as well as explicit comparative n-grams like "surgery vs radiation". The decision phase also has a high probability of queries for "active surveillance" and "watchful waiting"—options for non-treatment that do not apply to later phases, once treatment has started. The page n-grams are similar, with general terms regarding treatment options. The bigrams "clinical trial(s)" are highly probable in the secondary decision pages.

A top query trigram for the initial preparation phase is "what to expect", while many of the top query n-grams for initial post-treatments are variants of "after surgery" or "after prostatectomy". Searchers look for general recovery information, as well as information about performing various activities after treatment (e.g. "sex after") and treatment side effects (e.g. "incontinence after"). The n-grams from retrieved pages for these two phases both include a number of treatment side effects ("erectile dysfunction", "urinary incontinence"), as well as n-grams containing the word "catheter".

The top search n-grams for all secondary phases include medications used in hormonal therapies (e.g. "lupron", "zytiga"), and "adjuvant radiation", referring to a type of radiation that is given after the initial surgery. The top page n-grams for the secondary phases have terms related to drugs and their side effects.

We see that `youtube.com` is the top domain name for initial preparation. In general, videos are associated with the initial preparation and decision phases. 26.2% and 28.2% of users visited pages with "video(s)" in the title or URL during initial preparation and decision sessions, while only 8.3% of users visited such pages during the initial post-treatment sessions. Almost no users visited video pages during the secondary phases.

We also observe that the initial recovery phase contains many n-grams containing first person pronouns in the top page content n-grams, and `cancerforums.net` is the top domain name. There is an association of forums with the initial post-treatment phase. 48.8% of users visited pages with "forum(s)", "discussion(s)", or "community" in the title or URL during this phase. This is substantially higher than the percentage during the initial decision (35.9%) or secondary decision (37.1%) phases, which had the next highest percentages of such visits.

The top domain names associated with the background distribution in the mixture model (the distribution independent of phase) are `webmd.com`, `cancer.org`, `cancer.gov`, `ask.com`, and `ehow.com`. These are the most probable domains visited, even though many of these are not associated with particular phases, and so do not appear in Table 3.

5.2 Evolution of Queries on Treatments

We now focus specifically on the "initial decision" phase, with the goal of seeking an understanding of the sequential patterns of information gathering about treatments and outcomes during decision making.

Initial Decision	Initial Preparation	Initial Post-treatment	Secondary Decision	Secondary Prep.	Secondary Post.
Search queries					
prostate cancer	after prostate	after prostate	after a	adjuvant radiation	seed implants
cancer treatment	surgery for	after prostatectomy	a radical	how much	hdr treatment
proton therapy	robotic prostatectomy	prostate surgery	psa of	taking lupron	pain in
best treatment	after prostatectomy	after surgery	radical prostatectomy	seed implants	cause pain
for prostate	on the	after radical	what are	lupron injections	radiation burns
cancer treatments	da vinci	radical prostatectomy	after radical	i stop	treatment cause
treatment options	what to	psa after	are the	stop taking	lupron treatment
pros and	home on	incontinence after	radiation after	i do	after seed
and cons	the same	how to	radiation therapy	can i	not effective
surgery for	vinci prostate	sex after	cancer treatment	treatment after	psa after
active surveillance	same day	after a	adjuvant radiation	will i	flomax after
da vinci	go home	after robotic	the side	to avoid	protectomy and
surgery vs	davinci prostate	after prostectomy	radiation be	prostate seed	after lupron
watchful waiting	for radical	radical prostectomy	treatment after	with catheter	radical protectomy
vs radiation	to expect	do i	whats next	zytiga cost	enlarged abdomen
treatment for	day of	what to	treatment options	catheter in	for high
cyberknife prostate	life after	on lupron	radiation what	lupron treatment	after medications
cons of	is surgery	levels after	if radiation	radiation after	medications not
prostate treatment	cryotherapy surgery	blood in	be next	taking casodex	long will
the best	kegel exercises	long does	post psa	on lupron	i take
Page content					
early stage	da vinci	prostate surgery	side effects	side effects	of radiation
stage prostate	prostate surgery	after surgery	advanced prostate	the radiation	how long
surgery and	surgery and	the catheter	radiation therapy	medical advice	side effects
cancer treatment	robotic surgery	surgery and	prostate cancer	hormone therapy	therapy is
cancer treatments	the catheter	the penis	early stage	call your	able to
da vinci	robotic prostatectomy	after prostate	hormone therapy	should not	may also
for prostate	surgery the	surgery the	of radiation	that you	cause the
radiation therapy	cancer surgery	surgery is	treatment of	radiation therapy	effects and
the tumor	an erection	the urethra	clinical trials	dose of	the radiation
robotic surgery	able to	an erection	the drug	do not	used to
side effects	erectile dysfunction	able to	treatment with	radiation oncology	weeks after
of urology	after prostate	the surgery	the treatment	used in	dose of
a treatment	of urology	after a	therapy for	your doctor	doctor if
diagnosed with	robotic prostate	most men	has spread	weeks after	talk with
minimally invasive	is removed	da vinci	cancer that	is given	your treatment
prostate surgery	the penis	catheter is	of treatment	list of	after treatment
the latest	minimally invasive	after radical	therapy is	to treat	do not
cancer surgery	the da	is removed	clinical trial	does not	change in
with prostate	most men	i had	of cancer	diagnosis or	have been
robotic prostatectomy	the bladder	incontinence after	psa level	radiation oncologist	the effects
Domain names					
cancer.gov	youtube.com	cancerforums.net	provenge.com	rxlist.com	chemocare.com
cancerfightingstrategies.com	aicr.org	urology.jhu.edu	pcf.org	crmc.org	cancerresearchuk.org
cancercenter.com	mayoclinic.org	healingwell.com	healthyliving.msn.com	uptodate.com	rxlist.com
seattlecca.org	surgery.about.com	medhelp.org	mciverclinic.com	medicinenet.com	radonc.ucla.edu
davinciprostatectomy.com	prostatecancer.org.au	livestrong.com	zytiga.com	cpmc.org	lvhn.org
internationalhifu.com	seer.cancer.gov	hisprostatecancer.com	cancer.net	link.springer.com	philaurology.com
davincisurgery.com	prostate-cancer-institute.org	uptodate.com	search.ask.com	zytiga.com	oncolink.org
provenge.com	ucomparehealthcare.com	healthcentral.com	lifescript.com	nature.com	healthline.com
iuhealth.net	prostatecancercare.com	simonfoundation.org	hisprostatecancer.com	patient.varian.com	ucsfhealth.org
seattlecancerwellness.com	urology.jhu.edu	myprostatedoc.blogspot.com	medscape.org	goodrx.com	hisprostatecancer.com

Table 3: Most probable bigrams associated with each of the six phases of treatment queries. Bigrams are estimated from the relevant search queries and text content and domain names of pages visited following those queries.

Number and Specificity of Treatments.

To understand the progression of treatment-related searches, we examine the average depth of the treatments searched (as defined in the treatment hierarchy displayed in Table 1) and the average cumulative number of treatments searched, as functions of the number of treatment queries conducted. These metrics can provide insights about the decision-making process, including changes over time in the specificity of treatment-related searches and the overall number of different treatments studied by the average user.

Figure 1 shows these values averaged across users for the first 11 initial decision queries, which is the average (10.9) number of queries in this phase (median 8).

We find that the first query is, on average, the broadest, with an average depth below 1, which means the bulk of initial queries contained general terms such as "treatment options". The depth increases nearly monotonically for the first 11 queries, showing that searchers ask for progressively more specific information. Beyond 11 queries, this trend levels off and becomes noisier, as the results are averaged among fewer users.

The average cumulative number of treatments searched in the initial query is 0.65, which means that only 65% of searchers specified a treatment initially, and the remaining 35% conducted a general query such as "best treatment options". After 11 queries, the average user has searched for 2.4 different treatments.

Treatment Comparisons.

We next consider treatments that are referenced together within the same query. Queries with multiple treatments are likely comparative, and we indeed observed a number of queries with explicit comparative language such as "vs", as highlighted in our n-gram characterization of the initial decision phase in the previous subsection.

We found that 9.6% of initial decision treatment queries contained more than one treatment in the same query, and 43.6% of users searched at least one query with multiple treatments. Examining the treatments that co-occurred, we found that 75% of such queries contained surgery and radiation, 7.3% contained different types of surgery, 7.3% con-

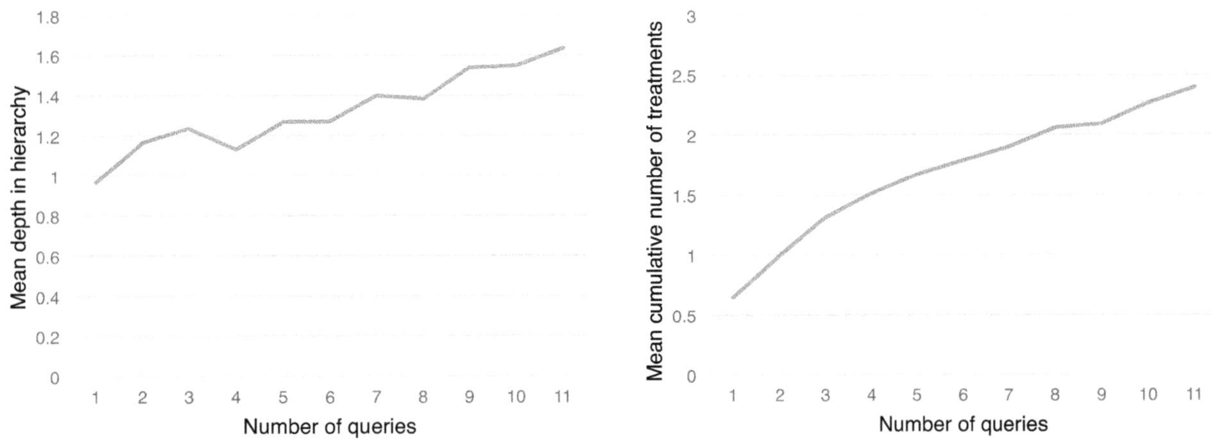

Figure 1: Left: Specificity of treatments searched over time by the average user during the initial decision phase, as given by each treatment query's depth in the treatment hierarchy in Table 1. Right: Cumulative number of different treatments searched over time by the average user. We use the mean number of queries in the decision phase (11 queries) as the range of the x axis.

tained surgery and observation, 6.3% contained radiation and hormone therapy, and 4.2% contained different types of radiation. Of the co-occurrences of surgery and radiation, 65.3% were for the most general terms (e.g., "surgery vs radiation"), while the others contained more specific types (e.g., "robotic surgery or seed implants").

Transitions among Treatments.

Finally, we examined the transition structure among different treatment types by analyzing the sequences of treatments that appear in consecutive queries within the same search session. These experiments were undertaken to pursue insights about how searchers refine their queries as they explore treatment options.

We examined how successive queries progress through the treatment hierarchy in Table 1. We found that 68.8% of the time, the same treatment is searched as in the previous query. In 12.7% of the cases, the subsequent query is more specific than the previous one, going deeper down the same branch in the hierarchy (e.g., searching "robotic surgery" after searching "surgery"), while the subsequent query is coarser (higher up along the branch) in 9.5% of cases. We found that 9.0% of subsequent queries are situated in an entirely different branch of the hierarchy (e.g. searching radiation after searching surgery).

We also explored *which* treatments are likely to be searched after a preceding treatment query. We construct a transition graph, where treatment categories are nodes, and directed edges are weighted by the number of times that one treatment was searched after the other. The graph includes a dummy START node, whose outgoing edges to each treatment node are weighted by the number of times that each treatment was in a user's *initial* query. To show a concise visualization of the typical transitions among treatments, we compute the maximum directed spanning tree of this dense graph, using the Chu-Liu-Edmonds algorithm [7, 12].

The induced tree is shown in Figure 2. The general treatment category (e.g., for non-specific queries such as "treatment options") and the coarsest surgery category follow from START. This may be taken as intuitive as our results above

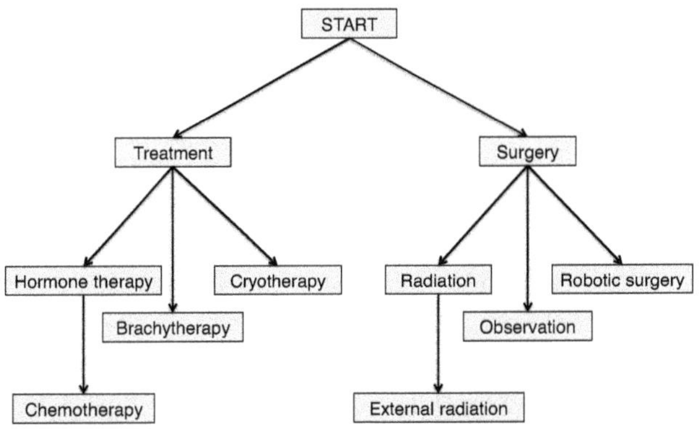

Figure 2: Maximum directed spanning tree induced from the treatment query transition graph.

showed that search histories most often begin with the general treatment category, and searches for surgery are the most common of all specific treatment types. Many of the edges are the same as those captured by the curated treatment hierarchy in Table 1: hormone therapy and cryotherapy following the general treatment category, robotic surgery following surgery, and external beam radiation following radiation. Other edges do not follow the natural hierarchy, but instead illustrate a typical order of treatments that searchers pursue via their queries. For example, searches for radiation and observation are most likely to follow surgery searches, which might be expected in light of the finding above that the most common comparative searches contain surgery and radiation, or surgery and observation.

The lowest-weight edges (weight of 3) are excluded to keep the tree concise, and because very low weight edges are likely to introduce noise. (Recall that edge weights are the number of times each treatment category was searched after the other.) One edge was from "Treatment" to "HIFU", which fits with the hierarchy in Table 1. The other edge was from START to "Open surgery", which is not a sensible result, but open surgery happened to be searched in the first query (3 times) more than after other queries.

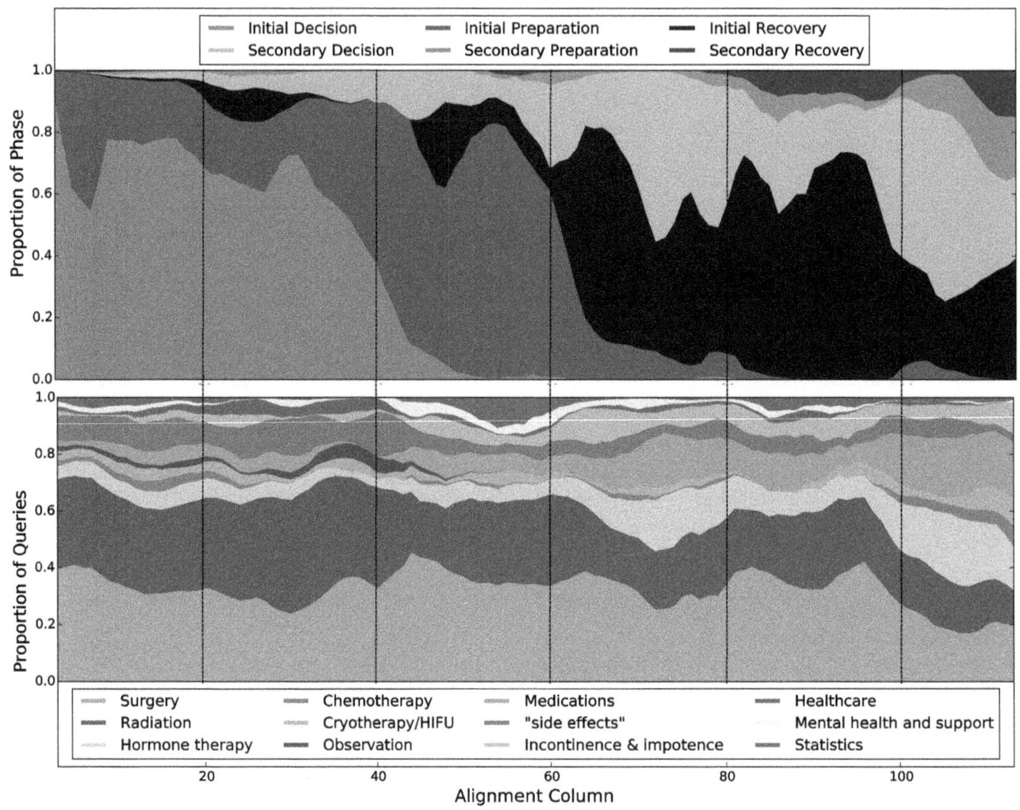

(a) Distribution over non-gap phases and content categories in each alignment column.

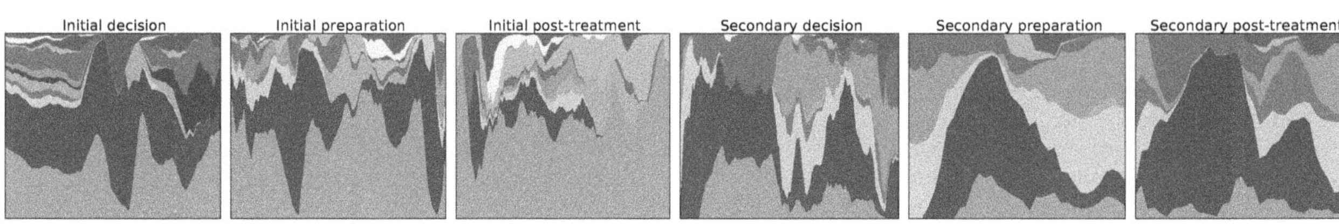

(b) The distribution over content categories in each alignment column, restricted to each particular phase.

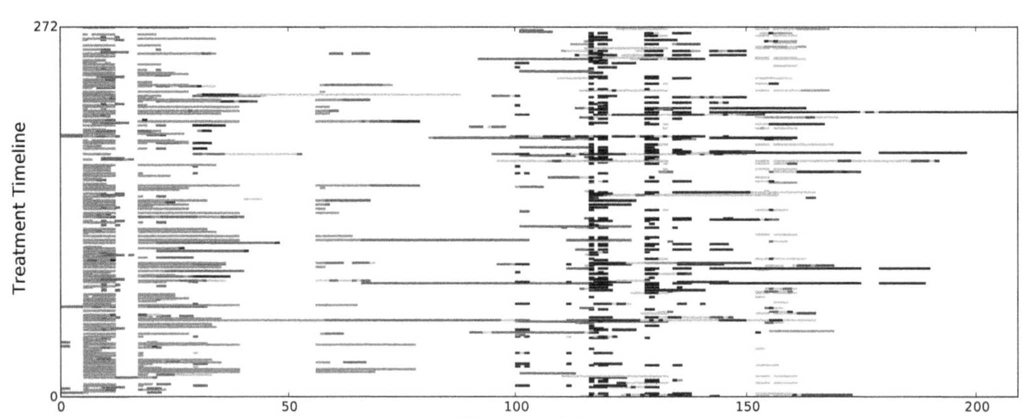

(c) Multiple sequence alignment of 272 treatment timelines. Colored dots represent the label in each row/column, using the legend at the top of (a). White space represents gaps.

Figure 3: Different visualizations of treatment timeline alignments.

5.3 Progression of Phases and Search Content

We focused in the previous section on temporal patterns within the initial decision phase. We now seek to understand the temporal patterns across all phases. We wish to visualize how the phases progress over time, and how the content of treatment queries evolves over time within each phase and across entire timelines.

No individual tagged search history contained all six phases described in Section 4.4. However, we can align and stitch together the partial timelines to visualize an "average" complete timeline, aggregated across the hundreds of histories.

Toward this goal, we computed a *multiple sequence alignment* of the timelines. Multiple sequence alignment (MSA) methods were developed in computational biology and are typically used to build a molecular sequence via alignment of smaller sequence snippets. Alignments are scored based on how well symbols at each position align, penalizing gaps and mismatches. The optimization problem is then to solve for a single alignment that gives the highest score.

Solving for the best alignment between two sequences can be done efficiently with dynamic programming, using the same procedure that is used to compute string edit distance. The size of the dynamic programming table increases exponentially with the number of sequences, making this problem NP-hard for an arbitrary number of sequences [18], and impractical for more than a few. Many methods have been developed in computational biology to approximately solve for an MSA efficiently, such as the merging of pairwise alignments. For this experiment, we used ClustalW (from `clustal.org`), a software package for aligning protein sequences [22]. While protein alignments typically use domain-specific scoring functions, we created custom scores appropriate for our task.

Each treatment timeline was considered to be a sequence, and each phase label in the timeline was treated to be a symbol in the sequence. The most likely label was chosen in cases where annotators listed more than one possibility, using the annotators' highest-ranked choice. We created special symbols for the first query with each phase label in the timeline, to encourage the start of each phase to align, so that they are not aligned to arbitrary positions. This means that there are 12 total symbols and 272 sequences.

Alignments are scored such that each position in the alignment is given a score of 1 if the symbols match. A score of 0.1 is given if the phases match, but one of the symbols is the special 'first time' indicator and the other is not. No credit is given for aligning different phases. We did not apply strong penalties for gaps, preferring alignments where different phases do not overlap. We used a penalty of 0.1 for gap creation, to discourage gaps with all other options being equal, with no penalty for introducing successive gaps.

Figure 3(c) shows the resulting MSA of the timelines. We see that the left is dominated by initial phases (blue) while the right is dominated by secondary phases (green), though the phases do not progress monotonically. We note that the initial post-treatment and secondary decision phases are often interleaved, as searchers tend to search for recovery or side effects following the initial treatment at the same time as they search for the next steps.

To more clearly see the phase progression, Figure 3(a) shows the distribution of the phases after gaps are removed for each column. To reduce noise, we excluded columns with less than ten non-gap symbols. This roughly halves the number of columns included in the visualization. The values are smoothed by averaging the values from the preceding/following three columns.

Age	Sample	Filtered	Classified	Expected
20s	16.4%	7.3%	4.9%	0.0%
30s	17.0%	5.2%	2.8%	0.0%
40s	13.5%	9.0%	5.6%	1.4%
50s	18.8%	14.6%	12.7%	15.3%
60s	17.8%	39.1%	42.3%	43.1%
70s	8.1%	14.9%	23.9%	24.1%
80s	8.4%	9.8%	7.7%	16.1%

Table 4: The distribution of ages associated with searches from a 2-month sample of logs (left), the filtered set of searchers who searched "prostate cancer", and the set of positively classified users. The right column shows the expected distribution in the logs of real cancer diagnoses, based on ground truth incidence rates.

In addition to the distribution of phases, the figure also shows the distribution over various categories of search terms in each column. The categories are based on the term ontology (Section 4.1), including terms referencing treatments and side effects, as well as searches for healthcare providers, search terms referencing mental health or seeking social or emotional support, and searches that are aimed at retrieving statistics such as prognosis or success rates. We see some variation over time in the content. Searches for hormone therapy and prostate cancer medications (many of which are hormonal therapies, but categorized separately for this visualization) increase over time, while searches for observation only appear in the first half. The general term "side effects" is prominent initially and declines, and more specific terms for side effects (related to incontinence and impotence) begin to rise. This highlights a shift from a general interest in learning about side effects to more specific concerns.

Many of the differences in the category distributions over time are smoothed over due to overlapping phases at each point. Figure 3(b) shows the content distribution within each phase in isolation, clarifying the differences. For these images, we did not require a minimum number of non-gap values, other than excluding columns with only gaps. This reveals differences among the phases. For example, searches for healthcare (dark green) appear mostly in the initial decision phase, while searches describing mental health (yellow) appear mostly in the initial post-treatment phase. The treatment distribution differs between the initial and secondary phases, with fewer references to surgery and more references to hormone and chemotherapy in the latter.

6. AGE COMPOSITION OF SEARCHERS

We now present a final experiment focused on examining ages inferred for the experiential searchers in our dataset. We performed this experiment to understand the demographic composition of the dataset, as well as to provide an auxiliary form of validation, to determine whether the searchers in our dataset exhibit similar demographics as patients diagnosed with prostate cancer. Since rates of cancer are higher in older age groups than in the general population, we would expect to see a shift toward this demographic in our classified dataset, should our classifier be capturing a higher proportion of people experiencing cancer.

We associated age groups with searchers by looking for references to ages in search queries. Specifically, we matched queries against expressions of the form "at/age _", "_ year(s) old", and "in my/his/her _s" for different numeric values. A similar self-reporting methodology was used to estimate the stage in pregnancy of expectant mothers or the age of newborns, based only on search logs [13]. If a search history included multiple such expressions, the majority age group was chosen. We were able to associate ages with 142 user identifiers (out of the set of 1,413 classified).

We computed the distribution of age groups for the search histories identified by the classifier. For comparison, we computed the age distribution for the larger set of histories from our initial filter (those who searched "prostate cancer" three times), and the entire set of search logs from the most recent two months. From the two month sample, we estimated the expected distribution of ages in the logs among those diagnosed with prostate cancer in the United States (US). We computed this estimate using Bayes' theorem: $\propto P(cancer|age)P(age)$, where $P(cancer|age)$ is defined by the age-specific prostate cancer incidence rates from the US National Cancer Institute (NCI),[2] and $P(age)$ is the distribution in the sample of logs (first column of Table 4).

Table 4 shows the distribution of age groups from 20s to 80s (the NCI data does not list rates for specific age groups beyond 80s) for the three sets of log data as well as the expected distribution from incidence rates.

The age distribution among positively classified searchers is strikingly similar to the expected distribution, particularly for the ages of 60s and 70s, which are each within 1 percent of the expected rate. The Pearson correlation between these two distributions is highly significant ($r = .959$, $p < .001$). The distribution among users passing through our initial filter (three queries for prostate cancer) skews toward the older ages as might be expected. However, after applying the experiential classifier, the percentages further increase for the age groups with the highest incidence rates (people in their 60s and 70s) and decrease for the youngest age groups. We believe this provides additional evidence that many of the classified searchers included in our study were likely to be experiencing a diagnosis of prostate cancer.

7. DISCUSSION AND IMPLICATIONS

A limitation of using search log analysis to learn about Web-based decision support is that we lack the larger context that frames the information-seeking activity. To address this shortcoming, we are developing methodologies to connect long-term log behaviors with self-reported data from consenting search participants. This approach would provide details on the context behind the search and retrieval activity appearing in logs of online activity. This information would allow us to understand the influence of Web content on a patient's decision-making and details such as the resources that were helpful in deliberating about care decisions, whether a decision aligned with a doctor's recommendation, and the outcome following a decision. Many of these details are impossible to infer from the observed activities in logs alone. Engaging directly with patients, and aligning online activity with patients' clinical situations, would enable us to perform rich analyses grounded in detailed patient reports. While we hope to conduct such a study as future work, we also believe that there is complementary value in the lightweight, large-scale analyses presented in this paper.

We believe that there are opportunities to leverage the reported findings to inform the design of search and retrieval systems for supporting healthcare decision making. Given the focus of this paper, we are especially interested in enhancing the ability of Web search engines to serve as decision support systems, per the expectations that people appear to have when they turn to the Web for critical assistance with challenging treatment decisions under uncertainty. The different phases of treatment appear to be identifiable, with distinctive n-gram associations and timing characteristics. This suggests that search output can be tailored to the user's current phase. For example, a searcher during a decision-making phase may find it helpful to gain access to results that include comparisons of treatments. We found that comparative queries are common, with nearly half of users conducting an explicit comparison, and from our experiments, we know which comparisons are most common. These insights could be used to return results, or interface treatments such as direct answers using data pulled from external sources, that include relevant comparisons even if the query did not explicitly include a comparison. We also now have data on the progression of queries on treatments, including the depth over time and transitions between treatments, which can be used to model treatment search behavior. Such models could be used by search providers for important tasks such as appropriately suggesting or expanding queries.

Beyond tailoring results to a current phase of search aligned with a phase of care, it may be valuable to provide searchers with content that is typically viewed in later phases of an illness. For example, searchers making a decision may find it useful to read the content that is commonly viewed by those in a post-treatment phase, in order to understand the expected recovery process and side effects from particular treatments. Our analyses showed that many people may seek out discussions of the personal experiences of patients (e.g. through forums) during the post-treatment phase, and surfacing the concerns and issues of others could provide searchers facing decisions with more context than traditional decision-making materials. Such content might not be discovered in the course of normal searching in an early phase without designing a system for such proactive retrieval, as queries in the initial decision phase tend to be broad.

Promising future directions include adapting the annotations, classifiers, and overall methodology to understand the information needs and to guide decision support for treatment decisions for other illnesses. Beyond the pursuit of enhancing search for decisions about treatments, we can employ the methods to enhance search and retrieval for other healthcare needs, such as selecting a care provider.

8. REFERENCES

[1] S. L. Ayers and J. J. Kronenfeld. Chronic illness and health-seeking information on the internet. *Health*, 11(3), 2007.

[2] J. Bader and M. Theofanos. Searching for cancer information on the internet: Analyzing natural language search queries. *JMIR*, 5(4), 2003.

[3] E. V. Bernstam, J. R. Herskovic, and W. R. Hersh. Query log analysis in biomedicine. 2009.

[2] http://seer.cancer.gov/csr/1975_2011/browse_csr.php?sectionSEL=23&pageSEL=sect_23_table.07.html

[4] P. Black and D. Penson. Prostate cancer on the internet – information or misinformation? *Journal of Urology*, 175(5):1836–1842, 2006.
[5] M.-A. Cartright, R. W. White, and E. Horvitz. Intentions and attention in exploratory health search. In *SIGIR*, 2011.
[6] K. Castleton, T. Fong, A. Wang-Gillam, M. Waqar, and *et al.* A survey of internet utilization among patients with cancer. *Support Care Cancer*, 2011.
[7] Y. Chu and T. Liu. On the shortest arborescence of a directed graph. *Science Sinica*, 14:1396–1400, 1965.
[8] J. Chuang, C. D. Manning, and J. Heer. Termite: Visualization techniques for assessing textual topic models. In *Advanced Visual Interfaces*, 2012.
[9] R. J. W. Cline and K. M. Haynes. Consumer health information seeking on the internet: the state of the art. *Health Education Research*, 16(6), 2001.
[10] D. Downey, S. Dumais, and E. Horvitz. Models of searching and browsing: languages, studies, and applications. In *IJCAI*, 2007.
[11] G. E. Dupret and B. Piwowarski. A user browsing model to predict search engine click data from past observations. In *SIGIR*, 2008.
[12] J. Edmonds. Optimum branchings. *J. Res. Nat. Bur. Standards*, 71(B):233–240, 1967.
[13] A. Fourney, R. W. White, and E. Horvitz. Exploring time-dependent concerns about pregnancy and childbirth from search logs. In *CHI*, 2015.
[14] S. Fox and M. Duggan. Health online 2013. Technical report, Pew Internet and American Life Project, 2013.
[15] C. M. Gaston and G. Mitchell. Information giving and decision-making in patients with advanced cancer: A systematic review. *Soc Sci Med*, 61(10), 2005.
[16] J. Ginsberg, M. Mohebbi, R. Patel, L. Brammer, and *et al.* Detecting influenza epidemics using search engine query data. *Nature*, 2008.
[17] Y. Goto and T. Nagase. Oncology information on the Internet. *Jpn J Clin Oncol*, 42(5):368–374, 2012.
[18] D. Gusfield. *Algorithms on Strings, Trees, and Sequences.* Cambridge University Press, 1997.
[19] P. R. Helft. Patients with cancer, internet information, and the clinical encounter: A taxonomy of patient users. In *American Society of Clinical Ontology*, 2012.
[20] R. Islamaj Dogan, G. C. Murray, A. Névéol, and Z. Lu. Understanding PubMed user search behavior through log analysis. *Database*, 2009:bap018, 2009.
[21] L. Klotz. Active surveillance for low-risk prostate cancer. *F1000 Med Reports*, 4(16), 2012.
[22] M. Larkin, G. Blackshields, N. Brown, C. R., P. McGettigan, and *et al.* Clustal W and Clustal X version 2.0. *Bioinformatics*, 23:2947–2948, 2007.
[23] T. Lau and E. Horvitz. Patterns of search: analyzing and modeling web query refinement. In *7th International Conference on User Modeling*, 1999.
[24] G. Lin, D. Aaronson, S. Knight, P. Carroll, and R. Dudley. Patient decision aids for prostate cancer treatment. *CA Cancer J Clin*, 59:379–390, 2009.
[25] A. M. O'Connor, V. Fiset, C. DeGrasse, I. D. Graham, and *et al.* Decision aids for patients considering options affecting cancer outcomes. *JNCI Monographs*, 1999(25):67–80, 1999.
[26] A. M. O'Connor, A. Rostom, V. Fiset, J. Tetroe, and *et al.* Decision aids for patients facing health treatment or screening decisions. *BMJ*, 319(7212), 1999.
[27] Y. Ofran, O. Paltiel, D. Pelleg, J. M. Rowe, and E. Yom-Tov. Patterns of information-seeking for cancer on the internet. *PLOS One*, 7(9), 2012.
[28] R. Overberg. *Breast cancer stories on the internet: improving search facilities to help patients find stories of similar others.* PhD thesis, Leiden University, 2013.
[29] H. Patel, S. Mirsadraee, and M. Emberton. The patient's dilemma: Prostate cancer treatment choices. *Journal of Urology*, 169(3):828–833, 2003.
[30] M. Paul and R. Girju. Cross-cultural analysis of blogs and forums with mixed-collection topic models. In *EMNLP*, 2009.
[31] M. J. Paul, R. W. White, and E. Horvitz. Search and breast cancer: On disruptive shifts of attention over life histories of an illness. Technical report, 2014.
[32] S. Pautler, J. Tan, G. Dugas, N. Pus, and *et al.* Use of the Internet for self-education by patients with prostate cancer. *Urology*, 57(2):230–233, 2000.
[33] G. Peterson, P. Aslani, and K. A. Williams. How do consumers search for and appraise information on medicines on the internet? *JMIR*, 5(4), 2003.
[34] M. Richardson. Learning about the world from long-term query logs. *ACM TWEB*, 2(4), 2009.
[35] L. J. F. Rutten, N. K. Arora, A. D. Bakos, N. Aziz, and J. Rowland. Information needs and sources of information among cancer patients. *Patient Educ Couns*, 57(3), 2005.
[36] M. J. Satterlund, K. D. McCaul, and A. K. Sandgren. Information gathering over time by breast cancer patients. *J Med Internet Res*, 5(3), 2003.
[37] A. Sidana, D. J. Hernandez, Z. Feng, A. W. Partin, and *et al.* Treatment decision-making for localized prostate cancer. *The Prostate*, 72(1):58–64, 2012.
[38] M. I. Trotter and D. W. Morgan. Patients' use of the internet for health related matters. *Health Informatics*, 14(3), 2008.
[39] R. J. Volk, S. T. Hawley, S. Kneuper, E. W. Holden, and *et al.* Trials of decision aids for prostate cancer screening. *Am J Prev Med*, 33(5):428–434, 2007.
[40] T. Weninger, W. H. Hsu, and J. Han. Cetr: Content extraction via tag ratios. In *WWW*, 2010.
[41] R. W. White and S. M. Drucker. Investigating behavioral variability in web search. In *WWW*, 2007.
[42] R. W. White and E. Horvitz. Cyberchondria: Studies of the escalation of medical concerns in web search. *ACM TOIS*, 27(4), 2009.
[43] R. W. White and E. Horvitz. From health search to healthcare: explorations of intention and utilization via query logs and user surveys. *JAMIA*, 2013.
[44] R. W. White, N. P. Tatonetti, N. H. Shah, R. B. Altman, and E. Horvitz. Web-scale pharmaco-vigilance: Listening to signals from the crowd. *JAMIA*, 20(3), 2013.
[45] C. Zhai and J. Lafferty. Two-stage language models for information retrieval. In *SIGIR*, pages 49–56, 2002.
[46] S. Ziebland, A. Chapple, C. Dumelow, J. Evans, and *et al.* How the internet affects patients' experience of cancer: a qualitative study. *BMJ*, 328(7439), 2004.

PocketTrend: Timely Identification and Delivery of Trending Search Content to Mobile Users

Gennady Pekhimenko
Carnegie Mellon University
Pittsburgh, PA
gpekhime@cs.cmu.edu

Dimitrios Lymberopoulos, Oriana Riva,
Karin Strauss, Doug Burger
Microsoft Research, Redmond, WA
{dlymper,oriana,kstrauss,dburger}@microsoft.com

ABSTRACT

Trending search topics cause unpredictable query load spikes that hurt the end-user search experience, particularly the mobile one, by introducing longer delays. To understand how trending search topics are formed and evolve over time, we analyze 21 million queries submitted during periods where popular events caused search query volume spikes. Based on our findings, we design and evaluate *PocketTrend*, a system that automatically detects trending topics in real time, identifies the search content associated to the topics, and then intelligently pushes this content to users in a timely manner. In that way, PocketTrend enables a client-side search engine that can instantly answer user queries related to trending events, while at the same time reducing the impact of these trends on the datacenter workload. Our results, using real mobile search logs, show that in the presence of a trending event, up to 13–17% of the overall search traffic can be eliminated from the datacenter, with as many as 19% of all users benefiting from PocketTrend.

Categories and Subject Descriptors

H.3.3 [**Information Search and Retrieval**]: Information Filtering

Keywords

Web search; trend detection

1. INTRODUCTION

Search portals like Google and Yahoo are among the top daily visited websites, indicating how crucial these services are to end users. In response to their popularity, search engine providers have put tremendous effort in optimizing their infrastructure, usually either through server-side [2, 29, 4, 7, 18] or client-side caching [15], to enable the fastest possible search user experience.

Unfortunately, these optimizations can be rendered ineffective or costly due to the unpredictable nature of the search query volume. Important events that take place in the physical world can instantly translate into significant, and often unpredictable, spikes in search requests. Figure 1 shows Bing's normalized hourly mobile query volume during the week of the 2012 presidential elections in the United States. The blue line represents the actual query volume, while the red dotted line shows the estimated query volume

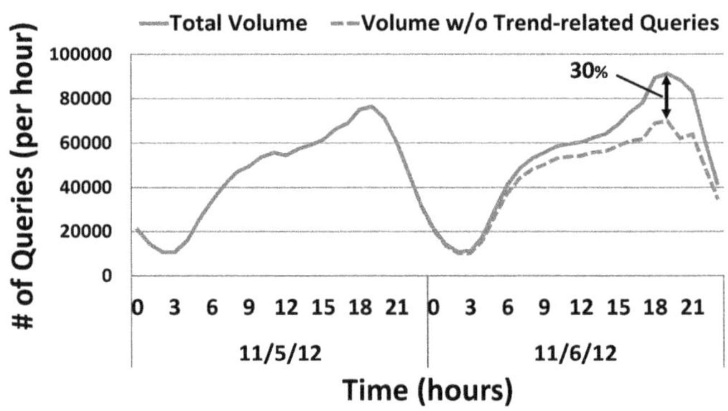

Figure 1: Normalized hourly query volume during the week of U.S. president elections (11/6/2012) with (blue line) and without (red dotted line) the election-related queries.

when all queries related to the elections were manually filtered out. On the election day, the search volume increased by roughly 30% compared to the previous days, and remained that high for several hours. When all queries related to elections are filtered out, the search volume falls back to the same volume levels as the previous days, indicating that the volume spike was due to the elections.

Even though not happening daily, search volume spikes as in Figure 1 have significant impact on the end user experience. First, in the presence of such unpredictable events, end users lose the benefit of real-time search experience delivered by previously proposed approaches for client-side search index caching [15] that is orders of magnitude faster than the actual service call. These approaches have focused on periodically (e.g., daily) caching the static part of the search index, and therefore cannot handle fresh content that might spike during the day. The impact on the end user experience is particularly crucial to mobile devices, where cellular links are limited by lengthy connection setup times [8].

Second, even though server-side caching techniques [19, 29, 4, 7, 3] can help smoothen out the datacenter's computation overhead due to these search volume spikes, they do nothing about reducing the number of search requests reaching the search backend. As the number of requests simultaneously hitting the backend increases, the datacenter load gets closer to its capacity limits. This usually causes a slower user experience, makes the search engine more susceptible to common Denial of Service (DoS) attacks, and in the worst case can bring the whole service down incurring a large revenue loss. To overcome these risks, search engines invest heavily on over-provisioning their datacenters' capacity by adding more servers than they actually need on a daily basis which leads to significant increase in datacenters' cost.

WWW 2015, May 18–22, 2015, Florence, Italy.
ACM 978-1-4503-3469-3/15/05.
http://dx.doi.org/10.1145/2736277.2741641 .

In this work, we study the feasibility of enabling a real-time search experience for trending search topics without overwhelming the search backend with an excessive number of search requests. We envision search engines that can timely detect and efficiently propagate trending search content (i.e., search queries and corresponding search results) to users' mobile devices to enable a real-time search experience at a lower cost for the datacenter. With such a mechanism in place, in the case of the 2012 U.S. presidential elections (Figure 1), 30% of users' queries could be instantly served locally (e.g., through the web browser or a dedicated search application), without sending a request to the search engine. Likewise, 30% of the overall query volume could be eliminated from the search backend at peak time.

To enable this type of user experience, the search backend must address three challenges. First, it needs to detect, in real-time, search query volume spikes due to trending events. Second, it must identify the part of the search index associated to these events. Third, it must proactively and efficiently propagate the identified trending search content to end users in a timely manner. Note that the proactive dissemination of trending content to end users can introduce additional request and/or bandwidth overheads if not done properly. For instance, proactively pushing trending content to every single user of the search engine is not an option as it would cause the number of connections and bandwidth consumed by the datacenter to explode. Instead, the search backend should be able to intelligently decide *which* users and *when* should be updated with the appropriate content to avoid increasing the number of search requests and to keep the bandwidth overhead as low as possible.

To address these challenges, we conduct a data-driven design exploration study. To understand how trending search topics are formed and how they evolve over time, we analyze 21 million mobile search queries submitted to Bing during periods where real events led to search query volume spikes. Using this dataset, we quantify the benefit and bandwidth overhead of different approaches to proactively pushing trending search content to end users. Based on our findings, we design *PocketTrend*, an architecture for enabling real-time search experience for trending topics. Its design is based on key observations of the search log analysis:

- Only a small number of search queries and search results is responsible for the majority of a trending event's query volume. PocketTrend leverages this observation to employ a two-step algorithm for identifying the small part of the search index that corresponds to the trending event, reducing the footprint of the data to be pushed to users to roughly 1 MB.

- Many users access the search engine with queries unrelated to the trending event, *after* the trending event has been detected. PocketTrend leverages this finding to opportunistically update these users by piggybacking the trending search content along with the requested search results. In that way, the datacenter does not need to establish any new connections to deliver the trending content. Using this approach, we show that up to 13-17% of the overall search traffic (roughly 50% of the trending search traffic) can be answered locally on the users' devices with a reasonable bandwidth overhead.

- Frequent users that accessed the search engine right before the trending event started are likely to search for the trending event in the future. However, we show that the overhead of pushing trend content to these users in terms of number of connections that the datacenter must maintain and bandwidth it must consume makes this approach infeasible.

Event	Log dates	#users	#queries
U.S.Pres.Elections, 11/6/12	2–9 Nov.12	700K	7.7M
PopeElection, 3/13/13	13–17 Mar.13	550K	7.0M
BostonMarathonBomb, 4/15/13	14–21 Apr.13	660K	6.7M

Table 1: Details of the mobile search dataset used to study users' search behavior around trending topics.

2. SEARCH LOG ANALYSIS

Timely detecting and propagating trending search content to end users poses three fundamental challenges: *What* content to push, *When* to push it, and *Whom* to push it. Addressing these challenges requires first understanding how trending topics are formed and evolve over time. To gain insight on how mobile users search for trending events, we analyzed more than 21 million search queries, submitted by roughly 2 million unique users in the United States. All queries were submitted through mobile devices to Bing. In particular, we leverage three week-long datasets, each corresponding to a significant physical event that resulted into a major trending topic as shown in Table 1. The events are U.S. president elections, pope election, and Boston marathon bombing.

Each entry in the search logs has 6 fields: user ID, search query submitted by the user, timestamp, list of search results that were clicked by the user, and all search results that were shown, but were not clicked by the user. A search result consists of a URL and a snippet describing the URL.

To prevent disclosing sensitive information about Bing's exact query volume, at given times for the commercial search engine that collected these logs, the query volumes have been properly normalized. This normalization does not affect the results presented throughout the paper as we look at relative gains.

2.1 What to Push

First, it is necessary to automatically detect trending events near real time, and also identify the portion of the search index that is related to these events. This portion of the search index will become the actual search content (search queries and corresponding search results) that will be pushed to end users. The feasibility of this approach depends on how concentrated the search content associated to a trending topic is. If users' clicks are evenly distributed over a large number of search results, then identifying the trending part of the search index can be quite difficult. Conversely, if most users click on a small number of search results when searching for trending topics, then the trending search content is more compacted and therefore ideal for client-side caching.

Figure 2 shows the cumulative coverage achieved by the most popular 50 search results for the three trending events we studied. To generate these data, we extracted all queries related to each trending event, and then identified the most popular (most often clicked) search results. We find that the single most popular search result accounts for anywhere between 4% and 7% of the overall trend-related search result clicks depending on the trending event. All together, the 50 most popular search results cover anywhere between 24% and 30% of the overall trend-related search results that were clicked by users. In other words, simply pushing the top 50 search results associated to a trending topic to end users, could result in 30% of users' queries related to the trending event being answered instantly on their mobile devices without the need to reach the search engine.

When considering domains instead of absolute URLs (e.g., cnn.com/story1.html and cnn.com/story2.html are mapped to the same domain cnn.com), the entropy of the search results is even smaller. The top 50 domains account for 52%–59% of the over-

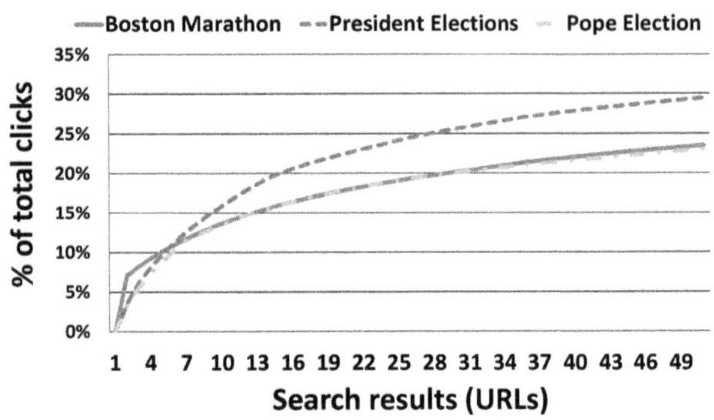

(a)

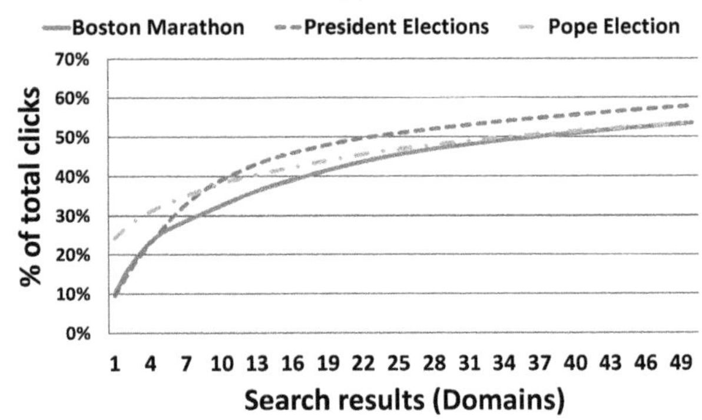

(b)

Figure 2: The cumulative percentage of the overall trending search results for the 50 most often clicked trending search results when considering: (a) absolute URLs, and (b) URL domains.

all query volume depending on the event, suggesting that caching most popular URLs can be efficient.

Summarizing, Figure 2 shows that a small number of search results (URLs) accounts for the majority of the trending search volume, indicating the feasibility of the proposed approach. Section 3.2 describes how PocketTrend exploits this trend to identify a small set of trending search queries and search results to push to users. The larger the size of the content pushed to the users, the more likely the case of satisfying users' search requests locally (on the device) in real time. We evaluate this tradeoff in Section 4.5.

2.2 When to Push

Assuming the set of search queries and corresponding search results is identified, a decision about when to push this content to end users needs to be made. Even though a trending event can be detected quite early (within 20 minutes), the content related to the event might evolve over time, especially in the very beginning. Hence, pushing the trending data too early could be ineffective as crucial content might be missing.

Figure 3 sheds light on the distribution of all trend-related queries over time for pope and U.S. president elections. In particular, this figure shows the percentage of the total hourly query volume that corresponds to trend-related search queries over the lifetime of the event. For both events the peaks have durations that span several hours. However, it is clear that different trends evolve in different manners. During the pope election event, there is an immediate sharp 3-hour window where the event is mostly active, and then it stabilizes and slowly decays over time. On the other hand, the U.S. president election event starts with a moderate spike and

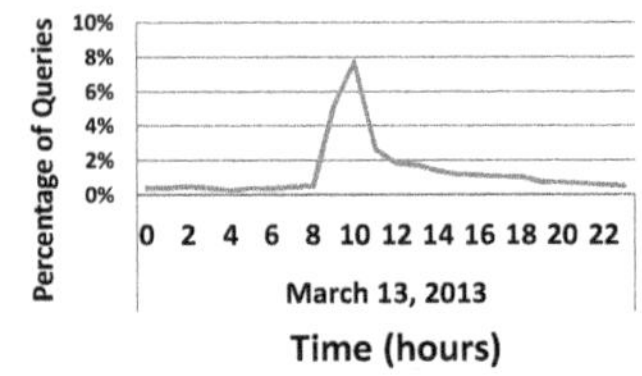

(a) Pope election

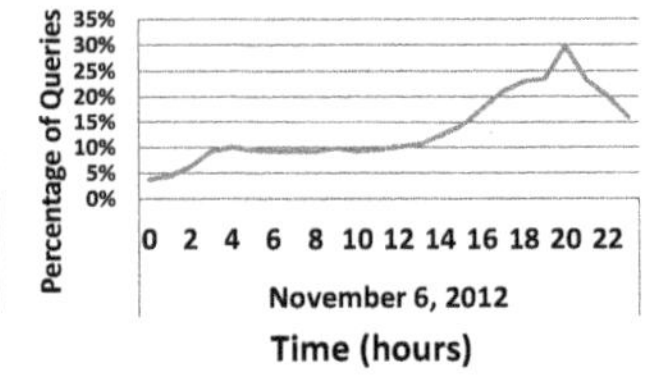

(b) U.S. president elections

Figure 3: Percentage of the total hourly query volume that is related to the trending event over time.

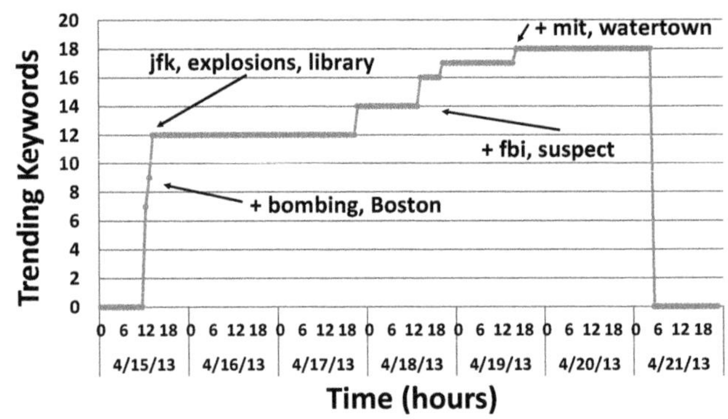

Figure 4: Evolution of trends' keywords over time for the Boston Marathon bombing event.

remains stable for multiple hours until it reaches its peak that lasts roughly 8 hours. We also observe that most trend-related queries are submitted during each event's peak that lasts a few to several hours. Hence, the window of opportunity for pushing trend content to users is only a few hours.

Finally, the trending content can evolve during the trending event lifetime. Figure 4 shows the number of keywords over time for the Boston Marathon bombing event; in the first 2 hours, 7 keywords have been detected, but, by the time the event has stabilized, 18 keywords have been detected.

Summarizing, to address the constant evolution of trending events, PocketTrend needs to continuously scan the search logs to identify the freshest trending search content and push it to users. In Section 3, we propose various techniques to achieve this goal.

2.3 Whom to Push to

Identifying which users, and in what order, will be updated with the detected trending search content is crucial. This is not a trivial task as commercial search engines have hundreds of millions of unique users. Attempting to simultaneously update every user with the trending search content will overwhelm the data center, creating a bigger problem than the one PocketTrend solves.

Mobile users can be updated "actively" or "passively". Active updates require the datacenter to track each user and preemptively push the trending search content when it becomes available. Such an approach, however, can lead to pushing content to large numbers of users out of which only few might eventually search for it.

Given that, if not highly accurate, active pushing can further stress the datacenter's I/O resources, we also explore passive, opportunistic updates. Each time a user submits a query to the search engine and a trending search topic is currently active, the search engine can opportunistically update the user with the latest trending search content along with providing the search results to the

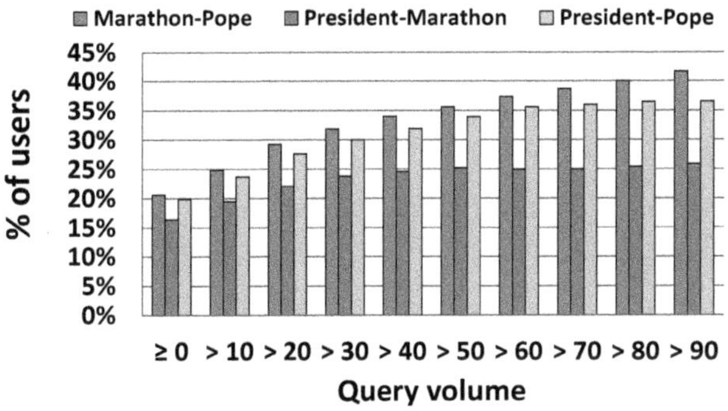

Figure 5: Percentage of users that searched for both trending events for every pair of the three trending events we studied. Users are categorized by query volume.

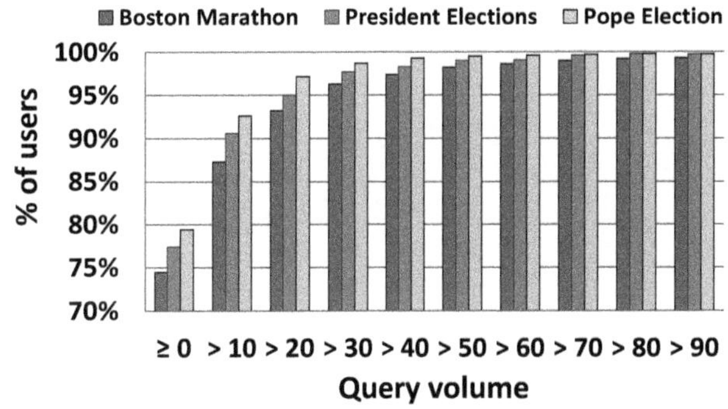

Figure 6: Percentage of users that submitted a search request within 2 hours before the trending event happened, and then searched for the event itself after it happened.

(non-trend-related) query. In that way, no extra requests need to be submitted to the datacenter and no user-tracking is required.

To understand who should be updated with the trending search content and how, we leveraged the search logs to explore the feasibility of both active and passive approaches.

Active Content Pushing. First, we opted to identify loyal users of the search engine since loyal users are more likely to come back and search for trending topics. We defined loyal users as users that had submitted a large number of queries in the past and they had also searched for at least one trending event. The intuition is that if a user searched for a trending event in the past, then most probably that user will also search for the next trending event. Figure 5 shows the percentage of users that searched for both trending events as a function of user query volume, for every pair of the three trending events we study. Note that as the user query volume increases, the percentage of users that searched for both trending events becomes higher (indicating a stronger correlation). However, the user intersection between trending events is rather low; about 25% of the users that searched for a previous trending event will search for a future one. This could be because some users might search for trending content on multiple devices, may not be interested in all trending topics, or may have already read about the event in the news. As a result, updating users that previously searched for a trending event would result into lots of user updates to the benefit of only a small fraction (≈25%) of users.

The second approach to identifying whom to push to the trending search content was based on the assumption that users that recently submitted a search query in the search engine are likely to search for the trending content as soon as they find out. Figure 6 shows the percentage of users that submitted a search query within 2 hours before the trending event started, and they also searched for the trending event after the event took place. Again, the higher the query volume of a user, the higher the probability that the user will eventually search for the trending topic. However, in this case, more than 80% of the users submitting a query within the last 2 hours will return to search for the trending topic.

Summarizing, high volume recent users are ideal candidates for pushing the trending search content. The number of users a search engine can push content to ultimately depends on the datacenter's bandwidth available for PocketTrend updates. We analyze this tradeoff in Section 4.2.

Passive Content Pushing. Table 2 shows the percentage of mobile users that submitted an unrelated query after the trending event happened, and then returned to search for the trending topic. For these users, the unrelated query can be used to piggyback trending search content. Surprisingly, up to 26% of all the users that searched for something while the trending event was active later search for the trending event as well. This corresponds to 79% of the users that eventually searched for the trending event. This correlation demonstrates the opportunity to exploit simple and low-cost passive updates to opportunistically push trending content to users.

Summarizing, passive updates could complement or even replace active updates to enable a real-time search user experience with a lower impact on the datacenter's bandwidth requirements. In Section 4.3 we analyze this tradeoff.

Event	% of returning users out of	
	all users	users that searched the trend
U.S. president elections	18.2%	77.4%
Pope election	3.1%	79.4%
Boston marathon bombing	26.3%	74.5%

Table 2: Percentage of users that searched for an unrelated topic when the trending event was ongoing and then came back to search for the actual trending event.

3. POCKETTREND ARCHITECTURE

The design of the PocketTrend architecture is driven by the findings of the search log analysis described in the previous section. As shown in Figure 7, PocketTrend runs on the search backend and consists of three major components: *trend event detection*, *trending content identification*, and *trending content delivery* to end users.

First, like in previous work [20, 24, 9], PocketTrend detects trending keywords by analyzing the frequency at which these keywords are used in the search queries. The goal is to detect keywords that are searched significantly more frequently than normal (e.g., five times more frequently than during the same hour the day before). The detected trending keywords are grouped together to form trending events. A trending event at this stage is nothing more than a collection of frequently-searched keywords.

At the next stage (trending content identification in Figure 7), PocketTrend scans the search logs to identify all queries that contain a significant number of trending keywords, and marks these queries as trending. A subset of these, the ones that have the highest search rates and the highest number of clicks, is selected to form the trending search content to be pushed to users. Likewise, the most clicked search results for the selected trending queries are also added to the trending content. This strategy ensures that only the most relevant trending search content will be propagated to users' devices, saving bandwidth and storage resources.

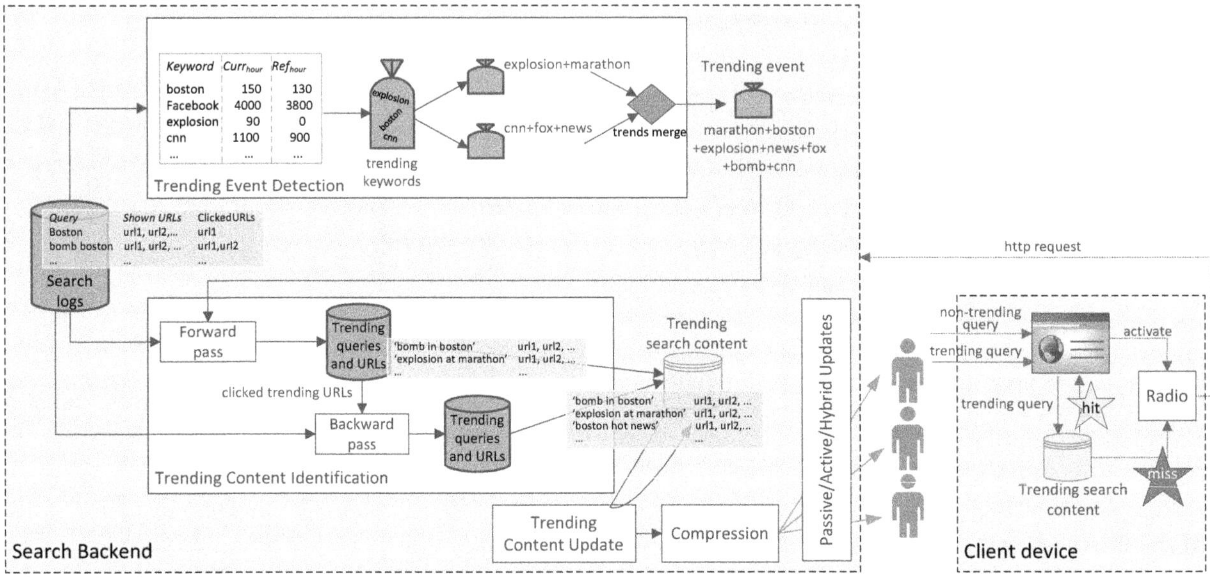

Figure 7: PocketTrend overview.

Trend event detection and trend content identification continuously run in the search backend. In the last stage, the freshest trending search content is pushed to end users actively or passively (see Section 2). To reduce the bandwidth consumed for pushing the trending search content, PocketTrend also uses data compression techniques [31].

At the client side, the trending search content can be used to enable real-time query suggestion or query auto-completion. Since both queries and search results are pushed to the client devices, query suggestions or auto-completions can be accompanied with the relevant search results that the user can instantly click on. If these are not satisfactory the user can still select a query or manually enter his own to get the freshest search results from the search backend. In that way, PocketTrend does not replace the search engine, but it rather works along with it to enable the fastest possible search experience for end users.

In the following, we describe all PocketTrend components in detail.

3.1 Trending Event Detection

Trending events are identified in two steps. First, an initial set of trending keywords is identified, and then trending keywords are grouped together to form events.

3.1.1 Trending Keyword Detection

As in related work on trend detection [20, 24, 9], we leverage the observation that in the absence of active global trends, the same keyword within the same hour (but for different days) tends to have similar numbers of appearances in search queries. We define a keyword to be trending if the number of appearances within a specific hour in the current day is significantly higher (e.g., 5x more) than in the same hour during a reference day.[1] Formally, a keyword is defined to be frequent if

$$\frac{Curr_{hour}}{Ref_{hour}} \geq KeywordRatioThreshold \qquad (1)$$

[1]We use a previous day as reference point to identify trending keywords. We also tested time periods smaller than an hour and a "sliding window" approach, and achieved identical performance.

where $Curr_{hour}$ is the number of appearances of a keyword in the current hour and Ref_{hour} is that of the same keyword in the same hour in a reference day.[2]

$KeywordRatioThreshold$ in formula 1 is an empirically defined threshold that separates random, small frequency variations of keywords that can happen across days, from significant frequency variations that indicate a trending event. We are interested in major trending events that result into significant search volume spikes as in Figure 1, so finding an appropriate value for $KeywordRatioThreshold$ becomes trivial. Based on our analysis of real user search logs, we found that keywords that appear more than 5 times more frequently than usual indicate the presence of strong trending events causing search volume spikes.

Even though Ref_{hour} in formula 1 has a non-zero value for most keywords, there are always keywords that appear suddenly due to a trending event. For instance, keywords like "pope" during Pope election, and "explosion" during the Boston marathon bombing were completely new keywords ($Ref_{hour} = 0$). To handle such cases, and to differentiate actual trending keywords from random new keywords, a keyword with $Ref_{hour} = 0$ becomes trending only if it is statistically important, in the sense that it is observed at least in 0.1% of all queries in the last hour.

3.1.2 Trending Keywords Grouping

Initially, every trending keyword is a trending event by itself. However, the detected trending keywords could belong to one or more trending events taking place at the same time. To properly group keywords together to form trending events, we examine how frequently trending keywords are searched together. Intuitively, the more often two keywords are searched together, the higher the probability they refer to the same topic. For example, for the Boston marathon bombing event we observed that the words "marathon" and "explosion" were searched together 93% of the time. Empirically, based on the analysis of millions of mobile search queries, we found that trending keywords that are searched

[2]There are other possible ways to define the word frequency, e.g., based on tf-idf metric [12, 25], but we found that those techniques usually incur higher computation overheads while generating same/similar list of keywords.

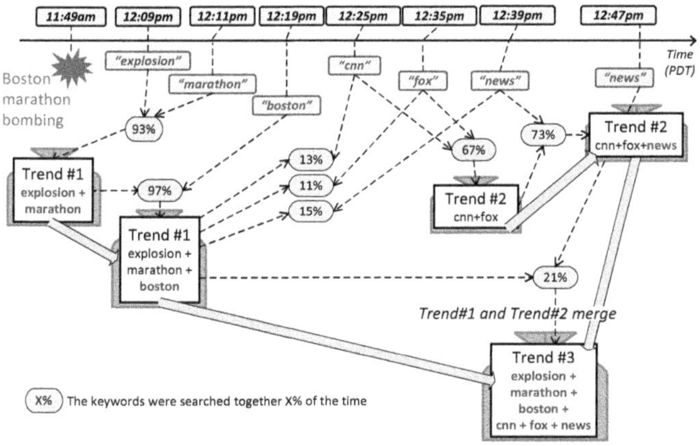

Figure 8: Detailed example of trend detection and trending keywords grouping (Boston marathon bombing).

together more than 20% of the overall times they appear in the search logs, they refer to the same trending event. As a result, every pair of trending keywords that is searched together at least 20% of the times they appear in the logs is merged to form a single trending event. Every new trending keyword is also evaluated against all the current trending keywords, and it either joins an active trending event or forms a new one.

The detected trending events are not considered as immediately active. They become active when the overall percentage of queries in the last hour that contains at least one of the trending event's keywords is higher than 1% of the overall search traffic. We impose this threshold to ensure that content is pushed to users only for events that are large enough to matter (for the user and for the datacenter).[3] The threshold could be adjusted depending on the datacenter's requirements.

To illustrate how trend detection works in practice, Figure 8 shows the trend evolution for the Boston marathon bombing event. The explosion happened at 11:49am PDT. Within 20 minutes, the keyword "explosion" is detected as trending, followed by "marathon" in 2 more minutes. This creates the first multi-keyword trend as these two keywords are searched together more than 90% of the time. In 8 more minutes, the keyword "boston" is detected as trending, and it is added to the initial trend. Later on, the keywords "cnn", "fox" and "news" are also detected as trending, but these keywords are not added to the existing trend #1, because they are not searched frequently enough together with the keywords from the current trend (13%, 11% and 15% correspondingly, at the time of detection as trending). At the same time, these trending keywords are frequently searched together, which allows us to create a new trend (trend #2). In 8 more minutes (at 12:47pm) the trending keyword "news" passes the threshold for intersection with trend #1, which leads to the same keyword being in two active trends. This leads to merging both trends into a single trend that is later used for identifying the trending search content.

3.2 Trending Content Identification

At this point, a trending event is a collection of trending keywords that are frequently searched together. PocketTrend leverages this collection of keywords to identify the search content related to the trending event. By search content, we mean all the search queries related to the trending event, and the search results associated to these queries. Detecting this content is quite challenging for two reasons. First, mobile users search for a specific topic in multiple different ways due to either the large number of synonyms used, or the typos and grammatical errors (e.g., "boeton explo"). Second, queries that look very similar can semantically be very different. For instance, the queries: "boston marathon", and "boston marathon bombing" could be very different as the former is an informational query about the event, while the latter focuses on the bombing incident.

3.2.1 Detecting Relevant Queries: Forward and Backward Passes

We address this problem with a two-step process, shown in Figure 9. First, a *forward pass* of the search logs takes place to identify a small set of queries that with high certainty are related to the trending event. Given this small set of highly relevant queries and the search results that users click on in response, PocketTrend identifies the core set of search results related to the trending event. At the second step, a *backwards pass* of the search logs takes place where we identify additional queries related to the trending event based on the set of search results identified in the first step. In particular, all queries that resulted into users clicking on a search result related to the trending event, are automatically assumed to be related to the trending event. This way, even infrequent and unconventional queries used to search for the trending event (e.g., "boston explode") can be captured.

Given that the goal of the *forward pass* step is to identify a small number of search queries that are relevant to the trending event with high probability, PocketTrend follows a conservative approach. All search queries in the past hour that contain 3 or more trending keywords are automatically assumed to be related to the trending event. Since mobile users' queries contain 3-4 or less keywords most of the time [13, 14], 3 trending keywords indicate a strong match.[4] All search queries that contain zero or just one trending keyword are ignored in this step, because even generic keywords such as "Boston", "cnn" or "news" can become trending. Search queries that contain exactly two trending keywords, the most common case in the mobile search logs, can be more complicated. For example, the queries: *"boston marathon results"* and *"explosion at boston today"* contain exactly two trending keywords for the Boston marathon bombing event. However, the first query is most probably not related to the bombing, because the user cares about the marathon results, and not the bombing incident.

To handle these cases, PocketTrend leverages the intuition behind techniques like tf-idf [25, 23], used for measuring how important a word is in a document. At a high level, the tf-idf value of an input text increases proportionally to the number of times the words composing it appear in a reference dictionary (term frequency), but is offset by the frequency of the words in the dictionary (inverse document frequency), which helps to control the fact that some words are generally more common than others. To achieve the same effect of inverse document frequency, we implement a matching algorithm where different trending keywords are given different weights in the matching process depending on how *unique* they are. For example, the keyword "boston" can be used in many different queries (e.g., "boston weather"), and hence its uniqueness is lower than the keyword "explosion". We can distinguish these two cases through the keyword frequency increase between the trending event's time period and a reference time period

[3]We admit that our methodology can potentially miss some trending events that do not exhibit significant increase in the search traffic, but we expect the effect of such relatively small trends on the datacenters to be minimal.

[4]In a more general case, the number of words for a strong match can be defined based on the relative number of words in the trending event.

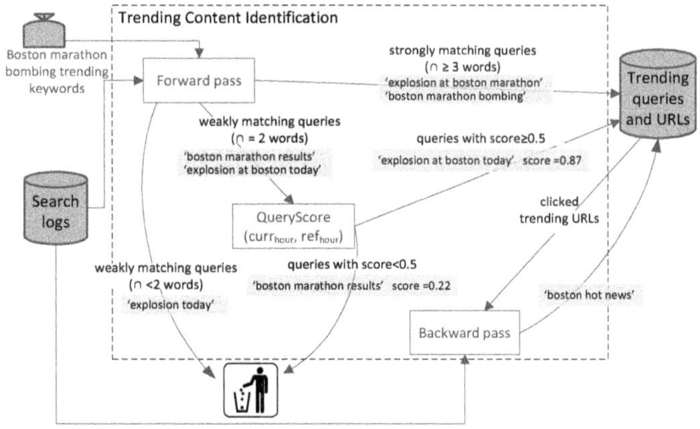

Figure 9: Trending content identification using forward and backward passes on top of search logs.

(formula 1). Keywords like "boston" usually have low increase ratios ($5x$–$8x$), while keywords like "explosion" can have ratios over $100x$.

Given this observation, PocketTrend computes a matching score $Query_{score}$ for every candidate search query:

$$Query_{score} = \frac{\sum_{Keyword-k_i InQuery} Uniqueness_{k_i} * Curr_{hour}^{k_i}}{\sum_{Keyword-k_j} Uniqueness_{k_j} * Curr_{hour}^{k_j}} \quad (2)$$

where $Uniqueness_k$ represents how unique keyword k is:

$$Uniqueness_k = \begin{cases} 1, & \text{if } 5 \le \frac{Curr_{hour}^k}{Ref_{hour}^k} \le 20 \\ 2, & \text{if } 20 < \frac{Curr_{hour}^k}{Ref_{hour}^k} \le 50 \\ 3, & \text{if } 50 < \frac{Curr_{hour}^k}{Ref_{hour}^k} \le 100 \\ 5, & \text{if } 100 < \frac{Curr_{hour}^k}{Ref_{hour}^k} \le 1000 \\ 10, & \text{if } 1000 < \frac{Curr_{hour}^k}{Ref_{hour}^k} \end{cases} \quad (3)$$

$Curr_{hour}^k$ and Ref_{hour}^k represent the number of queries in the past hour and in the reference hour respectively, that contained the trending keyword k. The higher the change in the appearance frequency of the keyword k in the search logs, the higher its uniqueness value. Note that the weight of a trending keyword (equation 2) takes into account both the uniqueness and absolute frequency of a keyword by multiplying them. For every query we find its matching weight as the total sum of the weights of all trending keywords that are contained in the query, normalized by the total weight of all available trending keywords. In that way, the matching score for a query is always a value between 0 and 1. Every query with a matching score above 0.5 is assumed to match the trending event.

At the *backward pass step*, we record all the search results that users clicked on after submitting queries that have been identified as trending. PocketTrend uses these results to identify additional queries that belong to the trending event. In particular, every query that resulted into a click on one of the search results identified in the *forward pass* step is added to the trending event.

3.2.2 Trending Content Cache Formation

After the trending event has been detected, a set of search queries associated to the event has been identified. By examining all the search results that users clicked after submitting these queries, the final set of search results (URLs and snippets) associated to the trending event can also be generated. When considering every single query and search result associated to the event, the total number of queries and search results can be quite large. For instance, in the case of U.S. presidential elections, the identified trending content includes 27,000 queries and 37,000 search results (Table 3). Pushing all this data to mobile users is not desirable due to the bandwidth requirements. However, as demonstrated in Section 2.1 (Figure 2), the majority of the search traffic related to the trending event is concentrated around a small set of these queries and corresponding search results (e.g., top-50 search results). As a result, PocketTrend leverages the most popular trending search queries (e.g., 1000 top queries) along with the corresponding search results to form the trending cache that is pushed to users. As we will show in Section 4.5, this approach ensures high, close to ideal, performance, while minimizing the bandwidth consumed.

Event	Queries	Results
U.S. Presidential Elections	27K	37K
Boston Marathon Bombing	13K	16K
Pope Election	1K	3K

Table 3: Number of unique trending search queries and search results for each trending event.

3.3 User Update Strategies

After the trending search content has been identified, PocketTrend needs to timely and efficiently propagate this content to users. PocketTrend explores two techniques for achieving this, based on the search log analysis described in Section 2.3.

First, it actively identifies a subset of the search engine's users that with high probability will search for the trending topic in the future, and pro-actively pushes the trending search content to these users. The selection of users is based on the analysis of the mobile search logs in Section 2.3 (Figure 6). PocketTrend identifies all users that submitted a query within two hours before the trending event took place, and pushes the trending search content to these users in descending order of their query volume. To limit the effect of active updates on the search backend and its bandwidth consumption, we enforce a maximum number of users to be updated every minute. In that way, PocketTrend does not overwhelm the datacenter by simultaneously pushing content to all users.

Second, based on the findings of the mobile search log analysis in Section 2.3, PocketTrend complements active content pushing with passive user updates. As Table 2 shows, a large percentage of users (up to 26%) submits queries unrelated to the trending event after the trending event has been detected. PocketTrend leverages this to opportunistically push the trending search content to these users along with the search results for the unrelated search query. In that way, PocketTrend can timely update users that might have never been updated through active updates, without increasing the datacenter's workload.

In the next section, we quantify the benefits and overhead for both active and passive updates, and study the feasibility of each technique in detail.

4. EVALUATION

In this section, we quantify the improvements PocketTrend can achieve and analyze the overhead paid by both the client and the server side. In particular, we leverage the search log traces from the 3 representative trending events described in detail in Section 2. On top of these 3 trending events, we also separately test a month

Trending event	% of unique users			
	PT-5k	PT-UpdatesOnly	PT-Unlimited	PT-Ideal
U.S.Pres.Elections	8.8%	10.7%	11.8%	13.7%
PopeElection	2.8%	2.3%	2.9%	4.5%
BostonMar.Bomb	19.6%	18.7%	21.5%	21.8%

Table 4: Percentage of users for which a trend cache hit is registered, when PocketTrend with active updates (5k), passive updates (UpdatesOnly), unlimited cache size (PT-Unlimited) or ideal cache (Ideal) is used.

of search logs data (from June 15th to July 15th 2013) and detected five small trends: Lil Wayne Hospitalization, Father's Day, Gandolfini's Death, USA Independence Day, and San Francisco Plane Crash).[5] By replaying these search logs, we know exactly which user searched for what, at what time, and what search result he/she clicked in response. At the same time, while replaying back the search logs, we run PocketTrend to identify trending search content and push it to end users. This enables us to know if the search query and search result clicked by a user when searching for the trending topic has already been pushed to the user's mobile device. If true, a cache hit is recorded meaning that this query did not have to reach the datacenter, and the user had an instant user experience. If either the query submitted by the user or the search result the user clicked on was not included in the pushed trending content, then a cache miss is recorded, and the query is assumed to hit the datacenter like any other search query. Note that in doing this we take into account the freshness of the search content. In fact, a user may have received trending search content but that may be too old to include the search result the user clicked on when doing the actual search, so a case like this would be recorded as a cache miss. Using this setup we evaluate PocketTrend when active or passive updates are used to push trending search content to end users.

4.1 Notation and Experiment Parameters

In our evaluation, we consider an active update mechanism (*PT-Xk*) which updates at most X thousand users every minute (e.g., *PT-5k* updates up to 5k users a minute), and a passive update mechanism (*PT-UpdatesOnly*) that opportunistically piggybacks the trending content on other pending queries' results (Section 3.3). Unless otherwise noted, in both cases every single detected trending query and search result is pushed to users (Table 3). We also compare PocketTrend's performance to a baseline system (*No-Caching*) with no client-side caching support, and to an ideal system (*PT-IdealCache*) which assumes that all users are updated with the freshest trending search content, irrespectively of its size, right before they submit their trend-related query. Note that such a system is not feasible and is only used for comparison purposes.

4.2 End user Search Experience

To understand the benefits PocketTrend can bring to users, we measured the fraction of users that received the trending search content, and subsequently searched for the trending topic by submitting a search query and clicking on a search result that was already pushed on their devices. Table 4 shows the percentage of all search engine users during the lifetime of the event that benefited at least once from PocketTrend in the case of active (*PT-5k*) and passive (*PT-UpdatesOnly*) updates. In both cases, we assume that the 1000 most popular trending search queries are pushed to the users. Results when all trending search content is pushed (*PT-Unlimited*), and when an ideal cache is used (*PT-IdealCache*) are also shown.

[5]We did this experiment to show that PocketTrend works for new testing data that was not used to define its design.

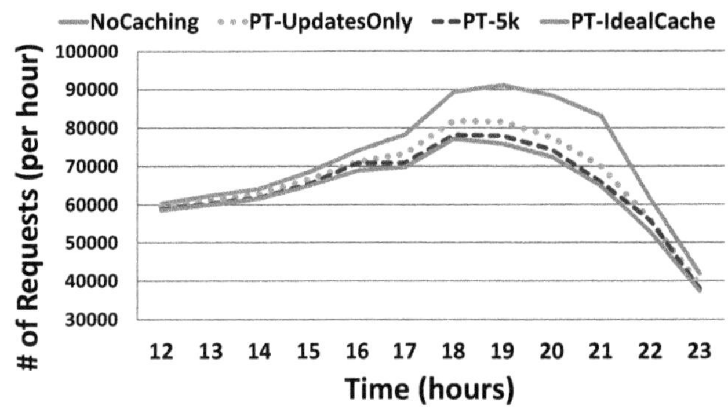

Figure 10: Search query volume reduction with PocketTrend (PT) for different update strategies (U.S. president elections).

For a large event like the Boston marathon bombing, even 20% of all unique users the search engine sees during the event lifetime benefit from PocketTrend. Given that search engines serve hundreds of millions of users on a daily basis, this percentage corresponds to several tens of million of mobile users. For smaller events like the pope election this percentage reduces to 3% of all unique users, but still corresponds to several million users. Surprisingly, passive updates only lightly reduce the effectiveness of PocketTrend, with anywhere between 2% and 19% of unique users being benefited. In the case of the U.S. president elections, passive updates actually outperform active updates. Due to the slow evolution of the trending event, active updates can push trending search content to users early during the trend development process. As the event evolves over time, updated users might search for the trending event but for content that was not captured in the active push (e.g., Ohio state election results were not rolling in when the content push took place). On the other hand, passive updates take place over time, as users come online, allowing them to use the freshest version of the trending search content, and therefore benefit more end users. This unexpectedly good performance of passive updates is crucial to make PocketTrend a low-cost mechanism for datacenters (more on this later).

Not only does the passive updates mechanism achieve similar performance to the active updates mechanism, but its performance is also very close to that of an ideal, but not practically feasible, implementation of the cache (freshest content is always available irrespectively of its size). As Table 4 shows, the ideal cache can only provide real-time search experience for an extra 2-3% of users.

4.3 Datacenter Query Load

PocketTrend not only benefits end users, but can also reduce the datacenter's query load by preventing trending search queries from hitting the backend. We evaluate the savings on the datacenter's side for different update mechanisms. In addition to *PT-UpdatesOnly* and *PT-5k* introduced above, we compare PocketTrend to a baseline system (*No-Caching*) with no client-side caching support and to an ideal system (*PT-IdealCache*) which assumes that all users are updated with the freshest trending search content right before they submit their trend-related query.

Figures 10 and 11 show the reduction in the overall search query volume for these four system designs, in the case of U.S. president elections and Boston marathon bombing, respectively. With active updates (*PT-5k*), PocketTrend is able to reduce the datacenter's query volume by 9–17%, depending on the trending event (at the trend's peak time). Note that this reduction of the query vol-

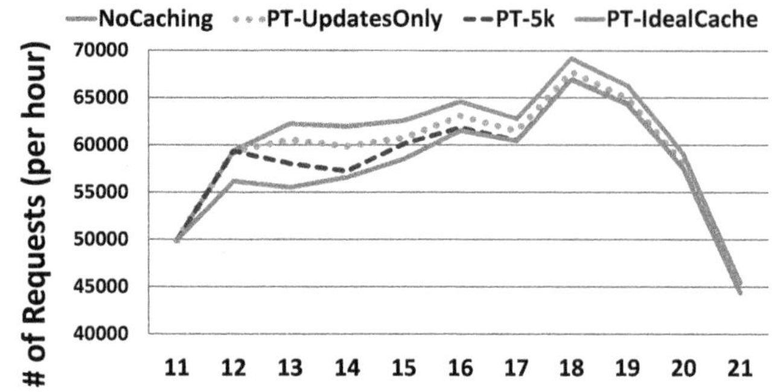

Figure 11: Search query volume reduction with PocketTrend (PT) for different update strategies (Boston marathon bomb).

ume lasts for several hours as the trending event evolves, and is progressively reduced over time as the trending event disappears.

Even more importantly, when passive updates are used (*PT-UpdatesOnly*), PocketTrend is still able to reduce the datacenter's query volume by 7–14%, depending on the trending event. Even though the benefit is lower compared to active updates, the fact that passive updates can achieve similar gains is important as they do not impose as high bandwidth requirements on the datacenter as active updates do (more about this in Section 4.4). However, there can be cases where active update strategies achieve significantly higher query volume reductions. For example, in the Boston marathon event (Figure 11), in the first two hours after the bombing (12pm – 2pm), *PT-5k* is almost twice more efficient than *PT-UpdatesOnly*. We believe that this has to do with the unpredictability of trending events. The Boston marathon bombing event was highly unexpected and dramatic for users, creating this instant spike in user query volume that only active updates can efficiently address initially. On the other hand, the U.S. president election was more expected, and it formed a trending event that slowly developed over time, providing enough time for passive updates to become almost as efficient as active updates[6].

When compared to the ideal cache implementation, both active and passive updates perform remarkably well, with the active strategy having a small edge over the passive one. This is especially noticeable in Figure 10 where *PT-5k* is always within 3% of *PT-IdealCache*. More importantly, *PT-UpdatesOnly* can get at least 63% (usually more) of the benefits provided by *PT-IdealCache*.

Note PocketTrend's 17% reduction of query volume in the case of president elections is lower than the potential reduction of 30% shown in Figure 1. This is due to two reasons. First, it is nearly impossible for PocketTrend to timely predict every single user that will search for the trending event. For some users, predictions cannot be made; some users might also get updated after they have searched for the trending event. Second, Figure 1 presents the results when all trend-related queries are manually selected. In this section, trend-related queries are detected through the PocketTrend's two-step trending content identification algorithm, which might not include every single trend-related query.

4.4 PocketTrend Overhead

Each time a search request is served locally at the client, one fewer request has to be processed by the datacenter. On the other hand, to avoid such requests the datacenter has to push trending content to the users, passively or actively. We quantify the overhead of PocketTrend on the datacenter with passive (*PT-UpdatesOnly*) or active (*PT-5k*) updates.

First, we measure the number of trending search content pushes performed by the datacenter. Figure 12(a) shows this for the U.S. president elections. For active updates, 5000 users are updated every minute with the trending search content. A large number of pushes takes place when the trending event is detected. After all users that submitted a search query within 2 hours before the trending event took place have been updated, no more pushes are initiated. With passive updates, pushes occur only for users that came to the search engine for other unrelated topics after the trending event was detected. Because of this, passive update pushes grow slowly over time, and at the end of the event's lifetime, they are half of the active update pushes.

Passive updates are not only fewer, but also more effective. For the same event, we compute the ratio between the number of search requests eliminated from the datacenter and the number of trending content pushes to end users. The higher this ratio is, the lower the overhead from the datacenter's point of view is. As Figure 12(b) shows, passive updates achieve a ratio of almost up to 20%, while active updates remain well below 4%.

Given that the passive and active update strategies provide comparable advantages to end users and to the datacenter, Figure 12 shows that passive updates can be a much more cost-effective approach for the datacenter and the end users. From the datacenter point of view, passive updates do not require any new requests to be

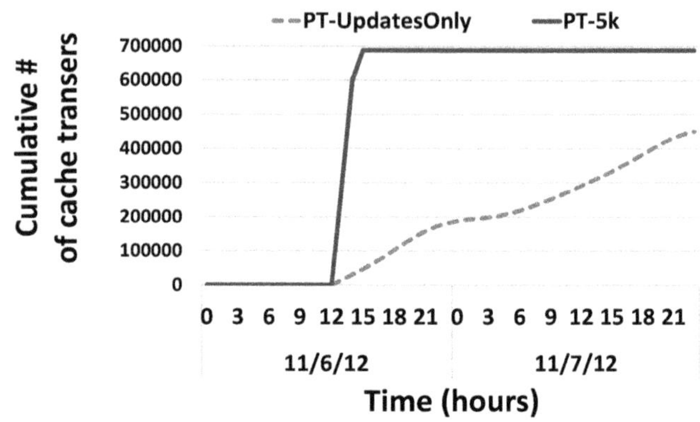

(a) Cache transfers

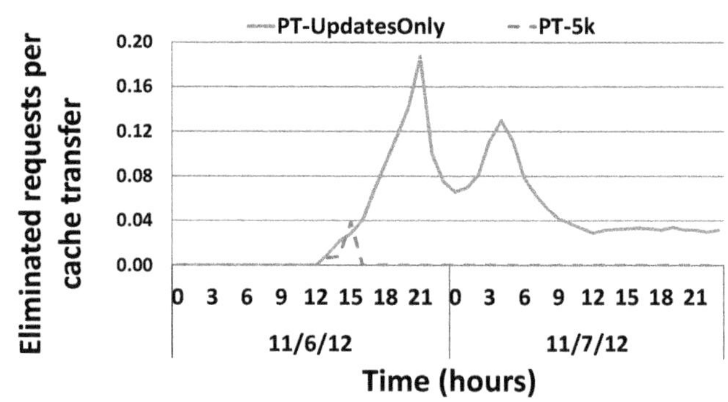

(b) Eliminated datacenter requests per cache transfer

Figure 12: PocketTrend overhead measured as cumulative number of cache transfers (a) and number of eliminated requests to the datacenter per cache transfer (b) (U.S. President Elections).

[6]When active and passive updates are combined, the reduction in the search query volume is only slightly higher than active updates.

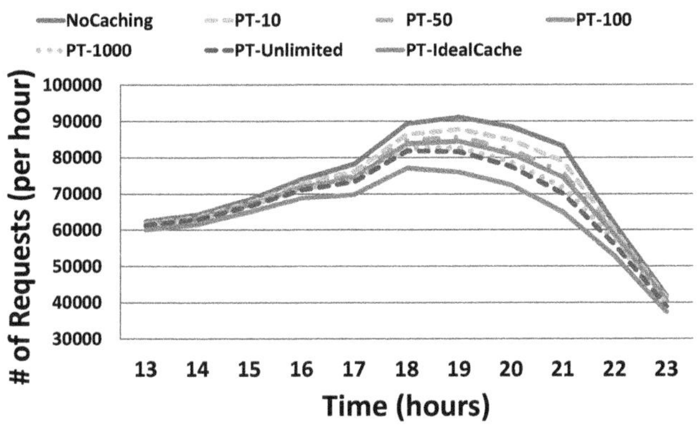

Figure 13: Effect of the size of the pushed trending search content on PocketTrend's query volume reduction (U.S. president elections).

submitted as trending search content is opportunistically pushed to end users, and the number of pushes is halved. From the user point of view, in contrast to active updates where a user's device needs to be explicitly activated to synchronize, passive updates only incur minor battery drain as the user's device radio is already powered up and connected to the search engine.

As we show in more detail in Section 4.5, each push shown in Figure 12(a) corresponds to the datacenter transferring approximately 1MB of additional data. Given the total number of pushes in Figure 12(a), active and passive updates require the datacenter to transfer an additional 680GB and 390GB, respectively. Note that the transfer of this data is distributed over the whole lifetime of a trending event. Given that trending events can last from several hours to tens of hours, this additional bandwidth does not stretch the bandwidth limits of the search backend.

4.5 Trending Content Size Effect

Figures 10 and 11 show the query volume reduction when every single trending search query and search result is pushed. To conclude our tradeoff analysis, we now analyze the PocketTrend's sensitivity on the size of the content pushed to users. We assume PocketTrend employs *UpdatesOnly*; similar results hold for active updates, but are not shown in the interest of space.

Figure 13 shows the overall query volume when the 10, 50, 100, and 1000 most popular trending search queries along with the top 10 most clicked search results for each trending query are pushed (labeled as *PT-** in the figure). As a reference, the results when all trending search queries (Table 3) and their corresponding search results are pushed is also shown (*PT-Unlimited*). Surprisingly, caching 1000 queries (*PT-1000*) provides most of the benefits of pushing every single trending query and search result (*PT-Unlimited*). As a result, PocketTrend can achieve its top performance while pushing a limited number of trending search queries ($\approx$ 1000) and results. Reducing the size of the pushed content to 100 entries significantly reduces the performance gain, while pushing the top 50 entries can halve PocketTrend's performance gain.

Considering that an average search result requires roughly 500 bytes (i.e., URL and data snippet), storing the top 10 search results (i.e., the first page of search results) for a trending query, requires about 5 kB. Hence, pushing 1000 trending search queries corresponds to pushing roughly 5 MB. Note that if PocketTrend were to push all trending search queries and search results (Table 3), more than 135 MB would be used. The size of the trending search content can be further reduced by leveraging data compression techniques. Given that the set of queries and search results pushed to end users relates to the same event, there is significant overlap across the 1000 entries. We experimentally verified that a simple compression algorithm based on bzip2 [27, 31] can achieve a significant compression ratio ranging from 4.5x to 5x. This means that the trending search content can be compressed from 5 MB to just 1 MB. This data size is less than the size of a simple application update on a smartphone today, and it could take place over WiFi links when the cost of cellular bandwidth is a concern.

5. RELATED WORK

Discovering trends in search is a well-studied problem [9]. Commercial search engines already offer products such as Google Trends [6]. Our trend detection approach leverages well-known techniques for trend analysis [20, 24], and is not the main contribution of this work. Instead, the contributions of this work lie on the findings of the search log analysis that show how mobile users search for trending topics. Specifically, the way these findings are leveraged to enable PocketTrend to automatically detect search content related to a trending event, and more importantly to efficiently push this content to users without significantly increasing the datacenter workload is the core contribution of this work.

Previous work on search engine optimization has focused primarily on server-side and client-side caching. In server-side caching [2, 29, 16, 7, 11], search results for popular queries are cached in the search backend. Incoming queries that are in the cache can be answered faster than other queries as there is no need to access the index, and perform any ranking in real-time. The reduction in user response time can be significant when the delay due to search backend's computation is the bottleneck between the user and the datacenter. This tends to be the case when users access search engines through very high speed links (e.g., desktops). Yet, as more and more people use their mobile devices to access search engines through slow cellular links that have high setup times [8], the bottleneck shifts from the datacenter to the cellular links. In this case, the benefit of server-side caching techniques is reduced.

Researchers have been exploiting client-side caching techniques to enable faster user experience in the case of web browsing [19, 30, 5, 17, 28], ad delivery [21], and more recently search result delivery [15]. Koukoumidis et al. [15] showed that a small set of queries and search results represents a significant fraction of the mobile query volume. By analyzing mobile search logs on a daily basis, authors identify the part of the search index that is most often accessed, and use it to create a search engine that lives on the mobile device, and it is able to instantly answer about 60% of the queries an individual user submits. The search results stored on the user's mobile device are only updated nightly when the phone is charging and connected to WiFi. Even though quite effective, this work is only limited to relatively static search content that can be predicted through periodic search log mining. This system cannot address unpredicted query volume spikes due to trending events taking place throughout the day as the necessary trending search content will not be available on the users' mobile devices. Moreover, the authors blindly update every user assuming that the updates take place during off-peak times (e.g., overnight), and over WiFi connections. This approach, in the case of trending events, would require the datacenter to simultaneously update hundreds of millions of users during peak time, creating a larger problem for the search backend than the one we solve.

Conversely, PocketTrend automatically detects trending events in real time, and identifies the search content associated to these events. The trending search content is then intelligently pushed either actively to a subset of users that with high probability will search for the trending event, or passively to any user that reaches the search engine after a trending event has been detected and is still active. In that way, PocketTrend addresses trending query volume spikes, without stressing even further the search engine's backend.

Unpredicted workload spikes is a reality for most web services [24], and are not limited to search engines [26]. As a result, there have been a lot of efforts to address these challenges directly at the networking level within datacenters [10, 22, 1]. These techniques are orthogonal to our work.

6. CONCLUSION

We have analyzed 21 million mobile search queries to understand how trending search topics are formed, and how they evolve over time. Based on our findings, we have designed and evaluated PocketTrend, a new architecture that is capable of servicing user queries related to trending events locally, improving both the user experience and the datacenter query load. Our evaluation using real mobile search logs, showed that in the presence of a trending event, up to 13%–17% of the overall traffic can be eliminated from the datacenter, impacting as many as 19% of all users.

Acknowledgements

We thank the reviewers for their valuable suggestions. Gennady Pekhimenko is supported by a Microsoft Research Fellowship and a Qualcomm Innovation Fellowship.

7. REFERENCES

[1] M. Alizadeh, A. Greenberg, D. A. Maltz, J. Padhye, P. Patel, B. Prabhakar, S. Sengupta, and M. Sridharan. Data Center TCP (DCTCP). In *Proc. of SIGCOMM*, pages 63–74, 2010.

[2] R. Baeza-Yates, A. Gionis, F. Junqueira, V. Murdock, V. Plachouras, and F. Silvestri. The impact of caching on search engines. In *Proc. of SIGIR*, pages 183–190, 2007.

[3] R. Baeza-yates, F. Junqueira, V. Plachouras, and H. F. Witschel. Admission policies for caches of search engine results. In *Proc. of the 14th String Processing and Information Retrieval Symposium*, volume 4726 of *LNCS*, pages 74–85, 2007.

[4] R. Baeza-Yates and F. Saint-Jean. A three level search engine index based in query log distribution. In *Proc. of the 10th String Processing and Information Retrieval Symposium*, volume 2857 of *LNCS*, pages 56–65, 2003.

[5] N. Balasubramanian, A. Balasubramanian, and A. Venkataramani. Energy consumption in mobile phones: a measurement study and implications for network applications. In *Proc. of IMC*, pages 280–293. ACM, 2009.

[6] H. Choi and H. Varian. Predicting the present with google trends. *Economic Record*, 88:2–9, 2012.

[7] T. Fagni, R. Perego, F. Silvestri, and S. Orlando. Boosting the performance of web search engines: Caching and prefetching query results by exploiting historical usage data. *ACM Trans. Inf. Syst.*, 24(1):51–78, Jan. 2006.

[8] H. Falaki, R. Mahajan, S. Kandula, D. Lymberopoulos, R. Govindan, and D. Estrin. Diversity in smartphone usage. In *Proc. of MobiSys*, 2010.

[9] N. G. Golbandi, L. K. Katzir, Y. K. Koren, and R. L. Lempel. Expediting Search Trend Detection via Prediction of Query Counts. In *Proc. of WSDM*, 2013.

[10] A. Greenberg, J. R. Hamilton, N. Jain, S. Kandula, C. Kim, P. Lahiri, D. A. Maltz, P. Patel, and S. Sengupta. VL2: a scalable and flexible data center network. In *Proc. of SIGCOMM*, pages 51–62, 2009.

[11] S. Jonassen, B. B. Cambazoglu, and F. Silvestri. Prefetching Query Results and Its Impact on Search Engines. In *Proc. of SIGIR*, 2012.

[12] K. S. Jones. A statistical interpretation of term specificity and its application in retrieval. *Journal of Documentation*, 28:11–21, 1972.

[13] M. Kamvar and S. Baluja. A large scale study of wireless search behavior: Google mobile search. In *CHI*, 2006.

[14] M. Kamvar, M. Kellar, R. Patel, and Y. Xu. Computers and iphones and mobile phones, oh my! In *WWW*, 2009.

[15] E. Koukoumidis, D. Lymberopoulos, K. Strauss, J. Liu, and D. Burger. Pocket Cloudlets. In *ASPLOS*, 2011.

[16] R. Lempel and S. Moran. Predictive caching and prefetching of query results in search engines. In *Proc. of WWW*, pages 19–28, 2003.

[17] D. Lymberopoulos, O. Riva, K. Strauss, A. Mittal, and A. Ntoulas. PocketWeb: instant web browsing for mobile devices. In *ASPLOS*, pages 1–12, 2012.

[18] H. Ma and B. Wang. User-aware Caching and Prefetching Query Results in Web Search Engines. In *Proc. of SIGIR*, 2012.

[19] E. P. Markatos and C. E. Chronaki. A top-10 approach to prefetching on the web. In *Proc. of INET*, 1998.

[20] M. Mathioudakis and N. Koudas. TwitterMonitor: trend detection over the twitter stream. In *Proc. of SIGMOD*, pages 1155–1158, 2010.

[21] P. Mohan, S. Nath, and O. Riva. Prefetching mobile ads: can advertising systems afford it? In *Proc. of EuroSys*, pages 267–280, 2013.

[22] D. Narayanan, A. Donnelly, E. Thereska, S. Elnikety, and A. I. T. Rowstron. Everest: Scaling Down Peak Loads Through I/O Off-Loading. In *OSDI*, pages 15–28, 2008.

[23] Pyevolve. Machine Learning - Text feature extraction (tf-idf). http://pyevolve.sourceforge.net/wordpress/?p=1589, 2014.

[24] K. Radinsky and E. Horvitz. Mining the Web to Predict Future Events. In *Proc. of WSDM*, 2013.

[25] A. Rajaraman and J. D. Ullman. *Mining of Massive Datasets*. Cambridge University Press, 2011.

[26] A. Saha and V. Sindhwani. Learning Evolving and Emerging Topics in Social Media: A Dynamic Nmf Approach with Temporal Regularization. In *Proc. of WSDM*, 2012.

[27] J. Seward. Bzip2 V. 1.0.6. http://www.bzip.org/, 2010.

[28] Z. Wang, F. X. Lin, L. Zhong, and M. Chishtie. How far can client-only solutions go for mobile browser speed? In *Proc. of WWW*, pages 31–40, 2012.

[29] Y. Xie and D. R. O'Hallaron. Locality in search engine queries and its implications for caching. In *INFOCOM*, 2002.

[30] L. Yin and G. Cao. Adaptive power-aware prefetch in wireless networks. *IEEE Trans. on Wireless Comms*, 2004.

[31] J. Ziv and A. Lempel. A Universal Algorithm for Sequential Data Compression. *IEEE Trans. Inf. Theory*, 1977.

Overcoming Relational Learning Biases to Accurately Predict Preferences in Large Scale Networks

Joseph J. Pfeiffer III[1], Jennifer Neville[1], Paul N. Bennett[2]
[1]Purdue University, [2]Microsoft Research
{jpfeiffer,neville}@purdue.edu, paul.n.bennett@microsoft.com

ABSTRACT

Many individuals on social networking sites provide traits about themselves, such as interests or demographics. Social networking sites can use this information to provide better content to match their users' interests, such as recommending scheduled events or various relevant products. These tasks require accurate probability estimates to determine the correct answer to return. Relational machine learning (RML) is an excellent framework for these problems as it jointly models the user labels given their attributes and the relational structure. Further, semi-supervised learning methods could enable RML methods to exploit the large amount of unlabeled data in networks.

However, existing RML approaches have limitations that prevent their application in large scale domains. First, semi-supervised methods for RML do not fully utilize all the unlabeled instances in the network. Second, the collective inference procedures necessary to jointly infer the missing labels are generally viewed as too expensive to apply in large scale domains. In this work, we address each of these limitations. We analyze the effect of full semi-supervised RML and find that collective inference methods can introduce considerable bias into predictions. We correct this by implementing a *maximum entropy* constraint on the *inference* step, forcing the predictions to have the same distribution as the observed labels. Next, we outline a massively scalable variational inference algorithm for large scale relational network domains. We extend this inference algorithm to incorporate the maximum entropy constraint, proving that it only requires a *constant* amount of overhead while remaining massively parallel. We demonstrate our method's improvement over a variety of baselines on seven real world datasets, including large scale networks with over five million edges.

Categories: H.2.8 [**Database Management**]: Database Applications - Data Mining
Keywords: Relational Machine Learning; Maximum Entropy Inference; Large Scale Networks

WWW 2015, May 18–22, 2015, Florence, Italy.
ACM 978-1-4503-3469-3/15/05.
http://dx.doi.org/10.1145/2736277.2741668.

1. INTRODUCTION

Many individuals on social networking sites provide information about their preferences and behaviors (e.g., profile and activity information). Social networking sites can use this information to better target relevant content to their users. For example, for scheduled events (e.g., concerts), the social networking site can determine whether the event is relevant to a user's interest and, if so, recommend it to the user. After some initial users have indicated whether they are/are not attending, the service can predict other interested users based on the *relational* information in the network (i.e., links among users). These types of prediction tasks occur in a variety of scenarios; for example, a site may be interested in estimating the number of users that will like a news article or buy a product, and users may be interested in estimated answers to *relational summarization* queries, such as "do my friends prefer rock or rap?" Methods that can make accurate predictions about unobserved user preferences are critical for estimation of user-level behaviors.

Common approaches to these types of tasks—where the goal is to accurately predict class probabilities for the set of unlabeled users in the network, given a small subset of labeled users—include conventional machine learning methods for independent and identically distributed (IID) data (e.g., logistic regression), or simple inference-only relational models such as label propagation (LP) [20, 10]. However, these approaches are limited in the sense that they only utilize either intrinsic information (e.g, attributes) or external sources (e.g., neighboring labels), and they do not *learn* how to combine them together.

Relational machine learning (RML) approaches focus on learning the relative importance of the relational information to the intrinsic information. Traditionally, the parameters for a *local conditional model* are maximized by solely learning from a labeled subgraph (Figure 1.a), where an observed vertex's label is conditioned on the observed neighbors' labels and intrinsic attributes. RML then "stitches together" a full joint model by collectively inferring all unlabeled instances. Semi-supervised learning (SSL) RML methods have been developed for partially-observed single network domains where the goal is *within-network* learning and inference [18, 12]. However, RML SSL methods have limited applicability for sparsely-labeled, large-scale networks due to their restricted performance gains and poor scalability.

More precisely, although IID learning algorithms for SSL usually treat the unlabeled data as weighted probabilistic samples, the same cannot be said for the general RML SSL approaches. Methods such as *relational* expectation maxi-

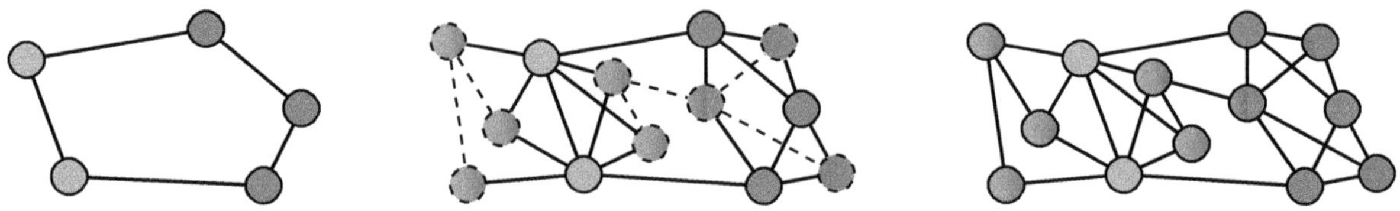

(a) Pseudolikelihood (G_L) (b) Composite Likelihood (G) (c) Pseudolikelihood (G)

Figure 1: (a) Pseudolikelihood over the labeled subgraph G_L. (b) Composite likelihood over the full graph G, where predicted labels for unlabeled (dashed) vertices are only considered as features of labeled vertices during learning and (dashed) links among unlabeled vertices are only used during collective inference. (c) Pseudolikelihood over the full graph G, where all vertices/edges are used for learning.

mization (relational EM, e.g., [18]) partly extend the view of traditional RML learning by utilizing the predictions of the *unlabeled* examples, incorporating these solely as attributes to the labeled examples (Figure 1.b). Note that in this example, the predictions for the dashed vertices are only considered as features during learning, *not* as labels. This is in contrast to IID SSL methods, which treats inferred predictions as *labels* that are used to relearn the parameters (see e.g., [13]) (Figure 1.c). In this case, learning corresponds to a weighted maximization problem, where the weights of the unlabeled corpus are equal to the previously inferred probabilities. Prior work on relational EM has generally not used this information, largely due to reductions in performance (although special exceptions exist, e.g. [12]).

In addition, although various approximations for *learning* RML models are generally the same order complexity as IID models, *inference* with RML models is generally viewed as a limiting factor for large scale implementations. RML methods require the use of *collective inference* to jointly infer label probabilities throughout large networks, and prior work has rarely been applied on networks with more than 10s of thousands of examples (see e.g., [14, 12]). This is in contrast to both IID learning and simple LP models that have previously been applied to large scale data and employ simple parallel inference algorithms.

In this work, we extend relational SSL approaches to address these two issues and apply them on sparsely-labeled, large-scale networks. In the first component of this work, we discuss how previous relational EM approaches can lead to extreme biases during inference—in particular, relearning from the inferred predictions in relational domains generally collapses all predictions to a singular prediction (e.g., all predict negatively labeled with high probability). To solve this, we augment the *inference* step of the EM algorithm to include a *maximum entropy* constraint. Our method (MaxEntInf) adjusts the label predictions at every step of collective inference so they adhere to maximum entropy constraints; namely, we force the predicted label proportions (i.e., percentage predicted positive vs. negative) to align with the proportions observed in the training set. Note the difference from typical maximum entropy approaches that augment the *learning* step of the algorithm; in this work, we adjust the *inference* step. Moreover, our approach provides a more general correction than [12], which requires a special model form and regularizer. MaxEntInf can be easily combined with any chosen RML conditional distribution, to keep predictions from collapsing to a singular value, and thus enables the use of more general SSL techniques.

In the second component of our work, we demonstrate that the collective inference step used by RML algorithms can easily be massively parallelized. In particular, we show that through *asynchronous* updates to variational inference methods, we can achieve linear speedup in terms of the number of cores. This speedup is largely attained due to the avoidance of synchronous updates to high degree vertices (common in real world networks in spite of their sparsity), which would effectively stop the parallelism. Our MaxEntInf algorithm is simple to extend to this massively parallel case and we prove that it requires only a constant overhead for both sequential and parallel algorithms (since it requires a bounded constant number of data samples to compute the correction).

The contributions of this work include the following:

- Identification of a bias with RML SSL learning algorithms in sparsely labeled networks.
- Development of *maximum entropy inference* (MaxEntInf) to correct the bias.
- Parallelized inference for RML and MaxEntInf.
- Proven error bounds for inference approximations, including both sequential and parallel cases. In particular, MaxEntInf correction can be employed with constant overhead.

We demonstrate the accuracy and scale of our correction and parallel algorithm on seven real world datasets. In particular, we find that our SSL methods using MaxEntInf outperform a variety of competing state-of-the-art baselines, both independent learners and simple relational-only models. We can use the accurate probabilities predicted by MaxEntInf for a variety of problems, including the relational summarization task described above. Notably, we apply our methods networks with over five million edges, demonstrating it scales to networks orders of magnitude larger than prior implementations.

2. RELATIONAL MACHINE LEARNING

Define a graph $G = \langle \mathbf{V}, \mathbf{E} \rangle$ to represent our social network, with $v_i \in \mathbf{V}$ corresponding to the individuals (vertices) and $\mathbf{E} \subseteq \mathbf{V} \times \mathbf{V}$ indicating the friendships (edges). Let $\mathbf{X}, \mathbf{Y}$ define the sets of attributes and labels. Every $v_i \in \mathbf{V}$ has a corresponding set of attributes $\mathbf{x}_i \in \mathbf{X}$ and a class label $y_i \in \mathbf{Y}$.

In a social network, a subset of items $\mathbf{V}_L$ are presumed labeled. Our task is to jointly predict the remaining unknown labels ($\mathbf{Y}_U$) using the known labels $\mathbf{Y}_L$, attributes

$\mathbf{X}$ and graph G. Within RML, we can express this statement as jointly inferring the unknown labels given the available information $P(\mathbf{Y}_U|\mathbf{Y}_L, \mathbf{X}, G)$. RML utilizes a local conditional model $\mathcal{C}$, with corresponding parameters $\Theta_\mathcal{C}$, to learn and infer labels within the network. A wide array of relational local conditional models $\mathcal{C}$ exist, and we can view most as a relational extension to common independent models (e.g., relational naive Bayes or relational logistic regression). As many instances are unavailable, traditional RML learns a function from the labeled subgraph G_L where all of the neighbors to all of the instances are known.

$$\hat{\Theta}_\mathcal{C} = \arg\max_{\Theta_\mathcal{C}} P(\mathbf{Y}_L|\mathbf{X}_L, G_L, \Theta_\mathcal{C}) \quad (1)$$

To make predictions, these parameters are then applied to jointly predict the unlabeled instances on the entire network (not just G_L):

$$P(\mathbf{Y}_U|\mathbf{Y}_L, \mathbf{X}, G, \hat{\Theta}_\mathcal{C})$$

To reduce clutter, in the remainder of this paper we drop references to $\mathbf{X}$: it is fixed and always conditioned on, regardless of the learning representation. RML utilizes *conditional independence* to simplify the above expressions. Let $\mathbf{Y}_{\mathcal{MB}_*(v_i)}$ indicate the labels of the Markov blanket of a vertex v_i, or the friends of an individual v_i, on a graph G_*. The full joint distributions are broken into local conditional distributions of the form:

$$P(y_i|\mathbf{Y}_{\mathcal{MB}_*(v_i)}, \Theta_\mathcal{C})$$

By maximizing the *pseudolikelihood* of the labeled subgraph G_L we can learn the local model parameters $\Theta_\mathcal{C}$ in a scalable fashion:

$$\hat{\Theta}_\mathcal{C} \approx \arg\max_{\Theta_\mathcal{C}} \sum_{v_i \in \mathbf{V}_L} \log P(y_i|\mathbf{Y}_{\mathcal{MB}_L(v_i)}, G_L, \Theta_\mathcal{C}) \quad (2)$$

Unlike independent models, we must perform *collective classification* for inference, due to the dependencies between the unlabeled instances in the network. To this end, the local conditional probabilities are combined with a global inference method (such as variational inference) to estimate the joint distribution over the unlabeled vertices, i.e:

$$P(\mathbf{Y}_U|\mathbf{Y}_L, G) \approx Q(\mathbf{Y}_U) = \prod_{v_i \in \mathbf{Y}_U} Q_i(y)$$

where each component $Q_i(y)$ is iteratively updated in a coordinate ascent algorithm:

$$Q_i(y) \propto \exp\left\{\mathbb{E}_{\mathbf{Y}_{U\setminus i}} f(y_i|\mathbf{Y}_{\mathcal{MB}(v_i)}, G, \Theta_\mathcal{C})\right\}$$

where $f(\cdot)$ is the unnormalized energy function. Throughout this work, let $\tilde{\mathbf{Y}}_U$ indicate the current joint probability estimates of the unlabeled instances that are iteratively updated via variational inference.

2.1 Semi-Supervised Learning

Many relational learning tasks involve learning and inference *within* a single large, partially-labeled network. In this case, a natural extension from the above RML methods utilizes the unlabeled data to make better predictions within the network. The most common form utilizes *expectation maximization* (EM; Algorithm 1). EM iteratively updates the parameter estimates by utilizing the expected values of the unlabeled examples to relearn the parameters and can be divided into two basic steps.

Algorithm 1 Relational-EM($\mathbf{Y}_L, \mathbf{X}, G_L, \mathcal{C}$)

1: $\hat{\Theta}_\mathcal{C}$ = InitialParameters($\mathbf{Y}_L, \mathbf{X}, G_L$)
2: **while** More Iterations *or* Not Converged **do**
3: $P(\mathbf{Y}_U)^t$ = UpdateInferences($\mathbf{Y}_L, \mathbf{X}, G, \hat{\Theta}_\mathcal{C}^{t-1}$)
4: $\hat{\Theta}_\mathcal{C}^t$ = UpdateParameters($\mathbf{Y}_L, P(\mathbf{Y}_U)^t, \mathbf{X}, G_L$)
5: **end while**
6: $P(\mathbf{Y}_U)$ = FinalizeInferences($\mathbf{Y}_L, \mathbf{X}, G, \hat{\Theta}_\mathcal{C}^T$)

E-Step: evaluate $P(\mathbf{Y}_U|\mathbf{Y}_L, G, \Theta_\mathcal{C}^{t-1})$ (3)

M-Step: learn $\Theta_\mathcal{C}^t$

$$\arg\max_{\Theta_\mathcal{C}} \sum_{\mathbf{Y}_U \in \mathcal{Y}_U} P(\mathbf{Y}_U|\mathbf{Y}_L, G, \Theta_\mathcal{C}^{t-1}) \log P(\mathbf{Y}_U, \mathbf{Y}_L|G, \Theta_\mathcal{C}) \quad (4)$$

We can compute the **E-Step** (Eq. 3) via RML collective classification methods; but, as with other RML optimizations, the **M-Step** (Eq. 4) is intractable to compute directly. Existing relational EM methods [18] simplify the expression by optimizing the *composite likelihood* (Eq. 6) instead:

E-Step: evaluate $P(\mathbf{Y}_U|\mathbf{Y}_L, G, \Theta_\mathcal{C}^{t-1})$ (5)

M-Step: learn $\Theta_\mathcal{C}^t$

$$\arg\max_{\Theta_\mathcal{C}} \sum_{\mathbf{Y}_U \in \mathcal{Y}_U} P(\mathbf{Y}_U|\mathbf{Y}_L, G, \Theta_\mathcal{C}^{t-1}) \sum_{v_i \in \mathbf{V}_L} \log P(y_i|\mathbf{Y}_{\mathcal{MB}(v_i)}, \Theta_\mathcal{C}) \quad (6)$$

By utilizing the additional relational information provided by the unlabeled instances, relational EM methods generally outperform traditional RML.

3. LIKELIHOOD APPROXIMATIONS

As discussed in the previous section, computing the full joint likelihood (Eq. 1) is not scalable to large datasets. Hence, RML maximizes the pseudolikelihood over the labeled graph G_L (Eq. 2) , while relational EM methods maximize the composite likelihood on the graph G (Eq. 6) . Note that although the composite likelihood over the graph G is similar to the pseudolikelihood, it is distinct as it only sums over the log conditional distributions of the *labeled* instances.

We graphically illustrate the differences between the learning approaches in Figure 1. Figure 1.a shows the traditional RML maximization problem, which uses the full pseudolikelihood of the labeled graph G_L. Relational EM methods use additional information from the *predicted* label values. In particular, the neighboring probabilities are incorporated as *attributes* for the label maximization step. This is shown in Figure 1.b, where the solid outlined instances are treated as labeled instances for maximization and the dashed instances are only used as attributes. Since this is only a partial pseudolikelihood, we refer to these learning algorithms as *composite likelihood* EM (CL-EM) methods.

Figure 1.c shows the full pseudolikelihood maximization, where every solid instance (including the unlabeled items) is used to update the parameter values. This corresponds to the critical component of EM that has been shown to work well for independent data/IID learners—incorporating probabilistic samples of the unlabeled instances into the training set allows the learners to observe new correlations between the various attributes and labels that were not present in the original labeled set. We formalize the generalized relational pseudolikelihood EM (PL-EM) approach as:

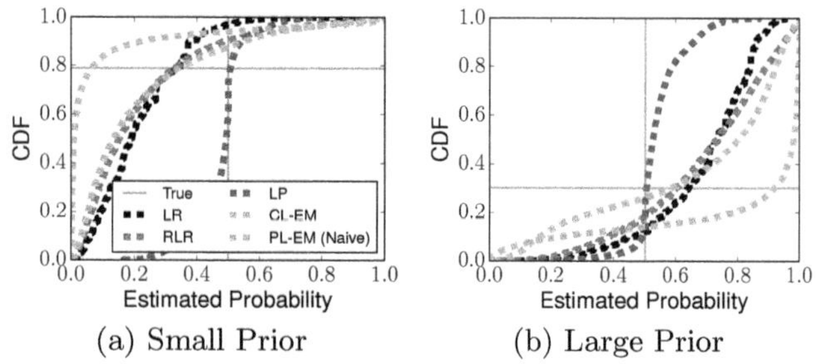

Figure 2: DVD: Naive application of the pseudo-likelihood exaggerates error produced by RML and CL-EM. (a) For small priors the probabilities are underestimated, while for (b) large priors the probabilities are overestimated.

$$\textbf{E-Step: } \text{evaluate } P(\mathbf{Y}_U|\mathbf{Y}_L, G, \Theta_C^{t-1}) \quad (7)$$

$$\textbf{M-Step: } \text{learn } \Theta_C^t$$

$$\arg\max_{\Theta_C} \sum_{\mathbf{Y}_U \in \mathcal{Y}_U} P(\mathbf{Y}_U|\mathbf{Y}_L, G, \Theta_C^{t-1}) \sum_{v_i \in \mathbf{V}} \log P(y_i|\mathbf{Y}_{\mathcal{MB}(v_i)}, \Theta_C) \quad (8)$$

Note the difference between PL-EM maximization (Eq. 8) and CL-EM maximization (Eq. 6). CL-EM maximizes strictly over the *labeled* data, while the PL-EM incorporates the estimates of the unlabeled instances as well. Thus, when new attribute combinations are observed in the unlabeled portion of the network, PL-EM can learn these values as well.

In Figure 2 we show the effect of a naive application of PL-EM to learning and inferring on the DVD dataset (discussed more in Sec. 6). As we can define the positive class label for DVD by thresholding at various Amazon sale ranks, we can examine the effect of RML, CL-EM and PL-EM in relation to the two different prior distributions (shown as the black horizontal lines). We use a relational logistic regression (RLR) as the base conditional model and then observe the distribution of final predictions produced by a variety of relational estimation and collective inference methods (CL-EM, PL-EM, LP). Deviations from where the prior (True) intersects with the vertical line at 0.5 predicted probability shows bias in the final predicted probabilities. The RLR model alone produces some bias in the predictions, which CL-EM roughly follows. However, naive application of PL-EM for estimation produces substantial bias away from the true prior. Since most class label variables in relational domains have a skewed prior, the true distribution of labels would be grossly misestimated by PL-EM.

Although some work in relational domains has augmented particular classifiers to account for this type of bias [12], they modify the optimization function via a regularizer and assume a specific form that is not applicable to all models. In the next section, we will outline a general correction to the *inference* step that is simple to implement in conjunction with any relational classifier. Further, we prove it is well approximated with constant overhead and demonstrate how to incorporate it into a massively parallel inference mechanism, allowing us to jointly learn and infer relational SSL models on large scale data.

4. MAXIMUM ENTROPY INFERENCE

In this section, we introduce our method to correct for the biases experienced by relational classifiers during their inference step; more generally, this will allow us to improve relational EM by utilizing the full pseudolikelihood over all unlabeled data during an EM process.

Note that given a labeled sample $\mathbf{V}_L \subseteq \mathbf{V}$, it is simple to compute the proportion of observed label types $P(y)$ (e.g., $P(-), P(+)$). We aim to satisfy the following maximum entropy constraint:

PROPOSITION 1. *The proportion of unlabeled items with predicted value y should equal the proportion of labeled items with value y.*

This forms the basis of our *maximum entropy inference* (MaxEntInf) approach, which will we will use to augment standard collective inference algorithms. We use variational mean field (VMF) inference as our example inference procedure, but the results are more general.

Recall that VMF assumes an approximating distribution $Q(\mathbf{Y}_U)$, such that $P(\mathbf{Y}_U|\mathbf{Y}_L, G, \Theta_C) \approx Q(\mathbf{Y}_U)$. For a possible $\mathbf{Y}_U \in \mathcal{Y}_U$, VMF assumes a fully factorized form $Q(\mathbf{Y}_U) = \prod_{v_i \in \mathbf{V}_U} Q_i(y)$, where (in a slight abuse of notation) we have a factorized probability of vertex v_i having label y. After each round of VMF, every $Q_i(y) \in Q(\mathbf{Y}_U)$ corresponds to the probability of an instance having a particular label. For example, for every unlabeled instance with $Q_i(+) \geq 0.5$ the corresponding predicted label $\hat{y}_i$ is $+$. MaxEntInf forces the proportion of unlabeled instances with $Q_i(+) \geq 0.5$ to be exactly $P(+)$. In more formal terms, MaxEntInf constrains the first moment of the predicted population to match the first moment of the observed population.

Our method will focus on a linear shift around an offset, which (without considerable checks) could result in probabilities lying outside $[0, 1]$—thus directly working with the probabilities themselves is problematic. To this end, we perform a transform of the current probabilities (i.e., every $Q_i(+)$) using the logit function (i.e., $\sigma^{-1}(x) = log[x/1-x]$):

$$z_i = \sigma^{-1}(Q_i(+)) = \log\left(\frac{Q_i(+)}{1 - Q_i(+)}\right)$$

The values $z_i \in Z$ take values in the range $[-\infty, +\infty]$, meaning that a linear transform within this space can then be transformed back into probability space through the logistic function (i.e., $\sigma(x) = (1 + e^{-x})^{-1}$).

Next let $z_{(r)}$ indicate the rth ranked value of Z (i.e., index r after Z are sorted). Let ϕ be our linear *pivot*—the index that will split the sorted range into two proportions, one approximately equal to $P(-)$ and the other approximately equal to $P(+)$ (i.e., $P(-) \cdot |\mathbf{V}_U|$). Formally, we have:

$$\phi = \arg\min_r \left(\frac{\sum_{i=1}^{|\mathbf{V}_U|} \mathbb{I}[i \leq r]}{|\mathbf{V}_U|} - P(-)\right)^2$$

Lastly, for all $z_i \in Z$ we subtract off the corresponding pivot value $z_{(\phi)}$. The result is then transformed back to the probability space to define $Q_i(y)$:

$$Q_i(+) = \sigma\left(z_i(y) - z_{(\phi)}\right) \qquad Q_i(-) = 1 - Q_i(+)$$

In particular, note that our transformation of $z_{(\phi)}$ is assigned $Q_{(\phi)}(y) = \sigma\left(z_{(\phi)} - z_{(\phi)}\right) = \sigma(0) = .5$, splitting the data into the two desired proportions to enforce the maximum entropy constraint. Further, the transformation is

Algorithm 2 MaxEntInf($G, \mathbf{V}_S, \tilde{\mathbf{Y}}_U, \mathcal{C}$)

```
1: P(−) = NegativeProportion(Y_L)
2: while Not Converged or More Iterations do
3:    Z = []
4:    for every v_i ∈ V_S do
5:       update variational Q_i(y)
6:       Z.insert(logit(Q_i(+))
7:    end for
8:    Z.sort()
9:    φ = P(−) * |Z|
10:   for every v_i ∈ V_S do
11:      Q_i(+) = logistic(logit(Q_i(+)) - Z[φ])
12:      Q_i(−) = 1 − Q_i(+)
13:      Ỹ_U.update(Q_i(y))
14:   end for
15: end while
```

lossless as it maintains a perfect ordering of the predicted label probabilities.

Our initial sequential VMF algorithm is described in Algorithm 2: as input to the sequential algorithm, we set $\mathbf{V}_S = \mathbf{V}_U$, meaning the single thread updates every unlabeled instance. The method begins by computing the prior $P(-)$. This is followed by a while loop that can either terminate upon convergence, or until some maximal number of iterations has been processed. The traditional VMF updates are computed in Lines 4-7, with each iteration performing the point wise update to the $Q_i(y)$ factor, followed by computing z_i. Lines 8-9 computes the corresponding offset, and then lines 10-13 calibrate the VMF estimates, storing the corrected result in $\tilde{\mathbf{Y}}_U$ for future iterations of the VMF algorithm.

Note that the correction does not require any assumptions about the conditional distribution form, as in prior work. All it requires is that the estimators return a set of probabilities.

Approximating MaxEntInf with Constant Sample Sizes

We can improve the runtime of the above sequential algorithm by sampling from the vector of logit values. In particular, we can prove that with a high confidence $(1-\delta)$, the chosen offset has provably small error (ϵ). Importantly, the size of sample does not depend on the data size; rather, it only depends on the amount of error and confidence we wish to have. Define $\mathbf{V}_S \subseteq \mathbf{V}_U$, $\phi^s = P(-) \cdot |\mathbf{V}_S|$ and $Z^s = \{z_i | z_i \in Z \cup v_i \in \mathbf{V}_S\}$. Then, we desire the following:

$$P\left(z^s_{(\phi^s)} \in z_{(\phi \pm \epsilon)}\right) \geq 1 - \delta$$

That is, of the full distribution $\mathbf{V}_U$, the $z_{(\phi^s)}$ we choose in the subsample $\mathbf{V}_S$ is no more than ϵ away from the $z_{(\phi)}$ in the full data. This error can be bounded using the Lemma 7 of Manku *et al.* [11]:

Lemma 1 (Lemma 7 of [11]). *Let $\mathbf{V}_S \subseteq \mathbf{V}_U$ be a uniformly random subset from the unlabeled vertices, ϕ be the index of our offset, ϵ be the amount of error in the chosen index we will allow, and δ be the probability bound. To satisfy $z^s_{(\phi^s)} \in z_{(\phi \pm \epsilon)}$ with $1-\delta$ probability, we must have:*

$$|\mathbf{V}_S| \geq \sqrt{\frac{1}{2\epsilon^2} \log\left(\frac{2}{\delta}\right)}$$

Thus, we require a constant number of samples from $\mathbf{V}_U$.

Algorithm 3 Parallel-MaxEntInf($G, \mathbf{Y}_L, \mathbf{V}_U, T, \mathcal{C}$)

```
[V_U^1, ··· , V_U^T] = RandomSplit(V_U, T)
Ỹ_U = SharedMemManager(Y_U)
for t ∈ 1, ··· , T do
   spawn R_t := MaxEntInf(G, Y_L, V_U^t, Ỹ_U, C)
end for
for t ∈ 1, ··· , T do
   join thread R_t upon completion
end for
return Ỹ_U
```

For example, if we set $\epsilon = .05$ to be the amount of error in the index and $\delta = .05$ as the probability bound, then to ensure 95% probability of success $(1-\delta)$, there only needs to be 28 samples in $\mathbf{V}_S$. Thus, as $|\mathbf{V}_U|$ grows $|\mathbf{V}_S|$ remains fixed, meaning our correction has a constant overhead.

Corollary 1 (Sequential Constant Overhead). *For a specified ϵ and δ, an approximation to the proposed sequential algorithm can be performed with constant overhead.*

Proof. From Lemma 1, we need only sample $|\mathbf{V}_S| = O(1)$ vertices from $\mathbf{V}_U$ to estimate the offset index ϕ. The sampling can be performed in constant time, and sorting and selection is therefore also in constant time. Although updating the probabilities requires $O(|\mathbf{V}_U|)$, the original variational inference algorithm required $O(|\mathbf{V}_U| + |\mathbf{E}|)$ time, thus our approach does not increase the order complexity. □

The fact that the approximation only requires a constant overhead makes it quite powerful for the sequential algorithm and big data problems in general. In the next section, we discuss parallelizing the method and prove that we retain a constant overhead in this scenario as well.

5. INFERENCE ON LARGE SCALE DATA

In this section, we discuss our scalable approach to VMF inference in parallel. This inference approach will allow us to apply relational machine learning at a scale not previously accomplished, and at the same time handle the MaxEntInf correction necessary for PL-EM.

To start, assume we have a set of T cores, with shared memory (or memory manager) syncing $\tilde{\mathbf{Y}}_U$ between the cores. We propose solving the joint inference process through an asynchronous and lock-free parallel VMF algorithm [2]. In particular, the unlabeled data is split into T segments, which are distributed amongst the T clients. Each client receives its corresponding portion of unlabeled data $\mathbf{V}^t_U$ and is tasked with updating the corresponding $Q(\mathbf{Y}^t_U) \subseteq Q(\mathbf{Y}_U)$. Along the way, the client estimates its own ϕ^t, computing its own offsets in the logit space, and calibrates its own MaxEntInf correction to the portion of the unlabeled data it is assigned. Each client uses the memory manager $\tilde{\mathbf{Y}}_U$, which is updated periodically with new label estimates as provided by the other clients. After a client finishes updating its corresponding segment of data, it pushes the newly estimated $Q_i(y)$ to the memory manager (maintaining $\tilde{\mathbf{Y}}_U$) for distribution amongst the other clients. When updating $Q_i(y)$ on a particular client, it is assumed that for every neighboring v_j some form of $Q_j(y)$ exists in $\tilde{\mathbf{Y}}_U$, although it may not be the most recent update. As high degree vertices are neighbors to most of the graph, synchronized updates would require them to lock a large portion of the unlabeled estimates, effectively shutting down the parallelism. By having asynchronous updates we avoid these locking issues, resulting in a massively scalable algorithm.

The parallel MaxEntInf inference approach is described in Algorithm 3. In Algorithm 3, the master devises a random split of the unlabeled data points and creates the shared memory (or memory manager) (Lines 1-2). Each client is then spawned, given the portion of data it should infer, along with the labeled data, the classifier and the memory manager. After each client has finished, the master collects the processes and returns the results (Line 6-9).

Line 4 calls Algorithm 2 for each processor. This algorithm differs from the initial MaxEntInf by: (a) the process only operates on a *subset* of the data and (b) the results after calibration are pushed to the memory manager for the other clients to use in their own inferences. Each client only calibrates on the subset of the data rather than the complete dataset. This is a fundamental shift from the sequential algorithm, where all instances are adjusted using the same offset value. Thus, we need to understand the impact of this approximation in comparison to the true correction.

Accuracy of Parallelizing MaxEntInf

Here we extend the notion of the constant sample size required to compute the correction (Lemma 1), to prove that each processor can independently compute its own offset without relying on other values. A natural extension to this is that the MaxEntInf correction again only requires a constant overhead to the parallel variational inference approach.

Let there be T threads, each thread $t \in \{1, \cdots, T\}$ receiving a portion of the data $\mathbf{V}_U^t$. Without loss of generality, assume all $|\mathbf{V}_U^t|$ are equal (if not, simply choose the smallest). Then, we wish to bound the error ϵ with probability $1-\delta$, i.e.:

$$P\left(z_{(\phi^t)} \in z_{(\phi \pm \epsilon)} \;\; \forall t \in \{1, \cdots, T\}\right) \geq 1-\delta$$

where $\phi^t = P(-) \cdot |\mathbf{V}_U^t|$ is the offset index for each subsample.

THEOREM 1 (PARALLEL SAMPLE SIZE). *Let $\mathbf{V}_U^1, \cdots \mathbf{V}_U^T \subseteq \mathbf{V}_U$ be disjoint uniformly random subsets of the unlabeled network vertices. Let ϕ be the true offset, ϵ be the amount of error in the chosen index ϕ^t for each subset T we will allow, and δ be the probability bound. If:*

$$|\mathbf{V}_U^t| \geq \sqrt{\frac{1}{2\epsilon^2} \log\left(\frac{2T}{\delta}\right)} \quad \forall 1, \cdots, T$$

then $\forall t \in \{1, \cdots, T\}$ $z_{(\phi^t)} \in z_{(\phi \pm \epsilon)}$ with $1-\delta$ probability.

PROOF. We wish to bound the following quantity:

$$P\left(z_{(\phi^t)} \in z_{(\phi \pm \epsilon)} \;\; \forall t \in \{1, \cdots, T\}\right) \geq 1-\delta$$

By the Union bound:

$$P\left(z_{(\phi^t)} \in z_{(\phi \pm \epsilon)} \;\; \forall t \in \{1, \cdots, T\}\right) \geq 1 - \sum_t P\left(z_{(\phi^t)} \notin z_{(\phi \pm \epsilon)}\right)$$
$$\geq 1 - T \cdot P\left(z_{(\phi^{t'})} \notin z_{(\phi \pm \epsilon)}\right)$$

where $\phi^{t'}$ is the offset index associated with the minimum $|\mathbf{V}_U^t|$. Then we have:

$$1 - T \cdot P\left(z_{(\phi^{t'})} \notin z_{(\phi \pm \epsilon)}\right) \geq 1-\delta$$
$$T \cdot P\left(z_{(\phi^{t'})} \notin z_{(\phi \pm \epsilon)}\right) \leq \delta$$

Applying Lemma 7 of [11] to $P(\phi_t' \notin \phi \pm \epsilon)$, we recover:

$$T \cdot P\left(z_{(\phi^{t'})} \notin z_{(\phi \pm \epsilon)}\right) \leq \delta$$
$$T \cdot 2\exp\{-2\epsilon^2 |\mathbf{V}_U^{t'}|^2\} \leq \delta$$
$$|\mathbf{V}_U^{t'}| \geq \sqrt{\frac{1}{2\epsilon^2} \log\left(\frac{2T}{\delta}\right)}$$

Thus if each subset has at least $\sqrt{\frac{1}{2\epsilon^2} \log\left(\frac{2T}{\delta}\right)}$ samples, then $z_{(\phi^t)} \in z_{(\phi \pm \epsilon)}$ $\forall t \in \{1, \cdots, T\}$ with probability $1-\delta$. □

This shows that the number of samples in each thread must only reach a certain threshold in order to have the desired accuracy, regardless of the total size of $\mathbf{V}_U$. Again using $\epsilon = .05$ and $\delta = .05$, if we have 10 cores available each core must only contain a minimum of 37 samples to achieve the desired accuracy. Similarly, if we have 100 cores each core must only contain 41 samples and for 1000 cores we must only have 47 samples per core. For big data problems, these thresholds are easy to achieve.

As with the sequential sampler, the parallel correction only has a constant amount of overhead in comparison to the uncorrected variational inference algorithm.

COROLLARY 2 (PARALLEL CONSTANT OVERHEAD). *Let $\mathbf{V}_U^1, \cdots \mathbf{V}_U^T \subseteq \mathbf{V}_U$ be disjoint uniformly random subsets of the unlabeled network vertices. For a specified ϵ and δ, an approximation to the parallel algorithm proposed can be performed with constant overhead.*

PROOF. From Theorem 1, we need only sample $|\mathbf{V}_S| = O(1)$ vertices from $\mathbf{V}_U^t$ to estimate the offset index ϕ^t. Again, the sampling can be performed in constant time, sorting and selection is therefore also in constant time, meaning that updating the estimates is again done in $O(|\mathbf{V}_U| + |\mathbf{E}|)$ time. □

6. EXPERIMENTS

In this section, we compare our proposed PL-EM framework against a variety of competing state-of-the-art methods. We test each method on seven real world datasets, three of which are an order of magnitude larger than any known prior application of RML.

6.1 Models

To control for variation due to knowledge representation, we compared models based on logistic regression, including independent logistic regression and relational methods that use logistic regression for the local conditional distribution in collective classification. For the relational approaches, three additional variables are incorporated into the conditional distribution: the proportion of positive neighbors, the proportion of negative neighbors, and the degree of the vertex. The parameter learning is done via iteratively reweighted least squares [4] where the least squares solution is solved using the tall/skinny streaming QR matrix factorization [3].

Logistic Regression [LR]: This is the independent logistic regression model. It does not consider any relational features, using only the vertex features to predict the label.

Logistic Regression EM [LR (EM)]: The independent logistic regression approach coupled with EM.

Relational Logistic Regression [RLR]: Logistic regression that incorporates relational features (positive proportions, negative proportions and degree). This method

Dataset	N_v	N_e	W	ρ	$P(+)$
Facebook	5,906	73,374	2	0.174	0.320
IMDB	7,934	122,230	28	0.207	0.164
DVD	16,118	75,596	28	0.208	0.210
Music	56,891	272,544	26	0.153	0.078
Comm.	881,187	5,302,712	50	0.710	0.059
Computers	881,187	5,302,712	50	0.815	0.169
Organic	881,187	5,302,712	50	0.486	0.021

Figure 3: Datasets compared. From left: dataset name, number of vertices, number of edges, number of attributes, label correlation, proportion positive.

does not perform EM and only the initial parameters are used for prediction. Predictions are not made collectively.

Label Propagation [LP]: This is a standard algorithm for inference in relational networks ([20, 10]). It does not learn a dependence on attributes and relational information; rather, the algorithm assumes high correlation and iteratively predicts label probabilities by averaging the current estimates of the relational neighbors. This iterative process repeats until convergence.

Composite Likelihood EM [CL-EM]: This is the traditional semi-supervised relational EM algorithm that maximizes the composite likelihood [18]. To allow for a comparison, we utilize our parallelized collective inference algorithm for efficiency. However, this method does not utilize the MaxEntInf correction proposed. It performs 10 rounds of variational inference for collective inference. As CL-EM is known to be unstable [14], we smooth the parameters at each iteration t. More specifically, we estimate $\Theta_{\mathcal{C}}^t = \alpha_t \Theta_{\mathcal{C}}^{new} + (1 - \alpha_t)\Theta_{\mathcal{C}}^{t-1}$ where $\alpha_t = \exp\{-0.125 \cdot t\}$. Further, for this method we report the average error between 10 and 11 rounds of EM.

Naive Pseudolikelihood EM [PL-EM (Naive)]: This method naively applies a semi-supervised relational EM that maximizes the pseudolikelihood rather than the composite likelihood. We again implement our parallelized collective inference algorithm for efficiency, but again omit the proposed MaxEntInf correction. It performs 10 rounds of variational inference for collective inference and, since the PL-EM is more stable than CL-EM, 10 rounds of EM.

MaxEntInf Pseudolikelihood EM [PL-EM (MaxEntInf)]: This is our proposed semi-supervised relational EM method that uses pseudolikelihood combined with the MaxEntInf approach to correct for relational biases. As with PL-EM (Naive), this method utilizes 10 rounds of variational inference for collective inference, 10 rounds of EM, and maximizes the full PL. However, this approach utilizes our proposed inference correction during each round of variational inference.

6.2 Datasets

We compare each of the methods on seven real world networks, gathered from various sources. Each network only includes vertices with degree greater than zero, and excludes the rest. A full listing of the statistics are given in Figure 3.

Smaller Datasets

The first four datasets are small in comparison to the last three. However, each provides a different type of network on which to compare the algorithms; further, they provide a means to evaluate scalability of our parallel inference.

Facebook: This is a snapshot of the Purdue University Facebook network. We include users who have listed their (a) political views, (b) religious views and (c) gender. The resulting network contains 5,906 vertices and 73,394 edges. We predict the political views, with the other two variables as features, resulting in a label correlation of 0.174 and positive proportion 0.32. This positive proportion is the largest observed in any dataset.

IMDB: This is a movie dataset release by the Internet Movie Database (www.imdb.com). The task is to predict whether a movie will have a gross revenue of $50 million (or greater). As features, we utilize the 19 provided movie genres: for each genre we define an indicator variable for whether the movie falls into the associated genre (these are not necessarily disjoint). In addition, we incorporate the user rating of the movie through 9 boolean indicator variables: each variable indicates whether the average movie rating is greater than the corresponding index. We connect movies through their producers: two movies that share two (or more) producers are linked. The resulting network has 7,934 vertices and 122,230 edges, with label correlation 0.207 and positive proportion 0.164.

DVD: This is a subset of the Amazon dataset gathered by [8], with items in the DVD classification. The prediction task is to determine whether an item has an Amazon salesrank < 7500. The attributes are the associated 24 genres that Amazon provides, as well as four boolean variables indicating whether the average number of stars is greater than the associated index. The edges are created through DVD *copurchases*, with an edge indicating that Amazon believes two items are frequently purchased together. The resulting network has 16,118 vertices and 75,596 edges, with a label correlation of 0.208 and positive proportion 0.21.

Music: This is another subset of the Amazon dataset gathered by [8], with items in the Music classification. As before, the prediction task is to determine whether an item has an Amazon salesrank < 7500. The attributes are the associated 22 styles of music that Amazon provides, as well as four boolean variables indicating whether the average number of stars is greater than the associated index. The resulting network has 56,891 vertices and 272,544 edges, with a label correlation of 0.153 and positive proportion 0.078. This is on the order of the largest datasets on which RML methods have previously been applied.

Larger Datasets

Our large scale network datasets are constructed from the publicly available NBER patents datasets (network structure [9], labelings [6][1]). For every patent that was published from 1990-2000, we queried the corresponding text from `http://patft.uspto.gov`, stripping out the claims and description for each patent. We removed English stop words [1] and took the top 50 most frequently occurring words. We weighted each document's words using TF-IDF [7], and each document feature vector was length normalized. The network has 881,187 vertices (patents) and 5,302,712 edges (citations between patents). We constructed three different classification tasks by considering the filing categories associated with each patent [6].

[1]http://www.nber.org/patents/subcategories.txt

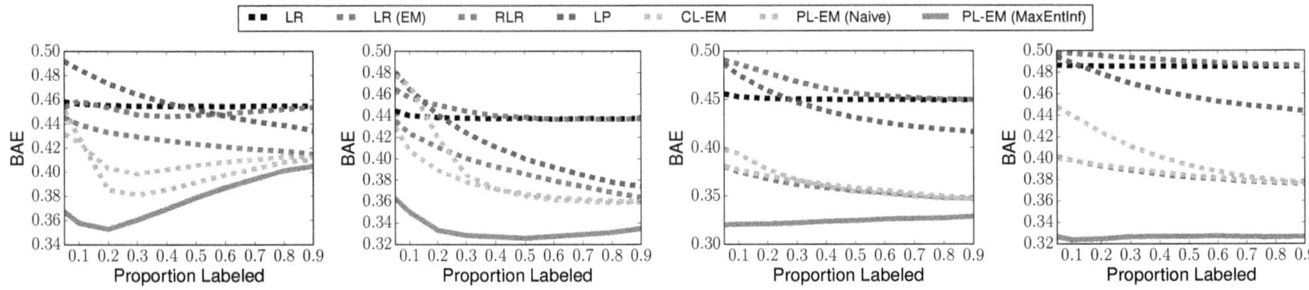

(a) Facebook (b) IMDB (c) DVD (d) Music

Figure 4: Results on the four smaller datasets. PL-EM with MaxEntInf outperforms each method.

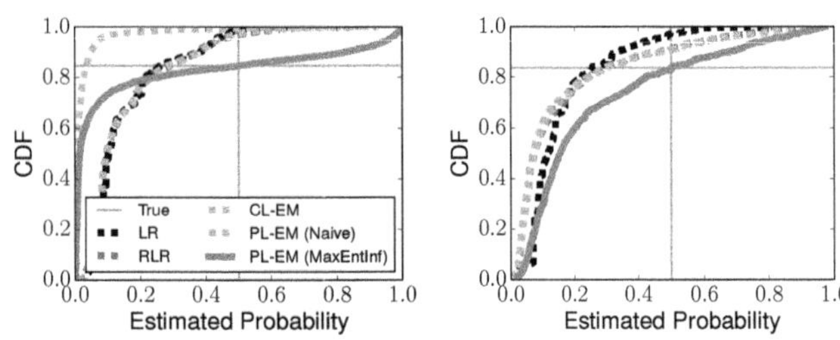

(a) 5% Labeled (b) 90% Labeled

Figure 5: IMDB: Distribution of predictions at varying labeled percentages. Note that at a high labeled percentage RLR, CL-EM, and Naive PL-EM continue to be poorly calibrated.

Communications: In this task, we considered whether patents were filed in "Primary Category 2, Subcategory 21" or not. The patents in this category are communications patents, involving computer communication infrastructure and technologies. Since this is a subcategory, the label has has considerable skew, with 0.059 positive proportion. However, label correlation is relatively high at 0.71.

Computers: In this task, we considered whether patents were filed in "Primary Category 2" or not. The patents in this category are related in some way to computers. Since it is a relatively large category, the positive proportion in 0.169. It has extremely high label correlation of 0.815.

Organic: In this task, we considered whether patents were filed in "Primary Category 1, Subcategory 14" or not. This category comprises chemical patents that relate to organic compounds. This is the most skewed dataset, with a positive proportion of 0.021. Label correlation is 0.486.

6.3 Methodology

For each dataset, we compare all methods. We repeat the experiments 100 times for the smaller datasets and 20 times for the larger datasets. Our error statistic is the *Balanced Absolute Error* (BAE) and we report the mean of the trials. The BAE measures the absolute error of a classifier $\mathcal{C}$, but normalizes the error across the classes:

$$err_{\mathcal{C}}(y) = \frac{\sum_{v_i \in \mathbf{V}_U} P_{\mathcal{C}}(y_i \neq y)\mathbb{I}[y_i = y]}{\sum_{v_i \in \mathbf{V}_U} \mathbb{I}[y_i = y]}$$

$$BAE_{\mathcal{C}} = \frac{\sum_{y \in \mathcal{Y}} err_{\mathcal{C}}(y)}{|\mathcal{Y}|}$$

This measure averages the balanced accuracy for all unlabeled instances. For the smaller datasets, we examine the BAE across a range of labeling percentages (0.05-0.9), while on the larger datasets we report accuracies on the more interesting sparser labeling percentages (0.001-0.1). Note that the extremely sparse labelings have only 880 instances out of nearly 900,000 labeled. All tests are paired across the various methods (i.e., each is given the same set of labeled instances).

Our tests were performed on a MacPro with two 2.66GHz 6-Core Intel Xeon processors, capable of 24 possible hyperthreads, with 48GB of RAM. The parallelized algorithms utilized all possible hyper threads, except for during the speedup tests.

6.4 Results

In Figure 4 we report the performance of the varying methods as the percentage of labeled data increases for each of the small datasets. In every instance, PL-EM with MaxEntInf outperforms all of the competing methods. Further, we find that vertex features alone are learned fairly accurately from a low label percentage, with little improvement as more data is gathered. This results in LR (EM) performing on par with LR, and each of these methods are outperformed by the relational methods as the proportion of labeled data increases. By incorporating both relational information and vertex information, RLR makes an initial gain over LP by utilizing the vertex information, then continues to improve at the same rate as LP. These gains are accentuated in the Amazon datasets, where the additional degree information leads to considerable gain over LR and LP. This is due to the salesrank of an item being heavily correlated to the degree (≈ -0.26) making the degree highly predictive. For each of these smaller datasets, PL-EM with MaxEntInf improves over the baselines.

We contrast the difference between the Naive PL-EM and PL-EM with MaxEntInf. In particular, the Naive application of PL-EM is nearly always outperformed by the more restrictive CL-EM, particularly for sparsely labeled domains. PL-EM (MaxEntInf) also slightly outperforms PL-EM (Naive) even at higher label percentages. This is due to Naive PL-EM continuing not to calibrate at the higher label percentages. We illustrate this in Figure 5. At the lower label percentage, Naive PL-EM strays far from the prior, as expected, while PL-EM (MaxEntInf) goes through the correct point. For the higher label percentage, PL-EM (Naive) has improved its estimates, but remains further from the

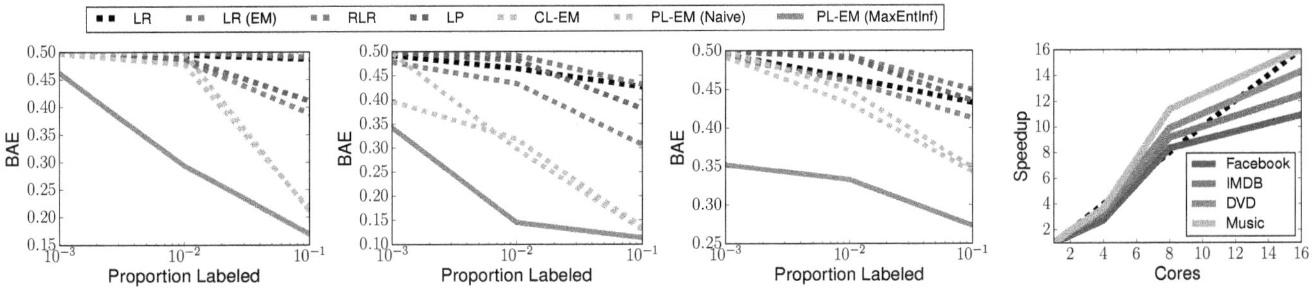

(a) Communication (b) Computers (c) Organic (d) Speedup

Figure 6: (a-c) Performance across each of the large scale datasets. (d) Speedup as we vary the number of processors available for each of the small datasets.

Percentage Labeled	No Correction	Correction
0.001	16.184	18.042
0.005	16.479	18.300
0.01	15.826	18.221
0.05	15.458	17.374
0.1	14.790	16.342
0.25	12.068	13.842

Figure 7: Total inference times on the large scale datasets (seconds).

correct prior than PL-EM (MaxEntInf). Thus, calibrating alone can decrease the error rate.

Next, Figures 6.a-c report performance results for the large scale datasets. PL-EM (MaxEntInf) produces significant performance improvements over the competing methods, with a substantial decrease in error. The effectiveness of LP largely depends on the dataset—as Communication and Computers have considerably more label correlation, LP performs the best on these datasets. Similarly, the attributes are largely ineffective on the Communication dataset, but helpful on both Computers and Organic. Thus, the RML methods perform best on Computers, with PL-EM (MaxEntInf) having an error of less than 0.1 with only 1/100 data points labeled. Again, PL-EM (Naive) is largely outperformed by CL-EM, but our correction allows the additional information provided by the pseudolikelihood to greatly improve the accuracy.

Figure 6.d examines the effect of parallelizing the inference algorithm on each of the smaller datasets. As expected, the algorithm scales at a linear rate. There are two slight irregularities in the curve. First, the algorithm appears to increase faster than linear up to 8 cores. This is an artifact of spawning the threads—these datasets are rather small, meaning the thread creation has a noticeable impact on the runtime. Second, after 8 cores the algorithm does not continue its rate and appears to slow. This is due to our machine only having 12 true cores, requiring the 16 thread test to utilize the hyper threads. Although we continue gaining, this hardware implementation has an impact on the gains.

Lastly, Figure 7 reports the total inference time (in seconds for each E-Step) for the large scale datasets with varying amounts of data. We provide the runtimes both with and without the MaxEntInf correction. Notably, the results show that we can solve the inference step with nearly 900,000 unlabeled documents, over 10 rounds of variational inference, within 20 seconds. This shows that the collective inference necessary for relational machine learning is no longer a significant burden.

6.5 Relational Summarization

As stated in the introduction, having more accurate probability estimates allows us to improve on a variety of tasks outside of simple prediction. So, we additionally compare on the alternative problem of relational summarization. For this we measure the *Friend BAE*, a measure that balances the error of individuals' friends for making predictions:

$$ferr_{\mathcal{C}}(y, v_i) = \sum_{v_j \in \{\mathcal{MB}(v_i) \cap \mathbf{V}_U\}} P_{\mathcal{C}}(y_j \neq y)\mathbb{I}[y_j = y]$$

$$FriendBAE_{\mathcal{C}}(y) = \frac{\sum_{v_i \in \mathbf{V}} \sum_{y \in \mathcal{Y}} err_{\mathcal{C}}(y)}{\sum_{v_i \in \mathbf{V}} \sum_{v_j \in \{\mathcal{MB}(v_i) \cap \mathbf{V}_U\}} \mathbb{I}[y_j = y]}$$

$$FriendBAE_{\mathcal{C}} = \frac{\sum_{y \in \mathcal{Y}} FriendBAE_{\mathcal{C}}(y)}{|\mathcal{Y}|}$$

These results are reported in Figure 8 on the DVD and Music datasets from Amazon, as well as the Communication and Computers large scale datasets. As with the original BAE, PL-EM with MaxEntInf outperforms all competing methods. Interestingly, PL-EM performs considerably better in the space on the DVD and Music datasets. This implies that Amazon generally has high degree instances connect with other high degree instances, making the prediction task easier due to the degree variable. In contrast, such effect does not occur in the Patents dataset, implying that the error is largely dispersed independent of degree. Overall, the PL-EM with MaxEntInf is able to outperform other estimators on a variety of tasks.

7. RELATED WORK AND DISCUSSION

Our work advances the field of relational machine learning (RML) [5] in two notable directions. First, we demonstrated that the error from the pseudolikelihood maximization learning approximation can be overcome by correcting the inference step of the algorithm. This approach allows any relational conditional distribution to be corrected on the fly solely by a small correction to the inference step, as well as allowing for the more general PL-EM algorithm to be used in conjunction with the chosen conditional. Second, we demonstrated that by using asynchronous variational mean field inference we can trivially parallelize the joint inference

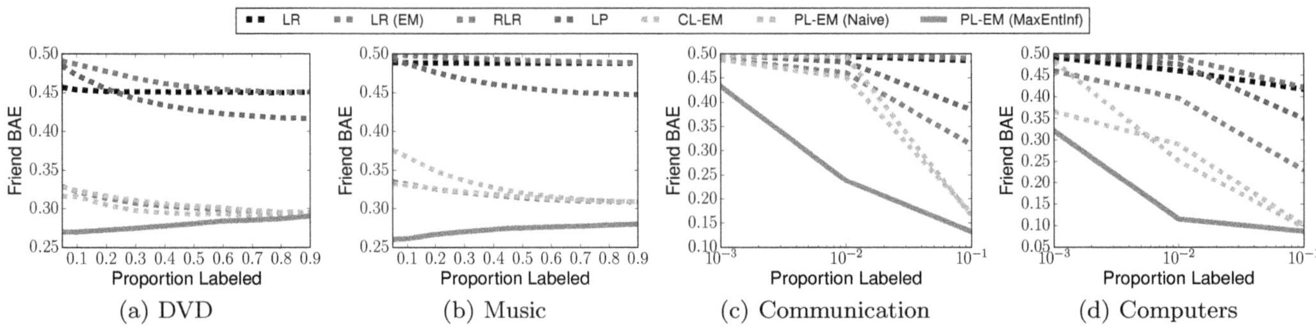

Figure 8: (a-d) Performance of methods on the Relational Summarization task, for the DVD, Music, Communication and Computers datasets.

algorithm, allowing for fast computations of the unlabeled probabilities. As part of this, we demonstrated that we can also parallelize the correction and we provided bounds on the error from this parallelization. The correction itself is similar to one proposed by [17] for IID EM learning, although we propose applying it in a considerably different domain and demonstrate it overcoming extreme inference biases. We also provided the error bounds for the sampled approach, proofs for the constant sampling overhead and demonstrated success in parallelizing the subsamples on large domains.

Seminal related work centers around relational Markov networks (RMNs) [16] and their first-order logic generalization Markov logic networks (MLNs) [15]. Both formalisms lie within the exponential family, meaning optimizing their corresponding MLEs will maximize their entropies. However, for large scale and complex network data these are also typically learned by maximizing the pseudolikelihood. The MPLE approximation provably over-propagates error for RMNs [19], similar to the extreme prediction biases observed in this work for the logistic regression conditionals. Hence, parameters learned from RMNs or MLNs likely suffer similar problems as the logistic regression formulation. This raises interesting theoretical questions on what characteristics a conditional form must have in order to avoid the over propagation error, which we leave for future work.

The most related work to ours is that of McDowell & Aha [12]. Their work first noted the differences between learning from the labeled vertices and the full network during the 'M'-step. However, their solution required the use of a special regularizer during the optimization step, and made use of a specific form of conditional. In contrast, our work pairs with any black box conditional distribution that provides label probabilities. Further, we demonstrated the power of parallelizing our inference step, allowing for our correction and inference method to scale to data orders of magnitude above previous relational algorithms.

Lastly, recent work on stochastic variants of the CL-EM algorithm has produced methods for *relational stochastic EM* and *relational data augmentation* [14]. These methods aggregate over a range of possible parameter values, resulting in significantly more stable estimates. However, each of these methods requires a maximization after a single round of Gibbs sampling. In [14], the authors proposed 1000 maximizations. In contrast, our MaxEntInf approach requires only 10 maximizations, and our estimation considers the full pseudolikelihood case. Coupled with our parallel algorithm, our approach is both more efficient and more general.

8. CONCLUSIONS

In this work, we proposed a novel maximum entropy constraint for inference during RML. Implementing this constraint is straightforward, allowing it to be used in conjunction with any relational learner. We proved the method has a constant overhead, making it ideally suited for big data problems. Additionally, we applied asynchronous variational mean field algorithms with success to relational inference problems. The maximum entropy inference correction is also ideally suited for this parallel implementation; as with the sequential case, we proved that it can be implemented with constant overhead. We demonstrated our approach on 7 real world network domains, showing that it outperformed a variety of baselines and competing methods. Further, we showed our parallel corrected inference procedure can be performed in under 20 seconds on networks with more than five million edges—an order of magnitude larger than prior works.

The methods presented here open multiple avenues for future work. First, the sampling approximation proofs are not limited to providing estimates on a per core basis: in many real world dataset we may wish to partition our data to reduce traffic overhead across the links while preserving an unbiased corrective estimate. However, these partitions may naturally introduce a bias on each core (e.g., geographic partitions). The included proofs provide evidence that the inference correction needs only a constant overhead between the cores, potentially greatly reducing the latency between the servers. Second, the proposed maximum entropy inference correction provides encouraging evidence that corrective inference methods can significantly improve relational machine learning methods, but is currently limited to the binary classification case. This approach should be expanded to include a larger number of possible label values. Third, these results raise interesting questions for which forms of conditionals are prone to bias and over propagation error effects. More theoretical work is necessary to determine when a relational classier might suffer from this bias and whether there are classifiers that are robust to these errors.

Acknowledgements

We thank David Gleich for his help with optimizing the maximization problem for the learning algorithms and Iman Alodah for her help with parts of the data processing. This research is supported by NSF under contract number(s) IIS-1149789 and IIS-1302172.

9. REFERENCES

[1] English stop words. http://www.textfixer.com/resources/common-english-words.txt.

[2] T. Broderick, N. Boyd, A. Wibisono, A. C. Wilson, and M. Jordan. Streaming variational bayes. In C. Burges, L. Bottou, M. Welling, Z. Ghahramani, and K. Weinberger, editors, *Advances in Neural Information Processing Systems 26*, pages 1727–1735. 2013.

[3] P. G. Constantine and D. F. Gleich. Tall and skinny qr factorizations in mapreduce architectures. In *Proceedings of the Second International Workshop on MapReduce and Its Applications*, MapReduce '11, pages 43–50, New York, NY, USA, 2011. ACM.

[4] J. Fox. Robust regression: Appendix to an r and s-plus companion to applied regression, 2002.

[5] L. Getoor and B. Taskar. *Introduction to Statistical Relational Learning*. The MIT Press, 2007.

[6] B. Hall, A. Jaffe, and M. Trajtenberg. The nber patent citations data file: Lessons, insights and methodological tools, 2001.

[7] K. S. Jones. A statistical interpretation of term specificity and its application in retrieval. *Journal of Documentation*, 28:11–21, 1972.

[8] J. Leskovec, L. A. Adamic, and B. A. Huberman. The dynamics of viral marketing. *ACM Trans. Web*, 1, 2007.

[9] J. Leskovec, J. Kleinberg, and C. Faloutsos. Graphs over time: Densification laws, shrinking diameters and possible explanations. In *Proceedings of the Eleventh ACM SIGKDD International Conference on Knowledge Discovery in Data Mining*, KDD '05, pages 177–187, New York, NY, USA, 2005. ACM.

[10] S. A. Macskassy and F. Provost. A simple relational classifier. In *MRDM-KDD*, 2003.

[11] G. S. Manku, S. Rajagopalan, and B. G. Lindsay. Approximate medians and other quantiles in one pass and with limited memory. In *Proceedings of the 1998 ACM SIGMOD International Conference on Management of Data*, SIGMOD '98, pages 426–435, New York, NY, USA, 1998. ACM.

[12] L. McDowell and D. W. Aha. Semi-supervised collective classification via hybrid label regularization. In *ICML*. icml.cc / Omnipress, 2012.

[13] K. Nigam, A. K. McCallum, S. Thrun, and T. Mitchell. Text classification from labeled and unlabeled documents using em. *Mach. Learn.*, 39(2-3):103–134, May 2000.

[14] J. J. Pfeiffer III, J. Neville, and P. Bennett. Composite likelihood data augmentation for within-network statistical relational learning. In *Proceedings of the 14th IEEE International Conference on Data Mining (ICDM 2014)*, 2014.

[15] M. Richardson and P. Domingos. Markov logic networks. *Mach. Learn.*, 62(1-2):107–136, Feb. 2006.

[16] B. Taskar, P. Abbeel, and D. Koller. Discriminative probabilistic models for relational data. In *Proceedings of the Eighteenth Conference on Uncertainty in Artificial Intelligence*, UAI'02, pages 485–492, San Francisco, CA, USA, 2002. Morgan Kaufmann Publishers Inc.

[17] Y. Tsuruoka and J. Tsujii. Training a naive bayes classifier via the em algorithm with a class distribution constraint. In *Proceedings of the Seventh Conference on Natural Language Learning at HLT-NAACL 2003 - Volume 4*, CONLL '03, pages 127–134, Stroudsburg, PA, USA, 2003. Association for Computational Linguistics.

[18] R. Xiang and J. Neville. Pseudolikelihood em for within-network relational learning. In *ICDM*, 2008.

[19] R. Xiang and J. Neville. Understanding propagation error and its effect on collective classification. In D. J. Cook, J. Pei, W. W. 0010, O. R. ZaŢane, and X. Wu, editors, *ICDM*, pages 834–843. IEEE, 2011.

[20] X. Zhu, Z. Ghahramani, and J. Lafferty. Semi-supervised learning using gaussian fields and harmonic functions. In *IN ICML*, pages 912–919, 2003.

Deriving an Emergent Relational Schema from RDF Data

Minh-Duc Pham[△] m.d.pham@vu.nl
Linnea Passing[□] passing@in.tum.de
Orri Erling[◇] oerling@openlinksw.com
Peter Boncz[⊙] boncz@cwi.nl

[△]Vrije Universiteit Amsterdam, The Netherlands
[□]Technische Universität München, Germany
[◇]OpenLink Software, UK [⊙]CWI, The Netherlands

ABSTRACT

We motivate and describe techniques that allow to detect an "emergent" *relational schema* from RDF data. We show that on a wide variety of datasets, the found structure explains well over 90% of the RDF triples. Further, we also describe technical solutions to the semantic challenge to give short names that humans find logical to these emergent tables, columns and relationships between tables. Our techniques can be exploited in many ways, e.g., to improve the efficiency of SPARQL systems, or to use existing SQL-based applications on top of any RDF dataset using a RDBMS.

Categories and Subject Descriptors

H.3 [**Information Storage and Retrieval**]: Miscellaneous

Keywords

RDF; Structure recognition; Relational schema

1. INTRODUCTION

RDF is the data model for the Semantic Web and Linked Open Data. It represents data as collection of <subject, property, object> triples. By providing flexibility for users to represent and evolve data without the need for a prior schema – sometimes called the "schema last" approach – and identifying properties and (references to) subjects uniformly using URIs, RDF has been gaining ground as the standard for global data exchange and interoperability, recently through the popularization of micro-formats such as RDFa, which are increasingly used embedded in web pages. This creates a need for database technologies that can query large amounts of RDF efficiently with SPARQL *or SQL*.

SQL-speaking relational database systems (RDBMS's) require to declare a schema upfront ("schema first") and can only store and query data that conforms to this schema. RDF systems typically rely on a "triple-store" architecture, which store all data in a single table containing `S`, `P` and `O` (subject, property, object) columns[1]. SQL systems tend to be more efficient than triple stores, because the latter need query plans with many self-joins – one per SPARQL triple pattern. Not only are these extra joins expensive, but because the complexity of query optimization is exponential in the amount of joins, SPARQL query optimization is much more complex than SQL query optimization. As a result, large SPARQL queries often execute with a suboptimal plan, to much performance detriment. RDBMS's can further store data efficiently e.g. using advanced techniques such as column-wise compression, table partitioning, materialized views and multi-dimensional data clustering. These techniques require insight in the (tabular) structure of the dataset and have so far not been applicable to RDF stores.

Semantic Web technology has its roots in Artificial Intelligence and knowledge representation, and we think it is seldom realized that its notion of "schema" in the term "schema last" differs from the corresponding "schema" notion in "schema first" for relational technology. Semantic Web schemas – *ontologies* and *vocabularies* – are intended to allow diverse organizations to consistently denote certain concepts in a variety of contexts. In contrast, *relational schemas* describe the structure of one database (=dataset), designed without regard for reuse in other databases.

Our work shows that actual RDF datasets exhibit (i) a very *partial* use of ontology classes and (ii) subjects share triples with properties from classes defined in *multiple* ontologies. To illustrate, (i) in the crawled WebDataCommons data there is information on less than a third of the ontology class properties in the actual triples, and (ii) we find in DBpedia that each subject combines information from more than *eight* different ontology classes on average. As such, when analyzing the actual structure of RDF datasets by observing which combinations of properties typically occur together with a common subject (called "**Characteristic Sets**" of properties [14]), any single ontology class tends to be a poor descriptor. Knowledge of the actual structure of a dataset is essential for RDBMS's to be able to store and query data efficiently. Our work allows RDF stores to automatically discover this actual structure, which we call the **emergent relational schema**. The emergent relational schema enables to internally store RDF data more like relational tables, allowing SPARQL query execution to use less self-joins, which also reduces the complexity of query opti-

[1]With "triple-store" we mean RDF or graph stores that use any data structure, be it a graph edge-list, B-tree, hash map, etc. that stores individual triples (or quads), or graph edges without exploiting their connection structure.

WWW 2015, May 18–22, 2015, Florence, Italy.
ACM 978-1-4503-3469-3/15/05.
http://dx.doi.org/10.1145/2736277.2741121.

mization [10]. Note that not all triples in a RDF dataset need to conform to this relational schema for these techniques to be effective, as long as the great majority does. Hence, RDF remains as flexible as ever in emergent relational schema aware systems.

There is also a usability advantage if the actual structure of an RDF dataset would be conveyed to a human user. A common problem when posing SPARQL queries is that queries come back empty if properties that one expects to occur given ontology knowledge, turn out not to be present in the data. Or, one may lack any ontology knowledge and thus have little to go by when querying. However, automatically deriving a human-friendly relational schema from a RDF dataset introduces additional challenges to recognizing its structure, since all the schema elements (tables, columns) should get correct and short *labels*, and the emergent relational schema must be *compact* to be understandable.

Our work presents a self-tuning algorithm that surmounts this challenge, which we tested on a wide variety of RDF datasets. We integrated our techniques in two open-source state-of-the art data management systems: the well-known RDF store Virtuoso and the MonetDB DBMS. The RDF bulkload in MonetDB now offers efficient SQL access to any RDF dataset via its emergent relational schema, allowing the wealth of SQL-based applications over ODBC and JDBC (e.g. Business Intelligence tools like Tableau) to be used. By doing so we are enriching RDBMS's with web standards, because these relational tables, columns and foreign key (FK) constrains are identifiable using ontology-based URIs, and even the primary key values and foreign key values themselves are URIs (RDF subjects resp. non-literal objects). As such, our work is a bridge between the Semantic Web and RDBMS's, enriching both worlds.

Contributions of our work are the following:

1) We identify an important difference between Semantic Web schema information (describing a knowledge universe) and relational schemas (describing one dataset), and argue that *both* should be available to data stores and their users.

2) We present methods for detecting the basic table structure and the relationships between them from an RDF dataset, and propose several approaches to semantically and structurally optimize the relational schema to make it compact.

3) We present techniques to assign human-friendly names to tables/columns and their FK relationships.

4) Our experiments on a wide variety of RDF datasets show that (i) over 90% of the triples in these conform to a compact emergent relational schema, (ii) our algorithms are efficient and can be executed during RDF bulk load with little overhead, (iii) RDF stores can improve both query optimization and execution by exploiting the emergent relational schema, and (iv) we illustrate with a user survey that the short human-readable labels we find have good quality.

2. EMERGING A RELATIONAL SCHEMA

The five steps of our emergent relational schema algorithm detect something akin to a UML class diagram by analyzing Characteristic Sets (CS's) [14] in an RDF input dataset:

1. Basic CS Discovery. We discover all occurring CS's from a bulk-loaded SPO table and count their frequencies. Then, we analyze properties in each CS that are not literals, i.e. refer to URIs (and hence to other CS's) in order to explore the relationships between CS's.

2. CS Labeling. We assign class, attribute and relationship labels (human-understandable names) to the recognized CS's using multiple methods.

3. CS Merging. We merge CS's that are semantically or structurally similar to each other, with the purpose of making the schema more *compact*. We re-run Steps 2 and 3 iteratively in order to *automatically tune* the similarity threshold parameter τ_{sim} to the nature of the dataset.

4. Schema Filtering. We filter low frequency CS's, but make sure to conserve highly referenced CS's (akin to relational "dimension tables"). As reference relationships can be indirect (via via) we use a PageRank-like algorithm to count how often referenced each CS is. We also filter out CS properties that are too sparsely populated.

5. Instance Filtering. We filter out instances (rows) to increase literal type homogeneity, and filter out individual triples to eliminate erroneously multi-valued attributes, and to improve foreign-key cardinality homogeneity.

The "class diagram" where each merged-CS that survived filtering is a class, is represented as a relational schema consisting of tables and foreign key relationships. Each class becomes one table, and its properties its columns, but relationships and multi-valued attributes lead to additional tables. Properties for which multiple literal types occur frequently, are represented by multiple table columns. The <10% triples that do not fit this schema remain stored in a separate SPO table. We now discuss the five steps in detail.

2.1 Basic CS Discovery

Given an RDF dataset R, the Characteristic Set of a subject s is defined as $cs(s) = \{p|\exists o : (s, p, o) \in R\}$ [14].

We first identify the basic set of CS's by analyzing all triples stored in an RDF table in SPO order. Such table is produced by a standard bulk load employed by triple stores. While loading the triples into this representation, the URIs get encoded in a dictionary, such that columns `S`, `P` and `O` are not URI strings, but integers called *object identifiers* (OIDs) pointing into this dictionary. This is a standard technique. These integer OIDs form a dense domain starting at 0.

We now make a single pass through the SPO table and fill a hash map where the key is the set of OIDs of properties that co-occur for each subject. Note that due to the SPO ordering these are easily found as the `P`'s of consecutive SPO triples with equal `S`. The key of the hash map is the offset in the SPO table where the CS first occurs. Its hash is computed by XOR-ing the hashes of all `P`'s (which are OIDs). The insert-order in the hash table (starting at 1) provides us with a dense numeric OID for each CS. Further, we remember in an array indexed by `S` which stores such CS-OIDs, to which CS each subject belongs (this array is part of the URI dictionary). Note that not all URIs in the dictionary may occur as a subject in the SPO table, for which case this array is initialized with zeros. After making the single pass over the SPO table, we will have all occurring *basic CS*-s in the hash map, and we also keep an occurrence count there.

Further we make a second pass over the SPO table, where we look at type information. For each triple with a literal object, we maintain a histogram of literal-type occurrences per property in a second hash map with key `[P,type]` and a count value. For each triple that is a non-literal, on the other hand, we look up to which CS its subject belongs (`srcCS`) and to which its object (`dstCS`) – this can be done efficiently using the array mentioned before. If there is a

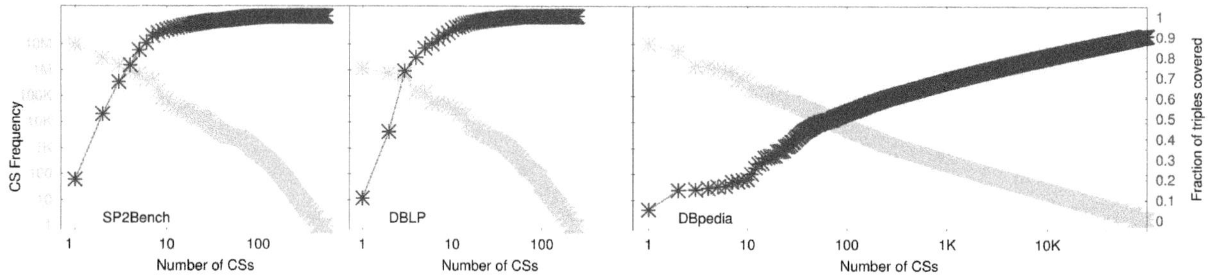

Figure 1: CS Frequency (light blue) vs. Cumulative number of covered triples (dark red)

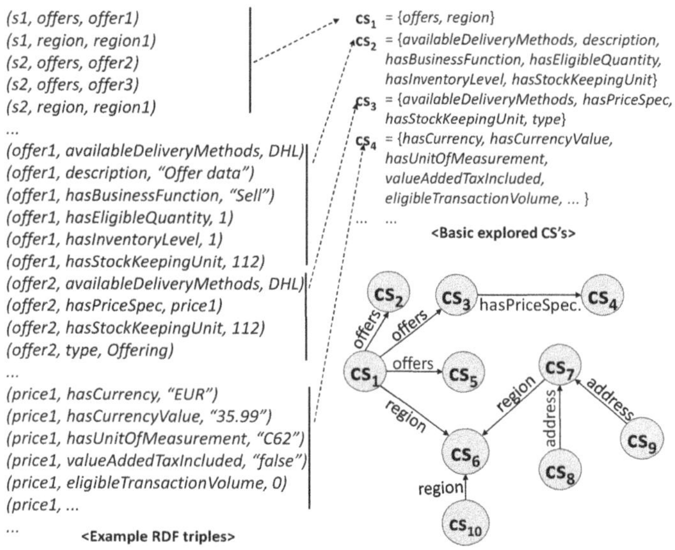

Figure 2: Example of basic CS's and their relationships

dstCS, we maintain another histogram stored in a third hash map with as key [srcCS,P,dstCS] and a count value. This histogram records how often basic-CS's refer to each other and over which property (relationship statistics).

These algorithms are all simple and obviously linear in average-case complexity, therefore we omit a listing or further analysis. Figure 2 shows an example of the found basic CS and their relationships after the exploration process.

Diversity of the basic CS's. Table 1 shows statistics on the basic CS's and their properties for the **synthetic** RDF benchmark datasets LUBM[2], SP2B[3],and BSBM[4], the originally **relational** datasets converted to RDF MusicBrainz[5], EuroStat[6], and DBLP[7], PubMed[8] and the **native** RDF datasets WebDataCommons[9] ("WebData.") and DBpedia[10]. The number of basic CS's can vary significantly regardless the number of input triples. If one would naively propose to store RDF data using a separate relational table for each

Datasets	#triples*	#CS's	#CS's to cover 90%	Avg. #prop.	#multi-type properties
LUBM	100M	17	7	5.71	0
BSBM	100M	49	14	12.61	0
SP2Bench	100M	554	7	9.8	0
synthetic	*data created by benchmark data generator*				
MusicBrainz	179M	27	10	4.7	0
EuroStat	70K	44	8	7.77	0
DBLP	56M	249	8	13.70	0
PubMed	1.82B	3340	35	19.27	0
relational	*RDF data from a relational database dump*				
WebData.	90M	13354	930	7.94	551
DBpedia	404M	439629	85922	24.36	1507
native	*real data originating as RDF*				

Table 1: Statistics on basic CS's.
(*: Number of triples after removing all duplicates)

basic CS, we now see that a complex RDF dataset like DBpedia would lead to an unacceptable number of small tables. As we can also see that while most of the datasets have a single literal type for each CS property, DBpedia and WebDataCommons have many properties with more than one literal type in its object values (i.e., multi-type properties), so native datasets appear to be both complex and "dirty".

Data coverage by basic CS's. Figure 1 shows the frequencies and the cumulative number of triples covered by the basic CS's sorted by their frequencies, for one of each kind of dataset (synthetic, relational, native). In this figure, the number of CS's needed for covering a large portion of the triples (e.g., 90%) can be significantly different between the datasets. We show for reference in Table 1, that 90% of the synthetic benchmark datasets can be covered by using a small number of CS's (e.g., 7 for SP2Bench). Many Linked Open Data datasets originate from existing sources whose data is kept in relational databases. We see that in such datasets a few CS's can cover almost all data. However, for complex datasets originally created as RDF (native), in order to cover 90% of the triples, many CS's are needed, in case of DBpedia more than 85,000.

2.2 CS Labeling

When presenting humans with a relational schema, short labels should be used as aliases for machine-readable and unique URIs for naming tables, columns and relationships between tables. For assigning labels to CS's, we exploit semantic information (ontologies) as well as structural information. Because not all ontologies follow the same structure, we developed a simple vocabulary to standardize minimal aspects of an ontology, namely classes and their properties, relationships between classes, their labels, as well as the subclass hierarchy. We expressed a large set of common ontolo-

[2]swat.cse.lehigh.edu/projects/lubm/
[3]dbis.informatik.uni-freiburg.de/forschung/projekte/SP2B/
[4]wifo5-03.informatik.uni-mannheim.de/bizer/berlinsparqlbenchmark/
[5]linkedbrainz.c4dmpresents.org/data/musicbrainz_ngs_dump.rdf.ttl.gz
[6]eurostat.linked-statistics.org
[7]gaia.infor.uva.es/hdt/dblp-2012-11-28.hdt.gz
[8]www.ncbi.nlm.nih.gov/pubmed
[9]A 100M triple file of webdatacommons.org
[10]dbpedia.org - we used v3.9

	mixed	partial
dataset	number of ontology classes used per CS	%ontology class properties used per CS
LUBM	1.94	37%
BSBM	3.96	3%
SP2Bench	4.94	4%
MusicBrainz	3.93	1%
EuroStat	3.14	84%
DBLP	6.58	8%
PubMed	4.94	-
WebData.	2.27	33%
DBpedia	8.35	5%

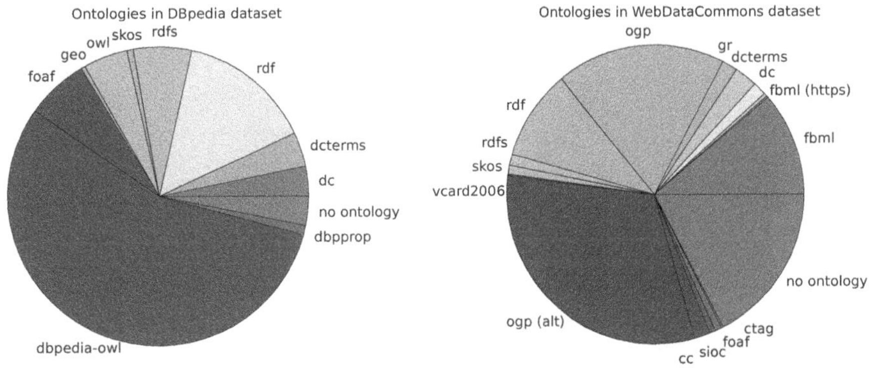

Figure 3: Partial & mixed ontology class usage in CS's (table–left), Ontologies used in native RDF datasets (graphs–right)

label of rdf:type	subjects CS %	all %
Thing	100	83
Organization	100	7
RadioStation	**97**	**0.2**
Company	1	4

Figure 4: Choosing a CS label from explicit RDF type annotations that refer to ontology classes in a hierarchy.

gies in this vocabulary. Our proposed system is extensible, as new ontology information can easily be added.

Figure 3 shows ontology class usage in the CS's and the percentage of triples corresponding to each ontology in several datasets. As shown in the graphs, each dataset contains a mix of multiple ontologies where even the most popular ontology covers less than 56% of the data. The first column in the table shows that properties from within *a single CS* typically stem from a number of different ontologies, e.g., the average number of ontologies used in each CS in DBpedia is 8.35. We also looked at the percentage of properties of each ontology class when used in a CS. Since an ontology class may be used in multiple CS's, we compute a weighted average (where the number of subjects in a CS is the weight). The second column in the table shows this percentage to be less than 10% in most of the datasets. In other words, the datasets make only very partial usage of the properties of each ontology class. The partial usage and mixing together mean that any individual ontology class is a poor descriptor of the structure of the data. Our emergent relational schema, aims to provide a better description.

Type properties. Certain specific properties explicitly specify the *concept* a subject belongs to. The most common RDF property with this role is `rdf:type`, where the `O` of triples with this property may be the URI identifying an ontology class. Recall that our first step is to find a good UML-like class diagram for the RDF dataset, where a CS roughly corresponds to an UML class, and specifically here we are trying to find a human-friendly short name (label) for each CS. Even though we stated above that any individual ontology class is a poor descriptor for the *structure* of a CS, ontologies do provide valuable clues for choosing a *label* (name) for the CS. The subjects that are member of a CS may have different `rdf:type` object values, this number is also variable (there can be zero such type annotations, but also multiple). To choose one, we look at the frequency of that type annotation. First, we use the global infrequent threshold τ_{inf} (e.g., 5%) to exclude infrequent type annota-

cs_4
dc:description
gor:validFrom
gor:validThrough
gor:hasCurrency
gor:hasCurrencyValue
gor:hasUnitOfMeasurement
gor:valueAddedTaxIncluded
gor:eligibleTransactionVolume

(prefix gor: http://purl.org/goodrelations/v1# prefix dc: http://purl.org/dc/elements/1.1/)

PriceSpecification
gor:description
gor:name
gor:eligibleTransactionVolume
gor:validFrom
gor:validThrough
gor:hasCurrency
gor:hasCurrencyValue
gor:hasUnitOfMeasurement
gor:valueAddedTaxIncluded
gor:hasMaxCurrencyValue
gor:hasMinCurrencyValue

Figure 5: Example CS vs. Ontology class

tions to be used for finding the CS class label. For the rest, we count (i) how many subjects in the CS have it, and (ii) how many subjects in the whole dataset have it. Similar to TF/IDF [18], dividing (i) by (ii) provides a reasonable ranking to choose an appropriate ontology class. Finally, if the ontology class has label information (and this information is typically available), we then use it as the label for the CS.

We should, however, in this ranking also take into account the class hierarchy information that an ontology provides. Thus, we account for missing superclass annotations by inferring them for the purpose of this ranking. In Figure 4, if a triple in some CS has `rdf:type Company`, but not `Organization` or `Thing` explicitly, we still include these annotations in the ranking calculation.

In this example, "RadioStation" is chosen as its coverage of the subjects in the CS is above τ_{inf} ($97 > 5$) and its ranking score (97/0.2=485) is the highest.

Discriminative Properties. Even if no type property is present in the CS, we can still try to match a CS to an ontology class. We compare the property set of the CS with the property sets of ontology classes using the TF/IDF similarity score [18]. This method relies on identifying "discriminative" properties, that appear in few ontology classes only, and whose occurrence in triple data thus gives a strong hint for the membership of a specific class. An example is shown in Figure 5. In this example, as cs_4 and the class `PriceSpecification` of the GoodRelations ontology[11] share discriminative properties like `gor:hasUnitOfMeasurement` and `gor:valueAddedTaxIncluded`, `PriceSpecification` can be used as the label of cs_4. Detailed computation of the TF/IDF-based similarity score between a CS and an ontology class can be found in [17]. An ontology class is considered to be matching with a CS if their similarity score exceeds the sim-

[11] purl.org/goodrelations/

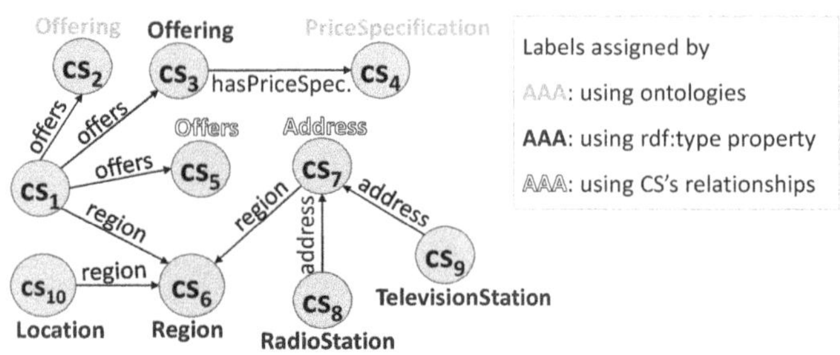

Figure 6: CS's with assigned labels

ilarity threshold τ_{sim}. The ontology class correspondence of a CS, if found, is also used to find labels for properties of the CS (both for relationships and literal properties).

Relationships between CS's. If the previous approaches do not apply, we can look at which other CS's refer to a CS, and then use the URI of the referring property to derive a label. For example, a CS that is referred as `Address` indicates that this CS represents instances of an `Address` class. We use the most frequent relationship to provide a CS label. For instance, in WebDataCommons 93532 instances refer to a CS via property `address` and only 3 via property `locatedAt`. Thus, `Address` is chosen as the label.

URI shortening. If the above solutions cannot provide us a link to ontology information for providing attribute and relationship labels, we resort to a practical fall-back, based on the observation that often property URI values do convey a hint of the semantics. That is, for finding labels of CS properties we shorten URIs (e.g., `http://purl.org/goodrelations/v1#offers` becomes `offers`), by removing the ontology prefix (e.g., `http://purl.org/goodrelations/v1#`), as suggested by [15].

Note that for CS's without any ontology match or relationships with other CS's, we may find no class label candidates, in which case a synthetic default label is used. Labels are intended to help users comprehend the data, but in any case should be overridable by manual labeling. A future approach might be to look for sources on the web, such as search engines; but for the moment we prefer to keep our techniques stand-alone, as these are part of RDF bulk-load.

Figure 6 shows the labels assigned to each CS in the example dataset by using different labeling methods (e.g., the label of cs_4 is assigned based on the matching between its property set and that of ontology classes, the label of cs_7 is derived from the CS's relationships, ...). In this example, cs_1 does not have any specific label as there is no sufficient information for assigning a good label to it.

2.3 CS Merging

After basic exploration, there may be thousands of CS's, in case of DBpedia even 100,000. This means the individual CS's have only a few subjects (=rows, in relational terms) in them, so that storing them in a relational table would incur overheads (e.g. tables not filling a disk page, large database catalog, expensive metadata lookup). Further, many of these basic CS's are very similar to each other (differing only in a few properties) and denote the same concept. When querying for that concept, one would have to formulate a UNION of many tables, which is cumbersome and also slows down queries. Finally, a relational schema with thousands of tables is just very hard to understand for humans. Therefore, the next step is to reduce the number of tables in the emergent relational schema by *merging* CS's, using either *semantic* or *structural* information.

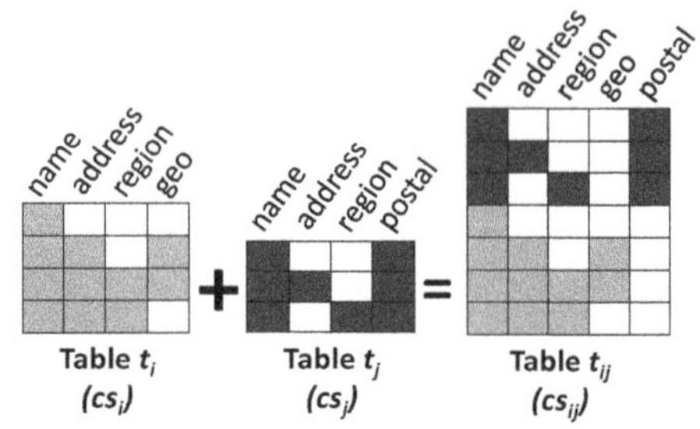

Figure 7: Example of merging CS's

Figure 7 shows an example of merging cs_i and cs_j. We note that all subjects that fall in a basic CS do so because there exist triples for all properties in that CS, such that a relational table representing the CS would have no NULL cells. In this example, cs_i and cs_j represent already the results of merging other CS's (the merging process is iterative) . As shown in the figure, the number of NOT-NULL cells in table t_{ij} is equal to the total number of NOT-NULL cells of the tables t_i and t_j, however, the number of NULL cells increases due to properties not in the intersection of the two CS's becoming padded with NULLs in the merged CS.

Semantic merging. We can merge two CS's on semantic grounds when both CS class labels that we found were based on ontology information. Obviously, two CS's whose labels were taken from the same ontology class URI represent the same concept, and thus can be merged. If the labels stem from *different* ontology classes we can examine the class hierarchy and identify the common concept/class shared by both CS's, if any, and then justify whether these CS's are similar based on the "generality" of the concept. Here the "generality" score of a concept is computed by the percentage of instances covered by it and its subclasses among all the instances covered by that ontology (Equation 1).

$$g_{score}(O_c) = \frac{\#instances\_coveredby(O_s)}{\#instances\_coveredby\_ontology} \quad (1)$$
$$where\ O_s\ is\ O_c\ or\ a\ subclass\ of\ O_c$$

Figure 4 showed an example of an ontology class hierarchy from DBpedia. Consider two CS labels such as `RadioStation` and `TelevisionStation` assigned by using ontology class names. By following the ontology's class hierarchy, it can be found that the corresponding classes of these labels share the same infrequent superclass `Broadcaster`. Therefore, these CS's can be considered as semantically similar, and could be merged with `Broadcaster` as new label.

More formally, there are two rules for semantic merging:

RULE 1. *If an ontology class URI exists equal to the labels of both cs_i and cs_j then merge cs_i and cs_j. (S1)*

RULE 2. *If there exists an ontology class O_c being an ancestor of the labels of cs_i and cs_j and $g_{score}(O_c)$ is less than $\frac{1}{Ub_{tbl}}$ then merge cs_i and cs_j. (S2)*

In $S2$, $\frac{1}{Ub_{tbl}}$ is used as the threshold for the generality score based on Ub_{tbl}, the upper bound for the number of tables in the schema – which is one of the only three parameters of emergent relational schemas, see Table 2.

Figure 8 demonstrates the modifications to the explored CS's of the example dataset and their relationships when sequentially applying merging rules $S1$ and $S2$. Here, since cs_2

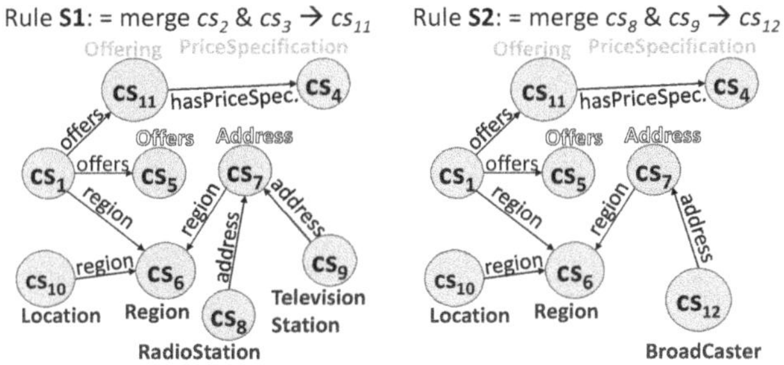

Figure 8: Example of merging CS's by using rules S1, S2

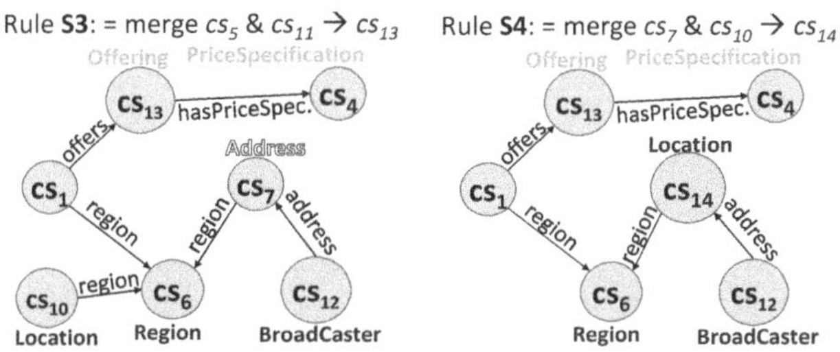

Figure 9: Example of merging CS's by using rules S3, S4

and cs_3 both derived their label `Offering` from the `Offering` class of the GoodRelation ontology, according to $S1$, they are merged into a new CS (cs_{11}). The references from/to cs_2 and cs_3 are also updated for cs_{11}. Besides, since the labels of cs_8 and cs_9 have `Broadcaster` as their non-general common ancestor in the ontology hierarchy, they are merged into cs_{12} according to S2. The label of cs_{12} is assigned by using the name of the common ancestor ontology class. The full description about updating the label of a CS after merging can be found in [17].

Structural merging. While semantic merging is a relatively safe bet, it may not always be applicable or effective enough to reduce the amount of merged CS's. Therefore, we also look at the *structure* of the CS's and their relationships to see if these can be merged. The idea here is to identify CS's that denote the same concept based on so-called "discriminative" properties, which are those with a high TF/IDF score (see the previous section). If the overlap between two CS's contains enough "discriminative" properties, we can merge them.

Figure 10 shows an example where the overlapping properties of cs_7 and cs_{10} indicate that these CS's both originate from the "Location" entity. Here, the property `rdfd:name` is not discriminative since it appears in most of the CS's. However, properties `rdfd:street-address` and `rdfd:region` give evidence that both represent a "Location".

Equations 2 and 3 formally show the detailed computations for the TF/IDF score of each property in a cs and the cosine similarity score (sim_{ij}) between two cs's (cs_i and cs_j), respectively. In these functions $total\#CSs$ is the total number of CS's, $\#containedCSs(p)$ is the number of CS having property p in their property list.

$$tfidf(p, cs) = \frac{1}{|D_p(cs)|} \times log \frac{total\#CSs}{1 + \#containedCSs(p)} \quad (2)$$

$$sim_{ij} = \frac{\sum_{p \in (cs_i \cap cs_j)} tfidf(p, cs_i) \times tfidf(p, cs_j)}{\sqrt{\sum\limits_{p_i \in cs_i} tfidf(p_i, cs_i)^2} \times \sqrt{\sum\limits_{p_j \in cs_j} tfidf(p_j, cs_j)^2}} \quad (3)$$

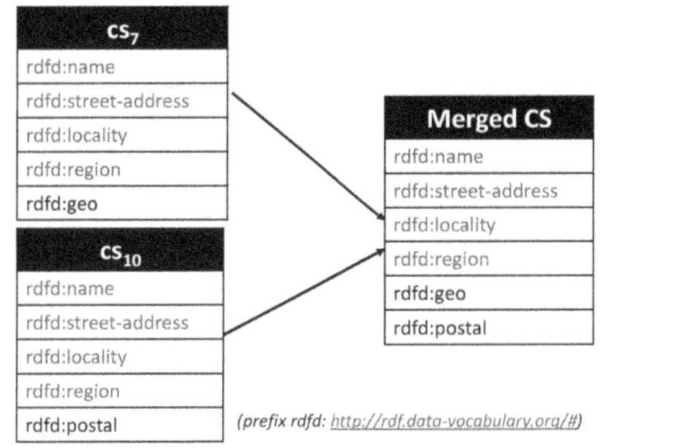

Figure 10: Merging CS's based on discriminative properties

In addition to the set of properties in a CS, incoming relationship references from other CS's can also be used as an evidence in identifying similar CS's. Normally, a subject refers to only one specific entity via a property. For example, the property `has_author` of the subject "Book" always refers to an "Author" entity. Thus, if one CS, e.g., cs_1, refers to several different CS's e.g., cs_2 and cs_3, via a property p, this hints at cs_2 and cs_3 being similar.

In summary, two CS's are considered *structurally similar* if they are both referred from the same CS via the same property (rule $S3$) or their property sets have a high TF/IDF similarity score (rule $S4$). In Rule 3, $ref(cs, p, cs_i)$ is the number of references from cs to cs_i via property p, and τ_{inf} is the infrequent threshold which is used to prevent non-frequent references from being considered in applying the rule $S3$. In Rule 4, τ_{sim} is the similarity threshold above which we decide to merge two CS's.

RULE 3. *If cs and p exist with* $\frac{ref(cs,p,cs_i)}{freq(cs)}$ *and* $\frac{ref(cs,p,cs_j)}{freq(cs)}$ *greater than* τ_{inf} *then merge* cs_i *and* cs_j. *(S3)*

RULE 4. *If the similarity score* sim_{ij} *between* cs_i *and* cs_j *is greater than* τ_{sim} *then merge* cs_i *and* cs_j. *(S4)*

Figure 9 shows the updates to the CS's and their relationships when we continue applying the rules $S3$ and $S4$. In this figure, cs_5 and cs_{11} are merged according to the rule $S3$ as they are both referred by cs_1 via the property `offers`. Besides, since cs_7 and cs_{10} have high similarity score (as shown in Figure 10), they are merged into cs_{14}.

We experimentally observed that the best order of applying the rules for merging CS's is $S1$, $S3$, $S2$, $S4$. Further details can be found in [17].

2.4 Schema Filtering

Our goal is to represent a large portion of the input triples in a compact, human-friendly, relational schema. After CS merging, most of these merged classes[12] cover a large amount of triples. However, it may happen that some classes still cover a limited number of RDF subjects, so if the merged CS covers $< min_t$ (e.g. 1000, see Table 2) subjects, it is removed from the schema; and we limit the UML class diagram to the merged Ub_{tbl} CS's with highest frequency. Note that omitting CS's with low frequency will only marginally reduce overall coverage.

Preserving Dimension Tables. However, for this removal of classes (merged CS's) we make one exception, namely

[12]At this stage, we also refer surviving merged CS's as classes, similar to UML classes.

we conserve CS's that – although small in terms of covered subjects – are referred to many times from other tables. The rationale is that such CS's thanks to the large amount of incoming references represent important information of the dataset that should be part of the schema. This is similar to a *dimension table* in a relational data warehouse, which may be small itself, but is referred to by many millions of tuples in large fact tables over a foreign key. Thus, combining the information of basic CS detection and relationship detection, we preserve CS's with a high frequency of incoming references. However, detecting dimension tables should not be handled just based on the number of *direct* relationship references. The relational analogy here are *snowflake* schemas, where a finer-grained dimension table like CITY refers to an even smaller coarse-grained dimension table COUNTRY. To find the transitive relationships and their relative importance, we use the PageRank [16] algorithm on the graph formed by all CS's (vertexes) and relationships (edges, regardless of direction). In each iteration, the score of a merged CS is computed based on the references from other merged CS's and their scores computed in the previous iteration. Equation 4 shows the formula for each iteration:

$$\begin{aligned} IR_k(cs_i) = \sum_{cs_j \rightarrow cs_i} & IR_{k-1}(cs_j) \times \frac{ref(cs_j, cs_i)}{refsTo(cs_i)} \\ & \times \frac{ref(cs_j, cs_i)}{freq(cs_j)} + refsTo(cs_i) \end{aligned} \quad (4)$$

$$\text{If}(IR_k(cs_i) \geq Ub_{tbl}) \rightarrow cs_i \textit{ is a dimension CS.}$$

The merged CS's having a score higher than a threshold Ub_{tbl} will be selected for inclusion in the schema. in which $IR_k(cs_i)$ is the indirect-referenced score of cs_i after k iterations, $ref(cs_j, cs_i)$ is the number of references from cs_j to cs_i, $freq(cs_j)$ is the frequency of cs_j, and $refsTo(cs_i)$ is the total number of direct references to cs_i.

Specifically, the number of iterations k is set the same as the diameter of the CS graph. It is because, with that value, after k iterations, the IR_k score of each CS will get computed from all the CS's. To compute the diameter of the graph, we implemented a fast and simple algorithm described by [3].

Minimizing the number of infrequent properties. A final step of schema filtering considers eliminating CS properties, which as column in a relational table would have many NULL values. If the property coverage ratio (see Equation 5) is less than the infrequent threshold τ_{inf}, that property is infrequent and it gets removed from the CS.

$$coverageRatio(p, cs) = \frac{freq(p, cs)}{freq(cs)} \quad (5)$$

2.5 Instance Filtering

The output after labeling, merging, and schema filtering is a compact relational emergent schema. In the instance filtering phase, all RDF triples are visited again, and either stored in relational tables (typically > 90% of the triples, which we consider *regular*), or (the remainder) separately in a PSO table. Hence, our final result is a set of relational tables with foreign keys between them, and a single triple table in PSO format. In principle, the regular triples are those belonging to a merged CS (that survived schema filtering). However, not all such triples are considered regular in the end, as we perform three types of *instance filtering*, described next.

Maximizing type homogeneity. Literal object values corresponding to each property in a CS can have several different types e.g., number, string, dateTime. The relational model can only store a single type in each column, so in case of type diversity, a relational system like MonetDB must use multiple columns for a single property. They contain the type-cast value of the literal, if possible, and NULL otherwise. The number of columns needed for representing the data from a cs_i hence is $\sum_{p \in cs_i} \#ofTypes(p)$. This number can be large just due to a few triples having the wrong type (dirty data). To minimize the number of such columns, for each property, we filter out all the infrequent literal types (types that appear in $< \tau_{inf}$ percent of all instances). All triples of class instances with infrequent types are moved to the PSO table.

Relationship Filtering. We further filter out *infrequent* or "dirty" relationships between classes. A relationship between cs_i and cs_j is infrequent if the number of references from cs_i to cs_j is much smaller than the frequency of cs_i (i.e., less than τ_{inf} percent of the CS's frequency). A relationship is considered dirty if the majority but not all the object values of the referring class (e.g., cs_i) refer to the instances of the referred class (cs_j). In the former case, we simply remove the relationship information between two classes. In the latter case, the triples in cs_i that do not refer to cs_j will be filtered out (placed in the separate PSO table).

We note that in the general case of *n-m* cardinality relationships, the relational model requires to create a separate *mapping table* that holds just the keys of both relations. However, in case one of the sides is $0 \ldots 1$, this is generally avoided by attaching a FK column to the table representing the other side. We try to optimize for this, by observing whether a multi-valued relationship is infrequent ($< \tau_{inf}$). If so, we remove the excess relationship to the separate PSO table, such that all remaining subjects in the class have maximally one relationship destination. Finally, if almost all instances of one class have *exactly* one match in the other class but a few ($< \tau_{inf}$) have none, we move *all* triples with that subject to the separate PSO table to preserve the exact *n*-1 cardinality (which keeps the FK column non-NULLable).

Multi-valued attributes. The same subject may have 0, 1 or even multiple triples with the same property, which in our schema leads to an attribute with cardinality > 1. While this is allowed in UML class diagrams, direct storage of such values is not possible in relational databases. Practitioners handle this by creating a separate table that contains the primary key (subject OID) and the value (which given literal type diversity may be multiple columns). The RDF bulk-loader of MonetDB does this, but only creates such separate storage if really necessary. That is, we analyze the mean number of object values (*meanp*) per property. If the *meanp* of a property p is not much greater than 1 (e.g., less than $(1+\tau_{inf}/100)$, we consider p as a single-valued property and only keep the first value of that property in each tuple while moving all the triples with other object values of this property to the non-structured part of the RDF dataset. Otherwise, we will add a table for storing all the object values of each multi-valued property.

$$\begin{aligned} meanp(p) &= \sum p(k) \times k \\ \text{where} \quad p(k) &= \frac{\#times\ p\ has\ k\ object\ values}{freq(p)} \end{aligned} \quad (6)$$

Parameter	Default	Description
Ub_{tbl}	1000	number of tables upper bound
min_t	1000	minimum table size
τ_{inf}	5%	infrequent threshold

Table 2: Emergent Relational Schema Detection Parameters

2.6 Parameter Tuning

An important question that we needed to address is how the various parameters guiding the recognition process should be set. Choosing improper parameters might result in a "bad" final schema with e.g., small data coverage, lots of NULLs, etc. Further, since each input dataset can have different characteristics, it would be unfeasible to find a fixed parameter set that works optimally for all datasets.

The most dataset sensitive parameter we found to be the τ_{sim}, used in labeling while matching ontologies using discriminative properties, as well as in the CS merging Rule 4 that determines up until which point merging should continue. It is a control on the strictness of finding equivalences between structures and ontologies, at 1 it is very strict while at 0 it is very lax. We evaluate the quality of the relational schema on two dimensions, namely (i) the number of tables (compactness of the schema) and (ii) its *precision*, which is the number of NOT-NULL cells, $fill(t)$, divided by the total number of cells, $cap(t)$, in all tables, as in Equation 7. There is a clear trade-off between having a compact schema and higher precision, depending on τ_{sim}.

Our auto-tuned algorithm iteratively re-runs the labeling and merging steps with different values of τ_{sim}. In each run, we measure the number of tables and the precision; we also compute a delta of these between successive values of τ_{sim}. In Equation 8, k is the total number of runs; nT_i ($nTnom_i$) and $prec_i$ ($prNom_i$) are the (normalized) number of tables and the schema precision at the ith run; $nTdelta_i$ and $prDelta_i$ are the relative change in the normalized number of tables and the precision at the ith run, respectively. We use the lowest value of $\tau_{sim} > 0$ where $nTdelta_i > prDelta_i$.

$$prec = \frac{\sum_t fill(t)}{\sum_t cap(t)} \quad (7)$$

$$\begin{aligned} nTnom_i &= \frac{nT_i - nT_1}{nT_k - nT_1} \qquad prNom_i = \frac{prec_i - prec_1}{prec_k - prec_1} \\ nTdelta_i &= nTnom_i - nTnom_{i-1} \\ prDelta_i &= prNom_i - prNom_{i-1} \end{aligned} \quad (8)$$

The left of Figure 11 shows normalized nT_i and $prec_i$ for WebData Commons as a function of τ_{sim} in steps of 0.05, while the right side shows the deltas between steps. Auto-tuning chooses the cross-over point of the deltas (τ_sim=0.7).

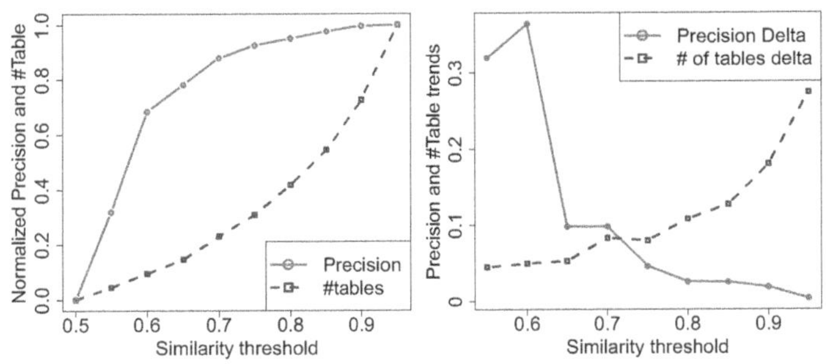

Figure 11: Left: τ_{sim} steps on X, #Tables&Precision on Y. Right: step deltas, auto-tuning selects cross-over (WebData)

labels	WebData.	DBpedia
top 3	3.6	3.8
final	4.1	4.6

Table 3: Human survey results on Likert scale

3. EXPERIMENTAL EVALUATION

Metrics. We propose several metrics for evaluating the quality of the emergent schema. These metrics rely on the fact that a structure is considered to be good if it is *compact* (few and thin tables), *precise* (few NULLs) and has *large coverage* (few triples that have to be moved to separate PSO storage). Given an RDF dataset R and its total number of triples $|R|$, the first performance metric, C, is the percentage of input triples covered by the schema:

$$C = \frac{\sum_1^n cov(t_i)}{|R|} \quad (9)$$

Each class in the structure is physically stored in a separate relational table. We define worth $w(t_i)$ of table t_i as:

$$w(t_i) = \overbrace{\frac{cov(t_i)}{\sum_1^n cov(t_i)}}^{(I)} \times \overbrace{\left(prec(t_i) + \frac{ref(t_i)}{\sum_1^n ref(t_i)}\right)}^{(II)} \quad (10)$$
$$where \;\; prec(t_i) = \frac{fill(t_i)}{cap(t_i)}$$

The precision $prec(t_i)$ of the table t_i is the fraction of non-NULL values in table ti, $cov(t_i)$ is the number of RDF triples stored in t_i; n is the number of tables and $ref(t_i)$ is the number of FK's referring to t_i. Here, (II) sums the precision and the relative importance of the table considering the relationships between tables, while (I) denotes the contribution of the table for the coverage of the schema. As the schema is only compact if n is small, the quality of the explored structure, Q, is defined as: $Q = \frac{\sum_1^n w(t_i)}{n}$.

3.1 Experimental Results

Labeling evaluation. We presented the emergent schemas of the DBpedia and WebDataCommons datasets to 19 humans and asked them to rate the labels.On a 5-point Likert scale from 1 (bad) to 5 (excellent) label quality, the top 3 labels of each table were scored by at least 3 persons. As shown in Table 3, the top 3 label candidates received an average rating of 3.6 for WebDataCommons and 3.8 for the DBpedia dataset. The finally chosen labels (one among the top 3) got better scores (4.1 and 4.6, respectively). We therefore conclude that the ordering of label candidates created by our algorithms produces encouraging results, as the chosen labels get higher ratings than the other candidates. Furthermore, our evaluation shows that 78% (WebDataCommons) and 90% (DBpedia) of the labels are rated with 4 points or better, hence are considered "good" labels by the users. The emergent relational schemas for the nine datasets we tested are too large to include in this paper, Figure 12 shows EuroStat, one of the simpler schemas.[13]

Merging/Filtering performance. Figure 13 and Table 4 show the performance of the proposed merging algorithms and the filtering techniques for detecting a compact relational emergent schema with high coverage. According to

[13]See `www.cwi.nl/~boncz/emergent` for the other datasets.

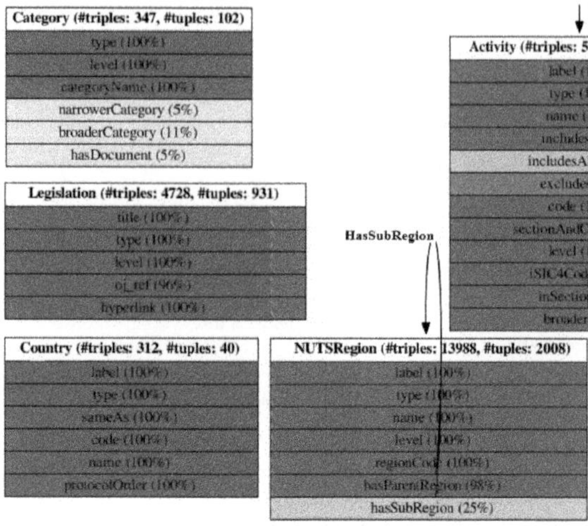

Figure 12: Final emergent schema for EuroStat – the lighter a column, the more NULLs (percentage in parentheses).

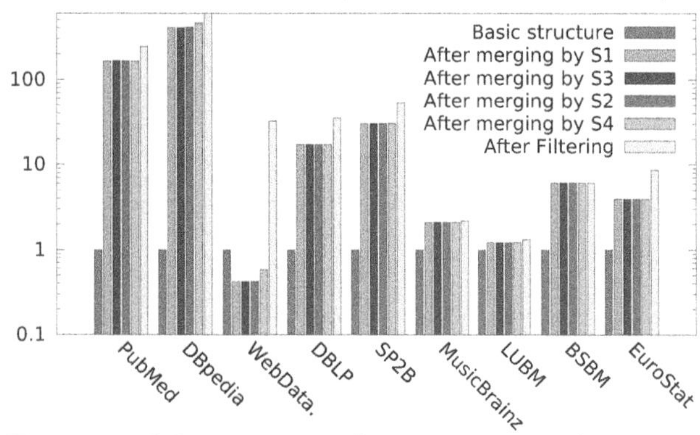

Figure 13: Schema quality Q during merging & filtering

Figure 13, the metric Q of the explored structure, except for WebDataCommons, always increases after the merging and filtering steps. For WebDataCommons, the value of Q decreases when merging CS's using rule S1. This stems from the fact that in WebDataCommons dataset each CS describing a certain entity such as `Website` may have many additional properties describing application attached to the website, and even use various properties for the same attribute (e.g., `ogp.me/ns#url`, `opengraphprotocol.org/schema/url`, `rdf.data-vocabulary.org/#url` for the website's URL), and thus, their merged CS's may contain properties with lots of NULLs values, causing the decrease of the metric Q. Nevertheless, the filtering step, by refining infrequent properties in the explored structure, can help addressing this issue and significantly increases the score of the metric Q. Comparing to the basic structure, the final schema of each experimental dataset is several orders of magnitude better in this metric.

Table 4 also shows that after the schema filtering, the final schema in all cases achieves very high coverage. We see that synthetic RDF benchmark data (BSBM, SP2B, LUBM) is fully relational, and also all dataset with non-RDF roots (PubMed, MusicBrainz, EuroStat) get > 99% coverage. Most surprisingly, the RDFa data that dominates WebDataCommons and even DBpedia is more than 90% regular. Further, a non-complete manual inspection of the < 10% irregular triples in these datasets appeared to show mainly mistyped properties, so our suspicion is that much of this irregularity is in fact data "dirtiness".

Computational cost. Figure 14 shows that the time for detecting the emerging schema is negligible compared to

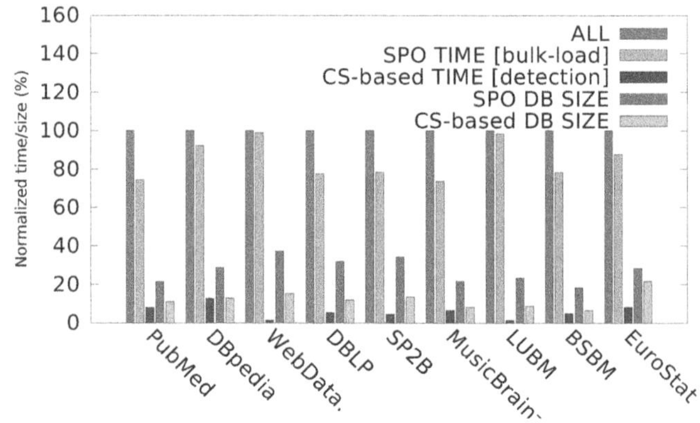

Figure 14: Building time & database size for single triple table (SPO) and reorganized relational tables (CS-based) (normalized by bulk-load time and database size for all six S,P,O table permutations (ALL)).

Datasets	Number of tables			Coverage – Metric C (%)		
	before merging	after merging	remove small tables	remove small tables	prune infreq. prop.	final schema
LUBM	17	13	12	100	100	**100.00**
BSBM	49	8	8	100	100	**100.00**
SP2B	554	13	10	99.99	99.65	**99.65**
MusicBrainz	27	12	12	100	99.9	**99.60**
EuroStat	44	10	5	99.73	99.53	**99.53**
DBLP	249	9	6	100	99.68	**99.60**
PubMed	3340	14	12	100	99.75	**99.73**
WebData.	13354	3000	253	98.17	94.37	**92.79**
DBpedia	439629	542	234	99.12	96.68	**95.82**

Table 4: #tables and metric C after merging & filtering

bulk-loading time for building a single SPO table as well as building all the six permutations of `S`, `P`, `O` (marked [ALL]). Thus, MonetDB integrates emergent schema detection into its RDF bulk-loading without recognizable delay.

Compression. Figure 14 shows that the database size stored using relational tables can be two times smaller than the database size of a single SPO triple table. The reason is that in the relational representation the `S` and `P` columns effectively get compressed away, only the `O` columns remain.

Query processing. As a proof that the recognized emergent schema can be easily integrated and boost the performance of existing RDF stores, we report on the effort at OpenLink to integrate emergent relational schema technology in one of the state-of-the-art RDF stores, Virtuoso [8][14] It was a few months work to integrate Characteristic Set based storage, query execution and query optimization in Virtuoso. We compare a classic Virtuoso RDF quad table (Virt-Quad) and this CS-based implementation (Virt-CS) on the BSBM benchmark at 10 billion triples scale.

The experimental results in Table 5 show that exploiting the emergent relational schema even in this very preliminary implementation already improves the performance of Virtuoso on a number of BSBM Explore queries by up to a factor of 5.8 (Q3, Hot run). Note that the Cold run is much slower comparing to the Hot run as most of the time goes in the statistics gathering, not in the execution. We see less gain from CS's in other queries, e.g., Q5, since the first condition on the BSBM products (on a range of numeric property) is selective, so the other columns of the CS (or self-joins to

[14]https://github.com/v7fasttrack/virtuoso-opensource

RDF Store	Q2			Q3			Q5			Q7			Q8		
	Cold	Hot	Opt.	Cold	Hot	Opt.	Cold	Hot	Opt.	Cold	Hot	Opt.	Cold	Hot	Opt.
Virt-Quad	11567	7	4.2	4210	53	40.2	3842	1350	18.6	19401	9	5.3	14644	9	4.4
Virt-CS	2485	6	3.5	2965	9	5.4	2130	712	4.2	11642	6	4.5	5370	5	3.3

Table 5: Query time (msecs) w/wo the recognized schema
(Cold: First query runtime after re-starting the server; Hot: Run the query 3 times and get the last runtime; Opt.: Query optimization time)

RDF quads) are done on a small fraction of the subjects of the first range check. In Q3 more single-valued properties are accessed per subject, resulting in much more gain.

By collapsing multiple triple patterns into a single abstract CS table, query optimization gets a plan search space of the same order as for the equivalent SQL. For Q3, the compilation time drops from 40.2 msecs to 5.4 msecs when using the recognized schema. In many RDF applications, e.g. Open PHACTS[15], query optimization time dominates and can run into the tens of seconds. Due to the extreme search space resulting from triple patterns, there are often ad hoc restrictions on plans, e.g. no hash join or no joins on hash build sides. With CS, a more thorough search of the plan space becomes again practicable and we expect qualitatively better plans to result.

4. RELATED WORK

We note that previous work has already proposed building relational-resembling RDF stores [22, 7, 12, 21, 4]. However, these proposals either demand the presence of an all-explaining ontology (which then gets remapped to relational tables), or ask the database system administrator to create and maintain "property tables" explicitly. Our approach, in contrast, does not require any form of explicit schema ingestion. Second, since these approaches just use the structure internally in the SPARQL engine to make things faster, they do not address the challenge of making the schema understandable to humans (compactness, finding short aliases). For the latter, a related line of work is creating summaries of the graph structure to aid query formulation [6], yet these do not focus on making RDF database systems faster, and typically require a cluster to compute, whereas our approach is cheap and can piggyback on RDF bulk-loading. Related to the automatic structure exploration from data is work on ontology mining [13] which discovers ontologies from unstructured text on the web. In our approach, we recognize the emergent structure in RDF data (e.g., mixing of ontologies), and do not change the semantics, and focus on providing a relational view of it.

Frequent itemset mining, which has been studied in many data mining papers [1, 5, 9], is equivalent to the basic CS recognition, originally proposed by [14]. We use this technique but go beyond that by finding a schema graph with cross-CS relationships, and we employ a host of techniques to make this schema graph compact and human-friendly (finding labels).

A recent study on the structure refinement for the RDF data, [2] proposed an integer linear programming (ILP)-based algorithm which allows an RDF dataset being partitioned into a number of "sorts" where each sort satisfies a predefined structured-ness fitting threshold. This approach, relying mainly on the similarity and correlation between the properties of sorts, may merge subjects describing unrelated entities but having many common properties into a single sort (as also shown in their experiment with Drug Company and Sultan), while our solution only merges related CS's together by exploiting the discriminating properties and the availability of the semantics/ontologies information. Besides, no relationship exploration as well as labeling for the sorts are considered in this work, and thus, no relational schema is recognized.

Consulting external resources for entity labeling is suggested by [20] in the context of table data reconstruction as well as by [19] a study on labeling hierarchical clusters. The former study shows that column names and table names usually cannot be found in table data itself. To reconstruct HTML table data they therefore rely on an external database with hyponym information. The latter study also mentions that documents often do not contain self-descriptive terms. To overcome this, they suggest using "anchor texts" as an additional resource in their document labeling task. Anchor texts are pieces of text on and next to hyperlinks to a specific document. The relational equivalent of anchor texts are names of foreign key relationships. In our case we rely on property names that refer to other tables for name suggestions, supplemented by ontology information when present.

5. CONCLUSIONS

In this paper, we introduced the notion of – and demonstrated practical techniques for – discovering an *emergent* relational schema in RDF datasets, that recovers a compact and precise relational schema with high coverage and useful labels as alias for all machine-readable URIs (which it preserves). The functional benefit of an emergent relational schema for RDF datasets is both in giving users better understanding of the structure of an RDF dataset, while also allowing the often > 90% of regular triples to be queried from existing SQL applications, which still dominate the IT industry. Our MonetDB RDF bulk loader enables this. We think that this also provides impetus to make SQL more semantic, e.g. stimulating usage of URIs in SQL metadata.

The emergent relational schema can also be used under the cover of an SPARQL engine as a new storage approach, where the 90% regular triples are stored in tabular structures and the rest in SPO format. We think that the knowledge of an emergent schema gives SPARQL engines just what they need to close the performance gap with SQL systems. This we demonstrated in Virtuoso, with gains both in compression, query execution and query optimization. The tabular structure opens up many opportunities to improve physical access patterns using (partial) clustered indexes, zone maps, table partitioning and even database cracking [11].

Looking ahead, the prospect of people supporting SQL applications on top of RDF data raises many new questions. Users will desire to tweak a found emergent schema by hand, e.g. by manually improving some labels. We propose making a found emergent schema explicit using a vocabulary, and researching techniques to control schema evolution to preserve schema stability while the emergent schema adapts over time to changes in the underlying RDF datasets.

[15]http://www.openphacts.org/

6. REFERENCES

[1] R. Agrawal et al. Fast algorithms for mining association rules. In *VLDB*, 1994.

[2] M. Arenas et al. A principled approach to bridging the gap between graph data and their schemas. In *VLDB*, 2014.

[3] K. Boitmanis et al. Fast and simple approximation of the diameter and radius of a graph. In *Experimental Algorithms*, pages 98–108. Springer, 2006.

[4] A. Bornea et al. Building an efficient RDF store over a relational database. In *SIGMOD*, 2013.

[5] D. Burdick et al. Mafia: A maximal frequent itemset algorithm for transactional databases. In *ICDE*, 2001.

[6] S. Campinas et al. Introducing RDF graph summary with application to assisted SPARQL formulation. In *DEXA Workshops*, 2012.

[7] E. Chong et al. An efficient SQL-based RDF querying scheme. In *VLDB*, 2005.

[8] O. Erling. Virtuoso, a hybrid RDBMS/graph column store. *IEEE Data Eng. Bull*, 2012.

[9] K. Gouda and M. Zaki. Efficiently mining maximal frequent itemsets. In *ICDM*, 2001.

[10] A. Gubichev and T. Neumann. Exploiting the query structure for efficient join ordering in SPARQL queries. In *EDBT*, 2014.

[11] S. Idreos, M. L. Kersten, and S. Manegold. Database cracking. In *Conference on Innovative Data Systems Research (CIDR)*, pages 68–78, Asilomar, California, 2007.

[12] J. Levandoski and M. Mokbel. RDF data-centric storage. In *ICWS*, 2009.

[13] Y. Li et al. Mining ontology for automatically acquiring web user information needs. *KDE*, 2006.

[14] T. Neumann and G. Moerkotte. Characteristic sets: Accurate cardinality estimation for RDF queries with multiple joins. In *ICDE*, 2011.

[15] R. Neumayer et al. When simple is (more than) good enough: Effective semantic search with (almost) no semantics. In *Advances in Information Retrieval*. Springer, 2012.

[16] L. Page et al. The pagerank citation ranking: Bringing order to the web. Technical report, Stanford, 1999.

[17] L. Passing. Recognizing, naming and exploring structure in RDF data. Master's thesis, Technische Universität München, 2014.

[18] G. Salton and M. J. McGill. Introduction to modern information retrieval. 1983.

[19] P. Treeratpituk and J. Callan. Automatically labeling hierarchical clusters. In *DGSNA*, 2006.

[20] P. Venetis et al. Recovering semantics of tables on the web. In *VLDB*, 2011.

[21] Y. Wang et al. Flextable: using a dynamic relation model to store RDF data. In *DASFAA*, 2010.

[22] K. Wilkinson. Jena property table implementation. Technical report, HP Labs, 2006.

The Digital Life of Walkable Streets

Daniele Quercia
University of Cambridge
dquercia@acm.org

Luca Maria Aiello
Yahoo Labs, Barcelona
alucca@yahoo-inc.com

Rossano Schifanella
University of Turin
schifane@di.unito.it

Adam Davies
Walkonomics
adam@walkonomics.com

ABSTRACT

Walkability has many health, environmental, and economic benefits. That is why web and mobile services have been offering ways of computing walkability scores of individual street segments. Those scores are generally computed from survey data and manual counting (of even trees). However, that is costly, owing to the high time, effort, and financial costs. To partly automate the computation of those scores, we explore the possibility of using the social media data of Flickr and Foursquare to automatically identify safe and walkable streets. We find that unsafe streets tend to be photographed during the day, while walkable streets are tagged with walkability-related keywords. These results open up practical opportunities (for, e.g., room booking services, urban route recommenders, and real-estate sites) and have theoretical implications for researchers who might resort to the use social media data to tackle previously unanswered questions in the area of walkability.

Categories and Subject Descriptors

H.4.m [**Information Systems Applications**]: Miscellaneous

General Terms

Experimental Study, Walkability, Urban Informatics

1. INTRODUCTION

What makes for a good city street? Some urban planners would say the "fabric": the collection of streets, blocks and buildings. In "Great Streets," the urbanist Alan Jacobs compared the layout of more than 40 world cities [19], and found that good streets tend to have narrow lanes (making them safe from moving cars), small blocks (making them comfortable), and architecturally-rich buildings (making them interesting). Intuitively, walking down a narrow, shop-lined street is a far safer, more comfortable, and more interesting experience than walking down an arterial between parking lots.

Despite its importance, good street design is necessary but not sufficient for the making of great streets. Streets, like communities, thrive on vitality [20]. It has been shown that the most meaningful indicator of that vitality is walkability [37]. This is a multi-faced concept. Recently, in his book "Walkable City," Jeff Speck outlines a "General Theory of Walkability," identifying the four key factors that make a city attractive to pedestrians:

> "The General Theory of Walkability explains how, to be favored, a walk has to satisfy four main conditions: it must be useful, safe, comfortable, and interesting. Each of these qualities is essential and none alone is sufficient. *Useful* means that most aspects of daily life are located close at hand and organized in a way that walking serves them well. *Safe* means that the street has been designed to give pedestrians a fighting chance against being hit by automobiles; they must not only be safe but feel safe, which is even tougher to satisfy. *Comfortable* means that buildings shape urban streets into 'outdoor living rooms', in contrast to wide-open spaces, which usually fail to attract pedestrians. *Interesting* means that sidewalks are lined by unique buildings with friendly faces and that signs of humanity abound."

The importance of walkability goes beyond aesthetic considerations. Walkable streets not only make a city beautiful but also greatly contribute to the wealth, health, and sustainability of the city. They contribute to wealth, not least because walkability can add 5 to 10 percent to house prices in the United States [9, 24]. They contribute to health so much so that walkability is considered to be at the heart of the cure to the health-care crisis in the States by many [23]. Finally, they contribute to environmental sustainability. A case in point is that replacing one's light-bulbs with energy saving once a year spares as much carbon as living in a walkable neighborhood does for a week [37].

The growing demand for walkable neighborhoods (especially from younger generations) has made websites that calculate walkability (e.g., **`walkonomics.com`**, **`walkscore.com`**) popular among real estate agents, health-care agencies, and environmentalists. However, to work, those sites need to process and gather a variety of datasets, which is financially-prohibitive.

To make walkability modeling cheap and scalable, one could resort to social media sites. That is because part of a street's vitality is, nowadays, captured in the digital layer: street dwellers take pictures and post them on Flickr, and, when they visit places, they share their whereabouts on Foursquare. It is therefore reasonable to assume that there might be digital footprints that distinguish walkable streets from unwalkable ones. As a result, we study whether digital activity on Flickr and Foursquare can help us identify walkable streets in London and, more generally, whether implicit social media data can provide walkability assessments without the need to manually collect expensive datasets.

WWW 2015, May 18–22, 2015, Florence, Italy.
ACM 978-1-4503-3469-3/15/05.
http://dx.doi.org/10.1145/2736277.2741631.

More specifically:

- We collect Flickr and Foursquare data for the 3,368 street segments in Central London (Section 3). One of the authors has created a web and mobile service called Walkonomics to produce safety and walkability scores for those streets (Section 4).
- To ensure experimental validity, we review the literature and spell out four main research questions concerning safety and walkability (Section 5).
- We answer those questions upon our datasets (Section 6). We find that unsafe streets tend to be photographed during the day but not at night; tend to be visited not only by males but also by females; and are identified by the presence of residential elements of the city that have no parks. By contrast, walkable streets are associated with residential areas and are identified by the presence of walkability-related photo tags with a correlation as high as $r = 0.89$.

Before concluding (Section 8), we discuss the theoretical and practical implications of our work (Section 7).

2. RELATED WORK

We have heavily borrowed from 1970s urban studies [1, 19, 20] and from the walkability literature, most of which has been recently summarized by Jeff Speck [37]. Our work is best placed within an emerging area of Computer Science research, which is often called 'urban informatics.' Researchers in this area have been studying large-scale urban dynamics [11, 12, 29], and people's behavior when using location-based services such as Foursquare [4, 10, 25].

More closely related to this work, computational methods that automatically mine a variety of data sources to predict economic indicators have been recently developed. Eagle *et al.* [15] used land-line phone records to predict socio-economic indicators in English neighborhoods. More recently, to predict those indicators in London, Smith *et al.* [36] used underground transit flows. Elvidge *et al.* analyzed satellite images to extract the total surface lit during night time, and found strong correlations with countries' Gross Domestic Product [16, 17]. Mao *et al.* used mobile phone records to predict economic indexes of ten areas of high economic activity in Cote d'Ivoire [27]. Traunmueller *et al.* also used mobile phone records but did so to test existing urban theories (from, e.g., Jane Jacobs' work) at scale [41].

The idea of testing traditional urban theories at web scale has recently received attention. It is well-known that the layout of urban spaces plugs directly into our sense of community well-being. The 20th century sociologist Kevin Lynch showed that everyone living in an urban environment creates their own personal "mental map" of the city based on features such as the routes they use and the areas they visit [26]. Lynch thus hypothesized that the more recognizable the features of a city are, the more navigable the city is. To put his theory to test, Quercia *et al.* built a web game that crowdsources Londoners' mental images of the city [32]. They showed that areas suffering from social problems such as housing deprivation, poor living conditions, and crime are rarely present in residents' mental images. The researchers then built another crowdsourcing game to determine which urban elements make city dwellers happy [31]. In that web game, users are shown ten pairs of urban scenes of London and, for each pair, a user needs to choose which one they consider to be most beautiful, quiet, and happy. Based on user votes, the researchers were able to rank all urban scenes according to these three attributes. By analyzing the scenes with image processing tools, they discovered that the amount of greenery in any given scene was associated with all the three attributes and that cars and fortress-like buildings were associated with sadness (they equated sadness to the low end of their 'spectrum' of happiness). In contrast, public gardens and Victorian and red brick houses were associated with happiness. Upon that work, practical innovations emerged: new mapping tools that return directions that are not only short but also tend to make urban walkers happy [33], and new web image ranking techniques that are able to identify memorable city pictures based on whether a neighborhood is predicted to be beautiful or to make people happy [45].

This stream of research requires access to datasets that are very difficult to get or entails the design of web engagement tools that are difficult to build. An alternative approach is to rely on more easily accessible social media data. English neighborhood deprivation has been related to Twitter topics [34] and sentiment [30], and a new way of redefining neighborhood boundaries has been proposed upon Foursquare check-ins [13].

In line with this last stream of research, we propose to use user-generated content to mine street safety and walkability. In the next section, we describe the datasets, before providing the details of our methodology.

3. DATASETS

Mapping Data. We consider the area of Central London, which consists of 3,368 street segments. To describe those segments, we rely on data gathered and distributed for free by OpenStreetMap (OSM) (a global group of volunteer cartographers who maintain free crowdsourced online maps) and by Ordnance Survey (the national mapping agency for Great Britain). To account for potential measurement errors when matching social media data with streets, we add a buffer of 22.5 meters around each street's polyline. This is common practice and has been done using the Vector Buffer Analysis tool provided by QGIS, a free and open-source desktop geographic information systems (GIS).

Foursquare Data. We collect information about all the ~8K Foursquare venues in London. In Foursquare, a venue is categorized within a multi-level taxonomy. Since there are hundreds of level-2 categories, categorizing venues at that level would result in a sparse dataset. To avoid that, our analysis categorizes venues with the top-level categories. That is, each venue belongs to one of these nine categories: *Arts & Entertainment*, *College & Education*, *Food*, *Nightlife*, *Outdoors & Recreation*, *Shops*, *Travel & Transport*, *Professional & Other Places*.

Flickr Data. We gather a random sample of ~7M geo-referenced Flickr pictures within the bounding box of Central London. For each picture, we summarize its popularity statistics of number of *views*, *favorites*, and *comments*. We also collect the owner's gender and age[1], and the picture's both human-generated *tags* (i.e., free-text annotations assigned by the photo's owner) and machine-generated tags[2]. The machine-generated tags are assigned by a computer vision classifier and describe the picture's subjects (e.g., bird, tree) and context (e.g., indoor, outdoor, night). Since we are interested in determining how many photos are taken at night on a street, we count the number of pictures that are classified as *night*, and the number of those that are classified otherwise. The machine-generated tags come with a confidence score in $[0, 1]$ that reflects the probability of the tag being correclty assigned to the picture. To make sure that the photo actually is taken at night, we consider only tags that are assigned with confidence greater than 0.95. We could

[1]These were available for around 55% of the owners in our sample.
[2]`http://www.fastcolabs.com/3037882`

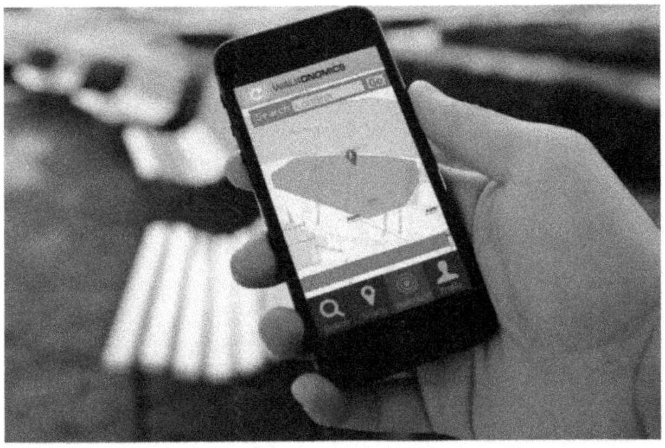

Figure 1: Walkonomics app with the *"WalkHood"* feature, which shows the areas one can walk to within five minutes from current location.

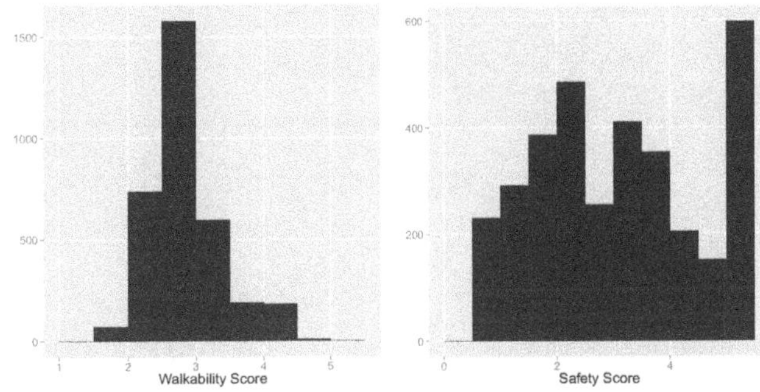

(a) Walkability (min:1.5, median:2.5, max:4.63) (b) Safety (min:0.5, median:3, max:5)

Figure 2: Frequency distributions of the walkability and safety scores at the level of street segment. The scores are defined from 1 to 5. The walkability scores in *(a)* are centered around a median of 2.5, while the safety ones in *(b)* are more uniformly distributed.

have used timestamps to do the same thing, but it has been shown that they are more unreliable than considering high-confidence machine tags [39].

4. WALKABILITY

One of the authors founded Walkonomics[3], a web platform and mobile app that maps and rates the pedestrian-friendliness of over 700,000 streets in England, San Francisco, Toronto and Manhattan. The mobile app has been installed in more than 8,000 devices and the website receives thousands of monthly unique visitors. Each street has five-level ratings in eight different categories. Those categories are the most important factors associated with walkability by public agencies [28, 40] and existing research [5, 37]:

Road safety. This measures pedestrian safety from vehicle traffic. It reflects the street's type, number and severity of road accidents [42].

Easy to cross. This measures how easy it is for a person to cross the street. Its score depends on the street's type (derived from OpenStreetMaps) and traffic activity. This activity is derived from the English Index of Multiple Deprivation, which is a composite score defined at the level of census area in England (Lower Super Output Area) and is computed by the UK Office of National Statistics [22].

Sidewalks. This measures the quality and width of the street's sidewalks, and is based on the street's type.

Hilliness. This measures how steep the street is. It is based on the street's slope [43].

Navigation. Its score reflects the provision of pedestrian "wayfinding" maps and signage on the street. Location information of pedestrian signage is publicly available [38].

Safety from crime. This measures safety from street crime. This is one of the domains of the English Index of Multiple Deprivation [22].

Smart and beautiful. This measures how attractive and green the street is. It is based on the number of trees on each street, and on whether the street is in or near a park. Information about trees and parks is extracted from OpenStreetMap.

Fun and relaxing. This measures whether a street is a fun and interesting place to be, and whether it is a relaxing environment or one dominated by vehicle traffic. Its score depends on the number of shops, bars, restaurants, and parks on the street (extracted from OpenStreetMap) and on the street's type.

The scores for all the categories are all extracted from public data that is updated periodically but not in real time. To correct any inaccuracies or errors in assessing streets, Walkonomics allows its web and mobile phone users to upload their own street reviews. To incentivize mobile phone users to do so on the spot, the mobile app allows them to: check the walkability of nearby streets and areas on a map; search by location, place name or post code; view search results on a map with colour-coded markers; read detailed reviews with star ratings for each category and user-generated photos; add their own ratings, reviews, photos and ideas for improvement; login using their Facebook, Twitter or email address and use their profiles to add street reviews; and see the Google StreetView of each street. The most popular feature of the app is the *"WalkHood"* map (Figure 1). This shows a polygon of the areas a user can walk to within 5 minutes from the current location.

The street's overall walkability score is the average of the eight categories, equally weighted. Since urban crime is the dimension among those provided by UK Office of National Statistics most related to walkability, we start with a few research questions about crime (which has been widely-studied in the urban context [35]) to then move on with questions about walkability.

The frequency distributions of walkability scores is shown in Figure 2 and the map of walkability scores in Central London is shown in Figure 3(a). For ease of comparison, in Figure 2 we also plot the distribution of "safety from crime" scores, that are as well displayed on the map of London in Figure 3(b).

5. METHOD

Critics might rightly say that we are not sure whether the scores we have just introduced actually measure what they are meant to measure (i.e., safety, walkability). To assess the validity of those scores, we need to theoretically derive hypotheses concerning, say, walkability (e.g., it is associated with the absence of cars) and test

[3] **http://www.walkonomics.com**

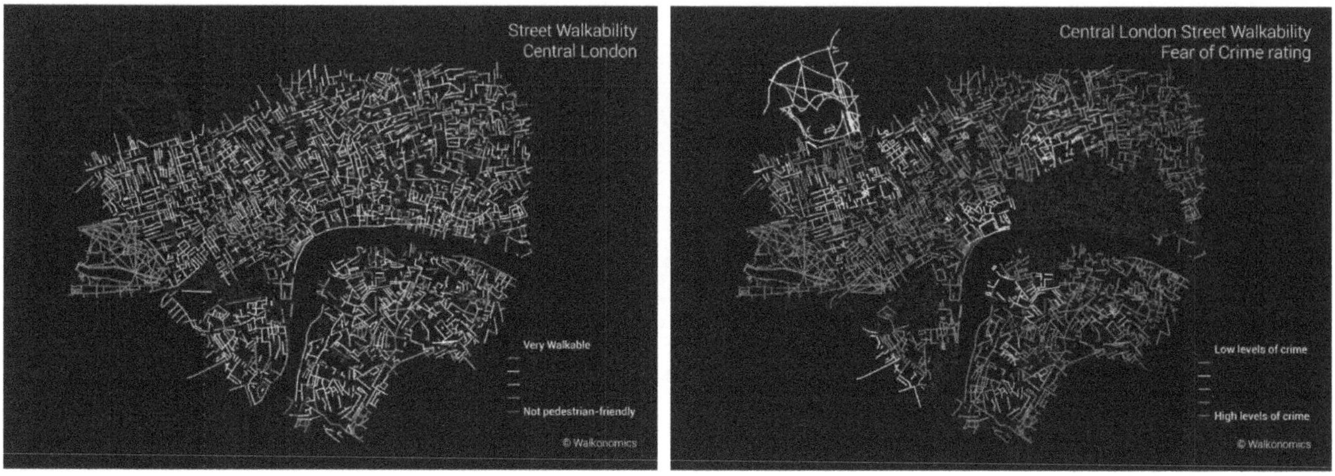

(a) Walkability scores of each street segment. Green segments are very walkable, while red ones are not pedestrian-friendly.

(b) Safety from crime scores of each street segment. Green segments have low levels of crime, while red ones have high levels.

Figure 3: Maps of Central London showing to which extent each street segment is *(a)* walkable, and *(b)* safe from crime.

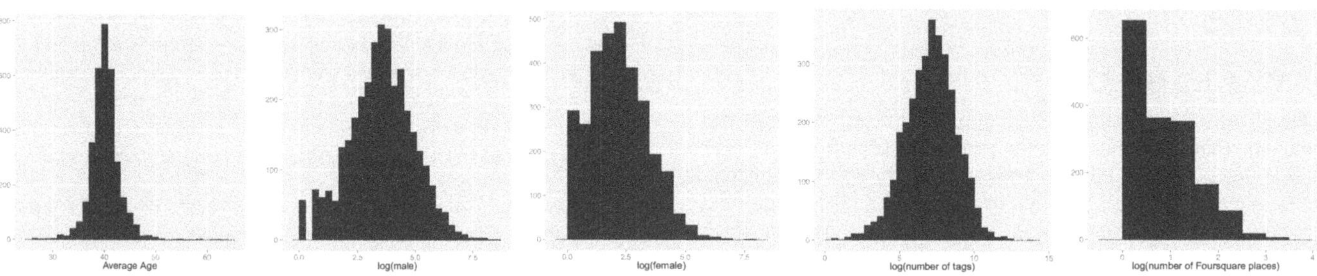

(a) Average Age (min:26, med:40, max:63) (b) Male (min:1,med:87,max:4564) (c) Female (min:1,med:20,max:2760) (d) Flickr tags (min:2,med:4.7K,max:968K) (e) Foursquare places (min:1,med:2,max:27)

Figure 4: Frequency distributions of Flickr and Foursquare activity features. Below the plot of each feature's frequency distribution, we report the minimum value, median value, and maximum value. All the features but age are log-transformed as the original values are skewed.

those hypotheses upon those scores. If the hypotheses receive support (e.g., the absence of cars is indeed found to be empirically associated with the walkability scores), then that speaks to the validity of the scores (concurrent validity). We thus derive hypotheses concerning safety and walkability next.

Research Questions on Safety

In the early 1960s, Jane Jacobs explored the relationships between urban decays, social interactions, and crime. She showed that nothing is safer than a city street that everybody uses, and called this phenomenon "the eyes on the street" [20].

In "The Ecology of Night Life," Shlomo Angel indeed showed that areas of very low or very high pedestrian density suffer from much less crime [2]. "At night, street crimes are most prevalent in places where there are too few pedestrians to provide natural surveillance, but enough pedestrians to make it worth a thief's while" [1]. Based on that, we posit our first research question:

R1: Can safe streets be identified by night activity?

In a similar vein, one could consider gender differences, in that, streets that men use might differ from those that women use in terms of safety from crime. However, it is unclear the nature of this relationship. One might hypothesize that safe streets are used by men and women alike, and unsafe ones are used by men only (women are likely to shy away). But one might also hypothesize the opposite: "to make it worth a thief's while" (as Alexander puts it), unsafe streets are so because they are predominantly used by women. Similar considerations go for age – streets that younger adults use might differ from those that older ones use in terms of safety. All this leads to our second research question:

R2: Can safe streets be identified by activity segmented by gender or age?

Jacobs' ideas about urban decays led to what urbanists now call "crime prevention through environmental design" [18]. This is based on the premise that the physical environment can be designed or manipulated to reduce fear of crime. One of the key strategies for crime prevention is activity support. The idea is that encouraging legitimate activity in public places (e.g., a basketball court, community center) helps discourage crime [6]. Therefore one expects that a safe street would offer places that encourage legitimate activity. Hence, our third research question:

R3: Can safe streets be identified by the presence of specific types of places?

Research Questions on Walkability

Recall that, in Jeff Speck's General Theory of Walkability, a walk has to satisfy four main conditions. It must be not only safe, comfortable, and interesting, but also useful [37]. By useful, he means that "most aspects of daily life are located close at hand." The most widely-used (albeit oversimplified) definition of walkability indeed concerns access to opportunities: the more miles one has to travel from a place for daily errands, the less walkable's the place [3]. This begs our next research question:

R4: Can walkable streets be identified by the presence of specific types of places?

The concept of walkability goes beyond the idea of access to opportunities though. To partly capture this richness, we gather the literature on walkability to produce a list of walkability-related keywords. With such a list, we aim at answering our final research question:

R5: Can walkable streets be identified by walkability-related photo tags?

The frequency distributions of the activity features we will use to answer those questions are summarized in Figure 4.

6. ANALYSIS

To answer the five research questions, we need to derive suitable Flickr and Foursquare activity features. However, before doing so, we need to ascertain whether those activity features are reliable. Without reliable measures of night activity on Flickr, of the presence of specific Foursquare places, and of the presence of Flickr photo tags, we cannot test our hypotheses. In general, there are three main types of error that reduce reliability: measurement error, specification error, and sampling error. To minimize the error that inevitably occurs in measuring Flickr and Foursquare activity (measurement error), we borrow measurement procedures from the literature [7, 39]. To minimize the effect of Flickr and Foursquare biases (e.g., Flickr pictures are taken predominantly during the day and by men), we borrow normalization measures (e.g., z-transformations) from previous studies [21]. Finally, to partly generalize our measurements to users not in our sample (sampling error), we will determine the minimum amount of data at the street level (e.g., number of photos per street) required to have measurements yielding the same results on repeated trials.

Research Question 1

Can safe streets be identified by night activity?

For each street segment i, we compute a *photo@night* score :

$$photo@night_i = \frac{n_i - \mu_n}{\sigma_n} - \frac{o_i - \mu_o}{\sigma_o},$$

where n_i (o_i) is the fraction of pictures taken at night (not at night) on street segment i; μ_m (μ_o) is the fraction of night (not night) pictures, averaged across all segments; and σ_n (σ_o) is the corresponding standard deviation. The resulting measurement is the z-score of the fraction of night pictures and accounts for the unbalances of pictures taken at night *vs.* day[4].

Having each street's score at hand, we can now correlate it with *safety from crime*. In so doing, we learn a strong positive correlation of $r = 0.60$: safe streets are photographed not only during the day but also at night, while unsafe ones mostly during the day. To further validate this statement, we group streets by their *photo@night* scores and test whether streets with higher scores are, on average, safer. By grouping streets into three bins, we find clear-cut evidence (Figure 5(a)): streets in the first bin (those photographed during the day) are far less safe (with a median fear of crime of 1.4) than streets in the last bin (those photographed mainly at night).

One might now wonder whether those results are observed only for Flickr-data-rich streets. To test that, we see how the previous correlation between safety and *photo@night* changes depending on the number of Flickr photos on each street. As one expects, it does change: the more photos, the higher the correlations. However, the amount of data needed to have a stable correlation is limited: aggregating all the streets with at least 30 photos results into stable correlations of $r > 0.6$ (Figure 5(b)). That number of photos is extremely low considering that the mean number of photos per street segment is 832, and the maximum goes up to 131K.

Research Question 2

Can safe streets be identified by activity segmented by gender or age?

For each street segment i, we compute a "manhood" score:

$$manhood_i = \frac{m_i - \mu_m}{\sigma_m} - \frac{f_i - \mu_f}{\sigma_f},$$

where m_i (f_i) is the fraction of male (female) users who have taken a picture on street segment i; μ_m (μ_f) is the fraction of male (female) users, averaged across all segments; and σ_m (σ_f) is the corresponding standard deviation. This is the z-score of the fraction of male users normalized to account for the unbalanced distribution of male and female users on Flickr.

By correlating manhood with safety (from crime), we find a positive correlation of $r = 0.58$, suggesting that safe streets tend to be visited by a predominantly male population. This parallels Alexander's suggestion that crime focuses on areas in which there are enough victims "to make it worth a thief's while" [1]. To further validate this finding, we group streets by their male scores and test whether streets with higher scores show, on average, higher safety. By binning streets into quartiles, that is exactly what we find (Figure 6(a)): streets in the lower quartile (those photographed more by females than males) are unsafer (with a median safety of 1.4) than streets in the last quartile (with a median of 4).

Our second hypothesized relationship for safety is that with dwellers' age. In our sample, users have a median age of 40 and are in the range [26,63] (Figure 2(a)). By averaging the age of users who took pictures on each street, we indeed find a positive correlation with safety ($r = 0.32$). The same correlation holds for median age.

To test whether those results are observed only for Flickr-data-rich streets, we see how the previous two correlations safety-manhood and safety-age change for streets that differ from the number of Flickr users they have. As one expects, the correlations do change (i.e., the more users, the higher the correlations) but it does not require many users to become stable: safety-manhood correlations become stable ($r > 0.5$) after collecting the gender of at least 380 users (Figure 6(b)), and safety-age ones become stable ($r > 0.3$) after collecting the age information for only 80 users (Figure 6(c)).

Research Question 3

Can safe streets be identified by the presence of specific types of places?

To determine the types of places on each street, we resort to Foursquare. We associate each place on Foursquare with the clos-

[4] On Flickr, pictures are taken more during the day than at night.

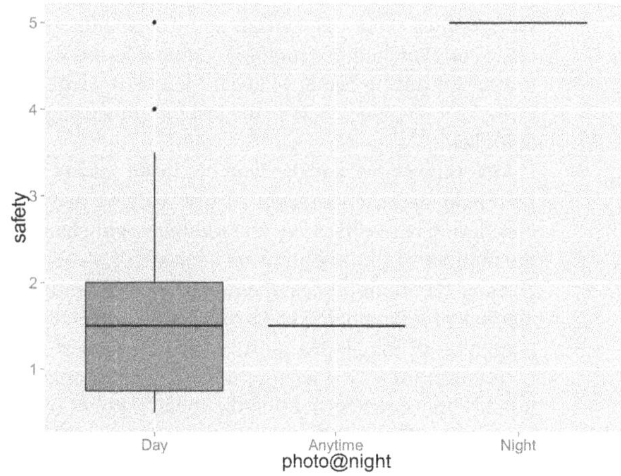

(a) Average street safety for street segments grouped by their *photo@night* scores in three bins. Safety increases for streets that are increasingly photographed at night. Whiskers represent the 2nd and 98th percentiles.

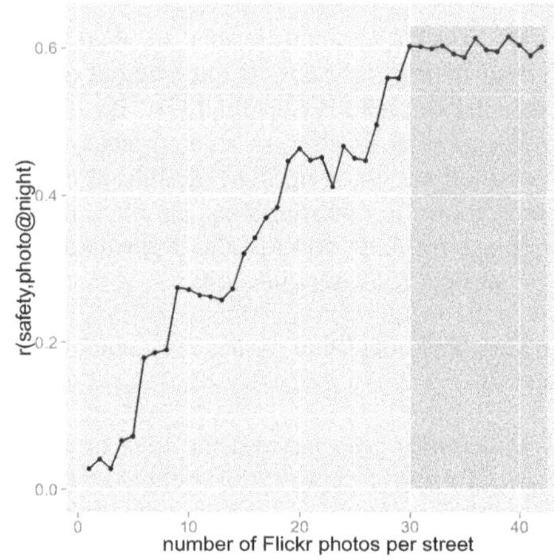

(b) Pearson correlation coefficient between street safety and *photo@night* as the number of photos on each segment increases. The shaded area indicates the number of photos per street segment after which the correlation becomes stable.

Figure 5: The digital life of safe streets: night activity. Safe streets tend to be photographed at night as well.

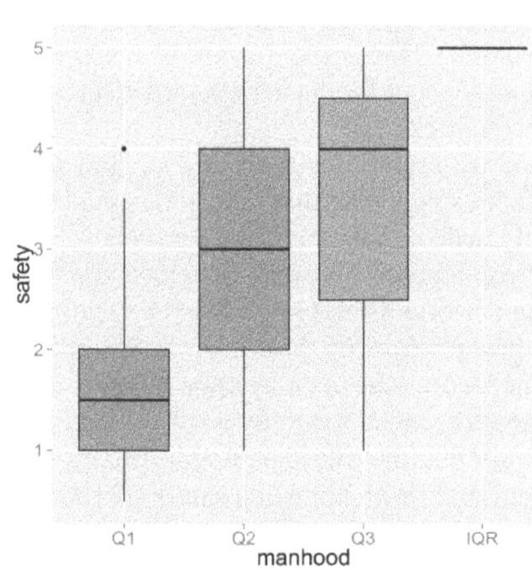

(a) Average safety score for street segments grouped by whether their manhood scores are in the lower quartile (Q1), second quartile (Q2), upper quartile (Q3), and interquartile range (IQR). Whiskers represent the 2nd and 98th percentiles

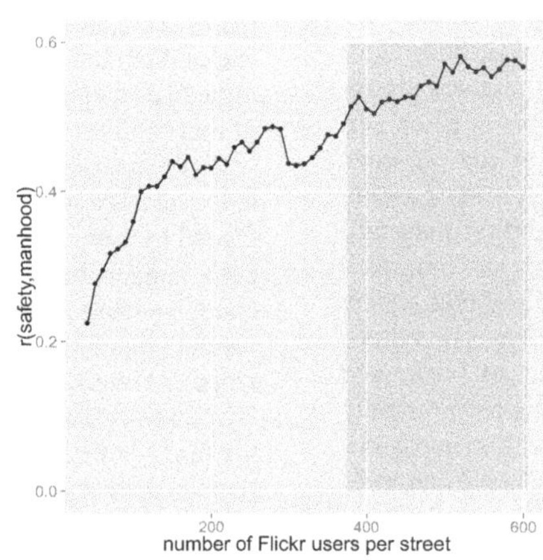

(b) Correlation coefficient r(safety, street's manhood) for segments of differing number of users. The shaded area indicates the number of users per street segment after which the correlation becomes stable.

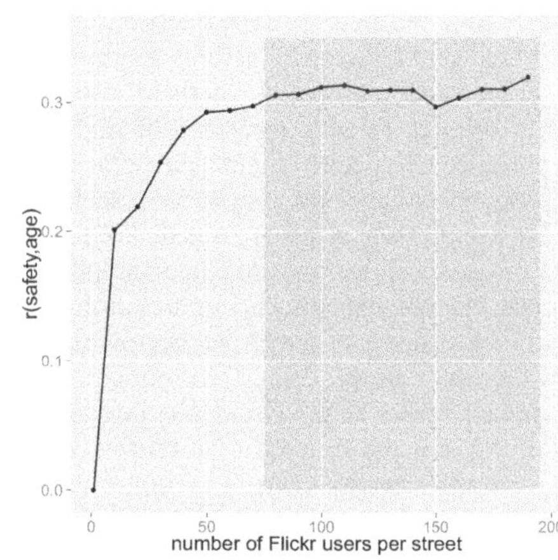

(c) Correlation coefficient r(safety, dwellers' average age) for segments of differing number of users. The shaded area indicates the number of users per street segment after which the correlation becomes stable.

Figure 6: The digital life of safe streets: gender and age. Safe streets tend to be increasingly photographed by men.

est street and categorize it using the first-level categories: arts, college, food, nightlife, outdoors, residential, shopping, and travel. We choose the first level to avoid data sparsity.

To test the extent to which safety is associated with the presence of specific places, we build the following linear model:

$$safety_i = \alpha + \beta_1 arts + \beta_2 college + \beta_3 food + \beta_4 nightlife + \\ +\beta_5 outdoors + \beta_6 residential + \beta_7 shopping, +\beta_8 travel + e,$$

to predict safety scores from the presence of first-level Foursquare categories. That is, a street's *predicted* safety score is computed from the fraction of places on it that fall into the different categories. It turns out that the regression shows an adjusted R^2 of 74%, suggesting that safety can be accurately predicted only from the presence of Foursquare venues. The corresponding beta coefficients (Table 1, column 3) suggest that safe streets tend to be associated with outdoor places (mainly parks), while unsafe ones with residential bits of central London that have no parks. This might appear surprising at first. However, further investigation shows that, in Central London, well-to-do residential areas are often associated with parks, while deprived areas are not. Therefore, this result

Predictive Variable	β (walkability)	β (safety)
Outdoors	1.701	16.543
Arts	6.303*	-13.036*
College	-4.812	13.820
Food	0.161	2.380
Nightlife	-8.947	-9.897*
Work	5.282*	8.731**
Residential	21.290**	-60.628
Shopping	-1.195	-0.370

Table 1: The predictive variables in the two linear models for walkability (column 2) and safety (column 3). Significance: ** $p < 0.001$, * $p < 0.01$, . $p < 0.05$.

can be explained by a strong interaction effect between residential streets and parks.

Research Question 4

Can walkable streets be identified by the presence of specific types of places?

Walkability and safety are related to each other. However, safe streets might not be necessarily walkable, and vice versa. In fact, the correlation between those two scores is as low as $r = 0.22$. Having answered the questions about safety, it is now interesting to explore those about walkability.

To test the extent to which walkability is associated with the presence of specific places, we regress a street's *predicted* walkability score with the fraction of places on it that fall into the different categories:

$$walkability_i = \alpha + \beta_1 arts + \beta_2 college + \beta_3 food + \beta_4 nightlife + \beta_5 outdoors + \beta_6 residential + \beta_7 shopping, + \beta_8 travel + e.$$

We find that the above model has an adjusted R^2 of 33%. That is, 33% of the variability of the walkability score can be explained only by the presence of specific Foursquare venues. The beta coefficients of the model are shown in Table 1 (column 2) and tell us that the presence of residential areas drives most of the predictive power of the regression.

Research Question 5

Can walkable streets be identified by walkability-related photo tags ?

To build the list of keywords associated with the concept of walkability, we hand-code relevant literature. We use the *Grounded Theory* approach [8], which is a systematic framework in the social sciences involving theory-driven content analysis that aims at identifying a set of words that best represent a certain concept. More specifically, we use *line-by-line* coding. This generates a set of words conceptually associated with walkability in three steps:

1. Collecting documents. The gold standard should cover the topic of walkability as comprehensively as possible. We collected a set of documents that fall into three categories: 1) recent news articles from online media; 2) academic papers; and 3) recent reports from public organizations or governments. This collection includes: 6 news articles, 8 academic papers, and 2 reports.

2. Annotating the documents. Three annotators coded the list of keywords. The annotators separately read each document line-by-line and highlighted any word they felt to be related to walkability. We then combined their annotations to generate two distinct lists: one *merges* the three sets of annotations, and the other *intersects* them.

3. Validating annotations. To quantitatively validate the two lists, we measure *agreement* among annotators defined as the ratio of the size of the merged word sets over the size of the intersected sets. The agreement is 84%, suggesting high agreements between the two lists.

High agreement emerges because the words that characterize walkability are quite well recognizable as such by different people, and therefore we can safely use them to identify photos related to the walkability concept. In our experiments, we adopt a very conservative approach and use the intersection list, which contains these terms: sidewalk, footway, street light, clean street, pedestrian, bench, resting, tree, greenery, art, architecture, historical, bike, private, hill, and social. One could informally see that those keywords indeed refer to the domain of walkability. However, those words by no means represent an exhaustive list and, as such, it is not clear whether we will observe any relationship between the presence of such keywords and walkability scores.

To balance those walkability tags (which mostly reflect positive associations), we create a list containing the tag 'car(s)'. That is because cars are often associated with poor walkability [1]. Having a single-term list might seem oversimplified. However, to appreciate the negative impact of cars on walkability, recall that for Jeff Speck's General Theory of Walkability, a walk has to satisfy four main conditions. It must be not only useful, comfortable, and interesting, but also safe [37]. By safe, he simply means that "the street has been designed to give pedestrians a fighting chance against being hit by automobiles." In later chapters, he adds: "Contrary to perceptions, the greatest threat to pedestrian safety is not crime, but the very real danger of automobiles moving quickly." In a similar way, Christopher Alexander notes: "Cars give people wonderful freedom and increase their opportunities. But they also destroy the environment, to an extent so drastic that they kill all social life." [1] The effect of cars on health and social life is well documented: higher traffic exposure results into more heart attacks [14], and hidden parking boosts retail sales, property values, appeal, and liveability [37, 44]. The entire aesthetic capital of a neighborhood can be squandered by the sole presence of cars [31].

Therefore, for each street segment i, we compute a z-transformed walkability score from Flickr tags:

$$z\text{-}walkability_i = \frac{w_i - \mu_w}{\sigma_w} - \frac{c_i - \mu_c}{\sigma_c},$$

where w_i (c_i) is the fraction of tags that match our walkability-related keywords (match 'car') on street segment i; μ_m (μ_o) is the fraction of tags that match our walkability-related keywords (match 'car'), averaged across all segments; and σ_w (σ_c) is the corresponding standard deviation.

Having those z-transformed scores, we can now correlate them with *walkability* (Figure 7(a)). We find strong correlations between walkability and presence of tags mentioning cars: the correlation with c_i is as high as -0.78. Given that the matching is done on a single term, this effect size is unexpectedly high, yet it speaks to the devastating effect of cars on walkability. As one expects, there is a positive correlation with the walkability-related tags (i.e., the correlation with w_i is 0.49). By then combining those two lists with the formula above, we obtain a correlation with $z\text{-}walkability_i$ of 0.89.

However, those correlations might hold only for data-rich streets. By binning streets whose number of tags fall into the same range together, we find that the correlation between walkability score and $z\text{-}walkability_i$ increases with the number of tags per segment and

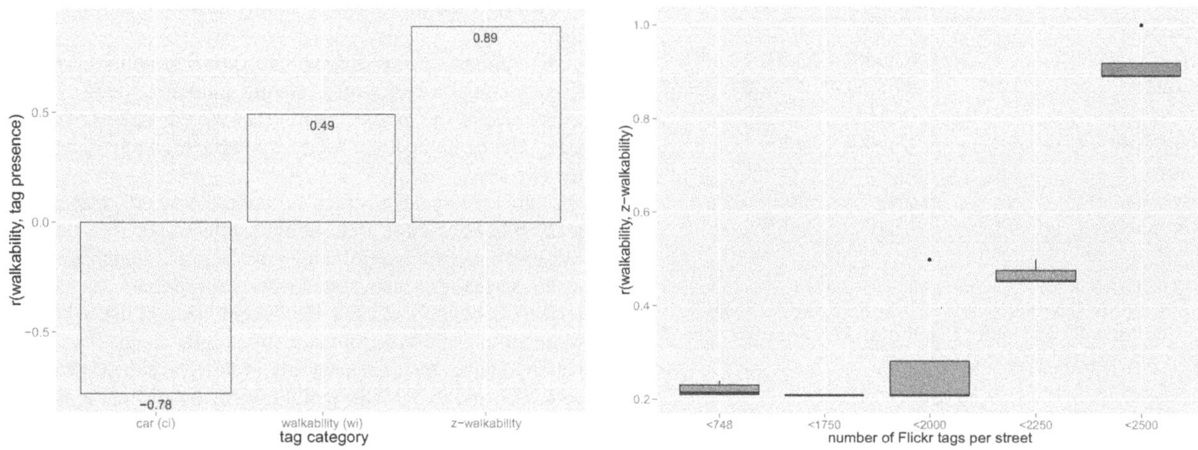

(a) Pearson correlations between walkability scores and presence of car tags (1st bar), of walkability tags (2nd bar), and of z-transformed combination of both (3rd bar).

(b) Pearson correlation coefficients between walkability scores and z-transformed presence of *walkability tags* for increasing number of photos per segment. Whiskers represent the 2nd and 98th percentiles.

Figure 7: The digital life of walkable streets. Walkable streets can be identified by the presence of walkability-related picture tags (panel *(a)*), but such an identification needs at least 2.2K tags per street segment (panel *(b)*).

tends to become stable ($r > 0.85$) after collecting at least 2500 tags per street (Figure 7(b)). This translates into a considerable number of pictures required for attaining a reasonable prediction accuracy (of the order of hundreds). That is likely because matching our keywords with Flickr tags yield sparse results. To partly fix that, in the future, one could either enrich our list of keywords or use unsupervised techniques to learn the statistical associations of Flickr tags with walkability score.

7. DISCUSSION

After successfully extracting social media metrics that reflect the walkability of physical streets, we now discuss a few open questions.

Practical Implications

We foresee many opportunities to practically apply walkability modeling, including:

Room booking. When tourists choose a place to stay, a system could make educated guesses about which places are walkable, and which are not. Walkability score might be a good indicator of whether they need to rent a car, for example.

Urban route recommendations. In the near future, new way-finding tools might well suggest not only shortest routes but also short ones that are pleasant and walkable [33]. However, the data needed by those tools is available only for a limited number of cities and, when available, is static. By contrast, our proposal allows for timely recommendations of routes at scale.

Real-estate. The use of walkability sites by real-estate agencies continues to grow [37]. With such a demand, many municipalities are under pressure to collect relevant data and make it easily accessible. For cash-strapped municipalities, it is usually difficult to obtain suitable data for computing walkability, owing to the high time, effort, and financial costs. Being based on social media mining, our approach promises to predict walkability scores at far lower cost.

Theoretical Implications

One contribution of this work to existing theory is the study of walkability dimensions as manifested in Flickr and Foursquare. As a result, we have ascertained the reliability of such sites for studying walkability. That is important, not least because it suggests that social media might offer unprecedented opportunities for theory. With real-time and fine-grained data, can we measure new indicators concerning walkability for which we have had no data (e.g., lifestyles and interests of individual street dwellers)?

Limitations

Our approach is not able to profile areas that have little Flickr activity[5]. Yet, it has two main advantages over the current state of the art: it adapts with time (unlike results from manual data collection efforts, that are costly to update), and it establishes smart defaults for places for which no census data is available. In the future, to design a system that works in a broader range of situations, one could augment our model with street design features, which have to be collected only once in while as they do not tend to massively change over time.

8. CONCLUSION

Our analysis has demonstrated that the relationship between behavioral features and walkability does not only hold in the offline world but also holds in the online world. This provides evidence that users' offline communities have a noticeable effect on their online interactions. To appreciate the importance of this insight, consider the relationship between the types of streets people experience in their cities and the social media content they generate while being on those streets. We have tested this relationship for the first time and found that, indeed, Flickr uploads from dwellers

[5]For Foursquare, activity is not required as the mere presence of venues suffice.

of walkable streets differ from those of unwalkable ones, mainly in terms of upload time and tagging.

More broadly, our results suggest that it is possible to effectively profile the walkability of city streets from their dwellers' social media posts in an unobtrusive way. Many opportunities open up from here for designers and researchers alike. Mobile app designers, for example, may create new recommendation services that combine walkability predictions with traditional mapping tools. On the other hand, comforted by our validation work, urban researchers might well be enticed to use social media to answer theoretical questions that could not have been tackled before because of lack of data.

9. ACKNOWLEDGMENTS

We thank Elizabeth Daly for her timely feedbacks on the manuscript.

10. REFERENCES

[1] C. Alexander, S. Ishikawa, and M. Silverstein. *A Pattern Language: Towns, Buildings, Constructions*. Oxford University Press, 1977.

[2] S. Angel. The Ecology of Night Life. *Center for Environmental Structure, Berkeley*, 1968.

[3] S. Ball. *Livable Communities for Aging Populations: Urban Design for Longevity*. Wiley, 2012.

[4] F. Bentley, H. Cramer, W. Hamilton, and S. Basapur. Drawing the city: differing perceptions of the urban environment. In *Proceedings of ACM Conference on Human Factors in Computing Systems (CHI)*, 2012.

[5] L. K. Brennan Ramirez. Indicators of Activity-Friendly Communities. *American Journal of Preventive Medicine*, 2006.

[6] Ceccato, V. *The Urban Fabric of Crime and Fear*. Springer, 2012.

[7] Z. Cheng, J. Caverlee, and K. Lee. Exploring millions of footprints in location sharing services. In *Proceedings of the AAAI International Conference on Webblogs and Social Media (ICWSM)*, 2011.

[8] J. M. Corbin. *Basics of Qualitative Research: Techniques and Procedures for Developing Grounded Theory*. Sage, 2008.

[9] J. Cortright. Walking the Walk: How Walkability Raises Home Values in U.S. Cities. *CEOs for Cities*, 2009.

[10] H. Cramer, M. Rost, and L. E. Holmquist. Performing a check-in: emerging practices, norms and 'conflicts' in location-sharing using foursquare. In *Proceedings of ACM Conference on Human Computer Interaction with Mobile Devices and Services (MobileHCI)*, 2011.

[11] D. J. Crandall, L. Backstrom, D. Huttenlocher, and J. Kleinberg. Mapping the world's photos. In *Proceedings of ACM Conference on World Wide Web (WWW)* , 2009.

[12] J. Cranshaw, R. Schwartz, J. Hong, and N. Sadeh. The Livehoods Project: Utilizing Social Media to Understand the Dynamics of a City. In *International AAAI Conference on Weblogs and Social Media (ICWSM)*, 2012.

[13] J. Cranshaw, R. Schwartz, J. I. Hong, and N. Sadeh. The Livehoods Project: utilizing social media to understand the dynamics of a city. In *Proc. of ICWSM*. AAAI, 2012.

[14] J. M. S. Diane R. Gold. Air Pollution, Climate, and Heart Disease. *Circulation*, 2013.

[15] N. Eagle, M. Macy, and R. Claxton. Network diversity and economic development. *Science*, 328:1029–1031, 2010.

[16] C. D. Elvidge, K. E. Baugh, E. A. Kihn, H. W. Kroehl, and E. R. Davis. Mapping city lights with nighttime data from the DMSP Operational Linescan System. *Photogrammetric engineering and Remote Sensing*, 1997.

[17] C. D. Elvidge, M. L. Imhoff, K. E. Baugh, V. R. Hobson, I. Nelsonc, J. Safran, J. B. Dietz, and B. T. Tuttle. Night-time lights of the world: 1994-1995. *Photogrammetry and Remote Sensing*, 2001.

[18] K. Hess. *Introduction to Private Security*. Cengage Learning, 2008.

[19] A. Jacobs. *Great Streets*. MIT Press, 1993.

[20] J. Jacobs. *The Death and Life of Great American Cities*. Random House, 1961.

[21] A. D. Kramer. An Unobtrusive Behavioral Model of "Gross National Happiness". In *Proceedings of ACM Conference on Human Factors in Computing Systems (CHI)*, 2010.

[22] M. Lad. English indices of deprivation 2010. Technical report, Department for Communities and Local Government, 2011.

[23] Lee, R.E. and McAlexander, K. and Banda, J. *Reversing the Obesogenic Environment*. Human Kinetics, 2011.

[24] C. B. Leinberger. Now Coveted: A Walkable, Convenient Place. *New York Times*, 2012.

[25] J. Lindqvist, J. Cranshaw, J. Wiese, J. Hong, and J. Zimmerman. I'm the mayor of my house: examining why people use foursquare - a social-driven location sharing application. In *Proceedings of ACM Conference on Human Factors in Computing Systems (CHI)*, 2011.

[26] K. Lynch. *The Image of the City*. Urban Studies. MIT Press, 1960.

[27] H. Mao, X. Shuai, Y. Y. Ahn, and J. Bollen. Mobile communications reveal the regional economy in Cote d'Ivoire. In *Proc. of NetMob*, 2013.

[28] R. Methorst, H. Monterde, R. Risser, D. Sauter, M. Tight, and J. Walker. Pedestrians' Quality Needs. *European Cooperation in Science and Technology (COST)*, 2010.

[29] A. Noulas, S. Scellato, R. Lambiotte, M. Pontil, and C. Mascolo. A Tale of Many Cities: Universal Patterns in Human Urban Mobility. *PLoS ONE*, 2012.

[30] D. Quercia, J. Ellis, L. Capra, and J. Crowcroft. Tracking Gross Community Happiness from Tweets. In *Proc. of ACM Conference on Computer Supported Cooperative Work (CSCW)*, 2012.

[31] D. Quercia, N. Ohare, and H. Cramer. Aesthetic Capital: What Makes London Look Beautiful, Quiet, and Happy? In *Proc. of ACM Conference on Computer Supported Cooperative Work (CSCW)*, 2014.

[32] D. Quercia, J. P. Pesce, V. Almeida, and J. Crowcroft. Psychological Maps 2.0: A web gamification enterprise starting in London. In *Proceedings of ACM Conference on World Wide Web (WWW)* , 2013.

[33] D. Quercia, R. Schifanella, and L. M. Aiello. The Shortest Path to Happiness: Recommending Beautiful, Quiet, and Happy Routes in the City. In *Proceedings of the 25th ACM Conference on Hypertext and Social Media (HT)*, 2014.

[34] D. Quercia, D. O. Séaghdha, and J. Crowcroft. Talk of the city: our tweets, our community happiness. In *Proc. of International AAAI Conference on Weblogs and Social Media (ICWSM)*. AAAI, 2012.

[35] R. J. Sampson. When Things Aren't What They Seem: Context and Cognition in Appearance-Based Regulation. *Harvard Law Review Forum*, May 2012.

[36] C. Smith, D. Quercia, and L. Capra. Finger on the pulse: identifying deprivation using transit flow analysis. In *Proc. of ACM ACM Conference on Computer Supported Cooperative Work (CSCW)*, pages 683–692, 2013.

[37] J. Speck. *Walkable City: How Downtown Can Save America, One Step at a Time*. Farrar, Straus and Giroux, 2012.

[38] Steer Davies Gleave. Legible London. *TfL Research Report*, 2014.

[39] B. Thomee, J. G. Moreno, and D. A. Shamma. Whose Time Is It Anyway? Investigating the Accuracy of Camera Timestamps. In *Proceedings of ACM Conference on Multimedia (MM)*, 2014.

[40] Transport for London. Attitudes towards Walking. *TfL Research Report*, March 2012.

[41] M. Traunmueller, G. Quattrone, and L. Capra. Mining Mobile Phone Data to Investigate Urban Crime Theories at Scale. In 6th *International Social Computing Conference (SocInfo)*, 2014.

[42] UK Department for Transport. Road accidents and safety statistics. Technical report, 2013.

[43] US Geological Survey. Shuttle Radar Topography Mission. 2010.

[44] J. S. Yan Song. Valuing spatial accessibility to retailing. *Journal of Retailing and Consumer Services*, 2007.

[45] V. Zambaldi, J. P. Pesce, D. Quercia, and V. Almeida. Lightweight Contextual Ranking of City Pictures: Urban Sociology to the Rescue. In *International AAAI Conference on Weblogs and Social Media (ICWSM)*, 2014.

Beyond Models: Forecasting Complex Network Processes Directly from Data

Bruno Ribeiro
Carnegie Mellon University
Pittsburgh, PA, USA
ribeiro@cs.cmu.edu

Minh X. Hoang
University of California,
Santa Barbara, CA, USA
mhoang@cs.ucsb.edu

Ambuj K. Singh
University of California,
Santa Barbara, CA, USA
ambuj@cs.ucsb.edu

ABSTRACT

Complex network phenomena – such as information cascades in online social networks – are hard to fully observe, model, and forecast. In forecasting, a recent trend has been to forgo the use of parsimonious models in favor of models with increasingly large degrees of freedom that are trained to learn the behavior of a process from historical data. Extrapolating this trend into the future, eventually we would renounce models all together. *But is it possible to forecast the evolution of a complex stochastic process directly from the data without a model?* In this work we show that model-free forecasting is possible. We present SED, an algorithm that forecasts process statistics based on relationships of statistical equivalence using two general axioms and historical data. To the best of our knowledge, SED is the first method that can perform axiomatic, model-free forecasts of complex stochastic processes. Our simulations using simple and complex evolving processes and tests performed on a large real-world dataset show promising results.

Categories and Subject Descriptors

H.2.8 [**Database Management**]: Database applications—*Data mining*

General Terms

Algorithms; Measurement

Keywords

Model-free Forecasting; Cascade Forecast

1. INTRODUCTION

Complex networked processes – such as information cascades and the spread of influence and viruses over online social networks – are hard to fully observe, model, and forecast. Self-reinforcing and latent effects can drive random and deterministic amplifications that are hard to predict without aggregate, large-population models. For instance, the way people react to social and monetary incentives can affect how information cascades spread over online social networks [12]; individuals also have evolving social interests [19, 24].

In our work we focus on forecasting statistics of complex network processes, such as the distribution of sizes of an epidemic process over a network. Recently, the availability of large-sample historical data – that details the evolution of similar processes in the past – has started a trend of forgoing parsimonious models in favor of models with increasingly large degrees of freedom that are trained over this historical data; these include latent Markovian infection models [24], auto-regressive models [20, 21], distance-based models for time series [14, 37], and classification-based approaches such as logistic regression [4] and naïve Bayes classifiers [13]. Hidden Markov models have also been proposed to replace parsimonious population models in ecology research [26].

Extrapolating this trend into the future, eventually we could renounce models all together. But is this possible? That is, *can we forecast statistics of complex network processes directly from the data without the help of models?* Such forecasting algorithm would be the *ultimate data-driven method.*

Contributions

In this work, we propose SED (Statistical Equivalence Digraph algorithm), an algorithm to forecast statistics of complex networked processes using general axioms that do not entail a model. Our algorithm works by extracting statistical information contained in the historical data through two axioms that define relationships of statistical equivalence between stochastic processes. To the best of our knowledge, our algorithm is the first that can perform (true) model-free forecast of network processes. Using simulation results and also a large real-world dataset, we show that SED is able to accurately forecast a variety of metrics under complex scenarios. We also show that accurate unbiased forecasting is limited to time horizons less than twice of that of the training data for a class of seemly simple infection processes. This proof further motivates our quest for forecasting directly from the data.

An important property of SED is its ability to adjust predictions according to the amount of evidence. Consider forecasting the distribution of sizes of hashtag cascades #A and #B on Twitter:

- We observe 20 hashtag seeds[1] of #A: ten seeds get cascades of size one and ten get cascades of size at least ten.

[1]Seeds are network nodes that are infected independently from other already infected nodes.

WWW 2015, May 18–22, 2015, Florence, Italy.
ACM 978-1-4503-3469-3/15/05.
http://dx.doi.org/10.1145/2736277.2741677.

- We also observe two seeds of #B generating cascades of size one and of size greater than ten, respectively.

Should we make the same forecast for #A and #B? As #B has less samples than #A we are more uncertain about #B's behavior. The lack of evidence prompts SED to assign greater uncertainty when forecasting metrics of #B, automatically adjusting forecasts to the amount of evidence.

Outline

Section 2 provides some definitions used throughout the paper. Section 3 explains the SED algorithm using the prediction of cascade statistics as an example. Section 4 presents the theory behind our approach. Section 5 tests the accuracy of SED using simulated data and shows an application of SED to forecast complex cascades over a large online social network dataset. Finally, Section 6 discusses the related work and Section 7 presents our conclusions.

2. DEFINITIONS

We first give a few definitions used throughout this work. In this paper we also often simplify our exposition by describing what are really general stochastic processes as an infection process on a network, a.k.a., a *cascade process.*

DEFINITION 2.1. *[Cascade Process] $\Psi^{(i)} \in \Omega$ is a cascade process with ID i, $i = 1, \ldots, |\Omega|$. For each cascade process $\Psi^{(i)} \in \Omega$ we observe a set of sample paths. The random variable $X^{(i)}_{\Delta t}$ is a measure over the sample paths of $\Psi^{(i)}$ over relative time interval $[0, \Delta t]$, where time zero is the time relative to the beginning of the cascade process. For instance, $X^{(i)}_{\Delta t}$ may be a random variable that gives the size of a cascade of $\Psi^{(i)}$ over time window $[0, \Delta t]$.*

The definition of $X^{(i)}_{\Delta t}$ allows us to be conservative and "mistakenly" merge two or more independent cascades of process $\Psi^{(i)}$ into a single larger cascade. This property is particularly useful when there is ambiguity to which independent cascade seed is responsible to infect a set of nodes.

DEFINITION 2.2. *[Forecasting] The process to forecast $\Psi^{(0)}$, has k_0 observations $x^{(0,1)}_{\Delta t_1}, \ldots, x^{(0,k_0)}_{\Delta t_1} \sim X^{(0)}_{\Delta t_1}$ over time window $[0, \Delta t_1]$, $\Delta t_1 > 0$, where time zero represents the time that the process starts. A forecast is an estimate of an statistic of $X^{(0)}_{\Delta t_2}$ where $\Delta t_2 > \Delta t_1$. A forecast assumes that all processes in Ω have been observed for at least Δt_2 time.*

For instance, ifΨ $^{(0)}$ is a viral marketing campaign we may want to forecast, using the observations of the first day of the campaign, what will be the average number of infected nodes per infected seed after a week, a statistic that predicts the performance of the campaign in the first week per user exposure.

DEFINITION 2.3. *[Historical Data] The historical data of process $\Psi^{(i)}$, $i = 0, \ldots,$ defined as $\mathcal{X}^{(i)}_{\Delta t} = \{x^{(i,1)}_{\Delta t}, \ldots, x^{(i,k_i)}_{\Delta t} \sim X^{(i)}_{\Delta t}\}$, is the set of all available observations of process $\Psi^{(i)}$ over time interval length Δt.*

In what follows we illustrate the SED algorithm. The theory behind the algorithm is explained in Section 4.

3. ALGORITHM

In this section, we present the SED Algorithm. Here we focus on the "how-to" solution. Our description of SED focuses on cascade processes to simplify our exposition; the algorithm for general networked processes is presented in Section 4, along with the justifications and the theory behind SED.

Algorithm 1 The SED Algorithm

Input: Historical data $\mathcal{X}^{(i)}_{\Delta t}$, $i = 1, \ldots, |\Omega|$, $\Delta t = \Delta t_1, \Delta t_2$ and $\mathcal{X}^{(0)}_{\Delta t_1}$;
α: Probability amplifier parameter;
n: Bootstrap resample size;
m: Number of bootstrap resamples;
Stat: Statistic of interest of $X^{(0)}_{\Delta t_2}$.

Output: Set of predicted observations of Stat($X^{(0)}_{\Delta t_2}$)

1: **for** $i := 0$ to $|\Omega|$ **do**
2: $\quad p_i \Leftarrow \frac{\sum_{j=0, j\neq i}^{|\Omega|} P_{\text{Kuiper}}(\mathcal{X}^{(i)}_{\Delta t_1}, \mathcal{X}^{(j)}_{\Delta t_1})}{|\Omega|}$
3: $\quad w(i \rhd 0) \Leftarrow \frac{P_{\text{Kuiper}}(\mathcal{X}^{(i)}_{\Delta t_1}, \mathcal{X}^{(0)}_{\Delta t_1})}{p_i}$
4: **end for**
5: $\vec{W} \Leftarrow [w(1 \rhd 0)^\alpha, ..., w(|\Omega| \rhd 0)^\alpha]$
6: $\vec{W} \Leftarrow \frac{1}{\|\vec{W}\|_1} \vec{W}$
7: $\hat{Y} \Leftarrow [\,]$
8: **for** $j = 1$ to m **do**
9: $\quad$ Sample i with probability $\vec{W}_i$, $i \in \{1, \ldots, |\Omega|\}$.
10: $\quad \hat{\mathcal{X}}^{(0)}_{\Delta t_2} \Leftarrow$ BoostrapSampling(src $= \mathcal{X}^{(i)}_{\Delta t_2}$, size $= n$)
11: $\quad \hat{Y}[j] \Leftarrow \text{Stat}(\hat{\mathcal{X}}^{(0)}_{\Delta t_2})$
12: **end for**
13: **return** $\hat{Y}$

The SED algorithm (Algorithm 1) takes as input the set of observations of each processΨ $^{(i)}$, over time interval lengths $\Delta t_1 > 0$ andΔ $t_2 > \Delta t_1$ for $i = 1, \ldots, |\Omega|$ and over interval lengthΔ t_1 for the process we want to forecast $i = 0$. The goal is to forecast a statistic ofΨ $^{(0)}$ over time interval length Δt_2. The algorithm also requires a parameter α that later we describe how to automatically optimize. For now it is enough to know that a large value of α indicates that the process to forecast behaves like an outlier in our dataset. Two other parameters are related to bootstrap sampling, n and m, where $n = m = 100$ should suffice for most applications but larger values always give more accurate results. The final input is the statistic we wish to forecast.

Step 2 of Algorithm 1 applies a two-sample Kuiper's test [16] to get the probabilities that the observations of two processes i and j, $i \neq j$, come from the same underlying distribution. Step 3 of Algorithm 1 computes the equivalence score $w(i \rhd 0)$ between processΨ $^{(i)}$ and the process to forecast $\Psi^{(0)}$. We call this equivalence score the *Equivalence Odds Ratio* (EOR), described in details in Section. 4.

With the EOR computed we build a weight vector $\vec{W}$ at step 5 of Algorithm 1, and normalize it using its $L1$-norm at step 6. The probability amplifier α (step 5) is a real number that is chosen automatically by another algorithm that we describe later. The next steps (9-11) forecast the statistic of interest using a two-step bootstrapping process with m and n resamples. These statistics may include, but are not limited to, the Complementary Cumulative Distribution Function (CCDF), mean, standard deviation and second moment of cascade sizes. We start by randomly sampling a process index i according to the weight in $\vec{W}$ (step 9). At step 10 we perform bootstrap sampling from the long-term observation $\mathcal{X}^{(i)}_{\Delta t_2}$ to obtain an estimate of the bootstrap resample of $\mathcal{X}^{(0)}_{\Delta t_2}$, where $|\hat{\mathcal{X}}^{(0)}_{\Delta t_2}| = n$. Finally, the statistics of the estimated $\hat{\mathcal{X}}^{(0)}_{\Delta t_2}$, e.g., the mean of $\hat{\mathcal{X}}^{(0)}_{\Delta t_2}$, are computed and stored in the vector $\hat{Y}$ (step 11). By repeating steps 9 to 11 m times we obtain the bootstrapped statistics, which provide the forecast of the statistic of interest over $X^{(0)}_{\Delta t_2}$.

3.1 Choosing Amplifier α and Sample Size n

To complete the algorithm, we also need to choose the amplification factor α and the sample size n. Larger values of n make the forecast more accurate, thus n is only limited by computational constraints. In our forecasts, however, we would like to compare our prediction with the ground truth of $X^{(0)}_{\Delta t_2}$, thus, we set $n = |X^{(0)}_{\Delta t_2}|$ to make the comparison easy. Finally, we determine α heuristically by minimizing the squared error in SED's prediction of the value of $\text{Stat}(X^{(0)}_{\Delta t_1})$, which we can easily get an estimate with $\text{Stat}(\mathcal{H}^{(0)}_{\Delta t_1})$.

4. THEORY

The framework of classical statistics, as developed by pioneers like R.A. Fisher [6], describes stochastic processes using models as building blocks. For instance, a process can be a Galton-Watson process, Markovian, auto-regressive, or a hierarchical combination of processes and non-parametric distributions. In 1933 Kolmogorov [15] laid the modern axiomatic foundations of probability theory that eliminated the necessity of models, although models are still useful in Kolmogorov's framework. To the best of our knowledge, our SED method is the first method able to perform forecasting using axioms rather than models.

Roadmap: In what follows (Section 4.1) we detail our axiomatic forecast framework and our SED method. Section 4.2 takes an in-depth look at the problem providing forecast accuracy bounds for a class of stochastic processes, proving that in some scenarios even for the best model cannot make accurate long-term forecasts of seemly simple processes.

4.1 SED: Axiomatic Forecasting

In what follows, we describe our SED method. SED performs forecasts using the following two axioms in lieu of a model. For the sake of conciseness and clarity, the definition of dynamic networked processes is given later in the text in Definition 4.1.

AXIOM 4.1. *The state of any dynamic networked process is unique at any time $t \geq 0$.*

Axiom 4.1 guarantees that at any given time t there is no ambiguity about the true state of the process, even if this true state is not observable.

AXIOM 4.2. *Let Ω be a set of processes with historical data and let $\Psi^{(0)}$ be the process that we wish to forecast. Each process $\Psi' \in \Omega$, where $\Omega' = \Omega \cup \{\Psi^{(0)}\}$, with the exception of at most one process, is equivalent to one and only one other process in Ω' besides itself according to a measure $\lambda : \mathcal{S} \to \mathbb{R}$, where $\mathcal{S}$ is the appropriate σ-algebra.*

Note that Axioms 4.1 and 4.2 do not entail a model. To illustrate the use of Axiom 4.2 in our method consider the following example.Ω' is the set of epidemic processes over the same graph $G = (V, E)$. We wish to forecast another epidemic$\Psi^{(0)}$ using multiple independent sample paths of the processes inΩ'. Let $\lambda(\sigma)$ as defined in Axiom 4.2 count the number of infected nodes in a sample path $\sigma \in \mathcal{S}$. The example also works if λ is another non-trivial metric, such as the cumulative number of infected nodes, the Wiener index, the reproduction number at time $t > 0$. Axiom 4.2 guarantees that the set of all observed infection processes Ω' is such that for any process$\Psi' \in \Omega'$ there is one and only one other process$\Psi'' \in \Omega'$ for which the distribution of the number of infected nodes is exactly the same.

Unless stated otherwise in what follows we simplify our exposition assuming thatΩ' has an even number of elements. Our method also can be readily extended to support $\lambda : \mathcal{S} \to \mathbb{R}^n$, $n > 1$, to incorporate complex features of the process. As we see later, the scenario with $n > 1$ requires the use of kernel two-sample tests [10] for the forecast. In what follows we consider $\lambda : \mathcal{S} \to \mathbb{R}$ unless stated otherwise.

Intuition: Axiom 4.2 goes at the heart of what it means to forecast the evolution of a process using historical data. We can only predict the future if, somehow, the present mimics what has happened in the past. When aided by models, there is a notion of behavior distance (e.g. likelihood function), which helps us find which processes in the past look similar to the process we are trying to forecast and use them to predict the future. Because models often have trouble assigning measures of similarity between two significantly different processes, many modern methods only consider "close enough distances", creating a manifold that is then used in the forecast. One of the challenges in manifold learning is determining a close enough distance where the model empirically works without being fooled by the data. Axiom 4.2 makes this distance precisely zero, which brings some advantages. First, the forecast does not need to learn parameters, often a computationally intensive task. Second, in a complex scenario it is probably better to state ignorance about process behavior than being very wrong. Network processes can be hard to forecast. In Section 4.2 we show that the statistical information used in the forecast of a seemly simple process cannot be extrapolated by models beyond the time horizon of the dataset (Δt_2).

Choice of λ: The measure λ can be thought of as a "fingerprint" of process behavior. With a bad choice of λ, too many "unrelated" processes have similar (but not equivalent) statistics, which in turn makes it hard to empirically distinguish them. In these cases SED assigns similar weights to most processes, and forecasting is performed conservatively (large confidence intervals). If the process to forecast has too few observations, SED also acts conservatively to reflect the uncertainty in the limited number of observations.

Violating Axiom 4.2: If no process in the historical data is equivalent to the process we wish to forecast (a reality in some scenarios), then one of two things can happen. If the process to forecast and most processes in the historical data have similar processes but not an equal process, then Axiom 4.2 provides a robust metric of process similarity. It is robust because it does not assume how processes behave and cannot be fooled by data. This shows well in our experiments with a real dataset. If most processes in the historical data are equal and the process to forecast is an outlier, SED will forecast in an uninformative way with large confidence intervals. This outlier status is easy to spot and stating the lack of confidence in the prediction is highly desirable.

Formal Definitions: In what follows, we use Random Marked Point Processes (RMPP) to formalize the networked process. Note that RMPPs allow us to avoid describing how the process evolves and, thus, no model is described. Let $G = (V, E)$ be a directed graph with node set V and edge set $E \subseteq V \times V$. Let $\mathcal{L}_V$ and $\mathcal{L}_E$ denote an arbitrary set of node and edge labels that will be used to define the state of the process at any time. As an example, in an epidemic process $\mathcal{L}_V = \{\text{infected}, \text{susceptible}\}$ and $\mathcal{L}_E = \emptyset$. The following generalization takes into account the complexity of real-world cascading processes.

DEFINITION 4.1. *[Cascade Process] Let $Z_k^{(i)} \subseteq V \times \mathcal{L}_V \times E \times \mathcal{L}_E$ denote the state of the i-th process after $k > 0$ events. Let $W_k^{(i)} > 0$ be the time between the k-th and the k + 1-st events. A dynamic networked process $\Psi^{(i)}$ is a simple Random Marked Point Process (RMPP) $\Psi^{(i)} = \{(Z_k^{(i)}, W_k^{(i)})\}_{k \in \mathbb{Z}^\star}$ operating over $V \times \mathcal{L}_V \times E \times \mathcal{L}_E$, where $\mathbb{Z}^\star$ is the set of non-negative integers. By convention,*

$$0 = T_0^{(i)} < T_1^{(i)} < \cdots$$

are the successive times at which the process evolves with $W_k^{(i)} := T_{k+1}^{(i)} - T_k^{(i)}$, $k \geq 0$.

Note that the dynamic networked process *need not follow the edges* of G. RMPPs are versatile stochastic models that allow arbitrary spatial and temporal correlations in process evolution. Also note that in real life we only have a finite number of realizations of the processes and, thus, we may not be able to distinguish some of them. In what follows, we define the measure λ precisely and introduce the notion of λ-stochastic equivalence.

DEFINITION 4.2 (λ-STOCHASTIC EQUIVALENCE). *We define two stochastic processes $\Psi^{(a)}$ and $\Psi^{(b)}$ as equivalent according to a Lebesgue measure $\lambda : \mathcal{S} \to \mathbb{R}$ at time window $[0, \Delta t]$, $\Delta t \in (0, \infty)$, if $X_{\Delta t}^{(a)} \stackrel{d}{=} X_{\Delta t}^{(b)}$, where $X_{\Delta t}^{(k)} \equiv \lambda(\sigma_k^{(\Delta t)})$ is a random variable, $\sigma_k = \{(Z_i^{(k)}, W_i^{(k)}) : 0 \leq T_i^{(k)} \leq \Delta t\}$ is a sample path of the stochastic process $\Psi^{(k)}$, $k \in \{a, b\}$, $\mathcal{S}$ is the appropriate σ-algebra, and the operator $\stackrel{d}{=}$ defines the random variables are equal in distribution.*

In what follows, we use Axioms 4.1 and 4.2 and the definition of λ-stochastic equivalence to build an equivalence digraph representing the equivalence relationships between all processes in Ω'.

4.1.1 Stochastic Equivalence Digraph

Axioms 4.1 and 4.2 state that the cascade process $\Psi \in \Omega'$ – e.g., the process of spreading a Twitter hashtagover the Twitter network – has one and only one λ-stochastic equivalent process $\Psi' \in \Omega'$. To create our forecast, all we need to do is to identify this process. This idea yields a simple statement wherein lies the answer to our practical forecasting problem:

THEOREM 4.1. *Any two-sample hypothesis test can be used to determine whether two processes $\Psi^{(i)}, \Psi^{(j)} \in \Omega'$ are λ-stochastic equivalent at time interval $\Delta t > 0$.*

PROOF. Axiom 4.1 states that sample paths are simple and thus admit a stochastic equivalence measure λ. From Axiom 4.2, we know that all processes in Ω' have a λ-stochastic equivalent process (except at most one process if $|\Omega'|$ is odd). The set of sample paths of $\Psi^{(i)}$ and $\Psi^{(j)}$ entail a set of independent observations of $X_{\Delta t}^{(i)}$ and $X_{\Delta t}^{(i)}$). Thus, λ-stochastic equivalence yields $X_{\Delta t}^{(i)} \stackrel{d}{=} X_{\Delta t}^{(i)}$. A two-sample hypothesis test assesses whether independent observations of the random variables $X_{\Delta t}^{(i)}$ and $X_{\Delta t}^{(i)}$ are drawings of the same underlying distribution. Hence, a two-sample hypothesis test is a tool to determine whether $\Psi^{(i)}$ and $\Psi^{(j)}$ are λ-stochastic equivalent at time $\Delta t > 0$. □

Interestingly, a test with low statistical power forces us to make conservative forecasts with large confidence intervals. The forecast uncertainty reflects the lack of statistical information. In such case, we can identify the problem as the test says that all processes in Ω' have a similar p-value. An interesting consequence of Axiom 4.2 and Theorem 4.1 is our ability to create a complete digraph whose nodes are the processes in Ω' and the weights represent the probability that they are λ-stochastic equivalent. We call the weights of the edges in this digraph the Equivalence Odds Ratio (EOR), defined as follows.

DEFINITION 4.3. *[Equivalence Odds Ratio (EOR)] The EOR, denoted $w_t(i \rhd j)$, $i \neq j$, under n observations $\mathcal{X}_{\Delta t}^{(i)} = \{x_{\Delta t}^{(i,1)}, \ldots, x_{\Delta t}^{(i,n)}\}$ of $X_{\Delta t}^{(i)}$ and m observations $\mathcal{X}_{\Delta t}^{(j)} = \{x_{\Delta t}^{(j,1)}, \ldots, x_{\Delta t}^{(j,m)}\}$ of $X_{\Delta t}^{(j)}$ is*

$$w_t(i \rhd j) = |\Omega'| \frac{P_{Kuiper}(\mathcal{X}_{\Delta t}^{(j)}, \mathcal{X}_{\Delta t}^{(i)})}{\sum_{\Psi^{(h)} \in \Omega' \setminus \{\Psi^{(j)}\}} P_{Kuiper}(\mathcal{X}_{\Delta t}^{(i)}, \mathcal{X}_{\Delta t}^{(h)})} \quad (1)$$

where $P_{Kuiper}(\cdot, \cdot)$ is the p-value of a two-sample Kuiper's test [16, 32], $\mathcal{X}^{(h)}$ are the observations of process $\Psi^{(h)}$, and with Ω' is as defined in Axiom 4.2 and $X_{\Delta t}^{(i)}$, $X_{\Delta t}^{(j)}$ as in Definition 4.2.

The Equivalence Odds Ratio (EOR) $w_t(i \rhd j)$ is the ratio between $p(\mathcal{X}_{\Delta t}^{(i)}, \mathcal{X}_{\Delta t}^{(j)})$ and the average p-value when i is compared to all other cascades in $\Omega' \setminus \{\Psi^{(j)}\}$. The EOR is not to be confused with a likelihood-ratio test, which compares the likelihood of two models given the data. In our framework there are no models.

DEFINITION 4.4 (STOCHASTIC EQUIVALENCE DIGRAPH). *Let $\mathcal{G}_{X_{\Delta t}}$ be a simple (no loops) complete digraph that connects all processes in Ω' with directed edge weights. For any two cascade processes $\Psi^{(i)}, \Psi^{(j)} \in \Omega'$, $i \neq j$, the weight of edge $i \to j$ is the EOR $w_t(i \rhd j)$.*

An EOR $w_t(i \rhd j) > 1$ suggests that process $\Psi^{(i)}$ is $w_t(i \rhd j)$ times more likely to be λ-stochastic equivalent to $\Psi^{(j)}$ than a random process selected from $\Omega' \setminus \{\Psi^{(j)}\}$. Note that the equivalence odds ratio is not symmetric, i.e., there can be processes $\Psi^{(i)}$ and $\Psi^{(j)}$ such that $w_t(i \rhd j) \neq w_t(j \rhd i)$. Note that Definition 4.4 does not impose the one-to-one equivalence required by Axiom 4.2. This is because the one-to-one equivalence is unnecessary and computationally expensive if Ω' is large, thus we assume we can safely approximate it through probabilistic matching. The Kuiper test in P_{Kuiper} can be also replaced by any two-sample hypothesis test such as Kolmogorov-Smirnov's test or extend our method to include P_{kernel} [10] that allows the use of a multi-dimensional λ through kernel two-sample tests. In one dimension, we choose Kuiper's test over Kolmogorov-Smirnov's test because the former gives equal importance to all domain values while the latter tends to be most sensitive around the median value [16, 32].

Next, we show how to use the *stochastic equivalence digraph* $\mathcal{G}_{X_{\Delta t}}$ to make predictions of cascade characteristics.

4.1.2 *Forecasting Procedure in Time*

Using the stochastic equivalence digraph $\mathcal{G}_{X_{\Delta t_1}}$ we can forecast$\Psi^{(i)}$ using an of estimate $P[X^{(i)}_{\Delta t_2} > x]$, $0 < \Delta t_1 < \Delta t_2$, obtained by the mixture

$$P[X^{(i)}_{\Delta t_2} > x] = \frac{1}{C} \sum_{\Psi^{(j)} \in \Omega' \setminus \{\Psi^{(i)}\}} w_{\Delta t_1}(j \rhd i) P[X^{(j)}_{\Delta t_2} > x],$$

where $C = \sum_{j \in \Omega'} w_{\Delta t_1}(j \rhd i)$ is a normalization constant. The above equation gives the first iteration of Sinkhorn's algorithm that finds probabilistic pairwise matches in a weighted graph [31]. For computational reasons we limit our matching to a single iteration. Sinkhorn's algorithm converges to a doubly stochastic matrix that defines the probability of pairwise matchings in a weighted graph, widely used in soft matching problems [40]. If the SED adjacency matrix is irreducible then the probabilistic matching is unique [31]. To increase estimation accuracy whenΩ' is large, we can add an exponential amplification factor:

$$P[X^{(i)}_{\Delta t_2} > x] = \frac{1}{C_\alpha} \sum_{\Psi^{(j)} \in \Omega' \setminus \{\Psi^{(i)}\}} w_{\Delta t_1}(j \rhd i)^\alpha P[X^{(j)}_{\Delta t_2} > x],$$

where $C_\alpha = \sum_{j \in \Omega'} w_{\Delta t_1}(j \rhd i)^\alpha$ and α is chosen as to minimize a regret function over the estimated distribution $P[X^{(i)}_{\Delta t'_2} > x]$ for$\Delta t'_2 \approx \Delta t_1$. Note that even for historical cascades$\Psi^{(j)} \in \Omega' \setminus \{\Psi^{(i)}\}$, we do not have the true function $P[X^{(j)}_{\Delta t_2} > x]$ that is used inside the sum. Therefore, we estimate $P[X^{(b)}_{\Delta t_2} > x]$ by bootstrapping the observations of $X^{(j)}_{\Delta t_2}$ in the historical cascades. In Section 5.2 we show that the estimates have good accuracy in practice.

4.2 A Big Data Forecast Paradox

In what follows we present a seemingly simple forecasting problem and prove that under conditions common to large social networks, no model or procedure is capable of extrapolating accurate unbiased cascade statistics beyond the time horizons of the historical data. This inability of models to extrapolate cascade statistics beyond what is already in the historical (training) data indicate that model-free forecasts can do as well as forecasts with perfect models.

Moreover, we also show the following paradox: As a the size of a power law network scales and increases both the historical data and the maximum cascade sizes, forecasts beyond the historical data horizon get more inaccurate while forecasts within the horizon get more accurate. This paradox poses a great challenge for big data analytics, where short-term forecasts can get increasingly better as the system and the historical data grow while long-term forecasts get worse.

This paradox happens because the present is a biased view of the future. More precisely, in the historical data we are more likely to see at least one infection from a cascade that will be larger in the future than a cascade that will be smaller. This bias is related to the inspection paradox [36] and depends on the observation window. The bias is so hard to correct for power law distributions that it denies us the ability to forecast beyond historical data horizons, where we have not yet recorded the bias. Moreover, our results are not confined to power laws; we consider all distributions (Type I, II, and III). The results apply to statistics such as the unbiased average of cascade sizes and the cascade size distribution.

Model: We collect data during time interval $[0, T]$ and seek to forecast statistics for interval $[0, cT]$, $c > 1$. Consider n independent cascades. Cascade infections arrive according to a constant-rate Poisson process with possibly distinct rates in the interval $[0, cT]$. The size of a cascade at time cT has distribution $\Lambda(cT) \sim \theta$, where θ is a distribution with support $\{1, \ldots, W\}$. Our initial goal is to estimate an unbiased average of the cascade sizes over the interval $[0, cT]$, $c > 1$. At first inspection the forecasting problem looks like a simple task and the impossibility results stated above seem surprising. We choose the Poisson process in our illustration precisely because its simplicity allows us to clearly understand why the forecasting problem is hard.

Our use of the Poisson process is also of interest because it connects the axiomatic framework with the classic model-based one. Poisson processes are arguably among the simplest and most widely used stochastic processes. Let N_t be the number of events in the time interval $[0, t]$. A Poisson process $\{\Lambda(\Delta t)\}$ with constant rate β is defined as an arrival process that satisfies the following three axioms:

A1. $\lim_{\epsilon \to 0} P[\Lambda(\Delta t) - \Lambda(\Delta t + \epsilon) = 1] = \beta\epsilon + o(\epsilon)$, and $\lim_{\Delta t \to 0} P[N_t - N_{t+\Delta t} > 1] = o(\Delta t)$; that is, no two events can happen at the same time;

A2. for all t, $s > 0$, $N_{t+s} - N_t$ is independent of the history up to t, $\{N_u, u \le t\}$;

A3. for all t, $s > 0$, $N_{t+s} - N_t$ is independent of t.

An equivalent constructive way to define the same process is: $P[N_t \ge k] = P[\sum_{i=1}^k X_i < t]$, where $\{X_1, \ldots, X_k\}$ are independent and identically distributed (i.i.d.) exponential random variables with parameter β.

Forecast Problem Definition. Let $\mathcal{O}_T$ denote the set of indices of the cascades in the historical data observed during interval $[0, T]$. The forecasting problem is defined as follows: We observe the cascades during time window $[0, T]$ and wish to forecast the average number of events we will observe in the window $[0, cT]$, $m_{cT} = \sum_{i=1}^n N^{(i)}_{cT}/n$.

4.2.1 *Forecast Accuracy Bounds*

In the following theorem, we prove that forecasting the average number of events in our mixture Poisson process is a hard problem.

THEOREM 4.2. *Let $\{N^{(i)}_{cT}\}_{i=1}^n$, $N^{(i)}_{cT} \sim (\theta_1, \ldots, \theta_W)$, be a set of observed events of a mixture of n Poisson processes during time interval $[0, cT]$. Let $|\mathcal{O}_T|$ denote the number of processes with at least one arrival in the interval $[0, T]$. Assume we are given the best unbiased forecast function $m_{cT|T}$ of the average number of events m_{cT}, where $m_{cT|T}$ takes as input the observations over time interval $[0, T]$. Then, the following conditions regarding the mean squared error $MSE(m_{cT|T}) = E[(m_{cT|T} - m_{cT})^2]$ hold:*

1. *If θ_W decreases faster than exponentially in W, i.e., $-\log \theta_W = \omega(W)$, then $MSE(m_{cT|T}) = \Omega(1/|\mathcal{O}_T|)$.*

2. *If θ_W decreases exponentially in W, i.e., $\log \theta_W = W \log b + o(W)$ for some $0 < b < 1$, then*

    (a) *$\log[MSE(m_{cT|T})] = \Omega(W - \log |\mathcal{O}_T|)$, provided $c > 1 + 1/b$,*

(b) $MSE(m_{cT|T}) = \Omega(W/|\mathcal{O}_T|)$, *provided* $c = 1 + 1/b$,
(c) $MSE(m_{cT|T}) = \Omega(1/|\mathcal{O}_T|)$, *provided* $c < 1 + 1/b$.

3. *If* θ_W *decreases more slowly than exponential, i.e.,* $-\log\theta_W = o(W)$, *then*
   (a) $\log[MSE(m_{cT|T})] = \Omega(W - \log|\mathcal{O}_T|)$, *provided* $c > 2$,
   (b) $MSE(m_{cT|T}) = \omega(1/|\mathcal{O}_T|)$, *provided* $c = 2$ *and* $\sum_{j=1}^{W} j^2\theta_j = \omega(1)$,
   (c) $MSE(m_{cT|T}) = \Omega(1/|\mathcal{O}_T|)$, *provided either* $c < 2$ *or* $c = 2$ *and* $\sum_{j=1}^{W} j^2\theta_j = O(1)$.

Proof of Theorem 4.2. Our proof of Theorem 4.2 shows that the forecasting mixtures of Poisson processes can be mapped into the set size distribution estimation problem; we then use our results on the hardness of estimating set size distributions from sampling [23] to prove the theorem. We start by showing how to map the forecasting mixtures of Poisson processes into the set size distribution estimation problem. Let $P[N_T^{(i)} = k|N_{cT}^{(i)}]$ be the probability that k events happen in the time window $[0, T]$ given the number of events at time cT is $N_{cT}^{(i)}$, $c > 1$. The distribution of $P[N_T^{(i)} = k|N_{cT}^{(i)}]$ is given in the following lemma.

LEMMA 4.1. *If* N_{cT} *is the number of events of a Poisson process at time* cT *and* N_T' *is the number of events that happened between* $[0, T]$, $c > 1$, *then* $P[N_T' = k|N_{cT}] = \binom{N_{cT}}{k} c^{-k}(1 - 1/c)^{N_{cT}-k}$.

PROOF. A Poisson process is defined as an arrival process that satisfies the three axioms listed above. Axiom A3 states that $\forall t$, $s > 0$, $N_{t+s} - N_t$ is independent of t. Thus, the counts of the number of events at a time interval $[0, T]$ is independent of the number of events at time interval $(T, cT]$ (axiom A2). Our Poisson process is time-homogeneous and thus the probability that an event lands in $[0, T]$ is proportional to $T/(cT) = 1/c$ (axiom A1). As the number of events between $[0, T]$ and $(T, cT]$ are independent, we have $P[N_T' = k|N_{cT}] = \binom{N_{cT}}{k} c^{-k}(1 - 1/c)^{N_{cT}-k}$. □

In what follows, we show that the timestamps of the past events in the interval $[0, T]$ are not relevant in the forecast.

LEMMA 4.2. *The event counts in the historical data provide all the statistical information collected in the interval* $[0, T]$ *w.r.t. the counts* $\{N_{cT}^{(i)}\}_{i=1}^{n}$ *in the interval* $[0, cT]$.

PROOF. Axiom A2 states that the exact timestamps of the events in the interval $[0, T]$ gives no statistical information about future events in $(T, cT]$. □

We are now ready for theorem that connects the forecast with an estimation problem that is known to be hard.

THEOREM 4.3. *The problem of forecasting any function* $g(\{N_{cT}^{(i)}\}_{i=1}^{n})$ *of the mixture Poisson sample paths described in Section 4.2 is equivalent to the set size estimation problem [23], where elements are randomly sampled from a collection of non-overlapping sets and we seek to recover the original set size distribution from the samples.*

PROOF. We prove the theorem by mapping the forecasting problem into the set size estimation problem. Let $\{N_{cT}^{(i)}\}_{i=1}^{n}$ be the sizes of n sets, whose elements are sampled independently with probability $1/c > 0$, leading to sampled set sizes that are binomially distributed as in Lemma 4.1. Finally, Lemma 4.2 shows that these non-zero sampled set sizes are the only information available to forecast the process. □

Theorem 4.3 shows that the present is a biased view of the future, as the set size problem suffers from the *inspection paradox* [23]. In what follows we prove our main theorem.

PROOF OF THEOREM 4.2. Using Theorem 4.3 we can construct a perfect map between the forecasting problem and the set size distribution problem. Theorem 4.2 follows from using Theorem 4.3 of our previous work (Murai et al. [23]) to this mapping, where we analytically compute the inverse of the Fisher information matrix of the data, giving rise to the error bounds in the theorem (through the Cramér-Rao bound). □

Theorem 4.2 shows clear limitations of forecasting with models. In realistic scenarios, where event sizes are large and have heavier-than-exponential distributions, no algorithm can obtain accurate unbiased forecasts of the average number of events beyond time interval $[T, 2T]$ if the dataset is limited to time horizon $[0, T]$. Fortunately, SED is not impacted by this problem as it limits its forecasts to the time horizons in the historical data. These results inspire the following apparent paradox.

4.2.2 A Big Network Data Paradox

When More Data Means Worse Forecasts. Theorem 4.2 creates an apparent paradox. The forecasting can become more inaccurate as the dataset $\mathcal{O}_T$ grows. The forecasting is not just more inaccurate, the forecast simply *breaks down*; as $\mathcal{O}_T$ grows, and the data time horizon remains the same $[0, T]$, there is nearly zero statistical (Fisher) information to forecast beyond horizon $[T, 2T]$.

To showcase the impact of this paradox, consider a growing network where the distribution of the size of events (cascade sizes) is Pareto with parameter $\beta > 1$. Our results hold generally but for illustration we use a scenario where the number of seeds increases proportionally with network size. In this scenario the relationship between the maximum number of events per seed W and the number of seeds $|\mathcal{O}_T| \gg 1$ is $E[W] \approx \sqrt[\beta]{|\mathcal{O}_T|}\,\Gamma(\beta - 1)$, a known result from extreme value theory [28]. Theorem 4.2 case 3(a) shows that the MSE error is lower bounded by $\log[\text{MSE}(m_{cT|T})] = \Omega(W - \log|\mathcal{O}_T|)$. As $E[W] \propto \sqrt[\beta]{|\mathcal{O}_T|}$ and $|\mathcal{O}_T|$ increases, so does W. We can think of the MSE lower bound growing roughly as $\exp(\sqrt[\beta]{|\mathcal{O}_T|})/|\mathcal{O}_T|$.

Thus, if the training data $\mathcal{O}_T$ has time horizon $[0, T]$ and event (cascade) sizes have a power law distribution, Theorem 4.2 cases 3(b-c) show that as the network grows the estimate in the interval $[T, 2T]$ gets more accurate. However, Theorem 4.2 case 3(a) shows that as the network grows the estimation error in the interval $(2T, cT]$, $c > 2$, grows exponentially with network size.

5. RESULTS

In this section we present our results. We start with our simulation results in Section 5.1. Section 5.2 shows our results over a large Twitter dataset.

5.1 Forecasting Using Simulated Data

In this section, we test the forecasts of SED on synthetic datasets. We test the performance of SED over two distinct models: the Poisson process and the Galton-Watson process. Recall that $\Omega' = \Omega \cup \{\Psi^{(0)}\}$ is the union of the historical processes Ω and the process to forecast $\Psi^{(0)}$. SED

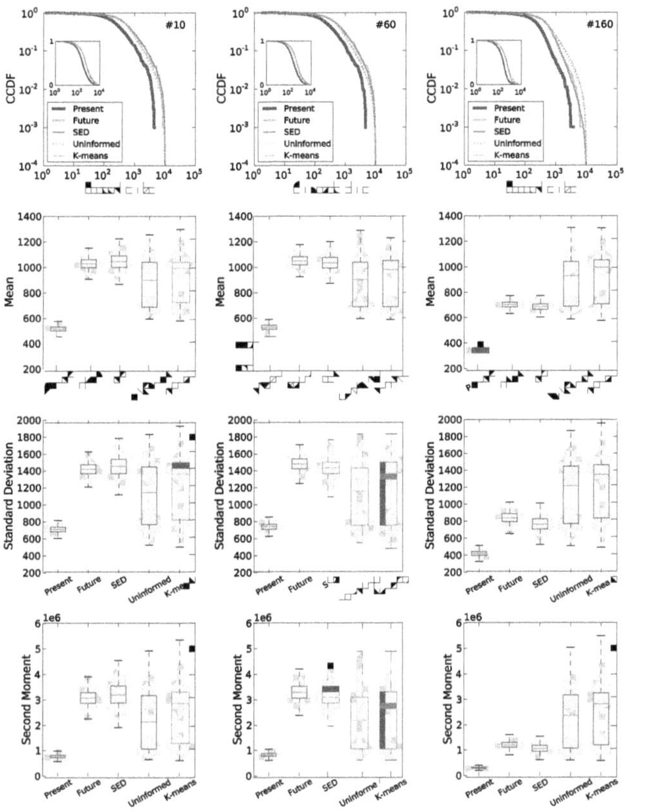

(a) ID 10 (b) ID 60 (c) ID 160

Figure 1: Prediction for mixture Poisson processes (Scenario 1) of the future CCDF, average, standard deviation, and second moment metrics. SED predictions match well the true future distributions and clearly outperform uninformed predictions.

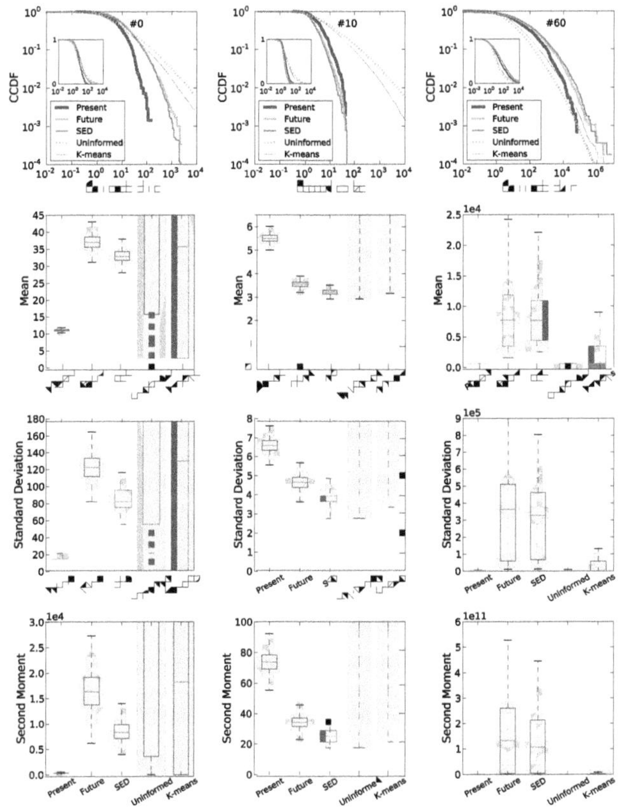

(a) ID 0 (b) ID 10 (c) ID 60

Figure 2: Prediction for Galton-Watson processes (Scenario 2) of the future CCDF, average, standard deviation, and second moment metrics. SED predictions again match well the future distributions and are clearly superior to uninformed predictions.

forecasts metrics of$\Psi^{(0)}$ at time intervalΔt_2 using data from time intervalΔt_1, $\Delta t_1 < \Delta t_2$ In addition to SED, we also have two baseline naive predictors: *uniformed prediction*, and *K-means prediction*. Uninformed prediction returns the bootstrapped statistics at time intervalΔt_2 of a randomly selected process in Ω. Whereas, K-means prediction first clusters the set of historical cascades using K-means algorithm and Euclidean distances between the CCDFs of cascade metrics (probability density functions, PDFs, give similar results). The number of cluster k is chosen using the elbow method, without making the clusters too small (k equals 10 for the two synthetic datasets, and 20 for the Twitter dataset). After that, given a new cascade$\Psi^{(0)}$, K-means prediction finds the cluster it belongs to, and returns the bootstrapped statistics at time intervalΔt_2 of a randomly selected process in that cluster.

For evaluation, we use violin plots to compare the predicted statistics with the bootstrap statistics from the ground-truth empirical distribution of$\Psi^{(0)}$ atΔt_2. A violin plot is a box plot combined with a kernel density estimate of the probability density function, giving a more detailed view of the data's variance. The box extends from the first quartile Q_1 to the third quartile Q_3 of the data, with a line at the median. The whiskers extend from the box to $Q_1 - 1.5 * \text{IQR}$ and $Q_3 + 1.5 * \text{IQR}$, where $\text{IQR} = Q_3 - Q_1$ is the inter-quartile range. The violin plots show the spread.

5.1.1 *Scenario 1: Mixture Poisson Processes*

Our mixture Poisson process is a Poisson process with random rate β that has support $(0, W]$, $W > 0$.

Data Generation: The simulated historical data $\mathcal{H}$ is generated through simulations from time zero until$\Delta t_2 = 1$ month from two sets of mixture Poisson processes. The first set has $n_1 = 100$ processes with rate distribution $\gamma_1 \propto \beta^{-2}$ and the second set has $n_2 = 100$ processes with rate distribution $\gamma_2 \propto \beta^{-3}$. Poisson rates are measured in number of events per month. Each process has $1,000$ infection seeds. The process to forecast$\Psi^{(0)}$ belongs to one of two sets and was observed from time zero until$\Delta t_1 = \Delta t_2/4$, approximately one week. In what follows we test how well SED can forecast$\Psi^{(0)}$. In Section 4.2 we show that estimating the Poisson rates is hard due to observation bias.

Results: For conciseness, Figure 1 shows only the results for three processes, one per column: processes 10, 60 (type 1), and 160 (type 2). The remaining results can be found in our technical report [29]. Four forecasts are evaluated: forecasting the CCDFs, mean, standard deviation, and second moment. For comparison baselines we use uninformed prediction – uniform matching weights – and matching using K-means with Euclidean distances, as the latter have been extensively and successfully used in mining and classifying time series [37]. For each process we present the true statistics atΔt_1 (Present) andΔt_2 (Future), and the predicted statistics atΔt_2, including SED, uninformed, and

K-means predictions. The Figure 1 shows that SED is the method that better represents, consistently, the true statistics at timeΔ t_2 under all scenarios (Future).

5.1.2 Scenario 2: Galton-Watson Process

The Galton-Watson process is a branching process $\{X_n\}$ such that $X_{n+1} = \sum_{j=1}^{X_n} \psi_j^{(n)}$, where $X_0 = 1$ and $\{\psi_j^{(n)} \sim Poisson(\lambda) : n, j \in \mathbb{N}\}$ is a set of i.i.d. natural number-valued random variables [22]. Intuitively, $\psi_i^{(n)}$ is the number of male children of the j-th descendants, and X_n is the number of descendants in the n-th generation. The total number of people with the considered family name at time t would be $\sum_{i=0}^{t} X_t$. A simple epidemic cascading on a network can be modeled as a Galton-Watson process.

To make this model harder to forecast, we replace the Poisson distribution of the number of children by a log-normal distribution. The purpose of the log-normal distribution is to skew the obtained distribution of the number of children, mimicking real life situation where the degree of a node in a network follows a heavy tail distribution. We call the values generated by the log-normal distribution the descendant effect of a node. Here is the model we use $X_{n+1} = \sum_{j=1}^{\lfloor X_n \rfloor} \psi_j^{(n)}$, where $X_0 = 1$ and $\{\psi_j^{(n)} \sim \text{log-normal}(\mu,\sigma^2) : n, j \in \mathbb{N}\}$. The operation $\lfloor X_n \rfloor$ is to get an integer-valued number of descendants.

Cascade Process Evolution: For each information cascade, we use a birth rate γ to generate new seeds over time. Given a single seed node ($X_0 = 1$), the total descendant effect up to time t in a Galton-Watson process, i.e., $\sum_{i=0}^{t} X_i$, will be used as the cascade size at time t for this seed. As a result, we obtain a sample of the cascade size per seed. To add more complexity to the model, we allow the parameters to change over time: $\mu_t = \mu_0 + t * \Delta_\mu$, $\sigma_t = \sigma_0 + t * \Delta_\sigma$, $\gamma_t = \gamma_0 + t * \Delta_\gamma$, where μ_t, σ_t, γ_t are the parameter values at time point t, andΔ $_\mu$, Δ_σ, Δ_γ are the amount of change at each time step.

Table 1 shows our parameter settings. We create 9 different cascade types, each one containing 10 cascades spanning a period of seven time units. These cascade types can be grouped into three big groups – small, medium and large – based on their mean μ in the log-normal distribution. Larger cascades have a larger variation (larger σ) and higher birth rate γ. For each of these big groups, we generate three subgroups with different evolutionary trends: increasing in size (inc), decreasing in size (dec), and constant size (const). Finally, we setΔ $t_1 = 2$ time units andΔ $t_2 = 7$ time units.

Results: Figure 2 shows the results of three processes: 0 (Small-inc), 10 (Small-dec) and 60 (Large-inc). We get similar results in the other processes. Note that the statistics of Present and Future are significantly different. Figure 2 shows that the uninformed and k-means forecasts are far from the truth that the confidence intervals do not fit in our plot. Over the same scenario SED accurately forecasts the mean, standard deviation and second moment as shown in the last three rows of Figure 2.

5.2 Forecasting Twitter Cascades

We study the Twitter dataset collected by Yang et al. [39][2], which contains 467 million Twitter posts from 20 million users covering a 7-month period from June 1st to December 31st, 2009. The underlying Twitter follower-followee network is obtained from Kwak et al. [18]. The fact that this Twitter dataset is only a sample of all tweets does not invalidate the dataset to test SED. SED is designed to make predictions over general dissemination processes, including sampled cascading processes such as our Twitter dataset.

[2]`http://snap.stanford.edu/data/twitter7.html`

		Parameters			Temporal delta		
Process Type	IDs	μ_0	σ_0	γ_0	Δ_μ	Δ_σ	Δ_γ
Small-inc	0..9				+0.2	+0.1	+30
Small-dec	10..19	1.5	1	300	-0.2	-0.1	-30
Small-const	20..29				0	0	0
Medium-inc	30..39				+0.2	+0.1	+30
Medium-dec	40..49	2	2	500	-0.2	-0.1	-30
Medium-const	50..59				0	0	0
Large-inc	60..69				+0.2	+0.1	+30
Large-dec	70..79	3	2.5	700	-0.2	-0.1	-30
Large-const	80..89				0	0	0

Table 1: Galton-Watson process simulation parameters.

Hashtag cascades

We are interested in the diffusion of a hashtag over the Twitter online social network. When an individual uses a hashtag in her tweet at a given time, if neither she nor any of her followees have tweeted the same hashtag for at least a week prior to the post timestamp, we consider her as a seed. The timestamp of the first tweet is the timestamp of a node hashtag "infection". Once the seed of a cascade has been identified, we start tracking the cascade over time. Note that our definition of seed is stringent and we may merge almost unrelated cascades into a single cascade. From our RMPP definition, metrics over merged cascade processes are allowed and, thus, we can be conservative to define independent cascades in our dataset.

If a hashtag was not been used for more than a week, we assume the cascade has ended. The first occurrence of the same hashtag after that would mark the beginning of a new cascade. Due to this one-week time window, hashtags appearing for the first time in the dataset during the first and last weeks of the monitored time frame are ignored. The time difference between the first and the last posts of an information cascade is defined as the duration of the cascade.

Cascade metric

In our case study, we are interested in the distribution of the number of infected descendants of a seed node for each hashtag in Twitter. In particular, given an infected seed node, we quantify how many of its descendants are "infected" by a hashtag complying with temporal infection order (infected children in the branching process must be infected after their parents). These quantities are obtained from the induced subgraph of the infected nodes over the original follower-followee network. Note that a user may have several followees who posted the same hashtag before she did. As a result, simply counting the number of infected descendants of an infected user does not guarantee the independence between samples required by our theory. To reduce the effect of these independence violations, we assume that two infected parents of an infected node are evenly responsible for the infection. Under this assumption we propose a normalized metric as follows.

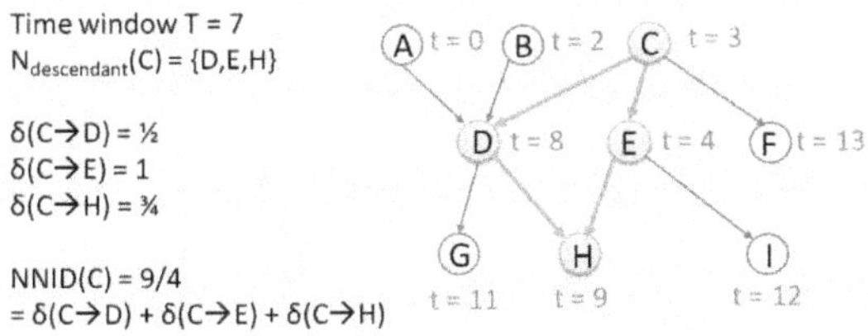

Figure 3: An example induced subgraphs of infected nodes and cascade metric. Node infection timestamps are shown in red.

DEFINITION 5.1. *Given a time window length T, the number of normalized infected descendants (NNID) of a node v are defined as:*

$$NNID(v) = \sum_{w \in N_{des}^T(v)} \delta(v \to w)$$

where $N_{in}^T(v)$ and $N_{des}^T(v)$ are the set of infected parents, and infected descendants of node v within the time window T respectively; $\delta(v \to v) = 1$; $\delta(v \to w)$ is the amount of infection spread from node v to w through all possible time-ordering paths, and is defined recursively as follows:

$$\delta(v \to w) = \frac{\sum_{u \in N_{in}^T(w) \cap N_{des}^T(v)} \delta(v \to u)}{|N_{in}^T(w)|}$$

We assume that if a node v is infected at time point t, then after time point $t+T$, its effect on other nodes will diminish to zero. Thus, the set of infected descendants of node v do not contains nodes infected after time $t+T$. To get a distribution of NNIDs for a cascade c at a given time point t, we first extract the induced subgraph $G_{ind} = (V_{ind}, E_{ind})$, where V_{ind} is the set of infected nodes of c up to time t. In addition, given two infected nodes u and v, if the edge $(u \to v) \in E$ and $t_{infect}(v) - t_{infect}(v) \leq T$, then $(u \to v) \in E_{ind}$, where $t_{infect}(v)$ is the timestamp at which v is infected in c. Next, for each seed node of the cascade, i.e., nodes with no infected parents within a time window T, we compute its NNID in G_{ind} using Definition. 5.1. In the end, we obtain a sample of NNID values, each for a seed in c, giving us an empirical distribution of NNIDs of c.

Example 1. *An induced subgraph of infected nodes is shown in Fig. 3. Given a time window $T = 7$, the descendant set of C is $\{D, E, H\}$; the infected parent sets of D and E are $\{B, C\}$ and $\{C\}$ respectively. Thus, $\delta(C \to D) = \frac{1}{2}$, and $\delta(C \to E) = 1$. The infection from C can spread to H following two different paths: $C \to D \to H$, and $C \to E \to H$. Thus, $\delta(C \to H) = \frac{\delta(C \to D) + \delta(C \to E)}{2} = \frac{3}{4}$. Finally, the number of normalized descendants of C is $NNID(C) = \delta(C \to D) + \delta(C \to E) + \delta(C \to H) = \frac{1}{2} + 1 + \frac{3}{4} = \frac{9}{4}$.*

Similarly, the set of seed nodes with no infected parents within a time window $T = 7$ is $\{A, B, C, F, I\}$, which gives a sample of NNIDs $\{1, \frac{3}{4}, \frac{9}{4}, 1, 1\}$ accordingly.

Twitter Results

For our tests, we identify the Twitter hashtag cascades that last at least 8 weeks. Using this dataset, we predict distribution of NNID (time window $T = 1$ week) at week 8 (Δt_2) using data from the week 2 (Δt_1). To guarantee that enough data is available for prediction, we only consider cascades that contain at least 300 infected users after 8 weeks and at least 30 infected users after one week. In the end, we are left with 1050 cascades split among the different hashtags. Similar to the simulations, besides the CCDF plots, we use violin plots to compare the predicted statistics (SED prediction and uninformed prediction) with the bootstrap statistics from the ground-truth sample atΔ t_2. It is worth noting that the uninformed prediction simply returns the average statistics of all cascades in Ω at timeΔ t_2.

The forecasting results for five Twitter hashtags are shown in Figure 4. Our technical report shows all other hashtag forecasts left out of this paper due to space constraints [29]. SED forecasts frequently outperform uninformed and k-means predictions. For example, all #FORASARNEY statistics differ considerably from those of uninformed and k-means predictions. Whereas SED accurately forecasts the average CCDFs and all three statistics, as observed by contrasting SED forecast violin plots against those of the ground truth (Future). For #H1N1, #FIERFOX and #SOUNDCLOUD, the uninformed forecasts are rather uncertain of the values of the mean, the standard deviation, and the second moment, leading to significantly lengthened violin plots. On the other hand, the SED forecasts are, once again, close to the ground truth. In the case of forecasting the mean of #JQUERY (last column, second row), the true mean (Future) is so close to the future average statistics (uninformed prediction), that SED shows no clear improvement over naive approaches. We include this #JQUERY example to show that in hard-to-forecast cases SED does no worse than uninformed and k-means. Note, however, that for standard deviation and the second moment of #JQUERY show SED superior to uninformed and k-means.

It must be noted that the hashtag Twitter dataset that we are using is noisy (cascades are not fully independent), making our forecasting task very difficult. Moreover, for many of the cascades in this dataset, the distribution at week 8 (Δt_2) is very close to the average prediction (uninformed prediction). Thus, more challenging datasets and further research are needed to further validate practical aspects of our approach.

6. RELATED WORK

Analyzing and predicting network processes in general, and information cascades in particular, has attracted much attention in recent years. Multiple works focus on building theoretical models (e.g., [8, 9, 38]) of dissemination processes. These models capture information diffusion at nodes through network topology as well as user interests and the information content [7, 27, 38]. Wang et al. [35] uses partial differential equations to predict information diffusion over both temporal and spatial dimensions. One challenge in this line of research is the gap between empirical data and theory. Building parsimonious models is a complex task and the resulting models are often not vetted against real data.

Most relevant to this paper are the works that predict cascade popularity. Some of these works predict the volume of aggregate activity, such as the number of votes on Digg stories [33], or Twitter hashtag usage [20]. A few works examine how information cascades grow in size depending on its content [19, 30] and user interests [2]. Other works make prediction using observations of a cascade during a given fixed time interval [17, 20, 34]. The cascade size prediction task is seen as a regression problem in a variety of works [3, 17, 33, 34]. Matsubara et al. [21] proposes a parsimonious model that captures the rise and fall patterns in information diffusion. In lieu of predicting the exact cascade sizes, many studies bin the cascades sizes and solve a binary

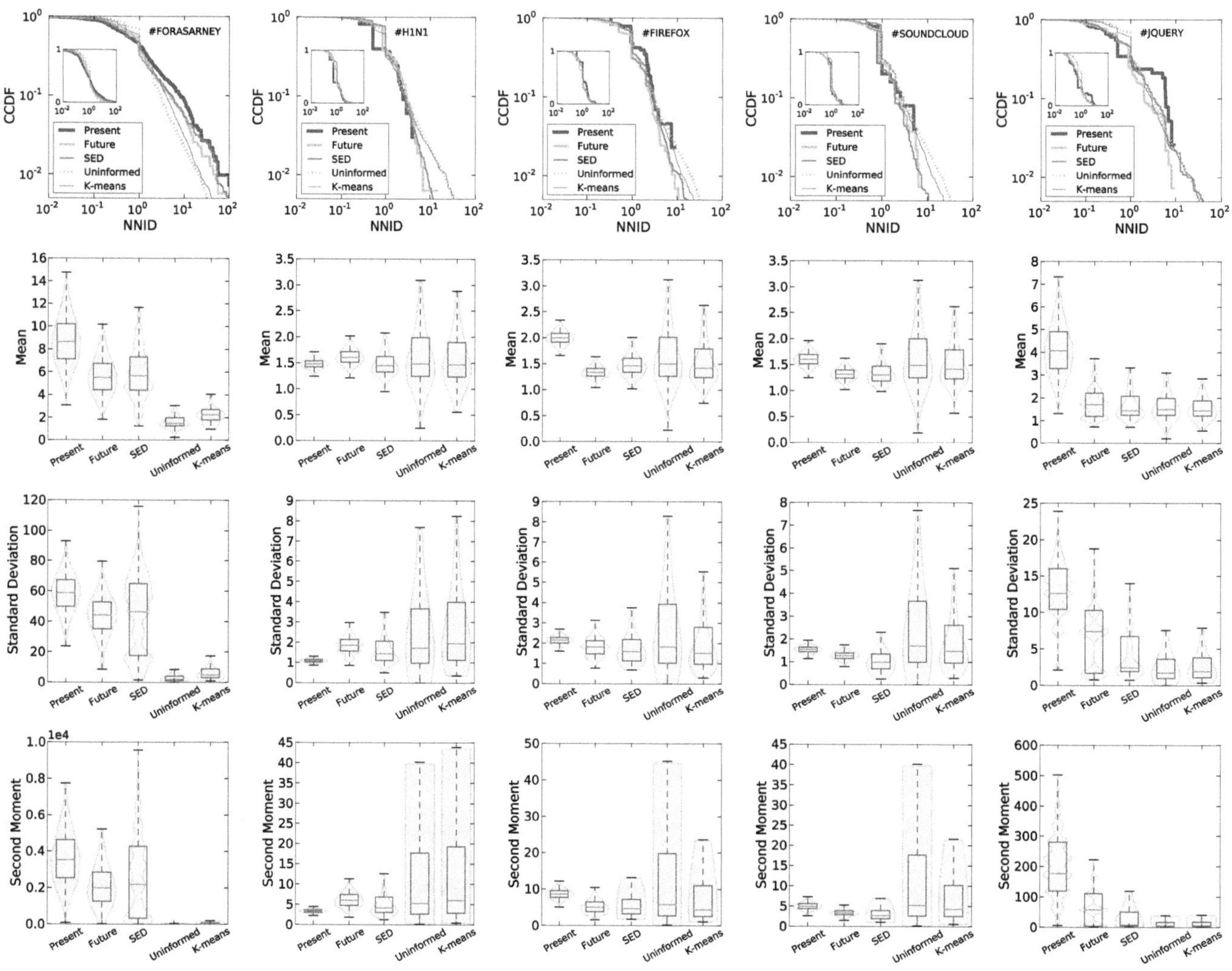

(a) FORASARNEY (b) H1N1 (c) FIREFOX (d) SOUNDCLOUD (e) JQUERY

Figure 4: Predictions of statistics of NNID for five example hashtags in Twitter.

classification problem of whether or not a cascade becomes viral [11,13,17] or if it doubles in size [4]. Instead of modeling the diffusion process, Najar et al. [25] directly predicts the final propagation state of the information given its initial state. Outside cascade sizes, Cheng et al. [4] also predicts structural features of the cascade sample paths. Our goal is different as we do not perform binary classification of the evolution of a sample path, or just predict cascade sizes. We propose a general axiomatic forecasting framework that is not tied to a specific set of cascade features or process and can be used off-the-shelf in any similar forecasting scenario.

Since we predict cascade statistics, our work also relates to research on fitting empirical data to parsimonious statistical models [1,5]. While the empirical data can be readily fitted to many known parsimonious models such as power laws, log-normal, or exponential, there is no guarantee that the fitted model can be used to predict the tail of the distribution or how the distribution changes with the observation window. Indeed, our experimental results using Twitter data show that cascade statistics can significantly change over time. Thus, the need to go beyond parsimonious models to design a data-driven statistical approach using axiomatic forecasting.

7. CONCLUSIONS

In this work we propose SED, a new algorithm for forecasting statistics of complex networked processes. SED is the first of its kind, a (true) model-free approach that uses axioms rather than models to extract statistical information from the data, pointing to a promising new direction of axiomatic forecasting. More importantly, we provide the underlying theory behind SED's model-free axiomatic forecasting approach. We test SED on two synthetic datasets and a large Twitter dataset, showing that SED can forecast accurately a variety of statistics under complex scenarios.

Acknowledgements

We thank C. Faloutsos and D. Towsley for their helpful comments. This work was partially supported by NSF grants CNS-1065133, IIS-1219254, and ARL Cooperative Agreement W911NF-09-2-0053. The views and conclusions contained in this document are those of the author and should not be interpreted as representing the official policies, either expressed or implied of the NSF, ARL, or the U.S. Government. The U.S. Government is authorized to reproduce and distribute reprints for Government purposes notwithstanding any copyright notation hereon.

8. REFERENCES

[1] Lada A Adamic. Zipf, power-laws, and pareto-a ranking tutorial. *Xerox Palo Alto Research Center*, 2000.

[2] Lars Backstrom, Dan Huttenlocher, Jon Kleinberg, and Xiangyang Lan. Group formation in large social networks: membership, growth, and evolution. In *Proc. SIGKDD*, 2006.

[3] Eytan Bakshy, Brian Karrer, and Lada A Adamic. Social influence and the diffusion of user-created content. In *EC*, 2009.

[4] Justin Cheng, Lada Adamic, P Alex Dow, Jon Michael Kleinberg, and Jure Leskovec. Can cascades be predicted? In *Proc. WWW*, 2014.

[5] Aaron Clauset, Cosma Rohilla Shalizi, and Mark EJ Newman. Power-law distributions in empirical data. *SIAM review*, 51, 2009.

[6] R. A. Fisher. *The design of experiments.* Oliver & Boyd, 1935.

[7] W Galuba, K Aberer, and D Chakraborty. Outtweeting the twitterers-predicting information cascades in microblogs. In *Proc. WOSN*, 2010.

[8] Michaela Goetz, Jure Leskovec, Mary McGlohon, and Christos Faloutsos. Modeling blog dynamics. In *ICWSM*, 2009.

[9] Amit Goyal, Francesco Bonchi, and Laks VS Lakshmanan. Learning influence probabilities in social networks. In *Proc. WSDM*, 2010.

[10] Arthur Gretton, Karsten M. Borgwardt, Malte J. Rasch, Bernhard Schölkopf, and Alexander Smola. A kernel two-sample test. *JMLR*, 13(1):723–773, March 2012.

[11] Liangjie Hong, Ovidiu Dan, and Brian D Davison. Predicting popular messages in twitter. In *Proc. WWW*, 2011.

[12] Ting-Kai Huang, Bruno Ribeiro, Harsha V Madhyastha, and Michalis Faloutsos. The socio-monetary incentives of online social network malware campaigns. In *Proc. COSN*, pages 259–270. ACM, 2014.

[13] Maximilian Jenders, Gjergji Kasneci, and Felix Naumann. Analyzing and predicting viral tweets. In *Proc. WWW*, 2013.

[14] Eamonn Keogh, Stefano Lonardi, and CA Ratanamahatana. Towards parameter-free data mining. *Proc. SIGKDD*, pages 206–215, 2004.

[15] A. N. Kolmogorov. *Foundations of the Theory of Probability.* Chelsea Publishing Co., 1950.

[16] N H Kuiper. *Tests concerning random points on a circle.* Proceedings of the Koninklijke Nederlandse Akademie, 1960.

[17] Andrey Kupavskii, Liudmila Ostroumova, Alexey Umnov, Svyatoslav Usachev, Pavel Serdyukov, Gleb Gusev, and Andrey Kustarev. Prediction of retweet cascade size over time. In *CIKM*, 2012.

[18] Haewoon Kwak, Changhyun Lee, Hosung Park, and Sue Moon. What is Twitter, a social network or a news media? In *Proc. WWW*, 2010.

[19] Jure Leskovec, Lars Backstrom, and Jon Kleinberg. Meme-tracking and the dynamics of the news cycle. In *Proc. SIGKDD*, 2009.

[20] Zongyang Ma, Aixin Sun, and Gao Cong. On predicting the popularity of newly emerging hashtags in twitter. *JASIST*, 64, 2013.

[21] Yasuko Matsubara, Yasushi Sakurai, B Aditya Prakash, Lei Li, and Christos Faloutsos. Rise and fall patterns of information diffusion: model and implications. In *Proc. SIGKDD*, pages 6–14, 2012.

[22] Fabricio Murai, Bruno Ribeiro, Don Towsley, and Krista Gile. Characterizing Branching Processes from Sampled Data. In *Proc. WWW Companion*, pages 805–811, 2013.

[23] Fabricio Murai, Bruno Ribeiro, Don Towsley, and Pinghui Wang. On Set Size Distribution Estimation and the Characterization of Large Networks via Sampling. *IEEE Journal on Selected Areas in Communications*, 31(6):1017–1025, 2013.

[24] Seth A Myers, Chenguang Zhu, and Jure Leskovec. Information diffusion and external influence in networks. In *Proc. SIGKDD*, 2012.

[25] Anis Najar, Ludovic Denoyer, and Patrick Gallinari. Predicting information diffusion on social networks with partial knowledge. In *Proc. WWW Companion*, pages 1197–1204. ACM, 2012.

[26] Charles T Perretti, Stephan B Munch, and George Sugihara. Model-free forecasting outperforms the correct mechanistic model for simulated and experimental data. *PNAS*, 110(13):5253–7, March 2013.

[27] Daniel Ramage, Susan T Dumais, and Daniel J Liebling. Characterizing microblogs with topic models. *ICWSM*, 10, 2010.

[28] Sidney I Resnick. *Extreme values, regular variation, and point processes.* Springer Science & Business Media, 2007.

[29] Bruno Ribeiro, Minh X. Hoang, and Ambuj K. Singh. Beyond models: Forecasting complex network processes directly from data. `http://www.cs.cmu.edu/~ribeiro/pdf/Ribeiro_etal_BeyondTR15.pdf`.

[30] Daniel M Romero, Chenhao Tan, and Johan Ugander. On the interplay between social and topical structure. In *ICWSM*, 2013.

[31] Richard Sinkhorn and Paul Knopp. Concerning nonnegative matrices and doubly stochastic matrices. *Pacific Journal of Mathematics*, 21(2):343–348, 1967.

[32] M A Stephens. Use of the Kolmogorov-Smirnov, Cramer–Von-Mises and related statistics without extensive tables. *J. of the Royal Statistical Society Series B*, 32, 1970.

[33] Gabor Szabo and Bernardo A Huberman. Predicting the popularity of online content. *Communications of the ACM*, 53, 2010.

[34] Oren Tsur and Ari Rappoport. What's in a hashtag?: content based prediction of the spread of ideas in microblogging communities. In *Proc. WSDM*, 2012.

[35] Feng Wang, Haiyan Wang, and Kuai Xu. Diffusive Logistic Model Towards Predicting Information Diffusion in Online Social Networks. *WINE*, cs.SI(June), August 2011.

[36] James R. Wilson. The inspection paradox in renewal-reward processes. *Operations Research Letters*, 2(1):27–30, April 1983.

[37] Zhengzheng Xing, Jian Pei, and Eamonn Keogh. A brief survey on sequence classification. *ACM SIGKDD Explorations Newsletter*, 12(1):40, November 2010.

[38] Jaewon Yang and Jure Leskovec. Modeling information diffusion in implicit networks. In *ICDM*, 2010.

[39] Jaewon Yang and Jure Leskovec. Patterns of temporal variation in online media. In *Proc. WSDM*, 2011.

[40] Ron Zass and Amnon Shashua. Probabilistic graph and hypergraph matching. In *CVPR*, pages 1–8. IEEE, 2008.

Weakly Supervised Extraction of Computer Security Events from Twitter

Alan Ritter
Computer Science and Engineering
The Ohio State University*
Columbus, OH
ritter.1492@osu.edu

Evan Wright
Software Engineering Institute
Carnegie Mellon University
Pittsburgh, PA
evanw@cmu.edu

William Casey
Software Engineering Institute
Carnegie Mellon University
Pittsburgh, PA
wcasey@cert.org

Tom Mitchell
Machine Learning Department
Carnegie Mellon University
Pittsburgh, PA
tom.mitchell@cmu.edu

ABSTRACT

Twitter contains a wealth of timely information, however staying on top of breaking events requires that an information analyst constantly scan many sources, leading to information overload. For example, a user might wish to be made aware whenever an infectious disease outbreak takes place, when a new smartphone is announced or when a distributed Denial of Service (DoS) attack might affect an organization's network connectivity. There are many possible event categories an analyst may wish to track, making it impossible to anticipate all those of interest in advance. We therefore propose a weakly supervised approach, in which extractors for new categories of events are easy to define and train, by specifying a small number of seed examples. We cast seed-based event extraction as a learning problem where only positive and unlabeled data is available. Rather than assuming unlabeled instances are negative, as is common in previous work, we propose a learning objective which regularizes the label distribution towards a user-provided expectation. Our approach greatly outperforms heuristic negatives, used in most previous work, in experiments on real-world data. Significant performance gains are also demonstrated over two novel and competitive baselines: semi-supervised EM and one-class support-vector machines. We investigate three security-related events breaking on Twitter: DoS attacks, data breaches and account hijacking.

A demonstration of security events extracted by our system is available at:
`http://kb1.cse.ohio-state.edu:8123/events/hacked`

*This Work was conducted at Carnegie Mellon

WWW 2015, May 18–22, 2015, Florence, Italy.
ACM 978-1-4503-3469-3/15/05.
http://dx.doi.org/10.1145/2736277.2741083 .

Categories and Subject Descriptors

I.2.7 [**Natural Language Processing**]: Language parsing and understanding; H.2.8 [**Database Management**]: Database applications—*data mining*

General Terms

Algorithms, Experimentation

1. INTRODUCTION

Social media presents a rich and timely source of information on events taking place in the world, enabling applications such as earthquake detection [41] or identifying the location of missing persons during natural disasters [29]. Previous work on event extraction has relied on large amounts of labeled data, or taken an open-domain approach [38, 2] in which general events are extracted without a specific focus. Often an information analyst might be interested in tracking a very specific type of event, for instance Denial of Service (Denial of Service (DoS)) attacks and might not have time or expertise to build an information extraction system from scratch in response to emerging incidents. To address this challenge we introduce an approach for rapidly training automatic extractors for the raw Twitter stream. As a proof of concept, we study three specific computer-security event categories: DoS attacks, data breaches, and account hijacking.

Our approach requires an analyst simply provide 10-20 historical seed examples of the event category of interest, for example seed instances of DoS attack events might include (*Spamhaus*, 3/18/2013). A bag of tweets which mention each seed event are then gathered, for instance Spamhaus is mentioned in the following tweet written on 3/18/2013:

> "The *Spamhaus* Project is currently under a major DDoS attack"

These seed events are used as training examples to automatically detect new events from a realtime Twitter stream.

Challenge: Data Sparsity Although many tweets mention computer security events, only a tiny proportion of the overall message volume is relevant. Because only a 1% sample of the Twitter stream is available through the public

API, without focusing the data collection, virtually no security events would be found in available data. To address this challenge we simply track a user-provided keyword associated with each event, for example we tracked *ddos* for DoS attacks, *hacked* for account hijacking, and *breach* for data breach events. When tracking relevant keywords, the Twitter API allows us to retrieve roughly the same total volume of data, however a much larger proportion is relevant to the security-related events of interest. Of course not all tweets mentioning a relevant keyword will describe the events of interest, we therefore leverage the seed events previously mentioned, to train a weakly supervised extractor.

Opportunity: Redundancy in Social Media While there has been much previous work on weakly supervised extraction of static relationships between entities [6, 5, 1], there have been few efforts focused on seed-based *event* extraction. Part of the reason is the reliance of weakly supervised learning methods on redundancy - many sentences on the web are likely to mention context independent relations, such as the headquarters of a company, however most events are only mentioned in a handful of articles written around the time of the event, making learning from a few seed instances very challenging [16, 36]. In the meantime, social networking websites such as Twitter have become an important complementary source of realtime information. When important events take place, many users independently turn to microblogs to share information, resulting in a huge number of redundant messages describing each significant event, and providing an opportunity to collect large amounts of training data for weakly supervised event extraction.

We cast *seed-based event extraction* as a unique semi-supervised learning problem in which only positive and unlabeled examples are available [9, 21, 19, 10]. A new approach to learning with positive and unlabeled data is introduced, which regularizes the label distribution over unlabeled examples towards a user-provided expectation [24, 25, 11].

A huge number of security events are reported in social media every day. These include everything from average users complaining about their email accounts being hijacked to massive data breaches involving international corporations. Many of these events are not sufficiently significant to be reported in the news, though they may still be of interest to a computer security analyst. The volume of security-related messages written on social media is simply too large to constantly monitor, leading to a situation of information overload.

Of course misinformation and rumors are prevalent in social media [35], we therefore preserve provenance for the extracted events, making it easy to display information sources to an analyst who can investigate further and make judgments about reliability.

This paper makes the following contributions:

- We demonstrate that social media is a valuable resource for information on security related events.
- We present a novel approach to extracting focused events from Twitter which requires only minimal supervision for each new event category.
- We cast seed-based weakly supervised information extraction as a learning problem with positive and unlabeled examples [9, 21] and propose a new approach which regularizes the label distribution over unlabeled examples towards a user-specified expectation of the label distribution for the keyword.

Given:

- An event type E of interest (e.g., Distributed denial of service attacks)
- A keyword or keyphrase, K, associated with this event type (e.g. "DDoS")
- A named entity recognizer which can identity entities mentioned in a tweet [37, 22, 20]
- A set of positive seed examples $e_1, e_2, \ldots, e_n$ of historical instances of E, where each seed example is represented by an entity involved in the event, plus the date of the event, for example: (*AT&T*, 2012/08/15)
- Access to the Twitter search interface to gather tweets mentioning the seed examples

Output:

- An extractor that can be applied to the Twitter stream filtered by keywords K to identify new instances of event type E as they are mentioned.

Figure 1: Summary of the weakly supervised event extraction problem.

2. WEAK SUPERVISION FOR EVENT EXTRACTION FROM TWITTER

Using a traditional annotate-train-test approach to information extraction [12, 17, 40] is problematic for our scenario, because significant time and effort would be required to develop extractors for each new event category of interest. In traditional IE, a large corpus of individual event triggers and their arguments must first be annotated in context. These annotations can then be used to train supervised machine learning models to extract new event instances. This approach has been quite successful, but requires a substantial annotation effort for each new type of event to be recognized.

A wide variety of different event types might interest an analyst, making it difficult or impossible to anticipate those which could be important and build extractors for them a-priori. This motivated us to investigate a *weakly supervised* approach to event extraction from Twitter in which new event categories are quickly defined by providing a small set of seed instances and relevant keywords.

The seed examples are used to train a classifier which is applied to a *candidate event*, to determine whether it describes a new instance of event type E. Candidate events are collected automatically by gathering tweets that match keywords of interest K, were written on the target date and mention a specific entity.

We now describe in detail the inputs and outputs of our algorithm. A summary is presented in Figure 1. We show how weakly supervised event extraction leads to a learning problem in which only positive and unlabeled examples

Figure 2: Example of gathering mentions of seed events. By querying for the event-type keyword, *hacked* and entity *Palin* in tweets on the event date ("sept. 8, 2008") we are able to obtain many high-quality mentions for the event.

are available [9, 21]. We propose a new approach to learning with positive and unlabeled data based on expectation regularization [24] in Section 3 which is experimentally compared against a variety of baselines in Section 6.

2.1 Event Representation

We define an event e as an (ENTITY, DATE) tuple, and a *mention* of e, m_e, to be any tweet which contains a reference to the ENTITY and is written on the specified DATE. Features for the event, are extracted from its mentions: $x_e = f(\{m_{e'}|e' = e\})$, which can be used to estimate the probability that the event belongs to category E,

$$p_{\theta^E}(y_e = 1|x_e) = \frac{1}{1 + e^{-\theta_E \cdot x_e}}$$

according to some parameters for the category, θ_E.

2.2 Seed Instances

To define a new event category, an information analyst provides a set of 10-20 seed events, represented as (ENTITY, DATE) tuples. Our seed lists for DoS attacks, account hijacking and data breach events are presented in tables 1, 2 and 3.

To gather mentions of a seed event (from which features

Victim	Date	# Mentions
spamhaus	2013/03/18	26
soca	2011/06/20	89
etrade	2012/01/05	76
interpol	2012/02/29	45
ustream	2012/05/09	911
virgin media	2012/05/08	15
pirate bay	2012/05/16	2,265
demonoid	2012/07/27	182
att	2012/08/15	2,743
sweden	2012/09/03	28
godaddy	2012/09/10	849
github	2013/07/29	102
reddit	2013/04/19	2,042
cia	2011/06/15	36
paypal	2010/12/10	57

Table 1: Seed instances for DDoS attacks

Victim	Date	# Mentions
associated press	2013/04/23	3,846
reuters	2012/08/05	607
us marines	2013/09/03	97
sarah palin	2008/09/18	5,460
mitt romney	2012/06/05	886
cnn	2014/01/23	597
justin bieber	2012/03/27	348
mutunga	2013/09/27	19
yes scotland	2013/08/20	212
zuckerberg	2013/08/18	229

Table 2: Seed instances for account hijacking attacks

can be extracted) we select tweets which reference the entity, and were written on the event's date. This can be accomplished by querying the Twitter search API[1] with the entity and keyword in addition to the specified date (see Figure 2).

2.3 Extracting Candidate Events

New candidate events are extracted from tweets gathered using the Twitter Streaming API[2]. As mentioned in Section 1 we track keywords associated with each event to avoid sparsity. In our experiments, we track the keywords: *hacked* for account hijacking, *ddos* for denial of service attacks, and *breach* for data breaches.

As tweets are gathered, we extract named entities using a Twitter-tuned NLP pipeline [37]. These extracted entities are then combined with the date on which the tweet was written to form new candidate event instances. Not every candidate will correspond to an event of interest. For instance, many tweets which mention the keyword *ddos*, are promoting products to mitigate Disributed Denial of Service (DDoS) attacks, or talk in general about the category of the event without mentioning a specific instance, e.g.:

> "NTP Amplification **DDoS** Attacks increased over the last few months."

or similarly for the *breach* keyword:

[1] `https://twitter.com/search-home`
[2] `https://dev.twitter.com/docs/streaming-apis`

Feature Category	Sample Feature	Event Category
keyword-context-left	`security` **`breach`**	Data Breach
victim-context-right	**`X`** `admits`	Data Breach
victim-context-right	**`X`** `data breach affecting`	Data Breach
keyword-context-both	`DT` **`ddos`** `attack`	DDoS
keyword-context-left	`NNP NNP hit IN` **`ddos`**	DDoS
victim-context-right	**`X`** `getting ddos'd`	DDoS
victim-context-both	`PRP hacked` **`X`** `POS account`	Account Hijacking
keyword-context-left	`POS email was` **`hacked`**	Account Hijacking
victim-context-right	**`X`** `POS NNP account`	Account Hijacking

Table 4: Examples of high-weight features. Context words other than nouns and verbs are replaced with their part-of-speech tags for better generalization.

Victim	Date	# Mentions
citi	2011/06/09	62
sony	2011/04/23	11
adobe	2013/10/03	1,192
evernote	2013/03/02	3,175
facebook	2013/06/21	1,026
steam	2011/11/07	49
zappos	2012/01/16	2,617
heartland	2009/01/20	28
utah	2013/03/29	12
rsa	2011/03/17	13
nyseg	2012/01/23	18

Table 3: Seed instances for account data breach

"**Breach** of ceasefire in central Syria delays aid convoy"

We therefore need to leverage the provided seed instances in order to determine which candidate event extractions fit the category and filter out distractors.

2.4 Classifying Unlabeled Events

The seed-based approach to event extraction described so far provides a natural interface for an information analyst to define new events, however it leads to a somewhat atypical learning problem. Instead of being provided a representative sample of positive and negative examples of the category of interest, we only have a small set of seed instances, in addition to a large sample of unlabeled events. Rather than heuristically assuming unlabeled examples are negative, we propose a learning objective which regularizes the label distribution towards a user-provided expectation in Section 3. In Section 6, we demonstrate that our approach outperforms a number of competitive baselines including semi-supervised EM and one-class support vector machines.

2.5 Feature Design

We define two sets of binary features as a basis for identifying security-related events. The first consists of a window of contextual words and parts of speech surrounding the entity which represents the candidate victim of the attack. The second feature set is composed of contextual features surrounding the tracked keyword. Context windows of 1-4 words to the left and right of the target are used. All words other than common nouns and verbs are represented by their part of speech tags for better generalization. Part of speech tagging is performed using a tagger which is adapted to Twitter [37]. Representative examples of high-weight features from our data are presented in Table 4.

3. LEARNING TO EXTRACT EVENTS WITH POSITIVE AND UNLABELED DATA

In Section 2 the task of weakly supervised event extraction was cast as a semi-supervised learning problem in which only positive and unlabeled data are available [9]. Motivated by this view on the problem we discuss a number of relevant approaches which are empirically evaluated on our task of security-related event extraction in Section 6.

3.1 Baseline 1: Heuristically Labeled Negative Examples

Perhaps the simplest approach is to use a *non-traditional* classifier to distinguish positive from unlabeled examples. This approach was theoretically analyzed by Elkan and Noto [9]. They noted a classifier trained on positive and unlabeled examples is proportional in expectation to a traditional classifier trained on both positive and negative examples, under the assumption that the observed positives are randomly selected. The approach of heuristically assuming unlabeled examples are negative has been used in previous work on weakly supervised relation extraction [26].

As we demonstrate in Section 6, the assumption that unlabeled examples are negative is too strong for our task of event extraction for two reasons: Firstly, only a small sample of positive seeds are available which are not sampled from the underlying distribution; secondly, the unlabeled examples contain a relatively large proportion of positives, leading to a challenging learning problem.

3.2 Expectation Regularization

Rather than heuristically assuming all unlabeled events are negative, and maximizing their likelihood, instead we propose asking an expert to provide an estimate of the proportion of genuine security events within the unlabeled data. Inspired by recent work on semi-supervised learning, [24] we augment the likelihood term over the positive-only seed instances with a term that encourages the expectation over model predictions on unlabeled data, $\hat{p}_\theta$, to match the user-provided target expectation, $\tilde{p}$.

The objective function combines conditional log likelihood of the (positive-only) labeled data, with an expectation regularization term and L^2 regularization, and is defined as follows:

$$O(\theta) = \underbrace{\sum_i^N \log p_\theta(y_i|x_i)}_{\text{Log Likelihood}} - \underbrace{\lambda^U D(\tilde{p}||\hat{p}_\theta^{\text{unlabeled}})}_{\text{Label regularization}} - \underbrace{\lambda^{L^2} \sum_j w_j^2}_{L^2 \text{ regularization}} \quad (1)$$

Where the parametric form of $p_\theta(y|x)$ was presented in Section 2.1.

The expectation regularization term is defined as the KL divergence between the empirical expectation of the model's posterior predictions on unlabeled data, $\hat{p}_\theta$, and the user-provided target expectation, $\tilde{p}$:

$$D(\tilde{p}||\hat{p}_\theta) = \tilde{p} \log \frac{\tilde{p}}{\hat{p}_\theta} + (1-\tilde{p}) \log \frac{1-\tilde{p}}{1-\hat{p}_\theta}$$

The gradient of the objective function is simply the sum of the gradient for logistic regression with L^2 regularization, combined with the gradient for the expectation regularization term. The derivative of the KL divergence is as follows:

$$\frac{\partial}{\partial \theta_k} D(\tilde{p}||\hat{p}_\theta) = \frac{\partial}{\partial \theta_k} \tilde{p} \log \frac{\tilde{p}}{\hat{p}_\theta} + (1-\tilde{p}) \log \frac{1-\tilde{p}}{1-\hat{p}_\theta}$$

Starting with the first term:

$$\begin{aligned}
\frac{\partial}{\partial \theta_k} \tilde{p} \log \frac{\tilde{p}}{\hat{p}_\theta} &= \frac{\partial}{\partial \theta_k} \underbrace{\tilde{p} \log \tilde{p}}_{\text{constant with respect to } \theta} - \tilde{p} \log \hat{p}_\theta \\
&= -\frac{\partial}{\partial \theta_k} \tilde{p} \log \hat{p}_\theta \\
&= -\frac{\tilde{p}}{\hat{p}_\theta} \frac{\partial}{\partial \theta_k} \hat{p}_\theta \\
&= -\frac{\tilde{p}}{\hat{p}_\theta} \frac{1}{N} \sum_{i=1}^N \frac{\partial}{\partial \theta_k} p_\theta(y_i = 1|x_i) \\
&= -\frac{\tilde{p}}{\hat{p}_\theta} \frac{1}{N} \sum_{i=1}^N \underbrace{p_\theta(y_i = 1|x_i)\,(1 - p_\theta(y_i = 1|x_i))\, x_{i,k}}_{\text{sigmoid derivative}}
\end{aligned}$$

The derivation of the gradient for the second term is similar; putting these together we get:

$$\frac{\partial}{\partial \theta_k} D(\tilde{p}||\hat{p}_\theta) =$$

$$\frac{1}{N} \left(\frac{1-\tilde{p}}{1-\hat{p}_\theta} - \frac{\tilde{p}}{\hat{p}_\theta} \right) \sum_{i=1}^N p_\theta(y_i = 1|x_i)(1 - p_\theta(y_i = 1|x_i)) x_{i,k}$$

This gradient makes sense intuitively: If the empirical label distribution matches the user-provided target expectation, then $\hat{p}_\theta = \tilde{p}$ and the gradient is 0. If $\hat{p}_\theta > \tilde{p}$ or $\hat{p}_\theta < \tilde{p}$, then the second factor is either positive or negative accordingly to push the parameters θ up or down. Also note that the terms for each unlabeled example $p_\theta(y_i = 1|x_i)(1 - p_\theta(y_i = 1|x_i)x_{i,k}$ will give more weight to uncertain cases, since the function $f(x) = x(1-x)$ has it's maximum at 0.5.

3.3 Baseline 2: Semi-Supervised EM with Constrained Class Priors

As a baseline we implemented a generative model based on Naïve Bayes which explicitly models unlabeled examples using latent variables [30]. We use EM to maximize likelihood, alternating between estimating the model's parameters, $\theta_k = p(x_k = 1|y)$, in the M-step, and updating the posterior distribution over unlabeled examples in the E-step, by applying Bayes' rule:

$$p_\theta(y_i|x_i) = \frac{p(x_i|y_i = 1)p(y_i = 1)}{p(x_i)}$$

Because only positive examples are observed, we constrain the prior distribution over positives to the same user-specified value as was used for label regularization, rather than re-estimating it from data in the M-step:

$$p(y_i = 1) = \tilde{p}$$

3.4 Baseline 3: One-Class SVMs

As an additional (novel) baseline for weakly supervised information extraction, we experimented with one-class SVMs [42], which are only trained on positive examples and ignore the unlabeled data. We used the one-class SVM implementation from LibSVM.[3] A linear kernel was used which is appropriate for our case due to the large number of features, where overfitting is a concern. We experimented with other kernel functions but found a linear kernel to have the best performance.

4. SECURITY RELATED EVENTS

Section 2 presented a generic framework for extracting targeted events from social media streams and section 3 presented a series of approaches for addressing the weakly supervised learning problem which it presented. Next we briefly define and describe the information security events we have investigated as a case study.

4.1 Denial of Service Attacks

The DoS is designed to deny the liveness properties (e.g. uptime) of a web service to other users. These attacks are most often accomplished by an agent who amplifies requests for a network service with no other intention but to saturate the service beyond some capacity of the resource(s) behind that device (e.g. bandwidth, processing or memory).

An Example: In March of 2013 an ongoing conflict between *Spamhaus* a large European spam blocking service and *Cyberbunker* a European internet service provider erupted into a massive and sustained DDoS attack. Beginning on March 18th of 2013 a distributed attack, that leveraged the Domain Name System (DNS) protocol to amplify the volume of the attack, was initialized from a set of hosts which requested DNS packets with a spoofed return addresses belonging to *Spamhaus*. During the attack (March 18th to 27th of 2013) significant side effects to internet users and services were experienced in Europe.

The use of social media to detect liveness properties of web services has been studied in [27], however we aim to take a step further to consider a specific cause of outage (i.e. DoS attack).

4.2 Data Breach

Data breach is an attack which implements sophisticated techniques to pilfer a collection of personal or digital credentials. The effects of a data breach if unmitigated may

[3]`http://www.csie.ntu.edu.tw/~cjlin/libsvm/`

result in fraudulent use of personal information; however, early detection may alert affected users to monitor for fraud and initialize preventative measures such as updating credentials. Data breach attacks my elicit signals from social media such as early discovery and warnings generated by affected users who discover fraud, further this may be useful to other users whose stolen personal information (e.g. credit card) has not yet been exploited.

An Example: On December 19, 2013, Target Brands Inc. announced that up to 40 million credit/debit cards of customers from Target stores during the time period November 27th 2013 to December 15th of 2013 may be affected by a databreach on their point of sale system. While stolen information may be used for fraudulent charges, the timely notification for affected customers allows for mitigation options.

4.3 Account Hijacking

Account hijacking may involve an intruder guessing, cracking, or using default passwords to gain unauthorized access to a user accounts or system privileges. Account hijacking usually focuses on the problem of determining an unknown user password by using techniques including brute force attacks, dictionary attacks (using frequently used passwords), Rainbow Tables [28] when hash values are available, or profiling an individual to boost other techniques.

An Example: On April 23, 2013, the Associated Press (AP) twitter account was hijacked and the intruders used the AP twitter account to falsely announce that the white house had been attacked and president Obama injured. The Dow Jones industrial average dropped immediately 143 points from 14,697 but quickly recovered. Phishing attacks (social engineering) on AP were alleged to have preceded the hijacked accounts. The Syrian Electronic Army (SEA) claimed responsibility for the intrusion. In addition to AP the hijackings of several high profile Twitter accounts have been reported [4] including: Financial Times (claimed by SEA), The Onion, The Guardian (claimed by SEA), North Korea (claimed by Anonymous), Burger King, Jeep, and Agence France-Presse (AFP).

5. DATA

5.1 Seed Events

To gather historical seed events the authors used targeted search queries, and several events they had in memory. The list of seeds is displayed in Tables 1, 2 and 3.

5.2 Unlabeled Events

Unlabeled event candidates were gathered by tracking keywords, and extracting named entity mentions as described in Section 2 using a set of NLP tools tuned to work on noisy Twitter data.[4] We gathered data over roughly a 1 month period from January 17 2014 until February 20. This resulted in roughly 14,610,000 raw tweets. Non-English tweets were filtered using `langid.py` [23], and named entities were extracted [37]. Events which are mentioned 3 or more times in the data were considered, that is: named entities mentioned in 3 or more tweets on the same day. This resulted in 4,014 extracted candidate account hijacking events, 570 candidate DDOS attacks and 1,738 data breaches.

[4]`https://github.com/aritter/twitter_nlp`

	Hijacking	DDOS	Data Breach
Logistic Regression	0.419	0.252	0.444
Expectation Reg.	**0.716**	**0.459**	**0.676**
Semi-Supervised EM	0.453	0.419	0.442
One-Class SVM	0.681	0.436	0.641

Table 5: Area under precision recall curve comparing various methods for learning with positive and unlabeled data. Our expectation-regularization based approach significantly outperforms all baselines in each event category according to a paired t-test with p value less than 0.05.

5.3 Features

We extract binary features from the bag of tweets associated with each event as described in Section 2.5. A sample of high-weight features inferred using our approach are listed in Table 4. We removed any features which did not appear in association with at least two distinct entities in the data. In total there are 52,995 features for account hijacking, 3,790 features for DoS attacks and 11,271 for data breach.

6. EVALUATION

To evaluate the ability of our models to extract new events, we manually annotated a random sample of candidate events for each category. We then compared the model's predictions against human judgments in order to measure precision and recall.

For each category one of the authors manually annotated 200 randomly sampled instances. In cases where the judgment was not immediately clear, the annotator followed any links in the tweets and used Google searches to determine whether the event did indeed correspond to an instance of the category.

We set the target expectation in each experiment to a value slightly larger than 0.5, and the L^2 regularization to 100. Following Mann et. al. [24], λ^U is set to 10 times the number of labeled examples.

6.1 Results

Precision and recall curves for account hijacking, DoS attacks and data breach are presented in Figures 3, 4, and 5. Several observations can be made: First the baseline of heuristically assuming unlabeled examples are negative results in generally poor performance. This is due to the unique nature of our problem: our seeds are not randomly sampled from the underlying distribution of positive examples, and the unlabeled examples contain a relatively high proportion of positives. While the one-class SVM presents a very strong baseline for this problem, our approach based on expectation regularization achieves significantly higher area under the precision-recall curve according to a paired t-test. Area under the curve for each method and event category is presented in Table 5. Examples of high-confidence extractions in each category are presented in Table 6.

6.2 Independent Validation with Computer Network Measurements

We consider validity by independently measuring the computer network traffic associated with one anecdotal confirmation of a discovered security event by our classification

Victim	Date	Category	Sample Tweet
namecheap	Feb-20-2014	DDoS	My site was down due to a DDoS attack on NameCheap's DNS server. Those are lost page hits man...
bitcoin	Feb-12-2014	DDoS	Bitcoin value dramatically drops as massive #DDOS attack is waged on #Bitcoin http://t.co/YdoygOGmhv
europe	Feb-20-2014	DDoS	Record-breaking DDoS attack in Europe hits 400Gbps.
barcelona	Feb-18-2014	Account Hijacking	Lmao, the official Barcelona account has been hacked.
adam	Feb-16-2014	Account Hijacking	@adamlambert You've been hacked Adam! Argh!
dubai	Feb-09-2014	Account Hijacking	Dubai police twitter account just got hacked!
maryland	Feb-20-2014	Data Breach	SSNs Compromised in University of Maryland Data Breach: https://t.co/j69VeJC4dw
kickstarter	Feb-15-2014	Data Breach	I suspect my card was compromised because of the Kickstarter breach. It's a card I don't use often but have used for things like that.
tesco	Feb-14-2014	Data Breach	@directhex @Tesco thanks to the data breach yesterday it's clear no-one in Tesco does their sysadmin housekeeping!

Table 6: Example high-confidence events extracted using our system.

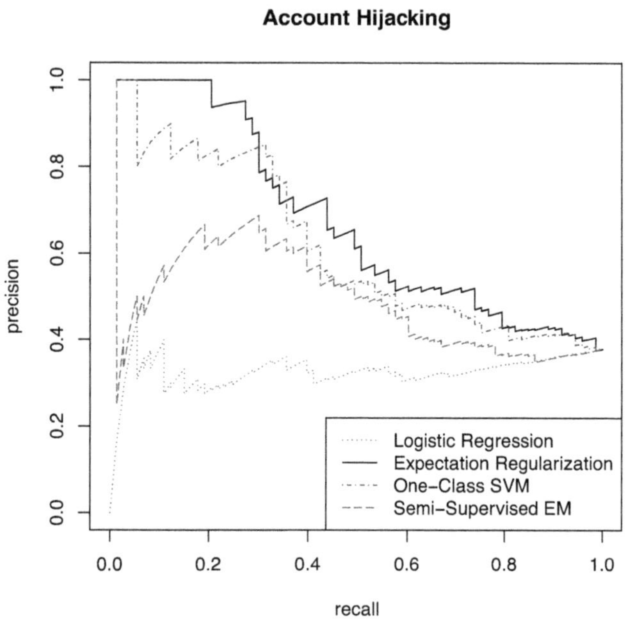

Figure 3: Precision and recall comparing various approaches to extracting events using only positive seeds and unlabeled data.

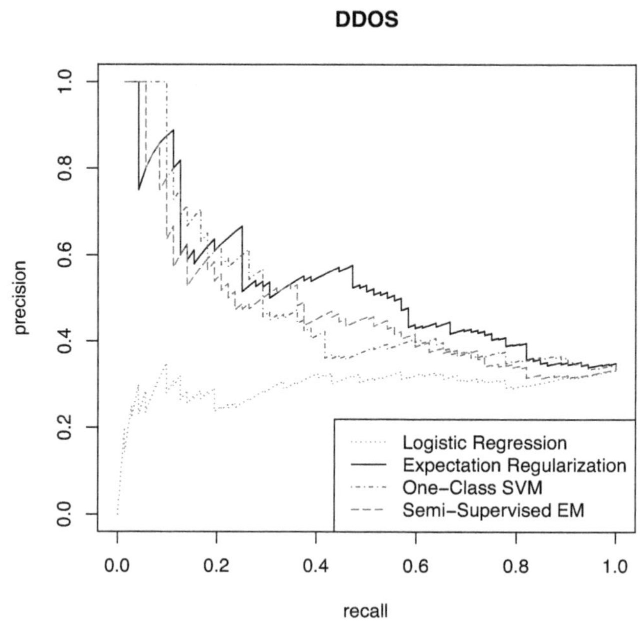

Figure 4: Precision and recall comparing various approaches to extracting events using only positive seeds and unlabeled data.

system. Our system identified *weasyl.com* in a DDoS attack on January 18. For example, without prior knowledge of *weasyl.com* or the attack date the classifier indicates the following messages as a DDoS event:

> "Over the last 24 hours, Weasyl has been subject to a few DDoS attacks on the site."

A popular data source to summarize large quantities of network data and network properties is network flow data, or *netflow* [8]. This data allows us to monitor network traffic and retrospectively identify events that occurred. Netflow data is gathered on routers or special-purposed devices, to account network activity. Netflow is valuable to understand traffic volume and actors as well as retrospectively accomplish network forensics.

Using netflow we measure the traffic between a large corporate network and *weasyl.com* during a nine day time period. Figure 6 shows the number of unique devices sending RST packets per hour to *weasyl.com*. The RST packet is the device's response to a malformed communication channel, including the case when the sender was spoofed. The spoofed communication channels are generated by the attacker and is a well-known technique in a DoS attack.

The traffic baseline is consistently under ten devices per hour, for the days before and after the DDoS event detected by our classifier. Yet, during the DDoS event we observe the number of devices with traffic communicating to *weasyl.com*

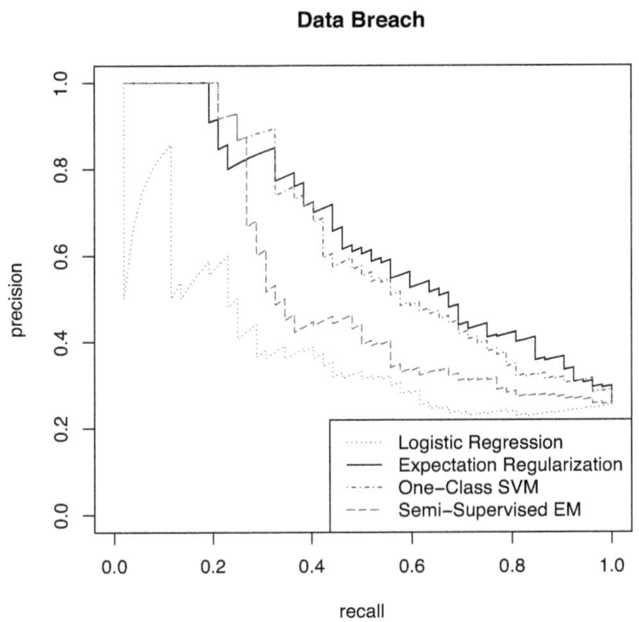

Figure 5: Precision and recall comparing various approaches to extracting events using only positive seeds and unlabeled data.

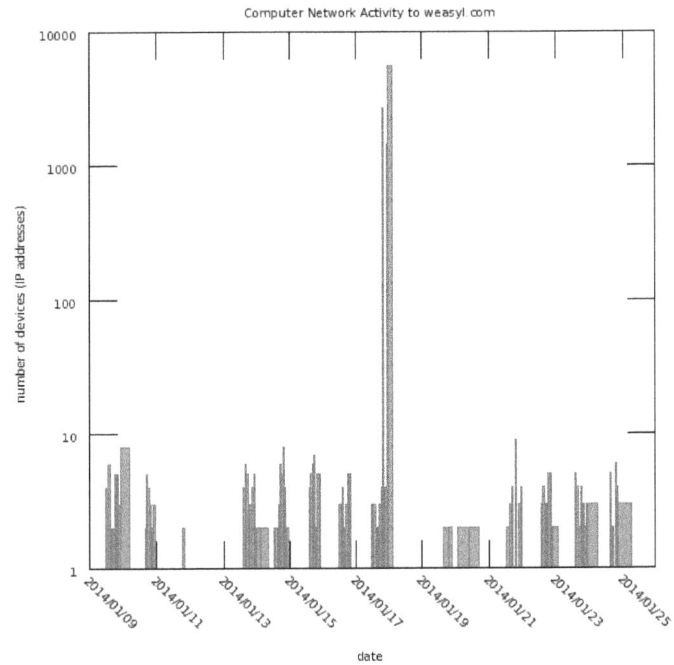

Figure 6: Network measurements (on log scale) for *weasyl.com* showing activity peak with DDoS detected by our classifier.

increasing by over three orders of magnitude. Further investigation of the network traffic led to identifying two distinct events approximately four hours apart. Both events were web-based SYN floods [33] where each of the source devices were randomly spoofed. Consequently, our detection of the event measured the backscatter [33] of responses from the webserver mistakenly responding to devices in our monitored network.

7. RELATED WORK

7.1 Weakly Supervised Relation Extraction

There has been substantial amount of work on weakly supervised relation extraction. Most previous work has focused on extracting static relations which remain relatively constant over time, for instance book authors [5, 1], class/instance pairs, named entities [31] or *hypernyms* [14, 32, 43]. The NELL system in particular [6] has pushed the boundaries of which relations are possible to extract.

Previous work on relation extraction has also addressed the challenge of false-positives in weakly supervised learning [44, 39]. We believe these approaches are not directly applicable for our scenario, however, as the multiple instance learning assumption they use is inappropriate for our event data. Typically all tweets mentioning an entity-date tuple are instances of the category, or all are false positives.

There has been much less work in contrast on weakly supervised *event extraction*, however, as newswire coverage of a specific event is generally too sparse to support seed-based learning. There are hundreds of thousands of sentences on the web which mention William Shakespeare as the author of Comedy of Errors, or that Nirvana plays grunge music, however there are typically only one or a handful of news articles that report on a specific event, such as a DoS attack.

Social media, however greatly lowers the barrier to publishing making it easy for anyone to comment on events as they take place. This leads to substantial redundancy of information, as many users will typically comment on events of interest. This redundancy on Twitter makes seed-based weakly supervised event extraction a feasible task because it is easy to find a large number of event mentions for an event category given a few seed instances.

7.2 Event Extraction

There has been growing interest in information extraction and event identification in Social Media [13]. Benson et al. [3] use distant supervision to train a relation extractor which identifies artists and venues mentioned within tweets of users who list their location as New York City. Sakaki et al. [41] train a classifier to recognize tweets reporting earthquakes in Japan; they demonstrate their system is capable of recognizing almost all earthquakes reported by the Japan Meteorological Agency. Ritter et. al. [38] demonstrate how to extract an open-domain calendar of events referenced in the future. Becker et. al. [2] link tweets to structured data sources describing events. Petrović et. al. present a streaming approach to identifying Tweets which are the first to report breaking news stories [34]. Chierichetti et. al [7] showed it is possible to detect high-volume events such as goals during the world cup using only non-textual evidence.

In contrast to previous work on event identification in social media, we take a weakly supervised approach to extracting focused event categories where only a few seed instances are provided. We also are the first to demonstrate the prevalence of security-related events reported on Twitter, and investigate how to automatically detect them.

A small amount of recent work has explored extracting security related information from text, such as understanding software vulnerability ontologies [18]. There has also been work demonstrating that private information can be inadvertently revealed on social media and studying how to prevent this [15]. In contrast we demonstrate Twitter is a valuable resource for information on security events, explore the challenges and opportunities presented by security event extraction in Twitter and focus on the goal of timely extraction of events as soon as they are reported. As far as we are aware this is the first work to explore extracting security-related events from social media.

8. CONCLUSIONS

Motivated by the wide variety of event categories which might be of interest to track, we proposed a weakly supervised seed-based approach to event extraction from Twitter. We showed how this leads to an unusual learning problem where only a small number of positive seeds and a sample of unlabeled candidate events are available. A number of approaches were investigated to address this challenge, including label regularization, constrained semi-supervised EM and one-class SVMs. We applied this approach to detect several security-related events including DoS attacks and account hijacking incidents, and demonstrated that a large number of security-related events are mentioned on Twitter.

9. ACKNOWLEDGMENTS

This research has been supported in part by DARPA (under contract number FA8750-13-2-0005) and the Department of Defense under Contract No. FA8721-05-C-0003 with Carnegie Mellon University for the operation of the Software Engineering Institute, a federally funded research and development center.

10. REFERENCES

[1] E. Agichtein and L. Gravano. Snowball: Extracting relations from large plain-text collections. In *Proceedings of the fifth ACM conference on Digital libraries*, pages 85–94. ACM, 2000.

[2] H. Becker, D. Iter, M. Naaman, and L. Gravano. Identifying content for planned events across social media sites. In *Proceedings of the fifth ACM international conference on Web search and data mining*, pages 533–542. ACM, 2012.

[3] E. Benson, A. Haghighi, and R. Barzilay. Event discovery in social media feeds. In *ACL*, 2011.

[4] B. Bishop. High-profile twitter account hijackings leave questions about security. web, May 2013.

[5] S. Brin. Extracting patterns and relations from the world wide web. In *The World Wide Web and Databases*. 1999.

[6] A. Carlson, J. Betteridge, B. Kisiel, B. Settles, E. R. Hruschka Jr, and T. M. Mitchell. Toward an architecture for never-ending language learning. In *AAAI*, 2010.

[7] F. Chierichetti, J. Kleinberg, R. Kumar, M. Mahdian, and S. Pandey. Event detection via communication pattern analysis. 2014.

[8] B. Claise. RFC 3954 - Cisco Systems NetFlow Services Export Version 9, Oct. 2004.

[9] C. Elkan and K. Noto. Learning classifiers from only positive and unlabeled data. In *Proceedings of the 14th ACM SIGKDD international conference on Knowledge discovery and data mining*, 2008.

[10] H. Fei, Y. Kim, S. Sahu, M. Naphade, S. K. Mamidipalli, and J. Hutchinson. Heat pump detection from coarse grained smart meter data with positive and unlabeled learning. In *Proceedings of the 19th ACM SIGKDD International Conference on Knowledge Discovery and Data Mining*, KDD '13, pages 1330–1338, New York, NY, USA, 2013. ACM.

[11] K. Ganchev, J. Graça, J. Gillenwater, and B. Taskar. Posterior regularization for structured latent variable models. *The Journal of Machine Learning Research*, 11:2001–2049, 2010.

[12] R. Grishman and B. Sundheim. Message understanding conference-6: A brief history. In *COLING*, 1996.

[13] W. Guo, H. Li, H. Ji, and M. T. Diab. Linking tweets to news: A framework to enrich short text data in social media. In *ACL (1)*, pages 239–249. Citeseer, 2013.

[14] M. A. Hearst. Automatic acquisition of hyponyms from large text corpora. In *Proceedings of the 14th conference on Computational linguistics-Volume 2*, pages 539–545. Association for Computational Linguistics, 1992.

[15] R. Heatherly, M. Kantarcioglu, and B. Thuraisingham. Preventing private information inference attacks on social networks. *Knowledge and Data Engineering, IEEE Transactions on*, 25(8):1849–1862, 2013.

[16] R. Huang and E. Riloff. Bootstrapped training of event extraction classifiers. In *Proceedings of the 13th Conference of the European Chapter of the Association for Computational Linguistics*. Association for Computational Linguistics, 2012.

[17] H. Ji and R. Grishman. Refining event extraction through cross-document inference. In *Proceedings of ACL-08: HLT*, Columbus, Ohio, 2008. Association for Computational Linguistics.

[18] A. Joshi, R. Lal, T. Finin, and A. Joshi. Extracting cybersecurity related linked data from text. In *Semantic Computing (ICSC), 2013 IEEE Seventh International Conference on*, pages 252–259. IEEE, 2013.

[19] W. S. Lee and B. Liu. Learning with positive and unlabeled examples using weighted logistic regression. In *ICML*, volume 3, pages 448–455, 2003.

[20] C. Li, J. Weng, Q. He, Y. Yao, A. Datta, A. Sun, and B.-S. Lee. Twiner: named entity recognition in targeted twitter stream. In *Proceedings of the 35th international ACM SIGIR conference on Research and development in information retrieval*, pages 721–730. ACM, 2012.

[21] X. Li and B. Liu. Learning to classify texts using positive and unlabeled data. In *IJCAI*, pages 587–592, 2003.

[22] X. Liu, S. Zhang, F. Wei, and M. Zhou. Recognizing named entities in tweets. In *Proceedings of the 49th Annual Meeting of the Association for Computational*

Linguistics: Human Language Technologies-Volume 1, pages 359–367. Association for Computational Linguistics, 2011.

[23] M. Lui and T. Baldwin. langid. py: An off-the-shelf language identification tool. In *Proceedings of the ACL 2012 System Demonstrations*, pages 25–30. Association for Computational Linguistics, 2012.

[24] G. S. Mann and A. McCallum. Simple, robust, scalable semi-supervised learning via expectation regularization. In *Proceedings of the 24th international conference on Machine learning*, pages 593–600. ACM, 2007.

[25] G. S. Mann and A. McCallum. Generalized expectation criteria for semi-supervised learning with weakly labeled data. *The Journal of Machine Learning Research*, pages 955–984, 2010.

[26] M. Mintz, S. Bills, R. Snow, and D. Jurafsky. Distant supervision for relation extraction without labeled data. In *Proceedings of the Joint Conference of the 47th Annual Meeting of the ACL and the 4th International Joint Conference on Natural Language Processing of the AFNLP: Volume 2-Volume 2*. Association for Computational Linguistics, 2009.

[27] M. Motoyama, B. Meeder, K. Levchenko, G. M. Voelker, and S. Savage. Measuring online service availability using twitter. *WOSNâĂŹ10*, pages 13–13, 2010.

[28] A. Narayanan. Fast dictionary attacks on passwords using time-space tradeoff. In *In ACM Conference on Computer and Communications Security*, pages 364–372. ACM Press, 2005.

[29] G. Neubig, Y. Matsubayashi, M. Hagiwara, and K. Murakami. Safety information mining-what can nlp do in a disaster-. In *IJCNLP*, pages 965–973, 2011.

[30] K. Nigam, A. McCallum, and T. Mitchell. Semi-supervised text classification using em. *Semi-Supervised Learning*, 2006.

[31] M. Paşca. Weakly-supervised discovery of named entities using web search queries. In *Proceedings of the Sixteenth ACM Conference on Conference on Information and Knowledge Management*, CIKM '07, pages 683–690, New York, NY, USA, 2007. ACM.

[32] P. Pantel and M. Pennacchiotti. Espresso: Leveraging generic patterns for automatically harvesting semantic relations. In *Proceedings of the 21st International Conference on Computational Linguistics and the 44th annual meeting of the Association for Computational Linguistics*, pages 113–120. Association for Computational Linguistics, 2006.

[33] T. Peng, C. Leckie, and K. Ramamohanarao. Survey of network-based defense mechanisms countering the dos and ddos problems. *ACM Comput. Surv.*, 39(1), April 2007.

[34] S. Petrović, M. Osborne, and V. Lavrenko. Streaming first story detection with application to twitter. In *Human Language Technologies: The 2010 Annual Conference of the North American Chapter of the Association for Computational Linguistics*, pages 181–189. Association for Computational Linguistics, 2010.

[35] V. Qazvinian, E. Rosengren, D. R. Radev, and Q. Mei. Rumor has it: Identifying misinformation in microblogs. In *Proceedings of the Conference on Empirical Methods in Natural Language Processing*, pages 1589–1599. Association for Computational Linguistics, 2011.

[36] K. Reschke, M. Jankowiak, M. Surdeanu, C. D. Manning, and D. Jurafsky. Event extraction using distant supervision. 2014.

[37] A. Ritter, S. Clark, O. Etzioni, et al. Named entity recognition in tweets: an experimental study. In *Proceedings of the Conference on Empirical Methods in Natural Language Processing*, 2011.

[38] A. Ritter, O. Etzioni, S. Clark, et al. Open domain event extraction from twitter. In *Proceedings of the 18th ACM SIGKDD international conference on Knowledge discovery and data mining*, pages 1104–1112. ACM, 2012.

[39] A. Ritter, L. Zettlemoyer, Mausam, and O. Etzioni. Modeling missing data in distant supervision for information extraction. *TACL*, 2013.

[40] K. Roberts, T. Goodwin, and S. M. Harabagiu. Annotating spatial containment relations between events. In *LREC*, 2012.

[41] T. Sakaki, M. Okazaki, and Y. Matsuo. Earthquake shakes twitter users: real-time event detection by social sensors. In *WWW*, 2010.

[42] B. Schölkopf, J. C. Platt, J. Shawe-Taylor, A. J. Smola, and R. C. Williamson. Estimating the support of a high-dimensional distribution. *Neural computation*, 2001.

[43] B. Wellner. Weakly supervised learning methods for improving the quality of gene name normalization data. In *Proceedings of the ACL-ISMB Workshop on Linking Biological Literature, Ontologies and Databases: Mining Biological Semantics*, ISMB '05, pages 1–8, Stroudsburg, PA, USA, 2005. Association for Computational Linguistics.

[44] W. Xu, R. Hoffmann, L. Zhao, and R. Grishman. Filling knowledge base gaps for distant supervision of relation extraction. In *ACL (2)*, 2013.

Groupsourcing: Team Competition Designs for Crowdsourcing

Markus Rokicki, Sergej Zerr, Stefan Siersdorfer
L3S Research Center, Hannover, Germany
{rokicki,siersdorfer,zerr}@L3S.de

ABSTRACT

Many data processing tasks such as semantic annotation of images, translation of texts in foreign languages, and labeling of training data for machine learning models require human input, and, on a large scale, can only be accurately solved using crowd based online work. Recent work shows that frameworks where crowd workers compete against each other can drastically reduce crowdsourcing costs, and outperform conventional reward schemes where the payment of online workers is proportional to the number of accomplished tasks ("pay-per-task"). In this paper, we investigate how team mechanisms can be leveraged to further improve the cost efficiency of crowdsourcing competitions. To this end, we introduce strategies for team based crowdsourcing, ranging from team formation processes where workers are randomly assigned to competing teams, over strategies involving self-organization where workers actively participate in team building, to combinations of team and individual competitions. Our large-scale experimental evaluation with more than 1,100 participants and overall 5,400 hours of work spent by crowd workers demonstrates that our team based crowdsourcing mechanisms are well accepted by online workers and lead to substantial performance boosts.

Categories and Subject Descriptors

H.1.2 [**Models and Principles**]: User / Machine Systems—*Human information processing, Human Factors*

General Terms

Algorithms, Experimentation, Human Factors

Keywords

crowdsourcing; competitions; groupsourcing; reward schemes; teams

WWW 2015, May 18–22, 2015, Florence, Italy.
ACM 978-1-4503-3469-3/15/05.
http://dx.doi.org/10.1145/2736277.2741097.

1. INTRODUCTION

The rapid development of information technologies, algorithms, and computer hardware has enabled the solution of many real life problems through efficient processing of large amounts of data and application of various methods in the area of artificial intelligence such as machine learning or decision theory. However, for many tasks such as semantic image annotation, mood analysis, or relevance ranking, humans still significantly outperform automatic methods. Projects such as Wikipedia or Open Street Maps which leverage collaborative human power have demonstrated that a large crowd of non-experts can, under certain conditions, be as effective and precise as a small group of experts [19, 17]. Information providers make implicit use of collaborative knowledge for improving their services: Search engines exploit query logs for determining the popularity and improving the automatic ranking of web pages or for suggesting queries and advertisements to their customers. Online shops like Amazon and auctions like eBay correlate information from buyers to recommend new items.

Games with a Purpose can help *intrinsically* motivating users to produce input in large quantities: In the ESP game [21, 22], for instance, online players compete in image annotation tasks; in this way, the images indexed by Google in 2004 could be annotated in just 31 days. On the other hand, platforms like Amazon's Mechanical Turk and CrowdFlower successfully make use of online workers and *monetary* incentives for accomplishing tasks such as the annotation of multimedia content, translation of texts, or generation of training sets for machine learning and other contexts [23, 25]. Such crowdsourcing platforms are based on a reward scheme where the payment of online workers is proportional to the number of accomplished tasks ("pay-per-task") which can be slow and costly. In our recent work [18] we successfully employed competitive scenarios to motivate users and reduce crowdsourcing costs, but can we obtain even more value for money?

Humans often collaborate in order to achieve a competitive advantage, and being a part of a team can additionally boost the motivation. Well organized teamwork can shorten the time required for completing a particular task by distributing the workload across team members; in addition, some complex tasks require diverse skills and can only be successfully solved by a group of people with expertise in different fields. Inducement prizes awarded for instance by companies like Microsoft, Google, or Yahoo for ideas or code, attract huge numbers of participants and create an enormous overall value. Participants often organize themselves in teams in order to increase their chances. In the DARPA Network Challenge [20] red weather balloons, spatially distributed in a large area in the US, had to be located. An overall prize of 40,000 USD was awarded to the winner and participants were allowed to form search teams. In this way each participant could increase his probability of a successful task completion, but on the other hand would have to share the prize with other team members. The Netflix Prize is another example for such an open competition, where 20,000 research teams were competing against each other, trying to implement the most effective collaborative filtering algorithm for a single prize of 1,000,000 USD; interestingly, some of the participating groups merged into one team ("The Ensemble"), combined their algorithms, and achieved competitive results. In our work [18] on crowdsourcing competitions we also noticed a tendency of some workers to cooperate in order to achieve a competitive advantage (manifesting in attempts to share accounts), which we had to prevent at that time due to our experimental design.

In this work we investigate how group mechanisms can be leveraged to improve the cost efficiency of crowdsourcing competitions. To this end, we first consider a strategy for team formation where workers are randomly assigned to one of a fixed set of teams, and teams compete against each other for a number of monetary prizes. Secondly, we explore an agglomerative strategy involving self-organization where workers (initially starting as one-man teams) can decide by themselves on which team they want to join, or whom to include in their team. Finally, we introduce and evaluate different combinations of team and individual competitions in a large-scale study.

Outline. The remainder of this paper is organized as follows: In Section 2 we discuss related work on games with a purpose and crowdsourcing designs. In Section 3 we formalize our crowdsourcing setting and describe our strategies for team competitions. The evaluation of our strategies is presented in Section 4 where we first describe the experimental setup along with the core results, and then delve deeper into details about team formation and worker dynamics. Finally, in Section 5 we conclude and describe directions of our future work.

2. RELATED WORK

Crowdsourcing has a wide range of applications, including the annotation of data sets, conduction of user surveys, and collaborative gathering of data collections. Since 2011, TREC offers a special trek "TrecCrowd" [1] addressing various issues related to gathering document-relevance labels for information retrieval systems [3, 4]. This includes human task design, user filtering, and the fusion of worker judgments. In this paper, we investigate how collaborative, game-based crowdsourcing designs, can increase the effectiveness of annotations.

Typically, crowd workers can have different qualifications and perform tasks of different types not equally well. In their seminal work [13] Kazai et al. study how payment, worker qualification, and required effort influence the output of tasks in Amazon Mechanical Turk. In the context of relevance labeling, the authors show that increasing the rewards, reducing the required effort, and filtering workers based on qualification requirements can increase the accuracy of the output. In [14] the same authors show the correlation between behavior and personality of workers and the accuracy of their work. In [16] the effect of the amount of micro-payments on quantity and quality of annotations is studied. In contrast, our work focuses on how competitive reward mechanisms in collaborative scenarios influence annotation behavior and the cost efficiency of crowdsourcing.

Gamification techniques can provide additional motivation for the workers. The authors in [2] have focused on principal aspects of game mechanics embedded in standard IR tasks including information seeking, crowdsourcing, and user engagement. He et al. [11] introduce a user interface for studying search behavior within a gamified setting where users receive points for finding relevant documents, and where scores are announced in leaderboards. Dinesh et al. [17] discuss additional incentive structures to encourage user activity within an online platform. A number of earlier works tackle the same problems. Eickhoff et al. [10] employ a game based approach for crowdsourcing of query result relevance labels and image cluster labels. The authors show that entertainment can be a powerful incentive in crowdsourcing and can partially replace financial rewards. In comparison, in this work we study non-linear reward distribution combined with team based strategies in order to increase the effectiveness of crowdsourcing.

There is a body of work on crowdsourcing theory in the area of business, economics, and e-commerce. For instance, [5] provides an analysis of crowdsourcing contests within the software development portal TopCoder[1]. In [9] the authors study the influence of the reward amount; they find that participation rates increase as a function of the offered reward. Other work shows that, while workers are generally attracted by high rewards, they also prefer tasks with low rewards that better suit their abilities and tend to maximize their outcome by balancing reward and workload [24]. In [12] this issue is further addressed by splitting the crowd into groups of workers with different abilities in a scenario where workers compete with each other in the context of bug detection. Although related to our research purposes, these works target crowd based software development contexts where just a *single* solution is selected at the end. In contrast, our work focuses on crowdsourcing of annotations in the context of information retrieval and data mining, where the workload and rewards are divided across multiple teams of workers.

A number of works have proposed theoretical stochastic models in the context of crowdsourcing. In [8] the authors introduce models for the effectiveness of winner-take-all scenarios, and consider aspects such as the optimal choice of the prize money. In [7] the same authors concentrate on scenarios where every non-zero effort of workers is rewarded and, similar to the scenario studied in this paper, the final output consists of the cumulative effort of all workers. Archak et al. [6] present a model for designing crowdsourcing contests with optimized reward distributions to improve the quality of the best submission. However, none of these works provide an experimental evaluation of their concepts.

Finally, in our previous work [18] we introduced non-linear payment strategies for *individual* crowdsourcing competitions in combination with different information policies for boosting the cost efficiency.

[1]`http://www.topcoder.com`

To the best of our knowledge, we are the first to examine *team based* crowdsourcing competitions, and to conduct systematic real-world studies on the effects of collaboration and uneven reward distributions on both quantity and quality of annotations.

3. DESIGN OF TEAM-BASED CROWDSOURCING COMPETITIONS

In this section, we formalize our crowdsourcing scenario and describe different strategies for distributing rewards among workers in team competitions. Furthermore, we describe the information policies (relating to information revealed about the own and other teams as well as fellow workers) we employed in our framework.

3.1 Problem Setting

We consider a scenario with a crowd consisting of n workers $W = \{w_1, \ldots, w_n\}$, and with a fixed (monetary) budget M for paying workers. This budget is distributed among the workers depending on the values $v(w_i)$ produced by them. These values $v(w_i)$ can, for instance, correspond to the number of correctly solved crowdsourcing tasks. A worker w_i receives a reward $r(w_i)$ with $\sum_{i=1}^{n} r(w_i) = M$. Our goal is to maximize the overall value $V = \sum_{i=1}^{n} v(w_i)$ produced by the workers in W.

3.2 Strategies for Reward Distribution

We start by describing two baseline approaches: The first is just a formalization of the usual "pay-per-task" strategy within our framework, the second is from our recent work on individual crowdsourcing competitions. We then extend the latter approach towards team competitions.

The Simple Baseline: Linear Reward Assignment. The commonly used strategy in crowdsourcing is to distribute rewards proportionally to the individual values produced by workers, i.e. each worker w_i receives a reward $r(w_i) = (v(w_i)/V) \cdot M$. In practice this is typically implemented by fixing a reward rate c (e.g. money per task solved) and an overall value $V = M/c$ to be produced (e.g. number of tasks to be solved), resulting in a reward $r(w_i) = v(w_i) \cdot c$ for worker w_i. This strategy corresponds to the usual payment scheme as, for instance, employed for Amazon Mechanical Turk HITs ("pay-per-task").

The Enhanced Baseline: Individual Competitions. In our own recent work [18] we explored various competitive as well as randomized strategies where workers are ranked according to their produced values, and the reward of a worker will depend on his rank. In the following, we describe the best performing of these strategies. Formally, let $rank(w_i) \in \{1, \ldots, n\}$ be the rank of worker w_i, with a rank of j corresponding to the jth highest value produced across all workers. The reward $r(w_i)$ is computed as a monotonically decreasing function $\Gamma(rank(w_i))$ of the worker's rank. Similar to "real world" competitions lower ranks are discounted, i.e. top performers receive more money per solved tasks, and Γ is a convex function. In practice, instead of mathematical functions in closed form, one would rather provide workers with an easy to understand payment scheme containing "round" numbers for rewards and number of winners (e.g. 50, 25, 15, 8, and 2 USD for the top-5).

Part of the leaderboard content is revealed to a worker; this "medium" *information policy* turned out to be most effective in our previous crowdsourcing competitions [18]. Specifically, workers are shown their scores and rank along with a snapshot consisting of their k neighbors above and below them in the leaderboard. The rationale is to trigger competitive behavior within part of the leaderboard while avoiding too much frustration for workers with lower scores. In [18], we showed that this form of competition clearly outperforms the conventional linear reward assignment described in the previous paragraph; therefore, we will compare our new methods in this paper to this enhanced baseline.

Balanced Team Strategy. In competitions among *individual* workers, relatively low performing workers (e.g. in terms of annotation speed) can quickly fall behind their competitors and become demotivated, resulting in a diminished overall value V produced. In this paper we introduce *team based* competitions as a means of motivating a larger number of lower performers, rather than just incentivizing a relatively small number of high-performing individuals.

We first consider a balanced strategy for team formation, where we set up a fixed number τ of teams (each with initial team size 0) and assign each new worker (from the stream of registering workers) uniformly at random to one of the teams containing the lowest number of workers. This guarantees an even distribution of workers across the (disjoint) teams in $T = \{t_1, \ldots, t_\tau\}$. In order to avoid large numbers of inactive team members we introduce a low initial threshold for the value produced by worker w_i before assigning him to a team. Instead of ranking individual workers, we now rank *teams* according to the sum of the values produced by their members, with $rank(t_i)$ defined analogous to the individual ranks described in the previous paragraph. A *team reward* $r(t_i)$ is assigned to each team, using, as for individual competitions, a monotonically decreasing, convex function. A worker w_j receives a reward $r(w_j)$ that is proportional to the contribution to his team $t(w_j)$ - more specifically: $r(w_j) = r(t(w_j)) \cdot v(w_j) / \sum_{w_l \in t(w_j)} v(w_l)$, where $v(w_j)$ is the value produced by w_j.

We carry the previously described information policy for individual competitions over to the team scenario, i.e. during a competition members of a team see their positions along with scores of the k neighbor teams above and below them in the leaderboard. In addition, workers are kept updated about their current shares of the team reward.

Self-Organizing Team Strategy. In order to avoid demotivation through team assignments imposed by the system, we also explore a strategy where workers can decide by themselves on which team they want to join, and whom to include in their team (or, alternatively, to stay single workers). Initially, each worker forms a one-man team and becomes its administrator. With the start of the competition begins the *team formation phase* where teams are built up in an agglomerative way as follows: The administrator of a team can invite the administrator of a second team; if the invitation is accepted both teams are merged and the inviting administrator becomes the (single) administrator of the whole team. This procedure can be repeated to form larger teams. The value produced by a team is equal to the sum of the values produced by its members during the whole competition, i.e.

values of merged teams are added up. Similar as for the balanced strategy, we require workers to produce a value above some low initial threshold before becoming involved in team formation activities. Note that workers (including administrators) are already actively involved in crowdsourcing tasks in the team formation phase. In order to support decision making, administrators gain access to statistics on the other teams - specifically, their sizes and produced values.

After the team formation phase and until the end of the competition no further merging of teams is possible, and administrators become "normal" workers without a dedicated view on team statistics. Except for administrators in the team formation phase, the information policy is the same as described for the balanced team strategy. We also rank teams and distribute rewards across workers in the same way as described in the previous paragraph.

Combining Teams and Individual Competitions. In order to account for different worker preferences we can combine team and individual strategies. To this end, the overall price money M is split into a part for a team competition and a separate part for an individual competition. Workers conduct crowdsourcing tasks as before and obtain scores corresponding to their values produced. From these scores both the individual ranks as well as team ranks and shares are computed. The overall reward of the worker is the sum of his individual reward and his team share.

4. EXPERIMENTS

In this section we evaluate the team strategies described in Section 3 using face recognition as crowdsourcing scenario. The objective of our evaluation was to study the cost efficiency of strategies, competitive behavior of workers, and team dynamics.

4.1 Setup

Crowdsourcing Task. We launched a *face recognition* task where workers were asked to identify a person on a given reference photo among a set of 10 test photos. The images were retrieved from the PubFig[2] database which was created for face verification [15]. Out of originally 58,797 images with faces of 200 celebrities, 37,004 images were available on the Web. We reviewed the dataset manually and removed 663 images showing placeholders as well as 135 images we deemed unsuitable because the correct person was not shown on the image. As a quality check mechanism we randomly introduced a "honeypot" task within each batch of 100 tasks that was manually selected beforehand. After workers finished a batch they were shown the honeypot and their own input for it. If workers solved the honeypot correctly, 100 points were added to their score, otherwise 20 points were subtracted (with a cut-off threshold of 0 for the score, i.e. we did not introduce negative scores).

Implementation and Settings. We announced the crowdsourcing tasks on the CrowdFlower platform and a mailing list consisting of participants from previous competitions about one day before the competition started. The workers were choosing the tasks autonomously, as common for crowdsourcing platforms such as CrowdFlower. As the tested reward strategies are not supported by Mechanical Turk or CrowdFlower, we ran the actual competition using an external application on servers at our institute. Each worker was assigned a user code upon registration which had to be submitted to the CrowdFlower task in order for the account to be activated, thus ensuring that each participant could be paid.

We started with two preliminary experimental rounds consisting of an individual competition and a group based competition. We observed an initial strong interest by workers for the novel type of scenario resulting in high participation rate, which quickly decline in the second experiment. Furthermore we received feedback from workers concerning the overlong duration of the experiments (originally six days) and missing communication features. To remedy these issues we reduced the experiment running time to three days and added automatic notifications for the chat. The final experiments were performed sequentially with a duration of three days per experiment (and one run per configuration) and a break of at least one day in between two competitions in order to avoid extensive user fatigue.

Tested Strategies. As a baseline, we chose the challenging "Individual Competition" strategy **ind** which has been shown to substantially outperform simple "pay-per-task" in [18]. We will provide evidence that reaching comparable performance using conventional "pay-per-task" would be unrealistic. We tested the team competition strategies "Balanced Teams" (**balanceTS**) and "Self-Organizing Teams" (**selfTS**) described in Section 3.2. For each strategy the prize money of $M = 100$ USD was divided into shares of 50, 25, 15, 8, and 2 USD for the top-5 performing teams or individuals. In addition, we conducted two experiments (coined **ind-balanceTS** and **ind-selfTS**) where we extended the team strategies with rewards for individual workers; to this end, the 100 USD prize money was equally divided into an individual and a team part with prizes of 25, 12, 7, 4, and 2 USD for the top-5 individuals/teams. Workers had to solve at least one batch correctly in order to qualify for participation in a team (for *balanceTS*) or for team formation activities (for *selfTS*). For all strategies we employed a medium information policy showing the scores of the three neighbor teams above and below the workers' teams in the leaderboard.

We chose a schedule with the most simple strategy at the beginning and incrementally increased the complexity over the course of the experimental series. More specifically, we conducted the experiments in the order *ind*, *balanceTS*, *ind-balanceTS*, *selfTS*, and *ind-selfTS*. Although this sequence of the experiments can have an influence on the outcomes, in contrast to a random order, it allows users to incrementally adapt to our scenarios and prevents a bias due to user fatigue which might have been in favor of our new strategies otherwise.

4.2 Results

In our experiments, overall 1.6 million images were matched correctly by 1,164 participants from 91 different countries (amounting to over 5,400 hours of work). The workers were accessing our competitions from several parts of the world, with a majority from Europe (38.0%) and Asia (34.7%). The country represented most numerously was India (14.4%), followed by Venezuela (6%) and the United States (4.2%).

[2] `http://www.cs.columbia.edu/CAVE/databases/pubfig/`

Experiment	No. Images	Cent / Hour	Cent / 100 Images
Baseline			
ind	298,332	9.895	3.352
Balanced Teams			
balanceTS	327,073	8.967	3.057
ind-balanceTS	391,620	8.059	2.553
Self-Organized Teams			
selfTS	282,942	9.346	3.534
ind-selfTS	295,158	9.929	3.388

Table 1: Aggregate outcomes of the experimental rounds.

Aggregate Results. Table 1 shows the number of correctly matched images for each of the reward strategies, along with the average amount of money spent per correctly annotated image (both measuring the produced value), and hours of work (measuring monetary recompense for the participants). The main results are the following:

- Using the enhanced baseline (*ind*), we obtained almost 300,000 correctly annotated images at an average cost of 33.5 cent for 1,000 correctly annotated images. Note that using the standard "pay-per-task" scheme, this would result in a task that requires a contributor to annotate over 30 images for a reward of only 0.01 USD.
- The winning strategy - balanced teams combined with individual rewards (*ind-balanceTS*) - clearly outperforms the other strategies, and beats the *ind* baseline by a margin of 30%. This reduces the amount paid for 100 correctly annotated images by almost 24%.
- The pure team strategy *balanceTS* still outperforms the baseline *ind* by around 10%, in terms of value produced as well as time invested by participants.
- The remaining self-organizing team strategies were performing similar to the baseline, without being able to beat it.

Overall, the balanced team strategy with automatic group formation consistently outperformed the self-organizing team strategy. One reason for this might be the additional overhead and complexity for workers due to activities such as team building, communication, and coordination for the *selfTS* and *selfTS-ind* strategies. For instance, our logs revealed that participants in the *selfTS* experiment spent more than 10% more time per value produced in comparison to the baseline. Another reason might be the formation of a very small number of large and dominant teams which we avoid in the balanced case. In section 4.3 we will analyze issues of team dynamics in more detail.

Worker Contributions. Figure 1 depicts the contributions of individual workers to the overall produced value (i.e. fraction of correctly annotated images by the top-10 ($1 \leq R \leq 10$) and the remaining ($R > 10$) participants). The team based strategies benefit from the "fat tail" of the contribution distribution, where lower ranked participants were motivated by the performance of their fellows and contributed more value compared to individual strategies. For self-organizing teams (*selfTS*) we observe that lack of individual

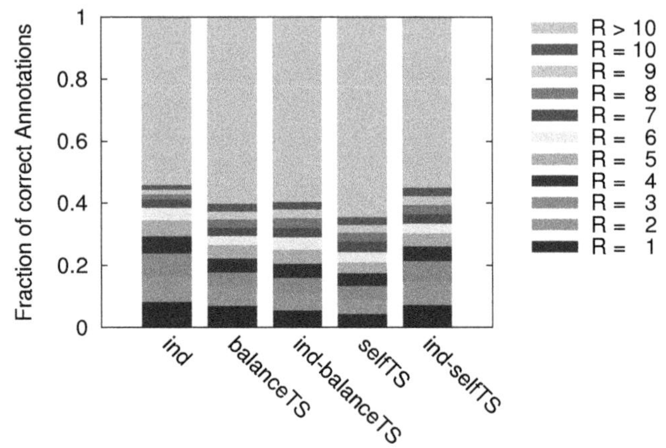

Figure 1: Individual worker contributions to the overall value in different experiments.

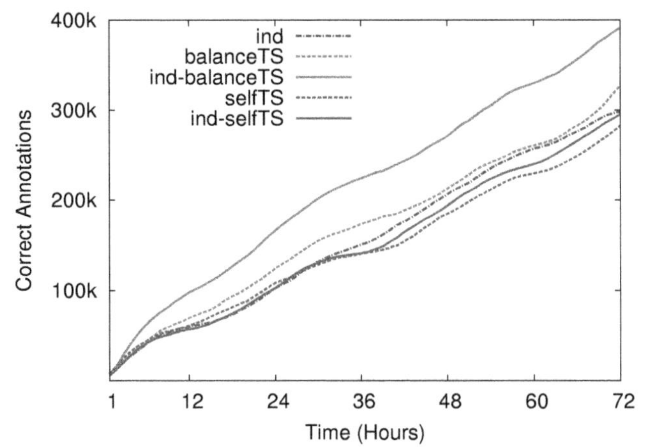

Figure 2: Cumulative number of correctly annotated images per experiment over time.

rewards and very large teams in the experiment can demotivate individual top performers. This effect can be remedied by combining group and individual competitions as shown for the *ind-selfTS* strategy.

Temporal Dynamics. Figure 2 illustrates the temporal evolution of the cumulative counts of correctly solved images aggregated over the whole set of workers. The numbers grow mostly linearly over time with higher increments at the beginning of the competitions and periodicities which are probably due to day cycles, similar to our findings in [18]. However, due to the larger and more diverse user base of CrowdFlower compared to Mechanical Turk in our previous work, the periodicity is less pronounced (for further illustration see the non-cumulative view for the individual competition *ind* and balanced team competition *balanceTS* in Figure 3). In addition, Figure 3b reveals fierce competitions between workers for the *balanceTS* strategy (e.g. for team ranks 1 and 3 towards the end of the contest), leading to a boost in the amount of annotations.

We also studied the contribution of individual workers over time. Figure 4 breaks the cumulative annotation counts down for the top-10 individual workers. Compared to indi-

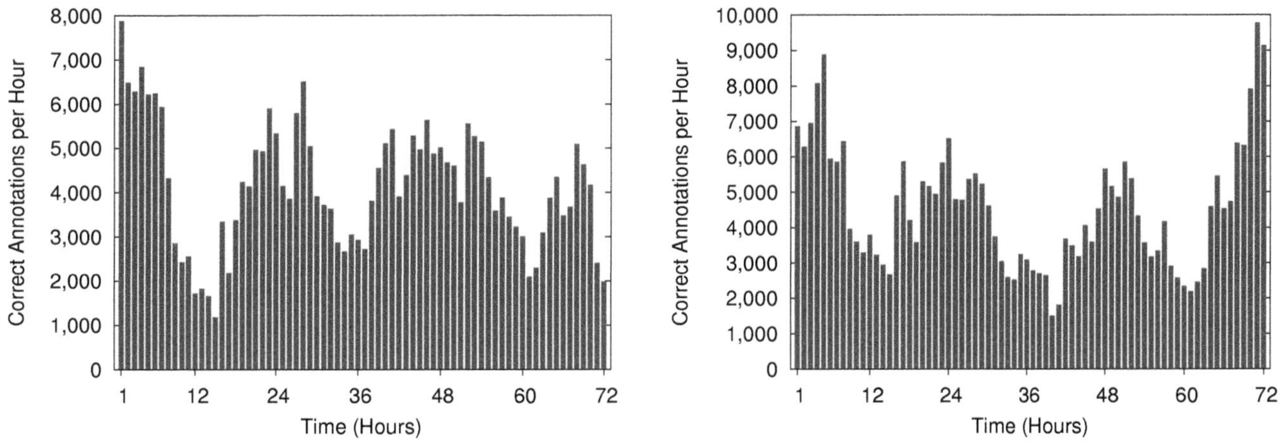

(a) ind (b) balanceTS

Figure 3: Temporal characteristics of annotations for individual competitions (*ind*) and balanced team competitions (*balanceTS*).

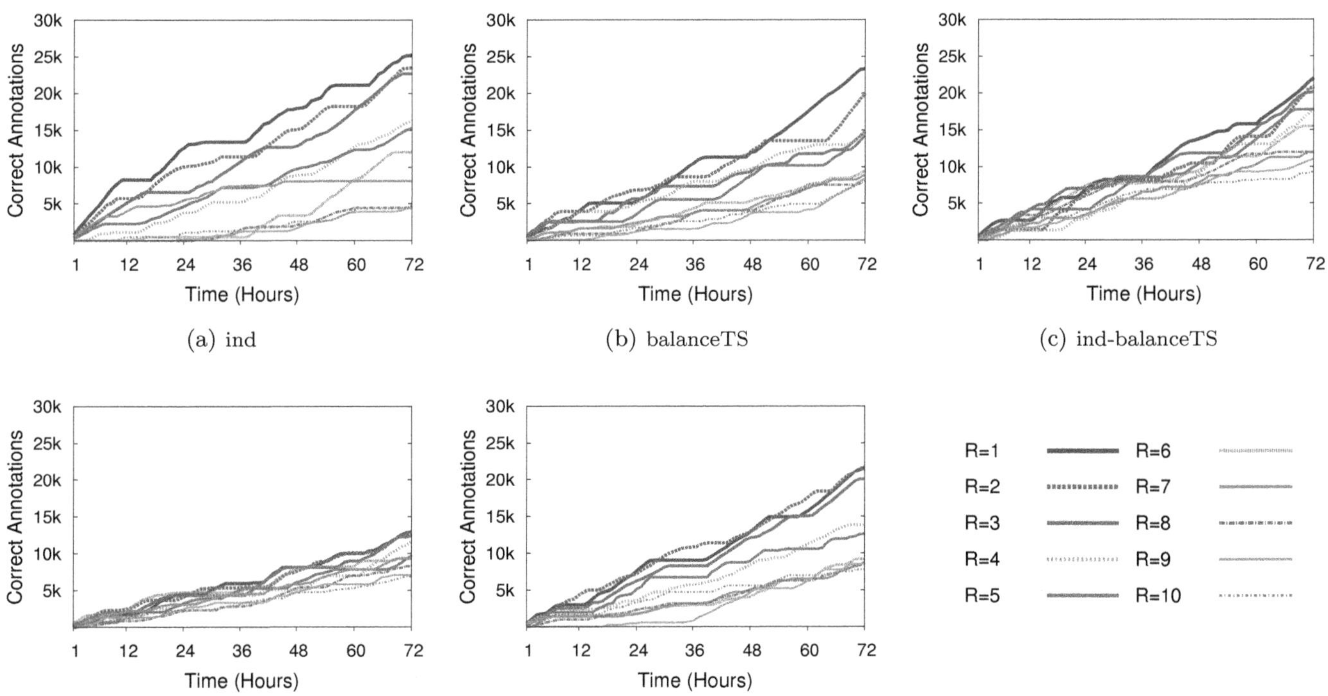

(a) ind (b) balanceTS (c) ind-balanceTS

(d) selfTS (e) ind-selfTS

Figure 4: Cumulative number of correctly annotated images for the top-10 participants over time.

vidual competitions we observe considerably higher scores for the lower ranked participants in team-based competitions. For our winning strategy (*ind-balanceTS*) in particular, the spread of the curves is much less pronounced, highlighting that in contrast to the individual competition *ind*, lower performers remain motivated even when confronted with stronger competitors. Except for the *selfTS* strategy, the top performers annotated more than 20,000 images each, indicating adequate motivation in the team scenarios.

Annotation Quality. In terms of correct annotations there is no noticeable difference between the baseline and any of our team-based strategies (see Table 2). For the large majority of batches with correctly solved honeypots the percentage of accurately recognized faces is over 95% for all of the strategies. The quality slightly increased in the course of our experimental runs, compensating to some degree the handicap of worker fatigue. Similarly, the number of batches with incorrectly solved honeypots declined over time as the

Exp.	Correct Honeypots: No. of batches	Correct Honeypots: Correctly matched faces	Incorrect Honeypots: No. of batches	Incorrect Honeypots: Correctly matched faces
ind	2,996	95.8%	85	81.0%
balanceTS	3,293	96.3%	81	74.6%
ind-balanceTS	3,964	96.6%	66	85.2%
selfTS	2,845	96.7%	65	82.8%
ind-selfTS	2,966	97.1%	41	83.7%

Table 2: Quality results.

users became more proficient at the task, whilst the fraction of correct annotations for these batches remained stable.[3]

4.3 Team Formation and Dynamics

In the following we examine team structures and temporal dynamics in order to shed further light on the performance differences between team strategies.

Team Composition. Figure 5 shows the contributions of workers to their team for the top-10 teams. We observe a strong competition between the top teams towards the end of the *selfTS* and *balanceTS* experiments, resulting in very similar performance characteristics for the competitors. For the combined strategy *ind-balanceTS*, especially participants in lower ranked teams were additionally engaged through individual rewards and contributed more value. Although some of the top workers seemed to be demotivated by the relatively weak performance of their teams, generally more participants were highly motivated in the group based strategies in comparison to the *ind* baseline.

For both of the self-organized team strategies the emerging team structure turned out to be suboptimal: the competitions were dominated by few very large teams, offering only small shares to strong performers. This issue was alleviated with the introduction of individual rewards in *ind-selfTS*, where the contributions of the top performers are about twice as high as for *selfTS*. Designing and testing team formation conditions (such as stronger restrictions on teams sizes) that lead to more competitive team scenarios is a challenging task for future work.

Team Formation Processes. Figure 6 visualizes team formation events (specifically the merging into larger teams) along with the development of the overall value produced by the top-5 teams for the group strategies *selfTS* and *balanceTS*. Over the course of the team formation phase, a large number of participants decided to join one of the leading teams - instead of collaborating with smaller teams in order to compete for the lower prize ranks ("winning team joining" pattern). However, we also observed occasional mergings of smaller teams if a higher rank in the leaderboard could be achieved in that way ("competitive merging" pattern). Finally, for both strategies fierce competitions occurred towards the end of the experiment (e.g. between rank 1 and 2 as well as rank 3 and 4). A dendrogram view of the team formation for the top-5 teams in both self-organized teams

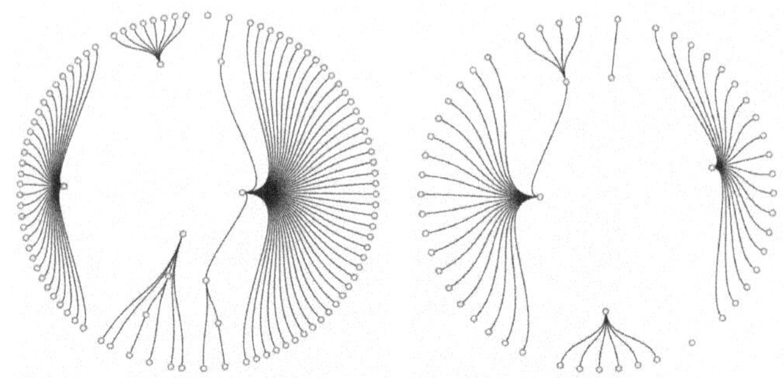

(a) selfTS (b) ind-selfTS

Figure 7: Team merging structure of top-5 teams for self-organizing team strategies (*selfTS* and *ind-selfTS*)

experiments is shown in Figure 7, where merges evolve from the outer to the inner part of the circles. The "winning team joining" pattern appeared in over 80% of all mergings.

In total, 550 and 284 invitations were posted for *selfTS* and *ind-selfTS*, where 75.4% and 57.3% were accepted after an average of 2.1 and 4.9 hours, respectively. These numbers exclude the invitations ignored or automatically canceled due to engagement in concurrent merging activities. The decline in the number of invitations in conjunction with the lower acceptance rate for subsequent experiments indicate that workers often preferred smaller teams after having participated in one of the very large teams before.

4.4 Worker Activity and Interaction

Worker Activity. Table 3 shows the number of participating contributors who solved at least one batch of 100 instances. The discrepancy between registered users and users who actually provided annotations is mostly due to particularities of CrowdFlower where each submission of a user code (i.e. registration) had to be rewarded with 1 cent[4]. Over the course of the experiments, we noticed user fatigue manifesting in a continuous, slight decrease in the number of participants, putting the baseline strategy at an advantage.

Figure 8 shows the number of workers with respect to the number of experiments they participated in; workers are further divided into the ones that won a monetary prize in at least one of the experiment and the ones who didn't. Similar to our observations in [18], workers who had won prizes in earlier rounds, were more motivated to participate in further rounds, with 11.5% of all workers engaged in at least 3 competitions.

User Feedback. During the experiments we continuously received feedback from the participants. Besides administrative issues (such as missing or inappropriate images), participants also suggested new features such as team chat functionalities which we implemented right after the preliminary rounds. User comments also provided us with valuable insights into details of the competition design. In a preliminary balanced team experiment, for instance, workers were assigned to a team immediately upon login, which was often

[3] The results for *balanceTS* are an exception: two of the workers tried to game the system by annotating randomly.

[4] During the *selfTS* and *ind-selfTS* experiments, we additionally observed periods without any registrations after the start of the competition due to technical problems of the platform.

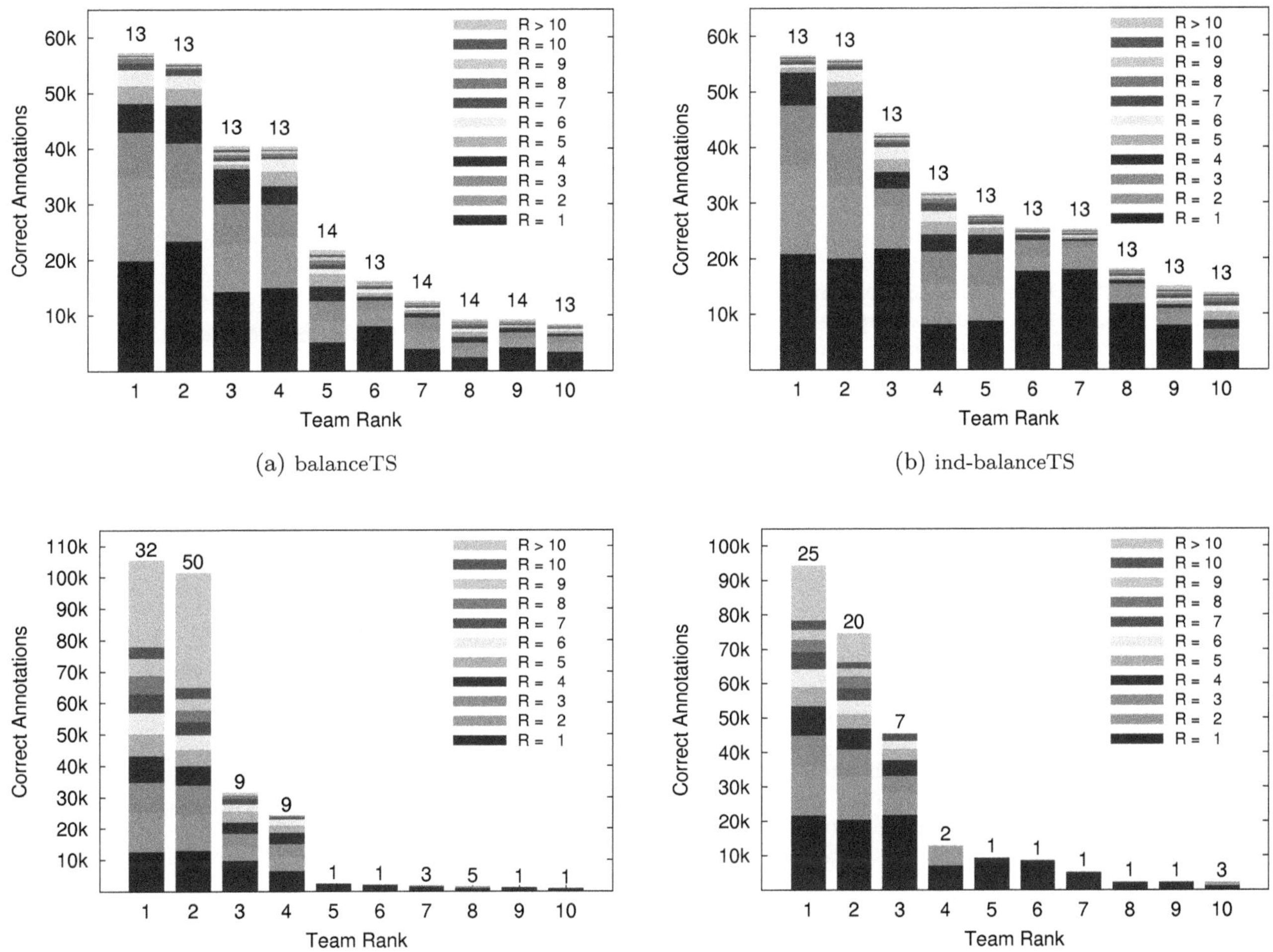

(a) balanceTS (b) ind-balanceTS

(c) selfTS (d) ind-selfTS

Figure 5: Contributions to the top-10 teams for the team based strategies. We show the number of correct annotations and the contribution of each individual team member (ordered by rank within the team). The size of each team is shown above the respective column.

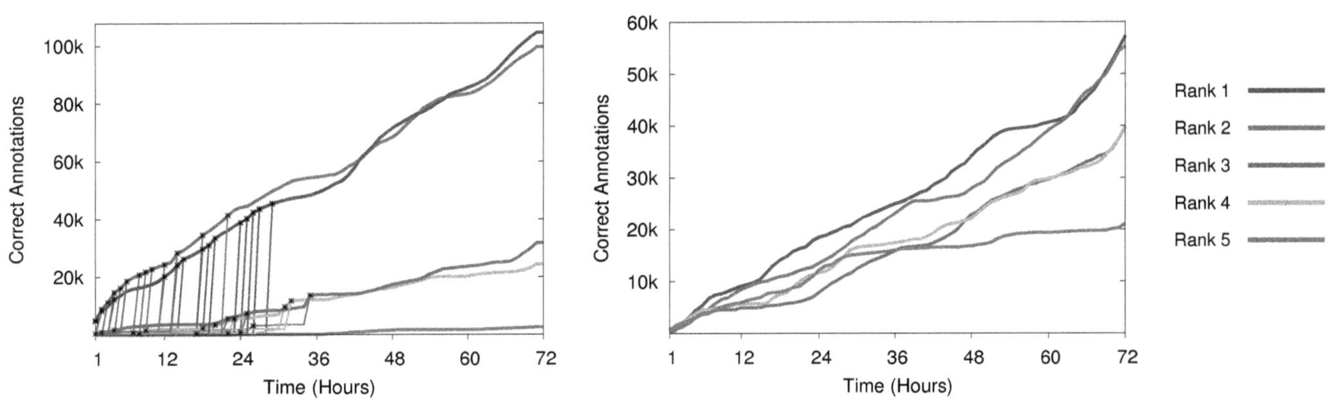

(a) selfTS (b) balanceTS

Figure 6: Temporal development of correct annotations of the top-5 teams for *selfTS* (left) and *balanceTS* (right). For *selfTS* we also show merging events during the team formation phase (i.e. in the first 36 hours).

Exp.	registered	annotated	solved batch
ind	839	448	300
balanceTS	785	382	282
ind-balanceTS	732	342	273
selfTS	586	219	181
ind-selfTS	763	316	222

Table 3: Participation statistics

not considered fair (“`we have a lot of members who has 0 points.(...) So we are at disadvantage!`”). Consequently, in our main series of experiments, users were only assigned to a team after first solving one batch of tasks. To ensure setup consistency throughout the experiments we had to discard numerous requests, such as the suggestion to adopt the interface for mobile devices.

Team Communication. Over the course of the experiments, about 2,500 messages were posted by over 200 of the participants. Conflicts, such as discussions about reward shares, were scant and most of the communication remained positive and friendly “`Thank you all for your hard work. May we meet again in another competition either as a team or a competitor. Good luck to you all.`”. Lots of messages were very constructive, including motivating statements like “`Let's go team !!! we are 5, team A are 3. We can reach them !!!`” and “`chat later, focus on work fast.`”.

Team members supported each other with working advice and clarification of the rules:

user 1: `What if I answer wrong?`
user 2: `we will lose 20 points :) go easy press F11 and than u will see better`

as well as discussing their own strategy with others:

user 3: `I'm trying to get to number 5 spot because he/she stopped clicking.`
user 2: `Yeah but u need 2000 thousand more buddy, and you know that he/she will be careful now :/ she will check again to see if you will attack and then he/she will start doing more [...]`
user 3: `good point`

Furthermore, many of the participants collaborated on team administration and coordination issues in a rather democratic way. For instance, team administrators sought out the opinions of their team members regarding new invitations and teams sizes (“`Ok. help me with the decisions`”, “`Don't invite anyone else so we don't have to split the reward with so many people! [...]`”). Team leaders received input from members about experiences made in previous competitions, such as suggestions for inviting former co-workers (“`<XXX> has worked with me.i still can watch the old competitions.he scored 8400 points,so you decide :)`”). Strategic decisions were discussed about catching up with competitors, defending the current position, or pausing to keep the share proportions stable.

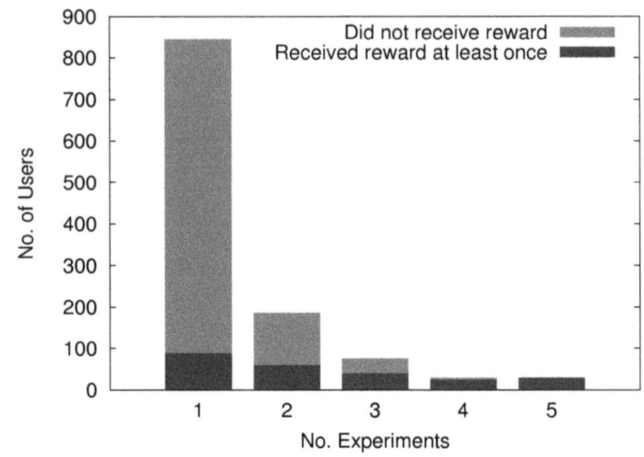

Figure 8: Worker participation.

Although some of the workers appreciated having control in the self-organizing team strategy (“`[...] this system.. it's stable and perfect.. all in our hands(public) but not of system automatically selecting arranging them in teams..`”), workers worried about inactive team mates (“`those people who haven't done much kinda piss me off`”). In our future work, we consider also offering a mechanism for democratically ruling out members.

5. CONCLUSIONS AND FUTURE WORK

We have studied various team competition strategies for crowdsourcing, including balanced teams, self-organizing teams, and combination of team and individual strategies. Our evaluation shows substantial performance boosts for team-based scenarios: Our best approach results in 30% more annotations than the recent state-of-the-art baseline, with no decrease in the quality of annotations. Our results indicate that balancing team sizes plays a crucial role in fostering engagement in competitions. In addition, the combination of team and individual competition helps to overcome declines in performance through weak teams. Our analysis of group formation processes, temporal dynamics in competitions, and user interactions sheds further light on worker motivation and behavior.

In our future work we aim to explore additional team formation mechanisms, including democratic decision processes, options for hiring and firing, and hierarchical worker structures. Furthermore, we plan to conduct more in-depth studies on the influence of parameters such as maximum team size, reward distribution, and duration of competitions. Finally, we want to study crowdsourcing scenarios that require closer collaboration and stronger expertise in different areas. To this end, we aim to introduce more sophisticated communication mechanisms that allow for effective coordination between team members and teams.

6. ACKNOWLEDGMENTS

This work is partly funded by the European Research Council under ALEXANDRIA (ERC 339233) and by the European Commission FP7 under QualiMaster (grant agreement No. 619525).

7. REFERENCES

[1] TREC Crowdsourcing Task. `https://sites.google.com/site/treccrowd/home`, 2013.

[2] *GamifIR '14: Proceedings of the First International Workshop on Gamification for Information Retrieval*, New York, NY, USA, 2014. ACM.

[3] O. Alonso and R. Baeza-Yates. Design and implementation of relevance assessments using crowdsourcing. In *Proceedings of the 33rd European Conference on Advances in Information Retrieval*, ECIR'11, pages 153–164, Berlin, Heidelberg, 2011. Springer-Verlag.

[4] O. Alonso and S. Mizzaro. Using crowdsourcing for trec relevance assessment. *Information Processing & Management*, 48(6):1053–1066, Nov. 2012.

[5] N. Archak. Money, glory and cheap talk: Analyzing strategic behavior of contestants in simultaneous crowdsourcing contests on topcoder.com. In *Proceedings of the 19th International Conference on World Wide Web*, WWW '10, pages 21–30, New York, NY, SA, 2010. ACM.

[6] N. Archak and A. Sundararajan. Optimal design of crowdsourcing contests. In *Proceedings of the International Conference on Information Systems*, ICIS 2009, Phoenix, Arizona, USA, 2009. Association for Information Systems.

[7] R. Cavallo and S. Jain. Efficient crowdsourcing contests. In *Proceedings of the 11th International Conference on Autonomous Agents and Multiagent Systems - Volume 2*, AAMAS '12, pages 677–686, Richland, SC, 2012. International Foundation for Autonomous Agents and Multiagent Systems.

[8] R. Cavallo and S. Jain. Winner-take-all crowdsourcing contests with stochastic production. In *Proceedings of the First AAAI Conference on Human Computation and Crowdsourcing*, Palm Springs, CA, USA, 2013. AAAI.

[9] D. DiPalantino and M. Vojnovic. Crowdsourcing and all-pay auctions. In *Proceedings of the 10th ACM Conference on Electronic Commerce*, EC '09, pages 119–128, New York, NY, USA, 2009. ACM.

[10] C. Eickhoff, C. G. Harris, A. P. de Vries, and P. Srinivasan. Quality through flow and immersion: Gamifying crowdsourced relevance assessments. In *Proceedings of the 35th International ACM SIGIR Conference on Research and Development in Information Retrieval*, SIGIR '12, pages 871–880, New York, NY, USA, 2012. ACM.

[11] J. He, M. Bron, L. Azzopardi, and A. de Vries. Studying user browsing behavior through gamified search tasks. In *Proceedings of the First International Workshop on Gamification for Information Retrieval*, GamifIR '14, pages 49–52, NY, USA, 2014. ACM.

[12] H. Jiang and S. Matsubara. Improving crowdsourcing efficiency based on division strategy. In *Proceedings of the 2012 IEEE/WIC/ACM International Joint Conferences on Web Intelligence and Intelligent Agent Technology*, volume 2, pages 425–429, Los Alamitos, CA, USA, 2012. IEEE Computer Society.

[13] G. Kazai. In search of quality in crowdsourcing for search engine evaluation. In *Proceedings of the 33rd European Conference on Advances in Information Retrieval*, ECIR'11, pages 165–176, Berlin, Heidelberg, 2011. Springer-Verlag.

[14] G. Kazai, J. Kamps, and N. Milic-Frayling. Worker types and personality traits in crowdsourcing relevance labels. In *Proceedings of the 20th ACM International Conference on Information and Knowledge Management*, CIKM '11, pages 1941–1944, New York, NY, USA, 2011. ACM.

[15] N. Kumar, A. C. Berg, P. N. Belhumeur, and S. K. Nayar. Attribute and Simile Classifiers for Face Verification. In *Proceedings of the 12th IEEE International Conference on Computer Vision*, ICCV 2009, pages 365–372, Piscataway, NJ, USA, 2009. IEEE Computer Society.

[16] W. Mason and D. J. Watts. Financial incentives and the "performance of crowds". *SIGKDD Explorations Newsletter*, 11(2):100–108, May 2010.

[17] D. Pothineni, P. Mishra, A. Rasheed, and D. Sundararajan. Incentive design to mould online behavior: A game mechanics perspective. In *Proceedings of the First International Workshop on Gamification for Information Retrieval*, GamifIR '14, pages 27–32, New York, NY, USA, 2014. ACM.

[18] M. Rokicki, S. Chelaru, S. Zerr, and S. Siersdorfer. Competitive game designs for improving the cost effectiveness of crowdsourcing. In *Proceedings of the 23rd ACM International Conference on Information and Knowledge Management*, CIKM '14, New York, NY, USA, 2014. ACM.

[19] N. Savage. Gaining wisdom from crowds. *Communications of the ACM*, 55(3):13–15, Mar. 2012.

[20] J. C. Tang, M. Cebrian, N. A. Giacobe, H.-W. Kim, T. Kim, and D. B. Wickert. Reflecting on the darpa red balloon challenge. *Commununications of the ACM*, 54(4):78–85, Apr. 2011.

[21] L. von Ahn and L. Dabbish. Labeling images with a computer game. In *Proceedings of the SIGCHI Conference on Human Factors in Computing Systems*, CHI '04, pages 319–326, New York, NY, USA, 2004. ACM.

[22] L. von Ahn and L. Dabbish. Designing games with a purpose. *Commununications of the ACM*, 51(8):58–67, Aug. 2008.

[23] P. Welinder and P. Perona. Online crowdsourcing: Rating annotators and obtaining cost-effective labels. In *Computer Vision and Pattern Recognition Workshops (CVPRW), 2010 IEEE Computer Society Conference on*, pages 25–32, June 2010.

[24] J. Yang, L. A. Adamic, and M. S. Ackerman. Crowdsourcing and knowledge sharing: Strategic user behavior on taskcn. In *Proceedings of the 9th ACM Conference on Electronic Commerce*, EC '08, pages 246–255, New York, NY, USA, 2008. ACM.

[25] M.-C. Yuen, I. King, and K.-S. Leung. A survey of crowdsourcing systems. In *Privacy, Security, Risk and Trust (PASSAT), IEEE Third International Conference on Social Computing (SocialCom)*, PASSAT/SocialCom 2011, pages 766–773. IEEE, 2011.

Authentication Melee: A Usability Analysis of Seven Web Authentication Systems

Scott Ruoti, Brent Roberts, Kent Seamons
Internet Security Research Lab
Brigham Young University
Provo, UT 84602
{ruoti, roberts}@isrl.byu.edu, seamons@cs.byu.edu

ABSTRACT

Passwords continue to dominate the authentication landscape in spite of numerous proposals to replace them. Even though usability is a key factor in replacing passwords, very few alternatives have been subjected to formal usability studies, and even fewer have been analyzed using a standard metric. We report the results of four within-subjects usability studies for seven web authentication systems. These systems span federated, smartphone, paper tokens, and email-based approaches. Our results indicate that participants prefer single sign-on systems. We report several insightful findings based on participants' qualitative responses: (1) transparency increases usability but also leads to confusion and a lack of trust, (2) participants prefer single sign-on but wish to augment it with site-specific low-entropy passwords, and (3) participants are intrigued by biometrics and phone-based authentication. We utilize the Systems Usability Scale (SUS) as a standard metric for empirical analysis and find that it produces reliable, replicable results. SUS proves to be an accurate measure of baseline usability. We recommend that new authentication systems be formally evaluated for usability using SUS, and should meet a minimum acceptable SUS score before receiving serious consideration.

Categories and Subject Descriptors

K.6.5 [**Management Of Computing And Information Systems**]: Security and Protection—*Authentication*; H.5.2 [**Information Interfaces and Presentation (e.g., HCI)**]: User Interfaces—*Evaluation/methodology*

Keywords

Authentication; security; usability; System Usability Scale

1. INTRODUCTION

Passwords continue to dominate the authentication landscape. Bonneau et al. [6] analyzed a broad collection of web authentication schemes designed to replace passwords. They demonstrated that passwords have a unique combination of usability, security, and deployability that has proven difficult to supplant. While Federated identity systems (i.e., Google OAuth 2.0, Facebook Connect) and password managers (e.g., LastPass) are seeing some success, these systems are designed to enhance passwords usage rather than disrupt it.

While Bonneau et al. presented a heuristic-based approach for evaluating the usability of authentication schemes, it is also imperative that authentication systems are subjected to empirical usability analysis. We survey the publications cited by Bonneau et al. and discover that only four of the twenty-three publications report the results of an empirical usability study [9, 15, 24, 29]. Moreover, Chiasson et al. [9] is the only study that compares its proposed system against another competing authentication system. Most troubling, none of the systems are analyzed using a standard usability metric, making it impossible to determine which of the four systems has the best usability. Without a standard metric, there is no means by which a new proposal can be evaluated to determine whether it has better usability than existing systems.

In this paper, we report the results of a series of within-subjects empirical usability studies for seven web authentication systems. The seven authentication systems are heterogeneous and span federated, smartphone, paper token, and email-based approaches. Our studies are the first to compare a heterogeneous collection of web authentication proposals. Our research goals are two fold:

1. *Determine which system has the best overall usability.* This is accomplished using the System Usability Scale (SUS) [7, 8], a standard usability metric that has been used in hundreds of studies [2, 3].

2. *Explore which authentication features users prefer and which features they dislike.* In our studies, participants use multiple authentication systems and provide feedback describing what they like and what they would change.

In the results of our studies, federated and smartphone-based single sign-on receive the best overall usability ratings. We also report insightful information from participants' qualitative responses. We find that systems with minimal user interaction are rated as highly usable, but are also described by participants as confusing and unworthy of trust. Although participants rate the usability of single sign-on highly, they are interested in augmenting it with additional low-entropy passwords. Our results also show that

WWW 2015, May 18–22, 2015, Florence, Italy.
ACM 978-1-4503-3469-3/15/05.
http://dx.doi.org/10.1145/2736277.2741683.

over half of participants are willing to use new authentication systems in their everyday life but they are most interested in adopting systems they perceive as different and innovative (e.g., biometrics, phone-based authentication).

Finally, our results validate SUS as an appropriate metric for comparing the usability of authentication systems because the SUS score for a given system is consistent across different participant groups and proves to be a strong indicator of users' preferences. We recommend that all new authentication proposals be formally evaluated for usability with SUS and that no proposal should receive serious consideration until it achieves a minimum acceptable SUS score.

2. AUTHENTICATION TOURNAMENT

In order to attain widespread deployment it is essential that new authentication systems not only be more secure than passwords, but must also provide tangible usability benefits that incentivize adoption. Very few web authentication systems have been evaluated using an empirical study. Fewer still have been analyzed using a standard usability metric or compared to alternative authentication systems. This makes it impossible to determine which of the existing systems is most usable.

As a first step to answering this question, we conduct empirical usability studies on seven web authentication systems. We use the System Usability Scale to determine which system is most usable. Also, we structure our usability studies as a tournament to gather qualitative data from participants regarding which authentication features are most important to them.

2.1 System Usability Scale

To address our first research goal, *which system has the best overall usability*, we measure each systems usability based on a standard usability metric. The System Usability Scale (SUS) [7, 8] is a standard metric from the usability literature that we adopt as part of our methodology. SUS has been used in hundreds of usability studies [3] and the original SUS paper [7] has been cited over 2,450 times.[1] Our prior work has also shown that a system's SUS score is consistent across different sets of users [20]. Moreover, Tullis and Stetson compare SUS to four other usability metrics (three standard metrics from the usability literature and their own proprietary measure) and determined that SUS gives the most reliable results [27].

The SUS metric is a single numeric score from 0, the least usable, to 100, the most usable, that provides a rough estimate of a system's overall usability. To calculate a system's SUS score, participants first interact with the system and then answer ten questions relating to their experience (see Table 1). Answers are given using a five-point Likert scale (*strongly agree* to *strongly disagree*). The questions alternate between positive and negative statements about the system being tested. Participants' answers are assigned a scalar value (see Table 2) and then summed to produce the overall SUS score, and the system with the highest average SUS score is the most usable.

SUS produces a numeric score for a non-numeric measure (i.e., usability), making it difficult to intuitively understand

[1] Citation count retrieved from Google Scholar on Feb 28, 2015.

1) I think that I would like to use this system frequently.
2) I found the system unnecessarily complex.
3) I thought the system was easy to use.
4) I think that I would need the support of a technical person to be able to use this system.
5) I found the various functions in this system were well integrated.
6) I thought there was too much inconsistency in this system.
7) I would imagine that most people would learn to use this system very quickly.
8) I found the system very cumbersome to use.
9) I felt very confident using the system.
10) I needed to learn a lot of things before I could get going with this system.

Table 1: The ten SUS questions

	Questions 1,3,5,7,9	Questions 2,4,6,8,10
Strongly Agree	10	0
Agree	7.5	2.5
Neither Agree or Disagree	5	5
Disagree	2.5	7.5
Strongly Disagree	0	10

Table 2: SUS score card

how usable a system is based solely on its SUS score. As part of an empirical evaluation of SUS, Bangor et al. [3] reviewed SUS evaluations of 206 different systems and compared these scores against objective measurements of the various systems' success in order to derive adjective-based ratings for SUS scores. These ratings and their correlation to SUS scores are given in Figure 1. We report these adjective-based ratings along with SUS scores to provide readers with a better intuition of each system's usability.

2.2 Tournament Structure

To address our second research goal, *which features of authentication do users prefer and which do they dislike*, we have participants use multiple authentication systems and then have them provide feedback on their experience. We believe that after participants have used multiple systems that they will be better able to articulate their opinions on authentication. One option would be to perform a full combinatorial comparison, but this would be prohibitive in terms of time and cost. For example, if each system is tested by 20 participants,[2] and an individual participant tests systems, it would require $\binom{7}{2} * 20 = 21 * 20 = 420$ participants, 27 person-days of effort, and \$4,200 USD to complete the study.[3] Alternatively, having each participant using all the authentication systems could result in study fatigue that would bias the results.

Instead, we model our study after a tournament bracket. We first arrange the seven web authentication systems into three groups based on common features. These groups are federated single sign-on, email-based, and QR code-based. For each of the groups we conduct a separate usability study, and the system with the highest SUS score in each study is selected as a winner. The three winners are then compared

[2] 20 participants is an average sample size used in security usability studies and is enough for statistical significance.

[3] The calculation assumes a 45-minute study at \$10 per user. These costs grow factorially in the number of systems tested.

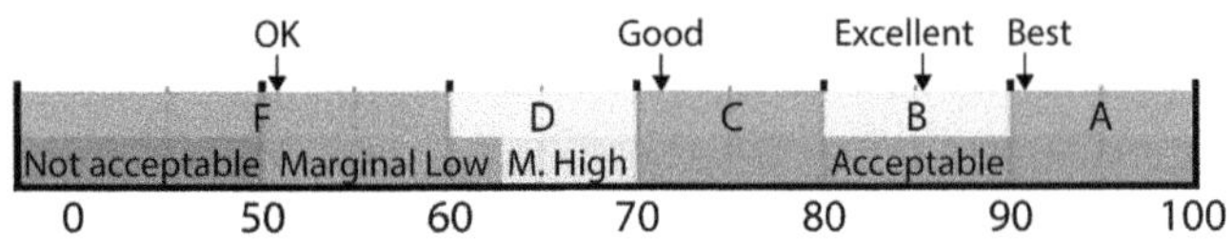

Figure 1: Adjective-based ratings to help interpret SUS scores

to each other in a championship round usability study. This methodology allows us to gather qualitative user feedback from participants who have tested similar systems and also participants who have tested dissimilar systems.

The breakdown of systems into the tournament bracket is given in Figure 2 and the remainder of this section describes the contestants in our authentication tournament.

2.2.1 *Federated Single Sign-on*

In federated single sign-on, all authentication responsibility is centralized in a single identity provider (IDP). Instead of websites maintaining their own collection of usernames and passwords, websites instead rely on the IDP to verify the identity of users visiting their website. The IDP is free to use whatever method it wants to authenticate users, though the three systems in our tournament all use usernames and passwords.

We select three federated single sign-on systems for inclusion in our tournament: Google OAuth 2.0, Facebook Connect, and Mozilla Persona. Google OAuth 2.0 and Facebook Connect are chosen because they are the only authentication systems other than current password-based authentication that are widely adopted. Since both Google and Facebook store personal information for users, it is possible that users might reject both systems for fear that their personal information will be leaked [18]. To address this concern, we also include Mozilla Persona, a federated single sign-on system that does not store users' personal information.

2.2.2 *Email-based Single Sign-on*

Email-based single sign-on is similar to federated single sign-on, but instead of centralizing authentication responsibilities into a single entity (e.g., Google, Facebook), they are instead delegated to email providers [13]. Users prove their identity by demonstrating their ability to either send or receive email. The advantage over federated single sign-on is that users have the freedom to choose which email providers they trust to be an identity provider.

We select two systems for this group: Simple Authentication for the Web (SAW) [28] and Hatchet. SAW was developed in our research group and was cited for this category in the Bonneau et al. survey. SAW authenticates a user by sending them an email with a link they can click to log in to the website. To increase the security of authentication, SAW requires the user to click the link on the device they want to be authenticated on. Hatchet is a variant of SAW that we developed for the purpose of this study. Hatchet replaces the link sent in SAW with a one-time password (OTP). This OTP is then entered into the website the user is logging in to.[4] Unlike SAW, Hatchet allows users to retrieve email on one device and be authenticated on another device.

2.2.3 *QR Code-based*

For our last group, we select the two most recent authentication proposals we are aware of: WebTicket [14] and Snap2Pass [12]. Both of these systems use QR codes and require a physical token to authenticate the user: a piece of paper and a smartphone respectively. In WebTicket, a user's credentials are encoded in a QR code that is printed and stored by the user (their WebTicket). The user authenticates to the website by scanning their WebTicket using their computer's webcam. WebTicket was originally presented as a browser plugin, but we have modified it to allow websites to deploy WebTicket for authentication. We believe that this is a more likely deployment scenario, as users have proven to be reticent to install browser plugins [20, 18].

Snap2Pass is a single sign-on authentication system where the user's phone acts as an IDP. The user first pairs their phone with the website by using the Snap2Pass application to scan a QR code provided by the website. Later, when the user authenticates to the website, they are presented with another QR code to scan. After scanning this QR code, the user's phones will verify the identity of the user to the website and the user is logged in.

3. METHODOLOGY

During the summer and fall of 2014, we conducted four IRB-approved studies analyzing the usability of seven web authentication systems. The studies varied as to which authentication systems were tested, but otherwise the content of the studies remained constant. This section gives an overview of the studies and describes the task design, study questionnaire, study development, and limitations.

3.1 Study Setup

The four studies were conducted between June and October 2014: June 24–July 12, July 28–August 23, October 7–October 11, and October 13–October 24. The first three studies evaluated the federated, email-based, and QR code-based groups respectively, and the fourth study is the championship round usability study. In the first study (federated), participants were randomly assigned two of the three authentication systems in the group, and in the second (email-based) and third studies (QR code-based) participants were assigned to use both systems in the group. In the fourth study (championship round), participants were assigned all three systems.[5]

In total, 106 individuals participated in our studies: 24 participants in the first study, 20 participants in the second study, [6] 27 participants in the third study, and 35 participants in the fourth study. Each individual was allowed to

[4]This use of OTPs is not unique to Hatchet [1], but to our knowledge there is no authentication system which employees OTPs and can be used to authenticate to arbitrary websites.

[5] We modified the study to assign participants three systems for two reasons: (1) in the first three studies participants showed no signs of study fatigue after evaluating two authentication systems and (2) we were interested in the qualitative responses of participants who had been assigned three heterogeneous authentication systems.

[6]We are unsure why fewer students signed up for the second study, though we speculate that it might be due to the

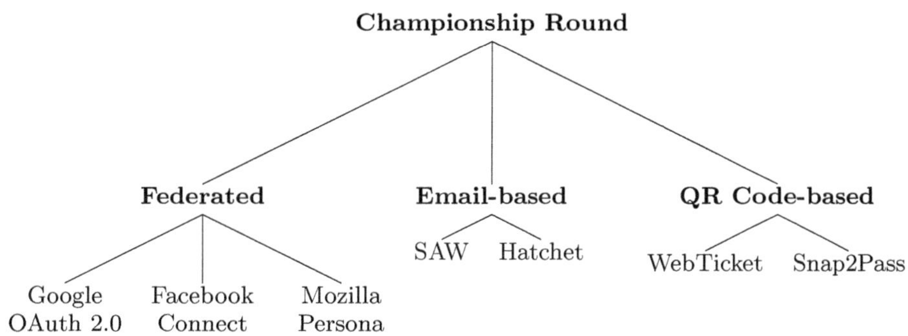

Figure 2: Authentication tournament bracket

participate in only one of the four studies. Participants took a minimum of 20 minutes and a maximum of 45 minutes to complete their study and were compensated $10 USD for their efforts. When using Snap2Pass, participants were provided with a Nexus 5 smartphone with the Snap2Pass application pre-installed. When using WebTicket, participants were provided with a black and white laser printer, a pair of scissors, and a 1080p webcam.

3.1.1 Quality Control

The results for eight participants are discarded for various reasons:

- Two participants, both in the second study (email-based), had the authentication emails generated by SAW marked as spam.[7] The survey coordinator was unable to resolve this problem and the participants were unable to complete the study.
- Three participants, one in the third study (QR code-based) and two in the fourth study (championship round), were non-native English speakers and were unable to understand the study's instructions.
- Three participants, one in the third study (QR code-based) and two in the fourth study (championship round), skipped a task and did not finish registering a necessary account. The study coordinator was unable to resolve this problem and the participants were unable to complete the study.

After removing results from these 8 participants we are left with results from 98 participants: 24 participants in the first study (federated), 18 in the second study (email-based), 25 in the third study (QR code-based), and 30 in the fourth study (championship round). The remainder of this paper will refer exclusively to these 98 participants.

3.1.2 Participant Demographics

We recruit participants for our study at Brigham Young University. All participants are affiliated with Brigham Young University,[8] with the overwhelming majority being undergraduate students: undergraduate students (93; 95%), graduate students (3; 3%), faculty (1; 1%), did not provide demographic information (1; 1%). Participants had a variety of majors, 51 in total, with the highest percentage studying exercise science (8 participants). No other major had more than five participants. We recruited broadly across campus to avoid attracting primarily technical majors. Participants were asked to self report their level of technical skill, with most reporting an intermediate level of knowledge. Table 3 contains a breakdown of participant demographics by study.

	Gender		Age		Technical Skill		
	Male	Female	18–24 years old	25–34 years old	Beginner	Intermediate	Advanced
Federated (n = 24)	58% 14	42% 10	83% 20	17% 4	13% 3	79% 19	8% 2
Email (n = 18)	67% 12	33% 6	78% 14	22% 4	28% 5	72% 13	0% 0
QR Code (n = 25)	52% 13	48% 12	88% 22	12% 3	12% 3	60% 15	28% 7
Championship (n = 30)[1]	67% 20	33% 10	77% 23	23% 7	13% 4	83% 25	4% 1
Total (n = 97)[1]	62% 59	38% 38	81% 79	29% 18	15% 15	75% 73	10% 9

[1] One participant in the QR code-based group did not provide demographic information, explaining the smaller number of participants reported in this table.

Table 3: Participant demographics

3.2 Task Design

We built two WordPress websites for the purpose of our studies: a **forum** website where users could get help with smartphones,[9] and a **bank** website.[10] We chose these two types of websites because they represented diametrically different information assurance needs. At a forum website there is little personal information stored, and so even if the user's account is stolen there is only minimal risk of harm. Conversely, users have been shown to be extremely cautious when it comes to online bank accounts [22]. Studying web-

fact that the majority of our participants were undergraduate students at Brigham Young University and finals for Summer term fell on August 13–14.

[7]We suspect that the emails were marked as spam because they contained both the words "bank" and "click on the link". Different wording could have avoided this problem.

[8]We did not require this affiliation.

[9]`https://forums.isrl.byu.edu`

[10]`https://bank.isrl.byu.edu`

sites with different information assurance needs allows us to examine whether users are amenable to a given authentication system being deployed to all websites, or only to websites that do not store personal information.

During the studies, participants are assigned two or three authentication systems in random order. For each authentication system, participants are given six tasks to complete (three for each website). For each task, participants are instructed on how to use the website to complete the task. Participants are not instructed on how to use any of the authentication systems, as one aspect of usability is how well an authentication system facilitates a novice user. Between each task, participants are logged out of both websites, ensuring that participants use the assigned authentication system for each task.

Below is a summary of the six tasks:

Task 1.
Participants create a new account at the **forum** website using the assigned authentication system.

Task 2.
Participants modify an existing **bank** account to allow login using the assigned authentication system.

Task 3.
Participants log into the **forum** website and create a post in the "New User" forum.

Task 4.
Participants log into the **bank** website and look up their checking account balance.

Task 5.
Participants log into the **forum** website and search for a specific post.

Task 6.
Participants log into the **bank** website and transfer money from one account to another.

3.2.1 Authentication System Implementation

For this study we implemented all seven authentication systems. We did this for two reasons: first, existing implementations of SAW, Hatchet, WebTicket and Snap2Pass are non-existent[11] and second, by implementing the systems ourselves we could assure a consistent user experience.

Source code for our implementations of these systems, as well as the **forum** and **bank** websites, is available at `https://bitbucket.org/isrlauth/battle-website`.

3.3 Study Questionnaire

We administer our study using Qualtrics' survey software. The survey begins with an introduction and a set of demographic questions.

Participants receive written instructions on how to complete the six study tasks for a particular authentication system. Participants use their own email and social network accounts to complete tasks. After completing the tasks, participants answer the ten SUS questions. Next, participants describe which features of the assigned authentication system they enjoy and which they would change. Lastly, participants indicate whether they would prefer to use the assigned authentication system over current password-based authentication and why. This process is then repeated for each assigned authentication system.

At the end of the survey, participants were asked several final questions. First, participants were asked what their favorite authentication system was: whether it was one of the systems they tested or current password-based authentication. They were also asked to explain why the selected system was their favorite. Lastly, participants were asked to describe their ideal authentication system. While most participants are not software engineers or user experience designers, we believe that asking this question serves two purposes: (1) it allows participants to synthesize all the systems they have used and extract what they consider the best from each and (2) it allows participants to mention authentication features that excite them but are not a part of any of the assigned systems.

3.4 Survey Development

After implementing the federated single sign-on systems, we developed the study tasks and questionnaire. We then had a convenience sample of nine individuals from our research institute complete the study. Based on their feedback we made some alterations to wording of the task instructions. After making these changes we began the first usability study (federated).

During this first study (federated), we noticed that a small number of participants were confused about how to complete the second task. In each case, the study coordinator was able to explain to them where to go on the **bank** website to complete the task and we did not need to discard any of the participant's responses. To avoid having participants ask the study coordinator for assistance in the three remaining studies we made a slight visual modification to the **bank** website. This change was universal for all the authentication systems and did not affect their functionality.

During the second usability study (email-based), Gmail began marking some of the authentication emails as spam. To our knowledge, four participants encountered this problem. This problem prevented the first two participants from completing the study and their results were discarded. For the latter two participants, the study coordinator was able to diagnose the problem and help them complete the study. In the fourth study, which once again included SAW, we added a note to the **bank** tasks to indicate to participants that this might occur and how to remedy the problem.

3.5 Limitations

While our studies included students with a diverse set of majors and technical expertise, it would be beneficial for future studies to test authentication systems using a non-student population. It is likely that a large number of participants are already familiar with Google OAuth 2.0 and Facebook Connect and this may have affected their opinions. A laboratory study only captures initial impressions. Participants might feel very differently after day-to-day use or discover new problems. Also, we only study seven authentication systems, which permits us to classify the usability of only a small fraction of existing authentication proposals. Future research could examine additional authentica-

[11] We contacted the authors of WebTicket and Snap2Pass and requested their implementations, but we received no reply.

		SUS			Better than Passwords		
		Mean	Standard Deviation	Median	Yes	Maybe	Is Participants Favorite System
n=16	**Google**	**72.0**	12.4	72.5	**31%**	38%	**31%**
	Facebook	71.4	13.5	72.5	13%	31%	25%
	Mozilla	71.8	10.8	71.3	**31%**	44%	25%
n=18	**SAW**	**61.0**	17.5	62.5	**28%**	28%	**44%**
	Hatchet	53.5	16.4	52.5	22%	44%	17%
n=25	WebTicket	57.9	16.9	60	20%	28%	4%
	Snap2Pass	**75.7**	17.8	82.5	**36%**	40%	**76%**
n=31	**Google**[1]	**75.0**	14.8	77.5	**26%**	32%	**29%**
	SAW[1]	53.2	16.2	55	6%	29%	0%
	Snap2Pass[1]	68.4	16.7	70	**26%**	39%	**29%**

The best performing system and metric for each usability study is given in **bold**. For the second, third, and fourth studies, participants used all available authentication systems and so $100\% - \Sigma(\textit{Favorite System})$ gives the percent of participants who preferred current password-based authentication to any of the assigned authentication systems.

[1] Championship round.

Table 4: SUS scores and participant preferences

tion systems in order to increase knowledge on the usability of authentication systems and help determine which systems are best-in-class and which system has the best overall usability.

4. RESULTS

In this section we report the quantitative results we gathered. Table 4 gives the SUS scores from the four usability studies and summarizes participants' authentication system preferences. Table 5 records whether the difference in the systems' SUS scores is statistically significant. Finally, Table 6 reports the mean time to authenticate for each system. The complete data set from the user study, including anonymous participant responses, is available in Ruoti's Master's Thesis [19].

The remainder of this section breaks down the individual results for each of the four usability studies. As mentioned in Section 2.1, in order to help the reader interpret the meaning of the SUS scores, we also report where these scores fall on Bangor's adjective-based scale [2, 3].

4.1 First Study – Federated

The SUS scores for Google OAuth 2.0, Facebook Connect, and Mozilla Persona were between 71 and 72, and the difference is not statistically significant. On Bangor's scale, all three systems are equal to or slightly above the "good" label, classified as acceptable, and receive a C grade.

Both Facebook Connect and Google OAuth 2.0 had similar registration and authentication times. In contrast, Mozilla Persona's registration and authentication times were two and four times greater, respectively. Even though there was a clear difference in mean time to authenticate, participants never mention this difference in their qualitative responses.

In deciding which authentication system they prefer, participants list trust in the federating party (i.e., Google, Facebook, Mozilla) as a key component. Many participants are hesitant to use Facebook Connect for fear that their social networking data would also be given to the website. Similarly, some participants are concerned that using Google OAuth 2.0 might increase the likelihood of their e-mail being hacked. There is little worry about Mozilla Persona in this regard.

According to our methodology, the winner of each usability study was decided based on highest SUS score. Since the difference of all three systems' SUS scores is not statistically significant, we attempt to break this tie based on which system has the highest number of participants who rate it as their favorite system. Once again, we find that all three systems perform similarly (Google – six participants, Facebook – five participants, Mozilla – five participants), and so we declare all three systems as winners. We still need a single system to move forward in the tournament and so we select Google OAuth 2.0, which had both the highest SUS score and the highest number of participants who rated it as their favorite system.

4.2 Second Study – Email-based

SAW's SUS score was higher than Hatchet's SUS score and this difference was statistically significant. As such, SAW is the winner of this round. Still, SAW's usability is not impressive. According to Bangor's scale, SAW's SUS score of 61 falls equidistant between the "excellent" and "good" label, is classified as having low-marginal acceptability, and given a D grade. Hatchet is slightly above the "OK" label, is classified as having low-marginal acceptability, and is given a failing grade.

While SAW was clearly the SUS champion in this category, participants using Hatchet and SAW took roughly equal amounts of time to register and authenticate (differences not statistically significant: registration — $p = 0.46$, authentication — $p = .27$).

4.3 Third Study – QR Code-based

Snap2Pass was the clear winner of this group, with a SUS score 17.8 points higher than WebTicket's SUS score (this difference was statistically significant). Additionally, only one participant indicated they would prefer WebTicket to Snap2Pass. According to Bangor's scale, Snap2Pass is slightly above the "good" label, is classified as acceptable, and receives a C grade. In contrast, WebTicket is between "OK" and "Good" (closer to "OK"), is classified as having low-marginal acceptability, and receives a D grade.

Participants' qualitative responses indicate that they felt both systems were fast, though comments made after the study indicate that they felt Snap2Pass was the faster of the two systems. These comments match the observations of the study coordinator who observed a significant number of participants struggle to authenticate quickly with WebTicket.

Two statistics in this study (QR code-based) vary significantly from the statistics in the other three usability studies. First, the median SUS score for Snap2Pass is significantly higher than its mean SUS score, indicating that their are several outliers who rate Snap2Pass very negatively, pulling its average down. In all the other results, including the fourth study when Snap2Pass is evaluated a second time, SUS scores are normally distributed. Second, 76% of participants in this study indicated that they are willing to replace current password-based authentication with Snap2Pass. In

	Google	Facebook	Mozilla	SAW	Hatchet	WebTicket	Snap2Pass	Google[1]	SAW[1]	Snap2Pass[1]
Google	—	.89	.94	.04	<.01	<.01	.47	.50	<.01	.45
Facebook	.89	—	.94	.06	<.01	.01	.42	.42	<.01	.54
Mozilla	.94	.94	—	.04	<.01	<.01	.43	.43	<.01	.47
SAW	.04	.06	.04	—	.05	.57	.01	<.01	.12	.15
Hatchet	<.01	<.01	<.01	<.05	—	.40	<.01	<.01	.96	<.01
WebTicket	<.01	.01	<.01	.57	.40	—	<.01	<.01	.30	<.01
Snap2Pass	.47	.42	.43	.01	<.01	<.01	—	.87	<.01	.12
Google[1]	.50	.42	.43	<.01	<.01	<.01	.87	—	<.01	.08
SAW[1]	<.01	<.01	<.01	.12	.96	.30	<.01	<.01	—	<.01
Snap2Pass[1]	.45	.54	.47	.15	<.01	<.01	.12	.08	<.01	—

2-tailed t-test. The participants for the second, third, and fourth study used all available authentication systems and within these groups statistical significance is calculated using the same population, while other significance values are calculated using equal variance. Only statistically significant results at the $p = .05$ level are shaded.

Row scheme scored higher than column scheme

Row scheme scored worse than column scheme

[1] Championship round.

Table 5: Comparison of system SUS scores

		Registration			Authentication				
		Task 1	Task 2	Average	Task 3	Task 4	Task 5	Task 6	Average
n=16	Google	46	43	44	3	10	2	2	**4**
	Facebook	53	23	**38**	7	6	3	4	**5**
	Mozilla	80	81	81	22	30	15	10	19
n=18	SAW	72	30	51	22	17	14	15	**17**
	Hatchet	51	29	**40**	27	20	19	17	21
n=31	Google[1]	51	38	**44**	3	2	2	2	**2**
	SAW[1]	55	34	**45**	62	42	17	25	36
	Snap2Pass[1]	76	-	76	13	14	13	11	13

All times are reported in seconds. We recorded participants' screens and use this data to calculate mean time to authenticate for all tasks except the second task of Snap2Pass. There are no results for the third study (QR code-based) due to video recording software failure.

[1] Championship round.

Table 6: Mean time to authenticate

the other three studies, only 60% of individuals indicated they were willing to replace current password-based authentication.

We are unsure as to what these anomalies mean, but report them in the interest of full disclosure. We are also unsure what caused these results, though we speculate it could be related to the fact that the second study had over a quarter of participants who rated themselves as having advanced technical skill (see Table 3).

4.4 Fourth Study – Championship Round

The championship round usability study consisted of the winners from the first three usability studies: Google OAuth 2.0, SAW, and Snap2Pass. The results are a tie between Google OAuth 2.0 and Snap2Pass, with SAW the clear loser. We apply the tie-break criteria from the first study (see Section 4.1), but the same number of participants chose Google OAuth 2.0 and Snap2Pass as their favorite system. For all three systems, there is no statistically significant difference between their scores in this study (championship round) and the previous three studies.

Since all three federated single sign-on systems tied in the first study, we declare federated single sign-on (collectively) and Snap2Pass to be the winners of our tournament.

5. DISCUSSION

In this section we begin with a discussion of SUS. We follow this with various insights gained from participants' qualitative responses. Finally, we report lessons learned while implementing the seven authentication systems.

5.1 System Usability Scale

SUS proves to be a highly reliable metric. SUS scores for Google OAuth 2.0, SAW, and Snap2Pass were consistent between the first three studies and the championship round study.[12] Within a single study, SUS scores for the systems are consistent regardless of the order in which participants use the systems, with all differences failing to be statistically significant.

Moreover, SUS is a good predictor of which system participants select as their favorite. In the first study (federated), all three federated systems had similar SUS scores, and an

[12]The differences in SUS scores is not statistically significant (see Table 5).

equal number of participants selected each of the three systems as their favorite. Likewise, in the second (email-based) and third (QR code-based) studies, when one system's SUS score was higher than the other system's SUS score, participants largely preferred the system with the higher SUS score. Most interesting, these preferences held between different sets of participants. The SUS scores for Google OAuth 2.0 and Snap2Pass are similar and the difference between the two is not statistically significant (see Table 5). This would indicate that an equal number of participants should prefer both systems, and this is indeed the case when they are evaluated in the championship round study (see Table 4).

While mean time to authenticate is reported in nearly every authentication usability study, our results indicate that mean time to authenticate is actually a poor measure of overall usability or participants' preferences. In the first study, Mozilla Persona had a much higher mean time to authenticate than either Google OAuth 2.0 or Facebook Connect, yet all three had similar SUS scores and were equally preferred by participants. Similarly, SAW and Hatchet did not differ significantly in mean time to authenticate, yet there was a clear distinction in both systems' SUS scores and participants' preferences.

Based on these results, we suggest that an empirical analysis using SUS be required for all future authentication system proposals. This allows new systems' SUS scores to be compared against existing proposals and validate whether these new proposals are improving upon the state-of-the-art. Additionally, we recommend that all new systems achieve a SUS score of 70 before they receive serious consideration. In our studies, only systems with a score of at least 70 (Google OAuth 2.0, Facebook Connect, Mozilla Persona, Snap2Pass) received consistently positive reviews from participants.

5.2 Transparency

Upon reviewing the results of the usability study (federated) we found that participants preferred systems that were transparent and required minimal interaction.[13] To verify that transparency improves usability, we administered a mini-study at the end of the second usability study (email-based). After completing the questionnaire for the second study, participants are then assigned a modified version of SAW. This modified version of SAW automates the process of retrieving and clicking links sent to user's email. Before beginning the six tasks, participants entered their email credentials into the new authentication system, and from then on whenever they click the login button they would immediately be logged into the website. Participants complete the same six tasks and answer the same questions as they did for all the other authentication systems.

The usability improvements of this modified version of SAW are striking. The modified version had a mean SUS score of 73.1, a standard deviation of 10.1, and median score of 75. This is an increase of 12.1 points over SAW's SUS score, and the difference is significant at the $p = 0.01$ significance level. This shows that transparency has a strong effect on perceived usability.

While these results demonstrate that transparency increases usability, transparency was not without its trade-offs. Minimal interaction with the authentication system prevents participants from understanding how the authentication system functioned and many participants have trouble trusting what they don't understand:

> *"I would like to understand more about how it works up-front. It doesn't feel secure."*

> *"If I understood how the system would prevent someone other than me from logging in I would use it."*

> *"I think it was very straightforward to use. Once again like with the other system, perhaps an explanation of how it protected information would give me more confidence in using it."*

This issue of transparency leading to confusion and lack of trust also appeared in our earlier research on secure webmail [20]. Future research could look closely at these trade-offs to discover what is an appropriate level of transparency in authentication.

5.3 Single Sign-on Protocols

Participants like the speed and convenience of single sign-on, though their qualitative responses also provide details about how existing systems could be improved.

5.3.1 Additional Low-entropy Passwords

Participants liked having a single account that was used to authenticate them to multiple websites. Still, some participants were worried about the risks associated with only having one account for all their websites:

> *"The simplicity is also a downside–after the first log-in, you only have to press 'log in' and it doesn't ask you any verifying information. That doesn't seem like a very secure system. For something inconsequential like a social media site or a blog, I wouldn't mind it, but I want a MUCH more secure authentication system for my bank account. If my google account gets hacked, I assume all the connected accounts that use it to log in can also be jacked. I don't want to take that risk with my important accounts."*

Participants suggest a novel approach to solving this problem. To increase the security of a website, participants propose augmenting single sign-on with a low-entropy password shared with the website (e.g., pin). Security is provided by the high-entropy password of the single sign-on account, yet in the case of an account compromise attackers would be unaware of the low-entropy passwords and be unable to gain access to the website. The cognitive burden for users is also low, as they only need to remember a single high-entropy password, while all other passwords are low-entropy and easily remembered. This is an interesting avenue for future research to explore.

5.3.2 Reputation

With federated single sign-on, the reputation of the provider was key. Qualitative responses from participants indicated that trust in a federated single sign-on system was based on the federating identity provider (IDP) (e.g., Google, Facebook). Participants often cite their opinions of the federating IDP when explaining why they prefer one system to another:

[13] Contrary to normal English usage, transparency in the usable security literature has the opposite meaning, and refers to hiding implementation details from users.

> *"I would be worried about security. I've heard that Facebook is 'relatively' easy to hack. I would want to be sure that it was all secure before I started using it."*

> *"I trust Google with my passwords."*

5.3.3 *Dedicated Identity Providers*

Some participants prefer that the IDP only handle authentication and not store sensitive information. For example, one participant stated,

> *"It would be it's own company (not tied to my email, or social network accounts) ..."*

If they were forced to use Google or Facebook as their IDP, one participant indicated that they would create a new account used for authentication only:

> *"I would make an account separate from my social network and mail specifically for functions like banking etc."*

5.4 The Coolness Factor

When participants described what authentication features they were most interested in, they often referred to the "coolness" of that feature. "Coolness" was often related to how different and innovative the technology was perceived to be when compared to current password-based authentication. For example, participants love that Snap2Pass allows them to use their smartphones and obviates the need for passwords:

> *"Man was that cool!"*

> *"Also, the feel of it made me enjoy doing it. I felt technologically literate and the app felt futuristic as a whole, which I enjoyed."*

> *"I thought the technology was cool. You can snap a code to sign yourself in!"*

5.4.1 *Biometrics*

None of the seven authentication systems we analyzed used biometric-based authentication; nevertheless, over a quarter of participants (28; 29%) discuss biometrics as part of their ideal authentication system. In nearly every case, biometrics were described as being "cool:"

> *"A fingerprint system would be cool."*

> *"retinal scanner so i just sit in front of my computer and it scans my eye. dope."*

Participants liked biometrics because they did not involve an authentication factor that could be forgotten, lost, or stolen:

> *"The ideal system would scan some part of my body - either eye or thumb - because these are literally ALWAYS with me."*

Participants also thought that biometrics were more difficult for hackers to compromise:

> *"People can hack accounts, but they can't fake your eye-scan pattern"*

The list of suggested biometrics is fingerprint, facial, retinal, and voice recognition. While participants may not understand all the implications of biometrics, these results indicate that there is significant interest in adopting biometric-based web authentication. Future research should examine how biometric-based authentication can be implemented on the web while still preserving users' privacy [5].

5.5 Physical Tokens

When using a physical token (i.e., WebTicket, smartphone), participants want to have a fallback mechanism. They are worried that they might lose their phone or WebTicket. They are also concerned with theft, especially when a single token could be used to log in to multiple different accounts or sites. For example, one user stated their concern with Snap2Pass,

> *"It would make me nervous having all the passwords I need on my phone. For instance, if I forgot or lost it somewhere I could be inconvenienced with having to then make a username and password for all the websites I need, or if it was stolen and the password on my phone compromised somebody could easily access all of my personal and financial information."*

Participants also voice concern that if they ever forgot to bring their physical token with them, then they would be unable to log into any websites. Alternatively, some participants also dislike that Snap2Pass requires a smartphone. One participant expresses both concerns in their responses:

> *"It seems unfortunate that you have to have a smart phone and you also have to have it with you."*

5.6 Implementation Lessons

As mentioned in Section 3.2.1, we implemented the seven authentication systems for our studies. We found existing software libraries for Google OAuth 2.0, Facebook Connect, Mozilla Persona, and Snap2Pass that aided our implementation. SAW, Hatchet, and WebTicket were implemented from scratch. The remainder of this section gives lessons learned from implementing the systems.

During authentication, Google OAuth 2.0, Facebook Connect, and SAW use `GET` requests. This caused problems with WordPress, which expects authentication to occur using `POST` requests. We were able to code around this limitation, but this still represents a significant impediment to a clean implementation. It would be best if web authentication proposals allow the use of `POST` requests, as this would reduce development costs.

Google OAuth 2.0 and Facebook Connect both require a security check to prevent impersonation attacks. Facebook Connect's software library handles this check for developers, but Google OAuth 2.0 library requires that developers implement the security check themselves. This check is easy to implement incorrectly, resulting in usability (e.g., failed authentication) and security problems (e.g., impersonation attacks). We recommend that authentication proposals provide publicly available implementations that handle security details for developers.

Implementing WebTicket was straightforward, but the webcam struggled to recognize QR codes. It is unclear if this problem was a limitation of the webcam or with the current state-of-the-art HTML5 QR code scanning libraries. Regardless, developers need to pay particular attention to this issue if they choose to implement WebTicket or a similar system.

6. RELATED WORK

The Bonneau et al. [6] framework for comparing web authentication schemes includes a set of eight usability benefits that center on convenience and ease-of-use. While a common framework supports a low-barrier method for subjective comparison of alternative system designs, our work emphasizes empirical results from formal user studies.

Dhamija et al. [11] proposed Deja Vu, a graphical password system. The evaluation of Deja Vu included a user study that compared Deja Vu to both passwords and pins. This is the earliest study we identified that compared a proposed authentication system against current password-based authentication. Similar to our work, the study required users in a laboratory to complete assigned tasks. The reported results were both quantitative (completion times and error rates) and qualitative. If a standard metric like SUS had also been included in their study, it would have enabled a direct point of comparison with our study. We want to see this cross comparison become standard practice going forward.

Chiason et al. [10] conducted a 26-person user study comparing two password managers: PwdHash and Password Multiplier. Even though both systems had considered usability issues in some detail in their original papers, the formal study was able to reveal several significant usability challenges. This is another example of why a formal user study must become the norm to complete any system evaluation.

Sun et al. [23] conducted a user study of OpenID, a single sign-on system. The study revealed design flaws in the OpenID login process that led to misconceptions and mistakes due to a lack of transparency of some security details. Similar to our results, some users expressed concern over a single point of failure at the IDP and concerns about the release of private information at the IDP.

To our knowledge, there are only four previous authentication usability studies that utilize SUS. Juang et al. [16] analyzed system-generated mnemonics for remembering passwords and found them more usable than user-generated or no mnemonics. Trewin et al. [26] analyzed three biometric modalities (face, voice, gesture) on mobile phones and compared them to passwords. Passwords were rated the most usable, with gesture and face biometrics slightly lower. Both voice and combinations of biometrics were found to be unusable. Tassabehji and Kamala [25] conducted a user study of a prototype online banking system using biometric authentication, and Bianchi et al. [4] analyzed a system for safely transferring a PIN from a mobile phone in order to authenticate to an ATM. Similar to our research, each of these four studies brought users into a laboratory environment to complete tasks using a prototype system. After using the system, users respond to survey questions about their experience.

Schaub et al. [21] completed a recent study of five graphical passwords systems. The study resulted in a number of helpful insights and guidelines for designers of graphical password systems. Similar to our studies, users were asked to complete a post-study questionnaire after hands-on experience with a system. The questionnaire utilized PSSUQ [17], a standard metric that is not as widely used as SUS.

7. CONCLUSION

Very few proposals for new authentication systems are accompanied by a formal user study. This leaves us with scant empirical data to determine a best-in-class system for the various types of authentication systems or to reason about how the usability of different authentication systems compare against each other. In this paper, we report the results of a series of within-subjects empirical usability studies for seven web authentication systems. Our studies are the first to compare a heterogeneous collection of web authentication proposals.

The result of our studies is that federated single sign-on systems (i.e., Google OAuth 2.0, Facebook Connect, Mozilla Persona) and Snap2Pass are rated as having the best overall usability. Our results validate SUS as an appropriate metric for comparing the usability of authentication systems, namely because the SUS score for a given system was consistent across different participant groups and proved to be a strong indicator of users' preferences.

Our usability studies also gathered insightful information from participants' qualitative responses. We found that transparent authentication systems are rated as usable but also lead to confusion and a lack of trust from users. Additionally, while participants rate the usability of single sign-on highly, they are interested in augmenting it with additional site-specific, low-entropy passwords. Our results show that over half of participants are willing to use new authentication systems in their everyday life, but that they are most interested in adopting systems that they perceive as different and innovative (e.g., biometrics, Snap2Pass).

Finally, our results have significant implications moving forward. First, the security and usability communities should collaborate more effectively on authentication proposals to ensure that new systems are rigorously evaluated in terms of both security and usability. Second, usability studies that incorporate SUS should become a standard practice for vetting all new authentication proposals. New authentication systems should meet a minimum SUS score before receiving serious consideration. Based on our experience and the literature on SUS, a minimum score of 70 is a reasonable expectation. Widespread adoption of these practices would lead to a significant leap forward for authentication.

8. ACKNOWLEDGEMENTS

The authors thank the anonymous reviewers, Jay McCarthy, Charles Knutson, and Daniel Zappala for feedback on earlier drafts of the paper.

9. REFERENCES

[1] Steam Guard. `https://support.steampowered.com/kb_article.php?ref=4020-ALZM-5519`. [Online; accessed 2014/11/20].

[2] A. Bangor, P. Kortum, and J. Miller. An empirical evaluation of the System Usability Scale. *International Journal of Human–Computer Interaction*, 24(6):574–594, 2008.

[3] A. Bangor, P. Kortum, and J. Miller. Determining what individual SUS scores mean: Adding an adjective rating scale. *Journal of Usability Studies*, 4(3):114–123, 2009.

[4] A. Bianchi, I. Oakley, and D. S. Kwon. Using mobile device screens for authentication. In *Proceedings of the 23rd Australian Computer-Human Interaction Conference*, OzCHI '11, pages 50–53, New York, NY, USA, 2011. ACM.

[5] J. Bonneau, E. W. Felten, P. Mittal, and A. Narayanan. Privacy concerns of implicit secondary factors for web authentication. In *SOUPS Workshop on "Who are you?!": Adventures in Authentication*, 2014.

[6] J. Bonneau, C. Herley, P. C. Van Oorschot, and F. Stajano. The quest to replace passwords: A framework for comparative evaluation of web authentication schemes. In *Symposium on Security and Privacy*, pages 553–567. IEEE, 2012.

[7] J. Brooke. SUS — a quick and dirty usability scale. In *Usability Evaluation in Industry*. CRC Press, 1996.

[8] J. Brooke. SUS: A retrospective. *Journal of Usability Studies*, 8(2):29–40, 2013.

[9] S. Chiasson, E. Stobert, A. Forget, R. Biddle, and P. C. Van Oorschot. Persuasive cued click-points: Design, implementation, and evaluation of a knowledge-based authentication mechanism. *IEEE Transactions on Dependable and Secure Computing*, 9(2):222–235, 2012.

[10] S. Chiasson, P. C. van Oorschot, and R. Biddle. A usability study and critique of two password managers. In *USENIX Security*, 2006.

[11] R. Dhamija and A. Perrig. Deja Vu — a user study: Using images for authentication. In *USENIX Security*, 2000.

[12] B. Dodson, D. Sengupta, D. Boneh, and M. S. Lam. Secure, consumer-friendly web authentication and payments with a phone. In *International Conference on Mobile Computing, Applications, and Services*, pages 17–38. Springer, 2012.

[13] S. L. Garfinkel. Email-based identification and authentication: An alternative to PKI? In *Symposium on Security and Privacy*, pages 20–26. IEEE, 2003.

[14] E. Hayashi, B. Pendleton, F. Ozenc, and J. Hong. WebTicket: Account management using printable tokens. In *SIGCHI Conference on Human Factors in Computing Systems*, pages 997–1006. ACM, 2012.

[15] R. Jhawar, P. Inglesant, N. Courtois, and M. A. Sasse. Make mine a quadruple: Strengthening the security of graphical one-time PIN authentication. In *International Conference on Network and System Security*, pages 81–88. IEEE, 2011.

[16] K. A. Juang, S. Ranganayakulu, and J. S. Greenstein. Using system-generated mnemonics to improve the usability and security of password authentication. In *Proceedings of the Human Factors and Ergonomics Society Annual Meeting*, volume 56, pages 506–510. SAGE Publications, 2012.

[17] J. R. Lewis. Ibm computer usability satisfaction questionnaires: psychometric evaluation and instructions for use. *International Journal of Human-Computer Interaction*, 7(1):57–78, 1995.

[18] C. Robison, S. Ruoti, T. W. van der Horst, and K. E. Seamons. Private facebook chat. In *International Conference on Privacy, Security, Risk and Trust and International Confernece on Social Computing*, pages 451–460. IEEE, 2012.

[19] S. Ruoti. Authentication melee: A usability analysis of seven web authentication systems. Master's thesis, Brigham Young University, 2015. `http://scholarsarchive.byu.edu/etd/4376/`.

[20] S. Ruoti, N. Kim, B. Burgon, T. Van Der Horst, and K. Seamons. Confused Johnny: When automatic encryption leads to confusion and mistakes. In *Symposium on Usable Privacy and Security*. ACM, 2013.

[21] F. Schaub, M. Walch, B. Könings, and M. Weber. Exploring the design space of graphical passwords on smartphones. In *Symposium on Usable Privacy and Security*. ACM, 2013.

[22] S. E. Schechter, R. Dhamija, A. Ozment, and I. Fischer. The Emperor's new security indicators. In *Security and Privacy*, pages 51–65. IEEE, 2007.

[23] S.-T. Sun, E. Pospisil, I. Muslukhov, N. Dindar, K. Hawkey, and K. Beznosov. What makes users refuse web single sign-on?: An empirical investigation of OpenID. In *Symposium on Usable Privacy and Security*. ACM, 2011.

[24] H. Tao. *Pass-Go, A New Graphical Password Scheme*. PhD thesis, University of Ottawa, 2006.

[25] R. Tassabehji and M. A. Kamala. Evaluating biometrics for online banking: The case for usability. *International Journal of Information Management*, 32(5):489–494, 2012.

[26] S. Trewin, C. Swart, L. Koved, J. Martino, K. Singh, and S. Ben-David. Biometric authentication on a mobile device: a study of user effort, error and task disruption. In *Proceedings of the 28th Annual Computer Security Applications Conference*, pages 159–168. ACM, 2012.

[27] T. S. Tullis and J. N. Stetson. A comparison of questionnaires for assessing website usability. Presented at *Usability Professional Association Conference*, 2004.

[28] T. W. van der Horst and K. E. Seamons. Simple authentication for the web. In *International Conference on Security and Privacy in Communications Networks and the Workshops*, pages 473–482. IEEE, 2007.

[29] D. Weinshall. Cognitive authentication schemes safe against spyware. In *Symposium on Security and Privacy*, pages 295–300. IEEE, 2006.

Finding the Hierarchy of Dense Subgraphs using Nucleus Decompositions

Ahmet Erdem Sarıyüce*
The Ohio State University
Columbus, OH, USA
sariyuce.1@osu.edu

C. Seshadhri
University of California
Santa Cruz, CA, USA
scomandu@ucsc.edu

Ali Pınar
Sandia National Labs
Livermore, CA, USA
apinar@sandia.gov

Ümit V. Çatalyürek
The Ohio State University
Columbus, OH, USA
umit@bmi.osu.edu

ABSTRACT

Finding dense substructures in a graph is a fundamental graph mining operation, with applications in bioinformatics, social networks, and visualization to name a few. Yet most standard formulations of this problem (like clique, quasi-clique, k-densest subgraph) are NP-hard. Furthermore, the goal is rarely to find the "true optimum", but to identify many (if not all) dense substructures, understand their distribution in the graph, and ideally determine relationships among them. Current dense subgraph finding algorithms usually optimize some objective, and only find a few such subgraphs without providing any structural relations.

We define the *nucleus decomposition* of a graph, which represents the graph as a *forest of nuclei*. Each nucleus is a subgraph where smaller cliques are present in many larger cliques. The forest of nuclei is a hierarchy by containment, where the edge density increases as we proceed towards leaf nuclei. Sibling nuclei can have limited intersections, which enables discovering overlapping dense subgraphs. With the right parameters, the nucleus decomposition generalizes the classic notions of k-cores and k-truss decompositions.

We give provably efficient algorithms for nucleus decompositions, and empirically evaluate their behavior in a variety of real graphs. The tree of nuclei consistently gives a global, hierarchical snapshot of dense substructures, and outputs dense subgraphs of higher quality than other state-of-the-art solutions. Our algorithm can process graphs with tens of millions of edges in less than an hour.

*Work done while the author was interning at Sandia National Laboratories, Livermore, CA.

WWW 2015, May 18–22, 2015, Florence, Italy.
ACM 978-1-4503-3469-3/15/05.
http://dx.doi.org/10.1145/2736277.2741640.

Categories and Subject Descriptors

F.2.2 [**Nonnumerical Algorithms and Problems**]: Computations on Discrete Structures; G.2.2 [**Graph Theory**]: Graph Algorithms

General Terms

Algorithms

Keywords

k-core; k-truss; graph decomposition; density hierarchy; overlapping dense subgraphs; dense subgraph discovery

1. INTRODUCTION

Graphs are widely used to model relationships in a wide variety of domains such as sociology, bioinformatics, infrastructure, the WWW, to name a few. One of the key observations is that while real-world graphs are often globally sparse, they are locally dense. In other words, the average degree is often quite small (say at most 10 in a million vertex graph), but vertex neighborhoods are often dense. The classic notions of transitivity [47] and clustering coefficients [48] measure these densities, and are high for many real-world graphs [35, 40].

Finding dense subgraphs is a critical aspect of graph mining [30]. It has been used for finding communities and spam link farms in web graphs [29, 20, 13], graph visualization [2], real-time story identification [4], DNA motif detection in biological networks [18], finding correlated genes [49], epilepsy prediction [26], finding price value motifs in financial data [14], graph compression [8], distance query indexing [27], and increasing the throughput of social networking site servers [21]. This is closely related to the classic sociological notion of group cohesion [6, 17]. There are tangential connections to classic community detection, but the objectives are significantly different. Community definitions involve some relation of inner versus outer connections, while dense subgraphs purely focus on internal cohesion.

1.1 The challenges of dense subgraphs

Our input is a graph $G = (V, E)$. For vertex set S, we use $E(S)$ to denote the set of edges internal to S. The *edge density* of S is $\rho(S) = |E(S)|/\binom{|S|}{2}$, the fraction of edges

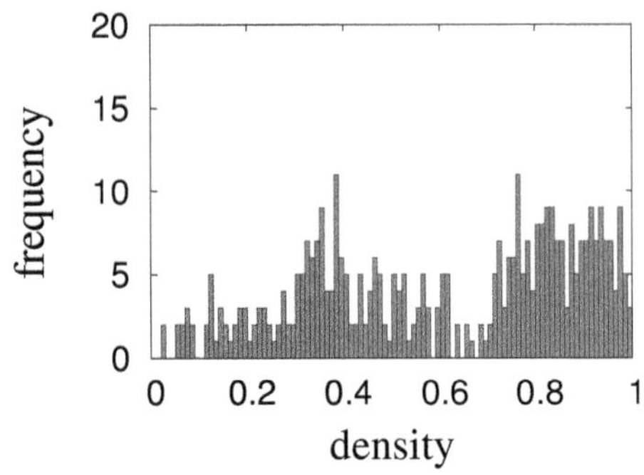

Figure 1: Density histogram of `facebook` (3, 4)-nuclei. 145 nuclei have density of at least 0.8 and 359 nuclei are with the density of more than 0.25.

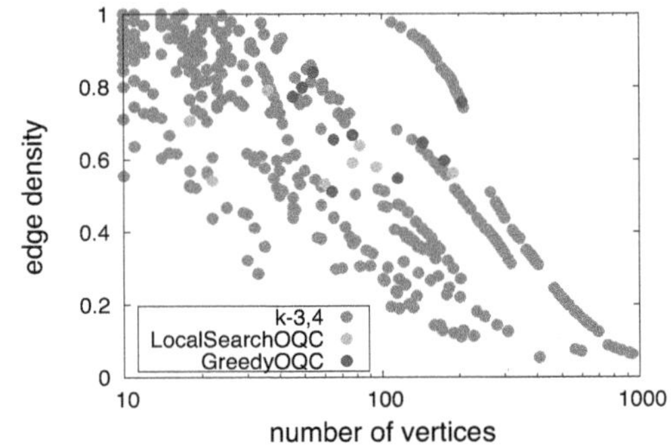

Figure 2: Size vs. density plot for `facebook` (3, 4)-nuclei. 50 nuclei are larger than 30 vertices with the density of at least 0.8. There are also 138 nuclei larger than 100 vertices with density of at last 0.25.

in S with respect to the total possible. The aim is to find a set S with high density subject to some size constraint. Typically, we are looking for large sets of high density.

In general, one can define numerous formulations that capture the main problem. The maximum clique problem is finding the largest S where $\rho(S) = 1$. Finding the densest S of size at least k is the k-densest subgraph problem. Quasi-cliques, as defined recently by Tsourakakis et al. [43], are sets that are almost cliques, up to some fixed "defect." Unfortunately, most formulations of finding dense subgraphs are NP-hard, even to approximate [24, 16, 28].

For graph analysis, one rarely looks for just a single (or the optimal, for whatever notion) dense subgraph. We want to find many dense subgraphs and understand the relationships among them. Ideally, we would like to see if they nest within each other, if the dense subgraphs are concentrated in some region, and if they occur at various scales of size and density. Our paper is motivated by the following questions.

- How do we attain a global, hierarchical representation of many dense subgraphs in a real-world graph?
- Can we define an efficiently solvable objective that directly provides *many* dense subgraphs? We wish to avoid heuristics, as they can be difficult to predict formally.

1.2 Our contributions

Nucleus decompositions: Our primary theoretical contribution is the notion of *nuclei* in a graph. Roughly speaking, an (r, s)-nucleus, for fixed (small) positive integers $r < s$, is a maximal subgraph where every r-clique is part of many s-cliques. (The real definition is more technical and involves some connectivity properties.) Moreover, nuclei that do not contain one another cannot share an r-clique. This is inspired by and is a generalization of the classic notion of k-cores, and also k-trusses (or triangle cores).

We show that the (r, s)-nuclei (for any $r < s$) form a hierarchical decomposition of a graph. The nuclei are progressively denser as we go towards the leaves in the decomposition. We provide an exact, efficient algorithm that finds all the nuclei and builds the hierarchical decomposition. In practice, we observe that (3, 4)-nuclei provide the most interesting decomposition. We find the (3, 4)-nuclei for a large variety of more than 20 graphs. Our algorithm is feasible in practice, and we are able to process a 39 million edge graph in less than an hour (using commodity hardware). The source code of our algorithms are available [1].

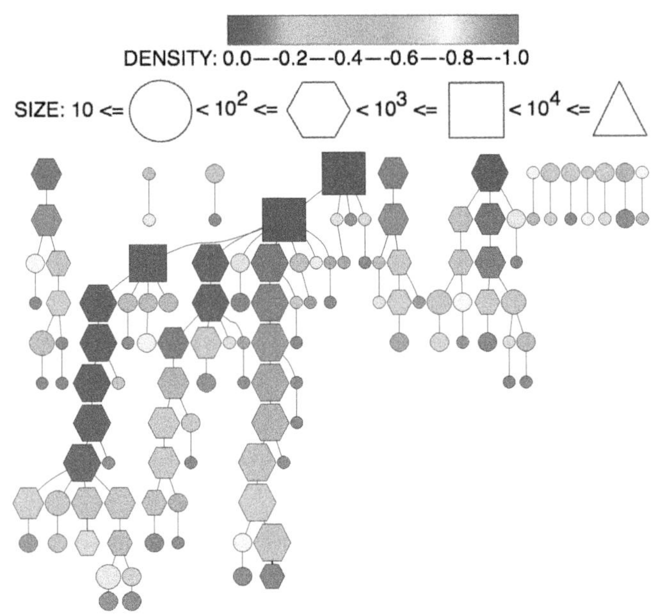

Figure 3: (3, 4)-nuclei forest for `facebook`. Legends for densities and sizes are shown at the top. Long chain paths are contracted to single edges. In the uncontracted forest, there are 47 leaves and 403 nuclei. Branching depicts the different regions in the graph, 13 connected components exist in the top level. Sibling nuclei have limited overlaps up to 7 vertices.

Dense subgraphs from (3, 4)-nuclei: The (3, 4)-nuclei provide a large set of dense subgraphs for range of densities and sizes. For example, there are 403 (3, 4)-nuclei (of size at least 10 vertices) in a `facebook` network of 88K edges. We show the density histogram of these nuclei in Fig. 1, plotting the number of nuclei with a given density. Observe that we get numerous dense subgraphs, and many with den-

[1] http://bmi.osu.edu/hpc/software/nucleus

sity fairly close to 1. In Fig. 2, we present a scatter plot of vertex size vs density of the $(3,4)$-nuclei. Observe that we obtain dense subgraphs over a wide range of sizes. For comparison, we also plot the output of recent dense subgraph algorithms from Tsourakakis et al. [43]. (These are arguably the state-of-the-art. More details in next section.) Observe that $(3,4)$-nuclei give dense subgraphs of comparable quality. In some cases, the output of [43] is very close to a $(3,4)$-nucleus.

Representing a graph as forest of $(3,4)$-nuclei: We build the forest of $(3,4)$-nuclei for all graphs experimented on. An example output is that of Fig. 3, the forest of $(3,4)$-nuclei for the `facebook` network. Each node of the forest is a $(3,4)$-nucleus, and tree edges indicate containment. More generally, an ancestor nucleus contains all descendant nuclei. By the properties of $(3,4)$-nuclei, any two incomparable nodes do not share a triangle. So the branching in the forest represents different regions of the graph. (All nuclei of less than 10 vertices are omitted. For presentation, we contract long chain paths in the tree to single edges, so the forest has less than 403 nodes.)

In the nuclei figures, densities are color-coded, with hotter colors indicating higher density. The log of sizes are coded by shape (circles comprise between 10 and 100 vertices, hexagons between 100 and 1000 vertices, etc.) For a fixed shape, relative size corresponds to relative size in number of vertices. We immediately see the hierarchy of dense structures. Observe the colors becoming hotter as we go towards to leaves, which are mostly red (density > 0.8). We see numerous hexagons and large circles of color between light blue to green. These indicate the larger parent subgraphs of moderate density (actually density of say 0.25 is fairly high for a subgraph having many hundreds of vertices).

The branching is also significant, and we can group together the dense subgraphs according to the hierarchy. We observe such branching in all our experiments, and show more such results later in the paper. The $(3,4)$-nuclei provide a simple, hierarchical visualization of dense substructures. They are well-defined and their exact computation is algorithmically feasible and practical.

We also want to emphasize the overlap between sibling nuclei. While sibling nuclei cannot share triangles, they can share edges, thus vertices. We observe roughly 20 pairs of $(3,4)$-nuclei having intersections of 4-6 vertices. For larger graphs, we observe many more pairs of intersecting nuclei (with larger intersections).

The rest of the paper is organized as follows: §2 summarizes the related work, §3 introduces the main definitions and the lemma about the nucleus decomposition, §4 gives the algorithm to generate a nucleus decomposition and provides a complexity analysis, §5 contains the results of extensive experiments we have, and §6 concludes the paper by discussing the future directions.

2. PREVIOUS WORK

Dense subgraph algorithms: As discussed earlier, most formulations of the densest subgraph problem are NP-hard. Some variants such as maximum average degree [22, 19] and the recently defined triangle-densest subgraph [44] are polynomial time solvable. Linear time approximation algorithms have been provided by Asashiro et al. [5], Charikar [9], and Tsourakakis [44]. There are numerous recent practical algorithms for various such objectives: Andersen and Chellapilla's use of cores for dense subgraphs [3], Rossi et al.'s heuristic for clique [34], Tsourakakis et al.'s notion of quasi-cliques [43]. These algorithms are extremely efficient and produce excellent output. For comparison's sake, we consider Tsourakakis et al. [43] as the state-of-the-art, which was compared with previous core-based heuristics and is much superior to prior art. Indeed, their algorithms are elegant, extremely efficient, and provide high quality output (and much faster than ours. More discussion in §5.4). These methods are tailored to finding one (or a few) dense subgraphs, and do not give a global/hierarchical view of the structure of dense subgraphs. We believe it would be worthwhile to relate their methods with our notion of nuclei, to design even better algorithms.

k-cores and k-trusses: The concepts of k-cores and k-trusses form the inspiration for our work. A k-core is a maximal subgraph where each vertex has minimum degree k, while a k-truss is a subgraph where each edge participates in at least k triangles. The first definition of k-cores was given by Erdős and Hajnal [15]. It has been rediscovered numerous times in the context of graph orientations and is alternately called the coloring number and degeneracy [31, 38]. The first linear time algorithm for computing k-cores was given by Matula and Beck [32]. The earliest applications of cores to social networks was given by Seidman [38], and it is now a standard tool in the analysis of massive networks. The notions of k-truss or triangle-cores were independently proposed by Cohen [11], Zhang and Parthasarathy [50], and Zhao and Tung [51] for finding clusters and for network visualization. They all provide efficient algorithms for these decompositions, and Cohen [11] and Wang and Cheng [45] explicitly focus on massive scale. In [46], Wang et al. proposed DN-graph, a similar concept to k-truss, where each edge should be involved in k triangles, and adding or removing a vertex from DN-graph breaks this constraint. Apart from the k-core and k-truss definitions, k-plex and k-club subgraph definitions have drawn a lot of interest as well. In a k-plex subgraph, each vertex is connected to all but at most $k-1$ other vertices [39], which complements the k-core definition. In a k-club subgraph, the shortest path from any vertex to other vertex is not more than k [33]. All these methods find subgraphs of moderate density, and give a global decomposition to visualize a graph.

3. NUCLEUS DECOMPOSITION

Our main theoretical contribution is the notion of nucleus decompositions. We have an undirected, simple graph G. We use K_r to denote an r-clique and start with some technical definitions.

DEFINITION 1. *Let $r < s$ be positive integers and $\mathcal{S}$ be a set of K_ss in G.*

- *$K_r(\mathcal{S})$ the set of K_rs contained in some $S \in \mathcal{S}$.*
- *The number of $S \in \mathcal{S}$ containing $R \in K_r(\mathcal{S})$ is the* $\mathcal{S}$-degree *of that K_r.*
- *Two K_rs R, R' are* $\mathcal{S}$-connected *if there exists a sequence $R = R_1, R_2, \ldots, R_k = R'$ in $K_r(\mathcal{S})$ such that for each i, some $S \in \mathcal{S}$ contains $R_i \cup R_{i+1}$.*

These definitions are generalizations of the standard notion of the vertex degree and connectedness. Indeed, setting $r = 1$ and $s = 2$ (so $\mathcal{S}$ is a set of edges) yields exactly that. Our main definition is as follows.

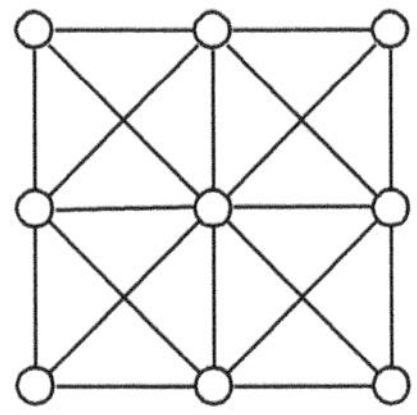

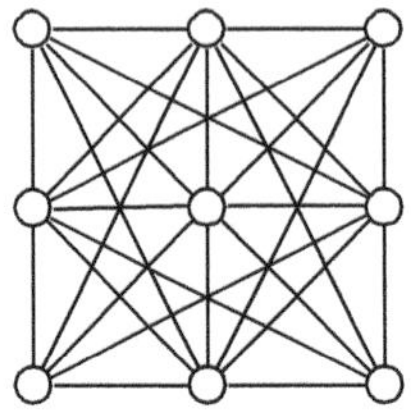

Figure 4: Having same number of vertices, 2-(2, 4) nucleus is denser than 2-(2, 3).

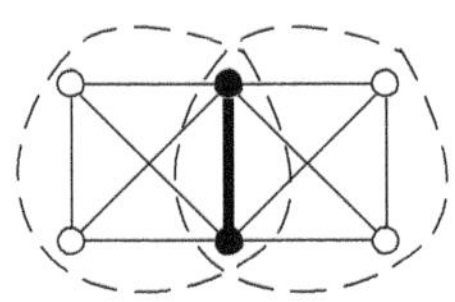

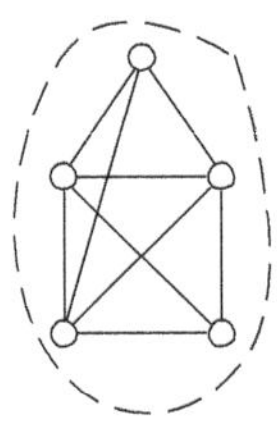

Figure 5: The left figure shows two (3, 4)-nuclei overlapping at an edge. The right figure has only one (3, 4)-nucleus

DEFINITION 2. *Let k, r, and s be positive integers such that $r < s$. A k-(r,s)*-nucleus *is a maximal union $\mathcal{S}$ of K_ss such that:*

- *The $\mathcal{S}$-degree of any $R \in K_r(\mathcal{S})$ is at least k.*
- *Any $R, R' \in K_r(\mathcal{S})$ are $\mathcal{S}$-connected.*

We simply refer to (r,s)-nuclei when k is unspecified. Note that we treat nuclei as a union of cliques, though eventually, we look at this as a subgraph. Our theoretical treatment is more convenient in the former setting, and hence we stick with this definition. In our applications, we simply look at nuclei as subgraphs.

Intuitively, a nucleus is a tightly connected cluster of cliques. For large k, we expect the cliques in $\mathcal{S}$ to intersect heavily, creating a dense subgraph. For a fixed k, r and same number of vertices, the density of the nuclei increases, as we increase s. Consider the example of Fig. 4, where there is a 2-(2, 3)-nucleus and a 2-(2, 4)-nucleus on the same number of vertices. Since in the latter case, we need every edge to participate in at least 2 K_4s, the resulting density is much higher.

As stated earlier, our definitions are inspired by k-cores and k-trusses. Set $r = 1, s = 2$. A k-(1, 2)-nucleus is a maximal (induced) connected subgraph with minimum vertex degree k. *This is exactly a k-core.* Setting $r = 2, s = 3$ gives maximal subgraphs where every edge participates in at least k triangles, and edges are triangle-connected. This is essentially the definition of k-trusses or triangle-cores.

So far we only discussed the degree constraint of nuclei. Note that a nucleus is not just connected in the usual (edge) sense, but requires the stronger property of being $\mathcal{S}$-connected. The standard definitions of trusses or triangle-cores omit the triangle-connectedness. For us, this is critical. Two cliques of distinct (r,s)-nuclei *can* intersect. For example, when $r > 2$, nuclei can have edge overlaps. This allows for finding even denser subgraphs, as Fig. 5 shows. In the left, cores, trusses, etc. pick up the entire graph. But there are actually 2 different 1-(3, 4)-nuclei (each K_4) intersecting at an edge. The (3, 4)-nuclei are denser than the graph itself. Note that any edge disjoint decomposition would not find two dense subgraphs.

Critically, the set of (r,s)-nuclei form a laminar family. A laminar family is a set system where all pairwise intersections are trivial (either empty or contains one of the sets).

LEMMA 1. *The family of (r,s)-nuclei form a laminar family.*

PROOF. Consider k-(r,s)-nucleus $\mathcal{S}$ and k'-(r,s)-nucleus $\mathcal{S}'$, where $k \leq k'$. Suppose they had a non-empty intersection, so some $K_s(\mathcal{S})$ is contained in both $\mathcal{S}$ and $\mathcal{S}'$. Observe that K_rs in $K_r(\mathcal{S})$ are connected to K_rs in $K_r(\mathcal{S}')$. Furthermore, the $(\mathcal{S} \cup \mathcal{S}')$-degree of member of $K_r(\mathcal{S} \cup \mathcal{S}')$ is at least k. Hence $\mathcal{S} \cup \mathcal{S}'$ satisfies the two conditions of being a nucleus, except maximality. By $\mathcal{S}$ is a k-(r,s)-nucleus, so $\mathcal{S} \cup \mathcal{S}' = \mathcal{S}$. So any non-empty intersection is trivial. □

Consider two nuclei that are not ancestor-descendant. By the above lemma, these two nuclei (considered as subgraphs of G) cannot share a K_s. Actually, the argument above proves that they cannot even share a K_r. This is the key disjointness property of nuclei.

Every laminar family is basically a hierarchical set system. Alternately, every laminar family can be represented by a forest of containment. For every nucleus $\mathcal{S}$, any other nucleus intersecting $\mathcal{S}$ is either contained in $\mathcal{S}$ or contains $\mathcal{S}$. Furthermore, all these sets are nested in each other. It makes sense to talk of the smallest sized nucleus containing $\mathcal{S}$. This leads to the main construct we use to represent nuclei.

DEFINITION 3. *Fix $r < s$. Define the* forest of (r,s)-nuclei *as follows. There is a node for each (r,s) nucleus. The parent of every nucleus is the smallest (by cardinality) other nucleus containing it.*

In our figures, we will only show the internal nodes of out degree at least 2, and contract any path of out degree 1 vertices into a single path. This preserves all the branching of the forest.

4. GENERATING NUCLEUS DECOMPOSITIONS

Our primary algorithmic goal is to construct the tree of nuclei. The algorithm is a direct adaptation of the classic Matula-Beck result of getting k-cores in linear time [32]. There are numerous technicalities involved in generalizing the proof. Intuitively, we do the following. Construct a graph $\mathcal{H}$ where the nodes are all K_rs of G and there is an edge connecting two K_rs if they are contained in a single K_s of G. We then perform a core decomposition on $\mathcal{H}$. Actually, this does not work. Edges of G (obviously) contain exactly 2 vertices of G, and the procedure above exactly produces nuclei for $r = 1, s = 2$. In general, a K_s contains $\binom{s}{r}$ K_rs, and the graph analogy above is incorrect. At some level, we are performing a hypergraph version of Matula-Beck. The proofs therefore need to be adapted to this setting.

Analogous to k-cores, the main procedure `set-k` (Algorithm 1) assigns a number, denoted by $\kappa(\cdot)$, to each K_r in G.

Algorithm 1: `set-k`(G, r, s)

1 Enumerate all K_rs and K_ss in $G(V, E)$;
2 For every K_r R, initialize $\delta(R)$ to be the number of K_ss containing R;
3 Mark every K_r as unprocessed;
4 **for each** *unprocessed* K_r R *with minimum* $\delta(R)$ **do**
5     $\kappa(R) = \delta(R)$;
6   Find set $\mathcal{S}$ of K_ss containing R;
7   **for each** $S \in \mathcal{S}$ **do**
8   **if** *any* K_r $R' \subset S$ *is processed* **then**
9   Continue;
10   **for each** K_r $R' \subset S$, $R' \neq R$ **do**
11   **if** $\delta(R') > \delta(R)$ **then**
12                 $\delta(R') = \delta(R') - 1$;
13   Mark R as processed;
14 **return** array $\kappa(\cdot)$;

It is convenient to denote the set of K_rs in G by $R_1, R_2, \ldots$, where R_i is the ith processed K_r in `set-k`. We will refer to this index as *time*. When we say "at time t", we mean at the beginning of the iteration where R_t is processed.

CLAIM 1. *The sequence $\{\kappa(R_i)\}$ is monotonically non-decreasing.*

PROOF. This holds because the loop goes R in non-decreasing order of $d(R)$ and Step 11 ensures that no new value of $\delta(\cdot)$ decreases below the current $\kappa(R)$. $\Box$

- Because of Claim 1, we can define *transition time* t_i to be the first time when the κ-value becomes i. Formally, t_i is the unique index such that $\kappa(R_{t_i}) = i$ and $\kappa(R_{t_i - 1}) < i$.
- We say K_s S is *unprocessed at time* t if all $R \in K_r(S)$ are unprocessed at time t. This set of K_ss is denoted by $\mathcal{S}_t$.
- The *supergraph* $\mathcal{G}_t$ has node set $K_r(\mathcal{S}_t)$, and $R, R' \in K_r(\mathcal{S}_t)$ are connected by a link if $R \cup R'$ is contained in some K_s of $\mathcal{S}_t$. Links are associated with elements of $\mathcal{S}_t$ (and there may be multiple links between R and R').

We prove an auxiliary claim relating the $\delta(\cdot)$ values to $\mathcal{S}_t$.

CLAIM 2. *At time t, for any unprocessed K_r R, $\delta(R)$ is at least the $\mathcal{S}_t$-degree of R. If $t = t_k$ (for some k), then $\delta(R)$ is exactly the $\mathcal{S}_t$-degree of R.*

PROOF. Pick unprocessed R'. The value of $\delta(R)$ is initially the number of K_ss containing R'. It is decremented only in Step 12, which happens only when a processed K_s containing R' is found. (Sometimes, the decrement will still not happen, because of Step 11.) Hence, the value of $\delta(R')$ at time t is at least the number of unprocessed K_ss containing R'.

Suppose $t = t_k$. For any preceding $\hat{t} < t$, the current $\kappa(\cdot)$ value is always at most k. For unprocessed (at time t) R, $\delta(R) > k$. Hence the decrement of Step 12 will always happen, and $\delta(R)$ is exactly the $\mathcal{S}_t$-degree of R. $\Box$

CLAIM 3. *Every k-(r, s)-nucleus is contained in $\mathcal{S}_{t_k}$.*

PROOF. Consider k-(r, s)-nucleus $\mathcal{S}$. Take the first $R \in K_r(\mathcal{S})$ that is processed. At this time (say t), no $S \in \mathcal{S}$ can be processed. Hence, $\mathcal{S} \subseteq \mathcal{S}_t$. By Claim 2, $d(R)$ is at least the $\mathcal{S}_t$-degree of R, which is at least the $\mathcal{S}$-degree of R. The latter is at least k, since $\mathcal{S}$ is a k-(r, s)-nucleus. By definition of t_k, $t \geq t_k$ and hence $\mathcal{S}_t \subseteq \mathcal{S}_{t_k}$. Thus, $\mathcal{S} \subseteq \mathcal{S}_{t_k}$. $\Box$

The main lemma shows that the output of `set-k` essentially tells us the nuclei.

LEMMA 2. *The k-(r, s)-nuclei are exactly the links (which are K_ss) of connected components of $\mathcal{G}_{t_k}$.*

PROOF. Consider k-(r, s)-nucleus $\mathcal{S}$. By Claim 3, it is contained in $\mathcal{S}_{t_k}$. By the nucleus definition, $\mathcal{S}$ is connected (as links) in $\mathcal{G}_{t_k}$. Let $\mathcal{S}'$ be the (set of links) connected component of $\mathcal{G}_{t_k}$ containing $\mathcal{S}$. By Claim 2, at time t_k, for any $R \in K_r(\mathcal{S}')$, $\delta(R)$ is exactly the $\mathcal{S}_{t_k}$-degree of R. Since $\mathcal{S}'$ is a connected component of $\mathcal{G}_{t_k}$, the $\mathcal{S}_{t_k}$-degree is the $\mathcal{S}'$-degree, which in turn is at least k. In other words, $\mathcal{S}'$ satisfies both conditions of being a k-(r, s)-nucleus, except maximality. By maximality of $\mathcal{S}$, $\mathcal{S} = \mathcal{S}'$. $\Box$

Building the forest of nuclei: From Lem. 2, it is fairly straightforward to get all the nuclei. First run `set-k` to get the processing times and the $\kappa(\cdot)$ values. We can then get all t_k times as well. Suppose for any K_r in G, we can access all the K_ss containing it. Then, it is routine to traverse $\mathcal{G}_{t_k}$ to get the links of connected components. To avoid traversing the same component repeatedly, we produce nuclei in reverse order of k. In other words, suppose all connected components of $\mathcal{G}_{t_{k+1}}$ have been determined. For $\mathcal{G}_{t_k}$, it suffices to determine the connected components involving nodes processed in time $[t_k, t_{k+1})$. Any time a traversal encounters a node in $\mathcal{G}_{t_{k+1}}$, we need not traverse further. This is because all other connected nodes of $\mathcal{G}_{t_{k+1}}$ are already known from previous traversals. We do not get into the data structure details here, but it suffices to visit all nodes and links of $\mathcal{G}_0$ exactly once.

4.1 Bounding the complexity

There are two options of implementing this algorithm. The first is faster, but has forbiddingly large space. The latter is slower, but uses less space. In practice, we implement the latter algorithm. We use $ct_r(v)$ for the number of K_rs containing v and $ct_r(G)$ for the total number of K_rs in G. We denote by $RT_r(G)$ the running time of an arbitrary procedure that enumerates all K_rs in G.

THEOREM 1. *It is possible to build the forest of nuclei in $O(RT_r(G) + RT_s(G))$ time with $O(ct_r(G) + ct_s(G))$ space.*

PROOF. This is the obvious implementation. The very first step of `set-k` requires the clique enumeration. Suppose we store the global supergraph $\mathcal{G} = \mathcal{G}_0$. This has a node for every K_r in G and a link for every K_s in G. The storage is $O(ct_r(S) + ct_s(G))$. From this point onwards, all remaining operations are linear in the storage. This is by the analysis of the standard core decomposition algorithm of Matula and Beck [32]. Every time we process a K_r, we can delete it and all incident links from $\mathcal{G}$. Every link is touched at most a constant number of times during the entire running on `set-k`. As explained earlier, we can get all the nuclei by a single traversal of $\mathcal{G}$. $\Box$

THEOREM 2. *It is possible to build the forest of nuclei in $O(RT_r(G) + \sum_v ct_r(v) d(v)^{s-r})$ time with $O(ct_r(G))$ space.*

PROOF. Instead of explicitly building $\mathcal{G}$, we only build adjacency lists when required. The storage is now only $O(ct_r(G))$. In other words, given a K_r R, we find all K_ss containing R only when R is processed/traversed. Each R

is processed or traversed at most once in set-k and the forest building. Suppose R has vertices $v_1, v_2, \ldots, v_r$. We can find all K_ss containing R by looking at all $(s-r)$-tuples in each of the neighborhoods of v_i. (Indeed, it suffices to look at just one such neighborhood.) This takes time at most $\sum_R \sum_{v \in R} d(v)^{s-r} = \sum_v \sum_{R \ni v} d(v)^{s-r} = \sum_v ct_r(v) d(v)^{s-r}$. □

Let us understand these running times. When $r < s \leq 3$, it clearly benefits to go with Thm. 1. Triangle enumeration is a well-studied problem and there exist numerous optimized, parallel solutions for the problem. In general, the classic triangle enumeration of Chiba and Nishizeki takes $O(m^{3/2})$ [10] and is much better in practice [12, 37, 42]. This completely bounds the time and space complexities.

For our best results, we build the (3,4)-nuclei, and the number of K_4s is too large to store. We go with Thm. 2. The storage is now at most the number of triangles, which is manageable. The running time is basically bounded by $O(\sum_v ct_r(v) d(v))$. The number of triangles incident to v, $ct_3(v)$ is $cc(v)d(v)^2$, where $cc(v)$ is the clustering coefficient of v. We therefore get a running time of $O(\sum_v cc(v)d(v)^3)$. This is significantly superlinear, but clustering coefficients generally decay with degree [35, 40]. Overall, the implementation can be made to scale to tens of millions of edges with little difficulty.

5. EXPERIMENTAL RESULTS

We applied our algorithms to large variety of graphs, obtained from SNAP [41] and UF Sparse Matrix Collection[1]. The vital statistics of these graphs are given in Tab. 1. All the algorithms in our framework are implemented in C++ and compiled with gcc 4.8.1 at -O2 optimization level. All experiments are performed on a Linux operating system running on a machine with two Intel Xeon E5520 2.27 GHz CPUs, with 48GB of RAM.

We computed the (r,s)-nuclei for all choices of $r < s \leq 4$, but do not present all results for space considerations. We mostly observe that the forest of (3,4)-nuclei provides the highest quality output, both in terms of hierarchy and density.

As mentioned earlier, we will now treat the nuclei as just induced subgraphs of G. A nucleus can be considered as a set of vertices, and we take all edges among these vertices (induced subgraph) to attain the subgraph. The *size* of a nucleus always refers to the number of vertices, unless otherwise specified. For any set S of vertices, the density of the induced subgraph is $|E(S)|/\binom{|S|}{2}$, where $E(S)$ is the set of edges internal to S. *We ignore any nucleus with less than 10 vertices. Such nuclei are not considered in any of our results.*

For brevity, we present detailed results on only 4 graphs (given in Tab. 1): facebook, soc-sign-epinions, web-NotreDame, and wikipedia-200611. This covers a variety of graphs, and other results are similar.

5.1 The forest of nuclei

We were able to construct the forest of (3,4)-nuclei for all graphs in Tab. 1, but only give the forests for facebook (Fig. 3), soc-sign-epinions (Fig. 6), and web-NotreDame (Fig. 7). For the web-NotreDame figure, we could not present the entire forest, so we show some trees in the forest that had nice branching. The density is color coded, from blue (density 0) to red (density 1). The nuclei sizes, in terms of vertices, are coded by shape: circles correspond to at most 10^2 vertices, hexagons in the range $[10^2, 10^3]$, squares in the range $[10^3, 10^4]$, and triangles are anything larger. The relative size of the shape, is the relative size (in that range) of the set.

Overall, we see that the (3,4)-nuclei provide a hierarchical representation of the dense subgraphs. The leaves are mostly red, and their densities are almost always > 0.8. But we obtain numerous nuclei of intermediate sizes and densities. In the facebook forest and to some extent in the web-NotreDame forest, we see hexagons of light blue to green (nuclei of > 100 vertices of densities of at least 0.2). The branching is quite prominent, and the smaller dense nuclei tend to nest into larger, less dense nuclei. This held in every single (3,4)-nucleus forest we computed. This appears to validate the intuition that real-world networks have a hierarchical structure.

The (3,4)-nuclei figures provide a useful visualization of the dense subgraph structure. The web-NotreDame has a million edges, and it is not possible to see the graph as a whole. But the forest of nuclei breaks it down into meaningful parts, which can be visually inspected. The overall forest is large (about 2000 nuclei), but the nesting structure makes it easy to absorb. We have not presented the results here, but even the wikipedia-200611 graph of 38 million edges has about a forest of only 4000 nuclei (which we were able to easily visualize by a drawing tool).

Other choices of r, s for the nuclei do not lead to much branching. We present all nucleus trees for $r < s \leq 4$ for the facebook graph in Fig. 8 (except (3,4) which is given in Fig. 3). Clearly, when $r = 1$, the nucleus decomposition is boring. For $r = 2$, some structure arises, but not as dramatic of Fig. 3. Results vary over graphs, but for $r = 1$, there is pretty much just a chain of nuclei. For $r = 2$, some graphs show more branching, but we consistently see that for (3,4)-nuclei, the forest of nuclei is always branched.

5.2 Dense subgraph discovery

We plot the density histograms of the (3,4)-nuclei for various graphs in Fig. 9. The x-axis is (binned) density and the y-axis is the number of nuclei (all at least 10 vertices) with that density. It can be clearly observed that we find many non-trivial dense subgraphs. It is surprising to see how many near cliques (density > 0.9) we find. We tend to find more subgraphs of high density, and other than the web-NotreDame graph, the mass of the histogram is shifted to the right. The number of subgraphs of density at least 0.5 is in the order of hundreds (and more than a thousand for wikipedia-200611).

An alternate presentation of the dense subgraphs is a scatter plot of all (3,4)-nuclei with size in vertices versus density. This is given in Fig. 2 and Fig. 10, where the red dots correspond to the nuclei. We see that dense subgraphs are obtained in all scales of size, which is an extremely important feature. Nuclei capture more than just the densest (or high density) subgraphs, but find large sets of lower density (say around 0.2). Note that 0.2 is a significant density for sets of hundreds of vertices.

5.2.1 Comparisons with previous art

How does the quality of dense subgraphs found compare to the state-of-the-art? In the scatter plots of Fig. 2 and Fig. 10, we also show the output of two algorithms of [43] in green

	|V|	|E|	Description	$\sum_v c_3(v)d(v)$	(3, 4) time (sec)	[43] Density (size)	(3,4)-nucleus Density (size)
dolphins	62	159	Biological	2.2K	< 1	0.68(8)	0.71(8)
polbooks	105	441	US Politics Books	23.8K	< 1	0.67(13)	0.62(13)
adjnoun	112	425	Adj. and Nouns	17.6K	< 1	0.60(15)	0.22(32)
football	115	613	World Soccer 98	26.3K	< 1	0.89(10)	0.89(10)
jazz	198	$2.74K$	Musicians	2.3M	< 1	1.00(30)	1.00(30)
celegans n.	297	$2.34K$	Biological	418K	< 1	0.61(21)	0.91(10)
celegans m.	453	$2.04K$	Biological	565K	< 1	0.67(17)	0.64(18)
email	$1.13K$	$5.45K$	Email	1.2M	< 1	1.00(12)	1.00(12)
facebook	$4.03K$	$88.23K$	Friendship	712M	93	0.83(54)	0.98(109)
protein_inter.	$9.67K$	$37.08K$	Protein Inter.	35M	< 1	1.00(11)	1.00(11)
as-22july06	$22.96K$	$48.43K$	Autonomous Sys.	199M	< 1	0.58(12)	1.00(18)
twitter	$81.30K$	$2.68M$	Follower-Followee	1.8B	396	0.85(83)	1.00(26)
soc-sign-epinions	$131.82K$	$841.37K$	Who-trust-whom	1.4B	242	0.71(79)	1.00(112)
coAuthorsCiteseer	$227.32K$	$814.13K$	CoAuthorship	2.1B	50.1	1.00(87)	1.00(87)
citationCiteseer	$268.49K$	$1.15M$	Citation	297M	3.4	0.71(10)	1.00(13)
web-NotreDame	$325.72K$	$1.49M$	Web	33.9B	671	1.00(151)	1.00(155)
amazon0601	$403.39K$	$3.38M$	CoPurchase	802M	23	1.00(11)	1.00(11)
web-Google	$875.71K$	$5.10M$	Web	11.4B	163	1.00(46)	1.00(33)
com-youtube	$1.13M$	$2.98M$	Social	451M	43	0.49(119)	0.92(24)
as-skitter	$1.69M$	$11.09M$	Autonomous Sys.	1.6B	1,036	0.53(319)	0.94(91)
wikipedia-2005	$1.63M$	$19.75M$	Wikipedia Link	741B	1,312	0.53(33)	0.82(14)
wiki-Talk	$2.39M$	$5.02M$	Wikipedia User	136B	605	0.48(321)	0.59(95)
wikipedia-200609	$2.98M$	$37.26M$	Wikipedia Link	2,015B	2,830	0.49(376)	0.62(103)
wikipedia-200611	$3.14M$	$39.38M$	Wikipedia Link	2,197B	3,039	1.00(55)	1.00(32)

Table 1: Important statistics for the real-world graphs of different types and sizes. Largest graph in the dataset has more than $39M$ edges. Times are in seconds. Density of subgraph S is $|E(S)|/\binom{|S|}{2}$ where $E(S)$ is the set of edges internal to S. Sizes are in number of vertices.

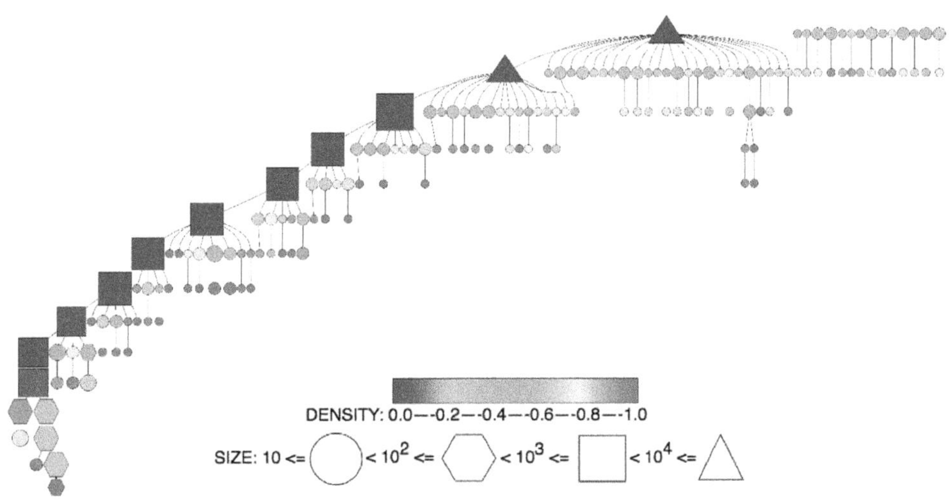

Figure 6: (3, 4)-nuclei forest for `soc-sign-epinions`. There are 465 total nodes and 75 leaves in the forest. There is a clear hierarchical structure of dense subgraphs. Leaves are mostly red (> 0.8 density). There are also some light blue hexagons, representing subgraphs of size ≥ 100 vertices with density of at least 0.2.

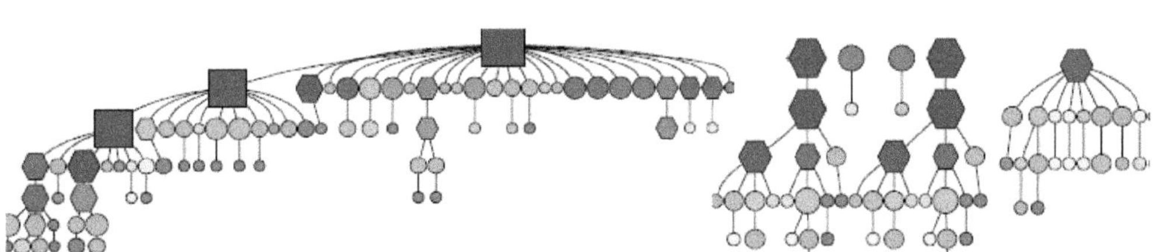

Figure 7: Part of the (3, 4)-nuclei forest for `web-NotreDame`. In the entire forest, there are 2059 nodes and 812 leaves. 79 of the leaves are clique, up to the size of 155. There is a nice branching structure leading to a decent hierarchy.

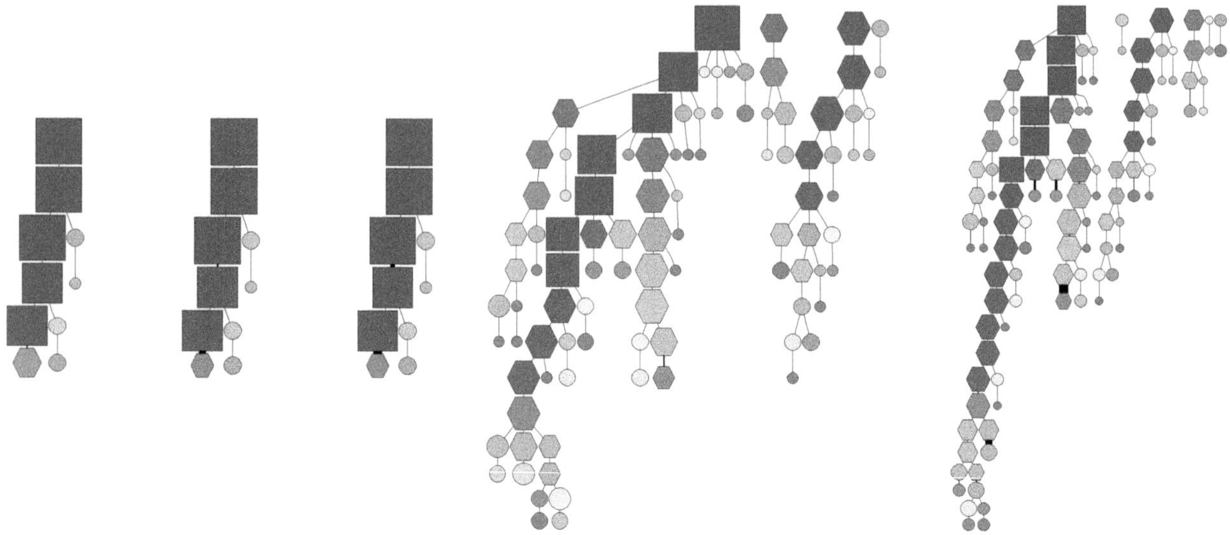

a: $(1,2)$-nuclei b: $(1,3)$-nuclei c: $(1,4)$-nuclei d: $(2,3)$-nuclei e: $(2,4)$-nuclei

Figure 8: (r,s)-nuclei forests for `facebook` when $r < s \leq 4$ (Except $(3,4)$, which is given in Fig. 3). For $r = 1$, trees are more like chains. Increasing s results in larger number of internal nodes, which are contracted in the illustrations. There is some hierarchy observed for $r = 2$, but it is not as powerful as $(3,4)$-nuclei, i.e., branching structure is more obvious in $(3,4)$-nuclei.

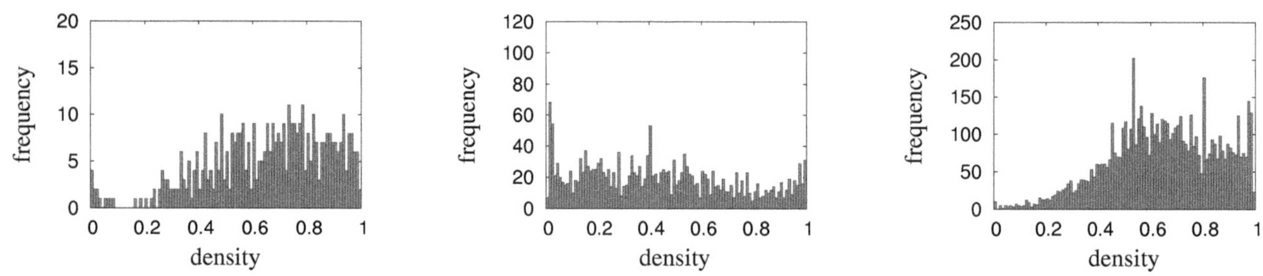

(a) `soc-sign-epinions` (b) `web-NotreDame` (c) `wikipedia-200611`

Figure 9: Density histograms for nuclei of three graphs. x-axis (binned) is the density and y-axis is the number of nuclei (at least 10 vertices) with that density. Number of nuclei with the density above 0.8 is significant: 139 for `soc-sign-epinions`, 355 for `web-NotreDame`, and 1874 for `wikipedia-200611`. Also notice that, the mass of the histogram is shifted to right in `soc-sign-epinions` and `wikipedia-200611` graphs.

and blue. The idea of [43] is to approximate *quasi-cliques*, and their result provides two every elegant algorithms for this process. (We collectively refer to them as OQC.) OQC algorithms only give a single output, so we performed multiple runs to get many dense subgraphs. This is consistent with what was done in [43]. OQC algorithms clearly beat previous heuristics and it is fair to say that [43] is the state-of-the-art.

The $(3,4)$-nucleus decomposition does take significantly longer than the algorithms of [43]. But we always get much denser subgraphs in all runs. Moreover, the sizes are comparable if not larger than the output of [43]. Surprisingly, in `facebook` and `soc-sign-epinions`, some of the best outputs of OQC are very close to $(3,4)$-nuclei. Arguably, the $(3,4)$-nuclei perform worst on `wikipedia-200611`, where OQC find some larger and denser instances than $(3,4)$-nuclei. Nonetheless, the smaller $(3,4)$-nuclei are significantly denser. We almost always can find fairly large cliques.

In Tab. 1, we consider the OQC output vs $(3,4)$-nuclei for all graphs. Barring 4 instances, there is a $(3,4)$-nucleus that is larger and denser than the OQC output. In all cases but one (adjnoun), there is a $(3,4)$-nucleus of density (of non-trivial size) higher than the the OQC output. The nuclei have the advantage of being the output of a fixed, deterministic procedure, and not a heuristic that may give different outputs on different runs. We mention that OQC algorithms have a significant running time advantage over finding $(3,4)$-nuclei, for a single subgraph finding.

5.3 Overlapping nuclei

A critical aspect of nuclei is that they can overlap. Grappling with overlap is a major challenge when dealing with

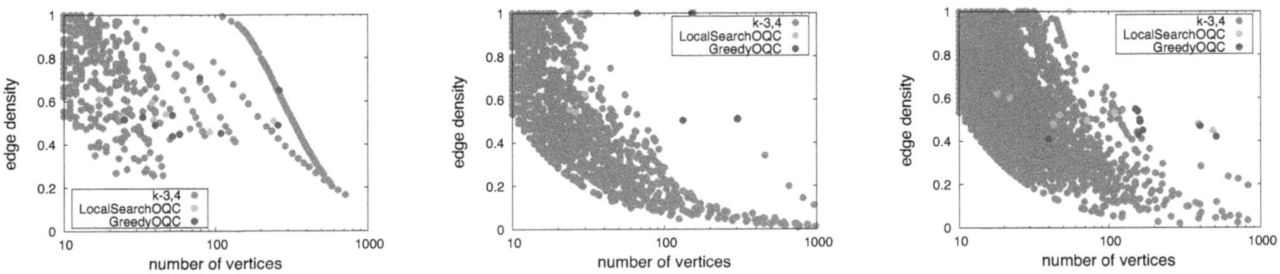

(a) `soc-sign-epinions` (b) `web-NotreDame` (c) `wikipedia-200611`

Figure 10: Density vs. size plots for nuclei of three graphs. State-of-the-art algorithms are depicted with OQC variants, and they report one subgraph at each run. We ran them 10 times to get a general picture of the quality. Overall, (3, 4)-nuclei is very competitive with the state-of-the-art and produces many number of subgraphs with high quality and non-trivial sizes.

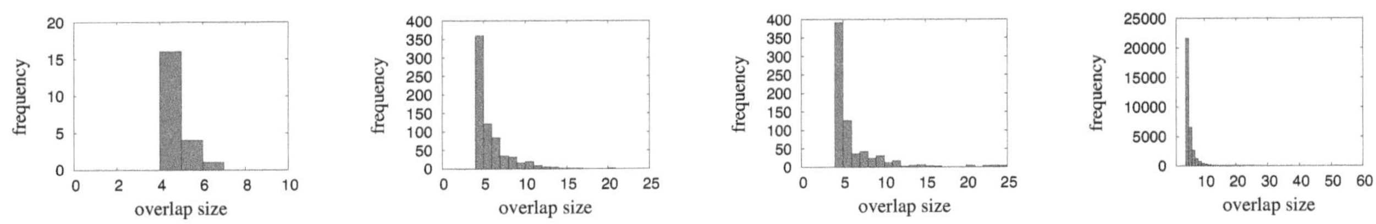

(a) `facebook` (b) `soc-sign-epinions` (c) `web-NotreDame` (d) `wikipedia-200611`

Figure 11: Histograms over non-trivial overlaps for (3, 4)-nuclei. Child-ancestor intersections are omitted. Overlap size is in terms of the number of vertices. Most overlaps are small in size. We also observe that $(2, s)$-nuclei give almost no overlaps.

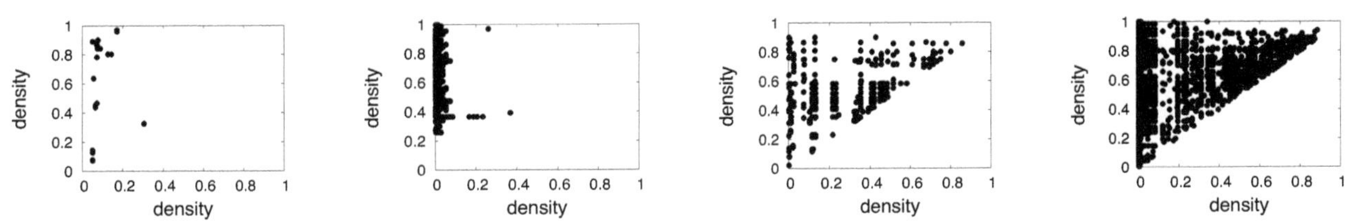

(a) `facebook` (b) `soc-sign-epinions` (c) `web-NotreDame` (d) `wikipedia-200611`

Figure 12: Overlap scatter plots for (3, 4)-nuclei. Each axis shows the edge density of a participating nucleus in the pair-wise overlap. Larger density is shown on the y-axis. (3, 4)-nuclei is able to get overlaps between very dense subgraphs, especially in `web-NotreDame` and `wikipedia-200611`. In `wikipedia-200611` graph, there are 1424 instances of pair-wise overlap between two nuclei, where each nucleus has the density of at least 0.8.

graph decompositions. We believe one of the benefits of nuclei is that they naturally allow for (restricted) overlap. As mentioned earlier, no two (r, s)-nuclei can contain the same K_r. This is a significant benefit of setting $r = 3, s = 4$ over other choices.

In Fig. 11, we plot the histogram over non-trivial overlaps for (3, 4)-nuclei. (We naturally do not consider a child nucleus intersecting with an ancestor.) For a given overlap size in vertices, the frequency is the number of pairs of (3, 4)-nuclei with that overlap. This is shown for four different graphs. The total number of pair-wise overlaps (the sum of frequencies) is typically around half the total number of (3, 4)-nuclei. We observed that the Jaccard similarities are less than 0.1 (usually smaller). This suggest that we have large nuclei with some overlap.

There are bioinformatics applications for finding vertices that are present in numerous dense subgraphs [25]. The (3, 4)-nuclei provide many such vertices. In Fig. 12, we give a scatter plot of all intersecting nuclei, where nuclei are indexed by density. For two intersecting nuclei of density $\alpha > \beta$, we put a point (α, β). We only plot pairs where the overlap is at least 5 vertices. Especially for `web-NotreDame` and `wikipedia-200611`, we get significant overlaps between dense clusters.

In contrast, for all other settings of r, s, we get almost no overlap. When $r = 2$, nuclei can only overlap at vertices, and this is too stringent to allow for interesting overlap.

5.4 Runtime results

Tab. 1 presents the runtimes in seconds for the entire construction. To provide some context, we describe runtimes for varying choices of r, s. For $r = 1, s = 2$ (k-cores), the decomposition is linear and extremely fast. For the largest graph (`wikipedia-200611`) we have, with $39M$ edges, it takes only 4.26 seconds. For $r = 2, s = 3$ (trusses), the time can be two orders of magnitude higher. And for $(3, 4)$-nuclei, it is an additional order of magnitude higher. Nonetheless, our most expensive run took less than an hour on the `wikipedia-200611` graph, and the final decomposition is quite insightful. It provides about 6000 nuclei with more than 10 vertices, most of them of have density of at least 0.4. The algorithms of [43] take roughly a minute for `wikipedia-200611` to produce *only one* dense subgraph.

The theoretical running time analysis of Thm. 2 gives a running time bound of $\sum_v c_3(v)d(v)$. In Tab. 1, we show this value for the various graphs. In general, we note that this value roughly correlates with the running time. For graphs where the running time is in many minutes, this quantity is always in the billions. For the large wiki graphs where the $(3, 4)$-nucleus decomposition is most expensive, this is in the trillions.

6. FURTHER DIRECTIONS

The most important direction is in the applications of nucleus decompositions. We are currently investigating bioinformatics applications, specifically protein-protein and protein-gene interaction networks. Biologists often want a global view of the dense substructures, and we believe the $(3, 4)$-nuclei could be extremely useful here. In our preliminary analyses, we wish to see if the nuclei pick out specific functional units. If so, that would provide strong validation of dense subgraph analyses for bioinformatics.

It is natural to try even larger values of r, s. Preliminary experimentation suggested that this gave little benefit in either the forest or the density of nuclei. Also, the cost of clique enumeration becomes forbiddingly large. It would be nice to argue that $r = 3, s = 4$ is a sort of sweet spot for nucleus decompositions. Previous theoretical work suggests that any graph with a sufficient triangle count undergoes special "community-like" decompositions [23]. That might provide evidence to why triangle based nuclei are enough.

A faster algorithm for the $(3, 4)$-nuclei is desirable. Clique enumeration is a well-studied problem [7], and we hope techniques from these results may provide ideas here. Of course, as we said earlier, any method based on storing 4-cliques is infeasible (space-wise). We hope to devise a clever algorithm or data structure that quickly determines the 4-cliques that a triangle participates in.

Last but not least, we seek for incremental algorithms to maintain the (r, s)-nuclei for a stream of edges. There are existing techniques for streaming k-core algorithms [36] and we believe that similar methods can be adapted for (r, s)-nuclei maintenance.

7. ACKNOWLEDGEMENTS

We are grateful to Charalampos Tsourakakis for sharing his code base for [43]. This work was funded by the DARPA GRAPHS program. Sandia National Laboratories is a multi-program laboratory managed and operated by Sandia Corporation, a wholly owned subsidiary of Lockheed Martin Corporation, for the U.S. Department of Energy's National Nuclear Security Administration under contract DE-AC04-94AL85000.

8. REFERENCES

[1] University of florida sparse matrix collection. http://www.cise.ufl.edu/research/sparse/matrices/.

[2] J. I. Alvarez-Hamelin, A. Barrat, and A. Vespignani. Large scale networks fingerprinting and visualization using the k-core decomposition. In *Advances in Neural Information Processing Systems 18*, pages 41–50, 2006.

[3] R. Andersen and K. Chellapilla. Finding dense subgraphs with size bounds. In *Workshop on Algorithms and Models for the Web-Graph (WAW)*, pages 25–37, 2009.

[4] A. Angel, N. Sarkas, N. Koudas, and D. Srivastava. Dense subgraph maintenance under streaming edge weight updates for real-time story identification. *Proc. VLDB Endow.*, 5(6):574–585, Feb. 2012.

[5] Y. Asahiro, K. Iwama, H. Tamaki, and T. Tokuyama. Greedily finding a dense subgraph. *J. Algorithms*, 34(2):203–221, Feb. 2000.

[6] D. J. Beal, R. Cohen, M. J. Burke, and C. L. McLendon. Cohesion and performance in groups: A meta-analytic clarification of construct relation. *Journal of Applied Psychology*, 88:989–1004, 2003.

[7] C. Bron and J. Kerbosch. Algorithm 457: Finding all cliques of an undirected graph. *Commun. ACM*, 16(9):575–577, Sept. 1973.

[8] G. Buehrer and K. Chellapilla. A scalable pattern mining approach to web graph compression with communities. In *Proc. of the 2008 International Conference on Web Search and Data Mining*, WSDM '08, pages 95–106, 2008.

[9] M. Charikar. Greedy approximation algorithms for finding dense components in a graph. In *Proc. of the Third International Workshop on Approximation Algorithms for Combinatorial Optimization*, APPROX '00, pages 84–95, 2000.

[10] N. Chiba and T. Nishizeki. Arboricity and subgraph listing algorithms. *SIAM J. Comput.*, 14:210–223, February 1985.

[11] J. Cohen. Trusses: Cohesive subgraphs for social network analysis. National Security Agency Technical Report, 2008.

[12] J. Cohen. Graph twiddling in a MapReduce world. *Computing in Science & Engineering*, 11:29–41, 2009.

[13] Y. Dourisboure, F. Geraci, and M. Pellegrini. Extraction and classification of dense communities in the web. In *Proc. of the 16th International Conference on World Wide Web*, WWW '07, pages 461–470, 2007.

[14] X. Du, R. Jin, L. Ding, V. E. Lee, and J. H. T. Jr. Migration motif: a spatial - temporal pattern mining approach for financial markets. In *Proc. of the 15th ACM SIGKDD International Conference on Knowledge Discovery and Data Mining*, 2009.

[15] P. Erdős and A. Hajnal. On chromatic number of graphs and set-systems. *Acta Mathematica Hungarica*, 17:61–99, 1966.

[16] U. Feige. Relations between average case complexity and approximation complexity. In *Proc. of Symposium on Theory of Computing*, pages 534–543, 2002.

[17] D. R. Forsyth. *Group Dynamics*. Cengage Learning, 2010.

[18] E. Fratkin, B. T. Naughton, D. L. Brutlag, and S. Batzoglou. Motifcut: regulatory motifs finding with maximum density subgraphs. In *ISMB (Supplement of Bioinformatics)*, pages 156–157, 2006.

[19] G. Gallo, M. D. Grigoriadis, and R. E. Tarjan. A fast parametric maximum flow algorithm and applications. *SIAM J. Comput.*, 18(1):30–55, Feb. 1989.

[20] D. Gibson, R. Kumar, and A. Tomkins. Discovering large dense subgraphs in massive graphs. In *Proc. of the 31st International Conference on Very Large Data Bases*, VLDB '05, pages 721–732, 2005.

[21] A. Gionis, F. Junqueira, V. Leroy, M. Serafini, and I. Weber. Piggybacking on social networks. *Proc. VLDB Endow.*, 6(6):409–420, 2013.

[22] A. V. Goldberg. Finding a maximum density subgraph. Technical report, Berkeley, CA, USA, 1984.

[23] R. Gupta, T. Roughgarden, and C. Seshadhri. Decompositions of triangle-dense graphs. In *Innovations in Theoretical Computer Science (ITCS)*, pages 471–482, 2014.

[24] J. Håstad. Clique is hard to approximate within $n^{(1-\epsilon)}$. In *Acta Mathematica*, pages 627–636, 1996.

[25] H. Hu, X. Yan, Y. Huang, J. Han, and X. J. Zhou. Mining coherent dense subgraphs across massive biological networks for functional discovery. *Bioinformatics*, 21(1):213–221, Jan. 2005.

[26] L. Iasemidis, D.-S. Shiau, W. Chaovalitwongse, J. Sackellares, P. Pardalos, J. Principe, P. Carney, A. Prasad, B. Veeramani, and K. Tsakalis. Adaptive epileptic seizure prediction system. *Biomedical Engineering, IEEE Transactions on*, 50:616–627, 2003.

[27] R. Jin, Y. Xiang, N. Ruan, and D. Fuhry. 3-hop: a high-compression indexing scheme for reachability query. In *SIGMOD Conference*, pages 813–826, 2009.

[28] S. Khot. Ruling out ptas for graph min-bisection, dense k-subgraph, and bipartite clique. *SIAM Journal on Computing*, 36(4):1025–1071, 2006.

[29] R. Kumar, P. Raghavan, S. Rajagopalan, and A. Tomkins. Trawling the web for emerging cyber-communities. In *Proc. of the Eighth International Conference on World Wide Web*, WWW '99, pages 1481–1493, 1999.

[30] V. E. Lee, N. Ruan, R. Jin, and C. C. Aggarwal. A survey of algorithms for dense subgraph discovery. In *Managing and Mining Graph Data*, volume 40. 2010.

[31] D. Lick and A. White. k-degenerate graphs. *Canadian Journal of Mathematics*, 22:1082–1096, 1970.

[32] D. Matula and L. Beck. Smallest-last ordering and clustering and graph coloring algorithms. *Journal of ACM*, 30(3):417–427, 1983.

[33] R. Mokken. Cliques, clubs and clans. *Quality and Quantity*, 13(2):161–173, 1979.

[34] R. A. Rossi, D. F. Gleich, A. H. Gebremedhin, and M. M. A. Patwary. A fast parallel maximum clique algorithm for large sparse graphs and temporal strong components. *CoRR*, abs/1302.6256, 2013.

[35] A. Sala, L. Cao, C. Wilson, R. Zablit, H. Zheng, and B. Y. Zhao. Measurement-calibrated graph models for social network experiments. In *WWW '10*, pages 861–870. ACM, 2010.

[36] A. E. Sarıyüce, B. Gedik, G. Jacques-Silva, K.-L. Wu, and Ü. V. Çatalyürek. Streaming algorithms for k-core decomposition. In *Proc. VLDB Endow.*, Aug 2013.

[37] T. Schank and D. Wagner. Finding, counting and listing all triangles in large graphs, an experimental study. In *Experimental and Efficient Algorithms*, pages 606–609. 2005.

[38] S. B. Seidman. Network structure and minimum degree. *Social Networks*, 5(3):269–287, 1983.

[39] S. B. Seidman and B. Foster. A graph-theoretic generalization of the clique concept. *Journal of Mathematical Sociology*, 1978.

[40] C. Seshadhri, A. Pinar, and T. G. Kolda. Triadic measures on graphs: The power of wedge sampling. *Statistical Analysis and Data Mining*, 7(4):294–307, 2014.

[41] SNAP. Stanford network analysis package. http://snap.stanford.edu/snap, retrieved March, 2014.

[42] S. Suri and S. Vassilvitskii. Counting triangles and the curse of the last reducer. In *WWW'11*, pages 607–614, 2011.

[43] C. Tsourakakis, F. Bonchi, A. Gionis, F. Gullo, and M. Tsiarli. Denser than the densest subgraph: Extracting optimal quasi-cliques with quality guarantees. In *Proc. of the 19th ACM SIGKDD International Conference on Knowledge Discovery and Data Mining*, KDD '13, 2013.

[44] C. E. Tsourakakis. A novel approach to finding near-cliques: The triangle-densest subgraph problem. *CoRR*, abs/1405.1477, 2014.

[45] J. Wang and J. Cheng. Truss decomposition in massive networks. *Proc. of the VLDB Endowment*, 5(9):812–823, 2012.

[46] N. Wang, J. Zhang, K.-L. Tan, and A. K. H. Tung. On triangulation-based dense neighborhood graph discovery. *Proc. VLDB Endow.*, 4:58–68, 2010.

[47] S. Wasserman and K. Faust. *Social Network Analysis: Methods and Applications*. Cambridge Univ Press, 1994.

[48] D. Watts and S. Strogatz. Collective dynamics of 'small-world' networks. *Nature*, 393:440–442, 1998.

[49] B. Zhang and S. Horvath. A general framework for weighted gene co-expression network analysis. *Statistical Applications in Genetics and Molecular Biology*, 4(1):Article 17+, 2005.

[50] Y. Zhang and S. Parthasarathy. Extracting analyzing and visualizing triangle k-core motifs within networks. In *Proc. of the 2012 IEEE 28th International Conference on Data Engineering*, ICDE '12, pages 1049–1060, 2012.

[51] F. Zhao and A. K. H. Tung. Large scale cohesive subgraphs discovery for social network visual analysis. In *Proc. VLDB Endow.*, pages 85–96, 2013.

Bringing CUPID Indoor Positioning System to Practice

Souvik Sen†, Dongho Kim†, Stephane Laroche‡, Kyu-Han Kim†, Jeongkeun Lee†
†HP Labs, ‡HP Networking
{souvik.sen, dongho.kim, stephane.laroche, kyu-han.kim, jklee}@hp.com

ABSTRACT

WiFi based indoor positioning has recently gained more attention due to the advent of the IEEE 802.11v standard, requirements by the FCC for E911 calls, and increased interest in location-based services. While there exist several indoor localization techniques, we find that these techniques tradeoff either accuracy, scalability, pervasiveness or cost – all of which are important requirements for a truly deployable positioning solution. Wireless signal-strength based approaches suffer from location errors, whereas time-of-flight (ToF) based solutions provide good accuracy but are not scalable. Recent solutions address these issues by augmenting WiFi with either smartphone sensing or mobile crowdsourcing. However, they require tight coupling between WiFi infrastructure and a client device, or they can determine the client's location only if it is mobile. In this paper, we present CUPID2.0 which improved our previously proposed CUPID indoor positioning system to overcome these limitations. We achieve this by addressing the fundamental limitations in Time-of-Flight based localization and combining ToF with signal strength to address scalability. Experiments from 6 cities using 40 different mobile devices, comprising of more than 2.5 million location fixes demonstrate feasibility. CUPID2.0 is currently under production, and we expect CUPID2.0 to ignite the wide adoption of WLAN-based positioning systems and their services.

Categories and Subject Descriptors

H.3.4 [**Information Systems and Retrieval**]: Systems and Software

Keywords

Wireless; Localization; Application; Indoor positioning

1. INTRODUCTION

Indoor positioning based services are recently attracting extensive interests from enterprises and consumers alike. While the primary goal of indoor positioning, notably in hospitals, malls and stadiums, is to provide navigation aid [1], others use indoor positioning to better market to customers [2], provide just-in-time information via audio for tours [3], connect people of interest in proximity to one another [4]; and ensure asset tracking and security in the enterprises [5]. The U.S. Federal Communications Commission (FCC) aims to use indoor positioning to provide timelier and more effective emergency services such as 911 calls [6]. The advent of IEEE802.11v standard, which allows location related information to be shared with the client from the WLAN network, has further propelled interest in the industry [7]. Several other standards activities involving access point location databases, navigation route representation, Geo-location APIs and accuracy testing, together can fuel pervasive adoption of indoor localization techniques [8]. While there exists numerous innovative solutions to improve the accuracy of indoor localization [9], we still face steep challenges to apply those techniques from research to practical scenarios due to various critical constraints such as accuracy, scalability, cost, energy and pervasiveness.

Accurate yet scalable and pervasive positioning is challenging. Manual WiFi fingerprinting [10–13] or additional infrastructure deployments [14, 15] achieve accuracy but are known to be costly propositions. Crowdsourcing solutions reduce the cost of fingerprinting [16, 17] but are slow to adapt to changes in the environment. Innovative triangulation and trilateration based schemes either require a high density of access points (APs) or sophisticated multi-antenna systems [18–21]. Sensing based solutions are limited to smartphones and tablets and can only locate the client after it has moved significantly [22–24]. In this paper, we rely on network-based positioning using only the WLAN infrastructure because it offers advantages in cost-efficiency (i.e., positioning uses the already available communication infrastructure), device-openness (i.e., any device compliant with the communication standards can be localized), energy-efficiency (i.e., client device need not continuously run any positioning software), and pervasiveness (i.e., requires only WiFi, a dominant technology across all end devices).

We present CUPID2.0 which achieves a mean localization error of $1.8m$, without requiring any fingerprinting or calibration, client coordination, software or mobility, and can locate hundreds of devices, every second with reasonable network overhead. We have implemented, deployed and analyzed CUPID2.0's performance at 6 cities across 2 different continents for more than 14 months. Extensive evaluation results comprising of 40 different mobile devices and more than 2.5 million location fixes demonstrate that CUPID2.0

WWW 2015, May 18–22, 2015, Florence, Italy.
ACM 978-1-4503-3469-3/15/05.
http://dx.doi.org/10.1145/2736277.2741686.

can enable large scale adoption and deployments. Consequently, CUPID2.0 has been productized and announced by HP Networking, as *HP Location Aware* [25,26].

To design CUPID2.0, we revisit on our previous proposals [24,27] with significantly different and realistic constraints. In our previous proposals, we observed that WiFi-based indoor positioning is primarily affected by multipath. Whenever the direct path [1] is relatively weak due to a blockage (figure 1), the signal strength or propagation time of the wireless signal is biased by the stronger reflected components that traverse longer distances than the direct path. Therefore, to eliminate the effect of multipath on distance estimation, we devised mechanisms to extract the *Energy of the Direct Path (EDP)* [27] and the *Time-of-Flight of the Direct Path (TFDP)* [24]. However, EDP is fundamentally susceptible to shadowing caused by blockages, and TFDP is not scalable as it requires several data-ACK exchanges between the AP and the client. In our earlier work we sidestepped these limitations by augmenting them with mobile sensing. However, this limited us to locate the client only after it has moved significantly. To eliminate the dependency on client mobility, in this paper we build CUPID2.0 as a WLAN-based solution that only uses AP-based trilateration techniques.

We find that unlike EDP, TFDP is largely unaffected by environmental variations. Apart from multipath, TFDP is also not susceptible to wireless shadowing. This is because, while any occlusions can absorb and reduce the energy of the direct path significantly, the propagation time of the direct path is affected only while it traverses through the blocking object, the dimensions of which are significantly lower than the distances traversed by the direct path through the air. Based on these observations, we focus primarily on TFDP to design CUPID2.0 and further investigate its challenges.

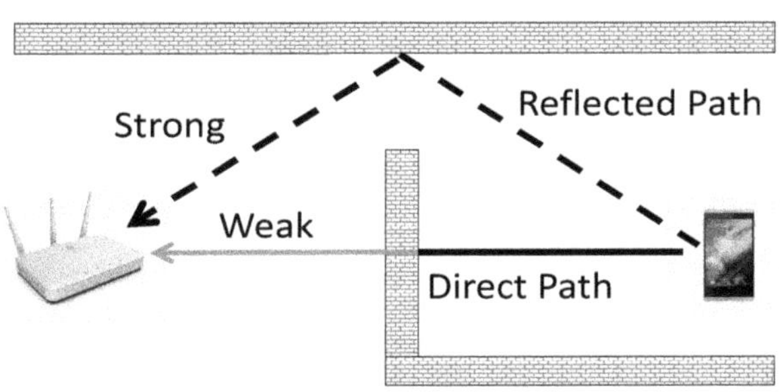

Figure 1: Wireless signal traverses through multiple paths, one direct, and a few reflected paths.

Although TFDP-based distance estimation is feasible, determining the client's location based on TFDP results into unique set of practical challenges:

- **Hardware noise:** Trilateration uses multiple APs for location estimation, thus often requiring distance computation from far-away APs. We find that if the received signal at the AP from the client is weak, the physical layer sometimes adds a fixed value to the correct TFDP, making distance estimation from distant APs difficult.
- **Client diversity:** TFDP estimation requires timely response to the AP's data packet from the client. We find that different client WiFi chipsets wait for different duration before responding to the AP's packet, making it difficult to correctly estimate the TFDP and therefore adversely affecting the pervasiveness of our solution.
- **Scalability:** TFDP measurements are inherently noisy because of the limited bandwidth of WiFi. The effect of random noise can be alleviated by aggregating the TFDP measurements from several data-ACK exchanges between the client and the AP [27]. However, this causes a large network overhead, particularly with multiple APs. Further, neighboring APs are typically configured on different channels, requiring channel switching for location estimation, adding to the network overhead.
- **Energy efficiency:** Apart from the AP to which the client is associated with, it may not respond to the other APs' data packets as its WiFi radio will mostly be off due to the use of power-save mode (PSM). Forcing the client to be awake will reduce its energy efficiency.

[1] Direct path signal is the signal component that traverses along the straight line joining the client and the AP.

In this paper we systematically address the challenges identified above to bring accurate WiFi-based indoor positioning to practice. Briefly, our solution combines complementary characteristics of TFDP and EDP to enable accurate yet scalable positioning (Section 3.5). We introduce smart packet overhearing and scheduling algorithms that reduce the network overhead and avoid the client's PSM problem (Section 3.2). We address the client heterogeneity and hardware noise issues via intelligent AP selection algorithms (Section 3.3,3.4). To the best of our knowledge, this paper is the first to present a year-long real-world deployment of a WiFi-based positioning system, and address the thus-learnt practical challenges. We believe that the implementation, deployment, testing and measurements of CUPID2.0 will help researchers and practitioners further develop indoor location-based systems, services, and applications.

2. BACKGROUND AND PROBLEM IDENTIFICATION

Trilateration based positioning using WiFi APs requires accurate distance estimation. We review two distance estimation techniques (signal strength and time-of-flight) and explain challenges and opportunities in using them.

2.1 Signal strength-based approach

Signal strength-based distance estimation approach [18,27–31] leverages the fact that the wireless signal suffers attenuation proportional to the distance between the transmitter and the receiver. If P_0 is the received signal strength (RSSI) at a distance of $1m$ from the client and P_R is the RSSI at the AP, then the distance between them can be calculated using the path-loss equation:

$$P_R = P_0 - 10\gamma log(d) \quad (1)$$

γ is a parameter called the path loss exponent that depends on the wireless multipath characteristics as well as any shadowing or occlusions created by walls, windows or even the human body. Since γ is susceptible to environmental variations, signal strength-based distance estimation using RSSI is known to be inaccurate [18]. To address the adverse effect of multipath on distance estimation, our previous work [27] primarily uses only the Energy of the Direct Path (EDP), ignoring the multipath reflections between the client and the AP. EDP improves performance over RSSI because RSSI includes the energy carried by multipath reflections which

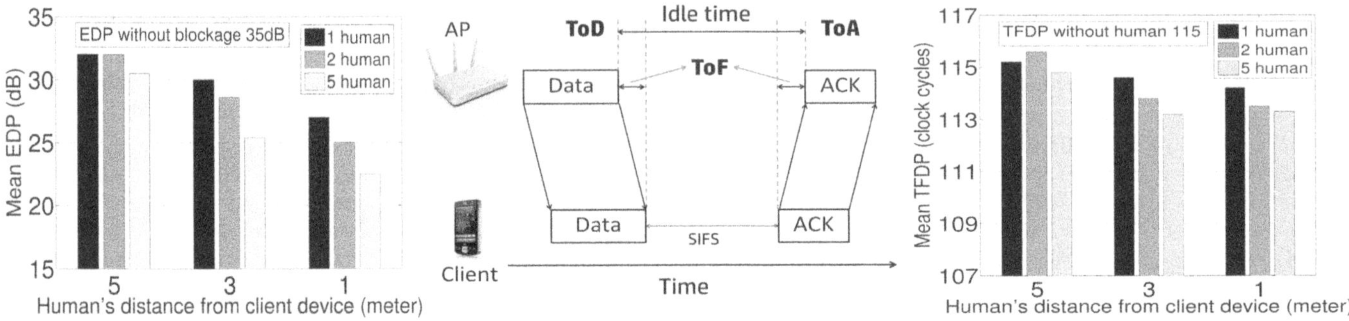

Figure 2: (a) EDP recorded at the AP for different shadowing scenarios. Client is $10m$ away. (b) ToF computation based on data-ACK exchange. (c) TFDP recorded at the AP for different shadowing scenarios.

Orientation	East	West	North	South
Vertical	42.3	43.8	39.7	39.3
Horizontal	36.2	36.5	33.8	34.9

Table 1: Mean EDP (dB) for different phone orientations at $5m$ distance. East implies facing the AP.

travel longer distances than the actual distance between the client and the AP (figure 1). However EDP is susceptible to shadowing. Figure 2(a) plots the average EDP values when the client-AP link is occluded by human bodies. The shadowing effect due to human bodies is hard to model as it depends not only on the number of human beings but also the proximity of the human to the client device. The modeling of the shadowing effect is even more complicated if such occlusions happen along with walls, pillars, windows and other building structures. More importantly, the effect of shadowing changes frequently due to environmental changes, making it difficult to estimate and track.

Signal strength based ranging also relies on the knowledge of the transmit power of the client. However, different mobile devices may use different transmit power values, making it difficult to apriori estimate the same [18] (table 5). P_0 in equation 1 also depends on the gain and polarization of the client's antenna. Therefore, even for the same device, different device orientations result into different P_0 values because orientation affects the antenna polarization as observed by the AP (table 1). It may be possible to adjust the value of P_0 depending on the orientation estimated from the client's gyroscope or compass [32]. However, such approaches are not client agnostic as they require application-level feedback at the client. Therefore, due to uncertainties in wireless shadowing, transmission power and antenna polarization, it is difficult to solely use the EDP to accurately estimate the distance between the client and the AP [24].

2.2 Time-of-Flight based approach

Time-of-Flight (ToF) captures the propagation time of a wireless signal from the client to the AP. It is proportional to the distance between the client and the AP because longer the distance greater will be the wireless propagation time. In the context of WiFi, ToF is measured using a round-trip data-ACK exchange [33]. The AP can precisely calculate the *Time-of-Departure* (ToD) of the data packet when it is sent out into the air by the physical (PHY) layer (figure 2(b)). It can also record the *Time-of-Arrival* (ToA) of the ACK packet based on preamble detection. According to the 802.11 standard, the client is expected to wait for a fixed time duration called Short Inter Frame Space (SIFS) between the data and the ACK packet. Therefore the AP can calculate the ToF and translate it to a distance estimate (d_{ToF}) as follows:

$$ToF = \frac{(ToA - ToD) - SIFS}{2} \quad (2)$$

$$d_{ToF} = c \times ToF \quad (3)$$

where c is the speed of light ($3.0 \times 10^8 m/s$).

As demonstrated in our earlier work [24], the ToF, obtained from the ToA and the ToD, actually captures the distance traversed by the strongest wireless propagation path between the client and the AP. Therefore, in order to calculate an accurate distance, we use the ToF of only the Direct Path (TFDP) [2]. Use of a stronger reflected signal otherwise causes significant error. The TFDP is generally less affected by shadowing and occlusions than the energy of the direct path (EDP). This is because any object blocking the direct path can significantly reduce its energy due to absorption. However, the propagation time of the direct path is affected only while it traverses through the blocking object, the dimensions of which are significantly lower than to the distance traversed by the direct path through the air. Our experiments show that TFDP is not affected by occlusions or proximity of human body (figure 2(c)) and the orientation of the client device (table 2). Even if the direct path is weak due to occlusions or blockage, as long as it is detectable at the AP, the TFDP can indicate the client's distance accurately.

Orientation	East	West	North	South
Vertical	115.1	114.7	115.4	114.2
Horizontal	114.2	114.9	115.8	115.2

Table 2: Mean TFDP (clock cycles) for different phone orientations. East implies facing the AP.

2.3 Challenges in TFDP based location estimation

Although TFDP-based distance estimation is more robust than signal strength based approach, location computation requires distance estimation from multiple APs. Since time-of-flight requires an active data-ACK exchange, this results into unique set of challenges as follows:

Overhead of determining TFDP: Time of Flight of Direct Path (TFDP) obtained from the PHY layer is inherently noisy due to the randomness of preamble detection time, which affects the Time-of-Arrival (ToA) timestamps. Our previous work [24] addresses this problem by leveraging the

[2]Mechanism of TFDP computation is elaborated in [24].

observation that the noise in TFDP values follows a Gaussian distribution and hence can be addressed by employing a Kalman filter [34]. However, as shown in figure 3 Kalman requires more than 10 data-ACK exchanges to estimate the correct TFDP value. This induces network overhead because each AP needs to send several data packets to estimate the client's distance. To solve the overhead problem, we exploit short NULL data packets. We further reduce channel airtime usage by scheduling the NULL packets back-to-back. If t_{NULL} and t_{ACK} are the time duration of the NULL and ACK packet respectively, t_{MAC} is the MAC layer contention time due to backoff and n is the number of NULL packets required to correctly obtain the client's distance from a single AP, then the total channel airtime usage (i.e., overhead) due to positioning is:

$$Overhead = N_c * N_{AP} * (n * (t_{NULL} + t_{SIFS} + t_{ACK}) + t_{MAC}) \quad (4)$$

where N_{AP} is the number of APs used to locate N_c number of clients. E.g., using only 4 APs to track 50 clients, every second, occupies 25% of the wireless airtime, which is prohibitive. Of course the number of NULL packets (n) can be smaller if the AP can leverage existing download traffic to the client. However, location tracking still needs to employ additional packets because the client may not have a continuous stream of traffic. Therefore, the TFDP overheads significantly limit the number of clients that can be tracked.

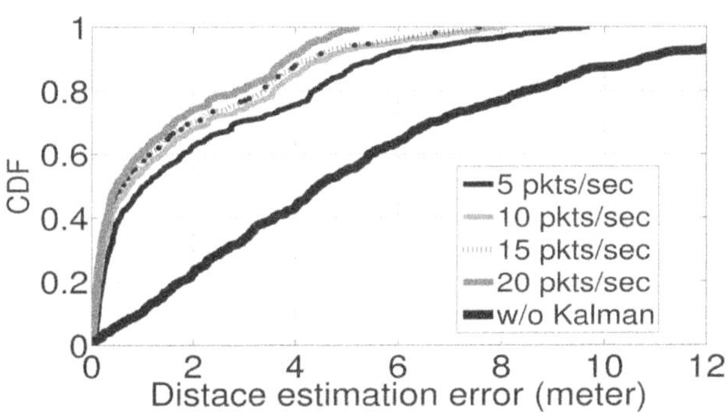

Figure 3: CDF of distance estimation error for different number of packets used by the Kalman filter.

Distance estimation complexity of neighboring APs: Location computation requires distance estimation from neighboring APs, apart from the AP to which the client is associated with. It is possible to obtain an ACK from the client if the neighboring AP impersonates the associated AP using MAC-address spoofing. However, the client may use the power-save mode (PSM) in which it may turn off its WiFi radio and hence it may not even receive the packets sent by the neighboring APs (figure 4). This is because a PSM client only follows the associated AP's beacons to determine when it should turn on its radio to receive the download packets. It ignores the beacons from all other APs. It is not possible to keep the client's WiFi radio always on without adversely affecting its battery life. Thus, to be energy-efficient, we need a solution that respects the client's PSM, yet enables distance estimation from neighboring APs.

Another challenge is that the neighboring APs may be on different channels than the client and its associated AP, requiring channel switching for location estimation. Such channel switchings further adds network overhead because

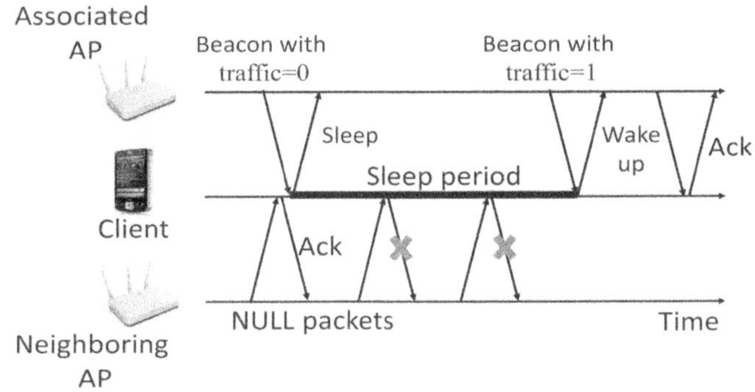

Figure 4: PSM clients will not respond to neighboring AP's packets during the sleep period.

it may consume upto 1ms [3]. We can amortize the channel switching overhead by measuring all the clients in the same channel back-to-back. However, this requires careful scheduling of the NULL packets among all APs. Therefore, TFDP based positioning needs a light-weight scheduling algorithm that ensures low channel-switching overheads.

Device heterogeneity: TFDP is calculated by measuring the time duration between the data-ACK exchange between the AP and the client. Ideally, the duration between the data and the ACK packet should capture only the ToF and an SIFS duration (equation 2). However, chipset manufacturers inculcate a random but fixed time duration to the SIFS [33]. This results into an additional time offset, which we call the *SIFS offset*. We find that the SIFS offset is a fixed number for each WiFi chipset type [33]. Caesar [33] addresses this problem by manually creating a database of per-chipset type and SIFS offset pair, and thereafter accounting for the SIFS offset in TFDP computation by using a lookup based on the client's MAC address. This approach is not scalable, as new chipsets are continuously introduced. More importantly, the MAC address of the client either indicates the mobile device or chipset manufacturer, and not the specific chipset type. Therefore, we need a mechanism that can automatically compute and account for the SIFS offset value, without requiring any manual intervention or relying on MAC-address based lookup.

Error due to signal normalization: Apart from client heterogeneity, another source of error in TFDP is the signal normalization operation in the PHY layer. The PHY layer in the AP can receive the client's ACK over a large range of signal strength values. It prefers to decode the wireless signal within a preferred range (PR) of signal strength. If the incoming signal is weaker or stronger than the PR, it is internally normalized. If the signal is too strong, the RF front-end is set in a low gain mode and the amplifier gain is decreased to avoid Analog to Digital Conversion (ADC) saturation. Weak signals are amplified to ascertain that the quantization noise of the ADC does not hamper correct detection. In our experiments we find that if the incoming ACK signal triggers signal normalization, the TFDP obtained from the PHY layer of Atheros 9390 chipsets is overestimated by a fixed value of 30 clock cycles.

The challenge is that we cannot determine the overestimation, based solely on the client's RSSI. In our experiments we find that the normalization of weak signals can occur between $0 - 16$dB, PR can occur between $10 - 48$dB and strong

[3]We have verified that Atheros' software-based Fast Channel Switch (FCS) feature switches channels within 1ms [35].

signal normalization can happen above 40dB. This implies that if the ACK packet's RSSI is between $10 - 16$dB or between $40-48$dB, additional signal normalization may or may not be invoked. RSSI is not a good indicator of signal normalization operation in the PHY layer because it depends on the incoming signal's peak-to-average power ratio [33]. Therefore, we need a robust scheme that can accurately determine the client's TFDP irrespective of its RSSI value.

3. SOLUTIONS

This section presents our solutions, called CUPID2.0, that address the limitations identified in the previous section. We begin with CUPID2.0's overall architecture.

3.1 Architecture

Figure 5 illustrates the architecture and operation of CUPID2.0. As shown in the figure, CUPID2.0 consists of a location server and multiple APs, each of which talks to a client. Given the architecture, CUPID2.0 employs trilateration to determine the client's location in the following steps. First, the location server instructs a set of selected APs to estimate and share the client's distance estimates. Let d_i is the estimated distance between a client and an AP i. Next, the location server estimates the location $< L_x, L_y >$ of the client by solving a set of trilateration equations using the Gauss-Newton [36] method:

$$d_i = \| < AP_{i,x}, AP_{i,y} > - < L_x, L_y > \| \quad (5)$$

where $< AP_{i,x}, AP_{i,y} >$ is the location coordinate of AP i, recorded apriori. Of course the above architecture entails selection of a minimal set of APs that can yield the client's location accurately and light-weight and robust distance estimation between the APs and the client. Our distance estimation approach is primarily based on the Time-of-Flight of the Direct Path (TFDP), as calculated from the data-ACK exchange between the AP and the client. However, we also combine TFDP with Energy of the Direct Path (EDP) to ensure scalability. In the following subsections we elaborate on the algorithms of CUPID2.0.

3.2 Distance estimation from multiple APs

CUPID2.0 requires multiple APs to conduct data-ACK exchanges adding to its wireless overhead. To address this overhead and to ascertain that neighboring APs can reliably obtain the TFDP information for PSM clients, we propose an overhearing-based scheme which enables neighboring APs to calculate the TFDP of the client without any active data-ACK exchange. Figure 5 shows a high level overview of our overhearing scheme. Whenever the location server needs to compute the client's location, it instructs the AP to which the client is associated with (called the *associated AP*) to begin multiple data-ACK exchanges. The associated AP (AP_2 in figure 5) transmits data packets right after its beacon to ensure that the client is awake. All other neighboring APs (AP_1 and AP_3 in figure 5) do not transmit any probe packets but overhears to compute the Time Of Arrival ($ToA_{2,i}$) of data packet's direct path from AP_2, as well as the ToA of ACK packet's direct path from the client C ($ToA_{C,i}$). The location server can determine the distance between the associated AP and the client using the TFDP between the two ($TFDP_{2,C}$ in figure 5). The location server can also mathematically compute the TFDP between the the ith neighboring AP and the client ($ToF_{i,C}$) as:

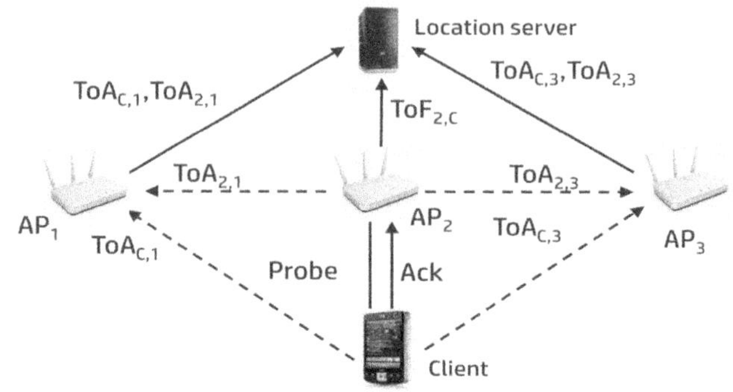

Figure 5: Neighboring APs can estimate the client's distance based on overhearing and recording the ToAs of the associated AP and the client's packets.

$$TFDP_{i,C} = ToA_{C,i} + d_{i,2}/c - ToA_{2,i} - TFDP_{2,C} - SIFS \quad (6)$$

Where $d_{i,2}$ is the distance between the associated AP AP_2 and AP_i and c is the speed of light.

The above overhearing technique does not require any clock synchronization between the APs. The ToA and TFDP values reported by a particular AP is according to its own clock. Equation 6 uses the known distance value between a neighboring AP and the associated AP ($d_{i,2}$), to align their clock values in the same frame of reference. However, the overhearing scheme does require the neighboring APs to switch channels and listen to the associated AP's data transmission. To achieve this, the location server sends distance measurement requests simultaneously to all the selected APs. On reception of the request, the associated AP transmits the NULL data packets right after its next beacon packet (figure 6). This ensures that the client is awake because it reads the beacon's Traffic Indication Map (TIM) and learns that the AP has traffic for itself. Neighboring APs switch its channel to coincide with the associated AP's beacon. In our scheme all APs know each other's beacon transmission times. This is accomplished by using the periodic background scanning operation of the RRM (radio-resource management) functions. During background scanning, an AP records the beacon arrival times of all other APs. Because beacons are transmitted periodically (every $100ms$), the same arrival time can be used to determine when the associated AP will transmit its next beacon.

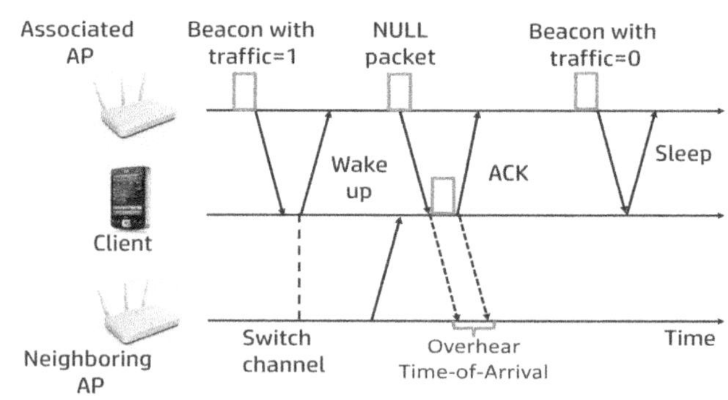

Figure 6: Scheduling NULL data packets after the associated AP's beacon.

3.3 SIFS offset estimation

Each wireless chipset type may have different SIFS offsets (δ_{sifs}) which needs to be accounted for correct TFDP estimation. Due to the δ_{sifs}, the estimated distance by the ith AP (m_i) will differ from the actual distance (d_i) by ϵ meters:

$$\epsilon = \frac{c \times \delta_{sifs}}{2} \quad (7)$$

$$m_i = d_i + \epsilon \quad (8)$$

Observe that the error in distance estimation (ϵ) is a constant and does not vary accross different APs. Therefore, it is possible to numerically estimate ϵ by including equation 8 with our original trilateration equation (5):

$$m_i - \epsilon = \| < AP_{i,x}, AP_{i,y} > - < L_x, L_y > \| \quad (9)$$

The above equation can estimate the location of the client as well as the constant distance error (ϵ), which can thereafter be used to determine the SIFS offset (δ_{sifs}) using equation 7. Because of the additional unknown variable (ϵ), unlike equation 5, the revised trilateration equations require measurements from at least 4 APs. However, once the SIFS offset is estimated, thereafter we use only 3 APs with equation 5 to locate the client.

Access Point Selection: Due to the SIFS offset and its estimation errors, CUPID2.0 needs to carefully choose the set of APs that can participate in trilateration. E.g., in figure 7, if the chosen APs (AP_1, AP_2, AP_3) are collinear with the client, the distance error due to the SIFS offset may add up, injecting errors in location estimation. However, if the chosen APs surround the client (AP_2, AP_3, AP_4), the individual distance errors will often cancel out resulting in a correct estimation of the client's location. To address this, we predetermine a set of triangles that can be formed by the neighboring APs. We begin tracking the client by using all the APs within the client's range. Once the client's location and SIFS offset values are known, we determine a set of 3 APs that surrounds the client. Thereafter, we track the client using the same APs with equation 5.

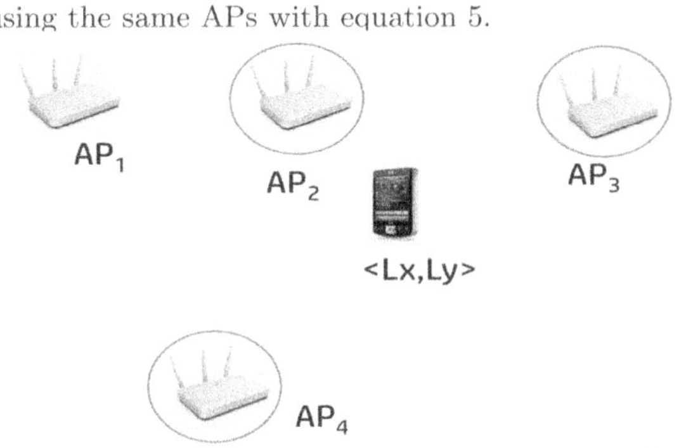

Figure 7: To address the error due to the SIFS offset, AP_2, AP_3 and AP_4 which surrounds the client, should be used for trilateration.

3.4 Dealing with signal normalization

As discussed in section 2, unless the RSSI of an ACK packet falls within 16 – 40 dB, the TFDP obtained from the PHY layer of the Atheros chipset can be biased by upto 30 clock cycles due to the additional time required for signal normalization. If the incoming ACK signal is received outside the 16–40 dB range, the TFDP values may or may not include a timing offset (figure 8(a)). Due to this uncertainty, initially when the client's previous location is not available, we locate the client by using only the APs who receive the client's ACK within the 16–40 dB range. However, once the client's location is known, we estimate its distance to the other weak or strong APs, denoted as the expected distance. The expected distance value can be used to determine if the TFDP reported by an AP is biased due to signal normalization. To elaborate further, we leverage the observation that the TFDP values recorded at a particular weak or strong AP may follow two distinct distributions(figure 8(a)). Therefore, we employ k-means clustering to distinguish them. If k-means suggest two distinct clusters, then the cluster with the smaller mean value captures the correct TFDP readings. However, if k-means suggests a single cluster, then all the TFDP readings reported by the AP can either be correct or be biased due to signal normalization. In such scenarios, we utilize the AP only if the expected distance of the client to the AP is close to the distance calculated from its TFDP values. Otherwise, we ignore the TFDP readings from the AP as they may be erroneous due to random noise.

3.5 Achieving scalability by combining TFDP with EDP

While our overhearing scheme (section 3.2) reduces overhead by eliminating the data-ACK exchanges from the neighboring APs, we further explore opportunities to improve scalability by reducing the number of packets from the associated AP, required for location estimation. We leverage the fact that EDP and TFDP has complimentary characteristics, which when combined can enable accurate yet scalable positioning. We observe that, unlike TFDP, EDP-based distance estimation is scalable because it mostly requires only a single response from the client. On there other hand, while TFDP is accurate, EDP-based localization is vulnerable to environmental changes. EDP-based distance estimation can be accurate if it is possible to correctly estimate the environment-related path-loss exponent (γ in equation 1) parameter. Since TFDP yields the accurate distance between the client an an AP, we can use it to determine the γ that the same AP should use to estimate the client's distance based only on EDP. However, it is important to periodically use the TFDP to recalibrate the path-loss exponent used by the AP, because the γ may change over time due to environmental variations, resulting into increase in distance estimation error (figure 8(b)).

Figure 8(c) illustrates our scalable distance estimation approach by combining TFDP with EDP. Our scheme operates in rounds of a few seconds, the length of which depends on the airtime overhead acceptable to the administrator. In the beginning of each round, we calculate the client's location using strictly the TFDP estimated from 10 data-ACK exchanges between each AP and the client. Thereafter, we use the TFDP based distance estimates to calculate the per-AP γ value. We calculate P_0 in equation 1 as twice the EDP observed by the strongest AP. This heuristic works reasonably well because the estimated γ is a normalized value based on the P_0 value used. For the remaining duration of each round, we use the previously estimated γ value to determine the client's distance and location strictly based on the EDP. The TFDP-based location estimation overhead (equation 4) therefore reduces to:

$$Overhead = N_c * (k * (n * (t_{NULL} + t_{SIFS} + t_{ACK}) + t_{MAC}) + (1 - k) * ((t_{NULL} + t_{SIFS} + t_{ACK}) + t_{MAC})) \quad (10)$$

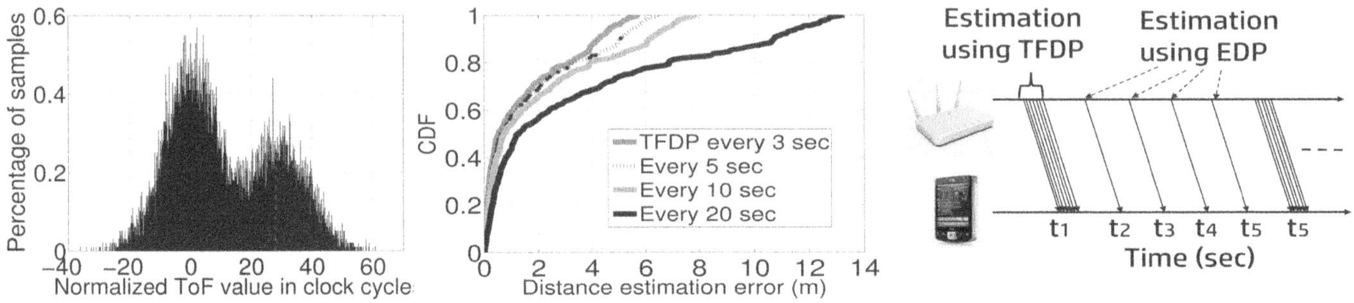

Figure 8: (a) Due to signal normalization, the TFDP recorded at weak or strong APs may fall in two distinct distributions. (b) Distance estimation error using EDP and path-loss exponent calculated using TFDP, at different intervals. (c) Scalable distance estimation using TFDP and EDP.

where k is a fraction indicating the frequency with which the TFDP is used to calculate the client's location. Observe that due to use of overhearing, CUPID2.0's overhead does not depend on the number of APs. As shown numerically in table 3, by using the TFDP every 5 sec, it is possible to locate upto 100 clients with less than 5% airtime overhead.

	No. of clients						
	10	20	30	50	100	150	200
TFDP only	5	10	15	25	50	75	100
CUPID2.0	0.43	0.87	1.31	2.2	4.4	6.6	8.8

Table 3: Percentage of wireless overhead of CUPID2.0 (TFDP every 5 sec) and TFDP-only scheme.

3.6 Scheduling for multiple clients

The scheduling algorithm in CUPID2.0 schedules NULL packet transmissions to each client every second under the wireless overhead constraints (e.g., airtime) given by a network administrator. We define CUPID2.0's airtime overhead as the fraction of airtime that the NULL packets occupy the wireless channel added with the neighboring AP's channel switching time, if applicable. To create an efficient schedule, CUPID2.0 divides the site into non-overlapping triangles formed by joining adjacent APs (figure 9). To locate the clients situated within a particular triangle, CUPID2.0 employs the APs forming the vertices of the same triangle. E.g., in figure 9, clients in $\triangle ABE$ are tracked by APs A, B and E, clients in $\triangle BEF$ are located by APs B, E,f and so on. To improve efficiency, CUPID2.0 needs to simultaneously locate as many clients as possible. This is analogous to scheduling as many triangles in figure 9 in parallel as possible. Two nearby triangles cannot be scheduled simultaneously because they may either share an AP or may be too close to each other, causing interference. But, clients belonging to nearby physical triangles, who do not share any APs, can be located simultaneously as long as they are on different channels. To accommodate this in our schedule, we further divide each physical triangle into upto 3 virtual triangles. Clients within a physical triangle who are all on the same channel belongs to the same virtual triangle. CUPID2.0 needs to create a schedule which will serve all the virtual triangles within the minimum possible time.

To solve the above scheduling problem, we treat each virtual triangle as a node in a conflict graph. An edge between two nodes means that they cannot be scheduled simultaneously. Finding the most efficient schedule of the virtual triangles is analogous to coloring the conflict graph using a minimum

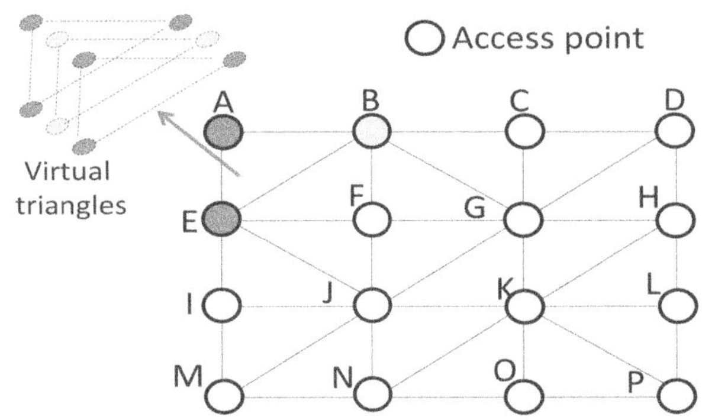

Figure 9: CUPID2.0's scheduling: Each physical triangle can be split into 3 virtual triangles. Virtual triangles who are not in conflict with each other can be scheduled simultaneously.

number of colors, which is known to be a NP-hard problem [37]. Therefore we use a greedy approximation called DSATUR [38] to color the conflict graph. The colors of the conflict graph determines the sequence with which each virtual triangle should be scheduled. Virtual triangles with the same color are scheduled in the same time slot, whereas those with different colors are scheduled in different time slots. The length of each time slot (t_s) depends on the overhead constraint given by the administrator:

$$t_s = \frac{Total\ available\ time}{Total\ no.\ of\ channels} < Overhead \qquad (11)$$

Using equations 10 and 11, we can determine the value of k, which yields the frequency with which the TFDP can be used to determine the location of all the clients in a particular slot. Using the TFDP frequency and the schedule based on the colors of the conflict graph, we can locate all clients, every second, without surpassing the overhead constraint. If there exists a large number of clients, we might not be able to find the value of k that satisfies the overhead constraint. In such scenarios, we use a default of $k = 0.05$, i.e, we use the TFDP every 20 seconds to find each client's location, and we use EDP otherwise.

4. IMPLEMENTATION AND EVALUATION

We evaluate CUPID2.0 using HP MSM 460 APs containing Atheros 9390 chipset tuned at different frequencies using a 40MHz bandwidth. The Atheros 9390 chipset uses a 88MHz clock and can export the Channel State Information (CSI) of any received packet. The reported CSI is a matrix containing one complex number per subcarrier and per receive antenna at the AP. Since the CSI captures the wireless

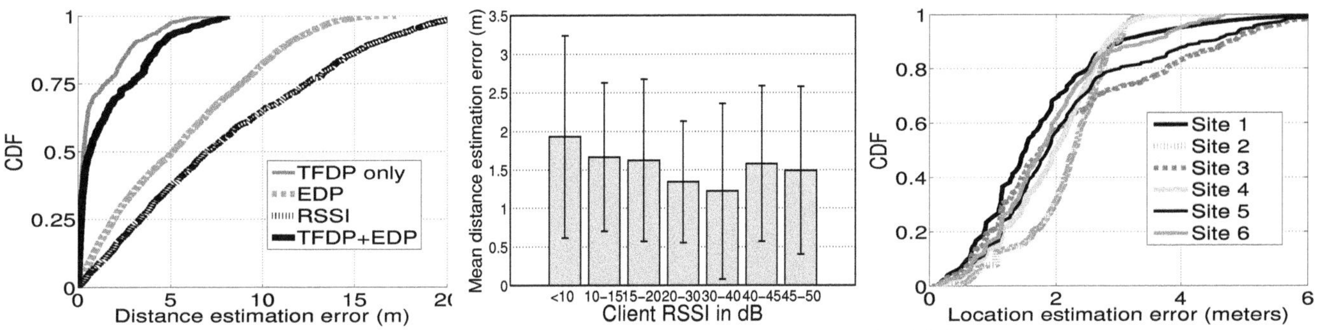

Figure 10: (a) Distance estimation error using different metrics. (b) CUPID2.0's distance estimation error does not vary significantly with signal strength. (a) CUPID2.0's location estimation error at different sites.

channel in the frequency domain, an Inverse Fast Fourier Transform (IFFT) provides the multipath components in the time domain. We determine the Energy of Direct Path (EDP) and Time-of-Flight of Direct Path (TFDP) using the time-domain multipath characteristics [24, 27]. The chipset also reports the Time-of-Departure (ToD) value, in terms of clock cycles, in the transmit-complete descriptor of any data packet. Similarly, it exports the Time-of-Arrival (ToA) and RSSI value of the ACK packet in its receive descriptor. For each data-ACK exchange, we estimate the ToF by using the ToA and ToD, as well as the chipset's clock frequency.

We implement several functions within the Atheros driver to enable packet scheduling, overhearing, channel switching, client admission, time-of-flight, RSSI and CSI reporting. A userspace module at the AP communicates with the AP's driver via netlink and with the location server using TCP sockets. The scheduling, distance and location estimation algorithms are implemented at the location server. It uses the client list from the APs, along with the target network overhead constraint from the administrator, to create a schedule which can report each client's location, every second. Depending on the schedule, the server uses 10 NULL data packets for TFDP or 1 packet for EDP computation.

Methodology

We have deployed the CUPID2.0 positioning system at a total of 6 sites (details in table 4). To evaluate CUPID2.0's performance we design several real-life experiments at each of the sites with APs installed at known locations. At each site, we evaluated CUPID2.0's performance at several locations whose ground truth coordinates were already known. To evaluate mobile scenarios, we asked the users to walk around arbitrarily in the building for an hour during normal office hours, with the smartphone in their pant pocket, or in hand. As each user walks, the AP estimates and stores her location coordinates. To collect ground truth, we pasted numbered markers at known locations. Whenever the user walked through a marker, she recorded its number and the current time. Since the locations of the markers are known, we did interpolation between the markers to obtain the ground truth. The distance between the ground truth and the estimated location is CUPID2.0's instantaneous localization error. CUPID2.0 has been tested by more than 200 users using more than 40 different mobile devices.

4.1 Distance estimation accuracy

CUPID2.0 computes the distance of the client by combining the time-of-flight and energy of her direct path, called TFDP and EDP respectively. CUPID2.0's distance estimation error depends on how frequently it uses the TFDP to recalibrate the EDP's path-loss exponent. Even with a TFDP computation every 5 seconds, mean distance estimation error is less than $1.5m$ (figure 10(a)). RSSI or EDP individually don't perform as well due to susceptibility to environmental variations and causes a mean error of $5.3m$ and $7.2m$ respectively. CUPID2.0's distance estimation accuracy may also depend on the signal strength of the client because of the effect of signal normalization on TFDP values (section 2.2). However by detecting and accounting for the signal normalization offset, CUPID2.0 maintains low errors for all clients, irrespective of signal strength (figure 10(b)).

Site	Site size sq. ft.	No. of deployed APs	No. of unique users	No. of location fixes	Mean error (m)
Site 1	21000	7	>100	~1.1M	1.7
Site 2	2420	4	>10	~50000	2.2
Site 3	4300	4	2	~50000	2.3
Site 4	10200	6	>20	~400000	1.7
Site 5	37000	14	>10	~110000	1.9
Site 6	12000	6	>100	~1.25M	2.0

Table 4: Description of sites where CUPID2.0 was tested, primarily using Galaxy S4 and iPhone 5.

4.2 Location estimation performance

We present CUPID2.0's location estimation performance using more than 500000 location fixes obtained from 6 different sites of varying sizes (details in table 4). Figure 10(c) plots the distribution of location estimation error, per site, when the clients are tracked by using TFDP estimates every 5 seconds and EDP values otherwise. Figure 11(a) compares CUPID2.0's positioning performance with RSSI, EDP, TFDP only techniques. CUPID2.0 demonstrates similar performance as TFDP, but reduces the wireless overhead by using TFDP less frequently. Figure 11(b) shows that CUPID2.0's positioning error is inversely proportional to the TFDP computation frequency. The frequency of TFDP estimation depends on the user specified wireless overhead. To understand the effect of overhead on location accuracy, we performed experiments using a 4300 square feet area at Site 1. Figure 11(c) shows the average location estimation error for different overhead constraints. The average positioning error under high density (40 clients) and low overhead (1% airtime usage) is approximately $3.2m$. The error will be lower if a higher overhead is acceptable ($1.7m$ with 5% overhead) because CUPID2.0 can utilize the TFDP more frequently to deal with the errors in EDP-based location estimation.

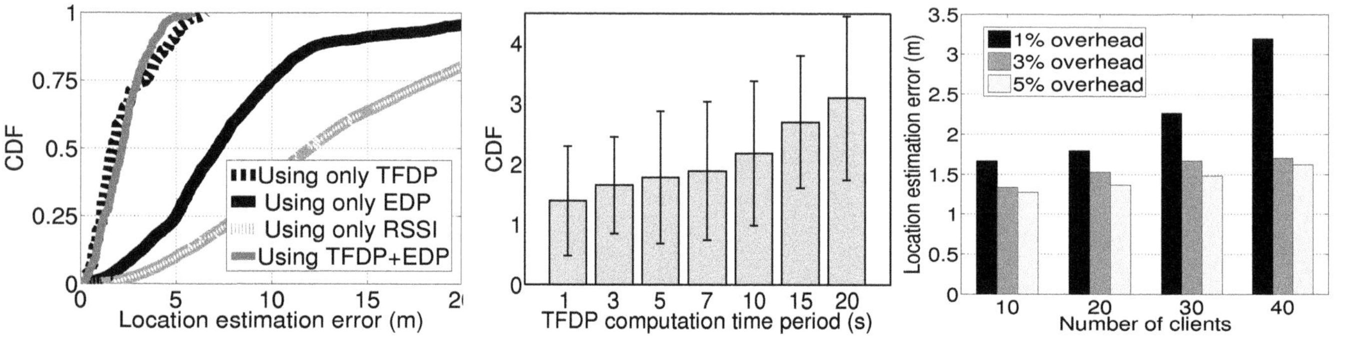

Figure 11: CUPID2.0's location estimation error (a) is similar to that of using only the TFDP and is significantly lower than EDP and RSSI; (b) depends on how frequently TFDP is used for positioning; (c) for different wireless overheads restrictions.

4.3 Effect of device heterogeneity

Device heterogeneity affects CUPID2.0's performance because different client chipsets add an unknown offset to the SIFS duration. CUPID2.0 accounts for the unknown offset by using intelligent access point selection. As a consequence it achieves the same performance as prior schemes which assumes that the SIFS offset is known apriori (figure 12(a)). Table 5 shows CUPID2.0's location estimation error for different mobile devices, as measured at Site 1, using the TFDP every 5 seconds and EDP otherwise. We find that if two mobile devices have the same chipset type, they demonstrate very similar error characteristics. Different chipsets have slightly different timing characteristics and may also use different clock speeds. E.g., Galaxy S3 has a 802.11n chipset containing a 88MHz clock where has Galaxy S4 is 802.11ac enabled with a 160MHz clock. Thus, different chipsets experience different location estimation errors, with the highest error recorded for Galaxy S3 (mean 2.2m).

4.4 Large-scale simulation

To understand CUPID2.0's performance in large venues (e.g., entire shopping mall, airport), we perform trace-driven simulation. In the simulation, we use a floor plan of 200,000 square meter, covered by 625 APs. We vary the number of users per AP as well as the wireless overhead constraint. For each client configuration and overhead constraint, using the scheduling algorithm, we measure how frequently a user can be located using TFDP. Thereafter we utilize our traces to determine her average localization error accordingly (using figure 11(b)). Figure 12(b) shows our simulation results. The mean localization error increases with increasing number of users or with tighter airtime constraint due to infrequent TFDP estimation. However, the localization error is still reasonable in all scenarios demonstrating that CUPID2.0 can achieve scale without sacrificing accuracy.

Device, device count Default count: 1	Chipset	P_0 (dB) (eqn. 1)	Mean error
Iphone 5, **total 8**	BCM4334	39.39	2.1m
Iphone 5S	BCM4334	39.39	2.1m
Ipad Mini	BCM4334	58.19	2.0m
Ipad Air	BCM4334	51.81	1.93m
Ipad 4	BCM4334	50.92	1.91m
Ipad Mini2	—	55.83	1.85m
Galaxy S3	BCM4330	40.29	2.23m
Galaxy S4, **total 7**	BCM4335	43.91	1.65m
Galaxy Note 3	BCM4339	55.83	1.67m
Galaxy Mega	WCN3680	48.89	1.51m
Galaxy Tab 3	Marvell 88W8787	55.54	1.86m
Galaxy Note 10.1	—	45.80	1.92m
HTC One M7	BCM4335	45.15	1.63m
Moto X	WCN3680	53.70	1.45m
Moto Droid Maxx	WL1285C	47.98	2.0m
LG G2	BCM4335	45.17	1.65m
Xperia Z1	—	52.77	1.78m
Kindle Fire	WG7310	53.61	2.1m
Lumia 1020	—	56.49	1.97m
Xperia ZL	—	40.04	1.81m
Kindle Fire HD	BCM43239	54.19	1.64m
Nexus 4	WCN3660	45.65	1.75
Blackberry Z30	—	34.24	2.12m
HTC One M8	—	44.24	1.65m
Lumia Icon	—	40.63	1.84m
Lumia 1520	—	43.81	1.81m
Xperia tab Z	—	48.53	1.78m

Table 5: Performance using different devices.

5. RELATED WORK

The literature about indoor localization is vast [9,39]. Given limited space, in this section, we choose only works relevant to our system to differentiate them from our work.

Signal strength based approach: Most WiFi based indoor positioning systems utilize the RSSI to determine the client's location. Common techniques include pattern matching where the client's location is determined by using a prior established RSSI fingerprint database [10–13] or trilateration based solutions where the client's distance is calculated from multiple APs and later combined to yield the client's location. However, RSSI is known to be a poor estimator of location [40] because it is vulnerable to environmental variations. EZ [18] deals with location errors using GPS fixes which is not guaranteed to be available all the time. Our previous work [27] and FILA [28] attempts to improve signal-strength based solutions using PHY layer solution. But they are still susceptible to wireless shadowing, errors due to client diversity and random phone placements.

Time-based approach: Early time-of-flight based localization schemes required clock synchronization [41] or additional hardware modules [15,42]. In the context of WiFi, the feasibility of computing time-of-flight based on regular data-ACK exchanges were first proposed in [43] and refined in [33]. Our previous work SAIL [24] demonstrated that it is important to eliminate the adverse effect of multipath in

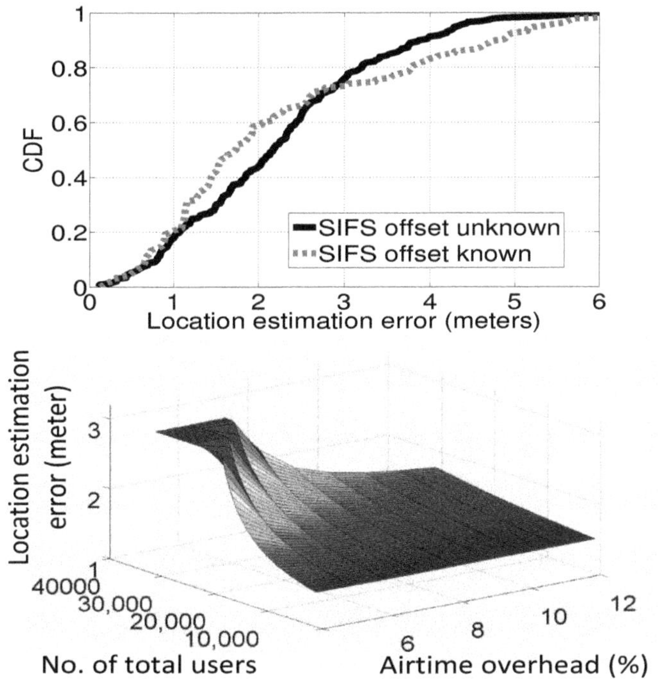

Figure 12: CUPID2.0's location estimation error (a) does not require knowledge of the SIFS offset; (b) for varying number of clients and overhead constraints.

ToF based distance estimation. However SAIL uses smartphone sensing to locate only mobile clients; and it does not address the overhead and deployment issues with ToF-based trilateration. In this paper we systematically identify and address challenges towards a practical and production-ready indoor positioning system based on WiFi.

Angle-of-Arrival (AoA)-based approach: Triangulation based approaches use estimation of the client's angle at multiple APs to localize the client [21,44–49]. However, most of these approaches are not readily deployable as they are accurate only if implemented using sophisticated antenna arrays. Angle estimation on commodity APs results into an average angle estimation error of 20° [27, 49] making them difficult to use for accurate positioning. Borealis [47], SpinLoc [50] and Ubicarse [48] calculates angles from commodity chipsets, but requires specific user actions and orientation information to compute the location of the mobile device.

Smartphone sensing based: Smartphone-based dead- reckoning techniques has often been used to improve the performance of WiFi-based localization [51]. However these approaches are vulnerable to random fluctuations in sensing data due to drift, compass errors, random phone placements etc. Recent approaches try to address these issues by using crowdsourcing techniques [16, 17, 22]. But, crowdsourcing either requires a strong user incentive model, or leads to coarse grained fingerprint information which reduces their accuracy. Crowdsourcing further cannot adapt to frequent, and automatic configuration changes as adopted by recent WLAN APs; the default update time settings found in [52] are 10mins and 4mins. Map based particle filtering [23, 53] also addresses noise in sensing information, but they rely on unique indoor walking paths such as long corridors, making them ineffective in open areas such as airport, auditorium etc.

6. DISCUSSION & ONGOING WORK

Energy efficiency: CUPID2.0 imposes minimal energy overhead on client devices. Unlike mobile sensing based solutions, it does not require any process to run at the client. Further, CUPID2.0's NULL data packet exchange involves only the PHY layer processing, and thus no other energy cost exists at the client.

Impact of wireless interference: In our year-long experiments, we did not witness any noticeable effect of interference on time-of-flight estimation. We believe this happens because at the AP, the time-of-arrival of the client's ACK packet is detected through sophisticated preamble detection čitelee2010improved. Further, the client does not carrier sense the channel before transmitting the ACK packet, resulting into no timing issues due to interfering signals.

Multi-floor positioning: CUPID2.0 identifies each floor by simply looking at the top three APs with respect to the received signal strength from the client's ACK. In our evaluation in Site 1, we find that the floor of the strongest 3 APs is always the same as the client's floor. However, this may not be true in atriums. We are currently investigating schemes to enable accurate 3D positioning, based on time-of-flight.

Device-based positioning: Device-based positioning will be possible by transposing CUPID2.0 from the infrastructure to the device. We are currently investigating its feasibility. However, there are advantages in computing the time-of-flight at the infrastructure. First, we may not be able to replicate our overhearing mechanism that improves scalability, at the client device. Second, mobile devices typically have a single antenna resulting into coarser multipath resolution and increased distance estimation error [24]. Third, to perform trilateration, mobile devices may need to scan multiple channels resulting to reduced battery life.

Improving accuracy with 802.11ac: The granularity of time-of-flight reported by the PHY layer depends on the chipset's clock frequency. Our current results use a 802.11n chipset that has a 88MHz clock, and hence provides a distance estimation granularity of 1.7m. We note that CUPID2.0's accuracy will further improve with upcoming 802.11ac based systems that uses a clock speed of 160MHz.

7. CONCLUSION

In this paper, we have presented CUPID2.0, a system that solves many practical challenges for WiFi-based indoor localization. As we explained, CUPID2.0 is the first system that demonstrates accuracy, scalability, low-cost, and energy efficiency in practical settings. Rather than using expensive fingerprinting or energy-hungry mobile sensing, CUPID2.0 uses Time-of-Flight (ToF) based trilateration to determine the user's location with less than 2m error. Furthermore, it combines ToF with signal strength and uses novel overhearing mechanisms to make location estimation scalable and practical. Large scale experimentation at 6 different cities, comprising of more than 240 users, 2.5M location fixes and 40 different mobile devices confirm the performance of CUPID2.0. We believe that our upcoming product called HP Location Aware, which is based on CUPID2.0, will be able to drive pervasive adoption of indoor positioning systems and extend the territory of location-based services and applications.

8. REFERENCES

[1] Techcrunch. How the 49ers are using beacons to help you find hot dogs. *URL http://techcrunch.com/2014/11/04/how-the-49ers-are-using-beacons-to-help-you-find-hot-dogs-and-beer/*, 2014.

[2] Shopkick. Shopkick retail platform. *URL http://www.shopkick.com/*.

[3] Techcrunch. Wifarer brings indoor navigation to the royal bc museum. *URL http://techcrunch.com/2012/08/01/wifarer-brings-indoor-navigation-to-the-royal-bc-museum/*, 2012.

[4] Lokast. Lokast mobile app platform. *URL http://www.lokast.com/*.

[5] ZoneDefense. Zonedefense location-based mobile security platform. *URL http://airpatrolcorp.com/products/zonedefense/*.

[6] FCC. Fcc proposes new indoor requirements and revisions to existing e911 rules. *URL http://www.fcc.gov/document/proposes-new-indoor-requirements-and-revisions-existing-e911-rules*.

[7] 802.11v.

[8] Qualcomm. Discussion of indoor location standards. *URL http://www.cwins.wpi.edu/workshop12/presentation/Standardization_panel/kirk.pdf*.

[9] Y. Gu et al. A survey of indoor positioning systems. *IEEE Communications Surveys & Tutorials*, 2009.

[10] V. Bahl et al. RADAR: An in-building rf-based user location and tracking system. In *INFOCOM*, 2000.

[11] S. Sen et al. Spot localization using phy layer information. In *MobiSys*, 2012.

[12] Yu-Chung et al. Accuracy characterization for metropolitan-scale wi-fi localization. In *MobiSys*, 2005.

[13] M. Youssef et al. The horus WLAN location determination system. In *MobiSys*, 2005.

[14] G. Borriello et al. Walrus: wireless acoustic location with room-level resolution using ultrasound. In *MobiCom*, 2005.

[15] N. Priyantha et al. The cricket location-support system. In *MobiCom*, 2000.

[16] Z. Yang et al. Locating in fingerprint space: wireless indoor localization with little human intervention. In *MobiCom*, 2012.

[17] A. Rai et al. Zee: zero-effort crowdsourcing for indoor localization. In *MobiCom*, 2012.

[18] K. Chintalapudi et al. Indoor localization without the pain. In *MobiCom*, 2010.

[19] J. Xiong et al. Arraytrack: A fine-grained indoor location system. In *NSDI*, 2013.

[20] R. Nandakumar et al. Centaur: locating devices in an office environment. In *MobiCom*, 2012.

[21] D. Niculescu et al. Ad hoc positioning system (APS) using AoA. In *INFOCOM*, 2003.

[22] H. Wang et al. Unsupervised indoor localization. MobiSys, 2012.

[23] F. Li et al. A reliable and accurate indoor localization method using phone inertial sensors. 2012.

[24] A. T. Mariakakis et al. Sail: single access point-based indoor localization. In *MobiSys*, 2014.

[25] HP. HP Location Aware - featuring HP Labs indoor location technology. *URL http://h30507.www3.hp.com/t5/Innovation-HP-Labs/HP-Location-Aware-featuring-HP-Labs-indoor-location-technology/ba-p/157850#.VF59uovF_Kc*.

[26] HP Networking. Sdn-enabled location technology delivers new revenue generation opportunities. *URL http://www8.hp.com/us/en/hp-news/press-release.html?id=1608266#.VF5-RIvF_Kc*.

[27] S. Sen et al. Avoiding multipath to revive inbuilding wifi localization. In *MobiSys*, 2013.

[28] K. Wu et al. Fila: Fine-grained indoor localization. In *INFOCOM*, 2012.

[29] N. Banerjee et al. Virtual compass: relative positioning to sense mobile social interactions. *Pervasive Computing*, 2010.

[30] K. Whitehouse et al. A practical evaluation of radio signal strength for ranging-based localization. *MC2R*, 2007.

[31] K.K. Chintalapudi et al. Ad-hoc localization using ranging and sectoring. In *INFOCOM*, 2004.

[32] Y. Chapre et al. Received signal strength indicator and its analysis in a typical wlan system. In *Local Computer Networks (LCN)*, 2013.

[33] D. Giustiniano et al. Caesar: carrier sense-based ranging in off-the-shelf 802.11 wireless lan. In *CoNEXT*, 2011.

[34] G. Welch et al. An introduction to the kalman filter, 1995.

[35] Qualcomm Atheros. Qualcomm atheros technology overview. *URL http://www.qca.qualcomm.com/wp-content/uploads/2013/11/AR9462.pdf*.

[36] J. Nocedal et al. *Numerical Optimizationn*. Springer series in operations research and financial engineering. Springer, 1999.

[37] M. R. Garey et al. Some simplified np-complete problems. In *STOC*, 1974.

[38] D. Brélaz. New methods to color the vertices of a graph. *Communications of the ACM*, 22(4):251–256, 1979.

[39] J. Hightower et al. Location systems for ubiquitous computing. *Computer*, 2001.

[40] A. J. Khan et al. Experiences with performance tradeoffs in practical, continuous indoor localization. In *WoWMoM*, 2013.

[41] M. Youssef et al. Pinpoint: An asynchronous time-based location determination system. In *Mobisys*, 2006.

[42] M. Ciurana et al. A ranging system with ieee 802.11 data frames. In *RWS*, 2007.

[43] D. McCrady et al. Mobile ranging using low-accuracy clocks. *IEEE Transactions on Microwave Theory and Techniques*, 38(6), 2000.

[44] J. Xiong et al. SecureAngle: improving wireless security using angle-of-arrival information. In *HotNets*, 2010.

[45] L. Cong et al. Hybrid tdoa/aoa mobile user location for wideband cdma cellular systems. *Wireless Communications, IEEE Transactions on*, 1(3):439–447, 2002.

[46] A. Tarighat et al. Improved wireless location accuracy using antenna arrays and interference cancellation. In *ICASSP*, 2003.

[47] Z. Zhang et al. I am the antenna: accurate outdoor ap location using smartphones. In *MobiCom*, 2011.

[48] S. Kumar et al. Accurate indoor localization with zero start-up cost. In *MobiCom*, 2014.

[49] J. Gjengset et al. Phaser: enabling phased array signal processing on commodity wifi access points. In *MobiCom*, 2014.

[50] S. Sen et al. Spinloc: Spin once to know your location. In *HotMobile*, 2012.

[51] R. Harle. A survey of indoor inertial positioning systems for pedestrians. 2013.

[52] Aruba Networks. Configuring adaptive radio management (arm) profiles and settings. Aruba Whitepaper.

[53] J. Hightower et al. Particle filters for location estimation in ubiquitous computing: A case study. *UbiComp*, 2004.

Early Detection of Spam Mobile Apps

Suranga Seneviratne†*, Aruna Seneviratne†*, Mohamed Ali Kaafar†,
Anirban Mahanti†, Prasant Mohapatra‡

†NICTA; *School of EET, UNSW; ‡ Department of CS, University of California, Davis

ABSTRACT

Increased popularity of smartphones has attracted a large number of developers to various smartphone platforms. As a result, app markets are also populated with spam apps, which reduce the users' quality of experience and increase the workload of app market operators. Apps can be "spammy" in multiple ways including not having a specific functionality, unrelated app description or unrelated keywords and publishing similar apps several times and across diverse categories. Market operators maintain anti-spam policies and apps are removed through continuous human intervention. Through a systematic crawl of a popular app market and by identifying a set of removed apps, we propose a method to detect spam apps solely using app metadata available at the time of publication. We first propose a methodology to manually label a sample of removed apps, according to a set of checkpoint heuristics that reveal the reasons behind removal. This analysis suggests that approximately 35% of the apps being removed are very likely to be spam apps. We then map the identified heuristics to several quantifiable features and show how distinguishing these features are for spam apps. Finally, we build an *Adaptive Boost* classifier for early identification of spam apps using only the metadata of the apps. Our classifier achieves an accuracy over 95% with precision varying between 85%–95% and recall varying between 38%–98%. By applying the classifier on a set of apps present at the app market during our crawl, we estimate that at least 2.7% of them are spam apps.

Categories and Subject Descriptors

H.4 [**Information Systems Applications**]: Miscellaneous

Keywords

Spam, Mobile Apps, Android, Spam Apps

1. INTRODUCTION

Recent years have seen wide adoption of mobile apps, and the number apps that are being offered are growing exponentially. As of mid-2014, Google Play Store and Apple App Store, each hosted approximately 1.2 million apps [48], with around 20,000 new apps being published each month in both of these app markets. These numbers are expected to significantly grow over the next few years [49].

Both Google and Apple have policies governing the publication of apps through their app markets. Google has an explicit spam policy [31] that describes their main reasons for considering an app to be "spammy". These include : i) apps that were automatically generated and published, and as such do not have any specific functionality or a meaningful description; ii) multiple instances of the same app being published to obtain increased visibility in the app market; and iii) apps that make excessive use of unrelated keywords to attract unintended searches. Overall, spam apps vitiate the app market experience and its usefulness.

At present, Google and Apple take different approaches to the spam detection problem. Google's approach is reactive. Google's app approval process does not check an app against its explicit spam app policy [42], and takes action only on the basis of customer complaints [46]. Such crowdsourced approach can lead to a considerable time lag between app submission and detection of spam behaviour. In contrast, Apple scrutinises the apps submitted for approval, presumably using a manual or semi-manual process, to determine whether the submitted app conforms to Apple's policies. Although this approach is likely to detect spam apps before they are published, it lengthens the app approval process. *With the ever increasing number of apps being submitted daily for approval, the app market operators need to be able to detect spam apps quickly and accurately.*

This paper proposes a methodology for automated detection of spam apps at the time of app submission. Our classifier utilises only features that can be derived from an app's metadata available during the publication approval process. It does not require any human intervention such as manual inspection of the metadata or manual testing of the app. We validate our app classifier, by applying it to a large dataset of apps collected between December 2013 and May 2014, by crawling and identifying apps that were removed from Google Play Store. We make the following contributions:

- We develop a manual app classification methodology based on a set of heuristic checkpoints that can be used to identify reasons behind an app's removal (Sections 3 and 4). Using this methodology we found that approximately 35% of the apps that were removed are spam apps; problematic content and counterfeits were the other key reasons for removal of apps.

WWW 2015, May 18–22, 2015, Florence, Italy.
ACM 978-1-4503-3469-3/15/05.
http://dx.doi.org/10.1145/2736277.2741084.

- We present a mapping of our proposed spam checkpoints to one or more quantifiable features that can be used to train a learning model (Section 5). We provide a characterisation of these features highlighting differences between spam and non-spam apps and indicate which features are more discriminative.
- We build an *Adaptive Boost* classifier for early detection of spam apps and show that our classifier can achieve an accuracy over 95% at a precision between 85%–95% and a recall between 38%–98% (Section 6).
- We applied our classifier to over 180,000 apps available in Google Play Store and show that approximately 2.7% of them are potentially spam apps (Section 6).

To the best of our knowledge, this is the first work to develop an early detection framework for identifying spam mobile apps and to demonstrate its efficacy using real world datasets. Our work complements prior research on detecting apps seeking *over-permissions* or apps containing *malware* [59, 22, 8, 45, 21].

2. RELATED WORK

In this section, we discuss related work in spam detection for web pages, email, and SMS, and the detection of malware apps and over-privileged apps.

Web spam refers to the publication of web pages that are specifically designed to influence search engine results. Using a set of manually classified samples of web pages obtained from *"MSN Search"*, Ntoulas et al. [41] characterise the web page features that can be used to classify a web page as spam or not. The features include top-level domain, language of the web page, number of words in the web page, and number of words in the page title etc.

Fetterly et al. [17] characterise the features that can potentially be used to identify *web spam* through statistical analysis. The authors analyse features such as *URL properties*, *host name resolutions*, and *linkage properties* and find that outliers within each of the properties considered are spam. Gyöngyi et al. [23] propose the use of the link structure in a limited set of manually identified non-spam web pages to iteratively find spam and non-spam web pages, and show that a significant fraction of the *web spam* can be filtered using only a seed set of less than 200 sites. Krishnan et al. [36] use a similar approach. Erdélyi et al. [15] show that a computationally inexpensive feature subset, such as the number of words in a page and the average word length, is sufficient to detect web spam.

Detection of *email spam* has received considerable attention [7]. Various *content related features* of mail messages such as *email header, text in the email body*, and *graphical elements* have been used together with machine learning techniques, such as naive Bayesian [44, 50, 38], support vector machines [14, 4, 51], and k nearest neighbour [3]. *Non-content related features* such as *SMTP path* [37] and *user's social network* [43, 11] has also been used in spam email detection.

Spam has also been studied in the context of *SMS* [20, 12], *product reviews* [34, 33, 10], *blog comments* [39], and *social media* [57, 6]. Cormack et al. [12] show that due to the limited size of SMS messages, bag of words or word bigram based spam classifiers do not perform well, and their performance can be improved by expanding the set of features to include orthogonal sparse word bigrams, and character bigrams and trigrams. Jindal et al. [34] identify spam product reviews using *review centric features* such as the number of feedback reports, textual features of the reviews, and *product centric features* such as price, sales rank as well as *reviewer centric features* such as the average rating given by the reviewer. Wang et al. [57] study detection of spammers in Twitter.

More recently, Malware mobile apps, over-privileged apps (i.e., apps with over-permissions), and similar apps (i.e., *clones:* similar apps by different developers and *rebranding:* similar apps by the same developer) have received attention [59, 22, 8, 45, 21, 56, 13]. Zhou et al. [59] propose *DroidRanger*, which uses permission-based behavioural fingerprinting to detect new samples of known Android malware families and heuristics-based filtering to identify inherent behaviours of unknown malware families. Gorla et al. [21] regroup app descriptions using a Latent Dirichlet Allocation and k-means clustering to identify apps that have unexpected API usage characteristics. Viennot et.al [56] clustered apps based on the Jaccard Similarity of app resources such as images and layout XMLs, to identify similar apps and used developer information such as the name and the certificate included in the app to differentiate clones from rebranding. Crussell et al. [13] clustered apps according to the code level similarity features to identify similar apps.

3. METHODOLOGY

3.1 Dataset

We use apps collected in a previous study [53], as a seed for collecting a new dataset. This initial seed contained 94,782 apps and was curated from the lists of apps obtained from approximately 10,000 smartphone users. The user base consisted of volunteers, Amazon mechanical turk users, and users who published their lists of apps in *social app discovery* sites such as *Appbrain*[1]. We crawled each app's Google Play Store page through a Java client that uses *jsoup*[2] HTML parser to discover: i) functionally similar apps; ii) other apps by the same developer. Then we collected metadata such as app name, app description, and app category for all the apps we discovered including the seed set. We discarded the apps with a non-English description using the language detection API, "*Detect Language*" [1]. We refer to this final set as the ***Observed Set*** - $\mathbb{O}$.

After identifying the ***Observed Set*** apps, we revisited Google Play Store to check the availability of each app. The subset of apps that were unavailable at the time of this second crawl is referred to as ***Crawl 1*** - $\mathbb{C}_1$. This process was repeated two times, ***Crawl 2*** - $\mathbb{C}_2$ and ***Crawl 3*** - $\mathbb{C}_3$ with at least one month gap between two consecutive crawls. Figure 1 illustrates data collection process and Table 1 summarises the datasets in use.

We identify temporary versus long-term removal of apps by re-checking the status of apps deemed to have been removed during an earlier crawl. For instance, all apps in ***Crawl 1*** were checked again during ***Crawl 2***. We found that only 85 (~0.13%) apps identified as removed in ***Crawl 1*** reappeared in ***Crawl 2***. Similarly, only 153 apps

[1] www.appbrain.com

[2] www.jsoup.org

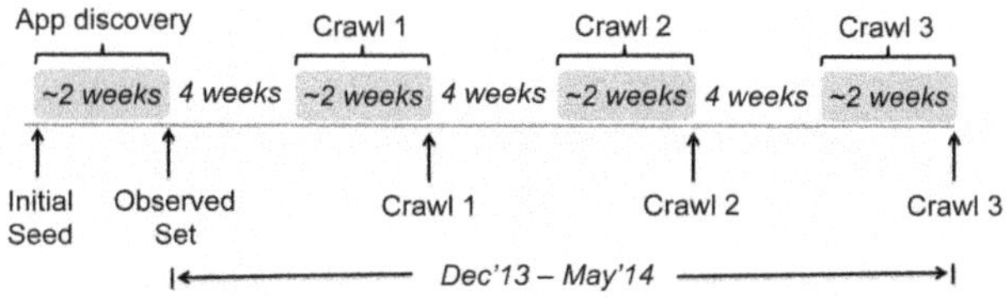

Figure 1: Chronology of the data collection

Table 1: Summary of the dataset

Set	Number of apps
Observed set ($\mathbb{O}$)	232,906
Crawl 1 ($\mathbb{C}_1$)	6,566
Crawl 2 ($\mathbb{C}_2$)	9,184
Crawl 3 ($\mathbb{C}_3$)	18,897

(~0.02%) identified as removed in ***Crawl 2*** reappeared in ***Crawl 3***. These apps were not included in our analysis.

3.2 App Labelling Process

For a subset of the removed apps in our dataset, our goal was to manually identify the reasons behind their removal.

We identified factors that lead to removal of apps from the market place by consulting numerous market reports [47, 25] as well as by examining the policies of the major app markets [31, 29, 27, 28, 30, 24]. We identified nine key **reasons**, which are summarised in Table 2. For each of these reasons, we formulated a set of heuristic checkpoints that can be used to manually label whether or not an app is likely to be removed. Owing to space limitations we do not provide the heuristic checkpoints for removed reasons except for spam. Full list of checkpoints for each reason can be found in our technical report [52]. Section 4 delves into the checkpoints developed for identifying spam apps.

Table 2: Key reasons for removal of apps

Reason	Description
Spam	These apps often have characteristics such as unrelated description, keyword misuse, and multiple instances of the same app. Section 4 presents details on spam app characteristics.
Unofficial content	Apps that provide unofficial interfaces to popular websites or services (E.g., an app providing an interface to a popular online shopping site without any official affiliation).
Copyrighted content	Apps illegally distributing copyrighted content.
Adult content	Apps with explicit sexual content.
Problematic content	Apps with illegal or problematic content. E.g., Hate speech and drug related.
Android counterfeit	Apps pretending to be another popular app in the Google Play Store.
Other counterfeit	A counterfeit app, for which the original app comes from a different source than Google Play Store (E.g., Apple App Store)
Developer deleted	Apps that were removed by the developer.
Developer banned	Developer's other apps were removed due to various reasons and Google decides to ban the developer. Thus all of his apps get removed.

From ***Crawl 1***, we took a random sample of 1500 apps and asked three independent reviewers to identify the ***highest likely*** reason behind the removal of each app using the heuristic checkpoints that we developed as a guideline. A reviewer's selection of a reason for app removal is subjective and it is based upon their judgement on the level of satisfaction of one or more checkpoints. If a reviewer could not conclusively determine the reasons behind a removal, she labelled those apps as ***unknown***.

Table 3: Reviewer agreement in labelling reason for removal

Reason	3 reviewers agreed	2 reviewers agreed	Total	Percent. (%)
Spam	292	259	551	36.73%
Unofficial content	65	127	192	12.80%
Developer deleted	68	56	124	8.27%
Android counterfeit	27	61	88	5.87%
Developer banned	24	54	78	5.20%
Copyrighted content	2	34	36	2.40%
Other counterfeit	11	23	34	2.27%
Adult content	8	4	12	0.80%
Problematic content	3	4	7	0.47%
Unknown	101	127	228	15.20%
Sub total	**601**	**749**	**1350**	90.00%
Reviewer disagreement	NA	NA	150	10.00%
Total Labelled	**NA**	**NA**	**1500**	100.00%

The reviewers were Android app developers and worked full time for 1.5 months at NICTA for this task. The manual labelling processing took approximately 20 working days (7 hours per day).

3.3 Agreement Among the Reviewers

We used majority voting to merge the results of the experts assessment, to arrive at the reason behind the app removal in our labelled dataset ($\mathbb{L}$). We decided not to crowdsource the labelling task to avoid issues with training and expertise.

Table 3 summarises reviewer agreement. For approximately 40% (601 out of 1500) of labelled apps, the three reviewers reached a consensus on the reason for removal and for 90% (1350 out of 1500) of the apps majority of the reviewers agreed on the same reason. For the remaining 10% of apps, reviewers disagreed about the reasons.

Table 3 also shows the composition of labelled dataset ($\mathbb{L}$) after majority voting-based label merging. We observe that *spam* is the main reason for app removal, accounting for approximately 37% of the removals, followed by *unofficial content* accounting for approximately 13% of the removals. Around 15% of the apps were labelled as *unknown*.

Figure 2 shows the conditional probability of the third reviewer's reasoning, given that the other two reviewers are in agreement. There is over 50% probability of the third reviewer's judgement of an app being spam, when two reviewers already judged the app to be spam. Other reasons showing such high probability are *developer deleted* and *adult content* apps.

Our analysis through the manual labelling process shows that the main reason behind app removal is them being *spam* apps. Furthermore, the reviewer agreement was high (more than 50%) when manually labelling *spam* apps indicating spam apps stand out clearly when looking at removed apps.

We release our labelled dataset to the research community [2] to stem further research in spam app detection.

4. MANUAL LABELLING OF SPAM APPS

This section introduces our heuristic checkpoints, which are used to manually label the spam apps. We also provide a characterisation of the reviewer agreement related to nine manual spam checkpoints and show that checkpoints are un-

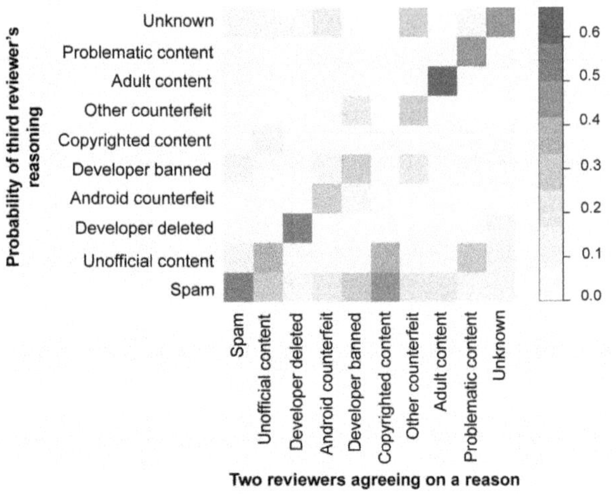

Figure 2: Probability of a third reviewer's judgement when two reviewers already agreed on a reason

ambiguous and suitable for manual labelling. Section 5 maps the defined checkpoints into automated features.

4.1 Spam Checkpoints

Table 4 presents the nine heuristic checkpoints used by the reviewers and those were derived based on Google's spam policy [31]. While we are unaware of Apple's spam policy, we note that Apple's app review guideline [24] includes certain provisions that match our spam checkpoints. For example, term 2.20 in the Apple app review guideline, *"Developers spamming the App Store with many versions of similar apps will be removed from the iOS Developer Program"* maps to our checkpoint S_6. Similarly, term 3.3 *"Apps with names, descriptions, screenshots, or previews not relevant to the content and functionality of the app will be rejected"* is similar to our checkpoint S_2.

Reviewers were asked not to deem the apps as spam when they simply observe an app satisfying a single checkpoint, but to consider making their decision based on matches with multiple checkpoints according to their domain expertise.

Note that Table 4 includes all checkpoints relevant to spam, including those that are considered only for manual labelling and not for automated labelling. In particular, checkpoints S_8 and S_9 are only used for manual labelling as features corresponding to these checkpoints are either not available at the time of app submission or require significant dynamic analysis for feature discovery. For instance, we do not use user "reviews" of the app (cf. checkpoint S_8), as user reviews are not available prior to the app's approval. Similarly, checking for excessive advertising (cf. checkpoint S_9) was also used only for manual labelling, as it requires dynamic analysis by executing it in a controlled environment.

4.2 Reviewer Agreement on Spam Checkpoints

Table 5 shows how often the reviewers agreed upon each checkpoint. Checkpoints S_2 and S_6 led to the highest number of 3-reviewers agreements and 2-reviewer agreements. Checkpoints S_1 and S_3 have moderate number of 3-reviewer agreements while having a high number of 2-reviewer agreements. The table also suggests that checkpoints S_1, S_2, S_3 and S_6 are the most dominant checkpoints.

Table 5: Checkpoint-wise reviewer agreement for spam

Checkpoint	S1	S2	S3	S4	S5	S6	S7	S8	S9
3 reviewers agreed	22	63	20	0	4	89	11	3	3
2 reviewers agreed	52	81	75	3	6	115	11	26	15
Disagreed	45								

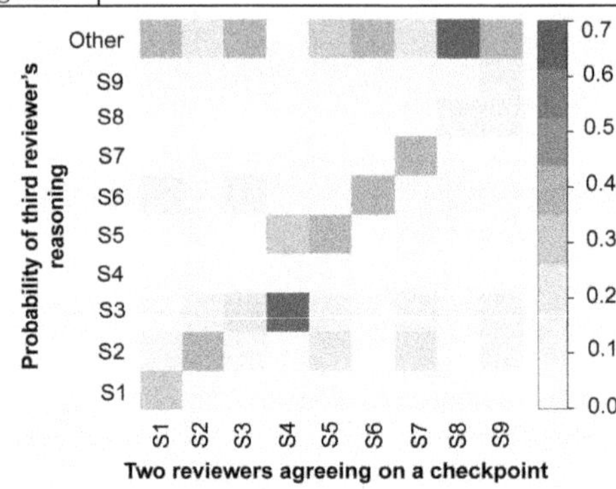

Figure 3: Probability of a third reviewer's judgement when two reviewers already agreed on a checkpoint

The sum of the cases where 3 reviewers agreed, 2 reviewers agreed, and reviewers disagreed shown in Table 5, is more than the total number of spam apps identified by merging the reviewer agreement (i.e., 551 apps) because one reviewer might mark an app as satisfying multiple checkpoints. For example, consider a scenario where reviewer-1 labels the app as satisfying checkpoints S_1, S_2 and reviewer-2 labels as S_1, S_2 and reviewer-3 labels only as S_1. This will cause one scenario of 3 reviewer agreement (for S_1) and another scenario of 2 reviewer agreement (for S_2).

Out of the 551 spam apps, three reviewers agreed on at least one checkpoint for 210 apps ($\sim$ 38%), and two reviewers agreed on at least one checkpoint for 296 apps ($\sim$ 54%). For 45 apps ($\sim$ 8%), the three reviewers gave different checkpoints (i.e. when the reviewers assess an app as spam, over 90% of the time they also agreed on at least one checkpoint).

Figure 3 illustrates the conditional probability of the third reviewer's checkpoint selection given two reviewers have already agreed on a checkpoint. We observe that for checkpoints S_1, S_2, S_5, S_6, S_7 and S_8, there is a high probability that the third reviewer indicates the same checkpoint when two of the reviewers already agreed on a checkpoint. There is, however, a noticeable anomaly for checkpoint S_4, for which it seems that reviewers are getting confused with S_3. This is due to the lower frequency of occurrences of checkpoint S_4. There were no 3-reviewer agreements for S_4 and there were only 3 cases where 2 reviewers agreed as shown in Table 5. In those 3 cases the other reviewer marked the checkpoint S_3 in 2 cases giving a high probability ($\sim$ 67%) for S_4 getting confused with S_3. Note that *Other* refers to all the checkpoints associated with reasons for app removals other than spam; the probability of *Others* being chosen is high because of the accumulated sum of probabilities of checkpoints associated with other reasons.

5. FEATURE MAPPING

Checkpoint heuristics for spam (cf. Table 4) need to be mapped into features that can be extracted and used for

Table 4: Checkpoints used for labelling of spam apps

Attribute	ID	Description and Examples
Description	S_1	Does the app description describe the app function clearly and concisely? ***E.g. Signature Capture App (Non - spam) - Description is clear on the functionality of the application*** *"SignIt app allows a user to sign and take notes which can be saved and shared instantly in email or social media."* ***E.g. Manchester (Spam) - Description contains details about Manchester United Football Club without any detail on the functionality of the app.*** *"Manchester United Football Club is an English professional football club, based in Old Trafford, Greater Manchester, that plays in the Premier League. ..... In 1998-99, the club won a continental treble of the Premier League, the FA Cup and the UEFA Champions League, an unprecedented feat for an English club."*
	S_2	Does the app description contain too much details / incoherent text / unrelated text for an app description? ***E.g. SpeedMoto (Non - spam) - Description is clear and concise about the functionality and usage.*** *"SpeedMoto is a 3d moto racing game with simple control and excellent graphic effect. Just swap your phone to control moto direction. Tap the screen to accelerate the moto. In this game you can ride the motorcycle shuttle in outskirts, forest, snow mountain,bridge. More and More maps and motos will coming soon"* ***E.g. Ferrari Wallpapers HD (Spam) - Description starts mentioning app as a wallpaper. However, then it goes into to details about Ferrari.*** *"*HD WALLPAPERS *EASY TO SAVE *EASY TO SET WALLPAPER *INCLUDES ADS FOR ESTABLISHING THIS APP FREE TO YOU THANKS FOR UNDERSTANDING AND DOWNLOADING =) Ferrari S.p.A. is an Italian sports car manufacturer based in Maranello, Italy. Founded by Enzo Ferrari in 1929, as Scuderia Ferrari, the company sponsored drivers and manufactured race cars before moving into production of street-legal ....."*
	S_3	Does the app description contain a noticeable repetition of words or keywords? ***E.g. English Chinese Dictionary (Non - Spam) - Keywords do not have excessive repetition.*** *"Keywords: ec, dict, translator, learn, translate, lesson, course, grammar, phrases, vocabulary, translation, dict"* ***E.g. Best live HD TV no ads (Spam) - Excessive repetition of words.*** *"Keywords: live tv for free mobile tv tuner tv mobile android tv on line windows mobile tv verizon mobile tv tv streaming live tv for mobile phone mobile tv stream mobile tv phone mobile phone tv rogers mobile tv live mobile tv channels sony mobile tv free download mobile tv dstv mobile tv mobile tv....."*
	S_4	Does the app description contain unrelated keywords or references? ***E.g. FD Call Assistant Free (Non - spam) - All the keywords are related to the fire department.*** *"Keywords: firefighter, fire department, emergency, police, ems, mapping, dispatch, 911"* ***E.g. Diamond Eggs (Spam) - Reference to popular games Bejeweled Blitz and Diamond Blast without any reason.*** *"Keywords : bejeweled, bejeweled blitz, gems twist, enjoy games, brain games, diamond, diamond blast, diamond cash, diamond gems, Eggs, jewels, jewels star"*
	S_5	Does the app description contain excessive references for other applications from the same developer? ***E.g. Kids Puzzles (Non - spam) - Description does not contain references to developer's other apps.*** *"This kids game has 55 puzzles. Easy to build puzzles. Shapes Animals Nature and more... With sound telling your child what the puzzle is. Will be adding new puzzles very soon. Keywords: kids, puzzle, puzzles, toddler, fun"* ***E.g. Diamond Snaker (Spam) - Excessive references to developer's other applications.*** *"If you like it, you can try our other apps (Money Exchange, Color Blocks, Chinese Chess Puzzel, PTT Web ....."*
	S_6	Does the developer have multiple apps with approximately the same description? ***The developer "Universal App" has 16 apps having the following description, with each time XXXX term is replaced with some other term.*** *"Get XXXX live wallpaper on your devices! Download the free XXXX live wallpaper featuring amazing animation. Now with "Water Droplet", "Photo Cube", "3D Photo Gallery" effect! Touch or tap the screen to add water drops on your home screen! Touch the top right corner of the screen to customise the wallpaper <>. To Use: Home -> Menu -> Wallpaper -> Live Wallpaper -> XXXX 3D Live Wallpaper To develop more free great live wallpapers, we have implemented some ads in settings. Advertisement can support our develop more free great live wallpapers. This live wallpaper has been tested on latest devices such as Samsung Galaxy S3 and Galaxy Nexus. Please contact us if your device is not supported. Note: If your wallpaper resets to default after reboot, you will need put the app on phone instead of SD card. "*
Identifier	S_7	Does the app identifier make sense and have some relevance to the functionality of the application or does it look like auto generated? ***E.g. Angry Birds Seasons & Candy Crush Saga (Non - spam) - Identifier give an idea about the app.*** *"com.rovio.angrybirdsseasons", "com.king.candycrushsaga"* ***E.g. Game of Thrones FREE Fan App & How To Draw Graffiti (Spam) - Identifiers appear to be auto generated.*** *"com.a121828451851a959009786c1a.a10023846a", "com.a13106102865265262e503a24a.a13796080a"*
Reviews	S_8	Do users complain about app being spammy in reviews? ***E.g. Yoga Trainer & Fitness & Google Play History Cleaner (Spam) - Users complain about app being spammy.*** *"Junk spam app Avoid", "More like a spam trojan! Download if you like, but this is straight garbage!!"*
Adware	S_9	Do the online APK checking tools highlight app having excessive advertising? ***E.g. Biceps & Triceps Workouts*** *"AVG threat labs" [26] gives a warning about inclusion of malware causing excessive advertising.*

Figure 6: Top-50 bigrams differentiating Spam and Top-1x

automatic spam detection during the app approval process. This section presents this mapping and a characterisation of these features with respect to ***spam*** and ***non-spam*** apps.

An app is considered ***spam*** if two-out-of-three reviewers labelled it as spam. We assumed that top apps with respect to the number of downloads, number of user reviews, and rating, are quite likely to be ***non-spam***. For example, according to this ranking, number one ranked app was *Facebook* and number 100 was *Evernote*[3], number 500 was *Tictoc*[4] and number 1000 was *Saavn*[5]. Thus, for ***non-spam*** apps, we selected top k times the number of labelled spam apps (551) from the set $\mathbb{O}$, except all removed apps, after ranking them according to total number of downloads, total number of user reviews, and average rating. We varied k logarithmically between 1 and 32, (i.e., 1x, 2x, 4x,..., 32x) to obtain 6 datasets of non-spam apps. At larger k values it is possible that spam apps are considered to be non-spam, as discussed later in this section.

As noted in Section 4.1, checkpoints S_8 and S_9 are not used to develop features as we intend to enable automated spam detection at the time of developer submission.

5.1 *Checkpoint S_1* - *Does the app description describe the app function clearly and concisely?*

We automate this heuristic by identifying word-bigrams and word-trigrams that are used to describe a functionality and are popular among either spam or non-spam apps.

First, we manually read the descriptions of top 100 non-spam apps and identified 100 word bigrams and word trigrams that describe app functionality, such as *"this app'*, *"allows you"*, and *"app for"*. Figure 4 shows the *cumulative distribution function (CDF)* of the number of bigrams and trigrams observed in app descriptions in each dataset. There is a high probability of spam apps not having these features in their app descriptions. For example, 50% of the spam apps had one or more occurrences of these bigrams whereas 80% of the top 1x apps had one or more of these bi- and tri-grams. The difference in distribution of these bigrams and trigrams between spam and non-spam apps decreases when more and more lower ranked apps are considered in the non-spam category. This finding is consistent across some of the features we discuss in subsequent sections and we believe this indicates lower ranked apps can potentially include spams that are as yet not identified by Google.

Second, as manual identification of bigrams and trigrams is not exhaustive, we identified the word-bigrams and word-trigrams that appear in at least 10% of the spam and 10% of the non-spam apps. We used each such word-bigram and word-trigram as features and the frequency of occurrence as the value of the feature. Figure 6 visualises top-50 bigrams (when ranked according to *information gain*); the size of the bigrams proportional to the logarithm of the *normalised information gain*. Note that bigrams such as *"live wallpaper"*, *"wallpaper on"*, and *"some ads"* are mostly present in spam whereas bigrams such as *"follow us"*, *"to play"* and *"on twitter"* are popular in non-spam.

[3]https://evernote.com
[4]http://www.tictoc.net
[5]http://www.saavn.com

Table 6: Features associated with **Checkpoint** S_2

	Feature
1	Total number of characters in the description
2	Total number of words in the description
3	Total number of sentences in the description
4	Average word length
5	Average sentence length
6	Percentage of upper case characters
7	Percentage of punctuations
8	Percentages of numeric characters
9	Percentage of non-alphabet characters
10	Percentage of common English words [9]
11	Percentage of personal pronouns [9]
12	Percentage of emotional words [40]
13	Percentage of misspelled words [58]
14	Percentage of words with alphabet and numeric characters
15	Automatic readability index (AR) [54]
16	Flesch readability score (FR) [18]

5.2 *Checkpoint S_2* - *Does the app description contain too much details, incoherent text, or unrelated text?*

We use writing style related "stylometry" features to map this checkpoint to a set of features anticipating spam and non-spam apps might have a different writing style. We used the 16 features listed in Table 6 for this checkpoint.

For characterisation, we select features using the *greedy forward feature selection in wrapper method* [35]. We use a decision tree classifier with maximum depth 10 and the feature subset was selected such that the classifier optimises the performance metric *asymmetric F-Measure*, $F_\beta = (1+\beta^2).\frac{precision.recall}{(\beta^2.precision)+recall}$, with $\beta = 0.5$. This metric was used since in spam app detection, precision is more important than recall [55]. This process identified the *Total number of words in the description, Total number of sentences in the description, Percentages of numeric characters, Percentage of non-alphabet characters,* and *Percentage of common English words* as the most discriminative features.

Figures 5a shows the CDF of the total number of words in the app description. Spam apps tend to have less wordy app descriptions than non-spam apps. For instance, nearly 30% of the spam apps have less than 100 words whereas approximately only 15% top-1x apps and top-2x apps have less than 100 words. As we inject more and more apps of lower popularity the difference diminishes. Figure 5b presents the CDF of the percentage of common English words [9] in the app description. It illustrates that spam apps typically use fewer common English words compared to non-spam apps.

5.3 *Checkpoint S_3* - *Does the app description contain a noticeable repetition of words or keywords?*

We quantify this checkpoint using the *vocabulary richness* (VR)$=\frac{\text{Number of unique words}}{\text{Total number of words}}$ metric. Figure 7 shows the CDF of the VR measure. We expected spam apps to have low VR due to repetition of keywords. However, we observe this only

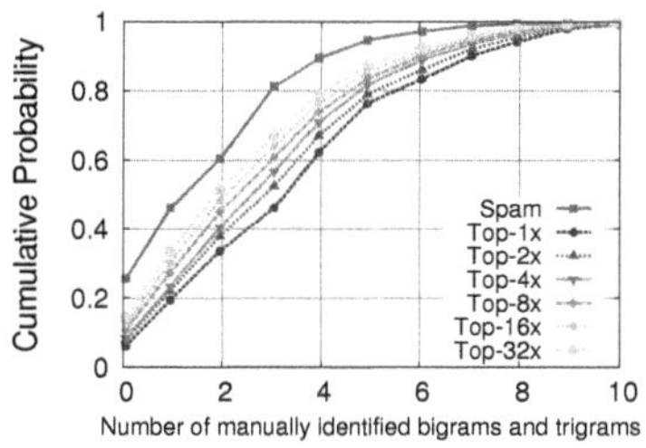

Figure 4: CDF of the frequency of manually identified word-bigrams and word-trigrams

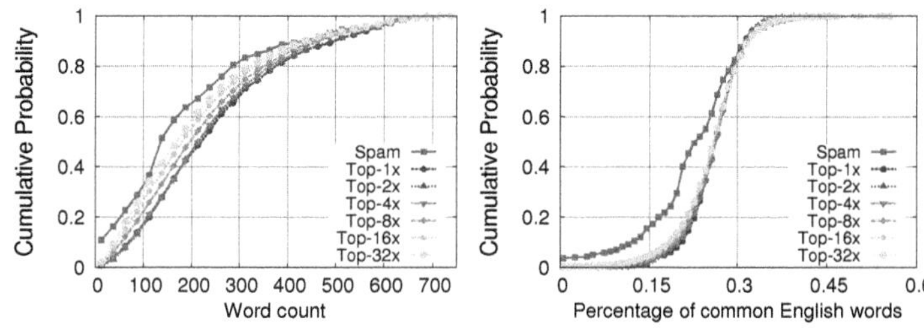

(a) (b)

Figure 5: Example features associated with **Checkpoint** S_2

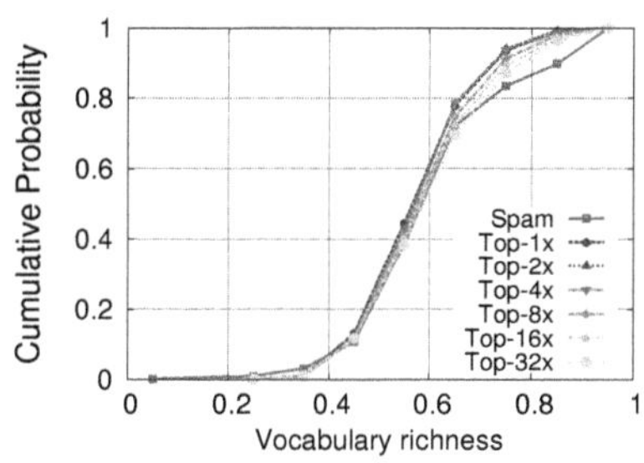

Figure 7: Vocabulary Richness

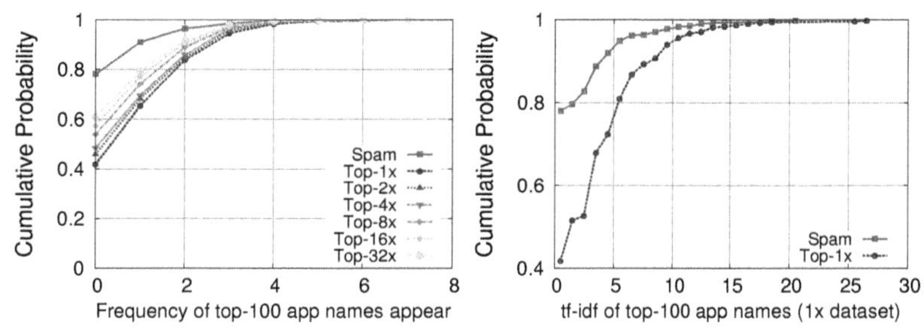

(a) (b)

Figure 8: Mentioning popular app names

in a limited number of cases. According to Figure 7, if VR is less than 0.3, an app is only marginally more likely to be spam. Perhaps the most surprising finding is that the apps with VR close to 1 are more likely to be spam. 10% of the spam apps had VR over 0.9 and none of the non-spam apps had such high VR values. When we manually checked these spam apps we found that they had terse app descriptions. We showed earlier that apps with shorter description are more likely to be spam under ***checkpoint*** S_2.

5.4 *Checkpoint S_4 - Does the app description contain unrelated keywords or references?*

Inserting unrelated keywords such that an app would appear in popular search results is a common spamming technique. Since the topics of the apps can vary significantly it is difficult to find when the terms included in the description are actually related to the functionality. In this study, we focussed on a specific strategy the developers might use, that is mentioning the names of the popular applications with the hope of appearing in the search results for these applications. For each app we calculated the number of mentionings of the top 100 popular app names in the app's description.

Figure 8a shows the distribution of the number of times the name of top-100 apps appear in the description. Somewhat surprisingly, we found that only 20% of the spam apps had more than one mention of popular apps, whereas 40%–60% of the top-kx apps had more than a single mention of popular apps. On investigation, we find that many top-kx apps have social networking interfaces and fan pages and as a result they mention the names of popular social networking apps. This is evident in Figure 6 as well where *Twitter* or *Facebook* are mentioned mostly in non-spam apps. To summarise, presence of social sharing features or availability of fan pages can be used to identify non spam apps.

Next, we consider the sum of the *tf-idf* weights of the top-100 app names. This feature attempts to reduce the effect of highly popular apps. For example, *Facebook* can have a high frequency because of its sharing capability and many apps might refer it. However, if an app refers to another app which is not as popular as *Facebook*, such as reference to popular games, it indicates a likelihood of it being a spam app. To discount the effect of the commonly available app names, we used the sum of *tf-idf* weights as a feature. For a given dataset let tf_{ik} where $i = 1:100$ be the number of times the app name of ith app (n_i) in top-100 apps appear in an app description of app k (a_k). Then we define IDF_i for i^{th} app in top-100 apps as, $IDF_i = \frac{N}{log(1+|\{n_i \in a_k\}|)}$ $\forall k$. Then feature $tf-idf(k)$ for k^{th} app is, $tf-idf(k) = \sum_{i=1}^{i=100} tf_{ik} \,.\, IDF_i$.

The calculation above is dataset dependent. Despite this, as Figures 8b shows, the CDF of top-1x dataset and the results still indicates that if popular app names are found in the app description, the app tends to be non spam rather than spam. We repeated the same with top-1000 app names and found that the results were similar.

5.5 *Checkpoint S_5 - Does the app description contain excessive references to other applications from the same developer?*

We use the *number of times a developer's other app names appear* as the feature corresponding to this checkpoint. However, none of the cases marked by the reviewers as matching checkpoint S_5 satisfied this feature because the description contained links to the applications rather than the app names and only 10 spam apps satisfied this feature (cf. Table 5). We do not use checkpoint S_5 in our classifier.

5.6 *Checkpoint S_6 - Does the developer have multiple apps with approximately the same description?*

For this checkpoint, for each app we considered the following features: (i) The total number of other apps the developer has, (ii) The total number of apps with an English language description which can be used to measure descriptions similarity and (iii) The number of other apps from the same developer having a description *cosine similarity(s)*, of over 60%, 70%, 80% and 90%.

To calculate the *cosine similarity* we first preprocess the app description text by converting the characters to lower case and removing punctuation symbols. Then we represent each document as a word frequency vector and calculate the cosine similarity between the two documents a and b as, $Cos(\mathbf{a}, \mathbf{b}) = \frac{\mathbf{a}.\mathbf{b}}{||\mathbf{a}|| \, ||\mathbf{b}||}$.

We observe that the features based on the similarity between app descriptions are the most discriminative. As examples, Figures 9a and 9b respectively show the CDF of number of apps with s over 60% and 90% by the same developer.

Figure 9a shows that only about 10%–15% of the non-spam apps have more than 5 other apps from the same developer with over 60% of description similarity. However, approximately 27% of the spam apps have more than 5 apps with over 60% of description similarity. This difference becomes more evident when the number of apps from the same developer with over 90% description similarity is considered, indicating that spam apps tend to have multiple clones with similar app descriptions.

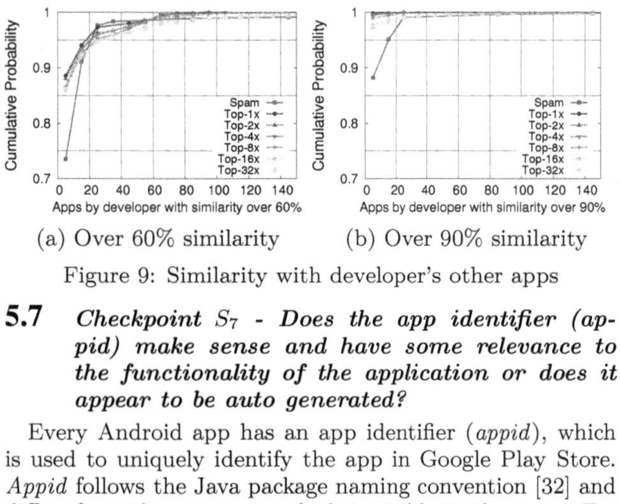

(a) Over 60% similarity (b) Over 90% similarity

Figure 9: Similarity with developer's other apps

5.7 *Checkpoint S_7 - Does the app identifier (appid) make sense and have some relevance to the functionality of the application or does it appear to be auto generated?*

Every Android app has an app identifier (*appid*), which is used to uniquely identify the app in Google Play Store. *Appid* follows the Java package naming convention [32] and differs from the app name which is visible to the users. For example, for the Facebook Android app, the app name is *Facebook* whereas the *appid* is *com.facebook.katana.*

Table 7 shows the features derived from the *appid.* We applied the feature selection method noted in Section 5.2 to identify the most discriminative features (*Number of words, Average word length, Percentage of bigrams with 2 non-letters*).

In Figure 10a we show the CDF of the number of words in the appid. The spam apps tend to have more words compared to non-spam apps. For example, 15% of the spam apps had more than 5 words in the appid where as only 5% of the non-spam had the same. Figure 10b shows the CDF of the average word length of a word in appid. For 10% of the spam apps the average word length is higher than 10 and it was so only for 2%–3% of the non-spam apps.

Table 7: Features associated with **Checkpoint** S_7

	Feature
1	Number of characters
2	Number of words
3	Average word length
4	Percentage of of non-letter characters to total characters
5	Percentage of upper case characters to total letter characters
6	Presence of parts of *app name* in *appid*
7	Percentage of bigrams with 1 non-letter to total bigrams
8	Percentage of bigrams with 2 non-letters to total bigrams
9	Percentage of bigrams with 1 or 2 non-letters to total bigrams
10	Percentage of trigrams with 1 non-letter to total trigrams
11	Percentage of trigrams with 2 non-letters to total trigrams
12	Percentage of trigrams with 3 non-letters to total trigrams
13	Percentage of trigrams with 1, 2 or 3 non-letters to total trigrams

Figure 10c shows the percentage of non-letter bigrams (e.g., *"01", "8_"*) among all character bigrams that can be generated from the appid. None of the non-spam apps had more 20% of non-letter bigrams in the appid, whereas about 5% of the spam apps had more than 20% of non-letter bigrams. Therefore, if an appid contains over 20% of non-letter bigrams out of all possible bigrams that can be generated, that app is more likely to be spam than non-spam.

5.8 Other Metadata

In addition to the features derived from the checkpoints, we added the metadata related features listed on Table 8.

Figure 11 shows the app category distribution in the spam and the top-1x categories. We note that approximately 42% of the spam apps belong to the categories *Personalisation* and *Entertainment.* We found a negligibly small number of spam apps in the categories *Communication, Photography, Racing, Social, Travel,* and *Weather.* Moreover, for categories *Arcade, Tools,* and *Casual,* the percentage of spam is significantly less than the percentage of non-spam. Qualitatively similar observations hold for these other top-kx sets.

Figure 12a shows the CDF of the length of the app name. Spam apps tend to have longer names. For example, 40% of the spam apps had more than 25 characters in the app name. Only 20% of the non-spam apps had more than 25 characters in their app names. Figures 12b shows the CDF of the size of the app in kilobytes. Spam apps tend to have a high probability of having a size in some specific ranges. For example if the size of the app is very low those apps are more likely to be non-spam. For example, 30% of the top-kx apps were less than 100KB in size and the corresponding percentage of spam apps is almost zero. Almost all the spam apps were having sizes less than 30MB whereas 10%–15% of the top-kx apps were more than 30MB in size. CDF of the spam app shows a sharp rise between 1000KB and 3000KB indicating there are more apps in that size range.

Table 9 shows the external information related features. For example, if a link to a developer web site or a privacy policy is given the app is more likely to be non-spam.

Table 8: Features associated with other app metadata

	Feature		**Feature**
1	App category	5	Developer's website available
2	Price	6	Developer's website reachable
3	Length of app name	7	Developer's email available
4	Size of the app (KB)	8	Privacy policy available

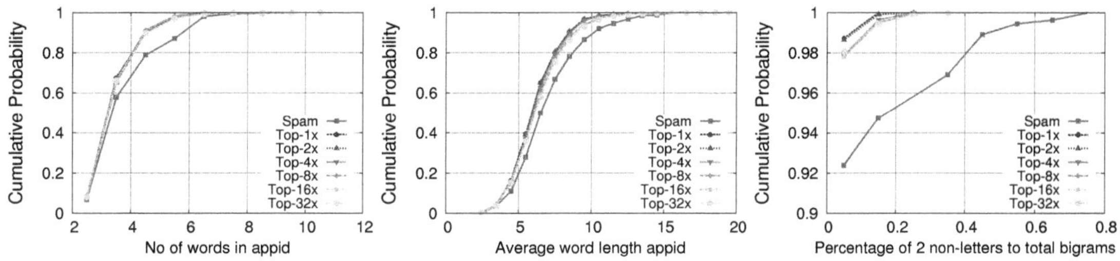

(a) (b) (c)

Figure 10: Example features associated with **Checkpoint** S_7

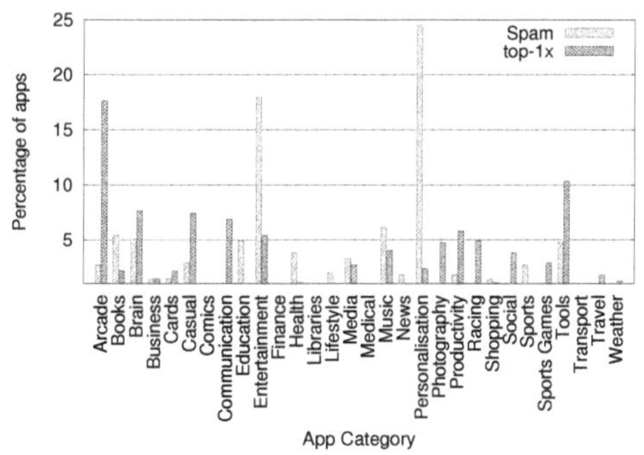

Figure 11: App category

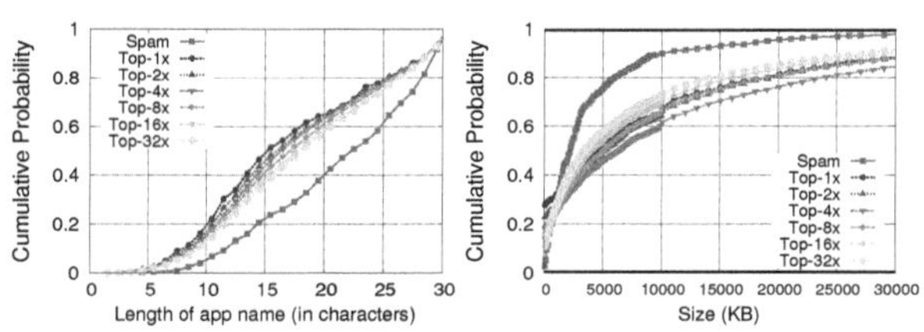

(a) (b)

Figure 12: Features associated with other app metadata

Table 9: Availability of developer's external information

	Spam	**top 1x**	**top 2x**	**top 4x**	**top 8x**	**top 16x**	**top 32x**
Website availa.	57%	93%	94%	93%	91%	89%	86%
Website reacha.	93%	98%	97%	97%	96%	96%	95%
Email availa.	99%	84%	89%	91%	93%	94%	95%
Priv. policy availa.	9%	56%	50%	48%	38%	32%	26%

6. EVALUATION

6.1 Classifier Performance

We build a binary classifier based on the *Adaptive Boost* algorithm [19] to detect whether or not a given app is spam. We use the spam apps as *positives* and apps from a top-kx set as *negatives*. Each app is represented by a vector of all the features listed in Section 5. The classifier is trained using 80% of the data and the remaining 20% of the data is used for testing. We repeat this experiment for $k = 1, 2, 4, \cdots, 32$.

Some of the features discussed in Section 5 depend on the other apps in the dataset rather than on the metadata of the individual apps. For such cases we calculate the features based only on the training set to avoid any information propagation from the training to the testing set that would artificially inflate the performance of the classifier. For example, when extracting the bigrams (and trigrams) that are popular in at least 10% of the apps, only spam and non-spam apps from the training set are used. This vocabulary is then used to generate feature values for individual apps in both training and testing sets.

Decision trees with a maximum depth of 5 are used as the weak classifiers in the *Adaptive Boost* classifier[6] and we performed 500 iterations of the algorithm. Table 10 summarises the results. Our classifiers, while varying the value of k, have precision over 85% with recall varying between 38%–98%. Notably, when k is small (e.g., when the total number of non spam apps represents $\leq$ 2x the number of spam apps) the classifier achieves up to 95% accuracy.

Recall drops when we increase the number of negative examples because larger k values implies inclusion of lower ranked apps as negative (non-spam) examples. Some of these lower ranked apps, however, exhibit some spam features and some may indeed be spam (not yet been detected as spam). As we have only a small number of spam apps in the training set, when unlabelled spam apps are added as non-spam, some spam related features become non-spam features as the number of apps satisfying that feature is high in non-spam. As a result recall drops when k increases.

As the number of negative examples increases the classifier becomes more conservative and correctly identifies a relatively small portion of spam apps. Nonetheless, even at $k = 32$ we achieve a precision over 85%. This is particularly helpful in spam detection, as marking a non-spam as spam can be more expensive than missing a spam.

Additionally, if the objective is to build an aggressive classifier that identifies as much spam as possible so that app market operators can flag these apps to make a decision later, a classifier built using smaller number of negative examples (i.e., $k = 1$ or $k = 2$) can be used. For example, in Table 11 we show the $k = 2$ classifier's performance in the higher order datasets. As can be seen, this classifier identifies nearly 90% of the spam. However, the precision goes down as we traverse down the app ranking because of increased number of false positives. Nonetheless, in reality some of these apps may actually be spam and as a result may not exactly be false positives.

6.2 Applying the Classifier in the Wild

To estimate the volume of potential spam that might be in Google Play Store, we used two of our classifiers to predict

[6] *Adaptive Boost* algorithm combines the output of set of weak classifiers to build a strong classifier. Interested readers may refer to [19].

Table 10: Classifier Performance

k	Precision	Recall	Accuracy	$F_{0.5}$
1	0.9310	0.9818	0.9545	0.9408
2	**0.9533**	**0.9273**	**0.9606**	**0.9480**
4	0.9126	0.8545	0.9545	0.9004
8	0.9405	0.7182	0.9636	0.8857
16	0.8833	0.4818	0.9658	0.7571
32	0.8571	0.3818	0.9793	0.6863

Table 11: Classifier Performance: $k = 2$ model

k	Precision	Recall	Accuracy	$F_{0.5}$
4	0.8080	0.9182	0.9400	0.8279
8	0.5549	0.9182	0.9091	0.6026
16	0.2730	0.9182	0.8513	0.3176
32	0.1164	0.9182	0.7862	0.1410

Table 12: Predictions on spam apps in Google Play Store

Dataset	Size	$k = 2$	$k = 32$
Crawl 1 ($\mathbb{C}_1$)	6,566	70.37 %	12.89 %
Crawl 2 ($\mathbb{C}_2$)	9,184	73.14 %	6.57 %
Crawl 3 ($\mathbb{C}_3$)	18,897	72.99 %	6.49 %
Others	180,627	54.59 %	2.69 %

whether or not an app in our dataset was spam. We selected a conservative classifier ($k = 32$) and an aggressive classifier ($k = 2$) to obtain a lower and upper bound.

We did this prediction only for the apps which were not used for training during the classifier evaluation phase to avoid classifier artificially reporting higher number of spam. Table 12 shows the results. $\mathbb{C}_1$, $\mathbb{C}_2$, and $\mathbb{C}_3$ are three sets of removed apps we identified as described in Section 3.1 and *Others* are the apps in $\mathbb{O}$ which were neither removed nor belong up to top-32x. Thus *Others* apps represent the average apps in Google Play Store and we know that they were there in the market for at least for 6 months, and by time we stopped monitoring they were still there in the market.

According to the results, more aggressive classifier ($k = 2$) predicted around 70% of the removed apps and 55% of the other apps to be spam. The conservative classifier ($k = 32$) predicted 6%–12% of the removed apps and approximately 2.7% of the other apps as spam; this can be considered as the lower bound for the percentage of spam apps currently available in Google Play Store.

7. CONCLUSIONS & FUTURE WORK

In this paper, we propose a classifier for automated detection of spam apps at the time of app submission. Our app classifier utilises only those features that can be derived from an app's metadata available during the publication approval process. It does not require any human intervention such as manual inspection of the metadata or manual app testing. We validate our app classifier, by applying it to a large dataset of apps collected between December 2013 and May 2014, by crawling and identifying apps that were removed from Google Play Store. Our results show that it is possible, to automate the process of detecting spam apps solely based on apps' metadata available at the time of publication and achieve both high precision and recall.

Our experiment suggests approximately 2.7% of the apps on Google Play Store are potentially spam. We plan to apply our rigorous manual labelling process to a sample of these apps and quantify the accuracy of our predictions. In this work, we used all the features mentioned in Section 5 to build the classifier while highlighting most discriminative features using *forward feature selection* on a manual checkpoint basis. Final weights of each features can be studied further to study the trade off between the number of features selected and the classifier's performance. Another interesting direction is to augment the proposed features with features extracted from the app binary and investigate whether the classifier performance can be enhanced.

The manual labelling challenge. In this work, we used a relatively small set (551) of labelled spam apps and used the top apps from the market place as proxies for non-spam apps. Our choices were dictated largely by the time consuming nature of the labelling process as mentioned in Section 3.2. Obviously, the performance of the classifier can be improved by increasing the number of labelled spam apps and further labelling non-spam apps through an extension of our manual effort.

One approach is to rely on crowdsourcing and recruit app-savvy users as reviewers. This in turn would require a major effort of providing individualised guidelines and interactions with the reviewers, and need to deal with assessment inconsistencies due to variable technical expertise. Nonetheless, from an app market provider perspective, this is a plausible option to consider. A framework that can quickly assess whether an app is spam, when the developers submit apps for approval will enable faster approvals whilst reducing the number of spam apps in the market.

Alternatively, hybrid schemes can be developed where apps are flagged during the approval process and removed based on a limited number of customer complaints. Another potential direction is to consider a mix of supervised and unsupervised learning, known as *semi-supervised learning* [5]. The basic idea behind semi-supervised learning is to use "unlabelled data" to improve the classification model that was previously being built using only labelled data. Semi-supervised learning has previously being successfully applied to real-time traffic classification problems [16].

The classification arms race. It is possible that spammers adapt to the spam app detection framework and change their strategies according to our selected features to avoid the detection. The relevant questions in this context are: i) how frequently should the classifier be retrained? and ii) how to detect when retraining is required? We believe that spam app developers will find it challenging and have significant cost overheads to adapt their apps to avoid features that allow discriminating between spam and non-spam apps. For instance, to avoid the similarity of descriptions of multiple apps, the spammer has to edit the different descriptions of the apps and to customise each of the app description to contain sufficient details and coherent text, etc. An important direction for future work is to study the longevity of our classifier. Additionally, we plan to investigate how the process of identifying retraining requirements can be automated. Prior work on traffic classification suggests that automated identification of retraining points is possible using semi-supervised learning approaches [16].

8. ACKNOWLEDGEMENTS

We thank the anonymous reviewers and our shepherd Lenin Ravindranath Sivalingam for constructive feedback on preparation of the final version of this paper.

9. REFERENCES

[1] Language Detection API. http://detectlanguage.com, 2013.
[2] PrivMetrics. http://privmetrics.org/publications, 2014.
[3] I. Androutsopoulos, G. Paliouras, V. Karkaletsis, G. Sakkis, C. D. Spyropoulos, and P. Stamatopoulos. Learning to filter spam e-mail: A comparison of a naive bayesian and a memory-based approach. *arXiv preprint cs/0009009*, 2000.
[4] H. B. Aradhye, G. K. Myers, and J. A. Herson. Image analysis for efficient categorization of image-based spam e-mail. In *Proc. of 8th ICDAR*, pages 914–918. IEEE, 2005.
[5] S. Basu, M. Bilenko, and R. J. Mooney. A probabilistic framework for semi-supervised clustering. In *Proc. of the 10th KDD*, pages 59–68. ACM, 2004.
[6] F. Benevenuto, G. Magno, T. Rodrigues, and V. Almeida. Detecting spammers on Twitter. In *Proc. of the 2010 CEAS*.
[7] E. Blanzieri and A. Bryl. A survey of learning-based techniques of email spam filtering. *Artificial Intelligence Review*, 29(1):63–92, 2008.
[8] I. Burguera, U. Zurutuza, and S. Nadjm-Tehrani. Crowdroid: Behavior-based malware detection system for Android. In *Proc. of the 1st SPSM*, pages 15–26. ACM, 2011.
[9] O. Canales, V. Monaco, T. Murphy, E. Zych, et al. A stylometry system for authenticating students taking online tests. Pace University, 2011.
[10] R. Chandy and H. Gu. Identifying spam in the iOS app store. In *Proc. of the 2nd WebQuality*, pages 56–59. ACM, 2012.
[11] P.-A. Chirita, J. Diederich, and W. Nejdl. Mailrank: Using ranking for spam detection. In *Proc. of the 14th CIKM*, 2005.
[12] G. V. Cormack, J. M. Gómez Hidalgo, and E. P. Sánz. Spam filtering for short messages. In *Proc. of the 16th CIKM*, 2007.
[13] J. Crussell, C. Gibler, and H. Chen. Andarwin: Scalable detection of semantically similar Android applications. In *Computer Security–ESORICS 2013*, pages 182–199. Springer.
[14] H. Drucker, S. Wu, and V. N. Vapnik. Support Vector Machines for spam categorization. *IEEE Transactions on Neural Networks*, 10(5):1048–1054, 1999.
[15] M. Erdélyi, A. Garzó, and A. A. Benczúr. Web spam classification: a few features worth more. In *Proc. of the 2011 WebQuality*, pages 27–34. ACM, 2011.
[16] J. Erman, A. Mahanti, M. Arlitt, I. Cohen, and C. Williamson. Offline/realtime traffic classification using semi-supervised learning. *Performance Evaluation*, 64(9-12):1194–1213, 2007.
[17] D. Fetterly, M. Manasse, and M. Najork. Spam, damn spam, and statistics: Using statistical analysis to locate spam web pages. In *Proc. of the 7th WebDB*, pages 1–6. ACM, 2004.
[18] R. Flesch. A new readability yardstick. *Journal of Applied Psychology*, 32(3):221, 1948.
[19] Y. Freund and R. E. Schapire. Experiments with a new boosting algorithm. In *Proc. of the 13th ICML*, 1996.
[20] J. M. Gómez Hidalgo, G. C. Bringas, E. P. Sánz, and F. C. García. Content based SMS spam filtering. In *Proc. of the 2006 DocEng*, pages 107–114. ACM, 2006.
[21] A. Gorla, I. Tavecchia, F. Gross, and A. Zeller. Checking app behavior against app descriptions. In *Proc. of the 36th ICSE*, pages 1025–1035, 2014.
[22] M. Grace, Y. Zhou, Q. Zhang, S. Zou, and X. Jiang. Riskranker: Scalable and accurate zero-day Android malware detection. In *Proc. of the 10th MobiSys*, pages 281–294. ACM, 2012.
[23] Z. Gyöngyi, H. Garcia-Molina, and J. Pedersen. Combating web spam with trustrank. In *Proc. of the 13th VLDB*, pages 576–587. VLDB Endowment, 2004.
[24] Apple. Inc. App store review guidelines. https://developer.apple.com/app-store/review/, 2014.
[25] Apple. Inc. Common app rejections. https://developer.apple.com/app-store/review/rejections/, 2014.
[26] AVG Threat Labs. Inc. Website safety ratings and reputation. http://www.avgthreatlabs.com/website-safety-reports, 2014.
[27] Google. Inc. Ads. http://developer.android.com/distribute/googleplay/policies/ads.html, 2014.
[28] Google. Inc. Google Play developer program policies. https://play.google.com/about/developer-content-policy.html, 2014.
[29] Google. Inc. Intellectual property. http://developer.android.com/distribute/googleplay/policies/ip.html, 2014.
[30] Google. Inc. Rating your application content for Google Play. https://support.google.com/googleplay/android-developer/answer/188189, 2014.
[31] Google. Inc. Spam. http://developer.android.com/distribute/googleplay/, 2014.
[32] Oracle. Inc. Naming a package. http://docs.oracle.com/javase/tutorial/java/package/namingpkgs.html, 2014.
[33] N. Jindal and B. Liu. Review spam detection. In *Proc. of the 16th WWW*, pages 1189–1190. ACM, 2007.
[34] N. Jindal and B. Liu. Opinion spam and analysis. In *Proc. of the 2008 WSDM*, pages 219–230. ACM, 2008.
[35] R. Kohavi and G. H. John. Wrappers for feature subset selection. *Artificial intelligence*, 97(1):273–324, 1997.
[36] V. Krishnan and R. Raj. Web spam detection with anti-trust rank. In *Proc. of the 2006 AIRWeb*.
[37] B. Leiba, J. Ossher, V. Rajan, R. Segal, and M. N. Wegman. SMTP path analysis. In *Proc. of the 2005 CEAS*.
[38] V. Metsis, I. Androutsopoulos, and G. Paliouras. Spam filtering with naive Bayes-which naive Bayes? In *Proc. of 2006 CEAS*.
[39] G. Mishne, D. Carmel, and R. Lempel. Blocking blog spam with language model disagreement. In *Proc. of the 2005 AIRWeb*.
[40] A. Mukherjee and B. Liu. Improving gender classification of blog authors. In *Proc. of the 2010 EMNLP*, pages 207–217. Association for Computational Linguistics, 2010.
[41] A. Ntoulas, M. Najork, M. Manasse, and D. Fetterly. Detecting spam web pages through content analysis. In *Proc. of the 15th WWW*, pages 83–92. ACM, 2006.
[42] J. Oberheide and C. Miller. Dissecting the Android bouncer. https://jon.oberheide.org/files/summercon12-bouncer.pdf, 2012.
[43] P. Oscar and V. Roychowdbury. Leveraging social networks to fight spam. *IEEE Computer*, 38(4):61–68, 2005.
[44] P. Pantel, D. Lin, et al. Spamcop: A spam classification & organization program. In *Proc. of AAAI-98 Workshop on Learning for Text Categorization*, pages 95–98, 1998.
[45] H. Peng, C. Gates, B. Sarma, N. Li, Y. Qi, R. Potharaju, C. Nita-Rotaru, and I. Molloy. Using probabilistic generative models for ranking risks of Android apps. In *Proc. of the 19th CCS*, pages 241–252. ACM, 2012.
[46] S. Perez. Developer spams Google Play with ripoffs of well-known apps again. http://techcrunch.com, 2013.
[47] S. Perez. Nearly 60K low-quality apps booted from Google Play Store in February. http://techcrunch.com, 2013.
[48] S. Perez. iTunes App Store now has 1.2 million apps, has seen 75 billion downloads to date. http://techcrunch.com, 2014.
[49] D. Rowinski. Apple iOS App Store adding 20,000 apps a month, hits 40 billion downloads. http://readwrite.com, 2013.
[50] M. Sahami, S. Dumais, D. Heckerman, and E. Horvitz. A Bayesian approach to filtering junk e-mail. In *Learning for Text Categorization: Papers from the 1998 workshop*, volume 62, pages 98–105, 1998.
[51] D. Sculley and G. M. Wachman. Relaxed online SVMs for spam filtering. In *Proc. of the 30th SIGIR*. ACM, 2007.
[52] S. Seneviratne, A. Seneviratne, D. Kaafar, A. Mahanti, and P. Mohapatra. Why my app got deleted: Detection of spam mobile apps. Technical report, NICTA, Australia, 2014.
[53] S. Seneviratne, A. Seneviratne, P. Mohapatra, and A. Mahanti. Predicting user traits from a snapshot of apps installed on a smartphone. *ACM SIGMOBILE MC2R*, 18(2):1–8, 2014.
[54] R. Senter and E. Smith. Automated Readability Index. Technical Report AMRL-TR-66-220, Aerospace Medical Research Laboratories, 1967.
[55] I. Soboroff, I. Ounis, J. Lin, and I. Soboroff. Overview of the TREC-2012 microblog track. In *Proc. of the 21st TREC*, 2012.
[56] N. Viennot, E. Garcia, and J. Nieh. A measurement study of Google Play. In *Proc. of the 2014 SIGMETRICS*. ACM, 2014.
[57] A. H. Wang. Don't follow me: Spam detection in Twitter. In *Proc. of the 2010 SECRYPT*, pages 1–10. IEEE, 2010.
[58] Wikipedia. Wikipedia:lists of common misspellings. http://en.wikipedia.org/wiki/, 2014.
[59] Y. Zhou, Z. Wang, W. Zhou, and X. Jiang. Hey, you, get off of my market: Detecting malicious apps in official and alternative Android markets. In *Proc. of the 2012 NDSS*.

N-gram IDF: A Global Term Weighting Scheme Based on Information Distance

Masumi Shirakawa
Osaka University
1-5 Yamadaoka, Suita
Osaka 565-0871, Japan
shirakawa.masumi@ist.osaka-u.ac.jp

Takahiro Hara
Osaka University
1-5 Yamadaoka, Suita
Osaka 565-0871, Japan
hara@ist.osaka-u.ac.jp

Shojiro Nishio
Osaka University
1-5 Yamadaoka, Suita
Osaka 565-0871, Japan
nishio@ist.osaka-u.ac.jp

ABSTRACT

This paper first reveals the relationship between Inverse Document Frequency (IDF), a global term weighting scheme, and information distance, a universal metric defined by Kolmogorov complexity. We concretely give a theoretical explanation that the IDF of a term is equal to the distance between the term and the empty string in the space of information distance in which the Kolmogorov complexity is approximated using Web documents and the Shannon-Fano coding. Based on our findings, we propose *N-gram IDF*, a theoretical extension of IDF for handling words and phrases of any length. By comparing weights among N-grams of any N, N-gram IDF enables us to determine dominant N-grams among overlapping ones and extract key terms of any length from texts without using any NLP techniques. To efficiently compute the weight for all possible N-grams, we adopt two string processing techniques, i.e., maximal substring extraction using enhanced suffix array and document listing using wavelet tree. We conducted experiments on key term extraction and Web search query segmentation, and found that N-gram IDF was competitive with state-of-the-art methods that were designed for each application using additional resources and efforts. The results exemplified the potential of N-gram IDF.

Categories and Subject Descriptors

H.1.1 [**Models and Principles**]: Systems and Information Theory—*information theory*; H.3.1 [**Information Storage and Retrieval**]: Content Analysis and Indexing

General Terms

Experimentation, Measurement, Theory

Keywords

Term Weighting; IDF; Multiword Expression; MED; Information Distance; Kolmogorov Complexity

WWW 2015, May 18–22, 2015, Florence, Italy.
ACM 978-1-4503-3469-3/15/05.
http://dx.doi.org/10.1145/2736277.2741628.

1. INTRODUCTION

Term weighting schemes as represented by TF-IDF [42], short for Term Frequency-Inverse Document Frequency, are fundamental technologies for text analysis. TF-IDF was originally introduced as a weighting factor of each word in document retrieval where a document is represented by a vector of words that occur in it. Afterwards TF-IDF has become a de facto standard of term weighting scheme for bag-of-words representation of text documents in information retrieval and text mining. Today it has been also used for explicitly highlighting key terms in texts in the area of natural language processing [19].

Term weighting schemes can be usually decomposed by two components: local term weighting scheme and global term weighting scheme. Local term weighting schemes give a weight to a term using its local document information such as term frequency and term co-occurrence in a target document. The local weight of a certain term varies depending on the document where the term occurs. Global term weighting schemes use global document information such as document frequency and total term frequency over documents. The global weight of a certain term is fixed, that is, it is independent from the target document in which the term occurs.

Representative term weighting schemes include TF-IDF, Okapi BM25 [37] and recently proposed TW-IDF [39]. Each weight for term t in document $d \in D$ is specifically computed as below

$$TF\text{-}IDF(t,d) = tf(t,d) \cdot \log \frac{|D|}{df(t)}$$

$$BM25(t,d) = \frac{(k_1+1) \cdot tf(t,d)}{k_1 \cdot (1 - b + b \cdot \frac{|d|}{avdl}) + tf(t,d)} \cdot \log \frac{|D|}{df(t)}$$

$$TW\text{-}IDF(t,d) = \frac{tw(t,d)}{1 - b + b \cdot \frac{|d|}{avdl}} \cdot \log \frac{|D|}{df(t)}$$

where $tf(t,d)$ is the term frequency of t in d, $df(t)$ is the document frequency of t over document set D, $|D|$ is the cardinality of D (i.e., total number of documents in D), $|d|$ is the length of d (i.e., total number of words in d), $avdl$ is the average length of documents in D, $tw(t,d)$ is a graph-based tf-like function, and k_1 and b are constant values[1]. Whereas they are very different regarding their local term

[1]Reasonable values are to set k_1 to a value between 1.2 and 2, and $b = 0.75$ [26].

weighting schemes, they use the same global term weighting scheme, i.e., IDF [21].

$$IDF(t) = \log \frac{|D|}{df(t)} \quad (1)$$

The reason why IDF is adopted in the representative term weighting schemes lies in its simplicity and robustness. The simplicity is easily understandable from Eq. (1). Even as the simplicity, IDF has proven to be justified and robust by the literature [2, 16, 27, 32, 36]. There are some choices of global term weighting schemes such as Residual IDF (RIDF) [8] and gain [32] other than IDF. IDF, however, has been chosen in many cases because of its simplicity (i.e., one can easily use it without the knowledge) and robustness (i.e., it works reasonably well for most applications).

One of the main drawbacks of IDF is that it cannot handle N-grams for $N > 1$, or phrases, which are composed of two or more words. IDF gives more weight to terms occurring in less documents. However, phrases occur in less documents when their collocations are more awkward. Consequently, awkward phrases unintentionally gain much weight. For example, estimated document frequencies of "Osaka University" and "Osaka be" using Google Search[2] were 1,890,000 and 6,160 respectively, resulting in that the latter gained far more IDF weight. The definition of IDF thus totally acts counter to the definition of good phrases.

Aside from term weighting schemes, a considerable number of studies have been made on extracting phrases, or Multiword Expressions (MWEs). Pointwise Mutual Information (PMI) [9] and Multiword Expression Distance (MED) [7] are representative solid schemes to measure a score that defines how likely a sequence of consecutive words is to compose a phrase. The score just indicates the compositionality of words, that is, it does not indicate how important the composed phrase is. To the best of our knowledge, there is no theoretical explanation that deals with both term weighting and multiword expression extraction. Weighting terms of any length so far requires heuristics.

This paper tackles a challenge of bridging the theoretical gap between term weighting and multiword expression extraction. In particular, we connect IDF and MED in the space of information distance [3]. Information distance is a universal metric defined by Kolmogorov complexity [22, 25]. MED is a theoretically justified information distance-based metric for multiword expression extraction that works better than PMI and several heuristic measures. We evince the relationship between IDF and information distance to connect it with MED. Our findings enable us to design schemes for handling both problems, i.e., term weighting and multiword expression extraction at the same time.

We also propose a term weighting scheme, *N-gram IDF*, that can handle terms of any length by combining IDF and MED in the space of information distance. N-gram IDF is capable of weighting phrases (i.e., N-grams for $N > 1$) as well as words in a sole theoretical scheme. It is therefore able to compare weights among words and phrases. Using N-gram IDF, we can obtain dominant N-grams among overlapping ones and extract key terms of any length from texts without using NLP techniques. We verify the simplicity and robustness of N-gram IDF by two applications: key term extraction and Web search query segmentation.

[2]Results were retrieved on November 9, 2014.

The remainder of this paper is organized as follows: Section 2 describes related work on term weighting and multiword expression extraction. Section 3 gives a yet another justification of IDF using Kolmogorov complexity and information distance. Based on our findings presented in Section 3, we propose N-gram IDF in Section 4. Section 5 illustrates how to compute N-gram IDF using efficient data structures that have been developed in the area of string processing. We show the potential of N-gram IDF on a couple of applications in Section 6. Finally, we conclude our work in Section 7.

2. RELATED WORK

Term weighting schemes are vital for text-related applications and hence have been well studied. TF-IDF [41] is the most popular (general-purpose) term weighting scheme among representative ones, followed by Okapi BM25 [37]. In addition to the effectiveness of TF-IDF in various applications such as information retrieval [46], document clustering [14], key term extraction [19] and object matching in videos [44], many theoretical explanations [2, 20, 36, 38] encourage researchers and developers to employ TF-IDF. Based on or inspired by TF-IDF, heuristically improved schemes such as TW-IDF [39] have been proposed.

The most popular global term weighting scheme is IDF [21], which has been adopted by TF-IDF, BM25 and TW-IDF. There are many alternatives such as x^I [5], z-measure [18], Residual IDF (RIDF) [8] and gain [32]. However, IDF is still a de facto standard of global term weighting scheme. This is due to the simplicity and robustness of IDF against the alternatives. Even as its simplicity of just computing $\log \frac{|D|}{df(t)}$, IDF has many justifications [2, 16, 27, 32, 36] to back up its robustness. In other words, it is difficult to beat IDF without using heuristics. Some reported that RIDF was superior to IDF in certain applications [31, 35]. This supports that RIDF can be a good alternative of IDF, though it is heuristic and the performance in other applications or datasets is not guaranteed. Specialized global term weighting schemes like Inverse Corpus Frequency (ICF) [34], designed for analyzing text stream, and Relevant Frequency (RF) [23], for text classification, can also be alternatives in the target applications.

As can be seen from the fact that there are many alternatives, IDF has some drawbacks to be improved. Among them, critical, but not solved one is that it is unable to handle phrases. Handling phrases requires the measurement of word compositionality, i.e., measuring how much the collocation is natural, as well as the term weighting. The measurement of the word compositionality, or Multiword Expression (MWE) extraction, has been an object of study for a long time. Pointwise Mutual Information (PMI) [9] and their variations are popular and effective for measuring the word compositionality [6, 12, 13, 43, 48]. Theoretically defined PMI was originally developed for measuring the association between a couple of words. Among 84 measures, PMI was the best for measuring the bi-gram compositionality [33]. When it comes to N-grams for $N > 2$, PMI needs to be extended to cope with them. Some literature heuristically extends PMI by computing the arithmetic average of [13, 12] or the best score among every possible separation [43]. Enhanced Mutual Information (EMI) [48] is another extension of PMI, measuring the cohesion of an N-gram by using the frequency of each word. Symmetric Conditional Probability (SCP) [12] is a measure similar to PMI and extended for N-grams for $N > 2$ by using the arithmetic average.

Recently proposed Multiword Expression Distance (MED) [7] is a theoretically justified measure of the word (non-)compositionality for N-grams for $N > 1$ based on information distance [3]. It has proven to be better than the heuristic extensions of PMI and SCP described above. Since MED is deeply related to our work, we minutely describe it in Section 3. At this time, we can conclude that MED is the most promising measure of the word compositionality based on a solid theory.

Term weighting and multiword expression extraction, as above, have been separately studied. One is for weighting terms and the other is for measuring the compositionality of consecutive words. No theoretical explanation, however, has been given to handle both problems. In this work, we first give a theoretical explanation that connects IDF, a global term weighting scheme, and MED, a measure for multiword expression extraction.

3. IDF AND INFORMATION DISTANCE

In this section, we uncover the relationship between IDF and information distance through explaining Kolmogorov complexity, information distance and Multiword Expression Distance (MED).

3.1 Kolmogorov Complexity

Kolmogorov complexity [22, 25] is a measure of the randomness of a (bit) string. It is also known as descriptive complexity, algorithmic entropy or program-size complexity, namely indicating the minimum amount of resources to describe a string on a universal Turing machine. We define $K(x)$ as the Kolmogorov complexity of string x. $K(x)$ is specifically the length of the shortest program that outputs x. For example, given strings x_1 and x_2,

$$x_1 = \text{“0101010101010101 00”}$$
$$x_2 = \text{“011101100010110010”}$$

x_1 can be shortly described as "01" ×8+ "00" whereas x_2 seems to be difficult to shorten. We can thus estimate that $K(x_1)$ is smaller than $K(x_2)$. Because the exact value of the Kolmogorov complexity is not computable, it is usually approximated by using compression algorithms [10] or Web documents [11].

We also define $K(x|y)$ as the conditional Kolmogorov complexity of string x given another string y. $K(x|y)$ is the length of the shortest program that outputs x from input y. Given that ϵ is the empty string, $K(x)$ can be written as $K(x|\epsilon)$. Given strings x_1, x_2 and y,

$$x_1 = \text{“010101010101010100”}$$
$$x_2 = \text{“011101100010110010”}$$
$$y = \text{“01110110001011001”}$$

x_2 can be efficiently described as $y+$ "0" using y. Consequently, $K(x_2|y)$ might be slightly smaller than $K(x_1|y)$. It is noteworthy that $K(x, y)$, the Kolmogorov complexity of the concatenated string of strings x and y, is expressed as

$$K(x, y) = K(x|y) + K(y) = K(y|x) + K(x) \quad (2)$$

up to an additive logarithmic term. Eq. (2) intuitively means that one string can be reused to describe the other.

3.2 Information Distance

Information distance [3] is a universal metric defined by the Kolmogorov complexity. It is an application-independent, unique objective distance just exactly like the distance in the physical world. It is actually the energy cost for transforming one string to the other. According to Landauer's principle [24], irreversibly processing one bit of information costs $1k\mathcal{T} \cdot ln(2)$ where k is the Boltzmann constant and $\mathcal{T}$ is the absolute temperature in Kelvin. Based on the Landauer's principle and the Kolmogorov complexity, information distance $E(x, y)$ between two strings x and y is defined as

$$E(x, y) = \max\{K(x|y), K(y|x)\} \quad (3)$$

up to an additive logarithmic term. Eq. (3) is transformed into the following equation using Eq. (2).

$$E(x, y) = K(x, y) - \min\{K(y), K(x)\} \quad (4)$$

Information distance has proven to be a metric, or a distance function, i.e., it satisfies non-negativity, identity of indiscernibles, symmetry and triangle inequality, which are respectively represented by the following formulas.

$$E(x, y) \geq 0$$
$$E(x, y) = 0 \Leftrightarrow x = y$$
$$E(x, y) = E(y, x)$$
$$E(x, z) \leq E(x, y) + E(y, z)$$

Moreover, information distance has been shown to be universal, or optimal. Distance $\mathcal{D}(x, y)$ is said to be admissible (i.e., an upper-semicomputable and normalized metric) if it satisfies the following density condition (Kraft's inequality).

$$\sum_{y:y \neq x} 2^{-\mathcal{D}(x,y)} \leq 1, \quad \sum_{x:x \neq y} 2^{-\mathcal{D}(x,y)} \leq 1$$

The density condition restricts the number of objects within a given distance from an object. When $\mathcal{D}(x, y)$ is admissible, there is a constant C for all x and y, and

$$E(x, y) \leq \mathcal{D}(x, y) + C.$$

Thus, $E(x, y)$ minorizes every admissible distance $\mathcal{D}(x, y)$ up to an additive constant, indicating that information distance is universal.

Information distance is generally utilized for measuring the similarity between two objects. Because the exact value of the information distance is not computable as well as the Kolmogorov complexity, it is computed using approximations such as Normalized Compression Distance (NCD) [10] and Normalized Google Distance (NGD) [11]. NCD measures the compression size of the concatenated string of x and y versus that of each string. NGD is intended for texts, counting the number of Web pages containing both terms x and y versus the number of Web pages containing each term. Cilibrasi and Vitányi [11] reported that the distance estimated by NGD was stable for the growing Web. It can be guessed that the stability comes from the universality of information distance.

3.3 Multiword Expression Distance

Multiword Expression Distance (MED) [7] is a universal metric for measuring the word compositionality based on the information distance. It in particular computes the information distance between the context and semantic of an N-gram. Inspired by Cilibrasi and Vitányi [11], Bu et al. [7] defined the context of an N-gram as the set of Web pages containing it and the semantic of an N-gram as the set of Web pages containing every word composing it. Obviously, the semantic of an N-gram subsumes the context of the N-gram. For example, the semantic of "football player" includes not only Web pages containing itself but also those containing "football" and "player."

Let us formulate MED according to Bu et al. [7]. We denote w as a word (uni-gram), W as a set of all words, g as an N-gram, $G \equiv W^+$ as a set of all N-grams, D as a set of all Web pages (documents), t as a search term that is an N-gram or the conjunction of search terms and T as a set of all search terms (namely, $G \subset T$). Let $\phi : T \to 2^D$ be the context function that maps a search term t to a set of Web pages containing all the N-grams in t, denoted by $\phi(t)$. Let $\theta : G \to T$ be the function that maps an N-gram $g = w_1 ... w_N$ to $\bigwedge_{i=1}^{N} w_i$, the conjunction of words composing g, denoted by $\theta(g)$. Let $\mu : G \to 2^D$ be the semantic function that is a composite function $\phi \circ \theta$, that is, $\mu(g) = \phi(\theta(g))$. From the definitions, we have $\phi(g) \subseteq \mu(g)$. Given an N-gram g, MED is defined as the information distance between $\phi(g)$, the context of g, and $\mu(g)$, the semantic of g. Using Eq. (4), MED is formulated as follows.

$$\begin{aligned} MED(g) &= E(\phi(g), \mu(g)) \\ &= K(\phi(g), \mu(g)) - \min\{K(\phi(g)), K(\mu(g))\} \end{aligned} \quad (5)$$

To approximately compute the Kolmogorov complexity $K(x)$, MED utilizes Shannon-Fano coding to encode the probability of x. We assume that all Web pages are equiprobable, i.e., the probability that a Web page is chosen is $\frac{1}{|D|}$. Let $p : \phi(T) \to [0, 1]$ be the context probability function where $\phi(T)$ is a set of all contexts, namely $\phi(T) \equiv \{x | \exists y \in T, x = \phi(y)\}$. Because each context is a set of Web pages, the probability of context c is defined as

$$p(c) = \frac{|c|}{M} \quad (6)$$

where $M = \sum_{c_i \in \phi(T)} p(c_i)$. This informally says that the probability that a set of Web pages c is chosen is proportional to the cardinality of c. Consequently, the Kolmogorov complexity K can be approximated by using the Shannon-Fano code [25] length associated with p.

$$K(x) \approx -\log p(x) \quad (7)$$

$$K(x, y) \approx -\log p(x, y) \quad (8)$$

Using Eqs. (6), (7) and (8), Eq. (5) is approximated as

$$\begin{aligned} &MED(g) \\ &\approx \max\{\log p(\phi(g)), \log p(\mu(g))\} - \log p(\phi(g), \mu(g)) \\ &= \max\{\log |\phi(g)|, \log |\mu(g)|\} - \log M \\ &\quad - \log |\phi(g) \cap \mu(g)| + \log M \\ &= \max\{\log |\phi(g)|, \log |\mu(g)|\} - \log |\phi(g) \cap \mu(g)|. \end{aligned} \quad (9)$$

Since $\phi(g) \subseteq \mu(g)$, Eq. (9) is finally

$$MED(g) \approx \log |\mu(g)| - \log |\phi(g)| = \log \frac{|\mu(g)|}{|\phi(g)|}. \quad (10)$$

Eq. (10) can be computed using the cardinality of $\phi(g)$ and $\mu(g)$. Specifically, $|\phi(g)|$ is the document frequency of g and $|\mu(g)|$ is the document frequency of $\theta(g)$, a conjunction of words composing g. In the literature [7], $|\phi(g)|$ and $|\mu(g)|$ are estimated by using a general search engine. The document frequency of $\theta(g)$ is obtained from the query of "logic and" of each word w_i in g.

3.4 Inverse Document Frequency

Here, we reveal the relationship between IDF and information distance based on the above discussions. Just like Eq. (1), we define IDF of an N-gram g as follows.

$$IDF(g) = \log \frac{|D|}{df(g)} = \log \frac{|D|}{|\phi(g)|} \quad (11)$$

We can be aware that IDF (Eq. (11)) and MED (Eq. (10)) are analogous to each other in their mathematical forms. The difference is that the numerator in the logarithmic term is $|D|$ in IDF contrast to $|\mu(g)|$ in MED. Are there any relationships between IDF and information distance? We further investigate the answer to this question.

Let us denote the empty string, or zero-gram, by ϵ. Define $\epsilon \in G$ and $G \equiv W^*$. $\phi(\epsilon)$ is a set of Web pages containing ϵ. Clearly, ϵ is contained in all Web pages. $\phi(\epsilon)$ is therefore equal to D, a set of all Web pages. We then derive the information distance between N-gram g and the empty string ϵ. $E(\phi(g), \phi(\epsilon))$ is specifically defined as

$$E(\phi(g), \phi(\epsilon)) = K(\phi(g), \phi(\epsilon)) - \min\{K(\phi(g)), K(\phi(\epsilon))\}. \quad (12)$$

As well as the derivation of MED, Eq. (12) can also be transformed into

$$\begin{aligned} &E(\phi(g), \phi(\epsilon)) \\ &\approx \max\{\log p(\phi(g)), \log p(\phi(\epsilon))\} - \log p(\phi(g), \phi(\epsilon)) \\ &= \max\{\log |\phi(g)|, \log |\phi(\epsilon)|\} - \log M \\ &\quad - \log |\phi(g) \cap \phi(\epsilon)| + \log M \\ &= \max\{\log |\phi(g)|, \log |\phi(\epsilon)|\} - \log |\phi(g) \cap \phi(\epsilon)|. \end{aligned} \quad (13)$$

Because apparently $\phi(g) \subseteq \phi(\epsilon)$, Eq. (13) becomes

$$\begin{aligned} E(\phi(g), \phi(\epsilon)) &\approx \log |\phi(\epsilon)| - \log |\phi(g)| \\ &= \log \frac{|\phi(\epsilon)|}{|\phi(g)|} \\ &= \log \frac{|D|}{|\phi(g)|} \\ &= IDF(g). \end{aligned}$$

We finally obtain the relationship between IDF and information distance, i.e., IDF of an N-gram g is equal to the information distance between $\phi(g)$ and $\phi(\epsilon)$.

Let us summarize our findings on IDF and information distance. In the space of information distance in which the Kolmogorov complexity is approximated using Web documents and the Shannon-Fano coding, the IDF of a term is equal to the distance between the term and the empty string, which is normally the base of the Kolmogorov complexity. The information distance can therefore be used as the global weight of terms. The farther a term is from the empty string in the space of information distance, the larger its weight is. We can henceforth design term weighting schemes in the space of information distance. Our findings are substantially useful because it becomes far easier to combine term weighting with MED, an information distance-based metric for multiword expression extraction. In next section, we show a theoretically justified combination of IDF and MED for weighting N-grams of any N.

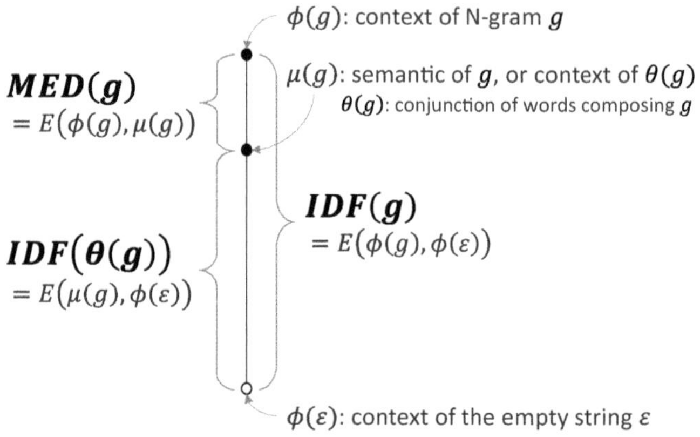

Figure 1: Relationship between IDF and MED in the space of information distance where the Kolmogorov complexity is approximated using Web documents and the Shannon-Fano coding. $\phi(g)$, $\mu(g)$ and $\phi(\epsilon)$ are on a line, i.e., the equity holds in the triangle inequity.

4. N-GRAM IDF

We propose a global term weighting scheme that is capable of handling terms of any length, namely N-grams for $N \geq 1$, based on the information distance. In Section 3, we revealed that the IDF of an N-gram is equal to the information distance between the N-gram and the empty string when the Kolmogorov complexity is approximated using Web documents and the Shannon-Fano coding. Similarly, the MED of an N-gram is the information distance between the N-gram and the conjunction of words composing the N-gram. Figure 1 shows the relationship between IDF and MED in the space of information distance. In this space, N-gram g, the conjunction of words $\theta(g)$ and the empty string ϵ are represented as the sets of Web pages $\phi(g)$, $\mu(g)$ and $\phi(\epsilon)$ respectively. Note that the equity holds in the triangle inequity, i.e., $E(\phi(g), \phi(\epsilon)) = E(\phi(g), \mu(g)) + E(\mu(g), \phi(\epsilon))$.

$$\begin{aligned} E(\phi(g), \mu(g)) + E(\mu(g), \phi(\epsilon)) &= \log \frac{|\mu(g)|}{|\phi(g)|} + \log \frac{|D|}{|\mu(g)|} \\ &= \log \frac{|D|}{|\phi(g)|} \\ &= E(\phi(g), \phi(\epsilon)) \end{aligned}$$

The challenge in this work is to theoretically connect the term weighting and multiword expression extraction, both of which have been separately studied for a long time. IDF gives too much weight to an N-gram for $N > 1$ when the collocation of the N-gram is awkward. In that case, MED should also be large since it exactly measures how much the collocation of the N-gram is awkward. Taken together, it seems reasonable to give more weight to an N-gram when its IDF is large and its MED is small. We can consider two of such schemes in the space of information distance (Figure 1): one is using $IDF(\theta(g))$ instead of $IDF(g)$ and the other is using both $IDF(\theta(g))$ and $MED(g)$.

$IDF(\theta(g))$ is the IDF of $\theta(g)$, the conjunction of words composing N-gram g. As can be seen in Figure 1, it is equivalent to $IDF(g) - MED(g)$. In other words, it is the information distance between $\theta(g)$ and the empty string ϵ. In particular, $IDF(\theta(g))$ is computed as

$$IDF(\theta(g)) = \log \frac{|D|}{|\mu(g)|} = \log \frac{|D|}{df(\theta(g))}. \tag{14}$$

This can give somewhat reasonable weight to N-grams. However, the weight monotonically grows as N increases, that is, the weight for N-grams of different N cannot be compared.

The other, and more promising, scheme is $IDF(\theta(g)) - MED(g)$. We can explain this by "how much the distance from the empty string to the semantic of g can be shortened by giving the context of g." In Section 3, we revealed that the distance in the space of information distance represents the weight of a term. Here, we measure the distance in an indirect manner. We name it N-gram IDF, and it is specifically computed as follows.

$$\begin{aligned} IDF_{N\text{-}gram}(g) &= IDF(\theta(g)) - MED(g) \\ &= \log \frac{|D|}{|\mu(g)|} - \log \frac{|\mu(g)|}{|\phi(g)|} \\ &= \log \frac{|D|}{|\mu(g)|} + \log \frac{|\phi(g)|}{|\mu(g)|} \\ &= \log \frac{|D| \cdot |\phi(g)|}{|\mu(g)|^2} \\ &= \log \frac{|D| \cdot df(g)}{df(\theta(g))^2} \end{aligned} \tag{15}$$

When $N = 1$, both $IDF_{N\text{-}gram}(g)$ and $IDF(\theta(g))$ correspond to $IDF(g)$ because $\theta(g) = g$, i.e., $df(\theta(g)) = df(g)$.

We found that the weight given by N-gram IDF (Eq. (15)) is surprisingly stable for any N. Table 1 shows examples of N-gram IDF for a couple of texts (the weight is computed in Section 5). An important feature of N-gram IDF is the comparability of weights among N-grams of different N. We can therefore establish the dominance relationship among weights of all N-grams in a text to handle overlapping N-grams. We define dominant N-grams as those having the maximum weight of at least one position (word) of a given text, except those having the maximum weight of a single stop word, as shown in Figure 2. It rarely occurs that overlapping N-grams have the same weight. We can introduce a simple rule that adopts longer and prefix match among them. The number of dominant N-grams does not exceed the length of the text because one position of the text corresponds to a dominant N-gram. From Table 1, we can confirm that N-gram IDF weights are stable regardless of N and dominant N-grams are well determined across different N.

5. IMPLEMENTATION

The computation of MED or N-gram IDF is not easy at all. Specifically, computing the document frequency of "logic and" of words requires much computational cost. Bu et al. [7] adopted an ad hoc approach that utilizes a general Web search engine to estimate the document frequency of the conjunction of words. However, it is difficult to compute them for all possible N-grams. Also, how to know all possible N-grams in a text corpus is an issue.

In order to solve the problems, we introduce two string processing techniques. First, we use enhanced suffix array [1] (as an alternative of suffix tree) to enumerate valid N-grams of any length. The idea originates from the equivalence class

Table 1: Examples of N-gram IDF. Dominant N-grams are indicated in boldface with asterisk. Detail of the dominant N-grams for the left text is represented in Figure 2.

Alice's Adventures in Wonderland - Kindle edition by Lewis Carroll		Fossil fuels must be phased out "almost entirely" by 2100 to avoid dangerous climate change	
***kindle edition**	12.043	***fossil fuels**	11.211
kindle	11.653	2100	10.772
***alice s adventures in wonderland**	11.496	fuels	9.752
adventures in wonderland	10.906	***phased**	9.391
s adventures in wonderland	10.804	phased out	9.291
wonderland	9.670	fossil	8.332
***lewis carroll**	9.498	***dangerous climate change**	8.249
alice s adventures	9.385	climate change	7.432
alice s adventures in	9.348	be phased out	6.828
in wonderland	8.762	by 2100	6.814
carroll	8.152	be phased	6.783
by lewis carroll	7.461	dangerous	6.749
alice	7.234	climate	6.575
adventures	7.101	dangerous climate	6.549
kindle edition by	6.739	***almost entirely**	6.118
lewis	6.192	***avoid**	6.063
edition	4.836	entirely	5.973
adventures in	4.280	to avoid	5.831
s adventures	3.586	2100 to	5.031
alice s	3.507	***must**	4.703
s adventures in	2.255	change	4.646
by lewis	1.768	almost	4.469
s	1.030	fuels must	4.283
by	0.820	must be phased	4.013
in	0.154	must be phased out	4.010
edition by	-0.875	must be	3.831
		fuels must be	3.478
		avoid dangerous	2.998
		out	2.612
		to avoid dangerous	2.575
		entirely by	2.055
		almost entirely by	1.984
		be	1.860
		by	0.820
		to	0.505
		out almost	-2.826

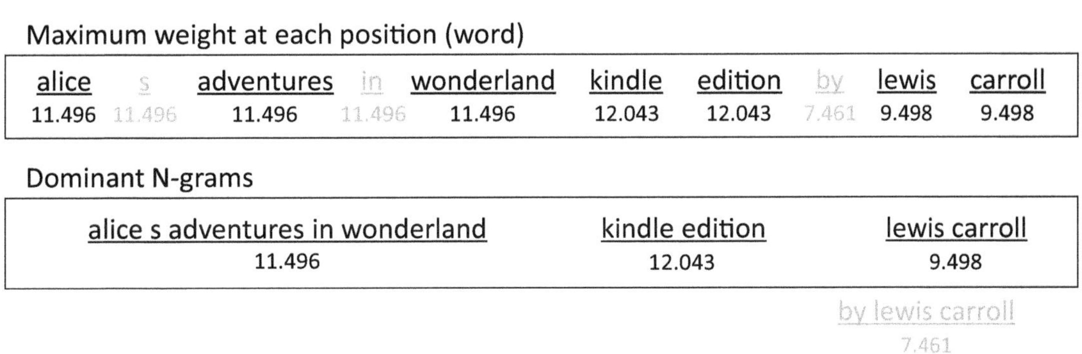

Figure 2: Example of dominant N-grams for the left text of Table 1. "by lewis carroll" is not a dominant N-gram because it only dominates single stop word "by."

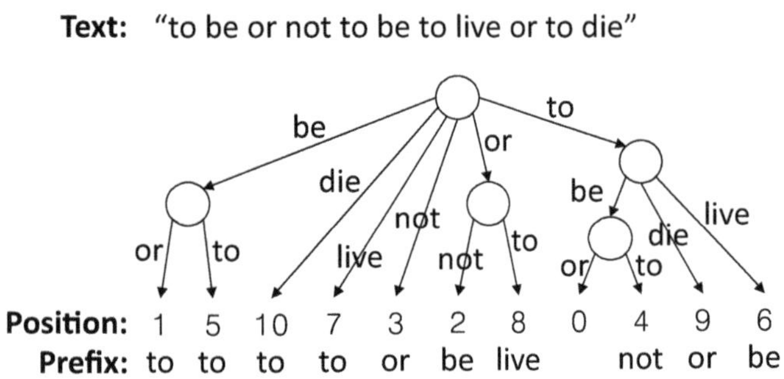

Figure 3: Example of enhanced suffix array (as an alternative of suffix tree). Intermediate nodes having multiple child nodes are candidates of the maximal substring ("be," "or," "to" and "to be"). Because maximal substring should also have multiple prefixes, "be" is not a maximal substring.

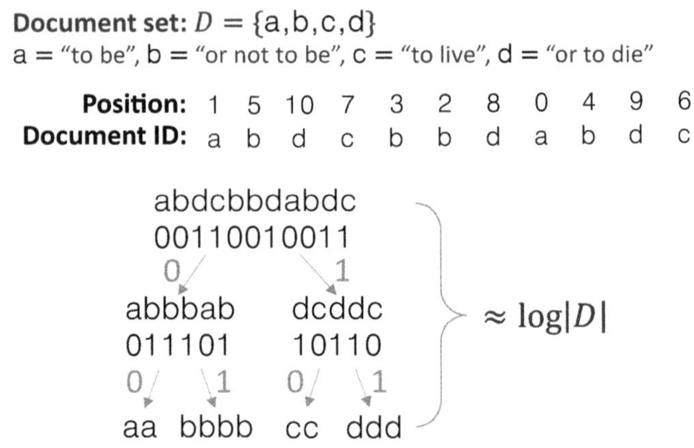

Figure 4: Example of wavelet tree for document IDs.

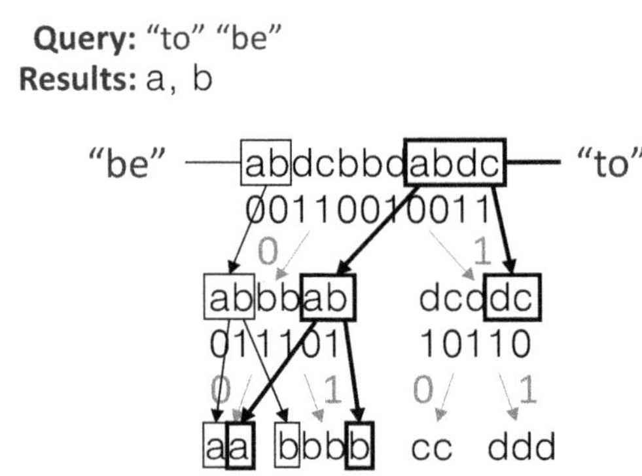

Figure 5: Example of wavelet tree-based document listing for the conjunction of words as a query.

of substrings that occur in (roughly) the same positions and have the same frequency [4]. It is guaranteed that the number of equivalence classes is less than twice of the length of a text. The literature [29, 30] proposed efficient algorithms to enumerate the longest substring (maximal substring) for every equivalence class in linear time using suffix tree or enhanced suffix array. Maximal substrings should be intermediate nodes having multiple child nodes in the suffix tree. Figure 3 illustrates an example of the suffix tree for text "to be or not to be to live or to die." Among all N-grams, "be," "or," "to" and "to be" have multiple child nodes. Maximal substrings should also have multiple prefixes. By memorizing prefixes for every N-gram, we can find that the prefix of "be" is unique, i.e., "to." Consequently, we obtain three maximal substrings "or," "to" and "to be." In this work, we adopt the algorithm [30] and library esaxx[3] to obtain all maximal substrings as valid N-grams.

Second, we utilize wavelet tree [17] for counting the document frequency of the conjunction of words. Wavelet tree is a succinct data structure that has recently been used for various purposes. Gagie et al. [15] showed that it can be used for document listing or counting the document frequency. While suffix array can be used for counting the document frequency of all N-grams [47], wavelet tree also enables us to count the document frequency of the conjunction of words. The time complexities are $O(df(g) \cdot \log|D|)$ for N-gram g and $O(N \cdot df(\theta(g)) \cdot \log|D|)$ for $\theta(g)$, the conjunction of words composing g. According to the literature [15], the latter time complexity is close to the lower bound. We adopt the document listing algorithm [15] and use library wat-array[4].

Let us describe the process flow to compute the N-gram IDF weight for all valid N-grams. Given a set of documents D as a single concatenated text[5], our implementation first enumerates valid N-grams by building the enhanced suffix array for the input text. Along with the first process, it obtains a list of document identifiers (document IDs) sorted by texts, not by document IDs. By doing this, we can represent all documents containing a certain N-gram by a region in the list. It next builds the wavelet tree for document IDs. Figure 4 illustrates an example of the wavelet tree. After sorting the concatenated text, i.e., "to be or not to be to live or to die" in Figure 3, the wavelet tree for the list of document IDs is constructed. Specifically, it is the full binary tree that classifies each document ID into either of the child nodes (0 or 1) until every child node contains a sole document ID, and keeps the order of the document IDs within a node. This enables us to find the corresponding position in a child node for a given position by using *rank* and *select* operations in $O(1)$ time [15]. Finally, it counts the document frequencies of the N-gram and the conjunction of words using the wavelet tree for every valid N-gram. Since all documents containing an N-gram is represented by a region in the list, the document frequency is counted by traversing the wavelet tree and counting the number of leaf nodes. Figure 5 shows how to list all documents containing multiple words using the wavelet tree that is built in Figure 4. Given multiple words "to" and "be" as a conjunctive query, it traverses the wavelet tree and finds leaf nodes "a" and "b" that can be reached from all the words in the query.

We coded a program that can process a set of documents to extract all valid N-grams and their N-gram IDF weight using esaxx and wat-array. Using the program, we processed English Wikipedia dump data as of Oct. 1, 2013. When

[3]https://code.google.com/p/esaxx/

[4]https://code.google.com/p/wat-array/

[5]Practically a control character is inserted between documents to identify the beginning and ending of each document.

processing it, we omitted the capitalization information. To further reduce the processing time, we introduced some techniques: $N \leq 10$ limitation, reuse of the results of overlapping N-grams and dynamic threshold of the document frequency, i.e., $\frac{1}{2000}$ of every constituent word. It still took 12 days using two high-memory (more than 60GB) machines to process 11GB of the Wikipedia corpus. Our program as well as the processed data, its demonstration page and datasets for key term extraction that are used in Section 6.1 can be found on the Web page[6].

6. EXPERIMENTS

We evaluated the robustness of N-gram IDF on two applications. To sum up, N-gram IDF achieved promising results for key term extraction and query segmentation. In fact, we also tried to use N-gram IDF as the bag-of-words feature in information retrieval, document clustering and document classification, though N-grams for $N > 1$ did not contribute to the performance regardless of the weighting scheme.

6.1 Key Term Extraction

We conducted experiments on key term extraction using Wikipedia datasets. In Wikipedia, key terms are highlighted as anchor texts that are linked to their Wikipedia articles. We hence used anchor texts as well as emphasized texts (bold texts) as correct key terms. Given a Wikipedia article, each method extracted terms from the text, calculated the weight for the terms and created a ranked list of key terms based on the weight. We then measured R-Prec, which is the precision of top R terms for R correct key terms. To reduce the effect of local term weighting schemes, we built a dataset using first paragraphs of randomly chosen articles. In short texts, $TF = 1$ challenge [45] exists, i.e., local term weighting scheme TF outputs 1 in most cases. We can therefore look into the performance of global term weighting schemes using short text datasets. The created dataset specifically contains 1,678 short texts in which there are 60.2 words (max: 291, min: 8) and 6.7 key terms[7] (max: 30, min: 3) on average.

Our N-gram IDF scheme can extract candidates of the key term and rank them based only on the weight. That is, dominant N-grams in a text are the candidates of the key term. The combination of TF and N-gram IDF, named N-gram TF-IDF, was employed in this experiment. As a comparative method, we employed POS tagging-based method using TF-IDF [19], which has proven to be robust. It first enumerates all noun phrases (NPs) by extracting consecutive words of NN* or JJ tags, and next measures the weight of NPs by summing the TF-IDF weight of each word. We named it TF-IDF sum with NPs. We also compared some versions of this: TF-IDF avg with NPs (using average IDF of all words) and TF-IDF with NPs (using IDF of the phrase). As the baseline, we used TF-IDF uni-gram, which only focuses on single words. All (single) stop words including numbers were removed from the candidates of the key term. Note that all global term weighting schemes except N-gram IDF are incapable of extracting key phrases by themselves. Even more, N-gram IDF is capable of extracting key terms other than simple noun phrases such as movie titles and television programs. We also evaluated POS tagging-based methods on decapitalized texts (No-Cap) to see the influence of the formality of the text.

Table 2: Performance of key term extraction on Wikipedia first paragraph dataset.

Method	R-Prec
N-gram TF-IDF	0.377
TF-IDF sum with NPs	0.386
TF-IDF sum with NPs, No-Cap	0.369
TF-IDF avg with NPs	0.367
TF-IDF avg with NPs, No-Cap	0.352
TF-IDF with NPs	0.369
TF-IDF with NPs, No-Cap	0.355
TF-IDF uni-gram	0.229

Table 3: Performance of key term extraction on Wikipedia full text dataset.

Method	R-Prec	Prec@10
N-gram TF-IDF	0.300	0.358
TF-IDF sum with NPs	0.317	0.427
TF-IDF sum with NPs, No-Cap	0.301	0.409
TF-IDF avg with NPs	0.283	0.359
TF-IDF avg with NPs, No-Cap	0.269	0.333
TF-IDF with NPs	0.282	0.355
TF-IDF with NPs, No-Cap	0.270	0.341
TF-IDF uni-gram	0.154	0.200

Table 2 shows the performance results of key term extraction. TF-IDF sum with NPs achieved the best precision of 0.386, followed by N-gram TF-IDF achieving 0.377. Among POS tagging-based methods, summing the TF-IDF weight was better than averaging the weight or directly using the weight of N-grams. TF-IDF uni-gram was apparently worse than the others because it did not extract any phrases, also resulting in extracting incorrect words (unigrams) that should compose phrases. It was surprising that N-gram TF-IDF was very competitive with the robust POS tagging-based method [19] by just using the term weight. When the capitalization information was missing, N-gram TF-IDF slightly outperformed TF-IDF sum with NPs. Taking it into consideration that the focus of text analysis has been shifting toward short and informal texts such as social media, N-gram IDF has advantages in real situations.

We also evaluated the methods on Wikipedia full text dataset containing 1,747 texts of whole articles. It contains 805.5 words (max: 16904, min: 102) and 36.8 key terms[8] (max: 999, min: 10) on average. Table 3 shows the results. Because there were many key terms in a single article, we also measured Prec@10, the precision of top 10 terms, along with R-Prec. On the Wikipedia full text dataset, the performance of N-gram TF-IDF was inferior to TF-IDF sum with NPs especially when focusing on the top 10 of ranked lists. This was mainly due to the local term weighting scheme. Whereas noun phrases are more likely to be key terms than words, words tend to occur more frequently in a long text than noun phrases. TF-IDF sum with NPs preferentially extracted key (noun) phrases because it prioritizes longer N-grams. Contrary to this, N-gram TF-IDF tried to acquire

[6]http://iwnsew.com

[7]We omitted short texts having less than three key terms.

[8]We omitted short texts having less than ten key terms.

Table 4: Performance of query segmentation on Roy et al. [40] dataset.

Method	nDCG@5	nDCG@10	MAP@5	MAP@10	MRR@5	MRR@10
N-gram IDF	0.730	0.742	0.900	0.893	0.582	0.593
Mishra et al.	0.706	0.737	0.895	0.892	0.529	0.542
Mishra et al. with Wikipedia	0.725	0.750	0.907	0.902	0.561	0.571
PMI-Q	0.716	0.736	0.898	0.892	0.567	0.577
PMI-W	0.670	0.707	0.860	0.863	0.493	0.506
Unsegmented	0.655	0.689	0.852	0.854	0.465	0.481
Human A	0.728	0.746	0.904	0.899	0.575	0.585
Human B	0.727	0.747	0.903	0.898	0.567	0.577
Human C	0.717	0.744	0.899	0.896	0.543	0.555
BQV	0.765	0.768	0.927	0.914	0.673	0.680

more key words since it fairly gives the weight to N-grams of any length, sacrificing the precision. In fact, the number of key words extracted with N-gram TF-IDF was 7,701, exceeding 7,030 obtained with TF-IDF sum with NPs. To apply N-gram IDF to long texts where not a few terms occur more than once, the local term weighting scheme should be well designed.

6.2 Query Segmentation

Query segmentation is another application of N-gram IDF. In this evaluation, we used an IR-based Web search query segmentation dataset [40]. The dataset contains 13,959 Web documents, 500 test queries and their qrels (query-relevance sets). The qrels were created by three human experts grading the query-document relevance score by 2 (highly relevant), 1 (relevant) or 0 (irrelevant). The average relevance score of the three experts was used as the gold standard in our evaluation. Given a query (e.g., "larry the lawnmower tv show"), each method segmented it into some words and phrases (e.g. "larry the lawnmower" and "tv show"). The words and phrases were then used to force the search system to match them exactly in documents. This is a Boolean query using double quotes in general Web search engines. After collecting documents that satisfy the Boolean query, we simply calculated the conventional TF-IDF weight for each document. Here, IDF was computed using the dataset documents. Because selecting which words or phrases should be quoted is a difficult problem, Roy et al. [40] measured evaluation scores for all possible quoted queries given a segmentation result obtained with each method. We followed their manner in our evaluation.

The dataset includes some results obtained with comparative methods: Mishra et al. [28], Mishra et al. with Wikipedia titles, PMI using query logs (PMI-Q) and PMI using Web documents (PMI-W). The thresholds of PMI-Q and PMI-W were adjusted by Roy et al. using their development set. It also provides three segmentation results by humans. Note that they were different from those who rated the qrels. We measured evaluation scores for them as well as unsegmented queries and (probably) the best quoted version of the queries (BQV)[9].

N-gram IDF was computed using the dataset documents because many queries and documents were informal and N-gram IDF computed in Wikipedia did not cover some N-grams in the dataset. Processing 283MB of the dataset documents took 40 minutes. We employed the same evaluation metrics as Roy et al.: normalized Discounted Cumulative Gain (nDCG), Mean Average Precision (MAP) and Mean Reciprocal Rank (MRR) for top 5 and 10 search results. Because computing MAP and MRR requires binary values of the qrel score, we regarded 2 and 1 as relevant when computing MAP, and only 2 as relevant for MRR.

Table 4 shows the performance results[10]. N-gram IDF was competitive with well-adjusted methods such as Mishra et al. with Wikipedia and PMI-Q, or human segmentation results, in all evaluation metrics. Let us recollect that N-gram IDF just has the weight of each N-gram like conventional IDF. Mishra et al. with Wikipedia leverages the human knowledge of Wikipedia and PMI-Q requires query logs and the threshold adjustment. Against these methods, N-gram IDF was able to achieve competitive performance by simply selecting dominant N-grams based on the weight. From these results, the simplicity and robustness of N-gram IDF were demonstrated.

7. CONCLUSIONS

This paper first time ever revealed the relationship between IDF and information distance. Specifically, the IDF of a term is equal to the distance between the term and the empty string in the space of information distance where the Kolmogorov complexity is approximated using Web documents and the Shannon-Fano coding. Our findings are helpful when designing a global term weighting scheme because the information distance can be regarded as the term weight. Based on our findings, we also proposed a global term weighting scheme, N-gram IDF, by incorporating IDF and MED, a universal information distance-based metric for measuring the word compositionality. N-gram IDF is able to handle N-grams of any N in a sole theoretical scheme. It enables us to compare the weight of words and phrases, and thus, select dominant N-grams among overlapping ones. We demonstrated the simplicity and robustness of N-gram IDF on key term extraction and Web search query segmentation tasks. N-gram IDF was able to achieve competitive perfor-

[9]BQV in the literature [40] may not be the best because it does not consider partly overlapping phrases such as "free solitaire" and "solitaire card games" for query "play free solitaire card games."

[10]Evaluation scores of the comparative methods were different from those reported by Roy et al. [40] because we used the TF-IDF weight that was computed using the dataset documents. We observed the same tendencies that did not contradict their results.

mance with state-of-the-art methods designed for each task using extra resources and efforts.

Our future work includes the development of approximation methods to shorten the processing time for handling large document sets. As the corpus size (the number of documents $|D|$) grows, the number of valid N-grams also increases linearly. The processing time for computing the N-gram IDF weight for all valid N-grams therefore becomes roughly $O(|D|^2)$. Fortunately, Bu et al. [7] reported that MED of a term was rather well measured by focusing on documents whose topics were related to the term. In order to manage the big text data and upgrade the quality of the weight, we plan to use small and biased document sets for measuring MED. Another future work is to handle texts written in languages without spaces between words such as Japanese and Chinese. Possible approaches to solve this problem are two: designing character-level N-gram IDF or introducing unsupervised word segmentation techniques. We will explore the possibility of both approaches.

8. ACKNOWLEDGMENTS

This work was supported in part by CPS-IIP Project (Integrated Platforms for Cyber-Physical Systems to Accelerate Implementation of Efficient Social Systems) in the research promotion program for national level challenges "research and development for the realization of next-generation IT platforms" and by the Grant-in-Aid for Scientific Research (A)(26240013) by MEXT, Japan.

9. REFERENCES

[1] M. I. Abouelhoda, S. Kurtz, and E. Ohlebusch. Replacing Suffix Trees with Enhanced Suffix Arrays. *Journal of Discrete Algorithms*, 2(1):53–86, Mar. 2004.

[2] A. Aizawa. An Information-Theoretic Perspective of TF-IDF Measures. *Information Processing and Management*, 39(1):45–65, Jan. 2003.

[3] C. H. Bennett, P. Gács, M. Li, P. M. Vitányi, and W. H. Zurek. Information Distance. *IEEE Transactions on Information Theory*, 44(4):1407–1423, July 1998.

[4] A. Blumer, J. Blumer, D. Haussler, R. M. McConnell, and A. Ehrenfeucht. Complete Inverted Files for Efficient Text Retrieval and Analysis. *Journal of the ACM*, 34(3):578–595, July 1987.

[5] A. Bookstein and D. R. Swanson. Probabilistic Models for Automatic Indexing. *Journal of the American Society for Information Science*, 25(5):312–318, Sept./Oct. 1974.

[6] G. Bouma. Normalized (Pointwise) Mutual Information in Collocation Extraction. In *Proceedings of International Conference of the German Society for Computational Linguistics and Language Technology (GSCL)*, pages 31–40, Sep./Oct. 2009.

[7] F. Bu, X. Zhu, and M. Li. Measuring the Non-compositionality of Multiword Expressions. In *Proceedings of International Conference on Computational Linguistics (COLING)*, pages 116–124, Aug. 2010.

[8] K. W. Church and W. A. Gale. Poisson Mixtures. *Natural Language Engineering*, 1(2):163–190, 1995.

[9] K. W. Church and P. Hanks. Word Association Norms, Mutual Information, and Lexicography. *Computational Linguistics*, 16(1):22–29, Mar. 1990.

[10] R. L. Cilibrasi and P. M. Vitányi. Clustering by Compression. *IEEE Transactions on Information Theory*, 51(4):1523–1545, Apr. 2005.

[11] R. L. Cilibrasi and P. M. Vitányi. The Google Similarity Distance. *IEEE Transactions on Knowledge and Data Engineering*, 19(3):370–383, Mar. 2007.

[12] J. F. da Silva and J. G. P. Lopes. A Local Maxima Method and a Fair Dispersion Normalization for Extracting Multi-word Units from Corpora. In *Proceedings of Meeting on Mathematics of Language (MOL)*, pages 369–381, July 1999.

[13] G. Dias. Mining Textual Associations in Text Corpora. In *Proceedings of ACM SIGKDD Workshop on Text Mining*, pages 20–23, Aug. 2000.

[14] B. C. Fung, K. Wang, and M. Ester. Hierarchical Document Clustering Using Frequent Itemsets. In *Proceedings of SIAM International Conference on Data Mining (SDM)*, pages 59–70, May 2003.

[15] T. Gagie, G. Navarro, and S. J. Puglisi. New Algorithms on Wavelet Trees and Applications to Information Retrieval. *Theoretical Computer Science*, 426–427:25–41, Apr. 2012.

[16] W. R. Greiff. A Theory of Term Weighting Based on Exploratory Data Analysis. In *Proceedings of International ACM SIGIR Conference on Research and Development in Information Retrieval (SIGIR)*, pages 11–19, Aug. 1998.

[17] R. Grossi, A. Gupta, and J. S. Vitter. High-Order Entropy-Compressed Text Indexes. In *Proceedings of ACM-SIAM Symposium on Discrete Algorithms (SODA)*, pages 841–850, 2003.

[18] S. P. Harter. A Probabilistic Approach to Automatic Keyword Indexing. Part I. On the Distribution of Specialty Words in a Technical Literature. *Journal of the American Society for Information Science*, 26(4):197–206, July/Aug. 1975.

[19] K. S. Hasan and V. Ng. Conundrums in Unsupervised Keyphrase Extraction: Making Sense of the State-of-the-Art. In *Proceedings of International Conference on Computational Linguistics (COLING)*, pages 365–373, Aug. 2010.

[20] D. Hiemstra. A Probabilistic Justification for Using TF×IDF Term Weighting in Information Retrieval. *International Journal on Digital Libraries*, 3(2):131–139, Aug. 2000.

[21] K. S. Jones. A Statistical Interpretation of Term Specificity and its Application in Retrieval. *Journal of Documentation*, 28:11–21, 1972.

[22] A. Kolmogorov. On Tables of Random Numbers. *Sankhyā Ser. A*, 25:369–376, 1963.

[23] M. Lan, C. L. Tan, J. Su, and Y. Lu. Supervised and Traditional Term Weighting Methods for Automatic Text Categorization. *IEEE Transactions on Pattern Analysis and Machine Intelligence*, 31(4):721–735, Apr. 2009.

[24] R. Landauer. Irreversibility and Heat Generation in the Computing Process. *IBM Journal of Research and Development*, 5(3):183–191, July 1961.

[25] M. Li and P. M. Vitányi. *An Introduction to Kolmogorov Complexity and Its Applications.* Springer, Berlin, 3rd edition, 2009.

[26] C. D. Manning, P. Raghavan, and H. Schütze. *Introduction to Information Retrieval.* Cambridge University Press, Cambridge, 2008.

[27] D. Metzler. Generalized Inverse Document Frequency. In *Proceedings of ACM Conference on Information and Knowledge Management (CIKM)*, pages 399–408, Oct. 2008.

[28] N. Mishra, R. S. Roy, N. Ganguly, S. Laxman, and M. Choudhury. Unsupervised Query Segmentation Using only Query Logs. In *Proceedings of International World Wide Web Conference (WWW)*, pages 91–92, Mar./Apr. 2011.

[29] K. Narisawa, S. Inenaga, H. Bannai, and M. Takeda. Efficient Computation of Substring Equivalence Classes with Suffix Arrays. In *Proceedings of Symposium on Combinatorial Pattern Matching (CPM)*, pages 340–351, July 2007.

[30] D. Okanohara and J. Tsujii. Text Categorization with All Substring Features. In *Proceedings of SIAM International Conference on Data Mining (SDM)*, pages 838–846, Apr./May 2009.

[31] C. Orăsan, V. Pekar, and L. Hasler. A Comparison of Summarisation Methods Based on Term Specificity Estimation. In *Proceedings of International Conference on Language Resources and Evaluation (LREC)*, pages 1037–1041, May 2004.

[32] K. Papineni. Why Inverse Document Frequency? In *Proceedings of Meeting of the North American Chapter of the Association for Computational Linguistics (NAACL)*, pages 1–8, June 2001.

[33] P. Pecina. An Extensive Empirical Study of Collocation Extraction Methods. In *Proceedings of ACL Student Research Workshop*, pages 13–18, June 2005.

[34] J. W. Reed, Y. Jiao, T. E. Potok, B. A. Klump, M. T. Elmore, and A. R. Hurson. TF-ICF: A New Term Weighting Scheme for Clustering Dynamic Data Streams. In *Proceedings of International Conference on Machine Learning and Applications (ICMLA)*, pages 258–263, Dec. 2006.

[35] J. D. M. Rennie and T. Jaakkola. Using Term Informativeness for Named Entity Detection. In *Proceedings of International ACM SIGIR Conference on Research and Development in Information Retrieval (SIGIR)*, pages 353–360, Aug. 2005.

[36] S. Robertson. Understanding Inverse Document Frequency: On theoretical arguments for IDF. *Journal of Documentation*, 60(5):503–520, 2004.

[37] S. Robertson, S. Walker, S. Jones, M. Hancock-Beaulieu, and M. Gatford. Okapi at TREC-3. In *Proceedings of Text Retrieval Conference (TREC)*, pages 109–126, 1994.

[38] T. Roelleke and J. Wang. TF-IDF Uncovered: A Study of Theories and Probabilities. In *Proceedings of International ACM SIGIR Conference on Research and Development in Information Retrieval (SIGIR)*, pages 435–442, July 2008.

[39] F. Rousseau and M. Vazirgiannis. Graph-of-word and TW-IDF: New Approach to Ad Hoc IR. In *Proceedings of ACM Conference on Information and Knowledge Management (CIKM)*, pages 59–68, Oct./Nov. 2013.

[40] R. S. Roy, N. Ganguly, M. Choudhury, and S. Laxman. An IR-based Evaluation Framework for Web Search Query Segmentation. In *Proceedings of International ACM SIGIR Conference on Research and Development in Information Retrieval (SIGIR)*, pages 881–890, Aug. 2012.

[41] G. Salton and M. J. McGill. *Introduction to Modern Information Retrieval.* McGraw-Hill, New York, 1983.

[42] G. Salton, A. Wong, and C.-S. Yang. A Vector Space Model for Automatic Indexing. *Communications of the ACM*, 18(11):613–620, 1975.

[43] P. Schone and D. Jurafsky. Is Knowledge-Free Induction of Multiword Unit Dictionary Headwords a Solved Problem? In *Proceedings of Conference on Empirical Methods in Natural Language Processing (EMNLP)*, pages 100–108, June 2001.

[44] J. Sivic and A. Zisserman. Video Google: A Text Retrieval Approach to Object Matching in Videos. In *Proceedings of IEEE International Conference on Computer Vision (ICCV)*, pages 1470–1477, Oct. 2003.

[45] M. Timonen. *Term Weighting in Short Documents for Document Categorization, Keyword Extraction and Query Expansion.* PhD thesis, University of Helsinki, 2013.

[46] H. C. Wu, R. W. P. Luk, K. F. Wong, and K. L. Kwok. Interpreting TF-IDF Term Weights as Making Relevance Decisions. *ACM Transactions on Information Systems*, 26(3):13:1–13:37, June 2008.

[47] M. Yamamoto and K. W. Church. Using Suffix Arrays to Compute Term Frequency and Document Frequency for All Substrings in a Corpus. *Computational Linguistics*, 27(1):1–30, Mar. 2001.

[48] W. Zhang, T. Yoshida, X. Tang, and T.-B. Ho. Improving Effectiveness of Mutual Information for Substantival Multiword Expression Extraction. *Expert Systems with Applications*, 36(8):10919–10930, Oct. 2009.

Query Suggestion and Data Fusion in Contextual Disambiguation

Milad Shokouhi
Microsoft
milads@microsoft.com

Marc Sloan*
University College London
marc.sloan.10@ucl.ac.uk

Paul N. Bennett
Microsoft
paul.n.bennett@microsoft.com

Kevyn Collins-Thompson*
University of Michigan
kevynct@umich.edu

Siranush Sarkizova*
Harvard University
ssarkizova@g.harvard.edu

ABSTRACT

Queries issued to a search engine are often under-specified or ambiguous. The user's search context or background may provide information that disambiguates their information need in order to automatically predict and issue a more effective query. The disambiguation can take place at different stages of the retrieval process. For instance, *contextual query suggestions* may be computed and recommended to users on the result page when appropriate, an approach that does not require modifying the original query's results. Alternatively, the search engine can attempt to provide efficient access to new relevant documents by injecting these documents directly into search results based on the user's context.

In this paper, we explore these complementary approaches and how they might be combined. We first develop a general framework for mining context-sensitive query reformulations for query suggestion. We evaluate our context-sensitive suggestions against a state-of-the-art baseline using a click-based metric. The resulting query suggestions generated by our approach outperform the baseline by 13% overall and by 16% on an ambiguous query subset.

While the query suggestions generated by our approach have higher quality than the existing baselines, we demonstrate that using them naïvely for injecting new documents into search results can lead to inferior rankings. To remedy this issue, we develop a classifier that decides when to inject new search results using features based on suggestion quality and user context. We show that our context-sensitive result fusion approach (Corfu) improves retrieval quality for ambiguous queries by up to 2.92%. Our approaches can efficiently scale to massive search logs, enabling a data-driven strategy that benefits from observing how users issue and reformulate queries in different contexts.

1. INTRODUCTION

An ambiguous query may be issued to a search engine when a user has an inexplicit information need or when the user enters only a few search terms in lieu of a longer, more complex query. A comprehensive study of two search logs found that between 7% and 23% of queries could be considered ambiguous, depending on how ambiguity is defined, and that such queries are typically short, averaging 1.02 to 1.23 terms [31]. In such cases, user context may help disambiguate the query and personalize search results [23]. For instance, a user searching for `[ eagles ]` with a recent history of sports-related queries may prefer the 'Philadelphia Eagles' American football team website over that of the rock band 'The Eagles'.

Table 1: Example contextual query suggestions

Session Context	User Query	Contextual Suggestion
Sports	`eagles`	`philadelphia eagles`
Music	`eagles`	`eagles band`
Physics	`pascal`	`pascal unit`
Computer Science	`pascal`	`pascal programming`
Video Games	`forge`	`minecraft forge`
Crafts	`forge`	`metal forge`

In this paper, we build on existing query disambiguation work by introducing user context. User context can encompass multiple aspects such as age, gender, topic, or location and can be short-term [9] or long-term [23]. In this work, we use categories from the Open Directory Project (ODP)[1] to represent the short-term topical context of a user's information need. In particular, by combining click information with categorized URLs retrieved for previous queries in the session, we can interpret the most probable category as the user's short-term *session context* [4]. We then use this inferred context together with observed query reformulations across query log sessions to mine contextual reformulations for query suggestion. Some examples of session context, original query, and the top ranked contextual suggestion are shown in Table 1.

We generate contextual query suggestion candidates using a similar utility-function based methodology to that employed by Ozertem et al. [27]. In this framework, candidates are found by extracting consecutive pairs of queries from sessions in search logs. These are then ranked according to the difference in utility value, where utility is a measure of the query's usefulness calculated using clicked documents. We also find that adding contextual features leads to significant gains in query suggestion quality particularly for ambiguous queries.

Moreover, we explore disambiguation approaches that go beyond simply offering contextual suggestions: we aim to improve the user's efficiency in a session by eliminating the need for a separate query reformulation altogether. Instead, we introduce methods for predicting *when* and *how* it is appropriate to incorporate

*Work performed while at Microsoft

[1]`http://www.dmoz.org/`

WWW 2015, May 18–22, 2015, Florence, Italy.
ACM 978-1-4503-3469-3/15/05.
http://dx.doi.org/10.1145/2736277.2741646.

context-driven results directly into the initial ranking. This goal is similar in motivation to previous work on whole-session relevance that merged in results from a user's predicted future queries for a task [28]. Toward this goal, we first learn to predict which queries are likely to benefit from this blending; then, given such a query, we use a data fusion technique [3, 32] to incorporate relevant results from the top ranking contextual suggestion with those of the original query. Finally, we show that this fusion approach significantly improves search results for ambiguous queries.

In particular, the problem of differentiating when a candidate contextual query reformulation is best left as a suggestion, versus when it is a good candidate for data fusion, is a key challenge unaddressed by previous work. Good suggestion candidates may not necessarily lead to a good result fusion. For example, the query suggestion `[ kmart ]` for the original query `[ target ]` is relevant and may help the user explore, but blending the results of the former into the Search Engine Results Page (SERP) of the latter would be confusing, as the *results* of the latter are not directly relevant to the original query. To mitigate this, we trained a novel classifier using session, context and query-based features to identify instances in which fusing results is beneficial over simply suggesting the query. Our experiments demonstrate that incorporating this fusion classifier by selectively choosing when to blend yields significant improvements in effectiveness.

In sum, the contributions of this work are as follows:

- The addition of contextual categorization (Section 2) to utility-based query suggestion generation, resulting in improved contextual query suggestions (Section 3).
- Investigating and demonstrating the need for selective blending by analyzing the failure cases of blindly fusing candidate suggestions with the original query in all cases (Section 4).
- The definition and evaluation of a fusion classifier that predicts whether to blend search results or suggest queries for contextual disambiguation (Section 5).

2. CONTEXTUAL QUERY DISAMBIGUATION

The aim of contextual query disambiguation is to use context to improve the search experience of a user who has issued an ambiguous query. Query suggestions provide the user with easily accessible reformulation options if they decide to issue a new query. As such, the quality and ranking of suggestions is important. Suggestions are used by users not only to disambiguate their original queries, but also in cases where the user wishes to broaden or narrow the scope of their initial query or otherwise adjust their search intent. Given this variability in usage, along with a relatively low engagement rate ($< 5\%$ on the Bing search engine), an attractive alternative to offering query suggestions as a separate interaction step is to directly blend their results with those for the initial query. This blending approach has at least two advantages. First, because blending can incorporate search results from multiple suggestions, the pool of potentially relevant documents is increased. Second, directly satisfying the user's query with a blended result decreases the total time required for a user to satisfy their information need. This not only saves time, but also potential frustration and abandonment.

Given a user query q, we seek a suitable contextual reformulation candidate q_c for suggestion or blending, where the context $o \in \Theta$ belongs to a finite, discrete set of contextual labels (such as topic, gender or location). Candidates are found by mining sessions in query logs for consecutive pairs of queries q_a, q_b. Sessions are defined as a series of queries issued by a single user over a period

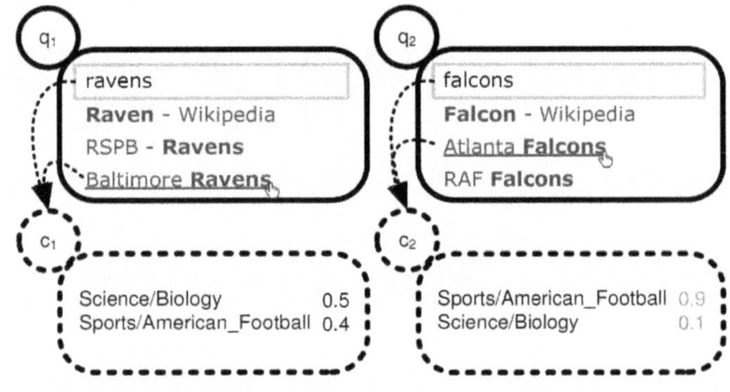

Figure 1: Session context (o^*) example. The queries and clicks observed throughout a session are used to update the context model (Θ). Suppose that the user had already clicked on a document related to Science/Biology in the previous query (q_0). Based on the clicks recorded on q_1, the context model is updated to c_1 which will become available at the time q_2 is submitted. Similarly, the context model is updated for the next query based on the clicks recorded on q_2.

of time, where we adopt the widely-used practice of demarcating session boundaries by 30 minutes of user inactivity [41].

We use the ODP taxonomy as our classification labels O as they are high quality, discrete and general enough for use on search log data. Nonetheless, it is worth noting that our technique is applicable to any classification space where meaningful labels can be attached to queries. In this study, we limit ourselves to the top two levels of the ODP hierarchy, giving us 17 topics (e.g. *Arts*, *Sport*) and 185 subtopics (e.g. *Arts/Music*, *Sports/Baseball*). This set of categories gives us enough granularity to distinguish the different contexts in which reformulations typically occur, while being broad enough to represent the topical meaning of most content, and general enough so that repeated similar behavior is pooled into statistically robust sets of observations.

To create the *context model* in a session, we directly implement the query classification technique used by Bennett et al. [4]. Their method uses a conventional topic classifier that assigns labels to individual URLs based on a given taxonomy. The classifier is applied to the clicked URLs from search results in a search log, where click information, dwell time and a number of query-URL features are combined to calculate a probability distribution over the 202 ODP categories described above. The session *context model* is then formed at each point by aggregating the ODP probability distributions of documents clicked for previous queries in the session.

We define *session context* (o^*) as the ODP category with highest probability (confidence) in this context model (Θ). Session context takes into account all URLs and interactions of the preceding queries meaning that it becomes more accurate and representative of the user's search intent as the session progresses.

Figure 1 gives an example of how session context is determined: suppose that the user has already clicked on a document related to *Science/Biology* in the previous query of the session. Once the user clicks on the third document for q_1 the context model is updated to also capture *Sports/American_Football* and in this case gives similar weights to the two subtopics (the weights assigned to the other 200 categories are negligible). The observed click on next query (q_2) increases the confidence score for *Sports/American_Football* subtopic in Θ for the future queries.

A drawback to using session context is that we cannot classify (and thus disambiguate) a user's query if it is the first in a session: in this case we simply return its usual results without modification. One potential way to alleviate this would be to classify queries in the user's longer-term search history in order to find personalization labels. A balance of short and long-term labels could be used to provide context from the start of a session, a topic explored more completely by Bennett et al. [5]. We leave this long-term scenario for future work.

3. QUERY SUGGESTION UTILITY

In this section we focus on query suggestion as a method for contextual query disambiguation. Inspired by previous work [27] we introduce a new utility function for measuring the effectiveness of query suggestion candidates for a given query. We then demonstrate how this function can be used to mine contextual (and non-contextual) query suggestion candidates from past search logs.

It is often the case that search logs are used to find and score query suggestions. The query-flow graph is one such example; its nodes are queries, its edges are query reformulations and their weights are the frequency of occurrence [7]. Variants include the click-bipartite graph which links queries with clicked URLs, and in both cases suggestion candidates can be found using random walks, clustering and other graph-based techniques [1, 11].

A simple approach for extracting query suggestions from logs is to mine query co-occurrences in search sessions [20]. For a given query q_a, suggestion candidates can then be ranked according to their maximum likelihood computed as

$$P(q_b|q_a) = \frac{P(q_b, q_a)}{P(q_a)} \quad (1)$$

where q_b is a query reformulation and $P(q_b, q_a)$ represents its co-occurrence probability with q_a based on past searches. We can extend this to include context by also conditioning on the contextual category, giving us

$$P(q_b|q_a, o) = \frac{P(q_b, q_a, o^*)}{P(q_a, o^*)}. \quad (2)$$

Here the session context (discussed earlier in Section 2) is denoted by o^*. At run-time the query and its session context are matched against this probability distribution for ranking candidates.

3.1 Reformulation Utility

Ranking query suggestions by maximum likelihood encounters two main issues. First, a suggestion candidate could be unrelated and biased towards popular navigational queries (topic drift). Second, the results for a suggestion may be low quality. Ozertem et al. [27] addressed the problem of reformulation quality by defining a relative utility function based on the click differences found in both the original query (q_a) and its reformulation (q_b). Suppose q_a and q_b have co-occurred consecutively[2] in a session. Using clicks from their impressions, they compute the utility of q_b as a query suggestion candidate for q_a using

$$\Delta = \sum_{d \in C(q_b)} \left(\frac{1}{\log r(q_b, d)} - \frac{1}{\log r(q_a, d)} \right). \quad (3)$$

[2]The authors showed that relaxing this constraint does not improve the results. Ozertem et al. also described an extended version of their technique enhanced with task boundary detection and supervised utility inference. Both of these extensions are orthogonal to our contributions and neither was reported to substantially improve the quality of the top suggestion which is what we are mostly concerned with in this work.

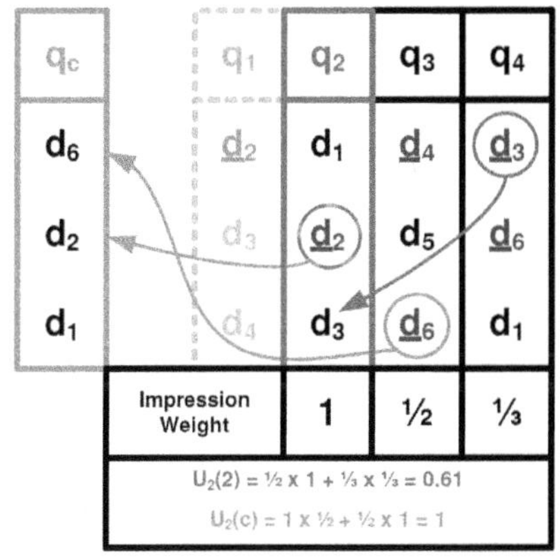

Figure 2: Example illustrating the utility function given by Equation 4. In this case, $q_a = q_2$ and its interactions are given in blue, whilst the candidate's q_c are given in green. Underlined documents represent SAT clicks.

Here $C(q_b)$ represents the clicked documents on the results returned for q_b in that session and the $r(q, d)$ function returns the position of document d in the results returned for query q. A candidate is found useful whenever it returns a clicked document that either did not exist in the ranked results for the original query, or did exist but at a relatively lower position. The authors then extended Equation 1 and ranked suggestions based on the probability $P(q_b|q_a, \Delta > 0)$.

In this work, we use their method as our baseline because (1) it is state-of-the-art and has been reported to significantly outperform other alternatives, (2) it applies a retrieval-based utility function which fits well with fusion scenarios that we discuss later in this work, and (3) we use a similar retrieval-based utility function that relies on clicks for computing suggestion utilities. However, we define a different relative utility function that unlike their approach does not ignore the clicks recorded on the original query. To alleviate data sparsity issues that arise when taking into account context we also use clicks that occur later in the session. We follow the common practice of considering clicks with longer dwell time than 30 seconds as satisfied clicks [4, 28]. Fox et al. [16] showed such clicked documents are highly likely to be relevant. In this paper, clicks *always* mean SAT clicks.

Our utility function measures the quality of queries and suggestion candidates based on the click-statistics of their results in the session and applies two reciprocal rank discounts, we thus refer to it as cumulative reciprocal rank (*CRR*). Suppose that the user has issued a query q_a, the I_ath query in the search session. Let us denote D_c as the documents in the ranking for query suggestion candidate q_c. We define the *CRR* of q_c with respect to q_a as

$$CRR_a(q_c) = \sum_{d \in D_c} \underbrace{\frac{1}{r(q_c, d)}}_{\text{Result Reciprocal Rank}} \times \underbrace{\frac{1}{(i(d, I_a) - I_a + 1)}}_{\text{Impression Reciprocal Rank}} \quad (4)$$

where $r(q, d)$ is as described above and I_a is the impression position of q_a in the session. The function $i(d, I_a)$ is the position in the session of the first query including or after q_a where d was clicked. If no such click exists in the session then i is set to $+\infty$.

In summary, the utility of a candidate query suggestion is a combined function of the relevance of a document (measured by whether it receives a click in the session at query q_a or after) and the position of the document in the ranking q_c (weighted by reciprocal rank).

We follow Sakai and Dou [30] and degrade the pseudo-relevance labels assigned to these documents by applying an impression reciprocal rank discount for clicks that occur later in the session, emphasizing the current information need. The relative utility between q_a and q_c is then simply

$$\Delta CRR(q_c, q_a) = CRR_a(q_c) - CRR_a(q_a). \quad (5)$$

This function is illustrated in Figure 2, where q_2 is the user's current query (so $I_a = 2$ in this case) in the session. The session context model at this point is formed based on the documents clicked for the previous queries in the session (q_1). The next two queries in the session (q_3, and q_4) are obviously unobserved at the time q_2 is submitted, but we use information about their clicked documents to generate pseudo-relevance labels in order to measure the utility of suggestion candidates. In this particular scenario, the underscore indicates that d_2 is the only document we have observed a *satisfied* click on for q_2. There are three more documents clicked later in this session (d_3, d_4 and d_6). While these documents can be regarded as pseudo-relevant under their respective queries (q_3 and q_4) their association with q_2 is weaker due to the potential topic drift.

In the example above, applying the impression discount allows us to consider d_3 as a relevant document for q_2 – albeit with discounted weight – although it has not been clicked under q_2 directly. We perform the same procedure for calculating *CRR* of the current query (q_2) and all suggestion candidates such as q_c. We compare suggestion candidates in terms of how they perform against the original query with respect to their ΔCRR (in this case $\Delta = +0.39$)[3]. Note that in this example, even though the user query ranks clicked document d_2 in the same position as q_c, q_c ranks d_6 (which is clicked in the next impression) very highly, which contributes to its improved score. By leveraging and weighting all of the clicks that occur in the remainder of the session we gain a broader view of the documents that are relevant to the query and can reward those candidates that find relevant documents that weren't returned for the original query (which may often lack clicks due to the query being ambiguous).

3.2 Ranking suggestions

For each given query (q_a, q_c) pair we compute the score as

$$P(q_c|q_a, \Delta CRR(q_c, q_a) > 0)$$

The probabilities are computed over historical logs and at run-time are used to rank suggestions accordingly. The contextual extension of our model considers the session category ($o*$) of each historical impression when computing these probabilities:

$$P(q_c|q_a, o^*, \Delta CRR(q_c, q_a) > 0)$$

At run-time, we match both query and its context against this probability distribution to rank candidates. We denote our approach *CosQus* (short for **Co**ntext **S**ensitive **Qu**ery **S**uggestion). We refer to the context-free version of our method that only computes probabilities over query-candidate *pairs* as *CosQus*(P), and to the contextual version that computes probabilities over query-category-candidate *triples* as *CosQus*(T). Note that we are only interested in the top-ranked suggestion in our experiments. We also propose a *hybrid* approach *CosQus*(H) that computes both of these probabilities and at run-time selects the candidate with the highest probability across the two.

[3]The top-ranked results for each candidate can be obtained by issuing that query, or from historical logs. In our work, we use the most recent SERP logged for a candidate in our logs.

3.3 Data

Our experiments are conducted over the query logs of the Bing search engine. We use log data for mining query suggestions, computing their utility values, evaluating the performance of different query suggestion approaches and later in the paper for training supervised result fusion classifiers. Therefore, it is important to carefully sample the logs at each stage to avoid the risk of leakage and overfitting. Figure 3 depicts the time periods of the search logs used in our work. For the query suggestion experiments in this part of the paper, we are only using the first three segments, and the purple and green boxes can be ignored.

Candidate generation. To generate the potential query suggestions for a given query, we mine all consecutive query reformulations submitted by Bing users between December 1st, 2012 and December 31st, 2013. Note that all our experiments are performed on the query logs of the *English-US* market. We reduced the space of query-candidates to a subset of up to 50 common reformulations by only including the top contextual and non-contextual suggestions based on Equations 1 and 2. For this, we selected the top 25 most probable reformulations without any context for the query (Equation 1). We also included the top 25 contextual reformulations for each query (Equation 2). It is worth noting that the same reformulation could appear for multiple contexts. Doing this allowed us to generate candidates at different topic granularities, capture instances where a non-contextual suggestion was ideal, and allowed us to try out different candidate selection strategies in our experiments. This pool of up to 50 unique candidates for a query effectively provides us with a framework for comparing different query suggestion rankings on the same dataset.

Utility computation. The blue box in Figure 3 specifies the period over which candidate utilities are computed for *CosQus* and our experimental baselines. We sampled 11.4 million search sessions from Bing logs between Feb. 1st, 2014 and Feb. 28th, 2014. In total there are roughly 23.5 million impressions in this set. We use the logs in this period to compute the utility values (e.g. $P(q_c|q_a, \Delta CRR(q_c, q_a) > 0)$ for *CosQus*(P)) over all reformulations that were extracted in the previous step.

Query suggestion evaluation. To compare the effectiveness of query suggestion techniques we sample another set of 5.7 million sessions (11.8 million impressions) from the query logs between March 1st, 2014 – March 14th, 2014. For each impression during this period we use the SAT-clicks in the session as previously described (Section 2) to assign pseudo-relevance labels to documents. These labels are later used to compute the *CRR* values for the query and all its candidates.

Ambiguous queries. We also targeted a subset of Wikipedia-derived ambiguous queries as ideal candidates for contextual query disambiguation. We first consider the title of all Wikipedia disambiguation pages[4] as ambiguous queries. We then used the Wikilinks dataset[5] containing millions of links and anchor text to Wikipedia articles extracted from webpages. We found instances where either different anchor text was used to link to the same Wikipedia article, or where the same anchor text was used to link to different Wikipedia articles. Combining all three approaches gave us a set of 1,319,309 ambiguous queries, of which around 1/3 matched queries in our candidate generation period. On our evaluation dataset,

[4]`en.wikipedia.org/wiki/Wikipedia:Disambiguation`
[5]`code.google.com/p/wiki-link/`

Table 2: The effectiveness of different query suggestion approaches according to cumulative reciprocal rank (*CRR*) on two experimental query sets ("Ambiguous" and "All"). The *suggestion utility* approach of [27] is used as a baseline. For reference we also provide the average *CRR* values for the original query $CRR_a(q_a)$ on the two datasets. All pairwise differences are statistically significant according to the t-test ($p < 0.01$).

Method	Queries	$CRR_a(q_a)$	$CRR_a(q_c)$	(% ▲/▼)
Baseline [27]			0.336	
Baseline+			0.318	(▼ 5.4%)
CosQus(P)	All	0.530	0.313	(▼ 6.8%)
CosQus(T)			0.358	(▲ 6.5%)
CosQus(H)			0.378	(▲13.0%)
Baseline [27]			0.259	
Baseline+			0.245	(▼ 5.4%)
CosQus(P)	Ambiguous	0.458	0.244	(▼ 5.8%)
CosQus(T)			0.278	(▲ 7.3%)
CosQus(H)			0.300	(▲16.0%)

we report the results on the subset of impressions that match these queries separately, as we find these queries to be most suitable for disambiguation by definition.

3.4 Experimental results

As stated earlier, the first contribution in our work is a new approach for ranking query suggestions. We compare our approach with the non-contextual utility function from Ozertem et al. [27] as our baseline. We also tested against a variant baseline (Baseline+) which incorporated the propagation of session clicks in a similar way to our *CRR* function. This was to make sure our comparison was fair and that both techniques had access to the same information for candidate ranking.

Our results in Table 2 show that the use of context (*CosQus*(T)) is clearly beneficial in helping to choose query suggestions, outperforming the three non-contextual methods. We can also observe significant gains by using the hybrid approach (*CosQus*(H)) and switching between contextual and non-contextual candidates based on their probabilities. Some additional conclusions we can draw from our results: (1) Using clicks from later in the session does not improve performance on non-contextual suggestions (Baseline+ and *CosQus*(P)), possibly because there is greater topic drift when not conditioning on context; (2) The biggest gains were seen with ambiguous queries, reinforcing our aim of contextual disambiguation, but we still made significant gains on all queries; and (3) Overall the *CRR* values were lower for ambiguous queries, most likely due to there being less high ranking clicks to learn from. Of note is the fact that results from the query suggestions were generally poorer than the original query. This will factor into our data fusion experiments and is discussed further in the next section.

4. DATA FUSION

While improving contextual query suggestions significantly is helpful, the level of user engagement with such suggestions is typically low. Therefore, we seek a way to translate these gains in suggestion quality to direct gains in result relevance and/or a reduction in user effort searching. In particular, users have been found to be more likely to click on suggestions when their query is rare or a single term, after they have clicked on several URLs, or when the suggestions themselves are unambiguous or a correction of the original query [21]. Instead of suggesting queries, we can directly perform contextual disambiguation by altering the search results of the user's query using data fusion.

In data fusion, we blend the search results from multiple rankings into one list. In our setting, these rankings result from multiple queries. This can range from injecting a single result into the original ranking to completely replacing the original ranking. The benefits are that we can find relevant documents from a number of sources and combine them into one list, but it is also possible to remove relevant documents in the process, so results blending must be done carefully. Search rankings can come from a number of sources. For instance, in federated search the same query is issued on multiple search engines and the results merged using a utility function [35]. LambdaMerge [33] uses a two-layer neural network to learn a ranking function for merging results lists for query reformulations based on query, document and reformulation features. Their focus is to optimize over a retrieval quality metric to produce effective merged lists whereas ours is on predicting when contextual blending is going to be effective; thus we adopt a simpler merging technique.

4.1 Contextual CombSUM

Our data fusion for contextual disambiguation method involves blending the results returned for a query with those returned for a related query suggestion. Running many queries in parallel is prohibitively costly in practice. Hence, we restrict ourselves to running only one additional suggestion candidate per query, and use the top candidate from *CosQus*(H) given its superior performance based on the results reported in the previous section.

CombSUM is a simple merging technique that sums normalized URL rank scores across queries, producing a new ranking in decreasing order of CombSUM scores [32]. The result is that highly ranked URLs which appear in multiple lists are more likely to appear in the merged list. For a given q_a, a query suggestion q_c, and a document d selected from one of their respective results, the CombSUM scores are computed as

$$\text{CombSUM}(d) = \frac{1+\epsilon}{r(q_a, d)} + \frac{1}{r(q_c, d)}. \quad (6)$$

The reciprocal rank takes the place of the rank score and ϵ is introduced to give a priority to the URLs that appear in the original ranking. We set a low weight for ϵ (0.01) primarily to serve as a tie-breaking mechanism in favor of the original ranking. After ranking the merged list by CombSUM, we keep the same number of results as the original ranking.

4.2 Naïve Fusion

We applied CombSUM data fusion to the rankings of every user query and *CosQus*(H) contextual query suggestion in our dataset (over the *memorization period*). Overall, we found the performance of these blended lists to be inferior to that of the original query with no blending. On average the *CRR* value dropped by about 7% on both datasets ("Ambiguous", and "All"). This is expected as we reported earlier, the *CRR* values for top query suggestions are substantially worse than the original queries (see Table 2); consequently the blended list will suffer.

To investigate whether the fusion between the results of a query and its suggestion candidate can improve search results we measured $\Delta CRR(q_c, q_a)$, and $\Delta CRR(f, q_a)$, where f signifies the CombSUM fusion ranking between query q_a and candidate q_c. We plotted ΔCRR for every suggestion and blended ranking in our scatterplot in Figure 4. Here, we observe a clear trend that shows that suggestions with good rankings (x-axis) lead to better blended rankings (y-axis), and bad suggestions hurt blending performance. There

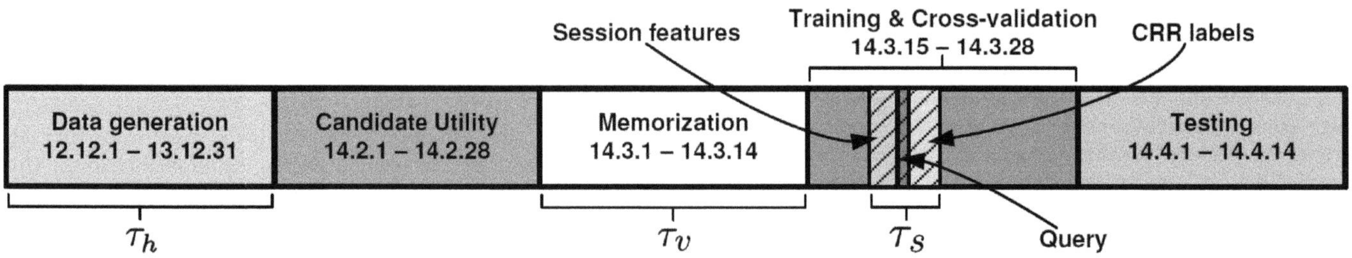

Figure 3: The timeline for the logs used in our feature generation and evaluation pipelines. Historical frequency features are computed between December 2012 and December 2013 (τ_h). Query suggestion utilities are computed based on the logs sampled in February 2014. Query suggestion techniques are evaluated against the logs sampled between March 1st, and March 14th, 2014. The same period is used for *memorizing* the effectiveness of blended result lists that are then used in our fusion baselines and as classification features (τ_v). The logs between March 15th, March 28th, 2014 are used for training (cross-validation) Corfu. The fusion models are compared based on their performance on our test data (first two weeks of April 2014). The red line shows an example query in our training period sampled from a session (τ_s) (represented by the shaded area). The data from the session before the query are used for computing the contextual session features, and the clicks observed for the query and later in the session are used for generating the pseudo-relevance labels in *CRR*.

are also more candidates with poor rankings than those with good (observable from histograms along the upper and right sides), which supports our finding in Table 2 that suggestion rankings on average did not perform as well as the original ranking.

The conclusions that can be drawn from this experiment are that the rankings for query suggestions can vary in quality with regard to the original query. In many cases (such as the case with our `[ kmart ]` example), a query suggestion may suffice as a form of contextual disambiguation and data fusion should not be applied naïvely across all such queries. The results are consistent with previous work [33] in suggesting that a more sophisticated data fusion technique may not necessarily lead to improvements due to low candidate quality.

5. FUSION CLASSIFIER

Based on the above findings, we developed a classifier to identify when a query suggestion's results should be fused with those of the original query. As we did in the previous section, we find candidate suggestions using *CosQus*(H). If our classifier indicates that it is better to fuse, we use CombSUM to merge the results of the suggestion with the original query: otherwise, we keep the original ranking We refer to our approach as **Co**ntextual **R**esult **Fu**sion (Corfu).

To generate training data for our classifier, we sampled 6.2 million sessions (13.2 million impressions) from Bing search logs between March 15th, 2014 and March 28th, 2014. This period is distinguished in a purple box in Figure 3. For each of these impressions we computed the ΔCRR value between the query and the top-ranked candidate suggested by *CosQus*(H). For training the classifier, instances with $\Delta > 0$ values are considered as positive examples, and those with $\Delta < 0$ are considered as negative examples. We trained both logistic regression and gradient boosted decision-tree models for classification (GBDT) [17]. Since GBDT consistently outperformed logistic regression, we focus here on the GBDT results only. We did a parameter sweep over the number of trees $\{20, 100, 500\}$, number of leaves $\{2, 4, 8, \cdots, 128\}$, minimum number of instances per leaf $\{1, 10, 50\}$, and learning rate $\{0.02, 0.05, 0.1, 0.4\}$ and picked the best model by 5-fold cross validation. We evaluate the performance of Corfu classifiers on test data comprising another mutually exclusive set of logs. Our test data is comprised of 13.7 million impressions sampled from 6.4 million Bing search log sessions between April 1st, 2014 and April 14th, 2014 (green box in Figure 3). We discard all impressions with zero gain or loss from our test data, leaving 2.2 million impressions, on which we report the final numbers.

5.1 Features

We trained our classifier using a range of query, context and session features: the full list is given in Table 3. Many of the features are self-explanatory and we give further insight into our choices below. Different subsets of the features were collected from different time periods in the Bing search logs owing to the different phases of candidate generation, utility scoring, training and validation. A breakdown of the timeline of the log, including when features were extracted, is given in Figure 3 and also discussed below.

Memorization. The *memorization* features are computed over the candidate utility computation period τ_v (white box in Figure 3). We averaged and recorded the blended $\Delta CRR_\mu(f, q_a)$ scores for each query pair (q_a, q_c) and contextual triple (q_a, q_c, o) (the values shown in Figure 4). From this we were able to create a white-list of queries where we found positive ΔCRR_μ. We use these white-lists as *static* fusion baselines against our Corfu classifier and respectively refer to them as Memorized(P) and Memorized(T). The experimental results summarized later in this section confirm that our classifier generalizes beyond what simple white-listing attains.

Session and context. Our session features are a mix of lexical and context-based attributes obtained from sessions τ_s containing q_a during the training and validation period (an example segment is given by the shaded area within the purple box in Figure 3). The lexical features measure the similarity of q_a and q_c with the queries preceding q_a in the session, an indicator of whether topic drift is occurring in the session. The context features revolve around the context model (Θ) at query time and the top category in this model (o^*) which represents the *session context*.

Historical. We derived our historical features over the candidate generation period τ_h captured over 13 months of query logs. These statistics capture the long-term frequency of q_a and q_c independently and together along with the typical overlap of their rankings.

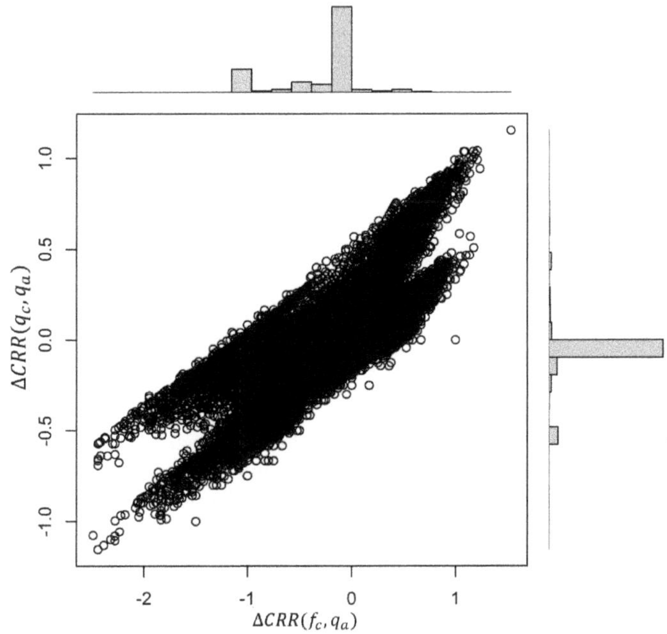

Figure 4: Scatterplot of the gain in *CRR* between the original query ranking and its suggestion against the gains between the original and the blended ranking.

Cross source. We also recorded the typical context model for q_c over τ_h and compared its similarity to that of Θ in τ_s, a measure of the topic alignment of q_c with q_a.

Next we show how a classifier trained based on these features can effectively decide when to blend the search results of a query with those returned for a related query suggestion.

5.2 Evaluation

Our evaluation results for Corfu and the Memorized variants are given in Table 4. We define *wins* and *losses* only on cases where fusion improves or hurts performance. That is, the correct cases of backing off to the original ranking do not contribute to the wins. Similarly, missing out on good fusion candidates does not count as a loss.[6] Using Corfu we were able to make significant gains over the original ranking, clearly alleviating the problems caused by naïvely using fusion on all query candidates. Our gains also apply across both ambiguous and general queries, although consistent with our previous experiments they are higher on the former set. This confirms our initial hypothesis that ambiguous queries should benefit more from contextual disambiguation. Simply memorizing good blendings was shown to not be an effective alternative. memorization generally leads to negative changes in all cases except a very slight gain in the case of context-independent memorization for ambiguous queries.

It is worth noting that the numbers in Table 4 are averaged over all impressions in our evaluation set. However, Corfu triggers fusion only in 5.68% of all impressions, and 9.52% over the ambiguous subset. This means that in a great majority of the cases, Corfu does back off to the ranking of the original query. If we average ΔCRR only over impressions that Corfu recommends for fusion,

[6]We ignore the costs associated with running an extra query here. In practice, zero gain might be considered as a slight loss.

Table 3: The features used for training the contextual blending classifier. Here, s is the search session containing the query q_a; $\mathcal{Q}_a$ represents all queries that appear in the session up until impression I_a; $\Theta(s,a)$ denotes the context model of s before receiving q_a which consists of pairs of ODP categories o and their associated confidence value $p(o)$. The category with the highest confidence value in Θ is distinguished by o^*, and the last query in $\mathcal{Q}_a$ is denoted by q_l.

Name	Description
Memorization (τ_v)	
$\Delta CRR_\mu(f, q_a)$	Average fusion utility of (q_a, q_c).
$\Delta CRR_\mu(f, q_a \vert o^*)$	Average fusion utility of (q_a, q_c, o^*).
Session and Context (τ_s)	
I_a	Position of query q_a in the session.
$p_\mu(o)$	Average category confidence values in Θ.
$p(o^*)$	Confidence of top category in Θ.
$H(\Theta)$	Entropy of category confidence values in Θ.
$Sim(q_a, q_l)$	Lexical similarity between q_a and q_l.
$Sim(q_c, q_l)$	Lexical similarity between q_c and q_l.
$Sim_\mu(q_a, \mathcal{Q}_a)$	Avg. text similarity of q_a and $\mathcal{Q}_a$ queries.
$Sim_\mu(q_c, \mathcal{Q}_a)$	Avg. text similarity of q_c and $\mathcal{Q}_a$ queries.
$Sim_{\max}(q_a, \mathcal{Q}_a)$	Max. text similarity of q_a and $\mathcal{Q}_a$ queries.
$Sim_{\max}(q_c, \mathcal{Q}_a)$	Max. text similarity of q_c and $\mathcal{Q}_a$ queries.
$\mathcal{I}(q_a \in \mathcal{Q}_a)$	Has q_a appeared previously in $\mathcal{Q}_a$?
$\mathcal{I}(q_c \in \mathcal{Q}_a)$	Has q_c appeared previously in $\mathcal{Q}_a$?
$\mathcal{I}(c^*, L1)$	Is c^* a 1st-level ODP category?
$\mathcal{I}(c^*, L2)$	Is c^* a 2nd-level ODP category?
$\mathcal{I}(q_a == q_l)$	Is q_a the same as q_l?
Historical (τ_h)	
$F(q_a)$	Historical query frequency for q_a.
$F(q_c)$	Historical query frequency for q_c.
$\Omega(q_a, q_c, 1)$	No. common docs in top-1 of q_a and q_c.
$\Omega(q_a, q_c, 5)$	No. common docs in top-5 of q_a and q_c.
$\Omega(q_a, q_c, 10)$	No. common docs in top-10 of q_a and q_c.
$F(q_a, q_c)$	Number of times q_a is followed by q_c.
$\delta F(q_a, q_c)$	$F(q_a) - F(q_c)$.
$\rho F(q_a, q_c)$	$F(q_a)/F(q_c)$.
Cross source ($\tau_{s,h}$)	
$\cos(\Theta, \Theta_h(q_c))$	Cosine similarity between Θ and $\Theta_h(q_c)$

we get a better picture of *f-segment* (fusion-segment) gains. On the *Ambiguous queries* dataset, Corfu achieves $\Delta CRR = 0.141$, improving over the results returned for the original query by 30.72%. Similarly, the f-segment ΔCRR on the *All-queries* dataset is 0.126 representing a 23.87% improvement over the no-fusion baseline.

Our results indicate that the causes of query ambiguity and fusion effectiveness are complex and it is not enough to simply memorize which contextual candidates work and which do not. Ranking the features from Corfu over ambiguous queries gives us insight into which are important when learning when to perform data fusion (Table 5). The ranking is based on the normalized reduction in residual squared error and the weights are normalized with respect to the top feature. The strongest feature is the Memorized utility score for query pairs, which is not surprising given the positive results for Memorized(P) on ambiguous queries. This demonstrates that Corfu is able to build on its success with the introduction of the other features. Of note is the fact that 3 of the top 5 features relate to the distribution of category confidence scores. The success of Corfu is strongly tied to the quality of the context model and a clear sign that context plays a part in determining whether data fusion will be successful during query disambiguation. Finally, the 2nd highest ranked feature is the frequency of q_c in τ_h, potentially a sign of confidence in q_c as a fusion candidate.

Table 4: The performance of different fusion methods on the testing dataset. The numerical columns respectively represent number of wins (#W), number of losses (#L), accuracy (Acc.) and ΔCRR. All numbers are computed with respect to the results of the original query (no fusion). All differences are statistically significant according to the paired t-test ($p < 0.01$). For reference, the *CRR* of a naïve system that always blends is about 7% worse than the no fusion baseline on both testbeds.

Method	#W	#L	Acc.	ΔCRR	(% ▲/▼)
All queries					
Memorized(P)	128K	144K	0.776	-0.007	(▼1.32%)
Memorized(T)	154K	199K	0.762	-0.021	(▼3.96%)
Corfu	50K	32K	0.803	0.007	(▲1.35%)
Ambiguous queries					
Memorized(P)	55K	53K	0.778	0.001	(▲0.21%)
Memorized(T)	69K	76K	0.768	-0.009	(▼1.96%)
Corfu	50K	26K	0.804	0.034	(▲2.92%)

Table 5: The top five most important features according to the Corfu model trained on *Ambiguous* queries. Similar trends can be found for the other dataset (not presented here). All feature weights are normalized with respect to the feature with the highest weight.

Feature	Weight	Description
$\Delta CRR_{\mu}(f, q_a)$	1.000	Memorized fusion utility of (q_a, q_c).
$F(q_c)$	0.572	Historical frequency of the candidate.
$p_{\mu}(o)$	0.433	Mean of confidence values in Θ.
$H(\Theta)$	0.285	Entropy of confidence values in Θ.
$p(o^*)$	0.200	Confidence of the top category in Θ.

Beyond CRR. The results presented so far confirm the effectiveness of Corfu in deciding when to apply contextual fusion, and demonstrate the improvements in retrieval quality as measured by *CRR*. However, evaluation metrics do have their shortcomings [29]. Given that our models are optimized for *CRR*, it would be reassuring to re-evaluate our results using alternative metrics. For this purpose, we define two metrics based on the first[7] and the last satisfied clicks in the session. We refer to the document that receives the last satisfied click in the session as $d_{\mathcal{L}}$. Likewise, the document that receives the first satisfied click is denoted by $d_{\mathcal{F}}$. Our first metric ($RR_{\mathcal{L}}$) measures the reciprocal rank of $d_{\mathcal{L}}$ in the original and blended rankings for a given query. This is inspired by observations in prior work that considered the last click of the session as a proxy for the user's intended destination [14, 42]. Our second metric ($RR_{\mathcal{F}}$) is similarly defined based on $d_{\mathcal{F}}$. Here, the idea is that boosting the position of these documents would allow users to satisfy their information needs more quickly.

The results are consistent with our previous findings. Corfu improves $RR_{\mathcal{L}}$ from $0.340 \rightarrow 0.351$ (▲2.3%) across all queries, and from $0.326 \rightarrow 0.338$ (▲3.6%) on the ambiguous subset. The f-segment gains are more substantial, as expected: $0.214 \rightarrow 0.351$ (▲64.2%) on all queries, and $0.232 \rightarrow 0.357$ (▲53.7%) on the ambiguous subset. The $RR_{\mathcal{F}}$ trends are consistent: Corfu improves $RR_{\mathcal{F}}$ from $0.535 \rightarrow 0.544$ (▲1.5%) across all queries, and from $0.541 \rightarrow 0.556$ (▲2.8%) on the ambiguous subset. The f-segment gains are: $0.477 \rightarrow 0.622$ (▲30.2%) on all queries, and $0.462 \rightarrow 0.621$ (▲34.3%) on the ambiguous subset. Overall, the $RR_{\mathcal{F}}$ numbers confirm that Corfu successfully places the first satisfied clicks higher in the ranking, allowing users to access high quality documents faster. The improved performance on $RR_{\mathcal{L}}$ also suggests that the blended rankings selected by Corfu are able to place these *target* documents higher in the ranking compared to the no-fusion baselines.

[7]That is the first satisfied click after issuing the current query. Clicks for previous queries in the session are excluded.

6. RELATED WORK

We group prior research by the three key problems we address in this paper: query disambiguation, finding effective query reformulations, and selectively blending results from multiple queries.

Contextual query disambiguation. Word disambiguation is an ongoing topic of research in Natural Language Processing and information retrieval (IR). In IR, disambiguation is usually applied to focus search results for queries that are either polysemous (have multiple senses) or that belong to a number of subtopic categories [36]. For instance, queries that are abbreviations and acronyms can be matched to their expanded forms by mining word associations in anchor text from a corpus and query reformulations from query logs [40]. Semantic graphs are commonly used to model word senses and are usually built using thesauri or lexical databases such as WordNet[8]. In these cases, supervised and unsupervised approaches such as PageRank, HITS or node similarity can be used to find alternative queries [24, 38]. While our approach is also unsupervised, we do not require an external ontology or corpus-learned language model. Similar work by Mihalkova and Mooney [25] makes use of prior queries within a session to perform disambiguation, although in their case at least 5 clicks on URLs with distinct hostnames are required before disambiguation can be achieved. They use a Markov logic network to re-rank for the user's ambiguous query, whereas in our fusion approach we can both re-rank and inject relevant URLs into the user's ranking. We note that intentionally ambiguous queries can be issued by users in a session when exploring an intrinsically diverse topic [28]: in these cases it would be beneficial to use session context to assist the user in narrowing or adjusting their information intent.

As well as disambiguation, web search ranking can be improved by incorporating user context. This context can include explicit features based on demographic identifiers such as age, gender, and location, or implicit features that are inferred from search behavior and history. For example, the predicted reading ability of a user, combined with an estimation of the technical difficulty of documents, can be used to improve search results, especially for educational documents [10]. Long-term user search histories can personalize search results [37] and even identify cases in which users are behaving atypically [15]. All of these categorical contextual markers can be used in our technique, both long-term and short-term. We focus our study on short-term, session subtopic categories as these are easy to interpret and useful in identifying the ambiguous queries from search logs that our method specifically targets.

Query reformulation. The prevalence of session search in query logs [19] has resulted in a wealth of research on the interpretation of query reformulations. While it has been found that as many as 10-20% of reformulations are simply spelling corrections [12], our underlying retrieval system helps correct for this with a robust spelling-correction system, meaning the observed reformulations are useful as observations of user progress and intent. Huang and Efthimiadis [18] performed an in-depth analysis of term-based query changes during a session in order to create a reformulation taxonomy. This was taken further by Kato et al. [22] who used a

[8]`http://wordnet.princeton.edu/`

questionnaire and search log analysis to define six cognitive search intents that users exhibit when reformulating queries, which they incorporated into a machine learning-based query expansion algorithm. In our work, we do not attempt to differentiate between reformulation types: we record effectiveness scores for all query-context-reformulation triples.

Early work on query reformulation involved query expansion, a classic IR technique that automatically replaces, re-weights or adds terms to queries to improve ranking and retrieval. Early methods searched for term co-occurrences within the document collection as candidates for expansion [26]. Modern techniques find term associations in thesauri, semantic graphs and query logs to create better expanded queries [13]. Typically, these expansion approaches replace the initial search results entirely with those of the expanded query, whereas our method can selectively fuse ranked results from multiple query variations.

A less intrusive method than query expansion, and one widely deployed for Web search, is to *suggest* new queries to the user. Two main avenues for providing new contextual queries to the user have been personalized query auto-completions [2, 34], which are estimated using previous queries from the same user, or query suggestions. Query suggestions occupy space on the SERP and are found by mining sessions in search logs [27], traversing query/click graphs [7, 11] or extracting phrases from corpora [6].

The query reformulation research most similar to ours is by Cao et al. [9], who proposed an unsupervised approach to cluster search log queries into unlabeled concepts and demonstrated their method's scalability by evaluating over a large search log. While their goal was to perform query suggestion, our goal is to find good reformulation candidates for contextual blending. In turn, our use of blending gives our method more fine-grained control over the nature of the final search results at the level of individual documents, whose rankings are influenced by the query disambiguation results. Our addition of a taxonomy to label concepts also makes interpreting query results easier. Finally, our technique has an even smaller computational footprint and we demonstrate its scalability in our evaluation over an even larger search log.

In later work, Cao et al. [8] use a taxonomy combined with click information, similar to our use of the ODP and clicks to create session context. While they also use other query and term features to train a prediction method offline to categorize search queries, their focus was on predicting faceted vs. vertical search, not performing selective blending of query suggestion results. Also, our method is trained offline but can be dynamically updated as searches occur in order to find new reformulations and reinforce established ones.

Other related reformulation work includes Wang and Zhai [39] that mined a search log for reformulations and then determined whether the user's original query under-specified (the user did not know which terms to use) or mis-specified (the user used the wrong terms) their search intent by mining term co-occurrences in a corpus. Ozertem et al. [27] followed a similar approach, but with query co-occurrences in a machine learning framework. Like these approaches, our method mines search logs for reformulations as a means for disambiguation, but does not operate on a term-by-term basis. In addition, the method in Ozertem et al. is mostly concerned with identifying effective individual terms and posits term suggestion as a potential use, whereas we directly learn reformulations to improve rankings for the user's original query.

Blending results from multiple queries. Data fusion techniques merge relevant results from related or expanded queries so as to improve the original ranking [32, 33]. While effective, these methods have not taken user context into account. Instead, state of the art research has investigated the blending of results from expanded queries; for instance, LambdaMerge is a supervised learning method that learns how to optimally blend results from query reformulations found using a click graph [33], whilst Xu et al. [43] implemented a kernel-based method for learning blending weights for results from query reformulations found using click-through data. Optimal blending strategies are an active area of research and not the focus of this paper, so we adopt a fixed blending strategy that allows us to evaluate the reformulation technique more effectively. Our novel contribution related to blending is the development of the contextual fusion classifier that uses session, context, historical and other features to learn when to selectively apply blending. To the best of our knowledge, ours is the first work to develop a context-based classifier of this type.

7. CONCLUSIONS

In this paper we investigated methods for improving the search experience for ambiguous queries by using user context. We defined user context as the topical categorization of the user's session and query. We began by focusing on contextual query suggestion. Unlike other methods which find suggestion candidates based on query/click graphs, we mined search logs for commonly co-occurring queries in sessions. We defined a utility function that accounted for the sparsity of clicks on ambiguous queries by including and weighting those that occur later in the session. Conditioning this utility on contextual categories and aggregating over search logs allowed us to rank and select a contextual query suggestion candidate. In our evaluation we found that a hybrid of both contextual/non-contextual queries (the *CosQus*(H) method) gave significant gains over a state-of-the-art baseline.

Next, we looked at data fusion as a means of directly improving search results for ambiguous queries. We blended results from our contextual query suggestions with those of the user's query and observed that naïvely blending on all suggestions led to poor overall performance. To resolve this, we proposed a novel fusion classifier (Corfu) that could distinguish when to perform data fusion and when to suggest a query instead. We trained it using session, context and query features extracted over a large-scale search log from `bing.com`. Our approach showed significant improvements over the rankings of the original query, for both ambiguous and general queries, and also made gains over simply memorizing which queries to blend on. An analysis of our feature set highlighted the importance that context plays in classifying when to use data fusion for contextual query disambiguation.

This work could be extended by exploring different types of contextual information for disambiguation. For instance, location would provide a suitable classification space and would lead to a different set of candidate queries and feature set for the classifier. Additionally, user history (rather than session context) could be used as a means for results personalization and a way to use context in the first query of a session. Also, more complex data fusion methods could be explored, potentially by taking context into account during the merging itself, though our approach of contextual query suggestion combined with a fusion classifier demonstrates that a simple fusion technique is sufficient.

References

[1] R. Baeza-Yates, C. Hurtado, and M. Mendoza. Query recommendation using query logs in search engines. EDBT'04, pages 588–596. Springer-Verlag, 2004.

[2] Z. Bar-Yossef and N. Kraus. Context-sensitive query auto-completion. WWW '11, pages 107–116. ACM, 2011.

[3] N. Belkin, P. Kantor, E. Fox, and J. Shaw. Combining the evidence of multiple query representations for information retrieval. *Information Processing and Management*, 31:431–448, 1995.

[4] P. N. Bennett, K. Svore, and S. T. Dumais. Classification-enhanced ranking. WWW '10, pages 111–120. ACM, 2010.

[5] P. N. Bennett, R. W. White, W. Chu, S. T. Dumais, P. Bailey, F. Borisyuk, and X. Cui. Modeling the impact of short- and long-term behavior on search personalization. SIGIR '12, pages 185–194. ACM, 2012.

[6] S. Bhatia, D. Majumdar, and P. Mitra. Query suggestions in the absence of query logs. SIGIR '11, pages 795–804. ACM, 2011.

[7] P. Boldi, F. Bonchi, C. Castillo, D. Donato, A. Gionis, and S. Vigna. The query-flow graph: Model and applications. CIKM '08, pages 609–618. ACM, 2008.

[8] H. Cao, D. H. Hu, D. Shen, D. Jiang, J.-T. Sun, E. Chen, and Q. Yang. Context-aware query classification. SIGIR '09, pages 3–10. ACM, 2009.

[9] H. Cao, D. Jiang, J. Pei, Q. He, Z. Liao, E. Chen, and H. Li. Context-aware query suggestion by mining click-through and session data. KDD '08, pages 875–883. ACM, 2008.

[10] K. Collins-Thompson, P. N. Bennett, R. W. White, S. de la Chica, and D. Sontag. Personalizing web search results by reading level. In *Proceedings of CIKM 2011*, pages 403–412. ACM, 2011.

[11] N. Craswell and M. Szummer. Random walks on the click graph. SIGIR '07, pages 239–246. ACM, 2007.

[12] S. Cucerzan and E. Brill. Spelling correction as an iterative process that exploits the collective knowledge of web users. In D. Lin and D. Wu, editors, *EMNLP 2004*, pages 293–300, Barcelona, Spain, 2004. Association for Computational Linguistics.

[13] H. Cui, J.-R. Wen, J.-Y. Nie, and W.-Y. Ma. Query expansion by mining user logs. *IEEE Trans. on Knowl. and Data Eng.*, 15(4):829–839, July 2003.

[14] D. Downey, S. Dumais, D. Liebling, and E. Horvitz. Understanding the relationship between searchers' queries and information goals. In *CIKM '08*, pages 449–458, Napa Valley, CA, 2008.

[15] C. Eickhoff, K. Collins-Thompson, P. N. Bennett, and S. Dumais. Personalizing atypical web search sessions. WSDM '13, pages 285–294. ACM, 2013.

[16] S. Fox, K. Karnawat, M. Mydland, S. Dumais, and T. White. Evaluating implicit measures to improve web search. *ACM Trans. Inf. Syst.*, 23(2):147–168, Apr. 2005.

[17] J. H. Friedman. Greedy function approximation: a gradient boosting machine. *Annals of Statistics*, pages 1189–1232, 2001.

[18] J. Huang and E. N. Efthimiadis. Analyzing and evaluating query reformulation strategies in web search logs. CIKM '09, pages 77–86. ACM, 2009.

[19] B. J. Jansen, A. Spink, and J. O. Pedersen. A Temporal Comparison of AltaVista Web Searching. *Journal of The American Society for Information Science and Technology*, 56:559–570, 2005.

[20] E. C. Jensen, S. M. Beitzel, A. Chowdhury, and O. Frieder. Query phrase suggestion from topically tagged session logs. FQAS'06, pages 185–196. Springer-Verlag, 2006.

[21] M. P. Kato, T. Sakai, and K. Tanaka. When do people use query suggestion? a query suggestion log analysis. *Inf. Retr.*, 16(6):725–746, Dec. 2013.

[22] M. P. Kato, T. Yamamoto, H. Ohshima, and K. Tanaka. Investigating users' query formulations for cognitive search intents. SIGIR '14, pages 577–586. ACM, 2014.

[23] F. Liu, C. Yu, and W. Meng. Personalized web search by mapping user queries to categories. CIKM '02, pages 558–565. ACM, 2002.

[24] C. Makris, Y. Plegas, and S. Stamou. Web query disambiguation using pagerank. *J. Am. Soc. Inf. Sci. Technol.*, 63(8):1581–1592, Aug. 2012.

[25] L. Mihalkova and R. Mooney. Search query disambiguation from short sessions. In *Beyond Search: Computational Intelligence for the Web Workshop at NIPS*, 2008.

[26] J. Minker. An evaluation of query expansion by the addition of clustered terms for a document retrieval system. *Information Storage and Retrieval*, 8(6):329–348, Dec. 1972.

[27] U. Ozertem, O. Chapelle, P. Donmez, and E. Velipasaoglu. Learning to suggest: A machine learning framework for ranking query suggestions. SIGIR '12, pages 25–34, Portland, OR, 2012.

[28] K. Raman, P. N. Bennett, and K. Collins-Thompson. Toward whole-session relevance: Exploring intrinsic diversity in web search. SIGIR '13, New York, NY, USA, 2013. ACM.

[29] T. Sakai. On the reliability of information retrieval metrics based on graded relevance. *Inf. Process. Manage.*, 43(2):531–548, Mar. 2007.

[30] T. Sakai and Z. Dou. Summaries, ranked retrieval and sessions: A unified framework for information access evaluation. SIGIR '13, pages 473–482, Dublin, Ireland, 2013.

[31] M. Sanderson. Ambiguous queries: Test collections need more sense. SIGIR '08, pages 499–506. ACM, 2008.

[32] J. A. Shaw and E. A. Fox. Combination of Multiple Searches. In *Text REtrieval Conference*, 1994.

[33] D. Sheldon, M. Shokouhi, M. Szummer, and N. Craswell. Lambdamerge: Merging the results of query reformulations. WSDM '11, New York, NY, USA, 2011. ACM.

[34] M. Shokouhi. Learning to personalize query auto-completion. SIGIR '13, New York, NY, USA, 2013. ACM.

[35] M. Shokouhi and L. Si. Federated search. *Foundations and Trends in Information Retrieval*, 5(1):1–102, 2011.

[36] R. Song, Z. Luo, J.-R. Wen, Y. Yu, and H.-W. Hon. Identifying ambiguous queries in web search. WWW '07, pages 1169–1170. ACM, 2007.

[37] J. Teevan, S. T. Dumais, and E. Horvitz. Personalizing search via automated analysis of interests and activities. SIGIR '05, pages 449–456. ACM, 2005.

[38] G. Tsatsaronis, I. Varlamis, and K. Nørvåg. An experimental study on unsupervised graph-based word sense disambiguation. In A. Gelbukh, editor, *Computational Linguistics and Intelligent Text Processing*, volume 6008 of *Lecture Notes in Computer Science*, pages 184–198. Springer Berlin Heidelberg, 2010.

[39] X. Wang and C. Zhai. Mining term association patterns from search logs for effective query reformulation. CIKM '08, pages 479–488. ACM, 2008.

[40] X. Wei, F. Peng, and B. Dumoulin. Analyzing web text association to disambiguate abbreviation in queries. SIGIR '08, pages 751–752. ACM, 2008.

[41] R. White and S. Drucker. Investigating behavioral variability in web search. In *WWW '07*, 2007.

[42] R. W. White, M. Bilenko, and S. Cucerzan. Studying the use of popular destinations to enhance web search interaction. In *SIGIR '07*, pages 159–166, Amsterdam, The Netherlands, 2007.

[43] J. Xu, W. Wu, H. Li, and G. Xu. A kernel approach to addressing term mismatch. WWW '11, pages 153–154. ACM, 2011.

Asymmetric Minwise Hashing for Indexing Binary Inner Products and Set Containment

Anshumali Shrivastava
Department of Computer Science
Computer and Information Science
Cornell University
Ithaca, NY 14853, USA
anshu@cs.cornell.edu

Ping Li
Department of Statistics and Biostatistics
Department of Computer Science
Rutgers University
Piscataway, NJ 08854, USA
pingli@stat.rutgers.edu

ABSTRACT

Minwise hashing (Minhash) is a widely popular indexing scheme in practice. Minhash is designed for estimating set resemblance and is known to be suboptimal in many applications where the desired measure is set overlap (i.e., inner product between binary vectors) or set containment. Minhash has inherent bias towards smaller sets, which adversely affects its performance in applications where such a penalization is not desirable. In this paper, we propose asymmetric minwise hashing (*MH-ALSH*), to provide a solution to this well-known problem. The new scheme utilizes asymmetric transformations to cancel the bias of traditional minhash towards smaller sets, making the final "collision probability" monotonic in the inner product. Our theoretical comparisons show that, for the task of retrieving with binary inner products, asymmetric minhash is provably better than traditional minhash and other recently proposed hashing algorithms for general inner products. Thus, we obtain an algorithmic improvement over existing approaches in the literature. Experimental evaluations on four publicly available high-dimensional datasets validate our claims. The proposed scheme outperforms, often significantly, other hashing algorithms on the task of near neighbor retrieval with set containment. Our proposal is simple and easy to implement in practice.

1. INTRODUCTION

Record matching (or linkage), data cleansing and plagiarism detection are among the most frequent operations in many large-scale data processing systems over the web. *Minwise hashing* (or minhash) [6, 7, 27] is a popular technique deployed by big data industries for these tasks. Minhash was originally developed for economically estimating the *resemblance* similarity between sets (which can be equivalently viewed as binary vectors). Later, because of its locality sensitive property [22], minhash became a widely used hash function for creating hash buckets leading to efficient algorithms for numerous applications including spam detection [6], collaborative filtering [4], news personalization [15], compressing social networks [13], graph sampling [14], record linkage [25], duplicate detection [21], all pair similarity [5], etc.

WWW 2015, May 18–22, 2015, Florence, Italy.
ACM 978-1-4503-3469-3/15/05.
http://dx.doi.org/10.1145/2736277.2741285 .

1.1 Sparse Binary Data, Set Resemblance, and Set Containment

Binary representations for web data are common, owing to the wide adoption of the "bag of words (n-gram)" representations for documents and images. It is often the case that a significant number of words (or combinations of words) occur rarely in a document and most of the higher-order n-grams in the document occur only once. Thus in practice, often only the presence or absence information suffices [9, 20, 24]. Leading search firms routinely use sparse binary representations in their large data systems, e.g., [8].

The underlying similarity measure of interest with minhash is the resemblance (also known as the Jaccard similarity). The resemblance similarity between two sets $x, y \subseteq \Omega = \{1, 2, ..., D\}$ is

$$\mathcal{R} = \frac{|x \cap y|}{|x \cup y|} = \frac{a}{f_x + f_y - a}, \tag{1}$$
$$\text{where } f_x = |x|, \;\; f_y = |y|, \;\; a = |x \cap y|.$$

Sets can be equivalently viewed as binary vectors with each component indicating the presence or absence of an attribute. The cardinality (e.g., f_x, f_y) is the number of nonzeros in the binary vector.

While the resemblance similarity is convenient and useful in numerous applications, there are also many scenarios where the resemblance is not the desired similarity measure [1, 11]. For instance, consider text descriptions of two restaurants:

1. "Five Guys Burgers and Fries Downtown Brooklyn New York"
2. "Five Kitchen Berkley"

Shingle (n-gram) based representations for strings are common in practice. Typical (first-order) shingle based representations of these names will be (i) {five, guys, burgers, and, fries, downtown, brooklyn, new, york } and (ii) {five, kitchen, berkley}. Now suppose the query is "Five Guys" which in shingle representation is {Five, Guys}. Suppose we hope to match and search the records, for this query "Five Guys", based on resemblance. Observe that the resemblance between query and record (i) is $\frac{2}{9}$ = 0.22, while that with record (ii) is $\frac{1}{4}$ = 0.25. Thus, simply based on resemblance, record (ii) is a better match for query "Five Guys" than record (i), which however should not be correct in this content.

Clearly the issue here is that resemblance penalizes the sizes of the sets involved. Shorter sets are unnecessarily favored over longer ones, which hurts the performance in (e.g.,) record matching [1]. There are other scenarios where such penalization is undesirable. For instance, in plagiarism detection, it is typically immaterial whether the text is plagiarized from a long or a short document.

To counter the often unnecessary penalization of the sizes of the sets with resemblance, a modified measure, the *set containment* (or Jaccard containment) was adopted [6, 1, 11]. Containment of set x and y with respect to x is defined as

$$\mathcal{J}_{\mathcal{C}} = \frac{|x \cap y|}{|x|} = \frac{a}{f_x}. \tag{2}$$

In the above example with query "Five Guys", the set containment with respect to query for record (i) will be $\frac{2}{2} = 1$ and with respect to record (ii) it will be $\frac{1}{2}$, leading to the desired ordering. It should be noted that for any fixed query x, the ordering under set containment with respect to the query, is the same as the ordering with respect to the intersection a (or binary inner product). Thus, near neighbor search problem with respect to $\mathcal{J}_{\mathcal{C}}$ is equivalent to the near neighbor search problem with respect to a.

1.2 Maximum Inner Product Search (MIPS) & Maximum Containment Search (MCS)

Formally, we state our problem of interest. We are given a collection $\mathcal{C}$ containing n sets (or binary vectors) over universe Ω with $|\Omega| = D$ (or binary vectors in $\{0,1\}^D$). Given a query $q \subset \Omega$, we are interested in the problem of finding $x \in \mathcal{C}$ such that

$$x = \arg\max_{x \in \mathcal{C}} |x \cap q| = \arg\max_{x \in \mathcal{C}} q^T x; \tag{3}$$

where $|\ |$ is the cardinality of the set. This is the so-called *maximum inner product search (MIPS)* problem.

For binary data, the MIPS problem is equivalent to searching with set containment with respect to the query, because the cardinality of the query does not affect the ordering and hence

$$x = \arg\max_{x \in \mathcal{C}} |x \cap q| = \arg\max_{x \in \mathcal{C}} \frac{|x \cap q|}{|q|}; \tag{4}$$

which we also refer to as the *maximum containment search (MCS)* problem.

1.3 Shortcomings of Inverted Index Based Approaches for MIPS (and MCS)

Owing to its practical significance, there have been many existing heuristics for solving the MIPS (or MCS) problem [31, 34, 12]. A notable recent work among them made use of the inverted index based approach [1]. Inverted indexes might be suitable for problems when the sizes of documents are small and each record only contains few words. This situation, however, is not always observed in practice. The documents over the web are large with huge vocabulary. Moreover, the vocabulary blows up very quickly once we start using higher-order shingles. In addition, there is an increasing interest in enriching the text with extra synonyms to make the search more effective and robust to semantic meanings [1], at the cost of a significant increase of the sizes of the documents. Furthermore, if the query contains many words then the inverted index is not very useful. To mitigate this issue several additional heuristics were proposed, for instance, the heuristic based on minimal infrequent sets [1]. Computing minimal infrequent sets is similar to the set cover problem which is hard in general and thus [1] resorted to greedy heuristics. The number of minimal infrequent sets could be huge in general and so these heuristics can be very costly. Also, such heuristics require the knowledge of the entire dataset before hand which is usually not practical in a dynamic environment like the web. In addition, inverted index based approaches do not have theoretical guarantees on the query time and their performance is very much dataset dependent. Not surprisingly, it was shown in [17] that simply using a sign of the projected document vector representation referred to as TOPSIG, which is also similar in nature to sign random projections (SRP) [18, 10], outperforms inverted index based approaches for querying.

1.4 Probabilistic Hashing

Locality Sensitive Hashing (LSH) [22] based randomized techniques are common and successful in industrial practice for efficiently solving NNS (*near neighbor search*). They are some of the few known techniques that do not suffer from the curse of dimensionality. Hashing based indexing schemes provide provably sub-linear algorithms for search which is a boon in this era of big data where even linear search algorithms are impractical due to latency. Furthermore, hashing based indexing schemes are massively parallelizable, which makes them ideal for modern distributed systems. The prime focus of this paper will be on efficient hashing based algorithms for binary inner products.

Despite the interest in set containment and binary inner products, there were no hashing algorithms for these measures for a long time and minwise hashing is still a popular heuristic [1]. Recently, it was shown that general inner products for real vectors can be efficiently solved by using asymmetric locality sensitive hashing schemes [35, 37]. The asymmetry is necessary for the general inner products and an impossibility of having a symmetric hash function can be easily shown using elementary arguments. Thus, binary inner product (or set intersection) being a special case of general inner products also admits provable efficient search algorithms with these asymmetric hash functions which are based on random projections. However, it is known that random projections are suboptimal for retrieval in the sparse binary domain [39]. Hence, it is expected that the existing asymmetric locality sensitive hashing schemes for general inner products are likely to be suboptimal for retrieving with sparse high dimensional binary-like datasets, which are common over the web.

1.5 Our Contributions

We investigate hashing based indexing schemes for the problem of near neighbor search with binary inner products and set containment. The impossibility of existence of LSH for general inner products shown in [35] also hold for the binary case.

Recent results on hashing algorithms for maximum inner product search [35] have shown the usefulness of asymmetric transformations in constructing provable hash functions for new similarity measures, which were otherwise impossible. Going further along this line, we provide a novel (and still very simple) asymmetric transformation for binary data, that corrects minhash and removes the undesirable bias of minhash towards the sizes of the sets involved. Such an asymmetric correction eventually leads to a provable hashing scheme for binary inner products, which we call *asymmetric minwise hashing (MH-ALSH)*. Our theoretical comparisons show that for binary data, which are common over the web, the new hashing scheme is provably more efficient that the recently proposed asymmetric hash functions for general inner products [35, 37]. Thus, we obtain a provable algorithmic improvement over the state-of-the-art hashing technique for binary inner products. The construction of our asymmetric transformation for minhash could be of independent interest in itself.

The proposed asymmetric minhash significantly outperforms existing hashing schemes, in the tasks of ranking and near neighbor search with set containment as the similarity measure, on four real-world high-dimensional datasets. Our final proposed algorithm is simple and only requires minimal modifications of the traditional minhash and hence it can be easily adopted in practice.

2. BACKGROUND

2.1 c-Approximate Near Neighbor Search and the Classical LSH

Past attempts of finding efficient algorithms, for exact near neighbor search based on space partitioning, often turned out to be a disappointment with the massive dimensionality of modern datasets [40]. Due to the curse of dimensionality, theoretically it is hopeless to obtain an efficient algorithm for exact near neighbor search. Approximate versions of near neighbor search problem were proposed [22] to overcome the linear query time bottleneck. One commonly adopted such formulation is the c-approximate Near Neighbor (c-NN).

DEFINITION 1. *(c-Approximate Near Neighbor or c-NN). [22] Given a set of points in a d-dimensional space $\mathbb{R}^d$, and parameters $S_0 > 0$, $\delta > 0$, construct a data structure which, given any query point q, does the following with probability $1-\delta$: if there exists an S_0-near neighbor of q in P, it reports some cS_0-near neighbor.*

The usual notion of S_0-near neighbor is in terms of distance. Since we are dealing with similarities, we define S_0-near neighbor of point q as a point p with $Sim(q,p) \geq S_0$, where Sim is the similarity function of interest.

The popular technique, with near optimal guarantees for c-NN in many interesting cases, uses the underlying theory of *Locality Sensitive Hashing* (LSH) [22]. LSH relies on a family of functions, with the property that similar input objects in the domain of these functions have a higher probability of colliding in the range space than non-similar ones. More specifically, consider $\mathcal{H}$ a family of hash functions mapping $\mathbb{R}^D$ to some set S.

DEFINITION 2. *(Locality Sensitive Hashing) A family $\mathcal{H}$ is called (S_0, cS_0, p_1, p_2) sensitive if for any two point $x, y \in \mathbb{R}^D$ and h chosen uniformly from $\mathcal{H}$ satisfies the following:*

- *if $Sim(x,y) \geq S_0$ then $Pr_{\mathcal{H}}(h(x)=h(y)) \geq p_1$*
- *if $Sim(x,y) \leq cS_0$ then $Pr_{\mathcal{H}}(h(x)=h(y)) \leq p_2$*

For approximate nearest neighbor search typically, $p_1 > p_2$ and $c < 1$ is needed. Note, $c < 1$ as we are defining neighbors in terms of similarity. To obtain distance analogy we can resort to $D(x,y) = 1 - Sim(x,y)$

FACT 1. *[22] Given a family of (S_0, cS_0, p_1, p_2) -sensitive hash functions, one can construct a data structure for c-NN with $O(n^\rho \log_{1/p_2} n)$ query time and space $O(n^{1+\rho})$, $\rho = \frac{\log 1/p_1}{\log 1/p_2} < 1$*

LSH trades off query time with extra preprocessing time and space that can be accomplished off-line. It requires constructing a one time data structure which costs $O(n^{1+\rho})$ space and further any c-approximate near neighbor queries can be answered in $O(n^\rho \log_{1/p_2} n)$ time in the worst case.

A particularly interesting sufficient condition for existence of LSH is the monotonicity of the collision probability in $Sim(x,y)$. Thus, if a hash function family $\mathcal{H}$ satisfies,

$$Pr_{h\in\mathcal{H}}(h(x)=h(y)) = g(Sim(x,y)), \tag{5}$$

where g is a monotonically increasing function, then the conditions of Definition 2 are automatically satisfied for all $c < 1$.

The quantity $\rho < 1$ is a property of the LSH family, and it is of particular interest because it determines the worst case query complexity of the c-approximate near neighbor search. It should be further noted, that the complexity depends on S_0 which is the operating threshold and c, the approximation ratio we are ready to tolerate. In case when we have two or more LSH families for a given similarity measure, then the LSH family with smaller value of ρ, for given S_0 and c, is preferred.

2.2 Minwise Hashing (Minhash)

Minwise hashing [6] is the LSH for the *resemblance*, also known as the *Jaccard similarity*, between sets. In this paper, we focus on binary data vectors which can be equivalent viewed as sets.

Given a set $x \in \Omega = \{1, 2, ..., D\}$, the minwise hashing family applies a random permutation $\pi : \Omega \to \Omega$ on x and stores only the minimum value after the permutation mapping. Formally minwise hashing (or minhash) is defined as:

$$h_\pi(x) = \min(\pi(x)). \tag{6}$$

Given sets x and y, it can be shown that the probability of collision is the resemblance $\mathcal{R} = \frac{|x\cap y|}{|x\cup y|}$:

$$Pr_\pi(h_\pi(x) = h_\pi(y)) = \frac{|x\cap y|}{|x\cup y|} = \frac{a}{f_x + f_y - a} = \mathcal{R}. \tag{7}$$

where $f_x = |x|$, $f_y = |y|$, and $a = |x \cap y|$. It follows from Eq. (7) that minwise hashing is (S_0, cS_0, S_0, cS_0)-sensitive family of hash function when the similarity function of interest is resemblance.

Even though minhash was really meant for retrieval with resemblance similarity, it is nevertheless a popular hashing scheme used for retrieving set containment or intersection for binary data [1]. In practice, the ordering of inner product a and the ordering or resemblance $\mathcal{R}$ can be different because of the variation in the values of f_x and f_y, and as argued in Section 1, which may be undesirable and lead to suboptimal results. We show later that by exploiting asymmetric transformations we can get away with the undesirable dependency on the number of nonzeros leading to a better hashing scheme for indexing set intersection (or binary inner products).

2.3 LSH for L2 Distance (L2LSH)

[16] presented a novel LSH family for all L_p ($p \in (0, 2]$) distances. In particular, when $p = 2$, this scheme provides an LSH family for L_2 distance. Formally, given a fixed number r, we choose a random vector w with each component generated from i.i.d. normal, i.e., $w_i \sim N(0,1)$, and a scalar b generated uniformly at random from $[0, r]$. The hash function is defined as:

$$h^{L2}_{w,b}(x) = \left\lfloor \frac{w^T x + b}{r} \right\rfloor, \tag{8}$$

where $\lfloor\rfloor$ is the floor operation. The collision probability under this scheme can be shown to be

$$Pr(h^{L2}_{w,b}(x) = h^{L2}_{w,b}(y)) = F_r(d), \tag{9}$$

$$F_r(d) = 1 - 2\Phi(-r/d) - \frac{2}{\sqrt{2\pi}r/d}\left(1 - e^{-r^2/(2d^2)}\right) \tag{10}$$

where $\Phi(x) = \int_{-\infty}^{x} \frac{1}{\sqrt{2\pi}} e^{-\frac{x^2}{2}} dx$ is the cumulative density function (cdf) of standard normal distribution and $d = ||x-y||_2$ is the Euclidean distance between the vectors x and y. This collision probability $F(d)$ is a monotonically decreasing function of the distance d and hence $h^{L2}_{w,b}$ is an LSH for $L2$ distances. This scheme is also the part of LSH package [2]. Here r is a parameter.

2.4 LSH for Cosine Similarity (SRP)

Sign Random Projections (SRP) or *simhash* is another popular LSH for the cosine similarity measure, which originates from the concept of **Sign Random Projections (SRP)** [18, 10]. Given a vector x, SRP utilizes a random w vector with each component generated from i.i.d. normal, i.e., $w_i \sim N(0,1)$, and only stores the sign of the projection. Formally simhash is given by

$$h^{sign}(x) = sign(w^T x). \tag{11}$$

It was shown in the seminal work [18] that collision under SRP satisfies the following equation:

$$Pr_w(h^{sign}(x) = h^{sign}(y)) = 1 - \frac{\theta}{\pi}, \tag{12}$$

where $\theta = cos^{-1}\left(\frac{x^T y}{||x||_2||y||_2}\right)$. The term $\frac{x^T y}{||x||_2||y||_2}$ is the popular **cosine similarity**. For sets (or equivalently binary vectors), the cosine similarity reduces to

$$\mathcal{S} = \frac{a}{\sqrt{f_x f_y}} \tag{13}$$

The recent work on *coding for random projections* [28] has shown the advantage of SRP (and 2-bit random projections) over L2LSH for both similarity estimation and near neighbor search. Interestingly, another recent work [39] has shown that for binary data (actually even sparse non-binary data), minhash can significantly outperform SRP for near neighbor search even as we evaluate both SRP and minhash in terms of the cosine similarity (although minhash is designed for resemblance). This motivates us to design asymmetric minhash for achieving better performance in retrieving set containments. But first, we provide an overview of asymmetric LSH for general inner products (not restricted to binary data).

2.5 Asymmetric LSH (ALSH)

The term "ALSH" stands for *asymmetric LSH*, as used in a recent work [35]. Through an elementary argument, [35] showed that it is not possible to have a Locality Sensitive Hashing (LSH) family for general unnormalized inner products.

For inner products between vectors x and y, it is possible to have $x^T y \gg x^T x$. Thus for any hashing scheme h to be a valid LSH, we must have $Pr(h(x) = h(y)) > Pr(h(x) = h(x)) = 1$, which is an impossibility. It turns out that there is a simple fix, if we allow asymmetry in the hashing scheme. Allowing asymmetry leads to an extended framework of asymmetric locality sensitive hashing (ALSH). The idea to is have a different hashing scheme for assigning buckets to the data point in the collection $\mathcal{C}$, and an altogether different hashing scheme while querying.

DEFINITION 3. *(Asymmetric Locality Sensitive Hashing (ALSH)) A family $\mathcal{H}$, along with the two vector functions $Q : \mathbb{R}^D \mapsto \mathbb{R}^{D'}$ (**Query Transformation**) and $P : \mathbb{R}^D \mapsto \mathbb{R}^{D'}$ (**Preprocessing Transformation**), is called (S_0, cS_0, p_1, p_2)-sensitive if for a given c-NN instance with query q, and the hash function h chosen uniformly from $\mathcal{H}$ satisfies the following:*

- *if $Sim(q,x) \geq S_0$ then $Pr_{\mathcal{H}}(h(Q(q))) = h(P(x))) \geq p_1$*
- *if $Sim(q,x) \leq cS_0$ then $Pr_{\mathcal{H}}(h(Q(q)) = h(P(x))) \leq p_2$*

Here x is any point in the collection $\mathcal{C}$. Asymmetric LSH borrows all theoretical guarantees of the LSH.

FACT 2. *Given a family of hash function $\mathcal{H}$ and the associated query and preprocessing transformations Q and P respectively, which is (S_0, cS_0, p_1, p_2) -sensitive, one can construct a data structure for c-NN with $O(n^\rho \log n)$ query time and space $O(n^{1+\rho})$, where $\rho = \frac{\log p_1}{\log p_2}$.*

[35] showed that using asymmetric transformations, the problem of **maximum inner product search (MIPS)** can be reduced to the problem of approximate near neighbor search in L_2. The algorithm first starts by scaling all $x \in \mathcal{C}$ by a constant large enough, such that $||x||_2 \leq U < 1$. The proposed ALSH family (**L2-ALSH**) is the LSH family for L_2 distance with the Preprocessing transformation $P : \mathbb{R}^D \mapsto \mathbb{R}^{D+m}$ and the Query transformation $Q : \mathbb{R}^D \mapsto \mathbb{R}^{D+2m}$ defined as follows:

$$P^{L2}(x) = [x; ||x||_2^2; ....; ||x||_2^{2^m}; 1/2; ...; 1/2] \tag{14}$$
$$Q^{L2}(x) = [x; 1/2; ...; 1/2; ||x||_2^2; ....; ||x||_2^{2^m}], \tag{15}$$

where [;] is the concatenation. $P^{L2}(x)$ appends m scalers of the form $||x||_2^{2^i}$ followed by m "1/2s" at the end of the vector x, while $Q^{L2}(x)$ first appends m "1/2s" to the end of the vector x and then m scalers of the form $||x||_2^{2^i}$. It was shown that this leads to provably efficient algorithm for MIPS.

FACT 3. *[35] For the problem of c-approximate MIPS in a bounded space, one can construct a data structure having $O(n^{\rho^*_{L2-ALSH}} \log n)$ query time and space $O(n^{1+\rho^*_{L2-ALSH}})$, where $\rho^*_{L2-ALSH} < 1$ is the solution to constrained optimization (16).*

$$\rho^*_{L2-ALSH} \tag{16}$$
$$= \min_{U<1, m\in N, r} \frac{\log F_r\left(\sqrt{m/2 - 2S_0\left(\frac{U^2}{V^2}\right) + 2U^{2^{m+1}}}\right)}{\log F_r\left(\sqrt{m/2 - 2cS_0\left(\frac{U^2}{V^2}\right)}\right)}$$
$$s.t. \quad \frac{U^{(2^{m+1}-2)}V^2}{S_0} < 1 - c,$$

Here the guarantees depends on the maximum norm of the space $V = \max_{x\in\mathcal{C}} ||x||_2$.

Quickly after, it was realized that a very similar idea can convert the MIPS problem in the problem of maximum cosine similarity search which can be efficiently solve by SRP leading to a new and better ALSH for MIPS **Sign-ALSH** [37] which works as follows: The algorithm again first starts by scaling all $x \in \mathcal{C}$ by a constant large enough, such that $||x||_2 \leq U < 1$. The proposed ALSH family (**Sign-ALSH**) is the SRP family for cosine similarity with the Preprocessing transformation $P^{sign} : \mathbb{R}^D \mapsto \mathbb{R}^{D+m}$ and the Query transformation $Q^{sign} : \mathbb{R}^D \mapsto \mathbb{R}^{D+2m}$ defined as follows:

$$P^{sign}(x) = [x; 1/2 - ||x||_2^2; ...; 1/2 - ||x||_2^{2^m}; 0; ...; 0] \tag{17}$$
$$Q^{sign}(x) = [x; 0; ...; 0; 1/2 - ||x||_2^2; ...; 1/2 - ||x||_2^{2^m}], \tag{18}$$

where [;] is the concatenation. $P^{sign}(x)$ appends m scalers of the form $1/2 - ||x||_2^{2^i}$ followed by m "0s" at the end of the vector x, while $Q^{sign}(x)$ appends m "0" followed by m scalers of the form $1/2 - ||x||_2^{2^i}$ to the end of the vector x. It was shown that this leads to provably efficient algorithm for MIPS.

As demonstrated by the recent work [28] on *coding for random projections*, there is a significant advantage of SRP over L2LSH for near neighbor search. Thus, it is not surprising that Sign-ALSH outperforms L2-ALSH for the MIPS problem. Similar to L2LSH, the runtime guarantees for Sign-ALSH can be shown as:

FACT 4. *For the problem of c-approximate MIPS, one can construct a data structure having $O(n^{\rho^*_{Sign-ALSH}} \log n)$ query time and space $O(n^{1+\rho^*_{Sign-ALSH}})$, where $\rho^*_{Sign-ALSH} < 1$ is the* *solution to constraint optimization problem*

$$\rho^*_{Sign-ALSH} = \min_{U,m,} \frac{\log\left(1 - \frac{1}{\pi}\cos^{-1}\left(\frac{S_0 \times \left(\frac{U^2}{V^2}\right)}{\frac{m}{4} + U^{2^{m+1}}}\right)\right)}{\log\left(1 - \frac{1}{\pi}\cos^{-1}\left(\min\{\frac{cS_0 U^2}{V^2}, z^*\}\right)\right)} \tag{19}$$

$$z^* = \left[\frac{(m - m2^{m-1}) + \sqrt{(m - m2^{m-1})^2 + m^2(2^m - 1)}}{4(2^m - 1)}\right]^{2^{-m}}$$

There is a similar asymmetric transformation [3, 32] which followed by sign random projection leads to another ALSH having very similar performance to Sign-ALSH. The ρ values, which were also very similar to the $\rho_{Sign-ALSH}$ can be shown as

$$\rho_{Sign} = \frac{\log\left(1 - \frac{1}{\pi}\cos^{-1}\left(\frac{S_0}{V^2}\right)\right)}{\log\left(1 - \frac{1}{\pi}\cos^{-1}\left(\frac{cS_0}{V^2}\right)\right)} \tag{20}$$

Both L2-ALSH and Sign-ALSH work for any general inner products over $\mathbb{R}^D$. For sparse and high-dimensional binary dataset which are common over the web, it is known that minhash is typically the preferred choice of hashing over random projection based hash functions [39]. We show later that the ALSH derived from minhash, which we call asymmetric minwise hashing (*MH-ALSH*), is more suitable for indexing set intersection for sparse binary vectors than the existing ALSHs for general inner products.

3. SAMPLING BASED ALSH FOR INDEXING BINARY INNER PRODUCTS

In [35], it was shown that there cannot exist any LSH for general unnormalized inner product. Using a slightly different argument it can be shown that even for binary data we cannot have any LSH scheme. Note, for binary inner product $x^T y \leq x^T x$ and therefore we cannot use exactly the same argument as before. But we can have x,y and z such that $x^T y \gg z^T z$. Now, $Pr(h(x) = h(y)) > Pr(h(z) = h(z)) = 1$ is again impossible. However, with asymmetry it is not difficult to construct a provable hashing scheme for binary inner product.

The construction is based on sampling. Simply sampling a random component leads to the popular LSH for hamming distance [33]. The ordering of inner product is different from that of hamming distance. The hamming distance between x and query q is given by $f_x + f_q - 2a$, while we want the collision probability to be monotonic in the inner product a. f_x makes it non-monotonic in a. Note that f_q has no effect on ordering of $x \in \mathcal{C}$ because it is constant for every query. To construct an LSH monotonic in binary inner product, we need an extra trick.

Given a binary data vector x, we sample a random co-ordinate (or attribute). If the value of this co-ordinate is 1 (in other words if this attribute is present in the set), our hash value is a fixed number 0. If this randomly sampled co-ordinate has value 0 (or the attribute is absent) then ensure that the hash value of the query never matches the hash value of the data. Formally,

$$\mathcal{H}_S(f(x)) = \begin{cases} 0 & \text{if } x_i = 1,\ i \text{ drawn uniformly} \\ 1 & \text{if f = Q (for query)} \\ 2 & \text{if f = P (while preprocessing)} \end{cases} \tag{21}$$

Note the asymmetry, i.e., the hash functions are different for query and the dataset. We can also write it down more formally using $P(.)$ and $Q(.)$ but we avoid it for the sake of simplicity.

THEOREM 1. *Given two binary vectors x and y, we have*

$$Pr(\mathcal{H}_S(P(x)) = \mathcal{H}_S(Q(y))) = \frac{a}{D} \tag{22}$$

PROOF. The probability that both $H_S(P(x))$ and $H_S(Q(y))$ have value 0 is $\frac{a}{D}$. They cannot be equal otherwise □

COROLLARY 1. *$\mathcal{H}_S$ is $(S_0, cS_0, \frac{S_0}{D}, \frac{cS_0}{D})$-sensitive ALSH for binary inner product with $\rho_{\mathcal{H}_S} = \frac{\log\left(\frac{S_0}{D}\right)}{\log\left(\frac{cS_0}{D}\right)} < 1$*

3.1 Shortcomings

The above ALSH for binary inner product is likely to be very inefficient for sparse and high dimensional datasets. For those datasets, typically the value of D is very high and the sparsity ensures that a is very small. For modern web datasets, we can have D running into billions (or 2^{64}) while the sparsity is only in few hundreds or perhaps thousands [8]. Therefore, we have $\frac{a}{D} \simeq 0$ which essentially boils down to $\rho_{\mathcal{H}_S} \simeq 1$. In other words, the hashing scheme becomes worthless in sparse high dimensional domain. On the other hand, if we observe the collision probability of minhash Eq.(7), the denominator is $f_x + f_y - a$, which is usually of the order of a and much less than the dimensionality for sparse datasets.

Another way of realizing the problem with the above ALSH is to note that it is informative only if a randomly sampled co-ordinate has value equal to 1. For very sparse dataset with $a \ll D$, sampling a non zero coordinate has probability $\frac{a}{D} \simeq 0$. Thus, almost all of the hashes will be fixed numbers which are not informative.

3.2 Why Is Minhash Reasonable?

In this section, we argue why retrieving inner product based on plain minhash is a reasonable thing to do. Later, we will show a provable way to improve it using asymmetric transformations.

The number of nonzeros in the query, i.e., $|q| = f_q$ does not change the identity of arg max in Eq.(4). Let us assume that we have data of bounded sparsity and define constant M as

$$M = \max_{x \in \mathcal{C}} |x| \tag{23}$$

where M is the maximum number of nonzeros (or maximum cardinality of sets) seen in the database. For sparse data seen in practice M is likely to be small compared to D. Outliers, if any, can be handled separately. By observing that $a \leq f_x \leq M$, we also have

$$\frac{a}{f_q + M - a} \leq \frac{a}{f_x + f_q - a} = \mathcal{R} \leq \frac{a}{f_q} \tag{24}$$

Thus, given the bounded sparsity, if we assume that the number of nonzeros in the query is given, then we can show that minhash is an LSH for inner products a because the collision probability can be upper and lower bounded by purely functions of a, M and f_q.

THEOREM 2. *Given bounded sparsity and query q with $|q| = f_q$, minhash is a $(S_0, cS_0, \frac{S_0}{f_q+M-S_0}, \frac{cS_0}{f_q})$ sensitive for inner products a with $\rho^q_{min} = \frac{\log \frac{S_0}{f_q+M-S_0}}{\log \frac{cS_0}{f_q}}$*

This explains why minhash might be a reasonable hashing approach for retrieving inner products or set intersection.

Here, if we remove the assumption that $|q| = f_q$ then in the worst case $\mathcal{R} \leq \frac{a}{f_q} \leq 1$ and we get log 1 in the denominator. Note that the above is the worst case analysis and the assumption $|q| = f_q$ is needed to obtain any meaningful ρ with minhash. We show the power of ALSH in the next section, by providing a better hashing scheme and we do not even need the assumption of fixing $|q| = f_q$.

4. ASYMMETRIC MINWISE HASHING

In this section, we provide a very simple asymmetric fix to minhash, named *asymmetric minwise hashing (MH-ALSH)*, which makes the overall collision probability monotonic in the original inner product a. For sparse binary data, which is common in practice, we later show that the proposed hashing scheme is superior (both theoretically as well as empirically) compared to the existing ALSH schemes for inner product [35].

4.1 The New ALSH for Binary Data

We define the new preprocessing and query transformations $P' : [0,1]^D \to [0,1]^{D+M}$ and $Q' : [0,1]^D \to [0,1]^{D+M}$ as:

$$P'(x) = [x; 1; 1; 1; ...; 1; 0; 0; ...; 0] \tag{25}$$

$$Q'(x) = [x; 0; 0; 0; ...; 0], \tag{26}$$

For $P'(x)$ we append $M - f_x$ 1s and rest f_x zeros, while in $Q'(x)$ we simply append M zeros.

At this point we can already see the power of asymmetric transformations. The original inner product between $P'(x)$ and $Q'(x)$ is unchanged and its value is $a = x^T y$. Given the query q, the new resemblance R' between $P'(x)$ and $Q'(q)$ is

$$R' = \frac{|P'(x) \cap Q'(q)|}{|P'(x) \cup Q'(q)|} = \frac{a}{M + f_q - a}. \tag{27}$$

If we define our new similarity as $Sim(x, y) = \frac{a}{M+f_q-a}$, then the near neighbors in this new similarity are the same as near neighbors with respect to either set intersection a or set containment $\frac{a}{f_q}$. Thus, we can instead compute near neighbors in $\frac{a}{M+f_q-a}$ which is also the resemblance between $P'(x)$ and $Q'(q)$. We can therefore use minhash on $P'(x)$ and $Q'(q)$.

Observe that now we have $M + f_q - a$ in the denominator, where M is the maximum nonzeros seen in the dataset (the cardinality of largest set), which for very sparse data is likely to be much smaller than D. Thus, asymmetric minhash is a better scheme than $\mathcal{H}_S$ with collision probability $\frac{a}{D}$ for very sparse datasets where we usually have $M \ll D$.

From theoretical perspective, to obtain an upper bound on the query and space complexity of c-approximate near neighbor with binary inner products, we want the collision probability to be independent of the quantity f_q. This is not difficult to achieve. The asymmetric transformation used to get rid of f_x in the denominator can be reapplied to get rid of f_q.

Formally, we can define $P'' : [0,1]^D \to [0,1]^{D+2M}$ and $Q'' : [0,1]^D \to [0,1]^{D+2M}$ as :

$$P''(x) = Q'(P'(x)); \quad Q''(x) = P'(Q'(x)); \tag{28}$$

where in $P''(x)$ we append $M - f_x$ 1s and rest $M + |f_x|$ zeros, while in $Q''(x)$ we append M zeros, then $M - f_q$ 1s and rest zeros

Again the inner product a is unaltered, and the new resemblance then becomes

$$R'' = \frac{|P''(x) \cap Q''(q)|}{|P''(x) \cup Q''(q)|} = \frac{a}{2M - a}. \tag{29}$$

which is independent of f_q and is monotonic in a. This allows us to achieve a formal upper bound on the complexity of c-approximate maximum inner product search with the new asymmetric minhash.

From the collision probability expression, i.e., Eq. (29), we have

THEOREM 3. *Minwise hashing along with Query transformation Q'' and Preprocessing transformation P'' defined by Equation 28 is a $(S_0, cS_0, \frac{S_0}{2M-S_0}, \frac{cS_0}{2M-cS_0})$ sensitive asymmetric hashing family for set intersection.*

This leads to an important corollary.

COROLLARY 2. *There exists an algorithm for c-approximate set intersection, with bounded sparsity M, that requires space $O(n^{1+\rho_{MH-ALSH}})$ and query time $O(n^{\rho_{MH-ALSH}} \log n)$, where*

$$\rho_{MH-ALSH} = \frac{\log \frac{S_0}{2M-S_0}}{\log \frac{cS_0}{2M-cS_0}} < 1 \tag{30}$$

Given query q and any point $x \in \mathcal{C}$, the collision probability under traditional minhash is $R = \frac{a}{f_x+f_q-a}$. This penalizes sets with high f_x, which in many scenarios is not desirable. To balance this negative effect, asymmetric transformation penalizes sets with smaller f_x. Note, that $M - f_x$ ones added in the transformations $P'(x)$ gives additional chance in proportion to $M - f_x$ for minhash of $P'(x)$ not to match with the minhash of $Q'(x)$. This asymmetric probabilistic correction balances the penalization inherent in minhash. This is a simple way of correcting the probability of collision which could be of independent interest in itself. We will show in our evaluation section, that despite this simplicity such correction leads to significant improvement over plain minhash.

4.2 Efficient Sampling

Our transformations P'' and Q'' always create sets with $2M$ nonzeros. In case when M is big, hashing might take a lot of time. We can use (improved) consistent weighted sampling [30, 23] for efficient generation of hashes. We can instead use transformations P''' and Q''' that makes the data non-binary as follows

$$P'''(x) = [x; M - f_x; 0] \tag{31}$$

$$Q'''(x) = [x; 0; M - f_x]$$

It is not difficult to see that the weighted resemblance (or weighted Jaccard similarity) between $P'''(x)$ and $Q'''(q)$ for given query q and any $x \in \mathcal{C}$ is

$$\mathcal{R}_W = \frac{\sum_i \min(P'''(x)_i, Q'''(q)_i)}{\sum_i \max(P'''(x)_i, Q'''(q)_i)} = \frac{a}{2M - a}. \tag{32}$$

Therefore, we can use fast consistent weighted sampling for weighted resemblance on $P'''(x)$ and $Q'''(x)$ to compute the hash values in time constant per nonzero weights, rather than maximum sparsity M. In practice we will need many hashes for which we can utilize the recent line of work that make minhash and weighted minhash significantly much faster [29, 36, 38, 19].

5. THEORETICAL COMPARISONS

For solving the MIPS problem in general data types, we already know two asymmetric hashing schemes, *L2-ALSH* and *Sign-ALSH*, as described in Section 2.5. In this section, we provide theoretical comparisons of the two existing ALSH methods with the proposed asymmetric minwise hashing (*MH-ALSH*). As argued, the LSH scheme described in Section 3 is unlikely to be useful in practice because of its dependence on D; and hence we can safely ignore it for simplicity of the discussion.

Before we formally compare various asymmetric LSH schemes for maximum inner product search, we argue why asymmetric minhash should be advantageous over traditional minhash for retrieving inner products. Let q be the binary query vector, and f_q denotes the number of nonzeros in the query. The $\rho_{MH-ALSH}$ for asymmetric minhash in terms of f_q and M is straightforward from the collision probability Eq.(27):

$$\rho^q_{MH-ALSH} = \frac{\log \frac{S_0}{f_q+M-S_0}}{\log \frac{cS_0}{f_q+M-cS_0}} \tag{33}$$

For minhash, we have from theorem 2 $\rho_{min}^q = \frac{\log \frac{S_0}{f_q+M-S_0}}{\log \frac{cS_0}{f_q}}$. Since M is the upper bound on the sparsity and cS_0 is some value of inner product, we have $M - cS_0 \geq 0$. Using this fact, the following theorem immediately follows

THEOREM 4. *For any query q, we have $\rho_{MH-ALSH}^q \leq \rho_{min}^q$.*

This result theoretically explains why asymmetric minhash is better for retrieval with binary inner products, compared to plain minhash.

For comparing asymmetric minhash with ALSH for general inner products, we compare $\rho_{MH-ALSH}$ with the ALSH for inner products based on sign random projections. Note that it was shown that Sign-ALSH has better theoretical ρ values compared to L2-ALSH [37]. Therefore, it suffices to show that asymmetric minhash outperforms sign random projection based ALSH. Both $\rho_{MH-ALSH}$ and ρ_{sign} can be rewritten in terms of ratio $\frac{S_0}{M}$ as follows. Note that for binary data we have $M = \max_{x \in C} ||x||^2 = V^2$

$$\rho_{MH-ALSH} = \frac{\log \frac{S_0/M}{2-S_0/M}}{\log \frac{cS_0/M}{2-cS_0/M}}; \quad \rho_{Sign} = \frac{\log\left(1 - \frac{1}{\pi}\cos^{-1}\left(\frac{S_0}{M}\right)\right)}{\log\left(1 - \frac{1}{\pi}\cos^{-1}\left(\frac{cS_0}{M}\right)\right)} \tag{34}$$

Observe that M is also the upper bound on any inner product. Therefore, we have $0 \leq \frac{S_0}{M} \leq 1$. We plot the values of $\rho_{MH-ALSH}$ and ρ_{sign} for $\frac{S_0}{M} = \{0.1,\ 0.2, ..., 0.8,\ 0.9,\ 0.95\}$ with c. The comparison is summarized in Figure 1. Note that here we use ρ_{Sign} based on the slightly more convenient transformation from [3, 32] instead of $\rho_{Sign-ALSH}$ for convenience although the two schemes perform essentially the same.

Clearly, irrespective of the choice of threshold $\frac{S_0}{M}$ or the approximation ratio c, asymmetric minhash outperforms sign random projection based ALSH in terms of the theoretical ρ values. This is not surprising, because it is known that minhash based methods are often significantly powerful for binary data compared to SRP (or simhash) [39]. Therefore ALSH based on minhash outperforms ALSH based on SRP as shown by our theoretical comparisons. Our proposal thus leads to an algorithmic improvement over state-of-the-art hashing techniques for retrieving binary inner products.

6. EVALUATIONS

In this section, we compare the different hashing schemes on the actual task of retrieving top-ranked elements based on set Jaccard containment. The experiments are divided into two parts. In the first part, we show how the ranking based on various hash functions correlate with the ordering of set containment. In the second part, we perform the actual LSH based bucketing experiment for retrieving top-ranked elements and compare the computational saving obtained by various hashing algorithms.

6.1 Datasets

We used four publicly available high dimensional sparse datasets: *EP2006*, *MNIST*, *NEWS20*, and *NYTIMES*. (Note that "EP2006" is a short name for "E2006LOG1P" from LIBSVM web site.) Except for MNIST, the other three datasets are binary "BoW" representation of the corresponding text corpus. MNIST is an image dataset consisting of 784 pixel image of handwritten digits. Binarized versions of MNIST are commonly used in literature. The pixel values in MNIST were binarized to 0 or 1 values. For each of the four datasets, we generate two partitions. The bigger partition was used to create hash tables and is referred as the *training partition*. The small partition which we call the *query partition* is used for querying. The statistics of these datasets are summarized in Table 1. The datasets cover a wide spectrum of sparsity and dimensionality.

Table 1: Datasets

Dataset	# Query	# Train	# Dim	nonzeros (mean $\pm$ std)
EP2006	2,000	17,395	4,272,227	6072 ± 3208
MNIST	2,000	68,000	784	150 ± 41
NEWS20	2,000	18,000	1,355,191	454 ± 654
NYTIMES	2,000	100,000	102,660	232 ± 114

6.2 Competing Hash Functions

We consider the following hash functions for evaluations:

1. **Asymmetric minwise hashing (Proposed):** This is our proposal, the asymmetric minhash described in Section 4.1.

2. **Traditional minwise hashing (MinHash):** This is the usual minwise hashing, the popular heuristic described in Section 2.2. This is a symmetric hash function, we use h_π as defined in Eq.(6) for both query and the training set.

3. **L2 based Asymmetric LSH for Inner products (L2-ALSH):** This is the asymmetric LSH of [35] for general inner products based on LSH for L2 distance.

4. **SRP based Asymmetric LSH for Inner Products (Sign-ALSH):** This is the asymmetric hash function of [37] for general inner products based on SRP.

6.3 Ranking Experiment: Hash Quality Evaluations

We are interested in knowing, how the orderings under different competing hash functions correlate with the ordering of the underlying similarity measure which in this case is the set containment. For this task, given a query q vector, we compute the top-100 gold standard elements from the training set based on the set containment $\frac{a}{f_q}$. Note that this is the same as the top-100 elements based on binary inner products. Give a query q, we compute K different hash codes of the vector q and all the vectors in the training set. We then compute the number of times the hash values of a vector x in the training set matches the hash values of query q defined by

$$Matches_x = \sum_{t=1}^{K} \mathbf{1}(h_t(q) = h_t(x)), \tag{35}$$

where $\mathbf{1}$ is the indicator function. t subscript is used to distinguish independent draws of the underlying hash function. Based on $Matches_x$ we rank all elements in the training set. This procedure generates a sorted list for every query for every hash function. For asymmetric hash functions, in computing total collisions, on the query vector we use the corresponding Q function (query transformation) followed by underlying hash function, while for elements in the training set we use the P function (preprocessing transformation) followed by the corresponding hash function.

We compute the precision and the recall of the top-100 gold standard elements in the ranked list generated by different hash functions. To compute precision and recall, we start at the top of the ranked item list and walk down in order, suppose we are at the pth ranked element, we check if this element belongs to the gold standard top-100 list. If it is one of the top 100 gold standard elements, then we increment the count of *relevant seen* by 1, else we move to $p+1$. By p^{th} step, we have already seen p elements, so the *total*

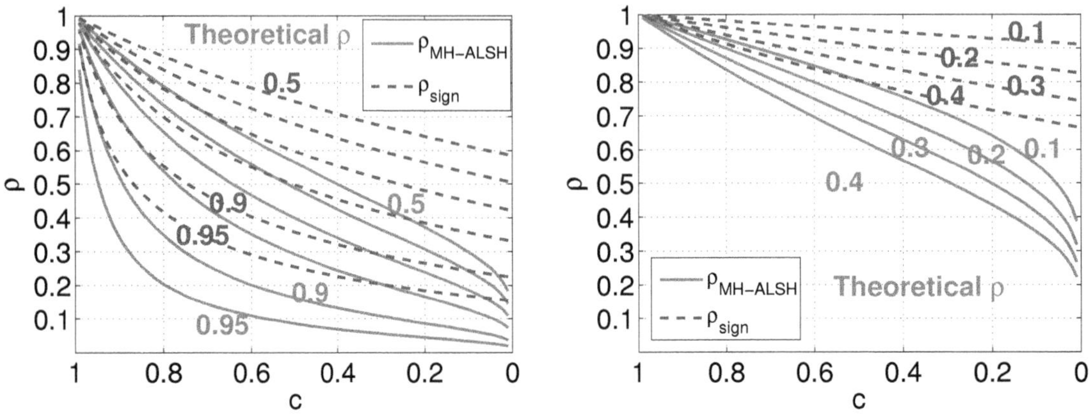

Figure 1: Values of $\rho_{MH-ALSH}$ and ρ_{sign} (lower is better) with respect to approximation ratio c for different $\frac{S_0}{M}$. The curves show that asymmetric minhash (solid curves) is noticeably better than ALSH based on sign random projection (dashed curves) in terms of their ρ values, irrespective of the choices of $\frac{S_0}{M}$ or c. For clarity, the results are shown in two panels.

elements seen is p. The precision and recall at that point is then computed as:

$$Precision = \frac{\text{relevant seen}}{p}, \qquad Recall = \frac{\text{relevant seen}}{100} \tag{36}$$

It is important to balance both. Methodology which obtains higher precision at a given recall is superior. Higher precision indicates higher ranking of the relevant items. We finally average these values of precision and recall over all elements in the query set. The results for $K \in \{32,\ 64,\ 128\}$ are summarized in Figure 2.

We can clearly see, that the proposed hashing scheme always achieves better, often significantly, precision at any given recall compared to other hash functions. The two ALSH schemes are usually always better than traditional minwise hashing. This confirms that fact that ranking based on collisions under minwise hashing can be different from the rankings under set containment or inner products. This is expected, because minhash in addition penalizes the number of nonzeros leading to a ranking very different from the ranking of inner products. Sign-ALSH usually performs better than L2-LSH, this is in line with the results obtained in [37].

It should be noted that ranking experiments only validate the monotonicity of the collision probability. Although, better ranking is certainly a good indicator of good hash function, it does not always mean that we will achieve faster sub-linear LSH algorithm. For bucketing the probability sensitivity around a particular threshold is the most important factor, see [33] for more details. What matters is the **gap** between the collision probability of good and the bad points. In the next subsection, we compare these schemes on the actual task of near neighbor retrieval with set containment.

6.4 LSH Bucketing Experiment: Computational Savings in Near Neighbor Retrieval

In this section, we evaluate the four hashing schemes on the standard (K, L)-parameterized bucketing algorithm [2] for sub-linear time retrieval of near neighbors based on set containment. In (K, L)-parameterized LSH algorithm, we generate L different meta-hash functions. Each of these meta-hash functions is formed by concatenating K different hash values as

$$B_j(x) = [h_{j1}(x); h_{j2}(x); ...; h_{jK}(x)], \tag{37}$$

where $h_{ij}, i \in \{1, 2, ..., K\}$ and $j \in \{1, 2, ..., L\}$, are KL different independent evaluations of the hash function under consideration. Different competing scheme uses its own underlying randomized hash function h.

In general, the (K, L)-parameterized LSH works in two phases:

i) **Preprocessing Phase:** We construct L hash tables from data by storing element x, in the training set, at location $B_j(P(x))$ in the hash-table j. Note that for vanilla minhash which is a symmetric hashing scheme $P(x) = x$. For other asymmetric schemes, we use their corresponding P functions. Preprocessing is a one time operation, once the hash tables are created they are fixed.

ii) **Query Phase:** Given a query q, we report the union of all the points in the buckets $B_j(Q(q))\ \forall j \in \{1, 2, ..., L\}$, where the union is over L hash tables. Again here Q is the corresponding Q function of the asymmetric hashing scheme, for minhash $Q(x) = x$.

Typically, the performance of a bucketing algorithm is sensitive to the choice of parameters K and L. Ideally, to find best K and L, we need to know the operating threshold S_0 and the approximation ratio c in advance. Unfortunately, the data and the queries are very diverse and therefore for retrieving top-ranked near neighbors there are no common fixed threshold S_0 and approximation ratio c that work for all the queries.

Our objective is to compare the four hashing schemes and minimize the effect of K and L, if any, on the evaluations. This is achieved by finding best K and L at every recall level. We run the bucketing experiment for all combinations of $K \in \{1, 2, 3, ...40\}$ and $L \in \{1, 2, 3, ..., 400\}$ for all the four hash functions independently. These choices include the recommended optimal combinations at various thresholds. We then compute, for every K and L, the mean recall of Top-T pairs and the mean number of points reported, per query, to achieve that recall. The best K and L at every recall level is chosen independently for different Ts. The plot of the mean fraction of points scanned with respect to the recall of top-T gold standard near neighbors, where $T \in \{5, 10, 20, 50\}$, is summarized in Figure 3.

The performance of a hashing based method varies with the variations in the similarity levels in the datasets. It can be seen that the proposed asymmetric minhash always retrieves much less number of points, and hence requires significantly less computations, compared to other hashing schemes at any recall level on all the four

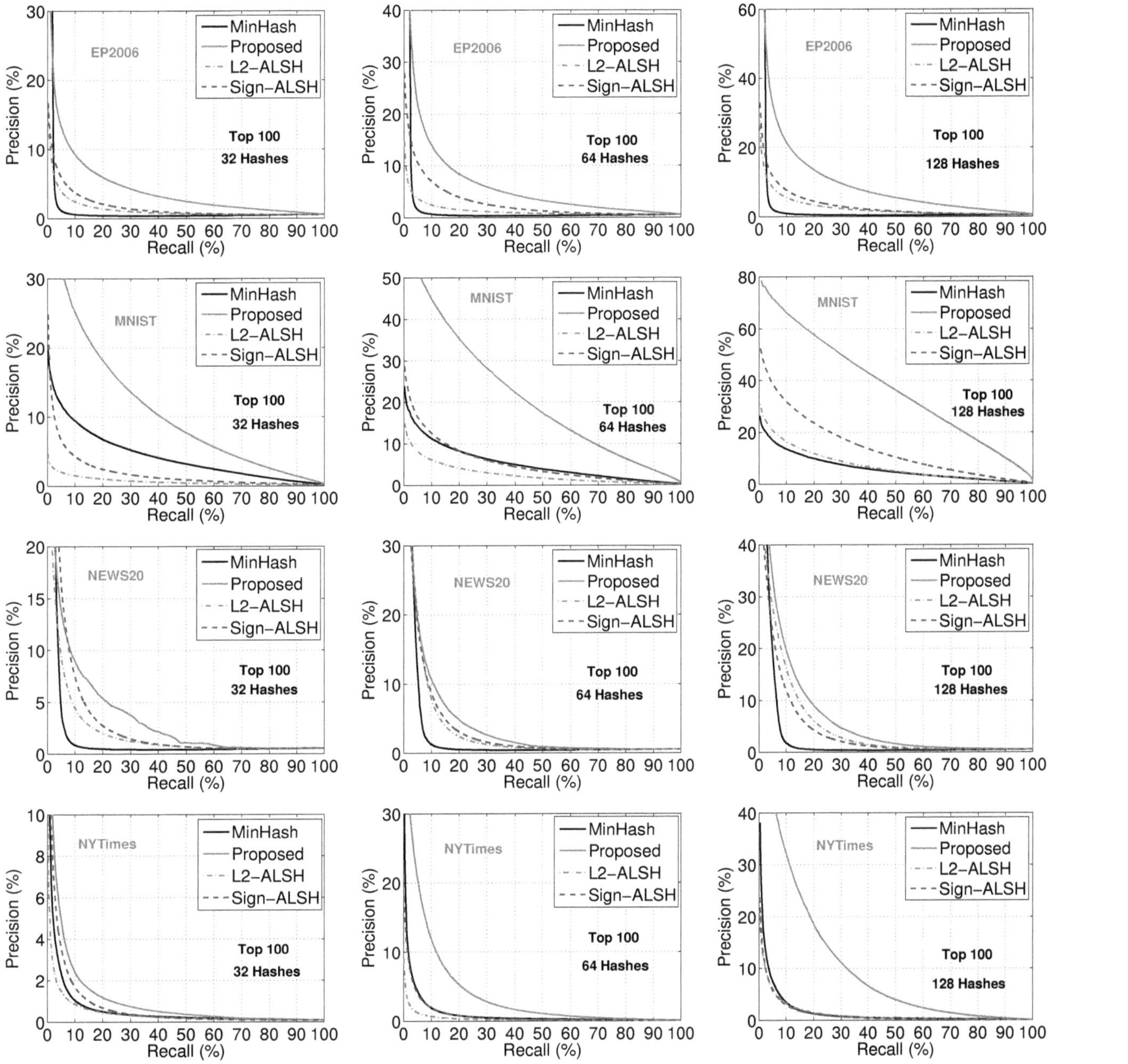

Figure 2: Ranking Experiments. Precision Vs Recall curves for retrieving top-100 items, for different hashing schemes on 4 chosen datasets. The precision and the recall were computed based on the rankings obtained by different hash functions using 32, 64 and 128 independent hash evaluations. Higher precision at a given recall is better.

datasets. Asymmetric minhash consistently outperforms other hash functions irrespective of the operating point. The plots clearly establish the superiority of the proposed scheme for indexing set containment (or inner products).

L2-ALSH and Sign-ALSH perform better than traditional minhash on EP2006 and NEWS20 datasets while they are worse than plain minhash on NYTIMES and MNIST datasets. If we look at the statistics of the dataset from Table 1, NYTIMES and MNIST are precisely the datasets with less variations in the number of nonzeros and hence minhash performs better. In fact, for MNIST dataset with very small variations in the number of nonzeros, the performance of plain minhash is very close to the performance of asymmetric minhash. This is of course expected because there is negligible effect of penalization on the ordering. EP2006 and NEWS20 datasets have huge variations in their number of nonzeros and hence minhash performs very poorly on these datasets. What is exciting is that despite these variations in the nonzeros, asymmetric minhash always outperforms other ALSH for general inner products.

The difference in the performance of plain minhash and asymmetric minhash clearly establishes the utility of our proposal which is simple and does not require any major modification over traditional minhash implementation. Given the fact that minhash is widely popular, we hope that our proposal will be adopted.

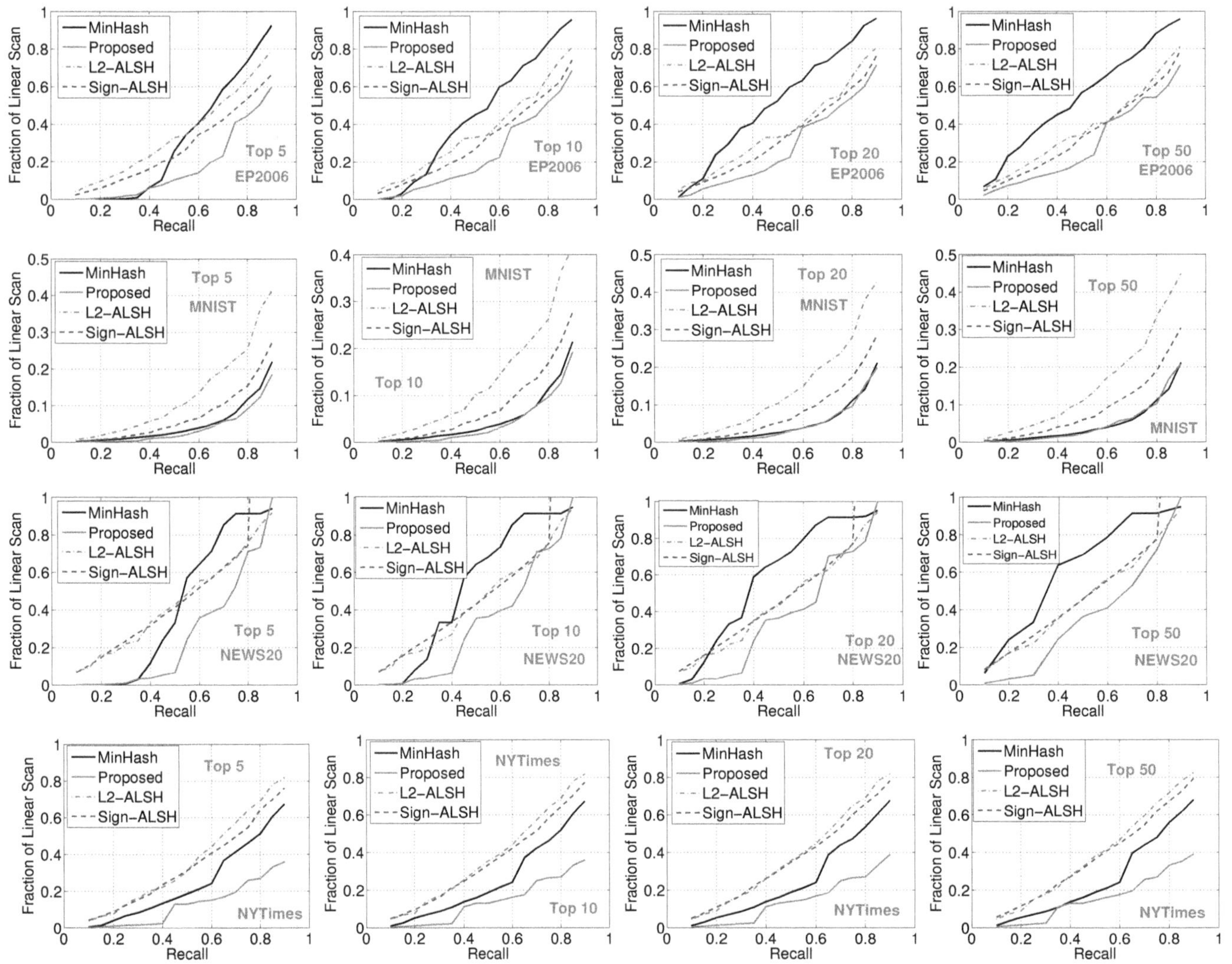

Figure 3: LSH Bucketing Experiments. Average number of points retrieved per query (lower is better), relative to linear scan, evaluated by different hashing schemes at different recall levels, for top-5, top-10, top-20, top-50 nearest neighbors based on set containment (or equivalently inner products), on four datasets. We show that results at the best K and L values chosen at every recall value, independently for each of the four hashing schemes.

7. CONCLUSION AND FUTURE WORK

Minwise hashing (minhash) is a widely popular indexing scheme in practice for similarity search. Minhash was originally designed for estimating set resemblance (i.e., normalized size of set intersections). In many applications the performance of minhash is severely affected because minhash has a bias towards smaller sets. In this study, we propose asymmetric corrections (asymmetric minwise hashing, or MH-ALSH) to minwise hashing that remove this often undesirable bias. Our corrections lead to a provably superior algorithm for retrieving binary inner products in the literature. Rigorous experimental evaluations on the task of retrieving maximum inner products clearly establish that the proposed approach can be significantly advantageous over the existing state-of-the-art hashing schemes in practice, when the desired similarity is the inner product (or containment) instead of the resemblance. Our proposed method requires only minimal modification of the original minwise hashing algorithm and should be straightforward to implement in practice.

Future work: One immediate direction for future work would be *asymmetric consistent weighted sampling* for hashing weighted intersection: $\sum_{i=1}^{D}\min\{x_i, y_i\}$, where x and y are general real-valued vectors. One proposal of the new asymmetric transformation is the following:

$$P(x) = [x; M - \sum_{i=1}^{D} x_i; 0], \qquad Q(x) = [x; 0; M - \sum_{i=1}^{D} x_i],$$

where $M = \max_{x \in \mathcal{C}} \sum_i x_i$. It is not difficult to show that the weighted Jaccard similarity between $P(x)$ and $Q(y)$ is monotonic in $\sum_{i=1}^{D}\min\{x_i, y_i\}$ as desired. At this point, we can use existing methods for consistent weighted sampling [30, 23, 19, 26]. on the new data after asymmetric transformations

Acknowledgement

The work is partially supported by NSF-DMS-1444124, NSF-III-1360971, ONR-N00014-13-1-0764, and AFOSR-FA9550-13-1-0137.

8. REFERENCES

[1] P. Agrawal, A. Arasu, and R. Kaushik. On indexing error-tolerant set containment. In *Proceedings of the 2010 ACM SIGMOD International Conference on Management of data*, pages 927–938. ACM, 2010.

[2] A. Andoni and P. Indyk. E2lsh: Exact euclidean locality sensitive hashing. Technical report, 2004.

[3] Y. Bachrach, Y. Finkelstein, R. Gilad-Bachrach, L. Katzir, N. Koenigstein, N. Nice, and U. Paquet. Speeding up the xbox recommender system using a euclidean transformation for inner-product spaces. In *RecSys*, 2014.

[4] Y. Bachrach, E. Porat, and J. S. Rosenschein. Sketching techniques for collaborative filtering. In *Proceedings of the 21st International Jont Conference on Artifical Intelligence*, IJCAI'09, 2009.

[5] R. J. Bayardo, Y. Ma, and R. Srikant. Scaling up all pairs similarity search. In *WWW*, pages 131–140, 2007.

[6] A. Z. Broder. On the resemblance and containment of documents. In *the Compression and Complexity of Sequences*, pages 21–29, Positano, Italy, 1997.

[7] A. Z. Broder, M. Charikar, A. M. Frieze, and M. Mitzenmacher. Min-wise independent permutations. In *STOC*, pages 327–336, Dallas, TX, 1998.

[8] T. Chandra, E. Ie, K. Goldman, T. L. Llinares, J. McFadden, F. Pereira, J. Redstone, T. Shaked, and Y. Singer. Sibyl: a system for large scale machine learning.

[9] O. Chapelle, P. Haffner, and V. N. Vapnik. Support vector machines for histogram-based image classification. *IEEE Transactions on Neural Networks*, 10(5):1055–1064, 1999.

[10] M. S. Charikar. Similarity estimation techniques from rounding algorithms. In *STOC*, pages 380–388, Montreal, Quebec, Canada, 2002.

[11] S. Chaudhuri, V. Ganti, and R. Kaushik. A primitive operatior for similarity joins in data cleaning. In *ICDE*, 2006.

[12] S. Chaudhuri, V. Ganti, and D. Xin. Mining document collections to facilitate accurate approximate entity matching. *Proceedings of the VLDB Endowment*, 2(1):395–406, 2009.

[13] F. Chierichetti, R. Kumar, S. Lattanzi, M. Mitzenmacher, A. Panconesi, and P. Raghavan. On compressing social networks. In *KDD*, pages 219–228, Paris, France, 2009.

[14] G. Cormode and S. Muthukrishnan. Space efficient mining of multigraph streams. In *Proceedings of the twenty-fourth ACM SIGMOD-SIGACT-SIGART symposium on Principles of database systems*, pages 271–282. ACM, 2005.

[15] A. S. Das, M. Datar, A. Garg, and S. Rajaram. Google news personalization: scalable online collaborative filtering. In *Proceedings of the 16th international conference on World Wide Web*, pages 271–280. ACM, 2007.

[16] M. Datar, N. Immorlica, P. Indyk, and V. S. Mirrokn. Locality-sensitive hashing scheme based on p-stable distributions. In *SCG*, pages 253 – 262, Brooklyn, NY, 2004.

[17] S. Geva and C. M. De Vries. Topsig: Topology preserving document signatures. In *CIKM*, pages 333–338, 2011.

[18] M. X. Goemans and D. P. Williamson. Improved approximation algorithms for maximum cut and satisfiability problems using semidefinite programming. *Journal of ACM*, 42(6):1115–1145, 1995.

[19] B. Haeupler, M. Manasse, and K. Talwar. Consistent weighted sampling made fast, small, and easy. Technical report, arXiv:1410.4266, 2014.

[20] M. Hein and O. Bousquet. Hilbertian metrics and positive definite kernels on probability measures. In *AISTATS*, pages 136–143, Barbados, 2005.

[21] M. R. Henzinger. Finding near-duplicate web pages: a large-scale evaluation of algorithms. In *SIGIR*, pages 284–291, 2006.

[22] P. Indyk and R. Motwani. Approximate nearest neighbors: Towards removing the curse of dimensionality. In *STOC*, pages 604–613, Dallas, TX, 1998.

[23] S. Ioffe. Improved consistent sampling, weighted minhash and L1 sketching. In *ICDM*, pages 246–255, Sydney, AU, 2010.

[24] Y. Jiang, C. Ngo, and J. Yang. Towards optimal bag-of-features for object categorization and semantic video retrieval. In *CIVR*, pages 494–501, Amsterdam, Netherlands, 2007.

[25] N. Koudas, S. Sarawagi, and D. Srivastava. Record linkage: similarity measures and algorithms. In *Proceedings of the 2006 ACM SIGMOD international conference on Management of data*, pages 802–803. ACM, 2006.

[26] P. Li. Min-max kernels. Technical report, arXiv:1503.0173, 2015.

[27] P. Li and A. C. König. Theory and applications b-bit minwise hashing. *Commun. ACM*, 2011.

[28] P. Li, M. Mitzenmacher, and A. Shrivastava. Coding for random projections and approximate near neighbor search. Technical report, arXiv:1403.8144, 2014.

[29] P. Li, A. B. Owen, and C.-H. Zhang. One permutation hashing. In *NIPS*, Lake Tahoe, NV, 2012.

[30] M. Manasse, F. McSherry, and K. Talwar. Consistent weighted sampling. Technical Report MSR-TR-2010-73, Microsoft Research, 2010.

[31] S. Melnik and H. Garcia-Molina. Adaptive algorithms for set containment joins. *ACM Transactions on Database Systems (TODS)*, 28(1):56–99, 2003.

[32] B. Neyshabur and N. Srebro. A simpler and better lsh for maximum inner product search (mips). Technical report, arXiv:1410.5518, 2014.

[33] A. Rajaraman and J. Ullman. *Mining of Massive Datasets*. http://i.stanford.edu/ ullman/mmds.html.

[34] K. Ramasamy, J. F. Naughton, and R. Kaushik. Set containment joins: The good, the bad and the ugly.

[35] A. Shrivastava and P. Li. Asymmetric LSH (ALSH) for sublinear time maximum inner product search (mips). In *NIPS*, Montreal, CA, 2014.

[36] A. Shrivastava and P. Li. Densifying one permutation hashing via rotation for fast near neighbor search. In *ICML*, Beijing, China, 2014.

[37] A. Shrivastava and P. Li. Improved asymmetric locality sensitive hashing (ALSH) for maximum inner product search (MIPS). *arXiv:1410.5410 (submitted to AISTATS)*, 2014.

[38] A. Shrivastava and P. Li. Improved densification of one permutation hashing. In *UAI*, Quebec City, CA, 2014.

[39] A. Shrivastava and P. Li. In defense of minhash over simhash. In *AISTATS*, 2014.

[40] R. Weber, H.-J. Schek, and S. Blott. A quantitative analysis and performance study for similarity-search methods in high-dimensional spaces. In *VLDB*, pages 194–205, 1998.

Language Understanding in the Wild: Combining Crowdsourcing and Machine Learning

Edwin Simpson
University of Oxford, UK
edwin@robots.ox.ac.uk

Matteo Venanzi
University of Southampton, UK
mv1g10@ecs.soton.ac.uk

Steven Reece
University of Oxford, UK
reece@robots.ox.ac.uk

Pushmeet Kohli
Microsoft Research, Cambridge, UK
pkohli@microsoft.com

John Guiver
Microsoft Research, Cambridge, UK
joguiver@microsoft.com

Stephen J. Roberts
University of Oxford, UK
sjrob@robots.ox.ac.uk

Nicholas R. Jennings
University of Southampton, UK
nrj@ecs.soton.ac.uk

ABSTRACT

Social media has led to the democratisation of opinion sharing. A wealth of information about public opinions, current events, and authors' insights into specific topics can be gained by understanding the text written by users. However, there is a wide variation in the language used by different authors in different contexts on the web. This diversity in language makes interpretation an extremely challenging task. Crowdsourcing presents an opportunity to interpret the sentiment, or topic, of free-text. However, the subjectivity and bias of human interpreters raise challenges in inferring the semantics expressed by the text. To overcome this problem, we present a novel Bayesian approach to language understanding that relies on aggregated crowdsourced judgements. Our model encodes the relationships between labels and text features in documents, such as tweets, web articles, and blog posts, accounting for the varying reliability of human labellers. It allows inference of annotations that scales to arbitrarily large pools of documents. Our evaluation using two challenging crowdsourcing datasets shows that by efficiently exploiting language models learnt from aggregated crowdsourced labels, we can provide up to 25% improved classifications when only a small portion, less than 4% of documents has been labelled. Compared to the six state-of-the-art methods, we reduce by up to 67% the number of crowd responses required to achieve comparable accuracy. Our method was a joint winner of the CrowdFlower - CrowdScale 2013 Shared Task challenge at the conference on Human Computation and Crowdsourcing (HCOMP 2013).

WWW 2015, May 18–22, 2015, Florence, Italy.
ACM 978-1-4503-3469-3/15/05.
http://dx.doi.org/10.1145/2736277.2741689.

General Terms

Crowdsourcing, machine learning, variational Bayes, classifier combination, text classification, sentiment analysis, human computation

1. INTRODUCTION

Social media provides an increasingly rich source of information about public opinion and current events, which can be valuable to professionals across a wide range of industries. For example, Twitter[1] can reflect the public's sentiment about the weather, such as in the data collected during the CrowdScale 2013 Shared Task challenge[2], opinion of major health emergencies such as the H1N1 flu pandemic [6], or knowledge of disaster events such as Typhoon Haiyan [5]. Mining this large body of unstructured data requires an understanding of the language used in each specific context. For example, the *sentiment* of a document, which reflects the author's attitudes or opinion of a subject, is captured in the language they use. However, that relationship between sentiment and language typically depends on factors such as the viewpoint and the gender of the authors and the context of their writing. For example, distinctive terms such as "love" and "dude" are more frequently used by female and male Twitter users, respectively, to refer to the same concept of a friend or a family member [15]. Similarly, reports posted by members of the public to Ushahidi after the 2010 Haiti earthquake used a type of language that is significantly different to that seen in other locations and other types of emergency [22]. This diversity in social media text inhibits the performance of any generic method for automated document classification "in the wild". However, this problem can be alleviated by human interpreters who can use their background knowledge and natural language understanding skills to recognise the sentiment of documents and adapt to the diverse language used in different contexts.

Interpreting sentiment or relevance of a piece of text is highly subjective and, along with variations in annotators' skill levels, it can result in disagreement. To overcome this

[1] `www.twitter.com`
[2] `www.crowdscale.org`

problem, existing methods for crowdsourced document classification require labels from multiple annotators for every document in the corpus [28, 26], which can be prohibitively costly or time consuming [22]. Fortunately, the occurrence of certain terms in each document also provides weak indications of the sentiment of a document, which can be used to reduce the cost of employing human interpreters to annotate the entire corpus. Therefore, we propose a hybrid approach to large scale document classification that integrates human intelligence with automated analysis of text.

In this paper we present *Bayesian Classifier Combination with Words (BCCWords)*, a framework for combining annotations from a crowd of workers with text features to classify a corpus of documents. This approach is an example of an emerging research area known as *human-agent collectives* [12]. We introduce a scalable Bayesian inference mechanism for BCCWords, which learns posterior distributions over the workers' reliability and document classifications, given the documents' text features and a set of crowdsourced annotations. Our method not only allows us to handle the varying error rates and bias of individual members of the crowd, but also allows us to annotate an entire set of documents when only a subset have been labelled by the crowd, by leveraging the inferred language model to automatically annotate the remaining documents.

In more detail, we make the following contributions to the state-of-the-art:

1. We present a novel generic model, BCCWords, that combines human and computer interpretations of free text documents and infers their sentiment.

2. We present a novel scalable variational Bayes inference algorithm, BCCWords–VB, for training the BCCWords model. This algorithm was first demonstrated at the CrowdScale 2013 Shared Task Challenge and was a joint winner.

3. We derive an efficient inference decomposition method that allows our algorithm to perform batch inference over hundreds of thousands of documents and demonstrate inference with 569,786 crowdsourced sentiment judgements for 98,979 documents in approximately 20 minutes on a standard laptop.

4. We present an exhaustive evaluation of our algorithm on two real datasets of text annotations and compare it against six state-of-the-art methods for crowd-based text classification and data aggregation. Specifically, our evaluation shows that our algorithm is up to 25% more accurate when only a small portion, less than 4% of the documents, have been labelled and that our algorithm reduces by up to 67% the amount of crowd labels required to achieve comparable accuracy with standard methods.

The paper is structured as follows. We review the literature on language modelling and aggregation models for crowdsourced judgements in Section 2. Section 3 presents our model in detail, then Section 4 provides mathematical details for our variational inference algorithm. Section 5 demonstrates the efficacy of our approach by comparing it against state-of-the-art benchmarks on two real world crowdsourcing datasets. Finally, we conclude and discuss future work in Section 6.

2. AGGREGATING JUDGEMENTS

Many applications in the literature have employed crowdsourcing, whereby multiple people process each document or data point [13, 1, 33]. A key challenge in such crowdsourcing applications is to mitigate the bias of subjective labellers. Previous work has addressed this problem by combining crowd responses to obtain reliable aggregate classifications. However, as yet, these methods have not exploited the language used in the text to further assist in interpreting the text. We propose to use the variations in language associated with sentiment to reduce errors and bias arise when employing members of the public to perform labelling tasks.

A further challenge with real world applications of document crowdsourcing is the cost of employing a sufficient number of annotators to rapidly label a large dataset. For example, the Ushahidi dataset comprises at least 40,000 text messages which had to be interpreted in the first month after the earthquake in Haiti, which proved to be infeasible [22]. However, a suitable language model would enable automated analysis at much greater scale and allows the annotators to focus their efforts on the most difficult documents. We therefore propose a learning method for harnessing the skills of human labellers to learn a bespoke language model from much larger sets of documents.

A number of methods have been used in the literature to address the challenge of aggregating annotations from the crowd, including the simple technique of *majority voting* [18]. However, simple majority voting treats all annotators as equally reliable and does not provide any meaningful measure of confidence in the combined decision to account for conflicts in judgement or low annotator skill levels. To overcome this problem, probabilistic methods have been developed which learn the skill levels or bias of each annotator and aggregate their decisions accordingly [26, 7, 32, 25, 31]. These methods are prone to error when only small amounts of gold labels are available as they do not consider uncertainty in skill levels and other model parameters. For example, when only one label is obtained from a worker, these methods may infer that the worker is either perfectly reliable or totally incompetent when, in reality, the worker is neither. This is a common problem with approaches to inference that use maximum likelihood or maximum a-posteriori solutions [4]. In order to overcome this limitation, algorithms for aggregating crowdsourced data including *SFilter* [8] and *Bayesian Classifier Combination (BCC)* [14, 30] capture the uncertainty in the workers' skill levels or bias, as well as the uncertainty in the aggregated labels. Unfortunately, these methods do not exploit the text features of documents, and consequently require each document to be labelled by the crowd, often multiple times, to obtain confident classifications.

Previous work has introduced methods for automatic text classification based solely on word content, such as the bag-of-words classifier [11]. Although such methods have been applied to automated sentiment analysis, they need a language model for each application context [21]. This often requires large amounts of training data and substantial effort by the system designer to cope with the diversity in language [17]. In contrast our approach uses a crowd of human annotators to learn a language model rapidly and cheaply. In the following sections we develop the BCCWords model and then demonstrate its efficacy with benchmark methods.

3. THE BCCWORDS MODEL

In this section we describe our novel BCCWords model. This model is an extension of the independent Bayesian classifier combination (IBCC) model presented in [28] which classified data points using only crowdsourced labels. BCWords models the crowd as multiple heterogeneous classifiers, and uses both the crowd's responses and the word structure of documents to classify them. An advantage of BCCWords is that it can be inferred in a *semi-supervised* or *unsupervised* manner. It does not require separate training and test phases but uses a single, combined learning phase over all available data. The semi-supervised approach simultaneously learns from labelled training data and the latent structure in the entire dataset, making it particularly suitable when gold-standard data is limited.

We start by introducing our notation. There is a crowd of K annotators expressing their judgement about the correct classification of N documents over a range of C possible classes. The classes may represent sentiment classes, topic labels, or other types of annotation. Each document, i, has an unknown true class $t_i \in C$. The judgement of annotator k for document i is denoted as label $l_i^{(k)}$, where $l_i^{(k)} \in C$. Also, we assume that the nth word, $w_{i,n}$, of document i takes a value d from a dictionary of size D words. For notational simplicity, we assume a dense set of judgements in which each annotator rates all N documents. However, as will become clear in section 4.1, our model naturally supports sparsity in the dataset, which is the case for the CrowdFlower dataset used in Section 5.

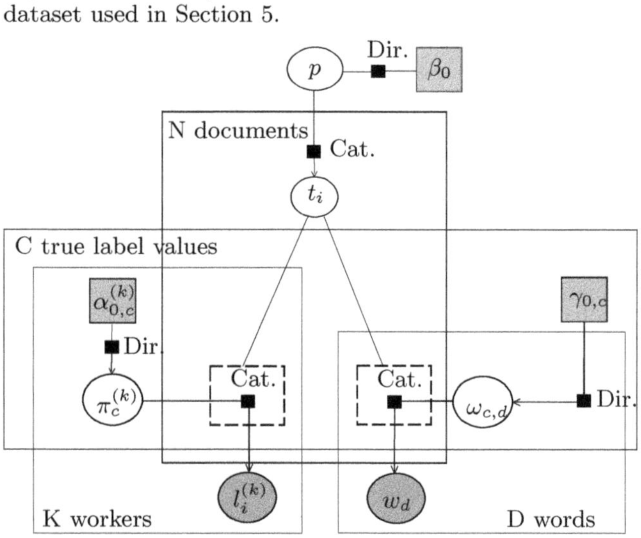

Figure 1: The factor graph of BCCWords. The circular, shaded nodes represent observed variables and the square, shaded nodes represent the hyperparameters. The plates describe (i) the set of K annotators, (ii) the N documents, (iii) the C possible true label values and (iv) the D words contained in the dictionary of terms used in the documents.

The factor graph of our Bayesian Combination Model, BCCWords, is shown in Figure 1, and the model is described as follows. We assume that each annotator draws judgements for documents of class $t_i = c$ from a categorical distribution with parameters $\boldsymbol{\pi}_c^{(k)}$:

$$l_i^{(k)} | \boldsymbol{\pi}_c^{(k)}, t_i \sim \mathrm{Cat}(\boldsymbol{\pi}_c^{(k)})$$

where $\boldsymbol{\pi}_c^{(k)}$ is the accuracy vector of annotator k for documents of class c. That is, each element of $\boldsymbol{\pi}_c^{(k)}$ specifies the probability that annotator k will give a judgement c' when presented with a document whose true class is c:

$$\pi_{c,c'}^{(k)} = p(l_i^{(k)} = c' | t_i = c)$$

where p is the Dirichlet distribution. The set of accuracy vectors $\boldsymbol{\pi}_c^{(k)}$ for all c is called the *confusion matrix* representing k's reliability. In Figure 1, the annotator confusion matrices are shown in the left-hand plate for all K annotators, depicting how the response of an annotator depends on the true class t_i of the document they are judging. The use of confusion matrices allows our model to combine annotators of very different skill levels, and is able to handle those who make random guesses or whose responses are the opposite of what we expect. Furthermore, a confusion matrix accounts for the personal bias of an annotator, since a tendency to select a more positive or negative judgment, c', than other members of the crowd, when presented with documents of true class c, will result in an increased likelihood, $\pi_{c,c'}^{(k)}$. A personal bias toward selecting judgement c' for all documents will result in high likelihoods $\pi_{c,c'}^{(k)}$ for all true classes c, thus the model will lean that the label c' from annotator k is less strongly discriminative.

Our language model is defined as follows. Given a document i of class c we assume that the probability that the nth word is d (i.e. $w_{i,n} = d$) follows a categorical distribution with parameters $\boldsymbol{\omega}_c = \{\omega_{c,d} \forall d\}$:

$$w_{i,n} | \omega_{c,d}, t_i \sim \mathrm{Cat}(\boldsymbol{\omega}_c),$$

where $\omega_{c,d} = p(w_{i,n} = d | t_i = c)$ is the probability that a randomly-drawn word from a document of class c is the word d. This probabilistic representation of text in documents corresponds to a mixture of bag-of-words model [11], where each mixture component is a bag-of-words model associated with one particular object class. The word distributions are represented in Figure 1 in the right-hand plate, showing the variables corresponding to the D words in the dictionary.

We assume that the true class label for each document, t_i, is drawn from a categorical distribution with parameters $\boldsymbol{\rho}$: $t_i | \boldsymbol{\rho} \sim \mathrm{Cat}(\boldsymbol{\rho})$. The parameters $\boldsymbol{\rho}$ can be regarded as the proportion of documents in each class, so that $\rho_c = p(t_i = c | \boldsymbol{\rho})$. These parameters are shown at the top of Figure 1.

To model the uncertainty in the latent variables in our model, we assign conjugate Dirichlet prior distributions to $\boldsymbol{\pi}_c^{(k)}$, $\boldsymbol{\omega}_c$ and $\boldsymbol{\rho}$, for each class $c \in C$ and annotator $k \in K$:

$$\boldsymbol{\pi}_c^{(k)} | \boldsymbol{\alpha}_{0,c}^{(k)} \sim \mathrm{Dir}(\boldsymbol{\alpha}_{0,c}^{(k)})$$
$$\boldsymbol{\rho} | \boldsymbol{\beta}_0 \sim \mathrm{Dir}(\boldsymbol{\beta}_0)$$
$$\boldsymbol{\omega}_c | \boldsymbol{\gamma}_{0,c} \sim \mathrm{Dir}(\boldsymbol{\gamma}_{0,c}),$$

where $\boldsymbol{\alpha}_{0,c}^{(k)}, \forall c$ is the per-annotator confusion matrix hyperparameter, and $\boldsymbol{\gamma}_{0,c}$ is the hyperparameter for the bag-of-words distribution for each class c. These hyperparameters have intuitive interpretations as prior *pseudo-counts*, meaning that their values are equivalent to a number of prior observations, which represent the strength of prior beliefs. When implementing BCCWords, the diagonal values of hyperparameters $\boldsymbol{\alpha}_{0,c}$ of the confusion matrices can be set to higher values than the off-diagonals, encoding the prior belief that annotators are expected to be better than random. The hyperparameters for the word distributions, $\boldsymbol{\gamma}_{0,c}$, and the class proportions, $\boldsymbol{\beta}_0$, can both be set so that the priors are uniform. This reflects an initial lack of information in the word structure of the documents and the class distribution of the documents.

To enable us to perform Bayesian inference over our model, we first specify the complete joint distribution:

$$p\left(\boldsymbol{l}, \boldsymbol{t}, \boldsymbol{\pi}_1^{(1)}, .., \boldsymbol{\pi}_C^{(K)}, \boldsymbol{\omega}_1, .., \boldsymbol{\omega}_C, \boldsymbol{\rho} | \boldsymbol{\alpha}_{0,1}^{(1)}, .., \boldsymbol{\alpha}_{0,C}^{(K)}, \boldsymbol{\beta}_0, \boldsymbol{\gamma}_{0,1}, .., \boldsymbol{\gamma}_{0,C}\right)$$
$$= \prod_{i=1}^{N} \left\{ \rho_{t_i} \prod_{k=1}^{K} \pi_{t_i, l_i^{(k)}}^{(k)} \cdot \prod_{n=1}^{W_i} \omega_{t_i, w_{i,n}} \right\} p(\boldsymbol{\rho}|\boldsymbol{\beta}_0)$$
$$\prod_{c=1}^{C} \left\{ p(\boldsymbol{\omega}_c | \boldsymbol{\gamma}_{0,c}) \prod_{k=1}^{K} p(\boldsymbol{\pi}_c^{(k)} | \boldsymbol{\alpha}_{0,c}^{(k)}) \right\} \quad (1)$$

where $\boldsymbol{l}$ is the set of labels from all annotators for all documents, and W_i is the number of words in document i. The next section describes a method that uses this joint distribution to estimate the posterior distribution over the unknown variables in our model.

4. EFFICIENT VARIATIONAL INFERENCE

The BCCWords model presented in the previous section is tuned, or *inferred*, by learning the parameters of the posterior distribution over its unknown variables, so that the model fits the data. In this section we describe an efficient method for inference using *variational Bayes* (VB) [4]. The next subsection presents details of the VB algorithm for BCCWords. Then, Section 4.2 describes how this BCCWords-VB algorithm can be extended to batch processing and subsequently can scale to large datasets when computer memory capacity is limited.

Variational Bayesian inference is an approximate method for obtaining a strict lower bound of the true (log) joint posterior. VB explicitly takes uncertainty into account at all levels of inference, allowing us to marginalise (albeit under the VB approximations) over unknown variables, rather than selecting the single most likely value. The approximation offers huge speed ups over Monte Carlo sampling based Bayesian methods [28], and the performance degradation appears small in BCC models. Hence, VB is our preferred algorithm for working with potentially large sets of documents. In our experiments we implement our VB algorithm using Infer.NET [20], which is a framework that enables rapid development and running of Bayesian inference in graphical models. In particular, the Infer.NET inference engine enables us to switch between alternative inference algorithms for BCCWords, including Gibbs sampling [9] and Expectation propagation [19], that are potentially more accurate but much slower than VB and less suitable for performing inference over large–scale datasets.

The variational Bayesian inference algorithm uses an approximation to the joint probability distribution, $q(\boldsymbol{t}, \boldsymbol{\theta}) = q(\boldsymbol{t})q(\boldsymbol{\theta})$, that factorises between the true classes of the documents, $\boldsymbol{t} = \{t_i \forall i\}$, and the set of model parameters, $\boldsymbol{\theta} = \{\boldsymbol{\pi}_c^{(k)} \forall c \forall k, \boldsymbol{\omega}_c \forall c, \boldsymbol{\rho}\}$. The algorithm iterates between updating the approximate posterior distribution over the true classes of the documents, $q(\boldsymbol{t})$, and the model parameters $q(\boldsymbol{\theta})$, until it converges. The theory behind variational inference guarantees that each iteration reduces the Kullback-Leibler divergence [16] between the approximate solution and the true posterior at each iteration, so that the approximation becomes closer to the exact solution with each iteration. The updates can be viewed as passing messages between the true class labels $\boldsymbol{t}$ and model parameters $\boldsymbol{\theta}$. As we will see in the detailed explanation below, the specific forms of the factors $q(\boldsymbol{t})$ and $q(\boldsymbol{\theta})$ arise naturally from the BCCWords model and its choice of distributions. The conditional independence relations in our model allow us to further factorise the distribution over the model parameters, $q(\boldsymbol{\theta})$ without additional approximation:

$$q(\boldsymbol{\theta}) = q(\boldsymbol{\rho}) \prod_{c \in C} \left\{ q(\boldsymbol{\omega}_c) \prod_{k \in K} q(\boldsymbol{\pi}_c^{(k)}) \right\}$$

This means we can update each subset of model parameters separately, and each of these factors will exchange different messages with $q(\boldsymbol{t})$. This type of algorithm is also known as *variational message passing (VMP)* and has an efficient scalable implementation which is described in Section 4.2.

4.1 The BCCWords–VB Algorithm

We now present the implementation of the variational inference approach to BCCWords described in the previous section. Specifically, we describe the details of the iterative updates within a step-by-step description of the inference algorithm based on the VB equations that we derive for BCCWords.

Inputs: the algorithm takes as input a data set of annotators' responses, $\boldsymbol{l}$, and where available, a set of known target labels which are gold-standard training labels. We note that gold labels are not necessary and the algorithm can operate in unsupervised mode. To run the algorithm, we must also select values for $\boldsymbol{\alpha}_{0,c}^{(k)}, \forall k$, $\boldsymbol{\beta}_0$ and $\boldsymbol{\gamma}_{0,c}$, as described above. A number of techniques can be used to initialise these hyperparameters when the choice of values is unclear [3].

Step 1. Initialisation: initialise approximate posterior distributions over the model parameters, $\boldsymbol{\theta}$. The choice of initial distributions affects the number of iterations required for convergence. In our implementation we initialise the posterior distributions over the model parameters by setting them to their prior distributions.

Step 2. Update true class predictions: update the approximate posterior $q(t_i)$ over the class of each document, $i \in N$. For any document i which has a gold label, the value of t_i is known so we do not need to update $q(t_i)$. Instead we set $q(t_i = c) = 1$ where c is the observed value of t_i, and $q(t_i \neq c) = 0$ for all other class values. For all other documents, we obtain the current estimate $q^*(t_i)$ of the probability that the true class of i is c:

$$q^*(t_i = c) = \frac{r_{i,c}}{\sum_{c' \in C} r_{i,c'}}, \quad (2)$$

where $r_{i,c}$ is the expectation of the likelihood, given by

$$r_{i,c} = \mathbb{E}_{\boldsymbol{\rho}, \boldsymbol{\pi}_c, \boldsymbol{\omega}_c}[\ln p(t_i = c, \rho_c, \boldsymbol{\pi}_c, \boldsymbol{l}, \boldsymbol{\omega}_c)]$$
$$= \mathbb{E}_{\boldsymbol{\rho}}[\ln \rho_c] + \sum_{k=1}^{K} \mathbb{E}_{\boldsymbol{\pi}_c^{(k)}}[\ln \pi_{c, l_i^{(k)}}^{(k)}] + \sum_{n=1}^{W_i} \mathbb{E}_{\boldsymbol{\omega}_c}[\ln \omega_{c, w_{i,n}}]. \quad (3)$$

The expectations in this equation are found using the current estimates of the distributions over the model parameters, and are defined explicitly in the subsequent steps of the algorithm. These terms can be seen as messages from the model parameters to the true class labels, $\boldsymbol{t}$.

Equation 2 can then be used to determine the messages to pass to the model parameters $\boldsymbol{\theta}$, which are expectations over the sufficient statistics of the set of true class labels for all documents. The message for $\boldsymbol{\rho}$ contains expected counts of each true class:

$$N_c = \sum_{i=1}^{N} q(t_i = c).$$

The message for the confusion matrices contains the counts of each judgement label $c' \in C$ given the true label $c \in C$:

$$N_{c,c'}^{(k)} = \sum_{i=1}^{N} \delta_{l_i^{(k)},c'}\ q(t_i = c) \tag{4}$$

where $\delta_{l_i^{(k)},c'}$ is the Kronecker delta and is unity if $l_i^{(k)} = c'$ and zero otherwise. Similarly, the message for the word distributions contains counts of word occurrences in each class:

$$N_{c,d} = \sum_{i=1}^{N} \sum_{n=1}^{W_i} \delta_{w_{i,n},d}\ q(t_i = c). \tag{5}$$

Step 3. Update confusion matrices: update the approximate posterior $q(\boldsymbol{\pi}_c^{(k)})$ for each class $c \in C$ and each annotator $k \in K$. The prior distributions over the confusion matrices are Dirichlet distributions, which are conjugate to the categorical distributions. This means that the posterior distributions over the confusion matrices are also Dirichlets, with updated parameters:

$$q^* \left(\boldsymbol{\pi}_c^{(k)}\right) = \text{Dir}\left(\boldsymbol{\pi}_c^{(k)} | \alpha_{c,1}^{(k)}, ..., \alpha_{c,L}^{(k)}\right), \tag{6}$$

where L is the cardinality of C and $\boldsymbol{\alpha}_c^{(k)}$ is calculated by adding counts from the true class label message to the prior pseudo-counts $\alpha_{0,c}^{(k)}$:

$$\alpha_{c,c'}^{(k)} = \alpha_{0,c,c'}^{(k)} + N_{c,c'}^{(k)}. \tag{7}$$

A more detailed derivation of these iterative update equations can be found in [28]. We can now calculate the message to send back to the true labels, which is the expectation term required for Equation (3):

$$\mathbb{E}\left[\ln \pi_{c,c'}^{(k)}\right] = \Psi\left(\alpha_{c,c'}^{(k)}\right) - \Psi\left(\sum_{b=1}^{L} \alpha_{c,b}^{(k)}\right), \tag{8}$$

where $\Psi(.)$ is the standard *digamma* function.

Step 4. Update word distributions: update the approximate posterior $q(\boldsymbol{\omega}_c)$ for each row $c \in C$ to current estimate $q^*(\boldsymbol{\omega}_c)$. Again, we have a posterior Dirichlet distribution due to the use of conjugate exponential-family distributions in our model:

$$q^* (\boldsymbol{\omega}_c) = \text{Dir}(\boldsymbol{\omega}_c | \gamma_{c,1}, ..., \gamma_{c,D}), \tag{9}$$

where the parameters are updated by $\gamma_{c,d} = \gamma_{0,c,d} + N_{c,d}$. The message to the true class labels, which is required for Equation (3), contains the terms:

$$\mathbb{E}[\ln \omega_{c,d}] = \Psi(\gamma_{c,d}) - \Psi\left(\sum_{d'=1}^{D} \gamma_{c,d'}\right). \tag{10}$$

Step 5. Update class proportions: update the approximate posterior $q(\boldsymbol{\rho})$ using the Dirichlet parameter update:

$$q^* (\boldsymbol{\rho}) = \text{Dir}(\boldsymbol{\rho} | \beta_1, ..., \beta_C) \tag{11}$$

where the parameters are updated by $\beta_c = \beta_{0,c} + N_c$. The message from this parameter is:

$$\mathbb{E}[\ln \rho_c] = \Psi(\beta_c) - \Psi\left(\sum_{b=1}^{L} \beta_b\right). \tag{12}$$

So, for one iteration of the algorithm, we calculate the updated parameters, distributions and expectation terms defined in steps 2 to 5.

Step 6. Check convergence: if the target label distributions $q^*(t_i = c)$ have not converged to a stable solution within a given tolerance, repeat the algorithm from Step 2.

Outputs: predictions of the document class labels, given by the current estimates of $q(t_i = c) \forall i \forall c$, their posterior expectations. The algorithm also outputs approximate posterior distributions over the model parameters, $q(\boldsymbol{\pi}_c^{(k)})$, $q(\boldsymbol{\omega}_c)$, and $q(\boldsymbol{\rho})$ for each row $c \in C$ and each annotator $k \in K$.

4.2 Scalability Through Inference Decomposition

Performing a task such as sentiment analysis or disaster report analysis can require us to work with extremely large datasets with vast memory requirements. A major source of memory usage is the large set of annotator confusion matrices that the inference algorithm must iteratively update. For example, the Ushahidi dataset, gathered after the Haiti earthquake, was interpreted by approximately 700 workers [22]. To resolve memory exhaustion difficulties of VB inference at scale, this section proposes a scalable version of the BCCwords-VB algorithm, *Scalable BCCwords* (ScalBCCWords), which can be run on a single computer. ScalBCCWords is identical to BCCWords except that we decompose the entire data set into a set of *batches* of data by distributing the annotators across P partitions. During each iteration of the VB inference algorithm ScalBCCWords switches each batch in and then out of memory in turn. Batches produce messages that summarise each portion of data and occupy considerably less computer memory than the entire data set.

We chose to distribute the workers between the batches so that each batch contains all the responses from workers in that batch. This partitioning criterion is sensible as each batch only has to represent a subset of annotators, and thus only represents a small set of confusion matrices. The splits can be chosen to meet memory constraints. The corresponding factor graph is shown in Figure 2, showing how all partitions share the same class distribution of documents and the word distributions conditioned on document class.

When batch p is processed, the pseudo counts $N_{c,c'}^{(k)}$ are calculated using Equation (4), for all $k \in p$. The log confusion matrix messages, $M_{p,c,i}$, for batch p for each class c and document i are calculated as follows,

$$M_{p,c,i} = \sum_{k \in p} \mathbb{E}\left[\ln \pi_{c,l_i^{(k)}}^{(k)}\right]$$

using Equation 8 to calculate the expected log confusion matrix. The log confusion matrix for batch p is then deleted

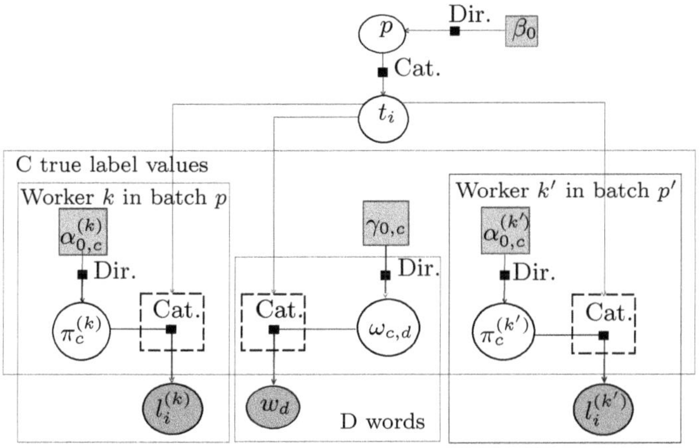

Figure 2: Factor graph for Scalable BCCwords. The four plates included in the graph describe (i) the set of workers K in the batch p, (ii) the set of workers K' in the batch p', (iii) the C possible true label values and (iv) the D words contained in the dictionary of terms used in the tweets. The plate for the N documents is omitted for simplification.

from memory. Once a message is obtained for each batch, the log true class prediction probability is calculated using,

$$r_{i,c} = \mathbb{E}_{\boldsymbol{\rho}}[\ln \rho_c] + \sum_{p \in P} M_{p,c,i} + \sum_{n=1}^{W_i} \mathbb{E}_{\boldsymbol{\omega}_c}[\ln \omega_{c,w_{i,n}}]$$

as per Equation 3. Hence, scalBCCWords is mathematically equivalent to BCCWords and both methods converge to the same solution. The remaining steps of the scalBCCWords algorithm are identical to those of BCCWords. We note that ScalBCCwords may process the batches in any order and not all the batches need be updated during each iteration of the VB algorithm. In our experiments, we provide an empirical evaluation of both our algorithms showing the advantage of ScalBCCWords-VB in memory occupancy.

5. EMPIRICAL EVALUATION

We evaluate the efficacy of our approach, ScalBCCWords, using two real-world datasets, comparing performance against the following five rival benchmark approaches. We note that BCCWords-VB and ScalBCCWords produce the same classifications as they are mathematically equivalent and therefore only ScalBCCWords results are shown.

Majority Voting (MV) is a popular and simple algorithm for obtaining a single decision from multiple opinions provided by a crowd [18, 29]. MV greedily assigns a class to each document by choosing the label with the most votes from the crowd. All votes are considered with uniform weight, thus treating all annotators as equally reliable. Typically, no measure of uncertainty in the final decision is provided.

Vote Distribution treats the fraction of votes in support of each class as the probability of that class. It therefore represents a simple technique for estimating the empirical probability that a document has a particular true label, assuming that all annotators are equally reliable.

Bag-of-words Classifier + MV trains a bag-of-words classifier by treating the majority vote as gold-labelled training data [11]. Therefore, this approach learns a language model that can be used to classify documents that have not yet been labelled by the crowd, but does not account for varying reliability of the crowd labellers when training the model.

Dawid & Skene is a model for combining labels from multiple classifiers, using confusion matrices to model the reliability of individual labellers [7]. The learning algorithm for Dawid & Skene does not account for uncertainty in the confusion matrices or other model parameters, which can lead to errors when gold-labelled data is limited.

Independent Bayesian Classifier Combination (IBCC) learns the confusion matrices using variational Bayes (VB). Therefore, in contrast to Dawid&Skene, it handles model uncertainty and can operate in unsupervised settings when gold-labelled examples are unavailable. However, this model does not consider text features and relies solely on labels provided by the crowd.

Community-Based Bayesian Classifier Combination (CBCC) is an extension of IBCC that models communities of workers with similar confusion matrices. It learns both the confusion matrices of each community and each worker but, like IBCC, it does not account for text features in the documents [30]. We run CBCC with three communities as suggested in the original paper, for both CF and SP.

In our experiments, we set the priors for IBCC, CBCC and ScalBCCWords as follows. For the class proportions, $\boldsymbol{\rho}$, we used unbiased priors by setting the values of $\beta_{0,c}$ to be equal for all classes. For the workers' confusion matrices, we used informative priors, setting the diagonal counts $\alpha_{0,c,c}^{(k)}$ to $C+1.5$, with the off-diagonals set to 1. This means that workers are initially assumed to be reasonably accurate. For ScalBCCWords, the word distributions were given uninformative priors, by setting uniform values for $\gamma_{0,c,d}$ for all words $d \in D$.

5.1 Datasets

We evaluate our approach using two crowdsourcing datasets, which provide real sentiment judgements obtained from human workers. The two datasets demonstrate our approach on two very different kinds of document, with distinct sentiment analysis problems.

The CrowdFlower dataset (CF) was provided by CrowdFlower[3] as part of the 2013 Crowdsourcing at Scale shared task challenge. The dataset contains 569,375 judgements for 98,980 tweets. This dataset includes 300 tweets with gold-standard sentiment labels, which correspond to 1,720 judgements from 461 workers. The judgements reflect the sentiment of tweets discussing the weather, and can take values from four sentiment categories: negative (0), neutral (1), positive (2), tweet not related to weather (4) and cannot tell (5). This dataset therefore concerns a multi-class labelling problem.

[3] www.crowdflower.com

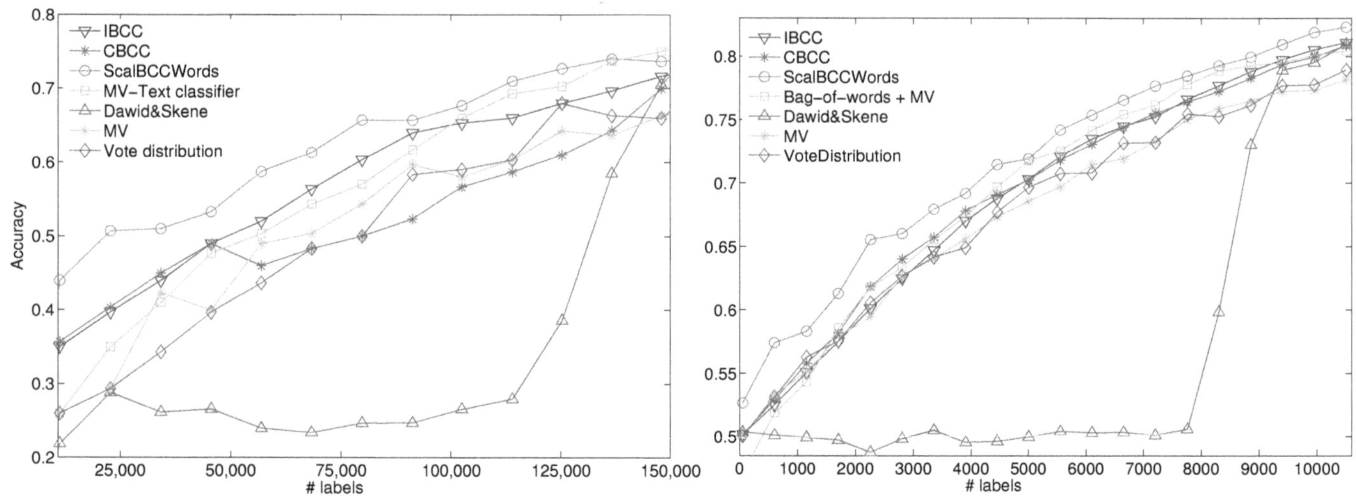

(a) CrowdFlower (CF)

(b) Sentiment Polarity (SP)

Figure 3: Accuracy of seven methods measured with increasing proportions of labels for both datasets.

The Sentiment Polarity dataset (SP) contains annotations for a set of 5,000 sentences from movie reviews, extracted by [23] from the website RottenTomatoes[4]. This dataset has gold-standard sentiment labels for all the movie reviews assigned by the website, which marked them as either "fresh" (positive) or "rotten" (negative). A set of 27,747 sentiment judgements were collected from 203 workers using Amazon Mechanical Turk (AMT)[5] by [27]. The SP dataset therefore presents a binary sentiment analysis problem, with workers forced to select either positive (1) or negative (0), with no option to express their uncertainty.

The vocabulary of a real-world text corpus is often extremely large, so most practical deployments of language modelling methods employ a set of heuristic pre-processing steps to remove noisy data that would otherwise add unnecessary computation and memory costs. In our experiments, the dictionary for both datasets was obtained using the standard approach of stemming the text through the Porter's stemmer algorithm [24], then removing common stop words, before extracting the 300 words with the highest term frequency x inverse document frequency (TF-IDF) score [2]. TF-IDF is a heuristic for selecting words that are important in distinguishing documents within a corpus, where term frequency is the number of occurrences of word d within the corpus, and inverse document frequency $= \log(N/N_d)$, where N_d is the number of documents containing d. While ScalBCCWords is agnostic to the type of features supplied, these standard text pre-processing steps are used to allow the experiments to focus on comparing crowdsourced sentiment classification methods.

5.2 Performance Comparisons

We investigated how the effectiveness of the language model learnt by ScalBCCWords varies with the number of labels supplied by the crowd. To do this we compared the performance of the alternative methods on our two datasets and evaluated the efficacy of each using four standard metrics:

Accuracy is the proportion of documents that were correctly labelled. For methods such as ScalBCCWords that output probabilities we assign the label with the highest probability.

Average recall is the mean across all classes of the recall rate, defined as the fraction of positive instances of a given class that were correctly labelled.

Negative log probability density (NLPD) is an error measure – the lower the better – based on how much weight a classifier gave to the correct class of each document as defined in [30].

AUC is the area under the curve of the receiver operating characteristic (RoC), which is the probability that a randomly-chosen positive example is assigned a higher probability than a randomly-chosen negative example [28]. This is a measure of an algorithm's ability to differentiate between classes, regardless of whether the classes are imbalanced. For the CF dataset, we provide the mean AUC over pairs of classes, using the method of [10].

The experiment is run iteratively, starting by running each method with 2% randomly-chosen judgements from the crowd, then evaluating the classification efficacy. We then increase the number of judgements by adding a further 2% randomly-selected labels from the crowd and re-running all the methods. This process is repeated until all crowdsourced labels have been used by the prediction methods.

Figure 3 shows the accuracy for the six methods for both datasets, which improves for all methods as they get more data. In particular, ScalBCCWords has highest accuracy for a small number of labels, demonstrating the added value of the language model. ScalBCCWords maintains the highest accuracy throughout, although IBCC, CBCC and Dawid & Skene catch up for large numbers of crowdsourced la-

[4] www.rottentomatoes.com
[5] www.mturk.com

Method	CF (20% labels) Accuracy	Avg. recall	NLPD	AUC	SP (20% labels) Accuracy	Avg. recall	NLPD	AUC
Majority vote	0.630	0.556	1.375	0.731	0.718	0.718	1.170	0.715
Vote distribution	0.653	0.592	1.227	0.749	0.706	0.706	0.945	0.738
Bag-of-words classifier + MV	0.670	0.608	2.280	0.755	0.726	0.726	0.642	0.792
Dawid&Skene	0.613	0.497	1.276	0.672	0.500	0.500	0.695	0.500
IBCC	0.693	0.553	0.950	0.811	0.738	0.738	**0.506**	0.833
CBCC	0.647	0.534	1.000	0.802	0.728	0.728	0.516	0.830
Scalable BCCwords	**0.717**	**0.578**	**0.909**	**0.836**	**0.755**	**0.755**	0.533	**0.843**

Table 1: Accuracy, average recall and negative log probability density score (NLPD) for the CF and the SP datasets for the six tested methods (one for each row) when using 20% crowdsourced labels. Using this subset of labels, 70% of the documents in both datasets have at least one crowdsourced label.

Method	CF (all labels) Accuracy	Avg. recall	NLPD	AUC	SP (all labels) Accuracy	Avg. recall	NLPD	AUC
Majority vote	0.840	0.764	0.921	0.852	0.885	0.885	0.797	0.885
Vote distribution	0.883	0.779	0.458	0.942	0.887	0.887	0.338	0.947
Bag-of-words classifier + MV	0.867	0.764	0.921	0.859	0.885	0.885	0.797	0.891
Dawid&Skene	0.830	0.745	0.459	0.897	0.914	0.914	**0.340**	**0.957**
IBCC	0.860	0.763	**0.437**	0.935	**0.915**	**0.915**	0.374	**0.957**
CBCC	0.886	0.746	0.526	**0.942**	**0.915**	**0.915**	0.383	**0.957**
Scalable BCCwords	**0.890**	**0.807**	0.591	0.877	**0.915**	**0.915**	0.389	**0.957**

Table 2: Accuracy, average recall and negative log probability density score (NLPD) for the CF and the SP datasets for the six tested methods (one for each row) when using all available crowdsourced labels.

bels. The accuracy of ScalBCCWords is 25% higher than CBCC (0.57 vs. 0.40) after 20,000 labels in CF and is 8% higher than CBCC (0.54 vs. 0.50) after 110 labels in SP. Importantly, in order to achieve the same accuracy, ScalBCCWords requires up to 56,935 fewer labels in CF and up to 440 fewer labels in SP compared to the benchmarks. Furthermore, Dawid & Skene initially infers a poor model of worker accuracy due to scarce labels, which leads to poor classification performance. Such a cold start phase is mitigated in the BCC methods by accounting for uncertainty in the workers' accuracy. Both MV and Vote Distributions are more accurate than Dawid & Skene in the initial phase but they are less accurate than all the other methods when a larger amount of crowd labels have been used.

Table 1 shows prediction metrics for both datasets when only 20% of the complete set of crowdsourced labels were used. Using this subset reduces the number of labels available for each document so that only 70% of documents have one or more crowdsourced labels. To classify the 30% of documents with no crowdsourced labels, ScalBCCWords and the bag-of-words classifier apply their language models, while other methods have no information about these documents and assign a default category to all unlabelled documents. ScalBCCWords has the highest accuracy and average recall on both datasets, significantly outperforming the bag-of-words model, which also uses a language model but does not model annotator bias and error rates.

Table 2 shows prediction metrics for both datasets, when all crowdsourced labels were used. ScalBCCWords has the highest accuracy and average recall on both datasets and competitive AUC and NLPD on the SP dataset. This demonstrates that ScalBCCWords performs well even when labels are plentiful (in this case, on average 6 labels per document).

5.3 Language Model

The language model inferred by ScalBCCWords represents the probabilities of each word in the dictionary conditioned on the sentiment classes. In Figure 4, the top row shows the Wordles (word clouds) with the most probable 27 words in the five sentiment classes of the CF dataset. ScalBCCWords is able to identify words that discriminate the sentiment classes, such as "love" and "perfect", which are more likely to occur in the positive sentiment class, whereas words such as "cold" and "hate" are more likely to appear in the negative class. We note that common words such as "day" are highly likely in both positive and negative classes and are therefore not good discriminators in this dataset. However, ScalBCCWords naturally uses the most discriminative words to infer the sentiment class through Equation 2. In the second row of Figure 4, the wordles show the words that most strongly indicate the class, i.e. the words d with highest probability $p(t_i = c|w_{i,n} = d)$ for class c. Here we can see that "day" is not indicative of sentiment class and there is little overlap between the word clouds for each class. Figure 5 shows the Wordles for the SP dataset, with the word "good" being equally likely in both sentiment classes, suggesting that words that seem intuitively positive may be poor discriminators, possibly because their meaning is highly context-dependent.

To validate the quality of the language model inferred by ScalBCCWords using the crowd labels, we compare it to a language model learned by training ScalBCCWords on the gold-standard labels. For both models, we rank words by their probabilities $\omega_{c,d}$ in each class c, to examine which terms the model has inferred are important to each class. Using the non-parametric Kendall's τ rank correlation test, we find a significant positive correlation between the rank-

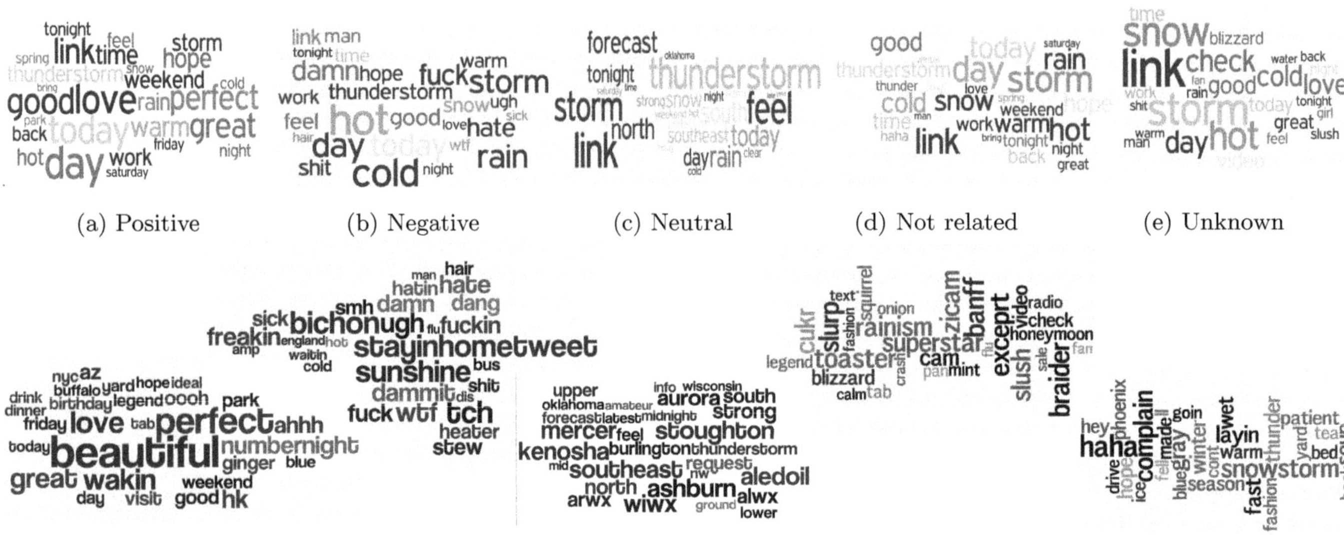

(a) Positive (b) Negative (c) Neutral (d) Not related (e) Unknown

(f) Positive (g) Negative (h) Neutral (i) Not related (j) Unknown

Figure 4: Top row (a) to (e): word clouds of the most probable 27 words from ScalBCCWords for the sentiment classes of the CF dataset. Word size is proportional to estimated likelihood given the true label class. Second row (f) to (j): word clouds for the most discriminative 27 words for three classes of the CF dataset. Word size is proportional to the class probability given the word. Colours are for legibility only.

	Positive		*Negative*		*Neutral*		*Unknown*		*Not related*	
	Gold	Crowd	Gold	Crowd	Gold	Crowd	Gold	Crowd	Gold	Crowd
Gold	1.0	0.384	1.0	0.337	1.0	0.423	1.0	0.403	1.0	0.373
Crowd	0.384	1.0	0.337	1.0	0.423	1.0	0.403	1.0	0.373	1.0

(a) CrowdFlower (CF)

	Positive		*Negative*	
	Gold	Crowd	Gold	Crowd
Gold	1.0	0.977	1.0	0.975
Crowd	0.977	1.0	0.975	1.0

(b) Sentiment Polarity (SP)

Table 3: The Kendall's τ rank correlation coefficients ($p < 10^{-5}$) for the word distributions, $\omega_{c,d}$, estimated by BCCWords using gold labels and crowd judgements. Colour intensity indicates the correlation strength.

(a) Positive (b) Negative

Figure 5: Word clouds of the most probable 27 words from ScalBCCWords for the sentiment classes of the SP dataset. Word size is proportional to estimated likelihood given the true label class. Colours are for legibility only.

ings obtained from the model trained on the crowdsourced data and the model trained on gold labels, as shown in Table 3 for both datasets. This indicates that ScalBCCWords can effectively train a language model using crowd labels when gold-standard data is unavailable. Kendall's τ is much higher for SP, which reflects the higher accuracy of ScalBCCWords on the SP dataset shown in Table 2. This suggests that the crowd's decisions may more accurately reflect the gold-labelled data when classifying the SP dataset, which has only two diametrically opposed classes, rather than the five less easily distinguished classes of CF.

5.4 Profiling Crowd Workers

Besides predicting document classifications and the language model, ScalBCCWords learns the confusion matrices that characterise the workers' skill levels across sentiment classes. Figure 6 shows example crowd members with very different confusion matrices. For example, subfigure (a) shows a competent annotator who provides accurate labels across all sentiment classes, hence the highly peaked likelihoods along the diagonals. Subfigure (b) shows an annotator whose reliability is inconsistent across the classes, with varying likelihoods of incorrect worker labels. This figure shows that we are able to detect annotators with very different behaviour within our two real-world datasets. The BCCWords model captures not just the overall skill level, but also the accuracy and bias of the annotator for each specific class, shown by the distribution in each row of Figure 6.

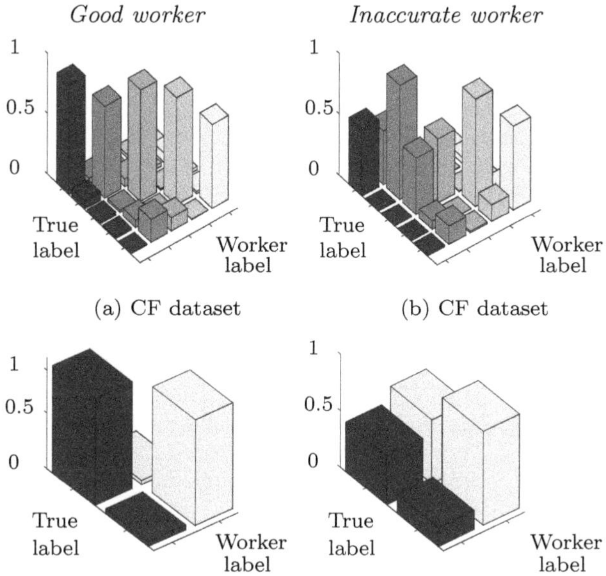

(a) CF dataset (b) CF dataset

(c) SP dataset (d) SP dataset

Figure 6: Confusion matrices of four workers, with the likelihood of worker label given true class on the vertical axis. These profiles show two workers who are very well calibrated in their opinions (left) and two workers who provide less accurate labels (right).

5.5 Memory Usage

We compared the memory usage of BCCWords-VB and ScalBCCWords on the CF dataset. Figure 7 shows a plot of memory demand when running the BCCWords-VB algorithm with increasing subsets of labels. In particular, we measured memory demand through the standard memory profiler available in .NET[6] that provides the approximate memory allocated on the garbage collection heaps to store the model instances of BCCWords. Despite the high noise of these counters, which explains the variability of the curves in the graph, we can still observe the general increasing trend of memory usage when using more labels. As shown in Figure 7, the ScalBCCWords algorithm uses up to 80% less memory than the standard implementation of BCCWords (1 GB vs. 200 MB) when the dataset includes 50,000 labels.

6. CONCLUSIONS

This paper presents BCCWords, a novel algorithm for combining crowdsourced annotations with text features in order to determine the sentiment of documents. We presented a scalable variational Bayes inference algorithm for BCCWords and demonstrated how it can be implemented for a large corpus annotated by crowd workers. Our analysis demonstrated that BCCWords is able to identify key differentiating text features, which produce more accurate sentiment classifications when crowdsourced labels are scarce. It is able to classify short messages such as tweets, despite the limited number of text features in these short messages.

[6] CLR Profiler, `clrprofiler.codeplex.com`

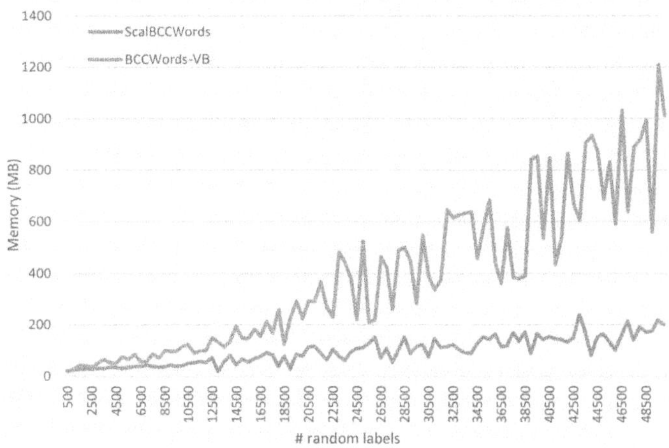

Figure 7: Memory usage of BCCWords (orange line) and the scalable implementation of BCCWords (blue line) measured on real data.

We compared our algorithm with six benchmark methods on two real-world crowdsourcing datasets and showed that our method can improve accuracy by 25% over both standard text classifiers and prominent aggregation models for crowdsourced data with annotations for a small portion of documents. Furthermore, our approach significantly reduces, by up to 67%, the amount of labels that must be obtained through crowdsourcing to achieve comparable accuracy with rival methods.

We are currently investigating other prominent applications of our method: identifying aid requirements in disaster response using reports from members of the public and first responders; evaluating investor sentiment towards companies expressed in free-text reports; and determining student sentiment from online forum postings to aid pastoral care. These domains provide vast amounts of unstructured data that can benefit from insights provided by human annotators and the scalability of automated methods. Future work will evaluate BCCWords with the different types of features available in these domains, including alternative text features, document metadata, and image features.

The way that BCCWords learns the annotator confusion matrices could be modified for problems with ordinal classes, such as those representing different strengths of sentiment, to take advantage of relationships between neighbouring classes when samples of annotator behaviour for each label and true class value are sparse.

7. ACKNOWLEDGMENTS

We thank Gabriella Kazai, Lumi, London, UK for initial discussions. This work was funded by the EPSRC ORCHID programme grant (EP/I011587/1) and Microsoft Research, Cambridge, UK.

8. REFERENCES

[1] Y. Bachrach, T. Graepel, T. Minka, and J. Guiver. How To Grade a Test Without Knowing the Answers – A Bayesian Graphical Model for Adaptive Crowdsourcing and Aptitude Testing. In *Proc. of the 29th Int. Conf. on Machine Learning*, pages 1183–1190. ACM, 2012.

[2] R. Baeza-Yates and B. Ribeiro-Neto. *Modern Information Retrieval*. Addison Wesley, 1999.

[3] J. Bergstra and Y. Bengio. Random Search for Hyper-Parameter Optimization. *The Journal of Machine Learning Research*, 13:281–305, 2012.

[4] C. Bishop. *Pattern Recognition and Machine Learning*. Springer, 4th edition, 2006.

[5] D. Butler. Crowdsourcing Goes Mainstream in Typhoon Haiyan Response. *Nature News*, doi:10.1038/nature.2013.14186, 2013.

[6] C. Chew and G. Eysenbach. Pandemics in the Age of Twitter: Content Analysis of Tweets during the 2009 H1N1 Outbreak. *PloS One*, 5(11):e14118, 2010.

[7] A. P. Dawid and A. M. Skene. Maximum Likelihood Estimation of Observer Error-Rates Using the EM Algorithm. *Journal of the Royal Statistical Society. Series C (Applied Statistics)*, 28(1):20–28, Jan. 1979.

[8] P. Donmez, J. Carbonell, and J. Schneider. A Probabilistic Framework to Learn from Multiple Annotators with Time-Varying Accuracy. In *Proc. of the Int. Conf. on Data Mining*, pages 826–837, 2010.

[9] A. Gelfand and A. Smith. Sampling-Based Approaches to Calculating Marginal Densities. *Journal of the American Statistical Association*, 85(410):398–409, 1990.

[10] D. J. Hand and R. J. Till. A Simple Generalisation of the Area Under the ROC Curve for Multiple Class Classification Problems. *Machine learning*, 45(2):171–186, 2001.

[11] Z. S. Harris. Distributional Structure. *Word*, pages 146–162, 1954.

[12] N. R. Jennings, L. Moreau, D. Nicholson, S. D. Ramchurn, S. Roberts, T. Rodden, and A. Rogers. On Human-Agent Collectives. *Communications of the ACM*, 2014.

[13] E. Kamar, S. Hacker, and E. Horvitz. Combining Human and Machine Intelligence in Large-Scale Crowdsourcing. In *Proc. of the 11th Int. Conf. on Autonomous Agents and Multiagent Systems*, pages 467–474, 2012.

[14] H. Kim and Z. Ghahramani. Bayesian Classifier Combination. In *Proc. of the 15th Int. Conf. on Artificial Intelligence and Statistics*, page 619, 2012.

[15] F. Kivran-Swaine, S. Brody, and M. Naaman. Effects of Gender and Tie Strength on Twitter Interactions. *First Monday*, 18(9), 2013.

[16] S. Kullback and R. A. Leibler. On Information and Sufficiency. *The Annals of Mathematical Statistics*, 22(1):79–86, 1951.

[17] A. Levenberg, S. Pulman, K. Moilanen, E. Simpson, and S. Roberts. Predicting Economic Indicators from Web Text Using Sentiment Composition. In *Int. Journal of Computer and Communication Engineering*, 2014.

[18] N. Littlestone and M. Warmuth. The Weighted Majority Algorithm. In *30th Annual Symposium on Foundations of Computer Science*, pages 256–261. IEEE, 1989.

[19] T. Minka. Expectation Propagation for Approximate Bayesian Inference. In *Proc. of the 17th Conf. on Uncertainty in Artificial Intelligence*, page 362, 2001.

[20] T. Minka, J. Winn, J. Guiver, and D. Knowles. Infer.NET 2.5. Microsoft Research Cambridge. *See http://research. microsoft. com/infernet*, 2013.

[21] K. Moilanen and S. Pulman. Sentiment composition. In *Proc. of the Recent Advances in Natural Language Processing Int. Conf.*, pages 378–382, 2007.

[22] N. Morrow, N. Mock, A. Papendieck, and N. Kocmich. Independent Evaluation of the Ushahidi Haiti Project. *Development Information Systems.*, 8:2011, 2011.

[23] B. Pang and L. Lee. A Sentimental Education: Sentiment Analysis using Subjectivity Summarization Based on Minimum Cuts. In *Proc. of the 42nd annual meeting on Association for Computational Linguistics*, page 271, 2004.

[24] M. F. Porter. An algorithm for suffix stripping. *Program: Electronic library and Information Systems*, 14(3):130–137, 1980.

[25] V. C. Raykar and S. Yu. Eliminating Spammers and Ranking Annotators for Crowdsourced Labeling Tasks. *Journal of Machine Learning Research*, 13:491–518, 2012.

[26] V. C. Raykar, S. Yu, L. H. Zhao, G. H. Valadez, C. Florin, L. Bogoni, and L. Moy. Learning From Crowds. *Journal of Machine Learning Research*, 11:1297–1322, 2010.

[27] F. Rodrigues, F. Pereira, and B. Ribeiro. Learning from Multiple Annotators: Distinguishing Good from Random Labelers. *Pattern Recognition Letters*, 34(12):1428–1436, 2013.

[28] E. Simpson, S. Roberts, I. Psorakis, and A. Smith. Dynamic Bayesian Combination of Multiple Imperfect Classifiers. In *Intelligent Systems Reference Library series: Decision Making and Imperfection*, pages 1–35. Springer, 2013.

[29] L. Tran-Thanh, M. Venanzi, A. Rogers, and N. R. Jennings. Efficient Budget Allocation with Accuracy Guarantees for Crowdsourcing Classification Tasks. In *Proc. of the 12th Int. Conf. on Autonomous Agents and Multiagent Systems*, pages 901–908, 2013.

[30] M. Venanzi, J. Guiver, G. Kazai, P. Kohli, and M. Shokouhi. Community-based Bayesian Aggregation Models for Crowdsourcing. In *Proc. of the 23rd Int. Conf. on World Wide Web*, pages 155–164, 2014.

[31] P. Welinder, S. Branson, P. Perona, and S. J. Belongie. The Multidimensional Wisdom of Crowds. In *Advances in Neural Information Processing Systems*, pages 2424–2432, 2010.

[32] J. Whitehill, T.-f. Wu, J. Bergsma, J. R. Movellan, and P. L. Ruvolo. Whose Vote Should Count More: Optimal Integration of Labels from Labelers of Unknown Expertise. In *Advances in Neural Information Processing Systems*, pages 2035–2043, 2009.

[33] K. W. Willett, C. J. Lintott, S. P. Bamford, K. L. Masters, B. D. Simmons, K. R. Casteels, E. M. Edmondson, L. F. Fortson, S. Kaviraj, W. C. Keel, et al. Galaxy Zoo 2: Detailed Morphological Classifications for 304,122 Galaxies from the Sloan Digital Sky Survey. *Monthly Notices of the Royal Astronomical Society*, 435(4):2835–2860, 2013.

HypTrails: A Bayesian Approach for Comparing Hypotheses About Human Trails on the Web

Philipp Singer
GESIS & Graz University of Technology
philipp.singer@gesis.org

Denis Helic
Graz University of Technology
dhelic@tugraz.at

Andreas Hotho
University of Würzburg
hotho@informatik.uni-wuerzburg.de

Markus Strohmaier
GESIS & University of Koblenz-Landau
markus.strohmaier@gesis.org

ABSTRACT

When users interact with the Web today, they leave sequential digital trails on a massive scale. Examples of such human trails include Web navigation, sequences of online restaurant reviews, or online music play lists. Understanding the factors that drive the production of these trails can be useful for e.g., improving underlying network structures, predicting user clicks or enhancing recommendations. In this work, we present a general approach called HypTrails for comparing a set of hypotheses about human trails on the Web, where hypotheses represent beliefs about transitions between states. Our approach utilizes Markov chain models with Bayesian inference. The main idea is to incorporate hypotheses as informative Dirichlet priors and to leverage the sensitivity of Bayes factors on the prior for comparing hypotheses with each other. For eliciting Dirichlet priors from hypotheses, we present an adaption of the so-called (trial) roulette method. We demonstrate the general mechanics and applicability of HypTrails by performing experiments with (i) synthetic trails for which we control the mechanisms that have produced them and (ii) empirical trails stemming from different domains including website navigation, business reviews and online music played. Our work expands the repertoire of methods available for studying human trails on the Web.

Categories and Subject Descriptors: H.5.3 **[Information Interfaces and Presentation]**: Group and Organization Interfaces—*Web-based interaction*
Keywords: Human Trails; Paths; Sequences; Hypotheses; Web; Sequential Human Behavior; Markov Chain; Bayesian Statistics

1. INTRODUCTION

The idea of human trails in information systems can be traced back to early work by Vannevar Bush ("As We May Think" [9]), in which he described a hypothetical system called *Memex*. Bush hypothesized that human memory operates by association, with thoughts defined by internal connections between concepts. The Memex itself was intended as users' extension of their memory, where common associative trails between documents can be stored, accessed and shared. Eventually, Bush's ideas led to the concept of Hypertext [27] and the development of the World Wide Web [4].

Today, the Web facilitates the production of human trails on a massive scale; examples include consecutive clicks on hyperlinks when users navigate the Web, successive songs played in online music services or sequences of restaurant reviews when sharing experiences on the Web. Understanding such human trails and how they are produced has been an open and complex challenge for our community for years. A large body of previous work has tackled this challenge from various perspectives, including (i) modeling [13, 31, 35], (ii) regularities and patterns [20, 42, 43] and (iii) cognitive strategies, finding that, for example, humans prefer to consecutively choose semantically related nodes [36, 45], humans participate in partisan sharing [2] or users benefit from following search trails [47]. In this paper, we are interested in tackling an important sub-problem of this larger challenge.

Problem. In particular, we take a look at the problem of expressing and comparing different *hypotheses* about *human trails* given empirical observations. We define a trail as *a sequence of at least two successive states*, and hypotheses as *beliefs about transitions between states*. An intuitive way of expressing such hypotheses is in the form of Markov transitions and our beliefs in them. For example, we might have various hypotheses about how humans consecutively review restaurants on Yelp. Figure 1 (a-c) shows three exemplary hypotheses for transitions between five restaurants (A-E) in Italy, and actual empirical transitions (d). The *uniform hypothesis* in Fig 1(a) expresses a belief that all transitions are equally likely (a complete digraph). In Fig 1(b), the *geo hypothesis* expresses a belief that humans prefer to consecutively review geographically close restaurants, while the *self-loop hypothesis* in Fig 1(c) expresses the belief that humans repeatedly review the same restaurant without ever reviewing another one. Other hypotheses are easily conceivable. What is difficult today is *expressing and comparing such hypotheses within a coherent research approach.* Such an approach would allow to make relative statements about the plausibility of different hypotheses given empirical data about human trails.

Objectives. We thus tackle the problem of *comparing a set of hypotheses about human trails given data.* We present a Bayesian approach—which we call *HypTrails*[1]—that provides a general solution to this problem.

[1]Portmanteau for Hyp(ertext/otheses) Trails

WWW 2015, May 18–22, 2015, Florence, Italy.
ACM 978-1-4503-3469-3/15/05.
http://dx.doi.org/10.1145/2736277.2741080.

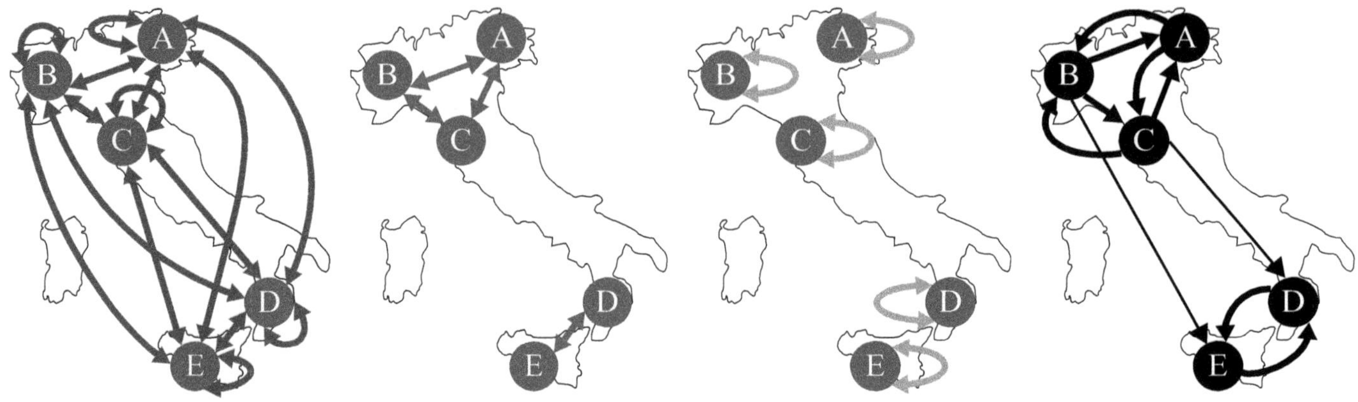

(a) *Uniform hypothesis:* all transitions are equally likely

(b) *Geo hypothesis:* regional node transitions are most likely

(c) *Self-loop hypothesis:* self-transitions are most likely

(d) *Empirical transitions:* obtained from real world data

Figure 1: *Example.* This figure illustrates three exemplary hypotheses (a), (b), and (c) about human trails as well as empirical observations obtained from real-world data (d). We look at trails of online restaurant reviews in Italy; nodes A–E represent restaurants. Hypotheses (a)–(c) are expressed via edges, with edge weights indicating strength of belief. For empirical data (d), edge weights correspond to actually observed transitions (how many times a restaurant has been reviewed before another restaurant). Our proposed approach compares evidences for different hypotheses given observed data (d). In this example, the geographic hypothesis (b) would be the most plausible one as we can mostly observe regional transitions between restaurants in the data (d).

Approach & Methods. The HypTrails approach utilizes a *Markov chain model* for modeling human trails and *Bayesian inference* for comparing hypotheses. The main idea is to (i) let researchers express hypotheses about human trails as adjacency matrices which are then used for (ii) eliciting informative Dirichlet priors using an adapted version of the (trial) roulette method. Finally, the approach (iii) leverages the sensitivity of Bayes factors on the priors for comparing hypotheses with each other. We experimentally illustrate our approach by studying synthetic datasets with known mechanisms which we then express as hypotheses. We demonstrate the general applicability of HypTrails by comparing hypotheses for empirical datasets from three distinct domains (Wikigame, Yelp, Last.fm).

Contributions. Our main contribution is the presentation of HypTrails, a general approach for expressing and comparing hypotheses about human trails. While the basic building blocks of HypTrails are well established (Markov chains, Bayesian inference), we combine, adapt and extend them in an innovative way that facilitates intuitive expression and elegant comparison of hypotheses. In particular, our adaption of the (trial) roulette method represents a simple way of eliciting priors for Markov chain modeling. We demonstrate the applicability of our framework in a series of experiments with synthetic and real-world data. Finally, to facilitate reproducibility and future experimentation, we make an implementation of HypTrails openly available to the community[2].

Structure. We present our approach in Section 2. Section 3 describes the synthetic and empirical data analyzed; corresponding experiments are presented in Section 4. We discuss our work in Section 5, present related work in Section 6 and conclude in Section 7.

2. THE HYPTRAILS APPROACH

We start with defining the problem setting and giving a short overview of the proposed approach in Section 2.1. We proceed with explaining the fundaments of our approach based on Bayesian Markov chain modeling in Section 2.2 where we also emphasize our main idea of incorporating hypotheses as Dirichlet priors and leveraging the sensitivity of Bayes factors for comparing hypotheses with each other. In Section 2.3 we thoroughly discuss the process of eliciting Dirichlet priors from scientific hypotheses.

[2]`https://github.com/psinger/HypTrails`

2.1 Problem Definition & Approach

We aim to produce a partial ordering O over a set of hypotheses $\mathbf{H} = \{H_1, H_2, ..., H_n\}$. We base the partial order on the plausibility of hypotheses given data D. Each hypothesis H describes beliefs about common transitions between nodes while data D captures empirically observed human trails. A hypothesis H can be expressed by an adjacency matrix Q where transitions $q_{i,j}$ with strong belief receive larger values than those with lower belief.

For generating the partial ordering O, our HypTrails approach resorts to Bayesian inference utilizing a Markov chain model. We incorporate a hypothesis H as informative Dirichlet priors into the inference process. For eliciting Dirichlet priors $Dir(\boldsymbol{\alpha})$ from a given hypothesis H expressed as matrix Q—i.e., for setting corresponding hyperparameters $\alpha_{i,j}$—HypTrails uses an adaption of the so-called (trial) roulette method. The partial ordering O is achieved by calculating marginal likelihoods $P(D|H)$ (weighted averages of likelihood, where the weights come from the parameters' prior probabilities) for competing hypotheses H which we then can compare with each other by determining Bayes factors B.

2.2 Bayesian Markov Chain Modeling

HypTrails is based on Bayesian Markov chain modeling. In the following, we only cover those fundamentals that are directly related to our approach, and point the reader to previous work [35, 38] for a more detailed treatise of the topic.

Markov chain definition. A Markov chain model represents a stochastic system that models transitions between states from a given state space $S = \{s_1, s_2, ..., s_m\}$ with $m = |S|$ (e.g., the distinct restaurants of our example in Figure 1). It amounts to a sequence of random variables $X_1, X_2, ..., X_t$. This random process is usually memoryless (the so-called Markov property, first-order) meaning that the next state only depends on the current state and not on a sequence of preceding states. Note though that Markov chain models can also be extended to incorporate higher orders; see Section 5 for a discussion. We can define the Markov property as:

$$P(X_{t+1} = s_j | X_1 = s_{i_1}, ..., X_{t-1} = s_{i_{t-1}}, X_t = s_{i_t}) = P(X_{t+1} = s_j | X_t = s_{i_t}) = p_{i,j}. \quad (1)$$

Markov chain models have been established as a robust method for modeling human trails on the Web in the past (e.g., [14, 35, 43]), specifically focusing on human navigational trails (e.g., [6, 31]) with Google's PageRank being the most prominent example [7]. Hence, the Markov chain model is a natural and intuitive choice for our approach as it lets us explicitly model human trails with a dependence of the next state on the current state. We also consider hypotheses as beliefs about transitions without memory.

A Markov model is usually represented by a stochastic transition matrix P with elements $p_{i,j} = P(s_j|s_i)$ which describe the probability of transitioning from state s_i to state s_j; the probabilities of each row sum to 1. The elements of this matrix are the parameters θ that we want to determine. For doing so we resort to Bayesian inference.

Bayesian inference. Bayesian inference refers to the Bayesian process of inferring the unknown parameters θ from data; it treats data and model parameters as random variables. For a more detailed discussion of Bayesian inference please refer to [35, 38]. Following Bayes' rule, the posterior distribution of parameters θ given data D and hypothesis H is then defined as:

$$\overbrace{P(\theta|D,H)}^{\text{posterior}} = \frac{\overbrace{P(D|\theta,H)}^{\text{likelihood}}\overbrace{P(\theta|H)}^{\text{prior}}}{\underbrace{P(D|H)}_{\text{marginal likelihood}}} \tag{2}$$

The *likelihood function* describes the likelihood that we observe data D with given parameters θ and hypothesis (model) H. The *prior* reflects our belief about the parameters before we see the data or, more technically, the prior *encodes* our hypothesis H. Thus, *we use the prior as a representation for different hypotheses about human trails.* More precisely, we model the data with different, mostly informative, priors. We use the conjugate prior of the categorical distribution as the prior of each row of the transition matrix P; i.e., the Dirichlet distribution $Dir(\boldsymbol{\alpha})$. The hyperparameters $\boldsymbol{\alpha}$ represent our prior belief of the parameters and can be seen as a vector of pseudo counts $\boldsymbol{\alpha} = [\alpha_1, \alpha_2, ..., \alpha_m]$. Given such a prior, the posterior distribution represents a combination of our prior belief and the actual data that we observe. For each row i of P we now have a posterior in the form of $Dir(n_{i,1} + \alpha_{i,1}, ..., n_{i,m} + \alpha_{i,m})$ where $n_{i,j}$ are the actual transition counts of the data between states s_i and s_j and $\alpha_{i,j}$ are the prior pseudo counts assigned to this transition. We provide a thorough description of how we elicit the needed Dirichlet priors from expressed hypotheses by researchers in Section 2.3.

Comparing hypotheses. Finally, the *marginal likelihood* (which we can also call evidence) expresses the probability of the data given a hypothesis H and plays a crucial role for comparing hypotheses;[3] it is defined as follows (for derivation please consult [35, 38]):

$$P(D|H) = \prod_i \frac{\Gamma(\sum_j \alpha_{i,j})}{\prod_j \Gamma(\alpha_{i,j})} \frac{\prod_j \Gamma(n_{i,j} + \alpha_{i,j})}{\Gamma(\sum_j (n_{i,j} + \alpha_{i,j}))} \tag{3}$$

Note that the hyperparameters $\alpha_{i,j}$ differ for various hypotheses H as we express them via different Dirichlet priors; the actual transition counts $n_{i,j}$ are the same for each hypothesis. For comparing the plausibility of two hypotheses, we resort to *Bayes factors* [21, 44]. Bayes factors are representing a Bayesian method for model comparison that include a natural *Occam's razor* guarding against overfitting. In our case, a model represents a hypothesis at interest with each having different priors with different hyperparameters that express corresponding beliefs. For illustrative purposes, we are now interested in comparing hypotheses H_1 and H_2 where $H_1, H_2 \in \mathbf{H}$, given observed data D. We can define the Bayes factor—note that we apply unbiased comparison assuming that all hypotheses are equally likely a priori—as follows:

$$B_{1,2} = \frac{P(D|H_1)}{P(D|H_2)} \tag{4}$$

$P(D|H)$ is the marginal likelihood (evidence) defined in Equation 3 and the Bayes factor [3] can be seen as a summary of the evidence provided by the data in favor of one scientific hypothesis over the other. HypTrails is not only suited for comparing two hypotheses with each other, but rather a set of hypotheses $\mathbf{H} = \{H_1, H_2, ..., H_n\}$. For determining the partial order O over $\mathbf{H}$, we order the evidences that data D provides in favor of hypotheses H; i.e., by ordering $P(D|H)$ using a less-than-equal binary relation. However, ordering the evidences is not enough as we need to check the significance of their ratios which we tackle by calculating Bayes factors. In case that the significance is not present, we consider two hypotheses as being equal. For determining the strength of the Bayes factor we resort to Kass and Raftery's [21] interpretation table.

Leveraging the sensitivity of Bayes factors. Throughout this section we have described our main idea of incorporating hypotheses in the form of informative Dirichlet priors into the inference process. We leverage marginal likelihoods and Bayes factors for making informed decisions about the relative plausibility of given hypotheses. Usually, one common critique of Bayes factors is that they are highly sensitive with regard to the choice of the prior [21]. In contrast, posterior measures ignore the influence of the prior the more data one observes which is why they are more ignorant to the choice of prior [39]. In our approach, we exploit the sensitivity of Bayes factors on the prior as *an elegant solution to the problem of comparing hypotheses.* As we express our different hypotheses in the form of priors, we are explicitly interested in using a measure that is sensitive to the choice of priors and hence, can give us insights into the relative plausibility of each hypothesis. Thus, in this case, marginal likelihoods and Bayes factors are an appropriate measure for comparing scientific hypotheses [39].

2.3 Eliciting Dirichlet Priors

This section explains in greater detail how we can express the hypotheses about human trails and how HypTrails elicits proper informative Dirichlet priors from these. First, we illustrate how the prior influences the evidence by studying several toy examples. Next, we present an intuitive way of eliciting the Dirichlet priors by introducing an adaption of the so-called *(trial) roulette method.*

Understanding influence of priors. In Section 2.2, we discussed that we use the sensitivity of Bayes factors with regard to the choice of prior (i.e., determined via marginal likelihoods) as a feature (or solution) rather than a limitation. It allows us to model hypotheses in the form of prior distributions which then can be compared by corresponding Bayes factors. But how exactly does the prior influence evidence (marginal likelihood)? Note that the posterior probability (see Equation 2) is a combination of our prior belief (pseudo counts) and the data we observe (transition counts) which is why both influence the evidence (see Equation 3).

To illustrate the influence, we apply several toy priors to human trail data. The choice of data is secondary and we observe the same behavior regardless of the underlying data; in this case we exemplary use navigation data (Wikigame dataset introduced in Section 3). First, we apply a *uniform prior*; i.e., $\boldsymbol{\alpha}$ has the same value for each row i and element j: $\alpha_{i,j} = 1 + c, \forall i, j$. By ranging the constant c over $0, 1, 3, 5, 10, 20$, we observe decreasing evidence (Figure 2(a)) which is not surprising as the uniform pseudo counts do not mirror the observed transition counts well. Technically, with increased c

[3] We calculate log-evidence utilizing logarithms of the gamma function for avoiding underflow.

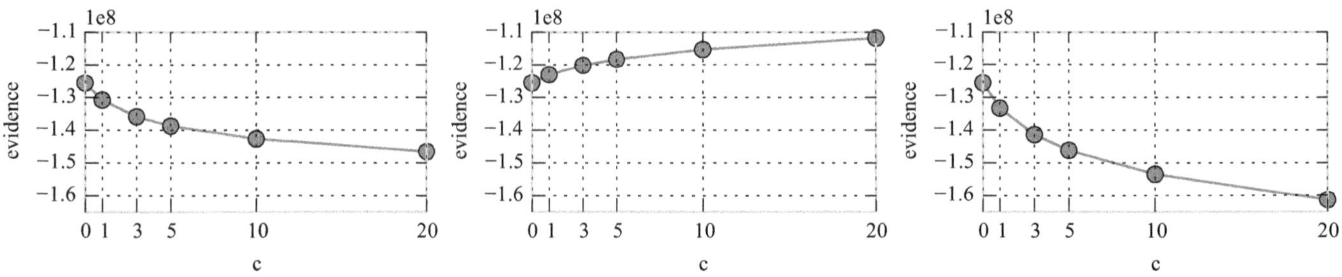

(a) Uniform prior (b) Empirically aligned prior (c) Empirically opposing prior

Figure 2: *Understanding influence of priors.* This figure shows how the choice of prior pseudo counts influences evidence; we apply several toy priors to navigation data (Wikigame, see Section 3). In (a) we use a uniform Dirichlet prior which means that for each row i, α has the same value for each element: $\alpha_{i,j} = 1+c, \forall i,j$. By increasing the constant c (x-axis), we can observe that the evidence (y-axis) is decreasing; the largest evidence is at $c = 0$. By using an empirically aligned prior (b) as $(n_{i,j} > 0 \rightarrow \alpha_{i,j} = 1+c) \wedge (n_{i,j} = 0 \rightarrow \alpha_{i,j} = 1), \forall i,j$, we end up with a larger evidence the larger c is. Finally, in (c) we intentionally set "bad" prior counts for the α values via $(n_{i,j} = 0 \rightarrow \alpha_{i,j} = 1+c) \wedge (n_{i,j} > 0 \rightarrow \alpha_{i,j} = 1), \forall i,j$ showing that the evidence becomes smaller as we increase c. The results indicate that the more a hypothesis is aligned with empirical data, the larger the evidence is, and vice versa.

the Dirichlet prior concentrates more and more of its probability mass on a uniform distribution of parameters, and thus, the weights of alternative parameter configurations become smaller. However, the likelihood is larger for the alternative parameter configurations (coming from the data) and this results in a smaller weighted average of the likelihood, i.e., in a smaller evidence.

On the other hand, if we provide some form of an *empirically aligned prior* as $(n_{i,j} > 0 \rightarrow \alpha_{i,j} = 1+c) \wedge (n_{i,j} = 0 \rightarrow \alpha_{i,j} = 1), \forall i,j$ we end up with a larger evidence the larger c is as we can see in Figure 2(b). This is because we actually increase the pseudo counts of transitions that we also observe in our data while we keep the pseudo counts for non-observed transitions at 1. In this case, we concentrate the prior probability mass on the parameter configuration that is very well aligned with the observations. As a consequence we give more weight for parameter configurations where the likelihood is anyhow large and this increases the evidence.

Finally, we illustrate the behavior of a toy prior that expressed an *empirically opposing prior* in the form of $(n_{i,j} = 0 \rightarrow \alpha_{i,j} = 1+c) \wedge (n_{i,j} > 0 \rightarrow \alpha_{i,j} = 1), \forall i,j$. In this example we intentionally set the prior pseudo counts to the opposite of what the actual data tells us. We assign low prior pseudo counts (1) to elements with large observed transition counts while we incrementally increase the pseudo counts of transitions that we do not observe in our data. As expected, Figure 2(c) shows that the evidence decays as we increase c. Technically, we assign the greatest weights for parameter configurations with the smallest likelihoods resulting in a steep decay of evidence with increasing values of c.

Note that $c = 0$ results in the same evidence for all three toy priors as in all cases $\alpha_{i,j} = 1, \forall i,j$. This refers to a Dirichlet prior that is uniformly distributed over the simplex which is a special form of a uniform prior and which we will refer to as a *flat prior*.

These toy examples show that if the prior is well aligned with data, the evidence is rising with the strength of the prior. The evidence is the largest if the prior and the likelihood are concentrated over the same parameter regions and it is the lowest if they concentrate on different regions [48]. Hence, we want to choose an informative prior that captures the same regions as the likelihood. This leads to the observation that if the prior choice represents a valid hypothesis about behavior producing human trails on the Web, the evidence should be larger than a uniform prior, or an unlikely hypothesis prior with an equal amount of pseudo counts. Thus, for fair comparison, we want to compare hypotheses with each other that exhibit the same amount of pseudo counts assigned. Next, we elaborate the (trial) roulette method for eliciting Dirichlet priors from hypotheses.

(Trial) roulette method. Our approach requires to define the hyperparameters of prior Dirichlet distributions by setting the pseudo counts $\alpha_{i,j}$ given the hypothesis at interest. However, the process of eliciting prior knowledge is no trivial problem and requires careful steps (see [18, 28] for a discussion). As a solution, we present an adaption of the so-called *(trial) roulette method* which was originally proposed in [19] and further discussed in [16, 28]. It is a graphical method that allows experts to express their subjective belief by distributing a fixed set of chips (think about casino chips you set on a roulette table) to a given grid (e.g., bins representing result intervals). The number of chips assigned to an element of the grid then reflect the experts' belief in the specific bin.

In our work we adapt the (trial) roulette method. The grid can be understood as a matrix Q where each element $q_{i,j}$ of the grid represents the belief of a given hypothesis about the transition from state s_i to state s_j. Values $q_{i,j}$ are set by researchers for expressing a hypothesis. They need to be positive values and larger values indicate stronger belief in a given transition. The prior of each row of the transition matrix P of the Markov chain model is defined as a Dirichlet distribution (cf. Section 2.2) with hyperparameters (pseudo counts) $[\alpha_{i,1}, \alpha_{i,2}, ..., \alpha_{i,j}]$ which we want to set given the hypothesis. Concretely, we want to automatically distribute a number of chips to the given pseudo counts (another grid) according to the values provided in matrix Q expressing a hypothesis H. We define the overall number of chips to distribute for a given hypothesis as:

$$\beta = \overbrace{m^2}^{\text{flat prior}} + \underbrace{k \cdot m^2}_{\text{additional informative prior}} \tag{5}$$

$m = |S|$ and m^2 amounts to the flat prior—i.e., we assign the same number of pseudo counts (1) to each transition—which is why the number of uniformly assigned chips is equal to the overall number of parameters of the Markov chain model. Additionally, we distribute $k * m^2$ informative pseudo clicks for the given hypothesis, where k describes a weighting factor for the informative part. The larger we set k, the more we concentrate the Dirichlet distributions according to a hypothesis at interest—see Section 5 for a discussion.

By and large, the goal of our adaption of the (trial) roulette method is to not only give researchers an intuitive way of expressing their hypotheses as matrices Q, but also to elicit informative Dirichlet distributions according to the values $q_{i,j}$ of Q. Next, we want to illustrate the process of expressing a hypothesis and assigning prior pseudo counts via the example shown in Figure 3 using the (trial) roulette method. Let us again focus on human trails over reviewed restaurants in Italy (see Figure 1) and illustrate the method using the

(a)

0.00	**1.00**	**0.00**	**0.00**	**0.00**	h_E
1.00	**0.00**	**0.00**	**0.00**	**0.00**	h_D
0.00	**0.00**	**0.00**	**1.00**	**0.90**	h_C
0.00	**0.00**	**1.00**	**0.00**	**0.70**	h_B
0.00	**0.00**	**0.90**	**0.70**	**0.00**	h_A
h_E	h_D	h_C	h_B	h_A	

(c_1)

0.00	3.47	0.00	0.00	0.00	h_E
3.47	0.00	0.00	0.00	0.00	h_D
0.00	0.00	0.00	3.47	3.12	h_C
0.00	0.00	3.47	0.00	2.43	h_B
0.00	0.00	3.12	2.43	0.00	h_A
h_E	h_D	h_C	h_B	h_A	

(d_1)

0.00	0.47	0.00	0.00	0.00	h_E
0.47	0.00	0.00	0.00	0.00	h_D
0.00	0.00	0.00	0.47	0.12	h_C
0.00	0.00	0.47	0.00	0.43	h_B
0.00	0.00	0.12	0.43	0.00	h_A
h_E	h_D	h_C	h_B	h_A	

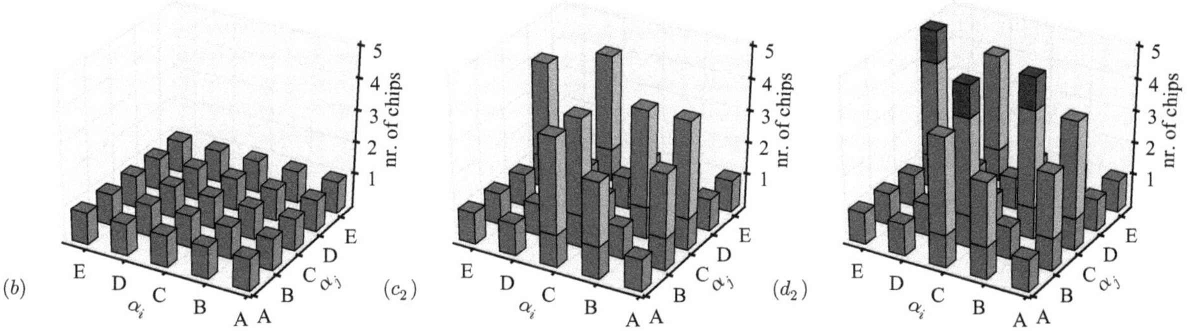

$\beta = 50 - 25 = 25$ chips left

$\beta = 25 - 22 = 3$ chips left

$\beta = 3 - 3 = 0$ chips left ✓

Figure 3: *Illustration of the (trial) roulette method.* In this figure the most important steps of our trial roulette method are visualized. We begin with a matrix expressing a researcher's hypothesis about human trails in (a)—in this case the exemplary geographic hypothesis for trails over businesses reviewed (cf. Figure 1). The (trial) roulette method proceeds with distributing a given number of chips (pseudo counts, in this case $\beta = 50$) to the Dirichlet priors. It starts by assigning one chip to each element (uniform) as can be seen in (b) before it proceeds by assigning the remaining chips according to their values of our given matrix in (a) as can be seen from (c) to (d). In each column, values of the matrices that receive at least one chip are marked bold and in the same color as the bars indicating chip assignments for the Dirichlet priors. In case of ties the ranking is produced in random fashion. For details please refer to the elaboration in Section 2.3.

geographic hypothesis given in Figure 1(b). For this visualization, we assume that we set $k = 1$ leading to $\beta = m^2 + m^2$ chips we want to distribute. The following steps are necessary:

(a) Expressing the hypothesis. Researchers start with expressing the hypothesis matrix Q with elements $q_{i,j}$ that capture the belief about transitions of underlying human trails; the matrix can be seen in Figure 3(a). In this example, we have five states (restaurants)—i.e., $S = A, B, C, D, E$ and $m = 5$ leading to $\beta = 50$ chips to distribute—and we express our geographic hypothesis about common transitions with values between 0 and 1. The precondition is that only positive values are used and larger values ($q_{i,j}$) always express stronger beliefs compared to smaller values. In this case, the closer a value is to 1, the closer two restaurants are geographically and the more we believe in corresponding transitions. As can be seen in Figure 1(b), both restaurant pairs B-C and E-D are the closest in geographical terms which is why we lay the strongest belief in these symmetric transitions; concretely, we set $q_{B,C} = 1.0$, $q_{C,B} = 1.0$, $q_{D,E} = 1.0$ and $q_{E,D} = 1.0$. The next closest restaurant pair is A-C which is why we also have strong beliefs in humans consecutively reviewing restaurant A after C and vice versa; we set $q_{A,C} = 0.9$ and $q_{C,A} = 0.9$. Finally, we set $q_{A,B} = 0.7$ and $q_{B,A} = 0.7$ as we also have some (lower) belief that humans consecutively review given restaurants. We set all other transitions to zero as we believe that given restaurants are too far away. One matrix Q represents one general hypothesis H about human trails—in a more realistic scenario one would want to express several of such matrices (such as for the other hypotheses given in Figure 1). Also note that we hand-pick values for this example and in a more rigorous investigation one would potentially use an automatic method for determining them (as we do in Section 4). The next steps are automatically performed by HypTrails for eliciting Dirichlet priors from such matrices, more specifically by the adapted (trial) roulette method.

(b) Initial uniform distribution. The (trial) roulette method starts with assigning uniform chips to each transition which can be seen as obtaining a flat prior ($\alpha_{i,j} = 1, \forall i, j$) and accounts to the left part (m^2) of Equation 5. The updated prior (i.e., hyperparameters for the Dirichlet distributions) can be seen in Figure 3(b) with black bars; all elements where one chip is assigned to are marked bold and black in Figure 3(a). By subtracting the distributed number of chips from β we have $\beta = 50 - 25 = 25$ chips left for the informative part described next.

(c) Informative distribution. Matrix Q gets normalized and then multiplied by the number of chips left: $Q = \frac{Q}{||Q||_1} * \beta$ where $||Q||_1$ is the ℓ_1-norm and $\beta = 25$. The resulting matrix can be seen in Figure 3(c_1). The method assigns as many chips to elements of the prior as the integer floored values of Q specify. So e.g., $q_{A,B} = 2.43$ and $\lfloor q_{A,B} \rfloor = 2$ leading to $\alpha_{A,B} += 2$ whereas $\lfloor q_{B,D} \rfloor = 0$ which is why the pseudo count for this transition is not increased. Overall, the method distributes 22 more chips marked bold and blue in Figure 3(c_1) leading to $\beta = 25 - 22 = 3$ chips left; the updated prior distributions (new chips marked blue) can be seen in Figure 3(c_2).

(d) Remaining informative distribution. Finally, the method subtracts the integer floored values from Q leading to the matrix illustrated in Figure 3(d_1) calculated by $Q = Q - \lfloor Q \rfloor$. It now needs to distribute the chips left (three in this case) according to the remaining values in Q. The method accomplishes this by ranking the values in descending order and assigning one chip to each element until none is left, starting from the largest and ending at the smallest. In case of a tie the ranking for the ties is produced in random fashion; hence, in this case $\alpha_{D,E}$ does not receive one more chip. We mark the elements that receive one further chip bold and red in Figure 3(d_1) and update our prior pseudo counts as can be seen in Figure 3(d_2) also in red color. Now, the (trial) roulette method has no chips left and is finished.

The final chip assignment shown in Figure 3(d_2) represents the prior (hypothesis). In detail, each row corresponds to a Dirichlet distribution with corresponding pseudo counts (hyperparameters) $\alpha_{i,j}$ (e.g., $\alpha_{C,B} = 5$). By proceeding, our HypTrails approach now uses these Dirichlet priors for Bayesian Markov chain modeling inference as described in Section 2.2. Concretely, in combination with the transitions $n_{i,j}$ observed from data they influence the marginal likelihood calculated as defined in Equation 3. See Figure 2 for a visualization of how the prior influences the evidence. By repeating the trial roulette method and evidence calculation for each hypothesis at interest, we can determine corresponding evidences and Bayes factors for comparing hypotheses with each other.

3. DESCRIPTION OF DATASETS

In this section, we introduce both synthetic as well as empirical datasets which we consider for our experiments. We produce *synthetic data* consisting of simulated human trails—in this case navigational trails—with known mechanisms from a generated (i.e., artificial) network. The introduced *empirical data* stems from three real-world datasets from different domains. The state space S investigated is always defined by the distinct elements the trails traverse over; e.g., if we observe trails over five distinct restaurants being reviewed (see Figure 1) we consider these five for the state space. As described in [35], we additionally add a reset state to the trails and state space of each dataset to ensure ergodicity.

3.1 Synthetic Datasets

We start by generating a directed random network using a generalized version of *Price's preferential attachment scale-free network model* [3, 32]. The network generation algorithm starts with a clique containing 11 nodes and proceeds to add nodes with an out-degree of 10 leading to an overall network size of 10,000 nodes. These parameters are arbitrary and could be set differently. Next, we simulate three different kinds of navigational trails, each consisting of exemplary 1,000 trails of length 5, as follows:

Structural random walk. For each trail we start at a random node of the network and perform a random walk through the network. The walker chooses the next node by randomly selecting one out-going link of the current node.

Popularity random walk. Again, the walker starts at a random node of the network, but now selects the next node by choosing the out-link according to the target's in-degree. The walker lays a softmax-like smoothing over the in-degrees of all target nodes ($e^{\deg^-(s)/10}$); it then chooses the next node according to given probability leading to a small stochastic effect. This is aimed at averting too long loops that would happen with simple greedy selection.

Random teleportation. Again, we start with a random node in the network for each trail. However, we now completely ignore the underlying topological link network and simply randomly choose any other node of the network—i.e., teleporting through the network.

3.2 Empirical Datasets

For our experiments we also consider three different empirical datasets which are described next.

Wikigame dataset. First, we study navigational trails over Wikipedia pages that are consecutively visited by humans. The dataset is based on the online game called Wikigame (`thewikigame.com`) where players aim to navigate to a given Wikipedia target page starting from a given Wikipedia start page using Wikipedia's link structure only. All start-target pairs are guaranteed to be connected in Wikipedia's topological link network and users are only allowed to click hyperlinks and use the browser's buttons such as refresh, but not use other features such as the search field. In this article, we study trails collected from users playing the game between 2009-02-17 and 2011-09-12. Overall, the dataset consists of 1,799,015 trails—where each trail represents the consecutive websites visited by one user for one game played—through Wikipedia's main namespace including 360,417 distinct pages with an average trail length of around 6. We use corresponding textual and structural Wikipedia article data for hypotheses generation. In particular, we use the Wikipedia dump dated on 2011-10-07[4].

Yelp dataset. Second, we study human trails over successive businesses reviewed by users on the reviewing platform *Yelp* (`yelp.com`)—we have used this setting as an example throughout this article (e.g., see Figure 1). For generating these trails we use a dataset publicly offered by Yelp[5]. Overall, we generate 125,365 trails—where each trail describes the subsequent review history of one single user—over 41,707 distinct businesses with an average trail length of 8. The data also includes further information about the businesses like the geographic location or category markers assigned, which we will use for hypotheses generation.

Last.fm dataset. Third, we study human trails that capture consecutive songs listened to by users on the music streaming and recommendation website *Last.fm* (`lastfm.com`). We use a publicly available dataset [11] for generating the trails at hand focusing on data from one day (2009-01-01). Overall, the dataset consists of 275 trails—where each trail captures the successive songs listened to by one user on a given day—over 11,166 distinct tracks with an average trail length of 52.8. For generating hypotheses, we consult the *MusicBrainz* (`musicbrainz.org`) API as described later.

4. EXPERIMENTS

To demonstrate HypTrails and its general applicability, we perform experiments with both synthetic as well as empirical datasets (as introduced in Section 3).

4.1 Experiments with Synthetic Data

Our first experiments focus on applying HypTrails to three synthetic trail datasets, generated by the following mechanisms: teleportation, a random walk and a popularity random walk (see Section 3). We look at these three datasets and compare three corresponding hypotheses (uniform, structural, popularity) that capture the generative mechanisms of each dataset. As we know from theory, HypTrails ranks the hypothesis that best captures the underlying mechanisms as the most plausible one. Next, we introduce the hypotheses in greater detail, before we discuss the experimental results.

Hypotheses. We now describe how we express the three hypotheses as matrices Q. Note that we only have to specify the hypothesis matrix Q (see Section 2.3) while the concrete pseudo count distribution for generating proper priors is handled by our approach.

Uniform hypothesis. This hypothesis has the intuition that trails have been purely generated by random teleportation and all transitions are equally likely. Thus, we equally believe in each transition and set each element of Q to an equal value (here 1).

Structural hypothesis. This hypothesis captures our belief that the trails have been generated by (only) following the underlying topological link structure. Hence, we believe that agents would always choose a random link leading from one node to another while traversing the network. We express this by setting $q_{i,j}$ of Q to 1 if a directed link between state s_i and state s_j exists in the topological network.

[4]This Wikipedia dump closely resembles the information available to players of the game for our given time period.

[5]`yelp.com/dataset_challenge`

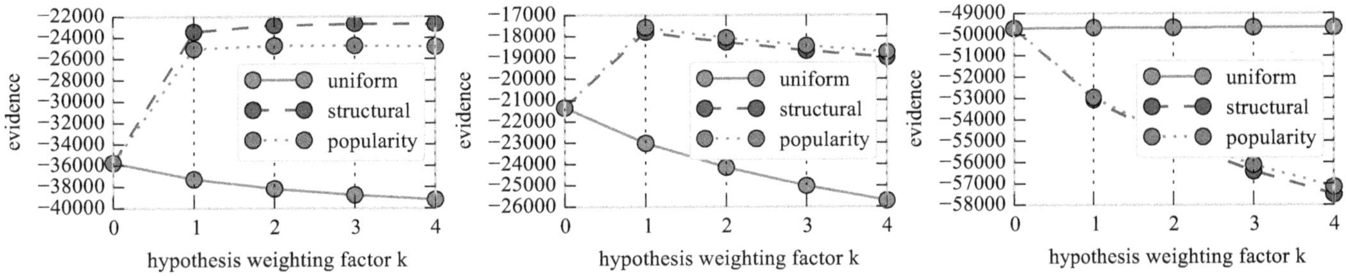

(a) Structural random walk (b) Popularity random walk (c) Random teleportation

Figure 4: *Experiments with synthetic data.* This figure depicts the results obtained when applying HypTrails to three synthetically generated trail corpora with known mechanisms (structural random walk (a), popularity random walk (b) and random teleportation (c)) comparing three different hypotheses: (i) uniform (solid, blue lines), (ii) structural (dashed, red lines) and (iii) popularity (dotted, purple lines). In each figure, the x-axis depicts the strength (weighting factor k) one assigns to a given hypothesis as defined in Equation 5 ($k = 0$ refers to a flat prior) while the y-axis shows the corresponding evidence (marginal likelihood) value. For simplicity, we can compare hypotheses with each other by comparing the evidence values (larger values mean higher plausibility) for the same values of k as all Bayes factors are decisive. The results illustrate what we know from theory as for each dataset the hypothesis that captures the mechanisms according to which the data has been produced best, is declared as the most plausible one.

Popularity hypothesis. This hypothesis also believes that the trails have been generated by following the links of the underlying link structure, but we have stronger beliefs in choosing large in-degree nodes compared to low in-degree nodes. Hence, we set $q_{i,j}$ to $\deg^-(s_j)$ if a directed link between state s_i and state s_j exists in the topological network.

Results. Figure 4 depicts the results for each hypothesis and dataset at interest. The x-axis denotes the weighting factor k for the number of pseudo counts assigned (cf. Equation 5). The y-axis denotes the corresponding Bayesian evidence (marginal likelihood). For $k = 0$ the evidence is the same for all hypotheses as in that case the flat prior is uniformly distributed over the simplex and no additional informative aspect is considered. The larger k gets, the more pseudo counts are assigned to the prior according to the given hypothesis and hence, the stronger our belief in specific transitions of a given hypothesis. We can compare hypotheses with each other by comparing the y-values (evidence) for the same x-values. According to Kass and Raftery's interpretation table of log-Bayes factors [21], we find that *all differences are decisive* which is why we refrain from presenting explicit Bayes factors. Hence, the larger the evidence for a given hypothesis is, the more plausible it is in comparison to the other hypotheses at interest. Across all three synthetic datasets, we can observe what we know from theory: the hypothesis that captures the underlying known mechanisms of the synthetic trails best is found to be the most plausible one. In the following we discuss the results of each dataset in detail:

Structural random walk. In Figure 4(a) we can see that the structural hypothesis is ranked as the most plausible one as it exhibits the highest evidences for $k > 0$. This result is as expected from theory as the trails are also produced according to a structural random walk only considering the underlying topological link network as expressed by the structural hypothesis. The reason why the popularity hypothesis is more plausible than the uniform hypothesis is because the former also incorporates structural information while the latter does not.

Popularity random walk. We show the results for our popularity random walk generated trails in Figure 4(b). In this case, the popularity hypothesis incorporating the in-degree (popularity) of potential structural target nodes is identified as the most plausible one as it captures the mechanisms according to which the trails have been generated.

Random teleportation. Finally, in Figure 4(c) we demonstrate the results for our trails generated via random teleportation. As expected, the uniform hypothesis is the most plausible one which accounts to our prior belief that all target nodes are equally likely to come next given a current node. Contrary, the structural and popularity hypotheses which both incorporate structural knowledge are less plausible hypotheses.

4.2 Experiments with Empirical Data

Our second kind of experiments focus on demonstrating the general applicability of the HypTrails approach by applying it to three real-world, empirical human trail datasets (Wikigame, Yelp and Last.fm) as introduced in Section 3. We compare *universal* as well as *domain-specific* hypotheses for each dataset which we describe next, before we discuss the experimental results.

Hypotheses. We now describe the universal and domain-specific hypotheses studied and how we express them. These are just exemplary hypotheses for illustrative purposes, researchers are *completely free to formulate other / their own hypotheses* accordingly.

Uniform hypothesis. We use the universal uniform hypothesis in a similar fashion as for our experiments with synthetic data in order to express our prior belief that each state is equally likely given a current state. Hence, we assign 1 to each element of the hypothesis matrix Q. We can see this hypothesis as a baseline for other hypotheses; if they are not more plausible than the uniform hypothesis, we cannot expect them to be good explanations about the behavior that is producing the underlying human trails.

Self-loop hypothesis. With the universal self-loop hypothesis we express our prior belief that humans never switch to another element in a trail. For example, for a navigational scenario this would mean that if a user currently is on a specific Wikipedia page, she would always just refresh the current one and never switch to another one. We set the diagonal to 1 in the corresponding hypothesis matrix Q and leave all other elements zero.

Similarity hypothesis. This hypothesis expresses our belief that humans consecutively target nodes in trails that are in some way (e.g., semantically) related to each other. We now aim at modeling this hypothesis for all three datasets. However, due to their given nature, the similarity hypothesis differs for each dataset which is why we describe the domain-specific similarity hypotheses next:

Wikigame similarity hypothesis. This hypothesis believes that humans prefer to consecutively access websites that are semantically related which has been observed and hypothesized in a series of previous works (e.g., [36, 45, 46]). Using the set of Wikipedia pages that users navigate over, we use the textual information of each site

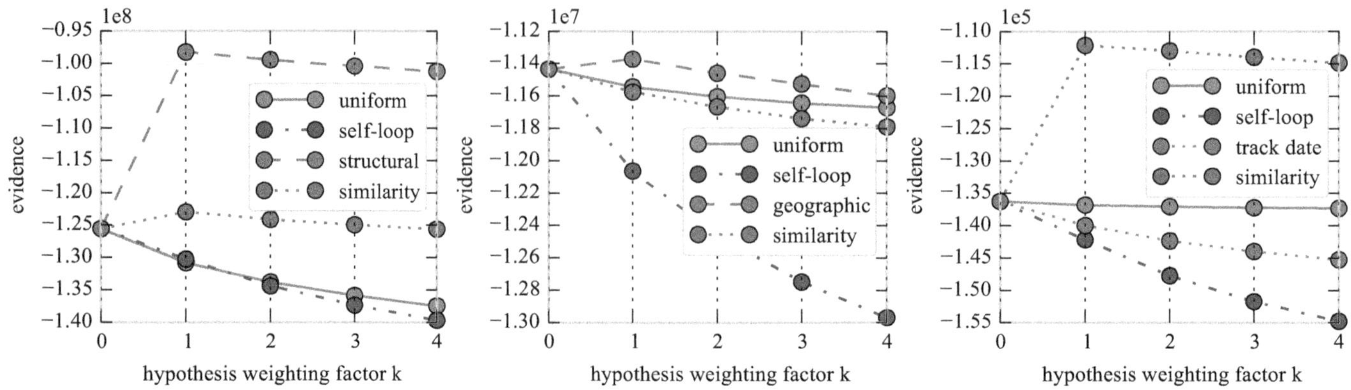

(a) Wikigame (b) Yelp (c) Last.fm

Figure 5: *Experiments with empirical data.* This figure depicts the results obtained from applying HypTrails to three different empirical human trail datasets (Wikigame (a), Yelp (b) and Last.fm (c)) for comparing a set of hypotheses. The x-axis depicts the strength (weighting factor k) one assigns to a given hypothesis as defined in Equation 5 ($k = 0$ refers to a flat prior) while the y-axis shows the corresponding evidence (marginal likelihood) value. For simplicity, we can compare hypotheses with each other by comparing the evidence values (larger values mean higher plausibility) for the same values of k as all Bayes factors are decisive. Several domain-specific hypotheses are declared as the most plausible ones for our three datasets: the structural hypothesis for the Wikigame trails (a), the geographic hypothesis for the Yelp trails (b) and the artist similarity hypothesis for our Last.fm trails (c).

provided by the corresponding Wikipedia dump (see Section 3) for calculating the semantic relatedness [33] between sites. We utilize a vector space model [33] for representing the documents (states) as vectors of identifiers using *tf-idf* [34] for weighing the terms of the vectors. We apply an automatic stop word removal process where we ignore all terms that are present in more than 80% of the documents in our corpus. Also, we use sub-linear term frequency scaling as a term that occurs ten times more frequently than another is not necessarily ten times more important [25]. Additionally, we perform a sparse random projection for reducing dimensionality while still guaranteeing Euclidian distance with some error [1, 24]. The final number of parameters is determined by the *Johnson-Lindenstrauss lemma* [15] that states that given our 360,417 number of samples (distinct Wikipedia pages), we only need 10,942 features while preserving the results up to a tolerance of 10%—which is also the tolerance level we use for dimensionality reduction. By doing so, we can reduce the number of tf-idf features from 2,285,489 to the specified 10,942. Finally, we calculate similarity between all pairs of pages (states) using *cosine similarity* between the described vector representations which define $q_{i,j}$ of our matrix Q. Each $q_{i,j}$ can now exhibit a final value between 0 and 1 where 1 means complete similarity and 0 means no relatedness at all. To increase sparsity we only consider similarities that are equal or larger than 0.1. Additionally, we set the elements of the diagonal of Q to 1.

Yelp similarity hypothesis. With this hypothesis we express our belief that humans choose the next business they review based on its similarity to the current business according to their categories (e.g., subsequently reviewing restaurants but not a barber after a restaurant). On Yelp, businesses can get assigned a list of categories that represent them (e.g., restaurant)—we leverage these categories for calculating similarity between businesses. Again, we use a vector space model for representing businesses as vectors of binary identifiers (category assigned or not assigned). For calculating all-pair similarity scores between businesses we utilize Jaccard similarity ranging from 0 to 1 which determine $q_{i,j}$ of the prior hypothesis matrix Q. The diagonal is set to zero as we do not believe in humans consecutively reviewing the same business.

Last.fm similarity hypothesis. This hypothesis believes that humans consecutively listen to songs on Last.fm if they are produced by the same artist—e.g., only listening to songs by Eros Ramazzotti. We set elements of the hypothesis matrix Q between two tracks to 1 only if they are from the same artist—the diagonal is set to zero.

Wikigame structural hypothesis. For Wikigame, we evaluate an additional domain-specific hypothesis that captures our prior belief that users navigate the Web (or in this case Wikipedia) primarily by using the underlying topological link structure. The corresponding hypothesis matrix Q can hence be built by looking whether links between sites of our states space S exist in the underlying topological link network G with directed edges $E(G)$ (derived from the Wikipedia dump as stated in Section 3.2). To be precise, the values of the elements $q_{i,j}$ of Q are determined by the number of hyperlinks linking from page s_i to page s_j; mostly, only one hyperlink links from one page to the other. Additionally, we set the diagonal of the matrix to 1 as users might also subsequently navigate the same page by e.g., clicking the refresh button of the browser.

Yelp geographic hypothesis. On Yelp, we also consider the domain-specific hypothesis that the next business a user reviews is one that is geographically close to the current one—we have used this as an example throughout this article (e.g., see Figure 1(b) or Figure 3). For doing so, we start by calculating the *haversine distance* [37] between the longitude and latitude values of all pairs of businesses. As the resulting value (in km) is smaller for geographic close businesses than for far businesses we normalize the values by dividing them by the maximum distance before subtracting them from 1. This leads to final values that range from 0 to 1 where 1 means geographically identical. We set the values of Q according to the calculated values while leaving the diagonal zero.

Last.fm date hypothesis. Finally, we specify a hypothesis that believes that successive tracks listened to on Last.fm are close regarding their original publication date (e.g., someone prefers to only listen to 80s songs). We determine the date of a track by using the Musicbrainz API and looking for the earliest release date available. Next, we calculate the difference between dates of two songs in years—we only consider track pairs for which we can retrieve a date for both tracks through the API. Similar to the Yelp dataset, we then divide each date difference value by the maximum and subtract it from 1 giving us scores between 0 and 1 where the latter means that two tracks are originally published in the same year. We set the transition values of Q according to the calculated values and leave the diagonal zero.

Results. The results for all datasets are shown in Figure 5. Again, all Bayes factors are decisive and we can simply interpret hypotheses having larger y-values (evidence, marginal likelihood) as more plausible. Across all datasets, we can identify some domain-specific hypotheses that are more plausible compared to the universal uniform hypothesis which we can see as a baseline. Hence, these hypotheses seem to capture some mechanisms well that human behavior exhibits while producing the human trails studied. Additionally, we find that throughout all datasets the universal self-loop hypothesis is the least plausible one with a small exception for the Wikigame dataset. We discuss the results for each dataset next.

Wikigame. First and foremost, the HypTrails results in Figure 5(a) show largest evidence for the domain-specific structural hypothesis. This indicates that users playing the Wikigame indeed seem to prefer to navigate Wikipedia by following links of the underlying topological link network. This is not too surprising as the Wikigame per definition only allows users to click on available hyperlinks for trailing through the Wikipedia space. Additionally, we can see that the domain-specific similarity hypothesis is more plausible than both the universal uniform as well as the self-loop hypotheses. This corroborates the theories and assumptions of previous work [36, 45, 46] which observed that humans tend to follow semantically related concepts successively.

We also see that the universal uniform and the self-loop hypotheses are the least plausible hypotheses at interest. Interestingly, for $k = 1$ the self-loop hypothesis exhibits larger evidence than the uniform prior which partly also demonstrates that self-loops are indeed an existing aspect of this dataset as also observed in previous work [35]. However, with larger k the evidence of the uniform hypothesis surpasses the self-loop hypothesis which may be explained by the fact that we weigh the informative part (i.e., only self-loops) too strongly while we ignore all other possible transitions.

Yelp. We depict the results for comparing the hypotheses at interest for our Yelp dataset (business reviews) in Figure 5(b). A first observation is that our approach indicates the domain-specific geographic hypothesis as the most plausible one. Hence, humans indeed seem to prefer to successively review businesses that are geographically close to each other on Yelp as captured by our dataset. Contrary, the other domain-specific similarity hypothesis is less evident compared to the uniform hypothesis which can be seen as a baseline. Consequently, from this exemplary analysis, we cannot assume that humans prefer to consecutively review the same businesses based on similar categoric descriptors, at least not based on the similarity of categorical descriptors given on Yelp. Finally, the self-loop hypothesis is indicated as the least plausible one which indicates that humans at maximum very seldom review the same business twice in a row in our dataset.

Last.fm. Finally, the Last.fm results depicted in Figure 5(c) highlight that the similarity hypothesis, expressing our prior belief that users consecutively listen to songs that stem from the same artist, is the most plausible one. This is visible as the evidence values are larger for all $k > 0$ compared to the other hypotheses of interest. Again, we observe that humans do not seem to prefer to listen to the same song over and over again (self-loop hypothesis) in our dataset. Also, for this example data, the track date hypothesis is less plausible compared to the universal uniform hypothesis.

5. DISCUSSION

The HypTrails approach represents an intuitive way of comparing hypotheses about human trails as we have demonstrated on synthetic as well as empirical data. However, there are some aspects—as partly exhibited throughout our experiments—that one should consider when applying HypTrails; we discuss them next.

Expressing hypotheses. When expressing hypotheses as matrices, choices have to be made regarding several factors such as (i) which transitions to believe in (e.g., about setting the diagonal) (ii) how to calculate values for representing a hypothesis (e.g., haversine distance for geographic closeness), (iii) how to normalize or (iv) availability of information (e.g., API restrictions). While several ways of doing this are conceivable, our approach does not constraint the researchers' choice in this regard. If in doubt, our advice is to express the uncertainty through another hypothesis (which reduces the problem) or through a set of other hypotheses (which focus on different representations). For example, in this article we first investigate the plausibility of a universal self-loop hypothesis compared to a uniform hypothesis before making a choice about the diagonal of other hypotheses. We find that for navigational trails (Wikigame), self-loops seem to play a role at least occasionally (cf. Figure 5(a)) which is why we also set the diagonals in other hypotheses to larger values than zero, while for both Yelp (cf. Figure 5(b)) as well as Last.fm (cf. Figure 5(c)) we cannot observe such behavior. Another choice to make is whether one wants to express hypotheses in a symmetric or asymmetric way—e.g., it might be useful to believe that transitioning from state A to state B is more relevant than from B to A. Following our advice, we would express a symmetric and asymmetric version of the hypothesis and compare them.

Behavior of hypothesis weighting factor *k*. Throughout our experimental results (see Figure 4 and Figure 5), we frequently observe that the evidence is falling with larger k. As pointed out in this article, the evidence is a weighted likelihood average and is largest if both the prior as well as the likelihood concentrate on the same parameter value regions. The larger we choose k, the larger we set the hyperparameters of the Dirichlet distributions and the more they get concentrated. Thus, only a few specific parameter configurations (single draw from the Dirichlet distribution) receive higher prior probabilities while many others receive low ones. As we cannot expect our hypotheses to concentrate on the exact same areas as the likelihoods as we did for our empirically aligned toy example in Figure 2(b), we sometimes see falling evidences with larger k as we reduce the scope of the prior. Even though we always want to compare hypotheses with each other for the same values of k, comparing marginal likelihoods for different weighting factors k might give further insights. For example, the flat prior for $k = 0$ might be seen as a further baseline to compare to. Also, the behavior of the evidence for single hypotheses with varying k can give insights into the strength we can assign to a given hypothesis.

Memoryless Markov chain property. Currently, HypTrails is memoryless, meaning that the next state only depends on the current one. Previous work has been contradictory in their statements about memory effects of human trails on the Web (see e.g., [14, 35]). While first order models have mostly been shown to be appropriate, it may be useful to extend HypTrails to also support memory effects in the future. This would mean that it would allow us to not only analyze hypotheses about how the current state influences the next one, but also how past ones (potentially) exert influence.

Future work. In this work, we have suggested first ways of expressing hypotheses as well as eliciting Dirichlet priors. Future work should further refine these methods as well as study the sensitivity and interpretability of expressed hypotheses and elicited priors with respect to HypTrails; e.g., by focusing on how to normalize hypothesis matrices (potentially row-based) and refining methods for eliciting priors (distribution of chips).

Furthermore, while we have showcased a certain variety of datasets and hypotheses that can be analyzed with HypTrails, we would like to encourage researchers to see these examples only as a stepping stone for more detailed experiments to be conducted. Additionally, in future work, multiple extensions and / or experimental variations are conceivable. For example, it could be useful to look at personalization or user group effects in data. Currently, the examples only demonstrate collective behavior, but one may assume that different groups of users produce human trails differently. One could segment the dataset according to some heuristic criteria and then analyze the same hypotheses on both sub-datasets. If one hypothesis is more plausible in one dataset than the other, one can assume differences in user behavior in different sub populations. One might also believe that human behavior changes over time [49]. This suggests to apply HypTrails to study the temporal evolution of hypotheses (and evidences for them). Furthermore, one can also think about combining hypotheses with each other to form new ones. For example, in Figure 5(a) we show that both the structural as well as the similarity hypotheses are very plausible to explain navigational behavior on Wikipedia. One could use a combination of both by weighing structural transitions according to their similarity.

6. RELATED WORK

Studies of human trails in information systems have been fueled by the advent of the WWW [4]. A fundamental way of interacting with the Web is navigating between websites. Such navigational trails have been extensively investigated in the past. An example of early work is by Catledge and Pitkow [10] who studied navigational regularities and strategies for augmenting the design and usability of WWW pages. Subsequent studies, e.g., the work by Huberman et al. [20] or Chi et al. [13], emphasize existing regularities and rationalities upon which humans base their navigational choices. These examples demonstrate the importance of better understanding sequential user behavior producing human trails on the Web. Apart from modeling [13, 31, 35] and the detection of regularities and patterns [20, 42, 43], researchers have also been interested in studying strategies humans follow when producing human trails on the Web. We highlight some exemplary findings next.

A prominent theory is the *information foraging theory* by Pirolli and Card [30] which states that human behavior in an information environment on the Web is guided by *information scent* which is based on the cost and value of information with respect to the goal of the user [13]. Another behavioral pattern is shown in [8] and [29] where the authors observed that semantics affect how users search visual interfaces on websites; the importance of semantics between subsequent concepts is also emphasized in [12, 36, 45, 46]. Amongst many others, further studies of human trails on the Web have focused on the detection of progression stages [49], trail prediction [22], the study of the value of search trail following for users [5, 47], partisan sharing [2] or the capture of trends in human trails [26].

While we have highlighted just an excerpt of related work, all these studies reveal interesting behavioral aspects that could be translatable into hypotheses about transitions over states. What is difficult, is to compare them within a coherent research approach. In this work, we have tackled this problem. Fundamentally, HypTrails is based on a Markov chain model which is prominently leveraged for modeling human trails on the Web. Google's PageRank, for example, is based on a first order Markov chain model [7] and a large array of further studies have highlighted the benefits of Markov chain models for modeling human trails on the Web (e.g., [17, 23, 31, 35, 43]). Given these advantages, and our interest in hypotheses about memoryless transitions, the Markov chain model represents a sensible choice for our approach. For deriving the parameters of models, we have utilized Bayesian inference [35, 38].

The main idea of our approach is to incorporate hypotheses as informative Dirichlet priors into the Bayesian Markov chain inference and compare them with Bayes factors. Bayes factors are known to be highly sensitive on the prior. This property of Bayes factors has been seen as a limitation in the past—as originally pointed out by Kass and Raftery [21]. However, as emphasized by Wolf Vanpaemel [39], if "models are quantitatively instantiated theories, the prior can be used to capture theory and should therefore be considered as an integral part of the model". In such a case, the sensitivity of Bayes factors on the prior *can be seen as a feature*—i.e., instrumental for gaining new insights into the plausibility of theories (or in our case hypotheses about human trails). Thus, marginal likelihoods and Bayes factors can be leveraged as an appropriate measure for evaluating hypotheses about human trails. The process of expressing theories as informative prior distributions over parameters has been discussed in follow-up work by Wolf Vanepaemel in [40] and in [41] where the author has tackled this task by using hierarchical methods. In this work, we have presented an adaptation of the so-called (trial) roulette method, which was first proposed in [19] and further discussed in [16, 28], for this task. With our adaption, we understand the grid as a hypothesis matrix where elements correspond to beliefs about transitions for a given hypothesis. Also, in our case, chips correspond to pseudo counts of Dirichlet priors which HypTrails automatically sets according to expressed hypotheses of researchers.

7. CONCLUSION

Understanding human trails on the Web and how they are produced has been an open and complex challenge for our community for years. In this work, we have addressed a sub-problem of this larger challenge by presenting HypTrails, an approach that enables scientists to compare hypotheses about human trails on the Web. HypTrails utilizes Markov chain models with Bayesian inference. The main idea is to incorporate hypotheses as Dirichlet priors into the inference process and leverage the sensitivity of Bayes factors for comparing hypotheses. Our approach allows researchers to intuitively express hypotheses as beliefs about transitions between states which are then used for eliciting priors.

We have experimentally illustrated the general mechanics of HypTrails by comparing hypotheses about synthetic trails that were generated according to controlled mechanisms. As derived from theory, HypTrails ranks those hypotheses as the most plausible ones, that best capture the mechanisms of the underlying trails. Additionally, we have studied empirical data to further show the general applicability of HypTrails. We have looked at human trails from three different domains: human navigational trails over Wikipedia articles (Wikigame), successive reviews of businesses (Yelp) as well as trails capturing songs that users consecutively listen to (Last.fm). Although the experiments presented in this work mainly serve to illustrate how one can apply the HypTrails approach, we hope that they also motivate and encourage researchers to conduct further, more in-depth studies of human trails on the Web in the future.

While we have developed HypTrails for comparing hypotheses about hypertext trails, the approach is not limited to Web data. It can be applied to any form of trails over states at interest in a straightforward manner; e.g., it could also be used to study human trails as recorded by GPS data. Insights gained by such studies can give a clearer picture of the underlying dynamics of human behavior that shape the production of human trails.

Acknowledgements. This work was partially funded by the DFG German Science Fund research project "PoSTs II" and by the FWF Austrian Science Fund research project "Navigability of Decentralized Information Networks". Furthermore, we want to thank Alex Clemesha for giving us access to the Wikigame data as well as Daniel Lamprecht and Paul Laufer for valuable input.

References

[1] D. Achlioptas. Database-friendly random projections. In *Symposium on Principles of Database Systems*, pages 274–281. ACM, 2001.

[2] J. An, D. Quercia, and J. Crowcroft. Partisan sharing: facebook evidence and societal consequences. In *Conference on Online Social Networks*, pages 13–24. ACM, 2014.

[3] A.-L. Barabási and R. Albert. Emergence of scaling in random networks. *Science*, 286(5439):509–512, 1999.

[4] T. Berners-Lee and M. Fischetti. *Weaving the Web: The original design and ultimate destiny of the World Wide Web by its inventor*. HarperInformation, 2000.

[5] M. Bilenko and R. W. White. Mining the search trails of surfing crowds: identifying relevant websites from user activity. In *International Conference on World Wide Web*, pages 51–60. ACM, 2008.

[6] J. Borges and M. Levene. Data mining of user navigation patterns. In *Web usage analysis and user profiling*, pages 92–112. Springer, 2000.

[7] S. Brin and L. Page. The anatomy of a large-scale hypertextual web search engine. In *International Conference on World Wide Web*, pages 107–117. Elsevier Science Publishers B. V., 1998.

[8] D. P. Brumby and A. Howes. Good enough but i'll just check: Web-page search as attentional refocusing. In *International Conference on Cognitive Modeling*, pages 46–51, 2004.

[9] V. Bush. As we may think. *The Atlantic Monthly*, 176(1):101–108, 1945.

[10] L. D. Catledge and J. E. Pitkow. Characterizing browsing strategies in the world-wide web. *Computer Networks and ISDN Systems*, 27(6):1065–1073, 1995.

[11] O. Celma. *Music Recommendation and Discovery in the Long Tail*. Springer, 2010.

[12] M. Chalmers, K. Rodden, and D. Brodbeck. The order of things: activity-centred information access. *Computer Networks and ISDN Systems*, 30(1):359–367, 1998.

[13] E. H. Chi, P. L. T. Pirolli, K. Chen, and J. Pitkow. Using information scent to model user information needs and actions and the web. In *Conference on Human Factors in Computing Systems*, pages 490–497. ACM, 2001.

[14] F. Chierichetti, R. Kumar, P. Raghavan, and T. Sarlos. Are web users really markovian? In *International Conference on World Wide Web*, pages 609–618. ACM, 2012.

[15] S. Dasgupta and A. Gupta. An elementary proof of a theorem of johnson and lindenstrauss. *Random Structures & Algorithms*, 22(1):60–65, 2003.

[16] C. Davidson-Pilon. *Probablistic Programming & Bayesian Methods for Hackers*. 2014.

[17] M. Deshpande and G. Karypis. Selective markov models for predicting web page accesses. *ACM Transactions on Internet Technology*, 4(2):163–184, May 2004.

[18] P. H. Garthwaite, J. B. Kadane, and A. O'Hagan. Statistical methods for eliciting probability distributions. *Journal of the American Statistical Association*, 100(470):680–701, 2005.

[19] S. Gore. Biostatistics and the medical research council. *Medical Research Council News*, 35:19–20, 1987.

[20] B. A. Huberman, P. L. T. Pirolli, J. E. Pitkow, and R. M. Lukose. Strong regularities in world wide web surfing. *Science*, 280(5360):95–97, Mar 1998.

[21] R. E. Kass and A. E. Raftery. Bayes factors. *Journal of the American Statistical Association*, 90(430):773–795, 1995.

[22] S. Laxman, V. Tankasali, and R. W. White. Stream prediction using a generative model based on frequent episodes in event sequences. In *International Conference on Knowledge Discovery and Data Mining*, pages 453–461. ACM, 2008.

[23] R. Lempel and S. Moran. The stochastic approach for link-structure analysis (salsa) and the tkc effect. *Computer Networks*, 33(1):387–401, June 2000.

[24] P. Li, T. J. Hastie, and K. W. Church. Very sparse random projections. In *International Conference on Knowledge Discovery and Data Mining*, pages 287–296. ACM, 2006.

[25] C. D. Manning, P. Raghavan, and H. Schütze. *Introduction to information retrieval*, volume 1. Cambridge university press Cambridge, 2008.

[26] Y. Matsubara, Y. Sakurai, C. Faloutsos, T. Iwata, and M. Yoshikawa. Fast mining and forecasting of complex time-stamped events. In *International Conference on Knowledge Discovery and Data Mining*, pages 271–279. ACM, 2012.

[27] T. H. Nelson. Complex information processing: a file structure for the complex, the changing and the indeterminate. In *National Conference*, pages 84–100. ACM, 1965.

[28] J. Oakley. Eliciting univariate probability distributions. *Rethinking Risk Measurement and Reporting*, 1, 2010.

[29] B. J. Pierce, S. R. Parkinson, and N. Sisson. Effects of semantic similarity, omission probability and number of alternatives in computer menu search. *International Journal of Man-Machine Studies*, 37(5):653–677, 1992.

[30] P. L. T. Pirolli and S. K. Card. Information foraging. *Psychological Review*, 106(4):643–675, 1999.

[31] P. L. T. Pirolli and J. E. Pitkow. Distributions of surfers' paths through the world wide web: Empirical characterizations. *World Wide Web*, 2(1-2):29–45, Jan 1999.

[32] D. d. S. Price. A general theory of bibliometric and other cumulative advantage processes. *Journal of the American Society for Information Science*, 27(5):292–306, 1976.

[33] H. Rubenstein and J. B. Goodenough. Contextual correlates of synonymy. *Communications of the ACM*, 8(10):627–633, 1965.

[34] G. Salton and C. Buckley. Term-weighting approaches in automatic text retrieval. *Information Processing & Management*, 24(5):513–523, 1988.

[35] P. Singer, D. Helic, B. Taraghi, and M. Strohmaier. Detecting memory and structure in human navigation patterns using markov chain models of varying order. *PloS one*, 9(7):e102070, 2014.

[36] P. Singer, T. Niebler, M. Strohmaier, and A. Hotho. Computing semantic relatedness from human navigational paths: A case study on wikipedia. *International Journal on Semantic Web and Information Systems*, 9(4):41–70, 2013.

[37] R. W. Sinnott. Virtues of the haversine. *Sky and Telescope*, 68(2):158, 1984.

[38] C. C. Strelioff, J. P. Crutchfield, and A. W. Hübler. Inferring markov chains: Bayesian estimation, model comparison, entropy rate, and out-of-class modeling. *Physical Review E*, 76(1):011106, Jul 2007.

[39] W. Vanpaemel. Prior sensitivity in theory testing: An apologia for the bayes factor. *Journal of Mathematical Psychology*, 54(6):491–498, 2010.

[40] W. Vanpaemel. Constructing informative model priors using hierarchical methods. *Journal of Mathematical Psychology*, 55(1):106–117, 2011.

[41] W. Vanpaemel and M. D. Lee. Using priors to formalize theory: Optimal attention and the generalized context model. *Psychonomic Bulletin & Review*, 19(6):1047–1056, 2012.

[42] S. Walk, P. Singer, and M. Strohmaier. Sequential action patterns in collaborative ontology-engineering projects: A case-study in the biomedical domain. In *International Conference on Conference on Information & Knowledge Management*. ACM, 2014.

[43] S. Walk, P. Singer, M. Strohmaier, T. Tudorache, M. A. Musen, and N. F. Noy. Discovering beaten paths in collaborative ontology-engineering projects using markov chains. *Journal of Biomedical Informatics*, 51:254–271, 2014.

[44] L. Wasserman. Bayesian model selection and model averaging. *Journal of Mathematical Psychology*, 44(1):92–107, 2000.

[45] R. West and J. Leskovec. Human wayfinding in information networks. In *International Conference on World Wide Web*, pages 619–628. ACM, 2012.

[46] R. West, J. Pineau, and D. Precup. Wikispeedia: An online game for inferring semantic distances between concepts. In *International Joint Conference on Artifical Intelligence*, pages 1598–1603. Morgan Kaufmann Publishers Inc., 2009.

[47] R. W. White and J. Huang. Assessing the scenic route: measuring the value of search trails in web logs. In *Conference on Research and Development in Information Retrieval*, pages 587–594. ACM, 2010.

[48] W. Xie, P. O. Lewis, Y. Fan, L. Kuo, and M.-H. Chen. Improving marginal likelihood estimation for bayesian phylogenetic model selection. *Systematic Biology*, 60(2):150–160, 2010.

[49] J. Yang, J. McAuley, J. Leskovec, P. LePendu, and N. Shah. Finding progression stages in time-evolving event sequences. In *International Conference on World Wide Web*, pages 783–794. ACM, 2014.

Exploiting Collective Hidden Structures in Webpage Titles for Open Domain Entity Extraction

Wei Song[†]*, Shiqi Zhao[‡], Chao Zhang[‡], Hua Wu[‡], Haifeng Wang[‡], Lizhen Liu[†], Hanshi Wang[†]

[†]College of Information Engineering, Capital Normal University, Beijing, China

[‡]Baidu Inc., Beijing, China

{wsong, lzliu, hswang}@cnu.edu.cn

{zhaoshiqi, zhangchao01, wu_hua, wanghaifeng}@baidu.com

ABSTRACT

We present a novel method for open domain named entity extraction by exploiting the collective hidden structures in webpage titles. Our method uncovers the hidden textual structures shared by sets of webpage titles based on generalized URL patterns and a multiple sequence alignment technique. The highlights of our method include: 1) The boundaries of entities can be identified automatically in a collective way without any manually designed pattern, seed or class name. 2) The connections between entities are also discovered naturally based on the hidden structures, which makes it easy to incorporate distant or weak supervision. The experiments show that our method can harvest large scale of open domain entities with high precision. A large ratio of the extracted entities are long-tailed and complex and cover diverse topics. Given the extracted entities and their connections, we further show the effectiveness of our method in a weakly supervised setting. Our method can produce better domain specific entities in both precision and recall compared with the state-of-the-art approaches.

Categories and Subject Descriptors

I.2.6 [**Artificial Intelligence**]: Learning—*Knowledge acquisition*; I.2.7 [**Artificial Intelligence**]: Natural language processing; H.3.1 [**Information Storage and Retrieval**]: Content Analysis and Indexing

General Terms

Algorithms, Experimentation

Keywords

Open domain entity extraction;Multiple sequence alignment;URL pattern;Template generation;Weak supervision

*This work was done when the first author was visiting Baidu.

WWW 2015, May 18–22, 2015, Florence, Italy.

ACM 978-1-4503-3469-3/15/05.

http://dx.doi.org/10.1145/2736277.2741107.

1. INTRODUCTION

A named entity (entity for short) is a contiguous sequence of textual tokens, which represents the name of an object of a certain class, such as a person or an organization. Entity extraction is a key subtask of Information Extraction (IE), and also a fundamental component for many Natural Language Processing (NLP) and Information Retrieval (IR) tasks. For example, relation extraction is based on identifying entities in advance. Word segmentation and parsing would be improved if one system already knows that a piece of text is an entity. Besides, search engines have been paying much attention on semantic and knowledge driven search beyond traditional keyword based search paradigm. In such scenario, mining and integrating new and long-tailed entities would benefit knowledge base construction and help understanding user intent.

The main challenge of entity extraction is to precisely determine the boundaries of entities [14]. It is challenging, especially for long and complex entities like book names and restaurant names. The forms of these names might be flexible, containing multiple words and even other entities. Almost all existing approaches attempt to solve this problem in different ways, among which supervised models are based on various syntactic and contextual features extracted from manually annotated training data [5, 11, 22], while semi (weakly)-supervised methods make use of class names, seeds or manually designed syntactic patterns to induce templates for determining the boundaries of entities [12, 15, 26]. Another alternative way is to make use of explicit structured data such as HTML tags [1, 19] and HTML tables of webpages [13, 17].

However, most of the above work relies on domain knowledge or human labor. Due to the necessity of training data, supervised methods only work well on predefined categories [18]. Semi-supervised methods simplify the training process, but don't get rid of prior knowledge either. The manual labor scales with the number of classes of interest. Because HTML patterns are usually website specific, it is impossible for people to enumerate HTML patterns or set seeds for every relevant website. Therefore, search engines and seeds are usually needed for retrieving webpages and inducing wrappers [19, 31]. Besides, some open entity extraction methods are proposed [14, 21], which attempt to extract entities without human intervention. But existing systems commonly utilize language dependent heuristics, which are difficult to be applied to other languages.

In this paper, we propose an open entity extraction method, which extracts entities and their connections from the web

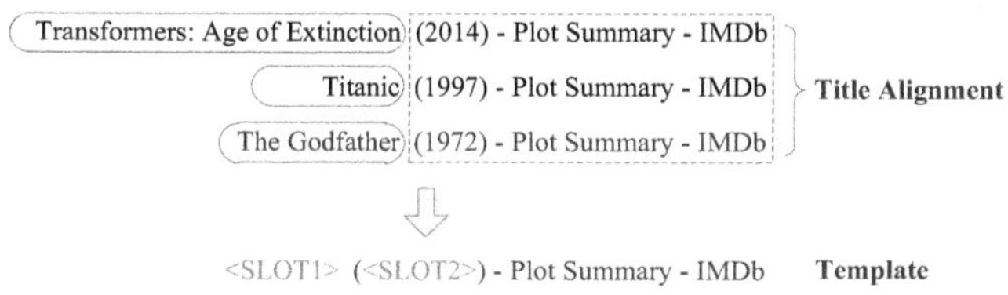

Figure 1: Webpage title alignment for inducing templates with substitutable slots.

without requiring prior knowledge, manual labor or sophisticated NLP techniques, and is language independent.

The key point is that we induce templates and extract entities by collectively identifying and aligning webpage titles with the same hidden textual structure. Our method is based on the following observation: **Parallel webpage titles that share the same hidden textual structures may contain certain classes of entities**. The term *hidden* here means that there is no explicit structure in an isolated webpage title, but if we align these titles together, the common structures among titles emerge naturally, such as the example shown in Figure 1. We can see that entities usually play a role as substitutable slot fillers within these titles. Therefore, the task to determine the boundaries of entities is actually casted to the task of inducing templates within parallel webpage titles and identifying substitutable slots in the templates.

Although the observation is obvious, the main challenges are two-fold: how to identify parallel webpage titles with the same hidden structures and how to induce and utilize the hidden structures for entity extraction.

For the first challenge, we identify webpage titles with the same or similar hidden structures by exploiting **generalized URL patterns**. We notice that webpage titles with similar URL morphology tend to share similar textual structures. Based on this strategy, we can collect large scale of parallel webpage titles, which are used as the data resource for entity extraction.

For the second challenge, we first apply the idea of **Multiple Sequence Alignment** (MSA) to align these webpage titles for inducing templates automatically. Then, we utilize search engine user behaviors and heuristic constraints to filter out invalid templates which fail to produce valid entities. Finally, for each target webpage title, we rank candidate templates based on the probability that they could correctly determine the entity boundary in this title and choose the most appropriate one for entity extraction.

To the best of our knowledge, we are the first to exploit webpage titles for entity extraction in an unsupervised manner. Figure 2 shows the working flowchart of the proposed approach. The system takes webpages as input and no additional manual labor is necessary. The system output includes extracted open domain entities and their connections. The connections are formed by recording from which templates each entity is extracted. Since the entities extracted by the same template are often of the same class, the connections reveal topic relatedness among entities and make it easy to incorporate distant or weak supervision.

In summary, the main contributions of this paper include:

- We exploit the hidden textual structures in webpage titles for open domain entity extraction. We propose algorithms for both discovering and utilizing these structures, which make our method get rid of manual labor.
- We demonstrate experimentally that: 1) Our method can extract large scale of open domain entities with high precision and topic coverage, many of which are long-tailed entities. 2) Based on the extracted entities and their connections, we can easily incorporate weak supervision for mining more accurate and complete domain specific entities. In both settings, our method outperforms the state-of-the-art approaches based on search engine query logs.

The rest of this paper is organized as follows. In Section 2, we propose our method. We show our experiments and results on open domain entity extraction in Section 3, and demonstrate its effectiveness on domain specific entity extraction in Section 4. We introduce the related work in Section 5 and conclude this paper in Section 6.

2. PROPOSED METHOD

2.1 Motivation

Our idea comes from the following simple observations:

- There are extensive entities of various topics existing in webpage titles, especially from vertical domain websites.
- The webpage titles, which are from the same website and contain the same class of entities, have similar hidden textual structures.
- Within the textual structures, entities play a role as substitutable slot fillers.

Numerous webpages are about entities. Because webpage titles summarize the key concepts of the content, if a webpage introduces an entity, it is natural that the title contains the entity. Considering the redundancy of the web, for one entity, it is quite likely that there is at least one webpage title containing it. Therefore, *webpage titles are valuable resources for entity extraction.*

The second and the third observations are also understandable. The webpages introducing the same classes of entities or their attributes are often organized in the same way within a website. As shown in Figure 1, it is easy to see that three titles share the same hidden structure:

$< moviename >$ ($< digit >$) - Plot Summary - IMDB

The hidden structure forms a **template**. The field like $< moviename >$ or $< digit >$ is substitutable, noted as a **slot**. The **slot fillers** are the text fragments which could be placed at the slot positions and expected to be some class of entities. This phenomenon becomes obvious when these titles are aligned together. Motivated by this, we aim to learn an extractor by aligning webpage titles with the same hidden textual structures collectively.

2.2 Generalized URL Patterns

A generalized URL pattern is a regular expression which could recognize a set of URLs. The webpage titles of URLs which could be recognized by the same generalized URL pattern are named as parallel webpage titles. We expect

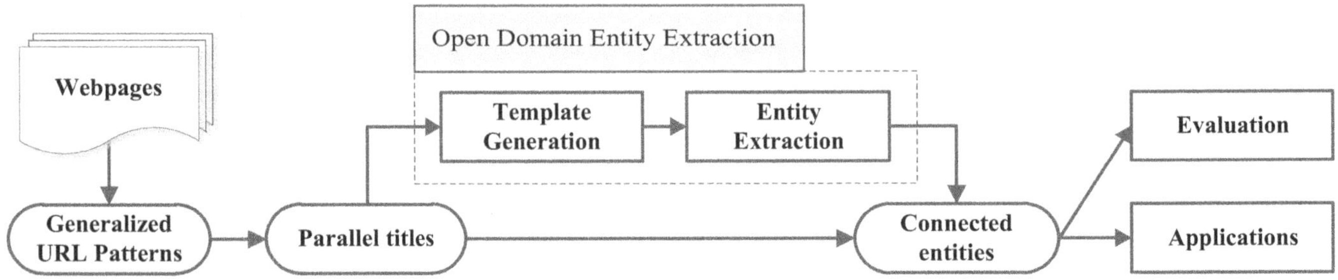

Figure 2: The flowchart of the proposed system.

that parallel webpage titles should have the same or similar hidden textual structures. The example below shows a generalized URL pattern and 2 URL instances.

$Pattern: \ http://www.imdb.com/title/tt\backslash d+/\$$

$URL1: \ http://www.imdb.com/title/tt0000001/$

$URL2: \ http://www.imdb.com/title/tt0000002/$

Exploiting generalized URL patterns for identifying parallel webpage titles is motivated by the idea that topic related webpages often form clusters and share the same URL pattern in a website [6, 32]. We learn the generalized URL patterns from a large scale URL database. The process is as follows:

Step 1: Segment the non-domain part of each URL with "/". We will generate candidate URL patterns by replacing one segment with a regular expression each time. For example, the candidate patterns for URL1 are $http://www.imdb.com/REG/tt0000001/\$$ and $http://www.imdb.com/title/REG/\$$, where REG is a special symbol to represent regular expressions.

Step 2: To determine whether a segment should be generalized, we accumulate all candidate patterns over the URL database. The ones with a frequency above a threshold are retained, such as
$http://www.imdb.com/title/REG/\$$.

Step 3: For each retained candidate pattern, the final generalized URL pattern is got by replacing the symbol REG with a regular expression based on the fillers of this segment. The resulting pattern for URL1 becomes $http://www.imdb.com/title/tt\backslash d+/\$$.

Given one generalized URL pattern, we can get corresponding parallel webpage titles which share the same or similar textual structures. These structures are difficult to be discovered if we deal with each title separately. We will show the structures could be discovered automatically by aligning them together in a collective way.

2.3 Open Domain Entity Extraction

Given parallel webpage titles of a generalized URL pattern, we aim to generate templates to uncover the hidden textual structures for entity extraction.

2.3.1 MSA based Template Generation

We view parallel titles as a set of word sequences and conduct alignment to induce templates. The textual structures of parallel titles in real data often have variations. There might be multiple templates, each of which matches a subset of the examined parallel titles. Therefore, we first adapt the Needleman-Wunsch algorithm [23] for pair-wise alignment to induce all possible templates.

Pairwise Alignment. We define the element set as $\Sigma = \mathcal{V} \bigcup \{\_\}$, where $\mathcal{V}$ refers to the word vocabulary, and "_" is used to represent an indel (suppose "_" $\notin \mathcal{V}$). Given two word sequences $A \in \mathcal{V}^*$ and $B \in \mathcal{V}^*$, an alignment can be represented as a 2-dimensional array $Align_{2\times I}^{A,B}$ that every word in one sequence is aligned to one word in the other sequence or to an indel which is caused by **inserting** a word into one sequence or **deleting** a word from the other. I is the number of aligned element pairs. A *substitution matrix* R is used to assign alignment scores, in which $R(a, b)$ represents the alignment score between a pair of elements $(a, b) \in \Sigma\times\Sigma$. A well aligned pair will be rewarded with a higher score. We define an overall score function $AlignScore(A, B)$ as the sum of the scores over all aligned element pairs in two sequences:

$$AlignScore(A, B) = \sum_{i=1}^{I} R(Align_{0,i}^{A,B}, Align_{1,i}^{A,B}) \quad (1)$$

Therefore, the task, as shown in Equation 2, is to find an optimal alignment with the best overall score.

$$Align^* = \arg\max_{Align_{2\times I}^{A,B}} AlignScore(A, B) \quad (2)$$

To achieve this, we should first define a proper substitute matrix R. In detail, $R(a, b)$ is defined as follows.

- Exact Match: $a \in \Sigma$ and $b \in \Sigma$ are exact matched if $a == b$. Define $R(a, a) = \alpha$, $\alpha > 0$, so that identical match is awarded. If two words are both delimiters, they are considered as an exact match as well.
- Mismatch: Include two types: normal word mismatch and gap penalty. If $a \in \mathcal{V}$ and $b \in \mathcal{V}$ are different normal words, define $R(a, b) = \beta$, $\beta < 0$. If $a \in \mathcal{V}$ and $b ==$ "_", define $R(a, b) = d$, $d < 0$.
- Forbiden Match: A normal word a is not allowed to be aligned with a delimiter b, for which we define $R(a, b) = -\infty$.

We construct a delimiter dictionary manually including "[", "|", "-" and so on. The delimiters and normal words together form the vocabulary $\mathcal{V}$. We specially consider delimiters, because delimiters are often used for segmenting different blocks in titles. Generally, delimiters shouldn't be part of an entity so that they shouldn't be aligned with normal words. Normal word mismatches are penalized by assigning a negative score, while gap mismatches are actually to penalize long distance alignment.

Given the substitute matrix R, we compute a matrix F by dynamic programming as described in Algorithm 1. The entries of F give the maximum scores among all possible alignments. Once the matrix F is computed, we backtrack the coming path starting from the bottom right corner of F and get the optimal alignment.

Algorithm 1 Computing Scoring Matrix for All Possible Alignments

Input:
Sequences A and B;
Substitution Matrix R and gap penalty d;
Output:
Score Matrix F;

```
/* Initialize matrix F_{(length(A)+1)×(length(B)+1)} with a
linear gap penalty. */
for i = 0 to length(A) do
    F_{i,0} = i * d;
end for
for j = 0 to length(B) do
    F_{0,j} = j * d;
end for
/* Compute optimal scores. */
for i = 1 to length(A) do
    for j = 1 to length(B) do
        MATCH ⟵ F_{i-1,j-1} + R(A_i, B_j);
        DELETE ⟵ F_{i-1,j} + d;
        INSERT ⟵ F_{i,j-1} + d;
        F_{i,j} = max{MATCH, DELETE, INSERT};
    end for
end for
return F;
```

Template Induction. Given a pairwise sequence alignment, we can induce a template for each sequence accordingly. We replace consecutive mismatch words in each sequence with a <*SLOT*> symbol which represents a template slot. The matched parts are considered as the backbone of the template. If one template does not contain <*SLOT*> or the template itself is <*SLOT*>, it is discarded, because this indicates two sequences are the same or completely different. An example is shown below.

Given two sequences A = "$w_1[w_2w_3]$", B = "$v_1(w_2w_3)$" respectively, the alignment result and corresponding templates are :

A:	w_1	-	[	w_2	w_3	]
B:	-	v_1	(	w_2	w_3	)
		⇓				
Template 1:	<SLOT>		[	w_2	w_3	]
Template 2:	<SLOT>		(	w_2	w_3	)

We accumulate all templates generated by pairwise alignment and remove the templates with low frequencies.

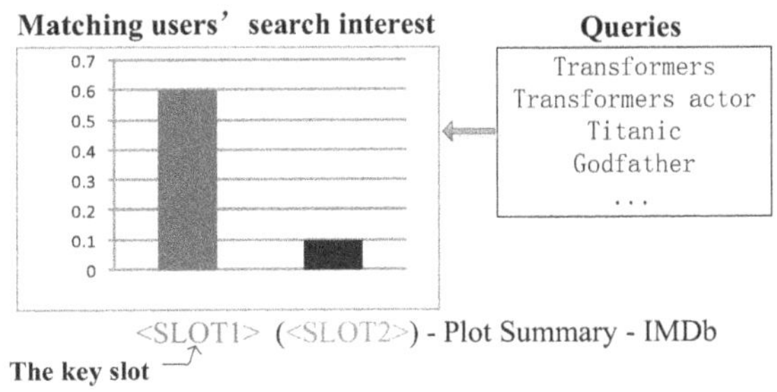

Figure 3: User behavior based slot selection, in which we can see that the slot for movie names is selected as the key slot, since it matches users' search interest when clicking on the corresponding titles.

User Behavior based Slot Selection. Some of the retained templates contain multiple slots. Such as the example shown in Figure 1, the slot fillers for movie names are what we really want. To select the right slot in a template, which is termed **key slot** in what follows, we take advantage of user click-through behaviors in search engines. Our assumption is that the key slot of a template is more likely to match users' search interest. In other words, for titles matched by the template, the fillers of the key slot are more likely to match users' search queries that click on these titles. A motivating example is shown in Figure 3.

We consider templates and user queries together through clicked URLs in query logs. Suppose a template T has m slots. One title x is matched by T and the corresponding slot fillers are $\{f_1(x), ..., f_m(x)\}$, where $f_i(x)$ is the slot filter of the ith slot s_i of the template T. If the title x is clicked by a searcher submitting query q, a title-query pair (x, q) forms. By accumulating all title-query pairs $\{(x, q)\}$ related to template T, the weight of the ith slot s_i to user queries could be measured as:

$$weight(s_i, T) = \sum_{(x,q)} Jaccard(f_i(x), q) \tag{3}$$

where $Jaccard(.,.)$ is the jaccard similarity between two word sets. We choose $s^* = \arg\max_i weight(s_i, T)$ as the key slot of template T, if $weight(s^*, T) > 0$. So if one template has more than one slot, we use all template slots for generalization, but extract slot fillers as candidate entities only from the key slot. This constraint asks help from searchers to guarantee the quality of entities.

Template filtering. We further filter out invalid templates by assessing the quality of extracted candidate entities. To this end, we first identify high-confident valid and invalid entity sets in a heuristic way and then design two indicators for template filtering.

- Lexicon based indicator: According to our observation, invalid candidate entities are often extracted from the titles of news or forum webpages. To filter out such candidates, we construct a stopword list including interrogative words and colloquial words like "where", "who", "ah" and some punctuation. If a candidate entity contains these words, it is considered as invalid.

- Redundancy based indicator: We figure out a set of valid entities based on redundancy. A candidate entity is more likely to be valid if it appears many times on the web. In this work, a candidate entity is considered as valid if it can be extracted more than 5 times by different templates.

Finally, a template is considered as a valid template, if it could produce at least J valid entities determined by the redundancy based indicator and less than K invalid entities determined by the lexicon based indicator.

2.3.2 Template based Entity Extraction

We apply the generated valid templates for entity extraction. One issue is that one title could be matched by more than one template at different granularity. For example, the title below can be matched by the following three templates.

Title: Stir Fried Beef Recipe - Website name

Template 1: <SLOT> Recipe - Website name

Template 2: <SLOT> - Website name

Template 3: <SLOT> Beef Recipe - Website name

To choose the best template for each title, we view it as a template ranking problem. Formally, given the titles $\mathcal{X} = \{x_1, ..., x_{|\mathcal{X}|}\}$ for one URL pattern, and a template set $\mathcal{T} = \{t_1, ..., t_{|\mathcal{T}|}\}$ associated with $\mathcal{X}$, we have to select the best template $t \in \mathcal{T}_x$ for each title $x \in \mathcal{X}$ for entity extraction, where $\mathcal{T}_x$ is a subset of $\mathcal{T}$ that can match x.

At first glance, some simple heuristics could be used for ranking:

- Common-First: Choose the template with the best coverage over all titles.
- Alignment-First: Choose the template with the best alignment score with the title.

The first heuristic will work for most titles, but may produce *super-entities* in some cases. For example, applying template 2 in the above example will extract "*Stir Fried Beef Recipe*" as a candidate entity. In contrast, alignment-first heuristic should be preferred for extracting clean entities. But sometimes, it may result in *sub-entities* such as "*Stir Fried*" which is extracted by applying template 3. Such templates are generated when two entities with common words happen to appear in paired titles.

To balance between the two extremes, we propose an **adaptive ranking (AdaRank)** function combining both alignment preference and popularity. Given title x, the probability of choosing $t \in \mathcal{T}_x$ as the perfect template can be represented as:

$$p(t|x) = \frac{p(x|t)p(t)}{p(x)} \tag{4}$$

$p(x|t)$ represents the likelihood that title x is generated using template t. Here, we approximate it using $\frac{1}{alRank(t,x)^{\rho}}$, where $alRank(t, x)$ is the rank of template t among $\mathcal{T}_x$ according to alignment scores. This means that templates with larger alignment scores with the title are more likely to generate the title. ρ is a positive value to control the punishment degree for the low rank templates. A larger value of ρ favors top ranked templates more. $p(t)$ can be seen as the prior probability of template t being a good template. We estimate $p(t)$ based on the global alignment information:

$$p(t) = \frac{\#(alRank(t, \cdot) == 1)}{|\mathcal{X}|} \tag{5}$$

where $\#(alRank(t, \cdot) == 1)$ represents the number of titles in $\mathcal{X}$ that template t has the largest alignment score with them. According to the probability ranking principle and removing constant factors, we compute the ranking score of the template t for the title x as:

$$rank(t|x) \equiv \frac{\#(alRank(t, \cdot) == 1)}{alRank(t, x)^{\rho}} \tag{6}$$

In summary, AdaRank integrates both the local alignment score and the global score of a template and achieves the best balance between them. It prefers the templates with both good alignment score and a certain size. Based on Equation 6, we use the top 1 ranked template for entity extraction and store the pair of the entity and the template for extracting it. The same procedure is applied to all titles as summarized in Algorithm 2.

Algorithm 2 Extracting Entities with Templates

Input:
A set of webpage titles $\mathcal{X}$ of certain URL pattern;
A set of templates $\mathcal{T}$;
Output:
A set of entity-template pairs, ET;

```
Initiate ET = ∅;
for each x in X do
    Get templates T_x which can match x;
    Rank T_x to get the best template t* for x;
    Extract the slot filler e from x which fills the key slot
    of t*;
    Add (e, t*) to ET;
end for
return ET;
```

3. EVALUATING OPEN DOMAIN ENTITY EXTRACTION

In this section we evaluate the quality of extracted entities. We first describe the data, then introduce the baseline our method is compared with. Finally, we report the experimental results on system comparisons and take a deep insight into the extraction results.

3.1 Experimental Settings

3.1.1 Data

The data we used for experiments include query logs and a webpage dataset. We use query logs from Baidu, which is the largest Chinese search engine in the world. In all, there are more than 1.9 billion queries and corresponding user clicked URLs. In our work, the query logs are used for selecting key slots. While the baseline (see Section 3.1.2) extracts entities directly from the queries.

Different methods extract entities from different resources. We constructed a webpage dataset according to the scale of query logs. First, generalized URL patterns were learned using the strategy described in Section 2.2 on 30 billion webpages. Then, we retained generalized URL patterns which

Table 1: Statistics of the data.

Webpage dataset	Volume
#generalized URL patterns	918,541
#webpages	11,056,478,017
query logs	**Volume**
#queries	1,929,617,042

Table 2: Performance on open entity extraction.

Method	#Entity	Precision	Coverage
OEQ (10, 0.1)	12419342	0.62	0.31
OEQ (100, 0.1)	930133	0.67	0.025
Ours	12375492	0.81	0.43

could recognize at least one user clicked URL in the query logs. Finally, we collected all webpages whose URLs can be recognized by one of the retained generalized URL patterns. We only used the titles of these webpages for entity extraction in our method. The statistics of query logs and webpage dataset are shown in Table 1.

Because we deal with Chinese, all webpage tiltes are segmented into words for further processing such as sequence alignment. Note that since online encyclopedias have URL patterns as well, our method could exhaust entries from them. To eliminate this effect of these websites, our method doesn't use URL patterns of three main Chinese online encyclopedias: Baidu Baike[1], Hudong Baike[2] and Chinese Wikipedia[3].

3.1.2 Baseline

The most common data resources for entity extraction are web documents and query logs. Extracting open domain entities from web documents without any supervision is hard and computationally expensive. As reported in both [21] and [25], entity extraction from query logs outperforms systems based on documents. In this work, we aim to show that by exploiting the hidden textual structures, entity extraction from webpage titles can achieve superior performance compared with approaches based on query logs.

We implemented a method which extracts open entities from queries [21], noted as OEQ. We adapt OEQ to Chinese: 1) We extract all text fragments segmented by blank characters from queries, since an entity should not cross 2 fragments separated by blank characters in Chinese. 2) We extract all k-grams in text fragments and count their frequencies. 3) We retain all k-grams, if they satisfy the representation and stand-alone constraints. Representation constraint is that the number of entity occurrence must exceed a threshold. Stand-alone means that one entity forms a query by itself, and stand-alone constraint is that the ratio of an entity occurring in a stand-alone way must exceed a threshold. Refer to [21] for more details.

3.1.3 Parameters

Our method has several parameters to be set. Due to the large size of dataset, we select a small portion of data to tune the parameters. For pairwise alignment, we define the substitute matrix by setting $\alpha = 2$, $\beta = -1$ and $d = -2$. The templates matching less than 20 titles were eliminated after template induction. For template filtering, we set parameter K to 20, and J to 30. For adaptive template ranking, ρ is set to 2.

For the baseline, we set the threshold for stand-alone score to 0.1 which is the same in [21], and tried several values of representation score threshold. We would report the performance when it is set to 10, with which OEQ produces a similar scale of entities to us. The quantity of produced entities reduces as the representation score threshold gets larger. We also report the results when the threshold is set to 100 as a reference.

3.2 Experimental Results

3.2.1 Overall Performance

Precision and Coverage. We randomly sampled 500 entities produced by each system respectively, and asked two annotators to judge whether the extracted ones are correct. The annotation standard is according to [28]. Entities that are names of specific objects or general concepts such as "低碳经济*(low-carbon economy)*" are all considered as correct. Inner-annotator agreement measured by Kappa coefficient [7] is 0.79. We adopt *Precision* as an evaluation metric to measure the ratio of correct entities, which is defined as $\frac{\#\text{correct extracted entities}}{\#\text{all extracted entities}}$. Because it is impossible to evaluate the recall, we evaluate the *Coverage* by comparing the system outputs against entries in Baidu Baike—the largest Chinese online encyclopedia, which has more than 6.5 million entries. We didn't consider entity alias so that the *Coverage* is measured based on exact string matching.

Table 2 shows the experimental results. We can see when producing similar quantity of entities, our method has higher precision compared with OEQ. This indicates that our method could produce large scale of entities with an acceptable precision. OEQ achieves higher precision when setting a larger threshold (100) for representation score at the price of a sharp decrease of coverage. But the precision is still obviously lower than our method. On coverage, our method outperforms OEQ as well. Because both methods could be applied to larger dataset, the coverage could be further improved.

Topic Analysis. We examine the topic distribution of extracted entities to see whether they cover a wide range of topics. To this end, we extract all entities with category tags from Baidu Baike. In detail, Baidu Baike maintains an entity category taxonomy, based on which entities can be assigned a category tag by users. The taxonomy contains 23 general topical categories and 90 sub-categories. In this experiments, if a Baidu Baike entity already has a subcategory tag, we will automatically assign its higher level general category to it. In this way, we collected about 1.1 million entities in Baidu Baike with general category labels. In Figure 4, the black bars show the number of entities each category has. We can see the distribution is unbalanced, person (PER), literature work (LITERATURE) and organization (ORG) are the most popular categories.

Among the 1.1 million entities, more than 0.59 million entities could be extracted by our method. The distribution over categories of our extracted entities are shown in Figure 4 as well. We can see that the distribution is consistent with that of the entities in Baidu Baike. The coverage ranges

[1]http://baike.baidu.com/
[2]http://www.baike.com/
[3]http://zh.wikipedia.org/

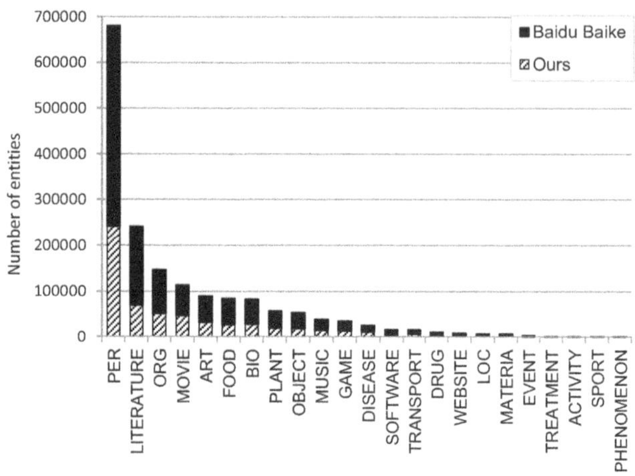

Figure 4: Entity category distributions.

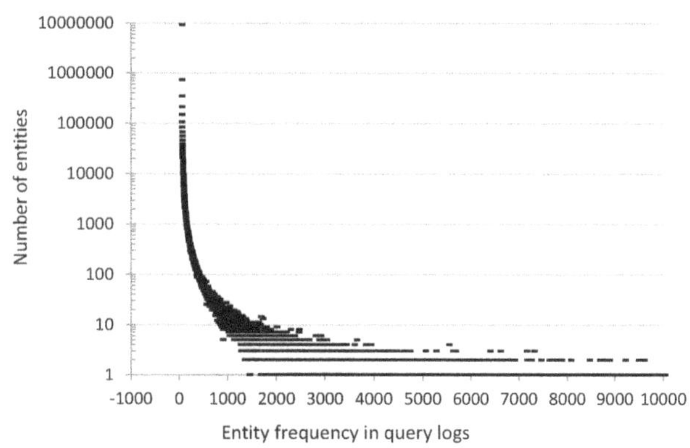

Figure 5: Number of entities with different frequencies in query logs.

from 41% (on LITERATURE) to 74% (on SPORT) across all categories. This indicates that the entities extracted by our method cover diverse topics.

Frequency Analysis. We analyse the frequencies of our extracted entities in query logs. Figure 5 illustrates the number of entities with different frequencies. We can see that about 9 million entities never occur in query logs which make up 73% of all entities. This indicates that our method is good at extracting long-tailed entities that are unable to be extracted from queries.

Length Analysis. Discovering complex multi-word entities is important and challenging. Thus we analyze the length (the number of words) of the extracted entities. Figure 6 shows the distribution of entities extracted by OEQ and by ours across different length intervals. We can see that OEQ extracts more simple entities with length no longer than 3, while our method extracts more long entities. From the outputs of our method and OEQ, we sampled 100 entities whose lengths are longer than 10 and evaluated the precision. Our method achieves a *Precision* of 77%, while OEQ gets a *Precision* of 52%. Many errors resulted by OEQ are long queries revealing some hot information need. Although they frequently appear on web, they are not entities.

Error Analysis. We also analyze the incorrect entities extracted by our method. The errors could be categorized

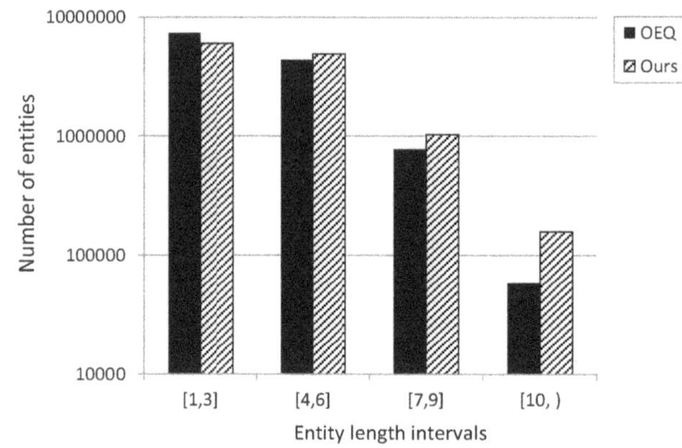

Figure 6: Number of entities across different length intervals.

into 3 types: 1) Too general classes. The extracted entities play a navigational function in webpage titles and usually are related to general information needs, such as "*关于爱国的作文(essays about patriotism)*". 2) Containing entity attribute or intent. The extracted candidates describe attributes or aspects of entities, such as "*北京景点(Attractions in Beijing)*". 3) User generated errors. Some webpage titles are generated by users. In some cases, although the titles share the same hidden structure, the slot fillers are noisy due to informality of users' edit.

Discussion. Based on the above analysis, we show that our method could extract massive, long-tailed entities with high precision and topic coverage. These entities have unique characteristics compared with the ones extracted from search queries and those already existing in encyclopedias: 1) The entities extracted from webpage titles are more formal. For example, we can extract complete full names of objects such as books, research papers and organizations. In contrast, many entities extracted from queries are shorten forms or alias of full names. 2) Large scale of entities are long-tailed. Less popular entities, which are difficult to be extracted based on redundancy, can be extracted by templates induced based on hidden structures. 3) Entities of some fine-grained domains can be extracted. For example, we can find names of rare plants, because our method can automatically discover and extract entities from vertical websites. These long-tailed fine-grained entities are potentially useful for development of vertical applications, for which we expect to exhaust all entities belonging to the application domain. On the other hand, although the entities in encyclopedias cover a wide range of domains, the coverage on long-tailed entities of certain domains is far from enough for satisfying the requirement of practical applications.

On the other side, we find that our method does not work well on extracting common concepts such as *climate*. The reason may be that few website collects and organizes common concepts together.

3.2.2 *Evaluating Generalized URL Patterns*

We randomly sampled 100 from the retained generalized URL patterns introduced in Section 3.1.1 and judged whether the corresponding titles have hidden structures. The results show that 78 out of 100 generalized URL patterns have hidden structures (though they might not produce correct enti-

Table 3: Performance on template ranking.

Method	Precision@1
Common-first	0.79
Alignment-first	0.84
AdaRank	0.93

ties). The parallel webpage titles that have no hidden structure can be divided into 2 categories: 1) All titles are the same. 2) All titles are totally different. Fortunately, our extractor can deal with both cases so that they cannot affect entity extraction. 26 among the 78 generalized URL patterns have a single hidden structure each, while the others have more hidden structures. This analysis indicates that generalized URL patterns are useful for identifying webpage titles with hidden textual structures.

After template filtering, 92,318 generalized URL patterns remain, which account for 10% of all. Each remained generalized URL pattern has 24 entity extraction templates on average. However, the most frequent template for each pattern can cover nearly 73% webpage titles. The number increases to 93%, if we take top-5 templates into account for each URL pattern. This further reveals that webpage titles with the same URL pattern truly have highly similar hidden textual structures.

3.2.3 Evaluating Entity Extractor

Evaluating Template Generation

Data and metrics. Here we also evaluate the entity extraction templates. Specifically, we evaluate whether we have correctly detected the key slot. For this purpose, we randomly sampled 200 templates, and asked two annotators to label the selected key slot as correct or not. To facilitate the annotation, we also provide 10 fillers for each slot in each template, so that the annotators can judge whether each examined slot can be used to extract correct entities. We use *Precision* as an evaluation metric, which is defined as $\frac{\text{\#correctly selected key slots}}{\text{\#selected key slots}}$.

The experimental results show that our method achieves a *Precision* of 81.5%. This indicates that user behavior based slot selection is effective for selecting high quality slots in templates for entity extraction.

Evaluating Template Ranking

Data and metrics. We randomly sampled 50 generalized URL patterns with more than 10 entity extraction templates after template generation phase (Section 2.3.1). From each URL pattern, we sampled 10 titles which could be matched by at least 2 templates. The resulting dataset consists of 500 titles which have 16 templates on average. For each title, we rank the templates using three ranking strategies introduced in Section 2.3.2: Common-first, Alignment-first and AdaRank. We use *Precision*@1 as a metric to see whether the top one template can correctly determine the boundary of the entity for each title.

Results. Table 3 shows the results. We can see that AdaRank obviously outperforms the other two strategies. This indicates that considering both local alignment and global popularity is effective for ranking entity extraction templates. Alignment-first heuristic performs better than common-first. All errors of alignment-first heuristic come from incorrect word alignment in multi-word entities, in which single words within two entities are aligned so that entities are incorrectly split into fragments.

4. INCORPORATING SUPERVISION

The extracted entity-template pairs can be viewed as a data resource for more specific tasks. Actually, the entity-template pairs form a bipartite graph. Therefore, the distant supervision (e.g. existing entries in knowledge bases) and weak supervision (e.g. manually provided seeds with labels) can be easily incorporated by propagating information through this graph. In this paper, we apply this data resource for set expansion of domain entities.

4.1 Set Expansion of Domain Entities

We focus on evaluating it in a weakly supervised setting as in [26]: **a few seeds S of a domain is given, the system should return more entities of the same domain.** This setting is useful for knowledge base expansion based on available resources.

We generate a subset of entities that are potentially relevant to the seeds from the entity-template pairs we have extracted and then rank these entities. This process involves the following steps:

Step 1: Extract all templates $\mathcal{T}$ that contain at least one of the seeds.

Step 2: Build a bipartite graph $\mathcal{G} = \{\mathcal{T} \cup \mathcal{E}, \mathcal{L}\}$, where $\mathcal{E}$ represents the set of entities that can be extracted by templates in $\mathcal{T}$. If an entity $e \in \mathcal{E}$ is extracted by a template $t \in \mathcal{T}$, there is an edge $l \in \mathcal{L}$ between them.

Step 3: An iterative algorithm is adopted to rank entities in this graph.

We use $TScore(t)$ to represent the relevance of a template t, use $EScore(e)$ to represent the relevance of an entity e, and use $Pri(e)$ to represent the prior relevance of e to the examined domain. We set the $Pri(e)$ for seed nodes as $\frac{1}{|S|}$ and 0 for all other entities. The iterative algorithm is motivated by the personalized PageRank [20]. It starts by initializing the $TScore^0(t)$ for all templates and the $EScore^0(e)$ for all entities as 0. Then in each iteration, the relevance scores of entities and templates in this graph are updated alternatively as follows.

$$EScore^{i+1}(e) = \mu Pri(e) + (1-\mu)\sum_t p(e|t)TScore^i(t) \quad (7)$$

$$TScore^{i+1}(t) = (1-\mu)\sum_e p(t|e)EScore^i(e) \quad (8)$$

where $p(e|t)$ is the probability that a template t extracts an entity e. If t extracts e, $p(e|t) = \frac{1}{\text{\#entities extracted by } t}$, otherwise $p(e|t) = 0$. Similarly, $p(t|e)$ is set to $\frac{1}{\text{\#templates that extract } e}$, if t extracts e, otherwise $p(t|e) = 0$. μ is a real value between 0 and 1 for a linear combination of the prior relevance of an entity and the sum of the relevance scores of the templates that can extract it. The algorithm will iterate for a predefined number of iterations.

We can find from the whole process that the hidden structures represented by templates play important roles for propagating information.

4.2 Experimental Settings

4.2.1 Baseline

We compare our domain specific entity expansion method with the method proposed in [26], which is the state-of-the-art weakly supervised method for domain specific entity extraction based on web search logs, noted as WSLOG. This algorithm makes use of seeds of a given domain to find patterns from queries of a search engine and further mines and ranks entities matching the patterns.

4.2.2 Data and Metrics

We conducted experiments on 10 domains that are the same as those examined in [26]. For each domain, 5 seeds are given. We re-implemented WSLOG and conducted experiments using the query log data introduced in Section 3.1.1. Our method runs on the entity-template pairs extracted by our open entity extraction module. The parameter μ is set to 0.5, and the algorithm iterates 10 times.

For each domain, we chose the top ranked 500 expanded entities from each method and pooled them together. We asked two annotators to judge the quality of these pooled entities of each domain. One entity that can be annotated as correct must satisfy: 1) It is a correct entity. 2) It belongs to the examined domain. The Kappa value of annotation is 0.82. We use $Precision(P)$, $Recall(R)$ and $F1$ as evaluation metrics. We define $P = \frac{\#\text{correct entities extracted by the system}}{\#\text{all extracted entities by the system}}$, $R = \frac{\#\text{correct entities extracted by the system}}{\#\text{all correct entities among pooled entities}}$ and $F1 = \frac{2 \times P \times R}{P+R}$.

4.3 Experimental Results

Table 4 shows the performance of our method and WSLOG. In most domains, our method outperforms WSLOG in both precision and recall.

The contextual templates extracted by WSLOG based on seeds sometimes cannot correctly determine the boundaries of entities in queries. For example, many templates for domain *University* can extract text fragments like "*2014北京大学(2014 Peking University)*" as candidate entities. In contrast, our method extracts entities collectively from parallel webpage titles. With the support of weak supervision, our method can better avoid incorrect entity boundaries.

In addition, WSLOG favors popular entities which appear enough times in query logs, but it can hardly mine long-tailed entities well. For the domain *Food*, WSLOG and our method both achieve good precision but low recall. It indicates that the correct entities extracted by two methods have a low overlap. WSLOG provides more short food names such as "*鱼(fish)*" and "*猪肉(pork)*", because these appear more often in queries. Even we use complex seeds like "*宫保鸡丁(Kung Pao Chicken)*", the simple food names still rank higher. In contrast, our method can provide more complex entities like "*西红柿炒鸡蛋(Scrambled Egg with Tomato)*".

Finally, the templates extracted by WSLOG are ambiguous in some cases. For example, the templates like "*<drug> 过敏(allergy)*" and "*<drug> 说明书(instruction)*" are important templates for domain *Drug*. However, these templates can extract entities of other domains such as *Cosmetics* as well. Actually, our method also faces the challenge on distinguishing entities from highly related domains. This is because the entities can be grouped together according to the purpose of the designers of the websites. For example, newspapers, TV programs and magazines are often organized together in some websites. That is why our performance on domain *Newspaper* is not so good. Extracting entities of fine-grained domains is necessary to be studied further.

Table 4: Comparison with WSLOG on set expansion of domain entities.

Domain	WSLOG			Ours		
Metrics	P	R	$F1$	P	R	$F1$
City	0.81	0.69	0.75	0.91	0.77	0.83
Country	0.1	0.31	0.15	0.30	0.94	0.46
Drug	0.49	0.52	0.5	0.75	0.81	0.78
Food	0.98	0.57	0.72	0.88	0.52	0.65
Location	0.84	0.66	0.74	0.99	0.78	0.87
Movie	0.64	0.54	0.59	0.92	0.77	0.84
Newspaper	0.11	0.46	0.18	0.17	0.72	0.27
Person	0.77	0.35	0.48	0.98	0.45	0.61
University	0.53	0.45	0.49	0.99	0.85	0.91
VideoGame	0.82	0.73	0.77	0.91	0.81	0.85
Average	0.61	0.53	0.54	0.78	0.74	0.71

5. RELATED WORK

In this section, we discuss the related work close to ours and highlight the main differences.

5.1 Entity Extraction

Traditional entity extraction is to identify and classify entities within domain-specific texts into predefined categories [5, 11, 12, 18, 22]. Our work is more related to entity discovery from massive web and user generated data. The differences among these studies lie in using different types of data resources and requiring different degrees of supervision.

5.1.1 Entity Extraction with Supervision

Extensive work extracts entities from different data resources with (weak) supervision.

Extraction from Documents. The mainstream work is to extract entities from web documents [8, 15]. For example, Etzioni et al. present a system that creates keyword queries for a given class and extracts entities from search result pages using predefined extracting rules. Although the system doesn't have to train a classifier using training data, it still needs domain knowledge as system input.

Extraction from Structured Data. Our work is also related to approaches that extract records from structured web data [1, 13, 17, 19, 24]. In [30], a semi-supervised method is proposed for combining information from both free texts and web tables. These methods identify tables for extraction based on explicit HTML tags or visually structured features. Instead, we exploit hidden collective textual structures. Besides, the outputs of record extraction usually are tuples containing various types of data, whereas our method focuses on extracting entities.

Extraction from Search Queries. Another body of research focuses on extracting entities from user search queries. For example, in [26], a weakly supervised method is proposed. A set of seeds are provided for an examined class. First, context patterns are learned from queries of a search engine based on the seeds. The class is represented with these patterns. Then these patterns are used to extract more entities from queries. Each entity is represented with a set of patterns which extract it. Finally, the entities are ranked according to the distance between the entity representation and the class representation.

5.1.2 Open Entity Extraction

Open Information Extraction (OIE) attempts to extract entities or relations without human intervention [2, 16].

Extraction from Documents. Banko et al. propose an open domain information extraction paradigm for entity extraction [2]. They first train a classier on a small amount of samples to classify a candidate as trustful or not, and then make a data driven pass over the corpus to extract candidate entities. Downey et al. also present a method to locate complex entities in texts [14]. They make use of capitalization information and measuring collocation to extract multi-word expressions as entities. However, the strategies for generating candidates are based on either sophisticated NLP techniques such as dependency parsing and noun phrase chunking, or language dependent heuristics.

Extraction from Query Logs. Parameswaran et al. propose a concept extraction algorithm based on statistical measures of support and confidence on k-grams [25]. But the complexity of this algorithm is high when k is large. So it could only extract concepts with limited length. Jain et al. present a method for open entity extraction from queries [21]. Like previous open entity extraction work on texts, this method also makes use of language dependent capitalization information to identify candidate entities. According to their experimental results, query log based methods outperform document based methods.

Our method follows the open entity extraction paradigm. It doesn't need any human labor or deep NLP techiniques. Unlike previous open entity extraction work, we focus on the most important field of a document, the title, instead of using document contents. Specifically, we identify and utilize the hidden structures in webpage titles and process them collectively. In this way, we significantly simplify the task of determining the boundaries of entities. In addition, we also discover the connections between entities based on the hidden structures, which provide new resources for potential applications.

5.2 Multiple Sequence Alignment (MSA)

Multiple sequence alignment technique is commonly used in computational biology for determining the commonalities within a collection of biological sequences, generally protein, DNA, or RNA [9, 23]. MSA is also applied to natural language processing for constructing concept mapping dictionary [3], identifying sentence level paraphrases [4] and modeling the organization of student essays [27]. Motivated by these work, we adapt MSA for one key component in our framework to infer the hidden structures within parallel webpage titles. In this way, textural templates can be learned automatically and unsupervisedly for extracting entities from large scale web data.

Some previous studies share similar ideas to ours. In [29], entities are mined from comparable news articles. We can view it as an alignment between different sources. But their approach is different from ours, and difficult to identify complex multi-word entities. In [1], record tuples are extracted from structured data by aligning HTML labels. Related work on template induction for IE (e.g., [31]) could be seen as a kind of alignment as well. In [10], clustering is adopted to learn templates automatically for event extraction.

Our method differs from previous work in the following aspects: 1) In previous work, the data to be aligned is provided in advance or retrieved based on seeds, and search engines are often used for searching for related data, while we identify data to be aligned automatically in web scale. 2) Instead of using explicit structured data, we deal with plain texts with collective hidden structures in webpage titles.

6. CONCLUSIONS

In this paper we put forward a novel method to extract entities by exploiting the hidden structures within webpage titles and applying the multiple sequence alignment technique for automatic template generation and entity extraction. Experimental results show that our method could extract large scale open domain entities with high precision. The extracted entities cover a wide range of topics, a large ratio of which is long-tailed and complex. Through the whole process, manual labor is unnecessary.

In addition, the generated title templates imply relatedness connections between entities. The extracted entity-template pairs can be used as a data resource, which can produce more precise domain specific entities by incorporating weak supervision.

Acknowledgments

This research is supported by the National Basic Research Program of China (973 Program, Grant No.2014CB340505), the National Natural Science Foundation of China (Grant No.61402304, Grant No.61303105) and the Beijing Municipal Natural Science Foundation (Grant No.4154065).

7. REFERENCES

[1] A. Arasu and H. Garcia-Molina. Extracting structured data from web pages. In *SIGMOD 2003*, pages 337–348. ACM, 2003.

[2] M. Banko, M. J. Cafarella, S. Soderland, M. Broadhead, and O. Etzioni. Open information extraction for the web. In *IJCAI*, volume 7, pages 2670–2676, 2007.

[3] R. Barzilay and L. Lee. Bootstrapping lexical choice via multiple-sequence alignment. In *EMNLP 2002*, pages 164–171. Association for Computational Linguistics, 2002.

[4] R. Barzilay and L. Lee. Learning to paraphrase: An unsupervised approach using multiple-sequence alignment. In *NAACL 2003 - Volume 1*, pages 16–23. Association for Computational Linguistics, 2003.

[5] D. M. Bikel, S. Miller, R. Schwartz, and R. Weischedel. Nymble: a high-performance learning name-finder. In *Proceedings of the fifth conference on Applied natural language processing*, pages 194–201. Association for Computational Linguistics, 1997.

[6] L. Blanco, N. Dalvi, and A. Machanavajjhala. Highly efficient algorithms for structural clustering of large websites. In *WWW 2011*, pages 437–446. ACM, 2011.

[7] J. Carletta. Assessing agreement on classification tasks: the kappa statistic. *Computational linguistics*, 22(2):249–254, 1996.

[8] A. Carlson, J. Betteridge, R. C. Wang, E. R. Hruschka Jr, and T. M. Mitchell. Coupled semi-supervised learning for information extraction. In *WSDM 2010*, pages 101–110. ACM, 2010.

[9] H. Carrillo and D. Lipman. The multiple sequence alignment problem in biology. *SIAM Journal on Applied Mathematics*, 48(5):1073–1082, 1988.

[10] N. Chambers and D. Jurafsky. Template-based information extraction without the templates. In *ACL 2011:Volume 1*, pages 976–986. Association for Computational Linguistics, 2011.

[11] H. L. Chieu and H. T. Ng. Named entity recognition: a maximum entropy approach using global information. In *COLING 2002:Volume 1*, pages 1–7. Association for Computational Linguistics, 2002.

[12] M. Collins and Y. Singer. Unsupervised models for named entity classification. In *Proceedings of the joint SIGDAT conference on empirical methods in natural language processing and very large corpora*, pages 100–110. Citeseer, 1999.

[13] B. B. Dalvi, W. W. Cohen, and J. Callan. Websets: Extracting sets of entities from the web using unsupervised information extraction. In *WSDM 2012*, pages 243–252. ACM, 2012.

[14] D. Downey, M. Broadhead, and O. Etzioni. Locating complex named entities in web text. In *IJCAI*, volume 7, pages 2733–2739, 2007.

[15] O. Etzioni, M. Cafarella, D. Downey, A.-M. Popescu, T. Shaked, S. Soderland, D. S. Weld, and A. Yates. Unsupervised named-entity extraction from the web: An experimental study. *Artificial Intelligence*, 165(1):91–134, 2005.

[16] O. Etzioni, A. Fader, J. Christensen, S. Soderland, and M. Mausam. Open information extraction: The second generation. In *IJCAI*, volume 11, pages 3–10, 2011.

[17] W. Gatterbauer, P. Bohunsky, M. Herzog, B. Krüpl, and B. Pollak. Towards domain-independent information extraction from web tables. In *WWW 2007*, pages 71–80. ACM, 2007.

[18] R. Grishman and B. Sundheim. Message understanding conference-6: A brief history. In *COLING*, volume 96, pages 466–471, 1996.

[19] R. Gupta and S. Sarawagi. Answering table augmentation queries from unstructured lists on the web. *Proceedings of the VLDB Endowment*, 2(1):289–300, 2009.

[20] T. Haveliwala, S. Kamvar, and G. Jeh. An analytical comparison of approaches to personalizing pagerank. 2003.

[21] A. Jain and M. Pennacchiotti. Open entity extraction from web search query logs. In *COLING 2010*, pages 510–518, Stroudsburg, PA, USA, 2010. Association for Computational Linguistics.

[22] A. McCallum and W. Li. Early results for named entity recognition with conditional random fields, feature induction and web-enhanced lexicons. In *NAACL 2003-Volume 4*, pages 188–191. Association for Computational Linguistics, 2003.

[23] S. B. Needleman and C. D. Wunsch. A general method applicable to the search for similarities in the amino acid sequence of two proteins. *Journal of molecular biology*, 48(3):443–453, 1970.

[24] Z. Nie, F. Wu, J.-R. Wen, and W.-Y. Ma. Extracting objects from the web. In *ICDE 2006.*, pages 123–123. IEEE, 2006.

[25] A. Parameswaran, H. Garcia-Molina, and A. Rajaraman. Towards the web of concepts: Extracting concepts from large datasets. *Proceedings of the VLDB Endowment*, 3(1-2):566–577, 2010.

[26] M. Paşca. Weakly-supervised discovery of named entities using web search queries. In *CIKM 2007*, pages 683–690. ACM, 2007.

[27] I. Persing, A. Davis, and V. Ng. Modeling organization in student essays. In *EMNLP 2010*, pages 229–239. Association for Computational Linguistics, 2010.

[28] S. Sekine, K. Sudo, and C. Nobata. Extended named entity hierarchy. In *LREC*, 2002.

[29] Y. Shinyama and S. Sekine. Named entity discovery using comparable news articles. In *COLING 2004*, page 848. Association for Computational Linguistics, 2004.

[30] P. P. Talukdar, J. Reisinger, M. Paşca, D. Ravichandran, R. Bhagat, and F. Pereira. Weakly-supervised acquisition of labeled class instances using graph random walks. In *EMNLP 2008*, pages 582–590. Association for Computational Linguistics, 2008.

[31] R. C. Wang and W. W. Cohen. Character-level analysis of semi-structured documents for set expansion. In *EMNLP 2009: Volume 3*, pages 1503–1512. Association for Computational Linguistics, 2009.

[32] C. Zhang, S. Zhao, and H. Wang. Bootstrapping large-scale named entities using url-text hybrid patterns. In *IJCNLP 2013*, pages 293–301, 2013.

ROCKER – A Refinement Operator for Key Discovery

Tommaso Soru
Institute of Computer Science,
University of Leipzig
tsoru@informatik.uni-leipzig.de

Edgard Marx
Institute of Computer Science,
University of Leipzig
marx@informatik.uni-leipzig.de

Axel-Cyrille Ngonga Ngomo
Institute of Computer Science,
University of Leipzig
ngonga@informatik.uni-leipzig.de

ABSTRACT

The Linked Data principles provide a decentral approach for publishing structured data in the RDF format on the Web. In contrast to structured data published in relational databases where a key is often provided explicitly, finding a set of properties that allows identifying a resource uniquely is a non-trivial task. Still, finding keys is of central importance for manifold applications such as resource deduplication, link discovery, logical data compression and data integration. In this paper, we address this research gap by specifying a refinement operator, dubbed ROCKER, which we prove to be finite, proper and non-redundant. We combine the theoretical characteristics of this operator with two monotonicities of keys to obtain a time-efficient approach for detecting keys, i.e., sets of properties that describe resources uniquely. We then utilize a hash index to compute the discriminability score efficiently. Therewith, we ensure that our approach can scale to very large knowledge bases. Results show that ROCKER yields more accurate results, has a comparable runtime, and consumes less memory w.r.t. existing state-of-the-art techniques.

Categories and Subject Descriptors

H.4.m [**Information Systems Applications**]: Miscellaneous; I.2.8 [**Computing Methodologies**]: Problem Solving, Control Methods, and Search

Keywords

Semantic Web; Linked Data; link discovery; key discovery; refinement operators

1. INTRODUCTION

The number of facts published in the Linked Data Web has grown considerably over the last years [3]. In particular, large knowledge bases such as LinkedTCGA [20] and LinkedGeoData [24] encompass more than 20 billion triples each. The architectural principles behind the Linked Data Web are akin to those on the Web. In particular, the decentral data publication process leads to facts on the same real-world entities being published across manifold knowledge bases. For example, information on *Austin, Texas* is distributed across several knowledge bases, including DBpedia[1], LinkedGeoData and GeoNames[2]. Given the size of the current Linked Data datasets, providing unique means to characterize resources within existing datasets would facilitate the use of these knowledge bases, for example within the context of entity search, data integration, linked data compression and link discovery [18]. Especially for the link discovery task, being provided with unique descriptions of resources in a knowledge base would allow for the more time-efficient computation of property matchings for link specifications, a task that has been pointed out to be particularly tedious in previous work [4].

In relational databases, keys are commonly either artificial or sets of columns that allow to describe each resource uniquely. Previous works [18, 2, 6] adopt this approach for uniquely describing RDF data and use properties instead of columns. Several problems occur when trying to detect keys for RDF data.

1. Resources from the same datasets might not all have the same properties. For example, in the fragment of DBpedia 3.9 shown in Figure 1, only 50% of the resources have a `:meshNumber`. Thus, while the `:meshNumber` is unique, it cannot be used as a key for this dataset.

2. The inverse problem exists for the `:graySubject`, which covers all resources but is not unique as the trigeminal nerve and the lacrimal nerve have the same `:graySubject`. For our toy dataset, only keys of size larger that 1 exist (e.g., {`:graySubject`, `:grayPage`}).

3. The key discovery problem is exponential in the number of properties n in the knowledge base, as the solution space contains $2^n - 1$ possible sets of keys. Thus, naïve solutions to the key discovery problem do not scale.

Moreover, depending on the use case, key discovery approaches have to be able to detect a single key (e.g., to link resources within a knowledge base) or to detect all keys for a resource (e.g., when integrating data across knowledge bases).

WWW 2015, May 18–22, 2015, Florence, Italy.
ACM 978-1-4503-3469-3/15/05.
http://dx.doi.org/10.1145/2736277.2741642.

[1]`http://dbpedia.org`
[2]`http://www.geonames.org/`

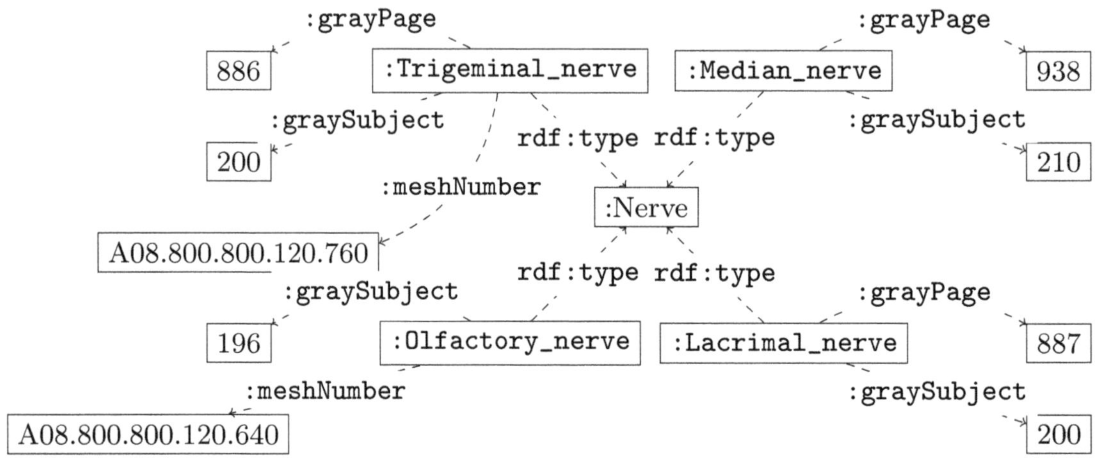

Figure 1: Fragment from a knowledge base on human nerves. The fragment was extracted from DBpedia 3.9.

In this paper, we address the three problems of key discovery within both settings of key discovery (i.e., finding all keys or almost-keys within a given threshold) by using a refinement operator dubbed ρ. This operator is able to detect sets of properties that describe any instance of a given class in a unique manner. By these means, it can generate n-tuples of property values that can be used as keys for resources which instantiate a given class. Our operator relies on a scoring function to compare sets of properties. Based on this comparison, it can efficiently detect single keys, all keys and even predict whether a key can be found in a given dataset. In addition to being finite, non-redundant and proper, our operator also scales well and can thus be used on large knowledge bases. Our contributions are:

- We provide the first refinement operator for key discovery on RDF knowledge bases.
- We prove that our operator is finite, non-redundant, proper, but not complete.
- We utilize the combination of a hash index to compute the discriminability score, i.e. the ability for a set of properties to distinguish their subjects, with two monotonicities of keys to prune the refinement tree and thus ensure that our operator scales.
- We show that our approach succeeds on datasets where current state-of-the-art approaches fail.
- We evaluate our operator on the OAEI instance matching benchmark datasets as well as on DBpedia classes with large populations. In particular, we measure the overall runtime, the memory consumption and the reduction ratio of our approach. Our results suggest that we outperform the state of the art w.r.t. correctness and memory consumption. Moreover, our results suggest that our approach terminates within an acceptable time frame even on very large datasets.

The rest of this paper is structured as follows: We begin by defining the problem at hand formally. Thereafter, we present our operator and prove its theoretical characteristics. After a discussion of related work, we evaluate our operator on synthetic and real data. We then conclude and present some future work.

2. PRELIMINARIES

In the following, we formalize the definition of keys that underlie this paper. This definition is used by our refinement operator to efficiently detect keys.

2.1 Keys

Let K be a finite RDF knowledge base containing instances which belong to a given class and their Concise Bounded Description (CBD).[3] K can be regarded as a set of triples $(s,p,o) \in (\mathcal{R} \cup \mathcal{B}) \times \mathcal{P} \times (\mathcal{R} \cup \mathcal{L} \cup \mathcal{B})$, where $\mathcal{R}$ is the set of all resources, $\mathcal{B}$ is the set of all blank nodes, $\mathcal{P}$ the set of all predicates and $\mathcal{L}$ the set of all literals. We call two resources $r_1, r_2 \in \mathcal{R}$ distinguishable w.r.t. a set of properties $P = \{p_1, \dots p_n\}$ iff $\exists p \in \{p_1, \dots p_n\} : \neg((r_1, p, o) \wedge (r_2, p, o))$. Given a knowledge base K, the idea behind *key discovery* is to find one or all sets of properties which make their respective subjects distinguishable in K.

Definition 1 (Key). *We call a set of properties $P \subseteq \mathcal{P}$ a* key *for a knowledge base K (short: key, denoted $key(P,K)$) if all resources in K are distinguishable w.r.t. P.*

Definition 2 (Minimal key). *We call P a* minimal key *(short: mkey) iff P is a key but none of its subsets is. Formally,*

$$mkey(P,K) \Rightarrow key(P,K) \wedge (\neg \exists P' \subset P : key(P',K)). \quad (1)$$

2.2 Discriminability

A *key* for an RDF knowledge base and a *primary composite key* for a database share the same aim. RDF properties represent the projection of database fields into the RDF paradigm, as well as each resource represents a tuple. However, while a tuple element has only one single value, a property might link a resource to more than one RDF objects. Therefore, two resources are distinguishable from each other w.r.t. a set of properties P if their sets of objects are different for at least one $p \in P$.

[3]For the definition of CBD, see `http://www.w3.org/Submission/CBD/`.

To the best of our knowledge, this particular feature of keys was not taken into account by previous works on key discovery for RDF data [18, 6, 2]. For instance, [18, 6] consider two resources r and r' as not distinguishable w.r.t. P if for each $p \in P$ they share at least one object.

Figure 2 shows an example of RDF data, as reported in [6]. Here, the authors claim that $P = \{p_1\} = \{$`:hasActor`$\}$ is not a key because `"G.Clooney"` is the object of more than one instance of `:Film`. We would instead consider P as a key, since every film is linked with a different set of objects ($sobj$), i.e.:

$sobj($`:f1`$, p_1) = \{$`"B.Pitt", "J.Roberts"`$\}$
$sobj($`:f2`$, p_1) = \{$`"G.Clooney", "B.Pitt", "J.Roberts"`$\}$
$sobj($`:f3`$, p_1) = \{$`"B.Pitt", "G.Clooney"`$\}$
$sobj($`:f4`$, p_1) = \{$`"G.Clooney", "N.Krause"`$\}$
$sobj($`:f5`$, p_1) = \{$`"F.Potente"`$\}$
$sobj($`:f6`$, p_1) = \varnothing$

Note that `:f6` is still distinguishable from the other resources w.r.t. P, since no other instance of `:Film` in the knowledge base has 0 actors. This particular case was not considered, for example, by the authors of [2].

2.3 Properties of a key

Keys abide by several monotonicities [18]. The first is the so-called *key monotonicity*, which is given by

$$key(P, K) \Rightarrow \forall P' : P \subseteq P' \Rightarrow key(P', K). \quad (2)$$

The reciprocal monotonicity is called the *non-key monotonicity*, which is given by

$$\neg key(P, K) \Rightarrow (\forall P' \subseteq P : \neg key(P', K)). \quad (3)$$

In other words, adding a property to a key yields another key, whilst removing a property to a non-key yields another non-key. In this paper, we present a key discovery approach based on refinement operators.

3. A REFINEMENT OPERATOR FOR KEY DISCOVERY

In this section, we present our refinement operator for key discovery and prove some of its theoretical characteristics. Our formalization is based on that presented in [8].

Let $P \subseteq \mathcal{P}$. Moreover, let $score : 2^{\mathcal{P}} \rightarrow [0, 1]$ be a function that maps each subset P of $\mathcal{P}$ to the fraction of subject resources from K that are distinguishable by using P.

Theorem 1 (Induced quasi-ordering). *The score function induces a quasi-ordering $\preceq$ over the set $\mathcal{P}$, which we define as follows:*

$$P_1 \preceq P_2 \Leftrightarrow \min_{p \in P_1} score(p) \leq \min_{q \in P_2} score(q). \quad (4)$$

The reflexivity and transitivity of $\preceq$ are direct consequences of the reflexivity and transitivity of $\leq$ in $\mathbb{R}$. Note that $\preceq$ is not antisymmetric as two sets of properties P_1 and P_2 can be different and contain the property with the lowest score, leading to $P_1 \preceq P_2$ and $P_2 \preceq P_1$.

Definition 3 (Refinement Operator). *Given a quasi-ordered space (S, op) an upward refinement operator r is a mapping from S to 2^S such that $\forall s \in S : s' \in r(s) \Rightarrow op(s, s')$. s' is then called a generalization of s.*

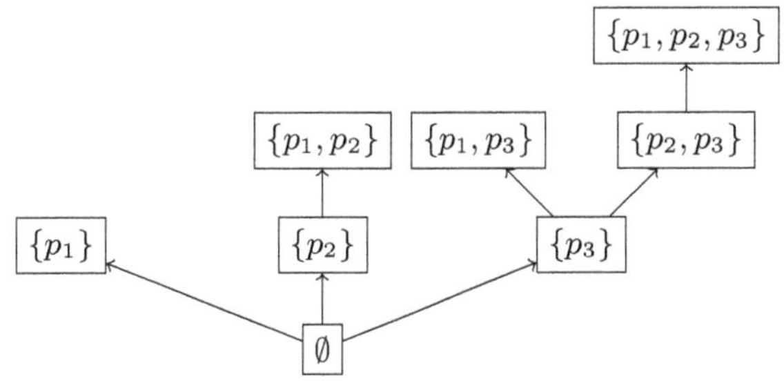

Figure 3: Complete refinement graph for $\mathcal{P} = \{p_1, p_2, p_3\}$. The nodes of the graph are subsets of $\mathcal{P}$. A directed edge (a, b) means $b \in \rho(a)$.

We define our refinement operator over the space $(\mathcal{P}, \preceq)$. First, we begin by ordering the elements of $\mathcal{P}$ according to their score in ascending order, i.e., $\forall p_i, p_j \in \mathcal{P}, i \leq j \Rightarrow score(p_i) \leq score(p_j)$. Then, we can define our operator as follows:

$$\rho(P) = \begin{cases} \mathcal{P} \text{ iff } P = \emptyset, \\ \{P \cup \{p_1\}, \ldots, P \cup \{p_i\}\} \text{ where } p_j \in P \Rightarrow i < j. \end{cases} \quad (5)$$

For example, the complete refinement graph for $\mathcal{P} = \{p_1, p_2, p_3\}$ is given in Figure 3. We use this operator in an iterative manner by only expanding the node with the highest score in the refinement graph. The intuition behind this approach to searching for key is that by ordering properties by their score, we can easily detect and expand the most promising sets of properties without generating redundant nodes. To prove some of the characteristics of ρ, we need to explicate the concept of a refinement chain:

Definition 4 (Refinement chain). *A set $P_2 \in \mathcal{P}$ belong to the refinement chain of $P_1 \in \mathcal{P}$ iff $\exists k \in \mathbb{N} : P_2 \in \rho^k(P_1)$, where $\rho^k(P) = \begin{cases} \mathcal{P} \text{ iff } k = 0, \\ \rho(\rho^{k-1}(P)) \text{ else}. \end{cases}$*

For example, a refinement chain exists between $\{p_3\}$ and $\{p_1, p_2, p_3\}$ in the example shown in Figure 3. There is yet no refinement chain between $\{p_1\}$ and $\{p_2\}$ in the same example.

A refinement operator r over the quasi-ordered space (S, op) can abide by the following criteria.

Definition 5 (Finiteness). *r is finite iff $r(s)$ is finite for all $s \in S$.*

Definition 6 (Properness). *r is proper if $\forall s \in S, s' \in r(s) \Rightarrow s \neq s'$.*

Definition 7 (Completeness). *r is said to be complete if for all s and s', $op(s', s)$ implies that there is a refinement chain between s and s'.*

Definition 8 (Redundancy). *A refinement operator r over the space (S, op) is redundant if two different refinement chains can exist between $s \in S$ and $s' \in S$.*

In the following, we show that ρ is finite, proper and non-redundant but not complete.

Theorem 2. *ρ is finite when applied to a finite knowledge base K.*

Dataset D1:
d1:Film(f1), d1:*hasActor*(f1," B.Pitt"), d1:*hasActor*(f1," J.Roberts"),
d1:*director*(f1," S.Soderbergh"), d1:*releaseDate*(f1," 3/4/01"), d1:*name*(f1," Ocean's 11"),
d1:Film(f2), d1:*hasActor*(f2," G.Clooney"), d1:*hasActor*(f2," B.Pitt"),
d1:*hasActor*(f2," J.Roberts"), d1:*director*(f2," S.Soderbergh"), d1:*director*(f2," P.Greengrass"),
d1:*director*(f2," R.Howard"), d1:*releaseDate*(f2," 2/5/04"), d1:*name*(f2," Ocean's 12")
d1:Film(f3), d1:*hasActor*(f3," G.Clooney"), d1:*hasActor*(f3," B.Pitt")
d1:*director*(f3," S.Soderbergh"), d1:*director*(f3," P.Greengrass"), d1:*director*(f3," R.Howard"),
d1:*releaseDate*(f3," 30/6/07"), d1:*name*(f3," Ocean's 13"),
d1:Film(f4), d1:*hasActor*(f4," G.Clooney"), d1:*hasActor*(f4," N.Krause"),
d1:*director*(f4," A.Payne"), d1:*releaseDate*(f4," 15/9/11"), d1:*name*(f4," The descendants"),
d1:*language*(f4," english")
d1:Film(f5),d1:*hasActor*(f5," F.Potente"), d1:*director*(f5," P.Greengrass"),
d1:*releaseDate*(f5," 2002"), d1:*name*(f5," The bourne Identity"), d1:*language*(f5," english")
d1:Film(f6),d1:*director*(f6," R.Howard"), d1:*releaseDate*(f6," 2/5/04"),
d1:*name*(f6," Ocean's twelve")

Figure 2: Example of RDF data, as reported in Symeonidou et al., 2014.

Proof. The finiteness of ρ is a direct result of K being finite. The upper bound of the number of properties in K is the number of triples in K. Thus, $|K| < \infty \Rightarrow |\mathcal{P}| < \infty$. Per definition, $|\rho(P)| \leq |\mathcal{P}|$. Thus, we can conclude that $\forall P \in \mathcal{P} : |\rho(P)| < \infty$. □

Theorem 3. *ρ is proper.*

Proof. The properness of ρ also results from the definition of ρ. As we always add exactly a property to P when computing $\rho(P)$, we know that $|\rho(P)| = |P| + 1$. Thus, $\rho(P) \neq P$ must hold. □

Theorem 4. *ρ is not complete.*

Proof. The incompleteness of ρ follows from the definition of $\rho(\emptyset)$. Let $\mathcal{P} = \{p_1, \ldots, p_n\}$. Then $\{p_1\} \preceq \{p_n\}$. Yet, there is clearly no refinement chain between $\{p_n\}$ and $\{p_1\}$ as any subset of $\mathcal{P}$ connected to p_n via a refinement chain must have a magnitude larger than one. Yet, the magnitude of $\{p_1\}$ is 1, which shows that $\{p_1\}$ cannot be connected to $\{p_n\}$ via a refinement chain. □

Theorem 5. *ρ is not redundant.*

Proof. ρ being redundant would mean that a pair of property sets (P, P') exist, where P is linked to P' by two distinct refinement chains C_1 and C_2. Given that these two chains begin and end at the same node, there must be a node N that is common to the two chains but has two distinct fathers N_1 and N_2 that are such that N_1 belongs to C_1 and not to C_2 while N_2 belong to C_2 but not to C_1. Now, N_1 being the father of N means $\exists p_i \in \mathcal{P} : N = N_1 \cup p_i$. Conversely, N_2 being the father of N also means that $\exists p_j \in \mathcal{P} : N = N_2 \cup p_j$. Now if $N_1 \neq N_2$, then we can assume wlog that $i < j$. For $N \in \rho(N_2)$ to hold, j resp. i must be less than the index of any element of N_2 resp. N_1. Moreover, for $N_1 \cup p_i = N_2 \cup p_j$ to hold, p_i would have to already be a element of N_2. However, by virtue of the construction of ρ, this means that $(N_2 \cup \{p_j\}) \notin \rho(N_2)$ given that $p_i \in N_2$ and $i < j$. Thus, we can conclude that there cannot be any to distinct refinement pairs between two subsets of $\mathcal{P}$. □

4. APPROACH

In this section, we present **ROCKER**, a refinement operator approach for key discovery. Our approach was designed with scalability in mind. To this end, it implements a scalable version of the discriminability *score* function based on a hash index. Moreover, we use the monotonicities of keys to check for the existence of keys as well as decide on nodes that need not be refined.

4.1 Implementation

In order to increase the scalability of our operator, we chose an hybrid approach using both in-memory and disk storage database. The following tasks are then performed by ROCKER:

1. the knowledge base model is built using the Apache Jena library;
2. for each class, its instances and properties are extracted;
3. this information is stored and indexed over a *B-tree* structure, whereas the instance URI is used as a key;
4. object values are sorted alphabetically, imploded into a string, indexed using hash codes, and stored into each tuple element;
5. the refinement operator starts from the empty-set node;
6. at each node, the discriminability score is computed by performing a query to the database;
7. the computation terminates according to some rule.

4.2 Definition of the score function

We firstly define the set of subjects of the knowledge base, i.e. the instances of a given class.

$$S = \{s : \exists(s, p, o) \in K\} \tag{6}$$

We then provide the definition of discriminability for two resources w.r.t. a set of properties P.

$$discr(s, s', P) \Leftrightarrow \tag{7}$$

$$\forall s \in S \; \forall p \in P \; \nexists s' \in S : sobj(s, p) \equiv sobj(s', p) \tag{8}$$

where *sobj* is the "set of objects" function introduced in Section 2.2. Finally, we define the score of P (denoted $score(P)$) as the number of subject resources of K that are distinguishable w.r.t. P by using the following formula:

$$score(P) = \frac{|\{s \in S : \forall s' \in S \; s \neq s' \Rightarrow discr(s, s', P)\}|}{|S|}. \tag{9}$$

The set P is a key if $score(P) = 1$, i.e., if P covers all subject resources from K and all resources are distinguishable w.r.t. P.

Basing the refinement on this scoring function has the advantage of allowing ROCKER to cover not only keys but also k-almost-keys [6], which are defined as follows: P is a k-almost-key if $\exists X \subseteq S : |X| \leq k \wedge \forall s, s' \in S \backslash X : discr(s, s', P)$. Consider for example the data shown in Figure 2. If `:f2` did not have `"J. Roberts"` in the list of its actors, then it would not be distinguishable from `:f3`. In this case, the set {`hasActor`} would be 2-almost-key. We can derive a minimal score α for a k-almost-key by simply using the maximal magnitude of X within $score(P)$:

$$|X| \leq k \rightarrow score(P) \geq \frac{|S| - k}{|S|} = \alpha. \quad (10)$$

Note that a key is a 0-almost-key. Moreover, every k-almost-key with $k \geq 0$ is also a $(k+1)$-almost-key.

In our implementation, the score function for P is thus calculated by querying the class table for the columns associated with the properties in P. For each row, the returned values are then concatenated and added to a sorted set, where duplicates are discarded automatically by virtue of the definition of set. The size of this final set represents the numerator for Equation 10.

4.3 Refinement Operator

The pseudo code of ROCKER's refinement operator is shown in Algorithm 1. Given a set of triples K and a set of properties $\mathcal{P}$, we begin by checking whether our ρ-based approach is able to find a key at all. This can be done by computing $score(\mathcal{P})$. If the score is less than 1 (i.e., if $\mathcal{P}$ is not a key), then we know no key exists by virtue of the non-key monotonicity. We can thus terminate and return $\varnothing$, unless a threshold $\alpha < 1$ is given. Under this setting, we terminate if $score(\mathcal{P}) < \alpha$. Now if $\mathcal{P}$ is a key, then some of its subsets might be minimal keys. We then begin by sorting the elements of $\mathcal{P}$ w.r.t. their score. This heuristic tries to make the refinement operator discover keys earlier, so that their descendants can be pruned from the refinement tree, thus decreasing the number of score calculations. A maximal-priority queue is then initialized, where the priority of an element is its score. The queue is initialized with the empty set with a priority of 0. We then take the element P of the queue with the highest priority iteratively and remove it from the queue. Thank to the non-redundancy of ρ, there is no need to check whether P has been seen before. P is refined to P', whose elements p are then checked iteratively. We thus evaluate the scores of all elements of P'. If their score is less than 1, then they are added to the queue. If their score is 1, then we add them to the solution and do not add them to the queue, as they do not need to be refined any further by virtue of the key monotonicity. We then return the set of all keys.

Our approach has several advantages due to the theoretical characteristics of ρ and the key monotonicities:

1. It terminates quickly if there is no key by virtue of using the non-key monotonicity.

2. It is guaranteed to find all existing minkeys by virtue of the key monotonicity.

3. Using a sorted queue, it encourages node pruning by evaluating the most promising nodes first.

4. It never visits the same node twice due to the non-redundancy of ρ.

5. It is ensured to find all existing keys.

Algorithm 1 ROCKER's algorithm for detecting all keys. The algorithm for detecting a single key does not require the solution variable. Instead, it returns the first P having $score(P) = 1$ it finds.

```
Require: Set of triples K
P = {p : ∃s, p with (s, p, o) ∈ K}
if score(P) < 1 then
  return ∅;
end if
P = sortByScore(P);
MaxPriorityQueue q = new Queue();
Set solution = new Set();
q.add(∅, 0); // add ∅ with priority 0
while ¬q.isEmpty() do
  P' = q.getFirst();
  q.removeFirst();
  P = ρ(P');
  for all p ∈ P do
    σ = score(p);
    if σ == 1 then
      solution.add(p);
    else
      q.add(p, σ);
    end if
  end for
end while
return solution;
```

4.4 Search Strategy

As already mentioned in [18], the number of nodes to visit in the key discovery problem is exponential w.r.t. the number of properties considered. More precisely, given n properties, the computational complexity of our algorithm is $O(2^n)$ in the worst case, i.e. when there exists one only key formed by all properties. We tackle this issue by introducing a *fast search* strategy, which can be enabled to speed up the computation. Within this optional setting, whenever a key is found, at the next iteration all branches containing parts of the key are pruned from the refinement tree. This strategy tries to improve the runtime while fostering diversity among the discovered keys. Moreover, we consider properties whose atomic candidate keys have a score greater than a threshold τ. This lets the algorithm discard properties that alone distinguish less instances, thus having a lower probability to be part of a key.

5. RELATED WORK

Key discovery is a rather new research field within the domain of Linked Data, although the issue of finding keys among fields has been inherited from relational databases. However, relational databases do not consider semantics (e.g., subsumption relations) which belong to the core of Linked Data. Previous work on key discovery for the Semantic Web can be found in [18, 2, 6]. For instance, KD2R is an automatic discovery tool for composite keys in RDF data sources that may conform to different schemata [18]. It relies on the creation of prefix trees, which serve for finding maximal undetermined keys and non-keys. However, state-of-the-art approaches as Linkkey and SAKey have shown to outperform KD2R on runtime and number of generated keys [2, 6]. To the best of our knowledge, not only is ROCKER the first refinement-operator-based approach for key discovery, it is also the first machine-learning-based approach for key discovery.

Independently on the application domain, the key discovery problem is a sub-problem of Functional Dependencies (FDs), as every element is distinguishable only by its attributes. Keys or FDs are widely used in ontology alignment, as well as in data mining [10], reverse engineering [5], and query optimization [9, 7]. In particular, blocking methods such as [12] utilize approximate keys to reduce the computational complexity of dataset joins. Unsupervised learning approaches aim at finding links among datasets by comparing datatype values of properties contained into minimal keys [22]. The so-called collective or global approaches of data linking use keys to generate identity links between instance joins for the final scope of enriching the ontology with the collected information [19, 1].

As previously mentioned, one of the main application areas of ROCKER is link discovery. Several approaches have been developed in previous works to detect matching properties and using them for link discovery. For example, [16] relies on the hospital-residents problem to detect property matches. Other approaches based on genetic programming (e.g., [17]) detect matching properties while learning link specifications, which currently implements several time-efficient approaches for link discovery. [15] proposes an approach based on the Cauchy-Schwarz inequality that allows discarding a large number of superfluous comparisons. HYPPO [13] and $\mathcal{HR}^3$ [14] rely on space tiling in spaces with measures that can be split into independent measures across the dimensions of the problem at hand. In particular, $\mathcal{HR}^3$ was shown to be the first approach that can achieve a relative reduction ratio r' less or equal to any given relative reduction ratio $r > 1$. In the ACIDS approach, similarity measures are performed on property values in order to yield features for machine-learning classifiers as support vectors machines [23]. Amongst other link discovery approaches, RDF-AI [21] relies on a five-step method that comprises the preprocessing, matching, fusion, interlink and post-processing of data sets.

6. EVALUATION

6.1 Experimental Setup

We evaluated ROCKER w.r.t. four characteristics: its runtime, RAM consumption, key extraction quality, and reduction ratio RR [18] between visited and total nodes.

$$RR(\alpha) = 1 - \frac{|vnodes(\alpha)|}{2^{|\mathcal{P}|}}. \quad (11)$$

Our approach was evaluated on data from twelve different datasets. The first two datasets were chosen in order to evaluate ROCKER on an existing artificial benchmark. Both `Restaurant 1` and 2 belong to the Ontology Alignment Evaluation Initiative (OAEI) benchmark. We then evaluated the scalability of ROCKER on ten other datasets generated from DBpedia. We built the datasets using the RDFSlice tool [11], so that each of them contains a class with its instances and their CBD. According to DBtrends[4], these classes rank among the top 20 of the most populated classes in DBpedia 3.9. The domains vary from geography (`Village`, `ArchitecturalStructure`) to professionals (`Artist`, `SoccerPlayer`) and abstract concepts (`PersonFunction`, `CareerStation`).

The generation of new evaluation datasets was preferred over the use of existing datasets due to the following reasons:

1. Datasets from the current state-of-the-art approaches contain a maximum of $1.6M$ triples, while ours scale up to $17.1M$ triples.

2. Some of the existing datasets were not formatted properly.

3. To the best of our knowledge, no key discovery benchmark has been created to date.

The lack of a manually-annotated gold standard for key discovery did not only affect the choice of the datasets. This led us to adopt the number of retrieved keys and the precision to measure the key extraction quality. In fact, while calculating the precision of a key discovery algorithm by annotating the retrieved keys is a feasible task, the set of all minimal keys needs to be known in order to compute the recall.

We compared ROCKER against two state-of-the-art approaches dubbed Linkkey [2] and SAKey [6]. While Linkkey is a tool able to retrieve keys, SAKey is more scalable and able to retrieve also k-almost keys (see Section 4.2).

ROCKER was implemented in Java as part of the link discovery framework LIMES.[5] The datasets and the algorithm source code are also available online.[6] We launched ROCKER with two different settings; the former aims at finding minimal keys ($\alpha = 1$), while the latter aims at finding minimal almost-keys ($\alpha < 1$). Both settings were set to use the *fast search* option with $\tau = 0.001$. For the sake of simplicity, we assigned the same value to α (0.999) for all datasets when retrieving almost-keys. All experiments were carried out on a 64-bit Ubuntu Linux machine with 16 GB of RAM and an octa-core 2.5 GHz CPU.

6.2 Results

Table 1 presents the results we obtained on the twelve datasets. Runtimes in milliseconds are reported for both tasks, i.e. "find minimal keys" and "find minimal almost-keys". For each dataset, the size in number of triples is also shown. As seen in table, all the computation runtimes for the artificial datasets lie within the same magnitude order of 1,000 milliseconds. Both ROCKER runs were slower than the other approaches, however this trend has been disproved by the following results. On the medium-sized datasets `PersonFunction`, `CareerStation` and `OrganisationMember`, our approach is the only one which completed all three tasks. In particular, Linkkey reached the Java heap space on the first two, while SAKey did not complete on the third one. On the seven remaining datasets whose size in NTriples format is larger than 1.5 GB, only our approach was able to finish the computation. This fact leads to consider ROCKER as the most scalable approach for key discovery at the state of the art.

[4]`http://dbtrends.aksw.org/`
[5]`http://limes.sf.net`
[6]`http://github.com/AKSW/rocker/`

As can be read in [2], Linkkey was evaluated on datasets smaller than all the DBpedia datasets we generated. We thus integrated the evaluation carried out by Linkkey's authors by running the tool on our new datasets. At the same time, the largest dataset SAKey was evaluated on is comparable with our medium-sized datasets [6]. Results shown in Table 1 are thus compatible with the evaluations performed by the respective state-of-the-art algorithms.

The node reduction ratio (RR) is shown in Table 2. RR expresses the rate of the number of nodes that were discarded by pruning subtrees, thus avoiding to compute their scores. The number of properties (i.e., the size of $\mathcal{P}$) and the number of visited nodes are also reported.

Table 3 reports the key extraction quality results. For each dataset we show the number of outcomes and the percentage of keys and minimal keys among them (i.e., precision). Many datasets have been omitted as no keys were found by any approach, or simply because the approach failed during the discovery (cf. Table 1). The most interesting results appear on the two OAEI datasets, where Linkkey was not able to recognise any key. On the other hand, SAKey was able to recognise all 3 minimal keys on `Restaurant 2`, yet it returned also 4 non-keys. SAKey was also able to find 2 out of 3 minimal keys, 3 non-minimal keys and 3 non-keys on `Restaurant 1`. Among the other datasets, 3 keys were found on `Village` by ROCKER only.

Table 3: Key extraction quality results.

Dataset	ROCKER	Linkkey	SAKey
Restaurant 1	3 (100%, 100%)	0 (0%, 0%)	8 (62%, 25%)
Restaurant 2	3 (100%, 100%)	0 (0%, 0%)	7 (42%, 42%)
Village	3 (100%, 100%)	-	-

Namespace prefixes and the sets of almost-keys found for `DBpedia ArchitecturalStructure` resp. `DBpedia Village`, using a threshold for the discriminability score $\alpha = 0.999$ are shown below. Reported are 10 almost-keys that were found on `DBpedia ArchitecturalStructure` and the first 20 almost-keys that were found on `DBpedia Village`. As can be seen, the algorithm found six atomic almost-keys. After these had been removed from the maximal-priority queue, the refinement operator followed a path of 109 refinements through the same branch of the refinement tree. Its climb ended on a node having a discriminability score greater than α, as well as a size of 110 properties. After removing this node and its descendants from the queue, the refinement resumed from the bottom of the graph, where ROCKER found 13 more almost-keys composed by 2 properties each. As our algorithm found 84 almost-keys for `DBpedia Village`, the big size of most of the almost-keys may be the reason for the longest computation.

Prefix	Namespace
dbo:	http://dbpedia.org/ontology/
dbp:	http://dbpedia.org/property/
dcterms:	http://purl.org/dc/terms/
rdfs:	http://www.w3.org/2000/01/rdf-schema#
geo:	http://www.w3.org/2003/01/geo/wgs84_pos#
foaf:	http://xmlns.com/foaf/0.1/
prov:	http://www.w3.org/ns/prov#

Size	Properties	Score
4	[foaf:name, geo:long, dbo:location, dbp:hasPhotoCollection]	0.99905
4	[foaf:name, geo:long, dbp:hasPhotoCollection, foaf:homepage]	0.99905
4	[foaf:name, geo:long, dbo:elevation, dbp:hasPhotoCollection]	0.99905
4	[foaf:name, geo:long, dbp:hasPhotoCollection, dbo:runwayLength]	0.99905
4	[foaf:name, geo:long, dbo:openingYear, dbp:hasPhotoCollection]	0.99905
4	[dbo:height, foaf:name, geo:long, dbp:hasPhotoCollection]	0.99905
4	[dbo:river, foaf:name, geo:long, dbp:hasPhotoCollection]	0.99905
4	[dbo:buildingStartYear, foaf:name, geo:long, dbp:hasPhotoCollection]	0.99905
4	[foaf:name, geo:long, dbp:hasPhotoCollection, dbo:part]	0.99905
4	[foaf:name, geo:long, dbp:hasPhotoCollection, dbo:primaryFuelType]	0.99905
1	[dbo:wikiPageID]	0.99995
1	[rdfs:label]	0.99995
1	[prov:wasDerivedFrom]	0.99995
1	[dbp:hasPhotoCollection]	0.99995
1	[foaf:isPrimaryTopicOf]	0.99995
1	[dbo:wikiPageRevisionID]	0.99995
110	[geo:lat, dbp:postalCode, dbp:imageFlag, dbp:northeast, ..., dbp:arname]	0.99997
2	[foaf:name, rdfs:comment]	0.99958
2	[geo:long, rdfs:comment]	0.99973
2	[geo:lat, rdfs:comment]	0.99968
2	[rdfs:comment, dbp:name]	0.99955
2	[dbo:wikiPageWikiLink, rdfs:comment]	0.99914
2	[rdfs:comment, dbp:wikiPageUsesTemplate]	0.99911
2	[dbo:isPartOf, rdfs:comment]	0.99901
2	[dbo:wikiPageLength, rdfs:comment]	0.99973
2	[rdfs:comment, dbo:wikiPageExternalLink]	0.99909
2	[rdfs:comment, dcterms:subject]	0.99902
2	[dbp:longd, rdfs:comment]	0.99904
2	[rdfs:comment, dbp:latd]	0.99900
2	[rdfs:comment, dbo:wikiPageOutDegree]	0.99900

7. DISCUSSION

As presented in the previous section, ROCKER improves the state of the art w.r.t. correctness and memory consumption. Other approaches Linkkey and SAkey have shown to require much more memory than ours, as they could not return any result on bigger datasets. In particular, the heap space of 16 GB was reached on 8 and 9 DBpedia datasets, respectively. Unlike the other approaches, ROCKER managed to remain below the heap space by storing the hash index on disk. In fact, in-memory-based algorithms Linkkey and SAKey were not able to handle indexes for datasets having more than 10 million triples.

Runtime results showed that SAKey is the fastest approach on small datasets, being 1.5 to 3 times faster than the others. This could be explained by the fact that the index creation task is quicker for in-memory-based algorithms. Moreover, the outcome analysis presented in Table 3 confirmed that Linkkey and SAKey found candidates that obey their respective key definitions. As mentioned before, the key definition introduced in this work is more correct. A stricter definition leads ROCKER to a farther exploration of the knowledge graph, whereas the other approaches stop. Thus, the runtime is affected. Nevertheless, as can be seen, the runtime is compensated by a substantial improvement in the quality of the results.

In order to analyse how the key discovery task varies w.r.t. the threshold α, we ran ROCKER on one chosen dataset `DBpedia Monument`. Figure 4 shows the number of minimal almost-keys found for values of α within the interval $[0.95, 1]$

Table 1: Runtime results in milliseconds for ROCKER, Linkkey and SAKey on all datasets.

Dataset	Triples	ROCKER(1.0)	ROCKER(0.999)	Linkkey	SAKey
OAEI 2011 Restaurant 1	$1.1K$	1,880	2,170	1,698	1,028
OAEI 2011 Restaurant 2	$7.5K$	2,424	2,833	2,278	885
DBpedia PersonFunction	$383K$	14,565	11,626	OutOfMemory	6,221
DBpedia CareerStation	$3.0M$	79,964	118,632	OutOfMemory	2,199,854
DBpedia OrganisationMember	$3.9M$	1,075,679	1,130,640	227,336	OutOfMemory
DBpedia Album	$11.4M$	1,948,767	366,147	OutOfMemory	OutOfMemory
DBpedia Artist	$12.0M$	203,764	168,049	OutOfMemory	OutOfMemory
DBpedia Village	$12.9M$	4,224,338	18,872,456	OutOfMemory	OutOfMemory
DBpedia Animal	$13.7M$	8,565,772	3,426,372	OutOfMemory	OutOfMemory
DBpedia SoccerPlayer	$13.9M$	314,853	317,285	OutOfMemory	OutOfMemory
DBpedia ArchitecturalStructure	$13.3M$	541,054	1,010,347	OutOfMemory	OutOfMemory
DBpedia MusicalWork	$17.1M$	2,524,120	2,634,869	OutOfMemory	OutOfMemory

Table 2: Reduction ratios for the two settings of ROCKER on all datasets.

Dataset	# properties	vnodes(1.0)	vnodes(0.999)	RR(1.0)	RR(0.999)
OAEI 2011 Restaurant 1	4	6	6	60.00%	60.00%
OAEI 2011 Restaurant 2	4	6	6	60.00%	60.00%
DBpedia PersonFunction	2	3	3	0.00%	0.00%
DBpedia CareerStation	3	4	4	42.86%	42.86%
DBpedia OrganisationMember	20	378	378	99.96%	99.96%
DBpedia Album	103	753	753	~100.00%	~100.00%
DBpedia Artist	205	928	928	~100.00%	~100.00%
DBpedia Village	116	1387	1700	~100.00%	~100.00%
DBpedia Animal	131	1188	1188	~100.00%	~100.00%
DBpedia SoccerPlayer	88	528	528	~100.00%	~100.00%
DBpedia ArchitecturalStructure	698	1622	3693	~100.00%	~100.00%
DBpedia MusicalWork	136	1201	1201	~100.00%	~100.00%

with a step of 0.005. As can be seen, values are not in scale, i.e. a minimal almost-key for α_0 does not necessarily belong to the set of minimal almost-keys for $\alpha_1 < \alpha_0$. This is because threshold α can "block" the computation before the following refinement. For instance, the highest value was reported for $\alpha = 0.955$, where 136 minimal almost-keys were found. Most of these keys are formed by a common root of two properties, which we call p_1 and p_2, in the form $\{p_1, p_2, p_i\}$ with $i = 3, \ldots, 96$. Since the discriminability score of $\{p_1, p_2\}$ is 0.953, it is not considered as minimal almost-key for $\alpha = 0.955$. However for $\alpha = 0.95$, $\{p_1, p_2\}$ will be a minimal almost-key and its descendants will not be visited, thus reducing the number of almost-keys and the runtime (see Table 6(a)).

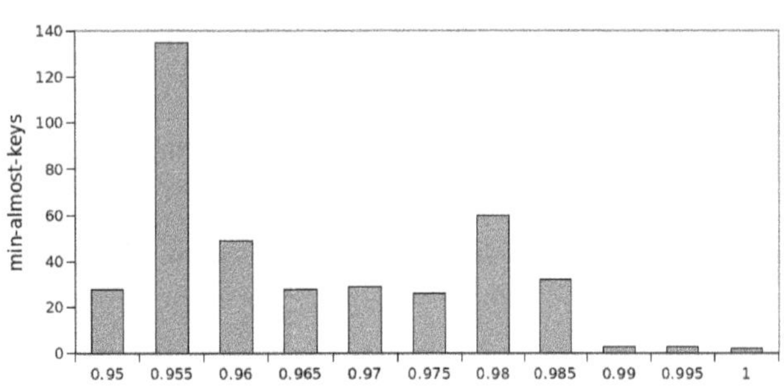

Figure 4: Number of minimal almost-keys found in function of threshold α for ROCKER on dataset `DBpedia Monument`.

Table 6(b) shows the memory consumption w.r.t. α. For $\alpha \geq 0.99$, ROCKER required less memory ($\sim$ 2 GB) than on the other experiments ($\sim$ 5.2 GB), because all the almost-keys were found before visiting the remaining refinement tree. The fact that no other almost-key exists is ensured by evaluating the score for the top element of the refinement tree, which contains all the remaining properties. Having this a score less than α, ROCKER ends the computation.

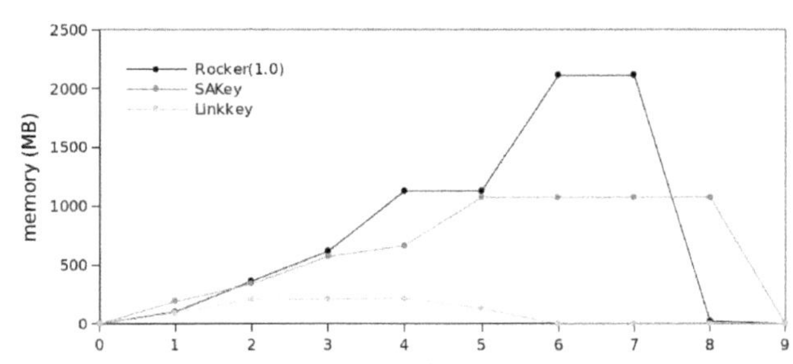

Figure 5: Linkkey showed the best runtime and RAM consumption performances on `DBpedia Monument`, confirming the results in Table 1.

8. CONCLUSION AND FUTURE WORK

In this paper, we presented the first refinement operator for key discovery. We showed that the operator is non-redundant, non-complete and finite. We implemented the operator within the ROCKER approach and showed how it can be extended to scale even on large knowledge bases. Our evaluation of ROCKER suggests that it goes beyond the state of the art with respect to its correctness and memory efficiency, while achieving comparable runtimes. Future directions include a study of the run times, number of keys and visited nodes w.r.t. the input threshold. Then, we will investigate on optimization by using in-memory storage for the hash tables, in order to decrease the query runtimes. Moreover, we will fully integrate the key discovery algorithm in LIMES and make it available in the next releases. We will then experiment with combining key discovery with the

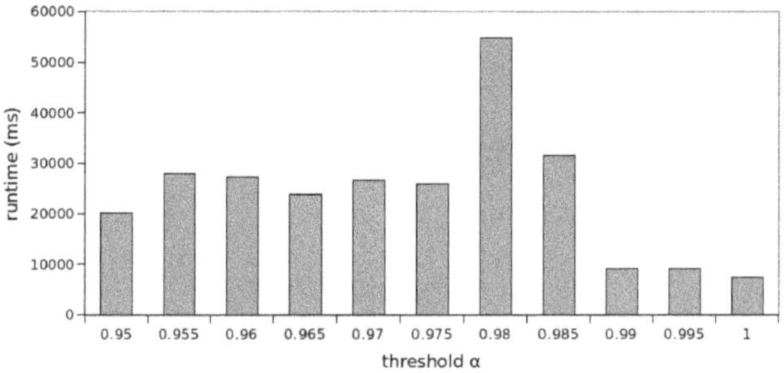

(a)

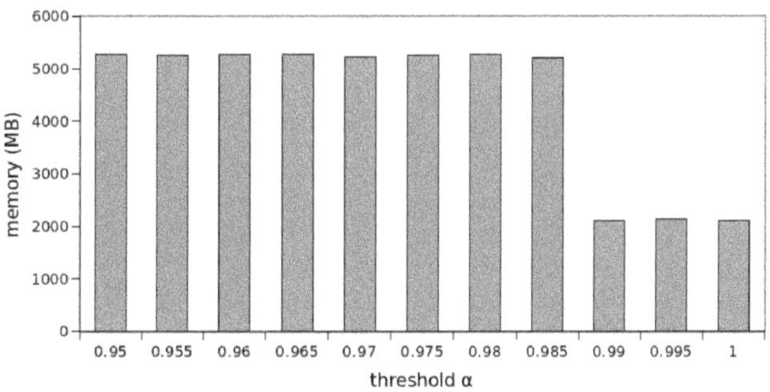

(b)

Figure 6: Run times (6(a)) and Random Access Memory consumption (6(b)) in function of threshold α for ROCKER on dataset `DBpedia Monument`.

detection of property alignments and use those alignments within the context of link discovery.

9. REFERENCES

[1] A. Arasu, C. Ré, and D. Suciu. Large-scale deduplication with constraints using dedupalog. In *Data Engineering, 2009. ICDE'09. IEEE 25th International Conference on*, pages 952–963. IEEE, 2009.

[2] M. Atencia, J. David, and J. Euzenat. Data interlinking through robust linkkey extraction. In T. Schaub, G. Friedrich, and B. O'Sullivan, editors, *Proc. 21st european conference on artificial intelligence (ECAI), Praha (CZ)*, pages 15–20, Amsterdam (NL), 2014. IOS press.

[3] S. Auer, J. Lehmann, and A.-C. N. Ngomo. Introduction to linked data and its lifecycle on the web. In *Reasoning Web*, pages 1–75, 2011.

[4] M. Cheatham and P. Hitzler. String similarity metrics for ontology alignment. In *The Semantic Web–ISWC 2013*, pages 294–309. Springer, 2013.

[5] R. H. Chiang, T. M. Barron, and V. C. Storey. Reverse engineering of relational databases: Extraction of an eer model from a relational database. *Data & Knowledge Engineering*, 12(2):107–142, 1994.

[6] N. P. Danai Symeonidou, Vincent Armant and F. Saïs. Sakey: Scalable almost key discovery in rdf data. In *ISWC 2014*, 2014.

[7] I. F. Ilyas, V. Markl, P. Haas, P. Brown, and A. Aboulnaga. Cords: automatic discovery of correlations and soft functional dependencies. In *Proceedings of the 2004 ACM SIGMOD international conference on Management of data*, pages 647–658. ACM, 2004.

[8] J. Lehmann and P. Hitzler. Concept learning in description logics using refinement operators. *Machine Learning*, 78(1-2):203–250, 2010.

[9] H. Mannila and K.-J. Räihä. Algorithms for inferring functional dependencies from relations. *Data & Knowledge Engineering*, 12(1):83–99, 1994.

[10] H. Mannila and H. Toivonen. Levelwise search and borders of theories in knowledge discovery. *Data Min. Knowl. Discov.*, 1(3):241–258, 1997.

[11] E. Marx, T. Soru, S. Shekarpour, S. Auer, A.-C. Ngonga Ngomo, and K. Breitman. Towards an efficient RDF dataset slicing. *International Journal of Semantic Computing*, 07(04):455–477, 2013.

[12] M. Michelson and C. A. Knoblock. Learning blocking schemes for record linkage. In *AAAI*, pages 440–445. AAAI Press, 2006.

[13] A.-C. Ngonga Ngomo. A Time-Efficient Hybrid Approach to Link Discovery. In *OM*, 2011.

[14] A.-C. Ngonga Ngomo. Link Discovery with Guaranteed Reduction Ratio in Affine Spaces with Minkowski Measures. In *ISWC*, pages 378–393, 2012.

[15] A.-C. Ngonga Ngomo and S. Auer. LIMES - A Time-Efficient Approach for Large-Scale Link Discovery on the Web of Data. In *IJCAI*, pages 2312–2317, 2011.

[16] A.-C. Ngonga Ngomo, J. Lehmann, S. Auer, and K. Höffner. RAVEN – Active Learning of Link Specifications. In *OM*, 2011.

[17] A. Nikolov, M. d'Aquin, and E. Motta. Unsupervised learning of link discovery configuration. In *ESWC*, pages 119–133, 2012.

[18] N. Pernelle, F. Saïs, and D. Symeonidou. An automatic key discovery approach for data linking. *Web Semantics: Science, Services and Agents on the World Wide Web*, 23:16–30, 2013.

[19] F. Saïs, N. Pernelle, and M.-C. Rousset. Combining a logical and a numerical method for data reconciliation. In *Journal on Data Semantics XII*, pages 66–94. Springer, 2009.

[20] M. Saleem, S. S. Padmanabhuni, A.-C. N. Ngomo, J. S. Almeida, S. Decker, and H. F. Deus. Linked cancer genome atlas database. In *Proceedings of the 9th International Conference on Semantic Systems*, pages 129–134. ACM, 2013.

[21] F. Scharffe, Y. Liu, and C. Zhou. Rdf-ai: an architecture for rdf datasets matching, fusion and interlink. In *Proc. IJCAI 2009 workshop on Identity, reference, and knowledge representation (IR-KR), Pasadena (CA US)*, 2009.

[22] D. Song and J. Heflin. Automatically generating data linkages using a domain-independent candidate selection approach. In *The Semantic Web–ISWC 2011*, pages 649–664. Springer, 2011.

[23] T. Soru and A.-C. Ngonga Ngomo. Active learning of domain-specific distances for link discovery. In *Proceedings of JIST*, 2012.

[24] C. Stadler, J. Lehmann, K. Höffner, and S. Auer. Linkedgeodata: A core for a web of spatial open data. *Semantic Web*, 3(4):333–354, 2012.

Random Walk TripleRush: Asynchronous Graph Querying and Sampling

Philip Stutz
Department of Informatics
University of Zurich
Zurich, Switzerland
stutz@ifi.uzh.ch

Bibek Paudel
Department of Informatics
University of Zurich
Zurich, Switzerland
paudel@ifi.uzh.ch

Mihaela Verman
Department of Informatics
University of Zurich
Zurich, Switzerland
verman@ifi.uzh.ch

Abraham Bernstein
Department of Informatics
University of Zurich
Zurich, Switzerland
bernstein@ifi.uzh.ch

ABSTRACT

Most Semantic Web applications rely on querying graphs, typically by using SPARQL with a triple store. Increasingly, applications also analyze properties of the graph structure to compute statistical inferences. The current Semantic Web infrastructure, however, does not efficiently support such operations. This forces developers to extract the relevant data for external statistical post-processing.

In this paper we propose to rethink query execution in a triple store as a highly parallelized asynchronous graph exploration on an active index data structure. This approach also allows to integrate SPARQL-querying with the sampling of graph properties.

To evaluate this architecture we implemented *Random Walk TripleRush*, which is built on a distributed graph processing system. Our evaluations show that this architecture enables both competitive graph querying, as well as the ability to execute various types of random walks with restarts that sample interesting graph properties. Thanks to the asynchronous architecture, first results are sometimes returned in a fraction of the full execution time. We also evaluate the scalability and show that the architecture supports fast query-times on a dataset with more than a billion triples.

1. INTRODUCTION

Use cases such as social network analysis, monitoring of financial transactions, or analysis of web pages and their links all require storage, retrieval, and analysis of large-scale graphs. To address this need, many have researched the development of efficient triple stores [1, 28, 21]. These systems borrow from the database literature to investigate efficient means for storing large graphs and retrieving subgraphs, which are usually defined via a pattern matching language such as SPARQL. Even though these systems process graphs, most of them leverage decades of research results in efficient processing of partial answer-sets by mapping the graphs into set-/array-style internal data structures. They are built like a centralized database, raising the question of scalability and parallelism within query execution.

To increase the parallelism of such graph-stores, modern solutions propose the use of parallel operators [30], sideways information-passing [20], or even pipelined operations and replication [8]. Other approaches focus on building triple stores based on specialized programming models for distributed systems: MapReduce [5] has been used to aggregate results from multiple single-node RDF stores in order to support distributed query processing [9] or to process whole SPARQL query execution pipelines (e.g., [14]). *Whilst these systems efficiently support the storage and retrieval, they mostly fall short on the support of graph-analytics. Hence, developers have to painstakingly retrieve the relevant data for statistical post-processing in a suitable tool.*

In this paper we rethink query execution within graph stores in the light of the changes of computer architectures. *We propose to exploit the large number of CPU-cores of modern servers via the parallel exploration of partial bindings.* Specifically, we explore each partial binding to a query in parallel akin to graph-exploration; this means (i) forking of the exploration whenever more than one binding is possible, (ii) returning the result when all variables of an exploration are bound, and (iii) aborting the exploration when it reaches a dead end (i.e., it cannot match a triple pattern).

This re-conceptualization of triple-stores has the side-effect that it can efficiently support numerous graph-analytic algorithms such as Random Walks with Restarts (RWR)—the basis of many approaches to information extraction and reasoning in noisy domains—or basic graph-algorithms such as shortest-path computations. This approach has the advantage to support the integration of statistical inference with SPARQL-based querying, which can provide better results in classification / learning [10], and simplifies the specification of restrictions on RWR via the re-use of SPARQL.

WWW 2015, May 18–22, 2015, Florence, Italy.
ACM 978-1-4503-3469-3/15/05.
http://dx.doi.org/10.1145/2736277.2741687.

We implemented *Random Walk TripleRush* (RW-TR)[1] to explore this architecture. RW-TR is built on the distributed graph processing system SIGNAL/COLLECT [24].[2] Whilst traditional stores pipe data through query processing operators, RW-TR asynchronously routes query descriptions through an active data-structure. For this reason, RW-TR does not use any joins in the traditional sense, but searches the index graph in parallel.

As a consequence, the contributions of this paper are the following: first and foremost, we propose a novel active index-structure that supports the parallel and distributed exploration of answers to SPARQL-queries. Second, we show how this architecture can be extended with support for RWR – an important graph-analytic approach. Third, we present an extensive evaluation of the architecture that includes (i) vertical-, horizontal-, and data-scalability experiments, (ii) an evaluation of the time until the first result is returned, which is sometimes computed much faster than the whole results set, (iii) a benchmark against two other triple stores in the single-node scenario, where RW-TR is on average more than 10 times faster, and (iv) a comparison with two other distributed triple stores at the billon-triples scale, where RW-TR is very competitive. Fourth and last, we show the effectiveness of our RWR computations via a use case.

In the following, we succinctly discuss the relevant related work, describe the novel distributed architecture, as well as the functionality and interactions of its building blocks. We then compare the architecture with traditional graph-store approaches. Next, we evaluate the approach on multiple benchmarks and show that it can offer competitive performance, as well as good scalability. We close with a discussion of the limitations.

2. RELATED WORK

Studies related to RW-TR can be divided into four categories: (i) distributed in-memory triple-stores, (ii) extensions to SPARQL, (iii) graph computation frameworks, and (iv) studies into RDF index structures.

Distributed in-memory triple stores: Most closely related to RW-TR are Trinity.RDF [30], which relies on parallel operators to improve SPARQL performance, and TriAD [8], which relies on pipelined operations and replication. Both systems are competitive in terms of SPARQL performance (see also Section 5.4) but are limited to pure SPARQL processing. In addition, both use a different approach to parallelization. Trinity.RDF relies on a distributed Bulk-Synchronous approach [27] whilst TriAD uses extensive pre-processing and replication of indices. RW-TR uses an asychronous querying approach, which allows efficient embedding of graph sampling.

SPARQL extensions: A number of projects have proposed extending SPARQL with additional functionality. Corese [3, 4] and iSPARQL [12], for example, provide support for approximate matching and SPARQL-ML [11] extends SPARQL with statistical relational learning operators. Whilst these approaches show how SPARQL could be extended, they typically do not do so efficiently. Only recently have benchmarks been proposed to integrate SPARQL processing with more traditional graph processing tasks.[3] We are unaware of any other system that combines efficient SPARQL processing with efficient graph sampling.

Distributed graph computation frameworks: A number of distributed graph processing frameworks have been proposed in recent years [16, 24, 6]. Whilst these systems provide a basis for building distributed analytic solutions, they do not provide a high-level (querying) language such as a SPARQL extension to answer analytic queries. Trinity.RDF [30], which is layered on top of Trinity, does offer SPARQL querying but does not provide any support for sampling queries or analytics, which would have to be implemented manually.

Sedge [29] introduces different graph partition management techniques to minimize inter-machine communication during query processing. The system's effectiveness is demonstrated by answering SPARQL queries. In contrast, the focus of our work is not to find better partitions of the graph or manage them effectively, but to propose a new way of thinking about distributed triple stores with sampling capabilities.

RDF index structures: RW-TR reflects the insights gathered about RDF indexing in the past years [21, 28] in that it builds a multi-level structure of increasingly specific nodes. It differs significantly from these investigations in that it proposes a query execution as a highly parallelized, asynchronous routing of partially bound results through the index. Some aspects of RW-TR have similarities with the pointer-chasing problem [18, 17, 13], where future references are prefetched to achieve locality. RW-TR's general query execution is, however, fundamentally different, as it routes (passive) partial solutions through an actively processing index structure rather than employing a (possibly parallelized) program that operates on an optimized but passive index structure. RW-TR does exploit locality when compressing lower-level lists with delta-encoding.

3. RW-TR ARCHITECTURE

RW-TR is built leveraging the large-scale, parallel and distributed graph processing framework SIGNAL/COLLECT[4] [24, 25]. It allows to specify graph computations in terms of vertex-centric methods. In contrast to other frameworks, SIGNAL/COLLECT allows for asynchronous execution, multiple vertex types, and the ability to change the graph structure during the execution. Conceptually, SIGNAL/COLLECT-vertices can be seen as actor-like active elements, where the framework handles messaging, parallelization and distribution.

The core idea of RW-TR is to build a triple store with three types of SIGNAL/COLLECT vertices: Each *index vertex* corresponds to a triple pattern, each *triple vertex* corresponds to an RDF triple, and *query vertices* coordinate query execution. Partially matched copies of queries are routed in parallel along different paths of this structure. The index graph is optimized for efficient routing of query descriptions to data and its vertices are addressable by an ID, which is a unique [subject predicate object] tuple.

We first describe how the graph is conceptually built and then explain the details of how this structure enables efficient parallel graph exploration.

[1] *RW-TR* is a significant redesign and extension of TripleRush [26], which was limited to parallelising basic-graph-pattern queries on a single machine.

[2] SIGNAL/COLLECT is similar to Pregel [19], GraphLab/PowerGraph [6], and Trinity [22].

[3] `http://ldbcouncil.org/benchmarks/snb`

[4] `http://uzh.github.io/signal-collect/`

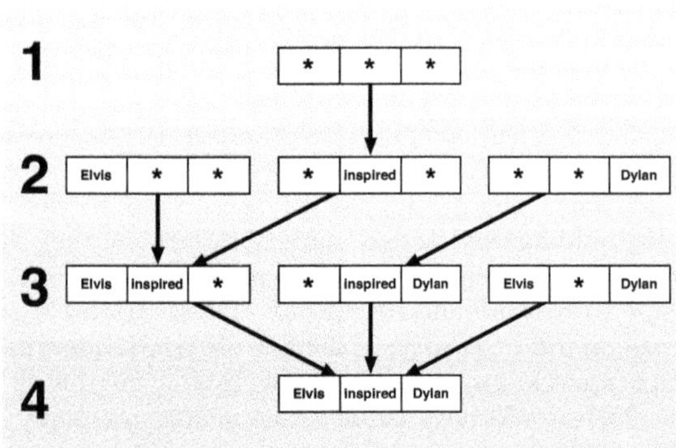

Figure 1: RW-TR index graph for the triple vertex [Elvis inspired Dylan].

3.1 Building the Index Graph

As mentioned before, RW-TR is a triple store with three types of SIGNAL/COLLECT vertices:

Triple vertices (level 4, Fig. 1) represent triples in the database. Each contains subject, predicate, and object information.

Index vertices (levels 1-3, Fig. 1) represent triple patterns and are responsible for routing partially matched copies of queries (referred to as *query particles*) towards triple vertices that match their respective patterns. They also contain subject, predicate, and object information, but one or several of them are wildcards.

Query vertices (Fig. 2) are added to the graph for each query that is being executed. A query vertex emits the first query particle that traverses the index structure. All query particles—successfully matched or not—get routed back to their respective query vertex and successful ones get reported as results. Once the query execution has finished, the query vertex removes itself from the graph.

The graph is built bottom-up, starting by creating a *triple vertex* for each RDF triple. These vertices are added to SIGNAL/COLLECT, which turns them into parallel processing units. A triple vertex will add its immediate *index vertices* (if they do not exist yet) and an edge from each of those vertices to itself. The construction process continues recursively for the index vertices until the parent vertex has already been added or the index vertex has no parent.

The index structure illustrated in Fig. 1 ensures that there is exactly one path from an index vertex to each triple vertex below it.

Observations: The number of predicates is usually much smaller than the number of distinct subjects or objects. Hence, storing edges from the root to [* P *] vertices requires the least amount of memory. The index graph we just described is different from traditional index structures, because it is designed for the efficient parallel routing of messages to triples corresponding to a given triple pattern. All vertices that form the index structure are active parallel processing elements that only interact via message passing.

3.2 Query Execution

We now look into how a query is executed, and then we follow with the description of the query optimizer.

Consider the subgraph shown in Fig. 2 and the query processing for the query: (unmatched = [?X inspired ?Y], [?Y inspired ?Z]; bindings = {}). The query execution starts by adding the query vertex to the TripleRush graph. After the query optimizer determines the execution order of the triple patterns, the query gets processed as follows:

1. The query vertex emits a single query particle, which is routed (by SIGNAL/COLLECT) to the index vertex that matches its first unmatched triple pattern. To determine when a query has finished processing, the initial query particle is endowed with a large number of tickets (Long.MaxValue). Should the tickets ever run out, new tickets could be acquired from the query vertex.[5]

2. When a query particle arrives at an index vertex, a copy of it is sent along each edge. The original particle evenly splits up its tickets among its copies.

3. Once a query particle reaches a triple vertex, the vertex attempts to match the next unmatched query pattern to its triple. If this succeeds, then a variable binding is created and the remaining triple patterns are updated with the new binding. The query particle gets sent to the index or triple vertex that matches its next unmatched triple pattern.

4. If all triple patterns are matched, then the query particle gets routed back to its query vertex.

5. If no vertex with a matching pattern is found, then a handler for undeliverable messages routes the failed query particle back to its query vertex.

6. Query execution finishes when the sum of tickets of all failed and successful query particles received by the query vertex equals the initial ticket endowment of the first particle that was sent out. The query vertex reports that all results have been delivered and removes itself from the graph.

Observations: Queries are often routed along downward edges in the index structure, and placing the index vertices in a way that achieves good locality means fewer messages are sent across machines. We found that the following scheme can achieve good locality, while at the same time ensuring a high degree of parallelism: If the subject of an index vertex is defined, then it is placed on a node determined by its subject. If the subject is a wildcard, then it is placed on a node determined by the object. If only the predicate is defined, then it is placed on a node determined by the predicate. The root index vertex is hardcoded to the last node. This scheme guarantees that particles are locally routed from [S * *] to [S P *] as well as from [* * O] to [* P O].

In addition, to assign a vertex to workers on a machine identified with the above assignment scheme, we compute the sum of its (encoded, see 3.5) IDs modulo the number of workers on the assigned node. In our tests, this scheme

[5]This feature is currently not supported by our system and was not necessary for any of our evaluations.

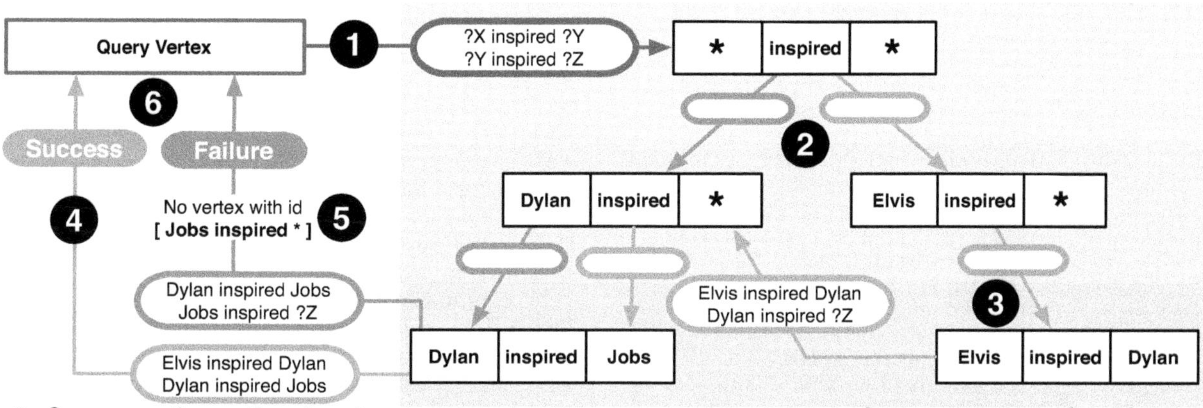

Figure 2: Query execution on the relevant part of the index that was created for the triples [Elvis inspired Dylan] and [Dylan inspired Jobs].

performed better than mixing the values with a collision-minimizing hash function. Signal/Collect uses the same mappings for vertex addressing and for routing messages to (potentially non-existent) index vertices.

3.3 Query Optimization

It has been highlighted [23] that the order in which patterns are explored affects the performance of query processing. When a triple pattern is matched at an index vertex, the bindings made in that vertex are forwarded to the index vertices responsible for subsequent triple patterns (unless there is no match). Since it is expensive to send particles, we explore the graph with a triple pattern ordering that considers both the number of particles to be sent and the branching factor for each particle when matching the next pattern. We estimate these costs by gathering several statistics on index vertices and predicates.

Statistics on the number of children are incrementally aggregated in the index vertices during graph loading. These statistics are cached and, if necessary, retrieved in parallel from the index vertices before optimization. We also compute predicate selectivity statistics after the loading is complete, by dispatching all required two-pattern queries [23] for all predicate combinations. In order to make this fast, we added special support and optimizations for queries that only compute the result count. When determining the number of bindings for the second pattern, the counts can be directly accessed in the index vertices. For the evaluated datasets, the predicate selectivity gathering is usually faster than the graph loading, but the number of dispatched queries is $O(|\ pred\ |^2)$, which could become a problem if a dataset contains many predicates. The optimizer also works, although not as well, when substituting missing selectivities with very large numbers (this was not necessary for any of the evaluated datasets).

In the remainder of this subsection we briefly introduce the cost model and discuss the optimization procedure.

3.3.1 *Cost Model*

We model a query q as a sequence of triple patterns p_i, indexed by $i \geq 1$. For a triple pattern p, we denote the subject, predicate, and object by $p.sub$, $p.pred$, and $p.obj$, respectively.

The cost of executing a query can now be defined as the sum of the costs of matching individual triple patterns in a given order:

$$Cost(q) = \sum_{p_i \in q} cost(p_i) \tag{1}$$

The cost $cost(p_i)$ of matching the ith triple pattern depends on two factors. First, we have to consider the number of bindings or query particles created by the previous triple pattern, which we call $frontier(p_{i-1})$, in accordance with graph search algorithms. $frontier(p_{i-1})$ can be seen as a worst-case estimate of the number of particles that might reach this stage of the exploration. Second, we need to account for the exploration cost $explore(p_i)$ of the index vertex corresponding to the triple pattern p_i. This can be seen as a worst-case estimate of the branching factor encountered per frontier particle that matches triple pattern p_i. Consequently, for $i \geq 1$, we estimate the cost of matching a pattern as: $cost(p_i) = frontier(p_{i-1}) \times explore(p_i)$.

In order to define these two functions we need the statistics defined in Table 1. Given these statistics we can estimate $frontier(p_{i-1})$ as:

$$frontier(p_{i-1}) = \begin{cases} 1, \text{ if } i = 1 \\ card(p_i), \text{ if } i = 2 \\ min(explore(p_i), \min_{\forall j<i} selectivity(p_j, p_i)), \\ \quad \text{otherwise (for all available selectivities)} \end{cases}$$

and $explore(p_i)$ is expressed as:

$$explore(p_i) = min(card(p_i), branch(p_i)),$$

where $branch(p_i)$, the branching factor of the index element associated with p_i, is estimated as follows:

$$branch(p_i) = \begin{cases} card(p_i), \text{ if } i = 1 \\ 1, \text{ if } p_i.sub,\ p_i.pred,\ p_i.obj \text{ are bound} \\ maxObj(p_i), \text{ if } p_i.sub,\ p_i.pred \text{ are bound} \\ maxSub(p_i), \text{ if } p_i.pred,\ p_i.obj \text{ are bound} \\ |\ pred\ |, \text{ if } p_i.sub,\ p_i.obj \text{ are bound} \\ edges(p_i) \times maxObj(p_i), \text{ if } p_i.pred \text{ is bound} \\ card(p_i), \text{ otherwise} \end{cases}$$

$card(p)$:	cardinality of triple pattern p, i.e., number of triples that can be reached following the vertex responsible for the triple pattern
$selectivity(p_i, p_j)$:	number of vertices that are connected by a predicate-pair ($p_i.pred$, $p_j.pred$), sharing a common subject/object (see [23])
$edges(p)$:	number of outgoing edges from the [* P *] vertex corresponding to $p.pred$ to all its [S P *] vertices (Figure 1)
$maxObj(p)$:	the maximum number of objects of any [S P *] vertex corresponding to the predicate $p.pred$
$maxSub(p)$:	the maximum number of subjects of any [* P *] vertex corresponding to the predicate $p.pred$
$\|pred\|$:	number of distinct predicates

Table 1: Statistics used in query optimization

3.3.2 *Query Optimizer*

The query optimizer uses uniform-cost search to find the plan with the best worst-case cost estimate. We employ a min-heap ordered by $Cost(q)$, which initially gets seeded with all possible 1-pattern plans. The optimizer then repeatedly removes the cheapest plan from the heap and computes all possible plan-extensions, which it then inserts into the min-heap.

To prevent the expansion of non-optimal (partial) plans, the optimizer maintains a map that uses the set of covered triple patterns as a key and the lowest cost ordering of the patterns as the value. Before expanding partial plans, the planner looks up their triple-pattern set in the map and only expands the partial plans that have no prior entries. Other plans are discarded as suboptimal.

If the optimizer finds a plan where $frontier(p_{i-1}) = 0$, then the optimizer reports that the query has no results and it is not executed. When the optimizer finds a plan that uses all patterns at the top of the heap, then it has found the cost-optimal plan to execute according to the model.

All operations on the planning heap and reference map take $O(log\ n)$ time, where n is the number of elements in the heap/map. In the worst case, the planning heap can contain almost all incomplete plans, which is exponential in the number of patterns in a query: one can create a (partial) plan by picking or not picking each of the $\mid q \mid$ patterns, resulting in a heap size and number of insert operations of $O(2^{|q|})$. This means that the search space exploration time complexity is $O(log(n) * 2^{|q|})$.

In order to prevent this exponential increase of the planning time for queries with many patterns, we use a greedy query optimizer when the number of patterns in the query is greater than a fixed number.[6] The greedy optimizer is described in [26].

3.4 Extension to Random Walks

Random Walks with Restarts (RWR) are a popular graph sampling technique that can be used for various tasks from computing the similarity between two nodes in a graph to retrieving novel relations [15]. Random walk based models have been applied to many problems such as ranking webpages and segmenting images. Conceptually, random walks can be seen as starting from a given vertex and then following a random edge to a neighboring vertex. There, the walker moves again to a randomly chosen neighbor, goes back to the vertex from which the walk started, or stops its walk based on a restart rule. Example restart rules are (i) walking for a finite number of steps from the starting node, (ii) walking for any number of steps and restarting when there is no outgoing edge, or (iii) at each vertex, restart with a given probability.

In order to add support for efficient sampling queries based on RWR, we have to modify three elements of the previously described architecture: First, we extend the query particles with the extra structures required for sampling. Second, we modify the routing of sampling query particles to adhere to the rules of random walks. And third, to sample correctly we need to store additional bookkeeping information inside the second-level indices (SIndex, PIndex, OIndex). Next we describe each of these modifications in more detail.

To allow for sampling queries we *extended the query particles* with a flag that indicates if the particle is currently executing a traditional (SPARQL) part of a query or a sampling element. In addition, we extended the particles' data structure to optionally include information about the constraints of the random walk, such as the directionality (subject -> object, object -> subject, or both), any constraints on the path (e.g., if it should only follow certain properties or some specified sequence of property types), and the stopping condition. This approach allows us to combine SPARQL and sampling queries within the same execution.

A naïve routing approach would route as many particles through the index as there are tickets. Whenever a particle would arrive at a triple vertex, it would test for its random walk constraints and decide whether to stop the exploration or continue. This would lead to a high overhead, as the same path would be followed multiple times. To improve on this approach, we route as follows: each query begins with a certain number of tickets provided to it. At each index level the particle is split and sent along each index path that qualifies according to the random walks' constraints. Tickets are assigned to each particle such that the sampling of the graph is not biased by the index structure. If there are not enough tickets to assign to all particles, then we randomly choose some paths to follow and abandon the others. As a result, RW-TR computes as many random walks in parallel as there are tickets.

Once the query reaches a triple vertex, the stopping condition gets evaluated. In case it applies and the query constraints are met, then the variable bindings to the subject, predicate, and/or object stored in the current vertex are added to the particle and reported to the query vertex as a success. In case the stopping condition applies and the query constraints fail, then it is reported as a failure. Else, the exploration continues.

To assign the tickets proportionally, additional bookkeeping information is stored in the second-level indices. We need to store the total number of outgoing edges that can be traversed by following the child vertices, and the sum of both outgoing and incoming edges of all child vertices. This information is calculated during the data loading phase. To assign the tickets proportionally to the particles sent to the child vertices, we need to know the outgoing edges per child index vertex. Precomputing these would increase the index

[6] In our experiments, we fixed this number to 8.

size considerably. We, therefore, ask the child index vertices for their number of outgoing edges via a special signal and can dispatch the particles as soon as the information arrives, as we know the total number of outgoing edges.

As an example, consider the sampling query

SAMPLE ?X FROM [Elvis inspired ?X]
CONSTRAINTS [maxhops = 3, tickets=10]

and the subgraph of Fig. 2. This is a neighborhood sampling query as it returns a sample of vertices reachable from Elvis by traversing edges labeled inspired for a maximum of three hops. Given that it uses 10 tickets, it uses 10 random walks along the inspired edges from the Elvis-vertex. We compute these random walks by starting at the vertex [Elvis inspired *], which has only one outgoing edge, leading to [Elvis inspired Dylan]. Given that Dylan is a correct answer to the random walk query, we would need to flip a coin to decide whether to return it as a correct answer or continue. As we are doing multiple random walks in parallel, it is efficient to do both. Hence, we assign half the tickets to the current answer and continue exploring with the other half (when we have an odd number of tickets we flip a coin to determine which path gets one more ticket). Hence, ⟨Dylan⟩, 5 is returned to the query vertex. Again, there's only one outgoing edge along which the remaining 5 tickets of the query are sent. At the vertex [Dylan inspired Jobs], the binding ⟨Dylan, Jobs⟩, 3 is returned to the query vertex, indicating that the path to reach Jobs went via the Dylan vertex. This is the second hop of the query, and according to the constraints set to the query, the query can make one more hop. But since there are no vertices that can be traversed from here, we will also return the two remaining tickets to the query vertex. The final result of our neighborhood sampling query will be the following distribution of bindings: [⟨Dylan⟩, 5; ⟨Dylan, Jobs⟩, 5].

3.5 RW-TR Optimizations

Just like parallel TripleRush [26], RW-TR contains some initial optimizations: a) we do dictionary encoding, b) we remove the triple vertices and fold them into the third index level, where each index vertex stores a compact representation of all the triples that match their pattern, c) we only send the tickets of the failed particles back to the query vertex, and d) we use bulk-messaging and message-combiners.

In addition to this, RW-TR contains improvements that address previous limitations with regard to insert performance and memory usage during loading, by adopting a new data structure for the index vertices. Next, we discuss the details and motivation of these changes.

Index Vertex Representation: In Fig. 1, one notices that the ID of an index vertex varies only in one position—the subject, the predicate, or the object—from the IDs of its children. To reduce the size of the edge representations, we do not store the entire ID of child vertices, but only the specification of this position consisting of one dictionary encoded number per child. We refer to these numbers as *ID-refinements*. The same reasoning applies to third level index vertices, where the triples they store only vary in one position from the ID of the binding index vertex.

Routing and binding only require a traversal of all ID-refinements. To support traversal and inserts in a memory-efficient way, we store the refinements in a special-tailored Splay tree, where the key of each node is an interval and each node stores the set of refinements contained in its interval. The data structure supports average case O(log(n)) inserts, low memory usage and fast traversal.

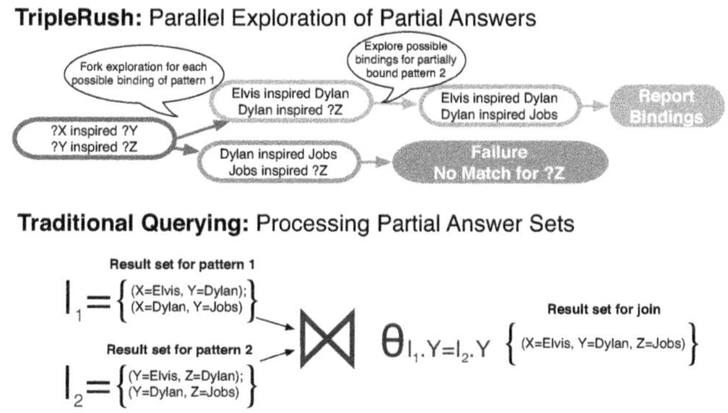

Figure 3: Comparison between query set processing and TripleRush parallel asynchronous partial answer exploration. Same query and data as in Fig. 2.

Index Graph Structure: Because we fold the triple vertices into the third index level, there is no longer an obvious place where one can verify if a fully bound pattern corresponds to a triple that exists inside the store.

To deal with this, RW-TR sends the particle that has to check for the existence of a fully-bound pattern to the corresponding [S * O] index vertex. These vertices do not store the ID-refinements into a Splay-tree, but into a sorted array. The existence is checked with binary search.We observe that most patterns have bound predicates, so these vertices are rarely used for anything but to check for the existence of a triple. We also observe that inserts into the array are O(n). In practice, this was not an issue, since there are usually very few predicates for a given subject/object pair.

4. PRELIMINARY ANALYSIS

As introduced in the last section and illustrated in Fig. 3, RW-TR processes SPARQL queries by exploring each partial binding asynchronously in parallel. Whenever an exploration encounters more than one possible partial binding, it forks the exploration and pursues both potential solutions in parallel ('green' and 'orange' explorations in the figure). When all variables of an exploration are bound, it returns a result ('green' path). Alternatively, when the remaining unbound variables of an exploration cannot be bound, it aborts that path ('orange' path). Essentially, RW-TR performs a parallel-asynchronous graph search.

Traditional DBMS use operators on indices and intermediate data structures (typically arrays or sets). Originally, these operators were executed synchronously, where each operator is executed until its full result set is available before the next operator is called (see also Figure 3). Parallelism is usually introduced by (i) executing independent operators in parallel (such as the scans that create the sets in the figure) and (ii) implementing parallelized operators resulting in a parallel but synchronous system (each operator has to find all its results before invoking the next one). Modern systems introduce additional parallelism via pipelining operators [8], which allow some operators to pass on partial results. Conceptually, these systems use parallelized approaches to process partial answer sets rather than exploring all possible partial solutions in parallel.

The central proposition of this paper is that RW-TR's parallel-asynchronous exploration approach may be a viable alternative graph store architecture for today's multi-core systems.
First, we believe that asynchronous-parallel query processing allows to exploit the many cores better than synchronous-parallel execution, as cores are less likely to wait for work during synchronization. RW-TR is built to exploit this asynchronicity. As mentioned, some current systems exploit a kind of asynchronicity via pipelining. Pipelining, however, comes at the cost of more complexity in both the operators and their coordination. Given that RW-TR does not require coordinating between its explorations, it does not incur such an overhead.
Second, we expect the exploitable performance improvement due to parallelism to be curbed by (i) the branching factor of the query, which is a function of the selectivity of the triple patterns and connectivity of the involved nodes (or join selectivity), as it limits the degree of parallelism and (ii) possible gains through locality, as forking explorations and moving them to other cores (possibly on other machines) can be costly operations.

RW-TR's index can be conceptualized as a vertical partition of the data into S-Index, P-Index, and O-Index, for subjects, predicates and objects, respectively, as well as three additional indices for each combination of two columns – SP-Index, PO-Index and SO-Index. In addition, the latter three indices are sharded by the subject key (for SP-Index and SO-Index) or object key (for PO-Index). Each shard is assigned to a processing unit in a distributed compute cluster.

5. EVALUATION

The goal of the evaluation was to explore the propositions that that RW-TR's parallel-asynchronous exploration approach is both competitive and scalable via the efficient exploitation of parallelism where possible, as well as to illustrate its capability to gain useful results via RWR. To that end we employ two standard benchmarks—LUBM and BSBM—and evaluate RW-TR's performance under different conditions, as well as a use case for RWR.
The experiments reported in subsection 5.3 and the distributed evaluations in subsection 5.4 were run on a cluster of 8 machines, each machine having 128 GB RAM and two E5-2680 v2 processors at 2.80GHz, with 10 cores per processor. The machines are connected with 40Gbps Infiniband. We used version 1.8.0_05-b13 of the Java Runtime. All other experiments were run on single machines of the same cluster.

We used both the LUBM[7] (Lehigh University Benchmark) and BSBM (Berlin SPARQL) [2] benchmarks. For LUBM, we used the queries used in the Trinity.RDF evaluation [30]. For BSBM, we generated the datasets and explore use case queries with the standard data generator and query test driver, but stripped the queries of advanced SPARQL features unsupported by RW-TR such as OPTIONAL or complex filters, and discarded queries 9 and 12 for relying on such features.

We executed ten runs of each LUBM query and in the diagrams report both the average and geometric mean over the fastest runs. For BSBM we executed the same ten generated queries from each category, computed the category average and reported the average and geometric mean over all categories. The measured total time for a run includes everything from query optimization until the result set is fully traversed, but the decoding of the results is not forced.

5.1 Vertical Scalability and First Results

The goal of this evaluation was to measure how well RW-TR scales with additional worker threads on a single machine of the cluster. Additionally, the first result is reported, in order to test our hypothesis that the fully asynchronous execution allows to deliver the first result much faster than the full result set. We ran this evaluation ten times on the LUBM 160 dataset with the Trinity.RDF queries and varied the number of worker threads between 1 and 20, because the hardware has 20 physical cores. We pre-planned the queries and ran them without the optimizer, in order to reduce overhead that is not directly associated with the execution engine.

In Figure 4 we see that adding more workers has a negative and at best neutral impact for queries L4, L5, and L6, which touch very little data and are answered in at most a millisecond. For queries L1, L3, and L7, which are more processing intense, the speedup for 20 workers relative to 1 worker is between 10 and 12, which is good, considering that query dispatch and result reporting is still handled by only one worker, and that all queries are answered in under 50ms at that point. Query 2 scales a bit up to 10 worker threads, but does not improve with more processing elements. This is likely due to its structure of only 2 triple-patterns, which offers RW-TR less potential for parallelization.

Figure 4(c) graphs time until the first result was reported relative to the total query execution time (Query 3 was omitted as it does not return results). For queries that profited from parallelization, the first answer was delivered in around a third of the time it took to compute the entire result. The relative benefit increased when going from 1 to 10 worker threads, but then remained approximately constant when going to 20 processing threads.

Overall, this evaluation shows that the architecture can take advantage of multicore architectures and that if there are enough workers available, then, for some queries, the asynchronous-parallel execution can deliver first results much sooner than the full results.

5.2 Data Scalability and Memory Usage

To measure the data scalability of RW-TR in the single-machine setup, we measured its performance for different sizes of the benchmark datasets. For comparison, we also supply the numbers for the in-memory backend of Sesame, as it is open-source and runs in the JVM, and for Virtuoso 7.1 as a comparison to on-disk approaches.

To make the comparison with the on-disk system Virtuoso fairer, we evaluated warm-cache runs and we configured it to make use of the processors and memory of the machine.

The two diagrams in Figure 5 show how the performance changes, when the LUBM and BSBM queries are executed on increasingly large datasets. On the BSBM dataset, the performance of all systems is comparable for small dataset sizes, but RW-TR scales better to large dataset sizes, for the largest BSBM dataset it is on average up to 10 times faster than Sesame and up to 25 times faster than Virtuoso. The geometric mean does not change dramatically, because most queries do not touch more data on a larger dataset.

[7]http://swat.cse.lehigh.edu/projects/lubm

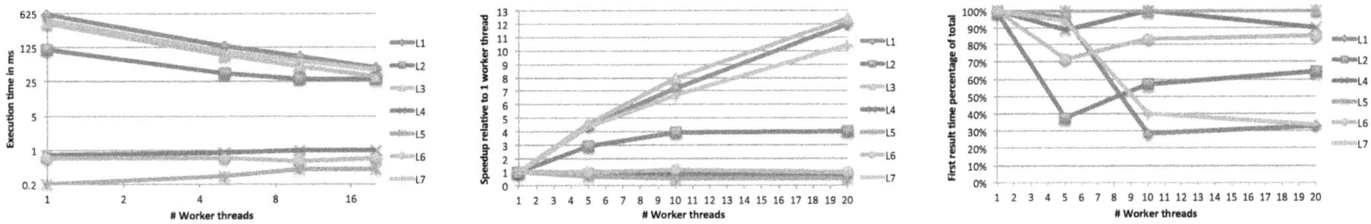

(a) (b) (c)

Figure 4: 4(a) shows the execution times of the different queries on a logarithmic scale on both axes, 4(b) shows the speedup relative to 1 worker thread for all queries, and 4(c) shows the time it took until the first result as a percentage of the total for the entire result.

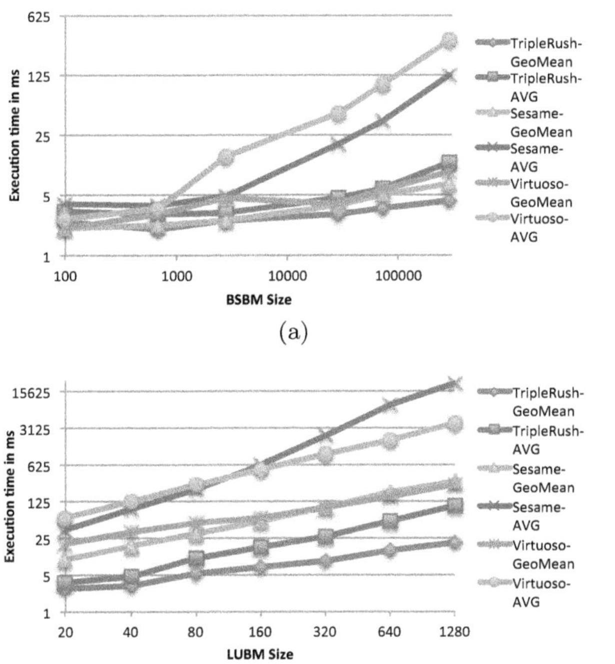

(b)

Figure 5: 5(a) and 5(b) compare the single-node scalability of execution times with increasing BSBM and LUBM sizes. Both axes are logarithmic.

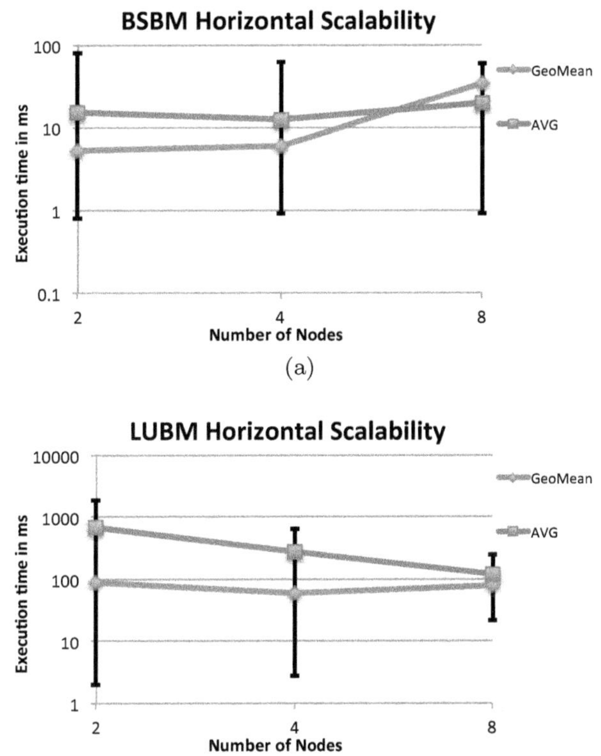

(b)

Figure 6: 6(a) and 6(b) compare the horizontal scalability of RW-TR with 2, 4, and 8 nodes for both BSBM 284'826 and for LUBM 1280. The aggregates are over all queries for that dataset, and for each query we used the fastest of 10 runs. Error bars indicate the runtimes for the fastest and slowest queries in the benchmark.

On the more processing intense LUBM queries, RW-TR shows better performance on any dataset size, up to more than 200 times faster for Sesame and 35 times faster for Virtuoso on average for the largest evaluated size.

We do not have any precise memory measurements, but we measured the used JVM memory, which can serve as an upper bound for the memory used by the index. We then look at the lowest such upper bound that we measured during any of the runs. For BSBM 284'826, RW-TR had a lowest upper bound of 39.7 GB, in contrast to 28.6 GB for Sesame. For LUBM 1280 RW-TR used 61.6 GB compared to the 34.7 GB used by Sesame. From this we conclude that the RW-TR index most likely uses more memory than Sesame's, but that the index size is still reasonable.

5.3 Horizontal Scalability

The goal of this evaluation was to measure RW-TR's scalability in the distributed setting. In particular, we wanted to explore if RW-TR's query evaluation approach would degrade when faced with messaging over the network rather than in-memory, or if the benefit of additional processors would dominate. For this, we measured the performance on large BSBM and LUBM data sets while varying the number of nodes used.

Figure 6 shows the results of these evaluations. We aggregated over the fastest runs of ten executions for each query, in order to reduce confounding factors (e.g. garbage collections). We found that for the BSBM dataset/queries the average execution time stays approximately the same, while the geometric mean slightly increases. For the LUBM dataset/queries the geometric mean stays approximately the same, whilst the average execution time decreases. Our interpretation is that for queries that do not require a lot of processing the added overhead and network latency reduces the performance, whilst for queries that require a lot of processing the benefit of the added processing elements can overcome this drawback. This explains why adding nodes tends to slow down the execution of the fastest millisecond-range queries, whilst improving the performance for the most processing-intense queries.

5.4 Comparison with Trinity.RDF and TriAD

Tables 2 and 3 compare the performance of RW-TR to the numbers reported in the Trinity.RDF [30] and TriAD [8] papers. We followed the evaluation procedure described to us by the Trinity.RDF authors, which includes a partitioning of rdf:type into a different type predicate for each class referred to as the object. The RW-TR distributed evaluation on LUBM 10240 with 1.36 billion triples was run on all 8 nodes of the cluster. The comparison of the numbers in these tables has many caveats, as the cited numbers were created with different hardware and cluster sizes and the approaches require different amounts of preprocessing. We believe this comparison at least shows that the RW-TR architecture is competitive in both the single-node and in the distributed scenario.

5.5 A Random Walk Use Case: Path Sampling

In this section we illustrate RW-TR's capability to run sampling queries based on random walks with restarts (RWR). Our goal is to show the simplicity with which Semantic Web developers using RW-TR can attain RWR results and how they can be combined with SPARQL queries. A more general discussion of the usefulness of RWRs is beyond the scope of our use case and can be found in [15].

Consider the need for establishing the relatedness of two entities. As an example, we could have a selection of sports teams—Liverpool, Manchester United, Chicago Bulls, and The Brooklyn Dodgers—and we would like to know what championship they compete in—the UEFA Cup, the World Series, or the NBA Finals—from a dataset of relationships extracted from a large text corpus. The dataset can be extremely noisy and may have misleading and/or conflicting relationships, such as the Manchester United team playing basketball. Indeed, for example, an October 2011 The Telegraph article connects a basketball player with Manchester United.[8]

RWR have been proposed to deal with these kinds of noisy settings. The rationale is the following: Intuitively, there are more short paths between nodes that are conceptually close to each other than between nodes that are further apart. Just picking the shortest path between two vertices may be mislead by a noisy connection. A sampling of random walks will unearth which vertices are closer via many connections and is, hence, less susceptible to false relations in the graph.

For our use case we use the Never Ending Language Learning (NELL) knowledge base (version 08m.845), which has about 2 million triples. NELL contains relations extracted from natural language text and it iteratively learns new relations based on what it learned in the previous iterations. This naturally leads to some ambiguous or false relations in the knowledge base. For example, NELL contains these two relations about Manchester United (the British soccer club), the first of which is clearly noise: ⟨sportsteam:man_united team-plays-sport sport:basketball⟩ and ⟨sportsteam:man_united team-plays-in-league sportsleague:fa⟩, where sportsleague:fa is the British Football Association cup.

To illustrate the capability of RW-TR to solve the task of finding the connectedness of a team with a championship, we ran queries of the following form:[9]

```
SAMPLE ?X FROM
   [ sportsteam:man_united ?X sportsleague:uefa]
CONSTRAINTS [maxhops = 5, tickets=100]
```

whilst varying the team, the championship, the maximum number of hops (we employed 5, 10, 20), and the number of tickets (we used 100, 1'000, and 10'000). By simulating multiple independent random walks from teams, we can count all walks that reach the respective championships and estimate or calculate information such as the number of walks reaching the goal, the path lengths, or the conditional probabilities of reaching the championships from a given team.

Figure 7 graphs some of the results. In the first graph on the left we show the distributions of reaching the UEFA Cup from all four teams for 1'000 tickets whilst varying the path length. As we can see, the distribution is extremely stable. Both Manchester United and Liverpool are clearly associated with the UEFA cup, whilst the two non soccer teams do not show any relations. This illustrates the small world phenomenon, where most entities that are related are close to each other in the graph and the longer paths actually do not lead to many additional relationships. This latter observation is supported by the actual number of arriving tickets in each of the classes.

The three graphs on the right of Figure 7 show the distributions of reaching each of the championships from the four teams. Given the stability of the results, we chose a path length of 5 and varied the number of walks (i.e., tickets initially assigned). The paths to the UEFA Cup and the World Series are very stable. Indeed, the number of arriving tickets (printed in the bars) are proportional to the number of initial tickets (or walks). The NBA graph on the far left tells a more subtle story. The more tickets we assign to the exploration, the more the result reflects the noisy extractions mentioned above. When using 1'000 or 10'000 tickets, we find a small number of connections between both Liverpool and Manchester United and the NBA finals — reflecting noisy connections. Hence, a higher number of tickets is more likely to follow noisy connections. Note that the total execution time for the thirty-six path sampling queries needed for the three graphs on the right of Figure 7 was less than a second.

6. LIMITATIONS AND CONCLUSION

In the following we discuss limitations and threats to validity, followed by the conclusion.

There are some limitations related to the RW-TR implementation being a prototype: (i) Encoded IDs cannot exceed 2^{31}, (ii) only a subset of SPARQL is supported, (iii) dictionary encoding/decoding is not distributed, and (iv) splay integer sets do not currently support deletions. These limi-

[8]http://www.telegraph.co.uk/sport/football/teams/liverpool/8826912/Liverpool-v-Manchester-United-basketball-star-and-Anfield-stakeholder-Lebron-James-jets-in-for-clash.html

[9]Note that this query almost uses the SPARQL SELECT syntax. We could support additional basic graph patterns in a WHERE clause employing the same semantics as in a SELECT statement.

Fastest of 10 runs	L1	L2	L3	L4	L5	L6	L7	Geo. mean
TripleRush	22.6	27.8	0.4	1	0.4	0.9	21.2	2.94
Trinity.RDF	281	132	110	5	4	9	630	46
TriAD	427	117	210	2	0.5	19	693	39
TriAD-SG	97	140	31	1	0.2	1.8	711	14

Table 2: Single-node, LUBM 160 (~21 million triples), time in ms. Comparison data from [30] and [8].

Fastest of 10 runs	L1	L2	L3	L4	L5	L6	L7	Geo. mean
TripleRush	3,111.2	1,457.9	0.7	3.5	9.5	29.1	1,165.8	62.1
Trinity.RDF	12,648	6,018	8,735	5	4	9	31,214	450
TriAD	7,631	1,663	4,290	2.1	0.5	69	14,895	249
TriAD-SG	2,146	2,025	1,647	1.3	0.7	1.4	16,863	106

Table 3: Distributed, LUBM 10240 (~1.36 billion triples), time in ms. Comparison data from [30] and [8].

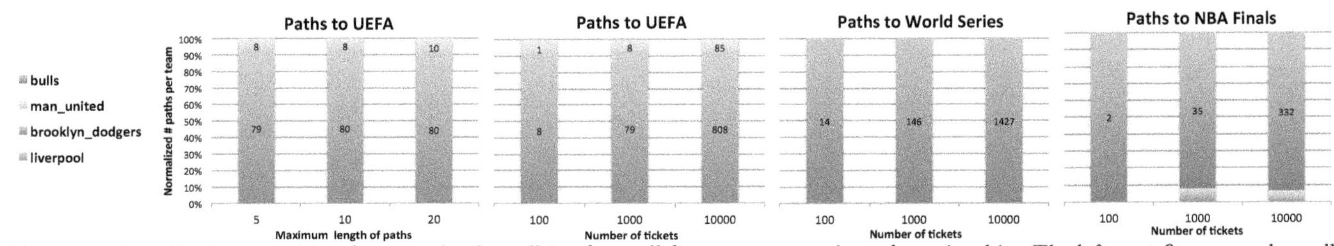

Figure 7: Distributions resulting from randomly walking from all four teams to a given championship. The leftmost figure graphs walks to UEFA whilst varying the maximum path-length when employing 1'000 tickets. The other graphs vary the number of tickets whilst fixing the path-length to 5.

tations are not inherent to the approach and resolving them is primarily a matter of engineering.

There are, however, limitations that are inherent to the approach: First, some operations, such as ordering the results, by definition require a synchronization. Our current approach can only handle them as post-processing steps, which is straightforward but inefficient. Second, an efficient execution of filters requires for an optimizer to be able to place them at any point during the query execution plan. Our current approach is limited to treating them as a post-processing step. More efficient handling would need to enable access to literals from inside the store.

Also, our evaluations have some limitations: Our benchmarking of RW-TR is limited to synthetic datasets, which means that the results might not generalize to real-world datasets. Furthermore, as mentioned in Section 5.4, we could not compare RW-TR's performance with Trinity.RDF and TriAD running on the same hardware, as those two software packages are not available. Nonetheless, we believe that our evaluation shows that RW-TR is competitive in those system's core strength—the evaluation of SPARQL queries—whilst also supporting sampling queries.

Our query optimizer can be improved to better deal with queries that have many patterns: typical SPARQL queries contain star-shaped patterns that can be optimized independently of others [7].

Finally, our RWR use-case is only one example and lacks a full efficiency evaluation. Also, the current version of RW-TR only supports sampling using RWR and no other analytics such as PageRank. The rationale for this limitation was that the main goal of this paper was to illustrate the versatility of our approach in supporting both SPARQL querying and RWR-style sampling. A full efficiency evaluation of RW-TR's RWR capability or an extension to other graph analytics, which would be supported by the underlying SIGNAL/COLLECT framework, is beyond the scope of this paper.

7. CONCLUSIONS

In this paper we proposed to exploit the large number of CPU-cores of modern servers via the parallel exploration of partial bindings implemented on a distributed graph processing system. In particular, we suggested to fork the exploration whenever more than one binding is possible, returning the result when all variables of an exploration are bound, and expiring the exploration when it reaches a dead end. This re-conceptualization of triple-stores has the side-effect that it can efficiently support random walks with restarts by tasking each parallel exploration to simultaneously explore as many random walks as it has tickets.

As such, RW-TR presents a new approach to building graph stores with integrated graph analytic operators such as sampling queries. Our evaluation shows that this architecture can serve as the basis for a graph store that is competitive with other systems. We hope that RW-TR can serve as a basis for further exploration that will help Semantic Web developers to efficiently and seamlessly analyze their graphs.

Acknowledgments.

We would like to thank the Hasler Foundation for the generous support of the SIGNAL/COLLECT project under grant number 11072 and Alex Averbuch, Cosmin Basca, Lorenz Fischer, Shen Gao, Tobias Grubenmann, and Katerina Papaioannou for their feedback.

8. REFERENCES

[1] D. Abadi, A. Marcus, S. Madden, and K. Hollenbach. Scalable Semantic Web Data Management Using Vertical Partitioning. In *Proceedings of the 33rd international conference on Very large data bases*, pages 411–422, 2007.

[2] C. Bizer and A. Schultz. The berlin sparql benchmark. *International Journal on Semantic Web and Information Systems (IJSWIS)*, 5(2):1–24, 2009.

[3] O. Corby, R. Dieng-kuntz, and C. Faron-zucker. Querying the semantic web with the corese search engine. pages 705–709. IOS Press, 2004.

[4] O. Corby, R. Dieng-Kuntz, C. Faron-Zucker, and F. Gandon. Ontology-based Approximate Query Processing for Searching the Semantic Web with Corese. Research Report RR-5621, 2006.

[5] J. Dean and S. Ghemawat. Mapreduce: simplified data processing on large clusters. *Communications of the ACM*, 51(1):107–113, 2008.

[6] J. E. Gonzalez, Y. Low, H. Gu, D. Bickson, and C. Guestrin. Powergraph: Distributed graph-parallel computation on natural graphs. In *USENIX Symposium on Operating Systems Design and Implementation (OSDI)*, pages 17–30, 2012.

[7] A. Gubichev and T. Neumann. Exploiting the query structure for efficient join ordering in sparql queries.

[8] S. Gurajada, S. Seufert, I. Miliaraki, and M. Theobald. Triad: a distributed shared-nothing rdf engine based on asynchronous message passing. In *Proceedings of the 2014 ACM SIGMOD International Conference on Management of Data*, SIGMOD '14, pages 289–300, 2014.

[9] J. Huang, D. J. Abadi, and K. Ren. Scalable sparql querying of large rdf graphs. *Proceedings of the VLDB Endowment*, 4(11):1123–1134, 2011.

[10] C. Kiefer, A. Bernstein, and A. Locher. Adding data mining support to sparql via statistical relational learning methods. In *Proceedings of the 5th European Semantic Web Conference on The Semantic Web: Research and Applications*, ESWC'08, pages 478–492, Berlin, Heidelberg, 2008. Springer-Verlag.

[11] C. Kiefer, A. Bernstein, and A. Locher. Adding Data Mining Support to SPARQL via Statistical Relational Learning Methods. In *Proceedings of the 5th European Semantic Web Conference (ESWC)*, Lecture Notes in Computer Science. Springer, 2008.

[12] C. Kiefer, A. Bernstein, and M. Stocker. The Fundamentals of iSPARQL: A Virtual Triple Approach for Similarity-Based Semantic Web Tasks. In *Proceedings of the 6th International Semantic Web Conference*, 2007.

[13] N. Kohout, S. Choi, D. Kim, and D. Yeung. Multi-chain prefetching: Effective exploitation of inter-chain memory parallelism for pointer-chasing codes. In *Parallel Architectures and Compilation Techniques, 2001. Proceedings. 2001 International Conference on*, pages 268–279. IEEE, 2001.

[14] S. Kotoulas, J. Urbani, P. A. Boncz, and P. Mika. Robust runtime optimization and skew-resistant execution of analytical sparql queries on pig. In *International Semantic Web Conference (1)*, volume LNCS 7649, pages 247–262, 2012.

[15] N. Lao and W. W. Cohen. Relational retrieval using a combination of path-constrained random walks. *Mach. Learn.*, 81(1):53–67, Oct. 2010.

[16] Y. Low, J. Gonzalez, A. Kyrola, D. Bickson, C. Guestrin, and J. M. Hellerstein. Graphlab: A new parallel framework for machine learning. In *Conference on Uncertainty in Artificial Intelligence (UAI)*, Catalina Island, California, July 2010.

[17] C.-K. Luk. Tolerating memory latency through software-controlled pre-execution in simultaneous multithreading processors. In *Computer Architecture, 2001. Proceedings. 28th Annual International Symposium on*, pages 40–51. IEEE, 2001.

[18] C.-K. Luk and T. C. Mowry. Compiler-based prefetching for recursive data structures. In *ACM SIGOPS Operating Systems Review*, volume 30, pages 222–233. ACM, 1996.

[19] G. Malewicz, M. H. Austern, A. J. C. Bik, J. C. Dehnert, I. Horn, N. Leiser, and G. Czajkowski. Pregel: a system for large-scale graph processing. In *Proceedings of the 2010 ACM SIGMOD International Conference on Management of data*, pages 135–146, 2010.

[20] T. Neumann and G. Weikum. Scalable join processing on very large rdf graphs. In *Proceedings of the 2009 ACM SIGMOD International Conference on Management of data*, pages 627–640, 2009.

[21] T. Neumann and G. Weikum. The RDF-3X engine for scalable management of RDF data. *The VLDB Journal*, 19(1):91–113, 2010.

[22] B. Shao, H. Wang, and Y. Li. The trinity graph engine. Technical report, Technical Report 161291, Microsoft Research, 2012.

[23] M. Stocker, A. Seaborne, A. Bernstein, C. Kiefer, and D. Reynolds. Sparql basic graph pattern optimization using selectivity estimation. In *Proceedings of the 17th international conference on World Wide Web*, pages 595–604. ACM, 2008.

[24] P. Stutz, A. Bernstein, and W. W. Cohen. Signal/Collect: Graph Algorithms for the (Semantic) Web. In *International Semantic Web Conference*, volume LNCS 6496, pages pp. 764–780. Springer, Heidelberg, 2010.

[25] P. Stutz, D. Strebel, and A. Bernstein. Signal/collect: Processing web-scale graphs in seconds. *The Semantic Web Journal – Interoperability, Usability, Applicability*, Forthcoming.

[26] P. Stutz, M. Verman, L. Fischer, and A. Bernstein. Triplerush: A fast and scalable triple store. In *9th International Workshop on Scalable Semantic Web Knowledge Base Systems (SSWS)*, volume 50, 2013.

[27] L. G. Valiant. A bridging model for parallel computation. *Communications of the ACM*, 33(8):103–111, 1990.

[28] C. Weiss, P. Karras, and A. Bernstein. Hexastore: sextuple indexing for semantic web data management. *Proceedings of the VLDB Endowment*, 1(1):1008–1019, 2008.

[29] S. Yang, X. Yan, B. Zong, and A. Khan. Towards effective partition management for large graphs. In *Proceedings of the 2012 ACM SIGMOD International Conference on Management of Data*, pages 517–528. ACM, 2012.

[30] K. Zeng, J. Yang, H. Wang, B. Shao, and Z. Wang. A distributed graph engine for web scale rdf data. *Proceedings of the VLDB Endowment*, 6(4):265–276, 2013.

Open Domain Question Answering via Semantic Enrichment

Huan Sun[†]*, Hao Ma[#], Wen-tau Yih[#], Chen-Tse Tsai[+], Jingjing Liu[#], Ming-Wei Chang[#]
huansun@cs.ucsb.edu
{haoma, scottyih, jingjl, minchang}@microsoft.com
ctsai12@illinois.edu
[†]University of California, Santa Barbara
[#]Microsoft Research
[+] University of Illinois at Urbana-Champaign

ABSTRACT

Most recent question answering (QA) systems query large-scale knowledge bases (KBs) to answer a question, after parsing and transforming natural language questions to KBs-executable forms (e.g., *logical forms*). As a well-known fact, KBs are far from complete, so that information required to answer questions may not always exist in KBs. In this paper, we develop a new QA system that mines answers directly from the Web, and meanwhile employs KBs as a significant auxiliary to further boost the QA performance.

Specifically, to the best of our knowledge, we make the first attempt to link answer candidates to entities in Freebase, during answer candidate generation. Several remarkable advantages follow: (1) Redundancy among answer candidates is automatically reduced. (2) The types of an answer candidate can be effortlessly determined by those of its corresponding entity in Freebase. (3) Capitalizing on the rich information about entities in Freebase, we can develop semantic features for each answer candidate after linking them to Freebase. Particularly, we construct answer-type related features with two novel probabilistic models, which directly evaluate the appropriateness of an answer candidate's types under a given question. Overall, such semantic features turn out to play significant roles in determining the true answers from the large answer candidate pool. The experimental results show that across two testing datasets, our QA system achieves an 18% $\sim$ 54% improvement under F_1 metric, compared with various existing QA systems.

Categories and Subject Descriptors: H.3.3 [Information Storage and Retrieval] Retrieval models; I.2.3 [Artificial Intelligence]Answer/reason extraction

Keywords: Question Answering; Knowledge Bases; Web Search

*This work was done when the first author was on a summer internship at Microsoft Research.

WWW 2015, May 18–22, 2015, Florence, Italy.
ACM 978-1-4503-3469-3/15/05.
http://dx.doi.org/10.1145/2736277.2741651.

1. INTRODUCTION

Open-domain question answering (QA), which returns exact answers to natural language questions issued by users, is a challenging task and has been advocated as the key problem for advancing web search [15]. Based on the information sources used to find answers, QA systems can be majorly categorized into *knowledge base (KB)-based* and *corpus-based.* A KB-based QA system answers a question by directly querying structured knowledge bases such as Freebase [6], whereas a corpus-based QA system mines answers from an unstructured corpus, such as news articles or other diversified forms of documents available on the Web.

Large-scale knowledge bases, such as Freebase [6], DBpedia [40], YAGO [38], Google's Knowledge Graph and Microsoft's Satori, contain a wealth of valuable information, stored in the form of relation triples, e.g., (*Obama*, *Place-of-Birth*, *Honolulu*). Recent blossom of such large-scale knowledge bases have enabled numerous QA systems to directly extract answers from KBs. For example, Berant et al. [2, 3] develop semantic parsing techniques that map natural language utterances into logical form queries, to execute on a knowledge base. The Paralex system [17] extracts relation tuples from general web corpora via information extraction tools (e.g., ReVerb [16]) and stores them as extracted KBs; during QA, it maps open-domain questions to queries over the extracted KBs. QA systems developed in [18] resort to both curated KBs such as Freebase and extracted KBs from general corpora, to answer a question. Figure 1(a) briefly illustrates the scheme of a KB-based QA system, where a question gets answered by being parsed and transformed to a specific form, suitable to execute on KBs.

However, despite their large size, existing knowledge bases are still far from complete and not updated in a timely fashion [14, 32, 42]. As a result, information required to answer a question may not always exist in KBs. Furthermore, although semantic parsing [2, 3] has been a hot research topic recently, the problem of mapping natural language utterances to logical-form queries is still considered largely unsolved, which limits the practical use of a KB-based QA system. In contrast, interesting or important facts and statements can often appear repeatedly in the rich web corpus including news articles, Wikipedia-like pages, community QA sites, blogs and forums. Driven by this observation of *web redundancy* [7], in this paper, we study the second category of QA systems, i.e., a corpus-based QA system, with the focus on directly mining answers from the Web.

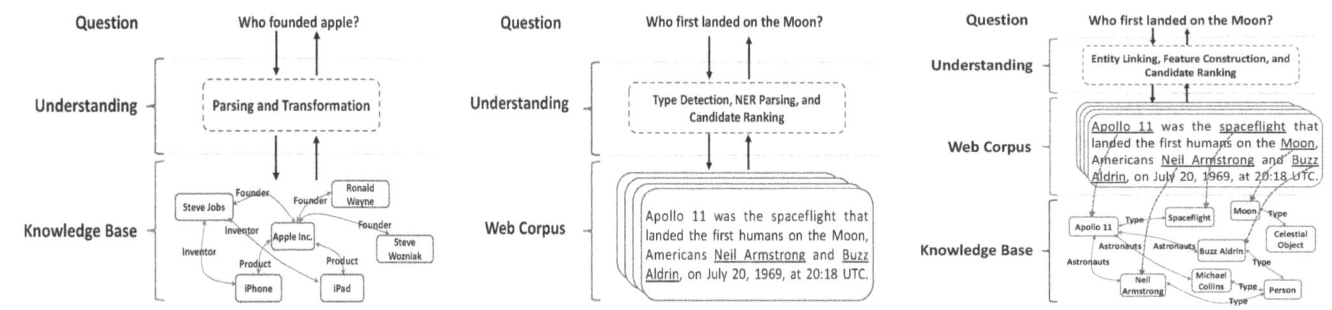

(a) KB-based QA Systems (b) Web-based QA Systems (c) Our Proposed QuASE

Figure 1: Process Diagrams of Different QA systems

Prior to the blossom of KBs, QA systems are generally viewed as a variation of information retrieval systems. This view can be exemplified by the TREC QA tracks [41], where each participant system is required to extract a small piece of text from a large collection of documents, as the answer to a natural language query. While most QA systems conduct sophisticated NLP analysis and try to integrate syntactic, semantic and pragmatic knowledge for achieving better performance (e.g., [22, 24]), systems like Mulder [26] and AskMSR [7] take a different path by leveraging the *crowd knowledge* from the Web. Without deep natural language analysis, such systems issue simple reformulations of the questions as queries to a search engine, and rank the repeatedly occurring N-grams in the top snippets as answers, based on named entity recognition (NER) [31] and heuristic answer type checking. Despite the simplicity of this strategy, the corpus-based QA systems, particularly, Web-based QA systems, are highly scalable and are among the top performing systems in TREC-10 [8]. A high-level view of such systems is illustrated in Figure 1(b).

One main weakness of such Web-based QA systems is its insufficient knowledge about the generated answer candidates. For instance, different mentions of the same entity such as "*President Obama*" and "*Barack Obama*" are viewed as different answer candidates, and will not be grouped together in most cases. Answer type checking, which verifies whether the type of an answer candidate matches the question, relies on a generic named entity recognition component that provides a small set of crude type labels. As a result, such systems are typically limited to answering questions in only a handful of categories.

To address this issue, we propose a new QA system framework, named **QuASE**, (i.e., question answering via semantic enrichment) in this work. Our system extends the traditional Web-based QA system by linking answer candidates in the search texts to a knowledge base. Figure 1(c) briefly illustrates how our system works, in contrast to the existing KB-based and Web-based QA systems respectively in Figure 1(a) and Figure 1(b). Specifically, given a question, QuASE first selects a set of most prominent sentences from web resources. Then from those sentences, we utilize entity linking tools [13] to detect answer candidates and link them to entities in Freebase. Once each answer candidate is mapped to the corresponding entity in Freebase, abundant information, such as their description texts and Freebase types, can be utilized for feature generation and modeling. A ranking algorithm is subsequently trained based on such features to rank correct answers as top choices.

By incorporating KBs as an important auxiliary in this manner, our system not only maintains the scalability of Web-based QA systems, but also will significantly enhance the QA performance: (1) Redundancy among answer candidates is automatically reduced. In the previous example, "*President Obama*" and "*Barack Obama*" shall be the same answer candidate, as both can be linked to the entity "*Barack Obama*" in Freebase; (2) Entity types stored in KBs can be naturally used to determine the types of an answer candidate. Freebase types vary at the thousands scale, allowing us to deal with more types of questions. (3) KBs contain a wealth of information about entities, which can be adopted for featuring answer candidates. Particularly, we utilize two kinds of information to develop semantic features: (a) description texts of an entity for evaluating whether an answer candidate contextually matches a question, and (b) Freebase entity types of an answer candidate for evaluating their type-matching degree with a question. Specifically, unlike existing QA systems, we build novel probabilistic models to directly evaluate the appropriateness of an answer candidate's Freebase types under a question, and treat the evaluation scores as features for downstream ranking.

Our main contributions in this work are three-fold:

(1) **New QA Framework** – We make the first attempt to incorporate entity linking in QA systems to ground answer candidates on entities in knowledge bases. Then we develop semantic features for each answer candidate based on their rich semantics in KBs, including entity description texts and types, when evaluating their possibility as true answers. Our proposed new architecture is very effective. Compared to existing QA systems, QuASE achieves an 18%$\sim$54% improvement in F_1 and 5% $\sim$ 20% in MRR, across different datasets.

(2) **Answer Type Checking Models** – In question answering, checking whether an answer candidate meets the expected answer types of a question is a crucial step. We develop two novel probabilistic models to directly evaluate the appropriateness of an answer candidate's types (available in KBs) given a question. To train the models, acquiring large-scale manually labeled data is generally very expensive; here, we propose a creative way to obtain labels from users' implicit behavioral data in query click logs. Our evaluations show that these two models can boost the QA performance by around 2% under all metrics. Combining these two models with other semantic features based on entity description texts, the performance can be boosted by 5%, indicating the advantages of leveraging rich semantics from KBs in question answering.

(3) **Extensive Experimental Evaluation** – In terms of testing data, we not only test our system on the well-known TREC dataset, which consists of well-formed questions, but also build a new testing question set, composed of free-form questions extracted from search engine query logs. Moreover, questions in this new dataset are from real online users instead of editors, which reflects more realistic information need than existing QA datasets. In addition to traditional Web-based QA systems, we also compare our system to the state-of-the-art KB-based QA systems. The results suggest that KB-based QA systems do not perform well, which coincides with our motivation that lots of knowledge is missing from current KBs. This observation also indicates the great importance of the Web-based QA system we are studying in this paper.

The rest of paper is organized as follows: we present our QA system framework in Section 2. Section 3 elaborates the features we have developed for ranking answer candidates. Two types of probabilistic models for extracting anwer-type related features are developed in Section 4 and 5. We conduct detailed experiments to verify the effectiveness of our system in Section 6. Section 7 reviews the related works. We finally conclude this work in Section 8.

2. METHODOLOGY

Figure 2 shows an end-to-end pipeline of our QA framework, which contains the following components in order: (1) Web Sentence Selection via Search Engine; (2) Answer Candidate Generation via Entity Linking; (3) Feature Generation and Ranking. We elaborate the details of each component as follows:

(1) **Web Sentence Selection via Search Engine**. Given a question, in order to find high-quality answer candidates, we design the following mechanism to retrieve highly relevant sentences from the Web that can potentially answer the question. We first submit the question as a query to a commercial search engine, and collect the top-50 returned snippets, as well as the top-50 documents. Since a query itself is generally short and contains only a few words, we compute the word count vector based on the returned snippets to represent the information for the query, denoted as w_q. For each sentence we parsed from the top-50 returned documents, we compute its word count vector w_s, and select those sentences with a high $\cos(w_s, w_q)$ into the high-quality sentence set. If the word vector w_s deviates far from w_q, the corresponding sentence can be regarded as irrelevant and thereby discarded.

(2) **Answer Candidate Generation via Entity Linking**. Once we obtain the sentence set, one of the state-of-the-art entity linking systems [13] is applied to identify answer candidates linked to Freebase. This system achieves the best scores at TAC-KBP 2013, by several novel designs such as postponing surface form boundary detections and discriminating concepts and entities in Wikipedia pages. Since the major target of this work is to verify that incorporating rich information from KBs will greatly boost the QA performance, we do not focus on constructing new entity linking tools in this paper. Moreover, for questions whose answers are not entities in Freebase, such as questions starting with "*when*", our system can be reduced to traditional Web-based QA systems without the auxiliary of KBs. In this paper, without loss of generality, we primarily focus on those questions targeted at certain entities in KBs.

(3) **Feature Generation and Ranking**. For each answer candidate, Freebase contains a wealth of information, such as their description texts and entity types. A set of semantic features shall be developed based on such rich information, and subsequently utilized in a ranking algorithm to evaluate the appropriateness of each candidate as the true answer.

Now we use an example to show how our system works. Given a question "*Who was the first American in space?*", we submit it to a search engine to return a set of relevant sentences {1. *On May 5, 1961, Shepard piloted the Freedom 7 mission...* ; 2. *Alan Shepard became the first American in space when the Freedom 7...*; ... }. On this sentence set, we apply entity linking to extract entities , such as *Freedom 7*, *Alan Shepard*, and *Sally Ride*, and link them to Freebase. Such linked entities are treated as answer candidates to the given question. For each answer candidate, semantic features are developed based on their rich information in Freebase, and subsequently integrated into a ranking algorithm, so that the true answer "*Alan Shepard*" will be ranked at the top of the candidate list.

Our QA system distinguishes itself from existing ones, in that it not only mines answers directly from the large-scale web resources, but also employs Freebase as a significant auxiliary to boost the performance. Freebase plays a significant role in both answer candidate generation and feature generation. As discussed in Section 1, by linking answer candidates to Freebase, our system is entitled with several unique advantages, such as reducing the redundancy among answer candidates and effortlessly granting answer candidates with Freebase entity types. Moreover, two kinds of rich information in KBs, entity description texts and entity types, will be naturally utilized to develop semantic features for downstream answer candidate ranking.

3. FEATURE DEVELOPMENT

Upon the generation of an answer candidate pool, effective features shall be developed in order to rank true answers as top choices. In this section, we elaborate the features developed for answer candidate ranking. Given a question, totally three categories of features are computed for each answer candidate. The features include both (1) non-semantic features: frequency that an answer candidate occurs in the retrieved sentence set, and (2) semantic features: Since we have linked each answer candidate to Freebase via entity linking, we are able to utilize their rich information in KBs to develop semantic features.

3.1 Count

The sentence set, returned by the sentence selection component, is considered quite related to the given question. The more frequent an answer candidate occurs in the sentence set, the more related it is to the question. Therefore, the *count* or *frequency* of each answer candidate serves as a significant indicator of being the correct answer or not. We compute the count of each answer candidate as one feature.

3.2 Textual Relevance

Given a question, the context where the true answer occurs and its descriptions in KBs should match the question. To evaluate the relevance of an answer candidate to a question, we first extract textual information from both the question side and the answer candidate side.

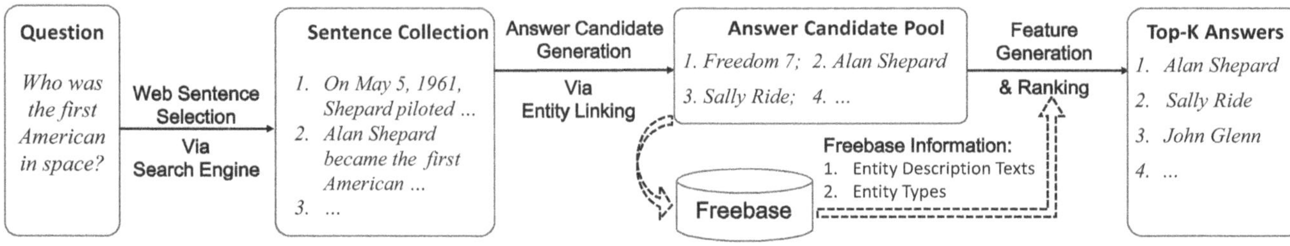

Figure 2: System Framework

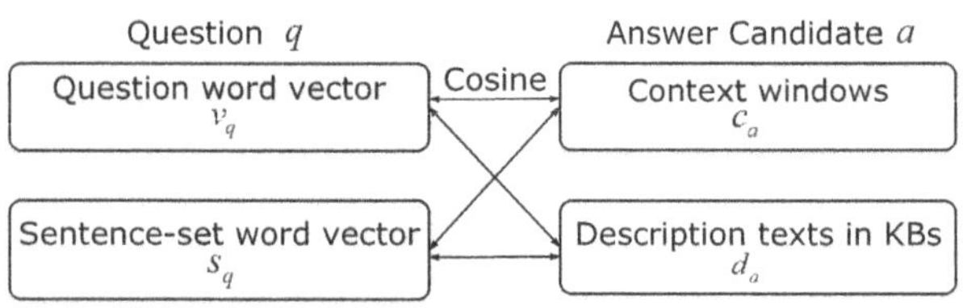

Figure 3: QA Textual Relevance Features

Textual Information on Question Side

(1) The set of words in question q;
(2) The relevant sentence set returned for question q.

Textual Information on Answer Candidate Side

(3) The context windows where an answer candidate a appears in retrieved sentences. Due to the general short length of a sentence, the size of a context window is set at 2, i.e., 2 words before and after answer candidate a compose the context where a occurs in a sentence. We collect all the context windows for each answer candidate in all the sentences.

(4) The description texts of answer candidate a in KBs. For example, Freebase describes entity "*Alan Shepard*", as "*Alan Bartlett 'Al' Shepard, Jr., was an American naval officer and aviator, test pilot, flag officer, one of the original NASA Mercury Seven astronauts ...*".

Based on the textual information for both questions and answer candidates, there can be many methods to measure the matching degree between a question and an answer candidate. We utilize a most intuitive method: For each piece of information (1) to (4), we compute the word frequency vector denoted as v_q, s_q, c_a, and d_a respectively. Then we apply cosine similarity measure between the textual information on the question side and that on the answer candidate side. As shown in Figure 3, we totally compute 4 features based on textual information for each <question, answer candidate> pair. Despite their simplicity, the features turn out to be very effective in improving QA performance. In fact, as future work, more complicated features can be developed and incorporated into our framework, such as deep semantic features learnt via deep learning [23].

3.3 Answer Type Related Features

Given a question "*the first American in space*", in the sentence set we selected, both the entity "*Alan Shepard*" (the astronaut) and the entity "*Freedom 7*" (the spaceflight) occur frequently. Both of them would be textually related to the question measured by features in Section 3.2. Therefore, the above count and textual relevance features turn out to be insufficient for such questions. However, by further checking the expected answer type of the question, it is obvious that the question is looking for a person instead of a spaceflight. Therefore, in order to find correct answers, there is a significant request for us to build answer-type related features, which evaluate the appropriateness of an answer candidate's types under a question.

There have been many works studying the expected answer types of a question [1, 27, 28, 33, 34, 35]. Directly applying their methodology to our setting is not trivial. First, previous type-prediction methods adopt a supervised learning methodology where they classify questions into a small set of types such as person and location. Such methods can hardly scale to thousands of entity types in Freebase, especially when the expected answer of a question is associated with multiple types in Freebase, e.g., entity "*Barack Obama*" associated with multiple types such as "*government.president*", "*people.person*", and "*celebrities.celebrity*". On the other hand, it is quite challenging, if not impossible, to build a mapping between the small set of types and an answer candidate's Freebase types, since Freebase contains thousands of fine-grained types while the types studied in previous methods are quite general and limited. In this paper, we directly handle thousands of Freebase types, and propose probabilistic models to directly measure the matching degree between a question and an answer candidate's Freebase types. The intuition behind such models is that words in a question should correlate with its answer types. Given a question q, we try to model the probability $P(t_a|q)$ or $P(q, t_a)$, where t_a is the set of Freebase types associated with answer candidate a. Answer candidate a with correct types should correspond to a higher $P(t_a|q)$ or $P(q, t_a)$. We will discuss two perspectives to model $P(t_a|q)$ and $P(q, t_a)$ respectively, and build our answer-type related features based on them. In Section 4, we first consider the type predictive power of a single word by modeling $P(t|w)$, where t is a single freebase type and w is a single word. Then different integration models based on $P(t|w)$ are explored, to predict $P(t_a|q)$. In Section 5, we simultaneously capture the joint associations among all the words in q and all the types in t_a, by building a unified generative model for $P(q, t_a)$.

4. WORD TO ANSWER TYPE MODEL

Now we first model the type predictive power of a single word, and then explore different models to integrate the

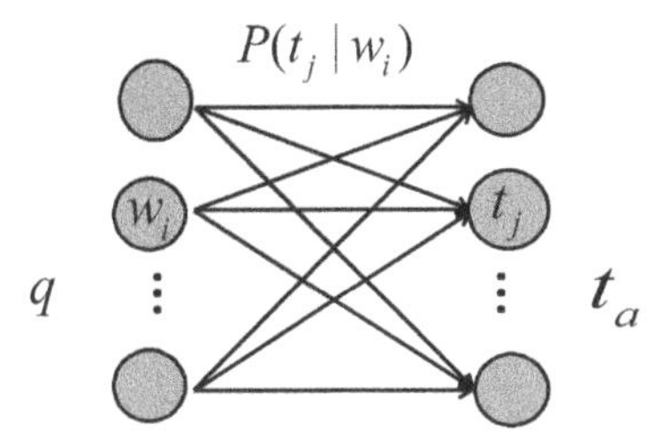

Figure 4: Word to Answer Type (WAT) Model

predictive power of each word in a question. To emphasize the separate consideration of each word in the first step, the underlying methods are named *word to answer type* (WAT) models.

In WAT, we define $P(t|w)$ as the conditional probability of observing Freebase type t as one answer type, if word w occurs in the question. To learn $P(t|w)$, we rely on a training set of questions, each of which is paired with its expected answer types. We will give more details on such training sets in our experiments. Given such a training set, we model $P(t|w)$ as follows:

$$P(t|w) = \frac{\#(w,t)}{\sum_t \#(w,t)} \tag{1}$$

where $\#(w,t)$ represents the co-occurrence frequency of word w and type t in the <question, answer types> pairs. The more frequently a type t co-occurs with a word w, the more likely the answer contains type t, if word w is in the question.

Given a question q with a set of words $\{w_i\}$ and answer candidate a with a set of Freebase types $t_a = \{t_j\}$, Figure 4 shows the point-wise word-to-type conditional probability, between the word set in q and the type set of a. Based on this point-wise conditional probability, the probability $P(t_a|q)$, can be estimated using the following different models.

1. Best Word-to-Type: Choose the highest point-wise conditional probability as $P(t_a|q)$.

$$P(t_a|q) = \max_{w_i \in q, t_j \in t_a} P(t_j|w_i) \tag{2}$$

2. Pivot Word: Choose the word in q that generates the highest productive conditional probability for all the types in t_a

$$P(t_a|q) = \max_{w_i \in q} \prod_{t_j \in t_a} P(t_j|w_i) \tag{3}$$

3. Pivot Word-to-Type: Choose the best set of point-wise conditional probabilities that generate the highest productive conditional probability for all the types in t_a.

$$P(t_a|q) = \prod_{t_j \in t_a} \max_{w_i \in q} P(t_j|w_i) \tag{4}$$

Now we define the WAT feature for answer candidate a based on the perplexity [5] of its type set t_a as:

$$\text{Perplexity}(t_a) = \exp\left(-\frac{\log(P(t_a|q))}{|t_a|}\right) \tag{5}$$

Where $|t_a|$ is the number of types in t_a. For Best Word-To-Type, since only one type is considered in the calculation, $|t_a| = 1$.

Perplexity has been applied for the evaluation of different topic models such as LDA [5], whereas in our work we use it as a matching measure between an answer candidate's Freebase types and words in a question. WAT model works based on the assumption that words in a question are predictive of the expected answer types. Based on golden pairs of questions and their expected answer types, we extract the distribution pattern of different types given a specific word in a question. For a new question and one answer candidate, if the answer candidate's types are expected, they should be better explained under the WAT models, i.e., associated with a higher $P(t_a|q)$, than otherwise. Correspondingly, WAT features for answer candidates with expected types should be lower than those with unmatched types. Overall three WAT features can be extracted, with $P(t_a|q)$ respectively instantiated by one of the three proposed models.

5. JOINT <QUESTION, ANSWER TYPE> ASSOCIATION

In this section, we consider the question "How likely can we observe a question and an entity with certain Freebase types, as a question-answer pair?" Different from WAT, we consider the predictive power of all the words simultaneously in a question. Given a question-answer pair, where answer a is associated with multiple Freebase types t_a, we build a generative model of the joint likelihood $P(q, t_a)$, to measure the matching of t_a with the question.

We assume the observation of a question q and its associated answer types t_a, can be explained by latent association patterns. One of such latent associations might be, words such as "*city*", "*place*", "*where*" will occur frequently in a question, if the expected answer type of the question is "*location*" in Freebase. The interplay of multiple latent associations can be captured by a generative model, named joint <question, answer type> association (JQA) model. Figure 5 shows the graphical representation of our generative model for JQA. We first clarify the notations in the figure as follows: (1) $\mathcal{D}$ is the set of <question, answer types> pairs while $|\mathcal{D}|$ denotes the set size. A plate means replicating a process for multiple times. (2) θ_i is the $K \times 1$ mixture weights of K latent association patterns, for the i-th <question, answer types> pair. (3) α, a $K \times 1$ vector, is parameters in a Dirichlet prior, and serves as a constraint of the mixture weights θ_i's. A Dirichlet prior for the mixture weights tends to alleviate over-fitting problems [5]. (4) Z_i is the hidden pattern label that can explain the joint observation of the current question and its answer types. Here we assume all the words in q and types in t_a are generated from the same latent association, since the number of words in a question, together with its associated types, is usually very small. (5) q^i and t_a^i respectively refer to the i-th question and its answer types. (6) β^Q, a $K \times |V^Q|$ matrix, defines the probability distribution over the word vocabulary V^Q, under K hidden patterns. β^T, a $K \times |V^T|$ matrix, defines the probability distribution over the Freebase type vocabulary V^T, under K hidden patterns. (7) The shaded variable w indicates one word observed in q^i while t represents one type in t_a^i.

Figure 5 conveys the generative process of a question and its answer types under multiple latent associations. Now we formally describe the generative process as follows:

For the i-th <question, answer types> pair in $\mathcal{D}$,

- Draw the mixture weights of K hidden association patterns: $\theta_i \sim \mathbf{Dir}(\alpha)$.

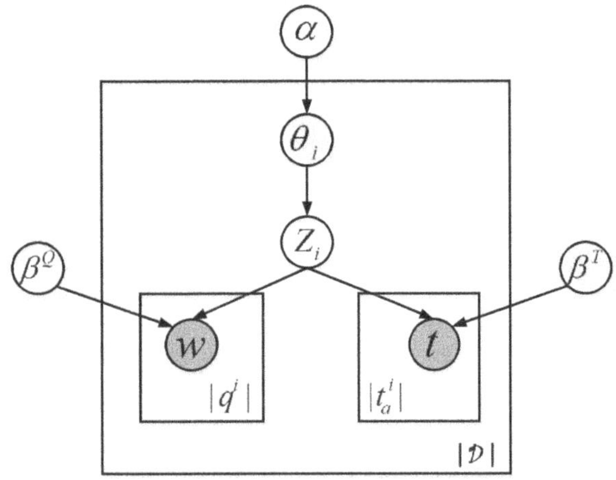

Figure 5: JQA Generative Model

– Draw a pattern label: $Z_i \sim \textbf{Mult}(\theta_i)$.
  * Draw a word for the question q^i from V^Q: $w \sim \beta^Q_{Z_i,:}$.
  * Draw a type for the answer a^i from V^T: $t \sim \beta^T_{Z_i,:}$.

We formulate the likelihood of observing all the question and its associated answer types as follows:

$$\begin{aligned}\mathcal{L} &= \prod_{i\in\mathcal{D}} P(q^i, t^i_a|\alpha, \beta^Q, \beta^T) \\ &= \prod_{i\in\mathcal{D}} \int_{\theta_i} P(\theta_i|\alpha)P(q^i, t^i_a|\theta_i, \beta^Q, \beta^T)\, d\theta_i\end{aligned} \tag{6}$$

Here,

$$\begin{aligned}&P(q^i, t^i_a|\theta_i, \beta^Q, \beta^T) \\ &= \sum_{Z_i} P(Z_i|\theta_i) \prod_{w\in q^i} P(w|Z_i, \beta^Q) \prod_{t\in t^i_a} P(t|Z_i, \beta^T)\end{aligned} \tag{7}$$

Finally, we resort to the maximum likelihood estimation approach to optimize the parameters in the model:

$$\arg\max_{\alpha,\beta^Q,\beta^T} \log\mathcal{L} \tag{8}$$

5.1 Model Solution

5.1.1 Variational Inference

Due to the interdependence of the latent variables, their true posterior distributions are computationally intractable. We introduce a variational distribution Q [4] in which the latent variables are independent of each other to approximate their true posterior distribution, *i.e.*, $Q(\theta, Z) = Q(\theta)Q(Z)$, where $\theta = \{\theta_i, \forall i \in \mathcal{D}\}$ and $Z = \{Z_i, \forall i \in \mathcal{D}\}$. According to the variational distribution, $Q(\theta_i) \sim \textbf{Dir}(\gamma_i)$, $Q(Z_i) \sim \textbf{Mult}(\phi_i)$, where γ_i and ϕ_i are $K \times 1$ variational parameters.

Instead of directly maximizing $\mathcal{L}$ which is intractable, we can maximize the lower bound of the log likelihood under the variational distribution and Jensen's inequality:

$$\log\mathcal{L} \geq E_Q \log P(\mathcal{D}, \theta, Z|\alpha, \beta^T, \beta^Q) + H(Q) = \lfloor\log\mathcal{L}\rfloor \tag{9}$$

where $\mathcal{D}$ denotes all the questions and their associated answer types. We expand the lower bound of the log likelihood as follows:

$$\begin{aligned}\lfloor\log\mathcal{L}\rfloor = &\sum_{i\in\mathcal{D}} E_Q \log P(\theta_i|\alpha) + \sum_{i\in\mathcal{D}} E_Q \log P(Z_i|\theta_i) \\ &+ \sum_{i\in\mathcal{D}} E_Q \log P(w \in q^i, t \in t^i_a|Z_i, \beta^Q, \beta^T) \\ &+ H(Q(\theta, Z))\end{aligned} \tag{10}$$

Each term on the right-hand side of the above equation, is a function over the model parameters as shown in Eqn. 11 to Eqn. 14.

$$\begin{aligned}&\sum_{i\in\mathcal{D}} E_Q \log P(\theta_i|\alpha) \\ &= -|\mathcal{D}| \cdot B(\alpha) + \sum_{i\in\mathcal{D}}\sum_k (\alpha_k - 1)[\psi(\gamma_{i,k}) - \psi(\sum_k \gamma_{i,k})]\end{aligned} \tag{11}$$

where $B(\alpha) = \frac{\prod_k \Gamma(\alpha_k)}{\Gamma(\sum_k \alpha_k)}$ is the normalization constant of the Dirichlet distribution $\textbf{Dir}(\alpha)$.

$$\sum_{\mathcal{D}} E_Q \log P(Z_i|\theta_i) = \sum_{i\in\mathcal{D}}\sum_k \phi_{i,k}[\psi(\gamma_{i,k}) - \psi(\sum_k \gamma_{i,k})] \tag{12}$$

The third term

$$\begin{aligned}&\sum_{i\in\mathcal{D}} E_Q \log P(w \in q^i, t \in t^i_a|Z_i, \beta^Q, \beta^T) \\ &= \sum_{i\in\mathcal{D}}\sum_k \phi_{ik}(\sum_{w\in q^i} N^{q^i}_w \log\beta^Q_{k,w} + \sum_{t\in t^i_a} \log\beta^T_{k,t})\end{aligned} \tag{13}$$

where $N^{q^i}_w$ is the frequency of word w in question q^i. The entropy term

$$\begin{aligned}&H(Q(\theta, Z)) \\ &= -\sum_{i\in\mathcal{D}} E_Q \log Q(\theta_i|\gamma_i) + \sum_{i\in\mathcal{D}} E_Q \log Q(Z_i|\phi_i) \\ &= \sum_{i\in\mathcal{D}}[\log B(\gamma_i) - \sum_k(\gamma_{i,k} - 1)(\psi(\gamma_{i,k}) - \psi(\sum_k \gamma_{i,k}))] \\ &- \sum_{i\in\mathcal{D}}\sum_k \phi_{ik}\log\phi_{ik}\end{aligned} \tag{14}$$

5.1.2 Parameter Estimation

The model parameters are estimated by using the variational expectation-maximization (EM) algorithm. In E-step, we update the variational parameters $\{\gamma\text{'s}, \phi\text{'s}\}$ while in M-step, we update the model parameters α, β^Q, and β^T so that $\lfloor\log\mathcal{L}\rfloor$ is maximized.

Specifically, E-step updates the variational parameters according to Eqn. 15 and 16.

$$\begin{aligned}\phi_{i,k} \sim \exp(&\sum_{w\in q^i} N^{q^i}_w \log\beta^Q_{k,w} + \sum_{t\in t^i_a} \log\beta^T_{k,t} \\ &+ \psi(\gamma_{i,k}) - \psi(\sum_k \gamma_{i,k}) - 1)\end{aligned} \tag{15}$$

$$\gamma_{i,k} = \alpha_k + \phi_{i,k} \tag{16}$$

During M-step, we maximize the lower bound over the parameter α, β^Q, and β^T, by utilizing the classic L-BFGS optimization algorithm [29]. The derivatives over the parameter α are calculated in Eqn. 17.

$$\frac{\partial \lfloor \log \mathcal{L} \rfloor}{\partial \alpha_k} = |\mathcal{D}|[-\psi(\alpha_k) + \psi(\sum_k \alpha_k)] + \sum_{i \in \mathcal{D}} [\psi(\gamma_{i,k}) - \psi(\sum_k \gamma_{i,k})] \tag{17}$$

We solve β^Q and β^T by $\beta^Q_{k,w} \propto \sum_{i \in \mathcal{D}} \phi_{i,k} N^{q^i}_w$ and $\beta^T_{k,t} \propto \sum_{i \in \mathcal{D}} \phi_{i,k}$.

We conduct E-step and M-step iteratively until the algorithm converges, indicating the current model parameters fit the observed training data.

5.2 JQA Feature Extraction

Now we discuss how to apply the learnt JQA model to evaluate the appropriateness of an answer candidate's types *w.r.t* a given question. Given a new question q_{new} and an answer candidate a_{new} with types $t_{a_{\text{new}}}$, we evaluate $P(q_{\text{new}}, t_{a_{\text{new}}} | \alpha, \beta^Q, \beta^T)$ using Eqn. 10. A standard inference procedure is employed to a new <question, answer types> pair [5]: α, β^Q, β^T are fixed as learnt from training data while variational parameters γ and ϕ are specifically estimated for the new pair according to Eqn. 15 and 16.

Similar to WAT, perplexity of observing question q_{new} and answer types $t_{a_{\text{new}}}$ is defined as:

$$\text{Perplexity}(q_{\text{new}}, t_{a_{\text{new}}}) = \exp(-\frac{\log(P(q_{\text{new}}, t_{a_{\text{new}}} | \alpha, \beta^Q, \beta^T))}{|q_{\text{new}}| + |t_{a_{\text{new}}}|})$$

This perplexity is named JQA feature for answer candidate ranking. The rationale behind JQA is similar to WAT. JQA assumes words in a question are associated with its expected answer types. We try to capture such associations by training JQA on golden pairs of questions and their expected answer types.

6. EXPERIMENTS

In this section, we are interested in evaluating QuASE in terms of the following aspects: (1) How do different feature combinations affect QuASE's performance? (2) How does QuASE compare to the state-of-the-art question answering systems? (3) What are the advantages of incorporating rich semantics in KBs into Web-based QA systems? (4) What are the advantages of our answer-type related features JQA and WAT? We further provide a detailed error analysis of different QA systems on questions they fail to answer.

6.1 Experimental Setup

QA Evaluation Datasets

We evaluate different question answering systems on two datasets: TREC questions and Bing queries. Table 1 shows statistics and example questions from each set.

TREC. The Text REtrieval Conference (TREC) had a QA track [41] since 1999. In the competition, editors first prepared some questions, and each participant system then finds answers from a big collection of news articles. TREC data have been publicly available, and become popular benchmarks for evaluating QA systems. We used factoid questions from TREC 8-12 as the TREC dataset in this work. Example questions are listed in Table 1. For questions to which answers are not entities in KBs, such as those starting with "*when*", QuASE can be reduced to traditional Web-based QA systems without incorporating KBs. Without loss of generality, we thus eliminate those questions from the original dataset. Among the remaining 1902 questions, 202 questions from TREC 12 are used for testing and 1700 from TREC 8-11 for training. Although answers to these questions are provided by TREC, they are incomplete or sometimes incorrect for two reasons. First, the provided answers were detected from the given corpus. It is possible that some correct answers do not occur in the corpus, and therefore not included. Second, the correct answers to some questions may have changed, such as "*Who is the prime minister of France?*". In order to have a fair evaluation, the answers were revised using Amazon MTurk (see [39] for detail).

Datasets	Example Questions
TREC	What are pennies made of?
1700 training	What is the tallest building in Japan?
202 testing	Who sang "Tennessee Waltz"?
Bing query	the highest flying bird
4725 training	indiana jones named after
1164 testing	designer of the golden gate bridge

Table 1: Two Question Sets in Our Experiments

Bing query. Although roughly 10% of the queries submitted to a search engine are with specific informational intent, only one fifth of them are formulated as well-formed questions (e.g., lack of Wh-words) [43]. Bing query dataset in Table 1 shows several such examples. We created Bing query dataset by selecting queries from Bing users: queries are not well-formed questions, but targeted at certain entities in Freebase. Questions in this dataset are from real search engine users and reflect more realistic information need than existing QA benchmark datasets. We crowd-sourced each question to at least three experienced human labelers for collecting correct entity answers in Freebase. Once all the labelers reach an agreement on the correct answers, we save the question paired with the correct answers. In the end, we gathered approximately 6000 question-answer pairs in total, from which we randomly select around 20% for testing and 80% for training.

Training Dataset for JQA and WAT

To train JQA and WAT proposed in Section 4 and 5, a sufficiently large training dataset with golden <question, answer types> pairs is indispensable. In reality, we do not have purified data available for training. Instead, we adopt a novel alternative way to obtain labels by joining users' implicit behavioral data in query click logs and the Freebase data. Specifically, we can obtain the <query, clicked url> pairs from the query click logs. Moreover, each entity in Freebase is also linked to some urls that are related to this entity (mostly Wikipedia pages or official web sites of this entity). Hence once a user issued a query and clicked on an entity related url, we can form a <question, answer types> pair: The question is the query given by the user, while we use the Freebase types of the entity corresponding to the clicked url as the answer types. Although such collected dataset is noisy in the sense that the clicked url might not be what the user truly look for, we will show that useful answer-type related features can still be learnt from the large amount of data to benefit the ultimate QA performance. Overall we collect a dataset of around **1.3 million** <question, answer types> pairs based on Bing query logs. We also tried directly using the training portion of each dataset in Table 1 to train the models. However, the training portions contain too limited questions, and features learnt from them can not perform as well as those learnt from the big query log dataset.

Answer Candidate Ranking

For each input question, our question answering pipeline produces an answer candidate pool. To rank these candidates, we first extract all the features discussed in Section 3 $\sim$ Section 5, and map an answer candidate to a feature vector representation *w.r.t* the question. Our ranker then assigns a score to each feature vector and orders the answer candidates accordingly. In our experiments, we use an inhouse fast implementation of the MART gradient boosting decision tree algorithm [9, 21] to learn our ranker using the training set of our data. This algorithm learns an ensemble of regression trees and has shown great performance in various search ranking tasks [10].

Evaluation Measures

We compare different QA systems on each dataset using the following metrics:

(1) Precision, Recall & F_1: As in [18], we treat the top ranked answer candidate as the answer returned to a question. Notice that because the answer candidate pool might be empty, it is possible that no answer is returned by a QA system. As usual, precision and recall are defined as #(*correct answers*)/#(*questions with answers returned*) and #(*correct answers*)/#*questions*. We also compute the F_1 score, which is the harmonic mean of precision and recall.

(2) Mean Reciprocal Rank (MRR). Given a question, Reciprocal Rank (RR) is the reciprocal of the highest ranking position of a correct answer [36]. MRR is the average of the reciprocal ranks over questions:

$$\text{MRR} = \frac{1}{N}\sum_{i=1}^{N}\frac{1}{r_i}, \tag{18}$$

where N is the number of questions and r_i is the highest ranking position of an answer to question i. If the true answer to a question is not detected, the RR for the question is 0.

Alternative QA systems

We compare QuASE with existing Web-based and KB-based QA systems. Due to unavailability of most existing QA systems, we select one representative from each category to compare.

(1) Web-based QA system: AskMSR+ [39]. As mentioned briefly in Section 1, early Web-based systems like Mulder [26] and AskMSR [7] have demonstrated that by leveraging the data redundancy in the Web, a simple system can be very competitive and outperform systems conducting sophisticated linguistic analysis of either questions or answer candidates[1]. We compare QuASE with AskMSR+ [39], an advanced version of AskMSR with two main changes. First, instead of reformulating a question according to some statement-like patterns as query terms to a search engine, AskMSR+ issues the question directly, as [39] found out that question reformulation no longer helps retrieve high-quality snippets. This may be due to the better performance of modern search engines, as well as the increased coverage of various community QA sites. Second, instead of using only N-grams extracted from snippets as answer candidates, AskMSR+ requires candidates to be specific types of named entities that can match the question. For instance, only a location entity can be a candidate to the "*where*" questions. With these design changes and other enhancements detailed in [39], AskMSR+ increases MRR by roughly 25% on the TREC dataset, compared to the original AskMSR system, and is thus a solid baseline.

(2) KB-based QA system: Sempre[2, 3]. Sempre[2] and ParaSempre[3] develop semantic parsers to parse natural language questions to logical forms, which are subsequently executed against knowledge bases. They have shown great performance for questions that are directly coined based on relation tuples in KBs. Here we test them on questions that are not necessarily answerable in KBs. The implementation of their systems is publicly available[2], as well as the pretrained systems. We applied the pre-trained systems to our evaluation datasets, and also re-trained the systems on our training datasets. We finally show the best performance we could obtain by these two systems.

6.2 Experimental Results

Results of different feature combinations in QuASE are summarized in Table 2. We have made the following observations: (1) As we discussed in Section 3.1, Count is a significant indicator of the true answer to a question. Although the simplest feature, it performs the best compared with other separated features. Such observation is consistent with the conclusion in [7] that based on data redundancy, simple techniques without complicated linguistic analyses can work well in QA systems. (2) Combined with the Textual Relevance (TR) features, Count+TR can further boost the performance by around 3% under F_1 and MRR, on both datasets. TR can be effective when some wrong answer candidates appear very frequently but their context information does not match the question. For example, given a question "*Who first landed on the moon?*", entity "*American*", which is the nationality of the astronaut, occurs quite frequently in the retrieved texts. However, the textual information related to "*American*" in Freebase can distinguish itself from the true answer, as its description is about American people, rather than people first landing on the moon. (3) Comparing Count+TR+WAT+JQA with Count+TR, our answer-type related features WAT and JQA turn out to be effective: they further improve the performance by around 2% on TREC and by 2% $\sim$ 5% on Bing query across all the metrics. (4) The advantages of incorporating rich semantics in KBs into QuASE can be observed by comparing Count+TR+WAT+JQA with Count+$\text{TR}^{-\text{KBs}}$, where $\text{TR}^{-\text{KBs}}$ denote the two textual relevance features without involving entity description texts from KBs, , i.e., $\cos(v_q, c_a) + \cos(s_q, c_a)$ in Figure 3. With around 5% improvements on both datasets, utilizing rich semantics in KBs can obviously benefit the QA performance.

Table 3 shows the performance of three QA systems. Compared with AskMSR+ system, which also utilized the count of an answer candidate for ranking, the single feature Count in QuASE, as shown in Table 2, performs better by at least 10% in terms of F_1. The potential reason is that through linking answer candidates to KBs, same answer candidates

[1]For instance, AskMSR is one of the top systems in TREC-10 [8].

[2]https://github.com/percyliang/sempre

	Bing query				TREC			
Features in QuASE	Precision	Recall	F_1	MRR	Precision	Recall	F_1	MRR
Count	0.5513	0.5262	0.5384	0.6111	0.5446	0.5446	0.5446	0.6224
TR	0.5243	0.5004	0.5121	0.5880	0.4554	0.4554	0.4554	0.5740
JQA	0.1358	0.1296	0.1326	0.2737	0.1980	0.1980	0.1980	0.3579
WAT	0.1709	0.1631	0.1669	0.3100	0.2624	0.2624	0.2624	0.4049
Count+TR	0.5674	0.5416	0.5512	0.6239	0.5644	0.5644	0.5644	0.6425
Count+TR+WAT	0.5926	0.5657	0.5788	0.6370	0.5693	0.5693	0.5693	0.6513
Count+TR+JQA	0.5764	0.5502	0.5630	0.6296	0.5743	0.5743	0.5743	0.6476
Count+TR+WAT+JQA	**0.5962**	**0.5691**	**0.5823**	**0.6402**	**0.5792**	**0.5792**	**0.5792**	**0.6532**
Count+TR^{-KBs}	0.5638	0.5382	0.5507	0.6187	0.5495	0.5495	0.5495	0.6281

Table 2: Comparison among Different Feature Combinations in QuASE

	Bing query				TREC			
QA Systems	Precision	Recall	F_1	MRR	Precision	Recall	F_1	MRR
QuASE	**0.5962**	**0.5691**	**0.5823**	**0.6402**	**0.5792**	**0.5792**	**0.5792**	**0.6532**
AskMSR+ [39]	0.3782	0.3760	0.3771	0.5337	0.4925	0.4901	0.4913	0.6223
Sempre [2, 3]	0.2646	01940	0.2239	0.2372	0.1567	0.1040	0.1250	0.1437

Table 3: Comparison among Different QA Systems

with different surface forms can be automatically merged, and therefore, redundancy and noise among answer candidates can be significantly reduced. On Bing query, QuASE with all the features can obtain around **54%** improvement on F_1 and **20%** improvement under MRR, while on TREC, it can achieve about **18%** improvement under F_1 and **5%** improvement under MRR. The great improvement further verifies the advantages of employing KBs as an auxiliary into Web-based QA systems. The improvement on F_1 measure is generally higher. MRR takes into account the entire candidate list while F_1 focuses on the first ranking position, implying AskMSR+ has a poor ability to rank the true answer at the top position. We will give more detailed analysis on QuASE and AskMSR+ in Section 6.3. Sempre systems formulate a question into logical forms to be executed against KBs. They are among the state-of-the-art KB-based QA systems on questions that are guaranteed answerable in KBs. However as shown in Table 2, the performance of Sempre is generally much lower than our system under all the measures. Similar performance of Sempre on TREC has also been reported in [18]. There are potentially two reasons why Sempre systems cannot perform well on Bing query and TREC dataset. First, the knowledge required to answer questions might not exist in KBs. For example, given one example question in TREC "*What color is indigo?*", there is no relationship between the true answer "*blue*" and "*indigo*" corresponding to "*alias*" or "*synonym*" although both entities "*blue*" and "*indigo*" exist in Freebase. Second, many questions, especially those not well-formed ones in Bing query, are generally hard to be transformed to logical forms and thereby unsuccessful to obtain answers by executing logical forms against KBs. Since Sempre turns out to be much less effective on both datasets, we will not include it in the following experiments.

To examine the sensitivity of the parameter K in JQA, we conducted 5-fold cross validation on each training set. Figure 6 shows that MRR does not vary too much as we vary K in JQA. The cross-validation result under F_1 observes a similar pattern, which is omitted here due to space constraints. Since larger K implies more numerical computations and larger complexities, we fixed $K = 3$ in all of our experiments.

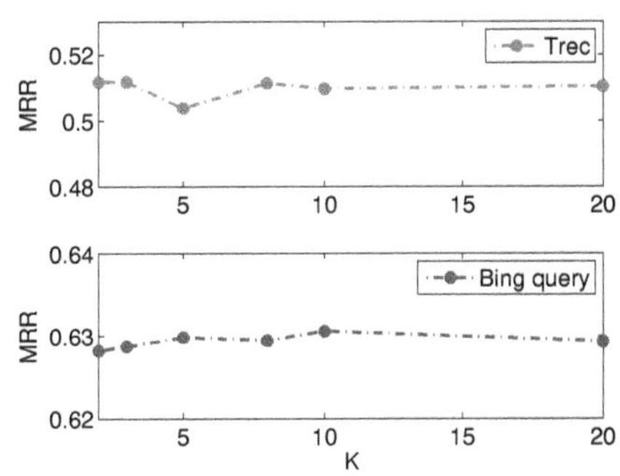

Figure 6: Cross Validation of Different K

6.3 System Comparison on Failed Questions

In this section, we provide detailed analysis of QuASE and AskMSR+ on their respective failed questions. We first define the failed questions for each system: AskMSR+'s failed questions are those where AskMSR+ ranks the true answer lower than QuASE, whereas QuASE's failed questions as those where QuASE ranks the true answer lower than AskMSR+. If there are multiple answers to a question, we consider the highest-ranked answer in defining failed questions.

Table 4 shows the rank distribution of the true answer given by each system on their failed questions. $r = \infty$ means the true answer is not in the candidate list. For those questions where QuASE performs worse than AskMSR+, in most cases, we do not have the answer in the candidate list, i.e., $r = \infty$. However, for those AskMSR+ performs worse, in most cases, AskMSR+ did find the true answer, but ranks it lower than QuASE. This result verifies that compared with AskMSR+, features in QuASE for ranking are effective as long as true answers are in the candidate list.

The distribution of QuASE's rank on failed questions					
Dataset	$r=\infty$	r=2	r=3	r=4	$r \geq 5$
Bing	**63.76%**	12.86%	7.62%	2.86%	11.90%
Trec	**53.57%**	14.29%	12.50%	3.57%	16.07%
The distribution of AskMSR+'s rank on failed questions					
Dataset	$r=\infty$	r=2	r=3	$r=4$	$r \geq 5$
Bing	13.82%	**27.88%**	21.66%	11.75%	**24.88%**
Trec	19.64%	**35.71%**	14.29%	10.71%	**19.64%**

Table 4: Error Analysis of QuASE and AskMSR+

Due to the imperfectness of any answer candidate generation technique, including entity linking or named entity detection, true answers to many questions might not be detected and included in the candidate list. Therefore, no matter how effective a ranking feature is, the performance on questions without true answers in the candidate list, cannot be boosted. For each method, we define the answerable question set as those questions with true answers included in their candidate list. Table 5 shows the performance of QuASE and AskMSR+ on their respective answerable question sets. Although the answerable questions by QuASE are slightly fewer than those by AskMSR+ system, the performance of QuASE is significantly better than AskMSR+ with a **17% ∼ 38%** improvement on MRR and a **31% ∼ 74%** improvement on F_1. For QuASE, how to improve entity linking performance, in order to include true answers in the candidate list, can be important to further improve QA performance. However the study of that problem is beyond the scope of this paper and we leave it as future work.

	Bing AQS		
Systems	MRR	F_1	|AQS|
QuASE	**0.8583**	**0.7629**	869
AskMSR+ [39]	0.6230	0.4388	998
	Trec AQS		
QuASE	**0.8195**	**0.7267**	161
AskMSR+ [39]	0.7023	0.5530	179

Table 5: Results on Answerable Question Sets

7. RELATED WORK

Our work is mainly related to previous studies in three categories: (1) KB-based QA systems; (2) Web-based QA systems; (3) Answer type prediction.

KB-based QA systems. The advances of large-scale knowledge bases (KBs) have enabled numerous QA systems to directly query KBs. Examples of the most recent KB-based QA systems include [2, 3, 18, 17, 40, 44, 45, 46]. Apart from [2, 3, 18, 17] discussed in Section 1, Unger et al. [40] relies on parsing a question to produce a SPARQL template, which mirrors the internal structure of the question. This template is then instantiated using statistical entity identification and predicate detection. Similarly, Yahya et al. [44] presents a methodology for translating natural language questions into structured SPARQL queries based on an integer linear program. Zou et al. [46] propose to represent a natural language question using a semantic graph query to be matched with a subgraph in KBs and reduce question answering to a subgraph matching problem. Yao et al. [45] proposes to associate questions patterns with answer patterns described by Freebase with the help of a web-scale corpus. Different from such KB-based QA systems, we take an alternative path to question answering by mining answers directly from the rich web corpus, instead of querying either curated KBs such as Freebase or extracted KBs from the Web as in [45].

Web-based QA systems. Prior to the availability and popularity of knowledge bases, most of early QA systems such as [7, 12, 25, 20, 37, 41], mine answers from TREC [41] document collections or the rich web corpus. Brill et al. [7] constructed the AskMSR QA system by utilizing the rich web resources. In [25], Ko et al. focus on a general model to estimate the correctness of answer candidates, instead of developing an entire QA system. Ferrucci et al. [20] gives an overview of IBM Watson system framework including question analysis, search, hypothesis generation, and hypothesis scoring. Most of existing web-based QA systems detect answer candidates via exploring N-grams or named entity recognition. However, we advocate linking answer candidates to Freebase via entity linking, which induces several remarkable advantages. Our system can be regarded as a fundamental and expandable QA system with the new concept to incorporate rich information in KBs into Web-based QA systems.

Answer Type Prediction. In our QA system, we develop features that evaluate the appropriateness of an answer candidate's types under a question. Previous works such as [1, 11, 27, 28, 30, 33, 34, 35] on predicting the expected answer types of a question are related. In [28], Li et al. classify questions into a hierarchy of classes. Question analysis and answer type validation in Watson QA system are detailed in [27, 33]. [34] utilizes WordNet [19] as the answer type taxonomy to do question classification while [1] addresses automatically annotating queries with target types from the DBpedia ontology. [30] develop answer type related features by finding what matters in a question. Researchers in [11, 35] model the answer types as latent variables to avoid the requirement of the predefined type taxonomies. Such methods simultaneously capture the "clustering" information of questions and model the answer relevance conditioned on latent variables. The significant differences between our models for answer-type related features and previous methods have been discussed in Section 3.3. Overall we directly work with thousands of freebase types and propose probabilistic models to measure the matching degree between a question and the Freebase types of an answer candidate.

8. CONCLUSION AND FUTURE WORK

In this paper, we develop a novel Web-based question answering framework with KBs as a significant auxiliary. Driven by the incompleteness problem of KBs, our system directly mines answers from the Web and shows great advantages on questions not necessarily answerable by KBs. Unlike existing Web-based QA systems, our system links answer candidates to KBs during answer candidate generation, after which, rich semantics of entities, such as their description texts and entity types in KBs, are utilized to develop effective features for downstream answer candidate ranking. Compared with various QA systems, our system framework has achieved an 18%∼54% improvement under F_1. As future work, other information reserved in KBs such as various relationships among entities, can also be explored as semantic features to be incorporated in our system.

9. REFERENCES

[1] K. Balog and R. Neumayer. Hierarchical target type identification for entity-oriented queries. In *CIKM*, pages 2391–2394. ACM, 2012.

[2] J. Berant, A. Chou, R. Frostig, and P. Liang. Semantic parsing on Freebase from question-answer pairs. In *EMNLP*, pages 1533–1544, 2013.

[3] J. Berant and P. Liang. Semantic parsing via paraphrasing. In *ACL*, 2014.

[4] C. Bishop et al. *Pattern recognition and machine learning*, volume 1. springer New York, 2006.

[5] D. Blei, A. Ng, and M. Jordan. Latent dirichlet allocation. *JMLR*, 3:993–1022, 2003.

[6] K. Bollacker, C. Evans, P. Paritosh, T. Sturge, and J. Taylor. Freebase: a collaboratively created graph database for structuring human knowledge. In *SIGMOD*, pages 1247–1250. ACM, 2008.

[7] E. Brill, S. Dumais, and M. Banko. An analysis of the AskMSR question-answering system. In *EMNLP*, pages 257–264, 2002.

[8] E. Brill, J. J. Lin, M. Banko, S. T. Dumais, and A. Y. Ng. Data-intensive question answering. In *TREC*, 2001.

[9] C. Burges. From RankNet to LambdaRank to LambdaMART: An overview. *Learning*, 11:23–581, 2010.

[10] C. Burges, K. M. Svore, P. N. Bennett, A. Pastusiak, and Q. Wu. Learning to rank using an ensemble of lambda-gradient models. In *Yahoo! Learning to Rank Challenge*, pages 25–35, 2011.

[11] S. Chaturvedi, V. Castelli, R. Florian, R. M. Nallapati, and H. Raghavan. Joint question clustering and relevance prediction for open domain non-factoid question answering. In *WWW*, pages 503–514, 2014.

[12] J. Chu-Carroll, J. Prager, C. Welty, K. Czuba, and D. Ferrucci. A multi-strategy and multi-source approach to question answering. Technical report, DTIC Document, 2006.

[13] S. Cucerzan and A. Sil. The msr systems for entity linking and temporal slot filling at TAC 2013. In *Text Analysis Conference*, 2013.

[14] X. Dong, K. Murphy, E. Gabrilovich, G. Heitz, W. Horn, N. Lao, T. Strohmann, S. Sun, and W. Zhang. Knowledge vault: A Web-scale approach to probabilistic knowledge fusion. In *SIGKDD*, pages 601–610, 2014.

[15] O. Etzioni. Search needs a shake-up. *Nature*, 476(7358):25–26, 2011.

[16] A. Fader, S. Soderland, and O. Etzioni. Identifying relations for open information extraction. In *EMNLP*, pages 1535–1545, 2011.

[17] A. Fader, L. Zettlemoyer, and O. Etzioni. Paraphrase-driven learning for open question answering. In *ACL*, pages 1608–1618, 2013.

[18] A. Fader, L. Zettlemoyer, and O. Etzioni. Open question answering over curated and extracted knowledge bases. In *SIGKDD*. ACM, 2014.

[19] C. Fellbaum. WordNet: An electronic lexical database. 1998. *http://www. cogsci. princeton. edu/wn*, 2010.

[20] D. Ferrucci, E. Brown, J. Chu-Carroll, J. Fan, D. Gondek, A. A. Kalyanpur, A. Lally, J. Murdock, E. Nyberg, J. Prager, et al. Building watson: An overview of the DeepQA project. *AI magazine*, 31(3):59–79, 2010.

[21] J. Friedman. Greedy function approximation: a gradient boosting machine. *Annals of Statistics*, pages 1189–1232, 2001.

[22] S. Harabagiu, D. Moldovan, M. Pasca, R. Mihalcea, M. Surdeanu, R. Bunescu, R. Girju, V. Rus, and P. Morarescu. FALCON: Boosting knowledge for answer engines. In *TREC*, volume 9, pages 479–488, 2000.

[23] G. Hinton and R. Salakhutdinov. Reducing the dimensionality of data with neural networks. *Science*, 313(5786):504–507, 2006.

[24] E. Hovy, L. Gerber, U. Hermjakob, M. Junk, and C. Lin. Question answering in Webclopedia. In *TREC*, volume 9, 2000.

[25] J. Ko, E. Nyberg, and L. Si. A probabilistic graphical model for joint answer ranking in question answering. In *SIGIR on Rearch and Development in IR*, pages 343–350. ACM, 2007.

[26] C. Kwok, O. Etzioni, and D. Weld. Scaling question answering to the Web. *TOIS*, 19(3):242–262, 2001.

[27] A. Lally, J. Prager, M. McCord, B. Boguraev, S. Patwardhan, J. Fan, P. Fodor, and J. Chu-Carroll. Question analysis: How watson reads a clue. *IBM Journal of Research and Development*, 56(3.4):2–1, 2012.

[28] X. Li and D. Roth. Learning question classifiers. In *ICCL*, pages 1–7, 2002.

[29] D. C. Liu and J. Nocedal. On the limited memory BFGS method for large scale optimization. *Mathematical programming*, 45(1-3):503–528, 1989.

[30] X. Luo, H. Raghavan, V. Castelli, S. Maskey, and R. Florian. Finding what matters in questions. In *HLT-NAACL*, pages 878–887, 2013.

[31] E. Marsh and D. Perzanowski. MUC-7 evaluation of ie technology: Overview of results. In *MUC-7*, volume 20, 1998.

[32] B. Min, R. Grishman, L. Wan, C. Wang, and D. Gondek. Distant supervision for relation extraction with an incomplete knowledge base. In *HLT-NAACL*, pages 777–782, 2013.

[33] J. W. Murdock, A. Kalyanpur, C. Welty, J. Fan, D. A. Ferrucci, D. Gondek, L. Zhang, and H. Kanayama. Typing candidate answers using type coercion. *IBM Journal of Research and Development*, 56(3.4):7–1, 2012.

[34] S. Na, I. Kang, S. Lee, and J. Lee. Question answering approach using a WordNet-based answer type taxonomy. In *TREC*, 2002.

[35] C. Pinchak and D. Lin. A probabilistic answer type model. In *EACL*, 2006.

[36] S. Robertson and H. Zaragoza. On rank-based effectiveness measures and optimization. *Information Retrieval*, 10(3):321–339, 2007.

[37] N. Schlaefer, P. Gieselmann, T. Schaaf, and A. Waibel. A pattern learning approach to question answering within the ephyra framework. In *Text, speech and dialogue*, pages 687–694. Springer, 2006.

[38] F. M. Suchanek, G. Kasneci, and G. Weikum. YAGO: a core of semantic knowledge. In *WWW*, pages 697–706. ACM, 2007.

[39] C. Tsai, W. Yih, and C. Burges. Web-based question answering: Revisiting AskMSR. Technical Report MSR-TR-2015-20, Microsoft Research, 2015.

[40] C. Unger, L. Bühmann, J. Lehmann, A. Ngonga Ngomo, D. Gerber, and P. Cimiano. Template-based question answering over RDF data. In *WWW*, pages 639–648. ACM, 2012.

[41] E. M. Voorhees and D. M. Tice. Building a question answering test collection. In *SIGIR on Rearch and Development in IR*, pages 200–207. ACM, 2000.

[42] R. West, E. Gabrilovich, K. Murphy, S. Sun, R. Gupta, and D. Lin. Knowledge base completion via search-based question answering. In *WWW*, pages 515–526, 2014.

[43] R. W. White, M. Richardson, and W. Yih. Questions vs. queries in informational search tasks. Technical Report MSR-TR-2014-96, Microsoft Research, 2014.

[44] M. Yahya, K. Berberich, S. Elbassuoni, M. Ramanath, V. Tresp, and G. Weikum. Natural language questions for the Web of data. In *EMNLP-CoNLL*, pages 379–390, 2012.

[45] X. Yao and B. Van Durme. Information extraction over structured data: Question answering with Freebase. In *ACL*, 2014.

[46] L. Zou, R. Huang, H. Wang, J. X. Yu, W. He, and D. Zhao. Natural language question answering over RDF: a graph data driven approach. In *SIGMOD*, pages 313–324. ACM, 2014.

All Who Wander: On the Prevalence and Characteristics of Multi-community Engagement

Chenhao Tan
Dept. of Computer Science
Cornell University
chenhao@cs.cornell.edu

Lillian Lee
Dept. of Computer Science
Cornell University
llee@cs.cornell.edu

ABSTRACT

Although analyzing user behavior *within* individual communities is an active and rich research domain, people usually interact with *multiple* communities both on- and off-line. How do users act in such multi-community environments? Although there are a host of intriguing aspects to this question, it has received much less attention in the research community in comparison to the intra-community case. In this paper, we examine three aspects of multi-community engagement: the *sequence of communities* that users post to, the *language* that users employ in those communities, and the *feedback* that users receive, using longitudinal posting behavior on Reddit as our main data source, and DBLP for auxiliary experiments. We also demonstrate the effectiveness of features drawn from these aspects in predicting users' future level of activity.

One might expect that a user's trajectory mimics the "settling-down" process in real life: an initial exploration of sub-communities before settling down into a few niches. However, we find that the users in our data continually post in new communities; moreover, as time goes on, they post increasingly evenly among a more diverse set of smaller communities. Interestingly, it seems that users that eventually leave the community are "destined" to do so from the very beginning, in the sense of showing significantly different "wandering" patterns very early on in their trajectories; this finding has potentially important design implications for community maintainers. Our multi-community perspective also allows us to investigate the "situation vs. personality" debate from language usage across different communities.

Categories and Subject Descriptors: J.4 [**Computer Applications**]: SOCIAL AND BEHAVIORAL SCIENCES; H.2.8 [**Database Applications**]: Data Mining

General Terms: Algorithms, Experimentation

Keywords: multiple communities; lifecycle; language; Reddit; DBLP

1. INTRODUCTION

树挪死，人挪活 (*People, unlike trees, thrive on relocation*).
—A Chinese saying

How people behave *within* a given community is a profound and broad question that has inspired work ranging from basic social-science research (e.g., [27]) to the design of online social systems (e.g., [21]). However, many settings offer an array of *multiple* possible interest sub-groups for users to engage in. In the offline world, for example, within the bounds of a single college campus, students can get involved with a variety of clubs, organizations, and social circles. And in the online case, there are many multi-community sites, such as Reddit, 4chan, Wikia, and StackExchange, all of which host a slew of topic-based sub-discussion forums. As the results in this paper show, multi-community settings exhibit many interesting and useful properties that are not manifested in within-community situations, and so *our main goal is to demonstrate that multi-community engagement is an exciting and underexploited research area*: we believe that such work will shed additional light on human behavior and on the design of social-media systems.

To demonstrate, we first tackle a seemingly foregone conclusion: that, analogously to the human life course [5, 14], a person first passes through an "adolescent" phase of trying out many different interests before "settling down". Indeed, the best-paper award at WWW 2013 was given to an excellent within-community study [9] demonstrating (among other things) that users' language use becomes more inflexible and out-of-step with the community's over time. But, contrary to this expectation, we find that even people with long histories of participation in a global community *continually* try out new sub-communities. Figure 1 depicts this for two very different settings: for Reddit and for the universe of computer-science conferences given by DBLP, the latter choice inspired by [3]. Note that despite their very different timescales (one can post to Reddit at any time, but submission deadlines only roll around every so often) and barriers to entry (conferences have gate-keepers, whereas posting on Reddit can be done essentially at will), they exhibit the same qualitative behavior. On average, Redditors post to 5 communities in their first 10 posts and then post to 2.5 *new* communities every 10 posts, while researchers publish at 5 *new* conferences every 10 papers (Fig. 1a and 1b). These exploration trends continue over the users' lifetimes (Fig. 1c, 1d). Thus, while within a single community "all users die old" [9], it seems that a multi-community setting keeps users young by offering them choices to explore as an alternative to opting out entirely.

Having established the prevalence of "wandering" behavior, we are led to investigate a host of related phenomena. *We believe that these phenomena are interesting in their own right, and at times quite surprising. Moreover, we also demonstrate that our findings inspire new kinds of features that are strongly predictive of users' future level of activity.*

Organization, further paper highlights and design implications. In Sections 2 and 3, we investigate three aspects of users' community trajectories: the communities they post to (§3.1), the language they use within a community (§3.2), and the feedback

WWW 2015, May 18–22, 2015, Florence, Italy.
ACM 978-1-4503-3469-3/15/05.
http://dx.doi.org/10.1145/2736277.2741661.

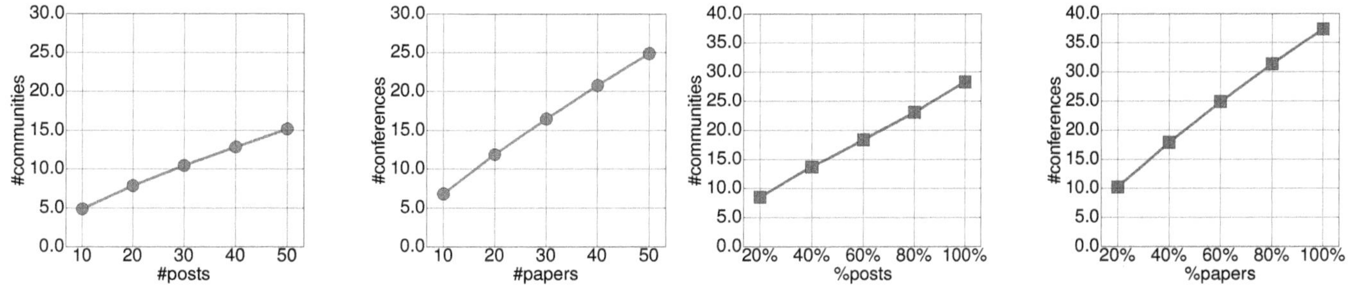

(a) 1st 50, Reddit (b) 1st 50, DBLP (c) lifetime, Reddit (d) lifetime, DBLP

Figure 1: Mean number of **unique** communities (subreddits for Reddit, conferences for DBLP) where people make their temporally first x contributions (left-hand plots) or their first x percent of contributions (right-hand plots), for "long-lived" people (50+ contributions overall). For Reddit (respectively, DBLP), contributions = posts (papers). Standard-error intervals are depicted, but very small, and trends for the median are consistent with the mean. Note that the left-hand plots depict long timespans: the average time to accumulate 50 contributions is 456.0 days on Reddit, 15.6 years on DBLP.

Example of a Redditor's first 50 subreddits, in the order posted to, first-time communities underlined: skyrim, aww, skyrim, aww, pics, aww, aww, pics, WTF, aww, pics, WTF, pokemontrades, funny, pokemontrades, pics, aww, AskReddit, pics, pokemon, fashion, AskReddit, aww, Scotland, fashion, aww, Scotland, pics, keto, keto, Fitness, keto, skyrim, pokemon, cats, aww, aww, pokemon, Scotland, AskReddit, fashion, keto, pokemon, ketouk, Scotland, keto, pics, ketouk, funny, gamecollecting.

Two DBLP examples: the set of venues of *James Harland*'s first 50 papers: LPAR, ACE, NACLP, TABLEAUX, DALT, ECOWS, CADE, Australian Joint Conference on Artificial Intelligence, IAT, ICLP, ICSOC, ILPS, "Workshop on Programming with Logic Databases (Book), ILPS", Future Databases, AAMAS, ACSE, EDBT, JICSLP, ACSC, ACAL, SAC, AAMAS (1), PRICAI, Computational Logic, CLIMA, ECAI, AMAST, ISLP, "Workshop on Programming with Logic Databases (Informal Proceedings), ILPS", KR, CATS.

Jure Leskovec's: INFOCOM, HT, AAAI, PKDD, ICDE, ECCV (4), KDD, ICDM, UAI, NIPS, ICML, CHI, VLDB, WWW, EC, WAW, WSDM, ICWSM, PAKDD, CIKM-CNIKM, JCDL, SDM, WWW (Companion Volume).

they receive from other members of the community (§3.3). Consistently, we see that — again, in contrast to the "older people become less adventurous" hypothesis — our users appear to continually seek out new and different communities, and adopt the language characteristics of the new communities. Another interesting point, albeit arguably less surprising, is that they tend to move to smaller communities (a fact noted by Redditors[1]), which might be a signal to site designers to make sure to offer a menu of narrowly-targeted options for users to choose from (or to ensure that sub-groups can arise organically). Finally, a complete surprise is that for users who made at least 50 posts, the patterns exhibited by those who end up departing the site altogether are *already* significantly different from those users who end up staying by *their first 10 posts*. The fact that future abandonment can be detected so early should be of interest to administrators of social-media systems. But, there is an unexpected factor potentially making this discrimination difficult: in our data, the eventually departing users are often most similar *not* to the least active users in our study, but to the *most* active users. We conjecture that our "dying" users are actively striving to remain engaged, but are not quite managing to explore enough to make their overall posting experience satisfactory. A design implication might be to include mechanisms in one's site that more proactively suggest new, diverse sub-communities for posting.

In Section 4, we show that the aforementioned differences in patterns are not "mere" correlations, but do indeed serve as features that are effective at predicting future activity level.

Again, our overall goal is to encourage further work on multi-community settings. As a spur to the imagination, and as a demonstration that this research domain is rich with possibilities, we discuss in sections 5 and 6 two additional questions that arise. First, what makes a user abandon a community and move on to new ones? We see that the positivity of initial feedback correlates with what groups users choose to return to, a finding that contradicts recent results on the power of negative feedback [6], albeit for commenting instead of posting. Second, we make a foray into the "situation vs. personality" debate in psychology [20, 12]: how much of our behavior is determined by fixed personality traits, versus how much is variable and influenced by the specific situation at hand? We consider this question from a linguistic perspective, and determine that *even after topic-specific vocabulary is discarded* (after all, it wouldn't be interesting to find that people use gym-related words at the gym that they don't use at work), users *do* employ different language patterns in different communities. This means that they are able to adapt even into "maturity" — a positive note to end on.

[1]One comment: "the longer you are on reddit, the more you get pulled into smaller subs".

2. EXPERIMENTAL SETUP

In the following, we first describe the data that we use and then propose an analysis framework for capturing the temporal dynamics of multi-community engagement.

2.1 Datasets.

The main dataset used in this paper is drawn from Reddit, a very active community-driven platform for submitting, commenting on, and rating posts[2] [30]. Reddit is organized into thousands of topic-based, user-created discussion forums called "subreddits", which users can post to essentially at will (modulo spam filtering, rate limits, and deletion of posts by moderators). Other users can "upvote" or "downvote" posts; the difference between the number of

[2]A Reddit post consists at a minimum of a title that serves as anchor-text for a link. The link may be to an offsite item ("link post") or to some text that the post's author places on Reddit ("text post"). The dataset with more detailed explanation is available at `https://chenhaot.com/pages/multi-community.html`.

upvotes and the number of downvotes, a difference that we henceforth refer to as *feedback*, is readily available.[3]

Relying primarily on RedditAnalytics[4], in February 2014 we collected all[5] 76.6M posts ever submitted to Reddit since its inception, together with their associated feedback values. We discarded the last month of posts, since their feedback values might not have had sufficient time to converge.

Since we need our users' community trajectories to be long enough to be *able* to exhibit significant wandering (whether or not they actually do), the set of users we consider are those who have made at least 50 posts, following the choice in [9]. We focus on the 157K *50+ posters* who first posted between January 2008 and January 2012 so that we have at least two years' worth (2012-2014) of observations for each of them. We chose to start from January 2008 because users were granted the ability to create their own subreddits at will then. Not only are the 50+ posters good objects of study because we have a lot of data on their behavior, but they also play a major role in determining the character of Reddit because they made 63% of the posts written by users who first posted in the time period under consideration.[6]

In order to ensure that our findings generalize beyond Reddit, we also consider a (more) physical-world multi-community situation: the set of conferences in computer science. Conferences generally correspond to topic areas within CS, and each can be thought of as representing a social group, at least to some degree. In this setting, we take "posting" to mean publishing a paper. We use the DBLP database[7] to find what papers appeared in which conferences, and refer to the resultant dataset as "DBLP". For DBLP, we do not consider an analog of Reddit's feedback, although citation or download counts could be used in future work.

It is important to note that program committees play a huge role in determining an author's conference trajectory. This property makes DBLP a less suitable domain for the questions of user choice that we focus on in this paper. We thus place our DBLP trajectory results in the Appendix (§9).

Statistics on the 50+ posters in Reddit and DBLP are given in Table 1.

Note 1: how we define "posting". In this paper, we use the term *posting* to refer to submitting an item to be voted or commented upon. We distinguish posting from *commenting on posts* for several reasons. First, posting is important for site designers to encourage since the site will presumably die without fresh conversation-starters. Second, posting is not affected by a confounding factor that commenting is subject to: Reddit influences commenting by how it presents potential targets for comments (e.g., by ranking them, or featuring targets on the Reddit home page). Third, the way that comments are presented on Reddit makes scraping the complete commenting history rather difficult. Nonetheless, looking at commenting in multi-community environments is an interesting direction for future research. We conjecture that it would lead to new findings since, for example, we do know that top posters are generally not top commenters, and vice versa.[8]

[3]The actual number of upvotes or downvotes is purposely inaccessible: `http://bit.ly/1xrciQY`.

[4]`http://redditanalytics.com/`

[5] Except that we filter out bots and banned users.

[6]Cross-posting (posting the same URL to multiple subreddits, with or without a title change) accounts for only 3% of the posts from the users that we consider in this paper — only 1.77% if we only consider their first 50 posts.

[7]`http://dblp.uni-trier.de`

[8]`http://bit.ly/1tendtD`

	Reddit	DBLP
Average number of posts	152.04	86.30
Median	89.	71.
Avg. no. of communities	28.85	38.08
Median	26.	34.
Mean avg. time gap btwn posts	10.47 days	3.36 mos

Table 1: Statistics for 50+ posters (157K in Reddit, 10K in DBLP).

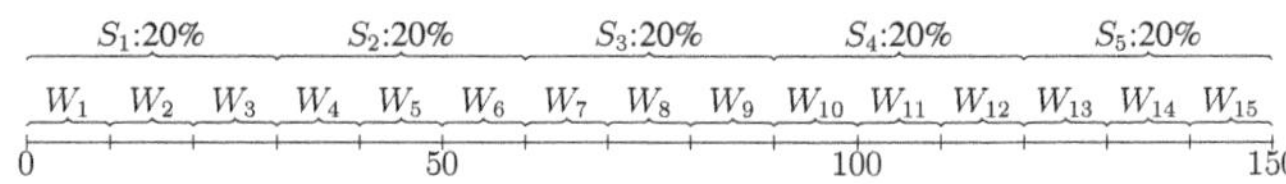

Figure 2: Illustration of windows and stages for window size $w = 10$, number of stages $S = 5$, number of posts $T = 150$, number of windows $T_w = 15$. W_i is a window; S_i is a stage.

2.2 Analysis framework.

We now set up terminology and concepts that facilitate discussion of users' trajectories among communities.

For each post by a given user, we store the timestamp, *time*, and the *community* (sometimes C for short). For Reddit data, we also store the post's *feedback* as of February 2014 and its *words* (the anchor-text plus any text written by the user, all tokenized and part-of-speech tagged using the Stanford NLP package[9]).

Several of the questions we are interested in pertain to properties of subsequences of trajectories. For example, suppose we want to know whether users are visiting a broader set of communities over time; one way to check is to look at how many communities they engaged with in their first w posts versus in their last w posts. Therefore, a basic element in our analysis is a *window*. Let variable t index the posts made by a user u, and suppose u has made T posts altogether. We split the entire index sequence $1, \ldots, T$ into non-overlapping consecutive windows W_i of size w, where i ranges from 1 to $T_w \stackrel{def}{=} \lfloor T/w \rfloor$. For example, in Fig. 2, W_6 would be the integers in the range $[51, 60]$. We use $w = 10$ throughout this paper. Our Reddit results were insensitive to choices of w.

We define functions F on windows W_i to summarize properties of that window and track how these properties change over time. We use two ways to define F. One way is to directly define F based on the entire window, for example, $F(W_i) = |\{C_t : t \in W_i\}|$, the number of unique communities in W_i. The other way is to define a function f for each index t — for example, $f(t)$ could be the number of words in the tth post — and let $F(W_i)$ be induced by f's average value over the indices in W_i, $F(W_i) = \frac{1}{w}\sum_{t \in W_i} f(t)$.

Given a window size w and a function of interest, F, we take two perspectives to track the trajectory of F: a *full-life view (all the user's posts)* and a *fixed-prefix view (50 posts)*. The rationals are as follows:

The first perspective, *full-life*, tracks users' entire lifetimes. Because the value of some functions is affected by choice of window size (e.g., the number of unique communities), we still fix the window size in the full-life view, but set an additional parameter S of the number of life stages that we want to examine, where each life stage contains the same number of windows, as depicted in Fig. 2. For each stage, we compute the average value over the windows in that stage.

A slight problem with the full-life view is that for different users, the value of the same life stage (say, the first 10% of one's life)

[9]`http://nlp.stanford.edu/software/corenlp.shtml`

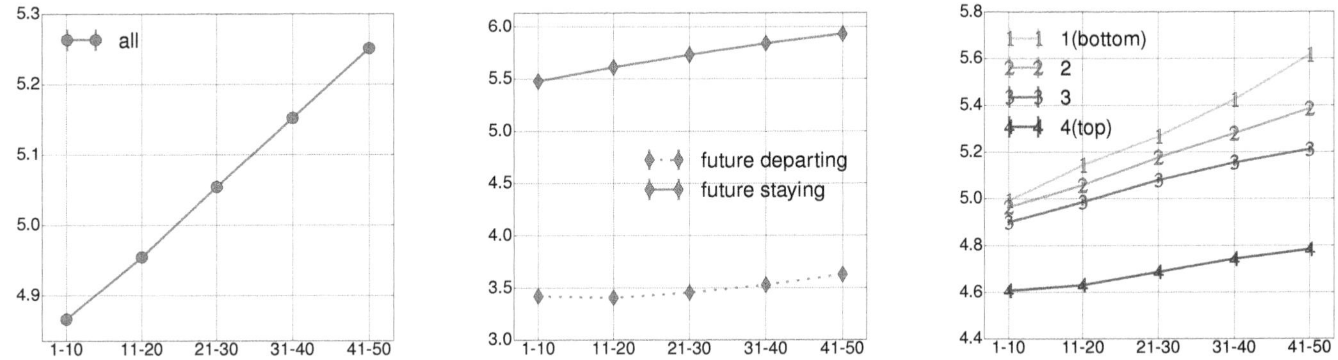

(a) Overall trend (b) Future departing status (c) Future activity quartile

Figure 3: Number of unique communities per window. x-axis: each of the first 5 windows. y-axis: number of unique communities appearing in the corresponding window. In Fig. 3b and Fig. 3c, users are categorized by their future state *after* the initial 50 posts. Standard-error intervals are depicted, but very small.

Note 2: y-axes scales, and other considerations regarding subsequent figures. Since many of the figures in Section 3 tend to support the same overall point as in Figure 3, we make the subsequent figures relatively small (labeling the y-axes in the captions), but use the same x-axis, legends, and line styles in all of them.
As in Figure 3, each of the other figures in Section 3 consists of three sub-figures. In each, we scale the y-axes according to the corresponding data's range in order to show significant changes (all figures show standard-error bars, which are tiny). But it should be noted that the lines when averaging over all users (leftmost sub-figure in the figures) would usually look flatter if plotted on the graphs that divide users by departure status (middle sub-figures) or activity quartile (rightmost sub-figures).

may be based on a significantly different number of posts (say, 10 for one user but 100 for another). The full-life view also includes information about the entirety of the user's life, and thus is not appropriate for prediction settings (for example, one does not ordinarily know at the time what percent of one's life has already passed). Thus we also take a *fixed-prefix* view, where *only* the initial 50 posts are examined. (Recall from the caption of Fig. 1 that this encompasses a long time span on average.) Thus, the same amount of data is used for every user and the induced features are valid for predicting future behavior. For space reasons, in the main paper we will focus on the fixed-prefix view, and place some full-life-view results in the Appendix (§9).

Future activity level. We further relate our analysis to users' future activity level, since future activity level is a useful quantity to predict. We employ two different ways to categorize users' future commitment: the two-way classification of whether a user eventually abandons the global community altogether or not, and a 4-way split based on the relative number of posts that a user eventually makes over his/her lifetime, as follows.

- Departing status. To determine which users should be considered to have abandoned the site, we define a date (specifically, 6 months before January 2014) as the start-of-future (SOF). We define *departing* users as those who stopped posting as of SOF; we define *lasting* users as non-departing users who additionally post at least once in the first 3 months and at least once in the second 3 months since SOF, so that they are consistently "active". There are 43,910 departing users and 75,708 lasting users. Note that they all made at least 50 posts before SOF.

- Activity quartile. We split users into four quartiles based on the number of posts that they make in their entire life after the initial 50 posts. (As it happens, the lasting/departing ratio is higher in the the higher-activity quartile.)

3. TRAJECTORY PROPERTIES

We have established in Fig. 1 that users do constantly "wander around" in multi-community environments. In this section, we apply the framework proposed in §2 to explore three aspects of this wandering process: (§3.1) the communities users post to; (§3.2) the language users employ in each community; (§3.3) the feedback that users receive from other community members. In §4, we will further validate the effectiveness of features based on these properties in prediction tasks.

3.1 Multi-community aspects

We have shown in §1 that users on average consistently post to 2.5 new communities every 10 posts (Fig. 1). But what else characterizes their patterns of movement among communities? The answers to this question have the design implications outlined in §1.

Section summary. *We find that over time, users span more communities every 10 posts, "jump" more, and concentrate less.*[10] *They enter smaller and less similar communities. Eventually-departing users seem consistently less "adventurous" than lasting users even, notably, from the very beginning. Curiously, eventually-departing users act similarly to users in the top activity quartile.*

In the following, we explain the metrics for understanding these properties and discuss related theories.

Users span more and more unique communities in a window, but relatively speaking, departing users span fewer unique communities. Figure 3 shows the per-window number of unique communities that users post to. The actual number is interesting: in Fig. 1, users post to 2.5 new communities every 10 posts; here on average, users post to around 5 communities every 10 posts, and thus only around 2.5 of them are ones that they have ever posted to. Given that users have more potential communities to go back

[10] The continual exploration is not simply an effect of the introduction of new communities over time. For instance, although new communities or options also emerge in real life, people seem to settle down and do not explore much.

to over time, this suggests that they do not tend to return to some previous communities. More discussion as to why users return to certain communities will be presented in §5.

Users "jump" between communities more and more "frequently", but departing users do so at around half the "rate". (Fig. 4) To understand how often users "jump", we count the number of "jumps" that users make per window. Formally, define $F(W_i) = \sum_{t,t+1 \in W_i} I(C_t \neq C_{t+1})$, where $I(x)$ is the indicator function: $I(x) = 1$ if x is true, 0 otherwise.

Note that the number of unique communities in a window of 10 does not determine how often users "jump". Given a window size of 10, users can jump as many as 9 times; given that users on average span 5 communities in a window, users can jump as few as 4 times. In fact, users make around 5.8 "jumps" per 10 posts.

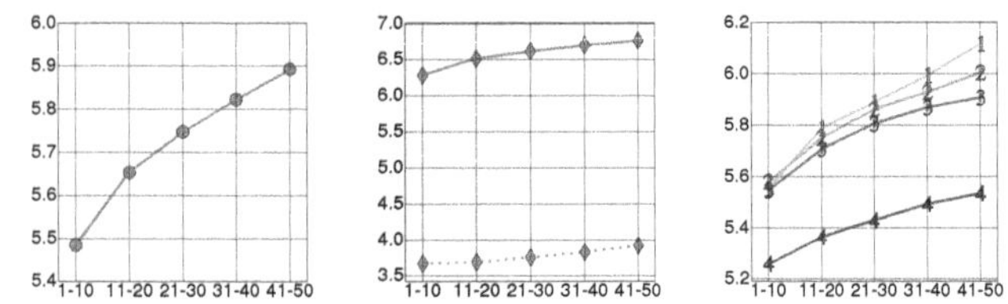

(a) Overall trend (b) Departing status (c) Activity quartile

Figure 4: Number of "jumps".

Users spread their posts out more and more evenly, but relatively speaking, departing users focus more. (Fig. 5) We employ entropy as a metric for concentration, following [1]. Entropy is based on the probability of a community appearing in a window W_i, $p_c = \frac{1}{w}\sum_{t \in W_i} I(C_t = c)$, and is defined as $-\sum_c p_c \log_2 p_c$ for W_i. It is an information-theoretic measure that grows as the intra-window community-posting distribution approaches the uniform distribution (minimum concentration) [26]. The same qualitative results hold if we use the Gini-Simpson index $(1 - \sum_c p_c^2)$, a commonly used metric in ecology for species concentration [16, 29].[11]

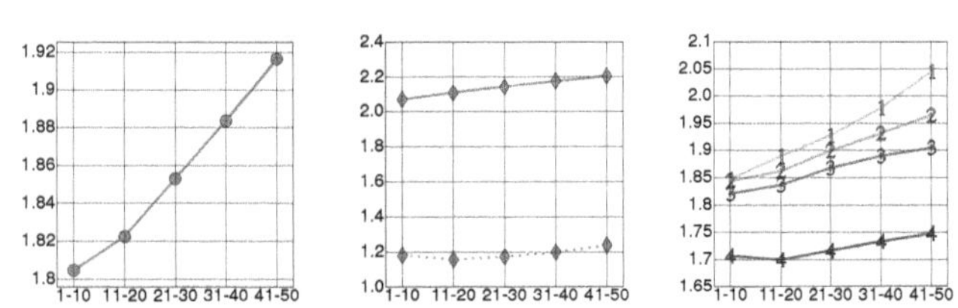

(a) Overall trend (b) Departing status (c) Activity quartile

Figure 5: Entropy of community-posting distribution.

Users enter smaller-looking communities (fewer posts per month), but relatively speaking, departing users prefer larger communities. (Fig. 6) Engaging with different communities entails a choice between communities of different sizes. A large community can encompass diverse community purposes and member preferences, leading to broader appeal, but at the same time, a large size may dilute personal connection and lead to more conflicts [24]. Or, size might not have any effect at all. To study this question, we set $f(t)$ to log of the number of posts made by the user in the community in month t as a simple metric of how "large" the active portion of a community looks to an incoming user.[12]

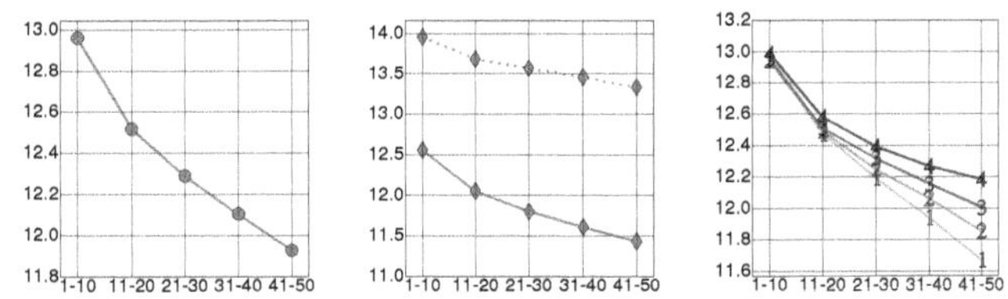

(a) Overall trend (b) Departing status (c) Activity quartile

Figure 6: Average $\log_2$(number of monthly posts in communities that a user posts to). Note that it is *not* the case that big subreddits are being abandoned as a whole: despite the availability over time of more and more small subreddits, the number of posts in the popular subreddits continues to increase.

We note that with respect to this metric of community size, the full-life view, shown in the Appendix (Fig. 16a), differs from the fixed-prefix perspective plotted above. In the full-life view, the higher-activity quartile users eventually enter smaller communities than lower-activity quartile users. It seems that they just move more slowly to such communities.

Users post to less similar communities over time, but relatively speaking, departing users prefer more similar ones. (Fig. 7) One hypothesis for how people select new communities is that they explore similar communities to those they have visited in the past, because they want more exposure to topics that they are already interested in. On the other hand, perhaps they choose new communities because their interests have changed, implying that they would choose more different communities.

We measure the dissimilarity between communities C_1 and C_2 based on poster overlap, restricting attention to just those communities with at least 1000 posts to ensure sufficient data. Denoting the set of users who ever posted in a community C as U_C, our measure is $1 - \frac{|U_{C_1} \cap U_{C_2}|}{|U_{C_1} \cup U_{C_2}|}$. Note that the dissimilarity between two communities is computed based on their eventual poster set, since we want to capture the "actual", eventual relationship between the two, and so does not change over time. For a window W_i, the overall community dissimilarity $F(W_i)$ is defined as the average of all the pairwise dissimilarities between the communities that the user posted at during that window W_i.

The same trends hold if we measure language dissimilarity between communities using the KL-divergence between community language models.

Different activity quartiles. For *all* of the above metrics, users of different *future* activity quartiles manifest significant differences even in their very earliest behavior, although the differences are not as dramatic as those between departing users and lasting users. The curves for the different quartiles always appear in either the

[11]An alternative hypothesis regarding the difference in activity quartiles is that there isn't really a difference, but perhaps users in the higher-activity quartile make several posts in a single community where a lower-activity user makes just one, e.g., $C_1C_1C_1C_2C_2C_2$ vs. C_1C_2. If this were so, we would observe a lower entropy simply due to accidentally choosing a window size that is small relative to the average burst size. However, we verified that this "burstiness" hypothesis does not hold, since the higher-activity users only change communities about 0.5 fewer times than lower-activity ones.

[12]Reddit does not provide directly applicable metrics: the number of subscribers or those "online now" can consist mostly of passive observers. The number of users who posted in a month is not presented at all, but we observe similar trends when extracting that as the metric.

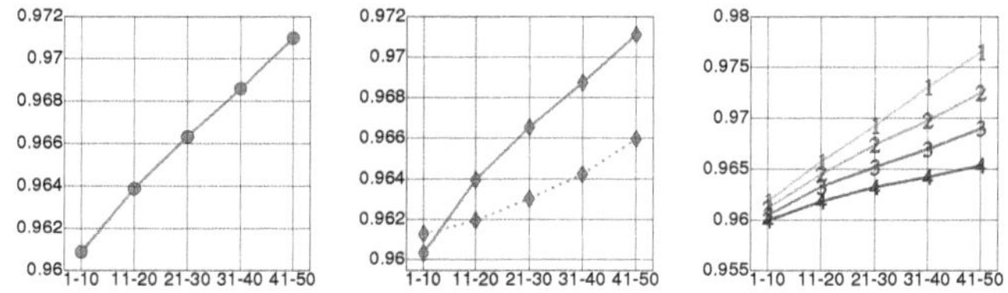

(a) Overall trend (b) Departing status (c) Activity quartile

Figure 7: Community dissimilarity based on poster overlap.

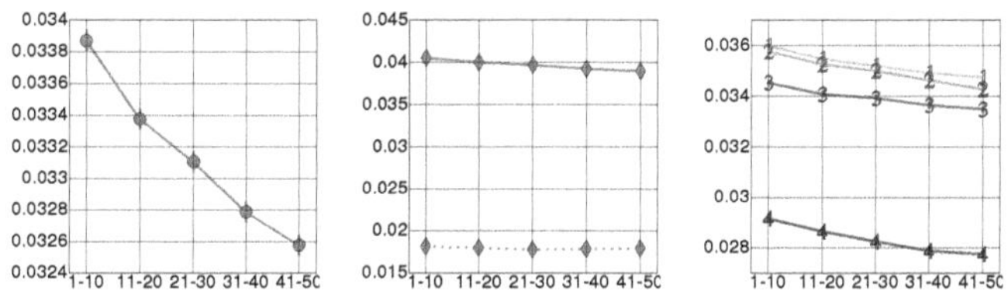

(a) Overall trend (b) Departing status (c) Activity quartile

Figure 8: Percentage of first singular person pronouns.

order 1,2,3,4 or 4,3,2,1, and the highest-activity quartile curves are always the closest to those for departing users.

3.2 Language aspects

The second aspect that we examine is the language that users employ within communities. This examination, and the formulation we apply below, are inspired by [9], which found that in single-community settings, users first pass through an "adolescent" phase where they learn linguistic norms, but after this phase stop adapting to new norms and become increasingly distant from the community. Our results indicate that this is *not* the case in the multi-community setting. Rather, with respect to part-of-speech tags or stopwords, users do not move farther and farther away from the community distribution; and when (frequent) content words are included, users seem to "stay young", continuously growing closer to the community's language. Surprisingly, departing users are better mimics of the community's language than lasting users are. The bulk of this section provides the experimental evidence, based on various forms of cross-entropy, from which we draw these conclusions.

Additionally, we, like [9], find that the usage of 1st-person-singular pronouns (e.g., I, me) declines over time,[13] which has been argued to indicate a greater sense of community affiliation [7, 28]. However, upon closer inspection, the fact that departing posters use these words *less* frequently than those users who end up staying seems problematic for such theories — although one could speculate that the cause is that our departing users start out with strong affiliation needs but become disappointed. These results are shown in Figure 8.

Cross-entropy with vocabulary-varying language models. We use cross-entropy to measure the distance between (a language model constructed from) a user's t^{th} post and a language model built from all the posts in the corresponding community, C, in that same month $m(t)$. Importantly, we will compute these models based on various choices of vocabulary V; this will reveal that although users' topical-word usage grows closer and closer to that of the community's, their usage in part-of-speech tags and stopwords stabilizes in terms of distance from the community's.

The first step of our V-dependent language-model construction is to replace every instance of any word not in V with the new token "<RARE>". Next, we define the community-based language model to be the distribution over $v \in V \cup \{\text{<RARE>}\}$ given by setting p^C to the relative frequency of v in the concatenation $words^{C,m(t)}$ of all the posts in C during the month $m(t)$. Then, we measure the cross-entropy by

$$f(t) = \frac{1}{|words_t|} \sum_{v \in words_t} \log_2 \frac{1}{p^C(v)}.$$

(This equation shows why we do not need to smooth the community language model: since $words_t$ is a component of $words^{C,m(t)}$, $p^C(v) > 0$ for $v \in words_t$.)

With all of this in hand, Figure 9 depicts representative evidence for the conclusions we drew at the beginning of this section. Specifically, the evidence consists of cross-entropy values for V chosen to be 46 parts-of-speech tags, the most frequent 100 words in Reddit, or the most frequent 1000 words in Reddit. Trends for V set to the 500 or 5000 most frequent words are similar to the most frequent 1000 words.

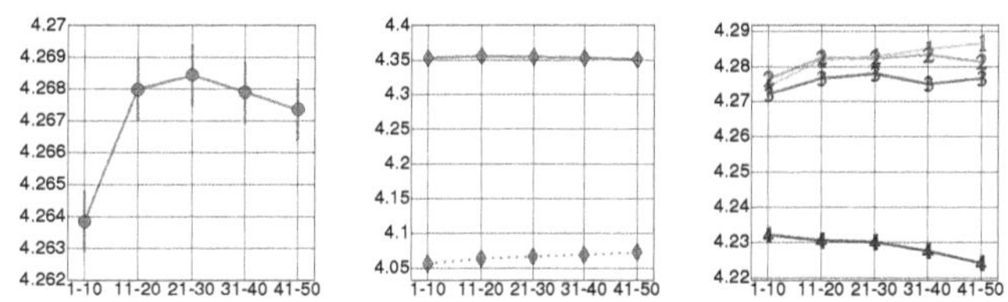

(a) Overall trend (b) Departing status (c) Activity quartile
V = part-of-speech tags

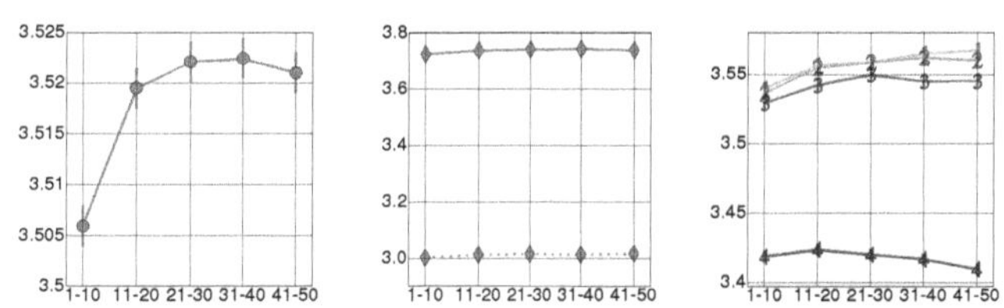

(d) Overall trend (e) Departing status (f) Activity quartile
V = stopwords (the 100 most frequent words in Reddit)

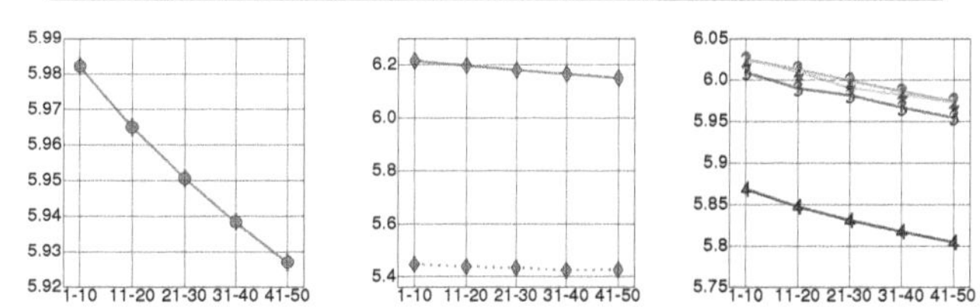

(g) Overall trend (h) Departing status (i) Activity quartile
V = stopwords + content words (1000 most frequent words)

Figure 9: Distance from the community language model. The rows indicate different choices of vocabulary V.

Technical aside: the potentially confounding factor of rare words interacting with community posting volume. We also used a "full" vocabulary that contains all words that appear more than 100 times in Reddit (180K types), but do not show the results here. This is due to the fact that for large vocabulary sizes, what appears to be differences in language matching can actually be merely a side-effect of one class of users posting in more-voluble communities. The argument runs as follows. The full vocabulary allows for many words v' with low frequency in the community — say, 1 — to contribute to the cross-entropy computation. The probability

[13] Acronyms such as "TIL" (for "today I learned") were not included.

estimate $p^C(v')$ for such words is $1/|words^{C,m(t)}|$ (where t is chosen appropriately). So, in groups where $|words^{C,m(t)}|$ is large, the contribution of such v' to the cross entropy is bigger than it would be for sub-communities where $|words^{C,m(t)}|$ is small.[14]

3.3 Feedback aspects

A final question that Reddit data allow us to easily answer is, how are users received by other members of the community? For each post, Reddit provides the difference between the number of upvotes and number of downvotes. Because the average value of this difference can vary among different communities, we measure the feedback that users get by the relative position of this difference among all posts in the community that month, i.e., how often the posts made by a user outperform the "median post" in a community. For each index t, we define $f(t)$ as $I(feedback_t > median(C_t, m(t)))$, where $median(C, m)$ represents the median vote difference in community C in month m.

Surprisingly, the feedback that 50+ posters receive is *continually* growing more positive, although the rate slows over time (Fig. 10). However, the growth is small compared to the drastic differences between departing users and lasting users. Even departing users get more-positive feedback over time, but the increase is not as great as for lasting users. Users in the top activity quartile also fare worse, although as shown in the relative perspective (Fig. 16b), they catch up in the later stages of their life. The results are consistent if we measure how often posts outperform 75% of the community's posts.

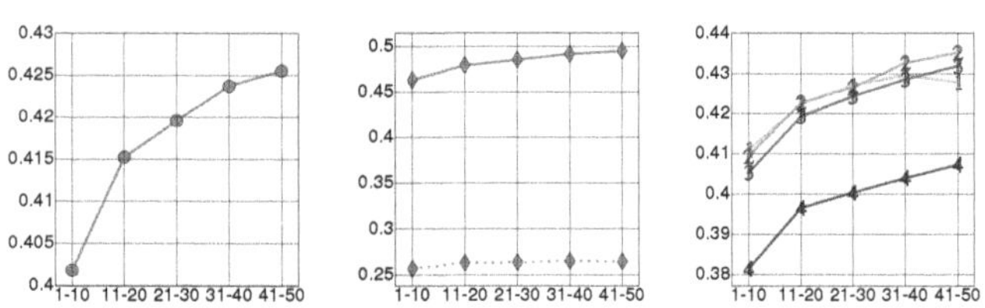

(a) Overall trend (b) Departure status (c) Activity quartile

Figure 10: Success rate at outperforming the median vote difference.

3.4 Recap

In all three aspects that we examined, users with different future activity levels manifest significant differences in their trajectories of multi-community engagement. Interestingly, users that eventually depart seem "destined" to do so even from the very beginning, since the curves for the departing vs. lasting users generally start out apart and maintain or increase that distance over time. Meanwhile, there are smaller but significant differences in these metrics between users at different activity quartiles. It is important to note that some metrics can be correlated (e.g., number of unique communities and entropy). However, none of the metrics determines another, so we believe discussing each one of them was valuable.

Another interesting phenomenon we consistently observe is that for all our metrics, users in the top activity quartile are the closest to the departing users in the first 50 posts (a direct comparison for language is shown in Fig. 11).

[14] This concern cannot be alleviated simply by sub-sampling a community's posts, since the true root of the problem is rare words, not just the length and number of posts in the community per se.

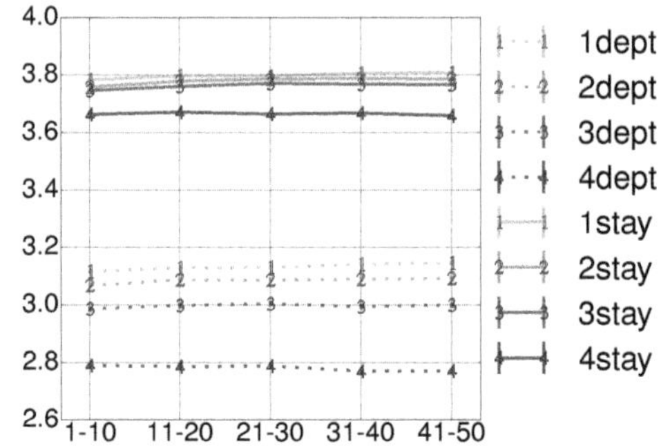

Figure 11: Interplay between departure status and activity quartiles. y-axis: distance from the corresponding monthly language model when setting the vocabulary to the 100 most frequent words. $i$dept refers to departing users in the i-th quartile; $i$stay refers to lasting users in the i-th quartile.

4. PREDICTING DEPARTURE AND ACTIVITY LEVELS

We have now seen many properties of multi-community engagement that correlate with user activity. To examine the effectiveness of these properties in prediction, we set up two different prediction tasks that correspond to how we measure users' future activity level in §2:

- Future departure status. In this task, we predict whether users abandon Reddit in the future. We use F1 for evaluation, with the minority class (departing users, as defined in §2) as the target class. We use weighted L2-regularized logistic regression as classifier.
- Future total number of posts. This is a regression task where the goal is, for a given user, to estimate $\log_2$(future number of posts). We employ L2-regularized support vector regression, and measure performance by root mean squared error (RMSE).

Each instance consists of a user's first 50 posts.

Baseline and features. We consider the following feature sets, where for window-based features we set the window size $w = 10$, thus deriving 50/10 = 5 values.[15]

- Average time-gap between posts. [9] states that this is an effective feature used in prior work on churn prediction [13, 34]. *Thus, this feature by itself serves as our (strong) baseline.*
- Multi-community aspects (henceforth "sub info"). This includes number of unique communities, number of "jumps", entropy, and Gini-Simpson index based on the user's community-posting distribution, as well as mean log "apparent" community size as defined in §3.1. Similarity between communities is not used because information about the future is incorporated in the way we compute it.
- Language aspects ("lang" for short). This includes cross-entropy with the monthly community language model for the following choices of vocabulary: part-of-speech tags; the top 100, 500, 1000, 5000, 10000 most frequent words;

[15] Alternatively, one could set $w = 50$, thus extracting features from all 50 posts in a single batch. This approach turns out to be poorer than using 5 windows because trend information is not captured.

and the full vocabulary as defined in §3.2. Additionally, we include the proportion of 1st-person-singular pronouns and post length in words.

- Feedback aspects. This includes the fraction of posts that outperform 50% and 75% of all of the corresponding month's worth of the community's posts in terms of positivity of feedback. Refer back to §3.3 for more information.

For entropy, Gini-Simpson index, and number of unique communities, we include the value for all 50 posts, since for these features, the values for all 50 posts are not simply the average of the values from 5 windows of 10 posts. We also use the index of the window with the largest value and the smallest value as features, following [9]. All features are linearly scaled to $[0, 1]$ based on training data.

Experiment protocol. In both tasks, we perform 30 randomized trials. In each trial, we randomly draw 20,000 users from our dataset as training data and a distinct set of 5,000 users as testing data. We use 5,000 users from the training data as validation set. We use LIBLINEAR [15] in all prediction tasks. For significance testing, we employ the paired Wilcoxon signed rank test [33].

The standard procedure for generating learning curves would be to only look at the *first* x posts as x varies, $x = 10, 20, 30, 40, 50$. A non-obvious but ultimately fruitful idea we introduce here is to contrast the effectiveness of the information in the early part of each 50-post instance with that of the late part of the 50-post instance. That is, we compare the performance if we use the *first* ("fst" in our plots) x posts with the performance of using the *last* x posts. (One might expect later periods to be more predictive, given that they are more recent. But surprisingly, we will see that when we predict departure status, we find that earlier information is more useful, which again suggests that departing users are "destined" to leave from the very beginning.)

4.1 Predicting departing status

Basic comparisons. (Figure 12a) Using all features outperforms a strong baseline that uses time-gap features by 18.3% — the difference between an F1 of .699 and an F1 of .591 — which shows the effectiveness of features drawn from multi-community engagement.

The performance of the first x posts is always above that of the last x posts. This suggests that the initial information is more predictive of eventual departure. Note that for 50+ posters, departure is quite "far away" from the initial posts. In fact, using all features drawn from only the first 10 posts outperforms time-gap features extracted from all 50 posts. Thus it may be very important for designers of social systems to make sure that users start well, perhaps through positive feedback or by recommending communities to post in (which can differ from the communities one might recommend that a user reads).

Feature-set analysis. (Figure 12b) In predicting departure, it is most useful to know how well users match a community's language. The second most useful features are the patterns of community visitation. Language-matching, community-trajectory, and community-feedback features all outperform time-gap information, which suggests that how users interact with different communities is more predictive than activity rate in predicting whether 50+ users will leave.

4.2 Predicting activity quartile

Comparisons with the baseline. (Figure 13a, 13b) In contrast to the case just discussed of predicting departure status, time-gap between posts is a much stronger feature in predicting future total

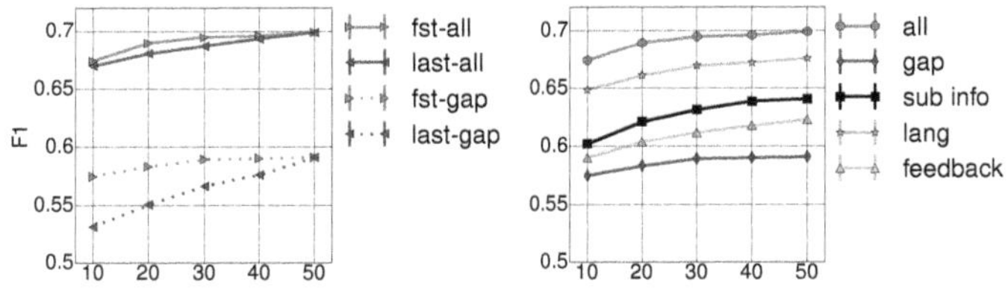

(a) Window comparison (b) Feature comparison

Figure 12: Results for predicting departing status. y-axis: F1 measure. In Fig. 12a, the dashed lines show the performance of the baseline, timing-based features; the solid lines show the performance of using all features. Red lines show the performance using the first x posts, while blue lines show the performance using the last x posts. Fig. 12b: performance of different feature sets. All differences for 50 posts are statistically significant according to the Wilcoxon signed rank test ($p < 0.001$).

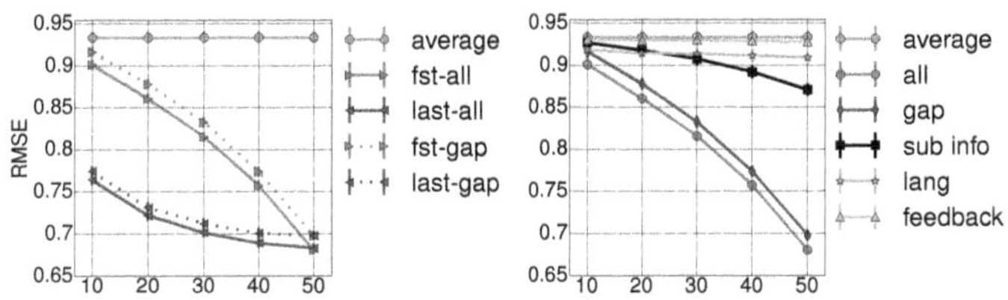

(a) Window comparison (b) Feature comparison

Figure 13: Results for predicting $\log_2$(future total number of posts). y-axis: RMSE, the smaller the better. The line styles are the same as in Fig. 12. "Average" shows a baseline that always predits the mean value in the training data. All differences for 50 posts are statistically significant according to the Wilcoxon signed rank test ($p < 0.001$).

number of posts. This is plausible because for these 50+ posters, time-gaps in posting determine how many posts that people can physically make. However, adding all the features based on multi-community engagement still improves the performance over timing information to a statistically significant degree. Prior work has shown that adding language features can lead to big improvements over timing-based features [9]; the relatively small improvement in our experiment may be due to the fact that the datasets in [9] have a longer history than ours.

Also, using the last x posts is much more effective than using the first x posts. There thus seems to be different factors affecting 50+ posters with respect to deciding whether to remain in a community versus deciding to be highly active in it.

5. WHEN DO USERS ABANDON THEIR POSTS?

We have already seen that (our) users constantly try out new communities, but we have not yet addressed a related question of practical importance to community maintainers, as well as of inherent social-scientific interest: how much and why do users *abandon* communities?

We can frame the "how much" issue succinctly by asking the following question. Suppose we partition the set of communities a user visits into (1) those that he or she abandons after just a single post, and (2) those that he or she posts at least twice to. Which set — the single-post communities or multiple-posts communities, is larger, on average? We claim that the answer is not a priori obvious[16]. But the data shows that users rack up more abandoned communities than return engagements, as depicted in the figure below. This suggests that although users are constantly willing to post to new groups, they are often only giving these new groups one shot.

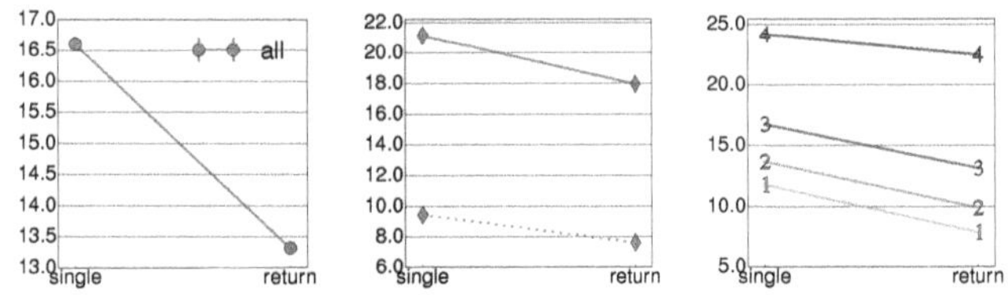

(a) Overall (b) Departing status (c) Activity levels

Figure 14: Comparison of the average number of communities where a user posts only once vs. more than once.

What is happening in the single-post communities that causes a user to stop posting in them immediately? We find that positivity of feedback (in Reddit, the difference in upvotes and downvotes) may play a substantial role, as shown by the figure below. Figure 15 is based on the *very first* post that a user makes in every community they posted in; it plots the percentage of such first posts that received a feedback score above that of the median feedback score in the respective community.

The reason that this is interesting to note is that our results contrast with previous findings of the power of *negative* feedback for predicting repeated commenting [6]; we conjecture that the difference is due to different impulses driving posting vs. commenting behavior.

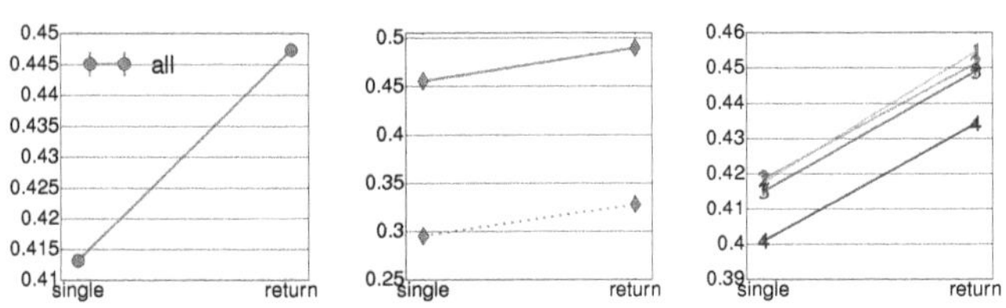

(a) Overall (b) Departing status (c) Activity levels

Figure 15: Users get better feedback for the first post in the communities that they eventually returned to than for the communities that they ended up making only a single post in. y-axis: average fraction of a user's post with feedback score better than the community's median. We exclude users that have only single-post communities or only multiple-posts communities, thus controlling for individual-user characteristics to some extent. All differences between connected points are statistically significant according to the paired t-test ($p < 0.001$).

6. DO USERS SPEAK DIFFERENTLY IN DIFFERENT COMMUNITIES?

So far we have revealed interesting and sometimes arguably counterintuitive properties of multi-community engagement, and demonstrated that they are effective cues in predicting a user's future activity level. But an additional fascinating and orthogonal question is: when users participate in multiple communities, to what degree are their actions stable *across* settings? To look at this question is to contribute another piece of evidence to the "situation vs. personality" debate [20, 12]: how much of our behavior is determined by fixed personality traits, versus how much is variable and influenced by the specific situation at hand? Or, to put it a bit more dramatically, are you fundamentally the same person at work as you are at the gym?

Here, we study the question with respect to language use. The overall message is, *even after topic-specific vocabulary is discarded* (after all, it wouldn't be interesting to find that people use gym-related words at the gym that they don't use at work), individuals *do* employ different language patterns in different communities. The way we determine this is conceptually straightforward: we check whether it's possible to tell which community a user's posts come from based just on the distribution of stopwords or non-content-words within their posts.

The rest of this section gives a quick sketch of our experiments. (Space constraints preclude a full discussion of the details.)

If we fix some vocabulary V of non-content words, then we can create classification instances from the 227K triples that exist in our data consisting of (1) a user u, (2) words of u's first 25 posts in some community C_1, and (3) words of u's first 25 posts in a different community C_2. Then, we compute the cross entropy of each post against the corresponding monthly language models, over the restricted vocabulary V, constructed from each of the two communities C_1 and C_2.[17] Add-1/|V| smoothing is applied to all language models concerned. We then use these non-content-word cross-entropies as features to guess which of (2) and (3) came from community C_1.

We run experiments for several choices of V: parts-of-speech, the 100 most frequent words in Reddit, and the 500 most frequent words in Reddit. The first two choices definitely do not include topic-specific words, and the latter will not include many (there are 180K words in the full Reddit vocabulary), and so these choices may be taken to represent a user's language *style* [2, 8]. If the user's style does not change from community to community, then the cross-entropy features mentioned above will not be helpful for determining that item (1) comes from C_1 and not C_2; thus, accuracy at matching language model to community would be 50%. But, as shown below, the average accuracies, utilizing logistic classification, of 30 random-split experiments (10K tuples for training and development, 2500 for testing) for each choice of V are (statistically) significantly above 50%:

V	accuracy
parts of speech	62.5%
most frequent 100 words	56.0%
most frequent 500 words	61.4%

7. RELATED WORK

Anthropologists, psychologists and sociologists have looked at some questions regarding multi-community engagement, often in the context of interaction with new social circles or cultures [5, 17, 4]. Recently, computer scientists have turned to examining multi-community engagement data available online [3, 1, 31, 32, 22]. Our work differs by focusing on the following specific problems: (a) characterizing full community-trajectory sequences, as opposed to looking at pairwise community transitions [3, 31, 32]; (b) revealing how properties of these trajectories correlate with a user's

[16] Recall the title of Duncan Watts' recent book "Everything Is Obvious: *Once You Know the Answer".

[17] Actually, we divide these 25 posts into windows of 5 posts and take the average cross entropy in each window, in order to be more robust and potentially capture trends, but it simplifies exposition to think of just a single post.

future cross-community activity — we incorporate but also go beyond language-based features, as inspired by previous within-community work [9, 25], and timing-based features [13]; (c) considering the effect of each community's positive and negative feedback, which may shed light on why users choose some communities over others.

Researchers have also been working on predicting users' survival (also known as churn prediction) [10, 13, 34] and activity level [11, 37]. They focus on the single-community setting. A number of studies examined community-level evolution or the success of individual communities (often websites) [18, 19, 23, 35, 36], whereas our work focuses on the life cycle of users.

8. CONCLUDING DISCUSSION

Summary. We have investigated properties of multi-community engagement; this is a setting that has not received much computational research attention before, and yet is important because it encompasses many online and physical situations. In this first large-scale study of the phenomenon, we have found a number of sometimes counterintuitive but robust properties — some involving choice of community, some involving language use within communities, and some involving feedback from communities — revolving around the discovery that users "wander" and explore communities to a greater extent than might have been previously suspected.

Limitations and further directions. We focused on posting, but commenting and other related behaviors are very interesting subjects for future study. Our study is quantitative and observational. Qualitative studies, or controlled experiments regarding the design implications in §1, can further improve our understanding.

It is important to note that our study is limited to "50+ posters" so that we would have enough history per user to observe a relatively long trajectory. This is an unusually engaged group of users that comprises 5.9% of our users. We have not addressed the question of how multi-community engagement is exhibited by users who are not as active.

The notion of considering users to exist in a multi-community setting can in principle be extended to looking at user behavior across multiple websites or apps. With the advent and adoption of multiple-website services such as OpenID, observing users at that scale of multi-community engagement may well become quite important in the future.

There are many more challenging questions that arise from taking a multi-community perspective. For example, are the particularly nomadic treated differently? What is multi-community engagement like in real life, considering the cost of switching? How can we extend current theories and principles in community design to a multi-community setting? Further understanding of these questions is crucial for on- and off-line community design and an exciting direction for future work.

9. APPENDIX

Full-life view for users in Reddit. In general, the overall trends and differences between departing users and staying users are the same as in the fixed-prefix view. But in terms of activity quartiles, there are some interesting differences. For example, the ordering of the activity quartiles with respect to mean $\log_2$(number of posts that month) completely reverses itself (compare Fig. 16a to Fig. 6c). For feedback, as users receive better feedback over time, users in the top activity quartile receive worse feedback in the beginning and catch up later in their life (Fig. 16b). These results are natural consequences of the trend developing over time. This suggests that the trends that we observe are robust over user life.

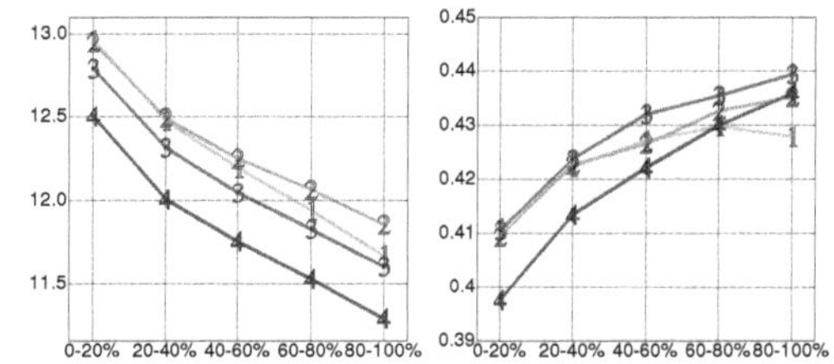

(a) (b)

Figure 16: Comparison of different Reddit activity quartiles from the full-life perspective. (a): mean $\log_2$(monthly number of posts). (b): fraction of posts that outperform the median value of feedback positivity in the corresponding month and community.

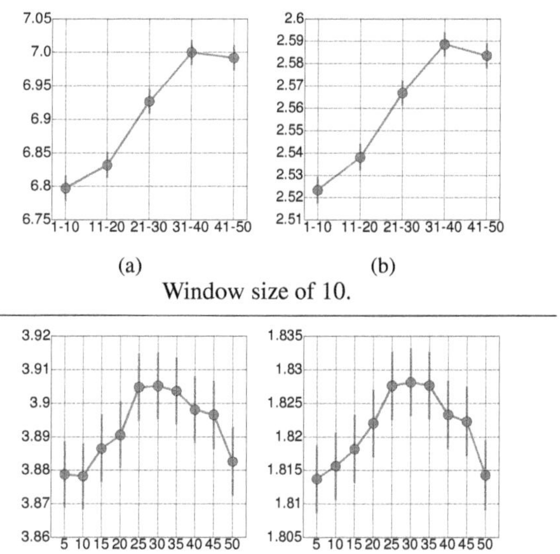

(a) (b)
Window size of 10.

(c) (d)
Window size of 5.

Figure 17: Fixed-prefix view for researchers in DBLP. (a,c): number of unique conferences per window. (b,d): entropy of the conference publishing distribution per window.

Fixed-prefix view for researchers in DBLP. In DBLP, authors span more conferences per window over time (Fig. 17a) in an increasingly scattered fashion (Fig. 17b), but in contrast to Reddit, there is saturation in the last two windows. Perhaps this suggests that as researchers become very senior, they publish more papers in some favorite set of venues.

When a very small window size is considered (w=5), the number of unique conferences and within-window entropy first increase and then decrease (Fig. 17c and 17d). But, changing the window size does *not* affect our central observation in Fig. 1 that 50+ researchers are publishing in new conferences at a relatively consistent rate over the years.

Acknowledgments. "Not all those who wander are lost" (J. R. R. Tolkien). We would have been lost without C. Danescu-Niculescu-Mizil, J. Hessel, A. Katiyar, J. Kleinberg, B. Pang, F. Radlinski, A. Sharma, K. Sridharan, A. Swaminathan, Y. Yue, the Cornell NLP seminar participants and the reviewers for their comments, and Jason Baumgartner for redditanalytics.com. This work was supported in part by NSF grant IIS-0910664 and a Google Research Grant.

References

[1] L. A. Adamic, J. Zhang, E. Bakshy, and M. S. Ackerman. Knowledge Sharing and Yahoo Answers: Everyone Knows Something. In *WWW*, 2008.

[2] S. Argamon and S. Levitan. Measuring the usefulness of function words for authorship attribution. In *Proceedings of the 2005 ACH/ALLC Conference*, 2005.

[3] L. Backstrom, D. Huttenlocher, J. Kleinberg, and X. Lan. Group Formation in Large Social Networks: Membership, Growth, and Evolution. In *KDD*, 2006.

[4] J. W. Berry. Immigration, Acculturation, and Adaptation. *Applied Psychology*, 46(1):5–34, 1997.

[5] C. Bühler. The curve of life as studied in biographies. *Journal of Applied Psychology*, 19(4):405, 1935.

[6] J. Cheng, C. Danescu-Niculescu-Mizil, and J. Leskovec. How Community Feedback Shapes User Behavior. In *ICWSM*, 2014.

[7] C. Chung and J. W. Pennebaker. The psychological functions of function words. *Social communication*, pages 343–359, 2007.

[8] C. Danescu-Niculescu-Mizil, M. Gamon, and S. Dumais. Mark my words! linguistic style accommodation in social media. In *WWW*, 2011.

[9] C. Danescu-Niculescu-Mizil, R. West, D. Jurafsky, J. Leskovec, and C. Potts. No Country for Old Members: User Lifecycle and Linguistic Change in Online Communities. In *WWW*, 2013.

[10] K. Dasgupta, R. Singh, B. Viswanathan, D. Chakraborty, S. Mukherjea, A. A. Nanavati, and A. Joshi. Social Ties and Their Relevance to Churn in Mobile Telecom Networks. In *EDBT*, 2008.

[11] M. De Choudhury, W. A. Mason, J. M. Hofman, and D. J. Watts. Inferring Relevant Social Networks from Interpersonal Communication. In *WWW*, 2010.

[12] M. B. Donellan, R. E. Lucas, and W. Fleeson, editors. *Personality and Assessment at Age 40: Reflections on the Past Person-Situation Debate and Emerging Directions of Future Person-Situation Integration [Special Issue]*. Number 43(2) in *Journal of Research in Personality*. 2009.

[13] G. Dror, D. Pelleg, O. Rokhlenko, and I. Szpektor. Churn Prediction in New Users of Yahoo! Answers. In *WWW (Companion)*, 2012.

[14] E. H. Erikson and J. M. Erikson. *The life cycle completed (extended version)*. WW Norton & Company, 1998.

[15] R.-E. Fan, K.-W. Chang, C.-J. Hsieh, X.-R. Wang, and C.-J. Lin. LIBLINEAR: A Library for Large Linear Classification. *J. Mach. Learn. Res.*, 9:1871–1874, 2008.

[16] C. Gini. *Variabilità e mutabilità*. C. Cuppini, Bologna, 1912.

[17] A. Hurtado. Understanding Multiple Group Identities: Inserting Women into Cultural Transformations. *Journal of Social Issues*, 53(2):299–327, 1997.

[18] A. Iriberri and G. Leroy. A Life-cycle Perspective on Online Community Success. *ACM Computing Surveys*, 41(2):11:1–11:29, 2009.

[19] S. R. Kairam, D. J. Wang, and J. Leskovec. The Life and Death of Online Groups: Predicting Group Growth and Longevity. In *WSDM*, 2012.

[20] D. T. Kenrick and D. C. Funder. Profiting from controversy: Lessons from the person-situation debate. *American Psychologist*, 43(1):23, 1988.

[21] R. E. Kraut and P. Resnick. *Building Successful Online Communities: Evidence-Based Social Design*. The MIT Press, 2012.

[22] H. Lakkaraju, J. McAuley, and J. Leskovec. What's in a Name? Understanding the Interplay between Titles, Content, and Communities in Social Media. In *ICWSM*, 2013.

[23] P. J. Ludford, D. Cosley, D. Frankowski, and L. Terveen. Think Different: Increasing Online Community Participation Using Uniqueness and Group Dissimilarity. In *CHI*, 2004.

[24] Y. Ren, R. Kraut, and S. Kiesler. Applying Common Identity and Bond Theory to Design of Online Communities. *Organization Studies*, 28(3):377–408, 2007.

[25] M. Rowe. Mining User Lifecycles from Online Community Platforms and their Application to Churn Prediction. In *ICDM*, 2013.

[26] C. E. Shannon. A Mathematical Theory of Communication. *Bell System Technical Journal*, 27(3):379–423, 1948.

[27] M. E. Shaw. *Group Dynamics: The Psychology of Small Group Behavior*. McGraw Hill, New York, 1971.

[28] J. C. Sherblom. Organization involvement expressed through pronoun use in computer mediated communication. *Communication Research Reports*, 7(1):45–50, 2009.

[29] E. H. Simpson. Measurement of diversity. *Nature*, 1949.

[30] P. Singer, F. Flöck, C. Meinhart, E. Zeitfogel, and M. Strohmaier. Evolution of Reddit: From the Front Page of the Internet to a Self-referential Community? In *WWW (Companion)*, 2014.

[31] B. Vasilescu, V. Filkov, and A. Serebrenik. StackOverflow and GitHub: Associations between Software Development and Crowdsourced Knowledge. In *Proceedings of SocialCom*, pages 188–195, 2013.

[32] B. Vasilescu, A. Serebrenik, P. Devanbu, and V. Filkov. How Social Q&A Sites Are Changing Knowledge Sharing in Open Source Software Communities. In *CSCW*, 2014.

[33] F. Wilcoxon. Individual Comparisons by Ranking Methods. *Biometrics Bulletin*, 1(6):80–83, 1945.

[34] J. Yang, X. Wei, M. S. Ackerman, and L. A. Adamic. Activity Lifespan: An Analysis of User Survival Patterns in Online Knowledge Sharing Communities. In *ICWSM*, 2010.

[35] H. Zhu, J. Chen, T. Matthews, A. Pal, H. Badenes, and R. E. Kraut. Selecting an Effective Niche: An Ecological View of the Success of Online Communities. In *CHI*, 2014.

[36] H. Zhu, R. E. Kraut, and A. Kittur. The Impact of Membership Overlap on the Survival of Online Communities. In *CHI*, 2014.

[37] Y. Zhu, E. Zhong, S. J. Pan, X. Wang, M. Zhou, and Q. Yang. Predicting User Activity Level in Social Networks. In *CIKM*, 2013.

LINE: Large-scale Information Network Embedding

Jian Tang[1], Meng Qu[2]*, Mingzhe Wang[2], Ming Zhang[2], Jun Yan[1], Qiaozhu Mei[3]
[1]Microsoft Research Asia, {jiatang, junyan}@microsoft.com
[2]School of EECS, Peking University, {mnqu, wangmingzhe, mzhang_cs}@pku.edu.cn
[3]School of Information, University of Michigan, qmei@umich.edu

ABSTRACT

This paper studies the problem of embedding very large information networks into low-dimensional vector spaces, which is useful in many tasks such as visualization, node classification, and link prediction. Most existing graph embedding methods do not scale for real world information networks which usually contain millions of nodes. In this paper, we propose a novel network embedding method called the "LINE," which is suitable for arbitrary types of information networks: undirected, directed, and/or weighted. The method optimizes a carefully designed objective function that preserves both the local and global network structures. An edge-sampling algorithm is proposed that addresses the limitation of the classical stochastic gradient descent and improves both the effectiveness and the efficiency of the inference. Empirical experiments prove the effectiveness of the LINE on a variety of real-world information networks, including language networks, social networks, and citation networks. The algorithm is very efficient, which is able to learn the embedding of a network with millions of vertices and billions of edges in a few hours on a typical single machine. The source code of the LINE is available online.[1]

Categories and Subject Descriptors

I.2.6 [**Artificial Intelligence**]: Learning

General Terms

Algorithms, Experimentation

Keywords

information network embedding; scalability; feature learning; dimension reduction

*This work was done when the second author was an intern at Microsoft Research Asia.

[1]`https://github.com/tangjianpku/LINE`

WWW 2015, May 18–22, 2015, Florence, Italy.
ACM 978-1-4503-3469-3/15/05.
http://dx.doi.org/10.1145/2736277.2741093.

1. INTRODUCTION

Information networks are ubiquitous in the real world with examples such as airline networks, publication networks, social and communication networks, and the World Wide Web. The size of these information networks ranges from hundreds of nodes to millions and billions of nodes. Analyzing large information networks has been attracting increasing attention in both academia and industry. This paper studies the problem of embedding information networks into low-dimensional spaces, in which every vertex is represented as a low-dimensional vector. Such a low-dimensional embedding is very useful in a variety of applications such as visualization [21], node classification [3], link prediction [10], and recommendation [23].

Various methods of graph embedding have been proposed in the machine learning literature (e.g., [4, 20, 2]). They generally perform well on smaller networks. The problem becomes much more challenging when a real world information network is concerned, which typically contains millions of nodes and billions of edges. For example, the Twitter followee-follower network contains 175 million active users and around twenty billion edges in 2012 [14]. Most existing graph embedding algorithms do not scale for networks of this size. For example, the time complexity of classical graph embedding algorithms such as MDS [4], IsoMap [20], Laplacian eigenmap [2] are at least quadratic to the number of vertices, which is too expensive for networks with millions of nodes. Although a few very recent studies approach the embedding of large-scale networks, these methods either use an indirect approach that is not designed for networks (e.g., [1]) or lack a clear objective function tailored for network embedding (e.g., [16]). We anticipate that a new model with a carefully designed objective function that preserves properties of the graph and an efficient optimization technique should effectively find the embedding of millions of nodes.

In this paper, we propose such a network embedding model called the "LINE," which is able to scale to very large, arbitrary types of networks: undirected, directed and/or weighted. The model optimizes an objective which preserves both the local and global network structures. Naturally, the local structures are represented by the observed links in the networks, which capture the *first-order* proximity between the vertices. Most existing graph embedding algorithms are designed to preserve this *first-order* proximity, e.g., IsoMap [20] and Laplacian eigenmap [2], even if they do not scale. We observe that in a real-world network many (if not the majority of) legitimate links are actually not observed. In other

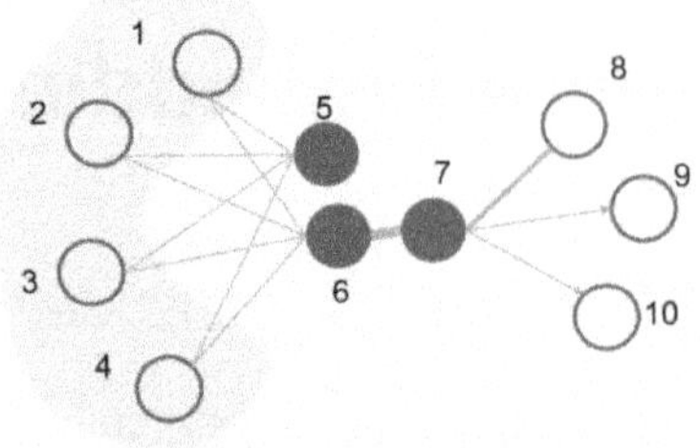

Figure 1: A toy example of information network. Edges can be undirected, directed, and/or weighted. Vertex 6 and 7 should be placed closely in the low-dimensional space as they are connected through a strong tie. Vertex 5 and 6 should also be placed closely as they share similar neighbors.

words, the observed *first-order* proximity in the real world data is not sufficient for preserving the global network structures. As a complement, we explore the *second-order* proximity between the vertices, which is not determined through the observed tie strength but through the shared neighborhood structures of the vertices. The general notion of the *second-order* proximity can be interpreted as nodes with shared neighbors being likely to be similar. Such an intuition can be found in the theories of sociology and linguistics. For example, "the degree of overlap of two people's friendship networks correlates with the strength of ties between them," in a social network [6]; and "You shall know a word by the company it keeps" (Firth, J. R. 1957:11) in text corpora [5]. Indeed, people who share many common friends are likely to share the same interest and become friends, and words that are used together with many similar words are likely to have similar meanings.

Fig. 1 presents an illustrative example. As the weight of the edge between vertex 6 and 7 is large, i.e., 6 and 7 have a high *first-order* proximity, they should be represented closely to each other in the embedded space. On the other hand, though there is no link between vertex 5 and 6, they share many common neighbors, i.e., they have a high *second-order* proximity and therefore should also be represented closely to each other. We expect that the consideration of the *second-order* proximity effectively complements the sparsity of the *first-order* proximity and better preserves the global structure of the network. In this paper, we will present carefully designed objectives that preserve the first-order and the second-order proximities.

Even if a sound objective is found, optimizing it for a very large network is challenging. One approach that attracts attention in recent years is using the stochastic gradient descent for the optimization. However, we show that directly deploying the stochastic gradient descent is problematic for real world information networks. This is because in many networks, edges are weighted and the weights usually present a high variance. Consider a word co-occurrence network, in which the weights (co-occurrences) of word pairs may range from one to hundreds of thousands. These weights of the edges will be multiplied into the gradients, resulting in the explosion of the gradients and thus compromise the performance. To address this, we propose a novel edge-sampling method, which improves both the effectiveness and efficiency of the inference. We sample the edges with the probabilities proportional to their weights, and then treat the sampled edges as binary edges for model updating. With this sampling process, the objective function remains the same and the weights of the edges no longer affect the gradients.

The LINE is very general, which works well for directed or undirected, weighted or unweighted graphs. We evaluate the performance of the LINE with various real-world information networks, including language networks, social networks, and citation networks. The effectiveness of the learned embeddings is evaluated within multiple data mining tasks, including word analogy, text classification, and node classification. The results suggest that the LINE model outperforms other competitive baselines in terms of both effectiveness and efficiency. It is able to learn the embedding of a network with millions of nodes and billions of edges in a few hours on a single machine.

To summarize, we make the following contributions:

- We propose a novel network embedding model called the "LINE," which suits arbitrary types of information networks and easily scales to millions of nodes. It has a carefully designed objective function that preserves both the first-order and second-order proximities.
- We propose an edge-sampling algorithm for optimizing the objective. The algorithm tackles the limitation of the classical stochastic gradient decent and improves the effectiveness and efficiency of the inference.
- We conduct extensive experiments on real-world information networks. Experimental results prove the effectiveness and efficiency of the proposed LINE model.

Organization. The rest of this paper is organized as follows. Section 2 summarizes the related work. Section 3 formally defines the problem of large-scale information network embedding. Section 4 introduces the LINE model in details. Section 5 presents the experimental results. Finally we conclude in Section 6.

2. RELATED WORK

Our work is related to classical methods of graph embedding or dimension reduction in general, such as multidimensional scaling (MDS) [4], IsoMap [20], LLE [18] and Laplacian Eigenmap [2]. These approaches typically first construct the affinity graph using the feature vectors of the data points, e.g., the K-nearest neighbor graph of data, and then embed the affinity graph [22] into a low dimensional space. However, these algorithms usually rely on solving the leading eigenvectors of the affinity matrices, the complexity of which is at least quadratic to the number of nodes, making them inefficient to handle large-scale networks.

Among the most recent literature is a technique called graph factorization [1]. It finds the low-dimensional embedding of a large graph through matrix factorization, which is optimized using stochastic gradient descent. This is possible because a graph can be represented as an affinity matrix. However, the objective of matrix factorization is not designed for networks, therefore does not necessarily preserve the global network structure. Intuitively, graph factorization expects nodes with higher first-order proximity are represented closely. Instead, the LINE model uses an objective that is particularly designed for networks, which preserves both the *first-order* and the *second-order* proximities. Practically, the graph factorization method only applies to undirected graphs while the proposed model is applicable for both undirected and directed graphs.

The most recent work related with ours is DeepWalk [16], which deploys a truncated random walk for social network embedding. Although empirically effective, the DeepWalk does not provide a clear objective that articulates what network properties are preserved. Intuitively, DeepWalk expects nodes with higher *second-order* proximity yield similar low-dimensional representations, while the LINE preserves both *first-order* and *second-order* proximities. DeepWalk uses random walks to expand the neighborhood of a vertex, which is analogical to a depth-first search. We use a breadth-first search strategy, which is a more reasonable approach to the *second-order* proximity. Practically, DeepWalk only applies to unweighted networks, while our model is applicable for networks with both weighted and unweighted edges.

In Section 5, we empirically compare the proposed model with these methods using various real world networks.

3. PROBLEM DEFINITION

We formally define the problem of large-scale information network embedding using *first-order* and *second-order* proximities. We first define an information network as follows:

DEFINITION 1. ***(Information Network)*** *An* ***information network*** *is defined as $G = (V, E)$, where V is the set of vertices, each representing a data object and E is the set of edges between the vertices, each representing a relationship between two data objects. Each edge $e \in E$ is an ordered pair $e = (u, v)$ and is associated with a weight $w_{uv} > 0$, which indicates the strength of the relation. If G is undirected, we have $(u, v) \equiv (v, u)$ and $w_{uv} \equiv w_{vu}$; if G is directed, we have $(u, v) \not\equiv (v, u)$ and $w_{uv} \not\equiv w_{vu}$.*

In practice, information networks can be either directed (e.g., citation networks) or undirected (e.g., social network of users in Facebook). The weights of the edges can be either binary or take any real value. Note that while negative edge weights are possible, in this study we only consider non-negative weights. For example, in citation networks and social networks, w_{uv} takes binary values; in co-occurrence networks between different objects, w_{uv} can take any non-negative value. The weights of the edges in some networks may diverge as some objects co-occur many times while others may just co-occur a few times.

Embedding an information network into a low-dimensional space is useful in a variety of applications. To conduct the embedding, the network structures must be preserved. The first intuition is that the local network structure, i.e., the local pairwise proximity between the vertices, must be preserved. We define the local network structures as the *first-order* proximity between the vertices:

DEFINITION 2. ***(First-order Proximity)*** *The* ***first-order*** *proximity in a network is the* ***local*** *pairwise proximity between two vertices. For each pair of vertices linked by an edge (u, v), the weight on that edge, w_{uv}, indicates the first-order proximity between u and v. If no edge is observed between u and v, their* ***first-order*** *proximity is 0.*

The *first-order* proximity usually implies the similarity of two nodes in a real-world network. For example, people who are friends with each other in a social network tend to share similar interests; pages linking to each other in World Wide Web tend to talk about similar topics. Because of this importance, many existing graph embedding algorithms such as IsoMap, LLE, Laplacian eigenmap, and graph factorization have the objective to preserve the *first-order* proximity.

However, in a real world information network, the links observed are only a small proportion, with many others missing [10]. A pair of nodes on a missing link has a zero *first-order* proximity, even though they are intrinsically very similar to each other. Therefore, *first-order* proximity alone is not sufficient for preserving the network structures, and it is important to seek an alternative notion of proximity that addresses the problem of sparsity. A natural intuition is that vertices that share similar neighbors tend to be similar to each other. For example, in social networks, people who share similar friends tend to have similar interests and thus become friends; in word co-occurrence networks, words that always co-occur with the same set of words tend to have similar meanings. We therefore define the *second-order* proximity, which complements the first-order proximity and preserves the network structure.

DEFINITION 3. ***(Second-order Proximity)*** *The* ***second-order*** *proximity between a pair of vertices (u, v) in a network is the similarity between their neighborhood network structures. Mathematically, let $p_u = (w_{u,1}, \ldots, w_{u,|V|})$ denote the first-order proximity of u with all the other vertices, then the* second-order *proximity between u and v is determined by the similarity between p_u and p_v. If no vertex is linked from/to both u and v, the* ***second-order*** *proximity between u and v is 0.*

We investigate both *first-order* and *second-order* proximity for network embedding, which is defined as follows.

DEFINITION 4. ***(Large-scale Information Network Embedding)*** *Given a large network $G = (V, E)$, the problem of* ***Large-scale Information Network Embedding*** *aims to represent each vertex $v \in V$ into a low-dimensional space R^d, i.e., learning a function $f_G : V \to R^d$, where $d \ll |V|$. In the space R^d, both the* ***first-order*** *proximity and the* ***second-order*** *proximity between the vertices are preserved.*

Next, we introduce a large-scale network embedding model that preserves both *first-* and *second-order* proximities.

4. LINE: LARGE-SCALE INFORMATION NETWORK EMBEDDING

A desirable embedding model for real world information networks must satisfy several requirements: first, it must be able to preserve both the *first-order* proximity and the *second-order* proximity between the vertices; second, it must scale for very large networks, say millions of vertices and billions of edges; third, it can deal with networks with arbitrary types of edges: directed, undirected and/or weighted. In this section, we present a novel network embedding model called the "LINE," which satisfies all the three requirements.

4.1 Model Description

We describe the LINE model to preserve the *first-order* proximity and *second-order* proximity separately, and then introduce a simple way to combine the two proximity.

4.1.1 LINE with First-order Proximity

The *first-order* proximity refers to the local pairwise proximity between the vertices in the network. To model the *first-order* proximity, for each undirected edge (i, j), we define the joint probability between vertex v_i and v_j as follows:

$$p_1(v_i, v_j) = \frac{1}{1 + \exp(-\vec{u}_i^T \cdot \vec{u}_j)}, \tag{1}$$

where $\vec{u}_i \in R^d$ is the low-dimensional vector representation of vertex v_i. Eqn. (1) defines a distribution $p(\cdot, \cdot)$ over the space $V \times V$, and its empirical probability can be defined as $\hat{p}_1(i, j) = \frac{w_{ij}}{W}$, where $W = \sum_{(i,j) \in E} w_{ij}$. To preserve the first-order proximity, a straightforward way is to minimize the following objective function:

$$O_1 = d(\hat{p}_1(\cdot, \cdot), p_1(\cdot, \cdot)), \tag{2}$$

where $d(\cdot, \cdot)$ is the distance between two distributions. We choose to minimize the KL-divergence of two probability distributions. Replacing $d(\cdot, \cdot)$ with KL-divergence and omitting some constants, we have:

$$O_1 = - \sum_{(i,j) \in E} w_{ij} \log p_1(v_i, v_j), \tag{3}$$

Note that the *first-order* proximity is only applicable for undirected graphs, not for directed graphs. By finding the $\{\vec{u}_i\}_{i=1..|V|}$ that minimize the objective in Eqn. (3), we can represent every vertex in the d-dimensional space.

4.1.2 LINE with Second-order Proximity

The *second-order* proximity is applicable for both directed and undirected graphs. Given a network, without loss of generality, we assume it is directed (an undirected edge can be considered as two directed edges with opposite directions and equal weights). The *second-order* proximity assumes that vertices sharing many connections to other vertices are similar to each other. In this case, each vertex is also treated as a specific "context" and vertices with similar distributions over the "contexts" are assumed to be similar. Therefore, each vertex plays two roles: the vertex itself and a specific "context" of other vertices. We introduce two vectors $\vec{u}_i$ and $\vec{u}_i'$, where $\vec{u}_i$ is the representation of v_i when it is treated as a vertex while $\vec{u}_i'$ is the representation of v_i when it is treated as a specific "context". For each directed edge (i, j), we first define the probability of "context" v_j generated by vertex v_i as:

$$p_2(v_j | v_i) = \frac{\exp(\vec{u}_j'^T \cdot \vec{u}_i)}{\sum_{k=1}^{|V|} \exp(\vec{u}_k'^T \cdot \vec{u}_i)}, \tag{4}$$

where $|V|$ is the number of vertices or "contexts." For each vertex v_i, Eqn. (4) actually defines a conditional distribution $p_2(\cdot | v_i)$ over the contexts, i.e., the entire set of vertices in the network. As mentioned above, the *second-order* proximity assumes that vertices with similar distributions over the contexts are similar to each other. To preserve the *second-order* proximity, we should make the conditional distribution of the contexts $p_2(\cdot | v_i)$ specified by the low-dimensional representation be close to the empirical distribution $\hat{p}_2(\cdot | v_i)$. Therefore, we minimize the following objective function:

$$O_2 = \sum_{i \in V} \lambda_i d(\hat{p}_2(\cdot | v_i), p_2(\cdot | v_i)), \tag{5}$$

where $d(\cdot, \cdot)$ is the distance between two distributions. As the importance of the vertices in the network may be different, we introduce λ_i in the objective function to represent the prestige of vertex i in the network, which can be measured by the degree or estimated through algorithms such as PageRank [15]. The empirical distribution $\hat{p}_2(\cdot | v_i)$ is defined as $\hat{p}_2(v_j | v_i) = \frac{w_{ij}}{d_i}$, where w_{ij} is the weight of the edge (i, j) and d_i is the out-degree of vertex i, i.e. $d_i = \sum_{k \in N(i)} w_{ik}$, where $N(i)$ is the set of out-neighbors of v_i. In this paper, for simplicity we set λ_i as the degree of vertex i, i.e., $\lambda_i = d_i$, and here we also adopt KL-divergence as the distance function. Replacing $d(\cdot, \cdot)$ with KL-divergence, setting $\lambda_i = d_i$ and omitting some constants, we have:

$$O_2 = - \sum_{(i,j) \in E} w_{ij} \log p_2(v_j | v_i). \tag{6}$$

By learning $\{\vec{u}_i\}_{i=1..|V|}$ and $\{\vec{u}_i'\}_{i=1..|V|}$ that minimize this objective, we are able to represent every vertex v_i with a d-dimensional vector $\vec{u}_i$.

4.1.3 Combining first-order and second-order proximities

To embed the networks by preserving both the *first-order* and *second-order* proximity, a simple and effective way we find in practice is to train the LINE model which preserves the *first-order* proximity and *second-order* proximity separately and then concatenate the embeddings trained by the two methods for each vertex. A more principled way to combine the two proximity is to jointly train the objective function (3) and (6), which we leave as future work.

4.2 Model Optimization

Optimizing objective (6) is computationally expensive, which requires the summation over the entire set of vertices when calculating the conditional probability $p_2(\cdot | v_i)$. To address this problem, we adopt the approach of negative sampling proposed in [13], which samples multiple negative edges according to some noisy distribution for each edge (i, j). More specifically, it specifies the following objective function for each edge (i, j):

$$\log \sigma(\vec{u}_j'^{T} \cdot \vec{u}_i) + \sum_{i=1}^{K} E_{v_n \sim P_n(v)}[\log \sigma(-\vec{u}_n'^{T} \cdot \vec{u}_i)], \tag{7}$$

where $\sigma(x) = 1/(1 + \exp(-x))$ is the sigmoid function. The first term models the observed edges, the second term models the negative edges drawn from the noise distribution and K is the number of negative edges. We set $P_n(v) \propto d_v{}^{3/4}$ as proposed in [13], where d_v is the out-degree of vertex v.

For the objective function (3), there exists a trivial solution: $u_{ik} = \infty$, for i=1, ..., $|V|$ and $k = 1, \ldots, d$. To avoid the trivial solution, we can still utilize the negative sampling approach (7) by just changing $\vec{u}_j'^T$ to $\vec{u}_j^T$.

We adopt the asynchronous stochastic gradient algorithm (ASGD) [17] for optimizing Eqn. (7). In each step, the ASGD algorithm samples a mini-batch of edges and then updates the model parameters. If an edge (i, j) is sampled, the gradient w.r.t. the embedding vector $\vec{u}_i$ of vertex i will be calculated as:

$$\frac{\partial O_2}{\partial \vec{u}_i} = w_{ij} \cdot \frac{\partial \log p_2(v_j | v_i)}{\partial \vec{u}_i} \tag{8}$$

Note that the gradient will be multiplied by the weight of the edge. This will become problematic when the weights of edges have a high variance. For example, in a word co-occurrence network, some words co-occur many times (e.g., tens of thousands) while some words co-occur only a few times. In such networks, the scales of the gradients diverge and it is very hard to find a good learning rate. If we select a large learning rate according to the edges with small weights, the gradients on edges with large weights will explode while the gradients will become too small if we select the learning rate according to the edges with large weights.

4.2.1 Optimization via Edge Sampling

The intuition in solving the above problem is that if the weights of all the edges are equal (e.g., network with binary edges), then there will be no problem of choosing an appropriate learning rate. A simple treatment is thus to unfold a weighted edge into multiple *binary* edges, e.g., an edge with weight w is unfolded into w *binary* edges. This will solve the problem but will significantly increase the memory requirement, especially when the weights of the edges are very large. To resolve this, one can sample from the original edges and treat the sampled edges as *binary* edges, with the sampling probabilities proportional to the original edge weights. With this edge-sampling treatment, the overall objective function remains the same. The problem boils down to how to sample the edges according to their weights.

Let $W = (w_1, w_2, \ldots, w_{|E|})$ denote the sequence of the weights of the edges. One can simply calculate the sum of the weights $w_{sum} = \sum_{i=1}^{|E|} w_i$ first, and then to sample a random value within the range of $[0, w_{sum}]$ to see which interval $[\sum_{j=0}^{i-1} w_j, \sum_{j=0}^{i} w_j)$ the random value falls into. This approach takes $O(|E|)$ time to draw a sample, which is costly when the number of edges $|E|$ is large. We use the alias table method [9] to draw a sample according to the weights of the edges, which takes only $O(1)$ time when repeatedly drawing samples from the same discrete distribution.

Sampling an edge from the alias table takes constant time, $O(1)$, and optimization with negative sampling takes $O(d(K+1))$ time, where K is the number of negative samples. Therefore, overall each step takes $O(dK)$ time. In practice, we find that the number of steps used for optimization is usually proportional to the number of edges $O(|E|)$. Therefore, the overall time complexity of the LINE is $O(dK|E|)$, which is linear to the number of edges $|E|$, and does not depend on the number of vertices $|V|$. The edge sampling treatment improves the effectiveness of the stochastic gradient descent without compromising the efficiency.

4.3 Discussion

We discuss several practical issues of the LINE model.
Low degree vertices. One practical issue is how to accurately embed vertices with small degrees. As the number of neighbors of such a node is very small, it is very hard to accurately infer its representation, especially with the *second-order* proximity based methods which heavily rely on the number of "contexts." An intuitive solution to this is expanding the neighbors of those vertices by adding higher order neighbors, such as neighbors of neighbors. In this paper, we only consider adding second-order neighbors, i.e., neighbors of neighbors, to each vertex. The weight between vertex i and its second-order neighbor j is measured as

$$w_{ij} = \sum_{k \in N(i)} w_{ik} \frac{w_{kj}}{d_k}. \quad (9)$$

In practice, one can only add a subset of vertices $\{j\}$ which have the largest proximity w_{ij} with the low degree vertex i.
New vertices. Another practical issue is how to find the representation of newly arrived vertices. For a new vertex i, if its connections to the existing vertices are known, we can obtain the empirical distribution $\hat{p}_1(\cdot, v_i)$ and $\hat{p}_2(\cdot|v_i)$ over existing vertices. To obtain the embedding of the new vertex, according to the objective function Eqn. (3) or Eqn. (6), a straightforward way is to minimize either one of the following objective functions

$$-\sum_{j \in N(i)} w_{ji} \log p_1(v_j, v_i), \text{ or } -\sum_{j \in N(i)} w_{ji} \log p_2(v_j|v_i), \quad (10)$$

by updating the embedding of the new vertex and keeping the embeddings of existing vertices. If no connections between the new vertex and existing vertices are observed, we must resort to other information, such as the textual information of the vertices, and we leave it as our future work.

5. EXPERIMENTS

We empirically evaluated the effectiveness and efficiency of the LINE. We applied the method to several large-scale real-world networks of different types, including a language network, two social networks, and two citation networks.

5.1 Experiment Setup

Data Sets.

(1) LANGUAGE NETWORK. We constructed a word co-occurrence network from the entire set of English WIKIPEDIA pages. Words within every 5-word sliding window are considered to be co-occurring with each other. Words with frequency smaller than 5 are filtered out. (2) SOCIAL NETWORKS. We use two social networks: FLICKR and YOUTUBE[2]. The FLICKR network is denser than the YOUTUBE network (the same network as used in DeepWalk [16]). (3) CITATION NETWORKS. Two types of citation networks are used: an author citation network and a paper citation network. We use the DBLP data set [19][3] to construct the citation networks between authors and between papers. The author citation network records the number of papers written by one author and cited by another author. The detailed statistics of these networks are summarized into Table 1. They represent a variety of information networks: directed and undirected, binary and weighted. Each network contains at least half a million nodes and millions of edges, with the largest network containing around two million nodes and a billion edges.

Compared Algorithms.

We compare the LINE model with several existing graph embedding methods that are able to scale up to very large networks. We do not compare with some classical graph embedding algorithms such as MDS, IsoMap, and Laplacian eigenmap, as they cannot handle networks of this scale.

- Graph factorization (GF) [1]. We compare with the matrix factorization techniques for graph factorization. An information network can be represented as an affinity matrix, and is able to represent each vertex with a

[2]Available at http://socialnetworks.mpi-sws.org/data-imc2007.html
[3]Available at http://arnetminer.org/citation

Table 1: Statistics of the real-world information networks.

	Language Network	Social Network		Citation Network	
Name	WIKIPEDIA	FLICKR	YOUTUBE	DBLP(AUTHORCITATION)	DBLP(PAPERCITATION)
Type	undirected,weighted	undirected,binary	undirected,binary	dircted,weighted	directed,binary
|V|	1,985,098	1,715,256	1,138,499	524,061	781,109
|E|	1,000,924,086	22,613,981	2,990,443	20,580,238	4,191,677
Avg. degree	504.22	26.37	5.25	78.54	10.73
#Labels	7	5	47	7	7
#train	70,000	75,958	31,703	20,684	10,398

low-dimensional vector through matrix factorization. Graph factorization is optimized through stochastic gradient descent and is able to handle large networks. It only applies to undirected networks.

- DeepWalk [16]. DeepWalk is an approach recently proposed for social network embedding, which is only applicable for networks with binary edges. For each vertex, truncated random walks starting from the vertex are used to obtain the contextual information, and therefore only *second-order* proximity is utilized.

- LINE-SGD. This is the LINE model introduced in Section 4.1 that optimizes the objective Eqn. (3) or Eqn. (6) directly with stochastic gradient descent. With this approach, the weights of the edges are directly multiplied into the gradients when the edges are sampled for model updating. There are two variants of this approach: LINE-SGD(1st) and LINE-SGD(2nd), which use *first-* and *second-order* proximity respectively.

- LINE. This is the LINE model optimized through the edge-sampling treatment introduced in Section 4.2. In each stochastic gradient step, an edge is sampled with the probability proportional to its weight and then treated as binary for model updating. There are also two variants: LINE(1st) and LINE(2nd). Like the graph factorization, both LINE(1st) and LINE-SGD(1st) only apply to undirected graphs. LINE(2nd) and LINE-SGD(2nd) apply to both undirected and directed graphs.

- LINE (1st+2nd): To utilize both *first-order* and *second-order* proximity, a simple and effective way is to concatenate the vector representations learned by LINE(1st) and LINE(2nd) into a longer vector. After concatenation, the dimensions should be re-weighted to balance the two representations. In a supervised learning task, the weighting of dimensions can be automatically found based on the training data. In an unsupervised task, however, it is more difficult to set the weights. Therefore we only apply LINE (1st+2nd) to the scenario of supervised tasks.

Parameter Settings.

The mini-batch size of the stochastic gradient descent is set as 1 for all the methods. Similar to [13], the learning rate is set with the starting value $\rho_0 = 0.025$ and $\rho_t = \rho_0(1-t/T)$, where T is the total number of mini-batches or edge samples. For fair comparisons, the dimensionality of the embeddings of the language network is set to 200, as used in word embedding [13]. For other networks, the dimension is set as 128 by default, as used in [16]. Other default settings include: the number of negative samples $K = 5$ for LINE and LINE-SGD; the total number of samples $T = 10$ billion for LINE(1st) and LINE(2nd), $T = 20$ billion for GF; window size $win = 10$, walk length $t = 40$, walks per vertex $\gamma = 40$ for DeepWalk. All the embedding vectors are finally normalized by setting $||\vec{w}||_2 = 1$.

5.2 Quantitative Results

5.2.1 Language Network

We start with the results on the language network, which contains two million nodes and a billion edges. Two applications are used to evaluate the effectiveness of the learned embeddings: word analogy [12] and document classification.

Table 2: Results of word analogy on WIKIPEDIA data.

Algorithm	Semantic (%)	Syntactic (%)	Overall (%)	Running time
GF	61.38	44.08	51.93	2.96h
DeepWalk	50.79	37.70	43.65	16.64h
SkipGram	69.14	57.94	63.02	2.82h
LINE-SGD(1st)	9.72	7.48	8.50	3.83h
LINE-SGD(2nd)	20.42	9.56	14.49	3.94h
LINE(1st)	58.08	49.42	53.35	2.44h
LINE(2nd)	**73.79**	**59.72**	**66.10**	2.55h

Word Analogy. This task is introduced by Mikolov et al. [12]. Given a word pair (a, b) and a word c, the task aims to find a word d, such that the relation between c and d is similar to the relation between a and b, or denoted as: $a : b \rightarrow c : ?$. For instance, given a word pair ("China","Beijing") and a word "France," the right answer should be "Paris" because "Beijing" is the capital of "China" just as "Paris" is the capital of "France." Given the word embeddings, this task is solved by finding the word d^* whose embedding is closest to the vector $\vec{u}_b - \vec{u}_a + \vec{u}_c$ in terms of cosine proximity, i.e., $d^* = \text{argmax}_d \cos((\vec{u}_b - \vec{u}_a + \vec{u}_c), \vec{u}_d)$. Two categories of word analogy are used in this task: semantic and syntactic.

Table 2 reports the results of word analogy using the embeddings of words learned on the WIKIPEDIA corpora (SkipGram) or the WIKIPEDIA word network (all other methods). For graph factorization, the weight between each pair of words is defined as the logarithm of the number of co-occurrences, which leads to better performance than the original value of co-occurrences. For DeepWalk, different cutoff thresholds are tried to convert the language network into a binary network, and the best performance is achieved when all the edges are kept in the network. We also compare with the state-of-the-art word embedding model SkipGram [12], which learns the word embeddings directly from the original Wikipedia pages and is also implicitly a matrix factorization approach [8]. The window size is set as 5, the same as used for constructing the language network.

We can see that LINE(2nd) outperforms all other methods, including the graph embedding methods and the SkipGram. This indicates that the *second-order* proximity bet-

Table 3: Results of Wikipedia page classification on WIKIPEDIA data set.

Metric	Algorithm	10%	20%	30%	40%	50%	60%	70%	80%	90%
Micro-F1	GF	79.63	80.51	80.94	81.18	81.38	81.54	81.63	81.71	81.78
	DeepWalk	78.89	79.92	80.41	80.69	80.92	81.08	81.21	81.35	81.42
	SkipGram	79.84	80.82	81.28	81.57	81.71	81.87	81.98	82.05	82.09
	LINE-SGD(1st)	76.03	77.05	77.57	77.85	78.08	78.25	78.39	78.44	78.49
	LINE-SGD(2nd)	74.68	76.53	77.54	78.18	78.63	78.96	79.19	79.40	79.57
	LINE(1st)	79.67	80.55	80.94	81.24	81.40	81.52	81.61	81.69	81.67
	LINE(2nd)	79.93	80.90	81.31	81.63	81.80	81.91	82.00	82.11	82.17
	LINE(1st+2nd)	**81.04****	**82.08****	**82.58****	**82.93****	**83.16****	**83.37****	**83.52****	**83.63****	**83.74****
Macro-F1	GF	79.49	80.39	80.82	81.08	81.26	81.40	81.52	81.61	81.68
	DeepWalk	78.78	79.78	80.30	80.56	80.82	80.97	81.11	81.24	81.32
	SkipGram	79.74	80.71	81.15	81.46	81.63	81.78	81.88	81.98	82.01
	LINE-SGD(1st)	75.85	76.90	77.40	77.71	77.94	78.12	78.24	78.29	78.36
	LINE-SGD(2nd)	74.70	76.45	77.43	78.09	78.53	78.83	79.08	79.29	79.46
	LINE(1st)	79.54	80.44	80.82	81.13	81.29	81.43	81.51	81.60	81.59
	LINE(2nd)	79.82	80.81	81.22	81.52	81.71	81.82	81.92	82.00	82.07
	LINE(1st+2nd)	**80.94****	**81.99****	**82.49****	**82.83****	**83.07****	**83.29****	**83.42****	**83.55****	**83.66****

Significantly outperforms GF at the: ** 0.01 and * 0.05 level, paired t-test.

ter captures the word semantics compared to the *first-order* proximity. This is not surprising, as a high *second-order* proximity implies that two words can be replaced in the same context, which is a stronger indicator of similar semantics than first-order co-occurrences. It is intriguing that the LINE(2nd) outperforms the state-of-the-art word embedding model trained on the original corpus. The reason may be that a language network better captures the global structure of word co-occurrences than the original word sequences. Among other methods, both graph factorization and LINE(1st) significantly outperform DeepWalk even if DeepWalk explores second-order proximity. This is because DeepWalk has to ignore the weights (i.e., co-occurrences) of the edges, which is very important in a language network. The performance by the LINE models directly optimized with SGD is much worse, because the weights of the edges in the language network diverge, which range from a single digit to tens of thousands, making the learning process suffer. The LINE optimized by the edge-sampling treatment effectively addresses this problem, and performs very well using either *first-order* or *second-order* proximity.

All the models are run on a single machine with 1T memory, 40 CPU cores at 2.0GHZ using 16 threads. Both the LINE(1st) and LINE(2nd) are quite efficient, which take less than 3 hours to process such a network with 2 million nodes and a billion edges. Both are at least 10% faster than graph factorization, and much more efficient than DeepWalk (five times slower). The reason that LINE-SGDs are slightly slower is that a threshold-cutting technique has to be applied to prevent the gradients from exploding.

Document Classification. Another way to evaluate the quality of the word embeddings is to use the word vectors to compute document representation, which can be evaluated with document classification tasks. To obtain document vectors, we choose a very simple approach, taking the average of the word vector representations in that document. This is because we aim to compare the word embeddings with different approaches instead of finding the best method for document embeddings. The readers can find advanced document embedding approaches in [7]. We download the abstracts of Wikipedia pages from `http://downloads.dbpedia.org/3.9/en/long_abstracts_en.nq.bz2` and the categories of these pages from `http://downloads.dbpedia.org/3.9/en/article_categories_en.nq.bz2`. We choose 7 diverse categories for classification including "Arts," "History," "Human," "Mathematics," "Nature," "Technology," and "Sports." For each category, we randomly select 10,000 articles, and articles belonging to multiple categories are discarded. We randomly sample different percentages of the labeled documents for training and use the rest for evaluation. All document vectors are used to train a one-vs-rest logistic regression classifier using the LibLinear package[4]. We report the classification metrics Micro-F1 and Macro-F1 [11]. The results are averaged over 10 different runs by sampling different training data.

Table 3 reports the results of Wikipedia page classification. Similar conclusion can be made as in the word analogy task. The graph factorization outperforms DeepWalk as DeepWalk ignores the weights of the edges. The LINE-SGDs perform worse due to the divergence of the weights of the edges. The LINE optimized by the edge-sampling treatment performs much better than directly deploying SGD. The LINE(2nd) outperforms LINE(1st) and is slightly better than the graph factorization. Note that with the supervised task, it is feasible to concatenate the embeddings learned with LINE(1st) and LINE(2nd). As a result, the LINE(1st+2nd) method performs significantly better than all other methods. This indicates that the first-order and second-order proximities are complementary to each other.

To provide the readers more insight about the first-order and second-order proximities, Table 4 compares the most similar words to a given word using *first-order* and *second-order* proximity. We can see that by using the contextual proximity, the most similar words returned by the *second-order* proximity are all semantically related words. The most similar words returned by the *first-order* proximity are a mixture of syntactically and semantically related words.

Table 4: Comparison of most similar words using 1st-order and 2nd-order proximity.

Word	Similarity	Top similar words
good	1st	luck bad faith assume nice
	2nd	decent bad excellent lousy reasonable
information	1st	provide provides detailed facts verifiable
	2nd	infomation informaiton informations nonspammy animecons
graph	1st	graphs algebraic finite symmetric topology
	2nd	graphs subgraph matroid hypergraph undirected
learn	1st	teach learned inform educate how
	2nd	learned teach relearn learnt understand

5.2.2 *Social Network*

Compared with the language networks, the social networks are much sparser, especially the YOUTUBE network. We evaluate the vertex embeddings through a multi-label

[4]`http://www.csie.ntu.edu.tw/~cjlin/liblinear/`

Table 5: Results of multi-label classification on the FLICKR network.

Metric	Algorithm	10%	20%	30%	40%	50%	60%	70%	80%	90%
Micro-F1	GF	53.23	53.68	53.98	54.14	54.32	54.38	54.43	54.50	54.48
	DeepWalk	60.38	60.77	60.90	61.05	61.13	61.18	61.19	61.29	61.22
	DeepWalk(256dim)	60.41	61.09	61.35	61.52	61.69	61.76	61.80	61.91	61.83
	LINE(1st)	63.27	63.69	63.82	63.92	63.96	64.03	64.06	64.17	64.10
	LINE(2nd)	62.83	63.24	63.34	63.44	63.55	63.55	63.59	63.66	63.69
	LINE(1st+2nd)	**63.20****	**63.97****	**64.25****	**64.39****	**64.53****	**64.55****	**64.61****	**64.75****	**64.74****
Macro-F1	GF	48.66	48.73	48.84	48.91	49.03	49.03	49.07	49.08	49.02
	DeepWalk	58.60	58.93	59.04	59.18	59.26	59.29	59.28	59.39	59.30
	DeepWalk(256dim)	59.00	59.59	59.80	59.94	60.09	60.17	60.18	60.27	60.18
	LINE(1st)	62.14	62.53	62.64	62.74	62.78	62.82	62.86	62.96	62.89
	LINE(2nd)	61.46	61.82	61.92	62.02	62.13	62.12	62.17	62.23	62.25
	LINE(1st+2nd)	**62.23****	**62.95****	**63.20****	**63.35****	**63.48****	**63.48****	**63.55****	**63.69****	**63.68****

Significantly outperforms DeepWalk at the: ** 0.01 and * 0.05 level, paired t-test.

classification task that assigns every node into one or more communities. Different percentages of the vertices are randomly sampled for training and the rest are used for evaluation. The results are averaged over 10 different runs.

Flickr Network. Let us first take a look at the results on the FLICKR network. We choose the most popular 5 communities as the categories of the vertices for multi-label classification. Table 5 reports the results. Again, LINE(1st+2nd) significantly outperforms all other methods. LINE(1st) is slightly better than LINE(2nd), which is opposite to the results on the language network. The reasons are two fold: (1) *first-order* proximity is still more important than *second-order* proximity in social network, which indicates strong ties; (2) when the network is too sparse and the average number of neighbors of a node is too small, the *second-order* proximity may become inaccurate. We will further investigate this issue in Section 5.4. LINE(1st) outperforms graph factorization, indicating a better capability of modeling the *first-order* proximity. LINE(2nd) outperforms DeepWalk, indicating a better capability of modeling the *second-order* proximity. By concatenating the representations learned by LINE(1st) and LINE(2nd), the performance further improves, confirming that the two proximities are complementary to each other.

Youtube Network. Table 6 reports the results on YOUTUBE network, which is extremely sparse and the average degree is as low as 5. In most cases with different percentages of training data, LINE(1st) outperforms LINE(2nd), consistent with the results on the FLICKR network. Due to the extreme sparsity, the performance of LINE(2nd) is even inferior to DeepWalk. By combining the representations learned by the LINE with both the *first-* and *second-order* proximity, the performance of LINE outperforms DeepWalk with either 128 or 256 dimension, showing that the two proximities are complementary to each other and able to address the problem of network sparsity.

It is interesting to observe how DeepWalk tackles the network sparsity through truncated random walks, which enrich the neighbors or contexts of each vertex. The random walk approach acts like a depth-first search. Such an approach may quickly alleviate the sparsity of the neighborhood of nodes by bringing in indirect neighbors, but it may also introduce nodes that are long range away. A more reasonable way is to expand the neighborhood of each vertex using a breadth-first search strategy, i.e., recursively adding neighbors of neighbors. To verify this, we expand the neighborhood of the vertices whose degree are less than 1,000 by adding the neighbors of neighbors until the size of the extended neighborhood reaches 1,000 nodes. We find that adding more than 1,000 vertices does not further increase the performance.

The results in the brackets in Table 6 are obtained on this reconstructed network. The performance of GF, LINE(1st) and LINE(2nd) all improves, especially LINE(2nd). In the reconstructed network, the LINE(2nd) outperforms DeepWalk in most cases. We can also see that the performance of LINE(1st+2nd) on the reconstructed network does not improve too much compared with those on the original network. This implies that the combination of *first-order* and *second-order* proximity on the original network has already captured most information and LINE(1st+2nd) approach is a quite effective and efficient way for network embedding, suitable for both dense and sparse networks.

5.2.3 Citation Network

We present the results on two *citation* networks, both of which are directed networks. Both the GF and LINE methods, which use *first-order* proximity, are not applicable for directed networks, and hence we only compare DeepWalk and LINE(2nd). We also evaluate the vertex embeddings through a multi-label classification task. We choose 7 popular conferences including AAAI, CIKM, ICML, KDD, NIPS, SIGIR, and WWW as the classification categories. Authors publishing in the conferences or papers published in the conferences are assumed to belong to the categories corresponding to the conferences.

DBLP(AuthorCitation) Network. Table 7 reports the results on the DBLP(AUTHORCITATION) network. As this network is also very sparse, DeepWalk outperforms LINE(2nd). However, by reconstructing the network through recursively adding neighbors of neighbors for vertices with small degrees (smaller than 500), the performance of LINE(2nd) significantly increases and outperforms DeepWalk. The LINE model directly optimized by stochastic gradient descent, LINE(2nd), does not perform well as expected.

DBLP(PaperCitation) Network. Table 8 reports the results on the DBLP(PAPERCITATION) network. The LINE(2nd) significantly outperforms DeepWalk. This is because the random walk on the paper citation network can only reach papers along the citing path (i.e., older papers) and cannot reach other references. Instead, the LINE(2nd) represents each paper with its references, which is obviously more reasonable. The performance of LINE(2nd) is further improved when the network is reconstructed by enriching the neighbors of vertices with small degrees (smaller than 200).

5.3 Network Layouts

An important application of network embedding is to create meaningful visualizations that layout a network on a

Table 6: Results of multi-label classification on the YOUTUBE network. The results in the brackets are on the reconstructed network, which adds second-order neighbors (i.e., neighbors of neighbors) as neighbors for vertices with a low degree.

Metric	Algorithm	1%	2%	3%	4%	5%	6%	7%	8%	9%	10%
Micro-F1	GF	25.43 (24.97)	26.16 (26.48)	26.60 (27.25)	26.91 (27.87)	27.32 (28.31)	27.61 (28.68)	27.88 (29.01)	28.13 (29.21)	28.30 (29.36)	28.51 (29.63)
	DeepWalk	39.68	41.78	42.78	43.55	43.96	44.31	44.61	44.89	45.06	45.23
	DeepWalk(256dim)	39.94	42.17	43.19	44.05	44.47	44.84	45.17	45.43	45.65	45.81
	LINE(1st)	35.43 (36.47)	38.08 (38.87)	39.33 (40.01)	40.21 (40.85)	40.77 (41.33)	41.24 (41.73)	41.53 (42.05)	41.89 (42.34)	42.07 (42.57)	42.21 (42.73)
	LINE(2nd)	32.98 (36.78)	36.70 (40.37)	38.93 (42.10)	40.26 (43.25)	41.08 (43.90)	41.79 (44.44)	42.28 (44.83)	42.70 (45.18)	43.04 (45.50)	43.34 (45.67)
	LINE(1st+2nd)	39.01* **(40.20)**	41.89 **(42.70)**	43.14 **(43.94**)**	44.04 **(44.71**)**	44.62 **(45.19**)**	45.06 **(45.55**)**	45.34 **(45.87**)**	45.69** **(46.15**)**	45.91** **(46.33**)**	46.08** **(46.43**)**
Macro-F1	GF	7.38 (11.01)	8.44 (13.55)	9.35 (14.93)	9.80 (15.90)	10.38 (16.45)	10.79 (16.93)	11.21 (17.38)	11.55 (17.64)	11.81 (17.80)	12.08 (18.09)
	DeepWalk	28.39	30.96	32.28	33.43	33.92	34.32	34.83	35.27	35.54	35.86
	DeepWalk (256dim)	28.95	31.79	33.16	34.42	34.93	35.44	35.99	36.41	36.78	37.11
	LINE(1st)	28.74 (29.40)	31.24 (31.75)	32.26 (32.74)	33.05 (33.41)	33.30 (33.70)	33.60 (33.99)	33.86 (34.26)	34.18 (34.52)	34.33 (34.77)	34.44 (34.92)
	LINE(2nd)	17.06 (22.18)	21.73 (27.25)	25.28 (29.87)	27.36 (31.88)	28.50 (32.86)	29.59 (33.73)	30.43 (34.50)	31.14 (35.15)	31.81 (35.76)	32.32 (36.19)
	LINE(1st+2nd)	**29.85** (29.24)	31.93 **(33.16**)**	33.96 **(35.08**)**	35.46** **(36.45**)**	36.25** **(37.14**)**	36.90** **(37.69**)**	37.48** **(38.30**)**	38.10** **(38.80**)**	38.46** **(39.15**)**	38.82** **(39.40**)**

Significantly outperforms DeepWalk at the: ** 0.01 and * 0.05 level, paired t-test.

Table 7: Results of multi-label classification on DBLP(AUTHORCITATION) network.

Metric	Algorithm	10%	20%	30%	40%	50%	60%	70%	80%	90%
Micro-F1	DeepWalk	63.98	64.51	64.75	64.81	64.92	64.99	64.99	65.00	64.90
	LINE-SGD(2nd)	56.64	58.95	59.89	60.20	60.44	60.61	60.58	60.73	60.59
	LINE(2nd)	62.49 **(64.69*)**	63.30 **(65.47**)**	63.63 **(65.85**)**	63.77 **(66.04**)**	63.84 **(66.19**)**	63.94 **(66.25**)**	63.96 **(66.30**)**	64.00 **(66.12**)**	63.77 **(66.05**)**
Macro-F1	DeepWalk	63.02	63.60	63.84	63.90	63.98	64.06	64.09	64.11	64.05
	LINE-SGD(2nd)	55.24	57.63	58.56	58.82	59.11	59.27	59.28	59.46	59.37
	LINE(2nd)	61.43 **(63.49*)**	62.38 **(64.42**)**	62.73 **(64.84**)**	62.87 **(65.05**)**	62.93 **(65.19**)**	63.05 **(65.26**)**	63.07 **(65.29**)**	63.13 **(65.14**)**	62.95 **(65.14**)**

Significantly outperforms DeepWalk at the: ** 0.01 and * 0.05 level, paired t-test.

Table 8: Results of multi-label classification on DBLP(PAPERCITATION) network.

Metric	Algorithm	10%	20%	30%	40%	50%	60%	70%	80%	90%
Micro-F1	DeepWalk	52.83	53.80	54.24	54.75	55.07	55.13	55.48	55.42	55.90
	LINE(2nd)	58.42 **(60.10**)**	59.58 **(61.06**)**	60.29 **(61.46**)**	60.78 **(61.73**)**	60.94 **(61.85**)**	61.20 **(62.10**)**	61.39 **(62.21**)**	61.39 **(62.25**)**	61.79 **(62.80**)**
Macro-F1	DeepWalk	43.74	44.85	45.34	45.85	46.20	46.25	46.51	46.36	46.73
	LINE(2nd)	48.74 **(50.22**)**	50.10 **(51.41**)**	50.84 **(51.92**)**	51.31 **(52.20**)**	51.61 **(52.40**)**	51.77 **(52.59**)**	51.94 **(52.78**)**	51.89 **(52.70**)**	52.16 **(53.02**)**

Significantly outperforms DeepWalk at the: ** 0.01 and * 0.05 level, paired t-test.

(a) GF (b) DeepWalk (c) LINE(2nd)

Figure 2: Visualization of the co-author network. The authors are mapped to the 2-D space using the t-SNE package with learned embeddings as input. Color of a node indicates the community of the author. Red: "data Mining," blue: "machine learning," green: "computer vision."

two dimensional space. We visualize a co-author network extracted from the DBLP data. We select some conferences from three different research fields: WWW, KDD from "data mining," NIPS, ICML from "machine learning," and CVPR, ICCV from "computer vision." The co-author network is built from the papers published in these conferences. Authors with degree less than 3 are filtered out, and finally the network contains 18,561 authors and 207,074 edges. Laying out this co-author network is very challenging as the three research fields are very close to each other. We first map the co-author network into a low-dimensional space with different embedding approaches and then further map the low-dimensional vectors of the vertices to a 2-D space with the t-SNE package [21]. Fig. 2 compares the visualization results with different embedding approaches. The visualization using graph factorization is not very meaningful, in which the authors belonging to the same communities are not clustered together. The result of DeepWalk is much better. However, many authors belonging to different communities are clustered tightly into the center area, most of which are high degree vertices. This is because DeepWalk uses a random walk based approach to enrich the neighbors of the vertices, which brings in a lot of noise due to the randomness, especially for vertices with higher degrees. The LINE(2nd) performs quite well and generates meaningful layout of the network (nodes with same colors are distributed closer).

5.4 Performance w.r.t. Network Sparsity

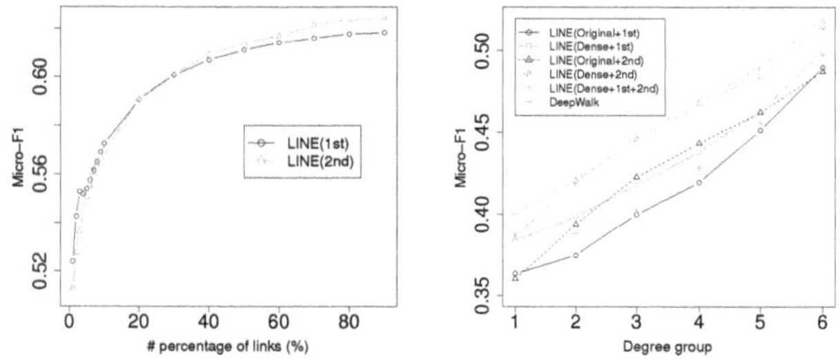

(a) Sparsity. (b) Degree of vertex.

Figure 3: Performance w.r.t. network sparsity.

In this subsection, we formally analyze the performance of the above models w.r.t. the sparsity of networks. We use the social networks as examples. We first investigate how the sparsity of the networks affects the LINE(1st) and LINE(2nd). Fig. 3(a) shows the results w.r.t. the percentage of links on the FLICKR network. We choose FLICKR network as it is much denser than the YOUTUBE network. We randomly select different percentages of links from the original network to construct networks with different levels of sparsity. We can see that in the beginning, when the network is very sparse, the LINE(1st) outperforms LINE(2nd). As we gradually increase the percentage of links, the LINE(2nd) begins to outperform the LINE(1st). This shows that the *second-order* proximity suffers when the network is extremely sparse, and it outperforms *first-order* proximity when there are sufficient nodes in the neighborhood of a node.

Fig. 3(b) shows the performance w.r.t. the degrees of the vertices on both the original and reconstructed YOUTUBE networks. We categorize the vertices into different groups according to their degrees including $(0, 1], [2, 3], [4, 6], [7, 12], [13, 30], [31, +\infty)$, and then evaluate the performance of vertices in different groups. Overall, the performance of different models increases when the degrees of the vertices increase. In the original network, the LINE(2nd) outperforms LINE(1st) except for the *first* group, which confirms that the *second-order* proximity does not work well for nodes with a low degree. In the reconstructed dense network, the performance of the LINE(1st) or LINE(2nd) improves, especially the LINE(2nd) that preserves the *second-order* proximity. We can also see that the LINE(2nd) model on the reconstructed network outperforms DeepWalk in all the groups.

5.5 Parameter Sensitivity

Next, we investigate the performance w.r.t. the parameter dimension d and the converging performance of different models w.r.t the number of samples on the reconstructed YOUTUBE network. Fig. 4(a) reports the performance of the LINE model w.r.t. the dimension d. We can see that the performance of the LINE(1st) or LINE(2nd) drops when the dimension becomes too large. Fig. 4(b) shows the results of the LINE and DeepWalk w.r.t. the number of samples during the optimization. The LINE(2nd) consistently outperforms LINE(1st) and DeepWalk, and both the LINE(1st) and LINE(2nd) converge much faster than DeepWalk.

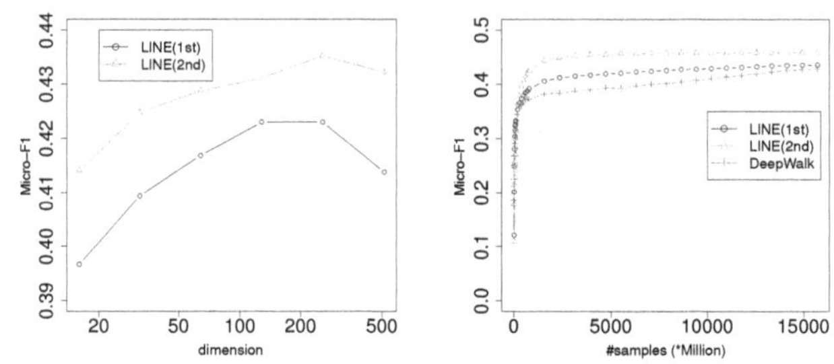

(a) #Dimension. (b) #Samples.

Figure 4: Sensitivity w.r.t. dimension and samples.

5.6 Scalability

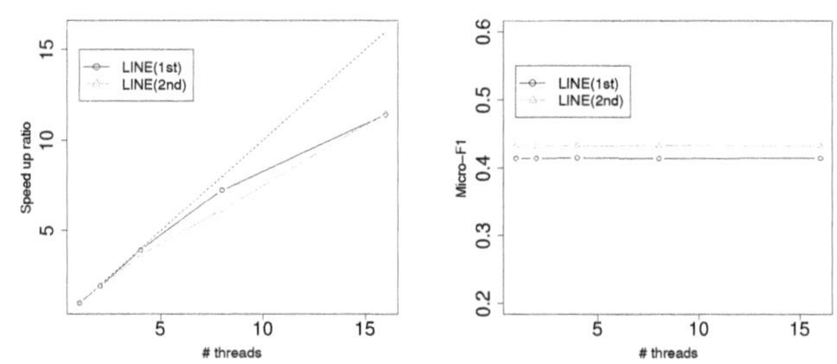

(a) Speed up v.s. #threads. (b) Micro-F1 v.s. #threads.

Figure 5: Performance w.r.t. # threads.

Finally, we investigate the scalability of the LINE model optimized by the edge-sampling treatment and asynchronous stochastic gradient descent, which deploys multiple threads for optimization. Fig. 5(a) shows the speed up w.r.t. the number of threads on the YOUTUBE data set. The speed up is quite close to linear. Fig. 5(b) shows that the classification performance remains stable when using multiple threads for model updating. The two figures together show that the inference algorithm of the LINE model is quite scalable.

6. CONCLUSION

This paper presented a novel network embedding model called the "LINE," which can easily scale up to networks with millions of vertices and billions of edges. It has carefully designed objective functions that preserve both the *first-order* and *second-order* proximities, which are complementary to each other. An efficient and effective edge-sampling method is proposed for model inference, which solved the limitation of stochastic gradient descent on weighted edges without compromising the efficiency. Experimental results on various real-world networks prove the efficiency and effectiveness of LINE. In the future, we plan to investigate higher-order proximity beyond the *first-order* and *second-order* proximities in the network. Besides, we also plan to investigate the embedding of heterogeneous information networks, e.g., vertices with multiple types.

Acknowledgments

The authors thank the three anonymous reviewers for the helpful comments. The co-author Ming Zhang is supported by the National Natural Science Foundation of China (NSFC Grant No. 61472006); Qiaozhu Mei is supported by the National Science Foundation under grant numbers IIS-1054199 and CCF-1048168.

7. REFERENCES

[1] A. Ahmed, N. Shervashidze, S. Narayanamurthy, V. Josifovski, and A. J. Smola. Distributed large-scale natural graph factorization. In *Proceedings of the 22nd international conference on World Wide Web*, pages 37–48. International World Wide Web Conferences Steering Committee, 2013.

[2] M. Belkin and P. Niyogi. Laplacian eigenmaps and spectral techniques for embedding and clustering. In *NIPS*, volume 14, pages 585–591, 2001.

[3] S. Bhagat, G. Cormode, and S. Muthukrishnan. Node classification in social networks. In *Social Network Data Analytics*, pages 115–148. Springer, 2011.

[4] T. F. Cox and M. A. Cox. *Multidimensional scaling.* CRC Press, 2000.

[5] J. R. Firth. A synopsis of linguistic theory, 1930–1955. *In J. R. Firth (Ed.), Studies in linguistic analysis*, pages 1–32.

[6] M. S. Granovetter. The strength of weak ties. *American journal of sociology*, pages 1360–1380, 1973.

[7] Q. Le and T. Mikolov. Distributed representations of sentences and documents. In *Proceedings of The 31st International Conference on Machine Learning*, pages 1188–1196, 2014.

[8] O. Levy and Y. Goldberg. Neural word embedding as implicit matrix factorization. In *Advances in Neural Information Processing Systems*, pages 2177–2185, 2014.

[9] A. Q. Li, A. Ahmed, S. Ravi, and A. J. Smola. Reducing the sampling complexity of topic models. In *Proceedings of the 20th ACM SIGKDD international conference on Knowledge discovery and data mining*, pages 891–900. ACM, 2014.

[10] D. Liben-Nowell and J. Kleinberg. The link-prediction problem for social networks. *Journal of the American society for information science and technology*, 58(7):1019–1031, 2007.

[11] C. D. Manning, P. Raghavan, and H. Schütze. *Introduction to information retrieval*, volume 1. Cambridge university press Cambridge, 2008.

[12] T. Mikolov, K. Chen, G. Corrado, and J. Dean. Efficient estimation of word representations in vector space. *arXiv preprint arXiv:1301.3781*, 2013.

[13] T. Mikolov, I. Sutskever, K. Chen, G. S. Corrado, and J. Dean. Distributed representations of words and phrases and their compositionality. In *Advances in Neural Information Processing Systems*, pages 3111–3119, 2013.

[14] S. A. Myers, A. Sharma, P. Gupta, and J. Lin. Information network or social network?: the structure of the twitter follow graph. In *Proceedings of the companion publication of the 23rd international conference on World wide web companion*, pages 493–498. International World Wide Web Conferences Steering Committee, 2014.

[15] L. Page, S. Brin, R. Motwani, and T. Winograd. The pagerank citation ranking: Bringing order to the web. 1999.

[16] B. Perozzi, R. Al-Rfou, and S. Skiena. Deepwalk: Online learning of social representations. In *Proceedings of the 20th ACM SIGKDD international conference on Knowledge discovery and data mining*, pages 701–710. ACM, 2014.

[17] B. Recht, C. Re, S. Wright, and F. Niu. Hogwild: A lock-free approach to parallelizing stochastic gradient descent. In *Advances in Neural Information Processing Systems*, pages 693–701, 2011.

[18] S. T. Roweis and L. K. Saul. Nonlinear dimensionality reduction by locally linear embedding. *Science*, 290(5500):2323–2326, 2000.

[19] J. Tang, J. Zhang, L. Yao, J. Li, L. Zhang, and Z. Su. Arnetminer: extraction and mining of academic social networks. In *Proceedings of the 14th ACM SIGKDD international conference on Knowledge discovery and data mining*, pages 990–998. ACM, 2008.

[20] J. B. Tenenbaum, V. De Silva, and J. C. Langford. A global geometric framework for nonlinear dimensionality reduction. *Science*, 290(5500):2319–2323, 2000.

[21] L. Van der Maaten and G. Hinton. Visualizing data using t-sne. *Journal of Machine Learning Research*, 9(2579-2605):85, 2008.

[22] S. Yan, D. Xu, B. Zhang, H.-J. Zhang, Q. Yang, and S. Lin. Graph embedding and extensions: a general framework for dimensionality reduction. *Pattern Analysis and Machine Intelligence, IEEE Transactions on*, 29(1):40–51, 2007.

[23] X. Yu, X. Ren, Y. Sun, Q. Gu, B. Sturt, U. Khandelwal, B. Norick, and J. Han. Personalized entity recommendation: A heterogeneous information network approach. In *Proceedings of the 7th ACM international conference on Web search and data mining*, pages 283–292. ACM, 2014.

Leveraging Pattern Semantics for Extracting Entities in Enterprises

Fangbo Tao[†], Bo Zhao[‡], Ariel Fuxman[♭], Yang Li[♮], Jiawei Han[†]
[*†]ftao2@illinois.edu, [‡]bozhao@linkedin.com, [♮]yangli@cs.ucsb.edu, [†]hanj@illinois.edu

[†]University of Illinois, Urbana, IL, USA
[‡]LinkedIn, Mountain View, CA, USA
[♭]Microsoft, Mountain View, CA, USA
[♮]UC Santa Barbara, Santa Barbara, CA, USA

ABSTRACT

Entity Extraction is a process of identifying meaningful entities from text documents. In enterprises, extracting entities improves enterprise efficiency by facilitating numerous applications, including search, recommendation, etc. However, the problem is particularly challenging on enterprise domains due to several reasons. First, the lack of redundancy of enterprise entities makes previous web-based systems like NELL and OpenIE not effective, since using only high-precision/low-recall patterns like those systems would miss the majority of sparse enterprise entities, while using more low-precision patterns in sparse setting also introduces noise drastically. Second, semantic drift is common in enterprises ("Blue" refers to "Windows Blue"), such that public signals from the web cannot be directly applied on entities. Moreover, many internal entities never appear on the web. Sparse internal signals are the only source for discovering them. To address these challenges, we propose an end-to-end framework for extracting entities in enterprises, taking the input of enterprise corpus and limited seeds to generate a high-quality entity collection as output. We introduce the novel concept of Semantic Pattern Graph to leverage public signals to understand the underlying semantics of lexical patterns, reinforce pattern evaluation using mined semantics, and yield more accurate and complete entities. Experiments on Microsoft enterprise data show the effectiveness of our approach.

Categories and Subject Descriptors

I.2.7 [**Artificial Intelligence**]: Natural Language Processing-text analysis; I.2.6 [**Artificial Intelligence**]: Learning- knowledge acquisition

*This work was done while the first four authors were employed at Microsoft. Fuxman's current affiliation: Google.

WWW 2015, May 18–22, 2015, Florence, Italy.
ACM 978-1-4503-3469-3/15/05.
http://dx.doi.org/10.1145/2736277.2741670.

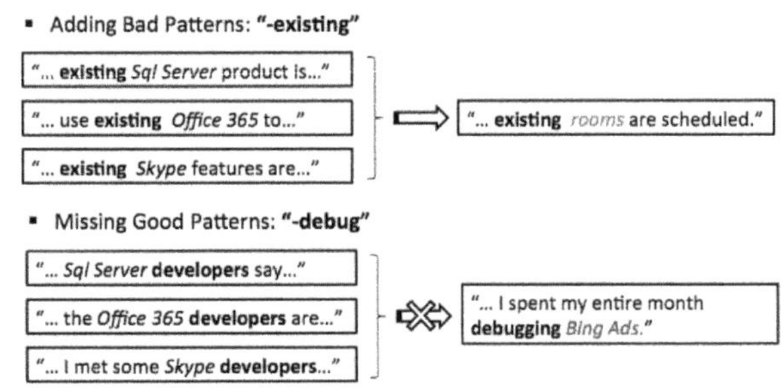

Figure 1: Two examples showing how sparsity makes entity extraction challenging in enterprises.

Keywords

Enterprise Entity Extraction, Semantic Pattern Graph, Enterprise Taxonomy

1. INTRODUCTION AND MOTIVATION

Access to an organized information network or knowledge base is critical for many real-world applications. Most real-world information is unstructured, interconnected, noisy, and often expressed in the form of text. This inspires constructing an organized, semi-structured knowledge base from the large volume of noisy text data. Such formal and structural representation of information has the advantage of being easy to manage and reason with, which can greatly facilitate many artificial intelligence applications, such as semantic search, reasoning and question answering. To achieve this goal, knowledge bases such as DBpedia [2] and Freebase [3] were manually constructed. However, due to the laborious, time consuming, and costly extracting and labeling process, these knowledge bases are often restricted by a very limited coverage. Recently, automatically constructed knowledge bases including YAGO [22], NELL [5] and Reverb [12] have emerged. However, it is still challenging to make such systems with both satisfactory coverage and quality. How to automatically construct a high-quality knowledge base from large amount of unstructured and noisy text data remains an open research problem.

Most previous studies on automatic knowledge base construction focus on open domain. Namely, they extract information from web-scale corpus and try to cover as many entities as possible. Despite the fact that these open domain efforts cover millions of entities, most lesser known or domain specific entities are not captured by them. Therefore, in closed domains (e.g., enterprises, governments, etc.), in order to better facilitate the knowledge-inspired applications, we have to build domain-specific knowledge bases. In this work, we focus on one particularly important domain, enterprises, and study the *Enterprise Entity Extraction* problem. Our goal is to harvest a comprehensive entity set from the enterprise corpus. The set should cover important entities within enterprises (e.g., products, teams, techniques, etc.) and provide categorical information for these entities. This can be seen as the first step towards building a complete enterprise knowledge base, which should eventually contain attributes, relations and brief summaries of these entities.

The *Enterprise Entity Extraction* task is very related to the Web Information Extraction [9, 5, 14, 21] problem, which aims to extract interesting entities (and potentially the relations among them) from Web corpus. Unfortunately, the techniques proposed for Web entity extraction can hardly be applied to enterprises. This is because enterprise corpora exhibit very different characteristics compared with the Web corpus, which leads to the following unique challenges for extracting entities in enterprises.

1. **Data Sparsity:** Enterprise entities exhibit much less redundancy than public entities in the Web. Therefore, the extracting techniques based on frequencies or statistics can hardly be utilized in enterprises.

2. **Semantic Drift:** Many entities in enterprises have special meanings different from the popular meanings in external world. For example, within Microsoft, "Blue" could mean "Microsoft Blue" instead of the color. Even for the same entities, the internal usage could be very different from the external usage. For example, for the entity "Windows", external usage mainly focuses how to install and use it, while internal usage cares more about implementation and design. Therefore, it is inappropriate to directly explore distributional semantics [17] for iteratively extracting enterprise entities.

3. **Low Public Coverage:** Most internal entities are not covered by public knowledge bases. Some are even not covered by the Web. Therefore, it is very hard to leverage public resources (e.g., Wikipedia, Google) to provide complementary information. For instance, the entity "Cloud ML" can only be found in Microsoft.

Data sparsity suggests to consider public data to alleviate deficient redundancy. However, due to Challenges 2 & 3, incorporating public signals on entities directly introduces much noise via Semantic Drift and also, not feasible for internal entities because of Low Public Coverage. Thus, instead of harvesting entity signals from public data, pattern-level approach is considered to tackle these challenges.

Most previous studies [9, 5, 14, 21] utilize general high precision/low recall patterns (e.g. Hearst Patterns) to extract entities. Namely, they extract lexical patterns, optionally with some fixed form (Hearst Patterns), from the contexts of seed entities, evaluate the patterns' precision, and promote only a few top ones for further entity extraction. While this is a good fit for the redundant Web corpus, it causes severe coverage issues in enterprise entity extraction since the enterprise corpus is very sparse. Based on our experiment on Microsoft corpus, under-utilizing these accurate patterns leads to less than 50% of enterprise entities being successfully extracted. That is to say, most entities in enterprise documents have contextual patterns with deficient mentions to be justified. But these patterns have

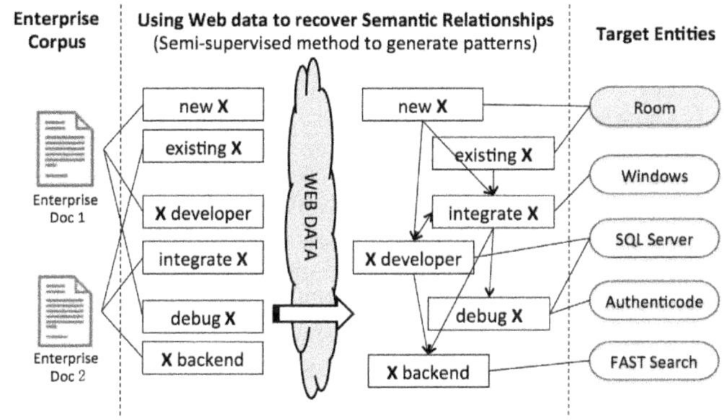

Figure 2: A toy example showing how we integrate enterprise corpus with web data to construct semantic pattern graph and improve entity quality.

highly relevant semantics to target entities, which we define as **Sparse Patterns**. Therefore, to better cover the remaining entities, some additional patterns (likely sparse) need to be incorporated.

Harvesting good patterns is very challenging, since the data sparsity issue makes it difficult to judge the quality of the patterns. As a result, the following two types of errors will emerge:

1. **Adding Bad Patterns:** Some bad patterns (e.g., very general patterns) may be wrongly judged as good ones. For example, as shown in Figure 1, pattern **"existing X"** is general enough for all kinds of entities, but it is mistakenly evaluated as a good pattern to distinguish "projects", due to the fact that **"existing X"** appears with all three positive seeds. Therefore, noun **"room"** would be implied as a "project" by the line "...*existing* **rooms** are scheduled...". Patterns like **"existing X"** are general enough to appear with any nouns. Using limited enterprise documents, we may not have enough signal to filter them out.

2. **Missing Good Patterns:** Some good patterns (especially sparse patterns) may be erroneously identified as bad. For instance, as shown in Figure 1, we already observe that **"X developer"** is a solid pattern since it appears with all the positive seeds. However, lexical pattern **"debug X"** was skipped by the extractor, since it never appears with seed entities. Therefore, the good pattern **"debug X"** is totally lost without any evidence to prove its efficacy. With enough background knowledge, any human expert can conclude that **"debug X"** has similar semantic to **"X developer"**. Moreover, an asymmetric relation holds here that **"X developer"** is more general than **"debug X"**. With high probability, an entity "X" that can be used as "debug X" can also be used as "X developer"; the other direction doesn't hold. This asymmetric relation implies that if **"X developer"** is a strong pattern to extract "projects", any noun "X" mentioned as **"debug X"** in the corpus should also be extracted as "projects" because the asymmetric relation makes the "X" possible to be used as **"X developer"**. However, using only enterprise corpus cannot discover the semantic relation

between these two patterns, which leads to poor performance of previous entity extractors.

To address these two problems, we developed a semi-supervised pattern extraction method and leverage Web data to understand the pattern semantics. As illustrated in Figure 2, semi-supervised pattern extraction can help extract more lexical patterns from enterprise text, while Web text can be used to build semantic relations between extracted patterns, which can be further utilized to induce sparse yet effective patterns. The built Semantic Graph helps to identify bad general patterns and good sparse patterns mentioned above, thus fixing the sparsity issue.

In this paper, we tackle the enterprise entity extraction problem via bootstrapping. We take a few seed entities plus an unlabeled enterprise corpus as input and produce a high-quality entity set as output. With insufficient knowledge of lexical patterns in enterprise corpus, we leverage public signals (i.e., Web text) to understand the underlying semantic relations among sparse lexical patterns. For this purpose, we propose a novel concept called Semantic Pattern Graph (SPG), which is a hierarchical graph structure describing the relations between lexical patterns. To the best of our knowledge, this is the first work that models semantic relations between lexical patterns for entity extraction.

Our contribution can be summarized as follows: (1) We develop an end-to-end framework for extracting entity in enterprises. (2) We propose the novel concept of Semantic Pattern Graph to utilize semantic relations between patterns for entity extraction. (3) We conduct comprehensive experiments on Microsoft enterprise corpus to justify the effectiveness of our system.

2. RELATED WORK

Recently, several open information extraction systems have been created. Most of them focus on entity and relation extraction on web-scale data. Knowitall [9, 10, 8] combined pattern-based and list-based extraction to achieve recall improvement. They used a set of generic, domain independent extraction patterns (mostly Hearst patterns [16]) to extend a set of seed concepts. NELL [5] is another open information extractor for harvesting entities and relations from the web. It used Coupled Pattern Learner [6], which extracts lexical patterns with part-of-speech (POS) restrictions from positively labeled data, to identify new entities. A restrict filtering constraint is applied to guarantee only high-precision/low-recall patterns are promoted. SPIED [14] used a similar way of pattern generation but scored patterns using both labeled and unlabeled entities. These three systems were designed to work with redundant entity mentions (e.g., web data) and performed poorly on sparse enterprise settings. In our tests of these pattern generators, we observe that high-precision/low-recall patterns they used can hardly cover 50% of our target entity set. We provide labeled data for SPIED and both precision and recall are quite unsatisfactory. Other open information extraction systems like ReVerb [12, 11] and OLLIE [21] used verbal patterns or some extraction templates, which may fail to work well in sparse environment. Moreover, Poon and Domingos [18] showed that open information extraction systems extracted low accuracy relational triples on a small corpus. Hence, two things are required in enterprise entity extraction: 1). More low-precision patterns need to be leveraged to cover more entities. 2). Open signals from the web need to be incorporated to improve accuracy of those sparse patterns.

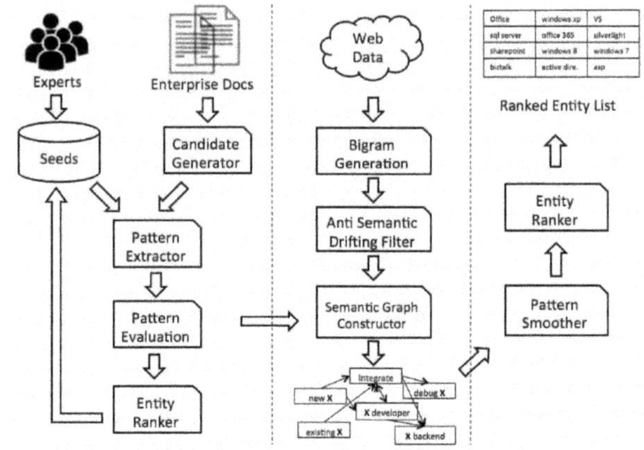

Figure 3: System Infrastructure

Our approach employs a semi-supervised bootstrap learning method, which begins with a small labeled set of target entities, trains a learning/ranking model, and uses that model to label more data and so on. Yarowsky [27] applied bootstrapped learning on word sense disambiguation. Later Riloff [19] used a set of seed entities to learn rules for entity extraction from unlabeled data and extended it to multi-class learning in [24]. Similar methods are also used in many set-expansion works. SEAL [25, 26] is a web-based set expansion system that uses wrappers (i.e., page-specific extraction rules) to extract more entities. It takes advantage of both page structure and text from webpages. For many cases where only text data is available, several IE systems [14, 1, 4, 20] also applied bootstrap method, specify a small set of domain-specific seed instances as input, then alternately learn patterns from seeds, and extend seeds from patterns. Our system inherits the semi-supervised bootstrap learning method for enterprise entity extraction.

A distinctive feature of our system is its use of Semantic Pattern Graph, which is derived from web-scale data, to re-score patterns and ease the sparsity issue. The pioneering work for pattern generation and scoring by Hearst [16] manually evaluated generated patterns to extract hypernym-hyponym pairs. Previous systems [13, 7, 23] used fully labeled corpus to score rules. Later, Carlson et al. [6] assessed patterns by precision and only promote patterns with high precision. We implemented their pattern assessment method in this paper for comparison and shown that his strategy works poorly on small corpus due to the coverage of high-precision patterns are very small. Gupta and Manning [15, 14] predicted labels of unlabeled entities to score patterns using features like distributional similarity and edit distances. None of the above works well enough in a enterprise setting due to the sparse and biased signals of patterns. Our system outperforms them by utilizing outside signals from the web to adjust the biased evaluation of patterns, which is computed merely using mentions in enterprise corpus.

3. APPROACH

We apply a set expansion framework to extract enterprise entities class by class. The reason is that letting domain experts provide a seed set for each entity class is relatively cheap. Moreover, in some enterprises (e.g., Microsoft), a partial taxonomy has been built by their employees, which can serve as the seed set directly. For ease of exposition, we present the approach below for extracting entities for one class C. It can easily be generalized to multiple classes. The bootstrapping process involves following steps (also shown in Figure 3).

1. Generating candidate pool and labeling data: By scanning all the documents in the enterprise corpus, a candidate pool containing all the possible enterprise entities is generated. Positive entity seeds from class C is also provided by enterprise insiders/experts. Negative seeds are automatically generated from the candidate pool using heuristics, i.e., capitalized ratio;
2. Pattern Extractor: Contextual patterns are created using context text around all the candidate entities in both seed set and candidate pool.
3. Evaluating patterns using Multinomial Naive Bayes model.
4. Ranking entities and adding top confident ones into seeds. A semi-supervised framework is used to extract more low-precision/sparse patterns. Each iteration adds the top positive/negative entities into the seed set and re-scores patterns, after certain amount of iterations.
5. Semantic Pattern Graph Construction: Bi-grams are first extracted from web text for semantic recovery. An Anti Semantic Drifting Filter is then applied to avoid inconsistency of single pattern's semantic in different domains. And with the extended pattern list generated in enterprise corpus, a Semantic Graph is built using bi-gram data and enterprise patterns. Details will be discussed in Section 4.
6. Smoothing pattern scores: A smoother is applied to re-evaluate each pattern based on their original score and graph structure, details will be discussed in Section 4.
7. Ranking entities: Smoothed patterns for the class are applied to the entity candidates. A Multinomial Naive Bayes classifier ranks the candidate entities and adds the top entities to C's dictionary.

In this section, we will explain steps 1-4 in detail. Steps 5-7 will be covered in the next section.

3.1 Generation of Candidate Pool

Different from the previous Web-scale entity extractors, we generate all possible entity candidates as our first step. Many enterprise entities and their patterns might be very sparse, such that using only seed patterns may never discover them. Finding these sparse entities first takes their sparse patterns into account in the process. Two restrictions are applied in the generation of candidate pool. First, the target term has a part-of-speech (POS) restriction, which is the POS tag sequence of the candidate phrase. Second, a noun phrase will be considered as a candidate only if the phrase appears at least once in the corpus as capitalized form.

In our framework, we automatically generate negative seeds from the candidate pool. For a candidate term t, sets C_t and U_t denote the capitalized and uncapitalized mention sets in the corpus. We require $\frac{|C_t|}{|C_t|+|U_t|} \leq threshold$ to consider t as a negative seed. We set $threshold = 0.1$ in our experiments.

3.2 Generation of Patterns

We use lexico-syntactic surface word patterns to extract entities from candidate pool. They are created using contexts of words or their lemmatized form within a window of one before or after a entity candidate in the candidate pool. Here we collect as many patterns as possible, even include those that never appear with any positive/negative samples. These "invisible" patterns might be quite useful after understanding its semantic relations in the smoothing phase. Therefore, we take them into account in every step. We generate flexible pattern by removing {"a", "an", "the"} when matching patterns to the text.

Two reasons are considered to pick one as the window size instead of two or more: 1) Bigger window size may introduce more noisy patterns that are irrelevant to the entity. 2) It is more interpretable to construct semantic pattern graph on unigram patterns.

To simplify the notation, we will use "+" or "−" to indicate the relative location of lexical patterns. "+" means the pattern appears after the entity and "−" means the pattern appears before the pattern. Thus, pattern **"existing X"** would be **"−existing"** and **"X developer"** would be **"+developer"** and so on.

3.3 Scoring Patterns using Semi-supervised NB

A Semi-supervised Naive-Bayes (**Semi-NB**) model is applied here as the ranker and classifier for our task. We treat lexical patterns as features and treat every candidate in the candidate pool as testing data. User-provided positive seed set and automatically generated negative seed set are training data in our Semi-NB setting. For each target entity e in both training and testing data, a feature vector is generated, each feature score on feature f is calculated as:

$$S(e, f) = \log\left(count(e, f) + 1\right)$$

The $count(e, f)$ here means the total mention count of target entity e with feature (pattern) f. With the real-valued feature scores, we use a multinomial Naive Bayes to calculate pattern scores and entity score. Entity scores $T(e)$ are calculated as follows:

$$T(e) = \log\frac{P(+|e)}{P(-|e)} = \log\frac{P(+)\prod_f P(f|+)^{S(e,f)}}{P(-)\prod_f P(f|-)^{S(e,f)}}$$
$$= \sum_f S(e, f)(\log P(f|+) - \log P(f|-)) + \log\frac{P(+)}{P(-)}$$

Where $P(f|+) = \frac{count(f,+)+1}{count(+)+|F|}$, $P(f|-) = \frac{count(f,-)+1}{count(-)+|F|}$. F is the set of all patterns. To evaluate each pattern, we also define normalized pattern score $R(f)$ as

$$R(f) = \lambda(\log P(f|+) - \log P(f|-))$$

Where λ is the normalization constant to normalize $R(f)$ to [-1, 1]. The value of λ is determined by the range of $\log P(f|+) - \log P(f|-)$ across all features. Positive $R(f)$ shows that pattern f is good signal for extracting enterprise entities, and vice versa. Therefore we rewrite $T(e)$ as:

$$T(e) = \sum_f S(e, f)R(f) + c$$

Moreover, to ease sparsity in this phase, we applied iterative semi-supervised mechanism into the process. As shown in Algorithm 1 and Figure 3, we iteratively add top positive

Pattern	Normalized Score
+developer	1.0
+infrastructure	0.82
-integrate	0.76
-existing	0.46
+implementation	0.40
-new	0.25
+documentation	0.23
...	...
+debugger	*0.15*
...	...
+verification	*-0.1*
-debug	*-0.3*
...	

Smoothing

Pattern	Normalized Score
+developer	1.0
+infrastructure	0.92
+debugger	*0.79*
+integrate	0.78
+documentation	0.50
+verification	*0.15*
-debug	*0.10*
+implementation	0.05
...	...
-existing	-0.16
-new	-0.2
...	...
...	...

Figure 4: Contrast of scores before and after smoothing. Red/bold patterns are the mistakenly highly ranked general patterns, and blue/italic patterns are "good" sparse patterns.

candidates and top negative candidates into the seed set. We re-calculate pattern scores after certain amount of iterations (here we chose 10 as our default iteration rounds) and use the new pattern scores to rank entities. Experimental results in Section 5 show that the semi-supervised mechanism works well for alleviating sparsity by adding more seeds and discover more patterns afterwards. M is chosen as 20 in our experiment.

Algorithm 1: Semi-NB for Enterprise Entity Extraction

```
Data: Enterprise Corpus
Result:
Initialization;
for i = 0, i < iteration#, i++ do
    Calculate pattern score using seed set;
    Rank entities in candidate pool;
    Add top M positive entities into the pos seed set;
    Add top M negative entities into the neg seed set;
Calculate pattern score using updated seed set;
Smooth patterns using SPG;
Rank entities in candidate pool;
```

3.4 Learning Enterprise Entities

After the smoothing phase (will be discussed in Section 4), we applied the learned patterns to the extracted entity candidates using the multinomial naive-bayes classifier. The candidates are ranked to indicate how possible it is as an enterprise entity. We then consider the top positive ones as our extracted entities and output them.

4. SEMANTIC PATTERN GRAPH

As discussed in Introduction, due to the lack of redundancy of entity mentions compared with web-scale data, enterprise entity extraction is especially challenging. To be more concrete, we show here the pattern scores we get without leveraging any public resources or smoothing in Figure 4. All the scores are normalized to scale [-1, 1]. On the left side, we show some selected pattern scores in the ranked list before leveraging Semantic Pattern Graph as a smoother. The numbers on the second column denote how much degree a pattern would tell a "good" enterprise entity. Positive number means the pattern is a positive signal for enterprise entity and vice versa. Clearly we can see three different types of patterns in Figure 4.

1. **Type I - Non-Sparse Good Patterns**: patterns like *"+develop"*, *"+infrastructure"* and *"−integrate"* belong to this category. These patterns are good indicators for chosen Enterprise Entity class C and usually rank pretty high in the pattern list. They appears frequently with positive seeds and infrequently with negative seeds, and they normally have rich semantics strongly correlated to class C;
2. **Type II - Bad General Patterns**: patterns like *"−existing"* and *"−new"* belong to this category. These patterns are bad indicators for C since they are too general. They usually do not have any semantics specifically correlated to class C. They happened to appear with most positive seeds and not too many negative seeds, which leads to their high ranks in the pattern list. Normally if the positive seeds that user provided are much more popular than negative seeds (which is commonly the case), bad general patterns will contaminate the pattern list severely. The problem of these patterns being ranked high is that they may discover non-enterprise entities and make our entity set less accurate.
3. **Type III - Sparse Good Patterns**: patterns like *"+debugger"*, *"+verification"* and *"−debug"* belong to this category. These patterns have semantics strongly correlated to class C but they are not as commonly used as Type I patterns. They are good indicators for extracting enterprise entities in class C. However, different from Type I patterns, they stand for more specific/less common operators for class C. In our example, every project can both be "debugged" and be "developed", but *"−develop"* is much more common. Therefore, Type III patterns usually can not rank very high and they may even possibly be on the negative side. Here, *"−debug"* has score -0.3 because it never appears with the pos seeds and appears with some neg seeds by accident.

Therefore, if we can demote Type II patterns and promote Type III patterns properly in the ranked pattern list, we can ease the trouble that sparsity brings and expect better quality of enterprise entities. To do so, a deeper understanding of the semantic relations between patterns is required. However, it cannot be obtained from enterprise corpus because of Sparsity again! The solution lies outside of the corpus: Web Data. It is possible to recover semantic structure from the web due to the fact that the patterns both enterprise entities and public entities use are shared. Here we define the key concept **Semantic Pattern Graph** as follows:

Definition 1. **Semantic Pattern Graph (SPG)**: A Semantic Pattern Graph is defined as a complete directed graph $G = (V, E)$, in which V is the pattern set and E contains edges representing relations between patterns. In **SPG**, every pair of distinct patterns is connected by a pair of edges.

A sample **SPG** is shown in Figure 5. The scores on the edges are defined as follows:

$$S_{p\to q} = \frac{|E_p \cap E_q|}{|E_p|}, \quad S_{q\to p} = \frac{|E_p \cap E_q|}{|E_q|}$$

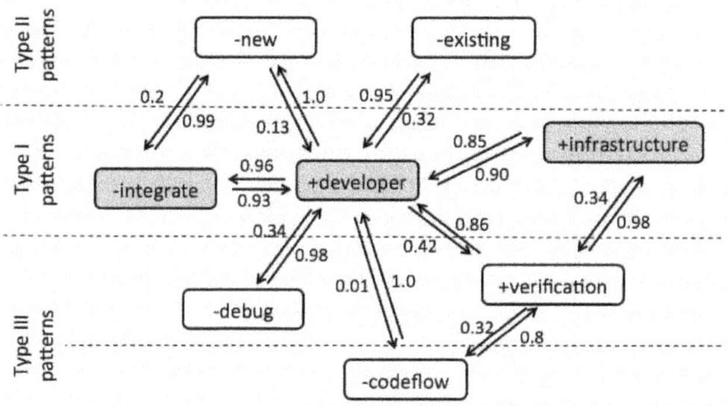

Figure 5: Toy Example of Semantic Pattern Graph from Microsoft dataset. For ease of exposition, only the edges between "+developer", "−integrate", "+infrastructure" and other patterns are shown in this example.

Here p, q are two distinct patterns. E_p, E_q denote the entity set that can appear with pattern p, q respectively in web data. If $S_{p\to q}$ is high, meaning that E_q is mostly covered by E_p, in other words, most entities that can appear with p, can also appear with q. Similarly, small $S_{p\to q}$ means that most entities that can appear with p, cannot appear with q. With such graph built, we can roughly divide semantic relations between patterns into three categories.

1. **Belonging:** If $S_{p\to q} \ll S_{q\to p}$, we say p is a general pattern of q. Semantically, q belongs to p. Examples are <"−new", "+developer"> and <"+developer", "−debug">, where "+developer" belongs to "−new" and "−debug" belongs to "developer".
2. **Equal:** If $S_{p\to q} \approx S_{q\to p}$ and both of them are large, we say p, q are semantically equal since E_p, E_q share most entities. Examples includes <"+developer", "−integrate"> and <"+developer", "+infrastructure">
3. **Independent:** If $S_{p\to q} \approx S_{q\to p}$ and both of them are small, we say p, q are semantically independent, because E_p and E_q have very little overlap.

Revisit Figure 4 and Figure 5, we observe that Type I pattern are usually in the central layer of SPG, Type II patterns are roughly in top layer and Type III patterns are in the bottom layer. The layers in Semantic Pattern Graph are defined by how general the patterns are. Thus, lower layer entities usually form a **Belonging** relation to higher layer entities, while entities in the same layer normally form **Equal** or **Independent** relations. In other words, Type I patterns **belong** to Type II patterns and Type III patterns **belong** to Type I patterns. Another observation from Figure 4 is that Type I patterns are usually top patterns in the ranked pattern list before smoothing, since they obtains sufficient positive signals from enterprise corpus. These observations inspire our design of smoothing algorithm.

4.1 SPG Construction

In this section, we explain how we construct the **SPG** like Figure 5 from web data. We use Microsoft Web N-gram data, especially bi-gram sub-portion to construct **SPG**. Web Bi-gram dataset contains all possible combinations of patterns and their unigram entities on the web. To avoid unnecessary computation, we construct **SPG** solely based on the patterns appeared in our target corpus. Since web bi-gram data contains much noise, PMI between patterns and entities are used on bi-gram frequency to filter out insignificant bi-grams using a threshold. As an example, PMI of bi-gram "**P E**" will be calculated as:

$$pmi(\mathbf{P},\mathbf{E}) = \log \frac{p(\mathbf{P},\mathbf{E})}{p(\mathbf{P})p(\mathbf{E})} = \log \frac{count(\mathbf{PE})}{\sum count(\mathbf{P}*) \sum count(*\mathbf{E})}$$

Here **P** refers to the pattern and **E** refers to the entity. $count(\mathbf{PE})$ denotes the count of bi-gram "**P E**" on the web. $\sum count(\mathbf{P}*)$ denotes the total counts of all bi-grams including pattern **P** and $\sum count(*\mathbf{E})$ is defined similarly.

Anti Semantic Drifting Filter: Another problem we need to address is Semantic Drift of the same pattern on different domains. For example, **"−express"** may have specific meaning (genetically express the gene) in biology domain, while have no such semantics in any other field. That is to say, if we use the whole bi-gram data for constructing SPG for a specific domain, the semantic relations may be contaminated by semantics from other fields. As an example, if we see **"−express"** in computer science corpus, we need to avoid linking this one to **"−translate"**, a pattern that has semantic drift as well in biology domain. In this regard, we apply a filter on web "pattern-entity" pairs to preserve semantics of the target domain as much as possible. We use the entity candidates generated in enterprise corpus only to filter the "pattern-entity" pairs for building SPG. Thus in the **"−express"** case, semantics from biology domain will be filtered out while constructing SPGs for other fields.

After we filter out all the bi-grams containing those patterns and entities. We then calculate score E_p for each pattern p and construct the complete directed graph based on the statistics.

4.2 Smoothing Algorithm

In this section, we introduce the algorithm of using SPG for pattern re-evaluation. Back to our "projects" extraction task for Microsoft internal corpus. We observe in Figure 5 that Type I patterns like **"+developer"** and **"−integrate"**, are in the central layer of a the constructed SPG. Also, we observe that type II patterns, like **"−existing"** and **"−new"**, are more general than Type I patterns in the graph, indicating their **Belonging** relations. Type I patterns are more general than Type III patterns, like **"−debug"** and **"+verification"** in the graph, which also indicates their **Belonging** relations. Based on those observation, a possible solution is to locate the Type I pattern in the graph, and demote their general patterns (Type II) and promote their specific patterns (Type III). Since we also know that Type I patterns, with high possibility, will rank top in the pattern list, we then take the top-K patterns in the ranked pattern list, locate them in the **SPG** and smooth the rest of the graph using an induced graph from SPG. The induced graph is defined as follows:

Definition 2. **Induced Smoothing Graph with Seeds (ISGwS)**: An Induced Smoothing Graph with Seeds is defined as a directed graph $G = (V, S, E)$, in which V is the pattern set, S is the seed set and E contains weighted edges representing smoothing score between patterns in S to patterns in V. Seed set S consists of top-K patterns in the ranked list before smoothing.

As an example, Figure 6 shows the **ISGwS** generated from Figure 5. The new graph contains three seeds **"+developer"**, **"−integrate"** and **"+infrastructure"**. We eval-

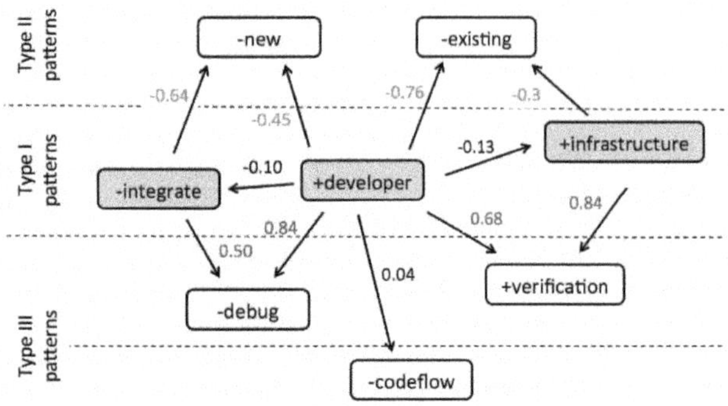

Figure 6: Toy Example of Induced Smoothing Graph with Seeds after scoring.

uate how strong the score of a pattern should be smoothed by top-K patterns using formula as follows:

$$T_{p \to q} = \kappa \cdot (S_{q \to p} - S_{p \to q}) \cdot S_{p \to q} \cdot S_{q \to p}$$

Here p is the top pattern, q can be any other patterns in the graph. $\kappa = 4$ is the normalization constant to scale $T_{p \to q}$ to $[-1, 1]$. First term $(S_{q \to p} - S_{p \to q})$ in the formula determine the sign of $T_{p \to q}$. Moreover, smoothing effect grows as the difference between $S_{q \to p}$ and $S_{p \to q}$ grows. The second and third terms $S_{p \to q}, S_{q \to p}$ convey two things. 1). The bigger direction $S_{p \to q}$ (or $S_{q \to p}$, depends on demoting or promoting) should be close to 1 to strongly show that there is a clear **Belonging** relation going on. For example, $S_{+developer \to -new}$ should be almost 1. 2). The smaller direction $S_{q \to p}$ (or $S_{p \to q}$) should also be big enough, such that the **Belonging** relation is not because of noise. For instance, pattern **"+codeflow"** in Figure 5 should not be promoted as much as **"−debug"** because that $S_{+developer \to +codeflow}$ is too small.

We get an Induced Smoothing Graph with Seeds by scoring the edges in Figure 5. The new graph is shown in Figure 6. By giving three top patterns, we strongly demote pattern "−new" and "−existing", promote pattern "−debug" and "+verification" and not do much to pattern "−integrate", "+infrastructure" and "+codeflow". The scoring approach satisfies our smoothing goal.

The last step is to average over all top-K patterns in the graph to smooth every other pattern, as follows:

$$R'(q) = (1 - \alpha)R(q) + \frac{\alpha}{K} \cdot \sum_{p \in top-K} T_{p \to q} \cdot R(p)$$

Here $R(q)$ and $R'(q)$ denote the pattern score before and after smoothing respectively. We use a linear combination of the original score and smoothed score to represent new score of pattern q. Moreover, we define the following form as *Smoothing Factor*:

$$SF(q) = \frac{1}{K} \sum_{p \in top-K} T_{p \to q} \cdot R(p)$$

After smoothing, we convert the pattern list in left side of Figure 4 to the right side list, as expected. A key problem here is how to choose α and K. α controls the balance between enterprise signals and public signals. K controls the effective size of trustworthy patterns using only local signals. Thorough experiment is conducted in Section 5 to answer this question.

5. EXPERIMENT

In this section, we evaluate the effectiveness of our framework for Enterprise Entity Extraction on real dataset from Microsoft. We will (1) Demonstrate the quality of discovered enterprise entities using several measurement capturing both precision and recall. (2) study the two key parameters α and K in Semantic Pattern Graph smoothing step and understand the philosophy of picking them properly. (3) study the entity coverage of using different pattern generation strategies, to show why it is necessary to consider much more patterns in enterprises than previous web-scale information extractors. (4) case study on 5 specific patterns of Type II and Type III to show the correctness of our analysis in Section 4. All the experiments, if not specifically mentioned, are conducted on a PC with 2.4GHz CPU and 16GB RAM.

5.1 Experimental Setup

We evaluate our system on extracting projects/products entities in Microsoft Internal Answer Forum corpus. The forum has 484,221 discussion threads by Microsoft employees concerning all kinds of technical problems and solutions from the years 2011 to 2014. For each thread, we concat the question and its answers together, and only keep the content for further analysis. We asked Microsoft employees to generate a complete list of projects/products with the help of Microsoft Internal Taxonomy. The list contains 2,080 entities. We randomly pick 57 out of them as the seed set. Some examples are shown in Table 1. After the Candidates Generation phase (Section 3.1), 62,708 candidates are extracted from our corpus. We consider all candidates with capitalized ratio $\frac{|C_t|}{|C_t|+|U_t|} < 0.1$ as negative seeds. Our object is to rank all candidates and make sure the 2,080 entities can rank higher with the 57 positive seeds and auto-generated negative seeds.

Microsoft Web N-gram services are used to build Semantic Pattern Graph. It is a cloud-based platform which extract N-grams from web-scale data of Bing. Since we only consider patterns within window size one, only the bi-gram portion of Web N-gram data is used in our experiment. We also filter out bi-grams with small relative counts such that arbitrary combinations would not contributes to the constructed **SPG**. For the major smoothing parameters, we set $\alpha = 0.3$ and $K = 50$ as default values.

All the large-scale experiments are done in Microsoft Cosmos platform.

office	windows xp	visual studio	sql server
office 365	silverlight	sharepoint 2013	windows 8
windows 7	biztalk	active directory	asp
azure	outlook	windows 2003	outlook

Table 1: Project/Product Seeds from Microsoft

5.2 Baselines and Evaluations

To show that our pipeline performs best for enterprise entity extraction, we compare our work with several baselines as follows. The comparison with existing entity extractors are not shown here due to 1) some of them are not public (e.g., Knowitall and NELL) and they rely mainly on Hearst pattern or high-precision/low-recall patterns, which leads to low coverage in enterprise setting 2) some of them are slow

Method	P@50	P@100	P@200	P@300	P@500
Count	0.38	0.36	0.385	0.383	0.37
Capi	0.16	0.16	0.165	0.15	0.138
Hybrid	0.46	0.61	0.615	0.613	0.59
NB	0.74	0.71	0.72	0.687	0.66
SmooNB	**0.88**	0.81	0.82	0.76	0.744
SemiNB	0.84	0.77	0.78	0.753	0.712
Our System	0.86	**0.85**	**0.84**	**0.843**	**0.824**

Table 2: Precision at top K results for project/product extraction

and performance on a small portion is not comparable (e.g., Spied from Stanford).

1. **Count:** Measure the ranking of the term solely by its count of capitalized form in the whole corpus, $score = \log(count + 1)$.
2. **Capi:** Measure the ranking of the term by Capitalized Ratio: $score = \frac{|C_t|}{|C_t|+|U_t|}$, where C_t and U_t denote the capitalized and uncapitalized mentions in the corpus.
3. **Hybrid:** Rank terms using both count and capitalized ratio: $score = \log(count + 1) * \frac{|C_t|}{|C_t|+|U_t|}$.

We applied both semi-supervised method and SPG-based smoothing to ease the sparsity problem. To study the effectiveness of both factors, we design several ablations as follows

1. **NB:** Use pure Naive Bayes model as the ranker and classifier to extract entities.
2. **SemiNB:** Use Semi-supervised Naive-Bayes model as the ranker and classier. The smoothing step is skipped.
3. **SmooNB:** Use pure Naive-Bayes as the ranker and classifier, apply smoothing after the weights of patterns are learned.
4. **Our System:** Use Semi-supervised Naive-Bayes model as the ranker and classier, and also apply smoothing after the weights of patterns are learned.

5.3 Extracting Projects/Products

In this section, we apply our framework on Microsoft Q/A Forum data and show the main result of projects/products extraction. We also conduct parameter study for Semantic Pattern Graph smoothing afterwards.

5.3.1 *Main Results*

Since we model Enterprise Entity Extraction problem in a ranking framework, several ranking-based evaluation measures are proposed to assess both precision and recall of the result. Two intuitions are emphasized for the result we yield: 1) The 2,080 entities should rank high on the whole, 2) The top results are real entities with high probability. These intuitions align with the natural of Enterprise Knowledge Base, that is with very high precision first being guaranteed, we then consider about coverage. Using this philosophy, we design three sets of evaluation measures as follows: a) Precision, evaluate the precision of top results from Prec@50 to Prec@500. b) Average Precision: AP@500, AP@1000, AP@2000 as

$$AP@n = \frac{\sum_{k=1}^{n} P(k)}{N}$$

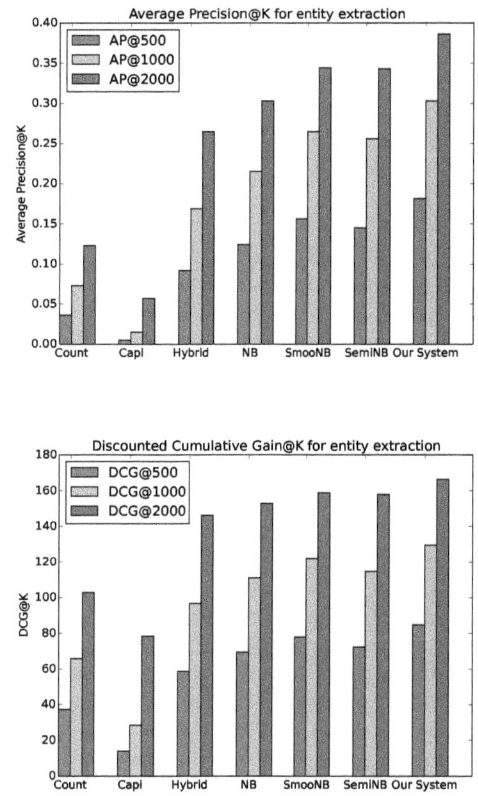

Figure 7: Average Precision and Discounted Cumulative Gain comparison

where $P(k)$ means the precision at cut-off k in the entity list, N means the number of relevant entities in total, and c) Discounted Cumulative Gain: DCG@500, DCG@1000 and DCG@2000 as

$$DCG@n = \sum_{k=1}^{n} \frac{\mathbb{1}(e_k \in \mathbb{E})}{\log_2(k+1)}$$

Where $\mathbb{1}(e_k \in \mathbb{E})$ is the indicator function showing if k-th item is an enterprise entity. Precision measurement emphasizes the top entity quality and AP/DCG measure the balance of both precision and recall. The result is shown in Table 2 and Figure 7.

From the result of Table 2, we observe that our system achieves above 80% precision even for top 500 results and the two baselines **Hybrid** and **NB** only achieves 59% and 66% respectively on top 500. To evaluate the Semi-supervised mechanism and Semantic Pattern Graph smoothing separately, we observe that both **SmooNB** and **SemiNB** can alleviate sparsity and enhance precision. It aligns with our intuition that Semi-supervised Learning can collect more patterns to capture entities with few mentions, while SPG leverage public signals to assign more accurate scores to each pattern. Table 2 also tells us that only applying smoothing can have better performance than only using semi-supervised learning. However, combing these two methods helps us to collect more low-precision patterns and assign them high confident scores, thus can yield best performance.

Figure 7 shows the performance on AP and DCG, with similar conclusion can be drew. AP and DCG are widely used to evaluate ranking qualities such as web search engines. We observe that using either Smoothing or Semi-learning outperforms the local ranker using only signals from corpus and positive seeds. Similar to precision, SPG smoothing improves more in terms of AP and DCG as well.

5.3.2 Parameter Study

In this section, we study the two major parameters used in our smoothing framework: 1) Smoothing weight α, 2) Top pattern size K. Changing α studies the balance between local signals from enterprise corpus and public signals from the web, while changing K studies the effective size of trustworthy patterns using only local signals.

We plot the 3-dimensional chart in Figure 8, in which we control α from 0 to 1 with size-0.03 steps and K from 10 to 200 with size-10 steps respectively, to evaluate precision of entities on top 500 results. We first observe that the performance goes up after we gradually apply smoothing to the patterns, and it reaches the best precision of 83.05% at $alpha = 0.32$ and $K = 50$. If we observe α curve standalone, we see that precision is positively correlated to α before it hits 0.32. After that, it keeps relatively high precision if $\alpha < 0.7$ and drops drastically if $\alpha > 0.7$. It makes sense in the sense that 1) Properly leveraged public signals can effectively alleviate sparsity and 2) Public signal itself cannot capture the unique semantics used in enterprise.

On the other hand, if we observe K curve standalone, we find the similar situation where the peak performance is achieved when K is reasonably large but not too large, say 50. As discussed before, our philosophy of picking K is to cover enough "high-precision/low-recall" patterns. If K is small, the top patterns can not capture most aspects of extracted class C, and therefore, smoothing phase may lead to strongly biased adjustment. As we can see from the figure 8, performance when $K = 10, \alpha = 0.32$ is even lower than the original one. If K is too large, due to sparsity issues, many $low - precision$ patterns may also be used as smoothing seeds and contaminate the rest of the Pattern Graph.

Currently we use intuitions to choose $K = 2\%$ of all patterns and $\alpha = 0.3$. More study on this issue will be covered in our future work.

5.4 Pattern Study

In this section, we conduct experiments to look closer to patterns and answer two questions: 1) Why previous entity extractors with high-precision/low-recall patterns will fail in enterprise setting? 2) How well the Semantic Pattern Graph performs to ease sparsity in a real case?

5.4.1 Pattern Coverage Study

To answer the first question, we implemented several pattern extractors used in previous systems: 1) NELL, 2) Knowitall and 3) SPIED. As discussed previously, NELL and SPIED used high-precision/low-recall patterns with part-of-speech (POS) restrictions to identify entities, while Knowitall uses mainly Hearst patterns and predefined templates for entity extraction. For Knowitall, we included all pattern templates mentioned in their paper [9]. For NELL, we strictly follow their Coupled Pattern Learner [6] approach, where the patterns follows its POS rules and at most 100

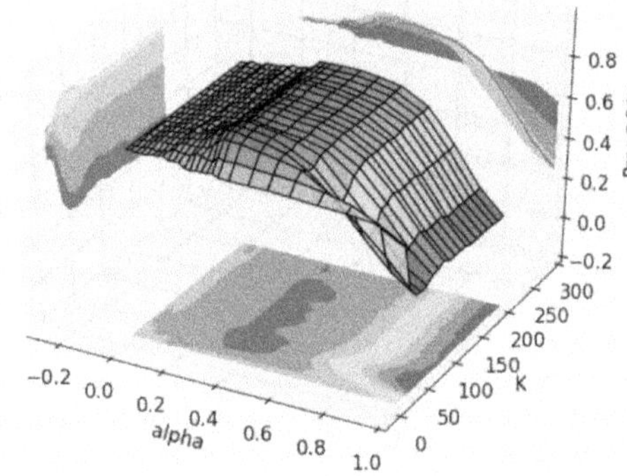

Figure 8: Parameter Study for smoothing weight α and top pattern size K. The performance is evaluated based on Precision@500

instances/entities and 5 patterns are promoted. Patterns are ranked by precision and instances are filtered out unless the number of times it co-occurs with promoted pattern is at least three times more than the number of times it co-occurs with patterns left. For Spied, since the extracting details are not disclosed in the paper, we use the same POS restrictions that NELL used to extract patterns.

System	Knowitall	NELL	Spied	Our System
Coverage (%)	21.5	54.4	54.3	**81.7**

Table 3: Coverage of projects/products using extracted lexical patterns

Table 3 shows the coverage of the 2,080 labeled projects using different lexical pattern set generated by four systems. We observe that our system can potentially extract more than 80% of target enterprise entities, while in the meantime, NELL/Spied/Knowitall can only find less than 55% entities. That is to say, in a sparse setting, even the best existing classifier/ranker would lose about half of the entities. Knowitall has the lowest coverage due to the limited pattern templates it uses. Hearst patterns have poor coverage in enterprise corpus. NELL and Spied use more general patterns confined by specific POS templates can yield better entity coverage than Knowitall, but are still deficient for a sparse setting. Because the POS constraints normally require verbs in the pattern or require explicit relations to another noun phrases. However, many enterprise entities lack of the redundancy of such patterns. For example in our system, two patterns "+platform" and "−native" are good signals for identifying enterprise entities, but will not be considered by precious web-scale extractors. Note that 20% of the entities in Microsoft are still unreachable by our patterns, some of them are never mentioned in the corpus and some of them are mentioned only a few times with non-informative patterns (the general patterns which are not exclusive to projects/products).

A reasonable concern of introducing less restricted patterns is that it potentially lower our confidence on judging every single pattern. Hence we introduced smoothing based on Semantic Pattern Graph to get accurate evaluation of each pattern.

Pattern	Score Before	Smo. Factor	Score After	Mention Count	Examples
+debugger	0.157	0.895	0.378	136	... from an attached **VS10** *debugger*. ...triggered the **jit** *debugger* dialog...
+backend	0.647	0.983	0.748	108	Both the **SQL Cluster** *Backend* and... ...instance of **FAST Search Server** *backend*...
+verification	-0.094	0.704	0.145	77	Failed **authenticode** *verification* of payload.
-existing	0.456	-0.532	0.160	1789	...migrate the *existing* **ORANGE** connection.. ..want all *existing* **assignments** such for...
-new	0.253	-0.995	-0.121	8239	...to create *new* **experience** I get... ...in *new* **Software Distribution** policies...

Table 4: Smoothed patterns along with the score before smoothing, smoothing factor and score after smoothing, and the example entities they appear with. Scores in columns 2-4 are normalized to [-1, 1], where positive score means it is good pattern for extracting product/project, and vice versa. Score After is the linear combination of Score Before and Smoothing Factor using $\alpha = 0.3$. Mention Count indicates how popular the pattern is in the corpus. Entity examples for the first three patterns are good enterprise entities which are promoted due to the promotion of their patterns, and the entities for last two patterns are the mistakenly classified entities which are demoted due to the demotion of their patterns.

5.4.2 SPG Smoothing evaluation

As discussed in previous sections, the SPG smoothing improves the pattern accuracy in two ways: 1) Demote Type II - Bad General Patterns. 2) Promote Type III - Sparse Good Patterns. Table 4 revisits the examples we have analyzed and shows the smoothing result for them and entities they extracted. '+debugger', '+backend' and '+verification' are Type III patterns, which are good indicators for projects/products but are underrated in our corpus. Some good patterns, like '+verification', are even evaluated as negative before smoothing. Since all these three patterns have clear **Belonging** relation with top patterns like '−develop' (they have highly correlated semantics to '−develop', but much more specific), their smoothing factor is usually pretty large. In the chart, we can see their scores after smoothing is promoted a lot and the entities appear with them can higher rank. On the other hand, '−existing' and '−new', as we analyzed, are Type II patterns with strongly biased signals. They don't indicate any semantics specifically correlated to project/product. However, they have large positive scores before smoothing due to the fact that they are commonly used with any positive seeds. For those general patterns, the top patterns, like '−develop', have clear **Belonging** relations with them. Therefore, their smoothing factor is pretty negative and the pattern is demoted after smoothing.

One more thing we need to notice is that, Type II patterns are just too general, the ideal case is that they should play no role in identifying enterprise entity nor non-enterprise entity. Therefore, the demoted score should be close to 0. And our method may potentially over-penalize general patterns if they happen to not appear with seed entities, with low probability (Positive seeds are usually very common entities in the corpus).

According to the mention count column, we can see that Type II patterns are much more common than Type III patterns when they appear with our enterprise entities. It complies with our intuition that 1) Type II patterns are too general that they may happen to appear with many positive seeds and 2) Type III patterns are too specific that positive seeds never appear with them. These examples, along with the performance comparison in Section 5.3, we conclude that Semantic Pattern Graph smoothing works well for resolving sparsity in enterprise setting.

6. CONCLUSION AND FUTURE WORK

This paper introduced our framework for enterprise entity extraction, which involves semi-supervised bootstrapping entity extraction framework using seed sets. It is the first work to introduce the concept of Semantic Pattern Graph into entity extraction problem and model the semantics between contextual patterns to enhance entity coverage and precision. With detailed analysis, we show that in a sparse setting, leveraging public web-scale data to understand semantic relations between lexical patterns can effectively alleviate the sparsity. Hence, many entities with very little evidence can be possibly correctly extracted. In the experiment part, we also show that the smoothing algorithm using SPG can significantly improve precision and recall of learned enterprise entities. We also conduct several other experiments to show our smoothed extractor outperforms methods without understanding pattern relations. Moreover, the Semantic Pattern Graph and its smoothing algorithm is general enough to be applied into many other Information Extraction tasks on closed-domain corpus (even other NLP tasks).

In future work, we plan to extend our size-1 patterns into more general patterns to adapt more complicated environment. Another research direction is to utilize Semantic Pattern Graph in a more complicated way. Conducting clustering on lexical patterns in a SPG may help us find several pattern groups with similar semantics, such that the way of picking seed patterns can be more balanced in different pattern groups. We also plan to generalize the Semantic Pattern Graph component into many other IE tasks, including relation extraction and entity typing.

7. ACKNOWLEDGEMENTS

Research was sponsored in part by the U.S. Army Research Lab. under Cooperative Agreement No. W911NF-09-2-0053 (NSCTA), the Army Research Office under Cooperative Agreement No. W911NF-13-1-0193, National Science Foundation IIS-1017362, IIS-1320617, and IIS-1354329, HDTRA1-10-1-0120, NIH Big Data to Knowledge (BD2K) (U54), and MIAS, a DHS-IDS Center for Multimodal Information Access and Synthesis at UIUC.

8. REFERENCES

[1] E. Agichtein and L. Gravano. Snowball: Extracting relations from large plain-text collections. In *ACM DL*, pages 85–94, 2000.

[2] S. Auer, C. Bizer, G. Kobilarov, J. Lehmann, R. Cyganiak, and Z. Ives. *Dbpedia: A nucleus for a web of open data*. Springer, 2007.

[3] K. Bollacker, C. Evans, P. Paritosh, T. Sturge, and J. Taylor. Freebase: a collaboratively created graph database for structuring human knowledge. In *SIGMOD*, pages 1247–1250, 2008.

[4] S. Brin. Extracting patterns and relations from the world wide web. In *The World Wide Web and Databases*, pages 172–183. Springer, 1999.

[5] A. Carlson, J. Betteridge, B. Kisiel, B. Settles, E. R. Hruschka Jr, and T. M. Mitchell. Toward an architecture for never-ending language learning. In *AAAI*, volume 5, page 3, 2010.

[6] A. Carlson, J. Betteridge, R. C. Wang, E. R. Hruschka Jr, and T. M. Mitchell. Coupled semi-supervised learning for information extraction. In *WSDM*, pages 101–110, 2010.

[7] W. W. Cohen and Y. Singer. A simple, fast, and effective rule learner. In *AAAI*, pages 335–342, 1999.

[8] D. Downey, O. Etzioni, S. Soderland, and D. S. Weld. Learning text patterns for web information extraction and assessment. In *AAAI*, pages 50–55, 2004.

[9] O. Etzioni, M. Cafarella, D. Downey, S. Kok, A.-M. Popescu, T. Shaked, S. Soderland, D. S. Weld, and A. Yates. Web-scale information extraction in knowitall:(preliminary results). In *WWW*, pages 100–110, 2004.

[10] O. Etzioni, M. Cafarella, D. Downey, A.-M. Popescu, T. Shaked, S. Soderland, D. S. Weld, and A. Yates. Methods for domain-independent information extraction from the web: An experimental comparison. In *AAAI*, pages 391–398, 2004.

[11] O. Etzioni, A. Fader, J. Christensen, S. Soderland, and M. Mausam. Open information extraction: The second generation. In *IJCAI*, pages 3–10, 2011.

[12] A. Fader, S. Soderland, and O. Etzioni. Identifying relations for open information extraction. In *EMNLP*, pages 1535–1545, 2011.

[13] D. Freitag. Toward general-purpose learning for information extraction. In *ACL*, pages 404–408, 1998.

[14] S. Gupta and C. D. Manning. Improved pattern learning for bootstrapped entity extraction. *CoNLL-2014*, page 98, 2014.

[15] S. Gupta and C. D. Manning. Spied: Stanford pattern-based information extraction and diagnostics. *Sponsor: Idibon*, page 38, 2014.

[16] M. A. Hearst. Automatic acquisition of hyponyms from large text corpora. In *Conference on Computational Linguistics*, pages 539–545, 1992.

[17] A. Lenci. Distributional semantics in linguistic and cognitive research. *Italian journal of linguistics*, 20(1):1–31, 2008.

[18] H. Poon and P. Domingos. Unsupervised ontology induction from text. In *ACL*, pages 296–305, 2010.

[19] E. Riloff. Automatically generating extraction patterns from untagged text. In *AAAI*, pages 1044–1049, 1996.

[20] E. Riloff, R. Jones, et al. Learning dictionaries for information extraction by multi-level bootstrapping. In *AAAI/IAAI*, pages 474–479, 1999.

[21] M. Schmitz, R. Bart, S. Soderland, O. Etzioni, et al. Open language learning for information extraction. In *EMNLP-CoNLL*, pages 523–534, 2012.

[22] F. M. Suchanek, G. Kasneci, and G. Weikum. Yago: a core of semantic knowledge. In *WWW*, pages 697–706, 2007.

[23] C. Sutton and A. McCallum. An introduction to conditional random fields for relational learning. *Introduction to statistical relational learning*, pages 93–128, 2006.

[24] M. Thelen and E. Riloff. A bootstrapping method for learning semantic lexicons using extraction pattern contexts. In *ACL*, pages 214–221, 2002.

[25] R. C. Wang and W. W. Cohen. Language-independent set expansion of named entities using the web. In *ICDM*, pages 342–350, 2007.

[26] R. C. Wang and W. W. Cohen. Iterative set expansion of named entities using the web. In *ICDM*, pages 1091–1096, 2008.

[27] D. Yarowsky. Unsupervised word sense disambiguation rivaling supervised methods. In *ACL*, pages 189–196, 1995.

Density-friendly Graph Decomposition

Nikolaj Tatti
Aalto University
nikolaj.tatti@aalto.fi

Aristides Gionis
Aalto University
aristides.gionis@aalto.fi

ABSTRACT

Decomposing a graph into a hierarchical structure via k-core analysis is a standard operation in any modern graph-mining toolkit. k-core decomposition is a simple and efficient method that allows to analyze a graph beyond its mere degree distribution. More specifically, it is used to identify areas in the graph of increasing centrality and connectedness, and it allows to reveal the structural organization of the graph.

Despite the fact that k-core analysis relies on vertex degrees, k-cores do not satisfy a certain, rather natural, density property. Simply put, the most central k-core is not necessarily the densest subgraph. This inconsistency between k-cores and graph density provides the basis of our study.

We start by defining what it means for a subgraph to be *locally-dense*, and we show that our definition entails a nested chain decomposition of the graph, similar to the one given by k-cores, but in this case the components are arranged in order of increasing density. We show that such a *locally-dense decomposition* for a graph $G = (V, E)$ can be computed in polynomial time. The running time of the exact decomposition algorithm is $\mathcal{O}(|V|^2|E|)$ but is significantly faster in practice. In addition, we develop a linear-time algorithm that provides a factor-2 approximation to the optimal locally-dense decomposition. Furthermore, we show that the k-core decomposition is also a factor-2 approximation, however, as demonstrated by our experimental evaluation, in practice k-cores have different structure than locally-dense subgraphs, and as predicted by the theory, k-cores are not always well-aligned with graph density.

Categories and Subject Descriptors

H.2.8 [**Database Management**]: Database Applications—*Data mining*

Keywords

community detection; k-core analysis; dense subgraphs

WWW 2015, May 18–22, 2015, Florence, Italy.
ACM 978-1-4503-3469-3/15/05.
http://dx.doi.org/10.1145/2736277.2741119 .

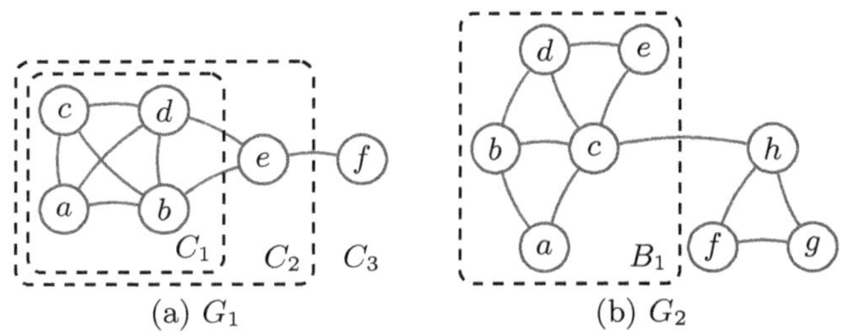

Figure 1: Toy graphs used in Example 1.

1. INTRODUCTION

Finding dense subgraphs and communities is one of the most well-studied problems in graph mining. Techniques for identifying dense subgraphs are used in a large number of application domains, from biology, to web mining, to analysis of social and information networks. Among the many concepts that have been proposed for discovering dense subgraphs, *k-cores* are particularly attractive for the simplicity of their definition and the fact that they can be identified in linear time.

The k-core of a graph is defined as a maximal subgraph in which every vertex is connected to at least k other vertices within that subgraph. A *k-core decomposition* of a graph consists of finding the set of all k-cores. A nice property is that the set of all k-cores forms a nested sequence of subgraphs, one included in the next. This makes the k-core decomposition of a graph a useful tool in analyzing a graph by identifying areas of increasing centrality and connectedness, and revealing the structural organization of the graph. As a result, k-core decomposition has been applied to a number of different applications, such as modeling of random graphs [8], analysis of the internet topology [12], social-network analysis [23], bioinformatics [6], analysis of connection matrices of the human brain [16], graph visualization [3], as well as influence analysis [19, 28] and team formation [9].

The fact that the k-core decomposition of a graph gives a chain of subgraphs where vertex degrees are higher in the inner cores, suggests that we should expect that the inner cores are, in certain sense, more dense or more connected than the outer cores. As we will show shortly, this statement is not true. Furthermore, in this paper we show how to obtain a graph decomposition for which the statement is true, namely, the inner subgraphs of the decomposition are denser than the outer ones. To quantify density, we adopt a classic notion used in the densest-subgraph problem [13, 15], where density is defined as the ratio between the edges and the vertices of a subgraph. This density definition can be also viewed as the average degree divided by 2.

Our motivating observation is that k-cores are not ordered according to this density definition. The next example demonstrates that the most inner core is *not* necessarily the densest subgraph, and in fact, we can increase the density by either adding or removing vertices.

EXAMPLE 1. Consider the graph G_1 shown in Figure 1, consisting of 6 vertices and 9 edges. The density of the whole graph is $9/6 = 1.5$. The graph has three k-cores: a 3-core marked as C_1, a 2-core marked as C_2, and a 1-core, corresponding the the whole graph and marked as C_3. The core C_1 has density $6/4 = 1.5$ (it contains 6 edges and 4 vertices), while the core C_2 has density $8/5 = 1.6$ (it contains 8 edges and 5 vertices). In other words, C_1 has lower density than C_2, despite being an inner core.

Let us now consider G_2 shown in Figure 1. This graph has a single core, namely a 2-core, containing the whole graph. The density of this core is equal to $11/8 = 1.375$. However, a subgraph B_1 contains 7 edges and 5 vertices, giving us density $7/5 = 1.4$, which is higher than the density of the only core.

This example motivates us to define an alternative, more density-friendly, graph decomposition, which we call *locally-dense decomposition*. We are interested in a decomposition such that (*i*) the density of the inner subgraphs is higher than the density of the outer subgraphs, (*ii*) the most inner subgraph corresponds to the densest subgraph, and (*iii*) we can compute or approximate the decomposition efficiently.

We achieve our goals by first defining a *locally-dense* subgraph, essentially a subgraph whose density cannot be improved by adding and deleting vertices. We show that these subgraphs are arranged into a hierarchy such that the density decreases as we go towards outer subgraphs and that the most inner subgraph is in fact the densest subgraph.

We provide two efficient algorithms to discover this hierarchy. The first algorithm extends the exact algorithm for discovering the densest subgraph given by Goldberg [15]. This algorithm is based on solving a minimum cut problem on a certain graph that depends on a parameter α. Goldberg showed that for a certain value α (which can be found by binary search), the minimum cut recovers the densest subgraph. One of our contributions is to shed more light into Goldberg's algorithm and show that the same construction allows to discover *all* locally-dense subgraphs by varying α.

Our second algorithm extends the linear-time algorithm by Charikar for approximating dense subgraphs [13]. This algorithm first orders vertices by deleting iteratively a vertex with the smallest degree, and then selects the densest subgraph respecting the order. We extend this idea by using the same order, and finding first the densest subgraph respecting the order, and then iteratively finding the second densest subgraph containing the first subgraph, and so on. We show that this algorithm can be executed in linear time and it achieves a factor-2 approximation guarantee.

Charikar's algorithm and the algorithm for discovering a k-core decomposition are very similar: they both order vertices by deleting vertices with the smallest degree. We show that this connection is profoundly deep and we demonstrate that a k-core decomposition provides a factor-2 approximation for locally-dense decomposition. On the other hand, our experimental evaluation shows that in practice k-cores have different structure than locally-dense subgraphs, and as predicted by the theory, k-cores are not always well-aligned with graph density.

The remainder of paper is organized as follows. We give preliminary notation in Section 2. We introduce the locally-dense subgraphs in Section 3, present algorithms for discovering the subgraphs in Section 4, and describe the connection to k-core decomposition in Section 5. We present the related work in Section 6 and present the experiments in Section 7. Finally, we conclude the paper with discussion in Section 8.

2. PRELIMINARIES

Graph density. Let $G = (V, E)$ be a graph with $|V| = n$ vertices and $|E| = m$ edges. Given a subset of vertices $X \subseteq V$, it is common to define $E(X) = \{(x, y) \in E \mid x, y \in X\}$, i.e., the edges of G that have both end-points in X. The *density* of the vertex set X is then defined to be

$$d(X) = \frac{|E(X)|}{|X|},$$

that is, half of the *average degree* of the subgraph induced by X. The set of vertices $X \subseteq V$ that maximizes the density measure $d(X)$ is the *densest subgraph* of G.[1]

The problem of finding the densest subgraph can be solved in polynomial time. A very elegant solution that involves a mapping to a series of minimum-cut problems was given by Goldberg [15]. As the fastest algorithm to solve the minimum-cut problem runs in $\mathcal{O}(mn)$ time, this approach is not scalable to very large graphs. On the other hand, there exists a linear-time algorithm that provides a factor-2 approximation to the densest-subgraph problem [4, 13]. This is a greedy algorithm, which starts with the input graph, and iteratively removes the vertex with the lowest degree, until left with an empty graph. Among all subgraphs considered during this vertex-removal process, the algorithm returns the densest.

Next we will provide graph-density definitions that relate pairs of vertex sets. Given two non-overlapping sets of vertices X and Y we first define the *cross edges* between X and Y as

$$E_\times(X, Y) = \{(x, y) \in E \mid x \in X, y \in Y\}.$$

We then define the *marginal edges* from X with respect to Y. Those are the edges that have one end-point in X and the other end-point in either X or Y, that is,

$$E_\Delta(X, Y) = E(X) \cup E_\times(X, Y).$$

The set $E_\Delta(X, Y)$ represents the additional edges that will be included in the induced subgraph of Y if we expand Y by adding X.

Assume that X and Y are non-overlapping. Then, we define the *outer density* of X with respect to Y as

$$d(X, Y) = \frac{|E_\Delta(X, Y)|}{|X|}.$$

Again, this is the "extra density" that we bring to Y if we expand it by appending X to it.

[1]We should point out that density is also often defined as $|E(X)|/\binom{|X|}{2}$. This is not the case for this paper.

We will be often dealing with the case where X and Y are overlapping and we would be interested in the outer density of vertices in X that are not already included in Y. Hence, we will expand the definition of outer density to a more general case by defining

$$d(X, Y) = d(X \setminus Y, Y).$$

k-cores. We briefly review the basic background regarding k-cores. The concept was introduced by Seidman [23].

Given a graph $G = (V, E)$, a set of vertices $X \subseteq V$ is a k-core if every vertex in the subgraph induced by X has degree at least k, and X is maximal with respect to this property. A k-core of G can be obtained by recursively removing all the vertices of degree less than k, until all vertices in the remaining graph have degree at least k.

It is not hard to see that if $\{C_i\}$ is the set of all distinct k-cores of G then $\{C_i\}$ forms a nested chain

$$\emptyset = C_0 \subsetneq C_1 \subsetneq \cdots \subsetneq C_\ell = V.$$

Furthermore, the set of vertices S_k that belong in a k-core but not in a $(k-1)$-core is called *k-shell.*

The *k-core decomposition* of G is the process of identifying all k-cores (and all k-shells). Therefore, the k-core decomposition of a graph identifies progressively the internal cores and decomposes the graph shell by shell. A linear-time algorithm to obtain the k-core decomposition was given by Matula and Beck [20]. The algorithm starts by provisionally assigning each vertex v to a core of index $\deg(v)$, an upper bound to the correct core of a vertex. It then repeatedly removes the vertex with the smallest degree, and updates the core index of the neighbors of the removed vertex. Note the similarity of this algorithm, with the 2-approximation algorithm for the densest-subgraph problem [13].

3. LOCALLY-DENSE GRAPH DECOMPOSITION

In this section we present the main concept introduced in this paper, the *locally-dense decomposition* of a graph. We also discuss the properties of this decomposition. We start by defining the concept of a *locally-dense subgraph.*

DEFINITION 2. *A set of vertices W is* locally dense *if there are no $X \subseteq W$ and Y satisfying $Y \cap W = \emptyset$ such that*

$$d(X, W \setminus X) \leq d(Y, W).$$

In other words, for W to be locally dense there should not be an X "inside" W and a Y "outside" W so that the density that Y brings to W is larger than the density that X brings.

Due to the notational simplicity, we will often refer to these sets of vertices as subgraphs.

Interestingly, the property of being locally dense induces a nested chain of subgraphs in G.

PROPOSITION 3. *Let U and W be locally-dense subgraphs. Then either $U \subseteq W$ or $W \subseteq U$.*

PROOF. Assume otherwise. Define $X = U \setminus W$ and $Y = W \setminus U$. Both X and Y should be non-empty sets. Then either $d(X, U \cap W) \leq d(Y, U \cap W)$ or $d(X, U \cap W) > d(Y, U \cap W)$. Assume the former. This implies

$$\begin{aligned} d(X, U \setminus X) &= d(X, U \cap W) \\ &\leq d(Y, U \cap W) \\ &\leq d(Y, U), \end{aligned}$$

which contradicts the fact that U is locally dense. For the first equality we used the fact that $U \setminus X = U \cap W$, while for the last inequality we used the fact that $E_\times(Y, U \cap W) \leq E_\times(Y, U)$.

The case $d(X, U \cap W) > d(Y, U \cap W)$ is similar. □

The proposition implies that the set of locally-dense subgraphs of a graph forms a nested chain, in the same way that the set of k-cores does.

COROLLARY 4. *A set of locally-dense subgraphs can be arranged into a sequence $B_0 \subsetneq B_1 \subsetneq \cdots \subsetneq B_k$, where $k \leq |V|$. Moreover, $d(B_i, B_{i-1}) > d(B_{i+1}, B_i)$ for $1 \leq i < k$.*

The chain of locally-dense subgraphs of a graph G, as specified by Corollary 4, defines the *locally-dense decomposition* of G.

We proceed to characterize the locally-dense subgraphs of the decomposition with respect to their *global* density in the whole graph G. We want to characterize the global density of subgraph B_i of the decomposition. B_i cannot be denser than the previous subgraph B_{i-1} in the decomposition, however, we want to measure the density that the additional vertices $S_i = B_i \setminus B_{i-1}$ bring. This density involves edges among vertices of S_i and edges from S_i to the previous subgraph B_{i-1}. This is captured precisely by the concept of *outer density* $d(B_i, B_{i-1})$ defined in the previous section. As the following proposition shows the outer density of B_i with respect to B_{i-1} is maximized over all subgraphs that contain B_{i-1}. In other words, B_i is the densest subgraph we can choose after B_{i-1}, given the containment constraint.

PROPOSITION 5. *Let $\{B_i\}$ be the chain of locally-dense subgraphs. Then $B_0 = \emptyset$, $B_k = V$, and B_i is the densest subgraph properly containing B_{i-1},*

$$B_i = \arg\max_{W \supsetneq B_{i-1}} d(W, B_{i-1}).$$

To prove the proposition we will use the following two following lemmas which we state without a proof.

LEMMA 6. *Let $X \subseteq Y$ be two sets of vertices. Assume $Z \cap Y = \emptyset$. If $d(Z, Y) \geq d(Y, X)$, then $d(Y \cup Z, X) \geq d(Y, X)$.*

LEMMA 7. *Let $X \subseteq Y$ be two sets of vertices. Assume $Z \subseteq Y \setminus X$. If $d(Z, Y \setminus Z) < d(Y, X)$, then $d(Y \setminus Z, X) > d(Y, X)$.*

PROOF OF PROPOSITION 5. Assume inductively that the proposition holds for all $j < i$.

Let $U = \arg\max_{W \supsetneq B_{i-1}} d(W, B_{i-1})$. We will first show that U is locally dense. We argue that there are no sets X and Y with $X \subseteq U$ and $Y \cap U = \emptyset$ that can serve as certificates for U being non locally-dense.

Fix any $X \subseteq U$. Define $X_j = X \cap (B_j \setminus B_{j-1})$ for $j < i$, and $X_i = X \cap (U \setminus B_{i-1})$. Define also $U_j = (U \setminus X) \cup B_{j-1}$ for $j \leq i$. Note that $B_j \subseteq U_j \cup X_j$.

If $X_i \neq \emptyset$, we have $d(X_i, U \setminus X_i) \geq d(U, B_{i-1})$, otherwise Lemma 7 implies that we can delete X_i from U and obtain a more dense subgraph.

Similarly, for $j < i$ with $X_j \neq \emptyset$, we have

$$\begin{aligned} d(X_j, U_j \setminus X_j) &\geq d(X_j, B_j \setminus X_j) \\ &\geq d(B_j, B_{j-1}) \\ &> d(U, B_{i-1}), \end{aligned}$$

where the first inequality follows from $B_j \setminus X_j \subseteq U_j \setminus X_j$, the second inequality is implied by Lemma 7 and the induction assumption on j, and the last inequality is implied by Lemma 6 and the induction assumption on $j+1, \ldots, i-1$.

These inequalities imply

$$\begin{aligned} d(X, U \setminus X) &= \sum_{j=1, X_j \neq \emptyset}^{i} \frac{|X_j|}{|X|} d(X_j, U_j \setminus X_j) \\ &\geq \sum_{j=1}^{i} \frac{|X_j|}{|X|} d(U, B_{i-1}) \\ &= d(U, B_{i-1}). \end{aligned}$$

Consider also any set Y with $Y \cap U = \emptyset$. Due to the optimality of U and Lemma 6 we must have $d(Y, U) < d(U, B_{i-1})$.

We conclude that for any X and Y with $X \subseteq U$ and $Y \cap U = \emptyset$ it is $d(X, U \setminus X) > d(Y, U)$, which shows that U is locally dense.

Assume now $U = B_j$ for $j \geq i$. We need to show that $j = i$. Assume otherwise. Since B_i is locally dense, we have $d(B_j \setminus B_i, B_i) < d(B_i, B_{i-1})$. With a simple calculation we can show that $d(B_j \setminus B_i, B_i) < d(B_j, B_{i-1})$. Lemma 7 implies that removing $B_j \setminus B_i$ produces a more dense subgraph which contradicts the optimality of U. □

As a consequence of the previous proposition we can characterize the first subgraph in the decomposition.

COROLLARY 8. *Let $\{B_i\}$ be a locally-dense decomposition of a graph G. Then B_1 is the densest subgraph of G.*

The above discussion motivates the problem of locally-dense graph decomposition, which is the focus of this paper.

PROBLEM 1. *Given a graph $G = (V, E)$ find a maximal sequence of locally-dense subgraphs*

$$\emptyset = B_0 \subsetneq B_1 \subsetneq \cdots \subsetneq B_k = V.$$

4. DECOMPOSITION ALGORITHMS

In this section we propose two algorithms for the problem of locally-dense graph decomposition (Problem 1). The first algorithm gives an *exact solution*, and runs in worst-case time $\mathcal{O}(|V|^2|E|)$, but it is significantly faster in practice. The second algorithm is a linear-time algorithm that provides a factor-2 approximation guarantee.

Both algorithms are inspired by corresponding algorithms for the densest-subgraph problem. The first algorithm by the exact algorithm of Goldberg [15], and the second algorithm by the greedy linear-time algorithm of Charikar [13].

4.1 Exact algorithm

We start our discussion on the exact algorithm for locally-dense graph decomposition by reviewing Goldberg's algorithm [15] for the densest-subgraph problem.

Recall that the densest-subgraph problem asks to find the subset of vertices W that maximizes $d(W) = |E(W)|/|W|$. Given a graph $G = (V, E)$ and a positive number $\alpha \geq 0$ define a function

$$f(\alpha) = \max_{W \subseteq V} \{|E(W)| - \alpha|W|\},$$

and the maximizer

$$F(\alpha) = \arg\max_{W \subseteq V} \{|E(W)| - \alpha|W|\},$$

where ties are resolved by picking the largest W. Note that the value of the function f decreases as α increases, and as α exceeds a certain value the function becomes 0 by taking $W = \emptyset$. Goldberg observed that the densest-subgraph problem is equivalent to the problem of finding the largest value of α^* for which $f(\alpha^*) \geq 0$ and the maximizer set $F(\alpha^*) = W^*$ is non empty.[2] The densest subgraph is precisely this maximizer set W^*. Furthermore, Goldberg showed how to find the vertex set $W = F(\alpha)$, for a given value of α. This is done by mapping the problem to an instance of the *min-cut problem*, which can be solved in time $\mathcal{O}(|V||E|)$, in a recent breakthrough by Orlin [22]. We will present an extension of this transformation in the next section, where we discuss how to speed-up the algorithm.

Thus, Goldberg's algorithm uses binary search over α and finds the largest value of α^* for which $f(\alpha^*) \geq 0$ and the maximizer set W^* is non empty. Each iteration of the binary search involves a call to a min-cut instance for the current value of α.

Our algorithm for finding the locally-dense decomposition of a graph builds on Goldberg's algorithm [15]. We show that Goldberg's construction has the following, rather remarkable, property: there is a sequence of values $\alpha^* = \alpha_1 \geq \ldots \geq \alpha_k$, for $k \leq n$, which gives all the distinct values of the function f. Furthermore, the corresponding set of subgraphs $\{F(\alpha_1), \ldots, F(\alpha_k)\}$ is exactly the set of all locally-dense subgraphs of G, and thus the solution to our decomposition problem.

Therefore, our algorithm is a simple extension of Goldberg's algorithm: instead of searching only for the optimal value $\alpha_1 = \alpha^*$, we find the whole sequence of α_i's and the corresponding subgraphs.

Next we prove the claimed properties and discuss the algorithm in more detail.

We first show that the distinct maximizers of the function F correspond to the set of locally-dense subgraphs.

PROPOSITION 9. *Let $\{B_i\}$ be the set of locally-dense subgraphs. Then*

$$B_i = F(\alpha), \text{ for } d(B_{i+1}, B_i) < \alpha \leq d(B_i, B_{i-1}).$$

PROOF. We first show that $U = F(\beta)$ is a locally-dense subgraph, for any β. Note that for any $X \subseteq U$, we must have $|E_\Delta(X, U \setminus X)| - \beta|X| \geq 0$, otherwise we can delete X from U and obtain a better solution which violates the optimality of $U = F(\beta)$. This implies that $d(X, U \setminus X) = E_\Delta(X, U \setminus X)/|X| \geq \beta$. Similarly, for any Y such that $Y \cap U = \emptyset$, we have $|E_\Delta(Y, U)| - \beta|Y| < 0$ or, equivalently, $d(Y, U) < \beta$. Thus, U is locally dense.

Fix i and select α s.t. $d(B_{i+1}, B_i) < \alpha \leq d(B_i, B_{i-1})$. Let $B_j = F(\alpha)$. If $j > i$, then, due to Corollary 4, $d(B_j, B_{j-1}) < \alpha$ which we can rephrase as

$$c = |E_\Delta(B_j \setminus B_{j-1}, B_{j-1})| - \alpha|B_j \setminus B_{j-1}| < 0.$$

If we delete $B_j \setminus B_{j-1}$ from U, then we increase the cost exactly by $-c$, that is, we obtain a better solution which violates the optimality of U. If $j < i$, then Corollary 4

[2]This observation is an instance of *fractional programming* [14].

Algorithm 1: ExactLD(G, X, Y)

input : Graph $G = (V, E)$
locally-dense subgraphs X and Y with $X \subsetneq Y$

$\alpha \leftarrow d(Y, X) + |V|^{-2}$;
$Z \leftarrow F(\alpha)$;
if $Z \neq X$ **then**
  output Z;
  ExactLD(G, X, Z);
  ExactLD(G, Z, Y);

implies that $d(B_{j+1}, B_j) \geq \alpha$, so we can add $B_{j+1} \setminus B_j$ to obtain a better solution. It follows that $B_i = F(\alpha)$. □

Next we need to show that it is possible to search efficiently for the sequence of α's that give the set of locally-dense subgraphs. To that end we will show that if we have obtained two subgraphs $B_x \subsetneq B_y$ of the decomposition (corresponding to values $\alpha_x \geq \alpha_y$), it is possible to pick a new value α so that computing $F(\alpha)$ allows us to make progress in the search process: we either find a new locally-dense subgraph $B_x \subsetneq B_z \subsetneq B_y$ or we establish that no such subgraph exists between B_x and B_y, in other words, B_x and B_y are consecutive subgraphs in our decomposition.

Proposition 10. *Let $\{B_i\}$ be the set of locally-dense subgraphs. Let $B_x \subsetneq B_y$ be two subgraphs. Set $\alpha = d(B_y, B_x) + |V|^{-2}$ and let $B_z = F(\alpha)$. If $x + 1 < y$, then $x < z < y$. If $x + 1 = y$, then $z = x$.*

Proof. A simple calculation shows that $\alpha > d(B_y, B_x) \geq d(B_y, B_{y-1})$. Proposition 9 now implies that $z < y$.

Assume that $x + 1 < y$. This implies that $d(B_y, B_{y-1}) < d(B_{x+1}, B_x)$ which implies that $d(B_y, B_x) < d(B_{x+1}, B_x)$. Let us write

$$a = E_\Delta(B_y \setminus B_x, B_x)\,, \qquad b = |B_y| - |B_x|,$$
$$c = E_\Delta(B_{x+1} \setminus B_x, B_x)\,, \text{ and } \qquad d = |B_{x+1}| - |B_x|.$$

Let us now bound the difference between the densities as

$$\begin{aligned} d(B_{x+1}, B_x) - d(B_y, B_x) &= \frac{a}{b} - \frac{c}{d} \\ &= \frac{ad - bc}{bd} \\ &\geq \frac{1}{bd} \\ &> \frac{1}{|V|^2}. \end{aligned}$$

This implies that $\alpha < d(B_{x+1}, B_x)$. Proposition 9 now implies that $z \geq x + 1 > x$.

Assume that $x+1 = y$. Since $d(B_y, B_{y-1}) < d(B_x, B_{x-1})$, the same argument as above shows that $z \geq x$, which guarantees that $x = z$. □

The exact decomposition algorithm uses Proposition 10 to guide the search process. Starting by the two extreme subgraphs of the decomposition, $\emptyset$ and V, the algorithm maintains a sequence of locally-dense subgraphs. Recursively, for any two currently-adjacent subgraphs in the sequence, we use Proposition 10 to check whether the two subgraphs are consecutive or not in the decomposition. If they are consecutive, the recurrence at that branch of the search is terminated. If they are not, a new subgraph between the two is discovered and it is added in the decomposition. The algorithm is named ExactLD and it is illustrated as Algorithm 1.

With the next propositions we prove the correctness of the algorithm and we bound its running time.

Proposition 11. *The algorithm* ExactLD *initiated with input $(G, \emptyset, V)$ visits all locally-dense subgraphs of G.*

Proof. Let $\{B_i\}$ be the set of locally-dense subgraphs. We will prove the proposition by showing that for $i < j$, the algorithm ExactLD(G, B_i, B_j) visits all monotonic subgraphs that are between B_i and B_j. We will prove this by induction over $j-i$. The first step $j = i+1$ is trivial. Assume that $j > i+1$. Then Proposition 10 implies that $B_k = F(\alpha)$, where $i < k < j$. The inductive assumption now guarantees that ExactLD(G, B_i, B_k) and ExactLD(G, B_k, B_j) will visit all monotonic subgraphs between B_i and B_j. □

Proposition 12. *The worst-case running time of algorithm* ExactLD *is $\mathcal{O}(|V|^2|E|)$.*

Proof. We will show that the algorithm ExactLD, initiated with input $(G, \emptyset, V)$ makes $2k-3$ calls to the function F, where k is the number of locally-dense subgraphs.

Let k_i be the number of calls of F when the input parameter $Y = B_i$. Out of these k_i calls one call will result in $F(\alpha) = X$. There are $k - 1$ such calls, since $Y = \emptyset$ is never tested. Each of the remaining calls will discover a new locally-dense subgraph. Since there are $k - 2$ new subgraphs to discover, it follows that $2k - 3$ calls to F are needed.

Since a call to F corresponds to a min-cut computation, which has running time $\mathcal{O}(|V||E|)$ [22], and since $k \in \mathcal{O}(|V|)$, the claimed running-time bound follows. □

4.2 Speeding up the exact algorithm

Our next step is to speed-up ExactLD. This speed-up does not improve to the theoretical bound for the computational time but, in practice, it improves the performance of the algorithm dramatically.

The speed-up is based on the following observation. We know from Proposition 10 that ExactLD(G, X, Y) visits only subgraphs Z with the property $X \subseteq Z \subseteq Y$. This gives us immediately the first speed-up: we can safely ignore any vertex outside Y, that is, ExactLD$(G(Y), X, Y)$ will yield the same output.

Our second observation is that any subgraph Z visited by ExactLD(G, X, Y) must contain vertices X. However, we cannot simply delete them because we need to take into account the edges between X and Z. To address this let us consider the following maximizer

$$F(\alpha; X) = \arg \max_{X \subseteq W \subseteq V} \{|E(W)| - \alpha |W|\}\,.$$

We can replace the original $F(\alpha)$ in Algorithm 1 with $F(\alpha; X)$. To compute $F(\alpha; X)$ we will use a straightforward extension of the Goldberg's algorithm [15] and transform this problem into a problem of finding a minimum cut.

In order to do this, given a graph $G = (V, E)$, let us define a weighted graph H that consists of vertices $V \setminus X$ and edges $E(V \setminus X)$ with weights of 1. Add two auxiliary vertices s and t into H and connect these vertices to every vertex in

$V \setminus X$. Given a vertex $y \in V \setminus X$, assign a weight of 2α to the edge (y, t) and a weight of

$$w(y) = \deg(y; V \setminus X) + 2\deg(y; X)$$

to the edge (s, y), where $\deg(y; U)$ stands for the number of neighbors of y in U. We claim that solving a minimum cut such that s and t are in different cuts will solve $F(\alpha; X)$. This cut can be obtained by constructing a maximum flow from s to t.

To prove this claim let $C \subsetneq V(H)$ be a subset of vertices containing s and not containing t. Let $Z = C \setminus \{s\}$ and also let $W = V \setminus (Z \cup X)$. There are three types of cross-edges from C to $V(H) \setminus C$: *(i)* edges from $x \in Z$ to t, *(ii)* edges from s to $x \in W$, and *(iii)* edges from $x \in Z$ to $y \in W$. The total cost of C is then

$$2|Z|\alpha + \sum_{y \in W} w(y) + |E_\times(Z, W)|.$$

We claim that the last two terms of the cost are equal to $2|E| - 2|E(X \cup Z)|$. To see this, consider an edge $e = (x, y)$ in $E \setminus E(X \cup Z)$. This implies that one of the end points, assume it is y, has to be in W. There are three different cases for x: *(i)* if $x \in W$, then e contributes 2 to the cost: 1 to $w(x)$ and 1 to $w(y)$, *(ii)* if $x \in X$, then e contributes 2 to $w(y)$, and *(iii)* if $x \in Z$, then e contributes 1 to $w(y)$ and 1 to the third term. Thus, we can write the cut as

$$\begin{aligned} &2|Z|\alpha + 2|E| - 2|E(X \cup Z)| \\ &\quad = 2|E| - 2|X|\alpha - 2(|E(X \cup Z)| - \alpha|Z \cup X|). \end{aligned}$$

The first two terms in the right-hand side are constant which implies that that finding the minimum cut is equivalent of maximizing $|E(X \cup Z)| - \alpha|Z \cup X|$. Consequently, if Z^* is the min-cut solution, then $F(\alpha) = X \cup Z^*$.

Note that the graph H does not have vertices included in X. By combining both speed-ups we are able to reduce the running time of ExactLD(X, Y) by considering only the vertices that are in $Y \setminus X$.

4.3 Linear approximation algorithm

As we saw in the last section, the exact algorithm can be significantly accelerated, and indeed, our experimental evaluation shows that it is possible to run the exact algorithm for a graph of millions of vertices and edges within 2 minutes. Nevertheless, the worst-case complexity of the algorithm is cubic, and thus, it is not truly scalable for massive graphs.

Here we present a more lightweight algorithm for performing a locally-dense decomposition of a graph. The algorithm runs in linear time and offers a factor-2 approximation guarantee. As the exact algorithm builds on Goldberg's algorithm for the densest-subgraph problem, the linear-time algorithm builds on Charikar's approximation algorithm for the same problem [13]. As already explained in Section 2, Charikar's approximation algorithm iteratively removes the vertex with the lowest degree, until left with an empty graph, and returns the densest graph among all subgraphs considered during this process.

Our extension to this algorithm, called GreedyLD, is illustrated in Algorithm 2, and it operates in two phases. The first phase is identical to the one in Charikar's algorithm: all vertices of the graph are iteratively removed, in increasing order of their degree in the current graph. In the second phase, the algorithm proceeds to discover approximate locally-dense subgraphs, in an iterative manner, from B_1 to B_k. The first subgraph B_1 is the approximate densest subgraph, the same one returned by Charikar's algorithm. In the j-th step of the iteration, having discover subgraphs $B_1, \ldots, B_{j-1}$ the algorithm selects the subgraph B_j that maximizes the density $d(B_j, B_{j-1})$. To select B_j the algorithm considers subsets of vertices only in the degree-based order that was produced in the first phase.

Algorithm 2: GreedyLD(G)

input : Graph $G = (V, E)$
output: Collection $\mathcal{C}$ of approximate locally-dense subgraphs

for $i = |V|, \ldots, 1$ **do**
  $w_i \leftarrow$ the vertex with the smallest degree;
  delete w_i from V;
$\mathcal{C} \leftarrow \{\emptyset\}$;
$j \leftarrow 0$;
while $j < |V|$ **do**
  $i \leftarrow \arg\max_{i > j} d(\{w_1, \ldots, w_i\}, \{w_1, \ldots, w_j\})$;
  add $\{w_1, \ldots, w_j\}$ to $\mathcal{C}$;
  $j \leftarrow i$;
return $\mathcal{C}$;

Discovering $\mathcal{C}$ from the ordered vertices takes $\mathcal{O}(n^2)$ time, if done naively. However, it is possible to implement this step in $\mathcal{O}(n)$ time. In order to do this, sort vertices in the reverse visit order, and define $\text{in}(v)$ to be the number of edges of v from the earlier neighbors. Then, we can we express the density as an average,

$$d(\{w_1, \ldots, w_i\}, \{w_1, \ldots, w_j\}) = \frac{1}{i - j} \sum_{k=j+1}^{i} \text{in}(v_k).$$

Consequently, we can see that recovering $\mathcal{C}$ is an instance of the following problem,

Problem 2. *Given a sequence $y_1, \ldots, y_n$, compute the maximal interval*

$$m(j) = \arg\max_{j \le i \le n} \frac{1}{i - j + 1} \sum_{k=j}^{i} y_k,$$

for every $1 \le j \le n$.

Luckily, Calders et al. [11] demonstrated that we can use the classic PAVA algorithm [5] to solve this problem for *every* value of j in total $\mathcal{O}(n)$ time.

To quantify the approximation guarantee of GreedyLD, note that the sequence of approximate locally-dense subgraphs produced by the algorithm are not necessarily aligned with the locally-dense subgraphs of the optimal decomposition. In other words, to assess the quality of the density of an approximate locally-dense subgraph B_j produced by GreedyLD, there is no direct counterpart in the optimal decomposition to compare. To overcome this difficulty we develop a scheme of "vertex-wise" comparison, where for any $1 \le i \le n$, the density of a the smallest approximate locally-dense subgraph of size at least i is compared with the density of a the smallest optimal locally-dense subgraph of size at least i. This is defined below via the concept of *profile*.

Definition 13. *Let $\mathcal{B} = (\emptyset = B_0 \subsetneq B_1 \subsetneq \cdots \subsetneq B_k = V)$ be a nested chain of subgraphs, the first subgraph being the* *empty graph and the last subgraph being the full graph. For an integer i,* $1 \leq i \leq n$ *define*

$$j = \min\{x \mid |B_x| \geq i\}$$

to be the index of the smallest subgraph in $\mathcal{B}$ *whose size is at least i. We define a* profile function $p : \{1, \ldots, n\} \to \mathbb{R}$ *to be*

$$p(i;\, \mathcal{B}) = d(B_j, B_{j-1})\,.$$

Our approximation guarantee is now expressed as a guarantee of the profile function of the approximate decomposition with respect to the optimal decomposition.

PROPOSITION 14. *Let* $\mathcal{B} = \{B_i\}$ *be the set of optimal locally-dense subgraphs. Let* $\mathcal{C} = \{C_i\}$ *be the subgraphs obtained by* GREEDYLD. *Then*

$$p(i;\, \mathcal{C}) \geq p(i;\, \mathcal{B})\,/2.$$

PROOF. Sort the set of vertices V according to the reverse visiting order of GREEDYLD and let $\text{in}(v)$ be the number of edges of v from earlier neighbors.

Fix k to be an integer, $1 \leq k \leq n$ and let B_i be the smallest subgraph such that $|B_i| \geq k$. Let v_j be the last vertex occurring in B_i. We must have $\text{in}(v_j) \geq d(v_j, B_i)$, and $d(v_j, B_i) \geq d(B_i, B_{i-1})$ as otherwise we can remove v_j from B_i and improve the density due to Lemma 7. We have

$$p(k;\, \mathcal{B}) = d(B_i, B_{i-1}) \leq \text{in}(v_j)\,.$$

Let C_x be the smallest subgraph such that $|C_x| \geq k$. Let v_z be the vertex with the smallest index that is still in $C_x \setminus C_{x-1}$. Let g_y be the degree of v_y right before v_j is removed during GREEDYLD. Note that $\text{in}(v_j) \leq g_y$, and we can easily show that $\sum_{y=z}^{j} g_y \leq 2 \sum_{y=z}^{j} \text{in}(v_y)$. We now have

$$\begin{aligned} p(k;\, \mathcal{C}) &= d(C_x, C_{x-1}) \\ &\geq \frac{1}{j-z+1} \sum_{y=z}^{j} \text{in}(v_y) \\ &\geq \frac{1}{2(j-z+1)} \sum_{y=z}^{j} g_y \\ &\geq \frac{\text{in}(v_j)}{2}, \end{aligned}$$

where the optimality of C_x implies the first inequality. □

We should point out that $p(1, \mathcal{B})$ is equal to the density of the densest subgraph, while $p(1, \mathcal{C})$ is equal to the density of the subgraph discovered by the Charikar's algorithm. Consequently, Proposition 14 provides automatically the 2-approximation guarantee of the Charikar's algorithm.

We should also point out that $p(i, \mathcal{C})$ can be larger than $p(i, \mathcal{B})$ but for the first index, say j, for which $p(j, \mathcal{C}) \neq p(j, \mathcal{B})$, Proposition 5 guarantees that $p(j, \mathcal{C}) < p(j, \mathcal{B})$.

5. LOCALLY-DENSE SUBGRAPHS AND CORE DECOMPOSITION

Here we study the connection of graph cores, obtained with the well-known k-core decomposition algorithms, with local-density, studied in this paper. We are able to show that from the theory point-of-view, graph cores are as good approximation to the optimal locally-dense graph decomposition as the subgraphs obtained by the GREEDYLD algorithm. In particular we show a similar result to Proposition 14, namely, a factor-2 approximation on the profile function of the core decomposition.

However, as we will see in our empirical evaluation, the behavior of the two algorithms, GREEDYLD and k-core decomposition are different in practice, with GREEDYLD giving in general more dense subgraphs and closer to the ones given by exact locally-dense decomposition.

Before stating and proving the result regarding k-cores, recall that a set of vertices $X \subseteq V$ is a k-core if every vertex in the subgraph induced by X has degree at least k, and X is maximal with respect to this property. A linear-time algorithm for obtaining all k-cores is illustrated in Algorithm 3.

Algorithm 3: CORE(G)

input : Graph $G = (V, E)$
output: Collection $\mathcal{C}$ of k-cores

$\mathcal{C} \leftarrow \{V\}$;
$k \leftarrow \min_w \deg(w)$;
for $i = |V|, \ldots, 1$ **do**
  $w_i \leftarrow$ the vertex with the smallest degree;
  if $\deg(w) > k$ **then**
    add V to $\mathcal{C}$;
    $k \leftarrow \deg(w)$;
  delete w_i from V;
return $\mathcal{C}$;

It is a well-known fact that the set of all k-cores of a graph forms a nested chain of subgraphs, in the same way that locally-dense subgraphs do.

PROPOSITION 15. *Let* $\{C_i\}$ *be the set of all k-cores of a graph* $G = (V, E)$. *Then* $\{C_i\}$ *forms a nested chain,*

$$\emptyset = C_0 \subsetneq C_1 \subsetneq \cdots \subsetneq C_l = V.$$

Similar to Proposition 14, k-cores provide a factor-2 approximation with respect to the optimal locally-dense subgraphs. The proof is in fact quite similar to that of Proposition 14.

PROPOSITION 16. *Let* $\mathcal{B} = \{B_i\}$ *be the set of optimal locally-dense subgraphs. Let* $\mathcal{C} = \{C_i\}$ *be the set of k-cores. Then*

$$p(i;\, \mathcal{C}) \geq p(i;\, \mathcal{B})\,/2.$$

PROOF. Sort V according to the reverse visiting order of CORE and let $\text{in}(v)$ be the number of edges of v from earlier neighbors.

Fix k to be an integer, $1 \leq k \leq n$ and let B_i be the smallest subgraph such that $|B_i| \geq k$. Let v_j be the last vertex occurring in B_i. We must have $\text{in}(v_j) \geq d(v_j, B_i)$, and $d(v_j, B_i) \geq d(B_i, B_{i-1})$ as otherwise we can remove v_j from B_i and improve the density due to Lemma 7. We have

$$p(k;\, \mathcal{B}) = d(B_i, B_{i-1}) \leq \text{in}(v_j)\,.$$

Let C_x be the smallest smallest core such that $|C_x| \geq k$. Let v_s be the vertex with the smallest index that is still in $C_x \setminus C_{x-1}$. Let v_l be the vertex with the largest index that is still in $C_x \setminus C_{x-1}$.

If $j > l$, then $\text{in}(v_j) < \text{in}(v_l)$ otherwise C_x is not a core. If $j < l$, then $\text{in}(v_j) \leq \text{in}(v_l)$, otherwise C_x would is not the smallest core as $j \geq k$. Hence, $\text{in}(v_j) \leq \text{in}(v_l)$.

Let g_y be the degree of v_y right before v_l is removed during CORE. We now have

$$\begin{aligned} p(k; \mathcal{C}) &= d(C_x, C_{x-1}) \\ &= \frac{1}{l-s+1}\sum_{y=s}^{l} \text{in}(v_y) \\ &\geq \frac{1}{2(l-s+1)}\sum_{y=s}^{l} g_y \\ &\geq \frac{\text{in}(v_l)}{2} \\ &\geq \frac{\text{in}(v_j)}{2}, \end{aligned}$$

which proves the proposition. □

6. RELATED WORK

Our paper is related to previous work on discovering dense subgraphs, clique-like structures, and hierarchical communities. We review some representative work on these topics.

Clique relaxations. The densest possible subgraph is a clique. Unfortunately finding large cliques is computationally intractable [17]. Additionally, the notion of clique does not provide a robust definition for practical situations, as a few absent edges may completely destroy the clique. To address these issues, researchers have come up with relaxed clique definitions. A relaxation, k-plex was suggested by Seidman and Foster [24]. In a k-plex a vertex can have at most $k-1$ absent edges. Unfortunately, discovering maximal k-plexes is also an **NP**-hard problem [7]. An alternative relaxation for a clique is the one of an n-clique, a maximal subgraph where each vertex is connected to every vertex with a path, possibly outside of the subgraph, of at most n-length [10]. So, according to this definition a clique is an 1-clique. As maximal n-cliques may produce sparse graphs, the concept of n-clans was also proposed by limiting the diameter of the subgraph to be at most n [21]. Since 1-clan corresponds to a maximal clique, discovering n-clans is a computationally intractable problem.

Quasi-cliques. For the definition of graph density we have chosen to work with $d(X)$, the average degree of the subgraph induced by X. While this is a popular density definition, there are other alternatives. One such alternative would be to divide the number of edges present in the subgraph with the total number of possible edges, that is, divide by $\binom{n}{2}$. This would give us a normalized density score that is between 0 and 1. Subgraphs that maximize this density definition are called *quasi-cliques*, and algorithms for enumerating all quasi-cliques, which can be exponentially many, have been proposed by Abello et al. [1] and Uno [29]. However, the definition of quasi-cliques is problematic. Note that a single edge already provides maximal density. Consequently additional objectives are needed. One natural objective is to maximize the size of a graph with density of 1, however, this makes the problem equivalent to finding a maximal clique which, as mentioned above, is a computationally-intractable problem [17].

Alternative definitions for density. Other definitions of graph density have been proposed. Recently, Tsourakakis proposed to measure density by counting triangles, instead of counting edges [26]. Interestingly enough, it is possible to find an approximate densest subgraph under this definition. An interesting future direction for our work is to study if the decomposition proposed in this paper can be extended for the triangle-density definition. Density definitions of the form $g(|E|) - \alpha h(|V|)$, where g and h are some increasing functions were studied by Tsourakakis et al. [27], with specific focus on $h(x) = \binom{x}{2}$. It not known whether the densest-subgraph problem according to this definition is polynomially-time solvable or **NP**-hard. Finally, a variant for $d(X)$ adopted for directed graph, along with polynomial-time discovery algorithm, was suggested by Khuller and Saha [18]. Such a definition could serve for defining decompositions of directed graphs, which is also left for future work.

Hierarchical communities. Discovering hierarchy of k nested communities with as homogeneous shells as possible with the constraint that inner communities are denser was studied by the authors of this paper [25]. Here, $|E|/\binom{|V|}{2}$ was used as density definition, and a heuristic algorithm was proposed. Unfortunately, no exact polynomial-time algorithm is known for this problem. As a potential future work it would be interesting to see whether the ideas presented in this paper can be merged with the idea of discovering k-homogeneous communities.

7. EXPERIMENTAL EVALUATION

We will now present our experimental evaluation. We test the two proposed algorithms, EXACTLD and GREEDYLD, for decomposing a graph into locally-dense subgraphs, and we contrast the resulting decompositions against k-cores, obtained with the CORE algorithm. We compare the three algorithms in terms of running time, decomposition size (number of subgraphs they provide), and relative density of the subgraphs they return. We also use the Kendall-τ to measure how similar are the decompositions in terms of the order they induce on the graph vertices.

7.1 Experimental setup

We perform our evaluation on 11 graphs of different sizes and densities. A short description of the graphs is given below, and their basic characteristics can be found in Table 1.

- `dolphins`: an undirected social network of frequent associations between dolphins in a community living off Doubtful Sound in New Zealand.
- `karate`: the social network of friendships between members of a karate club at a US university in the 1970.
- `lesmis`: co-appearance of characters in Les Miserables novel by Victor Hugo.
- `astro`: a co-authorship network among arXiv Astro Physics publications.
- `enron`: an e-mail communication network by Enron employees.
- `fb1912`: an ego-network obtained from Facebook.
- `hepph`: a co-authorship network among arXiv High Energy Physics publications.
- `dblp`: a co-authorship network among computer science researchers.
- `gowalla`: a friendship network of `gowalla.com`.

Table 1: Basic characteristics of the datasets and the running times of the algorithms. E stands for ExactLD, G for GreedyLD, and C for Core.

Name	$\|V\|$	$\|E\|$	running time C	G	E
dolphins	62	159	1ms	1ms	2ms
karate	34	78	1ms	1ms	2ms
lesmis	77	254	2ms	2ms	3ms
astro	18 772	396 160	0.4s	0.4s	2s
enron	36 692	183 831	0.3s	0.3s	2s
fb1912	747	30 025	44ms	44ms	0.2s
hepph	12 008	237 010	0.2s	0.2s	0.9s
dblp	317 080	1 049 866	2s	2s	14s
gowalla	196 591	950 327	2s	2s	9s
roadnet	1 965 206	5 533 214	7s	8s	1m6s
skitter	1 696 415	11 095 298	21s	21s	1m46s

- roadnet: a road network of California, where vertices represent intersections and edges represent road segments.
- skitter: an internet topology graph, obtained from traceroutes run daily in 2005.

The first three datasets are obtained from UCIrvine Network Data Repository,[3] and the remaining datasets are obtained from Stanford SNAP Repository.[4]

We apply Core, GreedyLD, and ExactLD to every dataset. We use a computer equipped with 3GHz Intel Core i7 and 8GB of RAM.[5]

7.2 Results

We begin by reporting the running times of the three algorithms for all of our datasets. They are shown in Table 1. As expected, the linear-time algorithms Core and GreedyLD are both very fast; the largest graph with 11 million edges and 1.7 million vertices is processed in 21 seconds. However, we are also able to run the exact decomposition for all the graphs in reasonable time, despite its running-time complexity of $\mathcal{O}(|V|^2|E|)$. It takes less than 2 minutes for ExactLD to process the largest graph. There are three reasons that contribute to achieving this performance. First, we need to compute the minimum cut only $\mathcal{O}(k)$ times, where k is the number of locally-dense graphs. In practice, k is much smaller than the number of vertices. Second, computing minimum cut in practice is faster than the theoretical $\mathcal{O}(|V||E|)$ bound. Third, as described in Section 4, most of the minimum cuts are computed using subgraphs. While in theory these subgraphs can be as large as the original graph, in practice these subgraphs are significantly smaller.

Next, we compare how well Core and GreedyLD approximate the exact locally-dense decomposition. In order to do that we compute the ratio

$$r(\mathcal{C}, \mathcal{B}) = \min_i \frac{p(i; \mathcal{C})}{p(i; \mathcal{B})}, \qquad (1)$$

[3]http://networkdata.ics.uci.edu/index.php
[4]http://snap.stanford.edu/data
[5]The implementation is available at http://research.ics.aalto.fi/dmg/software.shtml

Table 2: Smallest ratio of the profile function, and the profile function of the exact solution as defined in Equation (1), and the ratio of the most inner discovered subgraph versus the actual densest subgraph.

Name	$r(\mathcal{C}, \mathcal{B})$ Core	GreedyLD	$d(C_1)\,/d(B_1)$ Core	GreedyLD
dolphins	0.94	0.83	0.98	0.98
karate	0.95	0.99	0.95	0.99
lesmis	0.86	0.87	0.96	1.00
astro	0.85	0.85	0.87	0.92
enron	0.83	0.82	0.94	1.00
fb1912	0.69	0.74	0.91	1.00
hepph	0.74	0.75	1.00	1.00
dblp	0.80	0.86	1.00	1.00
gowalla	0.89	0.92	0.87	1.00
roadnet	0.81	0.87	0.84	0.87
skitter	0.73	0.84	0.84	1.00

Table 3: Sizes of the discovered decompositions and Kendall-τ statistics between the decompositions. E stands for ExactLD, G for GreedyLD, and C for Core.

Name	C	G	E	C-vs-E	G-vs-E	C-vs-G
dolphins	4	6	7	0.76	0.77	0.99
karate	4	3	4	0.80	0.95	0.78
lesmis	8	8	9	0.94	0.99	0.95
astro	52	83	435	0.93	0.93	0.99
enron	43	162	357	0.92	0.92	0.99
fb1912	87	55	75	0.95	0.98	0.97
hepph	64	63	283	0.93	0.93	0.98
dblp	47	97	1087	0.88	0.89	0.97
gowalla	51	161	899	0.97	0.96	0.98
roadnet	3	43	2710	0.57	0.80	0.68
skitter	111	266	3501	0.98	0.97	0.99

where $\mathcal{B}$ is the locally-dense decomposition and $\mathcal{C}$ is obtained by either from GreedyLD or Core. These ratios are shown in Table 2. We also compare $p(1; \mathcal{C})\,/p(1; \mathcal{B})$, that is, the ratio of density for the inner most subgraph in $\mathcal{C}$ against the density of $\mathcal{B}_1$, the densest subgraph. Propositions 14 and 15 guarantee that there ratios are at least 1/2. In practice, the ratios are larger, typically over 0.8. In most cases, but not always, GreedyLD obtains better ratios than Core. When comparing the ratio for the inner most subgraph, GreedyLD, by design, will always be better or equal than Core. We see that only in three datasets Core is able to find the same subgraph as GreedyLD.

Let us now compare the different solutions found by the three algorithms. In Table 3 we report the sizes of discovered communities and their Kendall-τ statistics, which compares the ordering of the vertices induced by the decompositions. In particular, the Kendall-τ statistic is computed by assigning each vertex an index based on which subgraph the vertex belongs. To handle ties, we use the b-version of Kendall-τ, as given by Agresti [2]. If the statistic is 1, the decompositions are equal.

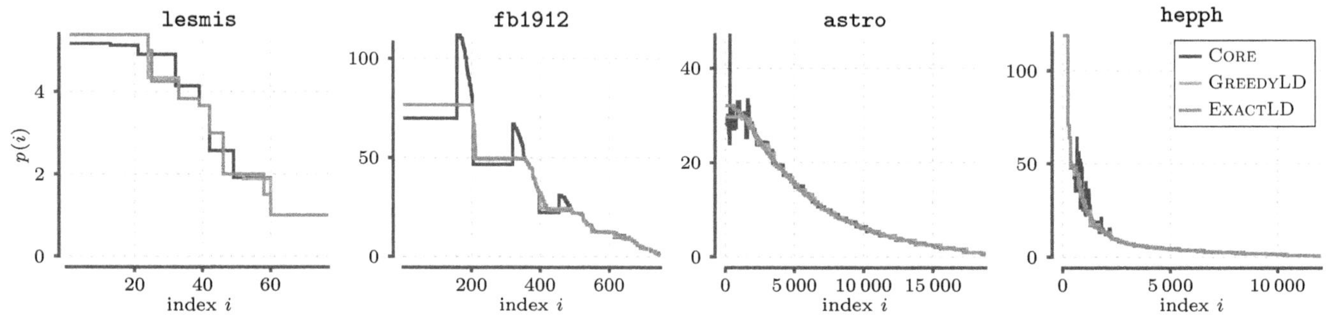

Figure 2: Profile functions for `lesmis`, `fb1912`, `astro`, and `hepph`.

Our first observation is that typically the locally-dense decomposition algorithms return more subgraphs than the k-core decomposition. As an extreme example, `roadnet` contains only 3 k-cores while GREEDYLD finds 43 subgraphs and EXACTLD finds 2710. This can be explained by the fact that the vertices in the graph have low degrees, which results in a very coarse k-core decomposition. On the other hand, EXACTLD and GREEDYLD exploit density to discover more fine-grained decompositions. This result is similar to what we presented in the Example 1 in the introduction.

The Kendall-τ statistics are typically close to 1, especially for large datasets suggesting that all 3 methods result in similar decompositions. The statistic between CORE and GREEDYLD is typically larger than to the exact solution. This is expected since CORE and GREEDYLD use the exact same order for vertices—the only difference between these two methods is how they partition the vertex order. In addition, decompositions produced by GREEDYLD are closer to the exact solution than the decompositions produced by CORE, which is also a natural result.

Let us now compare the solutions in terms of profile functions as defined in Definition 13. We illustrate several prototypical examples of such profile functions in Figure 2. From the figure we see that GREEDYLD produces similar profiles as the exact locally-dense decomposition. We also see that CORE does not respect the local density constraint. In **fb1912**, **astro**, and **hepph** there exist k-shells that are denser than their inner shells, that is, joining these shells would increase the density of the inner shell. GREEDYLD does not have this problem since by definition it will have a monotonically decreasing profile.

Finally, in Table 4 we present the decompositions obtained by the three algorithms for the **lesmis** graph. We see that GREEDYLD obtains very similar result to the exact solution, the only difference is the second subgraph and the third subgraph is merged and the 3rd last subgraph lends vertices to the 2nd last subgraph. While GREEDYLD has the same first subgraph as the exact solution, which is the densest subgraph, CORE breaks this subgraph into 3 subgraphs. Interestingly enough, the main character of the book, Jean Valjean, is not placed into the first shell by CORE.

Table 4: Decompositions of the `lesmis` dataset. The numbers represent the greedy peeling and the k-core decomposition, respectively. The names are ordered according to locally dense decomposition, the groups are marked with chanding color.

Valjean	1	2	Fameuil	2	3	Pontmercy	6	7
MmeThenardier	1	3	Blacheville	2	3	MotherInnocent	7	7
Thenardier	1	2	Favourite	2	3	Magnon	7	7
Javert	1	2	Dahlia	2	3	MmePontmercy	7	7
Eponine	1	2	Zephine	2	3	BaronessT	6	7
Gavroche	1	1	Fantine	2	3	Child1	7	7
Marius	1	1	Bamatabois	3	4	Child2	7	7
Mabeuf	1	1	Judge	3	4	Napoleon	8	8
Enjolras	1	1	Champmathieu	3	4	CountessDeLo	8	8
Combeferre	1	1	Brevet	3	4	Geborand	8	8
Prouvaire	1	1	Chenildieu	3	4	Champtercier	8	8
Feuilly	1	1	Cochepaille	3	4	Cravatte	8	8
Courfeyrac	1	1	Gillenormand	4	5	Count	8	8
Bahorel	1	1	MlleGillenormand	4	5	OldMan	8	8
Bossuet	1	1	LtGillenormand	4	5	Labarre	8	8
Joly	1	1	Simplice	5	6	MmeDeR	8	8
Grantaire	1	1	Anzelma	5	6	Isabeau	8	8
Gueulemer	1	2	Woman2	5	6	Gervais	8	8
Babet	1	2	Toussaint	5	6	Scaufflaire	8	8
Claquesous	1	2	Myriel	6	6	Boulatruelle	8	8
Montparnasse	1	2	MlleBaptistine	6	6	Gribier	8	8
Brujon	1	3	MmeMagloire	6	6	Jondrette	8	8
MmeHucheloup	1	3	Marguerite	7	7	MmeBurgon	8	8
Cosette	2	4	Fauchelevent	6	7	MlleVaubois	8	8
Tholomyes	2	3	Perpetue	7	7	MotherPlutarch	8	8
Listolier	2	3	Woman1	7	7			

8. CONCLUSIONS

Inspired by k-core analysis and density-based graph mining, we propose density-friendly graph decomposition, a new tool for analyzing graphs. Like k-core decomposition, our approach decomposes a given graph into a nested sequence of subgraphs These subgraphs have the property that the inner subgraphs are always denser than the outer ones; additionally the most inner subgraph is the densest one—properties that the k-cores do not satisfy.

We provide two efficient algorithms to discover such a decomposition. The first algorithm is based on minimum cut and it extends the exact algorithm of Goldberg for the densest-subgraph problem. The second algorithm extends a linear-time algorithm by Charikar for approximating the same problem. The second algorithm runs in linear time, and thus, in addition to finding subgraphs that respect better the density structure of the graph, it is as efficient as the k-core decomposition algorithm.

In addition to offering a new alternative for decomposing a graph into dense subgraphs, we significantly extend the analysis, the understanding, and the applicability of previous well-known graph algorithms: Goldberg's exact algorithm and Charikar's approximation algorithm for finding the densest subgraph, as well as the k-core decomposition algorithm itself.

9. REFERENCES

[1] J. Abello, M. Resende, and S. Sudarsky. Massive quasi-clique detection. In *LATIN 2002: Theoretical Informatics*, pages 598–612, 2002.

[2] A. Agresti. *Analysis of Ordinal Categorical Data*. John Wiley & Sons, 2nd edition, 2010.

[3] J. I. Alvarez-Hamelin, L. Dall'Asta, A. Barrat, and A. Vespignani. k-core decomposition: a tool for the visualization of large scale networks. *CoRR*, abs/cs/0504107, 2005.

[4] Y. Asahiro, K. Iwama, H. Tamaki, and T. Tokuyama. Greedily finding a dense subgraph. *SWAT*, pages 136–148, 1996.

[5] M. Ayer, H. Brunk, G. Ewing, and W. Reid. An empirical distribution function for sampling with incomplete information. *The Annals of Mathematical Statistics*, 26(4):641–647, 1955.

[6] G. Bader and C. Hogue. An automated method for finding molecular complexes in large protein interaction networks. *BMC Bioinformatics*, 4(1), 2003.

[7] B. Balasundaram, S. Butenko, and I. V. Hicks. Clique relaxations in social network analysis: The maximum k-plex problem. *Operations Research*, 59(1):133–142, 2011.

[8] B. Bollobás. The evolution of random graphs. *Transactions of the American Mathematical Society*, 286(1):257–274, 1984.

[9] F. Bonchi, F. Gullo, A. Kaltenbrunner, and Y. Volkovich. Core decomposition of uncertain graphs. In *Proceedings of the International Conference on Knowledge Discovery and Data Mining (KDD)*, pages 1316–1325, 2014.

[10] C. Bron and J. Kerbosch. Algorithm 457: Finding all cliques of an undirected graph. *Communications of the ACM*, 16(9):575–577, 1973.

[11] T. Calders, N. Dexters, J. J. M. Gillis, and B. Goethals. Mining frequent itemsets in a stream. *Information Systems*, 39:233–255, 2014.

[12] S. Carmi, S. Havlin, S. Kirkpatrick, Y. Shavitt, and E. Shir. A model of internet topology using k-shell decomposition. *Proceedings of the National Academy of Sciences*, 104(27):11150–11154, 2007.

[13] M. Charikar. Greedy approximation algorithms for finding dense components in a graph. *APPROX*, 2000.

[14] W. Dinkelbach. On nonlinear fractional programming. *Management Science*, 13(7):492–498, 1967.

[15] A. V. Goldberg. Finding a maximum density subgraph. *University of California Berkeley Technical report*, 1984.

[16] P. Hagmann, L. Cammoun, X. Gigandet, R. Meuli, C. J. Honey, V. J. Wedeen, and O. Sporns. Mapping the structural core of human cerebral cortex. *PLoS, Biology*, 6(7):888–893, 2008.

[17] J. Håstad. Clique is hard to approximate within $n^{1-\epsilon}$. In *Proceedings of the Annual Symposium on Foundations of Computer Science (FOCS)*, pages 627–636, 1996.

[18] S. Khuller and B. Saha. On finding dense subgraphs. In *Automata, Languages and Programming*, volume 5555, pages 597–608, 2009.

[19] M. Kitsak, L. K. Gallos, S. Havlin, F. Liljeros, L. Muchnik, H. E. Stanley, and H. A. Makse. Identification of influential spreaders in complex networks. *Nature physics*, 6(11):888–893, 2010.

[20] D. Matula and L. Beck. Smallest-last ordering and clustering and graph coloring algorithms. *Journal of the ACM*, 30(3):417–427, 1983.

[21] R. J. Mokken. Cliques, clubs and clans. *Quality and Quantity*, 13(2):161–173, 1979.

[22] J. Orlin. Max flows in $\mathcal{O}(nm)$ time, or better. In *Proceedings of the Annual ACM Symposium on Theory of Computing (STOC)*, pages 765–774, 2013.

[23] S. Seidman. Network structure and minimum degree. *Social Networks*, 5(3):269–287, 1983.

[24] S. B. Seidman and B. L. Foster. A graph-theoretic generalization of the clique concept. *Journal of Mathematical sociology*, 6(1):139–154, 2010.

[25] N. Tatti and A. Gionis. Discovering nested communities. In *Machine Learning and Knowledge Discovery in Databases—European Conference, ECML PKDD 2013*, pages 32–47, 2013.

[26] C. E. Tsourakakis. A novel approach to finding near-cliques: The triangle-densest subgraph problem. *CoRR*, 2014.

[27] C. E. Tsourakakis, F. Bonchi, A. Gionis, F. Gullo, and M. A. Tsiarli. Denser than the densest subgraph: extracting optimal quasi-cliques with quality guarantees. In *The 19th ACM SIGKDD International Conference on Knowledge Discovery and Data Mining, KDD 2013*, pages 104–112, 2013.

[28] J. Ugander, L. Backstrom, C. Marlow, and J. Kleinberg. Structural diversity in social contagion. *Proceedings of the National Academy of Sciences*, 109(16):5962–5966, 2012.

[29] T. Uno. An efficient algorithm for solving pseudo clique enumeration problem. *Algorithmica*, 56(1):3–16, 2010.

Crowd Fraud Detection in Internet Advertising

Tian Tian[†], Jun Zhu[†], Fen Xia[‡], Xin Zhuang[‡], Tong Zhang[‡]
[†]State Key Lab of Intelligent Technology & Systems; Tsinghua National TNLIST Lab
Department of Computer Science & Technology, Tsinghua University, Beijing 100084, China
[‡]Baidu Inc., No.10 Shangdi Street, Haidian, Beijing 100084, China
{tiant13@mails,dcszj@mail}.tsinghua.edu.cn, {xiafen,zhuangxin,tongzhang}@baidu.com

ABSTRACT

The rise of crowdsourcing brings new types of malpractices in Internet advertising. One can easily hire web workers through malicious crowdsourcing platforms to attack other advertisers. Such human generated *crowd frauds* are hard to detect by conventional fraud detection methods. In this paper, we carefully examine the characteristics of the group behaviors of crowd fraud and identify three persistent patterns, which are moderateness, synchronicity and dispersivity. Then we propose an effective crowd fraud detection method for search engine advertising based on these patterns, which consists of a constructing stage, a clustering stage and a filtering stage. At the constructing stage, we remove irrelevant data and reorganize the click logs into a surfer-advertiser inverted list; At the clustering stage, we define the sync-similarity between surfers' click histories and transform the coalition detection to a clustering problem, solved by a nonparametric algorithm; and finally we build a dispersity filter to remove false alarm clusters. The nonparametric nature of our method ensures that we can find an unbounded number of coalitions with nearly no human interaction. We also provide a parallel solution to make the method scalable to Web data and conduct extensive experiments. The empirical results demonstrate that our method is accurate and scalable.

Categories and Subject Descriptors

I.5.3 [**Computing Methodologies**]: Pattern Recognition—*Clustering*; K.4.4 [**Computers and Society**]: Electronic Commerce—*Payment schemes, Security*

Keywords

Fraud detection; Internet advertising; crowdsourcing

1. INTRODUCTION

As a way to use the Internet to deliver promotional marketing message to consumers, Internet advertising differs from broadcast and television advertising by its ability to carry out precision marketing. While at the same time it is exposed to greater risks of being influenced by precisely targeted attacks. For search engine advertising, advertisers can present their message to specific individual surfers selected according to their search queries or browsing histories. These advertisements are usually charged by the volume of clicks. However, this pay-per-click billing mechanism increases the risk of fraud since malicious ones can easily raise traffics on specific targets by technological means.

Conventional advertising frauds, such as malwares, auto clickers, etc, usually show specific characteristics on their individual behavior patterns, such as empty cookies, repetitive clicks or hit bursts. These phenomena can be effectively detected by well-studied anomaly detection methods [4, 16, 17]. Unfortunately, when new detection rules are proposed, fraudulent means evolves. Recently, crowdsourcing platforms that can distribute enormous tasks to a large group of web workers provide a more efficient way to handle various tasks including data collection and analysis [8, 10, 21]. Meanwhile, a new type of fraud clicks in Internet advertising has appeared on malicious crowdsourcing platforms[1], where attackers publish micro-tasks of searching and clicking advertisements on a certain search engine, and then web workers accomplish these tasks and are paid per task through the platform.

According to the statistics, expensive adwords on Google, such as insurance, loans, mortgage, etc, could cost an advertiser more than 50 US Dollars per click [11], while malicious platforms only need to pay about 0.1 US Dollars per click to the web workers. This big price gap has lead to a murky business of Internet advertising that attackers publish crowdsourced attacking tasks against competitors to raise their advertising expenses. We refer to these malicious behaviors as *crowd fraud*.

Since simple fraudulent means is well-studied and can usually be filtered out by search engine's anti-fraud mechanisms, crowd fraud has became one of the main sources of customer complaints to search engines and has caused tremendous damage to the marketing environment. There are many differences between the human-generated crowd fraud and the fraudulent behaviors automatically generated by machines, which pose new challenges to crowd fraud detection. For example, crowd fraud often arises from a vast number of attacking sources, but with low fraudulent traffic from each source. The fraudulent behaviors of web workers

[1]For example: http://www.adclickingjobs.com/; http://www.5iads.cn/ (in Chinese).

WWW 2015, May 18–22, 2015, Florence, Italy.
ACM 978-1-4503-3469-3/15/05.
http://dx.doi.org/10.1145/2736277.2741136.

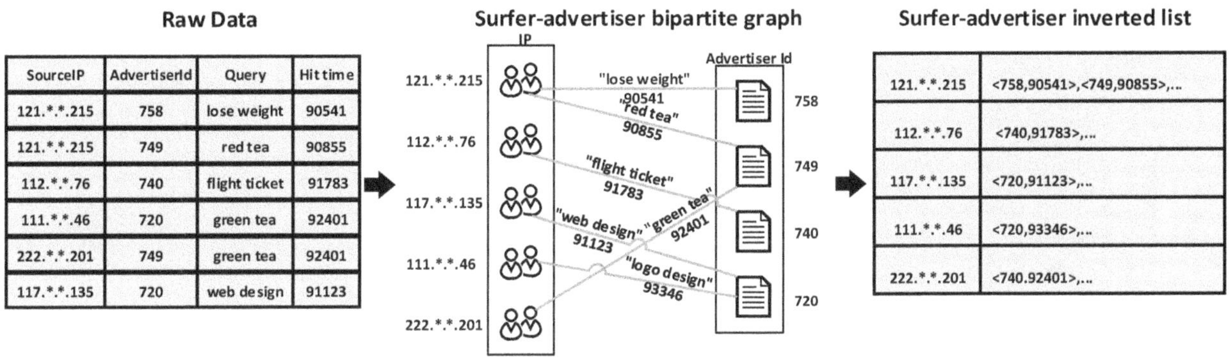

Figure 1: Example of the raw data, the constructed bipartite graph and the surfer-advertiser inverted list.

are noisy and have no distinct regularity, and the fraudulent traffic induced by each worker is often buried in his normal traffic. These differences mean that the short-term or individual behaviors of crowd fraud are almost normal. So conventional anti-fraud systems usually fail to detect crowd fraud. Current commercial crowd fraud detection strategies rely heavily on human interventions, such as the prior knowledge of suspicious queries and complicated artificial filtering rules. Such methods are labor intensive and become invalid rapidly since web workers can easily change their behavior patterns to avoid being detected.

To address the above challenges, we explore the group behaviors of crowd fraud. They are more persistent than the individual behaviors of each worker which may contain substantial randomness. By carefully analyzing the fraudulent behaviors confirmed to be crowd fraud by a commercial detection system, we find some general characteristics about the feature distributions and the network structures of crowd fraud: (1) **Moderateness**: Crowd fraud often aims at advertisers or queries that have moderate hit frequencies; (2) **Synchronicity**: Surfers involving in crowd fraud can usually be grouped into coalitions; in each coalition they usually attack a common set of advertisers; and most of their clicks toward a certain advertiser happen within a common short time period; and (3) **Dispersivity**: Crowd fraud surfers may simultaneously search a series of unrelated queries and click advertisements from different professions.

Based on the above characteristics, we investigate a novel crowd fraud detection method for search engine advertising. From the synchronicity characteristic we can see that crowd fraud has similar properties with coalition attacks. The success of graph based anomaly detection methods on detecting coalitions in many scenarios [13, 15] inspired us to develop our detection method based on the feature-enhanced graph structure of the click-through network. Our method consists of three major stages: (1) **Constructing**: we first remove the logs whose queries have extremely small or large hit frequencies based on the moderateness condition, and then construct a surfer-advertiser bipartite graph as in Fig. 1. Each edge of this graph represents one unique click log, and it contains features such as the hit time and searching query. We also generate the surfer to advertiser inverted list of this bipartite graph for the use of next stage. Each entry of this inverted list represents the click history of one unique surfer. (2) **Clustering**: to find surfer coalitions which exhibit synchronicity, we define a synchronization similarity between click histories and transform the coalition detection problem to a clustering problem. The number of clusters is determined using a nonparametric clustering algorithm, which is inspired by DP-means [12], a small-variance asymptotic version of Dirichlet process (DP) mixtures. (3) **Filtering**: We will find three types of coalitions after clustering, namely, small irrelevant coalitions, fraudulent coalitions, as well as some normal but large coalitions attracted by frequently-presented advertisements. The frequently-presented advertisements in one coalition come from similar business domains such as flight tickets or hospitals. So we examine all large coalitions and remove those with domain centralized advertisers.

Each step of our detection method is scalable with appropriate approximation, and the total number of detected fraudulent clusters is unbounded due to the nonparametric nature of our algorithm. We further implement a parallel version of this method and conduct extensive experiments to show its efficiency and accuracy.

To the best of our knowledge, this paper is the first to formulate the problem of crowd fraud detection in Internet advertising and provides a solution. Our main contributions can be summarized as follows:

1. We formally analyze the crowd fraud problem for Internet advertising, and identify three key characteristics, i.e., moderateness, synchronicity and dispersivity;
2. We present a solution to detect crowd fraud, in which we define a synchronization similarity between click histories and transform the coalition detection problem into a clustering problem, solved by a nonparametric clustering algorithm that automatically decides the number of clusters;
3. We make the method scalable for large-scale search engine advertising by parallelizing the nonparametric clustering algorithm. Extensive experiments are provided to show its effectiveness.

The rest of the paper is organized as: Sec. 2 analyzes the characteristics of crowd fraud; Sec. 3 and Sec. 4 present the detection system for search engine advertising and its parallel implementation; Sec. 5 presents empirical results; Sec. 6 discusses related work; and Sec. 7 provides concluding remarks.

2. CROWD FRAUD CHARACTERISTICS

We define *crowd fraud* as the phenomenon that a group of people driven by economic benefits work together to increase fraudulent traffic on certain targets. Crowd fraud differs from automatically generated fraudulent behaviors in several aspects: (1) The number of web workers involved in an attacking event from crowdsourcing platforms can be very large, while most conventional ways start from much fewer

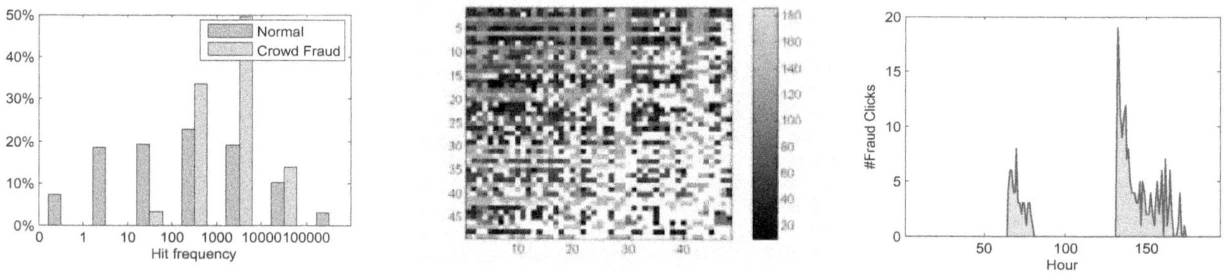

(a) Traffic moderateness (b) Target synchronicity (c) Temporal synchronicity

Figure 2: Characteristics of crowd fraud: (a) The histogram of the hit frequencies of various queries for both normal traffics and crowd fraud traffics; (b) A corner of the surfer-advertiser bipartite graph built from crowd fraud click relations, where different colors show different hit times and the white color means no click occurred; and (c) A snapshot of the fraudulent click number on one advertiser changes through time.

number of sources; (2) The total fraudulent traffic generated by each web worker in crowd fraud is limited, while other malpractices usually induce hit bursts; (3) Since crowd fraud clicks are generated by real humans, their behaviors have no distinct regularity, while the auto generated traffic usually has detectable repeatability; and (4) Besides the fraudulent traffic, each web worker may also have normal click behaviors, which is also different from automatic clicks. All these differences make the set of conventional features used to detect automatic fraudulent behaviors invalid for crowd fraud detection, which calls for a careful investigation to identify more distinctive and stable characteristics.

This paper focuses on the crowd fraud detection problem in search engine advertising. A main purpose of attackers is to raise fraudulent traffic on competitors to increase their promotional expenses. Thus the attacks usually aim at certain advertisers rather than advertisements.

To compare the differences between normal traffic and crowd fraud traffic, we collect a click dataset from a major Chinese search engine company. The raw click logs on the search engine maintain a history of all click actions that happened within a time period. We investigated the following attributes in the click logs. **Log Id:** We use log Id to identify a unique click log. **IP:** though both cookie Id and IP address can identify different surfers, cookie changes more frequently than IP. So we use the latter in our method, despite the network address translation. **Advertiser Id:** since malpractices mostly aim at certain advertisers, we use advertiser Id to identify their targets. **Hit time:** the time when the click happened. **Query:** the phrase that a surfer searched before his or her click action. We studied a subset of the click logs. After carefully examining the datasets we collected, we find similarities among the crowd fraud traffic on the moderateness, synchronicity and dispersivity characteristics, which provide strong hints to detect crowd fraud effectively. Below, we describe these characteristics in detail.

2.1 Moderateness

In a common search engine session, a surfer searches a query and the engine returns the most relevant results as well as advertisements in search engine results pages (SERPs). Then the surfer may click some links or advertisements which satisfy their requirements or preference. Advertisers can buy keywords from the search engine so that the system will display their message once a surfer's search query matches their keywords. As a result, the advertisers' intentions as well as their advertisement contents are expressed by the corresponding searching queries. We separately count the hit frequencies on each unique query appeared in the crowd fraud dataset and the full dataset, then plot the histogram of hit frequencies in Fig. 2(a).

We can see that most crowd fraud queries are clicked from 50 to 20,000 times during one week, while 50% queries of the full dataset lay outside this range. Thus, crowd fraud traffic differs from normal traffic in that the hit frequencies of its target queries will neither be too small nor too large. It is not too small may be because fraud practices always intend to raise click traffic, so they must click advertisements with considerable frequencies. It is not too large may be because normal traffics on frequently hit queries are very large, while crowd fraud traffics are usually relatively less since the human click efficiency is limited. So the effects of fraudulent traffics will be buried under the normal traffics.

2.2 Synchronicity

We characterize two types of crowd fraud's synchronicity. The first is the target synchronicity. Since crowd fraud starts from malicious crowdsourcing platforms, their behaviors can usually be grouped into sets. Workers on the same platform tend to accomplish similar tasks published on that platform, so their target advertisers are also likely to be similar. The click records can be viewed as a bipartite graph, with surfer vertices and advertiser vertices at two sides, as in Fig. 1, where each edge represents one unique click log, and it contains features such as the hit time and searching query. Then from the view of graph structure, although the click relation between surfers and advertisers forms a very sparse bipartite graph, the links between these crowd fraud workers from the same coalitions to the tasks on the same platform will be dense. To show this phenomenon, we select a dense corner of the bipartite graph built from the crowd fraud dataset, and plot the adjacency matrix of this subgraph in Fig. 2(b), where each cell represents one click from the surfer of the column to the advertiser of the row, and different colors represent different hit times. Our experimental results on real data also verify that these dense structures are common among fraudulent traffics.

The second is the temporal synchronicity. The different colors of cells in Fig. 2(b) show different hit times of the corresponding clicks. We can see that cells in the same row usually have similar colors, which means that the hit times of

Table 1: **Example queries, where each row represents the queries from one surfer.**

Queries from normal surfers	# Domains
eye cream, cleansing milk, skin care	1
electronic game, card game, game platform	1
headache, dizzy, light-headed	1
Queries from crowd fraud surfers	**# Domains**
franchised outlet, excavator, royal jelly	3
beach BBQ, hospital, calligraphy training	3
toy bear, stainless steel, gym	3

crowd fraud clicks on a same advertiser usually concentrate on a short period. We show this phenomenon more clearly by snapshotting the hit times of fraudulent clicks on one advertiser in Fig. 2(c). We can see that most clicks occurred within short time periods of several hours. This phenomenon also appears on other advertisers, We think this time period may be related to the task's publishing time on malicious crowdsourcing platforms, while their normal traffics usually show periodicity.

2.3 Dispersivity

As a more in-depth examination, we expand the click logs of some frequently appeared individual surfers of both the crowd fraud dataset and the full dataset. After comparison, we find differences between their target business domains. For normal surfers, their click targets during a short period usually focus on one certain business field or a few highly related fields, such as eye cream, cleansing milk, and skin care. However, crowd fraud surfers may click advertisements from many unrelated domains in a short period, such as franchised outlet, excavator and royal jelly. We think this is because web workers do not have real information demand, so if they do many tasks from different advertisers on crowdsourcing platforms, their searching queries as well as their target business domains show dispersivity. Some example searching queries and the number of domains are shown in Table 1.

In summary, the group behaviors of crowd fraud show strong regularities, including moderateness, synchronicity and dispersivity. These regularities differ crowd fraud traffic from normal traffic. Based on these observations, we develop an effective crowd fraud detection system in next section.

3. CROWD FRAUD DETECTION

Our method consists of three major stages: *constructing*, *clustering* and *filtering*, as outlined in Fig. 3.

3.1 Constructing Stage

This stage removes irrelevant data and reorganizes the logs into a surfer-advertiser inverted list.

We first filter out irrelevant logs based on their queries. According to the moderateness condition, click logs with queries whose hit frequency is extremely small or large are barely crowd fraud. So we choose a lower threshold S_L and an upper threshold S_U, and remove the logs with queries whose hit frequency falling outside the range $[S_L, S_U]$. The appropriate threshold values can be found from statistics of fraudulent traffic. Smaller Interval means less data left. This

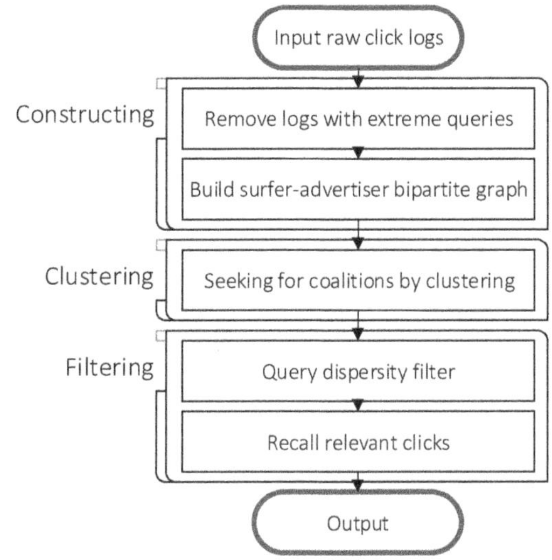

Figure 3: Workflow for crowd fraud detection.

pre-filtering can significantly reduce the data volume. In our experiments, it removes more than 70% click logs.

Then, we reorganize the remaining data as a surfer-advertiser inverted list. As shown in Fig. 1, the click logs represent a surfer-advertiser bipartite graph. The structure of this bipartite graph can be stored as a surfer-advertiser inverted list, which can express the surfers' behaviors more explicitly. In the sequel, we use $\mathcal{G}$ to denote an inverted list; $\boldsymbol{x}_i \in \mathcal{G}$ is the ith entry of $\mathcal{G}$, representing the click history of the ith surfer; each click history $\boldsymbol{x}_i$ consists of an undetermined number of click events; an event $x_{ij} \in \boldsymbol{x}_i$ consists of a target advertiser Id x^I_{ij} and a hit time x^T_{ij}, meaning that surfer i clicked an advertisement at time x^T_{ij}, and this advertisement belongs to an advertiser with Id x^I_{ij} . If surfer clicked advertisements belong to the same advertiser more than one time, we only record one click with the earliest hit time, which is sufficient to represent the intention of all this kind of clicks. A click history is of the form:

$$\{\{Id:74, time:456\}, \{Id:64, time:93\}, ...\}.$$

Suppose we have N unique IPs, M unique advertisers Ids and D click logs after pre-filtering, there will be N lines in $\mathcal{G}$, and each line will contains D/N events on average.

3.2 Clustering Stage

After pre-filtering the logs using the moderateness condition, we proceed to consider the synchronicity condition, which states that surfers involving in crowd fraud usually group into coalitions; in each coalition they usually attack a common set of advertisers; and most of their clicks toward a certain advertiser happen within a common short time period. We formulate the coalition detection as a clustering problem, and solve it by a nonparametric method that can automatically learn the unknown number of coalitions.

3.2.1 Problem Formulation

By the synchronicity property, we need to detect malicious surfer coalitions in which all surfers have similar behavior patterns. We define the *synchronization similarity* (sync-similarity for short) between each pair of click histories and the *coalition center* for every surfers coalition in order to formulize these coalitions.

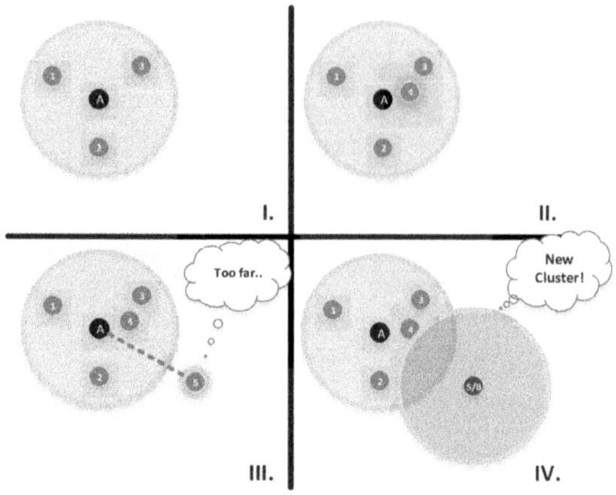

Figure 4: The nonparametric clustering procedure.

Definition 1. **[Sync-Similarity]** Given two click histories $\boldsymbol{x}_i, \boldsymbol{x}_j$ and a time window radius τ, the sync-similarity between them is given by

$$S_\tau(\boldsymbol{x}_i, \boldsymbol{x}_j) = \sum_{\substack{x_{is} \in \boldsymbol{x}_i \\ x_{jt} \in \boldsymbol{x}_j}} \mathbb{1}(x_{is}^I = x_{jt}^I, \ |x_{is}^T - x_{jt}^T| < \tau), \quad (1)$$

where $\mathbb{1}(\cdot)$ is the indicator function.

Numerically, the sync-similarity equals to the number of targets shared by two click histories. Here a common target not only requires a same advertiser Id appearing in both click histories, but also requires the hit times on this advertiser Id in the two click histories fall into a same time period.

Definition 2. **[Coalition Center]** The center $\boldsymbol{\mu_k}$ of coalition k has the same form as the click history. It consists of many click events, and each event μ_{ks} consists of two attributes, i.e., $\mu_{ks} = \{\mu_{ks}^I, \mu_{ks}^T\}$, where the advertiser Id μ_{ks}^I denotes a common attacking target of the coalition and the intrinsic hit time μ_{ks}^T denotes the average hit time of clicks on this advertiser induced by surfers in this coalition.

For all surfers in coalition k, if the sync-similarities between their click histories and the center $\boldsymbol{\mu}_k$ are larger than a similarity threshold T, their behaviors will be regarded as synchronized. Suppose there are K malicious coalitions, z_i denotes the coalition to which the ith surfer belongs, these coalitions should satisfy the following condition:

Condition 1. **[Synchronicity Condition]**

$$S_\tau(\boldsymbol{x}_i, \boldsymbol{\mu}_k) > T, \forall k, \ i, \ s.t. \ z_i = k, \quad (2)$$

where T is a similarity threshold.

Now our problem is to find coalitions that satisfy Eq. (2), as well as to find their centers. If we consider surfers who reside outside all coalitions as coalitions with only one surfer in it, the original detection problem will became a clustering problem. Each point for clustering represents the click history of one surfer; each cluster represents one coalition; and the cluster center represents the coalition center. For convenient calculation, we assume that all coalitions target on exact w advertisers. This assumption may lead to omit some coalitions which target on less than w advertisers, the reduction of flexibility brought by this assumption can be compensated by a propagation step in the final stage.

3.2.2 Clustering Algorithm

There are two main differences between our problem and an ordinary clustering problem. Firstly, the number of clusters is very hard to decide in advance, and it increases about linearly as the number of surfers increases. This is because most surfers behave normally, and then each of them belongs to one new cluster. Secondly, for each surfer in a cluster, the sync-similarity between it and the cluster center should be larger than a radius threshold. So we can not use classic clustering algorithms (e.g., K-means) directly. Inspired by DP-means [9, 12, 23], which is a small variance asymptotics of Dirichlet process mixtures [2], we present a nonparametric method, which solves the following problem:

$$\max_{\mathcal{C}, \{l_c\}_{c=1}^k} \sum_{c=1}^{k} \sum_{i \in l_c} S_\tau(\boldsymbol{x}_i, \boldsymbol{\mu}_c) - \lambda_w k, \quad (3)$$

where $\mathcal{C} = \{\boldsymbol{\mu}_c\}$ denotes all cluster centers, $l_c = \{i | z_i = c\}$ denotes all indexes of the surfers in cluster c, $\lambda_w = (1-\rho)w$ is a similarity threshold, and $\rho \in [0, 1]$ is a relaxing factor.

Problem (3) admits two properties: (1) The final cluster number is potentially unbounded and automatically determined by the data, and (2) The sync-similarity between each point to its most similar cluster center must be larger than ρw. To see the first property, since the cluster number k is also a variable in this objective, we need to learn the cluster number in real time. So the cluster number will increases when data grows, which is potentially unbounded. To see the second property, once the similarity between a point $\boldsymbol{x}_i$ to its most similar center $\boldsymbol{\mu}_c$ is smaller than ρw, we can create a new cluster whose center is composed by w events in $\boldsymbol{x}_i$, then the similarity between $\boldsymbol{x}_i$ and this new cluster center will be w, and the total change on the objective is $w - S_\tau(\boldsymbol{x}_i, \boldsymbol{\mu}_c) - \lambda_w = \rho w - S_\tau(\boldsymbol{x}_i, \boldsymbol{\mu}_c) > 0$.

These two properties provide us an iterative way to find a local optimum of problem (3). The final algorithm is similar as K-means' two-step update. For each iteration, we first assign each point into its nearest cluster, then update the cluster centers based on the assignments. The main difference between our algorithm and K-means is the assignment step. When a new point $\boldsymbol{x}_i$ comes, we find its most similar cluster center. If the similarity between $\boldsymbol{x}_i$ and this center is smaller than ρw, we generate a new cluster whose center is composed by w events in $\boldsymbol{x}_i$. Then we assign $\boldsymbol{x}_i$ to this new cluster. Fig. 4 illustrates this procedure. When converge, we maintain the remaining clusters whose size larger than a threshold n for the use of the next stage.

The algorithm is outlined in Alg. 1, which consists of a *UpdateCenter* subroutine that solves the subproblem

$$\max_{\boldsymbol{\mu}_c} \sum_{i \in l_c} S_\tau(\boldsymbol{x}_i, \boldsymbol{\mu}_c). \quad (4)$$

Though the problem can be solved by enumerating all the possible combinations of w events, the time complexity is $O(m^w)$, where m is the average number of unique events in points of this cluster, which is very large. Here we introduce an greedy algorithm, which is approximate but efficient. We sort all advertisers by their occurrence frequencies in all surfers' click histories in this coalition, then use the top w advertisers as the cluster center. The intrinsic hit times are the averages of click times on these advertisers.

As we shall see in experiments, the algorithm with greedy approximation still converges well and finds good solution-

Algorithm 1: Serial solution for coalition detection

Input: ρ, w, τ
Input: surfer-advertiser inverted list $\mathcal{G}$
$k = 0$, $\mathcal{C} = \varnothing$
while *not converged* **do**
  for $\boldsymbol{x}_i \in \mathcal{G}$ **do**
    $c = \arg\max_{c \in \{1,\cdots,k\}} S_\tau(\boldsymbol{x}_i,\ \boldsymbol{\mu}_c)$
    if $S_\tau(\boldsymbol{x}_i,\ \boldsymbol{\mu}_c) < \rho w$ **then**
      $\boldsymbol{\mu}' = \{$Select w events in $\boldsymbol{x}_i\}$
      $\mathcal{C} = \mathcal{C} \cup \{\boldsymbol{\mu}'\}$, $k = k + 1$
      $z_i = k$
    else $z_i = c$
  for $c \in \{1, \cdots, k\}$ **do** $\mu_c =$UpdateCenter(c)
Output: Accepted cluster centers $\mathcal{C}$

Procedure UpdateCenter(c)

$\boldsymbol{n} = \boldsymbol{t} = \varnothing$
for $\boldsymbol{x}_i \in \mathcal{G}$ *and* $z_i = c$ **do**
  for $j \in \{1, \cdots, |\boldsymbol{x}_i|\}$ **do**
    $r = x_{ij}^I$
    if $n_r \notin \boldsymbol{n}$ **then**
      Update $\boldsymbol{n}$ and $\boldsymbol{r}$
    $n_r = n_r + 1$
    $t_r = t_r + x_{ij}^T$
for $n_r \in \boldsymbol{n}$ **do** $t_r = t_r / n_r$ $\boldsymbol{y} = \{$the indexes of largest w elements in $\boldsymbol{n}\}$
Output: {events formed by $\boldsymbol{y}$ and times in $\boldsymbol{t}$}

s. By this approximation, the time complexity of *UpdateCenter* is reduced to $O(m\log(m))$, and it can be further reduced to $O(m\log(w))$. If $m \approx D/k$, the overall time complexity for one iteration of Alg. 1 is $O((k + \log(w))D)$. As analyzed above, most items belong to a cluster with size 1, so $k \approx N$. This causes the algorithm still very time consuming. We will describe an approximate and parallel algorithm that we use in practice in the next section.

3.3 Filtering Stage

Usually we can find many large coalitions after clustering, which may contain false alarms. For example, for hot businesses such as games or healthcare, normal surfers with similar information demands may also click a lot of common advertisers that provide similar services. Since the number of these kinds of surfers can be large, it is possible to appear groups of normal surfers which exhibit both the target synchronicity and the temporal synchronicity. This will cause false alarm detections. In order to distinguish these false alarms from real fraud coalitions, we build a query dispersity filter for clusters based on the dispersivity condition.

From our observations, although normal coalitions may exhibit synchronicity, their targets usually focus on one business domain or a few highly related domains, which invalid the dispersivity condition. To evaluate how dispersive a cluster is, we define the *domain coherence coefficient (DCC)* of a set of advertisers.

Definition 3. **[Domain Coherence Coefficient]** Given a set of advertisers $\mathcal{A}$. Let $\mathcal{A}'$ be its largest subset in which all advertisers belong to a same business domain. The domain coherence coefficient of this set is

$$R_{dcc}(\mathcal{A}) = \frac{|\mathcal{A}'|}{|\mathcal{A}|}. \tag{5}$$

Algorithm 2: Query dispersity filter

Input: $\mathcal{Q}$, λ, w
Input: candidate cluster centers $\mathcal{C}$
$\mathcal{F} = \varnothing$;
for $\boldsymbol{\mu}_i \in \mathcal{C}$ **do**
  $d_i = \max_{\boldsymbol{q}_j \in \mathcal{Q}} |\boldsymbol{\mu}_i^I \cap \boldsymbol{q}_j|$;
  if $d_i \leq \lambda w$ **then**
    $\mathcal{F} = \mathcal{F} \cup \{\boldsymbol{\mu}_i\}$;
Output: fraudulent cluster centers $\mathcal{F}$

Collecting domain information for all advertisers to calculate each cluster's DCC relies on a lot of external interventions. In our method, we choose a more straightforward way. We first build a query-advertiser inverted list $\mathcal{Q}$ from raw click logs. Each entry $\boldsymbol{q}_i \in \mathcal{Q}$ corresponds to a unique query, and the elements $q_{ij} \in \boldsymbol{q}_i$ represent advertisers that have displayed together with query $\boldsymbol{q}_i$. Since these advertisers are related to a common query, their business domains should be related. For cluster i, we use $\boldsymbol{\mu}_i^I = \{\mu_{is}^I | \mu_{is} \in \boldsymbol{\mu}_i\}$ to represent all advertisers targeted by surfers in this cluster, then if we find an entry $\boldsymbol{q}_j$ that satisfies $|\boldsymbol{\mu}_i^I \cap \boldsymbol{q}_j| = p_{ij}$, we can say at least p_{ij} advertisers in $\boldsymbol{\mu}_i$ are related. So by the definition of DCC, we can find a relation that

$$R_{dcc}(\boldsymbol{\mu}_i^I) \geq \max_{\boldsymbol{q}_j \in \mathcal{Q}} \frac{|\boldsymbol{\mu}_i^I \cap \boldsymbol{q}_j|}{|\boldsymbol{\mu}_i^I|}, \tag{6}$$

where $|\boldsymbol{\mu}_i^I|$ always equal to w in our setting. Since larger R_{dcc} means less dispersity, we can choose a threshold λ for R_{dcc} and remove clusters that invalid the dispersivity condition. Alg. 2 outlines the query dispersity filter.

After filtering, the remaining clusters represent the detected fraudulent coalitions. As a final step, we recall click logs that relate to them. For each coalition, the clicks happened between its surfers and the advertisers within its coalition center are recalled as crowd fraud clicks. Here we can also use our fraudulent centers as seeds of a bipartite graph propagation algorithm [14], then iteratively expand the set of suspicious surfers and the set of suspicious advertisers, as well as their intrinsic hit times. The propagation can compensate the reduction of flexibility brought by the assumption that every coalition center consists of w events, and it helps to increase the recall rate of the method.

4. PARALLELIZATION

The real world click logs can be very large, easily rendering a serial algorithm as above inapplicable. So we develop a parallel implementation to make it practical in real scenarios. The constructing stage and filtering stage are easy to parallelize under a distributed computing framework, such as MapReduce [6]. Our discussion will focus on the difficult nonparametric clustering step. We also provide some implementation details of our system.

4.1 Parallel Nonparametric Clustering

The nonparametric nature of our clustering algorithm causes difficulties in its parallelization. The main difficulty

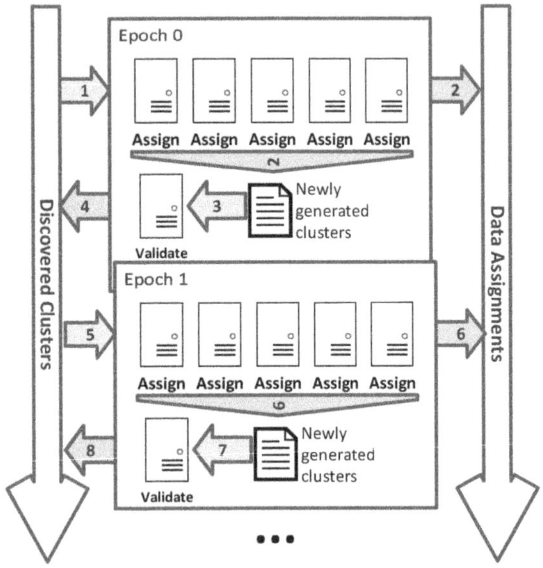

Figure 5: Parallel diagram for the assignment step.

lies in the assignment step, in which newly generated clusters are immediately used by other data points. So we cannot simply divide the assignment tasks to different computing nodes. Here, we use the optimistic concurrency control (OCC) technique [18] to make parallelization possible.

Fig. 4 shows a diagram of parallel assignment step. Using the OOC technique, we divide the assignment step into T epoches and equally partition the whole inverted list $\mathcal{G}$ into T parts denoted by $\mathcal{B}(t), t \in \{1, \cdots, T\}$.

Each epoch only processes one data portion. The newly generated clusters in an epoch are recorded for further use, but not used immediately. That is, each data point processed in this epoch only needs to be compared with clusters generated by the end of the last epoch. Since these clusters' information is known before the start of this epoch, the assignment tasks in one epoch can be distributed without communication. After each epoch, the new clusters generated by different nodes may overlap as they are not compared with each other. So a serial validation step is needed between each two epoches. During validation, running on a master node, every pair of the newly generated clusters are compared; and if their similarity is larger than the similarity threshold, we merge them as well as their associated data points. Pan, et al. [18] has proved this OOC algorithm for DP-means is equivalent to the serial algorithm. Their proof is also suitable for our algorithm.

For our problem, the total number of clusters approximately equals to the number of surfers. So both comparing a point with all cluster centers and delivering cluster center files from slave nodes to master nodes are very expensive. However, since most clusters are induced by normal surfers, they only contain one surfer per cluster and will be removed after clustering. So if the data points are randomly arranged, we can remove smaller clusters and maintain no more than K clusters after each epoch to speed up clustering. This reduction approximation may lead to remove some small fraudulent coalitions, but the algorithm can be speed up significantly. With OCC parallelization and reduction approximation, our final parallel solution for coalition detection is described in Alg. 3.

Algorithm 3: Parallel solution for coalition detection

Input: $T,\ \rho,\ w, K,\ \tau$
Input: $\mathcal{B}(t), t \in \{1 \cdots T\}$
$\mathcal{C} = \varnothing$
while *not converged* **do**
  $k = |\mathcal{C}|, \mathcal{Z} = \varnothing$;
  for *epoch* $t = 1$ *to* T **do**
    $\mathcal{C}' = \varnothing$
    for $\boldsymbol{x}_i \in \mathcal{B}(t)$ **do in parallel**
      $c = \arg\max_{c \in \{1, \cdots, k\}} S_\tau(\boldsymbol{x}_i,\ \boldsymbol{\mu}_c)$
      if $S_\tau(\boldsymbol{x}_i,\ \boldsymbol{\mu}_c) < \rho w$ **then**
        $\boldsymbol{\mu}' = \{$Select w events in $\boldsymbol{x}_i\}$
        $\mathcal{C}' = \mathcal{C}' \cup \{\boldsymbol{\mu}'\}$
        $z_i =$Ref$(\boldsymbol{x}_i)$ //Ref() is the reference function to the coalition center;
      else $z_i = c$
    Validate$(\mathcal{C}', \rho w)$
    $\mathcal{C} =\{K$ largest clusters in $\mathcal{C} \cup \mathcal{C}'\}$
  for $c \in \{1, \cdots, |\mathcal{C}|\}$ **do in parallel**
    $\boldsymbol{\mu}_c =$UpdateCenter(c)
Output: Accepted cluster centers $\mathcal{C}$

Procedure Validate$(\mathcal{C},\ \lambda)$

for $\mu_i \in \mathcal{C}$ **do**
  $c = \arg\max_{c \in \{1, \cdots, |\mathcal{C}| | c \neq i\}} S_\tau(\boldsymbol{\mu}_i, \boldsymbol{\mu}_c)$
  if $S_\tau(\boldsymbol{\mu}_i, \boldsymbol{\mu}_c) > \lambda$ **then**
    Ref$(\boldsymbol{\mu}_i)$=c
    $\boldsymbol{\mu}_i = \varnothing$

Remark 1. Intuitively, the majority of people behave normally, so almost all clusters in our problem are small clusters with only one data point in it, and the mistake induced by the reduction approximation will not be very high. In fact, under a relatively ideal setting that each point comes from an *i.i.d.* distribution, the false negative rate can be estimated as $\frac{n_i}{T}(1 - \frac{TK}{N})(e-1)^{-\frac{n_i}{T}}$, where n_i is the size of a suspicious large cluster i with more than one point in it. We defer the derivation details to Appendix. This result shows that a larger N leads to a larger false negative rate. Since the function xa^{-x} is monotonically decreasing when $x > 0$, a large cluster is less likely to be removed. Moreover, the larger K will lead to a smaller false negative rate, and if $K = N/T$ (i.e., no reduction), the false negative rate is 0.

4.2 Implementation Details

Both the clustering and filtering stages involve a lot of calculations on sync-similarity. To make this computation efficient, we sort every click history when constructing the surfer-advertiser inverted list. The events in a click history are ordered by their target advertiser Ids. When clusters are newly generated or updated, we maintain their orders. So when comparing two click histories, we can array in order all events belonging to them within linear time, and compute their sync-similarity by counting the number of adjacent and similar event pairs. The time complexity for this calculation is $O(d_1 + d_2)$, where d_1 and d_2 are the sizes of two click histories.

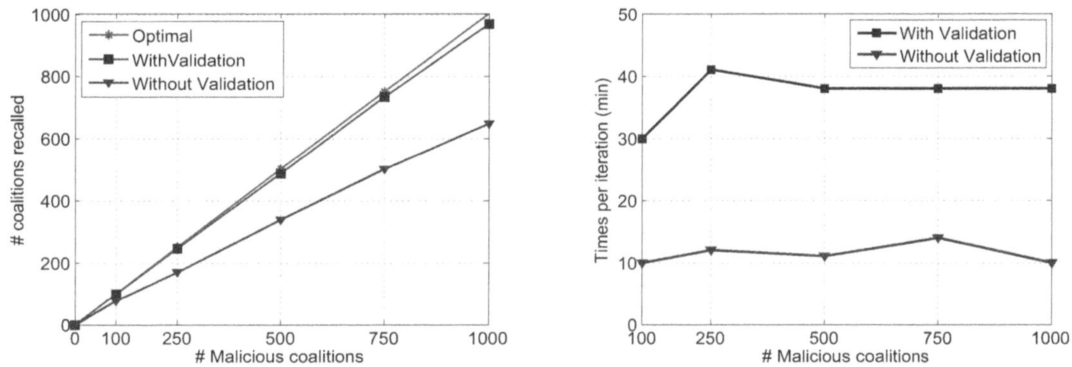

(a) Recall (b) Running speed

Figure 6: Performance on synthetic data: (a) the relation between the number of generated coalitions and the number of discovered coalitions; (b) the per iteration running time for the two clustering settings.

The validation procedure of OCC compares every pair of the newly generated clusters. This is a very time consuming bottleneck of the clustering algorithm. Meanwhile, we empirically found that only very few clusters can be merged during validation. So we can skip the validating procedure to further speed up the algorithm. Through evaluation in the next section, we can see this trick brings significant speed up and still holds an acceptable accuracy.

5. EXPERIMENTS

To verify the effectiveness of our crowd fraud detection system, we conduct a series of experiments on both synthetic and real click data and carefully evaluate its sensitivity, convergence, scalability and accuracy. Most of our algorithms are written in C++ ran under the streaming mode of a modified Hadoop [1] system. All the experiments are conducted on a Hadoop cluster with more than 4,000 nodes, and we use 1,000 mappers and 400 reducers. Raw click logs are stored on the HDFS.

5.1 Synthetic Data

Malpractices for Internet advertising is often hard to distinguish. To judge whether a single click log is malicious or not, an evaluator often needs to expand a lot of logs that correspond to the source IP or target advertiser Id of this log. Even an experienced researcher can only label about 50 logs per hour, so it is too labor intensive to label all the logs in a real large dataset. Thus, it is hard to evaluate the performance of our system, especially its recall rate.

In concern about this issue, we first provide results on synthetic data, where the truth is known, to check the sanity of our algorithms as well as evaluate the recall. Here, we generate several datasets, each of which consists of two parts: normal part and fraudulent part. For the normal part, we simulate 1 million surfers and 100 thousand advertisers. Each normal surfer randomly clicks 10 advertisers, and the hit times for these events are uniformly sampled from $[1, 240]$, which represents a time period of 240 hours. Since advertiser Ids and hit times are randomly sampled, it is unlikely to appear coalitions within this part of click logs. As for the fraudulent part, we generate L coalitions, each of which consists of 200 surfers and 5 advertisers and assigns each advertiser a random intrinsic hit time. Each surfer in a coalition clicks all the advertisers in that coalition, and the clicks target on each advertiser happen within a 6 hours time period centered at the advertiser's intrinsic hit time. In the experiment, we set L at 100, 250, 500, 750 and 1,000, leading to 5 different datasets.

The synthetic experiments only use the clustering stage of the system to evaluate recall rate, and due to the data generating mechanism, the coalition detection precision on this synthetic dataset should be near 100%. So we do not test the result precision on this dataset, and the evaluation on the system's precision is left to the real data experiments. As stated in Sec. 4.2, the validation procedure is the computational bottleneck, and only very few clusters can be merged in this procedure. So we test two types of clustering methods, one with the validation procedure and one without it. The parameters are set as: $T = 4$, $n = 50$, $w = 5$, $\tau = 8$, $K = 10,000$, that is, each iteration is divided into 4 epoch, the minimum number of surfers in one malicious coalition is 50, the minimum number of advertisers is 5, the time window radius is 8 hours, and the upper bound for the number of clusters maintained during learning is 10,000. Other small clusters are discarded on the fly. The discovered cluster numbers and the per-iteration running times for the 5 synthetic datasets with different numbers of fraudulent coalitions are shown in Fig. 6(a) and Fig. 6(b).

Sensitivity Fig. 6(a) shows the relation between the true number of coalitions and the number of coalitions discovered by the algorithm, where the diagonal line shows the optimal performance (i.e., the number of discovered coalitions equals to the true number of coalitions). We can see the number of discovered coalitions for both settings with/without the validation procedure increase about linearly when the number of true coalitions increase. The algorithm with validation achieves a recall rate of nearly 100% on average. This result shows the ability of our algorithm on detecting unknown crowd frauds. The recall rates of the algorithm without validation are relatively lower, e.g., it is about 82% on the dataset with 100 coalitions and 65% on the dataset with 1,000 coalitions. Since the occurrences of coalitions in real click logs are much rarer than the occurrences we defined in the synthetic datasets, the performance of the algorithm without validation is also acceptable.

Efficiency Fig. 6(b) shows the per iteration running time for the two types of clustering algorithms. We can see the

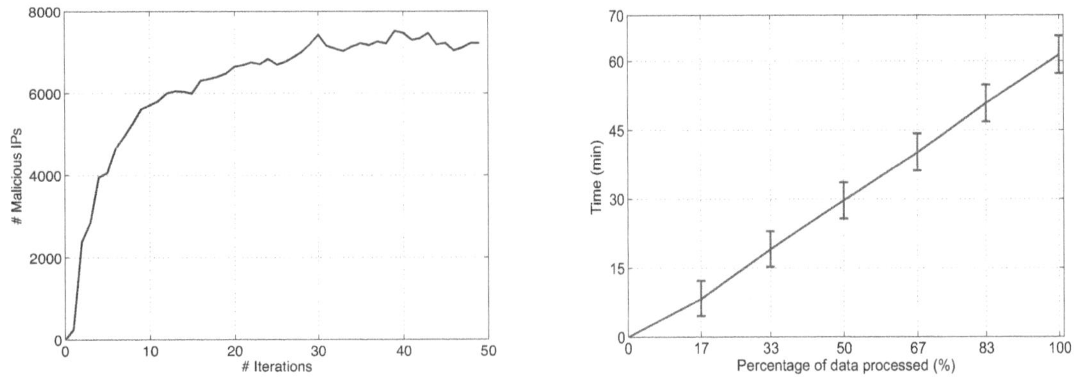

(a) Convergence (b) Scalability

Figure 7: Performance on real click data: (a) shows the number of malicious IPs we found during iterating. (b) shows the the overall running time after each epoch.

average running time for the algorithm with validation is about 3 times larger than that of the algorithm without validation. Considering the overhead time cost induced by the MapReduce implementation, the efficiency gap brought by the different algorithm strategies could be much larger. So when testing on the real click dataset, we use the clustering algorithm without validation for the clustering stage.

5.2 Real World Data

We applied our method to advertisement click logs of a major Chinese commercial search engine. We use the dataset in Sec. 2, which consists of around 400 million logs, and each log is composed by log Id, source IP, target advertiser Id, hit time and searching query.

At the constructing stage, we set $S_L = 50$ and $S_U = 10,000$ to remove queries whose hit frequencies are extremely small or large, these parameters are decided by the statistics of traffic moderateness on the collected crowd fraud dataset, such as in Fig. 2(a). Then we generate a surfer-advertiser inverted list for further use. At the clustering stage, we set parameters as $n = 3$, $w = 8$, $\rho = 0.8$, $\tau = 9$, that is, each malicious coalition needs to contain at least 3 surfers and 8 advertisers, and each surfer needs to click at least 80% of these advertisers during a time period of radius 9 hours. These parameters are selected to maximize the recall rate of coalitions on the given crowd fraud dataset. In the experiment, we run 50 iterations at the clustering stage. Each iteration is divided into 6 epoches and all validation procedures are skipped. As for the reduction approximation, we maintain 10,000 largest clusters at most during clustering, other small clusters are discarded in real time. So $T = 6$, $K = 10,000$. These parameters are decided by our computing resources, which make sure that the program stops running within a reasonable time period. For the filtering stage, we choose domain coherence coefficient threshold $\lambda = \frac{3}{8}$. For the ease of evaluating, the results are not expanded by propagation.

The experimental results are shown as following.

Convergence Fig. 7(a) shows the number of malicious IPs we found after each iteration. Since the numbers of target advertisers in each coalition are the same, this curve actually reflects the objective value of the problem. We can see this curve converges after about 30 iterations, which shows the convergence of our clustering algorithm.

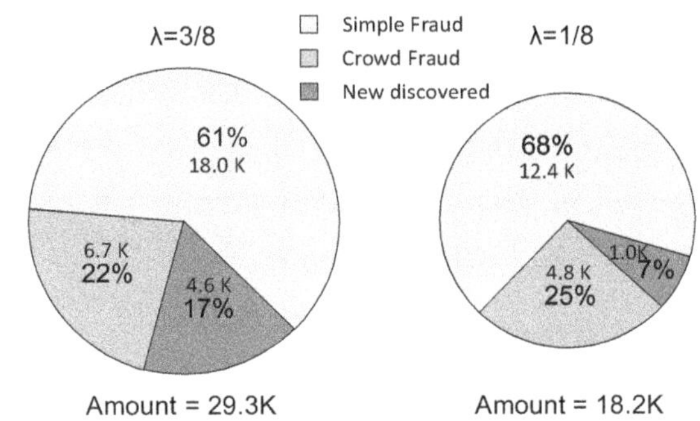

Figure 8: Diagram for the results on real data.

Scalability To show the running time of our system scales up linearly when data size scales up, we record the overall running time after each epoch among 50 iterations. Fig. 7(b) shows the average running times. We can see that the running time increases about linearly when the percentage of processed data increases. This result shows our detection system is scalable when data grows.

Accuracy To evaluate the accuracy of detected frauds, we compare our results with a rule-based system, which can distinguish simple automatically generated fraud and the crowd fraud in the full traffics. After the clustering stage, we found 231 malicious coalitions; after filtering stage, 210 coalitions are removed by query dispersity filter. The remaining 21 coalitions contain 29.3 thousand click logs in total. Through our observation, 20 of them satisfy the dispersivity condition, which correspond to 98.7% of click logs. The test results of these click logs are shown in Fig. 8.

24700 logs meet the results of the baseline system, which account for 83% of our results. 18000 of them are confirmed to be simple fraudulent clicks, they are caused automatically by malwares or spywares; 6700 of them are confirmed to be more hidden fraudulent clicks, they are very likely to be caused by crowd fraud behaviors. The rest 4600 logs are not found by the baseline methods. Since manual evaluating is very expensive, we randomly sampled 200 clicks among them to judge whether they are fraudulent clicks. The final manual evaluating result, provided by several domain experts, confirms that the accuracy on this subset is about 90%.

During manual evaluating, we find that all bad cases of previous trial are induced by one false alarm coalition. So we use a tighter query dispersity filter with $\lambda = \frac{1}{8}$, then all result coalitions satisfy the dispersivity condition. The evaluation of this result is also shown in Fig. 8. It shows that the overall accuracy of this trial is even higher than that of the last one.

6. RELATED WORK

Crowdsourcing is rising field that includes a series of problem solving strategies, business models or activities [7, 8, 20]. Online working platforms, such as Amazon Mechanical Turk (MTurk) [2], provide a new way to distribute enormous tasks to a crowd of workers, and each worker only needs to finish a small part of the entire task, resulting in faster and cheaper solutions. This mode is particularly suitable for large but repetitive tasks like labeling, evaluating, etc. However, the popularisation of crowdsourcing also gives rise to new types of security problems on the web. Crowdturfing [22] is the way to hire web workers through malicious crowdsourcing platforms to initiate fake campaigns. This phenomenon has brought serious problems to social networks and electronic commerce. In this paper, we focus on the fraudulent click problem for Internet advertising which also starts from malicious crowdsourcing platforms.

Anomaly Detection [4] is a well studied topic in various application domains. It aims to find patterns in data which do not conform to the expected behavior. Many methods have been developed for different applications such as fraud detection for credit cards, insurance, health care, intrusion detection for cyber-security, etc. Fraud detection for Internet advertising is an important application of anomaly detection. Rule-based methods such as detecting empty cookie and hit inflations [17] are useful to find simple attacks. Graph-based detection methods are also tried, e.g., people use co-clustering or prorogation methods [13] to find suspicious dense connections between surfers and targets. As for other related areas, CopyCatch [3] is a successful approach which focuses on detecting fake likes on Facebook. They provided a way to find coalitions who demonstrate steplock behavior. In our work, we build a detection system aimed at crowd fraud detection for Internet advertising which is unbounded and scalable.

Clustering is one fundamental problem in data mining. It groups a set of objects so that objects in the same group are more similar to each other than to those in other groups. K-means is one of the most popular clustering methods, but it needs to pre-specify the number of clusters. Many non-parametric methods has been studied to overcome this limitation, such as Dirichlet process mixtures (DPM) [2], which is the nonparametric version of the Gaussian mixture model and can learn the cluster number. Mean-shift clustering is an approach which merges clusters on the fly [5], with wide use in computer vision. DP means [12] is another nonparametric clustering method derived by a small variance asymptotics of DPM. It reserves the nonparametric essence and dramatically increases running speed compared to DPM. Similar small variance techniques have been extended to many other nonparametric Bayesian models [19, 23]. Inspired by DP-means, our work converts crowd fraud detection to clustering by defining the sync-similarity, and proposes a fast and parallel algorithm for real Internet advertising.

[2]http://www.mturk.com/.

7. CONCLUSIONS

We formalize the crowd fraud detection problem in Internet advertising, and carefully analyze the behaviors of crowd fraud to identify three important characteristics, including moderateness, synchronicity and dispersivity. Based on the findings, we further develop an effective detection system, which consists of three major steps, data constructing, clustering and filtering. One key step is convert the original coalition detection problem to a clustering problem. Our nonparametric clustering method ensures to learn the unknown number of coalitions, which is important for real-world applications. Finally, we build a parallel detection system for search engine advertising, and conduct extensive experiments to evaluate its performance on both synthetic and real click data. Results show that our system can find fraudulent clicks with a high accuracy, and it can be scaled up to large datasets.

In the future, we would like to do more analytical work on crowd fraud, and test the performance of our system on datasets of shorter time period. We'd also like to extend current algorithms to other fraud detection problems such as click fraud or social network spams.

Acknowledgments

The work was supported by the National Basic Research Program (973 Program) of China (No. 2013CB329403), National Natural Science Foundation of China (Nos. 61322308, 61332007), and the Tsinghua National Laboratory for Information Science and Technology Big Data Initiative.

APPENDIX

A. FALSE-NEGATIVE RATE ANALYSIS

Let s be the number of large clusters with size larger than 1, d be the number of small clusters with only one point in each cluster, and n_i be the size of the ith cluster. Assume that the N data points are *i.i.d.* sampled from a multinomial distribution with $s+d$ parameters $\epsilon_1, \epsilon_2, \cdots, \epsilon_s, \epsilon_0, \cdots, \epsilon_0$, where $\epsilon_i = \frac{n_i}{N}$ denotes the probability that a point is sampled from cluster i, and $\sum_{i=1}^{s} \epsilon_i + d\epsilon_0 = 1$. Since the number of clusters is large, each ϵ_i is small.

After the tth epoch, we maintain only K largest clusters and remove about $\frac{N}{T} - K$ small clusters, so the probability that a small cluster will be removed is $1 - \frac{TK}{N}$. For the ith cluster, the probability that its current size equals to one is $\frac{N}{T}\epsilon_i(1-\epsilon_i)^{t\frac{N}{T}-1} \approx \frac{N}{T}\epsilon_i \exp(-t\frac{N}{T}\epsilon_i) = \frac{n_i}{T}\exp(-t\frac{n_i}{T})$, where we use the fact that the binomial distribution converges towards the Poisson distribution as the number of trials goes to infinity while the product $N\epsilon_i$ remains fixed. Thus the probability that this cluster will be removed after this epoch is $(1 - \frac{TK}{N})\frac{n_i}{T}\exp(-t\frac{n_i}{T})$. Considering all T epoches, the probability that the ith cluster will be removed is $(1 - \frac{TK}{N})\frac{n_i}{T}\sum_{t=1}^{T}\exp(-t\frac{n_i}{T}) \leq (1 - \frac{TK}{N})\frac{n_i}{T}(e-1)^{(-\frac{n_i}{T})}$. Therefore, the false negative rate is the one as we sated in the Remark 1.

B. REFERENCES

[1] Apache hadoop. http://hadoop.apache.org/.

[2] C. E. Antoniak. Mixtures of Dirichlet processes with applications to Bayesian nonparametric problems. *The Annals of Statistics*, pages 1152–1174, 1974.

[3] A. Beutel, W. Xu, V. Guruswami, C. Palow, and C. Faloutsos. CopyCatch: stopping group attacks by spotting lockstep behavior in social networks. In *WWW*, 2013.

[4] V. Chandola, A. Banerjee, and V. Kumar. Anomaly detection: A survey. *ACM Computing Surveys (CSUR)*, 41(3):15, 2009.

[5] Y. Cheng. Mean shift, mode seeking, and clustering. *IEEE Trans. on PAMI*, 17(8):790–799, 1995.

[6] J. Dean and S. Ghemawat. MapReduce: simplified data processing on large clusters. *Communications of the ACM*, 51(1):107–113, 2008.

[7] A. Doan, R. Ramakrishnan, and A. Y. Halevy. Crowdsourcing systems on the world-wide web. *Communications of the ACM*, 54(4):86–96, 2011.

[8] J. Howe. The rise of crowdsourcing. *Wired magazine*, 14(6):1–4, 2006.

[9] K. Jiang, B. Kulis, and M. I. Jordan. Small-variance asymptotics for exponential family Dirichlet process mixture models. In *NIPS*, 2012.

[10] E. Kamar, S. Hacker, and E. Horvitz. Combining human and machine intelligence in large-scale crowdsourcing. In *AAMAS*, 2012.

[11] L. Kim. The most expensive keywords in Google adwords. http://www.wordstream.com/blog/ws/2011/07/18/most-expensive-google-adwords-keywords, 2011.

[12] B. Kulis and M. I. Jordan. Revisiting k-means: New algorithms via Bayesian nonparametrics. In *ICML*, 2012.

[13] X. Li, Y. Liu, M. Zhang, and S. Ma. Fraudulent support telephone number identification based on co-occurrence information on the web. In *AAAI*, 2014.

[14] X. Li, M. Zhang, Y. Liu, S. Ma, Y. Jin, and L. Ru. Search engine click spam detection based on bipartite graph propagation. In *WSDM*, 2014.

[15] A. Metwally, D. Agrawal, and A. El Abbadi. Detectives: detecting coalition hit inflation attacks in advertising networks streams. In *WWW*, 2007.

[16] A. Metwally, D. A. A. El Abbadi, and Q. Zheng. Hide and seek: Detecting hit inflation fraud in streams of web advertising networks. *Technical Report, University of California at Santa Barbara*, 2006.

[17] R. Oentaryo, E.-P. Lim, M. Finegold, D. Lo, F. Zhu, C. Phua, E.-Y. Cheu, G.-E. Yap, K. Sim, M. N. Nguyen, et al. Detecting click fraud in online advertising: a data mining approach. *JMLR*, 15(1):99–140, 2014.

[18] X. Pan, J. E. Gonzalez, S. Jegelka, T. Broderick, and M. Jordan. Optimistic concurrency control for distributed unsupervised learning. In *NIPS*, 2013.

[19] A. Roychowdhury, K. Jiang, and B. Kulis. Small-variance asymptotics for hidden Markov models. In *NIPS*, 2013.

[20] R. Snow, B. O'Connor, D. Jurafsky, and A. Y. Ng. Cheap and fast—but is it good?: evaluating non-expert annotations for natural language tasks. In *EMNLP*, 2008.

[21] Y. Tian and J. Zhu. Learning from crowds in the presence of schools of thought. In *SIGKDD*, 2012.

[22] G. Wang, C. Wilson, X. Zhao, Y. Zhu, M. Mohanlal, H. Zheng, and B. Y. Zhao. Serf and turf: crowdturfing for fun and profit. In *WWW*, 2012.

[23] Y. Wang and J. Zhu. Small-variance asymptotics for Dirichlet process mixtures of SVMs. In *AAAI*, 2014.

Provably Fast Inference of Latent Features from Networks

with Applications to Learning Social Circles and Multilabel Classification

Charalampos E. Tsourakakis
Harvard School of Engineering and Applied Sciences
babis@seas.harvard.edu

ABSTRACT

A well known phenomenon in social networks is homophily, the tendency of agents to connect with similar agents. A derivative of this phenomenon is the emergence of communities. Another phenomenon observed in numerous networks is the existence of certain agents that belong simultaneously to multiple communities. An understanding of these phenomena constitutes a central research topic of network science.

In this work we focus on a fundamental theoretical question related to the above phenomena with various applications: given an undirected graph G, can we infer efficiently the latent vertex features which explain the observed network structure under the assumption of a generative model that exhibits homophily? We propose a probabilistic generative model with the property that the probability of an edge among two vertices is a non-decreasing function of the common features they possess. This property is true for many real-world networks and surprisingly is ignored by many popular overlapping community detection methods as it was shown recently by the empirical work of Yang and Leskovec [44]. Our main theoretical contribution is the first provably rapidly mixing Markov chain for inferring latent features. On the experimental side, we verify the efficiency of our method in terms of run times, where we observe that it significantly outperforms state-of-the-art methods. Our method is more than 2 400 times faster than a state-of-the-art machine learning method [37] and typically provides non-trivial speedups compared to BigClam [43]. Furthermore, we verify on real-data with ground-truth available that our method learns efficiently high quality labelings. We use our method to learn social circles from Twitter ego-networks and perform multilabel classification.

Categories and Subject Descriptors

G.2.2 [**Graph Theory**]: Graph Algorithms; I.2 [**Artificial Intelligence**]: Learning

General Terms

Theory, Experimentation

Keywords

Machine learning; Markov chains; Graph Algorithms; Overlapping clustering; Social circles

1. INTRODUCTION

The major scientific concept of *pattern recognition* relies on finding the appropriate hidden variables in terms of which the patterns of a dataset are clearly described [34]. In the case of graph datasets, this major problem appears in various guises, e.g., [11, 13, 23, 32, 38] and has been attacked both by the algorithmic graph theory and the machine learning communities -among others- using different machinery. The former has focused on the ubiquitous graph clustering problem whereas the latter on learning latent classes and features. The difference between latent class models and latent feature models is that the former assume that each entity belongs exactly to a single cluster, whereas the latter allow for each entity to participate in multiple clusters. An analogous distinction also exists in the algorithmic graph theory community where the vertex set can be partitioned to either non-overlapping or overlapping sets [24].

Consider Figure 1. Each agent is represented as a vertex $v_i, i = 1, \ldots, 5$ and has three binary features associated with it. Each feature indicates whether the agent is interested in the news categories *business*, *technology* and *entertainment* respectively. The agents decide how to connect based on whether they share common interests. Specifically, Figure 1 shows the graph which emerges when each vertex connects to another vertex if and only if they share at least one common interest, namely a coordinate that is equal to 1 for both vertices. For instance, the single common feature between v_1 and v_2 is the *business* news. We refer to such coordinates as *common features* between the two vertices. It is clear from our toy example that given the vertex labelings and a rule on how vertices decide their connections, finding the resulting graph is easy. An interesting problem is to understand the other direction. Specifically, the question we focus on is the following:

Under the assumption that each agent has k latent binary features, and two agents form a connection with higher probability if they share more features, how can we learn efficiently the latent features?

Additionally to its theoretical importance, answers to this question have numerous applications. Applications of inter-

WWW 2015, May 18–22, 2015, Florence, Italy.
ACM 978-1-4503-3469-3/15/05.
http://dx.doi.org/10.1145/2736277.2741128 .

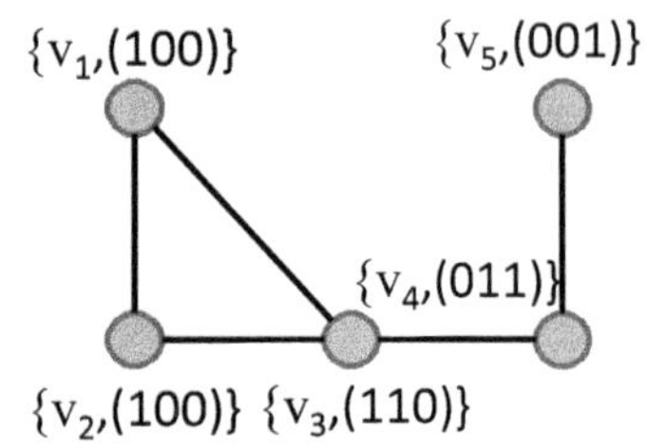

Figure 1: A graph $G(V,E)$ on five vertices. Each vertex v_i is labeled with three binary features and connects with other vertices that possess at least one common feature. For details, see text of Sections 1 and 3.

est include learning social circles [29, 43], distributed computation [7], detecting multifunctional proteins [12], mining collaboration, word-association and protein interaction graphs [36], link prediction [32, 37] and studying cancer [22] among many others.

Our main contributions are summarized as follows.

Modeling. We depart from the deterministic model we described above by introducing a simple probabilistic generative model with the following property: the probability of an edge between two vertices is a non-decreasing function of their common features. This property is motivated by the recent empirical work of Yang and Leskovec [44].

Hardness and Guarantees. We show that maximizing the log-likelihood function is NP-hard by proving that it subsumes as a special instance the overlapping correlation clustering problem [14]. We provide combinatorial insights by connecting the machine learning problem with specific graph sub-structures. Then, we provide a rapidly mixing Markov chain for learning latent features. To the best of our knowledge, this is the first rapidly mixing chain for learning latent features from network data. Furthermore, our method sheds light on the performance of the local heuristic due to Bonchi et al. [14].

Scalability. Our method is more than 2 400 faster than a state-of-the-art machine learning method due to Palla et al. [37] on small sized graphs. In larger graphs the speedup becomes even more pronounced. Also, our method is trivially parallelizable.

Accuracy and robustness to noise. Our method is able to learn high quality latent labelings, typically achieving more than 90% precision and recall. Furthermore, our method is able to recover latent labelings from noisy similarity graphs in contrast to BigClam [43].

Applications. Our proposed method is able to learn social circles from Twitter ego-networks successfully. It performs comparably well or outperforms BigClam [43], the best among various competitors we compared our method against. We also use our method to perform multilabel classification from nearest-neighbor and similarity graphs.

2. THEORETICAL PRELIMINARIES

In this Section we present the necessary theoretical background for our main theoretical result in Section 3. The interested reader may read the book of Levin, Peres and Wilmer [30] for a detailed exposition of the concepts that follow.

	$X_{uv}=0$	$X_{uv}=1$
$A_{uv}=0$	$1-q$	$1-p$
$A_{uv}=1$	q	p

Table 1: Conditional probabilities $\Pr[A_{uv}|X_{uv}]$. Indicator variable X_{uv} takes the value 1 if and only if vertices u,v share at least 1 out of k features, i.e., $\omega^T(u)\omega(v) \geq 1$. For details, see text of Section 3.

DEFINITION 1 (COUPLING). *A coupling of two probability distributions μ,ν is a pair of random variables X,Y defined on a single probability space such that the marginal distribution of X is μ and the marginal distribution of Y is ν.*

The mixing time measures the time required by a Markov chain to approach the stationary distribution. A precise definition follows. We remind the reader that the total variation distance between two probability distributions μ,ν is $|\mu-\nu|_{TV} = \frac{1}{2}\sum_{x\in\Omega}|\mu(x)-\nu(x)|$.

DEFINITION 2 (MIXING TIME). *The mixing time is defined as*

$$t_{mix}(\epsilon) = \min\{t : \max_{x\in\Omega}|P^t(x,\cdot)-\pi|_{TV} \leq \epsilon\}$$

where π is the stationary distribution and $P^t(x,\cdot)$ is the probability distribution of the state of the chain starting at state x after t steps.

We invoke the following result due to Bubley and Dyer in Theorem 2.

THEOREM 1 (PATH COUPLING [15]). *Suppose the state space Ω of a Markov chain is the vertex of a graph with length function l defined on edges. Let ρ be the corresponding path metric, namely*

$$\rho(x,y) = \min\{\textit{length of } P{:}P \textit{ a path from } x \textit{ to } y\}.$$

Suppose that for each edge $\{x,y\}$ there exists a coupling (X_1,Y_1) of the distributions $P(x,\cdot)$ and $P(y,\cdot)$ such that

$$\mathbb{E}[\rho(X_1,Y_1)|X_0=x,Y_0=y] \leq \rho(x,y)e^{-\alpha}.$$

Then, $t_{mix}(\epsilon) \leq \left\lceil \frac{-\log\epsilon+\log\left(diam(\Omega)\right)}{\alpha}\right\rceil$.

3. PROPOSED METHOD

Generative model. Consider again the example in Figure 1 and suppose for instance that the number of latent features is not a priori known. A simple argument shows that the smallest number of latent features k^* that can perfectly explain the observed graph is three. To see why, assume for the sake of contradiction $k^*=2$. Since there are no isolated vertices, there exist three possible labelings $\{(01),(10),(11)\}$. Notice that vertex v_5 cannot be labeled as (11) since it is not connected to every other vertex. Hence, without loss of generality it is labeled (01). Since v_1,v_2,v_3 are not connected with v_5, they have to be labeled by (10). But then since v_1,v_3 have the same label, they should see exactly the same (non)-neighborhood which contradicts the observed graph structure. As it is obvious from Figure 1(a), three labels suffice to explain perfectly the graph structure.

We depart from this deterministic generative model as follows. Let $\omega : V \to \{0,1\}^k$ be the latent vertex labeling. Define for each vertex v the set $\mathcal{C}(v)$ of non-zero coordinates. This set intuitively corresponds to the *interests* of v. Vertex v establishes its connections with other vertices based on the following simple rule: for each vertex u such that $|\mathcal{C}(v) \cap \mathcal{C}(u)| \geq r$ it adds an edge (u,v) with probability p. If $|\mathcal{C}(v) \cap \mathcal{C}(u)| \leq r-1$ it adds an edge (u,v) with probability $q < p$. Notice that under this model, a vertex v with no interests ($\mathcal{C}(v) = \emptyset$), connects to each $u \in V \backslash \{v\}$ independently with probability q. In the rest of the paper, we set $r = 1$, which results already in a simple yet non-trivial probabilistic model. We define for each pair of vertices u, v the indicator variable $X_{uv} = 1(\omega^T(u)\omega(v) \geq 1) = 1 - 1(\omega^T(u)\omega(v) = 0)$. Table 1 shows for any pair of vertices u, v the probability of the edge (u,v) conditioned on the value X_{uv}. Specifically, $\mathbf{Pr}[A_{uv} = 1 | X_{uv} = 1] = p \in (0,1)$ and $\mathbf{Pr}[A_{uv} = 1 | X_{uv} = 0] = q \in (0,1)$.

Maximum likelihood function. The likelihood function of a graph $G(V,E)$ given the latent labeling is

$$\mathbf{Pr}[G|\omega] = \prod_{(u,v)\in E(G)} p^{X_{uv}}(1-p)^{1-X_{uv}} \times \prod_{(u,v)\notin E(G)} q^{X_{uv}}(1-q)^{1-X_{uv}} \Leftrightarrow$$

$$\log_2\big(\mathbf{Pr}[G|\omega]\big) = C(n,m,p,q) + \sum_{(u,v)\in E(G)} X_{uv}\log_2\big(\frac{p}{1-p}\big) + \sum_{(u,v)\notin E(G)} (1-X_{uv})\log_2\big(\frac{1-q}{q}\big)$$

where $C(n,m,p,q) = m\log_2(1-p) + \big(\binom{n}{2} - m\big)\log_2 q$ is a constant that does not depend on the labeling ω. We show that maximizing $\mathbf{Pr}[G|\omega]$ over $\omega \in \Omega = 2^{[nk]}$, the set of all possible binary labelings of n vertices with k binary features, is in general NP-hard.

Objective Let's consider the special case $p = 1 - q = \frac{2}{3}$. Then, maximizing the likelihood function becomes equivalent to

$$\max_{\omega:V\to\{0,1\}^k} \sum_{(u,v)\in E(G)} 1(\omega^T(u)\omega(v) \geq 1) + \sum_{(u,v)\notin E(G)} 1(\omega^T(u)\omega(v) = 0) \qquad (1)$$

We refer to the function we aim to maximize as $h : \Omega \to \mathbb{R}$. This objective was introduced by Bonchi et al. [14] and is known as the overlapping correlation clustering (OCC) problem. Our analysis provides a probabilistic interpretation of OCC [14]. Furthermore, we directly obtain that maximizing the likelihood function for a given graph under our generative model is NP-hard. This is stated as the next lemma.

LEMMA 1 ([14]). *Optimizing 1 in general is NP-hard.*

In the following we study certain basic combinatorial aspects of Objective 1. First, notice that trivially the optimum of Objective 1 is at most $\binom{n}{2}$. We refer to this value as *perfect* score. Our first observation is that when the number of features k is at least the number of edges, we can achieve a perfect score. Specifically when $k \geq m$, for each edge $e = (u,v) \in E$ we create a binary feature f_e. We set the coordinate f_e to 1 only for the endpoints u, v. For the rest of the vertices, f_e is set to 0.

Consider the star graph $K_{1,n-1}$ on n vertices, an instructive special case. How many features are there needed to obtain a perfect score? Clearly, if we use $k = n-1$ features, then there is a labeling achieving perfect score. The center vertex is labeled as $\underbrace{1\ldots1}_{n-1 \text{ ones}}$ and for all $i = 1,\ldots,n-1$ the i-th leaf is labeled as e_i, where e_i is a vector whose coordinates are zero except for the i-th coordinate which is equal to 1. Can we use $k < n-1$ features and still have a perfect score? The answer is negative. To see why, assume that there exists $k < n-1$ such that we can label the vertices with k features and obtain a perfect score. We can assume without any loss of generality (otherwise the score is not perfect) that all the edges of the star tree are satisfied, namely each leaf shares at least one feature with the center vertex. Consider the labels of the $n-1$ leaves and specifically their non-zero coordinates that agree with the center vertex. By the pigeonhole principle, since $k < n-1$ at least one pair of leaves will have to share a common feature. But since these two leaves are not connected by an edge, at least one non-edge is not satisfied and hence the score cannot be perfect.

We wish to outline two facts. We observe that the latent labeling sheds light on the overlapping community structure of the graph. In the case of the star, we have $n-1$ communities overlapping on the center vertex, which is perfectly reflected by the labeling achieving a perfect score. Secondly, the argument above can be generalized to provide a lower bound on the number of features needed to obtain a perfect score. This is stated as the next lemma.

LEMMA 2. *Let $K_{\alpha,\beta}$ be an induced bipartite clique in $G(V,E)$. Then, at least $\alpha\beta$ features are required to achieve a perfect score.*

The proof is omitted as it is similar to the argument for the star graph $K_{1,n-1}$. The above lemma implies that if $K_{\alpha,\beta}$ is an induced bipartite clique that maximizes the product $\alpha\beta$ over all possible induced bipartite cliques, $\alpha\beta$ is a lower bound on the bound of features we need to explain the graph. On the other hand, as we noticed above m is an upper bound. Hence the bounds are tight, as we can see from the star graph $K_{1,n-1}$. Additionally, a simple corollary of Lemma 2 is that the number of features needed is at least the diameter of the graph, a computationally tractable graph parameter.

COROLLARY 1. *At least D features are required to achieve a perfect score, where D is the diameter of the graph.*

Finally, we observe that there exists a trivial constant factor approximation algorithm.

LEMMA 3. *For any $k \geq 1$ there exists a trivial constant approximation factor.*

PROOF. If $m = \Theta(n^2)$, then let $f(v) = \underbrace{1\ldots1}_{k \text{ ones}}$ for all $v \in V(G)$, otherwise let $f(v) = \underbrace{0\ldots0}_{k \text{ zeros}}$. □

Obtaining a polynomial time approximation scheme (PTAS) is an interesting direction. Here we design a rapidly mixing chain.

Algorithm 1 Metropolis Chain

Input: Graph G, mixing parameter c, number of steps T
1: Let $\omega_0 : V \to \{0,1\}^k$ be an arbitrary initial labeling.
2: **for** $t \leftarrow 1$ to T **do**
3: Choose a vertex u uniformly at random from $V(G)$ and a k-labeling x uniformly at random from $2^{[k]}$
4: Perform the transition from ω_{t-1} to ω_t such that $\omega_t(u) = x$ and $\omega_t(v) = \omega_{t-1}(v)\ \forall v \neq u$ with probability $\min\left(1, e^{c\left(h(\omega_t)-h(\omega_{t-1})\right)}\right)$.
5: **end for**
6: Output the best seen state.

Proposed method. Our proposed algorithm is shown in Algorithm 1. Our algorithm maximizes the function $h : \Omega \to \mathbb{R}$, see Equation (1), using a Metropolis chain, which takes as input the graph G, the number of steps T, and a parameter $c \geq 0$ which controls the trade-off between the search space efficiency and the quality of the optimization. In the following we interchangeably refer to a binary labeling as a state. For a state ω we denote with $\omega(v)$ the labeling of vertex v. The metric we choose is the Hamming metric. Specifically, the distance between two states $\omega_1 \neq \omega_2$ is the number of vertices in which the two states differ, i.e., $dist(\omega_1, \omega_2) = |\{u \in V : \omega_1(u) \neq \omega_2(u)\}|$. Notice that the diameter of the state space is exactly n, i.e., $diam(\Omega) = n$.

Even if Metropolis chains are treated in standard textbooks [30], it is worth explaining parameter c in further detail as it highlights the significance of our theoretical result. In the limit $c \to +\infty$ the chain resembles a deterministic hill climb algorithm and hence is limited by local optima which can result in a poor latent labeling. This is essentially the method of Bonchi et al. [14], even if it is not explicitly stated in their paper. This also explains the main drawback of their method, namely being prone to local optima. At the other extreme, as $c \to 0$ the search over the state space becomes efficient but in vain: the latent labelings we aim to find are not favored by the stationary distribution since the latter becomes uniform. Our main theoretical result is that there exists a non-trivial choice of c for which the Metropolis chain both *mixes rapidly* even if the state space is exponentially large and *favors the states that optimize our objective*. This is stated as Theorem 2. In the following, we assume that $k = \Theta(1)$ which results in a practical $\tilde{O}(n)$ algorithm.

THEOREM 2. *There exists a non-trivial range for the parameter $c = c(n)$ for which the Metropolis chain mixes rapidly, i.e., $t_{mix}(\epsilon) = O\left(n \log_2\left(\frac{n}{\epsilon}\right)\right)$ for any $\epsilon > 0$.*

PROOF. Let X_t, X'_t be two copies of the chain starting from states $\omega_1, \omega_2 \in \Omega$, such that $dist(\omega_1, \omega_2) = 1$. Let $u \in V$ be the single vertex for which $\omega_1(u) \neq \omega_2(u)$. We consider the following coupling:

- Chain X_t chooses a vertex v and a string $x \in \{0,1\}^k$, both uniformly at random.
- Chain X'_t chooses exactly the same vertex-string pair (v, x).

Let ω, ω' be the two new candidate states for the first (X_t) and the second chain (X'_t) respectively. Now we set the joint transition probability distribution in such a way that X_t, X'_t stay as close as possible while respecting the marginals.

Case I: $\mathbf{Pr}[\omega_1, \omega] \geq \mathbf{Pr}[\omega_2, \omega']$: If the first chain (X_t) performs the switch, then the second chain (X'_t) performs also a switch with probability $\frac{\mathbf{Pr}[\omega_2,\omega']}{\mathbf{Pr}[\omega_1,\omega]}$. If the first chain does not perform a switch, so does not the second chain too. Notice that the marginal for the second chain is correct. To see why, the probability that the second chain X'_t performs a switch is

$$\mathbf{Pr}[\omega_1, \omega]\frac{\mathbf{Pr}[\omega_2, \omega']}{\mathbf{Pr}[\omega_1, \omega]} + (1 - \mathbf{Pr}[\omega_1, \omega])0 = \mathbf{Pr}[\omega_2, \omega'] .$$

Case II: $\mathbf{Pr}[\omega_1, \omega] < \mathbf{Pr}[\omega_2, \omega']$: If the first chain (X_t) performs the switch, so does the second chain (X'_t). If the first chain does not perform a switch, the second chain performs a switch with probability $\frac{\mathbf{Pr}[\omega_2,\omega']-\mathbf{Pr}[\omega_1,\omega]}{1-\mathbf{Pr}[\omega_1,\omega]}$. Again, notice that the marginal for the second chain is correct. The probability that the second chain X'_t performs a switch is indeed what it should be:

$$\mathbf{Pr}[\omega_1, \omega] \times 1 + (1 - \mathbf{Pr}[\omega_1, \omega])\frac{\mathbf{Pr}[\omega_2, \omega'] - \mathbf{Pr}[\omega_1, \omega]}{1 - \mathbf{Pr}[\omega_1, \omega]} = \mathbf{Pr}[\omega_2, \omega'] .$$

Now we study the expected distance between the two chains after one step. Notice that the distance may remain the same, but it also may increase by 1, or decrease by 1. Let $\mathcal{I}, \mathcal{D}$ be the events for the two latter cases. Then, the expected distance after a single step of the chain is

$$\mathbb{E}[d_{t+1}|d_t = 1] = 1 + 2\mathbf{Pr}[\mathcal{I}] - \mathbf{Pr}[\mathcal{D}] .$$

Since we wish to upper bound $\mathbb{E}[d_{t+1}|d_t = 1]$, we appropriately bound $\mathbf{Pr}[\mathcal{D}]$ and $\mathbf{Pr}[\mathcal{I}]$. Before that, we make a simple observation that we use for both bounds. Consider any labeling $\omega : V \to \{0,1\}^k$ and suppose we change the labeling of a single vertex u, resulting in the new labeling ω'. Then, clearly $|h(\omega) - h(\omega')| \leq n - 1$ and the upper bound is tight.

Lower-bound $\mathbf{Pr}[\mathcal{D}]$: If the chosen vertex v is vertex u, then the distance cannot increase since $\omega = \omega'$. Specifically, the distance either remains 1 or decreases to 0. The latter happens when both chains perform the switch. Let this event be $\mathcal{S}$ Given our coupling the probability that both perform the switch is $\mathbf{Pr}[\mathcal{D}] = \min\left(\mathbf{Pr}[\omega_1, \omega], \mathbf{Pr}[\omega_2, \omega]\right)$. To see why, notice that if $\mathbf{Pr}[\omega_1, \omega] \geq \mathbf{Pr}[\omega_2, \omega]$ then the probability that both chains switch is due to our coupling $\mathbf{Pr}[\omega_1, \omega]\frac{\mathbf{Pr}[\omega_2,\omega]}{\mathbf{Pr}[\omega_1,\omega]} = \mathbf{Pr}[\omega_2, \omega]$. Similarly, if $\mathbf{Pr}[\omega_1, \omega] < \mathbf{Pr}[\omega_2, \omega]$ then the probability is $\mathbf{Pr}[\omega_1, \omega] \times 1$. To lower bound $\mathbf{Pr}[\mathcal{D}]$ we use the inequality $e^{-x} \geq 1 - x$ which is true for $x \geq 0$. Since the probability of choosing the vertex u on which the two states ω_1, ω_2 disagree is $\frac{1}{n}$, we obtain that $\mathbf{Pr}[\mathcal{S}] \geq \frac{1}{n}e^{-cn} \geq \frac{1}{n} - c$.

Upper bound $\mathbf{Pr}[\mathcal{I}]$: Suppose that the chosen vertex v is not u, i.e., i.e., the two chains agree on the labeling of v, $\omega_1(v) = \omega_2(v)$. Then, if both chains perform the switch the distance remains 1, otherwise if exactly only one of the two chains performs the switch the distance increases to 2. First we notice that if $\mathbf{Pr}[\omega_1, \omega] \geq \mathbf{Pr}[\omega_2, \omega']$ the probability that only the first chain performs the switch is $\mathbf{Pr}[\omega_1, \omega]\left(1 - \frac{\mathbf{Pr}[\omega_2, \omega']}{\mathbf{Pr}[\omega_1, \omega]}\right) = \mathbf{Pr}[\omega_1, \omega] - \mathbf{Pr}[\omega_2, \omega']$. If $\mathbf{Pr}[\omega_1, \omega] < \mathbf{Pr}[\omega_2, \omega']$ then the probability that only the second chain performs the switch is $\frac{\mathbf{Pr}[\omega_2, \omega'] - \mathbf{Pr}[\omega_1, \omega]}{1 - \mathbf{Pr}[\omega_1, \omega]}\Big(1 - \mathbf{Pr}[\omega_1, \omega]\Big) = \mathbf{Pr}[\omega_2, \omega'] - \mathbf{Pr}[\omega_1, \omega]$. We can write this in a compact way by saying that the probability that exactly one of the two chains performs the switch is

$$F = |\mathbf{Pr}[\omega_1, \omega] - \mathbf{Pr}[\omega_2, \omega']|.$$

We upper-bound F by considering one of the two probabilities as large as possible, namely 1, and the second as small as possible, namely e^{-cn}. Therefore,

$$F \leq 1 - e^{-cn} \leq cn.$$

Notice that the probability that we choose $v \neq u$ is $\frac{n-1}{n}$ and the probability we choose a labeling $x \in \{0,1\}^k$ such that $x \neq \omega_1(v) = \omega_2(v)$ is $\frac{2^k-1}{2^k}$. Therefore, we obtain

$$\mathbf{Pr}[\mathcal{I}] = \frac{n-1}{n}\frac{2^k-1}{2^k}F < F \leq cn.$$

Therefore, by choosing $c = \frac{1}{3n^2}$, for any $n \geq 4$ we obtain the following valid inequality

$$\begin{aligned}\mathbb{E}[d_{t+1}|d_t = 1] &= 1 + 2\mathbf{Pr}[\mathcal{I}] - \mathbf{Pr}[\mathcal{D}] \\ &\leq 1 + 2cn - \left(\frac{1}{n} - c\right) \leq 1 - \frac{1}{4n} = \beta.\end{aligned}$$

Therefore, by Theorem 1 we obtain that the mixing time

$$t_{\text{mix}}(\epsilon) \leq \frac{\log_2\left(\frac{n}{\epsilon}\right)}{1-\beta} = O\Big(n\log_2\left(\frac{n}{\epsilon}\right)\Big).$$

Finally, the states that maximize Objective 1 are favored by this choice of c. By Lemma 3, the optimal states achieve an objective of Dn^2 for some constant D. Hence, the Metropolis chain for $c = \frac{1}{3n^2}$ assigns to them value $e^{D/3}$. □

We remark that our method runs in polynomial time for $k \leq b\log_2 n$ where $b > 0$ is any constant. Specifically, for $k = b\log_2 n$ we obtain a $\tilde{O}(n^{b+1})$ algorithm due to the implicit $O(2^k)$ term in the search of labelings for any vertex.

4. EXPERIMENTAL RESULTS

4.1 Experimental Setup

Implementation and competitors. Our algorithm is implemented in MATLAB. We remove the random bits needed to select a vertex in each round uniformly at random by selecting an arbitrary ordering of vertices and considering changes in their labelings according to that order. Empirically this appears to have little effect -if any- on the results. Furthermore it avoids the coupon collector problem according to which $O(n\log n)$ draws of vertices are needed to consider all vertices at least once with high probability. A detailed understanding of this systematic scan is left as an interesting problem [33]. Finally, we set the maximum number of steps equal to $\lceil n\log n\rceil$. We terminate the chain either if it reaches the maximum number of steps or if for n steps it stays on the same state. We refer to our method as *FINLAnd* (Fast INference of LAtent features). We compare our method against methods that are publicly available: ILA [37] (MATLAB), BigClam [43] (C++) and CFinder [3] which is provided as a (.EXE) file. We received an improved MATLAB implementation of ILA than the one that is on the Web (as of 08/2014) upon contacting the authors of [37]. All methods were executed on a single machine with Intel Xeon CPU at 2.83GHz and 50GB RAM. As we describe below we used datasets with available ground-truth. In all executions the true number of latent features was passed as an argument to all methods. While there exist several heuristics to approximate the number of features k, we consider this problem worth a separate project.

Datasets. We used publicly available datasets in our experiments. Specifically, we use ego-networks from Twitter[1] [29], EMOTIONS and FLAGS, two Mulan[2] Multi-Label Learning datasets, and the MNIST digit database [1]. Specifically, EMOTIONS and FLAGS have (593, 6) and (194, 7) (points, features) respectively. We create a similarity graph out of each dataset by adding an edge between two points that share at least one common feature. From MNIST we extract a perfectly balanced dataset of 10 000 digits (1 000 digits for each digit 0,1,...,9). Each digit is a 28×28 matrix which is converted in a 1-dimensional vector with 784 coordinates. We create k'-nearest-neighbor graphs from this cloud of points for radically different k' values which result in graphs with $O(n^2)$ and $O(n)$ edges. Finally, all graphs were made *undirected* by replacing each directed edge within an undirected one and *simple* by removing multiple edges.

Evaluation. We use the well-known measures of precision (P) and recall (R) to evaluate the performance of the algorithms. Specifically, for any labeling $\omega : V \to \{0,1\}^k$ we define the set $\mathcal{F}(\omega) = \{(u,v) : \omega^T(u)\omega(v) \geq 1\}$. Also, let g be the ground-truth labeling. Then,

$$\mathrm{P}_\omega = \frac{|\mathcal{F}(\omega) \cap \mathcal{F}(g)|}{|\mathcal{F}(\omega)|} \quad \text{and} \quad \mathrm{R}_\omega = \frac{|\mathcal{F}(\omega) \cap \mathcal{F}(g)|}{|\mathcal{F}(g)|}.$$

We omit the indices when it is clear to which labeling ω we refer to.

4.2 Experimental findings

Before we present our findings in detail, we summarize them.

Mixing parameter c. By experimentation, we found that for the given number of steps that we run the chain, constant values of c, e.g., $c = 1/2$, achieve better performance than the value predicted by Theorem 2. This suggests that injecting a small amount of randomness in the deterministic hill climbing algorithm works well. This discrepancy between theory and practice indicates that either one has to increase the number of steps for which the chain runs or adopt a simulated annealing approach [25]. We experimented with the former approach and indeed we found that the output quality increases when $c = \frac{1}{3n^2}$ as we let the chain run for $b\lceil n\log n\rceil$ steps where $b > 0$ is a constant.

[1] http://snap.stanford.edu/data/egonets-Twitter.html
[2] mulan.sourceforge.net/datasets.html

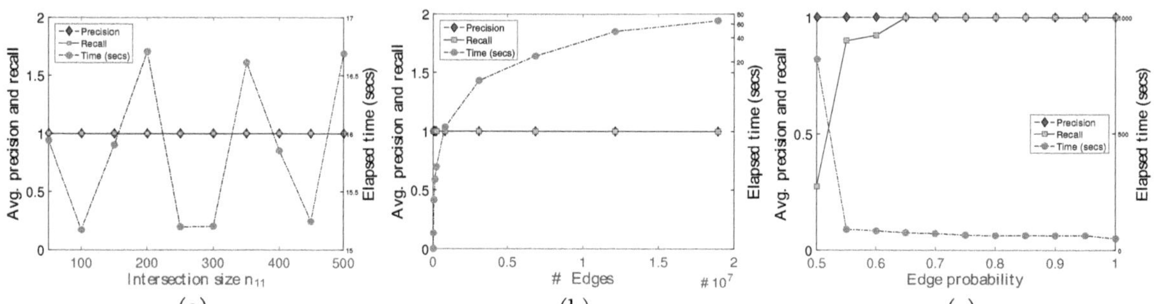

Figure 2: Average precision and recall (left y-axis) and average running time (right y-axis) versus (a) the intersection size n_{11}, (b) the number of edges and (c) the edge probability. Each point in the plots is the average over 25 experiments (5 randomly generated graphs $\times$ 5 random initial labelings). For details on each experiment, see text of Section 4.3

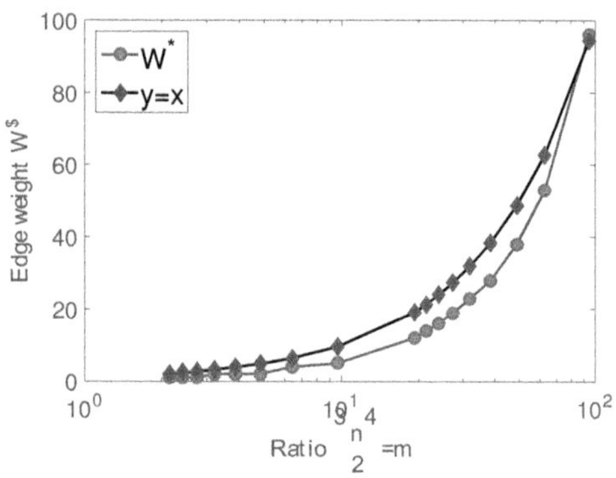

Figure 3: Figure plots in semilog the weight W^* for which we obtain at least 90% precision and recall at the same time versus the ratio $\binom{n}{2}/m$. Included is the plot of the identity function $W = \binom{n}{2}/m$ annotated properly in the legend. For details, see text of Section 4.3.

Efficiency. Our proposed method is able to learn latent features efficiently. For graphs with few hundreds of edges, our method is more than 2 400 times faster than the state-of-the-art ILA method [37]. The speedup becomes even more pronounced in large networks since ILA does not scale at all.

Robustness. Our proposed method is both robust to the initial labeling and to noise. Specifically, it is able to optimize the objective independently on how the vertices are initially labeled and furthermore even when a constant fraction of the edge set changes ($\sim 15\%$) our algorithm is able to recover the latent features with high accuracy. This is not always true for other competitors.

Best competitor. Our algorithm either outperforms or performs comparably well with BigClam [43], the best among the various methods we tried for the task of overlapping community detection. Surprisingly, even if our method is coded in MATLAB and BigClam in C++, it runs typically faster than BigClam.

Sparse graphs and a rule-of-thumb. Optimizing Objective 1 works well for dense graphs. To see why, consider the case of sparse graphs, namely $m = \tilde{O}(n)$. This is the typical case for most real-world networks. Since $m = o(n^2)$, the first term of Objective 1 is asymptotically vanishing, essentially contributing nothing to the optimal value. This means that even if we could optimize Objective 1 exactly, the optimal solution would not provide any insights. For this purpose, we propose for the case of sparse graphs a variation of Objective 1. Specifically, we introduce a positive real parameter W.

$$\max_{\omega: V \to \{0,1\}^k} \sum_{(u,v) \in E(G)} W 1(\omega^T(u)\omega(v) \geq 1) + \sum_{(u,v) \notin E(G)} 1(\omega^T(u)\omega(v) = 0) \quad (2)$$

We provide a surprisingly good rule-of-thumb on how to choose W. This value is equal to $\binom{n}{2}/m$. This value for W results in a normalized version of Objective 1.

Social circles. Using our rule-of-thumb we apply our Metropolis chain adapted for Objective 2 on the problem of clustering ego-networks. Notice that the only thing that changes in the pseudocode is function $h()$, which now becomes the function in Objective 2. We obtain *high* quality results for this graph mining problem, typically outperforming BigClam [43].

Detailed remarks about competitors. Among the numerous works for learning latent features that appear within the machine learning community, e.g., [16, 17, 20, 37], we choose the ILA method [37] as our competitor, since it was published fairly recently. We were able to run ILA only on graphs with few hundreds of edges. To be precise, the largest graph on which ILA produced results within a reasonable amount of time was a graph with 40 vertices and few hundreds of edges. Our algorithm required 0.02 seconds whereas ILA 49.1 seconds. It is worth outlining that not only our method is 2 455 times faster than ILA but also the output quality of our algorithm is better. For the record, ILA produced a good labeling achieving precision and recall equal to 0.99 and 0.93 respectively. For larger graphs, ILA fails completely to produce a labeling within a reasonable amount of time. For instance, ILA has not completed its execution on the EMOTION graph which has ~ 600 nodes after several days. The intermediate results are of poor quality, achieving less than 60% precision and recall.

For the task of finding overlapping communities, we experimented with CFinder [3], BigClam [43], a method based on nonnegative matrix factorization. The BigClam method is the best performing method. CFinder is unable to de-

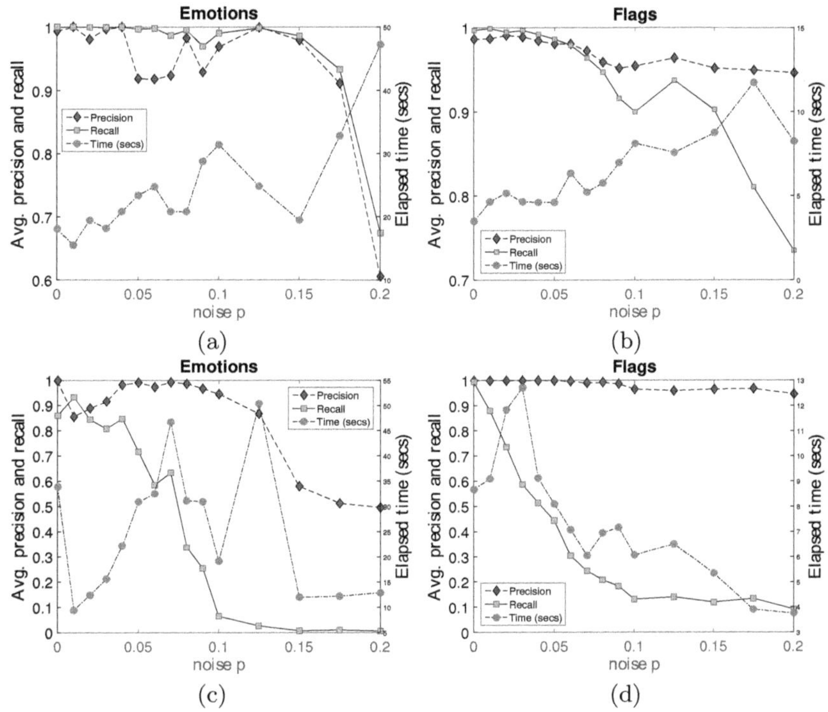

Figure 4: Average precision and recall (left y-axis) and average running time (right y-axis) versus sparsification parameter p on the Flags and Emotions similarity graphs. (a)(b) FINLAnd, (c)(d) BigClam. For details, see text of Section 4.4.

tect overlapping communities when the overlaps are dense, verifying the claim of Yang and Leskovec [44]. More importantly, CFinder does not scale to large graphs. Specifically, CFinder runs for hours on graphs with several thousands of edges, when other competitors are able to output within seconds. This is expected to happen when there exist strongly overlapping dense subgraphs, which as Yang and Leskovec point out is the typical case [44].

In the following sections which contain the results on real-world data, we include full results for [43], as it was the only competitor that could successfully complete for all experiments within a reasonable amount of time.

4.3 Tiles

Yang and Leskovec liken tiles and communities: characterizing precisely for each vertex to which communities it belongs to resembles the setting where some number of tiles are placed on the top of each other in an overlapping manner and the goal is to move them without breaking any of them [44].

Setting. We use two overlapping tiles or equivalently the 2-dimensional hypercube as our latent space. Specifically, we assume there exist two sets of vertices S_1, S_2 such that $|S_1| = n_{01}+n_{11}, |S_1| = n_{10}+n_{11}$ and $|S_\cap| = |S_1 \cap S_2| = n_{11}$. For each pair of distinct vertices u, v such that $u, v \in S_\cap$ we add an edge with probability p_{11}. For every other pair of vertices in S_1 (S_2) we add an edge with probability p_{01} (p_{10}). The latent labeling for vertices in $R_1 = S_1 \backslash S_\cap$, $S_\cap$, $R_2 = S_2 \backslash S_\cap$ is $(01), (11), (10)$ respectively. Notice that this labeling is not unique, the labels of R_1, R_2 can be exchanged. We explore various aspects of this setting.

Parameter n_{11} and scalability. We generate dense graphs with $O(n^2)$ edges by fixing $p_{01} = p_{10} = 0.75 < p_{11} = 0.95$ in order to simulate the "denser-overlaps" phenomenon [44]. The results are shown in Figures 2 (a),(b). Later, we show how to deal with sparse graphs successfully.

Specifically, Figure 2(a) ranges the intersection size $n_{11} \in \{1, 100 : 50 : 500\}$ where $a : b : c$ is the standard MATLAB notation for indicating the starting value a, the step b and the final value c. The total number of vertices is fixed to 5 000. For each value n_{11} we run our method *five* times on *five* randomly generated graphs. We compute for each of the 25 experiments the precision and recall and we plot the average precision and recall (left y-axis) versus n_{11}. Results are perfectly concentrated: average precision and recall (left y-axis) are always 1 for all n_{11} values. Furthermore, there does not appear to be any correlation between n_{11} and the average running time (right y-axis): running time fluctuations at the order of one second are most likely due to randomness.

Figure 2(b) shows the results we obtain as we increase the number of vertices in the graph, for a fixed intersection size $n_{11} = 50$. We range $n \in \{100, 250 : 250 : 1000, 2000 : 2000 : 10000\}$. On the left y-axis we plot again the average precision and recall versus the averaged number of edges over the five random graphs we generate for each value n. On the right y-axis the average running time. To emphasize the scalability we plot versus the number of edges (x-axis). Our method is able to recover the groundtruth labeling in all 25 experiments for all n values. Furthermore we observe that it scales well as the size of the graph grows.

Running time depends not only on size but structure as well. The following experiment outlines an interesting aspect of our method: its running time depends not only on the graph size but also on the graph structure. Equivalently, it is strongly indicated by our experimental results that if the graph cut structure exhibits good clustering properties, then our chain can find it easily and decide to stop within a linear number of steps. We use again the setting of two tiles. We set $p_{01} = p_{10} = p_{11} = p$ and the total number of vertices to $n = 10\,000$. We observe an interesting transition at $p = 1/2$.

Figure 2(c) plots the average precision and recall (left y-axis) and the average running time (right y axis) versus the edge probability p. We range p in the set $\{0.5 : 0.05 : 1\}$. The intersection size is fixed for all values of p to $n_{11} = 100$. Again, we perform for each value p, twenty-five experiments in total. When $p = 1/2$ the average running time is 820 seconds. Additionally to the slow performance for $p = 1/2$, the running time exhibits significant variance. Specifically, the standard deviation is 112 seconds. It is worth emphasizing that the datapoint corresponding to the average running time for $p = 1/2$ in Figure 2(c) is one of the two datapoints in all plots that does not exhibit strong concentration. The other one is the average recall, again for $p = 1/2$, which is equal to 0.27 with standard deviation equal to 0.06. Notice that that for all values of p greater than 1/2 the running time is significantly smaller even if the number of edges grows. For instance, when $p = 1$ the average running time is 49.4 seconds with a standard deviation of 0.29 seconds. This is happening because for $p = 1/2$ the existing density within the communities is not large enough, hence the optimal value of the objective does not correspond a latent labeling capturing the community structure. We deal with this immediately in the following.

Pair	FINLand			BigClam [43]		
	P	R	t	P	R	t
(0,1)	0.98	0.87	4.65	0.99	0.88	21.25
(0,7)	0.97	0.84	4.23	0.96	0.81	25.49
(0,8)	0.97	0.83	4.62	0.93	0.78	22.31
(0,9)	0.96	0.83	4.18	0.95	0.80	24.76
(1,4)	0.96	0.88	4.47	0.99	0.80	25.54
(1,6)	0.94	0.87	3.56	0.98	0.75	22.67
(1,7)	0.92	0.86	4.18	0.94	0.77	24.57
(1,9)	0.95	0.86	3.19	0.96	0.74	25.63
(3,4)	0.95	0.85	4.66	0.97	0.83	25.64
(3,6)	0.95	0.83	4.07	0.96	0.85	20.39
(3,7)	0.95	0.82	3.57	0.97	0.80	25.01
(6,7)	0.98	0.88	4.11	0.99	0.87	23.41
(6,9)	0.96	0.81	5.38	0.99	0.73	25.02

Table 2: Table shows the performance of FINLand and Bigclam in terms of precision (P), recall (R) and running time (t) for several pairs of digits. For details, see text of Section 4.4.

Sparse graphs and a rule-of-thumb. Lemma 3 shows that when the graph is sparse Objective 1 does not necessarily yield insightful solutions. As we have mentioned again, this happens since the first term corresponding to the summation over the edges is asymptotically negligible with respect to the second term in the regime when $m = o(n^2)$. For this purpose, we introduce Objective 2 which gives more importance satisfying an edge rather than a non-edge. This is achieved by the weight parameter $W \geq 1$. However, given a graph G it is not a priori clear how to choose W in order to learn a good latent vertex labeling. Here, we provide a simple yet well-performing rule-of-thumb on how to choose W. For this purpose we perform the following experiment. We generate two tiles on 1 000 vertices. We range $p_{01} = p_{10}$ in the set of values $\{0.01{:}0.01{:}0.1,.2{:}0.1{:}.9\}$. Notice we choose an increased level of granularity when $p_{01} = p_{10}$ is small. The intersection probability is $p_{11} = p_{01} + 0.1$ and the intersection size between the two equal-sized tiles is 20. For each value p_{01} we search for the value W^*_{true} that results in both precision and recall greater than 90%. Since every time that either the precision or the recall are less than 90%, we increase the weight W by one $|W^* - W^*_{\text{true}}| \leq 1$. Figure 3 plots in semilog W^* versus the inverse density ratio $\binom{n}{2}/m$ where m ranges as the edge probabilities change. We observe a striking phenomenon that we verified for various other settings of the parameters as well and that we exploit later on real data. Specifically, we plot the function $W^* = \binom{n}{2}/m$ which is very close to the observed measurements. Notice that this specific value of W^* results equivalently in a normalized version of our objective:

$$\max_{\omega: V \to \{0,1\}^k} \frac{1}{m} \sum_{(u,v)\in E(G)} 1(\omega^T(u)\omega(v) \geq 1) + \frac{1}{\binom{n}{2}} \sum_{(u,v)\notin E(G)} 1(\omega^T(u)\omega(v) = 0)$$

4.4 Classification

Digit classification. We choose several pairs of distinct digits. We obtain all datapoints corresponding to the two digits of each pair from the MNIST dataset. Then, we create a k'-nearest-neighbor graph. We choose two very different values of k', namely $k' = 300$ and $k' = 10$. The former value creates a dense nearest neighbor, resembling the regime of $O(n^2)$ edges, on which we optimize Objective 1. The latter values results in a sparse graph, resembling the regime with $O(n)$ edges, on which we optimize Objective 2 using our rule-of-thumb. The groundtruth here is defined by the MNIST labeling: there exist two latent features, each corresponding to whether a given image is the first or the second digit. Hence, each datapoint is labeled either as (01) or (10). Table 2 shows the results for $k' = 300$. The results for $k' = 10$ using our rule-of-thumb are qualitative the same. Indicatively, we report that for the pair of digits $(0, 7)$ precision and recall are $P = 0.9959$ and $R = 0.9821$ respectively. Similarly, for $(0, 8)$ we obtain $P = 0.9498, R = 0.8973$ respectively. A full evaluation of Objective 2 is shown in the next Section. As we see in Table 2 our method performs at least as well as BigClam. Furthermore, our method is typically at least 5 times faster than BigClam. It is worth outlining again that only BigClam among the competitors produced good quality results: CFinder produces poor quality results, verifying the claim of [44]. Finally, ILA does not complete after more than two days of running.

Multilabel classification and robustness to noise. For each of the EMOTIONS and FLAGS datasets we construct a similarity graph by placing an edge between two entities if and only if they share some common feature. Our experiments address the following two questions: (a) Can we recover the true labeling using this similarity graph? (b) Is our method robust to noise? We model noise as random deletions of edges. Specifically, for each value of the sparsification parameter p, we delete each edge independently from the rest with probability p. We searched for the first value of p for which either the precision or recall of our method is less than 90%. While p is less than 0.1 we use a search step equal to 0.01 whereas for larger p values we use a cruder search step of 0.025. Among the two resulting ranges we obtain, one for EMOTIONS and one for FLAGS, we use the superset for plotting purposes. Figure 4 presents the experimental results. We discuss them in detail in the following.

EMOTIONS: When $p = 0$, we perform 5 random experiments for our method, where the randomization is over the initial labelings ω_0. For BigClam, we perform a single experiment. For each value $p > 0$ we perform 25 experiments for our method (5 random initial labelings × 5 sparsified graphs) and 5 for BigClam, one for each sparsified graph. All obtained averages are well concentrated around the mean.

We observe that for $p = 0.175$ our method achieves average precision $P = 0.91$ and recall $R = 0.93$ with an average running time equal to 32.83 seconds. For $p = 0.2$ we obtain $P = 0.61$ and $R = 0.67$ with an average running time 47.19 seconds. Hence the resulting range for p is $\{0 : 0.01 : 0.1, 0.125 : 0.125 : 0.2\}$. Despite the fact that the total number of edges decreases as p increases, the average running time -even if not strictly increasing- exhibits an increasing trend. BigClam even for $p = 0$ is unable to recover the ground-truth. Specifically, it achieves $P = 0.998$ and $R = 0.857$ with running time equal to 33.85 seconds. For values of p up to 0.125 (included) the average precision is high $P \geq 0.867$ but the recall is extremely poor reaching the value $R = 0.026$. Above $p = 0.15$, precision drops as well. When $p = 0.20$, $P = 0.50$ and $R = 0.006$. The average speedup obtained by our method is 1.09. Notice that our method is not always faster than BigClam, specifically it is faster for 8 values of p.

FLAGS: We use the same number of experiments for each p value as for EMOTIONS. Our method for $p = 0$ achieves $P = 0.986$ and $R = 0.996$ with an average running time 3.48 seconds. BigClam achieves $P = 0.999$ and $R = 0.995$ with average running time 8.66 seconds. Even if BigClam outperforms slightly our method in this case, as soon as $p = 0.01$, its average recall drops below 90%. Specifically, $P = 0.999$ and $R = 0.879$ with an average running time 9.1 seconds. Our proposed method up to $p = 0.15$ achieves concurrently precision and recall greater than 90%. Specifically for $p = 0.15$ our method achieves average precision $P = 0.95$ and average recall $R = 0.90$. The average running time is 8.75 seconds. For the next value $p = 0.175$, the average recall drops below 90%. Specifically, $P = 0.95$ and $R = 0.81$. The running time is 11.74 seconds. The average speedup achieved is 1.38 and our method is faster than BigClam for 10 values of p.

4.5 Learning social circles from ego-networks

In this Section we focus on a special type of induced graph. Specifically, we consider *ego-networks*, namely graphs induced by a vertex and its neighbors. Ego-networks play an increasingly important role in many applications. including user identification [21], anomaly detection [5] and viral marketing [26].

The application of interest to us was introduced by Leskovec et al. [29, 43, 44]. Consider a given social media user who connects to other users. We expect most of the connections -unless the user is a spammer- to be due to the fact that the two users share some common feature. For instance, it could be their common interest in sports, their common ethnic background or because they work in the same space. This intuition is reflected on the structure of these networks. As Yang and Leskovec point out, the probability of an edge is a non-decreasing function of their common features [44].

The question that Leskovec et al. consider is the following: *can we recover the social circles of a user in social media based on the structure of the network?*

Their answer is positive. We use our method to perform the same task. We compare our method to BigClam [43] on ego-networks from Twitter with ground-truth available. The number of latent features is set equal to the number of social circles. BigClam is a successful method for finding overlapping communities and detecting social circles [44]. The results are shown in Table 3. The first two columns provide a description of the dataset in terms of the number of vertices and edges respectively. As we see our method typically outperforms BigClam, both in terms of the quality and the time efficiency.

Dataset		FINLand			BigClam [43]		
n	m	P	R	t	P	R	t
227	3860	0.85	1.00	0.009	1.00	0.38	0.26
14	70	1.00	1.00	0.001	1.00	1.00	0.06
222	5871	0.90	0.96	0.074	0.97	0.61	0.26
150	2503	0.91	1.00	0.018	1.00	0.61	0.17
213	3508	1.00	1.00	0.001	1.00	1.00	0.14
85	547	0.91	0.93	0.025	1.00	0.49	0.03
33	235	1.00	0.89	0.002	0.92	0.96	0.11
34	284	1.00	1.00	0.002	1.00	0.30	0.08
192	4190	0.89	1.00	0.054	1.00	0.55	0.05
120	577	1.00	0.92	0.002	1.00	0.55	0.37
99	1519	0.85	0.91	0.006	1.00	0.39	0.06
225	2602	1.00	0.96	0.018	0.96	0.75	0.19
56	665	0.87	0.96	0.038	0.96	0.39	0.30
113	1689	0.86	0.92	0.018	0.93	0.50	0.22
58	479	1.00	1.00	0.002	1.00	1.00	0.16

Table 3: Learning social circles from ego-networks from Twitter results. For details, see text of Section 4.5.

5. RELATED WORK

Learning Latent Features. The infinite relational model (IRM) is a prominent method among latent class models [23]. It assumes that each entity belongs to a single cluster or -equivalently in our terminology- it possesses a single feature. Edge probabilities depend solely on cluster assignments. Notice that this is reminiscent of McSherry's planted partition model [31]. However contrary to the planted partition model, IRM makes additional probabilistic assumptions. Specifically, it assumes that cluster assignments are drawn from the Chinese Restaurant Process [6]. In general, latent class models can model multiple participation to features, at the cost of combinatorial explosion: for each possible combination of features, create a new feature. Latent feature models allow multiple participation to features without the aforementioned cost [32]. Recently, Palla et al. [37] introduced the *infinite latent attribute* (ILA) model which yielded improvements over both [23] and [32]. Despite the accurate performance of ILA on small datasets, the method does not scale even to graphs with few hundreds of edges.

Overlapping clustering. Leskovec et al. showed that major non-overlapping clustering methods typically produce meaningful communities when their size is restricted to few tenths of vertices [28]. Recently, Yang and Leskovec show that overlapping communities can explain the core-periphery structure in networks [44]. Khandekar, Kortsarz and Mirrokni mathematically formalize this phenomenon and prove that overlapping clustering may yield significant benefits compared to the non-overlapping case [24]. A solid modeling approach to providing a theoretical model of communities that is also able to reproduce certain salient characteristics of real world networks is the affiliation networks model [27]. This model lies conceptually close to many research works including ours: the latent labelings our method produces can be seen as a bipartite graph where each vertex is afilliated to each feature it posseses. Anandkumar et al. provide guaranteed community recovery for the mixed membership Dirichlet model [4]. Gopalan and Blei use the same model [19] and probabilistic inference algorithms to detect overlapping communities. Arora et al. [9] can detect overlapping communities under other modeling assumptions. CFinder is a popular method for detecting overlapping communities using clique percolation [3]. CFinder does not scale well to large networks and more importantly it fails to find overlapping communities even in the context of two communities with a dense overlap. As Yang and Leskovec frequently this is the case on social networks [44]. It is worth mentioning that in the extreme case when the overlaps are complete, then it is known how to find these clique-separators in polynomial time [39]. However, the overlaps tend to be large near-cliques [40] rather than perfect cliques. Mcauley and Leskovec use overlapping community detection methods to discover social circles from ego-networks [29]. A subsequent method developed by Yang and Leskovec [43] is based on non-negative matrix factorization and scales better than [29]. As we saw in Section 4 our method outperforms [43], is significantly simpler and comes with solid theoretical guarantees. An interesting research direction is to understand the effects of recent developments in nonnegative matrix factorization [8] for detecting overlapping communities, since the underlying assumptions of Arora, Ge, Kannan and Moitra are -in many cases- realistic. Closely related to non-negative matrix factorization approaches is the geometric approach proposed in [41]. The concept of (α, β)-clusters is interesting within the context of overlapping communities but recent developments have shown that under a well-accepted conjecture finding even one (α, β)-cluster is intractable [10]. Finally, many other heuristics exist that are not well understood exist, e.g., [2, 14, 18, 35, 45]. As we discussed earlier our work sheds light on the heuristic method developed by Bonchi et al. [14] .

6. CONCLUSION

Summary. In this work we consider a fundamental problem with many important applications: can we learn efficiently and accurately latent features that explain a given graph? We propose a simple probabilistic model and a rapidly mixing Metropolis chain for optimizing the resulting maximum likelihood function. We use our method to perform successfully multilabel classification from similarity graphs and to learn social circles from Twitter ego-networks.

Open Problems. Our work opens numerous questions. What are the graph sub-structures that affect the performance of latent feature learning methods? Under our model, we showed that complete bipartite subgraphs play a key role. What about other models such as the ILA [37]? Combining such answers with the work of Ugander et al. [42] may shed light on the merits and limitations of such methods on real-world networks. Why does the simple probabilistic model we introduce perform so well on real world datasets? How do we include non-assortative features? Can we have a richer family of probabilistic models for undirected graphs for which we can have efficient (approximation) algorithms? Developing new probabilistic models and latent feature learning algorithms for directed graphs is also an interesting research direction. Finally, in future work we plan to use our method on other graph mining problems such as link prediction.

7. REFERENCES

[1] http://yann.lecun.com/exdb/mnist/. 4.1

[2] *Evolutionary algorithms for overlapping correlation clustering*, 2014. 5

[3] B. Adamcsek, G. Palla, I. J. Farkas, I. Derényi, and T. Vicsek. CFinder: locating cliques and overlapping modules in biological networks. *Bioinformatics*, 22(8):1021–1023, 2006. 4.1, 4.2, 5

[4] E. M. Airoldi, D. M. Blei, S. E. Fienberg, and E. P. Xing. Mixed membership stochastic blockmodels. In *NIPS'09*, pages 33–40, 2009. 5

[5] L. Akoglu, M. McGlohon, and C. Faloutsos. Oddball: Spotting anomalies in weighted graphs. In *Advances in Knowledge Discovery and Data Mining*, pages 410–421. Springer, 2010. 4.5

[6] D. J. Aldous. *Exchangeability and related topics.* Springer, 1985. 5

[7] R. Andersen, D. F. Gleich, and V. Mirrokni. Overlapping clusters for distributed computation. In *WSDM*, pages 273–282. ACM, 2012. 1

[8] S. Arora, R. Ge, R. Kannan, and A. Moitra. Computing a nonnegative matrix factorization–provably. In *STOC*, pages 145–162. ACM, 2012. 5

[9] S. Arora, R. Ge, S. Sachdeva, and G. Schoenebeck. Finding overlapping communities in social networks: toward a rigorous approach. In *ACM EC*, pages 37–54. ACM, 2012. 5

[10] M.-F. Balcan, C. Borgs, M. Braverman, J. T. Chayes, and S.-H. Teng. Finding endogenously formed communities. In *SODA '13*, pages 767–783, 2013. 5

[11] N. Bansal, A. Blum, and S. Chawla. Correlation clustering. *Machine Learning*, 56(1–3):89–113, 2004. 1

[12] E. Becker, B. Robisson, C. E. Chapple, A. Guénoche, and C. Brun. Multifunctional proteins revealed by overlapping clustering in protein interaction network. *Bioinformatics*, 28(1):84–90, 2012. 1

[13] P. Boldi and S. Vigna. The webgraph framework i: compression techniques. In *WWW'04*, pages 595–602, 2004. 1

[14] F. Bonchi, A. Gionis, and A. Ukkonen. Overlapping correlation clustering. In *ICDM '11*, pages 51–60, 2011. 1, 3, 1, 3, 5

[15] R. Bubley and M. Dyer. Path coupling: A technique for proving rapid mixing in markov chains. In *FOCS*, pages 223–231. IEEE, 1997. 1

[16] F. Doshi-Velez and Z. Ghahramani. Accelerated

sampling for the indian buffet process. In *ICML'09*, pages 273–280, 2009. 4.2

[17] F. Doshi-Velez and Z. Ghahramani. Correlated non-parametric latent feature models. In *UAI*, pages 143–150, 2009. 4.2

[18] T. Evans and R. Lambiotte. Line graphs, link partitions, and overlapping communities. *Physical Review E*, 80(1):016105, 2009. 5

[19] P. K. Gopalan and D. M. Blei. Efficient discovery of overlapping communities in massive networks. *Proceedings of the National Academy of Sciences*, 110(36):14534–14539, 2013. 5

[20] T. Griffiths and Z. Ghahramani. Infinite latent feature models and the indian buffet process. *TR 2005-001, Gatsby Comp. Neuroscience Unit.*, 2005. 4.2

[21] K. Henderson, B. Gallagher, L. Li, L. Akoglu, T. Eliassi-Rad, H. Tong, and C. Faloutsos. It's who you know: graph mining using recursive structural features. In *KDD*, pages 663–671. ACM, 2011. 4.5

[22] P. F. Jonsson and P. A. Bates. Global topological features of cancer proteins in the human interactome. *Bioinformatics*, 22(18):2291–2297, 2006. 1

[23] C. Kemp, J. B. Tenenbaum, T. L. Griffiths, T. Yamada, and N. Ueda. Learning systems of concepts with an infinite relational model. In *AAAI'06*, pages 381–388, 2006. 1, 5

[24] R. Khandekar, G. Kortsarz, and V. Mirrokni. On the advantage of overlapping clusters for minimizing conductance. *Algorithmica*, 69(4):844–863, 2014. 1, 5

[25] S. Kirkpatrick and C. D. Gelatt and MP. Vecchi. Optimization by simulated annealing In *Science*, 1983. 4.2

[26] S. Lattanzi and Y. Singer. The power of random neighbors in social networks. In *WSDM*, 2015. 4.5

[27] S. Lattanzi and D. Sivakumar. Affiliation networks. In *STOC*, pages 427–434, 2009. 5

[28] J. Leskovec, K. J. Lang, A. Dasgupta, and M. W. Mahoney. Statistical properties of community structure in large social and information networks. In *WWW*, pages 695–704. ACM, 2008. 5

[29] J. Leskovec and J. J. Mcauley. Learning to discover social circles in ego networks. In *NIPS*, pages 539–547, 2012. 1, 4.1, 4.5, 5

[30] D. A. Levin, Y. Peres, and E. L. Wilmer. *Markov chains and mixing times.* American Mathematical Soc., 2009. 2, 3

[31] F. McSherry. Spectral partitioning of random graphs. In *FOCS*, pages 529–537. IEEE, 2001. 5

[32] K. Miller, M. I. Jordan, and T. L. Griffiths. Nonparametric latent feature models for link prediction. In *NIPS*, pages 1276–1284, 2009. 1, 1, 5

[33] B. Morris, W. Ning and Y. Peres. Mixing time of the card-cyclic-to-random shuffle. The Annals of Applied Probability, 24:5, pages 1835–1849, 2014 4.1

[34] D. Mumford. Pattern theory: a unifying perspective. In *First European congress of mathematics*, pages 187–224. Springer, 1994. 1

[35] T. Nepusz, A. Petróczi, L. Négyessy, and F. Bazsó. Fuzzy communities and the concept of bridgeness in complex networks. *Physical Review E*, 77(1):016107, 2008. 5

[36] G. Palla, I. Derényi, I. Farkas, and T. Vicsek. Uncovering the overlapping community structure of complex networks in nature and society. *Nature*, 435(7043):814–818, 2005. 1

[37] K. Palla, D. A. Knowles, and Z. Ghahramani. An infinite latent attribute model for network data. In *ICML*. 2012. (document), 1, 4.1, 4.2, 4.2, 5, 6

[38] I. Psorakis, S. Roberts, M. Ebden, and B. Sheldon. Overlapping community detection using bayesian non-negative matrix factorization. *Physical Review E*, 83(6):066114, 2011. 1

[39] R. E. Tarjan. Decomposition by clique separators. *Discrete mathematics*, 55(2):221–232, 1985. 5

[40] C. Tsourakakis, F. Bonchi, A. Gionis, F. Gullo, and M. Tsiarli. Denser than the densest subgraph: extracting optimal quasi-cliques with quality guarantees. In *KDD*, pages 104–112. ACM, 2013. 5

[41] C. E. Tsourakakis. Toward quantifying vertex similarity in networks. *Internet Mathematics*, 10(3-4):263–286, 2014. 5

[42] J. Ugander, L. Backstrom, and J. Kleinberg. Subgraph frequencies: Mapping the empirical and extremal geography of large graph collections. In *WWW*, pages 1307–1318, 2013. 6

[43] J. Yang and J. Leskovec. Overlapping community detection at scale: a nonnegative matrix factorization approach. In *WSDM*, pages 587–596. ACM, 2013. (document), 1, 4.1, 4.2, 4.2, 4.2, 4.3, 4.5, 5

[44] J. Yang and J. Leskovec. Overlapping communities explain core-periphery organization of networks. Technical report, Stanford University, October 2014. (document), 1, 4.2, 4.3, 4.4, 4.5, 5

[45] Z.-Y. Zhang, Y. Wang, and Y.-Y. Ahn. Overlapping community detection in complex networks using symmetric binary matrix factorization. *Physical Review E*, 87(6):062803, 2013. 5

The K-clique Densest Subgraph Problem

Charalampos E. Tsourakakis
Harvard School of Engineering and Applied Sciences
babis@seas.harvard.edu

ABSTRACT

Numerous graph mining applications rely on detecting subgraphs which are large near-cliques. Since formulations that are geared towards finding large near-cliques are **NP**-hard and frequently inapproximable due to connections with the Maximum Clique problem, the poly-time solvable *densest subgraph problem* which maximizes the average degree over all possible subgraphs "lies at the core of large scale data mining" [10]. However, frequently the *densest subgraph problem* fails in detecting large near-cliques in networks.

In this work, we introduce the *k-clique densest subgraph problem*, $k \geq 2$. This generalizes the well studied *densest subgraph problem* which is obtained as a special case for $k = 2$. For $k = 3$ we obtain a novel formulation which we refer to as the *triangle densest subgraph problem*: given a graph $G(V, E)$, find a subset of vertices S^* such that $\tau(S^*) = \max_{S \subseteq V} \frac{t(S)}{|S|}$, where $t(S)$ is the number of triangles induced by the set S.

On the theory side, we prove that for any k constant, there exist an exact polynomial time algorithm for the *k-clique densest subgraph problem*. Furthermore, we propose an efficient $\frac{1}{k}$-approximation algorithm which generalizes the greedy peeling algorithm of Asahiro and Charikar [8, 18] for $k = 2$. Finally, we show how to implement efficiently this peeling framework on MapReduce for any $k \geq 3$, generalizing the work of Bahmani, Kumar and Vassilvitskii for the case $k = 2$ [10]. On the empirical side, our two main findings are that (i) the *triangle densest subgraph* is consistently closer to being a large near-clique compared to the *densest subgraph* and (ii) the peeling approximation algorithms for both $k = 2$ and $k = 3$ achieve on real-world networks approximation ratios closer to 1 rather than the pessimistic $\frac{1}{k}$ guarantee. An interesting consequence of our work is that *triangle counting*, a well-studied computational problem in the context of social network analysis can be used to detect large near-cliques. Finally, we evaluate our proposed method on a popular graph mining application.

WWW 2015, May 18–22, 2015, Florence, Italy.
ACM 978-1-4503-3469-3/15/05.
http://dx.doi.org/10.1145/2736277.2741128 .

Categories and Subject Descriptors

G.2.2 [**Graph Theory**]: Graph Algorithms; H.2.8 [**Database Applications**]: Data mining

General Terms

Theory, Experimentation

Keywords

Densest subgraph problem; Graph algorithms; Graph Mining; Near-clique extraction

1. INTRODUCTION

A wide variety of data mining applications relies on extracting dense subgraphs from large graphs. In bioinformatics dense subgraphs are used for detecting protein complexes in protein-protein interaction networks [9] and for finding regulatory motifs in DNA [24]. They are also used for detecting link spam in Web graphs [26], graph compression [17] and mining micro-blogging streams [6].

Among the various formulations for finding dense subgraphs, the *densest subgraph problem* (DS-PROBLEM) stands out for the facts that is solvable in polynomial time [28] and $\frac{1}{2}$-approximable in linear time [7, 18, 40]. To state the DS-PROBLEM we first introduce the necessary notation. In this work we focus on simple unweighted, undirected graphs. Given a graph $G = (V, E)$ and a subset of vertices $S \subseteq V$, let $G(S) = (S, E(S))$ be the subgraph induced by S, and let $e(S) = |E(S)|$ be the size of $E(S)$. Also, the *edge density* of the set S is defined as $f_e(S) = e(S)/\binom{|S|}{2}$. The DS-PROBLEM maximizes the degree density $\frac{e(S)}{|S|}$ over all subgraphs $S \subseteq V$. Notice that this is equivalent to maximizing the average degree[1]. The DS-PROBLEM is a powerful primitive for many graph applications including social piggybacking [27], reachability and distance query indexing [19, 37]. However, a large number of applications aims to find subgraphs which are large near-cliques rather than the subgraph that maximizes the average degree. Frequently the DS-PROBLEM fails in finding large near-cliques because it favors large subgraphs with low high edge density f_e. For

[1] In graph theory the term *edge density* refers by default to $f_e = e(S)/\binom{|S|}{2} \in [0, 1]$. However, since direct maximization of f_e is not a meaningful problem (even a single edge achieves the maximum possible edge density), the DS-PROBLEM maximizes the average degree. In the following, we refer to the average degree of a set as its *degree density*.

this reason other formulations have been proposed, see Section 2. Unfortunately, these formulations are **NP**-hard and also inapproximable due the connections with the Maximum Clique problem [32].

The main contribution of this work is a family of tractable formulations which attacks efficiently the problem of extracting large near-cliques and in contrast to well-performing heuristics comes with strong theoretical guarantees. In detail, our contributions are summarized as follows.

New formulation: We introduce the *k-clique densest subgraph problem* (K-CLIQUE-DS-PROBLEM) which generalizes the well-studied DS-PROBLEM [18, 25, 28, 40]. The goal is to maximize the average number of k-cliques induced by a set $S \subseteq V$ over all possible vertex subsets. Notice that the DS-PROBLEM is obtained as a special case for $k = 2$. We introduce also the special case obtained for $k = 3$ as the *triangle densest subgraph problem* (TDS-PROBLEM).

Exact algorithms. We present two exact algorithms for the TDS-PROBLEM. The algorithm which achieves the best running time is based on maximum flow computations and uses $O(n + t)$ space. It is worth outlining that Goldberg's network construction for the DS-PROBLEM which uses $O(n+m)$ space [25, 28] does not generalize to the TDS-PROBLEM. The slower one is based on supermodular maximization and uses linear space $O(n + m)$. Here, n, m, t are the number of vertices, edges and triangles in the input graph. Our algorithms can be modified to yield polynomial time algorithms for the K-CLIQUE-DS-PROBLEM when $k = \Theta(1)$.

Approximation algorithm. We propose a $\frac{1}{3}$-approximation algorithm for the TDS-PROBLEM which runs asymptotically faster than any of the exact algorithms. We also propose a $\frac{1}{3+3\epsilon}$-approximation algorithm for any $\epsilon > 0$ which can be implemented efficiently in MAPREDUCE. The algorithm requires $O(\log(n)/\epsilon)$ rounds and is MAPREDUCE efficient [39] due to the existence of efficient MAPREDUCE triangle counting algorithms, e.g., [48]. Our algorithms can be adapted to the K-CLIQUE-DS-PROBLEM for any $k = \Theta(1)$.

Experimental evaluation. We evaluate our exact and approximation algorithms on numerous real-world networks. Among our findings, we observe that the *optimal triangle densest subgraph* is consistently closer to being a large near-clique compared to the *optimal densest subgraph.* For instance, in the Football network (see Table 1 for a description of the dataset) the DS-PROBLEM returns the whole graph as the densest subgraph, with $f_e = 0.094$ whereas the TDS-PROBLEM returns a subgraph on 18 vertices with $f_e = 0.48$. We also observe that the peeling approximation algorithms for both $k = 2$ and $k = 3$ achieve on real-world networks approximation ratios closer to 1 rather than the pessimistic $\frac{1}{k}$ guarantee.

Graph mining application. We propose a modified version of the TDS-PROBLEM, the constrained triangle densest subgraph problem (CONSTRAINED-TDS-PROBLEM), which aims to maximize the triangle density subject to the constraint that the output should contain a specified set of vertices Q. We show how to solve exactly the TDS-PROBLEM. This variation is useful in various data-mining and bioinformatics tasks, see [49].

2. RELATED WORK

Since dense subgraph discovery constitutes a main research topic in graph analysis, a wide variety of related methods exists: heuristics [49, 52, 54], algorithmic contributions on **NP**-hard formulations [5, 12, 22, 40, **?**] and poly-time solvable formulations [18, 40, **?**]. We focus on the latter.

Densest Subgraph. In the densest subgraph problem we are given a graph G and we wish to find the set $S \subseteq V$ which maximizes the average degree [28, 38]. The densest subgraph can be identified in polynomial time by solving a maximum flow problem [25, 28]. Charikar [18] proved that the greedy algorithm proposed by Asashiro et al. [8] produces a $\frac{1}{2}$-approximation of the densest subgraph in linear time. A k-core is a maximal connected subgraph of G in which all vertices have degree at least k. It is worth remarking that the same algorithm provides a k-core decomposition of the graph and solves the problem of finding the degeneracy [11]. In the case of directed graphs, the densest subgraph problem is solved in polynomial time as well [18]. Khuller and Saha [40] provide a linear time $\frac{1}{2}$-approximation algorithm for the case of directed graphs among other contributions. Two interesting variations of the *DkS* problem were introduced by Andersen and Chellapilla [5]. The two problems ask for the set S that maximizes the density subject to $|S| \leq k$ (DamkS) and $|S| \geq k$ (DalkS). When restrictions on the size of S are imposed the problem becomes **NP**-hard [40]. Finally, the densest subgraph problem has been considered in various settings, including MAPREDUCE [10], the streaming [10], the dynamic setting [21, 45] and their combination recently [13].

Triangle Counting and Listing. The state of the art algorithm for *exact* triangle counting is due to Alon, Yuster and Zwick [4] and runs in $O(m^{\frac{2\omega}{\omega+1}})$, where currently the fast matrix multiplication exponent ω is 2.3729 [53]. Thus, their algorithm currently runs in $O(m^{1.4081})$ time. The best known listing algorithm until recently was due to Itai and Rodeh [33] which runs in $O(m\alpha(G))$ time, where $\alpha(G)$ is the graph arboricity. Since $\alpha(G) = O(\sqrt{m})$, the running time is always $O(m^{3/2})$. Recently, Björklund, Pagh, Williams and Zwick gave refined algorithms which are output sensitive algorithms [14]. Finally a wealth of approximate triangle counting methods exist [35, 41, 44, 51].

3. PROBLEM DEFINITION

We define the notion of average triangle density.

DEFINITION 1 (Triangle Density). *Let $G(V, E)$ be an undirected graph. For any $S \subseteq V$ we define its triangle density $\tau(S)$ as $\tau(S) = \frac{t(S)}{s}$, where $t(S)$ is the number of triangles induced by S and $s = |S|$.*

Notice that $3\tau(S)$ is the average number of (induced) triangles per vertex in S. The optimization problem we focus on follows.

PROBLEM 1 (TDS-PROBLEM). *Given $G(V, E)$, find a subset of vertices S^* such that $\tau(S^*) = \tau^*_G$ where $\tau^*_G = \max_{S \subseteq V} \tau(S)$.*

It is clear that the DS-PROBLEM and the TDS-PROBLEM in general can result in radically different solutions. Consider for instance a graph G on $2n + 3$ vertices which is the union of a triangle K_3 and of a bipartite clique $K_{n,n}$. The optimal solutions of the DS-PROBLEM and the TDS-PROBLEM are the bipartite clique and the triangle respectively. Therefore, the interesting question is whether maximizing the average degree and the triangle density result in different results in real-world networks. Our results in Section 5 indicate that the answer is positive since the triangle densest subgraph compared to densest subgraph is smaller which exhibits a stronger near-clique structure.

4. PROPOSED METHOD

Section 4.1 provides two algorithms which solve the TDS-PROBLEM exactly. Sections 4.2 and 4.3 provide two approximation algorithms for the TDS-PROBLEM. Finally, Section 4.4 provides a generalization of the DS-PROBLEM and the TDS-PROBLEM to maximizing the average k-clique density and shows how the results from previous Sections adapt to this problem.

4.1 Exact Solutions

Let n, m, t be the number of vertices, edges and triangles in graph G respectively. The algorithm presented in Section 4.1.1 achieves the best running time. We present an algorithm which relies on the supermodularity property of our objective in Section 4.1.2. The latter algorithm, even if slower, requires $O(n+m)$ space, whereas the former $O(n+t)$ space. In real-world networks, typically $m \ll t$. Finally, it is worth mentioning that Charikar's linear program, see §2 in [18], can be extended to a linear program (LP) which solves the TDS-PROBLEM, see [50] for the details.

4.1.1 An $O(m^{3/2}+nt+\min(n,t)^3)$-time exact solution

Algorithm 1 triangle-densest subgraph(G)

```
List the set of triangles T(G), t = |T(G)|
l ← t/n, u ← (n−1)(n−2)/6
S* ← ∅
while u ≥ l + 1/(n(n−1)) do
    α ← (l+u)/2
    H_α ← Construct-Network(G, α, T(G))
    (S, T) ← minimum st-cut in H_α
    if S = {s} then
        u ← α
    else
        l ← α
        S* ← (S\{s}) ∩ V(G)
    end if
    Return S*
end while
```

Algorithm 2 Construct-Network $(G, \alpha, \mathcal{T}(G))$

```
V(H) ← {s} ∪ V(G) ∪ T(G) ∪ {t}.
For each vertex v ∈ V(G) add an arc of capacity 1 to
    each triangle t_i it participates in.
For each triangle Δ = (u, v, w) ∈ T(G) add arcs to
    u, v, w of capacity 2.
Add directed arc (s, v) ∈ A(H) of capacity t_v for each
    v ∈ V(G).
Add weighted directed arc (v, t) ∈ A(H) of capacity 3α
    for each v ∈ V(G).
Return network H(V(H), A(H), w), s, t ∈ V(H).
```

Our main theoretical result is the following theorem. Its proof is constructive.

THEOREM 1. *There exists an algorithm which which solves the* TDS-PROBLEM *and runs in* $O(m^{3/2}+nt+\min(n,t)^3)$ *time.*

The first term $O(m^{3/2})$ comes from using the Itai-Rodeh algorithm [33] as our triangle listing blackbox. If we use the naive $O(n^3)$ triangle listing algorithm then the running time expression is simplified to $O(n^3+nt)$. On the other hand, if we use the algorithms of Björklund et al. [14] the first term becomes for dense graphs $\tilde{O}(n^{\omega}+n^{3(\omega-1)/(5-\omega)}t^{2(3-\omega)/(5-\omega)})$ and for sparse graphs $\tilde{O}(m^{2\omega/(\omega+1)}+m^{3\frac{\omega-1}{\omega+1}}t^{\frac{3-\omega}{\omega+1}})$, where ω is the matrix multiplication exponent. Currently $\omega < 2.3729$ due to [53]. We maintain [33] as our black-box to keep the expressions simpler. However, the reader should keep in mind that the result presented in [14] improves the total running time of the first term.

We work our way to proving Theorem 1 by first proving the next key lemma. Then, we remove the logarithmic factor.

LEMMA 1. *Algorithm 1 solves the* TDS-PROBLEM *and runs in* $O(m^{3/2}+(nt+\min(n,t)^3)\log(n))$ *time.*

Algorithm 1 uses maximum flow computations to solve the TDS-PROBLEM. It is worth outlining that Goldberg's maximum flow algorithm [28] for the DS-PROBLEM is based on a network construction that does not adapt to the case of the TDS-PROBLEM. Algorithm 1 returns an optimal subgraph S^*, i.e., $\tau(S^*)=\tau^*$. The algorithm performs a binary search on the triangle density value α. Specifically, each binary search query corresponds to querying *does there exist a set* $S \subseteq V$ *such that* $t(S)/|S| > \alpha$?. For each binary search, we construct a bipartite network H by invoking Algorithm 2. Let $\mathcal{T}(G)$ be the set of triangles in G. The vertex set of H is $V(H)=\{s\}\cup A\cup B\cup\{t\}$, where $A=V(G)$ and $B=\mathcal{T}(G)$. Notice that we overload the notation in order to use the frequently used notation for the sink vertex t. It should always be clear from the context to which entity (number of triangles vs. sink vertex) we refer to. For the purpose of finding $\mathcal{T}(G)$, a triangle listing algorithm is required [14, 33]. The arc set of graph H is created as follows. For each vertex $r \in B$ corresponding to triangle $\Delta(u,v,w)$ we add three incoming and three out-coming arcs. The incoming arcs come from the vertices $u, v, w \in A$ which form triangle $\Delta(u,v,w)$. Each of these arcs has capacity equal to 1. The outgoing arcs go to the same set of vertices u, v, w, but the capacities are equal to 2. In addition to the arcs of capacity 1 from each vertex $u \in A$ to the triangles it participates in, we add an outgoing arc of capacity 3α to the sink vertex t. From the source vertex s we add an outgoing arc to each $u \in A$ of capacity t_v, where t_v is the number of triangles vertex v participates in G. As we have already noticed, H can be constructed in $O(m^{3/2})$ time [33]. It is worth outlining that after computing H for the first time, subsequent networks need to update only the arcs that depend on the parameter α, something not shown in the pseudocode for simplicity. To prove that Algorithm 1 solves the TDS-PROBLEM and runs in $O(m^{3/2}+(nt+\min(n,t)^3)\log(n))$ time we proceed in steps.

For the sake of the proof, we introduce the following definitions and notation. For a given set of vertices S let $t_i(S)$ be the number of triangles that involve exactly i vertices from S, $i \in \{1,2,3\}$. Notice that $t_3(S)$ is the number of induced triangles by S, for which we have been using the simpler notation $t(S)$ so far.

We use the following claim as our criterion to set the initial values l, u in the binary search.

Claim 1. $\frac{t}{n} \leq \tau(S) \leq \frac{(n-1)(n-2)}{6}$ for any $S \subseteq V$.

The lower bound is obvious since $\tau(V) = \frac{t}{n}$. The upper bound also follows trivially by observing that $\tau(S) \leq \binom{n}{3}/n$ for any $\emptyset \neq S \subseteq V$. This suggests that the optimal value τ^* is always $O(n^2)$.

The next claim serves as a criterion to decide when to stop the binary search.

Claim 2 The smallest possible difference among two distinct values $\tau(S_1), \tau(S_2)$ is equal to $\frac{1}{n(n-1)}$.

To see why, notice that the difference δ between two possible different triangle density values is

$$\delta = \frac{t(S_1)|S_2| - t(S_2)|S_1|}{|S_1||S_2|}.$$

If $|S_1| = |S_2|$ then $|\delta| \geq \frac{1}{n} > \frac{1}{n(n-1)}$, otherwise $|\delta| \geq \frac{1}{|S_1||S_2|} \geq \frac{1}{n(n-1)}$. Notice that combining the above two claims shows that the binary search terminates in at most $\lceil 4 \log n \rceil$ queries. The following lemma is a structural lemma for the optimal $s-t$ cut the network H_α.

Lemma 2. *Consider any minimum st-cut (S,T) in the network H_α. Let $A_1 = S \cap A, B_1 = S \cap B$ and $A_2 = T \cap A, B_2 = T \cap B$. The cost of the min-cut is equal to*

$$\sum_{v \notin A_1} t_v + 2t_2(A_1) + t_1(A_1) + 3\alpha|A_1|.$$

Proof. Case I: $A_1 = \emptyset$: In this case the proposition trivially holds, as the cost is equal to $\sum_{v \in A} t_v = 3t$. It is worth noticing that in this case B_1 has to be also empty, otherwise we contradict the optimality of (S,T). Hence $S = \{s\}, T = A \cup B \cup \{t\}$.

Case II: $A_1 \neq \emptyset$: Consider the cost of the arcs from $A_1 \cup B_1$ to $A_2 \cup B_2$. We consider three different subcases, one per each type of triangle with respect to set A_1.

Type 3: If there exist three vertices $u, v, w \in A_1$ that form a triangle $\Delta(u,v,w)$, then the vertex $r \in B$ corresponding to this specific triangle has to be in B_1. If not, then $r \in B_2$, and we could reduce the cost of the min-cut by 3, if we move the triangle to B_1. Therefore the cost we pay for triangles of type three is 0.

Type 2: Consider three vertices u, v, w such that they form a triangle $\Delta(u,v,w)$ and $u, v \in A_1, w \in A_2$. Then, the vertex $r \in B$ corresponding to this triangle can be either in B_1 or B_2. In both cases we always pay 2 in the cut for each triangle of type two.

Type 1: Finally, in the case u, v, w form a triangle, $u \in A_1, v, w \in A_2$ the vertex $r \in B$ corresponding to triangle $\Delta(u,v,w)$ will be in B_2. If not, then it lies in B_1 and we could decrease the cost of the cut by 3 if we move it in B_2. Hence, we pay 1 in the cut for each triangle of type one.

Therefore the cost due to the various types of triangles with respect to A_1 is equal to $2t_2(A_1) + t_1(A_1)$.

Furthermore, the cost of the arcs from source s to T is equal to $\sum_{v \in A_2} t_v = \sum_{v \notin A_1} t_v$. The cost of the arcs from A_1 to T is equal to $3\alpha|A_1|$. Summing up the individual cost terms, we obtain that the total cost is equal to $\sum_{v \notin A_1} t_v + 2t_2(A_1) + t_1(A_1) + 3\alpha|A_1|$. □

The next lemma proves the correctness of the binary search in Algorithm 1.

Lemma 3. *(a) If there exists a set $W \subseteq V(G)$ such that $t_3(W) > \alpha|W|$ then any minimum st-cut (S,T) in H_α satisfies $S \backslash \{s\} \neq \emptyset$. (b) Furthermore, if there does not exists a set W such that $t_3(W) > \alpha|W|$ then the cut $(\{s\}, A \cup B \cup \{t\})$ is a minimum st-cut.*

Proof. (a) Let $W \subseteq V$ be such that

$$t_3(W) > \alpha|W|. \quad (1)$$

Suppose for the sake of contradiction that the minimum st-cut is achieved by $(\{s\}, A \cup B \cup \{t\})$. In this case the cost of the minimum st-cut is $\sum_{v \in A} t_v = 3t$. Now, consider the following (S,T) cut. Set S consists of the source vertex s, $A_1 = W$ and B_1 be the set of triangles of type 3 and 2 induced by A_1. Let T be the rest of the vertices in H. The cost of this cut is

$$cap(S,T) = \sum_{v \notin A_1} t_v + 2t_2(A_1) + t_1(A_1) + 3\alpha|A_1|.$$

Therefore, by our assumption that the minimum st-cut is achieved by $(\{s\}, A \cup B \cup \{t\})$ we obtain

$$3t \leq \sum_{v \notin A_1} t_v + 2t_2(A_1) + t_1(A_1) + 3\alpha|A_1|. \quad (2)$$

Now, notice that by double counting

$$\sum_{v \in A_1} t_v = 3t_3(A_1) + 2t_2(A_1) + t_1(A_1).$$

Furthermore, we observe

$$\sum_{v \in A_1} t_v + \sum_{v \notin A_1} t_v = 3t.$$

By combining these two facts, and the fact that $3t$ is the capacity of the minimum cut, we obtain the following contradiction of Inequality (1).

$$3t \leq \sum_{v \notin A_1} t_v + 2t_2(A_1) + t_1(A_1) + 3\alpha|A_1| \Leftrightarrow t_3(W) \leq \alpha|W|.$$

(b) By Lemma 2, for any minimum st-cut (S,T) the capacity of the cut is equal to $\sum_{v \notin A_1} t_v + 2t_2(A_1) + t_1(A_1) + 3\alpha|A_1|$, where $A_1 = A \cap S, A_2 = A \cap T$. Suppose for the sake of contradiction that the cut $(\{s\}, A \cup B \cup \{t\})$ is not a minimum cut. Therefore,

$$cap(\{s\}, A \cup B \cup \{t\}) = 3t > \sum_{v \notin A_1} t_v + 2t_2(A_1) + t_1(A_1) + 3\alpha|A_1|.$$

Using the same algebraic analysis as in (a), the above statement implies the contradiction $t_3(W) > \alpha|W|$, where $W = A_1$. □

Now we can complete the proof of Lemma 1.

Proof. The termination of Algorithm 1 follows directly from Claims 1, 2. The correctness follows from Lemmata 2, 3.

The running time follows from Claims 1,2 which show that the number of binary search queries is $O(\log(n))$ and each binary search query can be performed in $O\big(nt+\min(n,t)^3\big)$ time using the algorithm due to Ahuja, Orlin, Stein and Tarjan [3][2] or Gusfield's algorithm [31]. $\square$

The proof of Theorem 1 follows from Lemma 1 and the fact that the parametric maximum flow algorithm of Ahuja, Orlin, Stein and Tarjan [3], see also [25], s(h)aves the logarithmic factor from the running time.

4.1.2 An $O((n^5m^{1.4081}+n^6))\log(n))$-time exact solution

In this Section we provide a second exact algorithm for the TDS-PROBLEM. First, we provide the necessary theoretical background.

DEFINITION 2 (SUPERMODULAR FUNCTION). *Let V be a finite set. The set function $f : 2^V \rightarrow \mathbb{R}$ is supermodular if and only if for all $A, B \subseteq V$*

$$f(A \cup B) \geq f(A) + f(B) - f(A \cap B).$$

A function f is supermodular if and only if $-f$ is submodular.

Sub- and supermodular functions constitute an important class of functions with various special properties. In this work, we are primarily interested in the fact that *maximizing a supermodular function is solvable in strongly polynomial time* [30, 34, 42, 46]. For our purposes, we state the following result which we use as a subroutine in our proposed algorithm.

THEOREM 2 ([43]). *There exists an algorithm for maximizing an integer valued supermodular function f which runs in $O\big(n^5 EO + n^6)\big)$ time, where $n = |V|$ is the size of the ground set V and EO is the maximum amount of time to evaluate $f(S)$ for a subset $S \subseteq V$.*

We show in the following that when the ground set is the set of vertices V and $f_\alpha : 2^V \rightarrow \mathbb{R}$ is defined by $f_\alpha(S) = t(S) - \alpha|S|$ where $\alpha \in \mathbb{R}^+$, we can solve the TDS-PROBLEM in polynomial time.

THEOREM 3. *Function $f : V \rightarrow \mathbb{R}$ where $f(S) = t(S) - \alpha|S|$ is supermodular.*

PROOF. Let $A, B \subseteq V$. Let $t : 2^V \rightarrow \mathbb{R}$ be the function which for each set of vertices S returns the number of induced triangles $t(S)$. By careful counting

$$t(A\cup B) = t(A)+t(B)-t(A\cap B)+t_1(A : B\backslash A)+t_2(A : B\backslash A),$$

where $t_1(A : B\backslash A), t_2(A : B\backslash A)$ are the number of triangle with one, two vertices in A and two, one vertices in $B\backslash A$ respectively. Hence, for any $A, B \subseteq V$

$$t(A \cup B) + t(A \cap B) \geq t(A) + t(B)$$

and the function t is supermodular. Furthermore, for any $\alpha > 0$ the function $-\alpha|S|$ is supermodular. Since the sum of two supermodular functions is supermodular, the result follows. $\square$

[2]Notice that the network H_α has $O(n + t)$ arcs, therefore the running time of [3] is $O(\min(n,t)(n+t)+\min(n,t)^3) = O(nt + \min(n,t)^3)$.

Theorem 3 naturally suggests Algorithm 3. The algorithm will run in a logarithmic number of rounds. In each round we maximize function f_α using Orlin-Supermodular-Opt which takes as input arguments the graph G and the parameter $\alpha > 0$ [43]. We assume for simplicity that within the procedure Orlin-Supermodular-Opt function f is evaluated using an efficient exact triangle counting algorithm [4]. The algorithm of Alon, Yuster and Zwick [4] runs in $O(m^{2\omega/(\omega+1)})$ time where $\omega < 2.3729$ [53]. This suggests the $EO = O(m^{1.4081})$. The overall running time of Algorithm 3 is $O\big((n^5m^{1.4081} + n^6)\log(n)\big)$ and the space usage $O(n + m)$ rather than $O(n + t)$.

Algorithm 3 triangle-densest subgraph(G) [Supermodularity]

- $l \leftarrow 0, u \leftarrow \frac{(n-1)(n-2)}{6}, S^* \leftarrow V$
- **while** $u \geq l + \frac{1}{n(n-1)}$ **do**
  - $\alpha \leftarrow \frac{l+u}{2}$
  - $(val, S) \leftarrow$ Orlin-Supermodular-Opt(G, α)
  - **if** $val < 0$ **then**
    - $u \leftarrow \alpha$
  - **else**
    - $l \leftarrow \alpha$
    - $S^* \leftarrow S$
  - **end if**
  - Return S^*
- **end while**

4.2 A $\frac{1}{3}$-approximation algorithm

In this Section we provide an algorithm for the TDS-PROBLEM which provides a $\frac{1}{3}$-approximation. Our algorithm follows the peeling paradigm, see [8, 18, 40, 36]. Specifically, in each round it removes the vertex which participates in the smallest number of triangles and returns the subgraph that achieves the largest triangle density. The pseudocode is shown in Algorithm 4.

Algorithm 4 Peel-Triangles(G)

- Count the number of triangles t_v for each vertex $v \in V$
- $H_n \leftarrow G$
- **for** $i \leftarrow n$ to 2 **do**
  - Let v be the vertex of G_i of minimum number of triangles
  - $H_{i-1} \leftarrow H_i \backslash v$
- **end for**
- Return H_j that achieves maximum triangle density among H_is, $i = 1, \ldots, n$.

THEOREM 4. *Algorithm 4 is a $\frac{1}{3}$-approximation algorithm for the* TDS-PROBLEM.

PROOF. Let S^* be an optimal set. Let $v \in S^*, |S^*| = s^*$ and $t_A(v)$ be the number of induced triangles by A that v participates in. Then,

$$\tau_G^* = \frac{t(S^*)}{s^*} \geq \frac{t(S^*\backslash\{v\})}{s^*-1} \Leftrightarrow t_{S^*}(v) \geq \tau_G^*,$$

since $t(S^*\backslash\{v\}) = t(S^*) - t_{S^*}(v)$. Consider the iteration before the algorithm removes the first vertex v that belongs in S^*. Call the set of vertices W. Clearly, $S^* \subseteq W$ and for each vertex $u \in W$ the following lower bound holds $t_W(u) \geq t_W(v) \geq t_{S^*}(v) \geq \tau_G^*$ due to the greediness of Algorithm 3. This provides a lower bound on the total number of triangles induced by W

$$t(W) = \frac{1}{3}\sum_{u \in W} t_W(u) \geq \frac{1}{3}|W|\tau_G^* \Rightarrow \frac{t(W)}{|W|} \geq \frac{1}{3}\tau_G^*.$$

To complete the proof, notice that the algorithm returns a subgraph S such that $\tau(S) \geq \tau(W) \geq \frac{1}{3}\tau_G^*$. □

The key difference compared to the DS-PROBLEM peeling algorithm [18] is that when we remove a vertex, the counts of its neighbors may decrease more than 1. Therefore, when vertex v is removed, we update the counts of its neighbors in $O\big(\binom{deg(v)}{2}\big)$ time, by looking how many triangles each of its neighbors has after v is removed. Notice that $O(\sum_v \binom{deg(v)}{2}) = O(mn)$.

4.3 MapReduce Implementation

The MAPREDUCE framework [20] has become the *de facto* standard for processing large-scale datasets. In the following, we show how we can approximate efficiently the TDS-PROBLEM in MAPREDUCE. Before we describe the algorithm, we show that Algorithm 5 for any $\epsilon > 0$ terminates and provides a $\frac{1}{3+3\epsilon}$-approximation. The idea behind this algorithm is to peel vertices in batches [10, 29] rather than one by one.

Algorithm 5 `Peel-Triangles-in-Batches`$(G, \epsilon > 0)$

1: $S_{out}, S \leftarrow V$
2: **while** $S \neq \emptyset$ **do**
3: $\quad A(S) \leftarrow \{i \in S : t_S(i) \leq 3(1+\epsilon)\tau(S)\}$
4: $\quad S \leftarrow S \backslash A(S)$
5: $\quad$**if** $\tau(S) \geq \tau(S_{out})$ **then**
6: $\quad\quad S_{out} \leftarrow S$
7: $\quad$**end if**
8: **end while**
9: Return S_{out}.

LEMMA 4. *For any $\epsilon > 0$, Algorithm 5 provides a $\frac{1}{(3+3\epsilon)}$-approximation to the* TDS-PROBLEM. *Furthermore, it terminates in $O(\log_{1+\epsilon}(n))$ passes.*

PROOF. Let S^* be an optimal solution to the TDS-PROBLEM. As we proved in Theorem 4, for any $v \in S^*$ it is true that $t_{S^*}(v) \geq \tau_G^*$. Furthermore, in each round at least one vertex is removed. To see why, assume for the sake of contradiction that $A(S) = \emptyset$ for some S during the execution of the algorithm. Then, we obtain the contradiction that $3|S|\tau(S) = \sum_{v \in S} t_S(v) \geq (3+3\epsilon)|S|\tau(S)$. Consider the round where the algorithm for the first time removes a vertex $v \in S^*$. Let W be the corresponding set of vertices. Since $v \in A(W)$ is peeled off, we obtain an upper bound on its induced degree, namely $v \in A(W) \Rightarrow t_W(v) \leq (3+3\epsilon)\tau(W)$. Since $S^* \subseteq W$, we obtain

$$(3+3\epsilon)\tau(W) \geq t_W(v) \geq t_{S^*}(v) \geq \tau(S^*),$$

which proves that Algorithm 5 is a $\frac{1}{(3+3\epsilon)}$-approximation to the TDS-PROBLEM. To see why the algorithm terminates in logarithmic number of rounds, notice that

$$3t(S) > \sum_{v \in S\backslash A(S)} t_S(v) \geq (3+3\epsilon)\big(|S| - |A(S)|\big)\frac{t(S)}{|S|} \Leftrightarrow$$

$$|A(S)| \geq \frac{\epsilon}{1+\epsilon}|S| \Leftrightarrow |S\backslash A(S)| \leq \frac{1}{1+\epsilon}|S|.$$

Since S decreases by a factor of $\frac{1}{1+\epsilon}$ in each round, the algorithm terminates in $O(\log_{1+\epsilon}(n)) = O(\frac{\log(n)}{\epsilon})$ rounds. □

MAPREDUCE *Implementation:* Now we are able to describe our algorithm in MAPREDUCE. It uses any of the efficient algorithms of Suri and Vassilvitski [48] as a subroutine to count triangles per vertex in each round. The removal of the vertices which participate in less triangles than the threshold, is done in two rounds, as in [10]. For completeness, we describe the procedure here. The set of vertices S to be peeled off in each round are marked by adding a key-value pair $\langle v; \$\rangle$ for each $v \in S$. Each edge (u, v) is mapped to $\langle u; v\rangle$. The reducer receives all endpoints of the edges incident with v and the symbol \$ in case the vertex is marked for deletion. In case the vertex is marked, then the reduce task returns nothing, otherwise it copies its input. In the second round, we perform the same procedure with the only difference being that we map each edge (u, v) to $\langle v; u\rangle$. Therefore, the edges which remain have both endpoints unmarked. The algorithm runs in $O(\log(n)/\epsilon)$, as it takes $O(\log(n)/\epsilon)$ peeling off rounds, and in each peeling round, constant number of rounds is needed to count triangles per vertex, mark vertices for deletion and remove the corresponding vertex set.

4.4 k-clique Densest Subgraph

We outline that our proposed methods can be adapted to the following generalization of the DS-PROBLEM and the TDS-PROBLEM.

DEFINITION 3 (k-clique-densest subgraph). *Let $G(V, E)$ be an undirected graph. For any $S \subseteq V$ we define its k-clique density $h_k(S)$, $k \geq 2$ as $h_k(S) = \frac{c_k(S)}{s}$, where $c_k(S)$ is the number of k-cliques induced by S and $s = |S|$.*

PROBLEM 2 (K-CLIQUE-DS-PROBLEM). *Given $G(V, E)$, find a subset of vertices S^* such that $h_k(S^*) = h_k^*$ where $h_k^* = \max_{S \subseteq V} h_k(S)$.*

As in the triangle densest subgraph problem, we create a network H parameterized by the value α on which we perform our binary search. The procedure is described in Algorithm 6. The set $\mathcal{C}(G)$ is the set of k-cliques in G. We then invoke Algorithm 1, with the upper bound u set to n^k. Following the analysis of Theorem 1, we see that the K-CLIQUE-DS-PROBLEM is solvable in polynomial time. For instance, using Gusfield's algorithm [31] or [3] in each binary search query we get an overall running time $O\big(n^k + (n|\mathcal{C}(G)| + n^3)\log(n)\big) = O(n^{k+1}\log(n))$. Using the improved result due to Ahuja, Orlin, Stein and Tarjan for parametric max flows in unbalanced bipartite graphs [3], we save the logarithmic factor in the running time.
Furthermore, Algorithm 4 can also be modified, by removing in each round the vertex with the smallest number of k-cliques, to obtain Corollary 2. As the analogy of Theorem 4.

Algorithm 6 `Construct-Network-`k $(G, \alpha, \mathcal{C}(G), k)$

$V(H) \leftarrow \{s\} \cup V(G) \cup \mathcal{C}(G) \cup \{t\}$.
For each vertex $v \in V(G)$ add an arc of capacity 1 to each k-clique c_i it participates in.
For each k-clique $(u_{i_1}, \ldots, u_{i_k}) \in \mathcal{C}(G)$ add arcs to $u_{i_1}, \ldots, u_{i_k}$ of capacity $k-1$.
Add directed arc $(s, v) \in A(H)$ of capacity c_v for each $v \in V(G)$.
Add weighted directed arc $(v, t) \in A(H)$ of capacity $k\alpha$ for each $v \in V(G)$.
Return network $H(V(H), A(H), w), s, t \in V(H)$.

COROLLARY 1. *The algorithm which peels off in each round the vertex with the minimum number of k-cliques and returns the subgraph that achieves the largest k-clique density, is a $\frac{1}{k}$-approximation algorithm for the* K-CLIQUE-DS-PROBLEM.

Similarly, Algorithm 5 and the MAPREDUCE implementation can be modified to solve the K-CLIQUE-DS-PROBLEM. We omit the details.

COROLLARY 2. *The algorithm which peels off in each round the set of vertices with less than $k(1+\epsilon)h(S)$, where $h(S)$ is the k-clique density in that round, terminates in $O(\log_{1+\epsilon}(n))$ rounds and provides a $\frac{1}{k(1+\epsilon)}$-approximation guarantee for the* K-CLIQUE-DS-PROBLEM. *Furthermore, using [23], we obtain an efficient* MAPREDUCE *implementation.*

We illustrate an example where choosing a larger k value yields benefits. Let $G \sim G(n,p)$ be an Erdös-Rényi graph, where $p = p(n)$. Assume that we plant a clique K of size n^γ for some constant $\gamma > 0$. We wish to show a non-trivial range of $p = p(n)$ values such that the following conditions hold: $h_2(C) = \frac{|E(K)|}{|K|} = \frac{\binom{n^\gamma}{2}}{n^\gamma} < \frac{p\binom{n}{2}}{n} = \mathbb{E}[h_2(V)]$, and for $k \geq 3$ $h_k(C) = \frac{\binom{n^\gamma}{k}}{n^\gamma} > \frac{p^{\binom{k}{2}}\binom{n}{k}}{n} = \mathbb{E}[h_k(V)]$.
By simple algebraic manipulation we see that p satisfies both conditions if $O\big(n^{-(1-\gamma)}\big) < p < O\big(n^{-\frac{2}{k}(1-\gamma)}\big)$[3]. Clearly, for larger k values, we allow ourselves a larger range of p values for which we can find the hidden clique in expectation.

Our preliminary experimental results for $k = 4$ indicate that the 4-clique-densest subgraph gets closer to a large near-clique compared to the triangle densest subgraph. However, the gain of moving from the densest subgraph to the triangle densest subgraph with respect to extracting large near-cliques is larger than the gain of moving from the triangle densest subgraph to the 4-clique-densest subgraph.

5. EXPERIMENTAL EVALUATION

Before we present our findings in detail, we summarize them: (i) the TDS-PROBLEM and the proposed algorithms constitute new valuable graph mining primitives for finding large near-cliques, (ii) the $\frac{1}{3}$-approximation algorithm (Algorithm 4) achieves significantly better approximations than the pessimistic $\frac{1}{3}$ guarantee. Also it is significantly faster. (iii) Trying a small range of ϵ values for Algorithm 5 is in general a safer strategy compared to running experiments with fixed choice.

[3] Notice that for this range of p, the graph is connected and the clique number is constant with high probability [15]

5.1 Experimental Setup

The datasets we use are shown in Table 1. All graphs were made simple and undirected by ignoring the edge direction, when the graph is directed, and removing self-loops and multiple edges, if any. The experiments were performed on a single machine, with Intel(R) Core(TM) i5 CPU at 2.40 GHz, with 3.86GB of main memory. We have implemented Algorithm 1 in MATLAB R2011a using a maximum flow implementation due to Kolmogorov and Boykov [16] as our subroutine which runs in time $O(t(n+t)^3)$. This implementation is prohibitively expensive even for small graphs which have a large number of triangles. We have coded the peeling algorithm in C++ using priority queues. As our triangle listing algorithm, we use the simple node iterator algorithm which checks for each vertex the number of edges among its neighbors. The code is publicly available at `http://people.seas.harvard.edu/~babis/code.html`. We measure the quality of each extracted subgraph by two measures: the edge density of the extracted subgraph $f_e = e(S)/\binom{|S|}{2}$ and the output size $|S|$. Notice that when f_e is close to 1, the extracted subgraph is close to being a clique.

5.2 Main Findings

Table 2 shows the results obtained on several popular small- and medium-sized graphs. Each column corresponds to a dataset. The rows correspond to measurements for each method we use to extract a subgraph. Specifically, the first (DS), second ($\frac{1}{2}$-DS), third (TDS) and fourth ($\frac{1}{3}$-TDS) rows correspond to the subgraph extracted by Goldberg's exact algorithm [28] for the DS-PROBLEM, Charikar's $\frac{1}{2}$-approximation algorithm [18] for the DS-PROBLEM, Algorithm 1 and Algorithm 4 for the TDS-PROBLEM respectively. For each optimal extracted subgraph S, we show its size as a fraction of the total number of vertices, the edge density $f_e(S)$, the average degree $2\delta(S) = 2e(S)/|S|$ and the average number of triangles per vertex $3\tau(S) = 3t(S)/|S|$.

We observe that the triangle-densest subgraph is closer to being a near-clique compared to the densest subgraph. A pronounced example is the Football network where the optimal densest subgraph is the whole network with $f_e = 0.0094$, whereas the optimal triangle-densest subgraph is a set of 18 vertices with edge density 0.48. Finally, we observe that the quality of Algorithm's 4 output is very close to the optimal solution and sometimes even better. The same observation holds for the case of Charikar's $\frac{1}{2}$-approximation algorithm [18].

We use the C++ implementation of Algorithm 4 and a C++ implementation of Charikar's $\frac{1}{2}$-approximation algorithm on the rest of the datasets of Table 1. The results are shown in Table 3, up to two decimal digits of accuracy. The ca-HepTh dataset is an exception, as the optimal solutions coincide. We also notice that the run times appear the same for ca-HepTh due to using two decimal digits of accuracy. On other datasets, we observe differences between the two solutions. For instance, for the collaboration network ca-Astro the densest subgraph is a subgraph with 1 184 vertices and $f_e = 0.05$. The triangle-densest subgraph is a clique with 57 vertices. Overall, we verify the fact that the triangle-densest subgraph is closer to being a near-clique. Finally, the run times are shown. Notice that the run times reported for for Algorithm 4 include both the triangle counting and the peeling phase.

Name	Nodes	Edges	Description
Adjnoun	112	425	Generated by processing text data
AS-735	6 475	12 572	Autonomous Systems
AS-caida	26 475	53 381	Autonomous Systems
ca-Astro	17 903	196 972	Co-authorship
ca-GrQC	4 158	13 422	Co-authorship
ca-HepTh	11 204	117 619	Co-authorship
Celegans	297	4 296	Neural network of C. Elegans
DBLP	53 442	255 936	Co-authorship
Epinions	75 877	405 739	Social network
Enron	33 696	180 811	Email
EuAll	224 832	339 925	Email
Football	115	613	NCAA football game network
Karate	34	78	Social network
Lesmis	77	254	Generated by processing text data
Political blogs	1 490	16 715	Generated by processing sales data
Political books	105	441	Blog network
soc-Slashdot0811	77 360	469 180	Person to Person
soc-Slashdot0902	82 168	504 230	Person to Person
wb-cs-Stanford	8 929	26 320	Web Graph
web-Google	855 802	4 291 352	Web Graph
web-NotreDame	325 729	1 090 108	Web Graph
Wiki-vote	7 066	100 736	Wikipedia "who-votes-whom"

Table 1: Datasets used in our experiments.

Method	Measure	Adjnoun	Celegans	Football	Karate	Lesmis	Polblogs	Polbooks
DS	$\frac{\lvert S\rvert}{\lvert V\rvert}(\%)$	42.86	45.8	100	47.1	29.9	19.1	51.4
	2δ	9.58	17.16	10.66	5.25	10.78	55.82	9.40
	f_e	0.20	0.13	0.094	0.35	0.49	0.196	0.18
	3τ	14	45.93	21.12	5.64	41.61	768.87	22.68
$\frac{1}{2}$-DS	$\frac{\lvert S\rvert}{\lvert V\rvert}(\%)$	41.1	42.4	100	52.9	29.9	18.7	57.1
	2δ	9.57	17.1	10.66	5.2	10.78	55.8	9.3
	f_e	0.21	0.14	0.094	0.31	0.49	0.20	0.16
	3τ	14.16	46.5	21.12	5.16	41.61	774.6	22.68
TDS	$\frac{\lvert S\rvert}{\lvert V\rvert}(\%)$	36.6	10.4	15.7	17.7	16.9	8.1	19.1
	2δ	9.37	13.81	8.22	4.67	10.62	55.72	9.34
	f_e	0.23	0.46	0.48	0.93	0.89	0.46	0.50
	3τ	15	56.82	28	8.01	47.31	972.36	25.95
$\frac{1}{3}$-TDS	$\frac{\lvert S\rvert}{\lvert V\rvert}(\%)$	36.6	9.1	15.7	17.7	16.9	8.1	15.2
	2δ	9.37	13.56	8.22	4.67	10.62	55.72	9.13
	f_e	0.23	0.52	0.48	0.93	0.89	0.46	0.61
	3τ	15	56.55	28	8.01	47.31	972.36	25.5

Table 2: Comparison of the extracted subgraphs by the Goldberg's exact algorithm for the DS-PROBLEM (DS), Charikar's $\frac{1}{2}$-approximation algorithm ($\frac{1}{2}$-DS), our exact algorithm for the TDS-PROBLEM (TDS) and our $\frac{1}{3}$-approximation algorithm ($\frac{1}{2}$-TDS). Here, $f_e(S) = e(S)/\binom{|S|}{2}$ is the edge density of the extracted subgraph, $2\delta(S) = 2e(S)/|S|$ is the average degree and $3\tau(S) = 3t(S)/|S|$ is the average number of triangles.

5.3 Exploring parameter ϵ in Algorithm 5

In this Section we present the results of Algorithm 5 on the DBLP graph. This is particularly interesting instance as it indicates that instead of trying to select a good ϵ value, it is worth trying out at least few values, assuming computational resources are available. We range ϵ from 0.1 to 1.8 with a step of 0.1. Figure 1(a) plots the number of rounds Algorithm 5 takes to terminate as a function of ϵ. We observe that even for small ϵ values the number of rounds is 6. The reader should compare this to the upper bound predicted by Lemma 4 which exceeds 100. Figure 1(b) plots the relative ratio *Rel.* $\tau = \frac{\tau(S)}{\tau^*}$ where S is the output of Algorithm 5. For convenience, the lower bound $\frac{1}{3+3\epsilon}$ is plotted with red color.

Besides the ratio $\frac{f_e(S)}{f_e(S^*)}$, figure 1(c) plots also the relative ratio $\frac{f_t(S)}{f_t(S^*)}$ as a function of ϵ. Here $f_t(S) = \frac{t(S)}{\binom{|S|}{3}}$. As we observe, the quality of Algorithm 5 is close to the optimal solution except for $\epsilon = 0.7$ and $\epsilon = 0.8$. By inspecting why this happens we observe that the optimal triangle-densest subgraph is a clique of 44 vertices. It turns out that for $\epsilon = 0.7, 0.8$ the optimal subgraph which is found in the last

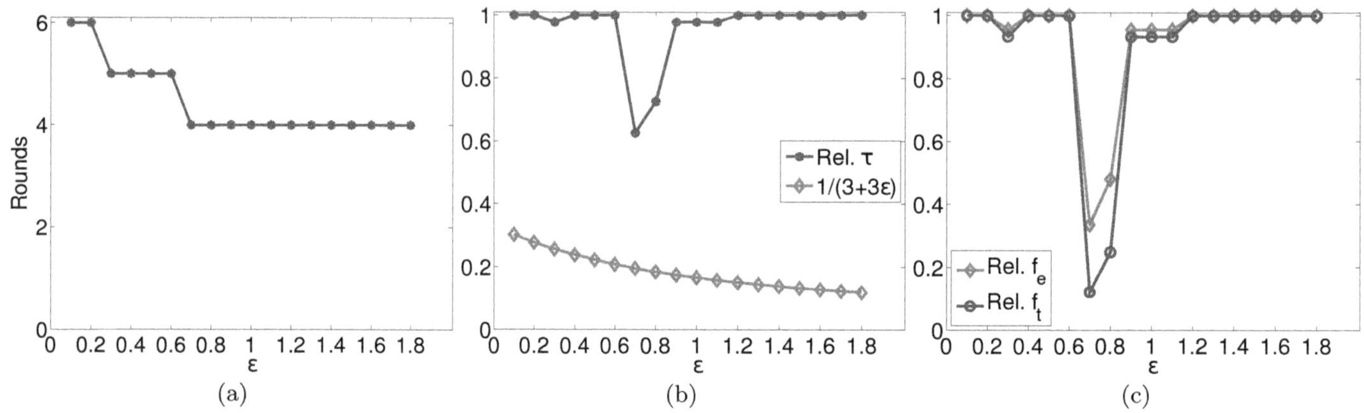

Figure 1: Exploring the trade-off between the number of rounds and accuracy as a function of the parameter ϵ for Algorithm 5. Let S, S^* be the extracted subgraphs by Algorithms 5 and 1 respectively. (a) Number of rounds, (b) relative average triangle density ratio $\frac{\tau(S)}{\tau^*}$ (blue $*$) and the approximation guarantee $1/(3+3\epsilon)$ (red $\diamond$), and (c) relative ratios $\frac{f_e(S)}{f_e(S^*)}, \frac{f_t(S)}{f_t(S^*)}$ as functions of ϵ.

	$\frac{1}{2}$-DS			$\frac{1}{3}$-TDS		
	$\lvert S\rvert$	f_e	T	$\lvert S\rvert$	f_e	T
AS-735	59	0.28	0.00	13	0.8	0.07
AS-caida	143	0.14	0.02	27	0.52	0.63
ca-Astro	1 184	0.05	0.06	57	1	1.42
ca-GrQC	42	0.79	0.00	14	0.89	0.02
ca-HepTh	32	1	0.02	32	1	0.02
Epinions	999	0.121	0.08	431	0.256	8.75
Enron	555	0.14	0.02	390	0.19	2.01
EuAll	507	0.13	0.08	200	0.29	9.52
soc-Slashdot0811	207	0.41	0.13	253	0.49	6.85
soc-Slashdot0902	219	0.40	0.16	173	0.50	7.72
wb-cs-Stanford	84	0.64	0.48	26	0.80	0.67
web-Google	240	0.23	2.54	120	0.44	79.5
web-NotreDame	1 367	0.115	0.50	457	0.345	16.3
Wiki-vote	846	0.11	0.00	464	0.80	0.19

Table 3: Comparison of the extracted subgraphs by the $\frac{1}{2}$-approximation algorithm of Charikar and the $\frac{1}{3}$-approximation algorithm, Algorithm 4. The respective run times are shown in seconds.

round of the execution of the algorithm (the latter happens for all ϵ values) consists of 98 and 74 vertices which contain as a subgraph the optimal K_{44}. For other values of ϵ, the subgraph in the last round is either the optimal K_{44} or close to it, with few more extra vertices. This example shows the potential danger of using a single value for ϵ, suggesting that trying out a small number of ϵ values can be significantly beneficial in terms of the approximation quality.

6. APPLICATION: ORGANIZING COCKTAIL PARTIES

A graph mining problem that comes up in various applications is the following: given a set of vertices $Q \subseteq V$, find a dense subgraph containing Q. We refer to this type of graph mining problems as *cocktail problems*, due to the following motivation, c.f. [47]. Suppose that a set of people Q wants to organize a cocktail party. How do they invite other people to the party so that the set of all the participants, including Q, are as similar as possible? A variation of the TDS-PROBLEM which addresses this graph mining problem follows.

PROBLEM 3 (CONSTRAINED-TDS-PROBLEM). *Given a graph $G(V, E)$ and $Q \subseteq V$, find the subset of vertices S^* that maximizes the triangle density such that $Q \subseteq S^*$,*

$$S^* = \arg \max_{Q \subseteq S \subseteq V} \tau(S).$$

The CONSTRAINED-TDS-PROBLEM can be solved by modifying our proposed algorithms accordingly. A useful corollary follows.

COROLLARY 3. *The* CONSTRAINED-TDS-PROBLEM *is solvable in polynomial time by adding arcs from s to $v \in A$ of large enough capacities, e.g., capacities equal to $n^3 + 1$ are sufficiently large. Furthermore, the peeling algorithm which avoids removing vertices from Q is a $\frac{1}{3}$-approximation algorithm for the* CONSTRAINED-TDS-PROBLEM.

In the following we evaluate the $\frac{1}{3}$-approximation algorithm on two datasets. The two experiments indicate two different types of performances that should be expected in real-world applications. The first is a positive whereas the second is negative case. Both experiments here serve as sanity checks[4]

Political vote data. We obtain Senate data for the first session (2006) of the 109th congress which spanned the period from January 3, 2005 to January 3, 2007, during the fifth and sixth years of George W. Bush's presidency [1]. In this Congress, there were 55, 45 and 1 Republican, Democratic and independent senators respectively. The dataset can be downloaded from the US Senate web page http://www.senate.gov. We preprocess the dataset in the following way: we add an edge between two senators if among the bills for which they both casted a vote, they voted at least 80% of the times in the same way. The resulting graph has 100 vertices and 2034 edges. We run the

[4] For instance, by preprocessing the political vote data from a matrix form to a graph using a threshold for edge additions, results in information loss.

$\frac{1}{3}$-approximation algorithm on this graph using as our set Q the first three republicans according to lexicographic order: Alexander (R-TN), Allard (R-CO) and Allen (R-VA). We obtain at our output a subgraph consisting of 47 vertices. By inspecting their party, we find that 100% of them are Republicans. This shows that our algorithm in this case succeeds in finding the large majority of the cluster of republicans. It is interesting that the 8 remaining Republicans do not enter the triangle-densest subgraph . A careful inspection of the data, c.f. [2], indicates that 6 republicans agree with the party vote on at most 79% of the bills, and 8 of them on at most 85% of the bills.

DBLP graph. We input as a query set Q a set of scientists who have established themselves in theory and algorithm design: Richard Karp, Christos Papadimitriou, Mihalis Yannakakis and Santosh Vempala. The algorithm returns at its output the query set and a set S of 44 vertices corresponding to a clique of (mostly) Italian computer scientists. We list a subset of the 44 vertices here: M. Bencivenni, M. Canaparo, F. Capannini, L. Carota, M. Carpene, R. Veraldi, P. Veronesi, M. Vistoli, R. Zappi. The output graph induced by $S \cup Q$ is disconnected. Therefore, this can be easily explained because of the following (folklore) inequality, given that $|Q| < |S|$ in our example.

Claim 1. *Let a, b, c, d be non-negative. Then,*

$$\max\left(\frac{a}{c}, \frac{b}{d}\right) \geq \frac{a+b}{c+d} \geq \min\left(\frac{a}{c}, \frac{b}{d}\right) \tag{3}$$

In our example, we get $a = t(S), c = |S|, b = t(Q), d = |Q|$. In such a scenario, where the output consists of the union of a dense subgraph and the query set Q, an algorithm which builds itself up from Q -assuming Q is not an independent set- to V by adding vertices which create as many triangles as possible and returning the maximum density subgraph, rather than peeling vertices from V down to Q should be preferred in practice, see also [49].

7. CONCLUSION

In this work we introduce the average triangle density as a novel objective for attacking the important problem of finding near-cliques. We propose exact and approximation algorithms. Furthermore, our techniques can solve the more general problem of maximizing the k-clique density. Experimentally we verify the value of the TDS-Problem as a novel addition to the graph mining toolbox.

Our work leaves numerous problems open, including the following: (a) Can we obtain a faster exact algorithm by improving the space usage of the network construction? (b) Can we use sparsification to obtain faster approximate solutions [44]?

8. REFERENCES

[1] http://tinyurl.com/bwgpka. 6

[2] http://tinyurl.com/zgdam. 6

[3] R. K. Ahuja, J. B. Orlin, C. Stein, and R. E. Tarjan. Improved algorithms for bipartite network flow. *SIAM Journal on Computing*, 23(5):906–933, 1994. 4.1.1, 2, 4.4

[4] N. Alon, R. Yuster, and U. Zwick. Finding and counting given length cycles. *Algorithmica*, 17(3):209–223, 1997. 2, 4.1.2

[5] R. Andersen and K. Chellapilla. Finding dense subgraphs with size bounds. In *WAW*, 2009. 2

[6] A. Angel, N. Sarkas, N. Koudas, and D. Srivastava. Dense subgraph maintenance under streaming edge weight updates for real-time story identification. *Proc. VLDB Endow.*, 5(6):574–585, Feb. 2012. 1

[7] Y. Asahiro, R. Hassin, and K. Iwama. Complexity of finding dense subgraphs. *Discr. Ap. Math.*, 121(1-3), 2002. 1

[8] Y. Asahiro, K. Iwama, H. Tamaki, and T. Tokuyama. Greedily finding a dense subgraph. *J. Algorithms*, 34(2), 2000. (document), 2, 4.2

[9] G. D. Bader and C. W. Hogue. An automated method for finding molecular complexes in large protein interaction networks. *BMC bioinformatics*, 4(1):2, 2003. 1

[10] B. Bahmani, R. Kumar, and S. Vassilvitskii. Densest subgraph in streaming and mapreduce. *Proceedings of the VLDB Endowment*, 5(5):454–465, 2012. (document), 2, 4.3, 4.3

[11] V. Batagelj and M. Zaversnik. An O(m) algorithm for cores decomposition of networks. *Arxiv*, arXiv.cs/0310049, 2003. 2

[12] A. Bhaskara, M. Charikar, E. Chlamtac, U. Feige, and A. Vijayaraghavan. Detecting high log-densities: an $O(n^{1/4})$ approximation for densest k-subgraph. In *Proceedings of the 42nd ACM symposium on Theory of computing*, pages 201–210. ACM, 2010. 2

[13] S. Bhattacharya, M. Henziger, D. Nanongkai, and C.E. Tsourakakis. Space- and time-efficient algorithms for maintaining dense subgraphs on one-pass dynamic streams. *STOC*, 2015. 2

[14] A. Björklund, R. Pagh, V. Williams Vassilevska, and U. Zwick. Listing triangles. In *Proceedings of 41st International Colloquium on Automata, Languages and Programming (ICALP)*, 2014. 2, 4.1.1, 4.1.1

[15] B. Bollobás. *Random graphs*, volume 73 of *Cambridge Studies in Advanced Mathematics*. Cambridge University Press, Cambridge, second edition, 2001. 3

[16] Y. Boykov and V. Kolmogorov. An experimental comparison of min-cut/max-flow algorithms for energy minimization in vision. *Pattern Analysis and Machine Intelligence, IEEE Transactions on*, 26(9):1124–1137, 2004. 5.1

[17] G. Buehrer and K. Chellapilla. A scalable pattern mining approach to web graph compression with communities. In *WSDM*, pages 95–106. ACM, 2008. 1

[18] M. Charikar. Greedy approximation algorithms for finding dense components in a graph. In *APPROX*, 2000. (document), 1, 2, 4.1, 4.2, 4.2, 5.2

[19] E. Cohen, E. Halperin, H. Kaplan, and U. Zwick. Reachability and distance queries via 2-hop labels. In *SODA*, 2002. 1

[20] J. Dean and S. Ghemawat. Mapreduce: simplified data processing on large clusters. *Commun. ACM*, 51(1):107–113, Jan. 2008. 4.3

[21] A. Epasto and S. Lattanzi and M. Sozio. Efficient Densest Subgraph Computation in Evolving Graphs. *WWW'15* (to appear), 2015. 2

[22] U. Feige, G. Kortsarz, and D. Peleg. The dense k-subgraph problem. *Algorithmica*, 29(3), 2001. 2

[23] I. Finocchi, M. Finocchi, and E. G. Fusco. Counting small cliques in mapreduce. *arXiv preprint arXiv:1403.0734*, 2014. 2

[24] E. Fratkin, B. T. Naughton, D. L. Brutlag, and S. Batzoglou. Motifcut: regulatory motifs finding with maximum density subgraphs. *Bioinformatics*, 22(14):e150–e157, 2006. 1

[25] G. Gallo, M. D. Grigoriadis, and R. E. Tarjan. A fast parametric maximum flow algorithm and applications. *SIAM Journal on Computing*, 18(1):30–55, 1989. 1, 2, 4.1.1

[26] D. Gibson, R. Kumar, and A. Tomkins. Discovering large dense subgraphs in massive graphs. In *VLDB*, 2005. 1

[27] A. Gionis, F. Junqueira, V. Leroy, M. Serafini, and I. Weber. Piggybacking on social networks. *Proc. VLDB Endow.*, 6(6):409–420, Apr. 2013. 1

[28] A. V. Goldberg. Finding a maximum density subgraph. Technical report, University of California at Berkeley, 1984. 1, 2, 4.1.1, 5.2

[29] M. T. Goodrich and P. Pszona. External-memory network analysis algorithms for naturally sparse graphs. In *Algorithms-ESA 2011*, pages 664–676. Springer, 2011. 4.3

[30] M. Grötschel, L. Lovász, and A. Schrijver. *Geometric algorithms and combinatorial optimization*. Springer, Berlin, 1988. 4.1.2

[31] D. Gusfield. Computing the strength of a graph. *SIAM Journal on Computing*, 20(4):639–654, 1991. 4.1.1, 4.4

[32] J. Hastad. Clique is hard to approximate within $n^{1-\epsilon}$. *Acta Mathematica*, 182(1), 1999. 1

[33] A. Itai and M. Rodeh. Finding a minimum circuit in a graph. *SIAM Journal on Computing*, 7(4):413–423, 1978. 2, 4.1.1, 4.1.1

[34] S. Iwata, L. Fleischer, and S. Fujishige. A combinatorial strongly polynomial algorithm for minimizing submodular functions. *Journal of the ACM (JACM)*, 48(4):761–777, 2001. 4.1.2

[35] M. Jha, C. Seshadhri, and A. Pinar. A space efficient streaming algorithm for triangle counting using the birthday paradox. In *Proceedings of the 19th ACM SIGKDD international conference on Knowledge discovery and data mining*, pages 589–597. ACM, 2013. 2

[36] J. Jiang, M. Mitzenmacher, and J. Thaler. Parallel peeling algorithms. *arXiv preprint arXiv:1302.7014*, 2013. 4.2

[37] R. Jin, Y. Xiang, N. Ruan, and D. Fuhry. 3-hop: a high-compression indexing scheme for reachability query. In *SIGMOD*, 2009. 1

[38] R. Kannan and V. Vinay. Analyzing the structure of large graphs, 1999. 2

[39] H. Karloff, S. Suri, and S. Vassilvitskii. A model of computation for mapreduce. In *SODA*, pages 938–948. Society for Industrial and Applied Mathematics, 2010. 1

[40] S. Khuller and B. Saha. On finding dense subgraphs. In *ICALP*, 2009. 1, 2, 4.2

[41] M. N. Kolountzakis, G. L. Miller, R. Peng, and T. C. E. Efficient triangle counting in large graphs via degree-based vertex partitioning. *Internet Mathematics*, 8(1-2):161–185, 2012. 2

[42] L. Lovász. Submodular functions and convexity. In *Mathematical Programming The State of the Art*, pages 235–257. Springer, 1983. 4.1.2

[43] J. B. Orlin. A faster strongly polynomial time algorithm for submodular function minimization. *Mathematical Programming*, 118(2):237–251, 2009. 2, 4.1.2

[44] R. Pagh and C.E. Tsourakakis. Colorful triangle counting and a mapreduce implementation. *Information Processing Letters*, 112(7):277–281, 2012. 2, 7

[45] A. D. Sarma, A. Lall, D. Nanongkai, and A. Trehan. Dense subgraphs on dynamic networks. In *Distributed Computing*, pages 151–165. Springer, 2012. 2

[46] A. Schrijver. A combinatorial algorithm minimizing submodular functions in strongly polynomial time. *Journal of Combinatorial Theory, Series B*, 80(2):346–355, 2000. 4.1.2

[47] M. Sozio and A. Gionis. The community-search problem and how to plan a successful cocktail party. In *KDD*, pages 939–948. ACM, 2010. 6

[48] S. Suri and S. Vassilvitskii. Counting triangles and the curse of the last reducer. In *WWW*, pages 607–614. ACM, 2011. 1, 4.3

[49] C.E. Tsourakakis, F. Bonchi, A. Gionis, F. Gullo, and M. Tsiarli. Denser than the densest subgraph: extracting optimal quasi-cliques with quality guarantees. In *KDD*, pages 104–112. ACM, 2013. 1, 2, 6

[50] C. E. Tsourakakis. A novel approach to finding near-cliques: The triangle-densest subgraph problem. *arXiv preprint arXiv:1405.1477*, 2014. 4.1

[51] C. E. Tsourakakis, M. N. Kolountzakis, and G. L. Miller. Triangle sparsifiers. *J. Graph Algorithms Appl.*, 15(6):703–726, 2011. 2

[52] N. Wang, J. Zhang, K.-L. Tan, and A. K. Tung. On triangulation-based dense neighborhood graph discovery. *Proceedings of the VLDB Endowment*, 4(2):58–68, 2010. 2

[53] V. V. Williams. Multiplying matrices faster than coppersmith-winograd. In *STOC*, pages 887–898. ACM, 2012. 2, 4.1.1, 4.1.2

[54] Y. Zhang and S. Parthasarathy. Extracting analyzing and visualizing triangle k-core motifs within networks. In *ICDE*, pages 1049–1060. IEEE, 2012. 2

GERBIL – General Entity Annotator Benchmarking Framework

Ricardo Usbeck*
Leipzig University, IFI/AKSW
Unister GmbH, Leipzig
usbeck@informatik.uni-leipzig.de

Michael Röder*
Leipzig University, IFI/AKSW
Unister GmbH, Leipzig
roeder@informatik.uni-leipzig.de

Axel-Cyrille Ngonga Ngomo*
Leipzig University, IFI/AKSW
Leipzig (Germany)
ngonga@informatik.uni-leipzig.de

ABSTRACT

The need to bridge between the unstructured data on the Document Web and the structured data on the Web of Data has led to the development of a considerable number of annotation tools. However, these tools are currently still hard to compare since the published evaluation results are calculated on diverse datasets and evaluated based on different measures. We present GERBIL, an evaluation framework for semantic entity annotation. The rationale behind our framework is to provide developers, end users and researchers with easy-to-use interfaces that allow for the agile, fine-grained and uniform evaluation of annotation tools on multiple datasets. By these means, we aim to ensure that both tool developers and end users can derive meaningful insights pertaining to the extension, integration and use of annotation applications. In particular, GERBIL provides comparable results to tool developers so as to allow them to easily discover the strengths and weaknesses of their implementations with respect to the state of the art. With the permanent experiment URIs provided by our framework, we ensure the reproducibility and archiving of evaluation results. Moreover, the framework generates data in machine-processable format, allowing for the efficient querying and post-processing of evaluation results. Finally, the tool diagnostics provided by GERBIL allows deriving insights pertaining to the areas in which tools should be further refined, thus allowing developers to create an informed agenda for extensions and end users to detect the right tools for their purposes. GERBIL aims to become a focal point for the state of the art, driving the research agenda of the community by presenting comparable objective evaluation results.

*Additional authors are listed at the end of the article.

WWW 2015, May 18–22, 2015, Florence, Italy.
ACM 978-1-4503-3469-3/15/05.
http://dx.doi.org/10.1145/2736277.2741626.

Categories and Subject Descriptors

I.2.7 [**Natural Language Processing**]: Text analysis

Keywords

Semantic Entity Annotation System; Reusability; Archivability; Benchmarking Framework

1. INTRODUCTION

The implementation of the original vision behind the Semantic Web demands the development of approaches and frameworks for the seamless extraction of structured data from text. While manifold annotation tools have been developed over the last years to address (some of) the subtasks related to the extraction of structured data from unstructured data [13, 17, 24, 25, 27, 32, 35, 41, 44], the provision of comparable results for these tools remains a tedious problem. The issue of comparability of results is not to be regarded as being intrinsic to the annotation task. Indeed, it is now well established that scientists spend between 60 and 80% of their time preparing data for experiments [14, 18, 31]. Data preparation being such a tedious problem in the annotation domain is mostly due to the different formats of the gold standards as well as the different data representations across reference datasets. These restrictions have led to authors evaluating their approaches on datasets (1) that are available to them and (2) for which writing a parser as well as of an evaluation tool can be carried out with reasonable effort. In addition, a large number of quality measures have been developed and used actively across the annotation research community to evaluate the same task, leading to the results across publications on the same topics not being easily comparable. For example, while some authors publish macro-F-measures and simply call them F-measures, others publish micro-F-measures for the same purpose, leading to significant discrepancies across the scores. The same holds for the evaluation of how well entities match. Indeed, partial matches and complete matches have been used in previous evaluations of annotation tools [7, 39]. This heterogeneous landscape of tools, datasets and measures leads to a poor repeatability of experiments, which makes the evaluation of the real performance of novel approaches against the state of the art rather difficult.

The insights above have led to a movement towards the creation of frameworks to ease the evaluation of solutions that address the same annotation problem [5, 7]. In this paper, we present GERBIL – a general entity annotator benchmark –, a community-driven effort to enable the continuous evaluation of annotation tools. GERBIL is an open-source and extensible framework that allows evaluating tools against (currently) 9 different annotators on 11 different datasets within 6 different experiment types. By integrating such a large number of datasets, experiment types and frameworks, GERBIL allows users to evaluate their tools against other semantic entity annotation systems (short: entity annotation systems) by using exactly the same setting, leading to fair comparisons based on exactly the same measures. While the evaluation core of GERBIL is based on the BAT-framework [7], our approach goes beyond the state of the art in several respects:

- GERBIL provides *persistent URLs* for experimental settings. Hence, by using GERBIL for experiments, tool developers can ensure that the settings for their experiments (measures, datasets, versions of the reference frameworks, etc.) can be reconstructed in a unique manner in future works.
- Through experiment URLs, GERBIL also addresses the problem of *archiving* experimental results and allows end users to gather all pieces of information required to choose annotation frameworks for practical applications.
- GERBIL aims to be a *central repository for annotation results* without being a central point of failure: While we make experiment URLs available, we also provide users directly with their results to ensure that they use them locally without having to rely on GERBIL.
- The results of GERBIL are published in a *machine-readable format*. In particular, our use of DataID [2] and DataCube [9] to denote tools and datasets ensures that results can be easily combined and queried (for example to study the evolution of the performance of frameworks) while the exact configuration of the experiments remains uniquely reconstructable. By these means, we also tackle the problem of *reproducibility*.
- Through the provision of results on different datasets of different types and the provision of results on a simple user interface, GERBIL also provides means to quickly gain an overview of the current performance of annotation tools, thus providing (1) developers with insights pertaining to the type of data on which their accuracy needs improvement and (2) end users with insights allowing them to choose the right tool for the tasks at hand.
- With GERBIL we introduce the notion of knowledge base-agnostic benchmarking of entity annotation systems through generalized experiment types. By these means, we allow benchmarking tools against reference datasets from any domain grounded in any reference knowledge base.

To ensure that the GERBIL framework is useful to both end users and tool developers, its architecture and interface were designed with the following principles in mind:

- **Easy integration of annotators**: We provide a wrapping interface that allows annotators to be evaluated via their REST interface. In particular, we integrated 6 additional annotators not evaluated against each other in previous works (e.g., [7]).
- **Easy integration of datasets**: We also provide means to gather datasets for evaluation directly from data services such as DataHub.[1] In particular, we added 6 new datasets to GERBIL.
- **Easy addition of new measures**: The evaluation measures used by GERBIL are implemented as interfaces. Thus, the framework can be easily extended with novel measures devised by the annotation community.
- **Extensibility**: GERBIL is provided as an open-source platform[2] that can be extended by members of the community both to new tasks and different purposes.
- **Diagnostics**: The interface of the tool was designed to provide developers with means to easily detect aspects in which their tool(s) need(s) to be improved.
- **Portability of results**: We generate human- and machine-readable results to ensure maximum usefulness and portability of the results generated by our framework.

In the rest of this paper, we present and evaluate GERBIL. We begin by giving an overview of related work. Thereafter, we present the GERBIL framework. We focus in particular on how annotators and datasets can be added to GERBIL and give a short overview of the annotators and tools that are currently included in the framework. We then present an evaluation of the framework that aims to quantify the effort necessary to include novel annotators and datasets to the framework. We conclude with a discussion of the current state of GERBIL and a presentation of future work. More information can be found at our project webpage `http://gerbil.aksw.org` and at the code repository page `https://github.com/AKSW/gerbil`. The online version of GERBIL can be accessed at `http://gerbil.aksw.org/gerbil`.

2. RELATED WORK

Named Entity Recognition and Entity Linking have gained significant momentum with the growth of Linked Data and structured knowledge bases. Over the last few years, the problem of result comparability has thus led to the development of a handful of frameworks.

The BAT-framework [7] is designed to facilitate the benchmarking of named entity recognition (NER), named entity disambiguation (NED) – also known as linking (NEL) – and concept tagging approaches. BAT compares seven existing entity annotation approaches using Wikipedia as reference. Moreover, it defines six different task types, five different matchings and six evaluation measures providing five datasets. Rizzo et al. [35] present a state-of-the-art study of NER and NEL systems for annotating newswire and micropost documents using well-known benchmark datasets, namely CoNLL2003 and Microposts 2013 for NER as well

[1] `http://datahub.io`

[2] Available at `http://gerbil.aksw.org`.

as AIDA/CoNLL and Microposts2014 [3] for NED. The authors propose a common schema, named the NERD ontology,[3] to align the different taxonomies used by various extractors. To tackle the disambiguation ambiguity, they propose a method to identify the closest DBpedia resource by (exact-)matching the entity mention.

Over the course of the last 25 years several challenges, workshops and conference dedicated themselves to the comparable evaluation of information extraction (IE) systems. Starting in 1993, the Message Understanding Conference (MUC) introduced a first systematic comparison of information extraction approaches [42]. Ten years later, the Conference on Computational Natural Language Learning (CoNLL) started to offer a shared task on named entity recognition and published the CoNLL corpus [43]. In addition, the Automatic Content Extraction (ACE) challenge [10], organized by NIST, evaluated several approaches but was discontinued in 2008. Since 2009, the text analytics conference hosts the workshop on knowledge base population (TAC-KBP) [22] where mainly linguistic-based approaches are published. The Senseval challenge, originally concerned with classical NLP disciplines, has widened its focus in 2007 and changed its name to SemEval to account for the recently recognized impact of semantic technologies [19]. The Making Sense of Microposts workshop series (#Microposts) established in 2013 an entity recognition and in 2014 an entity linking challenge thereby focusing on tweets and microposts [37]. In 2014, Carmel et al. [5] introduced one of the first Web-based evaluation systems for NER and NED and the centerpiece of the entity recognition and disambiguation (ERD) challenge. Here, all frameworks are evaluated against the same unseen dataset and provided with corresponding results.

GERBIL goes beyond the state of the art by extending the BAT-framework as well as [35] in several dimensions to enhance reproducibility, diagnostics and publishability of entity annotation systems. In particular, we provide 6 additional datasets and 6 additional annotators. The framework addresses the lack of treatment of NIL values within the BAT-framework and provides more wrapping approaches for annotators and datasets. Moreover, GERBIL provides persistent URLs for experiment results, unique URIs for frameworks and datasets, a machine-readable output and automatic dataset updates from data portals. Thus, it allows for a holistic comparison of existing annotators while simplifying the archiving of experimental results. Moreover, our framework offers opportunities for the fast and simple evaluation of entity annotation system prototypes via novel NIF-based [15] interfaces, which are designed to simplify the exchange of data and binding of services.

3. THE GERBIL FRAMEWORK

3.1 Architecture Overview

GERBIL abides by a service-oriented architecture driven by the model-view-controller pattern (see Figure 1). Entity annotation systems, datasets and configurations like experiment type, matching or measure are implemented as controller interfaces easily pluggable to the core controller. The output of experiments as well as descriptions of the various components are stored in a serverless database for fast deployment. Finally, the view component displays configuration options respectively renders experiment results delivered by the main controller communication with the diverse interfaces and the database.

[3]`http://nerd.eurecom.fr/ontology`

3.2 Features

Experiments run in our framework can be configured in several manners. In the following, we present some of the most important parameters of experiments available in GERBIL.

3.2.1 Experiment types

An experiment type defines the way used to solve a certain problem when extracting information. Cornolti et al.'s [7] BAT-framework offers six different experiment types, namely (scored) annotation (S/A2KB), disambiguation (D2KB) – also known as linking –, (scored respectively ranked) concept annotation (S/R/C2KB) of texts. In [35], the authors propose two types of experiments, focusing on highlighting the strengths and weaknesses of the analyzed systems. Thereby, performing *i)* entity recognition, i.e., the detection of the exact match of the pair entity mention and type (e.g., detecting the mention *Barack Obama* and typing it as a *Person*), and *ii)* entity linking, where an exact match of the mention is given and the associated DBpedia URI has to be linked (e.g., locating a resource in DBpedia which describes the mention *Barack Obama*). This work differs from the previous one for experimenting in entity recognition, and on annotating entities to a RDF knowledge base.

GERBIL reuses the six experiments provided by the BAT-framework and extends them by the idea to not only link to Wikipedia but to any knowledge base K. One major formal update of the measures in GERBIL is that in addition to implementing experiment types from previous frameworks, it also measures the influence of NIL annotations, i.e., the linking of entities that are recognized as such but cannot be linked to any resource from the reference knowledge base K. For example, the string **`Ricardo Usbeck`** can be recognized as a person name by several tools but cannot be linked to Wikipedia/DBpedia, as Ricardo does not have a URI in these reference datasets. Our framework extends the experiments types of [7] as follows: Let $m = (s, l, d, c) \in M$ denote an entity mention in document $d \in D$ with start position s, length l and confidence score $c \in [0, 1]$. Note that some frameworks might not return (1) a position s or a length l for a mention, in which case we set $s = 0$ and $l = 0$; (2) a score c, in which case we set $c = 1$.

We implement six types of experiments:

1. **D2KB**: The goal of this experiment type is to map a set of *given* entities mentions (i.e., a subset $\mu \subseteq M$) to entities from a given knowledge base or to NIL. Formally, this is equivalent to finding a mapping $a : \mu \rightarrow K \cup \{NIL\}$. In the classical setting for this task, the start position, the length and the score of the mentions m_i are not taken into consideration.

2. **A2KB**: This task is the classical NER/D task, thus an extension of the D2KB task. Here two functions are to be found. First, the entity mentions need to be extracted from a document set D. To this end, an extraction function $ex : D \rightarrow 2^M$ must be computed. The aim of the second step is then to match the results

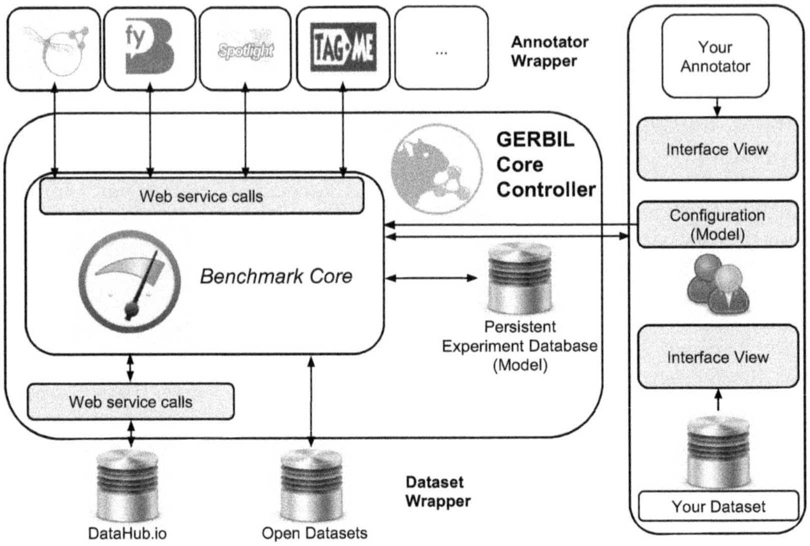

Figure 1: Overview of GERBIL's abstract architecture. Interfaces to users and providers of datasets and annotators are marked in blue.

of ex to entities from $K \cup \{NIL\}$ by devising a function a as in the D2KB task.

3. **Sa2KB**: Sa2KB is an extension of A2KB where the scores $c_i \in [0,1]$ of the mentions detected by the approach are taken into consideration. These scores are then used during the evaluation.

4. **C2KB**: The concept tagging task C2KB aims to detect entities when given a document. Formally, the tagging function tag simply returns a subset of K for each input document d.

5. **Sc2KB**: This task is an extension of C2KB where the tagging function returns a subset of $K \times [0,1]$ for each input document d.

6. **Rc2KB**: In this particular extension of C2KB, the tagging function returns a sorted list of resources from K, i.e., an element of K^*, where $K^* = \bigcup_{i=0}^{\infty} K^i$.

With this extension, our framework can now deal with gold standard datasets and annotators that link to any knowledge base, e.g., DBpedia, BabelNet [30] etc., as long as the necessary identifiers are URIs. We were thus able to implement 6 new gold standard datasets usable for each experiment type, cf. Section 3.3, and 6 new annotators linking entities to any knowledge base instead of solely Wikipedia like in previous works, cf. Section 3.2.4. With this extensible interface, GERBIL can be extended to deal with supplementary experiment types, e.g., entity salience [7], entity detection [39], typing [35], word sense disambiguation (WSD) [27] and relation extraction [39]. These categories of experiment types will be added to GERBIL in next versions.

3.2.2 *Matching*

A matching defines which conditions the result of an annotator has to fulfill to be a correct result. In case of existing redirections, we assume an implicit matching function to account for the many-to-one relation [7]. The first matching type M used for the C2KB, Rc2KB and Sc2KB experiments is the *strong entity matching*. Here, each mention is mapped to an entity of the knowledge base K via a matching function f with $f(m) \in K \cup \{NIL\}$. Following this matching, a single entity mention $m = (s,l,d,c)$ returned by the annotator is correct iff it matches exactly with one of the entity mentions $m' = (s',l',d,c')$ in the gold standard $G(d)$ of d [7]. Formally,

$$M(m,G) = \begin{cases} 1 & \text{iff } \exists m' \in G, f(m) = f(m'), \\ 0 & \text{else.} \end{cases} \quad (1)$$

For the D2KB experiments, the matching is expanded to the *strong annotation matching* and includes the correct position of the entity mention inside the document:

$$M_e(m,G) = \begin{cases} 1 & \text{iff } \exists m' \in G : f(m) = f(m') \wedge s = s' \wedge \\ & l = l', \\ 0 & \text{else.} \end{cases} \quad (2)$$

The strong annotation matching can be used for A2KB and Sa2KB experiments, too. However, in practice this exact matching can be misleading. A document can contain a gold standard named entity like "President Barack Obama" while the result of an annotator only marks "Barack Obama" as named entity. Using an exact matching leads to weighting this result as wrong while a human might rate it as correct. Therefore, the *weak annotation matching* relaxes the conditions of the strong annotation matching. Thus, a correct annotation has to be linked to the same entity and must overlap the annotation of the gold standard:

$$M_w(m,G) = \begin{cases} 1 & \text{iff } \exists m' \in G, f(m) = f(m') \wedge (\\ & (s \le s' \wedge (s+l) \le (s'+l')) \\ & \vee (s \ge s' \wedge (s+l) \ge (s'+l')) \\ & \vee (s \le s' \wedge (s+l) \ge (s'+l')) \\ & \vee (s \ge s' \wedge (s+l) \le (s'+l'))) \\ 0 & \text{else.} \end{cases} \quad (3)$$

3.2.3 Measures

Currently, GERBIL offers six measures subdivided into two groups and derived from the BAT-framework, namely the micro- and the macro-group of precision, recall and f-measure. At the moment, those measures ignore NIL annotations, i.e., if a gold standard dataset contains entities that are not contained in the target knowledge base K and an annotator detects the entity and links it to any URI, emerging novel URI or NIL, this will always result in a false-positive evaluation. To alleviate this problem, GERBIL allows adding additional measures to evaluate the results of annotators regarding the heterogeneous landscape of gold standard datasets.

3.2.4 Annotators

GERBIL aims to reduce the amount of work required to compare existing as well as novel annotators in a comprehensive and reproducible way. To this end, we provide two main approaches to evaluating entity annotation systems with GERBIL.

1. **BAT-framework Adapter**

   Within BAT, annotators can be implemented by wrapping using a Java-based interface. Since GERBIL is based on the BAT-framework, annotators of this framework can be added to GERBIL easily. Due to the community effort behind GERBIL, we could raise the number of published annotators from 5 to 9. We investigated the effort to implement a BAT-framework adapter in contrast to evaluation efforts done without a structured evaluation framework in Section 4.

2. **NIF-based Services**: GERBIL implements means to understand NIF-based [15] communication over webservice in two ways. First, if the server-side implementation of annotators understands NIF-documents as input and output format, GERBIL and the framework can simply exchange NIF-documents.[4] Thus, novel NIF-based annotators can be deployed efficiently into GERBIL and use a more robust communication format compared to the amount of work necessary for deploying and writing a BAT-framework adapter. Second, if developers do not want to publish their APIs or write source code, GERBIL offers the possibility for NIF-based webservices to be tested online by providing their URI and name only.[5] GERBIL does not store these connections in terms of API keys or URLs but still offers the opportunity of persistent experiment results.

[4]We describe the exact requirements to the structure of the NIF document on our project website's wiki as NIF offers several ways to build a NIF-based document or corpus.

[5]`http://gerbil.aksw.org/gerbil/config`

Currently, GERBIL offers 9 entity annotation systems with a variety of features, capabilities and experiments. In the following, we present current state-of-the-art approaches both available or unavailable in GERBIL.

1. **Cucerzan**: As early as in 2007, Cucerzan presented a NED approach based on Wikipedia [8]. The approach tries to maximize the agreement between contextual information of input text and a Wikipedia page as well as category tags on the Wikipedia pages. The test data is still available[6] but since we can safely assume that the Wikipedia page content changed a lot since 2006, we do not use it in our framework, nor we are aware of any publication reusing this data. Furthermore, we were not able to find a running webservice or source code for this approach.

2. **Wikipedia Miner**: This approach was introduced in [25] in 2008 and is based on different facts like prior probabilities, context relatedness and quality, which are then combined and tuned using a classifier. The authors evaluated their approach based on a subset of the AQUAINT dataset.[7] They provide the source code for their approach as well as a webservice[8] which is available in GERBIL.

3. **Illinois Wikifier**: In 2011, [34] presented an NED approach for entities from Wikipedia. In this article, the authors compare local approaches, e.g., using string similarity, with global approaches, which use context information and lead finally to better results. The authors provide their datasets[9] as well as their software "Illinois Wikifier"[10] online. Since "Illinois Wikifier" is currently only available as local binary and GERBIL is solely based on webservices we excluded it from GERBIL for the sake of comparability and server load.

4. **DBpedia Spotlight**: One of the first semantic approaches [24] was published in 2011, this framework combines NER and NED approach based upon DBpedia.[11] Based on a vector-space representation of entities and using the cosine similarity, this approach has a public (NIF-based) webservice[12] as well as its online available evaluation dataset.[13]

5. **TagMe 2**: TagMe 2 [13] was published in 2012 and is based on a directory of links, pages and an inlink graph from Wikipedia. The approach recognizes named entities by matching terms with Wikipedia link texts and disambiguates the match using the in-link graph and

[6]`http://research.microsoft.com/en-us/um/people/silviu/WebAssistant/TestData/`

[7]`http://www.nist.gov/tac/data/data_desc.html#AQUAINT`

[8]`http://wikipedia-miner.cms.waikato.ac.nz/`

[9]`http://cogcomp.cs.illinois.edu/page/resource_view/4`

[10]`http://cogcomp.cs.illinois.edu/page/software_view/33`

[11]`https://github.com/dbpedia-spotlight/dbpedia-spotlight/wiki/Known-uses`

[12]`https://github.com/dbpedia-spotlight/dbpedia-spotlight/wiki/Web-service`

[13]`http://wiki.dbpedia.org/spotlight/isemantics2011/evaluation`

the page dataset. Afterwards, TagMe 2 prunes the identified named entities which are considered as non-coherent to the rest of the named entities in the input text. The authors publish a key-protected webservice[14] as well as their datasets[15] online. The source code, licensed under Apache 2 licence can be obtained directly from the authors. The datasets comprise only fragments of 30 words and less of full documents and will not be part of the current version of GERBIL.

6. **AIDA**: The AIDA approach [17] relies on coherence graph building and dense subgraph algorithms and is based on the YAGO2[16] knowledge base. Although the authors provide their source code, a webservice and their dataset which is a manually annotated subset of the 2003 CoNLL share task [43], GERBIL will not use the webservice since it is not stable enough for regular replication purposes at the moment of this publication.[17] That is, the AIDA team discourages the use because they constantly switch the underlying entity repository, and tune parameters.

7. **NERD-ML**: In 2013, [11] proposed an approach for entity recognition tailored for extracting entities from tweets. The approach relies on a machine learning classification of the entity type given a rich feature vector composed of a set of linguistic features, the output of a properly trained Conditional Random Fields classifier and the output of a set of off-the-shelf NER extractors supported by the NERD Framework. The follow-up, NERD-ML [35], improved the classification task by re-designing the selection of the features. The authors assessed the NERD-ML's performance on both microposts and newswire domains. NERD-ML has a public webservice which is part of GERBIL.[18]

8. **KEA NER/NED**: This approach is the successor of the approach introduced in [41] which is based on a fine-granular context model taking into account heterogeneous text sources as well as text created by automated multimedia analysis. The source texts can have different levels of accuracy, completeness, granularity and reliability which influence the determination of the current context. Ambiguity is solved by selecting entity candidates with the highest level of probability according to the predetermined context. The new implementation begins with the detection of groups of consecutive words (n-gram analysis) and a lookup of all potential DBpedia candidate entities for each n-gram. The disambiguation of candidate entities is based on a scoring cascade. KEA is available as NIF-based webservice.[19]

9. **WAT**: WAT is the successor of TagME [13].[20] The new annotator includes a re-design of all TagME components, namely, the spotter, the disambiguator, and the pruner. Two disambiguation families were newly introduced: graph-based algorithms for collective entity linking based and vote-based algorithms for local entity disambiguation (based on the work of Ferragina et al. [13]). The spotter and the pruner can be tuned using SVM linear models. Additionally, the library can be used as a D2KB-only system by feeding appropriate mention spans to the system.

10. **AGDISTIS**: This approach [44] is a pure entity disambiguation approach (D2KB) based on string similarity measures, an expansion heuristic for labels to cope with co-referencing and the graph-based HITS algorithm. The authors published datasets[21] along with their source code and an API.[22] AGDISTIS can only be used for the D2KB task.

11. **Babelfy**: The core of this approach draws on the use of random walks and a densest subgraph algorithm to tackle the word sense disambiguation and entity linking tasks jointly in a multilingual setting [27] thanks to the BabelNet[23] semantic network [30]. Babelfy has been evaluated using six datasets: three from earlier SemEval tasks [33, 29, 28], one from a Senseval task [38] and two already used for evaluating AIDA [17, 16]. All of them are available online but distributed throughout the Web. Additionally, the authors offer a webservice that is limited to 100 requests per day which are extensible for research purposes [26].[24]

12. **Dexter**: This approach [6] is an open-source implementation of an entity disambiguation framework. The system was implemented in order to simplify the implementation of an entity linking approach and allows to replace single parts of the process. The authors implemented several state-of-the-art disambiguation methods. Results in this paper are obtained using an implementation of the original TagMe disambiguation function. Moreover, Ceccarelli et al. provide the source code[25] as well as a webservice.

Table 1 compares the implemented annotation systems of GERBIL and the BAT-Framework. While AGDISTIS has been in the source code of the BAT-Framework provided by a third-party after publication of Cornolti et al.'s initial work [7] in 2014, GERBIL's community effort led to the implementation of overall 6 new annotators as well as the before mentioned generic NIF-based annotator. The AIDA annotator as well as the "Illinois Wikifier" will not be available in GERBIL since we restrict ourselves to webservices. However, these algorithms can be integrated at any time as soon as their webservices are available.

3.3 Datasets

Table 2 shows the heterogeneity of datasets used for prior evaluations while Table 3 presents an overview of the datasets that were used to evaluate some well-known entity annotators in previous works. These tables make clear that the numbers and types of used datasets varies a lot, thus preventing a fast comparison of annotation systems.

[14] `http://tagme.di.unipi.it/`
[15] `http://acube.di.unipi.it/tagme-dataset/`
[16] `http://www.mpi-inf.mpg.de/yago-naga/yago/`
[17] `https://www.mpi-inf.mpg.de/departments/databases-and-information-systems/research/yago-naga/aida/`
[18] `http://nerd.eurecom.fr`
[19] `http://s16a.org/kea`
[20] `http://github.com/nopper/wat`
[21] `https://github.com/AKSW/n3-collection`
[22] `https://github.com/AKSW/AGDISTIS`
[23] `http://babelnet.org`
[24] `http://babelfy.org`
[25] `http://dexter.isti.cnr.it`

	Year	ACE	Wiki	AQUAINT	MSNBC	IITB	Meij	AIDA/CoNLL	N^3 collection	KORE 50	Wiki-Disamb30	Wiki-Annot30	Spotlight Corpus	SemEval-2013 task 12	SemEval-2007 task 7	SemEval-2007 task 17	Senseval-3	NIF-based corpus	Microposts2014	Software available?	Webservice available?
Cucerzan	2007				✓																
Wikipedia Miner	2008			✓*																	✓
Illinois Wikifier	2011	✓	✓	✓*	✓															✓	
Spotlight	2011												✓							✓	✓
AIDA	2011							✓												✓	✓**
TagMe 2	2012										✓	✓								✓	✓
Dexter	2013																			✓	✓
KEA	2013																				✓
WAT	2013																			✓	✓
AGDISTIS	2014			✓	✓	✓	✓	✓	✓	✓			✓							✓	✓
Babelfy	2014							✓		✓				✓	✓	✓	✓				✓
NERD-ML	2014							✓											✓	✓	✓
BAT-Framework	2013	✓	✓	✓	✓	✓	✓	✓*												✓	
NERD Framework	2014						✓	✓											✓	✓	✓
GERBIL	2014	✓	✓	✓	✓	✓	✓	✓*	✓	✓			✓					✓	✓	✓	✓

Table 3: Comparison of annotators and datasets with indication whether software or datasets respectively webservices are available for reproduction. $*$ indicates that only a subset has been used to evaluate this annotator. $**$ indicate that the webservice is not meant to be used within scientific evaluations due to unstable backends.

BAT allows evaluating the performance of different approaches using five datasets, namely AQUAINT, MSNBC, IITB, Meij and AIDA/CoNLL. With GERBIL, we activate one more dataset already implemented by the authors, namely ACE2004 from Ratinov et al. [34]. Furthermore, we implemented a dataset wrapper for the Microposts2014 corpus which has been used to evaluate NERD-ML [35]. The dataset itself was introduced in 2014 [3] and consists of 3500 tweets especially related to event data. Moreover, we capitalize upon the uptake of publicly available, NIF based corpora over the last years [40, 36].[26] To this end, GERBIL implements a Java-based NIF [15] reader and writer module which enables loading arbitrary NIF document collections, as well as the communication to NIF-based webservices. Additionally, we integrated four NIF corpora, i.e., the RSS-500 and reuters-128 dataset,[27] as well as the Spotlight Corpus and the KORE 50 dataset.[28]

The extensibility of the datasets in GERBIL is furthermore ensured by allowing users to upload or use already available NIF datasets from DataHub. However, GERBIL is currently only importing already available datasets. GERBIL will regularly check whether new corpora are available and publish them for benchmarking after a manual quality assurance cycle which ensures their usability for the implemented configuration options. Additionally, users can upload their NIF-corpora directly to GERBIL avoiding their publication in publicly available sources. This option allows for rapid testing of entity annotation systems with closed source or licenced datasets.

Some of the datasets shown in Table 3 are either not yet implemented due to size and server load limitations, i.e., Wiki-Disamb30 and Wiki-Annot30, or due their original experiment type. In particular, the Senseval-3 as well as the different SemEval datasets demand as experiment type word sense disambiguation and thereby linking to BabelNet [30] or Wordnet [12], which is not yet covered in GERBIL. Still, GERBIL offers currently 11 state-of-the-art datasets reaching from newswire and twitter to encyclopedic corpora of various amounts of texts and entities. Due to license issues we are only able to provide downloads for 9 of them directly but we provide instructions to obtain the others on our project wiki.

Table 4 depicts the features of the current datasets available in GERBIL. These provide a broad evaluation ground leveraging the possibility for sophisticated tool diagnostics.

3.4 Output

GERBIL's main aim is to provide comprehensive, reproducible and publishable experiment results. Hence, GERBIL's experimental output is represented as a table containing the results, as well as embedded JSON-LD[29] RDF data using the RDF DataCube vocabulary [9]. We ensure

[26]`http://datahub.io/dataset?license_id=cc-by&q=NIF`
[27]`https://github.com/AKSW/n3-collection`
[28]`http://www.yovisto.com/labs/ner-benchmarks/`

[29]`http://www.w3.org/TR/json-ld/`

Corpus	Topic	|Documents|	Avg. Entity/Doc.
ACE2004	news	57	4.44
AIDA/CoNLL	news	1393	19.97
AQUAINT	news	50	14.54
IITB	mixed	103	109.22
KORE 50	mixed	50	2.86
Meij	tweets	502	1.62
Microposts2014	tweets	3505	0.65
MSNBC	news	20	32.50
N^3 Reuters-128	news	128	4.85
N^3 RSS-500	RSS-feeds	500	0.99
Spotlight Corpus	news	58	5.69

Table 4: Features of the datasets and their documents.

		BAT-Framework	GERBIL	Experiment
[25]	Wikipedia Miner	✓	✓	SA2KB
[34]	Illinois Wikifier	✓	(✓)	SA2KB
[24]	Spotlight	✓	✓	SA2KB
[13]	TagMe 2	✓	✓	SA2KB
[17]	AIDA	✓	(✓)	SA2KB
[41]	KEA		✓	SA2KB
[32]	WAT		✓	SA2KB
[44]	AGDISTIS	(✓)	✓	D2KB
[27]	Babelfy		✓	SA2KB
[35]	NERD-ML		✓	SA2KB
[6]	Dexter		✓	SA2KB
	NIF-based Annotator		✓	any

Table 1: Overview of implemented annotator systems. Brackets indicate the existence of the implementation of the adapter but also the inability to use it in the live system.

Dataset	Format	Experiment
ACE2004	MSNBC	Sa2KB
Wiki	⋆	Sa2W
AQUAINT	⋆	Sa2KB
MSNBC	MSNBC	Sa2KB
IITB	XML	Sa2KB
Meij	TREC	Rc2W
AIDA/CoNLL	CoNLL	Sa2KB
N^3 collection	NIF/RDF	Sa2KB
KORE 50	NIF/RDF	Sa2KB
Wiki-Disamb30	tab-separated	Sa2KB
Wiki-Annot30	tab-separated	Sa2KB
Spotlight Corpus	NIF/RDF	Sa2KB
SemEval-2013 task 12	XML/⋆	WSD/Sa2KB
SemEval-2007 task 7	XML/⋆	WSD
SemEval-2007 task 17	XML/⋆	WSD
Senseval-3	XML/⋆	WSD
Microposts2014	Microposts2014	Sa2KB

Table 2: Datasets and their formats. A ⋆ indicates various inline or keyfile annotation formats. The experiments follow their definition in Section 3.2

a detailed description of each component of an experiment as well as machine-readable, interlinkable results following the 5-star Linked Data principles. Moreover, we provide a persistent and time-stamped URL for each experiment, see Table 5.

RDF DataCube is a vocabulary standard and can be used to represent fine-grained multidimensional, statistical data which is compatible with the Linked SDMX [4] standard. Every GERBIL experiment is modelled as `qb:Dataset` containing the individual runs of the annotators on specific corpora as `qb:Observations`. Each observation features the `qb:Dimensions` experiment type, matching type, annotator, corpus, and time. The six evaluation measures offered by GERBIL as well as the error count are expressed as `qb:Measures`. To include further metadata, annotator and corpus dimension properties link *DataID* [2] descriptions of the individual components.

GERBIL uses the recently proposed DataID [2] ontology that combines VoID [1] and DCAT [21] metadata with Prov-O [20] provenance information and ODRL [23] licenses to describe datasets. Besides metadata properties like titles, descriptions and authors, the source files of the open datasets themselves are linked as `dcat:Distributions`, allowing direct access to the evaluation corpora. Furthermore, ODRL license specifications in RDF are linked via `dc:license`, potentially facilitating automatically adjusted processing of licensed data by NLP tools. Licenses are further specified via `dc:rights`, including citations of the relevant publications.

To describe annotators in a similar fashion, we extended DataID for services. The class `Service`, to be described with the same basic properties as dataset, was introduced. To link an instance of a `Service` to its distribution the `datid:distribution` property was introduced as super property of `dcat:distribution`, i.e., the specific URI the service can be queried at. Furthermore, Services can have a number of `datid:Parameters` and `datid:Configurations`. Datasets can be linked via `datid:input` or `datid:output`.

Offering such detailed and structured experimental results opens new research avenues in terms of tool and dataset diagnostics to increase decision makers' ability to choose the right settings for the right use case. Next to individual configurable experiments, GERBIL offers an overview of recent experiment results belonging to the same experiment and matching type in the form of a table as well as sophisticated

Annotator	Dataset	F1-micro
DBpedia Spotlight	IITB	0.450
Babelfy	IITB	0.182
NERD-ML	IITB	0.489
WAT	IITB	0.202
DBpedia Spotlight	KORE50	0.265
Babelfy	KORE50	0.530
NERD-ML	KORE50	0.238
WAT	KORE50	0.523

Table 5: Results of an example experiment. It is accessible at http://gerbil.aksw.org/gerbil/experiment?id=201503050003

visualizations,[30] see Figure 2. This allows for a quick comparison of tools and datasets on recently run experiments without additional computational effort.

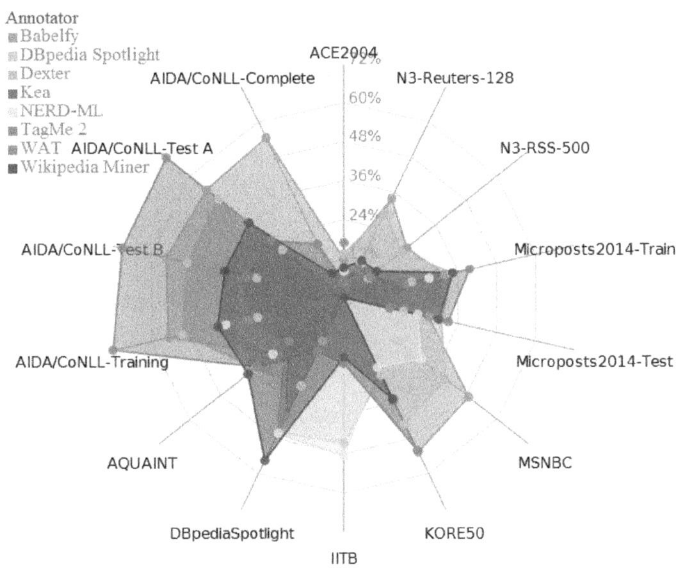

Figure 2: Example spider diagram of recent A2KB experiments with strong annotation matching derived from our online interface

4. EVALUATION

To ensure the practicability and convenience of the GERBIL framework, we investigated the effort needed to use GERBIL for the evaluation of novel annotators. To achieve this goal, we surveyed the workload necessary to implement a novel annotator into GERBIL compared to the implementation into previous diverse frameworks.

Our survey comprised five developers with expert-level programming skills in Java. Each developer was asked to evaluate how much time he/she needed to write the code necessary to evaluate his/her framework on a new dataset.

Overall, the developers reported that they needed between 1 and 4 hours to achieve this goal (4x 1-2h, 1x 3-4h), see Figure 3. Importantly, all developers reported that they needed

[30]http://gerbil.aksw.org/gerbil/overview

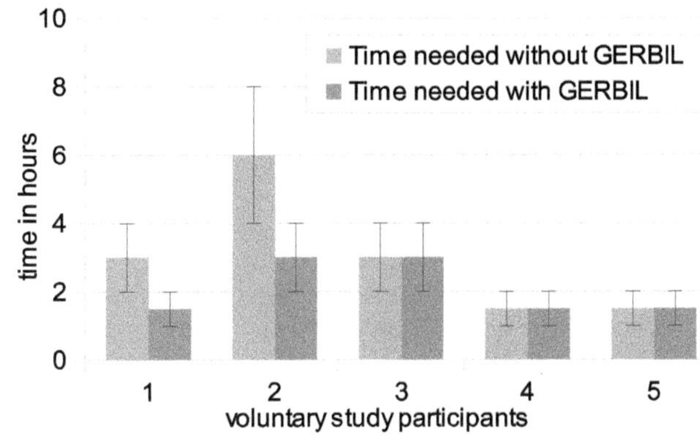

Figure 3: Comparison of effort needed to implement an adapter for an annotation system with and without GERBIL.

either the same or even less time to integrate their annotator into GERBIL. This result in itself is of high practical significance as it means that by using GERBIL, developers can evaluate on (currently) 11 datasets using the same effort they needed for 1, which is a gain of more than 1100%. Moreover, all developers reported they felt comfortable—4 points on average on a 5-point Likert scale between very uncomfortable (1) and very comfortable (5)—implementing the annotator in GERBIL. Further developers were invited to complete the survey, which is available at our project website. Even though small, this evaluation suggests that implementing against GERBIL does not lead to any overhead. On the contrary, GERBIL significantly improves the time-to-evaluation by offering means to benchmark and compare against other annotators respectively datasets within the same effort frame previously required to evaluate on a single dataset.

An interesting side-effect of having all these frameworks and datasets in a central framework is that we can now benchmark the different frameworks with respect to their runtimes within exactly the same experimental settings. These results are of practical concern for end users of annotation frameworks as they are most commonly interested in both the runtime and the quality of solutions. For example, we evaluated the runtimes of the different approaches in GERBIL for the A2KB experiment type on the MSNBC dataset. The results of this experiment are shown in Figure 4.

5. CONCLUSION AND FUTURE WORK

In this paper, we presented and evaluated GERBIL, a platform for the evaluation of annotation frameworks. With GERBIL, we aim to push annotation system developers to better quality and wider use of their frameworks. Some of the main contributions of GERBIL include the provision of persistent URLs for reproducibility and archiving. Furthermore, we implemented a generic adaptor for external datasets as well as a generic interface to integrate remote annotator systems. The datasets available for evaluation in the previous benchmarking platforms for annotation was extended by 6 new datasets. Moreover, 6 novel annotators were added to the platform. The evaluation of our framework by contributors suggests that adding an annotator to

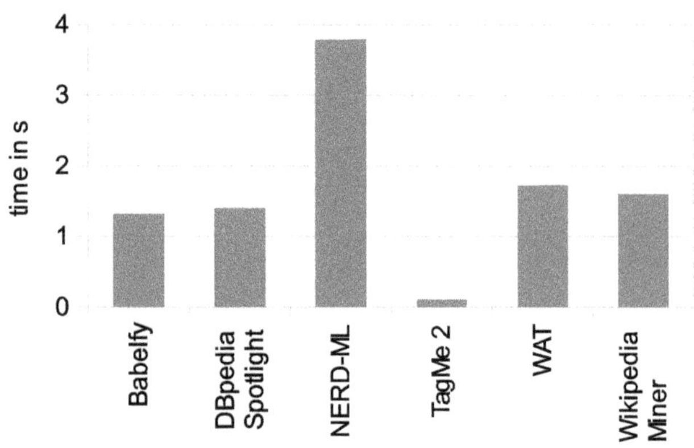

Figure 4: Runtime per document of different approaches in GERBIL for the A2KB experiment type on the MSNBC dataset.

GERBIL demands 1 to 2 hours of work. Hence, while keeping the implementation effort previously required to evaluate on a single dataset, we allow developers to evaluate on (currently) 11 times more datasets. The presented, web-based frontend allows for several use cases enabling laymen and expert users to perform informed comparisons of semantic annotation tools. The persistent URIs enhance the long term quotation in the field of information extraction. GERBIL is not just a new framework wrapping existing technology. In comparison to earlier frameworks, it extends the state-of-the-art benchmarks by the capability of considering the influence of NIL attributes and the ability of dealing with data sets and annotators that link to different knowledge bases. More information about GERBIL and its source code can be found at the project's website.

While developing GERBIL, we spotted several flaws in the formal model underlying previous benchmarking frameworks which we aim to tackle in the future. For example, the formal specification underlying current benchmarking frameworks for annotation does not allow using the scores assigned by the annotators for their results. To address this problem, we aim to develop/implement novel measures into GERBIL that make use of scores (e.g., Mean Reciprocal Rank). Moreover, partial results are not considered within the evaluation. For example, during the disambiguation task, named entities without Wikipedia URIs are not considered. This has a significant impact of the number of true and false positives and thus on the performance of some tools. Additionally, we will consider implementing a review function with which users can submit proposals for dataset changes to be evaluated by the GERBIL team. Furthermore, certain tasks seem to be too coarse. For example, we will consider splitting the Sa2KB and the A2KB tasks into two subtasks: the first subtask would measure how well tools perform at finding named entities inside the text (NER task) while the second would evaluate how well tools disambiguate those named entities which have been found correctly (similar to the D2KB task). In the future, we also plan to provide information about the point in time since when an annotator is stable, i.e., the algorithm underlying the webservice has not changed.

Acknowledgments. Parts of this work were supported by the ESF and the Free State of Saxony, the FP7 projects GeoKnow (GA No. 318159), LIDER (GA No. 610782), Apps4EU (GA No. 325090), LinkedTV (GA No. 287911), ERC Starting Grant MultiJEDI No. 259234, Italy PRIN ARS-Technomedia as well as by the German Government, Federal Ministry of Education and Research under the project number 03WKCJ4D.

6. ADDITIONAL AUTHORS

Ciro Baron (Leipzig University, Germany)
Andreas Both (R&D, Unister GmbH, Germany)
Martin Brümmer (Leipzig University, Germany)
Diego Ceccarelli (ISTI–CNR, Pisa, Italy)
Marco Cornolti (University of Pisa, Italy)
Didier Cherix (R&D, Unister GmbH, Germany)
Bernd Eickmann (R&D, Unister GmbH, Germany)
Paolo Ferragina (University of Pisa, Italy)
Christiane Lemke (R&D, Unister GmbH, Germany)
Andrea Moro (Sapienza University of Rome, Italy)
Roberto Navigli (Sapienza University of Rome, Italy)
Francesco Piccinno (University of Pisa, Italy)
Giuseppe Rizzo (EURECOM, France)
Harald Sack (HPI Potsdam, Germany)
René Speck (Institute for Applied Informatics, Germany)
Raphaël Troncy (EURECOM, France)
Jörg Waitelonis (HPI Potsdam, Germany)
Lars Wesemann (R&D, Unister GmbH, Germany)

7. REFERENCES

[1] K. Alexander, R. Cyganiak, M. Hausenblas, and J. Zhao. Describing linked datasets with the void vocabulary, 2011. http://www.w3.org/TR/void/.

[2] M. Brümmer, C. Baron, I. Ermilov, M. Freudenberg, D. Kontokostas, and S. Hellmann. DataID: Towards semantically rich metadata for complex datasets. In *10th International Conference on Semantic Systems 2014*, 2014.

[3] A. E. Cano Basave, G. Rizzo, A. Varga, M. Rowe, M. Stankovic, and A.-S. Dadzie. Making sense of microposts (#microposts2014) named entity extraction & linking challenge. In *Proceedings of 4th Workshop on Making Sense of Microposts (#Microposts2014)*, 2014.

[4] S. Capadisli, S. Auer, and A.-C. Ngonga Ngomo. Linked SDMX data. *Semantic Web Journal*, 2013.

[5] D. Carmel, M.-W. Chang, E. Gabrilovich, B.-J. P. Hsu, and K. Wang. ERD 2014: Entity recognition and disambiguation challenge. *SIGIR Forum*, 2014.

[6] D. Ceccarelli, C. Lucchese, S. Orlando, R. Perego, and S. Trani. Dexter: an open source framework for entity linking. In *Proceedings of the sixth international workshop on Exploiting semantic annotations in information retrieval*, 2013.

[7] M. Cornolti, P. Ferragina, and M. Ciaramita. A framework for benchmarking entity-annotation systems. In *22nd World Wide Web Conference*, 2013.

[8] S. Cucerzan. Large-scale named entity disambiguation based on wikipedia data. In *Conference on Empirical*

Methods in Natural Language Processing-CoNLL, 2007.

[9] R. Cyganiak, D. Reynolds, and J. Tennison. The RDF Data Cube Vocabulary, 2014. http://www.w3.org/TR/vocab-data-cube/.

[10] G. R. Doddington, A. Mitchell, M. A. Przybocki, L. A. Ramshaw, S. Strassel, and R. M. Weischedel. The automatic content extraction (ace) program-tasks, data, and evaluation. In *LREC*, 2004.

[11] M. V. Erp, G. Rizzo, and R. Troncy. Learning with the web: Spotting named entities on the intersection of NERD and machine learning. In *Proceedings of the Making Sense of Microposts (#MSM2013) Concept Extraction Challenge*, 2013.

[12] C. Fellbaum. *WordNet: An Electronic Lexical Database*. MIT Press, 1998.

[13] P. Ferragina and U. Scaiella. Fast and Accurate Annotation of Short Texts with Wikipedia Pages. *IEEE software*, 2012.

[14] Y. Gil. Semantic challenges in getting work done, 2014. Invited Talk at ISWC.

[15] S. Hellmann, J. Lehmann, S. Auer, and M. Brümmer. Integrating NLP using Linked Data. In *12th International Semantic Web Conference*, 2013.

[16] J. Hoffart, S. Seufert, D. B. Nguyen, M. Theobald, and G. Weikum. KORE: keyphrase overlap relatedness for entity disambiguation. In *Proceedings of CIKM*, 2012.

[17] J. Hoffart, M. A. Yosef, I. Bordino, H. Fürstenau, M. Pinkal, M. Spaniol, B. Taneva, S. Thater, and G. Weikum. Robust Disambiguation of Named Entities in Text. In *Conference on Empirical Methods in Natural Language Processing*, 2011.

[18] P. Jermyn, M. Dixon, and B. J. Read. Preparing clean views of data for data mining. *ERCIM Work. on Database Res*, 1999.

[19] A. Kilgarriff. Senseval: An exercise in evaluating word sense disambiguation programs. *1st LREC*, 1998.

[20] T. Lebo, S. Sahoo, D. McGuinness, K. Belhajjame, J. Cheney, D. Corsar, D. Garijo, S. Soiland-Reyes, S. Zednik, and J. Zhao. PROV-O: The PROV Ontology, 2013. http://www.w3.org/TR/prov-o/.

[21] F. Maali, J. Erickson, and P. Archer. Data Catalog Vocabulary (DCAT), 2014. http://www.w3.org/TR/vocab-dcat/.

[22] P. McNamee. Overview of the tac 2009 knowledge base population track. 2009.

[23] M. McRoberts and V. Rodríguez-Doncel. Open Digital Rights Language (ODRL) Ontology, 2014. http://www.w3.org/ns/odrl/2/.

[24] P. N. Mendes, M. Jakob, A. Garcia-Silva, and C. Bizer. DBpedia Spotlight: Shedding Light on the Web of Documents. In *7th International Conference on Semantic Systems (I-Semantics)*, 2011.

[25] D. Milne and I. H. Witten. Learning to link with wikipedia. In *17th ACM CIKM*, 2008.

[26] A. Moro, F. Cecconi, and R. Navigli. Multilingual word sense disambiguation and entity linking for everybody. In *Proc. of ISWC (P&D)*, 2014.

[27] A. Moro, A. Raganato, and R. Navigli. Entity Linking meets Word Sense Disambiguation: A Unified Approach. *TACL*, 2014.

[28] R. Navigli, D. Jurgens, and D. Vannella. SemEval-2013 Task 12: Multilingual Word Sense Disambiguation. In *Proceedings of SemEval-2013*, 2013.

[29] R. Navigli, K. C. Litkowski, and O. Hargraves. SemEval-2007 Task 07: Coarse-Grained English All-Words Task. In *Proc. of SemEval-2007*, 2007.

[30] R. Navigli and S. P. Ponzetto. BabelNet: The automatic construction, evaluation and application of a wide-coverage multilingual semantic network. *Artificial Intelligence*, 2012.

[31] R. D. Peng. Reproducible research in computational science. *Science (New York, Ny)*, 2011.

[32] F. Piccinno and P. Ferragina. From TagME to WAT: a new entity annotator. In *Proceedings of the first international workshop on Entity recognition & disambiguation*, 2014.

[33] S. S. Pradhan, E. Loper, D. Dligach, and M. Palmer. SemEval-2007 task 17: English lexical sample, SRL and all words. In *Proc. of SemEval-2007*.

[34] L. Ratinov, D. Roth, D. Downey, and M. Anderson. Local and global algorithms for disambiguation to wikipedia. In *ACL*, 2011.

[35] G. Rizzo, M. van Erp, and R. Troncy. Benchmarking the extraction and disambiguation of named entities on the semantic web. In *Proceedings of the 9th International Conference on Language Resources and Evaluation*, 2014.

[36] M. Röder, R. Usbeck, S. Hellmann, D. Gerber, and A. Both. N3 - a collection of datasets for named entity recognition and disambiguation in the nlp interchange format. In *9th LREC*, 2014.

[37] M. Rowe, M. Stankovic, and A.-S. Dadzie, editors. *Proceedings, 4th Workshop on Making Sense of Microposts (#Microposts2014): Big things come in small packages, Seoul, Korea, 7th April 2014*, 2014.

[38] B. Snyder and M. Palmer. The English all-words task. In *Proc. of Senseval-3*, pages 41–43, 2004.

[39] R. Speck and A.-C. N. Ngomo. Ensemble learning for named entity recognition. In *The Semantic Web – ISWC 2014*. 2014.

[40] N. Steinmetz, M. Knuth, and H. Sack. Statistical analyses of named entity disambiguation benchmarks. In *1st Workshop on NLP&DBpedia 2013*, 2013.

[41] N. Steinmetz and H. Sack. Semantic multimedia information retrieval based on contextual descriptions. In P. Cimiano, O. Corcho, V. Presutti, L. Hollink, and S. Rudolph, editors, *The Semantic Web: Semantics and Big Data*. 2013.

[42] B. M. Sundheim. Tipster/muc-5: Information extraction system evaluation. In *Proceedings of the 5th Conference on Message Understanding*, 1993.

[43] E. F. Tjong Kim Sang and F. De Meulder. Introduction to the CoNLL-2003 Shared Task: Language-Independent Named Entity Recognition. In *Proceedings of CoNLL-2003*.

[44] R. Usbeck, A.-C. Ngonga Ngomo, M. Röder, D. Gerber, S. Coelho, S. Auer, and A. Both. Agdistis - graph-based disambiguation of named entities using linked data. In *The Semantic Web – ISWC 2014*. 2014.

An Optimization Framework for Weighting Implicit Relevance Labels for Personalized Web Search

Yury Ustinovskiy
Yandex
Leo Tolstoy st. 16, Moscow, Russia
yuraust@yandex-team.ru

Gleb Gusev
Yandex
Leo Tolstoy st. 16, Moscow, Russia
gleb57@yandex-team.ru

Pavel Serdyukov
Yandex
Leo Tolstoy st. 16, Moscow, Russia
pavser@yandex-team.ru

ABSTRACT

Implicit feedback from users of a web search engine is an essential source providing consistent personal relevance labels from the actual population of users. However, previous studies on personalized search employ this source in a rather straightforward manner. Basically, documents that were clicked on get maximal gain, and the rest of the documents are assigned the zero gain. As we demonstrate in our paper, a ranking algorithm trained using these gains directly as the ground truth relevance labels leads to a suboptimal personalized ranking.

In this paper we develop a framework for automatic reweighting of these labels. Our approach is based on more subtle aspects of user interaction with the result page. We propose an efficient methodology for deriving confidence levels for relevance labels that relies directly on the objective ranking measure. All our algorithms are evaluated on a large-scale query log provided by a major commercial search engine. The results of the experiments prove that the current state-of-the-art personalization approaches could be significantly improved by enriching relevance grades with weights extracted from post-impression user behavior.

Categories and Subject Descriptors

H.3.3 [**Information Systems Applications**]

General Terms

Algorithms, Measurement, Experimentation

Keywords

Personalization; Click Prediction; Gradient Descent

WWW 2015, May 18–22, 2015, Florence, Italy.
ACM 978-1-4503-3469-3/15/05.
http://dx.doi.org/10.1145/2736277.2741105.

1. INTRODUCTION

Most of major search engines record detailed information about users' requests, including timestamps of actions, sets of retrieved documents, and detailed interactions of users with SERPs (search engine result pages), and store petabytes of such data. For these reasons, scalable methods of user logs processing and utilization are gaining an increasing interest in the IR community. The rapid development of these technologies made possible various practical applications of implicit feedback analysis, including evaluation of ranking quality [12], improvement of web search performance [1, 9], and web search personalization [4, 5, 6, 8, 11, 14, 16, 19, 21, 23].

Implicit feedback data are often employed as the source of implicit personalized relevance labels and thus become absolutely indispensable for personalization of web search. Such data allow the collection of a large-scale sample of judgements for a representative set of queries directly from users [14]. These judgements could be further used as the ground truth relevance labels for training and evaluating personalized rankers.

The most straightforward yet still prevalent approach treats clicked documents as relevant and non-clicked ones as totally irrelevant. However, clearly, not every click is an indicator of high personal document relevance and not every impression without a click indicates complete irrelevance. Noisy clicks may mislead learning to rank algorithm decreasing the quality of the trained ranking model. This raises the problem of identifying "reliable" clicks. A step toward solving this problem was made in [3, 4], where the authors considered only *satisfied clicks* (i.e., the last clicks on SERP and clicks followed by a dwell time exceeding some fixed threshold) as the evidence of relevance. Since satisfied clicks are less noisy than all clicks, it is expected that a personalized ranker trained on these gain values results in a better ranking.

In this paper we suggest a far-reaching generalization of this idea. Namely, 'satisfied clicks' approach to the collection of the personalized relevance labels still misses valuable information available in the click-through log. In particular, this approach (1) does not distinguish between skipped documents and not examined documents; (2) does not account for various types of satisfied clicks differently (e.g., multiple clicks, singleton clicks, first clicks, super long clicks); (3) does not take into account positional bias. We aim at improving personalized ranking by interpreting implicit feedback in a more sophisticated way than it has been done in the the current approaches to search personalization, see, e.g., [4, 11, 16]. The key component of our framework is an additional step which automatically extracts confidence levels of relevance labels from characteristics of user's actions on the SERP *prior* to training a personalized ranker. The relevance labels equipped with these *weights*, utilized by machine learning algorithm, are expected to improve the ranking quality.

To compare our method with the state-of-the-art approaches we need some fixed evaluation methodology. For this reason we use several popular implicit relevance labels to evaluate quality of personalized rankers and refer to these labels as *gains*.

To sum up, we make the following contributions:

- formulate the problem of weighting the implicit relevance labels for personalized search;
- propose a novel optimization framework for automatic training of confidence levels of implicit relevance labels as functions of characteristics of user behavior;
- provide new findings on user behavior modelling for web search personalization. In particular, we analyze the impact of dwell time and original ranking position on the confidence of the implicit personal relevance of the corresponding document.

We evaluate classical personalized relevance labels enriched with our confidence levels on the large-scale search log provided by Yandex[1] for the data mining challenge on web search personalization organized at `Kaggle.com`[2] in the scope of WSCD workshop held at WSDM 2014, [13]. The team that has won the challenge shared with us the dataset they used for training and testing their models. Our experiments prove that even given a very competitive personalization algorithm using a variety of strong state-of-the-art features and a powerful machine learning algorithm one can significantly improve the quality of its ranking by introducing weights of labels.

The remainder of the paper is organized as follows. In Section 2 we review related work on personalization, learning of user behavior models and semi-supervised learning. In Section 3 we fix some notations and give the formal statement of our problem. The core section of the paper is Section 4, where we define our algorithm for general and linear models. In Section 5 we give details of our experimental setup and list the features we use for learning. Results of the experiments are reported in Section 6. Finally, we discuss possible directions of future work and conclude the paper in Sections 7 and 8.

2. RELATED WORK

In numerous studies [4, 5, 6, 11, 14, 16, 23] appeared in the last decade, it has been demonstrated that personal and contextual information extracted from click-through logs has the potential to significantly improve personalized ranking quality. First papers on search personalization employ explicit relevance labels to learn ranking models. In [14] Shen *et al.* employed previous queries and clicks on the returned results to specify the actual information need of a searcher. The authors evaluated several context-sensitive language models on the TREC collection augmented with click-through data and used editorial relevance labels to tune and evaluate their algorithms. Tan *et al.* [17] collected search history from users to get information about users' search preferences. The approach turned out to be especially effective for recurring queries. All the experiments were evaluated on a set of manually labelled queries collected from volunteers. Matthijs and Radlinski [11] studied the effect of a set of personalized features extracted from a browsing history by tuning a few parameters. The authors reported results of both offline experiments on the labelled set of queries and online evaluations. As opposed to these studies, we train and evaluate all our algorithms on user clicks stored in search logs.

A large body of work has been devoted to search personalization algorithms using clicks for learning and evaluation. Bennett *et al.* [3] personalized web search by leveraging location information from both users and web sites. The authors re-ranked documents by training a location-sensitive model and evaluated it on a proprietary dataset collected via a browser plugin. They used *satisfied clicks* as an indicator of relevance and considered MRR (Mean Reciprocal Rank) of these clicks as the principal performance measure. The same labelling method and performance measures were chosen in [22]. In this paper White *et al.* improved ranking of results for the current user query by using behavioral data of the other users in the same cohort. In this study we consider the same evaluation methodology based on users' clicks. However, unlike the above papers, we propose to use these binary gain values to train a personalization ranker not directly. We develop a framework for systematic learning of numerically valued weights of these gains by analyzing different aspects of user interaction with the result page. We also emphasize that our goal is complementary to the one pursued in the above-mentioned studies on personalization mainly devoted to investigations of different sources of personalization features. Studies on personalization form a small portion of works employing implicit feedback to train machine learning algorithms. One of the pioneer works in this area is [9], where Joachims collects implicit feedback from a set users' clicks to improve the overall retrieval quality of a search engine. Agichtein *et al.* [1] collect features representing user implicit feedback and used them to learn a new ranking model. Authors employed manually assigned relevance labels to train and evaluate their model. Unlike these papers we do not aggregate clickthrough data to estimate document relevance, instead we estimate confidence in a personal relevance label of a document in a particular search session to a particular user.

The idea of our study is related to the one suggested in [26]. In that paper Yue *et. al.* improved conventional interleaving algorithms by interpreting users' actions in a more subtle way than it is defined in the state-of-the-art interleaving techniques. The authors suggested a machine learning approach that solves the *reverse problem* of hypothesis testing — it weights various types of clicks differently in order to improve the statistical power of the interleaving metrics. Our approach can also be considered a solution to the reverse problem of personalization, however, in contrast to that study, we (1) weight not only clicked documents and (2) focus on a completely different task: personalized web search ranking.

[1]`yandex.com`
[2]`kaggle.com/c/yandex-personalized-web-search-challenge`

An interesting theoretical machine learning approach to the general *reverse learning problem* was proposed in [25] by Xu *et al.* Similarly to our study, they combined two classes of features, one of which is known only for a subset of samples. To improve a standard linear machine learning model, authors estimated unknown feature values relying on the values of learning gains. Unlike that paper, in our problem statement, features describing user's interaction with the result page are available in training data only.

3. PROBLEM FORMULATION

3.1 Notations

In this section we fix notations and provide some insights into personalization framework. First, let us describe the data that are available in personalization learning.

Let $\mathcal{S} = \{t_1, \ldots, t_S\}$ be the *training dataset*, consisting of S samples t_i. Each sample t_i is a tuple $\{u, q, d\}$ corresponding to a user u, a query q issued by this user, and a document retrieved for the query. Let $\mathcal{Q}$ be the set of user-query pairs occurring in the training dataset $\mathcal{S}$. We assume that in dataset $\mathcal{S}$ for each pair $\{u, q\} \in \mathcal{Q}$, we have exactly 10 tuples t_i in $\mathcal{S}$, corresponding to the top $k = 10$ retrieved documents. These 10 tuples are further denoted as $\mathcal{S}_{u,q} \subset \mathcal{S}$.

Each sample t_i is characterized by an N-dimensional *personalization feature vector* $\mathbf{x}_i = (x_i^1, \ldots, x_i^N) \in \mathbb{R}^N$ that can be calculated based on the data available before the result page is shown to the user. Those may be any possible features that can be potentially used as components of a personalized ranking model. Among them, there could be both non-personal features, e.g., text relevance of document d to query q, and personal features, e.g., user-specific popularity of d or the match between the document's text and the user's interest profile. In what follows we denote by $\mathcal{X}$ the map that sends samples to their feature vectors:

$$\mathcal{X}\colon \mathcal{S} \to \mathbb{R}^N, \quad \mathcal{X}\colon t_i \mapsto (x_i^1, \ldots, x_i^N) \in \mathbb{R}^N.$$

The goal of the personalized web search is to re-rank for every query $\{u, q\} \in \mathcal{Q}$ the corresponding documents $\mathcal{S}_{u,q}$, on the basis of the personalization feature vectors. Typically, it is done by providing a *scoring function* $\mathcal{F}$, which maps the personalization features $\mathcal{X}(\{u, q, d\})$ to the ranking scores of the documents. Since the values of function $\mathcal{F}$ depend only on the feature vectors $\mathcal{X}(\{u, q, d\})$, we will further consider $\mathcal{F}$ as a function on the N-dimensional feature space $\mathbb{R}^N$:

$$\mathcal{F}\colon \mathbb{R}^N \to \mathbb{R}.$$

Hereby samples $t_i \in \mathcal{S}_{u,q}$ are ranked according to the values $f_i = \mathcal{F}(\mathcal{X}(t_i))$.

To evaluate the quality of a personalized ranker we need *gain values*, that is ground truth relevance labels assigned to all documents, retrieved for the queries $\{u, q\} \in \mathcal{Q}$. So, we define *gain* as a function

$$\mathcal{G}\colon \mathcal{S} \to \mathbb{R}.$$

In the classical information retrieval approach, editorial relevance labels are assigned to the query-document pairs by assessors and could be directly used to define the *gain function* $\mathcal{G}$. For example, the standard mapping used in DCG (Discount Cumulative Gain) or NDCG (Normalized Discount Cumulative Gain) takes values in $\{2^g - 1 | g = 0, 1, 2, 3, 4\}$.

The situation in the personalization of Web search is quite different: collecting a large-scale sample of personalized relevance labels from real users in the same manner is usually significantly more complicated and practically infeasible. The approach widely adopted in the existing studies on personalized search [4, 11, 16] is to use certain user actions as implicit indicators of a document's personal relevance, e.g., to consider clicked documents with dwell time >30 seconds as relevant and the rest of the documents as irrelevant: $\mathcal{G}(\{u, q, d\}) = \text{longclick}(d) := \{1 \text{ iff } d \text{ is clicked, and dwell time } {>}30\text{s}\}$. This methodology allows to collect large training datasets comprising data from click-through logs of commercial search engines.

Given a gain function $\mathcal{G}$, one defines the *performance measure* $\mathcal{O}\colon \text{Perm}(\mathcal{S}_{u,q}) \to \mathbb{R}$ on the set of rankings, i.e., permutations, of $\mathcal{S}_{u,q}$, in the following way:

$$\mathcal{O}(\sigma) = \sum_{t \in \mathcal{S}_{u,q}} \mathcal{G}(t) \cdot \text{discount}(\sigma(t)), \tag{1}$$

where $\sigma\colon \mathcal{S}_{u,q} \to \{1, \ldots, k\}$ is an ordering of documents in $\mathcal{S}_{u,q}$, $\sigma(\{u, q, d\})$ is the position of document d in the ranking, and $\text{discount}(k)$ is a positional discount (e.g., $1/\log_2(k+1)$ for DCG or $1/k$ for MRR).

Objective performance measure of a ranker $\mathcal{F}$ is the average of $\mathcal{O}(\{rank_{\mathcal{F}}(d)\}_{d \in \mathcal{S}_{u,q}})$ over all user-query pairs $\{u, q\} \in \mathcal{Q}$, where $rank_{\mathcal{F}}(d) \in \{1, \ldots, k\}$ is the rank of document d according to the value of the scoring function $\mathcal{F}(\mathcal{X}(\{u, q, d\}))$:

$$\mathcal{M}(\mathcal{F}) := \frac{1}{|\mathcal{Q}|} \sum_{\{u,q\} \in \mathcal{Q}} \mathcal{O}(\{rank_{\mathcal{F}}(d)\}_{d \in \mathcal{S}_{u,q}}) \to \max, \tag{2}$$

where $\mathcal{O}(\cdot)$ is introduced in Equation (1). The family of performance measures of the form (2) includes, as its special cases, both DCG-like measures in the case of multi-graded editorial relevance labels $\mathcal{G}$ and classical click measures (e.g., MRR or MAP) in the case of click-through-based gains $\mathcal{G}$.

3.2 Our approach

So far, we have the training set $\mathcal{S}$, the gain function $\mathcal{G}$, and the feature map $\mathcal{X}$. Our goal is to produce a scoring function $\mathcal{F}$ as optimal as possible in terms of the objective metric (2). With this formulation of personalization learning framework one can apply the majority of the state-of-the-art machine learning algorithms, including linear regression, polynomial regression, decision trees models, neural networks, etc.

Standard machine learning algorithms previously applied to search personalization assume that all learning samples $t_i \in \mathcal{S}$ carry equally important evidences for a machine learning algorithm. We argue that this straightforward approach leads to a suboptimal ranking. For example, assume, when evaluating ranker $\mathcal{F}$, only the documents, followed by a satisfied click, are treated as relevant answers, i.e., $\mathcal{G}(\{u, q, d\}) = $ (last click) OR (dwell time>30s). Let d be a document from the training set such that $20s <$ dwell time$(d) \leq 30s$. A standard machine learning algorithm utilizes the right inequality only. However, intuitively, the information that the click on document d has dwell time larger than 20s may carry an additional signal for the machine learning algorithm and could be also useful for training ranker $\mathcal{F}$. We may think of these documents as of something intermediate between non-clicked documents (or clicked with an insignificant dwell time) and documents with a sufficiently long dwell time, so they could be treated as potentially relevant by our algorithm $\mathcal{A}$. Hence our confidence in the label that marks them as irrelevant can be lower than for documents with the dwell time around 5s.

Another important distinctive property of the implicit relevance labelling that can adopted in search personalization is the existence of two types of non-relevant samples. The results of the first type are *skipped*, i.e., their snippets or titles were examined by a user and the results were deliberately not clicked. The results of the second type are *not examined*, i.e., neither their snippets, nor the documents themselves, were examined by a user. Clearly, skipped documents have, a priori, larger confidence in their negative label than not examined documents. Since we do not know for sure whether a given result was examined or not by a user, further we follow the widespread assumption: a user examines all snippets up to the last clicked document. In what follows, all not clicked results ranked above the last clicked result are referred to as 'skips' and the remaining not clicked results are said to be 'not examined'.

At this point we would like to stress that we do not deal with the problem of improving the evaluation methodology of personalized search defined by equation (2). On the contrary, we assume that there is some fixed metric $\mathcal{M}$ defined by some state-of-the-art gain function $\mathcal{G}$, e.g., based on the fact of a click or the fact of a satisfied click, as in most of the studies on personalization. Such a labelling is typically established by simple rules, and the gain values it produces turn out to be noisy, as we have discussed in the beginning of this section. That is, not every document with zero/positive label is useless/useful for a user. We argue that direct utilization of these gain values *for training* a personalization algorithm leads to a suboptimal (according to the metric $\mathcal{M}$) ranking.

To address this weakness of the state-of-the-art personalization approaches, we suggest introduction of *weights*, i.e., we equip every sample $t_i \in \mathcal{S}$ with a certain positive number $w_i \in \mathbb{R}$, which reflects the confidence in the corresponding gain value and the need for a machine learning algorithm to take into account the gain for this particular example. Classically this approach is applied when the observed measurements (gain values $\mathcal{G}(t_i)$) have different uncertainties [2]: the closer the weight w_i to zero is, the less confident about the gain value $\mathcal{G}(t_i)$ we are.

For the empirical use, the appropriate weight values w_i are not known and must be estimated. The core idea of the present paper is adding of an extra step in the machine learning, see Section 4, which trains the weight values $w_i \in [0;1]$ in advance.

As we have discussed above, in the traditional personalization learning each sample $t_i \in \mathcal{S}$ is equipped with feature vector $\mathcal{X}(t_i) \in \mathbb{R}^N$. The fundamental advancement of our weight-based personalization learning is the utilization of additional information gathered along with standard gain values $\mathcal{G}(t)$: post-impression features reflecting a more complete picture of the interaction between the user and the search system that resulted into particular gain values. Among them, there are, for instance, the total number of clicks on SERP, the indicator of the fact the document d was clicked by a user, the dwell time of a click, etc. Assume that each sample $t_i \in \mathcal{S}$ in the training dataset is characterized by M-dimensional *weight feature vector* $\mathbf{y}_i = (y_i^1, \dots, y_i^M)$. Let $\mathcal{Y}$ be the corresponding map:

$$\mathcal{Y}\colon \mathcal{S} \to \mathbb{R}^M, \quad \mathcal{Y}\colon t_i \mapsto (y_i^1, \dots, y_i^M) \in \mathbb{R}^M.$$

We emphasize that these features cannot be calculated before the result page is formed, thus do not participate in the ranking model. However, they are possibly useful during the training of the ranker $\mathcal{F}$, since they implicitly carry the information about *degree of relevance* of documents in $\mathcal{S}$. Unfortunately, state-of-the-art search personalization algorithms do not allow employment of features $\mathcal{Y}(t_i)$. For this reason we suggest to learn a *weight function* $\mathcal{W}$ on the space of $\mathcal{Y}$-features.

Namely, let $\mathcal{W}$ be the function mapping the space of $\mathcal{Y}$-features to the weights:

$$\mathcal{W}\colon \mathbb{R}^M \to [0;1], \quad \mathcal{W}\colon \mathcal{Y}(t_i) \mapsto w_i.$$

Assume that we are given a machine learning algorithm $\mathcal{A}$, which takes into account weights of samples. An example of such algorithm is a linear model minimizing weighted sum of residual squares, discussed in Section 4. Given the weight function $\mathcal{W}$, gain function $\mathcal{G}$ and such a machine learning algorithm, we assume that one uniquely determines the ranker $\mathcal{F}_\mathcal{W}$. Our aim is to provide such weight function $\mathcal{W}$ that the ranker $\mathcal{F}_\mathcal{W}$ maximizes the overall ranking quality $\mathcal{M}(\mathcal{F}_\mathcal{W})$:

$$\widehat{\mathcal{W}} = \operatorname*{argmax}_{\mathcal{W}} \mathcal{M}(\mathcal{F}_\mathcal{W}). \tag{3}$$

In the next section we show that, under additional assumptions on the machine learning algorithm $\mathcal{A}$ and on the set of possible weight functions, this problem can be solved via steepest gradient descent.

4. ALGORITHM

4.1 Assumptions

In this section we explain how to learn the weight function $\mathcal{W}$ introduced in Section 3.2. To solve the optimization problem (3), one has to reduce the set of all possible functions $\mathcal{W}\colon \mathbb{R}^M \to \mathbb{R}$ to some finite-dimensional parametric family. In order to learn the parameters of $\mathcal{W}$, we need to know the impact of each parameter on the objective function $\mathcal{M} = \mathcal{M}(\mathcal{F}_\mathcal{W})$. If there are few parameters, one can perform an exhaustive search in the parameter space. However, the computational complexity of this exhaustive search grows exponentially with the growth of the number of parameters. Since each step of the exhaustive search requires separate training of an algorithm, which is usually resource consuming, exhaustive search quickly becomes infeasible with the growth of parameter space dimension. Ideally, we would like to start a gradient descent optimization of $\mathcal{M}$ with respect to parameters of the weight function $\mathcal{W}$.

Weight function

First we fix the class of weight functions we are considering. Although our framework is applicable to various parametric families of weight functions, further in this paper we deal only with *logistic* weight functions:

$$\mathcal{W}_\beta(\mathbf{y}) = \operatorname{sigmoid}(\mathbf{y}\cdot\beta), \quad \operatorname{sigmoid}(z) = \frac{1}{1+e^{-z}}, \tag{4}$$

where $\mathbf{y} = (y^1, \dots, y^M) \in \mathbb{R}^M$ is a row vector of $\mathcal{Y}$-features, $\beta = (\beta_1, \dots, \beta_M)^T$ is a column vector of parameters, and $\mathbf{y}\cdot\beta = \sum y^i \beta_i$. Here and below superscript ^{T} stands for

X	$S \times N$ matrix with personalization features, its i-th row is feature vector $\mathbf{x}_i = \mathcal{X}(t_i)$ of sample t_i
Y	$S \times M$ matrix with weight features, its i-th row is feature vector $\mathbf{y}_i = \mathcal{Y}(t_i)$ of sample t_i
β	M-dimensional column vector of weight parameters
W_β	diagonal $S \times S$ matrix with $\mathcal{W}_\beta(\mathbf{y}_i)$ at the i-th position
$\mathbf{b}$	N-dimensional column vector of ranker $\mathcal{F}$ parameters
$\mathbf{f}$	S-dimensional column vector of the ranker values, its i-th coordinate is $f_i = \mathcal{F}(\mathcal{X}(t_i))$
$\mathbf{g}$	S-dimensional column vector of the gain values, its i-th coordinate is $g_i = \mathcal{G}(t_i)$
μ	L_2-regularization parameter

Table 1: Matrix notations.

matrix transposition. The choice of the sigmoid transform is convenient, since it automatically guarantees that the weight function takes its values in the unit interval $(0;1)$.

Learning-to-rank algorithm

In the most general setting, derivatives $\frac{\partial \mathcal{M}}{\partial \beta_i}$ required for steepest descend optimization could not be efficiently computed and even do not necessarily exist. To guarantee the existence of these derivatives and to be able to calculate them, we limit ourselves to the particular class of machine learning algorithms — *linear regression ranking models* — and use a smoothed variant of the performance measure $\mathcal{M}$: SoftRank smoothing [18].

Before we describe this algorithm, we fix *matrix* notations for some objects defined in Section 3 and introduce some additional notions specific for the algorithm, which are summarized in Table 1.

Linear ranker $\mathcal{F}$ is any ranker given by a linear function $\mathcal{F}\colon \mathbb{R}^N \to \mathbb{R}$, i.e., a function of the form

$$\mathcal{F}(\mathbf{x}) = \mathbf{x}\cdot\mathbf{b} = \sum_{i=1}^{N} x^i b_i, \quad \mathbf{x} = (x^1, \ldots, x^N), \tag{5}$$

where $\mathbf{b} = (b_1, \ldots, b_N)^T$ is a column vector of coefficients — parameters of the ranking function. Thus, in the matrix notation, the vector of ranker values is $\mathbf{f} = X \cdot \mathbf{b}$.

Regression learning is one of the possible pointwise approaches to the learning-to-rank problem. This type of algorithms predicts the gain value $g_i = \mathcal{G}(t_i)$ for each sample (point) $t_i \in \mathcal{S}$ separately. Typically, this is done by minimizing the *residual sum of squares*:

$$\mathrm{RSS} = \sum_{t_i \in \mathcal{S}} (g_i - f_i)^2 \to \min .$$

To incorporate weights into RSS optimization problem we use its weighted analogue: WRSS, by multiplying each residual square by the corresponding weight:

$$\mathrm{WRSS} = \sum_{t_i \in \mathcal{S}} w_i (g_i - f_i)^2 \to \min .$$

For the reduction of the overfitting to the training dataset we add L_2 regularization term to the WRSS minimization problem. The impact of the regularization on the final solution is controlled by the parameter $\mu \in \mathbb{R}$ (L_2RSS is defined analogously):

$$L_2\mathrm{WRSS} = \sum_{t_i \in \mathcal{S}} w_i (g_i - f_i)^2 + \mu ||\mathbf{b}||^2 \to \min \tag{6}$$

Further in the paper we assume that the machine learning algorithm $\mathcal{A}$ solves this minimization problem. We would like to point out that although the framework described below solves the weight optimization problem (3) only for linear regression algorithm, the learned weight function $\mathcal{W}$ itself could be used in a more complicated algorithms. For example, our experimental results in Section 6 prove that the weight function learned for a simple linear regression problem (solution to (3) for ranker (5)) significantly improves a decision tree model.

4.2 Gradient computation

In the case of L_2WRSS regression problem (6), we have $f_i = \mathbf{x}_i \cdot \mathbf{b}$ and linear learning has the explicit solution:

$$\mathbf{b} = (X^T W_\beta X + \mu \mathrm{Id})^{-1} X^T W_\beta \mathbf{g}; \tag{7}$$

the vector of ranker values is:

$$\mathbf{f} = X\mathbf{b} = X(X^T W_\beta X + \mu \mathrm{Id})^{-1} X^T W_\beta \mathbf{g}. \tag{8}$$

For our choice of the weight function, see (4), the elements of the matrix W_β smoothly depend on the parameter vector β, so together with equation (8) this gives smooth dependence of the vector $\mathbf{f}$ on parameters β, and we can compute all the derivatives $\frac{\partial \mathbf{f}}{\partial \beta_k}$ for $i = 1, \ldots, M$. Setting $Z_\beta = X^T W_\beta X + \mu \mathrm{Id}$ and differentiating the equality $Z_\beta \mathbf{b} = X^T W_\beta \mathbf{g}$ with respect to β_i, one obtains:

$$\frac{\partial \mathbf{b}}{\partial \beta_i} = Z_\beta^{-1} X^T \frac{\partial W_\beta}{\partial \beta_i} \mathbf{g} - Z_\beta^{-1} \frac{\partial Z_\beta}{\partial \beta_i} \mathbf{b} = \\ = Z_\beta^{-1} X^T \frac{\partial W_\beta}{\partial \beta_i} (\mathbf{g} - \mathbf{f}). \tag{9}$$

Here $\frac{\partial W_\beta}{\partial \beta_i}$ is the elementwise derivative of matrix W_β, i.e., the diagonal $S \times S$ matrix with $y_k^i\, \mathrm{sigmoid}'(\mathbf{y}_k \cdot \beta)$ at k-th position.

To finish the computation of the derivatives $\frac{\partial \mathcal{M}}{\partial \beta_i}$ we need to find $\frac{\partial \mathcal{M}}{\partial f_j}$. Although in the straightforward interpretation of the metric $\mathcal{M}$ described above, this derivative never exists, there are effective methods to cope with this problem. Indeed, ordering of documents $\mathcal{S}_{u,q}$ defined by the values of the ranking function $\mathcal{F}$ is locally constant and changes discontinuously as scores $f_i = \mathcal{F}(\mathcal{X}(t))$ vary, so does the objective function $\mathcal{M}$. A standard method of turning $\mathcal{M}$ into a smooth function is a probabilistic smoothing of the ranking measure, see [18, 20, 24]. Further we employ *SoftRank* approach from [18]. In a nutshell, this method replaces each score f_i with a random variable with a normal distribution with the mean f_i and computes the expectation value $E\mathcal{M}$ instead of the true value $\mathcal{M}$. We refer to [18, Section 3] for technical details and explicit formulas. By abuse of notation we continue writing simply $\mathcal{M}$ instead of $E\mathcal{M}$.

Now we have all ingredients to start steepest descend in the space of parameters β. Let $\beta^j \in \mathbb{R}^M$ be the vector of weight function parameters at j-th iteration. The pseudocode in Algorithm 1 summarizes iterative steepest descend learning of the weight function $\mathcal{W}_\beta$ in the case of linear ranker $\mathcal{F}$, see equations (5) and (6).

Input: feature matrices X, Y, vector of gain values $\mathbf{g}$
Parameters: number of iterations J, step size regularization ϵ, parameter of L_2 regularization μ
Initialization: $\beta^0 = (0, \dots, 0)^T$
for $j = 0$ *to* J **do**

$\mathbf{f} = X(X^T W_{\beta^j} X + \mu \mathrm{Id})^{-1} X^T W_{\beta^j} \mathbf{g}$ (see (8));

$\text{step} = \frac{\partial \mathcal{M}}{\partial \mathbf{f}} \cdot \frac{\partial \mathbf{f}}{\partial \beta}\Big|_{\beta=\beta^j} = \sum_{i=1}^{S} \frac{\partial \mathcal{M}}{\partial f_i} \cdot \frac{\partial f_i}{\partial \beta}\Big|_{\beta=\beta^j}$ (see (9));

$\beta^{j+1} = \beta^j + \epsilon\,\text{step};$

end
Output: optimized vector β^J

Algorithm 1: Steepest descend optimization of β.

4.3 Computational complexity

In this section we give an upper bound on the complexity of one iteration of Algorithm 1. In what follows, we assume that $M, N \ll S$, since in the personalization framework it is usually very easy to collect a training set of arbitrarily large size, and, typically, in studies on personalization [3, 4, 15], the number of samples in the training set is several orders of magnitude larger than the number of features. Under these assumptions we estimate the complexity of our algorithm with a sigmoid weight function $\mathcal{W}$ and a linear ranker $\mathcal{F}$ (see equations (4) and (5)).

To calculate the derivatives (9) we first compute the $S \times S$ matrix with the numbers $\text{sigmoid}'(\mathbf{y}_k \cdot \beta), k = 1\dots, S$, on the diagonal. Then compute M matrices $\frac{\partial W_\beta}{\partial \beta_i}$ multiplying diagonal by numbers y_k^i and matrix W_β, which requires $O(MS)$ operations. After this, using the fact that matrix W_β is diagonal, we compute matrix Z_β, in $O(SN^2)$ operations.

Recall that computation of a product of two matrices of sizes $A \times B$ and $B \times C$ requires $O(ABC)$ operations, and finding a solution of a linear system of a size $A \times A$ requires $O(A^3)$ operations. Hence, to multiply right-hand sides of equations (8) and (9) from the right to left one requires

$$\begin{aligned} &O(S) + O(NS) + O(N^3) + O(NS) + \\ &\quad + M\big(O(S) + O(NS) + O(N^3) + O(NS)\big) = \\ &\qquad = O(SNM) + O(N^3 M) \end{aligned}$$

operations. Taking into account the fact that $M, N \ll S$, we obtain the estimate $O(SMN) + O(SN^2)$ operations to compute the vectors $\frac{\partial \mathbf{f}}{\partial \beta_i}$, see (9).

The complexity of the procedure of smoothing the objective function is described in [18, Section 3.6]. The computation of the derivatives $\frac{\partial M}{\partial f_j}$ for one user-query pair requires $O(k^3)$ operations, where k is the number of documents retrieved for a given query q (assumed to be constant across different queries in our case). So, the computation of all the derivatives of the objective function $\mathcal{M}$ over all scores $f_i, i = 1, \dots, S$ requires $\frac{S}{k} O(k^3) = O(Sk^2)$ operations.

All in all the computation of the gradients $\frac{\partial \mathcal{M}}{\partial \beta}$ requires:

$$O(SNM) + O(SN^2) + O(Sk^2)$$

operations. Note that the complexity of our framework is linear with respect to the number of samples in the training dataset and the number of iterations.

5. EXPERIMENTAL SETUP

In this section we describe the dataset and the features that are used to train both the personalized ranker and the weight function used in our learning framework.

5.1 Data

In the experiments we verify our theoretically grounded framework on the large-scale log of a popular commercial search engine. Namely, we use a sample from the publicly available dataset shared by Yandex with the participants of 'Personalized Web Search Challenge' on `Kaggle.com`.This dataset contains user sessions collected during 30 days including user ids, their queries, query terms, SERPs, and clicks. All queries with no clicks on the result page were eliminated. The sessions from the first 27 days were intended for training and are supplied with all available data, while the sessions from the last three days are not accompanied by information about clicks and were used to find the winners of the challenge. While the clicks for the latter sessions had not become publicly available even after the challenge, we use the former sessions for our experiments, also used by all participants of the challenge to train and test their solutions. The stream of user actions stored in the dataset is pre-segmented into *search sessions*. As described below, we use this segmentation to compute some of the weight features. All data including texts of queries are fully anonymized and encoded by numerical values. An original production ranking recorded in this dataset, which was presented to real users, will be further referred to as *non-personalized baseline*.

5.2 Personalization features

The core component of any personalization algorithm is the set of features $\mathcal{X}$ used for training a personalized ranker. Note that the specific choice of features $\mathcal{X}$ is out of the scope of our study, and the framework we suggest could be applied regardless of a feature set. However, to prove effectiveness of our methodology on the real data, we conduct our experiments by using a competitive collection of personalization features. Namely, we use the evaluation dataset provided by team `pampampampam`, the winner of the Personalized Web Search Challenge.

This evaluation dataset $\mathcal{S}$ consists of 280K queries uniformly sampled from the 27th day in the original raw Kaggle log for training and testing purposes. For each query-document pair, personalization features are computed based on the information available prior to the moment this query was issued (including the information from the first 26 days of the Kaggle dataset).

We briefly enlist the types of features extracted from the Yandex dataset. For every sample $\{u, q, d\} \in \mathcal{S}$ we used 165 features covering most of the existing sources of signal for personalization investigated in previous studies on personalization [4, 16, 21]. Since some data used in these studies is unavailable in our case, as we use the above mentioned publicly available dataset, we use simplified versions of some features, e.g., we do not have any information on *topics* of documents, *stopwords* in queries and IDF's (inverse document frequencies) of words.

- Features based on the user behavior aggregated over all users, e.g., various click-through rates of document d, the number of times document d was shown, the number of times document d was skipped.
- Features reflecting the short-term search context of a given query, e.g., the number of times the document was shown/clicked/skipped by the user in the current search session. These features are analogous to the **Query-Doc-User Features** from [4] based on URL-match with decay.
- Features intended for long-term personalization (see [4, 16]) computed during the first 26 days, e.g., the number of times the document/host was shown/clicked/skipped by the user in the past. These features are analogous to the **Query-Doc-User Features** from [4] based on URL-match without decay.
- Characteristics of query q, e.g., word count, query popularity, click entropy, sum of inverse frequencies of its terms. These features include all **Query features** from [4].
- The original position of document d assigned by the default non-personalized ranker (The **Query-Doc** feature from [4]).

During evaluation of our personalization system we perform the following version of cross-validation by proceeding the following splitting of the dataset five times. We divide the whole dataset $\mathcal{S}$ containing 2.8M samples into two parts on the basis of unique user id: (1) part $\mathcal{S}_1$ containing 1/3 of query-document pairs is used for learning of personalization models and weights as it is described in Algorithm 1; (2) the remaining part $\mathcal{S}_2$ is used for evaluation. We did this type of splitting following the state-of-the-art studies on personalization [3, 15, 19] to prevent user-specific overfitting and to ensure that the model we learned is applicable to users not seen in the training dataset. All performance values reported below are averaged over these five splittings.

5.3 Weight features

The core part of our experiments is the choice of the set of weight features $\mathcal{Y}$. These features characterise user behavior on the result page and are used only as components of the function $\mathcal{W}_\beta$ trained with the procedure described in Section 4. They do not participate in training a personalization ranker, since these features cannot be calculated before the search results are shown to the user. The basic features of user interaction with SERP are reported in Table 2. There are two types of features: the first ones depend on the particular query-document pair and the second ones depend on the whole SERP. All the non-binary features are

Feature	Description
	Document level features
click*	1 iff d was clicked
dwell	dwell time of a click, 0 if click(d)=0
long*	1 iff dwell(d) > 30
last*	1 iff click(d) = 1 and d is the last clicked document
first*	1 iff click(d) = 1 and d is the first clicked document
sat*	last(d) = 1 or long = 1
position	original position of the document
skip*	d was skipped
skipprev*	the previous document in the ranking list was skipped
skipabove	the number of skipped documents above d
	SERP level features
topclick	the highest position among all clicks
bottomclick	the lowest position among all clicks
numclick	total number of clicks on the result page
numclick3	number of clicks at top 3 results
numskips	total number of skipped documents on the result page
lastquery*	query q is the last query in the session
examtime	time to the first click on SERP

Table 2: Basic weight features (* indicates binary)

Feature	#	Discretization levels
dwell	10	0–5–15–30–50–90–150–300–750–3000–∞
position	10	1, 2, 3, 4, 5, 6, 7, 8, 9, 10
skipabove	3	0, 1, 2–∞
numclick	2	1, 2–∞
numclick3	4	0, 1, 2, 3
numskips	3	0, 1, 2–∞
examtime	10	0–5–15–30–50–90–150–300–750–3000–∞

Table 3: Discretization of non-binary features.

Feature	#
click=x AND numclick=y AND position=1	4
click=x AND numclick=y AND position>1	4
last=1 AND numclick=x	2
first=1 AND numclick=x	2
skip=0 AND click=0	1
skipprev=1 AND click=1	1

Table 4: Composite weight features and their counts.

turned into the binary ones as it is reported in Table 3. The set of binary features we choose was motivated by the basic binary features used in [26] for improving the statistical power of interleaving algorithms. From the binary features we combine more complex ones as described in Table 4. To sum up, we take binary features from Tables 2 and 3 and the ones presented in Table 4 (64 features in total).

Besides improving the quality of the personalized ranker, we expect that the values of weight function will help answering the following questions:

Q1 How does the time the user has spent on the clicked document d affect the confidence in its positive gain value?

Q2 How does *positional bias* of users' clicks affect the weights of the gain values?

Q3 Do all the non-clicked documents indicate non-relevance to the same extent?

6. RESULTS

In this section we report the results of various experiments we conduct on training weight functions $\mathcal{W}$ on the Yandex dataset. Below we compute re-ranking performances on all the queries in the test set, which, in particular, includes many of the queries not affected by the personalization. Although averaging improvements over all queries, instead of affected ones, decreases change in MRR*, it also provides more insight into the overall effect of our method.

We conclude this section by analyzing the learned weight function in the scope of the stated research questions and provide some insight into interpreting the user behavior.

6.1 Evaluation methodology

To evaluate the quality of our framework we used five simplest and widely used [1, 9, 22], 'basic' binary gains $\mathcal{G}$:

click, first click, last click, long click, satisfied click.

We fix the positional discount function: $\text{discount}(k) = 1/k$ and compute the corresponding objective measures as in equations (1) and (2) for each of the gains. Further these five performance metrics are referred to as MRR* (where * stands for one of the gains: click, first, last, long or sat).

Relying on the unique user identifier, we randomly divide part $\mathcal{S}_1$ into three equal parts: $\mathcal{S}_1 = \mathcal{S}_1^1 \sqcup \mathcal{S}_1^2 \sqcup \mathcal{S}_1^3$. First, we adjust the regularization parameter and use it in the subsequent experiments: $\mu = \text{argmax}_\mu \mathcal{M}(\mathcal{F})$, where the performance metric $\mathcal{M}$ is computed over $\mathcal{S}_1^2$ and the ranker $\mathcal{F}$ is trained via L_2-regularized RSS linear model on $\mathcal{S}_1^1$. Step regularization parameter ϵ was set to the trivial default value $\epsilon = 1$ and was not tuned. Smaller values of ϵ could possibly improve the quality of our framework, however, at the same time, they would increase the optimal number of iterations and thus, the runtime of the steepest descent algorithm. After that we run Algorithm 1 and find the best iteration count according to the performance $\mathcal{M}(\mathcal{F}_\mathcal{W})$ measured on the set $\mathcal{S}_1^2$. The resulting ranker trained on the set $\mathcal{S}_1^1$ is evaluated on the set $\mathcal{S}_2$.

The remaining set $\mathcal{S}_1^3$ is further used to tune the parameters of the decision tree model, see Section 6.3.

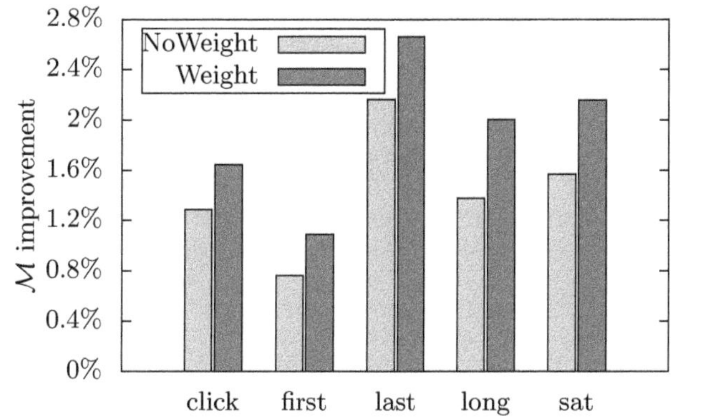

Figure 1: Relative improvements of MRR* of various gains for linear models trained without and with weights over the non-personalized baseline.

	MRR* improvement in %				
WRSS \ gain $\mathcal{G}$	click	first	last	long	sat
$\mathcal{W}$ for 'first'	+1.17	**+0.98**	+1.54	+1.24	+1.32
$\mathcal{W}$ for gain $\mathcal{G}$	**+1.68**	**+0.98**	**+2.66**	**+2.00**	**+2.16**

Table 5: MRR* improvements over the non-personalized baseline of the linear rankers learned with weights trained for 'first' gain and for the corresponding gain.

6.2 Linear model

In this section we compare two personalization algorithms: linear regression model learned with the identical weights (L_2RSS) and linear regression model learned with the weight function optimized with our framework (L_2WRSS). The improvements of both learning algorithms over non-personalized baseline according to five binary gains are demonstrated in Figure 1. For every gain, weighted L_2WRSS model significantly outperforms the corresponding L_2RSS model.

To demonstrate that the weight function $\mathcal{W}$ trained with our framework essentially depends on the choice of the evaluation metric $\mathcal{M}$, and, therefore, on the gain function $\mathcal{G}$, we also conduct the following experiment. We trained weight function $\mathcal{W}$ relying on the 'first' gain, and the corresponding ranker $\mathcal{F}_\mathcal{W}$ was evaluated according to the other basic gains.

In Table 5 we report the performance of this ranker in comparison with the rankers trained by utilizing weight functions optimized by Algorithm 1 for the corresponding gains. One can see that for 'click' 'last', 'long' and 'sat' gains the weight function trained for the 'first' gain is significantly outperformed. This proves that the choice of the performance measure strongly affects the weight function provided by our algorithm. Another argument supporting this claim will be discussed in Section 6.4.

6.3 Decision tree model

To understand whether the weights provided by our framework are specific for linear machine learning algorithms only or could be used for more complicated models, we used them at the top of a proprietary implementation of Friedman's gradient boosted decision tree-based machine learning algorithm [7] with the WRSS loss function.

Alg.\ gain $\mathcal{G}$	MRR* improvement in %				
	click	first	last	long	sat
RSS	+1.95	+1.50	+2.75	+2.11	+2.22
WRSS	**+2.02**	**+1.60**	**+2.81**	**+2.23**	**+2.34**

Table 6: MRR* improvements over the non-personalized baseline of the decision-tree rankers learned without (RSS) and with (WRSS) trained weights. All WRSS rankers significantly (p<0.05) outperform RSS rankers according to the Student t-test.

Alg.	Fraction of queries in%			
	meas diff	plus	minus	plus/minus
RSS	26.94	15.65	11.30	1.38
WRSS	28.50	16.67	11.83	1.41

Table 7: Fractions of affected ('meas diff'), improved ('plus'), deteriorated ('minus') queries and robustness rate ('plus/minus') for the decision-tree rankers learned for 'sat' gain without (RSS) and with (WRSS) trained weights.

Namely, given the gain function $\mathcal{G}$, we train a weight function, as in Section 6.2. For the trained weights, we learn the gradient boosted decision tree model on the set $\mathcal{S}_1^1 \sqcup \mathcal{S}_1^2$. Note that in Section 6.1 we have trained weights w_i using the same dataset $\mathcal{S}_1^1 \sqcup \mathcal{S}_1^2$, this ensures that the model trained with the use of our weights has accessed the same set of labelled samples as the model trained using baseline identical weights.

We would like to point out that the decision tree training model based on RSS loss function we use in this section coincides with the training model used by the winners of the Personalized Web Search Challenge. Thus it represents very strong personalization benchmark and any statistically significant improvement is valuable and important.

The resulting improvements are summarized in Table 6. Although the corresponding weight functions were trained under the assumption that machine learning algorithm $\mathcal{A}$ is linear (see Section 4.1), the utilization of these weights inside the decision tree model significantly improves its performance for all five basic gains. This indicates, that trained weights are universal and, being applicable to any algorithm based on minimizing WRSS loss function, they improve various machine learning algorithms.

For a better understanding of the magnitude of our improvements, we compare them with other studies on personalization. Most papers [3, 4, 5, 15, 22] report improvement of the order of a tenth of a percent up to a few percent *over the non-personalized baseline*. However, all these papers employ some *new sources of data* for personalization, e.g., short-term and long-term history, task-aggregation, geographical data, browsing data, etc. On the contrary, in our experiments we (1) achieve the improvements by changing the machine learning framework only, rather then by incorporating new signals for personalization and (2) evaluate our methodology against a very strong personalization baseline. This observation proves that weight learning framework indeed a notable improvement of the existing approaches.

Another important property of any re-ranking algorithm is its *robustness*. The fractions of affected queries, i.e., measurably different from the baseline performance, improved,

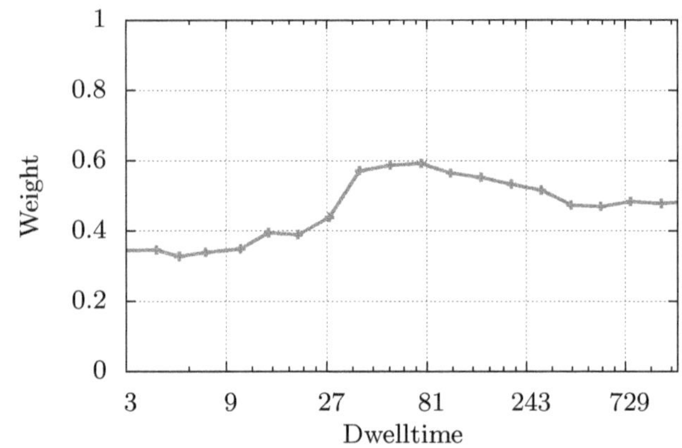

Figure 2: Average trained weight (for satisfied clicks gain) of clicked documents as a function of dwell time.

deteriorated queries are common characteristic of re-ranking models, see, e.g, [3, 11, 16]. A robust algorithm not only improves the average quality, but also does not "hurt much", i.e., has low fraction of deteriorated and improved queries. From Table 7 one can see that the personalization model learned with weights affects more queries and has a better improvement/deterioration ratio.

To conclude this section, we would like to mention that web search personalization is known as one of the most challenging learning tasks. For instance, the additional improvement of 0.12% over the baseline (e.g., the same as the WRSS achieved over RSS according to MRR with 'sat' gain) would allow the team that took the 3rd place in Kaggle competition become a winner[3]. Given that, by applying our framework, we managed to improve even the ranking system that won the challenge, we consider this improvement as an important and convincing motivation for opening a new research direction of optimizing weight functions of personalized labels introduced in our paper.

6.4 Analyzing weight function

Now we address the research question Q1 by analyzing the effect the dwell time has on the trained weight values w_i. Dwell time is a common measure of conversion, so it has been widely studied from different perspectives [10]. Figure 2 depicts the average weight of documents with a given interval of dwelltime on the logscale. One could conclude that the average weight values increase in the neighbourhood of point 30, justifying this threshold for satisfied clicks. In fact, it works in the opposite direction. Namely, these weights dramatically increase at 30, since they were optimized for a metric MRR-SAT, where only satisfied clicks are relevant. This observation again proves (as Table 5) that the weight function essentially depends on the choice of the evaluation metric $\mathcal{M}$. We stress that choice of the 'right' metric $\mathcal{M}$ lies out of the scope of our study and could not be done solely using data available in our experiments.

To answer both questions Q2 and Q3, we demonstrate the average of the trained weight values over clicked/skipped/not examined documents ranked at the various fixed positions in Figure 3. The weights of a skipped

[3]http://www.kaggle.com/c/yandex-personalized-web-search-challenge/leaderboard

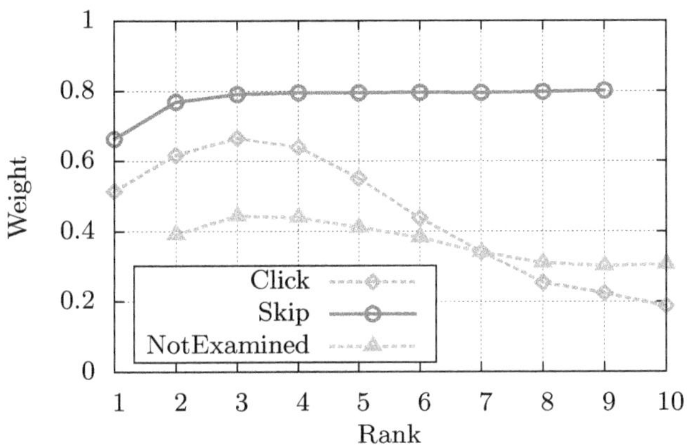

Figure 3: Average trained weight (for satisfied clicks gain) of clicked, skipped and not examined documents as a function of ranking position.

document at position 10 and a not examined document at position 1 are not presented, since (by definition) there are no such documents.

As we have expected, the average confidence in the negative label of 'skipped' documents is noticeably larger than of 'not examined' ones. Interestingly, confidence in the positive label of clicked documents increases up to position 3 and decreases after it. There are two possible explanations of this behavior. The first one is related to *positional bias*: users tend to click on the top-ranked documents despite their relevance, so clicks at first positions are often noisy. The second effect is that the queries with clicks at low ranked documents are typically complex and ambiguous so do not have a single relevant result, unlike, e.g., navigational queries. Confidence in the relevance of a particular result retrieved in a response to such complex query is lower.

7. FUTURE WORK

Improving personalized ranking is the focus of our study. However, our framework and the tuned weight function itself could be applied in a wide variety of settings, and, hence, there are various directions for future work.

Given a set of query-document pairs equipped with editorial labels, we can use the method proposed in our study to learn confidence levels of these labels, taking into account query, document and assessor features. Besides it, the weights we learn potentially provide a valuable signal for automatic evaluation of search engine performance. Namely, similarly to classical click-based metrics like MRR and MAP, it is possible to use measures of the form (1) that would incorporate the tuned weights w_i into the gain function $\mathcal{G}$. At last, as we have briefly discussed in Section 6.4, the weight values and coefficients β_i of the trained weight functions $\mathcal{W}_\beta$ encode important information about user's behavior patterns and provide useful insights for its modelling and analysis.

Besides diverse possible applications of our framework, there is a large room for its development and improvement. Probably the most essential direction for future research is to extend our algorithm, which is primarily intended for linear regression models, to more complicated machine learning models, e.g., neural networks and decision trees. The gap between improvements demonstrated in the linear and decision tree model cases, see Figure 1 and Table 6, suggests that the solution to this *extension problem* will likely substantially improve the overall effectiveness of our framework.

8. CONCLUSION

In this paper, following the most studies on personalization of web search, we deal with a training of a personalized ranker on the basis of user clicks. The state-of-the-art approaches to personalization employ very simple and noisy implicit personal relevance labels, missing vast amount of useful information. We have presented an optimization framework for training the confidence levels of these labels. Given a click-through dataset and a fixed evaluation methodology, our algorithm extracts weights of relevance labels from various features characterising user interaction with the result page. These weights could be utilized in the majority of machine learning algorithms.

Our experiments with the large-scale publicly-available dataset demonstrate that rankers trained via both simple linear models and the state-of-the-art decision trees machine learning algorithms significantly benefit from the employment of the trained weight function.

Acknowledgements

We are grateful to the team `pampampampam` and its members, who have shared their learning dataset with us. Also we would like to thank Igor Kuralenok for valuable discussions and advice on this research.

9. REFERENCES

[1] E. Agichtein, E. Brill, and S. Dumais. Improving web search ranking by incorporating user behavior information. In *Proceedings of the 29th Annual International ACM SIGIR Conference on Research and Development in Information Retrieval*, SIGIR '06, pages 19–26, New York, NY, USA, 2006. ACM.

[2] A. Aitken. On least squares and linear combination of observations. volume 55 of *Proc. R. Soc. Edinb*, pages 42–48, 1934.

[3] P. N. Bennett, F. Radlinski, R. W. White, and E. Yilmaz. Inferring and using location metadata to personalize web search. In *Proceedings of the 34th International ACM SIGIR Conference on Research and Development in Information Retrieval*, SIGIR '11, pages 135–144, New York, NY, USA, 2011. ACM.

[4] P. N. Bennett, R. W. White, W. Chu, S. T. Dumais, P. Bailey, F. Borisyuk, and X. Cui. Modeling the impact of short- and long-term behavior on search personalization. In *Proceedings of the 35th International ACM SIGIR Conference on Research and Development in Information Retrieval*, SIGIR '12, pages 185–194, New York, NY, USA, 2012. ACM.

[5] K. Collins-Thompson, P. N. Bennett, R. W. White, S. de la Chica, and D. Sontag. Personalizing web search results by reading level. In *Proceedings of the 20th ACM International Conference on Information and Knowledge Management*, CIKM '11, pages 403–412, New York, NY, USA, 2011. ACM.

[6] Z. Dou, R. Song, and J.-R. Wen. A large-scale evaluation and analysis of personalized search

strategies. In *Proceedings of the 16th International Conference on World Wide Web*, WWW '07, pages 581–590, New York, NY, USA, 2007. ACM.

[7] J. H. Friedman. Stochastic gradient boosting. *Comput. Stat. Data Anal.*, 38(4):367–378, Feb. 2002.

[8] D. Jiang, K. W.-T. Leung, and W. Ng. Context-aware search personalization with concept preference. In *Proceedings of the 20th ACM International Conference on Information and Knowledge Management*, CIKM '11, pages 563–572, New York, NY, USA, 2011. ACM.

[9] T. Joachims. Optimizing search engines using clickthrough data. In *Proceedings of the Eighth ACM SIGKDD International Conference on Knowledge Discovery and Data Mining*, KDD '02, pages 133–142, New York, NY, USA, 2002. ACM.

[10] C. Liu, R. W. White, and S. Dumais. Understanding web browsing behaviors through weibull analysis of dwell time. In *Proceedings of the 33rd International ACM SIGIR Conference on Research and Development in Information Retrieval*, SIGIR '10, pages 379–386, New York, NY, USA, 2010. ACM.

[11] N. Matthijs and F. Radlinski. Personalizing web search using long term browsing history. In *Proceedings of the Fourth ACM International Conference on Web Search and Data Mining*, WSDM '11, pages 25–34, New York, NY, USA, 2011. ACM.

[12] F. Radlinski, M. Kurup, and T. Joachims. How does clickthrough data reflect retrieval quality? In *Proceedings of the 17th ACM Conference on Information and Knowledge Management*, CIKM '08, pages 43–52, New York, NY, USA, 2008. ACM.

[13] P. Serdyukov, G. Dupret, and N. Craswell. Log-based personalization: The 4th web search click data (wscd) workshop. WSDM '14, pages 685–686, New York, NY, USA, 2014. ACM.

[14] X. Shen, B. Tan, and C. Zhai. Context-sensitive information retrieval using implicit feedback. In *Proceedings of the 28th Annual International ACM SIGIR Conference on Research and Development in Information Retrieval*, SIGIR '05, pages 43–50, New York, NY, USA, 2005. ACM.

[15] M. Shokouhi, R. W. White, P. Bennett, and F. Radlinski. Fighting search engine amnesia: Reranking repeated results. In *Proceedings of the 36th International ACM SIGIR Conference on Research and Development in Information Retrieval*, SIGIR '13, pages 273–282, New York, NY, USA, 2013. ACM.

[16] D. Sontag, K. Collins-Thompson, P. N. Bennett, R. W. White, S. Dumais, and B. Billerbeck. Probabilistic models for personalizing web search. WSDM '12, pages 433–442, New York, NY, USA, 2012. ACM.

[17] B. Tan, X. Shen, and C. Zhai. Mining long-term search history to improve search accuracy. In *Proceedings of the 12th ACM SIGKDD International Conference on Knowledge Discovery and Data Mining*, KDD '06, pages 718–723, New York, NY, USA, 2006. ACM.

[18] M. Taylor, J. Guiver, S. Robertson, and T. Minka. Softrank: Optimizing non-smooth rank metrics. In *Proceedings of the 2008 International Conference on Web Search and Data Mining*, WSDM '08, pages 77–86, New York, NY, USA, 2008. ACM.

[19] Y. Ustinovskiy and P. Serdyukov. Personalization of web-search using short-term browsing context. In *Proceedings of the 22Nd ACM International Conference on Conference on Information and Knowledge Management*, CIKM '13, pages 1979–1988, New York, NY, USA, 2013. ACM.

[20] M. N. Volkovs and R. S. Zemel. Boltzrank: Learning to maximize expected ranking gain. In *Proceedings of the 26th Annual International Conference on Machine Learning*, ICML '09, pages 1089–1096, New York, NY, USA, 2009. ACM.

[21] R. W. White, P. N. Bennett, and S. T. Dumais. Predicting short-term interests using activity-based search context. In *Proceedings of the 19th ACM International Conference on Information and Knowledge Management*, CIKM '10, pages 1009–1018, New York, NY, USA, 2010. ACM.

[22] R. W. White, W. Chu, A. Hassan, X. He, Y. Song, and H. Wang. Enhancing personalized search by mining and modeling task behavior. In *Proceedings of the 22Nd International Conference on World Wide Web*, WWW '13, pages 1411–1420, Republic and Canton of Geneva, Switzerland, 2013. International World Wide Web Conferences Steering Committee.

[23] B. Xiang, D. Jiang, J. Pei, X. Sun, E. Chen, and H. Li. Context-aware ranking in web search. In *Proceedings of the 33rd International ACM SIGIR Conference on Research and Development in Information Retrieval*, SIGIR '10, pages 451–458, New York, NY, USA, 2010. ACM.

[24] J. Xu, T.-Y. Liu, M. Lu, H. Li, and W.-Y. Ma. Directly optimizing evaluation measures in learning to rank. In *Proceedings of the 31st Annual International ACM SIGIR Conference on Research and Development in Information Retrieval*, SIGIR '08, pages 107–114, New York, NY, USA, 2008. ACM.

[25] L. Xu, M. White, and D. Schuurmans. Optimal reverse prediction: A unified perspective on supervised, unsupervised and semi-supervised learning. In *Proceedings of the 26th Annual International Conference on Machine Learning*, ICML '09, pages 1137–1144, New York, NY, USA, 2009. ACM.

[26] Y. Yue, Y. Gao, O. Chapelle, Y. Zhang, and T. Joachims. Learning more powerful test statistics for click-based retrieval evaluation. In *Proceedings of the 33rd International ACM SIGIR Conference on Research and Development in Information Retrieval*, SIGIR '10, pages 507–514, New York, NY, USA, 2010. ACM.

A First Look at Tribal Web Traffic

Morgan Vigil
Dept. of Computer Science
UC Santa Barbara
Santa Barbara, CA
mvigil@cs.ucsb.edu

Matthew Rantanen
Southern California
Tribal Chairmen's Association
Pala, CA
mrantanen@sctdv.net

Elizabeth Belding
Dept. of Computer Science
UC Santa Barbara
Santa Barbara, CA
ebelding@cs.ucsb.edu

ABSTRACT

With broadband penetration rates of less than 10% per capita, Tribal areas in the U.S. represent some of the most underserved communities in terms of Internet access [4]. Although numerous sources have identified this digital divide, there have been no empirical measurements of the performance and usage of services that do exist in these areas. In this paper, we present the characterization of the Tribal Digital Village (TDV) network, a multi-hop wireless network currently connecting 13 reservations in San Diego county. This work represents the first traffic analysis of broadband usage in Tribal lands. After identifying some of the unique purposes of broadband connectivity in indigenous communities, such as language revitalization and cultural development, we focus on the performance of popular applications that enable such activities, including Youtube and Instagram. Though only a fraction of the bandwidth capacity is actually used, 30% of Youtube uploads and 24% of Instagram uploads fail due to packet loss on the relay and access links that connect the reservations to the TDV backbone. Although failure rates are prohibitive to the contribution of locally generated media (particularly videos), our analysis of Instagram media interactions and engagement in the TDV network reveals a high locality of interest. Residents engage with locally created media 8.2× more than media created by outside sources. Furthermore, locally created media circulates through the network two days longer than non-local media. The results of our analysis point to new directions for increasing content availability on reservations.

1. INTRODUCTION

Even as global broadband coverage continues to increase, Tribal communities remain largely unconnected to broadband services, with less than 10% of the population residing on Tribal lands having access to broadband–a stark contrast to the rest of the United States where the average broadband penetration rate is 70% [4]. The lack of broadband access for these communities is caused by a convergence of challenges, including geographic obstacles, funding, and complex network policy standards. Tribal communities represent some of the final frontiers of the digital divide in the U.S. and a disparity in the accessibility of critical opportunities, including education, health, and financial services. Even after issues of connectivity are resolved, content-related issues become apparent: web content does not reflect Tribal interests; indigenous languages are not represented in web media and are at risk of extinction; and indigenous people play a limited role in how they are represented in media in general. To this end, social media has been cited as a key factor in establishing digital sovereignty, identity, and cultural resilience in Tribal communities [25].

Despite the U.S. government's concern with making broadband more accessible to Tribal communities and anecdotal evidence supporting the importance of online services in preserving Tribal identity and culture, there have been no quantitative studies exploring how Tribal communities utilize existing broadband connectivity. Likewise, little has been done to understand Tribal use of social media from a networking perspective, even though this insight could motivate innovative technical solutions for bringing access to more people. This research represents some of the first work in characterizing web usage in Tribal communities.

Using network traffic collected from the Tribal Digital Village (TDV) network in rural San Diego County, we gain insight into web usage in Tribal America [10]. Our data represents Internet usage over a period of two months, from June 23 to August 20, 2014. The TDV network provides 13 previously unconnected Indian reservations[1] with affordable residential broadband services over a long-distance multi-hop wireless backbone that terminates in a high speed fiber connection to the Internet. Surprisingly, our work reveals that Instagram, not Facebook or Google, is the most requested application in the network, generating over 2 million requests in two months. Additionally, it is one of the top five most bandwidth-consuming applications in the network. Unlike other popular social networking platforms, such as Facebook or Twitter, Instagram focuses exclusively on the processes of creating, sharing, and interacting with media, which makes it especially relevant for understanding how social media functions within a Tribal context. Likewise, Instagram has been cited as one of the top social networking platforms of 2014 with one of the most diverse and engaged user bases [19]. While it has been studied in the context of data visualization [21] and participatory crowd-sensing [27],

WWW 2015, May 18–22, 2015, Florence, Italy.
ACM 978-1-4503-3469-3/15/05.
http://dx.doi.org/10.1145/2736277.2741645 .

[1] An area of land reserved for a Tribe or Tribes under treaty or other agreement with the United States for use as permanent tribal homelands. http://www.bia.gov/FAQs/

to the best of our knowledge, there has been no study of its usage and performance within the context of a particular community. Thus, our work in Section 5 is the first to use Instagram as a lens through which to understand media prevalence and locality in a community context.

This paper leverages the Instagram social network along with traffic traces from a wireless network to better understand web usage and social media behavior in the unique context of Tribal America. We add the caveat that "Tribes" refers to a set of indigenous people who represent a wide variety of languages, cultures, and perspectives across the U.S.; our study provides measurements for only a small fraction of this population. However, with 13 individual Tribes represented in our study, our findings present a unique opportunity to get a diverse perspective on Tribal traffic. This work presents the following contributions:

- One of the first characterizations of web traffic in a Tribal community
- An evaluation of media performance in a network topology commonly used to bring initial access to developing regions
- An analysis of Instagram media popularity and locality within the context of the TDV network as a whole and within six individual reservations

Our analysis shows that while the usage patterns observed in the TDV network are consistent with reported usage patterns in other Tribal communities and content delivered over the TDV network is very socially and locally oriented, the technologies used to present, store, and share this content are not amenable for use in vastly disconnected environments.

We begin by reviewing related work in Section 2 and move to describing the TDV network and the uniqueness of the Tribal networking context in Section 3. We proceed to discuss general usage and media performance in Section 4. In Section 5, we explore media popularity and locality using Instagram network traces. We discuss our findings and future work in Section 6 and end with our concluding remarks.

2. RELATED WORK

There are several important measurement studies focused on initial analysis of usage and performance in developing contexts [22][14][18]. When it comes to measuring wireless networks in developing contexts, our work is most similar to [18] and [22]. While we look at the performance of media applications and approach network analysis through a cultural lens, our work is distinct in three major ways. First, the TDV network is unlike the networks studied in the aforementioned work in that it is not a highly latent or bandwidth-limited network. Rather, this work provides a first look at web traffic generated by a disenfranchised population that is unique in terms of political status, age demographics, and geographic context in a developed and well-connected nation. Second, our work focuses on the relationship between physical proximity and social closeness in an online social network, including the strength of social connections as well as the popularity of social media. Our focus on social media was informed by interview studies of First Nations (Tribal) broadband usage by Molyneaux et al.[25]. While Molyneaux et al. also focus on characterizing broadband use in Tribal communities, the study involves no analysis of measured network usage or performance and is based exclusively on survey responses. Our work is complementary to this approach and we find that our analysis supports many of the observations made by Molyneaux et al., including the significance of social media, the popularity of audio and video media as well as online gaming.

A significant body of work explores the diffusion of information in social networks, including characterization and modeling of diffusion patterns through various online social networks, including Twitter, Facebook, and Flickr [23] [12] [13]. Most relevant to our analysis is work focusing on information diffusion in social networks over time and space. Cha et al. study the role media popularity and the strength of social links play in the rate that media diffuses the Flickr social network [13]. In contrast, we study media diffusion and social bonds with respect to geographic locality. Also relevant to our work is research exploring the connection between location and social connections [16]. Cho et al. connect information from an underlying physical data network to those in an online social network. This work focuses on understanding the social motivation behind human mobility while our work seeks insight into the impact social bonds in geographic communities have on media in their online counterparts.

3. BACKGROUND

Most of the challenges for broadband accessibility on reservations stem from a centuries-long history of conflict between the U.S. government and indigenous Americans. This history includes removal of indigenous people from their ancestral homelands and forced assimilation and deculturization in Western boarding schools, resulting in a generation disenfranchised from their indigenous cultures and languages. However, Tribes have been resilient and view broadband technologies as a way to communicate, share, and develop indigenous identity as never before. Rejuvenation of disappearing languages and culture in addition to the growth and development of contemporary cultural identities are major motivators for broadband access in Tribal communities [25]. Demonstrating the breadth of the issue, Figure 1 highlights U.S. counties containing Tribal areas with absolutely no access to fixed or mobile broadband (i.e. 3G, 4G, LTE). As Tribes in the U.S. seek to cultivate broadband infrastructure within their communities, they must contend with national telecommunications policy, coordinate with neighboring deployment strategies and regulatory bodies, and find sustainable revenue sources. Issues of resource allocation and use are rendered even more complex by their status as sovereign nations. For instance, Tribes cannot use Tribal land as collateral on loans to subsidize the build-out of communications infrastructure as sovereign land cannot be repossessed. Additionally, attitudes regarding the ownership and control of digital content as well as the impact of Internet content on culture and community have caused some Tribal leaders to hesitate in the deployment of broadband infrastructure in their communities [17].

In spite of the challenges, several Tribes have taken action to increase broadband connectivity in their communities. Our research focuses on a high-speed wireless network established by the Southern California Tribal Chairmen's Association (SCTCA). As recently as 2001, none of the Tribal land represented by the SCTCA had access to broadband

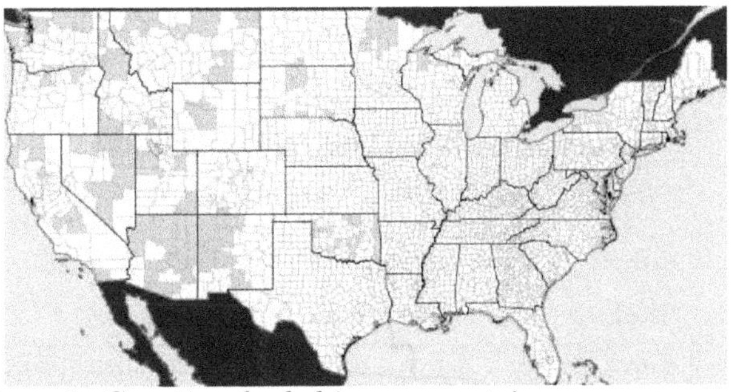

Figure 1: Counties shaded in gray contain one or more census blocks that do not have 3G or better mobile broadband coverage[2].

services. As a solution, the SCTCA launched the Tribal Digital Village (TDV) network. The ultimate goal of the project is to provide affordable Internet access to the over 3,000 disconnected homes located on Tribal land. Our study of the TDV network provides insight into how initial connectivity is being used and how future technologies and information services might be designed to best serve these emerging networks.

3.1 Description of the network

Since its inception thirteen years ago, the TDV network has provided coverage to half of the 3,050 homes located on 13 of the 17 reservations that comprise the Southern California Tribal Chairmen's Association. While 576 homes have adopted Internet services at some point over the past thirteen years, only 354 homes currently utilize Internet provided by the TDV network. The lack of broadband adoption and attrition occurs for various reasons, including residents' inability to pay for services or lack of satisfaction with the quality of services. Currently, the TDV network offers two service packages: \$34.95 per month for 2 Mbps and \$64.95 per month for 3 Mbps. In addition to providing broadband access to homes, the TDV network provides access to Tribal municipalities, schools, libraries, and learning centers free of charge. Figure 2a gives an overview of the geographic location of the TDV network and the reservations it connects. Figure 2b shows the network architecture, where the TDV headquarters is denoted as 'Gateway' and tower masts associated with broadband access points are named after the reservations they serve. We note that the spatial positioning of relay tower masts in Figure 2b does not correspond with their actual geolocations, and instead serves to give the reader a sense of the network topology. The incoming access link provides 500 Mbps over fiber and terminates at the TDV headquarters, located on the Pala reservation. A wireless backbone comprised of five solar-powered, point-to-point microwave (11 GHz and 18 GHz) links connects 13 reservations to the gateway. Reservations connect to the backbone by way of point-to-point links over unlicensed 2.4 GHz and 5 GHz. Access links extending from relay towers into individual homes and municipality buildings are point-to-multipoint links operating over WiFi. Of the 500 Mbps of bandwidth at the gateway, 200 Mbps remain in Pala to support operations at headquarters and the Pala relay link while the remaining 300 Mbps are used to provide services

[2]Tribal Mobility Fund Phase I Eligible Areas Map. Credit: FCC. http://www.fcc.gov/maps/tribal-mobility-fund-phase-1-eligible-areas

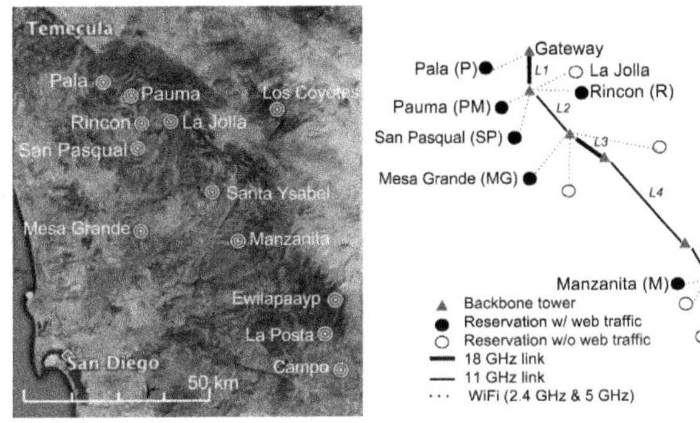

(a) (b)

Figure 2: Maps of (a) San Diego County with reservations covered by TDV network marked by circles and (b) TDV network topology.

to access points that connect to the Internet over the backbone. Overall, the TDV network consists of over 815 km of wireless links– the shortest link (L1) in the backbone spans 1.6 kilometers and the longest link (L4) spans 38.8 kilometers.

3.2 Data collection

Our point of collection is located at the Internet gateway of the TDV network. We collect data by attaching a traffic monitoring server to the switch that bridges the gateway and the TDV network. A mirror port is configured to capture all packets traversing the network. We capture packet headers with tcpdump and use Bro to collect flow-level statistics for network applications [5]. Overall, we collected 5.5 TB of traffic representing 52.8 billion IP packet headers. Data collection methodology and subsequent analysis received IRB and SCTCA approval prior to collection. All MAC addresses and IP addresses are anonymized using TraceAnon [9].

4. GENERAL TRAFFIC ANALYSIS

We begin our analysis by looking at general usage and performance patterns. Relevant findings include:

- Performance bottlenecks are associated with relay and access links rather than the main backbone
- Packet loss leads to high rates of failure for media downloads and uploads

All tables and figures are derived from the entire two-month measurement period, with the exception of Figure 6.

As discussed in Section 3, major points of connectivity are located at municipality buildings including schools, libraries, and learning centers. The majority of these buildings close for the day between 4 pm and 6 pm, rendering their Internet connectivity inaccessible to the public. In order to gauge the impact of municipality connectivity on daily traffic load, we look at the average hourly traffic volume associated with web uploads and downloads across our entire sample (shown in Figure 3). We observe that even after the typical closing times (between hours 16 and 18), the hourly traffic volume maintains its level. We verify that the majority of traffic is attributable to residential access points by identifying traffic associated with municipality buildings. Overall, we find that 99% of the observed traffic volume is associated with residential access points.

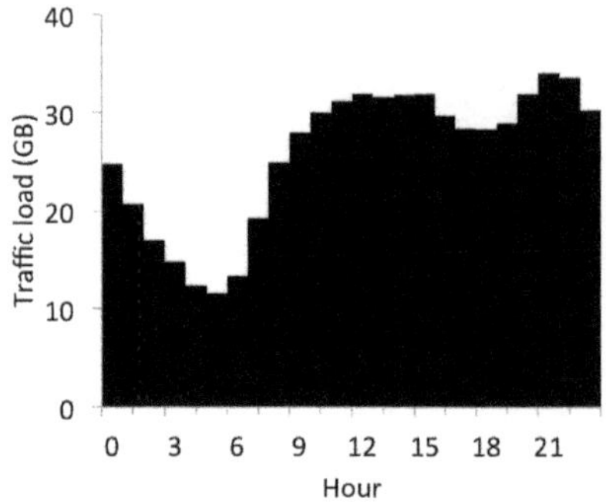

Figure 3: Average hourly traffic volume.

Table 1: Devices used in TDV network.

Mobile devices		**411**
	iOS	42.9%
	Android	35.2%
	Windows	11.5%
Desktop devices		**131**
	Mac OS X	23.1%
	Linux	11.9%
	Windows	45.0%

Table 1 provides an overview of unique devices used to access the Internet over the TDV network. These devices were identified using the user agent field of HTTP traffic headers. The majority of users access web content using mobile devices (smart phones, tablets, e-readers) as opposed to stationary devices (desktops, laptops, and gaming consoles). Additionally, gaming consoles account for 11% of desktop devices in the TDV network.

In order to characterize traffic, we examine network performance both as a whole and associated with each reservation. Figure 4 compares the traffic load averaged over the entire measurement period with the service level agreement (SLA). We see that the traffic load rarely exceeds the 500 Mbps SLA. This differentiates the TDV network from previously studied networks in developing contexts, as its bandwidth capacity is not a limiting factor on traffic usage and performance. In Table 2, we report performance statistics associated with each reservation relay link. The 'Link' column in the table is associated with the backbone link that connects to each relay tower and reservations are noted using their associated abbreviations from Figure 2b. Retransmission rate is calculated according to the number of retransmitted segments in a flow divided by the total number of segments transmitted. We observe high retransmission and failure rates at all relay links. Pala, which connects to the gateway via a single relay link, has the highest failure and retransmission rates. Exemplified by Pauma, Rincon, and San Pasqual, performance can vary in terms of packet loss and flow failure even for reservations connecting to the backbone via the same link. Likewise, reservations that are multiple hops away from the gateway, such as Mesa Grande and Manzanita, do not experience performance degradation in proportion to the number of backbone hops they must travel. Based on these observations, we conclude that performance degradation occurs either over the relay links between backbone towers and individual reservations or over the access links that extend connectivity from relay links into homes and municipality buildings. Our current measurement configuration does not allow us to pinpoint the exact location of packet loss, but based on our findings and our knowledge of the network topology, we suspect that packet loss is either due to low signal strength between the backbone towers and relay points or due to interference between access links connecting to the same relay point.

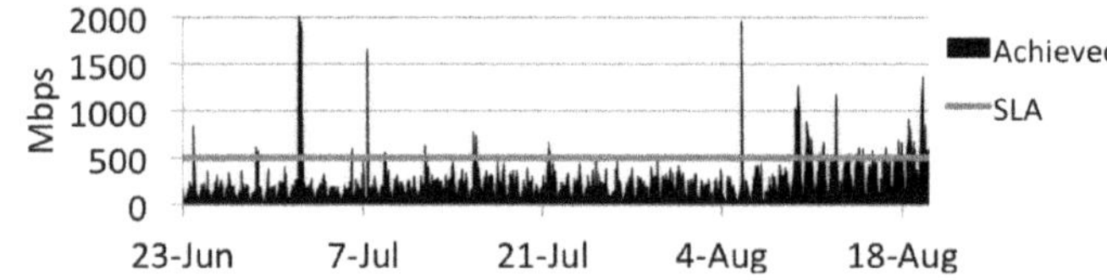

Figure 4: Achieved throughput compared to SLA.

Table 2: TCP statistics for each reservation.

	Link	% Failed requests	% Retransmitted	RTT (ms)	IAT (s)
P	–	25.6	5.9	140	0.37
PM	L1	24.0	5.7	89	0.26
R	L1	28.8	4.6	93	0.26
SP	L1	33.9	4.9	94	0.30
MG	L2	25.7	4.8	71	0.15
M	L5	23.1	5.1	79	0.27

4.1 Overview of web applications

Figure 5 reveals that Instagram is the most requested web application, with over 12.1 million requests over the measurement period. This is surprising given current measurements of web usage in the U.S., which have revealed Facebook as the most dominant social media presence, followed by Twitter, LinkedIn, and Pinterest [8]. We are also surprised by the high levels of gaming traffic represented by PlayStation and Xbox. While Xbox is not ranked as one of the top 10 most requested applications in the network, it is ranked in the top 15. Similar to what we observed with the rank of Instagram traffic, the popularity of PlayStation is unexpected; it ranks as the sixth most popular web site in the TDV network compared to 1,089th in the U.S. [8]. In terms of popularity, Youtube is second only to Instagram with 1.8 million requests during the measurement period. This is similar to the rest of the U.S. where Youtube is ranked as the third most popular web site [8]. Surprisingly, e-commerce sites like Amazon and Ebay are not even ranked in the top 30 most accessed websites in the TDV network, despite ranking as the 4th and 8th most accessed websites in the U.S. When searching for an explanation for this dearth, we find that sovereignty plays a role. Many e-commerce sites rely on U.S. Postal Services for shipping; however, as reservation roads are not maintained by the county, U.S. Postal Services will not deliver to homes that must be accessed through these roads. Similarly, other major shipping companies (i.e. UPS and FedEx) reserve the right not to deliver to all areas and do not guarantee delivery to all addresses. In short, online ordering and shipping can be a significant challenge on reservations and the lack of e-commerce traffic in the TDV network reflects this.

Figure 5b shows the top 10 most bandwidth-consuming web sites observed in the TDV network. We find that streaming media sites represent the greatest bandwidth consumers in the network, accounting for 44% of the overall web traffic volume. This is consistent with streaming media usage in the rest of the U.S., where streaming media accounts for 34-50% of peak traffic bandwidth [6]. Likewise, the composition of streaming media mirrors that of the U.S., where Netflix accounts for 60% of streaming media. We also notice that video gaming sites such as playstation.com and xbox.com

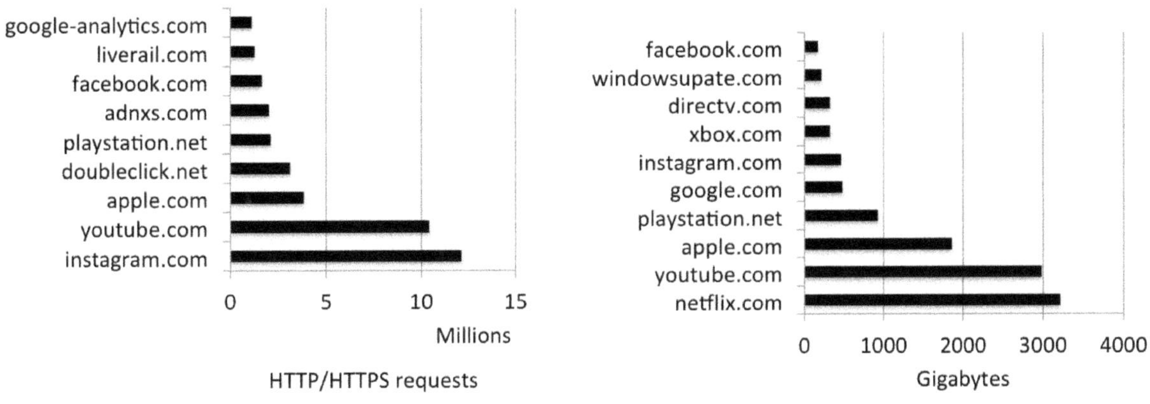

(a) (b)

Figure 5: Overview of the most popular URLs by (a) number of HTTP requests and (b) traffic volume.

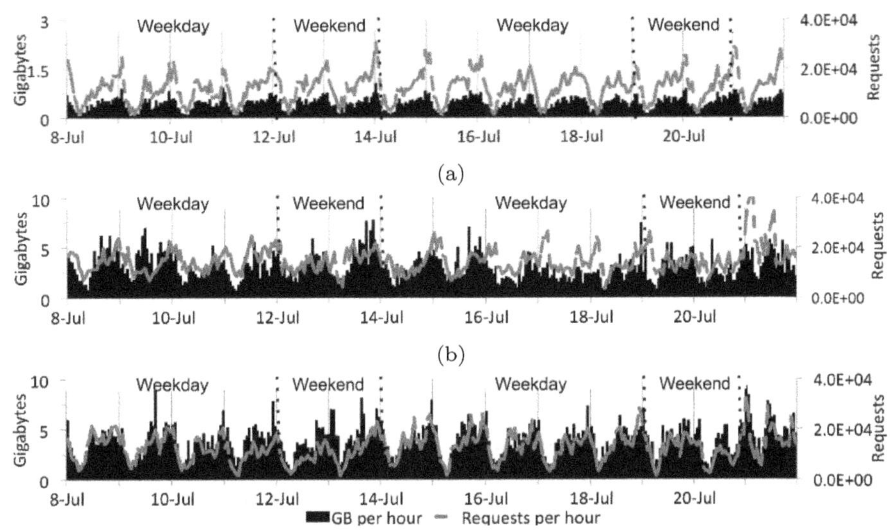

(c)

Figure 6: Hourly traffic demand for (a) Instagram, (b) Youtube, and (c) Netflix from July 8 to July 21.

rank among the top 10 web sites in terms of bandwidth and overall, gaming traffic accounts for 8.9% of web traffic volume. Social media comprises a much smaller portion of traffic volume, counting for only 4.5% of the total bandwidth consumed by web traffic. Finally, media and software downloads from online stores such as the Google PlayStore and the iTunes Store account for 23% of web traffic volume. This is in contrast to global mobile traffic patterns, which measure app store downloads as accounting for less than 18% of mobile traffic [6]. In total, media represents over 70% of observed web traffic by volume. Given the popularity of media-oriented applications in terms of HTTP requests and proportion of traffic volume, as well as Tribal interests in leveraging broadband for the development of cultural media, we focus the remainder of this paper on understanding media performance and usage in the TDV network.

4.2 Media performance

Previous studies of emergent wireless networks have observed connections between usage patterns and network performance [22][28][15]. Based on the high levels of media traffic in the network in addition to the popularity of media-based sites, we look specifically at the performance of media applications in the TDV network to identify the presence of performance bottlenecks that might impact user behavior. In order to do this, we look to the performance of three applications: Youtube, Netflix, and Instagram. These three applications are representative of the predominant media transaction types (streaming and bulk transfer). We select each application based on its high traffic volume in the network and the different ways that it allow users to interact with media. We begin by studying the daily usage of each application. In Figure 6 we show the daily traffic volume and web requests generated by Instagram, Netflix, and Youtube over a two-week period which we verify as representative of the entire sampling period (note the different y-axis scales). Traffic volume per hour was calculated by summing the total number of bytes per hour; the number of HTTP requests per hour was calculated by summing the total number of HTTP requests per hour. While weekend and weekday traffic are not significantly different for any of the applications, all three applications exhibit anthropocentric patterns in their usage over time.

We now look at media performance for Instagram, Youtube, and Netflix. Table 3 reports performance statistics for each application including the retransmission rate, download fail-

Table 3: TCP statistics for Instagram photos (I-P), Instagram videos (I-V), Youtube (Y), and Netflix (N).

	% Retransmitted	% Failed downloads	% Failed uploads	RTT (ms)	IAT (s)
I-P	3.2	11.6	24.9	91	0.22
I-V	3.8	31.0	25.0	91	0.29
Y	2.9	32.3	30.1	73	0.18
N	3.4	75.0	NA	94	0.34

ure rate, upload failure rate (when applicable), round trip time (RTT), and packet inter-arrival time (IAT). Round trip times and packet inter-arrival times associated with each application were calculated by taking the average round trip time and packet inter-arrival time for each TCP flow and averaging them over all TCP flows. The retransmission rate for each application represents the percentage of segments retransmitted per TCP flow averaged across all TCP flows.

4.2.1 *Video downloads*

Understanding the user experience with regards to the network performance of these platforms can highlight areas of improvement in terms of network infrastructure and application design. Overall, we find relatively high rates of download failure for Youtube, Netflix, and Instagram videos. We find that Netflix has the highest failure rate of all, with 75.0% of video downloads ending in a failure. In comparison, 32.3% of Youtube downloads fail, and Instagram video downloads experience a failure rate of 31%. In exploring failures associated with video downloads, we find that the predominant cause of failure for all applications is a TCP RST sent by the client. This type of failure causes 63% of download failures for Youtube, 60% of download failures for Netflix, and 58% of download failures for Instagram videos. This type of failure is indicative of a poor user experience, often due to packet loss [22].

To assess the impact of retransmission rate on download performance, we compare the distributions of successful video downloads to failed video downloads for Netflix (N), Youtube (Y), and Instagram (I) in Figure 7. As an example of our notation in Figures 7 and 8, we use "N-S" to signify successful Netflix flows and "N-F" for failed Netflix flows. We find that for all three applications, retransmission rates are higher for failed downloads than for successful downloads, and on average, failed flows experience 8.2-9.7% loss. For streaming video applications, such as Youtube and Netflix, this type of loss rate would negatively impact the user quality of experience and termination of download mid-stream (triggering a client-sent RST) is consistent with our findings of cause of failure. To assess how failure impacts user interaction with streaming video applications, we study the distributions of flow size and flow duration for successful and unsuccessful Netflix and Youtube downloads using Tstat [1]. Figure 8a graphs the distribution of flow sizes for failed and successful flows for both Youtube and Netflix and Figure 8b shows the distribution of flow duration for failed and successful flows for the two applications. For the size of a flow, we report the goodput rather than the total size including retransmitted data. We find that for both applications, failed flows are on average 83% larger and last 28% longer than their successful counterparts. While we have established that failed downloads are associated with higher retransmission rates, we note that these failures correspond to longer, lengthier downloads, which are more likely to experience losses resulting in

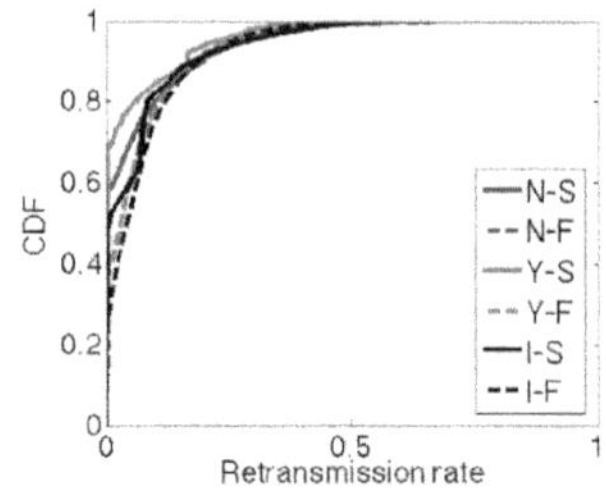

Figure 7: Distribution of retransmission rates for downloads.

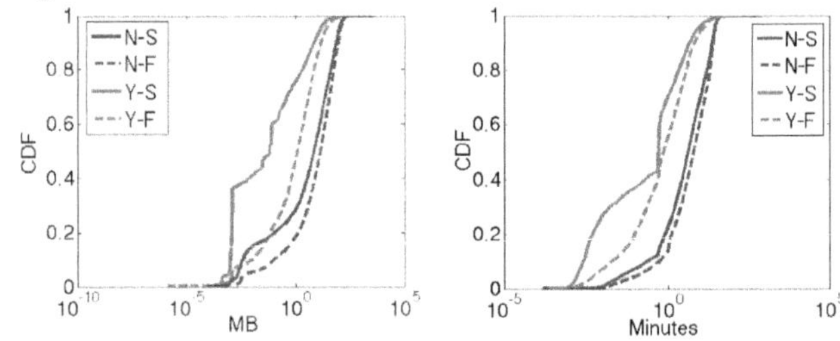

(a) (b)

Figure 8: Distributions of (a) flow size and (b) duration for Netflix and Youtube downloads.

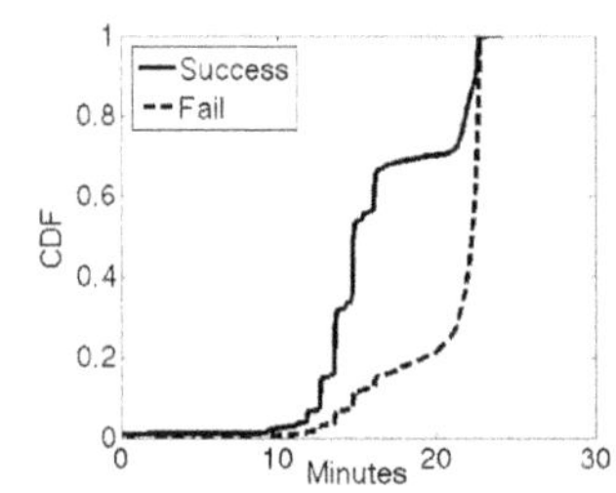

Figure 9: Distribution of flow duration for Instagram video downloads.

a poor user experience. However, we are surprised to find that although Instagram videos are smaller than Youtube and Netfix downloads and experience shorter flow duration, this application experiences the highest retransmission rate for both failed and successful downloads. One reason for the high retransmission rate for successful Instagram video downloads is that it downloads media in bulk, rather than as a stream–so quality of experience is not impacted by the number of packet losses. However, packet loss impacts the length of time it takes to download a video before a user can watch it. In Figure 9, we compare the distributions of flow duration for successful and failed Instagram video downloads. We find that download times are 62% longer for failed downloads than for successful downloads. This is expected as packet loss leads to more retransmissions that result in longer download times. Overall, 40% of downloads require over 15 minutes.

4.2.2 *Video uploads*

We now investigate upload performance for Youtube and Instagram videos. Upload performance in these applications is particularly important in the context of the TDV network given many of the goals Tribal communities have for broadband connectivity, including cultural content creation, dissemination, and engagement. Overall, 504 video files were uploaded to Instagram compared to 444 uploaded to Youtube. 25% of Instagram video uploads failed and 30% of Youtube uploads failed. When examining the predominant cause of failure for uploads, we find that for Instagram, 85% of failures were due to an unresponsive client (no data packets or control packets were observed coming from the client) and 11% of failures were caused by an RST sent by the server. For Youtube, 55% of upload failures are caused by a timeout-triggered RST sent by the server and 36% of failures are caused by an unresponsive client.

While packet loss over relay and access links can be a contributing factor to failure, we also consider that all Instagram uploads and 98% of Youtube uploads are initiated from mobile devices. Uploading from a mobile device increases the likelihood of a user inadvertently moving from a space of high connection quality to low connection quality, particularly if upload times are extensive. On average, successful Instagram video uploads take 1.4 minutes and successful Youtube video uploads take 4.9 minutes. Failed Instagram uploads take 2.1 minutes before termination and failed Youtube uploads take 5.7 minutes before termination. We believe that this short upload duration, facilitated by lower retransmission rates for upstream traffic, is what allows for Instagram video uploads to be more successful than video downloads. The average uploaded Instagram video is only 0.24 MB compared to the average uploaded Youtube video, which is 11.2 MB. This difference is unsurprising given the restrictions Instagram places on video length (15 seconds), dimension (640×640 pixels), and resolution. This is in contrast to Youtube, which limits video uploads at 11 hours or 128 GB. Increased video sizes have negative consequences for upload failure, as they typically take longer to upload and are more likely to experience packet loss. We also find that on average, failed Instagram uploads are retried 1.3 times and failed Youtube uploads are retried 1.7 times. 3% of retried Instagram video uploads and 7% of retried Youtube uploads are never successfully completed. For each of these failed retries, we find that each final attempted retry takes 10 minutes on average before the attempt is terminated. We also find that repeatedly failed Instagram video uploads require 3 more minutes than video uploads that eventually succeed; repeatedly failed Youtube uploads require 3.6 more minutes than video uploads that eventually succeed.

4.2.3 *Images*

With the largest number of uploaded files and a platform that lends itself to media sharing and collaboration, Instagram embodies much of the community enrichment potential of broadband connectivity. Unlike Youtube, it enables users to upload images as well as videos. Because the Instagram app was designed exclusively for mobile devices, it imposes limitations on its media formats and as a result provides a higher likelihood of successful media transfers. This primarily manifests as limited upload file dimensions (640×640 pixels). Once an image has been uploaded to Instagram, three standardized versions are created: small image ($\geq$10 KB), medium image ($\geq$20 KB), and large image ($\geq$100 KB). For uploaded videos, small, medium, and large images are generated from the first frame of the video. When the Instagram app is active, images are downloaded from content servers where large versions of the image correspond with images that are more relevant to users, medium images correspond with images that are less relevant, and small images are used for metadata reports. In Table 4, we show the failure rates associated with small, medium, and large downloaded, as well as uploaded Instagram images. 76% of download failures and 86% of upload failures are caused by unresponsive clients after a TCP connection has been established.

Table 4: Failure rates for Instagram images.

	Total #	Failure rate (%)
Small images	5,450,807	13.9
Medium images	2,880,253	15.0
Large images	2,345,020	17.6
Uploaded images	10,677	23.6

Table 5: Overview of TDV Instagram data.

	Total	Local
Media objects	150,368	4,807
Content creators	1,180	164
Media interactions	277,309	19,099
Social interactions	144,721	11,159
Instagram users	NA	238

5. SOCIAL MEDIA AND LOCALITY

Discussions from Section 3 highlight the importance of digital media to Tribal interests in preserving and sharing cultural knowledge. Moreover, studies of emergent networks in under-served communities note the importance of local content sharing for establishing a digital culture that emphasizes locally relevant information. In the previous section, we evaluated the performance of media transactions in three of the most popular web applications in the network. As we would expect, packet loss has a negative impact on both streaming and bulk media downloads alike. Media uploads fail due to timeouts and unresponsive clients. We are surprised that Instagram is so vulnerable to loss, given its design for mobile environments. In this section, we analyze media practices in the TDV network to determine whether we can distinguish localized usage patterns. Due to its surprising popularity in the TDV network and its publicly accessible API, we use Instagram network traces to answer questions about media locality in a Tribal context. Our analysis reveals that the locality of interest in the TDV network is very high compared to non-indigenous communities, with the top 10% of users' strongest social connections spanning less than 10 km [20]. This is expected given the social values observed in indigenous communities that focus heavily on developing intra-community relationships [26]. In Section 6, we discuss the implications of these findings for improving connectivity.

Table 5 provides an overview of the Instagram data we observe, including information about media interactions and users involved in the TDV Instagram network. In Table 5, "content creators" refer to Instagram users who have uploaded media to Instagram. We note that media interactions differ from social interactions: a media interaction includes user-explicit actions such as liking, commenting on, or viewing a media object, while a social interaction only includes user-explicit actions that are announced on the acting user's social feed, such as liking and commenting on a media object.

We find that media views comprise nearly half of all media interactions. This means that only about half of the media interactions that occur in the network are publicly broadcast through the Instagram social network. We also find that only 7% of media interactions occur between a user from the TDV network and media created by a user from the TDV network; only 8% of social interactions are between a TDV user and media created by a TDV user. This is consistent with the fact that only 3% of the media objects we observed were created by local users.

Table 6: Definitions of Instagram interaction types.

Media interactions	User-explicit actions (i.e. liking, commenting on, and viewing a media object).
Social interactions	User-explicit actions that are broadcast to a user's followers (i.e. liking and commenting on a media object).

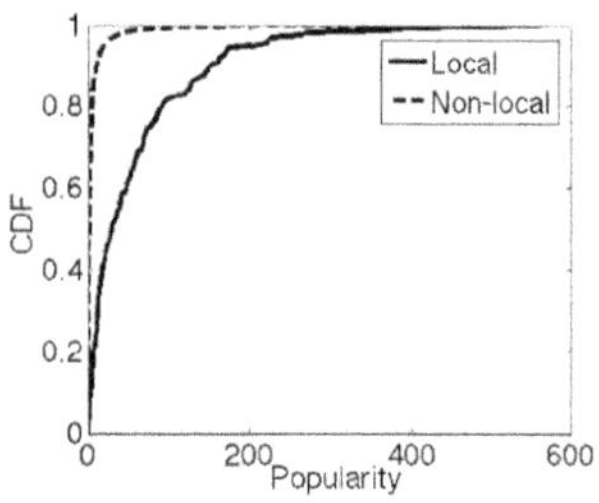

Figure 10: Distributions of media interactions associated with local and non-local content creators.

At first glance, this low proportion of local interaction seems to indicate a low level of local interest. However, when we look to interactivity based on content creator locale, we find a much higher proportion of social interactions associated with content creators from within the TDV network. We are able to identify the media associated with a content creator based on the media's identifier, which contains a unique ten digit identifier concatenated to the user identifier of its creator. In Figure 10, we show the "popularity" of each content creator we observe in the TDV network. Here, we define "popularity" as the total number of media interactions (see Table 6) associated with media created by each observed content creator. On average, the TDV community interacts with locally created media 57 times while it interacts with non-locally created media only five times. So while there are far more non-local media objects to interact with, TDV users are much more engaged with content created by local content creators than with content created by non-local content creators.

Based on previous work exploring the connection between social media and cultural resilience in indigenous communities, we study the underlying social structure of the TDV Instagram network [25].We begin by defining a social connection between a given pair of Instagram users u_i and u_j as:

$$C_{u_i} = \sum_{j=0}^{n} P_{u_i}(u_j) \quad (1)$$

where $P_{u_i}(u_j) = 1$ if there exists any social interaction between user u_i and media created by user u_j and $P_{u_i}(u_j) = 0$ if no such social interaction exists between user u_i and media created by user u_j. In Figure 11a, we show the number of social connections (C) between each user and all other users in the same reservation ($n = \{11, 17, 25, 69, 114\}$[3][4]), in the TDV network ($n = 238$), and outside the TDV network ($n = 33,183$). As users interact with other users from broader circles of the Instagram network, the number of social connections associated with individual users increases. In addition to the number of social connections, we measure the strength (S) associated with a connection, or the

[3]The value of n is dependent on which reservation u_i is associated.

[4]We exclude users from Manzanita in these calculations as $n = 2$ for this reservation and skews the distribution.

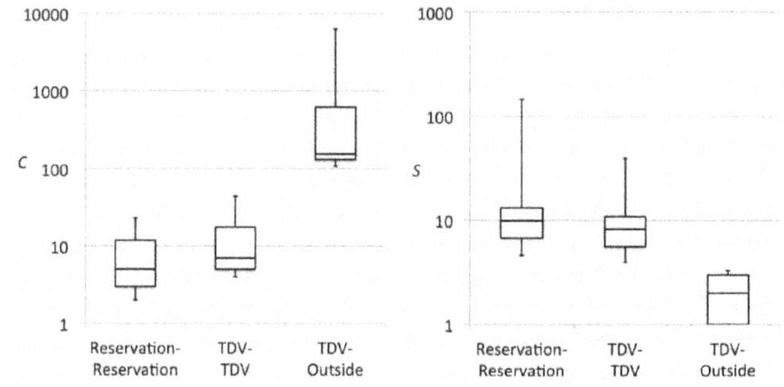

(a) (b)

Figure 11: (a) Number of social connections and (b) strength of social connections per user.

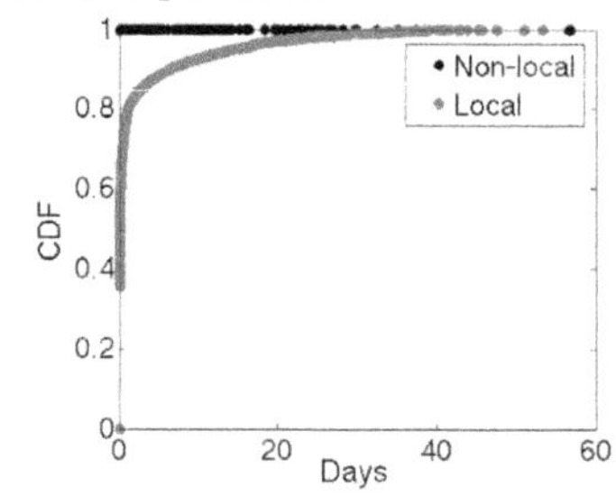

Figure 12: Circulation times of local and non-local media.

number of social interactions that exist between user u_i and media created by user u_j:

$$S_{u_i,u_j} = I_{u_i,u_j} + I_{u_j,u_i} \quad (2)$$

where I_{u_i,u_j} is the number of social interactions between u_i and media created by u_j. Figure 11b illustrates the distribution of S for each user in association with other users from the same reservation, from the TDV network, and from outside the TDV network. While we observe a greater number of social connections between local and non-local users in Figure 11a, Figure 11b reveals that the strength of these connections is weak. In contrast, Figure 11b shows that the more proximate users are in the network, the stronger the social connections are between them. Thus, we find that the TDV Instagram network is composed of a dense core of a few strong local connections and expands out via numerous weak connections. Based on this finding, we expect to see a high locality of interest with respect to media.

5.1 Media prevalence

In addition to the popularity of media, we examine interactions over time to identify how long media circulates in the TDV Instagram network. We measure this by identifying the time delta between a media object's initial appearance in the TDV network and its final appearance in the network across all media interactions (defined at the beginning of Section 5). We have already established that the number of non-local media far exceeds the number of local media present in the network (see Table 5); however in Figure 12, we see that locally created content circulates for much longer within the TDV network than non-local media. Looking more closely, we find that 99.6% of the 145,561 non-local media occur only once in the TDV network. Half of the 4,807 local media objects circulate for over 4.2 hours and are liked or commented on an average of 5 times, while 382 local media objects circulate for over a week and are liked or commented on an average of 7 times. Intuitively, longer circulation times should correspond to an increased level of social engagement; however, circulation time is based on media interactions, not just social interactions. This means that media views, which account for 50% of all media interactions, contribute significantly to a media object's circulation time. Therefore, not only is local media more socially popular than non-local media (see Figures 10 and 11), but it is relevant over a longer period of time.

6. DISCUSSION

6.1 Bonds and bridges

Work in the social sciences has identified the importance of online social networks (OSNs) to Tribal identity and cultural preservation [25]. In particular the formation of "bonds" and "bridges" within Tribal OSNs has significant impact on the strength and resilience of indigenous culture [26]. Bonding relations within a community help members make sense of negative experiences and look forward to a more positive future, creating cultural continuity that connects the traditional culture of the past to the development of a new culture of the present. Bridging connections between different communities allows for communal empowerment and influence on the wider society. In Section 5, we investigated various dimensions of local versus non-local media prevalence and propagation in the TDV Instagram network. With respect to media interactions on Instagram, our findings show that there are many weak bridging connections and a dense core of strong bonding connections. This leads us to believe that social media in Tribal functions to strengthen and maintain bonding connections; however, it is unclear whether bridging connections exert any quantifiable influence over outside communities.

The high locality of interest with respect to locally created media presents opportunities to improve bonding connections in several ways. Current connectivity can be improved by storing locally created content locally, which would prevent users from uploading media over lossy relay and access links that extend upload completion times, improving upload success rates. This strategy would also improve download performance (particularly for videos), as user quality of experience could be improved by avoiding lossy links. Moreover, if locality of media interest corresponds to spatial closeness, social bonds could be used as a means of extending connectivity via opportunistic encounters with peers. This way, users who have access to spaces of ubiquitous connectivity might serve as media vectors, transferring relevant media over Bluetooth, WiFi Direct, or NFC to other users as they come into contact geographically.

6.2 Nations within a nation

While previously studied networks in developing contexts typically reside within greater regions of development, Tribal communities in the U.S. are positioned within a developed nation. In many ways, the effects of the digital divide are amplified in this context and citizens without broadband access are marginalized at an accelerated rate. With high broadband penetration rates in the non-Tribal U.S., many services now assume ubiquitous broadband accessibility, and with this assumption come expectations that cannot be met on Tribal lands with the current state of broadband accessibility. As funding and infrastructure licensing processes move online, Tribes are increasingly alienated from the means by which necessary infrastructures are established. In Section 4, we show that even with sufficient bandwidth capacity, the wireless links used to extend connectivity over long distances are prone to average packet loss rates of 5%, which degrade media performance in both the up-link and down-link directions. Packet loss is caused by limitations in 802.11, which make it sub-optimal for transmitting over long-distance wireless links. Even though the WiFi spectrum is inappropriate for the distance requirements of the TDV network, the spectrum is unlicensed and helps reduce the cost of using the network. If Tribes were able to project their sovereignty over radio frequency in Tribal land, software defined networks leveraging unlicensed or opportunistically available spectrum could significantly increase the penetration and affordability of broadband services. These spectrum rights have been recommended by the FCC and are currently under discussion as becoming part of spectrum access policy in the U.S. [2].

6.3 Attitudes towards technology

Broadband is generally recognized as a means to increase the number of available communication pathways. However, there are various concerns surrounding the Internet and Internet technologies. Some of these concerns exist in both Tribal and non-Tribal contexts, including online engagement detracting from face-to-face interactions, the abundance of "negative" and "pornographic" content online, and the dissonance between offline and online identities [25]. Other concerns are more specific to the Tribal context; these include issues of acculturation and protecting American Indian intellectual property on the Internet. Age demographics also play an important role in Tribal broadband usage. Reservations have younger populations than the surrounding U.S.; the median age on reservations is 26 years, whereas the median age in the U.S. is 37.2 years [7]. Reasons for the skew in ages on reservations include: higher mortality rates due to health conditions, accidents, and suicide; and lack of employment and educational services on reservations which cause working-age populations to seek school and job opportunities outside reservations [3] [11]. In Figure 5, we observe the impact of the age skew in the types of applications that are popular, such as the prevalence of online gaming sites (Playstation and Xbox) and niche social media platforms (Instagram). Dissolving the digital divide in a way that benefits Tribal communities involves understanding inter-generational Tribal attitudes and concerns regarding broadband technologies and allowing Tribes to be actively involved in navigating how those concerns should impact network deployment and technological design in their communities. In this context, we note that localized content storage not only presents a solution that reduces the impact of packet loss, but also presents an opportunity for Tribes to impose tighter control on their intellectual content.

7. CONCLUSION

Internet usage in the TDV network is distinct from the U.S. context in which it resides, especially with respect to the prevalence of niche social media traffic, as well as the influence utility infrastructures have on traffic patterns, exemplified in the lack of online shopping traffic due to unreliable delivery infrastructure. Our work empirically supports trends identified in survey studies regarding Tribal broadband usage: we show that social media is the most popular application in the network in addition to other media-oriented applications like Netflix, Youtube, and iTunes. While packet loss negatively impacts media performance, we use Instagram traffic to identify strong social connections between users within the same reservations and we find that locally created media receives significantly more interactions than non-local media. By exploiting these patterns, architectures that combine local storage, user mobility, and offline social encounters can improve and extend current connectivity.

Tribes in the U.S. are not the only indigenous groups facing issues of disenfranchisement. While issues of sovereignty, funding, lack of political power, and geographic isolation exist for indigenous people around the world, where it is available, broadband connectivity has been shown to strengthen indigenous identity and further collective goals as cultural practices and struggles are communicated between indigenous groups at a transnational scale [24]. By understanding indigenous usage of broadband as well as the technical barriers to broadband deployment, indigenous communities can focus on developing and extending connectivity in ways that make sense for their unique political, geographical, and community contexts.

8. ACKNOWLEDGMENTS

This work was funded through NSF Network Science and Engineering (NetSE) Award CNS-1064821. We would like to thank Joseph Peralta and Geoff Herrin of the Southern California Tribal Digital Network for assisting us with information collection and analysis.

9. REFERENCES

[1] TCP Statistics and Analysis Tool. `http://tstat.tlc.polito.it/index.shtml`, 2008.

[2] Taking Additional Steps to Make U.S. Spectrum Policy More Comprehensive. `http://www.broadband.gov/plan/5-spectrum/#s5-3`, March 2010.

[3] American Indian and Alaska Native Populations. `http://www.cdc.gov/minorityhealth/populations/REMP/aian.html`, July 2013.

[4] Tribal Initiatives. `http://transition.fcc.gov/indians/`, March 2013.

[5] The Bro Network Security Monitor. `https://www.bro.org/`, October 2014.

[6] Mobile broadband, smartphones, apps, fixed networks. `https://itunews.itu.int/En/4958-Mobile-broadband-smartphones-apps-fixed-networks.note.aspx`, February 2014.

[7] National Congress of American Indians, Demographics. `http://www.ncai.org/about-tribes/demographics`, July 2014.

[8] Top Sites in United States. `http://www.alexa.com/topsites/countries/US`, October 2014.

[9] Traceanon. `http://www.wand.net.nz/trac/libtrace/wiki/TraceAnon`, May 2014.

[10] Tribal Digital Village. `http://sctdv.net/`, July 2014.

[11] A. Austin. Native Americans Are Still Waiting for an Economic Recovery. `http://www.epi.org/publication/native-americans-are-still-waiting-for-an-economic-recovery/`, October 2013.

[12] E. Bakshy, I. Rosenn, C. Marlow, and L. Adamic. The Role of Social Networks in Information Diffusion. In *Proceedings of the 21st International Conference on World Wide Web*, WWW '12, pages 519–528, Lyon, France, May 2012.

[13] M. Cha, A. Mislove, and K. P. Gummadi. A Measurement-driven Analysis of Information Propagation in the Flickr Social Network. In *Proceedings of the 18th International Conference on World Wide Web*, WWW '09, pages 721–730, Madrid, Spain, May 2009.

[14] J. Chen, D. Hutchful, W. Thies, and L. Subramanian. Analyzing and Accelerating Web Access in a School in Peri-urban India. In *Proceedings of the 20th International Conference on World Wide Web*, WWW '11, pages 443–452, Hyderabad, India, May 2011.

[15] J. Chen, L. Subramanian, and J. Li. RuralCafe: Web Search in the Rural Developing World. In *Proceedings of the 18th International Conference on World Wide Web*, WWW '09, pages 411–420, Madrid, Spain, May 2009.

[16] E. Cho, S. A. Myers, and J. Leskovec. Friendship and Mobility: User Movement in Location-based Social Networks. In *Proceedings of the 17th ACM SIGKDD International Conference on Knowledge Discovery and Data Mining*, KDD '11, pages 1082–1090, San Diego, California, USA, 2011.

[17] T. Davis and M. Trebain. Shaping the Destiny of Native American People by Ending the Digital Divide. In *EduCause Review*, pages 38–46, January 2001.

[18] B. Du, M. Demmer, and E. Brewer. Analysis of WWW Traffic in Cambodia and Ghana. In *Proceedings of the 15th International Conference on World Wide Web*, WWW '06, pages 771–780, Edinburgh, Scotland, May 2006.

[19] M. Duggan and A. Smith. Social Media Update 2014. `http://www.pewinternet.org/2015/01/09/social-media-update-2014/`, January 2015.

[20] E. Gilbert, K. Karahalios, and C. Sandvig. The Network in the Garden: An Empirical Analysis of Social Media in Rural Life. In *Proceedings of the SIGCHI Conference on Human Factors in Computing Systems*, CHI '08, pages 1603–1612, Florence, Italy, April 2008.

[21] N. Hochman and R. Schwartz. Visualizing Instagram: Tracing Cultural Visual Rhythms. In *Proceedings of the Workshop on Social Media Visualization (SocMedVis) in conjunction with the Sixth International AAAI Conference on Weblogs and Social Media (ICWSM '12)*, pages 6–9, Dublin, Ireland, June 2012.

[22] D. L. Johnson, V. Pejovic, E. M. Belding, and G. van Stam. Traffic Characterization and Internet Usage in Rural Africa. In *Proceedings of the 20th International Conference Companion on World Wide Web*, WWW '11, pages 493–502, Hyderabad, India, May 2011.

[23] H. Kwak, C. Lee, H. Park, and S. Moon. What is Twitter, a Social Network or a News Media? In *Proceedings of the 19th International Conference on World Wide Web*, WWW '10, pages 591–600, May 2010.

[24] D. McCaskill and J. Rutherford. Indigenous peoples of South-East Asia: poverty, identity and resistance. In R. Eversole, J.-A. McNeish, and A. D. Cimadamore, editors, *Indigenous Peoples and Poverty: An International Perspective*, pages 126–157. Zed Books, London, UK, December 2005.

[25] H. Molyneaux, S. O'Donnell, C. Kakekaspan, B. Walmark, P. Budka, and K. Gibson. Social Media in Remote First Nation Communities. *Canadian Journal of Communication*, 39(2), 2014.

[26] D. Narayan-Parker. *Bonds and Bridges: Social Capital and Poverty*, volume 2167. World Bank Publications, 1999.

[27] T. Silva, P. de Melo, J. Almeida, J. Salles, and A. Loureiro. A Picture of Instagram is Worth More Than a Thousand Words: Workload Characterization and Application. In *2013 IEEE International Conference onDistributed Computing in Sensor Systems (DCOSS)*, pages 123–132, Cambridge, MA, USA, May 2013.

[28] M. Zheleva, P. Schmitt, M. Vigil, and E. Belding. The Increased Bandwidth Fallacy: Performance and Usage in Rural Zambia. In *Proceedings of the 4th Annual Symposium on Computing for Development*, ACM DEV-4 '13, pages 11–21, Cape Town, South Africa, December 2013.

A Weighted Correlation Index for Rankings with Ties

Sebastiano Vigna*
Dipartimento di Informatica
Università degli Studi di Milano, Italy

ABSTRACT

Understanding the correlation between two different scores for the same set of items is a common problem in graph analysis and information retrieval. The most commonly used statistics that quantifies this correlation is Kendall's τ; however, the standard definition fails to capture that discordances between items with high rank are more important than those between items with low rank. Recently, a new measure of correlation based on *average precision* has been proposed to solve this problem, but like many alternative proposals in the literature it assumes that there are *no ties* in the scores. This is a major deficiency in a number of contexts, and in particular when comparing centrality scores on large graphs, as the obvious baseline, indegree, has a very large number of ties in social networks and web graphs. We propose to extend Kendall's definition in a natural way to take into account weights in the presence of ties. We prove a number of interesting mathematical properties of our generalization and describe an $O(n \log n)$ algorithm for its computation. We also validate the usefulness of our weighted measure of correlation using experimental data on social networks and web graphs.

1. INTRODUCTION

In the analysis of social networks and web graphs, one is often faced with different scores[1] assigned by different centrality measures (e.g., indegree and Bavelas's closeness [1]) to the same graph. Analogously, in information retrieval one has the lists of documents returned by different search engines and their associated relevance scores, or the lists of query recommendation returned by different algorithms.

In most of the literature, the scores are assumed to be without ties, thus inducing a *ranking* of the elements. At that point, correlation statistics such as Spearman's rank correlation coefficient [25] and Kendall's τ [12] can be used to evaluate the similarity of the rankings. Spearman's correlation coefficient is equivalent to the traditional linear correlation coefficient computed on ranks of items. Kendall's τ, instead, is proportional to the number of pairwise adjacent swaps needed to convert one ranking into the other.

For a number of reasons, Kendall's τ has become a standard statistic to compare the correlation between two ranked lists. Such reasons include fast computation ($O(n \log n)$, where n is the length of the list, using Knight's algorithm [14]), and the existence of a variant that takes care of ties [13].

The explicit treatment of ties is of great importance when comparing scores assigned by different graph centrality measures. The baseline of such scores is indegree. More sophisticated approaches include Bavelas's closeness [1], Katz's index [10], PageRank [22], and countless variants. Due to the highly skewed indegree distribution, a very large number of documents share the same indegree, and the same happens of many other scores: it is thus of uttermost importance that the evaluation of correlation takes into account ties as first-class citizens. Breaking ties randomly, for instance, leads to the paradoxical results that the score made by half zeroes, half ones has with any other equivalent score an expected τ of $n/(2(n-1)) \approx 0.5$ instead of one.

On the other hand, Kendall's τ has some known problems that motivated the introduction of several weighted variants. In particular, a striking difference often emerges between the anecdotal evidence of the top elements by different scores being almost identical, and the τ value being quite low. This is due to a known phenomenon: the scores of important items tend to be highly correlated in all reasonable rankings, whereas most of the remaining items are ranked in slightly different ways, introducing a large amount of noise, yielding a low τ value.

This problem motivates the definition of correlation statistics that consider more important correlation between highly ranked items. In particular, recently Yilmaz, Aslam and Robertson introduced a statistics, named *AP (average precision) correlation* [27], which aims at considering more important swaps between highly ranked items. The need for such a measure is very well motivated in the introduction of their paper, and we will not repeat here their detailed discussion.

In this paper, we aim at providing a measure of correlation in the same spirit of the definition of Yilmaz, Aslam and Robertson, but taking smoothly ties into account. We will actually define a general notion of weighting for Kendall's τ, and develop its mathematical properties. Since it is important that such a statistics is computable on very large data sets, we will provide a generalization of Knight's algorithm that can be applied whenever the weighting depends additively or multiplicatively on a weight assigned to each

*Sebastiano Vigna has been supported by the EU-FET grant NADINE (GA 288956).

[1] We purposely and consistently use "score" to denote real numbers associated to items, and "rank" to denote ordinal positions induced by the scores. The two terms are used somewhat interchangeably in the literature, but in this paper the distinction is important as we assume that scores of different items can be identical.

WWW 2015, May 18–22, 2015, Florence, Italy.
ACM 978-1-4503-3469-3/15/05.
http://dx.doi.org/10.1145/2736277.2741088.

item. The same algorithm can be used to compute AP correlation in time $O(n \log n)$.

All data and software used in this paper are available as part of the LAW software library under the GNU General Public License.[2]

2. RELATED WORK

Shieh [24] wrote the one of the first papers proposing a generic weighting of Kendall's τ. She assumes from the very start that there are no ties, and assign to the exchange between i and j a weight w_{ij}. Her motivation is the *fidelity evaluation of software packages for structural engineering*, in which a set of variables is ranked in two different ways, and one would like to emphasize agreement on the most important ones. In particular, she concentrates on weights given by the product of two weights associated with the elements participating in the exchange. Our work can be seen as a generalization of her approach, albeit we combine weights differently.

Kumar and Vassilvitskii [16] study a definition that extends Shieh's taking into account *position weights* and *similarity between elements*. Again, they assume that ties are broken arbitrarily, which is an unacceptable assumption if large sets of elements have the same score. Fagin, Kumar and Sivakumar [5] use instead *penalty weights* to apply Kendall's τ just to the top k elements of two ranked lists (with no ties). Exchanges partially or completely outside the top k elements obtain different weights.

Finally, the recent quoted work by Yilmaz, Aslam and Robertson [27] on AP correlation is the closest to ours in motivation and methodology, albeit targeted at ranked lists with no ties. Melucci [?] extends their definition to include a probabilistic weight assigned to items, remarking that both approaches are actually specific instances of Shieh's.

We note that analogous research exists in association with Spearman's correlation: Iman and Conover [9], for example, study the usage of *Savage scores* [23] instead of ranks when comparing ranked lists. Savage scores for a ranked list of n elements are given by $\sum_{j=i}^{n} 1/j$, where i is the rank (starting at one) of an element. Spearman's correlation applied to Savage scores considers more important elements at the top of a ranked list.

A fascinating proposal, entirely orthogonal to the ones we discussed, is the idea of weighting Kemeny's distance between permutations proposed by Farnoud and Milenkovic [6]. In this proposal, Kemeny's distance between two permutations π and σ is characterized as the minimum number of *adjacent transpositions* (i.e., transpositions of the form $(i\ i+1)$) that turn π into σ. At this point, one can define a *weight* associated to each adjacent transposition, and by assigning larger weights to adjacent transpositions with smaller indices one can make differences in the top part of the permutations more important than differences in the bottom part. The right notion of weighted distance turns out to be the minimum sum of weights of a sequence of adjacent transposition that turn π into σ. The interesting property of this approach is that avoids the need for a *ground truth* (an intrinsic notion of importance of an element), which is necessary, implicitly or explicitly, to weigh an exchange in the approaches of [24, 27] and in the one discussed in this paper. The main drawbacks, presently, are that the weight assignment is not very intuitive (as it is related to positions, rather than to elements) and that more work is needed to extend the distance into a proper correlation index in the case of ties.

3. MOTIVATION

The need for weighted correlation measures in the case of ranked list has been articulated in detail in previous work. Here we will focus on the case of centrality measures for graphs. Consider the graph of English Wikipedia (more precisely, `enwiki-2013`, a dataset available at the LAW web site), which has about four million nodes and one hundred million arcs. In this graph, 99.95% of the nodes have the same indegree of some other node—for example, more than a half million node has indegree one. It is clearly mandatory, when computing the correlation of other scores with indegree, that ties are taken into consideration in a systematic way (e.g., not broken arbitrarily).

We will consider four other commonly used scores based on the adjacency matrix A of the Wikipedia graph. One is PageRank [22], which is defined by

$$\mathbf{1}/n \sum_{k\geq 0} (\alpha \bar{A})^k,$$

where $\alpha \in [0\,..\,1)$ is a *damping factor* and $\bar{A}$ is a stochasticization of A: every row not entirely made of zeroes is divided by its sum, so to have ℓ_1 norm one.

The other index we consider is Katz's [10], which is defined by

$$\mathbf{1} \sum_{k\geq 0} (\alpha A)^k,$$

where $\alpha \in [0\,..\,1/\lambda)$ is an attenuation factor depending on λ, the dominant eigenvalue of A [20]. In both cases, we take α in the middle of the allowed interval (using different values does not change the essence of what follows, unless they are extreme).

A different kind of score is provided by Bavelas's *closeness*. The closeness of x is defined by

$$\frac{1}{\sum_{d(y,x)<\infty} d(y,x)},$$

where $d(-,-)$ denotes the usual graph distance. Note that we have to eliminate nodes at infinite distance to avoid zeroing scores. By definition, the closeness of a node with indegree zero is zero. Finally, we consider *harmonic centrality* [2], a modified version of Bavelas's closeness designed for directed graphs that are not strongly connected; the harmonic centrality of x is defined by

$$\sum_{y\neq x} \frac{1}{d(y,x)}.$$

These scores provide an interesting mix: indegree is an obvious baseline, and entirely local. PageRank and Katz are similar in their definition, but the normalization applied to A makes the scores quite different (at least in theory). Finally, closeness and harmonic centrality are of a completely different nature, having no connection with dominant eigenvectors or Markov chains.[3]

Our first empirical observation is that, looking just at the very top pages of Wikipedia (Table 1; entries in boldface are unique to the list they belong to, here and in the following), we perceive these scores as almost identical, except for closeness, which displays almost random values. The latter behavior is a known phenomenon: nodes that are almost isolated obtain a very high closeness score (this is why harmonic centrality was devised). We note also that harmonic centrality has a slightly different slant, as it is the only ranking including Latin, Europe, Russia and the Catholic Church in the top 20.

The problem is that these facts are not reflected in any way in the values of Kendall's τ shown in Table 3. If we exclude closeness,

[2] `http://law.di.unimi.it/`

[3] It is interesting to remark that, in spite of these rankings being real-valued, more than 20% of the nodes have the same score of some other node.

	Ind.	PR	Katz	Harm.	Cl.
Indegree	1	0.75	0.90	0.62	0.55
PageRank	0.75	1	0.75	0.61	0.56
Katz	0.90	0.75	1	0.70	0.62
Harmonic	0.62	0.61	0.70	1	0.92
Closeness	0.55	0.56	0.62	0.92	1

Table 3: Kendall's τ between Wikipedia centrality measures.

	Ind.	PR	Katz	Harm.	Cl.
Indegree	1	0.31	0.63	0.24	0.06
PageRank	0.31	1	0.27	0.10	0.10
Katz	0.63	0.27	1	0.50	0.20
Harmonic	0.24	0.10	0.50	1	0.65
Closeness	0.06	0.10	0.20	0.65	1

Table 4: Kendall's τ between Wikipedia centrality measures, restricted to nodes of indegree 1 and 2.

with the exception of the correlation between indegree and Katz, all other correlation value fail to surpass the 0.9 threshold, usually considered the threshold for considering two rankings equivalent [26]. Actually, they are below the threshold 0.8, under which we are supposed to see considerable changes. The correlation of closeness with harmonic centrality, moreover, is even more pathological: it is the *largest* correlation.

An obvious observation is that, maybe, the score is lowered by a large discordance in the rest of the rankings. Table 2 tries to verify this intuition by listing the top pages that are associated with the Wordnet category "scientist" in the Yago2 ontology data [8]. These pages have considerably lower score (their rank is below 300), yet the first three rankings are almost identical. Harmonic centrality is still slightly different (Linnaeus is absent, and actually ranks 21), which tells us that the Kendall's τ is not giving completely unreasonable data. Nonetheless, closeness continues to provide apparently random results.

We have actually to delve deep into Wikipedia, beyond rank 100 000 using the category "cocktail" to see that, finally, things settle down (Table 5). While closeness still displays a few quirks, the rankings start to stabilize.

To understand what happens in the very low-rank region, in Table 4 we provide Kendall's τ as in Table 3, but *restricting the computation to nodes of indegree 1 and 2*. As it is immediately evident, after stabilization the low-rank region is fraught with noise and all correlation values drop significantly.

The very high correlation between closeness and harmonic centrality is, actually, not strange: on the nodes reachable from giant connected component of our Wikipedia snapshot (89% of the nodes) they agree almost exactly, as closeness is the reciprocal of a denormalized *arithmetic* mean, whereas harmonic centrality is the reciprocal of a denormalized *harmonic* mean [2]. Even if the remaining 11% of the nodes is completely out of place, making closeness useless, Kendall's τ tells us that it should be interchangeable with harmonic centrality. At the same time, Kendall's τ tells us that indegree is very different from PageRank, which again goes completely against our empirical evidence (and also against theoretical considerations [7]).

In the rest of the paper, we will try to approach in a systematic manner these problems by defining a new weighted correlation index for scores with ties.

4. A WEIGHTED CORRELATION INDEX

In his 1945 paper about ranking with ties [13], Kendall, starting from an observation of Daniels [4], reformulates his correlation index using a definition similar in spirit to that of an inner product, which will be the starting point of our proposal: we consider two real-valued vectors $\boldsymbol{r}$ and $\boldsymbol{s}$ (to be thought as scores) with indices in n;[4] then, let us define

$$\langle \boldsymbol{r}, \boldsymbol{s} \rangle := \sum_{i<j} \operatorname{sgn}(r_i - r_j) \operatorname{sgn}(s_i - s_j),$$

where

$$\operatorname{sgn}(x) := \begin{cases} 1 & \text{if } x > 0; \\ 0 & \text{if } x = 0; \\ -1 & \text{if } x < 0. \end{cases}$$

Indices of score vectors in summations belong to n throughout the paper. Note that the expression above is actually an inner product in a larger space of dimension $n(n-1)/2$: each score vector $\boldsymbol{r}$ is mapped to the vector with coordinate $\langle i, j \rangle$, $i < j$, given by $\operatorname{sgn}(r_i - r_j)$.[5] We have the property

$$\langle \boldsymbol{r}, \alpha \boldsymbol{s} \rangle = \langle \alpha \boldsymbol{r}, \boldsymbol{s} \rangle = \operatorname{sgn}(\alpha) \langle \boldsymbol{r}, \boldsymbol{s} \rangle,$$

which reminds of the analogous property for inner products, and that $\langle \boldsymbol{r}, - \rangle = \langle -, \boldsymbol{r} \rangle = 0$ if $\boldsymbol{r}$ is constant. Following the analogy, we can define

$$\|\boldsymbol{r}\| := \sqrt{\langle \boldsymbol{r}, \boldsymbol{r} \rangle},$$

so

$$\|\alpha \boldsymbol{r}\| = |\operatorname{sgn}(\alpha)| \cdot \|\boldsymbol{r}\|.$$

The norm thus defined measures the "untieness" of $\boldsymbol{r}$: it is zero if and only if $\boldsymbol{r}$ is a constant vector, and it has maximum value $\sqrt{n(n-1)/2}$ when all components of $\boldsymbol{r}$ are distinct.

Since $\langle \boldsymbol{r}, \boldsymbol{s} \rangle$ is an inner product on a larger space, we have a Cauchy–Schwartz-like inequality:

$$|\langle \boldsymbol{r}, \boldsymbol{s} \rangle| \leq \|\boldsymbol{r}\| \|\boldsymbol{s}\|.$$

This property makes it possible to define Kendall's τ between two vectors $\boldsymbol{r}$ and $\boldsymbol{s}$ with nonnull norm as a normalized inner product, in a way formally identical to cosine similarity:

$$\tau(\boldsymbol{r}, \boldsymbol{s}) := \frac{\langle \boldsymbol{r}, \boldsymbol{s} \rangle}{\|\boldsymbol{r}\| \cdot \|\boldsymbol{s}\|}. \tag{1}$$

We recall that if $\boldsymbol{r}$ and $\boldsymbol{s}$ have no ties, the definition reduces to the classical "normalized difference of concordances and discordances", as the denominator is exactly $n(n-1)/2$. The definition above is exactly that proposed by Kendall [13], albeit we use a different formalism.

The form of (1) suggests that to obtain a weighted correlation index it would be natural to define a *weighted* inner product

$$\langle \boldsymbol{r}, \boldsymbol{s} \rangle_w := \sum_{i<j} \operatorname{sgn}(r_i - r_j) \operatorname{sgn}(s_i - s_j) w(i, j),$$

where $w(-,-) : n \times n \to \mathbf{R}_{\geq 0}$ is some nonnegative symmetric weight function. We would have then a new norm

$$\|\boldsymbol{r}\|_w = \sqrt{\langle \boldsymbol{r}, \boldsymbol{r} \rangle_w}$$

[4]Throughout the paper, we use von Neumann's notation: if n is a natural number, $n = \{0, 1, \ldots, n-1\}$.

[5]We thank Ravi Kumar for this useful observation. Note that the map from the original space to the larger space is *not* linear.

Indegree	PageRank	Katz	Harmonic	Closeness
United States	United States	United States	United States	**Kharqan Rural District**
List of sovereign states	Animal	List of sovereign states	United Kingdom	**Talageh-ye Sofla**
Animal	List of sovereign states	United Kingdom	World War II	**Talageh-ye Olya**
England	France	France	France	**Greatest Remix Hits (Whigfield album)**
France	Germany	Animal	Germany	**Suzhou HSR New Town**
Association football	Association football	World War II	Association football	**Suzhou Lakeside New City**
United Kingdom	England	England	English language	**Mepirodipine**
Germany	India	Association football	China	**List of MPs ... M–N**
Canada	United Kingdom	Germany	Canada	**List of MPs ... O–R**
World War II	Canada	Canada	India	**List of MPs ... S–T**
India	Arthropod	India	**Latin**	**List of MPs ... U–Z**
Australia	Insect	Australia	World War I	**List of MPs ... J–L**
London	World War II	London	England	**List of MPs ... C**
Japan	Japan	Italy	Italy	**List of MPs ... F–I**
Italy	Australia	Japan	**Russia**	**List of MPs ... A–B**
Arthropod	Village	New York City	**Europe**	**List of MPs ... D–E**
Insect	Italy	English language	Australia	**Esmaili-ye Sofla**
New York City	Poland	China	**European Union**	**Esmaili-ye Olya**
English language	English language	Poland	**Catholic Church**	**Levels of organization (ecology)**
Village	**National Reg. of Hist. Places**	World War I	London	**Jacques Moeschal (architect)**

Table 1: Top 20 pages of the English version of Wikipedia following five different centrality measures.

Indegree	PageRank	Katz	Harmonic	Closeness
Carl Linnaeus	Carl Linnaeus	Carl Linnaeus	Aristotle	**Noël Bernard (botanist)**
Aristotle	Aristotle	Aristotle	Albert Einstein	**Charles Coquelin**
Thomas Jefferson	Thomas Jefferson	Thomas Jefferson	Thomas Jefferson	**Markku Kivinen**
Margaret Thatcher	Charles Darwin	Albert Einstein	Charles Darwin	**Angiolo Maria Colomboni**
Plato	Plato	Charles Darwin	Thomas Edison	**Om Prakash (historian)**
Charles Darwin	Albert Einstein	Karl Marx	**Alexander Graham Bell**	**Michel Mandjes**
Karl Marx	Karl Marx	Plato	**Nikola Tesla**	**Kees Posthumus**
Albert Einstein	Pliny the Elder	Margaret Thatcher	**William James**	**F. Wolfgang Schnell**
Vladimir Lenin	Vladimir Lenin	Vladimir Lenin	Isaac Newton	**Christof Ebert**
Sigmund Freud	Johann Wolfgang von Goethe	Isaac Newton	Karl Marx	**Reese Prosser**
J. R. R. Tolkien	Margaret Thatcher	Ptolemy	**Charles Sanders Peirce**	**David Tulloch**
Johann Wolfgang von Goethe	Ptolemy	Johann Wolfgang von Goethe	Noam Chomsky	**Kim Hawtrey**
Spider-Man	Sigmund Freud	Pliny the Elder	**Enrico Fermi**	**Patrick J. Miller**
Pliny the Elder	Isaac Newton	Benjamin Franklin	Ptolemy	**Mikel King**
Benjamin Franklin	Benjamin Franklin	J. R. R. Tolkien	**John Dewey**	**Albert Perry Brigham**
Leonardo da Vinci	J. R. R. Tolkien	Thomas Edison	Johann Wolfgang von Goethe	**Gordon Wagner (economist)**
Isaac Newton	Immanuel Kant	Sigmund Freud	**Bertrand Russell**	**George Henry Chase**
Ptolemy	Leonardo da Vinci	Immanuel Kant	Plato	**Charles C. Horn**
Immanuel Kant	**Pierre André Latreille**	Leonardo da Vinci	**John von Neumann**	**Paul Goldstene**
George Bernard Shaw	Thomas Edison	Noam Chomsky	Vladimir Lenin	**Robert Stanton Avery**

Table 2: Top 20 pages of Wikipedia following five different centrality measures and restricting pages to Yago2 Wordnet category "scientist". The global rank of these items is beyond 300.

and a new correlation index

$$\tau_w(\boldsymbol{r}, \boldsymbol{s}) := \frac{\langle \boldsymbol{r}, \boldsymbol{s} \rangle_w}{\|\boldsymbol{r}\|_w \cdot \|\boldsymbol{s}\|_w}.$$

Note that still $\langle \boldsymbol{r}, - \rangle_w = \langle -, \boldsymbol{r} \rangle_w = 0$ if $\boldsymbol{r}$ is constant.

4.1 Properties

We say that two score vectors $\boldsymbol{r}$ and $\boldsymbol{s}$ are *equivalent* if $\operatorname{sgn}(r_i - r_j) = \operatorname{sgn}(s_i - s_j)$, *opposite* if $\operatorname{sgn}(r_i - r_j) = -\operatorname{sgn}(s_i - s_j)$ for all i and j. Since $\langle \boldsymbol{r}, \boldsymbol{s} \rangle$ is a *semi-definite inner product* on a larger space (due the possibility of zero weights), the Cauchy-Schwarz inequality still holds, even if we need positive definiteness for the necessary condition on equality:

Theorem 1 $|\langle \boldsymbol{r}, \boldsymbol{s} \rangle_w| \leq \|\boldsymbol{r}\|_w \|\boldsymbol{s}\|_w$. *A sufficient condition for equality to hold is that the two vectors are equivalent or opposite. The condition is necessary if w is strictly positive and $\|\boldsymbol{r}\|_w, \|\boldsymbol{s}\|_w \neq 0$ or $\|\boldsymbol{r}\|_w, \|\boldsymbol{s}\|_w = 0$*

Note that the two last conditions are necessary: when w is the constant zero weight we have equality for all vectors, and if one of the vector has null norm while the other has not the necessary linearity condition for equality is moot.

Interestingly, even if our "inner product" is neither additive nor linear, we can still prove directly the triangular inequality for the induced "norm":

Theorem 2 $\|\boldsymbol{r} + \boldsymbol{s}\|_w \leq \|\boldsymbol{r}\|_w + \|\boldsymbol{s}\|_w$.

PROOF.

$$\begin{aligned}
\|\boldsymbol{r} + \boldsymbol{s}\|_w^2 &= \langle \boldsymbol{r} + \boldsymbol{s}, \boldsymbol{r} + \boldsymbol{s} \rangle_w \\
&= \sum_{i<j} \operatorname{sgn}(r_i + s_i - r_j - s_j)^2 w(i, j) \\
&\leq \sum_{i<j} (|\operatorname{sgn}(r_i - r_j)| + |\operatorname{sgn}(s_i - s_j)|)^2 w(i, j) \\
&= \langle \boldsymbol{r}, \boldsymbol{r} \rangle_w + \langle \boldsymbol{s}, \boldsymbol{s} \rangle_w + \sum_{i<j} |\operatorname{sgn}(r_i - r_j) \operatorname{sgn}(s_i - s_j)| w(i, j).
\end{aligned}$$

We now notice that

$$\sum_{i<j} |\operatorname{sgn}(r_i - r_j)\operatorname{sgn}(s_i - s_j)| w(i,j)$$
$$\leq \sum_{i<j} \operatorname{sgn}(r_i - r_j)^2 w(i,j) = \langle \boldsymbol{r}, \boldsymbol{r}\rangle_w = \|\boldsymbol{r}\|_w^2,$$

and analogously for $\|\boldsymbol{s}\|_w$. We conclude that $\|\boldsymbol{r}+\boldsymbol{s}\|_w^2 \leq \|\boldsymbol{r}\|_w^2 + \|\boldsymbol{s}\|_w^2 + 2\|\boldsymbol{r}\|_w\|\boldsymbol{s}\|_w = (\|\boldsymbol{r}\|_w + \|\boldsymbol{s}\|_w)^2$. □

The triangular inequality has a nice combinatorial interpretation: adding score vectors can only *decrease* the amount of "untieness". There is no way to induce in a sum vector more untieness than the amount present in the summands.

Finally, we gather systematically the properties of τ_w:

Theorem 3 *Let $w : n \times n \to \mathbf{R}$ be a nonnegative symmetric weight function. The following properties hold for every score vector $\boldsymbol{t}$ and for every $\boldsymbol{r}$, $\boldsymbol{s}$ with nonnull norm:*

- *if $\boldsymbol{t}$ is constant, $\|\boldsymbol{t}\|_w = 0$;*
- $-1 \leq \tau_w(\boldsymbol{r},\boldsymbol{s}) \leq 1$;
- *if $\boldsymbol{r}$ and $\boldsymbol{s}$ are equivalent, $\tau_w(\boldsymbol{r},\boldsymbol{s}) = 1$;*
- *if $\boldsymbol{r}$ and $\boldsymbol{s}$ are opposite, $\tau_w(\boldsymbol{r},\boldsymbol{s}) = -1$;*

Moreover, if w is strictly positive:

- *if $\|\boldsymbol{t}\|_w = 0$, $\boldsymbol{t}$ is constant;*
- *if $\tau_w(\boldsymbol{r},\boldsymbol{s}) = 1$, $\boldsymbol{r}$ and $\boldsymbol{s}$ are equivalent;*
- *if $\tau_w(\boldsymbol{r},\boldsymbol{s}) = -1$, $\boldsymbol{r}$ and $\boldsymbol{s}$ are opposite.*

As a result, if w is strictly positive and we obtain correlation ± 1 the equivalence classes formed by tied scores are necessarily in a size-preserving bijection that is monotone (increasing or decreasing, depending on the sign) on the scores.

4.2 Decoupling rank and weight

The reader has probably already noticed that the dependence on the weight on the *indices* associated to the elements has no meaning: a trivial request (see, for instance [11]) on a correlation measure is that, like Kendall's τ, it is *invariant by isomorphism*, that is, it does not change if we permute the indices of the vector. This currently doesn't happen because we are using the numbering of the element as *ground truth* to weigh the correlation between $\boldsymbol{r}$ and $\boldsymbol{s}$. While there is nothing bad in principle (we can stipulate that elements are indexed in order of importance using some external source of information), we think that a more flexible approach decouples the problem of the ground truth from the problem of weighting. We thus define the *ranked-weight* product

$$\langle \boldsymbol{r}, \boldsymbol{s}\rangle_{\rho,w} := \sum_{i<j} \operatorname{sgn}(r_i - r_j)\operatorname{sgn}(s_i - s_j) w(\rho(i), \rho(j)),$$

where $\rho : n \to n \cup \{\infty\}$ is a ranking function associating with each index a *rank*, the highest rank being zero. We admit the possibility of rank ∞, given that the weight function provides a meaningful value in such a case, to include also the case of *partial ground truths*. The definition of the ranked-weighted product induces, as in (1), a correlation index $\tau_{\rho,w}$, and the machinery we developed applies immediately, as $w(\rho(-), \rho(-))$ is just a different weight function.

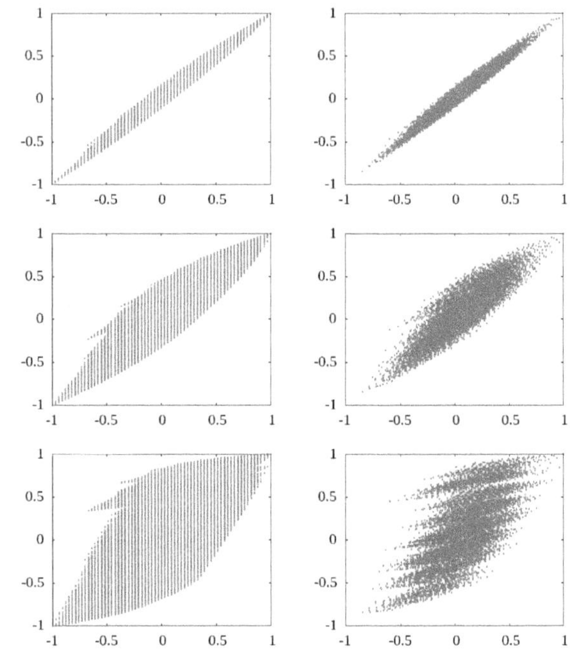

Figure 1: Scatter plots between Kendall's τ and the additive weighted τ. The rows, from top to bottom, represent logarithmic, hyperbolic and quadratic weighting. The plots are generated correlating a permutation of 12 elements versus the identity permutation (left), or a permuted set of scores with skewed distribution w.r.t. the same scores in descending order (right).

What if there is no ground truth to rely on? Our best bet is to use the rankings induced by the vectors $\boldsymbol{r}$ and $\boldsymbol{s}$. Let us denote by $\rho_{\boldsymbol{r},\boldsymbol{s}}$ the ranking defined by ordering elements lexicographically with respect to $\boldsymbol{r}$ and then $\boldsymbol{s}$ in case of a tie (in descending order), and analogously for $\rho_{\boldsymbol{s},\boldsymbol{r}}$. If two elements are at a tie in both vectors, their can be placed in any order, as their rank does not influence the value of $\tau_{\rho,w}$. We just take the average of the two possible correlations and define

$$\tau_{\bullet,w}(\boldsymbol{r},\boldsymbol{s}) := \frac{\tau_{\rho_{\boldsymbol{r},\boldsymbol{s}},w}(\boldsymbol{r},\boldsymbol{s}) + \tau_{\rho_{\boldsymbol{s},\boldsymbol{r}},w}(\boldsymbol{r},\boldsymbol{s})}{2}. \tag{2}$$

The same approach has been used in [27] to make AP correlation symmetric.

This is the definition used in the rest of the paper. It should be noted that the theory developed in Section 4.1 about $\|-\|_w$ has no counterpart for $\tau_{\bullet,w}$, but the relevant parts of Theorem 3 can be trivially extended, and those are the basic properties that we want to hold.

4.3 Choosing a weighting scheme

There are of course many ways to choose w. For computational reasons, we will see that it is a good idea to restrict to a class of weighting schemes in which w is obtained by combining additively or multiplicatively a one-argument weighting function $f : n \to \mathbf{R}_{\geq 0}$ applied to each element of a pair.

Shieh [24], for instance, combines weights multiplicatively, without giving a motivation. We have, however, two important motivations for *adding* weights. First and foremost, unless weights are scaled in some way that depends on n (which we would like to avoid), the largest weight will be some constant, and then weight

Indegree	PageRank	Katz	Harmonic	Closeness
Martini (cocktail)	Martini (cocktail)	Irish coffee	Irish coffee	**Magie Noir**
Piña colada	Caipirinha	Caipirinha	Caipirinha	**Batini (drink)**
Mojito	Mojito	Martini (cocktail)	Kir (cocktail)	**Scorpion bowl**
Caipirinha	Piña colada	Piña colada	Martini (cocktail)	**Poinsettia (cocktail)**
Cuba Libre	Irish coffee	Kir (cocktail)	Piña colada	Irish coffee
Irish coffee	Kir (cocktail)	Mojito	Mojito	Caipirinha
Singapore Sling	Cosmopolitan (cocktail)	Mai Tai	Beer cocktail	Kir (cocktail)
Manhattan (cocktail)	Manhattan (cocktail)	Cuba Libre	Shaken, not stirred	Martini (cocktail)
Windle (sidecar)	IBA Official Cocktail	Singapore Sling	Pisco Sour	Piña colada
Cosmopolitan (cocktail)	Beer cocktail	Long Island Iced Tea	Mai Tai	Mojito
Mai Tai	Mai Tai	Shaken, not stirred	Spritz (alcoholic beverage)	Beer cocktail
IBA Official Cocktail	Singapore Sling	Beer cocktail	Long Island Iced Tea	Shaken, not stirred
Kir (cocktail)	Cuba Libre	Manhattan (cocktail)	Sazerac	Mai Tai
Shaken, not stirred	**Tom Collins**	Cosmopolitan (cocktail)	Fizz (cocktail)	Spritz (alcoholic beverage)
Beer cocktail	Long Island Iced Tea	Windle (sidecar)	Flaming beverage	Pisco Sour
Pisco Sour	Sour (cocktail)	Pisco Sour	Cuba Libre	Long Island Iced Tea
Long Island Iced Tea	Shaken, not stirred	White Russian (cocktail)	Wine cocktail	Sazerac
Sour (cocktail)	**Negroni**	IBA Official Cocktail	Singapore Sling	Flaming beverage
White Russian (cocktail)	Flaming beverage	Moscow mule	Moscow mule	Fizz (cocktail)
Vesper (cocktail)	**Lillet**	Vesper (cocktail)	White Russian (cocktail)	Wine cocktail

Table 5: Top 20 pages of Wikipedia following five different centrality measures and restricting pages to Yago2 Wordnet category "cocktail". The global rank of these items is beyond 100 000.

will decrease monotonically with importance. As a result, an exchange between the first and the last element would be assigned an extremely low weight. Second, adding weights paves the way to a natural measure for *top k correlation* [5] by assigning rank ∞ to elements after the first k. The definition of such a measure in the multiplicative case is quite contrived and ends up being case-by-case.

For what matters f, we are particularly interested in the *hyperbolic* weight function $f(r) := 1/(r+1)$. This function gives more importance to elements of high rank, and weights zero only pairs in which both index have infinite rank. Using a hyperbolic weight has a number of useful features. First, it reminds the well-motivated weight given to exchanges by AP correlation. Second, it guarantees that as n grows the mass of weight grows indefinitely. Using a function with quadratic decay, for instance, might end up in making the influence of low-rank element vanish too quickly, as it is summable. For the opposite reason, a *logarithmic* decay might fail to be enough discriminative to provide additional information with respect to the standard τ.

We try to make this intuition more concrete in Figure 1, where we display a number of scatter plots showing the correlation between Kendall's τ and the additive weighted τ defined by (2) under different weighting schemes. The left half of the plots correlates all permutations on 12 elements with the identity permutation. The right half correlates all score vectors made of 15 values with skewed distribution (there are $t+1$ elements with score $0 \leq t \leq 4$) with the same vector in descending order. A visual examination of the plots suggests, indeed, that logarithmic weighting restricts too much the possible divergence from Kendall's τ, whereas quadratic weighting ends up in providing answers that are too uncorrelated. We will return to these consideration in Section 6.

5. COMPUTING $\tau_{\rho,w}$

Our motivations come from the study of web and social graphs. It is thus essential that our new correlation measure can be evaluated efficiently. We now describe a generalization of Knight's algorithm [14] that makes it is possible to compute $\tau_{\rho,w}$ in time $O(n \log n)$ under some assumptions on w. Our first observation is that, similarly to the unweighted case, each pair of indices i, j with $i < j$ belongs to one of five subsets; it can be

- a *joint tie*, if $r_i = r_j$ and $s_i = s_j$;
- a *left tie*, if $r_i = r_j$ and $s_i \neq s_j$;
- a *right tie*, if $r_i \neq r_j$ and $s_i = s_j$;
- a *concordance*, if $\operatorname{sgn}(r_i - r_j)\operatorname{sgn}(s_i - s_j) = 1$;
- a *discordance*, if $\operatorname{sgn}(r_i - r_j)\operatorname{sgn}(s_i - s_j) = -1$.

Let J, L, R, C and D be the overall weight of joint ties, left ties, right ties, concordances and discordances, respectively. Clearly,

$$J + L + R + C + D = \sum_{i<j} w(\rho(i), \rho(j)) = T.$$

The first requirement for our technique to work is that T can be computed easily. This is possible if weights are computed additively or multiplicatively from some single-argument function f. In the additive case,

$$T = \sum_{i<j} \bigl(f(\rho(i)) + f(\rho(j))\bigr) = (n-1)\sum_i f(\rho(i)). \quad (3)$$

Also the multiplicative case is easy, as

$$2T = 2\sum_{i<j} f(\rho(i)) f(\rho(j)) = \Bigl(\sum_i f(\rho(i))\Bigr)^2 - \sum_i f(\rho(i))^2. \quad (4)$$

The same observation leads to a simple $O(n \log n)$ algorithm to compute L: sort the indices in n by $\boldsymbol{r}$, and for each block of consecutive $k > 1$ elements with the same score apply (3) or (4) restricting the indices to the subset. In the same way one can compute R and J.

We now observe that, as in the unweighted case,

$$\langle \boldsymbol{r}, \boldsymbol{s} \rangle_{\rho,w} = C - D = T - (L + R - J) - 2D.$$

This can be easily seen from the fact that C is given by the total weight T, minus the weight of discordances D, minus the number of ties, joint or not, which is $L + R - J$ (we must avoid to count twice the weight of joint ties, hence the $-J$ term). In particular,

$$\langle \boldsymbol{r}, \boldsymbol{r} \rangle_{\rho,w} = T - L \qquad \langle \boldsymbol{s}, \boldsymbol{s} \rangle_{\rho,w} = T - R,$$

as in this case there are just concordances and all ties are joint.

We are left with the computation of D. The core of Knight's algorithm is an *exchange counter*: an $O(n \log n)$ algorithm that given a list of elements and an order $\preceq$ on the elements of the list computes the number of exchanges that are necessary to $\preceq$-sort the list. The algorithm is a modified MergeSort [15]:[6] during the merging phase, whenever an element is moved from the second list to the temporary result list the current number of elements of the first list is added to the number of exchanges. The number of discordances is then equal to the number of exchanges (as we evaluate whether there is a discordance on i and j only for $i < j$).

Our goal is to make this computation weighted: for this to happen, it must be possible to keep track incrementally of a *residual weight* r associated with the first list, and obtain in constant time the weight of the exchanges generated by the movement of an element from the second list.

If weights are computed multiplicatively or additively starting from a single-argument function f this is not difficult: it is sufficient to let r be the sum of the values of f applied to the elements currently in the first list. In the additive case, moving an element i from the second list increases the weight of exchanges by the residual r plus the weight $f(\rho(i))$ multiplied by the length of the first list. In the multiplicative case, we must instead use the weight $f(\rho(i))$ multiplied by the residual r. When we move an element from the first list we update the residual by subtracting its weight.

The resulting recursive procedure (for the additive case) is Algorithm 1. The final layout of the computation of $\tau_{\rho,w}$ is thus as follows:

- Consider a list $\mathscr{L}$ initially filled with the integers $[0\,..\,n)$.
- Sort stably $\mathscr{L}$ using $\boldsymbol{r}$ as primary key and $\boldsymbol{s}$ as secondary key.
- Compute T and L using $\mathscr{L}$ to enumerate elements in the order defined by $\boldsymbol{r}$ and $\boldsymbol{s}$.
- Apply Algorithm 1 to $\mathscr{L}$ using $\boldsymbol{s}$ to define the order $\preceq$, thus computing D and sorting stably $\mathscr{L}$ by $\boldsymbol{s}$.
- Compute R using $\mathscr{L}$ to enumerate elements in the order defined by $\boldsymbol{s}$.
- Compute T and put everything together.

The running time of the computation is dominated by the sorting phases, and it is thus $O(n \log n)$.

5.1 The asymmetric case and AP Correlation

It is easy to adapt Algorithm 1 for the case in which $w(i, j)$ is given by a combination of *two* different one-argument functions, one, f, for the left index and one, g, for the right index. The only modification of Algorithm 1 is the replacement of f with g at line 14, so that we combine the residual computed with f with a weight computed with g.

The formulae for computing T can be updated easily for the additive case:

$$T = \sum_{i<j}\bigl(f(\rho(i)) + g(\rho(j))\bigr) = \sum_{i \neq 0} i\bigl(f(\rho(n-1-i)) + g(\rho(i))\bigr)$$

[6] In principle, any stable algorithm that sorts by comparison could be used. This is particularly interesting as entirely on-disk algorithms, such as *polyphase merge* [15], could be used to count exchanges using constant core memory.

Algorithm 1 A generalization of Knight's algorithm for weighing exchanges.

Input: A list $\mathscr{L}$, a comparison function $\preceq$ for the elements of $\mathscr{L}$, a rank function ρ, and a single-argument weight function f that will be combined additively. e is a global variable initialized to 0 that will contain the weight of exchanges after the call weigh(0, $|\mathscr{L}|$). The procedure works on a sublist specified by its starting index $0 \le s < |\mathscr{L}|$ and its length ℓ. $\mathscr{T}$ is a temporary list.
Output: the sum of $f(\rho(-))$ on the specified sublist.

```
0   function weigh(s : integer, ℓ : integer)
1     if ℓ = 1 then return f(ρ(L[s])) fi
2     ℓ0 ← ⌊ℓ/2⌋
3     ℓ1 ← ℓ − ℓ0
4     m ← s + ℓ0
5     r ← weigh(s, ℓ0)
6     w ← weigh(m, ℓ1) + r
7     i, j, k ← 0
8     while j < ℓ0 and k < ℓ1 do
9       if L[s + j] ⪯ L[m + k] then
10        T[i] = L[s + j++]
11        r ← r − f(ρ(T[i]))
12      else
13        T[i] = L[m + k++]
14        e ← e + f(ρ(T[i])) · (ℓ0 − j) + r
15      fi
16      i++
17    od
18    for k = ℓ0 − j − 1, . . . , 0 do
19      L[s + i + k] ← L[s + j + k]
20    od
21    for k = 0, . . . , i − 1 do L[s + k] ← T[k] od
22    return w
23  end
```

and for the multiplicative case:

$$T = \sum_{i<j} f(\rho(i))g(\rho(j)) = \sum_{i} f(\rho(i)) \sum_{i<j} g(\rho(j)).$$

Both formulae can be computed in linear time using a suitable loop.

Given this setup, it is easy to compute AP correlation: as it can be checked from the very definition [27], the AP correlation of $\boldsymbol{r}$ w.r.t. $\boldsymbol{s}$, where both vectors have no ties, is simply $\tau_{w,\rho_s}(\boldsymbol{r}, \boldsymbol{s})$, where ρ_s is the ranking induced by $\boldsymbol{s}$ and the weight function w is computed additively from two weight functions $f(r) = 0$, $g(r) = 1/r$. In this case, $T = n - 1$, $J = L = R = 0$ (we are under the assumption that there are no ties) and Algorithm 1 can be considerably simplified, as the residual r is always zero.[7]

[7] Of course, it is possible to forget that we are computing AP corre-

Algorithm 2 The replacement for lines 9–15 of Algorithm 1 to compute AP correlation.

```
9   if L[s + j] ⪯ L[m + k] then
10    T[i] = L[s + j++]
11  else
12    T[i] = L[m + k++]
13    e ← e + (ℓ0 − j)/ρ(T[i])
14  fi
```

	Ind.	PR	Katz	Harm.	Cl.
Indegree	1	0.95	0.98	0.90	0.27
PageRank	0.95	1	0.96	0.92	0.65
Katz	0.98	0.96	1	0.93	0.26
Harmonic	0.90	0.92	0.93	1	0.28
Closeness	0.27	0.65	0.26	0.28	1

Table 6: τ_h on Wikipedia.

Algorithm 2 makes explicit the change to the selection statement of Algorithm 1 that is sufficient to compute AP correlation. Since keeping track of the residual is no longer necessary, the recursive function can be further simplified to a recursive procedure that does not return a value. The value e computed by the modified algorithm is all we need to compute AP correlation using the formula $(T - 2e)/T$.

	Ind.	PR	Katz	Harm.	Cl.
Indegree	1	0.76	0.90	0.63	0.55
PageRank	0.76	1	0.76	0.62	0.56
Katz	0.90	0.76	1	0.70	0.62
Harmonic	0.63	0.62	0.70	1	0.91
Closeness	0.55	0.56	0.62	0.91	1

	Ind.	PR	Katz	Harm.	Cl.
Indegree	1	1.00	1.00	1.00	0.22
PageRank	1.00	1	1.00	1.00	0.85
Katz	1.00	1.00	1	1.00	0.18
Harmonic	1.00	1.00	1.00	1	0.07
Closeness	0.22	0.85	0.18	0.07	1

Table 7: The logarithmic (top) and quadratic (bottom) additive τ on Wikipedia.

6. EXPERIMENTS

We now return to our main motivation—understanding the correlation between centralities on large graph. In this section, we gather the results of a number of computational experiments that help to corroborate our intuition that τ_h, the *additive hyperbolic weighted* τ, or in short, the *hyperbolic* τ, works as expected. We will find also an interesting surprise along the way.

Note that judging whether a new measure is useful for such a purpose is a difficult task: to be interesting, a new measure must highlight features that were previously undetectable or badly evaluated, but those are exactly those features on which a systematic assessment is problematic.

Table 6 reports the value of τ_h on the Wikipedia graph. We finally see data corresponding to the empirical evidence discussed in Section 3: indegree, Katz and PageRank are almost identical, harmonic centrality is highly correlated but definitely less than the previous triple, which matches our empirical observations. Closeness is not close to any ranking (and in particular, not to harmonic centrality) due to its pathological behavior.

There is of course a value that immediately stands out: the suspiciously high correlation (0.65) between closeness and PageRank. We reserve discussing this value for later.

In Table 7 we show the same data for logarithmic and quadratic weights. The intuition we gathered from Figure 1 is fully confirmed: logarithmic weights provides results almost indistinguishable from Kendall's τ (compare with Table 3), and quadratic weighs make the influence of the tail so low that all non-pathological scores collapse.

To gather a better understanding of the behavior of τ_h we extended our experiments to two very different datasets: the *Hollywood co-starship graph*, an undirected graph (2 million nodes, 229 million edges) with an edge between two persons appearing in the Internet Movie Data Base if they ever worked together, and a *host graph* (100 million nodes, 2 billion arcs) obtained from a large-scale crawl gathered by the Common Crawl Foundation[8] in the first half of 2012.[9] As (unavoidably anecdotal) empirical evidence we report the top 20 nodes for both graphs.

Table 8 should be compared with Table 10. PageRank and harmonic centrality turns to be less correlated to indegree than Katz in Table 8, and indeed we find many quirk choices in the very top PageRank actors (Ron Jeremy is a famous porn star; Lloyd Kaufman is an independent horror/splatter filmmaker and Debbie Rochon an actress working with him). Harmonic centrality provides unique names such as Malcolm McDowell, Robert De Niro, Anthony Hopkins and Sylvester Stallone, and drops all USA presidents altogether. Kendall's τ values, instead, suggest that PageRank and harmonic centrality are entirely uncorrelated (whereas we find several common items), and that harmonic and closeness centrality should be extremely similar.

We see analogous results comparing Table 9 with Table 11. Here τ_h separates in a very strong way harmonic centrality from the first three, and indeed we see a significant difference in the lists, with numerous sites that have a high indegree and appear in at least two of the three lists because of technical or political reasons (`gmpg.org`, `rtalabel.org`, `staff.tumblr.com`, `phpbb.com`, `miibeian.gov.cn`,) disappearing altogether in favor of sites such as `apple.com`, `amazon.com`, `myspace.com`, `microsoft.com`, `bbc.co.uk`, `nytimes.com` and `guardian.co.uk`, which do not appear in any other list. If we look at Kendall's τ, we should expect PageRank and Katz to give very different rankings, whereas more than half of their top 20 elements are in common.

6.1 PageRank and closeness

It is now time to examine the mysteriously high τ_h between PageRank and closeness we found in all our graphs. When we first computed our correlation tables, we were puzzled by its value. The phenomenon is interesting for three reasons: first, it has never been reported—using standard, unweighted indices this correlation is simply undetectable; second, it was known for techniques based on singular vectors [17]; third, we know *exactly* the cause of this correlation, because the only real difference between harmonic and closeness centrality is the score assigned to nodes unreachable from

lation and use the weight matrix just described combined with the machinery of Section 4 to define an "AP correlation with ties". In this case, J, L and R should be computed using the formulae for the asymmetric case, and the probabilistic interpretation would be lost. Such an index would most likely yield a notion of correlation very similar to τ_h, but we find more natural and more in line with Kendall's original definition to introduce the weighted τ as a symmetric index in which both ends of an exchange are relevant in computing the exchange weight. Moreover, as discussed in the conclusions, our approach naturally paves the way to a weighted notion of top-k correlation.

[8] `http://commoncrawl.org/`

[9] The crawl contains 3.53 billion web documents; we are using the associated host graph, which has a node for each host and an arc between two hosts x and y if some page in x points to some page in y. More information about the graph can be found in [19], and the complete host ranking can be accessed at `http://wwwranking.webdatacommons.org/`.

Indegree	PageRank	Katz	Harmonic	Closeness
Shatner, William	Jeremy, Ron	Shatner, William	Sheen, Martin	**Östlund, Claes Göran**
Flowers, Bess	Hitler, Adolf	Sheen, Martin	Clooney, George	**Östlund, Catarina**
Sheen, Martin	**Kaufman, Lloyd**	Hanks, Tom	Jackson, Samuel L.	**von Preußen, Oskar Prinz**
Reagan, Ronald (I)	Bush, George W.	Williams, Robin (I)	Hopper, Dennis	**von Preußen, Georg Friedrich**
Clooney, George	Reagan, Ronald (I)	Clooney, George	Hanks, Tom	**von Mannstein, Robert Grund**
Jackson, Samuel L.	Clinton, Bill (I)	Reagan, Ronald (I)	Stone, Sharon (I)	**von Mannstein, Concha**
Williams, Robin (I)	Sheen, Martin	Willis, Bruce	Brosnan, Pierce	**von der Busken, Mart**
Hanks, Tom	**Rochon, Debbie**	Jackson, Samuel L.	Hitler, Adolf	**van der Putten, Thea**
Jeremy, Ron	**Kennedy, John F.**	Stone, Sharon (I)	**McDowell, Malcolm**	**de la Bruheze, Joel Albert**
Hitler, Adolf	Hopper, Dennis	Freeman, Morgan (I)	Williams, Robin (I)	**de la Bruheze, Emile**
Willis, Bruce	**Nixon, Richard**	Flowers, Bess	**De Niro, Robert**	**te Riele, Marloes**
Clinton, Bill (I)	**Estevez, Joe**	Brosnan, Pierce	Willis, Bruce	**de Reijer, Eric**
Freeman, Morgan (I)	Shatner, William	Douglas, Michael (I)	**Hopkins, Anthony**	**des Bouvrie, Jan**
Hopper, Dennis	Jackson, Samuel L.	Madonna (I)	Madonna (I)	**de Klijn, Judith**
Stone, Sharon (I)	**Stewart, Jon (I)**	Travolta, John	**Lee, Christopher (I)**	**de Freitas, Luís (II)**
Madonna (I)	**Carradine, David (I)**	Hopper, Dennis	Douglas, Michael (I)	**de Freitas, Luís (I)**
Bush, George W.	Asner, Edward	Ford, Harrison (I)	**Sutherland, Donald (I)**	**Zuu, Winnie Otondi**
Harris, Sam (II)	**Zirnkilton, Steven**	Asner, Edward	Freeman, Morgan (I)	**Zuu, Emmanuel Dahngbay**
Brosnan, Pierce	**Colbert, Stephen**	**MacLaine, Shirley**	**Stallone, Sylvester**	**Zilbersmith, Carla**
Travolta, John	**Madsen, Michael (I)**	Clinton, Bill (I)	Ford, Harrison (I)	**Zilber, Mac**

Table 10: Top 20 pages of the Hollywood co-starship graph.

Indegree	PageRank	Katz	Harmonic	Closeness
wordpress.org	gmpg.org	wordpress.org	youtube.com	**0-p.com**
youtube.com	wordpress.org	youtube.com	en.wikipedia.org	**0-0-0-0-0-0-0.indahiphop.ru**
gmpg.org	youtube.com	gmpg.org	twitter.com	**0-0-1.i.tiexue.net**
en.wikipedia.org	**livejournal.com**	en.wikipedia.org	google.com	**0-00cigarettes.info**
tumblr.com	tumblr.com	tumblr.com	wordpress.org	**0-0mos00.hi5.com**
twitter.com	en.wikipedia.org	twitter.com	flickr.com	**0-0new0-0.hi5.com**
google.com	twitter.com	google.com	facebook.com	**0-0sunny0-0.hi5.com**
flickr.com	**networkadvertising.org**	flickr.com	**apple.com**	**0-1.i.tiexue.net**
rtalabel.org	**promodj.com**	rtalabel.org	vimeo.com	**0-1.sxsy.co**
wordpress.com	**skriptmail.de**	wordpress.com	creativecommons.org	**0-2.paparazziwannabe.com**
mp3shake.com	**parallels.com**	mp3shake.com	**amazon.com**	**0-311.cn**
w3schools.com	**tistory.com**	w3schools.com	**adobe.com**	**0-360.rukazan.ru**
domains.lycos.com	google.com	creativecommons.org	**myspace.com**	**0-5days.com**
staff.tumblr.com	miibeian.gov.cn	staff.tumblr.com	**w3.org**	**0-5days.net**
club.tripod.com	phpbb.com	domains.lycos.com	**bbc.co.uk**	**0-5kalibr.pdj.ru**
creativecommons.org	**blog.fc2.com**	club.tripod.com	**nytimes.com**	**0-9-0-4-4-9.promoradio.ru**
vimeo.com	**tw.yahoo.com**	vimeo.com	**yahoo.com**	**0-9-0-9.dbass.ru**
miibeian.gov.cn	w3schools.com	miibeian.gov.cn	**microsoft.com**	**0-9-0-9.promodj.ru**
facebook.com	wordpress.com	facebook.com	**guardian.co.uk**	**0-9-1125.i.tiexue.net**
phpbb.com	domains.lycos.com	phpbb.com	**imdb.com**	**0-9-7-16.software.informer.com**

Table 11: Top 20 hosts of the Common Crawl host graph.

	Ind.	PR	Katz	Harm.	Cl.
Indegree	1	0.42	0.93	0.55	0.43
PageRank	0.42	1	0.36	0.10	0.18
Katz	0.93	0.36	1	0.61	0.49
Harmonic	0.55	0.10	0.61	1	0.86
Closeness	0.43	0.18	0.49	0.86	1

	Ind.	PR	Katz	Harm.	Cl.
Indegree	1	0.90	0.98	0.91	0.10
PageRank	0.90	1	0.88	0.81	0.64
Katz	0.98	0.88	1	0.92	0.11
Harmonic	0.91	0.81	0.92	1	0.18
Closeness	0.10	0.64	0.11	0.18	1

Table 8: Kendall's τ (top) and τ_h (bottom) on the Hollywood co-starship graph.

	Ind.	PR	Katz	Harm.	Cl.
Indegree	1	0.71	0.89	0.61	0.54
PageRank	0.71	1	0.66	0.50	0.50
Katz	0.89	0.66	1	0.69	0.59
Harmonic	0.61	0.50	0.69	1	0.86
Closeness	0.54	0.50	0.59	0.86	1

	Ind.	PR	Katz	Harm.	Cl.
Indegree	1	0.91	0.96	0.72	0.20
PageRank	0.91	1	0.90	0.81	0.69
Katz	0.96	0.90	1	0.78	0.15
Harmonic	0.72	0.81	0.78	1	0.35
Closeness	0.20	0.69	0.15	0.35	1

Table 9: Kendall's τ (top) and τ_h (bottom) on the on the Common Crawl host graph.

the giant component. We thus expect to discover an unsuspected correlation between the way PageRank and closeness rank these nodes.

To have a visual understanding of what is happening, we created Figure 2, 3 and 4 in the following way: first, we isolated the nodes that are unreachable from the giant component (in the case of Hollywood, which is undirected, these nodes form separate components), omitting nodes which have indegree zero, modulo loops (as all measures give the lowest score to such nodes); then, we sorted the nodes in order of decreasing closeness rank, and plotted for each node its rank following the other measures (we average ranks on block of nodes so to contain the number of points in the plots). A point of high abscissa in the figures implies a high rank.

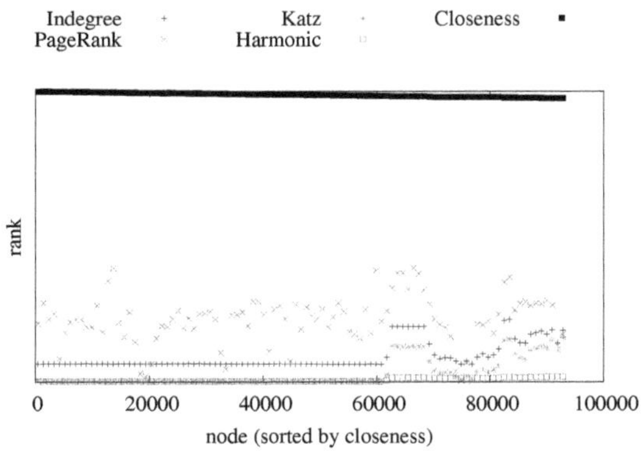

Figure 2: Ranks of components unreachable from the giant component of the Wikipedia graph.

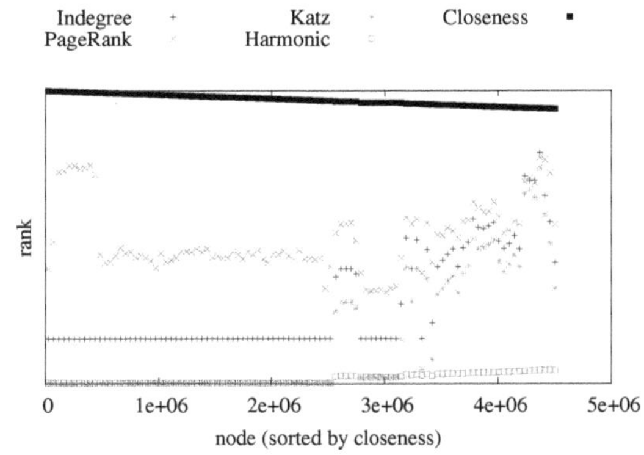

Figure 4: Ranks of components unreachable from the giant component of the Common Crawl host graph.

All three pictures show clearly that *PageRank assigns a preposterously high rank to nodes belonging to components that are unreachable from the giant component*. This behavior is actually related to PageRank's well-known *insensitivity to size* [2]: for instance, in a graph made of two components, one of which is a 3-clique and the other a k-clique, the PageRank score of all nodes is $1/(3+k)$, independently of k. The same phenomenon is at work when the community around Lloyd Kaufman's production company (very small and very dense) is attributed such a great importance that its elements make their way to the very top ranks. Dually, harmonic centrality, the only score sensitive to size among those we are considering, sports consistently the lowest ranks on such nodes.

We remark that the gap in rank is lower in the case of Wikipedia, but this is fully in concordance with the higher baseline value of Kendall's τ.

7. CONCLUSIONS

In this paper, motivated by the need to understand similarity between score vectors, such as those generated by centrality measures on large graphs, we have defined a weighted version of Kendall's τ starting from its 1945 definition for scores with ties. We have developed the mathematical properties of our generalization following a mathematical similarity with internal products, and showing that for a wide range of weighting schemes our new measure behaves as expected, providing a correlation index between -1 and 1, and hitting boundaries only for opposite or equivalent scores.

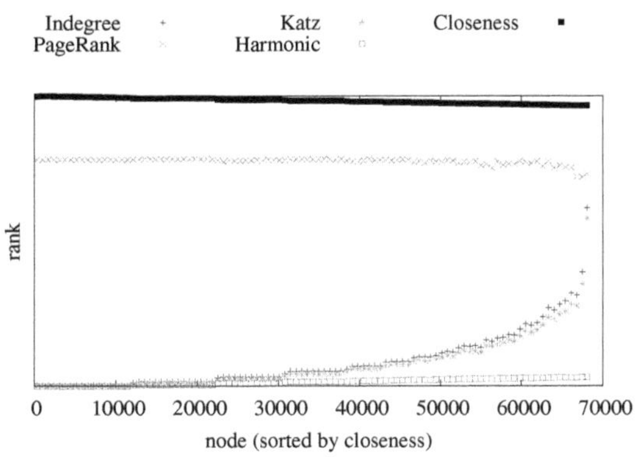

Figure 3: Ranks of components of the Hollywood co-starship graph, excluding the giant component.

We have then proposed families of weighting schemes that are intuitively appealing, and showed that they can be computed in time $O(n \log n)$ using a generalization of Knight's algorithm, which makes them suitable for large-scale applications. The fact that the main cost of the algorithm is a modified stable sort makes it possible to apply standard techniques to run the algorithm exploiting multicore parallelism, or a in distributed environment. The algorithm can be also used to compute AP correlation [27].

In search for a confirmation of our mathematical intuition, we have then applied our measure of choice τ_h (which uses additive hyperbolic weights) to diverse graph such as Wikipedia, the Hollywood co-starship graph and a large host graph, finding that, contrarily to Kendall's τ, τ_h provides results that are consistent with an anecdotal examination of lists of top elements.

Our measure was also able to discover a previously unnoticed correlation between PageRank and closeness on small components that are unreachable from the giant component, providing a quantifiable account of the strong bias of PageRank towards small-sized dense communities. This bias might well be the cause of the repeatedly assessed better performance of indegree w.r.t. PageRank in ranking documents [21, 3], as in all our experiments the τ_h between PageRank and indegree is above 0.9.

A generalization similar to the one described in this paper can be also applied to *Goodman–Kruskal's* γ, which in the notation of Section 5 is just $(C-D)/(C+D)$. The problem with γ is that the contribution of ties is only implicit (they are simply not counted). Thus, the value of w on tied pairs does not appear at all in the above formula. This "forgetful" behavior can lead to unnatural results: for instance, the γ correlation between the score vectors $\langle 1,2,3\rangle$ and $\langle 1,2,2\rangle$ is one, independently of the weights (i.e., even if we let w_{12} go to infinity). This behaviour suggests the Kendall's τ is a better candidate for this approach—the τ correlation is $\sqrt{2/(2+w_{12})}$, which is 1 when $w_{12}=0$, $\sqrt{2/3}$ with uniform weights, and goes to zero as w_{12} goes to infinity.

We remark that an interesting application of additive hyperbolic weighting is that of measuring the correlation between top k lists. By assuming that the rank function ρ returns ∞ after rank k, we obtain a correlation index that weighs zero pairs outside the top k, weights only "by one side" pairs with just one element outside the top k, and weights fully pairs whose elements are within the top k. Formula (2) could provide then in principle a finer assessment than, for instance, the modified Kendall's τ proposed in [5], as the position of each element inside the list, beside the fact that it appears in the top k or not, would be a source of weight. We leave the analysis of such a correlation measure for future work.

8. REFERENCES

[1] Alex Bavelas. Communication patterns in task-oriented groups. *J. Acoust. Soc. Am.*, 22(6):725–730, 1950.

[2] Paolo Boldi and Sebastiano Vigna. Axioms for centrality. *Internet Math.*, 10(3-4):222–262, 2014.

[3] Nick Craswell, David Hawking, and Trystan Upstill. Predicting fame and fortune: PageRank or indegree? In *In Proceedings of the Australasian Document Computing Symposium, ADCS2003*, pages 31–40, 2003.

[4] Henry E. Daniels. The relation between measures of correlation in the universe of sample permutations. *Biometrika*, 33(2):129–135, 1943.

[5] Ronald Fagin, Ravi Kumar, and D. Sivakumar. Comparing top k lists. *SIAM Journal on Discrete Mathematics*, 17(1):134–160, 2003.

[6] F. Farnoud and O. Milenkovic. An axiomatic approach to constructing distances for rank comparison and aggregation. *IEEE Trans. on Information Theory*, 60(10):6417–6439, October 2014.

[7] Santo Fortunato, Marián Boguñá, Alessandro Flammini, and Filippo Menczer. On local estimations of pagerank: A mean field approach. *Internet Math.*, 4(2):245–266, 2007.

[8] Johannes Hoffart, Fabian M. Suchanek, Klaus Berberich, and Gerhard Weikum. YAGO2: A spatially and temporally enhanced knowledge base from Wikipedia. *Artificial Intelligence*, 194:28–61, 2013.

[9] Ronald L. Iman and W. J. Conover. A measure of top-down correlation. *Technometrics*, 29(3):351–357, 1987.

[10] Leo Katz. A new status index derived from sociometric analysis. *Psychometrika*, 18(1):39–43, 1953.

[11] John G. Kemeny. Mathematics without numbers. *Daedalus*, 88(4):577–591, 1959.

[12] Maurice G. Kendall. A new measure of rank correlation. *Biometrika*, 30(1/2):81–93, 1938.

[13] Maurice G. Kendall. The treatment of ties in ranking problems. *Biometrika*, 33(3):239–251, 1945.

[14] William R. Knight. A computer method for calculating Kendall's tau with ungrouped data. *Journal of the American Statistical Association*, 61(314):436–439, June 1966.

[15] Donald E. Knuth. *Sorting and Searching*, volume 3 of *The Art of Computer Programming*. Addison-Wesley, second edition, 1997.

[16] Ravi Kumar and Sergei Vassilvitskii. Generalized distances between rankings. In *Proceedings of the 19th International Conference on World Wide Web*, pages 571–580. ACM, 2010.

[17] Ronny Lempel and Shlomo Moran. The stochastic approach for link-structure analysis (SALSA) and the TKC effect. *Computer Networks*, 33(1):387–401, 2000.

[18] Massimo Melucci. On rank correlation in information retrieval evaluation. *SIGIR Forum*, 41(1):18–33, June 2007.

[19] Robert Meusel, Sebastiano Vigna, Oliver Lehmberg, and Christian Bizer. Graph structure in the web — Revisited, or a trick of the heavy tail. In *WWW'14 Companion*, pages 427–432. International World Wide Web Conferences Steering Committee, 2014.

[20] Carl D. Meyer. *Matrix analysis and applied linear algebra*. Society for Industrial and Applied Mathematics, 2000.

[21] Marc Najork, Hugo Zaragoza, and Michael J. Taylor. HITS on the web: how does it compare? In Wessel Kraaij, Arjen P. de Vries, Charles L. A. Clarke, Norbert Fuhr, and Noriko Kando, editors, *SIGIR 2007: Proceedings of the 30th Annual International ACM SIGIR Conference on Research and Development in Information Retrieval, Amsterdam, The Netherlands, July 23-27, 2007*, pages 471–478. ACM, 2007.

[22] Lawrence Page, Sergey Brin, Rajeev Motwani, and Terry Winograd. The PageRank citation ranking: Bringing order to the web. Technical Report SIDL-WP-1999-0120, Stanford Digital Library Technologies Project, Stanford University, 1998.

[23] I. Richard Savage. Contributions to the theory of rank order statistics—the two-sample case. *The Annals of Mathematical Statistics*, 27(3):590–615, 1956.

[24] Grace S. Shieh. A weighted kendall's tau statistic. *Statistics & Probability Letters*, 39(1):17–24, 1998.

[25] Charles Spearman. The proof and measurement of association between two things. *The American journal of psychology*, 15(1):72–101, 1904.

[26] Ellen M. Voorhees. Evaluation by highly relevant documents. In *Proceedings of the 24th annual international ACM SIGIR conference on Research and development in information retrieval*, pages 74–82. ACM, 2001.

[27] Emine Yilmaz, Javed A. Aslam, and Stephen Robertson. A new rank correlation coefficient for information retrieval. In *Proceedings of the 31st annual international ACM SIGIR conference on Research and development in information retrieval*, pages 587–594. ACM, 2008.

Gathering Additional Feedback on Search Results by Multi-Armed Bandits with Respect to Production Ranking

Aleksandr Vorobev[1], Damien Lefortier[1,2], Gleb Gusev[1], and Pavel Serdyukov[1]

[1]Yandex, Moscow, Russia,
{alvor88,damien,gleb57,pavser}@yandex-team.ru
[2]University of Amsterdam, Amsterdam, The Netherlands

ABSTRACT

Given a repeatedly issued query and a document with a not-yet-confirmed potential to satisfy the users' needs, a search system should place this document on a high position in order to gather user feedback and obtain a more confident estimate of the document utility. On the other hand, the main objective of the search system is to maximize expected user satisfaction over a rather long period, what requires showing more relevant documents on average. The state-of-the-art approaches to solving this exploration-exploitation dilemma rely on strongly simplified settings making these approaches infeasible in practice. We improve the most flexible and pragmatic of them to handle some actual practical issues. The first one is utilizing prior information about queries and documents, the second is combining bandit-based learning approaches with a default production ranking algorithm. We show experimentally that our framework enables to significantly improve the ranking of a leading commercial search engine.

1. INTRODUCTION

A common search system is usually based on a deterministic ranking model that aggregates both *pre-feedback* features describing the content of web pages and *implicit feedback* features based on user behavior data stored in query logs. This leads to the following iterative process of interaction with users that repeatedly submit a particular query. At the first stage, when the query is relatively new to the system, it ranks documents by the scores using their pre-feedback information only. Further, at the second stage, it corrects this ranking with respect to implicit feedback data, while it is being collected. During this stabilizing phase, scores of top ranked documents which get negative user feedback become lower, so these documents are exchanged with other documents with high pre-feedback based scores. After the algorithm found enough documents getting mostly positive user feedback, the ranking is not being changed anymore by two reasons: first, the algorithm continues to receive only redundant confirmation of the top documents' relatively high relevance, and, second, no documents lacking implicit feedback have scores higher than those which were lucky to get some. At the same time, pre-feedback information cannot fully reflect all the aspects of the documents that potentially impact user satisfaction, therefore, some of those documents lacking user feedback can be more relevant than those ranked higher. However, the customary scheme of user–system interaction just described cannot find the additional evidence for that, since these low ranked documents are very unlikely to ever receive user feedback. Therefore, it may be of use to have other mechanisms to place some lower ranked documents on the upper positions to attract more user feedback to them. In this way, we may degrade the query performance for a short period of time, by taking the risk of showing some less relevant documents on the top positions, but improve it in the long term, by giving a chance to get user feedback (and, hence, improve their scores) for more potentially highly relevant documents.

Thus, there are two different ranking strategies: the exploitative one, aiming, at each step, to maximize the ranking performance for the current query issue , and the exploratory one, allowing to collect more user feedback on lower ranked documents even at the cost of degrading the ranking performance for some query issues. It is especially important to achieve the optimal interplay between these two strategies that maximizes the cumulative quality of a series of consecutive query issues. We refer to this problem as *Online Learning to Rank with Exploration and Exploitation (OL-REE)* problem in this paper. It is a particular case of the well-known exploration–exploitation trade-off problem formalized most appropriately in the Stochastic Multi-Armed Bandit (SMAB) setting [2]. This setting originates from a problem of a gambler facing a row of casino slot machines, sometimes known as "one-armed bandits". Here we briefly describe the problem setup.

There is a set of *arms* $A = \{a_i\}$. At each *step* t, an algorithm chooses an arm $a(t) \in A$, receives its *reward* R_t, which is a sample from an unknown arm-associated distribution with an unknown expectation $r_{a(t)}$ (we call r_a the arm *gain* throughout the paper), and updates the stored information about $a(t)$. The algorithm goal is to maximize the cumulative reward $\mathbf{R}(T)$ over the first T steps: $\mathbf{R}(T) = \mathbf{E}\left(\sum_{t=1}^{T} R_t\right)$, where $\mathbf{E}$ denotes expectation. The general idea underlying

WWW 2015, May 18–22, 2015, Florence, Italy.
ACM 978-1-4503-3469-3/15/05.
http://dx.doi.org/10.1145/2736277.2741104.

a bandit algorithm is the following. It stores information about each arm a, which includes not only an estimate of r_a on the basis of the observed user behaviour, but also the confidence in this estimate which can be represented, for example, as its standard deviation or as a distribution over values of r_a. Then, at each step, an algorithm balances between a purely exploratory choice (the arm with the lowest confidence) and a purely exploitative choice (the arm with the highest estimated r_a).

In this paper, we investigate one of the most promising ways to formulate the OLREE problem in the SMAB terms. We consider a repeatedly submitted query as a separate bandit problem setting, each query submission as one step, a ranking system as a gambler, and each document as an arm. Examination of a document by a user is considered as pulling of the corresponding arm, and the reward of the arm is then determined by the user satisfaction with the examined document. As we discuss in Section 8, this approach allows us to apply SMAB theory more appropriately in practice than do the other known applications of this theory to OLREE. Unlike in the original SMAB formulation, within this approach, a gambler is able to choose not one but several arms for pulling. Their number is upper-bounded by the capacity of the search engine result page (SERP). However, after an arm is chosen for pulling (so, a document is included into the ranking), the gambler has no control over it and whether it will be eventually pulled or not depends entirely on the user who issued the query. Moreover, due to the limitations of logging mechanisms, while estimating the gain r_d of a document d and the confidence in this estimate, the gambler does not often know whether the pulling of the arm actually took place. In this case, the SMAB formulation and the known bandit algorithms cannot be directly applied to the OLREE task and should be adopted to it.

To the best of our knowledge, the only existing adoption that attempts to solve the mentioned problems was suggested by Sloan and Wang [31]. It is based on utilizing a click model to infer information about the document gain from the user behavior and takes position bias into account. However, this pioneering study did not address another problem, whose solution would actually make this promising "document=arm" approach practically useful: no real-world search engine can afford to ignore the initial guess about the document relevance made on the ground of the *prior* information that is already available before the exploration starts. Neither it is reasonable and feasible to explore all documents available to the search system, as such intense exploration will severely degrade user experience, what is highly undesirable even for a very short period. Thus, we need to explore only the documents, in whose scores the ranking system is least confident. The prior estimation of both r_d and our confidence in this estimate and smooth introduction of a bandit-based ranking algorithm into a default ranking system are the essential problems that have not been addressed so far.

In this paper, we propose an approach to marry a state-of-the-art default ranking model with the above-described bandit-based formulation. Particularly, we develop an approach for setting prior values of r_d estimates and of confidences in them based on both the document features available to the default ranking system and the ranked list of documents it produces. This approach relies on two techniques that have not been previously applied to the OLREE problem: constructing a regression model for error prediction and applying isotonic regression to adjust regression to ranking. We show experimentally that incorporation of our bandit-based algorithm into a highly optimized production ranker of a major commercial search engine remarkably increases the performance of the latter during a 10-day period.

To sum up, our contributions are:

- A new formulation of the OLREE problem in the terms of the SMAB problem (Section 2).
- An approach to utilizing prior information in the OLREE problem by estimating prior distributions of documents' relevances (i.e., the confidences in their prior estimates) (Section 4),
- An algorithm for combining a state-of-the-art ranking model with a bandit-based ranking approach (Section 5).

Besides, we present experimental results in Section 7, review related work on application of bandit-based methods to IR tasks in Section 8, and make conclusions in Section 9.

2. PROBLEM FORMALIZATION

We suggest the following SMAB formulation for the OLREE problem which leads to the optimization problem considered in [31, Eq. 1]. Given a unique query, we associate it with a dedicated bandit algorithm which makes a step per each query issue. This algorithm treats each document related to the query as an arm. At each step, in order to choose the list of arms for pulling, the algorithm generates a SERP in response to the current query issue and observes some user behavior on it. The main difference of our OLREE setting from the ordinary SMAB problem described in Section 1 and from the approaches of all the related studies, except for [31], is that an arm chosen by the algorithm for pulling can be both *pulled* or *not pulled* depending on whether the user, who issued the query, actually *examined* or *did not examine* the corresponding document on the SERP (similar events $\{S_i = j\}, j = 1, 2$ were used in [31, Sec. 3.2]). This leads to the notion of document *trial* which means the fact of pulling the corresponding arm. Each examined document provides a reward to the algorithm, which equals 1, if the user is *satisfied* with the document, and 0 otherwise (*unsatisfied*). We also assume that the reward of a document d is a Bernoulli random variable with a probability of success r_d.

In the scope of this paper, we define satisfaction as a click with a long enough dwell time or the last click on the SERP (see Section 6.2 for details). In this way, the cumulative reward of our bandit algorithm over the first T query issues equals the cumulative number of satisfied clicks, as in [31] (in their study, each click was considered to be satisfied). We also assume that user behavior on search result pages is consistent with the following conditions (which are implied by the examination hypothesis [11]): a search result can be clicked by the user only if it is examined by her, the examination probability does not depend on the document, and, given the fact of examination, the click probability depends on the document only. So, it is reasonable to consider that an arm is pulled if and only if the user examined the snippet of the corresponding document. Thus, the cumulative reward over T issues of a query could be represented as

$$\mathbf{R}(T) = \sum_{t=1}^{T} \sum_{i=1}^{k} P(E^t_{d_i(t)} = 1) P(C^t_{d_i(t)} = 1 | E^t_{d_i(t)} = 1),$$

where the binary variables E^t_d and C^t_d indicate the examination of the document snippet ($E^t_d = 1$) and the satisfied click on the document ($C_d^t = 1$) at step t respectively, k is the number of documents on each SERP, and $d_i(t)$ is the document placed on position i by our algorithm at step t.

As long as one can never be sure that the user will examine a particular document, unless it is shown on the first position, the number of document trials that will actually take place during the period of T query issues is a random variable. It is the principal difference of our approach and that of [31] (their "effective" number of impressions is similar to our number of trials, see their Section 3.2) from the other SMAB formulations of the OLREE problem we are familiar with.

On the other hand, SMAB algorithms essentially use the information of which arms were pulled. Therefore, their application to the OLREE problem requires to infer which snippets on the SERP were examined. In Section 3.3, we describe both a binary inference approach, which unambiguously defines if the snippet was examined or not, and a probabilistic inference approach, which obtains the probability of examination and performs better in practice.

3. APPROACH

3.1 Background on SMAB algorithms

Our approach to OLREE problem relies on a SMAB algorithm B of the following type. In the course of the game, it stores a vector of real-valued parameters $F_t(a) \in \mathbb{R}^I$ for each arm a, where t denotes the step number, $\mathbb{R}^I$ is an algorithm-specific parameter space and I is the set of parameter indices. At each step t, algorithm B calculates scores

$$S_t(a) := S_{B,t}(F_t(a)),$$

where $S_{B,t}$ is either a random or deterministic scoring function on $\mathbb{R}^p$ depending on particular algorithm B. Algorithm B chooses an arm $a_t^* \in \arg\max_a(S_t(a))$, observes its reward, and calculates $F_{t+1}(a_t^*)$ according to some rule U_B on the basis of $F_t(a_t^*)$ and the observed reward. It sets $F_{t+1}(a) = F_t(a)$ for other arms a.

In the next two sections, we describe two SMAB algorithms we adopt to the OLREE problem in Section 3.2. Below we also describe a class of SMAB algorithms, which can be easily applied within our approach.

3.1.1 UCB-1

First, we adopt the state-of-the-art algorithm **UCB-1** [2], which was applied to the OLREE problem in the main related studies [27, 31], where it outperformed its competitors. Following UCB-1, at step t,

$$S_t(a) = \widehat{r}_{a,t} + \alpha\sqrt{\frac{2ln\ t}{\gamma_{a,t}}}, \quad (1)$$

where $\widehat{r}_{a,t} = \frac{W_{a,t}}{\gamma_{a,t}}$ is the maximum likelihood estimate of r_a after step $(t-1)$, $\gamma_{a,t}$ is the number of trials of the arm a during the first $(t-1)$ steps, $W_{a,t}$ is the number of successful trials among them, α is a parameter controlling the exploration rate (to be fitted on a training data). Thus, $F_t(a)$ consists of two components, $W_{a,t}$ and $\gamma_{a,t}$. The rule U_B increments $\gamma_{a,t}$ by 1 when a is pulled ($\gamma_{a,t+1} = \gamma_{a,t} + 1$) and increments $W_{a,t}$ by 1 when this pulling is successful.

3.1.2 Bayesian bandits

In the case of the standard SMAB problem, bandit algorithms following the Bayesian approach, namely, Bayesian-UCB [19] and Thompson sampling [20], have stronger theoretically grounded guarantees and achieved better performance in experiments with other tasks [19, 20] than the pointwise alternatives such as UCB-1. However, to the best of our knowledge, they have not been applied to the OLREE problem earlier. We further describe *Bayesian bandits* algorithm, which generalizes both Bayesian-UCB and Thompson sampling. It relies on the posterior probability density function $p_{a,t}(r), r \in [0,1]$, of gain r_a. This posterior probability is updated by rule U_B to be specified below. At step t, algorithm samples α uniformly from the set $[\alpha_{low}(t), \alpha_{up}(t)]$ ($\alpha_{low}(t)$ and $\alpha_{up}(t)$ are parameters of the algorithm) and then sets $S_t(a)$ to the α-quantile of $p_{a,t}(r)$ (i.e., $\int_0^{S_t(a)} p_{a,t}(r)dr = \alpha$). Thus, $F_t(a)$ coincides with $\{p_{a,t}(r)\}_{r\in[0,1]}$. At step t, with observed reward R_t, rule U_B keeps $p_{a,t+1}(r) = p_{a,t}(r)$ for $a \neq a_t^*$ and updates $p_{a,t}(r)$ for $a = a_t^*$ as follows:

$$\begin{aligned} p_{a,t+1}(r) &= p_{a,t}(r|R_t) \propto P(R_t|r_a = r)p_{a,t}(r) = \\ &= r^{R_t}(1-r)^{1-R_t}p_{a,t}(r) \propto \\ &\propto r^{W_{a,t+1}}(1-r)^{\gamma_{a,t+1}-W_{a,t+1}}p_{a,0}(r). \quad (2) \end{aligned}$$

Thus, Bayesian bandit, in contrast to UCB-1, requires some initialization, i.e., prior distribution $p_{a,0}(r)$ for each arm a. In the case of $\alpha_{low}(t) = \alpha_{up}(t)$, this algorithm coincides with Bayesian-UCB [19], and if $\alpha_{low}(t) = 0, \alpha_{up}(t) = 1$, it reduces to Thompson sampling [20]. Note that we can store $\{\gamma_{a,t}, W_{a,t}, \{p_{a,0}(r)\}_{r\in[0,1]}\}$ instead of $\{p_{a,t}(r)\}_{r\in[0,1]}$ and update only $\gamma_{a,t}$ and $W_{a,t}$ when we run Bayesian bandits in practice.

Since the SMAB problem is to maximize the expectation of the cumulative reward, the rational exploitative strategy is to choose the arm a with the maximum mean of the posterior distribution $p_{a,t}(r)$. This motivated us to consider the following modifications of Bayesian bandits and UCB-1 (we call them MeanBayes and MeanUCB-1 respectively) whose exploitative settings rank documents by the posterior mean values. The algorithm MeanBayes uses the following scoring function similar to Equation 1: $S_t(a) = \overline{r}_{a,t} + \alpha \cdot \sigma_{a,t}$, where $\overline{r}_{a,t}$ and $\sigma_{a,t}$ are the mean and the standard deviation of the posterior distribution $p_{a,t}(r)$ respectively.

The modification MeanUCB-1 calculates $\widehat{r}_{a,t}$ by the following modified rule: $\widehat{r}_{a,t} = \frac{W_{a,t}+1}{\gamma_{a,t}+2}$. While the original rule takes the maximum likelihood estimate of r_a, which corresponds to the mode of the posterior distribution $p_{a,t}(r)$, the estimate of the modified rule corresponds to its mean in the assumption that $p_{a,t}(r)$ is a beta distribution (see Section 4).

Now we describe our general approach to the OLREE problem, which is capable of adopting a variety of known SMAB algorithms, including the above-mentioned methods.

3.2 General Approach to OLREE

In our framework, we assume that any algorithm solving the OLREE problem (*OLREE algorithm* below) works for each query independently and deals with a limited set of candidate documents which are chosen for exploration on the ground of the pre-feedback information.

Adopting any SMAB algorithm B to the OLREE problem requires answers to two questions: how to choose not one but the list of documents for the SERP and how to update parameters $F_t(d)$ of each document on the ground of the user feedback. The first problem has a very natural solution which is to rank documents by their scores $S_t(d)$ at step t. In order to solve the second problem, Sloan and Wang [31] suggested to update $F_t(d)$ by a specific rule U which, for each document d from the SERP, estimates the posterior probability that d was examined, relying on a click model. Then, this probability is considered as a weight of the document trial taken into account when updating $F_t(d)$. It is obviously implied that $F_{t+1}(d) = F_t(d)$ for each document d not presented on the SERP at step t. We call this adoption of the SMAB algorithm B (see Algorithm 1) as a **Bandit-Based Ranking Algorithm (BBRA)**.

Algorithm 1: Bandit-Based Ranking Algorithm (BBRA)

Data: set of documents D for a given query, number of query issues T, prior $F_0(d)$ for each $d \in D$;

for $t = 0$ **to** $T - 1$ **do**
  foreach $d \in D$ **do**
    $S_t(d) = S_{B,t}(F_t(d))$;
  end
  Sort D by decreasing S_t: $\{d_1(t), d_2(t), \ldots\}$;
  Display documents $\{d_1(t), \ldots, d_k(t)\}$ to the user;
  Observe user behavior C on the SERP;
  for $i = 1$ **to** k **do**
    $F_{t+1}(d_i(t)) = U(F_t(d_i(t)), C)$;
  end
end

Result: Ranking for each query issue: $\{d_i(t)\}_{i=1..k}^{t=1..T}$

Now we describe the specific rules U for updating parameters $F_t(d)$ utilized by each of the SMAB scoring functions studied in this paper. Note that any SMAB algorithm with parameters $F_t(d)$ which could be calculated on the basis of $\left\{W_{a,t}, \gamma_{a,t}, \{p_{a,t}(r)\}_{r\in[0,1]}\right\}$ can easily be used within BBRA with the below-described update rules.

3.3 Update rule for OLREE

All the updated rules we experiment with rely on the Dependent Click Model (DCM) [15], since it was used in different studies on bandit algorithms in web search ranking [17, 31] and outperformed the alternative models in the experiments in [31]. To replace DCM with any other click model, one should specify an update rule based on it. However, any of the below-described general methods for constructing update rules (EM-algorithm for updating parameters of UCB-1, Bayesian inference for Bayesian bandits) can be applied to any click model.

As most of state-of-the-art click models, DCM is based on the cascade hypothesis. In terms of variables $d_i(t)$, E_d^t and C_d^t introduced in Section 2, DCM is described by the following equations:

$$P(E^t_{d_1(t)} = 1) = 1,\ P(E^t_{d_{i+1}(t)} = 1|\ C^t_{d_i(t)} = 1) = \lambda_i,$$
$$P(E^t_{d_{i+1}(t)} = 1|\ E^t_{d_i(t)} = 1, C^t_{d_i(t)} = 0) = 1,$$
$$P(C_d^t = 1|E_d^t = 1) = r_d. \quad (3)$$

Naturally, we assume that satisfied clicks (i.e., C_d^t) are directly observed by the search engine, and examinations (i.e., E_d^t) are not, as it occurs in practice. Thus, E_d^t are hidden variables of the constructed Bayesian network. As in [15], we do not infer anything from abandoned sessions with no clicks, because such sessions cannot be explained by DCM in the case of real user behavior and the reasons of abandonment are often unknown. The cascade hypothesis allows to regard the documents above (and on) the lowest click position as examined, while updating parameters $F_t(d)$ on the ground of the user feedback. Further, we use two approaches to estimate the values E_d^t and, on the basis of these estimates, to update parameters $F_t(d)$ for the documents d placed below the lowest click. Within the first, *honest*, approach, for each of such documents, we follow [31] and estimate the posterior probability that it was examined. When updating $F_t(d)$, we use this probability as the weight of the document trial (see Equation 4). The second one, *negligent*, is to regard these documents as not examined by the user. It takes into account less information but requires much less computations than does the honest approach. We experiment with both approaches to verify if the complex computations of the latter one are indeed justified by its performance. Specifically, we have the following update rules U.

1) The **negligent** approach unambiguously defines which documents were examined at each step t. Thus, we can just use rule U_B (corresponding to the chosen SMAB algorithm B described in Section 3.1) to update $F_t(d)$ for each examined d. In terms of that section, $\gamma_{d,t} = |\{\tau < t : E_d^\tau = 1\}|$, $W_{d,t} = |\{\tau < t : C_d^\tau = 1\}|$ (here $|A|$ is the size of set A).

2) Now we describe the update rules for UCB-1 and Bayesian bandits specifically (which are also applicable to their modifications MeanUCB-1 and MeanBayes) in the case of the **honest** inference approach.

• The **point estimate** $\widehat{r}_{d,t}$ and its confidence $\gamma_{d,t}$ for UCB-1 are calculated by the expectation–maximization (EM) algorithm which maximizes the likelihood of the observed user behavior. This approach was suggested in [31] in combination with ranking by UCB-1.

At the **E-step**, we estimate the hidden variables E_d^t by calculating posterior probabilities of examinations $P(E_d^t = 1|\,UB_t)$, where UB_t is the user behavior observed at step t (see Appendix for details).

Further, we use them at the **M-step**:

$$\gamma_{d,t+1} = \sum_{\tau=1}^{t} P(E_d^\tau = 1|\,UB_t), \quad W_{d,t+1} = \sum_{\tau=1}^{t} C_d^\tau. \quad (4)$$

• Calculation of the **posterior distribution** $p_{d,t}(r)$ for Bayesian bandits relies on the Bayesian inference, see Appendix for details.

Note that parameters $F_t(d)$ updated by the proposed rules aggregate all the user feedback observed on a document d in response to a query q. Hence, ranking by decreasing $S_{B,t}(F_t(d))$ (see Alg. 1) utilizes all the user feedback observed in response to q. In contrast, Radlinski et al. [27, Alg. 2] used a dedicated instance of the SMAB algorithm for each position of the SERP, i.e., took into account only the user feedback on that position while choosing the document for it. While it was appropriate for the problem they solved (increasing the SERP diversity), it may be not the best solution for our case. Indeed, position and previous documents influence only the examination probability of the document d (not r_d) under the examination hypothesis, and our update rules take this influence into account. Hence, aggregation of user feedback on d over all the contexts within the same query seems to be rational. In order to include the approach from [27] in the set of baseline algorithms we experiment with, we adopted it to our problem setup by the following modification of BBRA.

Adoption of [27]. The algorithm stores a dedicated set of parameters $F_{t,i}(d)$ for each position i. The document $d_i(t)$

for the position i is then chosen from the documents which are not chosen for the previous positions, by maximizing $S_{B,t}(F_{t,i}(d))$, and the user feedback on $d_i(t)$ (clicked or not) is used to update only the parameters $F_{t,i}(d_i(t))$.

Adoption of ϵ-greedy. To test the effectiveness of exploration provided by Algorithm 1 with different scoring functions S, we compare them with ϵ-greedy [34], which is the simplest and widely used way to add exploration to any ranking algorithm. We apply it to our exploitative algorithms (see Section 7): for each position i, we choose the top document from the exploitative ranking that was not chosen for the previous positions with probability $1-\epsilon$, and choose a random document from D that was not chosen for the previous positions with probability ϵ.

4. PRIOR DISTRIBUTION PREDICTION

In this section, we discuss setting prior values F_0 of parameters, which is needed for initialization of the BBRA algorithm (see Algorithm 1). Note that we use variables r, W_t, γ_t, F_t, $\{p_t(r)\}_{r\in[0,1]}$ to denote the parameters associated with the pair (q,d) under consideration. While estimation of r is a standard task, prediction of confidence of this estimate is a rather novel problem. Diaz et al. [13, 12] used arm-specific prior estimation of r and set confidence of this estimate to be constant over arms, when considering search verticals as arms. Zhu et al. [37] formulated the problem of confidence prediction in another context and suggested an approach to it when r is defined by a language model based retrieval model. In contrast, our below-described approach assumes that the estimate r is generated by a ranker learned on hundreds of features, which is more realistic for a large-scale search engine, and proposes a set of features useful specifically for such type of prediction.

In our task, without this prediction, the BBRA algorithm would consider all the estimates of r as equally confident and would explore all the documents equally, either placing even clearly irrelevant documents on the top positions or minimizing exploration and so reducing to the standard exploitative ranking. The former case may lead to a short-term but dramatic drop in query performance and irrevocably decrease the market share of the web search engine. Thus, defining documents whose exploration would be the most effective is critical for incorporation of the BBRA algorithm into a web search system. Note that this practical problem was not considered in any related studies on bandit algorithms. For the case of the BBRA algorithm based on Bayesian bandits or UCB-1, we propose the following solution for it.

In the case of Bayesian bandits, we suggest to set $\{p_0(r)\}_{r\in[0,1]}$ to be a beta distribution for each query-document pair, as it was done in [13, 12] for a query-vertical pair, because it brings the following substantial advantages to our framework. First, a beta distribution is determined by only two parameters, α and β. From the viewpoint of our task, it is important to set just two independent principal parameters, estimate of r and its confidence. In terms of distribution, they can be considered as a mean value and a mean absolute deviation from the mean, respectively, which, in the case of the beta distribution, can be expressed through α and β in the following way:

$$\begin{cases} Er = \frac{\alpha}{\alpha+\beta} \\ E|r-E(r)| = \frac{2\alpha^\alpha\beta^\beta}{B(\alpha,\beta)(\alpha+\beta)^{\alpha+\beta+1}} \end{cases} \quad (5)$$

Thus, after estimation of Er and $E|r-E(r)|$ for a particular query-document pair, we are able to set a beta distribution for it by obtaining α and β as solutions of the system of Equations 5 by computational techniques. We use the downhill simplex algorithm [26] here.

Second, when we start with a beta distribution within the negligent Bayesian inference approach (see Equation 2), the posterior distribution $p_t(r)$ we obtain at each step of the inference is also some beta distribution. This allows us to represent the posterior distribution by only two numbers in our memory storage. Moreover, if $p_0(r)$ is uniform on the interval $[0,1]$ in Equation 2, the parameters of the posterior distribution of r are $\alpha = W_t+1, \beta = \gamma_{t+1} - W_t + 1$. It means that we can interpret our prior beta distribution as if the arm corresponding to the query-document pair was pulled $(\alpha+\beta-2)$ times with $(\alpha-1)$ of them successfully. Then, it is straightforward to use this distribution also for setting prior values of UCB-1 parameters γ and W according to their definition in Section 3.1.1: $\gamma_0 = \alpha+\beta-2, W_0 = \alpha-1$.

Now, the only open question is how to predict the mean value and the mean absolute deviation for each query-document pair. For this purpose, we use a vector $x = x_{q,d}$ of several hundred ranking features of the production ranker of Yandex[1], a popular search engine used by millions of people from different countries. For prediction of $E(r|x)$, we just relied on a model M_1 based on gradient boosted decision trees (GBDT) [14] and trained by minimizing MSE. The straightforward choice of a ground truth would be to use values of r_d inferred from logs for each query-document pair separately. However, we infer an aggregate value of r_d for all the pairs with the same relevance label manually assigned by professional judges hired by Yandex, since, in our experiments, the user feedback is generated on the basis of these aggregated r_d values (see Section 6 for details).

At the next step, we calculate predictions $M_1(x)$ for examples of a held-out part of the training data and train a new model M_2 to predict absolute errors $|r - M_1(x)|$ of predictions $M_1(x)$ also minimizing MSE. Then, we consider $M_2(x)$ as an estimate of $E(\Big|r - E(r|x)\Big|\,|x)$. Note that the signed error $(r - M_1(x))$ of prediction $M_1(x)$ cannot be predicted at any reasonable quality level: if we could do so, we would just improve $M_1(x)$ by correcting it by that prediction of the signed error. On the contrary, the absolute error of prediction turns out to be predictable. In our experiments, M_2 trained on the same features as M_1 outperformed a simple baseline by 19.6% in terms of MSE. This baseline predicts the same constant value for all the query-document pairs, which is equal to the average absolute error over all the pairs from the training set.

However, it is reasonable to expect that our prediction of M_1 error may be significantly strengthened by some features which are not useful for M_1 itself. We consider several ones based on predictions by M_1, which are closely related to their errors. Namely, for a query-document pair (d,q), we use: 1) $M_1(d,q)$; 2) the rank of d according to $M_1(d,q)$ among all the documents for q from the training data set, denote their subset by D_q; 3) $Avg(M_1,q)$ and 4) $StDev(M_1,q)$ are the average and the standard deviation of $M_1(d',q)$ over $d' \in D_q$ respectively; 5) $(M_1 - Avg(M_1,q))$; 6) $(M_1 - Avg(M_1,q))/StDev(M_1,q)$. Experimental results in Table 1 show that each new feature strengthens M_2 in terms

[1]yandex.com

Table 1: Gain in MSE for new features of M_2, %

Comparison with	1	2	3	4	5	6	All
baseline	6.95	1.83	0.19	1.19	3.57	2.70	8.19
baseline + all others	1.55	0.00	0.02	0.64	0.24	0.00	-

of MSE if added to the baseline vector of features (used for M_1) and each, except for features 2 and 6, does if added to the baseline features supplemented by all other new ones. All the differences, except for zeroes, are significant ($p < 0.05$). Thus, prediction $M_1(q,d)$ and its distribution over all the documents for q make its error prediction much more precise. In further experiments, we use the best of our versions of M_2, i.e., trained on all the baseline and new features.

The key point of both predictions is the choice of the loss function. Now we explain why minimizing merely MSE while training M_1 and M_2 allows us to reach a good estimate of $E(r|x)$ and $E(\left|r - E(r|x)\right| |x)$, respectively. It is well-known from statistics that the solution of the optimization problem

$$f^* = \arg\min_f E(h - f(x))^2$$

is $f^*(x) = E(h|x)$. Further, training of GBDT model tends to minimize MSE of prediction on the training data set, i.e., to minimize $E_{data}(h - f(x))^2$ where expectation is taken over the joint distribution of all the values of (h, x) in the training data set. Since our data set is supposed to be a large enough uniform sample from the real joint distribution of (h, x), $E_{data}(h - f(x))^2$ is close to $E(h - f(x))^2$. Therefore, it is reasonable to expect that the trained model provides an unbiased estimate of $E(h|x)$. Finally, we apply this reasoning to M_1 with $h = r$ and to M_2 with $h = \left|r - E(r|x)\right|$. In Section 7, we confirm the positive effect of these predictions on the cumulative query performance by experimental results.

5. INTRODUCTION OF BANDITS TO LTR

A modern ranking system is usually based on hundreds of features incorporated into a scoring function $f(q,d)$ trained to maximize some ranking quality measure. In Sec. 4, we use these features to train models $M_1(q,d), M_2(q,d)$ that predict the mean value of r_d and its deviation from the mean. When we switch from using ranking based on $f(q,d)$ to the ranking method produced by Alg. 1, we may observe a drop of ranking performance for the first several issues of each query. This drop is caused by two different reasons, one is inevitable and acceptable, and another one cannot be accepted.

First, Algorithm 1 allows some exploration whose rate is controlled by the exploration parameter. At the start of running Algorithm 1, this exploration leads to performance decrease that pays off, however, by the increase in quality aggregated at some horizon. This is in line with the main objective of OLREE to reach the best cumulative performance. Another reason of the performance drop is that the exploitative component of Algorithm 1 can be worse than $f(q,d)$. In fact, fully exploitative version of Algorithm 1 ranks documents by the outcomes of $M_1(q,d)$, which is trained via minimization of MSE in a pointwise manner. At the same time, well-known pairwise and listwise learning-to-rank algorithms, which are directly focused on finding the best ranking, are known to often outperform pointwise methods [24] and are widely used in search systems. Therefore, we expect that M_1 has lower ranking quality than $f(q,d)$ in general.

On the other hand, we cannot substitute $M_1(q,d)$ by $f(q,d)$ in Alg. 1, since scores $f(q,d)$ cannot serve as reasonable estimates of r_d in the general case. In fact, the values of $f(q,d)$ can be much greater or much smaller than the values of r_d for a given query q, despite producing the best achievable ranking (from the viewpoint of exploitation). This section is devoted to the problem of incorporating both $f(q,d)$ and $M_1(q,d)$ in a single model $M_{LTR}(q,d)$ that would have both advantages: (1) it should estimate r_d as precisely as possible, (2) it should produce the best possible exploitative ranking.

If we had a model that perfectly predicts r_{d_j}, the outcome scores would also provide the ideal ranking of documents d_j, $j = 1, 2, \ldots, k$. Therefore, when improving the quality of a predictive model, we expect that its ranking quality will be also improved (the intuition of all pointwise ranking models). Our approach is based on the reverse reasoning: when improving ranking quality of a model, we usually expect to increase or, at least, not decrease its predictive quality. Since $f(q,d)$ is supposed to produce the best achievable exploitative ranking, we suggest to correct $\widehat{r}_d = M_1(q,d)$ in such a way that the ranking produced according to corrected estimates $\widetilde{r}_d = M_{LTR}(q,d)$ would coincide with the ranking by $f(q,d)$. At the same time, we tend to minimize deviation of $\widetilde{r}_d$ from $\widehat{r}_d$, as it is regarded as the best possible pointwise estimate of r_d. This formulation naturally leads to the following particular case of the isotonic regression problem with a complete order [5, Section 1].

Assume $d_1, d_2, \ldots, d_n$ is the ranking produced by f, that is, $f(q,d_1) \geq f(q,d_2) \geq \ldots \geq f(q,d_n)$. The task is to find $\widetilde{r}_{d_j} = x_j$, $j = 1, 2, \ldots, n$, such that

$$\begin{cases} x_1 \geq x_2 \geq \ldots \geq x_n \\ \sum_{i=1}^{n} (x_i - \widehat{r}_{d_i})^2 \to \min \end{cases}$$

Applying the necessary Karush-Kuhn-Tucker conditions implies (see [5, Section 2] for details) that the unique solution of this problem has the following form. All the documents are to be divided into consecutive groups $\{d_1, \ldots, d_{k_1}\}, \ldots, \{d_{k_m+1}, \ldots, d_n\}$ to have the identical values $\widetilde{r}_d$ inside each group: $\widetilde{r}_{d_1} = \ldots = \widetilde{r}_{d_{k_1}} = \frac{\widehat{r}_{d_1} + \ldots + \widehat{r}_{d_{k_1}}}{k_1}, \ldots, \widetilde{r}_{d_{k_m+1}} = \ldots = \widetilde{r}_{d_n} = \frac{\widehat{r}_{d_{k_m+1}} + \ldots + \widehat{r}_{d_n}}{n - k_m}$. The optimal partition of the document set into such groups can be found by the Pool Adjacent Violators algorithm [5, Section 3] which has a linear complexity $O(n)$. It starts with regarding each document as a separate group and iteratively merges neighbor groups, if the average of $\widehat{r}_d$ in the upper group is less than in the lower one. In order to keep ranking produced by LTR, we break ties in each group in accordance with the ranking scores $f(q,d)$: $\widetilde{r}_d := \widetilde{r}_d + 0.0001 \cdot f(q,d)$.

While correcting the $\widehat{r}_d$ values, we keep their confidence constant for simplicity. Thus, we have the following **Procedure of LTR-correction** of $F_0(d)$:

- transform $\widehat{r}_d$ to $\widetilde{r}_d$ by isotonic regression with breaking ties,
- keep the customary γ_d.

Our experiments show that, as we expected, this correction increases performance not only in terms of NDCG@10 up to the level of the production baseline LTR currently used in Yandex (by 0.79%), but also in terms of MSE by 1.1%.

There are several ways to make use of this scheme in practice. First, we can combine any LTR ranking with our prior distributions of r_d before the start of the BBRA. Then the BBRA starts from the performance of LTR ranking and further improves it in accordance with the collected information. Second, it is possible to periodically update the user behavior features participating in the LTR model by making use of clicks gathered by BBRA and correct the current posterior distribution in accordance with the updated LTR ranking. We can expect that this periodical correction will strengthen our approach, because the LTR algorithm could exploit user feedback more effectively than the BBRA, which, on the other hand, defines the rate of exploration needed for improving LTR. In particular, it may use query-document features to get information for other query-document pairs from observations for a particular pair, i.e., propagate this information over documents or queries. Third, it is also possible to re-train the LTR algorithm periodically on the ground of the fresh values of user behavior features. Because of the large number of other settings varying in our experiments, we implement only the first idea and show that it gives us a remarkable advantage over both LTR and BBRA working separately.

6. EXPERIMENTAL SETTINGS

Here, we describe our experimental setup to evaluate and compare different OLREE algorithms described in Section 3.

6.1 Data set

We collected the log of the live stream of search queries submitted to Yandex during two weeks of November, 2013 (referred as *Logs* below). We randomly sampled 0.003% of query issues from it. Since our algorithm can hardly explore r_d for very rare queries and hence these queries may introduce noise into our analysis, we filtered out the queries whose frequency estimated on *Logs* is less than 3 issues per day on average. As a result, we obtained a data set of 28 746 query issues, which represent 37.5% of the search traffic. For each query q from the data set, we united sets of top-10 results provided by different production rankers (we also use the best of them further and refer to it as *LTR* below) for this query to obtain the final set D_q of documents to assess. All the documents from D_q were assessed for relevance using the 5-grade scale (Perfect, Excellent, Good, Fair, Bad). In Section 7, we experiment with sets of top-ranked documents D (see Algorithm 1) of different predefined sizes m (from 5 to 30), which can exceed D_q for some queries q. Since, in reality, we always have as many documents to experiment with as we need, in such cases we added several documents to D_q (to make its size equal to m) by sampling them from all the Bad documents in the data set and labeling them as Bad with respect to the query q.

Further, we randomly split all the queries from the data set into several parts: $Train_1$ (25% of all the queries), $Train_2$ (25%), $Train_3$ (20%), and $Test$ (30%). We used the sets $Train_1$ and $Train_2$ to train the predictors M_1 and M_2, introduced in Section 4, correspondingly. As we described in Section 3, OLREE algorithms depend on a few parameters defining the exploration rate. Another parameter influencing the exploration rate is the number $|D|$ of the top documents the bandit algorithm works with. We used $Train_3$ to find their optimal values for each algorithm by exhaustive search in the parameter space. Finally, we tested M_1, M_2, LTR-correction and different OLREE algorithms on $Test$.

6.2 Realistic simulation of production

Since it is very risky for the search engine's market share to experiment with exploratory algorithms on real users, most of related studies [17, 27, 30] performed only experiments with simulated user feedback. In our experiments, we try to simulate a production environment much more realistically than they did. First, in contrast to [27, 30], we use not artificial but real queries and documents. It is especially important for our approach, because, for each query-document pair, we need not only its value of r_d but also its vector of features.

Second, we are the first to take into account different query frequencies while evaluating an effect of OLREE algorithms on the aggregated quality of the web search system during a fixed period by means of simulations, whereas all the previous papers used simulations of the equal number of query issues for each query. It is well-known that the more steps a bandit algorithm is able to make, the more effective it is in comparison with an exploitative strategy in terms of the cumulative reward. Therefore, for appropriate evaluations, it is required to simulate realistic query frequencies. We perform this as follows.

Let us consider a query issue i from $Test$ referring to a query q whose frequency estimated on Logs is I_q issues per 10 days. Naturally, we simulate I_q consequent submissions of q, run a tested algorithm on them. We repeat this simulation 5 times and consider the average query performance (see Section 6.3 for the description of our metrics) over all these issues as an estimate of the query performance of i, since i represents a random sample from these issues in $Test$. Then, to evaluate the overall performance of the algorithm, we average the obtained results over all the query issues from $Test$. Besides this cumulative performance, we also evaluate the *final* quality the algorithm is able to provide after 10 days by measuring the quality of ranking produced by the exploitative version of the algorithm (see Section 7) on the basis of all information it obtained during I_q issues of q and averaging this value over all the query issues from $Test$.

Third, for each simulated query issue, the tested algorithm provides the list of $k = 10$ documents, and we simulate the user feedback on them by DCM (see Section 3). For this purpose, we assume $\lambda_i = \lambda$ in Equation 3 and assign the same r_d values to all the query-document pairs with the same relevance judgments, as it was done in [17, 31]. However, unlike in these studies, we do not set λ and r_d to extreme ad-hoc values, but infer more realistic estimates by maximizing the likelihood of the user feedback on queries from $Train_1$ + $Train_2$ stored in *Logs* under the DCM model adapted in the following way. In terms of Equation 3, we substitute r_d, which is attributed to each individual document d, with r_j (where $j \in \{1, 2, \ldots, 5\}$ identifies the relevance label of d), as it was done in [9]. We also use the standard way to identify satisfied clicks on logs [3, 4, 10]. The inferred values r_j, $j = 1, 2, \ldots, 5$, are also used as the ground truth for training M_1 and M_2 (see Section 4).

Several studies [23, 32, 21] also suggested an alternative approach to offline experiments with bandit algorithms, which is called the replay method and is based on utilizing logs of the user-system interaction. However, it was applied only to bandit algorithms choosing one arm at each step (e.g., by recommending one news article) and is effective only when each arm was chosen by the logging policy a sufficient number of times. The first problem we would face when trying to apply this method to our task is that our OLREE algorithms regularly suggest the permutations of top-10 documents which are absent in the logs at all. Indeed, even just 10 documents can be ranked in $10! = 3628800$ ways. Collecting a "random bucket" (as it was done in [18, 23, 21]) for such a number of permutations will be possible only for a tiny set of extremely popular queries, will take lots of time and will leave lots of users dissatisfied with low-quality rankings. Second, one of our goals is not only to find the best permutation of a given top-10, but also to increase its overall relevance by introducing more relevant but currently lower ranked documents into it. It means that the replay method would be infeasible even for popular queries.

6.3 Metrics

In our evaluations, we use the following two measures of query performance. First, we consider the widely used NDCG measure. For this purpose, we assign an NDCG-wise relevance gain $\frac{2^g-1}{2^4}$ [8] to each query-document pair, where $g \in \{0, 1, 2, 3, 4\}$ corresponds to its relevance judgment (from Bad to Perfect). Because of the proprietary nature of the *LTR* algorithm, we do not report absolute values of measures, but instead report absolute changes in measure value with respect to the LTR ranking in percentages: $\Delta NDCG = (NDCG@10 - NDCG@10_{LTR}) \cdot 100\%$. Second, we are interested in the number of satisfied clicks on the top 10 positions, since this metric is the underlying objective of our bandit ranking approach described in Section 2. We present it in the form of *regret* which is the common metric (to be minimized) in the SMAB problem. In our case, it equals the difference between the cumulative reward of the ranking by true r_d values and the cumulative reward of the tested algorithm. After averaging regret over all queries, we measure its relative change: $\Delta Reg = \frac{regret - regret_{LTR}}{regret_{LTR}} \cdot 100\%$.

Since the optimal exploration rate of a bandit-based algorithm strictly depends on the number of steps which is defined by the query frequency in our experiments, we split $Test$ into 4 frequency groups of the same size in order to tune exploration rate and to compare different algorithms separately on each group. The corresponding frequency intervals (number of issues per 10 days) are $[30, 150), [150, 750), [750, 5500), [5500, 1.5 \cdot 10^6)$ for Groups 1-4 respectively. To define a frequency group in practice, one can utilize methods of query frequency prediction, e.g., on the basis of historical data [29].

7. EXPERIMENTAL RESULTS

We first describe different methods we experimented with. Each one consists of the following basic components with options, which are denoted as follows:

• OLREE algorithm (see Section 3): U (MeanUCB-1 by default, UCB-1 is indicated by the postfix *orig*) or B (MeanBayes), which include scoring function $S_t(d)$ and update rule; additional options (see Section 3.3): *10* means that a dedicated instance per each position is used (adoption of [27]), e stands for an exploitative version ($\alpha = 0$ in Equation 1 for UCB-1, MeanUCB-1 and MeanBayes, $\alpha_{low} = \alpha_{up} = 0.5$ for Bayesian bandits), ϵ denotes ϵ-greedy applied to the exploitative version, n means that the negligent inference approach is used (honest approach is applied by default);

• prediction of prior r and γ (see Section 4): the best constant (over all query-document pairs) estimate of r and $\gamma = 1$ (setting from [31]) are used by default, R stands for prediction of r by M_1 and the best constant estimate of γ, prediction of r by M_1 and prediction of γ by M_2 are denoted by P;

• correction of prior estimates by LTR (see Section 5) is marked by L and is not used by default. Each method is denoted by the combination of its options.

Besides the production LTR ranking, we consider the following two baselines, which do not take into account prior information on relevance the search system possess: U_orig is our implementation of the method suggested in [31], U10_orig is our adoption of Algorithm 2 from [27] to our task.

We observed that, for any query with more than 10 000 submissions within a simulated 10-day period (82% of Group 4), each method with optimal settings (see details below) is able to provide nearly optimal ranking after 10 000 submissions if switches to exploitation. Therefore, in response to all further issues of each such query, we showed the constant document list that is provided by the exploitative version of the method under consideration on the basis of all information it obtained during the first 10 000 issues. Note that the related studies [27, 14] modeled 1000 steps of bandit algorithms at maximum.

Although each SMAB algorithm we adopted to the OLREE problem has an *exploration parameter* that controls the exploration rate (α for UCB-1, MeanUCB-1 and MeanBayes, $(\alpha_{low}, \alpha_{up})$ for Bayesian bandits and ϵ for ϵ-greedy), it may be not sufficient to find the optimal strategy for the OLREE problem, which requires to choose many documents at each step. Thus, it may be useful to manually restrict the number of documents $m = |D|$ the OLREE algorithm explores. We tune $m \in \{5, 10, 15, 20, 25, 30\}$ and the exploration parameter for each method to be tested and for each frequency group on $Train_3$ individually. In the case of $m = 5$, we place documents assigned to positions 6-10 by the LTR ranking on the same positions on the SERP at each query issue.

As Figure 1 and Table 2 show, expectedly, the optimal m increases with query frequency and with complexity of the method. The optimal m for the best methods is 15 or higher, what confirms that the exploration of documents normally placed out of the first page has a high potential for ranking improvement. The optimal values of α range from 0.01 to 0.44 for different MeanUCB-1 methods and from 0 to 1.32 for MeanBayes methods.

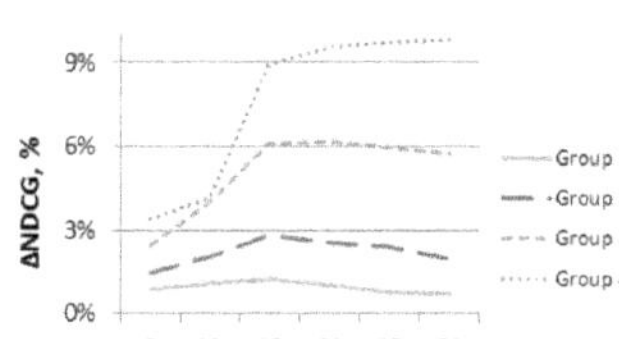

Figure 1: Setting m for UPL

Method	Frequency groups			
	1	2	3	4
U10_orig	5	5	5	15
U_orig, U	5	5	15	20
UR	5	10	15	25
UP	10	15	15	25
UPL	15	15	15	30
UePL	15	15	15	25
UϵPL	0	0	0	15
UnPL	5	5	10	10
BR	5	5	15	20
BP	5	10	15	30
BPL	15	15	15	30

Table 2: Optimal m

We conducted experiments with all the methods on $Test$ according to the procedure described in Section 6 and used Student's paired t-test to compare the obtained results. Each of the methods based on MeanUCB-1 or MeanBayes outperformed its analog, where UCB-1 (Bayesian Bandits correspondingly) was used and the other options were the same. Therefore, we present results only for MeanUCB-1-based and MeanBayes-based methods in comparison with the baselines U10_orig and U_orig. The results observed in the experiments with the methods based on UCB-1 and Bayesian bandits are analogous. The performance on $Test$ in terms of cumulative ΔNDCG (for each frequency group and aggregately), final ΔNDCG, and ΔReg (see Section 6.3) is reported in Table 3. First, we see that among two baselines *U10_orig* and *U_orig*, which do not use any prior information, *U_orig* performs significantly better according to each column of the table

Table 3: **Performance evaluation of the previous bandit algorithms and our methods based on priors**

Method	ΔNDCG,%						ΔReg,%
	cumulative					final	
	G.1	G.2	G.3	G.4	All	All	All
U10_orig	-1.77	0.05	1.22	6.88	2.26	4.75	-17.3
U_orig[31]	-0.40	1.16	3.87	9.40	4.21	7.59	-25.0
U	-0.36	1.17	4.07	9.40	4.27	7.64	-24.8
UR	0.01	1.27	4.23	9.66	4.55	7.76	-25.2
UP	0.34	1.99	5.57	10.13	5.25	8.51	-29.8
UPL	0.93	**2.98**	**6.12**	**10.35**	**5.78**	**8.91**	**-31.5**
UePL	0.84	2.84	5.61	9.16	5.21	7.98	-25.9
UϵPL	0.84	2.84	5.61	9.64	5.37	8.31	-28.3
UnPL	0.65	1.25	1.46	2.70	2.04	3.00	-0.9
BR	-0.08	1.35	3.97	9.21	4.33	7.50	-21.6
BP	0.38	1.88	5.42	9.38	4.94	8.03	-27.0
BPL	**0.94**	2.98	6.05	9.72	5.53	8.53	-30.4

($p < 0.01$). Being based on an estimate of the mean, U is only slightly better than *U_orig*.

Second, we observe that our approach to utilizing prior information from the current production system allows to remarkably increase the cumulative performance. The method UR using prediction of r_d significantly outperforms the former three methods in terms of ΔNDCG according to each column ($p < 0.05$). The prediction of γ by M_2 used in UP and BP remarkably strengthens ($p < 0.01$) each of the methods UR and BR, and, then, the LTR-correction provides the additional notable increase in quality ($p < 0.01$ for UPL vs UP, BPL vs BP).

Now we examine how the deterioration of each component of the best method (UPL) affects its performance. The exploitative version UePL is significantly weaker ($p < 0.01$) than UPL and BPL, except for Group 1. Within Group 1, the number of submissions of a query is too small to significantly gain from exploration. Next, random exploration by ϵ-greedy (UϵPL) turned out to be effective only for Group 4 and with low exploration rate (optimal $\epsilon = 0.04$), because of the high cost of each exploratory choice (a high risk of choosing irrelevant document), and does not still reach the performance of UPL or BPL. Finally, the negligent inference approach (UnPL) performs very poorly (especially for frequent queries) due to the low learning rate. This emphasizes the importance of applying an appropriate model of user behavior to infer as much information from logs as possible.

Figure 2 presents the dynamics of the cumulative ΔNDCG on Group 1 (left) and Group 4 (right) for the principally different methods: the best exploitative one (UePL), the best method with the negligent inference (UnPL), and the best methods with the different prior settings (U, UR, UP, UPL). We see that prior information plays a critical role for queries with low frequency, and learning rate defined by an OLREE algorithm becomes much more important for more frequent queries. However, given the OLREE algorithm, the prior settings notably influence its performance even for Group 4.

Another aspect of search quality, which cannot be directly measured by the cumulative NDCG, is the frequency of significant drops in query performance in comparison with other search engines. In the case of the method U, 14.4% and 5.1% of query issues during the first day have ΔNDCG less than −10% and −20% respectively, while these shares are only 2.4% and 0.33% for UPL. It means that, in the case of U, much more users would be negatively affected by the severe degradations of the quality and could completely switch to another search engine.

Finally, the analysis of UPL performance for individual queries confirms a clear idea: the gain of proper OLREE

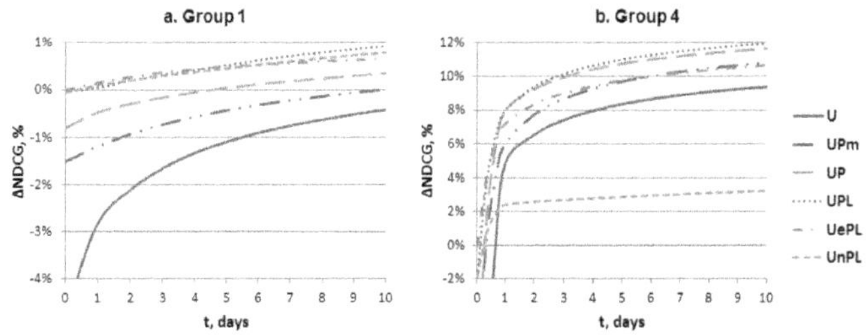

Figure 2: Dynamics of cumulative ΔNDCG over t days (at 1st step for $t = 0$)

algorithms over the LTR ranking they start with depends on the quality of the latter. Figure 3 presents the cumulative ΔNDCG of UPL averaged over all queries of a known frequency whose initial LTR performance lies within a given range. Naturally, it crucially decreases with the growth of LTR quality, because chances of each exploration action to be successful (i.e., to find a new relevant document) decrease. It means that taking current ranking quality into account while setting the exploration rate for the query has a high potential to increase performance of OLREE algorithms. In practice, methods of query performance prediction [16, 36] can be used for this purpose.

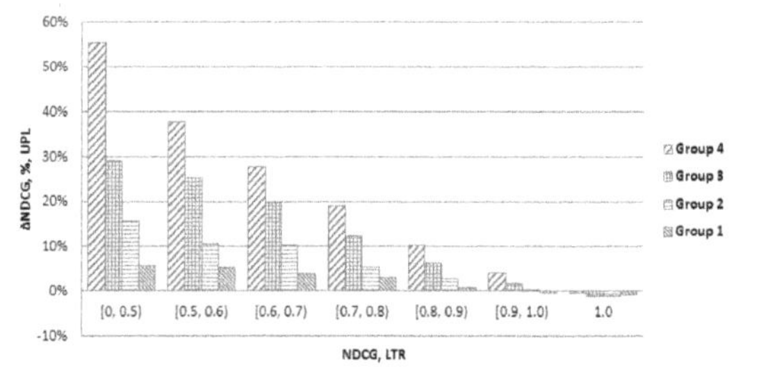

Figure 3: Dependence of ΔNDCG of UPL on LTR quality

8. RELATED WORK

Almost all the attempts to represent the OLREE task as the SMAB problem (exceptions are discussed below) could be divided into the following three types, each giving its own definition for a bandit problem, an arm, its trial and its reward. The first two types rely on the contextual bandit approach and regard submissions of all the queries as an entire bandit problem. The first one considers each submission as a trial and a linear ranking algorithm parametrized by a weight vector ω as an arm. The reward is then defined by the whole user behavior on the SERP (for example, it can be opposite to abandonment). As long as arms here are vectors, these approaches [35, 28] apply boosting rather than standard bandit algorithms to find an optimal value of ω. The second interpretation [22, 25] considers a query-document as an arm, the fact of an arm trial consists in two conditions: the corresponding document was presented on SERP and was examined by the user, and the reward is a click (reward=1) or a skip (reward=0). By assuming that the click probability linearly depends on a number of features of the query-document pair, one is able to estimate this probability and confidence in this estimate for each pair. One major problem of these two approaches is that linear rankers are known to be suboptimal with respect to such state-of-the-art LTR approaches as neural networks [6] and decision trees [7]. Another major weakness of these approaches is their low degree of freedom, which does not allow to derive the best possible ranking for each individual query.

Within the third type of approaches, a separate bandit problem setup corresponds to issues of each query (or even more locally, see description of [27]). Definitions of an arm and a trial are the same as in the second approach. While considering each query separately and each document as an arm, these approaches allow to reach the best ranking for each of the relatively frequent queries individually. If we assume that the first result is always examined and the lower results are never examined, as it was made in [22], this approach reduces to the ordinary SMAB formulation: the document on the first position is the chosen arm. However, in web search ranking, user satisfaction significantly depends on the lower documents, thus maximizing relevance of only the first document is suboptimal.

A more appropriate method was proposed in [27] for the problem of web search diversification. There was considered a dedicated instance of bandit algorithm for each position within issues of a fixed query. As we discussed in Section 3.3 and showed experimentally in Section 7, our method is more effective in our framework.

Sloan and Wang [31] proposed to use one bandit algorithm instance for one query, which accounts for all clicks on different positions. However, they could not obtain any profit from exploration in terms of NDCG. In this paper, we significantly strengthen their approach by incorporating it into the production ranking and by utilizing prior information.

There were also different attempts to reduce the OLREE problem to the SMAB problem [30, 33, 1], which do not formally correspond to the above described classes of approaches. The work of Slivkins et al. [30] belongs to the second type of approaches, excluding the linear model assumption, and considers a "perfect world" scenario: given a query, all the documents are assumed to be represented by points of a metric space with such a metric $D(x, y)$ that the probability r_d of a click on a document d satisfies the following inequality: $|r_{d_1} - r_{d_2}| \leq D(d_1, d_2)$. It allows to develop and theoretically justify a contextual bandit algorithm which propagates inferred information from one document to the other ones positioned close to this document in the metric space. However, the practical realization of such a space construction remains an open question. In fact, it requires an accurate estimation of differences between click probabilities of each two documents. It is not even clear if this problem is simpler than ranking of documents by their click probability, the problem which we actually solve.

9. CONCLUSIONS

In this paper, we investigate a new formulation of the exploration–exploitation dilemma in online learning to rank (OLREE) in terms of the SMAB problem. It represents a general approach to applying a variety of SMAB algorithms to the OLREE problem. Further, previous methods proposed in the literature for this problem did not consider the following critical practical issue: any commercial search engine is based on a highly optimized ranking algorithm which utilizes hundreds of features and can not be just substituted with a principally new one. Thus, an OLREE algorithm should be "married" with the current production ranker and handle all its advantages. To address this issue, we developed a general framework for introducing our bandit-based learning method into any default ranking system. Finally, we applied the whole scheme to several SMAB algorithms and experimentally demonstrated that it enables to notably increase the performance of a major search system in terms of NDCG measure averaged over a 10 day period.

We plan to extend this work by making our OLREE algorithm more contextual, i.e., able to effectively aggregate user feedback over different contexts to produce the optimal (in OLREE terms) ranking in the current context at each step.

Appendix

We give here some details about the update rules described in Section 3.3. We introduce random events $A_l = \{C^t_{d_j} = 0 \text{ for } j = l+1 \text{ to } k\}$ that there was no click below position l at query issue t. We also denote the lowest click position observed at query issue t by $l(t)$ (to be considered not as a random variable, but as a fixed value determined by the observed user behavior after the query issue t). In the equations below we assume all the probabilities under the condition $C^t_{d_{l(t)}(t)} = 1$ and under the condition that the current estimates of r_d (point estimate $\widehat{r}_d$ or $\overline{r}_d$ in the cases of UCB-1, MeanUCB-1 and Bayes-UCB, posterior distribution $p_{d,t}(r)$ in the case of Bayesian bandits) are true values for all the documents. For brevity, we omit these conditions and use d_j instead of $d_j(t)$ below. Now, we describe update rules specific for UCB-1 and Bayesian bandits:

- In the case of UCB-1, E-step is the following. For $i = 1, \ldots, l(t)$, we obviously put $P(E^t_{d_i} = 1 | UB_t) = 1$. For $i > l(t)$, we obtain:

$$
\begin{aligned}
P(E^t_{d_i} = 1 | UB_t) &= P(E^t_{d_i} = 1 | A_{l(t)}) = \\
&= P(\bigcap_{j>l(t)} \{E^t_{d_j} = 1\} | A_{l(t)}) = \\
&= \frac{P\left(A_{l(t)} \cap \bigcap_{j>l(t)} \{E^t_{d_j} = 1\}\right)}{P\left(A_{l(t)} \cap \bigcap_{j>l(t)} \{E^t_{d_j} = 1\}\right) + P\left(A_{l(t)} \cap \bigcap_{j>l(t)} \{E^t_{d_j} = 0\}\right)} = \\
&= \frac{P(E^t_{d_{l(t)+1}} = 1) \cdot \prod_{j>l(t)} P(C^t_{d_j} = 0 | E^t_{d_j} = 1)}{P(E^t_{d_{l(t)+1}} = 1) \cdot \prod_{j>l(t)} P(C^t_{d_j} = 0 | E^t_{d_j} = 1) + P(E^t_{d_{l(t)+1}} = 0)} \\
&= \frac{\lambda_{l(t)} \cdot \prod_{j>l(t)} (1 - \widehat{r}_{d_j,t-1})}{\lambda_{l(t)} \cdot \prod_{j>l(t)} (1 - \widehat{r}_{d_j,t-1}) + (1 - \lambda_{l(t)})}. \qquad (6)
\end{aligned}
$$

The first equality is valid because of the DCM assumptions (3): given that the last click is on position $l(t)$, document $d_{l(t)+1}$ was examined if and only if all the documents below $l(t)$ were examined. Otherwise, all the documents below $l(t)$ were not examined. We use it in the second equality in denominator.

This estimate is similar to the Equations 9 and 10 from [31] (S_i is equivalent to our E_{d_i}). However, authors use only observation of a click or its absence on the document d to estimate E_{d_i} while we utilize information about all the clicks on the SERP. As a result, we have more precise estimates for E_{d_i} under DCM assumptions. This difference is especially remarkable for documents above the lowest click: we exactly know that they were examined.

- In the case of Bayesian bandits, the update rule could be obtained in the similar way by applying the Bayesian inference.

10. REFERENCES

[1] A. Agarwal, D. Hsu, S. Kale, J. Langford, L. Li, and R. E. Schapire. Taming the monster: A fast and simple algorithm for contextual bandits. *arXiv preprint arXiv:1402.0555*, 2014.

[2] P. Auer, N. Cesa-Bianchi, and P. Fischer. Finite-time analysis of the multiarmed bandit problem. *Machine Learning*, 47(2-3):235–256, 2002.

[3] P. N. Bennett, F. Radlinski, R. W. White, and E. Yilmaz. Inferring and using location metadata to personalize web search. In *Proceedings of the 34th International ACM SIGIR Conference on Research and Development in Information Retrieval*, SIGIR '11, pages 135–144, New York, NY, USA, 2011. ACM.

[4] P. N. Bennett, R. W. White, W. Chu, S. T. Dumais, P. Bailey, F. Borisyuk, and X. Cui. Modeling the impact of short- and long-term behavior on search personalization. In *Proceedings of the 35th International ACM SIGIR Conference on Research and Development in Information Retrieval*, SIGIR '12, pages 185–194, New York, NY, USA, 2012. ACM.

[5] M. Best and N. Chakravarti. Active set algorithms for isotonic regression; a unifying framework. *Mathematical Programming*, 47(1-3):425–439, 1990.

[6] C. Burges, T. Shaked, E. Renshaw, A. Lazier, M. Deeds, N. Hamilton, and G. Hullender. Learning to rank using gradient descent. ICML'05, 2005.

[7] O. Chapelle, Y. Chang, and T.-Y. Liu. The yahoo! learning to rank challenge. *http://learningtorankchallenge.yahoo.com*, 2010.

[8] O. Chapelle, D. Metlzer, Y. Zhang, and P. Grinspan. Expected reciprocal rank for graded relevance. CIKM '09, pages 621–630, New York, NY, USA, 2009. ACM.

[9] A. Chuklin, P. Serdyukov, and M. De Rijke. Click model-based information retrieval metrics. In *Proceedings of the 36th international ACM SIGIR conference on Research and development in information retrieval*, pages 493–502. ACM, 2013.

[10] K. Collins-Thompson, P. N. Bennett, R. W. White, S. de la Chica, and D. Sontag. Personalizing web search results by reading level. In *Proceedings of the 20th ACM International Conference on Information and Knowledge Management*, CIKM '11, pages 403–412, New York, NY, USA, 2011. ACM.

[11] N. Craswell, O. Zoeter, M. Taylor, and B. Ramsey. An experimental comparison of click position-bias models. In *Proceedings of the 2008 International Conference on Web Search and Data Mining*, WSDM '08, pages 87–94, New York, NY, USA, 2008. ACM.

[12] F. Diaz. Integration of news content into web results. In *Proceedings of the Second ACM International Conference on Web Search and Data Mining*, pages 182–191. ACM, 2009.

[13] F. Diaz and J. Arguello. Adaptation of offline vertical selection predictions in the presence of user feedback. In *Proceedings of the 32nd international ACM SIGIR conference on Research and development in information retrieval*, pages 323–330. ACM, 2009.

[14] J. H. Friedman. Greedy function approximation: a gradient boosting machine. *Annals of Statistics*, pages 1189–1232, 2001.

[15] F. Guo, C. Liu, and Y. M. Wang. Efficient multiple-click models in web search. WSDM '09, pages 124–131, New York, NY, USA, 2009. ACM.

[16] B. He and I. Ounis. Query performance prediction. *Information Systems*, 31(7):585–594, 2006.

[17] K. Hofmann, S. Whiteson, and M. Rijke. Balancing exploration and exploitation in listwise and pairwise online learning to rank for information retrieval. *Information Retrieval*, 16(1):63–90, 2013.

[18] L. Jie, S. Lamkhede, R. Sapra, E. Hsu, H. Song, and Y. Chang. A unified search federation system based on online user feedback. KDD '13, pages 1195–1203, New York, NY, USA, 2013. ACM.

[19] E. Kaufmann, O. Cappe, and A. Garivier. On bayesian upper confidence bounds for bandit problems. In N. D. Lawrence and M. A. Girolami, editors, *AISTATS-12*, volume 22, pages 592–600, 2012.

[20] E. Kaufmann, N. Korda, and R. Munos. Thompson sampling: An asymptotically optimal finite-time analysis. In *Algorithmic Learning Theory*, volume 7568 of *Lecture Notes in Computer Science*, pages 199–213. Springer Berlin Heidelberg, 2012.

[21] L. Li, S. Chen, J. Kleban, and A. Gupta. Counterfactual estimation and optimization of click metrics for search engines. *CoRR*, abs/1403.1891, 2014.

[22] L. Li, W. Chu, J. Langford, and R. E. Schapire. A contextual-bandit approach to personalized news article recommendation. WWW '10, pages 661–670, New York, NY, USA, 2010. ACM.

[23] L. Li, W. Chu, J. Langford, and X. Wang. Unbiased offline evaluation of contextual-bandit-based news article recommendation algorithms. In *Proceedings of the Fourth ACM International Conference on Web Search and Data Mining*, WSDM '11, pages 297–306, New York, NY, USA, 2011. ACM.

[24] T.-Y. Liu. Learning to rank for information retrieval. *Found. Trends Inf. Retr.*, 3(3):225–331, Mar. 2009.

[25] T. Moon, W. Chu, L. Li, Z. Zheng, and Y. Chang. An online learning framework for refining recency search results with user click feedback. *ACM Trans. Inf. Syst.*, 30(4):20:1–20:28, Nov. 2012.

[26] J. A. Nelder and R. Mead. A simplex method for function minimization. *The computer journal*, 7(4):308–313, 1965.

[27] F. Radlinski, R. Kleinberg, and T. Joachims. Learning diverse rankings with multi-armed bandits. ICML '08, pages 784–791, New York, NY, USA, 2008. ACM.

[28] K. Raman, T. Joachims, P. Shivaswamy, and T. Schnabel. Stable coactive learning via perturbation. *ICML*, 2013.

[29] M. Shokouhi and K. Radinsky. Time-sensitive query auto-completion. SIGIR '12, pages 601–610, New York, NY, USA, 2012. ACM.

[30] A. Slivkins, F. Radlinski, and S. Gollapudi. Ranked bandits in metric spaces: Learning diverse rankings over large document collections. *J. Mach. Learn. Res.*, 14(1):399–436, Feb. 2013.

[31] M. Sloan and J. Wang. Iterative expectation for multi period information retrieval. In *WSDM Workshop on Web Search Click Data*, 2013.

[32] L. Tang, R. Rosales, A. Singh, and D. Agarwal. Automatic ad format selection via contextual bandits. In *Proceedings of the 22nd ACM international conference on Conference on information and knowledge management*, pages 1587–1594. ACM, 2013.

[33] H. P. Vanchinathan, I. Nikolic, F. De Bona, and A. Krause. Explore-exploit in top-n recommender systems via gaussian processes. In *Proceedings of the 8th ACM Conference on Recommender systems*, pages 225–232. ACM, 2014.

[34] C. J. C. H. Watkins. *Learning from delayed rewards.* PhD thesis, University of Cambridge, 1989.

[35] Y. Yue and T. Joachims. Interactively optimizing information retrieval systems as a dueling bandits problem. ICML '09, pages 1201–1208, New York, NY, USA, 2009. ACM.

[36] Y. Zhou and W. B. Croft. Query performance prediction in web search environments. In *Proceedings of the 30th annual international ACM SIGIR conference on Research and development in information retrieval*, pages 543–550. ACM, 2007.

[37] J. Zhu, J. Wang, I. J. Cox, and M. J. Taylor. Risky business: Modeling and exploiting uncertainty in information retrieval. In *Proceedings of the 32Nd International ACM SIGIR Conference on Research and Development in Information Retrieval*, SIGIR '09, pages 99–106, New York, NY, USA, 2009. ACM.

The E-Commerce Market for "Lemons": Identification and Analysis of Websites Selling Counterfeit Goods

John Wadleigh, Jake Drew and Tyler Moore
Darwin Deason Institute for Cyber Security
Southern Methodist University
Dallas, TX, USA
{jwadleigh,jdrew,tylerm}@smu.edu

ABSTRACT

We investigate the practice of websites selling counterfeit goods. We inspect web search results for 225 queries across 25 brands. We devise a binary classifier that predicts whether a given website is selling counterfeits by examining automatically extracted features such as WHOIS information, pricing and website content. We then apply the classifier to results collected between January and August 2014. We find that, overall, 32% of search results point to websites selling fakes. For 'complicit' search terms, such as "replica rolex", 39% of the search results point to fakes, compared to 20% for 'innocent' terms, such as "hermes buy online". Using a linear regression, we find that brands with a higher street price for fakes have higher incidence of counterfeits in search results, but that brands who take active countermeasures such as filing DMCA requests experience lower incidence of counterfeits in search results. Finally, we study how the incidence of counterfeits evolves over time, finding that the fraction of search results pointing to fakes remains remarkably stable.

Categories and Subject Descriptors

K.4.1 [**Public Policy Issues**]: Abuse and crime involving computers

Keywords

counterfeit goods; cybercrime measurement; binary classifier

1. INTRODUCTION

The economist George Akerlof won a Nobel Prize for his work describing markets with asymmetric information [2]. In such a market for "lemons", consumers cannot reliably distinguish between high- and low-quality goods. This inability triggers a market failure, where prices are driven down and inferior goods dominate.

More recently, Anderson argued that the market for secure software is also a lemons market, as buyers cannot reliably observe whether or not the software they are buying is in fact secure [4]. Researchers working in security economics now recognize that information asymmetry is one of the fundamental barriers facing cybersecurity today [5].

In this paper, we study a related market for lemons: the online sale of clothing and luxury goods. Miscreants selling knockoff versions of popular goods have proliferated online in recent years. Frequently, counterfeit-goods shops are manipulating search engines to get high placement in search results for legitimate terms, thereby duping consumers into thinking they can get a good deal on the real thing. If search engines cannot distinguish legitimate sellers from those selling counterfeits, why would we expect untrained people to be capable of doing so?

The online sale of knockoffs matters, and not just for those brands whose goods are impersonated. Bad experiences with e-commerce carry large indirect costs, in that they can turn people off from online participation and erode trust in the Internet [26]. Consequently, in this paper we set out to investigate the prevalence of counterfeit goods online. We make the following contributions:

- We present a methodology for collecting data on the prevalence of counterfeit goods in web search (Section 2).
- We build an accurate classifier using features automatically extracted from website content that distinguishes legitimate from fake sellers based upon data returned by search results (Section 3).
- We conduct extensive empirical analysis of data collected between January and August 2014 (Section 4). We apply the trained classifier and find that 5 407 websites are selling counterfeits, out of a total of 18 756 websites. Overall, 32% of search results point to fakes, and 79% of queries issued included at least one fake in the first page of results.
- We show that while search engines do refer customers to counterfeit sellers when the search terms ask for it, they also refer customers to counterfeit sellers in large numbers even when they give no indication that they want fakes.
- We present a linear regression that demonstrates that the higher the selling price is for fakes for a given brand, the more search results point to fakes. The regression also demonstrates that active enforcement (as measured by DMCA takedowns) can reduce the prevalence of fakes in search results by 9 %-pts.
- We show that the prevalence of fakes among brands is relatively stable over time, and furthermore that some sellers respond to their website dropping out of search results by adding copies registered at different URLs.
- We find that websites selling fakes are more likely to be registered in China and hosted in Estonia, Russia, or Sweden. Furthermore, counterfeit shops are less likely to be hosted in countries with industries targeted by counterfeiting, notably Italy, Switzerland and France.

WWW 2015, May 18–22, 2015, Florence, Italy.
ACM 978-1-4503-3469-3/15/05.
http://dx.doi.org/10.1145/2736277.2741658.

2. DATA COLLECTION METHODOLOGY

Researchers have extensively studied the online sale of unlicensed pharmaceuticals [15, 18, 19, 21], as well as the unauthorized acquisition of digital goods such as music, movies and software [14,28]. We decided to focus instead on the sale of counterfeit consumer physical goods, due to its prevalence and relative lack of attention from the research community.

2.1 Constructing search queries

We first had to decide on which brands to focus our investigation. We began by collecting data on five seed brands: Ugg, Coach, Rolex, Hermes, and Oakley. After gathering search results on associated queries, we scraped all product listing pages from 68 stores manually identified as selling counterfeits. We decided to focus on the 25 most observed brands in the inventories of the confirmed counterfeit stores.

We are very interested in measuring the extent to which consumers intending to buy from authorized retailers are instead presented with links to websites selling fakes. To that end, the 25 brands were then paired with search terms of varying levels of "innocence". We selected three search terms for each innocence level: innocent, grey, and complicit. We deem as innocent the keywords "fast delivery," "buy online" and the lack of keyword (meaning the query is only the product name). We deem the keywords "replica," "fake," and "knockoff" as complicit, as any shopper using those terms is clearly seeking out counterfeited goods. Between these extremes lie grey keywords "cheap," "discount," and "sale", since there is ambiguity as to the intention of the shopper. In total, we combine all 25 brands with each of the 9 keywords to yield 225 unique search queries.

2.2 Gathering website data

We automatically issued queries to the Google Custom Search API to obtain the top 100 results for each of the 225 terms.[1] We then visited the URLs using an automated browser, storing the HTML and a screenshot.

When the automated browser visited the search results, a script checked for the presence and properties of elements we believe to be indicative of malicious intent. The elements observed were IFrames, currencies, and pricing information.

We removed price outliers triggered by parsing errors or ambiguities in brand names (e.g., searches for Coach purses can also return advertisements for buses). We also converted non-US currency to US dollars for consistency.

Pricing data was found using regular expressions and a combination of currency symbols, and price associations were found (for example a product might contain both an "original price" and a "discount price") by locating individual prices and climbing the DOM structure. We also fetched the WHOIS data for each website, extracting the date and country of registration, as well as whether or not a privacy or proxy registration had been used [9].

We note that many shops attempt to hide their true nature to search engines by "cloaking" or by redirecting from a hacked website to a shop selling fakes. We deal with this problem by inspecting the destination website as presented to a browser. As described in the next section, we do build features that indirectly check for this malicious behavior, e.g., by also visiting the top-level page that is unlikely to be cloaked or to redirect elsewhere.

We gathered data in two distinct periods. An initial study carried out in January 2014 identified 21 646 search results and 6 979 distinct websites. To inspect for changes in behavior over time, we reissued the same queries weekly between June and August 2014.

[1] We note that the results returned by the Custom Search API are not identical to those obtained via Google's website. Because Google's Terms of Service prohibit automated collection of search results from its website, we elected to use the API instead. Given the advent of personalized search, it is impossible to collect the exact search results that will be presented to all users.

3. CLASSIFYING WEBSITES SELLING COUNTERFEITS

We first describe the features used in building the classifier in Section 3.1 and then outline the methods used in Section 3.2.

3.1 Feature selection and extraction

We constructed features after inspecting many websites selling counterfeit goods. We focus on three classes of features: URL-level, page-level, and website-level features.

URL-level features The least resource-intensive approach is to collect features based upon only the URL. This approach has been used to identify phishing websites [7] and malware [20].

1. **Replica in FQDN**
   This Boolean feature identifies when the term "replica" is contained as part of the web page's fully qualified domain name (FQDN). We also considered the term "knockoff", but that was often associated with articles and blogs decrying counterfeits.
2. **Length of FQDN**
   This numeric feature denotes the number of characters present in the URL's fully qualified domain name. Websites selling fakes frequently use subdomains concatenating several words.

Page-level features We also inspected the scraped HTML content to identify additional features indicating that counterfeits may be sold.

1. **Number of Currencies Seen**
   Unlike most big box retailers which offer custom websites for each country serviced, counterfeit goods websites typically offer a single unified site which is designed to service any number of countries. Furthermore, it is uncommon for these sites to implement their own custom payment vehicles. Most of the third party payment solutions deployed offer checkout alternatives which include providing payment in a large variety of currencies.
2. **Large IFrames**
   Unusually positioned and sized IFrames are used to obfuscate malicious scripts and redirections common in criminal websites [8, 25]. We define large IFrames as having unusually large height and width in addition to containing a different top level domain which is also not part of the Alexa top 1000 domains [3].
3. **Percent Savings Average**
   This numeric feature indicates the average percentage of savings for a given webpage. This is relevant for online stores whose pricing data we could automatically scrape and where we found two prices associated with one item (an "original" price and the discounted price). We report average savings percentage in order to identify counterfeit stores offering ludicrously high savings.
4. **Number of Times Duplicate Price Seen**
   This numeric feature specifies the number of times a duplicate price was seen on a given page. For example, a page with various products listed at prices $40, $45, $40, $50, $40,

and \$45 has 3 duplicate prices present (\$40 is repeated twice and \$45 is repeated once). This feature was included to catch lazy counterfeit store owners who copy and paste products, changing titles but not prices.

5. **Page Contains Webmail Address**
   This Boolean feature identifies when a webpage contains an email address which includes the text "@yahoo.com", "@gmail.com", or "@hotmail.com". It would be highly unusual for a legitimate brand reseller to utilize a free webmail account.
6. **Unique Brand Mention Count**
   The unique brand mention count represents the number of unique brand mentions identified within the webpage's HTML content. Counterfeit websites often stuff their pages with multiple brand mentions, in hopes of promoting the website in search results.
7. **Top-Level Page Mentions Brand**
   We also visited the top-level web page to look for the mention of any brand (a string search for any of the brands in the root page's text). It indicates that a website may have been hacked if the top-level page makes no mention of any brands while the page listed in the search results does. A website hacked to host or redirect to a store is almost certainly selling counterfeits.
8. **Content Consistent with Takedown Page**
   This Boolean feature identifies when a webpage has been taken down and replaced with content from brand-enforcement companies.

Website-level features The final category of features were those describing characteristics of the website itself, as opposed to the displayed content.

1. **Private or China-registered WHOIS**
   While legitimate companies use private and proxy WHOIS registrations [10], it is frequently employed by those conducting dubious operations such as selling counterfeit goods. Furthermore, we observed that many websites selling replicas have operations based in China.
2. **WHOIS Registration Age Under 1 Year**
   This Boolean feature identifies when a webpage is less than one year old. Counterfeit websites often rely on newly registered domains, which replace older ones that have been suspended.
3. **Website In Alexa Top 100K**
   This Boolean feature identifies when a webpage is ranked in the top one hundred thousand websites by Alexa based on the webpage's web traffic. We expect counterfeit pages to draw in less traffic than licensed retailers.

3.2 Building and evaluating the classifiers

Counterfeit websites were classified using Logistic Regression, Adaptive Boosting, and Support Vector Machine models. Each of the machine learning models were trained against our specialized features developed to identify counterfeit goods websites. Finally, the models were validated against a manually constructed ground truth dataset to assess each model's detailed classification accuracy characteristics.

We implemented the three models using the R programming language. Three of these packages include Support Vector Machines (SVM) [22], Generalized Linear Models (GLM) [27], and Adaptive Boosting (AdaBoost) [11]. While all three packages can be highly accurate for various types of classification problems, each package performs very differently when modeling (i.e. learning) different volumes of input data.

	GLM		SVM		ADA	
	#	%	#	%	#	%
TP	175	29.1%	180	29.9%	125	20.8%
TN	337	66.0%	340	56.5%	318	52.8%
FP	31	5.1%	28	4.7%	50	8.3%
FN	59	9.8%	54	9.0 %	109	18.1%
Accuracy	85.0%		86.4%		73.6%	
Precision	85.0%		86.5%		71.4%	
Recall	74.8%		76.9%		54.4%	

Table 1: Truth tables and accuracy measures for each classifier using 10-fold cross-validation.

Feature	Coef.	Odds ratio	p-value
Page Contains Webmail Address	0.697	2.007	0.1722
Unique Brand Term Count	0.167	1.182	< 0.0001
# Currencies Seen	0.240	1.272	0.0017
Large IFrames	5.320	204.3	< 0.0001
Private or China WHOIS	0.285	1.330	0.384021
Replica in FQDN	1.442	4.227	0.0002
WHOIS Registration < 1 Year	1.505	4.504	0.0001
Percent Savings Average	0.044	1.045	< 0.0001
# Times Duplicate Price Seen	0.005	1.005	0.4471
Top-Level Page Mentions Brand	-0.701	0.496	0.0097
Website on Takedown Page	2.892	18.05	0.0005
Length of FQDN	0.044	1.045	0.0782
Website in Alexa Top 100K	-2.626	0.072	< 0.0001

Table 2: Coefficients and odds ratios for the logistic regression classifier (terms in bold are statistically significant).

Ground Truth Identification One of the fundamental challenges to classifying logical copies of counterfeit goods websites is the lack of ground-truth data available for evaluating the accuracy of automated feature selection and classification methods. Some researchers have relied on expert judgment to assess similarity, (e.g., [16]) but most forego any systematic evaluation due to a lack of ground truth. We now describe a method for constructing ground truth datasets for samples of counterfeit goods websites.

In order to classify stores, 602 unique screenshot/HTML pairs were pulled at random from the data collected for manual inspection. The screenshots were then examined to determine whether the store appeared to be selling fakes – a task which is easier, and much slower, to do by hand. We relied on the judgment of a human reviewer who had viewed many manually curated examples of legitimate and counterfeit websites. Of the 602 stores sampled, 234 were determined to be counterfeit and 368 were determined to not be counterfeit.

Results We independently trained and evaluated logistic regression (GLM), Support Vector Machine (SVM) and, adaptive boosting (ADA) models using 10-fold cross-validation. Table 1 shows the detailed truth tables for each model, along with figures for accuracy, precision and recall. Logistic regression and SVM produced more accurate results than adaptive boosting.

To get a sense of the relative importance of different features in the classifier, we can examine the coefficients and odds ratios from the best-fit logistic regression trained on the ground-truth data. Table 2 presents the results, with terms that are statistically significant in the model highlighted in bold. As expected, the presence of a large IFrame loading an external website is highly associated with the website selling counterfeits. In fact, websites exhibiting this

	% Fake Search Results	# Fake Websites	% queries page 1 fake	% queries result 1 fake
Innocent	20%	631	64%	6%
Grey	35%	875	86%	28%
Complicit	39%	780	86%	49%
Overall	32%	1 587	79%	28%

Pairwise χ^2 comparison	% results fake adj. p	Sig.?	% queries page 1 fake adj. p	Sig.?	% queries result 1 fake adj. p	Sig.?
Innocent vs. Grey	0.0000	✓	0.0067	✓	0.0004	✓
Innocent vs. Complicit	0.0000	✓	0.0067	✓	0.0000	✓
Grey vs. Complicit	0.0000	✓	1.0000		0.0150	✓

Table 3: Comparing the prevalence of counterfeits by search query intent. The top table reports the results, while the bottom establishes whether or not the differences are statistically significant according to a pairwise χ^2 test with FDR-adjusted p-values.

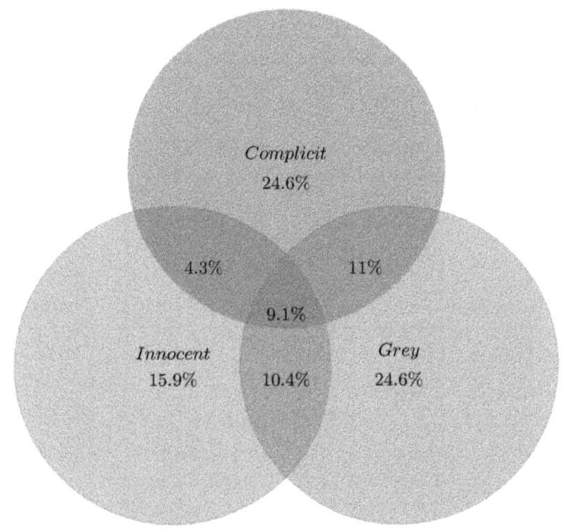

Figure 1: % unique counterfeit stores found through innocence level of query (not drawn to scale).

behavior face 204-times greater odds that they are selling counterfeits! Newly registered domains, using the term 'replica' in the FQDN, and appearing on a takedown page are all associated with selling fakes. The more currencies available on a website, the greater the advertised savings and the longer the FQDN, the more likely the website is to be fake. Surprisingly, however, a private or Chinese WHOIS registration address was not found to be statistically significant. Finally, two features are negatively associated with selling fakes – websites with a top 100,000 Alexa ranking and those whose top-level index page also mention the brand are less likely to sell fakes. The latter reflects the fact that the website is more likely to be an actual merchant and not a compromised host.

4. EMPIRICAL ANALYSIS

We now apply the best-performing SVM classifier to thousands of search results gathered between January and August 2014. In Section 4.1 we examine how the prevalence of stores selling fakes varies by brand and type of search query, while in Section 4.2 we describe a regression to help explain why the search results for some brands include more fakes than for others. In Sections 4.3 and 4.4 we study how knockoff search results vary over time. Finally, in Section 4.5 we examine characteristics of the fake websites themselves.

4.1 How prevalent are counterfeits in search?

Recall from Section 2 that in January 2014 we gathered up to the first 100 results to 225 queries spanning 25 brands targeted by counterfeiters. Overall, 32% of these search results linked to websites selling knockoffs, spanning 1 587 distinct websites. In 79% of the search queries, at least one link in the first page of results (top 10) pointed to fakes. Nearly one third of the time, the very first hit was to a website selling fakes!

Table 3 reports these overall measures, but it also breaks down the results by the intent of the search query: innocent (brand only, brand+"buy online", brand+"fast delivery) grey (brand+"cheap", "discount", or "sale"), or complicit (brand+"replica", "fake", or "knockoff"). Unsurprisingly, fewer innocent search queries linked to knockoffs than grey or complicit ones (20% vs. 35–39%). Nonetheless, it is striking that the fraction of fake results remains so high for obviously benign search terms, as well as how similar the proportion is for grey and complicit terms (e.g., "discount" vs. "replica").

The bottom rows of Table 3 report a statistical test for significance of the difference between these proportions using pairwise χ^2 tests. From these tests, we can see that the differences in proportion of fakes in search results across each query type are in fact statistically significant.

But what about the differences for high-ranking results? 64% of innocent queries have at least one fake result in the first page, compared to 86% for grey and complicit queries. The difference in page one fake prevalence between innocent and grey queries is statistically significant, but the difference between grey and complicit is not. Finally, in 6% of the innocent search queries the first result is fake, compared to 28% for grey and 49% for complicit queries (all differences statistically significant). Hence, we can conclude that regardless of the intent of the person issuing searches, there remains a good chance she will inadvertantly be exposed to a website selling knockoffs.

Another way to compare the results based on query intent is to check whether stores appearing in one type of query also appear in other query types. Figure 1 illustrates this overlap. While roughly 9% of the counterfeit sites appeared in the results of all three search categories, 65.1% were found under only one query type. In other words, many stores selling fakes may target different types of users: those targeting customers who know they are buying fakes may present a different shopping experience than to those selling to people who think what they are buying is legitimate.

We next examine the results broken down by brand. The first numerical column in Table 4 reports the proportion of search results pointing to fakes by brand in descending order. Bvlgari (or "Bulgari"), an Italian luxury goods company known for high-end watches, topped the list with 49.4% of its search results pointing to fake stores. Following close behind is Hublot, a Swiss luxury watchmaker. In fact, the nine brands with the most fakes are watch companies. By contrast, just 7.4% of results for Coach (maker of luxury handbags) point to fakes.

The brands with proportions listed in green bold-face with a minus sign experienced disproportionately low rates of counterfeit search results, according to a χ^2 test, while those at the top in red bold-face with a plus sign face disproportionately high rates of counterfeits in their search results. For the brands in the middle, the deviations from the 31.6% overall average are not statistically signficant.

In the next section, we present a linear regression that helps explain why we see such variation in search results across brands. From the right-hand columns in Table 4 we can already see some

Brand	% fake search results	# fake websites	% queries page 1 fake	% queries result 1 fake	# DMCA reports	Avg. fake site churn %	Median fake price
Bvlgari	(+) **49.4**	193	88.9	55.6	0	18.5	$588.30
Hublot	(+) **47.7**	201	100.0	77.8	8	20.0	$2060.42
Panerai	(+) **45.9**	188	100.0	55.6	18	18.6	$1381.99
Patek Philippe	(+) **44.8**	181	100.0	37.5	0	18.9	$3117.87
Tag Heuer	(+) **42.9**	171	100.0	25.0	5	19.4	$991.75
Breitling	(+) **42.6**	188	100.0	11.1	12	18.5	$1928.46
Cartier	(+) **39.8**	173	66.7	33.3	1	19.7	$1066.68
IWC	(+) **39.5**	179	100.0	50.0	3	21.1	$1339.76
Fendi	33.9	141	71.4	14.3	1	19.5	$279.47
Hermes	33.0	147	88.9	55.6	5	20.5	$261.33
Dior	32.4	183	66.7	33.3	39	22.7	$221.98
Gucci	29.7	178	77.8	22.2	16	23.9	$227.62
Rolex	28.9	120	100.0	62.5	33	21.7	$4316.39
Oakley	28.6	122	77.8	22.2	16	31.8	$112.85
Prada	28.6	150	88.9	22.2	23	24.8	$297.38
Versace	28.3	138	66.7	0.0	1	23.2	$182.95
Air Jordan	28.2	131	100.0	28.6	1439	29.4	$91.77
Armani	(-) **27.4**	153	66.7	11.1	1	20.9	$166.23
Burberry	(-) **27.1**	156	66.7	11.1	336	25.0	$210.45
Louis Vuitton	(-) **26.7**	147	77.8	33.3	93	29.6	$284.41
UGG	(-) **25.1**	95	77.8	11.1	10	28.7	$160.94
Nike	(-) **20.7**	125	55.6	0.0	1439	30.2	$88.99
Adidas	(-) **17.5**	99	50.0	0.0	9	23.3	$88.09
Chanel	(-) **14.9**	90	55.6	11.1	202	23.8	$630.27
Coach	(-) **7.4**	50	33.3	11.1	186	24.7	$223.07
Average	31.6	148.0	79.1	27.8	155.8	23.1	$812.78

Table 4: Counterfeit stores found in search results broken down by brand (left columns); additional per-brand characteristics such as DMCA enforcement activity anand the median advertised price among stores selling fakes (right columns). The entries in bold in the first column indicate a statistically significant difference in the brand's proportion of fakes in search results compared to the 31.6% average (using a χ^2 test with 95% confidence). Note that the reported percentage of fakes in result 1 and page 1 are based on results from the Google Custom Search API, which may differ from what users actually experience.

potential explanations. First, those brands at the top tend to not be as aggressive in pursuing infringers via DMCA notice-and-takedown requests. By contrast, many brands near the bottom have filed many such takedown requests for brand infringement. Furthermore, the right-most column reports the median sales price for goods sold on counterfeit websites for each brand. For the luxury watches at the top, even the fakes can sell for thousands of dollars. By contrast, for many of the less-targeted brands, the fakes sell for a few hundred dollars at most.

4.2 What explains the variation in counterfeit prevalence?

We have established that there is substantial variation in how prevalent stores selling fakes are in web search results (as low as 7.4% for Coach and as much as 49.4% for Bvlgari). We now describe a linear regression to help identify what characteristics may explain these differences.

Because much of the variation can be attributed to differences in brands, we group results together by brands for this regression. The response variable is the percentage of search results pointing to fakes (left-most column in Table 4). We have constructed a number of explanatory variables that we hypothesize influence the prevalence of fakes:

1. **Churn**: When search results exhibit lots of turnover, we expect that it is easier for websites selling unauthorized goods to penetrate the results using search-engine optimization. We measure the average weekly churn for the June–August data sample by computing each week's churn as the sum of the FQDNs added and dropped in the period divided by the total number of observed FQDNs in adjacent periods.
2. **Popularity**: We hypothesize that the popularity of a brand is corrleated with how many people will try to sell fakes. To estimate popularity, we used the Google Trends to compute the relative search popularity of every brand compared to Nike, which is the most popular brand we studied according to Google.
3. **Active DMCA Enforcement**: Some companies vigorously defend their brand online, while others do not. One countermeasure available to brandholders is to issue DMCA takedown requests on websites selling counterfeits because they display copyrighted images owned by the brandholder. We searched the Chilling Effects Database [2] of DMCA requests for each brand. If we observed more than 25 DMCA takedown notices associated with the brand, then we deemed the brand to be actively employing the DMCA in protecting its brand.[3]
4. **Average Counterfeit Sales Price**: The merchants peddling counterfeit goods have a strong financial incentive to sell fakes that command a higher street price. Hence, we computed for each brand the average asking price for all stores selling that brand's fakes.

Table 5 presents the results of the regression. Two explanatory variables are statistically significant. First, the presence of active DMCA enforcement is negatively correlated with the percentage of search results pointing to fakes. This is an encouraging result for any brand that has taken enforcement action but has wondered

[2]http://www.chillingeffects.org

[3]We selected 25 as the cutoff from inspecting the data. Brands with limited enforcement typically had fewer than 10 requests in the database, whereas those actively defending had at least 25.

	Coefficient	Std. Error	p-value
Intercept	6.81	21.6	0.756
Churn	0.286	0.896	0.753
Popularity	-0.218	0.164	0.1982
Active DMCA Enforcement	-8.59	4.02	0.002245
$\log_2$**(Counterfeit Price)**	2.88	1.11	0.00087
	$R^2 = 0.6546$ (adj. $R^2 = 0.5855$)		

Table 5: Linear regression on counterfeit prevalence by brand. Significant variables are shown in bold.

if it was a worthwhile endeavor or a futile game of whack-a-mole. These results indicate it's the former; more precisely, brands actively enforcing copyrights using the DMCA see an 8.6 percentage point reduction in the fraction of results that link to fakes. We note that the DMCA notices themselves may not be directly causing this reduction. Instead, sending DMCA requests indicates that the firm is taking steps to counter websites selling fakes, and that these strategies seem to be working.

The second significant explanatory variable is the counterfeit price. The greater the asking price for fakes, the more prevalent counterfeit stores are in the search results for a given brand. In particular, every doubling of the average asking price corresponds to a 2.88 percentage point increase in the proportion of fakes in search results. This points to a second potential intervention brands might consider: identifying ways to undermine the street price for fakes. While somewhat counterintuitive, allowing some fakes to be sold at very low prices might deter others from entering the market.

Finally, we note that despite the simplicity of the regression and the relatively small number of brands involved, a large amount of variation can be explained using this model. With an R^2 value of 0.6546, this indicates that 65% of variation in the percentage of results leading to fakes can be explained by this simple linear model.

4.3 How does the prevalence of counterfeits vary over time?

We now investigate how counterfeit peddling evolves over time by examining weekly collections of search results from June–August 2014. We first examine how the prevalence of fakes in search changes for brands over time. Figure 2 shows the relative position of each brand over the 12 week period, specifically charting their percent of counterfeit search results. The most striking observation from the bump chart is how consistent the positions were, despite moderate shifting. For example, UGG remained at the bottom throughout the period (though we note its position improved considerably since the January data collection described earlier). Meanwhile, Bvlgari stayed near the top position throughout the period. We do observe a few substantial movements, however. For example, Louis Vuitton fell four positions, from 16th to 20th most counterfeited, while Air Jordan rose from 20th to 15th most counterfeited brand.

Table 6 presents another way to look at the data, which may help reveal what is driving these fluctuations. It shows the average number of counterfeit websites added and removed, per brand, during the 12-week period. Brands that remove more fake websites than are added are likely to move down the rankings, while those who add more fake websites than are removed tend to rise in the rankings. The table shows this by plotting this delta, as well as the net change in rank from the first and last observation.

Overall, across brands the replacement-rate of counterfeit websites appears to be consistent over time, even within the top page of results. This suggests that whenever bad websites are taken down, they are consistently replaced by other bad websites rather than by legitimate ones.

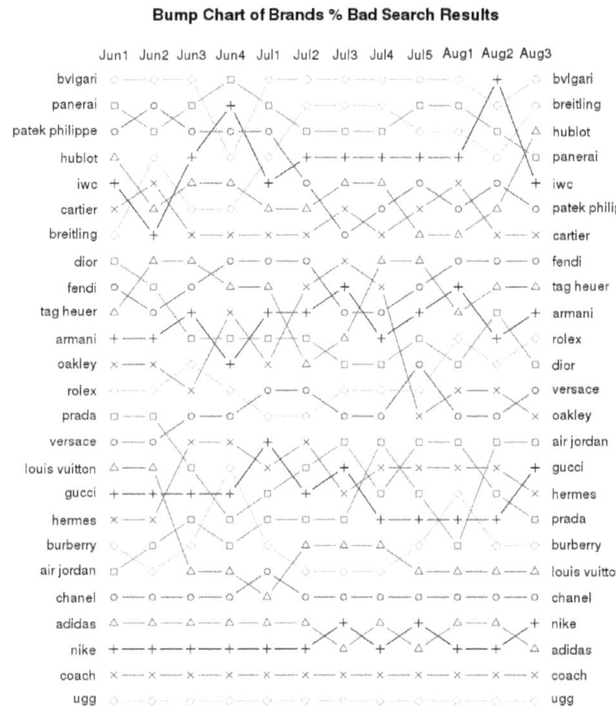

Figure 2: Bump chart tracking the prevalence of counterfeit search results in brands over time.

4.4 Does replicated content replace removed websites?

We have just established that there is substantial turnover in websites selling fakes. We now study the relationship between the old websites when they fall out of the search results and the new websites that replace them. To do that, we clustered the 3 622 websites in the June–August dataset that appeared in the results 4 weeks or less.

We clustered the websites based on image similarity. We compared vertical and horizontal similarity using luminosity histograms implemented using the Eye.Open image library for C#[4]. We then conservatively clustered websites together using hierarchical agglomerative clustering with cut-height of 25%. In total, 1 389 websites were placed into clusters of at least size 2.

Figure 3 plots the timing fake websites first appear and disappear in the search results, grouped by cluster, for all clusters containing at least 10 websites. Each group is assigned a different color and line style for a given cluster size. The purpose of this graph is to visualize the extent to which websites selling fakes are published in parallel or serialized. We can see, for example, that the cluster with 22 websites is highly parallel, with 14 near copies of the same page appearing in the search results at once. One of the clusters of size 16 (the blue dashed grouping), by contrast, has no more than four website copies in operation at once, suggesting a more serial operation of replacing websites that are removed.

We can quantify the tendency towards serial or parallel operations by calculating the maximum *depth* clusters have. Here depth is defined as the largest number of websites with overlapping time

[4] `https://similarimagesfinder.codeplex.com/`

	Avg # counterfeit stores per week				Avg # counterfeit stores per week (page 1)	
	added	removed	Δ stores	Δ rank	added	removed
Nike	32.4	27.8	4.6	1	1.6	1.2
Air Jordan	36.9	33.9	3.0	5	4.1	4.1
Hermes	28.1	25.6	2.5	1	4.1	3.8
Panerai	31.4	30.7	0.7	-2	4.6	4.3
Armani	39.1	38.5	0.6	1	4.4	3.6
Gucci	33.3	32.7	0.6	1	2.4	3.1
Louis Vuitton	35.8	35.3	0.5	-4	4.9	4.4
Fendi	32.7	32.3	0.4	1	2.2	2.2
Breitling	35.2	34.9	0.3	5	3.6	3.7
Hublot	34.1	33.8	0.3	1	3.8	4.4
Chanel	23.6	23.3	0.3	0	3.1	2.9
Versace	31.3	31.0	0.3	2	3.8	3.6
Bvlgari	36.2	36.0	0.2	0	4.9	4.6
Adidas	22.3	22.2	0.1	-1	2.1	2.4
Rolex	27.2	27.1	0.1	2	2.8	2.8
Coach	14.8	14.9	-0.1	0	2.2	1.8
UGG	12.9	13.0	-0.1	0	0.5	0.6
Tag heuer	29.2	29.4	-0.2	1	1.9	1.9
Cartier	34.4	34.9	-0.5	-1	3.0	2.9
Burberry	34.0	34.6	-0.6	0	4.0	4.2
Oakley	45.5	46.6	-1.1	-2	4.3	4.6
Patek philippe	30.3	31.5	-1.2	-3	2.7	3.0
IWC	41.9	43.2	-1.3	0	4.1	4.2
Dior	38.6	40.3	-1.7	-4	3.8	4.6
Prada	31.2	35.1	-3.9	-4	1.6	2.2
Average	31.7	31.5	0.2	0	3.2	3.2

Table 6: Turnover of bad stores by brand over 12 week collection.

intervals appearing in search results. Clusters with larger depths are more parallelized, while those with smaller depth values are more serialized. Table 7 reports the average depths for different cluster sizes. We can see that, in general, the average depth for clusters is much smaller than the cluster size (e.g., depth 2 for the 3 clusters of size 13). This suggests that a modestly parallel, but primarily serial, approach is being used by websites selling fakes. Once their websites drop out of the search results, they quickly replace them with new ones with content copied over from the dropped ones.

4.5 What are the characteristics of websites selling fakes?

Up to now, the analysis has focused on how the prevalence of counterfeits in search results varies. We now examine the counterfeit-hawking websites themselves to explore how they differ from websites that do not sell counterfeits.

First, Figure 4 plots the number of brands a given store appears in the search results for. Most stores were found by searching for only only one brand (969 stores), suggesting that most websites specialize in selling a single type of counterfeit good. This may reflect a search-engine optimization strategy moreso than a supply chain issue, as it is not expensive to create distinct storefronts. Some stores do sell multiple brands, however, which is to be expected when there are multiple brands in a given category (e.g., watches). Only a very small number of stores are like bazaars, however, selling more than 10 of the 25 brands we monitored.

We next study how the time since a website has been registered affects the likelihood that it will be selling counterfeits. Out of the 6 979 unique FQDNs encountered during data collection, we could extract the website's creation date from the WHOIS in 3 933 cases (56.35%). Figure 5 illustrates the subset of data for which this data was collected. Websites registered for less than a year were much more likely to be identified as selling counterfeits, whereas the websites identified as not selling counterfeits tended to be older. Note that despite the trend, there are a large number of exceptions to this rule.

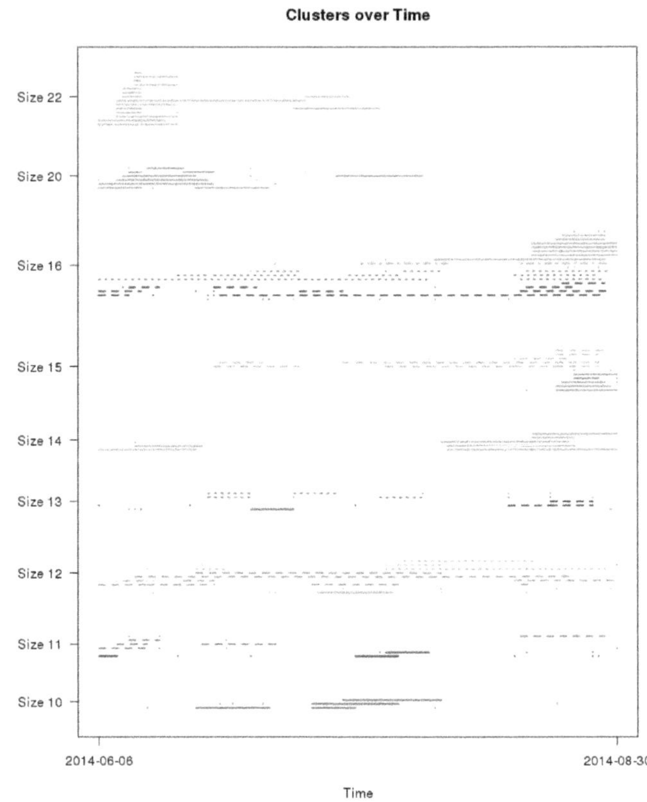

Figure 3: Clustered websites selling counterfeits grouped by order of appearance in the search results.

The last website-specific characteristic we study is its associated country. There are two ways to identify a website's geographic location. One is to use the IP address to find out where the website itself is hosted. Another approach is to identify the registrant's country from the WHOIS details. Of course, these countries need not be the same. It is quite common to register a web address in the owner's home country, but host the content elsewhere, particularly in countries with widespread web hosting infrastructure (e.g., the US, Netherlands and Germany).

Thus, we use both methods when examining all January search results for websites selling knockoffs and others. Table 8 presents odds ratios for the most popular countries from the results for both hosting and WHOIS countries associated with websites. The odds ratios are calculated relative to incidence of fake and legitimate websites hosted and registered in the US. Hence, any odds ratio greater than one (and highlighted in red bold font to indicate statistical significance at 95% confidence) indicate that the country is a positive risk factor for having counterfeit websites. Likewise, any odds ratio less than one (and highlighted in green bold font) is a negative risk factor for having counterfeit websites.

A number of trends are apparent from inspecting the odds ratios in Table 8. Websites selling fakes have 17-times greater odds of being registered in China than the US. However, while the fake website may be registered to a Chinese person or business, the website itself is only twice as likely to be hosted in China than in the US. Japan is also at much greater odds (8 times), but there are fewer Japanese websites in the results. Private and proxy WHOIS registrations are more likely to be associated with fakes, but at only 25% greater odds (and just outside statistical significance).

Cluster size	# in cluster	Avg. depth
1	2092	1.0
2	250	1.1
3	64	1.3
4	33	1.7
5	15	1.9
6	10	2.2
7	8	1.9
8	7	2.4
9	5	2.2
10	1	3.0
11	2	3.0
12	3	3.3
13	3	2.0
14	1	5.0
15	2	6.0
16	4	4.8
20	1	6.0
22	1	14.0

Table 7: Cluster sizes and average depths for similar fake websites appearing in search results between June–August.

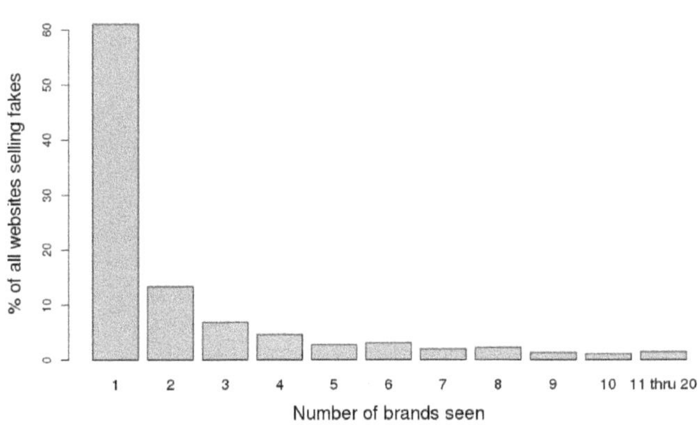

Figure 4: Brands per store (as measured by search queries).

Countries with large legitimate luxury goods industries (France, Italy, Switzerland) are much less likely to either host websites selling fakes or have them registered by entities in those countries. In contrast, countries with large web hosting industries (Netherlands, Estonia, Sweden) are more likely to host websites selling fakes, even though the websites are not likely to be registered there.

In sum, we can see that the infrastructure for supporting websites selling counterfeit goods is global, and that counterfeit producing countries (e.g., China) are more likely to register the websites and countries with strong IT infrastructures are more likely to host the websites.

5. RELATED WORK

In very recent work carried out concurrently to our own efforts, Wang et al. use clustering techniques to identify "campaigns" of similar websites advertising counterfeit goods [30], using methods described in [12]. They also issue search queries for brands, but they identify websites selling knockoffs by looking for signs that the hosting website has been hacked and is demonstrating cloaking behavior. Their analysis in turn focuses on linking together disparate websites into groupings. Our work complements theirs in

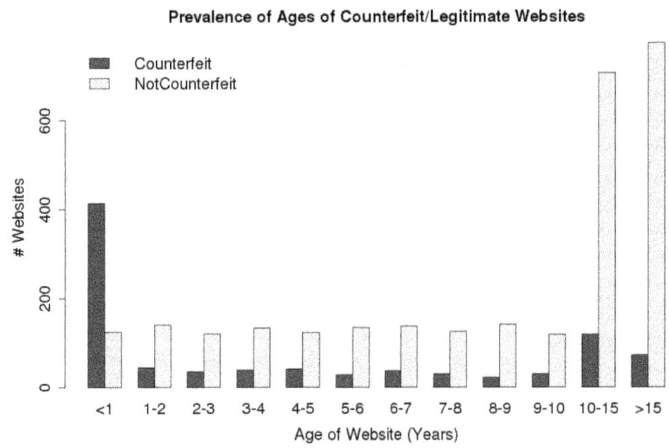

Figure 5: Websites' ages and counterfeit status.

that we focus on the more general problem of classifying all search results as selling knockoffs or not. Cloaking behavior is indicative of many, but certainly not all, of today's websites selling counterfeits. One way we can see this is to note that 45% of the websites we identified as selling counterfeits also mentioned the brand on their homepage. This suggests that many of these websites are not hacked or cloaking, but instead are brazenly selling fakes. Furthermore, we focus our analysis on examining differences in the prevalence of counterfeits in web search by user intent and brand characteristics.

More broadly, a number of papers have investigated abuse in search-engine results. Provos et al. presented a mechanism for identifying drive-by-downloads in web search results [25]. Moore et al. [23] and John et al. [13] report on the poisoning of trending search terms to distribute malware and host ad-laden, auto-generated content. Leontiadis et al. document search-poisoning by those peddling counterfeit pharmaceuticals [15]. The same authors recently reported on a longitudinal study of such search-engine poisoning promoting unlicensed pharmacies [17]. Notably, they compared the prevalence of search poisoning based upon the intent of the search queries, finding that both innocent and complicit queries turn up unlicensed pharmacies. This complements our own findings regarding the presence of knockoffs in search results, regardless of query intent.

A number of papers have proposed classifiers to identify malicious web content. Abu Nimeh et al. compare several methods for classifying phishing websites [1]. Many others have constructed features for classifying malicious web pages based upon website content or behavior [6, 8, 24, 29, 31]. Our paper continues in this tradition, but builds a classifier based upon features specific to websites selling knockoffs (e.g., selling in multiple currencies, pricing information).

6. CONCLUSION

The web has revolutionized commerce, giving consumers access to more choice at lower prices. Unfortunately, it can be hard to determine whether the great deal found online is truly a bargain or is actually cheap because the merchant is selling knockoffs. In this paper, we have conducted a large-scale empirical analysis of 25 counterfeit goods found through web search. We designed a purpose-built classifier to predict whether a given website found through search likely sells genuine merchandise or counterfeit goods.

Country	Hosting Country Odds ratio	Hosting Country 95% C.I.	WHOIS Country Odds ratio	WHOIS Country 95% C.I.
United States	1.00		1.00	
Australia	1.12	(0.666,1.81)	(+) **3.89**	(2.420,6.20)
Belgium			3.58	(0.874,12.99)
Canada	1.17	(0.713,1.86)	1.05	(0.496,2.02)
China	(+) **2.41**	(1.296, 4.38)	(+) **17.88**	(13.492,23.96)
Czech Republic	(+) **2.20**	(1.170, 4.01)	(+) **2.67**	(1.307, 5.18)
Denmark	1.73	(0.772, 3.62)	2.72	(0.539, 10.71)
Estonia	(+) **14.57**	(7.967,28.93)		
France	(-) **0.37**	(0.172, 0.70)	0.95	(0.468,1.76)
Germany	0.72	(0.492,1.04)	0.72	(0.343,1.34)
Hong Kong	0.43	(0.063, 1.50)	2.48	(0.851, 6.41)
India	1.23	(0.334, 3.60)	2.10	(0.903,4.46)
Ireland	1.62	(0.886, 2.85)		
Italy	(-) **0.48**	(0.196,0.99)	0.88	(0.400,1.72)
Japan			(+) **8.65**	(2.027,45.11)
Malaysia	(+) **9.42**	(4.804,19.89)		
Netherlands	(+) **4.57**	(3.293,6.37)	0.47	(0.070,1.61)
Panama	(+) **6.21**	(1.824,24.64)	(+) **6.55**	(4.281,10.09)
Russia	(+) **8.94**	(4.659,18.32)		
Singapore	1.31	(0.573, 2.74)		
Spain	0.85	(0.311, 1.95)	1.79	(0.693, 4.09)
Sweden	(+) **7.52**	(5.243,10.96)	0.38	(0.016, 1.85)
Switzerland	(-) **0.25**	(0.058,0.68)	(-) **0.19**	(0.045, 0.51)
Thailand			(+) **4.27**	(1.007, 16.84)
Turkey	(+) **3.61**	(1.302,9.98)		
United Kingdom	1.20	(0.936, 1.53)	(+) **1.96**	(1.496, 2.56)
Private/Proxy			1.25	(0.967, 1.60)

Table 8: Odds ratios indicating the relative prevalence of websites selling fakes compared to the US (for both hosting and WHOIS registration). Bold figures indicate statistically significant risk factors (plus signs indicate positive risk factors, minus signs negative risks).

We have found that 32% of inspected search results point to fakes overall, but we have also observed wide variation. Innocent queries such as "hublot buy online" are less likely to lead to fakes, but introducing the word "cheap" can lead to nearly 40% of the results pointing to stores selling counterfeits. Furthermore, some brands are targeted more often than others. Brands who sell high-end goods such as luxury watches tend to have their search results polluted with more knockoffs. Not all the news is bad for brands, however. We have presented a linear regression that indicates those who actively protect their brand (which we observe by a record of DMCA enforcement) experience much lower rates of fakes in search.

By and large, merchants selling fakes take advantage of reliable web hosting by operating in countries with strong infrastructure. They also tend to replace removed websites with copied content on new URLs.

In future work, we hope to continue measuring progress in combating the sale of counterfeit goods by carrying out longitudinal studies. More work can be done to improve the classifier's accuracy so that it can be used in an ongoing basis by operators in the field. We also hope to investigate similarities between websites selling fakes in greater depth.

Acknowledgments

We thank the anonymous reviewers for their constructive feedback.

This work was partially funded by the Department of Homeland Security (DHS) Science and Technology Directorate, Cyber Security Division (DHS S&T/CSD) Broad Agency Announcement 11.02, the Government of Australia and SPAWAR Systems Center Pacific via contract number N66001-13-C-0131. This paper represents the position of the authors and not that of the aforementioned agencies.

7. REFERENCES

[1] S. Abu-Nimeh, D. Nappa, X. Wang, and S. Nair. A comparison of machine learning techniques for phishing detection. In *Proceedings of the 2nd APWG eCrime Researchers Summit*, pages 60–69. ACM, 2007.

[2] G. A. Akerlof. The market for "lemons": Quality uncertainty and the market mechanism. *The Quarterly Journal of Economics*, 84(3):488–500, 1970.

[3] Alexa. Top 1 million websites. http://s3.amazonaws.com/alexa-static/top-1m.csv.zip.

[4] R. Anderson. Why information security is hard – an economic perspective. In *Proceedings of the 17th Annual Computer Security Applications Conference (ACSAC'01)*, New Orleans, LA, Dec. 2001.

[5] R. Anderson and T. Moore. The economics of information security. *Science*, 314(5799):610–613, Oct. 2006.

[6] S. N. Bannur, L. K. Saul, and S. Savage. Judging a site by its content: learning the textual, structural, and visual features of malicious web pages. In *Proceedings of the 4th ACM Workshop on Security and Artificial Intelligence*, pages 1–10. ACM, 2011.

[7] A. Blum, B. Wardman, T. Solorio, and G. Warner. Lexical feature based phishing URL detection using online learning. In *Proceedings of the 3rd ACM Workshop on Artificial Intelligence and Security*, AISec '10, pages 54–60, New York, NY, USA, 2010. ACM.

[8] D. Canali, M. Cova, G. Vigna, and C. Kruegel. Prophiler: a fast filter for the large-scale detection of malicious web pages. In *Proceedings of the 20th international conference on World wide web*, pages 197–206. ACM, 2011.

[9] R. Clayton. WHOIS data extracted from templates (deft-whois), 2014. http://www.deft-whois.com.

[10] R. Clayton and T. Mansfield. A study of WHOIS privacy and proxy service abuse. In *13th Workshop on the Economics of Information Security*, 2014.

[11] M. Culp, K. Johnson, and G. Michailidis. ada: An r package for stochastic boosting. *Journal of Statistical Software*, 17(2):9, 2006.

[12] M. F. Der, L. K. Saul, S. Savage, and G. M. Voelker. Knock it off: Profiling the online storefronts of counterfeit merchandise. In *Proceedings of the 20th ACM SIGKDD International Conference on Knowledge Discovery and Data Mining*, KDD '14, pages 1759–1768, New York, NY, USA, 2014. ACM.

[13] J. P. John, F. Yu, Y. Xie, A. Krishnamurthy, and M. Abadi. deseo: Combating search-result poisoning. In *USENIX Security Symposium*. USENIX Association, 2011.

[14] M. Kammerstetter, C. Platzer, and G. Wondracek. Vanity, cracks and malware: Insights into the anti-copy protection ecosystem. In *Proceedings of the 2012 ACM Conference on Computer and Communications Security*, CCS '12, pages 809–820, New York, NY, USA, 2012. ACM.

[15] N. Leontiadis, T. Moore, and N. Christin. Measuring and analyzing search-redirection attacks in the illicit online prescription drug trade. In *USENIX Security Symposium*, 2011.

[16] N. Leontiadis, T. Moore, and N. Christin. Pick your poison: pricing and inventories at unlicensed online pharmacies. In

Proceedings of the fourteenth ACM conference on Electronic commerce, pages 621–638. ACM, 2013.

[17] N. Leontiadis, T. Moore, and N. Christin. A nearly four-year longitudinal study of search-engine poisoning. In *Proceedings of the 2014 ACM SIGSAC Conference on Computer and Communications Security*, CCS '14, pages 930–941, New York, NY, USA, 2014. ACM.

[18] K. Levchenko, A. Pitsillidis, N. Chachra, B. Enright, M. Félegyházi, C. Grier, T. Halvorson, C. Kanich, C. Kreibich, H. Liu, D. McCoy, N. Weaver, V. Paxson, G. M. Voelker, and S. Savage. Click trajectories: End-to-end analysis of the spam value chain. In *Proceedings of the 2011 IEEE Symposium on Security and Privacy*, SP '11, pages 431–446, Washington, DC, USA, 2011. IEEE Computer Society.

[19] C. Littlejohn, A. Baldacchino, F. Schifano, and P. Deluca. Internet pharmacies and online prescription drug sales: a cross-sectional study. *Drugs: Education, Prevention, and Policy*, 12(1):75–80, 2005.

[20] J. Ma, L. K. Saul, S. Savage, and G. M. Voelker. Beyond blacklists: learning to detect malicious web sites from suspicious urls. In *Proceedings of the 15th ACM SIGKDD international conference on Knowledge discovery and data mining*, pages 1245–1254. ACM, 2009.

[21] D. McCoy, A. Pitsillidis, G. Jordan, N. Weaver, C. Kreibich, B. Krebs, G. Voelker, S. Savage, and K. Levchenko. Pharmaleaks: Understanding the business of online pharmaceutical affiliate programs. In *USENIX Security Symposium*, Bellevue, WA, Aug. 2012.

[22] D. Meyer. Support vector machines. *The Interface to libsvm in package e1071. e1071 Vignette*, 2012.

[23] T. Moore, N. Leontiadis, and N. Christin. Fashion crimes: trending-term exploitation on the web. In Y. Chen, G. Danezis, and V. Shmatikov, editors, *ACM Conference on Computer and Communications Security*, pages 455–466. ACM, 2011.

[24] A. Ntoulas, M. Najork, M. Manasse, and D. Fetterly. Detecting spam web pages through content analysis. In *Proceedings of the 15th international conference on World Wide Web*, pages 83–92. ACM, 2006.

[25] N. Provos, P. Mavrommatis, M. Rajab, and F. Monrose. All your iFrames point to us. In *USENIX Security Symposium*, Aug. 2008.

[26] M. Riek, R. Böhme, and T. Moore. Measuring the influence of perceived cybercrime risk on online service avoidance. *IEEE Transactions on Dependable and Secure Computing*, (to appear), 2015.

[27] G. Rodriguez. Generalized linear models, 2014. `http://data.princeton.edu/R/glms.html`.

[28] M. D. Smith and R. Telang. Competing with free: The impact of movie broadcasts on DVD sales and Internet piracy. *MIS Q.*, 33(2):321–338, June 2009.

[29] D. Wang, S. Savage, and G. Voelker. Cloak and dagger: Dynamics of web search cloaking. In *Proceedings of the 18th ACM Conference on Computer and Communications Security*, pages 477–490. ACM, 2011.

[30] D. Y. Wang, M. Der, M. Karami, L. Saul, D. McCoy, S. Savage, and G. M. Voelker. Search + seizure: The effectiveness of interventions on SEO campaigns. In *Proceedings of the 2014 Conference on Internet Measurement Conference*, IMC '14, pages 359–372, New York, NY, USA, 2014. ACM.

[31] S. Webb, J. Caverlee, and C. Pu. Predicting web spam with HTTP session information. In *Proceedings of the 17th ACM Conference on Information and Knowledge Management*, CIKM '08, pages 339–348, New York, NY, USA, 2008. ACM.

Concept Expansion Using Web Tables

Chi Wang, Kaushik Chakrabarti, Yeye He,
Kris Ganjam, Zhimin Chen, Philip A. Bernstein
Microsoft Research, Redmond, WA
{chiw, kaushik, yeyehe, krisgan, zmchen, philbe}@microsoft.com

ABSTRACT

We study the following problem: given the name of an ad-hoc concept as well as a few seed entities belonging to the concept, output all entities belonging to it. Since producing the exact set of entities is hard, we focus on returning a ranked list of entities. Previous approaches either use seed entities as the only input, or inherently require negative examples. They suffer from input ambiguity and semantic drift, or are not viable options for ad-hoc tail concepts. In this paper, we propose to leverage the millions of tables on the web for this problem. The core technical challenge is to identify the "exclusive" tables for a concept to prevent semantic drift; existing holistic ranking techniques like personalized PageRank are inadequate for this purpose. We develop novel probabilistic ranking methods that can model a new type of table-entity relationship. Experiments with real-life concepts show that our proposed solution is significantly more effective than applying state-of-the-art set expansion or holistic ranking techniques.

Categories and Subject Descriptors

H.3.3 [**Information Storage and Retrieval**]: Information Search and Retrieval; H.2.8 [**Database Management**]: Database applications—*Data mining*

Keywords

Concept Expansion; Web Table; Graph-based Ranking; Entity Extraction; Ontology Learning

1. INTRODUCTION

We study the following problem: *given the name of a concept as well as a few seed entities belonging to the concept, output all entities belonging to the concept.* This is referred to as the *concept expansion* problem. This problem has many applications.

• *Knowledgebase expansion*: A knowledgebase (e.g., Freebase [7], YAGO [25], Probase[32]) contains concepts (e.g., country), entities belonging to those concepts (e.g., USA, China, India for the concept 'country') and attributes of those concepts (e.g., population, capital city for the concept 'country'). They are used by web search engines for a variety of purposes: to answer search queries, understand short texts and annotate web tables [1, 27, 28]. While these knowledgebases have large numbers of entities for head concepts (e.g., country, city), they have very few entities for tail concepts (e.g., 'low-fertility country', 'emerging economies') [32, 33, 31]. There is a growing interest to extend the knowledgebase to cover tail concepts, entities and attributes.

• *Ad-hoc list creation*: Users often create lists for concepts of interest (e.g., dog breeds, beach vacation spots) using a spreadsheet (Excel, Google Sheets) or a note-taking application (e.g., OneNote, Evernote). Manually creating such lists is labor-intensive; approaches that automatically populate such lists or at least suggest some lists can be immensely beneficial.

Since producing the exact set of entities belonging to a concept is hard, a realistic goal is to return a ranked list of entities instead. This requires human effort to examine and admit the top-ranked entities, but still significantly less burdensome than manual population. Better the ranking, lower the human effort.

Prior work and limitation. Though abundant work has been done for the general concept expansion or set expansion problem, they either perform poorly or are not viable options for tail concepts. Set expansion approaches take a small set of "seed entities" as input, to discover 'similar' entities that appear in similar context [18, 29, 30, 16, 24, 21]. When expanding tail concepts, this approach is subject to the ambiguity in the input: given the seed entities 'Canon', 'Sony' and 'Nikon', it is difficult to know which concept the user has in mind, 'camera brands' or 'Japanese companies' or something else. It tends to mix entities belonging to different concepts during the expansion. This is known as the 'semantic drift' issue [11]. To prevent concept ambiguity and semantic drift, a common strategy is to populate negative examples from mutually exclusive concepts according to a reference ontology. This idea is used by Snowball [4], KnowItAll [15], NELL [10] etc. A similar setting is hard to set up for ad-hoc concepts. There is no reference ontology to provide comprehensive mutual-exclusiveness for constraining most tail concepts.

Our solution. To overcome these limitations, we take both a concept name and a small set of seed entities as input, but do not require negative examples or knowledge of other concepts. Furthermore, we propose to leverage *both structured data and text data* associated with millions of tables on the web. This setting has several unique benefits for expansion of tail concepts. First, a web table is often structured as rows about entities pertaining to a coherent, fine-grained concept. Second, the text mentioned in the caption, nearest headings etc. of a web table can help identify the tables about the user-input concept, providing opportunities for indexing and searching them with a web table search system (WTS) like Microsoft's Excel Power Query [3] or Google's Web Tables [2].

WWW 2015, May 18–22, 2015, Florence, Italy.
ACM 978-1-4503-3469-3/15/05.
http://dx.doi.org/10.1145/2736277.2741644.

t_1

Name	Windows	Linux
Oracle	Yes	Yes
MySQL	Yes	Yes
SQL Server	Yes	No
PostgreSQL	Yes	Yes

Operating systems support for top **database software**

t_2

Name	License
MySQL	GPL
PostgreSQL	PostgreSQL
Firebird	IPL
Berkeley DB	AGPLv3

List of open source **database software**

t_3

Vendor	Revenue
Oracle	11787 M
IBM	4870 M
Microsoft	4098 M
Teradata	882 M

Database software, 2011 revenue by vendor

t_4

Book	Price
Teach SQL in 10 mins	20.03
SQL Server for devs	38.13
Access 2013 Bible	32.17

Best selling books on **database software**

t_5

Name	Max row size
MySQL	64KB
Oracle	8KB
Firebird	64KB

Information about **database** size limits

t_6

Name	Developer
Oracle	Oracle
SQL Server	Microsoft
Office	Microsoft
Photoshop	Adobe

Best selling **software** in 2010

Figure 1: Tables returned by WTS for 'database software'. The text below the tables represent the caption/surrounding text/nearest headings

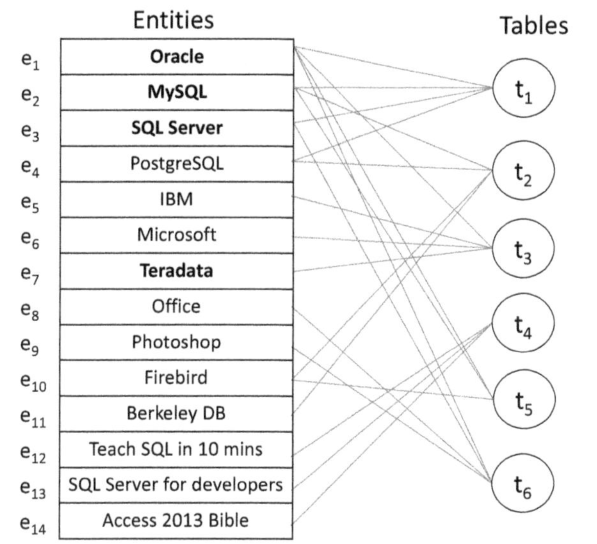

Figure 2: Bipartite graph of entities and tables. The seed entities are shown in bold

Once we retrieve the web tables from a WTS, we have two kinds of information at hand: (i) the seed entities and (ii) a ranked list of tables returned by the WTS that *roughly* reflects their relevance to the concept query. A viable approach of utilizing this information is to build a bipartite graph of all retrieved tables and the entities in them, and then run a graph-based ranking method like generalized Co-HITS [13]. Such a method can utilize prior knowledge on both the entity and table side, as well as the link structure. However, a traditional ranking method may fail tail concept expansion due to the abundance of *non-exclusive* tables.

EXAMPLE 1. *Consider the concept 'database software'. Figure 1 shows 6 tables returned by the WTS. The matching keywords found in column headers, captions, surrounding text etc., are shown in bold. The ranking order is $t_1, t_2, t_3, t_4, t_5, t_6$: t_1, t_2, t_3 and t_4 are ranked higher as they match both keywords while t_5 and t_6 are ranked lower as they match with only one keyword.*

Each table in such a system has a subject column. This column contains the set of entities the table is about, while the other columns represent binary relations or attributes of those entities; previous techniques can be used to accurately identify the subject column (the leftmost column in all the 6 tables in this case) [27, 28].

In this paper, we refer to an entity that belongs to the concept as relevant and others as irrelevant. A WTS returns two types of tables: those that exclusively contain relevant entities in their subject column (t_1, t_2, t_5) and those that do not (t_3, t_4, t_6). We refer to the former tables as exclusive and the latter as non-exclusive.

A bipartite graph can be built as in Figure 2. Suppose there are 4 seed entities (shown in bold). A generalized Co-HITS algorithm ranks entities and tables in the following order: Oracle, MySQL, SQL Server, Teradata, PostgreSQL, Firebird, Microsoft, IBM, Photoshop, Office, Berkeley DB...; $t_3, t_1, t_6, t_2, t_5, t_4$. Note that irrelevant entities like Microsoft, IBM, Photoshop and Office are ranked above a relevant entity like Berkeley DB.

Non-exclusive tables cause existing random-walk ranking algorithms to fail. Large non-exclusive tables about overlapping concepts (e.g., t_6) can accumulate high scores. Irrelevant entities that are popular in such non-exclusive tables will get higher scores than relevant but less popular entities, such as Berkeley DB. These relevant but less popular entities are often desirable for the application of concept expansion, since popular entities have a high chance to exist in a knowledgebase already. This analysis applies to all graph-based ranking methods that linearly aggregate scores from all neighboring vertices.

Our insight to resolving this semantic drift issue, is to model the *exclusivity* of tables. Using only exclusive tables to find relevant entities vastly boosts precision, without substantial loss of recall because: (i) it is common to retrieve from the WTS a large number of exclusive web tables for a tail concept such as t_1, t_2 and t_5 in Example 1; and (ii) most relevant entities appear in exclusive tables. *The core technical challenge is to identify exclusive tables.*

To infer exclusive tables and find relevant entities, our solution stems from the simple yet special entity-table relationship: *a table is exclusive if and only if all its subject entities are relevant, and an entity is relevant if it appears in at least one exclusive table.* Incorporating uncertainty, we propose a novel probabilistic model that holistically ranks the entities and tables. Our ranking method models the score of a table as 'how likely the entire table is exclusive' instead of 'the fraction of the table that is relevant,' and respects the asymmetric entity-table relationship: an exclusive table must contain only relevant entities while a relevant entity can appear in a non-exclusive table. The score from table to entity and entity to table is propagated in an asymmetric way, and aggregated nonlinearly to emulate taking 'all or none' from exclusive or non-exclusive tables. That is a key difference of our approach.

Our contributions can be summarized as follows:

• We propose a new problem setting to address the challenges of tail concept expansion using both the concept name and seed entities. We propose to leverage structured data and text data of millions of web tables for this problem (Section 2).

• We propose a novel holistic, probabilistic ranking model to rank entities based on their likelihood of belonging to the concept, and rank tables based on their likelihood of being exclusive to the concept. Specifically, we present properties that the score aggregation functions must satisfy in order to model the special table-entity relationship (Section 3). We develop a novel algorithm to perform the ranking, with guaranteed convergence for a broad class of aggregation functions (Section 4). We present concrete choices of aggregation functions and prior knowledge (Section 5).

• We perform extensive experiments on expanding a large scale concept-entity database. Our experiments show that our method produces significantly better quality results than three existing algorithms: a competitive set expansion algorithm using web tables, a probabilistic graphical model that propagates table scores via column similarities, and a generalized algorithm of personalized PageRank and Co-HITS. Our technique can increase the number of entities per concept by 1 to 2 orders of magnitude with close to 100% precision (Section 6).

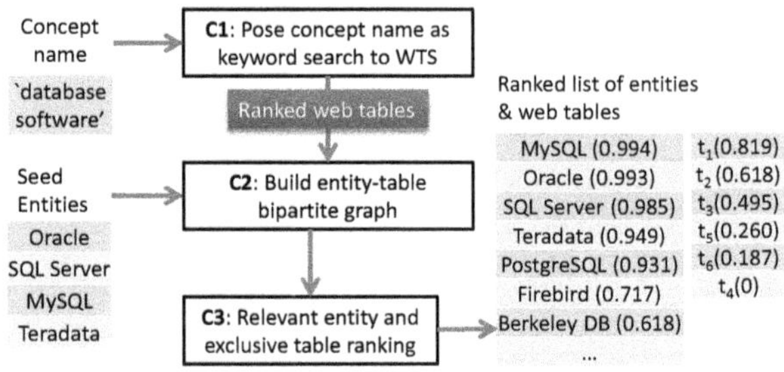

Figure 3: System architecture

Table 1: Example concepts and returned entities

asian country	third world country	trading partner
internet company	multiplayer game	national newspaper
adverse side effect	fitness class	flu-like symptom
antifungal agent	bacterial species	cytotoxic agent
grape variety	mammal species	memory card

Concept	**Seed entities**	**Returned entities**
adverse side effect	addiction, depression	headache, nausea, diarrhea, insomnia, dizziness, constipation...
grape variety	nebbiolo, barbera	ramisco, cornifesto, tinta carvalha, espadeiro, tinta barroca, tinta francisca...

2. PROBLEM STATEMENT AND SYSTEM ARCHITECTURE

2.1 System task

The end-to-end system task is: *given a concept name, seed entities and web tables, return a ranked list of relevant entities*. Recall that we refer to the entities belonging to the concept as relevant entities, and exclusive tables are defined as tables that contain only relevant entities in their subject columns.

This task is challenging for an ad-hoc tail concept. A tail concept can be defined as concepts with web mention frequency below a cut point, which partitions the sum of concept frequencies roughly into two equal parts. For example, the most frequent 350 concepts in Probase occupy 40% of the total frequency of all concepts. Any concept with lower frequency than them can be deemed a tail concept. This definition of tail concepts is similar to that of tail attributes by Yahya et al. [33].

Formally, we let C denote the concept name, S the set of seed entities, $T = \{t_j\}_{j=1}^{m}$ the set of web tables, $E = \{e_i\}_{i=1}^{n}$ the set of entities appearing in the subject columns of these web tables, and $\{x_i\}_{i=1}^{n}$ the entity ranking score indicating their relevance.

For convenience, we also use C to denote the set of relevant entities in the concept, and t_j the set of entities mentioned in the subject column of the table. The context disambiguates which meaning is used. For example, $e_i \in C$ means that entity e_i belongs to concept C, $e_i \in t_j$ means that entity e_i is mentioned in t_j's subject column, and $t_j \subset C$ means that t_j is an exclusive table.

We assume the seed entity set S is a subset of E; we ignore any seed entity not present in E.

2.2 System architecture

Figure 3 shows the architecture of the CONCEPTEXPAND system. It has 3 main components, namely C1, C2 and C3.

(C1) Pose concept name to Web Table Search system: This component retrieves the set of web tables from which the relevant entities can be identified. A quality set of retrieved tables should comprise (i) most of the tables containing relevant entities and (ii) few tables that contain no relevant entities at all.

One option is to develop custom algorithms for this purpose. A plausible algorithm is to obtain the tables whose subject column name matches with the concept name. While this works well for broad concepts (e.g., 'city', 'country'), it misses most tables for specific concepts. For example, we tried this algorithm for the 15 concepts shown in Table 1 (with both singular and plural variants). In a large fraction of the web snapshot, we found only 73 tables.

We resort to the rich content signals associated with web tables. For tables we aim to retrieve, the concept name typically appears in captions, nearest headings (h2, h3, h4), page titles, surrounding text, incoming anchor text and queries for which the page was clicked. These are the general criteria used by a web table search system (WTS) to return tables by keyword queries [27, 9]. Hence, we pose the ad-hoc concept name to a WTS and use the returned list of tables for further investigation. To obtain a reasonable amount of exclusive tables, we retrieve a large number of tables from WTS (such as 1,000). WTS rank positions are based on relevance, and they can be used as distant prior knowledge for exclusivity-aimed ranking. In the following, we assume t_j refers to the table ranked at position j by this WTS. We assume the WTS outputs the identity of the subject column for each returned table. All WTSs internally identify it by certain means [27, 28].

(C2) Build an entity-table bipartite graph: The inputs to this component are the set of seed entities and the tables returned by component C1. It identifies the set of distinct entities among the entity mentions in the subject columns of the input tables. It also identifies the seed entities among those distinct entities. In general, this is the entity resolution problem [6]. Since this is not the focus of the paper, we identify the distinct entities by simply grouping the entity mentions in the subject columns using a string matching module. We identify the seed entities amongst the distinct entities in the web tables using the same string matching module. The output of this component is a bipartite graph. It comprises the set of distinct entities on one side (with the seed entities identified) and the set of tables returned by WTS on the other side. An edge between an entity and a table indicates that the former is mentioned in the subject column of the latter. The bipartite graph for the example in Figure 1 is shown in Figure 2. Let $T(e_i) = \{t_j \ni e_i\}$ be the set of tables that are linked to e_i. $T(e_i)$ is referred to as *support table set*, and $|T(e_i)|$ as *support* of e_i. For example, $T(e_1) = \{t_1, t_3, t_5, t_6\}$.

(C3) Relevant entity and exclusive table ranking: The input to this component is the bipartite graph output by component C2, with seed entities and WTS table ranking included. The output is a ranked list of entities according to their relevance as well as a ranked list of tables according to their exclusivity. We perform ranking for both entities and tables because they are highly interdependent, as we will discuss in Section 3. The ranked list of tables can also complement the ranked list of entities and facilitate the investigation. Furthermore, the tables provide opportunities of adding relational attributes to the knowledgebase or spreadsheets, which is an important goal of knowledgebase expansion and ad-hoc list creation. It is formally defined as follows.

DEFINITION 1. *Given a concept C, ordered web tables $T = \{t_j\}_{j=1}^{m}$ that cover entities $E = \{e_i\}_{i=1}^{n}$, and a seed entity set $S \subset E$, rank these entities with score $\{x_i\}_{i=1}^{n}$, and the tables with score $\{y_j\}_{j=1}^{m}$, according to entities' relevance and tables' exclusivity, i.e., whether $e_i \in C$ and $t_j \subset C$.*

This component is the focus of the rest of the paper.

3. RANKING MODEL

We first state the principles for entity and table ranking. We then propose a probabilistic model following the principles.

Finding relevant entities and exclusive tables are highly interdependent tasks and can mutually enhance each other. It is due to the following relationship between them:

PRINCIPLE 1. *A table t_j is exclusive if and only if all the entities $e_i \in t_j$ are relevant.*

PRINCIPLE 2. *An entity e_i is relevant if it appears in at least one table t_j such that t_j is exclusive.*

Principle 2 is actually a straightforward corollary of Principle 1. We restate it in order to emphasize the assymetric relationship: An exclusive table must contain only relevant entities, but a relevant entity can appear in non-exclusive tables.

If we know either the complete set of relevant entities or the complete set of exclusive tables, we can leverage the two hard principles to obtain the other set. For example, if we know which entities belong to the concept C, we can deduce which tables belong to concept C using Principle 1. Conversely, we can deduce which entities belong to concept C using Principle 2 when the knowledge of tables is given. Note that in the latter case, false negatives are possible because some relevant entities may only appear in non-exclusive tables. Yet we assume this rarely happens given the large sample size of web tables and a reasonable performance of WTS

In reality, we do not have the complete knowledge on either side. The input provides partial prior information on both sides. If $e_i \in S$ is a seed entity, we have strong prior knowledge for e to belong to the concept C. If table t_j is ranked high (j is small) by WTS, we have weak prior knowledge for t_j to belong to concept C. The table prior is weak because the WTS does not rank tables according to their exclusivity. We can only assume that the WTS ranking is overall positively correlated with the exclusivity.

With the unavoidable uncertainty, we model the problem as a holistic entity and table ranking task that incorporates *soft counterparts* of the above principles.

Probabilistic ranking model: Let $x_i = p(e_i \in C) \in (0, 1]$ denote the likelihood of entity e_i belonging to concept C, and $y_j = p(t_j \subset C) \in [0, 1]$ denote the likelihood of table t_j belonging to concept C. We let $x_i > 0$ because we cannot assert an entity does not belong to concept C for sure, as we do not have negative evidence. We then model their relationship with soft counterparts of Principle 1 and 2. According to Principle 1, we model each y_j as an aggregation function $f_{E \to T}$ of $\{x_i, e_i \in t_j\}$. According to Principle 2, we model each x_i as an aggregation function $f_{T \to E}$ of $\{y_j, t_j \ni e_i\}$. Then, we solve the following equations to perform holistic entity and table ranking.

$$\begin{aligned} x_i &= f_{T \to E}(\{y_j, t_j \ni e_i\}) \\ y_j &= f_{E \to T}(\{x_i, e_i \in t_j\}) \end{aligned} \tag{1}$$

It is easy to incorporate the prior knowledge on entity and table side by adding pseudo tables and entities in the bipartite graph, which will be discussed in Section 5.2.

As we discussed in Section 1, symmetric, linear aggregation functions, like the random walk employed by PageRank, Co-HITS, etc. suffer from the semantic drift issue. The reason is that they do not consider the special relationship we are modeling between relevant entities and exclusive tables through Principle 1 and 2. We now discuss the design principle of the two aggregation functions $f_{E \to T}$ and $f_{T \to E}$, both of which should produce values between 0 and 1.

3.1 Entity to table aggregation function

Given x_i for $e_i \in E$, we model $y_j = p(t_j \subset C)$ as an aggregation function $f_{E \to T}$ of $\{x_i | e_i \in t_j\}$. This is the soft counterpart of the relationship expressed in Principle 1.

Principle 1 suggests that as long as one entity $e_i \in t_j$ is not in concept C, the whole table t_j is not in concept C. In our probabilistic model, we would like $f_{E \to T}$ to reflect the likelihood that all the entities in t_j belong to C. It should produce a low value if any $x_i | e_i \in t_j$ is low. Also, it should well distinguish tables that have small difference. We abstract the following two axiomatic properties:

1. Consider a table t_j. For any entity $e_i \in t_j$, its likelihood of belonging to C is an explanatory variable of the likelihood t_j belonging to C. When it is almost certain that the entity e_i does not belong to C, the table t_j is also almost certain to be non-exclusive. In contrast, if all the entities in t_j are certain to be relevant, the table t_j is also certain to be exclusive.

   PROPERTY 1 (ASYMPTOTIC PRINCIPLE 1). $\forall e_i \in t_j$, $\lim_{x_i \to 0} y_j = 0$*; Let* $\mathbf{x} = [x_i | e_i \in t_j]$, $y_j = 1$ *iff* $\mathbf{x} = \mathbf{1}$.

2. If two tables t_a and t_b are identical except two entities with equal support, the table containing the entity with a higher likelihood should have a higher likelihood of belonging to the concept (unless the likelihood for both is equal to zero).

   PROPERTY 2 (MONOTONICITY). *If* $t_a = t \cup \{e_1\}, t_b = t \cup \{e_2\}$, $|T(e_1)| = |T(e_2)|$ *and* $x_1 < x_2$*, then* $0 \le y_a \le y_b \le 1$ *(*$y_a = y_b$ *happens only when* $y_b = 0$*).*

As one example, the minimum value from $\{x_i | e_i \in t_j\}$, i.e.,

$$f_{E \to T}(\{x_i | e_i \in t_j\}) = \min_{e_i \in t_j} x_i \tag{2}$$

satisfies Property 1, but not Property 2. It is determined by a single element x^* in the set $\{x_i | e_i \in t_j\}$ and insensitive to other elements as long as they are not smaller than x^*.

EXAMPLE 2. *Consider the two tables t_1 and t_3 in Figure 1. t_1 contains 4 entities $e_1 = Oracle$, $e_2 = MySQL$, $e_3 = SQL\ Server$ and $e_4 = PostgreSQL$ and t_3 contains 4 entities $e_1 = Oracle$, $e_5 = IBM$, $e_6 = Microsoft$ and $e_7 = Teradata$. Suppose $x_1 = x_2 = x_3 = 0.9, x_4 = x_5 = x_6 = x_7 = 0.1$. Then Equation (2) produces identical y_j value for these two tables. But t_1 should be deemed more likely to belong to C than t_3 as it has more relevant entities.*

As another example, the random walk aggregation function, i.e.,

$$f_{E \to T}(\{x_i | e_i \in t_j\}) = \sum_{e_i \in t_j} \frac{x_i}{|T(e_i)|} \tag{3}$$

violates Property 1.

3.2 Table to entity aggregation function

Given y_j for $t_j \in T$, we model $x_i = p(e_i \in C)$ as an aggregation function $f_{T \to E}$ of $\{y_j | t_j \ni e_i\}$. This is the soft counterpart of the relationship expressed in Principle 2.

Principle 2 suggests that if an entity appears in one exclusive table, it is relevant. In our probabilistic model, we would like $f_{T \to E}$ to reflect the likelihood that at least one table $t_j \ni e_i$ in e_i's support set belongs to C. It should produce a high value if any $y_j(t_j \ni e_i)$ is high. Also, it should well distinguish entities that have slightly different support table sets. We abstract the following two axiomatic properties:

1. Consider an entity e_i and its arbitrary support table t_j. When the table t_j is certain to belong to C, the entity e_i is also certain to belong to C.

   PROPERTY 3 (PRINCIPLE 2). $x_i = 1$ *if* $\exists t_j \ni e_i, y_j = 1$.

   Note that Property 3 is unlike Property 1 in two aspects: (i) the limit ($\lim_{\mathbf{y} \to \mathbf{0}} x_i = 0$) is not true, because a relevant entity could occur in non-exclusive tables; and (ii) $x_i = 1$ if but not only if $\exists t_j \ni e_i, y_j = 1$, for the same reason.

2. If the support table sets of two entities e_a and e_b are identical except two equal sized tables, the entity contained in the table with a higher likelihood should have a higher likelihood of belonging to the concept (unless the likelihood for both is 1).

   PROPERTY 4 (MONOTONICITY). *If* $T(e_a) = T_0 \cup \{t_1\}$, $T(e_b) = T_0 \cup \{t_2\}$, $|t_1| = |t_2|$ *and* $y_1 < y_2$, *then* $0 < x_a \leq x_b \leq 1$ *(*$x_a = x_b$ *only when* $x_a = 1$*).*

As one example, the maximal value from $\{y_j | t_j \ni e_i\}$, i.e.,

$$f_{E \to T}(\{y_j | t_j \ni e_i\}) = \max_{t_j \ni e_i} y_j \tag{4}$$

satisfies Property 3 but violates Property 4.

As another example, the random walk aggregation function, i.e.,

$$f_{T \to E}(\{y_j | t_j \ni e_i\}) = \sum_{t_j \ni e_i} \frac{y_j}{|t_j|} \tag{5}$$

violates Property 3.

The concrete design of the aggregation functions following these principles will be presented in Section 5.1.

4. RANKING ALGORITHM

Based on the model proposed in Section 3, we develop an algorithm to perform joint inference for entity likelihood x_i and table likelihood y_j.

A simple idea is to find a solution that satisfies Equation (1), by iteratively applying the aggregation functions in Equation (1). This simple algorithm may fail to rank the relevant entities and exclusive tables ahead of irrelevant and non-exclusive ones when the following are both true: (i) there are a large number of tables in our bipartite graph that belong to a different concept C'; and (ii) these tables contain a similar set of entities. For example, in Figure 1, if there are many tables like t_4, the entities and tables about database books can amass high scores from each other.

To address this issue, we develop an algorithm, called CONCEPTEXPAND (Section 4.1). We give a formal theorem about the convergence condition of our algorithm in Section 4.2.

4.1 CONCEPTEXPAND algorithm

The main idea is to perform restricted propagation on a subset of entities and tables, instead of propagating scores among all entities and tables. We consider a two-phase algorithm. In the first phase, we identify such a subset. We begin with the seed entities, which are most likely to be relevant. We then gradually expand the set by iteratively adding the most plausible tables based on current estimation. We stop adding tables when the remaining tables all have low estimated likelihood of belonging to C. We collect entities with enough support, and remove tables with few entities in this collection. In the second phase, the iterative propagation will be performed within this set. The two-staged method prevents adding too many irrelevant tables all at once and impairing score propagation. During the first phase, only those high-confidence tables contribute to entities' likelihood computation. And the second phase will have a chance to refine the earlier estimation which was based on incomplete information.

As the starting point of the probabilistic reasoning, the score for the seed entities can be set according to the prior knowledge (i.e., they are very likely to be in C). For all the other entities, x_i is unknown, and they will not be computed until a table containing them is added to the reasoning set. To compute the score for a table t_j with missing entity score, we use the table prior π_j to replace the missing entities' score and feed to the aggregation function $f_{E \to T}$. The more knowledge we have of entities in a table, the less important the table prior is.

Algorithm 1: CONCEPTEXPAND

Input: Entity set E, table set T, seed entity set S, table likelihood threshold α
Output: entity score $\{x_i | e_i \in E\}$, table score $\{y_j | t_j \in T\}$

1 Initialize the support table set $T_0 \leftarrow \emptyset$;
2 Initialize the excluded entity set $U \leftarrow E \setminus S$;
3 Initialize seed entity score x_i using prior, for $e_i \in S$;
4 **repeat**
5   Update $y_j \leftarrow f_{E \to T}(\{x_i | e_i \in t_j, e_i \notin U\} \cup \{\pi_j | e_i \in t_j \cap U\})$ for $t_j \in T$;
6   Choose the optimal $(y^*, t^*) = \max_{t_j \notin T_0, |t \setminus U| > 0} y_j$;
7     $T_0 \leftarrow T_0 \cup \{t^*\}$;
8   Update $x_i \leftarrow f_{T \to E}(\{y_j | t_j \ni e_i, t_j \in T_0\})$ for $e_i \in t^*$;
9     $U \leftarrow U \setminus t^*$;
10 **until** $y^* < \alpha$ *or* $T_0 = T$;
11 **repeat**
12     $T_0 \leftarrow T_0 \setminus \{t \in T_0, |t \setminus U| < |t \cap U|\}$;
13     $U = U \cup \{e \in E \setminus U, |T(e) \cap T_0| \leq 1\}$;
14 **until** U *stops growing*;
15 **repeat**
16   Update $y_j \leftarrow f_{E \to T}(\{x_i | e_i \in t_j\})$ for $t_j \in T_0$;
17   Update $x_i \leftarrow f_{T \to E}(\{y_j | t_j \ni e_i\})$ for $e_i \in E \setminus U$;
18 **until** x_i*'s converge*;

We develop the CONCEPTEXPAND algorithm based on the above intuition. The pseudocode is shown in Algorithm 1. Lines 4–14 identify the table set and entity set for reasoning, by adding the most plausible table one by one, updating the estimation of both tables and entities, and removing the ones with low support. When adding a table, we require that the table contains some entity in the reasoning set (Line 6). This reduces the chance of adding a table simply because it has high prior. When removing tables and entities, we keep checking if any entity has no more than one support table (Line 13), and if any table has more than half of entities missing in the reasoning set (Line 12). Lines 15–17 solves the equations within the reasoning set, using a fixed-point iteration.

The parameter α can be set according to the precision-recall requirement. Lower α leads to higher recall but lower precision in general. When $\alpha = 0$, all the tables will be added to the reasoning set. $\alpha = 1$ filters out all tables. In general, one can set α automatically according to table prior scores $\{\pi_j\}$ (e.g., the median of $\{\pi_j\}$). See Section 6.3 for a study of its effect.

The algorithm has a complexity $O(mL)$, where m is the number of tables and L the total size of tables (i.e., the number of links in the table-entity bipartite graph). We show a running example of the algorithm in Section 5.3.

4.2 Convergence of algorithm

Given that the CONCEPTEXPAND algorithm requires iterative computation of y_j and x_i, a desirable property of the computation is that it converges after a limited number of iterations. In the following, we provide a condition for aggregation functions $f_{E\to T}$ and $f_{T\to E}$ which guarantees convergence.

PROPERTY 5 (DIMINISHING RETURN). *Let* $\mathbf{x} = [x_1, x_2, ..., x_n]$ *be an* n*-dimensional vector with entity score* x_i *as components. Let* $g(\mathbf{x})$ *be the entity score after one iteration of updates using* $f_{E\to T}$ *and* $f_{T\to E}$*. The aggregation generates diminishing return if (i) there exists a compact set* $\mathscr{C} \in [0,1]^n$ *such that* $g(\mathscr{C}) \subseteq \mathscr{C}$*, and (ii)* $\forall \mathbf{x}, \mathbf{z} \in \mathscr{C}(\mathbf{x} \neq \mathbf{z}), \max_{i\in[n]} |x_i - z_i| > \max_{i\in[n]} |g(\mathbf{x})_i - g(\mathbf{z})_i|$*.* $\mathscr{C}$ *is called the diminishing region of* g*.*

Discussions. The first part of Property 5 states that the aggregation has to produce proper probabilities in a compact region in $[0,1]^n$ if input are proper probabilities in the same region. The compact region can be $[0,1]^n$ itself, or a subset of it. This is a natural requirement since we want to output probabilities, and in some cases regularize them. For example, random walk requires the probabilities to be within a simplex $\sum_{i=1}^{n} x_i = 1$.

The second part of the property states that the maximum difference of probability for the same entity in $\mathbf{x}$ and $\mathbf{z}$ always diminishes after one iteration of $f_{E\to T}$ and $f_{T\to E}$. In particular, when we boost the initial belief of one entity by δ, the new belief will increase by less than δ after one iteration. Intuitively, this means that the initial boost will be "averaged out" by other entities and tables after iterative propagations. It is also a natural requirement because the change of inferred confidence should not surpass the change of original confidence.

We can in fact show that the condition holds in many common aggregation functions, when prior knowledge is incorporated as pseudo entities and pseudo tables. One example is to use arithmetic mean as aggregation functions for both $f_{E\to T}$ and $f_{T\to E}$, and add a pseudo entity with likelihood π_j to table t_j as prior knowledge (e.g., based on the ranking position in WTS).

PROPOSITION 1. *Let* $f_{E\to T}(\{x_i|e_i \in t_j\}) = \frac{\pi_j + \sum_{e_i\in t_j} x_i}{|t_j|+1}$, *and* $f_{T\to E}(\{y_j|t_j \ni e_i\}) = \frac{\sum_{t_j\ni e_i} y_j}{|T(e_i)|}$*, i.e., both* $f_{E\to T}$ *and* $f_{T\to E}$ *are arithmetic mean, then the aggregation generates diminishing return in* $[0,1]$*.*

There are other combinations of common aggregation functions that also enjoy Property 5, e.g., the random walk aggregation functions as in Equations (3) and (5). ■

Property 5 guarantees convergence.

THEOREM 1. *If aggregation functions satisfy Property 5 with diminishing region* $\mathscr{C}$*, then Algorithm 1 converges to the unique solution to Equation (1) in* $\mathscr{C}$*, with initial* $\mathbf{x} \in \mathscr{C}$*.*

To prove Theorem 1, we can essentially view $g(\mathbf{x})$ as a composite function from $f_{E\to T}$ and $f_{T\to E}$, and apply Banach's Fixed Point theorem [17] to ensure that a unique solution can be found for the system of Equation (1) using iterative computation.

Theorem 1 requires fairly simple properties to guarantee the convergence of CONCEPTEXPAND algorithm. Proposition 1 implies that common aggregation functions, such as smoothed arithmetic mean, guarantees convergence. Therefore, our computational framework is generic – any reasonable aggregation functions satisfying the required properties can be plugged in Equation (1) to model a particular application, and Algorithm 1 will converge to the solution of it.

5. RANKING DESIGN

We now discuss concrete choices of aggregation functions and prior knowledge encoding, which are functions that we plug into the generic framework outlined in Algorithm 1. We design these functions specifically for our problem. At the end of this section we will also present a running example.

5.1 Aggregation function

Entity to table aggregation. As discussed in Section 3.1, we need a function $f_{E\to T} : [0,1]^n \to [0,1]$ that satisfies the desirable Properties 1 and 2.

Property 2 (monotonicity) requires the function to be responsive to the change of every input element positively. Property 1 (asymptotic Principle 1) requires it to approach 0 when any input element approaches 0, and to approach 1 when all input elements approach 1. The three Pythagorean means, arithmetic mean, geometric mean, and harmonic mean satisfy the monotonicity, and the latter two satisfy Principle 1 asymptotically.

Between these two, we choose the one that fits Principle 1 most closely. We reemphasize that the table ranking score reflects whether *all* entities in the subject column of a table are within the concept. We prefer the score to be low even when there are only a small number of irrelevant entities in the table. Since the harmonic mean of a list of numbers tends strongly toward the least elements of the list, it tends (compared with the arithmetic and geometric mean) to mitigate the impact of large numbers (relevant entities) and magnify the impact of small ones (irrelevant entities). As such, we choose the harmonic mean as the aggregation function:

$$f_{E\to T}(\{x_i|e_i \in t_j\}) = \frac{|t_j|}{\sum_{e_i\in t_j} \frac{1}{x_i}} \tag{6}$$

Table to entity aggregation. As discussed in Section 3.2, we need a function $f_{T\to E} : [0,1]^n \to [0,1]$ that satisfies the desirable Properties 3 and 4.

Property 4 (monotonicity) requires the function to be responsive to the change of every input element positively. Property 3 (Principle 2) requires it to approach 1 when any input element approaches 1. The three Pythagorean means satisfy the monotonicity, but none of them satisfy Principle 2.

We derive a meaningful aggregation function from the probabilistic meaning of the score. If we assume the events '$t_j \subset C$' are independent for tables $t_j \in T(e_i)$ in the support set of e_i, we can use the 'noisy-or' model for table-to-entity score aggregation: $e_i \notin C$ only if none of its support tables belong to C.

$$\begin{aligned} f_{T\to E}(\{y_j|t_j \ni e_i\}) &= p(\vee_{t_j\ni e_i} t_j \subset C) \\ &= 1 - \prod_{t_j\ni e_i} p(t_j \not\subset C) = 1 - \prod_{t_j\ni e_i} (1 - y_j) \end{aligned} \tag{7}$$

The problem with this model is that it can accumulate weak evidences quickly to produce false positives, as illustrated by the following example.

EXAMPLE 3. *Consider two entities* Office *and* Berkeley DB. Berkeley DB *appears in one table* t_2*, with* $y_2 = 0.9$*. Suppose there are 6 other tables identical to* t_6 *(say,* $t_7, \ldots, t_{12}$*) and they all contain* Office*. Suppose* $y_6 = \cdots = y_{12} = 0.3$*. This is realistic because tables about popular yet non-target concepts (e.g., general software in this case) can dominate the WTS results. Equation (7) produces higher likelihood for* Office *than for* Berkeley DB *(0.92 vs 0.9) which is undesirable. Note that there is no table that strongly supports* Office *to be relevant; on the contrary, there is a table (*t_2*) that strongly supports* Berkeley DB *to be relevant.*

A similar issue is also discussed by Downey et al. [14], in a different scenario. They addressed the problem that when an entity is involved in a pattern for *multiple* times, the 'noisy-or' model will accumulate weak evidence. They proposed a *Urn* model for repetitive sampling of entities that allows replacement. In our case, each entity appears once in each table, so this model does not apply to our problem.

We propose a new heuristic solution. Given the collection of $\{y_j | t_j \ni e_i\}$, a few large values in it should contribute more to the aggregated value x_i than many small values. Based on that intuition, we sort the y_j's in a descending order $y_{j_1} \geq y_{j_2} \geq \cdots$, and assign a decreasing series of weights $1 \geq w_1 > w_2 > \ldots$ to them.

$$f_{T\to E}(\{y_j | t_j \ni e_i\}) = 1 - \prod_{t_{j_u} \ni e_i, y_{j_u} \geq y_{j_{u+1}}} (1 - y_{j_u})^{w_u} \quad (8)$$

So, the small values in $\{y_j | t_j \in T(e_i)\}$ have relatively small contribution to x_i. In other words, the number of support tables of e has a diminishing marginal utility. The more support tables we observe, the less important those small values are. When w_i's are all equal to 1, this function reduces to the 'noisy-or' model.

To determine w_i, we introduce a notion of *effective support*. For simplicity let us assume an entity appears in m tables with equal likelihood q. Then Equation (8) becomes: $f_{T\to E}(\{y_j | t_j \ni e_i\}) = 1 - (1-q)^{\sum_{i=1}^{m} w_i}$. We call $\sum_{i=1}^{m} w_i$ the effective support of x_i. In the 'noisy-or' model, the effective support is equal to the actual support m. By assigning the decaying weight $1 \geq w_1 > w_2 > \ldots$, we desire the effective support to grow sublinearly with m. The question is how slowly the effective support should grow with respect to m. A fast growing example is $\Theta(m^{\frac{m-1}{m}})$, which is close to linear when m is large. A extremely slow growing example is $\Theta(\ln(m))$, which almost does not grow in our scale with thousands of tables. A medium example is $\Theta(\sqrt{m})$, where support 100 is converted to effective support 10. In general, we can set $w_i = \frac{1}{i^p}, 0 < p < 1$, to obtain a asymptotic growth rate $\Theta(m^{1-p})$ of effective support ($p = 0$ and $p = 1$ correspond to linear and logarithmic growth respectively). The sequence $\{w_i\}$ in this case is referred to as p-series.

In this paper, we use the $\frac{1}{2}$-series as the decaying weight w_i. It resolves the issue in Example 3 to a large extent: the undesirable accumulation is much slower, with a square root growth rate of effective support.

PROPOSITION 2. *The rectified 'noisy-or' function with decaying weight, as in Equation* (8)*, satisfies both Property 3 and 4.*

We omit the proof due to limit of space.

5.2 Prior knowledge

Now we discuss how to incorporate prior knowledge for the specific task of concept expansion by adding pseudo entities or tables.
Prior on entity side: For seed entities, we have strong prior knowledge that they belong to concept C. We add one pseudo table for each seed entity $e_i \in S$ and link the pseudo table to the corresponding entity. The table has a fixed confidence score $1 - \epsilon_i$, where ϵ_i is a small error rate depending on the source of the entities. If the entities are provided by human curators, ϵ_i should reflect the error rate of the curators which is typically very low. If the entities come from a non-curated database such as web-extracted concept-entity pairs, ϵ_i should be set according to the precision of the database [32]. Furthermore, the different seed entities may have different confidence of belonging to C. For example, in Probase, an entity e_i has an integer support s_i about its occurrence with C. The larger s_i is, the more confident it is to be a correct seed entity for C. So we can set $\epsilon_i = \epsilon_C^{s_i}$, where ϵ_C is a small constant like 0.1.
Prior on table side: All WTSs return a ranked list of tables for a query. We assume the relevance of a table to the concept C degrades with their position in the ranked list returned by a WTS. Therefore, the prior estimation of the likelihood of a top ranked table belonging to C is higher than that of a lower ranked table. Since we retrieve a constant number of tables from WTS, we may retrieve tables that are partial matches to the concept name (like table t_6 in Figure 1). To account for that, we penalize tables that do not match all the tokens in the concept name. We define the table prior π_j as:

$$\pi_j = (\frac{1}{2})^{\text{\#missing tokens of } C \text{ in } t_j} \frac{1}{j+1} \quad (9)$$

Recall that j is the rank position of table t_j. When a table contains all tokens in C, its prior is $\frac{1}{j+1}$, which decays fast as the ranking position increases. Otherwise, its prior is penalized exponentially with respect to the number of missing tokens. We incorporate the prior by adding a pseudo entity with confidence π_j to link to each table t_j. In this way, the prior is just one value that participates in the aggregation function $f_{E\to T}$. The more knowledge of entities in a table we have, the less we rely on the table prior.

While it is possible to design more sophisticated prior score, we use this simple treatment that is general and easy to compute. The imperfect but reasonable prior score tests the ability of our reasoning framework of handling noise. Better prior score can be deigned in future work to exploit more information in web tables.

It can be verified that the chosen aggregation functions and prior score satisfy the convergence condition in Theorem 1. We leave detailed proofs to the full version of this paper.

5.3 Running example

EXAMPLE 4. *Consider the example in Figure 2. The prior of tables t_1 to t_6 are: 0.5, 0.33, 0.25, 0.2, 0.08, 0.07. For simplicity we set $\alpha = 0, \epsilon_i = 0.1$, and skip Line 13 of entity removal because in larger samples these entities occur more than once.*

Initially, $E \setminus U$ consists of $e_1 = Oracle$, $e_2 = MySQL$, $e_3 = SQLServer$ and $e_7 = Teradata$ and $T_0 = \emptyset$. In the first round, $y_1 = 0.68, y_3 = 0.35, y_5 = 0.15, y_6 = 0.11$. t_1 is selected and added to T_0. x_1 to x_4 are updated: $x_1 = 0.98, x_2 = 0.972, x_3 = 0.971, x_4 = 0.68$. $e_4 = PostgreSQL$ is removed from U. In the second round, t_2 is selected. t_3 is added in round 3, and t_5 in round 4. In round 5, t_6 is the last table to add into T_0, because t_4 has no entity in $E \setminus U$. With that we enter the second phase.

After the second phase, the scores converge to a fixed point. The entity scores from high to low are: MySQL (0.992), Oracle (0.991), SQL Server (0.984), Teradata (0.949), PostgreSQL (0.904), Firebird (0.683), Berkeley DB (0.608), IBM (0.495), Microsoft (0.495), Office (0.187), Photoshop (0.187). And the table scores from high to low are: $y_1 = 0.814, y_2 = 0.608, y_3 = 0.495, y_5 = 0.258, y_6 = 0.187, y_4 = 0$. The entity ranking is desired, while the table ranking has one mistake: t_5 is ranked after t_3. The main reason is that the table prior plays an important role when the table is small: $\pi_3 = 0.25 > \pi_5 = 0.08$. The real table size is typically much larger, and therefore the table prior would not dominate the table ranking as in this example.

6. EXPERIMENTAL EVALUATION

We present an experimental evaluation of the proposed algorithm. The goals of the experimental study are (i) to compare the ranking quality of different approaches in terms of precision and recall, and (ii) to understand the sensitivity of the proposed approach to different parameter settings.

6.1 Experimental Setup

6.1.1 Dataset

We use a production web table search engine (WTS) that indexes over 500M web tables extracted from a recent snapshot of the Microsoft Bing search engine. This is the same WTS that powers web table search in Excel PowerQuery [3]. We use concepts in Probase [32] as the testbed for expansion. We choose Probase instead of knowledgebases like YAGO [25] or Freebase [7] for the sake of better concept coverage, especially for tail concepts [32].

To prepare the set of concept queries, we acquired from Probase 9,926 concepts with sufficient popularity. In Probase, each concept-entity pair has a popularity value indicating the number of different domains it is found on the web. We chose concepts with popularity above 150 so that the concept is not too niche and the web-extracted concept-entity pairs are relatively reliable. Seed entities were sampled based on their popularity. We retrieved 1,000 tables for each concept, ending up with a dataset of 10M web tables.

6.1.2 Compared methods

• **Number of occurrences (# Occur).** In this baseline approach, we rank entities by their number of occurrences in the top ranked tables returned by WTS. Entities that occur more often in top tables are ranked higher.

• **Weighted number of occurrences (Weighted # Occur).** This approach enhances the previous one by weighting each occurrence of entity using the table prior. In addition, in order to utilize seed information, we only consider tables with 2 or more seeds. Entities are finally ranked by their aggregate weight across these tables.

• **SEISA [18].** Set expansion aims to automatically discover entities in the target concept using seed entities but not concept name as input. We implement the Dynamic Thresholding algorithm in the SEISA system [18], which is shown a competitive technique for set expansion using web lists.

• **Graphical Model [22].** We implement a graphical model-based table ranking method proposed in [22]. It takes column keywords as input and outputs a ranked list of relevant tables. The goal is similar with our table ranking when the input is a single concept name. We use the table prior as a feature for node potential and the column value overlap as edge potential in this graphical model.

• **Generalized Co-HITS (PageRank) [13].** Personalized PageRank and its variations have been adopted in set expansion systems like SEAL [29]. For our bipartite graph, the most appropriate variation to use is a generalized Co-HITS algorithm [13]. For brevity we still refer to it as PageRank. We set high restart probability on entity prior and low on table prior.

• **CONCEPTEXPAND.** This is our proposed method Algorithm 1, using aggregation functions discussed in Section 5.1. The threshold α for table filtering is simply set to 0, without any tuning.

• **CONCEPTEXPAND_PageRank.** To study the value of aggregation functions, we include a variation of CONCEPTEXPAND that uses random walk aggregation functions discussed in Section 3.

6.1.3 Evaluation

Ground truth preparation. Probase has an incomplete coverage of entities per concept, especially for tail concepts. We randomly checked 100 fine grained concepts and found that more than 90% of time the first relevant entity found in the web tables does not exist in Probase. We did a study for YAGO's fine grained concepts and found similar results. So simply using the existing Probase entities as ground truth leads to rather incomplete judgment. To obtain a reliable set of ground truth, we first identified 90 concepts for which Probase covers at least 4 entities in top-10 WTS tables.

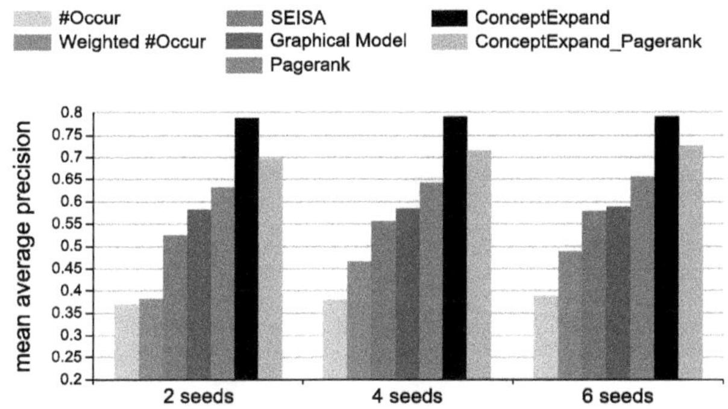

Figure 4: Mean average precision. Methods from left to right follow the order introduced in Section 6.1.2

Then we manually labeled a sample for 54 unambiguous concepts of them. Finally, we merge our labels and Probase entities to form a ground truth set. The final ground truth for each concept may still be incomplete, but is largely augmented upon Probase entities. This set has 18,232 relevant entities in total, with an average number of 338 entities per concept. The number of Probase entities per concept ranges from 4 to 60, with a mean of 23.

The labeled concepts span across multiple domains, such as geography, economy, business, healthcare and technology. Sample concepts and output from the algorithm are listed in Table 1.

Metrics. We use two metrics for evaluation:

• Mean average precision (MAP). This is the standard information retrieval measure for overall ranking performance.

• Relative recall[1] at a certain precision level. This is a metric more concerned with the practical value of the concept expansion task. It reflects the best recall one algorithm can achieve before falling below a precision level. Typically, the requirement for the precision in a knowledgebase is very high. Although we do not expect the expansion algorithm to return 100% correct results to directly populate into a knowledgebase, a high precision level such as 0.9 is helpful for easing the job of human curators in noise filtering.

6.2 Results

In this section we compare the 7 methods. Figure 4 and Figure 5 plot the mean average precision and relative recall at different precision levels. In both figures, the methods are sorted according to the order they are introduced in Section 6.1.2.

MAP performance. The overall ranking performance measured by MAP is consistent when using different number of seeds (Figure 4). The first six methods can be roughly partitioned into three groups according to their MAP: (i) baseline algorithms, # Occur and Weighted # Occur; (ii) existing methods adapted to this task, SEISA, Graphical Model and PageRank; and (iii) our proposed method CONCEPTEXPAND. The gap is large across groups. CONCEPTEXPAND outperforms existing algorithms by 20-50%. Note that the filtering parameter α for CONCEPTEXPAND has not been tuned in this experiment.

The last method CONCEPTEXPAND_PageRank is about halfway between CONCEPTEXPAND and PageRank. It shows that both the inference algorithm and the aggregation functions contribute to the superior performance of CONCEPTEXPAND.

CONCEPTEXPAND is not sensitive to the number of seeds. Without parameter tuning, it achieves a mean average precision of close to 80% with only two seeds per concept.

[1] $r = \frac{\# \text{ returned relevant entities}}{\# \text{ seed entities}}$

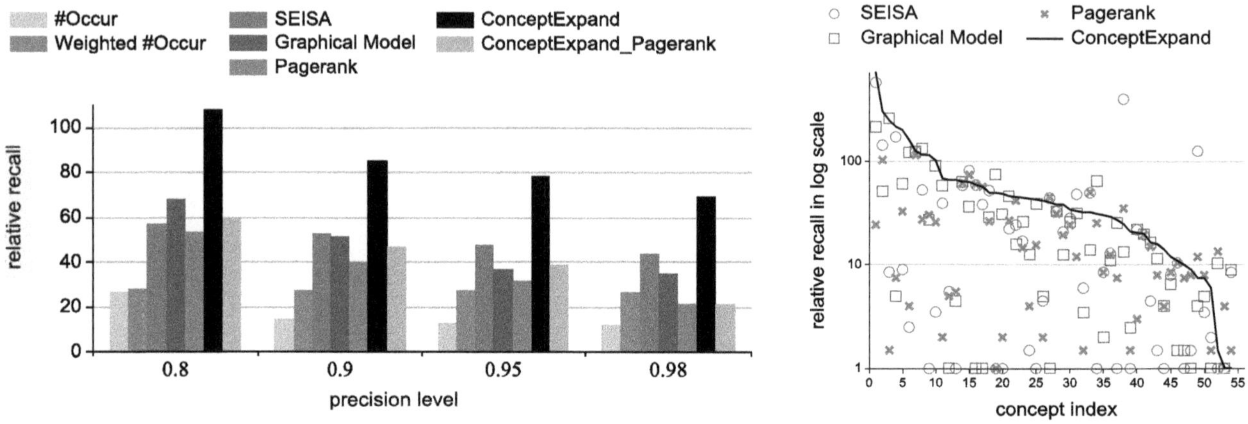

(a) Methods from left to right follow the order introduced in Section 6.1.2

(b) Scatter plot for precision level 0.98

Figure 5: Relative recall at certain precision levels (two seeds)

High precision performance. Regarding the relative recall at high precision levels, there is an even larger gap between CONCEPTEXPAND and competing algorithms (Figure 5). Though all methods can increase the entity coverage before the precision falls below a tolerable threshold, the degree of increase differs across the methods. For example, at precision level 0.98, PageRank increases the coverage by 20 times, SEISA does a better job and achieves 44 times expansion, none of which is comparable to the 70 times gain of CONCEPTEXPAND (Figure 5a). Figure 5b further visualizes the individual performance for these 54 concepts. With a few outliers, CONCEPTEXPAND dominates in the relative recall. When the requirement to precision gradually lowers down, CONCEPTEXPAND achieves even higher recall (108 times at precision level 0.8). Again, without parameter tuning, CONCEPTEXPAND shows strong superiority in its practical value.

When connecting the overall ranking performance (Figure 4) to the performance at high precision (Figure 5), we have two interesting observations.

First, CONCEPTEXPAND_PageRank improves the overall performance of PageRank algorithm by removing low confidence entities and tables, but the improvement is not much on the high precision end. In Figure 5a, CONCEPTEXPAND_PageRank's recall is as one third to one half as CONCEPTEXPAND's. Therefore, the high recall at high precision of CONCEPTEXPAND is mainly attributed to its asymmetric, non-linear score propagation following the special entity-table relationship, rather than the filtering.

Second, there is no clear winner among the three existing algorithms SEISA, Graphical Model and PageRank. Though PageRank has a better MAP than the other two, it poorly performs at high precision levels (lower than baseline at p-level 0.98). In contrast, SEISA does a good job at precision levels above 0.9, but underperforms Graphical Model at p-level 0.8, and eventually has a lowest MAP among the three. This observation reflects the limitations of existing algorithms. We take the concept 'public university' as an example to illustrate. The precision-recall curve is shown in Figure 6. Set expansion techniques like SEISA find most similar entities in the beginning, yet shift to different concepts (e.g., from public university to other universities) without constraining the expansion. Concept-name-based table ranking like Graphical Model does not utilize seed entities, and suffers from imperfect table ranking. For example, several tables about public university

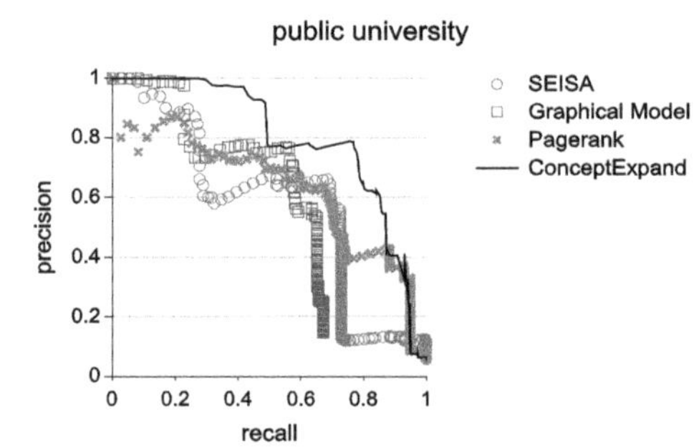

Figure 6: Precision-recall curve case study

cost, programs, salaries, faculty numbers are ranked among top 20. PageRank takes advantage of both concept names and seed information, but it tends to select popular entities from different tables and mix them because of the linear score aggregation. Popular irrelevant entities (e.g., New York University) are ranked high and inserted between relevant ones, thus it cannot produce contiguous high precision results.

6.3 Parameter study

In this section we study how the algorithm performs in response to varying parameter values.

Our algorithm has only one parameter, the stopping criterion α. Recall that this parameter controls the precision-recall trade-off, as it determines when the core table set stops expansion. We used $\alpha = 0$ for all previous experiments, which means all tables will be added to the table set. As we increase α, fewer tables will be added, which helps eliminating irrelevant tables. When α is equal or larger than 1, only one table will be added, leading to poor results.

In our experiments, we sort all table prior scores in descending order and set α to the score at certain positions of the ranked scores. For example, we use the lower quartile (denoted as lower 1/4), median (1/2), upper quartile (upper 1/4) and so on. Figure 7 shows the mean average precision and relative recall at different precision levels. It turns out that CONCEPTEXPAND works robustly in a wide range of α. In fact, the MAP has very small change when α varies from 0 to upper 1/16 quantile of table prior. The most sensitive metric is recall at precision level 0.8. It reaches the peak around 110 at

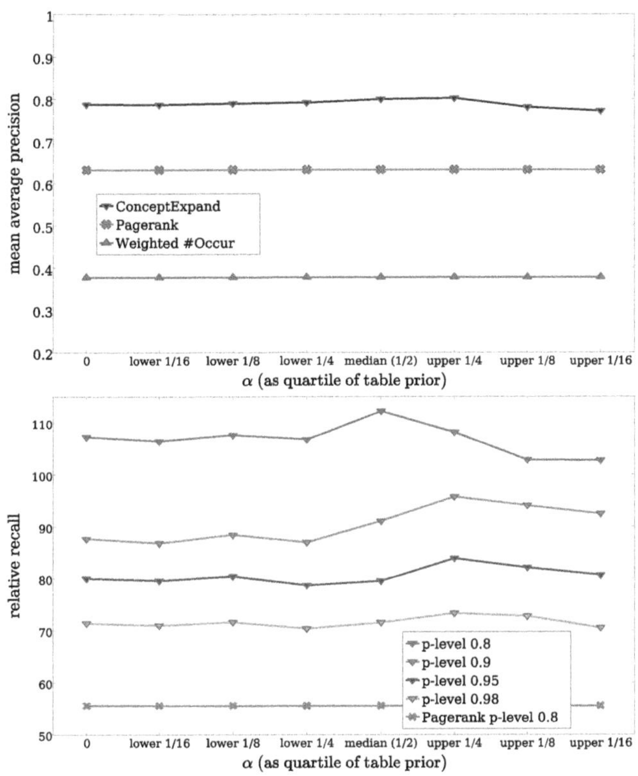

Figure 7: Vary filtering threshold α

median and declines when α further increases, but still above 100 when α is equal to upper quartile of table prior, where other three curves reach a high point. In the worst case in our test (α = upper 1/16 quantile), the recall at precision 0.98 is still much higher than PageRank's recall at precision 0.8. These results indicate a stop criterion ranging from median to upper quartile of table prior is a good choice, depending on the goal of precision. For higher precision a slightly higher α is preferred. As long as α is not too large to leave enough tables, stable performance can be expected thanks to the strong reasoning power of our method.

7. RELATED WORK

The concept expansion problem has been studied mainly in two settings: set expansion and multi-concept expansion. The former takes a set of seed entities as input to expand a single implicit concept, and the latter takes entities in two or more mutually exclusive concepts together and classify other entities.

Google Sets was an early set expansion system. It spawned quite a few set expansion techniques, such as Bayesian Sets [16], SEAL [30], SEISA [18] and others [24, 29, 21]. They mainly leverage the similarity between entities measured by their co-occurrences in web text, wrappers and lists. For example, SEISA employs iterative similarity aggregation and SEAL employs PageRank. Multi-concept expansion proposes to constrain the expansion by using negative examples from mutually exclusive concepts or type constraints [15, 10, 26]. This works well when expanding several mutually exclusive concepts in a reference ontology. None of the above methods are designed for ad-hoc tail concept expansion.

To put this problem in a broader context, the problem of knowledgebase expansion or completion has attracted a bulk of interest due to its practical value. Concept expansion is one main category, focusing on extending the number of entities (a.k.a. instances) belonging to each concept (a.k.a. type or class). Another main category is attribute completion, focusing on completing attributes (a.k.a. facts or relations) of entities. It is introduced as an annual competition in 2008 to the Text Analysis Conference. One can refer to Ji and Grishman [19] for an overview.

To differentiate the paradigm, West *et al.* [31] discusses the 'pull' mode and the 'push' mode for attribute completion. The 'pull' mode refers to extracting values for specific entities and attributes, while the 'push' mode refers to processing a large number of documents in batch and populates whatever facts it can find. A similar categorization applies to concept expansion. Set expansion works in the 'pull' mode and multi-concept expansion works in the 'push' mode. The 'pull' mode is found to better suit tail domains and tail entities. Our approach works in the 'pull' mode. Similar to West *et al.* [31] that leverages a web-search based question-answering system, we leverage a web table search system.

With regard to information source from which to harvest knowledge, the most popular sources are unstructured text [15, 21, 33, 31, 19], and semi-structured web wrappers, lists and tables [26, 18, 29]. Typically, textual patterns have good coverage for head entities, and the context helps identifying the concept. Semi-structured lists and tables contain both head entities and tail ones. A good strategy is to leverage both the semantics in text and the co-occurrence information in lists. For example, NELL [10] is a system for multi-concept expansion that combines textual signals and structure signals from separate sources respectively. In comparison, our work proposes to simultaneously utilizes text and structure from one source.

Our work is related to the holistic table ranking approach proposed by Pimplikar and Sarawagi [22], which takes concept keywords (column names) as input and returns relevant web tables. Though our method can rank tables as well, the ranking criteria is based on exclusivity rather than relevance. Other closely related studies about web tables include table column annotation [12, 20, 23, 27], and entity attribute discovery [8, 34, 35].

There is more work to which the ConceptExpand algorithm can be related. For example, ConceptExpand adds tables one by one to expand the viewpoint bipartite graph of reasoning. Therefore, techniques related to viewpoint network expansion, such as [5], can be considered as alternative ways for extracting a relevant viewpoint neighborhood.

8. CONCLUSION AND FUTURE WORK

In this paper, we studied the problem of finding entities belonging to a concept, given an ad-hoc concept name and a few seed entities. We resort to exclusive web tables and leverage both text signals and structure information. We formulate the task as a holistic ranking problem and develop a novel solution for probabilistic reasoning. It is the first method addressing the challenges for expansion of tail concepts, and experiments demonstrate its superiority to state-of-the-art approaches. Besides, the convergence guarantee of our simple unified framework works with many common aggregation functions (including generalized PageRank as special cases), rendering it generalizable to different problems.

This work can be extended in multiple directions. There is much more information in the knowledgebase and web tables that can be leveraged for concept expansion as well as attribute completion. First, one can utilize the relational attributes in web tables; tables belonging to the same concept often have similar attributes, and the missing attributes in knowledgebases can be potentially populated from them. Second, we distinguish exclusive tables and non-exclusive tables in this work since the latter is more risky to use for expansion. In future work, one can study how to select relevant portions in non-exclusive tables, e.g., via the attributes.

References

[1] Google Knowledge Graph. http://www.google.com/insidesearch/features/search/knowledge.html.

[2] Google Web Tables. http://research.google.com/tables.

[3] Microsoft Excel Power Query. http://office.microsoft.com/powerbi.

[4] E. Agichtein and L. Gravano. Snowball: Extracting relations from large plain-text collections. In *Proceedings of the Fifth ACM Conference on Digital Libraries*, 2000.

[5] S. Asur and S. Parthasarathy. A viewpoint-based approach for interaction graph analysis. In *KDD*, 2009.

[6] O. Benjelloun, H. Garcia-Molina, D. Menestrina, Q. Su, S. Whang, and J. Widom. Swoosh: a generic approach to entity resolution. *PVLDB*, 18(1):255–276, 2009.

[7] K. Bollacker, C. Evans, P. Paritosh, T. Sturge, and J. Taylor. Freebase: a collaboratively created graph database for structuring human knowledge. In *SIGMOD*, 2008.

[8] M. J. Cafarella, A. Y. Halevy, and N. Khoussainova. Data integration for the relational web. *PVLDB*, 2(1):1090–1101, 2009.

[9] M. J. Cafarella, A. Y. Halevy, D. Z. Wang, E. Wu, and Y. Zhang. Webtables: exploring the power of tables on the web. *PVLDB*, 1(1):538–549, 2008.

[10] A. Carlson, J. Betteridge, B. Kisiel, B. Settles, E. R. Hruschka, and T. M. Mitchell. Toward an architecture for never-ending language learning. In *AAAI*, 2010.

[11] J. R. Curran, T. Murphy, and B. Scholz. Minimising semantic drift with mutual exclusion bootstrapping. In *PAACL*, 2007.

[12] D. Deng, Y. Jiang, G. Li, J. Li, and C. Yu. Scalable column concept determination for web tables using large knowledge bases. In *PVLDB*, volume 6, pages 1606–1617, Aug. 2013.

[13] H. Deng, M. R. Lyu, and I. King. A generalized co-hits algorithm and its application to bipartite graphs. In *KDD*, 2009.

[14] D. Downey, O. Etzioni, and S. Soderland. Analysis of a probabilistic model of redundancy in unsupervised information extraction. *Artif. Intell.*, 174(11):726–748, July 2010.

[15] O. Etzioni, M. Cafarella, D. Downey, A.-M. Popescu, T. Shaked, S. Soderland, D. S. Weld, and A. Yates. Unsupervised named-entity extraction from the web: An experimental study. *Artificial Intelligence*, 165(1):91–134, 2005.

[16] Z. Ghahramani, Z. Ghahramani, and K. A. Heller. Bayesian sets. In *NIPS*, 2005.

[17] A. Granas and J. Dugundji. *Fixed Point Theory*. Springer-Verlag, 2003.

[18] Y. He and D. Xin. SEISA: set expansion by iterative similarity aggregation. In *WWW*, 2011.

[19] H. Ji and R. Grishman. Knowledge base population: Successful approaches and challenges. In *ACL*, 2011.

[20] G. Limaye, S. Sarawagi, and S. Chakrabarti. Annotating and searching web tables using entities, types and relationships. In *VLDB*, 2010.

[21] P. Pantel, E. Crestan, A. Borkovsky, A.-M. Popescu, and V. Vyas. Web-scale distributional similarity and entity set expansion. In *EMNLP*, 2009.

[22] R. Pimplikar and S. Sarawagi. Answering table queries on the web using column keywords. *PVLDB*, 5(10):908–919, 2012.

[23] G. Quercini and C. Reynaud. Entity discovery and annotation in tables. In *EDBT*, 2013.

[24] L. Sarmento, V. Jijkoun, M. de Rijke, and E. Oliveira. "more like these": growing entity classes from seeds. In *CIKM*, 2007.

[25] F. M. Suchanek, G. Kasneci, and G. Weikum. Yago: A core of semantic knowledge unifying wordnet and wikipedia. In *WWW*, 2007.

[26] P. Talukdar and F. Pereira. Experiments in graph-based semi-supervised learning methods for class-instance acquisition. In *ACL*, 2010.

[27] P. Venetis, A. Halevy, J. Madhavan, M. Pasca, W. Shen, F. Wu, G. Miao, and C. Wu. Recovering semantics of tables on the web. In *PVLDB*, volume 4, pages 528–538, 2011.

[28] J. Wang, H. Wang, Z. Wang, and K. Zhu. Understanding tables on the web. In *International Conference on Conceptual Modeling*, 2012.

[29] R. Wang and W. Cohen. Iterative set expansion of named entities using the web. In *ICDM*, 2008.

[30] R. C. Wang and W. W. Cohen. Language-independent set expansion of named entities using the web. In *ICDM*, 2007.

[31] R. West, E. Gabrilovich, K. Murphy, S. Sun, R. Gupta, and D. Lin. Knowledge base completion via search-based question answering. In *WWW*, 2014.

[32] W. Wu, H. Li, H. Wang, and K. Q. Zhu. Probase: A probabilistic taxonomy for text understanding. In *SIGMOD*, 2012.

[33] M. Yahya, S. E. Whang, R. Gupta, and A. Halevy. Renoun: Fact extraction for nominal attributes. In *EMNLP*, 2014.

[34] M. Yakout, K. Ganjam, K. Chakrabarti, and S. Chaudhuri. Infogather: entity augmentation and attribute discovery by holistic matching with web tables. *SIGMOD*, 2012.

[35] M. Zhang and K. Chakrabarti. Infogather+: Semantic matching and annotation of numeric and time-varying attributes in web tables. In *SIGMOD*, 2013.

User Latent Preference Model for Better Downside Management in Recommender Systems

Jian Wang
LinkedIn Corp
Mountain View, CA 94043 USA
jianwang@linkedin.com

David Hardtke
LinkedIn Corp
Mountain View, CA 94043 USA
dhardtke@linkedin.com

ABSTRACT

Downside management is an important topic in the field of recommender systems. User satisfaction increases when good items are recommended, but satisfaction drops significantly when bad recommendations are pushed to them. For example, a parent would be disappointed if violent movies are recommended to their kids and may stop using the recommendation system entirely. A vegetarian would feel steakhouse recommendations useless. A CEO in a mid-sized company would feel offended by receiving intern-level job recommendations. Under circumstances where there is penalty for a bad recommendation, a bad recommendation is worse than no recommendation at all. While most existing work focuses on upside management (recommending the best items to users), this paper emphasizes on achieving better downside management (reducing the recommendation of irrelevant or offensive items to users). The approach we propose is general and can be applied to any scenario or domain where downside management is key to the system.

To tackle the problem, we design a user latent preference model to predict the user preference in a specific dimension, say, the dietary restrictions of the user, the acceptable level of adult content in a movie, or the geographical preference of a job seeker. We propose to use multinomial regression as the core model and extend it with a hierarchical Bayesian framework to address the problem of data sparsity. After the user latent preference is predicted, we leverage it to filter out downside items. We validate the soundness of our approach by evaluating it with an anonymous job application dataset on LinkedIn. The effectiveness of the latent preference model was demonstrated in both offline experiments and online A/B testings. The user latent preference model helps to improve the VPI (views per impression) and API (applications per impression) significantly which in turn achieves a higher user satisfaction.

WWW 2015, May 18–22, 2015, Florence, Italy.
ACM 978-1-4503-3469-3/15/05. http://dx.doi.org/10.1145/2736277.2741126
.

Categories and Subject Descriptors

H.3.3 [**Information Storage and Retrieval**]: Information Search and Retrieval

General Terms

Algorithms, Design, Experimentation

Keywords

Recommender System; Downside Management; User Latent Preference Model

1. INTRODUCTION

Recommender systems are popular research topics in the information retrieval community. A host of academic and industrial incarnations of recommender systems exist in domains such as movies (Netflix), music (Pandora), and e-commerce product recommendations (eBay, Amazon). Most existing work focuses on upside management by finding the best items to recommend to a user. Better upside management can be achieved by leveraging state-of-art models such as collaborative filtering, matrix factorization, deep learning neural networks and so on. While it is essential to discover good items, it is equally important to avoid recommending irrelevant or offensive items to a user. User satisfaction is affected by both upside items and downside items. For example, a CEO in a mid-sized company would be interested in other executive positions while he would feel offended by receiving intern-level job recommendations. An item could be irrelevant or offensive for various reasons in different domains. It might be caused by wrong dining preference, wrong job location, wrong movie category and so on. In some cases, a single bad recommendation could cause a user to abandon the recommendation system completely.

One simple strategy for downside management is not to show an item when the predicted probability from recommender systems is too low: you just need to find an appropriate threshold. Such strategy is based on the assumption that an "ideal" recommender system could assign an appropriate probability for an item. In particular, the probability should indicate the user's willingness of accepting the item in different dimensions. Yet it is not the case in the real world. Most existing hybrid recommender systems (such as logistic regression, gradient boosting tree, etc.) consider all features together to predict a single probability for an item. The item might be recommended to a user according to its high probability if the content match is high even though the other contextual match is low. Users might not complain about a slight content mismatch. Yet they are less tolerant to be pushed with recommendations in the wrong location, wrong category or for other contextual reasons. Thus it would be hard to find the right threshold on a single probability from the existing recommender system if a downside item is about some specific dimension.

Downside management has been studied by some recent work [28, 29, 1, 8, 19, 25]. Researchers studied context-aware recommender systems [1, 8, 19, 25] to find items that match with the user's contexts. Contextual information could be leveraged in the pre-filtering stage, post-filtering stage, or in the contextual modeling. The concept of "context" is different from the "latent preference" in our model. The "context" is an explicit condition (for example, the current location of the user) that could be observed for each user while the "latent preference" is an implicit yet explainable factor that the model infers for each user (for example, the location of an item that the user would prefer). We study how the user's implicit preferences or interests would affect recommendations. This latent preference could be dietary restrictions of the user, the acceptable level of adult content in a movie, the geographical preference of a job seeker and so on.

In this work, we propose a general framework that predicts a user's latent preference and leverage it to filter out downside items. The core of the framework is multinomial regression that models a user's latent preference in a specific dimension. The user's preference could either be binary (for example, work at a nearby job, or take a job that requires relocation) or multi-class (for example, work as the intern level, senior level, staff level, or executive level). We assume that users in different groups tend to have different priors of preference choice. For example, job seekers around 22 years of old are more likely to relocate compared to older job seekers. To accommodate such differences in user segments, we propose to divide users in different segments and learn a multinomial regression for each segment. The segment could be based on the user's age, gender, seniority, region and so on. We further extend it with a hierarchical Bayesian framework to address the problem of data sparsity for those small segments. With this framework, different segments learn from each other by sharing the prior of the regression model. Detailed mathematical parameter inference steps are derived with the variational Bayesian algorithm. Items that would hurt the user satisfaction are filtered out in the recommendation stage.

While the framework we propose is general to any downside dimension in any domain, we apply it to the location dimension in the job domain in this paper. In other words, the model aims to avoid recommending jobs in locations where the job seeker would not want to work. In the experiments, we first evaluate the performance of the user latent preference model itself with traditional classification IR metrics. We then demonstrate the effectiveness of leveraging the user latent preference in recommender systems. The model was evaluated with both an offline anonymous job application dataset and real-world job seekers on LinkedIn. Experiments show that the user latent preference model helps to improve the VPI (views per impression) and API (applications per impression) metrics significantly. At the same time, the absolute number of applications and views remain stable in spite of fewer impressions. Such performance follows our intuition that the user latent preference model achieves better downside management which in turn results in higher user satisfaction. The major contributions of this paper include the following:

- Propose and study the problem of downside management in the field of recommender systems.
- Design the **User Latent Preference Model** to tackle the problem and leverage it in recommender systems. Propose to use the multinomial regression as the core model and extend it with a hierarchical Bayesian framework. Derive detailed parameter inference steps based on the variational Bayesian algorithm.
- Evaluate the model with both offline framework and online A/B testing on LinkedIn. Demonstrate its effect in achieving better downside management of recommender systems.

2. RELATED WORK

A major task of the recommender system is to present recommendations to the user. The task is usually conducted by first predicting a user's ratings for each item and then ranking all items in the descending order. There are two major recommendation approaches: content-based filtering and collaborative filtering. Content-based filtering [17, 22] assumes that descriptive features of an item indicate a user's preferences. Thus, a recommender system makes a decision for a user based on the descriptive features of other items the user likes or dislikes. Usually, the system recommends items that are similar to what the user liked before. Collaborative filtering [12, 24, 13, 16, 26, 21, 10] on the other hand assumes that users with similar tastes on some items may also have similar preferences on other items. Thus, the main idea is to use the behavior history from other like-minded users to provide the current user with good recommendations. Research on collaborative filtering algorithms reached a peak due to the 1 million dollar Netflix movie recommendation competition [4]. Factorization-based collaborative filtering approaches [7, 14, 27, 23], such as regularized Singular Value Decomposition, performed well on this competition, possibly better than Netflix's own well-tuned Pearson correlation coefficient algorithm. A common characteristic of these models is the introduction of user latent factors or/and item latent factors to solve the data sparsity issue.

Context-aware recommender systems [1, 8, 19, 25, 2, 11, 15] has become a hot topic in the research field recently. Most work focuses on using user contextual information or latent tastes to improve the upside management. For example, Weston et.al [30] proposed an advanced matrix factorization model to incorporate user's latent tastes. Hariri et. al [11] proposed a unified probabilistic model to integrate the user profile, item representations, and contextual information. They demonstrated the effectiveness of their model in the domain of article and music recommendation where tags were considered as contextual information. Zhang et. al [31] proposed the Explicit Factor Model (EFM) to generate explainable recommendations, meanwhile keeping a high prediction accuracy. Nguyen et.al [18] studied Gaussian Process Factorization Machines (GPFM) for context-aware recommendations using Gaussian processes. Different from this work, we leverage the user latent preference information to achieve better downside management.

Downside management has been studied in recent work of recommender systems. In [29], Wang et. al studied the influence of recommending jobs to users at the right time. They proposed to use a hierarchical proportional hazards model to push recommendations to a user only if the probability of a user applying to a job at the current time is higher than a threshold. In [27], Wang and Zhang proposed the concept of *utility* in the field of recommender system and explored to optimize the user's utility in the e-commerce domain. In [28], Wang and Zhang further studied the effect of finding the right time to push recommendations in the e-commerce domain. They proposed an opportunity model to discover the best opportunity to push recommendations to optimize for the user satisfaction. In this paper, we propose a more general framework for downside management and show the effectiveness of the model in finding the right location to recommend jobs. The framework is general which could be applied to any existing state-of-art recommender systems.

3. USER LATENT PREFERENCE MODEL

3.1 Problem Definition

In this paper, we aim to answer the following questions: 1) How do we discover the user's latent preference(s) 2) How do we leverage it for better downside management? The following notations are used in the paper.

- $u = 1, 2, ..., U$: the index of the user.
- $j = 1, 2, ..., J$: the index of the item.
- $m = 1, 2, ..., M$: the index of the segment for a user. A segment for a user could be determined by his age, gender, region, so on and so forth.
- $D = \{D_1, ..., D_m, ..., D_M\}$: The observed data of all segments from all users.
- $D_m = \{y_{m,i}, \mathbf{x_{m,i}}\}$: A set of observed data associated with segment m. Each segment m has N_m data observations from all users in that segment. Each observation $i = 1, ..., N_m$ in segment m is associated with two parts: the preference label $y_{m,i}$ and the feature vector $\mathbf{x_{m,i}}$.
- $y_{m,i}$: the preference label with the ith observation in segment m. It could be a binary choice (staying at the current location or not) or a multi-class choice (work in IT industry, financing industry, education industry, etc.). The index of the candidate choice is $k = 1, 2, ..., K$.
- $\mathbf{x_{m,i}}$: the d-dimensional vector of features associated with the ith observation in segment m. Features include both static demographic features and dynamic behavior features.

The goal of the model is to predict the probability that user u has the latent preference $y_{m,i} = k$, given that the user belongs to segment m and his feature vector is $\mathbf{x_{m,i}}$.

3.2 Review of Multinomial Regression

Before describing the hierarchical framework that we propose, we first briefly review the basics of multinomial regression.

Multinomial regression is widely used to solve multi-class classification problems with decent performance, e.g. predicting the probability of a user having the latent preference $y_{m,i} = k$ given the user feature vector $\mathbf{x_{m,i}}$. We consider a user's latent preference as a process to choose exactly one candidate at a time. The probability could be estimated based on all available features as follows:

$$p(y_{m,i} = k|\theta) = \frac{exp\{\theta_{\mathbf{k}}^{\mathbf{T}}\mathbf{x_{m,i}}\}}{\sum_{k'} exp\{\theta_{\mathbf{k'}}^{\mathbf{T}}\mathbf{x_{m,i}}\}}$$

where $\theta = \theta_1, ..., \theta_K$ is the model parameter to be learned from the training data. In a basic multinomial regression, all users share the same parameter θ.

Assuming that the prior distribution of each model parameter is a Gaussian centered on zero, the optimal parameters θ can be learned from the training data using the maximum a posteriori probability (MAP) estimation. The multinomial regression model reduces to logistic regression when the number of classes is 2 (positive and negative).

3.3 Model Extension with Bayesian Framework

In this paper we adopt multinomial regression as the core model for user latent preference model and use it to estimate $p(y_{m,i} = k)$. Users in different segments may have different priors for latent preferences. For example, young people tend to relocate more than old people. People in big cities tend to relocate less than those in small cities. Thus we propose to learn one regression model per user segment. Without loss of generality, we do not specify how to segment users in this paper. It could be determined by domain experts or offline experiments.

In the real world, a small number of user segments often have more users while most segments have few users. To address the problem of data sparsity, we follow a common practice and extend the multinomial regression with a hierarchical Bayesian framework as illustrated in Figure 1. This framework helps segments with few observations by borrowing information from other segments through a common prior for parameters of multinomial regression.

For each segment m, θ_m is sampled from a Gaussian distribution: $\theta_m \sim N(\mu_\theta, \mathbf{\Sigma}_\theta)$. We denote $\phi = (\mu_\theta, \mathbf{\Sigma}_\theta)$. For each ith observation in segment m with its observed features $\mathbf{x_{m,i}}$, its latent preference model $y_{m,i}$ is sampled from the multinomial regression model,

$$p(y_{m,i} = k|\theta_m) = \frac{exp\{\theta_{\mathbf{m,k}}^{\mathbf{T}}\mathbf{x_{m,i}}\}}{\sum_{k'} exp\{\theta_{\mathbf{m,k'}}^{\mathbf{T}}\mathbf{x_{m,i}}\}}.$$

Consider that data D consists of a series of observations from all segments. The latent preferences in the observations are generated by using a set of hidden variables $\theta = \{\theta_1, \theta_2 ..., \theta_M\}$. Note that the core model does not need to be multinomial regression. Other suitable models such as the proportional hazards model [29] could be leveraged here as well. θ_m contains all parameters in the core model. The data likelihood can be written as a function of $\phi = (\mu_\theta, \mathbf{\Sigma}_\theta)$. We use y_m to represent $\{y_{m,1}, ..., y_{m,i}, ..., y_{m,N_m}\}$, i.e., preference observations in segment m. Assuming that the data is independent identically distributed, we can present the

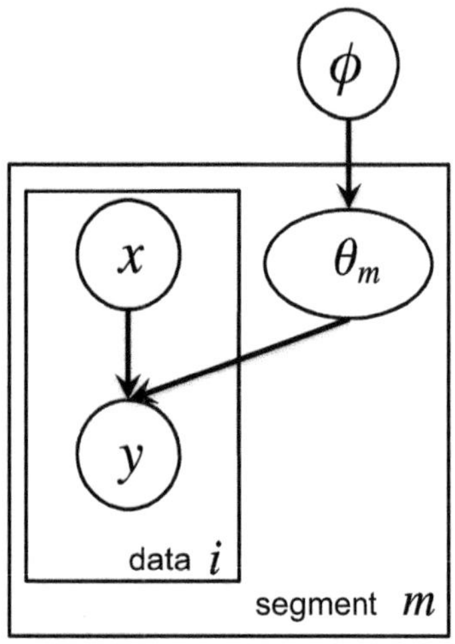

Figure 1: Illustration of dependencies of variables in the hierarchical Bayesian regression model. It shows the ith observation of segment m. $y_{m,i}$ is the label which is dependent on the regression model θ_m of segment m, as well as the observed features $\mathbf{x_{m,i}}$ of this user. Each segment m has its own parameters of multinomial regression θ_m. Models of each segment share information through the prior, $\phi = (\mu_\theta, \mathbf{\Sigma}_\theta)$.

data likelihood as

$$p(D|\phi) = \prod_{m=1}^{M} p(y_m|\phi) = \prod_{m=1}^{M} \int p(\theta_m, y_m|\phi) d\theta_m. \quad (1)$$

3.4 Parameter Inference with the Variational Bayesian Method

There is no closed-form solution for the estimation of model parameters. We follow the variational Bayesian method[3] for constrained (approximate) optimization to derive an iterative process to find an approximate solution. Maximizing the likelihood in Equation 1 is equivalent to maximizing the log likelihood $L(\phi)$,

$$L(\phi) = \ln p(D|\phi) = \sum_{m=1}^{M} \ln p(y_m|\phi) = \sum_{m=1}^{M} \ln \int p(\theta_m, y_m|\phi) \mathrm{d}\theta_m.$$

We can simplify the problem by introducing an auxiliary distribution $q(\theta_m)$ for each hidden variable θ_m [3]. In the variational approach, we constrain $q(\theta_m)$ to be a particular tractable form for computational efficiency. In particular, we assume that $q(\theta_m) = N(\mu_{\theta_m}, \Sigma_{\theta_m})$.

$$\begin{aligned} L(\phi) &= \sum_{m=1}^{M} \ln p(y_m|\phi) \\ &= \sum_{m=1}^{M} \ln \int q(\theta_m) \frac{p(\theta_m, y_m|\phi)}{q(\theta_m)} \mathrm{d}\theta_m \\ &\geq \sum_{m=1}^{M} \int q(\theta_m) \ln \frac{p(\theta_m, y_m|\phi)}{q(\theta_m)} \mathrm{d}\theta_m \\ &\equiv \boldsymbol{F}(q(\theta_1), ..., q(\theta_M), \phi). \end{aligned} \quad (2)$$

Note that $\boldsymbol{F}(q(\theta_1), ..., q(\theta_M), \phi)$ is the lower bound of $L(\phi)$. The process to infer parameters is to iterate between the E-step and M-step until convergence. In particular, the E step maximizes $\boldsymbol{F}(q(\theta_1), ..., q(\theta_M), \phi)$ with respect to $q(\theta_m)$ given the current parameter setting ϕ. The M step maximizes $\boldsymbol{F}(q(\theta_1), ..., q(\theta_M), \phi)$ with respect to ϕ given $q(\theta_m)$ learnt from the E step. Here are the detailed mathematical representation:

E step:

$$q(\theta_m) \leftarrow \arg\max_{q(\theta_m)} \boldsymbol{F}(q(\theta_1), ..., q(\theta_M), \phi), \forall m \in \{1, ..., M\} \quad (3)$$

M step:

$$\phi \leftarrow \arg\max_{\phi} \boldsymbol{F}(q(\theta_1), ..., q(\theta_M), \phi) \quad (4)$$

3.4.1 E-Step

In the **E-step**, maximizing $\boldsymbol{F}(q(\theta_1), ..., q(\theta_M), \phi)$ is equivalent to minimizing the following quantity to find each distribution $q(\theta_m)$.

$$\begin{aligned} q(\theta_m) &\leftarrow \arg\min_{q(\theta_m)} \int q(\theta_m) \ln \frac{q(\theta_m)}{p(\theta_m, y_m|\phi)} \mathrm{d}\theta_m \\ &= \arg\min_{q(\theta_m)} \int q(\theta_m) \ln \frac{q(\theta_m)}{p(\theta_m|\phi)} \mathrm{d}\theta_m - \int q(\theta_m) \ln p(y_m|\theta_m) \mathrm{d} \\ &= \arg\min_{q(\theta_m)} KL[q(\theta_m)||p(\theta_m|\phi)] - \int q(\theta_m) \ln p(y_m|\theta_m) \mathrm{d}\theta_m. \end{aligned} \quad (5)$$

The first part in Equation 5 is the KL-divergence between the posterior distribution $q(\theta_m)$ and the prior distribution $p(\theta_m|\phi)$. The KL-divergence between two Gaussian distributions is

$$\begin{aligned} KL[q(\theta_m)||p(\theta_m|\phi)] =& \frac{1}{2}[tr(\Sigma_\theta^{-1}\Sigma_{\theta_m}) + (\mu_\theta - \mu_{\theta_m})^T \Sigma_\theta^{-1} (\mu_\theta - \mu_{\theta} \\ & - \ln(\frac{\det \Sigma_{\theta_m}}{\det \Sigma_\theta}) - d]. \end{aligned}$$

The second part in Equation 5 is to maximize the likelihood of $y_m = \{y_{m,1}, ..., y_{m,i}, ..., y_{m,N_m}\}$ with the current θ_m,

$$\begin{aligned} & \sum_{i=1}^{N_m} \int q(\theta_m) \ln p(y_{m,i} = k|\theta_m) \mathrm{d}\theta_m \quad (6) \\ &= \sum_{i=1}^{N_m} [E(\theta_{m,k})^T \mathbf{x_{m,i}} - E(ln \sum_{k'} exp(\theta_{m,k'}^T \mathbf{x_{m,i}}))]. \end{aligned}$$

The expectation $E(\theta_{m,k})$ in the above equation is $\mu_{\theta_{m,k}}$. There is no closed form solution for the expectation $\delta = E(ln \sum_{k'} exp(\theta_{m,k'}^T \mathbf{x_{m,i}}))$. The moment generating function for the multivariate normal distribution is

$$E[exp(\theta_{m,k'}^T \mathbf{x_{m,i}})] = exp(\mu_{\theta_{m,k'}}^T \mathbf{x_{m,i}} + \frac{1}{2} \mathbf{x_{m,i}}^T \Sigma_{\theta_{m,k'}} \mathbf{x_{m,i}}). \quad (7)$$

By using this function, we get the upper bound of δ with the Taylor expansion as in the following equation,

$$E(ln \sum_{k'} exp(\theta_{m,k'}^T \mathbf{x_{m,i}})) \tag{8}$$
$$\leqslant \gamma \sum_{k'} exp(\mu_{\theta_{m,k'}}^T \mathbf{x_{m,i}} + \frac{1}{2} \mathbf{x_{m,i}}^T \Sigma_{\theta_{m,k'}} \mathbf{x_{m,i}}) - log(\gamma) - 1,$$

for every $\gamma \in \mathbb{R}^K$. Such approximation is widely used in literature [5] for other inference problems.

We can combine the above derivations with Equation 5, then find $q(\theta_m)$ with the conjugate gradient descent method.

3.4.2 M-Step

In the **M-step**, the goal is to maximize $\boldsymbol{F}(q(\theta_1), ..., q(\theta_M), \phi)$ in Equation 2 with respect to ϕ given all $q(\theta_m)$. It is same as to maximize the following quantity:

$$\phi \leftarrow \arg\max_{\phi} \sum_{m=1}^{M} \int q(\theta_m) \ln p(\theta_m, y_m|\phi) d\theta_m. \tag{9}$$

We derive the closed-form solution for μ_θ and Σ_θ:

$$(\mu_\theta, \Sigma_\theta) \leftarrow \arg\max_{\mu_\theta, \Sigma_\theta} \sum_{m=1}^{M} \int q(\theta_m) \ln p(\theta_m|\mu_\theta, \Sigma_\theta) d\theta_m$$
$$= \arg\max_{\mu_\theta, \Sigma_\theta} \sum_{m=1}^{M} \ln \frac{1}{\sqrt{(2\pi)^k |\Sigma_\theta|}} - \frac{1}{2} E[(\theta_m - \mu_\theta)^T \Sigma_\theta^{-1} (\theta_m - \mu_\theta)]. \tag{10}$$

By setting the first derivative to zero, we have the following closed form:

$$\mu_\theta = \frac{\sum_m^M \mu_{\theta_m}}{M}$$
$$\Sigma_\theta = \frac{\sum_m^M [\Sigma_{\theta_m} + (\mu_{\theta_m} - \mu_\theta)(\mu_{\theta_m} - \mu_\theta)^T]}{M}.$$

4. USAGE OF THE USER LATENT PREFERENCE MODEL

Let us denote $p(i,j)$ as the joint probability of user i accepting item j. It considers both the match from an existing recommender system and the prediction of the user's latent preference. $p(i,j)$ could be estimated by the following equation:

$$p(i,j) = p_{rec}(i,j) \sum_k [p(y_{m,i} = k) I_{j \in S(i,k)}]. \tag{11}$$

p_{rec} is the matching probability between user i and item j, which could be predicted by any state-of-art recommender systems. $p(y_{m,i} = k)$ is the probability of user i having a specific latent preference k. It is predicted by the user latent preference model, as shown in Equation 12. $S(i,k)$ contains all items that match with the user's preference. For example, if user i is predicted to seek jobs in his local area, $S(i, k = local)$ contains all local jobs. Note that the candidates of a user's preference $k = 1, 2, ..., K$ are all exclusive and item j can only belong to one set $S(i,k)$. I_* is a indicator function which equals to 1 if $*$ is true.

Table 1: The utility set of the recommender system. There are four types of utilities, depending on whether the system recommends the item to the user and whether the user accepts the item.

	show:Y	show:N
accept:Y	u_{TP}	u_{FN}
accept:N	u_{FP}	u_{TN}

$$p(y_{m,i} = k) = E[\frac{exp\{\theta_{\mathbf{k}}^{\mathbf{T}} \mathbf{x_{m,i}}\}}{\sum_{k'} exp\{\theta_{\mathbf{k'}}^{\mathbf{T}} \mathbf{x_{m,i}}\}}] \tag{12}$$
$$E[exp\{\theta_{\mathbf{k}}^{\mathbf{T}} \mathbf{x_{m,i}}\}] = exp\{\mu_{\theta_k}^T \mathbf{x_{m,i}} + \frac{1}{2} \mathbf{x_{m,i}}^T \Sigma_{\theta_k} \mathbf{x_{m,i}}\}.$$

The recommender systems aim to send recommendations to a user to increase user satisfaction. While a good recommendation (upside item) would increase the user satisfaction, a bad recommendation (downside item) would decrease the user satisfaction. Let us consider the utility for each type of recommendation as shown in Table 1. u_{TP} is the utility for a good recommendation that the user accepts. u_{FP} is the utility for a bad recommendation that the user doesn't accept. u_{FN} is the utility for missing a recommendation that the user would accept. u_{TN} is the utility of avoiding a bad recommendation. The utility for each type of recommendations (u_{TP}, u_{FP}, u_{FN}, and u_{TN}) could be set by domain experts in real-world applications. The user i's satisfaction of a recommendation set $utility_i$ is calculated by Equation 13.

$$utility_i = \sum (u_{TP} I_{show,accept} + u_{FP} I_{show,\bar{accept}} + u_{FN} I_{\bar{show},accept} + u_{TN} I_{\bar{show},\bar{accept}}). \tag{13}$$

To achieve a better user satisfaction/utility, the system with a filtering component should send recommendations only if the expected utility of an item is higher than zero. In other words, the system should send recommendations if the joint probability of a user accepting the item $p(i,j)$ is higher than the threshold α. The filtering threshold α is automatically determined by the utility set, which is a common practice as in [28, 29, 9]:

$$\alpha = \frac{u_{FP} - u_{TN}}{u_{FP} - u_{TN} + u_{FN} - u_{TP}}. \tag{14}$$

5. EVALUATION OF THE USER LATENT PREFERENCE MODEL

As described before, the user latent preference model could be applied to a single dimension in any domain. Without loss of generality, we evaluate it in the location dimension in the job domain in the experiment. We observe that some users have a strong preference of being a local user and would complain about receiving non-local job recommendations, and vice versa. *Local jobs* are defined as jobs within 50 miles of the user's current location (determined by his postal code). We treat *local users* as positive labels and *non-local users* as negative labels.

We first list all research questions, followed by the experimental setup, data analysis and performance analysis. Our major research questions for evaluating the user latent preference model include:

- How accurate is the prediction of the user latent preference model? What's the percentage of local users that the model could cover?

- How is the performance comparison for different user segments? Does the hierarchical Bayesian regression model have a better prediction power than the basic regression model?

5.1 Evaluation Metrics

As mentioned before, we label a user as the positive data if the user intends to stay at the current location and otherwise negative. It naturally reduces to a binary classification task. Traditional classification metrics are used to evaluate the prediction power of the user latent preference model: precision, recall and F1 measure. In the following equation, TP, FP and FN correspond to *true positive*, *false positive* and *false negative* respectively.

$$precision = \frac{TP}{TP + FP}$$

$$recall = \frac{TP}{TP + FN}$$

$$F1 = \frac{2}{\frac{1}{precision} + \frac{1}{recall}}$$

5.2 Models to Compare

In our experiments, we compare the basic regression model, as well as the hierarchical regression model with different segments. As shown in Table 2, *M-one* is the basic multinomial regression model with no segments. Other models segment users based on different features.

All models use the same set of features for the core regression model. Features include both the user static information (age, gender, region, current job, current industry, etc.) and the dynamic behavior information (# of local job applications in last month, # of non-local job applications in last month, last profile modification time, etc.). Extensive feature engineering could be explored to improve the model performance, which is beyond the scope of this paper.

5.3 Dataset

As mentioned earlier in the paper, we apply our model in the context of a job recommender system and use a real-world dataset from LinkedIn to evaluate our models. In order to build the user latent preference model, we random sampled from the job application data of United States users for three months from Jan 2014 to March 2014. The sample data contains around 530k users that applied to a reasonable number of jobs in that period [1]. If all jobs that a user applied to are local jobs, we label the user as a local user, and otherwise as a non-local user. In the dataset, 57.22% of users are labeled as local users (positive data) while 42.78% users are labeled as users that are willing to relocate (negative data). 10-cross validation is performed in the experiments. A significance level of 0.05 with the paired two-tailed t-test is used to compare two models.

We further analyze the data by dividing users into different segments (age, gender, region). In Figure 2, the bar plots the percentage of users in each segments. It shows that the data sparsity issue exists (in both age and region dimension). In addition, the line plots the percentage of local users, who only applied to local jobs. It indicates that users in different segments have different priors in relocating. This justifies our motivation for building a hierarchical Bayesian regression model that can 1) let different segments learn from each other to address the problem of data sparsity. 2) let each segment learn its own regression model based on users in the segment.

Some interesting observations include 1) Users around 22 years old are more likely to relocate. It follows the intuition that college graduates would like to change location when they apply for their first jobs. 2) The probability of staying in the same local area doesn't increase for older applicants. 3) Females are slightly more likely to stay in the same local area. 4) Applicants from the big cities/regions tend to stay in the same local area. Top 5 regions that users tend to be local users include San Francisco Bay Area, Greater New York City Area, Houston, Texas Area, Greater Denver Area, and Greater Seattle Area. 5) Applicants from small towns tend to relocate. Top regions that users tend to relocate usually associate with a university or college, including University of South Carolina, University of Wisconsin Madison, Syracuse university, Michigan State University and so on.

The findings from the LinkedIn job application data are consistent with results from demographic surveys [6]. 37% of American adults have never left their hometown, and 57% of American adults have never lived outside their home state. More educated individuals are more likely to have relocated during their lifetimes (77% of college graduates have changed communities at least once). People are most likely to move when they are young, and people from the midwest are less likely to move than those from the Western United States. People who have moved before are much more likely to relocate than those who have never moved. People with higher incomes are more likely to move for job opportunities, while lower income individuals cite different reasons for moving. The demographic data motivates our basic hypothesis that some people will not move under any circumstances, and these users should not be shown non-local job recommendations.

5.4 Performance Analysis

We evaluate the classification performance of different user latent preference models by treating the task as a classification task. We assume that the model predicts a user as a local user if the probability is higher than the classification threshold. We show the performance for different classification thresholds from 0.1 to 0.9. The left plot in Figure 3 shows the performance of the basic regression model *M-one*. It has decent performance in all metrics including precision, recall and F1. High precision ensures that we only filter out non-local jobs for local users. High recall ensures that we can discover most local users and achieve better downside management for these users. F1 metric balances the trade-off between the precision and recall metrics. As demonstrated in the right plot in Figure 3, it is clear that all hierarchical Bayesian regression models help to improve the precision performance significantly. As shown in Table 2, there are different ways of segmenting users. Among all models, *M-age* has the highest lift (5.82% for classification threshold 0.3) with 7 user segments. It is essential to choose the right user segments in the model. Models with too few segments

[1]Exact number is omitted for business concern

Table 2: **Different segmentation methods of the user latent preference model.**

Model	User segment	# of segments	Sample segments
M-one	none	1	N/A
M-age	age	7	<20 years old, 20-25 years old, 25-30 years old, ...
M-gender	gender	2	female, male
M-region	region	282	San Francisco bay area, Great New York area, ...
M-ageGender	(age, gender)	14	(<20 years old, female), ...
M-ageRegion	(age, region)	1974	(<20 years old, San Francisco bay area), ...
M-regionGender	(region, gender)	564	(San Francisco bay area, female), ...

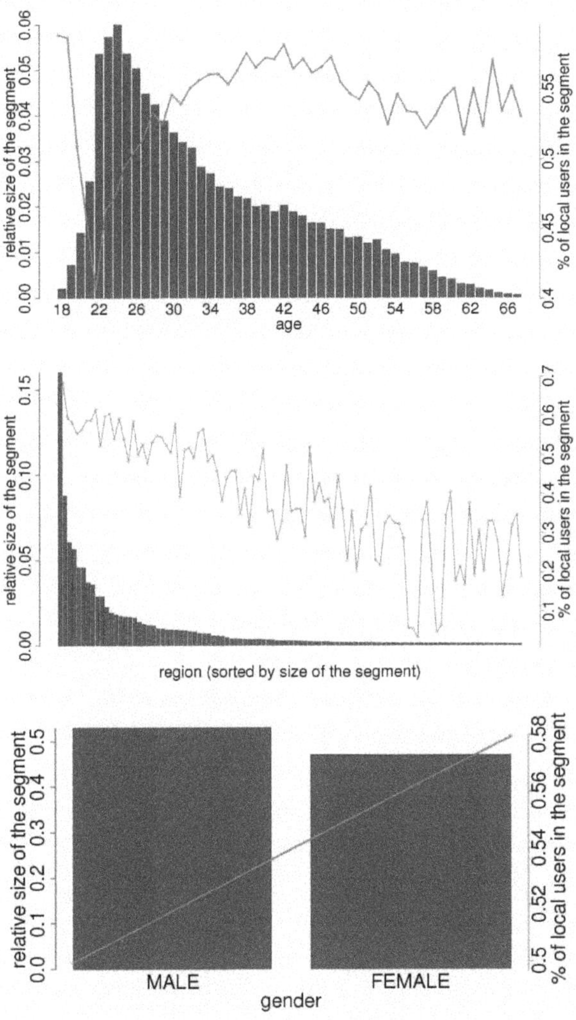

Figure 2: Data analysis of different user segments in the job domain. The bar plots the percentage of users in each segment with the left axis. The line plots the percentage of local users in each segment with the right axis. The three plots correspond to age segments, gender segments, and region segments respectively. Major observations include that 1) the data sparsity issue exists in some user segments 2) users in different segments have different priors in relocating.

(*M-gender*) or too many segments (*M-region, M-ageRegion, M-genderRegion, M-ageGender*) do not work as well as the *M-age* model.

6. EVALUATION OF THE RECOMMENDER SYSTEM

In this section, we incorporate the user latent preference model into the recommender system and evaluate its contribution in downside management. We first list all research questions that we intend to answer, followed by the experimental setup, and performance analysis. Major research questions include:

- Does it achieve higher user satisfaction by adding a filtering component to the basic recommender system?
- Could the user latent preference help to improve the downside management of recommender systems? Does it achieve even higher user satisfaction?
- How about using an extreme filter that filters out all non-local jobs for all users? Does it work as well? What's the contribution of using the prediction from the user latent preference model?

6.1 Models to Compare

In our offline and online experiments, we compare the following models. All models are trained with millions of job applications that were randomly sampled over months and tested with 17K users in the testing period. The threshold of the filtering component is determined by the utility set, as shown in Equation 14.

Baseline is the baseline recommender systems that select a set of items for the user, without considering the user latent preference. It could be any state-of-art recommendation model. We choose logistic regression here as an example. It is a common practice with decent performance and low time complexity [20, 29, 28]. The baseline recommender system does not have a filtering component. It always sends a set of top K items to each user (K is set to be 5). When we build the baseline logistic regression model, we leverage basic features including similarity-related features between the user profile (including the user's working experience, education information, etc) and the job information (including the job's title, description, etc), the user behavior features, and so on. Features include location-related features as well, such as the transition probability from the user's location to the job's location and so on.

Baseline.F applies a filter on the recommendation set from *Baseline* based on the recommendation probability $p_{rec}(i, j)$ without considering the user's latent preference.

Baseline+Latent.F applies a filter on the recommendation set based on the joint probability $p(i, j)$ which considers the user latent relocation preference. As a result, the model recommends local jobs to users that prefer to stay in the local area and non-local jobs to other users.

Baseline+AllLocal.F applies a filter on the recommendation set based on the joint probability $p(i, j)$. It assumes that all users are local users. In other words, it estimates $p(y_{m,i} = local) = 1$ for all users. As a result, the model recommends local jobs to all users.

6.2 Offline Testing Setup

As we discussed in Section 4, the user satisfaction is affected by both good recommendations and bad recommendations. The corresponding evaluation metric is the average utility which truly reflects the user satisfaction. Assume that there are U users to send recommendations in the testing period. The average utility/user satisfaction *utility* can be calculated as following: $utility = \frac{\sum_{i=1}^{U} utility_i}{U}$.

Unlike traditional metrics such as the number of applications/views, the utility metric considers both the positive effect of *good* recommendations and the negative effect of *bad* recommendations. The higher the utility, the better the model.

Table 3: Average utility of recommendations in the offline scenario. There are 17K users in the test dataset who applied to 2.12 jobs on average. *Rec coverage* is the percentage of users that are recommended at least one item. *Rec count* is the average number of unique recommendations that are pushed to each user.

utility set 1 u_{TP} = 2, u_{FN} = -1 u_{FP} = -1, u_{TN} = 0 Threshold = 0.25				
Model	Baseline	Baseline.F	Baseline+Latent.F	Baseline+AllLocal.F
Utility	0.590	1.300	**1.895**	1.235
Rec coverage	100%	98.4%	95.0%	74.8%
Rec count	5	4.282	3.488	2.852
utility set 2 u_{TP} = 2, u_{FN} = -1 u_{FP} = -2, u_{TN} = 0 Threshold = 0.4				
Model	Baseline	Baseline.F	Baseline+Latent.F	Baseline+AllLocal.F
Utility	-2.479	-0.206	**1.039**	0.500
Rec coverage	100%	96.6%	88.9%	74.2%
Rec count	5	3.882	2.969	2.831
utility set 3 u_{TP} = 2, u_{FN} = -2 u_{FP} = -1, u_{TN} = 0 Threshold = 0.2				
Model	Baseline	Baseline.F	Baseline+Latent.F	Baseline+AllLocal.F
Utility	0.393	0.951	**1.460**	0.486
Rec coverage	100%	99.0%	96.3%	75.6%
Rec count	5	4.460	3.729	2.854

6.3 Online A/B Testing Setup

In the online A/B testing, we evaluate the performance of recommender systems with real-world users on LinkedIn. We randomly select 5% United States users [2] that visit LinkedIn for each model and present the corresponding recommendations to each user group. The difference of the performance between two user buckets are reported in the performance analysis. A significance level of 0.05 with the paired two-tailed t-test is used to compare two models. We let each model to run for one week to burn in the novelty effect (active job seekers tend to apply to any new jobs they see due to a change in the recommendation model) and start the comparison after that.

In the LinkedIn product, summaries of job vacancy postings are shown to the user. We call this an **impression** (each job vacancy summary shown to the user is considered to be impressed). Job seekers can open a new page to view the entire job description, which we call as a **view** action. In addition, users will apply to the job if they wish to be considered for the position, which we call as an **apply** action. We report metrics that measure the model's performance in both upside management and downside management: the number of impressions, the number of views and applications, API ($\frac{\#\ of\ applications}{\#\ of\ impressions}$), and VPI ($\frac{\#\ of\ views}{\#\ of\ impressions}$).

[2]By the end of 2014, there are more than 111 million members in United States in LinkedIn.

6.4 Performance Analysis

6.4.1 *Offline Experiments*

We first evaluate all models in the offline scenario. The testing data include 17K users who applied to 2.12 jobs on average. Three different sets of utilities are tested, as shown in Table 3. Each set reflects different scenarios (depending on a user's tolerance to bad recommendations) and it could be tuned by domain experts in real-world applications.

In the *first* utility set, the utility u_{TP} for a good recommendation that the user applies to is set to 2. When the system shows a job and the user does not apply to it, the utility u_{FP} is -1. The penalty u_{FN} for missing a good recommendation is set as -1. The resulting filtering threshold is 0.25. Model that applies a filter all perform better than the *Baseline* model without filtering. Among all three models that have a filtering component, both *Baseline + Latent.F* and *Baseline + AllLocal.F* perform better than the *Baseline.F* model by filtering out many downside items (i.e., jobs that are not in the user's preferred area). It follows our intuition that the probability $p(i, j)$ with latent preference is a stronger signal than the pure recommendation probability $p_{rec}(i, j)$. In addition, *Baseline + Latent.F* model still keeps potentially good jobs that a non-local user wants to apply to, which leads to a higher utility than *Baseline + AllLocal.F* model. Note that the average number of recommendations of *Baseline + Latent.F* is significantly higher than the *Baseline + AllLocal.F* model.

In the *second* utility set, the utility u_{FP} is set to -2, indicating that the user is less tolerant to downside items. Thus the threshold of recommending an item is higher, being 0.4. Not surprisingly, the *Rec coverage* of *Baseline + Latent.F* decreases than that in the first set of utility. It still performs the best among all four models.

In the *third* utility set, u_{FN} is set to -2. It is the penalty for not recommending a good job that would be applied by the user. *Baseline + Latent.F* model still achieves the highest utility among all models. *Baseline + AllLocal.F* has a lower utility since it misses some potentially good recommendations for non-local users.

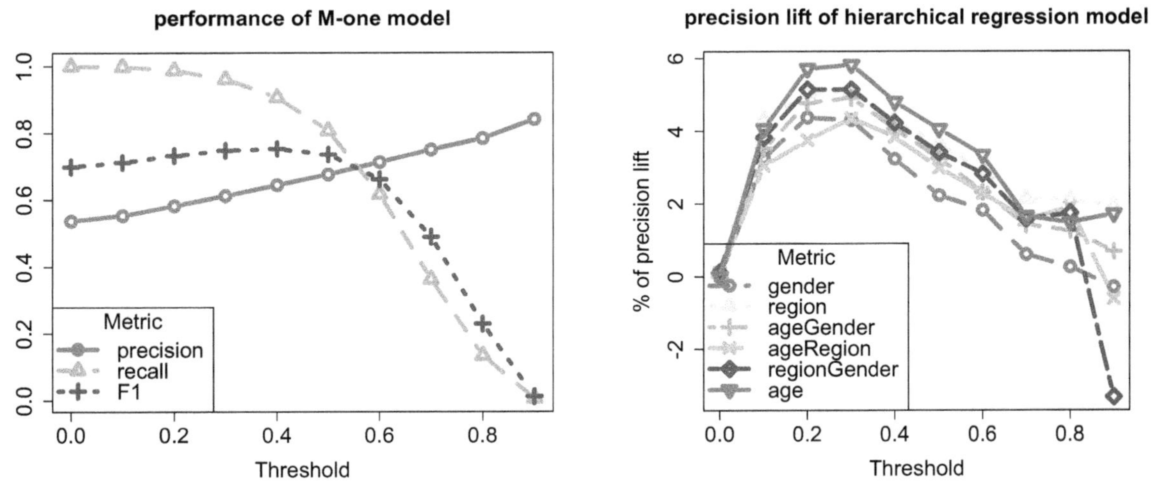

Figure 3: Performance of the user latent preference model in the classification task. The left plot shows the performance of the baseline multinomial regression in precision, recall and F1. The right plot shows the precision lift of hierarchical Bayesian regression models.

Table 4: The performance comparison of online A/B testing. The number shows the lift of the model. Numbers in bold are significantly better than the value in the corresponding baseline model. The absolute numbers are omitted for business concern.

Model	# of impressions	# of applications	# of views	API	VPI
Baseline+Latent.F vs. Baseline	**-11.1%**	+0.5%	-0.6%	**+12.9%**	**+11.7%**
Baseline+AllLocal.F vs. Baseline	**-18.4%**	**-10.4%**	**-6.1%**	**+9.7%**	**+15%**
Baseline+Latent.F vs. Baseline+AllLocal.F	**+8.9%**	**+12.1%**	**+5.8%**	+2.9%	-2.9%

6.4.2 Online Experiments

In the online A/B testing, the performance follows our intuition as shown in Table 4. *Baseline + Latent.F* model has a significantly better downside management than the *Baseline* model. In details, *Baseline + Latent.F* model shows less impressions to users. The corresponding API and VPI metrics increase significantly while the number of applications and views remain stable. It shows that downside items that are not interesting to users are removed from the recommendation set. The performance is consistent with that in offline experiments.

If we filter out non-local recommendations for all users, the performance of such model *Baseline+AllLocal.F* is shown in Table 4. As expected, it shows much fewer impressions. Although VPI and API increase significantly, the absolute number of applications and views drop. Such a model might filter out some good non-local recommendations for users who are willing to relocate. For example, recent college graduates would prefer to relocate to other cities for their first job. In this case, *Baseline+AllLocal.F* still recommends local jobs to these users. Yet the user latent preference model *Baseline + Latent.F* would treat these users as non-local users and recommend jobs in non-local areas.

For a real-world recommender system, one goal is to improve the upside management, which is reflected by the *# of applications* and *# of views* metrics. A good upside management helps users to discover items that they like, which saves users' time and effort. While good upside management lets users engage themselves with the system, it is equally important for a recommender system to have a good downside management. It aims to avoid showing those obviously terrible items to users. For example, if a user would like to stay in the San Francisco Bay Area, a good recommender system shouldn't recommend a job in the New York city even if the job is a perfect match. Good downside management is reflected in the high *API* and *VPI*. It makes recommendations more explainable and transparent to users, which in turn helps to increase the user satisfaction.

7. CONCLUSION AND FUTURE WORK

In this paper, we propose to develop the *user latent preference model* to predict the probability of a user having a specific preference. It is a general framework that could be applied to any existing recommender system in any domain (including job search, e-commerce, movie recommendations, etc.). The model uses multinomial regression to predict the user's preference among all candidates. We build a regression model for each user segment. In order to tackle the data sparsity issue, we further extend the model with the hierarchical Bayesian framework. The variational Bayesian inference algorithm helps to make the parameter estimation more computationally efficient. In the recommendation stage, we leverage the prediction of the user's latent preference to estimate the joint probability for a user accepting an item. We show the effectiveness of the user latent preference model in the context of recommending the right job at the right location. Both offline experiments and online A/B testing demonstrate that our proposed model has a better downside management, which leads to higher user satisfaction.

This is just the first step to tackle the downside management in recommender systems. In this paper, we propose to use multinomial regression as the core model in the user latent preference model. Other distributions or models could be explored for other dimensions. In addition, the current model predicts a user's latent preference in one dimension, such as time, location and so on. It would be interesting to explore how to integrate a user's latent preferences in multiple dimensions to provide better recommendations. Last but not least, the model could be evaluated in other domains to show its effectiveness in downside management.

8. REFERENCES

[1] G. Adomavicius and A. Tuzhilin. Context-aware recommender systems. In *Recommender systems handbook*, pages 217–253. Springer, 2011.

[2] L. Baltrunas and X. Amatriain. Towards time-dependant recommendation based on implicit feedback. In *Context-aware Recommender Systems Workshop at RecSys09*. ACM, 2009.

[3] M. Beal. *Variational algorithms for approximate Bayesian inference*. PhD thesis, University of London, 2003.

[4] J. Bennett and S. Lanning. The netflix prize. 2007.

[5] D. M. Blei and J. D. Lafferty. A correlated topic model of science. *The Annals of Applied Statistics*, pages 17–35, 2007.

[6] D. Cohn and R. Morin. Who Moves? Who Stays Put? Where's Home? Technical report, Dec 2008.

[7] P. Cremonesi, Y. Koren, and R. Turrin. Performance of recommender algorithms on top-n recommendation tasks. In *Proceedings of the fourth ACM RecSys 2010*, pages 39–46. ACM, 2010.

[8] L. Do and H. W. Lauw. Modeling contextual agreement in preferences. In *Proceedings of the 23rd International Conference on World Wide Web*, WWW '14, pages 315–326. International World Wide Web Conferences Steering Committee, 2014.

[9] C. Elkan. The foundations of cost-sensitive learning. In *Proceedings of the 17th IJCAI'01*, IJCAI'01, pages 973–978. Morgan Kaufmann Publishers Inc., 2001.

[10] N. Golbandi, Y. Koren, and R. Lempel. Adaptive bootstrapping of recommender systems using decision trees. In *Proceedings of the fourth ACM WSDM*, WSDM '11, pages 595–604. ACM, 2011.

[11] N. Hariri, B. Mobasher, and R. Burke. Query-driven context aware recommendation. In *Proceedings of the 7th ACM Conference on RecSys*, RecSys '13, pages 9–16, New York, NY, USA, 2013. ACM.

[12] J. L. Herlocker, J. A. Konstan, A. Borchers, and J. Riedl. An algorithmic framework for performing collaborative filtering. In *Proceedings of the 22nd annual international ACM SIGIR*, pages 230–237. ACM, 1999.

[13] R. Jin, L. Si, C. Zhai, and J. Callan. Collaborative filtering with decoupled models for preferences and ratings. In *Proceedings of the twelfth CIKM*, pages 309–316. ACM, 2003.

[14] Y. Koren. Factorization meets the neighborhood: a multifaceted collaborative filtering model. In *Proceeding of the 14th ACM SIGKDD international conference on Knowledge discovery and data mining*, KDD '08, pages 426–434. ACM, 2008.

[15] X. Liu and K. Aberer. Soco: A social network aided context-aware recommender system. In *Proceedings of the 22nd International Conference on World Wide Web*, WWW '13, pages 781–802. International World Wide Web Conferences Steering Committee, 2013.

[16] B. Marlin and R. S. Zemel. The multiple multiplicative factor model for collaborative filtering. In *Proceedings of the 21st ICML '04*, page 73. ACM, 2004.

[17] R. J. Mooney and L. Roy. Content-based book recommending using learning for text categorization. In *DL '00*, pages 195–204. ACM, 2000.

[18] T. V. Nguyen, A. Karatzoglou, and L. Baltrunas. Gaussian process factorization machines for context-aware recommendations. In *Proceedings of the 37th International ACM SIGIR Conference*, SIGIR '14, pages 63–72. ACM, 2014.

[19] U. Panniello, A. Tuzhilin, M. Gorgoglione, C. Palmisano, and A. Pedone. Experimental comparison of pre- vs. post-filtering approaches in context-aware recommender systems. In *Proceedings of the Third ACM Conference on RecSys*, RecSys '09, pages 265–268. ACM, 2009.

[20] D. Parra, A. Karatzoglou, X. Amatriain, and I. Yavuz. Implicit feedback recommendation via implicit-to-explicit ordinal logistic regression mapping. In *Proceedings of the CARS-2011*, 2011.

[21] D. Parra-Santander and P. Brusilovsky. Improving collaborative filtering in social tagging systems for the recommendation of scientific articles. *Web Intelligence and Intelligent Agent Technology*, 1:136–142, 2010.

[22] M. Pazzani, D. Billsus, S. Michalski, and J. Wnek. Learning and revising user profiles: The identification of interesting web sites. In *Machine Learning*, pages 313–331, 1997.

[23] E. Shmueli, A. Kagian, Y. Koren, and R. Lempel. Care to comment?: recommendations for commenting on news stories. In *Proceedings of the 21st WWW*, WWW '12, pages 429–438. ACM, 2012.

[24] L. Si and R. Jin. Flexible mixture model for collaborative filtering. In *Proceedings of ICML*, pages 704–711. AAAI Press, 2003.

[25] K. Verbert, N. Manouselis, X. Ochoa, M. Wolpers, H. Drachsler, I. Bosnic, and E. Duval. Context-aware recommender systems for learning: a survey and future challenges. *Learning Technologies, IEEE Transactions on*, 5(4):318–335, 2012.

[26] J. Wang, B. Sarwar, and N. Sundaresan. Utilizing related products for post-purchase recommendation in e-commerce. In *Proceedings of the fifth ACM conference on Recommender systems*, RecSys '11, pages 329–332. ACM, 2011.

[27] J. Wang and Y. Zhang. Utilizing marginal net utility for recommendation in e-commerce. In *Proceedings of the 34th international ACM SIGIR'11*, pages 1003–1012. ACM, 2011.

[28] J. Wang and Y. Zhang. Opportunity model for e-commerce recommendation: right product, right time. In *Proceedings of the 36th international ACM SIGIR Conference*, SIGIR '13. ACM, 2013.

[29] J. Wang, Y. Zhang, C. Posse, and A. Bhasin. Is it time for a career switch. In *Proceeding of the 22nd International Conference on World Wide Web*, WWW '13. ACM, 2013.

[30] J. Weston, R. J. Weiss, and H. Yee. Nonlinear latent factorization by embedding multiple user interests. In *Proceedings of the 7th ACM Conference on RecSys*, RecSys '13, pages 65–68. ACM, 2013.

[31] Y. Zhang, G. Lai, M. Zhang, Y. Zhang, Y. Liu, and S. Ma. Explicit factor models for explainable recommendation based on phrase-level sentiment analysis. In *Proceedings of the 37th International ACM SIGIR Conference*, SIGIR '14, pages 83–92. ACM, 2014.

The Role of Data Cap in Optimal Two-part Network Pricing

Xin Wang
University of Science and Technology of China
yixinxa@mail.ustc.edu.cn

Richard T. B. Ma
School of Computing, National University of Singapore
tbma@comp.nus.edu.sg

Yinlong Xu
University of Science and Technology of China
ylxu@ustc.edu.cn

ABSTRACT

Internet services are traditionally priced at flat rates; however, many Internet service providers (ISPs) have recently shifted towards two-part tariffs where a data cap is imposed to restrain data demand from heavy users and usage over the data cap is charged based on a per-unit fee. Although the two-part tariff could generally increase the revenue for ISPs and has been supported by the FCC chairman, the role of data cap and its revenue-optimal and welfare-optimal pricing structures are not well understood.

In this paper, we study the impact of data cap on the optimal two-part pricing schemes for congestion-prone service markets, e.g., broadband or cloud services. We model users' demand and preferences over pricing and congestion alternatives and derive the market share and congestion of service providers under a market equilibrium. Based on the equilibrium model, we characterize the two-part structures of the revenue-optimal and welfare-optimal pricing schemes. Our results reveal that 1) the data cap provides a mechanism for ISPs to transition from flat-rate to pay-as-you-go type of schemes, 2) with growing data demand and network capacity, the revenue-optimal pricing moves towards usage-based schemes with diminishing data caps, and 3) the structure of the welfare-optimal tariff comprises lower fees and data cap than those of the revenue-optimal counterpart, suggesting that regulators might want to promote usage-based pricing but regulate the per-unit fees. Our results could help providers design revenue-optimal pricing schemes and guide regulatory authorities to legislate desirable regulations.

Categories and Subject Descriptors

C.2.5 [**Computer-Communication Networks**]: Local and Wide-Area Networks—*Internet*; C.4 [**Performance of Systems**]: Modeling techniques

Keywords

Data Cap; Two-part Tariff; Revenue-optimal Pricing; Welfare-optimal Pricing

WWW 2015, May 18–22, 2015, Florence, Italy.
ACM 978-1-4503-3469-3/15/05.
http://dx.doi.org/10.1145/2736277.2741129.

1. INTRODUCTION

Traditionally, Internet service providers (ISPs) use flat-rate pricing [19] for network services, where users pay fixed monthly fees for unlimited data usage. Flat-rate pricing was widely adopted because it was easy for ISPs to implement and was preferred by users for its simplicity. However, with the rapid development and growing popularity of data intensity services, e.g., online video streaming and cloud-based applications, the Internet traffic keeps growing more than 50% per annum [13], which exposes some disadvantages of the flat-rate scheme. Because flat-rate does not count the users' data usage, "bandwidth hogs" [18] consume an unfair share of capacity and are subsidized by normal users, and ISPs cannot generate enough revenue to recoup their costs, especially for the mobile providers. As a consequence, most mobile LTE providers [17] and even broadband ISPs, e.g., Verizon [23] and AT&T [25], start to introduce a data cap and adopt a two-part tariff structure, a combination of flat-rate and usage-based pricing. Under such a two-part scheme, additional charges are imposed if a user's data demand exceeds the data cap and the exceeded amount is charged based on a per-unit fee.

Although prior work [5, 6, 8, 18] has shown that data-capped schemes could help ISPs generate higher revenue than that under the flat-rate pricing and the FCC chairman has recently backed usage-based pricing for broadband to penalize heavy Internet users [22], little is known about 1) the data cap's role and impact on a provider's optimal pricing structure, 2) the optimal two-part pricing structure and its dynamics under varying system parameters, e.g., the users' data values and demand, the capacity of providers and market competition, and 3) potential regulations on two-part pricing for protecting social welfare from monopoly providers. In this paper, we focus on a generic congestion-prone service market, e.g., mobile, broadband or cloud services, and study the data cap under two-part pricing schemes. Unlike physical commodities, the quality of network service is intricately influenced by a negative network effect (or network externality): the more users access the service simultaneously, the worse performance it provides. We model this service congestion as a function of providers' capacity and their data load. We characterize users by their demand and values on data usage, and analyze the market shares and congestion levels of the providers under varying pricing and market structures. Based on our model, we analyze the effect of data cap on the provider's optimal pricing structure and the resulting congestion and revenue. We also analyze and compare the revenue-optimal and welfare-optimal two-part schemes under varying system environments, and derive regulatory implications. Our main contributions and findings include the following.

- We model users' optimal data usages and preferences over various pricing schemes and exogenous levels of congestion.

We characterize the existence and uniqueness (Theorem 1) of a market equilibrium and show its monotonic dynamics (Theorem 2) under varying pricing and market structures.

- We analyze the impact of data cap on a provider's optimal pricing structure (Theorem 3) and find that data cap plays a transitional role between pay-as-you-go and flat-rate pricing and could increase the provider's revenue (Corollary 3).
- We characterize the dynamics of revenue-optimal two-part pricing (Theorem 4) under varying demand and values of users and capacities of providers. We find that with growing demand of users and capacity of providers, the structure of revenue-optimal solution moves closer to pay-as-you-go pricing with diminishing data cap, which provides a smooth transition from flat-rate to usage-based schemes. Although market competition drives pricing "cheaper", it does not necessarily change the structure of an optimal two-part tariff.
- We characterize the dynamics of welfare-optimal two-part pricing (Theorem 6) and find that welfare-optimal pricing imposes stricter data cap but lower fees than its revenue-optimal counterpart (Theorem 5). Our result implies that, to protect social welfare, regulators might want to encourage the use of two-part pricing with a limited data cap, while regulating the per-unit fee of the usage-based component.

We believe that our work provides new insights into the role of data cap in the optimal structure of two-part tariff. Our results could help service providers design revenue-optimal pricing schemes and guide regulatory authorities to legislate desirable regulations. The rest of this paper is organized as follows. Section 2 reviews related work. Section 3 models the behavior of users and characterizes the market equilibrium under providers' two-part pricing schemes. We analyze the impact of data cap and the revenue-optimal pricing in Section 4, and study the welfare-optimal pricing in Section 5, respectively. We draw some conclusions in Section 6.

2. RELATED WORK

As the demarcation between the lump-sum and usage-based fees, data cap plays a crucial role in the two-part tariff structures. From the perspective of economic theory, prior work [5–8, 18] demonstrated that data-capped schemes can increase providers' revenue compared with the traditional flat-rate pricing [19]. Odlyzko *et al.* [20] showed that ISPs could also reduce network congestion by imposing data caps. Our analysis and results also confirm these observations. Furthermore, we focus on understanding the impact of data cap on the structures of revenue-optimal and welfare-optimal tariffs. The impact and optimal design of data cap have been empirically studied. In a qualitative study of households users under bandwidth caps, Chetty *et al.* [4] studied how the uncertainties of user types and demand would impact the setting of data cap and operator's revenue, and proposed new tools to help users manage their caps. Poularakis *et al.* [12] proposed a framework to calculate the optimal data caps and empirically evaluated the gains of ISPs when they adopt data caps based on traffic datasets. Unlike these efforts, our work adopts an analytical approach to characterize the desirable data cap and the optimal structure of the two-part pricing schemes.

More generally, there have been several works that study the usage-based Internet pricing. Hande *et al.* [10] characterized the economic loss due to ISPs' inability or unwillingness to price broadband access based on the time of use. Li *et al.* [14] studied the optimal price differentiation under complete and incomplete information. Basar *et al.* [1] and our related work [27] devised a revenue-maximizing pricing under varying user scale and network capacity. Shen *et al.* [24] investigated optimal nonlinear pricing policy design for a monopolistic service provider and showed that the introduction of nonlinear pricing provides a large profit improvement over linear pricing. In this paper, we focus on the two-part pricing. Besides optimizing the revenue from the provider's perspective, we also look into the welfare-optimal solution, through which we derive regulatory implications.

From a modeling perspective, Chander [2], Reitman [21], Ma [15] and our work all consider the service market with congestion externalities. Chander [2] studied the quality differentiation strategy of a monopoly provider and Reitman [21] studied a multi-provider price competition. Both of them modeled the market as a continuum of non-atomic users, each of which is characterized by a quality-sensitivity parameter. However, this one-dimensional model only applies for flat-rate pricing and the distribution of users was often assumed to be uniform for analytical tractability. To faithfully characterize the utility of users under two-part tiered pricing, we establish a novel two-dimensional model that describes users by their data demand and valuation on data usage. Furthermore, we analyze a class of distributions, including the uniform distribution, to understand the impact of user demand and value on the optimal pricing structures of the providers. Ma [15] also considered a two-dimensional user model; however, the author only focused on the pay-as-you-go pricing, a special case of the two-part tariff structure studied in this paper.

3. MODEL

3.1 Model of Users and Their Data Demand

We model each user by two orthogonal characteristics: her average value of per-unit data usage v and desirable data demand u. The user's data demand is measured by what she is billed, e.g., the number of bits transmitted or the amount of time being online.

We denote q as the congestion level of an ISP. Given the network congestion q, we denote $\rho(u,q)$ as the user's achievable demand.

Assumption 1. *$\rho(u,q)$: $\mathbb{R}_+ \times \mathbb{R}_+ \mapsto \mathbb{R}_+$ is a continuous function, increasing in u and decreasing in q. It has an upper-bound $\rho(u,0) = u$ and satisfies $\lim_{q\to+\infty} \rho(u,q) = 0$.*

Assumption 1 states that a user's achievable data demand equals its desirable demand u under no congestion and decreases monotonically when the network congestion q becomes more severe.

Beside network congestion, the user's actual data demand also depends on her ISP's pricing. We consider an ISP that adopts a two-part tiered pricing structure $\theta = (g, f, p)$, where g, f and p denote a data cap, a lump-sum service fee and a per-unit usage fee, respectively. Under this scheme, we denote $t(y,\theta)$ as the user's charge when y units of data are consumed, defined as

$$t(y,\theta) \triangleq f + p(y-g)^+.$$

Intuitively, if a user's usage is below the data cap g, the ISP only collects the lump-sum fee f; otherwise, extra charges are imposed on the usage above the data cap with the per-unit usage fee of p. This two-part structure is also a generalization of flat-rate, i.e., $g = +\infty$, and pay-as-you-go [15] pricing, i.e., $f = 0$ and $g = 0$.

We denote $\pi(y)$ as the user's utility when she consumes y units of data, defined by $\pi(y) \triangleq vy - t(y,\theta)$, i.e., the total traffic value minus the charge. We assume that users determine their optimal data demands that maximize their utilities. In other words, each user tries to solve the following optimization problem:

$$\begin{aligned} \text{Maximize} \quad & \pi(y) = vy - t(y,\theta) \\ \text{subject to} \quad & 0 \le y \le \rho(u,q), \end{aligned} \tag{1}$$

where a user's actual data demand is constrained by the achievable demand $\rho(u,q)$ under the network congestion q. We define $\phi = (u,v)$ as the type of the user and denote $y^*(\phi,\theta,q)$ as its optimal demand under ISP's pricing scheme θ and congestion q. Due to the space limitation, proofs of some lemmas, theorems and corollaries are omitted, but are available in the technical report [26].

Lemma 1. *Given an ISP with pricing scheme θ and congestion q, a user of type ϕ has a unique solution y^* that maximizes her utility. This optimal demand satisfies*

$$y^*(\phi,\theta,q) = \rho(u,q) - \big[\rho(u,q) - g\big]^+ \mathbf{1}_{\{v<p\}} \tag{2}$$

and is non-increasing in p and q and non-decreasing in u, v and g.

Lemma 1 states that if a user's achievable demand $\rho(u,q)$ is beyond the data cap g and her value v is lower than the extra per-unit usage fee p, she would avoid consuming extra usage above g which would result in reducing her utility, and thus the optimal data demand equals the data cap, i.e., $y^* = g$; otherwise, the optimal data demand equals her achievable demand, i.e., $y^* = \rho(u,q)$. Lemma 1 also intuitively states that the optimal demand would increase if the user's value v or desirable demand u increases, or the provider's per-unit fee p or data cap g or congestion q alleviates.

3.2 Users' Preferences over Providers

We consider a market that comprises of a set $\mathcal{N}$ of providers. We denote $\boldsymbol{\theta} = (\theta_i : i \in \mathcal{N})$ and $\mathbf{q} = (q_i : i \in \mathcal{N})$ as the pricing strategy and congestion vectors of the providers. We define $y_i^*(\phi) \triangleq y^*(\phi,\theta_i,q_i)$ as the optimal demand of user type ϕ when it chooses provider i. For any two providers $i,j \in \mathcal{N}$, we denote $i \succ_\phi j$ if users of type ϕ prefer i over j. We denote Φ_i as provider i's market share, i.e., the set of user types that choose to use i, defined as follows.

Definition 1. *We denote $\pi_i(y)$ as the user's utility function when using provider i. For any $i,j \in \mathcal{N}$, $i \succ_\phi j$ if and only if 1) $\pi_i(y_i^*(\phi)) > \pi_j(y_j^*(\phi))$ or 2) $\pi_i(y_i^*(\phi)) = \pi_j(y_j^*(\phi))$ and i is chosen over j by the user based on any arbitrary tie-breaking condition. Thus, the market share of provider i is defined as*

$$\Phi_i(\boldsymbol{\theta},\mathbf{q}) = \{\phi : i \succ_\phi j, \forall j \in \mathcal{N}\backslash\{i\}\}.$$

Definition 1 assumes that users would choose the provider that induces the highest utility under their optimal data demand. However, a user's best provider might still induce negative utility. Thus, we allow users not to use any of the providers if they all induce negative utility as follows.

Assumption 2. *There exists a dummy provider $0 \in \mathcal{N}$ with fees $f_0 = p_0 = 0$ and congestion $q_0 = +\infty$.*

Under Assumption 2, users can choose the dummy provider to obtain zero utility and $\Phi_0(\boldsymbol{\theta},\mathbf{q})$ conveniently defines the set of users that do not use any of the real providers. Next, we show how providers' market shares $\Phi_i(\boldsymbol{\theta},\mathbf{q})$ $(i \in \mathcal{N})$ vary when the set of competing providers $\mathcal{N}$ or the pricing strategies $\boldsymbol{\theta}$ change.

Lemma 2. *For a set $\mathcal{N}$ of providers, if two pricing strategies $\hat{\boldsymbol{\theta}}$ and $\boldsymbol{\theta}$ satisfy $\hat{g}_i \ge g_i, \hat{f}_i \le f_i, \hat{p}_i \le p_i$ for some $i \in \mathcal{N}$ and $\hat{\theta}_j = \theta_j$ for all $j \neq i$, we have*

$$\Phi_i(\boldsymbol{\theta},\mathbf{q}) \subseteq \Phi_i(\hat{\boldsymbol{\theta}},\mathbf{q}) \quad \text{and} \quad \Phi_j(\boldsymbol{\theta},\mathbf{q}) \supseteq \Phi_j(\hat{\boldsymbol{\theta}},\mathbf{q}),\ \forall j \neq i.$$

For two sets $\mathcal{N}$ and $\mathcal{N}'$ of providers, if $\mathcal{N} \subseteq \mathcal{N}'$ and $(\theta_i', q_i') = (\theta_i, q_i)$ for all $i \in \mathcal{N}$, we have $\Phi_i(\boldsymbol{\theta}',\mathbf{q}') \subseteq \Phi_i(\boldsymbol{\theta},\mathbf{q})$, $\forall\, i \in \mathcal{N}$.

Lemma 2 states that under fixed levels of congestion $\mathbf{q}$, the market share of a provider would increase if the provider reduces its fees f or p, or raises its data cap g, unilaterally. Meanwhile, the market share of any other provider will decrease. It implies that monopolistic providers could use fees and data cap to trade off its market share and revenue; while, oligopolistic providers could compete for market shares by decreasing their fees and increasing data caps. Lemma 2 also implies that bringing new providers into the market will intensify market competition and existing providers' market shares will decrease, because some of their users might switch to the new providers.

Lemma 2 holds under the condition of fixed network congestion. However, a provider's congestion level depends on its market share and the data usage of its users. We discuss the dynamics of network congestion and equilibrium in the next subsection.

3.3 Network Congestion and Equilibrium

We denote U and V as the maximum desirable data demand and maximum per-unit data value of all users. Thus, the domain of users is defined as $\Phi = [0,U]\times[0,V]$. We model the set of all users by the measure space (Φ,μ), where μ denotes a product measure

$$\mu(E_1 \times E_2) = \mu_u(E_1) \times \mu_v(E_2), \quad \forall\, E_1 \subseteq [0,U], E_2 \subseteq [0,V],$$

where μ_u and μ_v are two continuous measures, defined by

$$\begin{aligned} \mu_u\left((u_1,u_2]\right) &= F_u(u_2) - F_u(u_1), \forall u_1 \le u_2, \text{ and} \\ \mu_v\left((v_1,v_2]\right) &= F_v(v_2) - F_v(v_1), \forall v_1 \le v_2, \end{aligned}$$

for some non-decreasing distribution functions F_u and F_v.

Based on the distribution of users, we denote d_i as provider i's data load, i.e., the aggregate data demand of users of i, defined by

$$d_i = D(\Phi_i(\boldsymbol{\theta},\mathbf{q});\theta_i,q_i) \triangleq \int_{\Phi_i(\boldsymbol{\theta},\mathbf{q})} y_i^*(\phi,\theta_i,q_i)d\mu \tag{3}$$

On the one hand, given congestion levels $\mathbf{q}$, provider i has an induced data load $d_i = D(\Phi_i;\theta_i,q_i)$. On the other hand, the provider's congestion level q_i is influenced by its data load d_i. We denote c_i as provider i's capacity and model its congestion q_i as a function $q_i = Q_i(d_i,c_i)$ of its data load d_i and capacity c_i.

Assumption 3. *$Q_i(d_i,c_i) : \mathbb{R}_+^2 \mapsto \mathbb{R}_+$ is continuous, increasing in d_i, decreasing in c_i and satisfies $Q_i(0,c_i) = 0$.*

Different forms of the congestion function Q_i can be used to model the different technologies used by the provider. Assumption 3 implies that a provider i's congestion increases (decreases) when its data load d_i (capacity c_i) increases, and no congestion exists when no user consumes data from the provider.

We denote $Q_i^{-1}(q_i,c_i)$ as the inverse function of $Q_i(d_i,c_i)$ with respect to d_i, which defines the implied load under the capacity c_i and an observed congestion level of q_i. By Assumption 3, we know that $Q_i^{-1}(q_i,c_i)$ is continuous, increasing in both q_i and c_i, and satisfies $Q_i^{-1}(0,c_i) = 0$. We denote $\mathbf{c} = (c_i : i \in \mathcal{N})$ as the vector of the capacities of all the providers. When the providers make exogenous pricing decisions $\boldsymbol{\theta}$ and capacity planning decisions $\mathbf{c}$, the resulting congestion $\mathbf{q}$ of the providers can be determined endogenously when users choose their best providers. We define such a market equilibrium of the system as follows.

Definition 2. *For a set $\mathcal{N}$ of providers with any fixed pricing strategies $\boldsymbol{\theta}$ and capacities $\mathbf{c}$, $\mathbf{q}$ is an equilibrium if and only if*

$$q_i = Q_i\Big(D_i\big(\Phi_i(\boldsymbol{\theta},\mathbf{q});\theta_i,q_i\big),c_i\Big), \quad \forall i \in \mathcal{N}.$$

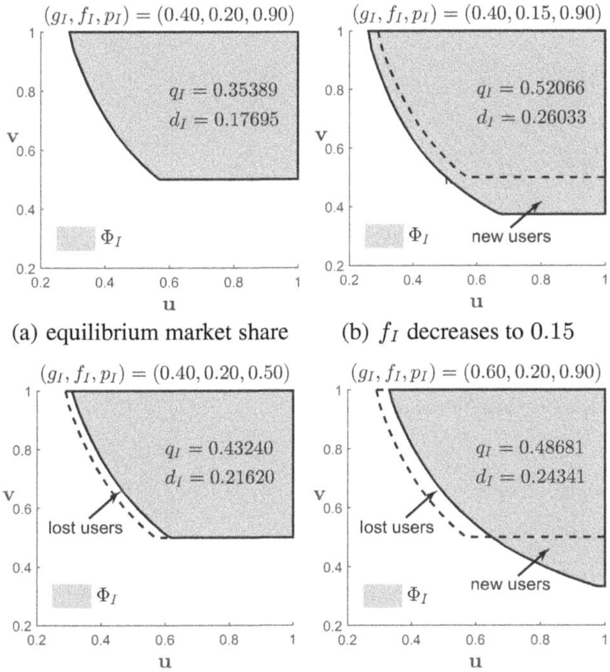

(a) equilibrium market share (b) f_I decreases to 0.15

(c) p_I decreases to 0.50 (d) g_I increases to 0.60

Figure 1: Shift of market share for a monopoly provider

To better understand the above definition, we can equivalently rephrase the above equality condition as $D_i(\Phi_i(\boldsymbol{\theta}, \mathbf{q}); \theta_i, q_i) = Q_i^{-1}(q_i, c_i)$, where the left-hand side is the induced data load of provider i given its market share $\Phi_i(\boldsymbol{\theta}, \mathbf{q})$, pricing strategy θ_i and congestion q_i and the right-hand side is its implied data load under capacity c_i. In equilibrium, both equal the actual aggregate user demand d_i. Because the equilibrium is depend on the pricing strategies $\boldsymbol{\theta}$ and capacities $\mathbf{c}$, we also denote it as $\mathbf{q}(\boldsymbol{\theta}, \mathbf{c})$.

Theorem 1. *Under Assumption 1-3, for any fixed pricing strategies $\boldsymbol{\theta}$ and capacities $\mathbf{c}$, there always exists a market equilibrium $\mathbf{q}$. In particular, when the market has only one (real monopoly) provider, the equilibrium is unique.*

Theorem 1 states that under minor assumptions of the demand (Assumption 1) and congestion (Assumption 3), the existence of a market equilibrium can be guaranteed. Besides, the equilibrium is unique in a market consisting of a monopoly provider. For this case, we denote I as the monopoly provider and define $\mathcal{I} = \{I\}$. The next theorem shows how a monopoly provider's congestion level varies when its pricing strategy θ_I and capacity c_I change, or other providers enter the market to compete.

Theorem 2. *In a monopoly market $\mathcal{I}$, provider I's unique level of congestion $q_I(\theta_I, c_I)$ in equilibrium is non-increasing in its fees f_I, p_I and capacity c_I, but is non-decreasing in its data cap g_I. When new providers enter and form a new market $\mathcal{N} \supseteq \mathcal{I} = \{I\}$, where provider I keeps its pricing θ_I and capacity c_I, if $q_I(\boldsymbol{\theta}, \mathbf{c})$ is I's congestion under an equilibrium, then $q_I(\boldsymbol{\theta}, \mathbf{c}) \leq q_I(\theta_I, c_I)$.*

Theorem 2 states that when the monopoly provider increases fees or decreases data cap, its induced congestion level will be alleviated, because its market share as well as data load will decrease. When the provider increases capacity, the congestion level will decrease, although the resulting market share and data load will increase. It also shows that with more competing providers, the existing monopoly's congestion will decrease, as users have more choices and may switch to other providers. This implies that competition could alleviate the congestion at the providers, because effectively more providers bring higher capacity to the entire market.

Under any market equilibrium $\mathbf{q}(\boldsymbol{\theta}, \mathbf{c})$, we denote R_i and S_i as the revenue and social welfare generated by provider i, defined as

$$R_i \triangleq \int_{\Phi_i} t(y_i^*(\phi), \theta_i)\, d\mu \quad \text{and} \quad S_i \triangleq \int_{\Phi_i} v y_i^*(\phi) d\mu, \tag{4}$$

where $y_i^*(\phi) = y^*(\phi, \theta_i, q_i)$ and $\Phi_i = \Phi_i(\boldsymbol{\theta}, \mathbf{q})$ are evaluated at the equilibrium $\mathbf{q}(\boldsymbol{\theta}, \mathbf{c})$.

3.4 Model Parameters and Properties

Although our model is built upon generic assumptions (Assumption 1 and 3), it does not yet capture the characteristics of network services. To this end, we carefully choose the model parameters, i.e., the congestion function $Q_i(d_i, c_i)$, the achievable demand function $\rho(u, q)$ and the measure space (Φ, μ) of user domain. We discuss the rationales and implications of our choices as follows.

First, we adopt the congestion function $Q_i(d_i, c_i) = d_i/c_i$, which models the *capacity sharing* [3] nature of network services. This form has been used in much prior work such as [3, 9, 11].

Corollary 1. *Suppose $Q_i(d_i, c_i) = d_i/c_i$ for all $i \in \mathcal{N}$ and $\mathbf{q}$ is an equilibrium of a system with capacities $\mathbf{c}$ and a measure μ of the users. For any scaled system with capacities $\hat{\mathbf{c}} = k\mathbf{c}$ and $\hat{\mu}(E) = k\mu(E)$ for all $E \subseteq \Phi$ for some $k > 0$, $\hat{\mathbf{q}} = \mathbf{q}$ is also an equilibrium, under which $\hat{d}_i = kd_i$ for all $i \in \mathcal{N}$.*

Corollary 1 states that when the providers' capacities and the user size scale linearly at the same rate, the market equilibrium does not change. Thus, by appropriately scaling the capacities, we can normalize the measure of the users to be $\mu(\Phi) = 1$, i.e., F_u and F_v can be normalized to probability distribution functions $F_u(U) = F_v(V) = 1$ without loss of generality.

Next, we choose a quintessential form $\rho(u, q) = ue^{-q}$ for the achievable demand function, which is used by prior work [16, 21]. Under this form, the user's achievable demand decays exponentially at a rate of q, i.e., the level of congestion.

Corollary 2. *If $\rho(u, q) = ue^{-q}$ and $Q_i(d_i, c_i) = d_i/c_i$ for all $i \in \mathcal{N}$, let $\mathbf{q}$ be an equilibrium under parameters $\boldsymbol{\theta}, \mathbf{c}, \Phi$ and μ. For another market with $\hat{\mathbf{f}} = \mathbf{f}/(UV)$, $\hat{\mathbf{g}} = \mathbf{g}/U$, $\hat{\mathbf{p}} = \mathbf{p}/V$, $\hat{\mathbf{c}} = \mathbf{c}/U$, $\hat{\boldsymbol{\Phi}} = [0, 1] \times [0, 1]$ and $\hat{\mu}([0, \hat{u}] \times [0, \hat{v}]) = \mu([0, U\hat{u}] \times [0, V\hat{v}])$ for all $(\hat{u}, \hat{v}) \in \hat{\Phi}$, we must have $\hat{\mathbf{q}} = \mathbf{q}$ as an equilibrium under which $\hat{d}_i = d_i/U$ for all $i \in \mathcal{N}$.*

Corollary 2 states that under the exponential form of achievable demand, any domain of the users can be normalized onto the domain $[0, 1] \times [0, 1]$. In particular, the equilibrium does not change when 1) the lump-sum fees, data caps, capacities and the users' desirable demands are normalized by U, or 2) the lump-sum and per-unit fees and users' values are normalized by V. Based on this result, we can focus on $U = V = 1$ without loss of generality and we will consider the forms $F_u(x) = x^\alpha$ and $F_v(x) = x^\beta$ for $x \in [0, 1]$, where α and β model the distribution of users with respect to their desirable data demands and values, respectively. For instance, when $\beta = 1$, user values are uniformly distributed; otherwise, they are leaning toward the high ($\beta > 1$) or low ($\beta < 1$) values in the domain $[0, 1]$. In summary, we will analyze the two-part tiered pricing of the providers with the following assumption.

Assumption 4. *Any provider i's congestion satisfies $Q_i(d_i, c_i) = d_i/c_i$, the users are distributed by $F_u(x) = x^\alpha$, $F_v(x) = x^\beta$ for $x \in [0, 1]$, and their achievable demands satisfy $\rho(u, q) = ue^{-q}$.*

When the level of congestion is exogenously given, Lemma 2 implies that the market share of a monopoly provider will decrease when it raises fees, e.g., f_I and p_I, or reduces data cap g_I. However, the higher fees or lower data cap would alleviate the provider's congestion in equilibrium by Theorem 2, which results in attracting more congestion-sensitive users to join. As a result, the dynamics of the provider's market share combines both effects and is not monotonic. Under Assumption 4, we illustrate an example in Figure 1 that shows how a monopoly provider's market share shifts when it changes the pricing strategy under equilibrium. In this example, the user distribution is parameterized by $\alpha = 4.0$ and $\beta = 0.8$ and the provider has a capacity of $c_I = 0.5$. In each subfigure, x-axis and y-axis vary the desirable data demand u and value v of the user types. In other words, each point in the subfigures represents a unique user type. In subfigure (a), we illustrate the market share Φ_I as the shaded area when the provider uses strategy $\theta_I = (g_I, f_I, p_I) = (0.4, 0.2, 0.9)$ and induces congestion $q_I = 0.35389$ and data load $d_I = 0.17695$ in equilibrium. Notice that the region of market share Φ_I has a flat-bottom on the right side where the desirable demand u is large. This flat boundary corresponds to the value of $v = f_I/g_I$, because if a user's per-unit value is lower than the effective average per-unit value for the capped amount data g_I, she would not use the provider. From subfigure (a) to (b), the provider decreases f_I from 0.2 to 0.15 and the cheaper lump-sum fee attracts a larger market share for the provider and induces higher data load and congestion in equilibrium. From subfigure (a) to (c), the provider decreases p_I from 0.9 to 0.5 and the cheaper per-unit usage fee induces higher load and congestion. However, the market share Φ_I shrinks, because higher congestion reduces the utility of some users, forcing them to leave the provider. From subfigure (a) to (d), the provider increases g_I from 0.4 to 0.6 and the larger data cap again induces higher data load and congestion in equilibrium. However, the resulting market share attracts more low-value heavy users and loses some high-value light users. Notice that although the changes in market share from subfigure (a) to subfigures (b) to (d) are not monotonic, the increase in congestion and data load in these cases are consequences of cheap prices and larger data caps stated in Theorem 2.

4. REVENUE-OPTIMAL PRICING

In this section, we study the revenue-optimal two-part pricing of the providers and characterize its dynamics under changes of system parameters, i.e., the distribution of users' demand and values, and the capacity of the providers. Because data cap is the demarcation between the lump-sum (for demand below the data cap) and usage-based (for demand above the data cap) charges, we first analyze the impact of data cap on the provider's pricing decisions and the corresponding data load, congestion and revenue, and then identify the role of data cap in the two-part pricing structure.

4.1 The Role of Data Cap

We start with a monopoly provider and assume that it chooses its pricing strategy, i.e., f_I and p_I, to maximize its revenue R_I. Given any fixed data cap g_I, we denote $f_I^*(g_I)$ and $p_I^*(g_I)$ as the optimal lump-sum and per-unit fee, respectively, and $d_I^*(g_I)$ and $R_I^*(g_I)$ as the resulting data load and maximum revenue. We study how various data caps influence its optimal pricing decisions, e.g., f_I^* and p_I^*, and the resulting optimal revenue R_I^*. In particular, we compare two-part schemes with the flat-rate pricing, a special case of an infinite data cap, i.e., $g_I = +\infty$. For simplification, we define the maximum revenue under the flat-rate as $R_\infty^* \triangleq \lim_{g_I \to \infty} R_I^*(g_I)$.

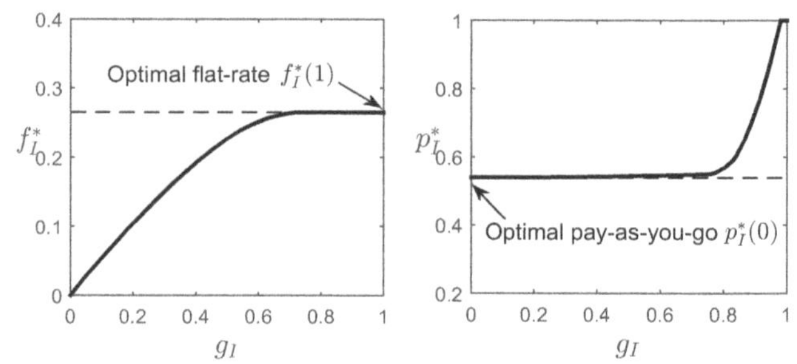

(a) optimal lump-sum fee (b) optimal per-unit fee

Figure 2: Optimal lump-sum fee $f_I^*(g_I)$ and per-unit fee $p_I^*(g_I)$ under varying data cap g_I.

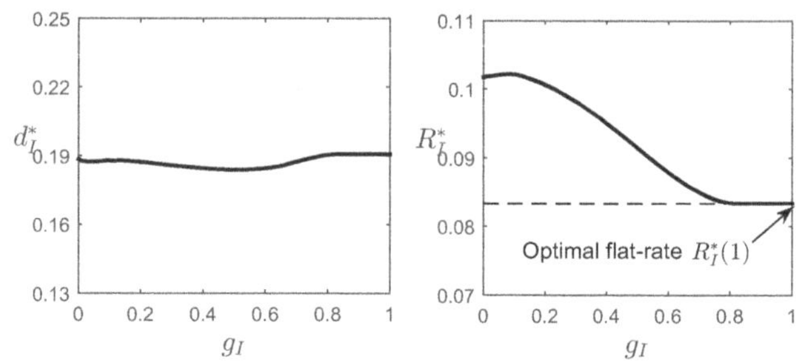

(a) corresponding data load (b) maximum revenue

Figure 3: Corresponding data load $d_I^*(g_I)$ and maximum revenue $R_I^*(g_I)$ under varying data cap g_I.

We consider the models under Assumption 4 where the maximum desirable demand is normalized as $U = 1$. As a result, an effective data cap g that might influence the users' demand has to be less than or equal to 1. In other words, when g_I is larger than 1, the two-part pricing is equivalent to a flat-rate scheme, i.e., $R_I^*(g_I) = R_\infty^* = R_I^*(1)$ for any $g_I \geq 1$. Thus, we will focus on $g_I \in [0, 1]$ without loss of generality.

Figure 2 plots the optimal lump-sum fee $f_I^*(g_I)$ and the optimal per-unit fee $p_I^*(g_I)$ as a function of the data cap g_I varying along the x-axis, respectively, where users are uniformly distributed, i.e., $\alpha = \beta = 1$, and the provider has a unit capacity, i.e., $c = 1$. We observe that both fees increase with the data cap; however, when g_I is small, $f_I^*(g_I)$ increases steeper and $p_I^*(g_I)$ is almost flat; when g_I is large, $f_I^*(g_I)$ becomes flatter and $p_I^*(g_I)$ increases steeper. This observation also illustrates that when g_I is small, the pricing structure is close to the pay-as-you-go pricing, where the lump-sum component is close to zero and the per-unit charge is close to the optimal pay-as-you-go price $p_I^*(0)$; when g_I becomes large, the pricing structure converges to the flat-rate scheme, where the lump-sum component converges to the optimal flat-rate $f_I^*(1)$ and the per-unit fee further increases to capture revenue from high-value users with large demands. The following theorem shows that our observed trends in the optimal fees are not particular to the model parameters, i.e., $\alpha = \beta = c = 1$.

Theorem 3. *Under Assumption 4, for any monopoly market with parameters $\alpha, \beta, c > 0$, the optimal lump-sum fee $f_I^*(g_I)$ is non-decreasing and concave in the data cap g_I, and the optimal per-unit fee $p_I^*(g_I)$ is non-decreasing and convex in the data cap g_I.*

Theorem 3 intuitively states that when the data cap is relaxed, a monopoly provider could compensate by increasing its prices so as to maximize revenue. Without adapting prices, larger data cap

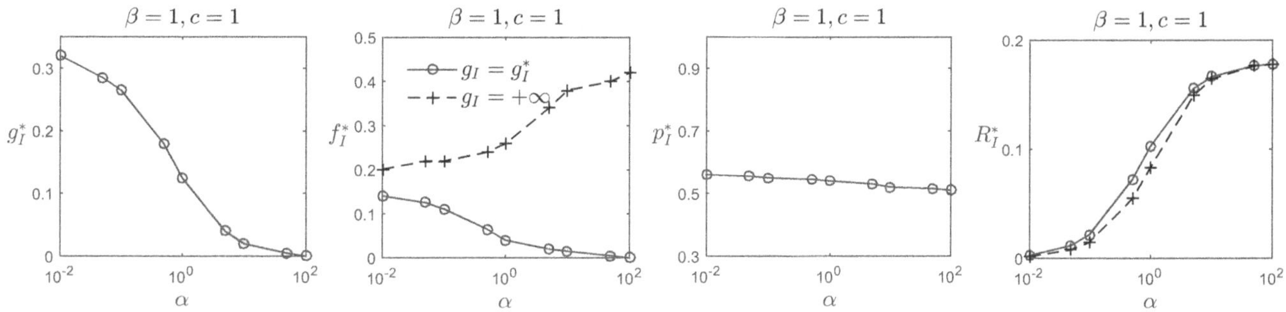

Figure 4: Optimal two-part pricing (g_I^*, f_I^*, p_I^*) and the resulting maximum revenue R_I^* under varying α.

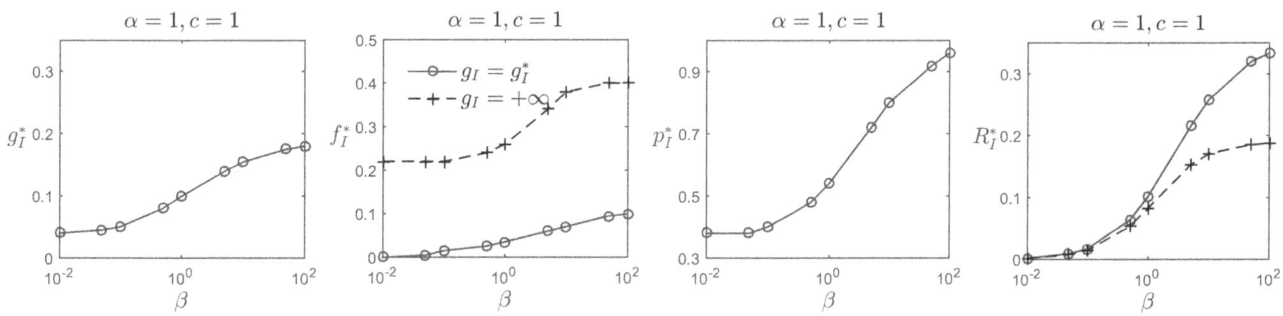

Figure 5: Optimal two-part pricing (g_I^*, f_I^*, p_I^*) and the resulting maximum revenue R_I^* under varying β.

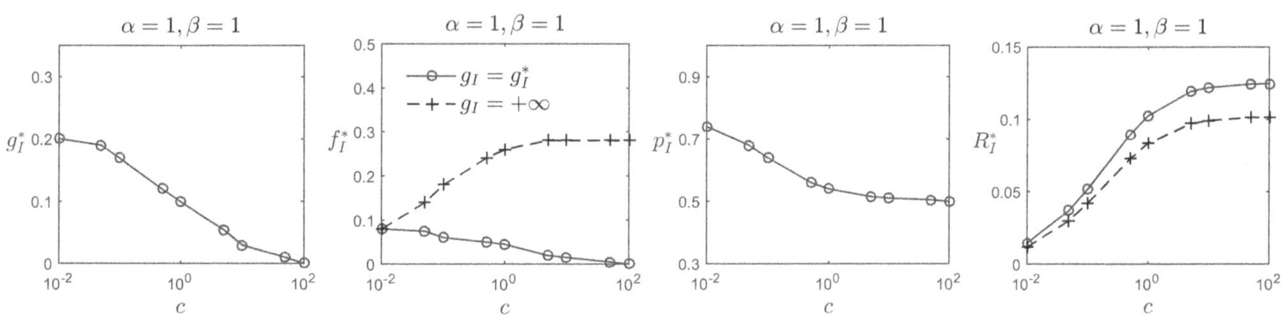

Figure 6: Optimal two-part pricing (g_I^*, f_I^*, p_I^*) and the resulting maximum revenue R_I^* under varying c.

will induce higher load and congestion in a new equilibrium by Theorem 2. However, the optimal tradeoff between prices and data load will induce an increase in prices, which oppositely results in a decrease in load as stated by Theorem 2. Under any fixed data cap g_I, if new providers enter the market, by Theorem 2, the existing provider's congestion and load will decrease. To increase load and maximize revenue under competition, it would need to reduce prices as compared to the prices in a monopoly market. Thus, under market competition, we would observe lower prices but similar pricing trends, e.g., when $g_I = 0$ and $g_I = 1$, the optimal per-unit and lump-sum prices will be lower than $p_I^*(0)$ and $f_I^*(1)$, respectively. The convexity of $p_I^*(g_I)$ and concavity of $f_I^*(g_I)$ shown in Theorem 3 also imply that the rate of change of the optimal per-unit and lump-sum fees are slow when the data cap is small and large, respectively. The reason is that in the regime of small (large) data cap, the two-part pricing structure is very close to that of the pay-as-you-go (flat-rate) scheme; and therefore, the revenue-optimal per-unit (lump-sum) fee is close to the optimal pay-as-you-go $p_I^*(0)$ (flat-rate $f_I^*(1)$) price. In general, the increase in data cap transitions a provider's pricing from a more pay-as-you-go structure to a more flat-rate structure regardless of the market structure.

Figure 3 plots the corresponding load $d_I^*(g_I)$ and maximum revenue $R_I^*(g_I)$, respectively. We observe that although the resulting data load under any data cap g_I does not vary much, the maximum revenue $R_I^*(g_I)$ varies significantly. In particular, when the pricing converges to the flat-rate structure as g_I goes to 1, the optimal revenue decreases to a minimum value. The following corollary shows that this observation is a very general result that does not depend on Assumption 4 of our model.

Corollary 3. *Under Assumption 1-3 and any monopoly market, the provider's revenue satisfies* $R_I^*(g_I) \geq R_\infty^*$, $\forall g_I \geq 0$.

Corollary 3 implies that the maximum revenue generated from any optimal two-part pricing under a fixed data cap $g_I \geq 0$ is no less than that under a flat-rate scheme. In other words, a provider could always be better off by switching from an optimal flat-rate scheme to an optimal two-part pricing scheme. Intuitively, under any fixed lump-sum f_I, the two-part structure generalizes the flat-rate scheme under which $p_I = 0$ and data cap does not play a role. Consequently, even without changing its flat-rate f_I, the provider could restrict g_I and increase p_I to trade off between higher usage revenue from high-value users' demand and its market share, which potentially lead to higher total revenue. This result is consistent with the views in prior work [5, 6, 8] that data cap could help providers extract higher revenue from the market. Although pure flat-rate is inferior to two-part schemes, Figure 3 shows that the maximum revenue does not always increase when the pricing struc-

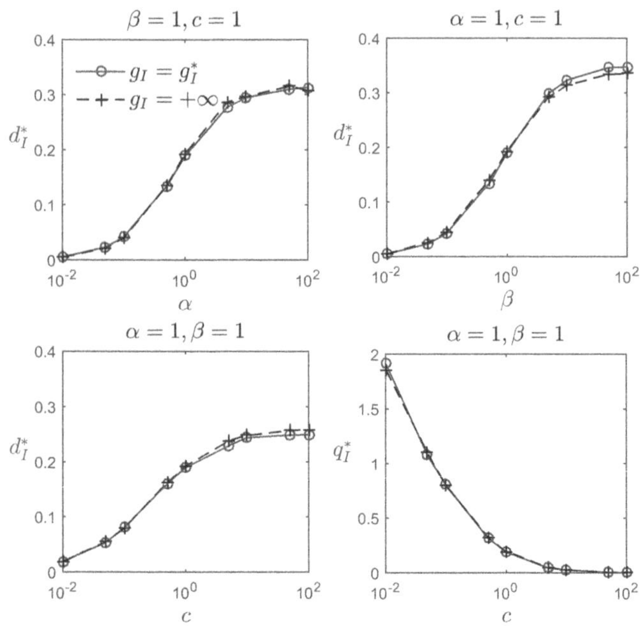

Figure 7: Resulting data load d_I^* under varying α, β and c, and congestion q_I^* under varying c.

ture moves towards the pure pay-as-you-go scheme, i.e., $g_I = 0$. In the next subsection, we further explore the optimal two-part pricing structure and its dynamics under various system parameters.

4.2 Optimal Two-Part Pricing Structure

In the previous subsection, we considered the revenue-optimal prices $f_I^*(g_I)$ and $p_I^*(g_I)$ under any fixed data cap g_I. In this subsection, we further explore revenue-optimal data cap g_I^*. Under any distribution of users specified by parameters α and β, and any fixed capacity c of the provider, we denote $\theta_I^* \triangleq (g_I^*, f_I^*, p_I^*)$ as the optimal two-part pricing that results in the maximum revenue R_I^*. We explore the dynamics of optimal two-part pricing θ_I^* when system parameters, i.e., α, β and c, change.

Figures 4 to 6 plot the optimal two-part pricing g_I^*, f_I^* and p_I^*, and the resulting maximum revenue R_I^* as functions of 1) parameter α of the distribution of users' demands, 2) parameter β of the distribution of users' values, and 3) parameter c of the provider's capacity, respectively. In each of the second and fourth subfigures, we also plot the optimal flat-rate price $f_I^*(1)$ and its corresponding revenue for comparison, respectively. We observe that as α, β and c increase, the maximum revenue increases under both the optimal flat-rate and optimal two-part schemes, where the latter induces higher revenue than the former as stated by Corollary 3. Intuitively, larger α, β and c imply higher users' demand, users' value and provider's capacity, respectively, where the provider is in a more advantageous position in extracting revenue. For example, we observe that the optimal flat-rate price $f_I^*(1)$ always increases under these changes. We also observe that when α or c increases, g_I^*, f_I^* and p_I^* all decrease; however, when β increases, g_I^*, f_I^* and p_I^* all increase. These monotonicities could be formally stated as follows.

Theorem 4. *Under Assumption 4, the data cap g_I^*, lump-sum fee f_I^* and per-unit fee p_I^* of the optimal two-part pricing are non-increasing in α and c, and are non-decreasing in β. The resulting maximum revenue R_I^* is non-decreasing in all α, β and c.*

By Theorem 3, we know that the optimal fees $f_I^*(g_I)$ and $p_I^*(g_I)$ increase with the data cap g_I when the provider's pricing structure transitions from pure pay-as-you-go to pure flat-rate pricing. Theorem 4 implies that when the demand of the users or/and the capacity of the provider increase, the optimal two-part pricing moves closer to a more pay-as-you-go type of structure; however, when the values of the users increase, it moves closer to a structure that has a bigger lump-sum component with a larger data cap. When the capacity increases, it reduces the network congestion and increases the achievable demand of the users. Because flat-rate pricing does not restrict the users' demand, it cannot effectively optimize the provider's revenue when the user demand increases; therefore, the provider will transition to impose a data cap and a per-unit fee so as to restrict demands from "bandwidth hogs". On the contrary, when the values of users tend to be concentrated towards the high-end, the provider could impose a high per-unit fee and also introduce a lump-sum component to capture users in the low-value and low-demand regime. The high per-unit fee does not affect these users as their demand is lower than the data cap.

Under market competition, if the provider keeps the same data cap g_I^*, it has to reduce the lump-sum and per-unit prices to capture market share and optimize revenue; however, it might be better off to increase data cap from g_I^* to attract more users rather than decreasing the fees too much. In general, all three components of the optimal two-part pricing under market competition have to be "cheaper" than those under a monopoly market. However, it does not alter the structure of the optimal two-part pricing, i.e., whether it is more like pay-as-you-go or flat-rate, in an obvious manner.

The implications of Theorem 4 also provide compelling explanations of why Internet service providers have shifted their pricing from the traditional flat-rate to the two-part structure recently. In the early years of the Internet, data demands were mostly for texts and used by small groups of advanced users with high-value tasks, e.g., scientific and business purposes. The network capacities were scarce before the emergence of fiber optics backbones. Under such conditions, flat-rate pricing could be used to effectively recoup costs and the maximum revenue under two-part pricing would not be much higher than that under an optimal flat-rate scheme. As a result, most providers adopted flat-rate pricing because of its simplicity. As mobile devices become a key means to access the Internet for end-users and multimedia content become more pervasive, together with the increase in network capacities, Internet traffic keeps growing more than 50% per annum [13]. As a result, providers now feel that flat-rate schemes cannot effectively influence users' demand and optimize their revenues; and therefore, start to adopt two-part pricing schemes. Furthermore, implied by Theorem 4, if these trends continue, we would expect that providers will further reduce the lump-sum component and data cap and move closer to pure pay-as-you-go pricing in the near future. In practice, the introduction of data cap in the two-part pricing also provides a means for providers to transition from flat-rate to pay-as-you-go smoothly, so that the changes will not be too abrupt for users and providers will not lose users due to the structural change of pricing schemes.

Figure 7 plots the corresponding data load under the optimal flat-rate and two-part pricing schemes when α, β and c increase, respectively. As the system congestion has the same trends as data load under fixed capacities, we only plot the corresponding network congestion in the lower-right subfigure when capacity c varies. We observe that the induced data load and network congestion do not differ much under the optimal two-part and flat-rate schemes. In general, increasing in users' desirable demand, users' values or provider's capacity will induce higher data load in the system; however, the congestion will decrease when the capacity becomes more abundant.

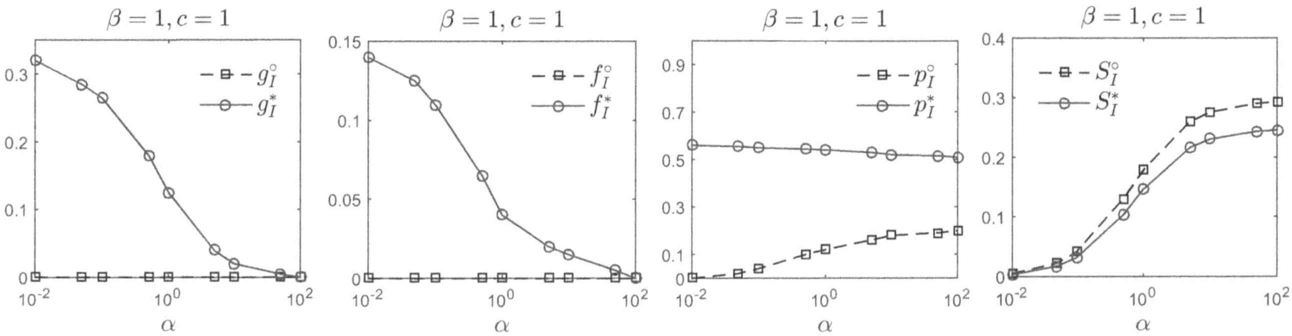

Figure 8: Welfare-optimal and revenue-optimal pricing schemes under varying α.

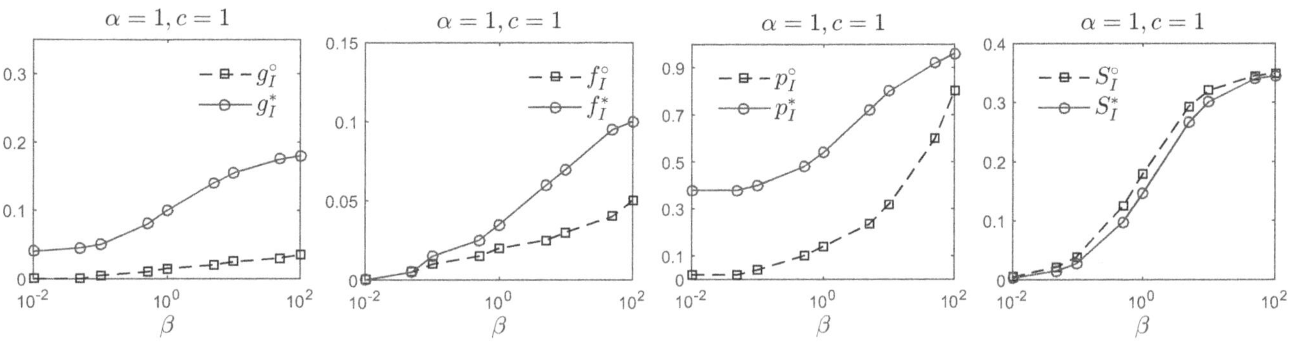

Figure 9: Welfare-optimal and revenue-optimal pricing schemes under varying β.

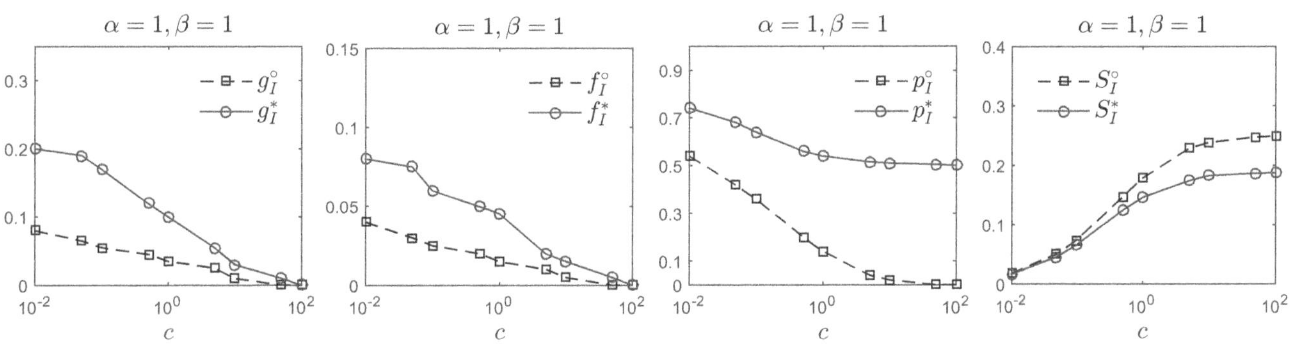

Figure 10: Welfare-optimal and revenue-optimal pricing schemes under varying c.

Corollary 4. *Under Assumption 4 and an optimal two-part pricing $\theta_I^* = (g_I^*, f_I^*, p_I^*)$, the provider's data load d_I^* is non-decreasing in α, β and c, and the corresponding network congestion q_I^* is non-decreasing in α and β, but is non-increasing in c.*

Corollary 4 implies that when the demand or values of users, or the capacity of the provider increases, under the optimal two-part pricing, the system will accommodate higher data load. The system congestion will decrease if the capacity increases; otherwise, it will increase. The increase in data load shows that revenue-optimal pricing is partially aligned with the users' welfare where the provider would adaptively serve more data demand. In the next section, we will explore how different the revenue-optimal pricing is from the welfare-optimal solution, through which we will obtain some insights on how monopolistic providers should be regulated for social welfare maximization.

In summary, the structure of revenue-optimal two-part pricing is largely influenced by the data cap, which plays a transitional role (mechanism) between flat-rate and pay-as-you-go pricing schemes. As users' demand and providers' capacity grow in the Internet, revenue objectives will drive providers to shift from flat-rate towards usage-based schemes, where data cap and both lump-sum and per-unit fees would decrease. Although market competition would force the providers to use "cheaper" schemes, i.e., higher data cap and lower lump-sum and per-unit fees, it does not necessarily change the structure of the optimal two-part pricing.

5. WELFARE-OPTIMAL PRICING

In the previous section, we studied the revenue-optimal pricing and showed that it accommodates higher data load when the users' demand or values, or the providers' capacities increase. However, the revenue-optimal solution does not maximize the social welfare, i.e., the total utility of the providers and their users. Although market competition could improve the social welfare, which would be maximized under a perfect competitive market, a large deviation from the maximum welfare would more likely happen in a monopoly market. In the section, we focus on a monopoly provider and compare its welfare-optimal and revenue-optimal solutions.

Under any distribution of users specified by parameters α and β, and any capacity c of the provider, we denote $\theta_I^\circ \triangleq (g_I^\circ, f_I^\circ, p_I^\circ)$ as the optimal two-part pricing that maximizes the social welfare S_I

(defined in Equation 4) and results in the maximum welfare S_I°. We denote the corresponding network congestion and data load as q_I° and d_I°, respectively. To make a comparison, we denote S_I^* as the social welfare achieved under the provider's revenue-optimal pricing θ_I^*. Similarly, we explore the dynamics of the welfare-optimal pricing θ_I° when system parameters, i.e., α, β and c, change.

Figures 8 to 10 plot the welfare-optimal solution g_I°, f_I° and p_I°, and the resulting maximum welfare S_I° as functions of 1) parameter α of the distribution of users' demands, 2) parameter β of the distribution of users' values, and 3) parameter c of the provider's capacity, respectively. As a comparison, we also plot the corresponding revenue-optimal solution g_I^*, f_I^* and p_I^*, and the resulting social welfare S_I^* in the four subfigures, respectively. We observe that the curves of the welfare-optimal pricing g_I°, f_I° and p_I° are always lower than those of the revenue-optimal pricing g_I^*, f_I^* and p_I^*, respectively. This observation can be formally shown as follows.

Theorem 5. *Under Assumption 4, for any monopoly market with parameters $\alpha, \beta, c > 0$, we have $g_I^\circ \le g_I^*$, $f_I^\circ \le f_I^*$ and $p_I^\circ \le p_I^*$.*

Theorem 5 implies that to shift the provider's two-part pricing from revenue-optimal to welfare-optimal, one should lower its fees, i.e., f_I and p_I; however, allow the provider to further throttle the data cap and move towards a usage-based structure. Besides revenue maximization, this result provides justifications for regulators, e.g., the US FCC, to encourage usage-based pricing for the Internet service providers. On the one hand, exorbitant fees reduce users' utilities and data demand, resulting lower social welfare; on the other hand, limiting the data cap will self-regulate the demand of low-value, and therefore, increase the social welfare.

When comparing the trends between the revenue and welfare-optimal solutions, we further observe that the welfare-optimal solution has the same trend as that of the revenue-optimal solution when β or c increases; however, this trend is reversed when α increases. These monotonicities could be formally stated as follows.

Theorem 6. *Under Assumption 4, the data cap g_I°, lump-sum fee f_I° and per-unit fee p_I° of the welfare-optimal two-part pricing are non-increasing in c, and are non-decreasing in α and β. The resulting revenue S_I° is non-decreasing in all α, β and c.*

Similar to the result of Theorem 4, Theorem 6 shows that when c increases, the welfare-optimal solution moves towards usage-based, but also reduces the per-unit fee to allow more user demand. However, when users' demand becomes more concentrated at the high-end as α increases, although the welfare-optimal solution is close to the pay-as-you-go scheme, the optimal per-unit fee increases so as to discourage the data demand from low-value users.

By comparing the maximum social welfare S_I° with S_I^*, we observe that the difference widens when α and c increases, but reaches largest as the values of users are uniformly distributed, i.e., $\beta = 1$. This implies that regulations are most in need when the capacity and users' demand become large. In both cases, we observe that both revenue and welfare-optimal solution tend to be pure pay-as-you-go, i.e., $g_I = 0$; however, the per-unit price for maximum welfare is lower than that of the revenue-optimal solution. This further implies that regulators could encourage usage-based pricing for the providers; however, price regulation on the per-unit fee might be needed to guarantee higher social welfare.

Add on to Figure 7, Figure 11 compares the data load and congestion under the revenue and welfare-optimal pricing schemes. We observe that the network congestion drops as the capacity c increases; however, when α or c becomes large, the achieved load from welfare-optimal pricing is much higher. This coincides with the large gaps in social welfare, where regulation is most in need.

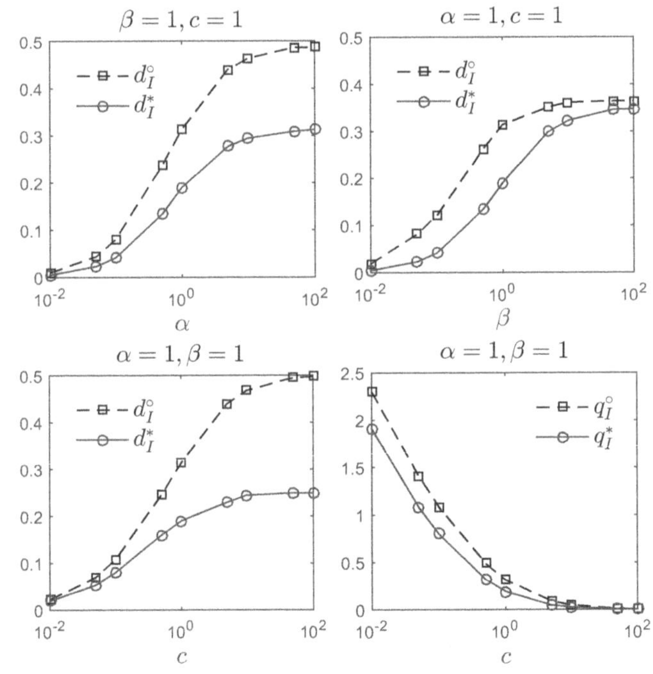

Figure 11: Resulting data load d_I^* and d_I° under varying α, β and c, and congestion q_I^* and q_I° under varying c.

The trends of d_I° and q_I° under the welfare-optimal pricing θ_I° are similar to those under the revenue-optimal pricing θ_I^* shown in Corollary 4, and can be shown as follows.

Corollary 5. *Under Assumption 4 and a welfare-optimal two-part pricing $\theta_I^\circ = (g_I^\circ, f_I^\circ, p_I^\circ)$, the data load d_I° is non-decreasing in α, β and c, and the corresponding network congestion q_I° is non-decreasing in α and β, but is non-increasing in c.*

Compared to the result of Corollary 4, Corollary 5 is even more intuitive: higher provider's capacity and users' demand and values will lead to higher social welfare when it is optimized.

In summary, our results suggest that regulatory authorities might want to regulate a monopoly market under heavy demand of users or abundant capacity of the provider. Under these scenarios, welfare-optimal solution will have lower fees and data cap than the revenue-optimal solution, forcing the pricing structure of the provider moving further towards usage-based. As the growth of users' demand and providers' capacities in the current Internet, our result further justifies from a welfare perspective that the regulators should encourage ISPs to shift towards two-part pricing with limited data caps; however, it also suggests that the per-unit fees might need to be regulated when market competition does not exist.

6. CONCLUSIONS

In this paper, we study the role of data cap in the optimal structure of two-part tariffs. We present a novel model of users' demand and preferences over pricing and congestion alternatives and derive the market share and congestion of the service providers under a market equilibrium. Based on the equilibrium model, we characterize the two-part structure of the revenue-optimal and welfare-optimal pricing schemes. We identify that the data cap provides a mechanism for service providers to transition from flat-rate to pay-as-you-go type of usage-based schemes. Our results reveal that with growing data demand and network capacity in the current Internet, revenue-optimal pricing will move towards usage-based schemes with diminishing data caps. Although market competition might drive pricing "cheaper", it does not necessarily change the optimal structure of the two-part tariff. From a perspective of social welfare, our results suggest that regulators might want to promote usage-based pricing but regulate the per-unit fees, because the structure of the welfare-optimal tariff comprises lower fees and data cap than those of the revenue-optimal counterpart.

Acknowledgments

This work is partially supported by the research grants for the HCCS project at ADSC from Singapore's Agency for Science, Technology and Research (A*STAR), Ministry of Education of Singapore AcRF grants T1 R-252-000-526-112 and R-252-000-572-112. This work is also supported in part by National Nature Science Foundation of China under Grant No. 61379038.

APPENDIX

A. PROOFS OF SELECTED RESULTS

Proof of Lemma 1: For any user type ϕ that uses the ISP with pricing scheme θ and congestion q, her utility is $\pi(y) = vy - f - p(y-g)^+$ from Equation 1. When $v \geq p$, the utility $\pi(y)$ is non-decreasing in $y \in \big[0, \rho(u,q)\big]$ and thus the optimal demand is $y^*(\phi,\theta,q) = \rho(u,q)$. When $v < p$, the utility $\pi(y)$ is non-decreasing in $y \in \big[0, g\big]$ and non-increasing in $y \in \big(g, \rho(u,q)\big]$, and thus the optimal demand is $y^*(\phi,\theta,q) = g$. In summary, we have $y^*(\phi,\theta,q) = \rho(u,q) - \big[\rho(u,q) - g\big]^+ \mathbf{1}_{\{v<p\}}$, and therefore, the optimal usage $y^*(\phi,\theta,q)$ is non-increasing in p and q and non-decreasing in u,v and g. ■

Proof of Lemma 2: For a set $\mathcal{N}$ of providers and any user type $\phi \in \Phi_i(\boldsymbol{\theta},\mathbf{q})$, we have $y^*(\phi,\hat{\theta}_i,q_i) \geq y^*(\phi,\theta_i,q_i)$. Because the optimal data usage y^* is non-increasing in p and non-decreasing in g from Lemma 1. Further, the utility function $\pi(y)$ is non-decreasing in the data usage y, thus it satisfies $\pi\big(y^*(\phi,\hat{\theta}_i,q_i)\big) \geq \pi\big(y^*(\phi,\theta_i,q_i)\big) \geq \pi\big(y^*(\phi,\theta_j,q_j)\big) = \pi\big(y^*(\phi,\hat{\theta}_j,q_j)\big)$ for $\forall j \neq i$. Then we have $\phi \in \Phi_i(\hat{\boldsymbol{\theta}},\mathbf{q})$ from Definition 1 and therefore $\Phi_i(\boldsymbol{\theta},\mathbf{q}) \subseteq \Phi_i(\hat{\boldsymbol{\theta}},\mathbf{q})$. Similarly, we can show that $\Phi_j(\boldsymbol{\theta},\mathbf{q}) \supseteq \Phi_j(\hat{\boldsymbol{\theta}},\mathbf{q}), \forall\, j \neq i$.

For two sets $\mathcal{N}$ and $\mathcal{N}'$ of providers and any provider $i \in \mathcal{N}$, for any user type $\phi \in \Phi_i(\boldsymbol{\theta}',\mathbf{q}')$, based on Definition 1, it satisfies that $\pi\big(y^*(\phi,\theta_i,q_i)\big) = \pi\big(y^*(\phi,\theta_i',q_i')\big) \geq \pi\big(y^*(\phi,\theta_j',q_j')\big) = \pi\big(y^*(\phi,\theta_j,q_j)\big), \forall j \in \mathcal{N}\backslash\{i\}$. Then we have $\phi \in \Phi_i(\boldsymbol{\theta},\mathbf{q})$ and therefore $\Phi_i(\boldsymbol{\theta}',\mathbf{q}') \subseteq \Phi_i(\boldsymbol{\theta},\mathbf{q}), \forall i \in \mathcal{N}$. ■

Proof of Theorem 1: We first prove the existence of equilibrium. By Definition 2, $\mathbf{q}$ is an equilibrium if and only if for all $i \in \mathcal{N}$,

$$q_i = Q_i\Big(D_i\big(\Phi_i(\boldsymbol{\theta},\mathbf{q});\theta_i,q_i\big),c_i\Big) = Q_i\big(D_i(\boldsymbol{\theta},\mathbf{q}),c_i\big).$$

Since $\boldsymbol{\theta}$ and $\mathbf{c}$ are constants, we omit them in the notation and write the above in a matrix form as $\mathbf{q} = Q\big(D(\mathbf{q})\big) = Q \circ D(\mathbf{q})$. Thus, we can view the composite function $Q \circ D$ as a mapping from the convex set $\mathbb{R}_+^{|\mathcal{N}|}$ to itself. By Assumption 3, we know that each $Q_i(d_i,c_i)$ is continuous in d_i and thus each $Q_i\big(D_i(\boldsymbol{\theta},\mathbf{q}),c_i\big)$ is continuous in $\mathbf{q}$. To this end, we know that $Q \circ D(\mathbf{q})$ is continuous in $\mathbf{q}$. By Brouwer fixed-point theorem, there always exists a fixed point that satisfies $Q \circ D(\mathbf{q}) = \mathbf{q}$ and is also an equilibrium.

We then prove the uniqueness of the equilibrium in a monopoly market by contradiction. Suppose there exist two equilibriums q_I and q_I' under fixed pricing strategy θ_I and capacity c_I. Without loss of generality, we assume that $q_I' > q_I$. For any user type $\phi \in \Phi_I\big(\theta_I,q_I'\big)$, we have $y^*(\phi,\theta_I,q_I) \geq y^*(\phi,\theta_I,q_I')$. Because the optimal data usage y^* is non-increasing in the congestion q_I from Lemma 1. Further, the utility function $\pi(y)$ is non-decreasing in the data usage y, thus it satisfies $\pi\big(y^*(\phi,\theta_I,q_I)\big) \geq \pi\big(y^*(\phi,\theta_I,q_I')\big) \geq 0$ implying that $\phi \in \Phi_I\big(\theta_I,q_I\big)$ from Definition 1. Thus we have $\Phi_I\big(\theta_I,q_I'\big) \subseteq \Phi_I\big(\theta_I,q_I\big)$. By Equation 3, we deduce $D_I\big(\theta_I,q_I\big) = \int_{\Phi_I(\theta_I,q_I)} y^*(\phi,\theta_I,q_I)d\mu \geq \int_{\Phi_I(\theta_I,q_I')} y^*(\phi,\theta_I,q_I')d\mu = D_I\big(\theta_I,q_I'\big)$. Because $Q_I(d_I,c_I)$ is non-decreasing in d_I from Assumption 3, we have

$$q_I = Q_I\Big(D_I\big(\theta_I,q_I\big),c_I\Big) \geq Q_I\Big(D_I\big(\theta_I,q_I'\big),c_I\Big) = q_I'$$

based on Definition 2, which is contradictory with the supposition that $q_I' > q_I$. Therefore, the equilibrium is unique in the market with only one real provider. ■

Proof of Theorem 2: We first prove the congestion $q_I(\theta_I,c_I)$ is non-increasing in the lump-sum fee f_I by contradiction. Suppose $q_I(\theta_I,c_I)$ is not non-increasing in f_I, there must exist pricing strategies $\theta_I' = (g_I,f_I',p_I)$ and $\theta_I = (g_I,f_I,p_I)$ satisfying $f_I' > f_I$ and $q_I(\theta_I',c_I) > q_I(\theta_I,c_I)$. For any user type $\phi \in \Phi_I\big(\theta_I',q_I(\theta_I',c_I)\big)$, because the optimal data usage y^* is non-increasing in the congestion q and the lump-sum fee f from Lemma 1, we have $y^*\big(\phi,\theta_I',q_I(\theta_I',c_I)\big) \leq y^*\big(\phi,\theta_I,q_I(\theta_I,c_I)\big)$. Furthermore, because the utility function π is non-decreasing in y and non-increasing in f, we have

$$\pi\Big(y^*\big(\phi,\theta_I,q_I(\theta_I,c_I)\big)\Big) \geq \pi\Big(y^*\big(\phi,\theta_I',q_I(\theta_I',c_I)\big)\Big) \geq 0$$

implying that $\phi \in \Phi_I\big(\theta_I,q_I(\theta_I,c_I)\big)$ from Definition 1. Thus we have $\Phi_I\big(\theta_I',q_I(\theta_I',c_I)\big) \subseteq \Phi_I\big(\theta_I,q_I(\theta_I,c_I)\big)$. From Equation 3, it satisfies $D_I\big(\theta_I',q_I(\theta_I',c_I)\big) \leq D_I\big(\theta_I,q_I(\theta_I,c_I)\big)$. Because $Q_I(d_I,c_I)$ is non-decreasing in d_I from Assumption 3, we have

$$\begin{aligned} q_I(\theta_I',c_I) &= Q_I\Big(D_I\big(\theta_I',q_I(\theta_I',c_I)\big),c_I\Big) \\ &\leq Q_I\Big(D_I\big(\theta_I,q_I(\theta_I,c_I)\big),c_I\Big) = q_I(\theta_I,c_I) \end{aligned}$$

by Definition 2, which is contradictory with the supposition that $q_I(\theta_I',c_I) > q_I(\theta_I,c_I)$. Therefore, $q_I(\theta_I,c_I)$ is non-increasing in f_I. Similarly, we can prove that $q_I(\theta_I,c_I)$ is non-increasing in the per-unit fee p_I, the capacity c_I and non-decreasing in the data cap g_I, and when new providers enter the market, the existing provider's congestion must be improved, i.e., $q_I(\boldsymbol{\theta},\mathbf{c}) \leq q_I(\theta_I,c_I)$. ■

Proof of Corollary 1: Given $\hat{\mathbf{c}} = k\mathbf{c}$, $Q_i(d_i,c_i) = d_i/c_i$ and $\hat{d}_i = kd_i$ for all $i \in \mathcal{N}$, we know that $\hat{q}_i = Q(\hat{d}_i,\hat{c}_i) = \hat{d}_i/\hat{c}_i = kd_i/kc_i = Q_i(d_i,c_i) = q_i$ and therefore $\hat{\mathbf{q}} = \mathbf{q}$. Thus, we only need to show that under $\hat{\mathbf{q}} = \mathbf{q}$, we must have $\hat{d}_i = kd_i$ for all $i \in \mathcal{N}$. Since $\boldsymbol{\theta}$ does not change and $\hat{\mathbf{q}} = \mathbf{q}$, we know that $\hat{\Phi}_i = \Phi_i$ and $y_i^*(\phi,\theta_i,\hat{q}_i) = y_i^*(\phi,\theta_i,q_i)$ for all $i \in \mathcal{N}$. Thus, we have $\hat{d}_i = \int_{\hat{\Phi}_i} y_i^*(\phi,\theta_i,\hat{q}_i)d\hat{\mu} = \int_{\Phi_i} y_i^*(\phi,\theta_i,q_i)dk\mu = kd_i$ for all $i \in \mathcal{N}$. ■

References

[1] T. Basar and R. Srikant. Revenue-maximizing pricing and capacity expansion in a many-users regime. *Proceedings of IEEE INFOCOM*, pages 294–301, 2002.

[2] P. Chander and L. Leruth. The optimal product mix for a monopolist in the presence of congestion effects: A model and some results. *International Journal of Industrial Organization*, 7(4):437–449, 1989.

[3] C.-K. Chau, Q. Wang, and D.-M. Chiu. On the viability of Paris Metro pricing for communication and service networks. *Proceedings of IEEE INFOCOM*, pages 1–9, 2010.

[4] M. Chetty, R. Banks, A. Brush, J. Donner, and R. Grinter. You're capped: understanding the effects of bandwidth caps on broadband use in the home. *Proceedings of the SIGCHI Conference on Human Factors in Computing Systems*, pages 3021–3030, 2012.

[5] F. O. I. A. Committee. Policy issues in data caps and usage-based pricing. *Annual Report*, 2013.

[6] W. Dai and S. Jordan. Design and impact of data caps. *IEEE Global Communications Conference*, pages 1650–1656, 2013.

[7] W. Dai and S. Jordan. How do ISP data caps affect subscribers? *Telecommunications Policy Research Conference TPRC*, 2013.

[8] R. Edell and P. Varaiya. Providing Internet access: What we learn from INDEX. *IEEE Network*, 13(5):18–25, 1999.

[9] R. Gibbens, R. Mason, and R. Steinberg. Internet service classes under competition. *IEEE Journal on Selected Areas in Communications*, 18(12):2490–2498, 2000.

[10] P. Hande, M. Chiang, R. Calderbank, and J. Zhang. Pricing under constraints in access networks: Revenue maximization and congestion management. *Proceedings of IEEE INFOCOM*, pages 1–9, 2010.

[11] R. Jain, T. Mullen, and R. Hausman. Analysis of Paris Metro pricing strategy for QoS with a single service provider. *Quality of Service IWQoS*, pages 44–58, 2001.

[12] J. C. L. T. K. Poularakis, I. Pefkianakis. Pricing the last mile: Data capping for residential broadband. *ACM SIGCOMM CoNEXT*, pages 295–306, 2014.

[13] C. Labovitz, D. McPherson, S. Iekel-Johnson, J. Oberheide, and F. Jahanian. Internet inter-domain traffic. *ACM SIGCOMM Computer Communication Review*, 41(4):75–86, 2011.

[14] S. Li, J. Huang, and S.-Y. Li. Revenue maximization for communication networks with usage-based pricing. *Global Telecommunications Conference*, pages 1–6, 2009.

[15] R. T. Ma. Pay-as-you-go pricing and competition in congested network service markets. *Proceedings of the 22nd IEEE International Conference on Network Protocols (ICNP)*, pages 257–268, 2014.

[16] R. T. Ma, J. C. Lui, and V. Misra. On the evolution of the Internet economic ecosystem. *Proceedings of the 22nd International World Wide Web Conference*, pages 849–860, 2013.

[17] M. Morgan. Pricing schemes key in LTE future. *Telecomasia.net. September 12*, 2011.

[18] P. Nabipay, A. Odlyzko, and Z.-L. Zhang. Flat versus metered rates, bundling, and "bandwidth hog". *6th Workshop on the Economics of Networks, Systems, and Computation*, 2011.

[19] A. Odlyzko. Internet pricing and the history of communications. *Computer networks*, 36(5):493–517, 2001.

[20] A. Odlyzko, B. S. Arnaud, E. Stallman, and M. Weinberg. Know your limits: Considering the role of data caps and usage based billing in Internet access service. *Public Knowledge*, April 23, 2012.

[21] D. Reitman. Endogenous quality differentiation in congested markets. *The Journal of Industrial Economics*, 39(6):621–647, 1991.

[22] A. Schatz and S. E. Ante. FCC chief backs usage-based broadband pricing. *Wall Street Journal*, December 2, 2010.

[23] L. Segall. Verizon ends unlimited data plan. *CNN Money. July*, 6, 2011.

[24] H. Shen and T. Basar. Optimal nonlinear pricing for a monopolistic network service provider with complete and incomplete information. *IEEE Journal on Selected Areas in Communications*, 25(6):1216–1223, 2007.

[25] P. Taylor. AT&T imposes usage caps on fixed-line broadband. *Financial Times. March*, 14, 2011.

[26] X. Wang, R. T. Ma, and Y. Xu. The role of data cap in optimal two-part network pricing. *Technical report*, 2015. `http://arxiv.org/pdf/1503.01514.pdf`.

[27] X. Wang, R. T. Ma, and Y. Xu. The role of data cap in two-part pricing under market competition. *4th Workshop on Smart Data Pricing*, 2015.

Tweeting Cameras for Event Detection

Yuhui Wang
NUS Graduate School for Integrative Sciences and Engineering
National University of Singapore, Singapore
wangyuhui@u.nus.edu

Mohan S. Kankanhalli
School of Computing
National University of Singapore, Singapore
mohan@comp.nus.edu.sg

ABSTRACT

We are living in a world of big *sensor* data. Due to the widespread prevalence of visual sensors (e.g. surveillance cameras) and social sensors (e.g. Twitter feeds), many events are implicitly captured in real-time by such heterogeneous "sensors". Combining these two complementary sensor streams can significantly improve the task of event detection and aid in comprehending evolving situations. However, the different characteristics of these *social* and *sensor* data make such information fusion for event detection a challenging problem. To tackle this problem, we propose an innovative multi-layer tweeting cameras framework integrating both physical sensors and social sensors to detect various concepts of real-world events. In this framework, visual concept detectors are applied on camera video frames and these concepts can be construed as "camera tweets" posted regularly. These tweets are represented by a unified probabilistic spatio-temporal (PST) data structure which is then aggregated to a concept-based image (Cmage) as the common representation for visualization. To facilitate event analysis, we define a set of operators and analytic functions that can be applied on the PST data by the user to discover occurrences of events and to analyse evolving situations. We further leverage on geo-located social media data by mining current topics discussed on Twitter to obtain the high-level semantic meaning of detected events in images. We quantitatively evaluate our framework with a large-scale dataset containing images from 150 New York real-time traffic CCTV cameras, university foodcourt camera feeds and Twitter data, which demonstrates the feasibility and effectiveness of our proposed framework. Results of combining camera tweets and social tweets are shown to be promising for detecting real-world events.

Categories and Subject Descriptors

H.4.m [**Information Systems Applications**]: Miscellaneous

WWW 2015, May 18–22, 2015, Florence, Italy.
ACM 978-1-4503-3469-3/15/05.
http://dx.doi.org/10.1145/2736277.2741634.

General Terms

Design; Experimentation; Performance

Keywords

tweeting cameras; social sensors; event detection; content analysis; social media

1. INTRODUCTION

We are witnessing a world of big *social* and *sensor* data. From visual sensors, wearable sensors, to humans as sensors [31], multiple sensor media streams constantly provide observations on the real world that are utilized in many aspects of our life: from industrial process control, robotics, surveillance, smart houses to situation awareness [34]. Examples of sensors include (a) ***physical sensors*** like cameras, accelerometers, gyroscopes, mobile phones, RFID tags, temperature sensors, humidity sensors and (b) ***social sensors*** like social networking sites containing user-generated content reporting events in all kinds of formats (text, image, video, etc.). On one hand, visual sensors, either static video cameras or mobile cameras embedded in smartphones, are rapidly increasing in numbers around the world. On the other hand, many types of social media platforms like Twitter, Weibo, Facebook, Wechat, Youtube, Flickr etc. allow humans as social sensors to report daily events or individual opinions, disseminate breaking news, discuss trending topics and discover social events. Therefore, our physical world is being monitored by these increasing numbers of physical and social sensors. These multi-modal streams of data can therefore facilitate event discovery since they implicitly capture the evolving situations around the world.

However, due to the diversity of these sources, physical sensors and social sensors capture information separately in their individual silos. The information captured by sensors of different modalities is not combined or fused which impedes event detection and understanding in a comprehensive manner. Since camera and social streams provide different facets of events or a situation, we argue that combining the two different but complementary streams would greatly improve event detection and further aid in comprehending evolving situations. Taking inspiration from the "things that tweet" [24, 13], we incorporate cameras into a social network to build a network of ***tweeting cameras***. This camera network "tweets" information to facilitate event detection – our key idea is to apply visual concept detectors on the camera data. The detected visual concepts at a camera can be considered as "tweets" posted by it. Multiple camera "tweet-

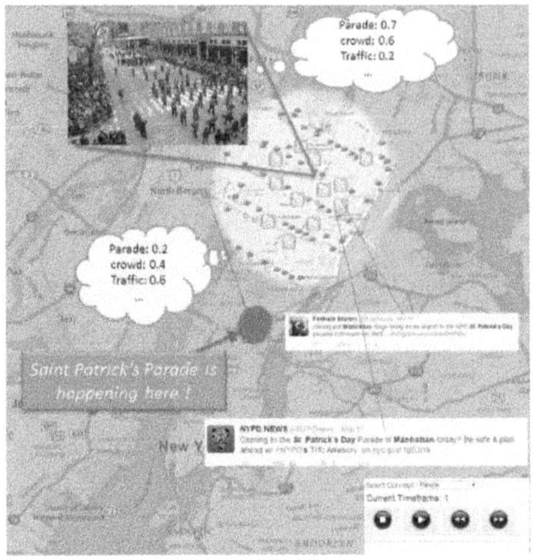

Figure 1: Tweeting Cameras and Twitter Tweets for Event Detection.

s" are then combined with twitter textual tweets from the vicinity to detect events occurring in that geographical area. The conceptual illustration of our idea is shown in Figure 1.

This introduces several challenging research problems:

1. How to integrate heterogeneous data from both physical sensors and social sensors to detect real-world events?

2. What kind of processing framework should be adopted in order to extract meaningful situational information from multi-modal media streams?

3. Given the intrinsic unreliability of individual camera data and the sheer volume of social media data, how can we handle the uncertainty and noise of these data?

In this work, we present an innovative approach to perform fusion of physical and social sensor data. In order to process social data and sensor data, we define a unified probabilistic spatio-temporal (PST) data structure to represent semantic concepts information, which aids handling the uncertainty and noise in sensor and social streams respectively. Concept detectors indicate the confidence of a detected concept in an image using a probability value. We consider these detected concepts as "Camera Tweets" with associated confidence values. Camera tweets at a particular geo-location can then be visualised as "concept pixels". Spatially aggregating such "concept pixels" creates a powerful and intuitive situation visualization interface, *concept-based image (Cmage)*, where both social information and sensor information are further fused to represent situations. For this purpose, we propose a multi-layer tweeting camera framework where tweets from cameras are analysed at different levels such that multi-level information is extracted and subsequently combined with social information to derive situational knowledge. In the first layer of the framework, we consider individual 'tweets' at the lowest level by applying a variety of concept detectors on the raw video data so as to extract low-level semantic information from visual features. After applying concept detectors on every camera in a spatial region, low-level semantic information is then represented by the proposed PST data structure and mapped to the *Cmage*. To facilitate pattern mining and mid-level information extraction, in the second layer, we aggregate all the processed low-level tweets and define a set of filtering operators and analytic functions which could be applied on the PST data to obtain mid-level processed camera tweets (e.g. concepts with high probabilities for a region). Mid-level tweets are aggregated information from several cameras which give insights into the overall situation pattern or general event trend by applying predefined analytic functions. At the highest level, information is extracted from social media (e.g. twitter data) to facilitate cross media analysis that provides the highest level semantic information about an event. The high-level processed 'tweets' analysed in the third layer allow us to infer the social meaning of a particular event. We tackle the social event detection problem with signal detection theory to separate the event 'signals' from social 'noise', and improve the detection accuracy by fusing the two complementary information sources (camera feeds and social feeds).

Contributions: To summarize, our main contributions in this work are:

1. Defining a unified probabilistic spatio-temporal data structure to handle uncertainty of physical sensors.

2. Proposing a multi-layer tweeting cameras framework containing innovative *concept image (Cmage)* and a set of filtering & analytic operators for user to query different levels of information from both physical and social sensors.

3. The aggregation of physical sensors and social sensors to overcome the unreliability of individual sensors and which improves the overall performance of event detection.

We demonstrate the feasibility of our work using three different datasets (New York real-time traffic camera feeds, NUS foodcourts' camera feeds and Twitter data from New York City), and conduct evaluation experiments with four instances of real-world events.

The remainder of the paper is organized as follows. Section 2 presents works related to our research. Section 3 describes the proposed multi-layer tweeting cameras framework. Section 4 elaborates on the details of defined operators and functions, signal detection theory for event detection, as well as the social information extraction algorithm. Section 5 gives qualitative demonstrations and comprehensive statistical evaluation on the data. Section 6 discusses issues related to our work and Section 7 concludes the paper.

2. RELATED WORK

Event Detection using Visual Sensors

With an increasing number of sensors having capabilities of sensing, processing, communicating, usage of sensors in event detection and situation awareness is spreading. Massively distributed visual sensors (webcams) are utilized for phenology study, scene and environment understanding [19, 6]. A multi-tier network SensEye of heterogeneous cameras has been proposed to overcome the disadvantage of single-tier networks in surveillance application, performing object detection, recognition and tracking tasks [25]. Distributed smart cameras [11], which combine video sensing, processing, and communication on a single embedded platform, are also being widely used in camera sensor networks to produce alerts if certain types of unusual behaviour [10] or abnormal events [1] occur. Event is an elementary concept not only for humans but also in multimedia applications. Several works propose event-related models [39], as well as the concept of atomic and compound events [5] in video application. Tasks of identifying and localizing specified spatio-temporal patterns in video, such as waving hands or picking up objects are tackled in crowd video event detection, where actions are matched with a predefined event template, which limits the general use of event detection in real-world scenarios [22]. In addition, unusual event detection has also drawn much attention. To bridge the gap between machine-oriented low level features and human-friendly high level semantics, a number of works concern image captioning [15, 21, 36] and video concept detection [20, 9], where the task is to assign concept labels to an input image/video along with their associated probabilities. However, this introduces uncertainty and confidence problems [8] in sensor readings. Moreover, multi-modal sensor fusion has been well studied for combining multiple physical sensor modalities for various multimedia tasks [4]. Since the fusion of video and text is not well explored, we contribute to this part by providing a unified spatio-temporal data representation that can easily incorporate social media text analysis.

Event Detection using Social Sensors
Many online social network services are prevalent nowadays by which users share personal opinions, breaking news and interesting stories. Twitter, as one of the most important social sensors, has attracted a large number of works for event detection [12], topic discovery [18], as well as content analysis [26]. A news processing system, TwitterStand [32], is built to capture and investigate latest breaking news. By analyzing news related tweets, it automatically obtains breaking news and current hot topics, filtering out noise that does not belong to the news domain. Also, Twitter users are regarded as social sensors [31] in detecting and tracking earthquakes, typhoons or traffic jams. Twitter streams with a specific set of keywords are monitored and classified into events and non-events. Events in the work, however, are only recognized for specific predefined keywords, which limits its usage for general automated event detection. Similarly, a framework constituted by event clustering, feature extraction and classification steps has been proposed to distinguish real-world event and non-event twitter messages [7]. [38] proposes a situation awareness algorithm to detect geospatial events in a given monitored geographic area, which offers good summary of events. However, the events detected are limited to a small local area. An overall situation cannot be inferred due to the geographic limitation. Aggregating large-scale social information streams from various locations into a unified platform allows users to understand evolving situation in a holistic view. Twitris [33] captures spatio-temporal-thematic properties in processing large scale social data, and integrates semantic context from multiple web resources, which facilitates social sensing in a broad variety of application domains. To understand various events, [35] takes social media data which express social interest of users as "social pixels" and spatially aggregates them into "Emage", an event data based analogy of image. Besides, data abstraction and tools are designed to analyze spatio-temporal pattern of situation. Based on the "Emage", a media-processing approach and a declarative query mechanism are defined for the end user to query and understand large scale social situation. Though many of these previous works on social sensors contribute to event detection, they do not consider the fusing of information from physical sensors (e.g. surveillance cameras) which we argue would offer complementary and powerful understanding of evolving situations. Besides, the fusion of mobile computing and social networking services for traffic anomaly detection has been proposed in [28], where GPS data are analysed for abnormal traffic patterns, and social information collected from

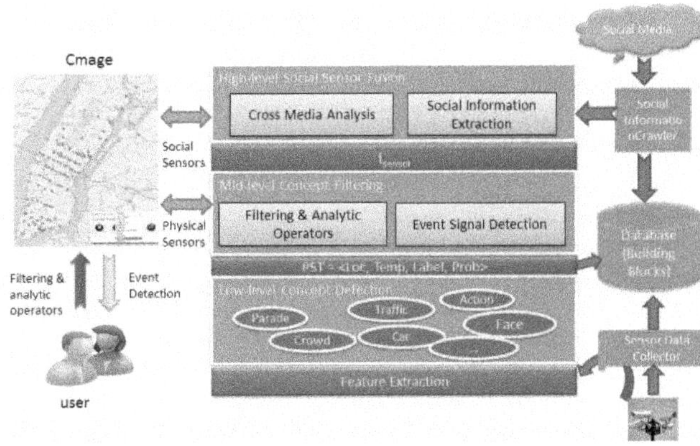

Figure 2: Overview of Proposed Multi-layer Tweeting Cameras Framework. In the first layer, low-level concepts are detected from raw sensor images through applying various concept detectors. A unified probabilistic spatio-temporal (PST) data structure represents the low-level concepts. Those camera "tweets" of low-level concepts are then aggregated and processed at the second layer using a set of predefined operators and functions. Signal detection theory is applied to detect abnormal patterns indicating occurring events. In the third layer, social information and the processed camera tweets are fused to derive high-level semantics.

microblogs are analysed to offer high-level semantic explanations for the anomalies. In addition, crowd-sourced sensing and collaboration systems over Twitter are designed and implemented which opens publish-subscribe infrastructure for sensors to be combined with social platform [14].

Summing up, many works have been done towards event detection using either visual sensors or social sensors. However, they explicitly consider either physical sensors or social sensors and do not deal with fusing these two types of sources. To the best of our knowledge, there is no previous work that builds a multi-layer tweeting camera framework that fuses both physical and social information for event detection, which is the main contribution of this paper.

3. TWEETING CAMERAS FRAMEWORK

In this section, we describe the proposed multi-layer tweeting cameras framework as shown in Figure 2. The framework consists of three layers, namely low-level concept detection layer, mid-level concept filtering layer, and high-level social sensor fusion layer. It provides an effective data processing pipeline to convert the raw media streams (either live camera feeds or real-time tweets) to different abstraction levels and finally facilitate event detection. By aggregating multiple individual sensor feeds via a common representation, the framework provides a visualization interface as well as information filtering tools for users to gain global understanding of the events occurring by manipulating a set of predefined analytic functions. In the following, we detail how (where, when, what) camera tweets are analysed and combined with social media data in this framework.

3.1 Data Collector and Storage

The data collector component is required for pulling in raw data, by which we crawl raw sensor data (e.g. image sequences from surveillance cameras), and obtain social media (e.g. tweets from Twitter) using their respective APIs. After obtaining the data, we use MongoDB to store the crawled images and tweets from Twitter. In addition, low-level concept information represented by the unified data structure (defined in Section 3.2) is also stored in the database for querying and further analysis.

3.2 Low-level Concept Detection

To bridge the gap between low-level features and human interpretable meaning, a wide variety of detectors have been created in many works to extract semantic information from images or videos. Concept detectors [20, 17], object detectors [16], face detectors [37] are examples of these advances. In the first layer, we incorporate a set of concept detectors to detect a variety of concepts from the camera feeds. Here the concepts could be faces, objects, actions or general entities with semantic meanings. These concept detectors, which are essentially statistical models or classifiers, assign text labels (tags) to the sensed data. Specifically, we adopt the VIREO-374 detectors [20] which can detect 374 general concepts defined in LSCOM [23] including "parade", "crowd", "traffic", "people marching" etc. These detectors, with a mean average precision of 16%, are not yet capable of providing accurate performance and are associated with uncertainty. The uncertainty is represented as a probabilistic confidence score indicating the probability that an observation is correctly classified into the concept category. If concept detectors are periodically applied to the camera data, we can consider the camera to be *tweeting* these labels and a set of cameras in a geographic region can be considered to be a *network of tweeting cameras*.

In addition, spatial and temporal aspects have been found to be critical for describing a situation or event [39]. Therefore, this layer models the outputs of concept detectors (camera tweets) in a unified data representation called probabilistic spatio-temporal data (PST data), which contains four elements, including camera location information, temporal information, label of the detected concept and the associated probability as the confidence value of the label. We consider the confidence of detecting a concept at any location to be like the intensity of pixels in an image, and term it as a "Concept Pixel". Such "Concept Pixel" represents a basic concept of an event, and is considered as small signal that provides a clue about the holistic situation. Therefore, spatially aggregated data from a set of cameras can be construed to be an image. Moreover, tweets represented by the PST data serve as the import for higher information filtering and are indexed in the repository (stored in MongoDB) for querying and pattern mining. Therefore, cameras whose feeds are analysed in the framework are constantly tweeting low-level concepts in the first layer and simultaneously pushing PST data in to database for indexing.

3.3 Mid-level Concept Filtering

In this layer, PST data from each camera is aggregated for the holistic representation. Specifically, "Concept Pixels" from a geographic region of interest are visualized in a map-based form called the "Concept Image" (Cmage). Concept filtering operators can then be applied on the Cmage to facilitate event detection.

3.3.1 Filtering Operators and Analytic Functions

A set of pre-defined filtering operators and analytic operators has been designed to analyse such integrated information. For example, a user can use filtering operators to query situational information about a specific concept from a particular location given specified time and probability threshold. In addition, we formally define basic analytic functions for statistics, such as min, max, sum, count, smooth, extremes, trend, abnormal, clustering and density function that can be applied on the PST data as well as the Cmage. For example, a user can check the weak signal trend of a particular concept, can obtain knowledge of when an event occurs and which region has a higher confidence of detecting specific concepts as well as how such concept confidence rises and falls with time.

3.3.2 Event Detection

Cameras in open environments do sensing under different and often noisy ambient conditions. Therefore, PST data is usually noisy. To overcome this problem, we use Signal Detection Theory [27] which models the detection task by checking objects/concepts being present or absent with the threshold set by "observers". It consists of two distributions, namely "noise" distribution and "signal + noise" distribution. We model detector results using Gaussian distributions where non-event results are considered as "noise", and event results are considered as "signals". Given this, we define event detection goal as separating the "signal" from "noise".

3.4 High-level Social Sensor Fusion

At the third level of this framework, we integrate both sensor information and social information so as to obtain a high-level semantic information of events which can be used for decision making and action. In such cross-media analysis, we try to leverage information from social media on to physical sensor data and vice versa. For example, when the tweeting cameras sense an unusual number of concepts from a specific location, we try to mine representative terms from the social media like the geo-located messages posted on Twitter. Tweets in the camera regions are collected and grouped into different clusters based on message content (topic, keywords, hash-tag, etc). We utilize the location and time information obtained from physical sensors to filter out non-concept related posts to enhance the efficiency. We then calculate the most dominant cluster (that contains most similar tweets) as the emerging topic in that particular location and compare current frequent terms in tweets with historical tweets to discover most discussed topics for the rising intensity of particular concept detector results (details provided in Section 4). Therefore, high-level knowledge is obtained in the form of social context (hot topics and messages in tweets) combined with mid-level information from physical sensors.

To summarise, in the proposed framework, camera tweets in the first layer are represented as probabilistic spatio-temporal data coming from multiple cameras, which describe low-level concepts and emit weak signals of events. Mid-level information is obtained at the second layer by aggregating and processing individual low level tweets using various filtering operators and analytic functions. High-level knowledge is derived by fusing both sensor information and social sensors information for situation understanding.

4. PROCESSING FRAMEWORK

In this section, we elaborate on the probabilistic spatio-temporal data structure, the aggregation format Cmage, as well as the analytic functions that can be applied on the data structure. We show how signal detection theory is leveraged upon to detect abnormal events. In addition, we illustrate how physical sensors and social sensors are utilised to complement each other for event detection.

4.1 Probabilistic Spatio-Temporal Data

Let D be a detection system that consists of a set of r concept detectors $D = \{D_1, D_2, \ldots, D_r\}$. Let l_i be the corresponding semantic label extracted by various concept detectors D_i, $L = \{l_1, l_2, \ldots, l_r\}$. For example, D can be VIREO-374 [20] where r = 374. The N cameras in the system are defined by $\mathbb{CAM} = \{CAM_1, CAM_2, \ldots, CAM_N\}$. As we assume that each concept detector D_i will assign a symbolic label l_i as well as the probability value p_i, we define $0 \leq p_j^{CAM_i t} \leq 1, (1 \leq i \leq N, 1 \leq j \leq r)$, be the confidence value of label l_j from by detector D_j, being applied to the raw media data captured by camera CAM_i at time t. Let $S = \{S_1, S_2, \ldots, S_n\}^t$ be the processed *probabilistic spatio-temporal stream* from whole camera network, where $S_i = \{(l_1^{CAM_i}, p_1^{CAM_i})^t, (l_2^{CAM_i}, p_2^{CAM_i})^t, \ldots, (l_r^{CAM_i}, p_r^{CAM_i})^t\}$ represents concept information detected from each individual camera.

Definition (PST: Probabilistic Spatio-Temporal Data) The fundamental building block for low-level concept representation is the probabilistic spatio-temporal element "pst".

$$pst = [loc, temp, label, prob, pointer] \quad (1)$$

where

- $loc = [lat, lon]$ represents the geo-location – latitude and longitude – of the camera location. We assume that the camera is static here but it naturally can be extended to mobile cameras as well.
- *temp* stores the time information of captured data.
- *label* represents semantic concept such as *car*, *human*, *crowd*, *parade*, etc., detected in the stream. Generally, these concepts express low-level abstraction of information which could be semi-reliably detected by existing detectors or classifiers.
- *prob* is the confidence value in [0,1] representing the output of a concept detector as a probability value.
- *pointer* points to actual raw data stream. While our intention is to abstract the raw data into a concept level data structure, it is also necessary to store the reference to the real data for further validation.

4.2 Cmage

Extending the idea of "Emage" which represents aggregated social interest of users [35], we project the probabilistic spatial temporal data with attached concepts onto the spatial map to form a *Cmage (concept image)*, to provide an intuitive visualization. The pixel intensity is the probability value of the concepts. Note that there is one Cmage for every concept. Let X be a 2D point set (lat, lon). A Cmage on X at a given time t is any probabilistic spatial temporal element $(L \times V)^X$, where L is the concept labels set and V is a probability value set of real values between 0 and 1. A Cmage is denoted as: $g^l = \{(x,p) | x \in X = \Re^2, 0 \leq p \leq 1, l \in L)\}$. A Cmage example is shown in Figure 3.

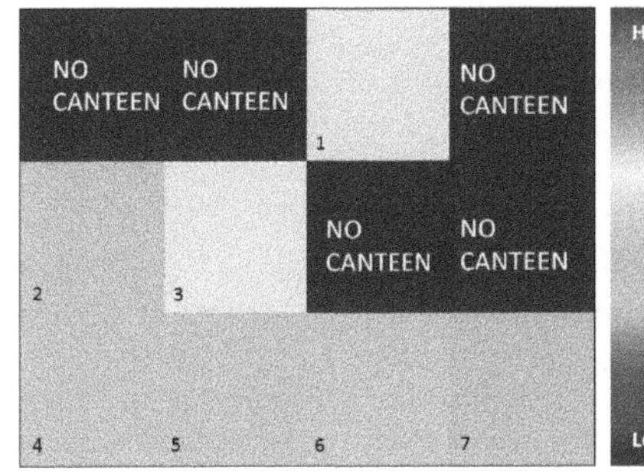

Figure 3: *Crowdedness* Cmage of NUS Foodcourts at 12:00 on 24th March 2014. The campus is divided into 3 × 4 grids. The 7 foodcourts are at cells numbered from 1 to 7. Higher pixels intensity means higher confidence of "Crowdedness" in that spatio-temporal location.

4.3 PST Data Filtering Operators

In order to efficiently retrieve relevant PST data by describing the data properties, we provide a set of basic operators for a user to query based on specific PST elements. The user can also apply analytic functions after obtaining the relevant subset of PST data. Hence the framework is envisaged to be used interactively by the user to gather insights.

4.3.1 Context-based Selection of Detector

Based on the prior knowledge of cameras (location, camera properties, history pattern or new information from other sources, e.g. social media), we define a concept selector τ_{task} to allow selecting a subset of cameras for achieving specific concept detection tasks.

$$\{T_1, T_2, \ldots, T_j\} = \tau_{task}\left(T, CAM_i, l_i\right), where: T_j \in T \quad (2)$$

4.3.2 Query Operators

Query operator Θ select a subset of data from the stream as a filter based on user specification. We use Predicate P as boolean function applied on a "pixel" (PST data point) of Cmage. Based on the four elements of PST data, we provide filtering by the functions indicated by $P\_filter(exp)$:

$$\Theta_{P\_filter(exp)}(S) = \{(l_j^{CAM_i}, p_j^{CAM_i})^t | P\_filter(exp) = True\} \quad (3)$$

where P_filter are predicates on an element of PST data.

These filtering functions can retrieve from the PST stream by taking user-defined pst related expression as parameter. Once the expression satisfies the predicate, a subset of $S' \subseteq S$ will be returned. Note that since the filter operations are based on predicates, we can combine multiple atomic predicates on pst data to form compositional queries.

Examples:
Show the March 17th data for the concept of "parade" at $5th$ Avenue with a confidence higher than 0.8:
Query: $\Theta_{P\_PROP \wedge P\_LAB \wedge P\_LOC \wedge P\_TEMP}(S)$
where: $P\_PROP = P\_prop(0.8 \leq p)$
$P\_LAB = P\_lab(label = traffic \vee parade)$
$P\_LOC = P\_loc(CAM_i) = 5^{th} Avenue)$
$P\_TEMP = P\_temp(t = March\ 17^{th})$

4.4 Data Analysis Functions

As the PST element is a numeric data presentation with spatial, temporal and symbolic information about going-on events or situations, we define a set of functions and arithmetic operations that could be applied on the PST values to extract characteristics or features of happening events.

4.4.1 Statistical functions

Statistical functions $\mathbb{S}_{func\_name}$ are used to analyse the PST dataset so as to explore the patterns or the nature of the stream by calculating extreme values, mean, trends, change points or other statistic-related indicator or parameters. The set of functions defined in our work is as follows:

a) `mean, max, min, sum`

$\mathbb{S}_{mean}(D)$ calculates the average value of a given set of data. Here we consider the data of the same label. The input data D could be a Cmage set $g_t^{\{l_1,l_2,...,l_k\}}$ or a subset of PST stream $S' \subseteq S$ of label l. The function gives an averaged Cmage g_t^m with pixels $cp = (lat, log, t, l, prob_{mean})$, where $prob_{mean}$ is calculated by taking the average probability value along the temporal axis. e.g. showing the average intensity of concept c in Cmage between t_1 and t_2 : $g_{t_1->t_2}^m = \mathbb{S}_{mean}(\Theta_{P\_lab(label=c) \wedge P\_tem(t_1 \leq t \leq t_2)}(S))$. $\mathbb{S}_{max}(D)$, $\mathbb{S}_{min}(D)$, and $\mathbb{S}_{sum}(D)$ are computed in a similar way.

b) `extremes`

Extended to the max and min functions, $\mathbb{S}_{extremes}(D)$ calculates the PST data's local minima and maxima along the temporal axis as well as among spatial regions, corresponding to the probability values. The results are computed by comparing current data points with nearby data in spatial region or with close data in temporal axis. The output are the PST data with a $tag_{extreme} \in \{crest, trough, plateau\}$.

Example: show the peak hours in foodcourt A.

$\mathbb{S}_{extremes}(D)(\Theta_{P\_lab(crowd) \wedge P\_loc(can_A)}(S))$

c) `trend`

A tweeting camera keeps sensing the environment at all times, so it would be helpful to design a function $\mathbb{S}_{trend}(D)$ to discover the social trend or changes from certain concepts pattern along time [2]. The function calculates the gradient of every data point along time series and returns every PST data with a $tag_{trend} \in \{ascending, descending, plateau\}$ as well as the trending rate $r \in \Re$.

Example: show the trend of crowdedness in foodcourt B.

$\mathbb{S}_{trend}(D)(\Theta_{P\_lab(crowd) \wedge P\_loc(can_B)}(S))$

d) `smooth`

Along with the temporal dimension, a concept detector (e.g. car detector) may be unreliable due to the environmental changes (e.g. illumination change or occlusion); therefore, the PST data generated by the sensor and hence the low-level concept detectors contain noise that may affect further analysis. The $\mathbb{S}_{smooth}(D)$ function smooths the PST data with Gaussian filter and convolution operator, so as to remove the noise in the data.

e) `outlier`

Abnormal data pattern is regarded as important information that deserves an alert for the tweeting camera system. A $\mathbb{S}_{outlier}(D)$ function is defined for extracting statistically abnormal data points from PST dataset. The function uses normal distribution model to fit the dataset and calculates the mean and variance of the observation. After that, it allows the user to specify a threshold as abnormal pattern in terms of σ.

Example: show the time when the crowd concept has an abnormal intensity during a particular period.

$\mathbb{S}_{outlier}(D, \sigma)(\Theta_{P\_lab(crowd) \wedge P\_tem(t_1 \leq t \leq t_2)}(S))$

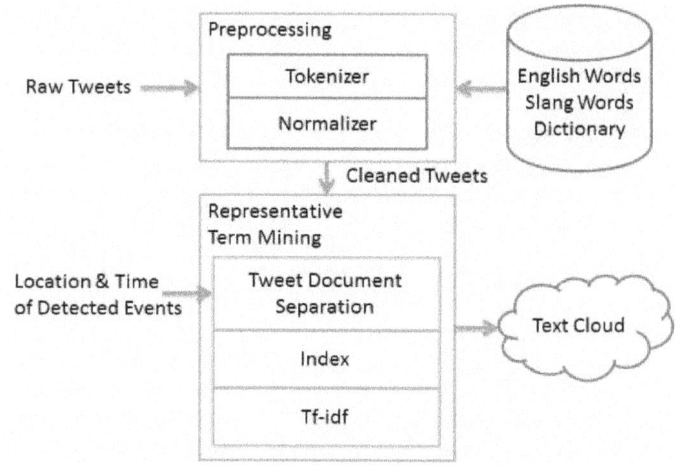

Figure 4: Architecture of Twitter Data Processing.

4.4.2 Data Mining with PST

Computing spatial clusters/segments helps in better characterizing the situation across regions [3]. We define the clustering function $\mathbb{CL}$ to group a set of PST data or 'pixels' of a Cmage in various dimensions (spatial, temporal, concept) based on the probability values of each data points. For example, $\mathbb{CL}_{loc}(\Theta_{P\_lab(c)}(S)) = \{loc_1^{gl}, loc_2^{gl}, \ldots loc_n^{gl}\}$ gives the locations of each group $gl \in \{gr_1, gr_2, gr_3\}$, where in gr_i the probability values of the subset data points $(l_r^{CAM_i}, p_r^{CAM_i})^t$ of concept l are close to each other.

4.4.3 Density Function

The Density Function $\mathbb{C}$ takes the PST dataset and calculates the number of elements that satisfy a predefined requirement. The set could be a Cmage, the whole PST dataset or a sub-stream of PST dataset selected by the filtering operations described in previous section. It can be used on various dimensions of data for deriving the characteristics of that particular dimension. For instance, when a specific event happens, the number of the cameras capturing the concept of this event gives us a intuitive information about the situation.

Example: calculate the number of cameras that detected "person" concept between time t_1 and t_2.

$\mathbb{C}_{CAM}(\Theta_{P\_lab(person) \wedge P\_pro(p=1) \wedge P\_tem(t_1 \leq t \leq t_2)}(S))$

4.5 Social Information Fusion

Once interesting PST data characteristics has been detected, camera location information is utilised to query social media tweets posted around the camera location, and the time interval during event (e.g. when an anomaly was detected (i.e., $[t_1, t_2]$)) is used to compare current highly frequent tweets with historical tweets, so as to obtain textual information that best describes an event using social media. The text analysis architecture including tweets preprocessing and representative term mining is shown in Figure 4.

All the tweets posted during $[t_1, t_2]$ are considered as a document denoted as T_C, and the historical tweets denoted by T_H refers to all the documents of other than the event time in the past days; tf-idf is used to analyse the relevance of each term among them once both T_H and T_C are obtained. Equation 4 adopted from [28] is used to calculate the weight of extracted terms that could best describe the event.

$$w_{term} = tf(term, T_C) \times idf(term, T_H)$$

$$s.t. \begin{cases} tf(term, T_C) = \dfrac{f(term, T_C)}{\max\{f(w, T_C), \forall w \in T_C\}} \\ idf(term, T_H) = \log \dfrac{|T_H|}{|\{th \in T_H : term \in th\}|} \end{cases} \quad (4)$$

where *tf* is the function to calculate the frequency of the term in the current tweet document (T_C), and *idf* refers to the calculation of inverse document frequencies in all the historical tweets documents (T_H). Therefore, terms with high weight mean that they are highly discussed in current document (event related topics) and less discussed in the whole collection of historical tweets.

To fuse information from both physical and social sensors, we define event signal $Es_e =< I_{se}(e), I_{so}(e) >$ where I_{se} stands for event sensor signal and I_{so} stands for event social signal. Here we take confidence value of a particular concept **c** as I_{se} and term weights of **tw** as I_{so}, in which **c** and **tw** are closely related or the same content. Then we adopt equation 5 to fuse them to derive final event signal intensity.

$$Es(e) = w_{se} * I_{se}(e) + w_{so} * I_{so}(e) \quad (5)$$

where w_{se} and w_{so} are considered as weights of sensors that can be specified by users.

4.6 Cameras Tweeting Rate

Since we use the polling method for fetching camera data, this determines how frequently a camera tweets. Currently we have set the cameras to regularly tweet once every 10 seconds. However, we provide flexibility to the user in setting this camera tweeting rate by $ctr = T(x)$ posts/second.

5. EXPERIMENTS

5.1 Datasets

5.1.1 NYC Traffic CCTV Camera

We have crawled live feeds from 150 public CCTV traffic cameras distributed on the roads all over the Manhattan district of New York City, which are under the management of the Department of Transportation. The live cameras provide frequently updated still images from several locations in the five boroughs. The update frequency varies from 1 second to 5 seconds.

We have collected our data (resolution of 352×240) during March 13 2014 to March 19 2014, June 24 2014 to August 20 2014, and October 3 2014 to October 22 2014, with a total size of data being 1.23 TB, to ensure sufficient variety. This dataset is denoted as NYC traffic in the remaining section.

5.1.2 NUS Foodcourt CCTV Camera

The NUS (National University of Singapore) foodcourt video dataset consists of feeds from 73 cameras located at 9 different foodcourts on the NUS campus. Each foodcourt has several cameras facing either seating area or the food stalls areas. The data has been recorded over six months.

5.1.3 Twitter Data

We have crawled tweets using Twitter Streaming API from October 08, 2014 to November 2, 2014, with the geographic bounding box of [40.698770, -74.021248, 40.872932, -73.905459] which includes Manhattan, and collected a total of 1,510,025 records. Each record is stored in the database with original set containing all data fields such as time of created, geo-location, text etc.

5.2 Evaluation Approach

In this study, we analyse the effectiveness and capacity of our framework to detect different events. We evaluate our framework by comparing detected events with ground truth shown in the next section, and illustrate the semantic meaning of the change of sensor data pattern by mining social information.

5.2.1 Events Ground Truth

We use the notices posted on the "Weekend Traffic Advisory" website of the New York City Department of Transportation for obtaining the ground truth.[1] This website details traffic alerts in terms of locations of road construction and other events that will affect the flow of traffic for the coming weekend. The ground truth for the events that we try to detect is shown in Table 1.

Table 1: Real-world Events Ground Truth

event	*date*	*time*	*location*
CBGB Music Festival	12 Oct	10am-7pm	Broadway 51 Street
Hispanic Parade	12 Oct	12pm-5pm	5th Avenue
Columbus Day Parade	13 Oct	11am-5pm	5th Avenue
Saint Patrick's Day Parade	17 Mar	12pm-5pm	5th Avenue
Million March NYC Protest	13 Dec	2pm-5pm	Washington Square Park, 5th Avenue, Foley Square

5.2.2 Measurement

To demonstrate the effectiveness of the framework, we consider the detection rate of each event listed in Table 1. As per the signal detection theory, the threshold for the corresponding concepts is evaluated in terms of detection rate.

5.3 Results

We evaluate our framework by examining the detection results and social information fusion results on the four events shown above. For event detection using sensors, we look at the concept results and demonstrate the usage of proposed analytic functions as well as visualization of Cmage. In the use of social information, we compare event relevant tweets during event happening time with ordinary non-event time in terms of the tf-idf values as word's importance weight.

5.3.1 Event Detection based on SDT

In order to model the noise and real signal of each camera, we consider concept confidence values as the signals for detection. We use noise and signal to model concept output values of non-event and event respectively and automatically select an optimal detection threshold. Note that the distribution is only valid between 0 and 1 since the confidence value is a probability value. Figure 5 shows the distribution of "parade" signal from camera in 5th Avenue 57 Street.

[1] http://www.nyc.gov/html/dot/html/motorist/wkndtraf.shtml

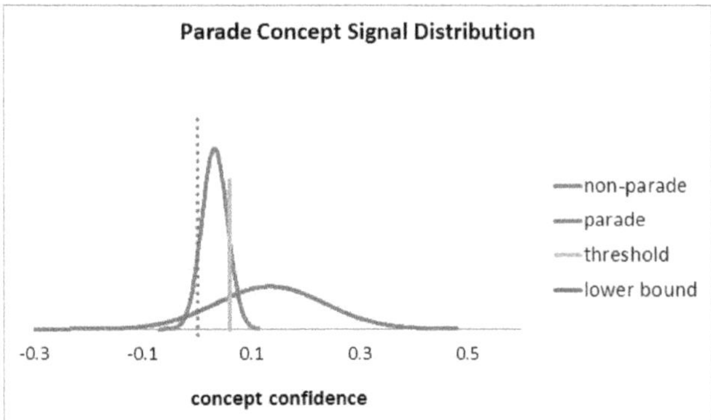

Figure 5: "Parade" Signal Distribution in 5 Ave @ 57 Street.

The distribution is determined by calculating mean and standard deviation of concept results from images captured on October 13, 2014, from 2pm to 3 pm to when a "Columbus Day Parade" event was happening. The non-parade curve depicts the concept results from same time but on different days when there are no parade events. These data are analysed to determine an optimal threshold for a particular concept detector for a camera. Note that since different cameras usually capture different scenes, optimal threshold of a particular detector are not always the same. Also, for a particular camera, varying the threshold would cause different hit rate as well as false alarm, as depicted in Figure 6.

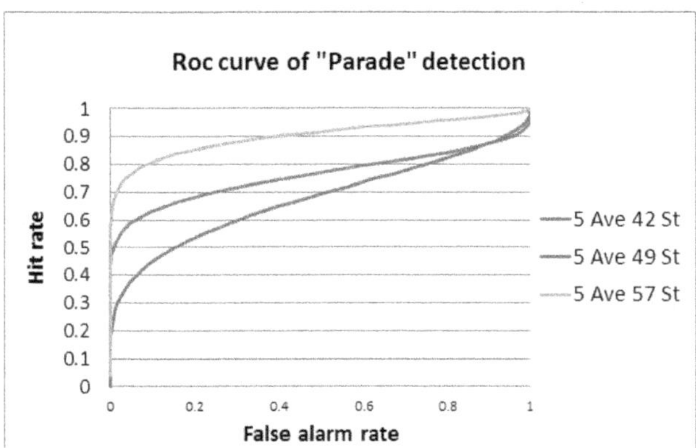

Figure 6: ROC Curve of "Parade" Signal in Three Locations.

This figure shows ROC curve of the parade detector for three different cameras. The threshold is set to the value that maximizes the hit rate as well as minimizes the false alarm rate. Therefore, the cusp point in the ROC curve i.e. the point that minimises false alarm while maximizing hit rate is chosen as the threshold. For example, the threshold for the parade concept in Camera of 5th Avenue 57 St is computed as 0.07. Once the threshold of concept detectors is set, it is fixed and applied on images to automatically trigger event alerts. However, the user can also manually reconfigure this threshold if required. Using this threshold, we examine the detection performance of two parade events in terms of f1-score; the analysis is shown in Figure 7 and 8 for two cameras.

We use the threshold to analyse the results of both "Columbus Day Parade" and "Hispanic Parade" event, and compare our thresholding results with baseline which is given by the detectors in the label field based on a fixed value 0.5 as

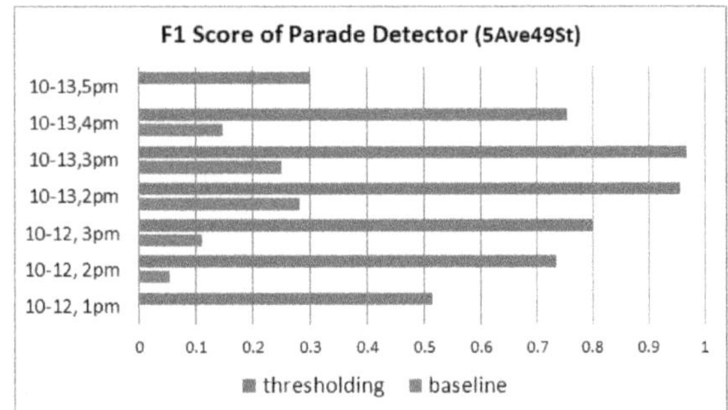

Figure 7: F1 Score for Camera in 5 Avenue at 49 Street

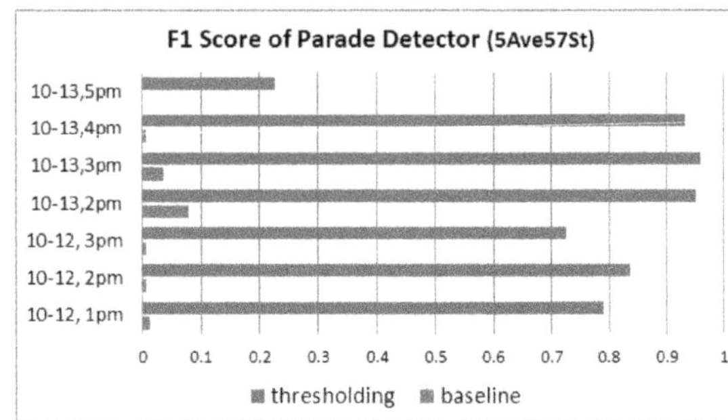

Figure 8: F1 Score for Camera in 5 Avenue at 57 Street

threshold. As can be seen, having an adaptive threshold significantly improves the performance.

5.3.2 Applying Analytic Functions

Once concepts' confidence is obtained for image snapshots of cameras, predefined analytic functions such as "smooth" , "extreme", "trend" can be applied to obtain meaningful information such as event pattern, concept trending by interacting with Cmage in the second layer of our framework.

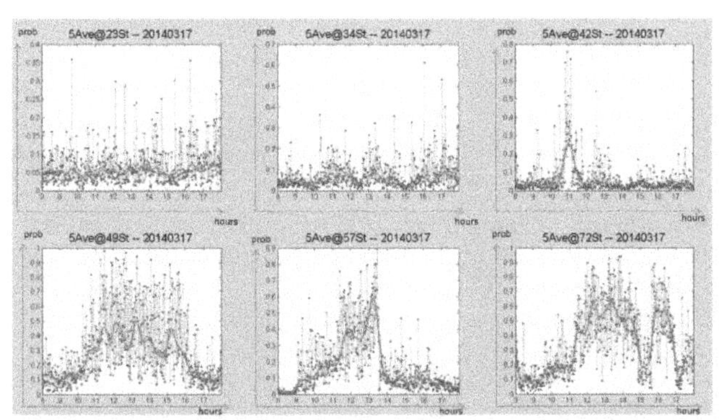

Figure 9: *People Marching* Concept Results from 8:00 to 18:00 in March 17th, during Saint Patrick's Day Parade Event

Figure 9 shows the *people marching* concept detailed results with smoothing function from 8:00 to 18:00 in March 17th Saint Patrick's Day. It is shown that the peaks occur from 11:00 in cameras at 5th Avenue 42, 49, 57 and 72 streets. This demonstrates that the function performs reasonably well in providing a smooth curve for the concept and effectively reducing the impact of sensor uncertainty.

The Foodcourt videos are separated into frames and the crowd volume index for the frames is calculated every 30 seconds through background subtraction. Given a snapshot taken at time t from Camera A, the crowd analyser will return a crowd index in the range of [0, 1], higher value representing higher intensity of crowdedness. Therefore, we are able to convert the image to the unified probabilistic spatio-temporal data point (loc_{cam_A}, t, "$crowd$", $probability$), where the location is the canteen having the camera. Therefore, the cameras would tweet crowd information twice every minute.

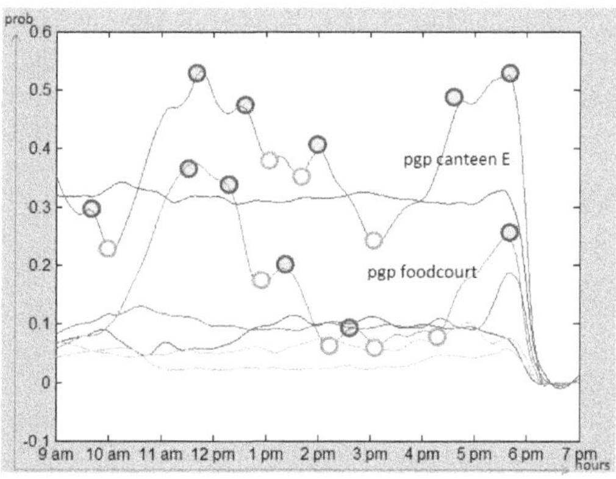

Figure 10: The Crowd Extremes at 7 Foodcourts on Sunday.

Figure 10 shows the crowd intensity on Sunday. Being applied with the *extreme* function, the two curves labelled with circles show extremes of the crowd intensity. These are foodcourts near student dorms. As can be seen, the curves match with real situation, sketching two major peaks at lunch time and dinner time and provide the information of foodcourts that remain open on Sundays so that user could have idea of where and when to go for lunch and dinner.

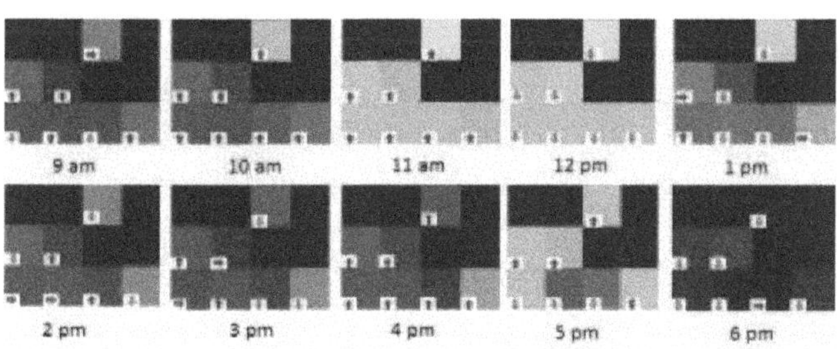

Figure 11: A Campus Foodcourt Cmage *Crowdness* with Arrows indicating Ascending, Descending and Plateau Trend.

In addition, we show the crowd density Cmage trend (with labels) of campus canteens from 9 am to 6 pm on 21th March 2014 in Figure 11. The *trend* function is applied after data are smoothed with the *smooth* function and the trend is calculated by taking the gradient value of a time point. If the gradient is below a given threshold t, the Cmage pixel will be labelled "plateau" at that time. If defined by user preference, a tweeting alert could be triggered with Cmage sending a notification to an end user.

5.3.3 Cross Media Analysis & Social Sensor Fusion

To extract the relevant semantic information from tweets in order to fuse with the camera information, we conduct term frequency analysis from social media by using tweets posted nearby the places where an event occurs. All the tweets are separated into different documents in terms of each hour and distance to a camera location. The time span of a document could be several hours depending on the start time and end time of detected events. For example, tweets posted from 1pm to 5pm within a geo-circle centered in 5th Avenue 42 Street are stored as one document. Here we set the radius as 0.01 in terms of coordinates. High frequency terms of a given location and tweets during the events are shown to the user through the framework interface. Examples are shown in Figure 12.

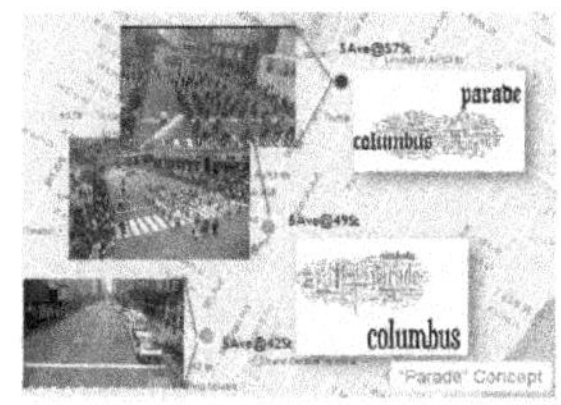

(a) Social Sensor Fusion for "Columbus Day Parade"

(b) Social Sensor Fusion for "Hispanic Parade" Event

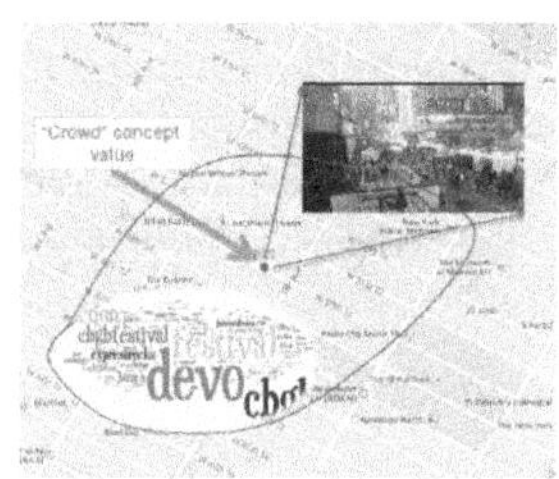

(c) Crowd Concept and Salient Topic Words during "CBGB Musical Festival"

(d) Sensor and Social Information of "Million March NYC" Protest Event

Figure 12: Social Sensor Fusion for Real-world Events

We calculate the term weight for each word posted from a specific location. Words of bigger size represent higher weight. As can be seen, most tweets posted near an event location are able to give high-level semantic meaning of the event, e.g. Figure 12 (a) and (b) confirm the events are indeed the "Columbus Day Parade" and "Hispanic Parade" events respectively. (c) offers details of musical band (DEVO) that participate in CBGB musical festival, and in (d) "Million March NYC" protest event is captured by both tweets and camera feeds in terms of "crowd" concept.

Table 2 shows the comparison between our approach of social information mining with baseline in terms of number of tweets. As represented, our framework utilize sensor information (where and when an event is detected) to significantly (from 10^5 to 10^3) reduce the noise in the tweets. The baseline TH and TC are the number of geo-tagged tweets crawled before and during the event respectively. Our approach TH and TC are the number of geo-tagged tweets crawled *around the event location* before and during the event respectively.

Table 2: Comparison based on Number of Tweets Analyzed

Event	Base line #tweets		our approach	
	$\|TH\|$	$\|TC\|$	$\|TH\|$	$\|TC\|$
Hispanic Parade	86,714	24,357	1,496	225
Columbus Day Parade	111,071	21,891	1,573	335
CBGB Musical Festival	86,714	24,357	1,321	369

As shown in Figure 13, according to the equation defined in section 4.5 the final parade event signal intensity is im-

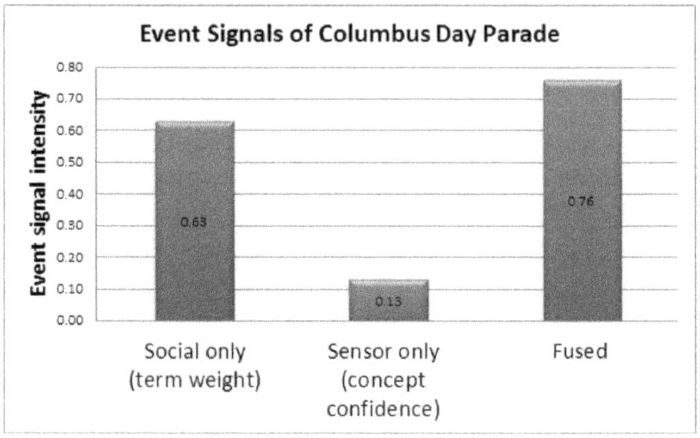

Figure 13: Comparison among Fused, Physical and Social Sensor Results of Detecting the "Columbus Day Parade" Event

proved when compared to using each individual sensor. Here the I_{se}(*"parade"*) here is the average confidence value in time span tweeted by the cameras. Though here only the "parade" is detected from both, this equation could also be generally applied when concepts discussed in two type of sensors are similar or correlated (e.g. a "crowd" concept detected could be related to a musical festival CBGB), which would be our future exploration.

To conclude, by automatically computing the concept detection threshold, we are able to improve the event detection rate and offer user the ability to analyse event patterns. Based on the spatial and temporal information provided by the sensors, we can leverage on the social information to give more detailed information of events.

6. DISCUSSION

Our experiments have verified the significant correspondence between physical sensors data and virtual social information. While the vocabulary of camera tweets is limited in our experiments, it can be scaled up. A more comprehensive set of concept detectors including face detectors and image caption labelers can be used in the first layer. Any improvement in the quality and scope of concept detectors will immediately benefit the proposed method. In the second layer, more filtering options and analytic operators to query various types of event can be provided. Without loss of generality, the framework is also able to detect unplanned events as long as the events emit visual and social signals. The occurrence of an unplanned event will then lead to changes in the observed signal levels, when compared to the times when there are no events occurring. The unified data representation for visual sensors and analytic operators allows users to flexibly specify events characteristic for detection. Thus outlier detection can potentially help detect unplanned events. For an unplanned (or planned) event that doesn't include visual information (e.g. video) the framework will have to rely on text processing only. While this can still be useful, it will not demonstrate the full power of the proposed approach. One of areas of improvement is the efficiency in performance. Concept detection requires considerable computation power and time to generate the camera tweets, which may not be able to keep up with the frame rate of camera feeds. Subsampling of the feeds could be one of the solutions. However, dropping of frames might lead to loss of critical information for events of short duration. Thus, improving the quality of camera tweets and generating them real-time is an open problem. Since we are exploring sensor data concerning real world situations, it is worth considering the degree of privacy loss for the people who happen to appear in the camera images. To prevent any breach of privacy, we currently use images of low resolution so that people's faces are not easily recognizable. For a more comprehensive approach towards privacy, the identity leakage model [29] could be used to calculate the privacy loss due to the face identity as well as the various side-channels. Furthermore, adaptive robust privacy protection methods [30] could be incorporated into our proposed framework.

7. CONCLUSIONS

In this work, we propose a novel *multi-layer tweeting cameras framework*, which uses visual sensors to tweet semantic concepts for event detection. We define a unified Probabilistic Spatio-Temporal (PST) data structure to integrate the low-level concepts from the network of visual sensors. A number of filtering operators and analytic operators are also defined for the user to apply on such PST data so as to derive mid-level concepts that are suitable for higher level data visualization. We also discussed how information from the physical sensors and social media sensors can be fused to infer high-level semantics. Experiments on three real-world datasets have confirmed the effectiveness of our proposed framework. More information is available on our project website[2] including code, data, and relsults.

For future work, we plan to integrate information from social media sensors, which include trend analysis and topic mining, to improve the quality of the camera tweets. In addition, we also would explore the possibility of creating an interactive framework that allows for the integration of other types of sensors into the framework. Finally, machine learning based approaches can be employed to learn the correlation between physical sensor tweets and social media tweets.

8. ACKNOWLEDGEMENT

This research was conducted at the NUS-ZJU SeSaMe Centre. It is supported by the Singapore NRF under its IRC@SG Funding Initiative and administered by the IDMPO. We thank the Ambient Intelligence Laboratory, NUS for sharing the NUS foodcourts camera data and associated analysis. We also would like to thank our SeSaMe colleague Dr. Christian Von Der Weth for his insightful comments and careful proof-reading.

9. REFERENCES

[1] A. Adam, E. Rivlin, I. Shimshoni, and D. Reinitz. Robust real-time unusual event detection using multiple fixed-location monitors. *In PAMI*, 30(3):555–560, 2008.

[2] T. Althoff, D. Borth, J. Hees, and A. Dengel. Analysis and forecasting of trending topics in online media streams. In *ACM Multimedia*, pages 907–916, 2013.

[3] P. Arbelaez, M. Maire, C. Fowlkes, and J. Malik. Contour detection and hierarchical image segmentation. *In PAMI*, 33(5):898–916, 2011.

[4] P. Atrey, M. Hossain, A. El Saddik, and M. Kankanhalli. Multimodal fusion for multimedia

[2]https://sites.google.com/site/fredyuhuiwang/home

analysis: a survey. *Multimedia Systems*, 16(6):345–379, 2010.

[5] P. K. Atrey, M. S. Kankanhalli, and J. B. Oommen. Goal-oriented optimal subset selection of correlated multimedia streams. *ACM Trans. Multimedia Comput. Commun. Appl.*, 3(1), 2007.

[6] R. Babari, N. Hautiere, E. Dumont, N. Paparoditis, and J. Misener. Visibility monitoring using conventional roadside cameras - emerging applications. *Transportation Research Part C: Emerging Technologies*, 22(0):17 – 28, 2012.

[7] H. Becker, M. Naaman, and L. Gravano. Beyond trending topics: Real-world event identification on twitter. In *International Conference on Weblogs and Social Media, Barcelona, Catalonia, Spain*, 2011.

[8] C. Bhatt and M. Kankanhalli. Probabilistic temporal multimedia data mining. *ACM Trans. Intell. Syst. Technol.*, 2(2):17:1–17:19, 2011.

[9] C. A. Bhatt, P. K. Atrey, and M. S. Kankanhalli. A reward-and-punishment-based approach for concept detection using adaptive ontology rules. *ACM Trans. Multimedia Comput. Commun. Appl.*, 9(2):10:1–10:21, 2013.

[10] O. Boiman and M. Irani. Detecting irregularities in images and in video. *International Journal of Computer Vision*, 74(1):17–31, 2007.

[11] M. Bramberger, A. Doblander, A. Maier, B. Rinner, and H. Schwabach. Distributed embedded smart cameras for surveillance applications. *Computer*, 39(2):68–75, 2006.

[12] M. Cataldi, L. Di Caro, and C. Schifanella. Emerging topic detection on twitter based on temporal and social terms evaluation. In *International Workshop on Multimedia Data Mining*, pages 4:1–4:10, 2010.

[13] H. Cramer and S. Buttner. Things that tweet, check-in and are befriended. two explorations on robotics amp; social media. In *HRI*, pages 125–126, 2011.

[14] M. Demirbas, M. Bayir, C. Akcora, Y. Yilmaz, and H. Ferhatosmanoglu. Crowd-sourced sensing and collaboration using twitter. In *WoWMoM*, pages 1–9, 2010.

[15] C. Farabet, C. Couprie, L. Najman, and Y. LeCun. Learning hierarchical features for scene labeling. *PAMI*, 35(8):1915–1929, Aug 2013.

[16] R. B. Girshick, P. F. Felzenszwalb, and D. A. McAllester. Object detection with grammar models. In *Advances in Neural Information Processing Systems*, pages 442–450, 2011.

[17] A. Habibian, K. E. van de Sande, and C. G. Snoek. Recommendations for video event recognition using concept vocabularies. In *ICMR*, pages 89–96, 2013.

[18] L. Hong, A. Ahmed, S. Gurumurthy, and et al. Discovering geographical topics in the twitter stream. In *WWW*, pages 769–778, 2012.

[19] N. Jacobs and et al. The global network of outdoor webcams: Properties and applications. In *ACM SIGSPATIAL*, pages 111–120, 2009.

[20] Y.-G. Jiang, J. Yang, C.-W. Ngo, and A. Hauptmann. Representations of keypoint-based semantic concept detection: A comprehensive study. *IEEE Transactions on Multimedia*, 12(1):42–53, 2010.

[21] A. Karpathy, A. Joulin, and F. Li. Deep fragment embeddings for bidirectional image sentence mapping. In *Advances in Neural Information Processing Systems 27*, pages 1889–1897. 2014.

[22] Y. Ke, R. Sukthankar, and M. Hebert. Event detection in crowded videos. In *ICCV*, pages 1–8, 2007.

[23] L. Kennedy and A. Hauptmann. Lscom lexicon definitions and annotations (version 1.0). 2006.

[24] M. Kranz, L. Roalter, and F. Michahelles. Things that twitter: Social networks and the internet of things. In *What can the Internet of Things do for the Citizen (CIoT) Workshop at International Conference on Pervasive Computing*, 2010.

[25] P. Kulkarni, D. Ganesan, P. Shenoy, and Q. Lu. Senseye: A multi-tier camera sensor network. In *ACM Multimedia*, pages 229–238, 2005.

[26] J. Lehmann, B. Gonçalves, J. J. Ramasco, and C. Cattuto. Dynamical classes of collective attention in twitter. In *WWW*, pages 251–260, 2012.

[27] D. Los Angeles Thomas et al. *Elementary signal detection theory.* Oxford University Press, 2001.

[28] B. Pan, Y. Zheng, D. Wilkie, and C. Shahabi. Crowd sensing of traffic anomalies based on human mobility and social media. In *ACM SIGSPATIAL*, pages 344–353, 2013.

[29] M. Saini, P. Atrey, S. Mehrotra, and M. Kankanhalli. W3-privacy: understanding what, when, and where inference channels in multi-camera surveillance video. *Multimedia Tools and Applications*, 68(1):135–158, 2014.

[30] M. Saini, P. K. Atrey, S. Mehrotra, and M. Kankanhalli. Adaptive transformation for robust privacy protection in video surveillance. *Advances in Multimedia*, page 14, 2014.

[31] T. Sakaki, M. Okazaki, and Y. Matsuo. Earthquake shakes twitter users: Real-time event detection by social sensors. In *WWW*, pages 851–860, 2010.

[32] J. Sankaranarayanan, H. Samet, B. E. Teitler, M. D. Lieberman, and J. Sperling. Twitterstand: News in tweets. In *ACM SIGSPATIAL*, pages 42–51, 2009.

[33] A. Sheth, A. Jadhav, P. Kapanipathi, and et al. Twitris: A system for collective social intelligence. In *Encyclopedia of Social Network Analysis and Mining*, pages 2240–2253. 2014.

[34] J. Shin and et al. Asap: A camera sensor network for situation awareness. *Principles of Distributed Systems*, 4878:31–47, 2007.

[35] V. K. Singh, M. Gao, and R. Jain. Social pixels: Genesis and evaluation. In *ACM Multimedia*, pages 481–490, 2010.

[36] O. Vinyals and et al. Show and tell: A neural image caption generator. *CoRR*, abs/1411.4555, 2014.

[37] P. Viola and M. Jones. Robust real-time face detection. *In IJCV*, 57(2):137–154, 2004.

[38] M. Walther and M. Kaisser. Geo-spatial event detection in the twitter stream. In *European Conference on Advances in Information Retrieval*, pages 356–367, 2013.

[39] U. Westermann and R. Jain. Toward a common event model for multimedia applications. *IEEE MultiMedia*, 14(1):19–29, Jan. 2007.

Mining Missing Hyperlinks from Human Navigation Traces: A Case Study of Wikipedia

Robert West
Stanford University
west@cs.stanford.edu

Ashwin Paranjape
Stanford University
ashwinp@cs.stanford.edu

Jure Leskovec
Stanford University
jure@cs.stanford.edu

ABSTRACT

Hyperlinks are an essential feature of the World Wide Web. They are especially important for online encyclopedias such as Wikipedia: an article can often only be understood in the context of related articles, and hyperlinks make it easy to explore this context. But important links are often missing, and several methods have been proposed to alleviate this problem by learning a linking model based on the structure of the existing links.

Here we propose a novel approach to identifying missing links in Wikipedia. We build on the fact that the ultimate purpose of Wikipedia links is to aid navigation. Rather than merely suggesting new links that are in tune with the structure of existing links, our method finds missing links that would immediately enhance Wikipedia's navigability. We leverage data sets of navigation paths collected through a Wikipedia-based human-computation game in which users must find a short path from a start to a target article by only clicking links encountered along the way. We harness human navigational traces to identify a set of candidates for missing links and then rank these candidates. Experiments show that our procedure identifies missing links of high quality.

Categories and Subject Descriptors

H.5.4 [**Information Interfaces and Presentation**]: Hypertext/Hypermedia—*Navigation*

General Terms

Algorithms, Experimentation, Human Factors

Keywords

Navigation; browsing; Wikipedia; Wikispeedia; human computation; link prediction

1. INTRODUCTION

The success of the World Wide Web hinges on the hyperlinks that weave its many billions of documents together. It is this fact that gave rise to its very name. Hyperlinks are essential for several reasons. From a human–computer interface perspective, they allow users to explore the available information in a natural way by effortlessly following pointers to references. For instance, the act of clicking a Wikipedia link is negligible compared to the cumbersome effort of flipping through countless pages of a paper encyclopedia, or even finding another volume on yet another shelf in a physical library. Links are also important from an information management perspective. They are among the most prominent features used by search engines, both for indexing and ranking. When building a Web index, anchor texts serve as informative descriptors of the target page they point to, oftentimes more so than page titles and content [21]. Moreover, in search-result ranking, several standard methods, such as PageRank [6] and HITS [18], rely on the Web graph induced by the hyperlinks. And finally, links are important from a content provider perspective, since they make content discoverable to users and search engines. If a document has no incoming links, it cannot be accessed by a browsing user, nor can it be crawled and indexed by a search engine.

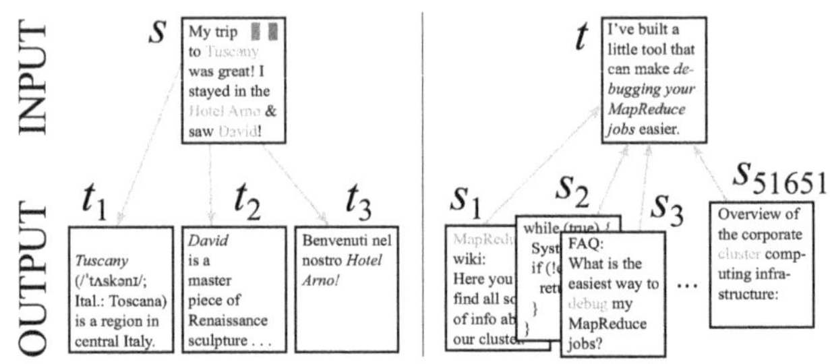

(a) Target prediction (b) Source prediction

Figure 1: In scenario (a) a source s is given, and the aim is to find mentions of relevant concepts in the source page and link them to appropriate targets. Here the set of candidate anchors is limited to the source document. In scenario (b) a target article t is given, and the aim is to identify sources that contain relevant mentions of t and could benefit from linking to it. Here every document mentioning the target is a potential source.

Source vs. target prediction. While maintaining a good hyperlink structure is important, it is also difficult and time-consuming. We distinguish two tasks that typically arise during webpage maintenance, which we term *target prediction* and *source prediction:*

- In the *target prediction* task (Fig. 1(a)), a source document s is given, and the goal is to find mentions of relevant concepts in s and link them to appropriate targets t.
- In the *source prediction* task (Fig. 1(b)), a target document t is given, and the goal is to identify sources s that contain relevant mentions of t and would benefit from referencing t.

WWW 2015, May 18–22, 2015, Florence, Italy.
ACM 978-1-4503-3469-3/15/05.
http://dx.doi.org/10.1145/2736277.2741666.

To illustrate these two abstract tasks, consider the following concrete scenarios (schematized in Fig. 1).

Target prediction: In a typical target prediction scenario, a traveler might write a blog post about his recent trip to Tuscany, in which he mentions several places, foods, landmarks, and historical persons. To provide more context, he wants to link these mentions to external resources, such as Wikipedia articles, online recipes, or hotel websites. Manually identifying the relevant concepts and linking them to the most appropriate target pages can be a tedious process [11, 28].

Source prediction: A typical source prediction scenario might involve a software engineer in a large company who has just finished a piece of code that could increase the productivity of many colleagues. She also created a documentation and tutorial page, but for it to be visible, she needs to link to it from other pages that colleagues interested in her code are likely to visit, such as company-internal wikis, Q&A fora, etc. Along the same lines, consider a Wikipedia editor who has just written a new article. The article is of little use if it is not reachable from other articles, so the editor wants to plant links into other articles to point to the new article.

Identifying appropriate sources for a given target is even more difficult than identifying appropriate targets for a given source: In target prediction, the set of candidate anchors is limited and can be identified by inspecting the source document. In source prediction, on the contrary, the set of candidate sources is practically unbounded, as any page on the Web is a potential candidate to link to the target.

Existing approaches. Automatic methods for detecting missing links would be important and useful. Previous work has proposed methods mainly for the target prediction problem; *i.e.*, they annotate a given source document with links to external resources, primarily Wikipedia articles. One class of techniques can process arbitrary plain-text documents. Here the text of the input document is combined with background knowledge from Wikipedia's textual content as well as graph structure to predict outgoing links [22, 23, 26]. A second group of approaches takes Wikipedia articles as input and uses the already existing links (and possibly the text content) to predict further outgoing links for the input article, *e.g.*, based on adjacency-matrix factorization [44, 45], information retrieval techniques [13, 51], or machine learning [29].

With regard to the source prediction problem, a very simple approach would be to first collect all anchor texts in the document collection that frequently link to the target t and to then link all as yet unlinked occurrences of these anchor texts to t as well. Unfortunately, this method is too simplistic and suffers from some major drawbacks: first, a phrase might not be link-worthy in every context (*e.g.*, 'flower' is a good link anchor in the context of botany, but not in that of a wedding, where the concept of a flower needs no further explanation); second, the disambiguation problem is not addressed (*e.g.*, 'Florence' should link to FIRENZE in most contexts, but to FLORENCE, ALABAMA in the context of Lauderdale County, Alabama). Hence more sophisticated algorithms are required for solving the source prediction task.

Independent of whether the source or target prediction task is considered, what is largely missing from the picture is the realization that, beyond text content and graph structure, there are additional sources of data that could be utilized in order to detect missing links more accurately. In particular, one such source of data that has remained mostly unexplored is human navigational traces on websites. Such traces are captured by the usage logs recorded on the server side by many websites, and the question arises: How can human click trails be harnessed in order to detect missing links?

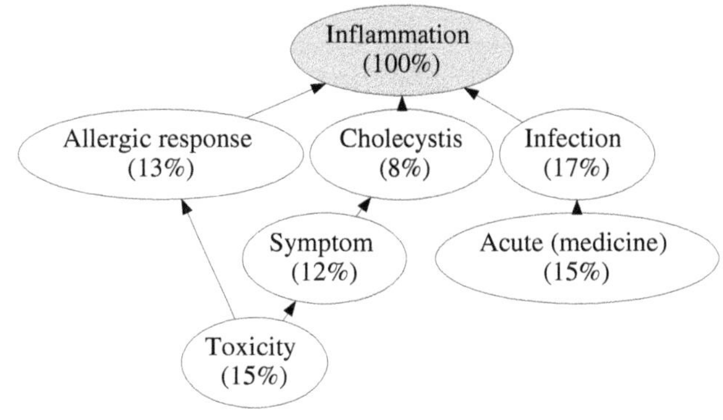

Figure 2: The final portions of several navigation paths with the same target t = INFLAMMATION. The unfilled nodes are Wikipedia articles that appeared on paths to t. The number in each node indicates the percentage of paths with target t that passed through that node.

Present work: Navigation logs for mining missing links. In this paper we explore the use of human navigational traces for detecting missing links in websites like Wikipedia. Logs of website navigation contain strong signals with regard to which existent hyperlinks are useful: from a user interface perspective, if a link is traversed often by humans then it is useful, and if it is never traversed by humans then it is redundant (although from a search engine's perspective it could still be useful for indexing and ranking). Hence we expect such logs to also contain clues into whether an as yet non-existent link *should* be there or not. For instance, if we often observe users going through page s and ending up in page t, although s does not directly link to t, then it might be a good idea to introduce a 'shortcut' link from s to t.

As an analogy, consider the task of improving a road network. A civil engineer would not just look at the existing road segments and try to infer which road segments to build next. Rather, she would take into account how heavily each road segment is used and would then decide where it would make sense to add a shortcut, an extra lane, or a traffic light. We argue that similarly we should consider how the Web's hyperlink structure is used and decide on that basis what hyperlinks to add next. The *raison d'être* of hyperlinks is to enable navigation, so by creating hyperlinks that aid navigation, we are optimizing the right objective.

Proposed approach to source prediction. Here we propose a method for using navigational data to discover missing links following the above intuitions, thereby addressing the source prediction problem; *i.e.*, given a target page, we find good sources to link to the target. We demonstrate the effectiveness of our approach using Wikipedia. We chose Wikipedia as our proof-of-concept domain because high-quality navigation logs are available for it, collected via a class of human-computation games known under names such as *The Wiki Game* [9] or *Wikispeedia* [39, 43]. In these games, users are given two Wikipedia articles—a *start* and a *target*—and need to find a short path from the start to the target by traversing links encountered in the visited articles. The underlying graph structure is unknown to users; they only see the outgoing links of the page they are currently on. But, crucially, they also have expectations on which pages should link to which other pages, based on their commonsense and expert knowledge about the world, and are guided by these expectations toward articles they consider likely to contain links to the target.

We consider our approach to be general and applicable to websites other than Wikipedia. Also note that we simply use navigational traces from the Wikipedia games since they are readily available to us. Obtaining raw, passively collected browsing logs of Wikipedia is much harder due to privacy considerations. However, we are encouraged to believe that our approach will generalize to passively collected browsing logs as well.

Building on the above intuition about humans browsing the Web, we reason as follows: if page s is traversed by many users in search of target t, then this is an indicator that users expect the link from s to t to exist. So if s does not link to t yet (or not any more, for that matter), but contains a phrase that could be used as an anchor for t, then we should consider the link (s,t) for addition.

As a concrete example, consider Fig. 2. The figure summarizes several navigational paths, all with the target $t =$ INFLAMMATION. Paths progress from bottom to top, and only the last few clicks are shown per path. Each node s also contains the fraction of all paths with target INFLAMMATION that passed through s. For instance, we see that 17% of times INFLAMMATION was reached from INFECTION and 13% of times it was reached from ALLERGIC RESPONSE. A considerable fraction of paths (15%) passed through ACUTE (MEDICINE), which does not link to t, although it mentions t several times and could clearly benefit from a link to it.

The central part of our approach is that we mine many link candidates (s,t) from a large number of navigation traces for each target t and then rank these candidates by relevance.

We perform a set of experiments using automatically (and thus only approximately) defined ground-truth missing links, as well as an evaluation involving human raters. In our automatically defined ground truth, we consider as positive examples of missing links such links that existed for a substantial amount of time but are missing from the latest Wikipedia snapshot. In our evaluation by humans, raters labeled the identified missing links as relevant or not. Experiments show that restricting the candidate set to pairs observed in paths and then ranking those candidates using a simple heuristic performs better than applying more sophisticated ranking methods to the set of all possible candidates (*i.e.*, including those not observed in paths). The reason why simple ranking methods suffice is that the 'heavy lifting' is done by the users before ranking, by using vast amounts of world knowledge to select the pages that are best-suited to link to the target.

The remainder of the paper is structured as follows. Sec. 2 provides details about the navigation trace data set and our methods for candidate selection and ranking. We present experimental results in Sec. 3 and provide further discussion and perspectives in Sec. 4. Related work is reviewed in Sec. 5, and Sec. 6 concludes the paper.

2. USING HUMAN NAVIGATION LOGS FOR MINING MISSING LINKS

In this paper we address the source prediction task of Fig. 1(b): Given a target page t, we suggest a good list of source pages s that should link to t. Although this paper is focused on the special case of Wikipedia, we believe that our approach is general enough to be applied to other websites beyond Wikipedia. We discuss implications and requirements of this extension in Sec. 4.

We selected Wikipedia as our domain because, first, it constitutes an important and relevant special case due to its reliance on the links between articles, and because, second, high-quality navigation traces are available for it. In this section we first describe how these data were collected and then give a detailed account of how we use them for source prediction.

2.1 Data sources

Our data sets of Wikipedia navigation traces were collected via a popular online game that is generically known as 'Wikiracing' [50]. Several websites offer versions of this game, such as *The Wiki Game* [9] or *Wikispeedia* [39, 43], but they all share the same general idea: a user is given two Wikipedia articles—a *start* and a *target*—and is asked to navigate from the start to the target by exclusively clicking hyperlinks contained in the visited pages. We also refer to start–target pairs as *missions*. In our experiments we use data from both The Wiki Game (Sec. 3.1) and Wikispeedia (Sec. 3.2). Before describing how exactly we do so, we provide more details about the two data sets.

The Wiki Game. In The Wiki Game, users may choose from five challenges: 'least clicks' (minimize the number of clicks), 'speed race' (minimize time), 'five clicks [or fewer] to Jesus' (find JESUS in five or fewer clicks, minimizing time), 'no United States' (minimize time while avoiding the USA article), and 'six degrees of Wikipedia' (minimize time while finding a path of exactly six clicks). In each challenge, several players compete for the same mission simultaneously, navigating the full Wikipedia. We pool the paths collected from all five challenges between 2009 and 2012, thus obtaining a data set of 974k paths grouped into 364k distinct missions (start–target pairs); *i.e.*, there are 2.7 paths per mission on average. The number of distinct targets is 3,219, *i.e.*, we have 303 paths per target on average, with a median of 208. Targets with many paths are quite frequent; *e.g.*, there are 2,087 targets with at least 100, and 698 targets with at least 500, paths. In the following, we focus on the 2,087 targets (65% of all targets) that have at least 100 paths.

Wikispeedia. Unlike The Wiki Game, Wikispeedia is a single-player game. Once a mission is successfully completed, the user may enter her name into a high-score table associated with that mission, where users are ranked by number of clicks, with ties broken by time. The game is played on a reduced, static snapshot of Wikipedia containing 4,604 of the most important articles [48]. The data set we work with is publicly available [40] and comprises 51k paths collected from 2009 to 2014, grouped into 29k distinct missions, for an average of 1.8 paths per mission. The number of distinct targets is 3,326; *i.e.*, we have 15 paths per target on average, with a median of 10.

Comparing the two data sets, we notice that The Wiki Game, on the one hand, has the advantage of more data, in particular more paths per target. Wikispeedia, on the other hand, has the advantage of using a static Wikipedia snapshot (while The Wiki Game fetches pages from live Wikipedia on the fly and caches them for some time [10]), which allows for a different kind of evaluation (Sec. 3.2), and of being publicly available, which makes our experiments reproducible.

2.2 Source candidate selection

Our method for source prediction consists of four steps, as illustrated in Fig. 3. (The fourth step, ranking, is covered in Sec. 2.3.)

Step 1: Collect paths. We start by collecting navigation paths with the given target t, up to time T.

Step 2: Generate pairs. For each path $p = \langle p_0, \ldots, p_n = t \rangle$, the initial set of candidates is $\{(p_i,t) : 0 < i < n\}$, *i.e.*, every direct link from any page along the path to the target t is initially a candidate. (The start page p_0 is exempt, since it is selected randomly and is therefore unlikely to be a useful candidate.) There are in general many paths for the same target t (upper left box in Fig. 3), so we take the union of the candidate sets resulting from all these paths (lower left box) as the initial candidate set for t.

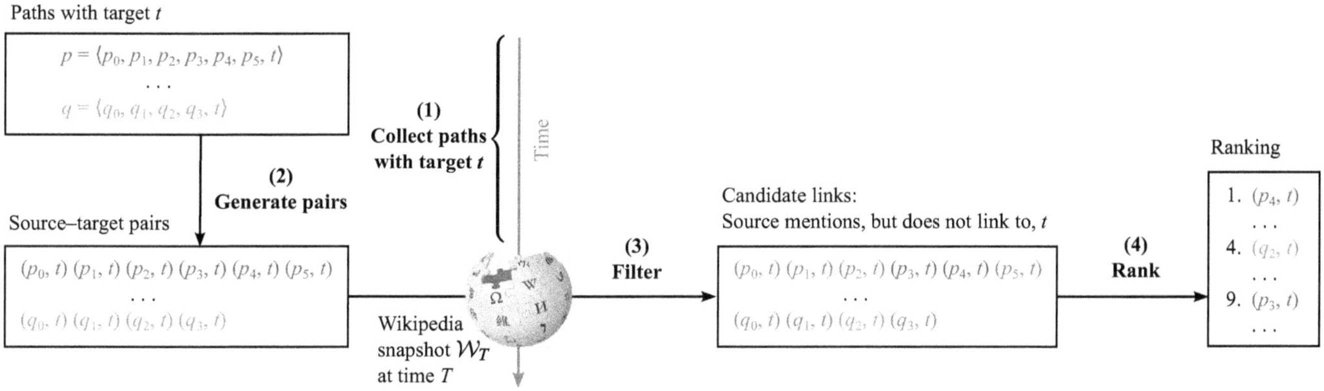

Figure 3: Overview of our approach for mining missing hyperlinks to a given target t from human navigation traces. (1) Collect paths with target t up to time T, and capture the reference Wikipedia snapshot $\mathcal{W}_T$ at time T. (2) Generate source–target pairs. (3) Filter the pairs based on $\mathcal{W}_T$: a pair (s,t) becomes a candidate if s mentions, but does not link to, t in $\mathcal{W}_T$; also exclude (s,t) if s tends to appear in the second half of paths with target t. (4) Rank the candidate links.

Step 3: Filter. Next, we filter this initial set using the Wikipedia version $\mathcal{W}_T$ at time T, which serves as our *reference snapshot.* A link (s,t), where $s \in \{p_1,\dots,p_{n-1}\}$, can be suggested only if it does not already exist in $\mathcal{W}_T$. Further, the source s should contain a phrase that could serve as the anchor for a link to t; in other words, s should mention t in $\mathcal{W}_T$.

To detect pages that mention the target t, we construct the set $\mathcal{A}_t$ of all phrases that serve as anchor texts for t across all articles in the reference Wikipedia snapshot[1] and subsequently define that s mentions t if it contains any phrase from $\mathcal{A}_t$.

Previous work [42] has shown that navigation traces tend to consist of a 'getting-away-from-the-start' phase, in which the user attempts to reach a hub article that is well-connected in the network of pages, and a 'homing-in-on-the-target' phase, in which the user actively seeks out pages related to t. Guided by this finding, we apply one additional filtering step and include in our final candidate set (the box labeled 'candidate links' in Fig. 3) only sources that tend to appear in the second half of paths with target t. More precisely, we first define the *relative path position* of p_i along the path $p = \langle p_0,\dots,p_n = t\rangle$ to be i/n, and then discard the pair (s,t) if the relative path position of s on paths with target t is less than or equal to 0.5 on average.

2.3 Source candidate ranking

Source candidate selection yields an unordered set of candidates for each target t. The goal of the next (and final) step in our pipeline is to turn this set into a meaningful ranking (step 4 in Fig. 3). Since the source prediction task (Fig. 1(b)) asks for sources for a given target t, we produce a separate ranking for each t. Several ranking methods are conceivable:

1. **Ranking by relatedness.** It seems reasonable to rank source candidates s by their relatedness to t, since clearly a link is more relevant between articles with topical connections.[2]

   Since we deal with Wikipedia as our data set, we choose relatedness measures based on Wikipedia (see below).

2. **Ranking by path frequency.** Navigation traces provide us with statistics about how frequently a source s was traversed by users searching for target t. Based on this, we compute the *path frequency* of s given target t, defined as the fraction of paths that passed through s, out of all the paths with target t. Intuitively, pages s that were traversed more frequently on paths to t should be better sources for links to t.

We experiment with two relatedness measures for case 1 above. The first is due to Milne and Witten [25] and is based on the inlink sets $\mathcal{S}$ and $\mathcal{T}$ of s and t, respectively. It calculates the distance between s and t as the negative log probability of seeing a link from $\mathcal{S} \cap \mathcal{T}$ when randomly sampling a link from the larger one of the sets $\mathcal{S}$ and $\mathcal{T}$ (normalized to approximately lie between 0 and 1), and the relatedness as one minus that distance:

$$\mathrm{MW}(s,t) = 1 - \frac{\log(\max\{|\mathcal{S}|,|\mathcal{T}|\}) - \log(|\mathcal{S}\cap\mathcal{T}|)}{\log(N) - \log(\min\{|\mathcal{S}|,|\mathcal{T}|\})}, \quad (1)$$

where N is the total number of Wikipedia articles.

The second relatedness measure is due to West *et al.* [44] and works by finding a low-rank approximation of Wikipedia's adjacency matrix via the singular-value decomposition (SVD). The pair (s,t) corresponds to an entry $A[s,t]$ in the adjacency matrix A and to an entry $A_k[s,t]$ in the rank-k approximation A_k obtained from A via SVD. If $A[s,t] = 0$ and $A_k[s,t] \gg 0$ then s does not link to t yet but is a good candidate. Therefore we define the SVD-based relatedness as

$$\mathrm{SVD}(s,t) = A_k[s,t] - A[s,t]. \quad (2)$$

In our experiments on The Wiki Game, we use the reduced rank $k = 1{,}000$. Since the adjacency matrix is much smaller for Wikispeedia (Sec. 2.1), we use the smaller value of $k = 256$ there.

2.4 Exploratory analysis of link candidates

Having introduced the data set and our source prediction method, we now explore the data set of human navigation traces to build intuitions on strengths and potential weaknesses of our approach.

We use the Wikipedia version as of T = 2014-01-02 as our reference snapshot $\mathcal{W}_T$ in all experiments.

[1] In practice, we exclude (1) phrases that rarely (less than 6.5% of all cases [26]) serve as link anchors for any target, which excludes, *e.g.*, 'A' as an anchor for AMPERE, and (2) anchor texts for which t is seldom (less than 1% of all cases) the target, which excludes, *e.g.*, 'Florence' as an anchor for FLORENCE, ALABAMA.

[2] According to the Wikipedia linking guidelines [49], links should correspond to 'relevant connections to the subject of another article that will help readers understand the article more fully.'

Number of pages on a path mentioning the target. We count for each path $p = \langle p_0, \ldots, p_n = t \rangle$ how often the target t is mentioned across all visited nodes $p_1, \ldots, p_{n-1}$ (excluding the randomly selected start page p_0) and find that, on average, t is mentioned on 1.7 pages per path. Since p_{n-1} contains a link to t, it is very likely to also mention t (for our definition of a mention, *cf.* Sec. 2.2), which means that, on average, each path contains 0.7 additional pages that mention t.

Now consider the subset of visited pages that mention t. Out of these, 73% contain a link to t in the reference Wikipedia snapshot $\mathcal{W}_T$. The remaining 27%, which do not link to t in $\mathcal{W}_T$, are potentially good candidate sources to link to t, since these pages were actively chosen by the user while searching for t.

Properties of pages along paths. We also investigate which parts of a path carry most value for source prediction. Consider Fig. 4(a), which aggregates all paths and shows for each part of the path how likely the pages in that part are to mention t. In order to be able to aggregate paths of variable length, we adopt the notion of relative path position (Sec. 2.2). Fig. 4(a) uniformly buckets the range $[0,1]$ into five intervals and plots the average for each interval. We only include paths of at least five clicks, such that each path contributes to each bucket, and the page p_{n-1} just before the target always falls into the last bucket.

We see that target mentions become more frequent as paths progress (the black curve in Fig. 4(a)): two-thirds of pages with relative path positions in the interval $[0.6, 0.8)$ mention the target, while at positions in $[0.8, 1.0)$ nearly all pages (91%) do. We are particularly interested in mentions that are not accompanied by a link to t (the magenta curve in Fig. 4(a)), since these are our source candidates. The figure tells us that candidates are more likely to appear towards the end of paths: at relative path positions in the interval $[0.6, 0.8)$, 30% of pages without a link to t mention t, and for the interval $[0.8, 1.0)$, the fraction is as high as 46%.

We note that these curves are in tune with previous work [42], which has shown that humans tend to follow a 'semantic gradient' during information network navigation, passing through articles that get ever more related to the target. In this light it makes a lot of sense that the rate of target mentions should increase as paths progress.

2.5 Obtaining ground truth based on Wikipedia evolution

In order to form intuitions about how meaningful our suggestions are, we would ideally like to evaluate for each relative path position how good the source candidates at that position are. However, ground-truth data is hard to come by; in order to make strong claims, we need to ask humans how good our predictions are. We do so later on (Sec. 3.1.2), but since obtaining human ratings is expensive and time-consuming, we preliminarily adopt a notion of ground truth that is approximate and biased, but nevertheless allows us to gain some initial insights. In this subsection, we define this approximate ground truth and analyze our navigation traces in terms of it.

We obtain a weak notion of ground truth from the evolution of Wikipedia's graph structure as follows. First we define the *link rate* of (s,t) as the fraction of time s contained a link to t since s was created. (We compute these values based on Wikipedia's complete edit history.) Then we choose a *link-rate threshold* $\alpha \in [0\%, \ldots, 100\%]$ and label a candidate link (s,t) as positive if its link rate is greater than α. Candidates with a positive label correspond to links that existed for a substantial amount of time, but got deleted before the reference Wikipedia snapshot $\mathcal{W}_T$ (*cf.* step 3 of Sec. 2.2).

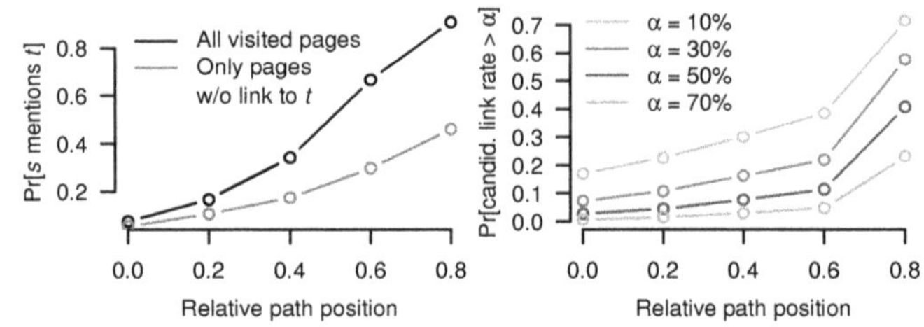

(a) Fraction of target mentions (b) Fraction of good candidates

Figure 4: (a) Fraction of sources s mentioning target t, as a function of the relative path position of s; the magenta curve is conditioned on s not linking to t. (b) Fraction of candidates that are positive according to the automatically generated ground truth, as a function of relative path position, for several link-rate thresholds α (Sec. 2.5); source candidates mention, but do not link to, the target and are considered positive if their link rate is greater than α.

That is, such links could have been valuable for navigation, yet were removed at some point in time, so we argue that reintroducing them is likely to improve Wikipedia.

Consider a candidate (s,t) labeled as positive according to the above definition. The link (s,t) may (case 1), or may not (case 2), have existed during the game from which it was mined. Further, if it existed during the game, it may (case 1a), or may not (case 1b), have been clicked by the user. These three cases correspond to the following scenarios. If the link (s,t) existed during the game and was clicked by the user (case 1a), but has been deleted since (as required for (s,t) to be a candidate), then it is probably a good idea to suggest it for reintroduction. If the link existed during the game, but was not clicked by the user (case 1b), this means that she did not see it in her rush to reach t as fast as possible (or else she would have clicked on it to immediately win the game); so either the user found another promising way to continue the search before seeing the link to t, or the link was too hard to find in the text of s, which is a signal that we should reintroduce that link and make it more obvious. Finally, if (s,t) did not exist during the game (case 2) then the user could not possibly have taken it, although she might have intended to do so (since she actively navigated to s while searching for t); in this case, too, (s,t) might be a good link suggestion.

We refer to our automatically obtained labels as 'weak' because, by definition, they contain many *false negatives*. Wikipedia is an evolving organism, and an important part of our task is to suggest links which never existed. However, by the above link-rate threshold criterion, these links will be counted as negative examples. For an example of such a false negative, consider again Fig. 2, where the article on ACUTE (MEDICINE) should clearly link to INFLAMMATION, as it explains a concept critical to understanding the term ACUTE as used in medicine, but the link from ACUTE (MEDICINE) to INFLAMMATION is labeled as negative by the automatic ground truth, since ACUTE (MEDICINE) has never linked to INFLAMMATION in Wikipedia's history. In other words, the automatically obtained ground truth has high precision, but low recall of truly positive examples. Nonetheless, this weak ground truth is useful during development because it provides us with many labeled examples for free and allows for relative comparisons between different methods.

Fig. 4(b) captures this approximate notion of candidate quality, again broken up by relative path position. The graph shows that the fraction of positives obtained from the automatically obtained ground truth becomes higher for pages appearing later on in paths.

We conclude that not only are mentions at later positions more frequent (Fig. 4(a)), but that they also correspond to better link anchors. (We try several values for the link-rate threshold α, but the same trend holds for all thresholds.) This provides additional justification for our decision to include in our set of source candidates only sources that tend to appear in the second half of navigation traces with the given target (Sec. 2.2).

3. EVALUATION

In our experiments we compare five methods: Given a target t, we can either consider as source candidates the set of *all* articles that mention t but do not link to it (across our entire reference Wikipedia snapshot $\mathcal{W}_T$); or we can subselect candidate sources based on whether we observe them in navigation paths (Sec. 2.2). Further, we consider two relatedness measures for ranking (Sec. 2.3). This yields four combinations of candidate selection methods ('none' and 'path-based') and relatedness measures ('MW' and 'SVD'). The fifth method requires no external relatedness measure but simply ranks candidates with respect to their frequency among paths with target t (Sec. 2.3).

To sum up, we consider the following five methods for predicting missing links to a given target page t:

- **No selection, rank by MW:** Use all candidate sources and rank them based on the MW method (Eq. 1).
- **No selection, rank by SVD:** Use all candidate sources and rank them based on the SVD method (Eq. 2).
- **Path-based selection, rank by MW:** Only use candidates appearing in navigational traces and rank them based on the MW method.
- **Path-based selection, rank by SVD:** Only use candidates appearing in navigational traces and rank them based on the SVD method.
- **Path-based selection, rank by frequency:** Only use candidates appearing in navigational traces and rank them based on the frequency with which they appear in paths (*cf.* Sec. 2.3 for our definition of *path frequency*).

Ground truth. We perform a twofold evaluation, one based on the automatically obtained and approximate labels defined in Sec. 2.5 (we use the link-rate threshold $\alpha = 30\%$ throughout), the other based on labels obtained from human raters. For our human evaluation, we select a subset of targets, predict sources for them using the methods that performed best during the development phase on the automatic ground truth, and ask raters on Amazon Mechanical Turk [3] to label the top predictions. Here we get rid of the shortcomings of the automatic ground truth, on which we cannot obtain absolute performance numbers (mainly due to the high false-negative rate; Sec. 2.5), but have less data to work with.

We perform an evaluation by humans only on the predictions obtained on data from The Wiki Game.

Evaluation metric. As our evaluation metric, we use precision@k for $k = 1, \ldots, K$. We first calculate the K precision values for each target separately and then compute the aggregate value for each k by averaging over all targets. This means we can only include targets for which our methods find at least K source candidates (which naturally shrinks the set of test targets). We use $K = 10$ for The Wiki Game, which defines our evaluation set of 699 targets. Since the Wikispeedia data set contains fewer paths, we are less restrictive here and choose $K = 5$, obtaining an evaluation set of 181 targets.

Candidate selection	Rank by MW	Rank by SVD	Rank by path freq.
None	39%	20%	N/A
Path-based	43%	32%	39%

Table 1: Area under the precision@k curve for no candidate selection versus path-based candidate selection for all ranking measures (The Wiki Game; Fig. 5(a)). Note that path frequency is only applicable for path-based candidate selection.

The bulk of our experiments is performed in Sec. 3.1 on data from The Wiki Game. Subsequently, Sec. 3.2 completes the evaluation by demonstrating that our algorithm works equally well on Wikispeedia.

3.1 Evaluation on The Wiki Game

We start by evaluating our algorithm on data from The Wiki Game, first based on the automatically obtained ground truth, then by asking human raters.

3.1.1 Evaluation using automatically obtained ground truth

The precision@k curves for all five methods as evaluated on The Wiki Game are displayed in Fig. 5(a), and their performance is summarized in terms of the area under the precision@k curve in Table 1.

Overall, we achieve good performance, especially given that our ground truth is of high precision but low recall, with many false negatives. Even though the precision@k lies in the range between 0.4 and 0.5 (for path-based candidate selection and MW ranking), manual error inspection revealed that most suggested links make sense and are truly missing, and that, in fact, the Wikipedia community has simply never included these links into the Wikipedia graph so that they could have made their way into our ground truth (*e.g.*, (ACUTE (MEDICINE), INFLAMMATION) in Fig. 2).

Comparing the different methods, we observe that path-based candidate selection performs better than doing no subselection for both relatedness measures used in ranking. Path-based selection improves performance by a particularly large margin for the SVD-based ranking method, which has much lower precision@k than the other methods. This establishes the fact that there is a lot of value in path-based candidate selection especially when the ranking measure does not excel by itself.

The margin between path-based selection and no selection is larger for smaller k, which means that considering navigational paths is particularly useful for predicting the top link sources.

Note that both relatedness measures (MW and SVD) use the high-quality link structure of the Wikipedia page graph (Sec. 2.3). If we wanted to generalize our approach to domains beyond Wikipedia, we can easily imagine scenarios where no such high-quality relatedness measures are readily available (*e.g.*, when pages are not as topically coherent as Wikipedia articles, or pages have scarce content and are poorly interlinked). With such situations in mind, it is encouraging to see that our fifth measure ('rank by frequency' in combination with path-based candidate selection; the yellow curve in Fig. 5(a)) performs quite competitively. Recall that that ranking method does not rely on any external relatedness measure but simply ranks source candidates with respect to the frequency with which they appeared on paths with target t. This is an important observation because it means our method has the potential to generalize well to use cases where a good relatedness measure is not readily available.

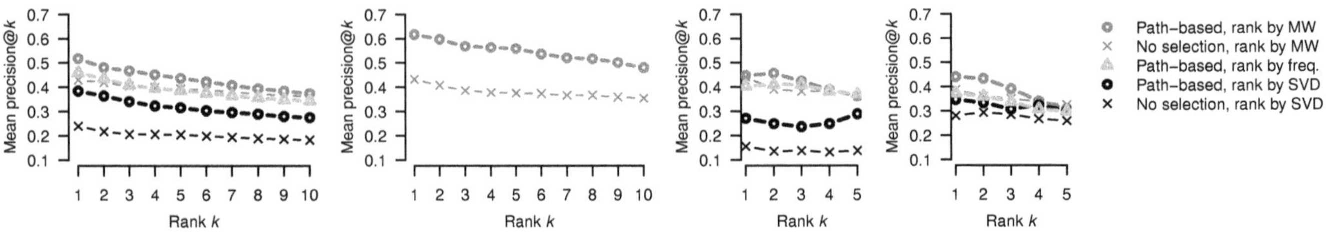

(a) The Wiki Game (b) The Wiki Game (c) Wikispeedia (d) Wikispeedia

Figure 5: Performance in terms of precision@k for different source selection and ranking methods on our two data sets. Bold lines represent path-based candidate selection. (a) The Wiki Game, automatically obtained ground truth (Sec. 3.1.1). (b) The Wiki Game, human ground truth (Sec. 3.1.2); only the MW ranking method was used in the human evaluation. Note that performance as evaluated by humans exceeds the estimate from the automated evaluation (Fig. 5(a)), *i.e.*, the latter underestimates the actual quality of suggested links. (c) Wikispeedia, automatically obtained ground truth, same evaluation methodology as applied to The Wiki Game ('standard evaluation'; Sec. 3.2). (d) Wikispeedia, automatically obtained ground truth, stricter evaluation (Sec. 3.2).

Reintroduction of valuable but deleted links. By construction, the last click on a path always leads into the target. The fact that a user looked for, found, and clicked on this link is a very strong signal that the link is useful for navigation. Removing such links from Wikipedia is particularly harmful from a user-interface perspective, and it is desirable that a source prediction method suggest them for reintroduction. To see if our path-based candidate selection method meets this desideratum, Fig. 6(a) plots, for each rank k, the fraction of predicted links that were also the last link on the paths they were mined from. We observe that, while most suggested links were not clicked by humans (most likely because they were not present in the version of the Wikipedia page used by The Wiki Game), a substantial fraction (between 20% and 35%) correspond to links that existed at game time and were chosen by the user but do not exist in the reference snapshot any more. We conclude that our top suggestions are often links that were taken by the user as the last click to the target but have since been removed, and thus our method rightfully reintroduces such links back into Wikipedia.

Total volume of added links. So far we have conducted a per-target evaluation, by first computing precision@k values for each target and then averaging over all targets for each rank k. But it is also interesting to consider the total number of links we can suggest at a given precision level, across all targets, since this gives us an idea of the potential number of improvements we could make to Wikipedia by deploying our system. The results of this evaluation are presented in Fig. 6(b), which shows that we can make 1,000 link suggestions at a precision of 42%, and 10k suggestions at a precision of 30% (ranking candidates by frequency and assuming the same link-rate threshold $\alpha = 30\%$ used in our automated evaluation, corresponding to the red curve in Fig. 6(b)).

3.1.2 Evaluation by human raters

Wikipedia is a continuously evolving entity. Although the link history, on the basis of which we defined our automatic ground truth, captures this evolution, it can only tell us which links are positive examples (because they persisted throughout a long period of time). However, there are many links that should be, but have never been, added to Wikipedia, and if our method suggests such a link, then the previous evaluation would count it as a bad suggestion. Therefore the above notion of ground truth suffers from false negatives. To combat this problem, we perform a more accurate evaluation by human raters in this section. Having done so, we can also confirm the prevalence of false negatives *post hoc* (see the end of this subsection).

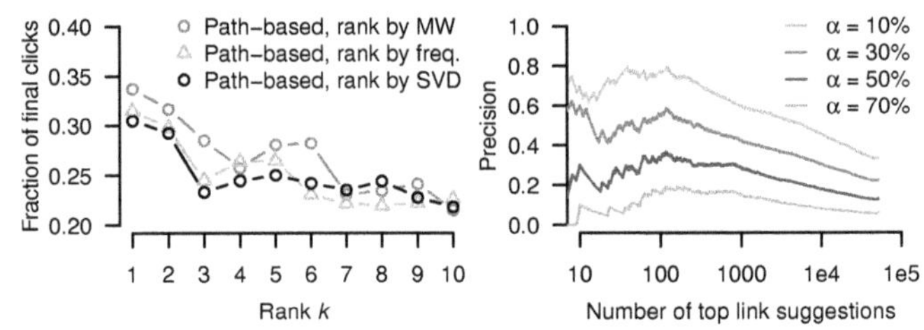

(a) Fraction of final clicks (b) Volume vs. precision

Figure 6: (a) Fraction of clicks that were the final click along their respective path, as a function of rank. If a suggestion corresponds to the final click along a path, the suggested link must have existed at game time, so a useful link is effectively reintroduced into Wikipedia by that suggestion. (b) Precision as a function of the total number of top link suggestions made by our method across all targets, where suggestions are ranked by frequency (Sec. 2.3). Positive suggestions are those whose link rate lies above the respective link-rate threshold α (Sec. 2.5).

Methods compared via human evaluation. In our human evaluation, we compare two of the top-performing methods: (1) path-based candidate selection with MW ranking and (2) no candidate selection with MW ranking. By using the same ranking method and only switching whether path-based candidate selection was performed, we can gauge the impact of the latter on performance.

Target sampling. In order to select targets on which to evaluate the predictions of the two methods, we stratify the base set of 699 targets by the number of paths observed per target and select ten targets from each decile, for a total of 100 test targets. The rationale behind stratification is that we want to avoid being biased towards targets for which the path-based candidate selection method can make a particularly large number of good predictions (because more data are available for those targets).

Obtaining ratings through Amazon Mechanical Turk. We use Amazon Mechanical Turk [3] for recruiting human raters. As in the automatic evaluation, our goal is to assess the precision@k, where $k = 1,\dots,10$, for the two compared methods. In each rating task, the human evaluator was presented with a target t and a set of 14 candidate sources and was asked to indicate which of the candidates should contain a link to the target article. There were no constraints

Candidate selection	Automatic ground truth	Human-labeled ground truth
None	39%	38%
Path-based	43%	55%

Table 2: Area under the precision@k curve for MW ranking, comparing the automated (Fig. 5(a)) and human (Fig. 5(b)) evaluations of our method run on data from The Wiki Game.

on the number of source articles the rater could choose. The set of 14 candidate sources comprised the following entries:

1. Five predictions from each of the two compared methods (either suggestions 1 through 5 or suggestions 6 through 10 from each method).
2. Two control sources, sampled randomly from the set of all Wikipedia articles that link to the target t.
3. Two control non-sources, sampled randomly from the set of all Wikipedia articles and hence highly unlikely to link to t.

In cases where the two methods agreed on a suggestion, that suggestion was included only once in the set of source candidates, thereby making the presented list shorter than the maximum of 14 items. Also, to prevent any ordering bias, we shuffled the order of sources in the presented list. The task description is reproduced *verbatim* in Appendix A.

We paid 5¢ per task, and each task was presented to ten different workers. We consider a source to be a positive example if over half of the ten raters labeled it as such.

Fig. 5(b) presents the results. We observe that path-based candidate selection followed by MW ranking outperforms MW ranking on the set of all candidates by a large margin. Table 2, which summarizes the performance of both compared methods on the human-labeled ground truth (again as the area under the precision@k curve) and compares it to the performance obtained on the automatically labeled ground truth, shows that the area under the precision@k curves for path-based candidate selection increases by 12%, compared to the automatically obtained ground truth. On the other hand, when doing no candidate selection, the area under the curve decreases by 1%.

The reasons for the increased performance on the human-labeled ground truth are twofold. First, the automatically obtained ground truth uses only a historical notion of correctness in which many actually positive examples are mislabeled as negative. Second, MW relatedness alone, without performing path-based candidate selection, might not capture the notion of human-intuition–based similarity well. Path-based selection, on the contrary, captures exactly that quality by design, and it is thus not surprising that it prevails on a human-labeled ground truth by such a large margin.

Out of the controls that represent randomly selected sources already linking to the target page (item 2 in the above list of source-candidate types presented to raters), only 9% are labeled as positive by more than five of the ten raters, a value much lower than even our precision@10 of about 50%. This tells us that the links we suggest are better than the average pre-existing link to the target.

Finally, out of the random control non-sources (item 3 in the above list), only one pair (GEOGRAPHY OF KOREA to SOUTH KOREA) was rated positive by more than five of the ten raters (we happened to sample a connected pair here). This statistic confirms that human labeling was not random.

False negatives in the automated ground truth. Now that we have human-labeled data, we can quantify the prevalence of false negatives in the automatically constructed ground truth. For this purpose, consider Fig. 7, which shows a histogram of the average human labels for the candidates that were labeled as negative according to the automatic ground truth. Here, 'average human label' refers to the average of the binary labels obtained from the ten human raters for each candidate. We see that a large fraction of the examples labeled as negative according to the automated ground truth are in fact positive examples according to the more reliable human ground truth.

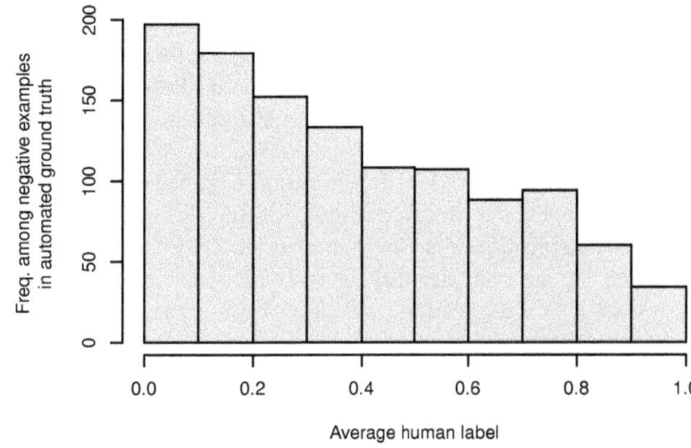

Figure 7: Histogram of average human labels for examples labeled as negative by the automatically obtained ground truth, highlighting the prevalence of false negatives in the latter.

3.2 Evaluation on Wikispeedia

To conclude the evaluation, we present results on the second data set of navigation paths, collected via Wikispeedia. Recall from Sec. 2.1 that, while The Wiki Game has the advantage of more data, it also has a slight drawback: it does not use a static Wikipedia snapshot but rather fetches articles from live Wikipedia on the fly and caches them for some time [10], which means that we do not know the exact version of the article the user saw at game time; the versions used in different games may be different from each other and from the reference snapshot $\mathcal{W}_T$. Hence, our evaluation on The Wiki Game could not account for what a source article s looked like at game time. Instead, we allowed for suggestion all links (s,t) not present in the reference snapshot $\mathcal{W}_T$, regardless of whether they existed during the respective game, and our automated evaluation counted a suggestion (s,t) as positive if the link was present for a substantial fraction of the entire lifetime of s. We call this the *standard evaluation.*

Wikispeedia, on the contrary, uses a static Wikipedia snapshot $\mathcal{W}$ [48], so we know exactly which links existed during the game. In the notation of Sec. 2.2 and Fig. 3, the snapshot $\mathcal{W}_T$ is replaced by $\mathcal{W}$, which is identical to the snapshot used in all games. This in turn allows for a stricter evaluation methodology: By allowing for suggestion only those links that were not present in $\mathcal{W}$, we permit only links that did not exist during the game and that the user could thus not possibly have clicked. Further, we count a suggestion as positive only if it has been present in the live Wikipedia for a substantial amount of time *after* the date of the static snapshot $\mathcal{W}$. If a suggested link did not exist during the game, but was added afterwards, this is an even stronger signal that the suggestion is good. Hence we call this the *stricter evaluation.*[3]

[3]When applying the standard evaluation to Wikispeedia, we use the same reference snapshot $\mathcal{W}_T$ also used for The Wiki Game in order

Now, if we can show that the stricter evaluation yields similar results to the standard evaluation on Wikispeedia, then we may argue by analogy that the stricter evaluation would likely give similar results on The Wiki Game, too, if such an evaluation were possible on that data set.

The results are displayed in Fig. 5(c) and Fig. 5(d). As for The Wiki Game, we use the link-rate threshold (Sec. 2.5) $\alpha = 30\%$ for deciding if a suggestion is positive, and as described in the beginning of Sec. 3, we consider targets for which our algorithm can make at least $K = 5$ suggestions and show the average precision@k for $k = 1, \ldots, 5$.

Our first observation is that the standard-evaluation results are similar for Wikispeedia (Fig. 5(c)) and The Wiki Game (Fig. 5(a)). In particular, the orderings of methods by performance are identical. (The results are somewhat less clean for Wikispeedia, due to the smaller amount of data.) Further, the outcome of the stricter evaluation (Fig. 5(d)) is similar to that of the standard evaluation (Fig. 5(c)), the main difference being that SVD ranking performs better under the stricter evaluation.

We therefore have reason to believe that the performance would also remain high on The Wiki Game under the stricter evaluation if this kind of evaluation were possible on that data set, which corroborates the result that our algorithm finds good new links.

4. DISCUSSION

This paper introduces an effective method for the source prediction problem (Fig. 1(b)), in which a target page t is given, and the task is to find and rank sources s that should link to t. Prior work (Sec. 5) has primarily addressed the complementary target prediction problem (Fig. 1(a)), where s is given and t to be found. We consider source prediction more challenging than target prediction, since in the latter the set of link candidates is immediately given by the phrases contained in the source page s, whereas, in the former, every page could potentially be a source, so the set of source candidates must first be retrieved in a candidate selection step.

Computational feasibility. To illustrate this point, we briefly report on an experiment we had initially planned on doing. We intended to compare the performance of our method to the link predictions made by Milne and Witten's [26] machine-learned target prediction algorithm, but this was computationally infeasible: In order to use this target prediction method in a source prediction setting, we first had to find all articles s mentioning t (this required a full scan of a 44GB Wikipedia dump). Next, we intended to annotate each source s with outgoing links and then rank s according to the score it gives to t. However, each annotation takes on the order of several seconds [27], and nearly every article mentions at least one of the targets we want to evaluate, so we would have had to annotate essentially all of Wikipedia, which would have taken several million seconds, or several thousands of hours. One reason for the computational complexity of Milne and Witten's algorithm is that they (as well as other target prediction methods [22, 23, 51]) tend to spend significant effort on mention disambiguation.

On the contrary, in our approach we neither have to scan Wikipedia for articles that mention t, nor do we need to do any sophisticated disambiguation or ranking. We simply use as source candidates all pages seen in our navigation traces, look for mentions only in this small subset of all Wikipedia pages, and rank according to a simple precomputed metric or simple frequency counts. This is possible because the brunt of the computational effort is done by humans: since they actively seek out pages that are likely to link to the target, these pages tend to already be good source candidates, and issues such as disambiguation are much less critical.

Applications beyond Wikipedia. Now we address the question if and how our technique could apply beyond the realm of Wikipedia. We envision two ways forward.

The first idea would be to gamify arbitrary websites. One could imagine a framework, *e.g.*, written in JavaScript, that would wrap the website of interest, recruit players, and ask them to navigate to the targets we are interested in linking to. This would require adding at least some initial links pointing to t manually, such that t is reachable by navigating. Furthermore, our method for finding valid anchors for the target, which is currently based on anchor-text/target-page pairs mined from Wikipedia (Sec. 2.2), would need to be adapted to the new domain. Possibilities would include the use of prevalent phrases from the target's title and content as anchor texts, or, akin to our current method, the use of anchor texts that are already being used in other pages to refer to the target.

The second approach we envision is to use passively rather than actively collected log data for source candidate selection and ranking. It might be possible to simply use the logs that are kept by webservers anyway. The added challenge here would be that we do not know what target (if any) a user tried to reach, whereas the target is always given explicitly to the user in the human-computation setup. However, we believe that reasoning along the following lines might be promising: if users that ended up in t often went through s, then the shortcut from s to t might be promising. An alternative heuristic might be to collect instances where a user navigates to s, issues a keyword query into the website's search box (if it exists), and clicks to t from the search-engine result page.

On Wikipedia, the linking guidelines are explicitly stated [49], so links are fairly consistent. Further, each page is typically about a single, well-defined topic. These are among the reasons why machine-learning methods can infer powerful models for linking to Wikipedia articles. Websites other than Wikipedia are less likely to have the above properties, so it will be more difficult for statistical models to predict meaningful links. We expect methods for mining missing links directly from navigational traces to suffer less from this problem, since they do not take the detour through modeling the static structure of the link graph, but instead directly optimize navigability as the objective.

What we find especially promising in this light is a result from Fig. 5, namely that our method does not crucially rely on any measure of relatedness between pages: ranking our source candidates simply by the frequency with which they occurred in navigational traces for the given target (the yellow curves of Fig. 5) constitutes a competitive method. We believe that this makes our approach a strong candidate for the source prediction task on websites other than Wikipedia, where a notion of relatedness between pages might be much harder to obtain.

5. RELATED WORK

We find missing links by observing humans navigating a network during a human-computation game. There has been related work on several aspects of our approach: the link prediction problem, human network-navigation behavior, and games with a purpose.

Link prediction. The link prediction problem in networks comes in many flavors and variants. Unsupervised methods for link prediction in social networks were extensively evaluated by Liben-Nowell and Kleinberg [19], who found the Adamic–Adar measure [1] to perform best. More recently approaches based on network community detection [8, 15, 16] and random walks [4] were considered for predicting missing links. Supervised link predic-

to decide whether a source mentions, or links to, a target. Under the stricter evaluation, the static snapshot $\mathcal{W}$ is used for this purpose.

tion [20] was also studied by the relational-learning community [31, 34], but scalability remains a challenge with these approaches.

While the above works focused mostly on the identification of missing links in social networks, there is also a rich line of work on the identification of missing links among Wikipedia articles [13, 29, 44, 51] and on linking existing webpages to Wikipedia [22, 23, 26]. Generally these approaches focus on building models of Wikipedia's graph structure, while also performing keyword extraction and word-sense disambiguation.

Human navigation in networks. This line of research is rooted in Milgram's seminal small-world experiment [24], which asked participants to forward a letter to a friend such that it could finally reach a predestined target person. The game through which our data was collected is similar to this task in that a target must be reached in the absence of prior information about the underlying network. It is different in that our setup has the same user staying in control from the start all the way to the target, whereas, in the small-world experiment, every step is executed by a new, autonomous participant. Kleinberg [17] investigated the algorithmic aspects of the small-world problem, showing that efficient search is only possible when the probability of long-range links decays as a power law with a specific exponent.

Much research has followed in Kleinberg's wake, so we focus on the most directly related projects: data sets such as ours were previously analyzed by West and Leskovec, who characterize human strategies in successful navigation tasks [42] and train machine-learning models capable of navigating automatically [41], and by Helic *et al.* [14] and Trattner *et al.* [36], who explore heuristic navigation algorithms based on hierarchical knowledge representations.

A related line of work pertains to the analysis of so-called 'click trails'. Research here primarily studies the click paths on which users embark starting from search-engine result pages. In early fundamental work, Chi *et al.* [7] coin the notion of 'information scent', operationalized by Olston and Chi [30] in a system for supporting users by combining query- and click-based navigation strategies. White and Huang [46] establish that click trails add value to the information contained in the ultimate target page, and Teevan *et al.* [35] show that users frequently prefer click-based navigation to querying. Downey *et al.* [12] investigate the benefits of navigating versus querying further, finding that navigating is particularly useful when the information need is rare. Work by White and Singla [47] is relevant in that it explores how different trail topologies (such as stars, trees, and linear chains) are observed in different search scenarios (informational versus navigational). Click trails have also been used to predict whether users will give up in information network navigation [32], to compute the semantic relatedness of concepts [33, 43], and to identify relevant websites from user activity [5]. Our work continues this line of work and attempts to use navigational trails as a rich source of data for detecting missing links in networks.

Games with a purpose. 'Games with a purpose' [38] were popularized by von Ahn and colleagues, a seminal early example being the *ESP Game* for labeling images [37]. Wikispeedia was originally designed as a game with a purpose for computing the semantic relatedness between concepts [43]. Further relevant work was done by Ageev *et al.* [2], who developed a human-computation game for collecting data in which users are asked to find the answers to as many factual questions (*e.g.*, 'What is the highest peak in the Western Hemisphere?') as possible within a given amount of time, using Web-search queries that may optionally be followed by click-based navigation. As in our navigation data sets, the goal is explicitly known here, but not in the form of a specific target page but rather in the form of a specific answer string.

6. CONCLUSION

In this paper we study the problem of identifying missing links in Wikipedia. We build on the fact that the ultimate purpose of Wikipedia links is to aid navigation. Our method harnesses human navigation traces and finds missing links that would immediately enhance Wikipedia's navigability. We analyze click trails to detect a set of missing-link candidates and then rank these candidates. We evaluate our method on both automatically labeled ground truth as well as ground truth obtained from human annotators. Overall, our algorithm performs at a level that would make our system useful in practice.

There are many interesting avenues for future work. For instance, extending the method to passively collected Web-browsing logs would be a natural next step. Furthermore, it would also be worthwhile to think about gamifying general websites beyond Wikipedia.

In summary, our paper makes contributions to the rich line of work on detecting missing hyperlinks between documents. We hope that future work will draw on our insights to build more user-friendly websites and make the Web more navigable as a whole.

Acknowledgments. This research has been supported in part by NSF IIS-1016909, IIS-1149837, IIS-1159679, CNS-1010921, NIH R01GM107340, Boeing, Facebook, Volkswagen, Yahoo, and SDSI. Robert West acknowledges support by a Stanford Graduate Fellowship and a Facebook Graduate Fellowship, and thanks the Wikimedia Foundation for sharing their office space. Finally, we would like to thank Alex Clemesha for sharing data from The Wiki Game.

7. REFERENCES

[1] L. Adamic and E. Adar. Friends and neighbors on the Web. *Social Networks*, 25(3):211–230, 2003.

[2] M. Ageev, Q. Guo, D. Lagun, and E. Agichtein. Find it if you can: A game for modeling different types of Web search success using interaction data. In *SIGIR*, 2011.

[3] Amazon.com. Mechanical Turk. Website, 2014. `http://www.mturk.com` (accessed Nov. 10, 2014).

[4] L. Backstrom and J. Leskovec. Supervised random walks: Predicting and recommending links in social networks. In *WSDM*, 2011.

[5] M. Bilenko and R. W. White. Mining the search trails of surfing crowds: Identifying relevant websites from user activity. In *WWW*, 2008.

[6] S. Brin and L. Page. The anatomy of a large-scale hypertextual Web search engine. *Computer Networks and ISDN Systems*, 30(1):107–117, 1998.

[7] E. H. Chi, P. Pirolli, K. Chen, and J. Pitkow. Using information scent to model user information needs and actions and the Web. In *CHI*, 2001.

[8] A. Clauset, C. Moore, and M. E. J. Newman. Hierarchical structure and the prediction of missing links in networks. *Nature*, 453(7191):98–101, 2008.

[9] A. Clemesha. The Wiki Game. Website, 2009. `http://www.thewikigame.com` (accessed Nov. 10, 2014).

[10] A. Clemesha. Personal communication, Jan. 14, 2014.

[11] P. Devanbu, Y.-F. Chen, E. Gansner, H. Müller, and J. Martin. Chime: Customizable hyperlink insertion and maintenance engine for software engineering environments. In *ICSE*, 1999.

[12] D. Downey, S. Dumais, D. Liebling, and E. Horvitz. Understanding the relationship between searchers' queries and information goals. In *CIKM*, 2008.

[13] S. Fissaha Adafre and M. de Rijke. Discovering missing links in Wikipedia. In *LinkKDD*, 2005.

[14] D. Helic, M. Strohmaier, M. Granitzer, and R. Scherer. Models of human navigation in information networks based on decentralized search. In *HT*, 2013.

[15] K. Henderson and T. Eliassi-Rad. Applying latent Dirichlet allocation to group discovery in large graphs. In *SAC*, 2009.

[16] M. Kim and J. Leskovec. The network completion problem: Inferring missing nodes and edges in networks. In *SDM*, 2011.

[17] J. Kleinberg. The small-world phenomenon: An algorithmic perspective. In *STOC*, 2000.

[18] J. M. Kleinberg. Authoritative sources in a hyperlinked environment. *JACM*, 46(5):604–632, 1999.

[19] D. Liben-Nowell and J. Kleinberg. The link-prediction problem for social networks. *JASIST*, 58(7):1019–1031, 2007.

[20] R. N. Lichtenwalter, J. T. Lussier, and N. V. Chawla. New perspectives and methods in link prediction. In *KDD*, 2010.

[21] C. D. Manning, P. Raghavan, and H. Schütze. *Introduction to Information Retrieval*. Cambridge University Press, 2008.

[22] E. Meij, W. Weerkamp, and M. de Rijke. Adding semantics to microblog posts. In *WSDM*, 2012.

[23] R. Mihalcea and A. Csomai. Wikify! Linking documents to encyclopedic knowledge. In *CIKM*, 2007.

[24] S. Milgram. The small world problem. *Psychology Today*, 2(1):60–67, 1967.

[25] D. Milne and I. H. Witten. An effective, low-cost measure of semantic relatedness obtained from Wikipedia links. In *WIKIAI*, 2008.

[26] D. Milne and I. H. Witten. Learning to link with Wikipedia. In *CIKM*, 2008.

[27] D. Milne and I. H. Witten. An open-source toolkit for mining Wikipedia. *Artificial Intelligence*, 194:222–239, 2013.

[28] C. Nentwich, L. Capra, W. Emmerich, and A. Finkelstein. Xlinkit: A consistency checking and smart link generation service. *TOIT*, 2(2):151–185, 2002.

[29] T. Noraset, C. Bhagavatula, and D. Downey. Adding high-precision links to Wikipedia. In *EMNLP*, 2014.

[30] C. Olston and E. H. Chi. ScentTrails: Integrating browsing and searching on the Web. *TCHI*, 10(3):177–197, 2003.

[31] A. Popescul, R. Popescul, and L. H. Ungar. Statistical relational learning for link prediction. In *SRL*, 2003.

[32] A. T. Scaria, R. M. Philip, R. West, and J. Leskovec. The last click: Why users give up information network navigation. In *WSDM*, 2014.

[33] P. Singer, T. Niebler, M. Strohmaier, and A. Hotho. Computing semantic relatedness from human navigational paths on Wikipedia. In *WWW*, 2013.

[34] B. Taskar, M. F. Wong, P. Abbeel, and D. Koller. Link prediction in relational data. In *NIPS*, 2003.

[35] J. Teevan, C. Alvarado, M. S. Ackerman, and D. R. Karger. The perfect search engine is not enough: A study of orienteering behavior in directed search. In *CHI*, 2004.

[36] C. Trattner, D. Helic, P. Singer, and M. Strohmaier. Exploring the differences and similarities between hierarchical decentralized search and human navigation in information networks. In *i-KNOW*, 2012.

[37] L. von Ahn and L. Dabbish. Labeling images with a computer game. In *CHI*, 2004.

[38] L. von Ahn and L. Dabbish. Designing games with a purpose. *CACM*, 51(8):58–67, 2008.

[39] R. West. Wikispeedia. Website, 2009. `http://www.wikispeedia.net` (accessed Nov. 10, 2014).

[40] R. West. Wikispeedia project website, 2014. `http://snap.stanford.edu/data/wikispeedia.html` (accessed Nov. 10, 2014).

[41] R. West and J. Leskovec. Automatic versus human navigation in information networks. In *ICWSM*, 2012.

[42] R. West and J. Leskovec. Human wayfinding in information networks. In *WWW*, 2012.

[43] R. West, J. Pineau, and D. Precup. Wikispeedia: An online game for inferring semantic distances between concepts. In *IJCAI*, 2009.

[44] R. West, D. Precup, and J. Pineau. Completing Wikipedia's hyperlink structure through dimensionality reduction. In *CIKM*, 2009.

[45] R. West, D. Precup, and J. Pineau. Automatically suggesting topics for augmenting text documents. In *CIKM*, 2010.

[46] R. W. White and J. Huang. Assessing the scenic route: Measuring the value of search trails in Web logs. In *SIGIR*, 2010.

[47] R. W. White and A. Singla. Finding our way on the Web: Exploring the role of waypoints in search interaction. In *WWW*, 2011.

[48] Wikipedia. 2007 Wikipedia Selection for Schools. Website, 2007. `http://schools-wikipedia.org` (accessed Aug. 3, 2008).

[49] Wikipedia. Wikipedia:Manual of Style/Linking. Website, 2014. `http://en.wikipedia.org/w/index.php?title=Wikipedia:Manual_of_Style/Linking&oldid=632571069` (accessed Nov. 10, 2014).

[50] Wikipedia. Wikiracing. Website, 2014. `http://en.wikipedia.org/w/index.php?title=Wikiracing&oldid=630702489` (accessed Nov. 10, 2014).

[51] F. Wu and D. S. Weld. Autonomously semantifying Wikipedia. In *CIKM*, 2007.

APPENDIX

A. HUMAN-RATER INSTRUCTIONS ON AMAZON MECHANICAL TURK

The following description of the evaluation task was given to human raters on Amazon Mechanical Turk:

"Here's the deal! Our good friend Wikipedia is having self-doubts and wants you to help improve its links.

You are given a Wikipedia article (referred to as the target) and a list of other Wikipedia articles (referred to as source articles). You have to tell Wikipedia if the source article should contain a link to the target. And of course, if you are unsure of what the source or target article means, you can always click on the article name to open it in a new tab.

But remember that Wikipedia is a sensitive fellow and will be mad if you don't play by the rules: There should be a link from the source to the target if and only if (1) the target article has some relevant information about the source article and could help readers understand the source more fully, or (2) the target article describes a proper name which is likely to be unfamiliar to readers."

Semantic Annotation of Mobility Data using Social Media

Fei Wu[†1], Zhenhui Li[†2], Wang-Chien Lee[‡3],Hongjian Wang[†4], and Zhuojie Huang[§5]
[†]College of Information Sciences and Technology
[‡]Department of Computer Science and Engineering
[§]GeoVISTA Center
Pennsylvania State University, University Park, PA, USA
{[1]fxw133, [2]jessieli, [4]hxw186 }@ist.psu.edu, [3]wlee@cse.psu.edu, [5]seenhzj@gmail.com

ABSTRACT

Recent developments in sensors, GPS and smart phones have provided us with a large amount of mobility data. At the same time, large-scale crowd-generated social media data, such as geo-tagged tweets, provide rich semantic information about locations and events. Combining the mobility data and surrounding social media data enables us to semantically understand *why a person travels to a location at a particular time* (e.g., attending a local event or visiting a point of interest). Previous research on mobility data mining has been mainly focused on mining patterns *using only the mobility data.* In this paper, we study the problem of using social media to annotate mobility data. As social media data is often noisy, the key research problem lies in using the right model to retrieve only the relevant words with respect to a mobility record. We propose frequency-based method, Gaussian mixture model, and kernel density estimation (KDE) to tackle this problem. We show that KDE is the most suitable model as it captures the locality of word distribution very well. We test our proposal using the real dataset collected from Twitter and demonstrate the effectiveness of our techniques via both interesting case studies and a comprehensive evaluation.

Categories and Subject Descriptors

I.7.m [**Computing Methodologies**]: DOCUMENT AND TEXT PROCESSING

Keywords

Heterogeneous data; Mobility data; Microblogs; Semantics; Annotation; Keneral Density Estimation;

1. INTRODUCTION

With the rapid advancement of positioning technology and wide availability of mobile devices, we can now easily collect large-scale mobility data from mobile users. Given the location history of a mobile user, one of the most fundamental and important questions one may ask is: *What is the* ***purpose*** *for this person to visit a certain location at a particular time*? In other words, we wish to *understand the* ***semantics*** *of a person's mobility data.* Generally, the semantics could be the landmark information (e.g., a museum or a shopping mall) or information about the events attended (e.g., basketball game, movies or exhibition). The semantics provide us with richer and much more interpretable information about a mobile user, therefore can greatly benefit many applications such as advertisement targeting, personalized recommendation, and future movement prediction.

Mining mobility data has gained increasing interests recently. Researchers have studied various mobility patterns, such as frequent patterns [21], periodic behaviors [18], representative behaviors [13, 10], activity recognition [19, 15, 27, 31, 37]. However, all these patterns and activities are extracted *purely from the mobility data.* While they are useful for understanding the inherent moving behaviors of a mobile user, they do not provide any *contextual semantics* required for understanding the intended activities of the user.

To understand the contextual semantics of the mobility data, it is necessary to harness *external surrounding locational data.* The external information considered in previous work [3, 1, 27, 32] is mostly *static*, such as landmarks [3, 1], landscapes [27], land-use categories [32]. The previous studies assume a spatial point (e.g., a location) always carries the same semantics regardless of the time. The static annotation will miss the important *dynamic event information.* For instance, Madison Square Garden, a well-known multi-purpose arena in New York City, holds both Knicks[1] and Rangers[2] games as well as many other events such as concerts and exhibitions. Different people (and even the same person) may visit Madison Square Garden for different purposes at different times. Consequently, simply using "Madison Square Garden" to annotate a user's location record could fail to reveal the complete purpose of his visit. Therefore, it is critical to examine the *dynamic events* associated with this location and use them for annotation.

Motivated by the example above, in this paper, we study the problem of annotating a user's location history with dynamic semantics, that reflect a user's interest or purpose at a particular location and time. To achieve our goal, an issue we face is to find the sources for time-sensitive information related to locations. Fortunately, popular location-based social media services, such as Twitter and Foursquare, facili-

[1]Knicks is a basketball team based in New York City
[2]Rangers is an ice hockey team based in New York City

WWW 2015, May 18–22, 2015, Florence, Italy.
ACM 978-1-4503-3469-3/15/05.
http://dx.doi.org/10.1145/2736277.2741675.

Input: Location history of a mobile user

Record ID	Time	Longitude	Latitude
r_1	2013-1-20	40.75051	-73.99349
r_2	2013-2-10	40.68312	-73.97597
r_3	2013-2-19	40.75051	-73.993499

Input: Geo-tagged tweets from the crowd

Time	Longitude	Latitude	Tweets
2013-1-20	40.75051	-73.99349	LETS GO RANGERS
2013-1-20	40.61219	-74.15814	I'm at Buffalo Wild Wings
2013-1-20	40.75050	-73.99350	I'm @ Madison Square Garden for Pittsburgh Penguins vs New York Rangers

Annotation

Record ID	Annotations
r_1	madison, garden, rangers, penguins
r_2	nets, barclays, center, nba
r_3	rangers, madison, square, montreal, canadiens

Figure 1: An example of semantic annotation on location history using social media.

tate mobile users to voluntarily generate enormous amount of spatiotemporal text. Such human-powered sensing data brings us rich and comprehensive information of dynamic local events.

In this paper, our goal is to annotate the location history of a mobile user using the spatiotemporal documents collected from social media, such as geo-tagged tweets. As illustrated in Figure 1, we assume two inputs: (i) the location history of a mobile user, represented by a sequence of $\langle time, location \rangle$ pairs; and (ii) a set of documents from social media with the time and location information attached. For each entry in a user's location history, we aim to derive a list of words that best describes the purpose of the user's visit to that location at that time. We name this word list as an *annotation document.* For example, in Figure 1, location record r_1 is annotated with words related to a Rangers' game with Penguins at Madison Square Garden. The annotation documents of a user can latter be used to create a profile of that user. For example, Figure 1 shows that the user has interests in the hockey team Rangers and the basketball team Brooklyn Nets.

However, the use of time-sensitive social media data for dynamic annotation comes with a price. Specifically, in the previous studies on static annotation [3, 1, 27, 32], a set of *clean, predefined and fixed* attributes is often provided as an input. Therefore, one can simply annotate the *closest* location attribute to a given location. But for our problem, we need to automatically and dynamically model the spatial distributions of words from social media and use only the words that are relevant to local venues and events for annotation. This brings several challenges in practice. First, social media data (e.g., tweets) are extremely *noisy*, containing numerous irrelevant documents about casual chatting with friends, retweeting news, and posting personal opinions. Second, as there are many landmarks and various events nearby, the word frequency in the neighborhood is often dominated by a small number of popular venues and events. Therefore, in order to discover the true semantics of a querying location record, we need to find a suitable model to identify the relevant words.

In this paper, we first look into two simple methods for annotation: a frequency based method and a Gaussian mixture model based method. We will discuss the limitations of these methods and justify the reason of choosing a more suitable model - Kernel Density Estimation (KDE) model for our problem. In essence, KDE model well captures both the *locality* and the *relevance* of the words w.r.t. a given location record. Further, as the estimated spatial distribution by the KDE model is controlled by a bandwidth parameter h, we will analyze several options of choosing the parameter h. Finally, we conduct extensive experiments to demonstrate the effectiveness of our proposed method.

In summary, the main contributions of this paper are:

- We study an interesting problem of inferring a user's interests and purposes from his location history using external contextual information (e.g., tweets). To the best of our knowledge, we are the first to use time-sensitive social media data to generate dynamic annotations for the mobility data.
- We propose to study different methods and identify the most suitable model for semantic annotation using noisy and dynamic social media data.
- The effectiveness of our method is demonstrated using both quantitative evaluations and case studies on a large geo-tagged tweet data.

The rest of the paper is organized as follows. We first review the related work in Section 2. The semantic annotation problem is then formulated in Section 3. We describe our proposed method in Section 4. Case studies and quantitative evaluations on real data are presented in Section 5. We further discuss an application of our method to user interest profiling in Section 6, and conclude the paper in Section 7.

2. RELATED WORK

Mobility Pattern Mining. In literature, numerous methods have been proposed to extract patterns from the mobility data. Representative works include stop and move detection [3, 2, 24], activity recognition (e.g., biking and walking) [19, 15, 27, 31, 37], significant place extraction [39, 24, 38, 7] and frequent regular pattern discovery [21, 13, 18, 10], just to name a few. These works mainly focus on the inherent *trajectory patterns.* While the patterns describe the mobility records, they do *not* explore external source to discover the contextual semantics.

Static Annotation. To mine contextual semantics of mobility data, existing methods have been using various types of *static information* including landmarks [3, 1], landscape and environment [27], and land-use categories [32, 34]. In these papers, a location (i.e., a point, a region, or a road segment) is associated with a set of *predefined and fixed* attributes, such as a landmark (e.g., "Eiffel tower") or a land type (e.g., residential area or business center). A location on the trajectory is then annotated using the attributes of nearby locations [3, 27]. Yan et al. [32, 34, 33] extend the point-based annotation to three kinds of objects: points, lines, and regions based on spatial join, using direction, distance, and topological spatial relations such as intersection. In addition to landmarks and land-use categories, Yan et al. [32, 33] further consider transportation modes to determine the type of POIs for trajectory annotations via a hidden Markov model. While the contextual semantics used in these studies are static, the contextual semantics in our problem need to be *dynamically extracted* from social media data and contain richer location information.

Local Word Detection. There have been extensive studies in mining geo-tagged social media data. One line of research work that is highly relevant to our problem is local word detection. The general premise is that local words should have concentrated spatial distributions around their location centers. Based on this observation, Backstrom et al. [4] proposes a spatial variation model to detect local words. This method has been used in [9] to detect local words in tweets. Meanwhile, [22] uses spatial discrepancy to detect spatial bursts. In these work, to determine whether the word is local or not, each word is assigned with a locality score. In our problem setting, local word detection may serve as a filter to select only important local words for annotation. However, as shown in our experiment results in Section 5.5, this filtering step is *not necessary* and could even be *erroneous*.

Microblogs Summarization. Our problem is also related to the microblogs summarization problem. On documents, researchers have developed summarization methods based on word frequency [26, 30], cluster of sentences [25, 29], and graph of sentences [14, 23]. As microblogs are short and contain informal use of the language, methods based on word frequency have been shown to perform the best [17, 8]. However, the summarization methods do not model the spatial characteristics of words, which is essential in our problem. While the concept of using frequency may be applied, we will discuss the problem with of frequency based methods in Section 4.1 and experiments.

3. PRELIMINARIES

3.1 Problem Definition

In this paper we consider location data of one mobile user as a set of spatiotemporal points, $U = \{r_1, r_2, ..., r_n\}$, where each record $r_i = (loc_i^U, t_i^U)$. The location loc_i^U is a geographic coordinate, and t_i^U is the timestamp. Location data can be collected from a variety of platforms such as mobile phones and web services.

We consider the external context data as a set of spatiotemporal documents $\mathcal{D} = \{d_1, d_2, ..., d_m\}$. Each document d_j can be represented as a (W_j, loc_j^D, t_j^D) tuple, where W_j is the set of words in d_j, loc_j^D is a geographic coordinate, and t_j^D is a timestamp. We define $\mathcal{W} = \bigcup_j W_j$ as the set of all words (uni-gram) in $\mathcal{D}$. Examples of external context documents are geo-tagged tweets or other spatiotemporal documents from location-based services (e.g., Flickr). For simplicity, we only consider uni-gram in this paper. However, our model is also applicable for N-grams.

Given the location history of a user U and a source of external context documents $\mathcal{D}$, our goal is to obtain an annotation document that is potentially associated with a mobility record $r_i \in U$. Formally, an annotation document for a mobility record r_i is a set of relevant words, $\mathcal{A}(r_i) = \{(w, s_w(r_i)) | w \in \mathcal{W}, s_w(r_i) > \theta\}$, where $s_w(r_i)$ is a function that measures the relevance of a word w to the record r_i.

3.2 Problem Analysis

The key research problem is to find a relevance function $s_w(r_i)$ for a given location record r_i. A straightforward solution is to use the words frequently appearing near the location of r_i for annotation. However, setting the distance threshold (for defining near) is non-trivial. Another issue with this approach is that all the words within the distance threshold are treated equally regardless of their distances to the location record r_i.

To avoid setting a hard distance threshold, an alternative idea is to model the distribution of words in order to annotate the words based on their probabilities (or densities) at the given location r_i. One frequently-used model for spatial distribution in practice is the Gaussian mixture model [10]. While we have adopted it as the second proposed method, we suspect that Gaussian model may suffer from several potential drawbacks. First, the number of components in Gaussian mixture model may vary considerably across different words. For example, there could be 3 museums but 10 parks in a city. Second and more importantly, the true distribution of a word may not necessarily follow a mixture of Gaussian. In fact, the social media data generated by the crowd are constrained by the underlying city maps and natural landscapes, such as road networks, downtowns, lakes, and mountains, thus may deviate significantly from a Gaussian distribution.

We propose to use kernel density estimation (KDE) to model the distribution of words. KDE has been applied to location-based social networks [36], check-in data [16], human mobility [20], epidemiology [5], ecology [18], and marketing [12]. In particular, [36, 20] have demonstrated the advantages of KDE over Gaussian model under their problem settings. We propose to adapt KDE, aiming to capture both the locality of a word distribution and the relevance of a word to a given location record r_i. In the following section, we provide a detailed discussion of our proposed methods.

4. SEMANTIC ANNOTATION METHODS

The essence of the annotation problem boils down to measuring the *locality* of a word with respect to the location of a record r_i. The locality can be represented by a local density measure.

The annotation should be time-sensitive, as the same location may hold different events at different time. Therefore, for a location record $r_i = (loc_i^U, t_i^U)$, we consider the documents within a time window τ of t_i, i.e., $[t_i - \tau, t_i + \tau]$. We define the set of documents that fall into this time window as $\mathcal{D}_i = \{d_j | t_i - \tau \le t_j^D \le t_i + \tau\}$. Accordingly, the word set for documents in this time window is defined as $\mathcal{W}_i = \bigcup_{d_j \in \mathcal{D}_i} W_j$. For each $w \in \mathcal{W}_i$, we further let $L_i(w)$ be the set of locations of all tweets in $\mathcal{D}_i$ which contain the word w: $L_i(w) = \{loc_j^D | w \in W_j, d_j \in \mathcal{D}_i\}$. In this section, we only discuss annotation problem within one time window.

4.1 Frequency Based Method

One simple but intuitive measure is to count the occurrence of word w near the given location record. More specifically, given a mobility record r_i, the score $s_w^F(r_i)$ is defined as:

$$s_w^F(r_i; L_i(w), \delta) = |\{loc_j^D \in L_i(w) : dist(loc_i^U, loc_j^D) < \delta\}|,$$

where δ is a spatial threshold and $dist()$ is a distance function between two geographic points.

It is clear that the frequency measure can not find words that are specific to the locations. To alleviate this problem, we weight the word frequency by the inverted document frequency. The resulting relevance score inherits the same idea as the *tf-idf* score which is widely used in information retrieval for evaluating word importance over a collection of documents. Mathematically, given a mobility record r_i, the

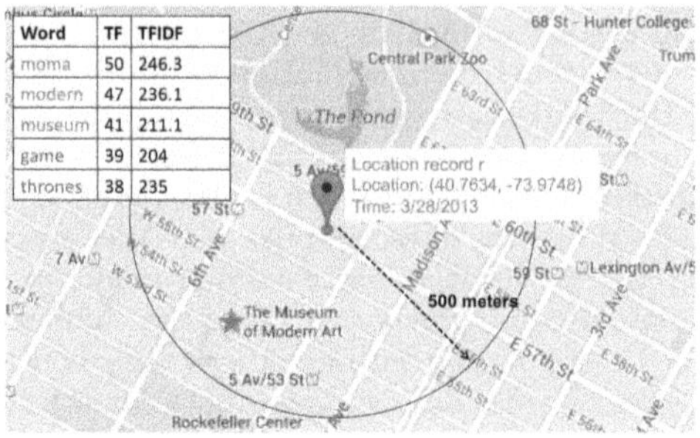

Figure 2: An example illustrating the problem of frequency based methods. The true user's intention of this location record is to attend the Game of Thrones event. But since MOMA is a more popular venue nearby, frequency-based methods will incorrectly use words "moma" and "modern" for annotation.

score $s_w^{tf-idf}(r_i)$ is defined as follows:

$$s_w^{tf-idf}(r_i; L_i(w), \delta) = s_w^F(r_i; \delta) \cdot \log \frac{|\mathcal{D}|}{|\{d_j \in \mathcal{D} : w \in W_j\}|}.$$

However, there are two problems with the above measure. First, it does not consider the *distance* from the user's location record to the center of the word. As a result, it favors nearby popular events, i.e., those events located within the spatial proximity. We illustrate this problem of $s^F(r_i;\delta)$ and $s^{tf-idf}(r_i;\delta)$ in Figure 2 with a real example. In this example, the user was attending the Game of Thrones (a TV series) exhibition. The original tweet is: "with @jedafrank (@ Game of Thrones Exhibition w/ 14 others) http://t.co/U5ztm1RWRu". The event location is very close to the Museum of Modern Art (MOMA). If we look at all the nearby tweets by setting the distance threshold $\delta = 500$ (meters), the highest ranked words are "moma" and "modern", since MOMA is a very popular location.

Second, the frequency based measure needs a threshold δ, which is not easy to set. Choosing a large threshold δ may include irrelevant words, whereas choosing a small threshold may result in a loss of useful information.

4.2 Gaussian Model

Using word probability addresses the problem of a hard threshold. The word probability at one location can be obtained from a two-dimensional Gaussian model fitted using the locations of all the occurrences of word w (i.e., $L_i(w)$). Therefore, we can define the relevance score as follows:

$$\begin{aligned} s_w^G(r_i; L_i(w)) &= f^G(r_i; \mu_w, \Sigma_w) \\ &= \frac{1}{2\pi|\Sigma_w|^{\frac{1}{2}}} e^{-\frac{1}{2}(loc_i^U - \mu_w)'\Sigma_w^{-1}(loc_i^U - \mu_w)}, \end{aligned}$$

where μ_w is a two-dimensional mean vector, and Σ_w is a 2×2 covariance matrix. In practice, a finite mixture of C Gaussian densities are often used for modeling multimodal distributions. The Gaussian mixture model (GMM) has been previously applied to model human mobility [10], as well as served as the underlying generative model to detect spatially related words [35]. Using the Gaussian mixture model, we can define the relevance score as follows:

$$s_w^{GMM}(r_i; L_i(w)) = \sum_{k=1}^{C} \pi_w^k f^G(r_i; \mu_w^k, \Sigma_w^k),$$

where μ_w^k, Σ_w^k, and π_w^k are the mean, covariance matrix, and weight of the k-th component, respectively, and $\sum_{k=1}^{C} \pi_w^k = 1$.

The mixture model still has several drawbacks. First, the assumption that the underlying probability is a mixture of Gaussians may not hold. Figure 3(a) show 100 tweet locations in NYC mentioning word "museum". It is easy to see the density of the word occurrences exhibits complex variations on the map . We use Gaussian mixture model to fit the points by setting component number $C = 2$. As shown in Figure 3(b), the density contours estimated according to the Gaussian mixture model tend to be over-smoothed. Second, even if the underlying distribution of a word follows the Gaussian mixture model, choosing the number of components is non-trivial. More importantly, the number of components for each word may vary significantly. Manually setting number of components for each word is not feasible.

4.3 Kernel Density Estimation

From the above discussion, we conclude that a good annotation framework should satisfy two main properties. First, it should model the effect of *distance*. Second, a good word density estimation at a location should only depend on the data points that are *local* to the location. With these properties in mind, we propose to use Kernel Density Estimation (KDE) methods to model the spatial density of the word occurrences.

KDE is a non-parametric model for estimating density from sample points. Following the kernel density model, we define the relevance score for a word w at r_i as follows:

$$s_w^{KDE}(r_i; L_i(w), H) = \frac{1}{|L_i(w)|} \sum_{loc_j^D \in L_i(w)} K_H(loc_i^U - loc_j^D).$$

Here, we define

$$K_H(x) = |H|^{-1/2} K(H^{-1/2}(x)), \tag{1}$$

where $K(x)$ is a kernel function of choice and H is a bandwidth matrix. The bandwidth matrix H has a strong influence on the estimated density. For our problem, we assume that the dimensions of the geographic coordinate are independent of each other. Further, we treat the two dimensions equally and use the same bandwidth h for both dimensions, i.e., $H = hI$ where I is the identity matrix. It is obvious that the estimated density will be sharply peaked around the sample points when h is small and overly smoothed when h is large.

In practice, the method is known to be less sensitive to the choice of kernel function than the bandwidth matrix H [11]. Further, it is desirable that a word occurrence contributes equally to all locations that are at the same distance from it. Therefore, we let $K(x)$ be the Gaussian kernel with matrix I as the covariance matrix. We can re-write Eq. (1) as:

$$K_H(x) = \frac{1}{2\pi|H|^{-\frac{1}{2}}} e^{-\frac{1}{2}x'H^{-1}x} = \frac{1}{2\pi h} e^{-\frac{1}{2h}x'x}.$$

Indeed, the KDE method satisfies the properties we have for a good annotation framework. First, the kernel density

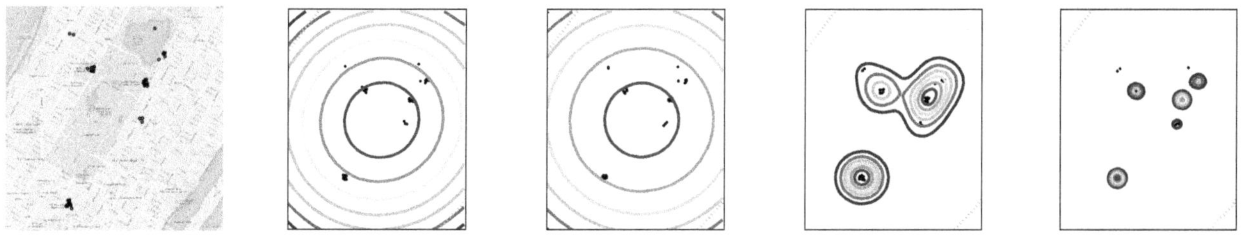

(a) Locations on map (b) GMM ($C = 2$) (c) KDE ($h = 0.01$) (d) KDE ($h = 0.003$) (e) KDE ($h = 0.001$)

Figure 3: Example of different models on word distribution for word "museum".

function $K_H(loc_i^U - loc_j^D)$ quantifies how much each document $d_j \in \mathcal{D}_i$ contributes to r_i. It is easy to see that the function decays as a function of distance between r_i and d_j. Second, the parameter h controls the range of effect one sample point has on the geographic space. By tuning h, we can make sure that each sample only contributes to its nearby locations. Next we discuss how to determine the bandwidth parameter h for our annotation problem.

4.3.1 Determining the Bandwidth h

It is well known that the resulting density estimate can be highly sensitive to the value of the bandwidth h, producing densities sharply peaked when h is too small, and producing an overly smooth estimate when h is too large. Figure 3(c)-(d) show the density maps with different values of h.

In general, there are two classes of approaches to selecting the bandwidth parameter h: reference rule approach and data-driven approach. While these approaches typically aim to find a fixed h, it is possible to estimate an adaptive bandwidth h which depends on the density at each sample point. Below we introduce these approaches in detail.

Reference rule approach. The *reference rule* approach derives h from assumptions of the underlying distribution. One commonly used reference rule, namely, *the Scott's rule of thumb*, is derived from the assumption that the underlying density being estimated is Gaussian. For location data, we assume that the longitude and latitude are independent. The Scott's rule can be written as:

$$H_w = n^{-2/(d+4)} \Sigma_w,$$

where Σ_w is the variance matrix of location of all the occurrences of word w (i.e., $L_i(w)$) and d is the dimension ($d = 2$ for our problem). The estimate is optimal (i.e., minimizes the mean integrated squared error) if the true underlying density is Gaussian. However, as we pointed out earlier, this assumption may not necessaries be true at a fine-granularity in our problem.

Cross validation approach. From a data-driven perspective, cross validation can be applied to choose h_w which fits the data best. In general, cross validation fits the model to a part of the data (i.e., training data), and then evaluates the goodness of the model on the rest of the data (i.e., testing data). The model that has the best performance on the testing data are picked based on our evaluation metric. We use log-likelihood as the metric to choose a proper h_w. The log-likelihood is given by:

$$\mathcal{L}(h_w) = \frac{1}{|L_i^{test}(w)|} \sum_{l \in L_i^{test}(w)} \log s_w^{KDE}(l; L_i^{train}(w), h_w),$$

where $L_i^{train}(w)$ and $L_i^{test}(w)$ are partitions of $L_i(w)$. Larger value of $\mathcal{L}(h_w)$ indicates a better goodness of fit.

KDE with adaptive bandwidth. The bandwidth parameter h_w picked via aforementioned approaches is fixed. Another variation of KDE is to use an adaptive bandwidth, where h_w depends on each sample point. Breiman et al. [6] suggested adapting h_w to each sample point $loc_j^D \in L_i(w)$, and set it to be the distance between loc_j^D and its k-th nearest neighbor, where the optimal value of k can be determined via cross validation.

5. EXPERIMENT

In this section, we conduct both quantitative evaluations and case studies to verify the effectiveness of the proposed method on real datasets.

5.1 Datasets

We use three datasets of geo-tagged tweets from three major cities in U.S.A, i.e., New York City, Chicago, and Los Angeles. The statistics of the datasets is summarized in Table 1. Each tweet is of the form $\langle timestamp, userid, latitude, longitude, content \rangle$. We split the spatiotemporal documents by each day, as period for most events spans a day. In addition, events span multiple days can also be observed within each day.

City	#tweets	Time range
New York City (NYC)	15,612,712	11/2012-7/2013
Chicago (CHI)	11,269,220	10/2011-7/2013
Los Angeles (LA)	10,989,333	11/2012-7/2013

Table 1: Statistics of datasets.

To generate the other input of our method, i.e., the **location history** of a user, we gather all the pairs of GPS coordinate (longitude and latitude) and timestamp from the geo-tagged tweets of the user. We consider those check-in points as stop point. In practice, we may also use different sources to obtain the location history data, such as mobile services or GPS devices. For such densely sampled raw trajectory, a stopping point detection method can be applied first [38]. In this paper, we use the location history extracted from the geo-tagged tweets because the content of the corresponding

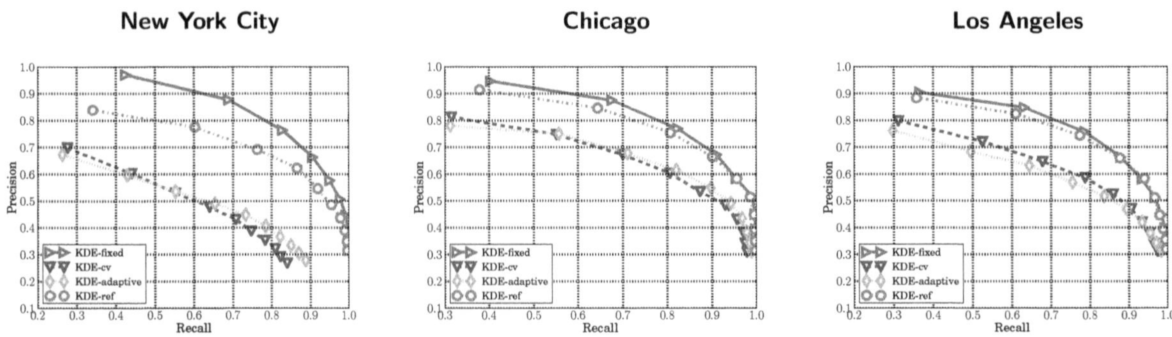

Figure 4: Precision-recall curves of different methods for choosing bandwidth h.

tweets provides a means for evaluation. We emphasize that *these tweets are excluded from the external contextual documents and are used for evaluation purpose only.*

5.2 Evaluation Method

Ground truth annotation dataset. Given a location record r of a user, the ground truth annotation document should consist of the relevant words that describe the true intentions of this user visiting location r. Since most of the tweets are not location-specific, our first step toward building a ground truth annotation dataset is to identify the location records that are relevant to some local events. To this end, we use the tweets that are posted through Foursquare check-ins. Foursquare is a location-based social network, where users can check-in at venues and events. When a user checks-in at a venue/event, it automatically generates a post containing the name of the venue/event along with a clause indicating the number of users that check-in at the same time, e.g., " w/ 400 others". Below we show an exemplar check-in tweet:

"Daddy's home!!!! LETS GO RANGERS (@ Madison Square Garden for Pittsburgh Penguins vs New York Rangers w/ 90 others)"

We gather check-in tweets that have more than 50 users checking-in at the same time, as those check-ins are more likely to contain event information. We manually filter the irrelevant words in each tweet and use the remaining words to construct the ground truth annotation document. For example, for the exemplar tweet above, the relevant words are: { "rangers", "madison", "square", "garden", "pittsburgh", "penguins"}.

For experiments in this paper, we have prepared 1,540 ground truth annotation documents for New York City, 697 for Chicago, and 623 for Los Angeles.

Evaluation metric. We use precision and recall as the metric to evaluate our annotation methods. The precision and recall are commonly used in information retrieval systems to evaluate the quality of the search result. Given a location record r with ground truth annotation document $\mathcal{G}(r) = \{w_{g1}, w_{g2}, ..., w_{gt}\}$, and an annotation document $\mathcal{A}(r)$ obtained by a method under evaluation, the precision and recall are defined as follows:

$$P(\mathcal{A}(r)) = \frac{|\mathcal{G}(r) \bigcap \mathcal{A}(r)|}{|\mathcal{A}(r)|},$$

$$R(\mathcal{A}(r)) = \frac{|\mathcal{G}(r) \bigcap \mathcal{A}(r)|}{|\mathcal{G}(r)|}.$$

Since each method returns a ranked word list, we only keep top-k words in the list as the annotation document $\mathcal{A}(r)$. By varying k, we can plot a precision-recall curve for each method.

5.3 Determining Bandwidth h

In this section, we study different approaches to determining the bandwidth h in the KDE model. Note that, the choice of h relates to the granularity of the annotation. For our task, we aim to find a small h that gives us annotations at a fine granularity. For applications that need more coarse-level annotations (e.g., annotation by names of the cities), a larger h may compensate for the data sparsity issue and provide more robust result.

In addition to the three approaches introduced in Section 4.3.1, namely the reference rule (KDE-ref), cross validation (KDE-cv), and adaptive bandwidth (KDE-adaptive), we also consider a fourth option which uses a fixed h for all the words (KDE-fixed).

For KDE-adaptive and KDE-cv, we split the datasets as 70% for training and 30% for testing. We select the parameter h_w for each word that yields the highest log-likelihood on the test data. For KDE-fixed, we empirically choose $h = 10^{-4}$ as it performs the best in practice among a set of different values. Here we emphasize that for KDE-fixed, all the words share the same bandwidth h, whereas for all the other methods we compute a h_w for each word.

Figure 4 shows the precision-recall curves for all methods. It is easy to see that for all three cities, KDE-ref and KDE-data perform much worse than KDE-fixed and KDE-ref. One possible explanation is that the bandwidth h_w obtained by maximizing the log-likelihood $\mathcal{L}(h_w)$ is often unreliable when the samples are sparse [11, 20], which is indeed the case for many words in our dataset. In such cases, the estimated h_w tends to take a large value, resulting in an over-smoothed density estimate.

In addition, we have observed that the value of bandwidth h_w estimated by KDE-ref takes value around 10^{-4} for most of the words. This explains why KDE-ref and KDE-fixed have very similar results. This also suggests that it is not necessary to estimate h_w for each word separately for our problem. Thus we simply set $h = 10^{-4}$ for the remaining experiments.

5.4 Compare with Other Annotation Methods

In this section, we compare the performance of our proposed measures s^{KDE}, s^{F}, s^{tf-idf}, and s^{GMM}. We name those measures, KDE, FREQ, TFIDF, and GMM, respectively.

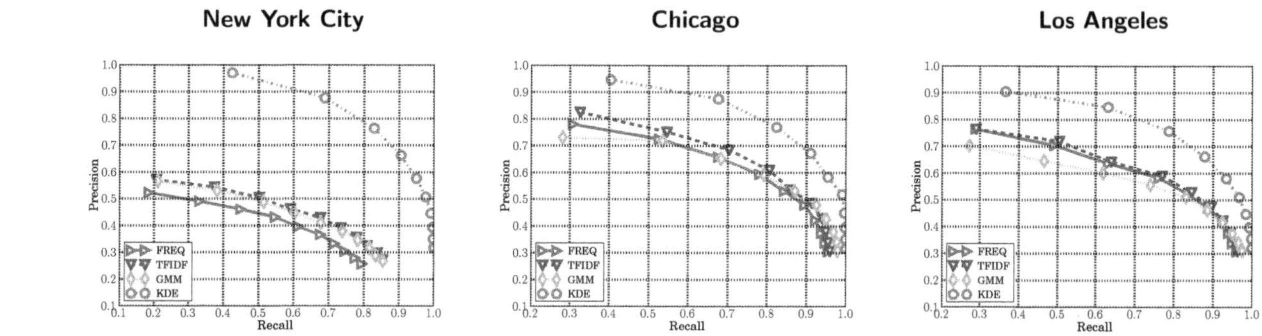

Figure 5: Comparison of Precision-recall curves for methods FREQ,TFIDF,GMM and KDE on three datasets.

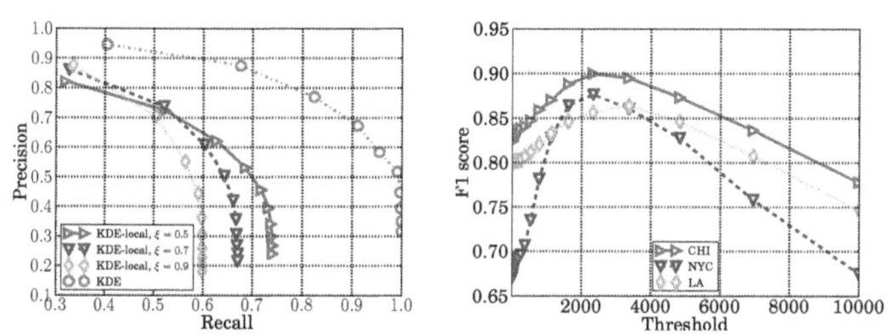

(a) (b)

Figure 6: (a) Comparison of Precision-recall curves of using threshold to filtering non-local words first on the Chicago dataset. (b) F_1 score w.r.t. to threshold.

We set $\delta = 1$ (kilometer) for FREQ and TFIDF, and $C = 5$ for GMM, as those parameters return the best result. We run this experiment on all three datasets.

Figure 5 summarizes the performance of four methods. We can see that KDE clearly outperforms other three methods. Especially for NYC dataset, KDE has a precision close to 0.95, when maintain a recall of 0.4. Meanwhile, all other methods only have precision value less than 0.6 under the same recall value. For CHI and LA datasets, KDE consistently has better precision over the other three methods. The KDE method has better performance on NYC dataset, as most large events are located at Manhattan area of New York City. There are more irrelevant tweets near places holding events. As a result, FREQ, TFIDF, and GMM perform poorly, as the measures they used are not local enough. In CHI and LA datasets, many events are held at less populated areas. FREQ, TFIDF, and GMM are less affected by irrelevant tweets.

5.5 Comparison with Filtering non-local Words

As we discussed earlier, local word detection method can be applied as a pre-processing step to filter non-local word first. However, for our annotation problem this pre-processing step can be *erroneous*. In this section, we compare KDE with KDE using local word detection method.

To model locality of words (query), Backstrom et al. [4] propose a model based on the intuition that a local word should have a high local focus. In addition, the frequency of this word should drop rapidly as the distance to the center increases, reflecting a strong association to the center location. The model uses a fast decaying function in the form of $Cd^{-\alpha}$ to capture the intuition, where d is the distance to its center. The center corresponds to the location where the word appears most frequently. The parameter is determined using the following likelihood function:

$$f(C, \alpha) = \sum_{l_i \in L(w)} \log C d_{l_i}^{-\alpha} + \sum_{l_i \notin L(w)} \log(1 - C d_{l_i}^{-\alpha}).$$

The C captures the center frequency and α measures the speed of decaying. We use the center of the most frequent grid as the word center and follow the center finding step as suggested by [9]. Then, a grid search is used to determine C and α that maximize the likelihood function. We set a threshold ξ on α to filter non-local words.

Figure 6(a) shows the precision-recall curve as we vary ξ from 0.5 to 0.9. It is clear that as the threshold ξ increases the performance decreases. The result indicates that many words describing the user intentions have a low α. For example, word "knicks" (name of a professional basket ball team) will be frequently mentioned at the arena where the game is held at a game day. However, many users may watch the game at some local bars and tweet about the event. The word density will have multiple peaks. Therefore, using a single modal model to fit the occurrences will result in a small α. For our annotation problem, words occurrences often express such multiple modality at a fine-granularity.

5.6 Threshold Study

In real applications, we can set a threshold parameter θ for KDE score to pick relevant words for annotation. We want to study what is the optimal threshold and whether this optimal value is consistent over different datasets. For a given threshold, we calculate the average F_1 score for the location records: $F_1 = 2 \cdot \frac{precision \cdot recall}{precision + recall}$. Figure 6(b) shows the F_1 score on three datasets. For CHI, NYC, and LA datasets, KDE method achieves the best performance at ($F_1 = 0.90, \theta = 2300$) , ($F_1 = 0.87, \theta = 2300$), and ($F_1 = 0.90, \theta = 3300$), respectively. When the threshold is in the range of $[2000, 3000]$, the F_1 score is greater than 0.85 on the three datasets. The results suggest that a reasonable range for selecting θ should fall in the range of $[2000, 3000]$. We set $\theta = 2000$ for the following case studies.

5.7 Case Studies

In this section, we perform several case studies over three different cities to demonstrate the effectiveness of our method in generating time- and space-sensitive semantic *annotations* for the mobile users' location records. For comparison, we

(a) Annotation documents using tweets (our method)

r_1: (40.7505, -73.9934), 1/20/13

Word	Relevance Score
madison	99778
garden	95544
square	76263
penguins	49841
rangers	48560

r_2: (40.6831, -73.9760), 2/10/13

Word	Relevance Score
barclays	86572
center	64970
spurs	40781
nets	34046
antonio	92677

r_3: (40.7505, -73.9934), 3/24/13

Word	Relevance Score
madison	57783
garden	57440
square	45425
penn	25696
rangers	10096

r_4: (40.7634, -73.9748), 3/28/13

Word	Relevance Score
exhibition	26179
thrones	26102
game	23634
day	1002
others	978

r_5: (40.8295, -73.9270), 4/18/13

Word	Relevance Score
yankee	104122
stadium	104087
diamondbacks	42027
yankees	40528
arizona	33577

r_6: (40.8295, -73.9269), 6/5/13

Word	Relevance Score
yankee	96293
stadium	91471
yankees	28911
indians	27710
cleveland	24590

(b) Locations on the map

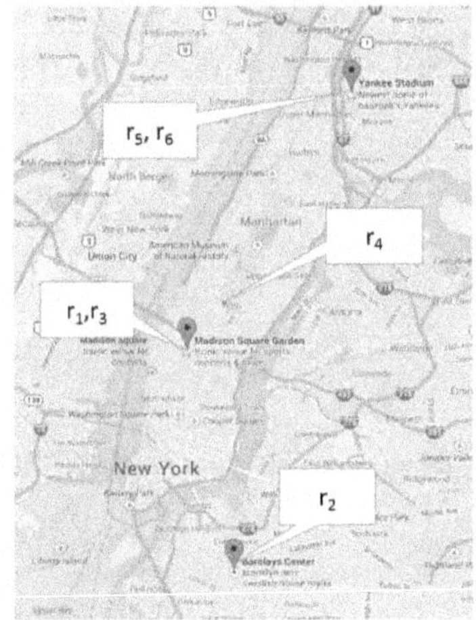

(c) Annotation by static POI information (method for comparison)

r_1, r_3: (40.7505, -73.9934)

POI	Distance
Madison Square Garden	3
Auntie Anne's Pretzels	9
Forest Electric Corporation	16
Auntie Anne's Pretzels	21
Event Bar	31

r_2: (40.6831, -73.9760)

POI	Distance
Barclays Center	72
Burlington Coat Factory	79
Jean-Baptiste Gary E MD	84
National Vision	98
Wellness Center	99

r_5, r_6: (40.8259, -73.9269)

POI	Distance
New York Yankees	34
Yankees Audi Club	37
Johnny Rockets	64
Yankee Stadium	78
Apple Bank For Saving	129

r_4: (40.7634, -73.9748)

POI	Distance
Manhattan Dental Health	9
Och-Ziff Capital Management Group	23
Oz Management Group	23
Summit Rock Advisors	23
Ingres Corporation	23

(d) Tweets as ground truth:

r_1: Daddy's home!!!! LETS GO RANGERS (@ Madison Square Garden for Pittsburgh Penguins vs New York Rangers) [pic]: http://t.co/cUYIVcRx
r_2: I'm at Barclays Center for San Antonio Spurs vs Brooklyn Nets (Brooklyn, NY) w/ 69 others http://t.co/UgJxCvlX
r_3: Let's do it. (@ Madison Square Garden - @thegarden for @washcaps vs @NYRangers w/ 44 others) http://t.co/oaaE4f1t9n
r_4: with @jedafrank (@ Game Of Thrones Exhibition w/ 14 others) http://t.co/U5ztm1RWRu
r_5: I'm at Yankee Stadium - @mlb for Arizona Diamondbacks vs New York Yankees (Bronx, NY) w/ 129 others [pic]: http://t.co/MnHVcn17OP
r_6: I'm at Yankee Stadium - @mlb for Cleveland Indians vs New York Yankees (Bronx, NY) w/ 143 others http://t.co/KTidl9wtEv

Figure 7: Case study for user #901.

also show annotation results using nearby POI information. The POI information is gathered via Google Places API[3].

Case User #901. In this case, we examine the location history of user #901, who lives in Staten Island (based on his user profile) and visits New York City frequently. We pick six location records from this user. Figure 7(a) shows the top-5 words extracted by our method for each record.

For the location records $\mathbf{r_5}$ and $\mathbf{r_6}$, our method ranks the words "yankee", "stadium" and "yankees" as the top three words with the relevance scores higher than 90. Figure 7(d) shows tweets from this user at those location records. We can see that this user was indeed watching Yankees' games on these two days, as he tweeted about the games. In addition, the location information of these two records on the map (Figure 7(b)) shows that the user was physically present at the Yankee Stadium, instead of watching the games at home.

Similarly, for location records $\mathbf{r_1}$ and $\mathbf{r_3}$, we can infer from the tweets in Figure 7(d) and locations in Figure 7(b) that the user was attending Rangers' hockey game at Madison Square Garden. Our method correctly ranks the words "madison", "garden", "square" and "rangers" at the top of the list. Further, word "penguin" from $\mathbf{r_1}$ corresponds to the team that Rangers was competing with on that day. We also note that, in overall, these words have lower scores than those related to the Yankees, because Rangers' games are relatively smaller events compared to Yankees' games.[4]

In addition, we find that this user went to see the NBA game between San Antonio Spurs and Brooklyn Nets on 02/10/2013 at Barclays Center ($\mathbf{r_2}$) and the Game of Thrones exhibition on 3/28/2013 ($\mathbf{r_4}$).

Figure 7(c) shows the annotation by static POI information. For records $\mathbf{r_1}, \mathbf{r_2}, \mathbf{r_3}, \mathbf{r_5}, \mathbf{r_6}$, the static annotation correctly identifies location names. However, such annotation does not include dynamic event information, such as "rangers", "penguin", "spurs" and "nets" in $\mathbf{r_1}$ and $\mathbf{r_2}$.

Case User #115. Now we look at another user #115, who lives in New York City. We also pick six location records from this user and show the corresponding annotation documents in Figure 8(a). This user is also a fan of the Yankees, as indicated by record $\mathbf{r_4}$. For record $\mathbf{r_2}$ on 5/6/2013, our method ranks the words "art", "metropolitan" and "museum" as the top-3 words followed by the words "metgala" and "met". As the first three words indicate that this user was at the Metropolitan Museum of Art, the words "gala" and "metgala" further reveal the specific event this user was attending. As confirmed by the corresponding tweets in Figure 8(d) and the actual locations in Figure 8(b), this user indeed attended the Met Gala event, an annual affair to celebrate the opening of the Metropolitan Museum's fashion exhibit. Meanwhile, annotation by POI information cannot reveal such rich contextual information. As shown in Figure 8(c), the static POI annotation only identifies road and landmark names around the location. For record $\mathbf{r_5}$, our method detects a soccer game with "field", "citi", "israel" and "honduras" as the most relevant words. At the same time, annotation by POI information does not contain this event information as shown in Figure 8(c). Other than these big events, annotation using our method indicates the user's visit to Museum of Modern Art (MOMA) in $\mathbf{r_1}$ and an ice-skating event near Central Park in $\mathbf{r_3}$.

Case User #329. Finally, we study user #329 from Chicago. Similar results are observed and reported in Figure 9. The actual tweets and our annotations in Figure 9(a) reveal three activities of the user. $\mathbf{r_1}, \mathbf{r_3}$ records two different marathon that user #329 participated in. Although the en route check-ins do not have a specific POI, our method can associate the nearby tweets at that time and location and identify the "marathon" as a top word in annotation. Records $\mathbf{r_2}, \mathbf{r_6}$ are baseball matches of Chicago White Sox. The "United Center" and "hawks" in the annotations of $\mathbf{r_4}, \mathbf{r_5}$ reveal the

[3]https://developers.google.com/places/

[4]Yankee Stadium has a capacity of 50,291, whereas Madison Square Garden has a capacity of 18,200.

(a) Annotation documents using tweets (our method)

r_1: (40.7583, -73.9854), 5/5/13

Word	Relevance Score
modern	20607
art	16814
museum	15975
moma	3272

r_2: (40.778, -73.962), 5/6/13

Word	Relevance Score
metropolitan	54272
museum	46360
art	44129
punk	10156
metgala	7279

r_3: (40.7684, -73.9745), 5/13/13

Word	Relevance Score
wollman	12690
skating	10909
rink	10405
ice	10123
fox	4497

r_4: (40.8294, -73.9269), 5/15/13

Word	Relevance Score
yankee	102144
stadium	98309
game	16975
yankees	14301

r_5: (40.7564, -73.8460), 6/5/13

Word	Relevance Score
citi	40914
field	40416
honduras	13359
israel	12631

(b) Locations on the map

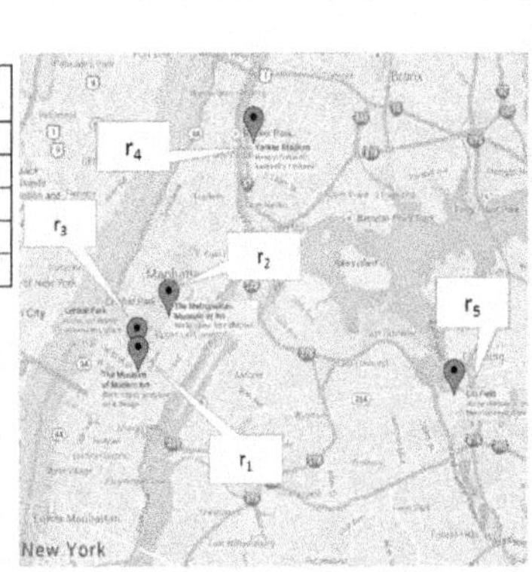

(c) Annotation by static POI information (method for comparison)

r_1 : (40.7583, -73.9854)

POI	Distance
Forever 21	26
Disney Store	26
Hodgson Russ LLP	30
00 Commercial Blinds	33
New York Society of Security analysts	35

r_2: (40.778, -73.962)

POI	Distance
995 Fifth Avenue	56
Frank E. Campbell – The Funeral Chapel	56
Thomas W. Loeb, MD	59
Olive & Bettes	70
Universal Funeral Chapel	70

r_3: (40.7684, -73.9745)

POI	Distance
Victorian Garden Amusement Park	66
Wollman Ice Skating Park	70
Central Park Carousel	174
Central Park Zoo	174
The Arsenal	282

r_5: (40.7564, -73.8460)

POI	Distance
Citi Field	9
Shea Stadium Home Run Apple	138
Mama's of Corona	151
Mets Plaza	170
NYC Parks & Recreation	183

*r_4: (40.8295, -73.9269): Annotation by POI is the same as r_5, r_6 in Figure 8.

(d) Tweets as ground truth:

r_1: katyperry @ Museum of Modern Art (MoMA) http://t.co/j9ql2faeRw

r_2: .emmyrossum #MetGala #PunkFashion @ The Metropolitan Museum of Art http://t.co/T11YQfm6KG

r_3: @minkakelly #foxupfront @ Wollman Park http://t.co/56dcTzx5YJA

r_4: @bearpascoee @4stillrunning @ruebenrandle #bleachercreatures #rollcall yankees #204 @ Yankee Staduim http://t.co/PIGxyatsF9

r_5: Houduras vs. Israel http://t.co/kUxOy8hozw

Figure 8: Case study for user #115.

fact that the United Center is the home arena of ice hockey team Chicago Blackhawks. In Figure 9(b), we show the actual POIs of each tweets, which are consistent with out annotation.

In summary, the above case studies show that our method can correctly annotate the semantics (including landmarks and events) to a user's location records. Further, our clustering results on the annotation documents well represent the user's interests in local events.

6. PROFILING USER AS AN APPLICATION

Given the annotation document $\mathcal{A}(r_i)$ for each location record r_i of a user U, we can discover the interests of the user by examining the similarities of all the annotation documents. For example, a New York City sports fan may have several annotation documents related to the sport events in New York City. Therefore, assuming there are K underlying interests for this user, the annotation documents should be partitioned into K groups so that each cluster represents one interest.

6.1 Profiling Method

A potential solution is to apply some clustering algorithms. In order to do this, a distance measure between two documents must be specified. In the literature, the cosine similarity is frequently used to measure the document similarity due to its length invariance [28]. However, in our problem, the absolute scores in a document are important in differentiating the event days and the normal days. For example, suppose we have annotation documents on two location records: $\mathcal{A}(r_1) = \{(nets, 150), (nba, 100), (others, 1)\}$ and $\mathcal{A}(r_2) = \{(nets, 10), (nba, 8), (others, 5)\}$, where record r_1 is on a game day. The cosine similarity will then consider these two documents as very similar: $Cos(\mathcal{A}(r_1), \mathcal{A}(r_2)) = 0.93$. Therefore, we propose to use the Euclidean distance as our similarity measure, which better preserves the original relevance scores. Indeed, the Euclidean distance between the two documents in the previous example is large: $Euc(\mathcal{A}(r_1), \mathcal{A}(r_2)) = 173.26$.

Various clustering methods, such as K-means and hierarchical clustering, can be applied to cluster the annotation documents based on the proposed similarity measure. In this paper, we simply use the K-means method.

6.2 Case Studies

We run the user profiling method on user #901 and user #115 in Section 5.7. We use all the location records of a user and cluster all the annotation documents to profile the user's interests. There are 33 location records of user #901 and 250 records of user #115.

Case User #901. In Figure 10, we report the top-5 words (based on the sum of relevance scores) for each document cluster and the ground truth profile of this user. K is set as 5 in the K-means clustering algorithm. We can see that Cluster 1 and Cluster 4 both contain annotation documents that are related to Yankees' games, and the words "stadium", "yankee" and "bronx" also appear in the user's reference interest profile. Taking a closer look at Cluster 4, we see that it is about a special event, namely the Old-Timers' Day. This is a popular event held annually to celebrate the accomplishments of Yankees' former players. Our method is able to differentiate it from Yankees' regular games (Cluster 1). In addition, Cluster 2 corresponds to the user's interest in Rangers. The annotation document of record $\mathbf{r_2}$ forms a cluster (Cluster 3) by itself, as this NBA basketball game differs from other sports games that this user attended. Finally, we note that Cluster 5 has the largest number of documents (23 out of 33 total documents). This is because, in practice, most tweets are not related to specific events. The annotation documents for those records tend to include arbitrary words with low relevance scores and typically form one cluster.

Figure 10(b) shows the words from this user's tweets ranked by tf-idf score. Note that our annotation method only uses the tweets from the crowd (excluding the tweet from this target user). The sports related terms are frequently seen in this person's tweets, indicating he is a sports fan. Words describing routine behaviors of a user also have high tf-idf scores, such as "staten" and "island" (home of this user).

Case User #115. We use K-means with $K = 7$ in this case and report the top-5 words of each cluster in Figure 11. We only show 3 clusters in the figure as we exclude the clusters of background words. In Figure 11(a), we can see that Cluster 1 corresponds to this user's interest in the Met Gala event and Cluster 2 corresponds to this user's interest in Yankees' game. Meanwhile, Cluster 3 summarizes terms

(a) Annotation documents using tweets (our method)

r_1: (41.8783,-87.6207), 10/9/11

Word	Relevance Score
bank	109512
america	105554
marathon	41678
chicago	20740

r_2: (41.8301, -87.6341), 9/17/12

Word	Relevance Score
cellular	147857
filed	55661
white	52603

r_3: (41.8762, -87.6271), 10/7/12

Word	Relevance Score
marathon	1977
photo	1657
chicago	1193
posted	1107

r_4: (41.8806, -87.6741), 4/30/13

Word	Relevance Score
united	137381
center	54741
hawks	14107
game	9243

r_5: (41.8806, -87.6741), 2/25/13

Word	Relevance Score
edemonton	150778
oilers	140648
united	139282
blackhawks	101182

r_6: (41.8301, -87.6341), 4/7/13

Word	Relevance Score
cellular	114981
field	95051
white	46879
chicago	4606

(b) Locations on the map

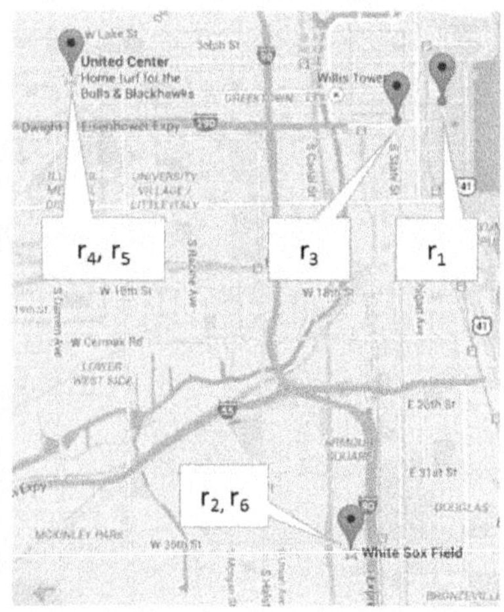

(c) Tweets as ground truth:

r_1: I'm at Bank of America Chicago Marathon (300 S Columbus, Chicago) w/ 85 others http://t.co/WPrsOpMe

r_2: I'm at U.S. Cellular Field for Detroit Tigers vs Chicago White Sox (Chicago, IL) w/ 49 others http://t.co/1xsPh6jk

r_3: I'm at Chicago Marathon (Chicago, IL) w/ 166 others http://t.co/pGOZGKCL

r_4: Let's go hawks (at @UnitedCenter w/ 138 others) http://t.co/M6qxZgvO0o

r_5: Let's go hawks (at @unitedcenter for Edmonton Oilers vs Chicago Blackhawks w/ 185 others) http://t.co/NVXZuuRVSu

r_6: Let's go sox (@ U.S. Cellular Field - @mlb for Seattle Mariners vs Chicago White Sox w/ 139 others) [pic]: http://t.co/MgUrGC29YG

Figure 9: Case study for user #329.

Cluster	Top-5 words
1	yankee, stadium, yankees, bronx.
2	garden, madison, square, rangers, penguins.
3	barclays, center, brooklyn, nets, spurs.
4	yankee, stadium, yankees, old, oldtimersday.
5	public, island, plaza, staten, drinking.

(a)

Word	tf-idf
staten	13.43
stadium	13.08
rpx	12.22
hylan	11.18
island	11.16
drinking	7.57
rangers	7.44
yankee	6.32
bronx	5.58
plaza	5.22
madison	4.64
garden	4.81
photo	4.42
ale	4.15

(b)

Figure 10: Interest profiles for user #901. (a) Top words in each cluster of the annotation documents. (b) Words from tweets ranked by tf-idf scores.

Cluster	Top-5 words
1	art, metropolitan, museum, metgala, punkfashion.
2	yankee, mets, sox, stadium, orioles.
3	citi, field, mets, edcny, subwayseries.

(a)

Word	tf-idf
metgala	42.09
punkfashion	42.09
yankee	33.87
stadium	31
bagatelle	28.30
citi	27.19
field	25.41
metropolitan	24.57
marquee	22.73
bleacher	18.83
creatures	15.95
superstudio	15.68
art	14.37
museum	14.10

(b)

Figure 11: Interest profiles for user #115. (a) Top words in each cluster of the annotation documents. (b) Words from tweets ranked by tf-idf scores.

that are related to events held at the Citi Field, including the Electric Daisy Carnival festival and the baseball games. Our results are consistent with this user's interests inferred from his tweets as shown in Figure 11(b).

These two case studies show that our interest profiling using annotation documents can reveal the real interests of this user inferred from the tweets.

7. CONCLUSION

In this paper, we address a novel problem of annotating dynamic semantics to the mobility data using external contextual data. The proposed solution enables us to understand the purposes and interests of a user from his location history, which could benefit a wide range of applications in real world. To this end, we study different methods for annotation and have discussed their advantages and disadvantages. We show that KDE is the best model to capture both the locality and the relevance of words. The effectiveness of our method has been verified through quantitative evaluations and case studies.

There are a number of extensions that could be further explored. First, our current method does not explicitly differentiate between landmark words and event-related words. An event-related word tends to have high density at its center only when the event occurs, whereas a landmark word always has high density at its center. Considering such temporal characteristic may help us differentiate these two types of words. Second, our current method will generate the same annotation for different users, as long as their location records have the same timestamps and locations. Considering the personal location history may enable us to further refine the results. For example, we can promote words which appear in the annotation documents of multiple location records of a user. Third, the semantics at a uni-gram level may be shallow. We can apply multiword expression methods for more interpretable annotations. Finally, as an interesting direction for future work, we plan to explore other types of external contextual data to compensate for the data sparsity data. Potential data sources include environment data, news data, and crime data.

8. REFERENCES

[1] L. O. Alvares, V. Bogorny, B. Kuijpers, J. A. F. de Macedo, B. Moelans, and A. Vaisman. A model for enriching trajectories with semantic geographical information. In *Proc. ACM GIS*, 2007.

[2] N. Andrienko and G. Andrienko. Designing visual analytics methods for massive collections of movement data. *Cartographica: The International Journal for Geographic Information and Geovisualization*, 2007.

[3] D. Ashbrook and T. Starner. Using gps to learn significant locations and predict movement across multiple users. *UbiComp*, 2003.

[4] L. Backstrom, J. Kleinberg, R. Kumar, and J. Novak. Spatial variation in search engine queries. In *Proc. WWW*, 2008.

[5] J. Bithell. An application of density estimation to geographical epidemiology. *Statistics in medicine*, 9(6):691–701, 1990.

[6] L. Breiman, W. Meisel, and E. Purcell. Variable kernel estimates of multivariate densities. *Technometrics*, 1977.

[7] X. Cao, G. Cong, and C. S. Jensen. Mining significant semantic locations from gps data. *Proc. VLDB*, 2010.

[8] D. Chakrabarti and K. Punera. Event summarization using tweets. *ICWSM*, 11:66–73, 2011.

[9] Z. Cheng, J. Caverlee, and K. Lee. You are where you tweet: a content-based approach to geo-locating twitter users. In *Proc. ACM CIKM*, 2010.

[10] E. Cho, S. A. Myers, and J. Leskovec. Friendship and mobility: user movement in location-based social networks. In *Proc. ACM KDD*, 2011.

[11] K. Dehnad. Density estimation for statistics and data analysis. *Technometrics*, 29(4):495–495, 1987.

[12] N. Donthu and R. T. Rust. Note-estimating geographic customer densities using kernel density estimation. *Marketing Science*, 8(2):191–203, 1989.

[13] N. Eagle, A. Pentland, and D. Lazer. Inferring friendship network structure by using mobile phone data. In *Proc. PNAS*, 2009.

[14] G. Erkan and D. R. Radev. Lexrank: graph-based lexical centrality as salience in text summarization. *Journal of Artificial Intelligence Research*, 2004.

[15] B. Guc, M. May, Y. Saygin, and C. Körner. Semantic annotation of gps trajectories. In *Proc AGILE*, 2008.

[16] S. Hasan, X. Zhan, and S. V. Ukkusuri. Understanding urban human activity and mobility patterns using large-scale location-based data from online social media. In *UrbComp*, 2013.

[17] D. Inouye and J. K. Kalita. Comparing twitter summarization algorithms for multiple post summaries. In *PASSAT and SocialCom*. IEEE, 2011.

[18] Z. Li, B. Ding, J. Han, R. Kays, and P. Nye. Mining periodic behaviors for moving objects. In *Proc. ACM KDD*, 2010.

[19] L. Liao. *Location-based activity recognition*. PhD thesis, University of Washington, 2006.

[20] M. Lichman and P. Smyth. Modeling human location data with mixtures of kernel densities. In *Proc. SIGKDD*. ACM, 2014.

[21] N. Mamoulis, H. Cao, G. Kollios, M. Hadjieleftheriou, Y. Tao, and D. Cheung. Mining, indexing, and querying historical spatiotemporal data. In *Proc. ACM KDD*, 2004.

[22] M. Mathioudakis, N. Bansal, and N. Koudas. Identifying, attributing and describing spatial bursts. In *Proc. VLDB*, 2010.

[23] R. Mihalcea and P. Tarau. Textrank: Bringing order into texts. ACL, 2004.

[24] A. T. Palma, V. Bogorny, B. Kuijpers, and L. O. Alvares. A clustering-based approach for discovering interesting places in trajectories. In *Proc. SAC*, 2008.

[25] D. Radev, T. Allison, S. Blair-Goldensohn, J. Blitzer, A. Celebi, S. Dimitrov, E. Drabek, A. Hakim, W. Lam, D. Liu, et al. Mead-a platform for multidocument multilingual text summarization. 2004.

[26] B. Sharifi, M.-A. Hutton, and J. Kalita. Summarizing microblogs automatically. In *Proc NAACL*, 2010.

[27] S. Spaccapietra, C. Parent, M. L. Damiani, J. A. de Macedo, F. Porto, and C. Vangenot. A conceptual view on trajectories. *Trans. IEEE TKDE*, 2008.

[28] A. Strehl, J. Ghosh, and R. Mooney. Impact of similarity measures on web-page clustering. In *AAAI Workshop for Web Search*, 2000.

[29] H. Takamura, H. Yokono, and M. Okumura. Summarizing a document stream. In *Advances in Information Retrieval*, pages 177–188. Springer, 2011.

[30] L. Vanderwende, H. Suzuki, C. Brockett, and A. Nenkova. Beyond sumbasic: Task-focused summarization with sentence simplification and lexical expansion. *Information Processing & Management*, 2007.

[31] K. Xie, K. Deng, and X. Zhou. From trajectories to activities: a spatio-temporal join approach. In *Proc. LBSN*, 2009.

[32] Z. Yan, D. Chakraborty, C. Parent, S. Spaccapietra, and K. Aberer. Semitri: a framework for semantic annotation of heterogeneous trajectories. In *Proc. EDBT*, 2011.

[33] Z. Yan, D. Chakraborty, C. Parent, S. Spaccapietra, and K. Aberer. Semantic trajectories: Mobility data computation and annotation. *ACM Trans. TIST*, 4(3):49, 2013.

[34] Z. Yan, N. Giatrakos, V. Katsikaros, N. Pelekis, and Y. Theodoridis. Setrastream: semantic-aware trajectory construction over streaming movement data. In *SSTD*. Springer, 2011.

[35] Z. Yin, L. Cao, J. Han, C. Zhai, and T. Huang. Geographical topic discovery and comparison. In *Proc. WWW*, 2011.

[36] J.-D. Zhang and C.-Y. Chow. igslr: personalized geo-social location recommendation: a kernel density estimation approach. In *Proc. SIGSPATIAL*. ACM, 2013.

[37] Y. Zheng, Y. Chen, Q. Li, X. Xie, and W.-Y. Ma. Understanding transportation modes based on gps data for web applications. *Trans. ACM TWEB*, 2010.

[38] Y. Zheng, L. Zhang, X. Xie, and W.-Y. Ma. Mining interesting locations and travel sequences from gps trajectories. In *Proc. WWW*, 2009.

[39] C. Zhou, D. Frankowski, P. Ludford, S. Shekhar, and L. Terveen. Discovering personally meaningful places: An interactive clustering approach. *TOIS*, 2007.

Automatic Web Content Extraction by Combination of Learning and Grouping

Shanchan Wu, Jerry Liu, Jian Fan
HP Labs
1501 Page Mill Road, Palo Alto, CA, 94304
{shanchan.wu, jerry.liu, jian.fan}@hp.com

ABSTRACT

Web pages consist of not only actual content, but also other elements such as branding banners, navigational elements, advertisements, copyright etc. This noisy content is typically not related to the main subjects of the webpages. Identifying the part of actual content, or clipping web pages, has many applications, such as high quality web printing, e-reading on mobile devices and data mining. Although there are many existing methods attempting to address this task, most of them can either work only on certain types of Web pages, e.g. article pages, or has to develop different models for different websites. We formulate the actual content identifying problem as a DOM tree node selection problem. We develop multiple features by utilizing the DOM tree node properties to train a machine learning model. Then candidate nodes are selected based on the learning model. Based on the observation that the actual content is usually located in a spatially continuous block, we develop a grouping technology to further filter out noisy data and pick missing data for the candidate nodes. We conduct extensive experiments on a real dataset and demonstrate our solution has high quality outputs and outperforms several baseline methods.

Categories and Subject Descriptors

H.3.3 [**Information Storage and Retrieval**]: Information Search and Retrieval—*Retrieval models, Information filtering*

General Terms

Algorithms, Experimentation, Performance

Keywords

Content Extraction; Information Extraction; Web Page Segmentation; Noise Removal; Information Retrieval; Web Mining

1. INTRODUCTION

As more and more information is published on the World Wide Web, the influence of the World Wide Web increases. Thus, discovering knowledge from web and providing users with useful information have become important and popular. For this purpose, main content in a web page must be identified. This is a challenging task, since the main content in a web page is often accompanied by a lot of additional and often distracting content such as branding banners, navigation elements, advertisements and copyright etc, and the web pages in the World Wide Web are highly heterogeneous. To extract useful knowledge from a web page and to provide users clean content to read, this additional information should be treated as noise and removed from the main content.

The task of extracting the main content from web pages has attracted many research works [4, 10, 12, 13, 18]. However, most of these previous works focus on article web pages, such as news articles, and blog posts. These article pages show some similar layout patterns, although the styles are usually different from website to website. Thus some heuristics from the visual features can be used to extract these informative items with pretty high accuracy [4].

As article news pages are likely be are generated from some underlying structured sources, some template-based solutions make the assumption that there exists a template structure in news pages for a specific news website. Some template based approaches such as Tree Edit Distance (TED) exploit the similarities of the structures in HTML pages and generate wrappers [14]. However, the generated wrappers can only work properly for news pages which are constructed on a template that has been seen in the training data. Furthermore, any small changes in the underlying HTML structures will be very likely to invalidate the wrappers, and it is computationally and resource expensive to maintain up-to-date wrappers for the huge amount of news websites.

Besides article pages, there are also a large volume of non-article web pages, such as online shopping pages and recipe pages. The layout patterns of the non-article web pages are more difficult to be generalized. These previous solutions that were only demonstrated to work for article web pages are not very likely to work for non-article web pages. To help users to get more accurate main content, the tool of Smart Print provides for Web page printing [10] provides users an option to manually select the informative areas of a web page in an interactive interface. The more manual work that needs to get involved in the tool, the worse the user experience would be. A good extraction solution that works well for all kinds of web pages will reduce manual work and hence would help to improve user experience.

There are some previous learning approaches to classify web page regions as actual content regions and noisy regions based on some features extracted from the regions [18]. Usually the output for a region with either "YES" or "NO" does not take the surrounding areas into consideration, i.e. an isolated binary decision. A region by itself may look like or be classified as a noisy or non-noisy region. However, after taking the surrounding areas into consideration, a region which was classified as a non-noisy region may

WWW 2015, May 18–22, 2015, Florence, Italy.
ACM 978-1-4503-3469-3/15/05.
http://dx.doi.org/10.1145/2736277.2741659.

turn out to be a noisy region, and vice versa. Furthermore, most of the previous approaches are focused on article web pages, which are relatively simpler to extract actual content from compared with general webpages. In general, web pages may contain tables, figures or other visual formats for actual content in addition to text. Hence, regions of general web pages are more likely to be misclassified than those of article web pages. We expect that incorporating some techniques that take the surrounding areas into consideration would help to improve the classification accuracy.

We propose a novel approach for automatic extraction of web content in a webpage by combination of learning and grouping. We formulate the problem as a DOM tree node selection problem. To train a learning model, we develop multiple features by utilizing the DOM tree node properties. We consider the features of positions, areas, fonts, text, tags and links. We calculate and adjust the feature values into the formats more suitable for the learning model. After the learning model is trained, it is used to score the nodes and select the candidate nodes. We compact the candidate nodes by removing the redundant nodes. With the observation that the actual content is usually located in a spatially continuous block, we develop a grouping technology to further filter out noisy data and pick missing data for the candidate nodes. We conduct extensive experiments on a real dataset and demonstrate our solution has high quality outputs and outperforms several baseline methods.

2. RELATED WORK

Extracting web content from web pages has received substantial interest by researchers [13, 4, 6, 10, 12, 18, 21, 8, 17, 9, 19, 16]. Most of existent working has focused on article web pages. For example, Pasternack et. al. [13] proposed a method based on utilizing maximum subsequence segmentation to extract the text of articles from HTML documents using features of tri-grams and tags. Wang et al. [18] proposed an approach by learning a template-independent wrapper for news article extraction to identify one minimum sub-tree containing title and and one minimum sub-tree containing article body content. Luo et al. [12] utilized line-break features to generate text segments corresponding to paragraphs and then find the range of text body by the maximum subsequence algorithm. They also proposed some heuristic rules to filter out the noisy data within the text body. Fan et al. [4] proposed a system to extract titles, main text body, content- related images and image captions from news- and blog-like article web pages. Kohlschutter et al. [8] analyzed shallow text features - number of words and link density - to distinguish main content from other parts of information from news article web pages.

Weninger et al. [19] proposed the Content Extraction via Tag Ratios (CETR) method to extract content text from diverse web pages using HTML tag ratios. They computed the tag ratio for each line and then clustered the resulting histogram into content and noise areas. Sun et al. [17] proposed Content Extraction via Text Density (CETD) to extract content from web pages, based on the observation that the content is usually containing more text and simply formatted, while noise is usually highly formatted and contains less text with short sentences.

One approach for content extraction is the Template Detection (TD) algorithms [1, 3, 7, 11, 20] which applies collections of documents with the same templates to learn common structures. Bar-Yossef et al. presented an approach to automatically detect templates by counting the frequent pagelet item sets, where each pagelet is a self-contained logical regions in a web with a well defined topic or functionality[1]. Lin et al. partitioned a web page into several blocks by HTML tag <table>, and utilized entropy measure to partition blocks into informative or redundant by a set of word based features [11]. Yi et al. introduced a site style tree (SST) structure to distinguish noisy blocks and main content blocks of the Web site [20], based on the observation that noisy blocks are more likely to share some common contents and presentation styles, while the main content blocks of the pages are more likely to be diverse in their actual contents and/or presentation styles. Chen et al. proposed a two-stage template detection method to combine template detection and removal with the index building process of a search engine. They segmented web pages into blocks, and blocks are clustered according to their style features. The blocks with similar layout style and content were detected and identified as templates [3]. All these template detection algorithms generally try to identify the main content by removing common parts found in different web pages. This is based on the assumption that the noisy parts such as advertisements are more likely to be repeated across different web pages. As different web sites are designed with different styles, in order to more successfully identify the main content different template models need to be built for different web sites. Even each website is provided with a unique template model, it would meet difficulties when different design styles are used in different web pages in the same website. Furthermore, the update of the layout or structure of the pages in the web site will invalidate the template model.

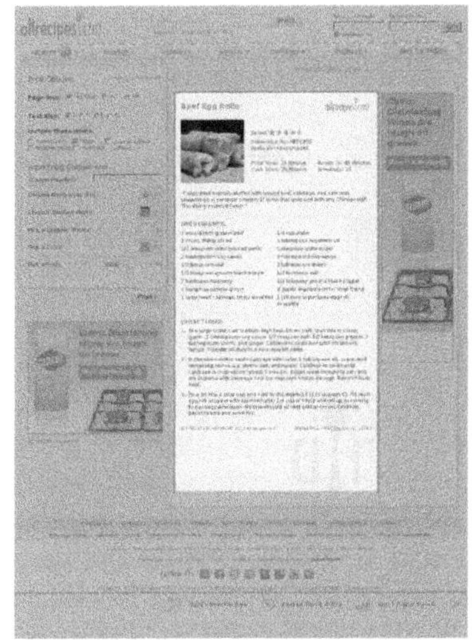

Figure 1: An example of extracting the main content from a webpage. The area with light red background is the main content area.

Cai et al. [2] proposed the Vision-based Page Segmentation (VIPS) technique to segment a web page into semantically related content blocks from its visual presentation, based on some heuristic rules on the visual information. They constructed a tree structure for a web page, where the nodes to the tree are visually grouped blocks. Based on the VIPS technique, Song et al. [15] presented an approach to rank block importance for web pages by learning from block features (including spatial features and content features). Fernandes et al. [5] proposed a different method to compute block importance of a web page by assigning weights to classes of structurally similar blocks.

3. PROBLEM FORMULATION AND SOLUTION

The task of extracting main content from a web page is to select a set of informative areas in the web page. Figure 1 shows an ex-

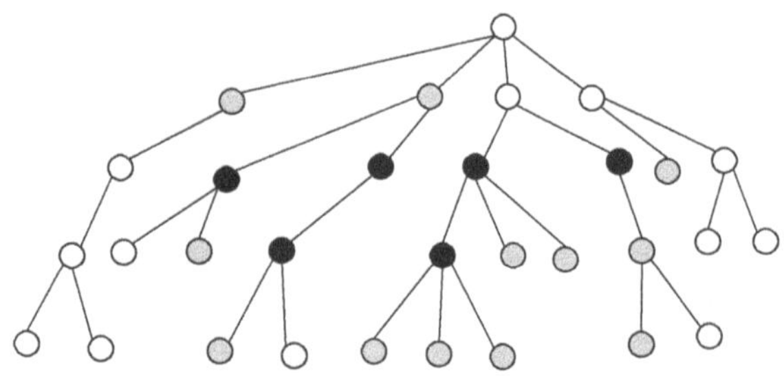

Figure 2: DOM tree.

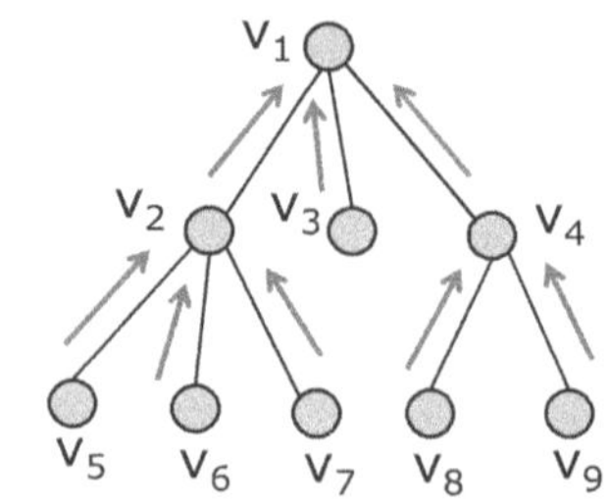

Figure 3: Feature calculation.

ample of extracting the main content from a recipe web page. Web pages are encoded by the HTML language and a rendering engine can render it to a DOM tree structure. Figure 2 shows a simple DOM tree structure. For most of the web pages, the sizes of their DOM trees are usually much bigger than the size of the DOM tree in this example. Each node in the DOM tree can be labeled with a HTML tag, e.g. "TITLE", "P", "A", "HEAD", and each node is associated with other properties, like position information, font information, text information etc. To simplify the expression, we use a DOM tree node to represent the a block of content of this node and all of its descendant nodes. The task of extracting main content from a web page may be formulated as a problem of node selection from its DOM tree of the web page.

To solve this problem, we propose a solution with two major steps as following.

The first step is the learning step. In this step we train a learning model using the training data. Based on the learning model, we assign a score to each node in the DOM tree of a web page. The scores represent how likely the corresponding nodes are part of the main content, i.e., the content which we recommend to users and interest users. We select the candidate nodes by a threshold.

The second step is the grouping step. As the output from the learning step is not perfect, in this step we group candidate nodes, remove the noisy groups, and refine the selected group by further removing noisy nodes and picking up missing nodes.

We will describe more details about the solution in the following sections.

4. FEATURE SELECTION

In this section, we describe how we select and calculate features for DOM tree nodes that will be used for a learning model.

As we use a node in the DOM tree to represent the regions covered by this node and all its descendants, we set the features of a node to be able to represent the aggregated properties of this node and all its descendants. For a feature, we have three types of values: one is absolute value, one is relative value, and one is adjusted value. The absolute value is the real value of this feature, for example, the area size in square inches. The relative value is the value that is the normalized value of this feature. For example, the relative value of the area size feature of a node is the area size covered by this node and all its descendants divided by the area size of the whole page. The adjusted value is the value that is transformed from the relative value to a format more suitable for a learning model. For some features, we can just set the adjusted value to be the same as the relative value, and use it for the learning model.

For a node v_i, the absolute value of its feature x is recursively set to be the union of its original x property value and the absolute values of the feature x of all its children:

$$F_x(v_i) = F'_x(v_i) \bigcup \left\{ \bigcup_{v_j \in Children(v_i)} F_x(v_j) \right\} \quad (1)$$

In equation (1), $F_x(v_i)$ is the absolute value of feature x for node v_i and $F'_x(v_i)$ is the original x property value of node v_i, and $F_x(v_j)$ is the absolute value of feature x for node v_j. If a node does not have any children, the absolute values of all its features are set to be its corresponding original property values. The property values of a node are directly available after the web page is rendered by a rendering engine, e.g., Webkit. For different features, the union operation in equation (1) is slightly different. For the number of characters, the union operation is mathematical addition. For font color and font size, the union operation is merging the pairs of key and values, e.g., $\{red : 4, green : 2\} \bigcup \{red : 3, blue : 1\} = \{red : 7, green : 2, blue : 1\}$, where $red : 4$ means the number of red characters is 4. For left, right, top and bottom positions, the union operation is to get the corresponding left most or top most or right most or top most or bottom most positions. For area size, the union operation calculates the area size of the union regions, rather than adding them up since there might be some overlap.

Figure 3 shows the way about how the absolute feature values are calculated. In the DOM tree, the absolute feature values are calculated by traversing the tree from the bottom level to the top level, level by level. In Figure 3, the absolute feature values of nodes v_5, v_6, v_7, v_8, v_9 which are in the bottom level are first calculated, and then the absolute feature values of the nodes v_2, v_3, v_4 which are in one upper level are calculated, and at last the feature values of root node v_1 are calculated. After getting all of the absolute feature values, we can get the relative feature values and the adjusted feature values by visiting each node once more.

We are considering position features, area features, font features, text, tag and link features.

4.1 Position and Area Features

For the position features, we consider the left, right, top, bottom, horizontal center and vertical center positions. As we have mentioned earlier, for the left, right, top, bottom positions of a node, we calculate its absolute value using equation (1). Since there are no original horizontal center and vertical center position properties from the rendering output, their absolute values are the mean value of the absolute value of the left position and the absolute value of right position, or the the mean value of the absolute value of the top position and bottom position. We can easily get the relative values of these positions by normalization with the page width or the page height, depending on the types of the positions.

After we get the relative values of the positions, we then calculated the adjust values based on a measure of how good are the positions. For left position, a "perfect" relative left position value is the average value of the relative left positions of all of the ground truth blocks in the training dataset. Suppose this "perfect" value is $BEST\_LEFT$. Then we calculate the adjusted value of left position feature of a node as follows:

$$POS\_LEFT = 1 - |BEST\_LEFT - LEFT|$$

where POS_LEFT is the adjusted value of the left position feature and $LEFT$ is the relative value of the left position. The value is in the range of [0,1] and the higher the better. Similarly we can calculate the adjusted values of left, right, top, bottom, horizontal center and vertical center positions, which we label as POS_LEFT, POS_RIGHT, POS_TOP, POS_BOTTOM, $POS\_CENTERX$, and $POS\_CENTERY$.

We add one feature to capture the distance between the center of a node to the "perfect" center position, which only has the adjusted value. The calculation is based on the relative values of the center positions and we label this adjusted feature value as POS_DIST.

For area features, we consider the area size. We set the adjusted value of area size to be the same as the relative value, i.e., the normalization of the area size of a node, which we label as $AREA\_SIZE$.

We also add one feature to capture how close is the area size to the "perfect" area size, which only has the adjusted value. A "perfect" relative area size value is the average value of the relative area size values of all of the ground truth blocks in the training dataset. If we use the difference between the relative area size value of a node and the "perfect" relative area size value to measure the closeness, then a very big area size will almost always be worse than a very small area size, which is not fair. So we calculate the logarithm value of the relative area size value and the logarithm value of the "perfect" value, and use the difference of these two values to measure the closeness, which is more reasonable. We label this adjusted feature value as $AREA\_DIST$.

4.2 Font Features

For font features, we consider font color and font size. The absolute value of the color feature of node k has a form of a set of pairs of key and value, i.e., $\{c_1 : m_{k1},\ c_2 : m_{k2},\ \cdots,\ c_i : m_{ki},\ \cdots,\}$, where c_i is the color ID and m_{ki} is the number of characters with color c_i in that node. As we have shown previously, this absolute value can be calculated by the union operation from bottom level of the DOM tree to upper level of the DOM tree. level by level. After we have the absolute value, we can calculate the relative value in the similar format of $\{c_1 : \varphi_{k1},\ c_2 : \varphi_{k2},\ \cdots,\ c_i : \varphi_{ki},\ \cdots,\}$, where c_i is the color ID and φ_{ki} is the percentage of characters with color c_i in node k, with $\varphi_{ki} = \frac{m_{ki}}{\sum_j m_{kj}}$.

Based on font color, we introduce a feature to capture how much the colors of the characters in a node matches the majority of the colors of the characters in the whole page. We call this feature as font color popularity, which only has the adjusted value. We note that the relative value of the color feature of the root node r, $\{c_1 : \varphi_{r1},\ c_2 : \varphi_{r2},\ \cdots,\ c_i : \varphi_{ri},\ \cdots,\}$, can also represent distribution of the colors of the characters in the whole page. We calculate the font color popularity value of node k as:

$$FONT\_COLOR\_POPULARITY = \sum_i \varphi_{ki}\varphi_{ri}$$

Similar to font color, for font size, we can calculate the relative value of the font size of node k in the format of $\{z_1 : \rho_{k1},\ z_2 : \rho_{k2},\ \cdots,\ z_i : \rho_{ki},\ \cdots,\}$, where z_i is the font size with size value z_i and ρ_{ki} is the percentage of characters with font size z_i in node k. Suppose the minimum font size in the webpage is z_{min} and maximum font size in the webpage is z_{max}. We calculate the font size adjusted value as:

$$FONT\_SIZE = \sum_i \frac{\rho_{ki}(z_i - z_{min})}{(z_{max} - z_{min})}$$

Similar to font color popularity, for font size, we also have font size popularity to capture how much the character sizes in node k matches the majority of the character sizes in the whole page (represented by root node r), which is calculated as:

$$FONT\_SIZE\_POPULARITY = \sum_i \rho_{ki}\rho_{ri}$$

4.3 Text, Tag and Link Features

For text, we consider the number of visible characters and the text area size. After we get the absolute value of the number of visible characters of a node, its relative value is normalized by the total number of visible characters in the page. We set the adjusted value of the number of visible characters to be the same as the relative value and label it as $VISIBLE\_CHAR$.

We can also calculate the absolute value of text area size and the absolute value of image area size for each node. We want to have a feature to capture whether a node has more text area or more image area. This feature only has adjusted value and is calculated as:

$$TEXT\_RATIO = \frac{A_{text}}{A_{text} + A_{image} + 1}$$

where A_{text} is the text area size of a node (absolute value) and A_{image} is the image area size of a node. 1 is added to the denominator to avoid zero value.

For tag, we want a feature to capture how likely an HTML tag could indicate whether a node associated that tag is a ground truth node. This feature value is trained from the training data by a simple statistical calculation. we label this feature as TAG_SCORE.

We also consider tag density. The intuition is that main content and noisy content would be likely to have different tag density in a webpage. Suppose $numTags$ is the number of tags of a node (absolute feature value), and $numChars$ is the number of visible characters of a node (absolute feature value). We calculate the tag density as follows:

$$TAG\_DENSITY = \frac{numTags}{numChars + 1}$$

For link, we consider the link density. The intuition is that main content and noisy content would be likely to have different link density in a webpage. Suppose $numLinks$ is the number of links of a node (absolute feature value). We calculate the link density as follows:

$$LINK\_DENSITY = \frac{numLinks}{numTags + 1}$$

Now totally we have 17 features with adjusted values to learn a model. We will talk about how to learn a model in the next section.

5. LEARNING

To train the model, we need some labeled data. For a webpage, the ground truth regions could be marked by a set of DOM tree

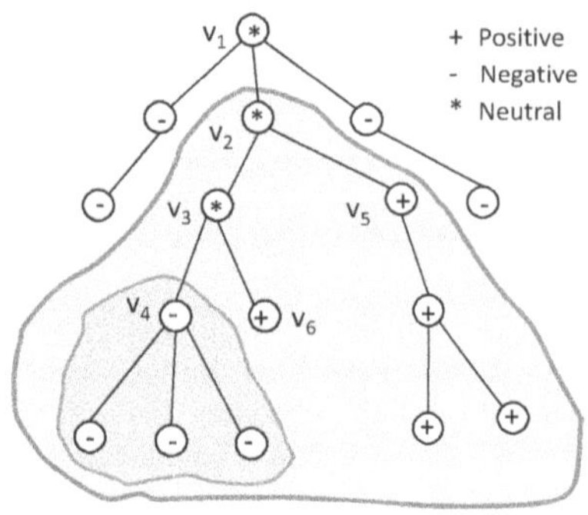

Figure 4: An example of DOM tree node labeling.

nodes. For some more sophisticated ground truth, inside the ground truth regions, there may be non-ground truth sub-regions, with each sub-region represented by a DOM tree node. As an example in Figure 4, node v_2 is marked by a user as a node to cover the region that he wants to select, and node v_4 is marked by the user as a node to represent the sub-region inside the selected region that he wants to cut off. The path from the root node to node v_2 is $[v_1 \rightarrow v_2]$, and the path from the root node to node v_4 is $[v_1 \rightarrow v_2 \rightarrow v_3 \rightarrow v_4]$. We define a positive node as the node which is part of ground truth for which all its descendant nodes are also part of the ground truth. We define a negative node as the node which is part of non ground truth and all its descendant nodes are also part of the non ground truth. The rest of the nodes in the DOM tree are the neutral nodes.

The following rules can be used to label the DOM tree nodes.

(a) A node which is deselected by the user must be labeled a negative node.

(b) All descendants of a negative node must also be labeled as negative nodes.

(c) A node is labeled as positive node if and only if one of its ancestors(including itself) is selected by the user and does not have a descendant which is deselected by the user.

(d) All descendant and ancestor nodes of a selected node (including itself) which are not labeled as negative or positive nodes by any of the rules in (a),(b) and (c) must be labeled as neutral nodes.

(e) The rest of the nodes which the rules in (a),(b), (c) and (d) do not apply to must be labeled as negative nodes.

Figure 4 is an example that shows the results after labeling the DOM tree nodes by applying the above rules. In this example, node v_2 is selected by the user and node v_4 is deselected by the user.

The "perfect" relative values of the position and area features for the ground truth regions, which we mentioned in Section 4.1, such as $BEST\_LEFT$, are set to be the average values of those relative feature values of all of the "top" ground truth nodes in the training data. A node is a "top" ground truth node if and only if it is a positive node and its parent is not a positive node. In Figure 4, nodes v_5 and v_6 are "top" ground truth nodes.

With a training dataset and the feature values, there are many classification models that could be trained to classify the nodes of a DOM tree. One of the strongest classification methods is SVM. However, even a very strong classification method would tend to misclassify many nodes, which we will demonstrate in Section 7.

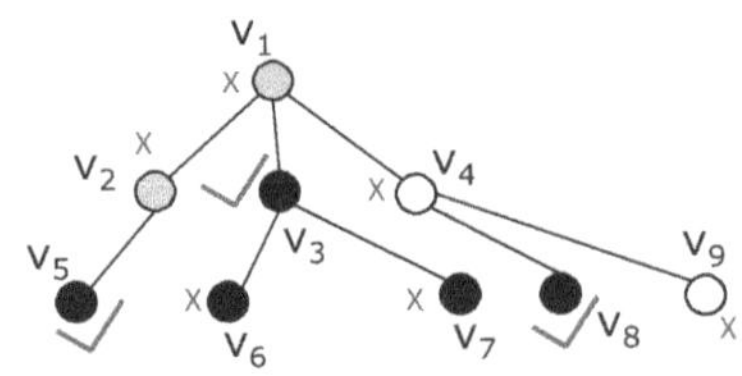

Figure 5: An example of candidate node compaction. The dark black nodes are the original candidate nodes with scores greater than the threshold.

So we want to choose a model with the ability of assigning good probability scores, rather than a binary classification. These scores will be used in the next steps for further selection and filtering before the final output. Hence the scores that can represent the probabilities are important. Although many methods can also generate scores along with classification, most of them are highly skewed, e.g., SVM. The Logistic Regression method can generate scores that are pretty much close to probability values. So we choose the Logistic Regression model in the learning step. We separate the training nodes into two classes for this model, with the positive nodes being one class and the rest nodes being the other class. After training the model, we can use the model to assign a score for each node. Assuming $x_1, \cdots, x_n$ are the feature values of a node v, after training a Logistic Regression model, its score can be set as:

$$p(v) = \frac{1}{1 + e^{-(\beta_0 + \beta_1 x_1 + \cdots + \beta_n x_n)}}$$

The parameters $\beta_0, \beta_1, \cdots \beta_n$ are the model parameters trained from training dataset. The score $p(v)$ represents how likely node v is a ground truth (positive) node.

Candidate Node Selection

After obtaining the scores of all of the nodes in the DOM tree from the learning model, we select the initial candidate nodes with scores greater than a threshold. As we have mentioned earlier, a node can represent a region area covered by this node and all of its descendants. We can compact the candidate node set by removing those nodes with any of its ancestors being included in the original candidate node set. Figure 5 shows one example. v_3, v_5, v_6, v_7, v_8 are the original candidate nodes with scores greater than the threshold. Since v_6 and v_7 are descendants of v_3 which is also part of the candidate nodes, we remove them and only keep v_3, v_5 and v_8 as the candidate nodes.

6. GROUPING AND REFINING

6.1 Grouping

If we have a perfect score output and perfect score threshold, we can return the candidate nodes from the learning step and we are done here. However, web pages are full of noise and we would not be able to get perfect score output. There are very likely some noisy regions that are mistakenly picked and some missing regions. To further remove the noisy nodes and pick up the missing nodes, we apply a grouping technology. The heuristic is that users tend to select spatially consecutive regions, rather than picking regions here and there. This is also consistent with general web designs which usually put the main content and the advertisements and navigation bars in different spacial locations, rather than mixing them together. The candidate nodes from the output of a learning model

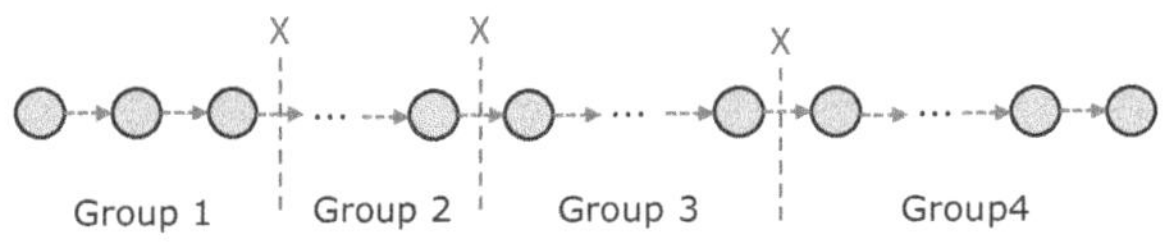

Figure 6: Separating the candidate nodes into different groups.

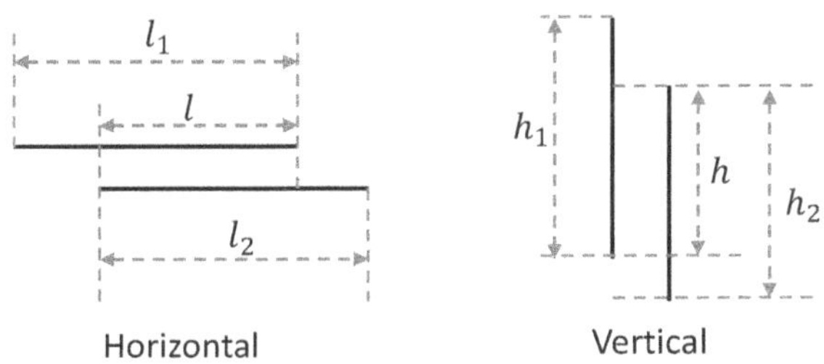

Figure 7: Horizontal and vertical position overlaps of two nodes.

may not all part of the main content, and some of them may belong to some other parts like advertisements. Our grouping idea is to use the physical spatial information and logical spatial information to try to separate the candidate nodes into different groups, with the target to put the nodes with close spatial connection into the same group, and then select a group with the highest possibility to be the main content.

First, we sort the candidate nodes by their positions in the depth first search of the DOM tree. We note that the depth first traverse of the DOM tree generally matches the same sequence of the nodes appearing in the webpage. In Figure 5, the candidate nodes after compaction are sorted in the ordered sequence of $[v_5 \rightarrow v_3 \rightarrow v_8]$. We can create links to connect consecutive nodes in the ordered sequence. To separate the nodes into different groups, we just need to break some of the links. In the end, those nodes which are still linked in the same sub-sequence are clustered into the same group. For this purpose, we just need to find the breaking points to break the ordered sequence to different sub-sequences. Figure 6 shows an example to use three breaking points to separate the candidate nodes into four groups.

To find the breaking points, we consider whether there is some overlap area for the neighborhood nodes in the ordered sequence, and how the horizontal and vertical projected positions of the neighborhood nodes overlap. Intuitively, if two neighborhood nodes have overlap area (which is very rare), they should be grouped together. Otherwise, we consider the projection overlap ratio. Figure 7 explains the projection overlap ratio. The horizontal lengths of the two nodes are l_1 and l_2, with projection overlap length l. The horizontal projection overlap ratio is set to be $min(\frac{l}{l_1}, \frac{l}{l_2})$. The vertical lengths of the two nodes are h_1 and h_2, with projection overlap length h. The vertical projection overlap ratio is set to be $min(\frac{h}{h_1}, \frac{h}{h_2})$. We define the projection overlap ratio (POR) to be the maximum value of the vertical projection overlap ratio and the horizontal projection overlap ratio. Intuitively, if POR of two nodes is high, they are aligned in positions and should be grouped together. Formally, for two nodes v_1 and v_2 in Figure 7,

$$POR_{1,2} = \max\left(min(\frac{l}{l_1}, \frac{l}{l_2}), min(\frac{h}{h_1}, \frac{h}{h_2})\right)$$

Suppose v_{i-1}, v_i, v_{i+1} and v_{i+2} are four consecutive nodes in the ordered sequence. With a predefined threshold T, we will break

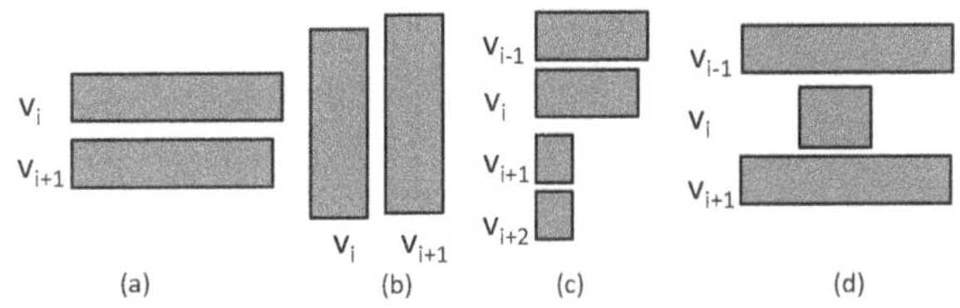

Figure 8: Projection overlap examples. v_i and v_{i+1} in both (a) and (b) have high projection overlap ratios; v_{i-1} and v_i, v_{i+1} and v_{i+2} have high projection overlap ratios in (c); v_{i-1} and v_{i+1} have high projection overlap ratios in (d).

the link between v_i and v_{i+1} if none of the four following conditions holds:

(1) v_i and v_{i+1} contain overlap area or $POR_{i,i+1} > T$.

(2) v_i and v_{i+1} have the same parent in the DOM tree.

(3) v_i and v_{i+2} contain overlap area or $POR_{i,i+2} > T$.

(4) v_{i-1} and v_{i+1} contain overlap area or $POR_{i-1,i+1} > T$.

Condition (2) allows two consecutive nodes with "logical alignment", i.e. they have the same parent, to be grouped together. Conditions (3) and (4) allow the node that is misaligned with its exact previous and its exact next neighbor nodes which are aligned to be grouped with its neighbors.

Figure 8 shows several examples for different projection overlap ratios. For (a) and (b) in Figure 8, since v_i and v_{i+1} have high projection overlap ratio, there will not be a breaking point between v_i and v_{i+1} in (a) and (b). For (c), since v_i and v_{i+1}, v_i and v_{i+2}, v_{i-1} and v_{i+1} do not have high projection overlap ratios, if v_i and v_{i+1} do not have the same parent in the DOM tree, then there will be a breaking point between v_i and v_{i+1} in (c). For (d), since v_{i-1} and v_{i+1} have high projection overlap ratio, there will not be a breaking point between v_i and v_{i+1} in (d)

One additional advantage for our grouping technology is that we only need to set one parameter, i.e. the projection overlap ratio, rather than considering a lot of parameters and features. Other useful features have been considered in the learning step. To make a good separation in the grouping step, the learning step and the candidate node compaction are necessary. After learning, a lot of noisy nodes have been discarded. And, after candidate node compaction, the redundant nodes have also been discarded. If the redundant nodes and too many noisy nodes are kept, it would be difficult to make a good separation in the grouping step.

6.2 Group Selection

After we separate the candidate nodes into different groups, we would need to further separate the groups into two category, one category for groups that belong to the main content, the other category for groups that belong to noisy content. As we notice that the main content is more likely to be spatially and logically a whole part, a good strategy is to select the best group. As the candidate nodes are generated from a learning approach, the majority area covered by the candidate nodes should belong to the main content. Otherwise it would indicate that the learning approach is not good and we need to improve the learning approach or switch to another learning approach. For the scores assigned by the learning approach, from the statistical point of view, the nodes that are more likely to be parts of contents should have higher scores. Hence we leverage both the area sizes and the scores to find the best group.

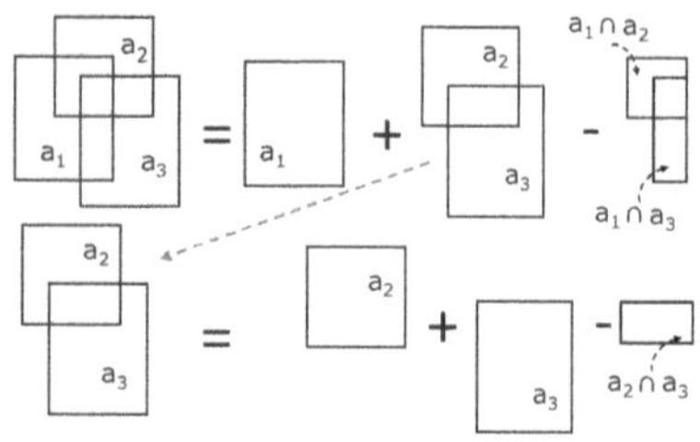

Figure 9: Example for computing area size.

For each group, we calculate the average score $\overline{P}$ of all its nodes from the Logistic Regression function output, and calculate the covered area size S. Then we pick up the best group by the largest value $\overline{P} \cdot S$.

To precisely calculate the covered area size S, first we collect all of the rectangles covered by the group. Suppose a_1, a_2, $\cdot$, a_n are the rectangles, $R_{a_1,a_2,\cdots,a_n}$ is the region covered by a_1, a_2, $\cdot$, a_n, and $f(R_{a_1,a_2,\cdot,a_n})$ is the area size of the region $R_{a_1,a_2,\cdot,a_n}$. Considering there may be some overlap between different rectangles, to calculate the covered area size by these rectangles, we can recursively apply the following equation:

$$\begin{aligned} & f(R_{a_1,a_2,\cdots,a_n}) \\ & = f(R_{a_1}) + f(R_{a_2,a_3,\cdots,a_n}) - f(R_{a_1} \cap R_{a_2,a_3,\cdots,a_n}) \\ & = f(R_{a_1}) + f(R_{a_2,a_3,\cdots,a_n}) - f(R_{a_1 \cap a_2, a_1 \cap a_3, \cdots, a_1 \cap a_n}) \end{aligned}$$

As $a_1 \cap a_2, a_1 \cap a_3, \cdots$, and $a_1 \cap a_n$ are also rectangles, both $f(R_{a_2,a_3,\cdots,a_n})$ and $f(R_{a_1 \cap a_2, a_1 \cap a_3, \cdots, a_1 \cap a_n})$ can be further recursively decomposed using the above equation. Figure 9 shows an example to calculate the area size for three overlapped rectangles. The area size of region R_{a_1,a_2,a_3} is equal to the area size of region R_{a_1} plus the area size of region R_{a_2,a_3} minus the area size of region $R_{a_1 \cap a_2, a_1 \cap a_3}$. And the area size of region R_{a_2,a_3} is equal to the area size of region R_{a_2} plus the area size of region R_{a_3} minus the area size of region $R_{a_2 \cap a_3}$. Similarly, the area size of region $R_{a_1 \cap a_2, a_1 \cap a_3}$ is equal to the area size of region $R_{a_1 \cap a_2}$ plus the area size of region $R_{a_1 \cap a_3}$ minus the area size of region $R_{a_1 \cap a_2 \cap a_1 \cap a_3}$.

6.3 Refining

After the "Best Group" is selected, most of the noisy nodes are expected to be removed. However, the selected group may not always be able to contain all of the nodes of the main content. One part of the reasons is that It is impractical to train a perfect learning model for this problem. The better the output from the learning model, the less likely it would be to miss the nodes of the main content in the selected group. Another part of the reasons comes from diversity of the web page designs. The grouping technique would not be able to perfectly work for all kinds of web pages. However, based on the criterion of group selection, the nodes in the"Best Group" still have the highest possibility to be the main content among all of the groups. As we have already mentioned, the main content tends to be logically and spatially a whole part. So, to pick the missing nodes of the main content, we can expand from the "Best Group".

Our strategy is to expand the group by replacing the nodes with their common lowest ancestor if the area size of the "Best Group" is too small. And, we recursively replace the common lowest ancestor with its parent if the area size covered by the node is still too small and it is not very close to the root node. If area size of the common lowest ancestor or a higher level of ancestor that is selected is too big, it might be likely to introduce new noisy content. We then recursively drill down to replace with the child node with the biggest area size among all of children so long as the area size is not too big. Then, from the the siblings of the child node and the child node itself, we pick up the best node by considering both score and area size. Algorithm 1 describes the details of the refining process. We select the parameters in the algorithm based on the statistical analysis of the training data. We will explain with more details in Section 7.

After the refining steps, we also do some minor checking to see if the title is obviously missing from the selection. If it is missing, we add the title node into the final selection. There are some literature work for title detection [6]. We only check *H1* to *H6* tags, where *H1* is most preferred and *H6* is least preferred. If a most preferred title candidate node exists in the location of the top of the main content selection, we add it to the final selection.

Algorithm 1 Refining the candidate nodes

Input: A list of candidate nodes, DOM tree
Parameters: area size ratios $\theta_1, \theta_2, \theta_3, \theta_4$; level depth d
Output: A list of DOM tree nodes

1. Get the common lowest ancestor v of the candidate nodes in the DOM tree. Calculate the overall covered area size S_1 of node v, i.e. $S_1 = s(v)$
2. If $S_1 < \theta_1 \cdot S_{page}$, where S_{page} is the area size of the whole web page, repeat: $v \leftarrow parent(v)$, $S_1 = s(v)$, until $S_1 \geq \theta_2 \cdot S_{page}$.
3. Get the refined nodes differently according to different conditions:
   (a) If the depth of node v in the DOM tree greater than d, or $S_1 \leq \theta_3 \cdot S_{page}$, return node v as the output and stop here.
   (b) Else if $S_1 \geq \theta_4 \cdot S_{page}$:
      (i) Repeat: $v \leftarrow \arg\max_{v'} \{s(v') | v' \in children(v)\}$, $S_2 = f(v)$, until $S_2 < \theta_4 \cdot S_{page}$
      (ii) $v_{out} \leftarrow \arg\max_{v'} \{p(v') \cdot s(v')\}$, where $v' \in siblings(v) \cup \{v\}$
      (iii) return v_{out} as the output
   (c) Else, return the original candidate nodes.

7. EXPERIMENTAL EVALUATION

7.1 Evaluation Data Set and Metrics

Evaluation Data Set

We use the log data from the real product HP SmartPrint for evaluation. The log data records the clip activities of those users who agree to provide their clip data to SmartPrint for the purpose of improving the user experience of the product. In the log data, the information includes clip paths, the urls of the web pages etc. We downloaded and parsed the webpages using the webkit rendering engine. We chose the clip data that have been manually selected by users. As the web pages may have been changed since the clip data is recorded, we excluded the data with any of clip paths not matching any of the paths in the web page. With this preliminary step of filtering, we filtered some noisy data. Then we asked people

Table 1: Statistics of the data set

Total number of pages	2000
Number of training pages	1335
Number of testing pages	665
Number of websites (domains)	805

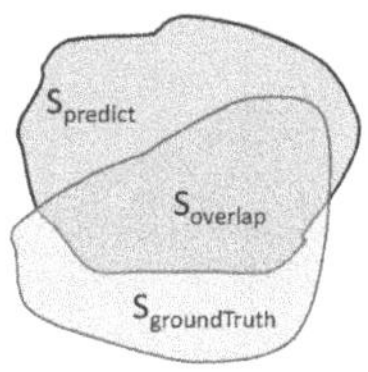

Figure 10: The region overlap.

to examine the ground truth and filter out the obviously non-ground truth data which might be caused by non-intentional user behaviors. At last, we have a clean dataset for training and evaluation. The total number of pages is 2000, which comes from 805 websites, i.e., there are 805 domain names in this dataset, making it to be sufficiently diversified rather than being biased on a small number of websites. We used two thirds of the dataset with 1335 pages as the training dataset and one third of the dataset with 665 pages as the testing dataset. The statistics of the dataset are shown in table 1.

Evaluation Metrics and Parameters

The recommended content regions are the output from the algorithm. The effectiveness of the recommendation can be measured by how close the recommended regions and the ground truth regions are matched. We use the precision and recall and F-measure as the evaluation metrics. To show how to calculate the metrics, we create an example as shown Figure 10. The light blue area refers to the region selected by a user and the light red area refers to the region recommended by a method. Suppose the overlap area size is $S_{overlap}$, and the area size selected by the user is $S_{groundTruth}$, and the area size recommended by the method is $S_{predict}$. Then we can calculate the precision and recall and F-measure as the follows:

$$P = \frac{S_{overlap}}{S_{predict}},\ R = \frac{S_{overlap}}{S_{groundTruth}},\ F_1 = \frac{2PR}{P+R}$$

The parameters we choose are as follows:

Logistic Regression Score Threshold = 0.55, Projection Overlap Ratio Threshold = 0.70. We will report on a sensitivity analysis for these two parameters in the next subsection.

$\theta_1 = 0.05$, $\theta_2 = 0.2$, $\theta_3 = 0.4$, $\theta_4 = 0.9$, $d = 3$ in Algorithm 1. Based on the training dataset, we found that around 1% of the pages have the ground truth area size which is less than 5% of the page area size; less than 2% of the pages have the ground truth area size greater than 90% of the page size; and the ground truth area size distribution has the highest distribution density in the range from 20% to 40% of the page area size. That's the reason why we pick these parameters for the refining step in Section 6.3. d value is based on the general web page designs, where we observe that the levels of the main content nodes are usullay not the top 3 levels.

7.2 Comparison with the Baseline Methods

We consider the following baseline methods:

- **LR_A:** This baseline method applies the logistic regression learning model to compute the scores for all of the nodes of the DOM tree for a webpage, and only selects the node with the highest score as the output node.
- **SVM_A:** This baseline method applies the linear SVM learning method to learn a linear model and utilizes the model to compute the scores for all of the nodes of the DOM tree for a webpage, and only selects the node with the highest score as the output node.
- **LR:** This baseline method applies the logistic regression learning model to compute the scores for all of the nodes of the DOM tree for a webpage, and only selects the nodes with the scores higher than the threshold and removes the redundant nodes. As mentioned previously, a redundant node is a node in which at least one ancestor node is included in the candidate node set.
- **SVM:** This baseline method applies the SVM learning method to classify the nodes of the DOM tree for a webpage and selects the nodes that are classified as positive with redundant nodes removed. We select the linear kernel for SVM since we have totally 964380 training nodes which is huge and it is computationally expensive to train an SVM model on a large training items with a nonlinear learning kernel.
- **MSS:** This baseline method applies the Maximum Subsequence Segmentation algorithm proposed in [13]. We use the implementation of this method in [4] for comparison.

We label our proposed method, which utilizes the combination of learning and grouping, as **CLG**. The use the same features as described in Section 4 for all methods except *MSS*. For method *MSS*, we use the set of features described in literature [4]. We use the identical score threshold parameter for *LR* and *CLG*. We will further analyze the parameters in the next subsection.

Figure 11 reports on the precision and recall values for all of the methods, i.e., *LR_A*, *SVM_A*, *MSS*, *LR*, *SVM* and our proposed method *CLG*. As expected, since *LR_A* and *SVM_A* pick only one node that has the highest score from the learning models, they have higher precision values than all other methods. However, their recall values and F_1 values are very low, this is because the area of the node with the highest score is very likely to be just a small fraction of the whole ground truth area. So, *LR_A* and *SVM_A* are not the good solutions. Method *MSS* show pretty much lower recall value and F_1 value than *LR*, *SVM*, and *CLG*, although its precision value is kind of close to the precision values of other methods. As shown in literature [13, 4], this method works very well for article webpages. However, our experiment shows that it is not that good for general webpages. This tells us that a method that works well for article web pages might not work well for general web pages. Method *CLG* has higher F_1 value than all of the baseline methods. Method *CLG* also has higher precision, recall and F_1 values than methods *LR* and *SVM* both of which utilize learning step only. The learning model for *CLG* and *LR* are identical. This demonstrates that the grouping step is valuable and helps to significantly further improve the results from the learning step.

Figure 12 is an example that shows the selected regions by different methods for an identical recipe web page. For this web page, users would be interested in the main content in the middle region. Methods *LR* and *SVM* are both able to pick the majority of the main content, but at the same time, they also pick pretty many noisy content regions which are scattered around the page. If a tool makes human effort capable to further clean the selection, that would be pretty much work to remove the scattered noisy content regions.

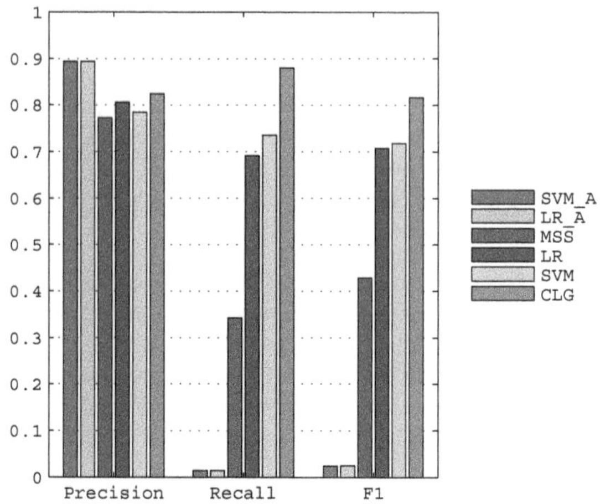

Figure 11: Precision, recall and F_1 measure for different methods.

MSS method is able to pick up some regions that are almost logically continuous, from part of the middle block, to the right and then to to the bottom blocks. Continuous regions are good for users to do further manual selection. However, *MSS* method misses more actual content and mistakenly picks more noisy content. Method *CLG* selects exactly the main content for this web page, which is continuous and complete. This example further demonstrates that our solution has higher quality of content selection than the baseline methods.

As *CLG* tends to select the regions which are spatially a single part, even if the output is not exactly what a user wants, it will be easy for the user to make further manual selection, which is convenient for clipping webpages for e-reading or other purposes.

7.3 Parameter Sensitivity Analysis

We want to analyze how the parameters will impact the results.

Sensitivity Analysis for Score Threshold

Figure 13 shows the curve of the precision and recall values with respect to different score thresholds to pick up the original candidate nodes for the method *CLG*. As expected, when the threshold value increases, the precision value increases and the recall value decreases. However, the curve does not show steep shape. Especially when the score threshold is greater than 0.4, the precision and recall values are pretty stable, which means that the precision and recall values are not sensitive to the score threshold value. We select the threshold value to be 0.55 for a good balance. Figure 14 compares the F_1 values for the methods *LR* and *CLG* with respect to different score thresholds for the learning step. The figure shows that *CLG* has higher F_1 values for all score thresholds, and the F_1 values of *CLG* are much more stable than the F_1 values of *LR*. The F_1 value of *LR* shows significant decrease when the score threshold value is greater than 0.6. This demonstrates that the grouping step of *CLG* helps to make the selection output more accurate and less sensitive to the score threshold parameter.

Sensitivity Analysis for Projection Overlap Ratio Threshold

For the projection overlap ratio threshold described in Section 6.1, we would expect that when the threshold value increases, noisy nodes and actual content nodes would be less likely to be grouped into the same group, which would help to increase the precision. However, with the increase of the projection overlap ratio threshold, actual content nodes would be more likely to be grouped into

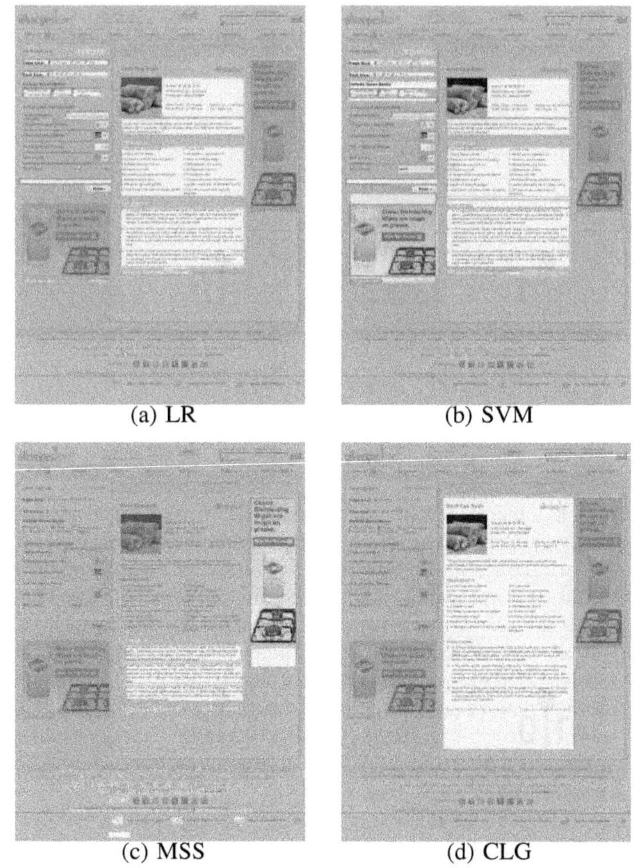

Figure 12: An example of selection output by *LR*, *SVM*, *MSS*, and *CLG*. The regions with light red background are the selected regions.

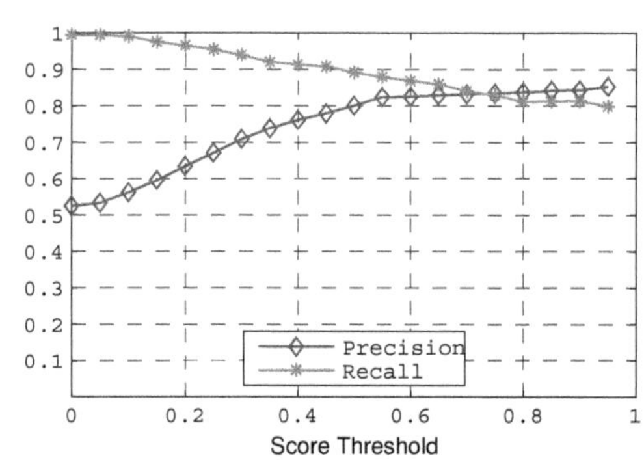

Figure 13: Precision and recall values for *CLG* with respect to different logistic regression thresholds.

different groups. We should pick a good threshold value to make a good balance. Figure 15 reports on the precision and recall values for *CLG* with respect to different projection overlap ratio thresholds. For a good balance, we have picked a threshold value of 0.7 for other experiments. As expected, When the threshold increases, the precision value increases and the recall value decreases. We also notice that both values do not change significantly. This demonstrates that the output of *CLG* is not sensitive to the projection overlap ratio threshold.

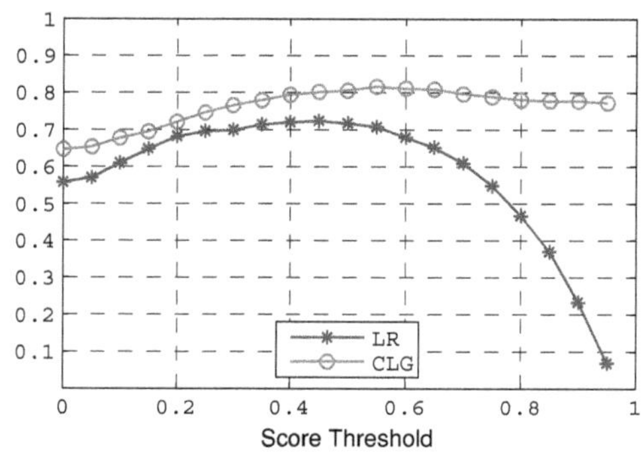

Figure 14: F_1 values for *LR* and *CLG* with respect to different logistic regression thresholds.

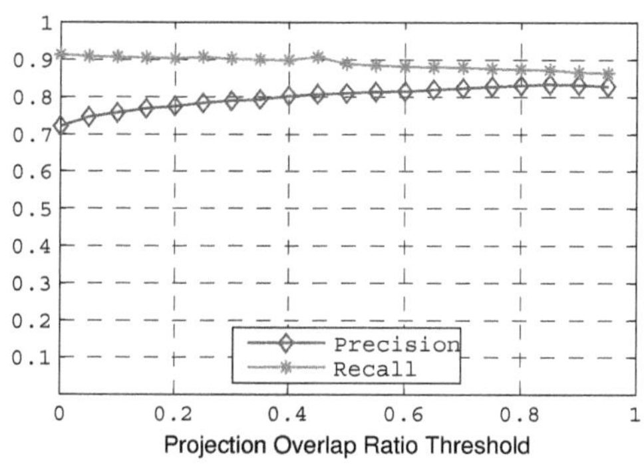

Figure 15: Precision and recall for *CLG* with respect to different projection overlap ratio thresholds.

8. CONCLUSIONS

In this paper, we propose an effective approach by combination of a learning model and a grouping technology to identify actual content from web pages. We generate multiple features by utilizing DOM tree node properties to train a machine learning model and select candidate nodes based on the learning model. With the observation that the actual content is usually located in a spatially continuous block, we develop a grouping technology to further process the candidate nodes by filtering out noisy data and picking missing data. We show the effectiveness of our solution in a real dataset.

9. REFERENCES

[1] Z. Bar-Yossef and S. Rajagopalan. Template detection via data mining and its applications. In *Proceedings of the 11th international conference on World Wide Web*, WWW '02, pages 580–591, 2002.

[2] D. Cai, S. Yu, J.-R. Wen, and W.-Y. Ma. Extracting content structure for web pages based on visual representation. In *Proceedings of the 5th Asia-Pacific web conference on Web technologies and applications*, APWeb'03, pages 406–417, Berlin, Heidelberg, 2003.

[3] L. Chen, S. Ye, and X. Li. Template detection for large scale search engines. In *Proceedings of the 2006 ACM symposium on Applied computing*, SAC '06, pages 1094–1098, 2006.

[4] J. Fan, P. Luo, S. H. Lim, S. Liu, P. Joshi, and J. Liu. Article clipper: a system for web article extraction. In *Proceedings of the 17th ACM SIGKDD international conference on Knowledge discovery and data mining*, KDD '11, pages 743–746, 2011.

[5] D. Fernandes, E. S. de Moura, B. Ribeiro-Neto, A. S. da Silva, and M. A. Gonçalves. Computing block importance for searching on web sites. In *Proceedings of the sixteenth ACM conference on Conference on information and knowledge management*, CIKM '07, pages 165–174, 2007.

[6] Y. Hu, G. Xin, R. Song, G. Hu, S. Shi, Y. Cao, and H. Li. Title extraction from bodies of html documents and its application to web page retrieval. In *Proceedings of the 28th annual international ACM SIGIR conference on Research and development in information retrieval*, SIGIR '05, pages 250–257, 2005.

[7] H.-Y. Kao, S.-H. Lin, J.-M. Ho, and M.-S. Chen. Mining web informative structures and contents based on entropy analysis. *IEEE Trans. on Knowl. and Data Eng.*, 16(1):41–55, Jan. 2004.

[8] C. Kohlschütter, P. Fankhauser, and W. Nejdl. Boilerplate detection using shallow text features. In *Proceedings of the third ACM international conference on Web search and data mining*, WSDM '10, pages 441–450, 2010.

[9] C. Kohlschütter and W. Nejdl. A densitometric approach to web page segmentation. In *Proceedings of the 17th ACM conference on Information and knowledge management*, CIKM '08, pages 1173–1182, 2008.

[10] S. H. Lim, L. Zheng, J. Jin, H. Hou, J. Fan, and J. Liu. Automatic selection of print-worthy content for enhanced web page printing experience. In *Proceedings of the 10th ACM symposium on Document engineering*, DocEng '10, pages 165–168, 2010.

[11] S.-H. Lin and J.-M. Ho. Discovering informative content blocks from web documents. In *Proceedings of the eighth ACM SIGKDD international conference on Knowledge discovery and data mining*, KDD '02, pages 588–593, 2002.

[12] P. Luo, J. Fan, S. Liu, F. Lin, Y. Xiong, and J. Liu. Web article extraction for web printing: a dom+visual based approach. In *Proceedings of the 9th ACM symposium on Document engineering*, DocEng '09, pages 66–69, 2009.

[13] J. Pasternack and D. Roth. Extracting article text from the web with maximum subsequence segmentation. In *Proceedings of the 18th international conference on World wide web*, WWW '09, pages 971–980, 2009.

[14] D. C. Reis, P. B. Golgher, A. S. Silva, and A. F. Laender. Automatic web news extraction using tree edit distance. In *Proceedings of the 13th international conference on World Wide Web*, WWW '04, pages 502–511, 2004.

[15] R. Song, H. Liu, J.-R. Wen, and W.-Y. Ma. Learning block importance models for web pages. In *Proceedings of the 13th international conference on World Wide Web*, WWW '04, pages 203–211, 2004.

[16] A. Spengler and P. Gallinari. Document structure meets page layout: loopy random fields for web news content extraction. In *Proceedings of the 10th ACM symposium on Document engineering*, DocEng '10, pages 151–160, 2010.

[17] F. Sun, D. Song, and L. Liao. Dom based content extraction via text density. In *Proceedings of the 34th international ACM SIGIR conference on Research and development in Information Retrieval*, SIGIR '11, pages 245–254, 2011.

[18] J. Wang, C. Chen, C. Wang, J. Pei, J. Bu, Z. Guan, and W. V. Zhang. Can we learn a template-independent wrapper for news article extraction from a single training site? In *Proceedings of the 15th ACM SIGKDD international*

conference on Knowledge discovery and data mining, KDD '09, pages 1345–1354, 2009.

[19] T. Weninger, W. H. Hsu, and J. Han. Cetr: content extraction via tag ratios. In *Proceedings of the 19th international conference on World wide web*, WWW '10, pages 971–980, 2010.

[20] L. Yi, B. Liu, and X. Li. Eliminating noisy information in web pages for data mining. In *Proceedings of the ninth ACM SIGKDD international conference on Knowledge discovery and data mining*, KDD '03, pages 296–305, 2003.

[21] L. Zhang, L. Tang, P. Luo, E. Chen, L. Jiao, M. Wang, and G. Liu. Harnessing the wisdom of the crowds for accurate web page clipping. In *Proceedings of the 18th ACM SIGKDD international conference on Knowledge discovery and data mining*, KDD '12, pages 570–578, 2012.

Executing Provenance-Enabled Queries over Web Data

Marcin Wylot
eXascale Infolab
University of Fribourg
Switzerland
marcin.wylot@unifr.ch

Philippe Cudré-Mauroux
eXascale Infolab
University of Fribourg
Switzerland
pcm@unifr.ch

Paul Groth
Elsevier Labs
p.groth@elsevier.com

ABSTRACT

The proliferation of heterogeneous Linked Data on the Web poses new challenges to database systems. In particular, because of this heterogeneity, the capacity to store, track, and query provenance data is becoming a pivotal feature of modern triple stores. In this paper, we tackle the problem of efficiently executing provenance-enabled queries over RDF data. We propose, implement and empirically evaluate five different query execution strategies for RDF queries that incorporate knowledge of provenance. The evaluation is conducted on Web Data obtained from two different Web crawls (The Billion Triple Challenge, and the Web Data Commons). Our evaluation shows that using an adaptive query materialization execution strategy performs best in our context. Interestingly, we find that because provenance is prevalent within Web Data and is highly selective, it can be used to improve query processing performance. This is a counterintuitive result as provenance is often associated with additional overhead.

Categories and Subject Descriptors

H.2.8 [**Information Systems**]: Data Management—*Database Applications*

General Terms

Algorithms, Design, Experimentation

Keywords

Provenance Queries; RDF; Linked Data; RDF Data Management; Web Data; Provenance

1. INTRODUCTION

A central use-case for Resource Description Framework (RDF) data management systems is data integration [20]. Data is acquired from multiple sources either as RDF or converted to RDF; schemas are mapped; record linkage or entity resolution is performed; and, finally, integrated data is exposed. There are a variety of systems such as Karma [23] and the Linked Data Integration Framework [31] that implement this integration process. To establish trust and transparency, the support of provenance within these systems is a key feature [31]. For example, users may want to tailor their queries based on the source of information; e.g., find me all the information about Paris, but exclude all data sourced from commercial websites.

To support these use-cases, the most common mechanism used within RDF data management is named graphs [5]. This mechanism was recently standardized in RDF 1.1. [29]. Named graphs associate a set of triples with a URI. Using this URI, metadata including provenance can be associated with the graph. While named graphs are often used for provenance, they are also used for other purposes, for example, to track access control information. Thus, while RDF databases (i.e., triple stores) support named graphs, there has only been a relatively small amount of works specifically focused on provenance within the triple store itself and much of it has been focused on theoretical aspects of the problem [9, 13].

Given the prevalence of provenance in Web Data ($\tilde{3}6\%$ of data sets) [30] and the use of named graphs[1], the aim of this paper is to investigate how RDF databases can *effectively* support queries that include provenance conditions (i.e., provenance-enabled queries). Specifically, we pose the following research question: **What is the most effective query execution strategy for provenance-enabled queries?**

To answer this question, we define 5 provenance-aware query execution strategies. These are then tested on a state-of-the-art triple store (TripleProv [33]) that implements specific provenance-aware storage models and collocation strategies. Experiments are performed on Web data taken from the Billion Triple Challenge and the Web Data Commons datasets. We also perform a dataset analysis and develop a cost model that provide insight into why particular strategies are effective for Web Data. Unexpectedly, we find that, because of the selectivity properties of provenance within Web Data, the speed of query execution can be increased significantly by incorporating knowledge of provenance.

Concretely, the contributions of this paper are four-fold:

1. A characterization of provenance-enabled queries with respect to Named Graphs (Section 3);
2. Five provenance-oriented query execution strategies (Section 4);

[1]See analysis at `http://gromgull.net/blog/2012/07/some-basic-btc2012-stats/`

WWW 2015, May 18–22, 2015, Florence, Italy.
ACM 978-1-4503-3469-3/15/05.
http://dx.doi.org/10.1145/2736277.2741143 .

3. An implementation of these strategies within a state-of-the art triple store (Section 5);
4. An experimental evaluation of our query execution strategies and an extensive analysis of the datasets used for the experimental evaluation in the context of provenance data (Section 6).

2. RELATED WORK

There are two areas of related work that we build upon: provenance query systems and dynamic query execution.

Provenance Query Systems: Miles defined the concept of *provenance query* [24] in order to only select a relevant subset of all possible results when looking up the provenance of an entity.

A number of authors have presented systems for specifically handling such provenance queries. Biton *et al.* showed how user views can be used to reduce the amount of information returned by provenance queries in a workflow system [4]. The RDFProv [6] system focused on managing and enabling querying over provenance that results from scientific workflows. Similarly, the ProQL approach [22] defined a query language and proposed relational indexing techniques for speeding up provenance queries involving path traversals. Glavic and Alonso [14] presented the Perm provenance system, which was able of computing, storing and querying relational provenance data. Provenance was computed by using standard relational query rewriting techniques.Recently, Glavic and his team have built on this work to show the effectiveness of query rewriting for tracking provenance in database that support audit logs and time travel [1]. The approaches proposed in [4, 22] assume a strict relational schema whereas RDF data is by definition schema free. Our approach is different in the way that we tailor the proposed techniques for Semantic Web data, thus we do not take advantage of a predefined schema. Our approach also looks at the execution of provenance queries in conjunction with standard queries within an RDF database.

In that respect, our work is related to the work on annotated RDF [32, 35], which developed SPARQL query extensions for querying over annotation metadata (e.g., provenance). Halpin and Cheney have shown how to use SPARQL Update to track provenance within a triple store without modifications [18]. The theoretical foundations of using named graphs for provenance within the Semantic Web were established by Flouris et al. [12]. Here, our focus is different since we propose and empirically evaluate different execution strategies for running queries that take advantage of provenance metadata.

Our focus on provenance is motivated by the increasing availability of provenance using common models for provenance such as W3C PROV [16].

Dynamic Query Execution: Dynamic query execution has been studied in different contexts by database researchers. Graefe and Ward [15] focused on determining when re-optimizing a given query that is issued repeatedly is necessary. Subsequently, Colde and Graefe [8] proposed a new query optimization model which constructs dynamic plans at compile-time and delays some of the query optimization until run-time. Kabra and DeWitt [21] proposed an approach collecting statistics during the execution of complex queries in order to dynamically correct suboptimal query execution plans. Ng *et al* [28] studied how to re-optimize suboptimal query plans on-the-fly for very long-running queries in database systems. Avnur and Hellerstein proposed Eddies [2], a query processing mechanism that continuously reorders operators in a query plan as it runs, and that merges the optimization and execution phases of query processing in order to allow each tuple to have a flexible ordering of the query operators. Our work is different in the sense that we dynamically examine or drop data structures during query execution depending on provenance information.

Our approach builds on TripleProv [33], our previous work on storing and tracking provenance information within triple stores. TripleProv, however, does not support provenance-enabled queries, which is the focus of this work.

3. PROVENANCE-ENABLED QUERIES

"Provenance is information about entities, activities, and people involved in producing a piece of data or thing, which can be used to form assessments about its quality, reliability or trustworthiness" [16]. The W3C PROV Family of Documents[2] defines a model, corresponding serializations and other supporting definitions to enable the interoperable interchange of provenance information in heterogeneous environments such as the Web. In the paper, we adopt the view proposed in those specifications. We also adopt the terminology of Cyganiak's original NQuads specification[3], where the *context value* refers to the provenance or source of the triple[4]. We note that context values often are used to refer to the named graph to which a triple belongs. Based on this background, we introduce the following terminology used within this paper:

Definition 1. A **Workload Query** is a query producing results a user is interested in. These results are referred to as *workload query results.*

Definition 2. A **Provenance Query** is a query that selects a set of data from which the workload query results should originate. Specifically, a *Provenance Query* returns a set of *context values* whose triples will be considered during the execution of a *Workload Query.*

Definition 3. A **Provenance-Enabled Query** is a pair consisting of a *Workload Query* and a *Provenance Query*, producing results a user is interested in (as specified by the *Workload Query*) and originating only from data pre-selected by the *Provenance Query.*

As mentioned above, provenance data can be taken into account during query execution through the use of named graphs. Those solutions are however not optimized for provenance, and require rewriting all workload queries with respect to a provenance query. Our approach aims to keep workload queries unchanged and introduce provenance-driven optimization on the database system level.

We assume a strict separation of the workload query on one hand and the provenance query on the other (as illustrated in Figure 1)[5]. Provenance and workload results are

[2]`http://www.w3.org/TR/prov-overview/`

[3]`http://sw.deri.org/2008/07/n-quads/`

[4]The W3C standard defines N-quads statements as a sequence of RDF terms representing the subject, predicate, object and graph label of an RDF Triple and the graph it is part of in a dataset.

[5]We note that including the provenance predicates directly in the query itself is also possible, and that the execution

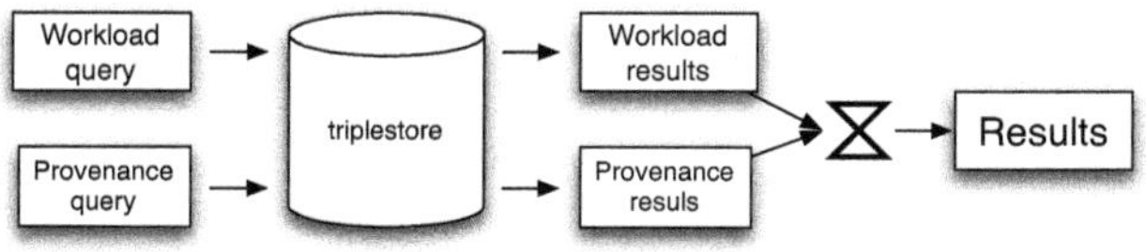

Figure 1: Executing provenance-enabled queries; both a workload and a provenance query are given as input to a triplestore, which produces results for both queries and then combine them to obtain the final results.

joined to produce a final result. A consequence of our design is that workload queries can remain unchanged, while the whole process of applying provenance filtering takes place during query execution. Both provenance and workload queries are to be delivered in the same way, preferably using the SPARQL language or a high-level API that offers similar functionality. The body of the provenance query specifies the set of context values that identify which triples will be used when executing the workload queries.

To further illustrate our approach, we present a few provenance-enabled queries that are simplified versions of use cases found in the literature. In the examples below, *context values* are denoted as *?ctx*.

Provenance-enabled queries can be used in various ways. A common case is to ensure that the data used to produce the answer comes from a set of trusted sources [25]. Given a workload query that retrieves titles of articles about "Obama":

```
SELECT  ?t WHERE  {
  ?a <type> <article> .
  ?a <tag> <Obama> .
  ?a <title> ?t . }
```

One may want to ensure that the articles retrieved come from sources attributed to the government:

```
SELECT ?ctx WHERE {
  ?ctx   prov:wasAttributedTo <government> . }
```

As per the W3C definition, provenance is not only about the source of data but is also about the manner in which the data was produced. Thus, one may want to ensure that the articles in question were edited by somebody who is a "SeniorEditor" and that articles where checked by a "Manager". Thus, we could apply the following provenance query while keeping the same "Obama" workload query:

```
SELECT ?ctx WHERE {
  ?ctx prov:wasGeneratedBy <articleProd>.
  <articleProd> prov:wasAssociatedWith ?ed .
  ?ed rdf:type <SeniorEdior>  .
  <articleProd> prov:wasAssociatedWith ?m .
  ?m rdf:type <Manager> . }
```

A similar example, albeit for a curated protein database, is described in detail in [7]. Another way to apply provenance-enabled queries is for scenarios in which data is integrated from multiple sources. For example, we may want to aggregate the chemical properties of a drug (e.g., its potency) provided by one database with information on whether it has regulatory approval provided by another:

```
SELECT ?potency ?approval WHERE {
  ?drug <name> ''Sorafenib'' .
  ?drug ?link ?chem.
  ?chem <potency> ?potency .
  ?drug <approvalStatus> ?approval }
```

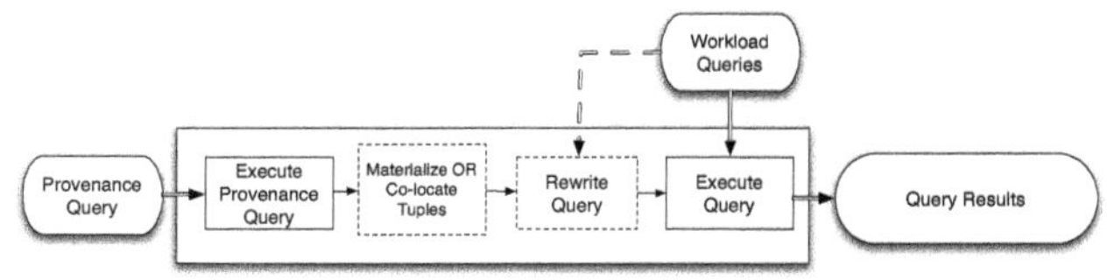

Figure 2: Generic provenance-enabled query execution pipeline, where both the workload queries and the provenance query get executed in order to produce the final results

Here, we may like to select not only the particular sources that the workload query should be answered over but also the software or approach used in establishing the links between those sources. For instance, we may want to use links generated manually or for a broader scope than those generated through the use of any type of string similarity. Such a use-case is described in detail in [3]. Below is an example of how such a provenance query could be written:

```
SELECT ?ctx WHERE {
{ ?ctx prov:wasGeneratedBy ?linkingActivity.
  ?linkingActivity rdf:type <StringSimilarity> }
UNION { ?ctx prov:wasDerivedFrom <ChemDB>}
UNION { ?ctx prov:wasDerivedFrom <DrugDB>} }
```

In the following, we discuss approaches to processing these types of queries.

4. PROVENANCE & QUERY EXECUTION

There are several ways to execute provenance-enabled queries in a triple store. The simplest way is to execute the RDF query and the provenance query independently, and to join both result sets based on context values. One also has the option of pre-materializing some of the data based on the provenance specification. Another way is through dynamic query rewriting; in that case, the workload query is rewritten using the provenance query (or some of its results) and only then to execute the query. The query execution strategies presented in this section can be implemented in practically any triple store—provided that it offers some support for storing and handling context values. We discuss our own implementation based on TripleProv in Section 5.

4.1 Query Execution Pipeline

Figure 2 gives a high-level perspective on the query execution process. The provenance and workload queries are provided as input; the query execution process can vary depending on the exact strategy chosen, but typically starts by executing the provenance query and optionally pre-materializing or co-locating data; the workload queries are then optionally rewritten—by taking into account some results of the provenance query—and finally get executed. The process returns as output the workload query results, restricted to those which are following the specification expressed in the provenance query. We give more detail on this execution process below.

4.2 Generic Query Execution Algorithm

Algorithm 1 gives a simplified, generic version of the provenance-enabled query execution algorithm. We start by executing the provenance query, which is processed like an ordinary query (*ExecuteQuery*) but *always* returns

strategies and models we develop in the rest of this paper would work similarly in that case.

Algorithm 1 Generic executing algorithm for provenance-enabled queries

```
ctxSet = ExecuteQuery(ProvenanceQuery)
materializedTuples = MaterializeTuples (ctxSet) OPTIONAL
collocatedTuples = fromProvIdx(ctxSet) OPTIONAL
for all workload queries do
    ExecuteQuery(queryN, ctxSet)
end for
```

sets of context values as an output. Subsequently, the system optionally materializes or adaptively co-locates selected tuples[6] containing data related to the provenance query. We then execute workload queries taking into account the context values returned from the previous step. The execution starts as a standard query execution, but optionally includes a dynamic query rewriting step to dynamically prune early in the query plan those tuples that cannot produce valid results given their provenance.

4.3 Query Execution Strategies

From the generic algorithm presented above, we now introduce five different strategies for executing provenance-enabled queries and describe how they could be implemented in different triplestores.

Post-Filtering: this is the baseline strategy, which executes both the workload and the provenance query independently. The provenance and workload queries can be executed in any order (or concurrently) in this case. When both the provenance query and the workload query have been executed, the results from the provenance query (i.e., a set of context values) are used to filter *a posteriori* the results of the workload query based on their provenance (see Algorithm 2). In addition to retrieving the results, the database system needs in this case to track the lineage of all results produced by the workload query. More specifically, the system needs to keep track of the context values of all triples that were involved in producing a valid result. We discussed how to come up and how to compactly represent such lineage using *provenance polynomials* in our previous work [33]. Tracking lineage during query execution is however non-trivial for the systems which, unlike TripleProv, are not provenance-aware. For quadstores, for instance, it involves extensively rewriting the queries, leading to more complex query processing and to an explosion of the number of results retrieved, as we discussed in detail in Section 8.6 of [33].

Query Rewriting: the second strategy we introduce executes the provenance query upfront; then, it uses the set of context values returned by the provenance query to filter out all tuples that do not conform to the provenance results. This can be carried out logically by rewriting the query plans of the workload queries to add provenance constraints (see Algorithm 3, *is present in ctxSet*). This solution is efficient from the provenance query execution side, though it can be suboptimal from the workload query execution side (see Section 6). It can be implemented in two ways by the triplestores, either by modifying the query execution process, or by rewriting the workload queries in order to include constraints on the named graphs. We note that the query rewriting is very different from the case discussed above (for post-filtering, the queries may have to be rewritten to keep track of the lineage of the results; in this case, we know what context values we should filter on during query execution, which makes the rewriting much simpler.)

Full Materialization: this is a two-step strategy where the provenance query is first executed on the entire database (or any relevant subset of it), and then materializes all tuples whose context values satisfy the provenance query. The workload queries are then simply executed on the resulting materialized view, which only contains tuples that are compatible with the provenance specification. This strategy will outperform all other strategies when executing the workload queries, since they are executed *as is* on the relevant subset of the data. However, materializing all potential tuples based on the provenance query can be prohibitively expensive, both in terms of storage space and latency. Implementing this strategy requires either to manually materialize the relevant tuples and modify the workload queries accordingly, or to use a triplestore supporting materialized views.

Pre-Filtering: this strategy takes advantages of a dedicated *provenance index* collocating, for each context values, the ids (or hashes) of all tuples belonging to this context. This index should typically be created upfront when the data is loaded. After the provenance query is executed, the provenance index can be looked up to retrieve the lists of tuple ids that are compatible with the provenance specification. Those lists can then be used to filter out early the intermediate and final results of the workload queries (see Algorithm 4). This strategy requires to create a new index structure in the system (see Section 5 for more detail on this), and to modify both the loading and the query execution processes.

Adaptive Partial Materialization: this strategy introduces a tradeoff between the performance of the provenance query and that of the workload queries. The provenance query is executed first. While executing the provenance query, the system also builds a temporary structure (e.g., a hash-table) maintaining the ids of *all* tuples belonging to the context values returned by the provenance query. When executing the workload query, the system can then dynamically (and efficiently) look-up all tuples appearing as intermediate or final results, and can filter them out early in case they do not appear in the temporary structure. Further processing is similar to the *Query Rewriting* strategy, that is, we include individual checks of context values inside the tuples. However those checks, joins, and further query processing operations can then be executed faster on a reduced number of elements. This strategy can achieve performance close to the *Full Materialization* strategy while avoiding to replicate the data, at the expense of creating and maintaining temporary data structures. The implementation

[6]We use *tuples* in a generic way here to remain system-agnostic; tuples can take the form of atomic pieces of data, triples, quads, small sub-graphs, n-ary lists/sets or RDF molecules [33, 34] depending on the database system used.

Algorithm 2 Algorithm for the *Post-Filtering* strategy.

```
Require: WorkloadQuery
Require: ProvenanceQuery
(ctxSet) = ExecuteQuery(ProvenanceQuery)
(results, polynomial) = ExecuteQuery(WorkloadQuery) {independent execution of ProvenanceQuery and WorkloadQuery}
for all results do
   if ( polynomial[result].ContextValues ⊈ ctxSet ) then
      remove result
   else
      keep result
   end if
end for
```

Algorithm 3 Algorithm for the *Rewriting* strategy.

```
Require: query: workload query
Require: ctxSet: context values; results of provenance query
tuples =q.getPhysicalPlan (FROM materializedTuples for materializes scenario)
for all tuples do
   for all entities do
      if ( entity.ContextValues ⊈ ctxSet) then
         nextEntity
      else
         inspect entity
      end if
   end for
end for
```

Algorithm 4 Algorithm for the *Pre-Filtering* strategy.

```
Require: query: workload query
Require: ctxSet: context values; results of provenance query
tuples =q.getPhysicalPlan
for all tuples do
   for all ctxSet do
      ctxTuples = getTuplesFromProvIdx(ctx)
      if ( tuple ⊈ ctxTuples) then
         nextTuple
      end if
   end for
   for all entities do
      if ( entity.ContextValues ⊈ ctxSet) then
         nextEntity
      else
         inspect entity
      end if
   end for
end for
```

of this strategy requires the introduction of an additional data structure at the core of the system, and the adjustment of the query execution process in order to use it.

5. STORAGE MODEL & INDEXING

We implemented all the provenance-enabled query execution strategies introduced in Section 4 in TripleProv, our own triplestore supporting different storage models to handle provenance data. Both TripleProv[7] and the extensions implemented for this paper[8] are available online. In the following, we briefly present the implementation of the provenance-oriented data structures and indices we used to evaluate the query execution strategies described above. We note that it would be possible to implement our strategies in other systems, using the same techniques. The effort to do so, however, is beyond the scope of the paper.

[7]`http://exascale.info/tripleprov`

[8]`http://exascale.info/provqueries`

Algorithm 5 Algorithm for the *Partial Materialization* strategy.

```
Require: query: workload query
Require: ctxSet: context values; results of provenance query
Require: collocatedTuples: collection of hash values of tuples related to the result of the provenance query (ctxSet)
tuples =q.getPhysicalPlan
for all tuples do
   if ( tuple ⊈ collocatedTuples) then
      nextTuple
   end if
   for all entities do
      if ( entity.ContextValues ⊈ ctxSet) then
         nextEntity
      else
         inspect entity
      end if
   end for
end for
```

5.1 Provenance Storage Model

We use the most basic storage structure of Diplodocus[RDF] [34] and TripleProv [33] in the following: 1-scope RDF molecules [34], which collocate objects related to a given subject and which are equivalent to property tables. In that sense, any *tuple* we consider is composed of a subject, and a series of predicate and object related to that subject.

TripleProv supports different models to store provenance information. We compared those models in [33]. For this work, we consider the "SLPO" storage model [33], which collocates the context values with the predicate-object pairs, and which offers good overall performance in practice. This avoids the duplication of the same context value, while at the same time collocating all data about a given subject in one structure. The resulting storage model is illustrated in Figure 3. In the rest of this section, we briefly introduce the secondary storage structures we implemented to support the query execution strategies of Section 4.

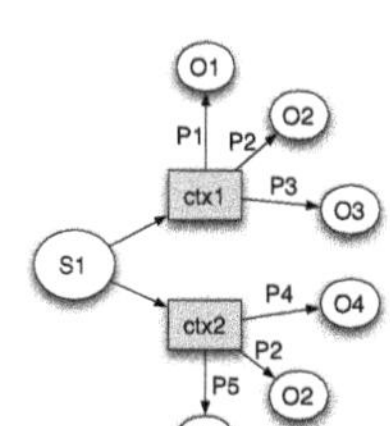

Figure 3: Our storage model for collocating context values (ctx) with predicates and objects (PO) inside an RDF molecule.

5.2 Provenance Index

Our base system supports a number of vertical and horizontal data collocation structures. Here, we propose one more way to collocate molecules, based on the context values. This gives us the possibility to prune molecules during query execution as explained above. Figure 4 illustrates this index, which boils down, in our implementation, to lists of collocated molecule identifiers, indexed by a hash-table whose keys are the context values the triples stored in the molecules belong to. We note that a given molecule can appear multiple times in this index. This index is updated upfront, e.g., at loading time.

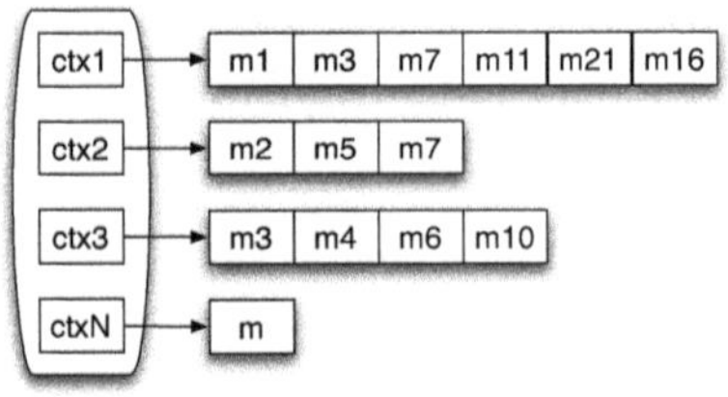

Figure 4: Provenance-driven indexing schema

5.3 Provenance-Driven Full Materialization

To support the provenance-driven materialization scheme introduced in Section 4.3, we implemented some basic view mechanisms in TripleProv. These mechanisms allow us to project, materialize and utilize as a secondary structure the portions of the molecules that are following the provenance specification (see Figure 5 for a simple illustration.)

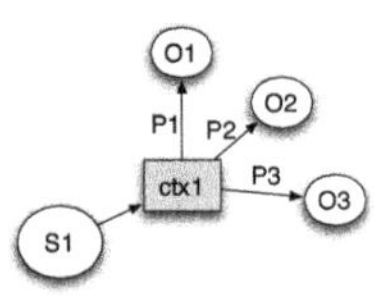

Figure 5: The molecule after materialization, driven by a provenance query returning only one context value (ctx1).

5.4 Adaptive Partial Materialization

Finally, we implement a new, dedicated structure for the adaptive materialization strategy. In that case, we collocate all molecule identifiers that are following the provenance specification (i.e., that contain *at least* one context value compatible with the provenance query). We explored several options for this structure and in the end implemented it through a *hashset*, which yields constant time performance to insert molecules when executing the provenance query and to query for molecules when executing workload queries.

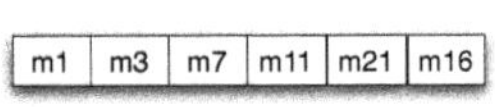

Figure 6: Set of molecules which contain at least some data related to a provenance query.

6. EXPERIMENTS

To empirically evaluate the query execution strategies discussed above in Section 4.3, we implemented them all in TripleProv. In the following, we experimentally compare a baseline version of our system that does not support provenance queries to our five strategies executing provenance-enabled queries. We perform the evaluation on two different datasets and workloads.

Within TripleProv, queries are specified as triple patterns using a high-level declarative API that offers similar functionality to SPARQL.[9] The queries are then encoded into a logical plan (a tree of operators), which is then optimized into a physical query plan as in any standard database system. The system supports all basic SPARQL operations, including "UNION" and "OPTIONAL"; at this point, it does not support "FILTER", however.

6.1 Implementations Considered

Our goal is to understand the various tradeoffs of the query execution strategies we proposed in Section 4.3 and to assess the performance penalty (or eventual speed-up) caused by provenance queries. We use the following abbreviations to refer to the different implementations we compare:

TripleProv: the vanilla version of [33], without provenance queries; this version stores provenance data, tracks the lineage of the results, and generates provenance polynomials, but does not support provenance queries;

Post-Filtering: implements our post-filtering approach; after a workload query gets executed, its results are filtered based on the results from the provenance query;

Rewriting: our query execution strategy based on query rewriting; it rewrites the workload query by adding provenance constraints in order to filter out the results;

Full Materialization: creates a materialized view based on the provenance query, and executes the workload queries over that view;

Pre-Filtering: uses a dedicated provenance index to pre-filter tuples during query execution;

Adaptive Materialization: implements a provenance-driven data co-location scheme to collocate molecule ids that are relevant given the provenance query.

6.2 Experimental Environment

Hardware Platform: All experiments were run on a HP ProLiant DL385 G7 server with an AMD Opteron Processor 6180 SE (24 cores, 2 chips, 12 cores/chip), 64GB of DDR3 RAM, running Ubuntu 12.04.3 LTS (Precise Pangolin). All data were stored on a recent 3 TB Serial ATA disk.

Datasets: We used two different datasets for our experiments: the Billion Triples Challenge (BTC)[10] and the Web Data Commons (WDC)[11] [26]. Both datasets are collections of RDF data gathered from the Web. They represent two very different kinds of RDF data. The Billion Triple Challenge dataset was created based on datasets provided by Falcon-S, Sindice, Swoogle, SWSE, and Watson using the MultiCrawler/SWSE framework. The Web Data Commons project extracts all Microformat, Microdata and RDFa data from the Common Crawl Web corpus and provides the extracted data for download in the form of RDF-quads or CSV-tables for common entity types (e.g., products, organizations, locations, etc.).

Both datasets represent typical collections of data gathered from multiple and heterogeneous online sources, hence applying some provenance query on them seems to precisely address the problem we focus on. We consider around 40 million triples for each dataset (around 10GB). To sample the data, we first pre-selected quadruples satisfying the set of considered workload and provenance queries. Then, we randomly sampled additional data up to 10GB.

For both datasets, we added provenance specific triples (184 for WDC and 360 for BTC) so that the provenance queries we use for all experiments do not modify the result sets of the workload queries, i.e., the workload query results are always the same. We decided to implement this

[9]We note that our current system does not parse full SPARQL queries at this stage. Adapting a SPARQL parser is currently in progress.

[10]`http://km.aifb.kit.edu/projects/btc-2009/`

[11]`http://webdatacommons.org/`

to remove a potential bias when comparing the strategies and the vanilla version of the system (in this way, in all cases all queries have exactly the same input and output). We note that this scenario represents in fact a worst-case scenario for our provenance-enabled approaches, since the provenance query gets executed but does not filter out any result. Therefore, we also performed experiments on the original data (see Section 6.3.4), where we use the dataset as is and where the provenance query modifies the output of the workload queries.

Workloads: We consider two different workloads. For BTC, we use eight existing queries originally proposed in [27]. In addition, we added two queries with UNION and OPTIONAL clauses, which we thought were missing in the original set of queries. Based on the queries used for the BTC dataset, we wrote 7 new queries for the WDC dataset, encompassing different kinds of typical query patterns for RDF, including star-queries of different sizes and up to 5 joins, object-object joins, object-subject joins, and triangular joins. We also included two queries with UNION and OPTIONAL clauses. In addition, for each workload we prepared a complex provenance query, which is conceptually similar to those presented in Section 3.

The datasets, query workloads and provenance-queries presented above are all are available online[12].

Experimental Methodology: As is typical for benchmarking database systems (e.g., for tpc-x[13] or our own OLTP-Benchmark [11]), we include a warm-up phase before measuring the execution time of the queries in order to measure query execution times in a steady-state mode. We first run all the queries in sequence once to warm-up the system, and then repeat the process ten times (i.e., we run 11 query batches for each variant we benchmark, each containing all the queries we consider in sequence). We report the average execution time of the last 10 runs for each query. In addition, we avoided the artifacts of connecting from the client to the server, of initializing the database from files, and of printing results; we measured instead the query execution times inside the database system only.

6.3 Results

In this section, we present the results of the empirical evaluation. We note that our original RDF back-end Diplodocus (the system TripleProv extends) has already been compared to a number of other well-known triple stores(see [34] and [10]). We refer the reader to those previous papers for a comparison to non-provenance-enabled triple stores. We have also performed an evaluation of TripleProv and different physical models for storing provenance information in [33]. In this paper, we focus on a different topic and discuss results for *Provenance-Enabled Queries.* Figure 7 reports the query execution times for the BTC dataset, while Figure 8 shows similar results for the WDC dataset. We analyze those results below.

6.3.1 Datasets Analysis

To better understand the influence of provenance queries on performance, we start by taking a look at the dataset, provenance distribution, workload, cardinality of intermediate results, number of molecules inspected, and number of basic operations for all query execution strategies. The analysis detailed below was done for the BTC dataset and workload.

First, we analyze the distribution of context values among triples. There are 6'819'826 unique context values in the dataset. Figure 9 shows the distribution of the number of triples given the context values (i.e., how many context values refer to how many triples). We observe that there are only a handful of context values that are widespread (left-hand side of the figure) and that the vast majority of the context values are highly selective. On average, each context value is related to about 5.8 triples. Collocating data inside molecules further increases the selectivity of the context values, we have on average 2.3 molecules per context value then. We leverage those properties during query execution, as some of our strategies prune molecules early in the query plan based on their context values.

6.3.2 Discussion

Our implementations supporting provenance-enabled queries overall outperform the vanilla TripleProv. This

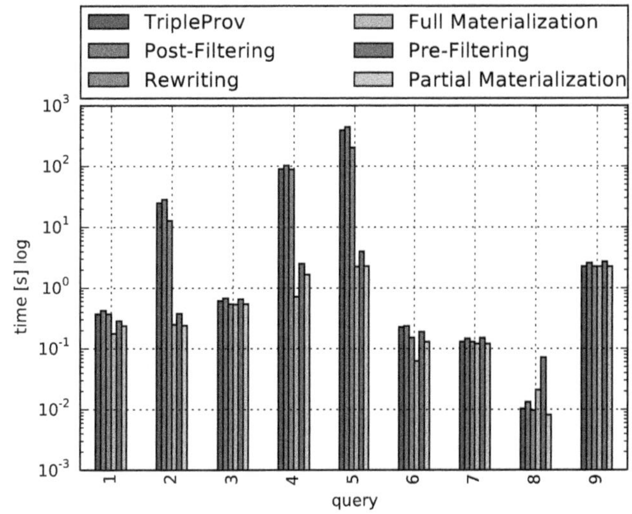

Figure 7: Query execution times for the BTC dataset (logarithmic scale)

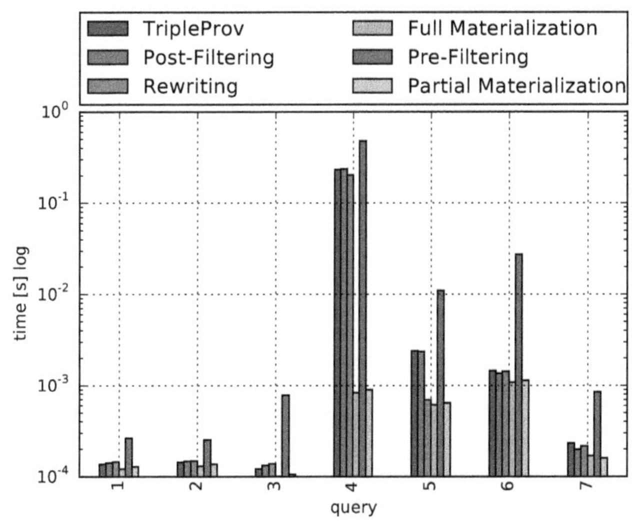

Figure 8: Query execution times for the WDC dataset (logarithmic scale).

[12]`http://exascale.info/provqueries`
[13]*http://www.tpc.org/*

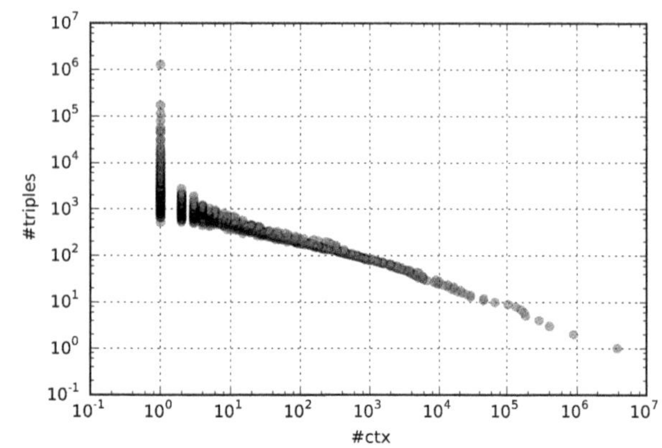

Figure 9: Distribution of number of triples for number of context values for the BTC dataset.

is unsurprising, since as we showed before the selectivity of provenance data in the datasets allows us to avoid unnecessary operations on tuples which do not add to the result.

The *Full Materialization* strategy, where we pre-materialize all relevant subsets of the molecules, makes the query execution on average 44 times faster than the vanilla version for the BTC dataset. The speedup ranges from a few percents to more than 200x (queries 2 and 5 of BTC) over the vanilla version. The price for the performance improvement is the time we have to spend to materialize molecules, in our experiments for the BTC it was 95 seconds (the time increases with data size), which can however be amortized by executing enough workload queries (see Section 6.4). This strategy consumed about 2% more memory for handling the materialized data.

The *Pre-Filtering* strategy performs on average 23 times faster than the vanilla version for the BTC dataset, while the *Adaptive Partial Materialization* strategy performs on average 35 times faster for the BTC dataset. The advantage over the *Full Materialization* strategy is that for *Adaptive Partial Materialization*, the time to execute a provenance query and materialize data is 475 times lower and takes only 0.2 second.

The *Query Rewriting* strategy performs significantly slower than the strategies mentioned above for the BTC dataset, since here we have to perform additional checking over provenance data for each query. However, even in this case, for some queries we can observe some performance improvement over the vanilla version of the system; when the provenance query significantly limits the number of tuples inspected during query execution (see Section 4), we can compensate the time taken by additional checks to improve the overall query execution time—see queries 2 and 5 for BTC. Those queries can be executed up to 95% faster than the vanilla version as they require the highest number of tuple inspections, which can significantly limit other strategies (see Section 6.3.3).

We note that the *Post-Filtering* strategy performs in all cases slightly worse than TripleProv (on average 12%), which is expected since there is no early pruning of tuples; queries are executed in the same way as in TripleProv, and in addition the post-processing phase takes place to filter the results set.

For the WDC dataset we have significantly higher cardinality of context values set (10 times more elements), which results in significantly worse performance for *Pre-Filtering*, since this strategy performs a loop over the set of context values. The provenance overhead here is not compensated on workload query execution since they are already quite fast (below 10^{-2} second for most cases) for this dataset. For this scenario the time consumed for *Full Materialization* was 60 seconds while it took only 2ms for *Adaptive Partial Materialization.* The *Adaptive Partial Materialization* strategy outperforms other strategies even more clearly on the WDC dataset.

The WDC workload shows an even higher predominance of the *Adaptive Partial Materialization* strategy over other strategies.

6.3.3 Query Performance Analysis

We now examine the reasons behind the performance differences for the different strategies, focusing on the BTC dataset. Thanks to materialization and collocation, we limit the number of molecule look-ups we require to answer the workload queries. The tables below explain the reasons behind the difference in performance. We analyze the number of inspected molecules, the number of molecules after filtering by provenance, the cardinality of intermediate results, and the number of context values used to answer the query:

#r - number of results

#m - total number of molecules used to answer the query, before checking against context values

#mf - total number of molecules after pruning with provenance data

#prov - total number of provenance context values used to answer the query (to generate a polynomial)

#im - intermediate number of molecules used to answer the query, before checking against context values

#imf - intermediate number of molecules after pruning with provenance data

#i - number of intermediate results, used to perform joins

#ec - number of basic operation executed on statements containing only constraints in a query

#er - number of basic operation executed on statements containing projections in a query

The total number of executed basic operations (*#bos*) equals *#ec* + *#er*.

We prepared the provenance query to ensure that the results for all variants are constant, therefore we avoid the bias of having different result sets.

query #	#r	#m	#mf	#prov	#im	#imf	#i	#ec	#er
1	2	4	4	2	0	0	0	84039	470
2	9	203	203	4	0	0	0	3698911	8392
3	13	32	32	7	0	0	0	18537	5580
4	5	1335	1335	5	1	1	1	44941143	4048
5	5	3054	3053	8	3052	3052	3	79050305	37040
6	2	137	133	6	136	132	374	22110	8365
7	2	20	6	5	2	2	18	438	7239
8	237	267	251	287	0	0	0	752	0
9	17	32	32	8	0	0	0	18537	101420

Table 1: Query execution analysis for TripleProv and the *Post-Filtering* strategy.

Table 1 shows the baseline statistics for the vanilla version, TripleProv.

Table 2 give statistics for the *Rewriting.* We observe at this level already that we inspect data from on average 50x fewer molecules, which results on average in a 30% boost in performance. However, executing the provenance query also has its price, which balances this gain in performance for simpler queries (e.g., 7-9).

query #	#r	#m	#mf	#prov	#im	#imf	#i	#ec	#er
1	2	4	2	2	0	0	0	5438	470
2	9	203	1	4	0	0	0	832980	6176
3	13	32	32	6	0	0	0	9715	3990
4	5	1335	22	5	1	1	1	1666409	3304
5	5	3054	18	8	3052	17	3	2163812	8008
6	2	137	98	6	136	97	6	13434	5506
7	2	20	2	5	2	1	18	399	7211
8	237	267	237	287	0	0	0	580	0
9	17	32	32	7	0	0	0	9715	52220

Table 2: Query execution analysis for the *Rewriting* strategy.

query #	#r	#m	#mf	#prov	#im	#imf	#i	#ec	#er
1	2	1	1	2	0	0	0	4660	466
2	9	1	1	4	0	0	0	832426	4144
3	13	31	31	6	0	0	0	2801	2826
4	5	8	8	5	1	1	1	87716	2386
5	5	16	15	8	14	14	3	1865699	4662
6	2	102	98	6	101	97	6	10279	4513
7	2	15	2	5	1	1	14	284	7102
8	237	237	237	287	0	0	0	435	0
9	17	31	31	7	0	0	0	2801	5114

Table 3: Query execution analysis for the *Full Materialization* strategy.

Table 3 gives statistics for our second variant (*Full Materialization*). The total number of molecules initially available is in this case reduced by 22x. Thanks to this, the total number of molecules used to answer the query ('#m') decreases on average 63x; we also reduce the number of molecules inspected after pruning with provenance data ('#mf') by 33% compared to the baseline version. This results in a performance improvement of 29x on average. For some queries (3, 7 and 9), the number of inspected molecules remains almost unchanged, since the workload query itself is very selective and since there is no room for further pruning molecules before inspecting them. Those queries perform similarly as for the baseline version. For queries 2, 4, and 5, we observe that the reduction in terms of the number of molecules used is 200x, 166x, and 190x, respectively, which significantly impacts the final performance. The price to pay for these impressive speedups is the time spent on the upfront materialization, which was 95 seconds for the dataset considered.

query #	#r	#m	#mf	#prov	#im	#imf	#i	#ec	#er
1	2	2	2	2	0	0	0	5436	470
2	9	1	1	4	0	0	0	832680	6176
3	13	32	32	6	0	0	0	9715	3990
4	5	22	22	5	1	1	1	1663384	3304
5	5	19	18	8	17	17	3	2159510	8008
6	2	102	98	6	101	97	6	13353	5506
7	2	15	2	5	1	1	18	393	7211
8	237	237	237	287	0	0	0	537	0
9	17	32	32	7	0	0	0	9715	52220

Table 4: Query execution analysis for the *Pre-Filtering* and *Adaptive Partial Materialization* strategies.

Table 4 gives statistics for our last two implementations using *Pre-Filtering* and *Adaptive Partial Materialization*. The statistics are similar for both cases (though the structures used to answer the queries and the query execution strategies vary, as explained in Sections 4 and 5). Here the cardinality of the molecule sets remains unchanged with respect to the vanilla version, and the total number of molecules used to answer the query is identical to molecules after provenance filtering for the naive version, but all molecules we inspect contain data related to the provenance query ('#m' and '#mf' are equal for each query). In fact, we inspect a number of molecules similar to *Full Materialization*, which yields performance of a similar level, on average 14x (*Pre-Filtering*) and 22x (*Adaptive Partial Materialization*) faster than the *Rewriting* strategy. The

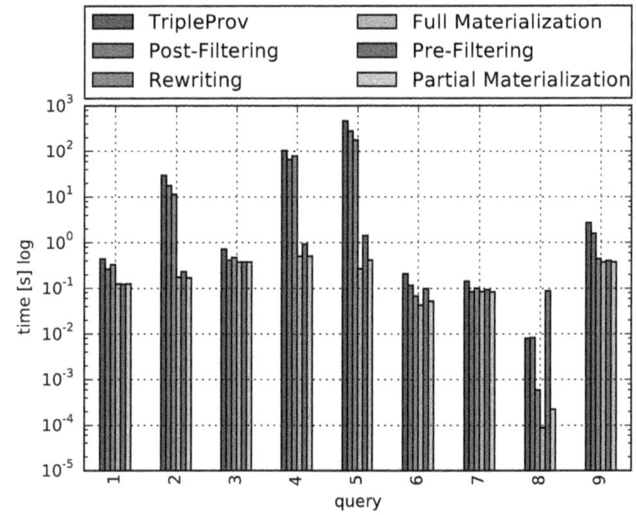

Figure 10: Query execution times for the BTC dataset (logarithmic scale), Representative Scenario.

cost of materialization for *Adaptive Partial Materialization* is much lower than for *Full Materialization*, however, as the strategy only requires 0.2 extra second in order to dynamically co-locate molecules containing data relevant for the provenance query.

6.3.4 Representative Scenario

As we mentioned above, our experiments so far aimed at comparing the execution times for different strategies fairly, thus we prepared an experimental scenario where the final output remains unchanged for all implementations (including vanilla TripleProv). In this section, we present a microbenchmark depicting a representative scenario run on the original BTC dataset (without any triples added), where the output changes due to constraints imposed on the workload by the provenance query. This dataset is also available online on the project web page.

Table 5 shows the corresponding query execution analysis. The number of results is in this case smaller for many queries as results are filtered out based on their context values.

query #	#r	#m	#mf	#prov	#im	#imf	#i	#ec	#er
1	2	1	1	1	0	0	0	2166	222
2	8	1	1	2	0	0	0	604489	5064
3	10	4	4	4	0	0	0	2002	2970
4	5	8	8	3	1	1	1	82609	2768
5	3	5	5	4	4	4	1	1381357	6364
6	1	4	4	4	3	3	1	5601	2523
7	1	15	2	3	1	1	18	297	4079
8	5	5	5	4	0	0	0	5	0
9	10	4	4	4	0	0	0	2002	2970

Table 5: Query execution analysis for the Pre-Filtering and Partial Materialization strategies for the Representative Scenario.

Figure 10 shows query performance results for the original BTC dataset.

As shown on Figure 10, the performance gains for all provenance-enabled strategies are higher in this more realistic scenario where we did not modify the original data. The speedup is caused by the smaller number of *basic operations* (*#ec+#er*) executed, which results from fewer intermediate results. For queries for which the results remain the same (2 and 4), the improvement is directly related to the smaller number of *basic operations* performed caused by the limited number of context values resulting from the provenance query.

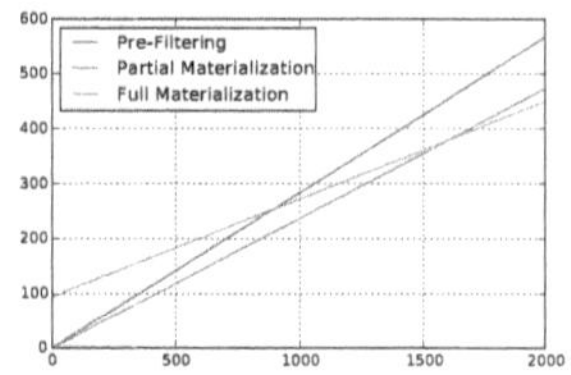

Figure 11: Cumulative query execution time including time of materialization for 2'000 repetitions of query 1 for BTC.

6.4 End-to-End Workload Optimization

Having devise several query execution strategies, it is interesting to understand which ones perform better under what circumstances. Specifically, when it pays off to use a strategy which has a higher cost for executing the provenance query and when this is not beneficial. Ideally, the time consumed on the execution of the provenance query (including some potential pre-materialization) should be compensated when executing the workload queries. Let i and j denote two different query execution strategies and P and W denote the time taken to execute the provenance and the workload queries, respectively. If: $P_i + W_i < P_j + W_j$, then strategy i should be chosen since it yields an overall lower cost for running the entire provenance-enabled workload.

As an illustration, Figure 11 shows the cumulative query execution time for query 1 of BTC including the time overhead for the provenance query execution and data materialization. We observe that the *Partial Materialization* strategy compensates the overhead of running the provenance query and of materialization after a few repetitions of the query already, compared with the *Pre-Filtering*, which has a lower cost from a provenance query execution perspective, but which executes workload queries slower. For the case of *Full Materialization*, which has a significantly higher materialization overhead, it takes about 900 workload query repetitions to amortize the cost of running the provenance query and pre-materializing data in order to beat the *Pre-Filtering* strategy. The *Full Materialization* strategy outperforms the *Partial Materialization* strategy only after more than 1'500 repetitions of the query.

In the end, the optimal strategy depends on the data, on the exact mixture of (provenance and workload) queries, and of their frequencies. Given those three parameters, one can pick the optimal execution strategy using several techniques. If the provenance and the workload queries are known in advance or do not vary much, one can run a sample of the queries using different strategies (similarly to what we did above) and pick the best-performing one. If the queries vary a lot, then one has to resort to an approximate model of query execution in order to pick the best strategy, as it is customary in traditional query optimization. Different models can by used in this context, like the very detailed main-memory model we proposed in [17], or the system-agnostic model recently proposed in [19].

As observed above, however, the performance of our various strategies are strongly correlated (with a correlation coefficient of 95%) to the number of basic operations (e.g., molecule look-ups) performed—at least as run in our system. Hence, we propose a simple though effective model in our context based on this observation. We fit a model based on experimental data giving the time to execute a varying number of basic operations. In our setting, the best model turns out to be $e^{(a * \ln bos + b)}$ (the logarithm comes from the cost of

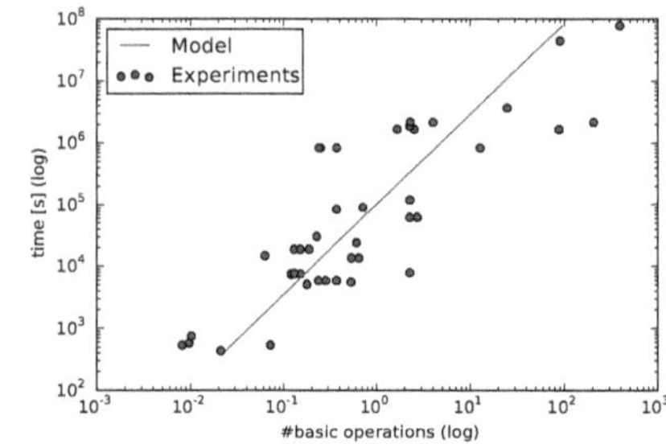

Figure 12: Query execution time vs. number of basic operations from experimental results and for our model, where the model parameters a and b were fit to 0.85 and -9.85, respectively.

preparing a query, such as translating strings into identifiers and building the query plan, which gets amortized with a higher number of subsequent basic operations). Figure 12 shows the performance of this model in practice. Using this model and statistics about the predicates in the queries, we can successfully predict the winning strategy, i.e., *Partial Materialization* for the scenarios discussed above.

7. CONCLUSIONS

In this paper, we considered the following research question: "What is the most effective query execution strategy for provenance-enabled queries"? In order to answer the research question above, this paper made the following contributions: a characterization of provenance-enabled queries, a description of five different query execution strategies, an implementation of these strategies in TripleProv, as well as a detailed performance evaluation.

The ultimate answer to this question depends on the exact data and queries used, though based on our experimental analysis above, we believe that an adaptive materialization strategy provides the best trade-off for running provenance-enabled queries over Web Data in general. Our empirical results show that this strategy performs best when taking into account the costs of materialization, both on Web Data Commons and on Billion Triple Challenge data. A key reason for this result is the selectivity of provenance on the Web of Data. Hence, by leveraging knowledge of provenance, one can execute many types of queries roughly 30x faster than a baseline store.

Building on the results of this work, we see a number of avenues of future work. The investigation of how provenance can be used to improve performance within data management systems. The development of an analytics environment which allows users to adjust provenance without changing the workload queries. Finally, the diffusion of these results to further settings and systems.

Acknowledgements

This work was supported by the Swiss National Science Foundation under grant number PP00P2_128459 and by the Dutch national program COMMIT.

References

[1] B. Arab, D. Gawlick, V. Radhakrishnan, H. Guo, and B. Glavic. A generic provenance middleware for queries, updates, and transactions. In *6th USENIX Workshop on the Theory and Practice of Provenance (TaPP 2014)*, Cologne, June 2014. USENIX Association.

[2] R. Avnur and J. M. Hellerstein. Eddies: Continuously adaptive query processing. *SIGMOD Rec.*, 29(2):261–272, May 2000.

[3] C. R. Batchelor, C. Y. A. Brenninkmeijer, C. Chichester, M. Davies, D. Digles, I. Dunlop, C. T. A. Evelo, A. Gaulton, C. A. Goble, A. J. G. Gray, P. T. Groth, L. Harland, K. Karapetyan, A. Loizou, J. P. Overington, S. Pettifer, J. Steele, R. Stevens, V. Tkachenko, A. Waagmeester, A. J. Williams, and E. L. Willighagen. Scientific lenses to support multiple views over linked chemistry data. In *ISWC 2014 - 13th International Semantic Web Conference, Riva del Garda, Italy, October 19-23, 2014. Proceedings, Part I*, pages 98–113, Oct. 2014.

[4] O. Biton, S. Cohen-Boulakia, and S. B. Davidson. Zoom*userviews: Querying relevant provenance in workflow systems. In *Proceedings of the 33rd International Conference on Very Large Data Bases*, VLDB '07, pages 1366–1369. VLDB Endowment, 2007.

[5] J. J. Carroll, C. Bizer, P. Hayes, and P. Stickler. Named graphs, provenance and trust. In *Proceedings of the 14th International Conference on World Wide Web*, WWW '05, pages 613–622, New York, NY, USA, 2005. ACM.

[6] A. Chebotko, S. Lu, X. Fei, and F. Fotouhi. Rdfprov: A relational rdf store for querying and managing scientific workflow provenance. *Data Knowl. Eng.*, 69(8):836–865, Aug. 2010.

[7] C. Chichester, P. Gaudet, O. Karch, P. Groth, L. Lane, A. Bairoch, B. Mons, and A. Loizou. Querying neXtProt nanopublications and their value for insights on sequence variants and tissue expression. *Web Semantics: Science, Services and Agents on the World Wide Web*, (0):–, 2014.

[8] R. L. Cole and G. Graefe. Optimization of dynamic query evaluation plans. *SIGMOD Rec.*, 23(2):150–160, May 1994.

[9] C. V. Damásio, A. Analyti, and G. Antoniou. Provenance for SPARQL queries. In *Proceedings of the 11th international conference on The Semantic Web - Volume Part I*, ISWC'12, pages 625–640, Berlin, Heidelberg, 2012. Springer-Verlag.

[10] G. Demartini, I. Enchev, M. Wylot, J. Gapany, and P. Cudre-Mauroux. BowlognaBenchâĂŤBenchmarking RDF Analytics. In K. Aberer, E. Damiani, and T. Dillon, editors, *Data-Driven Process Discovery and Analysis*, volume 116 of *Lecture Notes in Business Information Processing*, pages 82–102. Springer Berlin Heidelberg, 2012.

[11] D. E. Difallah, A. Pavlo, C. Curino, and P. Cudré-Mauroux. Oltp-bench: An extensible testbed for benchmarking relational databases. *PVLDB*, 7(4):277–288, 2013.

[12] G. Flouris, I. Fundulaki, P. Pediaditis, Y. Theoharis, and V. Christophides. Coloring rdf triples to capture provenance. In *Proceedings of the 8th International Semantic Web Conference*, ISWC '09, pages 196–212, Berlin, Heidelberg, 2009. Springer-Verlag.

[13] F. Geerts, G. Karvounarakis, V. Christophides, and I. Fundulaki. Algebraic structures for capturing the provenance of sparql queries. In *Proceedings of the 16th International Conference on Database Theory*, ICDT '13, pages 153–164, New York, NY, USA, 2013. ACM.

[14] B. Glavic and G. Alonso. The perm provenance management system in action. In *Proceedings of the 2009 ACM SIGMOD International Conference on Management of Data*, SIGMOD '09, pages 1055–1058, New York, NY, USA, 2009. ACM.

[15] G. Graefe and K. Ward. Dynamic query evaluation plans. *SIGMOD Rec.*, 18(2):358–366, June 1989.

[16] P. Groth and L. Moreau (eds.). PROV-Overview. An Overview of the PROV Family of Documents. W3C Working Group Note NOTE-prov-overview-20130430, World Wide Web Consortium, Apr. 2013.

[17] M. Grund, J. Krüger, H. Plattner, A. Zeier, P. Cudré-Mauroux, and S. Madden. HYRISE - A main memory hybrid storage engine. *PVLDB*, 4(2):105–116, 2010.

[18] H. Halpin and J. Cheney. Dynamic Provenance for SPARQL Updates. In *The Semantic Web âĂŞ ISWC 2014*, volume 8796 of *Lecture Notes in Computer Science*, pages 425–440. Springer International Publishing, 2014.

[19] R. Hasan and F. Gandon. Predicting SPARQL query performance. In *The Semantic Web: ESWC 2014 Satellite Events - ESWC 2014 Satellite Events, Anissaras, Crete, Greece, May 25-29, 2014, Revised Selected Papers*, pages 222–225, 2014.

[20] T. Heath and C. Bizer. *Linked Data: Evolving the Web into a Global Data Space.* Synthesis Lectures on the Semantic Web. Morgan & Claypool Publishers, 2011.

[21] N. Kabra and D. J. DeWitt. Efficient mid-query re-optimization of sub-optimal query execution plans. *SIGMOD Rec.*, 27(2):106–117, June 1998.

[22] G. Karvounarakis, Z. G. Ives, and V. Tannen. Querying data provenance. In *Proceedings of the 2010 ACM SIGMOD International Conference on Management of data*, pages 951–962. ACM, 2010.

[23] C. A. Knoblock, P. Szekely, J. L. Ambite, S. Gupta, A. Goel, M. Muslea, K. Lerman, M. Taheriyan, and P. Mallick. Semi-automatically mapping structured sources into the semantic web. In *Proceedings of the Extended Semantic Web Conference*, Crete, Greece, 2012.

[24] S. Miles. Electronically querying for the provenance of entities. In L. Moreau and I. Foster, editors, *Provenance and Annotation of Data*, volume 4145 of *Lecture Notes in Computer Science*, pages 184–192. Springer Berlin Heidelberg, 2006.

[25] L. Moreau and G. Paul. *Provenance: An Introduction to PROV.* Morgan and Claypool, September 2013.

[26] H. Mühleisen and C. Bizer. Web data commons - extracting structured data from two large web corpora. In C. Bizer, T. Heath, T. Berners-Lee, and M. Hausenblas, editors, *LDOW*, volume 937 of *CEUR Workshop Proceedings*. CEUR-WS.org, 2012.

[27] T. Neumann and G. Weikum. Scalable join processing on very large RDF graphs. In *Proceedings of the 2009 ACM SIGMOD International Conference on Management of data*, pages 627–640. ACM, 2009.

[28] K. Ng, Z. Wang, R. R. Muntz, and S. Nittel. Dynamic query re-optimization. In *Scientific and Statistical Database Management, 1999. Eleventh International Conference on*, pages 264–273, Aug 1999.

[29] D. W. R. Cyganiak and M. L. (Ed.). RDF 1.1 Concepts and Abstract Syntax. W3C Recommendation, February 2014. http://www.w3.org/TR/rdf11-concepts/.

[30] M. Schmachtenberg, C. Bizer, and H. Paulheim. Adoption of the linked data best practices in different topical domains. In *The Semantic Web–ISWC 2014*, pages 245–260. Springer, 2014.

[31] A. Schultz, A. Matteini, R. Isele, C. Bizer, and C. Becker. LDIF - Linked Data Integration Framework. In *COLD*, 2011.

[32] O. Udrea, D. R. Recupero, and V. Subrahmanian. Annotated rdf. *ACM Transactions on Computational Logic (TOCL)*, 11(2):10, 2010.

[33] M. Wylot, P. Cudre-Mauroux, and P. Groth. Tripleprov: Efficient processing of lineage queries in a native rdf store. In *Proceedings of the 23rd International Conference on World Wide Web*, WWW '14, pages 455–466, Republic and Canton of Geneva, Switzerland, 2014. International World Wide Web Conferences Steering Committee.

[34] M. Wylot, J. Pont, M. Wisniewski, and P. Cudré-Mauroux. dipLODocus[RDF]: short and long-tail RDF analytics for massive webs of data. In *Proceedings of the 10th international conference on The semantic web - Volume Part I*, ISWC'11, pages 778–793, Berlin, Heidelberg, 2011. Springer-Verlag.

[35] A. Zimmermann, N. Lopes, A. Polleres, and U. Straccia. A general framework for representing, reasoning and querying with annotated semantic web data. *Web Semant.*, 11:72–95, Mar. 2012.

Understanding Malvertising Through Ad-Injecting Browser Extensions

Xinyu Xing
Georgia Institute of Technology
xxing8@gatech.edu

Wei Meng
Georgia Institute of Technology
wei@gatech.edu

Byoungyoung Lee
Georgia Institute of Technology
blee@gatech.edu

Udi Weinsberg
Facebook Inc.
udi@fb.com

Anmol Sheth
A9.com/Amazon
anmolsheth@gmail.com

Roberto Perdisci
University of Georgia
perdisci@cs.uga.edu

Wenke Lee
Georgia Institute of Technology
wenke@cc.gatech.edu

ABSTRACT

Malvertising is a malicious activity that leverages advertising to distribute various forms of malware. Because advertising is the key revenue generator for numerous Internet companies, large ad networks, such as Google, Yahoo and Microsoft, invest a lot of effort to mitigate malicious ads from their ad networks. This drives adversaries to look for alternative methods to deploy malvertising.

In this paper, we show that browser extensions that use ads as their monetization strategy often facilitate the deployment of malvertising. Moreover, while some extensions simply serve ads from ad networks that support malvertising, other extensions maliciously alter the content of visited webpages to force users into installing malware. To measure the extent of these behaviors we developed Expector, a system that automatically inspects and identifies browser extensions that inject ads, and then classifies these ads as malicious or benign based on their landing pages. Using Expector, we automatically inspected over 18,000 Chrome browser extensions. We found 292 extensions that inject ads, and detected 56 extensions that participate in malvertising using 16 different ad networks and with a total user base of 602,417.

Categories and Subject Descriptors

H.3.5 [**Online Information Services**]: Web-based services; K.6.2 [**Installation Management**]: Performance and usage measurement; K.6.5 [**Security and Protection (D.4.6, K.4.2)**]: Invasive software (e.g., viruses, worms, Trojan horses)

General Terms

Security, Design, Experimentation

WWW 2015, May 18–22, 2015, Florence, Italy.
ACM 978-1-4503-3469-3/15/05.
http://dx.doi.org/10.1145/2736277.2741630.

Keywords

Malvertising; Browser Extension; Adware

1. INTRODUCTION

Online advertising is a powerful way to deliver brand messages to potential customers. To monetize their online services and applications, most modern websites act as ad *publishers* and reserve ad space on their web pages where online ads are displayed to their visitors. Ad networks work as brokers between advertisers and publishers. Joining an ad network frees websites from having to set up their own ad servers and invest in tracking software. Consequently, some ad networks attract a very large number of publishers and produce huge revenues.

As online advertising became increasingly popular and pervasive, miscreants have started to abuse this convenient channel to conduct malicious activities. Malvertising is one of such activities, where an attacker maliciously uses advertising to distribute various forms of malware. Malvertising can result in serious consequences, because an attacker can purchase ad space to publish malicious ads on many popular websites. Therefore, the maliciously crafted content could reach a very large audience. In addition, users may be unaware of the fact that they could encounter malicious content while browsing highly reputable websites, which may put them at an even higher risk.

Recent reports indicate that some ad networks have started to offer browser extension developers an opportunity to monetize their "free" work [3, 9]. In other words, some ad networks are extending their business by connecting advertisers to browser extension developers. Given this new business trend and little studies on malvertising in this new context, we conduct a comprehensive study on malvertising activities of ad-injecting extensions, which insert ads on webpages without user consents. In particular, we aim to answer a number of fundamental questions: How many ad-injecting extensions are present on popular repositories like the Chrome Extension store? How many extensions are conducting malvertising activities? What are the characteristics of malvertising via ad-injecting extensions?

To answer the aforementioned questions, we developed `Expector` (Extension Inspector), a tool that is able to automatically identify ad-injecting extensions. We ran `Expector` on extensions served by the Chrome Extension store, and observed several interesting behaviors. First, compared to ads "naturally" published (without any browser extension intercession) by popular websites, ad-injecting extensions tend to serve a larger fraction of malicious ads. We attribute this to the observation that popular websites partner with large reputable ad networks, whereas extensions utilize smaller ad networks that devote insufficient efforts to identifying and mitigating malicious advertisers. Second, in contrast to previous studies that found only a low fraction of malicious ads, we observed that some ad networks serve only malicious ads. This is presumably because these ad networks and miscreants collude to conduct malvertising, or because miscreants effectively own these ad networks and use them for serving malicious ads. Finally, we found that ad-injecting extensions can make malvertising more detrimental, because some ad networks are unscrupulous on abusing the privileges that ad-injecting extensions offer.

In summary, the main contributions of this paper are as follows:

- We present a comprehensive study that exposes and quantifies the extent to which browser extensions facilitate malvertising. Furthermore, we show that the high privileges granted to extensions are often abused to increase the likelihood of infecting users with malware, e.g., through click hijacking.
- We present `Expector`, a measurement framework that automatically identifies browser extensions that inject ads on webpages. Our evaluation shows that `Expector` has both low false positives (3.6%) and low false negatives (3%).
- We ran `Expector` on all extensions available on the Chrome extension store (almost 18,000), and identified 292 extensions that embed ad-injection capabilities. Of these, 56 deliver ads that lead users to sites that host malware, and have an overall user base of 602,417. Furthermore, we found 16 unique ad-network domains that inject malicious ads, leading users to 117 distinct malware-serving domains.
- We show that a user installing an ad-injecting extension is more likely to be exposed to malvertising threat, compared to users that do not install such browser extensions.

The rest of this paper is structured as follows. We begin with the discussion of related work in Section 2. In Section 3 we provide essential background. We detail the design of `Expector` and show the results from applying it to the Google Chrome extension store in Section 4. We then perform a detailed study for malvertising extensions identified by `Expector` in Section 5 and 6. Finally, we conclude the paper in Section 7.

2. RELATED WORK

In this section, we discuss three lines of work most related to ours – (1) malvertising, (2) misbehaving browser extension, and (3) adware.

Malvertising. Malvertising has been a growing concern for many ad networks. Prior research on this threat has shown the rampancy of malvertising through normal Web browsing [21, 26, 28, 30]. Provos *et al.* [28] studied various channels for distributing drive-by downloads. The authors found that 2% of the landing sites deliver malware via advertisements, which were often reached through multiple ad syndication. Ford *et al.* [21] studied malware distribution through Flash ads and developed a tool for malicious Flash ad detection. According to recent studies [26,30], researchers found that about 1% ads lead users to malicious content. In addition, Zarras *et al.*observed that smaller ad networks are more prone to serving malicious advertisements, and ad arbitration (syndication) process can facilitate the distribution of malicious advertisements. Different from these previous studies, we focus on unraveling those characteristics of malvertising unique to ad-injecting browser extensions.

Browser Extension. Though not considered malicious, ad-injecting activities of browser extensions are misbehaving practice. A series of issues in misbehaving browser extensions have been studied for years, mostly focusing on preventing user data leakage through malicious extensions [20,24,25,27,29] and protecting against privilege abuse of extensions [22]. The security model of Chrome extensions was criticized in [27]. The authors showed that extensions introduce attacks on the Chrome browser itself, and proposed a enforcing micro-privileges at the DOM element level. Egele *et al.* [20,24] proposed several detection solutions to spyware that silently steals user information. By leveraging both static and dynamic analysis techniques the authors show that it is possible to track the flow of sensitive information as it is processed by the web browser and any extension installed. [22] showed that many Chrome extensions are over-privileged, which can potentially cause security risks. To address the shortcomings of existing extension mechanisms, the authors propose a comprehensive new model for extension security. Our work differs from these studies because we focus on a little studied yet important issue in misbehaving browser extensions – ad injection.

A pioneering work in this problem space is Hulk [23], a dynamic analysis system that automatically detects Chrome browser extensions with malicious behaviors. Using Hulk, Kapravelos *et al.*found thousands of suspicious extensions including those with ad-injecting practice. Despite effectiveness on identifying misbehaving browser extensions, Hulk cannot provide us only with a corpus of ad-injecting extensions for studying their malvertising activities because it is designed for identifying various misbehaviors in Chrome extensions. In addition, our study needs not only a tool to identify ad-injecting extensions but also an automatic solution to categorize ads placed by these extensions. Considering the limitation of Hulk as well as our unique requirement, we built a customized measurement tool – `Expector`– to facilitate our study.

In addition to Hulk, other tools have been recently developed to assist users in identifying ad-injecting Chrome extensions [6, 7]. These tools operate by comparing extensions installed by a user against a list, oftentimes crowd-sourced, of known adware, and alerting the user if such extensions are found. Such an approach is limited by the accuracy and completeness of its list, and cannot handle new adware that was not yet reported. Therefore, our study does not rely on manually curated lists.

Adware. As an ad-injecting browser extension is one instance of adware, analysing malvertising activities of ad-injecting extensions also falls under the category of the study on adware. Edelman *et al.* [18] provide an overview of the adware ecosystem, studying the ad networks, exchanges, and practices used by ad injectors. In a more recent work [19], the same authors study fraud in online affiliate marketing, and how adware takes part of such frauds. Both works focus more on the business aspects of the ecosystem, and unlike our work, they do not attempt to conduct a comprehensive analysis of adware, but instead extract the participants of manually selected adware extensions.

3. AD-INJECTING EXTENSIONS

Browser extensions are programs that enhance the functionalities of the browser. These programs are written using a combination of HTML, JavaScript, and CSS, and are typically hosted in online stores, such as the Chrome web store [10] and Mozilla Ad-

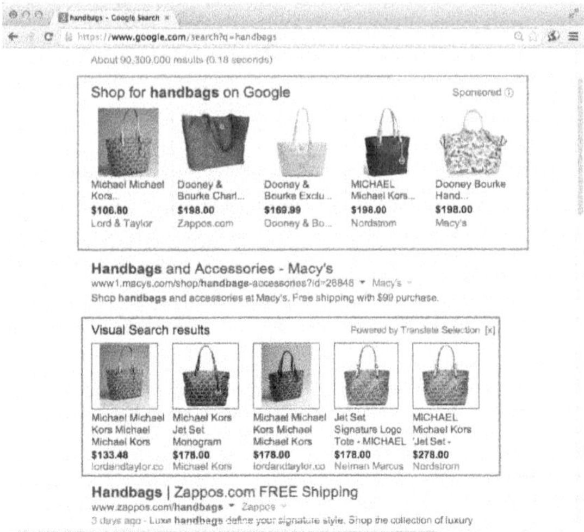

Figure 1: A Google search injected with ads from "Translate Selection" Chrome extension.

Ons store [8]. Extensions interact with the current webpage loaded in the browser by injecting JavaScript to read or modify the DOM structure of the webpage, communicating with external servers using `XMLHttpRequest`, and leveraging the browser APIs and features. The permissions requested by the extension are listed in a manifest file that is reviewed by the user at installation time. As is evident from this description, browser extensions hold significant privileges, thus leaving the door open to malpractices and security and privacy risks. In the rest of the section we describe three primary types of ad injection malpractices that we observed through our study of Chrome browser extensions. Then, we briefly introduce JavaScript libraries used by ad-injecting extensions.

3.1 Ad Injection Practices

Ad Injection on Search Result Pages. Consider the screenshot in Figure 1, showing the result page of a Google search for the query "bags". The user has installed the "Translate Selection" Chrome extension whose primary purpose is to help users quickly translate the selected text between different languages. However, this extension bundles with it the functionality to inject ads in the search results returned to the user. The top highlighted region in Figure 1 shows the standard Google sponsored ads. The bottom highlighted region shows another set of ads of bags with links to online stores.

Ad Injection on Retail Websites. Another type of ad injection practice is related to injecting ads on webpages related to online retail (amazon.com, ebay.com, etc.). When a potential shopper browses a product on an online retail website, the extension sends the context of a browsing session to a third-party advertisement service, which retrieves similar or related products. These products are shown in the form of an ad to the user, overlayed on the existing website content.

Ad Injection on Unrelated Websites. The third type of ad injection practice consists of extensions that aggressively insert ads on almost every webpage that the user browses. This practice can often degrade the user's experience by shown pop-ups or other forms of annoying ads.

3.2 JavaScript Libraries for Ad Injection

It is relatively straightforward for extension developers to monetize their extensions through ad injection. Similar to existing ad networks and ad exchanges, there exists a thriving market of ad networks that provide JavaScript ad injection libraries for extension developers to integrate with their applications. These libraries inject ads on webpages by modifying the DOM structure of the HTML and inserting additional HTML `iframe`'s that contain the injected ad content. The ad provider may trigger the ad injection only on specific websites (e.g., retail websites), and/or inject ads when a user performs a specific operations (e.g., mouse hover on a product image).

4. EXPECTOR

In this section, we provide details for the design and implementation of `Expector`, our browser extension analysis and measurement framework that aims to automatically detect and characterize ad-injection practices used by browser extensions. We then discuss how we use `Expector` to detect ad-injecting extensions (with either "regular" ads or malvertising) in the Chrome Extension store.

4.1 Design

Identifying Triggering Websites. Some ad-injecting extensions inject ads only when the user visits a specific set of websites. Therefore, `Expector` needs to identify the websites that may trigger the ad injection functionalities of each extension to be analyzed. To identify such websites, `Expector` performs static analysis of the extension's code. As some of the ad injection code may be loaded from third-party library at runtime, `Expector` also spawns a browser with the extension installed to intercept all the scripts transmitted via the network. More specifically, `Expector` installs a virtual proxy between the browser's JavaScript engine and the extension. Using the remote debugging protocols supported by browsers (e.g., Chrome [12]), the virtual proxy intercepts all the function invocations related to JavaScript executions. Once the JavaScript code executed by the extension is obtained, it searches for references to one of the ten most popular top-level domains (TLDs) [17] (e.g., `.com`, `.net`, `.org`). We limit the search to these top-ten TLDs because we assume that extensions will most likely target popular websites, almost all of which are registered under the top-ten TLDs.

Triggering Events for Ad Injection. Besides injecting ads based on websites the user visits, extensions also inject ads on specific user generated events. For example, the extension code may register an event listener on a product image of a retail site and listen to the "MouseOver" event. The callback for injecting ads of similar products is only executed when the user hovers his mouse on this image. In order to effectively identify ad injection extension, `Expector` tries to trigger as many as possible potential events that the extension might be interested in. To this end, for all DOM elements that have a JavaScript event handler to process user events, like onClick, onMouseOver, etc., we instruct the browser to execute the corresponding JavaScript function.

A caveat to the above described event trigger mechanism is that some extensions inject ads only after some time has elapsed since the user installed the extension. We assume these practices are used to reduce user dissatisfaction from the injected ads and to reduce the chance to be detected by an extension reviewer. We therefore "tricked" these extensions by setting the system clock before we install an extension to a random long enough time backwards, then install the extension, launch the browser and then set the system clock back.

Identifying Extension-Injected Elements. As a first step for detecting injected ads, the measurement framework should identify the suspicious DOM elements that are potentially inserted by the extension for ad injection. A naive approach is to directly compare the HTML source of two different pages – one with the extension loaded, and another one without. However this approach will result in a large number of false positives as most webpages load a large amount of dynamic content that can be served by different hosts on each reload of the webpage. For example, each reload of a webpage can potentially result in ads served from different ad providers.

To address this, `Expector` uses *both* the DOM structure as well as the content of the DOM elements to identify potential extension-injected elements. This is achieved by the following steps:

1. We assume that all hosts that serve content on the webpage *without* the extension installed are trusted and generate a list of trusted host names by loading the webpage multiple times without the extension. The reason we trust such existing hosts is that extensions use different ad networks than mainstream websites, mostly due to restrictions enforced by the large ad networks [2].

2. We load the webpage using two instances of the browser (with and without the extension loaded) and record the DOM tree.

3. We trigger user events in the instance with extension installed as described above.

4. The DOM tree structure is flattened into a list of elements by performing a pre-order traversal over the corresponding DOM tree, i.e., for each node in the list, its descendants are located at its right side and its ancestors are at the left side of the node. Each item in the list consists of the tag name of the DOM element and the domain associated with the DOM element (if such domain exists). For example, an iframe tag like `<iframe src='http://www.amazon.com/product/B00BWYQ9YE/'/>` is encoded as a two tuple (`'iframe'`, `'www.amazon.com'`) after transformation.

5. In order to compute the difference between the two lists, we used a variant of the *longest common subsequence* (LCS) algorithm. The modified LCS algorithm outputs nodes that are present only in the webpage loaded with the extension installed.

6. Finally, these elements are further processed and only the elements whose host name is not presented in the trusted list are labeled as potential injected ad elements. Although extensions might use domains in the trusted list to serve ads, we find in practice it is rare as popular and reputable ad networks (e.g. Google AdSense) disallow their usage in extensions [2].

The above process enables us to identify DOM elements that are only added by the extension. As DOM tree manipulation might be a legitimate functionality for some extensions, `Expector` needs to apply further checks to identify DOM elements that are ads.

Identifying Extension-Injected Ads. A unique characteristic of online ads is that users who click the ad are usually redirected to multiple other sites before eventually reaching the landing page. These redirections enable ad networks to monitor ad clicking for analytics and billing purposes. This redirection pattern is unique to ads and simply detecting it is sufficient to identify that the corresponding DOM element is advertisement. We use these observations for distinguishing ad elements from other non-ad elements.

To this end, `Expector` visits the ad landing pages potentially associated with the identified DOM elements through redirects. For all elements that have a URL associated with them, we instruct the browser to visit the URL. Note that we ignore `iframe`'s, since the URL points to the source of the iframe. For the remaining elements (`iframe`'s or elements with no URLs), we instruct the browser to trigger a click event to emulate a user clicking inside the element. For all the above cases, if the element contains an ad, the advertiser's website will be loaded usually through a series of redirects, first to one or more ad networks, and then to the ad landing page.

To detect such redirection patterns, we implemented a lightweight Chrome extension, which is loaded before the other extension is installed, that logs all HTTP requests made by the browser. HTTP requests issued as a result of the above process are analyzed for searching redirections. A redirection is detected when a visit (click) results in more than one domain in the traffic trace, and the last domain (e.g., the ad landing page) is not the same as the original web site. If such redirection is identified, the extension is labeled for further inspection.

4.2 Implementation

We implement `Expector` using Node.js [11] and Selenium [14]. We use Node.js to spawn a Chrome instance and load a Chrome extension for pre-parsing (identifying triggering websites). Using the remote debugging protocol of Chrome, we configure a virtual proxy working as a Chrome Developer Tool that intercepts all the JavaScript function invocations. Specifically, we listen on all *Debugger.scriptParsed* events and log all the JavaScript code parsed by the `V8` JavaScript engine. The rest of the components of `Expector` are implemented with Selenium and the LCS algorithm is implemented in Python.

To ensure fast and scalable processing of a large number of Chrome extensions, we deploy `Expector` across 60 Linux Debian 7 virtual machines running on a 32 core server with 128 GB RAM. This setup enabled us to process all 18,030 extensions in the Chrome webstore in less than three days.

4.3 Evaluation

In order to assure the completeness of our study on the Chrome extensions store, we evaluate the accuracy of `Expector` to detect ad injecting extensions by characterizing the false positive and negative rates using two different datasets:

Measuring false positives. We evaluate the false positive rate of `Expector` by testing all the available extensions on the Chrome web store followed by manual verification. To this end, we developed a crawler that downloads all extensions that are listed on the Chrome Web Store [10] along with the extension's meta data, i.e., developer account, extension category, number of active users, rating, description, and user reviews. We ran our crawler during March 2014, and obtained 18,030 Chrome extensions[1].

Out of the 18,030 extensions downloaded from the Chrome web store, 108 extensions (0.6%) failed to be processed by `Expector`. By inspecting the code of these extensions we found that these extensions utilize native binary code [13] that was not ported by the extension developer to Linux. All other 17,922 extensions were successfully evaluated by `Expector` using the setup within three days highlighting the ability of `Expector` to scale to a large number of extensions.

`Expector` reported 303 extensions as adware, which accounts for 1.7% extensions on Google Chrome store. We manually installed each of these and inspected their source code, and found that 292 of these are indeed adware, which is notably higher (9×)

[1] In [23], Kapravelos *et al.*evaluated Hulk using a larger dataset containing 48,332 Chrome extensions presumably because they collected their extension samples through different channels.

than the crowd-sourced approach used by Extension Defender [6]. This indicates a very low false positive rate of 3.6%. We further analyzed the 11 extensions that Expector incorrectly identified and find that Expector flagged them as users were re-directed to webpages controlled by the extension developer that contained ads. For example, parental control extensions like *Anti-Porn Pro* and *No Xvideos* maintain a blacklist of websites. When users navigate to these webpages, the extension re-directs the user to a webpage hosted by the extension developer showing a warning message along with a few ads. This webpage hosts ads which are detected by Expector and consequently the corresponding extension is flagged as adware.

Measuring false negatives. In order to study the false negative rate of Expector we use a crowdsourced list of Chrome extensions that are tagged as adware. This list is provided by Extension Defender [1] that enables users to submit extensions as potential adware which are reviewed and verified manually by the curators of this list. In March 2014, this Extension Defender had 78 Chrome extensions that were tagged as adware.

We first manually verify the crowdsourced list of extensions tagged as adware. Surprisingly, we found that out of the 78 extensions only 34 of them were manually verified as adware. This initial analysis highlights the limitations of the crowdsourced approach where curators cannot manually check every update to the extension source code and verify user complaints. Consequently, we postulate that these 44 extensions may have disabled the ad injection functionality after being flagged as adware, and Extension Defender failed to remove them from their list.

Out of the 34 manually verified adware extensions, Expector was able to correctly detect 32 of these. We further analyzed the two extensions that Expector missed. The first one uses a Windows DLL file, which is not compatible on Linux, but could have been processed if Expector was deployed on Windows. We do not count this as a false negative. The second extension operates on Facebook, and uses a more sophisticated triggering method. It requires the user to visit Facebook.com, scroll to the bottom of the page, and wait for 10 seconds before injecting ads. Expector correctly identified the triggering website and the timeout event, but failed to detect the required scroll event. These complex triggering events are difficult to identify. However, as our analysis shows, they are quite rare as they target a very specific user interaction, thus reducing the number of ads the extension injects (and lowering their revenue). In summary, Expector has a low false negative rate of 3.0% (1/33).

5. STUDYING MALVERTISING IN A CONTROLLED ENVIRONMENT

In this section, we expose and characterize malvertising activities by interacting with those ad-injecting extensions that Expector identifies.

5.1 Methodology

As described in Section 4, Expector detects 292 ad-injecting extensions. To study their malvertising activities, we need to be able to classify the ad as being malicious, i.e., an ad that leads the user to a malware hosting domain. To this end we use the following process.

Each ad-injecting extension identified by Expector, is automatically installed in a browser and instrumented so that it injects ads. Expector then browses a set of pages and activates a "click" event on all ads (both injected by the extension and those appearing on the page regardless of the extension) that appear during this browsing session and logs the landing pages.

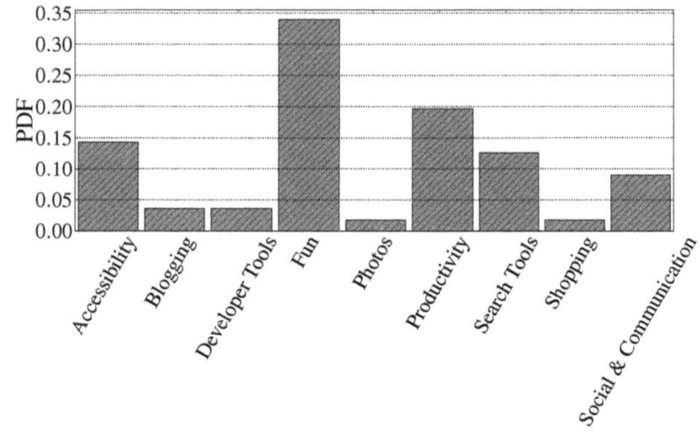

Figure 2: The distribution of ad-injecting Chrome extensions with malvertising practice across different categories.

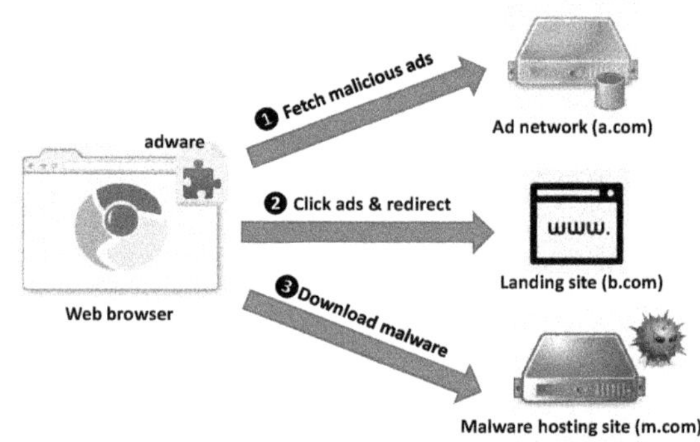

Figure 3: The malvertising flow of an ad-injecting extension, showing a common pattern of three different domains – 1) ad network domain for serving the ad, 2) a landing domain reached after the ad is clicked, and 3) the domain hosting the malware executable.

All of the "safe browsing" APIs that we tested (including Google Safe Browsing API and www.bluecoat.com) failed to detect the majority of ad landing pages in our study, probably because the ad landing URLs are constructed dynamically. As a result, we visit each of the ad landing pages and observe whether it hosts an executable or contains links that enable to download an executable. In such cases, the executable is downloaded and uploaded to an online service (VirusTotal [16]) to check whether it is a malware. Based on the returned results we classify the ad as either malicious or non-malicious.

5.2 Results

We studied malvertising activities by setting the set of pages that Expector visits to the top-1000 Alexa websites. We observed that ad-injecting extensions operate similarly to standard websites and use APIs provided by an ad network for injecting ads. We group together ad-injecting extensions based on the ad networks which they use for fetching ads.

As described above, Expector provides all the ads appearing on each website (separated to organic ads and those injected by the extension), and we classified the ads injected by the ad-injecting extensions based on whether an ad redirects a user to a landing page where malware can be downloaded. As shown in Table 1, we found that 16 out of the 67 (24%) ad network domains deliver malicious

Table 1: Characteristics of ad networks, i.e., domains that serve ads to the ad-injecting extensions in our study.

Ad network domain	Number of extensions	Number of malware hosting domains	Fraction of malvertising	Number of unique ads
toparcadehits.com	1	66	1.0	119
a.kaytri.com	5	50	1.0	137
my-uq.com	8	4	1.0	12
go.webfind.pw	15	1	1.0	3
pchealthcheckup.net	15	3	1.0	3
onlinewebfind.com	14	4	1.0	11
premiumvideoupdates.com	17	2	1.0	12
feeds.webmakerplus.info	8	14	1.0	27
search.buzzdock.com	7	1	1.0	1
simplyfwd.com	5	2	1.0	3
search.privitize.com	2	4	1.0	7
www.freedailydownload.com	1	1	1.0	7
speedtestbeta.com	2	34	1.0	61
adfishmedia.go2cloud.org	1	7	0.640	46
nym1.ib.adnxs.com	17	2	0.153	54
lax1.ib.adnxs.com	2	1	0.490	14

Table 2: The top-5 most popular ad-injecting extension that delivered malicious ads. Notice that the top four hijack all mouse-click events and constantly serve malicious ads.

Ad-injecting extension name	User base	Fraction of malvertising	Malicious activities
HD-Total-Plus	183,470	1.0	Hijacking click events
DownloadTerms	114,851	1.0	Hijacking click events
BetterSurf	97,250	1.0	Hijacking click events
Expresso Smileys and Emoticons	3,392	1.0	Hijacking click events & adding hyperlinks
memeticons2	2,358	0.49	Simple ad injection

ads (i.e., engage in malvertising) – when clicking ads delivered by these ad networks, users are redirected to landing pages that manipulate the users into downloading malicious executables. These 16 ad network domains are used by 56 extensions out of the 292 ad-injecting extensions that we studied (19%). Overall we found 16 unique executables, all of which are labeled as *Trojan*.

Figure 2 plots the distribution of the 56 malvertising extensions across the different extension categories. Interestingly, the majority of these extensions (over 35%) fall under the "Fun" category, perhaps trying to capture many users that might be less tech-savvy and are more likely to be manipulated into installing malware.

For these 16 ad network domains, we note that malicious executables are typically not hosted on the same site as the landing pages of the malicious ads. A common case we observed is depicted in Figure 3 where the ad-injecting extension fetches ads from an ad network (a.com). When a user clicks the ad, she is redirected to a landing page residing on a different domain – a malicious ad landing domain (b.com). Finally, the malware itself is typically hosted on a third domain (m.com). We assume that this is because separating ad landing domains from malware hosting domains makes it more difficult for browser companies, such as Google (via their Safe browsing API), Firefox and Apple from labeling the malicious landing sites as malware site.

Table 1 lists the 16 ad network domains, i.e., the sites that deliver ads to extensions that are used for malvertising. We observe that they are not the popular ad networks, with the exception of `nym1.ib.adnxs.com` and `lax1.ib.adnxs.com` that use AppNexus, a large and very popular ad network [5]. The large ad networks generally prohibit using their network for displaying ads on domains not owned by the publisher, essentially disallowing extensions to inject ads on arbitrary domains [2]. Furthermore, they ban all forms of malvertising [4]. It is thus surprising that AppNexus hosts malvertising. While this might be attributed to AppNexus not being strict enough regarding their advertisers, it might be the result of a compromised legitimate advertiser – clicking the ad redirects to an advertiser's page that might have been compromised by hackers, and they redirected to a malicious page hosting malware [15].

Table 1 also lists the number of domains actually hosting a downloadable malware. As the table shows, some host the malware in many different domains, reaching well over 30. We assume that this is to make it more difficult for browser companies to mark these domains as malicious. Finally, the table also provides the fraction of malicious ads delivered by each domain during `Expector`'s visits to the top-1000 Alexa websites. A key observations is that the extension-inserted ads are mostly malicious for almost all the 16 ad network domains – 13 out of the 16 ad network domains delivered only malicious ads leading users to download malware. This is in clear contrast to the organic ads embedded on webpages, where we did not observe any malicious ad. This is presumably because the top-1000 alexa websites entertain business with large reputable ad networks, which have already deployed effective defense mechanisms against malvertising and serve nearly no malicious ads. In contrast, Chrome extensions employ small – maybe malicious – ad networks, which may collude with malicious advertisers, primarily serve malicious ads and offer extension developers higher rate than those reputable ones.

Table 2 provides details for the top-5 most popular ad-injecting extension we identified as participating in malvertising. The table shows that 4 out of 5 of these extensions engage solely in malvertising, meaning they only serve malicious ads to users. Furthermore their user base is fairly large, with hundreds of thousands of active victim users.

Table 3: The HTTP request patterns originated from ad-injecting extension for each ad network. The table shows the purpose of the request (fetch an ad or report that a user clicked on an ad), the field used to identify the affiliate (extension), and the method used by the ad network to track the user.

Ad network	Request pattern	Request type	Affiliate ID field
txtsrving.info	cdncache1-a.akamaihd.net/loader/...pid=...	fetch ad	pid
	i.txtsrving.info/kwdu?...subid=...	fetch ad	subid
	p.txtsrving.info/click?..subid=...	click	subid
superfish.com	www.superfish.com/ws/findByUrl.action?...userid=...dlsource=...	fetch ad	dlsource
	www.superfish.com/ws/offerURL.action?...userid=...dlsource=...	click	dlsource
imgclck.com	www.imgclck.com/supp0rt/www/delivery/afr.php?...&beacon=...	fetch ad	beacon
xtensionplus.com	xtensionplus.com/display.htm?...&pi=...	fetch ad	pi

Table 4: Relationships between malicious ad network domains and corresponding malware hosting domains.

Ad network domain	Average correlation between ad network domains & identified malware domain lookups	Average correlation between ad network domains & other malware domain lookup	Fraction of overlapping IPs per day
a.kaytri.com	0.870	0.220	0.006
my-uq.com	0.810	0.121	0.009
go.webfind.pw	0.819	0.161	0.470
pchealthcheckup.net	0.840	0.122	0.153
premiumvideoupdates.com	0.925	0.063	0.098
feeds.webmakerplus.info	0.851	0.209	0.153
simplyfwd.com	0.917	0.082	0.326
search.privitize.com	0.848	0.201	0.332
www.freedailydownload.com	0.676	-0.419	0.286

5.3 Summary

During our study, none of the ads originally embedded on the top-1000 Alexa websites were malicious, whereas we found that roughly 4% of extension-injected ads on these websites were malicious. This implies that a user installing an ad-injecting extension is more likely to be exposed to malvertising, even though she only visits highly popular websites.

6. MALVERTISING IN THE WILD

In this section, we continue to explore malvertising activities of ad-injecting extensions. In particular, we are interested in the following questions. (1) For many ad networks shown in Table 1, why are the served ads primarily malicious, whereas a prior study [30] indicates the proportion of malicious ads on an ad network is up to around 40%? (2) We demonstrated that a user could be tricked into clicking malicious ads injected by extensions, visiting the landing pages and eventually downloading malware; however, are there any users actually tricked into downloading malware in the real world? (3) If so, how likely do users click malicious ads injected by extensions and eventually download malware? Using datasets obtained from large real-world networks, we answer these questions in the subsequent sections.

6.1 Dataset

In order to perform the study on malvertising through extensions, we use two datasets provided to us by a large ISP network, a security company, and two universities, all of which monitor their users' network traffic.

HTTP Traffic. We obtained the HTTP traffic log of tens of thousands of users from two university networks and tens of enterprise network during the entire month of May 2014. For each HTTP request, we obtained a source identifier, the destination IP address, and the complete HTTP request header including the user's cookie identifier (if present), requested URL path and referrer.

DNS Traffic. A large ISP provided us the DNS queries performed to the domains we study during the 30 days in May 2014. The DNS traffic log contains A-type DNS records from around 20 million machines located in the US. Each DNS query contains an identifier for the requesting host and the requested domain.

6.2 Analysis of Ad Networks

To tackle the first question described above, we restrict our study to the ad networks shown in Table 1. Then we identify patterns in the URLs that each ad-injecting extension generates by inspecting the source code, and extract the affiliate IDs which are unique IDs used for tracking ad-injecting extensions. Table 3 lists some traffic pattern examples used by ad-injecting extensions, along with the fields we use to identify the affiliate IDs (leading us to the corresponding ad-injecting extension) contained in the HTTP requests.

We used the aforementioned HTTP dataset and observed the HTTP traffic to each ad network. For the ad networks shown in Table 4, we surprisingly found that, all HTTP traffic to these ad network matches the traffic patterns that the corresponding extensions generate. Furthermore, we inspected the referrer fields of the HTTP traffic by visiting the referrer pages. We searched the corresponding ad network domain names in the referer pages and found that none of the referrers contain these ad network domains. These observations imply that the ad network domains that appear in the traffic logs are accessed due to displaying an ad injected by an extension rather than some other method (e.g., email links or organic web ads). In other words, the ad networks in Table 4 only entertain business with advertisers and extension developers rather than website owners (publishers). Presumably, this is the reason why the prior study does not identify ad networks that primarily serve malicious ads. In addition, this serves as an evidence that some ad

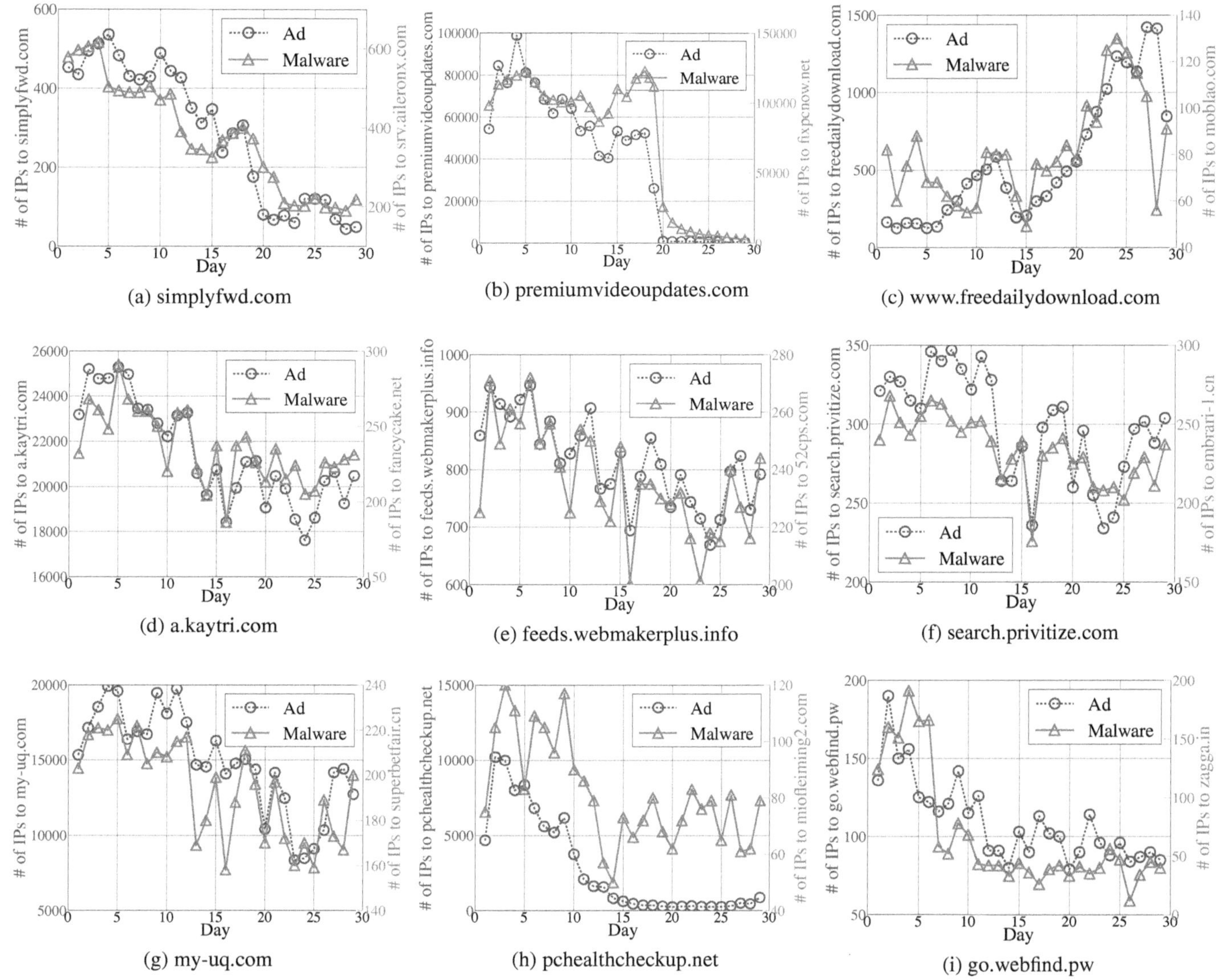

(a) simplyfwd.com (b) premiumvideoupdates.com (c) www.freedailydownload.com

(d) a.kaytri.com (e) feeds.webmakerplus.info (f) search.privitize.com

(g) my-uq.com (h) pchealthcheckup.net (i) go.webfind.pw

Figure 4: Number of unique sources resolving malicious ad network domains ("Ad") and the number of unique sources resolving one of the corresponding malware hosting domains ("Malware"). The plots clearly show visible positive correlation between the two metrics.

networks are malicious and legit websites never have business with them.

6.3 Correlation Between Ad-Injecting Extensions and Malware

We explore the second question by considering our DNS dataset, and looking for correlations between users resolving the ad network domains and those resolving the domains hosting the downloadable malware (meaning, users that actually download the malware, not only clicked an ad and visited the landing domain). We restrict this study to ad networks that we found to be used solely by extensions and participate in malvertising. Table 4 lists the 9 ad networks matching these criteria.

Ideally, we would like to show causality relationship between downloading malware and receiving ads from the extensions. However, to this end one must obtain complete temporal HTTP flows of many users, which we do not have. Instead, we use our DNS dataset and show strong temporal correlation between the users that resolve the ad network domains and the malware hosting domains.

Figure 4 shows the number of unique sources that resolve an ad network domain and one of malware hosting domains a corresponding ad redirects to. Overall, the plots show a clear correlation between the two. Specifically consider the plot corresponding to `premiumvideoupdates.com`, the curves exhibit a similar temporal pattern, but moreover both curves exhibit a sharp decrease in the number sources on the 20th day of the month. This date is actually the date that Google took down a few popular extensions that used `premiumvideoupdates.com` as their ad network domain. While the domain `fixpcnow.net` still existed after the removal of the extensions, the fact that the extension became unusable reduced its visit count to almost zero. Although we cannot claim causality, this example does serve as a strong evidence for causality. Moreover, the inverse causality argument cannot be made, i.e., even if Google marked the domain `fixpcnow.net` as unsafe, bringing its visitors count to zero, this will not have an impact on the ads served by the malicious extension (and thus the number of users resolving its ad serving domain).

(a) Malvertising on cnn.com. (b) Media player updates. (c) Trojan drops.

Figure 5: Extension Plus-HD 1.3 inserts a malicious ad on cnn.com, pop ups media update warning and drops a Trojan on the unwary user machine.

In order to study the correlation beyond a few illustrative examples, we further computed the Pearson correlation values between monthly DNS lookups of each ad network domain and all of its corresponding malware hosting domains. Table 4 shows the average Pearson correlation values for each ad network domain over all its malware hosting domains. The table shows that the average correlation is very high (1 indicates perfect positive correlation and -1 indicates perfect negative correlation).

To strengthen our belief that these correlations can indicate causality, we computed the correlation of DNS resolutions for our ad networks with 44 other malware domains, which are identified as hosting malware by Google safe browsing API, and are not a part of the malware hosting domains that we identified. Table 4 shows that average Pearson correlation values between the ad network domain lookups and these arbitrary malware domain lookup is significantly lower than the correlation with the malware domains we observe through extensions malvertising. This serves as another evidence that the extensions are indeed correlated with the specific malware domains reached through ads injected by the extensions and not to any arbitrary malware hosting domains.

6.4 Malicious Ad Conversion

Finally, we seek to assess the probability that a user of a malvertising extension will download malware. To this end we consider the overlapping source identifiers in our DNS dataset that resolve both an ad network domain and a corresponding malware hosting domain. Recall that the DHCP churn rate of the ISP is extremely low in a daily basis and the majority of the ISP customers that provided this data are home users, it is very likely that the sources that resolve both originate from a single user (host). Overall, the fraction of overlapping source identifiers indicates the infection rate of malware delivered by extensions that use the identified ad network.

Table 4 shows this fraction, ranging from as low as 0.6% to an astonishing 47% (meaning, almost 1 in 2 sources that resolve the ad network domain also resolve a malware domain). In order to better understand the high variance in this fraction we installed the extensions corresponding to each overlap ratio and studied their methods for injecting malicious ads. As expected, we found that the extensions exhibiting low overlap ratios use much more subtle methods that resemble standard online ads, whereas those exhibiting the high overlap ratios use dubious techniques, such as abusing extension privilege to hijack all mouse click events (essentially resulting in a click-through-rate of 100%). The reason that the overlap never reaches 100% is that we measure DNS resolution of the download page, and users oftentimes understand that they are being manipulated and avoid downloading the malware.

For example, Figure 5 shows the consequences of installing a Chrome extension called *Plus-HD 1.3* (now removed from the Chrome extensions store). When the user visits a page, such as `www.cnn.com`, a popup is injected at the bottom of the browser window (not the bottom of the page!). When an unwary user that clicks anywhere on the page (not only on the buttons), a new tab opens up, showing as if a video is ready for watching, but indicates that the user needs to download and install a "Media Downloader". If the user indeed clicks, the malware is downloaded and the user is prompted to execute it. Table 2 provides the details of ad injection behavior for the top popular malicious extensions.

Overall, these overlap ratios indicate that these clearly malicious practices of extension developers actually pay off in the short run, since users that install them cannot really avoid being directed to the download page, and as we show, many of them actually download the malware (hopefully, not all of them install it). In the long run such behavior might not be the best course of action for the attackers because they can easily be detected by many users, reported to the extension store and get quickly disabled and removed from the store.

7. CONCLUSIONS

In this paper, we performed the first in-depth study on malvertising in the context of ad-injecting browser extensions. We showed that the increasing efforts of large ad networks to mitigate malvertising from their networks cause browser extensions to become a new avenue for malicious malvertising activities. We found that users of ad-injecting extensions are more likely to be exposed to the malvertising threat even though they only visit malicious-ad free popular websites. We also found that an ad-injecting extension can significantly facilitate malvertising and make this activity more harmful especially when miscreants abuse the privilege that ad-injecting extensions offer. Though we only observed roughly 20% of ad-injecting extensions that conduct malvertising, other ad-injecting extensions can easily go beyond the grey area because they leave the door open to malpractices. As part of future work we plan on extending `Expector` beyond Chrome, so that it can process extensions of other popular browsers. Furthermore, our study lies on the foundations to the analysis of web apps, which are very similar to extensions for increasingly popular browser-based OSes, such as Chrome OS and FireFox OS.

Acknowledgments

The authors would like to thank the anonymous reviewers and the IBM researcher, Yunhui Zheng, for their help and feedback. This material is based in part upon work supported by the National Science Foundation under Grants No. CNS-1017265, CNS-0831300 and CNS-1149051, by the Office of Naval Research under Grant No. N000140911042, by the Department of Homeland Security under contract No. N66001-12-C-0133, and by the United State Air Force under Contract No. FA8650-10-C-7025. Any opinions, findings, and conclusions or recommendations expressed in this material are those of the authors and do not necessarily reflect the views of the National Science Foundation, the Office of Naval Research, the Department of Homeland Security, or the United States Air Force.

8. REFERENCES

[1] Abusive extension submission. http://extensiondefender.com/submit.php.

[2] Ad placement policies. https://support.google.com/adsense/answer/1346295#Ads_on_the_same_page_or_site_as_another_publisher.

[3] Adware companies are buying up popular chrome add-ons. http://www.omgchrome.com/malware-buying-google-chrome-extensions/.

[4] Anti-malvertising.com. http://www.anti-malvertising.com/.

[5] Appnexus. http://www.appnexus.com/.

[6] Extension defender. http://extensiondefender.com/.

[7] Extshield notifies you if you're running an adware extension. http://lifehacker.com/chrome-protector-notifies-you-if-youre-running-an-adwa-1505371480.

[8] Firefox add-ons. https://addons.mozilla.org/en-US/firefox/.

[9] Get ready, chrome users - you're about to start seeing ads inside of extensions. http://thenextweb.com/google/2012/07/03/get-ready-chrome-users-youre-about-to-start-seeing-ads-inside-of-extensions/.

[10] Google Chrome Web Store. https://chrome.google.com/webstore/.

[11] Node.js. http://nodejs.org/.

[12] Remote Debuggin Protocol, Google Developers. https://developers.google.com/chrome-developer-tools/docs/debugger-protocol.

[13] Saying goodbye to our old friend npapi. http://blog.chromium.org/2013/09/saying-goodbye-to-our-old-friend-npapi.html.

[14] Selenium automates browsers. http://docs.seleniumhq.org/.

[15] Tips for publishers. http://www.anti-malvertising.com/tips-for-publishers.

[16] Virustotal. https://www.virustotal.com/.

[17] Web Technology Surveys. http://w3techs.com/technologies/overview/top_level_domain/all.

[18] B. Edelman and W. Brandi. The ad networks and advertisers that fund ad injectors. http://www.benedelman.org/injectors/, 2013.

[19] B. Edelman and W. Brandi. Information and incentives in online affiliate marketing. In *HBS Working Paper*, 2013.

[20] M. Egele, C. Kruegel, E. Kirda, H. Yin, and D. Song. Dynamic spyware analysis. In *2007 USENIX Annual Technical Conference on Proceedings of the USENIX Annual Technical Conference*, ATC'07, pages 18:1–18:14, Berkeley, CA, USA, 2007. USENIX Association.

[21] S. Ford, M. Cova, C. Kruegel, and G. Vigna. Analyzing and detecting malicious flash advertisements. In *Proceedings of the 2009 Annual Computer Security Applications Conference*, ACSAC '09, pages 363–372, Washington, DC, USA, 2009. IEEE Computer Society.

[22] A. Guha, M. Fredrikson, B. Livshits, and N. Swamy. Verified security for browser extensions. In *Proceedings of the 2011 IEEE Symposium on Security and Privacy*, SP '11, pages 115–130, Washington, DC, USA, 2011. IEEE Computer Society.

[23] A. Kapravelos, C. Grier, N. Chachra, C. Kruegel, G. Vigna, and V. Paxson. Hulk: Eliciting malicious behavior in browser extensions. In *23rd USENIX Security Symposium (USENIX Security 14)*, San Diego, CA, Aug. 2014. USENIX Association.

[24] E. Kirda, C. Kruegel, G. Banks, G. Vigna, and R. A. Kemmerer. Behavior-based spyware detection. In *Proceedings of the 15th Conference on USENIX Security Symposium - Volume 15*, USENIX-SS'06, Berkeley, CA, USA, 2006. USENIX Association.

[25] Z. Li, X. Wang, and J. Y. Choi. Spyshield: Preserving privacy from spy add-ons. In *Proceedings of the 10th International Conference on Recent Advances in Intrusion Detection*, RAID'07, pages 296–316, Berlin, Heidelberg, 2007. Springer-Verlag.

[26] Z. Li, K. Zhang, Y. Xie, F. Yu, and X. Wang. Knowing your enemy: Understanding and detecting malicious web advertising. In *Proceedings of the 2012 ACM Conference on Computer and Communications Security*, CCS '12, pages 674–686, New York, NY, USA, 2012. ACM.

[27] L. Liu, X. Zhang, V. Inc, G. Yan, and S. Chen. Chrome extensions: Threat analysis and countermeasures. In *Proceedings of 19th Network and Distributed System Security Symposium*, NDSS '12, 2012.

[28] N. Provos, P. Mavrommatis, M. A. Rajab, and F. Monrose. All your iframes point to us. In *Proceedings of the 17th Conference on Security Symposium*, SS'08, pages 1–15, Berkeley, CA, USA, 2008. USENIX Association.

[29] M. Ter Louw, J. Lim, and V. Venkatakrishnan. Enhancing web browser security against malware extensions. *Journal in Computer Virology*, 4(3):179–195, 2008.

[30] A. Zarras, A. Kapravelos, G. Stringhini, T. Holz, C. Kruegel, and G. Vigna. The dark alleys of madison avenue: Understanding malicious advertisements. In *Proceedings of Internet Measurement Conference*, IMC '14, Vancouver, BC, Canada, 2014. ACM.

E-commerce Reputation Manipulation: The Emergence of Reputation-Escalation-as-a-Service

Haitao Xu*†, Daiping Liu*, Haining Wang*, Angelos Stavrou‡

*University of Delaware
Newark, DE 19716, USA
{hxu,dpliu,hnw}@udel.edu

†College of William and Mary
Williamsburg, VA 23187, USA
hxu@cs.wm.edu

‡George Mason University
Fairfax, VA 22030, USA
astavrou@gmu.edu

ABSTRACT

In online markets, a store's reputation is closely tied to its profitability. Sellers' desire to quickly achieve high reputation has fueled a profitable underground business, which operates as a specialized crowdsourcing marketplace and accumulates wealth by allowing online sellers to harness human laborers to conduct fake transactions for improving their stores' reputations. We term such an underground market a *seller-reputation-escalation (SRE) market.* In this paper, we investigate the impact of the SRE service on reputation escalation by performing in-depth measurements of the prevalence of the SRE service, the business model and market size of SRE markets, and the characteristics of sellers and offered laborers. To this end, we have infiltrated five SRE markets and studied their operations using daily data collection over a continuous period of two months. We identified more than 11,000 online sellers posting at least 219,165 fake-purchase tasks on the five SRE markets. These transactions earned at least $46,438 in revenue for the five SRE markets, and the total value of merchandise involved exceeded $3,452,530. Our study demonstrates that online sellers using SRE service can increase their stores' reputations at least 10 times faster than legitimate ones while only 2.2% of them were detected and penalized. Even worse, we found a newly launched service that can, within a single day, boost a seller's reputation by such a degree that would require a legitimate seller at least a year to accomplish. Finally, armed with our analysis of the operational characteristics of the underground economy, we offer some insights into potential mitigation strategies.

Categories and Subject Descriptors

K.4.4 [**Electronic Commerce**]: Security; H.3.5 [**Online Information Services**]: Web-based services

Keywords

E-commerce; reputation manipulation; fake transaction

1. INTRODUCTION

Due to its convenience and ubiquitous nature, online shopping has become one of the primary means for purchasing goods. In many cases, due to its global nature, lower cost, and fast delivery, online shopping is the preferred or even the exclusive means of acquiring a product. A large number of online shopping markets including Amazon and eBay have incorporated reputation systems. The primary purpose of these reputation systems is to offer a means for users to give feedback on a product and its seller. Moreover, this process encourages sellers to provide better products because through the scoring process they are rewarded with higher reputation, which in turn can attract more business. For instance, sellers with higher reputations are usually listed at the front by online market search engines, and shoppers are biased towards sellers with higher reputations [34]. Thus, online sellers have strong motivation to improve reputations as quickly as possible.

In the majority of reputation systems, sellers' reputations are dominated by the number of transactions they complete and the number of positive customer ratings (or reviews) they receive. Depending on the size and popularity of a product, it usually takes a long time for a seller to accumulate high reputation. As a result, a non-negligible number of insincere sellers have attempted to subvert the reputation systems using opinion spam and artificial ratings, among others. Several recent works [21,30,31] have aimed to tackle these problems. However, the known reputation manipulation techniques are only the tip of the iceberg of an emerging underground industry that employs sophisticated methods to cater to online sellers who want to quickly boost their online reputations. We refer to such enterprises as *seller-reputation-escalation (SRE) markets.*

SRE markets operate in the crowdsourcing model, where online sellers hire inexpensive human laborers to carry out fake purchase campaigns to accelerate reputation accumulation. By fake purchases, we mean purchases that although they appear legitimate and complete as far as the online system is concerned, no real product or at most an empty package is delivered by a seller. This approach is far more elaborate and much more difficult, if not infeasible, to detect because a buyer appears to have genuinely purchased a product as opposed to just leaving a review or score for the product and its seller. Moreover, multiple individuals that do not know each other are involved in the process.

For insincere sellers, fake purchases can significantly increase their transaction volumes, product ratings, and positive reviews. The boost in reputation attracts legitimate customers and at the same time cements the seller's ability to handle negative reviews. Furthermore, the process is fairly scalable, and the seller may post up to hundreds of such tasks each day, thus quickly improving the store reputation. Therefore, SRE markets are seriously endangering existing reputation systems widely deployed in current e-commerce platforms. Although SRE markets have appeared for several years, we still lack insights into the basic characteristics of this underground enterprise.

WWW 2015, May 18–22, 2015, Florence, Italy.
ACM 978-1-4503-3469-3/15/05.
http://dx.doi.org/10.1145/2736277.2741650.

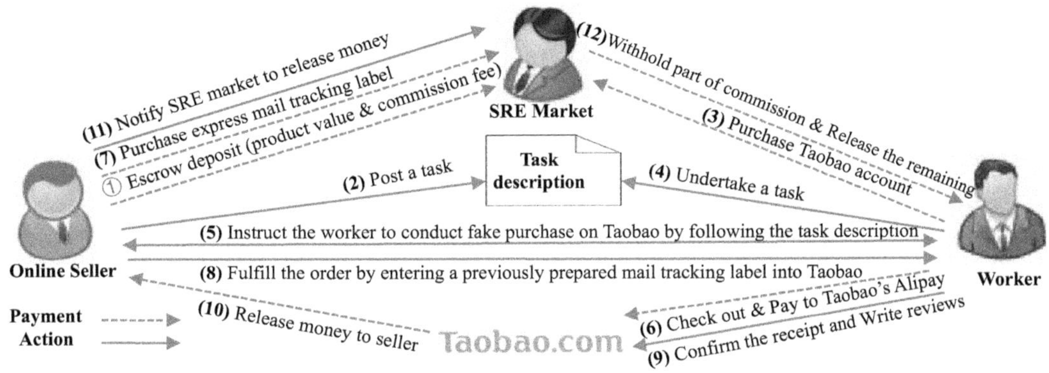

Figure 1: Lifecycle of a fake-purchase task on the SRE market.

In this paper, we present an empirical analysis of the prevalence of the SRE markets by infiltrating five popular SRE markets, which specialize in providing reputation-escalation services to sellers on the Taobao marketplace [1], the largest consumer-to-consumer (C2C) online marketplace in China. We conducted daily crawls of these five markets for two months and collected 219,165 tasks posted by more than 11,000 online sellers[1] and continuously monitored these sellers' activities on these markets. For approximately 4,000 sellers, we were able to identify their IDs on the Taobao marketplace. To validate our findings, we randomly selected a set of 4,000 legitimate Taobao sellers to act as our control group. We evaluate the effect of SRE services on escalating seller reputations by comparing the two groups' growth curves of their store reputations. We characterize the sellers and workers involved, and we estimate the revenue generated and fake-transaction volume handled by these markets. Furthermore, we report a more threatening service recently launched by one SRE market where Taobao sellers can increase their reputation scores significantly within a single day by paying less than $100 to the SRE market operators. Given our insights into the SRE operations, we propose possible intervention approaches from the perspective of defenders.

In summary, our main contributions are threefold:

- To our knowledge, we are the first to analyze in depth the operations of SRE markets and perform the empirical study of them. We estimate that the five SRE markets we infiltrated generated at least $46,438 in revenue and handled at least $3,452,530 in fake-transaction volume during the two months we monitored.
- We investigate the effect of SRE markets on online store reputation escalation. We find that online sellers using SRE services can increase their store reputations 10 times faster than legitimate ones, and only a small portion (2.2%) of them are detected and penalized.
- We discover a newly launched service on one SRE market that can boost a seller's reputation score within one day by such a degree that would require a legitimate seller at least one year to accomplish.

The remainder of the paper is organized as follows. Section 2 provides a brief introduction to Taobao and an overview of the business model of SRE markets. Section 3 describes our data collection. Section 4 presents the results from our infiltration of five SRE markets. Section 5 evaluates the effectiveness of SRE services. Section 6 discusses possible defensive interventions. Section 7 surveys the related work, followed by our conclusions in Section 8.

[1] A Taobao seller earns one reputation score for each completed transaction with good ratings.

2. BACKGROUND

The increasingly thriving e-commerce has drawn forth a large number of online sellers. For instance, eBay, the online marketplace giant, has 25 million sellers globally [2]. SRE markets have emerged to satisfy online sellers' demands for high reputation. We identified five SRE markets which provide SRE services exclusively to online sellers on the Taobao marketplace. In this section, we first briefly introduce the Taobao online marketplace and then provide an overview of how a typical SRE market works.

2.1 Taobao Overview

Taobao, launched by Alibaba Group [3] in 2003, is the largest consumer-to-consumer (C2C) online marketplace in China with more than 8.5 million sellers, over one billion product listings, and around 500 million registered users as of March 2015 [4,5]. Taobao has achieved great success with 60 million daily visitors and 50,000 sales per minute, and is ranked 9th globally by Alexa [6] as of this writing. In 2013, the total gross merchandise traded on Alibaba was more than Amazon and eBay's gross sales combined [7].

To facilitate shopping on Taobao, Alibaba operates Alipay and AliWangWang. Alipay serves as an online payment system which provides escrow services for buyers — holding buyer's payment until the buyer is happy with the goods received. AliWangWang is an embedded instant messaging program, commonly used for Taobao buyers to communicate with sellers prior to the purchase.

The great success of Taobao makes it an ideal host for miscreants such as the operators of SRE markets, which accumulate wealth by providing reputation-escalation services to Taobao sellers. Though not yet reported, the other major online marketplaces such as Amazon may also suffer from fake transactions conducted through SRE markets.

2.2 How a Typical SRE Market Works

SRE markets operate in the crowdsourcing mode and are at the center of the shadowy ecosystem, which connects insincere online sellers who desire for high reputation with people who want to earn extra money. However, unlike other crowdsourcing markets such as Amazon Mechanical Turk (MTurk), these SRE markets only accommodate one kind of task: conducting fake transactions on the specified Taobao stores. According to the terminology of crowdsourcing markets, sellers on SRE markets act as task requesters while people undertaking fake-purchase tasks act as task workers.

Figure 1 shows a typical lifecycle of a fake-purchase task on a SRE market, including five stages: (1) task creation, (2)

Qualification Types
Q1: The worker must have an amount of guaranteed money held by the SRE market.
Q2: The Taobao account used by the worker for taking tasks must be verified and pre-aged.
Q3: The worker's Taobao account must not be used a lot for fake purchases on the SRE market.
Q4: The worker should be proficient, reflected by her score value on the SRE market.
Q5: The worker should be located in the geographic region specified in the task.
Q6: The worker never undertakes prior tasks posted by this seller.

Table 1: Qualification types

task undertaken, (3) conducting fake purchase on Taobao, (4) order fulfillment, and (5) commission realization.

Task Creation. The lifecycle of a fake-purchase task begins with an online seller creating a task on an SRE market. To this end, the seller must first deposit money into the SRE market at the amount equivalent to the sum of the goods' value designated in the task and the commission fee calculated by the SRE market (**Step 1**). Then, the seller creates a task and customizes an associated qualification requirement to limit which workers are qualified to undertake this task (**Step 2**).

Qualification Requirement. The qualification requirement is composed of several qualification types predefined by an SRE market. Table 1 lists the qualification types provided by an SRE market. Each one describes a qualification that a worker must have in order to take on the task and is believed to help the seller reduce the risk of being penalized by Taobao for fake transactions. Qualification Q1 requires a worker to have an amount of money held by the SRE market in case a dishonest worker intentionally complains about the seller to Taobao and requests a refund for her purchase even though she gets rewarded for making the fake purchase. Q2 requires the Taobao buyer account used by the worker for undertaking tasks to be verified and pre-aged[2], which allows the seller to evade simple detection heuristics used by Taobao for suspending freshly minted accounts based on weak signs of misbehavior. Q3 requires the worker's Taobao account to not get involved in too many fake purchases because such accounts are probably being closely monitored by Taobao. Q4 requires the worker to be familiar with the task flow. Q5 highlights the requirement for workers' geographical distribution represented by IP address to make the fake purchase appear more real. Q6 reflects the seller's effort to diversify the workers to avoid triggering any Taobao alarms.

Task Undertaken. In light of the qualification requirements, a professional worker usually has several pre-aged Taobao accounts on hand and takes turns using them to avoid using one account too often. The demand for Taobao accounts has inspired another service provided by SRE markets. Each SRE market serves as an account merchant that stockpiles a multitude of Taobao accounts and can sell them to workers at a whim. The prices for Taobao accounts range from $0.2 to $0.5 each depending on the account's age and purchase history. After purchasing a specific number of Taobao accounts from the SRE market (**Step 3**), the worker chooses a qualified task to work on (**Step 4**).

Conducting Fake Purchase on Taobao. After attaching a Taobao account to the task, the worker first starts chatting with the seller posting the task through a third-party Instant Messaging (IM) program on the SRE site. After further checking the worker's Taobao account against the qualification requirements, the seller instructs the worker to

[2]Pre-aged Taobao account refers to the account that has been created for some time and ever used for real purchases.

Class	Detail
Goods	Type (physical or virtual), Selling price
Commission	Commission fee offered for this task
Browsing behavior	Search first on Taobao by the keywords given, randomly choose three other stores to browse before finally entering the seller's store.
	Like the store and add it to favorites.
	Stay on the page for 5 minutes and scroll down to the bottom before adding to cart.
	Feign chat with the seller via Taobao's built-in IM program AliWangWang.
Payment method	The worker pays either for herself or using the e-Gift card provided by the seller.
Shipping address	Use the shipping address designated by the seller for the order placed.
Confirmation & reviews	Confirm the delivery and leave good ratings and positive reviews after a predefined waiting time.

Table 2: A typical task description

follow the task description and behave like a real buyer on Taobao (**Step 5**). Table 2 enumerates a typical task description. It describes the type of goods to purchase (physical or virtual), its selling price, and the commission fee offered. It also details the required browsing behaviors on Taobao before checking out, the payment method, shipping address, as well as the timing for delivery confirmation and leaving positive reviews.

Order Fulfilment. After finishing all the required actions listed in the task description, the worker gets to the checkout step and provides payment to Taobao's escrow-based system Alipay using either her own form of allowed payment or the e-Gift card provided by the seller (**Step 6**). Then the seller arranges to fulfill the order. For virtual goods such as software and prepaid phone cards, the order is directly fulfilled via the Internet, and the worker is required to confirm the receipt and leave good ratings immediately after checkout. For physical goods such as clothes, the seller never ships out the ordered goods but is required by Taobao to provide a mail tracking label for package tracking. To evade detection, for each task with physical goods, the seller purchases one express mail tracking label from the SRE market at a price of $0.4-0.7, depending on the shipment companies (**Step 7**). SRE markets usually partner with shipment companies to get a stable supply of fresh and unscanned express tracking labels. With the label purchased, the seller inputs the label number into Taobao and hence fulfills the order (**Step 8**). Some sellers may ship an empty package to the designated shipping address while most ship nothing.

Commission Realization. After a predefined wait time elapses, the worker confirms the receipt of the goods on Taobao (**Step 9**). In addition, the worker must rate the seller with a full score and write positive reviews with the contents either specified in the task description or composed by the worker. Then the worker requests Alipay to release money from her Alipay account to the seller's Alipay account (**Step 10**). Subsequently, the seller notifies the SRE market to release the money pre-deposited on the market when posting the task to the worker (**Step 11**). Upon request, the SRE market withholds a portion (typically 20%) of the commission fee offered for the task and then releases the remaining money (the remaining 80% commission fee, along with the reimbursement if the worker paid for the goods with her own money) to the worker (**Step 12**). To this point, the lifecycle of a typical fake-purchase task is completed.

In summary, the worker typically needs a verified and aged Taobao account, invests several minutes and tens of US dollars in purchasing goods, and receives a reward of several dollars after about 3 days; the seller needs to purchase an express mail tracking label if the goods in the task is physical and pays a small commission fee in return for accumulating a transaction and a good rating (review); the SRE market earns money from each task by withholding a part of the

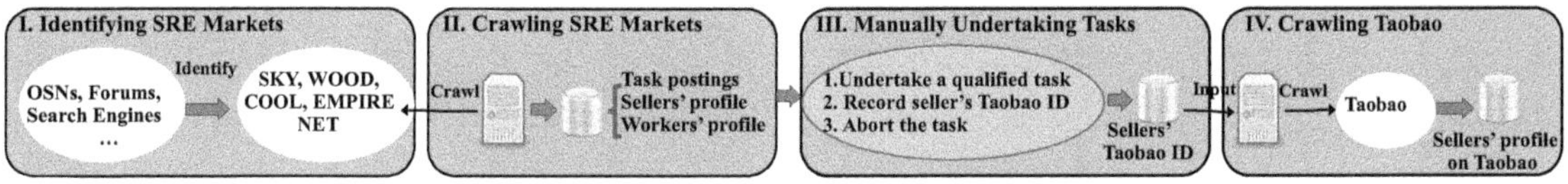

Figure 2: Procedure of data collection.

commission fee, selling mailing labels to sellers and Taobao accounts to workers. In the lifecycle of a task, two escrow-based payment services, Taobao's Alipay and the SRE market's payment system, play a key role in guaranteeing that the worker completes all required actions to earn the commission and that the seller pays a commission fee to the worker for the fake transaction.

3. DATA COLLECTION

In this section, we describe our crawling mechanism and summarize the dataset.

3.1 Crawling Mechanism

Figure 2 briefly illustrates the procedure of our data collection. First, we identified SRE markets (**I**). Then web crawlers were developed to automatically crawl the identified SRE markets for task postings and the profiles of users (i.e., sellers and workers) on the SRE markets (**II**). In order to recognize those sellers' IDs on the Taobao marketplace, we manually undertook tasks for one month (**III**). For those sellers with their Taobao IDs recognized, we then crawled Taobao for their sales and reputation information to evaluate the impact of their misconducts done through the SRE markets upon the Taobao stores (**IV**). Note that steps **I** and **III** are manual operations and the others are fully automated. We detail these steps as follows.

Identifying SRE Markets. SRE markets usually advertise themselves to attract new Taobao sellers and workers through online social networks, public forums, IM group chat, search engines, etc. We investigated these common haunts and identified five SRE markets in total. They are SKY [8], WOOD [9], EMPIRE [10], COOL [11], and NET [12]. All five markets have nearly identical web layout and source code. Whois domain lookup reveals that they have been created for two to four years. We do not claim that our study covers all SRE markets, which is very challenging if not impossible. However, we believe that the five SRE markets we studied represent a reasonable coverage since they are some of the most active and popular SRE markets.

Crawling SRE Markets. In early February 2014, we first registered an account on each market, then performed a few test crawls, and finally developed automated crawlers which exploit the cookies stored locally by SRE markets to bypass their CAPTCHA mechanisms and login prompts. During the two months from February 21, 2014 to April 21, 2014, we conducted a comprehensive crawl of the five chosen SRE markets. Our crawled data includes task postings and the profiles of both sellers and workers on the SRE markets.

In an attempt to record all task postings, we had to crawl the SRE markets continuously 24-hours/7-days because a task may immediately become invisible once undertaken by a worker. A task posting specifies what kind of workers are qualified for the task (see Table 1 for a list of qualification types) and provides a detailed description of the task including the goods involved, its price, commission fee offered, browsing behaviors required, payment method, and many more listed in Table 2. From the collected task postings, we extracted the involved sellers' usernames on a SRE market and further employed the application programming interface (API) provided by the SRE market to crawl once daily for the sellers' profiles on the market. A profile mainly contains the number of tasks ever posted on the market by the seller and when the seller first and last posted tasks. However, the publicly accessible worker-related data is only restricted to a list of the top 10 workers on each market, which is published and daily updated as an excitation mechanism. We crawled once daily for the list of the top 10 workers and further collected their profile information. A worker's profile includes the total number of tasks undertaken, as well as the first and the last time of undertaking a task.

Undertaking Tasks. In order to examine the impact that a seller's posting fake-purchase tasks on a SRE market has upon her online store in the Taobao marketplace, we had to figure out the corresponding Taobao ID of the SRE seller. We soon realized that only undertaking her task postings allows us to record her Taobao ID. Unfortunately, we cannot recognize a seller's associated Taobao ID unless we undertake her tasks *manually*. To undertake a task, a Taobao account is required and we used our own legitimate Taobao account. During the month between February 21, 2014 and March 21, 2014, we conducted numerous attempts to undertake a task and then abort the task immediately after the associated Taobao seller ID is recorded. In this way, we were able to identify more than 4,000 Taobao seller IDs. We failed to identify more seller IDs because either our Taobao account, SRE market account, or geographic IP does not satisfy the qualification requirements of many tasks.

Crawling Taobao. With the identified Taobao seller IDs, we were able to monitor the daily variation in transaction volume and reputation of each of those Taobao stores. To this end, we developed another web crawler and employed the API provided by Taobao to crawl Taobao once daily for those sellers' profile information. A seller's profile on Taobao mainly contains the following information: her seller ID, the major business she runs, the store start date, the current store reputation score, the transaction volume in the recent week (month, semi-year, and year), and customers' rating.

We took a similar recipe as in [18] to make sure our continuous crawl unnoticed by both SRE market operators and Taobao marketplace. Specifically, neither our IP nor accounts on SRE markets were blocked during the period of measurement. Also, we were not contacted by any operator or Taobao to inquire about our browsing activities. So, we believe that our crawled data is valid and not tainted by SRE market operators. With the collected data from SRE markets and Taobao, we were able to examine the SRE market characteristics, evaluate the impact of SRE services upon Taobao stores, and offer insights for designing a robust fake-transaction detection mechanism.

3.2 Data Summary

Table 3 summarizes the dataset collected on the five SRE markets we infiltrated. Specifically, it enumerates the measurement period, the total number of task postings, the number of active sellers, and the number of sellers with Taobao IDs successfully identified. As a result of the two-month collection of the five SRE markets, we collected 219,165 tasks in total, contributed by 11,130 Taobao sellers. Of them, 4,162 sellers' Taobao IDs were identified through our manually undertaking tasks for one month. A comparison of Taobao seller IDs across the five markets shows that 52 of 4,162 sellers posted tasks on more than one SRE markets. Excluding

Market	Period	Task Posts	Active Sellers	Identified Sellers
SKY	02/21-04/21	63,343	2,789	1,332
WOOD	02/21-04/21	54,824	2,968	1,232
EMPIRE	02/21-04/21	48,120	2,016	706
COOL	03/07-04/21*	39,823	2,419	657
NET	02/21-04/21	13,055	938	235
Total	—	219,165	11,130	4,162

Table 3: List of the SRE markets we infiltrated, the months monitored, total task postings, active sellers during the time frame, and Taobao ID identified sellers. *This market went down between 02/21 and 03/06.

the overlapping seller IDs, we identified 4,109 unique Taobao seller IDs altogether.

4. SRE MARKET CHARACTERISTICS

Now we present our measurement results of the five SRE markets. We first examine the popularity of SRE markets. Then we investigate the strategies formulated by SRE markets to circumvent Taobao's detection of fake transactions. Next we characterize two key players on SRE markets: sellers and workers. Finally, we estimate the generated gross revenue and the total fake-transaction volume handled by the five SRE markets during our two-month monitoring.

4.1 SRE Market Popularity

We first attempt to measure how attractive SRE markets are to Taobao sellers, in terms of daily active sellers, daily task postings, and how fast a task is undertaken. By active sellers we mean those sellers who post at least one task on a specific day. Table 4 lists the statistics of these metrics for each of the five SRE markets. All five markets but NET have more than 200 active sellers per day on average, and as many as 517 active sellers can be observed on the COOL market on a single day. In addition, hundreds of new tasks are posted every day on each market, and the average number of new tasks on the SKY market has almost reached 1,000 per day. The peak number of new daily tasks is observed on the COOL market, with 1,843 posts. Moreover, a newly posted task is usually undertaken very quickly. The average time for a new task to be undertaken is less than 300 seconds (5 minutes) on all five markets. It is even faster on the COOL market at less than 2 minutes on average. The minimum time for new tasks to be undertaken is within 2 seconds. All these results indicate that SRE markets serve as popular distributors for fake transactions targeting the Taobao marketplace.

	Daily active sellers		Daily new tasks		Time to undertake (seconds)	
Market	Avg.	Max	Avg.	Max	Avg.	Min
SKY	224	313	951	1481	230	2
WOOD	297	381	816	1132	260	1
EMPIRE	222	310	689	1035	243	1
COOL	233	517	663	1843	95	2
NET	59	102	138	276	288	1

Table 4: Statistics of daily active sellers, daily new tasks, and the time to undertake a task on the five SRE markets.

4.2 Strategies to Evade Taobao Detection

The high popularity of SRE markets among Taobao sellers benefits from those sellers' confidence that they will not be detected or penalized by Taobao for fake transactions, or at least the risk is quite low. Indeed, all five markets provide a set of similar guidelines for sellers to follow when posting tasks in order to circumvent Taobao's detection system. Next we investigate Taobao's detection mechanism and SRE markets' tit-for-tat strategies.

Restriction	SKY	WOOD	EMPIRE	COOL	NET
IVA & Aged	7.48	17.65	21.99	23.22	10.98
Use Frequency	15.26	36.78	38.47	39.97	23.20

Table 5: Fraction (%) of tasks with restrictions on workers' Taobao accounts.

The details about the implementation of Taobao's detection algorithm are not publicly available, but many parameters have been learned from previous penalty from Taobao posed for fake transactions. The detection mechanism is believed to cover all steps in a purchase transaction.

Taobao Buyer Accounts. According to Taobao's report, more than 90% of registered Taobao buyer accounts are ID-verified accounts (IVAs). Non-IVA accounts and newly registered ones would receive special attention. In addition, Taobao buyer accounts with too many purchases within a short time may have been put in some gray lists by Taobao for close monitoring. A Taobao store with a large portion of transactions from non-IVA accounts, newly generated accounts, or accounts in gray lists would become a suspect of fake transactions. Correspondingly, SRE markets have restricted the number of tasks each Taobao buyer account can undertake per day to be less than six. Also, Taobao sellers on SRE markets can enforce extra restrictions on Taobao buyer accounts. Table 5 lists the fraction of tasks with restrictions on Taobao accounts among the total 215,292 tasks we crawled. Note that on the COOL market, 23.22% of tasks require that the workers' Taobao buyer accounts must be IVA and pre-aged, and about 40% have restrictions on the frequency that a worker's Taobao account can be used to undertake tasks.

Geographic Distribution & Shipping Address. Without a diverse pool of IP addresses and shipping addresses, fake transactions could be easily spotted by Taobao's detection system. To avoid detection, workers on SRE markets are required to change IP addresses and clean up browser cookies between two consecutive tasks. In addition, Taobao sellers can also set geographical preferences of the workers or require the workers to fill in the shipping addresses of sellers' choice to make fake transactions appear geographically distributed. Table 6 lists the fractions of tasks with geographic preference and shipping addresses (SA) designated. It shows that a small portion of tasks have restrictions on geographic distribution or shipping address, which is reasonable considering that workers on the crowdsourcing platform have already been very diverse.

Restriction	SKY	WOOD	EMPIRE	COOL	NET
Geographic dist.	0.59	9.89	1.87	3.92	1.44
Designated SA	10.09	19.72	8.03	7.68	12.17

Table 6: Fraction (%) of tasks with geographic preference and shipping address (SA) designated.

Imitating a Real Purchase on Taobao. In addition to buyers' Taobao accounts, IP, and shipping addresses, their browsing behaviors throughout the purchase are also closely monitored. To imitate a real purchase, the majority of tasks on SRE markets require workers to show some of the following actions. (1) *Search to enter*: Search on Taobao for the designated goods with given keywords and locate the seller's store; randomly choose three other stores to browse first and then enter the seller's store. (2) *Browse the store*: Browse several other goods first, then browse the designated goods page; scroll down to the bottom of the page and stay five minutes. (3) *Like the store*: Add the store to favorites. (4) *Start a fake chat:* Talk with the seller via Taobao's built-in IM tool AliWangWang. Finally check out the goods. Table 7 summarizes the fraction of tasks with the required actions. Clearly, a large portion of tasks on SRE markets require workers to show at least one kind of browsing behavior of

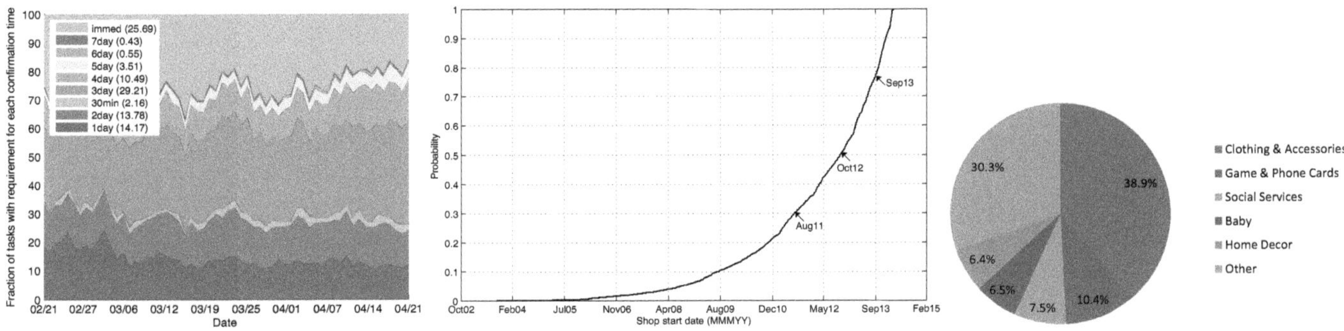

(a) (b) (c)

Figure 3: (a) A breakdown of when to confirm the receipt. Numbers in parentheses in the legend denote the fraction of the total 219,165 tasks crawled on the five SRE markets. (b) CDF of shop start date of the identified Taobao sellers. (c) Top 5 main businesses run by the 4,109 Taobao sellers.

a real buyer. For instance, more than 73% of tasks on all five markets require workers to present at least one of the four actions. And "search to enter" is the most required action. More than 47% of tasks on all five markets require the workers to enter the stores by first searching on Taobao with given keywords. Our results indicate that SRE markets have paid significant attention to evade human behavior based detection. Thus, defenders should not rely on only one kind of human behavior and should combine human behaviors with other features for accurate detection.

Requirement	SKY	WOOD	EMPIRE	COOL	NET
Search to enter	66.80	51.81	53.43	68.34	47.38
Browse the store	17.69	17.11	41.14	28.42	54.31
Like the store	42.41	30.25	27.85	27.23	28.21
Fake chat	33.32	43.65	34.06	41.21	41.48
One or more	79.46	73.99	80.33	81.80	82.61

Table 7: Fraction (%) of tasks with requirements for each kind of browsing behavior before checking out. "One or more" denotes the tasks with at least one required action.

Payment. When checking out, a worker pays for the ordered products with either an e-Gift card provided by the seller or her own debit card. Credit card payment is usually not recommended on SRE markets to prevent insincere workers from disputing a credit card refund after completing the task. Tasks with e-Gift payment are often undertaken quickly due to no need of monetary investment. Table 8 lists the fractions of tasks with the requirements for e-Gift payment and no credit card payment. It is clear that tasks with e-Gift card payment are quite limited, which is reasonable since too many transactions with e-Gift payment on a store may trigger alarm. Also, as expected, tasks with a declaration of no credit card payment are limited, as well. One possible explanation is that credit card payment is not very popular in China, and sellers try to avoid credit card dispute issues. This observation indicates that most workers pay with their debit cards.

Requirement	SKY	WOOD	EMPIRE	COOL	NET
e-Gift payment	0	0.27	6.12	0	0.59
No credit card	4.73	2.32	0	0	0

Table 8: Fraction (%) of tasks with requirements for e-Gift card payment or no credit card payment.

Requirement	SKY	WOOD	EMPIRE	COOL	NET
Empty package	6.87	2.02	0	0	0

Table 9: Fraction (%) of tasks declaring shipment of empty package.

Shipping. Taobao monitors package tracking information as well. For each transaction involving physical goods, a seller needs to submit one package tracking number to Taobao for buyer tracking. To create a fake illusion of shipment, a seller purchases a tracking label from an SRE market and submits the tracking number to Taobao. However, no real product or at most an empty package is delivered by the seller. Table 9 lists the fraction of tasks declaring to ship empty packages. We found that most tasks ship nothing to buyers, which means a fake tracking number is enough to avoid detection. This may be because it is difficult for online marketplaces to verify the shipment of a package since goods are usually delivered using third-party shipping services.

Receipt Confirmation and Writing Positive Reviews. The last step to complete an online purchase is to confirm the receipt and write reviews. For workers on SRE markets, they must give the highest scores and leave positive reviews. The wait time for receipt confirmation is specified in each task and has nine possible values: immediately, 30 minutes, 1 day, 2 days, 3 days, 4 days, 5 days, 6 days, and 7 days. Figure 3a shows a breakdown of wait time of the total 219,165 tasks crawled on the five SRE markets. More than 50% of tasks require workers to confirm the receipt two to four days after placing the order with an attempt to match the typical shipping speed. Slightly more than a quarter of tasks require immediate confirmation of receipt, and a close scrutiny indicates that nearly all of them are tasks with virtual goods, which is reasonable due to no need for shipping.

Requirement	SKY	WOOD	EMPIRE	COOL	NET
Email & phone	1.16	2.42	0.26	1.56	0.02
Confirm on AliW.	11.65	0	0	0	1.97
Guarantee $	19.10	5.13	1.26	23.96	4.21

Table 10: Fraction (%) of tasks requiring leaving email address and phone number, confirmation on AliWangWang, and guarantee money.

Preparation for Appeal to Taobao against Penalization. Although elaborately conducted, a fake purchase may still be detected, and the sellers involved may be penalized by Taobao. However, sellers have the right to appeal against penalties by presenting evidence of real transactions. Although an express tracking label usually serves as strong evidence, to collect more evidence, some sellers require task workers to leave their phone numbers or email addresses in the placed orders. Some workers are also required to confirm the receipt of goods on other channels like AliWangWang. Moreover, to prevent malicious workers from reporting fake transactions to Taobao after getting rewarded, some tasks require workers to have guarantee money held by SRE markets. Table 10 lists the fractions of tasks with each of these requirements. Although only a small portion of tasks have

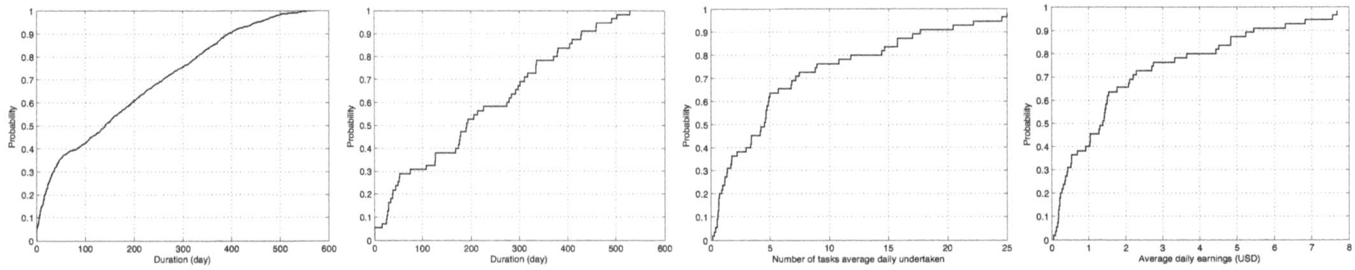

(a) (b) (c) (d)

Figure 4: (a) CDF of active duration of sellers on the COOL market. (b) CDF of active duration of the top workers on the COOL market. (c) CDF of average tasks undertaken daily by the top workers on the COOL market. (d) CDF of average daily earnings of the top workers on the COOL market.

these requirements, they reflect the sophistication of SRE markets against Taobao detection.

SRE markets' strategies have turned out to be quite effective in evading Taobao's detection of fake transactions. Among the 4,109 identified Taobao sellers involved in fake transactions, only 89 (2.2%) sellers were detected and penalized by Taobao, in the form of either having store reputation reduced to zero or having the store forcibly shut down.

4.3 Seller Characteristics

Over the two months of measurement, we observed 11,130 Taobao sellers with at least one task posted on the five SRE markets. By manually undertaking tasks for one month from February 21, 2014 to March 20, 2014, we identified 4,109 unique Taobao seller IDs and subsequently crawled their profiles on Taobao.

Store Start Date. The last day we manually undertook tasks was March 20, 2014. We chose this day as a reference date to calculate the age of those sellers' stores. Figure 3b shows the cumulative distribution function (CDF) of the store's start date for the 4,109 identified sellers. The plot shows that about 70% of those sellers opened their stores after August 2011, within 2.5 years; 50% of stores have an age of no more than 1.5 years; 25% of stores were opened for less than half a year. This indicates that SRE markets are more popular among new sellers since they usually have a stronger desire to improve their stores' reputation.

Main Business. Each Taobao store has one main business. The 4,109 identified stores fall into nine categories based on their main businesses. Figure 3c shows the top 5 main businesses, which account for 69.7% of the 4,109 stores. Specifically, nearly 40% of stores sell clothing and accessories, which conforms to the fact that apparel is the most popular buying category on the Taobao marketplace. About 10% of stores sell game and phone cards.

Active Duration. We crawled the 11,130 sellers' profiles on SRE markets. However, only the COOL market provides the consistent and correct information, while the other SRE markets have shown strange variation in sellers' profiles over time. For instance, the total number of tasks posted by a seller on those markets does not monotonically increase over time but fluctuates irregularly. Thus, we only consider the profile dataset crawled from the COOL market. A seller is considered to be active throughout the period from her first posted task to the last one. The length of this time period is counted as the seller's active duration on the market. Figure 4a shows the CDF of active durations for the 2,419 sellers on the COOL market. About 57% of sellers stay active on the COOL market for more than 100 days, 40% for more than 200 days, and about 2% for more than 500 days. Based on the articles on the COOL market and Whois query results, we conjecture that the COOL market was founded on August 2012. Our results imply that most sellers on the COOL market may post tasks for several months or years, and a small portion have remained active since shortly after the market was formed.

Daily Tasks Posted per Seller. We also investigate how many tasks a seller posts daily. Table 11 lists the average number of tasks posted daily per active seller on the five SRE markets during the two months we crawled. It is obvious that the sellers on the SKY market are the most active, with 4.2 tasks posted daily on average per seller, while the sellers on the NET market are the least active, with an average of 2.2 tasks posted daily per seller.

	SKY	WOOD	EMPIRE	COOL	NET
Avg. task #	4.2	2.7	3.1	2.4	2.2

Table 11: Average number of tasks posted daily per seller on each SRE market.

4.4 Worker Characteristics

The only publicly accessible data about workers on each market is a list of the top 10 workers. In addition, only the COOL market provides consistently reasonable profile information. For instance, all the SRE markets but COOL set the first time of sellers to post tasks to be January 1, 2014. Thus, we use the 55 unique workers appearing in the top 10 worker list on the COOL market for analysis. We examine their active durations, average tasks undertaken daily, and average daily earnings. We compute average daily earnings by multiplying average tasks undertaken daily by 80% of average commission fee per task (because 20% of commission fee is withheld by the market). Figure 4b plots the CDF of the active durations for the 55 workers on the COOL market. The active duration of a worker is the length of the time period during which the worker undertakes tasks. The CDF plot shows that about 70% of workers have been active for more than 100 days, about 30% of workers for more than 300 days, and about 2% for more than 500 days, which demonstrates that the top workers could remain active on the markets for several years. Figure 4c shows the CDF of average tasks undertaken daily by the top workers. About 40% of workers undertake more than 5 tasks daily, about 25% undertake more than 10 tasks daily, and about 10% undertake more than 20 tasks daily. It takes about 5 minutes to undertake a task as revealed by the chat contents on SRE markets. Thus, nearly all workers only spend less than 2 hours in taking tasks on SRE markets, which implies that most workers may take tasks only in their spare time. We do not have statistics about the demographics of workers, but close monitoring of the IM chat groups on each market reveals that most workers are college students, housewives, and freelancers. Figure 4d shows the CDF of average daily earnings of the 55 workers on the COOL market. More than one third can earn more than \$2 daily, and about 5% earn more than \$7 daily. The daily earnings seems quite low, but it is still attractive considering that the completion of a task only costs about 5 minutes, and the per capita daily income for a Chinese person is about $16 according to the World Bank statistics [13].

4.5 Estimating Revenue and Fake-Transaction Volume

We estimate how much revenue these five SRE markets generated and how large of a transaction volume they handled during the two-month period we monitored. The revenue generated by each market consists of the withheld commission fee from task postings on that market and the earnings from express tracking label sales. For each task, SRE markets withhold 20% of the associated commission fee. And for each physical goods, the corresponding seller needs to purchase from the SRE market one express tracking label to complete the transaction. Each express tracking label is charged at a price of $0.4-0.7 depending on the shipment company. SRE markets cooperate with shipment companies to provide tracking labels for sale. We do not know how they split the revenue from each sold tracking label and assume a 50/50 basis. Thus, the revenue generated by a market could be calculated based on the formula: 20% × CPT × (total task number) + 50% × label price × (total physical tasks), where CPT denotes the average commission fee per task, ranging from $0.28 to $0.38 depending on the five markets. In addition, we calculate the fake-transaction volume handled by an SRE market by adding together the goods' value in each task we crawled over the course of two months. This metric reflects the total value of fake transactions conducted through SRE markets during our observation time period.

	SKY	WOOD	EMPIRE	COOL	NET
Revenue($)	11,805	12,369	9,938	9,189	3,137
Trans. Vol.($)	815,130	1,121,700	674,300	714,730	126,670
CPT($)	0.32	0.32	0.28	0.38	0.30
# tasks	63,343	54,824	48,120	39,823	13,055
# phys. tasks	38,753	44,301	36,216	30,811	11,768
Label price($)	0.4	0.4	0.4	0.4	0.4

Table 12: Estimated revenue and transaction volume

Based on the two-month crawled data, Table 12 lists our estimation of the revenue generated and the fake transaction volume handled by each market during the two months, along with the parameters involved in the formula for calculating revenue. We estimate that WOOD generated a revenue of at least $12,369 during the two months. SKY, EMPIRE, and COOL all generated more than $9,000 revenue. The revenue generated by NET is slightly more than $3,000. One main reason for the relatively low revenue of NET is that our crawler missed a large portion of task postings due to the quick cookie expiration. Based on the statistics for the COOL market, we estimate that its annual revenue will be more than $74,000. Note that we did not catch all the task postings on SRE markets, and all five SRE markets simultaneously profit from a variety of other services like selling Taobao accounts and the TRUSTEE service (see Section 5). Therefore, the estimated results likely represent only a lower bound of their overall revenues.

We estimate that the fake transaction volume handled by each market is enormous. For instance, the COOL market handled at least $1,121,700 during the two months, and its estimated annual transaction volume is more than $6,700,000. The operators of SRE markets accumulate such a large amount of wealth in a short time, and they may make off with money that sellers and workers deposit into the markets. Actually, at least two SRE markets have been reported to make off with millions of dollars, and the involved sellers and workers suffered heavy financial losses [14, 15].

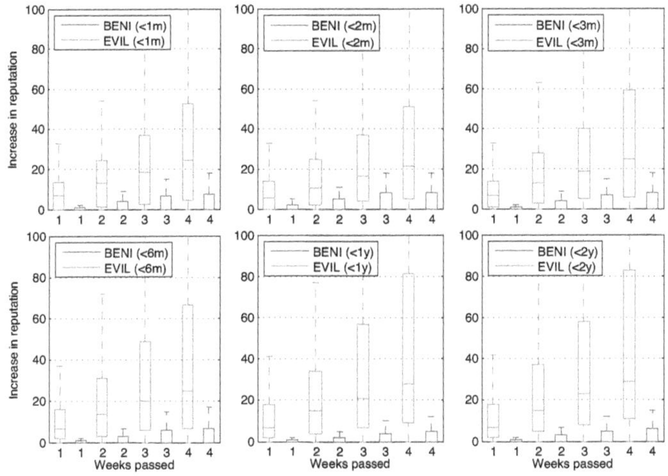

Figure 5: Comparison of the reputation growth distribution between BENI and EVIL stores with varying store ages over the course of one month.

5. EFFECTIVENESS OF SRE SERVICES

In this section, we first evaluate the effectiveness of a typical SRE service for sellers to post tasks on SRE markets. Then, we present a more worrisome service newly launched by one SRE market and evaluate its effectiveness.

5.1 Effect of Posting Tasks on SRE Market

By manually undertaking tasks for one month, we identified 4,109 unique Taobao sellers, denoted as "EVIL" sellers. One interesting question is whether posting tasks on SRE markets could indeed improve sellers' reputations on Taobao. Or, can a seller using SRE services increase her store reputation remarkably faster than a fellow Taobao seller who has the same store age, sells the same categories of goods, but does not use SRE services? To address this question, we randomly selected 4,000 legitimate Taobao sellers who follow the same distribution of store ages and main businesses as those 4,109 SRE sellers. We denote these random sellers as "BENI", standing for benign sellers, which is arguably a fine assumption since the possibility that a randomly selected Taobao seller performs fake transactions on the SRE markets is extremely small considering the order of magnitude of active sellers on Taobao. We compare the two groups' growth curves in their store reputations to evaluate the effectiveness of SRE services.

Set	1	2	3	4	5	6
Store age	<1m	<2m	<3m	<6m	<1y	<2y

Table 13: The store ages based on which we partition EVIL and BENI sellers. "<1m" denotes a store age of less than 1 month while "<1y" denotes less than 1 year.

We argue that only the comparison in reputation growth between the two stores with similar ages and selling the same category of goods makes sense. Thus, for the two groups of sellers, EVIL and BENI, we only consider those selling clothing and accessories (the most popular business run by the Taobao sellers identified for using SRE services, see Figure 3c). We further partition each group into six sets based on store age. Table 13 enumerates the store ages used for partition. We focus on the sellers with store ages not exceeding 2 years because they represent a majority of Taobao sellers on SRE markets (see Figure 3b).

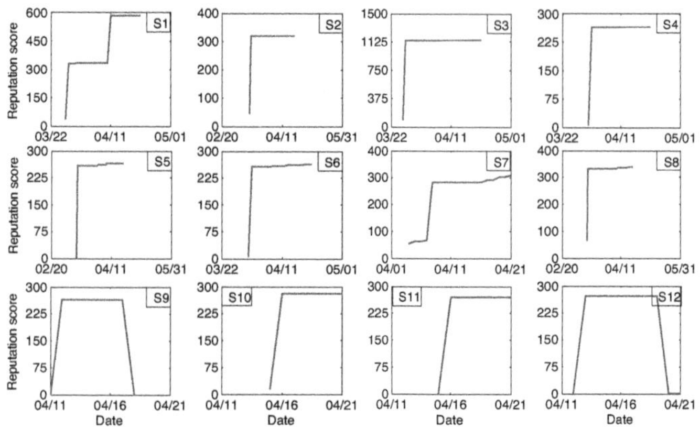

Figure 6: Reputation changes over time for the 12 Taobao sellers identified to use TRUSTEE service.

In Figure 5, we use boxplots to compare the distribution of reputation growth across one month between EVIL stores and BENI stores with varying store ages. Note that for each box, its bottom corresponds to the reputation increase of the Taobao seller on the 25th percentile, its top corresponds to that of the seller on the 75th percentile, and the line across the box corresponds to that of the seller in the median.

These boxplots clearly show that the reputations of EVIL stores increase much faster than those of BENI stores, regardless of the store age and time interval. Within one week, EVIL stores increase their reputation scores by a median value (represented by the median line of each magenta box) of 6 to 8, and by a median value of 22 to 30 within four weeks. The top 25% of EVIL stores (represented by the whiskers on top of magenta boxes) increase their reputation scores by 14 to 18 at least (depending on store ages) within one week, and by 50 to 82 at least within one month. In contrast, the reputation scores of BENI stores with different store ages increase at a much slower rate. The median line of each blue box representing BENI stores overlaps with the x axis, implying that the median increase in reputation scores of BENI stores with different store ages is zero. It indicates that about 50% of BENI stores have not completed any transactions during the entire month. In addition, the top 25% of BENI stores (represented by the whiskers on top of the blue boxes) increase their reputation scores by 1 at least within one week and by 5 to 8 at least within one month, which is merely one-tenth of the reputation increase of the top 25% EVIL stores within one month. For all six kinds of store ages, the reputation increase of EVIL stores within one week (represented by the first magenta box in each subplot) is much larger than that of BENI stores within one month (represented by the last blue box in each subplot).

In summary, Taobao stores can remarkably increase their reputation scores by posting tasks on SRE markets, achieving higher ratings up to 10 times faster than legitimate stores. Actually, the effectiveness of SRE services is directly related to the Taobao's reputation computation method, which could be boiled down to one sentence that a Taobao seller earns one reputation score for each completed transaction with good ratings. And the three main inputs to the Taobao's reputation computation method—transaction volumes, product ratings, and customer reviews—are exactly what an unscrupulous seller gains from fake-purchase activities conducted through SRE markets.

5.2 An Emerging Service and Its Effectiveness

A new service was launched by the EMPIRE market on March 7, 2014. Different from the typical SRE service discussed above, this service does not require sellers to post tasks but demands full control of sellers' Taobao stores during the service time. The market operator does not disclose how this service is implemented but guarantees to increase sellers' reputation scores by up to 10,000 within several days. This service is quite attractive, since a legitimate seller may need several years to achieve the same reputation level, and even an insincere seller must tediously post about 10,000 tasks on SRE markets. We refer to this service as the *TRUSTEE service*.

Desired Grade	Reputation Δ	Fee (USD)	Days
1 diamond	251	96	3
2 diamonds	501	192	5
3 diamonds	1,001	384	7
4 diamonds	2,001	720	9
5 diamonds	5,001	1,200	11
1 crown	10,001	2,080	13

Table 14: TRUSTEE service expense standard: list of desired Taobao grade, corresponding reputation score increase, charged fees, and days needed to complete.

Table 14 presents the expense standard of the TRUSTEE service. The charged fees vary with desired Taobao grades[3]. According to the expense standard, a seller can obtain a diamond grade (i.e., increasing reputation by 251) within 3 days at the cost of \$96 while gaining a crown grade (i.e., increasing reputation by 10,001) requires \$2,080 and 13 days.

We crawled the EMPIRE market once daily for the list of customers who purchased this service from March 9, 2014 to April 21, 2014 and collected 108 Taobao sellers using this service. However, their Taobao IDs are not included in the crawled data and cannot be recognized by manually undertaking tasks, due to no task postings from those sellers. To reveal their Taobao IDs, we leverage one observation that some Taobao sellers use their Taobao IDs as their SRE account names. Thus, we crawled the Taobao marketplace and examined whether a Taobao store whose ID matches an existing SRE account. In this way, we successfully identified the Taobao IDs for 12 sellers. Subsequently, we performed daily crawling of these stores on Taobao to monitor their reputation changes.

Figure 6 shows the dynamics of the reputation scores of these 12 sellers, denoted as S1-S12, during and after their use of the TRUSTEE service. Each subplot depicts one seller's reputation change. In each subplot, a steep increase corresponds to one use of the TRUSTEE service. We make several observations from this figure. First, the use of the TRUSTEE service can significantly increase sellers' store reputations by a desired amount. We observed that each of these 12 sellers increased their reputation scores after receiving the TRUSTEE service by 251 or 1,001, corresponding to one diamond and three diamonds in Table 14, respectively. Second, some sellers may use the TRUSTEE service more than once. For instance, seller S1 used the TRUSTEE service twice within two weeks and requested an increase of 251 each time. Third, each request for the TRUSTEE service can be fulfilled within one day. Note that seller S3 requested an increase of 1,001 in reputation and was also satisfied within one day. Forth, it seems that the TRUSTEE service cannot guarantee a continuous increase in reputation nor an instant increase in sales. For each seller, the curve remains flat in the following 10 to 15 days after using the

[3]Taobao sellers have twenty grades going from one to five hearts, then one to five diamonds, then one to five crowns, and lastly one to five golden crowns. Taobao sellers need a specific number of transactions completed with positive reviews to progress to higher grades.

service. Fifth, only two sellers were observed to be penalized by Taobao. The reputation scores of two sellers S9 and S12 were reduced to zero in 7 to 10 days after their use of the TRUSTEE service. We conjecture that the two sellers were penalized by Taobao for their reputation manipulation. Lastly, four of those 12 Taobao stores using the service were newly opened within the past six months. Especially, two stores began using the service just a few days after their opening. It seems that this service is quite popular among new Taobao stores.

6. POTENTIAL MITIGATION STRATEGIES

Although reputation manipulation is known for a long time in e-commerce, there is no open literature studying this specific SRE problem and we are the first to term the SRE markets and investigate them. Existing attacks against reputation systems include self-promoting, whitewashing, slandering, orchestrated attack, and denial-of-service attack [16]. Compared to those known attacks, the newly emerging SRE problem is much more sophisticated in three aspects: (1) much more organized (in the form of crowdsourcing), (2) much more severe (about tens of thousands of sellers and workers are involved during a short window of two months), and (3) much harder to detect (SRE market operators have formulated elaborate strategies for each step involved in a purchase transaction). In addition, our study shows that only 2.2% of the fraudulent sellers were detected, indicating that the Taobao's existing proprietary fake-transaction detection mechanisms fail in the face of the SRE problem.

Moreover, we believe that most existing detection mechanisms are vulnerable to SRE reputation escalation because the existing detection mechanisms do not consider the factor of shipping. In fact, whether the ordered products are delivered or not is the only difference between fake purchases conducted through SRE markets and real purchases.

We realize that the booming SRE business depends on four components: a highly available website to connect Taobao sellers and workers; express mail tracking labels sold to sellers; Taobao buyer accounts sold to task workers; and an escrow mechanism to resolve disputes between sellers and workers. Accordingly, defenders could develop a set of intervention approaches.

Domain Registrar and Web Hosting. If registrars were to suspend SRE markets' domains and web hosting service providers were to take down SRE market sites, the business of SRE markets would be interrupted immediately. We note that even temporary unavailability of SRE sites causes panic among involved sellers and workers greatly since they worry about their deposits on the SRE markets.

Shipping. Taobao could identify the shipment companies colluding with SRE markets and pressure them to terminate the cooperation. In addition, Taobao could collaborate with shipment companies to identify fake tracking numbers.

Taobao Accounts. To undertake tasks, a professional worker may need tens of Taobao accounts. Taobao accounts on SRE markets serve as the essential tools to conduct fake transactions, which highlights the need for Taobao account abuse detection at registration time.

Escrow Service Provided by SRE Markets. Escrow services used by SRE markets are all based on Alipay, the escrow system provided by Taobao. Actually, each SRE market operator has a publicly visible Alipay account to accept the money from a seller before posting tasks and to release money to task workers after the completion of tasks. Thus, suspending Alipay accounts used by SRE markets would dramatically demonetize the underlying enterprise.

In addition, by targeting SRE markets' evasion strategies revealed in this work, Taobao can further improve its current detection mechanism. A high risk of being penalized for fake transactions would cause Taobao sellers to abandon SRE services. In addition, the especially high popularity of SRE markets with new Taobao stores indicates that some measures should be taken by online marketplaces to help new stores to promote without hurting the fairness to established stores.

7. RELATED WORK

Over the past few years, many researchers have focused their studies on underground markets. Several works studied the underground economy related to Twitter, including markets for selling fraudulent accounts [35,36] and Twitter followers [33]. McCoy et al. examined the role of payment processing in the underground economy [26]. Motoyama et al. studied the social dynamics of underground forums [29] and investigated the market for CAPTCHA-solving services [28]. Franklin et al. [19] measured the commoditization of fraudulent activities on an underground market. Christin [18] performed a similar measurement on Silk Road, an anonymous online marketplace. Caballero et al. [17] and Grier et al. [25] studied the pay-per-install market and exploit-as-a-service model for malware distribution. In [20,27], the authors studied the markets for online pharmaceutical sales. Park et al. [32] leveraged magnetic honeypot ads to study Nigerian scams on Craigslist.

Reputation systems are important to the e-commerce ecosystem. Several works [22–24,31] investigated the online review manipulation, and some others [21,30,34] proposed methods to detect deceptive opinion spam, i.e. fake reviews written to deliberately mislead readers. In this study, we examined a newly emerging underground industry in which a potentially unbounded number of inexpensive human laborers are hired to conduct fake purchases for reputation inflation. This way of tainting the reputation system is more advanced and beyond the attacks known previously.

8. CONCLUSION

We have conducted the first systematic study of a seller-reputation-escalation (SRE) ecosystem by infiltrating five SRE markets. These markets specialize in accommodating online marketplace sellers to post fake-purchase tasks for escalating their business reputations. We performed daily crawls for two months and observed that more than 11,000 online sellers posted nearly 220,000 tasks on the five SRE markets. Each new task could be undertaken within seconds. SRE markets turn out to be quite popular with online sellers. In addition, we examined the tactics formulated by SRE markets for evading the online marketplace defenders' detection mechanism of fake transactions. Those tactics are so sophisticated that only 2.2% of illegitimate online sellers were detected and penalized for fake transaction. Moreover, we characterized the online sellers involved in fake transactions and discovered that most of them run new stores and mainly sell clothing or game cards on the online marketplace. Furthermore, we evaluated the effectiveness of SRE services and revealed that the illegitimate sellers using SRE services can increase their reputations 10 times faster than legitimate ones. In addition, we investigated a newly launched SRE service and found that the service can increase sellers' reputations by up to thousands within one day. We estimated that an SRE market can generate annual revenue of over $70,000 and handle annual fake-transaction volume of over $6,700,000. Finally, we discussed possible intervention approaches and proposed that the joint interventions at the domain, web hosting, shipping, account registration, and payment tiers are probably the most viable defense strategy.

9. REFERENCES

[1] http://en.wikipedia.org/wiki/Taobao.

[2] http://blog.ebay.com/ebay-marketplaces-introduces-new-logo/.

[3] http://en.wikipedia.org/wiki/Alibaba_Group.

[4] http://blogs.wsj.com/chinarealtime/2015/03/03/cat-and-mouse-game-alibaba-exec-on-fake-transactions/

[5] http://www.jamaicaobserver.com/business/Alibaba--China-s-Internet-behemoth_17598819.

[6] http://www.alexa.com/topsites/global.

[7] http://venturebeat.com/2014/03/31/alibaba-plunks-down-692m-to-push-into-offline-retail/.

[8] http://www2.88sxy.com/.

[9] http://www.ntyjy.com/.

[10] http://www.shuazuanshuaxinyu.com/.

[11] http://www.kus.cc/Index.html.

[12] http://www.shuakewang.com/.

[13] http://data.worldbank.org/indicator/NY.GDP.PCAP.CD.

[14] http://bbs.tianya.cn/post-law-438844-1.shtml.

[15] http://weitao.taobao.com/tzh/feed/feed_detail_display.htm?feedId=100505423&wsnsUid=2054965595.

[16] K. Hoffman, D. Zage, and C. Nita-Rotaru. A survey of attack and defense techniques for reputation systems. In *ACM Computing Surveys (CSUR)*, 2009.

[17] J. Caballero, C. Grier, C. Kreibich, and V. Paxson. Measuring pay-per-install: The commoditization of malware distribution. In *Proceedings of the 20th USENIX Security Symposium*, 2011.

[18] N. Christin. Traveling the silk road: A measurement analysis of a large anonymous online marketplace. In *Proceedings of the 22nd International Conference on World Wide Web (WWW)*, 2013.

[19] J. Franklin, V. Paxson, A. Perrig, and S. Savage. An inquiry into the nature and causes of the wealth of internet miscreants. In *Proceedings of the 14th ACM Conference on Computer and Communications Security (CCS)*, 2007.

[20] K. Levchenko, A. Pitsillidis, N. Chachra, B. Enright, M. Felegyhazi, C. Grier, T. Halvorson, C. Kanich, C. Kreibich, H. Liu, D. McCoy, N. Weaver, V. Paxson, G. M. Voelker, and S. Savage. Click trajectories: End-to-end analysis of the spam value chain. In *Proceedings of the 32nd IEEE Symposium on Security and Privacy*, 2011.

[21] J. Li, M. Ott, and C. Cardie. Identifying manipulated offerings on review portals. In *Proceedings of the Conference on Empirical Methods in Natural Language Processing (EMNLP)*, 2013.

[22] D. Mayzlin, Y. Dover, and J. Chevalier. Promotional reviews: An empirical investigation of online review manipulation. in *National Bureau of Economic Research, No. w18340*, 2012.

[23] C. Nosko, and S. Tadelis. The limits of reputation in platform markets: An empirical analysis and field experiment. *Working paper*, 2014

[24] C. Dellarocas, and C.A. Wood. The sound of silence in online feedback: Estimating trading risks in the presence of reporting bias. *Management Science*, 54(3):460-476, 2008

[25] C. Grier, L. Ballard, J. Caballero, N. Chachra, C. J. Dietrich, K. Levchenko, P. Mavrommatis, D. McCoy, A. Nappa, A. Pitsillidis, N. Provos, M. Z. Rafique, M. A. Rajab, C. Rossow, K. Thomas, V. Paxson, S. Savage, and G. M. Voelker. Manufacturing compromise: The emergence of exploit-as-a-service. In *Proceedings of the 19th ACM Conference on Computer and Communications Security (CCS)*, 2012.

[26] D. McCoy, H. Dharmdasani, C. Kreibich, G. M. Voelker, and S. Savage. Priceless: The role of payments in abuse-advertised goods. In *Proceedings of the 19th ACM Conference on Computer and Communications Security (CCS)*, 2012.

[27] D. McCoy, A. Pitsillidis, G. Jordan, N. Weaver, C. Kreibich, B. Krebs, G. M. Voelker, S. Savage, and K. Levchenko. Pharmaleaks: Understanding the business of online pharmaceutical affiliate programs. In *Proceedings of the 21st USENIX Security Symposium*, 2012.

[28] M. Motoyama, K. Levchenko, C. Kanich, D. McCoy, G. M. Voelker, and S. Savage. Re: CAPTCHAS - Understanding CAPTCHA-solving services in an economic context. In *Proceedings of the 19th USENIX Security Symposium*, 2010.

[29] M. Motoyama, D. McCoy, K. Levchenko, S. Savage, and G. M. Voelker. An analysis of underground forums. In *Proceedings of ACM SIGCOMM Conference on Internet Measurement Conference (IMC)*, 2011.

[30] A. Mukherjee, A. Kumar, B. Liu, J. Wang, M. Hsu, M. Castellanos, and R. Ghosh. Spotting opinion spammers using behavioral footprints. In *Proceedings of the 19th ACM SIGKDD International Conference on Knowledge Discovery and Data Mining (KDD)*, 2013.

[31] M. Ott, C. Cardie, and J. Hancock. Estimating the prevalence of deception in online review communities. In *Proceedings of the 21st International Conference on World Wide Web (WWW)*, 2012.

[32] Y. Park, J. Jones, D. McCoy, E. Shi, and M. Jakobsson. Scambaiter: Understanding targeted Nigerian scams on Craigslist. In *Proceedings of the Network and Distributed System Security Symposium (NDSS)*, 2014.

[33] G. Stringhini, G. Wang, M. Egele, C. Kruegel, G. Vigna, H. Zheng, and B. Zhao. Follow the green: Growth and dynamics in Twitter follower markets. In *Proceedings of ACM SIGCOMM Conference on Internet Measurement Conference (IMC)*, 2013.

[34] G. Swamynathan, K. C. Almeroth, and B. Y. Zhao. The design of a reliable reputation system. In *Electronic Commerce Research*, 10.3-4 (2010): 239-270.

[35] K. Thomas, C. Grier, V. Paxson, and D. Song. Suspended accounts in retrospect: An analysis of Twitter spam. In *Proceedings of ACM SIGCOMM Conference on Internet Measurement Conference (IMC)*, 2011.

[36] K. Thomas, D. McCoy, C. Grier, A. Kolcz, and V. Paxson. Trafficking fraudulent accounts: The role of the underground market in Twitter spam and abuse. In *Proceedings of the 22nd USENIX Security Symposium*, 2013.

Effective Techniques for Message Reduction and Load Balancing in Distributed Graph Computation

Da Yan, James Cheng, Yi Lu
Dept. of Computer Science and Engineering
The Chinese University of Hong Kong
{yanda, jcheng, ylu}@cse.cuhk.edu.hk

Wilfred Ng
Dept. of Computer Science and Engineering
The Hong Kong University of Science and Technology
wilfred@cse.ust.hk

ABSTRACT

Massive graphs, such as online social networks and communication networks, have become common today. To efficiently analyze such large graphs, many distributed graph computing systems have been developed. These systems employ the "think like a vertex" programming paradigm, where a program proceeds in iterations and at each iteration, vertices exchange messages with each other. However, using Pregel's simple message passing mechanism, some vertices may send/receive significantly more messages than others due to either the high degree of these vertices or the logic of the algorithm used. This forms the communication bottleneck and leads to imbalanced workload among machines in the cluster. In this paper, we propose two effective message reduction techniques: (1)vertex mirroring with message combining, and (2)an additional request-respond API. These techniques not only reduce the total number of messages exchanged through the network, but also bound the number of messages sent/received by any single vertex. We theoretically analyze the effectiveness of our techniques, and implement them on top of our open-source Pregel implementation called Pregel+. Our experiments on various large real graphs demonstrate that our message reduction techniques significantly improve the performance of distributed graph computation.

Categories and Subject Descriptors

D.4.7 [**Organization and Design**]: Distributed systems

General Terms

Performance

Keywords

Pregel; distributed graph computing; graph analytics

1. INTRODUCTION

With the growing interest in analyzing large real-world graphs such as online social networks, web graphs and semantic web graphs, many distributed graph computing systems [1, 5, 10, 11, 13, 18, 21, 23] have emerged. These systems are deployed in a shared-nothing distributed computing infrastructure usually built on top of a cluster of low-cost commodity PCs. Pioneered by Google's Pregel [13], these systems adopt a vertex-centric computing paradigm, where programmers think naturally like a vertex when designing distributed graph algorithms. A Pregel-like system also takes care of fault recovery and scales to arbitrary cluster size without the need of changing the program code, both of which are indispensable properties for programs running in a cloud environment.

MapReduce [3], and its open-source implementation Hadoop, are also popularly used for large scale graph processing. However, many graph algorithms are intrinsically iterative, such as the computation of PageRank, connected components, and shortest paths. For iterative graph computation, a Pregel program is much more efficient than its MapReduce counterpart [13].

Weaknesses of Pregel. Although Pregel's vertex-centric computing model has been widely adopted in most of the recent distributed graph computing systems [1, 11, 10, 18] (and also inspired the edge-centric model [5]), Pregel's vertex-to-vertex message passing mechanism often causes bottlenecks in communication when processing real-world graphs.

To clarify this point, we first briefly review how Pregel performs message passing. In Pregel, a vertex v can send messages to another vertex u if v knows u's vertex ID. In most cases, v only sends messages to its neighbors whose IDs are available from v's adjacency list. But there also exist Pregel algorithms in which a vertex v may send messages to another vertex that is not a neighbor of v [24, 19]. These algorithms usually adopt pointer jumping (or doubling), a technique that is widely used in designing PRAM algorithms [22], to bound the number of iterations by $O(\log|V|)$, where $|V|$ refers to the number of vertices in the graph.

The problem with Pregel's message passing mechanism is that a small number of vertices, which we call *bottleneck vertices*, may send/receive much more messages than other vertices. A bottleneck vertex not only generates heavy communication, but also significantly increases the workload of the machine in which the vertex resides, causing highly imbalanced workload among different machines. Bottleneck vertices are common when using Pregel to process real-world graphs, mainly due to either (1)high vertex degree or (2)algorithm logic, which we elaborate more as follows.

We first consider the problem caused by high vertex degree. When a high-degree vertex sends messages to all its neighbors, it becomes a bottleneck vertex. Unfortunately, real-world graphs usually have highly skewed degree distribution, with some vertices having very high degrees. For example, in the *Twitter* who-follows-who graph[1], the maximum degree is over 2.99M while the average degree is

[1] http://law.di.unimi.it/webdata/twitter-2010/

WWW 2015, May 18–22, 2015, Florence, Italy.
ACM 978-1-4503-3469-3/15/05.
http://dx.doi.org/10.1145/2736277.2741096.

only 35. Similarly, in the *BTC* dataset used in our experiments, the maximum degree is over 1.6M while the average degree is only 4.69.

We ran *Hash-Min* [17, 24], a distributed algorithm for computing connected components (CCs), on the degree-skewed *BTC* dataset in a cluster with 1 master (Worker 0) and 120 slaves (Workers 1–120), and observed highly imbalanced workload among different workers, which we describe next. Pregel assigns each vertex to a worker by hashing the vertex ID regardless of the degree of the vertex. As a result, each worker holds approximately the same number of vertices, but the total number of neighbors in the adjacency lists (i.e., number of edges) varies greatly among different workers. In the computation of *Hash-Min* on *BTC*, we observed an uneven distribution of edge number among workers, as some workers contain more high-degree vertices than other workers. Since messages are sent along the edges, the uneven distribution of edge number also leads to an uneven distribution of the amount of communication among different workers. In Figure 1, the taller blue bars indicate the total number of messages sent by each worker during the entire computation of *Hash-Min*, where we observe highly uneven communication workload among different workers.

Bottleneck vertices may also be generated by program logic. An example is the *S-V* algorithm proposed in [24, 22] for computing CCs, which we will describe in detail in Section 3.4. In *S-V*, each vertex v maintains a field $D[v]$ which records the vertex that v is to communicate with. The field $D[v]$ may be updated at each iteration as the algorithm proceeds; and when the algorithm terminates, vertices v_i and v_j are in the same CC iff $D[v_i] = D[v_j]$. Thus, during the computation, some vertex u may communicate with many vertices $\{v_1, v_2, \ldots, v_k\}$ in its CC if $u = D[v_i]$, for $1 \leq i \leq k$. In this case, u becomes a bottleneck vertex.

We ran *S-V* on the USA road network in a cluster with 1 master (Worker 0) and 60 slaves (Workers 1–60), and observed highly imbalanced communication workload among different workers. In Figure 2, the taller blue bars indicate the total number of messages sent by each worker during the entire computation of *S-V*, where we can see that the communication workload is very biased (especially at Worker 0). We remark that the imbalanced communication workload is not caused by skewed vertex degree distribution, since the largest vertex degree of the USA road network is merely 9. Rather, it is because of the algorithm logic of *S-V*. Specifically, since the USA road network is connected, in the last round of *S-V*, all vertices v have $D[v]$ equal to Vertex 0, indicating that they all belong to the same CC. Since Vertex 0 is hashed to Worker 0, Worker 0 sends much more messages than the other workers, as can be observed from Figure 2.

In addition to the two problems mentioned above, Pregel's message passing mechanism is also not efficient for processing graphs with (relatively) high average degree due to the high overall communication cost. However, many real-world graphs such as social networks and mobile phone networks have relatively high average degree, as a person is often connected to at least dozens of people.

Our Solution. In this paper, we solve the problems caused by Pregel's message passing mechanism with two effective message reduction techniques. The goals are to *(1)mitigate the problem of imbalanced workload by eliminating bottleneck vertices*, and to *(2)reduce the overall number of messages exchanged through the network*.

The first technique is called **mirroring**, which is designed to eliminate bottleneck vertices caused by high vertex degree. The main idea is to construct mirrors of each high-degree vertex in different machines, so that messages from a high-degree vertex are forwarded to its neighbors by its mirrors in local machines. Let

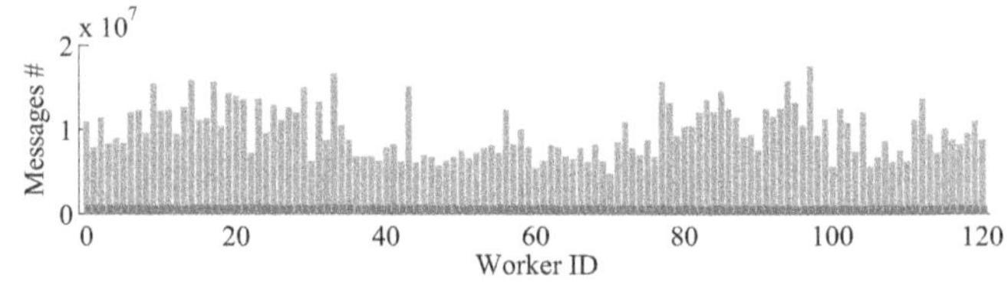

Figure 1: *Hash-Min* on BTC (with/without mirroring)

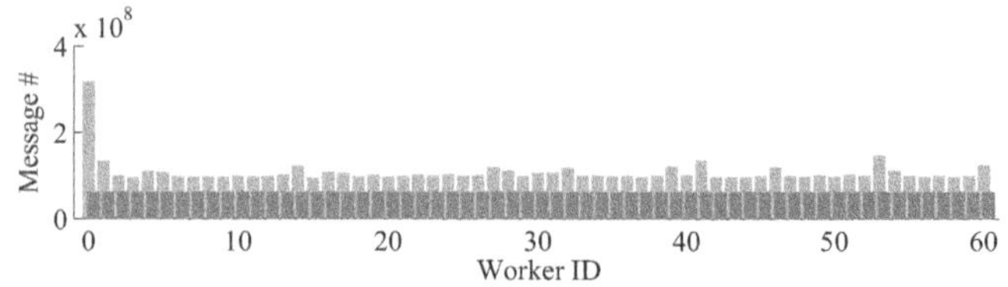

Figure 2: *S-V* on USA (with/without request-respond)

$d(v)$ be the degree of a vertex v and M be the number of machines in the cluster, mirroring bounds the number of messages sent by v each time to $\min\{M, d(v)\}$. If v is a high-degree vertex, $d(v)$ can be up to millions, but M is normally only from tens to a few hundred. We remark that ideas similar to mirroring have been adopted by existing systems [11, 18], but we find that mirroring a vertex does not always reduce the number of messages due to Pregel's use of message combiner [13]. Hence, we provide a theoretical analysis on which vertices should be selected for mirroring in Section 5.

In Figure 1, the short red bars indicate the total number of messages sent by each worker when mirroring is applied to all vertices with degree at least 100. We can clearly see the big difference between the uneven blue bars (without mirroring) and the even-height short red bars (with mirroring). Furthermore, the number of messages is also significantly reduced by mirroring. We remark that the algorithm is still the same and mirroring is completely transparent to users. Mirroring reduces the running time of *Hash-Min* on BTC from 26.97 seconds to 9.55 seconds.

The second technique is a new **request-respond paradigm**. We extend the basic Pregel framework by an additional request-respond functionality. A vertex u may request another vertex v for its attribute $a(v)$, and the requested value will be available in the next iteration. The request-respond programming paradigm simplifies the coding of many Pregel algorithms, as otherwise at least three iterations are required to explicitly code each request and response process. More importantly, the request-respond paradigm effectively eliminates the bottleneck vertices resulted from algorithm logic, by bounding the number of response messages sent by any vertex to M. Consider the *S-V* algorithm mentioned earlier, where a set of k vertices $\{v_1, v_2, \ldots, v_k\}$ with $D[v_i] = u$ require the value of $D[u]$ from u (thus there are k requests and responses). Under the request-respond paradigm, all the requests from a machine to the same target vertex are merged into one request. Therefore, at most $\min\{M, k\}$ requests are needed for the k vertices and at most $\min\{M, k\}$ responses are sent from u. For large real-world graphs, k is often orders of magnitude greater than M.

In Figure 2, the short red bars indicate the total number of messages sent by each worker when the request-respond paradigm is applied. Again, the skewed message passing represented by the blue bars are now replaced by the even-height short red bars. In particular, Vertex 0 now only responds to the requesting workers instead of all the requesting vertices in the last round, and hence the highly imbalanced workload caused by Vertex 0 in Worker 0 is now evened out. The request-respond paradigm reduces the running time of *S-V* on the USA road network from 261.9 seconds to 137.7 seconds.

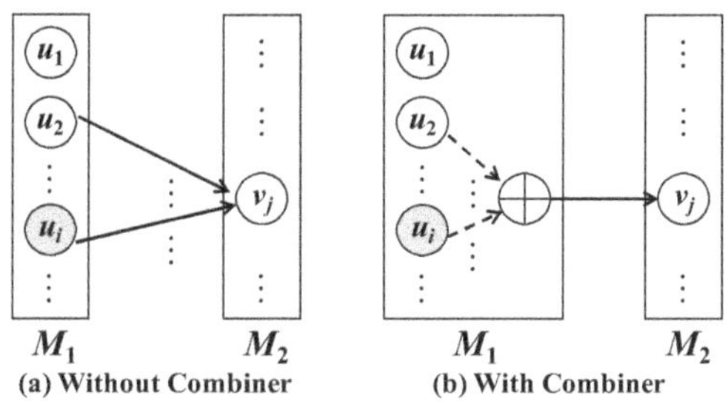

Figure 3: Illustration of combiner

Finally, we remark that our experiments were run in a cluster without any resource contention, and our optimization techniques are expected to improve the overall performance of Pregel algorithms more significantly if they were run in a public data center, where the network bandwidth is lower and reducing communication overhead becomes more important.

The rest of the paper is organized as follows. We review existing parallel graph computing systems, and highlight the differences of our work from theirs, in Section 2. In Section 3, we describe some Pregel algorithms for problems that are common in social network analysis and web analysis. In Section 4, we introduce the basic communication framework. We present the mirroring technique and the request-respond functionality in Sections 5 and 6. Finally, we report the experimental results in Section 7 and conclude the paper in Section 8.

2. BACKGROUND AND RELATED WORK

We first review Pregel's framework, and then discuss other related distributed graph computing systems.

2.1 Pregel

Pregel [13] is designed based on the bulk synchronous parallel (BSP) model. It distributes vertices to different machines in a cluster, where each vertex v is associated with its adjacency list (i.e., the set of v's neighbors). A program in Pregel implements a user-defined *compute*() function and proceeds in iterations (called *supersteps*). In each superstep, the program calls *compute*() for each active vertex. The *compute*() function performs the user-specified task for a vertex v, such as processing v's incoming messages (sent in the previous superstep), sending messages to other vertices (to be received in the next superstep), and making v vote to halt. A halted vertex is reactivated if it receives a message in a subsequent superstep. The program terminates when all vertices vote to halt and there is no pending message for the next superstep.

Pregel numbers the supersteps so that a user may use the current superstep number when implementing the algorithm logic in the *compute*() function. As a result, a Pregel algorithm can perform different operations in different supersteps by branching on the current superstep number.

Message Combiner. Pregel allows users to implement a *combine*() function, which specifies how to combine messages that are sent from a machine M_i to the same vertex v in a machine M_j. These messages are combined into a single message, which is then sent from M_i to v in M_j. However, combiner is applied only when commutative and associative operations are to be applied to the messages. For example, in the PageRank computation, the messages sent to a vertex v are to be summed up to compute v's PageRank value; in this case, we can combine all messages sent from a machine M_i to the same target vertex in a machine M_j into a single message that equals their sum. Figure 3 illustrates the idea of combiner, where the messages sent by vertices in machine M_1 to the same target vertex v_j in machine M_2 are combined into their sum before sending.

Aggregator. Pregel also supports aggregator, which is useful for global communication. Each vertex can provide a value to an aggregator in *compute*() in a superstep. The system aggregates those values and makes the aggregated result available to all vertices in the next superstep.

2.2 Pregel-Like Systems in JAVA

Since Google's Pregel is proprietary, many open-source Pregel counterparts are developed. Most of these systems are implemented in JAVA, e.g., Giraph [1] and GPS [18]. They read the graph data from Hadoop's DFS (HDFS) and write the results to HDFS. However, since object deletion is handled by JAVA's Garbage Collector (GC), if a machine maintains a huge amount of vertex/edge objects in main memory, GC needs to track a lot of objects and the overhead can severely degrade the system performance. To decrease the number of objects being maintained, JAVA-based systems maintain vertices in main memory in their binary representation. For example, Giraph organizes vertices as main memory pages, where each page is simply a byte array object that holds the binary representation of many vertices. As a result, a vertex needs to be deserialized from the page holding it before calling *compute*(); and after *compute*() completes, the updated vertex needs to be serialized back to its page. The serialization cost can be high, especially if the adjacency list is long. To avoid unnecessary serialization cost, a Pregel-like system should be implemented in a language such as C/C++, where programmers (who are system developers, not end users) manage main memory objects themselves. We implemented our Pregel+ system in C/C++.

GPS [18] supports an optimization called large adjacency list partitioning (LALP) to handle high-degree vertices, whose idea is similar to vertex mirroring. However, GPS does not explore the performance tradeoff between vertex mirroring and message combining. Instead, it is claimed in [18] that very small performance difference can be observed whether combiner is used or not, and thus, GPS simply does not perform sender-side message combining. Our experiments in Section 7 show that sender-side message combining significantly reduces the overall running time of Pregel algorithms, and therefore, both vertex mirroring and message combining should be used to achieve better performance. As we shall see in Section 5, vertex mirroring and message combining are two conflicting message reduction techniques, and a theoretical analysis on their performance tradeoff is needed in order to devise a cost model for automatically choosing vertices for mirroring.

2.3 GraphLab and PowerGraph

GraphLab [11] is another parallel graph computing system that follows a design different from Pregel. GraphLab supports asynchronous execution, and adopts a data pulling programming paradigm. Specifically, each vertex actively pulls data from its neighbors, rather than passively receives messages sent/pushed by its neighbors. This feature is somewhat similar to our request-respond paradigm, but in GraphLab, the requests can only be sent to the neighbors. As a result, GraphLab cannot support parallel graph algorithms where a vertex needs to communicate with a non-neighbor. Such algorithms are, however, quite popular in Pregel as they make use of the pointer jumping (or doubling) technique of PRAM algorithms to bound the number of iterations by $O(\log |V|)$. Examples include the *S-V* algorithm for computing CCs [24] and Pregel algorithm for computing minimum spanning forest [19]. These algorithms can benefit significantly from our request-respond technique. Recently, several studies [8, 12] reported that GraphLab's asynchronous execution is generally slower than its synchronous mode (that simulates Pregel's model) due to the high locking/unlocking overhead. Thus, we mainly focus on Pregel's computing model in this paper.

GraphLab also builds mirrors for vertices, which are called ghosts. However, GraphLab creates mirrors for every vertex regardless of its degree, which leads to excessive space consumption. A more recent version of GraphLab, called PowerGraph [5], partitions the graph by edges rather than by vertices. Edge partitioning mitigates the problem of imbalanced workload as the edges of a high-degree vertex are handled by multiple workers. Accordingly, a new edge-centric Gather-Apply-Scatter (GAS) computing model is used instead of the traditional vertex-centric computing model.

3. PREGEL ALGORITHMS

In this section, we describe some Pregel algorithms for problems that are common in social network analysis and web analysis, which will be used for illustrating important concepts and for performance evaluation.

We consider fundamental problems such as (1)computing connected components (or bi-connected components), which is a common preprocessing step for social network analysis [14, 15]; (2)computing minimum spanning tree (or forest), which is useful in mining social relationships [15]; and (3)computing PageRank, which is widely used in ranking web pages [16, 9] and spam detection[7].

For ease of presentation, we first define the graph notations used in the paper. Given an undirect graph $G = (V, E)$, we denote the neighbors of a vertex $v \in V$ by $\Gamma(v)$, and the degree of v by $d(v) = |\Gamma(v)|$; if G is directed, we denote the in-neighbors (out-neighbors) of a vertex v by $\Gamma_{in}(v)$ ($\Gamma_{out}(v)$), and the in-degree (out-degree) of v by $d_{in}(v) = |\Gamma_{in}(v)|$ ($d_{out}(v) = |\Gamma_{out}(v)|$). Each vertex $v \in V$ has a unique integer ID, denoted by $id(v)$. The diameter of G is denoted by δ.

3.1 Attribute Broadcast

We first introduce a Pregel algorithm for *attribute broadcast*. Given a directed graph G, where each vertex v is associated with an attribute $a(v)$ and an adjacency list that contains the set of v's out-neighbors $\Gamma_{out}(v)$, *attribute broadcast* constructs a new adjacency list for each vertex v in G, which is defined as $\widehat{\Gamma}_{out}(v) = \{\langle u, a(u)\rangle | u \in \Gamma_{out}(v)\}$.

Put simply, *attribute broadcast* associates each neighbor u in the adjacency list of a vertex v with u's attribute $a(u)$. *Attribute broadcast* is very useful in distributed graph computation, and it is a frequently performed key operation in many Pregel algorithms. For example, the Pregel algorithm for computing bi-connected components [24] requires to relabel the ID of each vertex u by its preorder number in the spanning tree, denoted by $pre(u)$. *Attribute broadcast* is used in this case, where $a(u)$ refers to $pre(u)$.

The Pregel algorithm for *attribute broadcast* consists of 3 supersteps: in superstep 1, each vertex v sends a message $\langle v\rangle$ to each neighbor $u \in \Gamma_{out}(v)$ to request for $a(u)$; then in superstep 2, each vertex u obtains the requesters v from the incoming messages, and sends the response message $\langle u, a(u)\rangle$ to each requester v; finally in superstep 3, each vertex v collects the incoming messages to construct $\widehat{\Gamma}_{out}(v)$.

3.2 PageRank

Next we present a Pregel algorithm for PageRank computation. Given a directed web graph $G = (V, E)$, where each vertex (page) v links to a list of pages $\Gamma_{out}(v)$, the problem is to compute the PageRank, $pr(v)$, of each vertex $v \in V$.

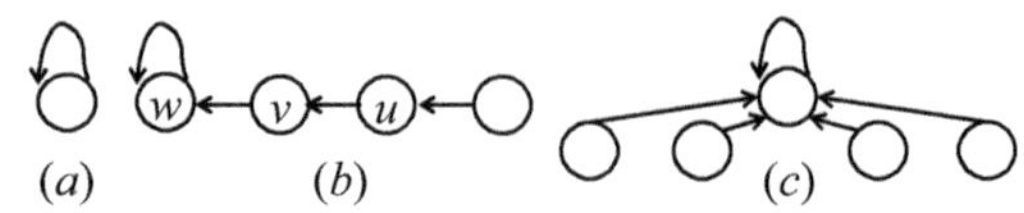

Figure 4: Forest structure of the *S-V* algorithm

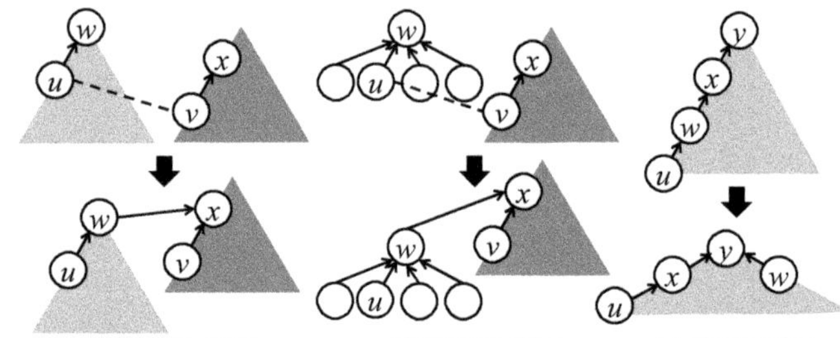

Figure 5: Key operations of the *S-V* algorithm

Pregel's PageRank algorithm [13] works as follows. In superstep 1, each vertex v initializes $pr(v){=}1/|V|$ and distributes the value $\langle pr(v)/d_{out}(v)\rangle$ to each out-neighbor of v. In superstep i ($i{>}1$), each vertex v sums up the received values from its in-neighbors, denoted by sum, and computes $pr(v){=}0.15/|V| + 0.85 \times sum$. It then distributes $\langle pr(v)/d_{out}(v)\rangle$ to each of its out-neighbors.

3.3 Hash-Min

We next present a Pregel algorithm for computing connected components (CCs) in an undirected graph. We adopt the *Hash-Min* algorithm [17, 24]. Given a CC C, let us denote the set of vertices of C by $V(C)$, and define the ID of C to be $id(C) = \min\{id(v) : v \in V(C)\}$. We further define the *color* of a vertex v as $cc(v) = id(C)$, where $v \in V(C)$. *Hash-Min* computes $cc(v)$ for each vertex $v \in V$, and the idea is to broadcast the smallest vertex ID seen so far by each vertex v, denoted by $min(v)$. When the algorithm terminates, $min(v) = cc(v)$ for each vertex $v \in V$.

We now describe the *Hash-Min* algorithm in Pregel framework. In superstep 1, each vertex v sets $min(v)$ to be $id(v)$, broadcasts $min(v)$ to all its neighbors, and votes to halt. In superstep i ($i{>}1$), each vertex v receives messages from its neighbors; let min^* be the smallest ID received, if $min^* < min(v)$, v sets $min(v) = min^*$ and broadcasts min^* to its neighbors. All vertices vote to halt at the end of a superstep. When the process converges, all vertices have voted to halt and for each vertex v, we have $min(v) = cc(v)$.

3.4 The S-V Algorithm

The *Hash-Min* algorithm described in Section 3.3 requires $O(\delta)$ supersteps [24], which can be slow for computing CCs in large-diameter graphs. Another Pregel algorithm proposed in [24] computes CCs in $O(\log|V|)$ supersteps, by adapting Shiloach-Vishkin's (*S-V*) algorithm for the PRAM model [22]. We use this algorithm to demonstrate how algorithm logic generates a bottleneck vertex v even if $d(v)$ is small.

In the *S-V* algorithm, each vertex u maintains a pointer $D[u]$, which is initialized as u, forming a self loop as shown Figure 4(a). During the computation, vertices are organized into a forest such that all vertices in a tree belong to the same CC. The tree definition is relaxed a bit here to allow the tree root w to have a self-loop, i.e., $D[w] = w$ (see Figures 4(b) and 4(c)); while $D[v]$ of any other vertex v in the tree points to v's parent.

The *S-V* algorithm proceeds in rounds, and in each round, the pointers are updated in three steps (illustrated in Figure 5): (1)*tree*

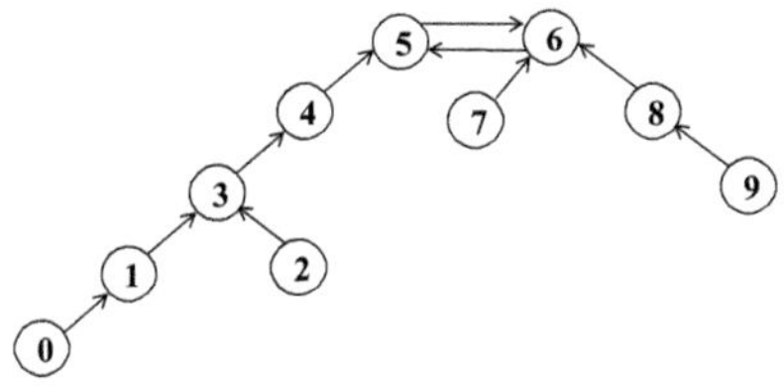

Figure 6: Conjoined Tree

hooking: for each edge (u, v), if u's parent $w = D[u]$ is a tree root, hook w as a child of v's parent $D[v]$, i.e., set $D[D[u]] = D[v]$; (2)*star hooking*: for each edge (u, v), if u is in a star (see Figure 4(c) for an example of star), hook the star to v's tree as in Step (1), i.e., set $D[D[u]] = D[v]$; (3)*shortcutting*: for each vertex v, move vertex v and its descendants closer to the tree root, by hooking v to the parent of v's parent, i.e., setting $D[v] = D[D[v]]$. The above three steps execute in rounds, and the algorithm ends when every vertex is in a star.

Due to the shortcutting operation, the *S-V* algorithm creates flattened trees (e.g., stars) with large fan-out towards the end of the execution. As a result, a vertex w may have many children u (i.e., $D[u] = w$), and each of these children u requests w for the value of $D[w]$. This renders w a bottleneck vertex. In particular, in the last round of the *S-V* algorithm, all vertices v in a CC C have $D[v] = id(C)$, and they all send requests to the vertex $w = id(C)$ for $D[w]$. In the basic Pregel framework, w receives $|V(C)|$ requests and sends $|V(C)|$ responses, which leads to skewed workload when $|V(C)|$ is large.

3.5 Minimum Spanning Forest

The Pregel algorithm proposed by [19] for minimum spanning forest (MSF) computation is another example that shows how algorithm logic can generate bottleneck vertices. This algorithm proceeds in iterations, where each iteration consists of three steps, which we describe below.

In Step (1), each vertex v picks an edge with the minimum weight. The vertices and their picked edges form disjoint subgraphs, each of which is a conjoined-tree: two trees with their roots joined by a cycle. Figure 6 illustrates the concept of a conjoined-tree, where the edges are those picked in Step (1). The vertex with the smaller ID in the cycle of a conjoined-tree is called the supervertex of the tree (e.g., vertex 5 is the supervertex in Figure 6), and the other vertices are called the subvertices.

In Step (2), each vertex finds the supervertex of the conjoined-tree it belongs to, which is accomplished by pointer jumping. Specifically, each vertex v maintains a pointer $D[v]$; suppose that v picks edge (v, u) in Step (1), then the value of $D[v]$ is initialized as u. Each vertex v then sends request to $w = D[v]$ for $D[w]$. Initially, the actual supervertex s (e.g., vertex 5 in Figure 6) and its neighbor s' in the cycle (e.g. vertex 6 in Figure 6) see that they have sent each other messages and detect that they are in the cycle. Vertex s then sets itself as the supervertex (i.e., sets $D[s] = s$) due to $s < s'$, before responding $D[s] = s$ to the requesters (while $D[s'] = s$ remains for s' since $s' > s$). For any other vertex v, it receives response $D[w]$ from $w = D[v]$ and updates $D[v]$ to be $D[w]$. This process is repeated until convergence, upon when $D[v]$ records the supervertex s for all vertices v.

In Step (3), each vertex v sends request to each neighbor $u \in \Gamma(v)$ for its supervertex $D[u]$, and removes edge (v, u) if $D[v] = D[u]$ (i.e., v and u are in the same conjoined-tree); v then sends the remaining edges (to vertices in other conjoined-trees) to the supervertex $D[v]$. After this step, all subvertices are condensed into their supervertex, which constructs an adjacency list of edges to the other supervertices from those edges sent by its subvertices.

We consider an improved version of the above algorithm that applies the Storing-Edges-At-Subvertices (SEAS) optimization of [19]. Specifically, instead of having the supervertex merge and store all cross-tree edges, the SEAS optimization stores the edges of a supervertex in a distributed fashion among all of its subvertices. As a result, if a supervertex s is merged into another supervertex, it has to notify its subvertices of the new supervertex they belong to. This is accomplished by having each vertex v send request to its supervertex $D[v] = s$ for $D[s]$. Since smaller conjoined-trees are merged into larger ones, a supervertex s may have many subvertices v towards the end of the execution, and they all request for $D[s]$ from s, rendering s a bottleneck vertex.

4. BASIC COMMUNICATION FRAMEWORK

When considering on which system we should implement our message reduction techniques, we decided to implement a new *open-source Pregel system in C/C++*, called **Pregel+**, to avoid the pitfalls of a JAVA-based system described in Section 2.2. Other reasons for a new Pregel implementation include: (1)Giraph has been shown to have inferior performance in recent performance evaluation of graph-parallel systems [2, 4, 6, 8, 20]; (2)GPS does not perform sender-side message combining, while our work studies effective message reduction techniques in a system that adheres to Pregel's framework, where message combining is supported; (3)other systems such as GraphLab and PowerGraph are also not suitable as discussed in Section 2.3.

We first introduce the basic communication framework of Pregel+. Our two new message reduction techniques to be introduced in Sections 5 and 6 further extend the basic communication framework.

We use the term "worker" to represent a computing unit, which can be a machine or a thread/process in a machine. For ease of discussion, we assume that each machine runs only one worker but the concepts can be straightforwardly generalized.

In Pregel+, each worker is simply an MPI (Message Passing Interface) process and communications among different processes are implemented using MPI's communication primitives. Each worker maintains a *message channel*, Ch_{msg}, for exchanging the vertex-to-vertex messages. In the *compute*() function, if a vertex sends a message msg to a target vertex v_{tgt}, the message is simply added to Ch_{msg}. Like in Google's Pregel, messages in Ch_{msg} are sent to the target workers in batches before the next superstep begins. Note that if a message msg is sent from worker M_i to vertex v_{tgt} in worker M_j, the ID of the target v_{tgt} should be sent along with msg, so that when M_j receives msg, it knows which vertex msg should be directed to.

The operation of the message channel Ch_{msg} is directly related to the communication cost and hence affects the overall performance of the system. We tested different ways of implementing Ch_{msg}, and the most efficient one is presented in Figure 7. We assume that a worker maintains N vertices, $\{v_1, v_2, \ldots, v_N\}$. The message channel Ch_{msg} associates each vertex v_i with an incoming message buffer I_i. When an incoming message msg_1 directed to vertex v_i arrives, Ch_{msg} looks up a hash table T_{in} for the incoming message buffer I_i using v_i's ID. It then appends msg_1 to the end of I_i. The lookup table T_{in} is static unless graph mutation occurs, in which case updates to T_{in} may be required. Once all incoming messages are processed, *compute*() is called for each active vertex v_i with the messages in I_i as the input.

A worker also maintains M *outgoing message buffers* (where M is the number of workers), one for each worker M_j in the cluster, denoted by O_j. In *compute*(), a vertex v_i may send a message msg_2

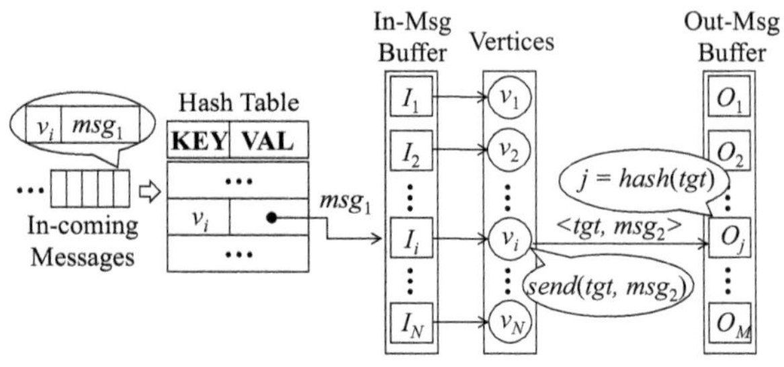

Figure 7: Illustration of Message Channel, Ch_{msg}

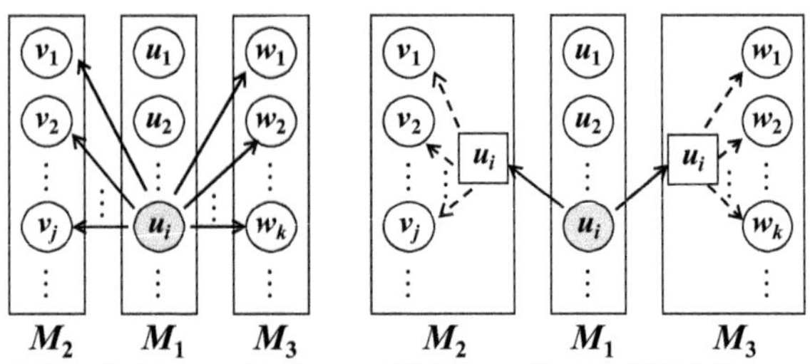

(a) Pregel's Message Passing **(b) Message Passing With Mirrors**

Figure 8: Illustration of Mirroring

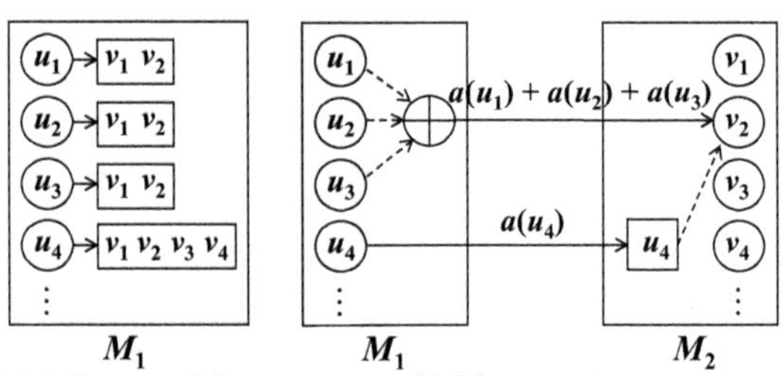

(a) Adjacency Lists **(b) Messages to v_2**

Figure 9: Mirroring v.s. Message Combining

to another vertex with ID tgt. Let $hash(.)$ be the hash function that computes the worker ID of a vertex from its vertex ID, then the target vertex is in worker $M_{hash(tgt)}$. Thus, msg_2 (along with tgt) is appended to the end of the buffer $O_{hash(tgt)}$. Messages in each buffer O_j are sent to worker M_j in batch. If a combiner is used, the messages in a buffer O_j are first grouped (sorted) by target vertex IDs, and messages in each group are combined into one message using the combiner logic before sending.

5. THE MIRRORING TECHNIQUE

The mirroring technique is designed to eliminate bottleneck vertices caused by high vertex degree.

Given a high-degree vertex v, we construct a mirror for v in any worker in which some of v's neighbors reside. When v needs to send a message, e.g., the value of its attribute, $a(v)$, to its neighbors, v sends $a(v)$ to its mirrors. Then, each mirror forwards $a(v)$ to the neighbors of v that reside in the same local worker as the mirror, without any message passing.

Figure 8 illustrates the idea of mirroring. Assume that u_i is a high-degree vertex residing in worker machine M_1, and u_i has neighbors $\{v_1, v_2, \ldots, v_j\}$ residing in machine M_2 and neighbors $\{w_1, w_2, \ldots, w_k\}$ residing in machine M_3. Suppose that u_i needs to send a message $a(u_i)$ to the j neighbors in M_2 and k neighbors in M_3. Figure 8(a) shows how u_i sends $a(u_i)$ to its neighbors in M_2 and M_3 using Pregel's vertex-to-vertex message passing. In total, $(j + k)$ messages are sent, one for each neighbor. To apply mirroring, we construct a mirror for u_i in M_2 and M_3, as shown by the two squares (with label u_i) in Figure 8(b). In this way, as illustrated in Figure 8(b), u_i only needs to send $a(u_i)$ to the two mirrors in M_2 and M_3. Then, each mirror forwards $a(u_i)$ to u_i's neighbors locally in M_2 and M_3 without any network communication. In total, only two messages are sent through the network, which not only tremendously reduces the communication cost, but also eliminates the imbalanced communication load caused by u_i.

We formalize the effectiveness of mirroring for message reduction by the following theorem.

THEOREM 1. *Let $d(v)$ be the degree of a vertex v and M be the number of machines. Suppose that v is to deliver a message $a(v)$ to all its neighbors in one superstep. If mirroring is applied on v, then the total number of messages sent by v in order to deliver $a(v)$ to all its neighbors is bounded by* $\min\{M, d(v)\}$.

PROOF. The proof follows directly from the fact that v only needs to send one message $a(v)$ to each of its mirrors in other machines and there are at most $\min\{M, d(v)\}$ mirrors of v. □

Mirroring Threshold. The mirroring technique is transparent to programmers. But we can allow users to specify a mirroring threshold τ such that mirroring is applied to a vertex v only if $d(v) \geq \tau$ (we will see shortly that τ can be automatically set by a cost model following the result of Theorem 2). If a vertex has degree less than τ, it sends messages through the normal message channel Ch_{msg} as usual. Otherwise, the vertex only sends messages to its mirrors, and we call this message channel as the *mirroring message channel*, or Ch_{mir} in short. In a nutshell, a message is sent either through Ch_{msg} or Ch_{mir}, depending on the degree of the sending vertex.

Figure 9 illustrates the concepts of Ch_{msg} and Ch_{mir}, where we only consider the message passing between two machines M_1 and M_2. The adjacency lists of vertices u_1, u_2, u_3 and u_4 in M_1 are shown in Figure 9(a), and we consider how they send messages to their common neighbor v_2 residing in machine M_2. Assume that $\tau = 3$, then as Figure 9(b) shows, u_1, u_2 and u_3 send their messages, $a(u_1)$, $a(u_2)$ and $a(u_3)$, through Ch_{msg}, while u_4 sends its message $a(u_4)$ through Ch_{mir}.

Mirroring v.s. Message Combining. Now let us assume that the messages are to be applied with commutative and associative operations at the receivers' side, e.g., the message values are to be summed up as in PageRank computation. In this case, a combiner can be applied on the message channel Ch_{msg}. However, the *receiver-centric* message combining is not applicable to the *sender-centric* channel Ch_{mir}. For example, in Figure 9(b), when u_4 in M_1 sends $a(u_4)$ to its mirror in M_2, u_4 does not need to know the receivers (i.e., v_1, v_2, v_3 and v_4); thus, its message to v_2 cannot be combined with those messages from u_1, u_2 and u_3 that are also to be sent to v_2. In fact, u_4 only holds a list of the machines that contain u_4's neighbors, i.e. $\{M_2\}$ in this example, and u_4's neighbors v_1, v_2, v_3 and v_4 that are local to M_2 are connected by u_4's mirror in M_2.

It may appear that u_4's message to its mirror is wasted, because if we combine u_4's message with those messages from u_1, u_2 and u_3, then we do not need to send it through Ch_{mir}. However, we note that a high-degree vertex like u_4 often has many neighbors in another worker machine, e.g., v_1, v_3 and v_4 in addition to v_2 in this example, and the message is not wasted since the message is also forwarded to v_3 and v_4, which are not the neighbors of any other vertex in M_1.

Choice of Mirroring Threshold. The above discussion shows that there are cases where mirroring is useful, but it does not give any formal guideline as to when exactly mirroring should be applied.

To this end, we conduct a theoretical analysis below on the interplay between mirroring and message combining. Our result shows that mirroring is effective even when message combiner is used.

THEOREM 2. *Given a graph $G = (V, E)$ with $n = |V|$ vertices and $m = |E|$ edges, we assume that the vertex set is evenly partitioned among M machines (e.g., by hashing as in Pregel) and each machine holds n/M vertices. We further assume that the neighbors of a vertex in G are randomly chosen among V, and the average degree $deg_{avg} = m/n$ is a constant. Then, mirroring should be applied to a vertex v if v's degree is at least $(M \cdot \exp\{deg_{avg}/M\})$.*

PROOF. Consider a machine M_i that contains a set of n/M vertices, $V_i = \{v_1, v_2, \ldots, v_{n/M}\}$, where each vertex v_j has ℓ_j neighbors for $1 \leq j \leq n/M$. Consider a specific vertex v_j in M_i, and infer how large ℓ_j should be so that applying mirroring on v_j can reduce the overall communication even when a combiner is used.

Consider an application where all vertices send messages to all their neighbors in each superstep, such as in PageRank computation. Further consider vertex $u \in \Gamma_{out}(v_j)$. If another vertex $v_k \in V_i \setminus \{v_j\}$ sends messages through Ch_{msg} and v_k also has u as its neighbor, then v_j's message to u is wasted since it can be combined with v_k's message to u. We assume the worst case where all vertices in $V_i \setminus \{v_j\}$ send messages through Ch_{msg}. Since the neighbors of a vertex in G are randomly chosen among V, we have

$$\Pr\{u \in \Gamma_{out}(v_k)\} = \ell_k/n,$$

and therefore,

$$\begin{aligned}&\Pr\{v_j\text{'s message to } u \text{ is not wasted}\}\\ =& \prod_{v_k \in V_i \setminus \{v_j\}} \Pr\{u \notin \Gamma_{out}(v_k)\} = \prod_{v_k \in V_i \setminus \{v_j\}} \left(1 - \frac{\ell_k}{n}\right).\end{aligned}$$

We regard each ℓ_k as a random variable whose value is chosen independently from a degree distribution (e.g., power-law degree distribution) with expectation $E[\ell_k] = m/n = deg_{avg}$. Then, the expectation of the above equation is given by

$$\begin{aligned}& E\left[\prod_{v_k \in V_i \setminus \{v_j\}} \left(1 - \frac{\ell_k}{n}\right)\right] = \prod_{v_k \in V_i \setminus \{v_j\}} E\left[1 - \frac{\ell_k}{n}\right]\\ =& \prod_{v_k \in V_i \setminus \{v_j\}} \left(1 - \frac{E[\ell_k]}{n}\right) = \prod_{v_k \in V_i \setminus \{v_j\}} \left(1 - \frac{deg_{avg}}{n}\right)\\ \geq& \prod_{v_k \in V_i} \left(1 - \frac{deg_{avg}}{n}\right) = \left(1 - \frac{deg_{avg}}{n}\right)^{n/M}.\end{aligned}$$

For large graphs, we have

$$\begin{aligned}&\Pr\{v_j\text{'s message to } u \text{ is not wasted}\}\\ \approx& \lim_{n \to \infty} \left(1 - \frac{deg_{avg}}{n}\right)^{n/M} = \exp\left\{-\frac{deg_{avg}}{M}\right\},\end{aligned}$$

where the last step is derived from $\lim_{n\to\infty}(1 - 1/n)^n = e^{-1}$.

According to the above discussion, the expected number of v_j's neighbors that are not the neighbors of any other vertex(es) in M_i is equal to $\ell_j \cdot \exp\{-deg_{avg}/M\}$. In other words, if mirroring is not used, v_j needs to send at least $\ell_j \cdot \exp\{-deg_{avg}/M\}$ messages that are not wasted. On the other hand, if mirroring is used, v_j sends at most M messages, one to each mirror. Therefore, mirroring reduces the number of messages if $\ell_j \cdot \exp\{-deg_{avg}/M\} \geq M$, or equivalently, $\ell_j \geq M \cdot \exp\{deg_{avg}/M\}$. To conclude, choosing $\tau = M \cdot \exp\{deg_{avg}/M\}$ as the degree threshold reduces the communication cost. □

Theorem 2 states that the choice of τ depends on the number of workers, M, and the average vertex degree, deg_{avg}. A cluster usually involves tens to hundreds of workers, while the average degree deg_{avg} of a large real world graph is mostly below 50. Consider the scenario where $M = 100$ and $deg_{avg} \leq 50$, then $\tau \leq 100e^{0.5}$=165. This shows that mirroring is effective even for vertices whose degree is not very high. We remark that Theorem 2 makes some simplified assumption (e.g., G being a random graph) for ease of analysis, which may not be accurate for a real graph. However, our experiments in Section 7.1 show that Theorem 2 is effective on real graphs.

Mirror Construction. Pregel+ constructs mirrors for all vertices v with $\Gamma_{out}(v) \geq \tau$ after the input graph is loaded and before the iterative computation, although mirror construction can also be pre-computed offline like GraphLab's ghost construction. Specifically, the neighbors in v's adjacency list Γ_{out} is grouped by the workers in which they reside. Each group is defined as $N_i = \{u \in \Gamma_{out}(v) \mid hash(u) = M_i\}$. Then, for each group N_i, v sends $\langle v; N_i \rangle$ to worker M_i, and M_i constructs a mirror of v with the adjacency list N_i locally in M_i. Each vertex $v_j \in N_i$ also stores the address of v_j's incoming message buffer I_j so that messages can be directly forwarded to v_j by v's mirror in M_i.

During graph computation, a vertex v sends message $\langle v, a(v) \rangle$ to its mirror in worker M_i. On receiving the message, M_i looks up v's mirror from a hash table using v's ID (similar to T_{in} described in Section 4). The message value $a(v)$ is then forwarded to the incoming message buffers of v's neighbors locally in M_i.

Handling Edge Fields. There are some minor changes to Pregel's programming interface for applying mirroring. In Pregel's interface, a vertex calls *send_msg*(tgt, msg) to send an arbitrary message msg to a target vertex tgt. With mirroring, a vertex v sends a message containing the value of its attribute $a(v)$ to all its neighbors by calling *broadcast*$(a(v))$ instead of calling *send_msg*$(u, a(v))$ for each neighbor $u \in \Gamma_{out}(v)$.

Consider the algorithms described in Section 3. For PageRank, a vertex v simply calls *broadcast*$(pr(v)/|\Gamma_{out}(v)|)$; while for *Hash-Min*, v calls *broadcast*$(min(v))$.

However, there are applications where the message value is not only decided by the sender vertex v's state, but also by the edge that the message is sent along. For example, in Pregel's algorithm for single-source shortest path (SSSP) computation [13], a vertex sends $(d(v) + \ell(v, u))$ to each neighbor $u \in \Gamma_{out}(v)$, where $d(v)$ is an attribute of v estimating the distance from the source, and $\ell(v, u)$ is an attribute of its out-edge (v, u) indicating the edge length.

To support applications like SSSP, Pregel+ requires that each edge object supports a function *relay*(msg), which specifies how to update the value of msg before msg is added to the incoming message buffer I_i of the target vertex v_i. If msg is sent through Ch_{msg}, *relay*(msg) is called on the sender-side before sending. If msg is sent through Ch_{mir}, *relay*(msg) is called on the receiver-side when the mirror forwards msg to each local neighbor (as the edge field is maintained by the mirror). For example, in Figure 9, *relay*(msg) is called when msg is passed along a dashed arrow.

By default, *relay*(msg) does not change the value of msg. To support SSSP, a vertex v calls *broadcast*$(d(v))$ in *compute*(), and meanwhile, the function *relay*(msg) is overloaded to add the edge length $\ell(v, u)$ to msg, which updates the value of msg to the required value $(d(v) + \ell(v, u))$.

Summary of Contributions. GPS does not use message combining, and therefore, its LALP technique are not as effective as our mirroring technique that is reinforced with message combiner. GraphLab's ghost vertex technique creates mirrors for all vertices regardless of the vertex degree, and thus it is also not as effective as our mirroring technique. As far as we know, this is the first work that considers the integration of vertex mirroring and message combining in Pregel's computing model. In addition, we also identified the tradeoff between vertex mirroring and message combining in message reduction, and provided a cost model to automatically select vertices for mirroring so as to minimize the number of messages. As we shall see in our experiments in Section 7.1, the mirroring threshold computed by our cost model in Theorem 2 achieves near-optimal performance. In addition, we also cope with the case where the message value depends on the edge field, which is not supported by GPS's LALP technique.

6. THE REQUEST-RESPOND PARADIGM

In Sections 1, 3.4 and 3.5, we have shown that bottleneck vertices can be generated by algorithm logic even if the input graph has no high-degree vertices. For handling such bottleneck vertices, the mirroring technique of Section 5 is not effective. To this end, we design our second message reduction technique, which extends the basic Pregel framework with a new *request-respond* functionality.

We illustrate the concept using the algorithms described in Section 3. Using the request-respond API, *attribute broadcast* in Section 3.1 is straightforward to implement: in superstep 1, each vertex v sends requests to each neighbor $u \in \Gamma_{out}(v)$ for $a(u)$; in superstep 2, the vertex v simply obtains $a(u)$ responded by each neighbor u, and constructs $\widehat{\Gamma}_{out}(v)$. Similarly, for the *S-V* algorithm in Section 3.4, when a vertex v needs to obtain $D[w]$ from vertex $w = D[v]$, it simply sends a request to w so that $D[w]$ can be used in the next superstep; for the MSF algorithm in Section 3.5, a vertex v simply sends a request to its supervertex $D[v] = s$ so that $D[s]$ can be used to update $D[v]$ in the next superstep.

Request-Respond Message Channel. We now explain in detail how Pregel+ supports the request-respond API. The request-respond paradigm supports all the functionality of Pregel. In addition, it supplements the vertex-to-vertex message channel Ch_{msg} with a *request-respond message channel*, denoted by Ch_{req}.

Figure 10 illustrates how requests and responses are exchanged between two machines M_i and M_j through Ch_{req}. Specifically, each machine maintains M request sets, where M is the number of machines, and each request set $S_{\text{to } k}$ stores the requests to vertices in machine M_k. In a superstep, a vertex v in machine M_j may call *request*(u) in its *compute*() function to send request to vertex u for its attribute value $a(u)$ (which will be used in the next superstep). Let $hash(u) = i$, then the requested vertex u is in machine M_i, and hence u is added to the request set $S_{\text{to } i}$ of M_j. Although many vertices in M_j may send request to u, only one request to u will be sent from M_j to M_i since $S_{\text{to } i}$ is a (hash) set that eliminates redundant elements.

After *compute*() is called for all active vertices, the vertex-to-vertex messages are first exchanged through Ch_{msg}. Then, each machine sends each request set $S_{\text{to } k}$ to machine M_k. After the requests are exchanged, each machine receives M request sets, where set $S_{\text{from } k}$ stores the requests sent from machine M_k. In the example shown in Figure 10, u is contained in the set $S_{\text{from}j}$ in machine M_i, since vertex v in machine M_j sent request to u.

Then, a response set $R_{\text{to}k}$ is constructed for each request set $S_{\text{from } k}$ received, which is to be sent back to machine M_k. In our example, the requested vertex, $u \in S_{\text{from}j}$, calls a user-specified function *respond*() to return its specified attribute $a(u)$, and adds the entry $\langle u, a(u) \rangle$ to the response set $R_{\text{to}j}$.

Once the response sets are exchanged, each machine constructs a hash table from the received entries. In the example shown in Figure 10, the entry $\langle u, a(u) \rangle$ is received by machine M_j since it is in the response set $R_{\text{to}j}$ in machine M_i. The hash table is available for the next superstep, where vertices can access their requested value in their *compute*() function. In our example, vertex v in machine M_j may call *get_resp*(u) in the next superstep, which looks up u's attribute $a(u)$ from the hash table.

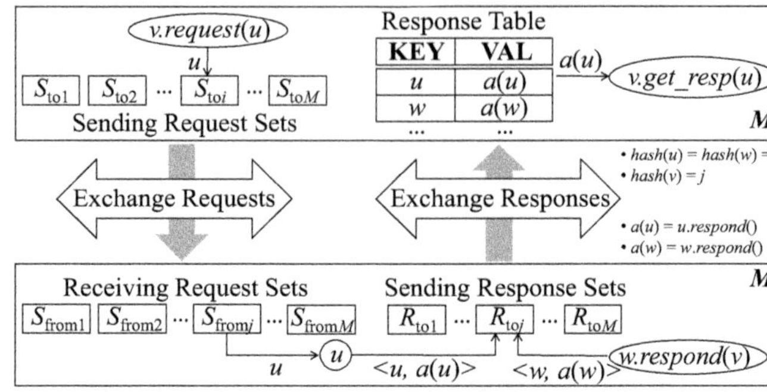

Figure 10: Illustration of request-respond paradigm

The following theorem shows the effectiveness of the request-respond paradigm for message reduction.

THEOREM 3. *Let* $\{v_1, v_2, \ldots, v_\ell\}$ *be the set of requesters that request the attribute* $a(u)$ *from a vertex* u. *Then, the request-respond paradigm reduces the total number of messages from* 2ℓ *in Pregel's vertex-to-vertex message passing framework to* $2\min(M, \ell)$, *where* M *is the number of machines.*

PROOF. The proof follows directly from the fact that each machine sends at most 1 request to u even though there may be more than 1 requester in that machine, and that at most 1 respond from u is sent to each machine that makes a request to u, and that there are at most $\min(M, \ell)$ machines that contain a requester. □

In the worst case, the request-respond paradigm uses the same number of messages as Pregel's vertex-to-vertex message passing. But in practice, many Pregel algorithms (e.g., those described in Sections 3.4 and 3.5) have bottleneck vertices with a large number of requesters, leading to imbalanced workload and long elapsed running time. In such cases, our request-respond paradigm effectively bounds the number of messages to the number of machines containing the requesters and eliminates the imbalanced workload.

Explicit Responding. In the above discussion, a vertex v simply calls *request*(u) in one superstep, and it can then call *get_resp*(u) in the next superstep to get $a(u)$. All the operations including request exchange, response set construction, response exchange, and response table construction are performed by Pregel+ automatically and are thus transparent to users. We name the above process as *implicit responding*, where a responder does not know the requester until a request is received.

When a responder w knows its requesters v, w can explicitly call *respond*(v) in *compute*(), which adds $\langle w, w.\textit{respond}() \rangle$ to the response set $R_{\text{to } j}$ where $j = hash(v)$. This process is also illustrated in Figure 10. Explicit responding is more cost-efficient since there is no need for request exchange and response set construction.

Explicit responding is useful in many applications. For example, to compute PageRank on an *undirected* graph, a vertex v can simply call *respond*(u) for each $u \in \Gamma(v)$ to push $a(v) = pr(v)/|\Gamma(v)|$ to v's neighbors; this is because in the next superstep, vertex u knows its neighbors $\Gamma(u)$, and can thus collect their responses. Similarly, in *attribute broadcast*, if the input graph is undirected, each vertex v can simply push its attribute $a(v)$ to its neighbors. Note that

Data	Type	|V|	|E|	AVG Deg	Max Deg
WebUK	directed	133,633,040	5,507,679,822	41.21	22,429
LiveJournal	directed	10,690,276	224,614,770	21.01	1,053,676
Twitter	directed	52,579,682	1,963,263,821	37.34	779,958
BTC	undirected	164,732,473	772,822,094	4.69	1,637,619
USA Road	undirected	23,947,347	58,333,344	2.44	9

Figure 11: Datasets (M = million)

data pushing by explicit responding requires less messages than by Pregel's vertex-to-vertex message passing, since responds are sent to machines (more precisely, their response tables) rather than individual vertices.

Programming Interface. Pregel+ extends the vertex class in Pregel's interface [13] by requiring users to specify an additional template argument <*R*>, which indicates the type of the attribute value that a vertex responds.

In *compute*(), a vertex can either pull data from another vertex v by calling *request*(v), or push data to v by calling *respond*(v). The attribute value that a vertex returns is defined by a user-specified abstract function *respond*(), which returns a value of type <*R*>. Like *compute*(), one may program *respond*() to return different attributes of a vertex in different supersteps according to the algorithm logic of the specific application. Finally, a vertex may call *get_resp*(v) in *compute*() to get the attribute of v, if it is pushed into the response table in the previous superstep.

7. EXPERIMENTAL RESULTS

We now evaluate the effectiveness of our message reduction techniques. We ran our experiments on a cluster of 16 machines, each with 24 processors (two Intel Xeon E5-2620 CPU) and 48GB RAM. One machine is used as the master, while the other 15 machines act as slaves. The connectivity between any pair of nodes in the cluster is 1Gbps.

We used five real-world datasets, as shown in Figure 11: (1)*WebUK*[2]: a web graph generated by combining twelve monthly snapshots of the .uk domain collected for the DELIS project; (2)*LiveJournal* (*LJ*) [3]: a bipartite network of LiveJournal users and their group memberships; (3)*Twitter*[4]: Twitter who-follows-who network based on a snapshot taken in 2009; (4)*BTC*[5]: a semantic graph converted from the Billion Triple Challenge 2009 RDF dataset; (5)*USA*[6]: the USA road network.

LJ, *Twitter* and *BTC* have skewed degree distribution; *WebUK*, *LJ* and *Twitter* have relatively high average degree; *USA* and *WebUK* have a large diameter.

Pregel+ Implementation. Pregel+ is implemented in C/C++ as a group of header files, and users only need to include the necessary base classes and implement the application logic in their subclasses. Pregel+ communicates with HDFS through libhdfs, a JNI based C API for HDFS. Each worker is simply an MPI process and communications are implemented using MPI communication primitives. While one may deploy Pregel+ with any Hadoop and MPI version, we use Hadoop 1.2.1 and MPICH 3.0.4 in our experiments. All programs are compiled using GCC 4.4.7 with -O2 option enabled.

[2]http://law.di.unimi.it/webdata/uk-union-2006-06-2007-05
[3]http://konect.uni-koblenz.de/networks/livejournal-groupmemberships
[4]http://konect.uni-koblenz.de/networks/twitter_mpi
[5]http://km.aifb.kit.edu/projects/btc-2009/
[6]http://www.dis.uniroma1.it/challenge9/download.shtml

All the system source codes, as well as the source codes of the algorithms discussed in this paper, can be found in `http://www.cse.cuhk.edu.hk/pregelplus`.

7.1 Effectiveness of Mirroring

Figure 12 reports the performance gain by mirroring. We measure the gain by comparing with (1)Pregel+ without both mirroring and combiner, denoted by **Pregel-noMC**; (2)Pregel+ with combiner but without mirroring, denoted by **Pregel-noM**; and (3)GPS [18] with and without LALP. The request-respond technique is not applied in Pregel+ for this set of experiments. As a reference, we also report the performance of Giraph 1.0.0 [1] (with combiner) and GraphLab 2.2 (which includes PowerGraph [5]).

We test the mirroring thresholds 1, 10, 100, 1000, and the one automatically set by the cost model given by Theorem 2 (which is 199, 165, 62, 126, for *WebUK*, *Twitter*, *LJ*, *BTC*, respectively). But for the *USA* road network, its maximum vertex degree is only 9 and thus we do not apply mirroring with large thresholds. For GPS, we follow [8] and fix the threshold of LALP as 100. This is a reasonable choice, since [8] reports that this threshold achieves good performance in general, and we find that the best performance after tuning the threshold is very close to the performance when the threshold is 100. We also report the preprocessing time of constructing mirrors for Pregel+ and that of LALP for GPS in rows marked by "Preproc Time". We also report the number of messages sent by Pregel+ and GPS (note that Giraph does not report the number of messages, but the number should be the same as that of Pregel-noMC and Pregel-noM; while GraphLab does not employ message passing).

We ran PageRank on the three directed graphs, and *Hash-Min* on the two undirected graphs in Figure 11. For PageRank computation, we use aggregator to check whether every vertex changes its PageRank value by less than 0.01 after each superstep, and terminate if so. The computation takes 89, 89 and 96 supersteps on *WebUK*, *Twitter* and *LJ*, respectively, before convergence. We do not run GraphLab in asynchronous mode for PageRank, since its convergence condition is different from the synchronous version and hence leads to different PageRank results.

Mirroring in Pregel+. As Figure 12 shows, mirroring significantly improves the performance of Pregel-noM, in terms of the reduction in both running time and message number. The improvement is particularly obvious for the graphs, *Twitter*, *LJ*, and *BTC*, which have highly skewed degree distribution. Thus, the result also demonstrates the effectiveness of mirroring in workload balancing.

Mirroring is not so effective for PageRank on *WebUK*, for which Pregel-noM has the best performance. The number of messages is only slightly decreased when mirroring threshold $\tau = 1000$, and yet it is still slower than Pregel-noM. This is because messages sent through Ch_{mir} are intercepted by mirrors which incurs additional cost. Since the degree of the majority of the vertices in *WebUK* is not very high, mirroring does not significantly reduce the number of messages, and thus, the additional cost of Ch_{mir} is not paid off.

The results also show that the mirroring threshold given by our cost model achieves either the best performance, or close to the performance of the best threshold tested. The one-off preprocessing time required to construct the mirrors is also short compared with the computation time.

Comparison with Other Systems. Figure 12 shows that Pregel+ without mirroring (i.e., Pregel-noM) is already faster than both Giraph and GraphLab, which verifies that our Ch_{msg} implementation is efficient, and thus the performance gain by mirroring is not an over-claimed improvement gained over a slow implementation.

		Pregel+		Pregel+ with Mirroring Mirroring Thresholds					GPS		Giraph	GraphLab	
		noM	noMC	1	10	100	1000	Cost Model	Basic	LALP		Sync	Async
PageRank on *WebUK*	Comput Time	*2669**	7732	5603	5561	3475	2784	2935	3909	4020	4834	4262	
	Preproc Time	—		162.29	143.00	46.68	32.79	26.66	—	663.34	—	—	
	# of Msgs	120107	490184	319614	314212	168317	*119889**	134734	487285	377687			
PageRank on *Twitter*	Comput Time	1575	3131	1621	1648	1177	1381	1048	1343	*750.11**	1567	1762	
	Preproc Time	—		40.74	41.34	24.13	8.63	14.31	—	74.95	—	—	—
	# of Msgs	62276	174730	68430	65770	40980	48616	*38873**	174730	78904			
PageRank on *LJ*	Comput Time	316.26	541.53	251.98	255.26	212.35	243.32	216.05	316.45	*197.28**	312	662	
	Preproc Time	—		9.95	7.72	3.75	1.07	3.94	—	8.17	—	—	
	# of Msgs	6429	21563	5949	*3949**	4209	5162	4359	21563	9665			
Hash−Min on *BTC*	Comput Time	26.97	44.28	29.95	15.53	*9.55**	10.69	9.85	37.99	33.00	93	83	155
	Preproc Time	—		20.74	6.63	5.92	5.56	5.41	—	3.52	—	—	
	# of Msgs	1189	2419	1294	259.4	126.1	152.4	*122.5**	1525	716.4			
Hash−Min on *USA*	Comput Time	546.86	546.66	*542.69**	—				1205	—	5714	2982	627
	Preproc Time	—		4.52					—		—	—	
	# of Msgs	8353	8485	8305					8485				

Figure 12: Effects of mirroring (⋆: best result; Comput/Preproc time: Computation/Preprocessing time in sec; # of Msgs: # of messages in millions)

Compared with GPS, the reduction in both message number and running time achieved by *the integration of mirroring and combiner* in Pregel+ is significantly more than that achieved by *LALP alone* in GPS, which can be observed from (1)Pregel+ with mirroring vs. Pregel-noMC, and (2)GPS with LALP v.s. GPS without LALP. In contrast to the claim in [18] that message combining is not effective, our result clearly demonstrates the benefits of integrating mirroring and combiner, and hence highlights the importance of our theoretical analysis on the tradeoff between mirroring and message combining (i.e., Theorem 2).

However, we notice that GPS is sometimes faster than Pregel+ even though much more messages are exchanged. We found it hard to explain and so we studied the codes of GPS to explore the reason, which we explain below. GPS requires that vertex IDs should be integers that are contiguous starting from $0, 1, \cdots, |V|$; while other systems allow vertex IDs to be of any user-specified type as long as a hash function is provided (for calculating the ID of the worker that a vertex resides in). As a result of the dense ID representation, each worker in GPS simply maintains the incoming message buffers of the vertices by an array, and when a worker receives a message targeted at vertex tgt, it is put into tgt's incoming message buffer (i.e., I_{tgt}) whose position in the array can be directly computed from tgt. On the contrary, systems like Pregel+ and Giraph need to look up I_{tgt} from a hash table using key tgt, which has extra cost for each message exchanged.

We remark that there are good reasons to require vertex IDs to take arbitrary type, rather than to hard-code them as contiguous integers. For example, the Pregel algorithm in [24] for computing bi-connected components constructs an auxiliary graph from the input graph, and each vertex of the auxiliary graph corresponds to an edge (u, v) of the input graph. While we can simply use integer pair as vertex ID in Pregel+, using GPS requires extra effort from programmers to relabel the vertices of the auxiliary graph with contiguous integer IDs, which can be costly for a large graph. We note that, if one desires, he can easily implement GPS's dense vertex ID representation in Pregel+ to further improve the performance for certain algorithms, but this is not the focus of our work which studies message reduction techniques.

7.2 Effectiveness of Request-Respond Technique

Figure 13 reports the performance gained by the request-respond technique. We test the three algorithms in Section 3 to which the request-respond technique is applicable: *attribute broadcast*, *S-V* and minimum spanning forest. We also include Giraph and GPS

	Pregel+	ReqResp	Giraph	GPS	Pregel+	ReqResp	Giraph	GPS
	Attribute Broadcast on *WebUK*				S-V on *USA*			
Time	178.4 s	84.53 s	169.28 s	*83.71 s**	261.93 s	*137.69 s**	690 s	189.77 s
Msg #	11015 M	*2699 M**	-	10950 M	6598 M	*3789 M**	-	6598M
	Attribute Broadcast on *BTC*				S-V on *BTC*			
Time	16.33 s	13.31 s	54.76 s	*8.69 s**	408.78 s	*190.55 s**	1531 s	286.22 s
Msg #	772.8 M	*393.2 M**	-	772.8 M	22393 M	*11232 M**	-	22393M
	Attribute Broadcast on *LJ*				Minimum Spanning Forest on *USA*			
Time	11.66 s	9.09 s	11.56 s	*6.43 s**	*19.95 s**	25.20 s	259.63 s	85.15 s
Msg #	449.2 M	*131.9 M**	-	449.2 M	387.1 M	*162.2 M**	-	387.1 M
	Attribute Broadcast on *Twitter*				Minimum Spanning Forest on *BTC*			
Time	59.84 s	*29.65 s**	71.35 s	29.93 s	83.36 s	*36.56 s**	350.15 s	209.92 s
Msg #	3927 M	*1396 M**	-	3927 M	2424 M	*1110 M**	-	2424 M

Figure 13: Effects of the request-respond technique

as a reference. We do not include GraphLab since the algorithms cannot be easily implemented in GraphLab (e.g., it is not clear how a vertex v can communicate with a non-neighbor $D[v]$ as in *S-V* and minimum spanning forest).

The results show that Pregel+ with request-respond, denoted by **ReqResq**, uses significantly less messages. For example, for *attribute broadcast* on *WebUK*, ReqResq reduces the message number from 11,015 million to only 2,699 million. ReqResq also records the shortest running time except in a few cases where GPS is faster due to the same reason given in Section 7.1. Another exception is when computing minimum spanning forest on *USA*, where Pregel+ is faster without request-respond. This is because vertices in *USA* have very low degree, rendering the request-respond technique ineffective, and the additional computational overhead is not paid off by the reduction in message number.

8. CONCLUSIONS

We presented two techniques to reduce the amount of communication and to eliminate skewed communication workload. The first technique, mirroring, eliminates communication bottlenecks caused by high vertex degree, and is transparent to programming. The second technique is a new request-respond paradigm, which eliminates bottlenecks caused by program logic, and simplifies the programming of many Pregel algorithms. Our experiments on large real-world graphs verified that our techniques are effective in reducing the communication cost and overall computation time.

Acknowledgments. We thank the anonymous reviewers for their constructive comments. This work is supported by SHIAE Grant (No. 8115048).

9. REFERENCES

[1] Apache Giraph. http://giraph.apache.org/.

[2] Z. Cai, Z. J. Gao, S. Luo, L. L. Perez, Z. Vagena, and C. M. Jermaine. A comparison of platforms for implementing and running very large scale machine learning algorithms. In *SIGMOD*, pages 1371–1382, 2014.

[3] J. Dean and S. Ghemawat. Mapreduce: Simplified data processing on large clusters. In *OSDI*, pages 137–150, 2004.

[4] B. Elser and A. Montresor. An evaluation study of bigdata frameworks for graph processing. In *BigData Conference*, pages 60–67, 2013.

[5] J. E. Gonzalez, Y. Low, H. Gu, D. Bickson, and C. Guestrin. Powergraph: Distributed graph-parallel computation on natural graphs. In *OSDI*, pages 17–30, 2012.

[6] Y. Guo, M. Biczak, A. L. Varbanescu, A. Iosup, C. Martella, and T. L. Willke. How well do graph-processing platforms perform? an empirical performance evaluation and analysis. IPDPS, 2013.

[7] Z. Gyöngyi, H. Garcia-Molina, and J. O. Pedersen. Combating web spam with trustrank. In *VLDB*, pages 576–587, 2004.

[8] M. Han, K. Daudjee, K. Ammar, M. T. Özsu, X. Wang, and T. Jin. An experimental comparison of Pregel-like graph processing systems. *PVLDB*, 7(12):1047–1058, 2014.

[9] G. Jeh and J. Widom. Scaling personalized web search. In *WWW*, pages 271–279, 2003.

[10] Z. Khayyat, K. Awara, A. Alonazi, H. Jamjoom, D. Williams, and P. Kalnis. Mizan: a system for dynamic load balancing in large-scale graph processing. In *EuroSys*, pages 169–182, 2013.

[11] Y. Low, J. Gonzalez, A. Kyrola, D. Bickson, C. Guestrin, and J. M. Hellerstein. Distributed graphlab: A framework for machine learning in the cloud. *PVLDB*, 5(8):716–727, 2012.

[12] Y. Lu, J. Cheng, D. Yan, and H. Wu. Large-scale distributed graph computing systems: An experimental evaluation. *PVLDB*, 8(3):281–292, 2014.

[13] G. Malewicz, M. H. Austern, A. J. C. Bik, J. C. Dehnert, I. Horn, N. Leiser, and G. Czajkowski. Pregel: a system for large-scale graph processing. In *SIGMOD Conference*, pages 135–146, 2010.

[14] A. Mislove, M. Marcon, P. K. Gummadi, P. Druschel, and B. Bhattacharjee. Measurement and analysis of online social networks. In *SIGCOMM Conference on Internet Measurement*, pages 29–42, 2007.

[15] J. Niu, J. Peng, C. Tong, and W. Liao. Evolution of disconnected components in social networks: Patterns and a generative model. In *Performance Computing and Communications Conference (IPCCC), 2012 IEEE 31st International*, pages 305–313. IEEE, 2012.

[16] L. Page, S. Brin, R. Motwani, and T. Winograd. The pagerank citation ranking: Bringing order to the web. 1999.

[17] V. Rastogi, A. Machanavajjhala, L. Chitnis, and A. D. Sarma. Finding connected components in map-reduce in logarithmic rounds. In *ICDE*, pages 50–61, 2013.

[18] S. Salihoglu and J. Widom. GPS: a graph processing system. In *SSDBM*, page 22, 2013.

[19] S. Salihoglu and J. Widom. Optimizing graph algorithms on pregel-like systems. *PVLDB*, 7(7):577–588, 2014.

[20] N. Satish, N. Sundaram, M. M. A. Patwary, J. Seo, J. Park, M. A. Hassaan, S. Sengupta, Z. Yin, and P. Dubey. Navigating the maze of graph analytics frameworks using massive graph datasets. In *SIGMOD Conference*, pages 979–990, 2014.

[21] Z. Shang and J. X. Yu. Catch the wind: Graph workload balancing on cloud. In *ICDE*, pages 553–564, 2013.

[22] Y. Shiloach and U. Vishkin. An o(log n) parallel connectivity algorithm. *J. Algorithms*, 3(1):57–67, 1982.

[23] D. Yan, J. Cheng, Y. Lu, and W. Ng. Blogel: A block-centric framework for distributed computation on real-world graphs. *PVLDB*, 7(14):1981–1992, 2014.

[24] D. Yan, J. Cheng, K. Xing, Y. Lu, W. Ng, and Y. Bu. Pregel algorithms for graph connectivity problems with performance guarantees. *PVLDB*, 7(14):1821–1832, 2014.

Tackling the Achilles Heel of Social Networks: Influence Propagation based Language Model Smoothing

Rui Yan
Baidu Inc.
No. 10, Shangdi 10th Street,
Beijing 100085, China
yanrui02@baidu.com

Ian E.H. Yen
Dept. of Computer Science
University of Texas at Austin
Austin, TX 78712, USA
ianyen@cs.utexas.edu

Cheng-Te Li
Academia Sinica
No 128, Academia Road,
Taipei 11529, Taiwan
ctli@citi.sinica.edu.tw

Shiqi Zhao
Baidu Inc.
No. 10, Shangdi 10th Street,
Beijing 100085, China
zhaoshiqi@baidu.com

Xiaohua Hu
College of Info. Sci. and Tech.
Drexel University
Philadelphia, PA 19104, USA
xh29@drexel.edu

ABSTRACT

Online social networks nowadays enjoy their worldwide prosperity, as they have revolutionized the way for people to discover, to share, and to distribute information. With millions of registered users and the proliferation of user-generated contents, the social networks become "giants", likely eligible to carry on any research tasks. However, the giants do have their Achilles Heel: extreme data sparsity. Compared with the massive data over the whole collection, individual posting documents, (e.g., a microblog less than 140 characters), seem to be too sparse to make a difference under various research scenarios, while actually they are different. In this paper we propose to tackle the Achilles Heel of social networks by smoothing the language model via influence propagation. We formulate a socialized factor graph model, which utilizes both the textual correlations between document pairs and the socialized augmentation networks behind the documents, such as user relationships and social interactions. These factors are modeled as attributes and dependencies among documents and their corresponding users. An efficient algorithm is designed to learn the proposed factor graph model. Finally we propagate term counts to smooth documents based on the estimated influence. Experimental results on *Twitter* and *Weibo* datasets validate the effectiveness of the proposed model. By leveraging the smoothed language model with social factors, our approach obtains significant improvement over several alternative methods on both intrinsic and extrinsic evaluations measured in terms of perplexity, nDCG and MAP results.

Categories and Subject Descriptors

H.3.1 [**Information Storage and Retrieval**]: Content Analysis and Indexing—*Text mining*; J.4 [**Social and Behavioral Sciences**]: Miscellaneous

WWW 2015, May 18–22, 2015, Florence, Italy.
ACM 978-1-4503-3469-3/15/05.
http://dx.doi.org/10.1145/2736277.2741673.

General Terms

Algorithms, Experimentation, Performance

Keywords

Language model smoothing; influence propagation; social network

1. INTRODUCTION

Along with the prosperity of Web 2.0, online social networks have emerged as a brand new medium in spotlight and revolutionized the way for people to discover, to share and to propagate information via peer-to-peer interactions [13]. Among the popular websites which provide social services, big names cover nearly every corner of online social life and events: *Facebook*[1] encourages photo/video/blog sharing and leaving comments among friends, *Twitter*[2] provides succinct, fast spreading microblogs for news feeds, *Foursquare*[3] is a location based mobile social network which provides comments generally about places of interest.

In this sense, we are living in an era with "giants": with incredibly large number (in billions [1]) of affiliated users and the proliferation of user-generated contents, the online social networks are the mighty giants of our times, plausibly invincible and eligible to carry on any kind of research tasks. In fact, people have conducted a series of studies on social networks, such as search and retrieval [31], information recommendation [36, 5], link prediction [12, 7] and summarization [16, 38].

Although powerful as giants, social networks still suffer from their weakness: extreme sparsity. For many textual related researches such as retrieval, mining or recommendation etc., accurate estimation of document language models are likely to be an essential part to the success of new methods and models. More observed data generally allow people to establish a more accurate statistical model. However, due to the real-time propagation on social networks, the posted documents are sometimes officially limited within a restricted length to facilitate fast spreading (e.g., 140 characters per tweet on Twitter). In this case, we have to estimate the language model based on a small piece of texts (e.g., a tweet), while given

[1]https://www.facebook.com
[2]https://www.twitter.com
[3]https://www.foursquare.com

limited data sampling, the language model estimation usually encounters with severe zero count problem: the maximum likelihood estimator would give unseen terms a zero probability rather than a reliable approximation. Therefore, sparsity actually becomes the Achilles Heel of social networks for texts related studies, and we aim at tackling the bottleneck.

Statistical language models have attracted much attention in the information retrieval community due to their solid theoretical background as well as their success in a variety of tasks [25, 14]. Language model smoothing is proposed to address the sparsity problem, and has been demonstrated to affect retrieval performance significantly [40]. The quality of textual related tasks heavily relies on proper smoothing of the document language model. Although much work on language model smoothing has been investigated, the intuitions behind are generally related to two major concerns: 1) semantic association [34, 18, 30] and 2) positional proximity [41, 19, 34]. However, for social networks, there is much more information hidden in social factors, which could be utilized to measure language model smoothing. Therefore, social interaction could be a third direction to investigate better language modeling.

The key idea for language model smoothing is to propagate term counts via certain ways of projection to other places where they originally do not really exist. Hence we propose a socialized factor graph model to investigate various factors which could have impacts on language models, and measure the influence propagated along the factor graph. According to the influence estimated, we propagate the term occurrence in discounted counts and hence smooth the original language models. To the best of our knowledge, we are the first one to mapping social influence onto the textual dimension to facilitate socialized language model smoothing. Our 1st contribution is to fuse a series of social attributes with textual information and form an integrated objective function to balance both. Intuitively, a smoothed language model should enhance the coherence between terms with semantic association, and analogously for those through social interactions. In other words, the terms that are associated via close friends based on the social linkage could have similar (or smoothed) probabilistic distributions: stronger social ties could also lead to more similar smoothed language models.

Another main technical challenge lies in how to define the attributes, factors and formulate the propagation functions to model the joint probabilistic factor graph. We explore several different factors captured from posting document pairs and user pairs, and evaluate their dependencies on each other. To be more specific, we have examined features such as text similarity, text quality, social status and social interactions and so on, and then grouped them as factor functions. Factor functions are finally formulated into one objective function to calculate the estimated influence and hence to smooth the language model accordingly.

In this paper, we define the problem of Socialized Language Model Smoothing (SLMS) based on the factor graphs. We evaluate the effectiveness of our proposed language model smoothing method using two different social network datasets from *Twitter* and *Weibo*[4]. Both of them are mainstream microblogs, one in English and the other one in Chinese. We apply intrinsic evaluation measured in perplexity and extrinsic evaluation measured in nDCG and MAP in our experimental setups. Experimental results show that our proposed influence propagation based language model smoothing on factor graphs consistently outperforms the baseline smoothing methods, and the improvement is significant, which indicates the effectiveness of our approach. In other words, the social factors along with the textual information in combination could to some extent tackle the Achilles Heel of social networks.

The rest of the paper is organized as follows. We start by introducing the problem definition and then the influence propagation based language model smoothing on factor graphs, using textual and social information in combination. We describe the experiments and evaluation in Section 4, review previous works in Section 5 and finally draw the conclusions.

[4]https://www.weibo.com

2. PROBLEM FORMULATION

In this section, we introduce some notations and representations necessary for language modeling and smoothing on social networks, and then elaborate the problem of Socialized Language Model Smoothing (SLMS) via factor graph model.

Definition 1. (Document and Collection.) Given a posting document d_0 to smooth, we have a whole document collection $D = \{d_1, d_2, \dots, d_n\}$ as the background set to smooth d_0.

In the context of web documents on social networks, e.g. Twitter or Weibo, etc., each posting document is written by a particular user. Compared with traditional documents that are defined merely based on plain texts, these posting documents are associated with more interesting elements. For instance, social networks support particular *relationships* established among users, i.e., *follower-followee* on Twitter. Also, there are social interactions spread between the posting documents, e.g., *replying*, *sharing* and *reposting* documents. We hence have a hidden network structure behind the document collection. User activities implicitly reflect more information behind the documents to model the textual properties. We believe that the social relationships would help to better describe the text information. Thus, integrating the document contents and social information can disclose a more accurate estimation of the document language model to smooth. In this paper, we mainly employ the microblogging service as the basis for our study and hence make a good utilization of its characteristics for illustration.

Specifically, given a posting document d_i, and its associated user u_i, together with the associated user networks, we give the following definition of socialized augmentation network.

Definition 2. (Socialized Augmentation Network.) We have the heterogeneous graph of posting documents and their corresponding users. We denote the whole graph G as a collection of nodes V and edges E, and have G=(V, E)=$(V_u, V_d, E_u, E_d, E_{u,d})$. It is obvious to see that there are three kinds of relationships associated: 1) (V_d, E_d) is a weighted directed graph between posting document pairs, where $V_d = \{d_i | d_i \in D\}$ is the posting collection with a size of $|D|$, and E_d is the set of relationships, indicating the influence from source postings to the target postings, which is our goal to estimate; 2) (V_u, E_u) is also a weighted directed graph indicating the social ties between users. $V_u = \{u_i | u_i \in V_u\}$ is the set of users with a size of $|V_u|$. E_u is established by the social behavior among users, which will be described in Section 3.2; 3) $(V_{u,d}, E_{u,d})$ is the unweighted bipartite graph representing authorship of posting documents and users. $V_{u,d}$ = $V_u \cup V_d$. Edges in $E_{u,d}$ connect each posting document with all of its authors and help mapping from social dimension to textual dimension. Usually a posting document d is written by only one user u.

Now we give a formal definition of our proposed SLMS problem:

Input: Given the entire document set D, and the socialization augmentation networks, we aim to smooth the language model of the target document, denoted as $P(w|d_0)$, based on the influence from all other documents d_i where $\{d_i|d_i \in D\}$.

Output: The smoothed language model of $P(w|d_0^+)$ for every original document d_0.

With these preliminaries, we show that relationships from document pairs, user pairs and user-document pairs can be all formulated and hence mapped as the instances on the factor graph using potential functions to form a combined objective function.

3. METHODOLOGY

In this section, we propose a socialized factor graph to compute influence propagation, and formulate the socialized language model smoothing problem into a unified learning framework. The model simultaneously incorporates all resources (i.e., texts and social information) into the augmentation contexts to generate high-quality estimation for document language models after smoothing.

The socialized language model smoothing problem contains several sub-problems: 1) document pair influence measurement, 2) user pair influence measurement, and 3) variable pair influence measurement. We aim to quantify the correlation between document pairs based on semantic association derived from contents, while also we intend to augment the pairwise relationship between documents from the interactions of users on social level. Social contexts contain rich information about the document pairs. We also analyze the dependency of variables on each other based on the same authorship. Finally, we use the estimated influence propagation on the documents to smooth the original language model, and then apply to a series of related research tasks. The framework is illustrated in Figure 1, and the details are explained later.

3.1 Proposed Model

Factor graph assumes observation data are cohesive on both features and relationships between each other [11]. It has been successfully applied in many applications, such as social influence analysis [28, 27], social relationship mininig [7, 33], and linked data disambiguation [12, 32]. In this work, we formulate the social features and associated networks into the factor graph model, which is shown in Figure 1. Given the document pairs, let E_d be the pairwise links between two posting documents, and E_u be the user social ties. The input of the factor model is the whole document collection and the socialized augmentation contexts, and a target document d_0 to smooth. Both pairs are digested into the attribute factors, which are observable. There is also a set of hidden variables $Y = \{y_i\}_{i=1}^n$, representing the influence inferred from the observed pairs and coordination among the hidden variables.

We define two feature functions in the proposed factor model: *attribute factor* and *dependency factor*.

• **Attribute Factor**. The influence from a posting document to another could be estimated by some attributes (represented as $\mathbf{x}$), which refer to features that are inherent to the documents and their authors. In general, we define a series of features for the document pairs and user pairs. These features include the textual based contents such as text quality, similarity and popularity, as well as the social ties such as user relationships, interactions, authoritativeness and so on. Details of the defined features are given in the next section. We use the feature function $f(y_i, \mathbf{x}_i)$ to represent the posterior probability of label y_i given $\mathbf{x}_i$ contained in the pairwise information among the heterogenous nodes.

We define this type of potential function as a linear exponential function and to estimate the significance of each feature, we introduce a vector of weight variable α for each feature c, and formally we could define the attribute factors as the local entropy as follows:

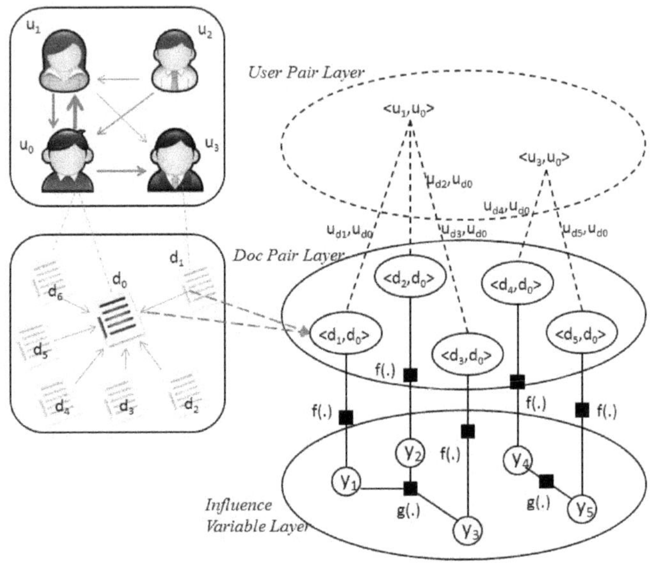

Figure 1: Graphical representation of the socialized augmentation factor graph. The left part shows the heterogeneous graph, consisting of the document collection and users with social ties. The right part indicates the decomposable factor graph. The top layer shows the user pairs, which could be instantiated into several user pairs identified by different document pairs on the middle layer. The lower layer indicates the influence to estimate between document pairs. There are factor functions within the same layer ($g(.)$) and factor functions across layers ($f(.)$). In the final step, The language models are smoothed based on the influence estimated on the lower layer. Some links between documents and users are omitted to keep concise.

$$f_i(y_i, \mathbf{x}_i) = \frac{1}{Z_\alpha} \exp\{\sum_c \alpha_c f_{i,c}(y_i, x_{i,c})\} \tag{1}$$

where $x_{i,c}$ is the c-th attribute to calculate the influence. $f_c(.)$ is the function to calculate the result from the c-th feature and α_c is the corresponding weight. Z_α is a normalization factor.

• **Dependency Factor**. As proposed, we introduce factors that are capable of handling multiple hidden variables on the variable layer, to characterize the dependencies among the posting documents generated by the same user. The dependency factor is to propagate the social influence among all posting documents from the same user. The heuristics is that if document d_0 is influenced by document d_i. It is highly possible to be influenced by the document d_k from the same user, which is actually a belief propagation.

To capture this intuition, we define the potential function to model the correlation of a candidate variable y_i with another candidate variable y_k in the factor graph. The function is defined as:

$$g(y_i, y_k) = \frac{1}{Z_{ik,\beta}} \exp\{\beta_k g_k(y_i, y_k)\} \tag{2}$$

where $g(.)$ is a function indicating whether two variables are correlated or not. Note that if $g(y_i, y_k)$=0, there will be no dependency between the two variables. In other words, the two variables are not correlated. Actually we can group the document set into clusters and each cluster is associated with one user, and we use Y_i to denote the cluster where y_i is in. Hence, for $\forall y_k \in Y_i$, y_i has dependency on y_k. We further revise Equation (2) as:

$$g_i(y_i, Y_i) = \prod_{y_k \in Y_i} g(y_i, y_k) = \frac{1}{Z_\beta} \exp\{\sum_{y_k \in Y_i} \beta_k g_k(y_i, y_k)\} \quad (3)$$

Again, Z_β is the normalization factor.

In this way, the influence estimation could be viewed as a sequence labeling process [38], i.e., the judgment on a certain pair is affected by the "similar" pairs (i.e., the documents written by the same user in this work), which is exactly the intuition for language model smoothing [21].

• **Objective Function**. In general, the attribute factors capture the potential influence from document/user pairs and the dependency factor captures correlations between variables. In Equation (1) we define the features $f_c(.)$ for all attributes, where α_c is the corresponding weight. In Equation (3), we define the correlation where β_k indicates the weights. Let Y and X be the sets of candidate variables and attribute variables respectively, we define a conditional probability encoded within the factor graph model by multiplying all potential functions and can be written as

$$P_\theta(Y|X) = \prod_i f_i(y_i, \mathbf{x}_i) g_i(y_i, Y_i) \quad (4)$$

Hence, by integrating the defined factor functions, and also following the labeling assumption [10], we can define the following log-likelihood over all the undetermined labels of all instances, i.e., $Y=\{y_i\}_{i=1}^n$, where the objective function summing up likelihood:

$$\mathcal{O}(\theta) = \log P_\theta(Y|X)$$
$$= \sum_i \sum_c \alpha_c f_{i,c}(y_i, x_{i,c}) + \sum_{y_k \in Y_i} \beta_k g_k(y_i, y_k) - \log Z \quad (5)$$

$Z = Z_\alpha Z_\beta$ is the normalization factor, which sums up the conditional likelihood of P_θ over all instances. θ is the collection of parameters indicating weights, i.e., $\theta = \{\alpha\} \cup \{\beta\}$.

Calculating the marginal distribution for each factor (in deriving the log-gradient of the objective function) requires a loopy sum-product inference algorithm. With the learned parameters, we may estimate an undetermined influence between document pairs in the test set by inferring the influence propagated and then smooth language models accordingly. The inference algorithm is introduced in section 3.3.

3.2 Function Definitions

Many features have been designed for document correlation and social associations among users in previous literature. In this paper, we investigate 8 features or factors. Besides, some features that are widely used in traditional text analysis, we also utilize several features extracted from users' social interactions, for instance, following behaviors, social status, and other statistics. We start from the feature definition first.

3.2.1 Attributes

We use the potential functions in the factor graph model to learn the potential influence for a document d_i to shade on d_0. Referring to Equation (1), we define the attribute functions as follows:

Text Similarity. It is intuitive that the textual similarity between two documents play an important role in language model smoothing [34, 18, 30]. Similar documents should be smoothed with higher weights since it is more consistent with their existing models. We use the cosine similarity between two unigram models:

$$f_{sim} = \frac{d_0 \cdot d_i}{||d_0||||d_i||} \quad (6)$$

Text Quality. We also measure the text quality of document d_i. It is not a good idea to smooth the target language model using a piece of text with low quality. Hereby we use the Out-Of-Vocabulary (OOV) ratio to measure the textual quality. The lower OOV ratio, the higher quality would be. Against the vocabulary from the official news corpora [42], OOV in microblogs often refers to a set of misspellings, informal terminologies, and irregular symbols.

$$f_{oov} = 1 - \frac{|\{w|w \in (d_i \cap \text{OOV})\}|}{|d_i|} \quad (7)$$

Technically, the measurement of *text quality* is not a pairwise function strictly between d_0 and d_i, but the criteria is indeed a practical indicator to decide whether or not to propagate the influence from d_i to d_0. We also include similar criteria for user pairs.

Posting Popularity. It is intuitive that a popular posting document is more likely to influence on many other posting documents. We use the aggregated numbers of social interaction (i.e., replies and retweets) as the approximation of popularity for d_i.

Social Status. Since micro-blogging service requires no reciprocal linkage among users, it is natural to assume that the social status is asymmetric between two users. A followee is more likely to influence the followers. This feature is represented by nominal values, e.g., '1' - the user of d_0 follows the user who writes d_i; '-1' - the user of d_0 is followed by the user who writes d_i; '0' - the two users have no direct follow behaviors.

User Similarity. We presume that people within the same social circle will have a larger probability to influence each other. Still, due to the asymmetry, we measure the Jaccard distance of the common followees of two users as their similarity. We use function $\mathcal{F}(u)$ to denote the social circle set for the user u. The $\mathcal{F}(.)$ of "followee" can be replaced by "followers" or extended to "friends".

$$f_{usim} = \frac{|\mathcal{F}(author(d_0)) \cap \mathcal{F}(author(d_i))|}{|\mathcal{F}(author(d_0)) \cup \mathcal{F}(author(d_i))|} \quad (8)$$

Interaction Strength. We also include the strength of interactions between the user pairs. It is possible that if two users have frequent social interactions, they are likely to share the writing preference on the term usage. Due to the asymmetrical social relationship, we only count the times for $author(d_0)$ to repost from $author(d_i)$ to measure how likely for the user to be influenced.

User Impacts. On social networks, some users are intrinsically have much larger influence on the others, e.g., sports stars, political celebrities, etc. Their words are usually copied, quoted and spreaded. There are many different ways to evaluate the user impacts, while we use the classic PageRank [23] scores to denote user impacts. The linkage based PageRank algorithm is quite suited to the scenario of user impact measurement. With a large number of in-links, the user is almost guaranteed to have high social impacts.

3.2.2 Dependency

As for the dependency function between candidate variables, referring to Equation (3), we define the function $g(.)$ for two candidate variables associated by the same user authorship in Y_i, and let the corresponding variables be y_i and y_k, respectively. The dependency function aims at encoding the influence propagation between posting documents from the same user, defined as follows.

$$g_k(y_i, y_k) = \mathcal{I}\{author(d_i) = author(d_k)\} \times f_{sim}(d_i, d_k) \\ = \mathcal{I}\{author(d_i) = author(d_k)\} \times \frac{d_i \cdot d_k}{||d_i||||d_k||} \tag{9}$$

The boolean indicator $\mathcal{I}(.)$ is 1 when $author(d_i)$=$author(d_k)$ and 0 otherwise. We assume that two candidate variables will have higher correlation if they represent documents written by the same user. The correlation should also be affected by text similarity.

3.3 Model Inference

There are two scenarios for parameter estimation. If we do not have any labels of influence values among the candidate random variables, we can only propose to optimize the factor graph model via a two-step iterative procedure. At first, all of the model parameters (i.e., θ) are randomly initialized. Given the parameters, we infer the marginal probabilities of candidate variables. Then, given the marginal probabilities, we are able to evaluate experimental performance (Section 4.3) with respect to a set of held-out validation data, and search for better model parameters until convergence.

Unfortunately, this inference algorithm is way too indirect, depending on external evaluation metrics. Besides, it takes a longer time to converge. It is impossible to manually label influence values, but we do have partial labels available due to the special phenomenon of *repostings* on Twitter and Weibo! For each retweeted pairs, they have exactly the same contents and hence we label the influence as 1. With the partially labeled variables, we can now estimate the parameter configuration $\theta = \{\alpha, \beta\}$ to maximize the log-likelihood objective function $\mathcal{O}(\theta) = \log P_\theta(Y|X)$ approximately with gradient based methods, e.g., stochastic gradient descent [2].

$$\theta^* = \text{argmax}_\theta \ \mathcal{O}(\theta) \tag{10}$$

Algorithm 1: Learning algorithm on the factor graph

Input: a factor graph G, and the learning rate η.
Output: Estimated parameters $\theta = \{\alpha, \beta\}$.
Initialize all elements in $\theta \leftarrow 1$
begin
  repeat
    Compute potential function values S according to Equations (1)-(9)
    Run inference method using current θ to get $P_\theta(Y|X)$
    for $\{\alpha, \beta\} \in \theta$ **do**
      Compute gradient of $\frac{\partial \mathcal{O}(\theta)}{\partial \theta}$ using S according to Equation (13).
      $\frac{\partial \mathcal{O}(\theta)}{\partial \theta} = \mathbb{E}_{P_\theta(Y|Y^L)}S - \mathbb{E}_{P_\theta(Y)}S$
      Update parameter θ with the learning rate η:
      $\theta = \theta + \eta \cdot \frac{\partial \mathcal{O}(\theta)}{\partial \theta}$
  until *Convergence*;

Based on Equations (5), the probability distribution $P(Y|X)$ can be written in a more brief format as follows:

$$P(Y|X) = \frac{1}{Z}\exp\{\theta \sum_i s(y_i)\} = \frac{1}{Z}\exp\{\theta \cdot S\} \tag{11}$$

where $s(y_i) = (f_i(y_i, \mathbf{x}_i), g_i(y_i, Y_i))$ and $S = \sum_i s(y_i)$.

In this way, the objective function could be written as

$$\mathcal{O}(\theta) = \log P(Y^L|X) = \log \sum_{Y|Y^L} \frac{1}{Z}\exp\{\theta S\} \\ = \log \sum_{Y|Y^L} \exp\{\theta S\} - \log \sum_{Y} \exp\{\theta S\} \tag{12}$$

where Y^L denotes the known labels and $Y|Y^L$ is a labeling configuration of Y inferred from Y^L. In order to maximize the objective function, we adopt the gradient decent method. We calculate the gradient for each parameter θ.

$$\frac{\partial \mathcal{O}(\theta)}{\partial \theta} = \frac{\partial(\log \sum_{Y|Y^L}\exp\{\theta S\} - \log\sum_Y \exp\{\theta S\})}{\partial \theta} \\ = \frac{\sum_{Y|Y^L}\exp \theta S \cdot S}{\sum_{Y|Y^L}\exp \theta S} - \frac{\sum_Y \exp \theta S \cdot S}{\sum_Y \exp \theta S} \\ = \mathbb{E}_{P_\theta(Y|Y^L)}S - \mathbb{E}_{P_\theta(Y)}S \tag{13}$$

$\mathbb{E}_{P_\theta(Y|Y^L)}S$ and $\mathbb{E}_{P_\theta(Y)}S$ are two expectations of S. The value of S can be obtained naturally using approximated inference algorithms, such as Loopy Belief Propagation (LBP) algorithm [39], Gibbs Sampling [4] or Contrastive Divergence [3]. One challenge here is that the graphical structure in the model can be arbitrary and may contain cycles, which makes it intractable to directly calculate the marginal distribution. We chose Loopy Belief Propagation due to its ease of implementation and effectiveness. It should be noted that the proposed ranked-margin algorithm can be exploited not just for graphical models, but also for other learning models as long as the gradient of the expected difference can be calculated. The general idea is to use two steps, one step for calculating $\mathbb{E}_{P_\theta(Y|Y^L)}S$ and the other step for calculating $\mathbb{E}_{P_\theta(Y)}S$, to estimate the gradient of a parameter θ w.r.t. the objective function.

With the marginal probabilities, the gradient can be obtained by summing over all undetermined labels. It is worth noting that we need to perform the LBP process twice in each iteration, one time for estimating the marginal distribution of unknown variables y_i = ?, and the other time for marginal distribution over all variables. Finally with the gradient, we update each parameter with a learning rate η. The learning algorithm is summarized in Algorithm 1. After learning the optimal parameters θ, we need to apply the inference algorithm again to compute the marginal probability to infer the unknown labels by finding a label configuration which maximizes the probability $P(Y|X)$. Finally, each node in the factor graph is assigned with label that maximizes the marginal probability.

$$Y^* = \text{argmax}_{Y|Y^L} \ P(Y|X) \tag{14}$$

3.4 Distributed Learning

As a social network may contain millions of users and hundreds of millions of posting documents generated by users, it is beneficial to learn the factor graph from the full social network data using multiple machines rather than a single one. To address this challenge, we deploy the learning task on a distributed system under the map-reduce programming model [6]. Within every individual framework, our target is to smooth the document d_0 based on the subset of influential variables (e.g., group of variables as Y_i), which makes the graph easy to divide: it is natural to extend the individual-centric method to a distributed environment.

Map-Reduce is a programming model for distributed processing of large data sets. In the map stage, each machine (called a process

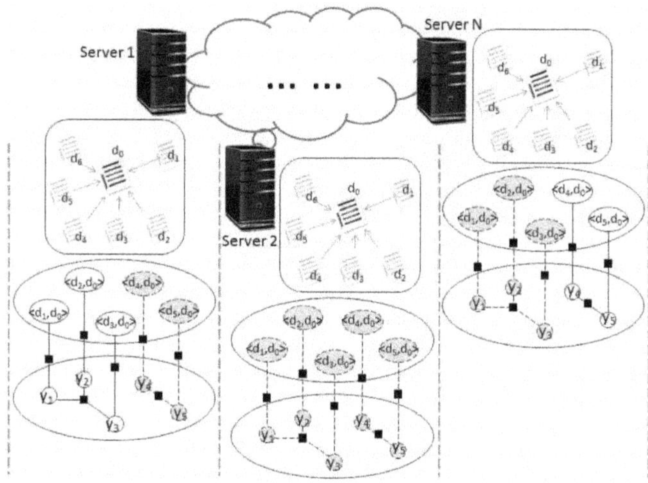

Figure 2: Distributed experimental environment setups. The whole graph is distributed to several computing nodes and the shaded nodes indicate inactive document pairs on that node.

node) receives a subset of data as input and produces a set of intermediate values. In the reduce stage, each process node merges all intermediate values associated with the same target documents and outputs the final computation results. Users specify a map function that generates a set of intermediate values, and a reduce function that merges all intermediate values.

In the process of distributed learning, the whole graph is first divided into several subgraphs that are assigned to slave nodes. Then LBP is performed on each slave to compute the marginal probabilities and the parameter gradient. There is a master node collects and sums up all gradients from subgraphs, and updates parameters by gradient descent method. For details, please refer to [29, 28].

3.5 Language Model Smoothing

Given the estimated influence from all other posting documents, we now propose a term-level language model smoothing approach based on influence propagation. Each word propagates the evidence of its occurrence to other documents based on the estimated influence. To capture the *proximity* heuristics used in language model smoothing [21, 19, 30, 34], we assign "close-by" words with higher propagated counts than those ones which are "far away" from each other. In other words, most propagated counts come from "nearby" terms, while higher influence indicates closer proximity [37, 35, 43]. Theoretically, all positions can have a full vocabulary with different term distributions: each word has a certain non-zero probability to occur in each of the posting document, as if all words had appeared with a variety of discounted counts, while in practical scenarios, we still choose to filter noisy terms with extremely low counts.

In general, we smooth a specific posting document using the background information from the document collection. Consider the traditional way of concatenating the document language model $P(w)$ and the background $P_B(w)$ in a weighted linear combination, i.e., $P'(w)$=$(1-\lambda)P(w)$+$\lambda P_B(w)$. The tradeoff is balanced by the damping factor λ. Compared with this arbitrary and equal weighting for all documents, our socialized language model smoothing based on propagated influence is in a finer-granularity.

The idea for term projection is that if a word w occurs at an influential posting document, we would like to assume that the highly influenced document will also have the words occurred, with a discounted count. The larger the influence estimated, the larger the propagated term counts there will be. Note that each propagated count has a value less than 1.

Let $d_O = \{w_1, w_2, \dots, w_{|d_O|}\}$ where $|d_O|$ is the length of the document. We use $c(w, d_O)$ to denote the original term count within document d before smoothing. If w does not occur in d_O, $c(w, d_O)$ will be 0, which is a zero count problem. We have calculated the values of Y=$\{y_i\}_{i=1}^n$ from the last section, indicating the influence from the d_i to the document d_O to smooth. The function actually serves as a discounting factor for terms measured in pairwise. We use $c'(w, d_O)$ to denote the total propagated count of term w from its occurrences in all other documents, i.e.,

$$c'(w, d_O) = (1-\lambda)c(w, d_O) + \lambda \sum_{y_i \in Y} y_i \cdot c(w, d_i) \qquad (15)$$

Even if $c(w, d_O)$ is 0, $c'(w, d_O)$ may be greater than 0.

Based on term propagation, we have a term frequency vector $\{c'(w_1, d_O), \dots, c'(w_v, d_O)\}$ for the virtual document d_O^+ extended from document d_O. We can see that term information with calculated influence has been stored in this vector. Thus the language model of this new **smoothed** virtual document can be estimated as

$$P(w|d_O^+) = \frac{c'(w, d_O^+)}{\sum_{w' \in V} c'(w', d_O^+)} \qquad (16)$$

where V is the vocabulary set and $\sum_{w' \in V} c'(w', d_O^+)$ is the length of the virtual document after smoothing.

4. EXPERIMENTS AND EVALUATION

4.1 Datasets and Experimental Setups

Utilizing the data crawled from the online social networks through the following linkage, we construct 2 datasets of microblogs and the corresponding users, which form the heterogeneous network. The crawler monitored Twitter data from 3/25/2011 to 5/30/2011, and Weibo data from 9/29/2012 to 11/30/2012. We use roughly one month as the training set and the rest as testing set. The details of the data are listed in Table 1 and #Repost denotes the number of reposting (namely "retweeting" in Twitter or "转发" in Weibo) which we used as labels in our training.

Table 1: Statistics of the social network datasets.

	#User	#Document.	#Link	#Repost	Lang
Twitter	9,449,542	364,287,744	596,777,491	55,526,494	EN
Weibo	3,923,021	216,302,309	258,543,931	101,024,128	CN

Pre-processing. Basically, the social network factor graph can be established from all posting documents and all users, however, the data is noisy. We first pre-filter the pointless babbles [1] by applying the the linguistic quality judgements (e.g., OOV ratio) [24], and then remove inactive users that have less than one follower or followee and remove the users without any linkage to the remaining posting documents. We remove stopwords and URLs, perform stemming and segmentation (for Chinese texts), and build the graph after filtering, and run LBP to obtain the marginal probabilities. We establish the language model smoothed by the estimated influence.

Hashtag Clusters	Numbers	Notes
1. apple	42,528	Tech: apple products
2. nfl	40,340	Sport: American football
3. travel	38,345	General interst
4. mlb	38,261	Sport: baseball
5. fashion	30,053	General interest
1. 中国好声音	72,184	TV show: voice of China
2. 舌尖上的中国	71,169	Food: Chinese foods
3. 微博	63,154	Tech: Microblog service
4. 爱情公寓	57,783	TV drama: culture
5. 小米	49,428	Tech: smart phone

Table 2: Clusters of hashtag topics explored in our study.

4.2 Algorithms for Comparison

To illustrate the performance of our approach, we implement several alternative algorithms as baselines to compare with our method. The baselines include naive smoothing, smoothing by semantics, and positional smoothing from very recent studies. For fairness we conduct the same pre-processing procedures for all algorithms.

The first baseline is based on the traditional language model: **LM** is the language model without smoothing at all. We include the plain smoothing of **Additive** (also known as Add-δ) smoothing and **Absolute Discouting** which decreases the probability of seen words by subtracting a constant [22]. We also implement several classic strategies smoothed from the whole collection as background information: **Jelinek-Mercer** applies a linear interpolation, and **Dirichlet** employs a prior on collection influence [40, 14].

Beyond these simple heuristics, we also examine a series of semantic based language model smoothing. The most representative two semantic smoothing methods are the Cluster-Based Document Model (**CBDM**) proposed in [18], and the Document Expansion Language Model (**DELM**) in [30]. Both methods use semantically similar documents as a smoothing corpus for a particular document: CBDM clusters documents beforehand and smooths a document with the cluster where it belongs to, while DELM finds nearest neighbors dynamically for the document as the smoothing cluster. However, both methods are only based on document-level semantic similarity. We also include Positional Language Model (**PLM**) proposed in [19], which is the state-of-art positional proximity based language smoothing. PLM mainly utilizes positional information without semantic information. We implemented the best reported PLM configuration. We compare our proposed social language model smoothing (**SLMS**) against these baselines.

4.3 Evaluation Metric

It is generally difficult to examine the effect of language model directly. For most of the language model smoothing research, the performance is measured based on extrinsic evaluations (e.g., retrieval) [34, 30, 19]. We include two extrinsic evaluations in this study, i.e., standard posting document retrieval and recommendation, but first we aim to evaluate the information contained in the language itself. Hence we use language *perplexity* to evaluate the smoothed language model.

4.3.1 Intrinsic Evaluation

Our first set of experiments involved intrinsic evaluation of the "perplexity" approach based on a clustering scenario. The experimental procedure is as follows: we manually selected 10 topics (5 for each dataset) based on popularity (measured in the number of postings) and to obtain broad coverage of different types: sports, technology, cultures, and general interests. These topics are shown in Table 1. We group the posting documents with the same hashtag '#' into clusters, and then we remove the hashtags and compute its *perplexity* with respect to the current topic, defined as

$$\text{pow}\left[2, -\frac{1}{N}\sum_{w_i \in V} \log P(w_i)\right]$$

Perplexity is actually an entropy based evaluation. In this sense, the lower perplexity within the same topic cluster, the better performance in purity the topic cluster would have.

4.3.2 Extrinsic Evaluation

In addition to the intrinsic perplexity-based measurements on hashtag clusters, we also evaluate the effectiveness of our smoothed language models on the tasks of microblog search, and information recommendation. Here are a few more details about our experimental setups. For the retrieval task, to avoid the laborious work of building a test collection by hand, we focus our evaluation efforts on documents that contained at least one hashtag. Given the 10 topics mentioned above, we process all documents with hashtags as follows: first, the ground truth labels (i.e., the hashtags) are removed from the documents. We then use the hashtag terms as queries to search for relevant posting documents. The ones originally with the hashtag are regarded as relevant while others not. Note that, the retrieval performance under this experimental setting is to some extent a lower bound, since some of the retrieved documents could be false negative: they do not contain the hashtag but they are indeed relevant.

For the microblog recommendation task, we apply the recommendation framework described in [36] using the same experimental setups. For a specific user, we recommend posting documents based on their previous posting documents and their social behaviors using the graph co-ranking algorithm [36]. The language models for the documents are established after smoothing, and the recommendation list predicts which documents will be reposted in the test data. Again, to save the efforts by human evaluators, we use the automatic evaluation of microblog recommendation. The performance is evaluated by comparing with the ground truth, which indicates whether the posting has been retweeted or not. Also the automatic evaluation sketched above does not assess the full potential of the recommendation system. For instance, it is possible for the algorithm to recommend documents of interest to users but without recommendation, the documents are outside of their scope.

For both the retrieval and the recommendation task, we return the results as a ranking list given a search *query* or a designated *user*, and the ranking list is check by examining the *relevant* documents or the *reposted* documents. We measured ranking performance using the normalized Discounted Cumulative Gain (nDCG) [9].

$$nDCG(k) = \frac{1}{N_\Delta}\sum\nolimits_{|\Delta|} \frac{1}{Z_\Delta}\sum_{i=1}^{k} \frac{2^{r_i}-1}{\log(1+i)}$$

where N_Δ denotes the total numbers of queries or users (Δ=q for queries and Δ=u for users), k indicates the top-k positions in a ranked list, and Z_Δ is a normalization factor obtained from a perfect ranking for a particular query/user. r_i is the judge score (i.e., 1: relevant/reposted, 0: irrelevant/unretweeted) for the i-th posting document in the ranking list for the query/user.

Topic	EN-1	EN-2	EN-3	EN-4	EN-5	CN-1	CN-2	CN-3	CN-4	CN-5
LM	15851	11356	10676	7584	8257	22306	17441	10204	16887	9237
Additive	15195	10035	10342	7198	7924	19139	16221	10108	16342	9003
Absolute	15323	10123	10379	7230	8093	19403	16932	9984	16681	9111
Jelinek-Mercer	14115	10011	10185	9818	8003	20025	16201	10049	16001	8728
Dirichlet	13892	9516	10138	7124	7345	19712	16361	9119	15886	8550
PLM	13730	9925	10426	6913	7512	19965	15230	9865	14219	8981
CBDM	12931	9845	9311	6893	7510	19129	15194	9323	15113	7906
DELM	11853	9820	9513	7133	7348	18809	14165	9510	13985	7621
SLMS	10788*	9539*	8408*	5817*	7109*	18169*	15375*	9194*	13212*	6919*

Table 3: Perplexity of language models under different hashtag topic clusters. '⋆' indicates that we accept the improvement hypothesis of SLMS over the best rival baseline by Wilcoxon test at a significance level of 0.01.

We also evaluate the system in terms of Mean Average Precision (MAP) [20] under a similar judge assumption as above:

$$MAP = \frac{1}{N_\Delta} \sum\nolimits_{|\Delta|} \frac{1}{Z_\Delta} \sum_{i=1}^{k} P_i \times r_i$$

Here N_Δ is the number of documents associated with the query or user, Z_Δ is the number of relevant documents retrieved or recommended, and P_i is the precision at i-th position for the query/user.

4.4 Overall Performance

We compare the performance of all methods of language model smoothing in the two datasets, measured in the intrinsic evaluation of perplexity, as well as the extrinsic evaluation of retrieval and recommendation. Table 3-5 list the overall results against all baseline methods. Our proposed method SLMS shows clearly better performance than the baseline methods. On average, SLMS achieves an average +23.8% improvement compared with other methods in terms of nDCG and MAP, and an average -18.6% improvement in terms of language perplexity in hashtag topic clustering. The advantage of our proposed method mainly comes from the two dimensions of textual influence and social influence propagated through the documents on social networks. We use a myriad of attribute factors and dependencies to control the influence propagation on the factor graph to make a more reliable estimation.

Language model without any smoothing performs worst as expected, and once again demonstrates the severe weakness of data sparsity on social networks - the *Achilles Heel*! Simple intuition based methods such as additive smoothing does not help a lot, since it only arbitrarily modifies the given term counts straightforward to avoid zero occurrence, which is proved to be insufficient. Absolute smoothing has a comparable performance as additive, due to the similar idea to reduce term counts naively. Jelinek-Mercer and Dirichlet methods are more useful since they include the information from the whole collection as background language models, but they fail to distinguish documents from documents and use all of them equally into smoothing. PLM offers a strengthened language model smoothing strategy within each posting document based on positions, and smooth the terms outside of the posting document formulating the background collection into a Dirichlet prior. The performance of CBDM and DELM indicates a prominent improvement, and proves that semantic attributes included into the smoothing process really make a difference. Both of the smoothing methods cluster documents, and use the clustered documents as a better background. However, none of these methods has made use of the social factors during the language model smoothing, while our method suggests social attributes, such as interactions and relationships, do have an impact on texts through influence propagation.

Having demonstrated the effectiveness of our proposed methods, we carry the next move to investigate more analysis on parameter settings, factor contributions, convergence and distributed learning analysis, which lead to some interesting observations.

	nDCG@5	nDCG@25	nDCG@50	MAP
LM	0.271	0.298	0.319	0.328
Additive	0.295	0.320	0.331	0.385
Absolute	0.283	0.328	0.378	0.367
Jelinek-Mercer	0.331	0.376	0.361	0.503
Dirichlet	0.365	0.387	0.408	0.555
PLM	0.392	0.413	0.399	0.532
CBDM	0.388	0.397	0.426	0.546
DELM	0.404	0.438	0.489	0.566
SLMS	0.463*	0.492*	0.503*	0.600*

Table 4: Retrieval performance against baselines. '⋆' indicates that we accept the improvement hypothesis of SLMS over the best baseline by Wilcoxon test at a significance level of 0.01.

	nDCG@5	nDCG@25	nDCG@50	MAP
LM	0.506	0.534	0.570	0.603
Additive	0.521	0.572	0.583	0.632
Absolute	0.525	0.581	0.585	0.635
Jelinek-Mercer	0.543	0.583	0.591	0.646
Dirichlet	0.562	0.609	0.621	0.639
PLM	0.558	0.602	0.619	0.653
CBDM	0.538	0.616	0.647	0.651
DELM	0.557	0.645	0.669	0.660
SLMS	0.617*	0.662*	0.689*	0.673*

Table 5: Recommendation performance. '⋆' indicates that we accept the improvement hypothesis of SLMS over the best rival baseline by Wilcoxon test at a significance level of 0.01.

4.5 Analysis and Discussions

4.5.1 *Parameter Settings*

In the experiments, as we crawled data from two consecutive months, we learn parameters $\theta=\{\alpha, \beta\}$ on the data from the first month, using the labels by the reposting behavior, and examine the performance on the testing data from the next month. There is another free parameter λ in Equation (15) to balance the origi-

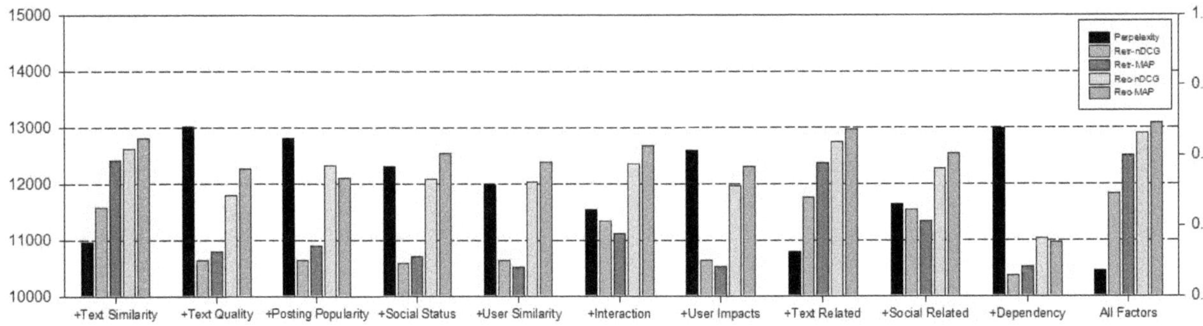

Figure 3: Performance comparison measured in perplexity, nDCG@25, and MAP in hashtag topic clustering, retrieval and recommendation tasks for feature analysis. "+factor(s)" means the performance of individual factor (group) in isolation.

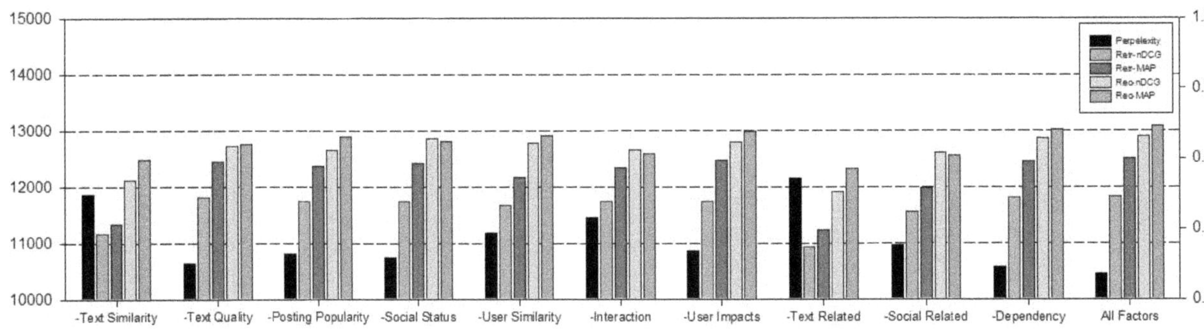

Figure 4: Performance comparison measured in perplexity, nDCG@25, and MAP in hashtag topic clustering, retrieval and recommendation tasks. "-factor(s)" means the performance of individual factor (group) when dropped out from the all-feature model.

nal language model and the smoothing language model. As we opt for more or less generic parameter value as we do not want to tune our method too much to suit the specific datasets at hand, we experiment with value ranging from 0 to 0.9, with a step size of 0.1. By examining the performance of perplexity, we find $\lambda \in [0.3, 0.4]$ yields the best results for the two datasets, hence we set λ=0.35.

4.5.2 *Factor Contributions*

We further analyze the contribution or all factors. We conduct to a detailed experiment on all separate factors and visualize the result in Figure 3-4. In the factor graph for socialized language model smoothing, we consider 8 different attributes and factors: (i) text similarity, (ii) text quality, (iii) posting popularity, (iv) social status, (v) user similarity, (vi) social interactions, (vii) user impacts and (viii) variable dependency. Besides, we combine factors (i)-(iii) as *text related* ones and (iv)-(vii) as *social related* ones. We also list the performance of SLMS which employs all components here for comparison. Here we examine the contribution of the different factors defined in our model. To be specific, we show the performance of all the factors in isolation and then leave-one-out from the full combination of all features, one at a time.

From Figure 3 and 4, we see that all of the individual factors have positive contributions to our evaluation tasks. The first result in Figure 3 is performed using the correspond component only and the second group of results in Figure 4 is performed using the full factor combination exempting the corresponding component, using a leave-one-out manner. For the individual factor analysis, we could see that on average *text similarity* still contributes most in isolation and its absence leads to unfavorable decrease. As to the social related features, *interaction* is the most important social factor for measuring the propagated influence, and gets a clear drop on the performance when left out from full factor combination. It is natural to see through the reposting behavior, the language model for a particular user is influenced by others. We also examine the three aspects of feature groups, i.e., text related factors, social related factors and variable dependencies. Text related factors are proved to be more useful while the social group yields better performance when integrate the factors together. Dependency factor seems to be the least powerful predictor. It is understandable that dependency factor is not deterministic but just to balance the label values. In general, the combination of all factors will be beneficial to improve the performance, as directly compared in Figure 3 and 4, which indicates that our method works well by combining the different factor functions and each factor in our method contributes to the overall improvements.

4.5.3 *Convergence Property*

We conduct an experiment to see the effect of the number of the loopy belief propagation iterations. Figure 5 (a) illustrates the convergence analysis results of the learning algorithm. We see on both test cases, the LBP-based learning algorithm can converges in less than 10 iterations. After only 6-7 learning iterations, the performance in terms of perplexity on both test cases becomes stable. This suggests that learning algorithm is very efficient and has a good convergence property.

4.5.4 *Distributed Scalability*

The distributed learning environment can typically achieve a significant reduction of the CPU time on the large-scale social networks. On the moderate scaled network after filtering and pre-

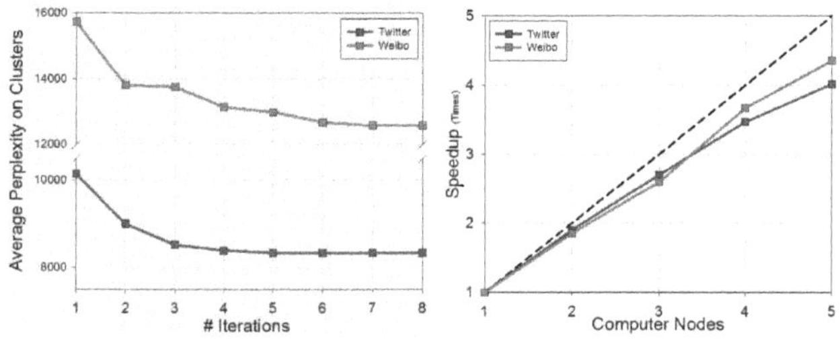

(a). Convergence performance. (b). Distributed computing speedups.

Figure 5: Experimental analysis illustrations.

processing, the speedup of the distributed influence learning is about 3-4 times. However, under the scenario of real world applications without human supervised filtering or pre-processing, the distributed learning framework can generally scale up with a speedup of 10-15 times or more [28].

In particular, we further conduct a scalability experiment with our distributed learning environment. We evaluate the speedup of the distributed learning algorithm on the 5 computer nodes using the two datasets. It can be seen from Figure 5 (b) that when the size of the data set is sufficiently large, the distributed learning shows a good parallel efficiency (speedup>3). In the figure, the dashed line denotes the perfect speedup ideally. The result confirms that the benefits to apply the distributed algorithm on the divisible subgraphs and that the distributed learning like many distributed learning algorithms is good on large-scale data sets.

5. RELATED WORK

Language models have been paid high attention to during recent years [25]. Many different ways of language modeling have been proposed to solve different research tasks. Better estimation of query language models [14, 15] and more accurate estimation of document language models [18, 30] have long been proved to be of great significance in information retrieval and text mining, etc. Language models are typically implemented based on traditional retrieval models, such as text weighting and normalization [40], but with more elegant mathematical and statistical foundations [26].

There is one problem for language models. Given limited data sampling, a language model estimation sometimes encounters with the zero count problem: the maximum likelihood estimator would give unseen terms a zero probability, which is not reliable. Language model smoothing is proposed to address this problem, and has been demonstrated to affect performance significantly [40, 14].

Many approaches have been proposed and tested. There are several ways of to smooth the original language model. The information of background corpus has been incorporated using linear combination [25, 40]. In contrast to the simple strategy which smoothes all documents with the same background, recently corpus contents have been exploited for more accurate smoothing. The basic idea is to smooth a document language model with the documents similar to the document under consideration through clustering [34, 18, 30]. Position information has also been used to enrich language model smoothing [41, 19] and the combination of both strategies of position and semantics [34]. In their work, the key idea is to define a language model for each position within a document, and score it based on the language models on all positions: hence the effect of positional adjacency is revealed. Beyond the semantic and/or position related smoothing intuitions, structural based language model smoothing is an alternative direction to investigate. A graph based language model smoothing method has been proposed utilizing structural adjacency only between neighboring nodes [21, 8].

There is a study in [17] which smoothes document language models of tweets for topic tracking in online text streams. Basically, it applies general smoothing strategies (e.g., Jelinek-Mercer, Dirichlet, Absolute Discounting, etc.) on the specific tracking task, while we have proposed a unified factor graph model based framework which incorporates a series of social factors as well as the text information on language model smoothing, which is a novel insight. To the best of our knowledge, we are the pilot study which maps the social influence onto the textual dimension and hence to estimate the influence between posting documents. Language model is smoothed by the influence propagated on the factor graph.

6. CONCLUSIONS

Online social networks are massive, useful and of great potentials, but have a severe bottleneck of textual data sparsity. To tackle such an Achilles Heel of social networks, we present an influence propagation based language model smoothing method to solve the zero count phenomenon for online social networks. The social influence is estimated based on a factor graph model, by utilizing a series of attributes and dependency factors from both textual and social dimensions. In this way, we propagate the term occurrence along the networks with a discounted counts according to the estimated pairwise influence between documents, and finally smooth the sparse language model accordingly.

We examine the effect of our proposed language model smoothing method on a series of intrinsic and extrinsic evaluation metrics based on the Twitter dataset (in English) and Weibo dataset (in Chinese). Our proposed method consistently and significantly outperforms the alternative baselines (with -18.6% improvement in terms of perplexity and +23.8% improvement in nDCG and MAP). Furthermore, we have investigated factor contributions as well as a series of experimental analysis for convergence and distributed learning. In general, all features facilitate the smoothing performance, while text similarity and social interaction are proved to have a stronger contribution. In the future, we will include more flexible social factors and make our model adaptive to diversified online social networks, e.g., structures with reciprocal linkage (e.g., Facebook) or documents without reposting behaviors (e.g., Foursquare).

7. ACKNOWLEDGMENTS

This work was partially done when the first author was in University of Pennsylvania. We thank all the anonymous reviewers for their valuable and constructive comments.

8. REFERENCES

[1] P. Analytics. Twitter study–august 2009. 15, 2009.

[2] L. Bottou. Online learning and stochastic approximations. *On-line learning in neural networks*, 17:9, 1998.

[3] M. A. Carreira-Perpinan and G. E. Hinton. On contrastive divergence learning. In *Artificial Intelligence and Statistics*, volume 2005, page 17, 2005.

[4] G. Casella and E. I. George. Explaining the gibbs sampler. *The American Statistician*, 46:167–174, 1992.

[5] K. Chen, T. Chen, G. Zheng, O. Jin, E. Yao, and Y. Yu. Collaborative personalized tweet recommendation. In *SIGIR '12*, pages 661–670, 2012.

[6] J. Dean and S. Ghemawat. Mapreduce: Simplified data processing on large clusters. pages 107–113, 2004.

[7] J. Hopcroft, T. Lou, and J. Tang. Who will follow you back?: Reciprocal relationship prediction. In *CIKM '11*, pages 1137–1146, 2011.

[8] Y.-Y. Huang, R. Yan, T.-T. Kuo, and S.-D. Lin. Enriching cold start personalized language model using social network information. In *ACL '14*, pages 611–617, 2014.

[9] K. Järvelin and J. Kekäläinen. Cumulated gain-based evaluation of ir techniques. *ACM Trans. Inf. Syst.*, 20(4):422–446, 2002.

[10] R. Kindermann, J. L. Snell, et al. *Markov random fields and their applications*, volume 1. American Mathematical Society Providence, RI, 1980.

[11] F. R. Kschischang, B. J. Frey, and H.-A. Loeliger. Factor graphs and the sum-product algorithm. *Information Theory, IEEE Transactions on*, 47(2):498–519, 2001.

[12] T.-T. Kuo, R. Yan, Y.-Y. Huang, P.-H. Kung, and S.-D. Lin. Unsupervised link prediction using aggregative statistics on heterogeneous social networks. In *KDD '13*, pages 775–783, 2013.

[13] H. Kwak, C. Lee, H. Park, and S. Moon. What is twitter, a social network or a news media? In *WWW '10*, pages 591–600, 2010.

[14] J. Lafferty and C. Zhai. Document language models, query models, and risk minimization for information retrieval. In *SIGIR '01*, pages 111–119, 2001.

[15] V. Lavrenko and W. B. Croft. Relevance based language models. In *SIGIR '01*, pages 120–127, 2001.

[16] C. Lin, C. Lin, J. Li, D. Wang, Y. Chen, and T. Li. Generating event storylines from microblogs. In *CIKM '12*, pages 175–184, 2012.

[17] J. Lin, R. Snow, and W. Morgan. Smoothing techniques for adaptive online language models: Topic tracking in tweet streams. In *KDD '11*, pages 422–429, 2011.

[18] X. Liu and W. B. Croft. Cluster-based retrieval using language models. In *SIGIR '04*, pages 186–193, 2004.

[19] Y. Lv and C. Zhai. Positional language models for information retrieval. In *SIGIR '09*, pages 299–306, 2009.

[20] C. D. Manning, P. Raghavan, and H. Schütze. *Introduction to information retrieval*, volume 1. 2008.

[21] Q. Mei, D. Zhang, and C. Zhai. A general optimization framework for smoothing language models on graph structures. In *SIGIR '08*, pages 611–618, 2008.

[22] H. Ney, U. Essen, and R. Kneser. On the estimation ofsmall'probabilities by leaving-one-out. *Pattern Analysis and Machine Intelligence, IEEE Transactions on*, 17(12):1202–1212, 1995.

[23] L. Page, S. Brin, R. Motwani, and T. Winograd. The pagerank citation ranking: bringing order to the web. 1999.

[24] E. Pitler, A. Louis, and A. Nenkova. Automatic evaluation of linguistic quality in multi-document summarization. In *ACL '10*, pages 544–554, 2010.

[25] J. M. Ponte and W. B. Croft. A language modeling approach to information retrieval. In *SIGIR '98*, pages 275–281, 1998.

[26] F. Song and W. B. Croft. A general language model for information retrieval. In *CIKM '99*, pages 316–321, 1999.

[27] J. Tang, T. Lou, and J. Kleinberg. Inferring social ties across heterogenous networks. In *WSDM '12*, pages 743–752, 2012.

[28] J. Tang, J. Sun, C. Wang, and Z. Yang. Social influence analysis in large-scale networks. In *KDD '09*, pages 807–816, 2009.

[29] W. Tang, H. Zhuang, and J. Tang. Learning to infer social ties in large networks. In *ECML/PKDD '11*, pages 381–397. 2011.

[30] T. Tao, X. Wang, Q. Mei, and C. Zhai. Language model information retrieval with document expansion. In *HLT-NAACL '06*, pages 407–414.

[31] J. Teevan, D. Ramage, and M. R. Morris. #twittersearch: A comparison of microblog search and web search. In *WSDM '11*, pages 35–44, 2011.

[32] Z. Wang, J. Li, Z. Wang, and J. Tang. Cross-lingual knowledge linking across wiki knowledge bases. In *WWW '12*, pages 459–468, 2012.

[33] S. Wu, J. Sun, and J. Tang. Patent partner recommendation in enterprise social networks. In *WSDM '13*, pages 43–52, 2013.

[34] R. Yan, H. Jiang, M. Lapata, S.-D. Lin, X. Lv, and X. Li. Semantic v.s. positions: Utilizing balanced proximity in language model smoothing for information retrieval. In *IJCNLP'13*, pages 507–515, 2013.

[35] R. Yan, L. Kong, C. Huang, X. Wan, X. Li, and Y. Zhang. Timeline generation through evolutionary trans-temporal summarization. In *EMNLP '11*, pages 433–443, 2011.

[36] R. Yan, M. Lapata, and X. Li. Tweet recommendation with graph co-ranking. In *ACL '12*, pages 516–525, 2012.

[37] R. Yan, X. Wan, J. Otterbacher, L. Kong, X. Li, and Y. Zhang. Evolutionary timeline summarization: A balanced optimization framework via iterative substitution. In *SIGIR'11*, pages 745–754, 2011.

[38] Z. Yang, K. Cai, J. Tang, L. Zhang, Z. Su, and J. Li. Social context summarization. In *SIGIR '11*, pages 255–264, 2011.

[39] J. S. Yedidia, W. T. Freeman, Y. Weiss, et al. Generalized belief propagation. In *NIPS*, volume 13, pages 689–695, 2000.

[40] C. Zhai and J. Lafferty. A study of smoothing methods for language models applied to ad hoc information retrieval. In *SIGIR '01*, pages 334–342, 2001.

[41] J. Zhao and Y. Yun. A proximity language model for information retrieval. In *SIGIR '09*, pages 291–298, 2009.

[42] W. X. Zhao, J. Jiang, J. Weng, J. He, E.-P. Lim, H. Yan, and X. Li. Comparing twitter and traditional media using topic models. In *ECIR '11*, pages 338–349. 2011.

[43] X. W. Zhao, Y. Guo, R. Yan, Y. He, and X. Li. Timeline generation with social attention. In *SIGIR '13*, pages 1061–1064, 2013.

A Game Theoretic Model for the Formation of Navigable Small-World Networks*

Zhi Yang[§] and Wei Chen[†]
[§]Computer Science Department, Peking University, Beijing, China
[†]Microsoft Research, Beijing, China
yangzhi@net.pku.edu.cn, weic@microsoft.com

ABSTRACT

Kleinberg proposed a family of small-world networks to explain the navigability of large-scale real-world social networks. However, the underlying mechanism that drives real networks to be navigable is not yet well understood. In this paper, we present a game theoretic model for the formation of navigable small world networks. We model the network formation as a game in which people seek for both high reciprocity and long-distance relationships. We show that the navigable small-world network is a Nash Equilibrium of the game. Moreover, we prove that the navigable small-world equilibrium tolerates collusions of any size and arbitrary deviations of a large random set of nodes, while non-navigable equilibria do not tolerate small group collusions or random perturbations. Our empirical evaluation further demonstrates that the system always converges to the navigable network even when limited or no information about other players' strategies is available. Our theoretical and empirical analyses provide important new insight on the connection between distance, reciprocity and navigability in social networks.

Categories and Subject Descriptors

G.2.2 [**Discrete Mathematics**]: Graph Theory—*Network problems*

General Terms

Theory

Keywords

small-world network, game theory, navigability, reciprocity

1. INTRODUCTION

In 1967, Milgram published his work on the now famous small-world experiment [30]: he asked test subjects to forward a letter to their friends in order for the letter to reach a person not known to the initiator of the letter. He found that on average it took only six hops to connect two people in U.S., and coined the term *six-degree of separation*. This seminal work inspired numerous researches on the small-world phenomenon and small-world models, which last till the present day of information age.

In [36] Watts and Strogatz investigated a number of real-world networks such as film actor networks and power grids, and showed that many networks have both low diameter and high clustering (meaning two neighbors of a node are likely to be neighbors of each other), which is different from randomly wired networks. They thus proposed a small-world model in which nodes are first placed on a ring or a grid with local connections, and then some connections are randomly rewired to connect to long-range contacts in the network. The local and long-range connections can also be viewed as strong ties and weak ties respectively in social relationships originally proposed by Granovetter [14, 13].

Kleinberg notices an important discrepancy between the small-world model of Watts and Strogatz and the original Milgram experiment: the latter shows not only that the average distance between nodes in the network are small, but also that nodes can efficiently navigate in the network with only local information. To address this issue, Kleinberg adjusted Watts-Strogatz model so that the long-range connections are selected not uniformly at random among all nodes but inversely proportional to a power of the grid distance between the two end points of the connection [21].

More specifically, Kleinberg modeled a social network as composed of n^k nodes on a k-dimensional grid, with each node having local contacts to other nodes in its immediate geographic neighborhood. Each node u also establishes a number of long-range contacts, and a long-range link from u to v is established with probability proportional to $d_M(u,v)^{-r}$, where $d_M(u,v)$ is the grid distance between u and v, and $r \geq 0$ is the model parameter indicating how likely nodes prefer to connect to remote nodes, which we call *connection preference* in the paper. Watts-Strogatz model corresponds to the case of $r = 0$, and as r increases, nodes are more likely to connect to other nodes in their vicinity. Kleinberg modeled Milgram's experiment as decentralized greedy routing in such networks, in which each node only forwards messages to one of its neighbors with coordinate closest to the target node. He showed that when $r = k$, greedy routing can be done efficiently in $O(\log^2 n)$ time in expectation, but for any $r \neq k$, it requires $O(n^c)$ time for some constant c depending on r. Therefore, the small world at the critical value of $r = k$ is meant to model the real network, and we call it the *navigable small-world network*.

*The work is done when the first author is a visiting researcher at Microsoft Research Asia.

WWW 2015, May 18–22, 2015, Florence, Italy.
ACM 978-1-4503-3469-3/15/05.
http://dx.doi.org/10.1145/2736277.2741110.

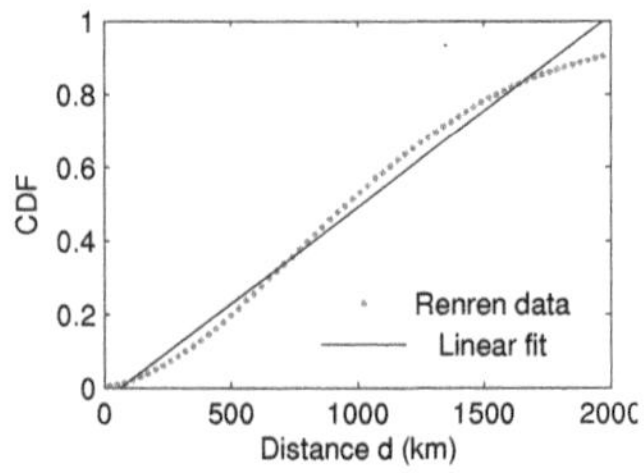

Figure 1: The fraction of nodes within distance d in Renren.

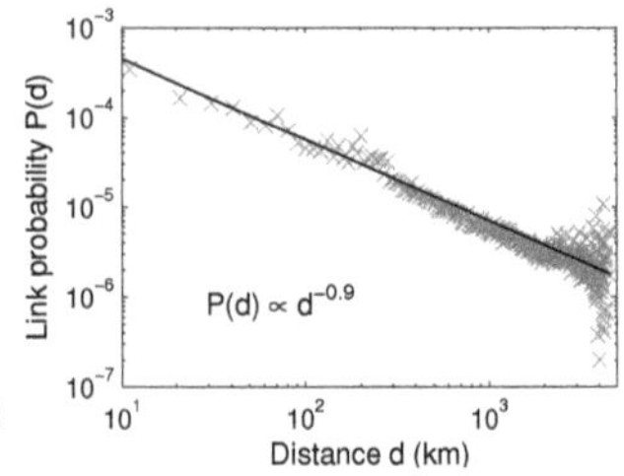

Figure 2: Friendship probability vs. distance in Renren.

After Kleinberg's theoretical analysis, a number of empirical studies have been conducted to verify if real networks indeed have connection preference close to the critical value that allows efficient greedy routing [28, 1, 7, 10, 34]. Since real network population is not evenly distributed geographically as in the Kleinberg's model, Liben-Nowell et al. [28] proposed to use the *fractional dimension* α, defined as the best value to fit $|\{w : d_M(u, w) \leq d_M(u, v)\}| = c \cdot d_M(u, v)^\alpha$. They showed that when the connection preference $r = \alpha$, the network is navigable. They then studied a network of 495,836 LiveJournal users in the continental United States who list their hometowns, and find that $\alpha \approx 0.8$ while $r = 1.2$, reasonably close to α. We apply the same approach to a ten million node Renren network [19, 38], one of the largest online social networks in China. We map the hometown listed in users' profiles to (longitude, latitude) coordinates. The resolution of our geographic data is limited to the level of towns and cities and thus we cannot get the exact distance of nodes within 10km. We found that $\alpha \approx 1$ (Figure 1) and $r \approx 0.9$ (Figure 2) in Renren network. Other studies [1, 7, 10, 34] also reported connection preference r to be close to 1 in other online social networks (including Gowalla, Brightkite and Facebook). Even though they did not report the fractional dimension, from both the LiveJournal data in [28] and our Renren data, it is reasonable to believe that the fractional dimension is also close to 1. Therefore, empirical evidences all suggest that the real-world social networks indeed have connection preference close to the critical value and the network is navigable.

A natural question to ask next is how navigable networks naturally emerge? What are the forces that make the connection preference become close to the critical value? As Kleinberg pointed out in his survey paper [22] when talking about the above striking coincidence between theoretical prediction and empirical observation, "it suggests that there may be deeper phenomena yet to be discovered here". There are several studies trying to explain the emergence of navigable small-world networks [29, 16, 8, 33, 5], mostly by modeling certain underlying node or link dynamics (see related work for more details).

In this paper, we tackle the problem in a novel way using game-theoretic approach, which is reasonable in modeling individual behaviors in social networks without central coordination. One key insight we have is that connection preference r is not a global preference but individual's own preference — some prefer to connect to more faraway nodes while others prefer to connect to nearby nodes. Therefore, we establish *small-world formation games* where individual node u's strategy is its own connection preference r_u (Section 3). This game formulation is different from most existing network formation games where individuals' strategies are creating actual links in the network (c.f. [35]). It allows us to directly explore the entire parameter space of connection preferences and answer the question on why nodes end up choosing a particular parameter setting leading to the navigable small world.

In terms of payoff functions, we first consider minimizing greedy routing distance to other nodes as the payoff, since it directly corresponds to the goal of navigable networks. However, Gulyás et al. [15] prove that with this payoff the navigable networks cannot emerge as a equilibrium for the one-dimensional case. Our empirical analysis also indicates that nodes will converge to random networks ($r_u = 0, \forall u$) rather than navigable networks for higher dimensions. Our empirical analysis further shows that if we adjust the payoff with a cost proportional to the grid distance of remote connections, the equilibria are sensitive to the cost factor.

The above unsuccessful attempt suggests that besides the goal of shortening distance to remote nodes, some other natural objective may be in play. Reciprocity is regarded as a basis mechanism that creates stable social relationships in a person's life [12]. A number of prior works [18, 28, 31] also suggest that people seek reciprocal relationships in online social networks. Therefore, we propose a payoff function that is the product of average distance of nodes to their long-range contacts and the probability of forming reciprocal relationship with long-range contacts. We call this game distance-reciprocity balanced (DRB) game. In practice, increasing relationship distance captures that individuals attempt to create social bridges by linking to "distant people", which can help them search for and obtain new resources. Meanwhile, increasing reciprocity captures that individuals look at social bonds by linking to "people like them", which could help them preserve or maintain resources. Therefore, the DRB game is natural since it captures sources of bridging and bonding social capital in building social integration and solidarity [9].

Even though the payoff function for the DRB game is very simple, our analysis demonstrates that it is extremely effective in producing navigable small-world networks as the equilibrium structure. In theoretical analysis (Section 4), we first show that both navigable small world ($r_u = k, \forall u$) and random small world ($r_u = 0, \forall u$) are the only two uniform Nash equilibria of the DRB game. Although we do not know whether non-uniform equilibria exist, we prove that the navigable small world is a strong Nash equilibrium, which means that it tolerates collusion of any size trying to gain better payoff, and it also tolerates arbitrary deviations (without the objective of increasing anyone's payoff) of large groups of random deviators. In contrast, any non-navigable equilibrium such as the random small world or possible non-uniform equilibria does not tolerate either collusions or random perturbations of a small group of nodes. Our theoretical analysis provides strong support that navigable small-world network is the unique stable equilibrium that would naturally emerge in the DRB game.

We further conduct empirical evaluations to cover more realistic game scenarios not covered by our theoretical analysis (Section 5). We first test random perturbation cases and show that arbitrary initial profiles always converge to the navigable equilibrium in a few steps, while a very small random perturbation (less than theoretical prediction) of the random small world causes it to quickly converge back to the navigable equilibrium. Next, we simulate more realistic scenarios where nodes have limited or no information about other nodes' strategies. We show that if they only learn their friends' strategies (with some noise), the system still converges close to the navigable equilibrium in a small number of steps. Finally, even when the node has no information about other players' strategies and can only use its obtained payoff as feedback to search for the best strategy, the system still moves close to the navigable equilibrium within a few hundred steps (in the 100×100 grid). These empirical results further demonstrate the robustness of the navigable small world in the DRB game.

In summary, our contributions are the following: (a) we propose the small-world formation game and design a balanced distance-reciprocity payoff function to explain the navigability of real social networks; (b) we conduct comprehensive theoretical and empirical analysis to demonstrate that navigable small world is a unique robust equilibrium that would naturally emerge from the game under both random perturbation and strategic collusions; and (c) our game reveals a new insight between distance, reciprocity and navigability in social networks, which may help future research in uncovering deeper phenomena in navigable social networks. To our best knowledge, this is the first game theoretic study on the emergence of navigable small-world networks, and the first study that linking relationship reciprocity with network navigability.

Additional related work. We provide additional details of prior works on explaining the emergence of navigable small-world networks, and other related studies not covered in the introduction.

Some studies try to explain navigability by assuming that nodes form links to optimize for a particular property. Mathias et al. [29] assume that users try to make trade-off between wiring and connectivity. Hu et al. [16] assume that people try to maximize the entropy under a constraint on the total distances of their long-range contacts. These works rely on simulations to study the network dynamics. Moreover, the navigability of a network is sensitive to the weight of wiring cost or the distance constraint, and it is unlikely that navigable networks as defined by Kleinberg [21] would naturally emerge.

Another type of works propose node/link dynamics that converge to navigable small-world networks. Clauset and Moore [8] propose a rewiring dynamic modeling a Web surfer such that if the surfer does not find what she wants in a few steps of greedy search, she would rewire her long-range contact to the current end node of the greedy search. They use simulations to demonstrate that a network close to Kleinberg's navigable small world will emerge after long enough rewiring rounds. Sandberg and Clarke [33] propose another rewiring dynamic where with an independent probability of p each node on a greedy search path would rewire their long-range contacts to the search target, and provide a partial analysis and simulations showing that the dynamic converges to a network close to the navigable small world. Chaintreau et al. [5] use a move-and-forget mobility model, in which a token starting from each node conducts a random walk (move) and may also go back to the starting point (forget), and use the distribution of the token on the grid as the distribution of the long-range contacts of the starting node. They provide theoretical analysis showing that the move-and-forget model with a particular harmonic forget function converges close to the navigable small world. However, it is unclear if the harmonic forget function used is natural in practice and what is the effect of other forget functions.

The approach taken by these studies can be viewed as orthogonal and complementary to our approach: they aim at using natural dynamics (rewiring or mobility dynamics) to explain navigable small world, while we focus on directly exploring the entire parameter space of connection preferences of nodes and use game theoretic approach to show, both theoretically and empirically, that the nodes would naturally choose their connection preferences to form the navigable small world. Moreover, all the prior studies only show that they converge approximately to the navigable small world, while in our game the navigable small world is precisely the only robust equilibrium. Finally, none of these works introduce reciprocity in their model and we are the first to link reciprocity with navigability of the small world.

Some studies use hyperbolic metric spaces or graphs to try to explain navigability in small-world networks (e.g. [4, 32, 23, 24, 6]). However, they do not explain why connection preferences in real networks are around the critical value and how navigable networks naturally emerge. In particular, Chen et al. [6] show that the navigable small world in Kleinberg's model does not have good hyperbolicity.

A number of network dynamics are proposed to address general network evolution, but they do not address network navigability in particular. For example, models in [3, 27, 26, 11] leverage preferential attachment or triangle closure mechanisms to capture power-law degree or high clustering coefficient, and other models [2, 20] capture spatial effects using a gravity model, balancing the effect of spatial distance with other node properties (e.g., node degree).

2. PRELIMINARIES

In this section, we present the Kleinberg's small-world model and some basic concepts of a noncooperative game.

2.1 Kleinberg's Small-World Model

Let $V = \{(i,j) : i,j \in [n] = \{1,2,\ldots,n\}\}$ by the set of n^2 nodes forming an $n \times n$ grid. For convenience, we consider the grid with wrap-around edges connecting the nodes on the two opposite sides, making it a torus. For any two nodes $u = (i_u, j_u)$ and $v = (i_v, j_v)$ on this wrap-around grid, the *grid distance* or *Manhattan distance* between u and v is defined as $d_M(u,v) = min\{|i_v - i_u|, n - |i_v - i_u|\} + min\{|j_v - j_u|, n - |j_v - j_u|\}$.

The model has two universal constants $p, q \geq 1$, such that (a) each node has undirected edges connecting to all other nodes within lattice distance p, called its *local contacts*, and (b) each node has q random directed edges connecting to possibly faraway nodes in the grid called its *long-range contacts*, drawn from the following distribution. Each node u has a *connection preference* parameter $r_u \geq 0$, such that the i-th long-range edge from u has endpoint v with probability proportional to $1/d_M(u,v)^{r_u}$, that is, with probability $p_u = d_M(u,v)^{-r_u}/c(r_u)$, where $c(r_u) = \sum_{\forall v \neq u} d(u,v)^{-r_u}$ is the normalization constant. Let $\mathbf{r}$ be the vector of r_u values on all nodes. We use $\mathbf{r} \equiv s$ to denote $r_u = s, \forall u \in V$.

Greedy routing on the small-world network from a source node u to a target node v is a decentralized algorithm starting at node u, and at each step if routing reaches a node w, then w selects one node from its local and long-range contacts that is closest to v in grid distance as the next step in the routing path, until it reaches v. In [21], Kleinberg shows that when $\mathbf{r} \equiv 2$, the expected number of greedy routing steps (called *delivery time*) is $O(\log^2 n)$, but when $\mathbf{r} \equiv s \neq 2$, it is $\Omega(n^c)$ for some constant c related to s.

The above model can be easily extended to k dimensional grid (with wraparound) for any $k = 1, 2, 3, \ldots$, where each long range contact is still established with probability proportional to $1/d_M(u,v)^{r_u}$. It is shown that $\mathbf{r} \equiv k$ is the critical value allowing efficient greedy routing. Henceforth, we call Kleinberg's small world with $\mathbf{r} \equiv k$ the *navigable small world*. Another special network is $\mathbf{r} \equiv 0$, in which every node's long-range contacts are selected among all nodes uniformly at random, and we refer it as the *random small world*. We use $K(n, k, p, q, \mathbf{r})$ to refer to the class of Kleinberg random graphs with parameters n, k, p, q, and $\mathbf{r}$.

2.2 Game and Solution Concepts

A game is described by a system of players, strategies and payoffs. We denote a game by $\Gamma = (S_u, \pi_u)_{u \in V}$, where V represents a finite set of players, S_u is the set of strategies of player u, and $\pi_u : \mathcal{S} \to \mathbb{R}$ is the payoff function of node u, with $\mathcal{S} = S_1 \times S_2 \times \ldots \times S_n$. An element $\mathbf{s} = (s_1, s_2, \ldots, s_n) \in \mathcal{S}$ is called a *strategy profile*.

Let $\mathcal{C} = 2^V \setminus \emptyset$ denote the set of all coalitions. For each coalition $C \in \mathcal{C}$, let $-C = V \setminus C$, and if $C = \{u\}$, we denote $-C$ by $-u$. We also denote by $\mathcal{S}_C$ the set of strategies of players in coalition C, and $\mathbf{s}_C$ the partial strategy profile of $\mathbf{s}$ for nodes in C.

DEFINITION 1 (BEST RESPONSE). *Player u's strategy $s_u^* \in S_u$ is a best response to the strategy profile $\mathbf{s_{-u}} \in \mathcal{S}_{-u}$ if*

$$\pi_u(s_u^*, \mathbf{s_{-u}}) \geq \pi_u(s_u, \mathbf{s_{-u}}), \forall s_u \in S_u \setminus \{s_u^*\},$$

Moreover, if "$\geq$" above is actually "$>$" for all $s_u \neq s_u^*$, then s_u^* is the unique best response to $\mathbf{s_{-u}}$.

Nash equilibrium (NE) for a strategic game is a strategy profile such that each player's strategy is a best response to the other players' strategies.

DEFINITION 2 (NASH EQUILIBRIUM). *A strategy profile $\mathbf{s}^* \in \mathcal{S}$ is a Nash equilibrium if for every player $u \in V$, s_u^* is a best response to $\mathbf{s}_{-u}^*$; $\mathbf{s}^*$ is a strict Nash equilibrium if for every player $u \in V$, s_u^* is the unique best response to $\mathbf{s}_{-u}^*$.*

While in an NE no player can improve its payoff by unilateral deviation, some of the players may benefit (sometimes substantially) from forming alliances/coalitions with other players. The *strong Nash equilibrium (SNE)* is a strategy profile for which no coalition of players has a joint deviation that improves the payoff of each member of the coalition.

DEFINITION 3 (STRONG NASH EQUILIBRIUM). *For a real number $f \in (0, 1]$, a strategy profile $\mathbf{s}^* \in \mathcal{S}$ is an f-strong Nash equilibrium if for all $C \in \mathcal{C}$ with $|C| \leq f|V|$, there does not exist any $s_C \in \mathcal{S}_C$ such that*

$$\forall u \in C, \pi_u(\mathbf{s}_C, \mathbf{s}_{-C}^*) \geq \pi_u(\mathbf{s}^*), \exists u \in C, \pi_u(\mathbf{s}_C, \mathbf{s}_{-C}^*) > \pi_u(\mathbf{s}^*).$$

When $f = 1$, we simply call $\mathbf{s}^*$ the strong Nash equilibrium.

When restricting $|C| = 1$, SNE falls back to NE; when restricting $C = V$, SNE means *Pareto-optimal*, which requires that no player can improve her payoff without decreasing the payoff of someone else. Therefore, SNE is a very strong equilibrium concept allowing collusions of any size.

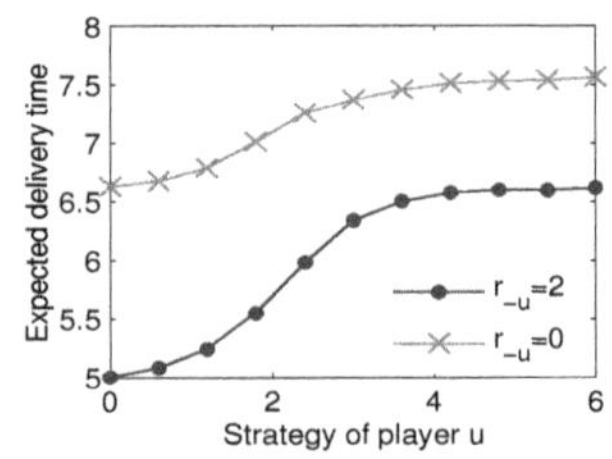

Figure 3: The expected delivery time for a player u with different strategy.

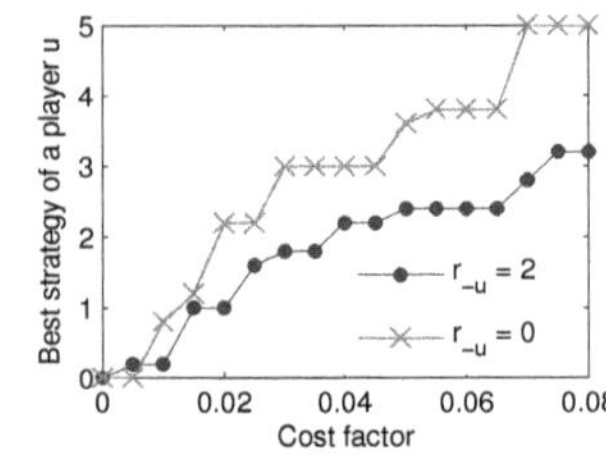

Figure 4: The best response of a player u given different cost factor.

3. SMALL-WORLD FORMATION GAMES

Connection preference r_u in Kleinberg's model reflects u's intention in establishing long-range contacts: When $r_u = 0$, u chooses its long-range contacts uniformly among all nodes in the grid; as r_u increases, the long-range contacts of u become increasingly clustered in its vicinity on the grid. Our insight is to treat connection preference as node's strategy in a game setting and study the game behavior.

More specifically, we model this via a non-cooperative game among nodes in the network. First, we assume that each r_u is taken from a discrete set $\Sigma = \{0, \gamma, 2\gamma, 3\gamma, \ldots, \}$, where γ represents the granularity of connection preference and is in the form of $1/g$ for some positive integer $g \geq 2$. Using discrete strategy set avoids nuances in continuous strategy space and is also reasonable in practice since people are unlikely to make infinitesimal changes. Next, we model the small-world network formation as a game $\Gamma = (\Sigma, \pi_u)_{u \in V}$, where V is the set of nodes in the grid, connection preference $r_u \in \Sigma$ is the strategy of a player u, and π_u is the payoff function of u. Our objective is to study intuitively appealing payoff functions π_u and find one that would allow the navigable small-world network to emerge.

3.1 Routing-based Payoff

As navigable small world achieves best greedy routing efficiency, it is natural to consider the payoff function as the expected delivery time to the target in greedy routing. Given the strategy profile $\mathbf{r} \in \mathcal{S}$, let $t_{uv}(r_u, \mathbf{r}_{-u})$ be the expected delivery time from source u to target v via greedy routing. The payoff function is given by:

$$\pi_u(r_u, \mathbf{r_{-u}}) = -\sum_{\forall v \neq u} t_{uv}(r_u, \mathbf{r}_{-u}). \quad (1)$$

We take a negation on the sum of expected delivery time because nodes prefer shorter delivery time.

Although the above payoff function is intuitive and simple, it has some serious issues. Prior work [15] has already proved that, with the length of greedy paths as the payoff, player u's best response is to link uniformly (i.e., $r_u = 0$) for the one-dimensional case. For high dimensions, Figure 3 shows the expected delivery time for a single node u at a 100×100 grids, where each node generates $q = 10$ links. We see that when other nodes fixed their strategy (e.g., $\mathbf{r}_{-u} \equiv 2$), the best strategy of a single node u is 0. More tests on different initial conditions reach the same result that the system will converge to the random small-world networks. The intuitive reason is that to reach other nodes quickly, it is better for a node to evenly spread its long-range contacts in the network.

This is inconsistent with empirical evidence that real-world networks are navigable ones. ([28, 7, 1, 10, 25, 17]).

In practice, creating and maintaining long-range links have higher costs, so one may adapt the above payoff function by adding the grid distances of long-range contacts as a cost term in the payoff function:

$$\pi_u(r_u, \mathbf{r_{-u}}) = -\sum_{\forall v \neq u} t_{uv}(r_u, \mathbf{r}_{-u}) - \lambda \sum_{v \neq u} p_u(v, r_u) d_M(u, v), \quad (2)$$

where λ is a factor controlling the long range cost. A larger λ means users are more concerned with distance costs. Figure 4 shows that the best strategy of a user u is significantly influenced by the cost factor. Similar result is also shown in [15]. Thus, it is unclear if the navigable small-world network can naturally emerge from this type of games.

3.2 Distance-Reciprocity Balanced Payoff

The previous section demonstrates that seeking short routing distance alone cannot explain the emergence of navigable small world, and thus people in the social network must have some other objective to achieve. Reciprocity is regarded as a basis mechanism that creates stable social relationships in the real world [12]. Several empirical studies [18, 28, 31] also show that high reciprocity is also a typical feature present in real small-world networks (such as Flickr, YouTube, LiveJournal, Orkut and Twitter).

Therefore, we consider the payoff of a user u as the following balanced objective between distance and reciprocity:

$$\pi_u(r_u, \mathbf{r_{-u}}) = \left(\sum_{\forall v \neq u} p_u(v, r_u) d_M(u, v) \right) \times \left(\sum_{\forall v \neq u} p_u(v, r_u) p_v(u, r_v) \right), \quad (3)$$

where $\sum_{\forall v \neq u} p_u(v, r_u) d_M(u, v)$ is the mean grid distance of u's long-range contacts, and $\sum_{\forall v \neq u} p_u(v, r_u) p_v(u, r_v)$ is the mean probability for u to form bi-directional links with its long-range contacts, i.e., reciprocity. We refer the small-world formation game with payoff function in Eq.(3) the *Distance-Reciprocity Balanced (DRB)* game.

The payoff function in Eq.(3) reflects two natural objectives users in a social network want to achieve: first, they want to connect to remote nodes, which may give them diverse information as in the famous "the strength of weak tie argument" by Granovetter [14]; second, they want to establish reciprocal relationship which are more stable in long term. However, these two objectives can be in conflict for a node u when others prefer linking in their vicinity (i.e., other nodes v choosing positive exponent r_v). In this case, faraway long-range contacts are less likely to create reciprocal links. Therefore, node u should obtain the maximum payoff when it achieves a balance between the two objectives. We use the simple product of distance and reciprocity objectives to model this balancing behavior.

4. PROPERTIES OF THE DRB GAME

In this section, we conduct theoretical analysis to discover the properties of the DRB game. When player u's strategy r_u is the unique best response to a strategy profile $\mathbf{r}_{-u}$, we denote this unique best response as $B_u(\mathbf{r}_{-u})$.

4.1 Equilibrium Existence in DRB Game

We first show that navigable small-world network is a Nash Equlibrium of the DRB game.

THEOREM 1. *For the DRB game in a k-dimensional grid, the following is true for sufficiently large n:* [1] *For every node $u \in V$, every strategy profile $\mathbf{r}$, and every $s \in \Sigma$, if $\mathbf{r}_{-u} \equiv s$, then u has a unique best response to $\mathbf{r}_{-u} \equiv s$:*

$$B_u(\mathbf{r}_{-u} \equiv s) = \begin{cases} k & \text{if } s > 0, \\ 0 & \text{if } s = 0. \end{cases}$$

PROOF (SKETCH). The intuition is as follows. When $s > 0$, all other nodes prefer long-range contacts in their vicinity. In this case, when node u chooses $0 \le r_u < k$, it achieves good average grid distance to long-range contacts but its long-range contact v is unlikely to have the reciprocal link to u because u is not likely to be in the vicinity of v. On the other hand, if u chooses $r_u > k$, it achieves good reciprocity but its average grid distance to long-range contacts is low. The case of $r_u = k$ provides the best balance between grid distance to long-range contacts and reciprocity. The detailed proof is included in Appendix A.

When $s = 0$, all others nodes link uniformly. In this case, the reciprocity for node u becomes a constant independent of its strategy r_u. Thus, r_u should be selected to maximize average distance of u's long-range contacts, which leads to $r_u = 0$. The detailed proof for the case of $s = 0$ is included in [37]. □

Theorem 1 shows that when all other nodes use the same nonzero strategy s, it is strictly better for u to use strategy k; when all other nodes uniformly use the 0 strategy, it is strictly better for u to also use 0 strategy. When setting $s = k$ and $s = 0$, we have:

COROLLARY 2. *For the DRB game in the k-dimensional grid, the navigable small-world network ($\mathbf{r} \equiv k$) and the random small-world network ($\mathbf{r} \equiv 0$) are the two strict Nash equilibria for sufficiently large n, and there are no other uniform Nash equilibria.*

The above analysis shows that DRB game has two uniform Nash equilibria $\mathbf{r} \equiv k$ and $\mathbf{r} \equiv 0$, corresponding to navigable and random small-world networks, respectively. Other non-uniform equilibria may exist. Given that multiple equilibria exist, we need to further investigate if the navigable small world possess further properties making it the likely choice in practice. This is the task of the remaining sections.

4.2 Equilibrium Stability in DRB Game

In this section, we show the important results that the navigable small-world network is stable in terms of tolerating both collusions of any group of players and arbitrary deviations of random players' strategies, while other non-navigable equilibria do not tolerate either collusions or random perturbations of a small group of players.

We first show that the navigable small-world network tolerates collusion of players of any size.

[1] Technically, a statement being true for sufficiently large n means that there exists a constant $n_0 \in \mathbb{N}$ that may only depend on model constants such as k and γ, such that for all $n \ge n_0$ the statement is true in the grid with parameter n.

THEOREM 3. *For the DRB game in the k-dimensional grid, the navigable small-world network ($\mathbf{r} \equiv k$) is a strong Nash equilibrium for sufficiently large n.*

PROOF (SKETCH). We prove a slightly stronger result — any node u in any strategy profile $\mathbf{r}$ with $r_u \neq k$ has strictly worse payoff than its payoff in the navigable small world. Intuitively, when u deviates to $0 \leq r_u < k$, its loss on reciprocity would outweigh its gain on link distance; when u deviates to $r_u > k$, its loss on link distance is too much to compensate any possible gain on reciprocity. The detailed proof is in Appendix B. □

The above theorem shows that the navigable small-world equilibrium is not only immune to unilateral deviations, but also to deviations by coalitions, and in particular it is Pareto-optimal, such that no player can improve her payoff without decreasing the payoff of someone else.

Next, we would like to see if the navigable equilibrium can also tolerate deviations of a random set of players, even if the deviations could be arbitrary and there is no guarantee that deviated players are better off. To do so, we define the following δ-deviation Nash equilibrium, which intuitively means that even if each player has an independent probability of $p \leq \delta$ to deviate to an arbitrary strategy, the unique best response of every node u after the deviation is still $\mathbf{r}^*_u$.

DEFINITION 4 (δ-DEVIATION NASH EQUILIBRIUM). *Let $D_p \subseteq V$ be a random set of nodes where each node $u \in V$ is independently selected to be in D_p with probability p. An NE $\mathbf{r}^* \in \mathcal{S}$ is a δ-deviation NE if for any $0 < p \leq \delta$, with probability at least $1 - 1/n$, for all $u \in V$, all $r_u \in \Sigma \setminus \{r^*_u\}$, all $\mathbf{r}'_{\mathbf{D_p}} \in \Sigma^{|D_p|}$,*

$$\pi_u(r^*_u, \mathbf{r}^*_{V\setminus(D_p\cup\{u\})}, \mathbf{r}'_{\mathbf{D_p}}) > \pi_u(r_u, \mathbf{r}^*_{V\setminus(D_p\cup\{u\})}, \mathbf{r}'_{\mathbf{D_p}}),$$

where the probability is taken from the probability space of D_p.

The equilibrium is more robust when δ is larger. With the above definition, we have the following theorem:

THEOREM 4. *For the DRB game in a k-dimensional grid ($k > 1$), For any constant ε with $0 < \varepsilon < \gamma/4$, there exists $n_0 \in \mathbb{N}$ (depending only on k, γ, and ε), for all $n \geq n_0$, the navigable small-world network ($\mathbf{r} \equiv k$) is a δ-deviation NE for $\delta = 1 - n^{-\varepsilon}$.*

PROOF (SKETCH). The independently selected deviation node set D_p satisfies that with high probability, for any node u, at sufficiently many distance levels from u there are enough fraction of non-deviating nodes. We then show that u obtains higher order payoff just from these non-deviating nodes than any possible payoff she could get from any possible deviation. The full proof is in [37]. □

Notice that δ is close to 1 when n is sufficiently large, meaning that the navigable equilibrium tolerates arbitrary deviations from a large number of random nodes.

After showing that the navigable small-world is very stable, we now examine the stability of other possible equilibria.

THEOREM 5. *For the DRB game in a k-dimensional grid ($k > 1$), For any constant ε with $0 < \varepsilon < \gamma/4$, there exists $n_0 \in \mathbb{N}$ (depending only on k, γ, and ε), for all $n \geq n_0$, any possible NE $\mathbf{r} \not\equiv k$ is not an f-strong NE for $f = 2/n^{\varepsilon}$. Moreover, we can find a class of coalition sets C such that every node $u \in C$ would deviate to $r_u = k$, and then the best response of all nodes in the next step is to select k.*

PROOF (SKETCH). The proof is based on Theorem 4. We notice that a large random set D of nodes deviating arbitrarily from $\mathbf{r} \equiv k$ can be viewed as a small random set $V \setminus D$ of nodes collude together to deviate to $\mathbf{r}_D \equiv k$ from an arbitrary strategy profile. We then bound the size of coalition $|V \setminus D|$ using Chernoff bound. The full proof is in [37]. □

When n is sufficiently large, we see that f is close to 0, which means that the collusion by a small portion of players could drive the system out of the current non-navigable equilibrium and make the system quickly converge to the navigable equilibrium. Therefore, non-navigable equilibria are not stable under collusions of small groups of nodes.

In terms of random perturbation, a symmetric view of Theorem 4 already implies that if a small number of random nodes could perturb to strategy k from an arbitrary strategy profile, then the best response of all nodes after the perturbation is to select k. In addition, we show below that for the random small-world network, which is shown to be another NE, it does not tolerate a small set of random nodes randomly perturbing to a finite set of other strategies (not necessarily including k). Again, in this case the unique best response for every node after the perturbation is to select k.

THEOREM 6. *For the DRB game in a k-dimensional grid ($k > 1$) with the initial strategy profile $\mathbf{r} \equiv 0$ and a finite perturbed strategy set $S \subset \Sigma$ with at least one non-zero entry ($0 < \max S \leq \beta$), for any constant ε with $0 < \varepsilon < \gamma$, there exists $n_0 \in \mathbb{N}$ (depending only on k, γ, and ε), for all $n \geq n_0$, if for any $u \in V$, any $s \in S \setminus \{0\}$, r_u is perturbed to s with independent probability of $p \geq 1/n^{\frac{(k-1)\varepsilon}{k+\beta}}$, then with probability $1 - 1/n$,*

$$B_u(\mathbf{r}'_{-u}) = k, \forall u \in V,$$

where $\mathbf{r}'$ is the strategy profile after the perturbation.

PROOF (SKETCH). We consider the gain of a node u when selecting $r_u = k$ separately from each group of nodes with the same strategy after the perturbation, and then apply the results in Theorem 1. See [37] for details. □

An example of the above perturbation assumption is that each node is selected independently with probability $|S|/n^{\frac{(k-1)\varepsilon}{k+\beta}}$ for perturbation, and perturbed strategy is selected from S uniformly at random. Note that $|S|/n^{\frac{(k-1)\varepsilon}{k+\beta}}$ is very small for large enough n and a finite perturbed strategy set S, which implies that the best response of any node u in the perturbed profile becomes $r_u = k$ as long as a small number of random nodes are perturbed to a finite set of nonzero strategies. Suppose that every node chooses his/her best response against others simultaneously, the random small-world NE ($\mathbf{r} \equiv 0$) would be switched to the navigable small-world NE ($\mathbf{r} \equiv k$) in just one step after the perturbation.

4.3 Implications from Theoretical Analysis

Combining the above theorems together, we obtain a better understanding of how the navigable small-world network is formed. From any arbitrary initial state, best response dynamic drives the system toward some equilibrium, with the navigable small world as one of them (Corollary 2). Even if the systems temporarily converges to a non-navigable equilibrium, the state will not be stable — either a small-size

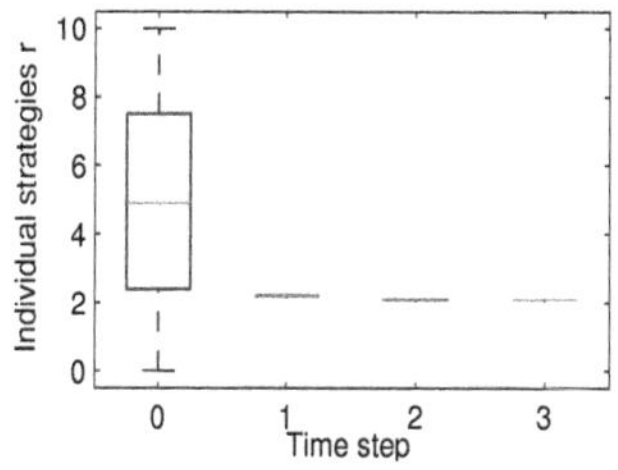

Figure 5: The return to navigable small-world NE (perturbed probability p=1).

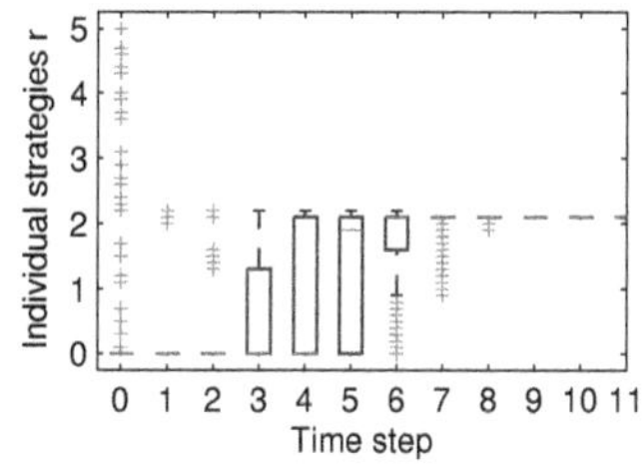

Figure 6: From random NE to small-world NE (perturbed probability p=0.01).

collusion (Theorem 5) or a small-size random perturbation (Theorem 6) would make the system leave the current equilibrium and quickly enter the navigable equilibrium. Once entering the navigable equilibrium, it is very hard for the system to move away from it — no collusion of any size would drive the system away from this equilibrium (Theorem 3), and even if a large random portion of nodes deviate arbitrarily the system still converge back to the navigable equilibrium in the next step (Theorem 4). These theoretical results strongly support that the navigable small world is the unique stable system state, which suggests that the fundamental balance between reaching out to remote people and seeking reciprocal relationship is crucial to the emergence of navigable small-world networks.

5. EMPIRICAL EVALUATION

In this section, we empirically examine the stability of navigable small-world NE. We simulate the DRB game on two dimensional grids, and consider nodes having full information, limited information, or no information of other players' strategies.

Before the main empirical evaluation, we also test the effect of the grid size on navigable equilibrium, since our theoretical results require sufficiently large grids. We found that for $\mathbf{r} \equiv 2.4$ for 10×10 grid and $\mathbf{r} \equiv 2.03$ for a 1000×1000 grid, with the granularity of $\gamma = 0.01$ (see [37] for more details). In our following experiments, we use a 100×100 grid with the navigable equilibrium $\mathbf{r} \equiv 2.1$.

5.1 Stability of NE under Perturbation

To demonstrate the stability of navigable NE, we simulate the DRB game with random perturbation. At time step 0, each player is perturbed independently with probability p. If the perturbation occurs on a player u, we assume that the player u chooses a new strategy uniformly at random from the interval $[0, 10] \cap \Sigma$. Notice that for strategy $r_u > 10$, the behavior of nodes is similar to $r_u = 10$ as nodes only connect to the 4 grid neighbors. We use a granularity of $\gamma = 0.1$ that covers the equilibrium $\mathbf{r} \equiv 2.1$ while reducing the simulation cost. Let $\mathbf{r}^0$ be the strategy profile at time 0 after the perturbation. At each time step $t \geq 1$, every player picks the best strategy based on the strategies of others in the previous step.

$$r_u^t = \operatorname*{argmax}_{r_u \in \Sigma \cap [0,10]} \pi(r_u, \mathbf{r}_{-u}^{t-1}), \forall u, \forall t > 1.$$

Figure 5 shows an extreme case where every player is perturbed when the initial profile is $\mathbf{r} \equiv 2$. The box-plot shows the distribution of players' strategies at each step. The figure shows that in just two steps the system returns to the navigable small-world NE. We tested 100 random starting profiles, and all of them converge to the navigable NE within two steps. This simulation result indicates that the navigable NE is very stable for random perturbations.

To contrast, we study the stability of the random small-world network in terms of tolerating perturbations. Figure 6 shows the result of randomly perturbing only 1% of players at the random NE, which are shown as the outliers at step 0. Note that 1% perturbation does not meet the requirement in Theorem 6. However, this small fraction of players would affect the decision of additional players in their vicinity, who can significantly improve the reciprocity by also linking in the vicinity. The figure clearly shows that in a few steps, more and more players would change their strategies, and the system finally goes to the navigable small-world NE.[2] We tested 100 random starting profiles, and all of them converge to the navigable NE within at most 12 steps.

These results show that the navigable small-world NE are robust to perturbations, while random small-world NE is not stable and easily transits to the small-world NE under a slight perturbation.

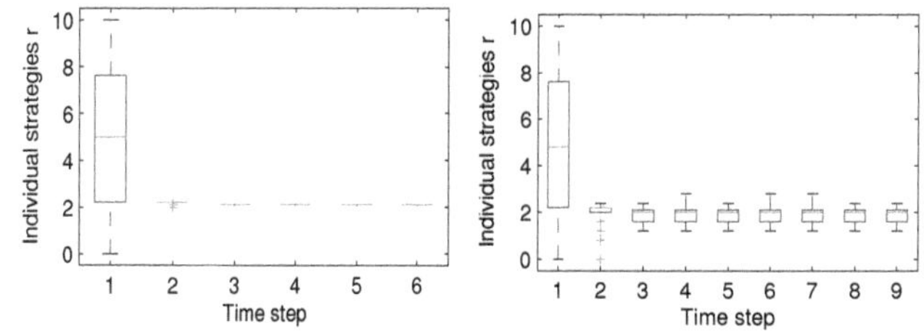

(a) Noise $\varepsilon = 0$. (b) Noise $\varepsilon \sim N(0, 0.5)$

Figure 7: Network evolution where each player only knows the strategies of their friends.

5.2 DRB Game with Limited Knowledge

Scenario 1: knowing friends' strategies. In practice, a player does not know the strategies of all players. So we now consider a weaker scenario where a player only knows the strategies of their friends. With these limited knowledge, a player can guess the strategies of all other players and pick the best response to the estimated strategies of all players.

To examine the convergence of navigable small-world NE in this scenario, we simulate the DRB game as follows. At time step 0, each player chooses an initial strategy uniformly at random from the interval $[0, 10] \cap \Sigma$. At every step $t \geq 0$, each player u creates q out-going long-range links based on her current strategy r_u^t, and learns the connection preferences of these q long-range contacts. Let F_u^t be the set of these q long-range contacts. We further allows a random noise term ε for each connection preference learned from the friends. Let r_v^t $(v \in F_u^t)$ be the learned (noisy) connection preference. Then based on these newly learned connection preferences, player u estimates the strategies of all other players. One reasonable estimation method is to assume that players close to one another in grid distance have similar strategy. More specifically, for a non-friend n-

[2]In step 1 and 2 in Figure 6, the number of outliers is larger than in step 0, even though the rendering make it seems they are less.

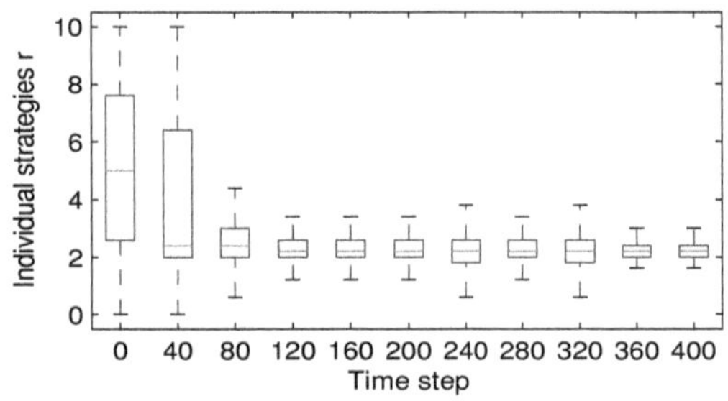

Figure 8: Network evolution where players have no knowledge of strategies of others.

ode $v \notin F_u^t$, u estimates the strategy of v by the average weight of known strategies:

$$r_v^t = \frac{\sum_{f \in F_u^t} r_{f,t-1}/d_M(v,f)}{\sum_{f \in F_u^t} 1/d_M(v,f)}.$$

Here we do not use the connection preferences learned in the previous steps and effectively assume that those old links are removed. This is both for convenience, and also reasonable since people could only maintain a limited number of connections and it is natural that new connections replace the old ones. Moreover, the connection preferences of those old connections may become out-dated in practice anyway. After the estimation procedure, player u use the strategy r_v^t from all other players (either learned or estimated) to compute its best response r_u^{t+1} for the next step.

In our experiment, we set $q = 30$. Figure 7(a) shows that when players have accurate knowledge of the strategies of their friends without noise, the system converges in just two steps. Even when the information on friends' strategies is noisy, the system can still quickly stabilize in a few steps to a state close to the navigable small-world NE, as shown in Figure 7(b). We tested 100 random starting profiles and also other estimation methods such as randomly choosing a connection preference based on friends' connection preference distributions, and results are all similar. This experiment further demonstrates the robustness of the small-world NE even under limited information on connection preferences.

Scenario 2: No information about others' strategies. We now consider the weakest scenario where each player has no knowledge about the strategies of other players. To get the payoff in this scenario, a player creates a certain number of links with the current strategy, and computes the payoff by multiplying the average link distance and the percentage of reciprocal links.

To make it even harder, we do not allow the player to try many different strategies at each step before fixing her strategy for the step. Instead, at each step each player only has one chance to slightly modify her current strategy. If the new strategy yields better payoff, the player would adopt the new strategy. So as the time goes on, the player could change the strategy towards the best one.

We simulate the DRB game as follows: At time step 0, each player chooses an initial strategy uniformly at random from the interval $[0, 10] \cap \Sigma$. Every player creates q outgoing links with her current strategy. At each time step $t \geq 1$, each player changes the strategy, i.e.,$r_u \leftarrow r_u + \delta$, and creates q new links with this new strategy, where δ is a random number determined as follows. First, for the sign of δ, in the first step it is randomly assigned positive or negative sign with equal probability; in the raining steps, to make the search efficient, we keep the sign of δ if the previous change leads to a higher payoff; otherwise we reverse the sign of δ. For the magnitude of δ, i.e. $|\delta|$, we sample a value uniformly at random from $(0, 1] \cap \Sigma$.

We simulate this system with $q = 30$. Figure 8 demonstrates that the system can still evolve to a state close to the navigable small-world NE in a few hundred steps, e.g., the strategies of 80.5% players fall in the interval $[1.8, 2.4]$, and the median of the strategies is the navigable NE strategy of 2.1. We test 50 random starting profiles, and take snapshots of the strategy profiles at the time step $t = 500$. On average, the strategies of 79.8% players in the snapshots fall in the interval $[1.8, 2.4]$.

In summary, our empirical evaluation strongly supports that our payoff function considering the balance between link distance and reciprocity naturally gives rise to the navigable small-world network. The convergence to navigable equilibrium will happen either when the players know all other players' strategies, or only learn their friends' strategies, or only use the empirical distance and reciprocity measure. Once in the navigable equilibrium, the system is very stable and hard to deviate by any random perturbation. Furthermore, other equilibria such as the random small world is not stable, in that a small perturbation will drive the system back to the navigable small-world network.

6. FUTURE WORK

Our study opens many possible directions of future work. For example, one may extend the current study to non-uniform population distributions on the grid and conduct theoretical and empirical analysis to see if the navigable small world would still emerge as a stable equilibrium. Another direction is to investigate deeper reasons or models on why individual's connection preference follows a power law form of $d_M(u,v)^{-r_u}$. Such studies may need to integrate prior studies on node and link dynamics and our game theoretic approach, and the integration may provide a more complete picture of the underlying mechanisms for navigable small-world networks.

7. ACKNOWLEDGMENTS

We thank the anonymous reviewers for their comments. This work was supported by the National Basic Research Program of China (Grant No. 2014CB340400), the National Science Foundation for Young Scholars of China (Grant No.61202423) and the Star Track Program of Microsoft Research Asia.

APPENDIX

A. PROOF OF THEOREM 1 FOR THE CASE OF $s > 0$

In all proofs in the appendix, for a given node $u \in V$, we denote $D(r_u) = \sum_{\forall v \neq u} p_u(v, r_u) d_M(u,v)$ as its average grid distance of its long range contacts (simply referred to as the *link distance*), and $P_u(r_u, \mathbf{r}_{-u}) = \sum_{\forall v \neq u} p_u(v, r_u) p_v(u, r_v)$ as its *reciprocity*. When $\mathbf{r}_{-u} \equiv s$, we simply use $P(r_u, s)$ to denote $P_u(r_u, \mathbf{r}_{-u} \equiv s)$. The subscript u in both $D(r_u)$ and $P(r_u, s)$ is omitted because their values are the same for all

$u \in V$. Let n_D be the longest grid distance among nodes in $K(n, k, p, q, \mathbf{r})$. We have that $n_D = k\lfloor n/2 \rfloor$. We denote $b_u(j)$ as the number of players at grid distance j from u. We can find two constants ξ_k^- and ξ_k^+ only depending on the dimension k, so that $\xi_k^- j^{k-1} \le b_u(j) \le \xi_k^+ j^{k-1}$ for $1 \le j \le \lfloor n/2 \rfloor$ and $1 \le b_u(j) \le \xi_k^+ j^{k-1}$ for $\lfloor n/2 \rfloor < j \le n_D$.[3] Note that the payoff function (Eq. (3)) for the DRB game is indifferent of parameters p and q of the network, so we treat $p = q = 1$ for our convenience in the analysis.

PROOF OF $B_u(\mathbf{r}_{-u} \equiv s) = k$ IF $s > 0$. Given $\mathbf{r_{-u}} \equiv s$, we now prove that the decision of $r_u = k$ is the unique best response of player u as long as $s > 0$.

Payoff of $r_u = k$: We have the lower bound for the link distance and the reciprocity:

$$D(r_u) \ge \frac{\sum_{j=1}^{n/2} b_u(j) \cdot j^{-k} \cdot j}{c(k)} \ge \frac{\xi_k^- n}{2c(k)}, \tag{4}$$

$$P(r_u, s) \ge \frac{\sum_{j=1}^{n/2} b_u(j) \cdot j^{-k} \cdot j^{-s}}{c(k)c(s)} \ge \xi_k^- \sum_{j=1}^{n/2} \frac{j^{-1-s}}{c(k)c(s)} \ge \frac{\xi_k^-}{c(k)c(s)}. \tag{5}$$

Notice that the normalization coefficient $c(k)$ can be bounded as:

$$c(k) = \sum_{\forall v \ne u} d_M(u,v)^{-k} \le \sum_{j=1}^{n_D} b_u(j) j^{-k} \le \xi_k^+ \sum_{j=1}^{n_D} \frac{1}{j} \le \xi_k^+ \ln(2kn). \tag{6}$$

Based on above inequalities, we can get the lower bound for the payoff of player u in the case of $r_u = k$:

$$\pi(r_u = k, \mathbf{r}_{-u} \equiv s) \ge \frac{(\xi_k^-)^2}{2(\xi_k^+)^2 c(s)} \frac{n}{\ln^2(2kn)}. \tag{7}$$

Payoff of $r_u < k$. We now turn to the player's payoff when $r_u < k$ and we write $\varepsilon = k - r_u$ ($\gamma \le \varepsilon \le k$). In this case, the upper bound for the link distance and reciprocity are as follows:

$$\begin{aligned} D(r_u) &\le \frac{\sum_{j=1}^{n_D} b_u(j) \cdot j^{-r_u} \cdot j}{c(r_u)} \le \frac{\xi_k^+ \int_1^{n_D+1} x^\varepsilon dx}{c(r_u)} \\ &\le \frac{\xi_k^+ (n_D+1)^{1+\varepsilon}}{(1+\varepsilon)c(r_u)} \le \frac{\xi_k^+ (kn)^{1+\varepsilon}}{c(r_u)}, \end{aligned} \tag{8}$$

$$P(r_u, s) \le \frac{\sum_{j=1}^{n_D} b_u(j) \cdot j^{-r_u} \cdot j^{-s}}{c(r_u)c(s)} \le \xi_k^+ \sum_{j=1}^{n_D} \frac{j^{\varepsilon-1-s}}{c(r_u)c(s)}. \tag{9}$$

In the case of $\varepsilon \ge 1 + s$, we have:

$$P(r_u, s) \le \xi_k^+ \int_{j=1}^{n_D+1} \frac{j^{\varepsilon-1-s}}{c(r_u)c(s)} \le \frac{\xi_k (n_D+1)^{\varepsilon-s}}{(\varepsilon - s)c(r_u)c(s)} \le \frac{\xi_k^+ (kn)^{\varepsilon-s}}{c(r_u)c(s)}. \tag{10}$$

In the case of $\varepsilon < 1 + s$, we have:

$$\begin{aligned} P(r_u, s) &\le \frac{\xi_k^+}{c(r_u)c(s)} \left(1 + \int_{j=1}^{n_D} j^{\varepsilon-1-s}\right) \\ &\le \begin{cases} \frac{\xi_k^+ ((kn/2)^{\varepsilon-s} + \varepsilon - s - 1)}{(\varepsilon-s)c(r_u)c(s)} & \text{if } \varepsilon \ne s, \\ \frac{2\xi_k^+ \ln(2kn)}{c(r_u)c(s)} & \text{if } \varepsilon = s. \end{cases} \end{aligned} \tag{11}$$

[3]The exact values of ξ_k^- and ξ_k^+ can be derived by the combinatorial problem of counting the number of ways to choose k non-negative integers such that they sum to a given positive integer j.

The coefficient $c(r_u)$ can be bounded as:

$$\begin{aligned} c(r_u) &= \sum_{\forall v \ne u} d_M(u,v)^{-r_u} \ge \sum_{j=1}^{n/2} b_u(j) j^{-r_u} \ge \xi_k^- \sum_{j=1}^{n/2} j^{\varepsilon-1} \\ &\ge \xi_k^- \int_1^{n/2} x^{\varepsilon-1} dx \ge \frac{\xi_k^-}{\varepsilon}\left(\frac{n}{2}\right)^\varepsilon - \frac{\xi_k^-}{\varepsilon} \ge \frac{\xi_k^-}{2\varepsilon}\left(\frac{n}{2}\right)^\varepsilon. \end{aligned} \tag{12}$$

The last inequality above relies on a loose relaxation of $\frac{1}{2}\left(\frac{n}{2}\right)^\varepsilon \ge 1$, which is guaranteed for all $n \ge 2^{1+1/\gamma}$ since $\varepsilon \ge \gamma$.

Combining Eq.(8), (10), (11), and (12), we have the payoff of node u in the case of $r_u < k$:

$$\pi(r_u = k - \varepsilon, \mathbf{r}_{-u} \equiv s) \le$$

$$\begin{cases} \text{if } \varepsilon > s, \\ \frac{(\xi_k^+)^2 2^{2\varepsilon+2} \varepsilon^2 k^{1+2\varepsilon-s}}{(\xi_k^-)^2 (\varepsilon-s) c(s)} n^{1-s} \le \frac{(\xi_k^+)^2 2^{2k+2} k^{2k+3}}{(\xi_k^-)^2 \gamma c(s)} n^{1-\gamma}, \\ \text{if } \varepsilon = s, \\ \frac{(\xi_k^+)^2 2^{2\varepsilon+3} 2\varepsilon^2 k^{1+\varepsilon} n^{1-\varepsilon} \ln(2kn)}{(\xi_k^-)^2 c(s)} \le \frac{(\xi_k^+)^2 2^{2k+3} k^{k+3}}{(\xi_k^-)^2 c(s)} n^{1-\gamma} \ln(2kn), \\ \text{if } \varepsilon < s, \\ \frac{(\xi_k^+)^2 2^{2\varepsilon+2} \varepsilon^2 k^{1+\varepsilon}}{(\xi_k^-)^2 c(s)} \left(1 + \frac{1}{s-\varepsilon}\right) n^{1-\varepsilon} \le \frac{(\xi_k^+)^2 2^{2k+3} k^{k+3}}{(\xi_k^-)^2 \gamma c(s)} n^{1-\gamma}. \end{cases} \tag{13}$$

The inequalities in the three cases above use the facts $\gamma \le \varepsilon \le k$, $s \ge \gamma$ (since $s > 0$), and $\varepsilon - s \ge \gamma$ when $\varepsilon > s$.

Comparing Eq.(13) with Eq.(7), the common denominator $c(s)$ can be ignored. For the rest terms, Eq.(7) is in strictly higher order in n than Eq.(13), which implies that we can find a large enough n_0 (only depending on model constants k and γ) such that for all $n \ge n_0$, $\pi(r_u = k, \mathbf{r}_{-u} \equiv s) > \pi(r_u = s', \mathbf{r}_{-u} \equiv s)$, for all $s \in \Sigma \setminus \{0\}$ and all $s' \in \Sigma$ with $s' < k$.

Payoff of $r_u > k$. We write $\varepsilon = r_u - k$ ($\varepsilon \ge \gamma$). The bound for the link distance is:

$$\begin{aligned} D(r_u) &\le \frac{\sum_{j=1}^{n_D} b_u(j) \cdot j^{-r_u} \cdot j}{c(r_u)} \le \xi_k^+ \sum_{j=1}^{n_D} \frac{j^{-\varepsilon}}{c(r_u)} \\ &\le \xi_k^+ \frac{1 + \int_1^{n_D} x^{-\varepsilon} dx}{c(r_u)} \le \begin{cases} \frac{\xi_k^+}{(1-\varepsilon)c(r_u)} (kn/2)^{1-\varepsilon} & \text{if } \varepsilon < 1, \\ \frac{\xi_k^+}{c(r_u)} \ln(2kn) & \text{if } \varepsilon \ge 1. \end{cases} \end{aligned} \tag{14}$$

The bound on the reciprocity is:

$$P(r_u, s) \le \frac{\sum_{j=1}^{n_D} b_u(j) \cdot j^{-r_u} \cdot j^{-s}}{c(r_u)c(s)} \le \frac{\sum_{j=1}^{n_D} b_u(j) j^{-r_u}}{c(r_u)c(s)} = \frac{1}{c(s)}. \tag{15}$$

On the other hand, the lower bound for the coefficient $c(r_u)$ is:

$$c(r_u) = \sum_{\forall v \ne u} d_M(u,v)^{-r_u} \ge \sum_{j=1}^{n/2} b_u(j) j^{-r} \ge b_u(1) \ge \xi_k^-. \tag{16}$$

Combining Eq.(14), (15), and (16), we get:

$$\pi(r_u = k + \varepsilon, \mathbf{r_{-u}} \equiv s) \le$$

$$\begin{cases} \frac{\xi_k^+ k^{1-\varepsilon}}{\xi_k^- (1-\varepsilon) c(s)} n^{1-\varepsilon} \le \frac{\xi_k^+ k}{\xi_k^- \gamma c(s)} n^{1-\gamma} & \text{if } \varepsilon < 1, \\ \frac{\xi_k^+}{\xi_k^- c(s)} \ln(2kn) & \text{if } \varepsilon \ge 1. \end{cases} \tag{17}$$

Comparing Eq.(17) with Eq.(7), the common denominator $c(s)$ can be ignored. For the rest terms, Eq.(7) is in strictly higher order in n than Eq.(17), which implies that we can find a large enough constant n_0 (only depending on model constants k and γ) such that for all $n \geq n_0$, $\pi(r_u = k, \mathbf{r}_{-u} \equiv s) > \pi(r_u = s', \mathbf{r}_{-u} \equiv s)$, for all $s \in \Sigma \setminus \{0\}$ and all $s' \in \Sigma$ with $s' > k$.

We complete the proof when combining the cases of $r_u < k$ and $r_u > k$. $\square$

B. PROOF OF THEOREM 3

We introduce some notations first. Given the strategy profile $\mathbf{r}$ and a node u with $r_u \neq k$, we partition the rest nodes $V \setminus \{u\}$ into three sets: $V_{<k} = \{u \in V \setminus \{u\} \mid r_u < k\}$, $V_{>k} = \{u \in V \setminus \{u\} \mid r_u > k\}$, $V_{=k} = \{u \in V \mid r_u = k\}$. For any $A \subseteq V$, Let $P_{u,A}(\mathbf{r}) = \sum_{v \in A} p_u(v, r_u) p_v(u, r_v)$ be the reciprocity u obtained from subset A. Then we have

$$\pi_u(\mathbf{r}) = D(r_u) \left(P_{u,V_{<k}}(\mathbf{r}) + P_{u,V_{>k}}(\mathbf{r}) + P_{u,V_{=k}}(\mathbf{r}) \right). \quad (18)$$

In this section, we actually prove a slightly stronger result: any node u in any strategy profile $\mathbf{r}$ with $r_u \neq k$ is strictly worse off than its payoff in the navigable equilibrium, when n is large enough. To prove this result, we first show the following key lemma, which will be used in later theorems too.

LEMMA 1. *In the k-dimensional DRB game, there exists a constant κ (only depending on model constants k and γ), for sufficiently large n (in particular $n \geq \max(e^4, 2k)$), the following statement holds: for any strategy profile $\mathbf{r}$, any node u with $r_u \neq k$, $\pi_u(r_u, \mathbf{r}_{-u}) \leq \kappa n^{1-\gamma}$.*

PROOF. We now consider the case of $r_u < k$ and $r_u > k$ separately.

Payoff of $r_u < k$. Let $\varepsilon = k - r_u$ ($\gamma \leq \varepsilon \leq k$). We first consider the reciprocity player u obtains from the players in $V_{<k}$. We have $c(r_v) \geq c(k-\gamma)$ for $\forall v \in V_{<k}$, since $r_v \leq k-\gamma$. Then we have:

$$P_{u,V_{<k}}(\mathbf{r}) = \sum_{v \in V_{<k}} \frac{d_M(u,v)^{-r_u - r_v}}{c(r_u)c(r_v)} \leq \sum_{v \in V_{<k}} \frac{d_M(u,v)^{-r_u}}{c(r_u)c(k-\gamma)}$$
$$\leq \frac{\sum_{\forall v \neq u} d_M(u,v)^{-r_u}}{c(r_u)c(k-\gamma)} = \frac{1}{c(k-\gamma)}. \quad (19)$$

Combining the above inequality with the bounds in Eq.(8) and (12), we get:

$$D(r_u)P_{u,V_{<k}}(\mathbf{r}) \leq \frac{\xi_k^+ 2^{\varepsilon+3} \varepsilon k^{1+\varepsilon}}{(\xi_k^-)^2} n^{1-\gamma} \leq \frac{\xi_k^+ 2^{k+3} k^{k+2}}{(\xi_k^-)^2} n^{1-\gamma}. \quad (20)$$

Next we examine the reciprocity that player u obtains from the players in $V_{>k}$. Note that for all $v \in V_{>k}$, $r_v \geq k + \gamma$. Using Eq.(16), we have:

$$P_{u,V_{>k}}(\mathbf{r}) = \sum_{v \in V_{<k}} \frac{d_M(u,v)^{-r_u - r_v}}{c(r_u)c(r_v)}$$
$$\leq \frac{\sum_{j=1}^n b_u(j) \cdot j^{-r_u} \cdot j^{-k-\gamma}}{\xi_k^- c(r_u)} = \frac{\xi_k^+ \sum_{j=1}^n j^{-1-r_u-\gamma}}{\xi_k^- c(r_u)}$$
$$\leq \frac{\xi_k^+ (1 + \int_1^n x^{-1-r_u-\gamma} dx)}{\xi_k^- c(r_u)} \leq \frac{\xi_k^+ (1 + r_u + \gamma)}{\xi^- (r_u + \gamma) c(r_u)} \leq \frac{\xi^+ (k+1)}{\xi^- \gamma c(r_u)}.$$

Based on the bounds in Eq.(8) and (12), we get:

$$D(r_u)P_{u,V_{>k}}(\mathbf{r}) \leq \frac{\xi_k^+ 2^{2\varepsilon+2} \varepsilon^2 (k+1) k^{1+\varepsilon}}{(\xi_k^-)^2 \gamma} n^{1-\varepsilon}$$
$$\leq \frac{\xi_k^+ 2^{2k+3} k^{k+4}}{(\xi_k^-)^2 \gamma} n^{1-\gamma}. \quad (21)$$

We now examine the reciprocity of player u from players in $V_{=k}$. Notice that the coefficient $c(k)$ can be bounded as:

$$c(k) \geq \xi_k \sum_{j=1}^{n/2} j^{-1} \geq \xi_k^- \int_1^{n/2} x^{-1} dx \geq \xi_k^- (\ln n - \ln 2) \geq \frac{\xi_k^- \ln n}{2}, \quad (22)$$

where the last inequality is true when $n \geq e^4$. Using Eq.(13) with $s = k$, together with Eq.(22), we get:

$$D(r_u)P_{u,V_{=k}}(\mathbf{r}) \leq \pi(r_u = k - \varepsilon, \mathbf{r}_{-u} \equiv k)$$
$$\leq \begin{cases} \frac{(\xi_k^+)^2 2^{2k+4} k^{k+3} \ln(2kn)}{(\xi_k^-)^3 \ln n} n^{1-\gamma} \leq \frac{(\xi_k^+)^2 2^{2k+5} k^{k+3}}{(\xi_k^-)^3} n^{1-\gamma} & \text{if } \varepsilon = k. \\ \frac{(\xi_k^+)^2 2^{2k+4} k^{k+3}}{\gamma (\xi_k^-)^3} \frac{n^{1-\gamma}}{\ln n} & \text{if } \varepsilon < k. \end{cases} \quad (23)$$

The last inequality in the case of $\varepsilon = k$ requires $n \geq 2k$.

Adding up results in Eq.(20), (21), (23), we obtain that

$$\pi(r_u, \mathbf{r}_{-u}) \leq \frac{3(\xi_k^+)^2 \cdot 2^{2k+5} k^{k+4}}{\gamma (\xi_k^-)^3} n^{1-\gamma} \leq \frac{(\xi_k^+)^2 2^{2k+7} k^{k+4}}{\gamma (\xi_k^-)^3} n^{1-\gamma}, \quad (24)$$

when $n \geq \max\{e^4, 2k\}$.

Payoff of $r_u > k$. Let $\varepsilon = r_u - k$ ($\varepsilon \geq \gamma$). For this case, we can relax the reciprocity $P_u(r_u, \mathbf{r}_{-u})$ to one and only upper bound link distance $D(r_u)$. Applying bounds in Eq.(14) and (16), we obtain:

$$\pi(r_u = k+\varepsilon, \mathbf{r}_{-u}) \leq \begin{cases} \frac{\xi_k^+}{\xi_k^- (1-\varepsilon)} (kn/2)^{1-\varepsilon} \leq \frac{\xi_k^+ k}{\xi_k^- \gamma} n^{1-\gamma} & \text{if } \varepsilon < 1, \\ \frac{\xi_k^+}{\xi_k^-} \ln(2kn) \leq 2n^{1-\gamma} & \text{if } \varepsilon \geq 1. \end{cases} \quad (25)$$

The last inequality in the above case of $\varepsilon \geq 1$ holds when $n \geq 2k$ and $\gamma \leq 1/2$.

Finally, the lemma holds when we combine Eq.(24) and (25) $\square$

PROOF OF THEOREM 3. Before derivation, a player u has the following payoff lower bound, according to Eq.(6) and (7).

$$\pi(r_u = k, \mathbf{r}_{-u} \equiv k) \geq \frac{(\xi_k^-)^2}{2(\xi_k^+)^3} \frac{n}{\ln^3(2kn)}. \quad (26)$$

Suppose that a coalition C deviates, and the new strategy profile is $\mathbf{r}$. Then some node $u \in C$ must select a new $r_u \neq k$. By Lemma 1, there is a constant κ such that for all sufficiently large n, $\pi(r_u, \mathbf{r}_{-u}) \leq \kappa n^{1-\gamma}$. Comparing with Eq. (26), we see that the payoff of u before the deviation is in strictly higher order in n than its payoff after the deviation. Therefore, for all sufficiently large n, u is strictly worse off, which means no coalition could make some member strictly better off while others not worse off. Hence, navigable small-world network ($\mathbf{r} \equiv k$) is a strong Nash equilibrium. $\square$

C. REFERENCES

[1] Adamic, L., and Adar, E. How to search a social network. *Social Networks 27* (2005).

[2] Allamanis, M., Scellato, S., and Mascolo, C. Evolution of a location-based online social network: Analysis and models. In *Proc. of IMC* (2012).

[3] Barabási, A., and Albert, R. Emergence of scaling in random networks. *Science 286*, 5439 (1999), 509–512.

[4] Boguñá, M., Krioukov, D., and Claffy, K. Navigability of complex networks. *Nature Physics 5* (2009), 74–80.

[5] Chaintreau, A., Fraigniaud, P., and Lebhar, E. Networks become navigable as nodes move and forget. In *Proc. of ICALP '08* (2008).

[6] Chen, W., Fang, W., Hu, G., and Mahoney, M. W. On the hyperbolicity of small-world and treelike random graphs. *Internet Mathematics 9*, 4 (2013), 434–491.

[7] Cho, E., Myers, S. A., and Leskovec, J. Friendship and mobility: User movement in location-based social networks. In *Proc. of KDD* (2011).

[8] Clauset, A., and Moore, C. How do networks become navigable. In *Arxiv preprint arXiv:0309.415v2* (2003).

[9] Gittell, R., and Vidal, A. *Community Organizing: Building Social Capital as a Development Strategy.* Sage publicaiton, 1998.

[10] Goldenberg, J., and Levy, M. Distance is not dead: Social interaction and geographical distance in the internet era. In *Arxiv preprint arXiv:0906.3202.* (2009).

[11] Gong, N. Z., Xu, W., Huang, L., Mittal, P., Stefanov, E., Sekar, V., and Song, D. Evolution of social-attribute networks: Measurements, modeling, and implications using google+. In *Proc. of IMC* (2012).

[12] Gouldner, A. W. The norm of reciprocity: a preliminary statement. *American Sociological Review 25*, 4 (1960), 161–178.

[13] Granovetter, M. *Getting a job: A study of contacts and careers.* Harvard University Press, 1974.

[14] Granovetter, M. S. The strength of weak ties. *American Journal of Sociology* (1973), 1360–1380.

[15] Gulyás, A., Korösi, A., Szabó, D., and Biczóki, G. On greedy network formation. *SIGMETRICS Perform. Eval. Rev.* (2012).

[16] Hu, Y., Wang, Y., Li, D., Havlin, S., , and Di, Z. Possible origin of efficient navigation in small worlds. *Phys Rev Letters* (2011).

[17] Illenberger, J., Nagel, K., and Flötteröd, G. The role of spatial interaction in social networks. *Networks and Spatial Economics 13* (2013).

[18] Java, A., Song, X., Finin, T., and Tseng, B. Why we twitter: understanding microblogging usage and communities. In *Proc. of WebKDD/SNA-KDD* (2007).

[19] Jiang, J., Wilson, C., Wang, X., Huang, P., Sha, W., Dai, Y., and Zhao, B. Y. Understanding latent interactions in online social networks. In *Proc. of IMC* (2010).

[20] Kaiser, M., and Hilgetag, C. C. Spatial growth of real-world networks. *Phys Rev Letters* (2004).

[21] Kleinberg, J. The small-world phenomenon: An algorithmic perspective. In *Proc. of 32nd ACM Symp. on Theory of Computing (STOC)* (2002).

[22] Kleinberg, J. Complex networks and decentralized search algorithms. In *Proc. of the International Congress of Mathematicians (ICM)* (2006).

[23] Krioukov, D., Papadopoulos, F., Kitsak, M., Vahdat, A., and Boguñá, M. Hyperbolic geometry of complex networks. *Physical Review E 82* (2010), 036106.

[24] Krioukov, D., Papadopoulos, F., Vahdat, A., and Boguñá, M. Curvature and temperature of complex networks. *Physical Review E 80* (2009), 035101(R).

[25] Lambiotte, R., et al. Geographical dispersal of mobile communication networks. *Physica A 387* (2008).

[26] Leskovec, J., Backstrom, L., Kumar, R., and Tomkins, A. Microscopic evolution of social networks. In *Proc. of KDD* (2008).

[27] Leskovec, J., Kleinberg, J. M., and Faloutsos, C. Graph evolution: Densification and shrinking diameters. *TKDD* (2007).

[28] Liben-Nowell, D., Novak, J., Kumar, R., Raghavan, P., and Tomkins, A. Geographic routing in social networks. *PNAS 102* (2005).

[29] Mathias, N., and Gopal, V. Small worlds: how and why. *Physical Review E 63*, 2 (2001).

[30] Milgram, S. The small world problem. *Psychology Today 2*, 1 (1967), 60–67.

[31] Mislove, A., Marcon, M., Gummadi, K. P., Druschel, P., and Bhattacharjee, B. Measurement and analysis of online social networks. In *Proc. of IMC* (2007).

[32] Papadopoulos, F., Krioukov, D. V., Boguñá, M., and Vahdat, A. Greedy forwarding in dynamic scale-free networks embedded in hyperbolic metric spaces. In *Proceedings of the 29th IEEE International Conference on Computer Communications (INFOCOM)* (2010), pp. 2973–2981.

[33] Sandberg, O., and Clarke, I. The evolution of navigable small-world networks. In *Arxiv preprint arXiv:cs/0607025* (2006).

[34] Schaller, M., and Latank, B. Distance matters: Physical space and social impact. *Personality and Social Psychology Bulletin 25* (1995).

[35] Tardos, E., and Wexler, T. Network formation games and the potential function method, 2007. In Algorithmic Game Theory.

[36] Watts, D. J., and Strogatz, S. H. Collective dynamics of 'small-world' networks. *Nature 393*, 6684 (1998), 440–442.

[37] Yang, Z., and Chen, W. A game theoretic model for the formation of navigable small-world networks, 2014. full technical report, Arxiv preprint arXiv:1411.4097.

[38] Yang, Z., Wilson, C., Wang, X., Gao, T., Zhao, B. Y., and Dai, Y. Uncovering social network sybils in the wild. In *Proc. of IMC* (2011).

A Scalable Asynchronous Distributed Algorithm for Topic Modeling

Hsiang-Fu Yu
Univ. of Texas, Austin
rofuyu@cs.utexas.edu

Cho-Jui Hsieh
Univ. of Texas, Austin
cjhsieh@cs.utexas.edu

Hyokun Yun
Amazon
yunhyoku@amazon.com

S.V.N Vishwanathan
Univ. of California, Santa Cruz
vishy@ucsc.edu

Inderjit S. Dhillon
Univ. of Texas, Austin
inderjit@cs.utexas.edu

ABSTRACT

Learning meaningful topic models with massive document collections which contain millions of documents and billions of tokens is challenging because of two reasons. First, one needs to deal with a large number of topics (typically on the order of thousands). Second, one needs a scalable and efficient way of distributing the computation across multiple machines. In this paper, we present a novel algorithm F+Nomad LDA which simultaneously tackles both these problems. In order to handle large number of topics we use an appropriately modified Fenwick tree. This data structure allows us to sample from a multinomial distribution over T items in $O(\log T)$ time. Moreover, when topic counts change the data structure can be updated in $O(\log T)$ time. In order to distribute the computation across multiple processors, we present a novel asynchronous framework inspired by the Nomad algorithm of [25]. We show that F+Nomad LDA significantly outperforms recent state-of-the-art topic modeling approaches on massive problems which involve millions of documents, billions of words, and thousands of topics.

Categories and Subject Descriptors

I.2.6 [**Artificial Intelligence**]: Learning—Parameter learning

General Terms

Algorithms, Experimentation

Keywords

Topic Models; Scalability; Sampling

1. INTRODUCTION

Topic models provide a way to aggregate vocabulary from a document corpus to form latent "topics." In particular, Latent Dirichlet Allocation (LDA) [3] is one of the most popular topic modeling approaches. Learning meaningful topic models with massive document collections which contain millions of documents and billions of tokens is challenging because of two reasons. First, one needs to deal with a large number of topics (typically on the order of thousands). Second, one needs a scalable and efficient way of distributing the computation across multiple machines.

Unsurprisingly, there have been significant attempts at developing scalable inference algorithms for LDA. To tackle large number of topics, [23] proposed a clever sparse sampling trick that is widely used in packages like MALLET and Yahoo! LDA. More recently, [11] proposed using the Alias table method to speed up sampling from the multinomial distribution. At the same time, there has also been significant effort towards distributing the computation across multiple processors. Some early efforts in this direction include [22] and [10], where the basic idea is to partition the documents across processors. During each inner iteration the words in the vocabulary are partitioned across processors and each processor only updates the latent variables associated with the subset of documents and words that it owns. After each inner iteration, a synchronization step is used to update global counts and to re-partition the words across processors. In fact, a very similar idea was independently discovered in the context of matrix completion by [6] and [15]. However, in the case of LDA we need to keep a global count synchronized across processors which significantly complicates matters as compared to matrix completion. Arguably, most of the recent efforts towards scalable LDA such as [16, 13] have been focused on the global count issue either implicitly or explicitly. Recently there is also a growing trend in machine learning towards asynchronous algorithms which avoid bulk synchronization after every iteration. For example, in the context of LDA see the work of [1], and in the more general machine learning context see *e.g.*, [7, 12].

In this paper, we propose a new asynchronous distributed topic modeling algorithm called F+Nomad LDA which simultaneously tackles the twin problems of large number of documents and large number of topics. In order to handle large number of topics we use an appropriately modified Fenwick tree. This data structure allows us to sample from a multinomial distribution over T items in $O(\log T)$ time. Moreover, when topic counts change, the data structure can be updated in $O(\log T)$ time. In order to distribute the computation across multiple processors, we present a novel asynchronous framework inspired by the Nomad algorithm

WWW 2015, May 18–22, 2015, Florence, Italy.
ACM 978-1-4503-3469-3/15/05.
http://dx.doi.org/10.1145/2736277.2741682.

of [25]. While we believe that our framework can handle variable update schedules of many different methods, in this paper we will primarily focus on Collapsed Gibbs Sampling (CGS). Our technical contributions can be summarized as follows:

- We identify the following key property of various inference methods for topic modeling: only a single vector of size k needs to be synchronized across multiple processors.
- We present a variant of the Fenwick tree which allows us to efficiently encode a multinomial distribution using $O(T)$ space. Sampling can be performed in $O(\log T)$ time and maintaining the data structure requires only $O(\log T)$ work.
- F+Nomad LDA: we propose a novel parallel framework for various types of inference methods for topic modeling. Our framework utilizes the concept of nomadic tokens to avoid locking and conflict at the same time. Our parallel approach is fully asynchronous with non-blocking communication, thus leading to good speedups. Moreover, our approach minimizes the staleness of the variables (at most k variables can be stale) for distributed parallel computation.
- We demonstrate the scalability of our methods by performing extensive empirical evaluation on large datasets which contain millions of documents and **billions** of words.

2. NOTATION AND BACKGROUND

We begin by very briefly reviewing Latent Dirichlet Allocation (LDA) [3]. Suppose we are given I documents denoted as $d_1, d_2, \ldots, d_I$, and let J denote the number of words in the vocabulary. Moreover, let n_i denote the number of words in a document d_i. Let w_j denote the j-th word in the vocabulary and $w_{i,j}$ denote the j-th word in the i-th document. Assume that the documents are generated by sampling from T topics denoted as $\phi_1, \phi_2, \ldots, \phi_T$; a topic is simply a J dimensional multinomial distribution over words. Each document includes some proportion of the topics. These proportions are latent, and we use the T dimensional probability vector θ_i to denote the topic distribution for a document d_i. Moreover, let $z_{i,j}$ denote the latent topic from which $w_{i,j}$ was drawn. Let α and β be hyper parameters of the Dirichlet distribution. The generative process for LDA can be described as follows:

1. Draw T topics $\phi_k \sim \texttt{Dirichlet}(\beta)$, $k = 1, \ldots, T$.
2. For each document $d_i \in \{d_1, d_2, \ldots, d_I\}$:
   - Draw $\theta_i \sim \texttt{Dirichlet}(\alpha)$.
   - For $j = 1, \ldots, n_i$
     - Draw $z_{i,j} \sim \texttt{Discrete}(\theta_i)$.
     - Draw $w_{i,j} \sim \texttt{Discrete}(\phi_{z_{i,j}})$.

2.1 Inference

The inference task for LDA is to characterize the posterior distribution $Pr(\phi_i, \theta_i, z_{i,j} \mid w_{i,j})$. In the Bayesian setting, we want an efficient way to draw samples from this posterior distribution. Collapsed Gibbs Sampling (CGS) [8] is a popular inference scheme for LDA. Define

$$n_{z,i,w} := \sum_{j=1}^{n_i} I\left(z_{i,j} = z \text{ and } w_{i,j} = w\right), \qquad (1)$$

$n_{z,i,*} = \sum_w n_{z,i,w}$, $n_{z,*,w} = \sum_i n_{z,i,w}$, and $n_{z,*,*} = \sum_{i,w} n_{z,i,w}$, where $I(\cdot)$ is the indicator function. The update rule for CGS can be written as follows

1. Decrease $n_{z_{i,j},i,*}$, $n_{z_{i,j},*,w_{i,j}}$, and $n_{z_{i,j},*,*}$ by 1.
2. Resample $z_{i,j}$ according to

$$\Pr\left(z_{i,j} | w_{i,j}, \alpha, \beta\right) \propto \frac{\left(n_{z_{i,j},i,*} + \alpha_{z_{i,j}}\right)\left(n_{z_{i,j},*,w_{i,j}} + \beta_{w_{i,j}}\right)}{n_{z_{i,j},*,*} + \sum_{j=1}^{J} \beta_j}. \qquad (2)$$

3. Increase $n_{z_{i,j},i,*}$, $n_{z_{i,j},*,w_{i,j}}$, and $n_{z_{i,j},*,*}$ by 1.

Although in this paper we will focus on CGS, note that there are many other inference techniques for LDA such as collapsed variational Bayes, stochastic variational Bayes, or expectation maximization which essentially follow a very similar update pattern [2]. We believe that the parallel framework proposed in this paper will apply to this wider class of inference techniques as well.

2.2 Review of Multinomial Sampling

Given a T-dimensional discrete distribution characterized by unnormalized parameters $\mathbf{p}$ with $p_t \geq 0$ such as in (2), many sampling algorithms can be applied to draw a sample z such that $\Pr(z = t) \propto p_t$.

- LSearch: Linear search on $\mathbf{p}$. **Initialization:** Compute the normalization constant $c_T = \sum_t p_t$. **Generation:** First generate $u = \texttt{uniform}(c_T)$, a uniform random number in $[0, c_T)$, and perform a linear search to find $z = \min\left\{t : \left(\sum_{s \leq t} p_s\right) > u\right\}$.
- BSearch: Binary search on $\mathbf{c} = \texttt{cumsum}(\mathbf{p})$. **Initialization:** Compute $\mathbf{c} = \texttt{cumsum}(\mathbf{p})$ such that $c_t = \sum_{s:s \leq t} p_s$. **Generation:** First generate the cumulated sum $u = \texttt{uniform}(c_T)$ and perform a binary search on $\mathbf{c}$ to find $z = \min\{t : c_t > u\}$.
- Alias method. **Initialization:** Construct an Alias table [19] for $\mathbf{p}$, which contains two arrays of length T: *alias* and *prob*. See [18] for a linear time construction scheme. **Generation:** First generate $u = \texttt{uniform}(T)$, $j = \lfloor u \rfloor$, and

$$z = \begin{cases} j+1 & \text{if } (u - j) \leq prob[j+1] \\ alias[j+1] & \text{otherwise} \end{cases}.$$

See Table 1 for a comparison of the time/space requirements of each of the above sampling methods.

3. FENWICK TREE SAMPLING

In this section, we first describe a binary tree structure F+tree for fast T-dimensional multinomial sampling. The initialization of an F+tree is linear in T and the cost to generate a sample is logarithmic in T. Furthermore, F+tree can also be maintained in logarithmic time for a single parameter update of p_t. We will explain how such properties of F+tree can be explored to significantly accelerate LDA sampling.

3.1 F+tree Sampling

F+tree, first introduced for weighted sampling without replacement [21], is a simplified and generalized version of Fenwick tree [5], which supports both efficient sampling and update procedures. In fact, Fenwick tree can be regarded as a compressed version of the F+tree studied in this paper.

Table 1: Comparison of samplers for a T-dimensional multinomial distribution $\mathbf{p}$ described by unnormalized parameters $\{p_t : t = 1, \ldots, T\}$.

	Data Structure Space	Initialization Time	Initialization Space	Generation Time	Parameter Update Time
LSearch	$c_T = \mathbf{p}^\top \mathbf{1}$: $O(1)$	$O(T)$	$O(1)$	$O(T)$	$O(1)$
BSearch	$\mathbf{c} = \mathtt{cumsum}(\mathbf{p})$: $O(T)$	$O(T)$	$O(1)$	$O(\log T)$	$O(T)$
Alias Method	$prob, alias$: $O(T)$	$O(T)$	$O(T)$	$O(1)$	$O(T)$
F+tree Sampling	$\mathtt{F.initialize}(\mathbf{p})$: $O(T)$	$O(T)$	$O(1)$	$O(\log T)$	$O(\log T)$

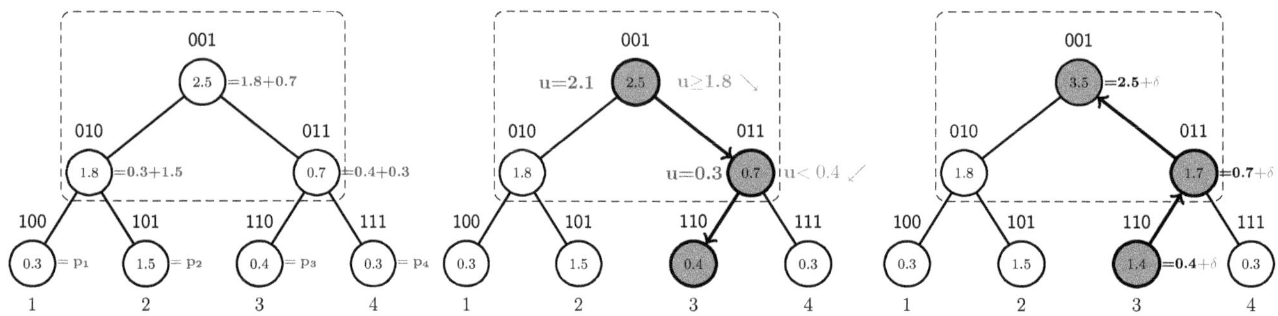

(a) F+tree for $\mathbf{p} = [0.3, 1.5, 0.4, 0.3]^\top$ (b) Sampling (c) Updating (with $\delta = 1.0$)

Figure 1: Illustration of sampling and updating using F+tree in logarithmic time.

For simplicity, we assume T is a power of 2. F+tree is a complete binary tree with $2T - 1$ nodes for a given $\mathbf{p}$, where

- each leaf node corresponds to a dimension t and stores p_t as its value, and
- each internal node stores the sum of the values of all of its leaf descendants, or equivalently the sum of values of its two children due to binary tree structure.

See Figure 1a for an example with $\mathbf{p} = [0.3, 1.5, 0.4, 0.3]$ and $T = 4$. Nodes in the dotted rectangle are internal nodes. Similar to the representation used in a heap [4], an array $\mathtt{F}$ of length $2T$ can be used to represent the F+tree structure. Let i be the index of each node, and $\mathtt{F}[i]$ be the value stored in the i-th node. The index of the left child, right child, and parent of the i-th node is $2i$, $2i + 1$, and $\lfloor i/2 \rfloor$, respectively. The 0/1 string along each node in Figure 1 is the binary number representation of the node index.

Initialization. By the definition of F+tree, given $\mathbf{p}$, the values of $\mathtt{F}$ be defined as follows:

$$\mathtt{F}[i] = \begin{cases} p_{i-T+1} & \text{if } i \geq T, \\ \mathtt{F}[2i] + \mathtt{F}[2i+1] & \text{if } i < T. \end{cases} \quad (3)$$

Thus, $\mathtt{F}$ can be constructed in $O(T)$ by initializing elements using (3) in reverse. Unlike the Alias method, there is no extra space required in the F+tree initialization in addition to $\mathtt{F}$.

Sample Generation. Sampling using a F+tree can be carried out as a simple top-down traversal procedure to locate $z = \min\left\{t : \left(\sum_{s:s\leq t} p_s\right) > u\right\}$ for a number uniformly sampled between $[0, \sum_t p_t)$. Note that $\sum_t p_t$ is stored in $\mathtt{F}[1]$, which can be directly used to generate $u = \mathtt{uniform}(\mathtt{F}[1])$. Let $\mathtt{leaves}(i)$ be the set of all leaf descendant of the i-th node. We can consider a general recursive step in the traversal with the current node i and $u \in [0, \mathtt{F}[i])$. The definition of F+tree guarantees that

$$u \geq \mathtt{F}[i.\mathtt{left}] \Rightarrow z \in \mathtt{leaves}(i.\mathtt{right}),$$
$$u < \mathtt{F}[i.\mathtt{left}] \Rightarrow z \in \mathtt{leaves}(i.\mathtt{left}),$$

This provides a guideline to determine which child to go next. If right child is chosen, $\mathtt{F}[i.\mathtt{left}]$ should be subtracted from u to ensure $u \in [0, \mathtt{F}[i.\mathtt{right}])$. Note that as half of the possible t values are removed from the set of candidates, it is clear that this sampling procedure costs only $O(\log T)$ time. The detailed procedure, denoted by $\mathtt{F.sample}(u)$, is described in Algorithm 1. A toy example with $u = 2.1$ is illustrated in Figure 1b.

Algorithm 1 Logarithmic time sampling: $\mathtt{F.sample}(u)$.

Input: $\mathtt{F}$: an F+tree for $\mathbf{p}$, $u = \mathtt{uniform}(\mathtt{F}[1])$.
Output: $z = \min\left\{t : \left(\sum_{s\leq t} p_s\right) > u\right\}$

- $i \leftarrow 1$
- While i is not a leaf
  - If $u \geq \mathtt{F}[i.\mathtt{left}]$,
    - $u \leftarrow u - \mathtt{F}[i.\mathtt{left}]$
    - $i \leftarrow i.\mathtt{right}$
  - Else
    - $i \leftarrow i.\mathtt{left}$
- $z \leftarrow i - T + 1$

Maintenance for Parameter Updates. A simple and efficient maintenance routine to deal with slight changes on the multinomial parameters $\mathbf{p}$ can be very useful in CGS for LDA (See details in Section 3.2). F+tree structure supports a logarithmic time maintenance routine for a single element change on $\mathbf{p}$. Assume the t-th component is updated by δ:

$$\bar{\mathbf{p}} \leftarrow \mathbf{p} + \delta \mathbf{e}_t,$$

Algorithm 2 Logarithmic time F+tree maintenance for a single parameter update: $\texttt{F.update}(t, \delta)$

Input: a F+tree $\texttt{F}$ for $\mathbf{p}$, t, δ.
Output: F+tree $\texttt{F}$ is updated for $\bar{\mathbf{p}} \equiv \mathbf{p} + \delta \mathbf{e}_t$

- $i \leftarrow \texttt{leaf}[t]$
- While i is a valid node
  - $\texttt{F}[i] = \texttt{F}[i] + \delta$
  - $i \leftarrow i.\texttt{parent}$

where $\mathbf{e}_t$ is the t-th column of the identity matrix of order T. A simple bottom-up update procedure to modify a F+tree $\texttt{F}$ for the current $\mathbf{p}$ to a F+tree for $\bar{\mathbf{p}}$ can be carried out as follows. Let $\texttt{leaf}[t]$ be the leaf node corresponding to t. For all the ancestors i of $\texttt{leaf}[t]$ (self included), perform the following delta update:

$$\texttt{F}[i] = \texttt{F}[i] + \delta.$$

See Figure 1c for an illustration with $t = 3$ and $\delta = 1.0$. The detailed procedure, denoted by $\texttt{F.update}(t, \delta)$, is described in Algorithm 2. The maintenance cost is linear to the depth of the F+tree, which is $O(\log T)$. Note that to deal with a similar change in $\mathbf{p}$, LSearch can update its normalization constant $c_T \leftarrow c_T + \delta$ in a constant time, while both BSearch and Alias method require to re-construct the entire data structure (either $\mathbf{c} = \texttt{cumsum}(\mathbf{p})$ or the Alias table: *alias* and *prob*), which costs $O(T)$ time in general.

See Table 1 for a summary of the complexity analysis for each multinomial sampling approach. Clearly, LSearch has the smallest update cost but the largest generation cost, and Alias method has the best generation cost but the worst maintenance cost. In contrast, F+tree sampling has a logarithmic time procedure for both operations.

Algorithm 3 F+LDA with word-by-word sampling

- $\texttt{F.initialize}(\mathbf{q})$, with $q_t = \frac{\beta}{n_t + \bar{\beta}}$
- For each word w
  - $\texttt{F.update}(t, n_{tw}/(n_t + \bar{\beta})) \quad \forall t \in T_w$
  - For each occurrence of w, say $w_{i,j} = w$ in d_i
    - $t \leftarrow z_{i,j}$
    - Decrease n_t, n_{td_i}, n_{tw} by one
    - $\texttt{F.update}(t, \delta)$ with $\delta = \frac{n_{tw}+\beta}{n_t+\bar{\beta}} - \texttt{F}[\texttt{leaf}(t)]$
    - $\mathbf{c} \leftarrow \texttt{cumsum}(\mathbf{r})$ (on T_w only)
    - $t \leftarrow \texttt{discrete}(\mathbf{p}, \texttt{uniform}(\alpha \texttt{F}[1] + \mathbf{r}^\top \mathbf{1}))$ by (6)
    - Increase n_t, n_{td_i}, n_{tw} by one
    - $\texttt{F.update}(t, \delta)$ with $\delta = \frac{n_{tw}+\beta}{n_t+\bar{\beta}} - \texttt{F}[\texttt{leaf}(t)]$
    - $z_{i,j} \leftarrow t$
  - $\texttt{F.update}(t, -n_{tw}/(n_t + \bar{\beta})) \quad \forall t \in T_w$

3.2 F+LDA = LDA with F+tree Sampling

In this section, we give details on applying F+tree sampling to CGS for LDA. Let us focus on a single CGS step in LDA with the current document id d_i, the current word w, and the current topic assignment t_{cur}. For simplicity of presentation, we further denote $n_{td} = n_{t,d_i,*}$, $n_{tw} = n_{t,*,w}$, and $n_t = n_{t,*,*}$ and assume $\alpha_t = \alpha, \forall t$, $\beta_j = \beta, \forall j$, and $\bar{\beta} = J \times \beta$. The multinomial parameter $\mathbf{p}$ of the CGS step in (2) can be decomposed into two terms as follows.

$$\begin{aligned} p_t &= \frac{(n_{td} + \alpha)(n_{tw} + \beta)}{n_t + \bar{\beta}}, \quad \forall t = 1, \ldots, T. \\ &= \beta \left(\frac{n_{td} + \alpha}{n_t + \bar{\beta}} \right) + n_{tw} \left(\frac{n_{td} + \alpha}{n_t + \bar{\beta}} \right). \end{aligned} \tag{4}$$

Let $\mathbf{q}$ and $\mathbf{r}$ be two vectors with $q_t = \frac{n_{td}+\alpha}{n_t+\bar{\beta}}$ and $r_t = n_{tw} q_t$. Some facts and implications about this decomposition:

(a) $\mathbf{p} = \beta \mathbf{q} + \mathbf{r}$. This leads to a simple two-level sampling for $\mathbf{p}$

$$\texttt{discrete}(\mathbf{p}, u) = \begin{cases} \texttt{discrete}(\mathbf{r}, u) & \text{if } u \leq \mathbf{r}^\top \mathbf{1}, \\ \texttt{discrete}(\mathbf{q}, \frac{u - \mathbf{r}^\top \mathbf{1}}{\beta}) & \text{otherwise,} \end{cases}$$

where $\mathbf{1}$ is the all-ones vector and $\mathbf{p}^\top \mathbf{1}$ denotes the normalization constant for $\mathbf{p}$, and $u = \texttt{uniform}(\mathbf{p}^\top \mathbf{1})$. This means that sampling for $\mathbf{p}$ can be very fast if $\mathbf{q}$ and $\mathbf{r}$ can be sampled efficiently.

(b) $\mathbf{q}$ is always dense but only two elements will be changed at each CGS step if we follow a document-by-document sampling sequence. Note $\mathbf{q}$ only depends on n_{td}. Decrement or increment of a single n_{td} only changes a single element of $\mathbf{q}$. We propose to apply F+tree sampling for $\mathbf{q}$ for its logarithmic time sampling and maintenance. At the beginning of CGS for LDA, a F+tree $\texttt{F}$ for $\mathbf{q}$ with $q_t = \frac{\alpha}{n_t + \bar{\beta}}$ is constructed in $O(T)$ time. When CGS switches to a new document d_i, perform the following updates

$$\texttt{F.update}(t, \frac{n_{td}}{n_t + \bar{\beta}}) \quad \forall t \in T_d := \{t : n_{td} \neq 0\}.$$

When CGS finishes sampling for this document, we can perform $\texttt{F.update}(t, \frac{-n_{td}}{n_t+\bar{\beta}})$ $\forall t \in T_d$. Both updates can be done in $O(|T_d| \log T)$. As $|T_d|$ is upper bounded by the number of words in this document, the amortized sampling cost for each word in the document remains $O(\log T)$.

(c) $\mathbf{r}$ is T_w sparse, where $T_w := \{t : n_{tw} \neq 0\}$. Unlike $\mathbf{q}$, all the elements of $\mathbf{r}$ change when we switch from one word to another word in the same document. Moreover, $\mathbf{r}$ is only used once to compute $\mathbf{r}^\top \mathbf{1}$ and to generate at most one sample. Thus, we propose to use BSearch approach to perform the sampling for $\mathbf{r}$. In particular, we only calculate the cumulative sum on nonzero elements in T_w. Thus, the initialization cost of BSearch is $O(|T_w|)$ and the sampling cost is $O(\log |T_w|)$.

Word-by-word CGS for LDA. Other than the traditional document-by-document CGS for LDA, we can also consider CGS using a word-by-word sampling sequence. For this sequence, we consider another decomposition of (4) as follows.

$$p_t = \alpha \left(\frac{n_{tw} + \beta}{n_t + \bar{\beta}} \right) + n_{td} \left(\frac{n_{tw} + \beta}{n_t + \bar{\beta}} \right), \quad \forall t. \tag{5}$$

For this decomposition (5), $\mathbf{q}$ and $\mathbf{r}$ have analogous definitions such that $q_t = \frac{n_{tw}+\beta}{n_t+\bar{\beta}}$ and $r_t = n_{td} q_t$, respectively. The corresponding three facts for (5) are as follows.

(a) $\mathbf{p} = \alpha \mathbf{q} + \mathbf{r}$. The two-level sampling for $\mathbf{p}$ is

$$\texttt{discrete}(\mathbf{p}, u) = \begin{cases} \texttt{discrete}(\mathbf{r}, u) & \text{if } u \leq \mathbf{r}^\top \mathbf{1}, \\ \texttt{discrete}(\mathbf{q}, \frac{u - \mathbf{r}^\top \mathbf{1}}{\alpha}) & \text{otherwise,} \end{cases} \tag{6}$$

Table 2: Comparison of various sampling methods for LDA. We use $\#MH$ to denote number of Metropolis-Hasting steps for Alias LDA. Note that in this table only the time complexity is presented—there are some hidden constants that also play important roles in practice. For example, the initialization cost of the Alias table is much more than linear search although they have the same time complexity.

	F+LDA		F+LDA		Sparse-LDA			Alias-LDA	
Sample Sequence	Word-by-Word		Doc-by-Doc		Doc-by-Doc			Doc-by-Doc	
Exact Sampling	Yes		Yes		Yes			No	
Decomposition	$\alpha\left(\frac{n_{tw}+\beta}{n_t+\bar{\beta}}\right)$	$+n_{td}\left(\frac{n_{tw}+\beta}{n_t+\bar{\beta}}\right)$	$\beta\left(\frac{n_{td}+\alpha}{n_t+\bar{\beta}}\right)$	$+n_{tw}\left(\frac{n_{td}+\alpha}{n_t+\bar{\beta}}\right)$	$\frac{\alpha\beta}{n_t+\bar{\beta}}$	$+\beta\left(\frac{n_{td}}{n_t+\bar{\beta}}\right)$	$+n_{tw}\left(\frac{n_{td}+\alpha}{n_t+\bar{\beta}}\right)$	$\alpha\left(\frac{n_{tw}+\beta}{n_t+\bar{\beta}}\right)$	$+n_{td}\left(\frac{n_{tw}+\beta}{n_t+\bar{\beta}}\right)$
Sampling method	F+tree	BSearch	F+tree	BSearch	LSearch	LSearch	LSearch	Alias	Alias
Fresh samples	Yes	Yes	Yes	Yes	Yes	Yes	Yes	No	Yes
Initialization	$O(\log T)$	$O(\|T_d\|)$	$O(\log T)$	$O(\|T_w\|)$	$O(1)$	$O(1)$	$O(\|T_w\|)$	$O(1)$	$O(\|T_d\|)$
Sampling	$O(\log T)$	$O(\log \|T_d\|)$	$O(\log T)$	$O(\log \|T_w\|)$	$O(T)$	$O(\|T_d\|)$	$O(\|T_w\|)$	$O(\#MH)$	$O(\#MH)$

(b) $\mathbf{q}$ is always dense but only very few elements will be changed at each CGS step using word-by-word sampling sequence. A F+tree structure $\mathtt{F}$ is maintained for $\mathbf{q}$. The amortized update time for each occurrence of a word is $O(\log T)$ and the sampling generation for $\mathbf{q}$ using $\mathtt{F}$ also costs $O(\log T)$. Thus, $\mathtt{discrete}(\mathbf{q}, u) := \mathtt{F.sample}(u)$.

(c) $\mathbf{r}$ is a sparse vector with $|T_d|$ non-zeros. BSearch is used to construct $\mathbf{c} = \mathtt{cumsum}(\mathbf{r})$ in $O(T_d)$ space and time. $\mathbf{c}$ is used to perform binary search to generate a sample required by CGS for the occurrence of the current word. Thus, $\mathtt{discrete}(\mathbf{r}, u) := \mathtt{binary\_search}(\mathbf{c}, u)$.

The detailed procedure of using word-by-word sampling sequence is described in Algorithm 3. Let us analyse the performance difference of F+LDA between two sampling sequences of a large number of documents. The amortized cost for each CGS step is $O(|T_d| + \log T)$ for the word-by-word sequence and $O(|T_w|+\log T)$ for the document-by-document sequence. Note that $|T_d|$ is always bounded by the number of words in a document, which is usually a much smaller number than a large T (say 1024). In contrast, $|T_w|$ approaches to T when the number of documents increases. Thus, we can expect that F+LDA with the word-by-word sequence is faster than the document-by-document sequence. Empirical results in Section 5.1 also confirm our analysis.

3.3 Related Work

SparseLDA [23] is the first sampling method which considered decomposing $\mathbf{p}$ into a sum of sparse vectors and a dense vector. In particular, it considers a three-term decomposition of p_t as follows.

$$p_t = \frac{\alpha\beta}{n_t + \bar{\beta}} + \beta\left(\frac{n_{td}}{n_t + \bar{\beta}}\right) + n_{tw}\left(\frac{n_{td} + \alpha}{n_t + \bar{\beta}}\right),$$

where the first term is dense, the second term is sparse with $|T_d|$ non-zeros, and the third term is sparse with $|T_w|$ non-zeros. In both SparseLDA implementations (Yahoo! LDA [16] and Mallet LDA [23]), LSearch is applied to all of these three terms. As SparseLDA follows the document-by-document sequence, very few elements will be changed for the first two terms at each CGS step. Sampling procedures for the first two terms have very low chance to be performed due to the observation that most mass of p_t is contributed from the third term. The choice of LSearch, whose normalization constant c_T can be updated in $O(1)$ time, for the first two terms is reasonable. Note that $O(T)$ and $O(|T_d|)$ initialization costs for the first two terms can be amortized. The overall amortized cost for each CGS step is $O(|T_w| + |T_d| + |T|)$.

AliasLDA [11] is a recently proposed approach which reduces the amortized cost of each step to $O(|T_d|)$. AliasLDA considers the following decomposition of $\mathbf{p}$:

$$p_t = \alpha\left(\frac{n_{tw} + \beta}{n_t + \bar{\beta}}\right) + n_{td}\left(\frac{n_{tw} + \beta}{n_t + \bar{\beta}}\right).$$

Instead of the "exact" multinomial sampling for $\mathbf{p}$, AliasLDA considers a proposal distribution $\mathbf{q}$ with a very efficient generation routine and performs a series of Metropolis-Hasting (MH) steps using this proposal to simulate the true distribution $\mathbf{p}$. In particular, the proposal distribution is constructed using the latest second term and a stale version of the first term. For both terms, Alias method is applied to perform the sampling. $\#MH$ steps decides the quality of the sampling results. The overall amortized cost for each CGS step is $O(|T_d| + \#MH)$. Note the initialization cost $O(|T|)$ for the first term can be amortized as long as the same Alias table can be used to generate T samples.

See Table 2 for a detailed summary for LDA using various sampling methods. Note that the hidden coefficient ρ_A in the $O(|T_d|)$ notation for the construction of the Alias table is larger than the coefficient ρ_B for the construction of BSearch and the coefficient ρ_F for the maintenance and sampling of F+tree. Thus as long as $T < 2^{\frac{\rho_A - \rho_B}{\rho_F}|T_d|}$, F+LDA using the word-by-word sampling sequence is faster than AliasLDA. Empirical results in Section 5.1 also show the superiority of F+LDA over AliasLDA for real-world datasets even using $T = 50{,}000$.

4. PROPOSED PARALLEL APPROACH

In this section we present our second innovation—a novel parallel framework for CGS. Note that the same technique can also be used for other inference techniques for LDA such as collapsed variational Bayes and stochastic variational Bayes [2] since they follow similar update patterns.

To explain our proposed approach, we find it instructive to consider a hypergraph G. Let $G = (V, E)$ be a hypergraph with $(I + J + 1)$ nodes:

$$V = \{\mathbf{d}_i : i = 1, \ldots, I\} \cup \{\mathbf{w}_j : j = 1, \ldots, J\} \cup \{\mathbf{s}\},$$

and hyperedges:

$$E = \{e_{ij} = \{\mathbf{d}_i, \mathbf{w}_j, \mathbf{s}\}\},$$

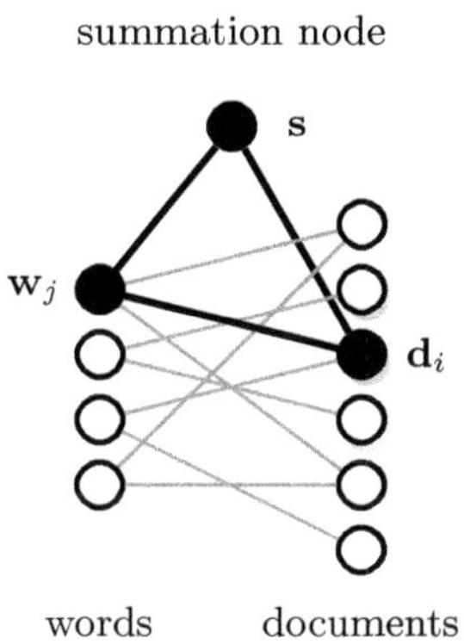

(a) Access graph for LDA

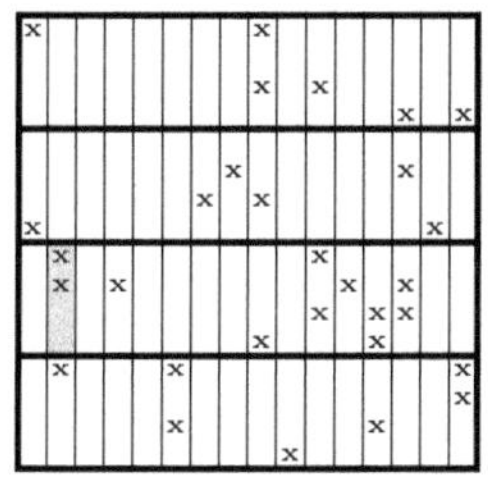

(b) Task and Data Partition

Figure 2: Abstract access graph for LDA

where $|E| = \sum_i n_i$. Note that G contains multi-edges, which means that the same hyperedge can appear more than once in E just as a single word can appear multiple times in a document. Clearly, G is equivalent to a bag-of-words representation of the corpus $\{d_1, \ldots, d_I\}$; each $\mathbf{d}_i$ is associated with the i-th document, each $\mathbf{w}_j$ is associated with the j-th vocabulary, and each hyperedge e_{ij} corresponds to one occurrence of the vocabulary w_j in the i-th document d_i. See Figure 2 (a) for a visual illustration; here, each gray edge corresponds to an occurrence of a word and the black triangle highlights a particular hyperedge $e_{ij} = \{\mathbf{d}_i, \mathbf{w}_j, \mathbf{s}\}$.

To further connect G to the update rule of CGS, we associate each node of G with a T-dimensional vector. In many inference methods, an update based on a single occurrence w_{ij} can be realized as a graph operation on G which accesses values of nodes in a single hyperedge e_{ij}. More concretely, let us define the t-th coordinate of each vector as follows:

$$(\mathbf{d}_i)_t := n_{t,i,*}, \quad (\mathbf{w}_j)_t := n_{t,*,w_j}, \text{ and } \quad (\mathbf{s})_t := n_{t,*,*}.$$

Based on the update rule of CGS, we can see that the update for the occurrence of w_{ij} only reads from and writes to the values stored in $\mathbf{d}_i$, $\mathbf{w}_{w_{ij}}$, and $\mathbf{s}$.

Interestingly, this property of the updates is reminiscent of that of the stochastic gradient descent (SGD) algorithm for matrix completion model. Similarly to LDA, matrix completion model has two sets of parameters $\mathbf{w}_1, \ldots, \mathbf{w}_J$ and $\mathbf{d}_1, \ldots, \mathbf{d}_I$, and each SGD update requires only one of $\mathbf{w}_j$ and one of $\mathbf{d}_i$ to be read and modified. Since each update is highly localized, there is considerable parallelism available; [25] exploits this property to propose an efficient asynchronous parallel SGD algorithm for matrix completion.

The crucial difference in the case of LDA, however, is that there is an additional variable $\mathbf{s}$ which participates in every hyperedge of the graph. Thus, if we change the update sequence from $(e_{ij}, e_{i'j'})$ to $(e_{i'j'}, e_{ij})$, then even if $i \neq i'$ and $j \neq j'$ the result of updates will not be the same since the value of $\mathbf{s}$ changes in the first update. Fortunately, this dependency is very weak; each element of $\mathbf{s}$ is a large number because it is a summation over the whole corpus and each update changes its value at most by one, therefore the relative change of $\mathbf{s}$ made in a short period of time is often negligible.

While existing approaches such as Yahoo! LDA [16] exploit this observation by introducing a parameter server and let each machine query the server to retrieve recent updates, it is certainly not desirable in a large scale system that every machine has to query the same central server. Motivated by the "nomadic" algorithm introduced by [25] for matrix completion, we propose a new parallel framework for LDA that is decentralized, asynchronous and lock-free.

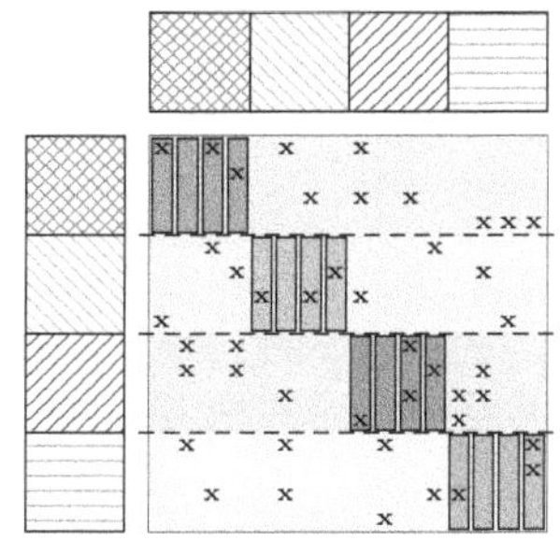

(a) Initial assignment of $\mathbf{w}_j$. Each worker works only on the diagonal active area in the beginning.

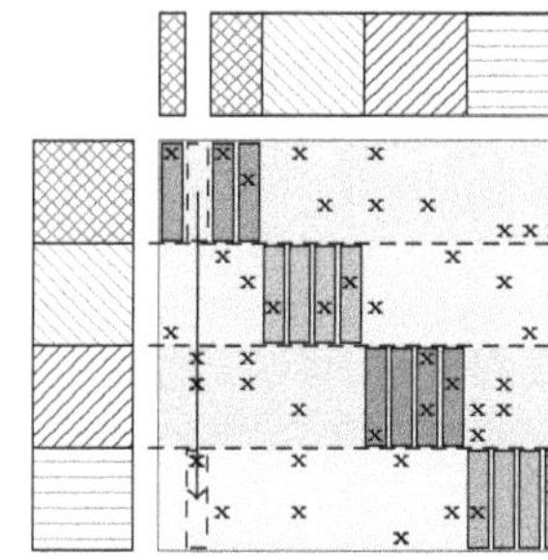

(b) After a worker finishes processing j, it sends the corresponding $\mathbf{w}_j$ to another worker. Here, $\mathbf{w}_2$ is sent from worker 1 to 4.

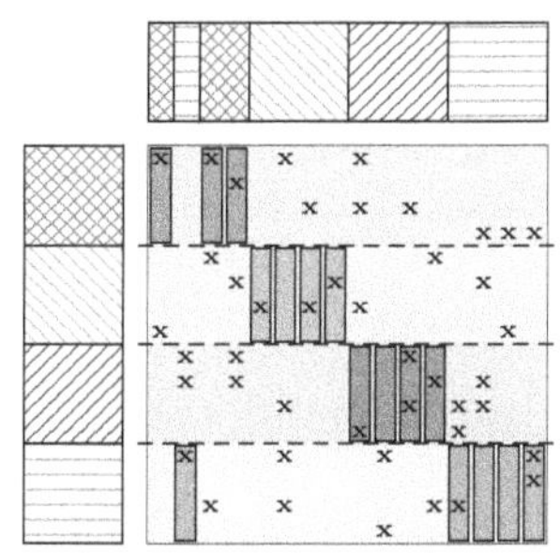

(c) Upon receipt, the $\mathbf{w}_j$ is processed by the new worker. Here, worker 4 can now process $\mathbf{w}_2$ since it owns it.

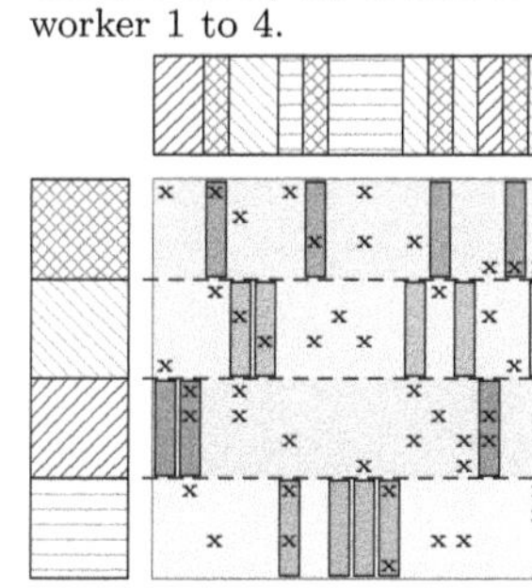

(d) During the execution of the algorithm, the ownership of the $\mathbf{w}_j$ changes.

Figure 3: Illustration of the Nomad LDA algorithm

Algorithm 4 The basic Nomad LDA algorithm

Given: initialized $\mathbf{s}_l$, $\bar{\mathbf{s}}$, and local queue $\mathbf{q}_l$

- **While** stop signal has not been received
  - If receive a token τ, $push(\mathbf{q}_l, \tau)$
  - $\tau \leftarrow pop(\mathbf{q}_l)$
  - If $\tau = \tau_s$
    - $\mathbf{s} \leftarrow \mathbf{s} + (\mathbf{s}_l - \bar{\mathbf{s}})$
    - $\mathbf{s}_l \leftarrow \mathbf{s}$
    - $\bar{\mathbf{s}} \leftarrow \mathbf{s}$
    - Send τ_s to another worker
  - Else if $\tau = \tau_j := (j, \mathbf{w}_k)$
    - Perform the j-th subtask
    - Send τ_s to another worker

4.1 Nomadic Framework for Parallel LDA

Let p be the number of parallel workers, which can be a thread in a shared-memory multi-core machine or a processor in a distributed memory multi-machine system.

Data Partition and Subtask Split. The given document corpus is split into p portions such that the l-th worker owns the l-th partition of the data, $D_l \subset \{1, \ldots, J\}$. Unlike the other parallel approach where each unit subtask is a document owned by the worker, our approach uses a fine-

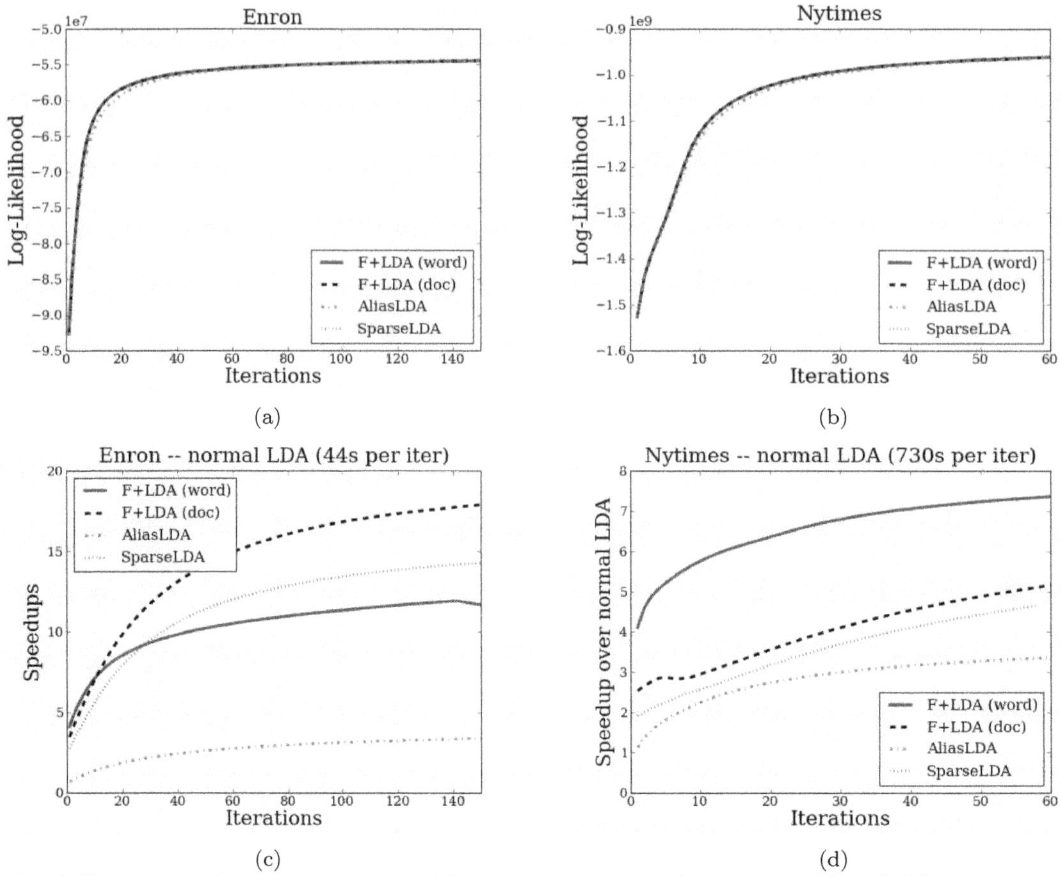

Figure 4: (a) and (b) present the convergence speed in terms of number of iterations. (c) and (d) present the sampling speed of each iteration—the y-axis is the speedup over the normal LDA implementation which takes $O(T)$ time to generate one sample. We observe all the sampling algorithms have similar convergence speed, while F+LDA(doc) is the fastest compared to other document-wise sampling approaches. Also, F+LDA(word) is faster than F+LDA(doc) for larger datasets, which confirms our analysis in Section 3.2.

grained split for tasks. Note that in the inference for LDA, each word occurrence corresponds to an update. Thus, we consider a unit subtask $\mathbf{t}_j$ as all occurrences of word w_j in all documents owned by the worker. See Figure 2b for an illustration in the data partition and task split. Each "x" denotes an occurrence of a word. Each block row (bigger rectangle) represents a data partition owned by a worker, while each smaller rectangle stands for a unit subtask for the worker.

Asynchronous Computation. It is known that synchronous computation would suffer from *the curse of last reducer* when the load-balance is poor. In this work, we aim to develop an asynchronous parallel framework where each worker maintains a local job queue $\mathbf{q}_l$ such that the worker can keep performing the subtask popped from the queue without worrying about data conflict and synchronization. To achieve this goal, we first study the characteristics of subtasks. The subtask $\mathbf{t}_j$ for the l-th worker involves updates on all occurrences of $\mathbf{w}_j$ in D_l, which means that to perform $\mathbf{t}_j$, the l-th worker must acquire permission to access $\{\mathbf{d}_i : i \in D_l\}$, $\mathbf{w}_j$, and $\mathbf{s}$. Our data partition scheme has guaranteed that two workers will never need to access a same $\mathbf{d}_i$ simultaneously. Thus we can always keep the ownership of $\mathbf{d}_i, \forall i \in D_l$ to l-th worker. The difficulty for parallel execution comes from the access to $\mathbf{w}_j$ and $\mathbf{s}$ which can be accessed by different workers at the same time. To overcome this difficulty, we propose to use a *nomadic token passing* scheme to avoid access conflicts. Token passing is a standard technique used in telecommunications to avoid conflicting access to a resource shared by many members. The idea is "owner computes": only the member with the ownership of the token has the permission to access the resource. Here we borrow the same idea to avoid the situation where two workers require access to the same $\mathbf{w}_j$ and $\mathbf{s}$.

Nomadic Tokens for $\mathbf{w}_j$. We have a token τ_j dedicated for the ownership of each word $\mathbf{w}_j$. These J tokens are nomadically passed among p workers. The ownership of a token τ_j means the worker can perform the subtask $\mathbf{t}_j$. Each token τ_j is a tuple $(j, \mathbf{w}_j)$, where the first entry is the index for the token, and the second entry is the latest value of $\mathbf{w}_j$. For a worker, a token τ means the activation of the corresponding inference subtask. Thus, we can guarantee that 1) the values of $\mathbf{w}_j$ used in each subtask is always up-to-date; 2) no two workers require access to a same $\mathbf{w}_j$.

Nomadic Token for $\mathbf{s}$. So far we have successfully kept the values of $\mathbf{d}_i$ and $\mathbf{w}_j$ used in each subtask latest, and avoid access conflicts by nomadic token passing. However, all subtasks depend on each other due to the need to access $\mathbf{s}$. Based on the summation property, we propose to deal with this issue by creating a special nomadic token $\tau_s = (0, \mathbf{s})$ for $\mathbf{s}$, where 0 is the token index for τ_s, and have two copies of $\mathbf{s}$ in each worker: $\mathbf{s}_l$ and $\bar{\mathbf{s}}$. $\mathbf{s}_l$ is a local shadow node for $\mathbf{s}$. The

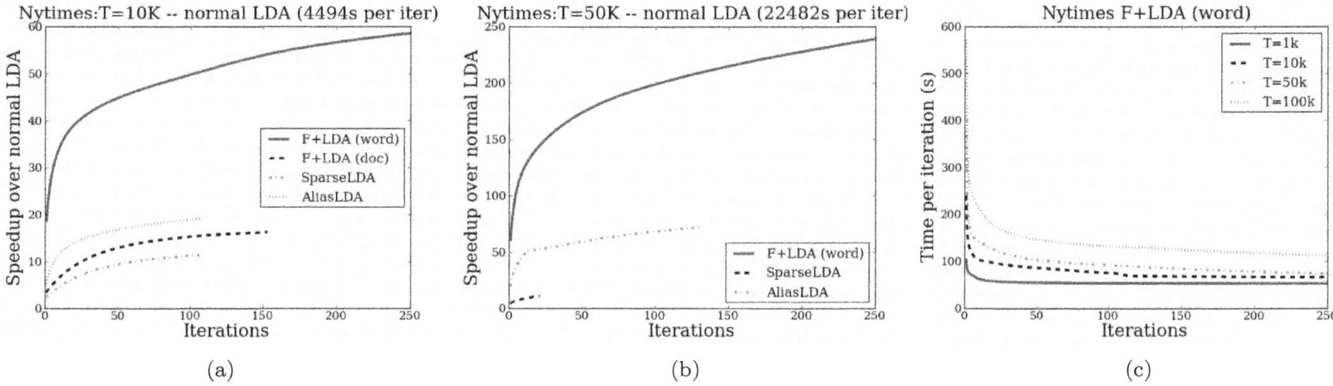

Figure 5: (a) and (b) present the sampling speed for $T = 10,000$ and $T = 50,000$. The superiority of F+LDA(word) is more significant when T is large. (c) shows the sampling speed for various T. The increase in sampling time is much smaller than the increase in the number of topics T. Note that the sampling time per iteration for $T = 100,000$ is only about twice as much as the time required for $T = 1,000$.

l-th worker always uses the values of $\mathbf{s}_l$ to perform updates and makes the modification to $\mathbf{s}_l$. $\bar{\mathbf{s}}$ was the snapshot of $\mathbf{s}$ from the last arrival of τ_s. Due to the additivity of $\mathbf{s}$, the delta $\mathbf{s}_l - \mathbf{s}$ can be regarded as the effort that has been made since the last arrival of τ_s. Thus, each time that τ_s arrives, the worker can perform the following operations to accumulate its local effort to the global $\mathbf{s}$ and update its local $\mathbf{s}_l$.

1. $\mathbf{s} \leftarrow \mathbf{s} + (\mathbf{s}_l - \bar{\mathbf{s}})$
2. $\bar{\mathbf{s}} \leftarrow \mathbf{s}$
3. $\mathbf{s}_l \leftarrow \mathbf{s}$

We present the general idea of Nomad LDA in Algorithm 4 and its illustration in Figure 3.

4.2 Related Work

Unlike the situation in the serial case, the latest values of $n_{z,*,w}$ and $n_{z,*,*}$ can be distributed among different machines in the distributed setting. The existing parallel approaches focus on developing mechanisms to communicate these values. We briefly review two approaches for parallelizing CGS in distributed setting: AdLDA [13] and Yahoo! LDA [16]. In both approaches, each machine has a local copy of the *entire* $n_{z,*,w}$ and $n_{z,*,*}$. AdLDA uses bulk synchronization to update its local copy after each iteration. At each iteration, each machine just uses the snapshot from last synchronization point to conduct Gibbs sampling. On the other hand, Yahoo! LDA creates a central parameter server to maintain the latest values for $n_{z,*,w}$ and $n_{z,*,*}$. Every machine asynchronously communicates with this machine to send the local update to the server and get new values to update its local copy. Note that the communication is done asynchronously in Yahoo! LDA to avoid expensive network locking. The central idea of Yahoo! LDA is that modest stale values would not affect the sampler significantly. Thus, there is no need to spend too much effort to synchronize these values. Note that for these two approaches, both values of $n_{z,*,w}$ and $n_{z,*,*}$ used in Gibbs sampling could be stale. In contrast, our proposed Nomad LDA has the following advantages:

- No copy of the entire $n_{z,*,w}$ is required in each machine.
- The value of $n_{z,*,w}$ used in the Gibbs sampling is always up-to-date in each machine.
- The computation is both asynchronous and decentralized.

Our Nomad LDA is close to a parallel approach for matrix completion [25], which also utilized the concept of nomadic variables. However, the application is completely different. [25] concentrates on parallelizing stochastic gradient descent for matrix completion. The access graph for this problem is a bipartite graph, and there is no variable that needs to be synchronized across processors.

5. EXPERIMENTAL EVALUATION

In this section we investigate the performance and scaling of our proposed algorithms. We demonstrate that our proposed F+tree sampling method is very efficient in handling large number of topics compared to the other approaches in Section 5.1. When the number of documents is also large, in Section 5.2 we show our parallel framework is very efficient in multi-core and distributed systems.

Datasets. We work with five real-world large datasets—Enron, NyTimes, PubMed, Amazon, and UMBC. The detailed data set statistics are listed in Table 3. Among them, Enron, NyTimes and PubMed are bag-of-word datasets in the UCI repository[1]. These three datasets have been used to demonstrate the scaling behavior of topic modeling algorithms in many recent papers [2, 16, 11]. In fact, the PubMed dataset stretches the capabilities of many implementations. For instance, we tried to use LDA code from `http://www.ics.uci.edu/~asuncion/software/fast.htm`, but it could not handle PubMed.

To demonstrate the scalability of our algorithm, we use two more large-scale datasets—Amazon and UMBC. The Amazon dataset consists of approximately 35 million product reviews from Amazon.com, and was downloaded from the Stanford Network Analysis Project (SNAP) home page. Since reviews are typically short, we split the text into words, removed stop words, and using Porter stemming [14]. After this pre-processing we discarded words that appear fewer than 5 times or in 5 reviews. Finally, any reviews that were left with no words after this pre-processing were discarded.

[1] https://archive.ics.uci.edu/ml/datasets/Bag+of+Words

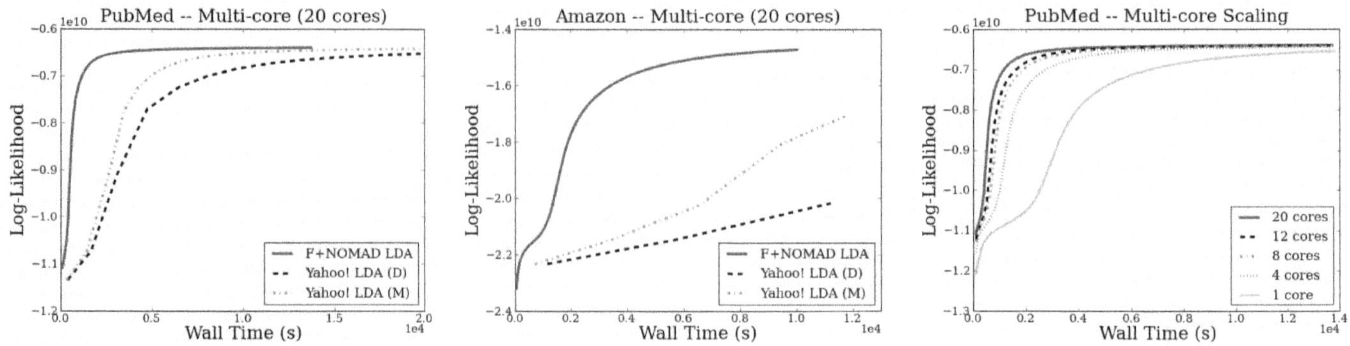

(a) (b) (c)

Figure 6: (a) and (b) show the comparison between Nomad LDA and Yahoo! LDA using 20 cores on a single machine. (c) shows the scaling performance of Nomad LDA as a function of number of cores.

Table 3: Data statistics.

	# documents (I)	# vocabulary (J)	# words
Enron	37,861	28,102	6,238,796
NyTimes	298,000	102,660	98,793,316
PubMed	8,200,000	141,043	737,869,083
Amazon	29,907,995	1,682,527	1,499,602,431
UMBC	40,599,164	2,881,476	1,483,145,192

This resulted in a corpus of approximately 30 million documents and approximately **1.5 billion** words.

The UMBC WebBase corpus is downloaded from `http://ebiquity.umbc.edu/blogger/2013/05/01/`. It contains a collection of pre-processed paragraphs from the Stanford WebBase[2] crawl on February 2007. The original dataset has approximately 40 million paragraphs and 3 billion words. We further processed the data by stemming and removing stop words following the same procedure in LibShortText [24]. This resulted in a corpus of approximately **1.5 billion** words.

Hardware. The experiments are conducted on a parallel platform at the Texas Advanced Computing Center (TACC), called Maverick[3]. Each node contains 20 Intel Xeon E5-2680 CPUs and 256 GB memory. Each job can run on at most 32 nodes (640 cores) for at most 12 hours.

Parameter Setting. Throughout the experiments we set the hyper parameters $\alpha = 50/T$ and $\beta = 0.01$, where T is the number of topics. Previous papers showed that this parameter setting gives good model qualities [9], and many widely-used software such as Yahoo! LDA and Mallet-LDA also use this as the default parameters. To test the performance with a large number of topics, we set $T = 1024$ in all the experiments except the ones in Figure 5.

Evaluation. Our main competitor is Yahoo! LDA in large-scale distributed setting. To have a fair comparison, we use the same training likelihood routine to evaluate the quality of model (see Eq. (2) in [16] for details).

5.1 Comparison of sampling methods: handling large number of topics

In this section, we compare various sampling strategies used for LDA in the serial setting. We include the following sampling strategies into the comparison (see Section 3 for details):

1. F+LDA: our proposed sampling scheme. Document-wise and word-wise sampling order are denoted by F+LDA(doc) and F+LDA(word), respectively.
2. SparseLDA: the approach that uses linear search on PDF to conduct document-wise sampling. This approach is used in Yahoo! LDA and Mallet-LDA.
3. AliasLDA: the approach that uses Alias method to do the sampling with document-wise sampling order. This approach is proposed very recently in [11].

To have a fair comparison focusing on different sampling strategies, we implemented the above three approaches to use the same data structures. We use two smaller datasets—Enron and NyTimes to conduct the experiments. Note that [11] also conducts the comparison of different sampling approaches using these two datasets after further preprocessing. Figure 4 presents the comparison results using $T = 1,024$, while in Figure 5 we show the results by varying T from $1,000$ to $100,000$.

We first compare F+LDA(doc), Sparse LDA, and Alias LDA, where all of the three approaches have the same document-wise sampling ordering. F+LDA(doc) and Sparse LDA follow the exact sampling distribution of the normal Gibbs sampling; as a result, we can observe in Figure 4a and 4b that they have the same convergence speed in terms of number of iterations. On the other hand, Alias LDA converges slightly slower than other approaches because it does not sample from the exact same distribution. Note that we found that this phenomenon becomes more clear when T is large. In terms of efficiency, Figures 4c and 4d indicate that F+LDA(doc) is faster than Sparse-LDA and Alias-LDA, which confirms our analysis in Section 3.

Next we compare the performance of document-wise and word-wise sampling for F+LDA. Figure 4a and 4b indicate that both orderings give similar convergence speed. As discussed in Section 3.2, using the F+tree sampling approach, the word-wise ordering is expected to be faster than document-wise ordering as the number of documents increases. This phenomenon is confirmed by our experimental results in Figures 4c, 4d, and 5a as F+LDA(word) is faster than F+LDA(doc) on the NyTimes dataset, which has a larger number of documents comparing to Enron. The experimental results also justify our use of word-wise sampling

[2]Stanford WebBase project: `http://dbpubs.stanford.edu:8091/~testbed/doc2/WebBase/`

[3]`https://portal.tacc.utexas.edu/user-guides/maverick`

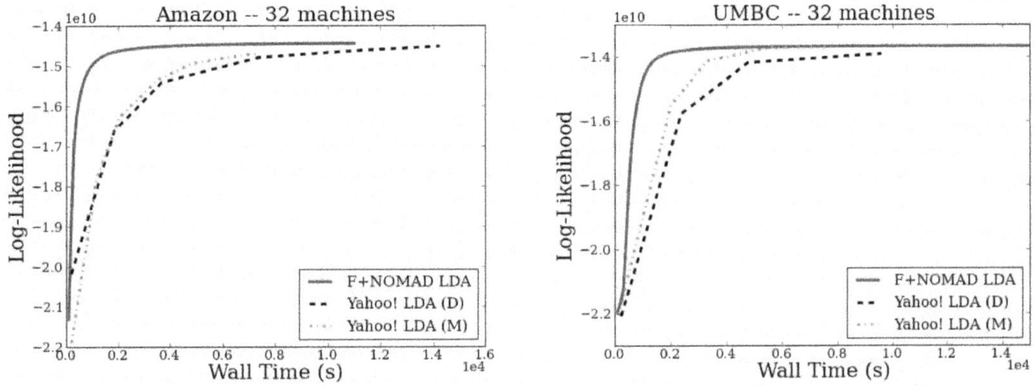

(a) (b)

Figure 7: The comparison between F+Nomad LDA and Yahoo! LDA on 32 machines with 20 cores per machine.

when applying the Nomad approach in multi-core and distributed systems.

Figure 5 shows the results for even larger T. As the length of the computing time is limited to 12 hours by the Maverick system, the number of iterations is different for all methods. We first observe that when $T \geq 10,000$, AliasLDA starts to outperform SparseLDA in Figures 5a and 5b. However, F+LDA(word) still outperforms these two methods significantly. In 5c, we can see that when T is increased from $1,000$ to $100,000$, the sampling time required by F+LDA(word) increases only by a factor of two. This can be explained by the logarithmic time complexity of F+LDA(word).

5.2 Multi-core and Distributed Experiments

Now we combine our proposed F+tree sampling strategy with the nomadic parallelization framework. This leads to a new F+Nomad LDA sampler that can handle huge problems in multi-core and distributed systems.

5.2.1 Competing Implementations.

We compare our algorithm against Yahoo! LDA for three reasons: a) It is one of the most efficient open source implementations of CGS for LDA, which scales to large datasets. b) [16] claims that Yahoo! LDA outperforms other open source implementation such as AD-LDA [13] and PLDA [20]. c) Yahoo! LDA uses a parameter server, which has become a generic approach for distributing large-scale learning problems. It is therefore interesting to see if a different asynchronous approach can outperform the parameter server on this specific problem. Yahoo! LDA is a disk-based implementation that assumes the latent variables associated with tokens in the documents are streamed from disk at each iteration. To have a fair comparison, in addition to running the disk-based Yahoo! LDA (denoted by Yahoo! LDA(D)), we further ran it on the `tmpfs` file system [17] which resides on RAM for the intermediate storage used by Yahoo! LDA. This way we eliminate the cost of disk I/O, and can make a fair comparison with our own code which does not stream data from disk; we use Yahoo! LDA(M) to denote this version.

5.2.2 Multi-core Experiments

Both F+Nomad LDA and Yahoo! LDA support parallel computation on a single machine with multiple cores. Here we conduct experiments on two datasets, Pubmed and Amazon, and the comparisons are presented in Figure 6. As can be seen from Figures 6a and 6b, F+Nomad LDA handsomely outperforms both memory and disk version of Yahoo! LDA, and gets to a better quality solution within the same time budget. Given a desired log-likelihood level, F+Nomad LDA is approximately 4 times faster than Yahoo! LDA.

Next we turn out attention to the scaling of F+Nomad LDA as a function of the number of cores. In Figure 6c we plot the convergence of F+Nomad LDA as the number of cores is varied. Clearly, as the number of cores increases the convergence speed is faster.

5.2.3 Distributed Memory Experiments

In this section, we compare the performance of F+Nomad LDA and Yahoo! LDA on two huge datasets, Amazon and UMBC, in a distributed memory setting. The number of machines is set to 32, and the number of cores per machine is 20. As can be seen from Figure 7, F+Nomad LDA dramatically outperforms both memory and disk version of Yahoo! LDA and obtains significantly better quality solution (in terms of log-likelihood) within the same wall clock time.

6. CONCLUSIONS

In this paper, we present a novel F+Nomad LDA algorithm that can handle large number of topics as well as large number of documents. In order to handle large number of topics we use an appropriately modified Fenwick tree. This data structure allows us to sample from and update a T-dimensional multinomial distribution in $O(\log T)$ time. In order to handle large number of documents, we propose a novel asynchronous and non-locking parallel framework, which leads to impressive speedups in multi-core and distributed systems. The resulting algorithm is faster than Yahoo! LDA and is able to handle datasets with billions of words. In future work we would like to include the ability to stream documents from disk, just like Yahoo! LDA does. It is also interesting to study how our ideas can be transferred to other sampling schemes such as CVB0.

Acknowledgments. We thank the anonymous reviewers for their constructive comments. We thank Alex Smola for help in implementing AliasLDA. We thank the Texas Advanced Computing Center for providing infrastructure and timely support for our experiments. This research was supported by NSF grants IIS-1219015, CCF-1320746, and CCF-1117055.

7. REFERENCES

[1] A. Asuncion, P. Smyth, and M. Welling. Asynchronous distributed learning of topic models. In *NIPS*, pages 81–88, 2008.

[2] A. Asuncion, M. Welling, P. Smyth, and Y. W. Teh. On smoothing and inference for topic models. In *UAI*, pages 27–34, 2009.

[3] D. Blei, A. Ng, and M. Jordan. Latent Dirichlet allocation. *Journal of Machine Learning Research*, 3:993–1022, Jan. 2003.

[4] T. H. Cormen, C. E. Leiserson, and R. L. Rivest. *Introduction to Algorithms*. MIT Press, Cambridge, MA, 1990.

[5] P. M. Fenwick. A new data structure for cumulative frequency tables. *Software: Practice and Experience*, 24(3):327–336, 1994.

[6] R. Gemulla, E. Nijkamp, P. J. Haas, and Y. Sismanis. Large-scale matrix factorization with distributed stochastic gradient descent. In *KDD*, 2011.

[7] J. E. Gonzalez, Y. Low, H. Gu, D. Bickson, and C. Guestrin. Powergraph: Distributed graph-parallel computation on natural graphs. In *OSDI*, 2012.

[8] T. Griffiths and M. Steyvers. Finding scientific topics. *PNAS*, 101:5228–5235, 2004.

[9] G. Heinrich. Parameter estimation for text analysis. Technical report, 2008.

[10] A. Ihler and D. Newman. Understanding errors in approximate distributed latent Dirichlet allocation. *IEEE TKDE*, 24(5):952–960, May 2012.

[11] A. Q. Li, A. Ahmed, S. Ravi, and A. J. Smola. Reducing the sampling complexity of topic models. In *KDD*, 2014.

[12] M. Li, D. G. Andersen, J. Park, A. J. Smola, A. Ahmed, V. Josifovski, J. Long, E. Shekita, and B. Y. Su. Scaling distributed machine learning with the parameter server. In *OSDI*, 2014.

[13] D. Newman, A. Asuncion, P. Smyth, and M. Welling. Distributed algorithms for topic models. *Journal of Machine Learning Research*, 10:1801–1828, 2009.

[14] M. Porter. An algorithm for suffix stripping. *Program*, 14(3):130–137, 1980.

[15] B. Recht and C. Ré. Parallel stochastic gradient algorithms for large-scale matrix completion. *Mathematical Programming Computation*, 5(2):201–226, June 2013.

[16] A. J. Smola and S. Narayanamurthy. An architecture for parallel topic models. *Proceedings of the VLDB Endowment*, 3(1):703–710, 2010.

[17] P. Snyder. tmpfs: A virtual memory file system. In *Proceedings of the Autumn 1990 European UNIX Users' Group Conference*, 1990.

[18] M. D. Vose. A linear algorithm for generating random numbers with a given distribution. *IEEE Transactions on Software Engineering*, 17(9):972–975, 1991.

[19] A. J. Walker. An efficient method for generating discrete random variables with general distributions. *ACM Transactions on Mathematical Software*, 3(3):253–256, Sept. 1977.

[20] Y. Wang, H. Bai, M. Stanton, W. Chen, and E. Chang. PLDA: Parallel latent Dirichlet allocation for large-scale applications. In *International Conference on Algorithmic Aspects in Information and Management*, 2009.

[21] C. K. Wong and M. C. Easton. An efficient method for weighted sampling without replacement. *SIAM Journal on Computing*, 9(1):111–113, 1980.

[22] F. Yan, N. Xu, and Y. Qi. Parallel inference for latent Dirichlet allocation on graphics processing units. In *NIPS*, pages 2134–2142, 2009.

[23] L. Yao, D. Mimno, and A. McCallum. Efficient methods for topic model inference on streaming document collections. In *KDD*, 2009.

[24] H.-F. Yu, C.-H. Ho, Y.-C. Juan, and C.-J. Lin. Libshorttext: A library for short-text classification and analysis. Technical report, 2013.

[25] H. Yun, H.-F. Yu, C.-J. Hsieh, S. V. N. Vishwanathan, and I. S. Dhillon. NOMAD: Non-locking, stOchastic Multi-machine algorithm for Asynchronous and Decentralized matrix completion. *Proceedings of the VLDB Endowment*, 7(11):975–986, 2014.

LightLDA: Big Topic Models on Modest Computer Clusters

Jinhui Yuan[1], Fei Gao[1],
Qirong Ho[3], Wei Dai[2], Jinliang Wei[2], Xun Zheng[2], Eric P. Xing[2],
Tie-Yan Liu[1], and Wei-Ying Ma[1]

[1]Microsoft Research
[2]School of Computer Science, Carnegie Mellon University
[3]Institute for Infocomm Research, A*STAR, Singapore

{jiyuan,feiga,tie-yan.liu,wyma}@microsoft.com,hoqirong@gmail.com,{wdai,jinlianw,xunzheng,epxing}@cs.cmu.edu

ABSTRACT

When building large-scale machine learning (ML) programs, such as massive topic models or deep neural networks with up to trillions of parameters and training examples, one usually assumes that such massive tasks can only be attempted with industrial-sized clusters with thousands of nodes, which are out of reach for most practitioners and academic researchers. We consider this challenge in the context of topic modeling on web-scale corpora, and show that with a modest cluster of as few as 8 machines, we can train a topic model with 1 million topics and a 1-million-word vocabulary (for a total of 1 trillion parameters), on a document collection with 200 billion tokens — a scale not yet reported even with thousands of machines. Our major contributions include: 1) a new, highly-efficient $\mathcal{O}(1)$ Metropolis-Hastings sampling algorithm, whose running cost is (surprisingly) agnostic of model size, and empirically converges nearly an order of magnitude more quickly than current state-of-the-art Gibbs samplers; 2) a model-scheduling scheme to handle the big model challenge, where each worker machine schedules the fetch/use of sub-models as needed, resulting in a frugal use of limited memory capacity and network bandwidth; 3) a differential data-structure for model storage, which uses separate data structures for high- and low-frequency words to allow extremely large models to fit in memory, while maintaining high inference speed. These contributions are built on top of the Petuum open-source distributed ML framework, and we provide experimental evidence showing how this development puts massive data and models within reach on a small cluster, while still enjoying proportional time cost reductions with increasing cluster size.

Categories and Subject Descriptors

H.3.4 [**Information Storage and Retrieval**]: Systems and Software—*Distributed Systems*; G.3 [**Probability and Statistics**]: Probabilistic algorithms (including Monte Carlo); G.4 [**Mathematical Software**]: Parallel and vector implementations

General Terms

Design, Algorithms, Experimentation, Performance

WWW 2015, May 18–22, 2015, Florence, Italy.
ACM ACM 978-1-4503-3469-3/15/05.
http://dx.doi.org/10.1145/2736277.2741115 .

Keywords

Large Scale Machine Learning; Distributed Systems; Topic Model; Model Scheduling; Data Parallelism; Metropolis-Hastings; Parameter Server; Petuum

1. INTRODUCTION

Topic models (TM) are a popular and important modern machine learning technology that has been widely used in text mining, network analysis and genetics, and more other domains [17, 5, 23, 24, 2]. Their impact on the technology sector and the Internet has been tremendous — numerous companies having developed their large-scale TM implementations [13, 1, 21], with applications to advertising and recommender systems. A key goal of contemporary research is to scale TMs, particularly the Latent Dirichlet Allocation (LDA) model [5], to web-scale corpora (Big Data). Crucially, Internet-scale corpora are significantly more complex than smaller, well-curated document collections, and thus require high-capacity parameter space featuring up to millions of topics and vocabulary words (and hence trillions of parameters, i.e. Big Models), in order to capture long-tail semantic information that would otherwise be lost when learning only a few thousands of topics [21].

To achieve massive data and model scales, a typical approach is to engineer a distributed system that can efficiently execute well-established parallelization strategies (e.g., split documents over workers, which have shared access to all parameters, possibly stored in a distributed manner) for LDA [16, 12, 21], while applying algorithmic speedups such as the SparseLDA [22] or AliasLDA [11] samplers to further decrease running time. Such efforts have enabled LDA models with tens of billions of parameters to be inferred from billions of documents, using up to thousands of machines [13, 1, 12, 21]. While such achievements are impressive, they are unfortunately costly to run: for instance, a cluster of thousands of machines will cost millions of dollars to set up (not to mention the future costs of power and regular maintenance). Alternatively, one might rent equivalent computation capacity from a cloud provider, but given the current typical price of $\geq$ \$1 per hour per research-grade machine, a single month of operations would cost millions of dollars. Neither option is feasible for the majority of researchers and practitioners, who are more likely to only have modest budgets.

Rather than insisting that big computing is the only way to solve large ML problems, what if we could solve large topic models with trillions of parameters in a more cost-effective manner, by providing an implementation that is efficient enough for modest clusters with at most tens of machines? We approach this problem at three levels: (1) We perform distributed cluster LDA inference in a *data-*

parallelism and *model-scheduling* fashion: in each iteration, every worker processes a subset of the training data, scheduling the fetch/use of a sub-model slice by slice. We do this in a memory- and network-efficient manner: we fix each data partition to a particular worker (i.e., data are never moved around), but we regularly change which model partitions each machine works on — specifically, we store the model in a distributed parameter server, and stream model partitions as needed to worker machines; (2) we develop a novel Metropolis-Hastings (MH) sampler with carefully constructed proposals that allows for $\mathcal{O}(1)$ amortized sampling time per word/token, resulting in a fast convergence (in terms of real time) that beats existing state-of-the-art LDA samplers by a significant margin [22, 11]; (3) we employ a differential data structure to leverage the fact that web-scale corpora exhibit both high-frequency as well as low-frequency words, which can be treated differently in storage (i.e., a hybrid internal representation). This gives a best-of-both-worlds outcome: the high memory efficiency of sparse data structures, with the high performance of dense data structures.

By realizing these ideas using the open-source Petuum framework (`www.petuum.org`) [9, 10, 6], we have produced a compute-and-memory efficient distributed LDA implementation, LightLDA, that can learn an LDA model with one trillion model parameters (one million topics by one million vocabulary words) from billions of documents (200 billion tokens in total), on a computer cluster with as few as 8 standard machines (whose configuration is roughly similar to a typical compute instance from a cloud provider) in 180 hours, which proportionally drops to 60 hours on 24 machines. In terms of parameter size, our result is two orders of magnitude larger than recently-set LDA records in the literature, which involved models with tens of billions of parameters and typically used massive industrial-scale clusters [12, 21, 1, 13]; our data size is also one order of magnitude larger than those same works[1]. We show that LightLDA converges significantly faster than existing implementations across several datasets and model settings (vocabulary size and number of topics). Notably, LightLDA's per-token computational complexity is independent of model size, hence it enjoys high throughput even under massive models.

Overall, LightLDA benefits both from a highly efficient Metropolis Hastings sampler built on a new proposal scheme, and a highly efficient distributed architecture and implementation built on Petuum. It represents a truly lightweight realization (hence its name LightLDA) of a massive ML program, which we hope will be easily accessible to ordinary users and researchers with modest resources. Compared to using alternative platforms like Spark and Graphlab that also offer highly sophisticated data- or model- parallel systems, or designing bespoke ground-up solutions like PLDA and YahooLDA, we suggest that our intermediate approach that leverages both simple-but-critical algorithmic innovation and lightweight ML-friendly system platforms stands as a highly cost-effective solution to Big ML.

2. CHALLENGES AND RELATED WORK

Before discussing the challenges, we briefly review the Latent Dirichlet Allocation (LDA) [5] model to establish nomenclature. Specifically, LDA assumes the following generative process for each document in a corpus:

- $\varphi_k \sim \text{Dirichlet}(\beta)$: Draw word distribution φ_k per topic k.
- $\theta_d \sim \text{Dirichlet}(\alpha)$: Draw topic distribution θ_d per document d.
- $n_d \sim \text{Poisson}(\gamma)$: For each document d, draw its length n_d (i.e., the number of tokens it contains).
- For each token $i \in \{1, 2, \ldots, n_d\}$ in document d:
  - $z_{di} \sim \text{Multinomial}(\theta_{di})$: Draw the token's topic.
  - $w_{di} \sim \text{Multinomial}(\varphi_{z_{di}})$: Draw the token's word.

[1][21] used 4.5 billion tokens, while [12] used 5 billion short documents of unspecified length.

To find the most plausible topics in a corpus and document-topic assignments, one must infer the posterior distribution of latent variables in LDA model, by using either a variational- or sampling-based inference algorithm. Sampling-based algorithms are known to yield very sparse updates that make them well-suited to settings with a massive number of topics and distributed implementation. In particular, the collapsed Gibbs sampler for LDA [7] is preferred. It works as follows: all variables except the token's topic indicator z_{di} are analytically integrated out, and we only need to Gibbs sample z_{di} according to

$$p(z_{di} = k|\text{rest}) \propto \frac{(n_{kd}^{-di} + \alpha_k)(n_{kw}^{-di} + \beta_w)}{n_k^{-di} + \bar{\beta}}, \tag{1}$$

where z_{di} follows a Multinomial distribution with K outcomes (i.e., K is the number of topics in the model), w is short for w_{di}, $\bar{\beta} := \sum_w \beta_w$, n_{kd}^{-di} is the number of tokens in document d that are assigned to topic k (excluding z_{di}), n_{kw}^{-di} is the number of tokens with word w (across all documents) that are assigned to topic k (excluding z_{di}), and n_k^{-di} is the number of tokens (across all docs) assigned to topic k (excluding z_{di}). To avoid costly recalculation, these counts (also called "sufficient statistics") are cached as tables, and updated whenever a token topic indicator z_{di} changes. In particular, the set of all counts n_{kd} is colloquially referred to as the *document-topic table* (and serves as the sufficient statistics for θ_d), while the set of all counts n_{kw} is known as the *word-topic table* (and forms the sufficient statistics for φ_k).

While training LDA model, the Gibbs sampler needs to scan the whole corpus for hundreds of times (i.e., iterations). In each iteration, it sequentially process all the tokens in the corpus according to Eq. 1 with an $\mathcal{O}(K)$ per-token complexity. Therefore, the amount of required computation for training LDA with Gibbs sampling depends on both the scale of corpus (specifically, the number of tokens) and the size of model (the number of topics). However, in many real-word applications especially the web-scale corpora, the problem exhibits billions of documents and thousands (even millions) of topics [21]. Much research has been invested on scaling LDA to ever-larger data and model sizes; existing papers usually show an algorithmic focus (i.e. better LDA inference algorithm speed) or a systems focus (i.e. better software to execute LDA inference on a distributed cluster) — or even both foci at once.

In any case, the inference algorithm is one limiting factor to efficiency. For example, the Peacock system [21] adopts the SparseLDA inference algorithm [22], which has a lower per-token computational complexity than the standard collapsed Gibbs sampler. We note that the recently developed AliasLDA algorithm [11] provides a further improvement on SparseLDA sampler. However, the per-token computational complexity of AliasLDA still depends on the document length and the sparsity of document-topic distribution, therefore in some settings, AliasLDA may not be a substantial improvement over SparseLDA. To tackle this challenge, we develop a new $\mathcal{O}(1)$-per-token Metropolis-Hastings sampler that is nearly an order of magnitude faster than the existing algorithms — which allows us to process the same quantity of data with fewer resources in a reasonable amount of time.

To tackle the Big Data and the Big Model challenges, algorithms alone are not enough, and we must also resort to an efficient distributed implementation. Recent large-scale implementations of LDA [13, 1, 21, 12] demonstrate that training is feasible on big document corpora (up to billions of documents) using large, industrial-scale clusters with thousands to tens of thousands of CPU cores. At a high level, the above large-scale LDA papers differ substantially in the degree to which they employ data-parallelism (commonly realized by splitting documents over machines) versus model-parallelism (often realized by splitting *word-topic* distributions over machines). Data-parallelism is a well-accepted solution to the Big Data problem, in which many distributed CPU cores can be used to sample thousands of tokens simultaneously. Furthermore, the total pool of memory across the cluster allows the entire (large) model to be persisted in a distributed fashion, hence supporting in-memory computation. This strategy addresses a key issue in the Big Model problem. Our distributed LDA implementation is based on a parameter server (PS) architecture [1, 9, 12]. PS architectures have shown appealing properties for distributed machine learning (e.g., allowing asynchronous communication in data-parallelism), and we use Petuum's PS for its theoretically-guaranteed SSP consistency model [9]. However, instead of using clusters with thousands of nodes, this paper aims to solve the Big Data and Big Model challenges with a modest computer cluster (i.e., tens of nodes).

In implementations that are predominately data-parallel [1, 12], the strategy is to make the *word-topic* distributions globally-shared, so that the inference algorithm can be agnostic to their physical layout across machines. The training data are partitioned and distributed to worker machines — that is, each worker only processes a subset of data — and the system schedules the inference computation on token topic indicators z_{di} in a document-centric manner. We do not expect either [1] or [12] to handle very large topic models with over 1 trillion parameters (the largest reported result was 10 billion parameters in [12]). In particular, [12] depends on the assumption that once the entire corpus has been distributed to sufficiently many machines, the local documents on each machine will only activate a small portion of the complete model, and therefore the memory required by each machine will not be too large. Consequently, their design cannot handle large topic models without a large computer cluster. The RLU cache technique used in an earlier version of Petuum [9] can partially resolve this issue and allow big models with data-parallel computing in small computer cluster: when sub-models corresponding to frequent words are accessed, they are likely to be in the local cache. However, for sub-models corresponding to long-tail words, the cache miss rate will be high, and a lot of network communication will be triggered.

The Peacock system [21] realizes both data- and model-parallel ideas, by grouping token topic indicators z_{di} according to their words w_{di}; this is beneficial because it reduces the proportion of the *word-topic* distributions that must be held at each worker machine. In particular, [21] adopted a grid-like model-parallel partitioning strategy, where each worker handles a subset of data and a part of the model. A shortcoming of this particular strategy is that workers only process one part of any particular document, so each document must be processed by several worker machines. Hence the system not only needs to synchronize the word-topic distributions among workers, but also the document-topic distributions — in other words, both training data and model need to be transferred among workers. In typical clusters, network bandwidth is often the largest bottleneck in the whole system, and the additional network overhead due to transmitting training data and doc-topic distributions will reduce efficiency.

3. A MODEL-SCHEDULING SCHEME FOR BIG MODEL

To tackle the aforementioned problems in classic parallelization schemes, we proposed a new scheme called *data-parallelism and model-scheduling*. As the name suggests, our scheme employs data-parallelism, by partitioning and distributing the training data into different worker machines; this ensures that each document

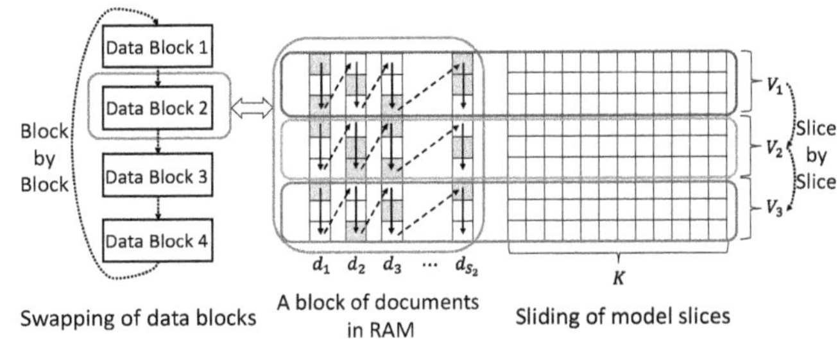

Figure 1: Model scheduling in each worker machine. The arrows across documents $d_1, d_2, \ldots$ indicate the token sampling order — observe that we sample tokens z associated with words v in the *word-topic table* (model) slice V_1, before moving on to tokens corresponding to V_2, and so forth. Once all document tokens in the data block have been sampled, the system loads the next data block from disk. Each document is sparse (with respect to the vocabulary): shaded cells indicate that the document has one or more tokens z corresponding to word v, whereas white indicate that the document has no tokens corresponding to word v (and are hence skipped over).

will be processed by one fixed worker, so training data and doc-topic distributions do not have to be synchronized among workers. Model scheduling refers to how we handle the distributed (big) model or word-topic table; we take extra steps to maximize memory and CPU efficiency. The basic idea is to split the *word-topic* distributions (the LDA model) into slices, and fetch/use the model from the parameter server slice-by-slice only when needed (like streaming). This new distribution scheme is more communication-efficient than the implementations of LDA mentioned in Section 2.

At minimum, any distributed LDA implementation must partition (1) the token topic indicators z_{di} and doc-topic table n_{kd} (collectively referred to as the data), as well as (2) the *word-topic table* n_{kw} (the model). When an LDA sampler is sampling a token topic indicator z_{di}, it needs to see the specific row $n_{kw_{di}}$ in the *word-topic table* (as well as the complete document d). However, naive partitioning can lead to situations where some machines touch a large fraction of the *word-topic table*: suppose we sampled every document's tokens in sequence, then the worker would need to see all the rows in *word-topic table* corresponding to words in the document. Using our fast Metropolis-Hastings sampler (described in the following section), each worker machine can sample thousands of documents per second (assuming hundreds of tokens per document); furthermore, we have empirically observed that a few million documents (out of billions in our web-scale corpus) is sufficient to activate almost the entire *word-topic table*. Thus, the naive sequence just described would rapidly swap parts of the *word-topic table* (which could be terabytes in size) in and out of each worker's RAM, generating a prohibitive amount of network communication.

The model-scheduling scheme proposed in this paper is meant to resolve the conflict between fast LDA sampling and limited memory capacity at each worker. The data partition assigned to a particular worker machine is most likely to be too big to reside in the worker machine's RAM. Therefore, the private data of each worker is further split into a few blocks. While generating the data blocks prior to running the LDA sampler, and we note that it is cheap to determine which vocabulary words are instantiated by each block. This information is attached as meta-data to the block. As shown in Figure 1, when we load a data block (and its meta-data) into local memory (denoted by the red rectangle), we choose a small set of words (say V_1 in the figure) from the block's local words. The set of words is small enough that the corresponding rows $n_{\cdot, w_{di}}$ in *word-topic table* can be held in the worker machine's local memory – we call this set of rows a "model slice". The worker fetches the model slice over the network, and the sampler only samples those tokens in the block that are covered by the fetched slice; all other tokens are not touched. In this manner, each worker only maintains a thin model slice in local memory, and re-uses it for all the documents in the current data block. Once all tokens covered by the slice have been sampled, the worker fetches the next model slice over the network (say V_2), and proceeds to sample the tokens covered by it. In this manner (similar to sliding windows in image processing or the TCP/IP protocol, but managed by a local scheduler), a worker processes all the tokens in a data block, one slice at a time, before finally loading the next block from disk. This swapping of blocks to and from disk is essentially out-of-core execution.

In addition to keeping worker memory requirements low, this model-scheduling also mitigates network communication bottleneck, in the following ways: (1) workers do not move onto the next model slice until all the tokens associated with the current slice have been sampled, hence we do not need to apply caching and eviction strategies to the model (which could incur additional communication, as model slices are repeatedly swapped in and out); (2) we overlap the computation and the loading (data blocks from disk, model slices from a distributed parameter server) with pipelining to hide I/O and network communication latency (further details in Section 6). We note that PLDA+ [13] makes use of pipelining in a similar (though not exactly identical) spirit. Finally, we point out that the model-scheduling strategy "sends the model to the data", rather than the converse. This is motivated by two factors: (1) the data (including tokens w_{di} and corresponding topic indicators z_{di}) are much larger than the model (even when the model may have trillions of parameters); (2) as the model converges, it gets increasingly sparse (thus lowering communication), while the data size remains constant. Other distributed LDA designs either adopt a "send data to model" strategy or have to communicate both data and model among workers [21], which is costly in our opinion.

4. A FAST MCMC ALGORITHM

As just discussed, model scheduling enables very large, trillion-parameter LDA models to be learned from billions of documents even on small clusters. However, it alone does not allow huge LDA models to be trained *quickly* or in acceptable time, and this motivates our biggest technical contribution: a novel sampling algorithm for LDA, which converges significantly faster than recent algorithms such as SparseLDA [22] and AliasLDA [11]. In order to explain our algorithm, we first review the mechanics of SparseLDA and AliasLDA.

SparseLDA. SparseLDA [22] exploits the observation that (1) most documents exhibit a small number of topics, and (2) most words only participate in a few topics. This manifests as *sparsity* in both the *doc-topic* and *word-topic* tables, which SparseLDA exploits by decomposing the collapsed Gibbs sampler conditional probability (Eq. 1) into three terms:

$$p(z_{di}=k|\text{rest}) \propto \underbrace{\frac{\alpha_k\beta_w}{n_k^{-di}+\bar{\beta}}}_{r} + \underbrace{\frac{n_{kd}^{-di}\beta_w}{n_k^{-di}+\bar{\beta}}}_{s} + \underbrace{\frac{n_{kw}^{-di}(n_{kd}^{-di}+\alpha_k)}{n_k^{-di}+\bar{\beta}}}_{t}. \quad (2)$$

When the Gibbs sampler is close to convergence, both the second term s and the third term t will become very sparse (because documents and words settle into a few topics). SparseLDA first samples one of the three terms r, s or t, according to their probability masses summed over all K outcomes. Then, SparseLDA samples the topic k conditioned upon which term r, s or t was chosen. If s or t was chosen, then sampling the topic k takes $\mathcal{O}(K_d)$ or $\mathcal{O}(K_w)$ time respectively, where K_d is the number of topics document d contains, and K_w is the number of topics word w belongs to. The amortized sampling complexity of SparseLDA is $\mathcal{O}(K_d+K_w)$, as opposed to $\mathcal{O}(K)$ for the standard collapsed Gibbs sampler.

AliasLDA. AliasLDA [11] proposes an alternative decomposition to the Gibbs sampling probability:

$$p(z_{di}=k|\text{rest}) \propto \underbrace{\frac{n_{kd}^{-di}(n_{kw}^{-di}+\beta_w)}{n_k^{-di}+\bar{\beta}}}_{u} + \underbrace{\frac{\alpha_k(n_{kw}+\beta_w)}{n_k+\bar{\beta}}}_{v}. \quad (3)$$

AliasLDA pre-computes an alias table [20] for the second term, which allows it to be sampled in $\mathcal{O}(1)$ time via Metropolis-Hastings. By re-using the table over many tokens, the $\mathcal{O}(K)$ cost of building the table is also amortized to $\mathcal{O}(1)$ per token. The first term u is sparse (linear in K_d, the current number of topics in document d), and can be computed in $\mathcal{O}(K_d)$ time.

4.1 Metropolis-Hastings Sampling

SparseLDA and AliasLDA achieve $\mathcal{O}(K_d+K_w)$ and $\mathcal{O}(K_d)$ amortized sampling time per token, respectively. Such accelerated sampling is important, because we simply cannot afford to sample token topic indicators z_{di} naively; the original collapsed Gibbs sampler (Eq. 1) requires $\mathcal{O}(K)$ computation per token, which is clearly intractable at $K = 1$ million topics. SparseLDA reduces the sampling complexity by exploiting the sparsity of problem, while AliasLDA harnesses the alias approach together with the Metropolis-Hastings algorithm [15, 8, 19, 3]. Our LightLDA sampler also turns to Metropolis-Hastings, but with new insights into the design of proposal distribution, which is most crucial for high performance. We show that the sampling process can be accelerated even further with a well-designed proposal distribution $q(\cdot)$ to the true LDA posterior $p(\cdot)$.

A well-designed proposal $q(\cdot)$ should speed up the sampling process in two ways: (1) drawing samples from $q(\cdot)$ will be much cheaper than drawing samples from $p(\cdot)$; (2) the Markov chain should mix quickly (i.e. requires only a few steps). What are the trade-offs involved in constructing a good proposal distribution $q(\cdot)$ for $p(\cdot)$? If $q(\cdot)$ is close to $p(\cdot)$, then the constructed Markov chain will mix quickly — however, the cost of sampling from $q(\cdot)$ might end up as expensive as sampling from $p(\cdot)$ itself. On the contrary, if $q(\cdot)$ is very different from $p(\cdot)$, we might be able to sample from it cheaply — but the constructed Markov chain may mix too slowly, and require many steps for convergence.

4.2 Cheap Proposals by Factorization

To design an MH algorithm that is cheap to draw from, yet has high mixing rate, we adopt a *factorized* strategy: instead of a single proposal, we shall construct a set of $\mathcal{O}(1)$ proposals, and alternate between them. To construct these proposals, let us begin from the true conditional probability of token topic indicator z_{di}:

$$p(k) = p(z_{di}=k|\text{rest}) \propto \frac{(n_{kd}^{-di}+\alpha_k)(n_{kw}^{-di}+\beta_w)}{n_k^{-di}+\bar{\beta}}. \quad (4)$$

Observe that it can be decomposed into two factors:

$$q(z_{di}=k|\text{rest}) \propto \underbrace{(n_{kd}+\alpha_k)}_{\text{doc-proposal}} \times \underbrace{\frac{n_{kw}+\beta_w}{n_k+\bar{\beta}}}_{\text{word-proposal}}. \quad (5)$$

Even if we exploit sparsity in both terms, sampling from this conditional probability costs at least $\mathcal{O}(\min(K_d, K_w))$. To do better, we utilize the following observation: the first term is document-dependent but word-independent, while the second term is doc-independent but word-dependent. Furthermore, it is intuitive to see that the most probable topics are those with high probability mass from both the doc-dependent term and the word-dependent term; hence, either term alone can serve as a good proposal q — because if p has high probability mass on topic k, then either term will also have high probability mass on k (though the converse

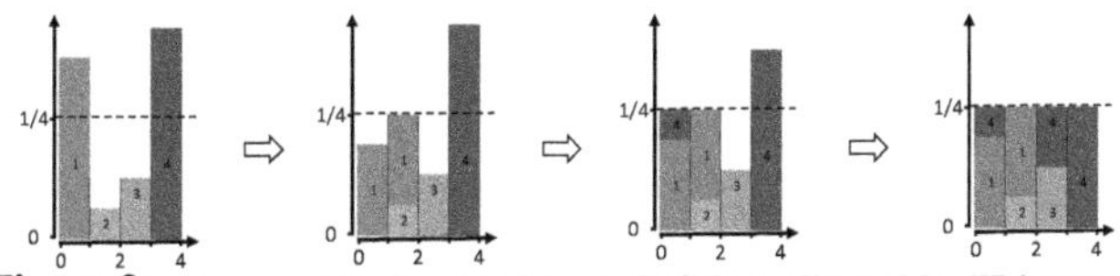

Figure 2: An example showing how to build an alias table. This procedure transforms a non-uniform sampling problem into a uniform sampling one. The alias table maintains the mass of each bin and can be re-used once constructed. More details about the alias method can be found in [14].

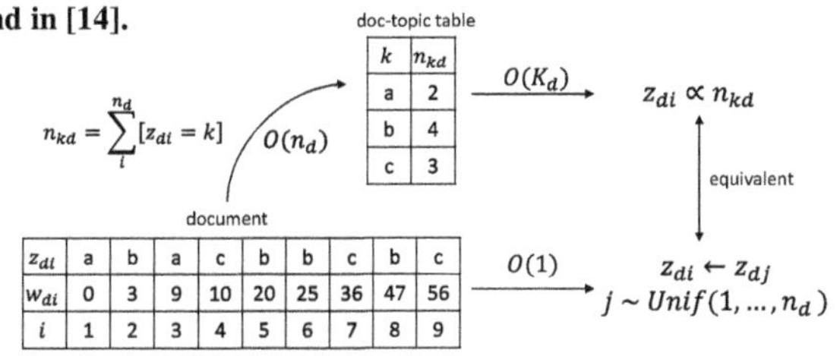

Figure 3: Illustration of how we sample the doc-proposal in $\mathcal{O}(1)$ time, without having to construct an alias table.

is not true). Just as importantly, both factors keep relatively stable during the sampling process[2], so that the alias method [14] (also used in AliasLDA [11]) can be applied to both factors to reduce the sampling cost from either proposal (where the cost of constructing the alias table is getting amortized). We now discuss the proposals individually.

Word-Proposal for Metropolis-Hastings. Define p_w as the word-proposal distribution

$$p_w(k) \propto \frac{n_{kw} + \beta_w}{n_k + \bar{\beta}}. \tag{6}$$

The acceptance probability of state transition $s \to t$ is

$$\min\{1, \frac{p(t)p_w(s)}{p(s)p_w(t)}\}. \tag{7}$$

Let $\pi_w := \frac{p(t)p_w(s)}{p(s)p_w(t)}$, we can show that

$$\pi_w = \frac{(n_{td}^{-di}+\alpha_t)(n_{tw}^{-di}+\beta_w)(n_s^{-di}+\bar{\beta})(n_{sw}+\beta_w)(n_t+\bar{\beta})}{(n_{sd}^{-di}+\alpha_s)(n_{sw}^{-di}+\beta_w)(n_t^{-di}+\bar{\beta})(n_{tw}+\beta_w)(n_s+\bar{\beta})}. \tag{8}$$

Once $t \sim p_w(t)$ is sampled, the acceptance probability can be computed in $\mathcal{O}(1)$ time, as long as we keep track of all sufficient statistics $n.$ during sampling. Intuitively, π_w is high (relative to topic s) whenever the proposed topic t is either (1) popular within document d, or (2) popular for the word w. Since the word-proposal tends to propose topics t which are popular for word w, using the word-proposal will help explore the state space of $p(k)$. We do not need to worry about the situation that the proposed state t is popular for word w but not for the true conditional probability $p(k)$, since in this case, t will be very likely to be rejected due to the low acceptance probability π_w used in the MH process. To sample from p_w in $\mathcal{O}(1)$, we use alias table similar to [11]. As illustrated by Figure 2, the basic idea of the alias approach is to transform a non-uniform distribution into a uniform distribution (i.e., alias table). Since the alias table will be re-used in MH sampling, the transformation cost gets amortized to $\mathcal{O}(1)$ [3].

Although the alias approach has low $\mathcal{O}(1)$ amortized time complexity, its space complexity is still very high, because the alias table for each word's proposal distribution stores $2K$ values: the splitting point of each bin and the alias value above that splitting point; this becomes prohibitive if we need to store a lot of words' alias tables. Our insight here is that the alias table can be sparsified; specifically, we begin by decomposing $p_w = \frac{n_{kw}}{n_k+\bar{\beta}} + \frac{\beta_w}{n_k+\bar{\beta}}$. We then draw one of the two terms, with probability given by their masses (this is known as a mixture approach). If we draw the first term, we use a pre-constructed alias table (created from n_{kw}, specific to word w) to pick a topic, which is sparse. If we draw the second term, we also use a pre-constructed alias table (created from β_w, common to all words w and thus amortized over all V words) to pick a topic, which is dense. In this way, we reduce both the time and space complexity of building word w's alias table to $\mathcal{O}(K_w)$ (the number of topics word w participates in).

Doc-Proposal for Metropolis Hastings. Define p_d as the doc-proposal distribution

$$p_d(k) \propto n_{kd} + \alpha_k. \tag{9}$$

The acceptance probability of state transition $s \to t$ is

$$\min\{1, \frac{p(t)p_d(s)}{p(s)p_d(t)}\}. \tag{10}$$

Let $\pi_d := \frac{p(t)p_d(s)}{p(s)p_d(t)}$, we can show that

$$\pi_d = \frac{(n_{td}^{-di}+\alpha_t)(n_{tw}^{-di}+\beta_w)(n_s^{-di}+\bar{\beta})(n_{sd}+\alpha_s)}{(n_{sd}^{-di}+\alpha_s)(n_{sw}^{-di}+\beta_w)(n_t^{-di}+\bar{\beta})(n_{td}+\alpha_t)}. \tag{11}$$

As with the word-proposal, we see that the doc-proposal accepts whenever topic t is popular (relative to topic s) within document d, or popular for word w. Again, we do not need to worry about the case that the proposed state t is popular within the document but not for the true conditional probability $p(k)$, since in this case, t will be very likely to be rejected due to the low acceptance probability π_d used in the MH process. We decompose $p_d(k) \propto \frac{n_{kd}}{n_d+\alpha} + \frac{\alpha_k}{n_d+\alpha}$ just like the word-proposal, except that when we pick the first term, we do not even need to explicitly build an alias table — this is because the document token topic indicators z_{di} serve as the alias table by themselves. Specifically, the first term n_{kd} counts the number of times topic k occurs in document d, in other words

$$n_{kd} = \sum_{i=1}^{n_d} [z_{di} = k], \tag{12}$$

where $[\cdot]$ is the indicator function. This implies that the array z_{di} is an alias table for the unnormalized probability distribution n_{kd}, and therefore we can sample from n_{kd} by simply drawing an integer j uniformly from $\{1, 2, \ldots, n_d\}$, and setting $z_{di} = z_{dj}$. Figure 3 uses a toy example to illustrate this procedure. Hence, we conclude that the doc-proposal can be sampled in $\mathcal{O}(1)$ non-amortized time (because we do not need to construct an alias table)[4].

4.3 Combining Proposals to Improve Mixing

While either the doc- or word-proposal alone can be used as an as efficient MH algorithm for LDA, in practice many MH-steps (repeatedly sampling each token) are required to produce proper mixing. With a small number of MH-steps, using the word-proposal alone encourages sparsity in word-topic distribution (i.e. each word belongs to few topics) but causes low sparsity in document-topic distributions (i.e. each document contains many topics). Conversely, using the doc-proposal alone with few MH-steps leads to sparsity in document-topic distribution but non-sparse word-topic dis-

[2]This is crucial because alias tables must be re-used to amortize computational complexity, which in turn requires the target distribution to be stable enough. This also explains why the decomposition in AliasLDA can not lead to an $\mathcal{O}(1)$ algorithm, that is, the first term in Eq. 3 involves the product of n_{kd} and n_{kw}, and is not stable enough to use alias approach.

[3]This strategy keeps the Metropolis-Hastings proposal p_w fixed over multiple documents, rather than changing it after every token. This is well-justified, since Metropolis-Hastings allows any proposal (up to some conditions) provided the acceptance probability can be correctly computed. We have already argued in Section 4.2 that the acceptance probability can be computed in $\mathcal{O}(1)$ time by simply keeping track of a few sufficient statistics $n_{\cdot\cdot}$.

[4]Unlike the word-proposal, p_d changes after every token to reflect the current state of z_{di}. Again, this is fine under Metropolis-Hastings theory.

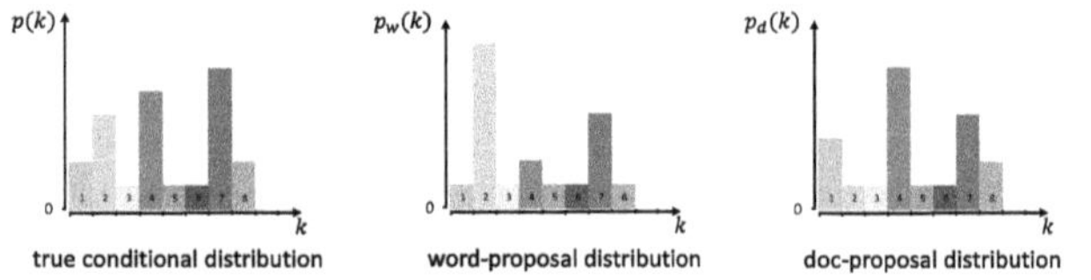

Figure 4: An example that explains why cycling two proposals helps mixing rate. The 2nd bin is a mode of $p(k)$, and $p_d(k)$ is obviously not a good proposal for this mode — but $p_w(k)$ is good at exploring it.

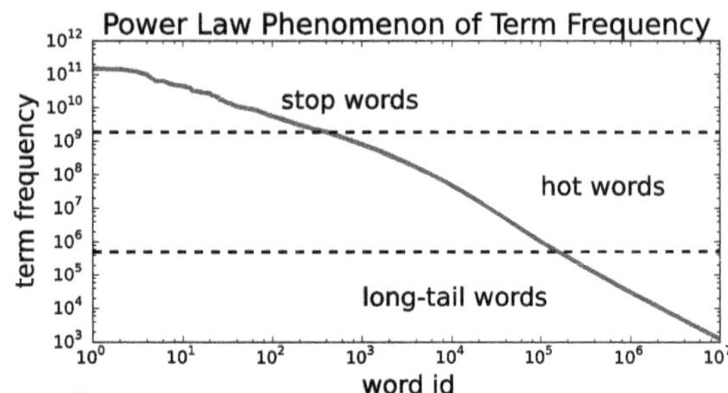

Figure 5: Word frequencies in topic modeling follow a power-law phenomenon (log-log plot). The great difference in the frequency of hot words versus long-tailed words makes selecting the right data structure difficult, as discussed in the text. This plot is obtained from 15 billion web pages, with over than 3000 billion tokens.

tributions. Therefore, while either proposal can sample tokens very quickly, they need many MH-steps to mix well.

The key to fast Metropolis-Hastings mixing is a proposal distribution that can quickly explore the state space, and reach all states with high probability (i.e., the modes). The word-proposal $p_w(k)$ is good at proposing only its own modes (resulting in concentration of words in a few topics), and likewise for the doc-proposal $p_d(k)$ (resulting in concentration of docs onto a few topics). As Figure 4 shows, with the word-proposal or doc-proposal alone, some modes will never be explored quickly.

How can we achieve a better mixing rate while still maintaining high sampling efficiency? If we look at $p(k) \propto p_w(k) \times p_d(k)$, we see that for $p(k)$ to be high (i.e. a mode), we need either $p_w(k)$ or $p_d(k)$ to be sufficiently large — but not necessarily both at the same time. Hence, our solution is to combine the doc-proposal and word-proposal into a "cycle proposal"

$$p_c(k) \propto p_d(k) p_w(k), \quad (13)$$

where we construct an MH sequence for each token by alternating between doc- and word-proposal. The results of [19] show that such cycle proposals are theoretically guaranteed to converge. By combining the two proposals in this manner, all modes in $p(k)$ will be proposed, with sufficiently high probability, by at least one of the proposals. Another potential benefit of cycling different proposals is that it helps to reduce the auto-correlation among sampled states, thus exploring the state space more quickly.

5. HYBRID DATA STRUCTURES FOR POWER-LAW WORDS

Even with carefully designed data parallelization and model scheduling, RAM capacity remains a critical obstacle when scaling LDA to very large number of topics. The LDA model, or *word-topic table* n_{kw}, is a $V \times K$ matrix, and a naive dense representation would require prohibitive amounts of memory. For example, for $V = K = 1$ million used in this paper's experiments, the model would be 4 terabytes in size assuming 32-bit integer entries. Even with reasonably well-equipped machines each with 128 gigabytes of RAM, just storing the matrix in memory would require 32 machines. In practice, the actual usage is often much higher due to other system overheads (e.g. cache, alias tables, buffers, parameter server).

A common solution is to turn to sparse data structures such as hash maps. The rationale behind sparse storage is that document words follow a power-law distribution (Figure 5). There are two implications: (1) after removing stop words, the term frequency of almost all meaningful words will not exceed the upper range of a 32-bit integer (2,147,483,647); this was measured on a web-scale corpus with 15 billion webpages and over 3000 billion tokens, and only 300 words' term frequencies exceed the 32-bit limit. For this reason, we choose to use 32-bit integers rather than 64-bit ones. (2) Even with several billion documents, the majority of words occur fewer than K times (where K may be up to 1 million in our experiments). This means that most rows $n_{k,\cdot}$ in the *word-topic table* are extremely sparse, so a sparse row representation (hash maps) will significantly reduce the memory footprint.

However, compared to dense arrays, sparse data structures exhibit poor random access performance, which hurts MCMC algorithms like SparseLDA, AliasLDA and LightLDA because they all rely heavily on random memory references. In our experiments, using pure hash maps results in a several-fold performance drop compared to dense arrays. How can we enjoy low memory usage whilst maintaining high sampling throughput? Our solution is a hybrid data structure, in which *word-topic table* rows corresponding to frequent words are stored as dense arrays, while uncommon, long-tail words are stored as open-addressing/quadratic-probing hash tables. In our web-scale corpus with several billion documents, we found that the top 10% frequent words in the vocabulary cover almost 95% of all tokens in the corpus, while the remaining 90% of vocabulary words are long-tail words that cover only 5% of the tokens. This implies that (1) most accesses to the hybrid *word-topic table* go to dense arrays, which keeps throughput high; (2) most rows of the *word-topic table* are still sparse hash tables[5], which keeps memory usage reasonably low. In our $V = K = 1$ million experiments, the hybrid *word-topic table* used 0.7TB, down from 4TB if we had used purely dense arrays. When this table is distributed across 24 machines, only 30GB per machine is required, freeing up valuable memory for other system components.

6. SYSTEM IMPLEMENTATION

Distributed implementations are clearly desirable for web-scale data: they reduce training time to realistic levels, and most practitioners have access to at least a small distributed cluster. However, existing distributed LDA implementations have only been shown to work at much smaller problem scales (particularly model size), or suggest the use of extremely large computer clusters (sometimes numbering in the thousands of machines) to finish training in acceptable time. What are the challenges involved in solving big LDA problems on just tens of machines? If we want to train on a corpus with billions of documents (each with at least hundreds of tokens) occupying terabytes of space, then on the data side, simply copying the data from disk to memory will take tens of hours, while transferring the data over the network also takes a similar amount of time. On the model side, storing 1 trillion parameters (1 million words by 1 million topics) can take up to terabytes of memory — necessitating distributed storage, which in turn requires inter-machine parameter synchronization, and thus high network communication cost. In light of these considerations, our goal is to design an architecture for LightLDA that reduces these data transmission and

[5]In order to further improve the throughput of the long tail words, we set the capacity of each hash table to at least two times the term frequency of a long-tail word. This guarantees a load factor that is ≤ 0.5, thus keeping random access performance high.

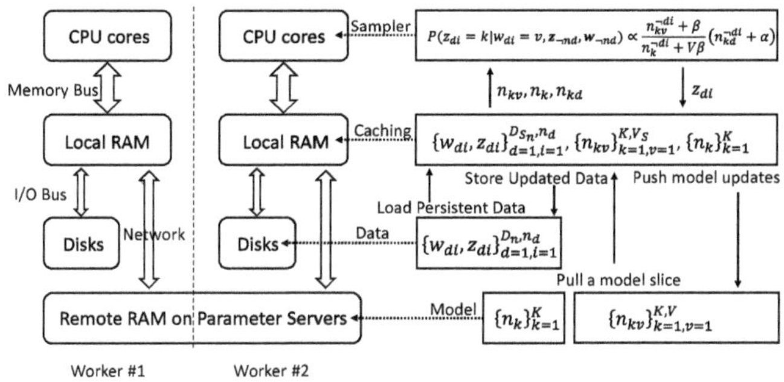

Figure 6: System architecture, data/model placement and logical flow.

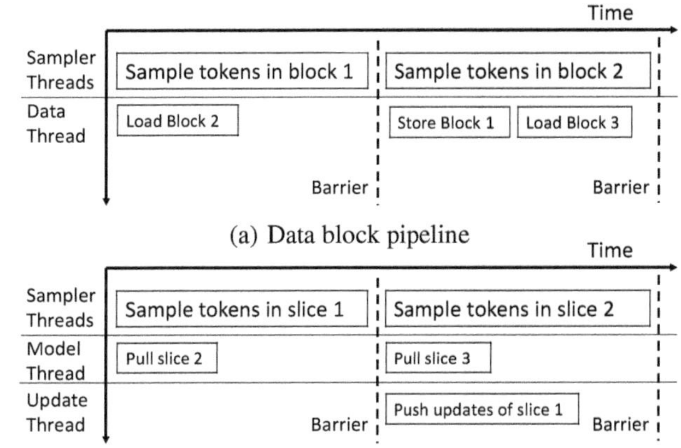

(a) Data block pipeline

(b) Model slice pipeline

Figure 7: Pipelines to overlap computation, disk I/O and network.

parameter communication costs as much as possible, thus making execution on small clusters realistic.

System Overview. We build LightLDA on top of an open-source framework for distributed large-scale ML, Petuum (`www.petuum.org`). We specifically make use of its parameter server [18, 9, 12] for bounded-asynchronous data-parallelism. We first introduce the general parameter server idea, and then describe our substantial enhancements to make big LDA models possible on small clusters.

Parameter Server and Data Placement. At the basic level, our parameter server (PS) presents a distributed shared memory interface [9], where programmers can access any parameter from any machine, agnostic to the physical location of the parameter. Essentially, the PS extends the memory hierarchy of a single machine (Figure 6); storage media closer to the CPU cores has lower access latency and higher transmission bandwidth, but has much smaller capacity. In the PS architecture, each machine's RAM is split into two parts: local RAM for client usage and remote RAM for distributed parameter storage (referred to as the "server" part). These hardware limitations, together with the requirements imposed by big topic model, strongly influence the manner in which we run our Metropolis-Hastings algorithm.

We use the PS to store two types of LDA model parameters: the *word-topic table* $\{n_{kv}\}_{k=1,v=1}^{K,V}$, which counts the number of tokens with word v assigned to topic k, and a length-K "summary row" $\{n_k\}_{k=1}^{K}$ which counts the total number of tokens assigned to topic k (regardless of word). 32-bit integers are used for the *word-topic table* (using a combination of dense arrays and sparse hash maps; see Section 5), and a 64-bit integer array for the summary row. We observe that as the LDA sampler progresses, the *word-topic table* becomes increasingly sparse, leading to lower network communication costs as time passes. Furthermore Petuum PS supports a bounded-asynchronous consistency model [9], which reduces inter-iteration parameter synchronization times through a staleness parameter s — for LightLDA, which is already a heavily-pipelined design, we found the optimal value to be $s = 1$.

Given that the input data are much larger than the model (and their volume remains unchanged throughout LDA inference), it is unwise to exchange data over the network. Instead, we shuffle and shard the corpus across the disks of all worker machines, and each worker machine only ever accesses the data in its local disk. In Figure 6, $\{w_{di}, z_{di}\}_{d=1,i=1}^{D_n,n_d}$ indicates a shard of training data in the n-th worker machine, where D_n represents the number of documents in the n-th worker, n_d indicates the number of tokens in document d. Each worker's local memory holds (1) the active working set of data $\{w_{di}, z_{di}\}_{d=1,i=1}^{D_{S_n},n_d}$, and (2) the model $\{n_{kv}\}_{k=1,v=1}^{K,V_S}$ required to sample the current set of tokens (using the Metropolis-Hastings sampler). During sampling, we update the token topic indicators z_{di}, and the *word-topic table*. The token-topic pairs $((w_{di}, z_{di})$ are local to the worker machine and incur no network communication, while the *word-topic table* is stored in the PS and therefore requires a background thread for efficient communication.

Token and Topic Indicator Storage. In data-parallel execution, each worker machine stores a corpus shard on its local disk. For web-scale corpora, each shard may still be very large — hundreds of gigabytes, if not several terabytes — which prohibits loading the entire shard into memory. Thus, we further split each shard into data blocks, and stream the blocks one at a time into memory (Figure 1 left). Data-structure-wise, we deliberately place tokens w_{di} and their topic indicators z_{di} side-by-side, as a vector of (w_{di}, z_{di}) pairs rather than two separate vectors for tokens and topic indicators (which was done in [1]). We do this to improve data locality and CPU cache efficiency: whenever we access a token w_{di}, we always need to access its topic indicator z_{di}, and the vector-of-pairs design directly improves locality. One drawback to this design is extra disk I/O, from writing the (unchanging) tokens w_{di} to disk every time a data shard gets swapped out. However, disk I/O can always be masked via pipelined reads/writes, done in the background while the sampler is processing the current shard.

We point out that our model-scheduling and disk-swapping (out-of-core) design naturally facilitates fault tolerance: if we perform data swapping to disk via atomic file overwrites, then whenever the system fails, it can simply resume training via warm-start: read the swapped-to-disk data, re-initialize the word-topic table, and carry on. In contrast, for LDA systems like PLDA+ [13] and YahooLDA [1] to have fault recovery, they would require periodic dumps of the data and/or model — but this incurs a nontrivial cost in the big data/model scenarios that we are trying to address.

Tuning the Model Scheduling Scheme. In Section 3, we introduced the high-level idea of model scheduling and its applications to LDA. There are still a number of improvements that can be employed to improve its efficiency. We present the most notable ones:

1. After completing a data block or a model slice, a worker machine's CPU cores need to wait for the next data block/model slice to be loaded from disk/network respectively. We eliminate this latency via pipelining (Figure 7). Specifically, the pipelining is achieved via a so-called double-buffering technique[4], which requires double memory quotas but can successfully overlap the computation and the communication (i.e., keeps the CPUs always busy). We caution that perfect pipelining requires careful parameter configuration (taking into consideration the throughput of samplers, size of data blocks, size of model slices).
2. To prevent data load imbalances across model slices, we generate model slices via sorting the vocabulary by word frequencies, and then shuffling the words. In this manner, each slice

will contain both frequent words and long tail words, improving load balance.

3. To eliminate unnecessary data traversal, when generating data blocks, we sort token-topic pairs (w_{di}, z_{di}) according to w_{di}'s position in the shuffled vocabulary, ensuring that all tokens belonging to the same model slice are actually contiguous in the data block (see Figure 1). This sorting only needs to be performed once, and is very fast on data processing platforms like Hadoop (compared to the LDA sampling time). We argue that this is more efficient than the "word bundle" approach in PLDA+ [13], which uses an inverted index to avoid data traversal, but at the cost of doubling data memory requirements.
4. We use a bounded asynchronous data parallel scheme [9] to remove the network waiting time occurring at the boundary of adjacent iterations. Note that, to pre-fetch the first slice of model for the next data block, we do not need to wait for the completion of the sampling on the current data block with the last slice of the model. This is exactly what we call Stale Synchronous Parallel (SSP) programming model.
5. We pre-allocate all the required memory blocks for holding data, model and local updates respectively. In other words, there is no any dynamic memory allocations during the whole training process. This helps remove the potential contention at the system heap lock. According to the specified memory quotas for either data or model, the system will automatically adjust the width of model slice for scheduling and streaming.

Multi-thread Efficiency. Our sampler is embarrassingly parallel within a single worker machine. This is achieved by splitting the in-memory data block into disjoint partitions (to be sampled by individual threads), and sharing the immutable in-memory model slice amongst the sampling threads. Furthermore, we make the shared model slice immutable, and all the updates to the model are firstly locally aggregated and then sent to be globally aggregated at the parameter server. By keeping the model slice immutable, we eliminate the race conditions of concurrent writing to a shared memory region, thus achieving near-linear intra-node scalability. While delaying model updates theoretically slows down the model convergence rate, in practice, it eliminates concurrency issues and thus increases sampler throughput, easily outweighing the slower convergence rate.

Modern server-grade machines contain several CPU sockets (each CPU houses many physical cores) which are connected to separate memory banks. While these banks can be addressed by all CPUs, memory latencies are much longer when accessing remote banks attached to another socket — in other words, Non-Uniform Memory Access (NUMA). In our experiments, we have found NUMA effects to be fairly significant, and we partially address them through tuning sampling parameters such as the number of Metropolis-Hastings steps (which influences CPU cache hit rates, and mitigates NUMA effects). That said, we believe proper NUMA-aware programming is a better long-term solution to this problem. Finally, we note that setting core affinities for each thread and enabling hardware hyper-threading on Intel processors can be beneficial; we observed a 30% performance gain when employing both.

7. EXPERIMENTAL RESULTS

We demonstrate that LightLDA is able to train much larger LDA models on similar or larger data sizes than previous LDA implementations, using much fewer machines — due to the carefully designed data parallelization and model scheduling, and especially the new Metropolis-Hastings sampler that is nearly an order of magnitude faster than SparseLDA and AliasLDA. We use several datasets (Table 7), notably a Bing "web chunk" dataset with 1.2 billion webpages (about 200 billion tokens in total). Our experiments show that (1) the distributed implementation of LightLDA has near-linear scalability in the number of cores and machines; (2) the LightLDA Metropolis-Hastings sampler converges significantly faster than the state-of-the-art SparseLDA and AliasLDA samplers (measured in a single-threaded setting); (3) most importantly, LightLDA enables very large data and model sizes to be trained on as few as 8 machines. Because LightLDA is significantly bigger in model size than previous topic models, and employs a new form of MH algorithm, a comparison on raw throughput (tokens or docs processed per second) that is not calibrated against the model size (as used in previous literature) is less meaningful. In this paper, we focus on absolute speed of convergence (measured by wall clock time to convergence) given the same machine setup, as a universal metric.

DATASET	V	L	D	L/V	L/D
NYTIMES	101636	99542125	299752	979	332
PUBMED	141043	737869083	8200000	5231	90
BING WEBC	1000000	200B	1.2B	200000	167

Table 1: Experimental datasets and their statistics. V denotes vocabulary size, L denotes the number of training tokens, D denotes the number of documents, L/V indicates the average number of occurrences of a word, L/D indicates the average length of a document. For the Bing web chunk data, 200B denotes 200 billion.

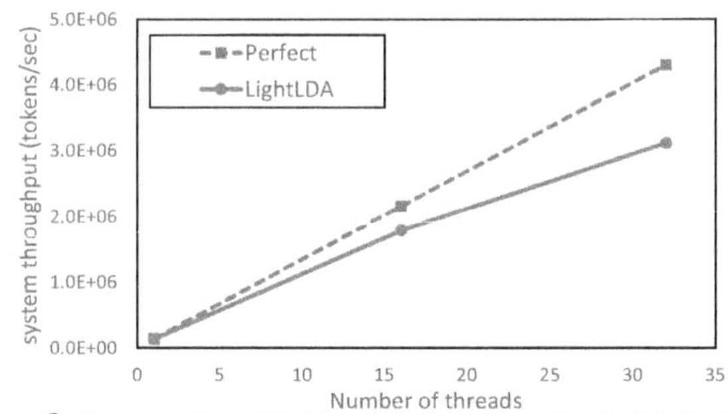

Figure 8: Intra-node scalability of LightLDA, using 1, 16, 32 threads on a single machine (no network communication costs).

7.1 Scalability of Distributed LightLDA

In these experiments, we establish that the LightLDA implementation scales almost linearly in computational resources. We begin with intra-node, single-machine multi-threaded scalability: to do this, we restrict the web chunk dataset to the 50,000 most frequent words, so that the model can be held in the RAM of a single machine. We then run LightLDA with 1, 16 and 32 threads (on a machine with at least 32 logical cores), training a model with 1 million topics on the web chunk dataset. To fully utilize the memory bandwidth, we set the number of Metropolis-Hastings steps as 16 in all the scalability experiments. We record the number of tokens sampled by the algorithm over 2 iterations, and plot it in Figure 8. The figure shows that LightLDA exhibits nearly linear scaling inside a single machine.

Next, we demonstrate that LightLDA scales in the distributed setting, with multiple machines. Using the same web chunk dataset with $V = 50,000$ vocabulary words and $K = 1$ million topics, we run LightLDA on 1, 8 and 24 machines (using 20 physical cores and 256GB RAM per machine[6]), and set the Petuum parameter server to use a staleness value of 1. A positive staleness value lets LightL-

[6]Such high-memory configurations can be readily purchased from cloud compute providers, but are not obligatory for LightLDA. The model-scheduling slices can be made thinner for small-memory machines, and the system will still work.

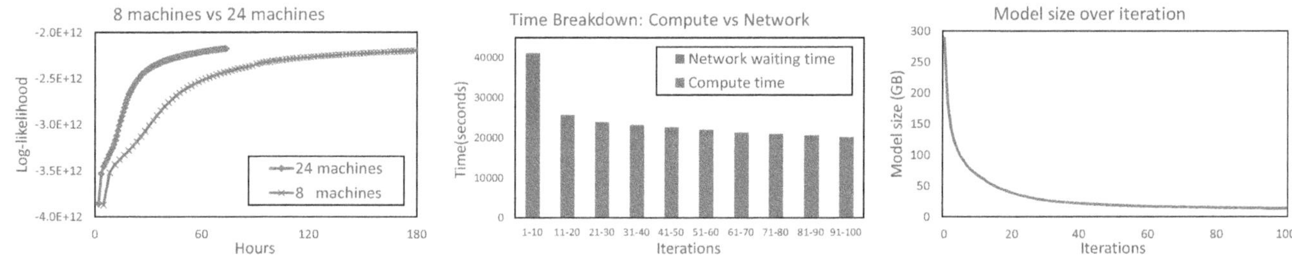

Figure 10: (a) Log-likelihood over running time with 8 and 24 machines, on Bing web chunk dataset, using $V = K = 1$ million (1 trillion parameters). (b) Compute time v.s. Network waiting time, as a function of iteration number. Observe that communication costs are significantly higher during the first 10 iterations, when the model is still dense. (c) Model si

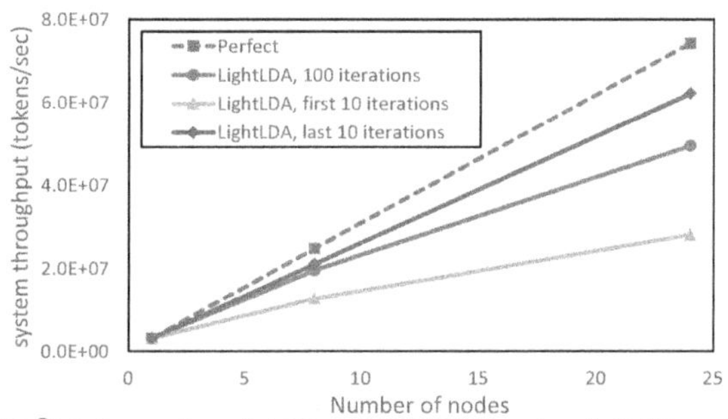

Figure 9: Inter-node scalability of LightLDA, using 1, 8, 24 machines.

DA mask the delay between iterations due to transferring model parameters over the network, yielding higher throughput at almost no cost to quality. This time, we record the number of tokens sampled over 100 iterations, and compute the average token throughput over the first 10 iterations, the last 10 iterations, and all 100 iterations. These results are plotted in Figure 9, and we note that scalability is poor in the first 10 iterations, but close to perfect in the last 10 iterations. This is because during the initial iterations, the L-DA model is still very dense (words and documents are assigned to many topics, resulting in large model size; see Figure 10(c)), which makes the system incur high network communication costs (Figure 10(b)) — enough to saturate our cluster's 1 Gbps Ethernet. In this situation, the pipelining (explained in Figure 7) does not mask the extra communication time, resulting in poor performance. However, after the first 10 iterations or so, the model becomes sparse enough for pipelining to mask the communication time, leading to near-perfect inter-node scalability (as shown in Figure 10(c)). To eliminate this initial communication bottleneck, we can initialize the model more sparsely, or we simply upgrade to 10 Gbps Ethernet (frequently seen in industrial platforms and cloud computing services) or better.

Finally, we demonstrate that LightLDA is able to handle very large model sizes: we restore the full $V = 1$ million vocabulary of the web chunk data and $K = 1$ million topics, yielding a total of one trillion model parameters on 200 billion tokens. We then run LightLDA on this large dataset and model using 8 and 24 machines, and plot the log-likelihood curves in (Figure 10(a)). Convergence is observed within 2 days on 24 machines (or 5 days on 8 machines), and it is in this sense that we claim big topic models are now possible on modest computer clusters. It is noteworthy that the system works well with no obvious performance drop on 8 machines even when the vocabulary size is extended from one million to 20 million (i.e., 20 trillion parameters in the model). This is due to the fact that all the extended words will be long-tail ones. With the help of hybrid data structure specifically designed for power-law words, increasing the vocabulary size does not introduce obvious memory footprint and performance load.

One might ask if overfitting happens on such large models, given

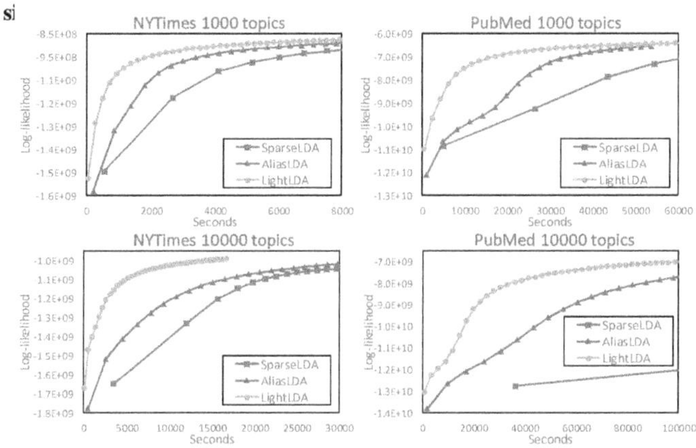

Figure 11: Log-likelihood versus running time for SparseLDA, AliasLDA, LightLDA.

that the number of parameters (1 trillion) is larger than the number of tokens (200 billion). We point out that (1) there is evidence to show that large LDA models can improve ad prediction tasks [21], and (2) the converged LDA model is sparse, with far fewer than 200 billion nonzero elements. As evidence, we monitored the number of non-zero entries in *word-topic table* during the whole training process, and observed that after 100 iterations, the model had only 2 billion non-zero entries (which is 1% of 200 billion tokens).

7.2 LightLDA Algorithm versus Baselines

We want to establish that our Metropolis-Hastings algorithm converges faster than existing samplers (SparseLDA and AliasLDA) to a high quality model. Using one computational thread, we ran LightLDA, SparseLDA and AliasLDA on two smaller datasets (NYTimes, PubMed) using $K = 1{,}000$ or 10,000 topics, and plotted the log-likelihood versus running time in Figure 11. We set the number of Metropolis-Hastings step to 2, for both AliasLDA and LightLDA. From the results, we make the following observations: AliasLDA consistently converges faster than SparseLDA (as reported in [11]), while LightLDA is around 3 to 5 times as fast as AliasLDA. To better understand the performance differences, we also plot the time taken by the first 100 iterations of each algorithm in Figure 12. In general, LightLDA has a consistently low iteration time and it does not suffer from slow initial iterations. AliasLDA is significantly faster than SparseLDA on datasets with short documents (PubMed[7]), but is only marginally faster on longer documents (NYTimes). This is reasonable since the per-token complexity of AliasLDA depends on the document length.

Although LightLDA is certainly faster per-iteration than SparseLDA and AliasLDA, to obtain a complete picture of convergence, we must plot the log-likelihood versus each iteration (Figure 14). We observe that SparseLDA makes the best progress per itera-

[7]Note that we use the whole PubMed data set in this experiment, whereas the AliasLDA paper [11] only considered 1% of the total PubMed data.

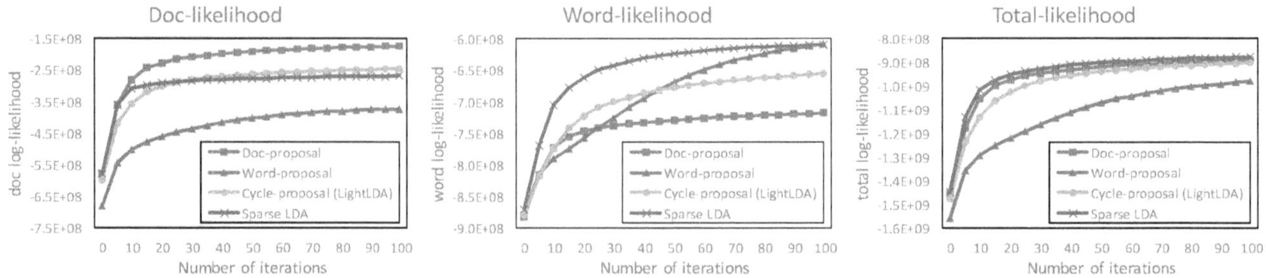

Figure 13: Performance of different LightLDA Metropolis-Hastings proposals, on the NYTimes data set with $K = 1000$ topics.

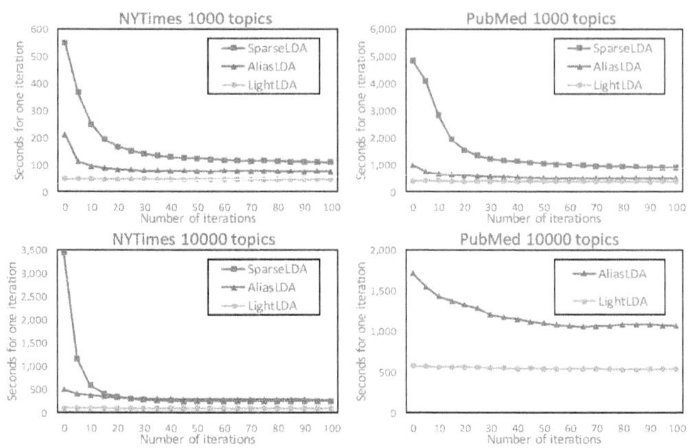

Figure 12: Running time for each of the first 100 iterations of SparseLDA, AliasLDA, LightLDA. The curve for SparseLDA was omitted from the $K = 10,000$-topic PubMed experiment, as it was too slow to show up in the plotted range.

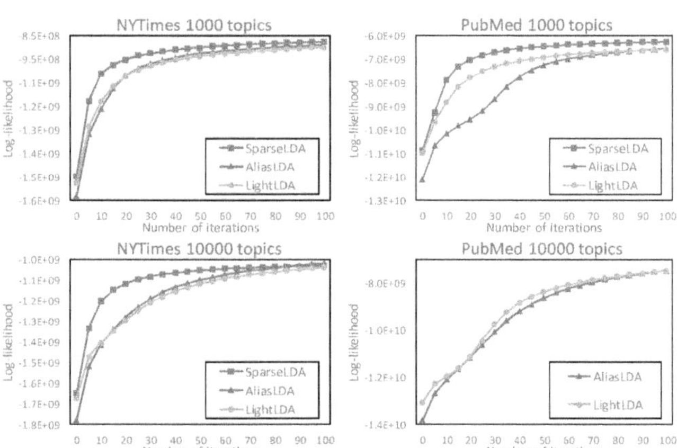

Figure 14: Log-likelihood versus iteration number for SparseLDA, AliasLDA, LightLDA.

tion (because it uses the original conditional Gibbs probability), while LightLDA is usually close behind (because it uses simple Metropolis-Hastings proposals). AliasLDA (another Metropolis-Hastings algorithm) is either comparable to LightLDA (on NYTimes) or strictly worse (on Pubmed). Because the per-iteration time taken for LightLDA and AliasLDA algorithm is very short (Figure 12), in terms of convergence to the same loss level *per time*, LightLDA and AliasLDA are significantly faster than SparseLDA (with LightLDA being the faster of the two, see Figure 11). In summary, LightLDA can achieve the same topic model quality in much less time than the other two algorithms.

Finally, we argue that the "cycle proposal" used in LightLDA, which alternates between the doc-proposal and word-proposal, would be highly effective at exploring the model space, and thus a better option than either proposal individually. To demonstrate this, in Figure 13, we plot the performance of the full LightLDA cycle proposal versus the doc- and word-proposals alone, as well as SparseLDA (which represents the gold standard for quality, being a non-Metropolis-Hastings Gibbs sampler). The plots are subdivided into (1) full likelihood, (2) document likelihood, and (3) word likelihood ([18] explains this decomposition in more detail). Intuitively, a high doc-likelihood shows that the learned topics compactly represent all documents, while a high word-likelihood indicates that the topics compactly represent the vocabulary. Although the doc- and word-proposals appear to do well on total likelihood, in actual fact, the word-proposal fails to maximize the doc-likelihood, while the doc-proposal fails to maximize the word-likelihood. In contrast, the full LightLDA cycle proposal represents both documents and vocabulary compactly, and is nearly as good in quality as SparseLDA. We note that, by trading-off between the word-proposal and doc-proposal, LightLDA allows explicit control of the word-topic distribution sparsity versus the doc-topic distribution sparsity. For real-world applications that require one type of sparsity or the other, this flexibility is highly desirable.

8. CONCLUSIONS

We have implemented a distributed LDA sampler, LightLDA, that enables very large data sizes and models to be processed on a small computer cluster. LightLDA features significantly improved sampling throughput and convergence speed via a (surprisingly) fast $\mathcal{O}(1)$ Metropolis-Hastings algorithm, and allows even small clusters to tackle very large data and model sizes thanks to the carefully designed model scheduling and data parallelism architecture, implemented on the Petuum framework. A hybrid data structure is used to simultaneously maintain good performance and memory efficiency, providing a balanced trade-off. On a future note, we believe the *factorization-and-combination* techniques for constructing Metropolis-Hastings proposals can be successfully applied to the inference of other graphical models[8], alongside the model scheduling scheme as a new enhancement over existing model partitioning strategies used in model-parallelism. It is our hope that more ML applications can be run at big data and model scales on small, widely-available clusters, and we hope that this work will inspire current and future development of large-scale ML systems.

9. ACKNOWLEDGMENTS

The authors thank the reviewers for their comments that helped improve the manuscript. This work is supported in part by DARPA FA87501220324, and NSF IIS1447676 grants to Eric P. Xing.

[8]Given that all probabilistic graphical models have an equivalent description as a factor graph, the factorization and cycling tricks can be used to speedup inference on general graphs when: (1) the factored proposal distribution is stable enough, so that it makes sense to apply the alias approach, and (2) the number of discrete states is so large that sampling from a Multinomial distribution becomes a computation bottleneck.

10. REFERENCES

[1] A. Ahmed, M. Aly, J. Gonzalez, S. Narayanamurthy, and A. J. Smola. Scalable inference in latent variable models. In *WSDM*, pages 123–132, 2012.

[2] E. Airoldi, D. Blei, S. Fienberg, and E. Xing. Mixed membership stochastic blockmodels. *J. Mach. Learn. Res.*, 9:1981–2014, 2008.

[3] C. Andrieu, N. D. Freitas, A. Doucet, and M. I. Jordan. An introduction to MCMC for machine learning. *Machine learning*, 50(1):5–43, 2003.

[4] M. Bauer, H. Cook, and B. Khailany. Cudadma: Optimizing gpu memory bandwidth via warp specialization. In *Proceedings of 2011 International Conference for High Performance Computing, Networking, Storage and Analysis*, pages 12:1–12:11, New York, NY, USA, 2011. ACM.

[5] D. M. Blei, A. Y. Ng, and M. I. Jordan. Latent dirichlet allocation. *J. Mach. Learn. Res.*, 3(30):993–1022, 2003.

[6] W. Dai, A. Kumar, J. Wei, Q. Ho, G. Gibson, and E. P. Xing. High-performance distributed ml at scale through parameter server consistency models. In *AAAI*, 2015.

[7] T. L. Griffiths and M. Steyvers. Finding scientific topics. *PNAS*, 101(1):5228–5235, 2004.

[8] W. K. Hastings. Monte Carlo sampling methods using Markov chains and their applications. *Biometrika*, 57(1):97–109, 1970.

[9] Q. Ho, J. Cipar, H. Cui, S. Lee, J. K. Kim, P. B. Gibbons, G. A. Gibson, G. Ganger, and E. Xing. More effective distributed ml via a stale synchronous parallel parameter server. In *NIPS*. 2013.

[10] S. Lee, J. K. Kim, X. Zheng, Q. Ho, G. A. Gibson, and E. P. Xing. On model parallelization and scheduling strategies for distributed machine learning. In *NIPS*, 2014.

[11] A. Li, A. Ahmed, S. Ravi, and A. J. Smola. Reducing the sampling complexity of topic models. In *KDD*, 2014.

[12] M. Li, D. G. Andersen, J. W. Park, A. Ahmed, V. Josifovski, J. Long, E. J. Shekita, and B.-Y. Su. Scaling distributed machine learning with the parameter server. In *OSDI*, pages 583–598, 2014.

[13] Z. Liu, Y. Zhang, E. Y. Chang, and M. Sun. Plda+: Parallel latent dirichlet allocation with data placement and pipeline processing. *ACM Transactions on Intelligent Systems and Technology (TIST)*, 2(3):26, 2011.

[14] G. Marsaglia, W. W. Tsang, and J. Wang. Fast generation of discrete random variables. *Journal of Statistical Software*, 11(3):1–11, 2004.

[15] N. Metropolis, A. Rosenbluth, M. Rosenbluth, A. Teller, and E. Teller. Equations of state calculations by fast computing machines. *J. Chem. Phys.*, 21:1087–1091, 1953.

[16] D. Newman, A. Asuncion, P. Smyth, and M. Welling. Distributed algorithms for topic models. *The Journal of Machine Learning Research*, 10:1801–1828, 2009.

[17] S. Shringarpure and E. P. Xing. mstruct: inference of population structure in light of both genetic admixing and allele mutations. *Genetics*, 182(2):575–593, 2009.

[18] A. Smola and S. Narayanamurthy. An architecture for parallel topic models. *Proc. VLDB Endow.*, 3(1-2), 2010.

[19] L. Tierney. Markov chains for exploring posterior distributions. *Annals of Statistics*, 22:1701–1762, 1994.

[20] A. J. Walker. An efficient method for generating discrete random variables with general distributions. *ACM Trans. Math. Softw.*, 3(3):253–256, 1977.

[21] Y. Wang, X. Zhao, Z. Sun, H. Yan, L. Wang, Z. Jin, L. Wang, Y. Gao, J. Zeng, Q. Yang, et al. Peacock: Learning long-tail topic features for industrial applications. *arXiv preprint arXiv:1405.4402*, 2014.

[22] L. Yao, D. Mimno, and A. McCallum. Efficient methods for topic model inference on streaming document collections. In *KDD*, 2009.

[23] J. Yin, Q. Ho, and E. P. Xing. A scalable approach to probabilistic latent space inference of large-scale networks. *NIPS*, 2013.

[24] J. Zhu, A. Ahmed, and E. P. Xing. Medlda: maximum margin supervised topic models for regression and classification. In *ICML*, pages 1257–1264, 2009.

A Novelty-Seeking based Dining Recommender System

Fuzheng Zhang[#†], Kai Zheng[*], Nicholas Jing Yuan[†],
Xing Xie[†], Enhong Chen[#], Xiaofang Zhou[*]
[†]Microsoft Research
[#]University of Science and Technology of China
[*]School of Information Technology & Electrical Engineering, University of Queensland
{v-fuz,nicholas.yuan,xingx}@microsoft.com,
{kevinz,zxf}@itee.uq.edu.au, cheneh@ustc.edu.cn

ABSTRACT

The rapid growth of location-based services provide the potential to understand people's mobility pattern at an unprecedented level, which can also enable food-service industry to accurately predict consumer's dining behavior. In this paper, by leveraging users' historical dining pattern, socio-demographic characteristics and restaurants' attributes, we aim at generating the top-K restaurants for a user's next dining. Compared to previous studies in location prediction which mainly focus on regular mobility patterns, we present a novelty-seeking based dining recommender system, termed **NDRS**, in consideration of both exploration and exploitation. First, we apply a Conditional Random Field (CRF) with additional constraints to infer users' novelty-seeking statuses by considering both spatial-temporal-historical features and users' socio-demographic characteristics. On the one hand, when a user is predicted to be novelty-seeking, by incorporating the influence of restaurants' contextual factors such as price and service quality, we propose a context-aware collaborative filtering method to recommend restaurants she has never visited before. On the other hand, when a user is predicted to be not novelty-seeking, we then present a Hidden Markov Model (HMM) considering the temporal regularity to recommend the previously visited restaurants. To evaluate the performance of each component as well as the whole system, we conduct extensive experiments, with a large dataset we have collected covering the concerned dining related check-ins, users' demographics, and restaurants' attributes. The results reveal that our system is effective for dining recommendation.

1. INTRODUCTION

Dining out has become one of the most distinctive aesthetic features of urban life [27]. With the rapid development of smart phones and positioning technology, the emerging location based services (e.g., Foursquare, Facebook Place, JiePang) can accurately record users' location information, which provides the potential to understand users' dining behavior at an unprecedented level.

In this paper, we aim at leveraging location records, users' socio-demographic characteristics, and restaurants' attributes to recommend restaurants for users' next dining. Actually, this problem is very similar to the location prediction problem, which has long been studied in traffic analysis [39], urban planning [42] and recommendation research [5]. Most of the previous studies in these fields put an emphasis on users' historical data and the proposed prediction methods heavily rely on repetitive mobility pattern in the past. However, due to the novelty-seeking tendency, which is biologically embedded into human brains according to the uncovered genetic roots and relations to the dopamine system [9], users would also be full of enthusiasm about exploring previously unvisited places. To be specific, more than 35% location visit is made at new places (previously unvisited) each day even after half a year according to the reported results in [6]. Actually, this neophilia characteristic is extremely outstanding in dining behavior, e.g., [3] discovered that an appropriate degree of novelty-seeking as well as attendant risk could be essential ingredients in entertainment and excitement for users' dining out motivation. [17] also stated that the physiological and psychological motivators which cannot be fulfilled in a user's normal daily life are likely to be satisfied by a sense of adventure, uniqueness of the setting, experience of different cultures and the opportunity of sampling new foods.

Given above, we present a framework, termed novelty-seeking based dining recommender system (**NDRS**), to generate the top-K restaurants for the next dining. At first, to infer a user's novelty-seeking status, we present a Conditional Random Field (CRF) to model the sequential dependency of novelty-seeking statuses in consideration of spatial, temporal and historical factors that would influence the novelty-seeking decision. Furthermore, as users' socio-demographic characteristics also have a profound and lasting impact on users' novelty-seeking tendency [37], we design these characteristics as additional constraints and incorporate them into CRF seamlessly. On the one hand, when a user is predicted to be novelty-seeking (exploring new restaurants), the recommendation candidates will be generated from tens of thousands of new restaurants which locate in the city this user resides. Then a context-aware collaborative filtering method is proposed to estimate the visit aspiration of these candidates by considering both user-restaurant-time's latent relationship and restaurants' contextual features (e.g., price, taste, service quality, etc.). On the other hand, when a user is predicted to be not novelty-seeking, the recommendation candidates are generated from the restaurants he has previously visited. We then present a Hidden Markov Model (HMM) with temporal regularity observations to estimate the visit probability for each candidate.

Our evaluation consists of multiple parts. First, we conduct several experiments on novelty-seeking status inference to evaluate the performance of our CRF with constraints method. Then, we show the results of recommending new restaurants and previously visited restaurants, respectively. Finally, we evaluate the effectiveness of our whole system by comparing with several competitive baselines.

WWW 2015, May 18-22, 2015, Florence, Italy.
ACM 978-1-4503-3469-3/15/05.
http://dx.doi.org/10.1145/2736277.2741095

To the best of our knowledge, our work is the first attempt to focus on recommending restaurants from the prospective of novelty-seeking. The key contributions of this paper include the following:

- We propose a framework which designs associated recommendation strategies based on different novelty-seeking statuses.
- We apply a CRF with constraints method to infer novelty-seeking status by considering spatial-temporal-historical features and users' socio-demographic characteristics.
- We present a context-aware collaborative filtering method to recommend new restaurants, and a HMM with temporal regularity to recommend visited restaurants.

The result of this paper is organized as follows. Section 2.2 introduces the preliminary concepts and present the dining recommendation problem. Section 3 first gives an analysis of novelty-seeking tendency and then presents the overview of our system. In Section 4, we discuss how to infer novelty-seeking status. The new and visited restaurant recommendation methods are presented in Section 5 and Section 6, respectively. The experimental results are discussed in Section 7, followed by a brief review of related work in Section 8 and a conclusion of this paper in Section 9.

2. PROBLEM STATEMENT

In this section, we first clarify some terms commonly used in this article, and then explicitly present our problem.

2.1 Preliminary

Point of Interest (POI) and **Restaurant**: A POI p refers to a specific point location that someone may find useful or interesting. It is described by a latitude, a longitude, and a category (such as restaurant, gas station, etc.). Note that a restaurant v is a particular POI with "Restaurant" category.

Check-In and **Dining Check-In**: A check-in record c is a triple $\langle u, p, t\rangle$ which indicates user $c.u$ visited POI $c.p$ at the particular time $c.t$. We use the term "dining check-in" to denote the check-in made in a restaurant.

Novel Restaurant, **Regular Restaurant**, **Novel Check-In**, **Regular Check-In**: For a user u at time t, a restaurant v is novel if this user has not visited this restaurant before time t, otherwise the restaurant v is regular if this user has already visited this restaurant before time t. A check-in in a novel restaurant is called novel check-in and similar to regular check-in.

Novelty-Seeking Status: Novlety-seeking status is an indicator to represent whether a user will like to visit new places. We use a binary value to indicate whether this user would visit a novel restaurant ($s = 1$) or a regular restaurant ($s = 0$) at a particular time.

2.2 The Dining Recommendation Problem

In this study, we consider the dining recommendation problem as follows: given a collection of users' check-in history including both dinning check-ins and check-ins at other POIs, socio-demographic characteristics (e.g., gender, age, education status) and restaurants' attributes (e.g., environment, price, rating), for the next dining of a user, assume the exact time is already known, we aim to recommend top-K restaurants he would most probably visit.

3. FRAMEWORK

In this section, we first present the analysis of novelty-seeking behavior in users' dining pattern, and then present the overview of our novelty-seeking based dining recommender system (**NDRS**).

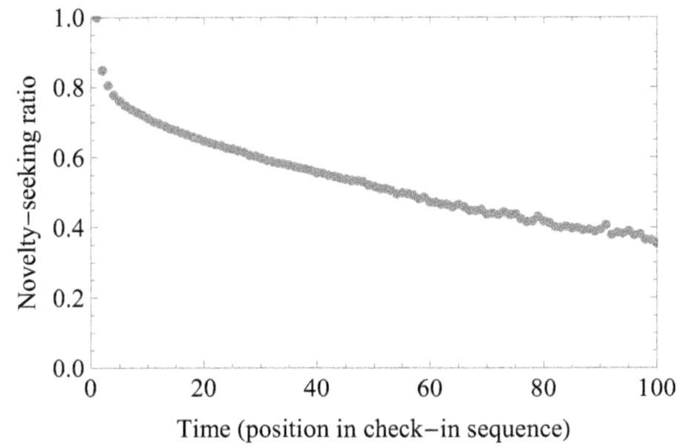

Figure 1: Novelty-seeking ratio w.r.t time

3.1 Novelty-Seeking Tendency Analysis

Before delving into the dining recommender system, a question concerned in this paper needs to be answered first: when a user dines out, will he prefers to try a novel restaurant for a certain level of freshness as well as risk-taking, or will he insist on a restaurant visited frequently in his past time? If a user frequently visits novel restaurants, the traditional statistical model based on his preference of historically visited restaurants would most probably fail. To have a deeper insight into the extent of user's exploration of novel restaurants, we define *novelty-seeking ratio* as the ratio of the number of dining check-ins with novelty-seeking status $s = 1$ to the number of total dining check-ins before a time t. As shown in Figure 1, at the beginning of dining behavior, it is obvious that almost all of them are novel. Over time, the novelty-seeking ratio declines as users will patronize the restaurants they have visited in the past. However, the novelty-seeking ratio declines slowly and it still remains about 0.4 even at the time stamp of the 100th dining visit. Such a significant part of novel dining check-ins indicates that users are keen on exploring new restaurants. On top of this, compared to traditional location recommendation techniques which mainly rely on each user's repetitive visit behavior, we should design the associated recommendation strategy in our system by taking users' novelty-seeking tendency into consideration.

3.2 System Overview

Our system is committed to generating the top-K restaurants a user would most probably visit in the next dining. In our system, by considering the influence of novelty-seeking tendency, a user's next dining decision is captured by first estimating his novelty-seeking status and then designing associated strategies to model the dining behavior for novel and regular restaurants, respectively. To infer the novelty-seeking status s of next dining, we propose a conditional random field (CRF) with additional constraints method which incorporates a CRF model with priori knowledge as constraints. Next, when the user is predicted to do exploration (novelty-seeking status $s = 1$), we propose a context-aware collaborative filtering to recommend novel restaurants. Otherwise, when the user is predicted to be backward-looking (novelty-seeking status $s = 0$), we present a Hidden Markov Model considering temporal regularity to recommend regular restaurants. Finally, the previous parts are integrated to generate the final recommendations. There are mainly three components in our system as shown in Figure 2.

- *Novelty-Seeking Status Inference*: This component presents a Conditional Random Field (CRF) with constraints model to predict the novelty-seeking status of next dining. In this method, we consider various factors that would influence the

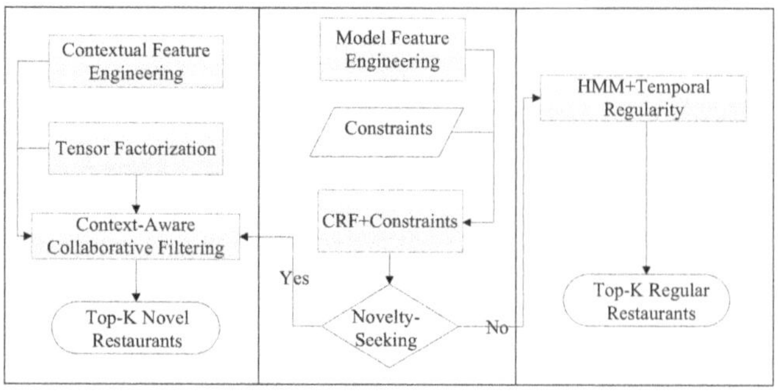

Figure 2: System overview.

novelty-seeking status, e.g., the previous novelty-seeking status, spatial-temporal limitation, users' socio-demographic characteristics, etc.

- *Novel Restaurant Recommendation*: In this component, by integrating the latent relationship in collaborative filtering and the effect of contextual features, we present a context-aware collaborative filtering method to recommend top-K novel restaurants.
- *Regular Restaurant Recommendation*: In this component, we use a Hidden Markov Model considering temporal regularity features to recommend top-K regular restaurants.

4. NOVELTY-SEEKING INFERENCE

4.1 Modeling Novelty-Seeking Behavior

According to the definition of novelty-seeking status in Section 2.1, we define our novelty-seeking status inference problem as follows: given the dining check-ins of a user, the novelty-seeking status inference problem aims to predict whether this user will visit novel restaurants (novelty-seeking status $s = 1$) or patronize regular restaurants (novelty seeking status $s = 0$) in his next dining.

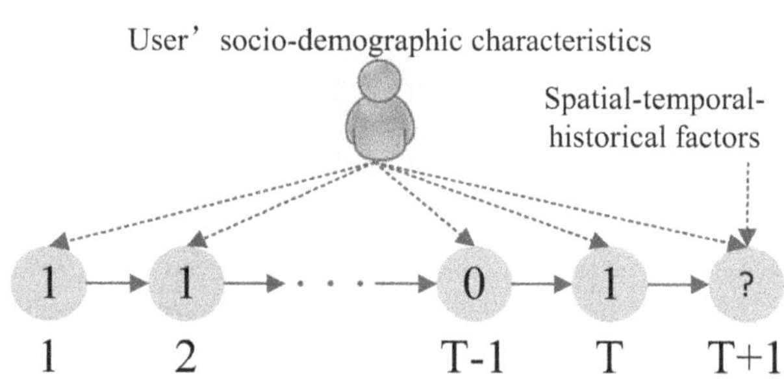

Figure 3: A user's novelty-seeking status sequence in dining check-ins, where each novelty-seeking status is influenced by the previous status, spatial-temporal-historical factors, and this user's socio-demographic characteristics.

A user's historical novelty-seeking statuses can be obtained based on the dining check-ins, and our goal is to predict the novelty-seeking status of next dining. For a user, we consider the novelty-seeking status of a check-in is influenced by the statuses of previous check-ins, since the fact that if this user has already done amount of explorations recently, he would likely have a rest and visit the company cafeteria which he is quite familiar with and vice versa. For simplicity and computational efficiency, we consider the first-order dependency as shown in Figure 3. Furthermore, various factors such as spatial-temporal limitation could also exert an effect on the novelty-seeking status. For example, the time of the dining out will influence the decision for exploration, a user will most probably have breakfast at a regular restaurant nearby his home and try some novel restaurants in the evening.

We first apply a conditional random field (CRF) to infer the next novelty-seeking status. Conditional Random Fields (CRFs) [21], which is a discriminative undirected probabilistic graphical model for parsing sequential data like natural language texts [31], has been successfully applied to sequential labeling problems in machine learning and data mining. To be specific, we first construct a linear chain CRF as shown in Figure 4. There are two kinds of nodes $\mathbf{G} = \{\mathbf{X}, \mathbf{Y}\}$, where the white nodes $\mathbf{Y} = \{Y_1, Y_2, \ldots, Y_T\}$ represent the hidden states to be inferred given the sequence of observations denoted by gray nodes $\mathbf{X} = \{X(1), X(2), \ldots, X(T)\}$. Note that in our scenario, Y_t indicates the novelty-seeking status at time t and $X(t) = (X_1(t), X_2(t), \ldots, X_m(t))$ is a vector which indicates the spatial-temporal-historical features (detailed in Section 4.2) we observe at that moment.

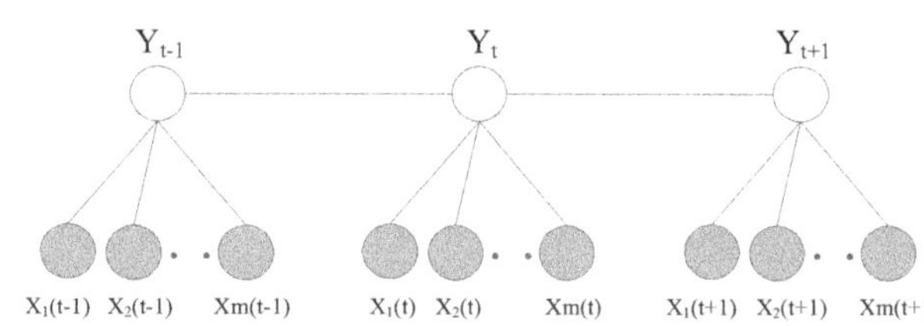

Figure 4: The graphic presentation of observations and labels in the liner chain CRF

With the labeled sequences dataset $\mathcal{D}$ with length N, CRF is typically trained by maximizing the penalized conditional log-likelihood as follows,

$$L(\lambda, \mathcal{D}) = \sum_{i=1}^{N} \log p(\mathbf{y}^{(i)}|\mathbf{x}^{(i)}) - \frac{\sum_k \lambda_k^2}{2\sigma^2}, \quad (1)$$

$$p_\lambda(\mathbf{y}|\mathbf{x}) = \frac{1}{Z(\lambda)} \exp\left(\sum_{t=1}^{T-1}\sum_{k=1}^{K} \lambda_k f_k(y_t, y_{t+1}, \mathbf{x})\right), \quad (2)$$

$$Z(\lambda) = \sum_{\mathbf{y}} \exp\left(\sum_{t=1}^{T-1}\sum_{k=1}^{K} \lambda_k f_k(y_t, y_{t+1}, \mathbf{x})\right). \quad (3)$$

where $f_k(y_t, y_{t+1}, \mathbf{x})$ is the feature function of the entire observation sequence and the labels at time t and $t+1$. The model assigns each feature function a numerical weight and combines them together to determine the probability of a certain value for Y_i. In addition, $\frac{\sum_k \lambda_k^2}{2\sigma^2}$ is the regularization term to avoid over-fitting.

4.2 Model Features Engineering

Based on the dining check-ins, for a user u at time t, we extract the spatial-temporal-historical features as follows,

Spatial features: As mentioned in [34], a user's novelty-seeking tendency is greatly influenced by the spatial limitation, here we consider two spatial features,

1) **Area Exploration Ratio**: this feature, which tends to reveal whether a user has fully explored the restaurants inside a area, is constructed with a procedure as like this: 1) First, we apply DBSCAN [10] (a density-based clustering algorithm) to a user's dining check-ins to detect his dining clusters. Note that each isolated

check-in is also treated as a cluster respectively. 2) Next, for each cluster, we identify a circular area which centres on the center of the cluster with a radius r (500m in our settings). In fact, there are also many other unvisited restaurants located in a discovered area 3) Finally, area exploration ratio is calculated as the ratio of the number of visited restaurants to the number of total restaurants (including both the visited and unvisited ones) located in all discovered areas. Actually, if a user prefers to explore as many restaurants as possible inside an area, it's most probably that he is enthusiastic about neophilia.

2) **Average Dining Distance** and **Dining Distance Variance**: Average dining distance measures the average distance of the previously visited restaurants, which indicates how far away a user would like to dine out. Dining distance variance calculates the variance of the distances between any two visited restaurants, which indicates whether this user would like to visit the restaurants concentrated in an area. These two quantities together can influence a user's novelty-seeking tendency to some extent in terms of the travel distance. To be more specific, if both average dining distance and dining distance variance are small, it strongly suggests that this user's dining behavior is limited to a small area (e.g., nearby to home or office), and thus the opportunity of exploring new restaurant will also be small. However, when both of these two quantities are large, it implies that this user would sometimes explore new restaurants in a faraway area.

Temporal features: The previous studies also imply that temporal status will influence a user's novelty-seeking tendency [30], here we consider three temporal features as follows,

1) **Total Time Interval**: This feature represents the time interval between this dining check-in and this user's first dining check-in, which is expressed as the number of days.

2) **Last Time Interval**: This feature represents the time interval between this check-in and the previous dining check-in, which is expressed as the number of hours.

3) **Hour of Week**: At different hours of a day, the probability of novelty-seeking might be different. In addition, the probability of novelty-seeking might also vary during different days of the week, e.g., people would prefer to explore new restaurant in weekend than in weekday. Therefore, we use a value from $\{0, \ldots, 167\}$ to represent the hour of the week.

Historical features: A user's dining history will influence his current novelty-seeking status. Accordingly, we identify two features,

1) **Visit Entropy**: This feature is calculated according to the previous visit frequency at each restaurant. To be more specific, for a user at a time, if the visit frequency of the previously visited restaurants are $f_1, f_2, \ldots, f_S$ respectively, his visit entropy is given as $H = -\sum_i \frac{f_i}{\sum_j f_j} \cdot \log_2 \frac{f_i}{\sum_j f_j}$. The visit entropy can be regarded as a kind of reference for novelty-seeking tendency, since a smaller value of this quantity implies this user's restaurant visit is more uniformly distributed on all the previously visited ones, and thus the probability of exploring new restaurant will be higher. The relationship between the entropy of a user's behavioral data and his novelty-seeking trait is also discussed in [43], which explicitly indicates that the novelty-seeking trait has a significant negative correlation with the entropy of behavioral data.

2) **Previous Novelty-Seeking Ratio**: It is calculated as the ratio of the number of novel dining check-ins to the number of total dining check-ins. This quantity measures this user's previous novelty-seeking tendency as a whole.

4.3 Constraints

However, except for these spatial-temporal-historical features and the dependency between adjacent labels contained in the single CRF, users' socio-demographic characteristics, have not been thoroughly leveraged in the model. Actually, psychologists have found that socio-demographic characteristics (i.e., age, gender, education status, etc.) have a great effect on users' novelty-seeking tendency [22]. These characteristics will influence a user's dining behavior as a whole, and thus they are more suited to be designed as a kind of priori knowledge for each user instead of the CRF's model features which mainly determine the instantaneous state. Therefore, we employ the Generalized Expectation Criterion [25] as an objective function to incorporate socio-demographic characteristics as prior knowledge. The General Expectation Criterion makes very natural an under-explored paradigm for incorporating the prior knowledge. Suppose we have already obtained the prior knowledge that the male is keen on exploring novel restaurants. To be more specific, the prior knowledge tells us desirable properties of the distribution over output variables. The distribution we want to match deriving from the prior knowledge is called target distribution, e.g., $p(s=1|\text{male}) = 0.6$, $p(s=0|\text{male}) = 0.4$. By carefully designing a constraint feature function denoted as $\phi(\mathbf{x}, \mathbf{y})$, the CRF model will also generate an expectation over the constraint feature function under the CRF's conditional distribution $p_\lambda(\mathbf{y}|\mathbf{x})$ as follows,

$$E_\lambda[\phi] = E_{p_\lambda(\mathbf{y}|\mathbf{x})}[\phi(\mathbf{x}, \mathbf{y})] = \sum_{\mathbf{y}} p_\lambda(\mathbf{y}|\mathbf{x})\phi(\mathbf{x}, \mathbf{y}). \quad (4)$$

The General Expectation Criterion encourages the gap (e.g., the square distance applied in this article) between the model expectation distribution $E_\lambda[\phi]$ and the target distribution is as small as possible. For the constraint feature functions, an example related to the relationship of the male and novelty-seeking status should be designed as

$$\phi_{\text{male,novel}}(\mathbf{x}, \mathbf{y}) = \sum_{t=1}^{T} \mathbb{I}(y_t = 1)\mathbb{I}(\mathbf{x}\ is\ \text{male}), \quad (5)$$

$$\phi_{\text{male,regular}}(\mathbf{x}, \mathbf{y}) = \sum_{t=1}^{T} \mathbb{I}(y_t = 0)\mathbb{I}(\mathbf{x}\ is\ \text{male}). \quad (6)$$

where $\phi_{\text{male,novel}}(\mathbf{x}, \mathbf{y})$ represents the constraint that the male would explore novel restaurant and $\phi_{\text{male,regular}}(\mathbf{x}, \mathbf{y})$ represents the constraint that the male visit regular restaurants. The indicator function $\mathbb{I}(\cdot)$ returns 1 if the statement in its parameter is true, and 0 otherwise.

To incorporate the General Expectation Criterion into the CRF model, the final objective function we intend to maximize is given by

$$L'(\lambda, \mathcal{D}) = L(\lambda, \mathcal{D}) - S(\tilde{\Phi}, E_{p_\lambda(\mathbf{y}|\mathbf{x})}[\Phi(\mathbf{x}, \mathbf{y})]). \quad (7)$$

where $\tilde{\Phi}$ is the empirical target distribution, $\Phi(\mathbf{x}, \mathbf{y})$ is the collection of constraint feature functions, and S is the score function expressing the distance (the square distance is applied in this article) between the model expectation and the target distribution. We follow the gradient-based methods mentioned in [8] to perform the optimization of Eq. (7).

For the constraint features, we consider a user's socio-demographic characteristics including gender, age and education status, where a user's education status is classified as college student and non-college student (college student are those who claim their college experience on the SinaWeibo profile while non-college students are on the opposite).

Ultimately, since both model features and constraint features needs categorical variables, each continuous variable is discretized to five categories according to the five-quantiles binning method.

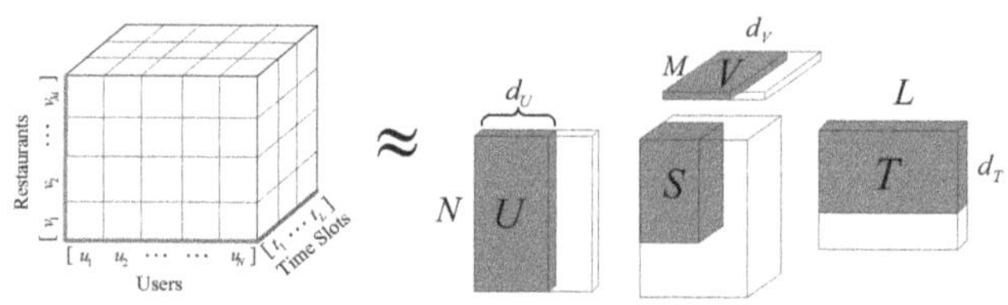

Figure 5: The illustration of tensor factorization, where the three dimensions of the tensor indicate user, restaurant and time slot. The value of each entry in the tensor indicates the visit frequency. The factorized three matrices indicate user feature, restaurant feature, and time slot feature in latent space, respectively.

5. NOVEL RESTAURANT RECOMMENDATION

Currently, if a user is predicted to be novelty-seeking ($s = 1$) in next dining, we will generate top-K recommendations from novel restaurants according to her historical dining behavior as well as other users' dining behavior. Futhermore, since the exact time of next dining is already known as mentioned in Section2.2, this scenario is similar to the user-item-time problem in a temporal-dynamic recommender system which will recommend users interested new items at a particular time. Given this, We present a context-aware collaborative filtering method to model users' preference for these novel restaurants at the given time in consideration of both latent user-restaurant-time relationship and restaurant's contextual features.

5.1 Context-Aware Collaborative Filtering

The goal of collaborative filtering method is to recommend novel restaurants to users at the next dining time according to their visit frequencies of regular restaurants. Considering user-restaurant-time as a three-dimensional tensor, denoted by $Y \in R^{N \times M \times L}$, where N is the number of users, M is the number of restaurants, and L is the number of hours in a day (for the time dimension, we divide a day into 24 hours). We apply tensor factorization, which is the state-of-the-art method used for collaborative filtering in the high dimensional situation [20]. For an entry C_{ijk} in the tensor Y, if the user i has visited the restaurant j at the time slot k in the historical data, we regard Y_{ijk} as being observed and use the frequency of this visit to denote the value. Therefore, our problem is then estimate the value of these unknown elements in the tensor.

We apply High Order Singular Value Decomposition (HOSVD) [7] to factorize the three-dimensional tensor into three matrices $U \in R^{N \times d_U}$, $V \in R^{M \times d_V}$, $T \in R^{L \times d_T}$ and one central tensor $S \in R^{d_U \times d_V \times d_T}$. The three matrices are compact representations of the three attributes in subspaces, where d_U, d_V, d_T are dimensionality parameters to balance the capability and generalization. The recosntructed value for user i, item j and time slot k is given as

$$F_{ijk} = S \times_U U_{i*} \times_V V_{j*} \times_T T_{k*}, \tag{8}$$

We regard the tensor matrix multiplication as $\times_U$, where the subscript denotes the direction, e.g., $C = S \times_P P$ is $C_{ijk} = \sum_{i=1}^{U} S_{ijk} \times P_{ij}$. The entries of the ith row of the matrix P is represented as P_{i*}.

Additionally, the single tensor factorization does not take full advantage of our data, since it only tries to find out user-restaurant-time's latent relationship in the feature space only through the observable visit frequencies. It does not consider other factors would also influence the users' dining preference for restaurants and time slots. Another important signal, the restaurant's contextual features, has not been well considered. Researchers in the hospitality management research has discovered that users' dining satisfaction and patronage is greatly influenced by the restaurant's contextual features, such as price, atmosphere and service quality [18]. Actually, an item's contextual features are often modeled into collaborative filtering to solve the uncertainty problems [2].

Assume that there are L contextual features, where the l-th feature has categorical values $1, 2, \dots, z_l$, and the value 1 means that the l-th contextual feature was unknown, while other index values are possible contextual conditions. By incorporating these contextual features into the tensor factorization, according to [42], the reconstructed value for an entry C_{ijk} is redefined as

$$F'_{ijk} = S \times_U U_{i*} \times_V V_{j*} \times_T T_{k*} + \sum_{l=1}^{L} B_{lc_{jl}} \tag{9}$$

where c_{jl} is the value of the l-th feature for restaurant j, and $B_{lc_{jl}}$ is the parameter modeling how the l-th contextual feature with condition c_{jl} will influence the value of entry C_{ijk}. These contextual feature parameters guarantee the fact that restaurants with similar contextual features tend to have similar number of visit frequency.

In order to generate estimations for these novel restaurants, the model parameters should be learned using the observable frequency of these visited restaurants at the corresponding time slots. We define the learning procedure as an optimization problem, which is given as

$$\min_{S,U,V,T,B} L(Y, F') + \Omega(S, U, V, T, B), \tag{10}$$

where $L(Y, F')$ is the loss function given as

$$L(Y, F') = \frac{1}{||S||_1} \sum_{i,j,k} Z_{ijk} \cdot (Y_{ijk} - F'_{ijk}), \tag{11}$$

where $Z \in 0, 1^{N \times M \times L}$ is a binary tensor with nonzero entries Z_{ijk} whenever Y_{ijk} is observed. Equation (11) indicates that we consider the reconstructed accuracy for the observed entries. In addition, $\Omega(S, U, V, T, B)$ is the regularization term to avoid overfitting, which is given as

$$\Omega(S, U, V, T, B) = \lambda \times (||S||^2_{Frob} + ||U||^2_{Frob} + ||V||^2_{Frob} + ||T||^2_{Frob} + ||B||^2_{Frob}), \tag{12}$$

Equation (10) guarantees that our context-aware collaborative filtering method can reconstruct the observations as accurately as possible and meanwhile maintain the capability of generalization. We use stochastic gradient descent [45] to solve this optimization problem.

Finally, after we obtain these parameters, for a user i, if the time slot of her next dining is k, the top-K novel restaurants will be recommended according to the preference ranking of the restaurants, which is given as

$$u_i : v_1 \succ v_2 \succ \cdots \succ v_M \longrightarrow F'_{i1k} > F'_{i2k} \cdots > F'_{iMk}, \tag{13}$$

5.2 Contextual Features Extraction

We consider four types of contextual features for restaurants as follows,

Popularity: This feature, which measures the popularity of a restaurant, is calculated as the sum of visit frequency in this restaurant for all users.

Area Popularity: This feature measures the overall popularity of an area where a restaurant locates in. It is natural to consider that when a restaurant locates in a more popular area, it has the potential to attract more consumers. For a restaurant, we first determine a circular area which centres on the center of this restaurant with a given radius (500m in our settings). The area popularity is then calculated as the sum of popularity for these POIs (including both restaurants and non-restaurants) locating in the identified area.

Area Attraction: We identify the area attraction feature according to what kind of POIs locate close to a restaurant. First, for each category C of the POIs, to determine its attraction to the restaurant category, we use the metrics defined in [16], which is given as

$$A_C = \frac{\#\text{co\_location}(C, \text{Restaurant})}{\#C} \tag{14}$$

where $\#\text{co\_location}(C, \text{Restaurant})$ refers to the frequency of co-location for category C with restaurant, while $\#C$ is the frequency of category C. Note that co-location indicates that the geographic distance between a restaurant and a POI with category C is less than 500m. The top 3 discovered POI categories are {Living Quarters, Shopping Mall, College}. Next, by aggregating nearby POIs, the area attraction of a restaurant j is given as

$$AA_j = \sum_C \#\text{co\_location}(C, j) \cdot A_C \tag{15}$$

where $\#\text{co\_location}(C, j)$ refers to the frequency of co-location for category C with this particular restaurant j.

Restaurant Attributes: We consider the following attributes for a restaurant: 1) *Restaurant Category*. There are total 49 restaurant categories in our dataset, such as Sichuan cuisine, Cantonese cuisine and Japanese cuisine. 2) *Price, Rating, Taste, Environment, Service Quality*. Since the restaurant in our check-in dataset is not described by these attributes, we crawl restaurant attributes from external sources and map them to the corresponding restaurant in our check-in dataset, which will be detailed in Section 7.1.

After obtaining these features, since the context-aware collaborative filtering model needs categorical feature variables, each feature with continuous value is discretized to five categories according to the five-quantiles binning method.

6. REGULAR RESTAURANT RECOMMENDATION

When a user is predicted to be not novelty-seeking ($s = 0$) in Section 4, we need to generate the top-K recommendations from a candidate pool of his regular restaurants.

In consideration of the sequential dependency widely discussed in location prediction [36] and the temporal influence on location visit [35], we apply a Hidden Markov Model (HMM) considering the temporal regularity to model a user's dining pattern. To be more specific, a user's visited restaurants in the dining check-in sequence are regarded as hidden states and the related temporal information are regarded as external observations. For the temporal information, we consider the hour of the day and distinguish weekday from weekend, thus each check-in's timestamp is mapped to a vector $t = \{h, w\}$, where $h \in \{0, 1, \ldots, 23\}$ and $w \in \{0, 1\}$.

For each user, a personalized HMM model is specified for him and we use supervised learning [24] to determine three types of parameters: emission probability, initial hidden state probability and state transition probability.

Emission probability $P(t|v)$ indicates the conditional dependency for a timestamp (observation) $t = \{h, w\}$ by a restaurant v. This probability is directly determined by maximum likelihood estimation with a Laplace smoothing as $P(h|v) = \frac{N(h,v)+1}{\sum_h N(h,v)+24}$ and $P(w|v) = \frac{N(w,v)+1}{\sum_w N(w,v)+2}$, where $N(h, v)$ is the frequency of check-ins in restaurant v at hour h and similar to $N(w, v)$. Furthermore, we observe that a user would only visit restaurants with 4.2 hour bins on average, e.g., a user might only visit restaurants at 7 a.m., 12 p.m. or 6 p.m.. To ensure nearby hours have similar conditional probabilities, the emission probability for hour h is further transformed by a Gaussian kernel smoothing function as follows,

$$P'(h|v) = \frac{\sum_{h'} \mathcal{N}(\frac{\text{dis}(h,h')}{\sigma_{h',v}}) P(h'|v)}{\sum_g \sum_{h'} \mathcal{N}(\frac{\text{dis}(g,h')}{\sigma_{h',v}}) P(h'|v)}. \tag{16}$$

where $\text{dis}(h, h') = \min(|h - h'|, 24 - |h - h'|)$ is the cyclic distance between hour h and h' in a day. $\mathcal{N}(\cdot)$ is a standard Gaussian distribution and $\sigma_{h',v}$ is set to be $N(h', v)^{-\frac{1}{5}}$ according to [33].

The initial state probability is estimated by maximum likelihood as $P(v) = \frac{N(v)}{\sum_v N(v)}$, where $N(v)$ is the check-in frequency in restaurant v. Similarly, the state transition probability can also be estimated by maximum likelihood with a Laplace smoothing as given by

$$P(v|v_p) = \frac{N(v_p, v) + 1}{2 \times \sum_{v'} N(v_p, v')} \tag{17}$$

where $N(v_p, v)$ indicates the frequency of visiting restaurant v right after restaurant v_p.

Given these parameters estimated, we generate the top-K regular restaurants according to the visit probability of a restaurant v as follows,

$$p(v|v_p, h, w) \propto p(v_p|v) \cdot p(h|v) \cdot p(w|v) \cdot p(v) \tag{18}$$

7. EXPERIMENTS

In this section, we first describe and analyze the data we collected from two specific websites. Based on this huge dataset, we then conducted extensive experiments to evaluate the performances of novelty seeking status inference, efficient novel restaurant recommendation, and regular restaurant recommendation, respectively. Finally, we validate the performance of our whole framework **NDRS**.

7.1 Data Collection and Description

We tested the performance of our system based on two publicly available websites: SinaWeibo and DianPing.

SinaWeibo, which is the largest social netowrk website in China, also provides location-based services such as check-ins. We crawled 135 million check-ins from 3 million users with the breath-first strategy using Lifespec crawling platform [41]. For each POI, we crawled its description including id, geographic coordinates and category. For each user, we also crawled his demographic information including gender, age and education status before 1st June 2014. To clean the datasets, we first filter the noisy data, e.g., repeated check-ins at the same place in quite a short interval (1hr is adopted in our setting). Next, since our system focuses on the dining check-ins of a user, we need sufficient restaurant visits. On top of this, we adopt two strategies to further filter the check-in dataset: 1) For a user, we only focus on the dining check-ins which are located in the city where she resides (note that we represent the city she resides is the place where most of her check-ins locate). The reason is our novel restaurant recommendation method only focus on the restaurants in her residence city. For example,

Table 1: Summarization of collected dataset for different cities (partially presented due to page limit).

City	Shanghai	Beijing	Chongqing	Guangzhou	Chengdu	Shenzhen	Nanjing	Tianjin	Xian	Shenyang
Users	183,239	69,412	6,787	42,694	10,788	9,462	12,760	10,137	7,807	6,015
Restaurants	34,127	27,120	6,948	18,625	12,074	9,931	8,570	7,349	7,095	5,268
Dining check-ins	2,582,914	895,120	89,749	542,563	152,227	135,302	167,826	120,802	86,651	65,841

Figure 6: A restaurant's description on DianPing

if a user resides in Beijing, it is actually difficult and meaningless to recommend restaurants in Shanghai if she does not visit Shanghai frequently. 2) We remove those users who have fewer than 10 dining check-ins, which is to ensure sufficient observable dining history. 3) For a city, if the number of users who reside in this city is smaller than 5,000 or the number of restaurants located in this city is smaller than 1000, we remove all the users who reside in this city and their related check-ins. The reason is that when we generate the Top-K novel restaurants for a user in Section 5, all the restaurant candidates are selected from the city he resides. For each city, the context-aware tensor factorization method is applied, respectively. Thus, we need enough users and restaurants in a city to ensure the user-restaurant-time tensor factorization.

After the filtering procedures, we eventually obtained a collection of 361,218 unique users from 21 cities all over China, with 4,941,060 dining check-ins. Table 1 summarizes the statistics of the final dataset for different cities.

Furthermore, since the restaurant in our SinaWeibo check-in dataset is only described by geographic coordinates and category, to obtain the restaurant attributes discussed in Section 5.2, we need to link external data sources. As shown in Figure 6, DianPing (similar to Yelp, the largest online review website in China) is such a desired website where the restaurants are described by sufficient attributes in detail. First, for each of the 21 cities from our SinaWeibo check-in dataset, we crawled all restaurants located in this city from DianPing by grabbing web pages directly, and extracted prices, ratings, tastes, environments and service qualities from the raw webpages. Then, we applied a two staged method described in [32] (including both geographic filtering and title string match) to map each restaurant from SinaWeibo to a restaurant from DianPing. Finally, we explicitly observed 500 paired results, where 91.5% of the pairs are correctly matched (the match precision is good enough for later process). In addition, we find that only 5.7% of restaurants from SinaWeibo can not be mapped to any restaurant from DianPing.

To evaluate the performance of our proposed methods, for each user, her previous 90% dining check-ins were used as training data and the remaining dining check-ins are used as testing data.

7.2 Experiments for Novelty-Seeking Inference

In this subsection, we study the performance of novelty-seeking status inference. First, for each constraint feature, we constructed the target distribution according to the empirical distribution in the training data. For example, if 60% of the dining check-ins generated by the male is novel and 40% is regular, the target distribution for constraint feature "male" is $p(s = 1|\text{male}) = 0.6, p(s = 0|\text{male}) = 0.4$. Next, we compared our method (CRF with model features, optimized with constraints), shortened as "**CRF(M)+C**" against the following baselines,

- **LR** (Logistic Regression): This algorithm uses both the model features and constraint features for the Logistic Regression.
- **CRF+C** (CRF with only constraints): This algorithm uses the same settings as **CRF(M)+C**, except that it does not incorporate model features.
- **CRF(M)** (CRF with only model features): This algorithm uses the same settings as **CRF(M)+C**, except that it does not incorporate constraints.
- **NSTM** (Novelty-Seeking Trait Model): This Bayesian model presented in [43] is a state-of-the-art method to model user's sequential behavior in consideration of novelty-seeking and preference. To accommodate our scenario, we set a user's novelty-seeking status as 0 or 1 (it is originally set from 1 to 5 in [43]).

Table 2: The results of novelty-seeking inference.

	Accuracy	True Positive Rate	False Negative Rate
CRF(M)+C	0.823	0.786	0.845
LR	0.641	0.593	0.667
CRF(M)	0.795	0.762	0.811
CRF+C	0.633	0.624	0.639
NSTM	0.748	0.767	0.719

If we consider novelty-seeking status $s = 1$ as positive and the other as negative, the results of true positive rate, false negative rate as well as accuracy are shown in Table 2, where accuracy indicates the percentage of correct prediction for all check-ins in the testing data, true positive rate indicates for these novel check-ins ($s = 1$) in the testing data, the percenrage of correct prediction, and false negative rate indicates for these regular check-ins ($s = 0$), the percenrage of correct prediction. It is clear that our method significantly outperforms competitors in all three criterions. For example, by using the constraints, our method achieves an improvement over **CRF(M)**. Compared our method with **CRF+C**, it is obvious that model features are significantly crucial to the detection of novelty-seeking status. We can see that **LR** performs worst due to the fact that this method does not take the sequential dependency of novelty-seeking statuses into consideration. In addition, the reason why **NSTM** is defeated by our method **CRF(M)+C** is that **NSTM** only considers a user's dining sequence, while our method incorporates various model features as well as users' socio-demographic characteristics as constraints. Since regular restaurant recommendation is easier than novel restaurant recommendation as shown in Section 7.3 and Section 7.4, to give a more accurate recommendation as a whole, we would expect that the False Negative Rate is as large as possible (if a user want to visit regular restaurants, we expect that the error of predicting her novelty-seeking status as $s = 1$ is as small as possible). In view of this, our method also outperforms these baselines evidently in the False Negative Rate criterion.

7.3 Experiments for Novel Restaurant Recommendation

In this subsection, we study the performance of our context-aware collaborative filtering model in various situations.

We compare our context-aware collaborative filtering method (**CACF** for short) against the following methods,

- **CF** (Collaborative Filtering): This algorithm uses the same settings as **CACF**, except that it does not incorporate contextual features.
- **LR** (Logistic Regression). This algorithm uses a Logistic Regression with all the contextual features in our **CACF**.
- **PPTM** (Personal Popularity Tendency Matching). This algorithm proposed in [28] gives an effective novel item recommendation by reasonably penalizing popular items while improving the recommendation accuracy, which is a state-of-the-art method in recommending novel items.

The evaluation method of novel recommendation is as follows: 1) For each city, we collect all the users who reside in this city and then use their training check-ins (the previous 90% check-ins mentioned in Section 7.1) to learn a model and then obtain a user's evaluation result on her novel check-ins in the testing data. Note that we only test the performance on novel check-ins in the testing data, therefore regular check-ins in the testing data are ignored. 2) The final result is the average value of the results from all users.

We used nDCG, a widely adopted metric in information retrieval, to evaluate the performance of novel restaurant recommendation. We first listed recommendation candidates in a descending order according to the estimation, and used $\mathrm{rel}_i = 1$ to indicate that the i-th recommended restaurant was just the one visited by the user and $\mathrm{rel}_i = 0$ otherwise. Next, we used nDCG@p to evaluate the performance given by

$$\mathrm{nDCG@p} = \frac{\mathrm{DCG_p}}{\mathrm{IDCG_p}}, \quad \text{where} \quad \mathrm{DCG_p} = \sum_{i=1}^{p} \frac{2^{\mathrm{rel}_i} - 1}{\log_2(i+1)}, \tag{19}$$

where IDCG_p is the value of DCG_p for a perfect ranking.

We used nDCG@10 in our reported results, which are shown in Figure 7, where dim means the feature dimension ($dim = d_U = d_V = d_T$) in the tensor factorization. The table shows that **CACF** outperformed the baselines in various situations. Compared **CACF** with **CF**, it shows that incorporating contextual features is effective for the recommendation. Compared **CF** with **LR**, it also implies that tensor factorization is more suitable for novel restaurant recommendation.

7.4 Experiments for Regular Restaurant Recommendation

In this subsection, we evaluate the performance of regular restaurant recommendation. We compared our temporal related Hidden Markov Model (**TM** for short) against the following baselines,

- **MC** (Markov Chain): This method models sequential behavior by learning the transition graph over restaurants. Actually, this algorithm only uses the transition probability in our **TM**.
- **TR** (Temporal Regularity): This method models the temporal regularity of restaurant visit. It only uses the emission probability in our **TM** to generate the recommendation list.

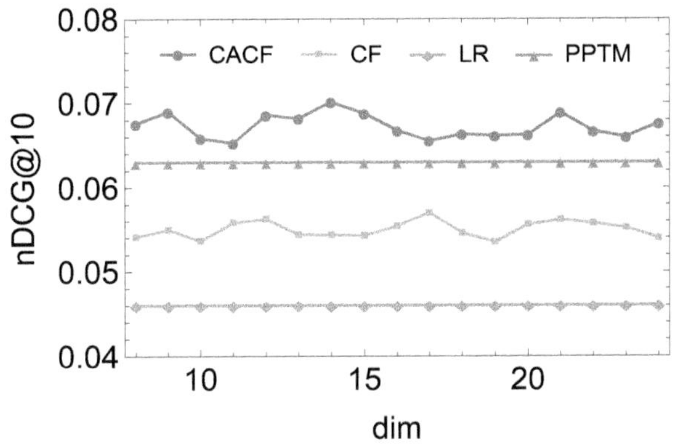

Figure 7: The results nDCG@10 of recommending w.r.t. latent dimension dim

- **OF** (Order by Frequency): This algorithm gives a recommendation list of restaurants according to this user's visit frequency in a restaurant.

The evaluation method of regular recommendation is as follows: 1) For each user, we use her training check-ins (the previous 90% check-ins mentioned in Section 7.1) to learn a model and then obtain this user's evaluation result on her regular check-ins in the testing data. Note that we only test the performance on regular check-ins in the testing data, therefore novel check-ins in the testing data are ignored. 2) The final result is the average value of the results from all users.

We also used nDCG@10 to evaluate the performance of each algorithm, and the results are shown in Table 3. It shows our **TM** outperforms the competitors greatly, which implies that the combination of Markov dependency and temporal regularity is more suitable for regular restaurant recommendation.

Table 3: The results nDCG@10 of recommending regular restaurants

TM	MC	TR	OF
0.374	0.327	0.313	0.332

7.5 Experiments for NDRS

In this subsection, we evaluate the performance of our whole system **NDRS**, which combines the results from the three components together to generate the final next dining recommendation list. We compared our system against the following baselines:

- **CACF+**: This method has the same settings as **CACF** mentioned before, except that for each user, the recommendation list is based on all the restaurants (including both novel and regular restaurants) located in the city. It does not emphasize the regularity in a user's previous dining pattern.
- **TM**: This method only use the regular restaurant recommendation as mentioned in Section 6, which does not consider recommending novel restaurants.
- **FPMC-LR**: This methods is proposed in [5], which embeds users' preference, personalized Markov chain, and localized region constraints into next POI recommendation.

Note that in this part, the testing data includes both novel and regular check-ins. We also employ nDCG@10 for the performance evaluation. As shown in Figure 8, our system **NDRS** enjoys the best performance compared to its competitors. Compared **NDRS** to

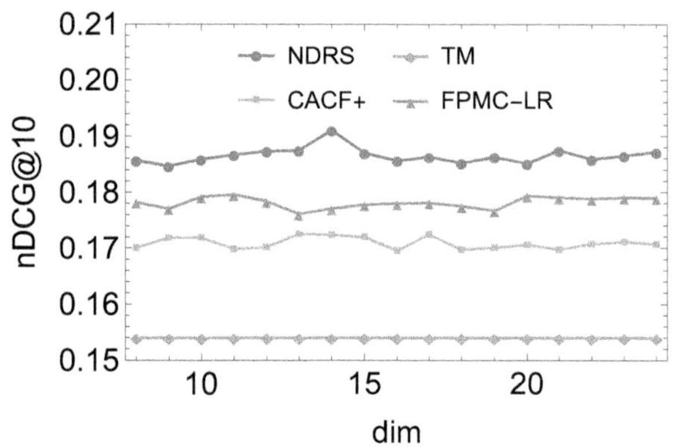

Figure 8: The results nDCG@10 of dining recommendation w.r.t. latent dimension dim

CACF+ and **TM**, it shows that integrating novel and regular restaurant recommendation together will give a better result. Compared **NDRS** to **FPMC-LR**, it also shows that using novelty-seeking status to determine whether recommending novel restaurants is effective for the dining recommendation scenario.

8. RELATED WORK

8.1 Location Recommendation

In recent years, with the rapid accumulation of spatial-temporal records in the check-in data and the prevalence of various interesting real-world applications [40], the location recommendation problem has received much attention. Ye et al. [38] exploited the social and geographical characteristics of users and location/places to generate the next location recommendation. Zheng et al. [47] used GPS data and users' comments at various locations to discover interesting locations and possible activities that can be performed for recommendation. Cheng et al. [4] first fused matrix factorization with geographical and social influence for POI recommendation.

Compared to previous works which mainly focus on regular mobility patterns, our work primarily aims at proposing a framework based on novelty-seeking status to predict whether a user will visit novel restaurants or regular restaurants.

8.2 Novelty-Seeking in Dining Behavior

Novelty seeking is also termed sensation seeking or neophilia. It has long been studied in psychology, consumer behavior and health science [11, 14, 23]. Acker and Mcreynolds [1] mentioned that novelty-seeking appears to be that through internal drive and external motivating force, the individual is then motivated to seek out novel information. There are two aspects to novelty-seeking that are likely to be correlated. The first aspect is seeking new and potentially discrepant information, which is emphasized by Fiske and Maddi [12]. The second aspect is the extent to which individuals would like to vary their choices among familiar contexts [13].

Novelty-seeking is closely related to dining behavior. Kivela et al. [17] proposed that with the dining experience, the quest to sample various food styles is one of many appealing experiences users aspire to achieve. Kivela and Chu [19] discovered that the adventure and hedonistic dishes found in a restaurant are sources of pleasure they help satisfy individuals' sensational desires particularly. Pizam et al. [29] moved forward to conclude that it is possible to predict the meal and types of food that tourists would prefer based on determining the relative level of novelty-seeking.

Compared to previous works which investigated this problem mainly by surveys or interviews, we present a computational framework to infer a user's novelty-seeking status and then use novelty-seeking status to provide insight for different recommendation strategies.

8.3 Novelty in Recommendation

It has been well acknowledged that novelty and diversity are important aspects in evaluating the performance of a recommender system [26]. Zhang et al. [46] addressed five measures to capture the novelty and redundancy of relevant documents in an adaptive information filtering system. Using these measures, the system can determine whether an item which is considered relevant contains any novel information to the user. Hurley and Zhang [15] took the view that novel items have greater utility and focus on strategies to recommend novel items. The authors formulated the trade-off between novelty and matching quality as a binary optimization problem and used an explicit control parameter to allow the tuning of this trade-off. Oh et al. [28] proposed an efficient novel-recommendation method which can help to diversify recommendations by reasonably penalizing popular items while improving the recommendation accuracy. Zhou et al. [48] presented an algorithm specifically to address the challenge of novelty and diversity, and showed it can be used to resolve the novelty-accuracy dilemma when combined in an elegant hybrid with an accuracy-focused algorithm. To better capture user's novelty tastes, Zhang and Hruley [44] proposed to partition the user profile into clusters of similar items and composed the recommendation list of items that match well with each cluster.

Compared with previous influential works that primarily aimed at recommending novel items, we step further to consider the novelty-seeking tendency of the user, which can help to understand the user's behavior at an intrinsic level.

9. CONCLUSION

This paper proposes a dining recommender system termed **NDRS**, which gives associated recommendation strategies according to different novelty-seeking statuses. Following the framework, we first design a CRF with constraints to infer novelty-seeking status. Next, a context-aware collaborative filtering method and a HMM with temporal regularity method are proposed for novel and regular restaurant recommendation, respectively. The extensive experiments we have conducted validated the effectiveness of our dining recommender system. Besides, this research sheds new light on other recommender systems such as POI and music recommendation, which can be used in more application scenarios.

References

[1] M. Acker and P. McReynolds. The" need for novelty": A comparison of six instruments. *The Psychological Record*, 1967.

[2] G. Adomavicius, R. Sankaranarayanan, S. Sen, and A. Tuzhilin. Incorporating contextual information in recommender systems using a multidimensional approach. *ACM Transactions on Information Systems (TOIS)*, 23(1):103–145, 2005.

[3] T. D. Andersson and L. Mossberg. The dining experience: do restaurants satisfy customer needs? *Food Service Technology*, 4(4):171–177, 2004.

[4] C. Cheng, H. Yang, I. King, and M. R. Lyu. Fused matrix factorization with geographical and social influence in location-based social networks. In *AAAI*, volume 12, page 1, 2012.

[5] C. Cheng, H. Yang, M. R. Lyu, and I. King. Where you like to go next: Successive point-of-interest recommendation. In *Proceedings of the Twenty-Third international joint conference on Artificial Intelligence*, pages 2605–2611. AAAI Press, 2013.

[6] E. Cho, S. A. Myers, and J. Leskovec. Friendship and mobility: user movement in location-based social networks. In *Proceedings of the 17th ACM SIGKDD international conference on Knowledge discovery and data mining*, pages 1082–1090. ACM, 2011.

[7] L. De Lathauwer, B. De Moor, and J. Vandewalle. A multilinear singular value decomposition. *SIAM journal on Matrix Analysis and Applications*, 21(4):1253–1278, 2000.

[8] G. Druck, G. Mann, and A. McCallum. Learning from labeled features using generalized expectation criteria. In *Proceedings of the 31st annual international ACM SIGIR conference on Research and development in information retrieval*, pages 595–602. ACM, 2008.

[9] R. P. Ebstein, O. Novick, R. Umansky, B. Priel, Y. Osher, D. Blaine, E. R. Bennett, L. Nemanov, M. Katz, and R. H. Belmaker. Dopamine d4 receptor (d4dr) exon iii polymorphism associated with the human personality trait of novelty seeking. *Nature genetics*, 12(1):78–80, 1996.

[10] M. Ester, H.-P. Kriegel, J. Sander, and X. Xu. A density-based algorithm for discovering clusters in large spatial databases with noise. In *Kdd*, volume 96, pages 226–231, 1996.

[11] R. Feng et al. Temporal destination revisit intention: The effects of novelty seeking and satisfaction. *Tourism management*, 28(2):580–590, 2007.

[12] D. W. Fiske and S. R. Maddi. Functions of varied experience. 1961.

[13] M. Givon. Variety seeking through brand switching. *Marketing Science*, 3(1):1–22, 1984.

[14] J. Hauser, G. J. Tellis, and A. Griffin. Research on innovation: A review and agenda for marketing science. *Marketing science*, 25(6):687–717, 2006.

[15] N. Hurley and M. Zhang. Novelty and diversity in top-n recommendation–analysis and evaluation. *ACM Transactions on Internet Technology (TOIT)*, 10(4):14, 2011.

[16] P. Jensen. Network-based predictions of retail store commercial categories and optimal locations. *Physical Review E*, 74(3):035101, 2006.

[17] J. Kivela and J. C. Crotts. Tourism and gastronomy: Gastronomy's influence on how tourists experience a destination. *Journal of Hospitality & Tourism Research*, 30(3):354–377, 2006.

[18] J. Kivela, R. Inbakaran, and J. Reece. Consumer research in the restaurant environment, part 1: A conceptual model of dining satisfaction and return patronage. *International Journal of Contemporary Hospitality Management*, 11(5):205–222, 1999.

[19] J. J. Kivelä and C. Y. H. Chu. Delivering quality service: Diagnosing favorable and unfavorable service encounters in restaurants. *Journal of Hospitality & Tourism Research*, 25(3):251–271, 2001.

[20] T. G. Kolda and B. W. Bader. Tensor decompositions and applications. *SIAM review*, 51(3):455–500, 2009.

[21] J. Lafferty, A. McCallum, and F. C. Pereira. Conditional random fields: Probabilistic models for segmenting and labeling sequence data. 2001.

[22] J. Lahti, K. Räikkönen, J. Ekelund, L. Peltonen, O. T. Raitakari, and L. Keltikangas-Järvinen. Socio-demographic characteristics moderate the association between drd4 and novelty seeking. *Personality and Individual Differences*, 40(3):533–543, 2006.

[23] M. Leyton, I. Boileau, C. Benkelfat, M. Diksic, G. Baker, and A. Dagher. Amphetamine-induced increases in extracellular dopamine, drug wanting, and novelty seeking: a pet/[11c] r-aclopride study in healthy men. *Neuropsychopharmacology*, 27(6):1027–1035, 2002.

[24] H. Mamitsuka. Predicting peptides that bind to mhc molecules using supervised learning of hidden markov models. *Proteins Structure Function and Genetics*, 33(4):460–474, 1998.

[25] G. S. Mann and A. McCallum. Generalized expectation criteria for semi-supervised learning of conditional random fields. 2008.

[26] S. M. McNee, J. Riedl, and J. A. Konstan. Being accurate is not enough: how accuracy metrics have hurt recommender systems. In *CHI'06 extended abstracts on Human factors in computing systems*, pages 1097–1101. ACM, 2006.

[27] M. Miele and J. Murdoch. The practical aesthetics of traditional cuisines: slow food in tuscany. *Sociologia Ruralis*, 42(4):312–328, 2002.

[28] J. Oh, S. Park, H. Yu, M. Song, and S.-T. Park. Novel recommendation based on personal popularity tendency. In *2013 IEEE 13th International Conference on Data Mining*, pages 507–516. IEEE, 2011.

[29] A. Pizam, G.-H. Jeong, A. Reichel, H. van Boemmel, J. M. Lusson, L. Steynberg, S. Volo, C. Kroesbacher, J. Kucerova, N. Montmany, et al. The relationship between risk-taking, sensation-seeking, and the tourist behavior of young adults: A cross-cultural study. *Journal of Travel Research*, 42(3):251–260, 2004.

[30] G. V. Rebec, J. R. Christensen, C. Guerra, and M. T. Bardo. Regional and temporal differences in real-time dopamine efflux in the nucleus accumbens during free-choice novelty. *Brain research*, 776(1):61–67, 1997.

[31] B. Roark, M. Saraclar, M. Collins, and M. Johnson. Discriminative language modeling with conditional random fields and the perceptron algorithm. In *Proceedings of the 42nd Annual Meeting on Association for Computational Linguistics*, page 47. Association for Computational Linguistics, 2004.

[32] T. Scheffler, R. Schirru, and P. Lehmann. Matching points of interest from different social networking sites. In *KI 2012: Advances in Artificial Intelligence*, pages 245–248. Springer, 2012.

[33] B. W. Silverman. *Density estimation for statistics and data analysis*, volume 26. CRC press, 1986.

[34] C. Song, T. Koren, P. Wang, and A.-L. Barabási. Modelling the scaling properties of human mobility. *Nature Physics*, 6(10):818–823, 2010.

[35] C. Song, Z. Qu, N. Blumm, and A.-L. Barabási. Limits of predictability in human mobility. *Science*, 327(5968):1018–1021, 2010.

[36] L. Song, D. Kotz, R. Jain, and X. He. Evaluating location predictors with extensive wi-fi mobility data. In *INFOCOM 2004. Twenty-third AnnualJoint Conference of the IEEE Computer and Communications Societies*, volume 2, pages 1414–1424. IEEE, 2004.

[37] P. A. Weaver, K. W. McCleary, L. Lapisto, and L. T. Damonte. The relationship of destination selection attributes to psychological, behavioral and demographic variables. *Journal of Hospitality & Leisure Marketing*, 2(2):93–109, 1994.

[38] M. Ye, P. Yin, and W.-C. Lee. Location recommendation for location-based social networks. In *Proceedings of the 18th SIGSPATIAL International Conference on Advances in Geographic Information Systems*, pages 458–461. ACM, 2010.

[39] J. Yuan, Y. Zheng, C. Zhang, W. Xie, X. Xie, G. Sun, and Y. Huang. T-drive: driving directions based on taxi trajectories. In *Proceedings of the 18th SIGSPATIAL International conference on advances in geographic information systems*, pages 99–108. ACM, 2010.

[40] N. J. Yuan, Y. Wang, F. Zhang, X. Xie, and G. Sun. Reconstructing individual mobility from smart card transactions: A space alignment approach. In *Data Mining (ICDM), 2013 IEEE 13th International Conference on*, pages 877–886. IEEE, 2013.

[41] N. J. Yuan, F. Zhang, D. Lian, K. Zheng, S. Yu, and X. Xie. We know how you live: exploring the spectrum of urban lifestyles. In *Proceedings of the first ACM conference on Online social networks*, pages 3–14. ACM, 2013.

[42] F. Zhang, D. Wilkie, Y. Zheng, and X. Xie. Sensing the pulse of urban refueling behavior. In *Proceedings of the 2013 ACM international joint conference on Pervasive and ubiquitous computing*, pages 13–22. ACM, 2013.

[43] F. Zhang, N. J. Yuan, D. Lian, and X. Xie. Mining novelty-seeking trait across heterogeneous domains. In *Proceedings of the 23rd international conference on World wide web*, pages 373–384. International World Wide Web Conferences Steering Committee, 2014.

[44] M. Zhang and N. Hurley. Novel item recommendation by user profile partitioning. In *Proceedings of the 2009 IEEE/WIC/ACM International Joint Conference on Web Intelligence and Intelligent Agent Technology-Volume 01*, pages 508–515. IEEE Computer Society, 2009.

[45] T. Zhang. Solving large scale linear prediction problems using stochastic gradient descent algorithms. In *Proceedings of the twenty-first international conference on Machine learning*, page 116. ACM, 2004.

[46] Y. Zhang, J. Callan, and T. Minka. Novelty and redundancy detection in adaptive filtering. In *Proceedings of the 25th annual international ACM SIGIR conference on Research and development in information retrieval*, pages 81–88. ACM, 2002.

[47] V. W. Zheng, Y. Zheng, X. Xie, and Q. Yang. Collaborative location and activity recommendations with gps history data. In *Proceedings of the 19th international conference on World wide web*, pages 1029–1038. ACM, 2010.

[48] T. Zhou, Z. Kuscsik, J.-G. Liu, M. Medo, J. R. Wakeling, and Y.-C. Zhang. Solving the apparent diversity-accuracy dilemma of recommender systems. *Proceedings of the National Academy of Sciences*, 107(10):4511–4515, 2010.

Daily-Aware Personalized Recommendation based on Feature-Level Time Series Analysis

Yongfeng Zhang[†‡],Min Zhang[†],Yi Zhang[‡],Guokun Lai[†],Yiqun Liu[†],Honghui Zhang[†],Shaoping Ma[†]
[†]State Key Laboratory of Intelligent Technology and Systems, Dept. of CS, Tsinghua University, China
[†]Tsinghua National Laboratory for Information Science and Technology (TNList)
[‡]School of Engineering, University of California, Santa Cruz, CA 95060, USA
yongfeng14@mails.tsinghua.edu.cn, z-m@tsinghua.edu.cn, yiz@soe.ucsc.edu
{laiguokun,zhhthu11}@gmail.com, {yiqunliu,msp}@tsinghua.edu.cn

ABSTRACT

The frequently changing user preferences and/or item profiles have put essential importance on the dynamic modeling of users and items in personalized recommender systems.

However, due to the insufficiency of per user/item records when splitting the already sparse data across time dimension, previous methods have to restrict the drifting purchasing patterns to pre-assumed distributions, and were hardly able to model them rather directly with, for example, time series analysis. Integrating content information helps to alleviate the problem in practical systems, but the domain-dependent content knowledge is expensive to obtain due to the large amount of manual efforts.

In this paper, we make use of the large volume of textual reviews for the automatic extraction of domain knowledge, namely, the explicit features/aspects in a specific product domain. We thus degrade the product-level modeling of user preferences, which suffers from the lack of data, to the feature-level modeling, which not only grants us the ability to predict user preferences through direct time series analysis, but also allows us to know the essence under the surface of product-level changes in purchasing patterns. Besides, the expanded feature space also helps to make cold-start recommendations for users with few purchasing records.

Technically, we develop the Fourier-assisted Auto-Regressive Integrated Moving Average (FARIMA) process to tackle with the year-long seasonal period of purchasing data to achieve daily-aware preference predictions, and we leverage the conditional opportunity models for daily-aware personalized recommendation. Extensive experimental results on real-world cosmetic purchasing data from a major e-commerce website (JD.com) in China verified both the effectiveness and efficiency of our approach.

Categories and Subject Descriptors

H.3.3 [**Information Search and Retrieval**]: Information Filtering; G.3 [**Mathematics of Computing**]: Probability and Statistic - *Time Series Analysis*

Keywords

Recommender Systems; Time Series Analysis; Collaborative Filtering; Sentiment Analysis

WWW 2015, May 18–22, 2015, Florence, Italy.
ACM 978-1-4503-3469-3/15/05.
http://dx.doi.org/10.1145/2736277.2741087.

1. INTRODUCTION

The vast amount of online products in various e-commerce websites make it an essential task to develop reliable Personalized Recommender Systems (PRS) [24]. One of the most extensively investigated approaches for personalized recommendation is to model user preferences according to his/her historical choices, as well as those of the others', leading to the success of Collaborative Filtering (CF) techniques [27].

However, both user preferences and item profiles may change dynamically over time [16, 34, 11], thus treating the historical decisions of a user or the received comments of an item as static, fixed, or long-term influential information sources can be infeasible in real-world applications. In the product domain of cosmetics for temperate area users, for example, one may buy a sun cream product in summer when the UV radiation is strong, while purchase nourishing creams in winter when it is cold and dry, as exposited in Fig.1. If the system simply treats the user's historical purchasing records as a whole without dynamic modeling of his/her preference, then the user may receive sun cream recommendations frequently in the cold winter, and vise versa. Similarly, an item can receive new reviews from users continuously in practical systems, which makes its profile drift dynamically over time, as a result, it would be unwise for the system to recommend items that no longer fit the user needs any more.

The dynamic nature of users and items requires the ability of time-dependent modeling in recommender systems. Researchers have been putting efforts to capture this nature and integrate time factors into the recommendation process, giving rise to the research of time-aware recommendation [5], which is also generally categorized into the research topic of Context-Aware Recommender Systems (CARS) [1].

The most early approaches for time-aware recommendation mainly focus on the dynamic modeling of user and item profiles [6, 2, 9]. However, recommendation based merely on content profiles may lack the ability to take advantage of the wisdom of crowds, which is proved effective in many CF approaches. This leads to two concurrent research lines. Koren [16] and Xiang [34] adopted the approaches of dynamic modeling through time bins on explicit feedbacks, and sessions on implicit feedbacks, respectively, which were further combined by Dror [11] into Yahoo! Music recommendation and achieved superior results in KddCup-2011; At the same time, Lu [19] and Shi [25], as well as Karatzoglou [15] and Gantner [13] adopted matrix/tensor factorization to model time as context information. Recently, Wang [32, 31] investigated users' subsequent purchasing behavior with opportunity models for recommendation.

However, both the profile-based and the dynamic modeling approaches attempt to model user preferences in the produce space according to user purchasing and rating histories, which suffer from the problem of data sparsity due to the fact that a single user may be only related to a small number of products, compared with the vast amount of products in a system [32]. As a result, many of the current approaches have to assume pre-defined distributions over time and conduct parameter estimation thereon for purchasing prediction. It is shown that considering content information, such as popularity, product names and categories, helps to alleviate the problem [9], but such information is either difficult to obtain and structure, or expensive for manual generation.

Fortunately, the increasing availability of textual user reviews and the ever developing text summarization and sentiment analysis techniques have made it possible to take advantage of this important information source besides numerical ratings [38]. In this work, we extract and summarize the domain knowledge (i.e., domain-specific product features like *anti-UV* or *nutrition* for cosmetics) automatically from the textual user reviews, and conduct feature-level dynamic modeling to capture the drifting user preferences and item profiles, thus to avoid the lack of data in previous product-level modeling approaches. This allows us to conduct direct time series analysis to predict the importance of each feature and to provide pre-time favoured recommendations. More importantly, by analyzing the seasonal, cyclic and trend factors of different features, we are able to understand in detail how users' preferences change over time.

In order for rapid track of the fashion and provide timely recommendation, we choose to model and predict the time series in daily resolution. This leads to nearly year-long period (up to 365) time series, making them difficult to model with standard Auto-Regressive Integrated Moving Average (ARIMA) process due to expensive computational costs. As a result, we develop the Fourier-assisted ARIMA (FARIMA) process that leverages Fourier terms to model the seasonal patterns and short-term ARIMA process to model the error. Based on the product features that have been predicted of different importances, we further adapt the conditional opportunity model for daily-aware recommendation. We conduct extensive experiments to exposit both the intuition of how user preferences drift over time in e-commerce, and the superior performance of our proposed method.

The following of the paper is organized as follows: we review the related work in Section 2, and provide the preliminary studies of time series for e-commerce in Section 3; we propose our model for daily-aware time series prediction and personalized recommendation in Section 4 and Section 5, respectively; in Section 6, we present the experimental results from different aspects on real-world purchasing dataset; and we conclude the work in Section 7.

2. RELATED WORK

With the ability to help discover items of potential interests, Personalized Recommender Systems (PRS) [24] have been widely integrated into many online applications, such as e-commerce, social networks, and online review services. Early systems for personalized recommendation rely on content-based approaches [21], which make recommendations by analyzing the item features or user demographics. Recently, the Collaborative Filtering (CF) [27] based approaches have gained great popularity due to their free from human efforts,

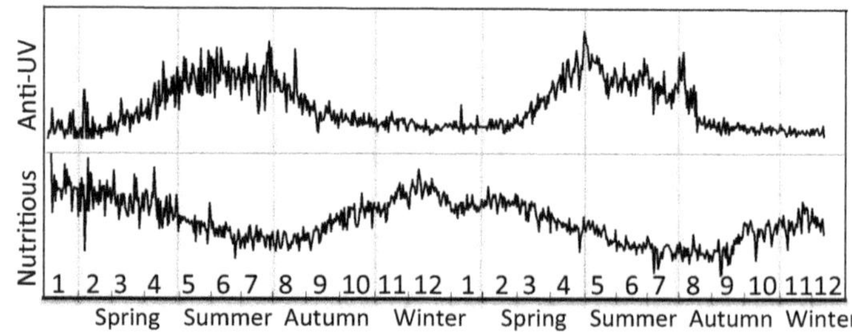

Figure 1: The frequency of two product features (Anti-UV and Nutritious) in user reviews over two consecutive years. The data is from JD.com, a major e-commerce website in China. One can see that Anti-UV seasonally prospers in summer, while Nutritious seasonally prospers in winter.

superior performance, and the ability to take advantage of the wisdom of crowds.

In real-world systems, however, it is usually observed that both user preferences and item profiles may dynamically drift over time [5], thus a static modeling of users/items that treats the historical purchases or reviews as fixed and long-term effective may be inappropriate to track users' interests. For example, a user may be less likely to buy an anti-UV suncream in winter, although she may well have bought one in summer; and a user who has purchased an SLR camera may not buy another one in a reasonably long period. As a result, the ability of time-aware modeling is of essential importance to practical systems [5].

In the early stage of the research on time-aware recommendation, researchers attempted to construct dynamic user or item profiles. Chen et al. [6] constructed a system that discovers, stores and updates private dynamic user profiles for personalized content recommendation; Baltrunas and Amatriain [2] proposed micro-profiling, which splits a user profile into several sub-profiles of different contexts; Chu and Park [9] combined both user and item profiles in a dynamic bilinear model for time-aware recommendation. A review of various user/item profiling techniques is provided in [14].

However, the profiling approaches usually require the presence of specific domain knowledge, which is usually expensive to obtain. Besides, it is difficult for them to leverage the wisdom of crowds. This drives researchers to investigate the CF approaches for time-aware recommendation.

Oku [20] and Yuan [37] integrated time factors into the similarity calculation of neighbour-hood based methods for time-aware CF; Koren [16] proposed timeSVD++ for dynamic CF with factor models by tracking the drifting user/item biases across different time bins; Xiang et al. [34] further extended the dynamic modeling to implicit feedback through random walk on sessions-based temporal graphs; Lu [19] and Shi [25] adapted the famous Matrix Factorization (MF) [28] approaches for time-aware CF, while Karatzoglou [15] and Gantner [13] leveraged tensor factorization to integrate the many contextual features. The topic modeling approaches are also investigated by Chen [7] and Vaca [30], while recently, Wang et al. [32, 31] borrowed the opportunity models from survival analysis to predict users' subsequent purchases for time-aware recommendation.

However, current approaches model the time-dependent user preferences in the product space directly, which suffers from the problem of data sparsity because a single user is usually related to only a small number of products compared with the huge product space in a system. Incorporating content information like product categories helps to build more accurate models [1, 9, 32], but such information is either absent in practical applications or difficult to generate and structure manually.

Fortunately, the ever developing phrase-level sentiment analysis techniques [18, 10, 36, 29] have made it possible to extract, summarize and structure the rich product features and user preferences automatically from free-text reviews, and have begun to be leveraged for personalized recommendation tasks [38, 33]. This also sheds light on the feature-level dynamic modeling for recommendation. Compared with product-level modeling, feature-level modeling is finer-grained because a user who made only a single review may well have commented on several product features. Besides, by investigating into the detailed features, we can obtain an intuitional understanding of how and why the user purchasing behaviors drift over time.

We adopt Time Series Analysis (TSA) [3, 26] for daily prediction of the trend of product features. Time series analysis has long been used in many scientific data analysis tasks, such as econometrics, bioinformatics, physics, and astronomy [26]. Recently, it has also begun to be applied to data mining tasks, such as epidemic prediction [35], and economic indicators prediction in Google Trends [8]. However, to the best of our knowledge, it has not been investigated in personalized recommendation tasks, perhaps because of the lack of per-user purchasing data as mentioned above. Nevertheless, as we will exposit in the following, the information-rich textual reviews have made such analysis practical in real-world systems, which helps not only in time-aware recommendation, but also a better understanding of user behaviors.

3. TIME SERIES IN E-COMMERCE

Before introducing the models for daily-aware recommendation, we execute an initial study of the time series in e-commerce to exposit the intuition. The data is from JD.com, a major e-commerce website in China, and the data consists of 5,524,491 reviews from 1,844,569 users towards 53,188 products since Jan. 1st, 2011 to Mar. 31st, 2014. We introduce the automatic extraction of product features from free-text reviews fist, and then focus on the trend, seasonal, cyclic and random effects of feature-level time series.

3.1 Product Feature Extraction

We extract a set of product features $\mathcal{F} = \{f_1, f_2, \cdots, f_r\}$ based on a review corpus from a product domain, *e.g.*, cosmetic products. We leverage the state-of-the-art phrase-level sentiment analysis techniques described in [18, 39, 22]. Generally, we adopt the Stanford Parser[1] to conduct part-of-speech tagging, morphological analysis and grammatical analysis on each of the reviews to construct the corresponding dependency tree, and then retain those Noun Phrases (NP) whose frequency are above a specific threshold as feature candidates. The candidates are further pruned by Pointwise Mutual Information (PMI) [22] to form the final feature set of this domain. In cosmetics for example, the extracted features include *anti-UV*, *nutritious*, *price*, *feeling*, etc. These features serve as the feature space in the following part of time series analysis, prediction, and personalized recommendation.

[1] http://nlp.stanford.edu/software/lex-parser.shtml

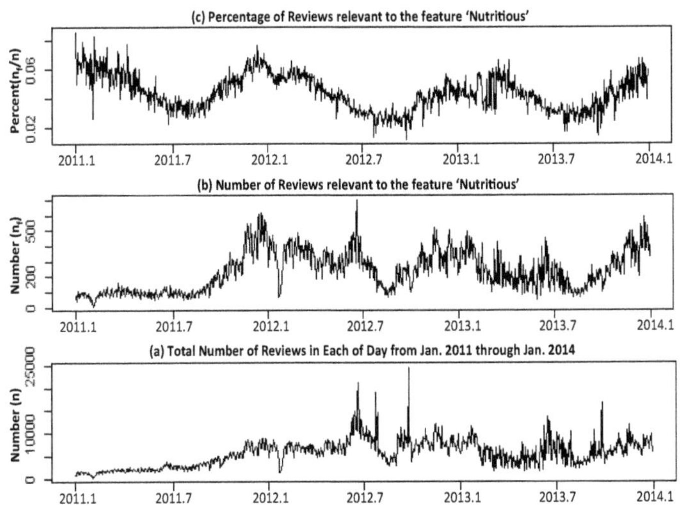

Figure 2: Three daily time series of the feature 'Nutritious': (a) The total number of reviews per day $N(t)$; (b) The number of reviews where 'Nutritious' is commented on per day $N_f(t)$; (c) The percentage of reviews $X_f(t) = N_f(t)/N(t)$ per day where 'Nutritious' is commented on.

The process of feature word extraction is fully automatic and requires no human efforts. Since the process is not the focus of this work, we refer the readers to the related literature [18, 39, 22] for more details. The quality evaluation of the extracted features will be reported in the experiments.

3.2 Feature-level Time Series

In this section, we investigate three candidate daily time series for each feature f to determine the appropriate one for dynamic user preference modeling and time-aware recommendation, as exampled in Fig.2 for the feature *nutritious*.

We first plot the total number of reviews per day $N(t)$ in Fig.2(a). This time series is an indicator of the total purchasing volume in the system, which is independent from a specific user, product or feature. After careful examination, we find that the peaks in $N(t)$ correspond to the online sales promotional campaigns carried out by the website. For example, on Oct. 1st in the year of 2012 and 2013, the website conducted sales promotion to celebrate the National Day.

As we aim to investigate the different time series patterns of different features, we further plot the number of reviews $N_f(t)$ per day where the target feature f is commented on, as shown in Fig.2(b). We expect to discover regular seasonal or cyclic patterns from the series, because the features tend to gain different degrees of attention over time. Unfortunately, this set of time series do not exhibit clear seasonal or cyclic patterns. Generally, they exhibit similar trends with the total number of reviews $N(t)$. The reason could be the magnitude-level difference between the total number of reviews and the number of reviews relevant to a feature, which diminishes the fluctuation of per-feature series.

This observation further inspires us to investigate the percentage of reviews relevant to each feature, which we denote as *percentage time series* $X_f(t) = N_f(t)/N(t)$, shown in Fig.2(c). As expected, the percentage time series exhibit explicit seasonal and cyclic patterns over three consecutive years on the feature *nutritious*.

3.3 Validating Percentage Time Series

To validate the seasonal effect of all product features on average rather than *nutritious* alone, we conduct time series decomposition on the percentage time series $X_f(t)$ for each of the r features $f \in \mathcal{F} = \{f_1, f_2, \cdots, f_r\}$. Without loss of generality, we use $X(t)$ to denote the time series of an arbitrary feature. In line with the literature [3, 26], we decompose a time series $X(t)$ into three components in an additive manner, which are trend-cycle $T(t)$, seasonal component $S(t)$, and random effect $R(t)$:

$$X(t) = T(t) + S(t) + R(t) \tag{1}$$

The trend-cyclic component $T(t)$ captures long-term increase or decrease in the data, as well as the rises and falls that are not of fixed period, and it is reconstructed with the Moving Average (MA) [3] process:

$$T(t) = \frac{1}{2s+1} \sum_{j=-s}^{s} X(t+j) \tag{2}$$

The seasonal component $S(t)$ captures the fixed period influence of seasonal factors like quarter, month, or day of a week, and it is estimated by averaging the difference values $X(t) - T(t) = S(t) + R(t)$ for a year over the (three) years provided in the data set. This is because the seasonal variation is by definition constant from one year to the next, and the white noise residual $R(t)$ can be averaged out.

Finally, the random effect $R(t) = X(t) - T(t) - S(t)$ is constructed by substracting trend-cyclic and seasonal effects from the time series.

Fig.3 shows the decomposition for the percentage time series of *nutritious*, where the scale used for moving average is half a year ($s = 182$ in Eq.(2)). The trend-cyclic component indicates that the overall attention towards the feature *nutritious* decreases first and then rises, while the seasonal component presents a clear and regular seasonal fluctuation over years. The amplitudes of the seasonal signal over years turn approximately equal when the trend basis is removed.

The seasonal component $S(t)$ comprises the major part of energy in the time series, and this is of key importance in the following part of time series estimation and prediction. As a result, we fit the seasonal component of each feature f by a simple one-order Fourier series with a fixed period $m = 365$ to investigate the seasonality of the features:

$$S(t) \approx \hat{S}(t) = a + A \sin\left(\frac{2\pi t}{m} + \varphi\right) \tag{3}$$

We estimate the parameters by minimizing the Akaike Information Criterion corrected (AICc) [4], which is a corrected version of AIC for finite size samples, and has long been used as a measure of the relative quality of a statistical model for a given set of data in time series analysis:

$$\text{AICc} = \underbrace{2k + n \ln\left(\frac{1}{n}\sum_{t=1}^{n}\left(S(t) - \hat{S}(t)\right)^2\right)}_{\text{AIC}} + \frac{2k(k+1)}{n-k-1} \tag{4}$$

where k is the number of parameters, and n is the total number of data instances. Here we set $k = 3$ because we use a simple one-order Fourier series with three parameters.

For the seasonal series $S_f(t)$ of each feature f, we calculate the percentage of energy that a simple one-order Fourier can capture from the total amount of energy therein, which is:

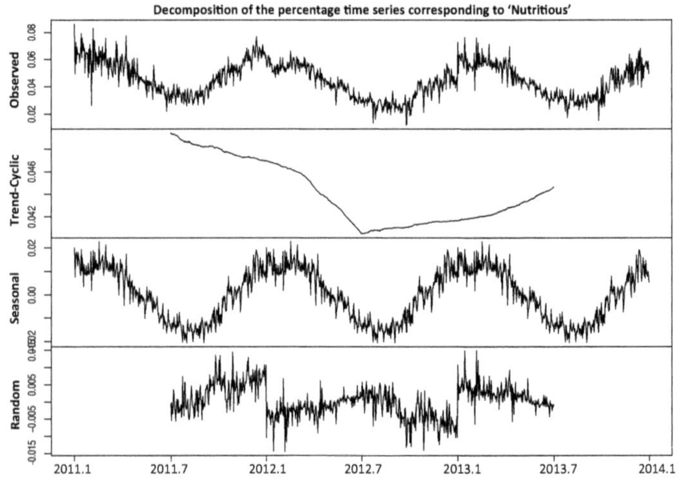

Figure 3: Decomposition of the percentage time series. From top to bottom are the original observed series, trend-cyclic component, seasonal component, and the random effect, respectively.

$$p_f = \sum_{t=1}^{n} |\hat{S}_f(t)|^2 \Big/ \sum_{t=1}^{n} |S_f(t)|^2 \tag{5}$$

According to Parseval's theorem, a full-order Fourier transformation from time domain to frequency domain will preserve the energy, namely, $p_f = 1$, while $p_f < 1$ for an under-ordered Fourier due to the loss of information. In this study, we retain $r = 58$ features primarily by selecting the feature set with the highest F_1-score, which will be exposited with more detail in the experiments. The distribution of p_f for the 58 features in $\mathcal{F}$ is shown in Table 1.

Table 1: Statistical distribution of p_f of the features.

p_f	$0.7 \sim 0.8$	$0.8 \sim 0.9$	$0.9 \sim 1.0$
#Features	7	35	16
Percent(%)	12.1	60.3	27.6

We find that a simple one-order fixed-period Fourier is able to preserve more than 70% of the energy, and 87.9% of the features even got 80% or more energy preserved. The minimum and maximum p_f among the features are 0.753 and 0.966, respectively, and the average is 0.874.

The decomposation analysis above indicates that the percentage time series is capable of capturing the trend, cyclic, seasonal and random effects of a feature over time, and the decomposed seasonal component can be easily modeled with Fourier terms, which serves as an important basis for model estimation and prediction in the following. We thus adopt the percentage time series of each feature f primarily to investigate the feature-level dynamic preference of the users.

4. DAILY-AWARE TIME SERIES ANALYSIS

In this section, we present our model for daily-aware time series prediction. The Auto-Regressive Integrated Moving Average (ARIMA) process is widely adopted for monthly or yearly time series analysis, however, the year-long period (around 365) of daily time series makes the ARIMA models infeasible in practice due to the huge computational cost. To address the problem, we adopt Fourier series to capture the seasonal effect in daily time series, and further leverage ARIMA process to model the residuals, which gives the Fourier-assisted ARIMA (FARIMA) model.

In the following, we briefly introduce the primary time series analysis (ARIMA) model first, and then integrate Fourier series into ARIMA to derive our FARIMA model.

4.1 Primary Time Series Analysis

The ARMA(p, q) process models a time series $X(t)$ with p Auto-Regressive (AR) terms and q Moving Average (MA) terms, which is given by:

$$\begin{aligned} X(t) &= \alpha_1 X(t-1) + \cdots + \alpha_p X(t-p) \\ &+ Z(t) + \beta_1 Z(t-1) + \cdots + \beta_q Z(t-q) \end{aligned} \tag{6}$$

where $Z(t) \overset{iid}{\sim} \Phi(0, \sigma^2)$ is independently identically sampled from a normal distribution with zero mean.

A simple example would be $X(t) \sim$ ARMA$(1, 0)$, which is $X(t) = \alpha_1 X(t-1) + Z(t)$ that models the next data point as the previous one plus a white noise.

The successful application of ARMA(p, q) process requires the time series $X(t)$ be *stationary*, namely, for any positive integer $k \geq 1$ and any integer τ, the two discrete processes:

$$\begin{aligned} &\{X(t_1), X(t_2), \cdots, X(t_k)\}, \text{and} \\ &\{X(t_1+\tau), X(t_2+\tau), \cdots, X(t_k+\tau)\} \end{aligned} \tag{7}$$

have the same point distribution:

$$F_{t_1, t_2, \cdots, t_k}(X_1, X_2, \cdots, X_k) = P(X(t_1) < X_1, \cdots, X(t_k) < X_k) \tag{8}$$

Unfortunately, many time series in practice do not hold the stationary property, however, the d-order difference time series $W(t) \doteq \nabla^d X(t)$ may be stationary, where 1-order difference series is $\nabla X(t) = X(t) - X(t-1)$, and higher-order differences are iteratively defined as $\nabla^d X(t) = \nabla(\nabla^{d-1} X(t))$.

When $W(t) \doteq \nabla^d X(t)$ is modeled by an ARMA(p, q) process in Eq.(6), we denote $X(t)$ as modeled by an ARIMA(p, d, q) process.

4.2 Fourier-assisted ARIMA Model

The prediction of a future data instance in ARIMA(p, d, q) process requires to borrow information from those instances of at least a period ago to model the seasonal and cyclic effect in data fluctuation, which means that the number of parameters (especially the value of p) should be at least comparable to the period of the time series.

This is fine when processing monthly, quarterly, or yearly series because the periods (and thus the number of parameters) are small, which are usually 12 for monthly data and 4 for quarterly data. However, the approximate period of 365 of daily series makes it impractical for model estimation in ARIMA. Fortunately, the results on energy analysis in the previous section make it possible for us to leverage Fourier series to enhance ARIMA models on daily time series.

To do so, we use Fourier terms to model the seasonal pattern while using short-term ARIMA time series for the dynamic error, which is given by:

$$\begin{aligned} X(t) \approx & \underbrace{a + \sum_{k=1}^{K} \left[\alpha_k \sin\left(\frac{2\pi kt}{m}\right) + \beta_k \cos\left(\frac{2\pi kt}{m}\right)\right]}_{F(t)} \\ & + \underbrace{\text{ARIMA}(p, d, q)(t)}_{E(t)} \doteq \hat{X}(t) = F(t) + E(t) \end{aligned} \tag{9}$$

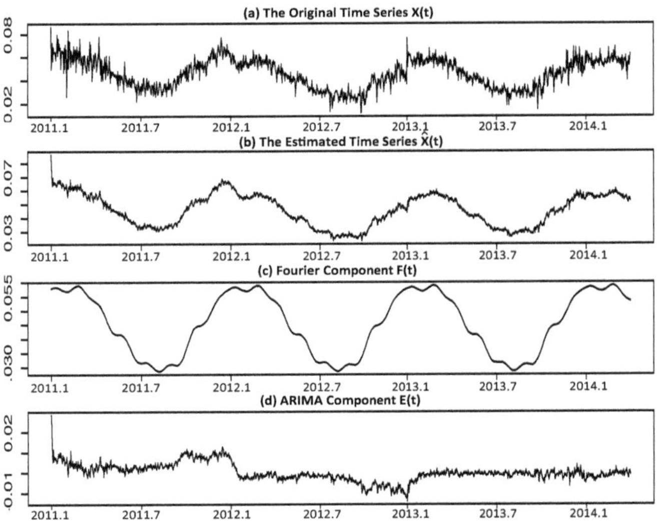

Figure 4: Fourier-assisted ARIMA estimation of a time series. (a) The original series $X(t)$; (b) The estimated series $\hat{X}(t) = F(t) + E(t)$; (c) The Fourier component $F(t)$; (d) The ARIMA component $E(t)$.

where $m = 365$ is the period, $F(t)$ is a K-order Fourier, and $E(t)$ is an ARIMA process that models the error of a Fourier approximation. The intuition here is that the annual seasonal shape is unchanged from year to year, so that Fourier terms can be used to model the annual seasonality, while the period of the residual series is reduced from $m = 365$ so that it can be modeled with a low-order ARIMA. This is shown in Fig.4, where the Fourier component $F(t)$ and ARIMA component $E(t)$ add up to the estimated series $\hat{X}(t)$.

The order of Fourier component K and ARIMA component (p, d, q) can be determined by minimizing the AICc, as shown by the procedure in Algorithm 1. The subroutines Fourier and Arima fit the given time series with the specified orders by minimizing the AICc, and return the fitted series together with the corresponding AICc value achieved. In this work, we choose the Fourier and Arima routines from the R language[2] in practical implementation.

5. DAILY-AWARE RECOMMENDATION

In this section, we leverage the predicted global preference (i.e., percentage time series) and the personal user/item preferences for daily-aware personalized recommendation. Table 2 lists the notations adopted for easy reference.

5.1 Feature Space Representation

The predicted percentage time series $\hat{X}_f(t)$ for each feature f is an indicator of the potential degree that users care about feature f at the given time t, which serve as the global preference of the users. There are many approaches in practice to describe the global preference of users towards the features based on the results of time series prediction. In this work, however, we adopt the approach of integrating $\hat{X}_f(t)$ into a vector of covariates directly to keep the simplicity, and also to fit with the conditional opportunity model in the following subsection. More precisely, we construct the *global covariate vector*:

$$\mathbf{x}^g(t) = [x_1^g(t), x_2^g(t), \cdots, x_r^g(t)]^{\mathrm{T}} \tag{10}$$

[2] http://www.r-project.org/

where the $k^{th}(1 \leq k \leq r)$ element $x_k^g(t) = \frac{1}{1+\exp(-\hat{X}_{f_k}(t))}$ is the sigmoid normalization of $\hat{X}_{f_k}(t)$ for feature $f_k \in \mathcal{F}$.

Besides, different users may concern about different features, and to profile a user u in the feature space, we consider all the historical reviews of the user. Suppose the kth feature f_k is mentioned for $w_k^u(t)$ times by user u, then we profile this user as a *user covariate vector*:

$$\mathbf{x}^u(t) = [x_1^u(t), x_2^u(t), \cdots, x_r^u(t)]^{\mathrm{T}} \tag{11}$$

where $x_k^u(t) = \frac{1}{1+\exp(-w_k^u(t))}$ is the normalization of $w_k^u(t)$.

Similarly, we profile an item as an *item covariate vector* according to its corresponding reviews:

$$\mathbf{x}^i(t) = [x_1^i(t), x_2^i(t), \cdots, x_r^i(t)]^{\mathrm{T}} \tag{12}$$

where $x_k^i(t) = \frac{1}{1+\exp(-w_k^i(t))}$, and item i is commented for $w_k^i(t)$ times on feature f_k.

Finally, we construct the covariate vector $\mathbf{x}(t)$ for user-item pair (u, i) by integrating the global preference $\mathbf{x}^g(t)$, personal user preference $\mathbf{x}^u(t)$, and item profile $\mathbf{x}^i(t)$:

$$\mathbf{x}(t) = \left[\mathbf{x}^g(t)^{\mathrm{T}}, \mathbf{x}^u(t)^{\mathrm{T}}, \mathbf{x}^i(t)^{\mathrm{T}}\right]^{\mathrm{T}} \tag{13}$$

In practical applications, our framework is flexible to integrate other available information into the covariate vector for model learning and prediction. Such information could be both user related (*e.g.* demographics), item related (*e.g.* content information), or even global factors.

5.2 Conditional Opportunity Model

To leverage the covariate vectors for prediction and recommendation in continuous rating scale, we adapt the conditional opportunity model used for follow-up purchase prediction in [32]. The probability density function of numerical rating y is modeled with a standard Weibull distribution:

$$p(y) = \gamma \lambda y^{\gamma-1} \exp(-\lambda y^{\gamma}) \tag{14}$$

Given the covariate vector $\mathbf{x}(t)$, we re-parameterize the scale parameter $\lambda = \exp(\boldsymbol{\theta}^{\mathrm{T}}\mathbf{x}(t))$ based on the regression parameter $\boldsymbol{\theta}$ and the covariates $\mathbf{x}(t)$ in the following opportunity model:

$$p(y) = \gamma \exp\left(\boldsymbol{\theta}^{\mathrm{T}}\mathbf{x}(t)\right) y^{\gamma-1} \exp\left(-\exp\left(\boldsymbol{\theta}^{\mathrm{T}}\mathbf{x}(t)\right) y^{\gamma}\right) \tag{15}$$

For each user u, we sample the regression parameter $\boldsymbol{\theta}_u$ from a Gaussian distribution $\boldsymbol{\theta}_u \sim \Phi(\boldsymbol{\mu}, \boldsymbol{\Sigma})$, and sample

Table 2: A summary of the notations used.

$\mathcal{F}$	$\mathcal{F} = \{f_1, f_2, \cdots, f_r\}$ is the product feature set
$\hat{X}_f(t)$	The value of the predicted percentage time series for feature f at time t
$\mathbf{x}(t)$	The integrated covariate vector that contains the global, user, and item covariates
λ, γ	Scale/shape parameter of Weibull distribution
$\boldsymbol{\theta}$	The regression parameter for covariate vectors
$\boldsymbol{\mu}, \boldsymbol{\Sigma}$	Gaussian distribution parameters for sampling $\boldsymbol{\theta}$
a, b	Gamma distribution parameters for sampling γ
ξ_u	$\xi_u = \{\boldsymbol{\theta}_u, \gamma_u\}$ is the hidden variables for a user u
D	$D = \{(y\|u, i, t)\}_{k=1}^n$ is a set of n data instances, where $(y\|u, i, t)$ is a data instance
y_u	$y_u = \{y_{u,1}, y_{u,2}, \cdots, y_{u,N_u}\}$ is the set of ratings in D rated by user u
$\hat{y}_{ui}(t)$	The predicted rating of user u to item i at time t

Algorithm 1: FARIMA$(X(t), m, \bar{K}, \bar{p}, \bar{d}, \bar{q})$

Input: Time series $X(t)$, Period $m = 365$,
Maximum possible order of Fourier: $\bar{K}$,
Maximum possible order of ARIMA: $\bar{p}, \bar{d}, \bar{q}$
Output: Fitted time series $\hat{X}(t)$

$minAICc \leftarrow \infty$; $\hat{F}(t)$;
for $K \leftarrow 1$ **to** $\bar{K}$ **do**
  $\{F(t), AICc\} \leftarrow$ FOURIER$(X(t), m, K)$;
  if $AICc < minAICc$ **then**
    $\hat{F}(t) \leftarrow F(t)$;
    $minAICc \leftarrow AICc$;
  end
end
$minAICc \leftarrow \infty$; $\hat{E}(t)$;
for (p, d, q) *in* $[0, \bar{p}] \times [0, \bar{d}] \times [0, \bar{q}]$ **do**
  $\{E(t), AICc\} \leftarrow$ARIMA$(X(t) - \hat{F}(t), p, d, q)$;
  if $AICc < minAICc$ **then**
    $\hat{E}(t) \leftarrow E(t)$;
    $minAICc \leftarrow AICc$;
  end
end
return $\hat{X}(t) \leftarrow \hat{F}(t) + \hat{E}(t)$;

the shape parameter γ_u from a Gamma distribution $\gamma_u \sim \Gamma(a, b)$. We use $D = \{(y|u, i, t)\}_{k=1}^n$ to denote a set of n user-item rating instances for model learning, where an instance $(y|u, i, t)$ means that user u rated item i with the rating y at time t. Based on this, we estimate the conditional probability of a single instance $(y|u, i, t)$ in the following conditional opportunity model:

$$\begin{aligned} & p(y|u, i, t) = p(y|\boldsymbol{\theta}_u, \gamma_u, \mathbf{x}(t)) \\ & = \gamma_u \exp\left(\boldsymbol{\theta}_u^{\mathrm{T}}\mathbf{x}(t)\right) y^{\gamma_u - 1} \exp\left(-\exp\left(\boldsymbol{\theta}_u^{\mathrm{T}}\mathbf{x}(t)\right) y^{\gamma_u}\right) \end{aligned} \tag{16}$$

Let $\phi = (\boldsymbol{\mu}, \boldsymbol{\Sigma}, a, b)$, and let $\xi_u = \{\boldsymbol{\theta}_u, \gamma_u\}$ be the hidden variables for user u; $y_u = \{y_{u,1}, y_{u,2}, \cdots, y_{u,N_u}\}$ be the ratings rated by user u, then the likelihood of the observations in D can be written as a function of ϕ:

$$p(D|\phi) = \prod_{u=1}^{|\mathcal{U}|} p(y_u|\phi) = \prod_{u=1}^{|\mathcal{U}|} \int p(\xi_u, y_u|\phi) d\xi_u \tag{17}$$

where $\mathcal{U}$ is the set of users in the system.

Maximizing the likelihood $p(D|\phi)$ is equivalent to maximizing the log-likelihood function $L(\phi) = \ln p(D|\phi)$. In this work, we adopt the same EM approach for model learning as in [32], which the reader may refer to for detailed derivation of the EM updating rules.

5.3 Rating Prediction and Recommendation

With the predicted covariate vector $\mathbf{x}(t)$ given by the FARIMA model, as well as the estimated regression parameters $\boldsymbol{\theta}_u$ and shape parameter γ_u for each user given by the conditional opportunity model, we make daily-aware rating prediction by selecting the y that maximizes the conditional probability $p(y|\boldsymbol{\theta}_u, \gamma_u, \mathbf{x}(t))$ in Eq.(16). The closed form solution can be easily found with the derivative of the Weibull distribution in Eq.(14):

$$p'(y) = \gamma \lambda y^{\gamma-2} \exp(-\lambda y^{\gamma})(\gamma - 1 - \lambda \gamma y^{\gamma}) \tag{18}$$

Table 3: **Cumulative statistical information in each quarter, where the statistics for a quarter represent the number of users, items and reviews in the system by the end of that quarter (included).**

Year	2011				2012				2013				2014
Quarter	Q_1	Q_2	Q_3	Q_4	Q_1	Q_2	Q_3	Q_4	Q_1	Q_2	Q_3	Q_4	Q_1
#Users	72,403	164,256	280,918	500,619	701,975	925,649	1,070,542	1,239,967	1,355,395	1,417,551	1,575,223	1,710,040	1,844,569
#Items	3,559	5,474	7,961	11,235	14,265	20,444	28,746	37,380	42,184	46,877	49,710	52,117	93,243
#Reviews	119,517	305,974	571,602	1,108,673	1,667,607	2,409,277	3,015,849	3,656,338	4,100,668	4,253,294	4,656,628	4,963,927	5,524,491

By setting $p'(y) = 0$ and $\lambda = \exp(\boldsymbol{\theta}_u^{\mathrm{T}}\mathbf{x}(t))$, the predicted rating for user u towards item i at time t will be:

$$\hat{y}_{ui}(t) = \left(\frac{\gamma_u - 1}{\gamma_u \exp(\boldsymbol{\theta}_u^{\mathrm{T}}\mathbf{x}(t))}\right)^{\frac{1}{\gamma_u}} \quad (19)$$

In practice, we construct the time-aware personalized recommendation list on daily resolution for user u by ranking the unreviewed items in descending order of the predicted ratings $\hat{y}_{ui}(t)$.

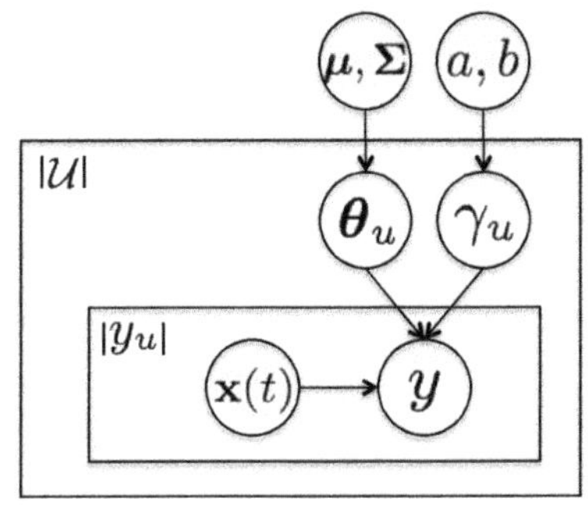

Figure 5: The dependency of variables for daily-aware recommendation. The ith rating $y_{u,i}$ of user u is dependent on the conditional opportunity model $\xi_u = \{\boldsymbol{\theta}_u, \gamma_u\}$ of user u and the integrated covariate vector $\mathbf{x}(t)$. Models of different users share information through the same prior $\phi = (\boldsymbol{\mu}, \boldsymbol{\Sigma}, a, b)$.

6. EXPERIMENTS

In this section, we conduct extensive experiments to evaluate the performance of product feature extraction, daily-aware time series prediction, dynamic personalized recommendation, and the performance of our framework in handling with cold-start users.

6.1 Experimental Setup

We obtained the real-world reviews in the cosmetic domain of JD.com, the second largest e-commerce website in China, from Jan. 1st, 2011 to Mar. 31st, 2014. The dataset covers all the reviews of three consecutive years and a quarter, which is sufficient for daily-aware time series modeling. The statistical information of cumulative per-quarter data is listed in Table 3, where the statistics of a specific quarter represents the total number of users, items, or reviews in the system until the end of that quarter.

To simulate the practical system operation over time, and also to evaluate the effectiveness of our framework over a whole year, we construct four time-dependent training-testing datasets $D_1 \sim D_4$ based on the last four quarters of data. Specifically, each of the dataset takes the reviews in one of the last four quarters (i.e. $Q_2 \sim Q_4$ of 2013, and Q_1 of 2014) as testing set, and takes the reviews in the previous quarters as training set, which is denoted in Table 4. In the following, we evaluate and report the performance of both time series prediction and personalized recommendation on each of the four datasets, as well as the average performance of the four quarters for the yearly performance.

In the following experiments, we set the maximum possible order of Fourier and ARIMA components as $\bar{K} = 10$ and $(\bar{p}, \bar{d}, \bar{q}) = (10, 3, 10)$ in Algorithm 1, respectively, as we find this is sufficient to achieve satisfactory performances. We introduce the comparative algorithms and evaluation metrics for each experimental task separately in the following, because the evaluation of time series prediction and personalized recommendation require different settings.

Table 4: Four time-dependent datasets constructed for model training and testing.

Dataset	Train	Test
D_1	$2011 + 2012 + Q_1, 2013$	$Q_2, 2013$
D_2	$2011 + 2012 + Q_1, Q_2, 2013$	$Q_3, 2013$
D_3	$2011 + 2012 + Q_1, Q_2, Q_3, 2013$	$Q_4, 2013$
D_4	$2011 + 2012 + 2013$	$Q_1, 2014$

6.2 Product Feature Extraction

We first extract product features in cosmetic domain based on all the textual reviews in the whole dataset. Similar with many other text mining tasks, the automatic extraction of product features from free-text reviews is inherently difficult and have to trade off between precision and recall.

In this work, we tune the parameters in the method introduced in [22, 39] and record the precision and recall. In line with the literature [18, 39], we construct the gold-standard feature set by sampling 1,000 reviews and presenting them to 3 human annotators for manual feature extraction. The gold-standard feature set is constructed by selecting the common features of the three manually extracted sets, and it is further used to evaluate the automatically extracted features. The averaged pair-wise agreement between annotators is 82.46%, and the evaluation results for several trials of automatic feature set extraction are shown in Table 5.

Table 5: Evaluation of automatic feature extraction when trading off between precision and recall.

Trial	1	2	3	4	5	6
#Features	32	44	58	66	79	95
Precision	**0.9063**	0.8864	0.8621	0.7879	0.6962	0.6316
Recall	0.3867	0.5200	0.6667	0.6933	0.7333	**0.8000**
F_1-score	0.5421	0.6555	**0.7519**	0.7376	0.7143	0.7059

We select the result with the highest F_1-score primarily (Trial #3), which contains 58 features. In general, we tend to keep a high precision while choosing an acceptable recall to reduce the probability of introducing noise into time series prediction and personalized recommendation. We adopt the automatically constructed feature set without incorporating any human annotation information in the following experiments, thus to guarantee that no manual effort is included in our framework.

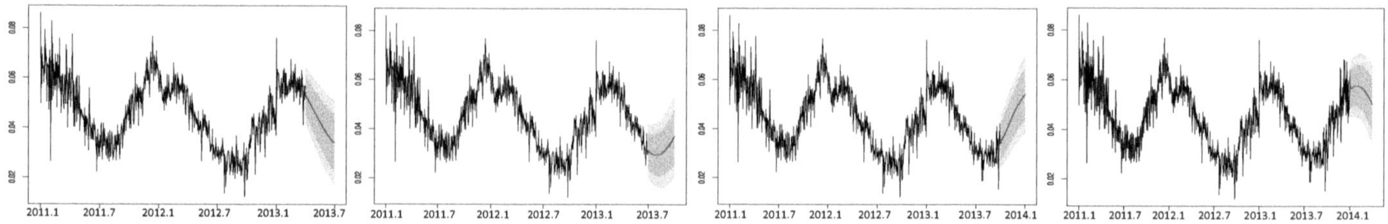

(a) $D_1 : K, p, d, q = 6, 4, 1, 3$ (b) $D_2 : K, p, d, q = 6, 4, 1, 5$ (c) $D_3 : K, p, d, q = 6, 3, 1, 2$ (d) $D_4 : K, p, d, q = 7, 3, 1, 2$

Figure 6: Exampled time series prediction results on the four datasets $D_1 \sim D_4$, where K is the final order of the Fourier component, and (p, d, q) is the order of ARIMA component. The orders are automatically selected by minimizing the AICc. The blue line is the predicted series for the testing set, and the dark grey and light grey boundaries are 80% and 95% prediction intervals of the random effect, respectively.

6.3 Daily-Aware Time Series Prediction

To evaluate the performance of FARIMA model in time series prediction, we conduct experiment on each of the four datasets $D_1 \sim D_4$. For each dataset, we adopt the training set for model learning based on Algorithm 1, and predict the time series of the following quarter in testing set. Figure 6 examples the time series prediction on the four datasets, where the listed Fourier order K and ARIMA order (p, d, q) are determined by minimizing the AICc automatically. We can see intuitionally that our FARIMA model is not only capable of capturing the future trends in rise and fall (*e.g.*, in Figure 6(a) and 6(c)), but also able to predict the future inflexions ahead of time (*e.g.*, in Figure 6(b) and 6(d)).

For numeral evaluation of the prediction accuracy, we adopt the Root Mean Square Error (RMSE) and Mean Absolute Percentage Error (MAPE), which are defined as:

$$\text{RMSE} = \sqrt{\frac{\sum_{t=1}^{n}(X(t) - \hat{X}(t))^2}{n}}, \text{MAPE} = \frac{1}{n}\sum_{t=1}^{n}\left|\frac{X(t) - \hat{X}(t)}{X(t)}\right| \tag{20}$$

where n is the number of instances in the testing set, $X(t)$ is the actual value and $\hat{X}(t)$ is the forecasted value. The RMSE is a measure of the absolute error of prediction that has been widely adopted in many tasks, however, in the task of time series prediction the values of $X(t)$ are not restricted to a fixed range; as a result, we further adopt MAPE as an indicator of relative prediction deviation. The averaged results over the features for each dataset as well as the total averages across datasets are shown in Table 6.

Table 6: Evaluation of time series prediction.

Dataset	D_1	D_2	D_3	D_4	Average
#Instance	4,253,294	4,656,628	4,963,927	5,524,491	4,849,585
RMSE	0.00406	0.00453	0.00704	0.00603	0.00541
MAPE	0.08012	0.11962	0.12580	0.07770	0.10081
~MAE	0.3205	0.4785	0.5032	0.3108	0.4032

The results on both RMSE and MAPE indicate that our FARIMA model is able to achieve quite accurate predictions of future time series. It may be easier for one to get a more intuitional understanding of the results by rescaling them into the frequently seen range of $1 \sim 5$ stars. By multiplying MAPE with the rating range (i.e., 4), we get the estimated MAE as shown in the last row of Table 6, which implies a superior result in prediction accuracy.

The results are statistically significant due to the huge amount of instances for testing. In the following experiments, we leverage the predicted percentage time series in each dataset for daily-aware recommendation.

6.4 Daily-Aware Rating Prediction

With the predicted daily time series on each feature, we preform daily-aware rating prediction and recommendation with the conditional opportunity model.

In real-world systems, the number of users and products are increasing with the business growth of the e-commerce. This is shown by the continuously growing number of users, item, and reviews in Table 3, which leads to the frequently noted problem of cold-start in recommender systems, especially when we are simulating the time effect by splitting training and testing sets according to time, because a user/item may have not even a single record in the training set, while we have to predict his/her ratings in the testing set, which may cause some comparative algorithms to fail.

As a result, for each dataset D_i, we only consider those users/items in the testing set that also exist in the training set. We will experiment on the performance of cold-start recommendation separately in the following sections.

We compare our daily-aware recommendation method based on Feature-level Time Series Analysis (FTSA) with the following comparative algorithms:

NMF: Non-negative Matrix Factorization [17] algorithm that is among the best MF algorithms in previous research [28]. This method is a baseline for time-independent CF.

timeSVD++: The state-of-the-art time-aware collaborative prediction method proposed by Koren [16]. For easy comparison, we adopt the open-source implementation provided by MyMediaLite [12].

Tensor: The tensor factorization approach [15] for time-aware prediction, which is widely adopted for context-aware recommendation. For daily prediction, we incorporate 366 days of a year as the time dimension of a tensor, and a user-item rating made on the ith day of a year is placed in the rating matrix on the ith layer.

EFM: The Explicit Factor Model for explainable recommendation proposed in [38], which is time-independent but it is the state-of-the-art CF method based on sentiment analysis on textual reviews as in this work.

To investigate the effect of incorporating different number of features r, we make use of the six sets of extracted features $\mathcal{F} = \{f_1, f_2, \cdots, f_r\}$ in the different trials on the experiment of product feature extraction (Table 5). Specifically, we tune $r = 32, 44, 58, 66, 79, 95$ in our FTSA approach by using the corresponding feature set for time series analysis and rating prediction. To ensure comparable model complexity, we take the same r as the number of latent factors in NMF, timeSVD++ and tensor factorization, and we use the same feature set in the EFM method.

We adopt the frequently used RMSE for evaluation. The hyper-parameters for each method are selected by grid search on the four datasets and retaining those with the best performance. The averaged RMSE of the four datasets is shown in Figure 7, and Table 7 shows the best RMSE achieved by each method on each dataset, as well as their averages.

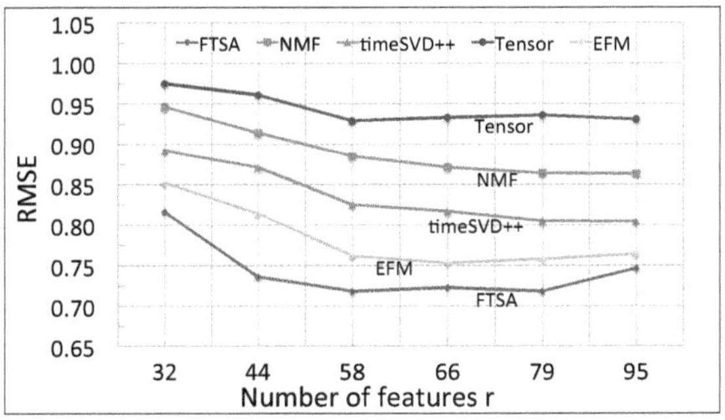

Figure 7: Averaged RMSE over $D_1 \sim D_4$ against the number of features/factors for different methods.

We see that for the latent factor based methods (NMF, timeSVD++ and Tensor), the RMSE decreases with the increase of the number of latent factors used r. However, we find that the time-aware tensor factorization approach did not gain superiority against the static NMF. This may be of the reason that splitting the rating records into the days of a year makes the training instances sparse, because the time-aware SVD (timeSVD++) gains superior results than NMF by integrating the advantages of time factors and latent factorization.

Surprisingly, a static model that takes advantage of textual reviews (EFM) is even better than a dynamic modeling approach (timeSVD++) that only makes use of the numerical ratings. This indicates the importance of incorporating textual reviews as an information source for CF. However, by further incorporating the time factors for dynamic CF through time series analysis on product features, our FTSA approach gains consistently better results than EFM.

We noticed that the performance of FTSA tends to drop slightly when the number of product features increases to 95, in which case too many noise features are incorporated (Table 5). As a result, it would be important to construct a reliable feature set for FTSA to gain the best performance in practical applications. However, our FTSA model achieves superior result in a large range of feature selections.

To validate the effect of our FARIMA model in time series prediction, we replace the predicted time series $\hat{X}_{f_k}(t)$ in Eq.(10) with the real value $X_{f_k}(t)$, and still conduct rating prediction with our conditional opportunity model. The results are shown by FTSA′ in Table 7. We find that our predicted percentage time series is even better than using the real values. This may indicate that the smoothing effect of our FARIMA model is important for noise filtering. For example, a feature may be commented for only a few times in a specific day due to the relatively fewer active users on that day. However, by leveraging the data accumulated through the previous years, we are able to model the dynamic user preferences more accurately.

6.5 Daily-Aware Top-K Recommendation

We also care about the performance of our method in top-K recommendation, as is important in real-world scenarios.

Table 7: The best RMSE achieved on four datasets and their averaged value for each method, standard deviations ≤ 0.015 for each experimental run.

Dataset	D_1	D_2	D_3	D_4	Average
NMF	0.857	0.866	0.851	0.878	0.863
timeSVD++	0.782	0.813	0.795	0.826	0.804
Tensor	0.912	0.937	0.916	0.951	0.929
EFM	0.733	0.768	0.742	0.769	0.753
FTSA	**0.706**	**0.729**	**0.711**	**0.726**	**0.718**
FTSA′	0.716	0.732	0.722	0.735	0.726

To evaluate top-K recommendation, we select those users who have 10 or more records in the testing set for each dataset D_i, and then conduct top-10 recommendation for them. Following [38, 23], we adopt the frequently used NDCG to evaluate top-10 recommendation, and we still use the NMF, timeSVD++, Tensor and EFM methods for performance comparison. We set $r = 58$ for all methods.

Table 8 shows the evaluation results on different datasets and their averages. It is shown that time-aware approaches (timeSVD++ and Tensor) are consistently better than static models (NMF and EFM). This indicates that considering the time factors may be more important for top-K recommendation than in rating prediction tasks. By taking advantage of both product features from textual reviews and dynamic time series analysis, our FTSA approach achieves the best NDCG among the comparative algorithms.

Table 8: The number of selected users and best NDCG on four datasets, standard deviations ≤ 0.01.

Dataset	D_1	D_2	D_3	D_4	Average
#Users	122,476	146,099	159,747	167,370	148,923
NMF	0.154	0.136	0.163	0.147	0.150
timeSVD++	0.228	0.241	0.236	0.233	0.235
Tensor	0.207	0.192	0.196	0.211	0.202
EFM	0.186	0.194	0.208	0.195	0.196
FTSA	**0.254**	**0.267**	**0.258**	**0.271**	**0.263**

This experimental result verifies our observations to some extent, that users tend to buy different categories/types of products at different time of a year, although they may make similar ratings towards the products. To further investigate users' purchasing behavior on different products, we conduct top-K recommendation for products of different popularities separately. To do so, we select those items that have more than L reviews in dataset D_i (including both training and testing set), and filter out the remaining 'low frequency' items. Based on the filtered items, we still select those users with 10 or more reviews in the testing set to conduct top-10 recommendation. The averaged NDCG of the four datasets under different filtering thresholds L is shown in Fig.8.

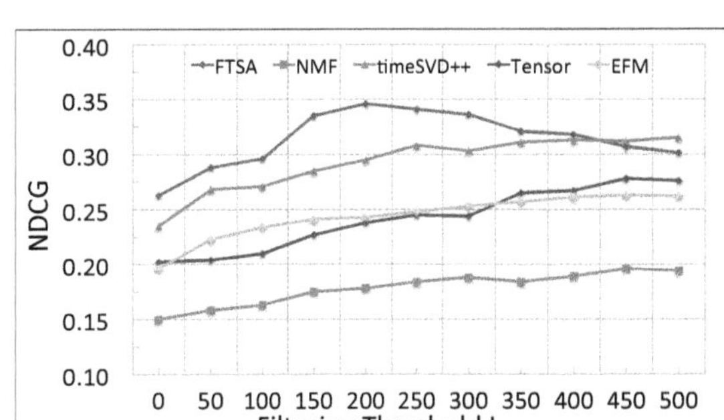

Figure 8: Averaged NDCG over $D_1 \sim D_4$ against the filtering threshold L for different algorithms.

We see that the results on NDCG for both dynamic algorithms (timeSVD++ and Tensor) and static methods (NMF and EFM) tend to rise gradually with the increase of filtering threshold L. This is not surprising because the training set becomes denser by selecting the popular items, which gives us more accurate predictions. Besides, it is generally easier to recommend popular items than long-tail ones. However, the results for FTSA is interesting because the performance tends to drop when L is too high. This indicates that our method achieves superior results against others for low- or mid-frequency items. After careful examination of the high frequency items, we find that they tend to be seasonally independent and are welcomed all over the year, *e.g.*, a major part of them are lipsticks. Thus forcing a seasonal factor on these products may result in inferior results. However, our method is still favoured in a large range of filtering thresholds. Besides, we usually need to consider all the products rather than only the popular ones in practical systems.

6.6 Recommendation for Cold-Start Users

Previous work of personalized recommendation usually filter out the cold-start users for evaluation, *e.g.*, those users that have less than 20 reviews. However, this may not be feasible for real-world systems because the most difficult users are not properly considered, although they may constitute a major part of the system. For example, [40] reported that about 49% of the users in Yelp made only a single review. As a result, we evaluate the performance on cold-start users separately in this section.

For each dataset D_i, we still conduct rating prediction and top-10 recommendation using the training set, but we only evaluate with the users that have at most one review in the training set. This setting fits with the real scenarios in practical systems, where we can adopt all the records in the system for model learning, and make recommendation for the cold-start users. The number of selected users for testing, as well as the RMSE for rating prediction and NDCG for top-10 recommendation are shown in Table 9.

Table 9: The number of users for evaluation, and the RMSE and NDCG on the four datasets, standard deviations ≤ 0.05 for RMSE and ≤ 0.02 for NDCG.

Metric	Dataset	D_1	D_2	D_3	D_4	Average
	#Users	527,328	637,965	613,904	712,003	622,800
R	NMF	1.729	1.693	1.732	1.706	1.715
M	timeSVD++	1.441	1.438	1.506	1.475	1.465
S	Tensor	1.763	1.779	1.725	1.769	1.759
E	EFM	1.383	1.362	1.360	1.389	1.374
	FTSA	**1.344**	**1.287**	**1.278**	**1.326**	**1.309**
N	NMF	0.067	0.073	0.061	0.066	0.067
D	timeSVD++	0.084	0.075	0.088	0.092	0.085
C	Tensor	0.046	0.054	0.044	0.048	0.048
G	EFM	0.093	**0.107**	0.095	0.087	0.096
	FTSA	**0.118**	0.098	**0.122**	**0.115**	**0.113**

In general, the prediction accuracy (RMSE) for cold-start users exhibits similar patterns with that of the total users (Table 7). The reviews-based approaches (EFM and FTSA) outperform the rating-based approaches (NMF, timeSVD++ and Tensor). The reason could be the inherent difficulty for rating-based methods to estimate accurate rating biases of a user with insufficient training data, thus they tend to predict the ratings of cold-start users around the global mean. For example, the regularization terms in NMF, timeSVD++ and tensor factorization actually force the predictions to be centred under a Gaussian prior, which makes the predictions less 'personalized'. However, by leveraging the product features embedded in reviews, we are able to expand the available information for prediction. We find that on average there are 0.66 ratings per user for the cold-start users, while the averaged number of features per user is 2.56, because a user may comment on more than one features in a single review. When taking time series factors into consideration, our FTSA approach achieves the best performance.

On the result of NDCG, we see that the static NMF approach is still better than the dynamic tensor factorization approach, which is different from the relatively 'warm-start' scenarios in Table 8. This is in fact not surprising because it is difficult for the tensors to learn time-shifting factors and even global time-specific mean ratings when so few as only a single rating is available on the time dimension. When the valid information is enriched with product features, our FTSA method gains superior results on most detests.

7. CONCLUSIONS

In this paper, we propose to leverage direct time series analysis for dynamic daily-aware recommendation. In order to overcome the problem of data insufficiency in previous product-level modeling approaches, we propose to extract product features automatically from user reviews, and thus to degrade product-level modeling to feature-level modeling. To make it computationally feasible for time series analysis on daily resolution, we develop the Fourier-assisted Auto-Regressive Integrated Moving Average (FARIMA) approach for percentage time series fitting and prediction, and we further adapt the conditional opportunity model for personalized rating prediction and recommendation.

For the first time, our analysis of time series in e-commerce characterizes the trend, seasonal, cyclic, and random effects of the product features that online users concern. The observation that a large amount of features exhibit clear seasonal and cyclic patterns may be inspiring for the construction of intelligent automatic marketing tools. Experimental results on both rating prediction and top-K recommendation, as well as cold-start performance verifies the superiority of our feature-level time series analysis approach.

This is a first step towards leveraging the rather mature technique of time series analysis in other research fields like Economics, to the research of personalized recommender systems, and there is much room for improvements. Apart from cosmetics, we will investigate other product domains with sufficient data, and even take geometrical information into consideration. Besides the conditional opportunity model, we can also develop other factorization, graphical, or even deep learning models to integrate feature-level time series for personalized recommendation. The cross-adaption of other models may even see more interdisciplinary research achievements between Economics and Artificial Intelligence.

Acknowledgement

This work was supported by National Key Basic Research Program (2015CB358700) and Natural Science Foundation (61472206, 61073071) of China, and Yi is sponsored by the National Science Foundation under grant CCF-1101741 and IIS-0953908. Yongfeng would also like to thank the Baidu and IBM Ph.D. Fellowship program, and the Siebel Scholar program for their kind supports.

8. REFERENCES

[1] G. Adomavicius, B. Mobasher, F. Ricci, and A. Tuzhilin. Context-Aware Recommender Systems. *Recommender systems handbook*, pages 217–253, 2011.

[2] L. Baltrunas and X. Amatriain. Towards Time Dependant Recommendation based on Implicit Feedback. *CARS*, 2009.

[3] G. E. P. Box, G. M. Jenkins, and G. C. Reinsel. Time Series Analysis: Forecasting and Control. *John Wiley & Sons*, 2013.

[4] K. P. Burnham and D. R. Anderson. Model Selection and Multimodel Inference: A Practical Information-Theoretic Approach. *Springer*, 2002.

[5] P. G. Campos, F. Díez, and I. Cantador. Time-aware Recommender Systems: A Comprehensive Survey and Analysis of Existing Evaluation Protocols. *User modeling & user-adapted interaction*, 24:67–119, 2014.

[6] T. Chen, W. Han, H. Wang, Y. Zhou, B. Xu, and B. Zang. Content Recommendation System based on Private Dynamic User Profiling. *ICMLC*, 2007.

[7] W. Chen, W. Hsu, and M. Lee. Modeling User's Receptiveness Over Time for Recommendation. *SIGIR*, pages 373–382, 2013.

[8] H. Choi and H. Varian. Predicting the Present with Google Trends. *Economic Record*, 88(s1):2–9, 2012.

[9] W. Chu and S. Park. Personalized Recommendation on Dynamic Content Using Predictive Bilinear Models. *WWW*, pages 691–700, 2009.

[10] X. Ding, B. Liu, and P. S. Yu. A Holistic Lexicon Based Approach to Opinion Mining. *WSDM*, 2008.

[11] G. Dror, N. Koenigstein, and Y. Koren. Yahoo! music recommendations: Modeling music ratings with temporal dynamics and item taxonomy. *RecSys*, 2011.

[12] Z. Gantner, S. Rendle, C. Freudenthaler, and L. Schmidt-Thieme. MyMediaLite: A Free Recommender System Library. *RecSys*, 2011.

[13] Z. Gantner, S. Rendle, and L. Schmidt-Thieme. Factorization Models for Context-/Time-Aware Movie Recommendations. *CAMRa*, pages 14–19, 2010.

[14] S. Gauch, M. Speretta, A. Chandramouli, and A. Micarelli. User Profiles for Personalized Information Access. *The Adaptive Web*, pages 54–89, 2007.

[15] A. Karatzoglou, X. Amatriain, L. Baltrunas, and N. Oliver. Multiverse Recommendation: N-dimensional Tensor Factorization for Context-aware Collaborative Filtering. *RecSys*, pages 79–86, 2010.

[16] Y. Koren. Collaborative Filtering with Temporal Dynamics. *KDD*, pages 447–455, 2009.

[17] D. D. Lee and H. S. Seung. Algorithms for Non-negative Matrix Factorization. *NIPS*, 2001.

[18] Y. Lu, M. Castellanos, U. Dayal, and C. Zhai. Automatic construction of a context-aware sentiment lexicon: An optimization approach. *WWW*, 2011.

[19] Z. Lu, D. Agarwal, and I. Dhillon. A Spatio Temporal Approach to Collaborative Filtering. *RecSys*, 2009.

[20] K. Oku, S. Nakajima, J. Miyazaki, S. Uemura, and H. Kato. A Recommendation Method Considering Users' Time Series Contexts. *ICUIMC*, 2009.

[21] M. J. Pazzani and D. Billsus. Content-Based Recommendation Systems. *The Adaptive Web LNCS*, pages 325–341, 2007.

[22] A. M. Popescu and O. Etzioni. Extracting Product Features and Opinions from Reviews. *EMNLP*, 2005.

[23] S. Rendle, C. Freudenthaler, Z. Gantner, and L. S. Thieme. BPR: Bayesian Personalized Ranking from Implicit Feedback. *UAI*, 2009.

[24] F. Ricci, L. Rokach, and B. Shapira. Introduction to Recommender Systems Handbook. *Springer US*, 2011.

[25] Y. Shi, M. Larson, and A. Hanjalic. Mining Mood-specific Movie Similarity with Matrix Factorization for Context-aware Recommendation. *CAMRa*, pages 34–40, 2010.

[26] R. H. Shumway and D. S. Stoffer. Time Series Analysis and Its Application. *Springer*, 2010.

[27] X. Su and T. M. Khoshgoftaar. A Survey of Collaborative Filtering Techniques. *Advances in Artificial Intelligence*, 4, 2009.

[28] G. Takacs, I. Pilaszy, B. Nemeth, and D. Tikk. Investigation of Various Matrix Factorization Methods for Large Recommender Systems. *Proc. ICDM*, 2008.

[29] D. Tang, F. Wei, B. Qin, M. Zhou, and T. Liu. Building Large-Scale Twitter-Specific Sentiment Lexicon: A Representation Learning Approach. *COLING*, pages 172–182, 2014.

[30] C. Vaca, A. Mantrach, A. Jaimes, and M. Saerens. A Time-based Collective Factorization for Topic Discovery and Monitoring in News. *WWW*, 2014.

[31] J. Wang and Y. Zhang. Is It Time For a Career Switch? *WWW*, pages 1377–1387, 2013.

[32] J. Wang and Y. Zhang. Opportunity Models for E-commerce Recommendation: Right Product, Right Time. *SIGIR*, pages 303–312, 2013.

[33] Y. Wu and M. Ester. FLAME: A Probabilistic Model Combining Aspect Based Opinion Mining and Collaborative Filtering. *WSDM*, pages 199–208, 2015.

[34] L. Xiang, Q. Yuan, S. Zhao, L. Chen, X. Zhang, Q. Yang, and J. Sun. Temporal Recommendation on Graphs via Long- and Short-term Preference Fusion. *KDD*, pages 723–731, 2010.

[35] D. Xu, Y. Liu, M. Zhang, S. Ma, A. Cui, and L. Ru. Predicting Epidemic Tendency through Search Behavior Analysis. *IJCAI*, pages 2361–2366, 2011.

[36] A. Yessenalina, Y. Yue, et al. Multi-level structured models for document-level sentiment classification. *EMNLP*, pages 1046–1056, 2010.

[37] Q. Yuan, G. Cong, Z. Ma, A. Sun, and N. M. Thalmann. Time-aware Point-of-interest Recommendation. *SIGIR*, pages 363–372, 2013.

[38] Y. Zhang, G. Lai, M. Zhang, Y. Zhang, Y. Liu, and S. Ma. Explicit Factor Models for Explainable Recommendation based on Phrase-level Sentiment Analysis. *SIGIR*, pages 83–92, 2014.

[39] Y. Zhang, H. Zhang, M. Zhang, Y. Liu, et al. Do Users Rate or Review? Boost Phrase-level Sentiment Labeling with Review-level Sentiment Classification. *SIGIR*, pages 1027–1030, 2014.

[40] Y. Zhang, M. Zhang, Y. Zhang, Y. Liu, and S. Ma. Understanding the Sparsity: Augmented Matrix Factorization with Sampled Constraints on Unobservables. *CIKM*, 2014.

Automatic Detection of Information Leakage Vulnerabilities in Browser Extensions

Rui Zhao
University of Colorado
Colorado Springs
rzhao@uccs.edu

Chuan Yue
University of Colorado
Colorado Springs
cyue@uccs.edu

Qing Yi
University of Colorado
Colorado Springs
qyi@uccs.edu

ABSTRACT

A large number of extensions exist in browser vendors' online stores for millions of users to download and use. Many of those extensions process sensitive information from user inputs and webpages; however, it remains a big question whether those extensions may accidentally leak such sensitive information out of the browsers without protection. In this paper, we present a framework, LvDetector, that combines static and dynamic program analysis techniques for automatic detection of information leakage vulnerabilities in legitimate browser extensions. Extension developers can use LvDetector to locate and fix the vulnerabilities in their code; browser vendors can use LvDetector to decide whether the corresponding extensions can be hosted in their online stores; advanced users can also use LvDetector to determine if certain extensions are safe to use. The design of LvDetector is not bound to specific browsers or JavaScript engines, and can adopt other program analysis techniques. We implemented LvDetector and evaluated it on 28 popular Firefox and Google Chrome extensions. LvDetector identified 18 previously unknown information leakage vulnerabilities in 13 extensions with a 87% accuracy rate. The evaluation results and the feedback to our responsible disclosure demonstrate that LvDetector is useful and effective.

Categories and Subject Descriptors

D.4.6 [**Software**]: Operating Systems—*Security and Protection.*; H.4.3 [**Information Systems**]: Communications Applications—*Information browsers*

Keywords

Web browser extension; JavaScript; Vulnerability analysis

1. INTRODUCTION

Popular web browsers all support extension mechanisms to help third-party developers extend the functionality of browsers and improve user experience. A large number of extensions exist in browser vendors' online stores for millions of users to download and use. Quite often, those extensions are written in JavaScript; they have higher privileges than regular webpages do, thus have become a popular vector for performing web-based attacks [1, 2].

Because many extensions have security vulnerabilities [1, 2, 3, 4, 11, 18, 22, 24] and some extensions are even malicious, browser vendors have taken stricter measures to control the extensions that can be installed on browsers. For example, Google bans Windows version chrome extensions found outside the Chrome Web Store starting from January 2014, and inspects the extensions in the Chrome Web Store to exclude the malicious ones.

Researchers have extensively studied privilege escalation related vulnerabilities in JavaScript-based extensions and shown that a lack of sufficient security knowledge in developers is one of the main reasons for many vulnerabilities [1, 2, 3, 18, 24]. However, an often overlooked problem is that extensions may accidentally leak users' sensitive information out of the browsers without protection.

Many browser extensions process sensitive information coming from either user inputs or webpages. For example, some extensions save users' website passwords, some extensions remember users' shopping preferences, and some extensions manage users' bookmarks. If such sensitive information is leaked out of the browser without protection, it can be used by unauthorized parties to illegally access users' online accounts, steal their online identities, or track their online behaviors. Therefore, banning extensions that may leak users' sensitive information is also necessary and important.

Yet detecting information leakage in JavaScript-based web browser extensions is especially challenging. One source of the challenges is JavaScript itself, an interpreted prototype-based object-oriented programming language with just-in-time code loading/generation [27, 28, 29, 41] and dynamic uses of functions, fields and prototypes [6, 21, 26]. The other source of the challenges is the highly complex interactions among browser extensions, internal components of browsers, and webpages [2, 3, 18, 24]. Only a handful of solutions have been proposed to address the problem of information leakage in JavaScript-based browser extensions [4, 11, 22]; however, they took either pure dynamic approaches or pure static approaches, thus suffering from many limitations (Section 5).

In this paper, we present a framework, LvDetector, that combines static and dynamic program analysis techniques for automatic detection of information leakage vulnerabilities in legitimate browser extensions. LvDetector focuses on legitimate browser extensions because lots of them are

WWW 2015, May 18–22, 2015, Florence, Italy.
ACM 978-1-4503-3469-3/15/05.
http://dx.doi.org/10.1145/2736277.2741134.

used by millions of users [14, 5], thus the impact level of their information leakage vulnerabilities is high. LvDetector does not aim to be sound at the whole program level (Section 3.1); it aims to be a practical and accurate utility by (1) using a dynamic scenario-driven call graph construction scheme to reduce the overall false positives in the analysis as much as possible, and (2) using static analysis based on each dynamically constructed call graph to extensively analyze the corresponding scenario. Extension developers can use LvDetector to locate and fix the vulnerabilities in their code; browser vendors can use LvDetector to decide whether the corresponding extensions can be hosted in their online stores; advanced users can also use LvDetector to determine if certain extensions are safe to use. Note that detecting potentially malicious code or intentional vulnerabilities is out of the scope of the current LvDetector framework.

The design of LvDetector is not bound to specific web browsers or JavaScript engines, and can adopt other program analysis techniques. We implemented LvDetector in Java and evaluated it on 28 popular Firefox and Google Chrome extensions. LvDetector identified 18 previously unknown information leakage vulnerabilities in 13 extensions with a 87% accuracy rate. The evaluation results and the feedback to our responsible disclosure demonstrate that LvDetector is useful and effective.

The main contributions of this work include: (1) a dynamic scenario-driven call graph construction scheme, (2) a formulation of transitive relations and function/program-level static analysis algorithms for effective exploration of information flow paths in browser extensions, (3) a unique framework that combines static and dynamic program analysis techniques for automatic detection of information leakage vulnerabilities in JavaScript-based browser extensions, and (4) an effectiveness evaluation of LvDetector.

The rest of the paper is organized as follows. Section 2 uses an example to illustrate the vulnerability analysis problem targeted by this paper. Section 3 presents the details of the LvDetector framework. Section 4 evaluates the effectiveness of LvDetector. Section 5 discusses the related work. Finally, Section 6 makes a conclusion.

2. MOTIVATING EXAMPLE

Many legitimate browser extensions process sensitive information coming from either user inputs or webpages. If such sensitive information is leaked out of the browser without protection, it can be used by unauthorized parties to illegally access users' online accounts, steal their online identities, or track their online behaviors. Figure 1 depicts a code excerpt of a real example browser extension that manages users' website passwords. In the code excerpt, this extension obtains the website password and username of a user in the save() function, encodes the password and username in the encode() function, and sends the encoded string to the remote server of the extension through the send() method of an XMLHttpRequest object in the post() function.

When this example extension was submitted to the extension web store of a browser vendor, the developers claimed that they cannot know users' website passwords. The browser vendor wants to verify this claim and identify potential information leakage vulnerabilities in this extension, but manually inspecting about 26,000 lines of code in this extension is time and effort consuming. The browser vendor can use LvDetector to easily perform this inspection task in three

```
function save() {
  var pwd = document.getElementById("pwd").value;
  var usr = document.getElementById("usr").value;
  var str = encode(pwd, usr);
  post(str);
}
...
function encode(pwd, usr) {
  return encodeURI(pwd) + encodeURI(usr);
}
...
function post(content) {
  var req = new XMLHttpRequest();
  var url = "https://www.remoteserver.com/"
  req.open("POST", url);
  req.send(content);
}
```

Figure 1: Code excerpt of a real example extension

steps: (1) runs LvDetector to instrument this extension, (2) executes a website password saving scenario using the instrumented extension, and (3) runs LvDetector to automatically detect potential information leakage vulnerabilities and generate a report. The browser vendor can also directly perform the third step by using the execution traces supplied by other LvDetector users (Section 3.2.1).

The generated vulnerability report contains a vulnerable information flow record: the website password assigned to the "pwd" variable in the save() function is propagated through the encode() function to the "content" variable in the post() function, and is leaked out in a send() method call. All the detailed operations in this vulnerable information flow are also provided in the report.

A user's website password should only be known by the user and the corresponding website - sending the unprotected website password to the remote server of the extension allows server-side attackers to directly obtain the user's website login information. LvDetector correctly identifies this vulnerability, providing evidence for the browser vendor to disprove the extension developers' claim.

3. OVERALL FRAMEWORK

Our key objective is to design LvDetector as a framework that can be easily used by ***analysts*** (extension developers, browser vendors, or advanced users) to automatically detect information leakage vulnerabilities in browser extensions.

3.1 Design Overview and Rationale

The overall workflow of LvDetector can be organized into three phases as shown in Figure 2.

The first phase, *call graph and variable use analysis*, starts with an *instrumentation* component that takes a browser extension as the input and instruments the extension for collecting execution traces. The *call graph analysis* component collects the traces generated from each scenario-driven execution of the instrumented extension to build a call graph. Meanwhile, the *SSA builder* component builds the SSA IR (Static Single Assignment form Intermediate Representation [10]) of each function in the extension source code, and the SSA IRs [10] in turn are fed into the *variable use analysis* component to generate variable use graphs. The variable use analysis component will automatically identify (1) commonly used cryptographic functions (e.g., AES encryption/decryption and SHA hash functions), (2) ***source variables*** that accept values from either user inputs or webpages

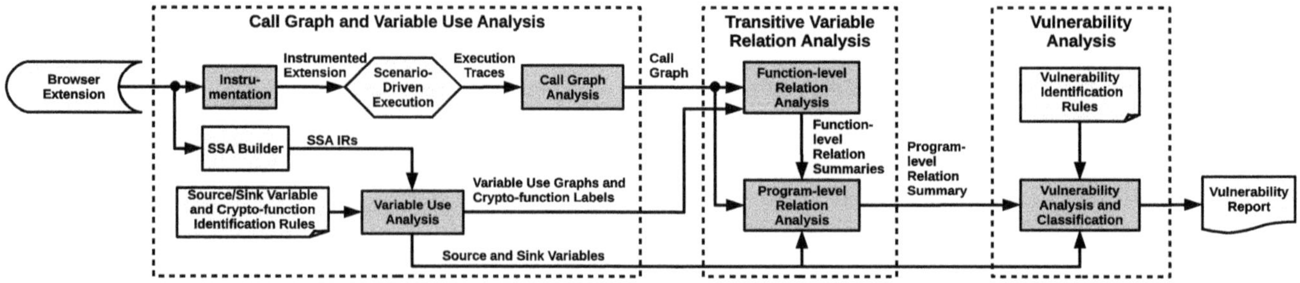

Figure 2: The overall workflow of the LvDetector framework (the shaded components are ours)

(e.g., through form fields), and (3) ***sink variables*** that contain values either saved to the local disk (e.g., through the setItem() method call of the localStorage object in HTML5) or sent across the network (e.g., through the send() method call of an XMLHttpRequest object). Sink variables are extracted from the sink statements, which are either common or specific to different browsers and are XMLHttpRequest, window object, SQLite database, file, local storage, bookmark, and password manager related statements. These criteria for identifying standard/nonstandard cryptographic functions, source variables, and sink variables in Google Chrome and Firefox extensions are included in a rule file.

The second phase, *transitive variable relation analysis*, computes a transitive summary of the relations among each pair of the source and sink variables. Specifically, the *function-level relation analysis* component iteratively computes a function-level relation summary for each function based on its variable use graph, the call graph, and the labeled cryptographic functions; the *program-level relation analysis* component computes the program-level relation summary based on the call graph and the function-level relation summaries.

Finally, the third phase, *vulnerability analysis*, identifies all the potential vulnerable information flows that may lead to sensitive information leakage. It analyzes vulnerabilities based on the program-level relation summary and the source-sink variable pairs, and generates an intuitive report with a list of classified vulnerability records for each scenario-driven execution.

The overall workflow takes a hybrid approach to analyze JavaScript browser extensions. It uses scenario-driven execution traces to dynamically and accurately construct a call graph; it then statically performs variable use analysis and transitive variable relation analysis based on SSA IR [10] to summarize the overall information flows among variables both within a single function and across function boundaries. The dynamic aspects of our approach accurately capture intricate across-function-boundary information flows that often occur in JavaScript extensions due to reflection, function objects, event handlers, asynchronous calls, DOM interactions, and so on. The static aspects of our approach extensively extract both explicit and implicit information flows within each function. This hybrid approach is superior to pure static approaches by effectively reducing false positives in the construction of call graphs [26], which are often the foundation of the overall program analysis. This approach is not bound to specific web browsers or JavaScript engines; it is superior to pure dynamic approaches by avoiding users' or browsers' responses to runtime alerts, incomplete information flow exploration, runtime overhead, and browser-specific instrumentation [1, 11, 31, 36].

Most analysis tools for statically typed programming languages choose to be sound rather than complete. However, due to the complexity and dynamic features of the JavaScript language (Section 1), achieving soundness in the static analysis of the full JavaScript language is very difficult or impossible [16, 25, 26]. Meanwhile, LvDetector bases its static analysis on the call graphs constructed from the scenario-driven execution traces, which may not cover all the possible execution paths in the program. Due to these reasons, LvDetector does not aim to be sound at the whole program level; it aims to be a practical and accurate utility. Note that scenario-driven execution traces can be more extensively collected as discussed in Section 3.2.1.

3.2 Call Graph and Variable Use Analysis

In this phase, LvDetector performs browser extension instrumentation, and call graph and variable use analysis.

3.2.1 Instrumentation and Call Graph Analysis

While call graph construction has been commonly used in whole program analysis of C and Java code [15, 38], accurately constructing call graphs for JavaScript code is very challenging due to its extremely dynamic (1) code loading and generation [27, 28, 29, 41], (2) uses of functions, fields, and prototypes [6, 21, 26], and (3) interactions with other components of the browsers and webpages [2, 3, 18, 24].

To accurately construct call graphs that are the foundation of the overall analysis, we take an instrumentation approach to dynamically extract call relations among different functions within a browser extension. As shown in Figure 2, this *instrumentation* component takes a browser extension as input, automatically inserts program tracing statements to the extension, and outputs the instrumented extension.

Specifically, it (1) formats the source code of the extension so that each line contains one JavaScript statement, (2) adds unique prototype names to the functions (including methods) that do not have explicit ones so that all the functions can be uniquely identified, (3) inserts print statements before each function/method call so that the detailed callsite information such as the prototype name of the caller, the call statement, and the callsite position can be recorded, and (4) inserts a print statement at the entry point of each function definition so that the detailed information about the callee can be recorded. Because these transformations are simple and minimal, they do not interfere with the original program functionality and semantics. In the cases that some extensions use the dynamic features of JavaScript such as the eval() function to obfuscate their original source code, this instrumentation component uses the Closure Compiler [7] and the ScriptEngine class in Java to evaluate the eval() statements and de-obfuscate the source code before performing the aforementioned transformations. The de-obfuscated extension source code does not further contain any eval() as observed in our experiments

(Section 4), indicating that JavaScript in legitimate browser extensions rarely uses multi-level obfuscation.

An analyst can install and run such an instrumented extension to generate the execution traces for each particular use scenario. Because the execution traces only contain the call relations and do not contain any information from users, they can also be shared (e.g., in a repository along with the extensions) among the analysts to further cover more execution paths of the extension. For example, extension developers can run LvDetector and contribute execution traces based on their test cases, browser vendors can run LvDetector and contribute execution traces based on their inspection tasks, and advanced users can run LvDetector and contribute execution traces based on their trial runs. All these traces can be leveraged to automatically perform or replicate the actual vulnerability analysis.

The *call graph analysis* component analyzes the dynamically generated execution traces to build a call graph that precisely reflects the actual call relations in the real use scenario. The output call graph is a directed graph. Its nodes and edges are all the functions and call relations traversed in a scenario-driven execution, respectively. Such a call graph can accurately capture the complex and dynamic function/method calls that often occur in JavaScript extensions due to reflection, function objects, event handlers, asynchronous calls, DOM interactions, and so on.

3.2.2 Variable Use Analysis

The purpose of this component is to construct a graph that precisely defines the immediate value flow relations among variables in each function, based on an SSA IR [10] constructed from the source code of the browser extension.

For each function, its ***variable use graph*** is a directed graph with nodes representing all the variables defined/used in the function, and edges representing the operations used to propagate values among variables. The direction of an edge represents the value flow direction. Since the input program is converted to its SSA IR, each variable is statically and precisely defined once and thus is associated with a single value. Therefore, the static definition and uses of every variable in the program can be precisely correlated.

Our *variable use analysis* directly employs the output from an existing SSA builder [8]. The IR output of the SSA builder contains mappings between SSA variables and the original JavaScript variables, and mappings between SSA instructions and the original JavaScript statements. This mapping information will be used in the *vulnerability analysis* phase to generate intuitive vulnerability reports.

The main step of the *variable use analysis* is to extract the operands and operators from the instructions in SSA IR. Each operand represents a unique variable in SSA IR, and each operator represents an operation that may propagate values among variables. The operations include object field reference, getters/setters, string operation, array access, binary/unary operation, global variable reference, assignment operation, Φ-function [10], and function call. The variable use graph is then constructed in a straightforward fashion to precisely record such immediate explicit and implicit (via Φ-functions) value flow relations. Meanwhile, a list of global variable references will also be maintained. This list will be used in the *transitive variable relation analysis* phase to compute information flows across functions. Based source/sink variable and crypto-function identification rules in the rule file (Section 3.1), this component also automatically identifies all the source/sink variables and cryptographic functions, and feeds them to the next two analysis phases.

Figure 3(a) illustrates the three variable use graphs for the code excerpt in Figure 1. Here the edge $v_{10} \xrightarrow{+} v_{13}$ in the variable use graph for the encode() function represents a value flow from v_{10} to v_{13} through a string concatenation operation, and the edge $v_3 \xrightarrow{encode()} v_7$ in the variable use graph for the save() function represents a value flow from v_3 to v_7 through the *encode*() function call.

3.3 Transitive Variable Relation Analysis

This phase summarizes the transitive relations between each pair of source and sink variables at both the function-level and the program-level.

3.3.1 Function-level Relation Analysis

This component iteratively computes a function-level relation summary for each function based on its variable use graph, the call graph, and the labeled cryptographic functions. Such a summary contains the transitive relations between each pair of variables in that function.

We formulate the dynamically generated ***call graph*** as G in Formula 1. We categorize the original operators in a variable use graph into a set of abstract operators, *Operator*, defined in Formula 2. For example, the string concatenation and substring operators are categorized as "STRING_OP", the arithmetic operators are categorized as "BINARY_OP", the calls to the labeled encryption functions are categorized as "ENCRYPT", the calls to the labeled decryption functions are categorized as "DECRYPT", the calls to the JavaScript global functions (e.g., encodeURI()) are categorized as "JS_GLOBAL", and the calls to all other JavaScript functions are initially categorized as "UNKNOWN". The Φ-function used in SSA IR [10] is categorized as "Φ". We define the ***updated variable use graph*** for function f as F^f in Formula 3, in which each original operator in a variable use graph is replaced with its corresponding abstract operator to simplify the graph representation. In Formula 4, E represents the updated variable use graphs of all the functions in the call graph G.

$$G = \{f_i \xrightarrow{s} f_j \mid s \text{ is a callsite from function } f_i \text{ to } f_j\} \quad (1)$$

$$\begin{aligned} Operator = \{&ENCRYPT,\ DECRYPT,\ JS\_GLOBAL, \\ &PROTOTYPE,\ CONSTRUCT,\ FIELD\_OP, \\ &ATTRIBUTE\_OP,\ ARRAY\_OP,\ STRING\_OP \\ &UNARY\_OP,\ BINARY\_OP,\ \Phi,\ UNKNOWN\} \end{aligned} \quad (2)$$

$$\begin{aligned} F^f = \{&x^f \xrightarrow{op} y^f \mid x,\ y \text{ are variables referenced in } f, \\ &f \in G,\ \text{relation } y = op(x) \text{ is in } f,\ op \in Operator\} \end{aligned} \quad (3)$$

$$E = \bigcup_{f \in G} F^f \quad (4)$$

The value of a variable in a caller function may be passed to a variable in a callee function; we use an abstract operator $CALL$ to represent this type of value passing operation, and define $C_{forward}$ in Formula 5 as the set of all such call value flows extracted from the call graph G. The value of a variable in a caller function may be also updated with the return value from a callee function; we use an abstract operator $RETURN$ to represent this type of value return operation, and define $C_{backward}$ in Formula 6 as the set of all such

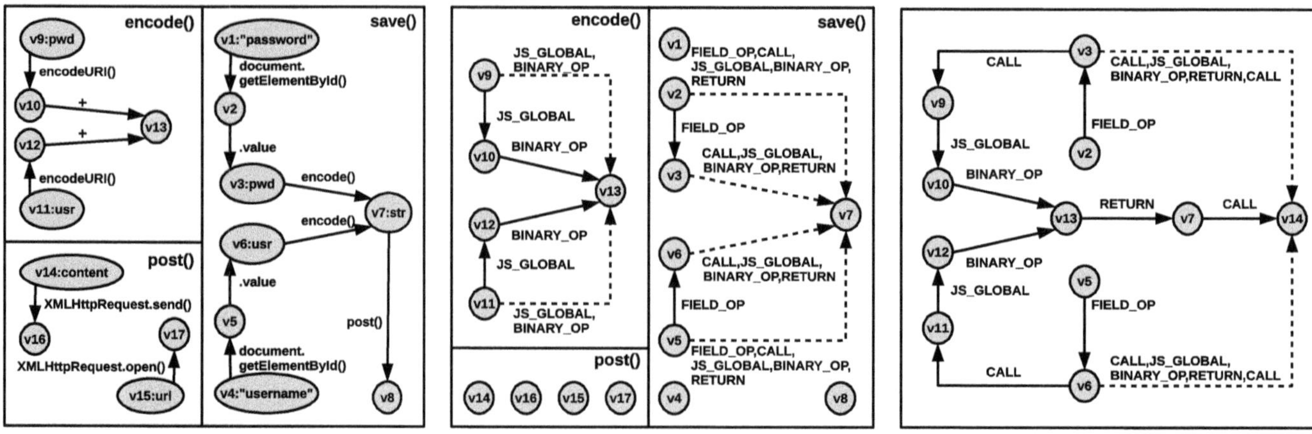

(a) Variable use graphs (b) Function-level relation analysis result (c) Program-level relation analysis result

Figure 3: The analysis results for the code excerpt in Figure 1. The dashed lines in (b) and (c) represent the computed transitive relations; to simplify the figure, we only kept the operators and omitted the variables in the labels of those dashed lines, and we only drew the two newly computed transitive relations in (c).

return value flows extracted from the call graph G. In Formula 7, E^+ defines the ***extended variable use graphs***, and it is the union of E, $C_{forward}$, and $C_{backward}$. In Formula 8, $Operator^+$ defines the extended set of abstract operators, and it is the union of $Operator$ and $\{CALL, RETURN\}$.

We use Formula 9 to define the transitive relation summary Q^f for function f, which is the set of transitive relations between each pair of variables x and y in the same function f. Each ***transitive relation*** is represented by a sequence of abstract operators and variables through which a value is passed from x to y. In Formula 10, Q defines the ***function-level relation summaries*** for all the functions in the call graph G.

$$C_{forward} = \{arg^{f_i} \xrightarrow{CALL} para^{f_j} \mid f_i \xrightarrow{s} f_j \in G, \; arg^{f_i} \textit{ is the argument of the callsite } s \textit{ in } f_i, \; para^{f_j} \textit{ is the corresponding parameter of } f_j\} \quad (5)$$

$$C_{backward} = \{ret^{f_j} \xrightarrow{RETURN} rec^{f_i} \mid f_i \xrightarrow{s} f_j \in G, \; ret^{f_j} \textit{ is the variable returned in } f_j, \; rec^{f_i} \textit{ accepts the returned value from callsite } s \textit{ in } f_i\} \quad (6)$$

$$E^+ = E \cup C_{forward} \cup C_{backward} \quad (7)$$

$$Operator^+ = Operator \cup \{CALL, \; RETURN\} \quad (8)$$

$$Q^f(x,y) = \{(x^f, op_1, v_1^{f_1}, op_2, v_2^{f_2}, \cdots, v_{k-1}^{f_{k-1}}, op_k, y^f) \mid f, f_1, f_2, \ldots, f_{k-1} \in G, \; op_1, op_2, \ldots op_k \in Operator^+, \; x^f \xrightarrow{op_1} v_1^{f_1}, \; v_1^{f_1} \xrightarrow{op_2} v_2^{f_2}, \; \ldots, \; v_{k-1}^{f_{k-1}} \xrightarrow{op_k} y^f \in E^+\} \quad (9)$$

$$\textit{Function level relation summaries } Q = \bigcup_{f \in G} Q^f \quad (10)$$

Figure 4 illustrates the function-level relation analysis algorithm for computing Q. The algorithm consists of two procedures. The Compute-ExtendedVariableUseGraphs procedure constructs the variable use graphs E (Formula 4) from line 2 to line 4, constructs $C_{forward}$ (Formula 5) from line 5 to line 8, constructs $C_{backward}$ (Formula 6) from line 9 to line 12, and finally returns the extended variable use graphs E^+ (Formula 7) at line 14.

The Compute-FunctionLevelRelations procedure initializes each transitive relation summary Q^f for function f with its updated variable use graph F^f at line 2 in the first for loop. In the following do-while loop, for each function f in the post-order traversal of G, this procedure updates Q^f with the newly computed transitive relations for each pair of variables in that function f from line 6 to line 7. The post-order traversal is used at line 5 so that callee functions are analyzed prior to their caller functions whenever possible. This update is an iterative process, and the do-while loop terminates when no more update occurs to any Q^f. The union of all the Q^fs is returned at line 10.

The *compute_transitive_summary* sub-procedure is capable of summarizing paths and cycles to compute transitive relations on a graph, based on the transitive operations defined for a given problem. In this sub-procedure, cycles are summarized using their equivalent directed acyclic graphs (DAGs) [40], and "UNKNOWN" operators are replaced with their corresponding transitive relations in the callee functions; therefore, the do-while loop from line 4 to line 8 ***must terminate***. Many existing transitive closure computation algorithms such as [40, 39] could be adapted to implement this sub-procedure. We implement this sub-procedure in our framework by adapting the algorithm in [40], which is an efficient algorithm with a time complexity linear to the number of nodes and edges in the input graph.

Figure 3(b) illustrates the *function-level relation analysis* result for the code excerpt in Figure 1. For example, the computed transitive relation from v_3 to v_7 is labeled with "CALL,JS_GLOBAL,BINARY_OP,RETURN"; we only kept these operators and omitted the variables in the label to simplify the figure.

3.3.2 Program-level Relation Analysis

The purpose of the *program-level relation analysis* is to compute program-level relation summary based on the call graph and the function-level relation summaries. Specifically, it aims to further summarize transitive relations between each pair of the specified source and sink variables, irrespective of whether the pair of variables are defined in the same function or in different functions.

It is important to note that partial cross-function relations (i.e., $C_{forward}$ and $C_{backward}$) have been included in the function-level relation analysis algorithm shown in Figure 4. Computing function-level relation summaries based on small-size and localized extended variable use graphs be-

```
Compute-ExtendedVariableUseGraphs (P, G)
    // P: program; G: call graph.
    E = C_forward = C_backward = ∅;
    for each function f ∈ G do
        F^f = get_updated_var_use_graph(P, f);
        E = E ∪ F^f;
    for each edge f_i --s--> f_j ∈ G do
        arg^{f_i} = argument_of_callsite(s);
        para^{f_j} = parameter_of_function(f_j);
        C_forward = C_forward ∪ (arg^{f_i} --CALL--> para^{f_j});
    for each edge f_i --s--> f_j ∈ G do
        ret^{f_j} = return_var_of_function(f_j);
        rec^{f_i} = accept_return_value_var(s);
        C_backward = C_backward ∪ (ret^{f_j} --RETURN--> rec^{f_i});
    E^+ = E ∪ C_forward ∪ C_backward;
    return E^+;

Compute-FunctionLevelRelations (P, G, E^+)
    // P: program; G: call graph;
    // E^+: extended variable use graphs.
    for each function f ∈ G do
        Q^f = F^f = get_updated_var_use_graph(P, f);
        vars^f = get_nodes_in(F^f);
    do
        for each function f in the post-order traversal of G do
            for each pair of variables src, dst ∈ vars^f do
                Q^f(src, dst) =
                    compute_transitive_summary(E^+, src, dst);
    while at least one Q^f is updated
    Q = ⋃_{f∈G} Q^f;
    return Q;
```

Figure 4: Function-level relation analysis algorithm

fore computing program-level relation summary is critical for the LvDetector framework to efficiently analyze large and complex extensions; otherwise, directly analyzing transitive relations on a program-level graph consisting of many extended variable use graphs with complex cycles and paths will be very inefficient. This is the key reason for us to explicitly divide the transitive variable relation analysis into two steps at the function-level and program-level.

The value of a variable in a function may be passed to another variable in another function through global variables or JavaScript events. We use an abstract operator $GLOBAL$ to represent the type of value passing through global variables, and define C_{global} in Formula 11 as the set of all such global value flows extracted from the whole program P; we use an abstract operator $MESSAGE$ to represent the type of value passing through JavaScript events, and define $C_{message}$ in Formula 12 as the set of all such message value flows extracted from the whole program P. In Formula 13, E' defines the further-extended variable use graphs, and it is the union of E^+, C_{global}, and $C_{message}$; in Formula 14, *Operator'* defines the further-extended set of abstract operators, and it is the union of $Operator^+$ and $\{GLOBAL, MESSAGE\}$.

Formula 15 defines the transitive relation summary, T^{f_i,f_j}, which is the set of transitive relations from any variable x in function f_i to any variable y in function f_j. Formula 16 defines the ***program-level relation summary***, T, which is the output of the program-level relation analysis component.

$$C_{global} = \{v^{f_i} \xrightarrow{GLOBAL} v^{f_j} \mid \textit{global variable } v \textit{ is defined in } f_i \textit{ and used in } f_j\} \quad (11)$$

$$C_{message} = \{arg^{f_i} \xrightarrow{MESSAGE} para^{f_j} \mid \textit{an event is dispatched in } f_i\textit{, and processed in } f_j\textit{, } arg^{f_i} \textit{ is the argument to this event, } para^{f_j} \textit{ is the corresponding parameter of } f_j\} \quad (12)$$

$$E' = E^+ \cup C_{global} \cup C_{message} \quad (13)$$

$$Operator' = Operator^+ \cup \{GLOBAL, MESSAGE\} \quad (14)$$

$$T^{f_i,f_j}(x,y) = \{(x^{f_i}, op_1, v_1^{f_1}, \cdots, v_{k-1}^{f_{k-1}}, op_k, y^{f_j}) \mid f_i, f_1, \ldots, f_{k-1}, f_j \in G,\ op_1, \ldots op_k \in Operator',\ x^{f_i} \xrightarrow{op_1} v_1^{f_1}, \ldots, v_{k-1}^{f_{k-1}} \xrightarrow{op_k} y^{f_j} \in E'\} \quad (15)$$

$$\textit{Program level relation summary } T = \bigcup_{f_i,f_j \in G} T^{f_i,f_j} \quad (16)$$

```
Compute-ProgramLevelRelations (P, Q, E^+, sVars, dVars)
       // P: program; Q: function-level relation summaries;
       // E^+: extended variable use graph;
       // sVars: a set of source variables;
       // dVars: a set of destination (sink) variables.
1      C_global = C_message = ∅;  T = Q;
2      for each global variable v in P do
3          defs = get_definitions(v); uses = get_uses(v);
4          for each pair of v^{f_i} ∈ defs and v^{f_j} ∈ uses do
5              C_global = C_global ∪ (v^{f_i} --GLOBAL--> v^{f_j});
6      for each event evt dispatched in f_i and processed in f_j do
7          arg^{f_i} = argument_of_event(evt);
8          para^{f_j} = parameter_of_function(f_j);
9          C_message = C_message ∪ (arg^{f_i} --MESSAGE--> para^{f_j});
10     E' = E^+ ∪ C_global ∪ C_message;
11     for each pair of src ∈ sVars and dst ∈ dVars do
12         T^{f_i,f_j}(src, dst) =        // src is in f_i, dst is in f_j
               compute_transitive_summary(E', src, dst);
13     return T;
```

Figure 5: Program-level relation analysis algorithm

Figure 5 illustrates the overall program-level relation analysis algorithm for computing T. It constructs C_{global} (Formula 11) from line 2 to line 5, constructs $C_{message}$ (Formula 12) from line 6 to line 9, builds the further-extended variable use graphs E' (Formula 13) at line 10, updates T with the newly computed transitive relations from line 11 to line 12 for each pair of variables constructed from the input sets $sVars$ and $dVars$, and finally returns T. The *compute_transitive_summary* sub-procedure at line 12 is the same one that is used in the function-level relation analysis algorithm (Figure 4). It is worth mentioning that in the program-level relation analysis, the number of edges ***will not increase exponentially*** because paths and cycles were summarized in the *compute_transitive_summary* sub-procedure, and the transitive relations computed in the function-level analysis will not be computed again in the program-level analysis.

Figure 3(c) illustrates the *program-level relation analysis* result for the code excerpt in Figure 1. The source variables are v_3 and v_6, and the sink variable is v_{14}. Two new transitive relations are computed from v_3 to v_{14} and from v_6 to v_{14}, respectively; both of them are labeled with "CALL,JS_GLOBAL,BINARY_OP,RETURN,CALL".

3.4 Vulnerability Analysis

The purpose of this phase is to analyze vulnerabilities based on the program-level relation summary and the source-destination (sink) variable pairs as shown in Figure 6. For all the relations from a source variable to a destination (sink) variable, currently LvDetector reports vulnerabilities based on two rules. One is that the ENCRYPT abstract operator does not appear in a relation (line 3); the other is that both the ENCRYPT and DECRYPT abstract operators appear in a relation, but no ENCRYPT abstract operator appears after the last DECRYPT abstract operator (line 5). Otherwise, LvDetector simply records a relation as a non-vulnerable information flow (line 8). Application developers may misuse cryptographic primitives as demonstrated by Egele et al. [13]. The current version of LvDetector does not further examine cryptographic misuses such as using constant keys or non-random initialization vectors in browser extensions, thus its vulnerability detection is more like a lower-bound analysis.

```
Analyze-Vulnerability (T, sVars, dVars)
    // T: program-level relation summary;
    // sVars: a set of source variables;
    // dVars: a set of destination (sink) variables.
1   for each pair of src ∈ sVars and dst ∈ dVars do
2       for each relation r ∈ T(src, dst) do
3           if the ENCRYPT operator does not appear in r then
4               report_vulnerability(r);
5           else if the DECRYPT operator appears in r but no
            ENCRYPT appears after the last DECRYPT then
6               report_vulnerability(r);
7           else
8               record_non_vulnerable_flow(r);
```

Figure 6: Vulnerability analysis algorithm

The report_vulnerability sub-procedure automatically classifies the source variables into two categories. All the source variables that accept sensitive information (e.g., the *password* type inputs, cookies, and bookmarks) either from user inputs or webpages are in the *sensitive* category, and the rest are in the *other* category. This sub-procedure also groups the sink variables into the *network* category and the *local disk* category, with their values sent across the network or saved to the local disk, respectively. It further classifies the reported vulnerabilities as *high-severity*, *medium-severity*, and *unranked* ones as shown in Table 1. Those vulnerabilities that leak information from the sensitive source variables to the network sink variables are classified as high-severity. Those vulnerabilities that leak information from the sensitive source variables to the local disk sink variables are classified as medium-severity because unprotected sensitive information on a user's local disk can also lead to security breaches due to, for example, bots [33]. The rest are classified as unranked because their source variables are not automatically classified as sensitive; an analyst can further classify these unranked ones based on whether the source variables can be considered as sensitive.

Each vulnerability report contains a list of high-severity, medium-severity, and unranked vulnerability records for each scenario-driven execution. Each record includes the complete information flow, and highlights the original variables and operations to provide more intuitive information. For example, for the code excerpt in Figure 1, the information flow from the variable "pwd" in the save() function to the

Table 1: Vulnerability classification

Source Vars \ Sink Vars	Network	Local disk
Sensitive	High-severity	Medium-severity
Other	Unranked	Unranked

variable "content" in the post() function is identified as a high-severity vulnerability, and the corresponding record is: $v_3(\boldsymbol{pwd}) \xrightarrow{CALL(encode())} v_9(\boldsymbol{pwd}) \xrightarrow{JS\_GLOBAL(encodeURI())} v_{10}() \xrightarrow{BINARY\_OP(+)} v_{13}() \xrightarrow{RETURN(encode())} v_7(\boldsymbol{str}) \xrightarrow{CALL(post())} v_{14}(\boldsymbol{content})$. Note that the contents in the parentheses such as "pwd", "+", and "encode()" are the original variables, operations, and function calls in the source code. In addition, the locations (i.e., file names, function names, and line numbers) of the original variables, operations, and function calls are also provided in each record. This intuitive information can help analysts easily locate the reported vulnerabilities in the extensions.

4. EVALUATION

We implemented LvDetector in Java. We also integrated two popular compilers into the LvDetector framework. In the instrumentation component, we used Closure Compiler [7] to identify all the functions and callsites. We chose WALA Compiler [8] as the SSA builder to generate SSA IRs. We evaluated LvDetector on 28 most popular or top rated extensions that belong to six categories as shown in Table 2; 17 of them were selected from the Firefox extension store [14], and 11 of them were selected from the Google Chrome extension store [5]. The main criteria for choosing these extensions are: they must use cryptographic functions; they must have sensitive source variables and network sink variables so that high-severity vulnerabilities may exist (Section 3.4). In the following subsections, we detail one case study, the overall analysis results for 28 extensions, the responsible disclosure and feedback, and the performance results; we also further discuss the false positives and false negatives.

4.1 Case Study of RoboForm

RoboForm (Lite) is a Firefox extension that can help users remember and auto-fill their website passwords [30]. It provides a master password mechanism to further protect users' website passwords. We used LvDetector to analyze RoboForm on six use scenarios.

Scenario 1: A user provides the master password in a 'password' type input field to RoboForm to protect the saved website passwords. The master password is automatically classified as sensitive; it should only be known by the user and should not be sent out even to the remote server of RoboForm. LvDetector identified one high-severity vulnerable information flow, in which the master password is leaked out through one sink statement, the send() method call of an XMLHttpRequest object, without the protection of any cryptographic function. We verified that this information flow is indeed vulnerable.

Scenario 2: A user allows RoboForm to save a website password to its remote server. The website password is automatically classified as sensitive; it should only be known by the user and the corresponding website. LvDetector identified two high-severity vulnerable information flows, in which the website password is leaked out through the same sink statement as in scenario 1 without the protection of any cryptographic function. They are two flows because they take different code branches. We verified that these two information flows are indeed vulnerable.

Scenario 3: A user allows RoboForm to save a website password to the local disk without using a master password. LvDetector identified one medium-severity vulnerable information flow, in which the website password is leaked out through one sink statement, the write() method call of a FileOutputStream object, without the protection of any cryptographic function. We verified that this information flow is indeed vulnerable.

Scenario 4: A user allows RoboForm to save a website password to the local disk with the protection of a master password. LvDetector identified two information flows and simply recorded them as non-vulnerable: one saves the website password to the local disk after performing an AES encryption, the other saves the master password to the local disk after performing a DES encryption. We verified that these two information flows are indeed non-vulnerable.

Scenarios 5 and 6: A user creates (scenario 5) and types (scenario 6) a RoboForm login account in a dialog box. The RoboForm login password is automatically classified as sensitive; it should only be known by the user and RoboForm. LvDetector identified one high-severity vulnerable information flow in each of the two scenarios. The RoboForm login password is leaked out through the same sink statement as in scenario 1 without the protection of any cryptographic function. However, these two information flows should not be identified as vulnerable because the RoboForm login password is sent only to the remote server of RoboForm.

4.2 Overall Results

Table 2 summarizes the overall analysis results on the 28 extensions. The second column lists the number of the use scenarios chosen in each extension. The third column lists the number of analyzed statements over the total number of statements in each extension. The fourth column lists the number of different cryptographic functions identified in each extension. The fifth column lists the number of the source variables in each extension for all the chosen scenarios. The sixth column lists the number of the sink variables in each extension for all the chosen scenarios. The seventh column lists the number of ***true positives (TP)*** that are vulnerable information flows correctly identified by LvDetector; correspondingly, the eighth column lists the number of ***false positives (FP)*** that include nonexistent flows and non-vulnerable existent flows. The ninth column lists the number of ***true negatives (TN)*** that are non-vulnerable information flows correctly identified by LvDetector; correspondingly, the last column lists the number of ***false negatives (FN)*** that are vulnerable information flows incorrectly identified by LvDetector as non-vulnerable. These TP/FP/TN/FN numbers come from our examination of the information flows reported/recorded by LvDetector (Figure 6).

For example, we chose six scenarios in the RoboForm case study (Section 4.1). LvDetector analyzed 6880 out of the total 26120 lines of code. LvDetector automatically identified six different cryptographic functions, and automatically identified seven source variables and 19 sink variables, LvDetector detected six vulnerable information flows with four true positives and two false positives, and recorded two non-vulnerable information flows with two true negatives and zero false negative.

The following five formulas present the precision, recall, F-measure, accuracy, and false positive rate calculations for the results in Table 2.

$$Precision(Pre) = \frac{TP(18)}{TP(18) + FP(6)} = 75\% \quad (17)$$

$$Recall(Rec) = \frac{TP(18)}{TP(18) + FN(0)} = 100\% \quad (18)$$

$$F - measure = \frac{2 \times Rec(100\%) \times Pre(75\%)}{Rec(100\%) + Pre(75\%)} = 86\% \quad (19)$$

$$Accuracy = \frac{TP(18) + TN(23)}{TP(18) + TN(23) + FP(6) + FN(0)} = 87\% \quad (20)$$

$$FalsePositiveRate = \frac{FP(6)}{FP(6) + TN(23)} = 21\% \quad (21)$$

A good analysis framework should achieve high precision and high recall. However, a tradeoff often exists between high precision and high recall because achieving one may compromise the other and vice versa. To combine precision and recall, the harmonic mean of them, F-measure, is often used. Accuracy is the overall success rate of the analysis.

From these calculations, we can conclude that LvDetector is an effective framework. It achieves a high precision rate (75%), indicating that the majority of the identified vulnerable flows are indeed vulnerable. It achieves a high recall rate (100%), indicating that LvDetector can identify the majority of the actually vulnerable flows for the executed scenarios. It also achieves a high F-measure rate (86%) and a high accuracy rate(87%). The false positive rate is 21%; however, the detection results of LvDetector will be used by analysts to more easily identify information flow vulnerabilities. This usage is different from that of other systems such as intrusion detection or online malware detection systems, in which the detection results will be used to make immediate decisions such as dropping network packets or removing malicious programs. Therefore, a 21% false positive rate will not cause too much inconvenience to the analysts.

Overall, LvDetector identified 18 true information leakage vulnerabilities in 13 extensions. These vulnerabilities are previously unknown, and they exist in 46% of the analyzed extensions. Nine of them are high-severity vulnerabilities, and seven of them are medium-severity vulnerabilities. The remaining two are unranked because their source variables that accept users' notes are not automatically classified as sensitive; they can be further classified as one high-severity and one medium-severity vulnerabilities, respectively, since users' notes and tasks may contain sensitive information. We examined that three main reasons account for those 18 vulnerabilities: developers did not realize the importance of protecting sensitive data before sending or saving them, protection was not applied to all the code branches for sensitive information flows, code had bugs such as sending or saving plaintext rather than ciphertext. These information leakage problems deserve serious attention from extension developers, browser vendors, researchers, and users.

4.3 Responsible Disclosure and Feedback

Among the 13 extensions that have vulnerabilities, 12 of them contain contact information on their websites or extension store webpages. We emailed those 12 developers asking if they would like to know the details about the vulnerabilities in their extensions, and received eight replies.

Table 2: Analysis results on 28 Firefox * and Google Chrome + extensions

Extensions	Num of Use Scenarios	Num of Statements (Analyzed / Total)	Num of Different Crypto Functions	Num of Variables		Num of Positives		Num of Negatives	
				Source	Sink	True (TP)	False (FP)	True (TN)	False (FN)
Feeds, News & Blogging									
1. Gmail Manager NG *	1	455 / 1482	4	1	3	0	0	1	0
2. Email Notifier *	1	212 / 1680	1	1	11	1	0	0	0
Shopping									
3. Shoptimate *	1	287 / 10612	1	1	2	2	0	0	0
4. EFT Pass +	1	735 / 4466	4	1	5	0	0	0	0
Privacy & Security									
5. Autofill Forms *	1	3490 / 3524	1	1	1	1	4	1	0
6. Cookies Manager *	1	419 / 3753	2	1	1	1	0	3	0
7. Secure Bookmarks +	1	2028 / 2569	2	1	5	0	0	6	0
8. Lazarus *	2	3525 / 7610	2	2	65	0	0	3	0
9. RoboForm *	6	6880 / 26120	6	7	19	4	2	2	0
10. QuickPasswords *	1	2082 / 2170	2	1	8	0	0	0	0
11. Link Password *	1	984 / 984	3	2	3	0	0	3	0
12. uPassword *	1	1467 / 3803	1	2	2	0	0	0	0
13. MD5 Reborned Hasher *	1	504 / 504	2	1	1	0	0	0	0
14. Encrypted Communication *	1	404 / 404	2	2	1	0	0	2	0
15. EverSync *	1	3868 / 6273	2	1	7	1	0	0	0
Productivity									
16. Add Tasks to Do It +	1	351 / 467	1	1	6	1	0	0	0
17. Tab Wrangler +	1	228 / 3659	1	1	1	1	0	0	0
18. Any.do +	3	442 / 12980	1	3	14	2	0	0	0
19. 123 Password +	1	128 / 418	2	1	1	0	0	0	0
20. ChromePW +	1	307 / 787	1	1	2	0	0	1	0
Social & Communication									
21. X-notifier +	1	846 / 5220	4	1	4	1	0	0	0
22. Simple Mail *	1	5013 / 9832	2	1	13	0	0	1	0
23. Inbox Ace +	1	15682 / 20251	1	1	19	0	0	0	0
24. Google Plus Follower Stats *	1	600 / 5532	1	1	1	0	0	0	0
25. FoxToPhone *	1	1342 / 1771	1	1	15	1	0	0	0
26. FB Chat History Manager *	1	102 / 560	3	1	1	0	0	0	0
Accessibility									
27. Smart Bookmarks +	1	1038 / 2818	1	1	1	1	0	0	0
28. AnnoPad +	1	566 / 10533	1	1	6	1	0	0	0
Total	36	53965 / 150783	18	40	218	18	6	23	0

We further provided the detailed vulnerabilities to the eight developers respectively. Two of them patched their extensions in the online stores; one of them removed his extension from the Google extension store; four of them did not further respond to us; one of them disagreed with our analysis result, and mentioned that tons of extensions persist much more sensitive data all over the place and his extension does not encrypt data because the browser's storage APIs do not provide encryption options.

4.4 Performance Results

We measured the running time of LvDetector in analyzing the vulnerabilities in each extension on a desktop computer with 2.83GHz CPU, 2.96GB memory, 32-bit Windows 7 operating system, and Java Runtime Environment 1.7. For the vulnerability analysis of the 36 use scenarios (Table 2), the maximum running time is about 48 minutes (corresponding to the scenario 1 of the RoboForm case study described in Section 4.1), the minimum running time is less than one minute, the median running time is six minutes, and the average running time is 12 minutes with a standard deviation of 13. Because LvDetector is an offline analysis framework, such a running time performance is quite acceptable. Note that the running time is not linear to the Lines of Code, and it is often related to the code complexity.

4.5 Discussion

False positives may come from a few sources. First, in the *variable use analysis*, the conditions in the control flow of the SSA IR are not currently considered; therefore, extra (i.e., nonexistent) information flows could be later included in the *function-level relation analysis*. Second, in the *variable use analysis*, the individual elements in a collection type of object such as array or linkedlist are not further differentiated from each other - the analysis granularity is only at the object level; therefore, extra information flows could be later included in the *function-level relation analysis*. Third, in the *program-level relation analysis*, all possible edges are created between global variable definitions and their uses; therefore, extra information flows could be included. Fourth, if the value of a sensitive variable is leaked to an intended remote server for further processing, this type of leakage should not be identified as vulnerable. Among the 6 false positives reported in our evaluation results (Section 4.2), four of them come from the first source, and the remaining two come from the fourth source as explained in the scenarios 5 and 6 of the RoboForm case study (Section 4.1). Although in our evaluation we did not observe any false positive coming from the second and the third sources, analysts should still pay attention to these sources when they use LvDetector.

False negatives may occur due to reasons such as the misuses of cryptographic primitives [13], which are not further examined by the current version of LvDetector (Section 3.4). In addition, because LvDetector builds call graphs from the scenario-driven execution traces, vulnerabilities will not be identified for the scenarios that are not executed by analysts.

In the future, we plan to consider the conditions in the control flow of the SSA IR, differentiate the elements in an Array from each other, and refine the mappings between global variable definitions and their uses; with these enhancements, we expect that false positives can be reduced. We also plan to investigate potential cryptographic misuses [13] in browser extensions and other path exploration techniques such as [23, 32] to see if LvDetector can identify more vulnerabilities.

5. RELATED WORK

Existing research on analyzing the security of JavaScript-based extensions mostly focused on identifying privilege escalation related vulnerabilities that could lead to web-based attacks or malware installation. Researchers applied static information flow analysis techniques [1] and dynamic taint analysis techniques [12] to identify privilege escalation related vulnerabilities in buggy browser extensions. Guha et al. proposed a new model for secure development, verification, and deployment of browser extensions to limit potential over-privilege problems [18]. Barth et al. designed a new extension system for Google Chrome that uses least privilege, privilege separation, and strong isolation mechanisms [2]. Carlini et al. manually reviewed and evaluated the effectiveness of those three mechanisms in a set of Google Chrome extensions [3]. Liu et al. revealed that malicious attacks can still violate the least privilege and privilege separation mechanisms of the Google Chrome extension system, and proposed some countermeasures [24].

Only a handful of existing solutions [4, 11, 22] aimed to address the same problem targeted by our LvDetector, but they took either pure dynamic approaches or pure static approaches. In [4], Chang and Chen proposed a framework, *iObfus*, to dynamically protect against the potential sensitive information leakage through browser extensions. iObfus marks sensitive web elements, obfuscates the sensitive information before performing any I/O operation, and de-obfuscates the information only for trusted domains. In [11], Dhawan and Ganapathy proposed a framework, *Sabre*, to dynamically track information flows in JavaScript-based Firefox extensions. Sabre associates security labels with JavaScript objects, tracks the propagation of those labels at runtime in the SpiderMonkey JavaScript engine of Firefox, and raises an alert if an object with a sensitive label is written to a low-sensitivity sink point. These frameworks are not publicly available for comparison. However, generally speaking, only using online dynamic techniques without performing a static analysis in advance suffers from ***three main drawbacks***: (1) asking users to respond to runtime alerts may not be wise, while using default response options may become too restrictive [1]; (2) it is not possible to detect all information flows dynamically [31, 36]; (3) performance and memory overhead can often be incurred to the system [1]. In addition, dynamic approaches are often browser-specific and require high instrumentation effort [11]. In [22], Kashyap and Hardekopf proposed an abstract interpretation approach to validate the pre-defined security signatures for browser extensions; however, pure static analysis of JavaScript-based extensions can often incur high false positives as we discussed in Section 3.1. Our LvDetector combines both static and dynamic program analysis techniques, and aims to automatically identify information leakage vulnerabilities in browser extensions before they are released to users.

Static and dynamic program analysis techniques have also been used to address other JavaScript security problems in web applications. On the one hand, static program analysis techniques have been used to detect JavaScript malware [6, 9], detect web application vulnerabilities such as injection and cross-site scripting [17], and examine a restricted version of JavaScript that enables the API confinement verification [34]. Static techniques can provide a comprehensive code coverage, but may over-estimate the actual execution paths and incur false positives. On the other hand, dynamic program analysis techniques have been used to enforce information flow security for a set of core features in JavaScript [19], detect privacy-violating information flows such as cookie stealing and history sniffing [20], and identify client-side code injection vulnerabilities [32]. Dynamic techniques can capture the precise program execution information, but may overlook certain potential execution paths and incur false negatives. Static and dynamic program analysis techniques have also been combined to prevent cross-site scripting attacks [35, 36], track information flow in JavaScript code injection attacks [21], and extract the dynamically generated code for analyzing script injection attacks [37]. Our LvDetector uses both static and dynamic program analysis techniques but focuses on addressing a different problem than those addressed by this body of work.

6. CONCLUSION

In this paper, we present a framework, LvDetector, that combines static and dynamic program analysis techniques for automatic detection of information leakage vulnerabilities in legitimate browser extensions. Extension developers can use LvDetector to locate and fix the vulnerabilities in their code; browser vendors can use LvDetector to decide whether the corresponding extensions can be hosted in their online stores; advanced users can also use LvDetector to determine if certain extensions are safe to use. LvDetector is not bound to specific web browsers or JavaScript engines; it follows a modular design principle, and can adopt other program analysis techniques. We implemented LvDetector in Java and evaluated it on 28 popular Firefox and Google Chrome extensions. The evaluation results and the feedback to our responsible disclosure demonstrate that LvDetector is useful and effective.

7. ACKNOWLEDGMENTS

The authors sincerely thank anonymous reviewers for their valuable suggestions and comments. The first two authors were supported in part by NSF grants CNS-1359542 and DGE-1438935. The third author was supported in part by NSF grant CCF-1261811.

8. REFERENCES

[1] S. Bandhakavi, S. T. King, P. Madhusudan, and M. Winslett. Vex: Vetting browser extensions for security vulnerabilities. In *Proc. of USENIX Security Symposium*, pages 339–354, 2010.

[2] A. Barth, A. P. Felt, P. Saxena, and A. Boodman. Protecting browsers from extension vulnerabilities. In *Proc. of NDSS*, 2010.

[3] N. Carlini, A. P. Felt, and D. Wagner. An evaluation of the google chrome extension security architecture. In *Proc. of USENIX Security Symposium*, 2012.

[4] W. Chang and S. Chen. Defeat information leakage from browser extensions via data obfuscation. In *Proc. of ICICS*, 2013.

[5] Google Chrome Extensions. `https://chrome.google.com/extensions/`.

[6] R. Chugh, J. A. Meister, R. Jhala, and S. Lerner. Staged information flow for javascript. In *Proc. of ACM PLDI*, pages 50–62. ACM, 2009.

[7] Closure Compiler. `https://developers.google.com/closure/compiler/`.

[8] WALA Compiler. `http://wala.sourceforge.net/wiki/index.php`.

[9] C. Curtsinger, B. Livshits, B. G. Zorn, and C. Seifert. Zozzle: Fast and precise in-browser javascript malware detection. In *Proc. of USENIX Security Symp.*, 2011.

[10] R. Cytron, J. Ferrante, B. K. Rosen, M. N. Wegman, and F. K. Zadeck. Efficiently computing static single assignment form and the control dependence graph. *ACM Trans. Program. Lang. Syst.*, 13(4), 10 1991.

[11] M. Dhawan and V. Ganapathy. Analyzing information flow in javascript-based browser extensions. In *Proc. of ACSAC*, pages 382–391, 2009.

[12] V. Djeric and A. Goel. Securing script-based extensibility in web browsers. In *Proc. of USENIX Security Symposium*, 2010.

[13] M. Egele, D. Brumley, Y. Fratantonio, and C. Kruegel. An empirical study of cryptographic misuse in android applications. In *Proc. of CCS*, 2013.

[14] Firefox Extensions. `https://addons.mozilla.org/`.

[15] D. Grove, G. DeFouw, J. Dean, and C. Chambers. Call graph construction in object-oriented languages. In *Proc. of ACM OOPSLA*, pages 108–124, 1997.

[16] S. Guarnieri and B. Livshits. Gatekeeper: Mostly static enforcement of security and reliability policies for javascript code. In *Proc. of USENIX Security Symposium*, pages 151–168, 2009.

[17] S. Guarnieri, M. Pistoia, O. Tripp, J. Dolby, S. Teilhet, and R. Berg. Saving the world wide web from vulnerable javascript. In *Proc. of ISSTA*, 2011.

[18] A. Guha, M. Fredrikson, B. Livshits, and N. Swamy. Verified security for browser extensions. In *Proc. of IEEE S&P Symposium*, pages 115–130, 2011.

[19] D. Hedin and A. Sabelfeld. Information-flow security for a core of javascript. In *Proc. of IEEE CSF*, 2012.

[20] D. Jang, R. Jhala, S. Lerner, and H. Shacham. An empirical study of privacy-violating information flows in javascript web applications. In *Proc. of CCS*, 2010.

[21] S. Just, A. Cleary, B. Shirley, and C. Hammer. Information flow analysis for javascript. In *Proc. of ACM PLASTIC Workshop*, pages 9–18, 2011.

[22] V. Kashyap and B. Hardekopf. Security signature inference for javascript-based browser addons. In *Proc. of IEEE/ACM CGO Symposium*, pages 219–229, 2014.

[23] C. Kolbitsch, B. Livshits, B. Zorn, and C. Seifert. Rozzle: De-cloaking internet malware. In *Proc. of IEEE S&P Symposium*, pages 443–457, 2012.

[24] L. Liu, X. Zhang, G. Yan, and S. Chen. Chrome extensions: Threat analysis and countermeasures. In *Proc. of NDSS*, 2012.

[25] B. Livshits, M. Sridharan, Y. Smaragdakis, O. Lhoták, J. N. Amaral, B.-Y. E. Chang, S. Z. Guyer, U. P. Khedker, A. Møller, and D. Vardoulakis. In defense of soundiness: A manifesto. *Commun. ACM*, 58(2):44–46, 2015.

[26] M. Madsen, B. Livshits, and M. Fanning. Practical static analysis of javascript applications in the presence of frameworks and libraries. In *Proc. of ESEC/FSE*, pages 499–509, 2013.

[27] N. Nikiforakis, L. Invernizzi, A. Kapravelos, S. Van Acker, W. Joosen, C. Kruegel, F. Piessens, and G. Vigna. You are what you include: Large-scale evaluation of remote javascript inclusions. In *Proc. of CCS*, pages 736–747, 2012.

[28] G. Richards, C. Hammer, B. Burg, and J. Vitek. The eval that men do - a large-scale study of the use of eval in javascript applications. In *Proc. of ECOOP*, 2011.

[29] G. Richards, S. Lebresne, B. Burg, and J. Vitek. An analysis of the dynamic behavior of javascript programs. In *Proc. of ACM PLDI*, 2010.

[30] RoboForm. `http://www.roboform.com/`.

[31] A. Sabelfeld and A. C. Myers. Language-based information-flow security. *IEEE JSAC*, 21(1), 2003.

[32] P. Saxena, D. Akhawe, S. Hanna, F. Mao, S. McCamant, and D. Song. A symbolic execution framework for javascript. In *IEEE S&P Symp.*, 2010.

[33] B. Stone-Gross, M. Cova, L. Cavallaro, B. Gilbert, M. Szydlowski, R. A. Kemmerer, C. Kruegel, and G. Vigna. Your botnet is my botnet: analysis of a botnet takeover. In *Proc. of CCS*, 2009.

[34] A. Taly, U. Erlingsson, J. C. Mitchell, M. S. Miller, and J. Nagra. Automated Analysis of Security-Critical JavaScript APIs. In *Proc. of IEEE S&P Symp.*, 2011.

[35] O. Tripp, P. Ferrara, and M. Pistoia. Hybrid security analysis of web javascript code via dynamic partial evaluation. In *Proc. of ISSTA*, pages 49–59, 2014.

[36] P. Vogt, F. Nentwich, N. Jovanovic, E. Kirda, C. Kruegel, and G. Vigna. Cross site scripting prevention with dynamic data tainting and static analysis. In *Proc. of NDSS*, 2007.

[37] S. Wei and B. G. Ryder. Practical blended taint analysis for javascript. In *Proc. of ISSTA*, 2013.

[38] W. E. Weihl. Interprocedural data flow analysis in the presence of pointers, procedure variables, and label variables. In *Proc. of ACM POPL*, 1980.

[39] M. Weiser. Program slicing. In *Proc. of ICSE*, 1981.

[40] Q. Yi, V. Adve, and K. Kennedy. Transforming loops to recursion for multi-level memory hierarchies. In *Proc. of ACM PLDI*, pages 169–181, 2000.

[41] C. Yue and H. Wang. A measurement study of insecure javascript practices on the web. *ACM Transactions on the Web*, 7(2):7:1–7:39, 2013.

Enquiring Minds: Early Detection of Rumors in Social Media from Enquiry Posts

Zhe Zhao
Department of EECS
University of Michigan
zhezhao@umich.edu

Paul Resnick
School of Information
University of Michigan
presnick@umich.edu

Qiaozhu Mei
School of Information
University of Michigan
qmei@umich.edu

ABSTRACT

Many previous techniques identify trending topics in social media, even topics that are not pre-defined. We present a technique to identify trending rumors, which we define as topics that include disputed factual claims. Putting aside any attempt to assess whether the rumors are true or false, it is valuable to identify trending rumors as early as possible.

It is extremely difficult to accurately classify whether every individual post is or is not making a disputed factual claim. We are able to identify trending rumors by recasting the problem as finding entire clusters of posts whose topic is a disputed factual claim.

The key insight is that when there is a rumor, even though *most* posts do not raise questions about it, there may be a *few* that do. If we can find signature text phrases that are used by a few people to express skepticism about factual claims and are rarely used to express anything else, we can use those as detectors for rumor clusters. Indeed, we have found a few phrases that seem to be used exactly that way, including: "Is this true?", "Really?", and "What?". Relatively few posts related to any particular rumor use any of these enquiry phrases, but lots of rumor diffusion processes have **some** posts that do and have them quite **early** in the diffusion.

We have developed a technique based on searching for the enquiry phrases, clustering similar posts together, and then collecting related posts that do not contain these simple phrases. We then rank the clusters by their likelihood of really containing a disputed factual claim. The detector, which searches for the very rare but very informative phrases, combined with clustering and a classifier on the clusters, yields surprisingly good performance. On a typical day of Twitter, about a third of the top 50 clusters were judged to be rumors, a high enough precision that human analysts might be willing to sift through them.

Categories and Subject Descriptors

H.3.3 [**Information Search and Retrieval**]: Text Mining

General Terms

Experimentation; Empirical Studies

WWW 2015, May 18–22, 2015, Florence, Italy.
ACM 978-1-4503-3469-3/15/05.
http://dx.doi.org/10.1145/2736277.2741637.

Keywords

Rumor Detection; Enquiry Tweets; Social Media

1. INTRODUCTION

On April 15th of 2013, two explosions at the Boston Marathon finish line shocked the entire United States. The event dominated news channels for the next several days, and there were millions of tweets about it. Many of the tweets contained rumors and misinformation, including fake stories, hoaxes, and conspiracy theories.

Within a couple of days, multiple pieces of misinformation that went viral on social media were identified by professional analysts and debunked by the mainstream media.[1] These reports typically appeared several hours to a few days after the rumor became popular and only the most widely spread rumors attracted the attention of the mainstream media.

Beyond the mainstream media, rumor debunking Websites such as Snopes.com and PolitiFact.org check the credibility of controversial statements.[2] Such Websites heavily rely on social media observers to nominate potential rumors which are then fact-checked by analysts employed by the sites. They are able to check rumors that are somewhat less popular than those covered by mainstream media, but still have limited coverage and even longer delays.

One week after the Boston bombing, the official Twitter account of the Associated Press (AP) was hacked. The hacked account sent out a tweet about two explosions in the White House and the President being injured. Even though the account was quickly suspended, this rumor spread to millions of users. In such a special context, the rumor raised an immediate panic, which resulted in a dramatic, though brief, crash of the stock market [10].

The broad success of online social media has created fertile soil for the emergence and fast spread of rumors. According to a report of the development of new media in China, rumors were detected in more than 1/3 of the trending events on microblog media in 2012.[3]

Rather than relying solely on human observers to identify trending rumors, it would be helpful to have an automated tool to identify potential rumors. The goal of such a tool would not be to assess

[1]Source: `http://www.cnn.com/2013/04/16/tech/social-media/social-media-boston-fakes/`, retrieved on March 7, 2015; and `http://www.scpr.org/blogs/news/2013/04/16/13322/boston-marathon-bombings-rumor-control-man-on-the/`, retrieved on March 7, 2015.

[2]Source: `http://www.snopes.com/politics/conspiracy/boston.asp`, retrieved on March 7, 2015.

[3]Ironically, this report was misinterpreted by a major news media source, which coined a new rumor that "more than 1/3 of trending topics on Weibo are rumors." Source: `http://truth.cntv.cn/erjiye/20/`, retrieved on March 7, 2015.

the veracity of claims made in the rumors, merely to identify when claims were being spread that some people were questioning or disputing. If such a tool can identify rumors **earlier** and with sufficiently high precision, human analysts such as journalists might be willing to sift through all the top candidates to find those that were worth further investigation. They would then assess the veracity of the factual claims. Important rumors might be responded to earlier, limiting their damage. In addition, such a tool could help to develop a large collection of rumors. Previous research on rumor diffusion has included case studies of individual rumors that spread widely (e.g., [16]), but a fuller understanding of the nature of rumor diffusion will require study of much larger collections, including those that reach only modest audiences, so that commonalities and differences between diffusion patterns can be assessed.

We propose a new way to detect rumors **as early as possible** in their life cycle. The new method utilizes the enquiry behavior of social media users as sensors. The key insight is that some people who are exposed to a rumor, before deciding whether to believe it or not, will take a step of information enquiry to seek more information or to express skepticism without asserting specifically that it is false. Some of them will make their enquiries by tweeting. For example, within 60 seconds after the hacked AP account sent out the rumor about explosions in the White House, there were already multiple users enquiring about the truth of the rumor (Figure 1). Table 1 shows some examples of these enquiry tweets.

(a) 60 seconds after the hacked twitter account sent out the White House rumor there were already sufficient enquiry tweets (blue nodes).

(b) Two seconds after the first denial from an AP employee and two minutes before the official denial from AP, the rumor had already gone viral.

Figure 1: Snapshots of the diffusion of the White House rumor. Red, yellow and blue nodes: Twitters spreading, correcting, and questioning the rumor.

Of course, not all tweets about a rumor will be such skeptical enquiries. As features for classifying *individual tweets*, enquiry signals are insufficient. Even if they yielded high precision, the recall would be far too low. As features for classifying *tweet clusters*, however, they provide surprisingly good coverage. Our technique for automatically detecting rumors is built around this signal.

Table 1: Examples of enquiry tweets about the rumor of explosions in the White House

Oh my god is this real? RT @AP: Breaking: Two Explosions in the White House and Barack Obama is injured
Is this true? Or hacked account? RT @AP Breaking: Two Explosions in the White House and Barack Obama is injured
Is this real or hacked? RT @AP: Breaking: Two Explosions in the White House and Barack Obama is injured
How does this happen? #hackers RT @user: RT @AP: Breaking: Two Explosions in the White House and Barack Obama is injured
Is this legit? RT @AP Breaking: Two Explosions in the White House and Barack Obama is injured

We make three contributions in this work. First, we develop an algorithm for identifying *newly emerging, controversial* topics that is scalable to massive stream of tweets. It is scalable because it clusters only *signal tweets* rather than all tweets, and then assigns the rest of the tweets only if they match one of the signal clusters. Second, we identify a set of regular expressions that define the set of signal tweets. This crude classifier of signal tweets based on regular expression matching turns out to be sufficient. Third, we identify features of signal clusters that are independent of any particular topic and that can be used to effectively rank the clusters by their likelihood of containing a disputed factual claim.[4]

The algorithm is evaluated using the Twitter Gardenhose (a 10% sample of the overall tweet stream) to identify rumors on regular uneventful days. We also evaluate it using a large collection of tweets related to the Boston Marathon bombing event. We compare the algorithm to various baselines. It is more scalable and has higher precision and recall than techniques that try to find all trending topics. It detects more rumors, and detects them much earlier than a related technique that treats only debunks or corrections as signals of rumors as well as techniques that rely on tracking all trending topics or popular memes. The performance is also satisfactory in an absolute sense. It successfully detects 110 rumors from the stream of tweets about the Boston Marathon bombing event, with an average precision above 50% among the top-ranked candidates. It also achieves a precision of 33% when outputting 50 candidate rumors per day from analysis of the Gardenhose data.

2. RELATED WORK

2.1 Detection Problems in Social Media

Although rumors have long been a hot subject in multiple disciplines (e.g., [9, 31, 22]), research on identifying rumors from online social media through computational methods has only begun in recent years. Our previous work has shown that particular known rumors can be retrieved with a high accuracy by training a machine learning classifier for each rumor [28]. Here we seek to identify new rumors, not necessarily retrieve all the tweets related to them.

Much previous research has tried to develop classifiers for a more challenging problem than ours, automatically determining whether a meme that is spreading is true or false ([35, 4, 14, 17]). Application domains have included "event rumors" in Sun et al. [33], and fake images on Twitter during Hurricane Sandy [16]. The "Truthy" system attempts a related classification problem, whether a spreading meme is spreading "organically" or whether it is being spread by an "astroturf" campaign controlled by a single person or organization [29, 30].

Identifying the truth value of an arbitrary statement is very difficult, probably as difficult as any natural language processing problems. Even if one knows what the truth is, the problem is related to textual entailment (recognizing whether the meaning of one given statement can be inferred from another given statement), the accuracy of the art of which is lower than 70% on balanced lab data sets [8]. This is even harder for short posts in social media.

Thus, most existing approaches that attempt to classify the truthfulness of spreading memes utilize information beyond the content of the posts, usually by analyzing the collective behavior of how users respond to the target post. For example, many studies identified the popularity of a post (e.g., number of posts that retweeted

[4]At the risk of redundancy, we emphasize that our technique does not make any attempt to assess whether rumors are true or not, or classify or rank them based on the probability that they are true. We rank the clusters based on the probability that they contain a *disputed* claim, not that they contain a *false* claim.

or replied to the post) as a significant signal. This information is used either directly as features of the "rumor" classifier (e.g., [4, 14, 35, 17, 33, 34]), or as filters to prescreen candidate topics (e.g., to only consider the most popular posts [15] or "trending topics" [4, 14]), or both [4, 14]. Other work identified burstiness [34], temporal patterns [17, 15], or the network structure of the diffusion of a post/topic [30, 4, 32, 17] as important signals.

Most of these features of the tweet collection can only be collected after the rumor has circulated for a while. In other words, these features only become meaningful when the rumor has already reached and been responded to by many users. Once these features become available, we also make use of them in our classifier that ranks candidate rumor clusters. However, since we have set ourselves the easier task of detecting controversial fact-checkable claims, rather than detecting false claims, we are able to rely for initial detection on content features that are available much earlier in a meme's diffusion.

Some existing work uses corrections made by authoritative sources or social media users as a signal. For example, Takahashi and Igata tracked the clue keyword "false rumor" [34]. Both Kwon et al. [17] and Friggeri et al. [13] tracked the judgments made by rumor debunking websites such as Snopes.com. Studies of rumors on Weibo.com also tracked official corrections made by the site [35, 33]. These correction signals are closer in spirit to those we employ. They suffer, however, from limited coverage and delays, only working after a rumor has attracted the attention of authoritative sources. In our experiments we will compare the recall and earliness of rumor detection through our system using both correction and enquiry signals to a more limited version of our system that uses only correction signals.

Another related problem is detecting and tracking trending topics [20] or popular memes [18]. Even if they are effective at picking up newly popular topics, they are not sufficiently precise to serve as trending rumor detectors, as most topics and memes in social media are not rumors. As an example, Sun et al. collected 104 rumors and over 26,000 non-rumor posts in their experiment [33]. Later in this paper, we will compare the precision of the candidate rumors filtered using our method and those filtered through trending topics and meme tracking.

2.2 Question Asking in Social Media

Another detection feature used in related work is question asking. Mendoza et al. found on a small set of cases that false tweets were questioned much more than confirmed truths [21]. Castillo et al. therefore used the number (and ratio) of question marks as a feature to classify the credibility of a group of tweets. The same feature is adopted by a few follow-up studies [14, 16].

In fact, the behavior of information seeking by asking questions on online social media has drawn interest from researchers in both social sciences and computer science (e.g., [6, 24, 25, 37]). Paul et al. analyzed a random sample of 4,140 tweets with question marks [25]. Among the set of tweets, 1,351 were labeled as questions by Amazon Mechanical Turkers. Morris et al. conducted surveys on if and how people ask questions through social networks. They analyzed the survey responses and presented findings such as how differently users ask questions via social media and via search engines, and how different cultures influence the behaviors [24, 23, 36]. These studies have proved that question asking is a common behavior in social media and provided general understanding of the types of questions people ask.

To study question asking behavior at scale, our previous work detected and analyzed questions from billions of tweets [37]. The analysis pointed out that the questions asked by Twitter users are tied to real world events including rumors. These findings inspired us to make use of question asking behavior as the signal for detecting rumors once they emerge.

Though inspired by the value of question marks as features for classifying the truth value of a post, for our purposes we need a more specific signal. Previous work has shown that only one third of tweets with question marks are real questions, and not all questions are related to rumors [25, 37]. In this paper, we carefully select a set of regular expressions to identify enquiry tweets that are indicative of rumors.

3. PROBLEM DEFINITION

3.1 Defining a Rumor

Many variations of the definition of rumors have been proposed in the literature of sociology and communication studies [26]. These different definitions generally share a few insights about the nature of rumors. First, rumors usually arise in the context of ambiguity, and therefore the truth value of a rumor appears to be uncertain to its audience. Second, although the truth value is uncertain, a rumor does not necessarily imply *false* information. Instead, the term "false rumor" is usually used in these definitions to refer to rumors that are eventually found to be false. Indeed, many pieces of *truthful* information spread as rumors because most people don't have first-hand knowledge to assess them and no trusted authorities have fact-checked them yet. Having such intuitions and following the famous work of DiFonzo and Bordia in social psychology [9], we propose a practical definition:

"A rumor is a controversial and fact-checkable statement."

We make the following remarks to further clarify this definition:

- "Fact-checkable": In principle, the statement has a truth value that could be determined right now by an observer who had access to all relevant evidence. This excludes statements that cannot be fact-checked or those whose truth value will only be determined by future events (e.g., "Chelsea Clinton will run for president in 2040.").
- "Controversial (or Disputed)": At some point in the life cycle of the statement, some people express skepticism (e.g., verifications, corrections, statements of disbelief or questions). This excludes statements that are fact-checkable but not disputed (e.g., "Bill Clinton tried marijuana," as Clinton himself has admitted it.).
- Any statement referring to a statement meeting the criteria above is also classified as a rumor. This includes statements that point to several other rumors (e.g., "Click the link `http://...` to see the latest rumors about Boston Bombing.").

The above definition of rumor is effective in practice. As we describe below, human raters were able to achieve high inter-rater reliability labeling statements as rumors or not.

3.2 The Computational Problem

Based on the conceptual definition, we can formally define the computational problem of real-time detection of rumors.

DEFINITION 1. *(Rumor Cluster). We define a rumor cluster R as a group of social media posts that are either declaring, questioning, or denying the same fact claim, s, which may be true or false. Let S be the set of posts declaring s, E be the set of posts questioning s, and C be the set of tweets denying s, then $R = S \cup E \cup C$. We say s is a candidate rumor if $S \neq \emptyset$ and $E \cup C \neq \emptyset$.*

Naturally, posts belonging to the same rumor cluster can either be identical to each other (e.g., retweets) or paraphrase the same fact claim. Posts that are enquiring about the truth value of the fact claim are referred to as *enquiry posts* (E) and those that deny the fact claim are referred to as *correction posts* (C).

DEFINITION 2. *(Real-time Rumor Detection). Consider the input of a stream of posts in social media,* $\mathcal{D} = \langle (d_1, t_1), (d_2, t_2) \dots \rangle$, *where* $d_i, i \in [1, 2, \cdots]$ *is a document posted at time* t_i. *The task of real-time rumor detection is to output a set of clusters* $\mathcal{R}_t = \langle R_{t,1}, R_{t,2}, \dots, R_{t,l} \rangle$ *at time t after every time interval* Δt, *where the fact claim* $s_{t,j}$ *of each cluster* $R_{t,j} \in \mathcal{R}_t$ *is a candidate rumor.*

Given any time point t where a new set of clusters are output, the clusters must satisfy that

$$\forall R_{t,j} \in \mathcal{R}_t, \exists (d', t') \in R_{t,j}\ s.t.\ t - \Delta t < t' \leq t$$

This means that the output rumor clusters at time t must contain at least one tweet posted in the past time interval Δt. Clearly, a cluster about a fact claim s can accumulate more documents over time, such that $R_{t_1,j} \subseteq R_{t_2,j}$ if $t_1 < t_2$ and $s_{t_1,j} = s_{t_2,j} = s$. Therefore, we can naturally define the first time (t_1 in the previous example) where a rumor cluster about a fact claim s is output as the *detection time* of the candidate rumor s. Our aim is to minimize the delay from the time when the first tweet about the rumor is posted to the detection time.

4. EARLY DETECTION OF RUMORS

We propose a real-time rumor detection procedure that has the following five steps.

1. **Identify Signal Tweets.** Using a set of regular expressions, the system selects only those tweets that contain skeptical enquiries: verification questions and corrections. These are the signal tweets.
2. **Identify Signal Clusters.** The system clusters the signal tweets based on overlapping content in the tweets.
3. **Detect Statements.** The system analyzes the content of each signal cluster to determine a single statement that defines the common text of the cluster.
4. **Capture Non-signal Tweets.** The system captures all non-signal tweets that match any cluster's summary statement, turning a signal cluster into a full candidate rumor cluster.
5. **Rank Candidate Rumor Clusters.** Using statistical features of the clusters that are independent of the statements' content, rank the candidate clusters in order of likelihood that their statements are rumors (i.e., controversial and fact-checkable).

The algorithm operates on a real-time tweet stream, where tweets arrive continuously. It outputs a ranked list of candidate rumor clusters at every time interval Δt, where Δt could be as small as the interval when the next tweet arrives. In practice, it will be easier to think of the time interval as, for example, an hour or a day, with many tweets arriving during that interval.

The system first matches every new tweet posted in that interval to rumor clusters detected in the past, using the same method of capturing non-signal tweets (component 4). Tweets that do not match to any existing rumors will go through the complete set of five components listed above, with a procedure described in Figure 2. If very short time intervals are used, signal tweets from recent past intervals that were not matched to any rumor clusters may also be included in this procedure. Below, each of the five steps are described in more detail.

Pattern Regular Expression	Type
is (that | this | it) true	Verification
wh[a]*t[?!][?1]*	Verification
(real? | really ? | unconfirmed)	Verification
(rumor | debunk)	Correction
(that | this | it) is not true	Correction

Table 2: Patterns used to filter Enquiries and Corrections

4.1 Identify Signal Tweets

The first module of our algorithm extracts enquiry tweets. Not all enquiries are related to rumors [37]. A tweet conveying an information need can be either of the following cases:

- It requests a piece of factual knowledge, or a verification of a piece of factual knowledge. Factual knowledge is objective and fact-checkable. For example: "According to the Mayan Calendar, does the world end on Dec 16th, 2013?"
- It requests an opinion, idea, preference, recommendation, or personal plan of the recipient(s), as well as a confirmation of such information. This type of information is subjective and not fact-checkable.

We hypothesize that only verification/confirmation questions are good signals for rumors. In addition, we expect that corrections (or debunks) are also good signals. To extract patterns to identify these good signals, we conducted an analysis on a labeled rumor dataset.

Discover patterns of signal tweets.

We analyzed 10,417 tweets related to five rumors published in [28], with 3,423 tweets labeled as either verifications or corrections. All tweets are lowercased and processed with the Porter Stemmer [27]. We extracted lexical features from the tweets: unigrams, bigrams and trigrams. Then we calculated the Chi-Square score for each feature in the data set. Chi-Squared test is a classical statistical test of independence and the score measures the divergence from the expected distribution if one assumes a feature is independent of the class label [12]. Features with high Chi-Square scores are more likely to appear only in tweets of a particular class. Patterns which appear excessively in verification and correction tweets but are underrepresented in other tweets were selected to detect signal tweets. From the patterns with high Chi-Square scores, human experts further selected those which are independent of any particular rumor. The patterns we selected are listed in Table 2.

As a way to identify all the tweets containing rumors, this set of regular expressions has relatively low recall. Even on the 3,423 tweets labeled as either verifications or corrections in our training data, only 572 match these regular expressions. In the signal tweet identification stage, however, it is far more important to have a high precision. Low recall of *signal tweets* may still be sufficient to get high recall of *signal clusters*. By identifying patterns that are more likely to appear only in signal clusters, even though these patterns only appear a few times inside each rumor cluster, our framework can make use of them to detect many rumors. Note that although current patterns are discovered from a data set containing only five rumors, we could in principle rerun this process after we have more rumors labeled by our rumor detection framework, shown as the dotted line in Figure 2.

4.2 Identify Signal Clusters

When a tweet containing a rumor emerges, many people either explicitly retweet it, or create a new tweet containing much of the

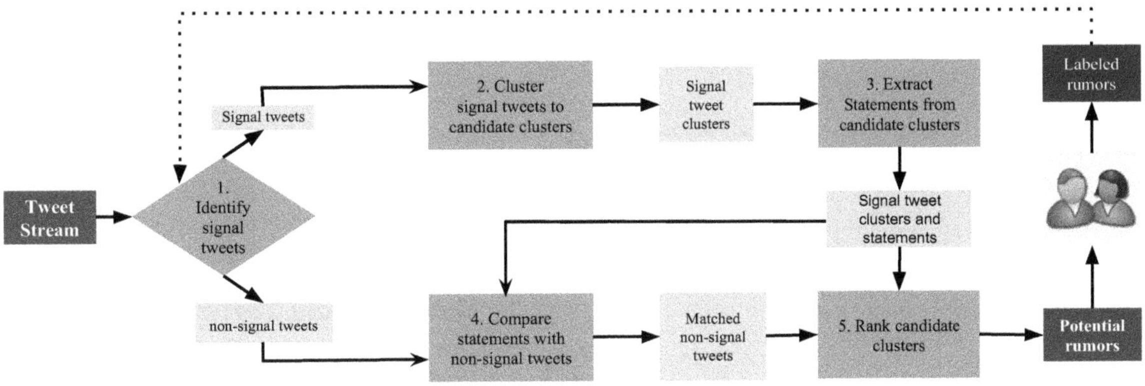

Figure 2: The procedure of real-time rumor detection.

original text. Therefore, tweets spreading a rumor are mostly near duplicates, as illustrated in Table 1. By clustering, we aim to group all the near duplicates, which are either retweets or tweets containing the original rumor content.

There are many different clustering algorithms such as the K-Means [19]. Many have a high computational cost and/or need to keep an $N \times N$ similarity matrix in memory. Given that we expect tweets about the same rumor to share a lot of text, we can trade off some accuracy for efficiency. In contrast to exploratory clustering tasks where documents may be merely similar, we want to cluster tweets that are near duplicates. Therefore, using an algorithm such as connected component clustering can be efficient and effective enough for our purposes. A connected component in an undirected graph is a group of vertices, every pair of which are reachable from each other through paths. An undirected graph of tweets is built by including an edge joining any tweet pair with a high similarity.

We use the Jaccard coefficient to measure similarity between tweets. Given two tweets d_a and d_b, the similarity between d_a and d_b can be calculated as:

$$J(d_a, d_b) = \frac{|Ngram(d_a) \cap Ngram(d_b)|}{|Ngram(d_a) \cup Ngram(d_b)|}$$

Here $Ngram(d_a)$ and $Ngram(d_b)$ are the 3-grams of tweets d_a and d_b. Jaccard distance is a commonly used indicator of the similarity between two sets. The similarity values from 0 to 1 and a higher value means a higher similarity.

To further improve efficiency, we use the Minhash algorithm [2] to reduce the dimensionality of the Ngram vector space, which makes calculating Jaccard similarity much faster. The Minhash algorithm is used for dimensionality reduction and fast estimation of Jaccard similarities. In our approach, we randomly generate 50 hash functions based on the md5 hash function. Then we use the 50 corresponding Minhash values to represent each tweet. In our implementation of the connected component clustering algorithm, we set the threshold for adding an edge at 0.6 (60% of the hashed dimensions for the two tweets are equal).

The connected components in this graph are the clusters. We create a cluster for each group of three or more tweets connected together. Connected components can be found by either breadth-first search or depth-first search, which has a linear time complexity $O(E)$, where E is the number of edges. Since we want to cluster tweets that are near duplicates, setting a high similarity threshold (0.6) yields a relatively small number of edges.

At this point, the procedure will have obtained a set of candidate rumor clusters $\mathcal{R}$. The next stage extracts, for each cluster R_i, the statement s_i that the tweets in the cluster promote, question, or attempt to correct. In our approach, for each rumor cluster, we extract the most frequent and continuous substrings (3-grams that appear in more than 80% of the tweets) and output them in order as the summarized statement. We keep the summarization component simple and efficient in this study, though algorithms such as LexRank [11] may improve the performance of text summarization.

4.3 Capture Non-signal Tweets

After the statement that summarizes the tweets in a signal cluster is extracted, we use that statement as a query to match similar non-signal tweets from the tweet stream, tweets that are related to the cluster but do not contain enquiry patterns. To be consistent, we still use the Jaccard similarity and select tweets whose similarity score with the statement is higher than a threshold (0.6 in our implementation). This step partially recovers from the low recall of signal tweet detection using limited signal patterns.

Note the efficiency gain that comes from matching the non-signal tweets only with the statements summarizing signal tweets. In particular, it is not necessary to compare each of the non-signal tweets with each other non-signal tweet. Non-signal tweets may form other clusters but we do not need to detect those clusters: they do not contain nuclei of three connected signal tweets and thus are unlikely to be rumor clusters.

4.4 Score Candidate Rumor Clusters

After we have complete candidate rumor clusters, including both signal and non-signal tweets, we score them. A simple way to output clusters is to rank them by popularity. The number of tweets in a cluster measures the statement's popularity. The most popular candidates, however, may not be the most likely to be rumors. There may be statistical properties of the candidate rumor clusters that are better correlated with whether they really contain disputed factual claims.

We extracted 13 statistical features of candidate clusters that are independent of any particular substantive content. We then trained classifiers using these features, to obtain a better ranking function. The features are listed as follows.

- Percentage of signal tweets (1 feature): the ratio of signal tweets to all tweets in the cluster.
- Entropy ratio (1 feature): the ratio of the entropy of the word frequency distribution in the set of signal tweets to that in the set of all tweets in the cluster.

- Tweet lengths (3 features): (1) the average number of words per signal tweet; (2) the average number of words per any tweet in the cluster; and (3) the ratio of (1) to (2).
- Retweets (2 features): the percentage of retweets among the signal tweets and the percentage of retweets among all tweets in the cluster.
- URLs (2 features): the average number of URLs per signal tweet and the average number per any tweet in the cluster.
- Hashtags (2 features): the average number of hashtags per signal tweet and the number per any tweet in the cluster.
- @Mentions (2 features): the average number of usernames mentioned per signal tweet and the number per any tweet in the cluster.

We use rumor clusters labeled by human annotators to train a classifier that ranks the candidate clusters by their likelihood of being rumors (detail described in section 5.3). We select two commonly used classifiers, the Support Vector Machine (SVM [7]) with the LIBSVM implementation [5], and the Decision Trees [1] with the Matlab implementation [5]. The detailed results are shown in Section 5.

5. EXPERIMENT SETUP

In this section, we present empirical experiments to evaluate the proposed method of early detection of rumors.

5.1 Data Sets

We first selected two different collections of tweets. One focuses on a specific high-profile event, i.e. the Boston Marathon bombing in April 2013. The other consists of a random sample of tweets from a month that was not unusually eventful.

BOSTON MARATHON BOMBING (BOSTON). Two bombs exploded at the finish line of the annual Boston Marathon competition on April 15th, 2013.[6] We chose this context as a typical example of unpredictable real-world events.

To obtain a complete set of tweets related to this event, we collected tweets containing keywords such as "Boston," "marathon," and "explosion" and their combinations, starting several hours after the explosion, using the official tracking API provided by Twitter. The tracking API returned all tweets containing those keywords after 23:29 GMT. To collect tweets posted before this time point, we used the Twitter search API to get tweets containing the same set of keywords. In summary, we collected 10,240,066 tweets through the search API (13:30 GMT, April 14 to 23:29 GMT, April 15) and 23,001,329 tweets through the tracking API (23:29 GMT, April 15 to May 10, 2013), adding up to 30,340,218 unique tweets in the entire data set.

GARDENHOSE. Besides the stream related to a major event, we are also interested in the performance of the proposed method in detecting rumors from everyday tweets. We thus collected a tweet stream in a random month of the year 2013 (November 1 to November 30, 2013), through the official stream API with Gardenhose access (10% sample of the real-time stream of all tweets). This data set contains 1,242,186,946 tweets. Although the size is forty times larger than the BOSTON set, we anticipated that the density of rumors in this everyday tweet stream may be lower.

To process such data sets of over a billion records, we implemented our methods in MapReduce and conducted the experiments on a 72 core Hadoop cluster (version 0.20.2). The main components of our framework, including filtering, clustering and retrieval algorithm are implemented using Apache Pig (version 0.11.1).

5.2 Baselines and Variants of Methods

To obtain a comprehensive understanding of the effectiveness of the overall method, the identifiers of signal tweets, and the algorithms used to rank statements, we tested six variants of the method. The first four variants all rank candidate rumors purely by popularity, the number of tweets in the cluster. They vary in the algorithm used to identify signal tweets. The last three variants all use both enquiry and correction tweets as signals. They vary in the algorithm used to rank the candidate rumor clusters.

Variant 1 (baseline 1): Trending Topics. This straightforward baseline method directly clusters all the input tweets. It treats all the tweets as signal tweets rather than selecting only a subset. This method echoes the common approaches to detecting trending topics and then identifying rumors among them [4, 14]. After tweets are clustered and statements are extracted, this baseline method simply outputs the top candidate clusters with the largest number of tweets.

Variant 2 (baseline 2): Hashtag Tracking. Hashtags are well recognized signals for detecting trending and popular topics and have been used previously in rumor detection [30, 34]. As a second baseline method, popular hashtags (i.e., those that appear more than 10 times) are used to filter the signal tweets. Tweets containing these hashtags are clustered and statements are extracted from these clusters. Again, clusters with the largest number of tweets are presented to the user.

Variant 3 (baseline 3): Corrections Only. One novel contribution of our approach is the utilization of enquiry tweets as early signals of rumors. To test the performance of these signals, we downgraded our identifier of signal tweets by only using correction tweets as filtering signals, i.e., tweets containing the correction patterns in Table 2, including "rumor," "debunk," or "(this|that|it) is not true." Certain correction patterns such as the phrase "false rumor" have been used previously in the literature to identify rumors [34]. The same clustering and statement detection procedures were applied to tweets filtered with the correction signals. The largest candidate rumor clusters are output by the system.

Variant 4: Enquiries and Corrections. Besides the baseline methods, we included three variants that treat both enquiries and corrections as signal tweets, using the complete set of patterns from Table 2. To enable comparison with the baselines, variant 4 still ranks the candidate rumor clusters purely by popularity.

Variant 5: SVM ranking. This version ranks the candidate rumor clusters based on their scores using the trained *SVM* classifier. Like Variant 4, it treats both enquiries and corrections as signal tweets.

Variant 6: Decision tree ranking. This version ranks the candidate rumor clusters based on their scores using the trained *Decision Tree* classifier. Like Variants 4 and 5, it treats both enquiries and corrections as signal tweets.

[5] `http://www.mathworks.com/help/stats/classificationtree-class.html`, retrieved on March 7, 2015.

[6] `http://en.wikipedia.org/wiki/Boston_Marathon_bombings`, retrieved on March 7, 2015.

5.3 Ground Truth

We recruited two human annotators to manually label candidate rumors (i.e. rumor clusters as defined in Section 3) as either a real rumor or not. The annotators made decisions based on the statement extracted from the cluster, actual tweets in the cluster, and other useful information about the statement through Web search. To train the annotators, we developed a codebook according to the definition of rumors discussed in Section 3 which includes both the definition and examples of rumor and non-rumor statements. After being trained, both annotators labeled all the top-ranked candidate rumor clusters extracted by either the *Popularity* method, the *Decision Tree* method, or the *Correction Signal* method, from the first week of the GARDENHOSE data set and the first two days and the eighth day of the BOSTON data set. At most 10 clusters per hour per method were annotated for the BOSTON data set and at most 50 clusters per day per method were annotated for the GARDENHOSE data set. These added up to 639 candidate rumor clusters. The inter-rater reliability was satisfactory, achieving a Cohen's Kappa score of 0.76. Such a high agreement also demonstrates the coherence of our definition of rumors. For the statements the two annotators did not agree on, an expert labeled them and broke the tie. Another 1,440 clusters generated by the first two baseline methods (*Trending Topics* and *Hashtags*) on the same 72 hours of the BOSTON data set were then labeled by one of the two annotators after they were well trained. It took an average about 80 hours for each annotator to finish the labeling task including training.

5.4 Evaluation Metrics

We selected several quantitative metrics to evaluate the effectiveness and efficiency of our proposed method. We calculated precision@N, which is the percentage of real rumors among the top N candidate rumor clusters output by the a method. Since it is not practical in general to manually label a complete data set with tens of millions of tweets and hundreds of thousands of clusters, we cannot directly evaluate the actual recall of a rumor detection method. However, the number of rumors each method returns can be an indirect way to understand whether one method can detect more rumors than another. Another important dimension of the effectiveness of a rumor detection system is how early a rumor can be detected. We calculated the detection time, the time when the algorithm was first able to identify it as a candidate rumor. Finally, we also evaluated the scalability of the proposed method by plotting the scale of the data against the running time of the algorithm.

6. EXPERIMENT RESULTS

6.1 Effectiveness of Enquiry Signals

We evaluated the effectiveness of rumor detection algorithms using different signals. We first compared the precision of the top-ranked candidate rumor clusters output by different methods. For a fair comparison, all methods ranked the candidate rumor clusters simply using the *popularity* (i.e. number of tweets in each cluster).

6.1.1 Precision of Candidate Rumor Clusters

We compared the precision of our proposed methods using both enquiry and correction signals with all three baseline methods on the BOSTON data set. Note that both the baselines 1 and 2 (*Trending Topics* and *Meme Tracking*) have to cluster a huge number of tweets, nearly all the incoming tweets of every time period, hence they cannot handle the scale of all tweets in the GARDENHOSE data set. Therefore, we compare the proposed methods with only Baseline 3 (*Correction Signals*) on the GARDENHOSE data set. These results are summarized in Table 3. Clearly, the use of both enquiry and correction signals typically detects more rumors than using no signal (trending topics) or using memes (meme tracking), and the top-ranked rumor clusters are much more precise. Using both enquiry and correction signals, our method detected 110 rumors from the stream of tweets related to the Boston Marathon bombing, with an average precision@10 above 50% (half of the top 10 candidate clusters output by the system are real rumors). On the stream of everyday tweets, this method detected 92 rumors from a random month of 2013, with the average precision@50 above 26% (one fourth of the top 50 clusters output by the system are real rumors).

Table 3: Precision of rumor detection using different signals. Candidate rumors ranked by popularity only. Maximum number of output rumor clusters: 10 per hour for BOSTON and 50 per day for GARDENHOSE.

Method	Data Set	Candidates Detected	Real Rumors	Precision
Trending Topics	BOSTON	720	71	0.099
Hashtag Tracking	BOSTON	720	35	0.049
Corrections only	BOSTON	109	52	0.466
Enquiries+ Corrections	BOSTON	194	**110**	**0.521**
Corrections only	GARDENHOSE	312	87	**0.279**
Enquiries+ Corrections	GARDENHOSE	350	**92**	0.263

Some interesting observations can be made from these results. Detecting trending topics or tracking popular memes can reveal some rumors, but they both suffer from a low precision among the candidate clusters (lower than 10%), and thus miss many rumors if the user can only check a certain number of candidates (i.e., 10 per hour or 50 per day). This is because both methods inevitably introduce many false positives, popular statements that are not disputed. Detection using correction signals only also misses half of the rumors in the Boston event, probably because the behavior of debunking rumors is less common than enquiries in social media, as it certainly requires more effort of the users.

Using correction signals achieves a high precision among detected candidates. This is not surprising as statements already explicitly corrected or referred in tweets as "rumors" are likely to in fact be disputed factual claims. Interestingly, using enquiry as well as correction signals yields a similar precision.

6.1.2 Earliness of Detection

One of the most important objectives of our study is to detect emerging rumors as early as possible so that interventions can be made in time. Correction signals may appear only in a later stage of a rumor's diffusion. If this is the case, detecting rumors using such signals may have less practical value, as the rumors may have already spread widely. To verify this and further understand the usefulness of enquiry signals, we measured the earliness of detection. We computed the difference between the time points at which the same rumor was first detected by different methods, assuming that the algorithms are run in batch mode to output results only once per hour. The results are summarized in Table 4.

We first compare the method which uses both enquiry and correction signals with Baseline 3 (correction signals only). Since different methods may yield different clustering results and/or statements for the same rumor, we manually matched the 52 rumors detected by *correction only* from the BOSTON data set with the 110

Table 4: Earliness of detection comparing to Enquiries+ Corrections: enquiry signals help to detect rumors hours earlier.

Method	Data Set	Rumors detected	Rumors matched	Average delay
Corrections only	BOSTON	52	46	+4.3h
Trending Topics	BOSTON	71	53	+3.6h
Hashtag Tracking	BOSTON	35	31	+2.8h

rumors detected by both *enquiries and corrections*. We obtained 46 rumors detected in the top 10 results per hour by both methods.

There are 27 rumors that *enquiries and corrections* detected at least one hour earlier than *correction only*. The two detected the rest of the 19 rumors in the same hour. The detection of a rumor using *enquiries and corrections* is on average 4.3 hours earlier.

For example, at 20:00 (GMT) April 15th the *enquiries and corrections* algorithm would have output the popular rumor that the police identified a Saudi national as the suspect. This was one hour earlier than people started to realize it was false and tweet corrections. For another widespread rumor about an 8-year-old girl who died in the explosion, *enquiries and corrections* identified it almost one day earlier than tracking correction signals only.

In theory, how early can rumors be detected through enquiry signals, if candidate rumors were output continuously rather than hourly? We marked the time points when the system captures **at least three** signal tweets. On average, a real-time system that tracks enquiry signals can *hypothetically* detect a rumor after its first appearance in 9.6 minutes. To collect at least three correction tweets, a method has to wait for 236.7 more minutes on average. Not all candidate rumor clusters are actually output by our algorithms, so precision would have to be sacrificed to detect all rumors that quickly.

We also compare *enquiries and corrections* with Baseline 1 (trending topics), and Baseline 2 (meme tracking), on the earliness of detection. For Baseline 1, we matched the 71 rumors detected by *trending topics* with 110 rumors detected by our method. We obtained 53 common rumors detected by both methods. On average these rumors were detected as trending topics 3.6 hours later than using enquiry+correction signals. For Baseline 2, we matched the 35 rumors detected by *meme tracking* with rumors detected by our method. 31 of them are matched. On average these rumors were detected as trending memes 2.8 hours later than using enquiry+correction signals. The earliness of our detection method compared to other methods passed paired-sample t-test at significance level of 0.01.

In brief, we see that the use of enquiry tweets as signals not only detects more rumors, but also detects them hours faster than tracking trending topics or popular memes. Tracking correction signals, although it yields high precision, is the latest among all methods.

6.2 Ranking Candidate Rumor Clusters

We assessed the benefits produced by ranking the candidate clusters, using the 13 statistical features described in the previous section. We tested the performance of ranking functions based on Support Vector Machines and Decision Trees compared with two other baseline methods. The first baseline ranks the clusters by the number of tweets inside each cluster, referred to as *Popularity*. The second baseline ranks the clusters based on the retweet ratio in the cluster of tweets, which was reported as an indicative feature of rumors [34]. The second baseline is referred to as *Retweet Ratio*.

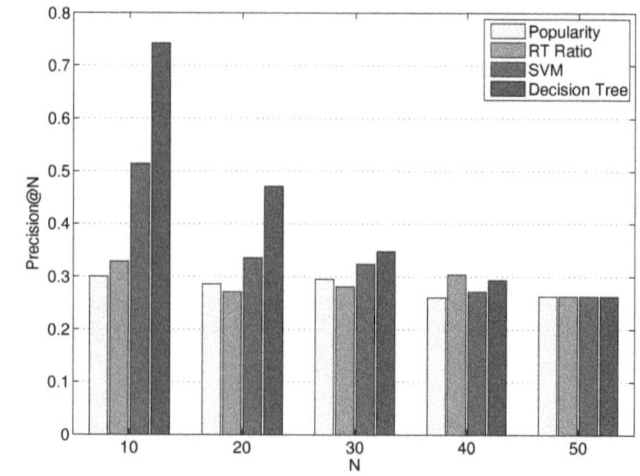

Figure 3: Precision@N of different ranking methods

We applied the ranking algorithms to the 350 candidate rumor clusters labeled by human annotators (the 50 most popular clusters for each of the seven days from 2013-11-1 to 2013-11-7 in GARDENHOSE data set). We used 6 days of labeled results to train the classifiers and the remaining day's results to test the algorithms. We did a 7-fold cross validation, holding out each of the seven days and computing the average performance. Figure 3 shows the results. We used Precision@N to evaluate different ranking algorithms. In this figure, we can see that *retweet ratio* has comparable performance to *popularity*, which remains about 0.3 no matter what N is. Our ranking algorithm significantly improves the Precision@N when N is small. The precision of the top 10 statements per day is above 0.7 using a Decision Tree, which outperforms SVM and the baseline methods. Of course, as N approaches 50, the precisions equalize since all the algorithms are essentially re-ranking the 50 most popular items. Note we are dealing with the classification task on only hundreds of examples and the 13 features we extracted are in different scales. In such case a decision tree is easier to tune than the more sophisticated SVM [3]; this may explain why the Decision Tree algorithm achieved a better performance than SVM. The improvement of Precision@10 and Precision@20 made by the decision tree compared to other methods passed the paired-sample t-test at significance level of 0.01.

Next, we tested whether the decision tree algorithm would find more rumors if it was able to suggest its own 50 top-ranked candidate clusters among all the candidates instead of reranking the most popular 50. In the previous figure, it was restricted to re-ranking the 50 most popular ones. We evaluated the performance using Precision@N. Figure 4 shows the results for the GARDENHOSE data set. We used tweets from 2013-11-1 to 2013-11-3 in the GARDENHOSE data set to train the decision tree and then used tweets from 2013-11-4 to 2013-11-7 to test, with popularity ranking as the baseline. Results show that we can not only improve Precision@N when N is small, but also find more rumors in 50 output statements. 33% of our output statements are rumors. The improvement of Precision@N when $N \leq 40$ made by our ranking algorithm passed the paired-sample t-test at significance level of 0.01.

In order to verify that the ranking algorithm is not overfitting only one data set, We also applied the decision tree trained using 7 days of labeled results in GARDENHOSE data set to rank rumor clusters detected hourly from BOSTON data set. We got similar results as in Figure 4. The average precision at 2, 4, 6, 8 an 10 in an hour is improved compared to *popularity* based ranking. The features used at the top levels of the decision tree include percentage of signal tweets and the average numbers of words, URLs and @mentions per any tweet in the cluster.

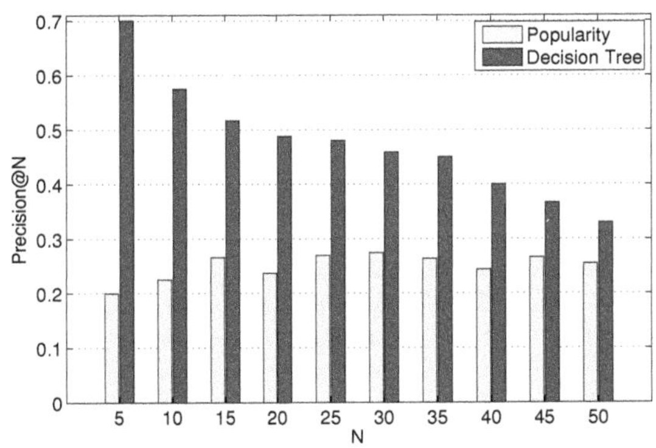

Figure 4: Precision@N if rumor clusters are ranked by the Decision Tree. One third of top 50 clusters are real rumors.

6.3 Efficiency of Our Framework

We have shown that our rumor detection algorithm is effective in detecting rumors in their early stage with reasonable precision. We now show that our framework is computationally efficient. Our framework first filters tweets with specific signals, then uses clustering to detect statements in this smaller group of tweets and at last outputs potential rumor statements. Compared to approaches that first generate trending topics and then identify rumors, we reduce the cost significantly in the detection process.

We first tested the time cost of our algorithm (*decision tree ranking* in Section 5.2 which uses both enquiry and correction signals) compared to baseline methods of running the algorithm on one batch of tweets from one time interval. We started from 1,000 tweet batches randomly sampled from tweets in our data set, then increased the number of tweets to 100,000,000 exponentially. Figure 5 shows the results. The x-axis shows the number of tweets to be processed in log scale. The baseline methods here are the Baseline 1 and 2 from Section 5.2, which try to detect trending topics or popular memes (hashtags) first. For baseline methods, we used the same clustering and ranking implementations as our method except they don't filter tweets with enquiry or correction signals and they don't have to retrieve tweets back after clustering. When the scale reaches one million tweets, Baseline 1 cannot finish in hours. Our method performs consistently and does not take much longer even at the 10 million scale: it can process 100 million tweets in about 80 minutes. It is intuitive that *Meme Tracking* achieves an intermediate performance. It clusters only those tweets that contain popular and trending hashtags, and thus scales somewhat better than clustering all tweets to find trending topics, but is still not as efficient as our method, which clusters a much smaller number of signal tweets.

We also tested our algorithm on one month's tweets from the GARDENHOSE data set, collected at November 2013. We set the time interval to be a day. The average number of tweets every day in the GARDENHOSE data set was about 40 million. As we would expect, experiment results indicate that the time cost does not increase significantly after processing several days, even with the accumulation of older rumor clusters. On average it took 28.77 minutes for our algorithm to finish detecting rumors each day and took 14.38 hours in total to process the 1.2 billion tweets in the entire month.

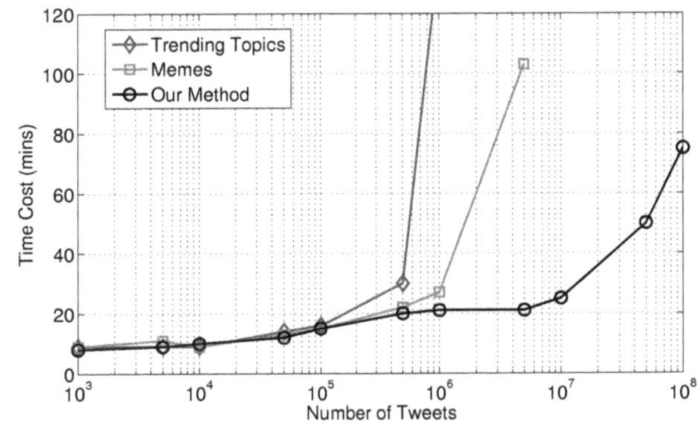

Figure 5: Running time vs. batch size.

6.4 Discussion

We have shown in the experiments that tweets asking verification questions or making corrections to controversial statements are very important signals of rumors early in their life cycle. Some users who have an information need of evaluating a rumor will post tweets either asking verification questions to express suspicions, or will correct the rumor after their investigation. Verification questions are particularly useful because they appear much sooner and thus facilitate earlier detection of rumors.

Not all clusters that include tweets that ask verification questions or use correction phrases are actually rumors. We identified 13 different statistical features of clusters of tweets, such as average tweet length and percentage of signal tweets, etc. By training a decision tree model, we built a powerful ranking algorithm that ranks tweet clusters by how likely they are to be rumors (i.e., controversial, fact-checkable claims). The precision we can achieve is much higher than without the ranking algorithm.

We demonstrated that our proposed framework can scale up well. By clustering only the small set of signal tweets, we avoided the computational cost of detecting popular statements or trending topics from the entire corpus. Our proposed framework is robust even if the number of tweets to be processed exceeds 100 million.

To give the readers a sense of the end-to-end operation of our system, we present the rumors detected in the two data sets. For the BOSTON data set, we identified the top 5 candidate rumor clusters each hour. Figure 6 plots the number of tweets hourly of each identified rumor statement. The dotted blue line in the background shows the number of tweets arriving in that hour.

Although the small set of regular expressions may yield a low recall of enquiry signals, when the candidate rumor clusters detected by our system are labeled by human experts, they can be used to enrich the set of signals. Indeed, using statistical feature selection techniques [12], one can extract features that are highly representative in the rumor clusters and underrepresented in the non-rumor clusters. These patterns can be approved by human experts and added into the pipeline to identify more signal tweets, thus improving precision and recall of rumor detection. By using rumors of our two data sets labeled by annotators, we have already discovered a few additional promising patterns such as "scandal?", or "fact check." We leave the iterative improvement of the signal patterns to future work.

One may be curious about what types of rumors are being circulated in a random week of tweets. From the GARDENHOSE data set, we output the 10 top-ranked rumors for each day and tracked them (Figure 7). We also show example statements extracted from

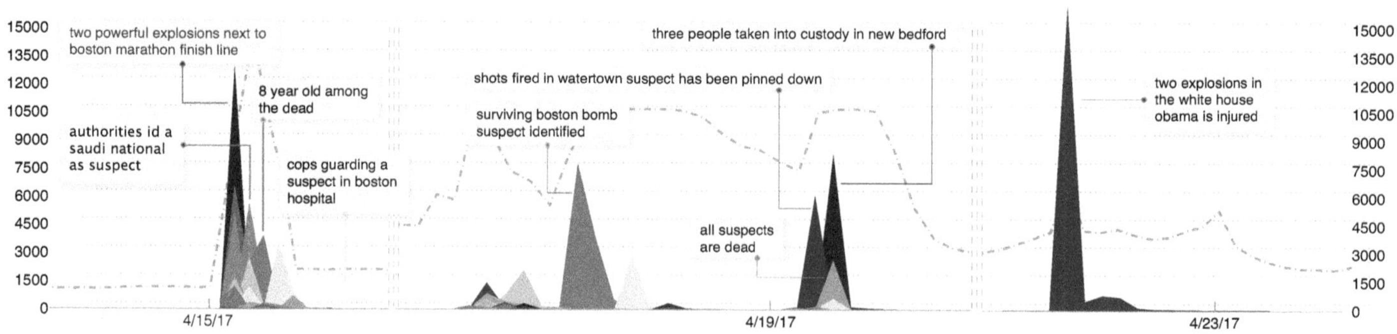

Figure 6: Tracking detected rumors about Boston Marathon bombing

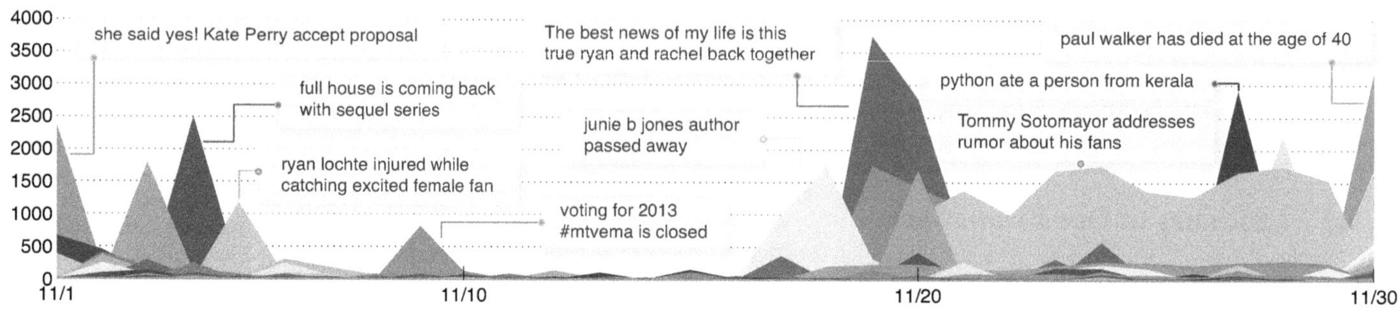

Figure 7: Tracking detected rumors in November 2013

the most popular rumor clusters. Most everyday rumors turn out to be gossip about celebrities, with occasionally emerging anecdotes like "python ate person."

7. CONCLUSION

One post of a rumor in social media can sometimes spread beyond anyone's control. A rumor about two explosions in the White House is a perfect example of how a single tweet out of more than 9,000 tweeted in the same second spreads and causes real damage.

In social media, users share information based on different types of needs, including the need to verify controversial information. We point out that such information needs can not only help spread rumors, but also provide the first clue for detecting them.

Based on this important observation, we designed a rumor detection approach. We cluster only those tweets that contain enquiry patterns (the signal tweets), extract the statement that each cluster is making, and use that statement to pull back in the rest of the non-signal tweets that discuss that same statement. We then rank the clusters based on statistical features that compare properties of the signal tweets within the cluster to properties of the whole cluster.

Extensive experiments show that our proposed method can detect rumors effectively and efficiently in their early stage. With a small Hadoop cluster, in about half an hour we process 10% of all the tweets posted in one day on Twitter. If we output 50 candidate statements, about one third of them are real rumors, and about 70% of the top ranked 10 clusters are rumors.

There is still considerable room to improve the effectiveness of the rumor detection method. We can improve the filtering of enquiry and correction signals by training a classifier rather than relying on manually selected regular expressions. We can further develop a method to automatically update the filtering patterns in real time to prevent potential spamming of the detection system. We can also explore more features for each statement and train a better ranking algorithm for candidate rumor clusters. Another direction is to adopt this method to detect rumors automatically and generate a large data set of rumors, which can benefit many potential analyses such as finding features that are potentially correlated to the truth value of a rumor, or analyzing general diffusion patterns or the life cycle of rumors.

8. ACKNOWLEDGMENT

We thank Cheng Li and Yuncheng Shen for generating the visualizations. This work is partially supported by the National Science Foundation under grant numbers IIS-0968489 and IIS-1054199. It is also partially supported by the DARPA under award number W911NF-12-1-0037.

9. REFERENCES

[1] L. Breiman, J. Friedman, C. J. Stone, and R. A. Olshen. *Classification and regression trees*. CRC press, 1984.

[2] A. Z. Broder. On the resemblance and containment of documents. In *Compression and Complexity of Sequences 1997. Proceedings*, pages 21–29. IEEE, 1997.

[3] R. Caruana and A. Niculescu-Mizil. An empirical comparison of supervised learning algorithms. In *Proceedings of the 23rd international conference on Machine learning*, pages 161–168. ACM, 2006.

[4] C. Castillo, M. Mendoza, and B. Poblete. Information credibility on twitter. In *Proceedings of the 20th international conference on World wide web*, pages 675–684. ACM, 2011.

[5] C.-C. Chang and C.-J. Lin. Libsvm: a library for support vector machines. *ACM Transactions on Intelligent Systems and Technology (TIST)*, 2(3):27, 2011.
[6] E. H. Chi. Information seeking can be social. *IEEE Computer*, 42(3):42–46, 2009.
[7] C. Cortes and V. Vapnik. Support-vector networks. *Machine learning*, 20(3):273–297, 1995.
[8] I. Dagan, O. Glickman, and B. Magnini. The pascal recognising textual entailment challenge. In *Machine learning challenges. evaluating predictive uncertainty, visual object classification, and recognising tectual entailment*, pages 177–190. Springer, 2006.
[9] N. DiFonzo and P. Bordia. *Rumor psychology: Social and organizational approaches.* American Psychological Association, 2007.
[10] P. Domm. False rumor of explosion at white house causes stocks to briefly plunge; ap confirms its twitter feed was hacked., April 2013.
[11] G. Erkan and D. R. Radev. Lexrank: graph-based lexical centrality as salience in text summarization. *Journal of Artificial Intelligence Research*, pages 457–479, 2004.
[12] G. Forman. An extensive empirical study of feature selection metrics for text classification. *The Journal of machine learning research*, 3:1289–1305, 2003.
[13] A. Friggeri, L. A. Adamic, D. Eckles, and J. Cheng. Rumor cascades. In *Proceedings of the Eighth International AAAI Conference on Weblogs and Social Media*, 2014.
[14] A. Gupta and P. Kumaraguru. Credibility ranking of tweets during high impact events. In *Proceedings of the 1st Workshop on Privacy and Security in Online Social Media*, page 2. ACM, 2012.
[15] A. Gupta, H. Lamba, and P. Kumaraguru. $1.00 per rt# bostonmarathon# prayforboston: Analyzing fake content on twitter. In *eCrime Researchers Summit (eCRS), 2013*, pages 1–12. IEEE, 2013.
[16] A. Gupta, H. Lamba, P. Kumaraguru, and A. Joshi. Faking sandy: characterizing and identifying fake images on twitter during hurricane sandy. In *Proceedings of the 22nd international conference on World Wide Web companion*, pages 729–736. International World Wide Web Conferences Steering Committee, 2013.
[17] S. Kwon, M. Cha, K. Jung, W. Chen, and Y. Wang. Prominent features of rumor propagation in online social media. In *Data Mining (ICDM), 2013 IEEE 13th International Conference on*, pages 1103–1108. IEEE, 2013.
[18] J. Leskovec, L. Backstrom, and J. Kleinberg. Meme-tracking and the dynamics of the news cycle. In *Proceedings of the 15th ACM SIGKDD international conference on Knowledge discovery and data mining*, pages 497–506. ACM, 2009.
[19] J. MacQueen et al. Some methods for classification and analysis of multivariate observations. In *Proceedings of the fifth Berkeley symposium on mathematical statistics and probability*, volume 1, pages 281–297. Oakland, CA, USA., 1967.
[20] M. Mathioudakis and N. Koudas. Twittermonitor: trend detection over the twitter stream. In *Proceedings of the 2010 ACM SIGMOD International Conference on Management of data*, pages 1155–1158. ACM, 2010.
[21] M. Mendoza, B. Poblete, and C. Castillo. Twitter under crisis: Can we trust what we rt? In *Proceedings of the first workshop on social media analytics*, pages 71–79. ACM, 2010.
[22] M. R. Morris, S. Counts, A. Roseway, A. Hoff, and J. Schwarz. Tweeting is believing?: understanding microblog credibility perceptions. In *Proceedings of the ACM 2012 conference on Computer Supported Cooperative Work*, pages 441–450. ACM, 2012.
[23] M. R. Morris, J. Teevan, and K. Panovich. A comparison of information seeking using search engines and social networks. *ICWSM*, 10:23–26, 2010.
[24] M. R. Morris, J. Teevan, and K. Panovich. What do people ask their social networks, and why?: a survey study of status message q&a behavior. In *Proceedings of the SIGCHI conference on Human factors in computing systems*, pages 1739–1748. ACM, 2010.
[25] S. A. Paul, L. Hong, and E. H. Chi. Is twitter a good place for asking questions? a characterization study. In *ICWSM*, 2011.
[26] S. C. Pendleton. Rumor research revisited and expanded. *Language & Communication*, 18(1):69–86, 1998.
[27] M. F. Porter. An algorithm for suffix stripping. *Program*, 14(3):130–137, 1980.
[28] V. Qazvinian, E. Rosengren, D. R. Radev, and Q. Mei. Rumor has it: Identifying misinformation in microblogs. In *Proceedings of the Conference on Empirical Methods in Natural Language Processing*, pages 1589–1599. Association for Computational Linguistics, 2011.
[29] J. Ratkiewicz, M. Conover, M. Meiss, B. Gonçalves, A. Flammini, and F. Menczer. Detecting and tracking political abuse in social media. In *ICWSM*, 2011.
[30] J. Ratkiewicz, M. Conover, M. Meiss, B. Gonçalves, S. Patil, A. Flammini, and F. Menczer. Truthy: mapping the spread of astroturf in microblog streams. In *Proceedings of the 20th international conference companion on World wide web*, pages 249–252. ACM, 2011.
[31] R. L. Rosnow. Inside rumor: A personal journey. *American Psychologist*, 46(5):484, 1991.
[32] E. Seo, P. Mohapatra, and T. Abdelzaher. Identifying rumors and their sources in social networks. In *SPIE Defense, Security, and Sensing*, pages 83891I–83891I. International Society for Optics and Photonics, 2012.
[33] S. Sun, H. Liu, J. He, and X. Du. Detecting event rumors on sina weibo automatically. In *Web Technologies and Applications*, pages 120–131. Springer, 2013.
[34] T. Takahashi and N. Igata. Rumor detection on twitter. In *Soft Computing and Intelligent Systems (SCIS) and 13th International Symposium on Advanced Intelligent Systems (ISIS), 2012 Joint 6th International Conference on*, pages 452–457. IEEE, 2012.
[35] F. Yang, Y. Liu, X. Yu, and M. Yang. Automatic detection of rumor on sina weibo. In *Proceedings of the ACM SIGKDD Workshop on Mining Data Semantics*, page 13. ACM, 2012.
[36] J. Yang, M. R. Morris, J. Teevan, L. A. Adamic, and M. S. Ackerman. Culture matters: A survey study of social q&a behavior. *ICWSM*, 11:409–416, 2011.
[37] Z. Zhao and Q. Mei. Questions about questions: An empirical analysis of information needs on twitter. In *Proceedings of the 22nd international conference on World Wide Web*, pages 1545–1556. International World Wide Web Conferences Steering Committee, 2013.

Improving User Topic Interest Profiles by Behavior Factorization

Zhe Zhao[1]* , Zhiyuan Cheng[2], Lichan Hong[2], Ed H. Chi[2]
[1]Department of EECS, University of Michigan, Ann Arbor, MI, USA
[2]Google Inc, Mountain View, CA, USA
zhezhao@umich.edu, zcheng@google.com, lichan@google.com, edchi@google.com

ABSTRACT

Many recommenders aim to provide relevant recommendations to users by building personal topic interest profiles and then using these profiles to find interesting contents for the user. In social media, recommender systems build user profiles by directly combining users' topic interest signals from a wide variety of consumption and publishing behaviors, such as social media posts they authored, commented on, +1'd or liked. Here we propose to separately model users' topical interests that come from these various behavioral signals in order to construct better user profiles.

Intuitively, since publishing a post requires more effort, the topic interests coming from publishing signals should be more accurate of a user's central interest than, say, a simple gesture such as a +1. By separating a single user's interest profile into several behavioral profiles, we obtain better and cleaner topic interest signals, as well as enabling topic prediction for different types of behavior, such as topics that the user might +1 or comment on, but might never write a post on that topic.

To do this at large scales in Google+, we employed matrix factorization techniques to model each user's behaviors as a separate example entry in the input user-by-topic matrix. Using this technique, which we call "behavioral factorization", we implemented and built a topic recommender predicting user's topical interests using their actions within Google+. We experimentally showed that we obtained better and cleaner signals than baseline methods, and are able to more accurately predict topic interests as well as achieve better coverage.

Categories and Subject Descriptors

H.2.8 [**Database applications**]: Data Mining

Keywords

Personalization, Behavior Factorization, User Profiles

1. INTRODUCTION

An important aspect of building content recommenders is the construction of personalized user profiles, which consists of two important sub-problems. One is feature engineering, which is the gathering of signals that indicate users' long-term and short-term interests. The other is the proper utilization of these signals using data mining and machine learning approaches. Due to the scale of today's social media platforms, we have a great number of users as well as topics/items. To build a user profile, signals are generally gathered and then aggregated directly to feed into topic modeling algorithms such as Latent Dirichlet Allocation (LDA) or matrix factorization.

Intuitively, different behavioral signals should be weighed differently in building user profiles. For example, users typically only publish posts or comment on topics that are more important to them, while a +1 on a post might also involve topics that are only somewhat interesting. As a concrete example, an academic research user might typically post about her research interests, and also comment on the latest politics and current events. However, she might tend to only +1 posts about bicycling, gardening, and parenting, preferring to keep her hobbies somewhat private. In fact, we might think of her as having multiple personalities, expressed through these actions.

Perhaps more importantly, different behavioral actions represent users' different publication and consumption interests. Since writing a post and resharing posts means the user is distributing information to her followers, these publishing acts can also be thought of as actions that curate a particular image to her audiences. Commenting and +1 actions are much more like reactions to others in a conversation, so these actions more likely represent topics that the user is interested in consuming from others. Obviously, there should be overlaps between the two sets of topic interests. These actions parallel ideas from a well-known social scientist Erving Goffman, whose seminal book called "*The Presentation of Self in Everyday Life*[5]" emphasizes how people are 'performing' for others like on a stage when they are in contact with others. Applied to social media, one can think of users as putting on a performance for her followers in order to control or guide the impression that others will form of her as a person.

Motivated by these ideas, we first performed an analysis on behavioral actions on Google+ social network. We will describe this analysis in more detail later in the paper, but in short, for each user, we gathered the two set of topics that she publishes and consumes separately. We found that the average Jaccard Index between the two sets is only 0.122, which suggests that users do tend to publish and consume information on somewhat different topics.

Because user have different topic interests depending on the behaviors, we wish to build different user profiles and make different topic interest predictions for different behaviors. As usual, we care most about recommending content for user to consume, but there are instances where we might want to recommend content that the user would want to reshare instead, for instance.

Here the main task is to predict the preferences of a user for a particular topical item, using observed implicit or explicit topical preferences. We model this recommendation task as a matrix completion problem, which can be solved using matrix factorization

*Work done while interning at Google

WWW 2015, May 18–22, 2015, Florence, Italy.
ACM 978-1-4503-3469-3/15/05.
http://dx.doi.org/10.1145/2736277.2741656 .

([16]) in three steps: 1. Learn a latent embedding space from the user-item matrix; 2. Represent both user and items in embedding space; 3. Compute the similarity of user to items as the preferences. Current state-of-the-art recommenders typically model user-item preferences using a single rating score for each observed user-item pair, due to scalability reasons.

Instead, in our approach, for each user, we use the embeddings built from factorization techniques to separately model the topic interests for different behaviors. We then use the embeddings to predict user preferences for different topics under different behavioral contexts. We call our approach "Behavioral Factorization".

To be precise, we first build a embedding model by separating each user's preferences into several preferences in different behavior contexts. This separation is key to getting a clean topic interest signals to train the embedding model. We then combine a user's topic preferences across different behaviors to make predictions of topical interests for, as an example, consumption. That is, our approach provides different recommendations for different behavioral engagement types. For example, given a user's activities on content topics such as creating post about "data mining", or +1 post about "video games", our prediction framework will recommend topics for different behavioral actions, e.g., recommend "minecraft" posts to consume, but "machine learning" posts to reshare.

The contributions of this work are:

- We introduce the general notion of separating the behavioral engagement types in the construction of an latent embedding model for user interest profiles.
- We develop a method to perform "behavioral factorization", in which we apply matrix factorization to the user-behavior by item matrix directly to construct an embedding space, which is used in the prediction of future topic interests.
- We evaluate behavioral factorization on a large-scale data set and show the amount of improvement obtained in building user profiles.

2. RELATED WORK

2.1 Building User Profiles

The diversity and volume of information shared on social media is overwhelming for many users. Therefore, the construction of topic interest profiles is an important part of personalized recommenders in social media systems. We are inspired by a wide variety of past personalization research that utilize behavioral signals.

Search engine researchers have utilized user profiles to provide personalized search results [9], [11], [4], [30], [35]. Usually user profiles are represented as vectors in a high dimensional space [1], [23], with vectors denoting users' preferences on different items, (e.g., web pages, movies, or social media posts.) or users' preferences on various topics (e.g., keywords representing topics, or topic categories from a taxonomy.)

2.1.1 Matrix Factorization & Embedding Models

In one family of recommender approach called Collaborative Filtering (CF) [26], systems typically model user preferences using a user-by-item matrix, with each entry representing a user's rating on a corresponding item. Therefore, a row in the input matrix is a particular user's expressed preferences of the items in the system. A user's unknown preference on a certain item is inferred using matrix completion and researchers have made great progress in using matrix factorization methods effectively for this problem [16], [17].

In our paper, instead of representing user profile by preferences of items (posts), we focus on inferring user's topical interests, and topics are represented as entities in Google Knowledge Graph [29], such as 'basketball' or 'video games'. Researchers have utilized matrix factorization to create embedding models, as well as generative models such as Latent Dirichlet Allocation (LDA) [2] to build user profiles [21]. Matrix factorization as well as generative models learn latent embedding spaces, where preferences can be calculated by similarity between user and item's latent embedding factors.

Compared to item-based approach, topic-based approach should be more scalable for applications in social media, where the number of actual items (posts) is large. Instead, we can make predictions of a user's interest in an item by calculating the relevance between the user's topic interests and the post's topics.

2.2 Personalized User Profiles in Social Media

Just as in other recommendation problem, social media researcher often treat building a user profile as the first task in building a personalized recommender. Researchers have applied matrix factorization and generative models such as LDA to modeling the user-topic matrix in social media and to building user profiles in particular [8], [7], [34], [3], [6], [15], [33], [27]. For example, Guy et al. built user profiles based on content and item preferences, and then provided personalized recommendations for social media items such as bookmarks and social software [7], [8]. Chen et al. built user topic profiles and provided personalized recommendation of conversations on Twitter. User profiles are also used to provide recommendations of friends [6], communities [33], and activities such as mentioning [33] and commenting [27], etc.

For a user profile, user preferences can be inferred using implicit feedback such as user's activities [8]. In contrast, in traditional recommender systems, CF usually requires user to have some explicit input on rating some items, e.g., movies and books, etc., which brings extra burden for users. For example, Hu et al. proposed a matrix factorization approach that leverages implicit feedback and was shown to be efficient with large-scale sparse data sets [13]. Extending on this idea, Noel et al. proposed a novel objective function in matrix factorization that considers feature-based similarity as well as user-user information in social media [24].

2.3 Contextual Personalization

Social media platforms also provide us rich contextual information such as who comments on who's post on what topic and when. Many recent works discussed how to make use of the rich context to learn better user profiles. Collective Matrix Factorization has been proposed by Singh et al. to provide recommendation in heterogeneous network where context information is used [28], [19]. Probably closest to our work are: (a) Liu et al. propose a social-aided context-aware recommender systems for books and movies, which makes use of rich context to partition user-item matrix into multiple matrices [20]; (b) Jamali et al. propose a context-dependent matrix factorization model to create user profiles for recommendation in social network [14].

Beyond matrix factorization techniques, context-aware generative models have been proposed by researchers to help creating user profiles and latent semantic models in social media platforms such as Twitter [25], [32], [36]. For example, Zhang et al. proposed a two-step framework that first discover different topic domains using generative models, and then provide recommendation within each domain using matrix factorization methods [37]. Their idea that different users may be interested in different domains is relevant to our work in differentiating user's behaviors. But we focus instead on how each user's topical interests are separated by different types of behaviors.

Researchers have also used content from a two or more different social media platform to build improved user profiles. Li et al. proposed a transfer learning approach that can factorize two matrices from two domains together using information from each other [18]. Hu et al. propose a triadic-factorization-based approach to factorize user-item-domain tensor to provide personalized recommendation across domains [12].

2.4 Behavioral Factorization

> "If we see perception as a form of contact and communion, then control over what is perceived is control over contact that is made, and the limitation and regulation of what is shown is a limitation and regulation of contact." — Erving Goffman, *The Presentation of Self in Everyday Life* [5].

Recent works have shown us that differentiating various contexts can improve the quality of user profiles. In our paper, we show that because social media users interact with different topics using different types of behaviors, we should use behavior types as an important context. We should also build multiple user profiles for different behavior types, then use these different profiles flexibly in different behavioral-dependent recommendation, e.g., recommend content to read, or recommend content to reshare, etc.

Sociologists have shown that people present different images to others in their everyday life and their everyday conversations engage in different topics with different audiences [5]. The emergence of social media has also drawn sociologists' interests to study this phenomenon in online communities. For instance, sociologists theorize that, because users do not have a clear idea of the exact audiences in public social media, they end up with blurred context boundaries [22]. However, because different types of behaviors, such as posting or commenting, affect very different audiences, our analysis below suggest that users still show different 'identities', exhibiting different types of behaviors around different topics in social media. By conducting qualitative study, Zhao et al. point out that users experience social media platforms such as Facebook as multiple different functional regions, similar to their multiple identities in real life [38]. To the best of our knowledge, our paper is the first work that utilizes users' different online presentations on a real-world social media platform.

3. GOOGLE+ BEHAVIORAL ANALYSIS

To motivate our work further, here we analyze users' online behaviors in Google+ using an anonymized data set. We first extract the topic entities in posts as our features to construct feature vectors for each post. For each users' behavioral actions on posts, we aggregate the corresponding post feature vectors to build an entity vector for each user-behavior combination. Then we coarsely measure the differences of topical interests represented by these user-behavior entity vectors. We show that there exists significant differences between these vectors, which motivates our approach to utilize behavioral factorization to model different behavioral types.

3.1 Dataset Description

We use anonymized Google+ users' public behaviors in May 2014 to conduct our analysis. We analyzed all user actions on all public posts, and each record is represented as a tuple: (u, b, E), where a user u (with an anonymized id) used behavior b to engage with a post containing E set of entities. There are four types of behaviors in our data: Create Post, Reshare, Comment, and +1.

Instead of using low-level features such as word tokens, we extract higher-level semantic concept from the post in the form of entities using Google's Knowledge Graph [29], which contains entities that represent concepts such as computer algorithms, landmarks, celebrities, cities, or movies. It currently contains more than 500 million entities, which provides both wide and deep coverage of topics.

Behavior	Comment	Plus One	Reshare	Create Post
Comment	1	0.092	0.050	0.102
+1	0.092	1	0.048	0.071
Reshare	0.050	0.048	1	0.012
Create Post	0.102	0.071	0.012	1

Table 1: Average Jaccard similarity between pairs of behavior types

Entity extraction is an open research problem and not a focus of our work here, but in a nutshell, we utilized an entity extractor based on standard entity recognition approaches that utilize prior co-occurrences between entities, likelihood of relatedness between entities, entities' positions within the text, and then finally ranking the topicality of the entity for the text.

Given a post, we use its corresponding Knowledge Graph entities as features to represent its topics. Therefore, each E in input tuple (u, b, E) is a set of Knowledge Graph entities. For example, if a user u_1 created a post with his dog's picture, this behavior might correspond to $(u_1, CreatePost, \{``Dog", ``Pet", \dots\})$. If another user u_2 commented on a post with a YouTube video about Minecraft on Xbox, this behavior might correspond to the tuple $(u_2, Comment, \{``Minecraft", ``Xbox", \dots\})$.

3.2 Measuring differences among behaviors

For each user, we aggregate the entities from the posts she interacted with using a particular type of behavior. In the end, for each user, we obtain four sets of topic entities corresponding to the four behavior types mentioned above.

We then use the Jaccard similarity index to measure the differences between the sets. Jaccard similarity index is a common metric for measuring the similarity between two sets and is calculated as follows given sets A and B: $J(A, B) = \frac{A \cap B}{A \cup B}$.

After we calculate Jaccard similarity scores of different behaviors for each user, we then average the scores across all users. We filter out users who have less than 10 entities as non-active. Table 1 shows the results of the average Jaccard similarities. We can see that the Average Jaccard Index between any two types of behaviors is low. Take user's commenting and +1 behaviors as an example, only 9% of the topics overlapped between these two behaviors. We also measure the difference between user's publishing and consuming behaviors. We combine the entities of user commenting and +1 behaviors as a set of entities of consuming, and we combine the entities of user creating post and resharing behaviors as a set of entities of publishing. The average Jaccard Index is 0.122. The low overlap rate of these Jaccard scores suggests that user acts differently in different behaviors.

3.3 Discussion

The results of the analysis show that, for each user, she typically have different topic interests with each behavior. That is, she will often create posts on topics that are different from the topics she comments on. The results suggest that general non-behavior-specific user profiles might not perform well in applications that emphasize different behavior types.

Content recommenders usually targets predicting contents for user to consume, which might be better reflected by behaviors such as commenting and +1. In other contexts, we might instead predict what topics users would create posts about. Therefore, by creating topic preferences for each behavior type separately, behavior-specific user profile might have better performance in different recommendation contexts.

In summary, users' various behaviors in social media contain important contextual information, which might help us improve the performance of user personalization profiles. We showed that users have significantly different topical interests reflected by their different behavior types in G+, and that building multiple profiles with separate behavior types allows us to tailor our content recommendation systems for various behavioral contexts.

4. PROBLEM DEFINITION

4.1 Input Behavioral Signals

Instead of building one single profile per user, we propose to build multiple profiles for a user to represent her different behavior types. Specifically, here we take users' behaviors on social media posts as input, and output a set of topic interest vectors to represent each user's different types of profiles.

Given a set of users $\mathfrak{U}$, a set of different behaviors types $\mathfrak{B}$, and a set of features that can represent social media content $\mathfrak{E}$, the input data can be represented as a set of tuples:

$$\mathfrak{T} = \{t_i = (u_i, b_i, E_i), i = 1, \ldots, N\}$$

where $u_i \in \mathfrak{U}$, $b_i \in \mathfrak{B}$, and $E_i \subset \mathfrak{E}$. Each t_i represents a user's action on a particular piece of social media content. For example, a t_i can be creating a post, or commenting on one. E_i is the set of features of that post. Here since we are building user topic profiles, we use entities from Google Knowledge Graph as our feature set. However, in general, $\mathfrak{E}$ can be any low-level (i.e., words) or high-level features (i.e., other entities, or even demographic features).

4.2 User Profiles

We define user profiles as sets of vectors in the feature space $\mathfrak{E}$:

$$\mathfrak{P} = \{P_u = \{\mathbf{V_{u_B}}\}\}$$

where $u \in \mathfrak{U}$, $B \subset \mathfrak{B}$, and P_u is the user profile for user u, and $\mathbf{V_{u_B}}$ is a vector of user u's preferences on features corresponding to her behavior types B. P_u can be thought of as a user tensor.

B can be either a single behavior type (e.g., creating a post), or a combination of behavior types (e.g., both creating a post and resharing a post). To be precise:

$$\mathbf{V_{u_B}} = (p^{e1}_{u_B}, p^{e2}_{u_B}, \ldots, p^{e_k}_{u_B}), e_j \in \mathfrak{E}$$

where $p^{e_j}_{u_B}$ is user u's behavior types B's preference on feature e_j, for $j = 1, \ldots, k$.

In the following sections, we propose our behavioral factorization approach to build user profiles, and compare the quality of the profiles with profiles built using the traditional matrix factorization technique.

5. OUR APPROACH

Here we introduce our behavior factorization approach to build user profiles for personalized recommendation, which includes three steps, as shown in Figure 1 and 2.

- Step 1: Given input user action tuples $\mathfrak{T}$ defined in Section 4, we first build matrices of different behavior types. This corresponds to the left part in Figure 1.
- Step 2: We factorize the matrices generated in step 1 to learn the latent embedding space. This corresponds to the right part in Figure 1
- Step 3: At last we build user profiles by making predictions of topics of interest utilizing the learned latent space. This creates profiles $P_u = \{\mathbf{V_{u_B}}\}$ for each user u. This corresponds to Figure 2.

We introduce each of these steps in turn below.

5.1 Step 1: Building matrices of different behavior types

In typical matrix factorization techniques, input user-item matrix R is represented as a $N \times K$ matrix, in which N is the number of users and K is the number of items. R is factorized into the product of two matrices, matrix X of $N \times L$, and matrix Y of $K \times L$. In other words, both row vector and column vector in R have been mapped into a L-dimensional latent embedding space. With this learned latent space, for any observed row vector in user-item matrix, the learned embedding space can be used to help complete the particular row vector to get complete estimated preferences of a user on items.

Since we are building user-topic-based profiles, instead users' interests on *items* ($N \times K$ user-item matrix) as input, we use users' interests on *topics* ($N \times K$ user-topic matrix) as input.

In addition, instead of using only one $N \times K$ matrix as input, we build and factorize multiple matrices as described below, including: (a) The traditional $N \times K$ matrix – referred to as Behavior Non-specific User-topic Matrix (**BNUM**); (b) Single Behavior-Specific User-topic Matrix (**SBSUM**); (c) Combined Behavior-Specific User-topic Matrix (**CBSUM**).

5.1.1 *Behavior Non-specific User-topic Matrix* BNUM

Here each entry indicates a user's implicit interests on a particular topic. Given input user tuples $\mathfrak{T} = \{t_i = (u_i, b_i, E_i), i = 1, 2, \ldots\}$, we first pull out the tuples $\mathfrak{T}_u$ involving user u:

$$\mathfrak{T}_u = \{t_j = (u_j, b_j, E_j)\}, t_j \in \mathfrak{T} \wedge u_j = u$$

Then we generate observed value for each user and topic pair:

$$r_{ui} = r(\mathfrak{T}_u, i)$$

That is, we first extract out all tuples $\mathfrak{T}_u$ involving user u and apply the function r to calculate implicit interests, given user u's tuples involving topic i. There are many possible forms of this function, and different weights can be trained for different behaviors. We use the following equation here in baseline methods as well as in later sections to calculate implicit interests:

$$r_{ui} = \frac{(\sum_{\mathfrak{T}_u} \sum_{e \in E_j} \sigma_i(e)) + 1}{(\sum_{\mathfrak{T}_u} \|E_j\|) + (\| \cup_{\mathfrak{T}_u} E_j \|)} \quad (1)$$

where $\sigma_i(e)$ is 1 if $i = e$ and 0 otherwise. That is, the implicit interest of topic i from user u is calculated by the number of occurrences of i in all user u's behaviors, divided by the sum of occurrences of all items. We smooth the value using additive smoothing.

5.1.2 *Single Behavior-Specific User-topic Matrix* SBSUM

Both **SBSUM** and **CBSUM** separate behavior types to generate separate user-topic matrices. Given a specific set of behavior types $B \subset \mathfrak{B}$, we want to build matrix $R_B = \{r^B_{ui}\}$, in which each entry represents the implicit interest only from behavior types in B.

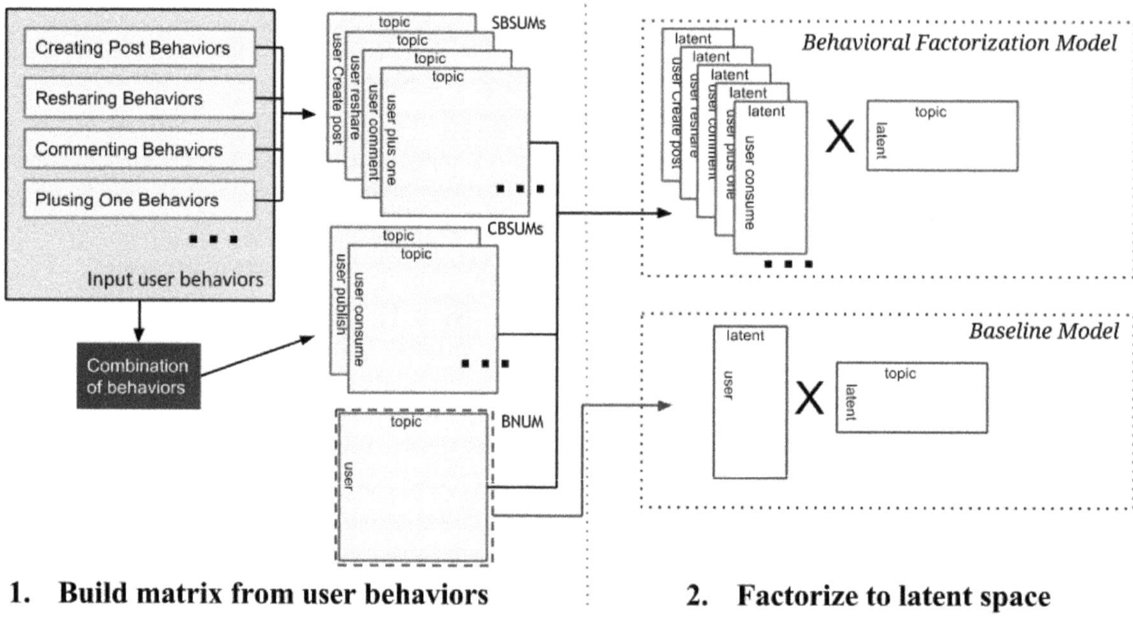

Figure 1: Framework of generating matrices and factorization.

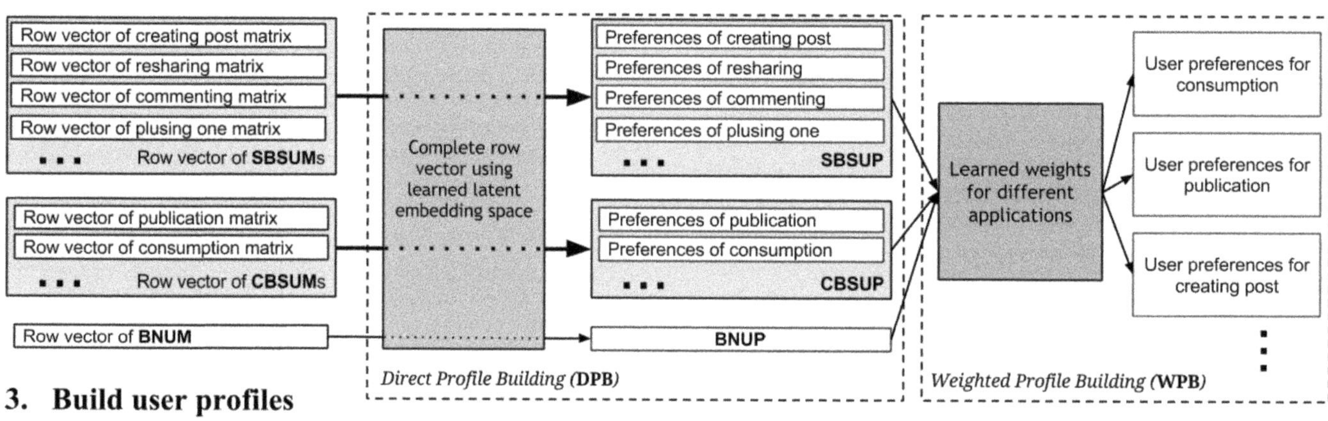

Figure 2: Building user profiles using latent embedding space.

We use the same method as in Equation 1, but add constraints to filter out behavior types not in B:

$$r_{ui}^{B} = \frac{(\sum_{\mathfrak{T}_u \wedge b_j \in B} \sum_{e \in E_j} \sigma_i(e)) + 1}{(\sum_{\mathfrak{T}_u \wedge b_j \in B} \|E_j\|) + (\| \cup_{\mathfrak{T}_u \wedge b_j \in B} E_j \|)} \tag{2}$$

Using this equation, for each B, we can build a matrix that represents users' observed implicit feedback with behavior types in B, which can be set as either a single behavior type, or a set of multiple behavior types. Therefore, based on the choices of B, we can build two types of behavior-specific user-topic matrices: Single Behavior-Specific User-topic Matrix **SBSUM**, and Combined Behavior Specific User-topic Matrix **CBSUM**.

First, we build one user-topic matrix for each behavior type, such as creating post, resharing, commenting or +1. The entry of each matrix is the observation value r_{ui}^{B} calculated by Equation 2, where B is a single behavior. Given $\mathfrak{B} = \{b_1, b_2, \ldots, b_M\}$ as a set of all behavior types, we generate the following M single behavior-specific user-topic matrices (**SBSUM**):

$$\begin{cases} R_{b_1} = \{r_{ui}^{B}\}, \;\; B = \{b_1, b_1 \in \mathfrak{B}\} \\ R_{b_2} = \{r_{ui}^{B}\}, \;\; B = \{b_2, b_2 \in \mathfrak{B}\} \\ \ldots \\ R_{b_M} = \{r_{ui}^{B}\}, \;\; B = \{b_M, b_M \in \mathfrak{B}\} \end{cases} \tag{3}$$

5.1.3 *Combined Behavior Specific User-topic Matrix* CBSUM

In building **SBSUM**, we create M matrices, each of which represents a single behavior type. However, we also want to capture topic interests of combinations of more than one related behavior types. For example, in G+, both creating and resharing posts generate content that is broadcast to followers, and these two behavior types can be combined together to represent the user's *publication*.

Meanwhile, commenting and +1'ing posts both indicate user's consumption of post. Combining them together can represent topics of interests in the user *consumption*. Therefore, given sets of behavior types, with each set being a subset of $\mathfrak{B}$, $\{B_1, B_2, \ldots, B_P\}$, we build P matrices, each of which represent user's combined behaviors in each set of behavior types.

$$\begin{cases} R_{B_1} = \{r_{ui}^B\}, \ B = \{B_1, B_1 \subset \mathfrak{B}\} \\ \dots \\ R_{B_P} = \{r_{ui}^B\}, \ B = \{B_P, B_P \subset \mathfrak{B}\} \end{cases} \tag{4}$$

5.2 Step 2: Learning latent embedding space

Here we introduce a matrix factorization technique for building user topic profile as the baseline method. In addition, we introduce our proposed method that extends the baseline algorithm to behavior factorization.

5.2.1 *Baseline model: Matrix factorization*

After building Behavior Non-specific User-topic Matrix (**BNUM**), we learn a latent embedding space that can be used to complete observed user-topic matrix to get predicted user-topic preferences. In recommender research, there are many efforts trying to improve matrix factorization techniques in both academia and industry. Here we use the factorization techniques as proposed in Hu et al. [13].

There is a very specific reason why we adopted Hu et al.'s approach. In social media platforms, implicit interest signals are easier to obtain for most users than explicit interest signals. There are just more implicit interest signals in the system. However, many recommender algorithms do not consider the potential differences between using explicit interest vs. implicit interest signals. Hu et al. [13] proposed a matrix factorization method that addressed this difference. It is worth noting that all other matrix factorization methods that work on user-item matrix can also be applied in our framework to build user profiles using behavior factorization. Note that 'topic' in user-topic matrix is the same as item in user-item matrix in the discussion below.

Given observation of the user-item matrix obtained from implicit interests from r_{ui}, Hu et al. splits observations into two variables: preference p_{ui} and confidence c_{ui}. Here p_{ui} is a binary variable that represents whether user u has interests in item i:

$$p_{ui} = \begin{cases} 1 & r_{ui} > 0 \\ 0 & r_{ui} = 0 \end{cases}$$

Confidence c_{ui} represents the confidence level of the preference p_{ui}. It indicates how confident we are in the interest value. It can be calculated in the following way: $c_{ui} = 1 + \alpha r_{ui}$.

Then the algorithm learns a latent embedding space and maps every user u and item i into that space (to $\mathbf{x_u}$ and $\mathbf{y_i}$ respectively). To learn that space, the algorithm tries to solve the following optimization equation:

$$\min_{x_*, y_*} \sum_{u,i} c_{ui}(p_{ui} - \mathbf{x_u^T y_i})^2 + \lambda(\sum_u \|\mathbf{x_u}\|^2 + \sum_i \|\mathbf{y_i}\|^2) \tag{5}$$

The results $\mathbf{x_u}$ and $\mathbf{y_i}$ will be used to complete the user-item matrix that estimates how likely a user will like an item. The proposed algorithm works well for implicit feedback/interest datasets as mentioned in Hu et al. [13].

At this point, we have built user-topic matrix using Equation 1, have adopted matrix factorization to learn a latent embedding space. Furthermore, we can model any user u's interests by estimating her preferences on all topics. For any new users who do not appear in the original user-topic matrix for training of the embedding space, we can still map them to the embedding space by using learned topic embedding vectors $\mathbf{y_i}$. We will discuss this in Section 5.3.

5.2.2 *Behavior Factorization model* (BF)

Different from the matrix factorization model introduced above, we want to separate user's different behavior types and generate topic preference for each user for different behaviors. So instead of factorizing one user-topic matrix, we factorize multiple user-topic matrices (**BNUM**, **SBSUM**, and **CBSUM**) generated in Step 1.

There are some early exploration on context-aware matrix factorization and tensor factorization techniques such as a social-network-aided context-aware recommender system proposed by Liu et al. [20], which creates multiple matrices and learns a latent space simultaneously. However, these techniques cannot be used directly in our behavior factorization problem, because we are building multiple user-topic matrices having the same column/topic space but having different rows/users. They build matrices having different items for different context, instead we use an implicit modeling approach, and also consider relations among behavioral contexts, i.e., such as combining publication behaviors and consumption behaviors.

Figure 1 shows the differences of our proposed Behavior Factorization (BF) approach as compared to the baseline model. In the first step of constructing matrix from user behaviors, instead of only constructing the Behavior Non-specific User-topic Matrix **BNUM**, we also construct two more types of matrices: Single Behavior Specific User-topic Matrix **SBSUM** and Combined Behavior Specific User-topic Matrix **CBSUM**.

Here in the second step, we factorize all generated matrices into the same latent embedding space. We learn a latent embedding space and map every user of each specific behavior types and every item into this space. Each entry in each matrix is the implicit interest value from user's behaviors, so we can extend the Baseline matrix factorization model as follows.

Here p_{ui}^B and c_{ui}^B represent the preference and confidence value for each matrix. Given all specific behavior types we used $\Gamma = \{B_1, B_2, \dots\}$ in Equation 3 and 4, we learn the embedding space by optimizing the following equation:

$$\min_{x_*, y_*} \sum_{B \in \Gamma} \sum_{u,i} c_{ui}^B(p_{ui}^B - \mathbf{x_u^B}^{\mathbf{T}} \mathbf{y_i})^2 + \lambda(\sum_{B \in \Gamma} \sum_u \|\mathbf{x_u^B}\|^2 + \sum_i \|\mathbf{y_i}\|^2) \tag{6}$$

By writing out the summation on Γ, we use a similar solution of the original Equation 5 to solve this optimization problem and learn embedding space for user-behavior and topics.

Compared to the original user-topic matrix, the embedding space learned by our approach might be better at measuring semantic similarity, because from previous analysis (Section 3), we know that the observed values in user-topic matrix are mixtures of multiple different interests from different behaviors. Separating the signals should therefore result in a cleaner topic model. This is also suggested by a recent paper studying how to learn generative graphical models such as LDA in social media [31]. In that work, they explored how to aggregate documents into corpus that represent a particular context. Since generative graphical model and matrix factorization both tries to learn latent space from data, this intuition can be shared in both techniques. Here our hypothesis is that building matrix at user-behavior level instead of user level can help us identify cleaner semantic alliances across topics, without increasing too much sparsity.

5.3 Step 3: Building user profiles

Finally, we introduce how we build user profiles using learned latent embedding spaces from previous steps. As shown in Figure 2, we introduce two methods: (i) direct profile building from input row vectors of profile matrices, and (ii) weighted profile building by merging different direct profiles using a set of weights learned from a regression model.

As defined in Section 4, for each user u, we will build $P_u = \{\mathbf{V_{u_B}}\}$. Each $\mathbf{V_{u_B}}$ is a vector of topic preferences of user u on specific behavior types B. We build three types of user profiles, corresponding to the three types of input matrices:

- **Behavior Non-specific User Profile (BNUP)**: By setting $B = \mathfrak{B}$, we build a single $\mathbf{V_u} = \mathbf{V_{u_B}}$ for user u as her profile. This profile does not differentiate behavior types. This profile is used in existing approaches for building user profile and personalized recommendation. Each user will have one preference on each topic of user-topic matrix.

- **Single Behavior-Specific User Profile (SBSUP)**: Setting B to only one behavior type, $\mathbf{V_{u_B}}$ represents users' preferences of topics with only behavior types in B.

- **Combined Behavior-Specific User Profile (CBSUP)**: By setting B to contain more than one behavior types, $\mathbf{V_{u_B}}$ that represents users' preferences of topics with the behavior types in B. In our paper, for example, we construct both the Publishing and Consumption CBSUP.

5.3.1 Direct Profile Building (DPB)

We use a user's embedding factors (i.e., vector $\mathbf{x_u}$ for user u in learned latent embedding space) to generate her complete user profiles of $\mathbf{V_{u_B}} \in P_u$. In **DPB**, the input will be observed row vectors in matrix R_B for any B in Γ, and we build user profile for each B.

Given a user u and B, we obtain embedding factor $\mathbf{x_u^B}$ and then use this embedding factor and topic embedding factors $Y = \{y_i\}$ to generate preference list of user u's behavior B by computing the dot product: $\mathbf{x_u^B}^\mathbf{T} Y$. Then for each user u, her output user profile can be represented as:

$$P_u = \{\mathbf{V_{u_B}} = \mathbf{x_u^B}^\mathbf{T} Y\}, B \in \Gamma \tag{7}$$

Specifically, given any B that is a subset of $\mathfrak{B}$, we use the following equation to generate user's **SBSUP** and **CBSUP**:

$$V_{u_B} = (p_{u_B}^{e_1}, p_{u_B}^{e_2}, \ldots, p_{u_B}^{e_K}),\ p_{u_B}^{e_i} = \mathbf{x_u^B}^\mathbf{T} \mathbf{y_i} \tag{8}$$

where x_u^B is the embedding factor of user u on behavior types B.

In summary, in **DPB**, different profiles are generated from different input row vectors, row vector of **BNUM** generates **BNUP**, row vector of **SBSUM** generates **SBSUP**, row vectors of **CBSUM** generates **CBSUP**. For example, to build **BNUP** for each user u, we set $B = \mathfrak{B}$, and use all her observed topic interest values to generate her embedding factor $\mathbf{x_u}$ in the embedding space. Then by calculating $\mathbf{x_u y_i}$ with every topic i, we get her **BNUP**.

$$\mathbf{V_u} = (p_u^{e1}, p_u^{e2}, \ldots, p_u^{eK}),\ p_u^{e_i} = \mathbf{x_u^T y_i} \tag{9}$$

For new users who are not in the learned embedding model, we can still generate their row input vectors using Equation 2, and then project the vector to an embedding factor.

5.3.2 Weighted Profile Building (WPB)

DPB generates a behavior profile for a user only if that user have exhibited that behavior in the past. By separating user's behavior types, we can generate profile for user u's behavior B using **DPB**, but this requires user u to have non-zero observed values with behavior B. For some users who do not have behaviors in B, $\mathbf{V_{u_B}}$ will be empty, which means that a user who do not exhibit the required behavior type actions will not have a user profile. This somewhat corresponds to the cold-start problem in recommender systems.

However, we can solve this by using user's profiles on other behavior types. We combine them to generate a combined preference vector on topics using weighted sum. This corresponds to a transfer learning problem.

Here, to generate preference vector $\mathbf{V_{u_B}}$ of user u's behavior types B, instead of directly using results of Equation 7, we use weighted sum of all preference vectors we generated for any behavior types in Γ using Equation 10:

$$\mathbf{V_{u_B}} = \sum_{B_t \in \Gamma} w_{B_t} \mathbf{x_u^{B_t}}^\mathbf{T} Y \tag{10}$$

The weights for different behavior types in Γ are model-level parameters, i.e., we learn one weight for each $B_t \in \Gamma$ for the entire dataset. Therefore, these weights can be learned using a supervised method from all users who have multiple types of behaviors in our dataset. Therefore, for users who have no B_t in their history, we can still build those profiles for them.

In our implementation, we use linear regression with stochastic gradient descent to learn these parameters. Therefore, **WPB** can be used to generate either **BNUP**, **SBSUP** or **CBSUP**, depending on particular applications. In most content recommendation applications, usually information consumption behaviors are most important, and thus, we use users' observed consumption behaviors to learn weights to build consumption profile.

Having described the steps in our modeling method, we now turn our attention to an evaluation of this method.

6. EVALUATION

In previous sections, we proposed the behavior factorization approach which can both learn a powerful latent space and build user profiles for multiple behavior types. In this experimental study section, we want to verify the following two hypotheses:

H1: The latent embedding model learned from our behavior factorization approach is better in building user profiles than the baseline matrix factorization model.

H2: By combining preference vectors from multiple behavior types, we improve the coverage of user profiles on specific behavior types.

In the rest of this section, we first describe how we set up our experiment, i.e., what datasets we use, and how we evaluate the performance of the output user profiles. Then we compare our Behavior Factorization model with baseline model. We also compare our two proposed methods in building user profiles to show that, by combining behavior types, we can improve user coverage with good quality.

6.1 Experiment Setup

To evaluate the performance of building user profiles, we examine how well different approaches do in predicting users' topical interests. We separate our dataset into two parts: training set and testing set. We train and build user profiles using only training set, and compare the performance of different models with the testing set. We consider an approach to be a better one if it completes the user-behavior-topic matrix more accurately.

6.1.1 Dataset

Our dataset contains public Google+ user behaviors in May and June 2014. How we generate the dataset is described in section 3.1. We train both baseline and our approach's matrix factorization model using Google+ user behaviors in May 2014. We use 20% randomly sampled behaviors in June 2014 to learn weights used in

Weighted Profile Building (**WPB**) of Section 5.3.2. We use the remaining 80% behaviors in June 2014 to evaluate the performances of different methods.

Input Matrices: In our dataset, we include all public posts created in May and June 2014. There are four types of behaviors on those posts: Creating post, Resharing, Commenting, and +1. We build different user-behavior-topic matrices by making sets of behavior types Γ contain the following behavior types:

- We directly use four behavior types in our dataset to build Single Behavior Specific User-topic Matrix (**SBSUM**).
- We want to capture users' interests in publishing information, so we group creating post and resharing together to build a publication Combined Behavior Specific User-topic Matrix (**Publication CBSUM**).
- We also want to understand users' interests in consuming information, so we group commenting and +1 to build a **Consumption CBSUM**.
- We also group all four behavior types together to generate a Behavior Non-specific User-topic Matrix (**BNUM**).

6.1.2 Evaluation Metrics

The user profile we built for a given behavior type B_t is a vector of preferences on topics, $\mathbf{V_{u_{B_t}}}$. The values in this vector estimate whether user u would like each topic with behavior B_t. This can be evaluated using implicit interests of $R_u^{B_t} = \{r_{ui}^{B_t},\ i \in \mathfrak{C}\}$ in testing set calculated using Equation 2.

Although the actual values in $\mathbf{V_{u_{B_t}}}$ and $R_u^{B_t}$ do not need to be identical, a good user profile of B_t should have the ranking order of topics in $\mathbf{V_{u_{B_t}}}$ similar to what we have observed in testing set.

To compare the orders of these two vectors, we transfer vectors $\mathbf{V_{u_{B_t}}}$ and $R_u^{B_t}$ into two ranked lists of topics in $\mathfrak{C}$: $L_{method} = (e_{r_1}, e_{r_2}, \ldots, e_{r_N})$ is the rank list of top N topics generated by profile building method, and $L_{observed} = (e_{o_1}, e_{o_2}, \ldots, e_{o_{N'}})$ is a rank list of all the observed topics. We use the following as evaluation metrics:

- **Recall@N**: indicates how many topics appearing in top N of L_{method} also appear in $L_{observed}$, divided by the actual number of observed topics.
- **NDCG@N**: Normalized Discounted Cumulative Gain (NDCG) is a widely used metric to evaluate two ranked lists. It is the discounted cumulative gain of current ranked list normalized by the ideal discounted cumulative gain[1].
- **Average Percentile@N**: Percentile denotes where each e_{r_j} in L_{method} appears in $L_{observed}$. Similar metric has been used in evaluating matrix completion tasks [13]. Here we use 100% to represent when e_{r_j} is at the top of $L_{observed}$ and 0% to represent when e_{r_j} is at the bottom of $L_{observed}$. Average percentile@N is the averaged position across all e_{r_j} in L_{method}.

6.1.3 Comparison Methods

Next we show our experiment results to verify our two hypotheses at the beginning of this section. The methods used are shown in Table 2.

For our first hypothesis H1, to evaluate the performance of the latent embedding model learned from our Behavior Factorization model (**BF**) against the one learned with traditional matrix factorization model (**Baseline**), we compare them on building user profiles using the Direct Profile Building (DPB) method. To do this, we generate user profiles (BNUP, SBSUP, or CBSUP) using Direct Profile Building (**DPB**) with input matrices of BNUM, SBSUM, or CBSUM, respectively. We then evaluate the profiles' performances with three evaluation metrics introduced above.

Subsequently, to verify our second hypothesis H2, we evaluate our proposed **WPB** by comparing its coverage and quality of user profiles against **DPB**. To do this, we use latent space of **BF** to build user profile for the specific behavior type of consumption (i.e., Commenting & +1), using both the Direct Profile Building **DPB** and Weighted Profile Building **WPB**.

Methods	Latent Model Training	Profile Building
Baseline + DPB	Baseline	Direct (DPB)
BF + DPB	Behavior Factorization	Direct (DPB)
BF + WPB	Behavior Factorization	Weighted (WPB)

Table 2: Method combinations used in our experiments.

6.2 Evaluation Results

6.2.1 H1: Baseline v.s. Behavior Factorization

To compare **BF** with Baseline matrix factorization approach, we first use the two latent embedding model learned from these two methods to build different user profiles (**BNUP**, **SBSUP** and **CBSUP**). Then, we compare their performances using our evaluation metrics. Since we are only comparing learned latent embedding models, we use **DPB** to build behavior-specific user profiles.

Performance of building **BNUP**.

Here we compare two approaches in building **BNUP**. Baseline model is learned using the method discussed in Section 5.2.1, and **BF** model is learned using the method discussed in Section 5.2.2. The comparison results are shown in Figure 3. From the figure we can see that our approach achieves significant improvement on all evaluation metrics. Compared to Baseline, Our **BNUP** has 89% improvement on NDCG, 93% improvement on Average Percentile and 82% improvement on Recall.

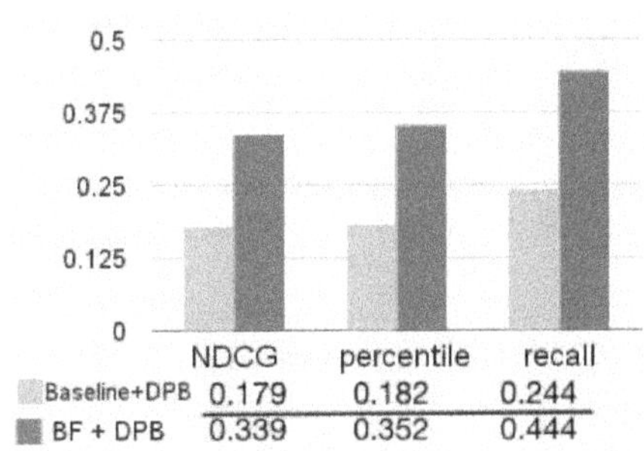

Figure 3: Comparison of BNUP outputs between Baseline and BF methods, given BNUM as input.

Performance of building **CBSUP**.

Next we evaluate the performance in building user's behavior specific profile, i.e., **CBSUP** for combined behavior types of Consumption and Publication. Results are shown in Figure 4(a) and Figure 4(b). We see significant improvement of our approach. We see that more improvement (about 100%) is on publication pro-

[1]http://en.wikipedia.org/wiki/Discounted_cumulative_gain

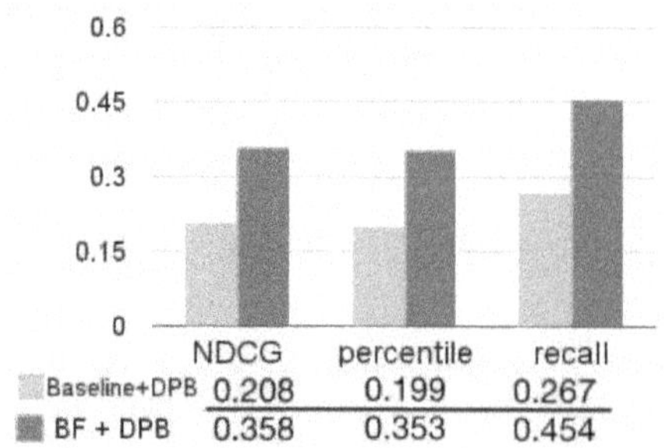

(a) **Consumption profile** output w/ **CBSUM** as input.

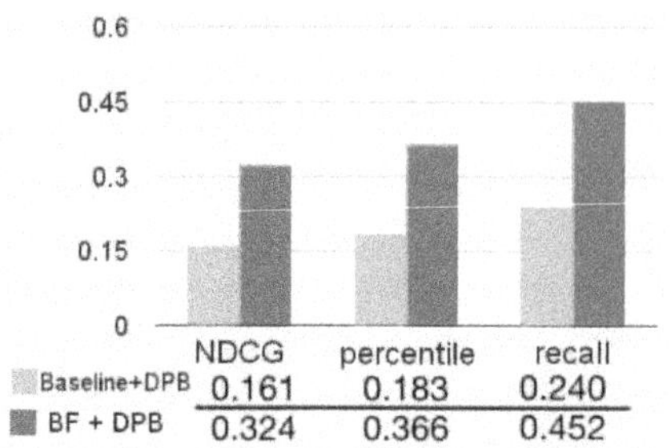

(b) **Publication profile** output w/ **CBSUM** as input.

Figure 4: Comparison of CBSUP between Baseline and BF.

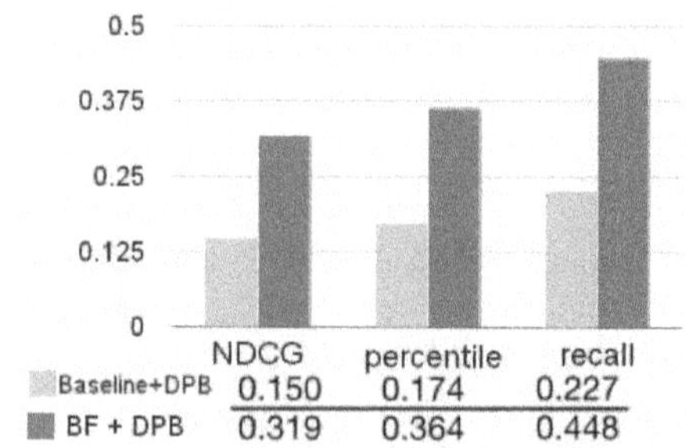

(a) **Create post profile** given **SBSUM**.

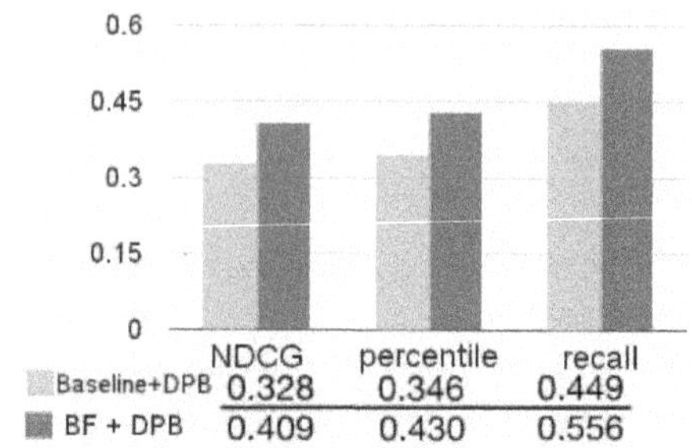

(b) **Reshare profile** given **SBSUM**.

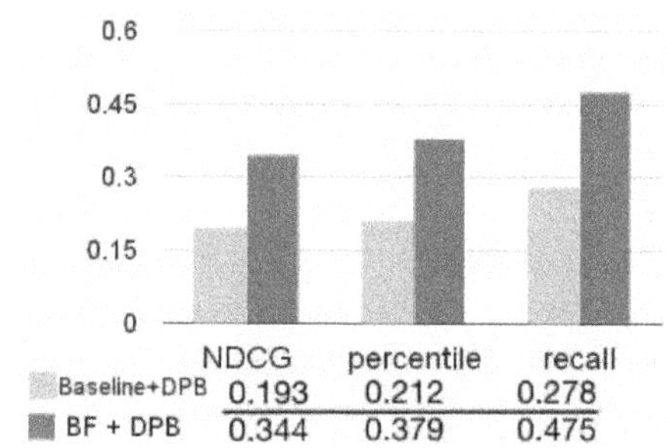

(c) **Comment profile** given **SBSUM**.

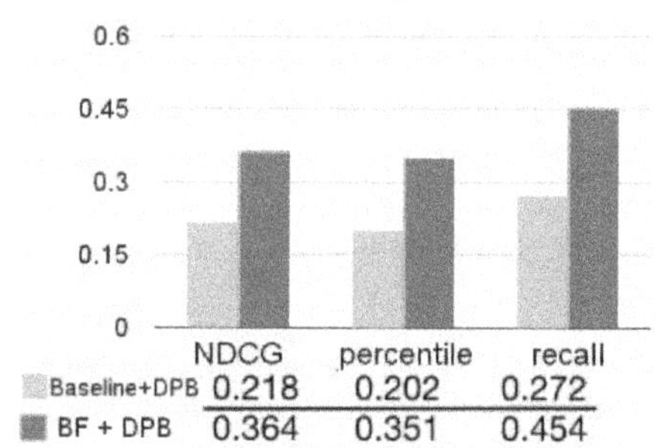

(d) **+1 profile** given **SBSUM**.

Figure 5: Comparison of SBSUP between Baseline and BF.

file than consumption profile. This aligns somewhat well with Goffman's work [5], because users usually have clearer idea about their audiences when they are publishing information. As a result, clearer personal topic interest representation appears in publication behaviors than consumption behaviors.

Performance of building **SBSUP**.

We build users' **SBSUP** for four single behavior types, and compare the performance between Baseline and our BF method. The results are shown in Figure 5. On average, our approach is about 80% better than Baseline. The greatest improvement is on creating post, followed by commenting. In these two behaviors, users usually know better about their audiences and have clearer goals, i.e., talking to his followers or creators of posts, as compared to resharing and +1. We can see that our approach learns better latent embedding models to build Single Behavior Specific User-topic Profiles. The improvement of using BF compared to using Baseline method passed paired-sample t-test with significant level $p < 0.01$.

6.2.2 *H2: Direct Profile Building* (**DPB**) *v.s. Weighted Profile Building* (**WPB**)

Next we verify our second hypothesis that Weighted Profile Building (**WPB**) improves coverage. We show that, compared to Direct Profile Building (**DPB**), generating user profile using WPB over all behavior types in Γ improves coverage for users without specific behavior types and with reasonable performance.

The left side of Figure 6 shows the user coverage of **Consumption CBSUP** built by **DPB** vs. **WPB**. Using **DPB** , we can only provide consumption profile for 30% of users in the testing set, because it requires users in the testing set to have comment and +1 histories in our training set. By using **WPB**, we improve the coverage to 49.7%, which is a 65.8% improvement.

The right side of Figure 6 shows the performance of user consumption profile of **DPB** and **WPB** for new and existing users: **Existing users:** For users who have comment and +1 behavior histories, **WPB** further improves the quality of their user consumption profiles by 6.7% on average on all three evaluation metrics, suggesting the interests of one types of behaviors can transfer to interests of another using behavioral factorization.

New Users: For users who have none of those behaviors in history, **WPB** still provides consumption profiles with reasonable performance, i.e., 79.2% of the performance of **DPB** on existing users, and 74.1% of the performance of **WPB** on existing users.

All Covered Users: We also calculated the average quality of profiles built by **WPB** on all 49.7% covered users who have or do

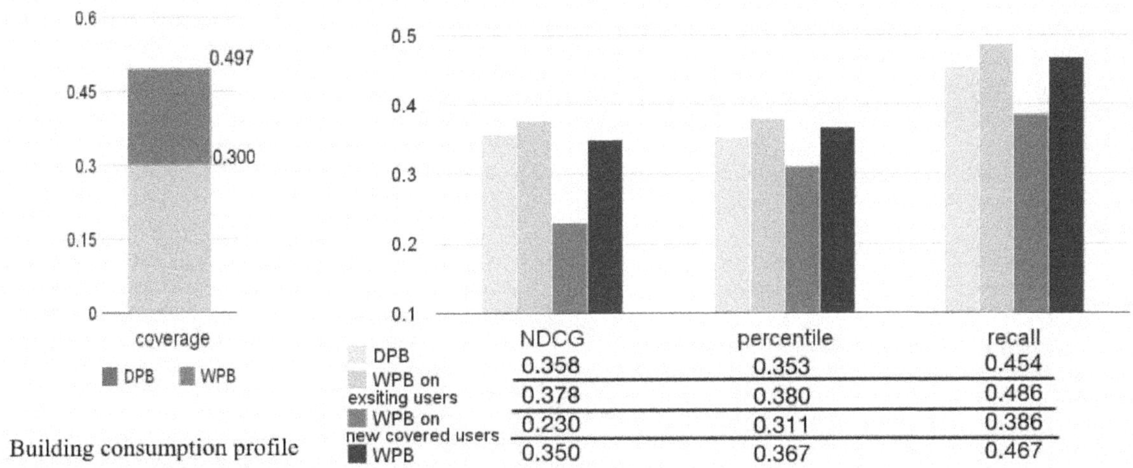

Figure 6: Comparison of consumption profile between DPB and WPB

not have consumption behaviors. The average percentile and recall are still slightly higher than profiles built by **DPB** on existing users.

Due to the limited space, here we only show our results on building profile for one specific set of behavior types—consumption of information, because, compared to other behavior types, the consumption topical interests of users is the most important.

However, besides consumption profile, we also tested **WPB** on building user profiles for other behavior types that we have examined in above experiments, such as **SBSUP** on commenting and +1, and we observed similar results. We can improve user coverage more than 70% for commenting and +1, while slightly improving the profile quality on average. The improvement of using **WPB** on existing users compared to DPB passed paired-sample t-test with significant level $p < 0.01$.

7. DISCUSSION

We have conducted experiments to evaluate our proposed Behavior Factorization approach to build either Behavior Non-specific user topic profiles or Behavior Specific user topic profiles. We demonstrated that it is important to build user profiles by separating types of behaviors. We also showed how this enables applications that target recommendations for different behaviors types.

7.1 Potential Applications

There are many applications can use the user profiles built by our method. Since we can map user's behaviors as well as different sets of items, e.g., posts, communities, or other users, into the same embedding model, the similarity between user's behavior and items can be used to generate rank lists for recommendation. Compared to conventional user profiles which don't separate user behaviors, our user profiles not only considers the content similarity between users and items, but also considers the context of different recommendation tasks. For example, consumption profile can be used to recommend relevant posts when a user is reading a post, publication profile can be used to recommend new friends after a user creates a post, etc.

7.2 Limitations and Future Work

As our results show, the proposed behavior factorization framework indeed improves the performance building users' interest profiles, however there are still some limitations. One limitation is that the framework depends on the fact that users' various behavior types inherently reveal users' different interests. It works well in building users' interest profiles in social media platforms (e.g., Google+), but may not generalize well for other domains where different behavior types do not necessarily reflect different user interests.

In addition, the results have shown that our method does not work as well when users have very sparse or no data for the target behavior type we are trying to predict. One reason is that these users may be less active than other users. The other reason is that our method optimizes multiple matrices which could lose the correlation across behavior types for the same user. To solve this problem, we are interested in applying tensor factorization techniques such as PARAFAC [10] on behavioral matrices. Our method can be thought of as an extension of an unfolding-based approach to tensor factorization, but a full Tucker3 decomposition might bring improvements in some modeling situations.

Furthermore, we would like to directly deploy the behavior factorization framework in real world recommendation systems and evaluate it via online live experiments.

8. CONCLUSION

In this paper, we proposed Behavior Factorization (**BF**) as a way to build user topic interest profiles in social media. To motivate our work, by analyzing a large quantity of behavior data from users in Google+, we showed that, for each user, topic interests exhibited by one type of behavior is different from other types.

To model users, we separate users' topic interests by their behaviors around those topics, and then constructing various combinations of novel user-behavior by topic matrices. Behavior Factorization first learns a latent embedding model by factorizing matrices separated by behaviors, then builds user topic profiles for different types of behaviors using this embedding model.

We verified our approach using large-scale Google+ data. Experiment results showed that BF improved our latent embedding model by about 80% in predicting user topic preferences, and by using Weighted Profile Building (**WPB**), we can improve coverage of consumption profile by 60%. Finally, it is our hope that our behavioral factorization approach might inspire other researchers to deeply think about how to model user context in topic modeling and recommender systems.

9. REFERENCES

[1] F. Abel, Q. Gao, G.-J. Houben, and K. Tao. Analyzing user modeling on twitter for personalized news recommendations. In *User Modeling, Adaption and Personalization*, pages 1–12. Springer, 2011.

[2] D. M. Blei, A. Y. Ng, and M. I. Jordan. Latent dirichlet allocation. *the Journal of machine Learning research*, 3:993–1022, 2003.

[3] J. Chen, R. Nairn, and E. Chi. Speak little and well: recommending conversations in online social streams. In *SIGCHI 2011*, pages 217–226.

[4] Z. Dou, R. Song, and J.-R. Wen. A large-scale evaluation and analysis of personalized search strategies. In *WWW 2007*, pages 581–590.

[5] E. Goffman. The presentation of self in everyday life. 1959.

[6] P. Gupta, A. Goel, J. Lin, A. Sharma, D. Wang, and R. Zadeh. Wtf: The who to follow service at twitter. In *WWW 2013*, pages 505–514.

[7] I. Guy, N. Zwerdling, D. Carmel, I. Ronen, E. Uziel, S. Yogev, and S. Ofek-Koifman. Personalized recommendation of social software items based on social relations. In *RecSys*, pages 53–60. ACM, 2009.

[8] I. Guy, N. Zwerdling, I. Ronen, D. Carmel, and E. Uziel. Social media recommendation based on people and tags. In *SIGIR 2010*, pages 194–201.

[9] A. Hannak, P. Sapiezynski, A. Molavi Kakhki, B. Krishnamurthy, D. Lazer, A. Mislove, and C. Wilson. Measuring personalization of web search. In *WWW 2013*, pages 527–538.

[10] R. A. Harshman. Foundations of the parafac procedure: Models and conditions for an" explanatory" multi-modal factor analysis. 1970.

[11] M. Hines. Google takes searching personally. cnet, 2004.

[12] L. Hu, J. Cao, G. Xu, L. Cao, Z. Gu, and C. Zhu. Personalized recommendation via cross-domain triadic factorization. In *WWW 2013*, pages 595–606.

[13] Y. Hu, Y. Koren, and C. Volinsky. Collaborative filtering for implicit feedback datasets. In *ICDM 2008*, pages 263–272.

[14] M. Jamali and L. Lakshmanan. Heteromf: recommendation in heterogeneous information networks using context dependent factor models. In *WWW 2013*, pages 643–654.

[15] Y. Kim, Y. Park, and K. Shim. Digtobi: a recommendation system for digg articles using probabilistic modeling. In *WWW 2013*, pages 691–702.

[16] Y. Koren. Factorization meets the neighborhood: a multifaceted collaborative filtering model. In *SIGKDD 2008*, pages 426–434.

[17] Y. Koren, R. Bell, and C. Volinsky. Matrix factorization techniques for recommender systems. *Computer*, (8):30–37, 2009.

[18] C.-Y. Li and S.-D. Lin. Matching users and items across domains to improve the recommendation quality. In *SIGKDD 2014*, pages 801–810.

[19] C. Lippert, S. H. Weber, Y. Huang, V. Tresp, M. Schubert, and H.-P. Kriegel. Relation prediction in multi-relational domains using matrix factorization. In *Proceedings of the NIPS 2008 Workshop: Structured Input-Structured Output, Vancouver, Canada.* Citeseer, 2008.

[20] X. Liu and K. Aberer. Soco: a social network aided context-aware recommender system. In *WWW 2013*, pages 781–802.

[21] A. Majumder and N. Shrivastava. Know your personalization: learning topic level personalization in online services. In *WWW 2013*, pages 873–884.

[22] A. E. Marwick et al. I tweet honestly, i tweet passionately: Twitter users, context collapse, and the imagined audience. *New media & society*, 13(1):114–133, 2011.

[23] N. Matthijs and F. Radlinski. Personalizing web search using long term browsing history. In *WSDM 2011*, pages 25–34.

[24] J. Noel, S. Sanner, K.-N. Tran, P. Christen, L. Xie, E. V. Bonilla, E. Abbasnejad, and N. Della Penna. New objective functions for social collaborative filtering. In *WWW 2012*, pages 859–868.

[25] M. Qiu, F. Zhu, and J. Jiang. It is not just what we say, but how we say them: LDA-based behavior-topic model. In *SDM*, pages 794–802. SIAM, 2013.

[26] P. Resnick, N. Iacovou, M. Suchak, P. Bergstrom, and J. Riedl. Grouplens: an open architecture for collaborative filtering of netnews. In *CSCW 1994*, pages 175–186.

[27] E. Shmueli, A. Kagian, Y. Koren, and R. Lempel. Care to comment?: recommendations for commenting on news stories. In *WWW 2012*, pages 429–438.

[28] A. P. Singh and G. J. Gordon. Relational learning via collective matrix factorization. In *SIGKDD 2008*, pages 650–658.

[29] A. Singhal. Google blog: Introducing the knowledge graph: Things, not strings, May 2012.

[30] B. Tan, X. Shen, and C. Zhai. Mining long-term search history to improve search accuracy. In *SIGKDD 2006*, pages 718–723.

[31] J. Tang, Z. Meng, X. Nguyen, Q. Mei, and M. Zhang. Understanding the limiting factors of topic modeling via posterior contraction analysis. In *ICML 2014*, pages 190–198.

[32] J. Tang, M. Zhang, and Q. Mei. One theme in all views: modeling consensus topics in multiple contexts. In *SIGKDD 2013*, pages 5–13.

[33] B. Wang, C. Wang, J. Bu, C. Chen, W. V. Zhang, D. Cai, and X. He. Whom to mention: expand the diffusion of tweets by@ recommendation on micro-blogging systems. In *WWW 2013*, pages 1331–1340.

[34] J. Wang, Z. Zhao, J. Zhou, H. Wang, B. Cui, and G. Qi. Recommending flickr groups with social topic model. *Information retrieval*, 15(3-4):278–295, 2012.

[35] R. W. White, W. Chu, A. Hassan, X. He, Y. Song, and H. Wang. Enhancing personalized search by mining and modeling task behavior. In *WWW 2013*, pages 1411–1420.

[36] H. Yin, B. Cui, L. Chen, Z. Hu, and Z. Huang. A temporal context-aware model for user behavior modeling in social media systems. In *SIGMOD 2014*, pages 1543–1554.

[37] X. Zhang, J. Cheng, T. Yuan, B. Niu, and H. Lu. TopRec: domain-specific recommendation through community topic mining in social network. In *WWW 2013*, pages 1501–1510.

[38] X. Zhao, N. Salehi, S. Naranjit, S. Alwaalan, S. Voida, and D. Cosley. The many faces of facebook: Experiencing social media as performance, exhibition, and personal archive. In *SIGCHI 2013*, pages 1–10.

Predicting Pinterest: Automating a Distributed Human Computation

Changtao Zhong, Dmytro Karamshuk, Nishanth Sastry
King's College London, UK
{changtao.zhong, dmytro.karamshuk, nishanth.sastry}@kcl.ac.uk

ABSTRACT

Everyday, millions of users save content items for future use on sites like Pinterest, by "pinning" them onto carefully categorised personal pinboards, thereby creating personal taxonomies of the Web. This paper seeks to understand Pinterest as a distributed human computation that categorises images from around the Web. We show that despite being categorised onto personal pinboards by individual actions, there is a generally a global agreement in implicitly assigning images into a coarse-grained global taxonomy of 32 categories, and furthermore, users tend to specialise in a handful of categories. By exploiting these characteristics, and augmenting with image-related features drawn from a state-of-the-art deep convolutional neural network, we develop a cascade of predictors that together automate a large fraction of Pinterest actions. Our end-to-end model is able to both predict whether a user will repin an image onto her own pinboard, and also which pinboard she might choose, with an accuracy of 0.69 (Accuracy@5 of 0.75).

Categories and Subject Descriptors

H.3.5 [**Online Information Services**]: Commercial Services, Data Sharing, Web-based services; I.4.9 [**Image Processing and Computer Vision**]: Applications; J.4 [**Social and Behavioral Sciences**]: Sociology

Keywords

Pinterest; Content Curation; Crowdsourcing; Image Analysis; Deep learning; User Behaviour; Supervised learning

1. INTRODUCTION

Following on the heels of the information glut created by the user-generated content revolution, an interesting new phenomenon that has been termed *content curation* has emerged: Rather than *create* new content, content curation involves *categorising* and *organising* collections of content created by others. For instance, on Pinterest, perhaps the most prominent content curation site, users can collect and categorise images (and the URLs of the webpages that contain them) by "pinning" them onto so-called "pinboards". Similarly, delicious.com (formerly del.icio.us) allows users to categorise URLs by tagging them.

A crucial aspect of such sites is that content curated by one user is also (by default) made available to the rest of the users to curate. For instance, on Delicious, links of another user can be copied onto one's own list, by tagging them. Users on Pinterest can copy images pinned by other users, and "repin" onto their own pinboards. Interestingly, such reappropriation and curation of content discovered by other users (termed as "repins") is by far the most common activity on Pinterest, constituting about 90% of user actions, as compared to directly discovering and pinning new images, which constitutes only 10% of actions[1].

Even if curating a content item that has already been categorised, users typically have to re-adjust it for their own collections: For instance, in tagging systems, multiple studies [9, 28, 25] have recognised that inter-user agreement can be low, and different users may choose different tags for the same URL (although an overall consensus vocabulary may emerge per-URL, due to tag imitation or background knowledge [9]). Similarly, users' pinboards are highly personal and idiosyncratic represntations of their taste, and furthermore, users are free to choose to repin any image onto any pinboard. Consequently, curation on Pinterest remains a highly manual process as well.

Our goal is to make it easier to re-appropriate and re-categorise content for personal use. Consider an image which has been introduced into Pinterest by an original pinner. Several other users may want to repin this onto their own pinboards. We are interested in automating this latter task: *Given a pin (image) and a user, we wish to predict whether the user would be interested in repinning the pin. Moreover, we wish to predict the pinboard onto which they would repin, and automatically suggest these to the user.*

Towards this end, we revisit the notion of agreement in the context of Pinterest. Unlike traditional social bookmarking, pinning on Pinterest does not involve creating an explicit vocabulary of tags to describe the image. However, each pinboard may be associated to one of 32 categories defined globally for all users by Pinterest. Thus, even though each pinboard may be exclusive to a user, the act of pinning *implicitly* categorises the image. In other words, *Pinterest users can be seen as performing a massive distributed human computation, categorising images found on the Web onto an (extremely coarse-grained) global taxonomy of 32 categories.*

We find that this lower dimension approximation of Pinterest has several desirable properties: First, for a given image, a remarkable ≈75% of repins tend to agree on the majority category, although the level of agreement varies with the category. This enables us to

[1]According to our dataset, collected originally in Jan 2013. This dataset, together with new image content-related features, is being made available to researchers at http://bit.ly/pinterest-dataset.

WWW 2015, May 18–22, 2015, Florence, Italy.
ACM 978-1-4503-3469-3/15/05.
http://dx.doi.org/10.1145/2736277.2741671.

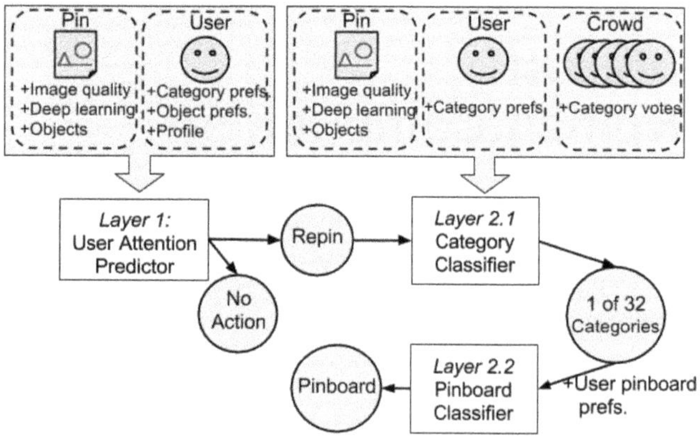

Figure 1: **Prediction cascade or pipeline to automate the manual curation of images on Pinterest**

robustly predict the category of an image. Second, users tend to specialise in a handful of categories; we use this to predict a personalised category, given the crowd "votes" for different categories. Third, most users appear to have one or two boards per category. Thus, given the category of an image, and the user, it is often trivial to predict the board to which the user would pin the image. Based on these observations, we are able to build classifiers that can predict the specific pinboard onto which the image would be repinned, if it is known that the user has pinned an image onto some pinboard.

Thus, the remaining problem is predicting whether the user would pay any attention to an image and repin it (onto some pinboard). We use the *content* of the image to build this predictor: we derive several thousands of image-content features (Table 1), ranging from basic visual and aesthetic features to features extracted from the layer right before the final classification layer of the state-of-the-art deep convolutional network in Caffe [18], and by recognising objects in the image, using the same convolutional neural network. Using these features, we construct a supervised machine learning model that is able to assign an image to the majority category. We also learn user preferences for these image features, and predict whether the image would be repinned by the user.

We compose these classifiers in a pipeline of three layers (Figure 1). The first layer predicts whether the user will pay attention to a pin; the second predicts the category that the user will choose for the pin; and the third predicts the pinboard chosen given the category. Together this pipeline or cascade of classifiers is able to predict curation actions on Pinterest with an accuracy of 69%. On the easier problem of suggesting up to five possible pinboards for each pin and user, the pipeline of Figure 1 can achieve an accuracy of 75% – in other words, the pinboard manually chosen by the user appears in the top five predictions of the pipeline of classifiers.

The paper is structured as follows. §2 presents related work. §3 gives a brief background of Pinterest and our dataset. §4 demonstrates properties in the dataset that are useful to predict repins. The rest of the paper develops a pipeline of predictors: §5 sets the stage, discussing the cascaded structure of the predictors and the features used. §6 develops a classifier to predict whether a user will pay any attention to a pin (Layer 1 in Figure 1). §7 then develops a two-stage multi-class classifier that predicts the board chosen by a user for a repin (Layers 2.1 and 2.2 in Figure 1). §8 puts it all together, showing that repins can be predicted, both in terms of whether users would be interested in repinning a pin and which of their boards they would place it onto. §9 ends by discussing implications for the wider research agenda.

2. RELATED WORK

Concurrent with the rapid rise of Pinterest, there have been several studies of Pinterest as a content curation platform [11, 38, 36, 27, 8, 37, 26, 3]. Using a variety of approaches ranging from qualitative user studies [36, 38] and textual or content analyses [8, 26], to large-scale exploratory data analysis [38, 12, 27, 3] and complex or multi-layer network studies [37], these works have shed light on a number of important aspects, such as the nature of its social network [38, 37], the relationship between Pinterest and other social networks such as Facebook [37] and Twitter [8, 26], the role of homophily and user specialisation [3], gender differences in activities [27, 8] and the motivations of content curators [38, 36, 12].

We believe this is the first work to extensively use a *machine learning approach* to automate content curation and thereby also try to obtain a *mechanistic understanding* of the *end-to-end process of social content curation* on Pinterest. Although Han *et al.* [12, §7] also explore pin prediction, the scope is a more limited problem of predicting 20 pins for each of 4667 users (in comparison, our dataset has 214K pins with 1.2M repins by 230K users) and checking whether these are in *any of* the user's pinboards after 125 days (our model performs a multi-class classification into specific pinboards). Also, the best Han *et al.* models obtain an average precision of 0.015; we are able to obtain much higher values (c.f. Table 6). Also using a supervised machine learning approach is the preliminary work of Kamath *et al.* [20], who propose a model for recommending boards to Pinterest users.

This paper also contributes to image analysis and understanding. This field has been well explored over the years, but the availability of user-generated image data on social sites such as Flickr, and annotated image databases such as ImageNet [6], have enabled significant advances in the recent past, answering relatively sophisticated questions such as what makes an image memorable [17], interesting [10] or popular [21]. Our paper contributes to this line of work, and aims to provide an understanding of how content curation happens, by collecting a large dataset of $> 200K$ images from Pinterest, and crucially, leveraging the category of the pinboards of these images to infer implicit label annotations.

Another related recent stream of research is concerned with using machine learning to predict the actions of a crowd. For instance, Blackburn and Kwak [1] predict crowdsourced decisions on toxic behavior in online games. [19] trains a model that predicts individual decision and consensus vote for the Galaxy Zoo classification problem and uses this to optimise task assignment for actual crowdsourcing. Here, we do the opposite: we use the actions of the crowd (agreement over the categories to assign a pin) to boost the performance of machine learning. Similar in spirit, but focused on a different task, is the model of Yin *et al.* [35], which takes actions of early voters as input and predicts eventual popularity of online items. An important difference is that this predicts a global trend whereas our focus is personalised predictions for individual users.

The properties of crowd agreement over item categories is a crucial element in our design. This has been studied widely in the context of social tagging (e.g., on delicious, citeulike, bibsonomy, etc.). Wetzker *et al.* [34] found that even if people share a common understanding about content, they may tag differently. It is known [31, 38] that tagging behaviour is driven by users' motivation to either categorise content for global use and easier navigation, or to describe content for personal use and to improve its searchability. Users employ different kinds of vocabularies depending on their motivation: a more compact but also a more informative vocabulary for categorisation, and a more diverse, yet more fine-grained vocabulary for descriptions [31]. Drawing on these results, we use fine-grained features, obtained by recognising objects in images,

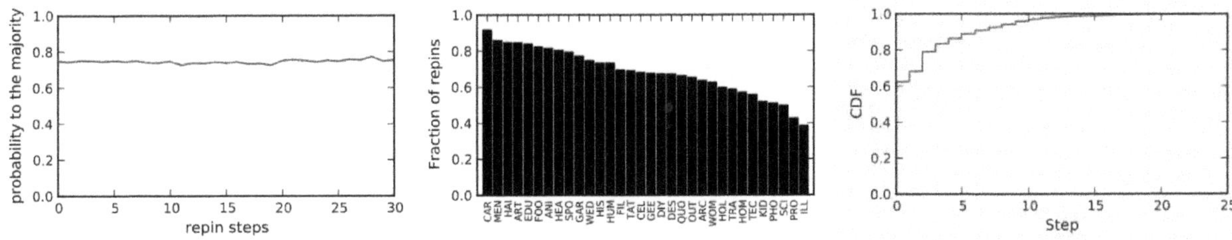

(a) Probability of majority pin (b) Levels of agreement in categories (c) No. pins for majority to appear

Figure 2: **Emergence of consensus in Pinterest**: (a) The category chosen by the ith pinner is independent of the category chosen by the previous $i-1$ pinners, and is the same as the category chosen by the majority of repinners with a remarkably high probability ($\approx$0.75). (b) The average fraction of pinners in the majority can vary across category, ranging from 91% (cars and motor cycles, or CAR), to 43% (Illustrations and Posters, or ILL). All except PRO (45%, Products) and ILL have a majority > 50%. (c) Cumulative distribution function (CDF) of the probability that the majority category that emerges at the ith pin remains the majority category after all repins have occured. For over 60% of pins, the category of the very first pin determines the majority category; in over 90% of cases, a stable majority has emerged after just 5 repins (all pins have >5 repins in our dataset).

to learn users' personal preferences, and the coarse-grained global taxonomy of 32 pre-defined categories for obtaining agreement.

3. PRELIMINARIES

We begin by briefly describing Pinterest, our terminology, and the dataset used in the rest of this paper:

Pinterest is a photo sharing website that allows users to organise thematic collections of images. Images on Pinterest are called pins and can be added in one of two ways. The first way is pinning, which imports an image from an external URL. The second is repinning, or copying an existing pin on Pinterest. Users can also like a pin or comment on it, but pining and repinning constitutes the vast majority ($\approx$92% in our dataset) of actions.

Terminology: We use the terms *pin* and *image* interchangeably; a pin or image may be *repinned* multiple times. In this paper, we are mostly concerned with how users categorise and organise their images or pins. All pins are organised into collections called *pinboards* (or *boards*), which belong to one of the 32 globally specified *categories* (excluding one category, 'other', for non-categorised boards). The user who introduces an image into Pinterest is its *pinner*; others who copy onto their own pinboards are *repinners*.

Dataset. Our dataset is derived from a previous study [38], and includes nearly all activities on Pinterest between Jan 3–21 2013. It was obtained by repeatedly crawling Pinterest: To discover new pins, each of the 32 category pages was visited once every 5 minutes, and the latest pins of that category were collected. Then, for every collected pin, we visited the homepage of the pin every 10 minutes. A pin's homepage would list the 10 most recent repins and 24 most recent likes[2], which we collected and stored along with the timestamp of the crawling pass. Through these regular visits, we captured almost all the activity during our observation period. We estimate that the fraction of visits which resulted in missed activities stands at 5.7×10^{-6} for repins and 9.4×10^{-7} for likes. Further details of our dataset may be found in [38].

In this paper, we wish to understand how the features of the pin and the pinner affect the activity of repinning. Therefore, we focus only on users with more than 10 pins in our original dataset, and on pins which have been repinned at least 5 times, ending up with a set of 214,137 pins, 237,435 users and 1,271,971 repins for analysis.

[2]This setting has been changed in April 2013.

4. PREDICTABILITY OF REPINS

Curation on Pinterest is currently a manual procedure: Users select images that they like, and categorise it amongst one of several thematic collections or pinboards that they curate. Over 85% of respondents in a previous user study considered their pinning activity to be highly personal, akin to personal scrapbooking [38].

This paper, however, aims to automate this procedure, as much as possible. To this end, we examine the extent to which properties of the pin, or the user, can assist in suggesting an appropriate pinboard of the user for the pin. We first take a pin-centric view, and ask whether repins of other users can help, and show that users tend to strongly agree on the *category* that they implicitly assign to a pin, via the category of the pinboard they choose. Next, we take a user-centric view, and show that users tend to be highly specialised in their choice of pinboards, focusing on a handful of categories, and also typically have very few boards within each category. We conclude by highlighting the implications of these findings, which we make use of in subsequent sections.

4.1 Pinterest users agree on image categories

Pinboards are personal to each user, and pinboards of different users typically share at most a handful of pins, if at all. However, each pinboard may be assigned to one of 32 categories which have been pre-determined by Pinterest. Therefore, we may regard a repin as implicitly assigning one-of-32 labels to an image, reminiscent of ESP game [32], a human computation task which greatly improved label prediction for images. We ask whether users agree on the category assignment for images in the context of Pinterest.

Formally, each repin by user u of a pin p to a pinboard b whose category is c is interpreted as an assignment of the category c to pin p by user u; we denote this as $repin\_cat(p,u)=c$. After users $1..i$ have repinned a pin, one can define the count of the category assignments of c to p: $count_i(p,c)=|\{k|repin\_cat(p,k)=c,\ \forall 1\le k\le i\}|$. We define the majority category of an image or a pin as the category chosen by the maximum number of repinners[3]. In other words, the majority category $\mathrm{maj}_i(p)$ after users $1..i$ have repinned a pin is the category with the maximum count: $\mathrm{maj}_i(p)=\mathrm{argmax}_c\, count_i(p,c)$. The final majority category $\mathrm{maj}_\infty(p)$ is the majority category after all r repins have been made. The consensus or agreement level after r repins can be com-

[3]Note that we do not require >50% of pinners agree on a category, although this often happens.

puted as the fraction of pins in the final majority category after r repins: $agreement_r(p) = count_r(p, \text{maj}_\infty(p))/r$.

Whereas other curation systems (such as social tagging on delicious.com) might push users towards agreement by suggesting tags [9], in Pinterest, a pin does not come with a category of its own, and no category is suggested by the system or other users. Indeed, it is quite difficult on Pinterest to discover the category of a pinboard: Visitors to a pinboard's webpage can only determine its category through a meta-property in the HTML source code[4]. Even the owner of the board is only shown the category on the page for editing a board's details (not normally seen when the owner views her board). Because of this UI design decision in Pinterest, we expect that a user's choice of the Pinterest category to associate with a pin is made independently of other users or the system itself. Furthermore, the category choice is made only implicitly, as a result of an explicit choice made on which pinboard to place the image in. Thus, we expect this decision to be influenced by, for instance, whether the image being pinned fits thematically with the other images in the pinboard, and not by other users.

We first test our expectation that users individually decide on an image's category. We ask what is the probability $P[repin\_cat(p,i) = \text{maj}_\infty(p)]$, that the ith repin of a pin agrees with the final majority category chosen for it. Confirming our intuition, Figure 2a shows that the ith repinner's choice appears to be unaffected (either positively or negatively) by the choices of all the previous $i-1$ repinners. Furthermore, we see that there is a remarkably high chance ($\approx$75%) that the category implicitly chosen by a user agrees with the majority. Figure 2b shows that the average levels of agreement can vary across pins of various categories, from 91% to 43%; and in all categories except Illustrations and Products, the final majority category has a clear majority of $> 50\%$ agreement.

Next, we ask how many pins it takes for the majority to emerge, *and stabilise*: Suppose we temporally order the pinners of a pin p, starting with the first pinner as *Repin 1*. We wish to know the number of repins required (smallest pinner number a) at which the majority category is the final majority category, and the consensus on the majority is unchanged by all subsequent pins. Formally, we want the smallest pin a such that $\text{maj}_k(p) = \text{maj}_\infty(p)$, $\forall k \geq a$. Figure 2c shows the cumulative distribution of the number of repins a required for stable agreement to emerge. In over 60% of images, this happens with the very first pin. After 5 repins, over 90% of images have reached consensus on the final majority category.

4.2 Pinterest users specialise in few categories

Having looked at a pin-centric view on predictability, we now look for user-specific patterns that can aid us in categorising their content automatically. Again we focus on categories. We first look at the distribution of categories per user and find that users are highly specialised: Figure 3 considers the fraction of a user's pins which are in the top-k categories of the user. This shows, for example, that about half the users have nearly half their pins in pinboards belonging to their the top category, and 80% users have *all* their pins in pinboards belonging to their top-5 categories. This indicates a high degree of specialisation.

We next consider how users choose to create pinboards. Figure 4 shows that most users have one or two pinboards in each category. Thus, it appears that users are mostly following the coarse-grained taxonomy developed by pinterest, and are in fact simply categorising images in this space, rather than on highly personalised pinboards.

[4]Users can repin images from the homepage of Pinterest, and may not even visit the board of the original pin. Thus they may not know the category assigned to it by the original pinner, even if they can read HTML.

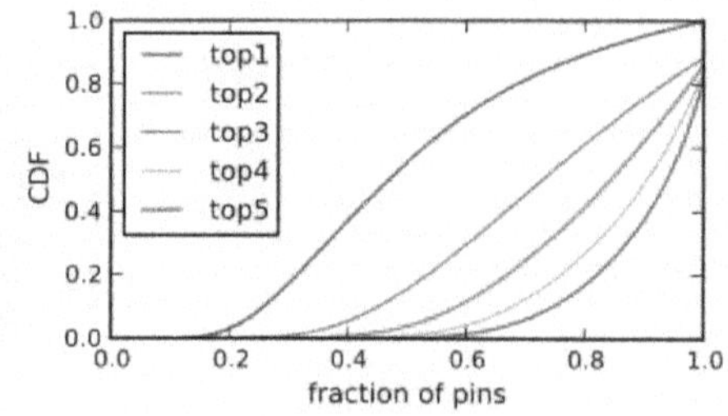

Figure 3: **Category concentration and user specialisation**. CDF of the fraction of users' pins in their top-k categories shows that each user specialises in a handful of categories.

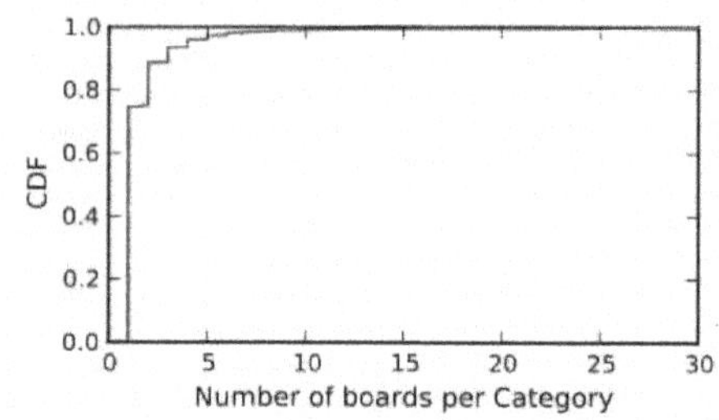

Figure 4: **Users' category choices can predict pinboard choices**. CDF of per-user number of boards per category shows that users tend not to have many boards in each category, implying that knowing the category assigned by a user, one can predict users' choice of pinboard for a pin.

4.3 Implication: Board prediction is easy

The results of §4.1 strongly suggest that most repinners agree on the category to assign to a pin, and furthermore, this majority category can be deduced just by observing the first few (say 5) repins. Secondly, since users' pins in different categories are highly skewed (Figure 3), users' own personal favourite categories can be predicted as a choice for the category used. In examining the corpus of repins, we find that, consistent with Figure 2, $\approx$87% of repins after the first five repins are made to the majority category. A further 4.7% of repins are made not to the majority category, but to the category in which the user has most of her pins. Thus, we expect that predicting the category of a particular pin based on these powerful signals can be an easy problem, and exploit these in §7.1.

Further, §4.2 suggests that users tend to have very few boards per category. Thus, once the category is predicted, we expect to be able to predict the actual pinboard chosen by the user as well. Finally, for the few cases when the user's pins are not in the majority category, we propose to use the fact that users specialise in a few categories to predict the correct category and thereby the board used. We explore the above two strategies in §7.2.

We conjecture that the high levels of agreement seen for a pin's category may in fact be a result of the high degree of user specialisation within categories: Since users choose to repin in very few categories, the fact that the user has paid any attention to a pin and repinned it is a strong indicator that the pin belongs to the given category. This may help explain the result of Figure 2a that nearly 8 out of 10 repinners agree on the category for a pin.

5. PREDICTING PINTEREST: AN OUTLINE

In the rest of this paper, we will use the notions of user category specialisation and agreement uncovered from the data, together with a number of user- and image-content related features to develop a model for predicting users' repins. Our ultimate goal, as stated earlier, is to automatically suggest, given a user and an image, whether the user will repin the image, and which pinboard it will be repinned to. In this section, we describe the features used, and our outline model for predicting content curation actions as a cascade of predictors. Later sections will use the dataset described in §3 to validate the different parts of the model.

5.1 Curation as a cascade of predictors

We model the process of curation as a cascade of predictors (Figure 1). A content curation action involves a user u who "repins" a pin onto one of her pinboards. The first prediction problem (§6) is to take a user u and a pin p, and predict an action $f_1 : (p, u) \rightarrow \{noaction, repin\}$. Next, the *repin* involves a further user-specific decision as to which pinboard the pin should be placed in (§7). We may formulate this problem as a classification task where a machine learning classifier f_2 is trained to recognise pinboard b_i to which user u is going to put repinned pin p, i.e., $f_2 : (p, u) \rightarrow \{b_1, b_2, ..., b_n\}$ where $\{b_1, b_2, ..., b_n\}$ is a set of user's u pinboards. However, taking cue from §4.1 and §4.2, we split this task into two. First, we predict the *category* that the user might implicitly choose for the image (§7.1), i.e., we train a classifier $f_{2.1}$ to recognise the category c_i in which user u is going to put the repinned pin p: Formally, we build a model to predict $f_{2.1} : (p, u) \rightarrow \{c_1, c_2, ..., c_n\}$ where $\{c_1, c_2, ..., c_n\}$ is a set of user's u categories. Then in §7.2, we train a classifier $f_{2.2}$ to predict the pinboard given the category as selected by the user. Formally, we develop the model $f_{2.2} : (c, u) \rightarrow \{b_1, b_2, ..., b_n\}$. As expected from Figure 4, this turns out to be an almost trivial problem.

5.2 Features

We tackle the above classification problems by incorporating both image- and user-related features (summarised in Table 1). In addition, we also use a feature derived from the "crowd" of other users repinning the image: the consensus agreement (§4.1) around the category of the image, as measured from the first five repins, serves as a powerful indicator of the category that other users might choose for the same image.

5.2.1 User-related features

We employ several user-related features which measure both the preferences as revealed by a user's repin history, and the user's extent of involvement with Pinterest, based on her profile.

User Image Preferences.

To describe users' preferences for particular types of content, we use two sets of features: *Category Preferences* and *Object Preferences*. The first set is a relatively coarse-grained approach wherein we measure how many images a user repins in each of the 32 different Pinterest categories. Object preferences are obtained by devising user-specific signatures from the visual features of those repins: We use the state-of-the-art approach in object recognition for images [6], deep convolutional networks [22], to extract a set of more fine-grained visual features. More specifically, we train a deep convolutional network using Caffe library [18] based on 1.3 million images annotated with 1000 ImageNet classes and apply it to classify Pinterest images. For each image, we can derive a 1000-long vector, representing Caffe's confidence levels in recognising the 1000 ImageNet classes it has been trained on. Then, for each user in our dataset, we derive a vector of 1000 features which represents the centroid of the vectors for each of their previous repins. This can be taken as an approximation of the user's preferences for different kinds of image objects.

User Profile Features.

We also take into account the extent of the user's activity on Pinterest by measuring different statistics from their profiles: number of followers, number of boards, number of repins, etc.

5.2.2 Image-related features

Image-related features are derived based on the content of the images. A more traditional approach is to use various metrics of the *quality* of the image. This is complemented by drawing a range of features using state-of-the-art object recognition for images.

Image Quality Features.

Firstly, we define 14 image quality features (*Image Quality-I and -II* in Table 1) to describe the content of an image. These include colour model-related *basic visual features* such as lightness, saturation, colourfulness, gray contrast, RMS contrast, naturalness, sharpness, sharp pixel proportion and left-right intensity balance. We also consider three *aesthetics-related features* that have been used previously in literature: simplicity, modified-simplicity and rule of thirds. Our goal is to assess how these image quality features can capture user preferences for a particular type of content.

We note that extraction of the majority of image quality features requires significant computational resources on the scale of 151K images. Therefore, we used a dataset of down-scaled images (i.e., with width equal to 200 pixels) to extract all image quality features, except lightness, saturation, colourfulness and naturalness for which performance was not an issue. Our experiment on a random subset of 1000 images showed that the Pearson's correlation coefficients between the features extracted from the original and rescaled images were over 0.90 across all features, suggesting that the error introduced by using the down-scaled images is reasonably small (an average absolute error of 0.01).

Object Recognition Features.

As described above, we train the Caffe library [18] using 1.3 million images annotated with 1000 ImageNet classes [6] and apply it to classify Pinterest images. Through this process, we extract two types of visual features: (1) *Deep neural network* features from the layer right before the final classification layer. These are known for a good performance in semantic clustering of images [7]; and (2) *Recognised objects* in the image, represented by a probability or confidence level for each of 1000 objects, as obtained from Caffe.

Pinner-related features.

In addition, we incorporate user-specific features of the original pinner of the image: Features such as number of followers are indicative of the status and reputation of the pinner, and might have a bearing on whether an image is repinned. Similarly, the taste and expertise of the original pinner may also indirectly influence the repinner, and are captured by the category preferences of the original pinner, and her activity levels (number of boards, repins etc.).

5.2.3 Crowd features

In addition to the above, driven by Figure 2c, we extract a simple but powerful feature: the majority category as seen after the first five repins. We then use these to predict the user-specific categories for repins beyond the first five (§7).

	features	dim	Description
User features (U or P)			**User Image Preference Features**
	Category Preferences	32	Users preferences towards different Pinterest categories, described by the fraction of images users have (re)pinned into each category since they signed up on Pinterest.
	Object Preferences	1000	User preferences for object classes as recognised by the Deep Neural Network Caffe [18] (see below for details) is computed as the centroid of the Caffe-generated object classes of all images (re)pinned by the user during a week-long training period in our dataset (3–9 Jan 2013).
			User Profile Features
	Pinboard count	1	Represents the number of personal pinboards of a user.
	Secret board count	1	Calculates the number of users' private pinboards, only accessible by the owner.
	Pin count	1	Represents the total number of pinned and repinned images.
	Like count	1	Measures the number of images a user has liked.
	Follower count	1	Accounts for the number of users who follow the user under consideration.
	Following count	1	Represents the number of users who are followed by the current user.
Image features (I)			**Image Quality-I: Basic Visual Features**
	Lightness	2	Derived directly from HSL colour space. The average and standard deviation of the lightness values of all the pixels in the image are derived as lightness features.
	Saturation	2	Derived directly from HSL colour space. The average and standard deviation of all the pixels are used.
	Colourfulness [14]	1	A measure of a image's difference against gray. It is calculated in RGB as [14]: $\sqrt{\sigma_{rg}^2 + \sigma_{yb}^2} + 0.3\sqrt{\mu_{rg}^2 + \mu_{yb}^2}$, where $rg = R - G$ and $yb = \frac{R+G}{2} - B$, and μ, σ denote mean and standard deviation respectively.
	Gray contrast [5]	1	This is measured as the relative variation of lightness across the image in HSL colour space. It is defined as the standard deviation of the normalised lightness $\frac{L(x,y)-L_{min}}{L_{max}-L_{min}}$ of all image pixels.
	RMS contrast [30, 33]	1	Defined by the standard deviation of all the pixel intensities relative to the mean image intensity.
	Naturalness [16]	1	A measure of the degree of correspondence between images and human perception of reality. It is described by grouping the pixels with $20 < L < 80$ and $S > 0.1$ in HSL colour space according to their H (hue) values into three sets: Skin, Grass and Sky. The naturalness score NS_i, $i \in \{Skin, Grass, Sky\}$, and the proportion of pixels NP_i are derived from the image as described in [16]. The final naturalness score is computed as the weighted average: $NS = \sum_i NS_i \times NP_i$.
	Sharpness [30]	1	A measure of the clarity and level of detail of an image. Sharpness can be determined as a function of its Laplacian, normalized by the local average luminance in the surroundings of each pixel.
	Sharp pixel proportion [4]	1	Photographs that are out of focus are usually regarded as poor photographs, and blurriness can be considered as one of the most important features for determining the quality of the photographs. The photographs are transformed from spatial domain to frequency domain by a Fast Fourier Transform, and the pixels whose values surpass a threshold are considered as sharp pixels (we use a threshold value of 2, following [4]). The sharp pixel proportion is the fraction of all pixels that are sharp.
	Intensity balance [4]	1	This measures how different the intensity is on the left side of the image compared to the right. We use OpenIMAJ [13], an open-source library for multimedia content analysis, to produce the intensity histograms of the left and right portions of the image and evaluate the similarities between them using Chi-squared distance.
			Image Quality-II: Aesthetic Features
	Simplicity-1 [23]	1	Simplicity in a photograph is a distinguishing factor in determining whether a photograph is professional. To compute this, the RGB channels are quantized respectively into 16 different levels and a histogram (H) of 4096=16^3 bins are generated for each RGB combination, and each pixel is put into the appropriate bin. Simplicity is defined as: $(\lvert S \rvert/4096) \times 100\%$, where $S = \{i \mid H(i) \geq \gamma h_{max}\}$, where $H(i)$ is the count of pixels in the ith bin, h_{max} is the maximum count in any bin, and $\gamma = 0.01$.
	Simplicity-2 [4]	1	A modified version of Simplicity-1. Instead of evaluating the simplicity of the whole image, Simplicity-2 extracts the subject region of a photograph and what remains is the background region. The colour distribution of the background is used to evaluate simplicity as above.
	Rule of Thirds [4]	1	This is a well-known photograph composition guideline. The idea is to place main subjects at roughly one-third of the horizontal or vertical dimension of the photograph. It is measured by how close the main subjects are placed near these "power points".
			Object Recognition Features
	Deep Neural Network (DNN) [7, 22]	4096	We use Caffe [18], an open-source implementation of deep convolutional neural networks [22] to train an eight-layer convolutional network on 1.3 million images annotated with 1000 classes, taken from the ImageNet [6, 22] image classification challenge. Then we extract 4096 features from the layer right before the final (following [7]), and use these as an abstract indication of objects in the image.
	Recognised Objects [22]	1000	We use the deep convolutional network described above to recognise object classes in Pinterest images and use them as 1000 Image Object features.

Table 1: **List of features used in the cascade of classifiers used to predict user curation actions on Pinterest**. The dimension (dim.) column gives the number of scalar values in a feature. User-specific features are used both to describe the user who is repinning the image (U) as well as the original pinner (P) who introduced the image on Pinterest. We also use the majority category as computed by the crowd of (the first 5) users pinning an image as a feature in §7. Image features (I) are based both on indicators of image quality, as well as object recognition using a Deep Convolutional Neural Network. User preferences among the recognised object classes is also captured as the user-specific feature "Object Preferences".

6. PREDICTING USER ATTENTION

Here we develop the first step of the cascade pipeline described in §5.1. We analyse the features which drive user attention towards a given pinned image and predict whether the user will take an action on it or not. Specifically, we consider two classes of signals: those of the pinned image and the user. The user u is described by the set of features U in Table 1, which depend on her category and object preferences as well as statistics of her user profile on Pinterest. The pin p is described by the set of image features I in Table 1, which may be attributed to the content of the pinned image. These are augmented by a set of features drawn from the Pinner who published the image, as various characteristics of the original Pinner, such as her "taste" of images, and how influential a user she is on Pinterest, may affect repinnability of the image.

We formalise the problem of predicting user attention as a classification problem where we train a binary classifier $f_1 : (p, u) \rightarrow \{repin, noaction\}$ to predict a binary output $\{repin, noaction\}$ for a given input (p, u). For the purpose of this analysis we have chosen a Random Decision Forest classifier[5] known for a good prediction performance in image classification problems [2].

6.1 Generating negative samples

One of the challenges in training a model for the system with the absence of explicit negative feedback (as there is no "dislike" button in Pinterest) is to generate realistic negative training samples. The fact that a pin was not repinned by a user does not necessarily mean they would not have liked to repin it. It might have been the case that a repin did not happen simply because the user didn't have a chance to see the pin, and had she seen the pin, she might have taken an action on it. To account for this variance when generating negative samples, we assume that pins published just before the time a user is taking an action are more likely to have been noticed by the user. Thus, for a user u who had n repin actions, we randomly select n negative samples[6], by choosing one pin published within *one hour of the time of each of the actions*, and which were not repinned by the user.

Note, that this approach is justified by the fact that over 80% of repins happen within one hour of the previous repin of the same image (Figure 5). A possible reason for this could be that pins which have not been curated recently are likely to be replaced on the Pinterest homepage (or category-specific pages) by more recent activities and would be less likely noticed by a user. We are not interested in the exact cause of this phenomenon; rather we wish to exploit it to generate negative samples of pins that may have been seen by a user but were not repinned. We also tried time windows of other sizes, ranging up to six hours before the time of repin. The precise window size does not appear to affect prediction results.

6.2 Validation

To assess the performance of the proposed model, we split the dataset into three consecutive time intervals: We use all pins from the first interval to learn users' preferences; all repin activity from the second one to train the model and all repins from the third one to test the model. Further, we consider two different experimental settings: when only category preferences of a user are taken into account and when both category preferences and visual object preferences are considered together. The results of the experiments are summarized in Table 2, and feature importances in Table 3.

Firstly, we note that, consistent with §4.2, the prediction performance is high (e.g. Accuracy=0.66) even when only user category preferences are considered (i.e., user object preferences are not considered). From Table 3 we also note that Category Preferences of users along with the image-related DNN and Recognised Objects features are the most important to predict user attention in this scenario. However, when we add User Object Preferences, prediction performance improves by 7-18% across all considered metrics (Accuracy, Precision, Recall, F1-Score). In this scenario, only ImageNet-related features are required, and none of the other sets of features contribute to more than 0.5% of samples. This suggests that the fine-grained object-related preferences are much more ef-

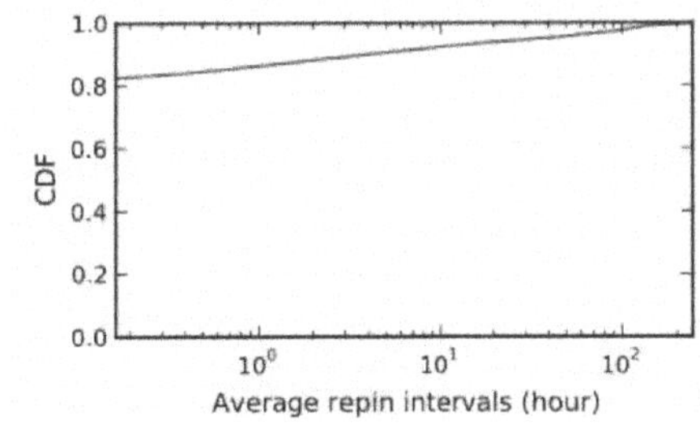

Figure 5: CDF of average time intervals between repins of an image showing that **repins are concentrated in time**.

Metric	Without Obj Prefs.	With Obj Prefs.
Accuracy	0.66	0.77
Precision	0.70	0.83
Recall	0.64	0.69
F1-Score	0.66	0.75

Table 2: **Performance of User Attention Prediction**: Given an image, the task is to predict whether the user will pay it any attention, i.e., whether the user will repin it or not. Two different settings are considered: when only user preferences for categories are known (i.e., without knowing user's object preferences), and when user preferences among the 1000 object classes recognisable by Caffe [18] are also taken into account.

Feature Type	Without Obj. Prefs.	With Obj. Prefs.
Object Preferences (U)	–	**0.40**
DNN (I)	0.37	0.32
Recognised Object (I)	0.21	0.26
Category Prefs (U)	**0.32**	**0.005**
Category Prefs (P)	0.005	0.005
Profile Features (U)	0.09	0.001
Profile Features (P)	0.001	0.001
Image Quality-I &-II (I)	0.001	0.001

Table 3: The relative importance of different classes of features for User Attention Prediction, measured as expected fraction of the samples that a feature contributes to, in the Random Decision Forests constructed for the two scenarios of Table 2. Feature classes correspond to Table 1, and are ordered in descending order of importance when object preferences are used. It may be observed that user category preferences become unimportant when more fine-grained object preferences are taken into account.

[5]We used the Random Forest implementation from the *SKLearn* package with $\sqrt{n_{features}}$ split and 500 estimators (other values from 10 to 1000 were also tested, but 500 showed the best tradeoff between speed and prediction performance).

[6]This means there are the same number of the positive and negative samples in our training set. We also evaluate our model in imbalanced cases (with positive/negative = 10/90) and observe similar performance (accuracy and AUC).

fective at capturing user preferences than the coarse-grained category preferences.

7. CATEGORY AND BOARD PREDICTION

In this section we elaborate our model by introducing the pinboard classifier which aims to predict a user's choice of a board for a repined image. We recall that a Pinterest user may have several different pinboards each assigned to one of 32 globally defined categories. Each of the images in the datasets are thus implicitly labeled by users with one of the 32 categories. In this section, we first develop a model to predict which category a user will choose, given that she will repin the image. We then refine this and predict which pinboard is used, if the category chosen by the user is known. The latter problem is trivial, as users tend to have very few pinboards per category (Figure 4). The former problem is aided enormously by deriving a straightforward category indication from the actions of the crowd (§4.1).

7.1 Category prediction

We design a multi-class Random Forest classifier[7] to learn which category a user will repin a given image into. Specifically, we consider three classes of signals:

User Because of user specialisation, we expect that most of the repin activities of the user is restricted to only a few categories, and furthermore, even amongst these categories, there may be a skewed interest favouring certain categories over others. Thus, given that the user has repinned an image, we can expect her underlying skew of interest amongst different categories to be a reasonable guess for the category chosen for the repinned image. Thus the user category preferences in Table 1 can be interpreted as the empirical probabilities $p_u(c_1), p_u(c_2), ..., p_u(c_{32})$ that a user u will repin an image into categories $c_1, c_2, ..., c_{32}$.

Image The decision of the repinner on which category to assign can be modulated by the features of the image, the objects in the image, and how closely the objects in the image match the interests of the user. Therefore, in this class of signals, we include all the Image features (I) (c.f. Table 1) as well as the matching object preferences of the user.

Crowd There is also a good agreement over category assignment amongst different users (c.f. §4.1). Thus, beyond any preferences that the user may have, the consensus or crowd vote on the category, e.g., as seen after the first five repins for the image, is a heuristic for the category that might be assigned by a given repinner.

As before, to evaluate performance of the proposed model, we split the dataset into three consecutive time intervals: We use all pins from the first interval to learn users' object preferences (this is common to §6 and is not repeated). We train the model based on activities in the second interval, and all repins from the last one are used to test the model.

The results of the experiments are summarised in Table 4. Firstly, we note that the prediction performance is quite high even when only using users' skew in their category preferences (Accuracy=0.42, compared with the baseline accuracy=0.19 obtained by randomly selecting a category among user's categories). When we add deep

[7]Again, we used the Random Forest implementation from the *SKLearn* package with $\sqrt{n_{features}}$ split and 500 estimators. We consider different combinations of features (as specified in Table 4), using χ^2 feature selection as indicated in Table 4.

Features	**ACC**
User	0.42
Image+User	0.77(*)
Crowd+Image+User	0.88(*)
Crowd+User	0.85
Random	0.19

Table 4: **Performance of Repin Category Prediction**: Given a user and an image repinned by her, the task is to predict which category she will repin the image into. The table shows performance in terms of Accuracy (ACC). Stars (*) indicate χ^2 feature selection is applied to select 200 most relevant features for the classification.

learning-based image recognition and image quality features to modulate user preferences amongst different categories, we see a dramatic improvement in accuracy to 0.77. Further adding information about the crowd-indicated category gives us an extremely accurate model with an accuracy of 0.88.

Given that the image features we consider are based on a state-of-the-art deep learning library, it is interesting to compare the performance of image-related features with a similar signal derived from the crowd. Table 4 shows that even by just using the user preferences among categories together with crowd-derived category information, we can obtain an accuracy of 0.85 (compared with 0.77 for Image+User features), suggesting that crowdsourced image categorisation is more powerful than current image recognition and classification technology.

7.2 Pinboard prediction

Next, we look at the way users select pinboards under each category. From Figure 4 we observe that the vast majority of users (75%) has only one board under each category, suggesting that in the most of the cases the problem of choosing a pinboard for a repinned image is similar to that of choosing a category. Nevertheless, some users may have more than one pinboard per category. To account for this, we combine the empirical probabilities of a user choosing a given category for an image (previously computed in §7.1) with the empirical probability of the user putting any given image into that pinboard (computed as the fraction of the user's images in the given pinboard).

This gives us a prediction score for each pinboard, allowing us to compute a ranked list of pinboards. We evaluate prediction power of our method by calculating accuracy at a given cut-off K of the top predicted categories (Table 5). Formally, we measure the performance using $Accuracy@K$, defined as a fraction of the experiments in which the ground truth pinboard was successfully predicted among the $top@K$ of the prediction list.

Comparing the $Accuracy@1$ results of the random benchmark in Table 5 with the random benchmark in Table 4, we note that pinboard prediction is just a slightly more difficult problem than that of predicting categories. The accuracy results of board prediction reflect those of the category prediction with an accuracy decrease of 15% (from 0.88 for category alone, to 0.73 for the more fine-grained board prediction). We also note that prediction performance for the Top-5 pinboards achieves 94% accuracy, which suggests that recommending a small set of possible boards for each pin can be a feasible implementation route for our method.

8. END-TO-END PERFORMANCE

To test the end-to-end performance of the proposed methods, we devise a cascaded-predictor (Figure 1) which sequentially combines individual classifiers introduced in the previous sections, i.e.,

A@k	Crowd+Image+User	Random
1	0.73	0.15
2	0.84	0.27
3	0.89	0.37
4	0.92	0.46
5	0.94	0.53

Table 5: Accuracy@K of predicting Top@K pinboards for pins.

the separately trained User Attention and Pinboard classifiers. We estimate the overall prediction performance of the system by calculating the accuracy, precision and recall of the proposed cascade predictor. These metrics are calculated as an outcome of an imaginary multi-class classifier $f : (u, p) \rightarrow \{noaction, b_1, b_2, ..., b_n\}$ where $b_1, b_2, ..., b_n$ denote users' pinboards. We also measure $Accuracy\ @K$, $Precison@K$ and $Recall@K$ at different cut-offs K of the $top@K$ pinboards predictions. We note that the testing set for these experiments is sampled such that the fraction of non-action and repin cases is set to 1:1, assuring that the number of positive and negative cases in attention prediction experiments are equal.

The results of the experiments presented in Table 6 suggest that the end-to-end performance remains on a high level of $Accuracy$ $@1 = 0.69$ for the $Top@1$ pinboard prediction and further increases to $Accuracy@5 = 0.75$ for the $Top@5$ users' pinboards. Since we need to predict among multiple users' boards, we define precision and recall by distinguishing between correct or incorrect classification of a user's board (defined as true/false positives) and correct or incorrect prediction of no action (defined as true/false negatives). From Table 6, we see that the end-to-end precision remains on a level of 0.60, and reaches 0.77 for predicting among the $Top@5$ users' pinboards, suggesting an overall high level of predictability of individual curation actions on Pinterest.

	@1	@2	@3	@4	@5
Accuracy	0.69	0.71	0.73	0.74	0.75
Precision	0.60	0.70	0.72	0.76	0.77
Recall	0.50	0.58	0.62	0.63	0.64

Table 6: End-to-end results for the cascade of predictors (Figure 1).

9. DISCUSSION AND CONCLUSIONS

Social bookmarking and curation is becoming increasingly important to the Web as a whole: Pinterest for instance has become an important source of referral traffic, second only to Facebook amongst all the major social networks [29]. Furthermore, Pinterest referral traffic is valuable for e-commerce sites, being 10% more likely to result in sales, with each sale being on average \$80, double the value of sales from Facebook referrals [15]. Therefore, understanding Pinterest can result both in fundamental insights into the nature of content curation, as well as commercially valuable applications such as recommending items that users are willing to buy, and optimising marketing campaigns for brand awareness and recall. Understanding what makes users curate an image could also help other applications such as more relevant image search.

This work takes first steps towards this research agenda by showing that although Pinterest users are curating highly personalised collections of content, they are effectively participating in a crowd-sourced categorisation of images from across the web, by their choices of pinboards. By exploiting the fact that user pinboards can have an associated category, we reinterpret the act of pinning as a distributed human computation that categorises images from across the Web into the 32 categories recognised on Pinterest. When viewed through this perspective, it becomes readily apparent that there is overwhelming agreement among users on how to categorise images. Additionally, we see that users tend to specialise in a handful of categories, and tend not to have several boards in the same category. Furthermore, even within their favourite categories, their attention is skewed towards the top 1-5 categories.

Based on these observations, we developed a cascade of predictors, that, given a pin and a user, is able to predict whether the user would repin it, and if so, to which of her pinboards. The three layers of the cascade could be conceived as providing a possible mechanistic understanding of content curation on Pinterest. Although alternate constructions may be possible, the behaviour and performance of the predictors we built serve to illuminate some of the factors involved in content curation: As can be expected, the first decision of whether the user repins the pin at all, depends to a large extent on the visual features of the image. In particular, the fine-grained object-related preferences extracted using a state-of-the-art deep neural network were much more effective at capturing user preferences than coarse-grained category preferences, highlighting that object recognition may play a central role in understanding what a user is interested in. The next layer in the cascade, predicting what category a user is likely to assign to a pin, is dominated by one factor: that most users agree on the category. Indeed, by looking at the first five repins of an image, we are able to predict other repins with $\approx 85\%$ accuracy, and although several other types of features, ranging from visual features of the image to features of the user were examined, only a marginal improvement of $\approx 3\%$ could be made over this single feature. We also found that this crowdsourced category was more powerful than image object recognition, at predicting personalised user category choices.

The final layer of predicting the board given the category turned out to be an almost trivial problem, suggesting that users, rather than showing complicated behaviours, appear to be "operating" just in the 32-dimension approximation of Pinterest global categories.

Because of the collective efforts of large numbers of Pinterest users, we have amassed an extensive annotated set of images (over 1.2 million category annotations for 214K pins). Although there is a great deal of agreement in general, individual users may have slightly different views about categorisation, and similarly, the categories may not be mutually exclusive (e.g., one user might classify an image of the Eiffel tower into an "Art" pinboard while another might choose "Architecture", both of which are standard Pinterest categories). We find that by incorporating user preferences, we are able to further improve the performance, evidence that users are "personalising" these categories by reinterpreting and reaggregating them through pinboards. Thus, this arrangement of allowing users the freedom to create pinboards suiting their own purposes, whilst at the same time associating the pinboards to a small number of standard categories appears to strike a good balance between the rigid taxonomies of an ontology and the free-for-all nature of so-called folksonomies [24], enabling a meaningful global categorisation (with enough power to predict image categories based on their visual features), whilst at the same time allowing user flexibility. We believe the image-based information in this dataset will be valuable in diverse other applications, and plan to make it available for researchers at `http://bit.ly/pinterest-dataset`.

Acknowledgements

This research was partially supported by the UK Engineering and Physical Sciences Research Council via Grant No. EP/K024914/1, and by the Henry Lester Trust.

10. REFERENCES

[1] Blackburn, J., and Kwak, H. Stfu noob!: predicting crowdsourced decisions on toxic behavior in online games. In *WWW* (2014).

[2] Bosch, A., Zisserman, A., and Munoz, X. Image classification using random forests and ferns. *ICCV* (2007).

[3] Chang, S., Kumar, V., Gilbert, E., and Terveen, L. G. Specialization, homophily, and gender in a social curation site: findings from pinterest. In *CSCW* (2014).

[4] Che-Hua Yeh, Yuan-Chen Ho, Brian A. Barsky, and Ming Ouhyoung. Personalized photograph ranking and selection system. In *ACM MM* (2010).

[5] Cheng, H., Zwol, R. v., Azimi, J., Manavoglu, E., Zhang, R., Zhou, Y., and Navalpakkam, V. Multimedia features for click prediction of new ads in display advertising. In *KDD* (2012), ACM.

[6] Deng, J., Dong, W., Socher, R., Li, L.-J., Li, K., and Fei-Fei, L. ImageNet: A large-scale hierarchical image database. In *CVPR* (2009).

[7] Donahue, J., Jia, Y., Vinyals, O., Hoffman, J., Zhang, N., Tzeng, E., and Darrell, T. DeCAF: A deep convolutional activation feature for generic visual recognition. *arXiv preprint 1310.1531* (2013). Subsequently published in ICML 2014.

[8] Gilbert, E., Bakhshi, S., Chang, S., and Terveen, L. I need to try this?: a statistical overview of pinterest. In *CHI* (2013).

[9] Golder, S. A., and Huberman, B. A. Usage patterns of collaborative tagging systems. *Journal of information science* (2006).

[10] Gygli, M., Grabner, H., Riemenschneider, H., Nater, F., and Gool, L. V. The interestingness of images. In *ICCV* (2013).

[11] Hall, C., and Zarro, M. Social curation on the website pinterest.com. *Proceedings of the American Society for Information Science and Technology* (2012).

[12] Han, J., Choi, D., Chun, B.-G., Kim, H.-c., and Choi, Y. Collecting, organizing, and sharing pins in pinterest: Interest-driven or social-driven? *SIGMETRICS* (2014).

[13] Hare, J. S., Samangooei, S., and Dupplaw, D. P. Openimaj and imageterrier: Java libraries and tools for scalable multimedia analysis and indexing of images. In *ACM MM* (2011).

[14] Hasler, D., and Suesstrunk, S. E. Measuring colorfulness in natural images. In *Proc. SPIE 5007, Human Vision and Electronic Imaging VIII* (2003).

[15] Hayes, M. How pinterest drives ecommerce sales. Available from http://www.shopify.com/blog/6058268-how-pinterest-drives-ecommerce-sales, 2012.

[16] Huang, K.-Q., Wang, Q., and Wu, Z.-Y. Natural color image enhancement and evaluation algorithm based on human visual system. *Computer Vision and Image Understanding* (2006).

[17] Isola, P., Xiao, J., Torralba, A., and Oliva, A. What makes an image memorable? In *CVPR* (2011).

[18] Jia, Y., Shelhamer, E., Donahue, J., Karayev, S., Long, J., Girshick, R., Guadarrama, S., and Darrell, T. Caffe: Convolutional architecture for fast feature embedding. *arXiv preprint 1408.5093* (2014). Subsequently published in ACM MM 2014.

[19] Kamar, E., Hacker, S., and Horvitz, E. Combining human and machine intelligence in large-scale crowdsourcing. In *AAMAS* (2012).

[20] Kamath, K. Y., Popescu, A.-M., and Caverlee, J. Board recommendation in pinterest. In *UMAP Workshops* (2013).

[21] Khosla, A., Sarma, A. D., and Hamid, R. What makes an image popular? In *WWW* (2014).

[22] Krizhevsky, A., Sutskever, I., and Hinton, G. E. Imagenet classification with deep convolutional neural networks. In *NIPS* (2012), pp. 1097–1105.

[23] Luo, Yiwen, and Tang, Xiaoou. Photo and video quality evaluation: Focusing on the subject. In *ECCV* (2008).

[24] Mathes, A. Folksonomies-cooperative classification and communication through shared metadata. *Computer Mediated Communication* (2004).

[25] Noël, S., and Beale, R. Sharing vocabularies: tag usage in citeulike. In *BCS-HCI* (2008).

[26] Ottoni, R., Las Casas, D., Pesce, J. P., Meira Jr, W., Wilson, C., Mislove, A., and Almeida, V. Of pins and tweets: Investigating how users behave across image-and text-based social networks. In *ICWSM* (2014).

[27] Ottoni, R., Pesce, J. P., Las Casas, D. B., Franciscani Jr, G., Meira Jr, W., Kumaraguru, P., and Almeida, V. Ladies first: Analyzing gender roles and behaviors in pinterest. In *ICWSM* (2013).

[28] Rader, E., and Wash, R. Influences on tag choices in del. icio. us. In *CSCW* (2008).

[29] Rose, K. Pinterest is sneaking up on twitter, facebook, and google. New York Magazine, Available from http://nymag.com/daily/intelligencer/2014/05/pinterest-is-sneaking-up-on-twitter-and-facebook.html, 2014.

[30] San Pedro, J., and Siersdorfer, S. Ranking and classifying attractiveness of photos in folksonomies. In *WWW* (2009).

[31] Strohmaier, M., Körner, C., and Kern, R. Why do users tag? detecting users' motivation for tagging in social tagging systems. In *ICWSM* (2010).

[32] Von Ahn, L., and Dabbish, L. Labeling images with a computer game. In *CHI* (2004).

[33] Webster, M. A., and Miyahara, E. Contrast adaptation and the spatial structure of natural images. *JOSA A* (1997).

[34] Wetzker, R., Zimmermann, C., Bauckhage, C., and Albayrak, S. I tag, you tag: translating tags for advanced user models. In *WSDM* (2010).

[35] Yin, P., Luo, P., Wang, M., and Lee, W.-C. A straw shows which way the wind blows: ranking potentially popular items from early votes. In *WSDM* (2012).

[36] Zarro, M., Hall, C., and Forte, A. Wedding dresses and wanted criminals: Pinterest. com as an infrastructure for repository building. In *ICWSM* (2013).

[37] Zhong, C., Salehi, M., Shah, S., Cobzarenco, M., Sastry, N., and Cha, M. Social bootstrapping: how pinterest and last. fm social communities benefit by borrowing links from facebook. In *WWW* (2014).

[38] Zhong, C., Shah, S., Sundaravadivelan, K., and Sastry, N. Sharing the loves: Understanding the how and why of online content curation. In *ICWSM* (2013).

Author Index

www.ingramcontent.com/pod-product-compliance
Ingram Content Group UK Ltd.
Pitfield, Milton Keynes, MK11 3LW, UK
UKHW051420290926
15471UKWH00009B/1700

9 781450 338608